THE GEOLOGICAL SOCIETY OF AMERICA
MEMOIR 134

BIBLIOGRAPHY
OF FOSSIL VERTEBRATES
1964 - 1968

C. L. Camp, R. H. Nichols,
B. Brajnikov, E. Fulton,
and J. A. Bacskai

Museum of Paleontology
University of California
Berkeley

1972

Published by
THE GEOLOGICAL SOCIETY OF AMERICA, INC.
Colorado Building, P.O. Box 1719
Boulder, Colorado 80302

Printed in the United States of America

The publication of this volume
is made possible
through the bequest of
Richard Alexander Fullerton Penrose, Jr.

CONTENTS

PREFACE

The closing date of the present volume (1968) marks the fortieth anniversary of this bibliography issued in five-year periods and covering the World literature. Previous numbers have appeared as: G. S. A. Special Papers nos. 27 and 42 and as G. S. A. Memoirs 37, 57, 84, 92 and 117. The O. P. Hay and A. S. Romer bibliographies provide nearly complete references for all the years before 1928. Our early volumes are now out-of-print.

Our bibliographies are more comprehensive than mere reference lists. They provide access to information such as new names, new discoveries, faunal lists, and other pertinent material, by means of index headings. The indexes have been largely constructed from our own abstracts of the original articles as prepared on cards filed under the authors' names. The indexes refer to citations in the Author Catalogue. The Systematic Synopsis of Classification finally brings into order the proposals for changes and additions to the classification of the Chordata. An attempt has been made to discover and index all new scientific names. There are limits to the powers of detection. If an author casually proposes a novelty without so indicating, the name can easily escape us. At the beginning we list the new periodicals with abbreviations and those with names changed since previous periods. The indexes provide the kind of information that would be conveyed by abstracts. It may be that the index form is handier than the usual abstract form entered in an Author Catalogue. We believe that the index form is preferable for future use, more direct and concise and easier to consult. This point may be argued.

We have continued to provide general Paleolithic archeological references and the sub-fossil records of the New World, Africa and Oceania as well. We don't attempt to separate fossil man from his background in vertebrate paleontology. Elimination of anthropological citations would reduce the bulk of this work by about forty per cent. The excessive bulk has resulted partly from the change in typographic style done for economy. This new style reduces the amount of material on each page by about one-fifth.

Among those who have contributed and helped most effectively in this work are the collaborators Mrs. Rachel H. Nichols, who has done much of the abstracting and who has compiled the Systematic Index as well, Dr. Boris Brajnikov, who has abstracted the voluminous Slavic literature as well as papers in other languages and who has paid special attention to geology, Mrs. Elizabeth Fulton followed by Mrs. Judith A. Bacskai, who have constructed the Subject Index, and furthermore, Mrs. Bacskai has helped Mrs. Nichols with the proof reading.

Koltype of Oakland, in their usual skillful way, have prepared the pages for the offset press. The National Science Foundation has provided substantial support, and the Geological Society of America has as always run the work through the press. Paleontologists, anthropologists, biologists and geologists in general should be grateful for this generous support of their researches.

Charles L. Camp
University of California
Berkeley, CA
September 9, 1971.

SUPPLEMENTARY LIST OF SERIALS

Call numbers are given for the University of California, Berkeley, Library and these largely agree with the Library of Congress system.

A Pedro Bosch Gimpera en el septuagésimo aniversario de su   not seen
   nacimiento.
      México.

Aarbøger for Nordisk Oldkyndighed og Historie   DL1.A2
   København.

Abh. Exact. Biol.   QH301.A2
   Abhandlungen zur exacten Biologie Herausgegeben von Prof.
      Dr. L. von Bertalanffy.
      Berlin: Gebr. Borntraeger Press

Abh. Sächsischen Akad. Wiss. Leipzig, Phil.-hist. Kl.   AS182.S33
   Abhandlungen der Sächsischen Akademie der Wissenschaften
      zu Leipzig.
      Philologisch-historische Klasse. Berlin.

Abh. Sächs. Akad. Wiss., Math.-Naturwiss. Kl.   AS182.S31
   Sächsische Akademie der Wissenschaften zu Leipzig
      Mathematisch-naturwissenschaftliche Klasse.
      Abhandlungen.

Abs. Ann. Meeting Amer. Anthrop. Assoc.   NST2
   Abstracts Annual Meeting.
      American Anthropological Association. Superceded by its
      Bulletin in 1968.

Abst., Program 1964 Ann. Meetings, Geol. Soc. Amer., et al.   QE1.G457
   Abstract Program 1964 Annual Meetings, The Geological Society
      of America, et al.

Acta Asiatica   Period.
   Bulletin of the Institute of Eastern Culture.
      The Tōhō Gakkai, Tokyo.

Acta Bernensia   DQ401.A25
   Bern.

Acta Biol., Acta Univ. Szeged.   QH301.A323
   Acta Universitatis Szegediensis, Acta Biologica, n. ser.,
      Hungary.

Acta, Geochim. Cosmochim.   QE515.A1G4
   Geochimica et Cosmochimica Acta Pergamon Press. Printed
      in Northern Ireland.

Acta Geol. Hispánica   QE1.A3188
   Acta Geologica Hispánica. Instituto Nacional de Geologia.
   Spain. Barcelona.

Acta Geol., Zagreb.   QE1.A3175
   Jugoslovenska Akademija Znanosti i Umjetnosti III Odjel
   za Prirodne Nauke. Acta Geologica.
   Subseries of Prirodoslovna Istraživanja.
   Summaries in English or German.
      Zagreb.

Acta Reg. Soc. Sci. Litt. Gothob., Zool.   not seen
   Göteborg.

Acta Theriologica   QL700.A3
   Polskiej Akademii Nauk. Bia Iowieża.

Acta Univ. Carolinae, Biol. Suppl.   Library of
   Acta Universitatis Carolinae, Biologica Supplementum.   Congress
   Prague.

Acta Zool., Budapest   QL1.A17
   Acta Zoologica Academiae Scientiarum Hungaricae
   Budapest.

Actas III Congr. Internat. Estud. Pirenaicos Gerona   not seen
   Zaragoza Inst. Estud. Pirenaicos

Actas V Congr. Panafr. Prehist. Estud. Cuaternario   GN700.P3
   Actas del V Congreso Panafricano de Prehistoria y de
   Estudio del Cuaternario.
   Santa Cruz de Tenerife, 1963.

Actes 18° Congr. Fédér. Soc.   not seen
   Acad. et Sav. Languedoc, Pyrénées, Gascogne à St. Gaudens.

Actes 2ème Congr. Internat. Spéléol.   Cave Res.
   Actes du Deuxième Congrès International de Spéléologie.   Assoc. Lib.
   Bari, Lecce, Salerno, 5-10 Octobre 1958.

Actes 3ème Congr. Internat. Spéléol.   Cave Res.
   Actes du Troisième Congrès International de Spéléologie.   Assoc. Lib.
   Wien — Obertraun — Salzburg 1961

Amer. Anthrop. Special Publ.   GN400.A1A66
   American Anthropologist. Special Publications.
   Published by the American Anthropological Association.

Amer. Psych.   BF1.A54
   American Psychologist

America   AQ.A4
   National Catholic Weekly Review.

An. Anthrop., Mexico   GN2.M45A5
   Anales de Antropologia, Universidad Nacional Autonoma
   de Mexico.

An. Mus. Nahuel Huapi   not seen
    Anales del Museo de Nahuel Huapi.
    San Carlos de Bariloche (Rio Negro Ter.), Argentina.
    Ministerio de obras públicas de la nación.
        Buenos Aires.

An. Ştiinţ. Univ. Cuza (n.s.), Sect. 2 (Ştiinţe Nat.), a. Biol.   QH301.J35A5
    Jassy. Universitatia. Analele Ştiinţifice ale Universităţii "Al.
      I. Cuza" din Iaşi (Serie nouă).
      Secţiunea II (Ştiinţe Naturale). a. Biologie.

An. Ştiinţ. Univ. Cuza (n.s.), Sect. 2 (Ştiinţe Nat.), b. Geol.-Geog. QE1.J33A5
    Jassy. Universitatia. Analele Ştiinţifice ale Universităţii "Al.
      I. Cuza" din Iaşi (Serie nouă).
      Secţiunea II (Ştiinţe Naturale). b. Geologie-Geografie.

An. Univ. Norte   not seen
    Anales de la Universidad del Norte.

Anal. Praehist. Leiden   GN700.A62
    Analecta Praehistorica Leidensia. (Inst. for Prehistory)
      Univ. Leiden.

Animals   not seen
    Animals, London.

Ann. Amer. Acad. Political Social Sci.   AQ.A45
    The Annals of the American Academy of Political and
      Social Science.

Ann. Archéol. Arabes Syrienne   DS94.5.A55

Ann. Assoc. rég. étude et rech. sci.   not seen
    Annales Association régionale pour l'étude et la recherche
      scientifique.
      Reims.

Ann. Comit. Geol. Républ. Popul. Romine   not seen
    Bucuresti

Ann. Guébhard   A46.I6
    Annales Guébhard-Séverine.
      Institut Adrien Guébhard-Séverine. Neuchatêl.

Ann. Mus. Roy. Afr. Cent., Sér. in 8°, Sci. Géol.   QE1.T47
    Annales, Musée Royal de l'Afrique Centrale, Tervuren, Belgique.
      Série in 8° — Sciences Geologiques.

Ann. Mus. Roy. Afr. Cent., Ser. in 8°, Sci. Zool.   QL337.K6T43
    Annales, Musée Royal de l'Afrique Centrale. Tervuren, Belgium.
      Série in 8° — Sciences Zoologiques.

Ann. Pal., Vert.   QE841.A1A6
    Annales de Paléontologie, Vertébrés. Paris (with v. 50, 1964,
      it was divided into Invertébrés et Vertébrés, with same vol.
      and fasc. nos. and dates).

Ann. Proc. Ass. Sci. Techn. Soc. South Afr.   not seen

Ann. Rept., Archeol. Surv., Dept. Anthrop., Univ. Calif., Los
Angeles
    California University. Los Angeles. Department of Anthropology.
    Archaeological Survey. Annual Report.

Ann. Rept., British Borneo Geol. Serv. Dept.   Doc. U. C.
    British Borneo Geol. Serv. Depart. Ann. Report.

Ann. Rept., Calif. Acad. Sci.   Reprint
    Annual Report of the California Academy of Sciences. San
    Francisco.

Ann. Rept. Ealing Microscopical Nat. Hist. Soc.   not seen
    Annual Report. Ealing Microscopical and Natural History
    Society.

Ann. Rept. Nairobi Nation. Mus. Formerly, Coryndon Mem. Mus.   QH71.N25A1

Ann. Spél.   Cave Res.
    Annales de Spéléologie   Assoc. Lib.
    Centre National de la Recherche Scientifique.
    Ariège.

Ann. Univ. Ferrara, Sez. 15   Period.
    Annale dell' Universita di Ferrara. Sezione 15.
    Paleontologia Umana e Paletnologia.

Ann. Univ. Saraviensis, Reihe Math.-Naturwiss. Fak.   Period.
    Saarbrücken. Universität. Annales universitatis saraviensis.
    Reihe: Mathematisch-naturwissenschaftliche Fakultät.
    Supercedes Ann. Naturwiss. Univ. Saarbrücken.

Antaios   AP30.A57
    Stuttgart: Ernst Klett Verlag.

Anthrop., Bratislava   not seen
    Anthropologica.
        Acta Facultatis Rerum Naturalium Universitatis Comenianae
        slovenské Pedagogické Nakladalel'stvo Bratislava.

Anthrop. Jour. Canada   GN1.A49
    Anthropological Journal of Canada. Quarterly Bulletin of the
    Anthropological Association of Canada.
    Gatineau, Quebec.

Anthrop. of the North   GN4.A75
    Anthropology of the North. Translations from Russian Sources.
    Arctic Institute of North America. University of Toronto
    Press.

Anthrop. Pap., Nation. Mus. Canada   E78.C2C25
    Anthropology Papers.
        National Museum of Canada.
        Ottawa.

Anthrop. Pap. Nev. State Mus.   F843.N38
    Anthropological Papers,
      Nevada State Museum, Carson City.

Antropología, Chile   F3069.A1A55
    Centro de Estudos Antropológicos Universidad de Chile.
      Santiago.

Arch. Hydrobiol., Suppl.   QH301.A65
    Archiv für Hydrobiologie. Supplement-Band.
      Berlin, Stuttgart.

Arch. Oral Biol.   RK1.A7
    Archives of Oral Biology.
      Permagon Press, Oxford, New York, London, Paris.

Arch., Publ. Cercle Recherch. Préhist. Renaisis   not seen

Arch. Russ. Anat. Histol. Embryol.   QL801.A84
    Archives russes d'anatomie, d'histologie et d'embryologie.

Archaeol. Cambrensis   Cave Res.
    Archaeologia Cambrensis Cambrian Archaeological Association.

Archaeol., Phys. Anthrop. in Oceania   GN58.O22A72
    Archaeology and Physical Anthropology in Oceania.

Argentina Austral.   Cambridge Scott
    Buenos Aires.   Polar Inst.

Arheoloogiline Kogumik   GN700.A8
    Arheoloogiline Kogumik. Eesti NSV Teaduste Akadeemia. Ajaloo
      Instituut. Talinn.
      Academy of Sci. of Estonian SSR. Inst. of History. In
      Estonian and Russian.

Ariz. Acad. Sci.   Q11.A677.J6
    Arizona Academy of Science, Journal.

Arkansas Amateur   E78.A8A65
    Northwest Arkansas Archeological Society.
      Prairie Grove, Ark.

Arkansas Archeologist   F413.A7
    The Arkansas Archeologist.
      Bulletin of the Arkansas Archeological Society. University
      of Arkansas.
      Fayetteville.

Arkheologiía, Sofia   Period.
    (formerly listed as: Archeologija, Sofia).
      Bulgarska Akademiía na Naukite, Arkheologicheski
      Institut i Muzei Bulgariau. French tables of
      contents. Sofia; Bulg. Akad. na Naukite Press.

Arnoldia   AM101.C35A4
   Arnoldia. National Museums of Southern Rhodesia. Series of
   miscellaneous publications.

Årsbok Statens Naturvetenskap Forskningsråds   Q180.S8A3
   Sweden. Svensk naturvetenskap.

Atlantic Nat.   not seen
   Atlantic Naturalist. Audubon Naturalist Society of the Central
   Atlantic States, Inc.

Atlántida, Madrid   A5301.A85

Atomes   Period.
   Paris. A monthly review, beginning 1946, of vulgarization on
   all scientific subjects.

Atti Accad. Fisiocritici Siena   not seen
   Siena

Atti VIII Congr. Naz. Spel.   not seen

Atti IX Congr. Naz. Spel.   not seen
   Atti del IX Congresso Nazionale di Speleologia. Trieste 1963.

Atti I Conv. Interr. Padano Paletnol.   not seen
   Atti I Conv. Interr. Padano Paletnologia.

Atti Soc. Peloritana Sci. Fis. Mat. Nat.   not seen
   Messina

Avisudkl. Berlingske Aftenavis   not seen

Azerb. neft. khoz.   TN4A9
   Azerbaidzhanskoe neftianoe khoziaistvo.
   Baku.

Basler Beiträge Geog. Ethnol., Ethnol. Reihe   GN4.B2
   Basler Beiträge Geographie und Ethnologie.
     Ethnologische Reihe. Geographisch-Ethnologische Gesell-
     schaft, Basel.

Beitr. Ur- und Frühgesch. Archäol. Mittelmeer-Kulturr.   GN705.B4
   Beiträge zur Ur- und Frühgeschichtlichen Archäologie des
     Mittelmeer-Kulturraumes. Institut für Ur- und Frühgeschichte
     der Universität Heidelberg.
     Bonn: Rudolf Habelt Verlag.

Ber. Deutsch. Ges. Geol. Wiss., Reihe A, Geol. Paläontol.   QE1.D45.B4
   Berichte der Deutschen Gesellschaft fur Geologische Wissen-
     schaften, Reihe A, Geologie und Paläontologie. Supercedes:
     Ber. Geol. Ges. Deutsch. Demokrat. Republik.
     Berlin: Akademie-Verlag.

Ber. Naturhist. Ges. Hannover
    Bericht der Naturhistorischen Gesellschaft zu Hannover.
      Hannover.
	QH5.N28

Ber. Naturw. Ver. Bielefeld u. Umgegend
    Naturwissenschaftlicher Verein für Bielefeld und Umgegend.
      Bericht.
	Calif. Acad. Sci.

Bib. Praehist. Hispana	DP91.B52

Biochimica et Biophysica Acta
    Biochimica et Biophysica Acta
      Amsterdam.
	QP501.B56

Biol. and Human Affairs	not seen

Biol. Jour., Linnean Soc. London
    Linnean Society London. Biological Journal.
      Formerly: Proc. Linnean Soc. London
	QH1.L61

Biol. Zbl.
    Biologisches Zentralblatt
      Leipzig: VEB Georg Thieme Verlag.
	QH301.B54

Biológiai vándorgyülés elöadásainak ismertetése. Budapest.	not seen

BioScience
    A.I.B.S. Bulletin
      American Institute of Biological Sciences.
	QH301.A13

Biulleten' Mezh Strat. Kom.
    Biulleten'. Mezhvedomstvennyĭ stratigraficheskiĭ komitet.
      Russia.
	Period.

Bol. Amer.
    Boletin Americanista.
      Universidad de Barcelona. Facultad de Filosofia y Letras.
	Period.

Bol. Bibliog. Cien. Hombre
    Boletín Bibliográfico de las Ciencias del Hombre.
      Centro de Estudios Arqueológicos y Antropológicos
      Americanos Dr. Paul Rivet.
      Montevideo, Uruguay.
	NST192

Bol. Centro Invest. Antrop. Mex.
    Boletín del Centro de Investigaciones Antropologicas de
      México.
      Mexico, D. F.
	F1201.C43

Bol. Inst. antropol. Univ. Antioquia
    Boletin del Instituto de antropologia del Universidad de
      Antioquia.
      Medellin, Colombia.
	not seen

Bol. Inst. Cien. Nat. Santa Maria   not seen
    Santa Maria, Brazil, (Rio Grande do Sul),
        Universidade Federal. Instituto de Ciencias Naturais.
        Boletim.

Bol. Inst. Nac. Anthrop. Hist., Mexico   F1219.M38
    Boletin instituto Nacional de Antropologia e Historia.
        Mexico (Republic)

Bol. Mus. Lab. Min. geol. Fac. cienc. Univ. Lisboa   Indiana
    Museu e Laboratório mineralógico e geológico. Faculdade de   Acad. Sci.
        ciencias.
        Universidade de Lisboa. Boletim.
        Lisboa (Lisbon, Portugal)

Bol. R. Soc. Espan. Hist. Nat., Sec. Biol.   QH301.S48
    Boletin de la Real Sociedad Española de Historia Natural.
        Seccion Biologica.
        Madrid.

Bol. Soc. Geog. Lima   G5.S6
    Boletin de la Sociedad Geográfica de Lima.

Bol. Univ. Chile   AS81.C52
    Boletin de la Universidad de Chile.

Boston Univ. Afr. Res. Studies.   DT1.B6
    Boston University African Research Studies, Boston University
        Press, Boston.

Brabants Heem.   not seen

Brain, behavior, evol.   QP376.A1B7
    Brain, behavior and evolution.
        Basel.

Bul. Inst. petrol, gaze şi geol.   not seen
    Buletinul Institutul de petrol, gaze şi geologie.
        Bucharest
        Summaries in Russian and English.

Bull. AAAS   Q1.A46
    Bulletin, American Association for the Advancement of
        Science.

Bull. Acad. polon. Sci., Sér. Sci. Géol.   QE1.P584.B8
    Polska Akademia Nauk. Bulletin de l'Académie Polonaise des
        Sciences. Série des sciences géologiques et géographiques.

Bull. Acad. Soc. Lorraines Sci.   Q46.A3538
    Academie et Société Lorraines des Sciences.
        Bulletin Trimestriel.

Bull. Assoc. Franç. Étude Quat.   Stanford
    Association Française pour l'Étude du Quaternaire, Bulletin.
        Paris.

Bull. Australian Bur. Min. Res. QE340.A32
 Australian Bureau of Mineral Resources. Bulletin. Geol.

Bull. Austral. Mammal Soc. not seen

Bull. Cercle Arch. Hesbaye-Condroz not seen

Bull. Correspondance Hellén. DF10.B8
 Bulletin de Correspondance Hellénique.
  École Francaise d'Athènes.

Bull. Geol. Soc. India. QE1.GA75B8
 Geological Society of India.
  Bulletin. Bangalore.

Bull. Geol. Surv. Indonesia QE301.A2345
 Geological Survey of Indonesia.
  Bulletin.

Bull. Georgia Acad. Sci. Q11.G42
 Bulletin of the Georgia Academy of Science.
  Athens, Georgia.

Bull. Ghana Geol. Surv. QE327.G6
 Ghana. Geological Survey.
  Bulletin. formerly Gold Coast Geol. Surv.

Bull. Grand Canyon Nat. Hist. Assoc. cat. by author
 Grand Canyon Natural History Association. Bulletin.
  Grand Canyon.

Bull. Groupement Archéol. Seine-et-Marne not seen
 Bulletin du Groupement Archéologique de Seine-et-Marne.

Bull. Groupement Internat. Recherch. Sci. Stomatol. Univ. Cal. Med.
 Bulletin du Groupement International pour la Recherche Lib.
  Scientifique en Stomatologie. Belgium. Liège.

Bull. Internat. Comm. Urgent Anthrop. Res. GN2.I64
 Bulletin of the International Committee on Urgent Anthropological Research.

Bull. Kanagawa Prefec. Mus. Sep.
 Kanagawa Prefectural Museum.
  Bulletin.

Bull. Los Angeles Co. Mus., Science. ESL
 Bulletin of the Los Angeles County Museum, Science.

Bull., Mus. Nat. Hist., Univ. Oregon QH1.O65B8
 Bulletin of the Museum of Natural History of the University
  of Oregon.
  Eugene, Oregon.

Bull. Nation. Mus. Canada, Geol. Ser. QE185.A72
 Bulletin, National Museum of Canada, Geological Series.

Bull., Rec. Trav. Stat. Mar. Endoume.   AMNH
  Aix-Marseille, Univerite d'Station Marine d'Endoume. Bulletin.
    Subseries of its Recueil des Travaux.

Bull. S. Plains Archeol. Soc.   NST126
  Bulletin of the South Plains Archeological Society.
    Floydada, Texas.

Bull. Soc. Amis Grand-Pressigny   not seen
  Bulletin de la Société des Amis Grand-Pressigny.

Bull. Soc. Archéol. Hist. Chelles   not seen
  Bull. Soc. Archéol. et Hist. de Chelles.

Bull. Soc. Étud. Sci. Nat. Vaucluse   not seen
  Bulletin de la Société française de Minéralogie et de
    Cristallographie.

Bull. Soc. Polymathique Moribihan   not seen
  Société Polymathique du Morbihan. Vannes.
    Bulletin.

Bull. Soc. Sci. Dauphiné   Period.
  Société Scientifique du Dauphiné.
    Bulletin.

Bull. Soc. Sci. Nat. Math.   not seen
  Cherbourg.

Bull. Southeast. Archaeol. Confer.   F211.S67.B8
  Bulletin. Southeastern Archaeological Conference.
    Cambridge, Massachusetts.

Bull. Ver. Schweiz. Petrol.-Geol.   not seen
  Basel.

Bull., Ward's Nat. Sci. Estab.   not seen
  Bulletin, Ward's Natural Science Establishment, Rochester, N.Y.

Bull. Zool. Nomen.   QL353.I54
  Bulletin of Zoological Nomenclature.
    International Commission on Zoological Nomenclature;
    London.

C. R. Congr. Nation. Soc. Savantes, Sec. Sci., Sci. Terre Biol. Méd. Q101.C55
  Comptes Rendus du Congrès National des Sociétés Savantes.
    Section des Sciences.
    Sciences de la Terre, Biologie-Médecine.
    France. Travaux Historiques et Scientifiques.

Cahiers Alsaciens Archéol. Art. Hist.   not seen
  Cahiers Alsaciens d'Archéologie, d'Art et d'Histoire.
    Strasbourg.

Cahiers Étud. Biol.   QH301.C15
    Cahiers d'Études biologiques.
       Paris: Lethielleux.

Cahiers de Tunisie   DT421.C26
    Les Cahiers de Tunisie Revue de Sciences Humaines.
       Université de Tunis.

Cahiers Hist. Mond.   D1.C25
    Cahiers d'Histoire Mondiale. Journal of World History.
       Cuadernos de Historia Mundial.
       Commission Internationale pour une Histoire du developpe-
       ment Scientifique et Culturel de l'Humanité. UNESCO.

Campus Rept. Univ. Calif.   Univ. Cal.
    Campus Report. The weekly newsletter/University of California,
       Berkeley.

Canadian Audubon.   QH1.C305

Canadian Jour. Earth Sci.   QE1.C33
    Canadian Journal of Earth Sciences. Ottawa.

Canadian Jour. Zool.   QL1.C33
    Canadian Journal of Zoology. Formerly: Canadian Journal
       of Research, Zool. Sci., v. 1-28.

Carib. Jour. Sci.   Q1.C34
    Caribbean Journal of Science.
       (Univ. Puerto Rico, Institute of Caribbean Studies).
       Mayaguez, P. R.

Carinthia II Naturwiss.   Q44.C37
    Beitr. Heimatk. Kärntens.

Carolina Jour. Anthrop.   not seen
    Carolina Journal of Anthropology.

Cas̆ Morav. Mus. Brn̆e, Sci. Nat.   AS142.B82
    C̆asopis Moravského Musea v Brn̆e Acta Musei Moraviae
       V̆edy Pr̆írodni - Scientiae Naturales.

Cas̆. Morav. Mus. Brn̆e, Sci. Social.   AS142.B82
    C̆asopis Moravského Musea v Brn̆e Acta Musei Moraviae
       V̆edy Spolec̆enske - Scientiae Sociales
       Brno: Moravske Museum Ed.

Cave Notes   GB601.A1C3
    Published by Cave Research Associates.

Cave Sci.   not seen

Caves and Karst   GB601.A1C3
    formerly Cave Notes. Name changed with 9:1.
       Publ. by Cave Research Associates, 3842 Brookdale
       Blvd., Castro Valley, Calif. 94546.

Chatterbox   AP201.C35
    Boston: Estes.

Chesopiean   NST.113
    The Chesopiean. A Journal of Atlantic Coast Archeology.

China Pictorial   fDS777.55.C514
    Peking.

"China Reconstructs"   not seen
    (China Welfare Institute)
    Peking.

Cimbebasia   QH1.C491
    Swa-Navorsig-Swa-Research-Swa-Forschong.
    South West Africa, Windhoek.

Coll. Pap. on the Quat.   not seen
    Collected Papers on the Quaternary (Chinese)

Collectanea Acta Geol. Lithuanica.   QE1.L45
    Collectanea Acta Geologica Lithuanica. Vilnius.
    (Festschrift).

Colloq. Internat. Cent. Nation. Recherch. Sci.   QE841.P75
    Colloques Internationaux du Centre National de la Recherche
    Scientifique.
    Paris, 6-11 June 1966. (Problemes Actuels de Paléontologie.
    Évolution des Vertébrés.) No. 163.

Com. Geol., Bucuresti   not seen
    Comunicari de Geologie, Bucuresti.

Com. Invest. Cien., La Plata   not seen
    Comisión de Investigación Científica.
    La Plata, Argentina.

Com. Mus. Argent. Cien. Nat., Geol.   QE1.B817.C6
    Comunicaciones, Museo Argentino de Ciencias Naturales
    "Bernardino Rivadavia,"
    Buenos Aires. Ser. Cien. Geol.

Compar. Biochem. Physiol.   U.C., Davis,
    Comparative Biochemistry and Physiology.   Riverside
    New York: Pergamon Press

Congr. Assoc. Géol. Carpato-Balkanique   QE267.C33K3
    Association Géologique Carpato-Balkanique Congrès
    5th, Bucuresti, 1961
    6th, Varşovia

39th Congr., ANZAAS   Q93.A8
    Australian and New Zealand Association for the Advancement
    of Science, 39th Congress
    Melbourne, Australia, 1967.

Constructor Mag.   not seen
    Constructor Magazine.

Contrib. Mus. Great Plains   F591.L394.C6
    Contribution of the Museum of the Great Plains.
    Great Plains Historical Association,
    Lawton, Oklahoma.

Cooperazione.   Sep.
    Cooperazione. Italy.

Coronet   not seen

COWA Surv. and Bibliog.   NST366
    COWA Surveys and Bibliographies.
    Published by Council for Old World Archaeology.
    Cambridge, Massachusetts.

Cuad. Inst. Hist., Ser. Hist.   QE508.N63
    Cuadernos del Instituto de Historia.
      Serie Histórica.
    Universidad Nacional Autonomo de México.
    México.

Darbai Lietuvos TSR, Ser. A   AS262.L45
    Lietuvos TSR Mokslų Akademija.
    Darbai. Serija A.

Darbai Lietuvos TSR, Ser. B   Q60.L5
    Lietuvos TSR Mokslų Akademijos.
    Darbai. Serija B. Vilnius.

Dǎri de seamǎ Comit. Inst. Geol.   QE287.R86
    Dǎri de seamǎ ale şedinţelor Comitetul Geologic Institutul
      Geologic. Republica Popularǎ Rominǎ.
    Bucureşti.

Deutsch. Jägerzeitung   not seen
    Melsungen.

Deutsch. Röntgenkongress, Baden-Baden   not seen
    Deutscher Röntgenkongress, Baden-Baden

Die Heimat. Heimatkalender Beil.   not seen
    "Rieder Volksz."
      Ried i. I.

Die Höhle   Cave Res.
    Zeitschrift für Karst- und Höhlenkunde.   Assoc. Lib.
    Wien.

Discovery, Yale   QH1.D5
    Peabody Museum, Yale University

Doc. Lab. Géol. Fac. Sci. Lyon   Period.
   Lyons (City). Université Faculté des sciences. Laboratoire
   de Géologie. Documents.

Doklady Akad. Nauk SSSR   AS262.A442
   Doklady Akademii Nauk SSSR
   formerly listed as C. R. Acad. Sci. URSS

Doklady Akad. Nauk Tadzhik. SSR   Q60.A57
   Doklady Akademiia Nauk Tadzhikskoi' SSR.
   Dushanbe; AN Tadzh. SSR Press.

Doklady Akad. Nauk Uzb. SSR   Q60.A65
   Doklady Akademiia Nauk Uzbekshoi SSR.

Drugi Jug. Speleol. Kongr., Split i Dal. zagora   Cave Res.
   Drugi Jugoslavenski Speleoloski Kongress, Split i Dalmatinska   Assoc. Lib.
   zagora.
   Zagreb, 1958.

"Du und Dein Werk" NR.   not seen
   Halle/s.

Earth Sci. Jour.   QE1.E195
   Earth Science Journal.
      The Waikato Geological Society. New Zealand.

Earth-Sci. Rev.   QE1.E2
   Earth-Science Reviews.
      International Magazine for Geo-Scientists.
      Amsterdam, London, New York. Elsevier Publishing Co.

El Comercio, Lima   not seen

El Comercio, Quito   not seen

El Libro y el Pueblo   F1225.M19L4
   Mexico.

El Minero Mexicano   not seen

Emilia Preromana   FILM.3954.DG
   Instituto Ferrarese di Paleontologia Umana.
      Modena, Italy.

Ergebn. Limnologie   QH96.E6
   Ergebnisse der Limnologie. Archiv für Hydrobiologie.
      Stuttgart.

Essex Nat.   not seen
   The Essex Naturalist.
      In J. B. Delair's personal collection.

Eugen. Rev.   HQ750.A1E9
   Eugenics Review. Eugenics education society, London.

Exc. Arqueol. en España   CC75.S83
    Excavaciones Arquelógicas en España.
    10 Servicio Nacional de Excavaciones Arqueológicas.
    Madrid.

Exkursionsführer zur Herbsttagung Geol. Ges. Deutsch.   not seen
    Demokratischen Rep., Exkursion B3, B5
    Exkursionsführer zur Herbsttagung der Geologischer Gesellschaft
    in der Deutschen Demokratischen Republik, Berlin.
    Exkursion B3 (Das Pleistozän im sächsich-thüringischen Raum).
    Berlin: Barendruck.

Ferienkurs fur schweizer Mittelschullehrer   not seen
    Zurich: Schulthess

Festschr. Deutsch. Biol. Hamburg   not seen
    Stuttgart: Wiss. Verlagsges.

Fieldiana: Zool. Mem.   QL3.C5
    Fieldiana: Zoology Memoirs.
    Published by Chicago Natural History Museum.

Folia Morphol.   QL801.C4
    Folia Morphologica. Czechoslovak Academy of Sciences.
    Previously called Ceskoslovenská Morfologie.

Fortschr. Evolutionforsch.   QH366.A1F66
    Fortschritte der Evolutionsforschung
    Stuttgart: Fischer Verl.

Fossilia   QE701.F66
    Revista de la Cátedra de Paleontologia de la Universidad
    Barcelona

Found. News   not seen
    Foundation News. Wellcome Foundation Ltd.

Fundber. Hessen   not seen
    Fundberichte aus Hessen.

Genetica   QH301.G4
    Nederlands Tijdschrift voor Erfelijkheids - en Afstammingsleer.
    Martinus Nijhoff/'s-Gravenhage.

Geobios   QE701.G35
    Paléontologie Stratigraphie Paléoécologie
        Edité par le Département des Sciences de la Terre,
        Faculté des Sciences, Université de Lyon.
        Supercedes "Travaux des Lab. de Géol. de Lyon"

Geochronicle   QC770.C4565
    The Geochronicle. Published by Geochron Laboratories, Inc.
      24 Blackstone St., Cambridge, Mass.

Geog. Helvetica   G1.G127
    Geographica Helvetica

Geokhimiĭa   QE515.A1G45
    Geokhimiĭa, Akademiĭa Nauk SSSR
      Moscow: Akad. Nauk SSSR Press.

Geol. i Geof.   QE1.G57427
    Geologiia i Geofizika
      Akademiia Nauk SSSR, Sibirskoe otdelenie
      Novosibirsk: "Nauka" Press

Geol. Markmed   Amer. Mus.
    Geologilised Markmed (Loodusuurijate selts)   Nat. Hist.
      Tallinn. Eesti NSV Teaduste Akademia.

Geol. News   not seen
    Geological News, London.

Geol. of Norfolk   not seen
    The Geology of Norfolk, a collection of papers assembled by
      the Paramoudra Club to mark its tenth anniversary.
      Norwich.

Geol. Prace, Bratislava   QE267.C8A223
    Geologicke prace, Ustredny ustav geologicky, redakcia
      Bratislava.

Geol. Soc. Amer., Cordilleran Sect., Pal. Soc., Pac. Coast   Earth Science
    Sect., Prog. 61st Ann. Meeting   Library
      The Geological Society of America, Inc. Cordilleran Section,
      The Palentological Society Pacific Coast Section, Program
      61st Annual Meeting, Fresno State College, April 15-17, 1965.

Geol. Surv. Canada Pap.   QE185.A37
    Canada. Geological Survey. Papers.

Geologica et Palaeontologica   QE1.G379
    Marburg: N. G. Elwert Verlag

Geologie   QE1.G5734
    Zeitschrift für das Gesamtgebiet der Geologie und Mineralogie
      sowie der angewandten Geophysik. Geologischen Wissen-
      schaften. Mit Beiheften. Berlin.

Geologie, Beiheft   QE1.G5734
    Zeitschrift für das Gesamtgebiet der Geologie und Mineralogie
      sowie der angewandten Geophysik.
      Beiheften. Berlin.

Geologist.   Earth Science
    The Geologist. Newsletter of the Geological Society of America. Library

Gerfaut   QL671.G4
    Le Gerfaut. Revue Beige d'Ornithologie.

Giorn. geol.   Cal Acad. Sci.
    Giornale di geologia
      (Bologna. R. Museo geologico)

Glas Acad. Serbe Sci., Classe Sci. Math. Nat.   AS346.S75
    Glas.
      Académie Serbe des Sciences. Class des Sciences Mathématiques
      et Naturelles.
      Srpska Akademija Nauka i Umetnosti, Belgrad.

Glasnik Zemaljskog Muz. u Sarajevu, Arheol.   DB231.S27
    Glasnik Zemaljskog Muzeja u Sarajevu, Arheologija.
    Sarajevo.

Godishnik Sof. Univers., Geol.-Geogr. Fak.   Period.
    Godishnik na Sofiiskiĭa Universitet Geologo-Geografski
    Fakultet, Kniga 1 - Geologiĭa.
    Sofia: "Nauka i Izkustvo" Press.

Golden Mag.   not seen
    The Golden Magazine for Boys and Girls.
    Publ. monthly by Golden Press, Poughkeepsie, N.Y.

Great Plains Jour.   E78.W5G73
    Great Plains Journal.
      Great Plains Historical Association.
      Lawton, Oklahoma.

Great Plains Newsletter   NST108
    Great Plains Newsletter.

Gregorianum   BX804.G7
    Pontificia Università Gregoriana
    Rome

Guidebk., 7th Inqua Congr.   QE1.I74
    Guidebooks for the 7th Inqua Congress, Boulder, Colo. 1965

Guidebk., New Mexico Geol. Soc., 13th Field Confr.   QE1.N446
    Guidebook of the Mogollon Rim Region, east-central Arizona.
    13th Field Conference, Oct. 18-20, 1962.

Guidebk., New Mexico Geol. Soc., 14th Field Confer.   QE1.N446
    Guidebook of the Socorro region, New Mexico. 14th Field
    Conference, Oct. 4-6, 1963.

Guidebk., New Mexico Geol. Soc., 15th Field Confer.   QE1.N446
    Guidebook of the Ruidoso Country. 15th Field Conference,
    Oct. 16-18, 1964.

Guidebk., New Mexico Geol. Soc., 16th Field Confer.   QE1.N446
    Guidebook of Southwestern New Mexico II. 16th Field
    Conference, Oct. 15-17, 1965.

Guidebk. Wyo. Geol. Assoc.   QE181.W8F5
    Wyoming Geological Association, Guidebook. Nineteenth Field
    Conference. 1965.

Gumma Daigaku Kiyo, Shizenkagakuhen.   not seen

Harvard Alumni Bull.   LD2180.H2

Heidenheimer Heimatbuch   not seen

Hercynia.   Q3.H45
    Martin-Luther-Universität.
    Leipzig. New ser.

Hespéris Tamuda   Period.
    Université Mohammed V.
    Faculté des Lettres et des Sciences Humaines.
    Rabat.

Hist. Today   AQ.H5
    History Today.
    London.

Höhlenkundliche Mitt.   not seen
    Höhlenkundliche Mitteilungen. Landesverein für Höhlenkunde
    in Wien und Niederösterreich.

Homenaje al profesor Cayetano de Mergelina   DP4.M87
    Junta de Gobierno de la Universidad [de Murcia].
    Murcia [Valencia] : Tipografía Moderna.

Humanitas   GN1.H85
    Boletin Ecuatoriano de Antropologia.

Hydrobiol.   QH301.H9
    Hydrobiologia.
        Acta Hydrobiologica, Hydrographica et Protistologica.
        Den Haag

Idaho Yesterdays   F741.I35

Ill. Biol. Monog.   QL1.I45
    Illinois Biological Monographs.
        University of Illinois. Urbana.

Ill. State Mus. Rept. Invest.   Amer. Mus.
    Illinois State Museum Report of Investigations.   Nat Hist.

Image   not seen
    Image. Published by Manitoba Hydro Commission.

Indian Min.   TN4.I55
   Indian Minerals
     India. Geological Survey. Mineral Information Bureau.

Inform. Circ., Idaho Bur. Mines, Geol.   TN24.I2A35

Informatsionnyi Sbornik   QE1.L395
   Leningrad (City) Vsesoiuznyi geologicheskii institut
   Informatsionnyi sbornik.

Inst. Ethiopien d'Archéol.   not seen
   Institut Ethiopien d'Archéologie. Cahiers. Addis-Ababa.

Inst. Geol. Nac. Colombia   QE239.A425
   Republica de Colombia. Ministerio de Minas y Petroless.
   Instituto Geologico Nacional Buletin Geologico.

Inst. Panamer. Geog. Hist., Plan Piloto del Ecuador, Sec. Antrop.   F3721.P36
   Instituto Panamericano de Geografia e Historia. Plan Piloto del
   Ecuador. Seccion de Antropologia.
   Mexico, D. F.

Interamer.   NST89
   The Interamerican.

7-th Internat. Congr. Anthrop. Ethnol. sci., Moscow, 1964   GN3.C75
   International Congress of anthropological and ethnological
   sciences Proceedings.
   Moscow; "Nauka" Press.

7th Internat. Congr., Internat. Assoc. Quat. Res., Abs.   QE696.A1I53
   VII International Congress, International Association for
   Quarternary Research.
   Abstracts. Boulder, Colo. 1965.

23rd Internat. Geol. Congr., Proc.   QE1.I6
   23rd International Geological Congress, Proceedings and
   Abstracts.
   Czechoslovakia, 1968
   Section 10, Tertiary/Quaternary Boundary.

Internat. Jour. Spel.   Cave Res.
   International Journal of Speleology.   Assoc. Lib.
     Began with v. 1:1-2, Dec. 1964

3 Internat. Kongress Spel.   Cave Res.
   Dritter Internationaler Kongress fur Speläologie.   Assoc. Lib.
   Wien.

Int. Res. Rept., Geochron. Lab., Univ. Ariz.   QE1.A75I5
   Interim Research Reports, Geochronology Laboratories,
   University of Arizona, Tucson.

Inventaria Archaeol. Africana   NST80
   Inventaria Archaeologica Africana. Panafrican Congress on Prehistory and Quaternary Studies. Musée Royal de l'Afrique Centrale.

Tervuren, Belgium.
General editor Jacques Nenquin.

Israel Jour. Zool.   QL1.I8
   Israel Journal of Zoology. Replaces Bull. Res. Council Israel,
   Sect. B, Zool.

Issled. Archeol. SSSR   DK30.L45
   Issledovaniia po Arkheologii SSSR. Studies in Archaeology
   presented to Professor M. I. Artamonov. Leningrad, 1961.

Istoriia Mater. Kul't. Uzbekistana   DK945.A5
   Istoriia Material'noĭ Kul'tury Uzbekistana.
   Institut Istorii i Arkheologii.
   Akademiia Nauk Uzbekskoĭ SSR
   Tashkent: Akad. Nauk Uzbek. SSR Press.

Izdanja Speleol. drustva Hrvatske, Zagreb.   not seen

Izv. Akad. Nauk Armian. SSR.   QE1.A345
   Nauki o zemle.

Izv. Akad. Nauk Azerb. SSR, Ser. Geol.-Geogr. Nauk. Seriia Nauk   QE1.A3457
   o Zemle. (Formerly: Izv. Akad. Nauk Azerbaĭdzhan. SSR,
   Ser. Geol.-Geogr. Sci.)
   Izvestiia Akademii Nauk Azerbaĭdzhanskoĭ SSR, Seriia
   Geologo-Geograficheskikh Nauk.

Izv. Akad. Nauk Kazakh. SSR, Ser. Geol.   QE1.A347
   Izvestiia Akademii Nauk Kazakhskoĭ SSR, Seriia Geologicheskaia.
   Alma-Ata; Akad. Nauk. Kaz. SSR Press.

Izv. Akad. Nauk Kazakh. SSR Seriia Obshch. Nauk   Period.
   Izvestiia Akademii Nauk Kazakhskoĭ SSR, Seriia Obshehestvennykh
   Nauk. Supercedes Seriia Istoricheskikh Arkheologicheskikh i
   Etnograficheskikh Nauk.
   Alma-Ata.

Izv. Akad. Nauk Kirgiz. SSR   Period.
   Izvestiia Akademii Nauk Kirgizskoĭ SSR, Frunze

Izv. Akad. Nauk Moldav. SSR, Ser. Biol. i Khim. Nauk   AS262.A3968
   Izvestiia Akademii Nauk Moldavskoĭ SSR, seriia Biologicheskikh
   i Khimicheskikh Nauk
   =Buletinul Akademieĭ de Shtiintse a RSS Moldovenesht'
   Kishinev; "Kartia Moldoveniaske" Press. Formerly Izvestiia
   Moldavskogo Filiala Akad. Nauk SSSR.

Izv. Akad. Nauk SSSR, ser. biol.   QH301.A374
   Izvestiia Akademii Nauk SSSR, seriia biologicheskaia.
   Moscow: "Nauka" Press, 6 issues yearly.

Izv. Akad. Nauk. SSSR, ser. geol.   QE1.A44
   Formerly listed as:
   Izv. Akad. Sci. USSR

Izv. Akad. Nauk Tadzhik. SSR Otd. Estestv. Nauk   Q60.573
   Izvestiia Akademiia nauk Tadzhikskoĭ SSR. Otdelenie estestvennykh
   nauk.

Izv. Akad. Nauk Tadzhik. SSR, otd. obshch. nauk.   Period.
   Izvestiia Akademii Nauk Tadzhikskoĭ SSR, otdelenie
   obshchestvennykh nauk
   Dushanbe: "Donish" Press.

Izv. Akad. Nauk Uz. SSR, ser. obshch. nauk   Period.
   Izvestiia Akademii Nauk Uzbekskoĭ SSR, seriia obshchestvennykh
   nauk.
   Tashkent.

Izv. Altaĭsk. otd. Geogr. Obshch. SSSR   not seen
   Izvestiia Altaĭskogo otdeleniia
   Geograficheskogo Obshchestva SSSR

Izv. Geogr. Obshch.   G23.R8
   Izvestiia Geograficheskoe obshchestvo SSSR
   Izvestiia Vsesoiuznogo Geograficheskogo Obshchestva
   Leningrad: Ak. Nauk SSSR Press

Izv. Kazan. Fil. AN SSSR, Ser. Geol.   QE1.A443
   Izvestiia Kazanskogo Filiala Akademii Nauk SSSR, Seriia
   geologicheskikh nauk
   Kazan'

Izv. Kiriz. Filiala Vses. Geogr. Obsh.   Period.
   Izvestiia Kirgizskogo filiala Vsesoiuznogo geograficheskogo
   obshchestva SSSR

Izv. Komi Fil. Vses. Geogr. Obshch.   Period.
   Izvestiia Komi Filiala Vsesoiuznogo Geograficheskogo Obshchestva
   Syktyvkar: Komi Press.

Izv. na Arkheol. Inst.   DR51.B85
   Izvestiia na Arkheologicheskiia Institut.
   Bulgaria - B"lgarska Akademiia na Naukite.

Izv. Rostovskogo Muz. Kraevedeniia   not seen
   Izvestia Rostovskogo Muzeia Kraevedeniia
   Rostov-on-Don (City)

Izv. Sib. Otd. Akad. Nauk SSSR, Ser. Obshch. Nauk   Period.
   Izvestiia Sibirskogo Otdeleniia Akademii Nauk SSSR, Seriia
   Obshchestvennykh Nauk.
   Novosibirsk; Sib. Otd. Ak. Nauk SSSR Press.

Izv. Vost.-Sib. Otd. Geogr. Obshch. SSSR   Period.
   Izvestiia Vostochno - Sibirskogo Otdela Geograficheskogo
   Obshchestva SSSR
   Irkutsk.

Izv. Vyssh. Uchebn. Zaved. Geol. i Razv.   QE1.I98
    Izvestiia Vysshikh Uchebnykh Zavedeniĭ, Geologiia i Razvedka
      Moscow: Mosk. Geologorazv. Inst. Press

Izvestiia Gosud. Akad. Ist. Mater. Kult. N.Y. Marra.   GN700.G6
    Izvestiia Gosudarstvennoĭ Akademii Istorii Material'noi Kul'tury
    imeni N.Y. Marra.
    Leningrad.

Jahrb. Verein. "Freunde der Universität Mainz"   not seen
    Jahrbuch der Vereinigung "Freunde der Universität Mainz"
    Mainz: Will und Rothe KG Verlag.

Jahresb. Bayer. Bodendenkmalpflege   not seen
    Jahresbericht der Bayerischen Bodendenkmalpflege
    München.

[?Jahresb.] Hist. Mus. Schloss. Thun   DQ30.T5
    Thun, Switzerland (Castle)
    Historisches Museum.
    [?Jahresbericht.]

James Arthur Lecture on the Evol. of the Human Brain, Amer.   QP376.A1J25
Mus. Nat. Hist.
    James Arthur Lecture on the Evolution of the Human Brain.
    American Museum of Natural History.
    New York.

Jap. Periodicals Index   Period.
    Japanese Periodicals Index
    Natural Sciences. Part 1: Science and Technology.
    Natural Diet Library, Tokyo.

J. Afr. Hist.   DT1.J6
    The Journal of African History.
    Edited by R. A. Oliver and J. D. Fage.
    Cambridge Univ. Press.

Jour. Animal Ecol.   QL750.J56
    Journal of Animal Ecology. Published by the British Ecological
    Society. London.
    British Ecological Society Jubilee Symposium, London, March,
    1963. Edited by A. Macfadyen and P. J. Newbould. A supple-
    ment to Journal of Ecology Vol. 52, and Journal of Animal
    Ecology Vol. 33.

Jour. Animal Morph. Physiol.   QL801.J54
    The Journal of Animal Morphology and Physiology.
    M. S. University, Dept. of Zoology.
    Baroda, India.

Jour. Anthrop. Soc. S. Australia   fGN2A67
    Journal of the Anthropological Society of South Australia.

Jour. Anthrop. Soc. Vidyodaya Univ.   not seen
    Journal of the Anthropological Society of Vidyodaya
       University.

Jour. Archaeol. Soc. Maryland   NST265
    Journal of the Archaeological Society of Maryland.

Jour. Arizona Acad. Sci.   Period.
    Journal of the Arizona Academy of Science.

Jour. Barbados Mus. Hist. Soc.   F2041.A1B35
    The Journal of the Barbados Museum and Historical Society.

Jour. Dental Res.   RK1.J6
    Journal of Dental Research.
       New York.

Jour. Fisheries Res. Board, Canada   QH1.C245
    Fisheries Research Board of Canada. Journal.

Jour. Inst. Polytech., Osaka City Univ., Geosci.   QE1.O8
    Journal of the Institute of Polytechniks, Osaka City University.
       Series G. Geoscience.

Jour. Minn. Acad. Sci.   Q181.A1M5
    Journal of the Minnesota Academy of Science.

Jour. Nat. Hist., London   QH1.J615
    Journal of Natural History, London.
       Supercedes Ann. Mag. Nat. Hist., Jan. 1967

Jour. Nation. Med. Assoc.   R15.N34

Jour. Res. Lepidoptera   QL541.J65
    Journal of Research on the Lepidoptera.
       Arcadia, California.

Jour. Roy. Microsc. Soc.   QH201.R63
    Journal of the Royal Microscopial Society.
       London.

Jour. Ultrastruct. Res.   QH573.J65
    Journal of Ultrastructure Research.
       N.Y. and London: Academic Press.

Jour. Zool., London   QL1.Z62
    Journal of Zoology. Proceedings of the Zoological Society of
       London. Name changed with vol. 146, 1965.

Karszt- és Barlangkutatás   Cave Res.
    A Magyar Karszt- és Barlangkutató Társulat Évkönyve   Assoc. Lib.
       (Official Organ of the Hungarian Speleological Society)
       Budapest

Kentucky Univ., Studies in Anthrop.   GN4.K4S8
   Kentucky University. Studies in Anthropology.
   University of Kentucky Press, Lexington.

Kexue tongbao   U.C.L.A.
   Other title: K'o Hsueh T'ung Pao
   Added Titles: Nauchnyĭ Vestnik; Scientia
   Table of contents: Russian and English.
   Peking.

Kirtlandia   QH1.K3456
   The Cleveland Museum of Natural History. Ohio, Cleveland.

Kleine Schrift. Karst- und Hohlenkunde   Cave Res.
   Kleine Schriften zur Karst- und Höhlenkunde.   Assoc. Lib.
   Verband der Deutschen Höhlen- und Karstforscher e. V.
   München.

Kodai Bunka   not seen

KoKogaku Techo   not seen

Kölnische Rundschau   not seen
   Köln.

Kolyma   not seen

Korrespondenzblatt Gesamt ver. Deutch. Ges.- und Altertumsver. DD2.G3
   Korrespondenzblatt des Gesamtvereins der Deutchen Geschichts-
   und Altertumsvereine.
   [Blätter fur Deutsche Landesgesichte]

"Kosmos" (Poland)   Q4.K6
   "Kosmos" Polskie Towarzystwo Przyrodnikov imienia Kopernika
   Seria A: Biologia
   Seria B: Przyroda Nieozywioka
   Warsaw.

Kraevedcheskii Sborn.   DK771.B8G46
   Kraevedcheskii Sbornik.
   Geograficheskoe obshchestvo SSSR.
   Buriatskiĭ filial.

Kraevedch. zapiski, Magadan   not seen
   Kraevedcheskie zapiski. Oblastnoĭ Kraevedcheskiĭ muzeĭ.
   Upravlenie Kul'tury Magadanskogo oblispolkoma.
   Magadan.

Kraglieviana   not seen
   Montevideo.

Kratk. Soobshch. BKNII SO AN SSSR   Period.
   Kratkie Soobshcheniia Buriatskogo Kompleksnogo Nauchno-
   Issledovatel'skogo Instituta
   Sibirskoe Otdelenie Akademii Nauk SSSR
   Ulan-Ude.

Lapidary Jour.   not seen
   The Lapidary Journal.

La Ric. Sci., Parte I: Riv.   Q4.R512
   Italy. Consiglio nazionale delle ricerche.
      La Ricerca Scientifica. Parte I: Rivista.

Las Cien. Asoc. Espan. Prog. Cien.   not seen

Latv. PSR Zināt. Akad. Vēstis   AS262.L27
   Latvijas PSR Zinātņu Akadēmijas Vēstis.
      Rigā.

Lauenburgische Heimat.   not seen
   Ratzeburg.

Ledetråd ved Folkelig Universitetsundervisning.   Cat. by author

Lethaia   QE701.L4
   An International journal of Palaeontology and stratigraphy.
      Oslo, Norway.

Listener.   Period.
   The Listener and BBC Television Review.

London Jour. Arts., Sci.   T1.N4
   See: Newton's London Journal of Arts and Sciences.

Lucrarile Inst. Spel. "Emil Racovita," Bucuresti   Cave Res.
   Lucrarile Institutului de Speleologie "Emil Racovita"   Assoc. Lib.
      Bucuresti.

Lynx   not seen
   Czechoslovakia

Mainzer Zeit.   DD901.M2M27
   Mainzer Zeitschrift
      Verlag des Mainzer Altertumsvereins.
      Mainz.

Man in Time and Space   not seen
   Człowiek w Czasie i Przestrzeni.
      Published quarterly by Polish Anthropological Society.
      Warszawa.

Man, Jour. Roy. Anthrop. Inst.   GN1.M3
   Man, the Journal of the Royal Anthropological Institute.
      (Supercedes Jour. Roy. Anthrop. Inst. and Man)

Manitoba Archaeol. Newsletter   NST102
   Manitoba Archaeological Newsletter.
      Manitoba Archaeological Society, Winnipeg, Manitoba.

Manual Austral. Inst. Aboriginal Studies   GN665.A1A85.M2
    Australian Institute of Aboriginal Studies Manual.
        Canberra.

Mat. i Prace Antrop.   GN4.M3
    Materiały i Prace Antropologiczne.
        Polskie Towarzystwo Antropologiczne.

Materialy Arkh. Evrop. Sev.-Vost.   Period.
    Materialy po Arkheologii Evropeiskogo Severo-Vostoka.
        Komi Filial Akademii Nauk SSSR.
        Komi Respublikanskiĭ Kraevedcheskiĭ Muzeĭ.
        Syktyvkar: Komi Book. Publ.

Materialy Geol. Inst. (VSEGEI)   QE1.L384
    Materialy Vsesoĭuznogo Nauchno-Issledovalel'skogo Geologicheskogo
        Instituta (VSEGEI); Ministerstvo Geologii i Okhrany Nedr
        SSSR.
        Leningrad.
        New Series: Quaternary Geology, Mineral Resources, etc.

Materialy Geol. Zap. Sibiri   QE315.M33
    Materialy po Geologii Zapadnoi Sibiri Zapadno-Sibirskoe
        Geologicheskoe Upravlenie
        Moscow: Gosgeoltekhizdat Press.

Materialy Ist. Sibiri, Drevn. Sibir.   DK757.A1D74
    Materialy po Istorii Sibiri, Drevniaia Sibir'.
        Akademiia Nauk SSSR, Sibirskoe Otdelenie, Novosibirsk.

MCZ Newsletter   not seen
    Museum of Comparative Zoology Newsletter, Harvard University.

Med. World News   Lane Med. Lib.
    Medical World News. The Newsmagazine of Medicine.

Meded. Geol. Sticht.   QE273.A1735
    Mededelingen van de Geologische Stichting. (Afd. Geologische
        Dienst te Haarlem en Afd. Geologische Bureao te Heerlen)
        Nieuwe serie.

Medical Opinion and Review   U.C. Med. Lib.

Mediz. Grundlagenforsch.   not seen
    Medizinische Grundlagenforschung
        Stuttgart.

Mem. Acc. Patav. SS. LL. AA., Cl. Sci., Math., Nat. Padova   AS222.A54

Mem. Amer. Anthrop. Assoc.   GN2.A22
    American Anthropological Association.
        Memoir.

Mém. Bur. Rech. Géol. Min.   QE1.F712
    Mémoires du Bureau de Recherches Géologiques et Minières.
        Paris.

Mém. Cent. Recherch. Anthrop., Préhist., Ethnog., Algiers   DT553.A4.H89
    Mémoires du Centre de Recherches Anthropologiques, Préhis-
       toriques et Ethnographiques.
       Algiers.

Mem. Dept. Archaeol. Pakistan   N7307.P4M3
    Memoirs of the Department of Archaeology (and Museums)
       Pakistan.

Mem. Geol. Soc. India   QE1.G475.M4
    Memoirs Geological Society of India.
       Bangalore: B. B. D. Power Press.

Mém. Inst. Franç. Afr. Noire   Doc. & Biol.
    Institut Francais d'Afrique Noire. Mémoires.

Mem. Kyushu Univ., Ser. D. Geol.   QE1.F8
    Kyushu University, Faculty of Science. Ser. D, Geology.
       Memoirs.
       Fukucka, Japan.

Mem. Mus. Civ. Stor. Nat., Verona   Univ. Florida
    Memorie del Museo Civico di Storia Naturale, Verona.

Mém. Mus. Nation. Hist. Nat., Paris, n.s. A., Zool.   QL1.P35
    Paris. Museum National d'Histoire Naturelle. Mémoires.
       Nouvelle Série. Série A. Zoologie.

Mem. Nasion. Mus. Bloemfontein.   DT.751.B56
    Nasionale Museum, Bloemfontein. Memoir.

Mem. R. Acad. Cien. Art. Barcelona   AS302.A405
    Memorias de la Real Academia de Ciencias y Artes de
       Barcelona.

Mem. S. Calif. Acad. Sci.   Q11.S62
    Memoirs Southern California Academy of Science.

Mém. Serv. Géol. Portugal   fQE284.A35
    Mémoires des Services Géologiques du Portugal.
       Mémoire no. 1 (nouvelle série)
       Lisbon, 1953

Mem. Soc. Amer. Archaeol.   E51.S75
    Memoirs of the Society of American Archaeology.
       (Issued as "Part II" of American Antiquity.)

Mém. Soc. Archéol. Hist. Charente   DC611.C51S6
    Mémoires de la Société Archéologique et Historique de la Charente.
       Angoulême.

Mém. Soc. Belge Géol. Pal. Hydrol.   QE1.S5212
    Mémoires de la Société Belge de Géologie, de Paléontologie et
       d'Hydrologie.
       Brussels.
       Serie in -8°.

Mem. Tokyo Archaeol. Soc.   not seen
    Tokyo Archaeological Society.
        Memoirs.

Mem. y Com., Sec. Geomorf.   not seen
    Memórias y Comunicaciones Instituto Jaime Almera.
        Investigaciones Geológicas, Sección Geomorfologia.
        Barcelona.

Mercian Geologist   U.C.L.A.
    (East Midlands Geological Society.)
        Nottingham.

Meyniana   QE23.M48
    Meyniana. Veröffentlichungen aus dem Geologischen Institut
    der Universität Kiel.

Min. Inform. Serv.   not seen
    Mineral Information Service.

Minn. Archaeol.   F608.M55
    The Minnesota Archaeologist.

Misc. Pap., Texas Archaeol. Salvage Project.   F388.A1T38
    Austin: Texas Archaeological Salvage Project, Miscellaneous
        Papers.

Misc. Publ. Mus. Zool. Univ. Mich.   QL1.M48
    Miscellaneous Publications of the Museum of Zoology.
        University of Michigan.

Misc. Rept. Res. Inst. Nation. Res.   7004.3327
    Miscellaneous Reports of the Research Institute for National
        Resources, Tokyo.
        (shigan Kagaku Kenkyusho Iho)

Missouri Archaeol.   F468.M55
    The Missouri Archaeologist.

Mitt. Geol. Inst. T. H. Hanover   not seen
    Mitteilungen, Geologisches Institut, Technische Hochschule,
        Hanover.

Mitt. Österreich. Arbeitsgemeinschaft Ur- und Frühgesch.   not seen
    Mitteilungen der Österreichischen Arbeitsgemeinschaft für
        Ur- und Frühgeschichte. Wien.

Mitt. U. A. G. Wien   not seen

Mitt. Verband Deutschen Höhlen- und Karstforscher, München   Cave Res.
    Verband der Deutschen Höhlen- und Karstforscher, München.   Assoc. Lib.
        Mitteilungen.

Moksliniai Pranešimai, Geol.-Geogr.   QE1.L44
    Lietuvos TSR Mokslų Akademija Geologijos ir Geografijos
        Institutas

Monatsschrift Baden-Württemberg	not seen

Monog. de Arte Rupestre. Arte Levantino.
  Monographías de Arte Rupestre. Arte Levantino.
    Inst. Prehist. Arqueol. Diputación Prov. Barcelona y
    Wenner-Gren Fund. Anthrop. Res. (n.y.), Barcelona
	not seen

Monog. Sch. Amer. Res., Santa Fe
  Santa Fe, New Mexico.
    School of American Research. Monograph.
	E51.S24

Monogr. Istanbul Üniv. Fen Fak.
  Istanbul Üniversitesi Fen Fakültesi.
    Monografileri.
	not seen

Mongol orny gazarzuin assudluud (Mongolia)	not seen

Münch. Univers.
  Münchener Universitätsreden
    München: Max Hueber Verlag.
	Earth Science
	Library

Munera Archaeol. Iosepho Kostrzewski
  Munera Archaeologica Iosepho
    Kostrzewski quinquagesinium annum optimarum artium
    studiis deditum peragenti ab amicis collegis descipulis oblata
    Poznán, 1963, 427 pp.
	GN845.P7P67

Munibe
  Suplemento de ciencias naturales del Boletín de la Real sociedad
    vascongada de los amigos del país.
    San Sebastián.
	QH7.M8

Mus. Notes, Texas Mem. Mus. Museum Notes. A publication of the Texas Memorial Museum.	Stanford

Museologist
  The Museologist: a Quarterly for the Museum Profession.
    Official publication. Northeast Conference of Museum,
    A. A. M. Rochester, N.Y.
	NST25

NSS News NSS News. National Speleological Society.	GB601.N2
N. Y. State Conservationist	HC107.N7A734
N. Y. Times Mag. The New York Times Magazine.	AQ.N732
Nachrichtenblatt fur Deutschen Vorzeit Leipzig	GN700.N3

Naše Jame
  Ljubljana: Društvo za Raziskovanje
    Jam Slovenije Press.
	x-GB608.67
	N2345

Nashville Speleonews   not seen

Nation. Mus. Canada, Bull., Anthrop. Ser.   GN4.C33
    National Museum of Canada. Bulletin. Anthropological Series.

Nation. Observer   Newspaper room

Nationzeitung, Basel   not seen

Natur und Technik   not seen

Natura (Biolog.)   QH301.N374
    Rumanian.

Naturalistes Belges   Amer. Mus.
    Bulletin mensuel. Brussels   Nat. Hist.

Naturens Verden   AMNH.5.06
                                                                      (48.9)A

Naturw. Wochenschrift   Q3.N55
    Naturwissenschaftliche
    Wochenschrift.
    Jena.

Naturwiss. und Med.   not seen
    Naturwissenschaft und Medizin.

Nauchn. Dokl. Vyssh. Shkoly, Biol. Nauki   QH301.N376
    Ministerstvo Vysshago i Srednego Spetsial'nogo obrazovaniia SSSR.
    Nauchnye Doklady Vysshei Shkoly, Biologicheskie Nauki (Table
    of contents in Russian and English)
    Moscow: "Vysshaia Shkola" Press.

Nauchn. Sess. Inst. Paleobiol. AN Gruz. SSR   QE721.A1A4.P5
    Akademiia Nauk Gruzinskoi SSR, Institut Paleobiologii, Nauchnaia
    Sessiia. Plan raboty i tezisy dokladov.
    Tbilisi; AN Gruz. SSR Press.

Nauchn. trudy Permsk. politekhn. inst.   not seen
    Nauchnye trudy Permskogo politekhnicheskogo instituta

Nauchn. Trudy Tashkent. Gos. Un.   Period.
    Tashkentskii gosudarstvennyi universitet im V. I. Lenina.
    Nauchnye Trudy.
    Tashkent.

Nauk. Zap. L'viv. prirod Muz., Ukranian.   QH7.A497
    Naukovo-pryrodoznavchi muzei, L'vov.
    Naukovi zapisky.

Nauka i Chelovechestvo   Q9.N34
    Nauka i Chelovechestvo
    "Znanie" Press, Moscow

Netherworld News   Cave Res.
    Pittsburgh Grotto.   Assoc. Lib.
      National Speleological Society
      Pittsburgh.

Neue Museumskunde   Libr. Congr.
    Halle, DDR, Ministerium für Kultur, Fachstelle für   Smithson.
    Heimatmuseen

Nev. State Mus. Pop. Ser.   Free on request
    Nevada State Museum Popular Series.   from Museum

New Jersey State Mus. Invest.   sep
    New Jersey State Museum Investigations.
    Trenton, New Jersey.

New Mexico Pap. Anthrop.   not seen
    New Mexico Papers in Anthropology.

Newsclub Mag.   not seen
    Newsclub Magazine, London
      (Part of an educational program circulated through magazines
      to London technical colleges and secondary schools. Now out
      of print. Copies rare.)

Newsletter, Archaeol. Soc. Virginia   NST110
    Newsletter of the Archaeological Society of Virginia.
    Richmond.

News Letter, Cranbrook Inst. Sci.   Period.
    News Letter, Cranbrook Institute of Science.

Newsletter Kansas Anthrop. Assoc.   NST181
    Kansas Anthropological Association Newsletter.
    Published by Kansas State College, Fort Hayes.

Nieuws-Bull. Koninklijke Ned. Oudheidk. Bond.   not seen
    Nieuws-Bulletin van de Koninklijke Nederlandse Oudheidkundige
    Bond

Nihon rekishi Koza   not seen
    Nihon rekishi koza,
      Iwanami Shoten. Tokyo.

Nordsk Hvalf. Tid.   SH381.A1N6
    Norsk Hvalfangst-Tidende

Norske Videns-Akad. Oslo, Mat.-Nat. Kl., Skrifter.   AS283.V57
    Norske Videnskaps-Akademi i Oslo. I. Matematisk-Naturvidenskapelig
    Klasse. Skrifter.
    Ny Serie.

Notes Mém. Moyen-Orient   QE318.A1N6
    Notes et Mémoires sur le Moyen-Orient.

O Arqueol. Port.   DP501.A6
  Nova serie.

Objets et Mondes   GN1.O2
  La Revue du Musée de l'Homme.
  Muséum National d'Histoire Naturelle.
  Paris.

Obshchie Vopr. Evoliuts. Paleobiol.   QE721.A1O2
  Obshchie Voprosy Evoliutsionnoi Paleobiologii
    Institut Paleobiologii Akademiia Nauk Gruzinskoi SSR
    Appears yearly under different editors.

Occ. Pap. Biol. Soc. Nevada   QH301.B528
  Occasional Papers, Biological Society of Nevada.

Occ. Pap., Brit. Columbia Provincial Mus.   QH71.V6A24
  Occasional Papers of the British Columbia Provincial Museum.

Occ. Pap. Calif. Acad. Sci.   Q11.C23
  Occasional Papers of the California Academy of Science.

Occ. Pap. Dept. Anthrop. Univ. Manitoba   GN4.M2303

Occ. Pap., Roy. Anthrop. Inst. Great Britain and Ireland   GN2.R64
  Occasional Papers of the Royal Anthropological Institute of
    Great Britain and Ireland.

Oceania   GN1.O4

Oceanus   GC1.O35
  The Woods Hole Oceanographic Institution. Mass.

Okhrana Prirody Moldavii   QH77.R8.O518
  Akademiia Nauk Moldavskoi SSR
    Kishinev: "Kartia Moldoveniaske" Press.

Oldsmobile Rocket Circle Mag.   Reprint
  Chicago, Ill. Oldsmobile dealers.

Opera Lilloana   F2801.T82
  Tucumán, Argentine Republic (City) Universidad.
    Instituto "Miguel Lillo."

Ore Bin   TN24.O7A5
  The Ore Bin. Oregon Department of Geology and Mineral
    Industries.

Ornitologiia   QL671.O867
  Ornitologiia
    Glavnoe Upravlenie Okhotnich'ego Khosiaistva i Zapovednikov
    pri Sov. Ministrov RSFSR Ministerstvo vysshego i srednego
    spetsial'nogo obrazovaniia SSSR i RSFSR
    Moscow: Mosk. Univ. Press
    English table of contents.

Orsz. Orvostörténeti Könyvtár Közleményei.   R131.A1B83
[Mitt. Landesbibl. für Geschichte der Medizin]. Budapest.

Osnovy Pal.   QE761.O8
Osnovy Paleontologii [Fundamentals of Paleontology.]
A set of fifteen unnumbered volumes. J. A. Orlov, gen. ed.
The Library has assigned arbitrary numbers according to the
list of volume titles included in each volume.

Ost-Europa Naturw.   not seen

Our Public Lands   HD181.L7A3
Official publication of the Bureau of Land Management, U. S.
Department of the Interior.

Pal. Abh., Abt. A.   QE701.P298.A2
Paläontologische Abhandlungen. Abteilung A: Paläozoologie.
Geologische Gesellschaft in der Deutschen Demokratischen
Republik.
Berlin.

Pal. geol. polezn. iskop. Moldavii   Period.
Paleontologiia, geologiia i poleznye iskopaemye Moldavii.
Kishinev; Akad. Nauk Moldav. SSR Press.

Pal. i Strat. Pribalt. Belorus   QE755.R8P25
Paleontologiia i stratigrafiia Pribaltiki i Belorussii
Ministerstvo Geologii SSSR, Institut Geologii (Vil'nius),
Institut Geologicheskikh Nauk (Minsk), Institut Geologii
(Riga)
Vil'nius: "Minitis" Press
Supercedes Pal. i Strat.

Pal. Sborn.   QE701.P2973
Paleontologicheskii sbornik.
L'vovskogo geologicheskogo obshchestva. Izdatel'stvo
L'vovskogo Universiteta.

Pal. Soc. Mem.   QE701.J6
The Paleontological Society Memoirs.
[Journal of Paleontology Supplements.]

Palaeogeog., Paleoclimatol., Palaeoecol.   QE500.P25
Palaeogeography, Paleoclimatology, Palaeoecology.
Elsevier Publ. Co.

PaleoBios   QE701.P38
Contributions from the University of California Museum of
Paleontology, Berkeley.

Paleovertebrata   QE841.A1P25
Université de Montpellier, France.

Panorama   Earth Science
   Sandoz, Ltd.   Library
     Basle, Switzerland

Pap. Anthrop., Anthrop. Club Univ. Oklahoma   GN1.P3
   Papers in Anthropology.
     Anthropology Club University of Oklahoma
     Norman, Oklahoma

Pap. Anthrop., Mus. New Mex.   E78N65S36
   Santa Fe, New Mexico.
     Museum of New Mexico.
     Papers in Anthropology.

Pap. Archaeol. Soc. N. Mex.   F791.A7P3
   Papers of the Archaeological Society of New Mexico.

Pap. Robert S. Peabody Found. Archaeol.   E51.P54
   Papers of the Robert S. Peabody Foundation for Archaeology.
     Phillips Academy, Andover, Massachusetts

Pap. Sacramento Anthrop. Soc.   GN4.S15.P3
   Sacramento Anthropological Society.
     Papers.

Pays Gaumais   not seen
   Le Pays Gaumais

Peruanistica, Ser.: Antrop.   GN4.P4S4
   Peruantistica, Serie: Antropología.
     Sociedad de Estudios Americanos.
     Lima.

Peshchery   Period.
   Peshchery caves, Permskiĭ Gosudarstvennyĭ Universitet, Perm'
     (Former Speleologicheskiĭ Biulleten')

Peshchery Gruzii   Period.
   Speleologicheskiĭ Sbornik
     Tbilisi; "Metsniereba" Press

Pfälzer Heimat   not seen

Pickups and Throwovers   not seen

Plains Anthrop.   E51.P585
   Plains Anthropologist.
     Journal of the Plains Conference.

Plaster Jacket   QE841.A1P5432
   The Plaster Jacket. Florida State Museum, University of Florida
     Gainesville.

Poeyana, ser. A.   QH301.P5
    Poeyana, serie A
       Comisión Nacional de la Academia de Ceincias de la República
       de Cuba.
       Instituto de Biologia
       Havana.

Polskie Towarzystwo Archeol., Popularn-onaukowa Biblioteka Archeol.   GN700.P66
    Polskie Towarzystwo Archeologiczne, Popularnonaukowa Biblioteka
       Archeologiczna.

Poročila, Solv. akad. znan. in umetn., Razr. prirodosl. in med. vede   UCLA
    Poročila,
       Slovenska Adademija Znanosti in Umetnosti, Razred za
       Prirodoslovne in Medicinske Vede
       Ljubljana, Yugoslavia

Prace Mat. Muz. Archeol. Etnog. Łodzí, Ser. Archeol.   GN700.L6
    Prace i Materialy Muzeum Archeologicznego i Etnograficznego
       w Łodzí. Seria Archeologiczna Łodź.

Priroda (Zagreb)   QH7.P63

Priroda i znanie   not seen
    Bulgarsko prirodizpitatelno druzhestvo
       Sofia

Prirodn. Obstan. i Fauny Proshl.   Period.
    Prirodnaia Obstanovska i Fauny Proshlogo, Institut Zoologii,
       Akademiia Nauk Ukrainskoi SSR.
       Kiev, Ukraine.

Problemy geografii Moldavii   Period.
    Kishinev

Problemy Severa.   GB395.P76
    Problemy Severa. Akademiia nauk SSSR.
       Komissiia po problemam severa soveta po izucheniiu
       proizvoditel'nykh sil. Moscow.

Proc. Alaskan Sci. Confer.   Q101.A5
    Proceedings of the Alaskan Science Conference of the National
       Academy of Sciences, National Research Council.
       Washington, Nov. 9-11, 1950
       (Bull. No. 122 of the National Research Council)

Proc. 1st European Bone and Tooth Symp.   QP88.2.A1E8
    Proceedings of the First European Bone and Tooth Symposium.
       Oxford, 1963.

Proc. 1st Internat. Congr. Africanists   DT1.I7
    Proceedings of the First International Congress of Africanists.
       Accra.

Proc. Internat. Congr. Americanists   E51.16
    Actas y Memorias 36th Congreso Internacional de
      Americanistas.
      España, 1964.

Proc. 2nd Internat. European Anat. Congr.   not seen
    Proceedings of the 2nd International European Anatomy Congress.

Proc. Israel Acad. Sci., Sect. Sci.   AS591.I8P7
    The Israel Academy of Sciences and Humanities. Section of
      Sciences. Proceedings.

Proc. K. Nederl. Akad. Wet., Ser. C.   QH301.A342
    Koninklijke Nederlandse Akademie van Wetenschappen. Proceedings.
      Series C: Biological and Medical Sciences.
      Amsterdam.

Proc. Somersetshire Archaeol. Nat. Hist. Soc.   DA670.S4956
    Proceedings of the Somersetshire Archaeological and Natural History
      Society.
      Taunton.

Procès-Verbaux, Soc. Linn. Bordeaux   QH3.S668P7
    Procès-Verbaux de la Société linnéenne de Bordeaux
    ceased publication with 101.

Proc. Trans. Dundee Nat. Soc. Scotland.   not seen

Program, 60th Ann. Meeting, Geol. Soc. Amer., Cordilleran Sec.   Earth Science
    Program, 60th Annual Meeting, The Geological Society of America,   Library
      Cordilleran Section, Univ. of Washington
      Seattle, Mar. 27-28, 1964

Program, 62nd Ann. Meeting, Geol. Soc. Amer., Cordilleran Sect.   Earth Science
    Program, 62nd Annual Meeting of the Geological Society of America, Library
      Cordilleran Section, the Seismological Society of America,
      and the Paleontological Society, Pacific Coast Section.
      Reno, Nev., April 6-9, 1966.

Program, 63rd Ann. Meeting. Geol. Soc. Amer., Cordilleran Sect.   Earth Science
    Program, 63rd Annual Meeting, the Geological Society of America,   Library
      Cordilleran Section. The Seismological Society of America,
      The Paleontological Society of America, Pacific Coast Section.
      Santa Barbara, Calif. Mar. 22-25, 1967.

Program, 64th Ann. Meeting, Geol. Soc. Amer., Cordilleran Sect.   Earth Science
    Program, 64th Annual Meeting, Geological Society of America.   Library
      Tucson, Ariz. April 11-13, 1968.

Program, 19th Ann. Meeting, Geol. Soc. Amer., Rocky Mt. Sect.   Earth Science
    Program, 19th Annual Meeting, Geological Society of America,   Library
    · Rocky Mountain Section
    Las Vegas, Nevada, May 11-14, 1966.

Program, 21st Ann. Meeting, Geol. Soc. Amer., Rocky Mt. Sect.   Earth Science
   1968 Ann. Meeting, Montana State Univ.   Library
   Bozeman, Mont., May 7-12, 1968

Program, 1966 Ann. Meeting. Geol. Soc. Amer.   Earth Science
   Program, 1966 Annual Meeting, The Geological Society of America,   Library
   San Francisco, Calif., Nov. 14-16, 1966

Program, 1967 Ann. Meeting, Geol. Soc. Amer.   Earth Science
   Program, 1967 Annual Meeting, The Geological Society of America,   Library
   New Orleans, Louisiana, Nov. 20-22, 1967.

Program, 1968 Ann. Meetings, Geol. Soc. Amer.   Earth Science
   Program with abstracts, 1968 Annual Meetings, the Geological   Library
   Society of America.
   Nov. 11-13, 1968, Mexico City, Mexico.

Program, Sect. E (Geol., Geog.), Amer. Assoc. Advanc. Sci., Meeting   Earth Science
   Dec. 26-31, 1965.   Library
   Program, Section E (Geology and Geography), American
   Association for the Advancement of Science, Meeting December
   26-31, 1965.
   Berkeley, California. Abstracts.

Publ., Amer. Geophys. Union, Antarctic Res. Ser.   Q115.A68
   American Geophysical Union of the National Academy of Sciences.
   Publications. [No. 1299]. Antarctic Research Series, [No. 6].

Publ. British Mus. (Nat. Hist.)   QL666.O6U45
   British Museum (Natural History), Publications.

Publ. Cent. Recherch. Zones Arides, Cent. Nation. Recherch. Sci.,   QE696.C534
   Ser. Geol.
   Publications du Centre de Recherches sur les Zones Arides. Centre
   National de la Recherche Scientifique. Serie: Geologie.
   Paris and Algiers.

Publ. Fort Burgwin Res. Center   F791.F6P8
   Fort Burgwin Research Center. Publications.

Publ. Inst. Hist., Univ. Nacion. Autónoma Mex.   GN62.G4
   Publicaciones del Instituto de Historia, Universidad Nacional
   Autónoma de México.

Publ. Inst. Panamer. Geog. Hist.   Cat. by author
   Instituto Panamericano de Geografía e Historia. Publicación.
   México, D. F.

Publ. Inst. Prov. de Invest. y Estud. Toledanos.   not seen
   Toledo.

Publ. Israel Acad. Sci. Human.   filed under author

Publ. Nation. Acad. Sci.   QH368.A1S92
   National Academy of Sciences, National Reserach Council,
   Washington, D. C. Publications.

Publ. Pal. Indonesia   not seen
   Indonesia, Direktorat Geologi.
      Publikasi Teknik (serie Paleontologi.) Bandung.

Publ. Serv. geol. Luxembourg   QE175.A3
   Publications du Service geologique du Luxembourg.

Publ. Tek. Ser. Pal., Bandung   QE701.I5678
   Republik Indonesia, Departemen Perindustrian Dasar/Pertambangan.
      Djawatan Geologi — Bandung.
      Publikasi Teknik Seri Paleontologi.

Publ. Univ. Tasmania, Dept. Geol.   Columbia Univ.
   Publication, University of Tasmania, Department of Geology.   D550.8.T18

Quart. Geol. Notes, Geol. Surv. S. Austral.   QE345.A38
   Quarterly Geological Notes, Geological Survey of South Australia.

Quart. Jour. Sci. Lit. Arts   Q1.Q8
   The Quarterly Journal of Science, Literature, and the Arts.
      Royal Institution of Great Britain.
      London.

Quart. Snow Mus. Nat. Sci.   not seen
   Quarterly, Snow Museum of Natural Science,
      Oakland, Calif.

Rassegna Spel. Ital.   Cave Res.
   Rassegna Speleologica Italiana.   Assoc. Lib.
      Organo ufficiale di stampa dei Gruppi Grotte Italiani.

Raymond Dart Lectures   GN29.R3
   Institute for the Study of Man in Africa.
      Johannesburg.

Rec. Queen Victoria Mus.   Univ. of
   Records of the Queen Victoria Museum.   So. Cal.
      Launceston, Tasmania. Edited by W. F. Ellis.

Referaty i Komunikaty, I Sympozjum   not seen
   Paleolityczne, Krakow.

Referaty Nauchno-Issl. Rab.   QE1.A436
   Referaty Nauchno-Issledovatel'skikh Rabot, Otdelenie Geologo-
      Geograficheskikh Nauk,
      Akademiia Nauk Souiza SSR.
      Moscow - Leningrad: Akad. Nauk Press.

Régészeti Tanulmányok, Budapest   not seen
   Régészeti Tanulmányok.
      Akadémiai Kiadó, Budapest

Regional Review   SB482.A14
    The Regional Review,
        U.S. Department of the Interior, National Park Service,
        Region One, Richmond, Va.

Rend. 1st. Lombardo, Sci. Biol. Med. B   AS222.I42
    Instituto Lombardo di Scienze e Lettere.
        Rendiconti. Scienze Biologiche e Mediche. B
        Milano

Rend. Soc. Cult. Preistor. Trentina.   not seen
    Rendiconti della Società di Cultura, Preistorica Trentina.
    Trento, Italy.

Rept. Faculty Sci., Kagoshima Univ.   7004.0724.1
    Reports of the Faculty of Science, Kagoshima University.
        Japan.

Rept. 22nd Internat. Geol. Congr.   QE1.I6
    International Geological Congress.
        Report of the twenty-second session, India, 1964.

Rept. Invest., Wash. State Univ., Lab. Anthrop.   NST385
    Washington State University, Laboratory of Anthrópology,
    Report of Investigations.

Rept. Res. Fac. Literature Meiji Univ., Archaeol.   not seen
    Reports on the Research by the Faculty of Literature, Meiji
        University, Archaeology.

Rept. Trans. Cardiff Nat. Soc.   QH1.C33
    Reports and Transactions of the Cardiff Naturalists' Society.
        National Museum of Wales, Cardiff.

Res. Bull. Chichibu Nat. Sci. Mus.   not seen

Rés. Com. Congr. Assoc. Franç. Avance. Sci.   not seen
    Rés. Communic. Congr.
        Association Française pour l'avancement des sciences.

Rev. Bras. Geog.   F2501.R4
    Revista Brasileira de Geografia Instituto Brasileiro de Geografia e
        Estatistica
        Conselho Nacional de Geografia
        Rio de Janeiro.

Rev. española Estomatología   not seen
    Revista española de Estomatología
        Madrid.

Rev. Fac. Ciên. Lisbon. Ser. 2, C   QH7.L55
    Revista de Faculdade de Ciências Universidade de Lisboa
        Lisbon

Rev. Hist. Sci.   not seen

Rev. Inst. Antrop., Univ. Nacion Litoral, Rosario
   Revista del Instituto de Antropología, Universidad Nacional
     del Litoral.
     Rosario, Argentine Republic (Santa Fe)
                     GN2.R58

Rev. Madagascar
   La Revue de Madagascar.
   Tananarive.
                     DT469.M21R4

Rev. Mens. Suisse Odonto-stomatol.
                     not seen

Rev. Micropal.
   Revue de Micropaléontologie.
     Paris. Université. Laboratoire de Micropaléontologie.
                     QE701.R46

Rev. Mus. Argent. Cien. Nat., Pal.
   Museo Argentino de Ciencias Naturales "Bernardino Rivadavia,"
     Revista del... Paleontologia
     Buenos Aires.
                     QE701.B6675

Rev. Roumaine Biol.
   Revue Roumaine de Biologie.
     Série de Zoologie, Supersedes Rev. Biol.,
     Bucarest, QH301, R426.
                     QL1.R35

Rev. Roumaine Géol. Géophys. Géogr., Sér. Géol.
   Revue Roumaine de Géologie, Géophysique et Géographie, série
     de Géologie.
     Bucarest: Éd. Académie de République Socialiste Roumaine.
                     QE1.R45

Rev. Soc. Sav. Haute-Normandie, Préhist.-Archéol.
   Rouen.
                     not seen.

Riv. Sci. preistor.
   Rivista di scienze preistoriche.
     Florence.
                     GN700.R55

Roczn. Polsk. Towarz. geol.
   Rocznik Polskiego towarzystwa geologiczne
     Krakov
                     UCLA

Roy. Dental Hospital Mag.
   London.
                     not seen

Roy. Ontario Mus. Ser.
   Royal Ontario Museum Series. Toronto.
                     Reprints

Roz. Ustred. Ustav. Geol.
   Rozpravy Ústredního ústavu geologického, Nakladatelství
     Ceskoslovenské Akademie věd.
     Prague.
                     QE267.C8A23

Rozp. Anthrop. Spolecnosti, Brno
   Rozpravy Anthropologicke Spolecnosti.
     Brno.
                     not seen

S.A.R.H. Mag.   not seen
   South African Railways and Harbours Magazine.
   Johannesburg. Cover title: S.A.R.H. Magazine.

S. Afr. Scope   not seen
   South African Scope.

Saito Ho-on Kai Mus., Res. Bull.   Q77.S32R4
   Saito Ho-on Kai Museum. Research bulletin.
   Sendai, Japan.

Salamandra.   QL640.S2
   Herausgegeben von der Deutchen Gesellshaft für Herpetologie und
   Terrarienkunde.

Sborn. Geol.-Geogr. Fak. Odessa Univ., Kiev   QE1.O453
   Sbornik Geologo-Geograficheskogo Fakulteta, Trudy Odesskogo
   Gosudarstvennogo Universiteta, Editor-Kiev Gos. Univ.

Sborn Geol. Věd. Rada A: Antropozoikum   QE755.C8P68
   Sborník Geologických Věd. Rada A: Antropozoikum.
   Ústřední Ústav Geologický.
   Prague.

Sborn. Geol. Věd. Rada G: Geologie   QE267.C8A26
   Sborník Geologických Věd Rada G: Geologie
   Ústřední Ústav Geologický
   Prague. Supercedes: Sborn. Geol. Úst. Čsl., odd.: Geol.

Sborn. Geol. Věd. Rada P: Paleontologie   QE755.C8P7
   Sborník Geologických Věd Rada P: Paleontologie
   Ústřední Ústav Geologický
   Prague. Supercedes: Sborn. Geol. Úst. Čsl., odd.: Paleon.

Sborník Národního Muzea v Praze. Rada B: Přírodni Vědy   QH7.P6
   (Acta Musei Nationalis Pragae)
     Prague: Narodni Muzeum Press Formerly listed as:
     Acta Mus. Nat. Pragae

Sborn. Východosloven. múzea v Košiciach, ser. A.   QH7.K67
   Sbornik Východoslovenského múzea v Košiciach.
     Acta musei Slovaciae Regionis Orientalis A- Historia naturalis
     Seria A Prírodné vedy
          Geologicke vedy − subtitle varies
   Košice, Slovakia: Museum Press

Schrift. Ver. Verbreitung Naturwiss. Kenntnisse Wien   Q44.V54
   Schriften der Vereines zur Verbreitung naturwissenschaftlicher
   Kenntnisse in Wien

Schwäbische Mus.   not seen
   Das Schwäbische Museum.
   Augsburg.

Sci. Club Mag.   not seen
    Science Club Magazine. London.
        (Part of an educational program circulated through magazines
        to London technical colleges and secondary schools. Now out
        of print. Copies rare.)

Sci. Jour., London   Q1.S414
    Science Journal. Publ. by Dorset House, London.

Sci. News Mag.   Q1.S417
    Science News Magazine. London.
        (Part of an educational program circulated through magazines
        to London technical colleges and secondary schools. Now out
        or print. Copies rare.)

Sci. Publ. Cleveland Mus. Natl. Hist.   QH1.C545
    Scientific Publications,
        Cleveland Museum of Natural History. Ser. 2.

Sci Publ. Foreign Cooperl.   not seen
    Center of Cent. Inst. Sci., Tech., Econ. Inform.
        Warsaw.

Sci. Publ. Sci. Mus., St. Paul, Minn.   not seen
    Scientific Publications of the Science Museum, Saint Paul, Minn.

Sci. Record, New. Ser.   Q1.S445
    Science Record, New Series
        Edited by the Publication Commission, Academia Sinica
        Peking: Science Press.

Sci. Rept. Yokosuka City Mus.   not seen
    The Yokosuka City Museum.
        Science Report.

Sci. S. Afr.   Period.
    Scientific South Africa
        Johannesburg.

Sci. Teacher   Q1.S46
    Science Teacher.

Science and Children   LB1585.A1S28

Sciences   not seen
    The Sciences
        New York Academy of Science

Ser. Biol., Acad. Cien. Cuba   QH301.A224
    Academia de Ciencias de Cuba
        Havana.
        Instituto de Biologia. Serie Biologica.

Shengwuxue tongbao   not seen
    Other title:
        Sheng Wu Hsueh T'ung Pao
        Peking

Shih Yu Tung Hsin	not seen
Shinano Kyoiku	not seen

Shizen Kagaku to Hakubutsu-kan
   Natural Science and Museums
     Tokyo.
	Cal. Acad.
	Sci.

Smolenice	not seen

Soobshch. Gosud. Ermitazha
   Soobshcheniia Gosudarstvennogo Ordena Lenina Ermitazha
     Leningrad-Moscow: "Sovetakii Khudozhnik" Press.
	Period.

Southeast. Mus. Conf. Notes
   Southeastern Museum Conference.
     Notes.
	NST177

Spatenforscher	not seen
Special Bull. Oklahoma Anthrop. Soc. Special Bulletin of the Oklahoma Anthropological Society.	F691.O4895

Spec. Publ., Amer. Soc. Mammal.
   American Society of Mammalogists.
     Special Publications.
	QL700.A53S63

Spelunca Mém. and Bull.
   Spelunca (4e Serie.) Mémoires.
     Société Spéléologique de France.
     Paris.
	Cave Res.
	Assoc. Lib.

Spisanie Bŭlg. Geol. Druzh.
   Spisanie na Bŭlgarskoto Geologichesko Druzhestvo
     Sofia; Bŭlg. Akad. Nauk. Press
	QE1.B6

Spisy Přirodov. Fak. Brno
   Spisy Přirodovecká Fakulta
     Universita Brno.
	Q44.B79

Stones and Bones Newsletter
   Alabama Archaeological Society.
     University, Alabama.
	NST85

Stud. Coal Geol. Geol. Sec. Hokkaido Assoc. Coal. Min. Technologists	not seen

Studia Univ. Babeş-Bolyai, ser. geol.-geogr.
   Studia Universitatis Babeş-Bolyai seria Geologia-Geografia
     Cluj, Transylvania, (Rumania)
	QE1.C557

Studien aus Alteuropa Köln-Graz	not seen
Studies from Res. Inst. for North. Culture, Hokkaido Univ. Sapporo, Japan.	not seen

Studies in Geol., Oregon State Univ.   QE1.O6
   Corvallis, Oregon State University.
      Studies in Geology.

Studies in Spel.   GB601.A1S8
   Studies in Speleology.
      Association of the Pengelly Cave Research Centre.
      London.

Struttgarter Zeitung   not seen

Südafr. Panorama   not seen
   Paris.

Sundai Shigaku   not seen

Sunset   F851.S95
   The Magazine of Western Living. Menlo Park, Calif.

I Symp. Paleolityczne, Kraków   not seen
   I Sympozjum Paleolityczne
      Kraków 11.-13. x. 1963.

Teruel   DP302.T31T47
   Instituto de Estudios Turolenses de la Excma. Diputacion
      Provincial de Teruel.
      Consejo Superior de Investigaciones Cientificas.
      Teruel, Spain.

This World   private copy
   San Francisco Sunday Chronicle

Ti chih lun-p'ing   U.S.G.S.
   (Geological notes edited by Geological Society of China)   Lib. of Congr.
      Peiping

Toimetised Eesti NSV Tead. Akad. ser. chem. geol.   AS262.E4
   Eesti NSV Teaduste Akademia Toimetised Keemia Geologia
      series chemistry and geology
      Tallinn

Totem Pole   GN1.T67
   The Totem Pole
      Bulletin of the Aboriginal Research Club. (Mimeographed.)
      Detroit, Michigan

Touring Plein Air   not seen
   Touring Club de France.
      Paris.

Trail and Timberline   F782.R6T7
   Colorado Mountain Club

Trans. Cave Res. Group, Great Britain
    Transactions of the Cave Research Group of Great Britain.

Cave Res.
Assoc. Lib.

Trans. Devon Archaeol. Explor. Soc.

not seen

Trans. Dumfries. Galloway Nat. Hist. Antiq. Soc.
    Transactions of the Dumfriesshire and Galloway Natural History
      and Antiquarian Society.

QH1.D8

Trans. Hunter Archaeol. Soc.
    Transactions of the Hunter Archaeological Society,
      Sheffield, England.

not seen

Trans. Proc. Pal. Soc. Japan
    Transactions and Proceedings of the Palaeontological Society
      of Japan. New Series.

QE701.P297

Trans. Roy. Soc. Arts
    Transactions of the Royal Society of Arts.
      London

not seen

Trans. Suffolk. Nat. Soc.
    Transactions, Suffolk Naturalists' Society.
      Norwich, England

not seen

Trav. Inst. Sci. Chérifien. Ser. Zool.
    Travaux de l'Institut Scientifique Chérifien.
      Série Zoologie.
      Rabat.

QL1.R16

Trav. Mus. Hist. Nat. "Grigore Antipa"
    Travaux du Museum d'Histoire Naturelle "Grigore Antipa"
      Muzeul National de Istorie Naturala "Grigore Antipa"
      Bucharest.
      Run as Trav. Mus. Hist. Nat., Bukarest in Vol. 7

QH7.B76

Treubia
    A Journal on Zoology and hydrobiology of the Indo-Australian
      Archipelago.
      National Biological Institute Museum Zoologicum Bogoriense
      Bogor, Indonesia

QL1.T7

Trudy Akad. Nauk Tadzhik. SSR
    Trudy L'Akademiia Nauk Tadzhikskoi SSR
      Zoologii i Parazitologii.

DK921.A55

Trudy Azerbaid. Inst. po dobyche nefti
    Trudy Azerbaidzhanskogo nauchno-issledovatel'skogo instituta
      po dobyche nefti. Baku. Aznefteizdat.

not seen

Trudy Geol. Inst.
    Trudy Geologicheskogo Instituta Akademii Nauk SSSR
      Moscow: "Nauka" Press

QE1.A381

Trudy Groznen. Neft. n.-i. Inst.   TN4.G76
   Trudy Groznenskiĭ Neftianoĭ nauchno-issledovatel'skiĭ Institut.
   Groznyĭ.

Trudy Iакut. fil. AN SSSR, Ser. Geol.   Period.
   Trudy Iakutskogo filiala Sibirskogo otdeleniia AN SSSR. (Seriia
   Geologicheskaia).
   Moscow: Akad. Nauk SSSR Press

Trudy Inst. Etnogr. Akad. Nauk SSSR   GN2.A148
   Substitutes: Trav. Inst. Ethnog. Acad. Sci. URSS

Trudy Inst. Geol. Akad. Nauk Tadzhik. SSR   QE1.A448
   Trudy Institute Geologii Akademiia Nauk Tadzhikskoĭ SSR.
   Dushanbe.

Trudy Inst. Geol. Arktiki   QE350.M67
   Moscow (City). Nauchno-issledovatel'skii institut geologii
   Arktiki. Trudy.
   Gosgeoltekhizdat, Moscow.

Trudy Inst. Geol. Geof.   QE1.A4436
   Trudy Instituta Geologii i Geofiziki Akademiia Nauk SSSR,
   Sibirskoe Otdelenie. Novosibirsk.

Trudy Inst. Geol., Kirg. Filial AN SSSR   Period.
   Trudy Instituta Geologii, Kirizskiĭ Filial Akademii Nauk SSSR.
   Frunze.

Trudy Inst. Geol., Komi fil. AN SSSR   Period.
   Trudy Instituta Geologii Komi filial, Akademiia Nauk SSSR
   Syktyvkar: Komi Press

Trudy Inst. Geol. Nauk AN URSR, ser. geomorf. ta chetvert. geol.   Period.
   Trudy Institutu Geologichnikh Nauk Akademiia Nauk Ukrains'skoi
   RSR Seriia geomorfologii ta chetvertinnoi geologii
   Kiev: Akad. Nauk Ukr. RSR Press

Trudy Inst. Istorii AN BSSR   DK507.A2A53
   Trudy Instituta Istorii, Akademii Navuk BSSR. Sektor Arkheologii.
   Materialy po arkheologii BSSR.
   Minsk: AN BSSR Press

Trudy Inst. Ist. Arkheol. Etnogr. Akad. Nauk Kazakh. SSR   DK901.A5
   Trudy Instituta Istorii, Arkheologii i Etnografii imeni Ch. Ch.
   Valikhanova
   Akademiia Nauk Kazakhskoĭ SSR, Alma-Ata.

Trudy Inst. Ist. Azerbaĭdzhan   DK511.A9A46
   Trudy Instituta Istorii
   Akademiia Nauk Azerbaidzhanskoĭ SSR Baku

Trudy Inst. Istorii Kirg. SSR   DK911.A5
   Trudy Instituta Istorii Akademii Nauk Kirgizskoĭ SSR
   Frunze.

Trudy Inst. miner. ress. Akad. Nauk URSR   U.C.
    Trudy Instituta mineral'nykh ressursov Akademii Nauk URSR
    Kiev.

Trudy Inst. Zemn. Kory SO AN SSSR   Period.
    Trudy Instituta Zemnoĭ Kory Sibirskogo Otdeleniia Akademii
    Nauk SSSR.
    Moscow: Akad. Nauk SSSR Press.
    Formerly Trudy Vost.-Sib. Fil. Ser. Geol.

Trudy Inst. Zool. AN Kazakh. SSR   QL1.A373
    Trudy Instituta Zoologii Akademiia Nauk Kazakhskoĭ SSR
    Alma-Ata: Akad. Nauk Press.

Trudy Inst. Zool. AN URSR   QL1.A486
    Trudy Institutu Zoologii̇ Kiev
    Akademia Nauk Ukraïns'koi RSR
    Kiev.
    Formerly run as Trav. Inst. Zool. Biol. Acad. Sci. Ukraine

Trudy Mosk. Obshch. Ispyt. Prirody, otd. biol.   QH7.M685
    Trudy Moskovskogo Obshchestva Ispytateleĭ Prirody, otdel
    biologicheskiĭ
    Moscow: Moscow University Press.
    Title, contents and summaries in English.

Trudy probl. temat. soveshch. Zool. Inst.   QL1.A47
    Trudy problemnykh i tematicheskikh soveshchaniĭ, Zoologicheskiĭ
    Institut, Akad. Nauk SSSR
    Leningrad - Moscow: Akad. Nauk Press

Trudy SNIGGIMS   QE315.S55
    Trudy Sibirskogo Nauchno-Issledovatel'skogo Instituta Geologii
    Geografii i Mineral'nogo Syr'ia
    Ministerstvo Geologii i Okhrany Nedr
    Leningrad.

Trudy Tuvin. Kompl. Eksp.   Period.
    Trudy Tuvinskoi Kompleksnoĭ Ekspeditsii
    Akademiia Nauk SSSR.
    Sovet po Izucheniiu Proizvoditel'nykh Sil.
    Moscow.

Trudy Vost.-Sib. Fil. Ser. Geol.   Period.
    Trudy Vostochno-Sibirskogo Filiala Sibirskogo Otdeleniia
    Akademii Nauk SSSR, Seriia Geologicheskaia.
    Irkutsk.

Trudy Vses. n.-i. geol. Inst.   QE1.L385
    Trudy Vsesoiuznogo nauchno-issledovatel'skogo geologicheskogo
    Instituta (VSEGEI), novaia seriia
    Ministerstvo Geologii SSSR
    Leningrad: "Nedra" Press.

Trudy Vses. Neft. Nauchn.-Issl. geologorazi. Inst. (VNIGRI)   TN4.L453
    Trudy Vsesoiuznogo Neftianogo Nauchno-Issledovatel'skogo

Geologorazvedochnogo Instituta (VNIGRI)
Leningrad: "Gostoptekhizdat" Press.

Trudy Vses. Paleont. Obshch.   QE775.R8V75
Trudy Vsesoi͡uznogo Paleontologicheskogo Obshchestva
Moscow: "Gosgeoltekhizdat" Press.

Tulane Studies Geol.   QE1.T815
Tulane Studies in Geology.
Tulane University of Louisiana.
New Orleans.

U.S. Geol. Surv. Water Supply Pap.   TC823.A3
United States Geological Survey. Water Supply Paper.
Washington.

Uch. Zap. Azerbaĭdzhan. Gos. Univ., ser. geol-geogr.   QE276.B26
Uchenye Zapiski Azerbaĭdzhanskogo Gosudarstvennogo Universiteta,
Serii͡a geologo-geograficheskai͡a.
Baku: Azerb. Gos. Univ. Press (6 issues yearly)

Uch. zapiski Azerb. med. inst.   not seen
Uchenye zapiski Azerbaĭdzhanskogo Meditsinskogo Instituta
Baku.

Uch. zapiski Azerb. Un., ser. biol.   QH301.B21
Uchenye Zapiski Azerbaĭdzhanskogo Universiteta, serii͡a
biologicheskikh nauk
Baku.

Uch. Zapiski Belorus. Univ.   Libr. Congr.
Uchenye Zapiski Belorusskogo Universiteta
Minsk

Uganda Mus. Occ. Paper   GN37.K3U35
Uganda Museum Occasional Paper.
Kampala.

Univ. Calif. In Memoriam   3082.H1
California, University, Berkeley, In Memoriam

Univ. Calif. Publ. Anthrop.   GN4.C28
University of California (State) Publications in Anthropology.

Univ. Colorado Studies, Ser. Earth Sci.   QE1.C577E2
University of Colorado Studies, Series in Earth Sciences.
Boulder, Colo., Univ. Colo. Press

Univ. Kansas Mus. Nat. Hist., Misc. Publ.   QH9.K3
University of Kansas Museum of Natural History, Miscellaneous
Publications.

Univ. Kans. Dept. Geol. Spec. Publ.   QE1.K34
   University of Kansas, Department of Geology, Special Publication
   No. 2 is Raymond C. Moore Comm. Vol.

Univ. Kans. Pal. Contrib., Pap.   QE701.K32
   University of Kansas Paleontological Contributions, Papers.

Univ. Méx.   not seen
   Universidad de México
     México.

Uppsala Univ. Årsskrift   AS284.U7
   Uppsala Universitet Årsskrift

Uzbek. Geol. Zhurnal   QE1.U9
   Uzbekshiĭ Geologicheskiĭ Zhurnal
     Tashkent: Ak. Nauk Uzbek. SSR Press

Varia Archaeol.   not seen
   Varia Archaeologica. Wilhelm Unverzagt zum 70.
     Geburtstag dargebracht. Festschrift.
     Berlin. 1964.

Verh. Deutsche Pathol. Gesellsch.   not seen
   Deutsche Gesellschaft für Pathology, Verhandlungen

Verh. Ned. Akad. Weten.   AS244.A55
   K. Nederlandse Akademie van Wetenschappen. Afd. Natuurk.
     Verhandelinge. Eerstereeks

Veröff. Zool. Staatsamml. München   QL1.M77
   Munich. Zoologische Staatssammlung, Veroeffentlichungen.

Vert. Pal. in Alberta, Univ. of Alberta   QE841.A1V4
   Vertebrate Paleontology in Alberta, University of Alberta, 1965.
     Report of a conference held at the University of Alberta
     Aug. 29 to Sept. 3, 1963.

Vesci Akad. Navuk BSSR, Ser. fiz.-tckh. Navuk   Period.
   Akademiia Navuk BSSR, Vestsi, Seryia
     Fizika-Energetychnykh Navuk.

Vest. Drevneĭ Ist.   D51.V4
   Vestnik Drevneĭ Istorii.
     Moscow.
     (Formerly listed as: Rev. Hist. Ancienne. Revue
     d'Histoire Ancienne.)

Vest. Ist. Mir. Kult.   CB3.V48
   Vestnik Istorii Mirovoĭ Kul'tury
     Akademiia nauk SSSR. Otdelenie istoricheskikh nauk.

Vestnik nauchn. inform. Zabaĭk. otd. Geogr. Obshch.   not seen
   Vestnik nauchnoĭ informatsii Zabaĭkal'skogo otdeleniia
     Geograficheskogo Obshchestva

Vestnik Leningrad. Univers.   AS262.L39
    Vestnik Leningradskogo Universiteta
    Leningrad (City): Univers. Press
    24 annual issues, four for each series. (Series: Biology,
    Geology and Geography.)
    English table of contents and summaries.

Vestnik Mosk. Univ., ser. biol.   QH301.M6733
    Vestnik Moskovskogo Universiteta seriiā Biologiiā
    Moscow: Mosk. Univ. Press

Vestnik Mosk. Univ., ser. IV, Geol.   QE1.M68
    Vestnik Moskovskogo Universiteta seriiā IV Geologiiā
    Moscow: Mosc. Univ. Press. Bimensual.

Věstnik Ústřed Úst. Geol.   QE267.C8A3
    Věstník Ústředního Ústavu Geologického
    Prague: (Czechoslovakia)
    Supercedes: Věst. Stát. Geol. Českosl. Republ.

Vestnik Zoologii   QL1.V35.B.
    Akademiiā Nauk Ukrainskoĭ SSR Institut Zoologii
    Kiev: "Naukova Dumka" Press

Vestsi Akad. Navuk BSSR ser. biiāl. Navuk   QH301.A3794
    Vestsi Akademii Navuk BSSR seryiā biiālagichnykh navuk
    Minsk: "Navuka i tekhnika" Press

Victorian Year Book   DU200.V6
    Melbourne, Australia

Vikram   AS471.V55
    Journal of Vikram University.
    Ujjain, India.

Viltrevy   QL1.V57
    Viltrevy, Swedish Wildlife.
    Published by Swedish Sportsmen's Association.

Visnik Kyivs'k. Univ., ser. geol. geogr.   Period.
    Visnik Kyivs'kogo Universitetu seriiā geologii ta geografii
    Kiev: University Press.

Voprosy Filosofii   B8.R8.V58
    Akademiiā Nauk SSSR Institut Filosofii
    Moscow: "Pravda" Press. Six issues yearly.

Voprosy Geol. Vost. Okrainy Russk. Plat.   QE.276.V67
    Voprosy Geologii Vostochnoĭ Okrainy Russkoĭ Platformy i
    Iuzhnogo Urala.
    Akad. Nauk SSSR. Bashkirskiĭ filial. Gorno-Geologicheskiĭ
    Institut. Ufa.

Vorzeit am Bodensee   not seen
    Vorzeit am Bodensee. Mitteilungen zur vor- und Frühgeschichte

und Heimatkunde des Bodenseeraumes.
Überlingen, Germany.

W. Afr. Archaeol. Newsletter   NST350
    The West African Archaeological Newsletter. Institute of African
    Studies. University of Ibadan, Nigeria
    Includes reports of conferences of West African Archaeologists.

W. Virginia Geol. and Econ. Surv. Educational Ser.   E78.W6.M3
    West Virginia Geological and Economic Survey. Educational
    Series.
    Morgantown.

Waldviertel   not seen
    Das Waldviertel.

Warera-no-Kóbutsu   not seen
    [Our minerals.]
    Kyoto.

Wash. Archaeol.   E78.W3W3
    Washington Archaeologist.
    Seattle.

Wildlife in Australia   QL338.A1W54
    (Wildlife Preserv. Soc. Queensland)
    Brisbane

Wiss. Beihefte Zeit. "Die Höhle"   Cave Res.
    Wissenschaftliche Beihefte zur Zeitschrift "Die Höhle"   Assoc. Lib.
        Landesverein für Höhlenkunde in Wien und Niederösterreich.
        Wien.

Wiss. Ergeb. Oldoway-Exped.   not seen
    Wissenschaftliche Ergebnisse der Oldoway-Expedizion.

Wyniki Badán Wykopaliskowych   not seen
    Wyniki badán wykopaliskowych prowadzonych w roku 1964.
        Universytet Jagiellónski, katedra archeologii Polski.
        Krakow.

Wyo. Geol. Assoc. Guidebk., Highway Geol. Wyo.   QE181.W8F5
    The Wyoming Geological Association, Technical Studies Committee.
    Highway Geology of Wyoming, 1964.

Yankee.
    Publ. by Yankee, Inc., Dublin, N. H.

Year Book, Amer. Philos. Soc.   B11.A6
    Year Book of the American Philosophical Society.

Yediot, Tel-Aviv.   Harvard
 Yediot.   Univ.

Zabergäu-Ver.   not seen
 Zabergäu-Verein.
  Güglingen, W. Germany

Zapiski Zabaĭkal'. Otd. Geogr. Obshch. SSSR   Period.
 Zapiski Zabaĭkal'skogo Otdela Geograficheskogo Obshchestva SSSR
  Chita: Transzheldorizdat Press

Zeit. Morph. Anthrop.   QM1.Z4
 Zeitschrift für Morphologie und Anthropologie.
  Stuttgart.

Zeit. Rhein. Naturf. Ges. Mainz   Libr. of Congr.
 Zeitschrift, Rheinische Naturforschende Gesellschaft, Mainz. Wyoming Univ.

Zeit. Zellforsch.   QH301.Z38
 Zeitschrift für Zellforschung und mikroskopische Anatomie
  Berlin: Springer-Verlag.

Zeit. Zool. Syst. Evolut.-Forsch.   QL1.Z33
 Zeitschrift für zoologische Systematik und Evolutionsforchung
  Hamburg-Berlin: Paul Parey Verlag

Zoo   Period.
 Revista del Parque Zoológico de Barcelona.

Zool. Afr.   QL1.Z602
 Zoologica Africana.
  Cape Town.

Zool. Gothoburgensis, Göteberg   QL1.Z603
 Zoologica, Gothoburgensis,
  Göteberg.

Zool. Zhurnal   QL1.Z648
 Zoologicheskiĭ Zhurnal Akademiia Nauk SSSR
  Moscow: "Nauka" Press.
  English contents and summaries. Monthly ed. Formerly listed
  as Zool. Jour. Moscow.

Zprávy. Geol. Vyzk.   QE1.Z65
 Zprávy o geologických výzkumech
  Prague. (Czech.)

Zprávy Geol. Výzkumech   QE1.Z65
 Zprávy o Geologických Výzkumech v Roce Československé
  Akademie Věd.
  Nakladatelství. (Slovakian)

Zprávy Oblastního Musea   not seen
   v Gottwaldově

Zpravy Vlastivedneho Ust.   not seen
   Olomouci.

AUTHOR CATALOGUE

AUTHOR CATALOGUE

A., J. A.
    1966   La prehistoria, la protohistoria y la arqueologia. Bol. Inf. Cien. Nac.
                Quito, 95, 25—55.

AALOE, A. O.
    1963   [On the stratigraphic position and conditions of sedimentation of strata
                containing Tremataspis mammillata.]
                Uurimused Eesti N SV Tead. Akad. Geol. Inst., 13, 83-90, 4 figs., (Rus-
                sian; Esthonian and English summaries).

ABELENTŜEV, V. I., and PUT', A. L.
    1966   [A student of Ukrainian fauna — I. G. Pidoplichko (to his 60th anniver-
                sary).]
                In: Voinstvenskiĭ, M. A., (ed.), 183—200, portr., (Ukrainian).

ABELSON, PHILIP H.
    1959A.   Geochemistry of organic substances.
                In: Abelson, P. H., (ed.), 1959B, 79—103, 4 figs.
    1959B.   (ed.) Researches in geochemistry. New York: Wiley, x + 511., illustr.
    1963   Geochemistry of organic acids.
                In: Breger, I. A., (ed.), 1963, 431—455, 4 figs., 11 tables.

ABELTEKOV, A. K., GAVRIŨSHENKO, P. P., ZAUROVA, E. Z., KOZHEMIÂKO,
P. P., KOZHOMBERDIEV, I. K., and IŨNUSALIEV, M. B.
    1968   [Archeological works in Kirgizia.]
                In: Rybakov, (ed.), 356—360, (Russian).

ABOUX, MARIE-LOUISE   See: Mortier and Aboux.

ABRAMOV, I. Ĩa.
    1960   [Carved ornamented bones from the village of Romankova.]
                Krat. Soob. Inst. Arkheol. Akad. Nauk. URSR, 10, 13—15, 1 fig., (Russian).

ABRAMOV, M. Ĩa.
    1964   [Point from Romankovo village.]   Arkheologiĩa, 16, 172, 1 fig., (Ukrain-
                ian; Russian summary).

ABRAMOVA, E. A.
    1966   [Local features of Siberian Paleolithic cultures.]
                In: Rybakov, (ed.), 46—55, (Russian).

ABRAMOVA, Z. A.
    1957   [New findings of Upper Paleolithic human sculptures in Central and West-
                ern Europe.]
                Sov. Arkheol. 1957:3, 245—248, 5 figs., (Russian).
    1958   [The cave lion in Paleolithic art.]
                Sov. Arkheol., 1958:3, 7—17, 5 figs., (Russian).
    1959   [The problem of feminine images in Magdalenian.]

Krat. Soob. Inst. Ist. Mat. Kult. SSSR, 76, ·103—107, 2 figs., (Russian).

1960   [Role and significance of Paleolithic art in ascertaining local peculiarities
of Upper Paleolithic culture in Eastern Europe.]
Sov. Arkheol., 1960:3, 6—16, 2 figs., (Russian).

1961   [Representation of animals from the Paleolithic site at Aleksandrovka.]
Krat. Soob. Inst. Ist. Mat. Kult. SSSR, 82, 97—103, 2 figs., (Russian).

1962A.   [Paleolithic art in the territory of the USSR.]
Arkheol. SSSR, Svod Arkheol-Istochnikov, 1, 84 pp. 5 charts, 62 pls.,
1 map, (Russian).
Rev.: Vencl in Archeol. Roz., 15, 515; 18:3, 347, (Czech.).

1962B.   [Records of the palaeolithical arts in the territory of U.S.S.R.]
Issel. Archeol. SSSR, 17—33, 4 figs., 1 table, (Russian).

1962C.   [Excavations at Paleolithic sites on the river Tashtyk in 1960.]
Krat. Soob. Inst. Ist. Mat. Kult. SSSR, 92, 65—70, 2 figs., (Russian).

1962D.   [Krasnyĭ Iar — a new Paleolithic site on Angara.]
Sov. Arkheol., 1962:3, 147—156, 5 figs., (Russian).
Abs.: Chard in Asian Perspectives, 7, 12.

1964A.   [Paleolithic site Druzhinikha on the Eniseĭ.]
Krat. Soob. Inst. Ist. Mat. Kult. SSSR, 101, 69—73, 1 fig., (Russian).

1964B.   [On hunt in Upper Paleolithic.]
Sov. Arkheol., 1964: 4, 177—180, 2 figs., (Russian).

1965   Krasnyĭ Iar — a new Palaeolithic site on the Angara, Arctic Anthrop.,
3, 122—128, 5 figs., (trans. from Sov. Arkheol., 1962, no. 3,
147—156).

1966A.   [Representations of man in the Paleolithic art of Eurasia.]
Moscow-Leningrad: "Nauka" Press. 221 pp., 30 figs., 29 pls., (Russian).
Rev.: Klein in Amer. Anthrop., 69, 534—535.

1966B.   [On local differences in Paleolithic cultures of Angara and Eniseĭ.]
Sov. Arkheol., 1966:3, 9—16, 2 figs., (Russian).

1967A.   Palaeolithic art in the U.S.S.R. Translated by Catherine Page. Edited by
Chester S. Chard.
Arctic Anthrop., 4:2, 1—179, 62 pls., 6 tables, 1 map.

1967B.   [Research on Paleolithic of Eniseĭ R.]
In: Rybakov, (ed.), 135—136, (Russian).

1967C.   [On inset tools in Eniseĭ Paleolithic.]
Krat. Soob. Inst. Arkheol. Akad. Nauk SSSR, 111, 12—18, 2 figs.,(Russian).

1967D.   L'art mobilier paléolithique en URSS.
Quartär, 18, 99—125, 6 figs., 9 pls.

1968   [Investigation of Eniseĭ Paleolithic.]
In: Rybakov, (ed.), 161—162, (Russian).

ABSOLON, K.
1957   Abs: Ipek, 20, 125.

ACCORDI, BRUNO
1955   Rev.: Parodi Bustos in Rev. Fac. Cien. Nat. Salta, 1:1, 70.
1962B.   Rev.: Vaufrey in L'Anthrop., 68, 403—404.
1963   Rapporti fra il "Milazziano" della costa iblea (Sicilia sud-orientale e la
comparsa di Elephas mnaidriensis. Geol. Romana, 2, 295—304,
6 figs., (English summary).
Rev.: Vaufrey in L'Anthrop., 68, 403—404.

ACCORDI, B., and COLACICCHI, R.
1962   Rev.: Vaufrey in L'Anthrop., 68, 403—404.

ACCORDI, B., and LEONARDI, A.
  1959   La diatomite miocenica ad ittioliti di Bessima (Enna).
            Boll. Accad. Gioenia Sci. Nat., Catania, 22—27, (French, English and
            German summaries).

ADAM, ELEANOR K.   See: Guilday and Adam; Guilday, Hamilton and Adam.

ADAM, KARL DIETRICH
  1953C.   Abs.: Raabe in Zbl. Geol. Pal., Teil 2, 1964, 803.
  1961C.   Die Tiere der Vorzeit in der Wilhelmina zu Bad Cannstatt.
            Natur, 69, 153—163, (not seen).
  1964   Die Grossgliederung des Pleistozäns in Mitteleuropa.
            Stuttgarter Beitr. Z. Naturk., no. 132, 1—12, 8 tables.
  1965A.   Die vermeintlichen Primaten-Funde W. Freudenbergs aus dem
            Altpleistozän von Mauer, Bammental und Lützelsachsen.   Fundber.
            Schwaben, 17, 199—213, 2 figs., pl. 48, 9 tables.
  1965B.   Neue Flusspferd-Funde am Oberrhein. Jahresh. Geol. Landesamt.
            Baden-Württemberg, 7, 621—631, figs. 101—102, pls. 32—36,
            tables 31—31a, (English summary).
  1966A.   Die Mammutreste.
            In: Ehrenberg, (ed.), 1966A, 39—60, 4 pls., 1 table.
  1966B.   Quartärforschung am Staatlichen Museum für Naturkunde in Stuttgart.
            Stuttgarter Beitr. Z. Naturk., 167, 14 pp., 11 figs., 4 tables.
  1966C.   Zur Grossgliederung des mitteleuropäischen Pleistozäns.
            Zeit. Deutsche. Geol. Ges., 115, 751—757, 4 tables.

ADAMENKO, O. M.
  1963   [The stratigraphy of Quaternary deposits of the Altai Plain in the
            region of the confluence of the rivers Biia and Katun.]
            Trudy Kom. Chet. Period., 22, 150—164, 2 tables, (Russian).
  1966A.   [On the question of geological age of South Siberian Paleolithic.]
            Biull. Kom. Izuch. Chetvert. Perioda, 31, 138—141, (Russian).
  1966B.   [Geological conditions on a Mousterian site in Siberia.]
            Sov. Geol., 9: 5, 156—159, 2 figs., (Russian).
  1967   [Main features of stratigraphy of Quaternary deposits in the upper
            OB' R. Basin.]
            In: Collected papers [Stratigraphy of the Mesozoic and Cenozoic of
            Middle Siberia], 184—191, (Russian).
            See: Okladnikov and Adamenko.

ADAMENKO, O. M., and GAĬDUK, I. M.
  1967   [New finds of Paleolithic artifacts in the Altai foothills.]
            Izv. Altaĭsk. otd Geogr. Obshch. SSSR, 1967: 8, 24—28, (Russian).

ADAMENKO, O. M., and ZAZHIGIN, V. S.
  1965   [The fauna of small mammals and the geological age of Kochkovsk
            formation in Southern Kulunda.]
            In: Nikiforova, (ed.), 1965B, 166—171, (Russian; English summary).

ADAMS, ROBERT McCORMICK
  1953   The Kimmswick bone bed.
            Missouri Archaeol., 15: 4, 40—56, illustr.

ADAMS, R. M., and MAGRE, F.
1939   Archaeological surface survey of Jefferson County, Missouri.
          Missouri Archaeol., 5: 2, 11—23, illustr.

ADAMS, R. M., MAGRE, F., and MUNGER, P.
1941   Archaeological surface survey of Ste. Genevieve County, Mo.
          Missouri Archaeol., 7: 1, 9—23, illustr.

ADROVER, RAFAEL
1962   Hallazgo de restos de mastodonte in las arcillas rojas de teruel. Nuevo
              yacimiento de "Las Pedrizas". Teruel, no. 27, 193—198.
1963   Estado actual de las investigaciones paleontológicas en la provincia de
              Teruel.
          Teruel, no. 29, 89—148, 6 pls.
          Rev.: L. de A. in Notas Comun. Inst. Geol. Min., no. 73, 291.
1964A.   Un yacimiento de coprolitos en el Pontiense de Teruel.
          Est. Geol. Inst. Invest., Lucas Mallada, 19, 205—209, 2 figs.
          Rev.: H.—P. in Bol. Soc. Espan. Hist. Nat., Sec. Geol., 62, 272.
1964B.   El primer Hipopótamo del mundo: el Hipopótamo Turolense.
          Teruel, 32, 245—251.
1966   Pequeno intento de lavado de las tierras de la cueva de Son Muleta y
              los resultados obtenidos.
          Bol. Soc. Hist. Nat. Baleares, 12: 1—4, 39—46.
1968   Los primeros Micromamíferos de la cuenca valenciana, en Buñol.
              (Nota preliminar).
          Acta Geol. Hispánica, 3: 3, 78—80, (French summary).
          See: Crusafont Pairo and Adrover; Crusafont Pairo, Adrover and
              Golpe; Gasull and Adrover; Thaler, Crusafont and Adrover.

ADROVER, R., and ANGEL, BASILIO DE LA SALLE
1966   Yacimiento del cuaternario continental, en Son Vida.
          Bol. Soc. Hist. Nat. Baleares, 12: 1—4, 107—110.

ADYALKAR, P. G.
1961   A note on the Palaeolithic and Neolithic cultures of Baripada,
              Mayurbhanj District, Orissa.
          Proc. Indian Sci. Congr., 48, 446, (abs.).

AFANAS'EV, A. V.
1960   [Zoogeography of Kazakhstan. (On the basis of mammals distribution).]
          Alma-Ata: Akad. Nauk Kazakh. SSR Press, 259 pp., ill., (Russian).

AGACHE, M. R.
1962   L'Abbé Henri Breuil.
          Bull. Trimestriel Soc. Antiq. Picardie, 1961, 59—60.

AGACHE, ROGER
1958F.   Aperçu des recherches sur le Paléolithique de la Somme depuis Victor
              Commont. Bull. Trimestrial Soc. Antiq. Picardie, 1958, 269—292.
1961   La "ballastiere hydraulique", une déplorable innovation pour les recherches
              archéologiques. Bull. Soc. Préhist., Paris, 57, 660—661.

AGACHE, R., BOURDIER, F., and PETIT, R.
1964   Le Quaternaire de la basse Somme: tentative de synthèse. Bull. Soc.
              Géol. France, 5, 422—442, 16 figs.

AGASSIZ, LOUIS
1967   Studies on glaciers. Preceded by the discourse of Neuchâtel. Translated
        and edited by Albert V. Carozzi. New York, London: Hafner,
        lxxi + 213 pp., frontispiece, 6 figs., 18 pls.
    Rev.: Flint in Science, 159, 520.

AGER, D. V.
1963B. Rev.: Beerbower in Amer. Sci., 52, 224A;   Birkelund in Meddel. Dansk
        Dansk Geol. Foren., 15, 398–399, (Danish);   Faegri in Naturen,
        88, 54–55, (Norwegian);   Livingstone in Ecology, 45, 424:   Manten
        in Palaeogeog., Palaeoclimatol., Palaeoecol., 1, 173–176;   Martinsson
        in Geol. Fören. Förh., 86, 114–115, (Swedish);   Miller in Co-
        peia, 1964, 730–731;   M.J.S.R. in Geol. Mag., 101, 191–192;
        Roscoe in Amer. Mid. Nat., 71, 251–253;   Rossi Ronchetti in
        Riv. Ital. Pal., 70, 156–157;   Skinner in Tulane Studies Geol.,
        2, 107;   v. V. in Geol. en Mijn., 43, 131–132, (Dutch);   Vogel
        in Zbl. Geol. Pal., Teil 2, 1964, 393–395.
1965   Serial grinding techniques. In: Kummel and Raup, (eds.), 1965, 212–
        224, 7 figs.

AGOGINO, GEORGE A.
1960A. The need for more state and federal aid for paleo-archaeology in the
        United States. New World Antiq., 7, 20–23.
1960B. Some pre-ceramic archaeological problems in the northern Plains and
        plateau area. New World Antiq., 7, 36–39.
1963C. Bison and the Paleo Indian. Anthrop. Jour. Canada, 1: 4, 2–3, 2 figs.
1963D. The Paleo-Indian relative age and cultural sequence. Great Plains Jour.,
        3, 17–24.
1964A. Recent progress at the Clovis site. Newsletter Okla. Anthrop. Soc., 12: 8,
        5–6.
1964B. A typological re-evaluation of the Paleo-Indian cultures of the High Plains.
        New World Antiq., 11, 98–106, 1 fig.
1964C. The Cody complex. New World Antiq., 11, 134–140, 1 fig.
1964D. The Cody complex. Wyo. Archaeol., 7: 2, 38–42, illustr.
1965A. The possibility of the pre-projectile Paleo-Indian. New World Antiq., 12,
        47–50.
1965B. The Blackwater Draw site and the people of New Mexico: a thirty year
        perspective. Wyo. Archaeol., 8: 1, 21–23.
1966   The Paleo-Indian chronology and cultural sequence. Wyo. Archaeol., 9: 2,
        18–25.
1967   An archaeologist's view of pre-projectile point cultures. Screenings, 16: 8,
        2–3, 2 figs.
1968   The experimental removal of preservatives from radiocarbon samples.
        Plains Anthrop., 13, 146–147.
    See: Brace 1964; Egan and Agogino; Haynes and Agogino; Irwin, Irwin
        and Agogino; Irwin, Irwin-Williams and Agogino; Irwin-Williams,
        Agogino and Irwin; Robbins and Agogino; Smith, Calvin, Runyan
        and Agogino; Smith, S. and Agogino; Tillson 1966.

AGOGINO, G. A. and FRANKFORTER, W. D.
1964   The Brewster site: a Paleo-Indian site in eastern Wyoming. Wyo. Archaeol.,
        7: 4, 7–11, illustr.

AGOGINO, G. A., and GALLOWAY, E.
   1965   The Sister's Hill site: a Hell Gap site in north-central Wyoming. Plains
             Anthrop., 10, 190–195, 4 figs.

AGOGINO, G. A., and ROVNER, I.
   1964   Palaeo-Indian traditions: a current evaluation. Archaeol., 17, 237–243,
             illustr.
   1965   Eastern New Mexico University excavations at Blackwater Draw: Locality
             number one. 7th Internat. Congr., Internat. Assoc. Quat. Res.,
             Abs., 1965, 3, (abs.).

AGOGINO, G. A., ROVNER, I., and IRWIN-WILLIAMS, C.
   1964   Early man in the New World. Science, 143, 1350–1352, 1 fig.

AGRON, SAM L.
   1965   Large fossil fish stolen. Rocks and Minerals, 40, 511, illustr.

AGUIRRE, EMILIANO de
   1963A.   Abs.: Lotze in Zbl. Geol. Pal., Teil 2, 1964, 687–688.
   1963B.   Abs.: Lotze in Zbl. Geol. Pal., Teil 2, 1964, 715.
   1963C.   Abs.: Lotze in Zbl. Geol. Pal., Teil 2, 1964, 715.
   1963D.   Abs.: Lotze in Zbl. Geol. Pal., Teil 2, 1964, 688.
   1964A.   Presencia en España de un félido del Neogeno chino, Metailurus Zdanski.
             Bol. Soc. Español. Hist. Nat., Sec. Geol., 62, 245–249, 2 figs.
   1964B.   Los elefantes de las terrazas medias de Toledo y la edad de estos
             depositos. Notas Comun. Inst. Geol. Min., 76, 295–296.
   1965   Studies on stratigraphic paleomammalogy in Pleistocene of Spain.
             7th Internat. Congr., Internat. Assoc. Quat. Res., Abs., 1965,
             4–5, (abs.).
   1968   Une interprétation Biomécanique de l'évolution de la région glabellaire
             dans l'anthropogenèse. Discussion. 7th Internat. Congr. Anthrop.
             Ethnol. Sci., Moscow, 1964, 3, 347–357, 13 figs.
             See: Crusafont Pairo, Aguirre and García; Esteras and Aguirre; Hoff-
             stetter, Crusafont and Aguirre; Howell, Butzer and Aguirre; Mar-
             tel San Gil and Aguirre.

AGGUIRRE, E. de, and BUTZER, K. W.
   1967   Problematical Pleistocene artifact assemblage from northwestern Spain.
             Science, 157, 430–431, 1 fig.

AGUIRRE, E. de, COLLINS, D., and CUENCA, J.
   1964   Perspectivas del Paleolitico inferior en España. Noticiario Arqueológico
             Hispánico, 6:1–3, 7–14.

AGGUIRRE, E. de, and MACORRA, LOUIS de la
   1964   Sobre las formaciones supraorbitarias en fósiles humanos. Bol. R. Soc.
             Española Hist. Nat., Sec. Biol., 62, 73–83, 6 figs., (English
             summary).

AHLÉN, INGEMAR
   1965A.   Studies on the red deer, Cervus elaphus L., in Scandinavia. I. History of
             distribution. Viltrevy, 3, 1–88, 13 figs., (Swedish summary).
   1965B   Studies on the red deer, Cervus elaphus L., in Scandinavia. II. Taxonomy
             and osteology of prehistoric and recent populations. Viltrevy, 3,
             89–176, 162 figs., (Swedish summary).

1965C.　　Studies on the red deer, Cervus elaphus L., in Scandinavia. III. Ecologi-
　　　　　cal investigations. Viltrevy, 3, 177—376, 93 figs., (Swedish sum-
　　　　　mary).

AIELLO, PAUL V.　See: Meighan, et al.

AIGNER, JEAN　See: Chia, Wang and Wang; Laughlin and Aigner.

AITKEN, M. J.
　　1961　　Rev.: Goodman in Ohio Archaeol., 15, 111—112.
　　　　　　Rev.: Matson in Amer. Anthrop., 66, 1211—1212.

AKERLEY, ROBERT L.　See: Neal and Akerley.

AKHUNDOV, F. M.
　　1963　　[Morphological differences of Necromites nestoris from the family Seman-
　　　　　　toridae (Mammalia, Pinnipedia).] Izv. Akad. Nauk, Azerbaidzhan,
　　　　　　SSR., 1963:3, 9—14, (Russian; Azerbaidzani summary).

AKIYAMA, M., ITO, Y., and SASAKI, S.
　　1968　　[Citric acid in fossil tusks of Elephas naumanni Makiyama.] Journ.
　　　　　　Geol. Soc. Japan, 74:4, 245—246, (Japanese).

AKSENOV, M. P., and MEDVEDEV, G. I.
　　1966　　[New data on Pre-Neolithic period of Angara region.] Izv. Vost.-Sib. Otd.
　　　　　　Geogr. Obshch. SSSR, 65, 153—165, 6 pls., 1 chart, (Russian).

ALARCAO, JORGE de
　　1965　　Palaeolithic cave paintings in Portugal. Archaeol., 18, 228—229, illustr.

ALBERS, HANS, and WEILER, W.
　　1964　　Eine Fischfauna aus der oberen Kreide von Aachen und neuere Funde,
　　　　　　von Fischresten aus dem Maestricht des angrenzenden belgisch —
　　　　　　holländischen Raumes. Neues Jahrb. Geol. Pal., Abh., 120, 1—33,
　　　　　　51 figs., 1 table.

ALBERT, ETHEL M.　See: Mandelbaum, Lasker and Albert.

ALBRECHT, P. W.
　　1967　　The cranial arteries and cranial arterial foramina of the turtle genera
　　　　　　Chrysemys, Sternotherus, and Trionyx: a comparative study with
　　　　　　analysis of possible evolutionary implications. Tulane Studies
　　　　　　Zool., 14, 81—99, 3 figs.

ALBRING, W.
　　1967　　[Mechanics and living beings.] Priroda, 1967:7, 58—65, 6 figs.,
　　　　　　(Russian).

ALBRITTON, CLAUDE C., JR.
　　1963　　Rev.: Roscoe in Amer. Mid. Nat., 71, 509—510.
　　1964　　Second bibliography and index for the philosophy of geology. Jour.
　　　　　　Grad. Res. Center, S. Methodist Univ., 33, 73—114.
　　1966　　Third bibliography and index for the philosophy of geology. Jour. Grad.
　　　　　　Res. Center, S. Methodist Univ., 35, 55—87.

ALBRITTON, C. C., Jr., and WENDORF, F.
1967   Geology of the Tushka archeological site in southern Egypt. Program,
        1967 Ann. Meeting, Geol. Soc. Amer., 1967, 3, (abs.).

ALCINA FRANCH, JOSÉ
1965   Manual de arqueología americana. Madrid: Aguilar, xx + 821 pp., 561
        figs., 26 tables, 36 maps.

ALDINGER, HERMANN
1965   Zur Ökologie und Stratinomie der Fische des Posidonienschiefers (Lias
        Epsilon). Senck. Lethaea, 46a, 1-12, 3 figs., 1 table, (English
        abstract).
        Abs.: Weiler in Zbl. Geol. Pal., Teil 2, 1966, 268-269.

ALEJO VIGNATI, MILCÍADES   See: Vignati, Milcíades Alejo.

ALEKPEROV, A. M.   See: Khozatskiĭ and Alekperov.

ALEKPEROVA, N. A.
1959   [Find of fossil remains of Cervus pliotarandoides Alessandri in Northern
        Caucasus.] Izv. Akad. Nauk Azerbaĭdzhan. SSR, Ser. Geol.-
        Geogr. Nauk, 1959: 2, 43-52, 2 figs., 2 tables, (Azerbaijanian;
        Russian summary).
1964   [The discovery of a new, for Azerbaĭdzhan, deer, Cervus (Rusa) from
        Upper Pliocene deposits.] Izv. Akad. Nauk Azerbaĭdzhan. SSR,
        1964: 2, 59-62, 2 fig., (Russian; Azerbaidzhani summary).
1966   [On the history of studies on fossil deer in Azerbaijan.] Uch. zapiski
        Azerb. Un., ser. biol., 1966: 1, 35-39, (Russian).

ALEKSANDROV, A. L.
1967   [Archeological finds on Kirenga R.] Izv. Vost.-Sib. Otd. Geogr. Obshch.
        SSSR, 65, 166-172, 3 pls., 1 map, (Russian).

ALEKSANDROV, V. A.
1965   [In memory of academician M. N. Tikhomirov.] Sovetskaĭa Etnografiĭa,
        1965: 6, 138-141, portr., (Russian).

ALEKSANDROVA, L. P.
1965A. [Fossil Eopleistocene voles (Rodentia, Microtinae) from South Moldavia
        and South-West Ukraine.]
        In: Nikiforova, (ed.), 1965B, 98-110, 24 figs., 1 table, (Russian; English
        summary).
1965B. [Rodents from Khazarian deposits of lower Volga region (Chernyĭ Iar).]
        In: Nikiforova, (ed.), 1965B, 149-157, 8 figs., (Russian; English summary).
1966   [New species of large fossil voles from Lower Quaternary sediments of
        southwestern Ukraine (Kotlovina vill.).] Biul. Kon. Izuch. Chetvert.
        Perioda, 32, 40-45, 4 figs., (Russian).
1967   [Rodents of Khaprovskiĭ faunistic complex.] Biull. Kom. Izuch. Chetvert.
        Perioda, 34, 87-98, 6 fig., (Russian).

ALEKSANDROVA, L. P., and TSEĬTLIN, S. M.
1965   [Occurrence of fossil remains of small mammals in Quaternary deposits
        of Nerl' R. Basin (Vladimir Province).]
        In: Nikiforova, (ed.), 1965B, 158-161, 4 figs., (Russian; English summary).

ALEKSEEV, M. N.
1961   Abs.: Mirtsching in Zbl. Geol. Pal., Teil 2, 1964, 672.
1961A.   [Materials on the stratigraphy of Cenozoic deposits and on geomorphology of the central part of Viliuĩ depression.] Trudy Ĩakut. fil. AN SSSR, Ser. Geol., 6, 180—226, 6 figs., 1 table, (Russian).
1961B.   [Stratigraphy of continental Neogene and Quaternary deposits of the Viliũsk depression and the valley of the lower Lena R.] Trudy Geol. Inst., 51, 117 pp., 35 figs., 8 tables, (Russian).
1964   [On the problem of zoning of sedimentation processes during the Anthropogene of Eastern Asia.] Izv. Akad. Sci. USSR, Geol. Ser., 1964:9, 65—83, 1 map, 1 table, (Russian).
        Rev.: Stoltenberg in Zbl. Geol. Pal., Teil 2, 1968, 24—25.
        See: Dubrovo and Alekseev; Gromov, V. I., et al.

ALEKSEEV, M. N., GITERMAN, R. E., KUPRINA, N. P., MEDIANTSEV, A. I., and KHOREVA, I. M.
1961   [Quaternary deposits of Ĩakutiĩa.]
        In: Gromov, V.I., et al., (eds.), 1961, 129—140, 1 table, (Russian; English summary).

ALEXEEV, M. N., KUPRINA, N. P., MEDIANTSEV, A. I., and KHOREVA, I. M.
1962   [Stratigraphy and correlation of Neogene and Quaternary deposits of the north-eastern part of the Siberian platform and its eastern folded margin.] Trudy Geol. Inst., 66, 126 pp., 37 figs., 10 tables, (Russian).

ALEKSEEV, M. N., RAVSKIĨ, E. I., and TSEĨTLIN, S. M.
1965   [Principles of Anthropogene geochronology in Eastern Siberia.]
        In: Nikiforova, (ed.), 1965A, 68—77, (Russian; English summary).
1966   [Fundamental geochronological stages of Anthropogene of the Siberian platform.] Izv. Akad. Nauk SSSR, ser. Geol., 1966:3, 101—103. 1 table, (Russian).

ALEKSEEV, V. A.
1959   [Some problems of anthropogenesis theory.] Voprosy Filosofii, 1959:11, 104—116, (Russian).
        See: Cherdyntsev, et al.

ALEKSEEV, V. A., IVANOVA, I. K., KIND, N. V., and CHERNYSH, A. P.
1964   [New data on the absolute age of Late Paleolithic levels of the site Moldova V on the Middle Dnestr.] Dokl. Akad. Nauk SSSR, 156: 2, 315—317, (Russian).

ALEKSEEV, V. P. (=Alexeev)
1960   [Some problems of the development of the wrist in the process of anthropogenesis (about the place of the Kiik-Koba man among Neanderthal forms).] Trudy Inst. Etnograf., 50, 179—209, 16 tables, (Russian).
1964   [Anthropological research in U.S.S.R.] Sovetskaiã Etnografiiã, 1964:4, 40—67, (Russian).
1965   [The 70-th anniversary of Ĩa. Ĩa. Roginskiĩ.] Sovetskaiã Etnografiiã, 1965: 3, 153—155, (Russian).
1966A.   [Osteometry. Methods for anthropological research.] Moscow: 251 pp., 71 figs., (Russian).
1966B.   [Hominids of the second half of Middle Pleistocene and of the Early Upper Pleistocene.] Trudy Inst. Etnogr. Akad. Nauk SSSR, 92, 143—181, 10 figs., 5 tables, (Russian).

1968A.   On the rate of evolution within the Hominidae family. Discussion. 7th
Internat. Congr. Anthrop. Ethnol. Sci., Moscow, 1964, 3, 433–440,
3 tables.

1968B.   [Contemporary state of craniological investigations in the domain of racio-
logy.] Voprosy Anthrop., 30, 17–37, 7 figs., 1 table, (Russian).

ALEKSEEVA, L. I. (=Aleksejewa, Alexeeva)

1959C.   [The significance of mammalian fauna from the Armavir formation for the
stratigraphy of the continental strata of the northern Caucasus.]
Trudy Geol. Inst., 32, 185–191, (Russian).

1961A.   [Oldest mammal fauna from Anthropogene of the South of European
part of USSR.]   Internat. Assoc. Quat. Res., Abs. Pap., 6-th Congr.,
125, (abs.; Russian).

1961B.   [Oldest mammalian fauna of the Anthropogene in the European South of
the USSR.]
In: Gromov, V. I. et al., (eds.), 1961, 31–40, 1 table, (Russian; English
summary).

1961C.   [On an early phase in the development of Quaternary Mammalian fauna
on the territory of the European part of USSR.]   Izv. Akad. Nauk
SSSR, Ser. Geol., 1961:12, 87–96, 2 tables, (Russian).
Abs.: Stoltenberg in Zbl. Geol. Pal., Teil 2, 1964, 184–185.

1964   [New finds of bones of monkeys of the Cercopithecidae family in the
South of the European part of USSR.]   Voprosy Anthrop., 16,
129–134, 2 figs., 3 tables, (Russian).

1965   [Stratigraphical review of the proboseideans of Eopleistocene (according
to the materials of the European South of the USSR).]
In: Gromov, V. I., et al., (eds.), 1965, 69–90, 5 pls., 8 tables, (Russian;
English summary).

1966   [New finds of sites of Eopleistocene mammalian fauna in Khar'kov province.] Biull. Kom. Izuch. Chetvert. Perioda, 31, 122–127, 2 figs.,
2 tables, (Russian).

1967A.   [Influence of temperature decrease on formation of Early Quaternary
mammalian complexes of the northern Black Sea region.]
In: Collected Papers, 1967. [Place and significance of fossil mammals of
Moldavia in the Cenozoic of USSR], 46–56 (Russian).

1967B.   [Moldavian complex of mammalian fauna.]   Pal. geol. polezn. iskop.
Moldavii, 2, 111–115, (Russian).

1967C.   [Contribution to the history of subfamily Bovinae in the Eopleistocene
of the European part of USSR.] Pal. geol. polezn. iskop. Moldavii,
2, 125–142, 2 figs., 3 tables, (Russian).
See: Aliman, M.-H. 1960B; Avakian and Alekseeva; Nikiforova and Alekseeva.

ALEKSEEVA, L. I., and GARUTT, V. E.

1965   [New data on the evolution of elephants of the genus Arkhidiskodon.]
Biull. Izuch. Chetvert. Perioda Akad. Nauk SSSR, No. 30,
161–166, 2 fig., (Russian).

ALEKSEEVA, L. I., and LOMIZE, M. G.

1960   [On the discovery of Pleistocene mammal fauna on the upper course of
Belaia R.] Izv. Vyssh. Uch. Zav., Geol. i Razv., 1960:2, 29–33,
1 fig., 2 tables, (Russian).

ALEKSEEVA, L. V. (= Alexeeva)
1968 [Certain problems of Primates phylogeny in relation to the study of
steroid hormones.] 7th Internat. Congr. Anthrop. Ethnol. Sci.,
Moscow, 1964, 3, 450—454, (Russian).

ALESSIO, M., BELLA, F., and CORTESI, C.
1964 University of Rome Carbon-14 dates II. Radiocarbon, 6, 77—90.

ALESSIO, M., BELLA, F., BACHECHI, F., and CORTESI, C.
1965 University of Rome Carbon-14 dates III. Radiocarbon, 7, 213—222.
1966 University of Rome Carbon-14 dates IV. Radiocarbon, 8, 401—412.
1967 University of Rome Carbon-14 dates V. Radiocarbon, 9, 346—367.

ALEXANDER, H. L., JR. See: Simons and Alexander.

ALEXANDER, JACK See: Wade, et al.

ALEXANDERSEN, V.
1963 Double-rooted human lower canine teeth.
In: Brothwell, D. R., (ed.), 1963, 235—244, 4 figs.
1967A. The pathology of the jaws and the temporomandibular joint.
In: Brothwell, Don, and Sandison, A. T., (eds.), 1967, 551—595, 17
figs., 4 tables.
1967B. The evidence for injuries to the jaws.
In: Brothwell, Don, and Sandison, A. T., (eds.), 1967, 623—629, 2 figs.

ALEXANDROVA, L. P. See: Ravskiĭ, Alexandrova, et al.; Vasil'ev, Iu. M. and
Alexandrova.

ALF, RAYMOND M.
1966 Mammal trackways from the Barstow formation, California. Bull. S.
Calif. Acad. Sci., 65, 258—264, 4 figs.

ALFORD, MALCOLM See: Lance, et al.

ALIEV, S. D. See: Gadzhiev and Aliev.

ALIMEN, MARIE-HENRIETTA (=Aliman, A.)
1955C. Rev.: Kühn in Ipek, 20, 122—123.
1960B. [Prehistoric Africa.] Trans. from French by L. I. Alekseeva, N. S.
Ivanova, O. L. Kasilova under the editorship of V. I. Gromov
and N. I. Kriger. Moscow: Izd-vo Foreign Literature, 503 pp.,
155 figs., 29 tables, (Russian, not seen).
Rev.: Alekseev and Fadeev of Russian trans. of L'Afrique préhistorique
in Sov. Etnog., 1962:2, 165—168; Debetz in Sov. Etnog., 1962:2,
169—172.
1962 Rev.: Dekeyser in Bull. Inst. Franç. Afr. Noire, Sér. B, 25, 478; Pericot in Zephyrus, 14, 146; D. de S. in L'Anthrop., 69:5—6,
536; Vallos in L'Anthrop., 68, 163—164.
1964A. La redoute des Hautes Bruyères. Bull. Assoc. Franç. Étude Quat., 1,
50—52, 2 figs.
1964B. La Celle — sous — Moret. Bull. Assoc. Franç. Étude Quat., 1, 53—58,
2 figs.

1964C. Considérations sur la chronologie de Quaternaire saharien. Bull. Soc. Géol.
France, 5, 627—634, 3 tables.
Rev.: R. V. in L'Anthrop., 70: 3—4, 351—352.

1964D. Le quaternaire des Pyrénées de la Bigorre. Mém. Expl. Carte Géol.
France, 386 pp., 117 figs., 12 pls., 24 tables (not seen).
Abs.: Anon. in Bull. Soc. Préhist. Franç. C.R. Séances Mens., 1964:8,
CLXXX — CLXXXI.
Rev.: Bonifay in L'Anthrop., 70: 1—2, 134—137.

1964E. Pyrénées centrales françaises. Préhistoire et données paléoclimatiques des
alluvions.
In: Ripoll Perelló, E., (ed.), 1964A, 101—111, 1 pl., (English summary).

1965A. Considérations sur les nucléus du Paléolithique ancien au Sahara Nord-
Occidental. Actas V Congr. Panafr. Prehist. Estud. Cuaternario,
1963: 1, 103—116, 4 figs., 3 pls.

1965B. Atlas de préhistoire. Tome I: généralités, méthodes de préhistoire. Rev.
and enlarged ed. Paris: Boubée (Collection L'Homme et ses
origines), 186 pp., 97 figs., 16 pls., 4 color pls., 1 map, 1 table.
Rev.: Anon. in La Nature, 93, 368; Boné in Anthropologica, 9, 97;
Bordaz in Science, 150, 333; Chavaillon in Bull. Assoc. Franç.,
Étude Quat., 3, 171—172; Furon in Rev. Gén. Sci., 73, 314;
Howell in Amer. Jour. Phys. Anthrop., 23, 453; Jeancolas in Bull.
Soc. Linn. Lyon, 35, 249—250; Martí Jusmet in Ampurias, 28,
315—316; Naber in Quartär, 17, 217—218; D. de S. in L'Anthrop.,
69: 5-6, 536—537; Sauter in Arch. Suiss. Anthrop. Gen., 30,
92—93.

.1965C. The Quaternary era in northwest Sahara. Spec. Pap. Geol. Soc. Amer.,
84, 273—291, 3 figs., (French summary).

1966 Généralités sur les faunes et les flores Quaternaires de l'Europe occidentale. In: Lavocat, R., (ed.), 1966, 13—38, figs. 1—4,
tables 1—4.

1967 The Quaternary of France. In: Rankama, K., (ed.), 1967, vol. 2, 89—
238, 33 figs., 14 tables.

1968 Chronologie des formations contenant des industries acheuléennes dite de
"Tabelbala-Tachenghit" (Sahara-nord-occidental). C. R. Acad.
Sci. Paris, Sci. Nat., 267, 839—842.

ALIMEN, MARIE-HENRIETTA   See: Arambourg 1965B; Biberson 1965A.

ALIMEN, M.-H., and CHAVAILLON, J.
1962 Position stratigraphique et évolution de la Pebble Culture au Sahara nord-
occidental. Proc. 4th Panafrican Congr. Prehist., Sec. 3, 3—26,
3 figs., 1 pl., 2 tables, (discussion by J. de Heinzelin, J. D.
Clark, L. S. B. Leakey, and C. Arambourg).

ALIMEN, H., CHAVAILLON, N., and KARPOFF, R.
1963 Nouveaux gisements paléolithiques dans l'Adrar des Iforas (Sahara). Bull.
Soc. Préhist., Paris, 60, 352—363, 3 figs., 4 pls.

ALIMEN, H., RĂDULESCO, C., and SAMSON, P.
  1968   Précisions paléontologiques et indices climatiques relatifs aux couches
          pléistocènes de la dépression de Braşov (Roumanie). C. R. Soc.
          Géol. France, 1968: 8, 272.

ALIZADE, K. A.
  1967   [Development of paleontological-stratigraphic research in Azerbaïdzhan.]
          Izv. Akad. Nauk Azerb. SSR, ser. Nauk o Zemle, 1967: 3–4,
          78–80, (Russian).

ALIZADE, A. N., ASADOV, S. M., and DERZHAVIN, A. N. (eds.)
  1951   [Animal life of Azerbaidzhan.] Baku: Izd. Akad. Nauk Azerb. SSR.,
          601 pp., 191 figs., 28 tables, 3 fold. maps, (Russian).

ALJTER, S. P.
  1960   [Zur Stratigraphie des Quartärs im Jenissej-Tal zwischen Krasnojarsk und
          Ustj-Pit.] Inform. Sbornik Vses. Geol. Inst., 39, 53–64, (Russian;
          not seen).
          Abs.: Mirtsching in Zbl. Geol. Pal., Teil 2, 1964, 700–701.

ALKER, JULIUS
  1966   A review of Eumys elegans Leidy, 1856 (Muridae: Mammalia). Proc.
          Neb. Acad. Sci., 76th Ann. Meeting, 1966, 12, (abs.).
  1968   The occurrence of Paracricetodon Schaub (Cricetidae) in North America.
          Jour. Mammal., 49, 529–530, 1 fig.

ALLCHIN, BRIDGET
  1959   The Indian Middle Stone Age: some new sites in central and southern
          India, and their implications. Bull. London Univ. Inst. Archaeol.,
          No. 2, 1–36, 7 figs.
  1964   Professor F. E. Zeuner [1905-1963]. Jour. Orient. Inst., 13, 163–164.
  1966   The stone-tipped arrow. Late Stone Age hunters of the tropical Old
          World. London: Phoenix House, xii + 224 pp., 43 figs., 16 pls.,
          4 maps.
          Rev.: Anon. in Mankind Quart., 7, 186; Binford in Amer. Anthrop., 70,
          412–413; Inskeep in Man, Jour. Roy. Anthrop. Inst., 2, 311;
          Mohapatra in E. Anthrop., 20, 280–283; Wainwright in Antiq. Jour.,
          47, 292.

ALLEGRANZI, A.   See: Leonardi, P., Allegranzi and Broglio.

ALLEN, J. R. L.
  1964   Pre-Pickwell Down age of the Plateau Beds (Upper Devonian) in South
          Wales. Nature, 204. 364–366, 2 figs.

ALLEN, JACK A.   See: Haynes, Doberenz and Allen.

ALLEN, K. A.   See: Pokorný 1965.

ALLIN, E. F.   See: Robinson, J. T. and Allin.

ALLISON, HARRIET J.   See: Camp, C. L., et al.

ALLISON, IRA S.
1966   Fossil Lake, Oregon: Its geology and fossil faunas.   Studies in Geol.,
        Oregon State Univ., no. 9, 48 pp., 3 figs., 23 pls., 5 tables.
        Rev.:   Whitmore in Jour. Pal., 41, 814–815.

ALMAGRO BASCH, MARTÍN
1960A.   Rev.:   González del solar in An. Arqueol. Etnol., Univ. Nac. Cuyo, 17–18,
          217–218.
1960B.   Rev.:   Berdichewsky S. in Antropología, 2:1, 127–128;   Pittioni in
          Archaeol. Austriaca, 33, 114.
1960C.   Las pinturas rupestres cuaternarias de la cueva de Maltravieso, en Caceres.
          Trab. Seminario Hist. Primitiva Hombre Univ. Madrid y Inst.
          Español. Prehist. Consejo Superior Invest. Cien., 1, 45 pp., 15 pls.,
          1 map.
          Rev.:   Carluci in Humanitas, 3:1, 91–92;   Sonneville-Bordes in L'Anthrop.,
          66, 348–349.
1963   Introducción al estudio de la prehistoria y de la arqueología de campo.
        2nd revised and enlarged ed.   Madrid: Ediciones Guadarrama,
        276 pp., (not seen).
        Rev.:   Llongueras Campaña in Ampurias, 28, 315;   Orellana Rodriguez
        in Antropología, 2:1, 125–127.
1964   El problema de la revisión de la cronología del arte rupestre cuaternario.
        In: Ripoll Perelló, E., (ed.) 1964A, 87–100.
1964-   Prof. Eduardo Hernández-Pacheco.   Ampurias, 26–27, 359–360.
1965
1966   Die bildende Kunst der jüngeren Altsteinzeit.
        In: Narr, (ed.), 269–297, 15 figs.

ALMAGRO BASCH, M. and ARRIBAS, A.
1956   Avance de la primera campaña de excavaciones realizadas en Los Millares
        (Almeria).
        In: Beltrán Martinez, A., ed., Congreso Internacional de Ciencias Prehis-
        tóricas y Protohistoricas, Actas IV Sesión, Madrid, 1954, 419–426,
        (not seen).

ALMEIDA, ANTÓNIO DE See: Breuil and Almeida.

ALMEIDA, ANTÓNIO DE, and CAMARATE FRANÇA, J.
1965   Le Magosien du Sud de l'Angola.   Actas V Congr. Panafr. Prehist. Estud.
        Cuaternario, 1963: 1, 117–126, 2 pls., 1 map.

[ALMELA SAMPER, ANTONIO]
1963   Doctor J. R. Bataller [1890-1962].   Bol. Inst. Geol. Min. España, 74,
        3–10, portr.

ALOISE, FRANK   See: Baldwin, G. C. 1963;   Ludovici 1963.

ALONSO DEL REAL Y RAMOS, CARLOS
1964   Notulae Breuilianae.
        In: Ripoll Perelló, E., (ed.), 1964, 113–121, (Spanish; English summary);

ALPYSBAEV, Kh. A.
1959A.   [Findings of Lower Paleolithic in South Kazakhstan.]   Trudy Inst. Ist.
          Arkheol. Etnogr. Akad. Nauk Kazakh. SSR, 7, 232—241. 10 figs.,
          (Russian).
1959B.   [Lower Paleolithic sites in the Little Karatau Mountains.]   Vestnik Akad.
          Nauk Kazakh. SSR, 1959:2, 64—70, 4 figs., (Russian).
1960   [Lower Paleolithic discoveries in Kazakhstan.]   Vestnik Akad. Nauk
          Kazakh. SSR, 1960:5, 59—6l.
1961A.   [Discovery of ancient and Late Paleolithic in South Kazakhstan.]   Sov.
          Arkheol., 1961: 1, 128—138, 11 figs., (Russian).
1961B.   [New Paleolithic sites in the Arystandy-Buryltaĭ (Boroldaĭ) rivers basin in
          South Kazakhstan.]   Trudy Inst. Ist. Arkheol. Etnogr. Akad. Nauk
          Kazakh. SSR, 12, 3—20, 8 plates, (Russian).
1962   [Discovery of Stone Age relics in Karatau ridge.]   Trudy Inst. Ist. Arkheol.
          Etnogr. Akad. Nauk Kazakh. SSR, 14, 12—37, 19 figs., (Russian).
1966   [Did primitive man have stone tools?]   Izv. Akad. Nauk Kazakh. SSR,
          seriia obshch. nauk, 1966: 4, 91—92, (Kazakh).
See: Kostenko, N. N. and Alpysbaev.

ALPYSBAEV, Kh. K.
1959   [Some results of the study of flint implements.]   Krat. Soob. Inst. Ist.
          Mat. Kult., 76, 10—16, 3 figs., (Russian).

AL'TER, S. P.
1960   [On the stratigraphy of Quaternary deposits of Eniseĭ R. valley between
          Krasnoĭarsk and Ust'-Pit.]   Informatsionnyĭ Sbornik, 39, 53—64,
          2 tables, (Russian).

ALTMEYER, HANS
1964   Fossilien aus den Rheinablagerungen der Umgebung Kölns. Aufschluss,
          15, 50—53, 3 figs.

ALTUNA, JESÚS
1963A.   Fauna de mamíferos del yacimiento prehistórico de Aitzbitarte IV. Munibe,
          15: 3—4, 105—124.
          Rev.:   H.-P. in Bol. Soc. Espan. Hist. Nat., Sec. Geol., 62, 273.
1963B.   Primer hallazgo de glotón (Gulo gulo L.) en la Península iberica.
          Munibe, 15: 3—4, 128.
1966A.   Las marmotas del yacimiento prehistorico de Lezetxiki (Guipúscoa).
          Munibe, 17: 1—4, 65—71, 3 figs., 2 pls., (English summary).
1966B.   Mamíferos de clima frio en los yacimientos prehistoricos del Pais Vasco.
          Munibe, 18, 65—68, (English summary).
See: Barandiarán and Altuna.

ALVAREZ, TICUL
1966   Roedores fossiles del Pleistoceno de Tequesquinahua, Estado de Mexico,
          Mexico. Acta Zool. Mex., 8: 3, 1-16, 5 figs., (English summary).
See: Packard and Alvarez.

ALVAREZ, T., and FERRUSQUIA V., I.
1967   New records of fossil marsupials from the Pleistocene of Mexico. Texas
          Jour. Sci., 19, 107.

ALVIN, K. L.   See: Patterson, C. and Greenwood.

AMADON, DEAN
　　1966　　Birds around the world: a geographical look at evolution and birds.
　　　　　　　New York: Natural History Press, xii + 175 pp., 30 figs.
　　　　　　　Rev.: Mayfield in Wilson Bull., 79, 123.

AMBLER, J. RICHARD　See: Lambert and Ambler.

AMBROSETTI, PIERLUIGI
　　1963　　An elephant tusk found near Ceprano (Southern Latium). Geol. Romana,
　　　　　　　2, 207—212, 4 figs., (Italian summary).
　　1964　　L'Elephas primigenius di Tarquinia. (Lazio settentrionale.) Geol. Romano,
　　　　　　　3, 367—377, 5 figs., 2 pls., tables, (English abstract).
　　　　　　　Rev.: Albanese in Riv. Ital. Pal., 72, 495—496.
　　1965　　Segnalazione di una fauna con Elephas antiquus nella zona di Ponte
　　　　　　　Galeria (Roma). Boll. Soc. Geol. Ital., 84: 1, 15—29, 3 figs., 2 pl.

AMODEO, SAVINA　See: Radmilli 1963D.

AN, CHIH-MIN
　　1959　　Finds at the Sanmen Gorge. Peking Rev., 2: 6, 21—22, illustr.
　　1961　　Old Stone Age cave found in Anyang. Peking Rev., 4: 31, 20—21, illustr.

AN, TSE-SEN　See: Ting, M.-l., et al.

AN, UZHI-SHEN
　　1964　　[New finds of fossil ostrich eggs in northern China and their preliminary
　　　　　　　microscopic study.] Vert. Palasiatica, 8:4, 374—386, 6 figs., 3
　　　　　　　pls., (Chinese; Russian summary).

ANASTAS'EVA, O. M.
　　1957　　[Remains of Bison priscus Boj. in the lower Dnepr valley.] Dop. ta povid.
　　　　　　　L'vivsk. Univ., 7: 3, 164—166, (Russian).

ANATI, EMMANUEL
　　1963　　Rev.: Contenson in Syria, 41, 164—167;　Parr in Antiq., 38,
　　　　　　　73—74.

ANATI, E., and HAAS, N.
　　1967　　A Palaeolithic site with pithecanthropian remains in the Plain of Esdrae-
　　　　　　　lon. Israel Explor. Jour., 17, 114—118, 4 figs.

ANATOL'EVA, A. I.
　　1960　　[Stratigraphy and some questions of paleogeography of Devonian of the
　　　　　　　Minusinsk intermontain downwarp.] Trudy Inst. Geol. Geof.,
　　　　　　　1960: 2, 52 pp., 11 figs., (Russian).

ANCIAUX DE FAVEAUX, DOM ADALBERT
　　1962　　Travaux d'approche pour une synthèse climatique, stratigraphique et archéo-
　　　　　　　logique des Plateaux des Biano. Proc. 4th Panafrican Congr. Pre-
　　　　　　　hist., Sec. 3, 165—178, 6 figs., 8 pls., 2 tables, (discussion by
　　　　　　　J. D. Clark, L. S. B. Leakey, and J. de Heinzelin).

1964   Un témoignage de l'Afrique centrale
          In: Ripoll Perelló, E., (ed.), 1964A, 137—152, 1 fig.

ANCION, N. See: Gilot, et al.

ANĐELKOVIĆ, JELENA
1962   [Contribution to the knowledge of Lower Sarmatian fishes of Belgrade
          region.] Ann. Géol. Pén. Balkan., 29, 115—128, 1 fig., 2 pls.,
          (Serbian; German summary).
          Abs.: Semaka in Zbl. Geol. Pal., Teil 2, 1966, 269.
1963   [Contribution to the knowledge of Lower Sarmatian fishes from Bosnia.]
          Ann. Géol. Pén. Balkan., 30, 87—96, 1 pl., (Serbian; German
          summary).
1964   [The genus Clupea from the Lower Sarmatian of Belgrade.] Ann. Géol.
          Pén. Balkan., 31, 161—167, 1 pl., 1 table, (Serbian; German
          summary).
1966   [Rhombus serbicus n. sp. from Lower Sarmatian of Servia.] Ann. Géol.
          Pén. Balkan., 32, 179—182, 1 pl., 1 table, (Serbian; English
          summary).
          Abs.: D. M. in Bull. Sci., Zagreb, Sec. A., 12: 5—6, 151, (English).

ANDERSEN, BJÖRN G.
1965   The Quaternary of Norway.
          In: Rankama, (ed.), 1965, 91—138, 23 figs., 2 tables.

ANDERSEN, RAOUL R.
1966   North Dakota archaeology 1966: a bibliography of general sources.
          Plains Anthrop., 11, 220—229.

ANDERSON, ADRIAN D. See: Leonhardy and Anderson.

ANDERSON, ALBERT J.
1965   Archaic on Staten Island. New World Antiq., 12, 50—57, illustr.

ANDERSON, DUANE C.
1966   The Gordon Creek burial. Southwestern Lore, 32, 1—9, 5 figs.

ANDERSON, EDWARD G.
1964   Nullarbor Expedition 1963-4. Helictite, 2, 121—134, 3 figs., pls. 10—11,
          2 maps, 1 table.

ANDERSON, ELAINE
1967   Equus conversidens from Wyoming. Jour. Mammal., 48, 660—663, 3
          tables.
1968   Fauna of the Little Box Elder Cave, Converse County, Wyoming. The
          Carnivora. Univ. Colorado Studies, Ser. Earth Sci., 6, 1—59, 8
          figs., 25 tables.

ANDERSON, J. E.
1962   The human skeleton. A manual for archaeologists. Illustrated by Tom
          Munro. Ottawa: Dept. of Northern Affairs and National Re-
          sources — National Museum of Canada, 164 pp., illustr.
          Rev.: Bauer in Mitt. Anthrop. Ges. Wien, 93—94, 180—181.

ANDERSON, J. M.
   1968A.   The confused state of classification within the family Procynosuchidae.
            Pal. Africana, 11, 77—84, 1 fig., 3 tables.
   1968B.   The cultural implications of the rhinoceros teeth from Limeworks, Maka-
            pansgat. Pal. Africana, 11, 85—97, 3 figs., 1 pl., 4 tables.

ANDERSON, MEGAN   See: Stokes, Anderson and Madsen.

ANDERSON, SYDNEY
   1967A.   Primates. In: Anderson, S., and Jones, (eds.), 1967, 151—177, figs. 24—26.
   1967B.   Introduction to the rodents. In: Anderson, S., and Jones, (eds.), 1967,
            206—209.

ANDERSON, S., and JONES, J. K., JR., (eds.)
   1967   Recent mammals of the world. A synopsis of families. New York: The
            Ronald Press Co., viii + 453 pp., 70 figs.
            Rev.: Guilday in Ecology, 49, 190;   Johaningsmeier in Amer. Sci., 56,
            75A;   Manville in Science, 157, 1421—1422;   Matthews in Nature,
            215, 1314—1315;   Southern in Jour. Animal Ecol., 37, 487—488.

ANDREESCU, I. See: Litiānu, Pricăjan, et al.

ANDREWS, ROY CHAPMAN
   1930   "An embarrassment of riches." Peking Leader Reprints, no. 51, 19—21.

ANDREWS, S. M., GARDINER, B. G., MILES, R. S., and PATTERSON, C.
   1967   Pisces. In: Harland, W. B., et al.,(eds.), 637—683.

ANDRIANOV, K. S.
   1960   [Results of the study of Quaternary deposits of TASSR, and purposes of
            further research.] Izv. Kazan. Fil. AN SSSR, ser. geol., 9, 225—239.
            1 table, (Russian).

ANDRIEU, P., and DUBOIS, J.
   1966   Travaux récents à la grotte éponyme de "Noailles". Bull. Soc. Préhist.
            Franç., C. R. Séances mens., 63, 167—180, 8 figs.

ANDRIEUX, C. See: Roussot, Andrieux and Chauffriasse.

ANDRIK, P., HANULÍK, M., and VITTEK, J.
   1963   Anomalien der Zahnzahl und ihre Beziehung zur Phylogenie. Acta Fac.
            Rer. Nat. Univ. Comen., Anthrop., 8, 17—38, 21 figs., (Czech;
            Russian and German summaries).

ANDRIST, ALBERT   See: Andrist, D., et al.

ANDRIST, DAVID, FLÜCKIGER, W., and ANDRIST, A.
   1964   Das Simmental zur Steinzeit. Acta Bernensia, 3, 211 pp., 50 figs., 20 pls.
            Rev.: Bosinski in Eiszeit. u. Gegenwart, 15, 237—238;   Ehrenberg in
            Die Höhle, 16, 30—31;   Jéquier in Bull. Soc. Prehist. Franç., C. R.
            seances mens., 1965:1, X11—X111;   Müller in Praehist. Zeit., 42,

191—194; Müller-Beck in Ur-Schweiz, 28:2, inside back cover;
M.-R.S. in L'Anthrop., 70:1—2, 148—151; Sauter in Arch. Suiss.
Anthrop. Gen., 29, 70—71; Valoch in Anthrop., 2:3, 90—91,
(Czech); Valoch in Archeol. Roz., 18:5, 595—596, (Czech);
[Zotz] in Quartär, 15—16, 213—214.

ANGEL, BASILIO DE LA SALLE
1962   Hallazgo del Myotragus en las canteras de Genova (Mallorca). Bol. Soc.
        Hist. Nat. Balear., 7.
1966   El Myotragus balearicus Bate considerado come vertebrado mamífero
        troglofilo. Bol. Soc. Hist. Natur. Baleares, 12: 1—4, 35—38.
        See: Androver and Angel; Crusafont Pairo and Angel; Crusafont Pairo,
        Angel and Cuerda.

ANGEL, J. LAWRENCE
1965   Early populations of northeast Greece. Abs. 64th Ann. Meeting Amer.
        Anthrop. Assoc., 1965, 5—6, (abs.).
1967   Palaeodemography in human evolution. Amer. Jour. Phys. Anthrop., 27,
        244, (abs.).

ANGELL, CARLTON WATSON
1964   Restorations of prehistoric life in co-operation with Ermine Cowles Case.
        Contrib. Mus. Pal. Univ. Mich., 13, 289—295, 3 pls.

ANGELOV, E. V.
1967   [Homo habilis, or "Able Man".] Priroda, 1967: 4, 47—50, 2 figs.,
        (Russian).

ANGELOV, N. See: Nikolova and Angelov.

ANGELROTH, HENRI
1960A. Pieces a tranchant retouche sur deux faces du silex. Bull. Soc. Roy.
        Belge Anthrop. Prehist., 71, 7—8, 3 figs.
1960B. Pointe mousterienne de Goyet brisee et retouchee ulterieurement. Bull.
        Soc. Roy Belge Anthrop. Prehist., 71, 11—12, 1 fig.
1961A. Rabots nucleiformes montois. Bull. Soc. Roy. Belge Anthrop. Prehist.,
        72, 81—85, 3 figs.
1961B. Pieces mousteriennes provenant des grottes de Goyet-Mozet. Bull. Soc.
        Roy. Belge Anthrop. Prehist., 72, 87—95, 5 pls.
1963   Les grottes prehistoriques de Goyet-Mozet. Essai de synthese. Bull. Soc.
        Roy. Belge Anthrop. Prehist., 73, 5—28.

ANGHI, CSABA G.
1960   The descendance of the Hungarian domestic horses from Eguus przewalskii
        Poljakoff and Equus gmelini Ant. Przeglad Zool., 4, 180—183,
        (Polish; English summary).

ANGRESS, SHIMON, and REED, C. A.
1962   An annotated bibliography on the origin and descent of domesticated
        animals. Fieldiana: Anthrop, 54, 1—143.
        Rev.: Herre in Zeit. Säugetierk., 29, 188; Lawrence in Amer. Jour.
        Sci., 262, 1136.

ANISIUTKIN, N. K.
  1966   [New Paleolithic site Stinka on the middle Dnestr R.]   Biull. Kom. Izuch.
          Chetvert. Perioda, 31, 131–136, 3 figs., (Russian).
  1968   [Two complexes on the Il'sk site.]   Sov. Arkheol., 1968: 2, 118–125,
          2 figs., 1 table, (Russian).

ANKEL, FRIDERUN VON
  1965   Der Canalis sacralis als Indikator für die Länge der Caudalregion der
          Primaten.   Folia Primat., 3, 263–276, 7 figs.
          Abs.: Preuschaft in Zbl. Geol. Pal., Teil 2, 1966, 341–342.

ANNELLI, F.
  1961   Prime ricerche paleontologiche nella Grotta della Masseria del Monte
          presse Conversano-Murgi di Bari.   Grotta d'Italia, 3, 87–113, 5 pls.,
          (not seen).

ANNIBALDI, G.   See: Leonardi, P., Annibaldi, et al.

ANOKHINA, Z. V.
  1965   [On the fauna of Paleolithic sites from the Mediterranean zone.]   Prirodn.
          Obstan. i Fauny Proshl., 2, 41–57, (Russian).

ANON.
  1828   Antediluvian footsteps.   London Jour. Arts, Sci., 14, 381–382, (not seen).
  1860   Pre-Adamite man; or, The story of our old planet and its inhabitants.
          London, (not seen).
  1956BS. Bibliographie préhistorique.   Maghreb-Sahara.   Année 1956.   Libyca, 4,
          359–369.
  1957CC. Dictionary of geological terms.   Prepared under direction of American
          Geological Institute.   Garden City, N. Y.:   Doubleday, Dolphin
          Books, x + 545 pp., (pb. ed.).
  1958AZ. La grotte des Striares.   Actes 2ème Congr. Internat. Spéléol., 1958,
          Appendice, 47–48, 1 fig.
  1958BA. Paul Rivet. 1876–1958.   Humanitas, 1: 108–109.
  1959BQ. British Caenozoic fossils (Tertiary and Quaternary).   Brit. Mus. (Nat.
          Hist.), vi + 130 pp., map, 44 pls.
  1959BR. [Field work of Uzbekistan Archeological Expedition in 1954–1955.]
          Historiia Mater. Kul't.   Uzbekistana, 1, 216–230, (Russian).
  1959BS. Bibliographie préhistorique.   Maghreb-Sahara.   Année 1957.   Libyca, 5,
          239–250.
  1959BT. "Men out of the past".   Mus. Talk, Santa Barbara Mus. Nat. Hist., 34, 6.
  1959BU. [Petr Petrovich Efimenko (75-th birthday).]   Sov. Arkheol., 1959:4,
          p. 153, portr., (Russian).
  1960CG. El mamut de Santa Elena, Veracruz.   Bol. Centro Invest. Antrop. Mex.,
          no. 10, 12.
  1960CH. Silver anniversary [Soc. for Amer. Archaeol.].   Bull. N. Y. State Archeol.
          Assoc., no. 19, 14–16.
  1960CI. Have you heard?   Bull. N. Y. State Archeol. Assoc., no. 20, 19–21.
  1960CJ Samwel Cave excavations.   Cave Notes, 2, 15.
  1960CK. News of Neanderthals.   Columbia Research News, 11: 1, 1–2, 1 fig.
  1960CL. Bibliographie préhistorique Maghreb-Sahara.   Année 1958.   Libyca, 6–7,
          263–270.

1960CM.   Bibliographie préhistorique Maghreb-Sahara. Année 1959. Libyca, 8, 311—318.
1960CN.   Ancestral man in the Far East. New World Antiq., 7, 87—89.
1960CO.   Some surprisingly early Russian datings. New World Antiq., 7, 155—156.
1960CP.   Three Neanderthal skeletons found in Shepherds' Cave in northern Iraq. NSS News, 18, 129.
1960CQ.   Liste des paléontologistes du monde. Paris: Union Paléontol. Internat., Serv. Inform. Géol. Bureau Recherch. Geol. et Minières, 237 pp.
1961CM.   Novos achados de Leakey em Olduvai. Anhembi, 43, 397—400, 2 figs.
1961CN.   Reproduções em tamanho natural das pinturas de Lascaux. Anhembi, 43, 403—404.
1961CO.   O abominável homen de carvão. Anhembi, 43, 643—645.
1961CP.   O rápido progresso da evolução humana. Anhembi, 44, 613—614.
1961CQ.   [Obit.] Henri Breuil. Anhembi, 45, 175.
1961CR.   Alberto Carlo Blanc [1906—1960]. Boll. Soc. Geog. Ital., ser. 9, 2, 396—398.
1961CS.   Memoria del año de 1953. In: Núñez Jiménez (ed.), 1961, 163—172, illustr.
1961CT.   Palaeontological Division of the Geological Survey of India. Indian Min., 15, 229—232, 6 figs.
1961CU.   Zamiatnin, S. N., 1899-1958. Krat. Soob. Inst. Ist. Mat. Kult. SSSR, 82, 3—4, portr., (Russian).
1961CV.   Altsteinzeitkulturen in Württemberg. Mitt. Verband Deutschen Höhlen- und Karstforscher, München, 7, 33.
1961CW.   The land bridge over the Bering Straits. New World Antiq., 8, 105.
1961CX.   Older than Peking man? Peking Rev., 4: 40, 20.
1961CY.   Rätselhafte Funde. Urania, 24, 53.
1961CZ.   Archäologische Entdeckungen in Rumänien. Urania, 24, 478.
1962CC.   Prazo da evolução humana. Anhembi, 45, 361.
1962CD.   Seria o zinjantropo menos velho? Anhembi, 45, 362—363.
1962CE.   Idade do zinjantropo. Anhembi, 45, 602.
1962CF.   A originalidade de Darwin. Anhembi, 46, 394—395.
1962CG.   Nôvo elo entre macaco e homen. Anhembi, 48, 148.
1962CH.   Notes and news from all over. Arkansas Archeologist, 3, 12.
1962CI.   General guide. Chicago: Chicago Nat. Hist. Mus., 47 pp., illustr.
1962CJ.   Comunicado de la Facultad de Ciencias de la Universidad Central de Venezuela con motivo del acto de homenaje al doctor José Royo y Gómez. Homenaje de los geologos colombianos en memoria del doctor José Royo y Gómez. Geos, Esc. Geol., Min. Met., Univ. Cent. Venezuela, no. 8, 23.
1962CK.   Kopie altsteinzeitlicher Höhlenmalerei von Altamira im Deutschen Museum in München fertiggestellt und zur Besichtigung freigegeben. Mitt. Verband Deutschen Höhlen- und Karstforscher, München, 8, 90—91.
1962CL.   Dr. Tilly Edinger als Gast im Senckenberg-Museum. Natur u. Mus., 92, 430.
1962CM.   Onderkaak Mosasaurus van Bemelen (Gem. Valkenburg). Natuurhist. Maandbl., 51, 161—162, illustr.
1962CN.   Is the Kwangsi "Giant ape" man or ape? Peking Rev., 5: 34, 20—21, illustr.
1962CO.   Commemorazione di Alberto Carlo Blanc [1906—1960]. Riv. Studi Liguri, 28, 346—349, portr.
1963BP.   Extinct moa is subject of archaeological study. Arkansas Amateur, 2, 12, 4.

1963BQ. Significant writings on life and man. Compiled and published under the directorates of General Education Reading Material Project, Aligarh Muslim University. Bombay: Asia Publishing House, xii + 69 pp., (not seen).
Rev.: Bose in Man in India, 44, 362.

1963BR. Essai sur la présence de l'homme du Paléolithique ancien et moyen dans la partie ouest du département de la Meuse. Bull. Acad. Soc. Lorraine Sci., 3: 1, 20–26, 4 figs.

1963BS. In memoriam Georg Lahner. Die Höhle, 14, 108.

1963BT. Radiocarbon dating. Geochronicle, 1, 4.

1963BU. [Academician Vladimir Afanase'vich Obruchev (the 100-th anniversary of the birthday).] Geol. i Geof., 1963: 10, 3–4, portr., (Russian).

1963BV. The Abo formation in the area around Socorro, New Mexico. Guidebk., New Mexico Geol. Soc., 14th Field Confer., 1963, 98–99.

1963BW. Professor Dr. Eugene Pittard [1867–1962]. Homo, 14, 191.

1963BX. Discussion on the antiquity of man in Australia. In: Sheils, H., (ed.), 1963, 79–85.

1963BY. Bibliographie Maghreb – Sahara. Anthropologie, préhistoire, ethnologie 1960–1961. Libyca, 9–10, 253–269.

1963BZ. Bibliographie Maghreb – Sahara. Anthropologie, préhistoire, ethnographie. 1962. Libyca, 11, 247–260.

1963CA. Field archaeology. Some notes for beginners issued by the Ordnance survey. 4th ed. London: Her Majesty's Stationery Office. (Ordnance Survey Professional Papers, New Series, No. 13), vii + 176 pp.
Rev.: Anon in Archaeol., 17, 303.

1963CB. "Museum Neandertal" bei Düsseldorf wieder eröffnet. Mitt. Verband Deutschen Höhlen- und Karstforscher, Müncher, 9, 45.

1963CC. Dienstjubiläum von Professor Dr. Wilhelm Schäfer. Natur u. Mus., 93, 194.

1963CD. Folsom Point. Newsletter Okla. Anthrop. Soc., 11: 1, 6, fig. C.

1963CE. News. Fayetteville, Ark. Fossil remains of prehistoric elephants, horses, bison and other animals found last summer in the Verdigris River may result in some significant contributions to scientific knowledge. Newsletter Okla. Anthrop. Soc., 11:1, 7–9.

1963CF. Paleo-Indian points. Ohio Archaeol., 13, 62–63, 2 figs.

1963CG. New ape-man fossil discovered. Peking Rev., 6: 45, 31, illustr.

1963CH. [The eggs of a dinosaur under the electron microscope]. Priroda, 52: 11, 117, (Russian).

1963CI. [Photograph of Alfred S. Romer, the President of the Congress.] Proc. 16th Internat. Congr. Zool., 5, opposite p. l.

1963CJ. [Photograph of V. Van Straelen (Belgium).] Proc. 16th Internat. Congr. Zool., 5, 65.

1963CK. Vertebrate paleo facility [Los Angeles County Museum]. Quart. Los Angeles Co. Mus. Nat. Hist., 2: 1, 20, 1 fig.

1963CL. New Associate Curator – Vertebrate Paleontology. Quart. Los Angeles Co. Mus. Nat. Hist., 2: 1, 22, portr.

1963CM. New facility [Los Angeles County Museum]. Quart. Los Angeles Co. Mus. Nat. Hist., 2: 2, 22.

1963CN. Had ancient Israelis Transvaal relatives? Sci. S. Afr., 1, 27, 2 portrs.

1963CO. Chad skull discoverer researching in republic. Sci. S. Afr., 1, 71–72.

1963CP. Single or multiple origin of man? Sciences, 2, 11 pp., (not seen).

1963CQ. [K. M. Polikarpovich. (3-18-1889–2-20-1963).] Sov. Arkheol., 1963: 4, p. 294, portr., (Russian).

1963CR.   Neue Funde von Neandertalen. Umschau, 60, 447.

1964A.   Francis Joseph Ryan, 1916–1963. Amer. Nat., 98, 259, portr.

1964B.   Vertebrate fossils. Ann. Rept. Carnegie Mus., 66, 15–16.

1964C.   Amphibians and reptiles. Ann. Rept. Carnegie Mus., 66, 21–22.

1964D.   Geology and anthropology. Ann. Rept. Santa Barbara Mus. Nat. Hist.,
          1963, 13–15.

1964E.   Investigation and research. Museum of Natural History. Paleobiology.
          Ann. Rept. U.S. Nation. Mus., 1964, 93–98, 1 fig.

1964F.   Seminar on Indian prehistory and protohistory. Antiq., 38, 304–305.

1964G.   Noticias sobre el XXXVI Congreso Internacional de Americanistas.
          Antropología, 2:2, 87–90.

1964H.   Films available for rent. Arkansas Archeologist, 5, 50.

1964I.   Expeditions 1964. Bull. Chicago Nat. Hist. Mus., 35: 4, 6.

1964J.   The Second Internation. Directory of Anthropological Institutions.
          Current Anthrop., 5, 213–280.

1964K.   New hypothesis on earliest man. Current Sci., 33, 443.

1964L.   A new link in human evolution? Discovery, 25: 5, 5.

1964M.   The evolution of man. Discovery, 25: 6, 32–33, fig. 1, cover illustr.

1964N.   La reproducción del techo de la cueva de Altamira en Madrid. Las
          Cien. Asoc. Españ. Prog. Cien., 29: 6.
          Rev.: [Hernández-Pacheco] in Bol. Soc. Españ. Hist. Nat., Sec. Geol.,
          63, 111.

1964O.   A mastodon at Novelty. Explorer, 6: 5, 10–12, illustr.

1964P.   Salvage of fossils. Explorer, 6: 6, 27.

1964Q.   World famous archeologist to lecture at Academy. Frontiers, 28, 128.

1964R.   Dinosaurs meet at World Fair. GeoTimes, 8: 7, 9, illustr.

1964S.   One of several prehistoric creatures reconstructed for the fair. Illustr.
          London News, 244, 773, fig.

1964T.   Summary of the Phanerozoic time - scale. In: Harland, W. B., et al,
          (eds.), 260–262.

1964U.   La reproducción del techo de la cueva de Altamira en Madrid. Las
          Ciencias, 29: 6, (not seen).

1964V.   Bibliographie Maghreb - Sahara. Anthropologie, Préhistoire, Ethnogra-
          phie, 1963. Libyca, 12, 351–360.

1964W.   British Palaeozoic fossils. London: British Museum, 208 pp., illustr.,
          (not seen).
          Rev.: Anon. in GeoTimes, 9:9, 22, 24.

1964X.   Od redakcji. Mat. Prace Antrop., 70, 5–6, portr.

1964Y.   Publikacje Jana Czekanowskiego w latach 1903-1963. Mat. Prace
          Antrop., 70, 33–47.

1964Z.   Paläontologische Funde in einer neuentdeckten Höhle bei Aufhausen
          (Schwäbische Alb). Mitt. Verband Deutschen Höhlen- und
          Karstforscher, München, 10, 119.

1964AA.   Neuer Fund prähistorischer Höhlenmalereien in Frankreich. Mitt. Ver-
          band Deutschen Höhlen- und Karstforscher, München. 10, 119.

1964AB.   Das "schlimme Grün", das die Malereien von Lascaux bedroht, ist im
          Rückzug. Mitt. Verband Deutschen Höhlen- und Karstforscher,
          München, 10, 119.

1964AC.   Urmenschenreste in einer Italienischen Höhle gefunden. Mitt. Verband
          Deutschen Höhlen- und Karstforscher, München, 10, 120.

1964AD.   Dalton points and the Dalton Complex in Alabama. Mo. Archaeol.
          Soc. Newsletter, no. 180, 3–6, 2 figs.

1964AE.   Dr. Vertress L. Vanderhoof. [3–10–1964.] Mus. Talk, Santa Barbara
          Mus. Nat. Hist., 39, 3.

1964AF.   Ornamental equines. Nat. Hist., 73: 2, 26–33, illustr.

1964AG.   Flint tools from southern Arabia. Nature, 201, 872.
1964AH.   Quaternary industries in Poland. Nature, 201, 1079.
1964AI.   British Palaeozoic fossils. Nature, 203, 818.
1964AJ.   Palaeontology in the U.S.S.R. Nature, 203, 1227.
1964AK.   Verslagen van de Maandvergaderingen te Maastrich op woensdag 1 juli
           1964. Natuurhist. Maandbl., 53, 103—105, illustr.
1964AL.   Did all Europeans come from Africa? New Sci., 21, 323, 1 map.
1964AM.   The rival ape-men of Olduvai Gorge. New Sci., 21, 659.
1964AN.   Prehistoric site rivals Olduvai. New Sci., 21, 797.
1964AO.   Mystery of an old Chinese jaw. New Sci., 22, 400—401.
1964AP.   Man's controversial ancestor. New Sci., 23, 12—13.
1964AQ.   Cave paintings found in Portugal. New Sci., 23, 365.
1964AR.   Earlier evolution of South African dinosaurs? New Sci., 23, 393.
1964AS.   Ancient elephants excavated in Essex. New Sci., 23, 423.
1964AT.   What were early hunters building? New Sci., 24, 11.
1964AU.   More proof of prehistoric man in Greece. New Sci., 24, 423.
1964AV.   A diamond saw for fossil footprints. New Sci., 24, 530, illustr.
1964AW.   Moon-watchers of the Ice Age. Comment by M. C. Jones. New Sci.,
           24, 559—560, 667.
1964AX.   Woman older than Peking Man? New Sci., 24, 857—858.
1964AY.   Homo habilis. Newsweek, April 13, 1964, 86, portr.
1964AZ.   A fluted point. Ohio Archaeol., 14, 16, 1 fig.
1964BA.   Shisha Pangma expedition found rare fossils. Peking Rev., 7: 29, 37.
1964BB.   Skull of early man found. Peking Rev., 7: 46, 26, illustr.
1964BC.   Conférence du professeur Luis Pericot, de l'Université de Barcelone.
           "Les problemes du Solutréen espagnol" Préhist. Spéléol. Arié-
           geoises, 19, 91—93.
1964BD.   The sounds of adventure. Quart. Los Angeles Co. Mus. Nat. Hist.,
           2: 3, 18—19, illustr.
1964BE.   Third preparator appointed for Vertebrate Paleontology. Quart. Los
           Angeles Co., Mus. Nat. Hist., 2: 3, 22, portr.
1964BF.   New preparators — Vertebrate Paleontology. Quart. Los Angeles Co.
           Mus. Nat. Hist., 2: 3, 23, portr.
1964BG.   Recent major gifts to the Museum. Quart. Los Angeles Co. Mus. Nat.
           Hist., 3: 1, 20, 1 fig.
1964BH.   South Dakota expedition. Quart. Los Angeles Co. Mus. Nat. Hist.,
           3: 1, 21.
1964BI.   Notes and news. S. African Jour. Sci., 60, 54, 104, 132, 340.
1964BJ.   Earlier men, earlier pre-men. Sci. Amer., 210: 5, 62.
1964BK.   Hominids and humans. Sci. Amer., 211: 2, 43—44.
1964BL.   Geological eras: reading the story of the earth's past. Sci. Digest,
           55: 2, 62—64, illustr.
1964BM.   Genus of extinct goose found in desert. Sci. News Letter, 85, 104.
1964BM.   Microscope reveals uses of Stone Age knives. Sci. News Letter, 85,
           264.
1964BO.   History of apes to be traced. Sci. News Letter, 86, 344.
1964BP.   1964 science review. Detailed highlights of achievements of the year
           reported and compiled by Science Service as a record of an
           eventful period of science, research and technology. Archaeology.
           Biology. Sci. News Letter, 86, 389—391, illustr.
1964BQ.   Man's ancestry — cautioning words. Sci. S. Afr., 1, 209—210.
1964BR.   Significance of Karroo fossils — another two eminent scientists investi-
           gating. Comment by J. P. Zeeman. Sci. S. Afr., 1, 166, 210,
           2 portrs.
1964BS.   Dinosaur evolution concepts revised. Sci. S. Afr., 1, 337.

1964BT.   Taungs skull anniversary. Sci. S. Afr., 2, 7, portr.
1964BU.   Election of AAAS officers: Alfred S. Romer. Science, 145, 1463,
            portr.
1964BV.   Arthur George Smith. "The Old Sarge". 1891–1964. Stones and
            Bones Newsletter, Nov. 1964, 6.
1964BW.   Pygmy progenitor? Time, 83; 17, 68.
1964BX.   The monster in the accelerator. Time, 84: 19, 38, illustr.
1964BY.   Dinosaurier auf Spitzbergen. Universum; Natur u. Tech., 19, 254.
            1 fig.
1964BZ.   The Hell Gap expedition: 1963. Wyo. Archaeol., 7: 2, 18–20, illustr.
1965A.   Doctora Noemí V. Cattoi, 1911–1965. Ameghiniana, 4, 3–5. portr.
1965B.   Vertebrate fossils. Ann. Rept. Carnegie Mus., 67, 15–16.
1965C.   Amphibians and reptiles. Ann. Rept. Carnegie Mus., 67, 20–21.
1965D.   Geology. Ann. Rept. Chicago Mus., 1964, 23–26, illustr.
1965E.   Anthropology and geology. Ann. Rept. Santa Barbara Mus. Nat. Hist.,
            1964, 13–15, illustr.
1965F.   Alabama's pebble tools. Anthrop. Jour. Canada, 3: 4, 17, 19, 21, 23,
            illustr.
1965G.   The U.S.S.R. Some excavations, discoveries and finds, 1964. A ceme-
            tery of dinosaurs. Upper Palaeolithic burial site found at
            Vladmir. Archaeol. News Letter, London, 7, 259.
1965H.   Ehrungen [Kurd von Bülow, Walter Hoppe, Werner Janensch, Hans
            Wehrli, Bruno Sander]. Ber. Geol. Ges. Deutsch. Demokratischen
            Republ., 10, 223–233, 5 portr.
1965I.   The Kyle woolly mammoth. Blue Jay, 23, 88–89, illustr.
1965J.   Reunion du lAvril 1964. Communications. Bull. Soc. Hist. Nat.
            Ardennes, 54, 5.
1965K.   Monsieur Guy Gaudron [1891–1965.]. Bull. Soc. Préhist. Franç.,
            C. R. séances mens., 1965: 4, cover.
1965L.   Who's got one? Conn. News, no. 91, 5–6, 1 pl.; no. 93, 8, 1 fig.
1965M.   Minutes of the annual meeting, May 1, 1965. Conn. News, no. 93,
            1–6.
1965N.   First reports on Clovis and Big Sandy points in Connecticut. Conn.
            News, no. 94, 2–4, 2 maps.
1965O.   D. Dwight Davis [1908-1965]. Copeia, 1965, 124.
1965P.   Six selected as candidates for 1965 Viking Medal. Current Anthrop.,
            6, 71–73.
1965Q.   Anthropological institutions, 1965. A list in preparation for the 3rd
            International Directory of Anthropological Institutions, including
            Institutional Associates in Current Anthropology and others
            who responded to a questionaire. Current Anthrop., 6, 485–
            568.
1965R.   Associates in Current Anthropology. Current Anthrop., 6, 569–638.
1965S.   Collagen analysis for archaeological dating. Current Sci., 34, 136.
1965T.   Not only dragons. Discovery, 26: 8, 6, 1 fig.
1965U.   Chinese ape-man. Discovery, 26: 10, 3.
1965V.   Desarrollo del Congreso. Actas V Congr. Panafr. Prehist. Estud. Cua-
            ternario, 1963: 1, 49–64, 66, (Spanish, French and English).
1965W.   Dayton Museum mastodon excavation. Explorer, 7: 4, 15, 2 figs.
1965X.   Prof. Eduardo Hernandez-Pacheco y Esteban. Fossilia, 1965: 2, 4.
1965Y.   Actividades. Fossilia, 1965: 5–6, 45–60.
1965Z.   Fossil sting ray: Palaeodasybatis discus Fowler. Frontiers, 30, 24,
            1 fig.
1965AA.   Bibliography of geochronology (revised). Geochronicle, 4, 1. 109
            items of the bibliography printed separately on 4 pp.

1965AB.   The preservation and dating of collagen in ancient bones. Geochronicle, 4, 3.
1965AC.   Bibliography of geochronology. Items 110—212. Geochronicle, 5, 5—8.
1965AD.   Arthur Holmes... Geochronicle, 6, 1.
1965AE.   Bibliography of geochronology. Items 213—315. Geochronicle, 6, 9—12.
1965AF.   On the cover. GeoTimes, 9:6, 3, cover photo.
1965AG.   A. S. Romer elected. GeoTimes, 9:6, 17.
1965AH.   Suplemento a la bibliografía del Abate Henri Breuil. In: Ripoll Perelló, E., (ed.), 1965B, XI—XII.
1965AI.   Necrologías del Abate Henri Breuil. In: Reipoll Perelló, E., (ed.), 1965B, XIII.
1965AJ.   List of publications of Professor Georg Haas. Israel Jour. Zool., 7—9.
1965AK.   [Sergei Vladimirovich Obruchev (1890-1965).] Izv. Geogr. Obshch., 97, 561—562, portr., (Russian).
1965AL.   Bericht des Staatlichen Museums für Naturkunde in Stuttgart für 1963 und 1964. Jahresh. Ver. Vaterland. Naturk. Württemberg; 120, 11—39, 4 figs.
1965AM.   Richesses en fossiles au Niger. La Nature, 93, 226.
1965AN.   Bibliographie Maghreb — Sahara. Anthropologie, Préhistoire, Ethnographie. 1964. Libyca, 13, 339—349.
1965AO.   Bibliography of Emerson F. Greenman. Mich. Archaeol., 11, 189—194.
1965AP.   Entdeckung neuer Höhlenmalerein in einer portugiesischen Höhle. Mitt. Verband Deutschen Höhlen- und Karstforscher, München, 11, 109.
1965AQ.   Some early points in the Disser collection. Mo. Archaeol. Soc. Newsletter, no. 188, 4—6, illustr.
1965AR.   NSF supports bone dig. NSS News, 23, 29.
1965AS.   Caves in the news. NSS News, 23, 119—120.
1965AT.   The Coryndon Memorial Museum, Nairobi. Nature, 207, 133.
1965AU.   Australian prehistory. Nature, 208, 835.
1965AV.   Glass dating by fission tracks. New Sci., 26, 81.
1965AW.   First primates lived with last dinosaurs. New Sci., 28, 392.
1965AX.   Stone Age glue from birch bark. New Sci., 27, 698.
1965AY.   What happened to the British hippo? New Sci., 28, 79.
1965AZ.   How the little dinosaurs run. New Sci., 28, 713—714.
1965BA.   Rich haul of "big lizards" from Gobi. New Sci., 28, 74l.
1965BB.   Two Clovis points from Iowa. Newsletter Iowa Archeol. Soc., No. 35, 15, illustr.
1965BC.   "Kay anthropological group uncovers three ancient bison skulls." Newsletter Okla. Anthrop. Soc., 13: 6, 3—4.
1965BD.   Yacimiento de mastodontidos en Corcoles. Notas Comun. Inst. Geol. Min., 78, 239.
1965BE.   Eduardo Hernandez-Pacheco y Esteban [1872-1965]. Notas Comun. Inst. Geol. Min., no. 79, 229.
1965BF.   Huellas fosilizadas de hace 140 millones de años. Notas Comun. Inst. Geol. Min., no. 79, 265.
1965BG.   "Pedigreed" fluted points. Ohio Archaeol., 15, 30, 1 fig.
1965BH.   In memoriam — Arthur George Smith. Ohio Archaeol., 15, 32—33.
1965BI.   Systematische Gesamt-Faunenliste. Hauptfundschicht Voigtstedt. Pal. Abh., Abt. A, 2, 687—689.
1965BJ.   Biggest dinosaur fossil ever found in China. Peking Rev., 8: 24, 27, illustr.
1965BK.   New findings on Lantian man. Peking Rev., 8: 24, 27.
1965BL.   A dinosaur in the foyer. Quart. Los Angeles Co. Mus. Nat. Hist., 3:3, 21, 1 fig.

1965BM.   Ancient fossil on display. Quart. Los Angeles Co. Mus. Nat. Hist.,
           3: 4, 23, 1 fig.
1965BN.   Citation read on the occasion of the conferment of the honorary degree
           of Doctor of Science on Sir Wilfrid Le Gros Clark, F.R.S. Ray-
           mond Dart Lectures, no. 2, VII—VIII.
1965BO.   Ratnapura National Museum. Pre-history and geology. Rept. Natl.
           Mus. Colombo, 1965, 21.
1965BP.   En feuilletant la Revue: biologie. Rev. Gén. Sci., 72, 111—113.
1965BQ.   Des origines de l'Homo sapiens. Rev. Gén. Sci., 72, 136—137.
1965BR.   Fossil Department. Rocks and Minerals, 40, 28—29, 108—109, 298—
           299, illustr.
1965BS.   New fossil hall opens to public. Santa Barbara Museum of Natural
           History, Santa Barbara, California. Rocks and Minerals, 40, 372.
1965BT.   Paleolithic funeral. Sci. Amer., 212: 2, 53—54.
1965BU.   The problem of man's emergence. Sci. Amer., 212: 5, 50, 52.
1965BV.   Dinosaur footprints on the ceiling. Sci. Digest, 57: 4, inside front
           cover, illustr.
1965BW.   Evolution controversy. Sci. Digest, 57: 6, 4.
1965BX.   Speech began with hunting. Sci. Digest, 57: 6, 72.
1965BY.   Early man in Borneo. Sci. Digest, 58: 3, 9.
1965BZ.   The tale of a dinosaur. Sci. on the March, 45: 1, 10—11, illustr.
1965CA.   Dr. Alfred S. Romer is AAAS President for 1965. Sci. News Letter,
           87, 37.
1965CB.   14-million-year-old mammal being prepared. Sci. News Letter, 87, 53,
           1 fig., cover illustr.
1965CC.   New species name of Homo suggested. Sci. News Letter, 87, 73.
1965CD.   20,000-year-old cave painting found. Sci. News Letter, 87, 184.
1965CE.   Coelacanth displayed for first time in U.S. Sci. News Letter, 87, 199.
           1 fig.
1965CF.   Fossil search aided by U.S. Public Roads. Sci. News Letter, 87, 231.
1965CG.   Third species questioned. Sci. News Letter, 87, 243.
1965CH.   Early tool [Folsom point]. Sci. News Letter, 87, 243, 1 fig.
1965CI.   Earth's oldest man now two million years old. Sci. News Letter, 87,
           244.
1965CJ.   Bering Strait studied as land and sea. Sci. News Letter, 87, 244.
1965CK.   Early man's teeth gave "survival" edge. Sci. News Letter, 87, 244.
1965CL.   Huge ancient tortoise unearthed in South China. Sci. News Letter,
           87, 376.
1965CM.   New species of dinosaur claimed by Chinese. Sci. News Letter, 88, 101.
1965CN.   Sharks once roamed rugged Israeli desert. Sci. News Letter, 88, 123.
1965CO.   Skull of apeman named most ancient human. Sci. News Letter, 88,
           297.
1965CP.   Seven ape-like teeth indicate new species. Sci. News Letter, 88, 324.
1965CQ.   Oldest great ape jaws found in Sahara Desert. Sci. News Letter, 88,
           359, illustr.
1965CR.   Past, modern man linked. Neanderthal man may have built structures,
           indicating that he was far more advanced than formerly believed
           and implying that he may have evolved into Cromagnon man.
           Sci. News Letter, 88, 359.
1965CS.   1965 science review. Detailed highlights of achievements of the year
           reported and compiled by Science Service as a record of an
           eventful period in science, research and technology. Anthropo-
           logy and archaeology. Sci. News Letter, 88, 389.
1965CT.   Cover. The lying stones. Science, 147, 533, 537, cover illustr.
1965CU.   Wilhelm Weiler zum fünfundsievzigsten Geburtstag. Senck. Lethaea,
           46a, iii-v, portr.

1965CV.   Skull session. This World, April 11, 1965, 25.
1965CW.   Verzeichnis der wissenschaftlichen Veröffentlichungen von Prof. Dr. Dr.
            h.c. Bernhard Rensch seit 1959. Zool. Jahrb., Abt. Syst. Ökol
            Geog. Tiere, 92, 193—194.
1966A.   A new hall of public exhibits — Fossil Hall — is nearing completion...
            Ann. Rept., Calif. Acad. Sci., 1965—1966, 15, 2 figs.
1966B.   Paleobiology. Ann. Rept. Smithson. Inst., 1966, 105—111, 128—129.
1966C.   Death takes Professor R. A. Stirton. Berkeley Daily Gazette, June 14,
            1966, 3.
1966D.   U.S. National Medal of Science. Bull. Geol. Soc. Amer., 77, P7—P8.
1966E.   The mighty Megatherium. Bull., Ward's Nat. Sci. Estab., 5: 36, 1—2,
            2 figs.; 6: 38, 4—5, illustr.
1966F.   A new center for prehistoric studies. Cahiers Hist. Mond., 9, 1025—
            1026.
1966G.   Paleontology museum. In a library of fossil bones, the skull and jaw
            of a diprotodont. Campus Rept., Univ. Calif., 1: 4, 2—3, 3 figs.
1966H.   An account of research expeditions of staff members, 1964—65. Dis-
            covery, Yale, 1: 2, 40—44, 3 figs.
1966I.   Walter G. Kühne... Discovery, Yale, 2:1, 43, portr.
1966J.   J. T. Robinson. Discovery, Yale, 2:1, 44, portr.
1966K.   After 120 million years — on its feet again. Explorer, 8:2, 11—13,
            illustr.
1966L.   Giant pig skull (Archaeotherium mortoni). Frontiers, 31, 54, 1 fig.
1966M.   Dirty Dolores gets first bath in nine years. Frontiers, 31, 60.
1966N.   On the accuracy of radiocarbon (C14) dates. Geochronology, 1966:2, 1.
1966O.   Maurice G. Mehl, 78... GeoTimes, 10:9, 30.
1966P.   Three fossil bird skeletons... GeoTimes, 11:1, 24.
1966Q.   William H. Matthews III... GeoTimes, 11:1, 31.
1966R.   Nikolai Nikolaevich Yakovlev [1869—1966]. GeoTimes, 11:1, 32.
1966S.   Bibliography & index of geology exclusive of North America. Geo-
            Times, 11:3, 29—30.
1966T.   Two paleontologists received Addison Every Verrill Medals on Oct. 28
            at Yale University. GeoTimes, 11:5, 32.
1966U.   Dinosaurs cutout. Golden Mag., 3: 1, 32—33, color illustr.
1966V.   [Vladimir Vladimirovich Bogachev (1881-1965).] Izv. Akad. Nauk
            Azerb. SSR, ser. Nauk o Zemle, 1966: 3, 141—142, (Russian).
1966W.   Werner-Reimers-Stiftungspreis 1966. Kosmos (Stuttgart), 62, *248.
1966X.   Le premier Mammifere secondaire trouvé en France. La Nature, no.
            3373, 192.
1966Y.   Frank H. H. Roberts [— 1966]. Mo. Archaeol. Soc. Newsletter,
            no. 199, 10.
1966Z.   The projectile points illustrated... Mo. Archaeol. Soc. Newsletter, no.
            199, 11, illustr.
1966AA.   Excavation at Rodgers Shelter. Mo. Archaeol. Soc. Newsletter, no. 203,
            9—10.
1966AB.   Divisional activities in the museum. Mus. Notes, Univ. Neb. News,
            no. 31, 3—4.
1966AC.   Golden anniversary [of Santa Barbara Museum of Natural History].
            Mus. Talk, Santa Barbara Mus. Nat. Hist., 41, 17—47, illustr.
1966AD.   Caves in the news. NSS News, 24, 33.
1966AE.   Notes and news. NSS News, 24, 218.
1966AF.   On the track of dinosaurs. Nat. and Sci., 4: 1, 6—8, illustr.
1966AG.   The names of early man. Nature, 209, 563.
1966AH.   Fossil mammals. Nature, 211, 337—338.
1966AI.   Dinosaurs in plenty. Nature, 212, 113.

1966AJ.   A relict marsupial. Nature, 212, 225, 1 fig.
1966AK.   Zwei fossile Reptilien. Naturwiss. Rund., 19, 162.
1966AL.   Otto H. Schindewolf (zur Vollendung des 70. Lebensjahres). Neues
          Jahrb. Geol. Pal., Abh., 125, Festband, IX—XXVII, portr.
1966AM.   Islands act as evolutionary traps. New Sci., 29, 8.
1966AN.   Assistant director appointed to state archeological program. Newsletter
          Iowa Archeol. Soc., no. 40, 5—6.
1966AO.   Hut remains may be oldest in America. Newsletter Okla. Anthrop.
          Soc., 14: 1, 4.
1966AP.   10,000-year-old houses discovered in Wyoming. Newsletter Okla. Anth-
          rop. Soc., 14: 4, 4—5.
1966AQ.   Stone Age sites are identified (New York Times, January 30, 1966).
          Newsletter Okla. Anthrop. Soc., 14: 6, 3—4.
1966AR.   Homo erectus. Newsletter Okla. Anthrop. Soc., 14:8, 10, 1 table.
1966AS.   Fluted point. Ohio Archaeol., 16, 34, 1 fig.
1966AT.   Paleo points. Ohio Archaeol., 16, 46, 1 fig.
1966AU.   [In memoriam L. N. Kudrin (1921-1966).] Pal. Sborn., 3: 2, 143—146,
          portr., (Russian).
1966AV.   A gift of old bones. Quart. Los Angeles Co. Mus., 5: 1, 23, illustr.
1966AW.   Prehistoric ground sloth now under preparation. Quart., Snow Mus.
          Nat. Sci., 1: 9, 2 pp., 2 figs.
1966AX.   Kurt Ehrenberg zum 70. Geburtstag am 22. November 1966. Quartär,
          17, iii, frontispiece portr.
1966AY.   Professor Matthew Robertson Drennan (1885-1965). S. African Jour.
          Sci., 62, 122—125.
1966AZ.   Homo erectus in Europe. Sci. Amer., 214: 1, 49—50.
1966BA.   Oldest New World Community. Sci. Amer., 214: 4, 51.
1966BB.   The oldest Australian. Sci. Digest, 59: 4, 26—27, illustr.
1966BC.   Artifact of Ice Age discovered in Illinois. Sci. News Letter, 89, 41.
1966BD.   Moa bird skeleton. Sci. News Letter, 89, 135, 1 fig.
1966BE.   "Missing link" found? A dinosaur skeleton 25 feet long that was
          found in the Big Horn Basin of Wyoming and Montana is approx-
          imately 116 million years old. Sci. News Letter, 89, 197, 1 fig.
1966BF.   "Two cultures". Sci. News Letter, 89, 339, 1 fig.
1966BG.   Bird believed extinct discovered on island. Sci. News Letter, 89, 477.
1966BH.   Man may owe hearing to ancient fish. Sci. News Letter, 89, 483,
          1 fig.
1966BI.   Alfred S. Romer honored by paleontologists. Science, 154, 1531.
1966BJ.   La grotte préhistorique des Fieux. Spelunca, 6: 2, 106—108, (English
          and German summaries).
1966BK.   Paleo-Indian points from middle Tennessee. Tenn. Archaeol., 22, 80,
          83, 3 figs., 1 table.
1966BL.   Paleo-Indian points from Hardin County. Tenn. Archaeol., 22, 81—83,
          4 figs., 1 table.
1966BM.   Man's oldest dwelling. Time, 87: 8, 102, 1 fig.
1966BN.   Gobi's treasure of bones. Time, 88: 4, 75, 1 fig.
1966BO.   Quatäre Verbeitung des Wasserfrosches. Umschau, 66, 200.
1966BP.   Discussions on terminology. W. Afr. Archaeol. Newsletter, no. 5, 39—
          53.
1966BQ.   Posts and training facilities. W. Afr. Archaeol. Newsletter, no. 5, 56—
          57.
1966BR.   Richard Estes. Grant no. 3665 — Penrose Fund (1964), $1,000. Ana-
          tomy and relationships of the primitive fossil snake Dinilysia.
          Year Book, Amer. Philos. Soc., 1966, 334—336.
1967A.   Bibliografia geologica española. Acta Geol. Hispanica, 2: 2, 25—52.

1967B.   Guide to the Museum of Paleontology, Earth Sciences Building, Univer-
                   sity of California, Berkeley. Berkeley: Univ. Calif. Press, 15 pp.
1967C.   Theodosius Dobzhansky. Discovery, Yale, 2:2, 35, portr.
1967D.   Ernst Mayr. Discovery, Yale, 2:2, 36, portr.
1967E.   Norman Dennis Newell. Discovery, Yale, 2:2, 37, portr.
1967F.   George Gaylord Simpson. Discovery, Yale, 2:2, 37, portr.
1967G.   Vertebrate paleontology. Discovery, 3:1, 58–59.
1967H.   Dr. Leakey's fabulous fossils. Frontiers, 31, 100–105, illustr.
1967I.   Dinah gets a bath. Frontiers, 32, 22–23, illustr.
1967J.   Mastodon teeth. GeoTimes, 12:1, 26.
1967K.   PS. [Paleontological Society.] GeoTimes, 12:1, 30.
1967L.   Henry Hurd Swinnerton. GeoTimes, 12:2, 32.
1967M.   Utah to close dig. GeoTimes, 12:3, 30–31.
1967N.   Richard F. Flint... GeoTimes, 12:3, 32.
1967O.   Gian Alberto Blanc. GeoTimes, 12:3, 33.
1967P.   Tilly Edinger [1898–May 27, 1967]. GeoTimes, 12:6, 31.
1967Q.   Prehistoric elephant for Nairobi Museum. Illustr. London News, 250:
                   6655, 8, illustr.
1967R.   General discussions, group B: principles of African Late Tertiary-
                   Quaternary stratigraphical nomenclature. In: Bishop, W. W.,
                   and Clark, J. D., (eds.), 397–407, 3 tables.
1967S.   Recommendations with French translations. In: Bishop, W. W., and
                   Clark, J. D., (eds.), 879–901, 2 tables.
1967T.   The Budapest skull. Interamer., 14: 3, 3.
1967U.   Wild man of Borneo [Tom Harrison]. Interamer., 14: 4, 7.
1967V.   Yukon Pleistocene. Interamer., 14: 5, 5.
1967W.   Australia: An archaeological dig... Interamer., 14: 7, 2.
1967X.   Grant for paleo research. Interamer., 14: 8, 3.
1967Y.   More Clovis. Interamer. 14: 8, 4.
1967Z.   Early man a hoax. Interamer. 14: 8, 5.
1967AA.   Mastodons. Interamer., 14: 8, 8.
1967AB.   Valsequillo finds well documented. Interamer., 14: 9, 7.
1967AC.   Aegyptopithecus zeuxis. Interamer., 14: 9, 8.
1967AD.   Professor M. Stekelis – 1898-1967. In memoriam. Israel Explor. Jour.,
                   17, 131–132.
1967AE.   Elwyn L. Simons... Nat. Hist., 76: 2, 5, portr.
1967AF.   Yuri Alexandrovich Orlov. 1893-1966. News Bull., Soc. Vert. Pal., 79,
                   62–63.
1967AG.   In memoriam. Tilly Edinger. 1897-1967. News Bull., Soc. Vert. Pal.,
                   80, [ii].
1967AH.   Iowa Clovis points. Newsletter Iowa Archeol. Soc., no. 41, 2, cover.
1967AI.   Iowa Sandia points. Newsletter Iowa Archeol. Soc., no. 43, 5, 1 fig.
1967AJ.   Allamakee County Paleo-Indian points. Newsletter Iowa Archeol. Soc.,
                   no. 44, 1, cover.
1967AK.   Sandia points near Mount Pleasant. Newsletter Iowa Archeol. Soc., no.
                   44, 2, 1 fig.
1967AL.   And what did John T. Scopes think about the whole thing? News-
                   letter Okla. Anthrop. Soc., 15: 2, 8–9.
1967AM.   A dating query. New World Antiq., 14, 15–16.
1967AN.   Brief history of the [Florida State] Museum. Plaster Jacket, 6, 9.
1967AO.   Underwater discovery. Plaster Jacket, 6, 10, 1 fig.
1967AP.   Connecticut... A vast number of dinosaur footprints were unearthed
                   near the town of Rocky Hill. Rocks and Minerals, 42, 45.
1967AQ.   Wyoming – Casper – Nearly 100 Cretaceous Mammal teeth... Rocks
                   and Minerals, 42, 45.

1967AR.　Canada — Quebec — Devonian armored fish Bothriolepis... Rocks and Minerals, 42, 45—46.

1967AS.　New Jersey — Carnegie Lake... Coelacanth and Semionoid fish. Rocks and Minerals, 42, 202.

1967AT.　Florida — Polk Co. — ... complete vertebrate fossils... Rocks and Minerals, 42, 282.

1967AU.　New Jersey — Boonton —... Semionotus and Coelacanthus... Rocks and Minerals, 42, 283.

1967AV.　Utah — The first whole dinosaur eggs found in the western hemisphere... Rocks and Minerals, 42, 283.

1967AW.　The Agate Fossil Beds National Monument Association. Rocks and Minerals, 42, 776.

1967AX.　New Jersey [Fort Lee phytosaur]. Rocks and Minerals, 42, 776.

1967AY.　Important find. Sci. Digest, 61: 3, 5.

1967AZ.　New World man [Mexico]. Sci. News Letter, 91, 447, 1 fig.

1967BA.　Ancient remains [Canada]. Sci. News Letter, 91, 510.

1967BB.　An interesting similarity. Tenn. Archaeol., 23, 38—39, 1 pl.

1967BC.　Two Cumberland points from middle Tennessee. Tenn. Archaeol., 23, 42—44, 2 figs., 1 table.

1967BD.　Additional Paleo-Indian points from east Tennessee. Tenn. Archaeol., 23, 43—44, 2 figs., 1 table.

1967BE.　Early projectile point types in North Carolina. Tenn. Archaeol., 23, 84, 1 fig.

1967BF.　Unpalatable man. Time, 89: 8, 46.

1967BG.　Fever chart for fossils. Time, 90: 10, 32—37.

1967BH.　Ancient ancestor. Time, 90: 21, 62.

1967BI.　Palaeontological Laboratory at Fort Lamy. W. Afr. Archaeol. Newsletter, no. 6, 53, (French summary).

1967BJ.　Resolutions on terminology. W. Afr. Archaeol. Newsletter, no. 7, 33—37, (French translation).

1967BK.　Mountains and plains: Denver's geologic setting. Washington, D.C., and Denver, Colo.: U.S. Geol. Surv., 23 pp., illustr.

1968A.　Early ape. GeoTimes, 13: 1, 24.

1968B.　Quaternary nomenclature. GeoTimes, 13: 5, 22—23.

1968C.　Man versus mammoth. Interamer., 15: 1, 2.

1968D.　Ancestor of man and ape. Interamer., 15: 1, 3.

1968E.　Gigantopithecus. Interamer., 15: 6, 3.

1968F.　Unusual point find. Interamer., 15: 6, 3.

1968G.　Early man. Interamer., 15: 7, 1.

1968H.　Eastern New Mexico University meeting. Interamer., 15: 7, 5.

1968I.　James Alfred Ford, 1911—1968. Interamer., 15: 7, 6.

1968J.　Early Jaw. Interamer., 15: 7, 8.

1968K.　Marmes needle. Interamer., 15: 8, 2.

1968L.　60,000 year old man in America. Interamer., 15: 9, 6.

1968M.　Museums and institutions that can be notified of fossil discoveries (revised March, 1966). Mo. Archaeol. Soc. Newsletter, no. 218, 6—7.

1968N.　Dr. Edwin H. Colbert. Nat. Hist., 77: 3, L — M, portr.

1968O.　Louis Dupree... Nat. Hist., 77: 5, 4, portr.

1968P.　C. Loring Brace... Nat. Hist., 77: 5, 4, portr.

1968Q.　Rare horses. Nature, 217, 901—902, 1 fig.

1968R.　Comparative anatomy at Harvard. Nature, 217, 1000—1001.

1968S.　New light on Jamoytius. Nature, 218, 1006.

1968T.　The first fishes. Nature, 219, 223—224.

1968U.　Rev. Dr. R. T. Wade. Nature, 219, 311.

1968V.   New discoveries and appraisals in palaeoanthropology. Nature, 219,
              820—824, 1 fig., 1 table.
1968W.   Where did marsupials start? Nature, 219, 1106—1107.
1968X.   Palaeoanthropologists at odds. Nature, 219, 1309.
1968Y.   Raking up the dead. Nature, 220, 123, 1 fig.
1968Z.   Swanscombe re-excavated. Nature, 220, 123—124, 1 fig.
1968AA.   Microsaurs and reptiles. Nature, 220, 331.
1968AB.   Leakey in Addis. Nature, 220, 639.
1968AC.   High Lodge Palaeolithic industry. Nature, 220, 1065—1066, 1 fig.
1968AD.   Teeth of Mesozoic mammals. Nature, 220, 1176.
1968AE.   Put teeth on old jawbone. Fossil found in Antarctica is 200,000,000
              years old. Rocks and Minerals, 43, 336.
1968AF.   The new surprise at L.A.'s Exposition Park. Sunset, May 1968, 40—42,
              illustr.
1968AG.   New life for Gondwanaland. Time, 91: 2, 51, 2 figs.
1968AH.   Died. James L. B. Smith, 70. Time, 91: 3, 88.
1968AI.   The man they ate for dinner. Time, 91: 19, 98, 1 fig.

ANTHONY, HAROLD
    1966   Childs Frick (1883-1965). News Bull., Soc. Vert. Pal., 77, 46—55,
                  portr.

ANTHONY, JEAN
    1961B.   Anatomie dentaire comparée. Paris: Claude Heimant, 119 pp.
    1966   Premières observations sur le moulage endocrânien des hommes fossiles
                  du Jebel Irhoud (Maroc). C.R. Acad. Sci. Paris, Sci. Nat., 262,
                  556—558.
                See: Fenart and Anthony; Millot and Anthony; Millot, Nieuwenhuys
                  and Anthony.

ANTHONY, JEAN, and ROBINEAU, D.
    1967   Le cercle céphalique de Latimeria (Poisson coelacanthidé). C.R. Acad.
                  Sci. Paris, Sci. Nat., 265, 343—346, 1 fig.

ANTIPCHUK, IÛ. P.
    1967   [Trends of lung evolution in the reptiles.] Dopovidi Akad. Nauk
                  URSR, ser. B, 1967: 7, 657—659, 2 figs., (Ukrainian; Russian
                  and English summaries).

ANTONIEWICZ, WLODZIMIERZ
    1964   Z rozwazan o poczatkach sztuki. In: Ripoll Perelló, E., (ed.), 1964A,
                  153—161, (Polish; French summary).

ANTUNES, MANUEL
    1965   Teilhard de Chardin, dez anos depois. Brotéria, Sér. Mensal, 80, 451—
                  460.

ANTUNES, MIGUEL TELLES See: Telles Antunes, Miguel.

ANUCHIN, D. N. See: Zalkind 1963.

AOKI, NAOAKI
    1967   Some fossil <u>Gobius</u> from Japan. Trans. Proc. Pal. Soc. Japan, no. <u>67,</u>
                  125—128, 6 figs., (Japanese summary).

AOKI, R.
    1915   [A contribution to the knowledge of the extinct sirenian <u>Desmostylus</u>
                  <u>hesperus</u> Marsh.] Jour. Geol. Soc. Japan, <u>22</u>, 412—419, (Japa-
                  nese).

APLONOVA, E. N. See: Saks, <u>et</u> <u>al</u>.

APOSTOL, LEONID
    1957   Contribution a la connaissance des mandibules de mammouth (<u>Mammon-</u>
                  <u>teus</u> <u>primigenius</u> Blumb.) du Quaternaire, de la region de Buca-
                  rest. Trav. Mus. Hist. Nat. "Grigore Antipa", <u>1</u>, 285—297, 3
                  pls., (Rumanian and Russian summaries).
    1962   Contribution à l'étude de <u>Mammonteus</u> <u>primigenius</u> (Blumb.) décélé
                  dans la Dobroudja. Trav. Mus. Hist. Nat. "Grigore Antipa", <u>3</u>,
                  501—512, 2 figs., 4 pls., (Rumanian and Russian summaries).
                  Abs.: Semaka in Zbl. Geol. Pal., Teil 2, 1964, 204.
    1963   Sur l'origine et l'évolution paléogéographique du de la relief de la dé-
                  pression de Braşov le long des montagnes méridionales, Trav.
                  Mus. Hist. Nat. "Grigore Antipa", 4, 521—531, 1 fig., (Ruma-
                  nian and Russian summaries).
    1965A.   Données préliminaires concernant un squelette de <u>Mammuthus</u> <u>trogon-</u>
                  <u>therii</u> (Pohlig) découvert dans la plaine de Mostiştea (Codreni,
                  Région de Bucureşti). Trav. Mus. Hist. Nat. "Grigore Antipa",
                  <u>5</u>, 443—453, 7 figs., (Rumanian and Russian summaries).
                  Rev.: Semaka in Zbl. Geol. Pal., Teil 2, 1967, 122.
    1965B.   Sur la présence d'<u>Anancus</u> <u>arvernensis</u> (Croizet et Jobert) et d'<u>Archi-</u>
                  <u>diskodon</u> <u>meridionalis</u> Nesti sur le territoire de Curtea de Argeş.
                  Trav. Mus. Hist. Nat. "Grigore Antipa", <u>5</u>, 455—463, 4 figs.,
                  1 pl., (Rumanian and Russian summaries).
                  Rev.: Semaka in Zbl. Geol. Pal., Teil 2, 1967, 122.
    1966   Sur la présence d'<u>Aceratherium</u> <u>incisivum</u> Kaup dans la région Coma-
                  nesti—Bacău. Trav. Mus. Hist. Nat. "Grigore Antipa", <u>6,</u>
                  357—361, 1 fig., 1 pl., (Rumanian and Russian summaries).
    1967A.   Étude des bovidés quaternaires de la région de Bucarest. Trav. Mus.
                  Hist. Nat. "Grigore Antipa", <u>7</u>, 449—462, 10 pls., 1 map, 7
                  tapes, (Rumanian and Russian summaries).
                  Rev.: Semaka in Zbl. Geol. Pal., Teil 2, 1968, 219.
    1967B.   Étude du rhinoceros à toison laineuse (<u>Coelodonta</u> <u>antiquitatis</u> Blumb.)
                  du Quaternaire de la région de Bucarest. Trav. Mus. Hist.
                  Nat. "Grigore Antipa", <u>7</u>, 463—473, 2 figs., 6 pls., (Rumanian
                  and Russian summaries).
                  Rev.: Semaka in Zbl. Geol. Pal., Teil 2, 1968, 219.

APOSTOL, L., and OLARU, V.
    1966   Sur la présence du <u>Mammuthus</u> <u>primigenius</u> Blumb. a Chiscani-Brăila,
                  region de Galatz. Trav. Mus. Hist. Nat. "Grigore Antipa", <u>6,</u>

363—367, 1 fig., 4 pls., 1 table, (Rumanian and Russian summaries).

APOSTOL, L., and POPESCU, A.
1963   Sur la présence d'Anancus arvernensis Croizet et Jobert a Covrigi, région
              d'Olténie. Trav. Mus. Hist. Nat. "Grigore Antipa", 4, 541—546,
              2 figs., 1 pl., (Rumanian and Russian summaries).

APPLEBY, ROBERT MILSON
1967   The reptile families Ichthyosauridae and Ophthalmosauridae. Proc.
              Geol. Soc. London, no. 1640, 137—138.

APPLEBY, R. M., CHARIG, A. J., COX, C. B., KERMACK, K. A., and TARLO,
L. B. H.
1967   Reptilia. In: Harland, W. B., et al., (eds.), 695—731, figs.

APPLEGATE, SKELTON P.
1964A.   First record of the extinct shark, Squalicorax falcatus, from California
              Bull. S. Calif. Acad. Sci., 63, 42—43, 1 fig.
1964B.   A shark tail from the Miocene of Palos Verdes Hills, California. Bull.
              S. Calif. Acad. Sci., 63, 181—184, 2 figs.
1965A.   A confirmation of the validity of Notorhynchus pectinatus; the se-
              cond record of this Upper Cretaceous cowshark. Bull. S. Calif.
              Acad. Sci., 64, 122—126, 2 figs.
1965B.   Tooth terminology and variation in sharks with special reference to the
              sand shark, Carcharias taurus Rafinesque. Contrib. Sci., Los
              Angeles Co. Mus., 86, 3—18, 5 figs., 2 tables.
              Abs.: Weiler in Zbl. Geol. Pal., Teil 2, 1966, 269—270.
              See: Fierstine and Applegate.

ApSIMON, A. M., and BOON, G. C.
1960   An exposure of the Bristol Avon Gravels at Shirehampton, near Bristol,
              June 1959. Proc. Spelaeol. Soc. Univ. Bristol, 9, 22—29.

AQUIRRE, E. S. J. DE
1963A.   Abs.: H.-P. in Bol. Soc. Espan. Hist. Nat., Sec. Geol., 61, 147.

ARAI, FUSAO
1962   [The Quaternary chronology of the northwestern Kanto District, Japan.]
              Gumma Daigaku Kiyo, Shizenkagakuhen, 10:4, (English summa-
              ry; not seen).

ARAI, J.
1953   New discovery of desmostylid (Cornwallius? sp.) in the Chichibu Basin
              (preliminary report). Res. Bull. Chichibu Nat. Sci. Mus., no. 3,
              65—84, pl. 85, (not seen).

ARAKELÎAN, B. N.
1961   [Archeological work in Armenia.]   Vestnik Akad. Nauk SSSR, 31:1,
              73—76, (Russian).

ARAMAYO, SILVIA A. See: Urquiola de de Carli and Aramayo.

ARAMBOURG, CAMILLE
1959   Titanopteryx philadelphiae nov. gen., nov. sp. Pterosaurien géant.

In: Arambourg, Dubertret, et al., 1959, 229—234, 3 figs., 1 pl.

1963B.   Rev.: Roth-Lutra in Anat. Anz., 116, 521—523; V [allois]
          in L'Anthrop., 68, 160—163.
1963E.   Abs.: Lotze in Zbl. Geol. Pal., Teil 2, 1964, 846.
1963G.   Découverte au Maroc d'un crâne de Neanderthalien. Bull. Soc. Préhist.,
          Paris, 59, 513—514.
1963H.   Les corrélations eurafricaines du quaternaire. Bull. Soc. Préhist., Paris,
          59, 740—744, 1 table.
1964A.   Le genre Bunolistriodon Arambourg 1933. Bull. Soc. Géol. France, 5,
          903—911, 3 figs., 2 text pls., pl. 24, 2 tables.
1964B.   Sur la présence d'un poisson du genre Hadrodus dans les phosphates maes-
          trichiens du Maroc. C. R. Soc. Géol. France, 1964, 318—319, 3
          figs.
          Rev.: Weiler in Zbl. Geol. Pal., Teil 2, 1968: 6, 640.
1965A.   Allocution prononcée par M. le Professeur Camille Arambourg dans la
          Séance d'overture. Actas V Congr. Panafr. Prehist. Estud. Cuater-
          nario, 1963: 1, 65, 67.
1965B.   Aperçu sur les résultats des fouilles du gisement de Ternifine. Discussion
          by I. Schwidetzky, H. Alimen and L. Balout. Actas V Congr. Pa-
          nafr. Prehist. Estud. Cuaternario, 1963: 1, 129—136, 2 figs.
1965C.   La Genese de l'Humanité. 7th edition. Paris: Presses Universitaires de
          France, 128 pp., 43 figs., (not seen).
          Rev.: Sauter in Arch. Suiss. Anthrop. Gen., 30, 88—89.
1965D.   Le gisement moustérien et l'Homme du Jebel Irhoud (Maroc). Quaterna-
          ria, 7, 1—7, 5 figs., (German and English summaries).
1965E.   Considérations nouvelles au sujet de la faune ichthyologique paléomédi-
          terranéenne. Senck. Lethaea, 46a, 13—17, 1 map.
          Abs.: Weiler in Zbl. Geol. Pal., Teil 2, 1966, 270—271.
1967   La deuxième mission scientifique de l'Omo. L'Anthrop., 71: 5—6, 562—
          566, 2 figs.
1968A.   Un Suidé fossile nouveau du Miocène supérieur de l'Afrique du Nord.
          Bull. Soc. Géol. France, 10, 110—115, 2 figs., 1 pl.
1968B.   Un Suidé fossile nouveau du Miocène supérieur de l'Afrique du Sud. C.
          R. Soc. Geol. France, 1968: 3, 104.

ARAMBOURG, C., and BALOUT, L.
1967   Algeria. In: Oakley, K. P., and Campbell, B. G., (eds.), 1—6.

ARAMBOURG, C., BIBERSON, P., COON, C. S., and ROCHE, J.
1967   Morocco. In: Oakley, K. P., and Campbell, B. G., (eds.) 37—44.

ARAMBOURG, C., CHAVAILLON, J., and COPPENS, Y.
1967   Premiers résultats de la nouvelle Mission de l'Omo (1967). C. R. Acad.
          Sci. Paris, Sci. Nat., 265, 1891—1896, 1 fig.

ARAMBOURG, C., and CHOUBERT, G.
1965   Les faunes de mammifères de l'étage Moghrebien du Maroc Occidental.
          Notes Mém. Serv. Géol. Maroc, 185, 29—33, 1 fig.

ARAMBOURG, C., and COPPENS, Y.
1967   Sur la découverte, dans le Pleistocène inférieur de la vallée de l'Omo
          (Éthiopie), d'une mandibule d'Australopithécien. C.R. Acad.

Sci. Paris, Sci. Nat., 265, 589—590, 1 fig.

1968   Découverte d'un australopithécien nouveau dans les gisements de l'Omo
(Ethiopie). S. African Jour. Sci., 64, 58—59, 2 figs., (English
summary).

ARAMBOURG, C., DUBERTRET, L., SIGNEUX, J., and SORNAY, J.

1959   Contribution à la stratigraphie et à la paléontologie du Crétacé et du
Nummulitique de la marge NW de la Péninsule Arabique. Notes
Mém. Moyen-Orient, 7, 193—262, 5 figs., 5 pls., 2 tables.

ARAMBOURG, C., and HOFFSTETTER, R.

1963   Rev.: Campbell in Nature, 206, 333;   Comas in An. Antrop.,
Mexico, 1966, 3, 249—251;   Pericot in Zephyrus, 14,
144—145;   Roth-Lutra in Anat. Anz., 116, 521—523;
Sauter in Arch. Suiss. Anthrop. Gén., 29, 74—75;   Vert.
Palasiatica, 8, 218, (Chinese).

ARAMBOURG, C., and MONTENAT, C.

1968   Le gisement de poissons fossiles du Miocène supérieur de Columbares
(Province de Murcia, Espagne). C. R. Acad. Sci. Paris, Sci. Nat.,
266, 1649—1651.

ARAMBOUROU, R. See: Jude and Arambourou.

ARAMBOUROU, R., and GENET-VARCIN, E.

1965   Nouvelle sépulture du Magdalénien final dans la grotte Duruthy à Sorde-
l'Abbaye (Landes). Ann. Pal., Vert., 51, 129—150, 11 figs.
Rev.: H.V.V. in L'Anthrop., 71: 3—4, 315—316.

ARAMBOUROU, R., and JUDE, P. E.

1964   Le gisement de la Chèvre à Bourdeilles (Dordogne). Périgueux; Imp.
R. et M. Magne, 136 pp., 13 figs., 2 pls.

D'ARAMENGO, CARLO BALBIANO

1966   Le Grotte di Sambughetto in Valstrona. Atti Soc. Ital. Mus. Civico,
Milano, 105, 265—279, 3 figs.

ARAPOV, A. A.

1965   [New observations on structural conditions of Balta suite in the cen-
tral part of the Moldavian SSR.] Izv. Akad. Nauk Moldav.
SSR., 1965: 8, 73—78, 2 figs., (Russian).
See: Negadaev-Nikonov and Arapov.

ARATA, ANDREW A.

1964   A mistaken report of a peccary from the Pleistocene of Louisiana.
Tulane Studies Geol., 2, 28, 1 fig.

1966   A Tertiary proboscidian from Louisiana. Tulane Studies Geol., 4, 73—
74, 1 fig.

1967   Muroid, gliroid, and dipodoid rodents. In: Anderson, S., and Jones,
(eds.), 1967, 226—253, figs. 34—38.

ARATA, A. A., and HARMANN, G. L.

1966   Fossil Ursus reported as early man in Louisiana. Tulane Studies Geol.,
4, 75—77, 2 figs.

ARATA, A. A., and HUTCHISON, J. H.
1964   The raccoon (Procyon) in the Pleistocene of North America. Tulane
          Studies Geol., 2, 21−27, 4 figs.

ARATA, A. A., and JACKSON, C. G. Jr.
1965   Cenozoic vertebrates from the Gulf Coastal Plain − 1. Tulane Studies
          Geol., 3, 175−177, 1 pl.

ARDASHNIKOVA, S. See: Postupal'skaĭa and Ardashnikova.

ARDREY, BERDINE See: Ardrey, Robert.

ARDREY, ROBERT
1961   Rev.: Havel in Amer. Anthrop., 66, 435−436;   Hugot in Bull.
          Inst. Franc. Afr. Noire, 29, 462−465.
1966   The territorial imperative. A personal inquiry into the animal
          origins of property and nations. New York: Atheneum,
          xiv + 390 pp., illustr. by Berdine Ardley.
          Rev.: Garrett in Mankind Quart., 7, 183−186;   Tuttle in Amer.
          Anthrop., 70, 171.

ARENDT, ĪU. A., and GORĪACHEVA, R. I.
1967   [Nikolaĭ Nikolaevich Ĭakovlev (1870-1966).] Mat. Biobibliog. Uchen.
          SSSR, ser. Biol. Nauk, Pal., iss. 2, 91 pp., portr., (Russian).

ARIAS, CLAUDIO
1964   La stazione di superficie a Piano di Santa Maria di Arabona. Atti Soc.
          Toscana Sci. Nat. Mem., Ser. A, 71, 40−50, 4 pls.

ARKELL, A. J.
1959   Abs.: Ipek, 20, 128.
1959B.   Preliminary report on the archaeological results of the British Ennedi
          Expedition, 1957. Kush, 7, 15−26, pls. 10−14, 1 map.
1960   Excavation possibilities in the Sudan: prehistory. Kush, 8, 272−274.
1964A.   A prehistoric site at Salvador near Tummo, between Hoggar and Ti-
          besti. Kush, 12, 291−292, 9 figs.
1964B.   Wanyanga. London: Oxford Univ. Press, 22 pp., 23 figs., 57 pls.,
          frontis. in color.
          Rev.: Mauny in Jour. Afr. Hist., 5, 458−459;   Inskeep in
          S. Afr. Archaeol. Bull., 20, 41;   Shinnie in Antiq.
          Jour., 45, 118;   Vaufrey in L'Anthrop., 69, 316−
          318.

ARKELL, A. J., and HEWES, G. H.
1967   Sudan. In: Oakley, K. P., and Campbell, B. G., (eds.), 101−103.

ARKELL, A. J., and SANDFORD, K. S.
1967   Egypt. In: Oakley, K. P., and Campbell, B. G., (eds.), 13−17.

ARKELL, W. J.
1951   Dorset geology, 1940-1950. Proc. Dorset Nat. Hist. Archaeol. Soc. 72,
          176−194, 2 pls.

ARKHIPOV, S. A.
1960   [Stratigraphy of Quaternary deposits, questions of neotectonics and
              paleogeography of the basin of the middle fork of the Eniseĭ R.]
              Trudy Geol. Inst., 30, 171 pp., 24 figs., 47 tables, (Russian).

ARKHIPOV, S. A., KORENEVA, E. V., and LAVRUSHIN, IŨ. A.
1960   [Stratigraphy of Quaternary deposits of the Eniseĭ region between the
              mouths of the Bakhta and Turukhan rivers.]   Trudy Geol. Inst.,
              26, 248—280, 16 figs., 1 table, (Russian).

ARMAND, D. L., GERASIMOV, I. P., DUMITRASHKO, N. V., KORZHUEV, S. S.,
MESHCHERIAKOV, IŨ. A., and MURZAEV, E. M.
1965   [Sergeĭ Vladimirovich Obruchev.]   Izv. Akad. Nauk, Ser. Geograf.,
              1965: 6, 143—144, (Russian).

ARMELAGOS, GEORGE J.
1964   A fossilized mandible from near Wadi Halfa, Sudan. Man, 64, 12—13,
              6 figs.
              Rev.: Preuschoft in Anthrop. Anz., 27, 136.
1965   The future of paleopathology. Abs. 64th Ann. Meeting Amer. Anthrop.
              Assoc., 1965, 6, (abs.).
              See: Greene, D. L., Ewing and Armelagos.

ARMELAGOS, G. J., EWING, G. H., GREENE, D. L., and PAPWORTH, M. L.
1965   Fossil evidence for prehistoric man in the Nile Valley. 7th Internat.
              Congr., Internat. Assoc. Quat. Res., Abs., 1965, 8, (abs.).

ARMENT, HORACE
1965   Desert artifacts. Screenings, 14: 12, 1—4, 9 figs.

ARMILLAS, PEDRO
1963   Programa de historia de America. Periodo indigena. Publ. Inst. Pana-
              mer. Geog. Hist., no. 226, (not seen).
              Rev.: Orellana Rodríguez in Antropología, 2: 2, 100—103.
1964   Northern Mesoamerica. In: Jennings and Norbeck (eds.), 1964, 291—
              329.

ARMSTRONG, M. H.
1963   Caves and hands — mutilated. NSS News, 21, 56—57, 2 photos.
1964   Lascaux and its future. NSS News, 22, 70—72, 4 figs.
1965   Recent speleological activities in France and Spain. NSS News, 23,
              118—119.

ARMSTRONG, W. G.
1966   Preparation of calcified and fossil hard tissues for amino acid analysis.
              4th Amino-acid colloquium. Technicon Instruments, 45—53,
              (not seen).

ARMSTRONG, W. G., and TARLO, L. B.
1966   Amino-acid components in fossil calcified tissues. Nature, 210, 481—
              482, 2 figs., 1 table.

ARNETTE, SIMONE
1965   L'archéologie en Pologne. Bull. Soc. Préhist. Franç., Étud. et Trav.,
              61, 3—10, 3 figs.

ARNHEIM, N. JR., COCKS, G. T., and WILSON, A. C.
1967   Molecular size of hagfish muscle lactate dehydrogenase. Science, 157,
            568–569, 1 fig., 1 table.

ARNOLD, HELLMUT
1964A.   Die Halterner Sande und ihre Fauna. Fortschr. Geol. Rheinland u.
            Westfalen, 7, 85–112, 9 figs., 1 table.
1964B.   Die Fossilführung des Bottroper Mergels in der Ziegelei Ridderbusch
            westlich Dorsten. Fortschr. Geol. Rheinland u. Westfalen, 7,
            199–212, 5 figs.
1964C.   Fossilliste für die Münsterländer Oberkreide. Fortschr. Geol. Rheinland
            u. Westfalen, 7, 309–330, 1 fig.

ARNOLD, H., and TASCH, K.-H.
1964   Das Oberkreide-Profil der Bohrung Prosper 4 nördlich Bottrop. Forts-
            chr. Geol. Rheinland u. Westfalen, 7, 635–648, 6 figs.

ARNOLD, H., WOLANSKY, D., HILTERMANN, H., and KOCH, W.
1964   Litho– und Biofazies der Oberkreide im südwestlichen Münsterland nach
            neuen Kernbohrungen. Fortschr. Geol. Rheinland u. Westfalen,
            7, 421–478, 13 figs., 3 tables.

ARREDONDO, OSCAR
1958C.   El Mesocnus torrei: un mamifero extinguido del Pleistoceno cubano.
            Scout, Havana, Cuba, May 1958, 2–3, 14, (not seen).
1961   Descripciones preliminares de dos nuevos generos y especies de edenta-
            dos del Pleistoceno Cubano. Bol. Grupo Explor. Cien., 1, 19–
            40, 5 figs., 1 pl.

ARRIBAS, ANTONIO
1967   Primer yacimiento de gastrolitos en España. Bol. Soc. Españ. Hist. Nat.,
            Sec. Geol., 65: 2, 151–156, 5 figs., (English summary).
            See: Almagro Basch, and Arribas.

ASADOV, S. M.   See: Alizade, A. N., et al.

ASCENZI, ANTONIO
1964   Microscopia e osso preistorico. Riv. Antrop., 51, 5–21, 2 figs., 1 pl.,
            (French, English and German summaries).

ASCHER, MARIA See: Ascher and Ascher.

ASCHER, ROBERT See: Clark, J. D., Ascher, et al.; Hockett and Ascher.

ASCHER, ROBERT, and ASCHER, M.
1965   Recognizing the emergence of man. Science, 147, 243–250, 6 figs.

ASHTON, E. H.   See: Zuckerman, et al.

ASIMOV, ISSAC
1964A.   A short history of biology. Garden City, N. Y.: Amer. Mus. Sci.
            Books, published for the Amer. Mus. of Nat. Hist., x + 183 pp.,
            7 figs.
            Rev.: Graubard in Science, 144, 670.
1964B.   The intelligent man's guide to the biological sciences. New York:
            Pocket Books, xii + 402 pp., 32 pls., (pb. ed.).

ASLANOVA, S. M.
1963   [The history of the study of fossil cetaceans on the territory of the
            Soviet Union.]   Izv. Akad. Nauk Azerbaidzhan. SSR., 1963: 5,
            11—20, (Russian; Azerbaidzhan, summary).
1965A.   [A seal from Lower Miocene sediments of Azerbaijan.]   Dokl. Akad.
            Nauk. Azerbaïd. SSR, 21: 6, 46—48, 1 fig., (Russian).
1965B.   [Some data on Perekishkiul' Maĭkop vertebrate fauna.]   Uch. zapiski.
            Azerb. Un., ser. biol., 1965: 2, 99—101, (Russian).

ASMUS, GISELA
1964   Kritische Bemerkungen und neue Gesichtspunkte zur jungpaläolithischen
            Bestattung von Combe Capelle Périgord.   Eiszeit. v. Gegenwart,
            15, 181—186, 1 fig., (French summary).
1965   Zur Datierungsfrage der paläolithischen Menschenreste aus Palästina.
            Anthrop. Anz., 29, 1—11.

ASO, MASARU   See: Serizawa, Nakamuro and Aso.

ASO, M. and ODA, S.
1966   Ikahata-mae site in Shizuoka Prefecture. Jour. Anthrop. Soc. Nippon,
            74: 749, 33—46, 6 figs., (Japanese; English summary).

ASTAKHOV, S. N.
1963   [Late Paleolithic station near Fediaevo village on Angara R.] Sov. Ark-
            heol., 1963: 3, 209—215, 3 figs., (Russian).
1966A.   [I. T. Savenkov collection from site Afontova Gora I.]   Materĩaly Ist.
            Sibiri, Drevn. Sibir', 2, 9—14, 2 figs., (Russian).
1966B.   [Late Paleolithic station Kokorevo IV.]   Sov. Arkheol., 1966: 2, 288—
            294, 2 figs., (Russian).
1967A.   [Research on Stone Age of Tuva.]   In: Rybakov, (ed.), 126—127,
            (Russian).
1967B.   [Adzes from Eniseĭ Late Paleolithic.]   Krat. Soob. Inst. Arkheol. Akad.
            Nauk SSSR, 111 19—23, 2 figs., (Russian).
1968   [Search for Stone Age relics in Tuva.]   In: Rybakov, (ed.), 159—161,
            1 fig., (Russian).

ASTRE, GASTON
1960D.   Abs.:   Brill in Zbl. Geol. Pal., Teil 2, 1962, 272.
1960E.   Abs.:   Brill in Zbl. Geol. Pal., Teil 2, 1962, 285.
1964A.   Remplissage pleistocène d'une fissure de Cassagnes-Comtaux. Bull. Soc.
            Hist. Nat. Toulouse, 99, 46—48.
1964B.   Le problème des aires d'affleurement du Stampien terminal au sommet
            des marno-mollasses tolosanes. Bull. Soc. Hist. Nat. Toulouse,
            99, 229—234.
1964C.   Aceratherium albigense (Rhinocéride) à Itzac (Tarn) dans le complex
            des Calcaires de Cordes (Oligocène). C. R. Soc. Géol. France,
            1964, 266—267.
1965A.   Nouvelle découverte d'une mutation ancienne d'Elephas antiquus au
            Viaduc du Viaur (Aveyron). Bull. Soc. Hist. Nat. Toulouse, 100,
            404—408, 1 fig.
1965B.   Brachyodus onoideus dans le Burdigalien du Cauzé (Tain-et-Garonne).
            Bull. Soc. Hist. Nat. Toulouse, 100, 469—472.
1966A.   Table centennale des matières (travaux scientifiques) du Bulletin de la

Société d'Histoire Naturelle de Toulouse durant son premier siècle (1866–1965). Bull. Soc. Hist. Nat. Toulouse, 101, 7–113.

1966B. Historique de la Société d'Histoire Naturelle de Toulouse durant son premier siècle. Bull. Soc. Hist. Nat. Toulouse, 101, 115–151.

1966C. Elephas antiquus du Bassin de Kozani-Ptolémais en Macédoine. Bull. Soc. Hist. Nat. Toulouse, 102, 292–294.

1966D. Faunes Magdalénienne, Mésolithique et Protohistorique des Escabasses (Lot). Bull. Soc. Hist. Nat. Toulouse, 102, 439–452, 2 figs.

1967A. Elephas trogontherii dans des graviers de Palaminy. Bull. Soc. Hist. Nat. Toulouse, 103, 19–29, 1 fig.

1967B. Pycnodonte du Kimeridgien de Saint-Cirice en Quercy. Bull. Soc. Hist. Nat. Toulouse, 103, 340–343, 1 fig.

1967C. La Société d'Histoire Naturelle de Toulouse et ses pourparlers de 1876 avec celle des Sciences Physiques et Naturelles. Bull. Soc. Hist. Nat. Toulouse, 103, 431–437.

ASTRUC, GUY
1965 La grotte-sanctuaire de Pergouset (Lot). Spelunca, Bull. 5: 4, 21–24, 2 figs.

ATKINSON, BROOKS
1966 Those 'forty dirty birds'. Audubon Mag., 68, 231–236, illustr.

ATLASOV, I. P.
1960 [Tectonics of the north-eastern section of the Siberian platform.] Trudy Inst. Geol. Arktiki, 106, 3–169, 28 figs., 1 table, (Russian).

ATTRIDGE, J. See: Charig, Attridge and Crompton.

ATTRIDGE, J., BALL, H. W., CHARIG, A. J., and COX, C. B.
1964 The British Museum (Natural History) — University of London joint Palaeontological Expedition to Northern Rhodesia and Tanganyika, 1963. Nature, 201, 445–449, 4 figs.
Abs.: Huene in Zbl. Geol. Pal., Teil 2, 1966, 300–301.

AUBEKEROV, B. ZH.
1967 [On the constitution of the second terrace above the flood-plain of the Irtysh R.] Izv. Akad. Nauk Kazakh. SSR, Ser. Geol., 1967: 2, 84–86, 1 fig., (Russian).

AUFFENBERG, WALTER
1964A. The Reddick 1 site, a Pleistocene fissure and cave complex. Guidebk., Soc. Vert. Pal. 1964 field trip, Fla., 1964, 31–50, 1 fig., 1 table.

1964B. A redefinition of the fossil tortoise genus Stylemys Leidy. Jour. Pal., 38, 316–324, 6 figs., pl. 51.

1964C. A new fossil tortoise from the Texas Miocene, with remarks on the probable geologic history of tortoises in eastern U.S. Pearce-Sellards Ser., Texas Mem. Mus., no. 3, 10 pp., 2 figs., 1 table.

1966A. The carpus of land tortoises (Testudininae). Bull. Florida State Mus., Biol. Sci., 10: 5, 159–192, 11 figs.

1966B. A new species of Pliocene tortoise, genus Geochelone, from Florida. Jour. Pal., 40, 877–882, 5 figs., pl. 102.
Rev.: Huene in Zbl. Geol. Pal., Teil 2, 1967, 103.

1967A. Further notes on fossil box turtles of Florida. Copeia, 1967, 319–325, 4 figs.

1967B.   Notes on West Indian tortoises. Herpetologica, 23, 34—44, 2 figs., 1
                table.
1967C.   The fossil snakes of Florida. Plaster Jacket, 3, 8 pp., 2 figs., 1 table.
1967D.   Fossil crocodilians of Florida. Plaster Jacket, 5, 6 pp., 3 figs.
1967E.   What is a plaster jacket? Plaster Jacket, 6, 7 pp., 12 figs.

AUFFENBERG, W., et al.
1964   Guidebook, 1964 field trip, Society of Vertebrate Paleontology in cen-
                tral Florida. Gainesville, Fla.: Univ. of Fla. and Fla. Geol.
                Surv., 52 pp., illustr.

AUFFENBERG, W., and MILSTEAD, W. W.
1965   Reptiles in the Quaternary of North America. In: Wright, H. E., and
                Frey, D.G., (eds.), 1965, 557—568, 1 fig., 3 tables.

AUGUSTA, JOSEF, and BURIAN, Z.
                Tiere der Urzeit. Prague: Artia Press, 48 pp., 60 pls.
1960B.   Menschen der Urzeit. Prague: Artia Press, 64 pp., 52 pls.
1962B.   Das Buch von den Mammuten. Hanau/Main: Artia-Verlag/Werner Dau-
                sien Verlag, 102 pp., illustr., (not seen).
1962C.   Das Buch von den Mammuten. Prague: Artia Press, 59 pp., 20 figs.,
                25 pls.
                Rev.: Bleich in Mitt. Verband Deutschen Höhlen- und Karstforscher,
                München, 10, 128;   Bogsch in Föld. Közlöny, 93,
                395—396, (Hungarian);   Guenther in Quartär, 18, 232—233;
                Thenius in Kosmos, (Stuttgart), 60, 448.
1962D.   Unter Urjägern. Transl. by Max A. Schönwälder und Frido Bunzl.
                Illustr. by Zdeněk Burian. Leipzig, Jena, Berlin: Urania-Verl.,
                159 pp., illustr., (not seen).
                Rev.: Pirker in Die Höhle, 13, 103—104.
1962E.   Flugsaurier und Urvögel. Prague: 104 pp., 38 pls.
                Rev.: Huene in Zbl. Geol. Pal., Teil 2, 1962, 301.
1963B.   Prehistoric reptiles and birds. 2nd impression. Translated by Margaret
                Schierl. London: Paul Hamlyn Ed., 104 pp., 22 black and
                16 color illustrs.
1964A.   An den Lagerfeuern der Altsteinzeit. 3rd ed. Translated by F. Bunzl
                and M. A. Schönwälder. Illustr. by Z. Burian. Leipzig, Jena,
                Berlin: Urania-Verlag, 218 pp., 44 illustr., (not seen).
                Rev.: Hatzl in Die Höhle, 16, 116.
1964B.   Saurier der Urmeere. Prague: Artia, 57 pp., 44 figs., 21 pls., (not seen).
                Rev.: Bogsch in Föld. Közlöny, 95, 331.
                Rev.: Huene in Zbl. Geol. Pal., Teil 2, 1965, 246.
1964C.   Prehistoric sea monsters. Translated by Margot Schierl. London: Paul
                Hamlyn, 67 pp., color pls., drawings, and photos.

AUMANN, GEORG
1957   Abs.: Schnitzer in Zbl. Geol. Pal., Teil 2, 1961, 369.
1960   Abs.: Schnitzer in Zbl. Geol. Pal., Teil 2, 1964, 136.

AUTLEV, P. U.
1964   [Paleolithic station of Gubsa R.] Sov. Arkheol., 1964: 4, 172—176,
                2 figs., (Russian).

AUTLEV, P. U., MURATOV, V. M., and FRIDENBERG, E. O.
1967   [New data on Dakhovskaĭa site.] In: Rybakov, (ed.), 65—66, (Ru-
              ssian).

AVAKIAN, L. A.
1959   [Quaternary fossil mammals of Armenia.] Erevan: Akad. Nauk Arm.
              SSR Press, 75 pp., 1 map, 12 pls., 9 tables, (Russian).

AVAKIAN, L. A., and ALEKSEEVA, L. I.
1966   [First find of Palaeoloxodon elephant in Armenian SSR.] Izv. Akad.
              Nauk Armian. SSR, Nauki O Zemle, 19: 1—2, 1 fig., 1 table,
              (Russian; Armenian summary).

AVDUSIN, D. A., and IANIN, V. L., (eds.)
1962   [Historic-archeological compendium.] Moscow; Mosc. Univ. Press,
              366 pp., illustr., (Russian).

AVELEYRA ARROYO DE ANDA, LUIS
1964A.   The primitive hunters. In: Wauchope, (ed.), 1964, 384—412, 14 figs.
1964B.   Handbook of Middle American Indians Vol. I. 11. The primitive
              hunters. In: West, R.C., (ed.), 1964, 384—412, 14 figs.
1965   The Pleistocene carved bone from Tequixquiac. With appendix by
              Eduardo Schmitter. Amer. Antiq., 30, 261—277, 9 figs.

AVNIMELECH, MOSHE
1959   Abs.: Weiler in Zbl. Geol. Pal., Teil 2, 1966, 271.
1962C.   Natural chalk cast of a fragment of the vertebral column of a Carcha-
              rodon (Selachii: Lamnidae) from the Eocene. Bull. Res.
              Council Israel, Sect. G, 11G, 42—44, illustr.
1966   Dinosaur tracks in the Judean hills. Proc. Israel Acad. Sci., Sect. Sci.,
              no. 1, 1—19, 3 figs., 8 pls.

AVRAM, E.   See: Panin and Avram.

AVRORIN, V. A. (ed.)
1964   [Archeology and ethnography of the Far East.] Materialy Ist. Sibiri,
              Drevn. Sibir', 1, 241 pp., 92 figs., 2 tables, (Russian).

AX, PETER
1964   Der Begriff Polyphylie ist aus der Terminologie der natürlichen, phy-
              logenetischen Systematik zu eliminieren. With comments by
              H. Frick, C. Kosswig, A. Kaestner, W. G. Kühne, E. Thenius,
              K. Krommelbein, W. Hennig, G. G. Wendt, and H. J. Becker.
              Zool. Anz., 173, 52—65, 2 figs.

AXELROD, DANIEL I.
1967A.   Drought, diastrophism, and quantum evolution. Evolution, 21, 201—
              209, 1 fig.
1967B.   Quaternary extinctions of large mammals. Univ. Calif. Publ. Geol.
              Sci., 74, vi + 42 pp., 12 figs., 1 table.
              Rev.: Guilday in Jour. Pal., 42, 1319.

AXELROD, D. I., and BAILEY, H. P.
1968   Cretaceous dinosaur extinction. Evolution, 22, 595—611, 5 figs., 2
              tables.

AYRES, HARVARD   See: Kelley, A. R. and Ayres.

AYRES, JAMES E.
1966   A clovis fluted point from the Kayenta, Arizona area. Plateau, 38,
            76—78, 1 fig.

AZZAROLI, AUGUSTO
1964A.   Rinoceronti pliocenici del Valdarno inferiore. Paleontogr. Ital., 57,
            11—20, pls. 6—15.
            Rev.: Fantini Sestini in Riv. Ital. Pal., 72, 495.
1964B.   Validità della specie Rhinoceros hemitoechus Falconer. Paleontogr.
            Ital., 57, 21—34, pls. 16—20.
            Rev.: Allasinaz in Riv. Ital. Pal., 72, 495
            Abs.: Dietrich in Zbl. Geol. Pal., Teil 2, 1964, 204
1965   The two Villafranchian horses of the Upper Valdarno. Palaeontogr.
            Ital., 59, 1—12, 3 figs., 10 pls., (Italian summary).
1966A.   La valeur des caractères crâniens dans la classification des éléphants.
            Eclog. Geol. Helvetiae, 59, 541—564, 28 figs.
            Rev.: Cita in Riv. Ital. Pal., 72, 1329.
1966B.   Pleistocene and living horses of the Old World. An essay of a classi-
            fication based on skull characters. Palaeontogr. Ital., 61, 1—15,
            pls. 1—46, (Italian summary).

B., G.
1966   Frederick Philip Mennell, F.G.S., M.I.M.M. [Feb. 1880 — April 18,
            1966]. Proc. Rhod. Sci. Assoc., 51, 14—16.

B., H.
1965   Das "Oreopithecus-Problem". Universum; Natur u. Tech., 20: 8, III.

B., L.
1967   Lothar F. Zotz. L'Anthrop., 71: 3—4, 335.
            Abbé A. Glory. L'Anthrop., 71: 3—4, 335—338.

BABAEV, A. M.
1962   [Discovery of fossil bones of rhinoceros, antelope, and horse in the
            Tadzhik depression.] Doklady Akad. Nauk Tadzhik. SSR. 5:
            4, 37—38, (Russian; Tadzhik summary).

BABKIN, P. S.
1964   [On some clinical versions in motor sphere of man in the light of
            phylogenetic evolution.] Voprosy Antrop., 16, 29—40, 1 fig.
            1 table, (Russian).

BABY, RAYMOND S., and POTTER, M. A.
1965   Four fluted points from Summit County, Ohio. Ohio Archaeol., 15,
            64—65, 1 fig.

BACH, HERBERT
1960   Neue vorgeschichtliche Funde. Urania, 23, 164.
1962   Krankheiten und Verletzungen des vor- und frühgeschichtlichen Menschen.
            Urania, 25, 134—140, 10 figs., (not seen).

BACHECHI, F. See: Alessio, Bella, Bachechi and Cortesi.

BACHINSKIĬ, G. A.
1965A.   [Taphonomic peculiarities of the Odessa cave sites of Middle Pliocene
            vertebrates.] Dopovidi Akad. Nauk URSR, Kiev, 1965: 6, 77⁴.–
            777, (Ukrainian; Russian and English summaries).
1965B.   [Principles of taphonomic classification of terrestrial vertebrate occur-
            rences in Neogene and Quaternary deposits of Ukraine.] Pal.
            Sborn., 2: 2, 65–72, (Russian; English summary).
1966   [Fossilization of bones of vertebrates, and new methods of determining
            their geological age.] In: Saks, (ed.), 1966, 460–467, 1 table,
            (Russian).

BACHINSKIĬ, G. A., and CHERNYSH, I. V.
1965   [New cave site of fossil vertebrates in the Ukrainian Carpathians.] Do-
            povidi Akad. Nauk U.R.S.R., Kiev, 1965: 12, 1631–1633, 1 fig.,
            1 table, (Ukrainian; Russian and English summaries).

BACHINSKIĬ, G. A., and DUBLIĀNSKIĬ, V. N.
1962   [Paleozoological characteristics of some subterranean karst cavities in
            the Crimean mountains.] Zbirn. Prats' Zool. Muz. Akad. Nauk
            URSR, 43–51, 8 figs., (Ukrainian; Russian summary).
1966   [New finds of fossil vertebrates in deep karst cavities of Mountain Cri-
            mea.] In: Collected papers [Ecology and history of Ukrainian
            vertebrate fauna], 110–117, (Ukrainian; Russian summary).
1968   [On the age and on paleogeographic environment of the formation of
            deep karstic cavities in Crimea.] Prirodn. Obstan. i Fauny
            Proshl., 4, 79–101, 2 figs., 2 tables, (Russian).

BACHINSKIĬ, G. A., DUBLIĀNSKIĬ, V. N., and LYSENKO, N. I.
1967   [History of formation of Krasnaiā Cave in the light of paleozoological
            data.] Vestnik zoologii, 1967: 4, 53–57, (Russian; English
            summary).

BACHINSKIĬ, G. A., DUBLIĀNSKIĬ, V. N., and SHTENGELOV, E. S.
1964   [Crystal Cave of Krivche in gypsum beds of Podoliiā.] Peshchery, 4,
            49–56, 1 fig., 2 tables, (Russian).

BACHINSKIĬ, G. A., and TATARINOV, K. A.
1966   [Taphonomical peculiarities of Nizhne Krivche spelean site of fossil ver-
            tebrates.] Dopovidi Akad. Nauk URSR, Kiev, 10, 1348–1351,
            1 fig., 1 table, (Ukrainian; Russian and English summaries).

BACHMAYER, FRIEDRICH
1964A.   Fossile Vogelfedern aus den jungtertiären Süsswasserablagerung von Wein-
            graben (Burgenland, Österreich). Ann. Naturhist. Mus. Wien,
            67, 175–180, 7 pls.
1964B.   Versteinertes Leben — die erdgeschichtlichen Dokumente. Veröff.
            Naturhist. Mus. Vienna, N.F. no. 5, 28–39, figs. 26–40.
1966   Ein bemerkenswerter Schildkrötenfund aus dem Ober-Pannon der
            Schottergrube "Heidfeld" Beim Flughafen Schwechat (Wien). Ann.
            Naturhist. Mus. Wien, 69, 101–103, 2 pls.
1967   Eine Riesenschildkröte aus den altpliozänen Schichten von Pikermi
            (Griechenland). Praktika Akad. Athenon, 42, 302–316, 3 figs.,
            6 pls., 2 tables.

BACHMAYER, F., and CORNELIUS-FURLANI, M.
1960   Die geologische Lage von Wien. Veröff. Naturhist. Mus. Vienna, N.F.
          No. 3, 30–32, 1 fig., 1 map. Reprinted in ibid, No. 5, 157–
          160, figs. 198–199, 1 map.

BACHMAYER, F., and WEINFURTE, E.
1965   Bregmaceros-Skelette (Pisces) mit in situ erhaltenen Otolithen aus den
          tortonischen Ablagerungen von Walbersdorf, Österreich. Senck.
          Lethaea, 46a, 19–33, pls. 1–3, (English abstract).
          Abs.: Weiler in Zbl. Geol. Pal., Teil 2, 1966, 271–272.

BACHMAYER, F., and ZAPFE, H.
1960A.   Paläontologische Ausgrabungen des Naturhistorischen Museums — Ersch-
          liessung einer neuen Fundstelle. Veröff. Naturhist. Mus. Vienna,
          N.F. No. 3, 21–23, 5 figs.
1960B.   Neue Funde aus einer eiszeitlichen Bärenhöhle. Veröff. Naturhist. Mus.
          Vienna, N.F. No. 3, 26–29, 5 figs.
          Abs.: Ehrenberg in Zbl. Geol. Pal., Teil 2, 1961 (1960), 544.
1964   Vor 10 Millionen Jahren. Hyänen im Burgenland. Universum; Natur
          u. Tech., 19, 206–208, 3 figs.
1966   Ein Lebensbild aus dem Tertiär. Rekonstruiert nach den Ausgrabungen
          bei Kohfidisch im Burgenland. Universum; Natur u. Tech., 21,
          80–81, 1 fig.

BACON, EDWARD, (ed.)
1963   Vanished civilizations; forgotten peoples of the ancient world. London:
          Thames and Hudson; New York: McGraw Hill, 360 pp., 539
          photos and drawings, 211 color illustr., maps.

BADEN-POWELL, D. F. W.
1965   Francis Henry Arnold Engleheart, J. P. [-1963]. Proc. Geol. Soc.
          London, 1618, 115.

BADER, N. O.
1961   [On the relationship between Upper Paleolithic and Mesolithic cultures
          of Crimea and Caucasus.] Sov. Arkheol., 1961: 4.
1964   [On the relationship between Upper Paleolithic and Mesolithic cultures
          of Crimea, Caucasus, and the Near East.] 7-th Internat. Congr.
          anthrop. ethnogr. sci., Moscow, (Russian).
1965   [Cultural variations at the end of Upper Paleolithic and in Mesolithic
          of Caucasus.] Sov. Arkheol., 1965: 4, 3–16, 5 figs., (Russian).
          See: Liubin, Bader and Markovin.

BADER, OTTO NIKOLAEVICH (= BAHDER, O. N.)
1940I.   Investigation of Mousterian site by Volch'ii Grot.] Krat. Soob. Inst.
          Ist. Mat. Kult. SSSR, 8, 90–96, 3 figs., (Russian).
1959   [Paleolithic station Sungir' on Kliaz'ma R.] Sov. Arkheol., 1959: 1,
          144–155, 13 figs., (Russian).
1961B.   [Unique Paleolithic figure from site at Sungir'.] Krat. Soob. Inst. Ist.
          Mat. Kult. SSSR, 82, 135–139, 3 figs., (Russian).
1962A.   [Discovery of Paleolithic cave paintings in the Urals.] In: Avdusin
          and Ianin, (eds.), 14–23, 6 figs., 1 col. pl., (Russian).
          Spanish translation by Barandiaran in Caesaraugusta, 23–24, 156–162,
          2 figs.

1962B.   [Archeological study of caves and rock shelters in Soviet Union.] In:
           Popov, (ed. in-chief), 1962, vol. 1, 177–193, 7 figs., (Russian).

1963   [Paleolithic paintings from Kapovaĩa cave (Shul'gan-Tash) in Urals.]
           Sov. Arkheol., 1963: 2, 125–134, 5 figs., 2 pls., (Russian).
           Rev.: [Valoch] in Anthrop., 1:3, 96;   Vencl in Archeol. Roz., 15,
           790 (Czech).

1964   The oldest burial? Illustr. London News, 245, 731, 3 figs.

1965A.   The Palaeolithic of the Urals and the peopling of the North. Arctic
           Anthrop., 3, 77–90, 14 figs., (trans. from Russian by Richard
           G. Klein).

1965B.   [Sungir' locality and its archeological outlook.] In: Bader, et al, (eds.),
           1965, 57–65, 3 figs., (Russian).

1965C.   [The Paleolithic of the Urals and its place in the ancient history of
           Eurasia.] In: Gromov, V. I., et al., (eds.), 1965, 129–141, 2 figs.,
           (Russian; English summary).

1965D.   [Kapovaĩa Cave. Paleolithic paintings.] Moscow: Nauka, Acad. Sci.
           USSR, Inst. Archeol., 35 pp., 14 figs., (Russian and French).
           Rev.: Balout in L'Anthrop., 72, 135–137.

1965E.   [Oldest Upper Paleolithic burials near Vladimir.] Vestnik Akad. Nauk
           SSSR, 1965: 5, 77–80, 3 figs., (Russian).

1966A.   [Paleolithic burial on Sungir' site.] In: Rybakov, (ed.), 44–45,
           (Russian).

1966B.   [Archeological research on caves and other karstic phenomena of the
           Russian Platform.] In: Collected Papers: "Problems of karst
           research on the Russian Plain", 121–126, (Russian; not seen).

1966C.   [Mysteries of the gray Urals.] Nauka i Chelovechestvo, 5, 94–117,
           illustr., (Russian).

1967A.   [Excavations on Sungir' site.] In: Rybakov, (ed.), 24–26, 1 fig.,
           (Russian).

1967B.   Die paläolithischen Höhlenmalereien in Osteuropa. Quartär, 18, 127–
           138, 4 figs., 2 pls.

1967C.   Eine ungewöhnliche paläolithische Bestattung in Mittelrussland. Quar-
           tär, 18, 191–193, 1 pl.

1967D.   [Burials in the Upper Paleolithic and the tomb on Sungir' site.] Sov.
           Arkheol., 1967: 3, 142–159, 7 figs., (Russian).

1968A.   [Northern Paleolithic expedition.] In: Rybakov, (ed.), 115, (Russian).

1968B.   [International symposium on the problem of Szeletian in Hungary.]
           Sov. Arkheol., 1968: 1, 309–313, (Russian).

1968C.   [In memoriam B. S. Zhukov.] Sov. Arkheol., 1968: 4, 234–238, portr.,
           (Russian).

           See: Shokurov and Bader; Sukachev, Gromov and Bader.

BADER, O. N., GROMOV, V. I., and SUKACHEV, V. N.
1961A.   [Upper Paleolithic station Sungir'.] Internat. Assoc. Quat. Res., Abs.
           Pap., 6th Congr., 134, (abs.; Russian).

1961B.   [Upper Paleolithic site Sungir'.] In: Gromov, V. I., et al., (eds.)
           1961, 64–66, (Russian; English summary).

BADER, O. N., IVANOVA, I. K., and VELICHKO, A. A., (eds.)
1965   [Stratigraphy and periodization of the Paleolithic of eastern and central
           Europe.] Moscow; "Nauka" Press, 232 pp., illustr., (Russian).

BADOUX, D. M.
1965   Probalilité d'une differenciation due au climat chez les Néandertaliens
           d' Europe. L'Anthrop., 69, 75–82, 1 table.

1966A.   A mandible of Sus scrofa L. from the River Lek, Netherlands. Säuge-
                tierkundl. Mitt., 14, 138—141, 1 fig., 2 tables.
1966B.   A mandible of the woolly rhinoceros, Coelodonta antiquitatis (Blumen-
                bach, 1803), from the Wieringermeer, Netherlands. Säugetier-
                kindl. Mitt., 14, 212—214, 1 fig.

BADOUX, M. H.
1964   La geólogie de la région des Rochers-de-Naye. Bull. Soc. Vaudoise Sci.
                Nat., 68, 539, (abs.).

BAER, JEAN G.
1964   Comparative anatomy of vertebrates. Translated by June Mahon.
                Washington: Butterworths, viii + 193 pp., 3 figs., 68 color and
                black and white pls.

BAERREIS, D. A.   See: Bender, et al.

BAGGERLY, CARMEN
1967   Further notes on the stone tools in the glacial drift of Michigan. New
                World Antiq., 14, 119—126.

BAI, HUI-YING   See: Woo and Bai.

BAI, YUN-ZHE   See: Dai and Bai.

BAIDA, URI   See: Picard and Baida.

BAÏGUSHEVA, V. S.
1964   [Khaprian fauna of the Liventsov sand-pit (Rostov region).] Biull. Kom.
                Izuch. Chetvert. Perioda. Akad. Nauk SSSR, no. 29, 44—50, 1
                table, (Russian).
                See: Dubrovo and Baigusheva.

BAILEY, EDWARD
1962   Rev.: Sandblad in Lychnos, 1963—1964, 417—419, (Swedish).

BAILEY, HARRY P.   See: Axelrod and Bailey.

BAILIT, HOWARD L., and FRIEDLANDER, J. S.
1965   Dental reduction in human evolution. Amer. Jour. Phys. Anthrop., 23,
                329, (abs.).
1966   Tooth size reduction: a hominid trend. Amer. Anthrop., 68: 3, 665—
                672, 2 figs.

BAILLIE, RALPH J.   See: Barrett, P. J. et al.

BAILLOUD, G.
1965   Les gisements paléolithiques de Melka-Kontouré. Inst. Ethiopien d'Ar-
                chéol., 1, 37 pp., 11· figs., 79 pls.
                Rev.: Chavaillon in L'Anthrop., 71: 5—6, 523—525.
                See: Leroi-Gourhan, Bailloud, et al.

BAIN, GEORGE W.
1966   A Laurasian looks at Gondwanaland. Trans. Proc. Geol. Soc. S. Africa,
                annexure to 67, 1—37, 13 figs.

BAIRD, DONALD
   1962A.   Abs.: Huene in Zbl. Geol. Pal., Teil 2, 1964, 160.
   1964A.   The aïstopod amphibians surveyed. Breviora, no. 206, 17 pp., 1 fig.
              Abs.: Program 1964 Ann. Meeting Geol. Soc. Amer., et al., 6—7.
              Abs.: Westphal in Zbl. Geol. Pal., Teil 2, 1965, 239—240.
   1964B.   Dockum (Late Triassic) reptile footprints from New Mexico. Jour. Pal., 38, 118—125, 3 figs.
              Abs.: Huene in Zbl. Geol. Pal., Teil 2, 1964, 980; 1965, 246—247.
   1964C.   Changisaurus reinterpreted as a Jurassic turtle. Jour. Pal., 38, 126—127, 1 fig.
              Abs.: Huene in Zbl. Geol. Pal., Teil 2, 1964, 985.
   1964D.   A fossil sea-turtle from New Jersey. New Jersey State Mus. Invest., no. 1, 26 pp., 9 figs.
              Abs.: Huene in Zbl. Geol. Pal., Teil 2, 1966, 301.
   1965A.   Paleozoic lepospondyl amphibians. Amer. Zool., 5, 287—294, 6 figs.
              Abs.: Westphal in Zbl. Geol. Pal., Teil 2, 1966, 292.
   1965B.   Footprints from the Cutler formation. In: Lewis and Vaughn, pp. C47—C50, fig. 14.
   1965C.   Aïstopod amphibians. Spec. Pap. Geol. Soc. Amer., 82, 6—7, (abs.).
   1966A.   New labyrinthondont amphibian from the Pennsylvanian of Kansas. Program, 1966th Ann. Meeting, Geol. Soc. Amer., 8—9, (abs.).
              Also: Spec. Pap. Geol. Soc. Amer., 101, 8—9, (abs.).
   1966B.   Affinities of the Paleozoic amphibian Subclass Lepospondyli. Spec. Pap. Geol. Soc. Amer., 87, 8—9, (abs.).
   1967   Age of fossil birds from the greensands of New Jersey. Auk, 84, 260—262.
              Rev.: Huene in Zbl. Geol. Pal., Teil 2, 1968, 209—210.
              Rev.: Kuhn in Zbl. Geol. Pal., Teil 2, 1968: 6, 657.
              See: Carroll, R. L. and Baird; Lewis, G. E. and Vaughn.

BAIRD, D., and CARROLL, R. L.
   1967A.   Captorhinus vs. Hypopnous (Reptilia, Captorhinomorpha). Jour. Pal., 41, 264—265.
   1967B.   Romeriscus, the oldest known reptile. Science, 157, 56—59, 3 figs.

BAIRD, D. and CASE, G. R.
   1966   Rare marine reptiles from the Cretaceous of New Jersey. Jour. Pal., 40, 1211—1215, 3 figs.
              Rev.: Huene in Zbl. Geol. Pal., Teil 2, 1967, 204; Huene in Zbl. Geol. Pal., Teil 2, 1968, 204.

BAIRD, D., and PATTERSON, O. F. III
   1967   Dicynodont-archosaur fauna in the Pekin formation (Upper Triassic) of North Carolina. Program, 1967 Ann. Meeting, Geol. Soc. Amer., 1967, 11, (abs.). Also: Spec. Pap. Geol. Soc. Amer., 115, 11, (abs.).

BAITSCH, H.
   1965   Professor Gieseler 65 Jahre alt. Anthrop. Anz., 29, vii—viii, portr.

BAKALOV, P., and NIKOLOV, Iv.
   1962   [Tertiary mammals. Vol. 10 of The Fossils of Bulgaria.] Sofia: Bulgarian Acad. of Sc. Press, 1962, 162 pp., 1 map, 82 plates, 26 tables, (Bulgarian; Russian and French summaries).

1963   Neuer Fund von <u>Trilophodon</u> (<u>Choerolophodon</u>) <u>pentelicus</u> in Bulgarien. Trudove Vŭrkhu Geol. Bŭlg., Ser. Pal., <u>5</u>, 229–240, 1 fig., 3 pls., (Bulgarian; Russian and German summaries).

1964   [Pleistocene mammals from Bulgaria.]   Trudove Vŭrkhu Geol. Bŭlg., Ser. Pal., <u>6</u>, 189–247, 20 pls., 1 table, (Bulgarian; Russian and German summaries).

BAKER, B. H.   See: McCall, Baker and Walsh.

BAKER, JAMES K.
1960   Evolution and speciation in the trodlodytic Plethodontidae of Texas. NSS News, <u>18</u>, 72, (abs.).

BAKER, JOHN R.
1968A.   Cro-Magnon man, 1868-1968.   Endeavour, <u>27</u>: 101, 87–90, 3 figs.
1968B.   Observations on the cranium of Broken Hill man, <u>Homo</u> <u>rhodesiensis</u> Woodward. Zeit. Morph. Anthrop., <u>60</u>, 121–127, 3 tables, (German summary).

BAKER, K.
1960   Early man in Carlsbad. NSS News, <u>18</u>, 47, 1 fig.

BAKER, M. J.   See: Callow, Baker, <u>et</u> <u>al.</u>

BAKER, PAUL T.
1967   The biological race concept as a research tool. Amer. Jour. Phys. Anthrop., <u>27</u>, 21–25.

BAKER, P. T., and WEINER, J. S., (eds.)
1966   The biology of human adaptability. New York: Oxford Univ. Press, xiii + 541 pp., (not seen).
            Rev.: Barnicot in Man, Jour. Roy. Anthrop. Inst., <u>2</u>, 307–308; Malina in Amer. Jour. Phys. Anthrop., <u>27</u>, 109–110.

BAKER, ROLLIN H.
1967   Perissodactyls. In: Anderson, S., and Jones, (eds.), 1967, 374–384, figs. 63–64.

BAKIROV, S. B., and KUZNETSOV, V. V.
1962   [Discovery of teeth of a cotylosaur in Malyĭ Karatau.] Vestnik Akad. Nauk Kazakh. SSR, 1962: 9, 84–85, 1 fig., (Russian).

BAKUN, N. N., and VANGENGEYM, E. A.
1963   Age of the Barktriy series of south-western Fergana based on paleontological data. Dokl. Acad. Sci. U.S.S.R., Earth Sci. Sect., <u>148</u>, 1–6.

BALABAĬ, P. P.
1956A.   [On the classification of the genus <u>Poraspis</u> Kiaer.] Nauk. Zap. Nauk.-pryr. Muz., <u>5</u>, 3–13, 9 figs., (Ukrainian; Russian summary).
1956B.   [Morphology and phylogenetical development of Agnatha.] Kiev: Ukrain. SSR Akad. Nauk Press, 141 pp., 84 figs., (Russian).
1956C.   [On the phylogenesis of Agnatha.] Zool. Zhurnal, <u>35</u>:6, 874–890. 12 figs., (Russian).
1959   [About the pteraspid fauna of the Podolsk shelf.] Geol. Zhurnal, Kiev, <u>19</u>:4, 87–90, 3 fig., (Ukrainian).

1960B.   [Research on pteraspids of the Lower Devonian of Podolia. Communication II.] Nauk. Zap. Nauk.-pryr. Muz., 8, 124—133, 2 figs., 1 table, (Ukrainian; Russian and English summaries).

1961   [Heterostraci of Upper Silurian of Podolia.] Nauk. Zap. Nauk.-pryr. Muz., 9, 3—11, 10 figs., (Ukrainian; Russian summary).

1962   [On the cephalaspid fauna of the Podolian shield.] Nauk. Zap. Nauk.-pryr. Muz., 10, 3—8, 11 figs., (Ukrainian; Russian summary).

BALAŠA, G.

1960   Fondation du département de préhistoire au Musée de Banská Bystrica. Archeol. Roz., 12, 904—905, (Czech; French summary).

BALÁZS, D.

1962   Beiträge zur Speläologie des südchinesischen Karstgebietes. Karst — és Barlangkutatás, 2, 3—82, 45 figs., 3 tables, (English and Russian summaries).

BALDAUF, RICHARD J.

1964A.   Aspects of anuran phylogeny as revealed by cranial morphology. Amer. Zool., 4, 395—396, (abs.).

1964B.   Is Calyptocephalella the most primitive living frog? Texas Jour. Sci., 16, 476—477, (abs.).

1965   Comments on the Lissamphibia. Amer. Zool., 5, 266.

BALDWIN, GORDON CURTIS

1963   The world of prehistory: the story of man's beginnings. Illustr. by Frank Aloise. New York: Putnam, 192 pp., illustr., maps, (not seen).

BALDWIN, PAUL H., and KOPLIN, J. R.

1966   The Boreal owl as a Pleistocene relict in Colorado. Condor, 68, 299—300, 1 fig.

BALDWIN, SAMUEL A.

1962   A tale of a dinosaur. Found. News, Dec. 1962, 14—15, 1 fig., (not seen).

BALL, H. W.   See: Attridge, et al.

BALLAND, RENÉ

1964A.   Le Quaternaire dans l'enseignement du second degré. Bull. Assoc. Franç. Étude Quat., 1, 13—14.

1964B.   Un gisement du Pleistocène inférieur aux environs de Bordeaux les argiles de Bruges (Gironde). Geol. en Mijn., 43, 77—82, 2 figs.

BALLAND, R., and ELHAÏ, H.

1965   Sur un gisement du Quaternaire moyen dans le Sud-Ouest de la France (Gironde). C.R. Acad. Sci. Paris, 261, 3439—3441.

BALLESIO, ROLAND

1962   Abs.: Doc. Lab. Géol. Fac. Sci. Lyon, no. 1, 25.

1963   Abs.: Doc. Lab. Géol. Fac. Sci. Lyon, no. 3, 14.

BALLESIO, R., BATTETTA, J., DAVID, L., and MEIN, P.

1965   Mise au point sur Aceratherium platyodon Mermier 1895. Doc. Lab. Géol. Fac. Sci. Lyon, 9, 51—95, 1 fig., 8 pls.

BALLIOT, MARCEL
1959   Récolte paléontologique dans une grotte du Bugey. Grotte du Pissoir
        (ou aux Ours) à Torcieu (Ain). Ann. Spel., 14, 238–239, 1
        fig.

BALOUT, LIONEL
1956   La préhistoire en Algérie (1956). Libyca, 4, 357–358.
1963   Voyages de l'Abbé Breuil en France, en Europe, à travers le monde
        (1897-1957). Libyca, 11, 9–42, 11 figs.
1964   L'industrie néandertalienne du Djebel Irhoud (Maroc). Bull. Soc. Pré-
        hist. Franç., C. R. séances mens., 1964:3, LXI–LXII, (abs.,
        and discussion).
1965A. L'Abbé Breuil, préhistorien de l'Afrique du Nord et du Sahara. Actas
        V Congr. Panafr. Prehist. Estud. Cuaternario, 1963: 1, 71–77.
1965B. La Basse-Tardoire grottes et abris paléolithique. C. Le Bois-du-Roc.
        Abri du Chasseur. Bull. Assoc. Franç. Étude Quat., 1965: 3–4,
        233–236, 1 fig., 1 table.
1965C. Abri André Ragout. Bull. Assoc. Franc. Étude Quat., 1965: 3–4,
        237–242, 5 fig.
1965D. La préhistoire. Leçon inaugurale de la Chaire de Préhistoire pronon-
        cée le 14 avril 1964. Bull. Mus. Hist. Nat. Paris, 37, 208–232.
1965E. Données nouvelles sur le problème du Moustérien en Afrique du Nord.
        Actas V Congr. Panafr. Prehist. Estud. Cuaternario, 1963:1,
        137–145, 5 pls.
1965F. Le Moustérien du Maghreb. Quaternaria, 7, 43–58, 6 figs., (English
        and Spanish summaries).
1967A. Deux problèmes de stratigraphie quaternaire en Tunisie. Discussion.
        In: Bishop, W.W., and Clark, J. D., (eds.), 357–358.
1967B. Introduction to part III. [Archaeological considerations.] A. Afrique
        du Nord et Sahara. In: Bishop, W. W., and Clark, J. D.,
        (eds.), 411–413.
1967C. Procédés d'analyse et questions de terminologie dans l'étude des en-
        sembles industriels du Paléolithique inférieur en Afrique du
        Nord. Discussion. In: Bishop, W. W., and Clark, J. D., (eds.),
        701–735, 15 figs., (English summary).
        See: Arambourg 1965B; Arambourg and Balout; Souville 1956B.

BALOUT, L., BIBERSON, P., and TIXIER, J.
1967   L'Acheuléen de Ternifine (Algérie), gisement de l'Atlanthrope. L'An-
        throp., 71: 3–4, 217–237, 16 figs.

BALSAC, HENRI HEIM DE
1966A. Faits nouveau concernant l'évolution crânio-dentaire des soricinés (Mam-
        mifères Insectivores). C. R. Acad. Sci. Paris, Sci. Nat., 263,
        889–892, 1 fig.
1966B. Évolution progressive et évolution régressive dans la denture des Sori-
        cinae (Mammifères Insectivores). C. R. Acad. Sci. Paris, Sci.,
        Nat., 263, 920–923.

BANDI, HANS GEORG
1961B. Rev.: Clark in Proc. Prehist. Soc. Cambridge, 32, 358–359; Fock
        in S. Afr. Archaeol. Bull., 19, 22.
1965A. Überlegungen zum Ursprung der Eskimokultur. Basler Beiträge Geog.
        Ethnol., Ethnol. Reihe, 2, 39–52.
1965B. Neue Ergebnisse archäologischer Forschungen in Alaska. Bull. Schweiz.
        Ges. Anthrop. Ethnol., 41, 11–12.

1965C.   Urgeschichte der Eskimo. Stuttgart: Fischer, ix + 171 pp., 67 figs.,
            6 tables.
    Rev.:   Gerhardt in Homo, 16, 193; Preuschoft in Anthrop. Anz.,
            28, 152; Resch in Umschau, 66: 3, IV.
    See: Hadleigh-West and Bandi.

BANDRABUR, T.   See: Litianu, Mihăilă and Bandrabur.

BANDRABUR, T., and GIURGEA, P.
1965   [Contribution to the study of Quaternary deposits of Siret R. in
            Bacău-Roman region.] Dări seamă şedinţ. Com. geol. RPR,
            51: 2, 67—83.

BANERJI, ADRIS
1964   Prehistoric foundations of Rajasthan. Jour. Orient. Inst., 14, 14—24.

BÁNESZ, LADISLAV
1959D.   Trouvailles paléolithiques du district de Sobrance en Slovaquie. Ar-
            cheol. Roz., 11, 577—580, figs. 225—226, (Czech., German sum-
            mary).
1960C.   Trouvailles aurignaciens de Seňa I en 1959. Archeol. Roz., 12, 428—
            430, (Czech; French summary).
1961C.   Paläolithische Objekte aus Kechnec III. Archeol. Roz., 13, 301—318,
            figs. 124—128, (Czech; German summary).
1961D.   Idole paléolithique et couches archéologiques à l'industrie d'obsidienne
            dans un ensemble de couches loessiques de Cejkov en Slovaquie.
            Archeol. Roz., 13, 765—774, figs. 264—270, (Czech; French
            summary).
1961E.   Fragment d'une figurine en terre cuite de la station paléolithique de
            Kašov en Slovaquie. Archeol. Roz., 13, 774—780, figs. 271—
            273, (Czech; French summary).
1964   Weitere Erforschung der paläolithischen Station Cejkov I. Archeol.
            Roz., 16, 317—323, figs. 90—91, (Czech; German summary).
1965A.   Zur chronologie des Aurignacien in der Tschechoslowakei. Archeol.
            Roz., 17, 393—419, figs. 122—128.
1965B.   [Considerations on the origin, subdivision, and extent of Aurignacian
            in Europe.] Sloven. Archeol., 13: 2, 261—318, 12 figs., (Slo-
            vakian; French summary).
1967A.   Paleolitické sídliskové objekty zbarce-svetlej III. Archeol. Roz., 19,
            285—295, figs. 83—90.
1967B.   Die altsteinzeitlichen Funde der Ostslowakei. Quartär, 18, 81—98, 7
            figs., 2 pls.
1968   Eine neue Aurignacien-Gruppe im oberen Theissgebiet. Archeol. Roz.,
            20, 47—55, 2 figs.

BANKS, MAXWELL R.
1965   Geology and mineral deposits. Publ., Univ. Tasmania, Dept. Geol., no.
            157, 12—17, figs. 14—17, map.

BANNER, JÁNOS
1960   Zu der Veröffentlichung des ersten paleolithischen Fundes in Mitteleu-
            ropa. Archeol. Roz., 12, 709—714.
1966   Die Anfänge der Paläolithikum-Forschung in Ungarn. Sborník Národ-
            niho Musea v Praze. Rada A: Historie, 20: 1—2, 201—206.

BANNER, J., and JAKABFFY, I.
1961   Rev.: Ruttkay in Archaeol. Austriaca, 33, 114–115.

BANNIKOV, A. G.
1954   [Mammals of Mongolian People's Republic.]   Trudy Mongol. Kom., 53
        669 pp., illustr., (Russian).

BANTA, BENJAMIN H.
1966   A check list of fossil amphibians and reptiles reported from the State
        of Nevada. Occ. Pap. Biol. Soc. Nevada, no. 13, 1–6.

BARABASHEV, E. V.   See: Shamsutdinov and Barabashev.

BARABASHEV, E. V., SIZIKOV, A. I., and FOMIN, I. N.
1963   [V. A. Obruchev in Transbaikalia. (Centenary of birthday).]   Zapiski
        Zabaikal'. Otd. Geogr. Obshch. SSSR, 21, 209–214, (Russian).

BARANDIARÁN, JOSÉ MIGUEL DE
1955   Exploración de la Cueva de Urtiaga. X campaña, 1954. Munibe,
        1955: 2, 69–80, (not seen).
1959   III Campaña de excavaciones en el yacimiento paleolítico de "Lezetxi-
        ki" y I campaña en el de "Kobatxo" (Garagarza-Mondragón).
        Munibe, 11: 1–2, 15–19, 3 figs.
1960   Exploración de la Cueva de Urtiaga. (XI y XII campañas). Munibe,
        12: 1, 3–18, 8 figs., 5 pls.
1961   Excavaciones en Aitzbitarte IV. (Trabajos de 1960). Munibe, 13:
        3–4, 183–285, 51 figs., 5 pls., 3 tables.
1962   Aitzbitarte. Exc. Arqueol. en España, no. 6, (not seen).
1963A.   Excavaciones en la caverna de Aitzbitarte IV (trabajos de 1961). Mu-
        nibe, 15: 1–2, 23–42, (not seen).
1963B.   Excavaciones en Aitzbitarte IV (campaña de 1962). Munibe, 15: 3–4,
        69–86, (not seen).
1964A.   Excavaciones en la caverna de Aitzbitarte (campaña 1963). Munibe,
        16: 1–2, 12–13, (not seen).
1964B.   Exploración de la Cueva de Lezetxiki en Mondragón (campaña de
        1961). Noticiario Arqueol. Hispánico, 6: 1–3, 25–30, 6
        figs.
1964C.   Exploración de la Cueva de Lezetxiki (campaña de 1962). Noticiario
        Arqueol. Hispanico, no. 6: 1–3, 31–42, 13 figs.
1965A.   Exploración de la cueva de Lezetxiki (Mondragón). (Campaña de
        1963.) Munibe, 17, 52–63, 16 figs.
        Rev.: H.-P. in Bol. Soc. Españ. Hist. Nat., Sec. Geol., 64: 3–4, 303.
1965B.   Excavaciones en Aitzbitarte IV (Campaña de 1964). Munibe, 17, 21–
        37, 18 figs.

BARANDIARÁN, J. M., and ALTUNA, J.
1965   Exploración de la cueva de Lezetxiki (Mondragón). (Campaña de 1964.)
        Munibe, 17, 38–51, 13 figs.
1966   Excavación de la cueva de Lezetxiki (Campaña 1965). Munibe, 18, 5–
        11, 8 figs.

BARANDIARÁN, J. M. DE, and ELÓSEGUI, J.
1962   Exploración de la Cueva de Urtiaga, en Itziar-Deva. Segunda época.
Noticiario Arqueol. Hispánico, 5, 50—57, 4 figs., 2 pls.

BARANDIARÁN, J. M. DE, and FERNÁNDEZ MEDRANO, D.
1957   Exploración de la Cueva de Lezetxiki en Mondragón (trabajos de 1956).
Munibe, 1957: 1—2, 34—48.
1960   Exploración de la Cueva de Lezetxiki en Mondragón (trabajos de 1957,
1959 y 1960). Munibe, 12: 4, 273—310, 29 figs., 7 pls.
1963   Exploración de la Cueva de Lezetxiki en Mondragón (campaña de
1962). Munibe, 15: 3—4, 87—102.
1964   Exploración de la cueva de Lezetxiki en Mondragón (Campaña de
1961). Munibe, 16: 1—2, 56—59.

BARANDIARÁN, J.-M. DE, and SONNEVILLE-BORDES, D. DE
1964   Magdalénien final et Azilien d'Urtiaga (Guipúzcoa): étude statistique.
In: Ripoll Perelló, E., (ed.), 1964A, 163—171, 5 figs., (Spanish
summary).

BARANDIARÁN MAESTU, IGNACIO M.a
1964   Estado actual de la investigación prehistórica en la Provincia de Guipúzcoa. Bilbao, (not seen).
1965A.   Paleolítico y Mesolítico en la Provincia de Guipúzcoa. Caesaraugusta,
23—24, 23—56, 10 figs.
1965B.   Notas sobre el Magdaleniense Final en la costa Cantábrica. Caesaraugusta, 25—26, 41—54, 6 figs.
1966   L'art rupestre paléolithique des provinces basques. Préhist. Spéléol.
Ariégeoises, 21, 47—73, 9 figs.

BARANOVA, IU. P. and BISKE, S. F.
1964   [Cenozoic stratigraphy and history of relief evolution of East-Siberian
lowlands.] Trudy Inst. Geol. Geof., 1964: 8, 41—63, 1 fig.,
(Russian).

BARAT, CAROL A.
1960   Profil géologique et données paleontologiques de la terrasse de Colen-
tina a nord-ouest de Bucarest. Trav. Mus. Hist. Nat. "Grigore
Antipa", 2, 295—306, 9 figs., (Rumanian and Russian summaries).
Abs.: Semaka in Zbl. Geol. Pal., Teil 2, 1962, 289.

BARBEY, C., and DESCAMPS, C.
1967   Note sur les formations Quaternaires de la Pointe de Fann (Dakar).
Notes Africaines, 114, 48—54, 9 figs.

BARBOUR, ERWIN H.   See: Matthew and Barbour

BARBOUR, GEORGE B.
1965A.   In the field with Teilhard de Chardin. New York: Herder and Herder, 160 pp., illustr.
1965B.   Teilhard de Chardin sur le terrain. Translated by Annie Bernard.
Paris: Éditions de Seuil, 184 pp., illustr., (not seen).
Rev.: M. C. in Fossilia, 1965: 3—4, 47—48; Delpech in Rev.
Synthèse, 88, 267—269.

BARBU, VIRGINIA
1964   [Remains of Anthracotherium in the coals of Ticu (Cluj region).]   Bul.
            Inst. petrol. gaze și geol., 11, 9—19, 2 pls., (Rumanian; Russian
            and English summaries).

BARDACK, DAVID
1964   A revision of fossil and living chirocentrid fishes. Diss. Abst., 24, 5618—
            5619.
1965A.   Anatomy and evolution of chirocentrid fishes. Univ. Kans. Pal. Con-
            trib., 40, 1—88, 27 figs., 2 pls., 3 tables.
1965B.   New Upper Cretaceous teleost fish from Texas. Univ. Kans. Pal. Con-
            trib., Pap., 1, 9 pp., 2 figs.
1965C.   Localities of fossil vertebrates obtained from the Niobrara formation
            (Cretaceous) of Kansas. Univ. Kansas Publ. Mus. Nat. Hist., 17:
            1, 1—14.
1967   Did some Cretaceous teleosts described by Cope as North American
            actually come from Lebanon? Jour. Pal., 41, 1274—1276, 1 fig.,
            1 table.
1968A.   Fossil vertebrates from the marine Cretaceous of Manitoba. Canadian
            Jour. Earth Sci., 5: 1, 145—153, 9 figs., 2 tables.
1968B.   Belonostomus sp., the first holostean from the Austin chalk (Cretace-
            ous) of Texas. Jour. Pal., 42, 1307—1309, 1 fig.

BARDACK, D., and ZANGERL, R.
1968   First fossil lamprey: a record from the Pennsylvanian of Illinois. Sci-
            ence, 162, 1265—1267, 4 figs., 1 table.

BARGHUSEN, HERBERT R.
1968   The lower jaw of cynodonts (Reptilia, Therapsida) and the evolutiona-
            ry origin of mammal-like adductor jaw musculature. Postilla,
            116, 1—49, 13 figs., 6 pls.

BARGMANN, W., and SCHADÉ, J. P., (eds.)
1964   Progress in brain research. Vol. 6. Topics in basic neurology. Amster-
            dam, London, New York: Elsevier Publ. Co., vi + 249 pp.,
            illustr.

BARKER, Mr.
1961   Potassium-argon dating. Antiq., 35, 59.

BARKER, H.
1967   Radiocarbon dating of bone. Nature, 213, 415.

BARLEY, M. W., and LUCAS, A. T., (eds.)
1958   [COWA surveys and bibliographies.]   Area 1 — British Isles. COWA
            Surv. and Bibliog., Area 1, no. 1, 12 + 7 pp.
1960   COWA surveys and bibliographies. Area 1 — British Isles. COWA Surv.
            and Bibliog., Area 1, no. 2, 13 + 9 pp.,

BARLOW, JON C.
1967   Edentates and pholidotes. In: Anderson, S., and Jones, (eds.), 1967,
            178—191, figs. 27—28.

BARLOW, NORA, (ed.)
1967   Darwin and Henslow. The growth of an idea. Letters 1831—1860.
            London: John Murray, xii + 251 pp., 8 pls., (not seen).

Rev.: G. G. Simpson in Nature, <u>215</u>, 1417; Zirkle in Science, <u>159</u>, 519—520.

BARNARD, K. H.
1954   A guide book to South African whales and dolphins. Cape Town: South African Mus., Guide no. <u>4</u>, ii + 33 pp.

BARNETT, LINCOLN, and EDITORS OF LIFE
1958   Prehistoric animals, dinosaurs and other reptiles. New York: Simon & Schuster, 56 pp., color illustr., (elemen. and junior high).

BARNETT, S. A., and McLAREN, A., (eds.)
1964   Penguin Science Survey 1964. Vol. B — Natural Science. London: Penguin Book Ltd., 251 pp., 45 figs.
        Rev.: Hart in S. African Jour. Sci., <u>61</u>, 62; S. in Current Sci., <u>34</u>, 570—571.

BARNHART, GEORGE W. See: Staley and Barnhart.

BARNICOT, N. A. See: Harrison, <u>et al.</u>

BARRADAS, LERENO
1967   Moçambique. In: Oakley, K. P., and Campbell, B. G., (eds.), 35—36.

BARRAL. L., and Simone, S.
1965   Nouvelles fouilles à la grotte du Prince (Grimaldi, Ligurie Italienne). Bull., Mus. Anthrop. Préhist. Monaco, <u>12</u>, 115—133, 11 figs.

BARRERA, ALFREDO
1967   The Museum of Natural History of the City of Mexico. Pac. Discovery, <u>20</u>: 5, 9—13, illustr.

BARRETT, PAUL H., (ed.)
1960   A transcription of Darwin's first notebook on "transmutation of species." Bull., Mus. Comp. Zool., Harvard Univ., <u>122</u>: 6, 247—296, 4 illustr.

BARRETT, PETER J., BAILLIE, R. J., and COLBERT, E. H.
1968   Triassic amphibian from Antarctica. Science, <u>161</u>, 460—462, 1 fig., 1 table.
        Rev.: Westphal in Zbl. Geol. Pal., Teil 2, 1969: 2, 207.

BARRIÈRE, CLAUDE
1961   Les fouilles de Rouffignac (Dordogne). Bull. Soc. Roy. Belge Anthrop. Préhist., <u>72</u>, 97—101, 1 diagram.
        See: Nougier and Barrière.

BARRIÈRE, C., and SAHLY, A.
1964   Les empreintes humaines de Lascaux. In: Ripoll Perelló, E., (ed.), 1964A, 173—180, 8 figs., (Spanish summary).

BARRIÈRE, JEAN, BOUTEYRE, G., LUMLEY, H. DE, RUTTEN, P., and VIGNERON, J.
1965   Relations entre deux surfaces rissiennes une plage tyrrhénienne et des industries paléolithiques en Languedoc méditerranéen (Montels, Hérault). Bull. Soc. Geol. France, <u>7</u>, 981—997, 7 figs.

Abs.: C. R. Soc. Geol. France, 1965, 271, (abs.)

BARRIÈRE, JEAN, and MICHAUX, JACQUES
  1968   Contribution à la connaissance de la stratigraphie du Pliocène de Mont-
             pellier: étude de gisement à Micromammifères de Vendargues.
             C. R. Soc. Géol. France, 1968: 9, 297—299, 1 fig.

BARRY, T. H.
  1965   On the epipterygoid-alisphenoid transition in the Therapsida. Ann. S.
             Afr. Mus., 48, 399—426, 22 figs.
  1967   The cranial morphology of the Permo-Triassic anomodont Pristerodon
             buffaloensis with special reference to the neural endocranium
             and visceral arch skeleton. Ann. S. Afr. Mus., 50: 7, 131—161,
             14 figs., pls. 10—11.

BÁRTA, JURAJ (= BARTA, ĨU.)
  1959B.   Venusplastik in der Westslowakei. Archeol. Roz., 11, 874—875, (Czech;
             German summary).
  1962B.   Nové poznatky k problematice kultury listovitých hrotov [w:] Referaty
             o pracovnich výsledich československých archeologu za rok 1961.
             Smolenice, 1, 49—60, (not seen).
  1963B.   Archäologische Kriterien bei der Stratifikation des slowakischen Quartärs.
             Geol. Prace, Bratislava, 64, 41—51, (Czech; German summary).
  1965A.   [Slovakian Paleolithic in the light of Pleistocene stratigraphy.] In:
             Bader, O. N., et al., (eds.), 1965, 7—11, 1 fig., (Russian).
  1965B.   Notes about the Paleolithic in Rumania. Sborník Geol. Věd, Řada A,
             Anthropozoikum, 3, 123—140, 4 pls., (Slovak; English and Rus-
             sian summaries).
  1965C.   Trenčin IV — eine neue jungpaläolithische Station in der Westslowakei.
             Sloven. Archeol., 13, 5—26, 9 figs., 4 pls., (Czech; German
             summary).
  1965D.   [Slovakia in Old and Middle Stone Age.] Bratislava: Slov. Akad.
             Ved Press, 232 pp., 46 pls., 3 maps, 2 tables, (Slovakian;
             German summary).
             Rev.: Ložek in Věstník Ústřed. Úst. Geol., 41: 1, 78, (Czech).
  1966   [Professor dr. Josef Skutil (1904—1965).] Sloven. Archeol., 14: 1, 227—
             229, portr., (Slovakian).
  1967   Stratigraphische Übersicht der paläolitischen Funde in der Westslowakei.
             Quartär, 18, 57—80, 11 figs., 2 pls.

BARTHOLOMAI, ALAN
  1966A.   The discovery of plesiosaurian remains in freshwater sediments in Queen-
             sland. Austral. Jour. Sci., 28, 437—438.
  1966B.   Fossil footprints in Queensland. Austral. Nat. Hist., 15, 147—150, 4
             figs.
  1966C.   The type specimens of some of De Vis' species of fossil Macropodidae.
             Mem. Queensland Mus., 14, 115—126, pls. 15—19.
  1967   Troposodon, a new genus of fossil Macropodinae (Marsupialia). Mem.
             Queensland Mus., 15, 21—33, 4 figs., 2 tables.
  1968   A new fossil koala from Queensland and a reassessment of the taxono-
             mic position of the problematical species, Koalemus ingens De
             Vis. Mem. Queensland Mus., 15, 65—72, 1 fig., pl. 9, 1 table.

BARTOLOMEI, GIORGIO
  1964   Mammiferi di brecce pleistoceniche dei Colli Berici (Vicenza). Mem. Mus.

Civ. Storia Nat. Verona, 12, 221—290, 20 figs., 1 table, (English summary).

1965   Primo rinvenimento di una Scimmia pleistocenica nell'Italia Settentrionale e considerazioni sul suo significato ecologico. Rend. Accad. Naz. Lincei, 39: 6, 533—535, 1 pl., (French summary).

BARTOLOMEI, G., and BROGLIO, A.
1964   Primi risultati delle ricerche nella Grotta Minore di San Bernardino nei Colli Berici. Ann. Univ. Ferrara, Sez. 15, 1: 8, 157—185, 9 figs., (French and English summaries).
    See: Leonardi, P., Annibaldi, Broglio and Bartolomei; Leonardi, P., Bartolomei and Broglio.

BARTON, P. L.
1968   Bibliography of New Zealand archaeology and related subjects, 1961—65. New Zealand Archaeol. Assoc. Newsletter, 11, 57—64.

BARTOSCH, SIEGFRIED
1962   Die Tierfährten von Nierstein. Aufschluss, 13, 57—60, 3 figs.

BAR YOSEF, O. See: Stekelis and Bar Yosef; Stekelis, Bar Yosef and Tchernov.

BASABE, JOSÉ MARÍA
1966   El húmero premusteriense de Lezetxiki (Guipúscoa). Munibe, 18, 13—31, 7 figs., 11 pls., 2 tables.
    Rev.: Vallois in L'Anthrop., 72: 3—4, 366—367.

BASCH, MARTIN ALMAGRO (= ALMAGRO BASCH, M.)
1964   Investigaciones arqueológicas en la China comunista. Atlantida, Madrid, 10, 424—432.

BASLER, ÐURO
1962   Der paläolithische Fund vom Visoko Brdo in Lupljanica (Nordbosnien). Glasnik Zemaljskog Muz. u Sarajevu, Arheol., n.s. 17, 5—13, 1 fig., 5 pls., (Serbo-Croatian; German summary).
1963   Abs.: P. in Bull. Sci., Zagreb, Sec. A, 10, 295.
1963B.   Gisements paléolithiques de la Bosnie du nord. Glasnik Zemaljskog Mus. u Sarajevu, Arheol., n.s. 18, 5—24, 6 figs. (Serbo-Croatian; French summary).

BASLER, Ð. and JANEKOVIĆ, Ð.
1961   Der paläolithische Funde von Kulaši. Glasnik Zemaljskog Muz. u Sarajevu, Arheol., n.s. 15—16, ,27—38, 4 figs., 6 pls. (Serbo-Croatian; German summary).

BASLER, Ð., MALEZ, M., and BRUNNACKER, K.
1966   Die Rote Höhle (Crvena Stijena) bei Bileća/Jugoslawien. Eiszeit. u. Gegenwart, 17, 61—68, 2 figs., 1 table, (English summary).

BASS, GEORGE F., and KATZEV, M. L.
1968   New tools for underwater archaeology. Archaeol., 21, 164—173, illustr.

BASS, W. M. See: Kerley and Bass.

BASSE DE MÉNORVAL, E., and BENEUT, G.
1964   Présence d'outillage denticulé de technique levalloisienne dans les alluvions anciennes de la Marne. Bull. Groupement Archéol. Seine-et-Marne, 4, 9, (not seen).

BASSOULLET, JEAN-PAUL, and ILIOU, J.
1967   Découverte de dinosauriens associés à des crocodiliens et des poissons dans le Crétacé inférieur de l'Atlas saharien (Algérie). C.R. Soc. Geol. France, 1967, 294–295.

BASTIAN, HARTMUT
1953   Weltall und Urwelt. Kurzweilige Himmelskunde und Erdgeschichte. Berlin: Safari-Verlag, 438 pp., 163 figs., (not seen).
1959   Rev.: Wirth in Die Höhle, 11, 82.
1964   And then came man. Translated by Desmond I. Vesey. New York: Viking Press. 354 pp., 73 figs., 32 pls., 4 tables.

BASTIAN, TYLER
1965   An archaeological survey of the Wichita Mountains in southwestern Oklahoma. Plains Anthrop., 10, 53, (abs.).

BASU, SCHINDRANATH
1963   Pragitihaser manus [Prehistoric man]. Calcutta: Mukhopadhya, 10 + 274 pp., (Bengali; not seen).
         Rev.: Bose in Sci. and Culture, 30, 277.

BATALLER, JOSÉ RAMON
1959   Paleontología del Garumniense. Est. Geol. Inst. Invest., Lucas Mallada, 15, 39–53.
         Abs.: Radig in Zbl. Geol. Pal., Teil 2, 1963, 898.

BATES, MARSTON
1967A.   A naturalist at large. Nat. Hist., 76: 7, 18, 20–22.
1967B.   Der Mensch und seine Umwelt. Stuttgart: Franckh'sche Verlagsbuchhandlung, 142 pp.
         Rev.: Hemmer in Homo, 18: 4, 265.

BATES, M., and EDITORS OF LIFE   LIFE
1964   The land and wildlife of South America. New York: Time, 200 pp., illustr.

BATTETTA, J.
1964   Les reconstitutions de fossiles – generalites (note préliminaire). Bull. Soc. Linn., Lyon, 33, 160–163.
1966   "Le cas Teilhard de Chardin," un livre qui demontre l'importance des methodes d'extractions et de reconstitutions des hommes fossiles. Bull. Soc. Linn. Lyon, 35, 444–445.
         See: Ballesio, et al., Viret, David, Mein and Battetta.

BATTISTINI, RENÉ
1965A.   Le Quaternaire littoral de l'extreme nord de Madagascar. Bull. Assoc. Franç. Étude Quat., 3, 133–144, 4 figs., (English summary).
1965B.   Sur la découverte de l'Aepyornis dans le Quaternaire de l'Extreme-Nord de Madagascar. C. R. Soc. Geol. France, 1965, 174–175.

1965C.   Une datation au radio-carbone des oeufs des derniers <u>Aepyornis</u> de l'extrême-Nord de Madagascar. C.R. Soc. Geol. France, 1965, 309.

1966   Un essai de datation par la méthode du radio-carbone du Lavanonian (dépôts du dernier "pluvial") de l'Extrême-Sud de Madagascar. C.R. Soc. Geol. France, 1966, 281–282.

BATTISTINI, R., and VÉRIN, P.

1967   Ecologic changes in protohistoric Madagascar. In: Martin, P. S., and Wright, H.E., (eds.), 1967, 407–424, 4 figs.

BATYROV, B.   See: Vereshchagin and Batyrov.

BAUCHOT, R., and STEPHAN, H.

1967   Encéphales et moulages endocraniens de quelques Insectivores et Primates actuels. Collog. Internat. Cent. Nation. Recherch. Sci., <u>163</u>, 575–587, 1 fig., 13 pls., (English and German summaries).

BAUDELOT, L.

1964   Description du <u>Cricetodon</u> <u>minus</u> de Sansan. Bull. Soc. Hist. Nat. Toulouse, <u>99</u>, 195–204, 2 figs.

BAUDELOT, SABINE

1965   Complément à l'étude de la faune des Rongeurs de Sansan: les glirides. C. R. Soc. Geol. France, 1965, 222, (abs.).

1966   Complément à l'étude de la faune des Rongeurs de Sansan: les glirides, Bull. Soc. Geol. France, <u>7</u>, 758–764, 2 figs.

1967   Sur quelques Soricidés (Insectivores) miocènes de Sansan (Gers). C. R. Soc. Geol. France, 1967, 290–292, 4 figs.

    Rev.: Fahlbusch in Zbl. Geol. Pal., Teil 2, 1969: 3, 291–292.

BAUDELOT, S., and DE BONIS, L.

1966   Nouveaux Glirides (Rodentia) de l'Aquitanien du bassin d'Aquitaine. C. R. Soc. Geol. France, 1966, 341–343, 1 fig.

    Rev.: Fahlbusch in Zbl. Geol. Pal., Teil 2, 1967, 518.

BAUDET, JAMES L.

1959C.   Les industries des plages suspendues (de 5 m) du Nord de la France. Bull. Soc. Anthrop. Paris, Ser. 10, <u>10</u>, 285–301, 7 figs.

1961C.   Image des dépots Pléistocènes et du développement palethnique en bordure de la plaine Flamande. Internat. Assoc. Quat. Res., Abs. Pap., 6th Congr., 134–135, (abs.).

1962A.   Silex paléolithiques de la région de Renaix. Arch., Publ. Cercle Recherch. Préhist. Renaisis, <u>3</u>, 18, (not seen).

1962B.   L'abbé Breuil. Spelunca, Bull., <u>2</u>:2, 7–10, portr.

1964   Vision Paléolithique septentrionale de l'Abbé Breuil. Observations ultérieures. In: Ripoll Perelló, E., (ed.), 1964A, 181–196, 3 figs., (Spanish summary).

1968   Le peuplement vieux paléolithique d'Europe septentrionale, problèmes et chronologie. C. R. Acad. Inscript. Belles-Lettres, 1967, 351–358, 2 figs., 1 table.

BAUER, F.   See: Schauberger, <u>et</u> <u>al.</u>

BAUMGARTEL, ELISE

1964   Note on F. Zorzi's 'Palaeolithic discoveries in the Grotta Paglicci.' Antiq., <u>38</u>, 139, pl. 23a.

BAUMHOFF, MARTIN A., and HEIZER, R. F.
1965   Postglacial cimate and archaeology in the Desert West. In: Wright,
            H. E., and Frey, D. G., (eds.), 1965, 697–707, 4 figs., 1 table.

BAUZÁ RULLÁN, JUAN
1964   Fauna de las formaciones del Terciario superior de La Puebla (Mallorca).
            Est. Geol. Inst. Invest., Lucas Mallada, 20, 187–220, 4 pls.
            Abs.: Weiler in Zbl. Geol. Pal., Teil 2, 1966, 272.
1966A.   Nueva contribución al conocimiento de los otolitos fosiles. Bol. Soc.
            Hist. Nat. Baleares, 12: 1–4, 111–113.
            Rev.: H.-P. in Bol. Soc. Espan. Hist. Nat., Sec. Geol., 65: 2, 199.
            Rev.: Weiler in Zbl. Geol. Pal., Teil 2, 1968: 6, 641–642.
1966B.   Contribuciones a la paleontologia de Baleares. Bol. Soc. Hist. Nat.
            Baleares, 12: 1–4, 133–137, 2 pls.
            Rev.: H.-P. in Bol. Soc. Espan. Hist. Nat., Sec. Geol., 65: 2, 199.
1968   Contributiones al conocimiento de la ictiologia fósil de España. Bol.
            Soc. Espan. Hist. Nat., Sec. Geol., 66, 29–33, 2 pls.
            Rev.: Weiler in Zbl. Geol. Pal., Teil 2, 1970: 3–4, 220.

BAUZÁ RULLÁN, J., QUINTERO, I., and REVILLA, J. DE LA
1963A.   Abs.: Radig in Zbl. Geol. Pal., Teil 2, 1964, 983; Weiler in Zbl.
            Geol. Pal., Teil 2, 1965, 217.
1963B.   Abs.: Weiler in Zbl. Geol. Pal., Teil 2, 1965, 217–218.

BAY, ROLAND
1966   Ausgrabungen villefranchien-zeitlicher Kulturen bei Ubeidiya im Jordan-
            tal, Israel. Bull. Schweiz. Ges. Anthrop. Ethnol., 42, 12–13.

BAYER, GERHARD
1964   Zur heutigen Lage in den Schieferbrüchen bei Holzmaden. Aufschluss,
            15, 168–169.

BAYLE DES HERMENS, R. DE
1964   Les industries préhistoriques de la Station de "La Pierre a Sacrifices"
            Tiaret (Algérie). Libyca, 12, 71–94, 11 figs., 2 tables.
1965A.   Les industries préhistoriques de la Cité Fronzy, Tiaret – Algérie. Bull.
            Soc. Préhist. Franç. Étud. et Trav., 61, 65–83, 8 figs.
1965B.   L'Atérien des vignes Deloche a Guertoufa–Tiaret. (Algérie.) Libyca,
            13, 59–81, 12 figs., 2 tables.
1966   Mission de recherches préhistoriques en République Centrafricaine. Note
            préliminaire. Bull. Soc. Préhist. Franç., Étud. et Trav., 63: 3,
            651–666, 6 figs.
1967   Premier aperçu du Paléolithique inférieur en République Centrafricaine.
            L'Anthrop., 71: 5–6, 435–466, 15 figs.

BAYLE DES HERMENS, R. DE, and CRÉMILLIEUX, A.
1966   L'abri préhistorique de Peylenc, commune de Saint-Pierre-Eynac (Hte-
            Loire). Note préliminaire. Bull. Soc. Préhist. Franç., Étud. et
            Trav., 63: 1, 208–219, 6 figs., 2 tables.

BAYLE DES HERMENS, R. DE, and LABORDE, A.
1965   Le gisement moustérien de la Baume-Vallée (Haute Loire). Étude pré-
            liminaire Bull. Soc. Préhist. Franç., Étud. et Trav., 62: 3, 512–
            527, 6 figs., 2 tables.

BAYLY, CLIFFORD   See: Shepherd 1962.

BAYROCK, L. A.
1964   Fossil Scaphiopus and Bufo in Alberta. Jour. Pal., 38, 1111—1112.
             See: Fuller and Bayrock; Trylich and Bayrock.

BAZAROV, D. B.
1965   [Quaternary Period in the Selenga medium height mountain region.]
             In: Saks, (ed.), 1965, 263—271, (Russian).

BAZHANOV, V. S.
1959B.   [Significance of Tertiary mammals and reptiles for subdivision of sedi-
             mentary series of Kazakhstan.]   Trudy Vses. Paleont. Obshch.,
             III sess., 108—112, (Russian).
1961C.   [Upper Cenozoic ostriches from Tian-Shan· region.]   Trudy Inst. Zool.
             AN Kazakh. SSR, 15, 5—11, 4 figs., (Russian).
1961D.   [First discovery of dinosaur egg shells in USSR.]   Trudy Inst. Zool.
             AN Kazakh. SSR, 15, 177—181, 2 figs., (Russian).

BAZHANOV, V. S., and KOSTENKO, N. N,
1960   [Fundamentals of Anthropogene stratigraphy of Kazakhstan and several
             other countrfies.]   Izv. Akad. Nauk Kazakh. SSR, ser. geol.,
             1960: 1, 3—18, 1 table, (Russian).

BAZHANOV, V. S., and KOZHAMKULOVA, B. S.
1960   [New paleozoological grounds concerning the paleogeography and stra-
             tigraphy of Kazakhstan.]   Vestnik Akad. Nauk Kazakh. SSR,
             1960: 3, 87—88, 2 figs., (Russian).

BAZHANOV, V. S., MATSUĬ, V. M., and MOS'KINA, O. D.
1968   [Stratotype cross-section of Lower Quaternary from "Ostraĭa Sopka,"
             Altaic Irtysh R. region.]   Izv. Akad. Nauk Kazakh. SSR, ser.
             geol., 1968: 2, 60—62, 1 fig., (Russian).

BAZILE, FRÉDÉRIC
1964A.   Harpons aziliens du Gard. Bull. Soc. Préhist. Franç., C. R. séances
             mens., 1964: 1, XVI—XVIII, 2 figs.
1964B.   Le pseudo harpon azilien de la grotte Labric Saint-Hippolyte du Fort
             (Gard). Bull. Soc. Préhist., Franç., C. R. séances mens., 1964: 6,
             CLV, 1 fig.
             See: Ravoux and Bazile.

BEALS, ALAN R.   See: Siegel and Beals.

BEALS, KENNETH L.
1966   A review of the role of the Paleo-Indian in the extinction of various
             North American Pleistocene mammals. Pap. Anthrop., Anthrop.
             Club Univ. Oklahoma, no. 7, 45—67.

BEALS, RALPH L., and HOIJER, H.
1963   Introduccíon a la antropología. (Transl. from 1953 ed.). Madrid:
             Aguilar Press, 719 pp., 130 figs.
             Rev.: Larrea in Arbor, 217, 129;   Vidart in Amerindia, 3,
                   85—87;   Vidart in Bol. Bibliog. Cien. Hombre, no. 2, 19—21.

1965   An introduction to anthropology. 3rd ed. New York: Macmillan, xxiii + 788 pp., illustr.

Rev.: Gruber in Amer. Jour. Phys. Anthrop., 23, 455—456.

Kaplan and Lasker in Amer. Anthrop., 68, 529—530.

BEARDSLEY, RICHARD K., (ed.)

1962   COWA surveys and bibliographies. Area 17 — Far East: Japan COWA Surv. and Bibliog., Area 17, no. 2, 5 + 14 pp.

BEARDSLEY, R. K., et al.

1956   Functional and evolutionary implications of community patterning. In: Wauchope, R., (ed.), 129—157, 2 figs.

BEARDSLEY, R. K., CHANG, K., and LOEHR, M., (eds.)

1959   COWA surveys and bibliographies. Area 17 — Far East. COWA Surv. and Bibliog., Area 17, no. 1, 11 + 43 pp.

BEATER, B. E.

1965   Later radial trimming of Middle Stone Age implements. S. Afr. Archaeol. Bull., 20: 78, 94, 1 fig.

1967A.   Middle Stone Age implements on aeolianite at Isipingo Beach, Natal. S. Afr. Archaeol. Bull., 22, 59.

1967B.   An engraved stone implement from the upper Mkomanzi River, Natal. S. Afr. Archaeol. Bull., 22, 157, 1 fig.

BEATTY, W. H.

1967   Atlatl weights or boatstones. Pap. Anthrop., Anthrop. Club Univ. Oklahoma, 8, 34—49.

BEAUCHÊNE, GUY DE

1963   La préhistoire du Gabon. Objets et Mondes, 3, 3—16, 10 figs.

1966   Prehistory and archaeology in Niger (and Togo, Upper Volta, Dahomey and the Ivory Coast). Discussion. W. Afr. Archaeol. Newsletter, no. 5, 6—9.

BEAUCHÊNE, GUY DE, and HUGON, M.

1964   Bibliographie africaniste. Jour. Soc. Africanistes, 34, 317—344.

BEAUMONT, GÉRARD DE

1961D.   Les chiens du "Puits de Ronze" à Orgnac (Ardèche) avec quelques remarques sur la variabilité dentaire chez les Canidae. Bull. Soc. Vaudoise Sci. Nat., 67, 369—386, 7 figs.

1964A.   Un crâne d'Amphicyon ambiguus (Filhol) (Carnivora) des Phosphorites du Quercy. Arch. Sci. Geneva, 17, 331—339, 3 figs., 1 pl.

1964B.   Note sur la région otique d'Ictitherium hipparionum (Gervais) (Carnivora). Arch. Sci. Geneva, 17, 339—342, 1 fig.

1964C.   Essai sur la position taxonomique des genres Alopecocyon Viret et Simocyon Wagner (Carnivora). Eclog. Geol. Helvetiae, 57, 829—836, 1 pl.

1964D.   Remarques sur la classification des Felidae. Eclog. Geol. Helvetiae, 57, 837—845.

1965A.   Une carnassière supérieure machairodontoïde du Burdigalien. Arch. Sci. Geneva, 18, 144—146, 1 fig.

1965B.   Les Viverravinae (Carnivora, Miacidae) de l'Éocène de la Suisse. Bull. Soc. Vaudoise Sci. Nat., 69, 133—146, 5 figs., 2 pls.

1965C.   Contribution a l'étude du genre <u>Cephalogale</u> Jourdan (Carnivora).
            Schweiz. Pal. Abh., <u>82</u>, 34 pp., 28 figs.
1966   Les Miacinae (Carnivora, Miacidae) de l'Eocène de la Suisse. Bull. Soc.
            Vaudoise Sci. Nat., <u>69</u>, 273—285, 2 figs., 1 pl.
1968   Observations sur les Herpestinae (Viverridae, Carnivora) de l'Oligocène
            supérieur avec quelques remarques sur des Hyaenidae du
            Néogène. Arch. Sci. Geneva, <u>20</u>, 79—107, 14 figs., 3 pls.

BEAUMONT, P. B.   See: Mason, R. J. and Beaumont.

BECK, WILLIAM S.   See: Simpson, G. G. and Beck.

BECKER, H. J.   See: Ax, 1964.

BECKETT, PETER
1957   Ancient occupied sites of the Paraparaumu district. Jour. Polynesian
            Soc., <u>66</u>, 357—364, 3 figs., 3 pls.

BECKSMANN, ERNST
1939C.   N. Steno (1638-1686) und sein Stellung in der Geschichte der Geolo-
            gie. Zeit. Deut. Geol. Ges., <u>91</u>, 329—336, 2 figs.

BEEBE, WILLIAM
1953   Unseen life of New York (City). New York: Duell, Sloan, and Pearce;
            Boston: Little, Brown.

BEER, GAVIN RYLANDS DE
1962C.   Reflections of a Darwinian: essays and addresses. London: Nelson,
            xi + 212 pp., portr., 4 maps.
1963A.   Rev.: Anon. in Sci. Amer., <u>211</u>: 4, 138;   Cain in Hist. Sci., <u>4</u>, 143—
            146;   Clampitt in Audubon Mag., <u>67</u>, 402—404;   Křiženecký
            in Anthrop., <u>2</u>: 2, 75, (Czech);   Montalenti in Scientia, <u>101</u>,
            285—286:   Zirkle in Science, <u>144</u>, 724—725.
1964A.   Other men's shoulders. Ann. Sci., <u>20</u>, 303—322.
1964B.   <u>Archaeopteryx.</u> In: Thomson, A. L., (ed.), 58—62.
1964C.   Ratites, phylogeny of. In: Thomson, A. L., (ed.), 681—685.
1964D.   Atlas of evolution. London: Nelson; New York: Thomas Nelson
            & Sons, 202 pp., 500 figs., 32 maps.
            Rev.: Anon. in Sci. Amer., <u>213</u>: 5, 138;   Bauer in Mitt. Anthrop.
            Ges. Wien, <u>95</u>, 355;   Fisher in Nature, <u>206</u>, 225;   Hughes in
            Man, Jour. Roy. Anthrop. Inst., <u>1</u>, 246;   Wolfe in Explorer, <u>8</u>,
            30.
1964E.   How Darwin came by his theory of natural selection. Comments by
            E. C. Peake. New Sci., <u>21</u>, 216—218, 365, 2 figs.
1964F.   The world of an evolutionist. Essay review. Science, <u>143</u>, 1311—1312,
            1317.
1965A.   Genetics and prehistory. The Rede Lecture. Cambridge: Cambridge
            University, 38 pp., 3 maps.
            Rev.: Roberts in Amer. Anthrop., <u>68</u>:4, 1085—1086; Wharton in
            Ohio Jour. Sci., <u>66</u>, 495.
1965B.   Bildatlas der Evolution. München, Basel, Wien: Bayerischer Landwirt-
            schaftsverlag, 202 pp., 500 figs., 16 color pls., 32 maps, (not
            seen).
            Rev.: Haltenorth in Säugetierkindl. Mitt., <u>14</u>, 232—233;   Kurth in
            Naturwiss. Rund, <u>19</u>, 212;   Reinig in Kosmos (Stuttgart), <u>62</u>,
            *109;   Schwidetzky in Homo, <u>17</u>: 3—4, 217.

1966A.   Portrait in science. Darwin's "Origin" today. Nat. Hist., 75: 7, 62,
              64–66, 68–71.
1966B.   Genetics: the centre of science. Proc. Roy. Soc. London, 164: 995,
              154–166.

BEER, G. DE, ROWLANDS, M. J., and SKRAMOVSKY, B. M., (eds.)
1967   Darwin's notebooks on transmutation of species. Part VI. Pages ex-
              cised by Darwin. Bull. Brit. Mus. (Nat. Hist.), Hist. Ser., 3: 5,
              131–176.

BEERBOWER, JAMES R.
1965   Search for the past. New Delhi: Prentice-Hall of India (Private) Ltd.,
              562 pp.
              Rev.: Misra in E. Anthrop., 20, 278–280.
1968   Search for the past. An introduction to paleontology. 2nd ed. En-
              glewood Cliffs., N. J.: Prentice-Hall, 544 pp., illustr.
              Rev.: Olson in Jour. Geol., 76: 6, 726–727.
              See: Clark, John and Beerbower; Clark, John, Beerbower and Kietzke.

BEETS, C.   See: Raaf, et al.

BEFU, HARUMI, CHARD, C. S., and OKADA, A.
1964   An annotated bibliography of the preceramic archaeology of Japan.
              Arctic Anthrop., 2, 1–83.

BEGINES RAMIREZ, A.   See: Gonzalez-Etchegaray, et al.

BEHM-BLANCKE, GÜNTER
1961B.   Das Paläolithikum in Thüringen. Internat. Assoc. Quat. Res., Abs. Pap.,
              6th Congr., 135, (abs.).
              Rev.: Kozlowski in L'Anthrop., 68, 597–598.
1967   Zur Datierung der altsteinzeitlichen Artefakte von Ehringsdorf bei Wei-
              mar. Ausgrabung. u. Funde, 12: 5, 247–251, 1 fig., 1 pl.

BEHN, FRIEDRICH
1962B.   Zur Problematik der Felsbilder. Abh. Sächsischen Akad. Wiss. Leipzig,
              Phil.-Hist. Kl., 54: 1, 89 pp., 64 pls.
              Rev.: [Beltran] in Caesaraugusta, 23–24, 155;   Ficker in Bayer. Vor-
              ges., 32: 1–2, 212–215;   Freund in L'Anthrop., 69, 110–111.

BEILEKCHI, V. S.
1966   [Archeological research in Moldavia in 1963.] Problemy geografii Mol-
              davii, 1, 128–132, (Russian).

BEISER, ARTHUR, and EDITORS OF LIFE
1962   The earth. New York: Time, 192 pp., illustr.

BELANGER
1963   Une dent d'hippopotame. Bull. Soc. Hist. Archéol. Périgord, 90, 70–
              71, 1 fig.

BELIAEVA, E. I. (=Beljaeva; Beliajeva)
1961   [Elasmotheriinae and their stratigraphic position.] Internat. Assoc.
              Quat. Res., Abs. Pap., 6th Congr., 126, (abs.; Russian).
1962A.   Abs.: Stoltenberg in Zbl. Geol. Pal., Teil 2, 1964, 994–995.

1964	[Some results of research on Tertiary land mammal faunas of Soviet Union.] In: Orlov, (ed.), 1964C, 14—26, 4 tables, (Russian; English summary).
1966	[Eopleistocene mammals of Western Transbaĭkalia. Order Perissodactyla. Family Rhinocerotidae.] Trudy Geol. Inst., 152, 92—143, 39 figs., 35 tables, (Russian).
	See: Gabuniĭa and Beliaeva.

BELIAEVA, E. I., and TROFIMOV, B. A.

1967	[Principal stages in evolution of Tertiary land mammals of the Asiatic part of the USSR.] In: Martinson, (ed.), 209—214, (Russian).

BELL, PETER ROBERT, (ed.)

1959	Abs.: Schindewolf in Zbl. Geol. Pal., Teil 2, 1962, 308—309.
1964	Darwin's biological work. Some aspects reconsidered. New York, London: Wiley, xi + 342 pp., illustr.
	Rev.: Bauchau in Rev. Questions Sci., 26, 445—446.

BELL, R. E.

1960C.	Guide to the identification of certain American Indian projectile points. Special Bull. Oklahoma Anthrop. Soc., No. 2, 105 pp., 51 pls.
1965A.	Bibliography of Oklahoma archaeology. Part I. Newsletter Okla. Anthrop. Soc., 13: 4, 3—8.
1965B.	Bibliography of Oklahoma archaeology. Part II. Newsletter Okla. Anthrop. Soc., 13: 5, 5—14.

BELL, W. A.

1960	Mississippian Horton group of type Windsor-Horton district, Nova Scotia. Canada Dept. Mines, Geol. Surv., Mem. 314, 112 pp., 24 pls., (French summary).

BELLA, F. See: Alessio, Bella et al.

BELLAIRS, ANGUS D'A.

1968	Reptiles. 2nd., revised edition. London: Hutchinson University Library, 200 pp., 12 figs.

BELLAIRS, A., and CARRINGTON, R.

1966	The world of reptiles. London: Chatto and Windus; New York: Amer. Elsevier Publ., 153 pp., illustr. with line drawings, 16 pls.
	Rev.: Bogert in Nat. Hist., 76: 2, 67—68.

BELLAIRS, A., and PARSON, T. S., (eds.)

1968	Biology of the Reptilia. Volume I: Morphology A. London: Academic Press.

BELOKRYS, L. S.

1959B.	[The problem of stratigraphic distribution of Zygolophodon borsoni Hays.] Izv. Vyssh. Uch. Zav., Geol. i Razv., 1959: 8, 48—52, 2 figs., (Russian).
1960D.	[New find of Trilophodon (Mastodon) ex. gr. angustidens Cuvier in Ukraine.] Izv. Vyssh. Uch. Zav., Geol. i Razv., 1960: 2, 34—40, 4 figs., (Russian).
1960E.	[On the remains of bunodont Mastodon from Lower Pliocene deposits of Krivoĭ Rog.] Izv. Vyssh. Uch. Zav., Geol. i Razv., 1960: 9, 13—26, 3 figs., 1 table, (Russian).

BELOKRYS, L. S., and RIZDVIANSKIĬ, K. F.
1958   [The problem of age of supra-ore clays in Nikopol' manganese ore-ba-
              sin.] Izv. Vyssh. Uch. Zav., Geol. i Razv., 1958: 8, 49—51,
              (Russian).

BELTRÁN, ANTONIO
1964A.   Novedades sobre pintura rupestre Prehistórica. Caesaraugusta, 21—22,
              168—173, 1 fig.
1964B.   El seminario de Arqueología en las cuevas con pinturas rupestres del
              Ariege (Francia). Caesaraugusta, 21—22, 178—184, 3 figs.
1964C.   Figuras relativas al culto de Fecundidad en Le Portel (Ariege). In: Ri-
              poll Perelló, E., (ed.), 1964A, 197—199, 3 figs., (English summa-
              ry).
1964D.   La grotte de Kapova (Oural du Sud) et ses peintures paléolithiques.
              Préhist. Spéléol. Ariégeoises, 19, 41—47, 1 fig.
1965   El seminario de Prehistoria y Protohistoria de la Universidad, en las
              cuevas con pinturas rupestres del Ariege y la Dordoña. Caesar-
              augusta, 23—24, 127—136, illustr.
            See: Gailli, et al.

BELTRÁN, A., ROBERT, R., and VÉZIAN, J.
1965   La Cueva de Le Portel, en Loubens (Ariege). Caesaraugusta, 25—26,
              5—38, 42 figs.
1966   La Cueva de Le Portel. Caesaraugusta, Anejo, 1966, 202 pp., 94
              pls., some color.
            Rev.: Jordá Cerdá in Zephyrus, 17, 148—150; Kühn in IPEK,
              22, 161;   Lhote in L'Anthrop., 72, 125—130;   KV in
              Archeol. Roz., 22:4, 477;   Ripoll Perelló in Ampurias, 28,
              323—324.

BELTRAO, R.
1966   Paleontologia de Santa Maria e Sao Pedro do Sul, Rio Grande de Sul,
              Brasil. Bol. Inst. Cien. Nat. Santa Maria, 2, 1—114, 57 figs.,
              (not seen).
            Rev.: Huene in Zbl. Geol. Pal., Teil 2, 1967, 103.

BELZ, C.
1963   On the trail of ancient man in Wyoming. Wyo. Archaeol., 6: 2, 11—13,
              1 fig.

BENAC, ALOJZ
1964   [Studies on Stone and Copper Ages in northwestern Balkans.] Saraje-
              vo: "Veselin Masleša" Press, 176 pp., 9 figs., 35 pls., (Jugosla-
              vian; French summary).

BENDA, LEOPOLD, with HEIMBACH, W., and MATTIAT, B.
1962   Uber die Anreicherung von Uran und thorium in Phosphoriten und Bo-
              nebeds des nördlichen Harzvorlandes. Geol. Jahrb., 80, 313—348,
              5 figs., pl. 29, (English and French summaries).

BENDER, MARGARET M., BRYSON, R. A., and BAERREIS, D. A.
1965   University of Wisconsin radiocarbon dates I. Radiocarbon, 7, 399—407.

BENDIX-ALMGREEN, SVEND ERIK
1962   De østgrønlandske perm-edestiders anatomi med saerligt henblik på Fade-

nia crenulata. Meddel. Dansk. Geol. Foren., 15:1, 152–153, (Danish).

1964   Palaeopathologien videnskaben der jagter sygdomssporene hos fortidens dyr. Naturens Verden, 1964, 129–141, 23 figs., (Swedish).

1966   New investigations on Helicoprion from the Phosphoria formation of south-east Idaho. Biol. Skrift. Danske Videnskab. Selskab, 14: 5, 1–54, 28 figs., 15 pls.

1967   On the fin structure of the Upper Permian edestids from East Greenland. Meddel. Dansk. Geol. Foren., 17, 147–149, 1 fig.

BENEUT, G.   See: Basse de Menorval and Beneut.

BENINGER, EDUARD
1936   Das Paläolithikum im Plateaulehm um Drosendorf. Waldviertel, 9: 4, 43–47, (not seen).

BENNETT, JOHN W.
1952   The prehistory of the northern Mississippi Valley. In: Griffin, J. B., (ed.), 108–123.

BENNETT, RICHMOND   See: Haynes, Grey, Damon and Bennett.

BENNINGHOFF, WILLIAM S.   See: Ray, Cooper and Benninghoff.

BERARD, G.   See: Lumley and Berard.

BERAUD, H. and J., VACHER, G., and VIGNARD, Ed.
1965   Le Périgordien Gravettien des Ronces dans les Gros-Monts de Nemours (Seine-et-Marne). Bull. Soc. Préhist. Franç., Étud. et Trav., 62: 1, 98–109, 3 figs.

BERDZENISHVILI, N. Z.
1964   [A new site of Stone Age in the Tskhaltsitela canyon.] Tbilisi; (Georgian; Russian summary; not seen).

BEREGOVAIA, N. A.
1960   Rev.: Formozov, in Sov. Arkheol., 1962: 3, 315–318, (Russian).

1966   Paleolithic sites in the USSR. Translated by Richard G. Klein. In: Beregovaia, N.A., Islamov, U., and Kalandadze, A.N., 1966, 1–79, 11 maps.

BEREGOVAIA, N. A., ISLAMOV, U., and KALANDADZE, A. N.
1966   Contributions to the archaeology of the Soviet Union: with special emphasis on Central Asia, the Caucasus and Armenia. Translated by R. G. Klein, E. M. Shimkin, and E. V. Prostov. Edited by Henry Field. Russ. Translation Ser., Peabody Mus. Archaeol. Ethnol., Harvard Univ., 3: 1, xvii + 177 pp., 31 figs., 12 maps.

BERG, DIETRICH E.
1964   Krokodile als Klimazeugen. Geol. Rund., 54, 328–333, 1 fig., (English and French summaries).

1965   Nachweis des Riesenlaufvogels Diatryma im Eozän von Messel bei Darmstadt/Hessen. Notizbl. Hess. Landesamt. Bodenforsch., 93, 68–72, 1 fig., pl. 8.

1966   Die Krokodile, insbesondere Asiatosuchus und aff. Sebecus?, aus dem
            Eozän von Messel bei Darmstadt/Hessen. Abh. Hess. L.-Amt.
            Bodenforsch., 52, 105 pp., 11 figs., 6 pls., (English and French
            summaries).
            Rev.: Hemmer in Zbl. Geol. Pal., Teil 2, 1967, 103–105.

BERG, FRIEDRICH
1966   Die prähistorischen Funde. In: Ehrenberg, (ed.), 1966A, 123–135,
            1 pl.

BERG, L. S., KAZANTSEVA, A. A., and OBRUCHEV, D. V.
1964   [Superorder Palaeonisci.] Osnovy Pal., [Agnathes. Pisces.], [11], 336–
            370, 64 figs., (Russian).

BERG, L. S., and OBRUCHEV, D. V.
1964   [Order Ospiida.] Osnovy Pal., [Agnathes. Pisces.], [11], 379–380, 1
            fig., (Russian).

BERGAMINI, DAVID, and EDITORS OF LIFE
1964   The land and wildlife of Australia. New York: Time Inc., 198 pp.,
            illustr.

BERGE, S.
1967   Nyere synspunkter over temmingen av våre husdyr. Naturen, 91, 105–
            115, (Norwegian).

BERGEIJK, WILLEN A. VAN
1966   Evolution of the sense of hearing in vertebrates. Amer. Zool., 6, 371–
            377, 4 figs.

BERGER, ANDREW J.   See: George, J. C. and Berger.

BERGER, FRANZ-ERNST
1959   Abs.: Schnitzer in Zbl. Geol. Pal., Teil 2, 1964, 205.

BERGER, RAINER   See: Leakey, Protsch and Berger; Orr, P. C. 1968; Wells, P. V.
            and Berger.

BERGER, R., FERGUSSON, G. J., and LIBBY, W. F.
1965   UCLA radiocarbon dates IV. Radiocarbon, 7, 336–371.

BERGER, R., HORNEY, A. G., and LIBBY, W. F.
1964   Radiocarbon dating of bone and shell from their organic components.
            Science, 144, 999–1001.

BERGER, R., and LIBBY, W. F.
1966   UCLA radiocarbon dates V. Radiocarbon, 8, 467–497.
1967   UCLA radiocarbon dates VI. Radiocarbon, 9, 477–504.

BERGMAN, S. HUGO   See: Wilf and Merlin.

BERGMANN, PAWEL
1965   Sagittal-arch indicators of the cerebral part of the skull as diagnostical
            features in anthropogenesis and systematics of primates. Prze-
            glad Anthrop., 31, 299–301, 2 figs., (French and English summa-
            ries).

BERGNER, GÜNTHER
1965 Geschichte der menschlichen Phylogenetik seit dem Jahre 1900. In: Heberer, (ed.), 1965, 20—55, 17 figs.

BERGOUNIOUX, FRÉDÉRIC-MARIE
1951 Abs.: Radig in Zbl. Geol. Pal., Teil 2, 1964, 519.
1960B. Interprétation géologique de la grotte de Bara—Bahau. Bull. Soc. Hist. Archéol. Périgord, 87, 105—109, 1 fig.
1964 Sur quelques castoridés du bassin Aquitaine. C. R. Soc. Géol. France, 1964, 168, (abs.)
1966 Primitive and prehistoric religions. New York: Hawthorn Books, 160 pp.

BERGOUNIOUX, F.-M., and CROUZEL, F.
1962B. Abs.: Dietrich in Zbl. Geol. Pal., Teil 2, 1964, 212—213.
1963 Migrations de mastodontes miocènes. C. R. 87e Congr. Nation. Soc. Savantes, Sec. Sci., 1962, 867—872.
1964 Les Pliopithecus de Sansan. C. R. Acad. Sci. Paris, 258, 3744—3746.
1965A. Les Pliopithèques de France. Ann. Pal., Vert., 51: 1, 43—65, 8 figs., 10 tables.
    Rev.: M. C. in Fossilia, 1965: 5—6, 69—70.
1965B. Chéloniens de Sansan. Ann. Pal., Vert., 51, 151—187, 18 figs.
1965C. Sur quelques castoridés du bassin d'Aquitaine. Bull. Soc. Geol. France, 6, 253—257, 1 fig.
1966A. Données complémentaires sur les mastodontes de Sansan. Bull. Soc. Hist. Nat. Toulouse, 102, 371—375, 1 fig.
1966B. Découverte d'un squelette d'Amphicyon major Blainville dans le Miocène moyen de Sansan (Gers). C. R. Acad. Sci. Paris, Sci. Nat., 262, 2015—2017, 1 pl.
1967A. Suoïdes de Sansan. Ann. Pal., Vert., 53, 1—24, 13 figs.
1967B. Un nouveau gisement fossilifère Burdigalien: Le lieu-dit Bézian à la Romieu (Gers). Bull. Soc. Hist. Nat. Toulouse, 103, 366—368.
1967C. Deux totues fossiles d'Afrique. C. R. Soc. Géol. France, 1967, 253.
1967D. Sansan et l'évolution de quelques groupes de mammifères. Colloq. Internat. Cent. Nation. Recherch. Sci., 163, 523—527, (English summary).

BERKA, ROLAND
1968 Fossilen aus dem Solnhofener Schiefer. Kosmos, 64, 197—199, 2 figs.

BERKNER, LLOYD V., and MARSHALL, L. C.
1965 Oxygen and evolution. New Sci., 28, 415—419, 3 figs. Comments by M. S. Glover, 28, 600.

BERMAN, DAVID S.
1967 Orientation of bradyodont dentition. Jour. Pal., 41, 143—146, 2 figs.
1968 Lungfish from the Lueders formation (Lower Permian, Texas) and the Gnathorhiza — lepidosirenid ancestry questioned. Jour. Pal., 42, 827—835, 4 figs.

BERMAN, Z. I. See: Zavadskiĭ and Berman.

BERNABO-BREA, LUIGI
1965A.   Segnalazioni di rinvenimenti paleolitici in Sicilia. Bull. Paletnol. Italy,
               n. ser. 16, 74, 7–22, 6 figs., (French and English summaries).
1965B.   Palikè. Giacimento paleolitico e abitato neolitico ed eneo. Bull. Pal-
               etnol. Ital., n. ser. 16, 74, 23–46, 17 figs., (French and English
               summaries).

BERNAL, IGNACIO
1961   La arqueología mexicana en 1960. Homenaje a Pablo Martínez del Río,
               229–235.
1964   Concluding remarks. In: Jennings and Norbeck, (eds.), 1964, 559–
               566.
1966A.   The National Museum of Anthropology, Mexico. Mus. UNESCO, 19,
               1–7, 9 figs.
1966B.   Le Musée national d'anthropologie de Mexico. Mus. UNESCO, 19, 8–
               14, 10 figs.

BERNARD, ANNIE   See: Barbour 1965B.

BERNDT, CATHERINE H.   See: Berndt and Berndt.

BERNDT, R. M., and BERNDT, C. H.
1964   The world of the first Australians. Sydney: Ure Smith, xxii + 509
               pp., (not seen).
               Rev.: Capell in Mankind, 6, 325–327;   Chaudhury in Man in India,
               47, 166;   Piddington in Jour. Polynesian Soc., 76, 239–240.
1965   Aboriginal man in Australia. Essays in honour of Emeritus Professor
               A. P. Elkin. Sydney, London, Melbourne: Angus and Robert-
               son, xviii + 491 pp., illustr., portr., bibliog.
               Rev.: Birdsell in Jour. Polynesian Soc., 75, 241–242;   Greenway in
               Amer. Anthrop., 69, 247–249.

BERNDT, R., and MEISE, W., (eds.)
1960   Naturgeschichte der Vögel. Vol. 2. Stuttgart: Franckh'sche Verlagshand-
               lung, 679 pp., 304 figs.

BERNSTEIN, LOWELL
1965   Fossil birds from the Dominican Republic. Quart. Jour. Florida Acad.
               Sci., 28, 271–284.

BERRILL, N. J.
1955   Rev.: Carter in Syst. Zool., 6, 187–192.

BERRY, WILLIAM B. N.
1968   Growth of a prehistoric time scale. Based on organic evolution. San
               Francisco: W. H. Freeman, 146 pp., 16 figs.
               Rev.: Anon. in Rocks and Minerals, 43, 621;   Swazey in Jour. Hist.
               Biol., 1: 2, 234.
               See: Rensberger and Berry.

BERSENEV, I. I., MOROZOVA, V. F., SALUN, S. A., SOKOLOVA, P. N., and
SOKHIN, V. K.
1962   [New data on stratigraphy of alluvial, lacustrine – alluvial and lacustri-
               ne Quaternary deposits of Maritime and Middle Amur regions.]
               Sov. Geol., 1962: 9, 78–86, 3 figs., 1 table, (Russian).

BERTALAN, KÁROLY   See: Vértes, Kretzoi and Bertalan.

BERTALAN, K., and KRETZOI, M.
1962   Die Höhlen des Tekeresvölgy bei Veszprém und das südlichste Vorkommen des Halsbandlemmings. Karszt -és Barlang kutatás, 2, 83—91, 5 figs., (Hungarian; German and Russian summaries).
1965   Die Bedeutung der ungarischen Karst- und Höhlensedimente fur die Geochronologie. 3. Internat. Kongress Spel., 4, 63—68, 3 figs.

BERTALANFFY, LUDWIG VON
1965   Professor Bernhard Rensch zum 65. Geburtstag. Naturwiss. Rund., 18: 2, 482—484, portr.

BERTHÉLEMY, A.
1960   La technique levalloisienne au cours du Tyrrhénien marocain. Hespéris Tamuda, 1, 253—272, 2 figs., 21 pls., 11 photos.

BERTHOLD, SARAH M.   See: Rubin and Berthold.

BERTRAM, B.
1967   The design of a new hall of fossils. Curator, 10, 164—175, 11 figs.

BERZI, A.
1966   L'orso di Gaville nel Valdarno superiore. Palaeontogr. Ital., 60, 19—32, pls. 6—9, (English summary).

BESSONNAT, GILBERT, LAPPARENT, A. F. DE, MONTENAT, C., and TERS, M.
1965   Découverte de nombreuses empreintes de pas de reptiles dans le Lias inférieur de la côte de Vendée. C. R. Acad. Sci. Paris, 260, 5324—5326.

BESTEL, M.
1967   Signale qu'il semble qu'une découverte paléontologique... Bull. Soc. Hist. Nat. Ardennes, 56, 31—32.

BETTS, CHARLES A.
1965A.   Man evolved like animals. Sci. News Letter, 87, 243, cover illustr.
1965B.   Man's tree — a new root? Sci. News Letter, 87, 346—347, illustr.

BEURLEN, KARL
1950   Abs.: Raabe in Zbl. Geol. Pal., Teil 2, 1964, 798.

BEZRUKOV, P. L.
1934   [Upper Cretaceous and Paleogene sediments of the upper basin of Tobol R.] Biull. Mosk. Obshch. Ispyt. Prirody, Otd. Geol., 42, 167—199, 7 figs., (Russian; German summary).

BHATIA, S. B.   See: Mohapatra, G. C., et al.

BI, CHU-ZHEN   See: Chao, T. and Bi.

BIBERSON, PIERRE
1961B.   Rev.: Jordá Cerdá in Zephyrus, 14, 143—144.
1961C.   Rev.: Jordá Cerdá in Zephyrus, 14, 143—144.
1964A.   Quelques précisions sur les classifications du Quaternaire marocain. Bull. Soc. Géol. France, 5, 607—616, 4 figs., 1 table.

1964B.   Nouvelles découvertes d'industries du Paléolithique inférieur, in situ dans le formations quaternaires de l'Adrar mauritanien. C. R. Acad. Sci. Paris, 258, 3074–3076.

1964C.   Torralba et Ambrona. Notes sur deux stations acheuléenes de chasseurs d'éléphants de la Vieille Castille. In: Ripoll Perelló, E., (ed.), 1964A, 201–248, 8 figs., 16 pls., (Spanish summary).

1965A.   Observations sur le Pléistocéne et la préhistoire de la province de Tarfaïa (Maroc occidental). Discussion by J. D. Clark, H. Alimen, and F. E. Zeuner. Actas V Congr. Panafr. Prehist. Estud. Cuaternario, 1963: 1, 157–171, 3 figs., 4 pls.

1965B.   Recherches sur le Paléolithique inférieur de l'Adrar de Mauritanie. Actas V Congr. Panafr. Prehist. Estud. Cuaternario, 1963:1, 173–189, 4 figs., 4 pls.

1965C.   Lower Paleolithic cultures of northwestern Africa. 7th Internat. Congr., Internat. Assoc. Quat. Res., Abs., 1965, 29, (abs.).

1965D.   La place des hommes du Paléolithique marocain dans la chronologie du Pléistocene atlantique. L'Anthrop., 68, 475–526.

1965E.   Essai sur l'évolution du Paléolithique inferieur de l'Adrar de Mauritanie. Quaternaria, 7, 59–78, 1 map, 2 tables, (English and Spanish summaries).

1966   Notes sur le Paléolithique du Maroc Méridional. Zephyrus, 17, 5–29, 1 map, 4 pls.

1967A.   Stratigraphical details of the Quaternary of northwest Africa. Discussion. In: Bishop, W. W., and Clark, J. D., (eds.), 359–364, 2 tables.

1967B.   Some aspects of the Lower Palaeolithic of northwest Africa. Discussion. In: Bishop, W. W., and Clark, J. D., (eds.), 447–475, 3 figs., 1 table, (French summary).

    See: Arambourg, Biberson, et al.; Balout, Biberson and Tixier; Carbonnel and Biberson.

BIBERSON, P., and AGUIRRE, E.
1965   Expériences de taille d'outils préhistoriques dans des os d'éléphant. Quaternaria, 7, 165–183, 15 pls., (Spanish and English summaries).

BIBERSON, P., and SOUVILLE, G.
1959   Le Cinquième congrès de l'INQUA: Madrid-Barcelone (septembre 1957). Libyca, 5, 251–264.

BIBIKOV, D. I. See: Gromov, I. M., et al.

BIBIKOV, S. N.
1940C.   [Paleolithic cave sites of the Íuriúzani river basin (southern Ural).] Krat. Soob. Inst. Ist. Mat. Kult. SSSR, 3, 35–39, 1 fig., (Russian).

1959   [Some problems concerning the peopling of Eastern Europe during the Paleolithic.] Sov. Arkheol., 1959: 4, 19–28, (Russian).

1961B.   [Concerning the original settlement of eastern Europe.] Krat. Soob. Ist. Arkheol. Akad. Nauk URSR, 11, 3–6, 3 figs., (Russian).

1963A.   [Archeological field work in the Ukraine in 1960–1961.] Arkheologiĩa, 15, 3–18, (Ukrainian; Russian summary).

1963B.   [Field studies of Ukrainian archeologists.] Vestnik Akad. Nauk SSSR, 1963: 7, 59–65, (Russian).

BIBIKOVA, V. I.
1966   [Bone tool from Kirillov Paleolithic site.] Arkheologiĩa, 20, 143–145, 1 fig., (Ukranian; Russian summary).

BIEDERMANN, HANS
1966   Magische Zeichen in Eiszeithöhlen. Universum; Natur u. Tech., 21, 82–
            84, illustr.

BIEN, GEORGE S.   See: Hubbs, et al.

BIGGERSTAFF, R. H.
1967   Time-trimmers for the Taungs child, or how old is "Australopithecus
            africanus"? Amer. Anthrop., 69, 217–220, 2 tables.

BILEWICZ, STANISLAW
1960A.   Enigmatic disappearance of famous bony remains of Sinanthropus.
            Przeglad Zool., 4, 145, (Polish).
1960B.   The structure and chemical composition of mammoth bones. Przeglad
            Zool., 4, 145, (Polish).

BILLY, G.   See: Vallois and Billy.

BILOKRIS, L. S.   See: Petrun' and Bilokris.

BINDER, HANS
1960   Bibliographie zur Karst- und Höhlenkunde in Deutschland für das Jahr
            1959. Kleine Schrift. Karst- und Höhlenkunde, no. 1, 10 pp.
1961A.   Bibliographie zur Karst- und Höhlenkunde in Deutschland für das Jahr
            1960. Kleine Schrift. Karst- und Höhlenkunde, no. 2, 14 pp.
1961B.   Die Grabung in der Grossen Grotte unter dem Rusenschloss bei Blau-
            beren (Kreis Ulm/Donau). Mitt. Verband Deutschen Höhlen- und
            Karstforscher, München, 7, 4–6.
1962A.   Bibliographie zur Karst- und Höhlenkunde in Deutschland für das Jahr
            1961. Kleine Schrift. Karst- und Höhlenkunde, no. 3, 14 pp.
1962B.   100 Jahre Urgeschichtsforschung in Württemberg und Hohenzollern.
            Mitt. Verband Deutschen Höhlen- und Karstforscher, München,
            8, 57–60, 2 pls.
1964   Zur Geschichte der Höhlenforschung auf der Schwäbischen Alb. Mitt.
            Verband Deutschen Höhlen- und Karstforscher, München, 10,
            9–16, 1 pl.
1965A.   Professor Dr. Florian Heller 60 Jahre alt. Mitt. Verband Deutschen Hö-
            hlen- und Karstforscher, München, 11, 68–70, portr.
1965B.   Urgeschichtliches Museum in Blaubeuren eröffnet. Mitt. Verband Deut-
            schen Höhlen- und Karstforscher, München, 11, 109.

BINDER, H., FRANK, H., and MÜLLER, K.
1960   Die Höhlen der Heidenheimer und der Ulmer Alb. Jahresh. für Karst-
            und Höhlenkunde, 1, 35–56, 27 figs.

BINFORD, LEWIS R.
1965   Radiometric analysis of bone and soil material from Lloyd's Rock Hole,
            Bedford County, Pennsylvania. In: Jelinek, A. J., and Fitting,
            J. E., (eds.), 1965, 32–40, 5 tables.

BINFORD, L. R., and BINFORD, S. R.
1966A.   The prodatory revolution: a consideration of the evidence for a new
            subsistence level. Amer. Anthrop., 68, 508–512, 1 fig.
1966B.   A preliminary analysis of functional variability in the Mousterian of
            Levallois facies. In: Clark, J. D., and Howell, F. C., (eds.),
            238–295, 12 figs., 10 tables.

BINFORD, SALLY R.
1965   Settlement systems and social groupings in the Mousterian. Abs. 64th
            Ann. Meeting Amer. Anthrop. Assoc., 1965, 8, (abs.).
1966A.   Me'arat Shovakh (Mugharet esh-Shubbabiq). Israel Explor. Jour., 16:1,
            20—32, 9 figs., 2 tables.
1966B.   Me'arat Shovakh (Mugharet esh-Shubbabiq). Israel Explor. Jour., 16:2,
            96—103.
1968   A structural comparison of disposal of the dead in the Mousterian and
            the Upper Paleolithic. Southwestern Jour. Anthrop., 24, 139—
            154, 4 tables.
            See: Binford and Binford.

BIRAM, BRENDA
1960   Dinosaurs. New York: Golden Press, 48 pp., illustr., (elemen. school).

BIRCH, L. C., and EHRLICH, P. R.
1967A.   Evolutionary history and population biology. Nature, 214, 349—352.
1967B.   Evolutionary history and taxonomy. Syst. Zool., 16, 282—285.

BIRD, JUNIUS B.
1965   The concept of a "pre-projectile point" cultural stage in Chile and Peru.
            Amer. Antiq., 31, 262—272, 6 figs., with reply by A. D. Krieger.

BIRDSELL, JOSEPH B., (ed.)
1959   COWA surveys and bibliographies. Area 22 — Australia. COWA
            Surv. and Bibliog., Area 22, no. 1, 4 + 11 pp.
1962   COWA surveys and bibliographies. Area 22 — Australia. COWA Surv.
            and Bibliog., Area 22, no. 2, 5 + 7 pp.
1967   Preliminary data on the trihybrid origin of the Australian Aborigines.
            Aborigines. Archaeol., Phys. Anthrop. in Oceania, 2, 100—155, 4
            figs., 6 pls., 7 tables.

BIRIUKOV, M. D., and KOSTENKO, N. N.
1965   [Concerning the "Obaily" mammal fauna of Zaisan basin.]   Vestnik
            Akad. Nauk Kazakh. SSR, 1965: 12, 75—77, 1 fig., (Russian).

BIRIUKOV, M. D., VOSKOBOŸNIKOV, M. E., KUZNETSOV, B. B., and NURUMOV,
T. N.
1962   [New data on the distribution of Aral formation with mammal fauna.]
            Vestnik Akad. Nauk Kazakh. SSR, 1962: 12, 77—79, 2 tables,
            (Russian).

BIRIUKOV, M. D., VOSKOBOŸNIKOV, M. E., and SAVINOV, P. F.
1968   [On the Neogene stratigraphy of Kazakhstan.] Izv. Akad. Nauk Kazakh.
            SSR, Ser. Geol., 1968: 2, 11—20, 1 table, (Russian).

BIRK, MARVIN
1967   "Fossil note." Rocks and Minerals, 42, 691.

BIRMAN, A. S., ZHEGALLO, V. I., RASTSVETAEV, L. M., KHOZATSKIŸ, L. I., and
SHEVYREVA, N. S.
1968   [Contribution to the history of vertebrates of the Eastern Kopet-Dag.]
            Authors' summary. Biull. Mosk. Obshch. Ispyt. Prirody, Otd.
            Geol., 43: 1, 159—160, (Russian).

BIRNEY, E. C.　See:　Choate and Birney.

BISHOP, W. W.
    1959B.　Recent palaeontological, Palaeolithic and stratigraphical research in
             Uganda. Uganda Mus. Occ. Paper, no. <u>4</u>, 2—3.
    1964A.　More fossil primates and other Miocene mammals from north-east Ugan-
             da. Nature, <u>203</u>, 1327—1331, 1 fig., 3 tables.
    1964B.　Mammalia from the Miocene volcanic rocks of Karamoja, East Africa.
             Discussion by K. A. Davies. Proc. Geol. Soc. London, <u>1617</u>, 91—
             94.
    1967A.　Introduction to part I. [Paleontological considerations.] In: Bishop,
             W. W., and Clark, J. D., (eds.), 3—5.
    1967B.　The Later Tertiary in East Africa — volcanics, sediments, and faunal in-
             ventory. Discussion. In: Bishop, W. W., and Clark, J. D., (eds.),
             31—56, 3 figs., 3 tables, (French summary).
    1967C.　Annotated lexicon of Quaternary stratigraphical nomenclature in East
             Africa. Discussion. In: Bishop, W. W., and Clark, J. D., (eds.),
             375—395, (French summary).

BISHOP, W. W., and CLARK, J. D., (eds.)
    1967A.　Background to evolution in Africa. "Systematic investigation of the
             African Later Tertiary and Quaternary." Chicago, London: Univ.
             Chicago Press, x + 935 pp., illustr.
             Rev.: Campbell in Sci. Jour., London, <u>4</u>: 4, 89—90; Fagan in Jour.
             Afr. Hist., <u>9</u>, 479—480; Fagg in Nature, <u>219</u>, 307—308; jf in
             Archeol. Roz., <u>21</u>: 3, 403, (Czech); A. W. G. in Jour. E. Afr.
             Nat. Hist. Soc., <u>27</u>: 3, 235—236; Hammen in Geol. en Mijn.,
             <u>48</u>: 2, 272; Hiernaux in Man, Jour. Roy. Anthrop. Inst., <u>3</u>, 666—
             667; Kurten in Amer. Jour. Phys. Anthrop., <u>29</u>, 450—452;
             Movius in Amer. Anthrop., <u>71</u>, 145—149. Nenquin in Antiq., <u>42</u>:
             168, 328—329; Simpson in Science, <u>159</u>, 182—183; White in
             Mankind, <u>7</u>: 3, 241—242.
    1967B.　Preface. In: Bishop, W. W., and Clark, J. D., (eds.), 1967A, v — vi.

BISHOP, W. W., GAUTIER, A., and HEINZELIN, J. DE
    1967　Appendix [to new observations on the Later Tertiary and Early Quater-
             nary in the Western Rift]. Revised stratigraphical nomenclature.
             In: Bishop, W. W., and Clark, J. D., (eds.), 82—83, 1 table.

BISKE, S. F.
    1959　[On the problem of burial of Berezovka mammoth.] Izv. Geogr. Obshch.,
             <u>91</u>, 66—73, 2 figs., (Russian).
    1964　[Conditions of deposition on Quaternary terraces in the Lena R. valley
             between Pokrovsk and Zhigansk.] Trudy Inst. Geol. Geof., <u>1964</u>:
             8, 5—40, 16 figs., (Russian).
             See: Baranova and Biske.

BISSET, J.　See:　Black, G. F. and Bisset.

BITIRI, MARIA
    1964　[Paleolithic station of Boineşti.] Studii şi Cercetări de Ist. Veche, <u>15</u>,
             167—186, 5 figs., (Rumanian; Russian and French summaries).
    1965A.　[Early stages of Upper Paleolithic in Rumania.] In: Bader, <u>et al</u>, (eds.).
             1965, 34—37, (Russian).

1965B.   Considérations sur le début du Paléolithique supérieur en Roumanie.
Studii şi Cercetări de Ist. Veche, 16, 5–16, (Romanian; Russian
and French summaries).

1965C.   [Considerations on certain forms of bifaced tools from Romanian Paleolithic stations.] Studii şi Cercetări de Ist. Veche, 16, 431–
449, 7 figs., (Romanian; Russian and French summaries).

1967A.   Paläolithische Blattspitzen in Rumänien. Quartär, 18, 139–155, 7 figs.

1967B.   [Some observations concerning the Paleolithic of Oaş and its periodization.] Studii şi Cercetări de Ist. Veche, 18, 623–643, 13 figs.,
(Romanian; French summary).

BJERRING, HANS C.
1967   Does a homology exist between the basicranial muscle and the polar
cartilage? Colloq. Internat. Cent. Nation. Recherch. Sci., 163,
223–267, 21 figs., 4 pls., 1 table, (French summary).

BJORK, PHILIP R.
1967   Latest Eocene vertebrates from northwestern South Dakota. Jour. Pal.,
41, 227–236, 1 fig., pls. 26–27, 4 tables.

BLACK, CRAIG C.
1963B.   Rev.: McKenna in Quart. Rev. Biol., 40, 191–192.

1965A.   Fossil mammals from Montana. Pt. 2. Rodents from the Early Oligocene Pipestone Local Fauna. Ann. Carnegie Mus., 38: 1, 48 pp.,
6 figs.

1965B.   New species of Heteroxerus (Rodentia, Sciuridae) in the French Tertiary. Verh. Naturf. Ges. Basel, 76: 1, 185–196, 5 figs.
Rev.: Hünermann in Zbl. Geol. Pal., Teil 2, 1967, 116–117.

1966   Tertiary Sciuridae (Mammalia: Rodentia) from Bavaria. Mitt. Bayer.
Staatssamml. Pal. Hist. Geol., 6, 51–63, pls. 4–6, 1 table, (Ger-
man summary).
Rev.: Fahlbusch in Zbl. Geol. Pal., Teil 2, 1967, 518–519.

1967   Middle and Late Eocene mammal communities: A major discrepancy.
Science, 156, 62–64.
Rev.: Fahlbusch in Zbl. Geol. Pal., Teil 2, 1968, 26–27.

1968A.   The Oligocene rodent Ischyromys and discussion of the family Ischyromyidae. Ann. Carnegie Mus., 39: 18, 273–305, 26 figs., 3
tables.

1968B.   The Uintan rodent Mytonomys. Jour. Pal., 42, 853–856, 1 fig., 1
table.
See: Robinson, Peter, Black and Dawson.

BLACK, C. C., and DAWSON, M. R.
1966A.   A review of the Late Eocene mamalian faunas from North America.
Amer. Jour. Sci., 264, 321–349, 4 figs., 2 tables.
Rev.: Fahlbusch in Zbl. Geol. Pal., Teil 2, 1967, 108.

1966B.   Paleontology and geology of the Badwater Creek area, central Wyoming.
Part 1. History of field work and geological setting. Ann. Carnegie Mus., 38: 13, 297–307, 1 table.

BLACK, DAVIDSON
1930H.   Explanation by Dr. Davidson Black. Peking Leader Reprints, no. 51,
11–13.

BLACK, D., and GRABAU, A.
1930   One big "Garden of Eden." Peking Leader Reprints, no. 51, 22–27.

BLACK, GEORGE F., and BISSET, J.
1894   Catalogue of Dr. Grierson's Museum, Thornhill. Edinburgh: (not seen).

BLACK, ROBERT F.
1966   Late Pleistocene to recent history of Bering Sea — Alaska coast and
              man. In: Laughlin, W. S., and Reeder, W. G., (eds.), 7—22, 3
              figs., 1 table.

BLACK, R. F., and LAUGHLIN, W. S.
1964   Anangula: A geologic interpretation of the oldest archeologic site in
              the Aleutians. Science, 143, 1321—1322, 1 fig., 1 table.

BLACKWELDER, RICHARD E.
1967   Taxonomy: A text and reference book. New York: John Wiley, 720
              pp., (not seen).
              Rev.: Brown in Science, 159, 184—185; Corgan in Bio Science, 18,
              830; Webb in Nature, 216, 895.

BLACKWOOD, BEATRICE   See: Penniman 1965.

BLACKWOOD, H. J. J., (ed.)
1964   Bone and tooth: proceedings of the first European symposium held at
              Somerville College, Oxford, April 1963. New York: Macmillan
              (Pergamon Press), xvii + 425 pp., illustr.
              Rev.: Moss in Amer. Jour. Phys. Anthrop., 23, 199—200.

BLAHA, CARL, JUNGWIRTH, J., and KROMER, K.
1966   Geschichte der Anthropologischen und der Prähistorischen Abteilung
              des Naturhistorischen Museums in Wien. Ann. Naturhist. Mus.
              Wien, 69, 451—461, 4 portrs.

BLAIR, W. FRANK
1965   Amphibian speciation. In: Wright, H. E., and Frey, D. G., (eds.),
              1965, 543—556, 4 figs.

BLAKE, MARTHA A.
1967   Bibliography of vertebrate paleontology and related subjects. Number
              21. The Society of Vertebrate Paleontology.

BLAKE, W., JR.   See: Dyck, Fyles and Blake.

BLAKE-PALMER, G.
1956   An Otago coastal occupation site with Dinornis remains. Jour. Polyne-
              sian Soc., 65, 161—163, 3 pls.

BLANC, ALBERTO CARLO
1959B.   Giacimenti musteriani con fauna ad Elefante, Rinoceronte e Leone,
              sulla scogliera del Capo di Leuca. La Zagaglia 1, 5—14, 3 figs.,
              (not seen).

BLANC, E.
1966   Prof. Barone Gian Alberto Blanc. Quaternaria, 8, 319.

BLANC, GIAN ALBERTO
    1958   La Grotte Romanelli. Actes 2ème Congr. Internat. Spéléol., 1958,
                Appendice, 35–46, 3 figs.

BLANCHARD, JACQUES
    1964   Selection intentionnelle des belles têtes de cerfs gravées et peintes. In:
                Ripoll Perelló. E., (ed.), 1964A, 249–258, 15 figs., (Spanish
                summary).
                Rev.: Sonneville-Bordes in L'Anthrop., 69: 5–6, 546–547.

BLEIBTREU, H. K.
    1967   Some problems in physical anthropology. In: Siegel, B. J., and Beals,
                A. R., (eds.), 252–305.

BLEICH, KLAUS EBERHARD
    1965   Prof. Dr. Gustav Riek 65 Jahre alt. Mitt. Verband Deutschen Höhlen-
                und Karstforscher, München, 11, 90.

BLIAKHER, L. IA.
    1962   [A sketch of the history of animal morphology.] Moscow: Akad.
                Nauk SSSR Press, 263 pp., 9 figs., 39 portrs., (Russian).

BLIZNETSOV, E. P.
    1964   [Subterranean Hunters' Cave.] Peshchery, 4, 27–33, 2 figs., (Russian).
    1968   [Survey of caves in the Perm' province.] In: Rybakov, (ed.), 116–
                117, (Russian).

BLOKH, A. M.
    1961   [Rare earths in the remains of Paleozoic fishes of the Russian Plat-
                form.] Geokhimiîa, 1961: 5, 390–400, 1 fig., 3 tables,
                Russian; English summary).
                See: Drozdova and Blokh.

BLOM, G. I.
    1966A.   [On the age of Romashkino suit.] In: Collected Papers [Materials on
                the geology of the eastern part of Russian Platform], issue I,
                190–193, (Russian).
    1966B.   [The Tananyk series in the south-east of the Russian platform.] Sov.
                Geol., 1966: 2, 133–137, (Russian).

BLOT, JACQUES
    1966A.   Note relative à la valeur specifique de Platax plinianus Massalongo 1859.
                ,   Mem. Mus. Civ. Stor. Nat., Verona, 14, 101–104, 3 pls.
    1966B.   Etude des palaeonisciformes du bassin houiller de Commentry (Allier,
                France). Paris; Cahiers de Paléontologie, Eds. CNRS, 99 pp.,
                30 figs., 18 pls., 2 tables.
    1967   Quelques remarques préliminaires concernant la faune ichthyologique
                du Monte Bolca (Italie). Colloq. Internat. Cent. Nation. Re-
                cherch. Sci., 163, 133–138, 2 pls., (English summary).
    1968   Le squelette interne de la nageoire anale et ses relations avec le sque-
                lette axial. C. R. Acad. Sci. Paris, Sci. Nat., 266, 1943–1946,
                2 figs.
                See: Lapparent and Blot.

BLOT, J., and HEYLER, D.
1964   Sur une particularité anatomique de certains poissons du Permo-Carbo-
            nifère des bassins de Commentry et Autun. Bull. Soc. Géol.
            France, 5, 64–69, 3 figs., pls. 7–9.

BLUMBERG, JOE M., and KERLEY, E. R.
1966   Discussion [of morphometry of bone in palaeopathology]. A critical
            consideration of roent-genology and microscopy in palaeo-patho-
            logy. In: Jarcho, S., (ed.), 150–170, 7 figs.

BLUNTSCHLI, HANS
1911   Die Bedeutung der Funde von fossilen Menschen und Affen für die
            Stammesgeschichte der Primaten. Ferienkurs für schweizer Mittel-
            schullehrer, (not seen).

BOAS, F.
1965   General anthropology. New York: Johnson Reprint Corp., 718 pp.,
            97 figs., 10 pls.
            Rev.: Schwidetzky in Homo, 18: 1, 59.

BOCA, BERNARDINO DEL
1961   Storia della antropología. Milano: Vallardi, xxv + 471 pp., 341 figs.,
            maps and graphs.
            Rev.: Holas in Bull. Inst. Franç. Afr. Noire, sér. B., 25, 184–185.

BOCCHINO R., ANDREINA
1964   Sobre un Pygidiidae (Pisces, Siluriformes) del Eoceno de Río Negro.
            Ameghiniana, 3, 185–189, 1 pl., (English summary).
1967   Luisiella inexcutata gen. et sp. nov. (Pisces, Clupeiformes, Dussumierii-
            dae) del Jurassico superior de la Provincia de Chubut, Argentina.
            Ameghiniana, 5: 2, 91–100, 3 figs., (English summary).

BOCK, W. J.
1963   The evolution of cranial kinesis in early tetrapods. Amer. Zool., 3,
            487, (abs.)

BOCK, WILHELM
1962   Systematics of dichotomy and evolution. Geol. Center Res. Ser., 2,
            300 pp., 506 figs.
1964   Permian and Triassic tracks. Proc. Penn. Acad. Sci., 38, 16, (abs.).

BOCQUET, AIMÉ, and MALENFANT, M.
1966   Un gisement prémoustérien près de Vinay (Isère). Trav. Lab. Geol. Fac.
            Sci. Univ. Grenoble, 42, 77–82, 1 fig.

BODIÁNSKIĬ, A. V.
1959   [The Mousterian camp-site by Orel cliff.] Krat. Soob. Inst. Arkheol.
            Akad. Nauk URSR, 9, 117–124, 3 fig., (Russian).

BODYLEVSKIĬ, V. I.
1958   [Jurassic and Lower Cretaceous fauna from 1–R bore in the Ust-Eni-
            seĭsk port region.] Trudy Inst. Geol. Arktiki, 93, 10–27, 5
            plates, (Russian).
1962   [A small atlas of leading fossils.] Leningrad: "Gostoptekhizdat" Press,
            256 pp., 9 figs., 91 plates, 13 tables, (Russian).

BOEDIHARTO, R.
1964   New finds of vertebrate bearing layers in the Wonogiri and Wonosari
            areas, central Java. Bull. Geol. Surv. Indonesia, 1, 47—49, 2 figs.

BOEKSCHOTEN, G. J.
1963   Abs.: Langer in Zbl. Geol. Pal., Teil 2, 1964, 676.
            See: Sondaar and Boekschoten.

BOEKSCHOTEN, G. J., and SONDAAR, P. Y.
1966   The Pleistocene of the Katharo basin (Crete) and its Hippopotamus.
            Bijdr. Dierkunde, 36, 17—44, 8 figs., 7 pls., 24 tables, (French
            and German summaries).

BOESSNECK, J.   See: Milojčić, et al.

BOESSNECK, VON JOACHIM
1967   Vor-und frühgeschichtliche Tierknochenfunde aus zwei Siedlungshügeln
            in der Provinz Granada/Südspanien. Säugetierkundl. Mitt., 15,
            97—109, 4 figs., 6 tables., (English summary).

BOEV, P. and MASLINKOV, D.
1965   [On the problem of paleopathology of jaws and teeth in the territory
            of the Bulgarian Peoples Republic.] Voprosy Antrop., 20, 102—
            114, 5 figs., 6 tables, (Russian).

BOGACHEV, V. V. (= Bogačew, W. W.)
1958B.   [Fishes of the Pontian sea.]   Doklady Akad. Nauk SSSR, 122: 4, 727—
            729, 1 fig., (Russian).
1959   [Remains of a cetacean from the Oligocene of Tsimliǎnskaǐa village.]
            Trudy Inst. miner. ress. Akad. Nauk URSR, 40—42, (Russian).
1960B.   [Meotian mountain goat from Crimea.]   Trudy Azerbaǐd. Inst. po
            dobyche nefti, 9, 64—70, (Russian).
1960C.   [New Pontian turtle from Crimea.]   Trudy Azerbaǐd. Inst. po dobyche
            nefti, 10, 88—92, (Russian).
1964   [Palaöntologische Notizen. Chaetodon penniger n. sp.]   Trudy Azer-
            baǐd. Inst. po dobyche nefti, 13, 123—133, 2 figs., (Russian).
            Abs.: Weiler in Zbl. Geol. Pal., Teil 2, 1965, 218—219.
1965   [Eocene fishes from Simferopol' Regional Museum collections.]   Ezhe-
            godnik Vses. Pal. Ob., 17, 268—275, 3 pls., (Russian).
            Rev.: Weiler in Zbl. Geol. Pal., Teil 2, 1967, 490—491.

BOGDANOV, A. A., SERGEEV, E. M., IAKUSHOVA, A. F., et al.
1966   [Iu. A. Orlov (1893-1966).]   Vestnik Mosk. Univ., Ser. IV, Geol., 1966:
            5, 1—2, (Russian).

BOGER, HORST
1966   Die marinen Niveaus über den Flözen Schieferbank und Sarnsbank
            (Grenze Namur C — Westfal A) im Ruhrgebiet. Fortschr. Geol.
            Rheinland u. Westfalen, 13:1, 1—38, 17 figs., 3 pls., (French and
            English summaries).

BÖHME, GOTTFRIED
1963   Abs.: Lotze in Zbl. Geol. Pal., Teil 2, 1964, 687.

BOHMERS, ASSIEN

1961B. Prandinge, gem. Ooststellingwerf (Friesland). Nieuws-Bull. Koninklijke Ned. Oudheidk. Bond, 6e s., 14, 234, (not seen).

1961C. Westerlee, gem. Scheemda (Groningen). Nieuws-Bull. Koninklijke Ned. Oudheidk. Bond, 6e s., 14, 235, (not seen).

1961D. Wijster, gem. Beilen (Drenthe). Nieuws-Bull. Koninklijke Ned. Oudheidk. Bond, 6e s., 14, 238, (not seen).

1961E. Steenwijk (Overijssel). Nieuws-Bull. Koninklijke Ned. Oudheidk. Bond, 6e s., 14, 239, (not seen).

1961F. Geldrop (Noord-Brabant). Nieuws-Bull. Koninklijke Ned. Oudheidk. Bond, 6e s., 14, 241, (not seen).

1961G. Brunsum (Limburg). Nieuws-Bull. Koninklijke Ned. Oudheidk. Bond, 6e s., 14, 242, (not seen).

BOHN, PETER

1966 Senonemys sümegensis nov. gen., nov. sp. – ein neuer Schildkrötenfund aus Ungarn. Föld. Közlöny, 96, 111–118, 2 figs., pl. 8, (Hungarian; German summary).

BOIARKINA, V. A., et al.

1966 [Vladimir Vladimirovich Obruchev.] Izv. Akad. Nauk SSSR, Ser. Geograf., 1966: 3, 154–155, (Russian).

BOITEAU, PIERRE

1964 Evolución de las concepciones biológicas. Translated by Raquel Rabiela De Gortani. México: Universidad Nacional Autónoma, 115 pp., (not seen).

Rev.: Anon. in Rev. Soc. Mexicana Hist. Nat., 25, 283.

BOITSOVA, E. P., and POKROVSKAIA, I. M.

1954 [Materials on stratigraphy of Oligocene and Miocene continental deposits of Turgai depression.] In: Pokrovskaia, (ed.), 1954, 86–109, 3 tables, (Russian).

BOK, I. I. See: Satpaev and Bok.

BÖKÖNYI, SÁNDOR

1959 Das Vorkommen des Vielfrasses (Gulo gulo L.) aus der heimatlichen Holozänzeit. Vert. Hungarica, 1, 226–235, 3 figs., (Hungarian; German summary).

BÖKÖNYI, S., KÁLLAI, L., MATOLCSI, J., and TARJÁN, R.

1965 Vergleichende Untersuchungen am Metacarpus des Urs- und des Hausrindes. Zeit. Tierzüchtung Züchtungsbiol., 81, 330–347, 9 figs., (English summary).

BOLLI, H. M. See: Kugler and Bolli.

BOLOMEY, ALEXANDRA

1965A. Die Fauna zweier villafrankischer Fundstellen in Rumänien. Ber. Geol. Ges. Deutsch. Demokratischen Republ., 10, 77–88, 9 figs.

1965B. Contribution à la connaissance de la morphologie de Pliotragus ardeus. Rev. Roumaine Biol., 10: 5, 315–323, 8 figs., 1 table.

BOLOTOVA, N. ÍA.
1966   [On the stratigraphy of Cenozoic sediments in northeastern Mongolia.]
             In: Marinov, (ed.), 1966, 79—85, (Russian).

BOLTIN, LEE   See: Gorenstein 1967.

BONADONNA, FRANCESCO PAOLO
1964   Studi sul Pleistocene del Lazio. II. Il bacino diatomitico di Cornazzano
             (Bracciano, Roma). Geol. Romana, 3, 383—404, 18 figs., 2 pls.
             Rev.: Orombelli in Riv. Ital. Pal., 72, 250.
1965A.   Resti di Hippopotamus amphibius Linné nei sedimenti del Pleistocene
             medio-inferiore della Via Portuense (Roma). Boll. Soc. Geol.
             Ital., 84: 1, 29—40, 5 figs.
             Rev.: Albanesi in Riv. Ital. Pal., 73, 396—397.
1965B.   Further information on the research in the Middle Pleistocene diatomite
             quarry of Valle dell' Inferno (Riano, Rome). Quaternaria, 7,
             279—299, 3 figs., 6 pls., (Italian and German summaries).
1967   Studi sul Pleistocene del Lazio. III. Linee di costa lungo il litorale di
             Tarquinia (Lazio settentrionale). Geol. Romana, 6, 121—135, 8
             figs., 1 table, (English summary).

BONAPARTE, JOSÉ F.
1962   Abs.: Huene in Zbl. Geol. Pal., Teil 2, 1964, 167.
1963A.   Abs.: Huene in Zbl. Geol. Pal., Teil 2, 1964, 983—984.
1963B.   Descripción del esqueleto postcraneano de Exaeretodon (Cynodontia-
             Traversodontidae). Acta Geol. Lilloana, 4, 5—52, 23 figs., 2 pls.,
             (English summary).
             Abs.: Huene in Zbl. Geol. Pal., Teil 2, 1964, 985—986.
1963C.   Descripción de Ischignathus sudamericanus n. gen. n. sp., nuevo cinodon-
             te gonfodonte del Triásico Medio Superior de San Juan, Argen-
             tina (Cynodontia-Traversodontidae). Acta Geol. Lilloana, 4, 111—
             128, 6 figs., (English summary).
             Abs.: Huene in Zbl. Geol. Pal., Teil 2, 1964, 986.
1963D.   Un nuevo cinodonte gonfodonte del Triásico Medio Superior de San
             Juan, Proexaeretodon vincei n. gen., n. sp. (Cynodontia — Tra-
             versodontidae). Acta Geol. Lilloana, 4, 129—133, 1 fig., (En-
             glish summary).
             Abs.: Huene in Zbl. Geol. Pal., Teil 2, 1964, 986.
1963E.   La familia Traversodontidae (Therapsida-Cynodontia). Acta Geol. Lillo-
             ana, 4, 163—194, 10 figs., (English summary).
             Abs.: Huene in Zbl. Geol. Pal., Teil 2, 1964, 987.
1966A.   Sobre las cavidades cerebral, nasal y otras estructuras del craneo de Ex-
             aeretodon sp. (Cynodontia-Traversodontidae). Acta Geol. Lilloa-
             na, 8, 5—31, 10 figs., 2 pls., (English summary).
1966B.   Sobre nuevos terapsidos triasicos hallados en el centro de la Provincia
             de Mendoza, Argentina. Acta Geol. Lilloana, 8, 91—100, 2 figs.,
             (English summary).
1966C.   Chiniquodon Huene (Therapsida-Cynodontia) en el Triasico de Ischigua-
             lasto, Argentina. Acta Geol. Lilloana, 8, 157—169, 4 figs., 1 ta-
             ble, (English summary).
1966D.   Una nueva "fauna" Triásica de Argentina (Therapsida: Cynodontia
             Dicynodontia) consideraciones filogenéticas y paleobiogeográficas.
             Ameghiniana, 4, 243—296, 29 figs., 2 pls., 2 charts, (English
             summary).
             Rev.: Huene in Zbl. Geol. Pal., Teil 2, 1967, 105.

1966E.   Chronological survey of the tetrapodbearing Triassic of Argentina.
           Breviora, no. 251, 13 pp., 2 tables.
1967   New vertebrate evidence for a southern transatlantic connexion during
           the Lower or Middle Triassic. Palaeontol., 10, 554—563, 7 figs.

BONAVÍA, DUCCIO
1966   Excavations of early sites in southern Peru. Current Anthrop., 7, 97.

BONCHEV, EKIM
1965   [Professor Petŭr Nikolov Bakalov.] Trudove Vŭrkhu Geol. Bŭlg., Ser.
           Pal., 7, 7—10, portr., (Bulgarian and French).

BONCH-OSMOLOVSKIĬ, G. A.
1940B.   [The grotto Kiik-Koba. Paleolithic of Crimea.]
           Rev.: Okladnikov in Krat. Soob. Inst. Ist. Mat. Kult. SSSR, 9, 125—
           128, (Russian).

BOND, GEOFFREY
1955B.   A note on dinosaur remains from the Forest Sandstone (Upper Karroo).
           Occ. Pap. Nation. Mus. S. Rhodesia, 2:20, 795—800, 1 pl., 2
           tables.
1957   The geology of the Khami Stone Age sites. Occ. Pap. Nation. Mus.
           S. Rhodesia, 3:21A, 44—55, 2 figs.
1965   Some new fossil localities in the Karroo system of Rhodesia. Arnoldia,
           2:11, 1—4.
1967   River valley morphology, stratigraphy, and palaeoclimatology in
           southern Africa. Discussion. In: Bishop, W. W., and Clark,
           J. D., (eds.), 303—312, (French summary).

BOND, W. R. G.
1932   The formation of the Dewlish Pliocene Elephant-bed Ravine. Proc.
           Dorset Nat. Hist. Archaeol. Soc., 53, 228—235, 1 pl.
1933   Further remarks on the Dewlish Elephant-bed Ravine. Particularly
           with regard to the date of its origin. Proc. Dorset Nat. Hist.
           Archaeol. Soc., 54, 173—180, 4 figs.

BONDARCHUK, V. G., and SHELKOPLIÂS, V. N. (eds.)
1965   [Materials on the Quaternary Period of the Ukraine. For the VII-th
           INQA Congress.] Kiev: "Naukova Dumka" Press, 332 pp.,
           illustr., (Russian; English summaries).

BONDE, NIELS
1966   The fishes of the Mo-clay Formation (Lower Eocene). Meddel. Dansk.
           Geol. Foren., 16:2, 198—202.

BONDESIO, PEDRO   See: Pascual and Bondesio.

BONÉ, EDOUARD L.
1962A.   Abs.: Kuhn-Schnyder in Zbl. Geol. Pal., Teil 2, 1964, 222—223.
1962B.   Rev.: Schaeuble in Zeit. Morph. Anthrop., 54, 113;   V [allois] in
           L'Anthrop., 68, 164—165.
1964A.   L'oeuvre paleontologique de Pierre Teilhard de Chardin. Rev. Questions
           Sci., 25, 47—76, 2 figs.
1964B.   Man's biological significance. S. Afr. Archaeol. Bull., 19, 51—56.
1965   Hipparion in Africa. 7th Internat. Congr., Internat. Assoc. Quat. Res.,
           Abs., 1965, 40, (abs.).

See: Singer and Bone.

BONE, E., and SINGER, R.
   1965   Hipparion from Langebaanweg, Cape Province and a revision of the
             genus in Africa. Ann. S. Afr. Mus., 48, 273—397, 15 figs., 13
             pls., 24 tables.

BONFIGLIO, L.
   1964   Su alcuni molari de elefanti fossili presso Vallaggio Paradiso a nord di
             Messina. Atti Soc. Peloritana Sci. Fis. Mat. Nat., 10, 157—164,
             (not seen).

BONHAM, JOHN C.
   1965   Indian "points" of the Niagara peninsula — "The Earthly Paradise of
             Canada". Totem Pole, 48:7, 64—77, 39 figs.

BONIFAY, EUGENE
   1962A.   Rev.: Freund in Quartär, 15—16, 220—224.
   1964A.   Pliocène et Pleistocène méditerraneens: vue d'ensemble et essai de
             corrélations avec la chronologie glaciarie. Ann. Pal., Vert., 50,
             195—226, 4 figs., 4 tables.
   1964B.   La grotte du Regourdou (Montignac, Dordogne). Stratigraphie et in-
             dustrie lithique moustérienne. L'Anthrop., 68, 49—64, 7 figs.
   1965   Moustérien et Premousterien de la grotte de Rigabe (Artigues, Var).
             Quartär, 15—16, 61—78, 9 figs.

BONIFAY, MARIE-FRANÇOISE
   1962   Abs.: Ehrenberg in Zbl. Geol. Pal., Teil 2, 1964, 192—193.
   1964   L'Equus hydruntinus de la Baume-Rousse (Lozère). L'Anthrop., 68,
             387—395, 2 figs., 5 tables.
   1966A.   La faune Villefranchienne. Aperçus anatomiques. In: Lavocat, R.,
             (ed.), 1966, 65—68, pl. 1.
   1966B.   Tableau d'anatomie comparée. In: Lavocat, R., (ed.), 1966, 106—108.
   1966C.   Les bovidés. In: Lavocat, R., (ed.), 1966, 233—243, fig. 58, pls. 25—
             31, table 15.
   1966D.   Les carnivores. In: Lavocat, R., (ed.), 1966, 337—396, figs. 65—67,
             pls. 69—102, tables 19—23.

BONIFAY, M.-F., and BONIFAY, E.
   1965   Age du gisement de mammifères fossile de Lunel-Viel (Hérault). C. R.
             Acad. Sci. Paris, 260, 3441—3444.

BONILLA LUNA, J.   See: Pichardo del Barrio, et al.

BONIN, GERHADT VON
   1963   Rev.: Anon. in Sci. Amer., 209:2, 137—138;   Roofe in Evolution, 18,
             138;   Roth-Lutra in Anat. Anz., 116, 307—308;   Webber in
             Amer. Jour. Phys. Anthrop., 23, 438—440.

BONIS, LOUIS DE
   1964   Étude de quelques mammifères du Ludien de la Débruge (Vaucluse).
             Ann. Pal., Vert., 50, 119—154, 7 figs., 5 pls.
   1966A.   Arrière-crânes et moulages endocrâniens de carnivores fossiles. Ann.
             Pal., Vert., 52, 141—162, 12 figs.

1966B.   Sur l'évolution du genre <u>Haplocyon</u> Schlosser (Carnivora). C. R. Soc.
              Geol. France, 1966, 143, (abs.).
1967   Sur l'évolution du genre <u>Haplocyon</u> Schlosser (Carnivora). Bull. Soc.
              Géol. France, <u>8</u>, 114–117, pl. 3, 1 table.
       Rev.: Fahlbusch in Zbl. Geol. Pal., Teil 2, 1967, 212–213;
              Fahlbusch in Zbl. Geol. Pal., Teil 2, 1968, 212–213.
1968   Remarques sur la position stratigraphique du "calcaire blanc de
              l'Agenais" et du gisement de Mammifères fossiles de
              Paulhiac (Lot-et-Garonne). C. R. Soc. Géol. France,
              1968:9, 316–318.
       See: Baudelot, S. and Bonis.

BONNAMOUR, LOUIS, and DESBROSSE, R.
1966   L'Abri gay a Poncin (Ain.): Fouilles 1965. Bull. Soc. Linn. Lyon,
              <u>35</u>, 319–328, 5 figs.

BONNER, JOHN TYLER
1968   Size change in development and evolution. Pal. Soc. Mem., <u>2</u>, 1–15,
              4 figs.

BONNET, ANDRÉ
1964   Nouvel essai de corrélation des terrasses rhodaniennes. Bull. Soc. Géol.
              France, <u>5</u>, 543–554, 5 figs., 1 table.
1965   Le Quaternaire des environs de St-Gilles (Gard). C. R. Soc. Géol.
              France, 1965, 174, (abs.).
1966   Le Quaternaire des environs de Saint-Gilles (Gard). Bull. Soc. Géol.
              France, <u>7</u>, 571–579, 2 figs., pl. 17.

BONNET, J.
1964   Contribution a la préhistoire en Charente. Mem. Soc. Archéol. Hist.
              Charente, <u>1962-1963</u>, 103–110, illustr.

BONNICHSEN, ROBSON   See: Swanson, Butler and Bonnichsen.

BONTÉ, ANTOINE
1966   Le Quaternaire de la Pointe aux Oies entre Wimereux et Ambleteuse
              (Pas-de-Calais). Ann. Soc. Geol. Nord, <u>86</u>, 183–186, 1 fig.
1967   Louis Dollo (1878–1965). Bull. Soc. Géol. France, <u>8</u>, 484–489, portr.

BOON, G. C.   See: ApSimon and Boon.

BOONSTRA, LIEUWE DIRK
1964   The girdles and limbs of the pristerognathid Therocephalia. Ann. S.
              Afr. Mus., <u>48</u>, 121–165, 50 figs., 1 pl.
       Abs.: Huene in Zbl. Geol. Pal., Teil 2, 1964, 987.
1965A.   The Russian dinocephalian <u>Deuterosaurus</u>. Ann. S. Afr. Mus., 48, 233–
              236.
       Abs.: Huene in Zbl. Geol. Pal., Teil 2, 1966, 301.
1965B.   The girdles and limbs of the Gorgonopsia of the <u>Tapinocephalus</u>-Zone.
              Ann. S. Afr. Mus., 48, 237–249, 11 figs.
       Abs.: Huene in Zbl. Geol. Pal., Teil 2, 1966, 301.
1965C.   The skull of <u>Struthiocephalus</u> <u>kitchingi</u>. Ann. S. Afr. Mus., 48, 251–
              265, 11 figs.

Abs.: Huene in Zbl. Geol. Pal., Teil 2, 1966, 302.

1966A.   The girdles and limbs of the Dicynodontia of the Tapinocephalus zone.
Ann. S. Afr. Mus., 50:1, 1–11, 6 figs.

1966B.   The dinocephalian manus and pes. Ann. S. Afr. Mus., 50:2, 13–26,
10 figs.

1967A.   An early stage in the evolution of the mammalian quadrupedal walking
gait. Ann. S. Afr. Mus., 50:3, 27–42, 11 figs.

1967B.   Langs verskillende weë. (Pareiasauria en Dicynodontia.) S. African
Jour. Sci., 63, 201–206, 6 figs., (Afrikaans; English summary).

1968   The terrestrial reptile fauna of Tapinocephalus-zone-age and Gondwanaland. S. African Jour. Sci., 64, 199–204, 3 tables.

BOPARDIKAR, B. P.   See: Joshi, et al.

BORDEN, CHARLES E.

1960   DjRi 3, an early site in the Fraser Canyon, British Columbia. Nation.
Mus. Canada, Bull. 162, Anthrop. Ser. no. 45, 101–118, 5 pls.

1961   Fraser River archaeological project. Progress report. April 20, 1961.
Anthrop. Pap., Nation. Mus. Canada, No. 1, 6 pp., 1 fig., 2 pls.

BORDES, FRANÇOIS

1961B.   Rev.: Jordá Cerda in Zephyrus, 13, 115–116;   Ripoll Perelló in
Ampurias, 24, 365.

1965A.   Utilisation possible des côtés des burins. Fundber. Schwaben, 17, 3–
4, 1 fig., pl. 30.

1965B.   A propos de typologie. L'Anthrop., 69, 369–377.

1965C.   A propos de la grotte de la Chaise (Charente). Quelques rectifications.
L'Anthrop., 69:5–6, 602–603.

1967   Considérations sur la Typologie et les techniques dans le Paléolithique.
Quartär, 18, 25–55, 7 figs., 8 pls.

1968   The Old Stone Age. Translated from the French by J. E. Anderson.
London: Weidenfeld and Nicolson; New York: McGraw-Hill,
255 pp., 78 figs.
Rev.:   Baldwin in Man, Jour. Roy. Anthrop. Inst., 3, 666;   Coles in
Antiq., 43:169, 79–80.
See: Gaussen 1964; Monméjean, et al.; Smith, P. E. 1966B.

BORDES, F., COMAS, J., and FRANCISCOLO, M. E.

1964   The Upper Palaeolithic and the New World. With reply by E. F. Greenman. Current Anthrop., 5, 321–324.

BORDES, F., and FITTE, P.

1964   Microliths du Magdalénien supérieur de la Gare de Couze (Dordogne).
In: Ripoll Perelló, E., (ed.), 1964A, 259–267, 5 figs., (Spanish
summary).
Rev.: D. de S. in L'Anthrop., 69:5–6, 537–538.

BORDES, F., and PRAT, F.

1965   Observations sur les faunes du Riss et du Würm I en Dordogne.
L'Anthrop., 69, 31–45, 3 figs., 4 tables.

BORDES, F., and SMITH, PH.

1965   Une sculpture du Solutréen inférieur de Laugerie-Haute. L'Anthrop.,
69, 99–102, 3 figs.

BORDES, F., and SONNEVILLE-BORDES, D. de
1966   Protomagdalénien, ou Périgordien VII? L'Anthrop., 70:1−2, 113−122,
            5 figs.
1967   Raymond Vaufrey (1890-1967). Quartär, 18, 1−8, portr.

BORGONIO, GUADALUPE   See: Maldonado-Koerdell and Borgonio.

BORHEGYI, STEPHAN F. de
1964   Pre-Columbian cultural similarities and differences between the High-
            land Guatemalan and Tropical Rainforest Mayas. Proc. Internat.
            Congr. Americanists, 1962:1, 215−224.

BORINA, E. I., and TIKHOMIROV, V. G.
1961   [New data on Devonian stratigraphy of Sarysu-Teniz watershed (Central
            Kazakhstan).] Uchen. Zap. Mosk. Univ., 192, 20−25, (Russian).

BORISENKO, Iu. A.
1966   [On the first finding of a vertebrate in the Upper Paleozoic deposits
            of the Donets Basin.] Dopovidi Akad. Nauk URSR, 1966:11,
            1493−1494, 2 figs., (Ukrainian; Russian and English summaries).

BORISENKO, T. I.   See: Cherdyntsev, Strashnikov, et al.

BORISKOVSKII, P. I. (=Boriskovsky, P. I.)
1955C.   [Excavations at Kostenki and some problems concerning the Late Paleo-
            lithic in the Ukraine.] Krat. Soob. Inst. Arkheol. Akad. Nauk
            URSR 4, 157−158, (Russian).
1959B.   [The excavation of the Valukinskii Paleolithic site (Kostenki XIX) in
            1956.] Krat. Soob. Inst. Ist. Mat. Kult., 73, 57−63, 3 figs.,
            (Russian).
1959C.   [Paleolithic hearth on Valunkinskii station (Kostenki XIX).] Sov.
            Arkheol., 1959:1, 246−248, 3 figs., (Russian).
1959D.   [Frantishek Proshek (9-20-1922 − 7-26-1958).] Sov. Arkheol., 1959:2,
            p. 301, portr., (Russian).
1960   [Some controversial problems regarding the Paleolithic at Kostenki.]
            Krat. Soob. Inst. Ist. Mat. Kult. SSSR, 78, 3−12, (Russian).
1961C.   [Flint workshops in the Valuiki area on the river Oskol.] Krat. Soob.
            Inst. Ist. Mat. Kult. SSSR, 82, 104−111, 4 figs., 1 table,
            (Russian).
1961D.   On the question of the most ancient digging tools. Issled. Archeol.
            SSSR, 12−16, (Russian).
1961E.   [New excavations at the Paleolithic Valukinskii site (Kostenki XIX).]
            Krat. Soob. Inst. Ist. Mat. Kult. SSSR, 84, 30−31, 1 fig.,
            (Russian).
1961F.   [Paleolithic site near Odessa.] Krat. Soob. Inst. Ist. Mat. Kult. SSSR,
            86, 28−35, 4 figs., (Russian).
1962A.   [Research on Stone Age relics in the Democratic Republic Vietnam in
            1960-1961.] Sov. Arkheol., 1962:2, 17−25, 4 figs., (Russian).
            English translation: Solheim II in: Asian Perspectives, 6, 23−
            30.
1962B.   [Archaeological discoveries in Vietnam.] Vestnik Akad. Nauk SSSR,
            1962:4, 98−101, 2 figs., (Russian).
1963   [Essays on the Paleolithic of the Don basin. Little known settlements
            of the Old Stone Age at Kostenki.] Mat. Issled. Arkheol. SSSR,
            no. 121, 3−191, 134 figs., (Russian).

Rev.: [Filip] in Archeol. Roz., 17, 117—118, (Czech).

1964A.   [Problem of the development of Late Paleolithic culture of the steppe region.] 7-th Internat. Congr. anthrop. ethnogr. sci., Moscow, (Russian).

1964B.   [Problems of the Late Paleolithic and Mesolithic of the northwestern Black Sea region.] Studii și Cercetări de Ist. Veche, 15, 5—17, 6 figs., (Romanian; Russian and French summaries).

1965   A propos des récents progrès des études paléolithiques en URSS. L'Anthrop., 69, 5—29, 7 figs.
Rev.: J. C. in Bull. Soc. Préhist. Franç., C. R. séances mens., 1965:7, 223—224.

1966   [Some problems of the Vietnam Stone Age.] Sbornik Národního Musea v Praze. Rada A: Historie, 20:1—2, 23—27, 1 pl., (Russian).

1967   [New research on Paleolithic of India.] Vestnik Akad. Nauk SSSR, 1967:9, 68—71, 2 figs., (Russian).

1968   [Sixtieth birthday anniversary of A. P. Okladnikov.] Sov. Arkheol., 1968:4, 157—160, portr., (Russian).

BORISKOVSKIĬ, P. I., and KRASKOVSKIĬ, V. I.
1961   [Relics of the most ancient human culture in the northwestern Black Sea region.] Publishers: Odesskoe Arkheologicheskoe Obshchestvo, 37 pp., 11 figs., (Russian).

BORISKOVSKIĬ, P. I., and PRASLOV, N. D.
1964   [The Paleolithic of the basin of the Dnieper and Asov region.] Arkheol. SSSR, Svod Arkheol. Istochnikov, 14, 56 pp., 1 fig., 31 pls., (Russian).
Rev.: Bánesz in Sloven. Archeol., 13:2, 467—468, (Slovakian);   Vencl in Archeol. Roz., 17, 118—119, (Czech).

BORISOGLEBSKAIA, M. B. (=Borissoglebskaya)
1967   [New genus of beaver from Oligocene of Kazakhstan.] Biull. Mosk. Obshch. Ispyt. Prirody, Otd. Biol., 72:6, 129—135, 4 figs., (Russian; English summary).

BORJA, CORINNE and ROBERT   See: Matthews 1964.

BORKHVARDT, V. G.
1966   [On the rise of vertebral centra in evolution of different vertebrates.] Vestnik Leningrad. Univers., 1966:15, 16—22, (Russian: English summary).

1967   [Structure and functional significance of vertebral centra in different animals.] Vestnik Leningrad. Univers., 1967:3, 19—25, 2 figs., (Russian; English summary).

BÓRMIDA, MARCELO
1960   Investigaciones paleontológicas en la region de Bolivar (Pcia. de Buenos Aires). Com. Invest. Cien., La Plata, 1, (not seen).

1965   Las industrias líticas precerámicas del Arroyo Catalán Chico y del Río Cuareim (Departamento de Artigas, R. O. del Uruguay). Riv. Sci. Preist., 19, 195—232, 24 figs., (Italian, French and English summaries).

BORNS, H. W., Jr.
1965   The Paleo-Indians' geography of Nova Scotia. 7th Internat. Congr.,
            Internat. Assoc. Quat. Res., Abs., 1965, 41, (abs.)
1966   The geography of Paleo-Indian occupation in Nova Scotia. Quaternaria,
            8, 49—57, 3 figs., (French and German summaries).

BOROVIKOV, L. I., and BORSUK, B. I.
1961   [Geology of Central and South Kazakhstan.] Materialy Geol. Inst.
            (VSEGEI), Nov. Ser., 41, 499 pp., (Russian).

BORSUK, B. I.   See: Borovikov and Borsuk.

BORSUK-BIAŁYNICKA, MAGDALENA
1966   On the Pleistocene rhinoceroses. Przeglad Zool., 10, 131—140, 8 figs.,
            2 tables, (Polish; English summary).

BORZATTI VON LÖWENSTERN, EDOARDO
1964   La Grotta di Uluzzo. Campagna di scavi 1963. Riv. Sci. Preist., 18,
            75—89, 5 figs., (French and English summaries).
1965A.   La Grotta di Uluzzo (Campagna di scavi 1964). Riv. Sci. Preist., 19,
            41—52, 3 figs., (French and English summaries).
1965B.   Selci paleolitiche raccolte all'aperto fra Torre dell'Alto e Torre di
            Uluzzo (S. Caterina-Lecce). Riv. Sci. Preist., 19, 281—288, 1
            fig., (French and English summaries).
            See: Palma di Cesnola and Borzatti von Löwenstern.

BOSCH, M. VAN DEN
1964A.   De Haaientanden uit de Transgressielagen in de Scharberg bij Elsloo.
            Natuurhist. Maanbl., 53, 19—25.
            Abs.: Weiler in Zbl. Geol. Pal., Teil 2, 1965, 219—220.
1964B.   De stratigrafie van het Mioceen in het oostelijke Noordzeebekken, naar
            aanleiding van een nieuw onderzoek naar de ouderdom van het
            Transgressieconglomeraat van Elsloo. Natuurhist. Maandbl., 53,
            36—40, 1 table, (German summary).
1964C.   Einige Haaientanden uit de Zanden van Grimmertingen. Natuurhist.
            Maandbl., 53, 131—138, 5 figs., (French summary).
            Abs.: Weiler in Zbl. Geol. Pal., Teil 2, 1965, 220.

BOSCH, M. v. d., and JANSSEN, A. W.
1965   Het Mioceen van Delden. Natuurhist. Maandbl., 54, 81—83, 1 map.

BOSCH-GIMPERA, PEDRO
1964A.   El arte rupestre de América. (A la memoria de Henri Breuil). An.
            Antrop., Mexico, 1, 29—45, 18 figs.
1964B.   El arte rupestre de América. In: Ripoll Perelló, E., (ed.), 1964A,
            269—282, 8 figs., 2 pls., (English summary).
1968   Europe, Asie, Amerique, au Paléolithique supérieur. C. R. Acad. In-
            script. Belles-Lettres, 1967, 455—462, 4 figs.

BOSELLINI, ALFONSO   See: Leonardi, P., Broglio and Bosellini.

BOSINSKI, GERHARD
1965   Abschläge mitt fazettierter Schlagflache in mittelpaläolithischen Funden.
            Fundber. Schwaben, 17, 5—10, pls. 1—6.

BOSS, EDWARD C.
[1965]   Bibliography of archaeological periodicals. McMurray, Pennsylvania:
                  privately printed, (not seen).
                  Rev.: Anon. in Current Anthrop., 7, 100.

BOSTANCI, ENVER Y.
1964   An examination of a Neanderthal type fossil skull found in the Chalci-
                  dique Peninsula. Bell. Türk. Tarih Kurumu, 28, 373—381, 4 pls.,
                  (Turkish and English).
1965   Fossil remains of Upper Paleolithic and Mesolithic Man in Beldibi and
                  Belbaşi rock shelters on the Mediterranean coast of Anatolia.
                  Ber. 8. Tagung Deutsch. Ges. Anthrop., 1963, 253—262, 3 pls.
                  Rev.: Vallois in L'Anthrop., 69, 312—313.

BOTOŞĂNEANU, LAZARE   See: Negrea, et al.

BOTTEMA, S.
1967   Appendix: a late Quaternary pollen diagram from Ioannina, north-
                  western Greece. In: Higgs, E. S., Vita-Frinzi, C., Harris, D. R.,
                  and Fagg, A. E., 26—29, 1 fig.

BOTTOMS, EDWARD
1964   The "Dime" site. Chesopiean, 2:6. 145—148.
1965   Kentucky Paleo-Indian projectile points. Chesopiean, 3:5, 117—123,
                  3 figs.
1966   The Richmond site: a Paleo-Indian locality in Chesterfield County,
                  Virginia. Chesopiean, 4:2, 40—49, 3 figs.
1967   The Continental Shelf of the eastern United States and its archaeologi-
                  cal possibilities. Chesopiean, 5, 57—59, 2 figs.
1968   Bertie Countie oolitic quartzite and its aboriginal utilization in eastern
                  Virginia and North Carolina. Chesopiean, 6, 32—43, 5 figs.
                  See: McAvoy and Bottoms.

BOTTOMS, E., and PAINTER, F.
1965   Facial grinding on Paleo-Indian projectile points. Chesopiean, 3:4, 95—
                  99, illustr.

BOUCHUD, JEAN
1964   Découverte d'un crâne de renne fossile dans la grotte Bernard (commune
                  de Saint-Martin-de-Caralp). C. R. Acad. Sci. Paris, 258, 4305—
                  4307, 1 pl.
1965A.   Le Cervus megaceros dans le sud et le sud-ouest de la France. Israel
                  Jour. Zool., 14, 24—37, 1 pl., 3 tables, (English summary).
1965B.   La faune wurmienne de Pont-du-Chateau (Puy-de-Dôme). Avec une
                  introduction géologique de A. Rudel et une analyse pollinique
                  de H. Elhai. Rev. Sci. Nat. Auvergne, 29, 71—99, 2 pls., 4
                  tables.
1966A.   La technique des fouilles. In: Lavocat, R., (ed.), 1966, 69—82.
1966B.   Les proboscidiens (Proboscidea). In: Lavocat, R., (ed.), 1966, 161—
                  173, fig. 53, pls. 2—3.
1966C.   Les rhinocéros. In: Lavocat, R., (ed.), 1966, 174—193, fig. 54, pls.
                  4—9, tables 11—13.
1966D.   Les artiodactyles non ruminant. In: Lavocat, R., (ed.), 1966, 216—
                  232, fig. 57, pls. 18—24.
1966E.   Les cervidés. In: Lavocat, R., (ed.), 1966, 244—277, figs. 59—60, pls.
                  32—47, tables 16—17.

1967	Etude d'un crâne de Renne fossile ("Rangifer guettardi" Desmarest) découvert dans le Sud de la France. Collog. Internat. Cent. Nation. Recherch. Sci., 163, 557—567, 2 pls., 3 tables, (English summary).
1968A.	Sur la présence de Crocuta crocuta sinensis Owen dans le Pléistocène inférieur de Phnom-Loang (Cambodge). C. R. Acad. Sci. Paris, Sci. Nat., 267:26, 2291—2293, 1 table.
1968B.	Les Cervidés et les Equidés du gisemen quaternaire des "Abîmes de La Fage" à Noailles (Corrèze). C. R. Soc. Géol. France, 1968: 6, 191—193.

BOUCOT, A. J., et al.

1960	A Late Silurian fauna from the Southerland River formation, Devonian Island, Canadian arctic archipelago. Bull. Geol. Surv. Canada, 65, x + 51 pp., 10 pls.

BOUILLON, EMILE

1963A.	Biface amygdaloïde à talon du Paléolithique ancien de Froidos (Meuse). Bull. Acad. Soc. Lorraine Sci., 3:1, 15—19, 2 figs.
1963B.	Contribution à l'étude du Paléolithique en Lorraine. Bull. Acad. Soc. Lorraine Sci., 3:2, 83—88, 4 figs., abs. on page 93.
1964	Vestiges de l'industrie moustérienne à Laneuville-devant-Nancy. Bull. Acad. Soc. Lorraine Sci., 3:4, 45—50, 3 figs.
1965	Quartzites taillées et grattoir-burin en silex paléolithiques à Flavigny-sur-Moselle. Bull. Acad. Soc. Lorraine Sci., 5:4, 286—294, 6 figs.

BOURDIER, FRANCK

1960C.	Evolution humaine et néotéme. Bull. Soc. Archéol. Hist. Chelles, 1960, 3—22, (not seen).
1960D.	Trois siècles d'hypothèses sur l'origine et la transformation des être vivants. Rev. Hist. Sci., 13, 1—44, (not seen).
1961	Le bassin du Rhone au Quaternaire: géologie et préhistoire. Tome I: texte. Paris: Editions du Centre National de la Recherche Scientifique, 364 pp.
1962C.	Le bassin du Rhone au Quaternaire: géologie et préhistoire. Tome II: figures, bibliographie, index. Paris: Éditions du Centre de la Recherche Scientifique, 295 pp., 297 figs.
	Rev.: Fink in Mitt. Geol. Ges. Wien, 57, 648—650; Hantke in Vierteljahreschr. Naturf. Ges. Zurich, 108, 486—487; Portmann in Ann. Guébhard, 40, 375.
1967	Préhistoire de France. Paris: Flammarion, 412 pp., 152 figs., (not seen).
	Rev.: Anon. in C. R. Soc. Géol. France, 1967:4, 146—147; Woldstedt in Eiszeit u. Gegenwart, 18, 242.
	See: Agache, Bourdier and Petit.

BOURDIER, F., and LACASSAGNE, H.

1964	Précisions nouvelles sur la stratigraphie et la faune du gisement villafranchien de Saint-Prest (Eure-et-Loir). Bull. Soc. Géol. France, 5, 446—453, 4 figs.

BOUSANI-BAUR, S. See: Portmann, A. 1965A.

BOUT, PIERRE

1964A.	Le Quaternaire du bassin supérieur de la Loire, des bassins moyen et

supérieur de l'Allier et de leurs marges.   Bull. Soc. Géol. France,
5, 472—482, 2 figs., 2 tables.

1964B.   Étude stratigraphique et paleogeographique du gisement de mammifères
fossiles Pléistocène moyen de Solilhac près le Puy-en-Velay
(Haute — Loire), France.   Geol. en Mijn, 43, 83—93, 3 figs.

BOUTEYRE, G.   See: Barrière, J. et al.

BOUVIER, EUGENE-LOUIS
1889   Les Cetaces souffleurs. Ecole superieure de pharmacie de Paris. These
presentee au concours d'agregation du 1er Mai 1889. Lille:
Bigot Freres, 218 + 1 pp.

BOUVIER, J.-M., and TRÉCOLLE, G.
1966   La frise gravée de Saint-Germain-la-Rivière. L'Anthrop., 70:5—6, 535—
540, 1 fig.

BOUYSSONIE, JEAN
1964   El Abate Henri Breuil. In: Ripoll Perelló, E., (ed.), 1964A, 283—287,
(English summary).

1966   Le film de Lascaux. Bull. Soc. Hist. Archéol. Périgord, 93, 204—205.

BOVA, BENJAMIN
1962   Giants of the animal world. Racine, Wis.: Whitman, 92 pp., illustr.,
(elemen. school).

1964   Reptiles since the world began. A Whitman Learn About Book. Illustrated by Stephan R. Peck. Racine, Wisconsin: Whitman Publ.
Co., 59 pp., color illustr.

BOWERS, ALFRED W., and SAVAGE, C. N.
1962   Primitive man on Brown's Bench — his environment and his record.
Inform. Circ., Idaho Bur. Mines, Geol., no. 14, 20 pp., 12 figs.,
4 tables, (not seen).

BOWLER, J. M., MULVANEY, D. J., CASEY, D. A., and DARRAGH, T. A.
1967   Green Gully burial. Nature, 213, 152—154, 2 figs.

BOWMAN, MERTON C.   See: Fox, R. and Bowman.

BOWMAN, ROBERT I., (ed.)
1966   The Galápagos. Proceedings of the Symposia of the Galápagos International Scientific Project. Berkeley, Calif.: Univ. Calif. Press,
xvii + 318 pp., illustr.
Rev.: Janzen in Syst. Zool., 16, 169—170.

BOYCE, A. J.
1964   The value of some methods of numerical taxonomy with reference to
hominoid classification. Publ. Syst. Assoc., no. 6, 47—65, 5 figs.

BOYER, DAVID S.
1966   Wyoming: high, wide, and windy. Natl. Geog. Mag., 129, 554—594,
illust.

BOYLAN, PATRICK J.
1967A.   Didermocerus Brooks, 1828, v. Dicerorhinus Gloger, 1841, (Mammalia:

Rhinocerotidae), and the validity of <u>A</u> <u>catalogue</u> <u>of</u> <u>the</u> <u>anatomi-</u><u>cal</u> <u>and</u> <u>zoological</u> <u>museum</u> <u>of</u> <u>Joshua</u> <u>Brookes,</u> 1828. Bull. Zool. Nomen., <u>124</u>, 55—56.

1967B.   Dean William Buckland, 1784 — 1856. A pioneer in cave science. Studies in Spel., <u>1</u>, 237—253, 3 figs., 1 pl.

BOYLE, MARY E.
1965   How the Duke of Berwick and Alba's English edition of <u>The</u> <u>Cavern</u> <u>of</u> <u>Altamira,</u> <u>at</u> <u>Santillana</u> <u>del</u> <u>Mar,</u> <u>Spain,</u> came to be written. In: Ripoll Perelló, E., (ed.), 1965B, XV — XXIII, 1 pl., (English and Spanish).

BOŽIČEVIĆ, S.   See: Malez and Božičević.

BR.
1961   Neandertaler — ein Schädelfund in Sud-China. Umschau, <u>61</u>, 44, 1 fig.

BRABANT, H.
1965   Observations sur l'évolution de la denture temporaire humaine en Europe occidentale. Bull. Groupement Internat. Recherch. Sci. Stomatol., <u>8</u>, 235—302, 20 figs., 14 tables. Rev.: Chamla in L'Anthrop, <u>70</u>:5—6, 562—564.
1967   Palaeostomatology. In: Brothwell, Don, and Sandison, A. T., (eds.), 538—550, 4 figs.

BRABANT, H., and KOVACS, I.
1961   Contribution à l'étude de la persistance du taurodontisme dans les races modernes et de sa parenté possible avec la racine pyramidale des molaires. Bull. Groupement Internat. Recherch. Sci. Stomatol., <u>4</u>, 232—286, 33 figs., (English, German and Spanish summaries).

BRABANT, H., and SAHLY, A.
1964   Etude des dents néanderthaliennes découvertes dans la grotte du Portel en Ariège (France). Bull. Groupement Internat. Recherch. Sci. Stomatol., <u>7</u>, 237—254, 7 figs., 6 tables, (English and German summaries). Rev.: ms in Archeol. Roz., <u>20</u>, 277.

BRABANT, H., and TWIESSELMANN, F.
1964   Observations sur l'évolution de la denture permanente humaine en Europe occidentale. Bull. Groupement Internat. Recherch. Sci. Stomatol., <u>7</u>, 11—84, 9 figs., 26 tables. Rev.: Chamla in L'Anthrop., <u>70</u>:5—6, 562—564.

BRACE, C. LORING
1964   The fate of the "Classic" Neanderthals: a consideration of hominid catastrophism, with comments by G. A. Agogino, D. R. Broth-well, W. E. Le Gros Clark, C. S. Coon, M. F. Farmer, S. Geno-vés T., R. D. Givens, F. C. Howell, W. W. Howells, G. H. R. von Koenigswald, G. Kurth, A. Montagu, H. Müller-Beck, K. J. Narr, A. Thoma, P. V. Tobias, and J. E. Weckler. Current Anthrop., <u>5</u>, 3—43, 10 figs., 2 tables.
1965A.   The dietary hypothesis and early hominid interpretations. Abs. 64th Ann. Meeting Amer. Anthrop. Assoc., <u>1965</u>, 9—10, (abs.).
1965B.   The dietary hypothesis and Australopithecine interpretations. Amer. Jour. Phys. Anthrop., <u>23</u>, 329, (abs.).

1967 The stages of human evolution: human and cultural origins. Englewood Cliffs, New Jersey: Prentice-Hall (Foundations of Modern
Anthropology Series), xi + 116 pp., illustr.
 Rev.: Campbell in Antiq., 42, 151—152; Davies in Mankind, 7:1, 75—
76; Simonds in Amer. Anthrop., 70, 1033.

1968 Ridiculed, rejected, but still our ancestor Neanderthal. Nat. Hist., 77:5,
38—45, illustr.

BRACE, C. L., HERSHKOVITZ, P., HAILMAN, J. P., KENNINGTON, G. S., and
OLSON, W. S.
1966 Whatever happened to hairy man? Science, 153, 362, 364.

BRACE, C. L., and MOLNAR, S.
1967 Experimental studies in human tooth wear: I. Amer. Jour. Phys.
Anthrop., 27, 213—221, 3 figs.

BRACE, C. L., and MONTAGU, M. F. A.
1965 Man's evolution: an introduction to physical anthropology. New York:
Macmillan, ix + 352 pp., 133 figs.
 Rev.: Ehrich in Human Biol., 38, 339—344; Hunt in Amer. Jour.
Phys. Anthrop., 24, 279—280.

BRADLEY, W. H.
1964 Geology of Green River Formation and associated Eocene rocks in
southwestern Wyoming and adjacent parts of Colorado and Utah.
U. S. Geol. Surv., Prof. Pap., 496A, 86 pp., 20 figs., 3 pls.

BRAGA, GIAMPIETRO
1966 Resti di pesci nei calcari dolomitici bituminosi del Trias superiore a sud
di Ampezzo Carnico (Alto Tagliamento). Atti Mem. Accad.
Patavina Sci. Let. Arti, Mem. Cl. Sci. Mat. Nat., 78:3, 329—337,
1 fig., 2 pls., (English summary).
 Rev.: Albanesi in Riv. Ital. Pal., 73, 388.

BRAIDWOOD, R. J., and HOWE, B.
1960 Rev.: Oates in Antiq., 35, 322—324.

BRAIN, C. K.
1965 Comments on a visit to Makapansgat Limeworks, December 1962. S.
Afr. Archaeol. Bull., 20:79, 110—111.
1967A. Procedures and some results in the study of Quaternary cave fillings.
Discussion. In: Bishop, W. W., and Clark, J. D., (eds.), 285—
301, 9 figs., 1 table, (French summary).
1967B. Part I. The site. In: Brain, C. K., and Cooke, C. K., 171—177, 5
figs.
1967C. Bone weathering and the problem of bone pseudo-tools. S. African
Jour. Sci., 63, 97—99, 3 figs.

BRAIN, C. K., and COOKE, C. K.
1967 A preliminary account of the Redcliff Stone Age cave site in Rhodesia.
S. Afr. Archaeol. Bull., 21, 171—182, 6 figs.

BRAIN, C. K., and MEESTER, J.
1964 Past climatic changes as biological isolating mechanisms in Southern
Africa. In: Davis, D. H. S., (ed.), Ecol. studies in So. Afr.,
332—340, 4 figs.

BRÄM, HEINRICH
1965   Die Schildkröten aus dem oberen Jura (Malm) der Gegend von Solo-
              thurn. Schweiz. Pal. Abh., 83, 1–190, 37 figs., 8 pls., 35 tables,
              (English summary).

BRAMLETTE, M. N.
1965   Mass extinctions of Mesozoic biota. Science, 150, 1240.

BRANDT, KARL
1966   Ein westfälischer Parallelfund zu den Spandauer Knochenartefakten.
              Berliner Jahrb. Vor – und Frühgesch., 6, 89–91, 1 pl.
1967   Halbierte Höhlenbärenfersen aus Westfalen und Süddeutschland. Eiszeit
              u. Gegenwart, 18, 110–112, 1 fig.
              Rev.: Ehrenberg in Zbl. Geol. Pal., Teil 2, 1969:6, 516.

BRANDTNER, F. J., et al.
1961   Abs.: Ebers in Zbl. Geol. Pal., Teil 2, 1964, 704–708.

BRANIŠA, LEONARDO, HOFFSTETTER, R., and SIGNEUX, J.
1964   Additions à la faune ichthyologique du Crétacé supérieur de Bolivie.
              Première partie. Caractères stratigraphiques, lithologiques et
              paléontologiques des gisements. Bull. Mus. Hist. Nat. Paris, 36,
              279–297, 3 figs., 1 pl.

BRANSON, CARL C.
1963*   Type species of Edestus Leidy. Okla. Geol. Notes, 23, 275–280, 3 figs.
1964A.   A Chinese edestid shark. Okla. Geol. Notes, 24, 78–80, 1 pl.
1964B.   Edestus giganteus Newberry is Edestus vorax Leidy. Okla. Geol. Notes,
              24, 103–106, 3 figs.
1964C.   Record of Edestus in Oklahoma. Okla. Geol. Notes, 24, 210, 1 fig.
1965A.   Geology of Byars fossil site. Okla. Geol. Notes, 25, 98.
1965B.   Petrodus in Oklahoma. Okla. Geol. Notes, 25, 274–275, 3 figs.
1966   Maurice G. Mehl – 1888 - 1966. Okla. Geol. Notes, 26, 139–140,
              portr.

BRASLIN, JOHN E.
1967   Sight plus sound at Yale's Peabody Museum. Museologist, no. 104,
              13–15.

BRATTSTROM, BAYARD H.
1964A.   Amphibians and reptiles from cave deposits in south-central New Mexico.
              Bull. S. Calif. Acad. Sci., 63, 93–103, 1 fig.
              Abs.: Nicholas in Internat. Jour. Spel., 1, 562–563.
1964B.   Evolution of the pit vipers. Trans. San Diego Soc. Nat. Hist., 13, 185–
              268, 41 figs.
1967   A succession of Pliocene and Pleistocene snake faunas from the high
              plains of the United States. Copeia, 1967, 188–202, 8 figs.,
              3 tables.

BRAUER, R.
1962   Abs.: Umschau, 63, 449.

BRAUN, PATRICK
1963   Formulaire technique d'anthropologie. 'Savoir en histoire naturelle',
              no. 26. Paris: Lechevalier, 262 pp., 50 figs., (not seen).

Rev.: Benoist in Anthropologica, 7:1, 157—158;   Furon in Rev. Gén.
Sci., 71, 184—185;   Hughes in Man, 65, 163—164;   Kaufmann
in Arch. Suiss. Anthrop. Gen., 30, 90.

BRAVO, T.   See: Zeuner and Bravo.

BRAY, ROBERT T.
1963   Comments on the preceramic in Missouri. Plains Anthrop., 8, 231—237.

BREED, WILLIAM J.
1967   Arizona's oldest amphibian. Plateau, 40, 68—71, 1 fig.

BREGER, IRVING A., (ed.)
1963   Organic geochemistry. Oxford: Pergamon, x + 658 pp., illustr.

BREITINGER, EMIL
1955C.   Der Saldanha Schädel aus der Kap-Provinz. Umschau, 55, 76—77, illustr.
1959   Rev.: Thenius in Zbl. Geol. Pal., Teil 2, 1959 (1960), 962—963.

BRENNAN, LOUIS A.
1960   Rev.: Bushnell in Antiq., 35, 70—71.
1963B.   Choppers: the Paleolithic strain. Bull. Eastern States Archeol. Fed.,
              no. 22, 10, (abs.).
1966   The earliest occupants — Paleo-Indian hunters. Bull. N. Y. State
              Archeol. Assoc., no. 36, 2—4.

BRESLER, JACK B., (ed.)
1966   Human ecology. Collected readings. Reading, Mass.: Don Mills; On-
              tario: Addison-Wesley, 472 pp., (not seen).
              Rev.: Bates in Amer. Anthrop., 69, 551—552; P. M. in Arch. Suiss.
              Anthrop. Gen., 31, 58.

BRETERNITZ, DAVID A.
1967   The prehistory of eastern Colorado, as seen from Boulder. Plains
              Anthrop., 12, 215, (abs.).

BREUIL, HENRI E. P.
1956G.   La caverne peinte de Lascaux, à Montignac (Dordogne). Cahiers Tech.
              de l'Art., 3:3, 5—16, 2 pls., (not seen).
1956H.   Objets inedits d'un gisement du Magdalénien VI de Limeuil (Dordogne).
              Mem. Serv. Invest. Arqueol. Asturias, 1, 119—121, 2 figs.
1960D.   Ma vie en Périgord, 1897-1959. Bull. Soc. Hist. Archéol. Périgord, 87,
              114—131.
1962B.   Les industries paléolithiques des plages quaternaires du Minho (La Sta-
              tion de Carreço). Avec la collaboration de A. Do Paço, O.
              Ribeiro, J. Roche, M. Vaultier, O. da Veiga Ferreira et G.
              Zbyszewski. Com. Serv. Geol. Portugal, 46, 53—131, pls. A—E,
              1—34.
1962C.   Théories et faits cantabriques relatifs au Paléolithique Supérieur et à
              son art des cavernes. Munibe, 14:3/4, 353—358.
1963B.   Théories et faits cantabriques relatifs au Paléolithique Supérieur et à
              son art A Pedro Bosch Gimpera en el septuagésimo aniversario
              de su nacimiento, 53—57, (not seen).
1964A.   Un grabado de reno posiblemente procedente del Bajo Aragón. In:
              Ripoll Perelló, E., (ed.), 1964A, xvii — xix, 1 fig.

1964B. L'Abbé Breuil visite les gisements préhistoriques du Congo Belge. In: Ripoll Perelló, E., (ed.), 1964A, 139—141.

1964C. Visite aux sites préhistoriques du Charbonnage de Luena. In: Ripoll Perelló, E., (ed.), 1964A, 142—144.

1964D. L'Abbé Breuil à Kansenia. In: Ripoll Perelló, E., (ed.), 1964A, 144—145.

1964E. Aperçu de la préhistoire du Congo austral en dehors du Katanga industriel. In: Ripoll Perelló, E., (ed.), 1964A, 145—152.

1965 Un terte retrouvé de l'abbé Breuil. L'Anthrop., 69, 386—388.

See: Cheynier and Breuil; Chollot 1964.

BREUIL, H., and ALMEIDA, A. de
1962 Introduction à la préhistoire de l'Angola. Proc. 4th Panafrican Congr. Prehist., Sec. 3, 203—205.

BREUIL, H., and LANTIER, R.
1959 Rev.: Vértes in Archaeol. Ert., 87, 99—100, (Hungarian).

1965 The men of the Old Stone Age (Palaeolithic and Mesolithic). Translated by B. B. Rafter. New York: St. Martin's Press, 272 pp., 16 pls.
Rev.: Anon. in Discovery, 27:2, 60; Coles in Antiq., 40, 237; Freeman in Amer. Anthrop., 68:4, 1075—1076; Sackett in Amer. Antiq., 32, 246.

BREWER, JESSE
1965 Suwannee point finds in Florida. Bull. Massachusetts Archaeol. Soc., 26, 17—19, 1 fig.

BRIEN, PAUL
1956 1856 - 1956. Acquisitions récentes de la paléontologie humaine. Naturalistes Belges, 37:4, 65—73.

1964A. Conclusions générales aux exposés de la journée du centenaire de la Société royale zoologique de Belgique. Ann. Soc. Roy. Zool. Belg., 94, 179—187.

1964B. Ethologie des Dipneustes en rapport avec les Vertébrés primitifs. Bull. Soc. Zool., France, 89, 271—310, 17 figs.

1967 L'évolution épigénétique. Référence à J. B. de Lamarck. L'Ann. Biol., 6, 465—482.

BRIGGS, J. E.
1961 Emendated generic names in Berg's Classification of Fishes. Copeia, 1961:2.

BRIGGS, L. CABOT
1956B. Initiation à l'anthropologie du squelette. Preface by H. Vallois. Libyca, 4, 9—56, 6 figs., 1 pl., 7 tables.

BRIGHT, ROBERT C.
1967 Late Pleistocene stratigraphy in Thatcher Basin, southeastern Idaho. Tebiwa, 10:1, 1—7, 2 figs.

BRIGOT, A., DUPORT, L., and GUILLIEN, Y.
1962 Découverte au Chatelard (commune de Puyréaux) d'un Elephas antiquus et d'un nucleus levallois. Note préliminaire. Mem. Soc. Archéol. Hist. Charente, 1961—1962, 47—51, 1 fig., 2 pls.

BRINK, ADRAIN SMUTS
1963A.   Abs.: Huene in Zbl. Geol. Pal., Teil 2, 1964, 987.
1963B.   Abs.: Huene in Zbl. Geol. Pal., Teil 2, 1964, 988.
1963C.   Abs.: Huene in Zbl. Geol. Pal., Teil 2, 1964, 988.
1963D.   Abs.: Huene in Zbl. Geol. Pal., Teil 2, 1964, 988–989.
1965A.   A new gomphodont cynodont from the Cynognathus zone of South
            Africa. Pal. Africana, 9, 97–105, figs. 41–43.
1965B.   On two new specimens of Lystrosaurus-zone cynodonts. Pal. Africana,
            9, 107–122, figs. 44–47.
1965C.   A new large bauriamorph from the Cynognathus-zone of South Africa.
            Pal. Africana, 9, 123–127, fig. 48.
1965D.   A new ictidosuchid (Scaloposauria) from the Lystrosaurus-zone. Pal.
            Africana, 9, 129–138, figs. 49–50.
1967   On monophyletic and polyphyletic origins of taxonomic groups. Colloq.
            Internat. Cent. Nation. Recherch. Sci., 163, 301–313, 5 figs.,
            (French summary).

BRINKMANN, ROLAND
1960   Geologic evolution of Europe. Translated by John C. Sanders. New
            York: Hafner, vi + 161 pp., 46 figs., 19 pls., 18 tables.

BRITT, CLAUDE, Jr.
1968   The Hopkins sites: multi-component sites in Miami County, Ohio.
            Ohio Archaeol., 18, 124–128, 3 figs., 3 tables.

BROCK, OSCAR W., Jr.
1967   Lamellar blades of possible Paleo-Indian provenience from Alabama.
            Jour. Ala. Archeol., 13, 99–109, 5 figs.

BROCK, O. W., Jr., and CLAYTON, M. V.
1966   Archaeological investigations in the Mud Creek-Town Creek drainage
            area of northwest Alabama. Jour. Ala. Archeol., 12, 79–137,
            31 figs., 11 tables.

BRÖCKELMANN, ST.   See: Koby and Bröckelmann.

BRODAL, ALF, and FÄNGE, R.
1963   The biology of Myxine. Oslo: Universitetsforlaget, xiii + 588 pp.,
            illustr.

BRODAR, MITJA
1962   Crvena stijena – 1958 und 1959. Glasnik Zemaljskog Muz. u Sara-
            jevu, Arheol., n.s. 17, 15–20, 4 pls. (Serbo-Croatian; German
            summary).
1963   Abs.: P. in Bull. Sci., Zagreb, Sec. A, 10, 296.
1965   [Chronology of Paleolithic cultures in Jugoslavia.] In: Bader, et al.,
            (eds.), 1965, 38–49, 5 figs., (Russian).

BRODAR, SREČKO
1955D.   Le Paléolithique du Karst yougoslave. In: Hadži (ed.), 1955, 79–87,
            (Jugoslavian; French summary).
1965   Traces de l'homme paléolithique dans la Grotte de Postojna. Bull. Sci.,
            Zagreb, Sec. A, 10, 325, (abs.).
1966   [Pleistocene deposits and Paleolithic findings in Postojnska Jama cave.]
            Poročila, Slov. akad. znan. in umetn., Razr. prirodosl. in med.

vede, <u>1966</u>:4, 51—138, figs., pls., tables, (Slovakian; German summary).

BRODKORB, PIERCE

1963C.   Abs.: Kuhn in Zbl. Geol. Pal., Teil 2, <u>1965</u>, 257—258.

1964A.   Catalogue of fossil birds: part 2 (Anseriformes through Galliformes). Bull. Florida State Mus., Biol. Sci., <u>8</u>, 195—335.
Rev.: Storer in Auk, <u>82</u>, 657—658.

1964B.   Fossil birds from Barbados, West Indies. Jour. Barbados Mus. Hist. Soc., <u>31</u>, 3—10, 1 pl.
Abs.: Kuhn in Zbl. Geol. Pal., Teil 2, <u>1966</u>, 311.

1964C.   A Pliocene teal from South Dakota. Quart. Jour. Florida Acad. Sci., <u>27</u>:1, 55—58, 1 fig.

1964D.   A new name for <u>Fulica minor</u> Shufeldt. Quart. Jour. Florida Acad. Sci., <u>27</u>, 186.
Abs.: Kuhn in Zbl. Geol. Pal., Teil 2, <u>1966</u>, 311.

1964E.   Notes on fossil turkeys. Quart. Jour. Florida Acad. Sci., <u>27</u>, 223—229, 1 pl.
Abs.: Kuhn in Zbl. Geol. Pal., Teil 2, <u>1966</u>, 311.

1965   New taxa of fossil birds. Quart. Jour. Florida Acad. Sci., <u>28</u>, 197—198.
Rev.: Kuhn in Zbl. Geol. Pal., Teil 2, <u>1967</u>, 210; Kuhn in Zbl. Geol. Pal., Teil 2, <u>1968</u>, 210.

1967   Catalogue of fossil birds. Part 3. (Ralliformes, Ichthyornithiformes, Chadariiformes). Bull. Florida State Mus., <u>11</u>, 99—220.
Rev.: Kuhn in Zbl. Geol. Pal., Teil 2, <u>1968</u>, 210.

BRODRICK, ALAN HOUGHTON

1963   Rev.: Burkitt in Nature, <u>202</u>, 942; Garrod in Antiq., <u>39</u>, 67—68; Gurnee in NSS News, <u>22</u>, 58; P. R. in Spelunca, Bull., <u>7</u>:2, 77; Sieveking in Archaeol. Jour., <u>123</u>, 226—227.

BROERS, C.-J.

1962   Quelques notions sur la morphologie de la région tympanale chez les Mammifères. C. R. Assoc. Anatomistes, no. <u>111</u>, 187—196, 6 figs.

BROGLIO, ALBERTO

1960B.   Ricerche statistiche sul Paleolitico superiore francese (Nota bibliografica). Rass. speleol. italiana, <u>12</u>, 206—209.

1961B.   Nota bibliografica sui problemi paletnologici e paleoantropologici connessi alla transizione dal Paleolitico medio al Paleolitico superiore. Rass. speleol. italiana, <u>13</u>, 54—64, 1 fig.

1964   Le industrie musteriane della Grotta del Broion. Mem. Mus. Civ. Storia Nat. Verona, <u>12</u>, 369—389, 9 figs., 3 pls., (French and English summaries).

1965   Il Riparo "Raffaello Battaglia" presso Asiago. Riv. Sci. Preist., <u>19</u>, 129—174, 23 figs., 2 tables, (French and English summaries).
See: Bartolomei and Broglio; Leonardi, P., Allegranzi and Broglio; Leonardi, P., Annibaldi, Broglio and Bartolomei; Leonardi, P., Bartolomei and Broglio; Leonardi, P. and Broglio; Leonardi, P., Broglio and Bosellini.

BROGLIO, A., LAPLACE, G., and ZORZI, F.

1963   I depositi quaternari del Ponte di Veia. Le industrie. Mem. Mus. Civ. Storia Nat. Verona, <u>11</u>, 325—367, 22 figs., 3 tables, (French and English summaries).

BROGLIO, A., and LEONARDI, P.
1964   Industria acheuleana in situ sul Monte Conero. Riv. Sci. Preist., 18,
              25–40, 11 figs., (French and English summaries).

BROIN, FRANCE de, and TAQUET, P.
1966   Découverte d'un crocodilien nouveau dans le Crétacé inferieur du Sahara.
              C. R. Acad. Sci. Paris, Sci. Nat., 262, 2326–2329, 1 fig.

BRONOWSKI, J.
1965   The identity of man. Garden City: The Natural History Press, xi +
              107 pp.

BRONOWSKI, V., and HAUTECOEUR, G.
1966A.   New sections of the Archaeological and Folklore Museum, Verviers,
              Belgium. Mus. UNESCO, 19, 62–63, 2 figs.
1966B.   Nouvelles sections au Musée d'archéologie et de folklore de Verviers
              (Belgique). Mus. UNESCO, 19, 63–64, 1 fig.

BROOKES, JOSHUA   See: Boylan 1967A.

BROOKS, H. K.
1965   Underwater paleontological collecting techniques. In: Kummel and
              Raup, (eds.), 1965, 168–175.

BROOKS, RICHARD A.   See: Heizer and Brooks.

BROOKS, RICHARD H.
1967   A comparative analysis of bone from Locality 2 (C1–245), Tule Springs,
              Nevada. In: Wormington, and Ellis, (eds.), 1967, 401–411, 2
              pls.

BROOKS, R. H., ORLINS, R., and WILLIAMS, P.
1967   Locality 2 (C1–245), Tule Springs, Nevada. In: Wormington, and
              Ellis, (eds.), 1967, 331–351, 7 figs., 5 pls.

BROSEMER, CHARLES V.   See: Duncan and Brosemer.

BROTHWELL, Don
1962B.   The scientific revolution in archaeology. Discovery, 23:8, 22–27, 5
              figs.
1963C.   Rev.: Bauer in Mitt. Anthrop. Ges. Wien, 93–94, 180; [Jelinek] in
              Anthrop., 2:1, 82, (Czech);   McCartney in Arkansas Archeolo-
              gist, 5, 74–78;   Morse in Jour. Ala. Archaeol., 9, 78–79:
              Preuschoft in Anthrop. Anz., 28, 38–39;   S. in Archeol. Roz.,
              17, 119, (Czech);   Schaeuble in Zeit. Morph. Anthrop., 54,
              112–113.
1963E.   Rev.: Brown in Mankind, 6:3, 141–142;   Keresztesi in Mitt. Anthrop.
              Ges. Wien, 93–94, 149–150;   Knussmann in Homo, 16, 120.
1965   On the accidental discovery of human remains in caves and rock-shelters.
              Studies in Spel., 1, 135–142, fig. 19, pl. 22.
1967   The bio-cultural background to disease. In: Brothwell, Don, and
              Sandison, A. T., (eds.), 56–68, 7 figs., 1 table.
              See: Brace 1964; Hughes and Brothwell.

BROTHWELL, D., and HIGGS, E., (eds.)

1963   Rev.: Anon. in Sci. Amer., 211:2, 113—114; Atkinson in Proc. Prehist. Soc. Cambridge, 31, 390—392; Barker in Mus. Jour., London, 64, 92—93; Corwin in Amer. Jour. Archaeol., 70, 199; Goodman in Ohio Archaeol., 15, 75; Meighan in Science, 143, 120—121; Palmer in Asian Perspectives, 8:1, 129—131; [Picard] in Rev. Archéol., 1965:1, 218—219; M. R. in Man in India, 47, 74—75; Stloukal in Anthrop., 2:3, 95.

BROTHWELL, D., and SANDISON, A. T., (eds.)

1967   Diseases in antiquity. A survey of the diseases, injuries and surgery of early populations. Springfield, Ill.: Thomas, xx + 766 pp., illustr.

      Rev.: Dastugue in L'Anthrop., 73:3—4, 291—293; Johnson in Amer. Anthrop., 71, 170—172; Kerley in Science, 161, 873—874; Krogman in Amer. Jour. Phys. Anthrop., 29, 105—106; MacConaill in Man, Jour. Roy. Anthrop. Inst., 3, 489; Vogel in Zeit. Morph. Anthrop., 60:3, 335.

BROUGH, MARGARET C., and BROUGH, J.

1967   Studies of early Tetrapods. I. The lower Carboniferous microsaurs. II. Microbrachis, the type microsaur. III. The genus Gephyrostegus. Phil. Trans. Roy. Soc. London, 252:776, 107—165, 10 figs.

BROUWER, A.

1967   General palaeontology. Translated by R. H. Kaye. Edinburgh and London: Oliver and Boyd, viii + 216 pp., illustr.

      Rev.: Ager in Earth-Sci. Rev., 3:4, A243—A245; Anon. in Earth Sci. Jour., 1, 181; G. Y. C. in Geol. Mag., 104, 412; Horowitz in Jour. Pal., 42, 604; House in Nature, 214, 1276—1277; Reed in Archaeol., 23:4, 351; Stehli in Palaeogeog., Palaeoclimatol., Palaeoecol., 4:1, 68—69; Voorthuysen in Geol. en Mijn., 47, 219.

BROWN, D. A. See: Irving and Brown.

BROWN, DONALD FREEMAN, (ed.)

1959A.   [COWA surveys and bibliographies.] Area 3 — western Europe. COWA Surv. and Bibliog., Area 3, no. 1, 24 + 34 pp.

1959B.   [COWA surveys and bibliographies.] Area 4 — western Mediterranean. COWA Surv. and Bibliog., Area 4, no. 1, 15 + 24 pp.

1962   COWA surveys and bibliographies. Area 3 — western Europe. COWA Surv. and Bibliog., Area 3, no. 2, 13 + 20 pp.

1964   COWA surveys and bibliographies. Area 4 — western Mediterranean. COWA Surv. and Bibliog., Area 4, no. 2, 23 + 24.

BROWN, JOHN ALLEN

1886B.   Report on the fossils of the district. Ann. Rept. Ealing Microscopical Nat. Hist. Soc., 1885—6, 2—5, (not seen).

1887   Palaeolithic man in N. W. Middlesex. London: Macmillan, iii + 227 + 4 pp., frontispiece + 8 pls.

BROWN, J. CLEVEDON

1957   Palaeolithic and other implements from the Shirehampton district. Proc. Univ. Bristol Speleol. Soc., 8, 43—44.

BROWN, JACK, and GOULD, R. A.
    1964   Column chromatography and the possibility of carbon-lens migration
              Amer. Antiq., 29, 387—389, 2 figs.

BROWN, LEWIS
    1968   The importance of proper tripods. Curator, 11, 7—32, 15 figs.

BROWN, ROLAND W.
    1962   Paleocene flora of the Rocky Mountains and Great Plains. U. S. Geol.
              Surv., Prof. Pap., 375, iv + 119 pp., 69 pls.

BROWNE, W. R.
    1963   Some problems of dating the past. In: Sheils, H., (ed.), 1963, 57—
              78.

BRUCE-MITFORD
    1961   Prehistoric and Romano-British antiquities in the British Museum. An-
              tiq., 35, 313—314.

BRUEMMER, FRED
    1968   Ill shapen beast. Nat. Hist., 77:3, 40—45, 3 figs., cover.

BRUES, ALICE M.
    1966   "Probable mutation effect" and the evolution of hominid teeth and
              jaws. Amer. Jour. Phys. Anthrop., 25, 169—170.

BRUES, A. M., and SNOW, C. C.
    1965   Physical anthropology. In: Siegel, B. J., (ed.), 1—39.

BRUIJN, H. de
    1966A.   Some new Miocene Gliridae (Rodentia, Mammalia) from the Calatayud-
               area (Prov. Zaragoza, Spain. I. II.) Proc. K. Nederl. Akad. Wet.,
               69, 58—78, 2 pls.
    1966B.   On the mammalian fauna of the Hipparion-beds in the Calatayud-Teruel
               Basin (Prov. Zaragoza, Spain). II. The Gliridae (Rodentia).
               Proc. K. Nederl. Akad. Wet., 69, 367—387, 2 pls.
               Rev.: Fahlbusch in Zbl. Geol. Pal., Teil 2, 1967, 117—118.
    1966C.   On the Pleistocene Gliridae (Mammalia, Rodentia) from Malta and
               Mallorca. Proc. K. Nederl. Akad. Wet., 69:4, 480—496, 3 figs.,
               3 pls.
               Rev.: Fahlbusch in Zbl. Geol. Pal., Teil 2, 1967, 519.

BRUIJN, H. de, and MEIN, P.
    1968   On the mammalian fauna of the Hipparion-beds in the Calatayud-Teruel
              Basin. V. The Sciurinae. Proc. K. Nederl. Akad. Wet., Ser. B,
              71:1, 73—90, 1 fig., 2 pls., 1 table.

BRUIJN, H. de, and MEURS, A. P. H. van
    1967   A biometrical study of the third premolar of Lagopsis and Prolagus
              (Ochotonidae, Lagomorpha, Mammalia) from the Neogene of the

Calatayud-Teruel basin (Aragon, Spain). I & II. Proc. K. Nederl. Akad. Wet., ser. B, 70:2, 113—125 and 126—143, 13 figs., 5 tables.

BRUN, R.
1960   Note sur quelques fossiles quaternaires de la sablière de Macé. Bull. Soc. Linn. Normandie., 10, 57—59.

BRUNA, M.
1963   De plaats van de mens in de natur. Natuurhist. Maandbl., 52, 153—155.

BRUNET, JEAN
1961   Le gisement de vertèbres miocènes de Beni Mellal (Maroc). Oiseaux. Notes Mém. Serv. Géol. Maroc, 155, 105—108, 4 figs.
1967   Geologic studies. In: Byers, D. S., (ed.), 66—90, 26 figs.
1968   The Pliocene rhinoceroses of Mexico. Program, 1968 Ann. Meetings, Geol. Soc. Amer., 1968, 40, (abs.).

BRUNET, MICHEL
1966   Les oiseaux. In: Lavocat, R., (ed.), 1966, 463—469, pls. 134—135.
1968   Découverte d'un crâne d'Anthracotheriidae, Microbunodon minimum (Cuvier), à la Milloque (Lot-et-Garonne). C. R. Acad. Sci. Paris, Sci. Nat., 267, 835—838, 1 pl.

BRUNET, M., and GUTH, C.
1968A.   Découverte d'un crâne de rhinocérotidé, Ronzotherium filholi, dans le Stampien inférieur de Villebramar (Lot-et-Garonne). C. R. Acad. Sci. Paris, Sci. Nat., 266, 573—575, 1 pl.
1968B.   Découverte d'un gisement de vertèbres dans le Calcaire de Castillon à Saint-Capraise-d'Eymet (Dordogne). C. R. Acad. Sci. Paris, Sci. Nat., 266, 2059—2060, 1 pl.

BRUNETT, FEL V.
1966   An archaeological survey of the Manistee River basin: Sharon, Michigan to Sherman, Michigan. In: Fitting, James E., (ed.), 169—182, 4 figs.

BRUNNACKER, KARL   See: Basler, Malez and Brunnacker; Heller, F. and Brunnacker.

BRYAN, ALAN LYLE
1964   New evidence concerning early man in North America. Man, 64, 152—153.
1965   Paleo-American prehistory. Occ. Pap. Idaho State Coll. Mus., no. 16, 247 pp., illustr.
        Rev.: Neuman in Plains Anthrop., 11, 231—233; Roosa in Mich. Archaeol., 12, 40; Stephenson in Amer. Antiq., 31, 589—590; Wendorf in Science, 151, 1212; Wood in Mo. Archaeol. Soc. Newsletter, no. 198, 3—4.
1967   The first people. In: Hardy, (ed.), 1967, 277—293, illustr.
    See: Swanson and Bryan.

BRYANT, LAURIE J.
1968   A new genus of mustelid from the Ellensburg formation, Washington. Contrib. Sci., Los Angeles Co. Mus., no. 139, 1—6, 2 figs., 2 tables.

BRYSON, R. A.   See: Bender, et al.

BRZOBOHATÝ, ROSTISLAV R.
1964A.   [Bemerkunger zur Erforschung der Fisch-Otolithen aus dem westkarpa-
                   thischen Tertiär.]   Zprávy Geol. Výzkumech Roce, 1963, 1,
                   275–276, (Czech.).
                   Abs.: Weiler in Zbl. Geol. Pal., Teil 2, 1965, 220.
1964B.   [Vorbericht über die Erforschung der Fisch-Otolithen aus den tertiären
                   Ablagerungen des Kartenblattes Zidlochovice-Seelowitz.]   Zprávy
                   Geol. Výzkumech Roce, 1963, 1, 236–238, (Czech.).
                   Abs.: Weiler in Zbl. Geol. Pal., Teil 2, 1965, 220.
1965   Fisch-Otolithen (Pisces, Teleostei) aus dem Karpatien von Nosislav (Mittel-
                   miozän, Südmähren). Čas. Morav. Mus. Brně, Sci. Nat., 50, 107–
                   128, 1 fig., 2 pls.
                   Abs.: Weiler in Zbl. Geol. Pal., Teil 2, 1966, 272–273.
1967A.   Die Fisch-Otolithen aus den Pouzdřany-Schichten. Čas. Morav. Mus.
                   Brně, Sci. Nat., 52, 121–168, 2 figs., 9 pls., 1 map, 3 tables,
                   (Czech. summary).
                   Rev.: Weiler in Zbl. Geol. Pal., Teil 2, 1968:6, 642.
1967B.   Ergebnisse der Erforschung von Fischotolithen aus dem Oligozän und
                   Miozän Südmährens. Spisy Přirodov. Fak. Brno, 1967:4, 152–
                   153.
                   Rev.: Weiler in Zbl. Geol. Pal., Teil 2, 1968:6, 643.

BUACHIDZE, Ts. I. (= Buatshidze, C.)
1968   [On the finding of fossil vole remains in the Shirak steppe.]   Soob.
                   Akad. Nauk Gruz. SSR, 52:2, 503–508, 3 figs., (Russian; Geor-
                   gian summary).

BUBENÍK, VON A., and WURTZINGER, H.
1967   Beidseitiger erster Prämolar im Unterkiefer des Rehes, Capreolus
                   capreolus Linné, 1758. Säugetierkundl. Mitt., 15, 35–39, 8 figs.,
                   (English summary).

BUBLICHENKO, N. L.
1961   [From past to present in paleontological study of Kazakhstan (40 years
                   of Soviet Union).]   Trudy Vses. Paleont. Obshch., IV sess., 125–
                   141, (Russian).

BUCHAN, S. H., CHALLINOR, A., HARLAND, W. B., and PARKER, J. R.
1965   The Triassic stratigraphy of Svalbard. Norsk Polarinst. Skrift., no. 135,
                   1–94, 27 figs.

BUDAY, T., CICHA, I., CTYROKY, P., and FEJFAR, O.
1964   Die Stellung des Neogens der Westkarpaten in der Paratethys. Cursillos
                   y Confer. Inst. "Lucas Mallada", 9, 109–116.

BUD'KO, V. D.
1964   [Concerning the dwellings on the Berdyzh Paleolithic site.]   Krat. Soob.
                   Inst. Ist. Mat. Kult. SSSR, 101, 31–34, 1 fig., (Russian).
1965   [Upper Paleolithic settlement Eliseevichi.]   Dokl. Akad. Nauk BSSR,
                   9:10, 705–707, 2 figs., (Russian).
1966   [Upper Paleolithic of the northwest of the Russian Plain.]   In:
                   Rybakov, (ed.), 38–40, (Russian).
1967A.   [A new construction of mammoth bones on the site Iudinovo I.]   Dokl.
                   Akad. Nauk BSSR, 11:7, 651–653, 2 figs., (Russian).

1967B.   [Iudinovo Upper Paleolithic site.] In: Rybakov, (ed.), 27—29, 2 figs.,
            (Russian).

1967C.   [Belorussian archeological expedition.] In: Rybakov, (ed.), 259—266,
            2 figs., (Russian).

1968   [Upper Paleolithic site Studenets.] In: Rybakov, (ed.), 244, (Russian).

BUDYKO, M. I.
1967   [Causes of extinction of some animals at the end of Pleistocene.] Izv.
            Akad. Nauk SSSR, ser. Geograf., 1967:2, 28—36, (Russian).

BUETTNER-JANUSCH, J., (ed.)
1963A.   Rev.: Bourlière in Terre et Vie, 112, 188—189; Barnicot in Sci.
            Progress, 52, 331; Erikson in Science, 145, 256—257; Gavan
            in Amer. Anthrop., 67, 511—513; Heberer in Anthrop. Anz.,
            27, 233—234; Roth-Lutra in Anat. Anz., 120, 102—103;
            Tappen in Human Biol., 38, 155—160; Tétry in L'Ann. Biol.,
            Ser. 4, 3, 585—586.

1964   Evolutionary and genetic biology of Primates. Vol. 2. New York and
            London: Academic Press, xii + 330 pp., illustr.
            Rev.: Ankel in Homo, 17:1, 62; Ferm in Quart. Rev. Biol., 40,
            379—380; Goustard in L'Ann. Biol., 5, 298—299.

1966   Origins of man: physical anthropology. New York: John Wiley &
            Sons, xxviii + 674 pp., illustr. with figs. and tables.
            Rev.: Givins in Amer. Jour. Phys. Anthrop., 25, 101—102; McKern
            in Human Biol., 39, 203—204; Miele in Mankind Quart., 7,
            61—62; Preuschoft in Anthropol. Anz., 31:1—2, 107—108;
            Roberts in Amer. Anthrop., 70, 167—168; Sunderland in Man,
            Jour. Roy. Anthrop. Inst., 1, 562; Vallois in L'Anthrop., 71:
            5—6, 525—527; Vogel in Zeit. Morph. Anthrop., 60:3, 334—
            335; Weiner in Nature, 212, 1521; Wheeler in Quart. Rev.
            Biol., 328—329; Wiener in Amer. Jour. Phys. Anthrop., 25,
            194—195.

1967   Hemoglobin and primate evolution. In: Starck, D., Schneider, R.,
            and Kuhn, H. J., (eds.), 357—361, 1 table.

BUGIANASHVILI, T. V., DEDABRISHVILI, SH. SH., PITSKHELAURI, K. N.,
RAMISHVILI, R. M., CHIKOIDZE, Ts. N., and GEZELISHVILI, I. A.
1968   [Research in the zone of upper Alazan' irrigation system under con-
            struction.] In: Rybakov, (ed.), 291—293, (Russian).

BUGYI, BLASIUS
1963   Zur Methodik einer Palaoendokrinologie des Menschen. Ber. 7.
            Tagung Deutsch Ges. Anthrop., 1961, 155—159.

BUKATCHUK, P. D., BURDENKO, B. V., NEGADAEV-NIKONOV, K. N. and
TAPTYKOVA, M. F.
1967   [On the stratigraphic position of the so-called Kuchurgan Sandstone.]
            Pal. geol. polezn. iskop. Moldavii, 2, 159—169, (Russian).

BUKATCHUK, P. D., and NEGADAEV-NIKONOV, K. N.
1968   [Alluvial Pliocene formations of Moldavian SSR.] Izv. Akad. Nauk
            Moldav. SSR, ser. Biol. i Khim. Nauk, 1968:3, 81—85,
            (Russian).

BULLEN, RIPLEY   See: Lazarus, Fairbanks and Bullen.

BULMER, SUSAN AND RALPH
1964   The prehistory of the Australian New Guinea Highlands. In: Watson,
            J. B., (ed.), 39–76, 4 figs.

BÜLOW, KURD VON
1962B.   Johannes Walther, der Begrunder der Biogeologie. Gedenkworte zu
            seinem 25. Todestag. Ber. Geol. Ges. Deutsch. Demokratischen
            Republ., 6, 373–382, portr.

BUNAK, VICTOR VALERIANOVICH
1959B.   Present state of the problem of the origin of speech and the early
            stages of its evolution. Cahiers Hist. Mond., 5, 312–324, 2
            tables.
1959C.   [The human skull and stages in its formation in fossil man and pres-
            ent-day races.]   Trudy Inst. Etnogr., 49, 283 pp., 89 figs.,
            35 tables, (Russian).
            Rev.: Ginsburg in Voprosy Antrop., no. 5, 144–150, (Russian);
            Schreider in L'Anthrop., 64, 347–349.
1966A.   [A short review of the taxonomic and phyletic schemes of hominids.]
            Trudy Inst. Etnog. Akad. Nauk SSSR, 92, 273–284, 3 figs.,
            3 tables, (Russian).
1966B.   [The braincase.]   Trudy Inst. Etnog. Akad. Nauk SSSR, 92, 285–309,
            12 figs., 3 tables, (Russian).
1966C.   [Speech and intellect, stages in their development in anthropogenesis.]
            Trudy Inst. Etnog. Akad. Nauk SSSR, 92, 497–555, 19 figs.,

            1 table, (Russian).

1968   [On the evolution of the form of human skull.]   Voprosy Antrop.,
            30, 3–16, 1 table, (Russian).

BUNAK, V. V., et al., (eds.)
1966   [Fossil hominids and the origin of man.]   Trudy Inst. Etnog. Akad.
            Nauk SSSR, 92, 558 pp., illustr., (Russian).
            Rev.: Krukoff in L'Anthrop., 71: 5–6, 537–539;   Schaeuble in Zeit.
            Morph. Anthrop., 59, 221–222;   Schwidetzky in Homo, 18:2,
            114;   Zalkind in Voprosy Antrop., 27, 182.

BUNZL, FRIDO   See: Augusta and Burian, 1962D, 1964A.

BURCHAK-ABRAMOVICH, M. O., and KOROTKEVICH, O. L.
1966   [Proboscidians of Hipparion fauna from Nova Emetovka village.] In:
            Voinstvenskiĭ, M. A., (ed.), 97–109, 6 figs., 2 tables, (Ukrainian;
            Russian summary).

BURCHAK-ABRAMOVICH, N. I.
1951D.   [History of terrestrial vertebrate fauna of Azerbaĭdzhan.] In: Alizade
            et al., (eds.), 7–33, 1 fig., (Russian).
1953C.   [Fossil ostriches from Caucasus and South of Ukraine.]   Trudy Estestv.-
            Istor. Muzeĭa Zardabi, 7, 206 pp., 18 pls., 22 tables, (Russian).
1958   [Tertiary birds from USSR.]   Uch. zapiski Azerb. Un., ser. biol., 1958:
            1, 81–88, 1 fig., (Russian).
1962B.   [New data on Binagady birds.]   Ornitologiĭa, 4, 458–464, (Russian).
1963B.   [Research on the causes of extinction of certain representatives of
            ratites.]   Nauchn. Sess. Inst. Paleobiol. AN Gruz. SSR, 9, 8–9,
            (Russian).

1964A. [Upper Tertiary beaver — Trogontherium (Trogontherium Cuvieri Fisch) in Azerbaidzhan (Guzun — Tapa).] Dokl. Akad. Nauk. Azerbaid. SSR, 20: 7, 43—46, 2 figs., 1 table, (Russian; Azerbaidzhani summary).

1964B. [History of evolution of oxen of subfamily Bovinae in the Caucasus and their relationship to oxen of adjoining countries.] In: Orlov, (ed.), 1964C, 27—36, (Russian; English summary).

1964C. [On progressive traits in the development of birds (Aves).] Nauchn. Sess. Inst. Paleobiol. AN Gruz. SSR, 10, 27—28, (Georgian and Russian).

1965A. [Research on intraspecific variations of Pleistocene Binagadi birds.] Nauchn. Sess. Inst. Paleobiol. AN Gruz. SSR, 11, 22—23, (Georgian and Russian).

1965B. [New species of fossil horned owl from Binagady.] Ornitologiia, 7, 452—454, (Russian).

1966A. [Binagady birds (some results of their study).] Biull. Mosk. Obshch. Prirody, Otd. Biol., 71:3, 129—132, (Russian).

1966B. [On the problem of extinction of some representatives of unkeeled birds in past and present.] Obshchie Vopr. Evoliuts. Paleobiol., 2, 30—48, 1 fig., 2 pls., (Russian; Georgian summary).

1966C. [Dinotherium in Caucasus.] Izv. Akad. Nauk Azerb. SSR, ser. Nauk o Zemle, 1966:2, 11—18, 2 figs., 1 table, (Russian).

1966D. [Birds of Gvardzhilas-Klde cave Late Paleolithic site in Imereti.] Peshchery Gruzii, 4, 93—110, 1 pl., 9 tables, (Russian; Georgian summary).

1966E. [Upper Tertiary birds of Caucasus.] Soob. Akad. Nauk Gruz. SSR, 44:3, 651—656, (Russian; Georgian summary).

1967 [Fossil primates from the USSR (Moldavia, Ukraine, Georgia) and the ecologic environment of their habitat.] In: Collected Papers: [Place and significance of fossil mammals of Moldavia in the Cenozoic of USSR], 89—99, (Russian).

BURCHAK-ABRAMOVICH, N. I., and DZHAFAROV, R. D.
1951 [On differences in metapodial bones (Mtp) of rhinoceros of the genus Rhinoceros.] Trudy Estestv.-Istor. Muzeia Zardabi, 4, 5—27, 14 figs., (Russian; Azerbaijan summary).

1965 [On the discovery of the species Sus apscheronicus in the Quaternary deposits of Apsheron.] Izv. Akad. Nauk Azerbaidzhan, SSR, Ser. Geol.-Geogr. Nauk, 1965:2, 19—30, 2 figs., 2 tables, (Russian; Azerbaijan summary).

BURCHAK-ABRAMOVICH, N. I., and GABASHVILI, E. G.
1968 [Primitive ox in Hipparion fauna of Udabno (East Georgia).] Pal. Zhurnal, 1968:1, 144—148, 4 figs., (Russian).

BURCHAK-ABRAMOVICH, N. I., and GADZHIEV, D. V.
1962 [Find of the river beaver Castor fiber L. in Azerbaijani.] Dokl. Akad. Nauk Azerbaid. SSR, 18:12, 63—67, 2 figs., 1 table, (Russian; Azerbaijani summary).

BURCHAK-ABRAMOVICH, N. I., and GAMBAROV, K. M.
1964 [New data on Archaeopteryx (discovery of a third skeleton).] Uch. zapiski Azerb. Un., ser. biol., 1964:3, 41—52, 3 figs., (Russian).

BURCHAK-ABRAMOVICH, N. I., and KON'KOVA, N. I.
1967   [Finds of fossil ostriches in Mold. SSR and other localities of USSR.]
             Pal. geol. polezn. iskop. Moldavii, 2, 146–156, (Russian).

BURCHAK-ABRAMOVICH, N. I., and SULTANOV, K. M.
1965   [Trogontherium-beaver (Trogontherium cuvieri Fisch.) in Western
             Azerbaidjan (Palan-Tiukan).]   Uch. Zap. Azerbaidzhan. Gos.
             Univ., ser. geol.-geogr., 1965:3, 3–7, 2 figs., 1 table, (Russian).

BURCHAK-ABRAMOVICH, N. O.
1950   [Orycteropus gaudryi F. M. in USSR and adjoining lands.] Izv. Akad.
             Nauk Armian. SSR, Ser. Biol.-Ist.-Kh., 3:10, 949–954, 1 fig.,
             1 table, (Russian; Armenian summary).

BURCHAK-ABRAMOVICH, N. O., and GABASHVILI, E. G.
1945   [A higher man-like ape from the Upper Tertiary of eastern Georgia.]
             Soob. Akad. Nauk Gruz. SSR, 6:6, 451–464, 7 figs., 1 table,
             (Georgian; Russian and English summaries).

BURDENKO, B. V.   See: Bukatchuk, Burdenko, et al.

BURGER, CARL
1965   All about elephants. Foreword by F. Osborn. New York: Random
             House, 132 pp., illustr., juv., (not seen).
             Rev.: Anon. in Sci. Amer., 213:6, 115.

BURIAN, ZDENEK   See: Augusta and Burian.

BURKITT, MILES
1963   Rev.: Smith in Anthropologica, n.s., 6, 253–255.
1964A.   The Abbé Breuil. In: Ripoll Perelló, E., (ed.), 1964A, 289–291,
             (Spanish summary).
1964B.   Archaeology in Sarawak. Nature, 201, 564.
1965   Philosophies of Pierre Teilhard de Chardin. Nature, 207, 139–140.

BURNABY, T. B.   See: Craig, G. Y. 1966B, C.

BURNS, ALICE M.
1967   Pebble tool traits on other than pebbles. Anthrop. Jour. Canada, 5:2,
             16–18, 1 fig.

BURR, WINTHROP A., and GERSON, D. E.
1965   Venn diagrams and human taxonomy. Amer. Anthrop., 67, 494–499,
             2 figs.

BURTON, MAURICE
1966   Ichthyosaur: 1811 and 1966. Illustr. London News, 249: 6637, 18.
             illustr.

BURTON, VIRGINIA LEE
1962   Life story. New York: Houghton Mifflin, 72 pp., color illustr., (pre-
             and elemen. school).

BURYKHIN, I. V.
1954   [Vladimir Afanas'evich Obruchev (90th birthday).]   Trudy Inst. Geol.,
             Kirg. Filial AN SSSR, 5, 3–7, (Russian).

BUSH, HELEN
    1960   Fossil discovery in Peru. Canadian Geog. Jour., 60, 176–181, illustr.
    1966   Mary Anning's treasures. Illustr. by P. A. Hutchinson. New York:
                McGraw-Hill, 144 pp., illustr., (not seen).
                Rev.: Anon. in Canadian Geog. Jour., $\underline{73}$:1, VI.

BUSHNELL, GEOFFREY
    1961   Radiocarbon dates and New World chronology. Antiq., $\underline{35}$, 286–291.

BUSHNELL, G. H. S.
    1966   Early Man in Peru. Antiq., $\underline{40}$, 63–64.

BUTLER, B. ROBERT
    1964   A recent Early Man point find in southeastern Idaho. Tebiwa, $\underline{7}$, 39–
                40, 1 fig.
    1965   Contributions to the archaeology of southeastern Idaho. Tebiwa, $\underline{8}$,
                41–48, 5 figs.
    1968   An introduction to archaeological investigations in the Pioneer Basin
                locality of eastern Idaho. Tebiwa, $\underline{11}$:1, 1–30, frontispiece,
                12 figs.

BUTLER, B. R., and FITZWATER, R. J.
    1965   A further note on the Clovis site at Big Camas Prairie, southcentral
                Idaho. Tebiwa, $\underline{8}$, 38–40, 2 figs.
                See: Swanson, Butler and Bonnichsen.

BUTLER, MARY   See: Sibley 1967.

BUTLER, PERCY MILTON
    1965A.   East African Miocene and Pleistocene chalicotheres. Brit. Mus. Nat.
                Hist., Fossil Mamm. Afr., no. $\underline{18}$, 163–237, 26 figs., 10 tables.
                Rev.: M. C. in Fossilia, $\underline{1965}$: 5–6, 70–71.
    1965B.   Chalicotheriidae. In: Leakey, et al, 1965, 26.
    1967A.   The prenatal development of the human first upper permanent molar.
                Arch. Oral Biol., $\underline{12}$, 551–563, 23 figs., (French and German
                summaries).
    1967B.   Relative growth within the human first upper permanent molar during
                the prenatal period. Arch. Oral Biol., $\underline{12}$, 983–992, 4 figs., 3
                tables, (French and German summaries).
    1967C.   Comparison of the development of the second deciduous molar and
                first permanent molar in man. Arch. Oral Biol., $\underline{12}$, 1245–1260,
                6 figs., 3 tables, (French and German summaries).
    1967D.   Dental merism and tooth development. Jour. Dental Res., $\underline{46}$, 845–
                850, 3 figs.
                See: Marshall and Butler; Van Valen, Butler, et al.

BUTLER, P. M., et al.
    1967   Mammalia. In: Harland, W. B., et al., (eds.), 763–787, 3 figs.

BUTLER, P. M., and GREENWOOD, M.
    1965   Insectivora. Chiroptera. In: Leakey, et al., 1965, 13–15.

BUTOMO, S. V.
1965   [Radiocarbon dating and construction of an absolute chronological scale for archeological relics.] In: Kolchin, (ed.), 1965, 28–34, 4 figs., (Russian).

BUTTIN, FRANÇOIS
1965   Les propulseurs de Léonard de Vinci. Bull. Soc. Préhist. Franç., Étud. et Trav., 61, 56–64, 4 figs.

BUTTS, LESLIE H.
1962   Photographic artifacts. Newsletter Okla. Anthrop. Soc., 10:4, 1–6, 4 figs.

BUTZER, KARL W.
1964   Environment and archeology: an introduction to Pleistocene geography. Chicago: Aldine, xviii + 524 pp., 84 figs., 19 tables.
        Rev.: Bourlière in Terre et Vie, 112, 297–298; Clark in Amer. Anthrop., 67, 1331–1333; Collins in Discovery, 27:1, 49–50; Cornwall in Proc. Prehist. Soc. Cambridge, 31, 389–390; Dimbleby in Man, Jour. Roy. Anthrop. Inst., 1, 108; Ehrich in Archaeol., 19, 221–222; Flannery in Amer. Jour. Archaeol., 69, 372–373; Heizer in Science, 148, no. 3669, 487–488; Higgs in Antiq., 40, 311–312; Jelinek in Mich. Archaeol., 12, 136–137; Merrifield in Mus. Jour., London, 66, 307–308; Moore in Austral. Nat. Hist., 15, 178; R. W. H. in Geol. Mag., 103, 186; Stearns in Amer. Sci., 53, 394A–395A; Wendorf in Amer. Antiq., 31, 286–287; Wright in Ecology, 47, 335– 336.
1965   Acheulian occupation sites at Torralba and Ambrona, Spain: their geology. Science, 150, 1718–1722, 3 figs., 1 table.
1967   Reply [to G. A. Wright: "On Late Pleistocene chronology"]. Current Anthrop., 8, 353–354.
        See: Aguirre and Butzer; Freeman, L. G. and Butzer; Howell, Butzer, and Aguirre.

BYERS, D. S.
1965   The position of the Debert site with respect to the eastern Paleo-Indian contribution of the Debert archaeological project. 7th Internat. Congr., Internat. Assoc. Quat. Res., Abs., 1965, 57, (abs.).
1966   The Debert archaeological project: the position of Debert with respect to the Paleo-Indian tradition. Quaternaria, 8, 33–47, 1 table, (French and German summaries).
1967   The prehistory of the Tehuacan Valley. Vol. 1. Environment and subsistence. Austin, London: Univ. of Texas Press, viii + 331 pp., 188 figs., 38 tables.
        Rev.: Bushnell in Antiq., 43:169, 69–71; Haberland in Archaeol., 22:3, 235–238.

BYERS, D., et al.
1965   Saturday morning roundtable. Bull. Southeast. Archaeol. Confer., 2, 24–51.

BYSTROV, A. P.
1959B.   [Microstructure of armor elements of Arthrodira.] Trudy Vses. Paleont. Obshch., III sess., 113–135, 25 figs., (Russian).

Ć.-G., M.
1965   Profesor Dr Olga Necrasova członek honorowy polskiego towarzystwa
            antropologicznego. Przegląd Antrop., 31, 191—192, portr.

CABAÇO, HIPÓLITO See: Do Paço and Cabaço.

CADENAT, P.
1960   Atlas préhistorique de l'Algérie, feuille n° 22 P: Ammi-Moussa. Libyca,
            6—7, 9—36.

CADEO, G. C.
1961   Risultati degli ultimi 15 anni di ricerche archeogiche, paletnologiche e
            paleontologiche nelle grotte lombarde. (Anni 1946—1960).
            Natura, Riv. Sci. Nat., 52, 20—28, 1 fig., (not seen).
1965A.   Breno (Valcamonica, Prov. di Brescia). Riv. Sci. Preist., 19, 295.
1965B.   Fiume Nevola, presso Senigallia (Prov. di Ancona). Torrette di Fano
            (Prov. di Pesaro). Riv. Sci. Preist., 19, 298—299.

CAHEN, L.
1966   Memorial to Arthur Holmes. [Jan. 14, 1890—Sept. 20, 1965.] Bull.
            Geol. Soc. Amer., 77, P127—P135, portr.

CAHN, THÉOPHILE
1962   La vie et l'oeuvre d'Etienne Geoffroy Saint-Hilaire. Paris: Presses
            Universitaires de France, 318 pp.
            Rev.: Wolff in L'Ann. Biol., ser. 4, 2, 391—393.

CAILLEUX, ANDRÉ (= Cayeux, André de)

1964A.   Datation absolue des principales industries préhistorique. Bull. Soc.
            Géol. France, 5, 409—413, 1 table.
1964B.   Trois milliards d'annès de vie. Paris: Encyclopédie planète, Édition
            Denoël, 256 pp., (not seen).
            Rev.: Bauchau in Rev. Questions Sci., 25, 436;   Martinsson in Geol.
            Fören Förh, 86, 319, (Swedish).

CAIN, ARTHUR JAMES
1964   Evolution. In: Thomson, A. L., (ed.), 254—257.
1966   Animal species and their evolution. London: Hutchinson Univ. Lib.,
            x + 190 pp., 5 figs.
            Rev.: King in Jour. Anat., 101, 390;   Megaw in Mankind, 6, 445.

CAINE, CHRISTY A. H.
1968   Big-game hunting artifacts from Minnesota. Plains Anthrop., 13, 87—
            89, 6 figs.

CALABY, J. H., and WHITE, C.
1967   The Tasmanian devil (Sarcophilus harrisi) in northern Australia in Re-
            cent times. Austral. Jour. Sci., 29, 473—475, 2 figs., 1 table.

CALDWELL, DAVID K.
1966   A Miocene needlefish from Bowden, Jamaica. Quart. Jour. Florida
            Acad. Sci., 28, 339—344, 1 fig.

CALDWELL, D. K., and CALDWELL, M. C.
    1965   The fossil who stayed alive. Quart. Los Angeles Co. Mus. Nat. Hist.,
                4:1, 14—15, illustr.

CALDWELL, JOSEPH R.
    1952   The archeology of eastern Georgia and South Carolina. In: Griffin,
                J. B., (ed.), 312—321.
    1966   (ed.) New roads to yesterday: essays in archaeology. New York:
                Basic Books, 556 pp., illustr., (not seen).
                Rev.: Bass in Amer. Jour. Phys. Anthrop., 27, 101—102; Ehrich in
                Science, 153, 856; Sackett in Amer. Anthrop., 69, 400—401.

CALDWELL, M. C.   See: Caldwell, D. K. and Caldwell.

CALLEJO SERRANO, C.
    1958   La cueva prehistórica de Maltravieso, junto a Cáceres. Publ. Bib. Pub.
                Ciudad Cáceres, (not seen).

CALLISON, GEORGE
    1967   Intracranial mobility in Kansas mosasaurs. Univ. Kansas Pal. Contrib.,
                Pap., 26, 1—15, 10 figs.

CALLOW, W. J., BAKER, M. J., and HASSALL, G. I.
    1965   National Physical Laboratory radiocarbon measurements III. Radio-
                carbon, 7, 156—161.

CALLOW, W. J., BAKER, M. J., and PRITCHARD, D. H.
    1964   National Physical Laboratory radiocarbon measurements II. Radiocar-
                bon, 6, 25—30.

CALVOCORESSI, DAVID
    1965   (ed.) COWA surveys and bibliographies. Area 11 — West Africa.
                COWA Surv. and Bibliog., Area 11, no. 3, 10 + 13 pp.
    1967   Comments on recommendations and discussions on terminology in
                African archaeology at Fourah Bay, June 1966. W. Afr.
                Archaeol. Newsletter, no. 7, 9—12, (French summary).

CAMARATE FRANÇA, JOSÉ   See: Almeida, and Camarate França; Roche, et al.

CAMARATE FRANÇA, J., ROCHE, J., and VEIGA FERREIRA, O. da
    1961   Rev.: J. R. in L'Anthrop., 69:5—6, 553.

CAMBRON, JAMES W., and HULSE, D. C.
    1961   A comparative study of some unfinished fluted points and channel
                flakes from the Tennessee Valley. Jour. Ala. Archaeol., 7, 88—
                105, 22 figs.
    1963   Fluted points found in situ. Jour. Ala. Archaeol., 9, 38—39, 1 fig.
    1964   Handbook of Alabama archaeology. Part I: point types. University,
                Ala.: Archaeol. Res. Assoc. of Ala., Inc., 143 pp., 74 figs.,
                115 drawings, (not seen).
                Rev.: Anon. in Ohio Archaeol., 15, 108—109; Story in Amer. Antiq.,
                31, 126.

CAMBRON, J. W., and RADFORD, R. D.
    1959   The Jacks site. Jour. Ala. Archaeol., 5, 75—76, pls. 10—11.

CAMP, CATHERINE CROOK   See: Camp, L. S.

CAMP, CHARLES L.
  1964   V. L. VanderHoof, 1904 - 1964. News Bull., Soc. Vert. Pal., no. 71,
              48—50, portr.
  1965A.   Memorial to V. L. VanderHoof (1904 - 1964). Bull. Geol. Soc. Amer.,
              76, P31—P35, portrait.
  1965B.   Obit. [Vertress Lawrence VanderHoof, 1904 - 1964.] Proc. Geol. Soc.
              London, no. 1618, 118—119.
  1966   Stories of fossils. Experimental edition. Berkeley: University of
              California Printing Department (Elementary School Science Pro-
              ject), 164 pp., illustr.
          See: Koch, J. and Camp.

CAMP, C. L., ALLISON, H. J., and NICHOLS, R. H.
  1964   Bibliography of fossil vertebrates 1954—1958. Geol. Soc. Amer., Mem.
              92, xxv + 647 pp.

CAMP, C. L., ALLISON, H. J., NICHOLS, R. H., and McGINNIS, H.
  1968   Bibliography of fossil vertebrates 1959—1963. Mem. Geol. Soc. Amer.,
              117, xlii + 644 pp.
          Rev.: Erdbrink in Geol. en Mijn., 49:3, 252—253; Ostrom in Jour.
              Pal., 44:5, 994—995; Romer in Earth-Sci. Rev., 6:1, A27—A28.

CAMP, C. L., CLEMENS, W. A., GREGORY, J. T., and SAVAGE, D. E.
  1967   Ruben Arthur Stirton, 1901 - 1966. Jour. Mammal., 48, 298—305,
              portr.

CAMP, C. L., GREGORY, J. T., and SAVAGE, D. E.
  1967A.   Ruben Arthur Stirton, 1901 - 1966. News Bull., Soc. Vert. Pal., 79,
              60—61, portr.
  1967B.   Ruben Arthur Stirton, 1901 - 1966. Univ. of Calif. In Memoriam,
              June 1967, 101—103.

CAMP, C. L., and KOCH, J. G.
  1966   Late Jurassic ichthyosaur from coastal Oregon. Jour. Pal., 40, 204—
              205, 2 figs. [Same as Koch and Camp, 1966.]

CAMP, L. SPRAGUE DE
  1964   Elephant. The fascinating life cycle of the world's largest land animal.
              New York: Pyramid Publ., 179 pp., 16 figs., 8 pls., (paperback).
  1968   The great monkey trial. New York: Doubleday, 538 pp., illustr.
          Rev.: Carson in Nat. Hist., 77:5, 68—69, 1 fig.

CAMP, L. S. DE, and CAMP, C. C. DE
  1968   The day of the dinosaur. Garden City, N. Y.: Doubleday, xvi + 319
              pp., illustr.
          Rev.: Asimov in Nat. Hist., 78:2, 107—108; Black in Carnegie Mag.,
              43:10, 263—265, 2 figs.

CAMPBELL, ALISTAIR H.
  1967   Aboriginal traditions and the prehistory of Australia. Mankind, 6, 476—
              481.

CAMPBELL, BERNARD GRANT

1964A.   Just another "man-ape"? Discovery, 25:6, 37—38, figs. 4—6. Discussion: see Napier, J., 1964A.

1964B.   Science and human evolution. Nature, 203, 448—451, 2 figs.

1965   The nomenclature of the Hominidae including a definitive list of hominid taxa. Occ. Pap. Roy. Anthrop. Inst. Great Britain and Ireland, 22, v + 34 pp., 2 tables.

    Rev.: Haltenorth in Säugetierkundl. Mitt., 17:3, 274; Coon in Human Biol., 38, 344—347; Hillaby in New Sci., 28, 915, illustr.; H. V. V. in L'Anthrop., 70:5—6, 558—559; Knussmann in Homo, 17:2, 121; Pohle in Berliner Jahrb. Vor- und Frühgesch., 8, 223—224; Simpson in Man, Jour. Roy. Anthrop. Inst., 1, 562.

    Abs.: Preuschoft in Zbl. Geol. Pal., Teil 2, 1966, 338—339.

1966-
1967   Human evolution. An introduction to man's adaptations. Chicago: Aldine; London: Heinemann Educational Books, xiv + 425 pp., illustr.

    Rev.: Angel in Jour. Pal., 42, 859—860; Billy in L'Anthrop., 71:5—6, 527—528; Cullen in Sci. Jour., 3:7, 94; Díaz Ungría in An. Antropol., Mexico, 5, 243—248; Haltenorth in Saügetierkundl. Mitt., 16:3, 262—263; Heberer in Homo, 18:2, 114; Helmuth in Zeit. Morph. Anthrop., 61:1, 117—118; Howells in Amer. Sci., 55, 324A, 326A; Hughes in Man, Jour. Roy. Anthrop. Inst., 3, 136; Marcozzi in Anthropos, 62:3/4, 575—577; Prost in Amer. Jour. Phys. Anthrop., 27, 225—227; Roth-Lutra in Anat. Anz., 124, 463—464; Sauter in Arch. Suiss. Anthropol. Gen., 32, 143—144; Shapiro in Nat. Hist., 76:6, 68—71; Stewart in Science, 160, 675; Tappen in Amer. Anthrop., 70, 636—637; Tuttle in Human Biol., 40:1, 98—101; Vogel in Anthrop. Anz., 30, 306—307.

1968   Inspiration and controversy: motives for research. S. African Jour. Sci., 64, 60—63.

    See: Oakley and Campbell.

CAMPBELL, C. B. G.

1966   Taxonomic status of three shrews. Science, 153, 436.

CAMPBELL, J. D.

1965   New Zealand Triassic saurians. New Zealand Jour. Geol., 8, 505—509, 2 figs.

CAMPBELL, JOHN M.

1961   The Kogruk Complex of Anaktuvuk Pass, Alaska. Anthropologica, n.s. 3, 3—20, 2 figs.

1962A.   (ed.) Prehistoric cultural relations between the Arctic and Temperate zones of North America. Montreal: Arctic Inst. of N. Amer., Tech. Pap. no. 11, 181 pp., illustr.

1962B.   Cultural succession at Anaktuvuk Pass, Arctic Alaska. In: Campbell, J. M., (ed.), 1962A, 39—54, 7 pls.

1963   Ancient Alaska and Paleolithic Europe. Anthrop. Pap. Univ. Alaska, 10:2, 29—49, 2 pls.

1965   Current research: Arctic. Amer. Antiq., 31, 291—295.

CAMPBELL, K. S. W.

1965   An almost complete skull roof and palate of the dipnoan Dipnorhynchus sussmilchi (Etheridge). Palaeontol., 8, 634—637, 1 fig., pl. 91.

CAMPBELL, T. D. and GOLDBY, F.
1942   Recent developments on later finds of pre-historic man. Mankind,
            3:3, 103.

CAMPION, DONALD R.
1965   The phenomenon of Teilhard. America, 112, 480–481.

CAMPS, G.
1964   Recherches récentes sur le Paléolithique inférieur des Hautes-Plaines
            Constantinoises. Libyca, 12, 9–42, 23 figs., tables.

CANTWELL, R. J.
1968   Fossil Sigmodon from southeastern Arizona. Program, 64th Ann. Meet-
            ing, Geol. Soc. Amer., 45, (abs.).

CĂPITANU, VIOREL See: Saraiman and Căpitanu.

CAPPETTA, HENRI, GRANIER, J., and LEDOUX, J.-C.
1967   Deux faunes de sélaciens du Miocène méditerranéen de France et leur
            signification bathymétrique. C. R. Soc. Geol. France, 1967,
            292–294.

CAPPETTA, H., RINGEADE, M., and THALER, L.
1966   Sur la signification stratigraphique des rongeurs nouvellement récoltés
            dans "l'Aquitanien" lacustre et laguno-marin du Bas-Languedoc.
            C. R. Soc. Geol. France, 1966, 187–188.
            Rev.: Fahlbusch in Zbl. Geol. Pal., Teil 2, 1967, 118.

CAPRON, P. C.   See: Gilot, et al.

CARBONELL, VIRGINIA M.
1965   The teeth of the Neanderthal child from Gibraltar: A re-evaluation.
            Amer. Jour. Phy. Anthrop., 23, 41–49, 2 pls.
            See: Dahlberg and Carbonell.

CARBONNEL, JEAN-PIERRE, and BIBERSON, PIERRE
1968   Industrie osseuse et présence humaine dans le gisement pléistocène in-
            férieur du Phnom-Loang (Cambodge). C. R. Acad. Sci. Paris,
            Sci. Nat., 267:26, 2306–2308.

CARBONNEL, J.-P., and GUTH, CHRISTIAN
1968   Le gisement pléistocène inférieur du Phnom Loang (Cambodge), stra-
            tigraphie et faune. C. R. Acad. Sci. Paris, Sci. Nat., 267:25,
            2077–2080.

CARDICH, AUGUSTO
1959   Los yacimientos de Lauricocha. Prologue by O. F. A. Menghin. Acta
            Praehist., 2, 1–65, 27 figs., 19 pls., (German summary).
1963   La prehistoria peruana y su profundidad cronologica. Bol. Soc. Geog.
            Lima, 80, 10–24, 1 table.
            Rev.: Kaltwasser P. in Antropología, 2:1, 129–130.
1964   Lauricocha. Fundamentos para una prehistoria de los Andes Centrales.
            Buenos Aires: Centro Argentino de Estudios Prehistoricos, (not
            seen).

CARLQUIST, SHERWIN
    1965   Island life. A natural history of the islands of the world. Garden
                 City, N. Y.: Natural History Press, xii + 451 pp., illustr.
                 Rev.: Bowman in Wilson Bull., 79, 356;   Grant in Evolution, 20,
                 245.

CARLSON, R. L.
    1967   Excavations at Khor Abu Anga and at sites in Nubia. Current Anthrop.,
                 8, 352.

CARLSTRÖM, DIEGO
    1963   A crystallographic study of vertebrate otoliths. Biol. Bull., 125, 441–
                 463, 5 figs., 1 table.
                 Abs.: Anon. in New Sci., 22, 70.
                 Rev.: Huppert in Naturwiss. Rund., 17, 448–449.

CARLUCI DE SANTIANA, MARÍA ANGÉLICA
    1961B.   La antigüedad del hombre en el Ecuador y los últimos descubrimientos
                 arqueológicos. El Comercio, Quito, Nov. 12, 1961, (not seen).

    1963   Puntas de proyectil. Tipos, tecnica y areas de distribution en el Ecua-
                 dor andino. Humanitas, 4:1, 5–56, 6 figs., 5 pls., 2 maps.
                 Rev.: Kaltwasser P. in Antropología, 2:2, 97.
                 See: Santiana and Carluci de Santiana.

CARMICHAEL, LEONARD
    1964   Report of the Secretary of the Smithsonian Institution. Ann. Rept.
                 Smithson. Instn., 1963, 1–26.
                 See: Taylor, F. A. and Carmichael.

CARMICHAEL, L., and LONG, J. C.
    1965   James Smithson and the Smithsonian story. New York: Putnam, 316
                 pp., illustr.

CAROZZI, ALBERT V.   See: Agassiz 1967, Lamarck 1964.

CARR, ARCHIE, and Editors of Life
    1963   Rev.: Grant in Frontiers, 28, 125;   Porter in Audubon. Mag., 66,
                 260–261.

CARR, G. V.
    1966   Facts and artifacts of the Chattahoochee. Bull. Georgia Acad. Sci.,
                 24:2, 73, (abs.).

CARRECK, J. N.
    1955   The Quaternary vertebrates of Dorset, fossil and subfossil. Proc. Dorset
                 Nat. Hist. Archaeol. Soc., 75, 164–188.

CARRERAS, FAUSTINO F.
    1960   La evolucion a 100 años de la teoria de Darwin. Rev. Fac. Cien. Nat.
                 Salta, 1:2, 43–49.

CARRINGTON, RICHARD
    1963   Rev.: Goodman in Ohio Archaeol., 15, 142;   Chowdhury in Man in
                 India, 44, 368–369.

1965 Dieses unser Leben. Die Geschichte des Menschen als Teil der Natur. München: Rütten u. Loening Verlag, 352 pp.
  Rev.: Kurth in Homo, 16:4, 252.
  See: Bellaires and Carrington.

CARRINGTON, R., and Editors of Life
1963 Rev.: Haltenorth in Säugetier Kundl.

CARROLL, ROBERT L.
1963 Abs.: Huene in Zbl. Geol. Pal., Teil 2, 1965, 247.
1964A. The relationships of the rhachitomous amphibian Parioxys. Amer. Mus. Novit., no. 2167, 11 pp., 5 figs.
  Abs.: Huene in Zbl. Geol. Pal., Teil 2, 1965, 240.
1964B. Early evolution of the dissorophid amphibians. Bull. Mus. Comp. Zool. Harvard, 131, 163—250, 25 figs., 2 pls.
  Abs.: Huene in Zbl. Geol. Pal., Teil 2, 1965, 238—239.
1964C. The earliest reptiles. Jour. Linn. Soc. London, Zool., 45, 61—83, 14 figs.
  Abs.: Huene in Zbl. Geol. Pal., Teil 2, 1965, 247.
1965A. Comments on Gregory's contribution. Amer. Zool., 5, 285—286.
1965B. Lungfish burrows from the Michigan coal basin. Science, 148, no. 3672, 963—964, 1 fig.
1966 Microsaurs from the Westphalian B of Joggins, Nova Scotia. Proc. Linn. Soc. London, 177, 63—97, 26 figs.
  Abs.: Huene in Zbl. Geol. Pal., Teil 2, 1966, 292—293.
1967A. An adelogyrinid lepospondyl amphibian from the Upper Carboniferous. Canadian Jour. Zool., 45, 1—16, 7 figs., 2 pls.
1967B. Labyrinthodonts from the Joggins formation. Jour. Pal., 41, 111—142, 26 figs., 1 table.
  Rev.: Westphal in Zbl. Geol. Pal., Teil 2, 1967, 508.
1967C. A limnoscelid reptile from the Middle Pennsylvanian. Jour. Pal., 41, 1256—1261, 3 figs.
1968A. The postcranial skeleton of the Permian microsaur Pantylus. Canadian Jour. Zool., 46, 1175—1192, 9 figs., 1 pl.
1968B. The origin of reptiles. In: Bellairs, A., et al., (eds.), 1, 1—44.
1968C. A ?diapsid (Reptilia) parietal from the Lower Permian of Oklahoma. Postilla, 117, 1—7, 3 figs.
  See: Baird and Carroll; Gregory, J. T. 1965A; Olson 1965B.

CARROLL, R. L., and BAIRD, D.
1967 Tuditanus [Eosauravus] and the distinction between microsaurs and reptiles. Program, 1967 Ann. Meeting, Geol. Soc. Amer., 1967, 34, (abs.). Also: Spec. Pap. Geol. Soc. Amer., 115, 34, (abs.).
1968 The Carboniferous amphibian Tuditanus [Eosauravus] and the distinction between microsaurs and reptiles. Amer. Mus. Novit., 2337, 1—50, 20 figs., 1 table.
  Rev.: Westphal in Zbl. Geol. Pal., Teil 2, 1969:2, 207—208.

CARROLL, WARREN B.
1964 A possible "Alberta" point found near Casper. Wyo. Archaeol., 7:2, 9, illustr.

CARSKADDEN, JEFF
1966 Paleo-Indian points from Muskingum County. Ohio Archaeol., 16, 4—5, 1 pl.

CARTER, GEORGE F.
1964A.	Stone circles in the deserts. Anthrop. Jour. Canada, 2:3, 2—6.
1964B.	Some thoughts on coastal archeology. Quart. Bull. Archeol. Soc. Virginia, 18, 46—55, 7 figs.
1966A.	That elephant from Bucks County, Pennsylvania. Anthrop. Jour. Canada, 4:3, 2—6, 2 figs.
1966B.	On pebble tools and their relatives in North America. Anthrop. Jour. Canada, 4:4, 10—19, 5 figs.
1966C.	Comments on Paleo-Indian components in the Shenandoah Valley of Virginia. Chesopiean, 4:5—6, 121—122.
1967A.	Artifacts and naturifacts: introduction. Anthrop. Jour. Canada, 5:1, 2—5.
1967B.	Some parallels between Japanese and American stonework. Anthrop. Jour. Canada, 5:1, 25—26, 1 fig.
1967C.	A warm interstadial in the Wisconsin? Anthrop. Jour. Canada, 5:2, 10—12.

CARTER, GEORGE STUART
1957C.	Chordate phylogeny. Syst. Zool., 6, 187—192.
1967A.	Structure and habit in vertebrate evolution. London: Sidgwick and Jackson, xiv + 520 pp.
1967B.	Structure and habit in vertebrate evolution. Seattle: Univ. Washington Press, xiv + 520 pp., 287 figs., 1 table, (Biology Series).
	Rev.: Bennett in Bio Science, 18, 741; George in Nature, 216, 413; Moody in Amer. Jour. Phys. Anthrop., 29, 110—111; Simpson in Science, 295.

CARTER, THERESA HOWARD   See: Simpson, W. K. and Carter.

CARUS, V.   See: Huxley, T. H. 1963.

CASAMIQUELA, RODOLFO M.
1960B.	Rev.: Parodi Bustos in Rev. Fac. Cien. Nat. Salta, 1:3, 86.
1961B.	Abs.: Huene in Zbl. Geol. Pal., Teil 2, 1964, 519—520.
1963A.	Abs.: Huene in Zbl. Geol. Pal., Teil 2, 1964, 989.
1964A.	Studies on ichnology. Problems and methods of ichnology with application to the study of Mesozoic footsteps (Reptilia, Mammalia) from Patagonia. Burenos Aires: Ministerio de Asuntos Sociales de la Province del Rio Negro, 229 pp., 71 figs., 26 pls., (Spanish; English summary).
	Rev.: Diaz in An. Soc. Cien Argent., 183, 144.
1964B.	Sobre un nuevo ejemplar de Aëtosauroides scagliai (Pseudosuchia, Aëtosauridae) de Ischigualasto (San Juan) y consideraciones acerca de la edad de los yacimientos triásicos de tetrápodos de la Argentina. Resumen. Ameghiniana, 3, 182—183, (abs.).
1964C.	Sobre la existencia de un nuevo macrotaxón de anfibios ultraevolucionados en el Carbonífero inferior de la Argentina (icnología). Resumen. Ameghiniana, 3, 183, (abs.).
1964D.	Sobre un dinosaurio hadrosáurido de la Argentina. Ameghiniana, 3:9, 285—312, 4 pls., 1 table, (English summary).
1964E.	Sobre el hallazgo de dinosaurios Triásicos en la Provincia de Santa Cruz. Argentina Austral., 35, 10—11, (not seen).
1965A.	Nuevos ejemplares de Shelania pasquali (Anura, Pipoidea) del Eoterciario de la Patagonia. Ameghiniana, 4, 41—51, 1 fig., 2 pls., 1 table, (English summary).

Abs.: Westphal in Zbl. Geol. Pal., Teil 2, 1966, 293.

1965B.   Estudios icnológicos. Analisis de "Orchesteropus atavus" Frenguelli y una forma afin, del Paleozoico de la Argentina. Rev. Mus. La Plata, sec. pal., 4:24, 187–245, 8 pls., 1 table, (English summary).

1965C.   Nota crítica A: A reevaluation of the early history of the frogs, según el Dr. M. K. Hecht (1962 - 63). Rev. Mus. La Plata, sec. pal., 4:27, 303–310.

1965D.   Nuevo material de Vieraella herbstii Reig. Reinterpretación de la ranita liasica de la Patagonia y consideraciones sobre filogenia y sistemática de los Anuros. Rev. Mus. La Plata, sec. pal., 4:27, 265–317, 3 figs., 5 pls., (English summary).

1965E.   Nota crítica preliminar a: The phylogeny of the Salientia, según el Dr. I. Griffiths. Rev. Mus. La Plata, sec. pal., 4:27, 310–314.

1966   Algunas consideraciones teóricas sobre los andares de los dinosaurious Saurisquios. Implicaciones filogenéticas. Ameghiniana, 4, 373–382, 3 pls., (English summary).

1967A.   Un nuevo dinosaurio ornitisquio triásico (Pisanosaurus mertii; Ornithopoda) de la formación Ischigualasto, Argentina. Ameghiniana, 5:2, 47–64, 4 pls., 1 table, (English summary).

1967B.   Sobre un nuevo Bufo fosil de la Provincia de Buenos Aires (Argentina). Ameghiniana, 5, 161–168, 1 fig., (English summary).

Rev.: Westphal in Zbl. Geol. Pal., Teil 2, 1968:6, 656.

CASE, ERMINE COWLES   See: Angell, 1964.

CASE, GERARD RAMON
1965A.   An occurrence of the sawfish, Onchopristis dunklei in the Upper Cretaceous of Minnesota. Jour. Minn. Acad. Sci., 32:3, 183, 1 fig.

1965B.   An occurrence of the sawfish, Onchopristis dunklei in the Upper Cretaceous of Minnesota. Proc. Minn. Acad. Sci., 32, 183, 1 fig.

1967   Fossil shark and fish remains of North America. New York: Grafco Press, 21 pp., 102 figs.

Rev.: Anon. in Rocks and Minerals, 42, 792;   Bottoms in Chesopiean, 5, 114.

See: Baird and Case.

CASE, G. R., and OWENS, W. A.
1966   The mound builders of the St. Johns River Valley – central Florida. Chesopiean, 4, 6–12, 12 figs., 5 pls.

CASE, JERRY
1964   Shark tooth hunting along the Calvert Cliffs of Maryland. Rocks and Minerals, 39, 467, 11 figs.

1965A.   Fossil hunting in central New Jersey. Rocks and Minerals, 40, 214–215, illustr.

1965B.   Hunting fossils in Florida's phosphate pits. Rocks and Minerals, 40, 294–295, illustr.

1965C.   Fossil Department. Rocks and Minerals, 40, 430–431, 509–510, 589–590, 668–669, 748–749, 834–835, 913–914, illustr.

1966A.   Fossil Department. Rocks and Minerals, 41, 56–57, 136–137, 204–205, 274–275, illustr.

1966B.   Localities for collecting teeth of the Miocene giant white shark. Earth Sci., 19:2, 65–68, 4 figs.

1968   The fossil fishes of Granton Quarry. Rocks and Minerals, 43, 169–172, 3 figs.

CASEY, D. A.   See: Bowler, et al.

CASEY, RAYMOND
1964   The Cretaceous period. In: Harland, W. B., et al., (eds.), 193–202,
              2 tables.

CASIER, EDGARD
1964   Contributions a l'etude des poissons fossiles de la Belgique. XIII –
              Présence de ganopristinés dans la Glauconie de Lonzée et le
              Tuffeau de Maestricht. Bull. Inst. Royal Sci. Nat. Belg., 40:11,
              25 pp., 9 figs., 2 pls.
              Abs.: Weiler in Zbl. Geol. Pal., Teil 2, 1965, 221.
1965   Poissons fossiles de la serie du Kwango (Congo). Ann. Mus. Congo
              Belge, Ser. in 8°, Sci. Geol., 50, x + 64 pp., 14 figs., 16 pls.
              Rev.: Weiler in Zbl. Geol. Pal., Teil 2, 1967, 491–493.
1966A.   Faune ichthyologique du London Clay. Appendice: Otolithes des
              poissons du London Clay par Frederick Charles Stinton. Preface
              by Errol White. London: Brit. Mus. (Nat. Hist.), 2 vols.: xiv
              + 496 pp., 82 figs., 7 tables; atlas, 68 pls.
              Rev.: Schaeffer in Quart. Rev. Biol., 42, 423–424; Tarlo in Nature,
              214, 637–638; Weiler in Zbl. Geol. Pal., Teil 2, 1967, 493–
              495.
1966B.   Sur la faune ichthyologique de la formation de Bissex Hill et de la
              série océanique, de L'Ile de Barbade, et sur l'âge de ces forma-
              tions. Eclog. Geol. Helvetiae, 59, 493–515, 3 pls., 2 tables.
1967   Poissons de l'Eocene inferieur de Katharinenhof-Fehmarn (Schleswig-
              Holstein). Bull. Inst. Royal Sci. Nat. Belg., 43:25, 1–23, 6 figs.,
              2 pls.
              Rev.: Weiler in Zbl. Geol. Pal., Teil 2, 1969:3, 282–283.

CASOLI, M.
1962   Abs.: Doc. Lab. Géol. Fac. Sci. Lyon, no. 1, 34–35.

CASSIDY, MARTIN W.
1964   Reinforced plastics: casting and laying up in latex rubber molds.
              Curator, 7, 63–79, 17 figs.

CASTELLANOS, ALFREDO
1965   Estudio fisiográfico de la Provincia de Corrientes. Publ. Inst. Fis. Geol.
              Univ. Nacion. Litoral, 49, 1–224, illustr.

CATTOI, NOEMI
1962   Un nuevo 'Xenarthra' del Terciario de Patagonia. Rev. Mus. Argent.
              Cien. Nat., Cien. Zool., 8, 123–134, 2 pls.

CAVE, A. J. E.   See: Straus and Cave.

CAVENDER, TED
1966A.   Systematic position of the North American Eocene fish, "Leuciscus"
              rosei Hussakof. Copeia, 66, 311–320, 6 figs.
1966B.   The caudal skeleton of the Cretaceous teleosts Xiphactinus, Ichthyo-
              dectes, and Gillicus, and its bearing on their relationship with
              Chirocentrus. Occ. Papers Mus. Zool. Univ. Mich., no. 650, 15
              pp., 4 figs., 1 pl.

CAYEUX, LOUIS
1967   La situation de la préhistoire en France et régionalement. Rev. Gén.
        Sci., 74, 97–100.

CERVERI, DORIS
1964   Giant footprint mystery. The Nevadan, 11-29-64, 24, illustr.

CHABREDIER, L.
1966   Étude méthodologique des relevés d'art pariétal préhistorique. Bull.
        Soc. Préhist. Franç., Étud. et Trav., 63:3, 501–512, 2 figs.

CHADWICK, LEIGH   See: Stümpke 1967.

CHAILLEY, JACQUES
1965   40,000 years of music. Translated from French by Rollo Myers. Pre-
        face by Virgil Thomson. New York: Farrar, Straus & Giroux,
        xvi + 229 pp., 15 figs., 37 pls.

CHAKRAVARTI, D. K.
1965   A geological, palaeontological and phylogenetic study of the Elephan-
        toidea of India, Pakistan and Burma. In: Jhingran, A. G.,
        et al., (eds.), 255–272.

CHALINE, JEAN P.
1961C.   Contribution à l'étude du remplissage des fissures de la Côte d'Or. La
          breche de Santeney et sa faune. Die Höhle, 12, 92, (abs.; Ger-
          man summary). Reprinted in Actes 2ème Congr. Internat.
          Spéléol, A, 60.
1962   Quelques résultats des recherches de microvertébrés dans les remplissages
          karstiques. Spelunca Mém., no. 2, 128–131, 2 tables.
1963   La faune à rhinocéros de Merck en Côte-d'Or. Bull. Sci. Bourgogne,
          21, 123–133, 3 figs., pl. 3, 4 tables.
1965A.   Problèmes posé par la découverte du lemming des steppes (Lagurus
          lagurus P.) dans la couche tayacienne de la Grotte de Fontéche-
          vade. Bull. Assoc. Franc. Étude Quat., 1965, 218, (English
          summary).
1965B.   Les rongeurs du Bois-du-Roc. (près de la Rochefoucault, Charente).
          Bull. Assoc. Franç. Étude Quat., 1965:3–4, 243–244, 1 table,
          (English summary).
1965C.   Contribution à l'étude du remplissage des fissures de la Côte d'Or.
          La breche de Santenay et sa faune. Discussion by J. Corbel.
          3. Internat. Kongress Spel., 4, 9–14, 3 tables.
1966A.   Un exemple d'évolution chez les Arvicolidés (Rodentia): les lignées
          Allophaiomys-Pitymys et Microtus. C. R. Acad. Sci. Paris, Sci.
          Nat., 263, 1202–1204, 1 fig.
1966B.   Recherche des micromammifères dans les sédiments. In: Lavocat, R.,
          (ed.), 1966, 83.
1966C.   Les lagomorphes et les rongeurs. In: Lavocat, R., (ed.), 1966, 397–
          440, pls. 103–125, tables 24–29.
1966D.   Les insectivores. In: Lavocat, R., (ed.), 1966, 441–450, pls. 126–129,
          table 31.
1966E.   Les chiroptères. In: Lavocat, R., (ed.), 1966, 451–462, pls. 130–133,
          table 32.
1967   Microtus mediterraneus n. sp., nouvel Arvicolidé (Rodentia) du Pléisto-
          cène moyen de France. C. R. Acad. Sci. Paris, Sci. Nat., 265,
          900–903, 2 tables.

Rev.: Fahlbusch in Zbl. Geol. Pal., Teil 2, 1969:3, 294–295.

CHALINE, J., and DELINGETTE, A.
1965   Un nouveau gisement fossilifère du Quaternaire ancien: la grotte des Valerots à Nuits-Saint-Georges (Côte-d'Or). C. R. Acad. Sci. Paris, 261, 4172–4174.

CHALINE, J., and MICHAUX, J.
1966   Résultats préliminaires d'une recherche systématique de micromammifères dans le Pliocène et le Quaternaire de France. C. R. Acad. Sci. Paris, Sci. Nat. 262, 1066–1069.

CHALLINOR, A.   See: Buchan, et al.

CHALUS, PAUL
1963   L'homme et la religion. Recherches sur les sources psychologiques des croyances. Du Paléolithique au premier millénaire avant notre ère. Paris: Michel, 510 pp., 22 figs., 12 color pls., 1 map.
Rev.: Bernard-Maitre in Arch. Philos., 28, 461–466.

CHALYSHEV, V. I.
1962A.   The marine Lower Triassic in the north Ural area. Dokl. Akad. Nauk SSSR, Earth Sci. Sect., 144, 129–131.
1962B.   [Finding of peculiar teeth of a stegocephalian.] Izv. Komi Fil. Vses. Geogr. Obshch., 7, 119–121, 2 figs., (Russian).
1966A.   (ed.) [Paleozoic sediments of northern Urals region.] Moscow: "Nauka" Press, 105 pp., 13 figs., 1 table, (Russian).
1966B.   [Upper Permian sediments of northern Urals region.] In: Chalyshev, (ed.), 1966A, 73–96, 3 figs., (Russian).

CHAMBERLAIN, BARBARA BLAU
1964   These fragile outposts. A geological look at Cape Cod, Martha's Vineyard, and Nantucket. Garden City, N. Y.: Natural History Press, xxii + 327 pp., 46 figs., (laymen).
Rev.: Clampitt in Audubon Mag., 67, 190.

CHAMBORD, EMM.
1964   Contribution à l'étude du Paléolithique dans le canton de Pleumartin (Vienne). Bull. Soc. Préhist. Franç., C. R. séances mens., 1964: 6, CXI–CXV, 2 pls.

CHAND, AMAR
1957   The Palaeolithic Period in the history of Orissa. Vikram, 1, 150–161.

CHAMNEY, T. POTTER   See: Russell, D. A. and Chamney.

CHANDRA, P. R.   See: Tripathi and Chandra.

CHANG, CHIH-KUO
1964   Pleistocene mammalian fossils from Wangching, Kirin Province. Vert. Palasiatica, 8:4, 402–413, 3 pls., (Chinese; English summary).

CHANG, HSI-CHIH
1964A.   New materials of mastodonts from the Yüshe Basin, Shansi. Vert. Palasiatica, 8, 33–41, 2 pls., (Chinese and English).

1964B.   On new material of _Palaeoloxodon namadicus_ of China, with discussion
           on the classification of some Pleistocene elephants of China.
           Vert. Palasiatica, 8, 269–287, 3 figs., 7 pls., (Chinese; English
           summary).

CHANG, HSI-CHIH, and LIU, H.
1964   On specimens of _Metailurus_ from Yushe, Shansi. Vert. Palasiatica, 8,
           182–188, 2 pls., (Chinese; English summary).

CHANG, KUO-JUI
1965   New antiarchs from the Middle Devonian of Yunnan. Vert. Palasiatica,
           9, 1–10, pls. 1–3, 1 table, (Chinese and English).
           Abs.: Sci. Abs. China, Earth Sci., 4, 10–11.
           See: Liu, H.-T., Su, et al.

CHANG, KWANG-CHIH,
1961   (ed.) COWA surveys and bibliographies. Area 17 – Far East. COWA
           Surv. and Bibliog., Area 17, no. 2, 14 + 45 pp.
1963C.   Rev.: Rudolph in Archaeol., 18, 242, 244.
1966   China 1962–1963. Asian Perspectives, 8:1, 69–75.
1968   Archeology of ancient China. Science, 162, 519–526, 6 figs., cover.
           See: Beardsley, Chang and Loehr.

CHANG, K., and KIDDER, J. E., (eds.)
1964   COWA surveys and bibliographies. Area 17 – Far East. COWA Surv.
           and Bibliog., Area 17, no. 3, 7 + 37 pp.

CHANG, YIN-YUN   See: Pei, Yuan, et al.

CHANG, YU-PING   See: Chow, M., Huang, et al.; Huang, Wan-po and Chang.

CHANG, YU-PING, HUANG, W., TANG, Y., CHI, H., and TING, S.
1964   The discussion of Cenozoic formation from Lantian, Shensi Province.
           Vert. Palasiatica, 8, 134–151, 10 figs., 3 pls., (Chinese).

CHANTELL, CHARLES J.
1964   Some Mio-Pliocene hylids from the Valentine formation of Nebraska.
           Amer. Mid. Nat., 72, 211–225, 4 figs.
1965   A Lower Miocene _Acris_ (Amphibia: Hylidae) from Colorado. Jour.
           Pal., 39, 507–508, 1 fig.
           Abs.: Westphal in Zbl. Geol. Pal., Teil 2, 1966, 293.
1966   Late Cenozoic hylids from the Great Plains. Herpetologica, 22, 259–
           264, 1 table.

CHAO, SI-TSZIN'
1962   Abs.: Huene in Zbl. Geol. Pal., Teil 2, 1964, 167–168.
1965   [The largest dinosaur of China – Khechzhou-Mamen dragon – discovered
           in the Sychzhou province.] Shengwuxue tongbao, 1965:4, 36–
           37, (Chinese).

CHAO, TZE-KUEI and BI, C.
1964   A simplified method of replicas of tooth surfaces. Vert. Palasiatica, 8,
           87–91, 2 pls., (Chinese; English summary).

CHAO, T. K., and LI, Y. H.
1960*   Reprinted in Chinese in Paleovert. et Paleoanthrop., 2:1, 97—99, (not seen).

CHAPMAN, CARL H.
1948   A preliminary survey of Missouri archaeology part IV. Ancient cultures and sequence. Missouri Archaeol., 10, 133—164, 6 figs.
1952   Culture sequence in the Lower Missouri Valley. In: Griffin, J. B., (ed.), 139—151.
1956   Preliminary salvage archaeology in the Table Rock Reservoir area, Missouri. Missouri Archaeol., 18: 1—2, 14—45, illustr.
1967A.   The archaeological survey of Missouri: fluted points. Mo. Archaeol. Soc. Newsletter, no. 213, 2, illustr.
1967B.   Fluted point survey of Missouri: an interim report. Mo. Archaeol. Soc. Newsletter, no. 215, 9—10, 1 fig., 1 map.
1967C.   Fluted point survey: addenda. Mo. Archaeol. Soc. Newsletter, no. 216, 6, 1 fig.

CHAPMAN, C. H., and CHAPMAN, E. F.
1964   Indians and archaeology of Missouri. Columbia, Missouri: University of Missouri Press (Missouri Handbook no. 6), 161 pp., illustr. Rev.: Anon. in Conn. News, no. 91, 8.

CHAPMAN, GAYNOR   See: Shepherd 1962.

CHAPMAN, John J.
1964   Elmer the mosasaur crops up again. GeoTimes, 8:6, 34—35.

CHAPOT, D.
1963   Contribution à l'étude de la faune des sables de Montchenu (Drôme) de l'Helvétien supérieur. Doc. Lab. Géol. Fac. Sci. Lyon, no. 3, 59—60, (abs.).

CHARD, CHESTER S.,
1957   (ed.) COWA surveys and bibliographies. Area 18 — northern Asia. COWA Surv. and Bibliog., Area 18, no. 1, 7 + 8 pp.
1960B.   COWA surveys and bibliographies. Area 18 — northern Asia. COWA Surv. and Bibliog., Area 18, no. 2, 9 + 7 pp.
1963D.   The Old World roots: review and speculations. Anthrop. Pap. Univ. Alaska, 10:2, 115—121.
1964A.   Northeast Asia. Asian Perspectives, 7, 8—15.
1964B.   Introduction. In: Michael, H. N., (ed.), 1964, ix—xvi.
1966   Northeast Asia. Asian Perspectives, 8:1, 10—20.
      See: Abramova 1967A; Befu, et al.; Oba and Chard; Okada, A., Okada and Chard.

CHARD, C. S., and WORKMAN, W. B.
1965   Soviet archaeological radiocarbon dates: II. Arctic Anthrop., 3, 146—150, 1 table.

CHARDIN, PIERRE TEILHARD DE
1930I.   A great reward for hard work. Peking Leader Reprints, no. 51, 13—14.
1959A.   Rev.: Heberer in Anthrop. Anz., 30, 195; Narr in Acta Praehist., 1961—1963, 5—7, 209—215.
1959B.   Rev.: Golota, in Voprosy Filosofii, 1967:9, 170—173, (Russian).

1962F.   Het verschijnsel mens. Translated by D. de Lange. Utrecht-Antwerpen:
           Het Spectrum, 265 pp., 4 figs., (not seen).
           Rev.: Visser in Geol. en Mijn., 25, 117—118.
1964A.   The future of man. Translated by Norman Denny. New York: Harper
           & Row; London: Collins, 319 pp.
           Rev.: Francoeur in Amer. Sci., 53, 216A.
1964B.   Fenomenet menneske. Translated by Lorentz Eckhoff. Oslo: Gylden-
           dal norsk forlag, 233 pp., (not seen).
           Rev.: [Faegri] in Naturen, 88, 316—318.
1965A.   Comparaisons des formations plio-pléistocènes de Birmanie et des
           contrées avoisinantes. L'Anthrop., 69, 209—218, 2 figs.
1965B.   The appearance of man. Translated by J. M. Cohen. Preface by Des-
           mond Collins. London: William Collins, 286 pp., 20 figs., portr.
           Rev.: Burkitt in Nature, 210, 71.
1965C.   Ecrits du temps de la guerre (1916 - 1919). Paris: Grasset, 448 pp.
           Rev.: Delpech in Rev. Synthèse, 88, 267—269.
1965D.   Science et Christ. Paris: Éditions du Seuil, 293 pp.
1968A.   Le Dieu de l'évolution. In: Chardin, et al., 1968, 11—17.
1968B.   Être plus. Paris: Éditions du Seuil, 158 pp.

CHARDIN, P. T. de, et al.
1965   Le Christ évoluteur. Socialisation et religion. Carrière scientifique.
           Paris: Éditions du Seuil, 167 pp.
1968   Le Dieu de l'évolution. Paris: Éditions du Seuil, 201 pp.

CHARIG, ALAN J.
1957   New Triassic archosaurs from Tanganyika including Mandasuchus and
           Teleocrater. Abstr. Diss. Univ. Cambridge, 1955—1956, 28—29.
1966   Yu. A. Orlov. [1893 - 1966.] Nature, 212, 460.
1967A.   A new Triassic mammal skull from Lesotho. Biol. and Human Affairs,
           32:3, 19.
1967B.   Fossil fishes. Nature, 215, 118—119.
           See: Appleby, et al.; Attridge, et al.

CHARIG, A. J., ATTRIDGE, J., and CROMPTON, A. W.
1965   On the origin of the sauropods and the classification of the Saurischia.
           Proc. Linn. Soc. London, 176, 197—221, 1 pl.
           Abs.: Huene in Zbl. Geol. Pal., Teil 2, 1966, 302.
           Rev.: M. C. in Fossilia, 1965: 5—6, 65—66.

CHARLES, ROBERT-P.
1963A.   A propos de la soi-disante "race de Grimaldi". Cahiers Ligures Préhist.
           Archéol., 12:2, 253.
1963B.   Nouvelles remarques sur le site à Néanderthaliens de Shanidar et sa
           datation. Cahiers Ligures Préhist. Archéol., 12:2, 271—281, 2
           tables.
1965A.   Le Néanderthalien de Pétralona. Bull. Correspondence Hellén., 89,
           810—814, figs. 1—3.
1965B.   Deux crânes du Paléolithique supérieur près de Lodève (Hérault).
           Cahiers Ligures Préhist. Archéol., 14:2, 143—149, 3 figs., 1 table.
1965C.   Le Néanderthalien de Pétralona en Chalcidique (Grèce). Cahiers Ligures
           Préhist. Archéol., 14:2, 182—194.
1966   Le crâne de l'homme fossile d'Ibalaghem (République du Mali). Actas V
           Congr. Panafr. Prehist. Estud. Cuaternario, 1963:2, 17—26, 1 fig.,
           1 pl., (English summary).

CHARRIER, G.
1965   Prima segnalazione di fossili dal territorio di Rio Branco (Brasile).   Atti
        Soc. Ital. Mus. Civico, Milano, 104, 41–54, 4 figs., 4 pls., (En-
        glish summary).
        Rev.: Albanesi in Riv. Ital. Pal., 72, 497.

CHASE, JOHN NEWLAND
1965   Neldasaurus wrightae, a new rhachitomous labyrinthodont from the
        Texas Lower Permian. Bull. Mus. Comp. Zool. Harvard, 133,
        153–225, 16 figs., 5 pls.

CHASE, JOHN W.
1956   The Halloka Creek site, Fort Benning, Georgia. Bull. Georgia Acad.
        Sci., 14:2, 37–38.

CHATTERJEE, SANKAR
1967   New and associated phytosaur material from the Upper Triassic Maleri
        formation of India. Bull. Geol. Soc. India, 4, 108–110.

CHAUCHARD, PAUL
1965   Le pensée scientifique de Teilhard. Paris: Éditions Universitaires, 270
        pp.
        Rev.: Delpech in Rev. Synthèse, 88, 267–269.

CHAUFFRIASSE, A.   See: Roussot, Andrieux and Chauffriasse.

CHAUVIRÉ, CÉCILE
1962   Les gisements fossilifères quaternaires de Châtillon-Saint-Jean (Drôme).
        Doc. Lab. Géol. Fac. Sci. Lyon, no. 1, 50–55, (abs.).
1963   Abs.: Doc. Lab. Géol. Fac. Sci. Lyon, no. 3, 16.
1963B. Caractères ostéologiques differentiels de quelques strigidés (oiseaux de
        proie nocturnes). Bull. Soc. Linn., Lyon, 32, 166–172, 2 figs.
        Abs.: Doc. Lab. Géol. Fac. Sci. Lyon, no. 3, 18.
1965A. Les oiseaux du gisement magdalénien du Morin (Gironde). C. R. 89e
        Congr. Nation. Soc. Savantes, Sec. Sci., Sci. Terre Biol. Méd.,
        1964, 255–266, 2 figs., 1 pl., 5 tables.
1965B. Note préliminaire sur les oiseaux du remplissage quaternaire des Abîmes
        de la Fage, à Noailles (Corrèze). C. R. Soc. Geol. France, 1965,
        8–10, 1 table.

CHAUVIRE, C., and WEISS, J.
1962   Abs.: Doc. Lab. Géol. Fac. Sci. Lyon, no. 1, 23–24.

CHAVAILLON, JEAN
1964   Étude stratigraphique des formations quaternaires du Sahara nord-occiden-
        tal (Colomb-Béchar à Reggane). Publ. Cent. Recherch. Zones
        Arides, Cent. Nation. Recherch. Sci., Sér. Géol., no. 5, 394 pp.,
        111 figs. and maps, 32 pls.
        Rev.: A. in Quaternaria, 7, 316–318;   A. G. in Arch. Suiss. Anthrop.
        Gen., 30, 93–94;   Alimen in Bull. Soc. Préhist., Franç., C. R.
        séances mens., 1964:9, ccxii–ccxiii;   Beauchêne in Jour. Soc.
        Africanistes, 34, 313–314;   Capot-Rey in Ann. Géog., 74, 488–
        490;   Keraudren in L'Anthrop., 69, 315–316;   Seddon in S.
        Afr. Archaeol. Bull., 20, 34–36;   Streit in Quartär, 15–16,
        229–231.

1965A.   Saharan prehistory and Pleistocene stratigraphy. 7th Internat. Congr.,
            Internat. Assoc. Quat. Res., abs., 1965, 63–64, (abs.).

1965B.   Regards sur la préhistoire Saharienne: les temps paléolithiques. Rev.
            Questions Sci., 26, 67–88, 1 fig.

1965C.   Fouilles paléolithiques en Ethiopie. Bull. Soc. Préhist. Franç., C. R.
            séances mens., 1965:6, cxcvii, (abs.).

1966A.   Campagne de fouilles 1966 du gisement de Melka Kontouré (Ethiopie).
            Bull. Soc. Préhist. Franc., C. R. séances mens., 63, 165–166.

1966B.   Préhistoire saharienne et stratigraphie pléistocène. Quaternaria, 8, 1–7,
            (English and Italian summaries).

            See: Alimen, and Chavaillon; Arambourg, Chavaillon and Coppens;
            Leroi-Gourhan, Bailloud, Chavaillon, et al.; Leroi-Gourhan and
            Chavaillon; Leroi-Gourhan, Chavaillon, N. and Chavaillon.

CHAVAILLON, J., and MALEY, JEAN
    1966   Une industrie sur galet de la vallée du Nil (Soudan). Bull. Soc. Préhist.
              Franç., C. R. séances mens., 63, 65–70, 3 figs.

CHAVAILLON, NICOLE
    1964   Note sur quelques dates intéressant la préhistoire du Sahara Nord-Oc-
              cidental. Bull. Soc. Préhist. Franç, C. R. séances mens., 1964:4,
              lxxxviii–xci, 1 fig. (Discussion: lxxxiii).

    1965   Une industrie post-atérienne de la vallée de la Saoura. Bull. Soc. Pré-
              hist. Franç., Etud. et Trav., 61, 84–104, 5 figs.

              See: Alimen, Chavaillon, and Karpoff; Leroi-Gourhan, Chavaillon and
              Chavaillon, J.

CHEATUM, E. P., and SLAUGHTER, B. H.
    1966   Notes on the alluvial history of the Lampasas River, Texas. Jour. Grad.
              Res. Center, S. Methodist Univ., 35, 48–54, 1 fig.

CHEBATAROFF, J.
    1960   Las terrazas del Catalán Chico. El Dia, Montevideo, suppl., Oct. 2,
              1960, (not seen).

CHEBOKSAROV, N. N.   See: Woo and Cheboksarov.

CHEBOTAREVA, N. S. (=Tschebotarewa, N. S.)   See: Gerasimov, I. P., Serebriãnny,
            and Chebotareva; Grichuk, Sammet, et al.

CHEBOTAREVA, N. S., KUPRINA, N. P., and KHOREVA, I. M.
    1957   [Geomorphology and stratigraphy of Quaternary deposits of the middle
              course of Lena and of the low course of Aldan.] Izv. Akad.
              Nauk SSSR, Ser. Geogr., 1957:3, 60–71, 4 figs., (Russian).
              Abs.: Mirtsching in Zbl. Geol. Pal., Teil 2, 1962, 297.

    1959   [Stratigraphy of Quaternary deposits of the upper course of Lena R.
              and lower Aldan R.] In: Markov and Popov, (eds.), 1959,
              498–509, 2 figs., 1 table, (Russian).
              English translation in: Michael, H. N., (ed.), 1964, 452–463, 2 figs.,
              1 table.

CHEDIIÃ, O. K.   See: Loskutov, et al.

CHEMEKOV, IÛ. F.
    1959   [Quaternary system of Khabarovsk region and Amur province.]

Materialy Geol. Inst. (VSEGEI), Nov. Ser. Chetv. Geol. i Geomorf., 27, 88–95, (Russian).
See: Gameshin, Zubakov, et al.

CHÊNG, TÊ-K'UN
1959   Rev.: Vasil'ev in Vest. Ist. Mir. Kult., 1960:1, 109–112, (Russian).
1964   New light on ancient China. Antiq., 38, 179–186.

CHEPALYGA, A. L. See: Dubrovo and Chepalyga; Gozhik and Chepalyga.

CHEPIKOV, K. R.
1944   [Stratigraphy of red Permian deposits of Volga-Urals province.]
                 Referaty Nauchno-Issl. Rab., 1945, 16–17, (Russian).
1945   [Stratigrapy of the red beds of Upper Permian in Transvolgian and
                 Kama regions.]   Referaty Nauchno-Issled. Rab., 1947, 27–28,
                 (Russian).

CHERDYNTSEV, V. V.
1961   [Absolute age determination of Quaternary fossil bones based on isotope
                 ratio of heavy elements.]   In: Gromov, V. I., et al., (eds.),
                 1961, 85–95, 5 tables, (Russian; English summary).
             See: Ivanova, Kind and Cherdyntsev.

CHERDYNTSEV, V V., ALEKSEEV, V. A., KIND, N. V., FOROVA, V. S., and
SULERZHITSKIĬ, L. D.
1964   [Radiocarbon data of the Laboratory GIN AN SSSR.] Geokhimiia,
                 1964:4, 315–324, 3 figs., (Russian; English summary).

CHERDYNTSEV, V. V., ALEKSEEV, V. A., KIND, N. V., FOROVA, V. S.,
ZABEL'SKIĬ, F. S., SULERZHITSKIĬ, L. D., and CHURIKOVA, I. V.
1965   [Radiocarbon data of the Laboratory of the Geological Institute (GIN)
                 AN SSSR.] Geokhimiia, 1965:12, 1410–1422, 6 tables, (Rus-
                 sian; English summary).

CHERDYNTSEV, V. V., STRASHNIKOV, N. S., BORISENKO, T. I., and
POLIAKOVA, L. M.
1961   [Absolute age determination on fossil Quaternary bones.]   Mat. Vses.
                 Sov. po Izuch. Chetvert. Perioda, 1, 266–272, 3 tables, (Russian).

CHERNIAKHOVSKIĬ, A. G.   See: Razumova and Cherniakhovskiĭ.

CHERNIGOVSKII, V. N.
1965   Some pathways in the evolution of interoceptive signalling. In: J. W.
                 S. Pringle, (ed.), 1965, 69–82, fig. 3.

CHERNOV, A. A., and SAMARIN, V. G.
1966   [Primeval Atlantida.] Priroda, 1966:10, 118–119, (Russian).

CHERNOV, S. A.
1959B.   [Reptiles. Fauna of Tadzhik SSR, vol. 18.] Trudy Akad. Nauk
                 Tadzhik. SSR, 98, 204 pp., 13 figs., (Russian; Tadzhik summary).

CHERNYSH, A. P.
1955B.   [Investigations of Late Paleolithic sites of the Middle Dniester region.]
                 Krat. Soob. Inst. Arkheol. Akad. Nauk URSR., 4, 159–160,
                 (Russian).

1957D.   [Representation of the human figure in the Upper Paleolithic.]   Krat. Soob. Inst. Ist. Mat. Kult., 67, 133—134, 2 figs., (Russian).

1959   Rev.: Bibikov, S. N., in Krat. Soob. Inst. Akheol. Akad. Nauk URSR, 10, 136—140, (Russian);   Žebera in Věstnik Stat. Geol. Českosl. Republ., 1961, 36:2, 151—152, (Czech).

1959B.   [Investigations at the site Molodova V in 1955.]   Krat. Soob. Inst. Ist. Mat. Kult., 73, 48—56, 3 figs., (Russian).

1960B.   [Concerning the problem of Mousterian dwellings.]   Krat. Soob. Inst. Arkheol. Akad. Nauk URSR, 10, 3—10, 5 figs., (Russian).

1960C.   [Remains of a dwelling of Mousterian time on the Dnestr.]   Sov. Etnogr., 1960:1, 149—152, 4 figs., (Russian).

1961C.   [Mousterian strata of the site at Molodovo V.]   Krat. Soob. Inst. Ist. Mat. Kult. SSSR, 82, 77—85, 4 figs., (Russian).

1961D.   [The Paleolithic settlement Molodove V.]   Kyjiv: Vydavnictvo Akad. Nauk Ukraj. RSR, 174 pp., 52 figs., (not seen).
       Rev.: [Filip] in Archeol. Roz., 14, 429 (Czech).

1965A.   [On the absolute age of Paleolithic relics from Dnestr region.]   In: Bader, O. N., et al., (eds.), 1965, 117—122, (Russian).

1965B.   [Early and Middle Palaeolithic of Dnestr region.]   Trudy Kom. Chet. Period., 25, 138 pp., 70 figs., 1 table, (Russian).

1967   [On the nomenclature of Late Paleolithic tools.]   Krat. Soob. Inst. Arkheol. Akad. Nauk SSSR, 111, 3—11, 3 pls., (Russian).

1968A.   [Paleolithic site Ataki I in the Dnestr R. region.]   Biull. Kom. Izuch. Chetvert. Perioda, Akad. Nauk SSSR, 35, 102—112, 6 figs., (Russian).

1968B.   [Excavations in Oselivka.]   In: Rybakov, (ed.), 1968, 202—203, (Russian).
       See: Alekseev, V. A., et al.; Ivanova and Chernysh.

CHERNYSH, E. K.   See: Grigor'eva, et al.

CHERNYSH, I. V.   See: Bachinskii and Chernysh.

CHEYNIER, ANDRÉ

1956F.   La Bombetterie. Station aurignacienne de plein air a Cublac (Correze). Mem. Serv. Invest. Arqueol. Asturias, 1, 95—106, 7 figs.

1960   Rev.: Pradel in Bull. Soc. Préhist., Paris, 57, 657.

1960B.   Les couches inférieures de Laugerie-Haute. Bull. Soc. Hist. Archéol. Périgord, 87, 132—136.

1963B.   Le Périgordien n'est qu'une "Theorie". Bull. Soc. Hist. Archéol. Périgord, 90, 23—26.

1964A.   La baguette gravée magdalénienne du Peyrat. Bull. Soc. Hist. Archéol. Périgord, 91, 25—27, 2 figs.

1964B.   Les "têtes de brochet", fossile directeur du "Saint-Germien", Proto-magdalénien II b. Bull. Soc. Préhist. Franç., C. R. séances mens., 1964:1, xi—xii, (Discussion: Tixier, Alimen, Lwoff).

1964C.   Les fouilles du Peyrat, campagne de 1964. Bull. Soc. Préhist. Franç., C. R. séances mens., 1964:7, clxix—clxx, (Discussion).

1965A.   Comment vivait l'Homme des cavernes a l'âge du Renne. Paris: Ed. du Scorpion, 227 pp., 27 figs.
       Rev.: Anon. in La Nature, no. 3372, 160;   Chavaillon in Bull. Soc. Préhist. Franc., C. R. séances mens., 1965:6, cxcv—cxcvi;   Kühn in IPEK, 22, 157;   Sauter in Arch. Suiss. Anthrop. Gen., 31, 64.

1965B.   L'abri Lachaud à Terrasson (Dordogne). Préhist., 16, 120 pp., 120 figs., 2 pls.

1966   Considerations sur le passage du Magdalénien à l'Azilien. Bull. Soc.
            Préhist. Franç., C. R. séances mens., 63, 135–138.
1967   Comment vivait l'homme des cavernes à l'âge du Renne. 2nd ed.
            Paris: R. Arnoux ed., 269 pp., 10 maps, 1 table, (not seen).
            Rev.: Vila in Spelunca, Bull., 7:3, 254–255.

CHEYNIER, A., and BREUIL, H.
1963   La caverne de Pair-non-Pair (Gironde). Bordeaux: Publ. de la Société
            archéologique de Bordeaux. Documents d'Aquitaine. 220 pp., 40
            figs., 15 pls.
            Rev.: Zotz in Quartär, 17, 207–208.

CHEYNIER, A., and GONZÁLEZ ECHEGARAY, J.
1964   La grotte de Valle. In: Ripoll Perelló, E., (ed.), 1964A, 327–345,
            13 figs., (Spanish summary).
            Rev.: D. de S.-B. in L'Anthrop., 69:5–6, 547.

CHI, HUNG-GIANG   See: Chang, Y., et al.; Dai and Chi.

CHI, TAO   See: Li, C.-K. and Chi.

CHIA, LAN-PO
1959D.   Reprinted in Chinese in Paleovert. et Paleoanthrop., 1:1, 21–26, (not
            seen).
1960   Reprinted in Chinese in Paleovert. et Paleoanthrop., 2:1, 45–50, (not
            seen).

CHIA, L.-P., and CHIU, C.-L.
1960   Reprinted in Chinese in Paleovert. et Paleoanthrop., 2:1, 64–68, (not
            seen).

CHIA, L.-P., WANG, T., and WANG, C.
1964   K'o Ho: an early Palaeolithic site in south-western Shansi Province.
            Summary translation [of Chia, Wang and Wang, 1962] with notes
            by Jean Aigner. Arctic Anthrop., 2, 105–117, 9 pls., 1 map.

CHIAPPELLA, G.
1965   Gli scavi nel giacimento di Palidoro (Roma). Quaternaria, 7, 307–308.

CHIAPPELLA, VIRGINIA G.
1964   Il paleolitico inferiore di Venosa. Bull. Paletnol. Ital., n. ser. 15, 73,
            6–23, 8 figs., (French and English summaries).

CHIARELLI, BRUNETTO
1968A.   Caryologie comparée et évolution chez les singes Catarrhina. Discussion.
            7th Internat. Congr. Anthrop. Ethnol. Sci., Moscow, 1964, 3,
            441–449, 2 figs., 2 tables.
1968B.   From the karyotype of the apes to the human karyotype. S. African
            Jour. Sci., 64, 72–80, 7 figs., 3 tables.
            See: Isetti and Chiarelli.

CHIBA, SHIGEO   See: Matsumoto, Ishii, et al.; Matsumoto, Mori, et al.

CHIGURIAEVA, A. A.
1960   [Microspores from a bed with bones of wild boar (Sus scrofa L.) on the

Minueshta creek in West Bashkiria.]   Voprosy Geol. Vost.
Okrainy Russk. Plat., <u>1960</u>:5, 127—128, 1 fig., (Russian).

CHIJI, M.   See: Ikebe and Chiji; Ikebe, Chiji and Ishida; Ikebe, Ishida and Chiji.

CHIKOIDZE, T̂S. N. See: Bugianashvili, <u>et al</u>.

CHILDE, VERE GORDON
1965   Man makes himself. 4th ed. Preface by Glyn Daniel. London: Watts,
            xvii + 244 pp., 11 figs.

CHIN, YOU-DI
1958   The Stone Age in Thailand. Jour. Pal. Soc. India, <u>3</u>, 205—210, 1 fig.,
            pl. 37, portr.

CHINZEI, KIYOTAKA
1966   The deposits at the Nekata Cave-site, Hamakita City, Shizuoka, and
            their geologic age. Jour. Anthrop. Soc. Nippon, <u>74</u>, 137—152,
            174—175, figs., tables, (Japanese; English summary).

CHIU, CHAN-SIANG See: Chow, M. and Chiu.

CHIU, CHUNG-LANG   See: Chia and Chiu.

CHKHIKVADZE, V. M. (= C̆khikvadze)
1968   [Sakyidae — a new family of fossil turtles.]   Pal. Zhurnal, <u>1968</u>:2,
            88—94, 2 figs., (Russian).

CHMIELEWSKA, MARIA
1961A.   Rev.: Vencl in Archeol. Roz., <u>17</u>, 563, (Czech).
1961C.   An encampment from the close of the Allerőd oscillation at Witów,
            District of Łęczyca. Prace Mat. Muz. Archeol. Etnog. Łodzi, Ser.
            Archeol., no. <u>6</u>, 9—71, 22 pls., (Polish; English summary).

CHMIELEWSKI, WALDEMAR (= Khmelevskiĭ, V.)
1958A.   Etat de conservation des ossements d'animaux recueillis dans la grotte
            Nietoperzowa de Jerzmanowice. Biul. Peryglac., no. <u>6</u>, 127—135,
            279—284, 379—383, 3 figs., 2 pls., (Polish, French and Russian).
1958B.   Gisement paléolithique de Dziadowa Skala près de Skarżyce (distr. de
            Zawiercie). Prace Mat. Muz. Archeol. Etnog. Łódźi. Ser. Archeol.,
            no. <u>3</u>, 5—61, 171—181, 10 figs., 14 pls., (Polish; French sum-
            mary).
1961A.   Ensembles du type tayacien en Pologne. Internat. Assoc. Quat. Res.,
            Abs. Pap., 6th Congr., 135—136, (abs.).
1961B.   Civilisation de Jerzmanowice. Wroclaw, Warszawa, Kraków: Zakład
            Narodowy Imienia Ossolińskich Wydawnictwo Polskiej Akademii
            Nauk, 93 pp., 24 pls.
1964   Middle Palaeolithic traditions in Upper Palaeolithic cultures of Central
            and Eastern Europe. Archaeol. Polona, <u>7</u>, 193—198, 3 figs.
1965A.   [Archeological cultures of Upper Pleistocene in Poland.] In: Bader,
            O. N., <u>et al</u>., (eds.), 1965, 15—23, 5 figs., (Russian).
1965B.   Archaeological research in northern Sudan. In: Wendorf, Fred, (ed.),
            1965A, 147—164, 12 figs.
            Rev.: ll in Archeol. Roz., 1967, <u>19</u>, 552, (Czechoslovakian).

1966   [Excavations of the Pleistocene and Early Holocene sites in Northern Sudan.] Archeol. Polski, 10:2, 407–430, 13 figs., (Polish; English summary).

1967   Studies on the deposits of Koziarnia cave at Sąspów in the Olkusz District. Archaeology. Folia Quaternaria, 26, 32–57, figs. 12–25, (Polish; English summary).

See: Kostrzewski, Chmielewski and Jażdżewski; Wendorf, Shiner, Marks, et al.

CHMIELEWSKI, W., and KUBIAK, H.
1962   Abs.: Dietrich in Zbl. Geol. Pal., Teil 2, 1964, 213.

CHOATE, JERRY R., and BIRNEY, E. C.
1968   Sub-Recent Insectivora and Chiroptera from Puerto Rico, with the description of a new bat of the genus Stenoderma. Jour. Mammal., 49, 400–412, 5 figs., 3 tables.

CHOLLOT, MARTHE
1964   Musée des Antiquités Nationales. Collection Piette. Preface by Henri Breuil. Introduction by André Varagnac. Paris: Editions des Musées Nationaux, 480 pp., 1 color pl., 1,225 photos., 8 maps., (not seen).
Rev.: St.-Mathurin in Antiq., 41, 331–332.

CHOPPY, B. and J.
1964   Spéléologie du nord de l'Espagne. Spelunca, Bull., 4:3, 38–43, 1 map.
1966   Peintures rupestres de la grotte de Salgues, Thémines (Lot). Spelunca, Bull., 6:1, 34–37, 3 figs.

CHOPRA, S. R. K.
1962   Abs.: Kuhn-Schnyder in Zbl. Geol. Pal., Teil 2, 1964, 223.

CHOU, VAN-AN
1960   [Quaternary studies in China.] Izv. Akad. Nauk, Ser. Geograf., 1960:2, 123–127, (Russian).

CHOUBERT, GEORGES   See: Arambourg and Choubert.

CHOUBERT, G., and FAURE-MURET, ANNE
1961   Le gisement de vertébrés miocènes de Beni Mellal (Maroc). Étude géologique. Notes Mém. Serv. Géol. Maroc, 155, 13–28, 2 figs.

CHOW, BEN-SHUN
1963A.   Abs.: Dietrich in Zbl. Geol. Pal., Teil 2, 1964, 204.
See: Chow, M. and Chow.

CHOW, MIN-CHEN
1960C.   Discovery of the Palaeocene mammal in Turfan Basin and summary of Cenozoic mammalian horizons of Sinkiang. Acta Pal. Sinica, 8, 155–158, 1 fig., (Chinese; English summary).
1962A.   Abs.: Dietrich in Zbl. Geol. Pal., Teil 2, 1964, 204.
1962B.   Abs.: Huene in Zbl. Geol. Pal., Teil 2, 1964, 168.
1964A.   A lemuroid primate from the Eocene of Lantian, Shensi. Vert. Palasiatica, 8:3, 257–262, 1 pl., (Chinese and English).

1964B.   Mammals of "Lantian Man" locality at Lantian, Shensi. Vert. Palasia-
                tica, 8:3, 301—311, 2 pls., (Chinese; English summary).
1965A.   [Characteristics of the zoological group Sinanthropus lantianensis Woo
                and epoch.] Kexue tongbao, 1965:6, 482—487, (Chinese).
1965B.   Mesonychids from the Eocene of Honan. Vert. Palasiatica, 9, 287—291,
                3 figs., (Chinese and English).
1965C.   New discoveries. Vert. Palasiatica, 9, 309—314, 1 fig., (Chinese and
                English).
1965D.   News from IVPP. Vert. Palasiatica, 9, 314.
                See: Tang and Chow; Yin, Chow and Hsu.

CHOW, M.-C., and Chiu, C.-S.
1964   An Eocene giant rhinoceros. Vert. Palasiatica, 8:3, 264—268, 1 pl.,
                (Chinese and English).

CHOW, M.-C., and CHOW, BEN-SHUN
1965   Notes on Villafranchian mammals of Lingyi, Shansi. Vert. Palasiatica,
                9, 223—234, 2 pls., (Chinese; English summary).

CHOW, M.-C., HU, CHANG-KANG, and LEE, YU-CHING
1965   Mammalian fossils associated with the hominid skull cap of Lantian,
                Shensi. Sci. Sinica, 14, 1037—1048, 2 figs., 3 pls.

CHOW, M.-C., HUANG, W.-P., CHANG, Y.-P., TANG, Y.-J., and HUANG, X.-S.
1965   Observations on the younger Cenozoic of SW Shansi. Vert. Palasiatica,
                9, 256—267, 6 figs., 2 pls., 1 table, (Chinese and English).

CHOW, M.-C., and LI, C.-K.
1965   Homogalax and Heptodon of Shantung. Vert. Palasiatica, 9, 15—22,
                2 figs., 1 pl., 1 table, (Chinese and English).

CHOW, M.-C., and TUNG, Y.-S.
1962   Abs.: Dietrich in Zbl. Geol. Pal., Teil 2, 1964, 204.
1965   A new coryphodont from the Eocene of Sinyu, Kiangsi. Vert. Palasia-
                tica, 9, 114—121, 2 figs., 2 pls., 1 table, (Chinese and English).

CHOW, M.-C., and WANG, B.
1964   Fossil vertebrates from the Miocene of northern Kiangsu. Vert. Palasia-
                tica, 8, 341—354, 3 figs., 2 pls., (Chinese and English).

CHOW, M.-C., and XU, Y.
1965   Amynodonts from the Upper Eocene of Honan and Shansi. Vert.
                Palasiatica, 9, 190—204, 3 figs., 4 pls., 2 tables, (Chinese and
                English).

CHOW, M.-C., XU, Y., and ZHEN, SHUO-NAN
1964   Amynodon from the Eocene of Lunan, Yunnan. Vert. Palasiatica, 8:4,
                355—361, 1 fig., 1 pl., 1 table, (Chinese; English summary).

CHOW, M.-C., and YEH, H.
1962   Abs.: Huene in Zbl. Geol. Pal., Teil 2, 1964, 168.

CHOWDHURY, TAPAN KUMAR ROY
1965   A new metoposaurid amphibian from the Upper Triassic Maleri forma-
                tion of Central India. Philos. Trans. Roy. Soc. London, Ser. B,
                250:761, 1—52, 20 figs., 3 pls., 5 tables.

Abs.: Westphal in Zbl. Geol. Pal., Teil 2, 1966, 293–294.
See: Jain, Robinson and Chowdhury.

CHU, XUAN-TSING   See: Ting, M.-L., et al.

CHUDINOV, PETER K. (= Tchudinov)
1964A.   [Subclass Cotylosauria.]   Osnovy Pal., [Amphibians, Reptiles, and
             Birds.], [12], 213–230, 24 figs., 1 table, (Russian).
1964B.   [Family Eotitanosuchidae.]   Osnovy Pal., [Amphibians, Reptiles, and
             Birds.], [12], 247–249, 2 figs., (Russian).
1964C.   [Family Estemmenosuchidae.]   Osnovy Pal., [Amphibians, Reptiles, and
             Birds.], [12], 252–253, 1 fig., (Russian).
1964D.   [Superfamily Venyukovioidea.]   Osnovy Pal., [Amphibians, Reptiles,
             and Birds.], [12], 287–289, 3 figs., (Russian).
1964E.   [Suborder Iguania.]   Osnovy Pal., [Amphibians, Reptiles, and Birds.],
             [12], 461–464, 4 figs., (Russian).
1964F.   [Suborder Scincomorpha.]   Osnovy Pal., [Amphibians, Reptiles, and
             Birds.] [12], 466–469, 1 fig., (Russian).
1964G.   [Superfamily Varanoidea (=Platynota).]   Osnovy Pal., [Amphibians,
             Reptiles, and Birds.], [12], 473–481, 12 figs., (Russian).
1964H.   [Suborder Cholophidia.]   Osnovy Pal., [Amphibians, Reptiles, and
             Birds.], [12], 481–482, 1 fig., (Russian).
1964I.   Some meetings of Soviet and foreign palaeontologists in 1963. Pal.
             Zhurnal, 1964:1, 142–143, (Russian).
1964J.   Contribution to knowledge of Deinocephalia of the USSR. Pal. Zhurnal,
             1964:2, 85–98, 4 figs., (Russian). Translation: Internat. Geol.
             Rev., 7, 1629–1639, 5 figs.
1965   New facts about the fauna of the Upper Permian of the USSR. Jour.
             Geol., 73, 117–130, 5 figs., pl. 1.
1966   [Unique site of Late Cretaceous reptiles in Baian-Khongor Aĭmak.]
             In: Marinov, (ed.), 1966, 74–78, 1 fig., (Russian).
1968A.   [On the skin structure of theromorph reptiles.] Doklady Akad. Nauk
             SSSR, 179:1, 207–210, 1 fig., 2 pls., (Russian).
1968B.   A new dinocephalian from the Cisuralian region (Reptilia, Therapsida;
             Upper Permian). Postilla, 121, 1–20, 4 figs.

CHUMAKOV, I. S. (= Tschumakow, Tchumakov)
1961A.   [On the use of micromammal fauna for subdivision of Quaternary de-
             posits.] Internat. Assoc. Quat. Res., Abs. Pap., 6th Congr., 127,
             (abs., Russian).
1961B.   [On the methods of paleontological study of Anthropogene deposits.]
             In: Gromov, V. I., et al., (eds.), 1961, 41–43, (Russian; En-
             glish summary).
1961C.   [Neogene and Pleistocene deposits of Rudnyĭ Altaĭ.] Mat. Vses. Sov.
             po Izuch. Chetvert. Perioda, 3, 110–116, (Russian).
             Abs.: Mirtsching in Zbl. Geol. Pal., Teil 2, 1964, 671–672.
1965   [The Cenozoic of the Rudnyĭ Altaĭ.] Trudy Geol. Inst., 138, 222 pp.,
             47 figs., 7 tables, (Russian).
1967   [Pliocene and Pleistocene deposits of the Nile valley in Nubia and
             Upper Egypt.] Trudy Geol. Inst., 170, 115 pp., 41 figs., 3 tables,
             (Russian).
             See: Deviatkin, Liskun and Chumakov; Vangengeim and Chumakov.

CHURAKOV, A. N., OBRUCHEV, V. V., and FINASHINA, G. N.
1965   [Vladimir Afanas'evich Obruchev.] Moscow: "Nauka", 231 pp.,
             frontispiece.

CHURCHER, C. S.

1965A. The affinities of Dinobastis serus Cope 1893. 7th Internat. Congr., Internat. Assoc. Quat. Res., Abs., 1965, 65, (abs.).

1965B. Camelid material of the genus Palaeolama Gervais from the Talara tar-seeps, Peru, with a description of a new subgenus, Astylolama. Proc. Zool. Soc. London, 145, 161—205, 31 figs., 3 pls.

1966A. Observaciones sobre el status taxonomico de Epieuryceros Ameghino 1889 y sus especies E. truncus y E. proximus. Ameghiniana, 4, 351—362, 13 figs., 1 table, (English summary).

1966B. The affinities of Dinobastis serus Cope 1893. Quaternaria, 8, 263—275, 1 fig., (German and French summaries).

1967 Smilodon neogaeus en las barrancas costeras de Mar del Plata, provincia de Buenos Aires. Publ. Mus. Mun. Cien. Nat. Trad. Mar del Plata, 1:8, 245—262, 14 figs., 2 tables, (English summary).

1968 Mammoth from the Middle Wisconsin of Woodbridge, Ontario. Canadian Jour. Zool., 46, 219—221, 1 pl.

See: Kenyon, W. A., and Churcher.

CHURCHER, C. S., and ZYLL DE JONG, C. G. VAN

1965 Conepatus talarae n. sp. from the Talara tar-seeps, Peru. Contrib. Roy. Ont. Mus., Life Sci. Div., no. 62, 15 pp., 8 figs.

CHURIKOVA, I. V. See: Cherdyn̂t̂sev, Alekseev, et al.

CHUVARDINSKIĬ, V. G.

1963 [On the problem of continental glaciations in Fennoscandia.] Prirodn. Obstan. i Fauny Proshl., 1, 66—96, (Russian).

CICHA, I. See: Buday, et al.

CIGLIANO, EDUARDO MARIO

1961 Noticia sobre una nueva industria precerámica en el valle de Santa Maria (Catamarca): el Ampajanguense. An. Arqueol. Etnol., Univ. Nac. Cuyo, 16, 169—179, 13 figs.

1962B. Industrias precerámicas de la Puna argentina. Ampurias, 24, 1—34, 6 figs., 8 pls.

1964 Algunos motivos en el arte rupestre del noroeste de la república Argen-tina. In: Ripoll Perelló, E., (ed.), 1964A, 293—308, 3 figs., 8 pls., (French summary).

CINQUABRE, P., and MAITRE, J.-P.

1964 Note sur une industrie Paléolithique de la région d'In-Eker (Ahaggar). Libyca, 12, 47—69, 23 figs., 5 tables.

CIPOVIĆ, V. See: Pavlović and Ćipović.

ĆIRIĆ, ALEKSANDAR

1960 Die Hios-Fauna von Prebreza (Serbien). Vesnik Geol., Beograd, Ser. A, 18, 109—132, 3 tables, (Croatian; German summary). Abs.: M. M. in Bull. Sci. Zagreb, 8, 151; Malez in Bull. Sci., Zagreb, 8, 151.

1962A. [On the finding of the species Mastodon (Bunolophodon) angustidens Cuv. form subtapiroidea Schles. in the lignite mine "Jarando" near Raška.] Vesnik, Beograd, ser. A, Geologija, 20, 103—106, 1 pl., (Servian; German summary).

Abs.: D. M. in Bull. Sci. Zagreb, Sec. A, 12:1—2, 21, (German).

1962B. [The "Steier" mammalian fauna from Lozovik near Svetozarevo.]
Vesnik, Beograd, ser. A, Geologija, 20, 107—119, 3 pls., (Servian
and German).
Abs.: in Bull. Sci. Zagreb, Sec. A, 12:1—2, 21, (German).

CLABAUGH, S. E.   See: Wilson, J. A., et al.

CLAIRAMBAULT, P.
1967   Le complexe strio-amygdalaire des Anoures. Colloq. Internat. Cent.
Nation. Recherch. Sci., 163, 281—294, 6 figs., 3 pls., (English
summary).

CLARACQ, P., and NOUGAREDE, F.
1959   Stations préhistoriques de l'Erg Bourarhet. Libyca, 5, 83—88, 1 fig.,
4 pls.

CLARK, DAVID L.
1968   Fossils, paleontology and evolution. Dubuque, Iowa: William C. Brown,
130 pp., illustr.
See: Rigby and Clark.

CLARK, GEORGE A.   See: Parkes and Clark.

CLARK, G. H. See: Grigor'ev, G. P. 1965A.

CLARK, JANET
1967   Bibliography of vertebrate paleontology and related subjects. 1965—1966.
The Society of Vertebrate Paleontology, no. 21, 82 pp.
1968   Bibliography of vertebrate paleontology and related subjects. 1966—1967.
The Society of Vertebrate Paleontology, no. 22, 84 pp.

CLARK, JOHN
1962   Field interpretation of red beds. Bull. Geol. Soc. Amer., 73, 423—428,
1 fig., 1 table.
1964   Weathermen to the past. Bull. Chicago Nat. Hist. Mus., 35:2, 6—7, 2
figs.
1966A.   Go to the ant. Bull. Field Mus. Nat. Hist., 37:6, 1, 2 figs.
1966B.   Status of the generic names Metacodon and Geolabis [insectivore].
Jour. Pal., 40, 1248—1251.
1967A.   The Slim Buttes formation. In: Clark, Beerbower, and Kietzke, 1967,
16—20, fig. 8.
1967B.   Paleogeography of the Scenic member of the Brule formation. In:
Clark, Beerbower, and Kietzke, 1967, 75—110, figs. 30—52.
1967C.   Interpretative summary. Conclusions. In: Clark, Beerbower, and
Kietzke, 1967, 138—143.

CLARK, J., and BEERBOWER, J. R.
1967   Geology, paleoecology, and paleoclimatology of the Chadron formation.
In: Clark, Beerbower, and Kietzke, 1967, 21—74, figs. 9—29.

CLARK, J., BEERBOWER, J. R., and KIETZKE, K. K.
1967   Oligocene sedimentation, stratigraphy, paleoecology and paleoclimatology
in the Big Badlands of South Dakota. Fieldiana, Geol. Mem.,
5, 158 pp., 56 figs.

Rev.: Hentzschel in Zbl. Geol. Pal., Teil 2, 1969:1, 5;   Macdonald in
Jour. Pal., 42, 1315—1317.

CLARK, J., and KIETZKE, K. K.
1967   Paleoecology of the lower nodular zone, Brule formation, in the Big
            Badlands of South Dakota. In: Clark, Beerbower, and Kietzke,
            1967, 111—137, figs. 53—56.

CLARK, JOHN B., DAWSON, M. R., and WOOD, A. E.
1964   Fossil mammals from the Lower Pliocene of Fish Lake Valley, Nevada.
            Bull. Mus. Comp. Zool. Harvard, 131, 29—63, 11 figs.

CLARK, JOHN DESMOND
1959B.   Rev.: Allchin in Jour. Afr. Hist., 2, 153—154;   Strouhal in Anthrop.,
            2:1, 84—85, (Czech).
1959D.   Reflections on the significance of prehistoric cultural influences in
            South West Africa. S. Afr. Mus. Assoc. Bull., 7:2, 37—45, (not
            seen).
1962F.   (ed.) COWA surveys and bibliographies. Area 12 — Equatorial Africa.
            COWA Surv. and Bibliog., Area 12, no. 2, 3 + 7 pp.
1962G.   (ed.) COWA surveys and bibliographies. Area 14 — East Africa. COWA
            Surv. and Bibliog., Area 14, no. 2, 2 + 16 pp.
1962H.   The Kalambo Falls prehistoric site: an interim report. Proc. 4th Pan-
            african Congr. Prehist., sec. 3, 195—201, 2 pls., 1 table, (dis-
            cussion by A. J. Arkell, and others).
1962I.   Carbon 14 chronology in Africa south of the Sahara. Proc. 4th Pan-
            african Congr. Prehist., sec. 3, 303—311, 1 table, (discussion by
            L. S. B. Leakey, and Ph. Tobias).
1963B.   Rev.: V [aufrey] in L'Anthrop., 68, 156—159;   White in S. Afr.
            Archaeol. Bull., 20, 38—39;   Willett in Jour. Afr. Hist., 5, 308—
            309.
1963D.   Fifth Pan-African Congress. Antiq., 37, 303—306.
1964A.   The Sangoan culture of Equatoria: the implications of its stone equip-
            ment. In: Ripoll Perelló, E., (ed.), 1964A, 309—325, 2 figs.,
            3 pls., (Spanish summary).
1964B.   The prehistoric origins of African culture. Jour. Afr. Hist., 5, 161—183,
            8 figs.
            Rev.: R. V. in L'Anthrop., 69:5—6, 554—556.
1964C.   The influence of environment in inducing culture change at the Kalambo
            Falls prehistoric site. S. Afr. Archaeol. Bull., 19, 93—101.
1965A.   The distribution of prehistoric culture in Angola. Actas V Congr.
            Panafr. Prehist. Estud. Cuaternario, 1963:1, 225—309, 17 figs.,
            2 pls.
1965B.   The atlas of African prehistory: a report on progress. Actas V Congr.
            Panafr. Prehist. Estud. Cuaternario, 1963:1, 311—328, illustr.
1965C.   (ed.) COWA surveys and bibliographies. Area 12 — Equatorial Africa.
            COWA Surv. and Bibliog., Area 12, no. 3, 3 + 11 pp.
1965D.   (ed.) COWA surveys and bibliographies. Area 14 — East Africa.
            COWA Surv. and Bibliog., Area 14, no. 3, 17 pp.
1965E.   The later Pleistocene cultures of Africa. Science, 150, 833—847, 13 figs.
            Rev.: R. V. in L'Anthrop., 70:3—4, 354—356.
1966A.   Acheulian occupation sites in the Middle East and Africa: a study in
            cultural variability. In: Clark, J. D., and Howell, F. C., (eds.),
            1966A, 202—229, 9 figs., 6 pls.

1966B.   Introduction [to Pleistocene fossiliferous lake beds of the Malawi
            (Nyasa) Rift]. In: Clark, J. D., Stephens, E. A., and Coryndon,
            S. C., 1966, 46–49.

1966C.   Initial investigation of the archeology of Karonga district, Malawi. In:
            Clark, J. D., Stephens, E. A., and Coryndon, S. C., 1966, 67–87,
            3 figs., 2 pls., 1 table.

1966D.   The distribution of prehistoric culture in Angola. Lisboa: companhia
            de Diamantes de Angola, Publicacões culturais, no. 73, 102 pp.,
            17 figs., 5 pls.
            Rev.: Fagan in Man, Jour. Roy. Anthrop. Inst., 1, 565.

1967A.   Atlas of African prehistory. Chicago, London: Univ. of Chicago Press,
            62 pp., 2 tables, 12 maps, 38 overlay maps.
            Rev.: Campbell in Sci. Jour., London, 4:4, 89–90; Cole in Amer.
            Anthrop., 71, 149–151; jf in Archeol. Roz., 21:3, 403, (Czech);
            Martin in Mankind, 7:1, 70–71; Strouhal in Archeol. Roz.,
            22:2, 215; Van der Merwe in Science, 159, 292.

1967B.   Introduction to part III. [Archaeological considerations.] B. Sub-
            Saharan Africa. In: Bishop, W. W., and Clark, J. D., (eds.),
            1967A, 413–416.

1967C.   Comments on the resolutions by Professor Desmond Clark. W. Afr.
            Archaeol. Newsletter, no. 7, 40–43.
            See: Anciaux de Faveaux 1962; Biberson 1965A; Bishop and Clark;
            Sharrock 1966; Willcox 1963.

CLARK, J. D., ASCHER, R., FREEMAN, L., et al.
    1965   Pleistocene culture and living sites. In: DeVore, P. L., (ed.), 1965,
            89–107.

CLARK, J. D., and FAGAN, B. M.
    1967   Zambia. In: Oakley, K. P., and Campbell, B. G., (eds.), 1967A, 121–
            125.

CLARK, J. D., and HOWELL, F. C., (eds.)
    1966A. Recent studies in paleoanthropology. Amer. Anthrop. Special Publ.,
            68:2, Part 2, vii + 394 pp., illustr.
            Rev.: kv in Archeol. Roz., 21:2, 256–257, (Czech).

    1966B. Preface [to recent studies in paleoanthropology]. In: Clark, J. D.,
            and Howell, F. C., (eds.), 1966A, v–vii.

CLARK, J. D., COLE, G. H., ISAAC, G. L., and KLEINDIENST, M. R.
    1966   Precision and definition in African archaeology. S. Afr. Archaeol. Bull.,
            21, 114–121.

CLARK, J. D., STEPHENS, E. A., and CORYNDON, S. C.
    1966   Pleistocene fossiliferous lake beds of the Malawi (Nyasa) Rift: a pre-
            liminary report. In: Clark, J. D., and Howell, F. C., (eds.),
            1966A, 46–87, illustr.

CLARK, J. D., and VAN ZINDEREN BAKKER, E. M.
    1964   Prehistoric culture and Pleistocene vegetation at the Kalambo Falls,
            Northern Rhodesia. Nature, 201, 971–975, 2 figs.
            Abs.: Anon. in New Sci., 22, 11.

CLARK, GRAHAME (= Clark, John Grahame Douglass)
    1960-
    1961   Archaeology and society. Reconstructing the prehistoric past. (Rev. ed.).

London: Methuen, University Paperbacks; New York: Barnes and Noble, 272 pp., 52 figs., 24 pls., frontis.

Rev.: Vincent in Sci. of Man, 1, 176.

1961A. Rev.: Braidwood in Antiq., 35, 321–322; Mossler in Mitt. Anthrop. Ges. Wien, 93–94, 148; Vaufrey in L'Anthrop., 68, 139–143.

1962 Rev.: Pittioni in Archaeol. Austriaca, 33, 115.

1964 Frühgeschichte der Menschheit. Stuttgart: W. Kohlhammer, 288 pp., 13 pls., 7 maps.

Rev.: Lippert in Mitt. Anthrop. Ges. Wien, 96–97, 378.

1966 Prehistory and human behavior. Proc. Amer. Philos. Soc., 110:2, 91–99.

1967 The Stone Age hunters. Preface by Stuart Piggott. New York, Toronto: McGraw-Hill, 143 pp., 137 illustrs.

Rev.: Bordes in Amer. Anthrop., 70, 628–629; Evans in Man, Jour. Roy. Anthrop. Inst., 3, 140–141; Gould in Mankind, 6, 525; Higgs in Antiq., 41, 333; Il in Archeol. Roz., 21:2, 256, (Czech); Lacaille in Antiq. Jour., 48:1, 104.

See: Garrod and Clark; McBurney 1967B.

CLARK, J. G. D., and PIGGOTT, S.

1965 Prehistoric societies. New York: Knopf, London: Hutchinson, 356 pp., 95 figs., 8 pls., 4 maps.

Rev.: Anon. in Mankind. Quart., 7, 128; Braidwood in Amer. Anthrop., 68, 1566–1568; Coles in Antiq., 40, 153–155; Dyson in Science, 152, 63–64; Goldman in Nat. Hist., 75:6, 64–65.

CLARK, J. M.

1964 Genesis and its underlying realities. Faith and Thought, 93, 146–158.

CLARK, ROBERT E. D.

1967 Darwin: Before and after. Exeter: Paternoster Press, 192 pp., (not seen).

Rev.: Bacon in Faith and Thought, 95:2, 72.

CLARK, SIR WILFRID EDWARD LE GROS

1960B. Rev.: Jordano in Bol. R. Soc. Españ. Hist. Nat., Sec. Biol., 59, 246.

1964A. The fossil evidence for human evolution. Second edition revised and enlarged. Chicago and London: Univ. Chicago Press, xii + 201 pp., 26 figs.

Rev.: Anon. in Scientia, 100 (Libri ricevuti), 113; Genovés in Amer. Jour. Phys. Anthrop., 27, 105–107; MacConaill in Man, 65, 197–198; Robinson in Amer. Anthrop., 67, 833–834; Swinton in Nature, 208, 1140; Vallois in L'Anthrop., 69, 324–325.

1964B. The origin of man. In: Barnett, S. A., and McLaren, (eds.), 1964, 30–45, fig. 3.

1965A. History of the primates; an introduction to the study of fossil man. 9th ed. London: Staples Printers, 127 pp., 45 figs.

1965B. There is a transcendence from science to science. Raymond Dart Lectures, 2, viii + 18 pp.

1966 The origin of the Hominidae. In: Genovés, S., et al., (eds.), 1966, 48–72, 4 figs., with comment by Thomas W. McKern.

1967A. Foreword. In: Leakey, L. S. B., (ed.), 1967A, xiii–xiv.

1967B. Man-apes or ape-men? The story of discoveries in Africa. New York and London: Holt, Reinhart and Winston, vii + 150 pp., 33 figs., 2 portrs.

Rev.: Day in Jour. Anat., 102, 565–566;   Day in Man, Jour. Roy. Anthrop. Inst., 2, 367;   Holloway in Human Biol., 40:3, 421–423;   Howell in Amer. Jour. Phys. Anthrop., 27, 95–101, 1 fig.; Manten in Earth-Sci. Rev., 4:3, A187–A188;   Napier in Nature, 214, 51;   Roth-Lutra in Anat. Anz., 124, 351–352;   Roth-Lutra in Anthropos, 62:3–4, 594–595;   Sauter in Arch. Suiss. Anthrop. Gen., 31, 56;   Smith in Nat. Hist., 76:8, 64–65;   Straus in Science, 156, 790–791;   Tobias in Jour. Afr. Hist., 10, 171–172;   Vallois in L'Anthrop., 72:3–4, 359–361;   Washburn in Amer. Anthrop., 70, 639–640;   Wheeler in Quart. Rev. Biol., 44:4, 449;   Wood in Mankind, 7:1, 78.

1968   Chant of pleasant exploration. Edinburgh and London: Livingstone, vii + 250 pp., (not seen).
Rev.: Dart in Nature, 220, 829–830.
See: Brace 1964; Leakey, et al. 1967A; Napier 1964A.

CLARKE, D. L.   See: Kerrich and Clarke.

CLARKE, DAVID T.-D.
1966   The Jewry Wall Museum. Mus. Jour., London, 66, 5–9, 4 figs.

CLARKE, JAMES W., et al.
1964   Bibliography of North American geology, 1960. U. S. Geol. Surv. Bull., 1196, 777 pp.

CLAVELL, E.   See: Crusafont Pairó, DeRenzi and Clavell.

CLAYTON, MARGARET V.
1965   Bluff shelter excavations on Sand Mountain. Jour. Ala. Archeol., 11, vi + 1–101 pp., 61 figs.
1967   The Boydston Creek Bluff Shelter. Jour. Ala. Archeol., 13, 1–35, 25 figs., 3 tables.
See: Brock and Clayton.

CLEGG, J. K.
1965   A note on the stone industry of Cathedral Cave, Carnarvon Gorge, Queensland. Mankind, 6, 237.

CLELAND, CHARLES EDWARD
1965A.   Barren ground caribou (Rangifer arcticus) from an Early Man site in southeastern Michigan. Amer. Antiq., 30:3, 350–351.
1965B.   The beta activity of four bone samples from Cueva Reclau, Gerona Province, Spain. In: Jelinek, A. J., and Fitting, J. E., (eds.), 1965, 62–63, 1 table.
1966   The prehistoric animal ecology and ethnozoology of the Upper Great Lakes region. Anthrop. Pap., Univ. Mich., no. 29, x + 294 pp., 5 figs., 40 tables.
Rev.: Ambrose in Mankind, 6:11, 610–611;   Baerreis in Science, 157, 1164;   Bryson and Baerreis in Wis. Archeol., 48, 262–265.

CLEMENS, WILLIAM A., JR.
1963C.   Abs.: Hünermann in Zbl. Geol. Pal., Teil 2, 1966, 322–323.
1964   Records of the fossil mammal Sinclairella, family Apatemyidae, from the Chadronian and Orellan. Univ. Kansas Publ. Mus. Nat. Hist., 14:17, 483–491, 2 figs., 1 table.

1965A. Marsupial evolution during the Cretaceous. Amer. Zool., 5:4, 681.
1965B. Collecting Late Cretaceous mammals in Alberta. 15th Ann. Field
        Confer. Guidebk., Alberta Soc. Petrol. Geol., pt. 1, 137—141,
        2 figs.
1966   Fossil mammals of the type Lance formation. Wyoming. Part II.
        Marsupialia. Univ. Calif. Publ. Geol. Sci., 62, 1—122, 77 figs.,
        24 tables.
        Abs.: B. B. in Przegl. Geol., 1967:3, 149.
        Rev.: Hünermann in Zbl. Geol. Pal., Teil 2, 1967, 110—111; Mac-
        Intyre and Graham in Quart. Rev. Biol., 43:1, 70; Russell
        in Jour. Pal., 41, 813—814.
1968A. A mandible of Didelphodon vorax (Marsupialia, Mammalia). Contrib.
        Sci. Los Angeles Co. Mus., no. 133, 1—11, 5 figs., 1 table.
1968B. Origin and early evolution of marsupials. Evolution, 22, 1—18, 5 figs.
        See: Jeletsky and Clemens.

CLEMENS, W. A., McKENNA, M. C., RUSSELL, D. E., SLOAN, R. E., and
VAN VALEN, L.
1964   Cimolestidae Marsh, 1889 (Mammalia): Proposed suppression under
        the plenary powers. Bull. Zool. Nomen., 21, 363.

CLEMENS, W. A., and RUSSELL, L. S.
1965   Mammalian fossils from the Upper Edmonton formation. Vert. Pal.
        in Alberta, Univ. of Alberta, 1965, 32—40, figs. 5—9, 1 table.

CLEMENT, JERRY T. See: Jakway and Clement.

CLIQUET, R.
1965   Antropologie. Herkomst, wezen, toekomst van de mens. Antwerpen:
        Uitgeverij de sikkel n.v., (not seen).
        Rev.: Walter in Homo, 16, 188.

CLYMER, ELEANOR
1962   Rev.: Anon. in Mankind. Quart. 5:1, 52—53.

COASH, J. R. See: Hoare, et al.

COBB, STANLEY, and EDINGER, T.
1962   The brain of the emu (Dromaeus novaehollandiae, Lath). Breviora,
        no. 170, 1—18, 4 figs.

COCKRUM, LENDELL See: Koopman and Cockrum.

COCKS, G. T. See: Arnheim, et al.

COCUDE-MICHEL, MARGUERITE
1964   Étude d'Eichstättisaurus digitatellus (= Homoeosaurus digitatellus Grier
        1914), saurien du Portlandien inférieur. C. R. Soc. Géol. France,
        1964, 420, (abs.).
1965   Étude d'Eichstättisaurus digitatellus (= Homoeosaurus digitatellus Grier
        1914) saurian du Portlandien inférieur de Solenhofen. Bull.
        Soc. Geol. France, 6, 704—706, pl. 20.
1967   Revision des rhynchocephales de la collection du Musee Teyler de
        Haarlem (Pays-Bas). I and II. Proc. K. Nederl. Akad. Wet.,
        Ser. B, 70, 538—555, 7 pls.

Rev.: Groiss in Geol. Bl. NO-Bayern, 19, 95.

COE, JOFFRE LANNING
1952   The cultural sequence of the Carolina Piedmont. In: Griffin, J. B.,
          (ed.), 1952A, 301–311.
1964   The formative cultures of the Carolina Piedmont. Trans. Amer. Philos.
          Soc., 54, part 5, 130 pp., 117 figs.
          Rev.: Bottoms in Chesopiean, 3:1, 25; MacCord in Bull. Archaeol.
          Soc. Virginia, no. 11, 5.
1965   The Paleo-Indian era: distribution of finds. North Carolina. Bull.
          Southeast. Archaeol. Confer., 2, 15–16A.

COE, WILLIAM R.   See: Stuckenrath, Coe and Ralph.

COGGI, LEONIDA
1964   Dente di Ptychodus latissimus Ag. nella scaglia cretacica delle Madonìe
          orientali (Sicilia centro-settentrionale). Atti Soc. Ital. Mus.
          Civico, Milano, 103, 118–128, 2 figs., (French and English
          summaries).
          Rev.: Guaitani Mazza in Riv. Ital. Pal., 71, 331–332.

[COHEN, DANIEL]
1963   The lying stones. Sci. Digest, 54:6, 64, illustr.
1965   Please explain. Is there a missing link? Sci. Digest, 58:3, 96–97,
          illustr.

COHEN, J. M.   See: Chardin 1965B.

COLBERT, EDWIN H.
1958J.   Abs.: Huene in Zbl. Geol. Pal., Teil 2, 1964, 138.
1963B.   Abs.: Huene in Zbl. Geol. Pal., Teil 2, 1964, 989.
1963E.   Abs.: Huene in Zbl. Geol. Pal., Teil 2, 1964, 989.
1963F.   Department of Vertebrate Paleontology. Ann. Rept. Amer. Mus. Nat.
            Hist., 94, 46–48, 1 pl.
1964A.   The Triassic dinosaur genera Podokesaurus and Coelophysis. Amer.
            Mus. Novit., 2168, 12 pp., 3 figs., 2 tables.
            Abs.: Huene in Zbl. Geol. Pal., Teil 2, 1964, 989–990.
1964B.   Relationships of the saurischian dinosaurs. Amer. Mus. Novit., no. 2181,
            24 pp., 6 figs.
1964C.   Department of Vertebrate Paleontology. Ann. Rept. Amer. Mus. Nat.
            Hist., 95, 54–57.
1964D.   The relevance of palaeontological data concerning evidence of aridity
            and hot climates in the past geologic ages. In: Nairn, ed. 1964,
            378–381.
1964E.   Climatic zonation and terrestrial faunas. In: Nairn, ed., 1964, 617–
            637, 642, 11 figs.
1964F.   Dinosaurs of the Arctic. Nat. Hist., 73:4, 20–23, illustr.
1964G.   Dinosaurs. Their discovery and their world. [4th printing of 1961E.]
            New York: E. P. Dutton, xvi + 300 pp., 51 figs., 100 pls.
1965A.   A phytosaur from North Bergen, New Jersey. Amer. Mus. Novit.,
            no. 2230, 25 pp., 9 figs., 1 table.
            Rev.: Huene in Zbl. Geol. Pal., Teil 2, 1967, 105.
1965B.   Department of Vertebrate Paleontology. Ann. Rept. Amer. Mus. Nat.
            Hist., 96, 55–59, 3 pls.
1965C.   The university in the museum. Curator, 8:1, 78–85.

1965D.   Old bones, and what to do about them. Curator, 8, 302–318, 12 figs.

1965E.   The age of reptiles. London: Weidenfeld and Nicolson; New York:
W. W. Norton, 228 pp., 67 figs., 20 pls., 15 tables. Also, p.b.
ed.

    Abs.: Huene in Zbl. Geol. Pal., Teil 2, 1966, 302–303.

    Rev.: Anon. in Discovery, 26:3, 58; Anon. in Sci. Amer., 214:1,
129; Charig in New Sci., 25, 659–660; Olson in Nat. Hist.,
74:10, 10; Romer in Quart. Rev. Biol., 41, 415–416; Whitmore
in GeoTimes, 10:6, 32.

1965F.   The appearance of new adaptations in Triassic tetrapods. Israel Jour.
Zool., 14, 49–62, 1 table.

    Rev.: Huene in Zbl. Geol. Pal., Teil 2, 1967, 106.

1965G.   Carl Sorensen. 1893 - 1965. News Bull., Soc. Vert. Pal., 74, 56–57,
portr.

1965H.   Die Evolution der Wirbeltiere. Eine Geschichte der Wirbeltiere durch
Zeiten. Transl. by G. Heberer. Stuttgart: Fischer, 426 pp.,
152 figs., (not seen).

    Abs.: Westphal in Zbl. Geol. Pal., Teil 2, 1966, 263.

    Rev.: Bauer in Mitt. Anthrop. Ges. Wien, 95, 369–370; Fischer in
Ber. Deutsch. Ges. Geol. Wiss., Reihe A, 11:3, 420; Haltenorth
in Säugetierkundl. Mitt., 14, 146; Knussmann in Homo, 16,
190; Krumbiegel in Geologie, 16, 864; Kurth in Naturwiss.
Rund., 18, 500; Marinelli in Verh. Zool.-Bot. Ges. Wien,
105–106, 190; Mertens in Natur u. Mus., 96, 121; Preuschoft
in Anthrop. Anz., 30, 306; Roth-Lutra in Anat. Anz., 121,
450–451; M. R. S. in Arch. Suiss. Anthrop. Gen., 30, 88;
Thenius in Kosmos (Stuttgart), 62, *277; Thenius in Mitt. Geol.
Ges. Wien, 58, 267–268; Thomas in Salamandra, 1, 78; Vallois
in L'Anthrop., 70:1–2, 168–169; Wetzig in Gegenbaurs Morph.
Jahrb., 108, 446; Zapfe in Ann. Naturhist. Mus. Wien, 70, 518.

1966A.   A gliding reptile from the Triassic of New Jersey. Amer. Mus. Novit.,
2246, 1–23, 10 figs.

    Rev.: Huene in Zbl. Geol. Pal., Teil 2, 1967, 105–106.

1966B.   Department of vertebrate paleontology. Ann. Rept. Amer. Mus. Nat.
Hist., 97, 62–64.

1966C.   Ancient reptile of Blue Bell. Frontiers, 31, 42–44, 2 figs.

1966D.   Rates of erosion in the Chinle formation — ten years later. Plateau,
38, 68–74, 1 fig., 2 tables.

1967A.   Adaptations for gliding in the lizard Draco. Amer. Mus. Novit., 2283,
20 pp., 6 figs., 2 tables.

1967B.   A new interpretation of Austropelor, a supposed jurassic labyrinthodont
amphibian from Queensland. Mem. Queensland Mus., 15, 35–
42, pl. 6, 1 table.

    Rev.: Westphal in Zbl. Geol. Pal., Teil 2, 1969:2, 208.

1967C.   New adaptations of Triassic reptiles. Proc. Israel Acad. Sci., Sect. Sci.,
5, 1–13, 9 figs.

1968A.   Men and dinosaurs. The search in field and laboratory. New York:
Dutton, xviii + 283 pp., illustr.

    Rev.: Cox in Nature, 222, 1307–1308; Eaton in Evolution, 22, 844;
Nelson in Isis, 60:4, 554–555; Olsen in GeoTimes, 14:2, 32;
Swazey in Jour. Hist. Biol., 2:2, 447; Wheeler in Science, 161,
348–349.

1968B.   Memorial to Charles Craig Mook (1887 - 1966). Proc. Geol. Soc. Amer.
for 1966, 1968, 309–315, portr.

    See: Barrett, P. J., et al.; Kay and Colbert; Seeley 1967.

COLBERT, E. H., and MERRILEES, D.
1967   Cretaceous dinosaur footprints from Western Australia. Jour. Roy.
            Soc. W. Australia, 50, 21–25, 1 fig., 2 tables.

COLBERT, E. H., and REEKIE, G.
1965   New space, new wings. Curator, 8, 212–222, 9 figs.

COLE, GLEN H.
1965   Recent archaeological work in southern Uganda. Uganda Jour., 29,
            149–161, 2 figs.
1967   The Later Acheulian and Sangoan of southern Uganda. Discussion.
            In: Bishop, W. W., and Clark, J. D., (eds.), 1967A, 481–528,
            18 figs., 6 tables, (French summary).
            See: Clark, J. D., Cole, et al.; Howell, Cole, et al.; Van Beck, Cole,
            and Jamme.

COLE, SONIA
1954C.   Rev.: Allchin in Jour. Afr. Hist., 2, 153–154.
1961B.   Forgeries and the British Museum. Antiq. 35, 103–106.
1963A.   Rev.: Pericot in Zephyrus, 14, 146–147; Souville in Hespéris Tamuda,
            4, 237–239.
1963B.   Rev.: Roth-Lutra in Anat. Anz., 116, 524–525; S. in Archeol. Roz.,
            17, 560–561, (Czech).
1963D.   The Stone Age of East Africa. In: Oliver, R., and Mathew, G., (eds.),
            1963, 23–57, 2 tables, 1 map.
1964A.   Ancient mammals of Africa. New Sci., 22, 606–609, 5 figs.
1964B.   The prehistory of East Africa. London: Weidenfeld and Nicolson,
            New York: Macmillan, 382 pp., 60 figs., 22 pls., 15 maps.
            Rev.: Chittick in Jour. Afr. Hist., 6, 123–125; Fagan in S. Afr.
            Archaeol., Bull., 20, 39–40; Heberer in Anthrop. Anz., 28,
            49–50.
1965   The prehistory of East Africa. New introduction. New York: New
            Amer. Lib., Mentor Book, xvii + 384 pp., 59 figs., 23 pls.,
            (paperback).
1966A.   Races of man. 2nd ed. London: Brit. Mus. (Nat. Hist.), 131 pp.,
            illustr.
1966B.   Animal ancestors: drawings and reconstructions by M. Maitland Howard.
            New York, and London: Dutton, and Phoenix House, 78 pp.,
            illustr., (not seen).
            Rev.: Shaw in Nat. Hist., 74:9, 16–17.

COLEMAN, WILLIAM
1964   Georges Cuvier zoologist. A study in the history of evolution theory.
            Cambridge, Mass.: Harvard Univ. Press, xii + 212 pp., illustr.,
            2 tables, frontispiece.
            Rev.: Ballard in Quart. Rev. Biol., 39, 376–377; Eriksson in Lychnos,
            1963–1964, 429–431, (Swedish); Zirkle in Science, 144, 166–
            167.

COLES, J. M.
1966   Functional archaeology. Nature, 210, 146–147.

COLIMORE, VINCENT   See: Cuénot 1965.

COLINVAUX, PAUL A.
1967   Bering Land Bridge: evidence of spruce in Late-Wisconsin times.
            Science, 156, 380–383, 3 figs., 2 tables.

COLLECTED PAPERS
1959   [Materials of the second conference of archeologists and ethnographers
            of Central Asia, Stalinabad, 1956.] Moscow-Leningrad: Akad.
            Nauk SSSR Press, 271 pp., illustr., (Russian).
1962-
1965A.   [Problems of ecology and practical significance of birds and mammals
            of Moldavia.] Kishinev: "Kartīa Moldovenīaske" Press, (Russian).
1965B.   Teilhard de Chardin et la pensée catholique. (Colloque de Venise).
            Paris: Editions du Seuil, 266 pp.
            Rev.: M. C. in Fossilia, 1965:3–4, 51–52.
1966A.   [Materials on the geology and economic ores of western Kazakhstan.]
            Alma-Ata: "Nauka" Press, (Russian).
1966B.   [Materials on the geology of the eastern part of Russian Platform.]
            Kazan': Kazan. Univ. Press, (Russian).
1966C.   [Solar activity and changes of climate.] Leningrad: Gidrometeoizdat
            Press, (Russian).
1966D.   [Materials on the geology and economic ores of the northwest of
            RSFSR.] Leningrad: "Nedra" Press, (Russian).
1966E.   [Problems of karst research on the Russian Plain.] Moscow: (Russian).
1966F.   [Materials of the IV Conference of pathologists-anatomists of Latviīa.]
            Riga: "Zinatne" Press.
1967A.   [Place and significance of fossil mammals of Moldavia in the Cenozoic
            of USSR.] Kishinev: Akad. Nauk Moldav. SSR, otd. pal. i
            strat., 116 pp., ill., (Russian).
1967B.   [Lower Pleistocene of glaciated regions of the Russian Plain.] Moscow:
            "Nauka" Press, (Russian).
1967C.   [Problems of paleogeographical regionalization in the light of paleonto-
            logical data.] Moscow: "Nedra" Press, (Russian).
1967D.   [Stratigraphy of the Mesozoic and Cenozoic of Middle Siberia.]
            Novosibirsk: "Nauka" Press, (Russian).
1967E.   [Problems of geology of Middle and Upper Paleozoic of Baltic regions.]
            Riga: "Zinatne" Press.
1967F.   [Problems of geology of South Urals and Povolzh'e.] Saratov: Saratov
            Univ. Press, (Russian).
1968   [Materials on the regional geology of Siberia]. Novosibirsk.

COLLETTE, BRUCE B.   See: Peters and Collette.

COLLIN, RICHARD O., and STOIBER, G. A.
1962   Fun with fossils. The how, why, and what for the young amateur
            collector. Illustrated by Lucy W. Muther. Phoenix, N. Y.:
            Frank E. Richards, 42 pp., illustr., (elemen. school).

COLLINS, CHARLES T.
1964   Fossil ibises from the Rexroad fauna of the Upper Pliocene of Kansas.
            Wilson Bull., 76, 43–49, 2 figs.

COLLINS, DESMOND M.
1965A.   Prehistoric art. Discovery, 26:5, 32–37, 5 figs.
1965B.   Seriation of quantitative features in Late Pleistocene stone technology.
            Nature, 205, 931–932, 3 tables.

Rev.: Vencl in Archeol. Roz., 18:3, 380–381, (Czech).
See: Aguirre, Collins and Cuenca; Chardin 1965B.

COLLINS, HENRY B., JR.
1951C.   Introductory statement [anthropology in Alaska]. Proc. Alaskan Sci.
         Confer., 1950, 43–44.
1963   Paleo-Indian artifacts in Alaska: an example of cultural retardation in
         the Arctic. Anthrop. Pap. Univ. Alaska, 10:2, 13–18.
1964   The Arctic and Subarctic. In: Jennings and Norbeck (eds.), 1964A,
         85–114, 4 figs.
         Rev.: Laughlin in Amer. Antiq., 30, 501–503.
1965   Eighty-first annual report of the Bureau of American Ethnology to the
         Secretary of the Smithsonian Institution. Ann. Rept. Bur. Amer.
         Ethnol., 81, 31 pp.

COLOM, G.
1966   Myotragus y la paleogeografia de su epoca. Bol. Soc. Hist. Nat. Baleares,
         12:1–4, 13–24.

COLWELL, JANE
1965   Dentine tubules in the South American family Leontiniidae. Geol. Soc.
         Amer., Cordilleran Sect., Pal. Soc., Pac. Coast Sect., Prog. 61st
         Ann. Meeting, 1965, 19, (abs.).

COMAS, JUAN
1961   El origen del hombre americano y la antropología física. Cuad. Inst.
         Hist., ser. Antrop., 13, 53 pp., 2 tables.
         Rev.: Anon. in Acta Praehist., 1966, 5–7, 294.
1962   Rev.: Anon. in Acta Praehist., 1966, 5–7, 287–288; Comas in An.
         Antrop., Mexico, 1964, 1, 211–220; M. G. in Anthropos, 61,
         959.
1966   Manual de antropologia fisica 2nd ed. México: Universidad nacional
         autónoma de México, Instituto de investigaciones históricas,
         Sección de antropología (Serie antropológica, 10), 710 pp., 122
         figs., 101 tables, (not seen).
         Rev.: Bunak in Voprosy Antrop., 27, 185–186; MacConaill in Man,
         Jour. Roy. Anthrop. Inst., 2, 309; Santos Jr. in Trab. Soc.
         Port. Anthrop. Etnol., 20:3–4, 390–391; Schwidetzky in Homo,
         18:2, 111.
1967   Unidad y variedad de la especie humana. México: UNAM, 145 pp.,
         illustr., (not seen).
         Rev.: Marquer in L'Anthrop., 73:3–4, 293; Sauter in Arch. Suiss.
         Anthropol. Gén., 32, 146; Wells in Man, Jour. Roy. Anthrop.
         Inst., 3, 317.
1968   (trans.) Definición del género humano. México: Instituto Nacional de
         Antropología e Historia, 129 pp., (not seen).
         Rev.: Wells in Man, Jour. Roy. Anthrop. Inst., 3, 662–663; Helmuth
         in Zeit. Morph. Anthrop., 61:1, 119.
         See: Bordes, Comas, et al.; Genovés and Comas.

COMASCHI CARIA, IDA
1965   L'Elefante nano del Quaternario di Gonnesa (Sardegna sud-occidentale).
         Rend. Semin. Fac. Sci. Univ. Cagliari, 35, 81–91, 3 figs., 4 pls.

COMBIER, JEAN
1967 Le Paléolithique de l'Ardèche dans son cadre paléoclimatique. Publ.
   Inst. Préhist. Univ. Bordeaux, Mém. no. 4, 462 + xvi pp., 175
   figs., 5 maps, 3 charts, 25 tables.
   Rev.: KV in Archeol. Roz., 21:2, 257, (Czech).

COMBIER, J., and DESBROSSE, R.
1964 Magdalénien final à pointe de Teyjat dans le Jura méridional. L'Anthrop.,
   68, 190–194, 1 fig.

COMBIER, M.
1966 L'Abbé Breuil. Bull. Soc. Linn. Lyon, 35, 262–265.

COMFORT, IRIS TRACY
1964 Earth treasures: rocks and minerals. Illustrated by Jan Fairservis.
   Englewood Cliffs, N. J.: Prentice-Hall, 72 pp., illustr., (Elemen.
   school).

COMISKEY, JEAN LOOK See: Look 1967

COMPTON, CARL B.
1960 America's first people. Ohio Archaeol., 10, 104–107.
   Reprint in: New World Antiq., 8, 22–28.
1963 The first Americans. Anthrop. Jour. Canada, 1:1, 2–5.
1964 Paleo-man in Texas. New World Antiq., 11, 22–28.

CONCI, CESARE
1966 Dono al Museo Civico di Storia Naturale di Milano della collezione
   paleontologica e paletnologica del Prof. Carlo Maviglia. Ricosti-
   tuzione presso il medesimo di un reparto paletnologico. Natura,
   Riv. Sci. Nat., 57, 60–62.

CONKLIN, DAVID A., (ed.)
1957 [COWA surveys and bibliographies.] Area 20 – Indonesia. COWA
   Surv. and Bibliog., Area 20, no. 1, 3 + 11 pp.

CONNAH, GRAHAM
1967A. Premier colloque international d'archéologie africaine. W. Afr. Archaeol.
   Newsletter, no. 6, 46–51.
1967B. "An apology for 'culture'." W. Afr. Archaeol. Newsletter, no. 7, 13–15,
   (French summary).

CONOLLY, J. R.
1965 The stratigraphy of the Hervey Group in Central New South Wales.
   Jour. Proc. Roy. Soc. N.S.W., 98, 37–83, 23 figs., 3 pls.

CONRAD, G.
1965 Stratigraphie du Quaternaire de l'Ahnet et du Mouydir (Sahara central).
   Quaternaria, 7, 91–100, 1 fig., 1 table, (Italian and German
   summaries).

CONTESCU, L. See: Macarovici, Motaş, and Contescu.

CONTRERAS, JULIO R.
1964 Datos acerca de la variación intrapoblacional de la morfología de los

molares de entidades de los géneros Galea y Microcavia (Rodentia, Caviidae). Ameghiniana, 3:8, 235–255, 3 figs., 2 pls., 1 table, (English summary).

CONVERSE, ROBERT N.
1963   Ohio flint types. Ohio Archaeol., 13, 77–120, illustr.
1967   Fossil shark teeth. Ohio Archaeol., 17, 105–106, 1 fig.

COOK, D. L.
1963A.   Abs.: R. in Helictite, 1, 62.

COOK, HAROLD J.
1965   Running Water formation, Middle Miocene of Nebraska. Amer. Mus. Novit., no. 2227, 1–8, 3 figs.

COOK, MARGARET C.
1965   Agate Fossil Beds National Monument, Cook Museum of Natural History, Harold J. Cook Research Center. News Bull., Soc. Vert. Pal., no. 75, 4–6, 3 photos.
1967   Agate Fossil Beds National Monument. News Bull., Soc. Vert. Pal., 79, 57–59, 3 figs.
1968   Agate Fossil Beds National Monument, Nebraska. News Bull., Soc. Vert. Pal., 83, 38.

COOK, MELVIN A.
1966   Prehistory and earth models. London: Olbourne, 368 pp., (not seen).

COOK, S. F.
1964   The nature of charcoal excavated at archaeological sites. Amer. Antiq., 29, 514–517.

COOK, S. F., and HEIZER, R. F.
1965   Studies on the chemical analysis of archaeological sites. Univ. Calif. Publ. Anthrop., 2, 102 pp., 15 figs., 17 tables.
               Rev.: Callen in Amer. Antiq., 32, 118–119.

COOKE, C. K.
1958   A comparison between the weapons in rock art in Southern Rhodesia and weapons known to have been used by Bushmen and later people. Occ. Pap. Nation. Mus. S. Rhodesia, 3:22A, 120–140, 12 figs.
1964A.   Some unusual implements from the area of the confluence of the Shashi and Shashani Rivers in Southern Rhodesia. Arnoldia, 1:8, 1–3, 2 figs.
1964B.   Animals in Southern Rhodesia rock art. Arnoldia, 1:13, 1–22, 10 figs.
1964C.   An introduction to the prehistory of the Rhodesias. Proc. Rhod. Sci. Assoc., 50, 50–58, 9 figs.
1964D.   Unusual implements from an open eroded site near Inyanga. Southern Rhodesia. S. Afr. Archaeol. Bull., 19, 17, 2 figs.
1966A.   Re-appraisal of the industry hitherto named the Proto-Stillbay. Arnoldia, 2:22, 1–14, 7 figs.
1966B.   The archaeology of the Mafungabusi area, Gokwe, Rhodesia. Proc. Rhod. Sci. Assoc., 51, 51–78, 7 figs., 14 tables, 1 map.
1967A.   A preliminary report on the Stone Age of the Nata River, Botswana. Arnoldia, 2:40, 1–10, 3 figs., 1 table.

1967B.   Part II. Archaeology and excavation. In: Brain, C. K., and Cooke, C. K., 1967, 177—182, 1 fig.

1967C.   Were the Late Stone Age people responsible for the cave art? S. African Jour. Sci., 63, 207—211.

   See: Brain and Cooke.

COOKE, C. K., and ROBINSON, K. R.

1954   Excavations at Amadzimba Cave, located in the Matopo Hills, Southern Rhodesia. Occ. Pap. Nation. Mus. S. Rhodesia, 2:19, 699—728, 13 figs.

COOKE, C. K., SUMMERS, R., and ROBINSON, K. R.

1966   Rhodesian prehistory re-examined. Part I: The Stone Age. Arnoldia, 2:12, 1—8.

COOKE, H. B. S.

1963C.   African mammals in the fossil record. Proc. 16th Internat. Congr. Zool., 4, 46—51, 1 fig., 1 table.

1964   The Pleistocene environment in Southern Africa. In: Davis, D. H. S., (ed.), 1964, 1—23, 11 figs.

1967   The Pleistocene sequence in South Africa and problems of correlation. In: Bishop, W. W., and Clark, J. D., (eds.), 1967A, 175—184, 1 table, (French summary).

1968   Evolution of mammals on southern continents. II. The fossil mammal fauna of Africa. Quart. Rev. Biol., 43, 234—264, 17 figs., 2 tables.

   See: Ewer and Cooke; Whitmore, Emery, et al.

COON, CARLETON STEVENS

1961   There are Neanderthals among us. N. Y. Times Mag., March 12, 1961, 32, 84, 86, illustr.

1962B.   Rev.: Chaplin in Bull. London Univ. Inst. Archaeol., 5, 91; Chowdhury in Man in India, 44, 92; Genovés in An. Antrop., Mexico, 1964 1, 220—222; Montagu in Montagu, M. F. A., (ed.), 1964, 228—241; Roginskiĭ in Sovetskaĭa Etnografiĭa, 1964:1, 170—175, (Russian); Simpson, G. G., in Perspectives Biol. Med., 6, 268—272; Trigger in Anthropologica, n.s., 7, 179—187.

1962C.   Rev.: Anon. in Archaeol., 17, 152; Bose in Man in India, 44, 361.

1967A.   Reply to Buettner-Janusch. Amer. Jour. Phys. Anthrop., 26, 359—360.

1967B.   Reply [to reviews of "The living races of man"]. Current Anthrop., 8, 123—125.

   See: Arambourg, Biberson, et al.; Brace 1964.

COON, C. S., and HUNT, E. E., JR.

1965   The living races of man. New York: Knopf, 352 pp.

   Rev.: Abbie, Angel, Barnicot, Bielicki, Brues, Darlington, Debetz, Hiernaux, Johnston, Kelso, Krogman, Lundman, Mavalwala, and Tappen in Current Anthrop., 8, 112—123; Bowles in Science, 154, 628—629; Buettner-Janusch in Amer. Jour. Phys. Anthrop., 25, 182—188; Harrison in Human Biol., 39, 330—333; Littlewood in Amer. Anthrop., 69, 260—261; H. V. V. in L'Anthrop., 71: 5—6, 532—536; Van Valen in Perspectives Biol. Med., 10, 320—321; Dobzhansky in Nature, 212, 879—880.

COOPER, BYRON N.
1964   New fossil finds at Saltville, Virginia. Mining Industries Jour., 10:4,
               1—3, 5 figs., (not seen).
           See: Ray, Cooper, and Benninghoff.

COOPER, G. ARTHUR, and WHITTINGTON, H. B.
1965   Use of acids in preparation of fossils. In: Kummel and Raup, (eds.),
               1965, 294—300.

COOPER, H. M.
1966   Archaeological stone implements from a lagoon bed, Kangaroo Island,
               South Australia. Rec. S. Austral. Mus., 15, 309—327, 21 figs.

COOPER, PETER P.
1967   Early points on the Upper Yadkin, N. C. Anthrop. Jour. Canada, 5:1,
               11, 1 fig.

COPPENS, YVES
1961B.   Actualités paléontologiques. Bull. Soc. Préhist., Paris, 57, 745—748,
               illustr.
1962C.   Rev.: Mauny in Bull. Inst. Franç. Afr. Noire, sér. B, 24, 310.
1963   De l'Australopithèque du Tchad au Pebbletool du Morbihan. Bull.
               Soc. Polymathique Morbihan, Déc. 1962 - Jan. 1963, 5—7, (not
               seen).
1964   Homo habilis et les nouvelles découvertes d'Oldoway. Bull. Soc. Pré-
               hist. Franç., C. R. séances mens., 1964:7, clxxi—clxxvi.
1965A.   L'Hominien du Tchad. Actas V Congr. Panafr. Prehist. Estud. Cuater-
               nario, 1963:1, 329—330.
1965B.   Les proboscidiens du Tchad. Leur contribution à la chronologie du
               Quaternaire African. Actas V Congr. Panafr. Prehist. Estud.
               Cuaternario, 1963:1, 331—387, 18 pls., 1 map, 1 table.
1965C.   L'Hominien du Tchad. C. R. Acad. Sci. Paris, 260, 2869—2871, 2 pls.
1965D.   Stratigraphic and antomic situation of Tchad hominian. 7th Internat.
               Congr., Internat. Assoc. Quat. Res., Abs., 1965, 75, (abs.).
1966A.   Les gisements de vertébrés quaternaires de l'Ouest africain. Bull. Inst.
               Franç. Afr. Noire, Ser. A, 28, 373—381, 2 figs.
1966B.   Le point des connaissances en Paléontologie humaine. Bull. Soc. Préhist.
               Franç., Etud. et Trav., 63:3, 475—484, 1 table.
1966C.   Le Tchadanthropus. L'Anthrop., 70, 5—16, 3 figs.
           Abs.: Anon. in Anthropos, 61, 900.
           Rev.: Comas in An. Antropol., Mexico, 5, 253—254.
1967A.   Essai de biostratigraphie du Quaternaire de la région de Koro-Toro
               (Nord-Tchad). Colloq. Internat. Cent. Nation. Recherch. Sci.,
               163, 589—595, 2 figs., (English summary).
1967B.   Les faunes de vertébrés Quaternaires du Tchad. Discussion. In: Bishop,
               W. W., and Clark, J. D., (eds.), 1967A, 89—97, 2 figs., 3 pls.,
               (English summary).
1967C.   Chad. In: Oakley, K. P., and Campbell, B. G., (eds.), 1967A, 7—8.
1968   Gisements paléontologiques et archéologiques découverts en 1961 dans
               le nord du Tchad au cours d'une seconde mission de trois mois.
               Bull. Inst. Franç. Afr. Noire, 30, 790—801, 5 figs.

See: Arambourg, Chavaillon and Coppens; Arambourg and Coppens; Ginsburg and Coppens.

COQUE, R., and JAUZEIN, A.
1966   Le Quaternaire de Tunisie. Quaternaria, 8, 139–154, 9 figs., (German summary).

CORAZZA, CLAUDIO
1964   Stazioni di superficie sul versante nord-ovest del Morrone. Atti Soc. Toscana Sci. Nat. Mem., Ser. A, 71, 95–112, 6 figs.

CORBEL, JEAN   See: Chaline 1965C.

CORBET, G. B., and MORRIS, P. A.
1967   A collection of Recent and sub-fossil mammals from southern Turkey (Asia Minor), including the doormouse Myomimus personatus. Jour. Nat. Hist., 1, 561–569, 2 figs.

CORDIER, GÉRARD
1965   Existe-t-il une pebble culture en Touraine? L'Anthrop., 69:1–2, 166–169, 1 fig.
        See: Jullien 1965B.

CORIN, F.
1965   Victor Van Straelen (14 juin 1889 - 29 février 1964). Bull. Soc. Belge Geol. Pal. Hydrologie, 74, 12–35, portr.

CORNELIUS-FURLANI, M.   See: Bachmayer and Cornelius-Furlani.

CORNELL, TOM
1964   Cumberland point. Jour. Ala. Archaeol., 10, 38, 1 fig.

CORNWALL, IAN W.
1964   The world of ancient man. London: Phoenix House; New York: John Day, xii + 271 pp., illustr.
        Rev.: Ashbee in Antiq. Jour., 45, 119;   Bose in Man in India, 44, 360;   Braidwood in Archaeol., 19, 302, 305;   Brothwell in Discovery, 25:12, 50;   Butzer in Man, Jour. Roy. Anthrop. Inst., 1, 251;   Cole in New Sci., 23, 49;   Lacaille in Mus. Jour., London, 263–264;   Pittioni in Archaeol. Austriaca, 39, 95;   S. in Archeol. Roz., 18, 213, (Czech);   Seddon in S. Afr. Archaeol. Bull., 20:79, 164;   Vaufrey in L'Anthrop., 69, 304–306.
1966   The world of ancient man. New York: New Amer. Lib., Mentor Book, xiv + 255 pp., 25 figs., (pb. ed.).
1968   Prehistoric animals and their hunters. Illustrated by M. M. Howard. London: Faber and Faber, 214 pp., illustr., (not seen).
        Rev.: Clark, W. E. LeGros, in Man, Jour. Roy. Anthrop. Inst., 3, 491;   Jarman in Prehist. Soc., Proc., 35, 384–385;   Kurtén in Science, 167, 1241–1242;   Martin in Nat. Hist., 79:3, 82–84;   Renfrew

in Nature, 221, 100–101.
See: Woolridge and Cornwall.

CORR, JAMES B.
1915   The fossils of Forfarshire. Proc. Trans. Dundee Nat. Soc., 1:2, 1–15,
           (not seen).

CORRENTI, V.
1968   Résultats de l'étude périgraphique des crânes de S. Teodoro (Sicile).
           7th Internat. Congr. Anthrop. Ethnol. Sci., Moscow, 1964, 3,
           393–406, 12 figs.

CORSIN, J.
1967   Quelques problèmes de morphogenèse du crâne chez les Urodèles.
           Collog. Internat. Cent. Nation. Recherch. Sci., 163, 295–300,
           3 figs., (English summary).
           Rev.: Westphal in Zbl. Geol. Pal., Teil 2, 1969:2, 208.

CORTESI, C.   See: Alessio, Bella, et al.

CORYNDON, S. C.
1966   Preliminary report on some fossils from the Chiwondo Beds of the
           Karonga district, Malawi. In: Clark, J. D., Stephens, E. A., and
           Coryndon, S. C., 1966, 59–66.
           See: Clark, J. D., Stephens, and Coryndon.

COSGRIFF, JOHN W.
1965   A new genus of Temnospondyli from the Triassic of Western Australia.
           Jour. Roy. Soc. W. Australia, 48, 65–90, 13 figs.
           Rev.: Westphal in Zbl. Geol. Pal., Teil 2, 1967, 101.
1967   Triassic labyrinthodonts from New South Wales. 39th Congr., ANZAAS,
           Melbourne, 1967, Sec. C, pp. K4–K5, (abs.).
           See: Welles and Cosgriff.

COTT, J., and SCHRADER, K.
1966   Eine Methode zum Abformen des Innenreliefs menschlicher Schädel.
           Neue Museumskunde, 9, 51–62, 13 figs.

COTTER, JOHN L.
1965A.   Current research. Northeast. Amer. Antiq., 30, 523–526.
1965B.   Current research. Northeast. Amer. Antiq., 31, 295–297.
           See: Mason, J. A. 1966B.

COTTLER, JOSEPH
1966   Alfred Wallace: explorer-naturalist. Illustrated by John Kauffman.
           New York: Little, Brown, 212 pp., illustr.
           Rev.: Batten in Nat. Hist., 75:9, 66.

COTTRELL, L., (ed.)
1960   Rev.: Macknight in Mankind, 6, 445.

COUCHARD, J.
1966   La stratigraphie du gisement de Badegoule-Ouest, commune du Lardin
           (Dordogne). L'Anthrop., 70:1–2, 17–28, 7 figs., 1 table.

COULONGES, L.
1964   A propos du terme "Saint-Germien." Bull. Soc. Préhist. Franç., C. R.
            séances mens., 1964:5, ciii—civ.

COULONGES, M. L.
1963   Magdalénien et Périgordien post-glaciaires: la grotte de la Borie del Rey
            (Lot-et-Garonne). Gallia-Préhist., 6, 1—29, 16 figs., 2 tables.
1966   A propos de l'Azilien. Bull. Soc. Préhist. Franç., C. R. séances mens.,
            63, 255—256.

COUREL, L., and DEMATHIEU, G.-G.-P.
1963   Les empreintes de pas fossiles dans le Trias de la bordure Est et Nord-
            Est du Massif Central. Bull. Sci. Bourgogne, 21, 73—92, 7 figs.,
            2 pls.

COURTIN, JEAN
1967   Récentes découvertes préhistoriques et protohistoriques au Tchad. W.
            Afr. Archaeol. Newsletter, no. 6, 17—19, (English summary).

COURVILLE, CYRIL B.
1967   Cranial injuries in prehistoric man. In: Brothwell, Don, and Sandison,
            A. T., (eds.), 1967, 606—622, 6 figs., 2 tables.

COUSSY, J.-P., and TAURISSON, P.
1965   Grotte de Roucadour (Lot). Spelunca, Bull., 5:1, 28.

COUSTÉ, RAOUL   See: Prot and Cousté.

COUTTS, P. J. F.
1966   Features of prehistoric campsites in Australia. Mankind, 6, 338—346.

COUTURIER, [M. A. J.]
1961   Le bouquetin fossile. Rés. Com. 79 ème Congr. Assoc. Franç. Avenc.
            Sci., Grenoble, 1960, 172, (not seen).

COWIE, JOHN WATSON
1964   The Cambrian period. In: Harland, W. B., et al., (eds.), 1964, 255—
            258, 1 fig., 1 table.

COWLES, JOHN
1960   Cougar Mountain Cave in south central Oregon. Rainier, Oregon:
            privately printed by John Cowles, 50 pp., 40 pls.

COX, A.
1961   Psychanalyse de Lascaux. Bull. Soc. Roy. Belge Anthrop., Préhist.,
            72, 103—120.

COX, C. BARRY
1964   On the palate, dentition, and classification of the fossil reptile Endothio-
            don and related genera. Amer. Mus. Novit., no. 2171, 25 pp.,
            6 figs.
            Abs.: Huene in Zbl. Geol. Pal., Teil 2, 1966, 303.
1965   New Triassic dicynodonts from South America, their origins and re-
            lationships. Philos. Trans. Roy. Soc. London, Ser. B, 248, 457—
            516, 30 figs.

1967A.   Changes in terrestrial vertebrate faunas during the Mesozoic. In: Harland, W. B., et al., (eds.), 1967A, 77—89, 1 fig., 1 table.

1967B.   Cutaneous respiration and the origin of the modern Amphibia. Proc. Linn. Soc. London, 78, 37—47, 1 fig.
Rev.: Westphal in Zbl. Geol. Pal., Teil 2, 1967, 508.
See: Appleby, et al.; Attridge, et al.

CRABTREE, DON E.
1966   A stoneworker's approach to analyzing and replicating the Lindenmeier Folsom. Tebiwa, 9:1, 3—39, 25 figs.

CRABTREE, D. E., and DAVIS, E. L.
1968   Experimental manufacture of wooden implements with tools of flaked stone. Science, 159, 426—428, 3 figs., 1 table.

CRACRAFT, JOEL
1968   First record of the turkey Meleagris gallopavo from the Pleistocene of Mexico. Condor, 70, 274.

CRAIG, DENNIS   See: Dart, R. A., and Craig.

CRAIG, GORDON YOUNGER
1966A.   Concepts in palaeoecology. Earth-Sci. Rev., 2, 127—155, 11 figs.
Rev.: Gaetani in Riv. Ital. Pal., 73, 711.

1966B.   Deterministic models of living and fossil populations of animals. Discussion by A. Hallam, and T. B. Burnaby. Proc. Geol. Soc. London, 1634, 136—137.

CRAIG, G. Y., and OERTEL, G.
1966   Deterministic models of living and fossil populations of animals. Quart. Jour. Geol. Soc. London, 122, 315—355, 19 figs., (discussion: A. Hallam and T. P. Burnaby).

CRAIG, M. JEAN
1965   Dinosaurs and more dinosaurs. Illustrated by George Solonevich. New York: The Four Winds Press, 96 pp., illustr., (juvenile).

CRAMER, HOWARD ROSS
1959   Darwin's effect on paleontology. Bull. Georgia Acad. Sci., 17, 171—174.
See: Gray, S. W., and Cramer.

CRAMER, H. R., and FALLS, D. L.
1966   A Mississippian shark from Dade Co., Georgia. Bull. Georgia Acad. Sci., 24:2, 75, (abs.).

CRANBROOK, EARL OF
1967   Bat remains from Niah Cave excavations, 1964. Sarawak Mus. Jour., 14, 224—228, 2 figs.

CRAIN, JAY B.
1966   Population dynamics, disease, and paleopathology. Program, Sixth Ann. Meeting Northeastern Anthrop. Assoc., 3.

CRANE, H. R., and GRIFFIN, J. B.
1964   University of Michigan radiocarbon dates IX. Radiocarbon, 6, 1—24.

1965   University of Michigan radiocarbon dates X. Radiocarbon, 7, 123—152.
1966   University of Michigan radiocarbon dates XI. Radiocarbon, 8, 256—
            285.

CRANE, JULES M., JR.
1966   Late Tertiary radiation of viperfishes (Chauliodontidae) based on a com-
            parison of Recent and Miocene species. Contrib. Sci., Los Angeles
            Co. Mus., no. 115, 29 pp., 13 figs., 3 tables.

CRAW, JULIA
1967   Nothing but elephants. Desert Mag., 30:1, 22—25, illustr.

CRAWFORD, DAYMOND D.
1965   The Granite Beach Site, Llano County, Texas. Bull. Texas Archeol.
            Soc., 36, 71—97, 10 figs.

CRAWFORD, ELLIS C.   See: Schultz, C. B., Tanner, et al.

CRAWFORD, J. R.
1965   A Middle Stone Age site from the Umoukwes, Southern Rhodesia. S.
            Afr., Archaeol. Bull., 20, 25—27, 8 tables.

CREER, K. M.
1964   A reconstruction of the continents for the Upper Palaeozoic from
            palaeomagnetic data. Nature, 203, 1115—1120, 7 figs., 2 tables.

CRÉMILLIEUX, A.   See: Bayle des Hermens and Crémillieux.

CREMONESI, GIULIANO
1964   Esplorazioni paletnologiche in Abruzzo — Anno 1963. Atti Soc. Tos-
            cana Sci. Nat. Mem., Ser. A, 71, 11—16, 1 fig.

CRESSMAN, L. S.
1964   The sandals and the cave. The Indians of Oregon. Portland, Oregon:
            Beaver Books, 81 pp., illustr.

CRISTESCU, M.   See: Necrasov and Cristescu.

CRNOLATAC, I.   See: Malez and Crnolatac.

CROFT, W. N., and WHITE, E. I.
1940   Swedish-Norwegian-British paleontological expedition to Spitsbergen,
            1939. Polar Rec., 3, 210—211.

CROIZAT, LÉON
1958   Rev.: Marcuzzi in Monitore Zool. Ital., 66, 251—258.

CROMPTON, ALFRED WALTER
1964A.   On the skull of Oligokyphus. Bull. Brit. Mus. (Nat. Hist.), Geol., 9,
            69—82, 17 figs., 1 pl.
1964B.   A preliminary description of a new mammal from the Upper Triassic of
            South Africa. Proc. Zool. Soc. London, 142, 441—452, 4 figs.
            See: Charig, Attridge, and Crompton.

CROMPTON, A. W., and CHARIG, A. J.
1962   Abs.: Huene in Zbl. Geol. Pal., Teil 2, 1964, 160.

CROMPTON, A. W., and HOTTON, NICHOLAS, III
1967   Functional morphology of the masticatory apparatus of two dicynodonts
            (Reptilia, Therapsida). Postilla, no. 109, 1–51, 7 figs., 2 tables.

CROMPTON, A. W., and JENKINS, F. A., JR.
1967   American Jurassic symmetrodonts and Rhaetic "pantotheres." Science,
            155, 1006–1008, 3 figs.
1968   Molar occlusion in Late Triassic mammals. Biol. Rev., 1968, 427–458,
            11 figs., 3 pls.

CROOK, J. H., and GARTLAN, J. S.
1966   Evolution of primate societies. Nature, 210, 1200–1203, 1 fig., 1 table.

CROOK, WILSON W., JR.
1964   Another radiocarbon date from Lewisville. Newsletter Okla. Anthrop.
            Soc., 12:6, 8–9.

CROSBY, ELEANOR
1968   An archaeological site survey near Taroom, South-eastern Queensland.
            Mem. Queensland Mus., 15, 73–82, 2 figs., pl. 10, 1 table.

CROSBY, J. L.
1967   Computers in the study of evolution. Sci. Progress, 55, 279–292.

CROSSLEY, WATSON
1964   Muskox skull found at Granview, Man. Blue Jay, 22, 34, 1 fig.
1965   Age of muskox skull found at Grand View, Manitoba. Blue Jay, 24,
            195, 1 fig.

CRUICKSHANK, A. R. I.
1964   Origin of the Triassic dicynodonts (Reptilia: Synapsida). Nature, 201,
            733.
1965   On a specimen of the anomodont reptile Kannemeyeria latifrons (Broom)
            from the Manda formation of Tanganyika, Tanzania. Proc. Linn.
            Soc. London, 176, 149–157, 5 figs.
1967   A new dicynodont genus from the Manda formation of Tanzania
            (Tanganyika). Jour. Zool., London, 153, 163–208, 23 figs.
1968A.   Tooth structure in Rhizodus hibberti Ag., a rhipidistian fish. Pal.
            Africana, 11, 3–13, 9 figs.
1968B.   A comparison of the palates of Permian and Triassic dicynodonts. Pal.
            Africana, 11, 23–31, 6 figs.

CRUSAFONT PAIRÓ, MIGUEL
1954F.   La zona pirenaica como filtro-barrera paleobiológico. Pirineos, 10:33–
            34, 317–332, (French, English, and German summaries).
1958F.   Abs.: Radig in Zbl. Geol. Pal., Teil 2, 1963, 904–905.
1958G.   Sobre la probable presencia del Mioceno continental en la cuenca del
            Ampurdan. Actas III Congr. Internat. Estud. Pirenaicos Gerona,
            57–65, (not seen).
1959D.   El yacimiento de mamíferos del villafranquiense superior de "Mestas
            de Con" (Asturias). Speleón, 10, 275–287, 1 pl., (French and
            English summaries).

1961E. [Principaux gisements de Mammifères en] Espagne. In: Piveteau, J., 1961A, Traité de Paléo., 6:1, 477—480, fig. 5.

1962B. Abs.: Radig in Zbl. Geol. Pal., Teil 2, 1963, 905.

1962D. Indarctos atticus, un nuevo carnivoro del Pikermiense español. Teruel, no. 27, 177—191, 1 pl.

1964A. Samuel Schaub-Glück (1882 - 1962). Bol. Soc. Espan. Hist. Nat., Sec. Geol., 62, 137—143, portrait.

1964B. La biota de Can Llobateres (Sabadell) y su significación biológica. Cursillos y Confer. Inst. "Lucas Mallada", 9, 177—179.

1964C. Los Mamiferos, y en especial los Primates, del Eoceno prepirenaico. Publ. Cat. Paleont. Univ. Barcelona, 2.

1964D. La ley recurrente de complejidad-consciencia, al dia. Discussion by S. A. Noguer. Mem. R. Acad. Cien. Art. Barcelona, no. 702, 135—201, 11 figs.
Rev.: J. M. G. in Fossilia, 1965:2, 48—49.

1964E. Proteognosia versus evolucionismo. Orb. Cathol., Barcelona, 6, 482—504, (not seen).

1965A. La V Semana sobre Teilhard de Chardin en Vezélay (Francia). Arbor, 60, 235—244.

1965B. Homenaje de la Santa Sede a la obra del Dr. Johannes Hürzeler. Arbor, 60, 507—510.

1965C. Neo-darwinismo y ortogeneticismo; un intento de conciliación. Atlantida, Madrid, 16, 394—401.

1965D. Zur Obergrenze des Villafranchiums in Spanien. Ber. Geol. Ges. Deutsch. Demokratischen Republ., 10, 19—48, (German and French; English summary).

1965E. Hesperidoceras, nuevo nombre para Hesperoceras Vill. et Crus., 1953. Bol. Soc. Espan. Hist. Nat., Sec. Geol., 63:2—3, 223—224.

1965F. Notas paleovertebrológicas. Fossilia, 1965:1, 8—28.

1965G. Un mecenazgo ejemplar. Fossilia, 1965:1, 29—34.

1965H. La variabilidad individual en el Myotragus balearicus Bate del Pleistoceno de Mallorca. Fossilia, 1965:3—4, 13—17, (French text).

1965I. Actividades. Fossilia, 1965:3—4, 23—45.

1965J. La biometria en el argumento evolutivo. Fossilia, 1965:5—6, 34—39.

1965K. Peritethyan relationships in the Upper Tertiary mammalian faunas. In: Jhingran, A. G., et al., (eds.), 1965, 301—305.

1965L. [. . . deceased in Spain at the age of 93 years . . . of Professor Eduardo Hernandez-Pacheco.] News Bull., Soc. Vert. Pal., 74, 54.

1965M. Los mamiferos, y en especial los primates del Eoceno prepirenaico. Notas Comun. Inst. Geol. Min., 77, 256; 78, 159—165.

1965N. Observations à un travail de M. Freudenthal et P. Y. Sondaar sur des nouveaux gisements à Hipparion d'Espagne. Proc. K. Nederl. Akad. Wet., Ser. B, 68, 121—126, 1 fig.

1965O. Notas paleovertebrológicas. Publ. Cat. Paleont. Univ. Barcelona, 4.

1965P. The Pontian mammalian-complex in Spain: its biological and biogeographical significance. XII Symposium of Vert. Pal. and Comp. Anat. Bristol, 1964, (not seen).

1966A. Notas paleomastológicas. Acta Geol. Hispanica, 1:1, 14—15.
Rev.: H.-P. in Bol. Soc. Espan. Hist. Nat., Sec. Geol., 64:2, 174.

1966B. Paleantropología: Un descubrimiento sensacional. Acta Geol. Hispanica, 1:1, 15.

1966C. Sobre el origen, evolución y relaciones del genero Myotragus. Bol. Soc. Hist. Nat. Baleares, 12:1—4, 7—12.

1966D. Caracterizacion del Pontiense en el afloramiento terciario de Campisábalos (Guadalajara). Notas Comun. Inst. Geol. Min., 85, 61—70, 1 fig., 1 pl., 1 table, (French and English summaries).

1967A.   Nuevos datos sobre la edad de los sedimentos terciarios de la zona de
             Utrillas-Montalbán. Acta Geol. Hispanica, 2, 115—116.
             Rev.: H.-P. in Bol. Soc. Españ. Hist. Nat., Sec. Geol., 66:2, 181.

1967B.   Sur quelques Prosimiens de l'Éocène de la zone préaxiale pyrénaique et
             un essai provisoire de reclassification. Collog. Internat. Cent.
             Nation. Recherch. Sci., 163, 611—632, 9 figs., 2 pls.
             See: Hernández-Pacheco and Crusafont Pairó; Hoffstetter, Crusafont,
             and Aguirre; Thaler, Crusafont, and Adrover.

CRUSAFONT PAIRÓ, M., and ADROVER, R.
  1965   El primer mamífero del Mesozoico español. Fossilia, 1965:5—6, 28—33,
             1 fig.

CRUSAFONT PAIRÓ, M., ADROVER, R., and GOLPE, J. M.
  1964   Découverte dans le Pikermien d'Espagne du plus primitif des hippopo-
             tames: Hippopotamus (Hexaprotodon) primaevus n. sp. C. R.
             Acad. Sci. Paris, 258, 1572—1575.

CRUSAFONT PAIRÓ, M., AGUIRRE, E. de, and GARCÍA, J.
  1968   Un nuevo yacimiento de mamíferos del Mioceno de la meseta española.
             Acta Geol. Hispánica, 3:1, 22—24, (French summary).
             Rev.: H.-P. in Bol. Soc. Españ. Hist. Nat., Sec. Geol., 66:3, 297.

CRUSAFONT PAIRÓ, M., and ANGEL, B.
  1966   Un Myotragus (Mammifère Ruminant), dans le Villafranchien de l'ile de
             Majorque: Myotragus batei nov. sp. C. R. Acad. Sci. Paris, Sci.
             Nat., 262, 2012—2014, 1 fig.

CRUSAFONT PAIRÓ, M., ANGEL, B., and CUERDA, J.
  1965A.   Una nueva especie de Myotragus en la Gran Balear. Fossilia, 1965:2,
             15—19.
  1965B.   Supervivencia del Myotragus en el Neolítico de las Baleares. Publ. Cat.
             Paleont. Univ. Barcelona, no. 5.

CRUSAFONT PAIRÓ, M., DE RENZI, M., and CLAVELL, E.
  1968   Les grands traits d'une coupure Crétacé-Paléocène-Éocène au Sud des
             Pyrénées (Isábena). Colloque sur l'Éocène, I. Mém. Bur. Rech.
             Géol. Min., 58, 591—596, 1 fig., (English summary).

CRUSAFONT PAIRÓ, M., GAUTIER, F., and GINSBURG, L.
  1966   Mise en évidence du Vindobonien inférieur continental dans l'Est de la
             province de Teruel (Espagne). C. R. Soc. Geol. France, 1966,
             30—32.
             Rev.: H.-P. in Bol. Soc. Españ. Hist. Nat., Sec. Geol., 64:2, 169.

CRUSAFONT PAIRÓ, M., GINSBURG, L., and TRUYOLS, J.
  1962   Abs.: Radig in Zbl. Geol. Pal., Teil 2, 1964, 843.

CRUSAFONT PAIRÓ, M., HARTENBERGER, J.-L., and HEINTZ, E.
  1964   Un nouveau gisement de mammifères fossiles d'âge villafranchien à la
             Puebla de Valverde (Province de Teruel, Espagne). C. R. Acad.
             Sci. Paris, 258, 2869—2871.

CRUSAFONT PAIRÓ, M., RIBA, O., and VILLENA, J.
  1966   Nota preliminar sobre un nuevo yacimiento de vertebrados aquitanienses

en Santa Cilia (rio Formiga; provincia de Huesca) y sus conse-
cuencias geologicas. Notas Comun. Inst. Geol. Min., 83, 7–13,
1 fig., (French and English summaries).
Rev.: H.-P. in Bol. Soc. Español. Hist. Nat., Sec. Geol., 64:2, 174.

CRUSAFONT PAIRÓ, M., and ROSELL SANUY, J.
1966   Primera datacion de los tramos superiores del Eoceno continental de la
         Cuenca de Ager (provincia de Lerida). Notas Comun. Inst. Geol.
         Min., 83, 79–91, 2 figs.

CRUSAFONT PAIRÓ, M., ROSELL SANUY, J., GOLPE, J.-M., and RENZI, M. de
1968   Le Paléogène de la vallée d'Ager et ses rapports avec celui de la Conca
         de Tremp (Pyrénées de la province de Lérida, Espagne). Colloque
         sur l'Eocène, I. Mém. Bur. Rech. Géol. Min., 58, 583–589,
         (English summary).

CRUSAFONT PAIRÓ, M., and RUSSELL, D. E.
1967   Un nouveau paroxyclaenidé de l'Eocène d'Espagne. Bull. Mus. Hist.
         Nat. Paris, 39, 757–773, 4 figs., (English summary).

CRUSAFONT PAIRÓ, M., and TRUYOLS SANTONJA, J.
1957B.   Abs.: Radig in Zbl. Geol. Pal., Teil 2, 1962, 558–559.
1960B.   Abs.: Radig in Zbl. Geol. Pal., Teil 2, 1962, 285.
1964A.   Aperçu chronostratigraphique des bassins de Calatayud-Teruel. Cursillos
         y Confer. Inst. "Lucas Mallada", 9, 89–92.
1964B.   Les mammifères fossiles dans la stratigraphie du Paléogène continental
         du Bassin de l'Ebre (Espagne). Mém. Bur. Rech. Géol. Min.,
         28:2, 735–740.
1966   Masterometry and evolution, again. Evolution, 20, 204–210.

CRUSAFONT PAIRÓ, M., TRUYOLS SANTONJA, J., and RIBA, O.
1966   Contribución al conocimiento de la estratigrafía del Terciario continen-
         tal de Navarra y Rioja. Notas Comun. Inst. Geol. Min., 90,
         53–76, 1 map.

CRUSAFONT PAIRÓ, M., VALENCIANO HORTA, A., and SANZ FUENTES, E.
1968   Un nuevo yacimiento de vertebrados en el Burdigaliense de Martorell
         (Provincia de Barcelona). Acta Geol. Hispánica, 3:2, 44–47,
         (French summary).

CRUSAFONT PAIRÓ, M., and VILLALTA COMELLA, J. F. de
1955C.   Una campaña paleontológica en la cuenca terciaria de Calatayud-Teruel.
         Teruel, no. 14, 218–221, 4 figs., [erroneously run as 1957 in
         Bibliog. Fossil Vert. 1954–1958].

CRUXENT, JOSÉ M.
1962   Les cultures lithique paléo-indiennes du Venezuela: Un curieux phéno-
         mène de convergence typologique et fonctionnelle avec les cultures
         forestières centrafricaines. Proc. 4th Panafrican Congr. Prehist.,
         Sec. 3, 257–259.
         See: Rouse and Cruxent.

CRUXENT, J. M., and ROUSE, I.
1961   Arqueologia cronologica de Venezuela. Vols. I and II. Washington,
         D. C.: Union Panamericana; Vol. I, xiv + 320 pp.; Vol. II,
         226 pp., 201 figs., 104 pls.

Rev.: Sykes in New World Antiq., <u>8</u>, 111.

ČTYROKÝ, PAVEL   See: Buday, et al.

ČTYROKÝ, P.,   FEJFAR, O., and HOLÝ, F.
1964A.   Neue paläontologische Funde im Untermiozän des nordböhmischen Braun-
kohlenbeckens. Neues Jahrb. Geol. Pal., Abh., <u>119</u>, 134–156,
11 figs., 6 tables, 1 map.
1964B.   Nové paleontologické nálezy ve spodním miocénu severočeské uhelné
pánve. Zprávy Geol. Výzkumech Roce, <u>1</u>, 201–203.

CUBILLAS PÉREZ, ISABEL
1961   Memorias del año 1950. In: Núñez Jiménez (ed.), 1961A, 155–162,
illustr.

CUENCA, J.   See: Aguirre, Collins, and Cuenca.

CUÉNOT, CLAUDE
1965   Teilhard de Chardin: a biographical study. Translated by Vincent
Colimore; edited by René Hague. Baltimore: Helicon; London:
Burns and Oates, vi + 492 pp., 16 illustr. + frontispiece.
Rev.: G. G. Simpson in New Haven Register, May 2, 1965.

CUERDA BARCELÓ, JUAN
1966   Sobre la edad de algunos yacimientos pleistocénicos de Baleares con
Myotragus. Bol. Soc. Hist. Nat. Baleares, <u>12</u>:1–4.
Rev.: H.-P. in Bol. Soc. Españ. Hist. Nat., sec. geol., <u>65</u>, 279–280.
See: Crusafont Pairó, Angel and Cuerda.

CUFFEY, ROGER J.,   JOHNSON, G. H., and RASMUSSEN, D. L.
1964   A microtine rodent and associated gastropods from the upper Pleistocene
of southwestern Indiana. Jour. Pal., <u>38</u>, 1109–1111, 1 fig.

CULLINGFORD, C. H. D., (ed.)
1953   British caving: an introduction to speleology. London: Routledge
and Kegan Paul Ltd., xvi + 468 pp., 87 figs., 48 pls., 12 tables.
1962   British caving: an introduction to speleology. 2nd rev. ed. London:
Routledge and Kegan Paul Ltd., xvi + 592 pp., 87 figs., 48 pls.,
12 tables.
Rev.: Binder in Mitt. Verband Deutschen Höhlen- und Karstforscher,
München, <u>8</u>, 85–86;   Fink in Die Höhle, <u>14</u>, 52.

CURL, R. L.
1962   The Pengelly Cave Research Center. NSS News, <u>20</u>, 182–184, 3 photos.

CURRY-LINDAHL, K.
1964   [History of the population of Scandinavia by vertebrate animals.]   Izv.
Akad. Nauk, Ser. Geograf., <u>1964</u>:1, 123–134, 9 figs., (Russian).

CURTET, ALBERT
1964   Moustérien de surface inédit dans les Deux-Sèvres. Bull. Soc. Préhist.,
Paris, <u>60</u>, 426–431, 2 figs.

CURTIS, GARNISS H.
1967   Notes on some Miocene to Pleistocene potassium/argon results. Discussion. In: Bishop, W. W., and Clark, J. D., (eds.), 1967A,
365–369.

See: Evernden, J. F., and Curtis; Evernden, J. F., Savage, Curtis, and James; Leakey, Evernden, J. H., and Curtis; Matthews and Curtis.

CURTIS, G. H., et al.
1965   Evaluation of the Olduvai discoveries. In: DeVore, P. L., (ed.), 1965, 20–38.

CURTIS, G. H., and EVERNDEN, J. F.
1965   Dating by potassium-argon technique. In: Leakey, et al, 1965, 90–91.

CUSCANI, POLITI P.
1963A.   Resto di Megaceros rinvenuto nel Senese. Atti Accad. Fisiocritici Siena, Sez. Agr., (2a), 9, 20 pp., 2 figs., 1 pl., (not seen).
    Rev.: Guaitani Mazza in Riv. Ital. Pal., 70, 151.
1963B.   Anche il Rhinoceros megarhinus nel Pliocene dei dintorni di Siena. Atti Accad. Fisiocritici Siena, Sez. Agr., (2a), 10, 27 pp., 1 fig., 3 pls., (not seen).
    Rev.: Guaitani Mazza in Riv. Ital. Pal., 71, 333.
1963C.   Prove paleontologiche della 'pliocenicita' della formazione argillosa in cui sono stati rinvenuti resti di Rhinoceros etruscus nel Senese. Atti Accad. Fisiocritici Siena (2e), 11, 39 pp., 3 figs., 4 pls., (not seen).
    Rev.: Guaitani Mazza in Riv. Ital. Pal., 70, 388.
1965   L'Ippopotamo (Hippopotamus amphibius var. major) di Poggio ai Venti (Massa Marittima). Atti Accad. Fisiocritici Siena, (2), 11, 71 pp., 1 fig., 6 pls., (not seen).
    Rev.: J. M. G. in Fossilia, 1965:5–6, 71–72; Guaitani Mazza in Riv. Ital. Pal., 72, 872.
1966   Resti di Ippopotami provenienti dalla zona di Chiusi. Atti Accad. Fisiocritici Siena, (2), 12, 32 pp., 2 figs., 3 pls., (not seen).
    Rev.: Albanesi in Riv. Ital. Pal., 73, 1048.
1967   Ancora sulla valutazione sistematica del grande ippopotamo (Hippopotamus amphibius var. major). Atti Accad. Fisiocritici Siena, (13), 16, 1–40.
    Rev.: Albanesi in Riv. Ital. Pal., 74:3, 992.

CUSHING, E. J., and WRIGHT, H. E., JR., (eds.)
1967   Quaternary paleoecology. New Haven, Conn.: Yale Univ. Press, 433 pp., illustr. (Vol. 7 of Proc. 7th Inqua Congr.).
    Rev.: Anon. in GeoTimes, 13:4, 34; Black in GeoTimes, 14:2, 34; Creel in Anthropol. Anz., 31:3, 233; Gadwin in Nature, 219, 1285–1287; A. A. M. in Earth-Sci. Rev., 4:3, A201–A202; Martin in Bio Science, 18, 1150, 1152; Mayer-Oakes in Amer. Anthrop., 71, 1227–1229; G. F. Mitchell in Antiq. Jour., 49:2, 397–398; Ritchie in Palaeogeog., Palaeoclimatol., Palaeoecol., 5, 372–374; Semken in Jour. Pal., 43:5, 1306–1307; Wilmsen in Amer. Jour. Archaeol., 73:1, 99–101.

CUTBILL, JOHN LOUIS, and FUNNELL, B. M.
1967   Numerical analysis of The Fossil Record. In: Harland, W. B., et al., (eds.), 1967A, 791–820, 22 figs.

CYS, JOHN M.
1967A.   Two new minor morphological features of Diadectes. Jour. Pal., 41, 256.
1967B.   The inability of dinosaurs to hibernate as a possible key factor in their extinction. Jour. Pal., 41, 266.

1967C.   Osteology of the pristerognathid Cynariognathus platyrhinus (Reptilia:
           Theriodontia). Jour. Pal., 41, 776—790, 6 figs., 1 table.
           Rev.: Huene in Zbl. Geol. Pal., Teil 2, 1968, 204.

CZEPPE, Z., et al.
1963   Rev.: Vaufrey in L'Anthrop., 69, 309—310.

CZYGAN, WOLFGANG W.
1963   Problematische Mikrofossilien (Otolithen oder Ossiculithen?) aus dem
           Stefan des Mittel-Schwarzwaldes. Ber. Naturf. Ges. Freiburg, 53,
           133—140, 3 figs.
           Abs.: Häntzschel in Zbl. Geol. Pal., Teil 2, 1964, 39; Weiler in Zbl.
           Geol. Pal., Teil 2, 1964, 148.

CZYZEWSKA, TERESA
1962   Abs.: Dietrich in Zbl. Geol. Pal., Teil 2, 1964, 204—205.

D., J.
1964   Reunion en l'honneur du professeur Antonio Beltran. Assemblée generale
           du 12 Decembre 1963. Préhist. Spéléol. Ariégeoises, 19, 89—91.
1965   Alden H. Miller: 1906 - 1965. Condor, 67, 545.

DABER, RUDOLF
1960   Bemerkungen zur Geschichte der Geologie in Berlin. Ber. Geol. Ges.
           Deutsch. Demokratischen Republ., 5, 147—159, 5 figs.
1965   Wilhelm Otto Dietrich. Ber. Geol. Ges. Deutsch. Demokratischen Re-
           publ., 10, 99—106, portr.

DACHEV, D.   See: Tsankov and Dachev.

DAGET, J.
1966   Bibliographie provisoire sur les Poissons du Quaternaire continental.
           Bull. Inst. Franç. Afr. Noire, Ser. A, 28, 401.

DAHLBERG, ALBERT A.
1966   Virginia M. Carbonell, 1920 - 1965. Amer. Jour. Phys. Anthrop., 24,
           276.

DAHLBERG, A. A., and CARBONELL, V. M.
1961   The dentition of the Magdalenian female from Cap Blanc, France. Man,
           61, art. 48, 49—50, 2 figs., 1 pl.
           Rev.: Talarczyk in Przeglad Antrop., 28, 229, (Polish).

DAHLBERG, A. A., and STALEY, R. N.
1965   Paleopathology of the dentition. Abs. 64th Ann. Meeting Amer. Anthrop.
           Assoc., 1965, 15, (abs.).

DAHM, HANS
1966   Das marine Niveau über Flöz Finefrau Nebenbank (Obere Wittener
           Schichten, Westfal A) im niederrheinisch-westfälischen Steinkohl-
           engebirge. Fortschr. Geol. Rheinland u. Westfalen, 13:1, 39—124,
           28 figs., 8 pls., 2 tables, (French and English summaries).

DAHR, ELIAS
1952   Craniology and taxonomy of the Australopithecinae. Årsbok Statens
            Naturvetenskap Forskningsråds, 5, (1950–51), 165–169, (Swedish;
            English summary).

DAI, ER-JIAN
1966   The paleoliths found at Lantian man locality of Gongwangling and
            vicinity. Vert. Palasiatica, 10, 30–32, 2 figs., 2 pls., (Chinese;
            English summary).

DAI, E.-j., et al.
1964   [Flaked stone tools from the desert of Alashan.]   Vert. Palasiatica, 8:4,
            414–419, 1 fig., 3 pls., (Chinese; Russian summary).

DAI, E.-j., and BAI, Y.-z.
1966   A paleolith found in one cave in Shantung. Vert. Palasiatica, 10, 82–
            84, 1 fig., 1 pl., (Chinese; English summary).

DAI, E.-j., and CHI, H.
1964   Discovery of palaeoliths at Lantian, Shensi. Vert. Palasiatica, 8, 152–
            161, 10 figs., 4 pls., (Chinese; English summary).

DAKARIS, S. I., et al.
1964   The climate, environment and industries of Stone Age Greece: Part I.
            Proc. Prehist. Soc. Cambridge, 30, 199–244, 26 figs., pls. xxi–xxvi.

DALES, GEORGE F., JR., (ed.)
1964   COWA surveys and bibliographies. Area 16 – southern Asia. COWA
            Surv. and Bibliog., Area 16, no. 3, 19 + 9 pp.

DALINKEVICIUS, J.
1960   On the problem of the Lower Cretaceous deposits in Lithuania. Collec-
            tanea Acta Geol. Lithuanica, 341–350, (English and Russian;
            Lithuanian summary).

DAL PIAZ, GIORGIO
1962   Cenni sulla vita e le opere di carattere geologico di Antonio Vallisneri
            senior. Atti Mem. Accad. Patavina Sci. Let. Arti, Mem. Cl. Sci.
            Mat. Nat., 73, suppl., 41–45.

DAL PIAZ, G., and MALARODA, R.
1966   Paleontologia. Volume secondo. Vertebrati. Padova: Ed. Cedam, 317
            pp., 521 figs.
            Rev.: Rossi Ronchetti in Riv. Ital. Pal., 73, 1391.

DALQUEST, WALTER W.
1961C.   Two species of Bison contemporaneous in early Recent deposits in Texas.
            Southwest. Nat., 6, 73–78.
1964A.   Equus scotti from a high terrace near Childress, Texas. Texas Jour. Sci.,
            16, 350–358, 4 figs.
1964B.   A new Pleistocene local fauna from Motley County, Texas. Trans.
            Kansas Acad. Sci., 67, 499–505, 4 figs.
1965A.   New Pleistocene formation and local fauna from Hardeman County, Texas.
            Jour. Pal., 39, 63–79, 2 figs., 2 tables.
1965B.   A turntable for examining small fossils under the microscope. News. Bull.,
            Soc. Vert. Pal., no. 75, 51, illustr.

1966   An unusual paleonisciform fish from the Permian of Texas. Jour. Pal.,
            40, 759–762, 1 fig.
            See: Hibbard and Dalquest.

DALQUEST, W. W., and HUGHES, J. T.
1965   The Pleistocene horse, Equus conversidens. Amer. Mid. Nat., 74, 408–
            417, 6 figs., 5 tables.
1966   A new mammalian local fauna from the Lower Pliocene of Texas.
            Trans. Kansas Acad. Sci., 69, 79–87, 6 figs., 3 tables.

DALY, ROSEMARY   See: Powers 1963.

DALZELL, BONNIE
1966   A new salmonid fish. Program, 62nd Ann. Meeting, Geol. Soc. Amer.,
            Cordilleran Sect., 1966, 31, (abs.). Also: Spec. Pap. Geol. Soc.
            Amer., 101, 300, (abs.).
            See: Mitchell, E. D. 1966B.

DAMBSKI, JERZY
1957   Contemporary views on the unity of the human species. Przeglad
            Antrop., 23, 160–181, (Polish; English and Russian summaries).

DAMON, PAUL E.
1964   The present status and future possibilities of geochemistry as applied
            to paleoecological research. Discussion. In: Hester, J. J., and
            Schoenwetter, J., (eds.), 1964, 77–84, fig. 28.
            See: Haynes, Damon, and Grey; Haynes, Grey, Damon, and Bennett.

DAMON, P. E., HAYNES, C. V., and LONG, A.
1964   Arizona radiocarbon dates V. Radiocarbon, 6, 91–107.

DAMOTTE, RENÉE   See: Toutin, Damotte, and Ginsburg.

DANI, AHMAD HASAN
1964   Prehistoric Pakistan. Asian Perspectives, 7, 183–188.

DANIEL, D. SCOTT   See: Sims and Daniel.

DANIEL, GLYN
1963A.   Rev.: Pittioni in Archaeol. Austriaca, 33, 114;   Powell in Archaeol.
            Jour., 119, 361.
1963C.   Editorial. Antiq., 37, 171–175, pl. 27.
1965   Introduction. In: Foster, I. L., and Daniel, G., (eds.), 1965, 1–15.
1966   Man discovers his past. London: Gerald Duckworth, 80 pp., 64 figs.,
            8 maps.
            Rev.: Evans in Man, Jour. Roy. Anthrop. Inst., 2, 312.
1967   The origins and growth of archaeology. Harmondsworth: Penguin
            Books, 304 pp., 7 pls., (not seen).
            Rev.: Heizer in Antiq., 42, 75–76.
            See: Childe 1965; Foster and Daniel.

DANIEL, G., and EVANS, J. D.
1967   The western Mediterranean. Rev. ed. Cambridge: Univ. Press, 72 pp.,
            illustrs., (not seen).
            Rev.: Barfield in Man, Jour. Roy. Anthrop. Inst., 2, 638–639.

DANIEL, RAOUL
1965A.   Présence de pièces Moustériformes dans le Protomagdalénien I de la
          Station de Beauregard près Nemours (S.-et-M.). Bull. Soc.
          Préhist. Franç., C. R. séances mens., 1965:1, xxiv–xxxi, 3 figs.
1965B.   Outils aurignaciens pour creuser et perforer la pierre, de la grotte de
          la Rochette (Dordogne). Bull. Soc. Préhist. Franç., C. R. séances
          mens., 1965:3, xcvi–xcix, 2 figs.
1965C.   Les stations mousteriennes des environs de Saint-Julien-de-la-Liègue
          (Eure). (Addendum aux anciens travaux de L. Coutil). Bull.
          Soc. Préhist. Franç., Etud. et Trav., 62:1, 22–30, 3 figs., 1 map,
          1 table.
1965D.   Présentation de silex mousteriens de Villejuif (Seine). Bull. Soc. Préhist.
          Franç., Etud. et Trav., 62:1, 63–69, 3 figs.
1965E.   La butte Saint-Martin-de-la-Roche commune d'Etrechy (Essonne). Ses
          differentes occupations aux temps préhistoriques. Bull. Soc.
          Préhist. Franç., Etud. et Trav., 62:3, 539–546, 3 figs.
1966   Les industries paléolithiques et néolithiques du Muret, commune de
          Mézières (Seine-et-Oise). Bull. Soc. Préhist. Franç., C. R. séances
          mens., 63:1, 20–26, 3 figs.

DANIELS, J. R. S.
1966   The site recording scheme. New Zealand Archaeol. Assoc. Newsletter,
          9, 42–44.

DANIELS, S. G. H.
1967   Comments on the terminology and typology recommendations of the
          Burg-Wartenstein conference (1965). W. Afr. Archaeol. News-
          letter, no. 7, 15–22, (French summary).
1968   A preliminary note on some multifactorial work. W. Afr. Archaeol.
          Newsletter, no. 8, 4–6, (French summary).

DANIELS, STEVE
1967   Statistics, typology and cultural dynamics in the Transvaal Middle Stone
          Age. S. Afr. Archaeol. Bull., 22, 114–125, 7 figs., 7 tables.

DANIELSSON, ULF
1965   The introduction of Darwinism in Sweden. I. Lychnos, 1963–1964,
          157–210, (Swedish).
1967   The penetration of Darwinism into Sweden. Lychnos, 1967, (for 1965–
          1966), 261–334, (English summary).

DANIL'CHENKO, P. G.
1962   Abs.: Weiler in Zbl. Geol. Pal., Teil 2, 1964, 149–150.

1964A.   [Superorder Holostei (Protospondyli-Halecostomi, pars).] Osnovy Pal.,
          [Agnathes. Pisces.], [11], 378–395, 27 figs., (Russian).
1964B.   [Superorder Teleostei.] Osnovy Pal., [11], 396–484, 97 figs., (Russian).
1968   Bony fishes of the Maikop deposits of the Caucasus. Translated from
          the Russian. Jerusalem: Israel Program for Scientific Translations,
          vii + 247 pp., 28 pls.
          Rev.: Patterson in Nature, 220, 936.

DANIL'CHENKO, P. G., and ÎAKOVLEV, V. N.
1964   [Order Pholidophorida.] Osnovy Pal., [Agnathes. Pisces.], [11], 392–
          395, 4 figs., (Russian).

DANILENKO, V. N.
1959   [M. Îa. Rudinskiĭ (10-16-1887 – 7-23-1959).]   Sov. Arkheol., 1959:4,
            p. 328, portr., (Russian).

DANILOV, N. N.
1960   [The avifauna of the central Urals and Transurals and the history of
            its origin.]   Trudy probl. temat. soveshch., Zool. Inst., 9, 73–80,
            (Russian).

DANILOVA, E. I.
1965   [Evolution of the hand.]   Kiev: "Naukova Dumka" Press, figs., pls.,
            22 tables, (Russian; not seen).
            Rev.: Khrisanfova in Voprosy Antrop., 26, 186.
1966   [The hand and the foot of hominids and of related forms.]   Trudy
            Inst. Etnog. Akad. Nauk SSSR, 92, 424–456, 8 figs., 10 tables,
            (Russian).

DANTE, JOHN H.   See: Frizzell and Dante.

DANTHINE, H., and FAIDER-FEYTMANS, G.
1963   Chronique. District G: Grand-Duché de Luxembourg et partie de la
            Belgique située à l'Est de la Meuse. 1957–1959. Helinium, 3,
            168–181, 2 maps.
1966   Chronique. District G (1960–62). Helinium, 6, 53–64, 1 map.

DARLINGTON, C. D.
1964   Contending with evolution. Sci. Progress, 52, 133–137.

DARLINGTON, PHILIP J., JR.
1965   Biogeography of the southern end of the world. Cambridge, Mass.:
            Harvard Univ. Press, viii + 236 pp., 38 figs., frontispiece.

DARNAY-DORNYAI, B.   See: Jánossy and Darnay-Dornyai.

DARRAGH, T. A.   See: Bowler, et al.

DART, MARJORIE
1968   Raymond A. Dart – list of publications 1920–1967. S. African Jour.
            Sci., 64, 134–140.

DART, RAYMOND A.
1928   Big game of prehistoric man in South Africa. S.A.R.H. Mag., Dec.,
            1928, 2010–2018, (not seen).
1960G.   Africa's place in the emergence of civilization. Johannesburg: South
            African Broadcasting Corporation, (The Van Riebeeck Lecture
            series), 96 pp., illustr.
1961D.   Africa's place in the evolution of man. Ann. Proc. Ass. Sci. Techn.
            Soc. South Afr., 1959–60, 21–41, (not seen).
1962H.   The continuity and originality of australopithecine osteodontokeratic
            culture. Proc. 4th Panafrican Congr. Prehist., sec. 3, 27–41,
            10 figs., (discussion by J. D. Clark, L. S. B. Leakey, and P.
            Tobias).
1964A.   The ecology of the South African man-apes. In: Davis, D. H. S.,
            ed., 1964, 49–66, 3 pls. Also in: Genovés, S., et al., (eds.),
            1966, 26–47, with comment by J. H. Prost.

1964B.	The Abbé Breuil and the osteodontokeratic culture. In: Ripoll Perelló, E., (ed.), 1964A, 347—370, 8 pls., (Spanish summary).
1964C.	The Associated Scientific and Technical Societies of South Africa. S. African Jour. Sci., 60, 129—131, 1 fig.
1965A.	Australopithecine acceptance, some of its effects. Presidential address. Ann. Proc. Ass. Sci. Tech. Soc. S. Afr., 1963/1964, publ. Sept. 1965.
1965B.	Australopithecine cordage and thongs. In: Genovés, (ed.), 1965C, 43—61, 10 figs.
1965C.	The unavoidable osteodontokeratic culture. In: Jhingran, A. G., et al., (eds.), 1965, 231—254, 6 pls.
1965D.	Pounding as a process and the producer of other artifacts. S. Afr. Archaeol. Bull., 20:79, 141—147, 6 figs.
1965E.	Recent discoveries during excavation preparations at Makapansgat. S. Afr. Archaeol. Bull., 20:79, 148—158, 10 figs.
1965F.	Beyond antiquity. A series of radio lectures on the origin of man. South African Broadcasting Corp., 119 pp. Also long-playing record pressed in 1966.
1965G.	"Olduvai Gorge 1951—1961: fauna and background" by L. S. B. Leakey. S. African Jour. Sci., 61, 226—228.
1965H.	Tree chopping with an elephant rib. S. African Jour. Sci., 61, 395—396, 2 figs.
1966A.	Les progrès de la recherche archéologique en Afrique du Sud. L'Anthrop., 70:1—2, 63—102, 8 figs.
1966B.	A tribute to Reginald Ruggles Gates. Mankind Quart., 7, 48—52.
1966C.	Comparison of three distal humeral objects from Fontéchevade with some from Makapansgat. S. African Jour. Sci., 62, 21—25, 6 figs.
1967A.	Amazing antiquity of mining in Southern Africa. Nature, 216, 407—408.
1967B.	A Chisenga kudu cranial chalice. S. African Jour. Sci., 63, 198—200, 1 fig.
1968A.	Australopithecus tool-user or tool-maker? Proc. Israel Acad. Sci., Sect. Sci., no. 8, 1—12, 12 pls.
1968B.	Australopithecus africanus: the man-ape of South Africa. S. African Jour. Sci., 64, 51—57, 6 figs., (reprinted from Nature, 7 February 1925).
	See: Galloway 1959.

DART, R. A., and CRAIG, D.

1962	Aventuras con el eslabon perdido. (Transl. from 1959 ed.). Mexico: Fondo de Cultura Económica Press, 382 pp., 22 figs., 16 pls.
	Rev.: Vidart in Amerindia, 2, 79—81; Vidart in Bol. Bibliog. Cien. Hombre, no. 2, 3—5.
1963	Dobrodruzstvi s "chybějícím clánkem". (Transl. of 1959 ed.) Praha: Mladá fronta, Edice Kolumbus, 300 pp., illustr., (not seen).
	Rev.: Vencl in Archeol. Roz., 16, 127—128.

DARWIN, CHARLES

1964	On the origin of the species. (Facsimile of lst ed., 1859). Introduction by Ernst Mayr. Cambridge, Mass.: Harvard Univ. Press, x + 502 pp.
	Rev.: Anon. in Sci. Amer., 212:2, 128, 130; Beer in Science, 146, 51—52; Rudolph in Ohio Jour. Sci., 66, 346; Sumner in Nature, 205, 218.
1966	Die Abstammung des Menchen. Stuttgart: Alfred Kröner, 367 pp., 4 figs.

Rev.: Knussmann in Naturwiss. Rund., 21, 37—38.

DASHZĔVĔG, DĔMBĔRĔLIIN
1964   On two Oligocene Hyaenodontidae from Erghilyin-Dzo (Mongolian
        People's Republic). Acta Pal. Polonica, 9, 263—274, 1 pl., (Polish
        and Russian summaries).
1965   Entelodon orientalis n. sp. from the Oligocene of the Gobi Desert,
        Mongolia. Acta Pal. Polonica, 10, 281—285, 1 pl., 1 table,
        (Polish and Russian summaries).
1966   [New data on Paleogene stratigraphy of Eastern Mongolia.] Doklady
        Akad. Nauk SSSR, 168:3, 647—649, 1 fig., (Russian).
1968   [New data on the age of Lower Paleogene deposits of Nemegetin basin
        in Mongolia.] Doklady Akad. Nauk SSSR, 182:2, 415—417,
        (Russian).

DASTUGUE, J.
1967   Pathologie des hommes fossiles de l'abri de Cro-Magnon. L'Anthrop.,
        71:5—6, 479—492, 7 figs.
        Rev.: Comas in An. Antropol., Mexico, 6, 314—316.

DAUGHERTY, RICHARD D.
1966   Current research: Northwest. Amer. Antiq., 31, 617—619.
        See: Fryxell and Daugherty; Wendorf, Daugherty and Waechter.

DAUMAS, J.-C., and LAUDET, R.
1968   Le trou Arnaud. Spelunca, Bull., 8:1, 14—18, 1 fig.

DAUMAS, MAURICE, (ed.)
1962   Histoire générale des techniques. Tome I. Les origines de la civilisation
        technique. Paris: Presses Universitaires de France, xvi + 652 pp.,
        illustr., 48 pls.

DAUX, GEORGES
1963   Chronique des fouilles et découvertes archéologiques en Grèce en 1962.
        Seconde partie. Travaux de l'Ecole française d'Athènes. Pélopon-
        nèse. Recherches préhistoriques. Bull. Correspondence Hellén.,
        87, 836—837.
1965   Chronique des fouilles et découvertes archéologiques en Grèce en 1964.
        Bull. Correspondence Hellén., 89, 683—1008, illustr.

DAVENPORT, GUY, (ed.)
1963   The intelligence of Louis Agassiz: a specimen book of scientific writ-
        ings. Foreword by Alfred S. Romer. New York: Beacon, 237
        pp., illustr., (not seen).

DAVID, A. I.
1962B. [Remains of Anthropogene mammals from Moldavia.] In: Collected
        Papers, 1962: Problems of ecology and practical significance of
        birds and mammals of Moldavia. (Russian).
1964   [Fossil horses from Moldavian Anthropogene.] Izv. Akad. Nauk Moldav.
        SSR, ser. Biol. i Khim. Nauk, 1964:7, 38—51, 3 figs., 8 tables,
        (Russian; Moldavian summary).
1965A. [Carnivorous mammals from Moldavian Anthropogene.] In: Collected
        Papers, 1965A: Problems of ecology and practical significance
        of birds and mammals of Moldavia, 2, (Russian).

1965B.   [Remains of <u>Spirocerus</u> antelope from Moldavia.]   Izv. Akad. Nauk
          Moldav. SSR, <u>1965</u>:5, 106–107, 1 fig., (Russian; Moldavian
          summary).

1965C.   [On remains of elephant from Karagash quarry.]   Izv. Akad. Nauk
          Moldav. SSR, <u>1965</u>:8, 7–9, 1 fig., 1 table, (Russian).

1965D.   [<u>Alces</u> <u>latifrons</u> from Moldavian Quaternary.]   Izv. Akad. Nauk Moldav.
          SSR, <u>1965</u>:8, 10–11, 1 fig., 1 table, (Russian).

1965E.   [New paleontological remains from Moldavia.]   Okhrana Prirody Moldavii,
          <u>3</u>, 133–136, (Russian).

1966   [A review of distribution of mammals in Moldavian Anthropogene and
          some paleogeographic inferences.]   Problemy geografii Moldavii,
          <u>1</u>, 141–154, 5 maps, (Russian).

1967A.   [On the Roussillon fauna of Moldavian mammals.]   Izv. Akad. Nauk
          Moldav. SSR, <u>1967</u>:4, 26–28, (Russian).

1967B.   [Some results of study on mammalian fauna of Moldavian Anthropogene.]
          Pal. geol. polezn. iskop. Moldavii, <u>2</u>, 170–177, (Russian).

1968A.   [Remains of large (hunting) mammalian species from the excavations in
          Brynzeny I cave.]   Izv. Akad. Nauk Moldav. SSR, ser. Biol. i
          Khim. Nauk, <u>1968</u>:3, 76–80, 3 tables, (Russian).

1968B.   [Mammalian fauna and natural environment in Moldavia during the
          Anthropogene epoch.]   Okhrana Prirody Moldavii, <u>5</u>, 79–88, 5
          figs., (Russian).

DAVID, A. I., and MARKEVICH, V. I.
1967   [Mammalian fauna from Novye Rusesh'ty I site.]   Izv. Akad. Nauk
          Moldav. SSR, <u>1967</u>:4, 3–25, 14 figs., 16 tables, (Russian).

DAVID, A. I., and TARABUKIN, B. A.
1967   [Skull of fossil rhinoceros (<u>Dicerorhinus</u> cf. <u>etruscus</u> Falc.) from
          Tiraspol' gravel.]   Pal. geol. polezn. iskop. Moldavii, <u>2</u>, 178–182,
          1 fig., 2 tables, (Russian).

DAVID, A. I., and VERESHCHAGIN, N. K.
1967   [Present state and further problems of the research on fossil mammalian
          faunas of Moldavia.]   In: Collected Papers, 1967A, [Place and
          significance of fossil mammals of Moldavia in the Cenozoic of
          USSR], 10–37, (Russian).

DAVID, L.
1962   (ed.) Rapport annuel 1962. Doc. Lab. Géol. Fac. Sci. Lyon, no. <u>1</u>,
          100 pp., 4 pls.

1963   (ed.) Rapport annuel 1963. Doc. Lab. Géol. Fac. Sci. Lyon, no. <u>3</u>,
          96 pp., 4 pls.

1964   (ed.) Geologie 1964. Doc. Lab. Géol. Fac. Sci. Lyon, no. <u>7</u>, 119 +
          13 pp., 6 maps.

1966   Baudran, nouveau gisement de vertebrés Quaternaires sur le causse de
          Martel. Doc. Lab. Géol. Fac. Sci. Lyon, <u>21</u>, 61–70, 7 figs.,
          (English abs.).

1967   La faune helvétienne des "sables de Saint-Fons" (Miocène-Rhône).
          Bull. Soc. Linn. Lyon, <u>36</u>:1, 9–13.

          See: Ballesio, et <u>al.</u>;   Viret, David, Mein and Battetta.

DAVID, PIERRE   See: Delporte and David.

DAVID, P., DUPLAIX, S., and GUILLIEN, Y.
  1965   La Basse-Tardoire grottes et abris paléolithique. B. La Chaise. La Chaise:
            terrasses, paleosols, hum, couches archéologiques. Bull. Assoc.
            Franç. Étude Quat., 1965:3–4, 219–221, 1 fig.

DAVID, P., and PRAT, F.
  1962   Sur la présence d'un cheval de grande taille dans certains horizons
            moustériens de la station de la Chaise de Vouthon (Charente).
            Mem. Soc. Archeol. Hist. Charente, 1961–1962, 63–82, 3 pls.,
            5 tables.
  1965   Considérations sur les faunes de La Chaise (commune de Vouthon,
            Charente), Abris Suard et Bourgeois-Delaunay. Bull. Assoc. Franç.
            Étude Quat., 1965:3–4, 222–231, 3 figs., 3 tables.

DAVID, ROGER   See: Delporte and David.

DAVIDOVICH, E. A.   See: Gulîamova, et al.

DAVIDSON, GEORGE
  1950   Prehistoric pageant. London, (not seen).

DAVIES, K. A.   See: Bishop 1964B.

DAVIES, OLIVER
  1961D.   Archaeology in Ghana. Edinburgh: Nelson (published on behalf of
            University College of Ghana), 45 pp., illustr.
            Rev.: Mauny in Bull. Inst. Franç. Afr. Noire, sér. B, 24, 307–308;
            Willett in Jour. Afr. Hist., 3, 154–155.
  1964   The Quaternary in the coastlands of Guinea. Glasgow: Jackson, xv +
            276 pp., 120 figs., 8 pls.
            Rev.: Biberson in L'Anthrop., 71:3–4, 338–351; Biberson in W. Afr.
            Archaeol. Newsletter, no. 9, 20–36, (French summary, 48–49);
            Clark in W. Afr. Archaeol. Newsletter, no. 9, 37–40, (French
            summary, 49);   Coles in Proc. Prehist. Soc. Cambridge, 32,
            369–370;   Folster in W. Afr. Archaeol. Newsletter, no. 9, 40–
            44, (French summary, 50);   Hill in Amer. Anthrop., 70, 156;
            R. V. in L'Anthrop., 69:5–6, 556–558.
  1965   The Lower and Middle Paleolithic in West Africa. Riv. Sci. Preist.,
            19, 1–21, 11 figs., (Italian and French summaries).
  1966   Report on Quaternary studies in Ghana. Bull. Inst. Franç. Afr. Noire,
            Ser. A, 28, 406–407.
  1967A.   The dates of the Late Pleistocene sea-levels. S. Afr. Archaeol. Bull.,
            22, 31.
  1967B.   Comments on the recommendations of the Burg-Wartenstein conference
            as set out in S.A.A.B. 21 (1966), pp. 114–21. W. Afr. Archaeol.
            Newsletter, no. 7, 23–26, (French summary).
  1967C.   West Africa before the Europeans: archaeology and prehistory. London:
            Methuen, xvii + 364 pp., 115 figs., 50 pls., 1 map.
            Rev.: Gabel in Amer. Anthrop., 70, 810–811;   Varley in Man, Jour.
            Roy. Anthrop. Inst., 3, 141–142.

DAVIES, WENDY
  1964   William Pengelly, F. R. S. 1812–1894. Studies in Spel., 1, 3–8, 1 pl.

DAVIES, WILLIAM E.
1966   The earth sciences and speleology. Bull. Nat. Spel. Soc., 28, 1—14.

DAVIS, D. DWIGHT
1964   The giant panda. A morphological study of evolutionary mechanisms.
             Fieldiana: Zool. Mem., 3, 339 pp., 159 figs.
             See: Hennig, W. 1966.

DAVIS, D. H. S., (ed.)
1964   Ecological studies in Southern Africa. The Hague: Junk, Monographiae
             Biologicae 14, xxiv + 415 pp., illustr.
             Rev.: Brown in S. Afr. Archaeol. Bull., 21, 55—56.

DAVIS, EMMA LOU
1964   An archaeological survey of the Mono Lake Basin and excavations of
             two rockshelters, Mono County, California. Ann. Rept., Archeol.
             Surv., Dept. Anthrop., Univ. Calif., Los Angeles, 1963—64, 251—
             390, 10 figs., 6 pls., 2 maps.
1967A.   Man and water at Pleistocene Lake Mohave. Amer. Antiq., 32, 345—
             353, 4 figs.
1967B.   Herschel C. Smith: 1907 - 1966. Amer. Antiq., 32, 389—390, 1 photo.
             See: Crabtree and Davis.

DAVIS, E. MOTT   See: Pearson, F. J., Davis, Tamers, and Johnstone; Pearson,
                    F. J., Davis and Tamers; Tamers, Pearson and Davis.

DAVIS, HESTER A.
1966   Current research: Southeast. Amer. Antiq., 31, 609—611.

DAVIS, JOHN
1967   In memoriam: Alden Holmes Miller. Auk, 84, 193—202, portr.

DAVIS, LARRY W.
1965   Shark teeth in Kansas. Ash Valley — Cedar Bluff — Russell. Rocks
             and Minerals, 40, 805—807, illustr.

DAVIS, P. R.
1964   Hominid fossils from Bed I, Olduvai Gorge. Nature, 201, 967—70.
             Reprint in Current Anthrop., 6, 417—419.

DAVIS, P. R., DAY, M. H., and NAPIER, J. R.
1964   Hominid fossils from Bed I, Olduvai Gorge, Tanganyika. A tibia and
             fibula. Nature, 201 967—968, 1 fig.

DAVITASHVILI, LEE SHIOVICH
1955   [The problem of ecogenesis in the organic world and its present state.]
             Nauchn. Sess. Inst. Paleobiol. AN Gruz. SSR, 2, 7—10, (Russian).
1956C.   [Louis Dollo and his role in elaboration of theoretical foundations of
             paleontology and historical geology.] Nauchn. Sess. Inst. Paleo-
             biol. AN Gruz. SSR, 3, 7—14, (Russian).
1956D.   [Our problems in the scope of theoretical foundations of palaeontology.]
             Trudy Inst. Paleobiol. Akad. Nauk Gruz. SSR, 3, 3—38, (Russian;
             Georgian summary).
1960   [The doctrine of Charles Darwin and the laws governing the historical
             development of organisms.] Bull. Mosk. Obshch. Ispyr. Prirody.
             Otd. Geol., 65:1, 25—46, (Russian; brief English summary).

1961A.   [Theory of sexual selection.]   Moscow; Akad. Nauk SSSR Press, 538
                    pp., illustr., (Russian).
                    Rev.: D. L. Stepanov in Bull. Mosk. Obshch. Ispyt. Prirody, Otd. Geol.,
                    67:4, 113–115, (Russian).

1961B.   [Significance of evolutionary progress doctrine for paleontology and
                    historical geology.]   Trudy Vses. Paleont. Obshch., IV sess., 167–
                    178, (Russian).

1964   [On the classification of assemblages of organisms and organic remains.]
                    Obshchie Vopr. Evoliuts. Paleobiol., 1, 5–18, (Russian; Georgian
                    and English summaries).

1966A.   [The contemporary status of evolutionary studies in the West.]   Moscow:
                    Acad. Sci. USSR, Div. Gen. Biol., Science Publ. House, 242 pp.,
                    (Russian).
                    Rev.: Galaktionov in Zhurnal Obshch. Biol., 29:4, 482–485, (Russian);
                    Olson in Evolution, 22, 426–436, (essay rev.).

1966B.   (ed.) [Cenozoic fauna of Georgia and its geohistorical significance.]
                    Tbilisi: "Metsnierela" Press, 104 pp., ill., (Russian; Georgic
                    summaries).

DAWSON, MARY R.
    1964   Late Eocene rodents (Mammalia) from Inner Mongolia.   Amer. Mus.
                    Novit., no. 2191, 15 pp., 8 figs.

    1965   Oreolagus and other Lagomorpha (Mammalia) from the Miocene of
                    Colorado, Wyoming, and Oregon.   Univ. Colorado Studies, Ser.
                    Earth Sci., 1, 1–36, 31 figs., 6 tables.
                    Rev.: Hünermann in Zbl. Geol. Pal., Teil 2, 1967, 118–119.

    1966   Additional Late Eocene rodents (Mammalia) from the Uinta Basin, Utah.
                    Ann. Carnegie Mus., 38:4, 97–114, 11 figs., 3 tables.
                    Rev.: Hünermann in Zbl. Geol. Pal., Teil 2, 1967, 119.

    1967A.   Fossil history of the families of Recent mammals.   In: Anderson, S.,
                    and Jones, (eds.), 1967, 12–53, fig. 2.

    1967B.   A register of the Tertiary mammal-bearing localities of Switzerland.
                    Jour. Pal., 41, 1278–1279.

    1967C.   Lagomorph history and the stratigraphic record. Univ. Kans. Dept.
                    Geol. Spec. Publ., 2, 287–316, 6 figs.
                    Rev.: Fahlbusch in Zbl. Geol. Pal., Teil 2, 1968, 214–215.

    1968A.   Oligocene rodents (Mammalia) from East Mesa, Inner Mongolia. Amer.
                    Mus. Novit., no. 2324, 1–12, 5 figs., 1 table.

    1968B.   Middle Eocene rodents (Mammalia) from northeastern Utah. Ann.
                    Carnegie Mus., 39:20, 327–370, 54 figs., 6 tables.
                    See: Black, C. C., and Dawson; Clark, J. B., Dawson and Wood;
                    Robinson, Peter, Black and Dawson.

DAWSON, WARREN R.
    1967   Foreword. In: Brothwell, Don, and Sandison, A. T., (eds.), 1967,
                    vii–x.

DAXNER, GUDRUN
    1967   Ein neuer Cricetodontide (Rodentia, Mammalia) aus dem Pannon des
                    Wiener Beckens. Ann. Naturhist. Mus. Wien, 71, 27–36, 3 figs.,
                    (English summary).
                    Rev.: Fahlbusch in Zbl. Geol. Pal., Teil 2, 1969:3, 296–297.

DAXNER, G., and FEJFAR, O.
    1967   Über die Gattungen Alilepus Dice, 1931 und Pliopentalagus Gureev,

1964 (Lagomorpha, Mammalia). Ann. Naturhist. Mus. Wien, 71, 37—55, 8 figs., 3 pls., 3 tables.

Rev.: Fahlbusch in Zbl. Geol. Pal., Teil 2, 1969:3, 295—296.

DAXNER, G., and THENIUS, E.
1965   Ergebnisse der Revision der altquartären Wildziegen (Bovidae, Mammalia) von Hundsheim in Niederösterreich. Anz. Österr. Akad. Wiss., math.-nat. Kl., 97—103.

Abs.: Kühn in Zbl. Geol. Pal., Teil 2, 1966, 333.

DAY, MICHAEL H.
1965   Guide to fossil man. A handbook of human palaeontology. Foreword by J. S. Weiner. London: Cassell, xvi + 289 pp., 94 figs.

Rev.: Campbell in Jour. Anat., 100, 916; Campbell in Nature, 210, 65—66; Coon in Human Biol., 38, 443—444; Davis in Man, Jour. Roy. Anthrop. Inst., 1, 401; Font in Ampurias, 26—27, 379; Knussmann in Homo, 17:3—4, 217; Lobdelle in Newsletter Okla. Anthrop. Soc., 14:9, 7; Pittioni in Archaeol. Austriaca, 39, 95—96; Robinson in Amer. Anthrop., 69, 539; Roth-Lutra in Anat. Anz., 124, 224—225.

1967   Olduvai hominid 10: a multivariate analysis. Nature, 215, 323—324, 3 figs.

1968   Guide to fossil man: a handbook of human paleontology. Cleveland: Meridian Books, 289 pp., illustr., (paperback).

See: Davis, P. R., Day and Napier.

DAY, M. H., and NAPIER, J. R.
1964   Hominid fossils from Bed I, Olduvai Gorge, Tanganyika. Fossil foot bones. Nature, 201, 969—970, 3 figs. Reprint in Current Anthrop., 6, 419—420.

1966   A hominid toe bone from Bed I, Olduvai Gorge, Tanzania. Nature, 211, 929—930, 4 figs.

DAYLEY, JON   See: Swanson and Dayley.

DEACON, H. J., (ed.)
1965   COWA surveys and bibliographies. Area 13 — South Africa. COWA Surv. and Bibliog., Area 13, no. 3, 7 + 12 pp.

1966   The dating of the Nahoon footprints. S. African Jour. Sci., 62, 111—113.

DEANE, ROGER E.   See: Tovell and Deane.

DEBELMAS, JACQUES
1963   L'origine de l'Homme. Bull. Soc. Sci. Dauphiné, 75:4 — 76:1, 2, 3, 3—8.

DEBÉNATH, ANDRÉ
1967   Découverte d'une mandibule humaine à la Chaise de Vouthon (Charente). C. R. Acad. Sci. Paris, Sci. Nat., 265, 1170—1171.

DEBETS, G. F. (= Debetz)
1939C.   [About the skull from Teshik-tash cave.]   Krat. Soob. Inst. Ist. Mat.
Kult. SSSR, 2, 9, 1 fig., (Russian).

1941   [The question of the settlement of north-western Siberia in the light
of paleoanthropological data.]   Krat. Soob. Inst. Ist. Mat. Kult.
SSSR, 9, 14–18, (Russian).

1955   [Paleoanthropologic findings in Kostenki.]   Sov. Etnog., 1955, 1, 44–
53, 2 figs., (Russian).

1956   Bilan d'ensemble des recherches paléoanthropologiques en U.R.S.S.
Communications de la délégation soviétique au 5e Congrès Inter-
national des Sciences Anthropologiques et Ethnologiques. Moscow:
Akad. Nauk SSSR Press, 17 pp., (Russian and French).

1961B.   [A skull from the Upper Paleolithic burial place in Pokrovskii ravine
(Kostenki XVIII).]   Krat. Soob. Inst. Ist. Mat. Kult., SSSR, 82,
120–127, 2 figs., 3 tables, (Russian).

1962   [Regarding the translation of the book by A. Aliman "L'Afrique préhistorique".]   Sov. Etnog., 1962:2, 169–173.

1964   [New data on the relationship of the pebble industry of australopithecine
apes and of the most ancient men.]   Sov. Etnog., 1964:5,
114–116, (Russian).

1967   [Skeleton of Upper Paleolithic man from Sungir' site burial.]   Sov.
Arkheol., 1967:3, 160–163, 2 figs., (Russian).

DEBRINE, B.,   SPIEGEL, Z., and WILLIAM, D.
1963   Cenozoic sedimentary rocks in Socorro Valley, New Mexico. Guidebk.,
New Mexico Geol. Soc., 14th Field Confer., 1963, 123–131, 1 fig.

DEBROSSE, RENÉ   See: Bonnamour and Debrosse.

DE CHABALIER
1963   Die Alge Chlorella bedroht die Bilder von Lascaux. Stuttgarter Zeitung.,
no. 92, 20, (not seen).

DECHASEAUX, COLETTE
1962D.   Rev.: Tétry in L'Ann. Biol., ser. 4, 2, 305–306;   Westphal in Zbl.
Geol. Pal., Teil 2, 1964, 137–138.

1963C.   Une forme européenne du groupe des Chameaux (Tylopedes): le genre
Xiphodon. C. R. Acad. Sci. Paris, 256, 5607–5609, 1 fig.

1964A.   L'encéphale de Neurogymnurus cayluxi insectivore des Phosphorites du
Quercy. Ann. Pal., Vert., 50, 81–100, 12 figs.

1964B.   Introduction. In: Piveteau, J., (ed.), 1964C, Traité de Paléo., 4:1, 1.

1964C.   Caractères généraux des cordés le problème des procordés. In: Piveteau,
J., (ed.), 1964C, Traité de Paléo., 4:1, 5–6.

1964D.   Urocordés. In: Piveteau, J., (ed.), 1964C, Traité de Paléo., 4:1, 9–17,
9 figs.

1964E.   Céphalocordés. In: Piveteau, J., (ed.), 1964C, Traité de Paléo., 4:1,
21–22.

1965A.   Cynohyaenodon et le problème de la pars orbitalis de l'ethmoïde. Ann.
Pal., Vert., 51:1, 25–41, 10 figs.

1965B.   Artiodactyles des Phosphorites des Quercy. 1. Étude sur le genre
Dichodon. Ann. Pal., Vert., 51, 189–208, 8 figs., 1 pl.

1967A.   Artiodactyls des Phosphorites du Quercy. II. Etude sur le genre
Xiphodon. Ann. Pal., Vert., 53, 25–47, 11 figs.

1967B.   Un castoridé du Pléistocène d'Europe, Trogontherium boisvilletti. Étude
du crâne-type et du moulage endocranien. Ann. Pal., Vert., 53,
119–162, 17 figs., 1 pl.

1967C.	Localisations cérébrales et paléoneurologie. Colloq. Internat. Cent. Nation. Recherch. Sci., <u>163</u>, 569–573, (English summary).
1968A.	Les débuts de l'histoire de la fissuration du néopallium chez les Carnivores fissipèdes et chez les Artiodactyles. C. R. Acad. Sci. Paris, Sci. Nat., <u>266</u>, 2320–2323, 2 figs.
1968B.	Le cerveau d'Archaeopteryx est-il de "type avien" ou de "type reptilien"? C. R. Acad. Sci. Paris, Sci. Nat., <u>267</u>:25, 2108–2110, 4 figs.

DECKERT, KURT, and KARRER, C.
| 1965 | Die Fischreste des Frühpleistozäns von Voigtstedt in Thüringen. Pal. Abh., Abt. A, <u>2</u>, 299–322, 49 figs., pls. 3–5, (Russian and English summaries). |
| | Abs.: Weiler in Zbl. Geol. Pal., Teil 2, <u>1966</u>, 273–274. |

DECONINCK, J.
| 1962A. | Quelques mots sur le gisement paléolithique du Mont de l'Enclus. Arch., Publ. Cercle Recherch. Préhist. Renaisis, <u>3</u>, 23–24, (not seen). |
| 1962B. | Découverte de reste de mammouth, sur le territoire de la commune de Dergneau près de Renaix. Autographie no 35 de E. Joly. Arch., Publ. Cercle Recherch. Préhist. Renaisis, <u>3</u>, 27, (not seen). |

DEDABRISHVILI, SH. SH.   See: Bugianashvili, <u>et al.</u>

DEDIEU, B.
| 1965 | La Grotte du djebel Zabaouine. Libyca, <u>13</u>, 99–126, 19 figs., 1 table. |

DEETZ, JAMES
| 1967 | Invitation to archaeology. New York: Natural History Press, x + 150 pp., 18 figs. |
| | Rev.: Chang in Amer. Jour. Archaeol., <u>72</u>:2, 200–201; Fowler in Amer. Anthrop., <u>70</u>, 1018; E.S.R. in Archaeol. Soc. N.J., News., <u>83</u>, 9; Rainey in Amer. Jour. Phys. Anthrop., <u>27</u>, 110–111. |

DEEVEY, EDWARD S., JR.
| 1967 | Introduction. In: Martin, P. S., and Wright, H. E., (eds.), 1967, 63–72. |

DeFORD, RONALD K.   See: Wilson, J. A., <u>et al.</u>

DEGEN, RUDOLF, (ed.)
| 1965 | Archäologischer Fundbericht. Altsteinzeit und Mittelsteinzeit. Jahrb. Schweiz. Ges. Urgesch., <u>51</u>, 71–87, figs. 1–16. |

DEGERBØL, MAGNUS
| 1964 | Some remarks on Late- and Post-glacial vertebrate fauna and its ecological relations in northern Europe. Jour. Animal Ecol., supplement to vol. 33, 71–85. |

DEGORCE, JEAN-PIERRE
| 1966 | Contribution a l'étude des pics du Paléolithique superieur. Bull. Soc. Hist. Archéol. Perigord, <u>93</u>, 261–263, 1 fig. |

DEHM, RICHARD
| 1962A. | Abs.: Dietrich in Zbl. Geol. Pal., Teil 2, <u>1964</u>, 185–186. |

1964   Die Spitzmäuse aus dem Alt-Burdigalium von Wintershof-West bei
Eichstätt in Bayern. Sitz.-Ber. Akad. Wiss. München, 1963, 17–
18.

1965   Klima und Wirbeltier-Entfaltung in Sudafrika während Perm und Trias.
Senck. Lethaea, 46a, 35–44, 5 figs.

1966   Über den Weinheimer Ovibos-Fund und die Niederterrassen-Sande. Mitt.
Bayer. Staatssamml. Pal. Hist. Geol., 6, 143–153, 2 figs., (English summary).

1967   Vorzeit und Leben. Münch. Univers., 42, 20 pp.

DEHM, R., OETTINGEN-SPIELBERG, TZU., and VIDAL, H.
1963   Abs.: Dehm in Sitz.-Ber. Akad. Wiss. München, 1963, 6–7;   Hünermann
in Zbl. Geol. Pal., Teil 2, 1965, 283–284.

DEINSE, A. B. Van
1963   Walvisnieuws over 1962. Lutra, 5, 31–35, (English summary).
1964A.   Walvisnieuws over 1963. Lutra, 6, 61–66, (English summary).
1964B.   De fossiele en recente walrussen van Nederland. Zool. Meded. Leiden,
39, 187–205, pl. 13.
1965   Lijst van publicaties van Dr. A. B. Van Deinse over walvisvaart, wal-
visachtigen en zeeroofdieren, [etc.]. Lutra, 7, 7–20.

DEINSE, A. V., and VERHEY, C. J.
1965   Vondsten van de Holeleeuw, Panthera spelaea (Goldfuss), in Nederland.
Lutra, 7, 27–31, pl. 4, (Dutch; English summary).

DeJARNETTE, DAVID L.
1964   Fluted projectile points in a stratified site in Marshall County, Alabama.
Bull. Eastern States Archeol. Fed., no. 23, 13–14, (abs.).
1967   Alabama pebble tools: the Lively Complex. Bull. Eastern States
Archeol. Fed., no. 26, 11–12, (abs.).
1968   The use of polyethylene in stratigraphic profiles. Jour. Ala. Archeol.,
14, 38–40, 2 figs.

DEKEYSER, P.-L.
1962B.   Morphologie et biologie des oiseaux de l'Ouest africain (Notes documen-
taires). V. Ardéiformes. Bull. Inst. Afr. Noire, (A), 24, 1190–
1241.

DEKIN, ALBERT A.
1966   A fluted point from Grand Traverse County. Mich. Archaeol., 12, 35–
36, 1 pl., 1 map.

De La CALLE, R.
1967   Cuban stamps commemorate "origin of man". Current Anthrop., 8,
476, illustr.

DELACOUR, JEAN T., and SCOTT, P.
1954-
1964   The waterfowl of the world. London: Country Life Ltd., 4 vols.
Rev.: O., P. J. S. in Ibis, 107, 262;   Parkes in Wilson Bull., 77, 305–
308.

DeLAET, SIGFRIED J.
1960   La arqueología y sus problemas. Notes and appendix by E. Ripoll
Perelló. Barcelona: Ed. Labor (colección "Biblioteca de

Iniciación Cultural", Sec. 6, no. 507–508), 216 pp., 9 figs., 16 pls., (not seen).

Rev.: Llongueras Campaña in Ampurias, 24, 359.

1963   et al. Bibliographie archéologique (Belgique, Pays-Bas, Grand-Duché de Luxembourg). Helinium, 3, 121–167.

1964   et al. Bibliographie archéologique (Belgique, Pays-Bas, Grand-Duché de Luxembourg). Helinium, 4, 167–190.

DeLAET, S. J., and THOMAS, H. L., (eds.)

1965   COWA surveys and bibliographies. Area 3 — Western Europe: Part I. COWA Surv. and Bibliog., Area 3, no. 3, 18 + 23 pp.

DeLAET, S. J., and TRIMPE BURGER, J. A.

1964   Kroniek. District E: Oostvlaandern, Westlaanderen en Zeeland (1960–1962). Helinium, 4, 56–70, 2 maps.

DELAIR, JUSTIN B.

1954   Some Wealden dinosaurs. Sci. Club Mag., Autumn, no. 4, 25, illustr., (not seen).

1955   Flying reptiles of the past. Sci. Club Mag., no. 7, 52, illustr., (not seen).

1956A.   Excavating an extinct reptile. Newsclub Mag., no. 7 (March-April), 2, (not seen).

1956B.   Monster sea saurians of long ago. Sci. News Mag., 14:3, 8–11, illustr., (not seen).

1959   New discoveries of fossils. Sci. Club Mag., no. 24, 244, (not seen).

1966A.   Unusual preservation of fibrous elements in an ichthyosaur skull. Nature, 212, 575–576, 3 figs.

Rev.: Anon. in Naturwiss. Rundschau, 20:4, 175; Huene in Zbl. Geol. Pal., Teil 2, 1968, 204.

1966B.   New records of dinosaurs and other fossil reptiles from Dorset. Proc. Dorset Nat. Hist. Archaeol. Soc., 87, 28–37, 2 figs.

1966C.   Fossil footprints from Dumfriesshire, with descriptions of new forms from Annandale. Trans. Dumfries. Galloway Nat. Hist. Antiq. Soc., 43, 14–30.

Rev.: Huene in Zbl. Geol. Pal., Teil 2, 1968, 200.

1967   Additional records of British Permian footprints. Trans. Dumfries. Galloway Nat. Hist. Antiq. Soc., 44, 1–5, 1 fig.

DELARUE, R., and VIGNARD, E.

1963C.   Le Protomagdalénien I du Bois "des Pins" dans les Beauregards de Nemours. Bull. Soc. Préhist., Paris, 60, 194–204, 3 figs.

DE LA TORRE, LUIS, and DYSART, M. P.

1966   A method for photographing teeth of small mammals. Jour. Mammal., 47, 515–518, 3 pls.

DELATTRE, A., and FENART, R.

1960   L'hominisation du crâne étudiée par la méthode vestibulaire. Paris: Centre National de la Recherche Scientifique, 418 pp., 179 figs., (English and German summaries).

DELFGAAUW, BERNARD

1964   Teilhard de Chardin und das Evolutionsproblem. München: C. H. Beck'sche Verlagsbuchhandlung, 120 pp., 4 figs., (not seen).

Rev.: Gieseler in Anthrop. Anz., 30, 294; Kurth. in Kosmos (Stuttgart), 62, *204.

1965   Geschichte als Fortschritt, II: Die Geschichte des Menschen, Statica-
                Dynamica. Köln: Bachem Verl., 266 pp., (not seen).
            Rev.: Pittioni in Archaeol. Austriaca, 40, 286.

DELIBRIAS, G., GUILLIER, M. T., and LABEYRIE, J.
    1964   Saclay natural radiocarbon measurements I. Radiocarbon, 6, 233—250.
    1965   Saclay natural radiocarbon measurements II. Radiocarbon, 7, 236—244.
    1966   GIF natural radiocarbon measurements. Radiocarbon, 8, 74—95.

DELINGETTE, ANNIE   See: Chaline and Delingette.

DELLING, MARILYN POWELL
    1966   A Folsom point from Boone County, Missouri. Plains Anthrop., 11,
                235, 1 fig.

DELMAS, ANDRÉ   See: Pineau and Delmas.

DELMAS, A., and PINEAU, H.
    1966   Poids des vertèbres présacrées et classification des Mammifères. C. R.
                Acad. Sci. Paris, Sci. Nat., 262, 2699—2702, 3 figs.

DELOFFRE, RAOUL
    1961   Ossicules de poissons dans l'Aptien supérieur pyrenéen. Rev. Micropal.,
                3, 227—229, 1 pl.
    1964   Sur l'âge du niveau à Leiodon mosasauroides découvert sur le territoire
                de la commune de Ledeuix (Basses-Pyrénées). C. R. Soc. Géol.
                France, 1964, 270—271.

DELORME, L. D.   See: Klassen, Delorme, and Mott.

DELPORTE, HENRI
    1962A.   Rev.: Sonneville-Bordes in L'Anthrop., 69, 105—108.
    1962C.   Note préliminaire sur la station de la Rochette. Le Périgordien
                supérieur. Bull. Soc. Etudes Rech. Préhist. Eyzies, 11, 39—49,
                3 figs., 2 tables.
    1962D.   Les niveaux aurignaciens de l'abri du Facteur à Tursac et l'évolution
                générale de l'Aurignacien en Périgord. Bull. Soc. Etudes Rech.
                Préhist. Eyzies, 11, 107—126, 3 figs..
    1963A.   Rev.: Sonneville-Bordes in L'Anthrop., 69, 105—108.
    1963C.   Rev.: Sonneville-Bordes in L'Anthrop., 69, 105—108.
    1963D.   Un "poignard" périgordien à l'abri du Facteur (Tursac, Dordogne).
                Bull. Soc. Etudes Rech. Préhist. Eyzies, 12, 58—63, 2 figs.
    1964A.   La Vénus de Krasniicar (Sibérie). Bull. Soc. Préhist. Franç., C. R.
                séances mens., 1964:6, cxxxiv.
    1964B.   Les niveaux aurignaciens de la Rochette. Bull. Soc. Études Rech.
                Préhist. Eyzies, 13, 52—75, 8 figs., 6 tables.
    1964C.   Oberservations sur les Vénus paléolithiques de Russie. In: Ripoll
                Perelló, E., (ed.), 1964A, 381—404, 2 figs., 6 pls., (Spanish sum-
                mary).
    1965   La statuette féminine de Krasnii Iar (Sibérie) et le Paléolithique de
                Sibérie. Bull. Soc. Préhist. Franç, Étud. et Trav., 62:1, 118—
                129, 2 figs.
    1966   Le Paléolithique dans le Massif Central: I. — Le Magdalénien des vallées
                supérieures de la Loire et de l'Allier. Bull. Soc. Préhist. Franç.,
                Étud. et Trav., 63:1, 181—207, 9 figs., 2 tables.

DELPORTE, H., and DAVID, R.
1965A.   Evolution du Mousterien à La Rochette, Saint-Léon-sur-Vézère, Dordogne.
           Bull. Soc. Préhist. Franç., C. R. séances mens., 1965:3, xc.
1965B.   L'évolution des industries moustériennes à La Rochette, Commune de
           Saint-Léon-sur-Vézère (Dordogne). Bull. Soc. Préhist. Franç.,
           Étud. et Trav., 62:1, 48−62, 9 figs.

DEL PUP, G.   See: Piccoli and Del Pup.

DEL REAL, CARLOS ALONSO
1963   Notas de Sociologia Paleolitica. Jour. World Hist., 7, 675−700.

DEMANGEOT, JEAN
1964   L'inter Mindel-Riss dans l'Apennin central. Bull. Soc. Géol. France, 5,
           597−602, 1 fig., 2 tables.

DEMANGEOT, J., and RADMILLI, A. M.
1966   Le gisement paléolithique de Valle Giumentina (Apennin central) et ses
           problèmes. Eiszeit. u. Gegenwart, 17, 159−199, 19 figs., 2 tables,
           (German summary).

DeMAR, ROBERT E.
1966A.   Longiscitula houghae, a new genus of dissorophid amphibian from the
           Permian of Texas. Fieldiana, Geol., 16, 45−53, 2 figs.
1966B.   The phylogenetic and functional implications of the armor of Dissorophi-
           dae. Fieldiana, Geol., 16, 55−88, 9 figs.
1967   Two new species of Broiliellus (amphibians) from the Permian of Texas.
           Fieldiana, Geol., 16:5, 117−129, 2 figs.
1968   The Permian labyrinthodont amphibian Dissorophus multicinctus, and
           adaptations and phylogeny of the family Dissorophidae. Jour.
           Pal., 42, 1210−1242, 18 figs., pl. 161, 1 table.
           Rev.: Westphal in Zbl. Geol. Pal., Teil 2, 1969:2, 209.

DEMARCQ, G., and TRUC, G.
1962   Abs.: Doc. Lab. Géol. Fac. Sci. Lyon, no. 1, 28.

DEMATHIEU, GEORGES-G.-P.
1964   Des empreintes de pas sur les grès triasiques du Mont d'Or lyonnais.
           Bull. Soc. Linn., Lyon, 33, 24−36, 5 figs., 1 pl.
1966   Rhynchosauroides petri et Sphingopus ferox, nouvelles empreintes des
           Reptiles des grès triasiques de la bordure Nord-Est du Massif
           Central. C. R. Acad. Sci. Paris, ser. D, 263, 483−486, 1 fig.
           See: Courel and Demathieu.

DEMEDIÙK, N. S.
1966   [New finds of vertebrate fauna in the Dnestr R. valley.] Pal. Sborn.,
           3:2, 135−136, (Russian; English summary).

DEMENT'EV, G. P.
1964   [Class Aves. Birds.] Osnovy Pal., [Amphibians, Reptiles, and Birds.],
           [12], 660−699, 40 figs., 1 table, (Russian).
           Abs.: Kuhn in Zbl. Geol. Pal., Teil 2, 1966, 311−312.

DENISON, ROBERT H.
1963B.   The early history of the vertebrate calcified skeleton. Clinical Ortho-
           paedics, 31, 141−152, 9 figs., (not seen).

1964A.   Armored fishes of Devonian seas. Bull. Chicago Nat. Hist. Mus., 35:3, 2, 8, 2 figs. and cover.

1964B.   The Cyathaspididae. A family of Silurian and Devonian jawless vertebrates. Fieldiana: Geol., 13:5, 309–473, figs. 90–161, 1 chart.
Rev.: Savage in Nature, 204, 735–736;
Abs.: Schmidt in Zbl. Geol. Pal., Teil 2, 1964, 756–757.

1966A.   The origin of the lateral-line sensory system. Amer. Zool., 6, 369–370, 2 figs.

1966B.   Cardipeltis, an Early Devonian agnathan of the Order Heterostraci. Fieldiana, Geol., 16:4, 89–116, 11 figs.

1967A.   Ordovician vertebrates from western United States. Fieldiana, Geol., 16:6, 131–192, 26 figs.

1967B.   A new Protaspis from the Devonian of Utah, with notes on the classification of Pteraspididae. In: Patterson, C., and Greenwood, P. H., (eds.), 1967, 31–37, 2 figs., 1 pl.

1968   Early Devonian lungfishes from Wyoming, Utah, and Idaho. Fieldiana: Geol., 17:4, 353–413, 26 figs.
See: Gupta, V. J. and Denison.

DENISOV, V. P., and OBORIN, V. A.
1968   [Studies in the Perm' and in the north of Sverdlovsk provinces.]   In: Rybakov, (ed.), 1968, 105–106, (Russian).

DENMAN, N. S.   See: Warburton and Denman.

DENNIS, EMILY
1967   A museum program in anthropology and archaeology for high school students. Mus. News, 45:6, 13–17, illustr.

DENNY, NORMAN   See: Chardin 1964A.

DE PORTA, J.
1965   Nota preliminar sobre la fauna de vertebrados hallada en Curití (Departamento de Santander, Colombia). Bol. Geol., Univ. Ind. Santander, S. A., 19, 111–114, 2 figs., 2 photos.

DERANIYAGALA, P. E. P.
1958A.   Rev.: Sahni in Jour. Pal. Soc. India, 4, 82.
1960F.   The extinct Hominoideae of Ceylon. Jour. Anthrop. Soc. Vidyodaya Univ., 2, 52–62, 3 figs., 3 pls., (not seen).

1964A.   Ceylon. Asian Perspectives, 7, 39–40.
1964B.   Prehistoric archaeology in Ceylon. Asian Perspectives, 7, 189–192, 3 pls.

1965   Some extinct hominoids and other Mammalia of Ceylon. In: Jhingran, A. G., et al., (eds.), 1965, 290–300, 2 pls., 1 table, 1 map.

DE RENZI, M.   See: Crusafont Pairó, DeRenzi and Clavell.

DE ROSNAY, J.
1965   La prévie ou l'évolution biochemique. Paris: Ronetypé, (not seen).

DERZHAVIN, A. N.
1951   [A sketch of the history of faunas of the Caspian Sea and the fresh water bodies of Azerbaïdzhan.] In: Alizade et al., (eds.), 1951, 34–83, 17 figs., 4 tables, (Russian).

See: Alizade, A. N., et al.

DESBROSSE, R.   See: Combier, J. and Desbrosse.

DESCAMPS, C.   See: Barbey and Descamps.

DES LAURIERS, JAMES R.
1965   A new Miocene tortoise from southern California. Bull. S. Calif. Acad.
            Sci., 64, 1–10, 3 figs., 4 tables.

DESMOSTYLUS RESEARCH COMMITTEE (DEREC)
1951   [The second skeleton of Desmostylus in Gihu Prefecture.] Jour. Geol.
            Soc. Japan, 57, 414, (Japanese).

DESPARMET, RAYMOND   See: Lapparent, Montenat and Desparmet.

DE SOLA, OSWALDO
1962   Palabras del Director de la Escuela de Geología, Minas y Metalurgia, en
            el acto de homenaje al profesor José Royo y Gómez. Geos,
            Esc. Geol., Min. Met., Univ. Cent. Venezuela, no. 8, 21–22.

DESROCHES, A.
1964   Catalogue raisonné des poissons fossiles du gisement de Cérin (Ain).
            Collections de l'Institut de Géologie de Lyon et du Muséum
            d'Histoire naturelle de la ville de Lyon. Doc. Lab. Géol. Fac.
            Sci. Lyon, no. 7, 41–42, (abs.).

DESTEXHE-JAMOTTE, J.
1964   Les burins accidentels. Bull. Soc. Roy. Belge Anthrop. Préhist., 74,
            37–42, 13 figs.

DEUEL, THORNE
1966   Origin of Man and culture. Trans. Ill. Acad. Sci., 59, 15–19.

DEVAMBEZ, PIERRE, (ed.)
1961   Encyclopédie de la pléiade. Histoire de l'art. I. Le monde non-chretien.
            Tours: Librairie Gallimard, xxii + 2205 pp., illustr.

DEVIATKIN, E. V.
1963   [Eopleistocene of South-Eastern Altaĭ.] Trudy Kom. Chet. Perioda,
            22, 32–63, 7 figs., 2 tables, (Russian).
1965   [Cenozoic deposits and neotectonics in Southeastern Altaĭ.] Trudy
            Geol. Inst., 126, 244 pp., 77 figs., 13 tables, (Russian).
            See: Nikiforova, K. V., Ravskiĭ and Deviatkin.

DEVIATKIN, E. V., and LISKUN, I. G.
1966   [On the stratigraphy of Cenozoic deposits of Western Mongolia.]
            Biull. Mosk. Obshch. Ispyt. Prirody, Otd. Geol., 41:5, 137–138,
            (Russian).
1967   [New materials on stratigraphy and fauna of Cenozoic deposits of
            West Mongolia.] Doklady Akad. Nauk SSSR, 176:1, 159–162,
            1 fig., (Russian).

DEVIATKIN, E. V., LISKIN, I. G., and CHUMAKOV, I. S.
1965   [Correlation of Eopleistocene deposits in the mountains of southern
            Siberia.] In: Nikiforova, (ed.), 1965A, 91–98, (Russian;
            English summary).

DEVIÁTKIN, E. V., ZAZHIGIN, V. S., and LISKUN, I. G.
1968   [First finds of small mammals in the Pliocene of Tuva and western
         Mongolia.] Dokl. Akad. Nauk SSSR, 183:2, 404–407, (Russian).

DEVILLERS, CHARLES   See: Grassé and Devillers.

DEVILLERS, C. and J.
1965   Une excursion aux gisements canadiens de dinosaures. Ann. Soc. Roy.
         Zool. Belge, 94, 227–239, 8 figs.

DEVIRTS, A. L.   See: Vinogradov, A. P., et al.

DE VISSCHER, JERRY   See: Fitting, DeVisscher and Wahla.

DE VISSCHER, J., and WAHLA, E. J.
1963   The DeVisscher Paleo II occupation site. Totem Pole, 46, 44–57,
         illustr.
1964A.   Paleo-II-W: a minor Paleo-Indian occupation site in Macomb County,
         Michigan. Mich. Archaeol., 10, 5–10, 48, 2 pls., 1 table.
1964B.   Paleo-II-W, a minor Paleo-occupation site in Macomb Co., Mich. Totem
         Pole, 47:8, 10 pp., 4 figs., 1 table.
1966   Part II: other Paleo-Indian sites along the Holcombe Beach. In: Fit-
         ting, J. E., DeVisscher, J., and Wahla, E. J., 1966, 83–107, 5 figs.,
         2 tables.

DE VORE, IRVEN
1964   The evolution of social life. In: Tax, S., (ed.), 1964, 25–36.
         See: Eimerl, DeVore, et al.; Washburn and DeVore.

DE VORE [B. I.] et al.
1965   Behavior as adaptation. In: DeVore, P. L., (ed.), 1965, 52–70.

DE VORE, PAUL L., (ed.)
1965   The origin of man. New York: The Wenner-Gren Foundation for
         Anthropological Research, vi + 151 pp., 2 photos.
1966   A symposium on the origin of man, April 2–4, 1965, Chicago, Illinois,
         U. S. A. Current Anthrop., 7, 97–99.

DEWEZ, M.
1960   Découvertes récentes d'objets du Paléolithique supérieur dans les déblais
         de la caverne de Spy. Bull. Soc. Roy. Belge Anthrop. Préhist.,
         71, 21–24, 5 figs.

DIAS DE ÁVILA PIRES, FERNANDO
1963   Seleção natural Centenário da comunicação de Darwin & Wallace sôbre
         a seleção natural. Publ. Avulsas Mus. Nac., no. 46, 20 pp.
         See: Souza Cunha and Dias de Ávila Pires.

DÍAZ GARCÍA, ARTURO
1961   Memoria del año 1946. In: Núñez Jiménez (ed.), 1961A, 123–130.

DIBBLE, DAVID S., and LORRAIN, D.
1965   Bonfire shelter: A stratified bison kill site in the Amistad Reservoir
         area, Val Verde County, Texas. Misc. Pap., Texas Archaeol.
         Salvage Project, no. 5, 128 pp., (not seen).

DIBNER, B.
1964   Darwin of The Beagle. New York: Blaisdell, x + 143 pp., (paperbound).
Rev.: MacFarlane in Austral. Jour. Sci., 28, 131.

DIBNER, V. D.
1957   [The geological structure of the islands of the central section of the
Karskiĭ sea.] Trudy Inst. Geol. Arktiki, 81, 97—104, (Russian).

DICKENSON, FRED
1968   Koalas — their fight for life. Walkabout, 34:8, 12—15, illustr.

DICKINSON, ALICE
1962   The first book of Stone Age man. New York: Franklin Watts, 82 pp.,
illustr., (ages 6—10).

DICKSON, DON R.
1962   Ozark prehistory. Arkansas Amateur, 1:2, 3—4.

DICKSON, JAMES A.
1967   A rock crystal fluted point from the Cumberland Valley, Pennsylvania.
Penn. Archaeol., 37, 1—4, 2 figs.

DICKSON, M. R.
1964   The skull and other remains of Prosqualodon marplesi, a new species
of fossil whale. New Zealand Jour. Geol. Geophys., 7, 626—635,
16 figs.

DIDKOVSKIĬ, V. ÎA   See: Svistun and Didkovskiĭ.

DIEBOLD, A. RICHARD   See: Slobin, Lancaster and Diebold.

DIEGO, FRANCISCO FERNANDEZ G. de
1962   Los "Bastones Perforados" del país Vasco. Munibe, 14:3/4, 370—413,
20 figs.

DIEHL, H.
1964   Eine neue Station paläolitischer Werkzeuge in Sudhessen: Dietzenbach,
Kr. Offenbach. Fundber. Hessen, 4, 142—144, (not seen).

DIELIS
1961   De vindplaats Bergeyk. Brabants Heem, 13, 141, (not seen).

DIETRICH, WILHELM OTTO
1916B.   Ist der afrikanische Elefant mit dem indischen verwandt? Naturw.
Wochenschrift, 31, 380—381.
1921B.   Über Kiefer- und Zahnwachstum und den "horizontalen Zahnwechsel".
Naturw. Wochenschrift, 36, 552—554.
1928F.   Pleistocäne, deutsch-ostafrikanische Hippopotamus-Reste. Wiss. Ergeb.
Oldoway-Exped., 3, 1—41, (not seen).
1948C.   Der Mensch. Herkunft und Zukunft. Natur und Technik, 2, 507—513,
(not seen).
1949   Die Pferdereihe. (Zum Mechanismus der Stammesgeschichte.) Forsch.
u. Fortschr., 25, 55—57.
1960   Geschichte der Sammlungen des Geologisch-Paläontologischen Instituts
und Museums der Humboldt-Universität zu Berlin. Ein Beitrag

zur Paläontologie-Geschichte. Ber. Geol. Ges. Deutsch.
Demokratischen Republ., 5, 247—289, 2 pls.

1965   Fossile Elefantenzähne von Voigtstedt in Thüringen. Pal. Abh., Abt.
A, 2, 521—536, 3 figs., pls. 32—35, 1 table, (Russian and English
summaries).

1968   Fossile Löwen im europäischen und afrikanischen Pleistozän. Pal. Abh.,
Abt. A, 3:2, 323—366, 1 fig., 8 pls., 13 tables, (Russian and
English summaries).
Rev.: Thenius in Zbl. Geol. Pal., Teil 2, 1969:6, 516—517.

DILKS, M. D., and REYNOLDS, G. M.
1965   A preliminary report on "A survey of fluted points in Maryland".
Jour. Archaeol. Soc. Maryland, 1:1, 1—3, 1 fig.

DINELEY, DAVID LAWRENCE
1963A.   Knoydart formation (Lower Devonian) of Nova Scotia. Geol. Soc.
Amer., Spec. Pap., 73, 138—139, (abs.).

1963B.   The "Red Stratum" of the Silurian Arisaig Series, Nova Scotia, Canada.
Jour. Geol., 71:3, 523—524.

1964A.   Armor-plated and jawless Devonian fish. Fossil record is clue to
pteraspid habitat. Nat. Hist., 73:7, 48—53, illustr.

1964B.   New specimens of Traquairaspis from Canada. Palaeont., 7, 210—219,
6 figs., pls. 38—39.

1965A.   Fossil harvest in the far north. Animals, 6, 254—260.

1965B.   An occurrence of Corvaspis (Ostracodermi) in Canada. Canadian Jour.
Earth Sci., 2, 93—97, 5 figs., 2 pls.

1965C.   Ostracoderms from the Siluro-Devonian of Somerset Island, Arctic Canada. Proc. Geol. Soc. London, no. 1624, 97—98, (Discussion
by L. B. Tarlo).

1966A.   Fossil vertebrates from the Read Bay and Peel Sound formations,
Somerset Island, District of Franklin. Geol. Surv. Canada Pap.,
1966:1, 12—13, (not seen).

1966B.   The Dartmouth beds of Bigbury Bay, south Devon. Discussion by
J. Shirley, B. C. King, L. B. H. Tarlo, and E. I. White. Proc.
Geol. Soc. London, 1629, 11—13.

1966C.   The Dartmouth beds of Bigbury Bay, south Devon. Quart. Jour. Geol.
Soc. London, 122, 187—217, 6 figs., pl. 10, 1 table.

1967A.   The Lower Devonian Knoydart faunas. In: Patterson, C., and Greenwood, P. H., (eds.), 1967, 15—29, 14 figs., 1 pl., 2 tables.

1967B.   Ancient fishes of Escuminac Bay. Nat. Hist., 76:1, 40—45, 8 figs.,
1 table.

DINESMAN, L. G.   See: Grosset, et al.

DINSDALE, TIM
1961   Loch Ness monster. London: Routledge and Kegan Paul, 248 pp.,
27 figs., 18 pls., (not seen).
Rev.: Tétry in L'Ann. Biol., ser. 4, 2, 497—498.

DIOP, Ch.-A.
1963   Histoire primitive de l'Humanité: Evolution du monde noir. Bull.
Inst. Franç. Afr. Noire, sér. B, 24, 449—541, 33 pls.

DI PESO, CHARLES C.
1963   Cultural development in northern Mexico. Smithson. Misc. Coll.,
146:1, 1—15.

1965   The Clovis fluted point from the Timmy site, northwest Chihuahua,
              Mexico. Kiva, 31, 83—87, 2 pls.

DJAMBAZOV, NIKOLAI   See: Dzhambazov, Nikolai.

DMITRIEVA, E. L.
1966   [Eopleistocene mammals of Western Transbaĭkalia. Order Artiodactyla.
              Subfamily Gazellinae.] Trudy Geol. Inst., 152, 144—153, 3 figs.,
              6 tables, (Russian).

DOBÁT, KLAUS
1963   "Höhlenalgen" bedrohen die Eiszeitmalerien von Lascaux. Die Höhle,
              14, 41—45, (French summary).

DOBEN-FLORIN, URSULA
1964   Die Spitzmäuse aus dem Alt-Burdigalium von Wintershof-West bei
              Eichstätt in Bayern. Abh. Bayer. Akad. Wiss., Math.-Nat. Kl.,
              117, 82 pp., 11 figs., 7 pls.

DOBERENZ, ALEXANDER R.   See: Haynes, Doberenz and Allen; Wyckoff, R. W.
              G. and Doberenz; Wyckoff, R. W. G., Doberenz and McCaughey;
              Wyckoff, R. W. G., McCaughey and Doberenz.

DOBERENZ, A. R., and LUND, R.
1966   Evidence for collagen in a fossil of the Lower Jurassic. Nature, 212,
              1502—1503, 2 figs.

DOBERENZ, A. R., and MATTER, P., III
1965   Nitrogen analysis of fossil bones. Comp. Biochem. Physiol., 16, 253—
              258, 3 tables.

DOBERENZ, A. R., and WYCKOFF, R. W. G.
1967A.   The microstructure of fossil teeth. Jour. Ultrastruct. Res., 18, 166—
              175, 8 figs., 1 table.
1967B.   Fine structure in fossil collagen. Proc. Nation. Acad. Sci., 57, 539—
              541, 5 figs.

DOBIE, JAMES L.
1968   A new turtle species of the genus Macroclemys (Chelydridae) from the
              Florida Pliocene. Tulane Studies Zool., 15, 59—63, 3 figs.

DOBKINA, E. I.   See: Vinogradov, A. P., et al.

DOBZHANSKY, THEODOSIUS
1958A.   Rev.: Firbas in Mitt. Anthrop. Ges. Wien, 96—97, 354—355.
1960C.   Die Ursachen der Evolution. In: Heberer, G., and Schwanitz, F., (eds.),
              1960, (see entry in Bibliog. of Fossil Verts. 1959—1963), 32—44.
1960D.   Evolution und Umwelt. In: Heberer, G., and Schwanitz, F., (eds.),
              1960 (see entry in Bibliog. of Fossil Verts. 1959—1963), 81—98.
1962   Rev.: Huxley in Perspectives Biol. Med., 6, 144—148; Montalenti in
              Scientia, 101, 285, 288—289.
1964A.   Mankind evolving. The evolution of the human species. 4th ed. New
              Haven and London; Yale Paperbound, 382 pp.
              Rev.: Kurth in Homo, 16:4, 252.

1964B.—
1965A.   Heredity and the nature of man. 1st ed. New York: Harcourt,
Brace and World, (1964); London: George Allen and Unwin,
(1965), x + 179 pp., 15 figs.
> Rev.: Bonné in Amer. Anthrop., 67, 1341—1343; Caspari in Amer.
> Sci., 54, 70A; Roberts in Man, Jour. Roy. Anthrop. Inst., 1,
> 246—247; Waddington in Nature, 208, 959—960.

1965B.   Dynamik der menschlichen Evolution. Gene und Umwelt. Frankfurt
am Main: S. Fischer Verlag, 442 pp., 10 figs., 27 tables, (not
seen).
> Rev.: Ehgartner in Mitt. Anthrop. Ges. Wien, 95, 366; Roth-Lutra in
> Anat. Anz., 121, 449—450; Schaeuble in Zeit. Morph. Anthrop.,
> 60:1, 116.

1965C.   Mendelism, Darwinism and evolutionism. Proc. Amer. Philos. Soc., 109,
205—215.

1966A.   Vererbung und Menschenbild. (Transl. by G. Heberer). Munich:
Nymphenburger Verl., 205 pp., 15 figs., 3 tables.
> Rev.: Grimm in Biol. Zbl., 88:4, 522—523; Kurth in Naturwiss.
> Rundschau, 19:11, 476; Tillner in Anthrop. Anz., 30, 191—192;
> Walter in Homo, 18:2, 111.

1966B.   L'Homme en évolution. Translation from English by Georges and Simon
Pasteur, of Mankind evolving, 1962. Paris: Flammarion, 432 pp.,
10 figs., 27 tables.
> Rev.: Boesiger in L'Ann. Biol., 6, 589—590.

1967   Changing man. Modern evolutionary biology justifies an optimistic view
of man's biological future. Science, 155, 409—415.

DOBZHANSKY, T., HECHT, M. K., and STEERE, W. G., (eds.)
1967   Evolutionary biology. Vol. I. New York: Appleton-Century-Crofts,
xi + 444 pp., 81 figs., 32 tables.
> Rev.: Alvarado in Bol. R. Soc. Españ. Hist. Nat., Sec. Biol., 65:3—4,
> 493—494; Buettner-Janusch in Amer. Anthrop., 70, 642—643;
> Clark, W. LeGros, in Man, Jour. Roy. Anthrop. Inst., 2, 632—
> 633; Hairston in Ecology, 48, 510—511; Kolosova in Zhurnal
> Obshch. Biol., 30:4, 505—507, (Russian); Olson in Quart. Rev.
> Biol., 43:2, 197—199; Schindewolf in Zbl. Geol. Pal., Teil 2,
> 1968:6, 561—563; Vallois in L'Anthrop., 72, 154—155;
> Walter in Anthropol. Anz., 31:3, 225—226.

DOCQUIER-HUART, J.
1961A.   Burin deterioré et utilisé comme retouchoir découvert à Amay au lieu
dit 'Paradis'. Bull. Cercle Arch. Hesbaye-Condroz, 2, 51, (not
seen).

1961B.   Quelques silex d'allure paléolithique supérieure recuellis en surface dans
les provinces de Liège et de Namur. Bull. Cercle Arch. Hesbaye-
Condroz, 2, 52—53, (not seen).

DOG, CHANG HAN   See: Ho, To You 1965.

DOIZE, R. L.
1960   Le grand harpon de Verlaine. (Belgique). Bull. Soc. Roy. Belge
Anthrop. Préhist., 71, 25—31, 5 figs.

DOKLÁDAL, MILAN
1960   Anthropologie na Balkane. Rozp. Anthrop. Spolecnosti, Brno, 8—9,
(not seen).

Rev.: Wokroj in Przegląd Antrop., 29, 86—94.

1965   Die Schädelform im Laufe der phylogenetischen und historischen Entwicklung des Menschen. Anthrop., 2:3, 19—35, 12 figs.

DOLAN, EDWARD M.

1966   Human skeletal materials and Pleistocene man in North America. New World Antiq., 13, 22—44, 5 tables.

DOLLFUS, OLIVIER

1964   Préhistoire et changements climatique post-Würmiens au Pérou. Bull. Assoc. Franç. Étude Quat., 1, 6—12.

DOMOSLAWSKA-BARANIECKA, MARIA DANUTA, and GADOMSKA, S.

1965   Geological position of the fossil bone remains of Elephas antiquus Falc. et Caut. in Warsaw. Kwart. Geol., 9, 641—648, 2 figs., (Polish; Russian and English summaries).

DONG, ZHI-MING

1965   A new species of Tinosaurus from Lushih, Honan. Vert. Palasiatica, 9, 79—82, 3 figs., (Chinese and English).

DONNAN, CHRISTOPHER B.

1964   A suggested sequence for the Providence Mountains (eastern Mohave Desert). Ann. Rept., Archeol. Surv., Dept. Anthrop., Univ. Calif., Los Angeles, 1963—64, 1—23, 1 map.

DONNER, J. J.

1965   The Quaternary of Finland. In: Rankama, (ed.), 1965, 199—272, 28 figs., 7 tables.

DONOHUE, MILDRED D., and GORDON, N. S.

1967   Fossil finds in Maryland: a retrospective bibliography. College Park, Md.: Univ. Maryland Libraries, iv + 248 pp.

DONOVAN, D. T.   See: Savage, R. J. G. and Donovan.

DO PAÇO, ALFONSO

1963   Paleolitico emeritense. Zephyrus, 14, 76—79, 3 figs.
         See: Breuil 1962B.

DO PAÇO, A., and CABAÇO, H.

1964   Paleolítico das Caldas da Rainha. Brotéria, Sér. Mensal, 78, 158—165, 6 figs.

DORF, ERLING

1959   Climatic changes of the past and present. Contrib. Mus. Pal. Univ. Mich., 13, 181—208, 3 figs., 1 pl., 7 maps.

DOROFEYEV, P. I.

1966   Flora of Hipparion epoch. Abstract by F. M. Hueber. Internat. Geol. Rev., 8, 1109—1117.

DORR, JOHN A., JR.

1964A.   Tertiary non-marine vertebrates in Alaska — the lack thereof. Bull. Amer. Assoc. Petrol. Geolog., 48, 1198—1203, 1 fig.

1964B.   Tertiary nonmarine vertebrates in Alaska — the lack thereof. Spec.
           Pap. Geol. Soc. Amer., 76, 307–308, (abs.)
1966   Wind-polished stones: two similar sites. Papers. Mich. Acad. Sci., 51,
           265–269, 1 fig., 1 pl.

DORR, J. A., JR., and MOSER, F.
1964   Ctenacanth sharks from the Mid-Mississippian of Michigan. Papers.
           Mich. Acad. Sci., 49, 105–113, 1 pl.

DORR, J. A., JR., and WHEELER, W. H.
1964   Cenozoic paleontology stratigraphy and reconnaissance geology of the
           Upper Ruby River Basin, southwestern Montana. Contrib. Mus.
           Pal. Univ. Mich., 13:12, 297–339, 4 figs., 2 pls.

DORSSER, H. J. VAN, and PELLETIER, H.
1965   Simples remarques sur les terrasses de l'Allier entre le Horst de Saint-
           Yvoine et Pont-du-Château. Rev. Sci. Nat. Auvergne, 29, 101–
           113, 2 figs.

DORT, WAKEFIELD, Jr.
1968   Paleoclimatic implications of soil structures at the Wasden site (Owl
           Cave). Tebiwa, 11:1, 31–36.

DORT, W., ZELLER, E. J., TURNER, M. D., and VAZ, J. E.
1965   Paleotemperatures and chronology at archeological cave site revealed by
           thermoluminescence. Science, 150, 480–481, 1 fig.
           Abs.: Simon in Naturwiss. Rund, 19, 245.

DORWIN, J. T.
1966   Fluted points and Late-Pleistocene geochronology in Indiana. Indianap-
           olis: Indiana Historical Society, (not seen). (Available from
           Indiana Historical Society, 408 State Library and Historical Bldg.,
           Indianapolis, Ind.).

DOUBLET, ROBERT
1966   L'atelier paléolithique de Férebrianges (Marne). Cahiers Archéol. Nord-
           Est, 9, 1–11, 7 figs.

DOUGHTY, PHILIP S.
1966   Giant Irish deer remains from Lough Neagh. Irish Nat. Jour., 15:7,
           187.

DOUGLAS, A. M., KENDRICK, G. W., and MERRILEES, D.
1966   A fossil bone deposit near Perth, Western Australia, interpreted as a
           carnivore's den after feeding tests on living Sarcophilus (Marsup-
           ialia, Dasyuridae). Jour. Roy. Soc. W. Australia, 49, 88–89,
           1 fig.

DOUMANI, GEORGE A., and LONG, W. E.
1962   The ancient life of the Antarctic. Sci. Amer., 207, 169–177, 180,
           182, 184, illustr.

DOVE, CHRISTOPHER
1967   Locality 4, (C1–247), Tule Springs, Nevada. In: Wormington, and
           Ellis, (eds.), 1967, 365–369, 1 pl.

DOWNEY, JOE S.   See: Lance, et al.

DOWNS, THEODORE
   1965   Pleistocene vertebrates of the Colorado Desert, California.   7th Internat.
               Congr., Internat. Assoc. Quat. Res., Abs., 1965, 107, (abs.).
   1967   Airlift for fossils. Quart. Los Angeles Co. Mus., 6:1, 20–25, illustr.
   1968   Fossil vertebrates of Southern Calif. Calif. Nat. Hist. Guides, 23, 61
               pp., 28 figs., 8 pls.
            Rev.: Whitmore in Jour. Pal., 43:5, 1307–1308.
            See: Tedford and Downs.

DOWNS, T., and WHITE, J. A.
   1965   Late Cenozoic vertebrates of the Anza-Borrego desert area, Southern
               California. Program, Sect. E (Geol., Geog.), Amer. Assoc.
               Advanc. Sci., Meeting Dec. 26–31, 1965, 10–11, (abs.).
   1966   Late Cenozoic vertebrates of the Anza-Borrego Desert Area, Southern
               California. Spec. Pap. Geol. Soc. Amer., 87, 310–311, (abs.).
   1968   A vertebrate faunal succession in superposed sediments from Late
               Pliocene to Middle Pleistocene in California. 23rd. Internat. Geol.
               Congr., Proc., 10, 41–47, 2 figs.

DRAGOO, DON W.
   1963   A third archaeological conference. Carnegie Mag., 37, 277–278.
   1965   Investigations at a Paleo-Indian site in Stewart County, Tennessee.
               Bull. Eastern States Archeol. Fed., 24, 12–13.
   1967A.   Early man in eastern North America. Bull. Eastern States Archeol.
               Fed., no. 26, 11, (abs.).
   1967B.   Who discovered America? Carnegie Mag., 41, 77–80, 2 figs.

DRĄGOWSKA-ZIEMIAŃSKA, LYDIA   See: Ziólkiewicz, et al.

DRAKE, ELLEN T.
   1966   Some notes on the beginnings of Peabody Museum. Discovery, Yale,
               2:1, 33–35, cover figs.
   1968   (ed.) Evolution and environment: A symposium presented on the
               occasion of the 100th anniversary of the foundation of Peabody
               Museum of Natural History at Yale University. New Haven:
               Yale Univ. Press, 470 pp., illustr.
            Rev.: Bernard in Palaeogeog., Palaeoclimatol., Palaeoecol., 7:3, 277–
               278;   Dobzhansky in Earth-Sci. Rev., 5:2, A97–A98;   T.N.G.
               in Geol. Mag., 106:3, 298–301;   McKenna in Science, 163,
               662–663;   Pojeta in Jour. Pal., 43:5, 1303–1304;   Williams
               in Quart. Rev. Biol., 45:1, 103–104.

DRAKE, FRANCIS, and KATHERINE
   1964   Earliest man on earth? Reader's Digest, Jan. 1964, 157–161, 163,
               3 figs.

DRAPER, WARWICK
   1923   Chiswick. London, (not seen).

DREIMANIS, ALEKSIS
   1958   Wisconsin stratigraphy at Port Talbot on the north shore of Lake Erie,
               Ontario. Ohio Jour. Sci., 58, 65–84, 2 figs., 6 tables.
            Abs.: Ebers in Zbl. Geol. Pal., Teil 2, 1963, 915–916.

1967A.   Mastodons, their geologic age and extinction in Ontario, Canada.
Canadian Jour. Earth Sci., 4, 663—675, 1 fig., 2 tables.

1967B.   Extinction of mastodons in eastern North America. A new climate-
environmental theory. Program, 1967 Ann. Meeting, Geol. Soc.
Amer., 1967, 51—52, (abs.). Also: Spec. Pap. Geol. Soc. Amer.,
115, 52, (abs.).

DRESNER, IAN G.   See: Wake and Dresner.

DREYER, DIETER
1962   Zur Entstehung und Paläontologie der Bonebedlagen im unteren Rät
Thüringens. Freiberger Forschungsh., Reihe C, 125, 127—155,
10 figs., 6 pls.

DRIVE, SCOTT   See: Mortine and Drive.

DROZDOVA, T. V., and BLOKH, A. M.
1966   [Aminoacids in bone remains of different geological age.] Geokhimiia,
1966:6, 709—714, 1 pl., 1 table, (Russian; English summary).

DRUETT, WALTER W.
1937   Pinner through the ages. Uxbridge, (not seen).

DRUMMOND, H. J. H.   See: Paterson and Drummond.

DRUSHITS, V. V., and OBRUCHEVA, O. P.
1962   [Paleontology.] Moscow: Moscow University Press, 379 pp., 238 figs.,
2 tables, (Russian).

DUARTE, LELIA   See: Silva Santos and Duarte.

DUARTE, PAULO
1961   Introdução à pré-história geral. I—X. Anhembi, 42, 483—517, 720—
745, 43, 84—95, 295—315, 515—535, 44, 77—95, 295—315,
503—546, 45, 66—95.
1962   Introdução à pré-história geral. XI—XIII. Anhembi, 45, 263—291,
484—502, 46, 72—95, 308—331.

DUBEĬKOVSKIĬ, S. G., and OCHEV, V. G.
1967   [On the remains of plesiosaurs from Jurassic and Cretaceous of the
upper Kama R.] In: Collected Papers, 1967F, [Problems of
geology of South Urals and Povolzh'e, 4:1], 97—103, 2 pls.,
(Russian).

DUBERTRET, LOUIS   See: Arambourg, Dubertret, et al.; Ejel and Dubertret.

DUBININ, V. B., and GARUTT, V. E.
1954   [On mammoth skeleton from Lena R. Delta.] Zool. Zhurnal, 33:2,
423—432, 9 figs., (Russian).

DUBINSKII, A. A.   See: Godina and Dubinskii.

DUBLIÁNSKII, V. N.   See: Bachinskii and Dubliánskii; Bachinskii, Dubliánskii, et al.

DUBOS, RENÉ
1965   Man adapting. New Haven and London: Yale Univ. Press, xxii +
                527 pp., 14 figs.
                Rev.: Pirie in Nature, 210, 978–979;   G. G. Simpson in Science, 152,
                1049.

DUBROVO, I. A.
1963D.   [New material on the Taman' vertebrate faunal complex.] Bull. Mosk.
                Obshch. Ispyt. Prirody. Otd. Geol., 68:6, 94–99, 3 figs., (Russian).
                Rev.: Stoltenberg in Zbl. Geol. Pal., Teil 2, 1967, 108–109.
1964A.   Elephants of the genus Archidiskodon in the USSR territory. Pal.
                Zhurnal, 1964:3, 82–94, 4 figs., 1 chart, (Russian).
1964B.   [On the subject of the existence of Protelephas planifrons on the ter-
                ritory of the U.S.S.R.]   Soob. Akad. Nauk Gruz. SSR., 34:3,
                599–603, (Russian; Georgian summary).
1965   Systematic position of Elephas wusti. (Translation of Dubrovo 1963C.)
                Internat. Geol. Rev., 7, 1110–1115, 3 figs., 1 table.
1966A.   [Systematic position of the elephant of Khozarian faunistic complex.]
                Biull. Kom. Izuch. Chetvert. Perioda, 32, 63–74, 2 figs., 5 tables,
                (Russian).
1966B.   [Pleistocene mammals from Middle and South Urals and their strati-
                graphic significance.] Nauchn. Trudy Permsk. politekhn. inst.,
                20, 125–135, (Russian).
1967   [New data on Upper Pliocene fauna of Urals.] Biull. Kom. Izuch.
                Chetvert. Perioda, 34, 127–131, 3 figs., (Russian).

DUBROVO, I. A., and ALEKSEEV, M. N.
1964   [About the stratigraphy of Quaternary deposits of the cis-Azov Region.]
                Biull. Kom. Izuch. Chetvert Perioda, Akad. Nauk SSSR, no. 29,
                35–43, 5 figs., (Russian).

DUBROVO, I. A., and BAĬGUSHEVA, V. S.
1964   [Elephants of Khaprovskiĭ faunistic complex (on materials of Livents-
                ovskiĭ quarry).] Biull. Mosk. Obshch. Ispyt. Prirody, Otd. Geol.,
                39:5, 133–136, 1 fig., 1 table, (Russian).
                Rev.: Stoltenberg in Zbl. Geol. Pal., Teil 2, 1967, 122–123.

DUBROVO, I. A., and CHEPALYGA, A. L.
1967   [Remains of fossil elephants from Dnestr R. terraces and their strati-
                graphic significance.] Pal. geol. polezn. iskop. Moldavii, 2, 191–
                203, 1 fig., 1 table, (Russian).

DUCROS, ALBERT
1967   Le chignon occipital, mesure sur le squelette. L'Anthrop., 71:1–2,
                75–96, 10 figs., 6 tables.

DUDLEY, MAY   See: Richardson and Dudley.

DUE ROJO, ANTONIO
1964   Notas paleontológicas. V. Notas Comun. Inst. Geol. Min., no. 75,
                249–274, (French and English summaries).
1965   Problemas y controversias paleontológicas. Notas Comun. Inst. Geol.
                Min., no. 79, 167–186, (English summary).

DUFF, ROGER
1950B.   Rev.: Bell in Mankind, 4:5, 213–214.

DUFFIELD, LATHEL F.   See: Nunley, Duffield and Jelks.

DUGES, ALFREDO
1892   Nota sobre un fosil de Arperos, Estado de Guanajuato.   El Minero
         Mexicano, 19, 233–235, (not seen).

DUGHI, RAYMOND, and SIRUGUE, F.
1964   Sur la structure des coquilles des oeufs des sauropsidés vivants ou fos-
         siles. Le genre Psammornis Andrews. C. R. Soc. Géol. France,
         1964, 149–150, (abs.).
1965   Sur la structure des coquilles des oeufs des sauropsidés vivants ou fos-
         siles; le genre Psammornis Andrews. Bull. Soc. Géol. France,
         6, 240–252, 1 fig., pls. 9–11.
         Abs.: Kuhn in Zbl. Geol. Pal., Teil 2, 1966, 312.
1966   Sur la fossilisation des oeufs de dinosaures. C. R. Acad. Sci. Paris,
         Sci. Nat., 262, 2330–2332.
1968   Marnes à oeufs d'Oiseaux du Paléocène de Basse-Provence. C. R. Soc.
         Géol. France, 1968:7, 219.

DUMITRASHKO, N. V.   See: Armand, et al.

DUMITRESCO, M., SAMSON, P., TERZEA, E., RADULESCO, C., and CHICA, M.
1965   Sur l'état actuel des fouilles paléontologiques dans la station pleistocene
         de la grotte "La Adam". 3. Internat. Kongress Spel., 4, 15–19.

DUMONT, ALLAN E., and RIFKIND, K. M.
1968   Evolutionary significance of the thoracic duct. Nature, 219, 1182–1183.

DUNBAR, C. O.
1966   The earth. Cleveland and New York: The World Publishing
         Co., xiii + 252 pp., 86 figs., 54 pls.
         Rev.: Batten in Nat. Hist., 76:7, 78–79.

DUNCAN, BION W., and BROSEMER, C. V.
1964   A Paint Rock Valley site. Jour. Ala. Archaeol., 10, 13–21, 7 figs.

DUNKLE, DAVID H.
1964A.   Museum awarded Foundation grant. Explorer, 6:3, 18–19, illustr.
1964B.   Preliminary description of a paleoniscid fish from the Upper Devonian
          of Ohio. Sci. Publ. Cleveland Mus. Nat. Hist., 3:1, 23 pp., 5
          figs., 4 pls.
1965   The presumed holocephalan fish Pseudodontichthys whitei Skeels. Sci.
          Publ. Cleveland Mus. Nat. Hist., 4:2, 10 pp., 2 figs., 1 pl.

DUNN, NORMAN L.
1964   New discoveries at Black Water Draw, Portales, New Mexico. Ohio
         Archaeol., 14, 57–63, 4 figs.

DUNN, STEPHEN P.
1966   Comments on Krader's review of "Peoples of Siberia". With reply by
         L. Krader. Amer. Anthrop., 68, 519–521.

DUPARC, GERMAINE
1960   L'outil et sa valeur fonctionnelle. Réflexions suggérées par un grattior
            aurignacien provenant de Brantome. Bull. Soc. Hist. Archéol.
            Périgord, <u>87</u>, 160—165, 3 figs.

DUPLAIX, S.   See: David, P., Duplaix and Guillien.

DUPORT, L.
1959   Le gisement moustérien de Puymoyen (Charente). Grotte René Simard.
            Mem. Soc. Archéol. Hist. Charente, <u>1958</u>, 35—40, 1 fig., 3 pls.
1961   [. . . le gisement Mousterien à denticulé, appelé Grotte Simard . . .]
            Mem. Soc. Archéol. Hist. Charente, <u>1960</u>, 23—24, (abs.).
            See: Brigot, <u>et</u> <u>al.</u>; Guillien and Duport.

DUPORT, L., and VANDERMEERSCH, B.
1961   Les gisements préhistoriques de la vallée des Eaux-Claires. V. — Indus-
            trie moustérienne de la Grotte René Simard et la découverte des
            pièces ostéologiques humaines. Mem. Soc. Archéol. Hist. Charente,
            <u>1960</u>, 127—128, 3 pls.
1962   Les gisements préhistoriques de la vallée des Eaux-Claires. Le gisement
            du Petit-Puymoyen. Etude archéologique. Mem. Soc. Archéol.
            Hist. Charente, <u>1961—1962</u>, 83—105, 4 figs., 9 pls.
1965   Geomorphologie et prehistoire au sud d'Angouleme. III. Les gisements
            mousteriens de l'Abri Commont, de la Grotte Simard et de la
            Grotte Castaigne. Bull. Assoc. Franç. Etude Quat., <u>1965</u>:3—4,
            189—192.

DUPRÉ, G.
1964   Contribution à l'étude des gisements préhistoriques du Saut-du-Perron
            (Loire). Nouvelles fouilles au Pré Brun. Doc. Lab. Geol. Fac.
            Sci. Lyon., <u>4</u>, 88 pp., 37 pls., 25 tables.
            Abs.: Doc. Lab. Géol. Fac. Sci. Lyon, no. <u>7</u>, 15.

DUPREE, A. HUNTER   See: Gray, A. 1963.

DUPREE, LOUIS
1964   Prehistoric archeological surveys and excavations in Afganistan:
                1959 - 1960 and 1961 - 1963. Science, <u>146</u>, 638—640, 2 figs.
1965   Archaeological reconnaissance in southern Tripolitania and northern
                Fezzan, Libya. Man, <u>65</u>, 147—149, 4 figs.
1968   The oldest sculptured head? Nat. Hist., <u>77</u>:5, 26—27, 2 figs.

ĐURKOVIĆ, RAD.   See: Pavlović and Đurković.

DURRELL, R. H.
1967   Invasion by sea and ice. Explorer, <u>9</u>:3, 12—16, illustr.

DURY, G. H.
1964   Australian geochronology: checklist 1. Austral. Jour. Sci., <u>27</u>, 103—
            109.

DUSTER, TOM
1967   Digging for fish in Wyoming. Olsmobile Rocket Circle Mag., <u>12</u>:1,
            20—22, illustr.

DUTRO, J. T.
1968   Paleontology [in 1967]. GeoTimes, 13, 17—18.

DUTUIT, JEAN-MICHEL
1964   Découverte de gisements fossilifères dans le Trias du couloir d'Argana
         (Atlas occidental marocain). C. R. Acad. Sci. Paris, 258, 1285—
         1287, 1 fig.
1965   Découverte de dicynodontes (Reptiles Thérapsides) dans le Trias du
         couloir d'Argana (Atlas occidental marocain). C. R. Acad. Sci.
         Paris, 260, 3447—3448.
1966   Apport des découvertes de vertébrés à la stratigraphie du Trias continen-
         tal du couloir d'Argana (Haut Atlas occidental, Maroc). Notes
         Mém. Serv. Géol. Maroc, 188, 29—31.
1967   Gisements de vertébrés triasiques de l'Atlas marocain. Collog. Internat.
         Cent. Nation. Recherch. Sci., 163, 427—428.

DYCK, WILLY
1967   Recent developments in radiocarbon dating: their implications for
         geochronology and archaeology. Current Anthrop., 8, 349—351,
         1 fig.

DYCK, W., FYLES, J. G., and BLAKE, W., Jr.
1965   Geological Survey of Canada radiocarbon dates IV. Radiocarbon, 7,
         24—46.

DYSART, MARGARET P.   See: De La Torre and Dysart.

DYSON, JAMES L.
1962   The world of ice. New York: Knopf, viii + 292 + xiii, 62 pls.
         Rev.: Sharp in Geog. Rev., 53, 635—636.

DYSON, ROBERT H., JR.
1958   (ed.) COWA surveys and bibliographies. Area 16 — southern Asia.
         COWA Surv. and Bibliog., Area 16, no. 1, 5 + 8 pp.
1960   (ed.) COWA surveys and bibliographies. Area 16 — southern Asia.
         COWA Surv. and Bibliog., Area 16, no. 2, 13 + 8 pp.
1964   On the origins of the Neolithic Revolution. Science, 144, 672—675.

DZHAFAROV, R. D.
1960   [The Binagada Rhinoceros.] Trudy Estestv.-Istor. Muzeĩa Zardabi, 12,
         5—99, 48 figs., 50 tables, (Russian).
1966   [Fossil vertebrate fauna of Binagady.] Izv. Akad. Nauk Azerb. SSR,
         Ser. Nauk o Zemle, 1966:1, 51—57, (Russian).
         See: Burchak-Abramovich, N. I., and Dzhafarov.

DZHAFAROVA, Zh. D.
1961   [Elephas (Archidiscodon) meridionalis from Zakavkaz'e.] Dokl. Akad.
         Nauk Azerbaid, SSR, 17, 1077—1080, 2 figs., (Russian;
         Azerbaijani summary).

1962   [Maikopian fishes from Akburun.] Dokl. Akad. Nauk Azerbaid. SSR,
         18:11, 47—51, 5 figs., (Russian; Azerbaijani summary).
         Abs.: Weiler in Zbl. Geol. Pal., Teil 2, 1966, 274.
1963   [About fossil fishes of the Shemakhin region.] Izv. Akad. Nauk
         Azerbaidzhan. SSR, 1963:3, 15—20, 9 figs., (Russian; Azerbaid-
         zhani summary).

Abs.: Weiler in Zbl. Geol. Pal., Teil 2, 1966, 274.

1964   [Clupeidae and Gadidae from Maikop deposits of the Shemakhin region.]
        Izv. Akad. Nauk Azerbaidzhan. SSR, 1964:4,-11–19, 11 figs.,
        (Russian; Azerbaidzhani summary).
        Abs.: Weiler in Zbl. Geol. Pal., Teil 2, 1966, 274.

1965   [Some data on ichthyofauna of Maĭkop suite of Azerbaĭdzhan.] Azerb.
        neft. khoz., 1965:4, 13–14, (Russian).

1966   [Flounders in Maĭkop deposits of Apsheron peninsula.] Dokl. Akad
        Nauk Azerbaĭd. SSR, 22:5, 73–76, 2 figs., (Russian; Azerbaĭdjan
        summary).

1967   [Ichthyofauna of Maĭkop series of Azerbaijan.] Trudy Azerbaĭd. Inst.
        po dobyche nefti, 19, 42–46, (Russian).
        Rev.: Weiler in Zbl. Geol. Pal., Teil 2, 1968:6, 644.

DZHAMBAZOV, NIKOLAĬ (= Djambazov)

1957   [The Peshch Cave near Staro village in the Vracha region.] Izv. na
        Arkheol. Inst., 21, 1–40, 15 figs., 16 tables, (Bulgarian; French
        summary).

1959A. [Excavations in the Samuilit͡sa II cave.] Arkheologii͡a, Sofia, 1:1–2,
        47–53, 6 figs., (Bulgarian).

1959B. [Excavations in the Morovit͡sa cave in 1955.] Izv. na Arkheol. Inst.,
        22, 15–28, 10 figs., (Bulgarian; French summary).

1960   [A new Paleolithic site in the Vit valley.] Arkheologii͡a, Sofia, 2:1,
        36–42, 7 figs., (Bulgarian).

1961   [Paleolithic site near Osenet͡s village, Razgrad district.] In: Mii͡atev
        and Mikov, (eds.), 1961, 397–402, 3 figs., (Bulgarian; French
        summary).

1962   [Excavations on the Paleolithic site near Beloslav village, Varna Province.]
        Arkheologii͡a, Sofia, 4:3, 53–60, 7 figs., (Bulgarian).

1963   [The Lovech caves.] Izv. na Arkheol. Inst., 26, 195–241, 36 figs.,
        1 table, (Bulgarian; French summary).

1964   [Research on Paleolithic and Mesolithic cultures in Bulgaria.] Arkheol-
        ogii͡a, Sofia, 6:3, 67–76, 13 figs., (Bulgarian).

1965   [New data on Paleolithic stratigraphy in Bulgaria.] In: Bader, et al.,
        (eds.), 1965, 50–56, 1 table, (Russian).

1967A. [Early Paleolithic findings near Svishchov.] Arkheologii͡a, Sofia, 1967:1,
        60–70, 6 figs., (Bulgarian).

1967B. Les pointes bifaciales dans les grottes Samouilitza I et II et les autres
        stations du Paléolithique récent en Bulgarie. Quartär, 18, 195–
        199, 1 pl.

1968   [Paleolithic site near Muselievo village, Pleven district.] Arkheologii͡a,
        Sofia, 1968:2, 54–64, 11 figs., (Bulgarian; French summary).
        See: Mikov and Dzhambazov.

DZHAMBAZOV, N., and MARGOS, A.

1960   [Concerning the study of Paleolithic culture in the region of Pobitite
        Kam'ni (Dikilitash).] Izv. na Arkheol. Inst., 23, 269–295, 20
        figs., (Bulgarian; French summary).

DZHANELIDZE, A. I.   See: Gamkrelidze 1959.

DZHAVRISHVILI, K. V.

1961   Man and caves. Die Höhle, 12, 94–95, (abs.). Reprinted in Actes
        3ème Congr. Internat. Spéléol., A, 62–63.

EASTMAN, C. R.   See: Zittel 1964A, B.

EATON, THEODORE HILDRETH
1960C.   Comparative anatomy of the vertebrates. (2nd ed.). New York: Harper.
1963   Caterpillar versus dinosaur? Jour. Res. Lepidoptera, 1, 114–116.
1964A.   A captorhinomorph predator and its prey (Cotylosauria). Amer. Mus.
          Novit, no. 2169, 3 pp., 1 fig.
          Abs.: Huene in Zbl. Geol. Pal., Teil 2, 1965, 247–248.
1964B.   Vertebrate paleontology. McGraw-Hill Yearbook. Sci. Tech., 1964,
          402–405, 2 figs.
          Abs.: Huene in Zbl. Geol. Pal., Teil 2, 1965, 248.
1965   A new Wyoming phytosaur. Univ. Kans. Pal. Contrib., Pap., 2, 6 pp.,
          2 figs.
          Abs.: Huene in Zbl. Geol. Pal., Teil 2, 1966, 303–304.
1968   Russell R. Camp. [12:21, 1904 – 9:2, 1967.] News Bull., Soc. Vert.
          Pal., no. 82, 67.
          See: Schaeffer, B. 1965A.

EBERZIN, A. G.
1966   [Vladimir Vladimirovich Bogachev (1881 - 1965).] Pal. Zhurnal, 1966:4,
          121–123, portr., (Russian).
1967   [Lavrentiĭ Nikolaevich Kudrin (1921 - 1966).] Pal. Zhurnal, 1967:2,
          140–141, portr., (Russian).

EBHARDT, VON HERMANN
1967A.   Zur Datierung einer Pferdedarstellung aus dem Fezzan. Säugetierkundl.
          Mitt., 15, 15–18, 3 figs., (English summary).
1967B.   Das Überleben des Ponytyps I bis in die Nacheiszeit und sein Auftauchen
          in der frühen Domestikation. Säugetierkundl. Mitt., 15, 18–35,
          12 figs., 4 tables, (English summary).

ECHEGARAY, JOAQUIN GONZÁLES   See: Gonzáles Echegaray, Joaquin.

ECKHOFF, LORENTZ   See: Chardin 1964B.

EDINGER, TILLY
1964A.   Midbrain exposure and overlap in mammals. Amer. Zool., 4:1, 5–19,
          9 figs.
1964B.   Recent advances in paleoneurology. In: Bargmann, and Schade, (eds.),
          1964, 147–160, 4 figs.
          Rev.: M. C. in Fossilia, 1965:3–4, 48.
1964C.   Characters in paleontology: Dollo. News Bull., Soc. Vert. Pal., no. 70,
          40–44, portr.
          Abs.: Häntzschel in Zbl. Geol. Pal., Teil 2, 1965, 6.
1966A.   Brains from 40 million years of camelid history. In: Hassler, and
          Stephan, (eds.), 1966, 153–161, 3 figs.
1966B.   A lesson on bones. MCZ Newsletter, 1966:1, 1 p.
1966C.   Shakespeare and V. P. News Bull., Soc. Vert. Pal., no. 78, 44.

EDITORIAL STAFF
1956   [Akademician Vladimir Afanas'evich Obruchev.] Izv. Akad. Nauk SSSR,
          ser. geograf., 1956:4, 3, portr., (Russian).
1965   [Iа̑. Iа̑. Roginskiĭ is 70 years.] Voprosy Antrop., 21, 181–185, portr.,
          (Russian).
1966   [Georgiĭ Frant͡sevich Debet͡s is 60 years.] Voprosy Antrop., 22, 168–
          171, portr., (Russian).

EDITORS
1963   [Centenary of the birth-date of Vladimir Afanas'evich Obruchev.]
                Uzbek. Geol. Zhurnal, 1963:5, 5–8, portr., (Russian).

EDITORS OF LIFE   See: Eimerl, DeVore and Editors of Life; Howell and Editors
                of Life; Moore, R. and Editors of Life; Ripley and Editors
                of Life; Stever, Haggerty and Editors of Life.

EARDLEY, ARMAND J.   See: Sharrock 1966.

EDMUND, A. GORDON
1962   Sequence and rate of tooth replacement in the Crocodilia. Contrib.
                Roy. Ont. Mus., Life Sci. Div., no, 56, 42 pp., 21 figs.
1965   A Late Pleistocene fauna from the Santa Elena Peninsula, Ecuador.
                Contrib. Roy. Ont. Mus., Life Sci. Div., no. 63, 21 pp., 9 figs.

EDWARDS, R. L.   See: Emery and Edwards.

EDWARDS, ROBERT   See: Mountford and Edwards.

EDWARDS, WILLIAM ELLIS
1965   The posture and antiquity of the earliest hominids. Amer. Jour. Phys.
                Anthrop., 23, 327–328, (abs.).
1966   Pleistocene extinction; A series of ten papers. Carolina Jour. Anthrop.,
                1, (not seen).
1967A.   Hominid muzzle reduction. Amer. Jour. Phys. Anthrop., 27, 245, (abs.).
1967B.   The Late-Pleistocene extinction and diminution in size of many mam-
                malian species. In: Martin, P. S., and Wright, H. E., (eds.),
                1967, 141–154.

EFIMENKO, P. P.
1958   Rev.: Bibikov in Sov. Arkheol., 1959:4, 258–261, (Russian).
1960   [Anterior-Asiatic elements in the monuments of Late Paleolithic of
                Northern Black Sea region.] Sov. Arkheol., 1960:4, 14–25,
                (Russian).

EFREMOV, I. A.
1961   [Some considerations on biological bases of paleozoology.] Trudy
                Vses. Paleont. Obshch., IV sess., 198–210, (Russian).
1968   [In memoriam Boris Pavlovich V'iushkov. (10th death anniversary).]
                Pal. Zhurnal, 1968:4, 107–108, portr., (Russian).

EGAN, GAIL N., and AGOGINO, G. A.
1965   Man's use of bison and cattle on the High Plains. Great Plains Jour.,
                5, 35–43, 1 fig.

EGIAZAROV, B. Kh.
1957   [A geological description of the Severnaĩa Zemlĩa Archipelago.] Trudy
                Inst. Geol. Arktiki, 81, 388–423, (Russian).
1958   [Devonian deposits of the western part of the Severnaĩa Zemlĩa
                Archipelago.] Trudy Inst. Geol. Arktiki, 67, 13–35, 1 fig.,
                (Russian).

EGOROV, A. G., and IVAN'EV, L. N.
1956   [Transbaĩkalian fossil sturgeon.] Priroda, 1956:3, 112, (Russian).

EGOROV, M. E., and LVOVA, A.
1962   [Paleontological discoveries in Chuvashia.]   Izv. Vsesoiûzn. Geogr.
          Obshch., 94, 347–349, 1 map, (Russian).

EGOZCUE, J., and VILARASAU De EGOZCUE, M.
1967A.   Chromosome evolution in the Cebidae. In: Starck, D., Schneider, R.,
           and Kuhn, H. J., (eds.), 1967, 150–154, 5 figs.
1967B.   The marked chromosomes of primates: origin and evolutionary signifi-
           cance. In: Starck, D., Schneider, R., and Kuhn, H. J., (eds.),
           1967, 164–166, 4 figs.

EHRENBERG, KURT
1960D.   Rev.: Schindewolf in Zbl. Geol. Pal., Teil 2, 1962, 303–304;   Zapfe
           in Die Höhle, 11, 115.
1961B.   Zum Lebensraum vom Höhlenbär und Höhlenbärenjäger. Die Höhle,
           12, 117, (abs.).   Reprinted in Actes 3ème Congr. Internat.
           Spéléol., A, 85.
1962B.   Abs.: Ehrenberg in Zbl. Geol. Pal., Teil 2, 1964, 193–194.
1962D.   Über weitere urzeitliche Fundstellen und Funde in der Salzofenhöhle,
           Steiermark. Archaeol. Austriaca, 32, 1–23, 7 figs.
1962E.   Georg Kyrles Wirken als Spel̈aologe und für die Spel̈aologie (Zu seinem
           75. Geburtstag und 25. Todestag). Die Höhle, 13, 33–39,
           (French summary).
1962F.   Höhlenbär und Höhlenbärenjäger. Neue Funde, neue Ergebnisse.
           Schrift. Ver. Verbreitung Naturwiss. Kenntnisse Wien, 102,
           125–143.
1963   Aus Österreichs spel̈aologischer Forschung seit 1945 – Ein Bildbericht.
           3. Internat. Kongress Spel., 1, 95–100.
1964A.   Ein Jungbärenskelett und andere Höhlenbärenreste aus der Bärenhöhle
           im Hartlesgraben bei Hieflau (Steiermark). Ann. Naturhist. Mus.
           Wien, 67, 189–252, 6 figs., 3 pls.
           Abs.: Ehrenberg in Zbl. Geol. Pal., Teil 2, 1965, 272–273.
1964B.   Berichte über Ausgrabungen in der Salzofenhöhle im Toten Gebirge.
           XVI. Grabungen und Forschungsergebnisse 1963. Anz. Akad.
           Wiss. Wien, 101, 55–73, 1 fig., 3 tables.
1965A.   Berichte über die Ausgrabungen in der Salzofenhöhle im Toten Gebirge.
           XVII. Grabungen und Ergebnisse der Salzofen – Expedition
           1964. Anz. Österr. Akad. Wiss., math.-nat. Kl., 102, 72–89.
           Abs.: Muckenhuber in Zbl. Geol. Pal., Teil 2, 1966, 326.
1965B.   Eindrücke und Beobachtungen auf einer Höhlenfahrt in die Dordogne.
           Die Höhle, 16, 73–77, (French summary).
1965C.   Zum Lebensraum von Höhlenbär und Höhlenbärenjäger. 3. Internat.
           Kongress Spel., 4, 21–25.
           Abs.: Ehrenberg in Zbl. Geol. Pal., Teil 2, 1966, 326.
1965D.   Florian Hellers bisheriges paläontologisches Schaffen. Ein Überblick
           zu seinem 60. Geburtstage. Mitt. Verband Deutschen Höhlen-
           und Karstforscher, München, 11, 71–80.
1966A.   (ed.) Die Teufels- oder Fuchsenlucken bei Eggenburg (NÖ). Denk.
           Akad. Wiss. Wien, 112, 158 pp., 6 figs., 15 pls., 19 tables.
           Rev.: Kühn in Zbl. Geol. Pal., Teil 2, 1967, 511–512.
1966B.   Die bisher veröffentlichten Ergebnisse über die Erforschung der Höhle
           und die Untersuchung ihrer Funde nebst einigen Ergänzungen.
           In: Ehrenberg, (ed.), 1966A, 7–14, 1 fig.
1966C.   Der Fundbestand in seiner Gesamtheit. Eine biospel̈aologisch-bio-
           historische Schlussbetrachtung. In: Ehrenberg, (ed.), 1966A,
           137–158, 1 fig., 5 tables.

1966D.   Die pleistozänen Bären Belgiens. III. Teil: Cavernes de Montaigle
         (Schluss), Cavernes de Walzin, Caverne de Freyr, Cavernes de
         Pont-a-Lesse. Mém. Inst. Roy. Sci. Nat. Belg., no. 155, 1—76,
         10 pls., tables.
         Abs.: Ehrenberg in Zbl. Geol. Pal., Teil 2, 1966, 326—328.

1966E.   Zum Problem der osteodontokeratischen Kultur. Quartär, 17, 177—181.

1967   Zum heutigen Stand des Problems intentioneller Depositionen eiszeitlicher
         Bärenjäger. Quartär, 18, 179—190.

EHRENBERG, K., and MAIS, K.

1966   Die Schlenken-Durchgangshöhle bei Vigaun (Salzburg) — Bericht über
         eine informative Grabung. Anz. Akad. Wiss. Wien, 103, 113—
         119.

1967   Über die Forschungen in der Schlenckendurchgangshöhle bei Vigaun im
         Sommer 1966. Anz. Akad. Wiss. Wien, 104, 22—30
         Rev.: Muckenhuber in Zbl. Geol. Pal., Teil 2, 1967, 513.

EHRHARDT, SOPHIE, and KENNEDY, K. A. R.

1965   Excavations at Langhnaj: 1944—63. Part III. The human remains.
         Poona: Deccan College. Building Centenary and Silver Jubilee
         Series (27), (not seen).
         Rev.: Bhattacharya in E. Anthrop., 20, 91—93; Fairservis and Possehl
         in Amer. Anthrop., 69, 536—537.

EHRICH, ROBERT W., (ed.)

1959   COWA surveys and bibliographies. Area 6 — Balkans. COWA Surv.
         and Bibliog., Area 6, no. 1, 16 + 23 pp.

1962   COWA surveys and bibliographies. Area 6 — Balkans. COWA Surv.
         and Bibliog., Area 6, no. 2, 25 + 34 pp.

1964   COWA surveys and bibliographies. Area 5 — central Europe. COWA
         Surv. and Bibliog., Area 5, no. 3, 14 + 45 pp.

1965   Chronologies in Old World archaeology. Chicago, London: Univ.
         Chicago Press, xii + 557 pp., illustr., maps.
         Rev.: Evans in Man, Jour. Roy Anthrop. Inst., 2, 135; Jelinek in
         Mich. Archaeol., 12, 137—138; Renfrew in Antiq., 40, 319—
         320; Rodden in Amer. Anthrop., 69, 93—94.

1966   COWA surveys and bibliographies. Area 6 — Balkans. COWA Surv.
         and Bibliog., Area 6, no. 3, 25 + 40 pp.

EHRICH, R. W., and GIMBUTAS, M., (eds.)

1957   COWA surveys and bibliographies. Area 5 — central Europe. COWA
         Surv. and Bibliog., Area 5, no. 1, 11 + 20 pp.

1960   COWA surveys and bibliographies. Area 5 — central Europe. COWA
         Surv. and Bibliog., Area 5, no. 2, 16 + 39 pp.

EHRLICH, P. R.   See: Birch and Ehrlich.

EHRLICH, P. R., and HOLM, R. W.

1963   Rev.: Cox in Nature, 203, 1208—1209; Montalenti in Scientia, 101,
         285—289.

EICKSTEDT, EGON FREIHERR VON

1964   Die Forschung am Menschen; einschliezlich Rassenkunde und Rassen-
         geschichte der Menschheit. Fasc. 17—18. Stuttgart: Enke,
         2193—2646, 63 figs., (not seen).

Rev.: H. V. V. in L'Anthrop., 69, 121–122.

EĬKHGORN, T. F.
1968   [Geographical distribution of Chimaerae in Mesozoic-Cenozoic seas of
the USSR.] Ezhegod. Vses. Pal. Obshch., 18, 366, (Russian).

EIMERL, SAREL, DeVORE, I., and the EDITORS OF LIFE
1965   The primates. New York: Time Incorporated, 200 pp., illustr.
Rev.: Buettner-Janusch in Amer. Sci., 53, 376A; Carpenter in Amer.
Anthrop., 69, 258–260; Krogman in Amer. Jour. Phys.
Anthrop., 28, 110.

EĬNOR, O. L.
1964   [Principles of geology of the USSR. Part II.] Kiev: Kiev University
Press, 335 pp., 98 figs., 3 tables, (Russian).

EISELE, CHARLES ROBERT
1964   Salvaging fossils in Nebraska. Mus. Notes, Univ. Neb. State Mus.,
no. 24, 1–5, 7 figs.
1965   Leptarctus, a primitive carnivore from the Early Pliocene of Nebraska.
Proc. Neb. Acad. Sci., 75, 15. (abs.).

EISELE, C. R., and SCHULTZ, C. B.
1965   The last niche in Elephant Hall. Mus. Notes, Univ. Neb. News, no. 27,
[3–4], figs. 5–6.

EISELEY, LOREN C.
1965   Man and novelty. Publ. Nation. Acad. Sci., 1469, 65–79.
See: Huxley, T. H. 1967.

EISENBUD, JULE
1964   A recently found carving as a breast symbol. Amer. Anthrop., 66,
141–147, 12 figs.

EISENTRAUT, MARTIN
1963   Die Wirbeltiere des Kamerungebirges. Hamburg and Berlin: Paul Parey,
365 pp., (not seen).
Abs.: Dietrich in Zbl. Geol. Pal., Teil 2, 1964, 186.

EJEL, FOUAD, and DUBERTRET, L.
1966   Sur l'âge précis du gisement de Poissons et de Crustacés cretacés de
Sahel Alma (Liban). C. R. Soc. Geol. France, 1966, 353–354,
1 fig.

EKLUND, RAY, JR.
1966   Fossils of the Badlands. Earth Sci., Midwest Fed. Min. Soc., 19, 259–
261, illustr.

ELGIN, KATHLEEN See: Farb 1962.

ELHAĬ, HENRI
1959B.   Découverte de deux silex taillés et d'une dent d'Equus caballus en Normandie. Bull. Soc. Linn. Normandie, 9, 35.

1965   Middle Quaternary deposits in southwest France. 7th Internat. Congr., Internat. Assoc. Quat. Res., Abs., <u>1965</u>, 125, (abs.).
See: Balland and Elhai; Bouchud 1965B.

ELHAĬ, H., and GRANGEON, P.
1964   Nouvelles recherches sur le gisement villafranchien de Senèze (Haute-Loire, France). Bull. Soc. Géol. France, <u>5</u>, 483–488, 2 figs., pl. 19.

ELHAĬ, H., and PRENANT, A.
1964   Présence et extension d'un niveau marin littoral interglaciaire sur la côte du Médoc. Bull. Soc. Géol. France, <u>5</u>, 495–507, 6 figs., 2 tables, pl. 20.

ELIAS, M. K. See: Hecker 1965A.

ELISEEV, V. I.
1961   [Cenozoic alluvial deposits of the northeastern margin of Chuĩa depression.] Trudy Geol. Inst., <u>56</u>, 191 pp., 65 figs., 41 tables (Russian).

ELKIN, A. P.
1966   A new venture. Archaeol., Phys. Anthrop. in Oceania, <u>1</u>, 1–4.
1967   Man and his past in Aboriginal Australia: a review of "Aboriginal man in Australia". Part I. Archaeol., Phys. Anthrop. in Oceania, <u>2</u>, 41–46.

ELLENBERGER, FRANÇOIS, and FUCHS, Y.
1965   Sur la présence de pistes de vertébrés dans le Lotharingien marin de la région de Sévérac-le-Château (Aveyron). C. R. Soc. Geol. France, <u>1965</u>, 39–40, 1 fig.

ELLENBERGER, F., and GINSBURG, L.
1966   Le gisement de dinosauriens triasiques de Maphutseng (Basutoland) et l'origine des sauropodes. C. R. Acad. Sci. Paris, Sci. Nat., <u>262</u>, 444–447.

ELLENBERGER, PAUL
1965   Découverte de pistes de vertébrés dans le Permien le Trias et le Lias inférieur, aux abords de Toulon (Var) et d'Anduze (Gard). C. R. Acad. Sci. Paris, <u>260</u>, 5856–5859, 1 fig.

ELLENBERGER, P., and GINSBURG, L.
1965   Sur le lieu d'origine du type de <u>Tritylodon</u> <u>longaevus</u> Owen. Bull. Mus. Hist. Nat. Paris, <u>37</u>, 190–191.
Rev.: J. M. G. in Fossilia, <u>1965</u>:5–6, 65.

ELLER, E. R.
1965A.   Paleozoic Hall. Carnegie Mag., <u>39</u>, 259–260, 1 fig.
1965B.   In the beginning . . . Carnegie Mag., <u>39</u>, 329–336, illustr.

ELLIS, DOROTHY See: Wormington and Ellis.

ELLISON, SAMUEL P., JR.
1966   Memorial to Maurice Goldsmith Mehl, (1887 - 1966). Bull. Geol. Soc. Amer., <u>77</u>, P219–P224, portr.

ELÓSEGUI, J.   See: Barandiaran and Elósegui.

ÉLOUARD, P.
1966   Découverte d'un archéocète dans les environs de Koalack. Notes
Africaines, 109, 8—10, 4 figs.

EL-TOUBI, M. R., KAMAL, A. M., and HAMMOUDA, H. G.
1965   The origin of Ophidia in the light of the developmental study of the
skull. Zeit. Zool. Syst. Evolut.-Forsch., 3, 94—102, (German
summary).

ELZINGA, G.
1960   Tietjerksteradeel (Friesland). Nieuws-Bull. Koninklijke Ned. Oudheidk.
Bond, 6e s., 13, 106, (not seen).
1961   Ruilverkaveling Koningsdiep. Nieuws-Bull. Koninklijke Ned. Oudheidk.
Bond, 6e s., 14, 182, (not seen).
1962   Tietjerksteradeel (Friesland). Nieuws-Bull. Koninklijke Ned. Oudheidk.
Bond, 6e s., 15, 49—50, (not seen).
1963   Chronique. District C: Overijssel, Gelderland, Zuiderzeepolders (1957—
1959). Helinium, 3, 60—91, 2 maps, (Dutch).

EMANUEL, WILLIAM H.
1968   The American "hand axe". Tenn. Archaeol., 24, 8—28, 12 figs.

EMERY, K. O.
1966A.   Underwater archaeology. Geochronicle, 1966:1, 1.
1966B.   Early man may have roamed the Atlantic Shelf. Oceanus, 12:2, 2—5,
illustr.
See: Whitmore, Emery, et al.

EMERY, K. O., and EDWARDS, R. L.
1966   Archaeological potential of the Atlantic continental shelf. Amer. Antiq.,
31, 733—737, 2 figs.

EMILIANI, CESARE
1965   Stratigraphic correlations and the Pleistocene epoch. Publ. Nation.
Acad. Sci., 1469, 56—62, 1 table.

EMLONG, DOUGLAS
1966   A new archaic cetacean from the Oligocene of northwest Oregon. Bull.
Mus. Nat. Hist., Univ. Oregon, no. 3, 51 pp., 15 figs., 5 tables.

EMORY, KENNETH P., (ed.)
1958   COWA surveys and bibliographies. Area 21 — Pacific Islands. COWA
Surv. and Bibliog., Area 21, no. 1, 7 + 6 pp.
1960   COWA surveys and bibliographies. Area 21 — Pacific Islands. COWA
Surv. and Bibliog., Area 21, no. 2, 8 + 5 pp.
1965   COWA surveys and bibliographies. Area 21 — Pacific Islands. COWA
Surv. and Bibliog., Area 21, no. 3, 1—8, 1—8.

ENDO, BANRI   See: Suzuki and Endo.

ENDO, KUNIHIKO   See: Kigoshi, Lin and Endo.

ENDO, SHINYA   See: Shimoda, Endo, Inoue and Ozaki.

ENGEL, FREDERIC (H. B.)
1964   Cadaveres de 8.830 años descubren en la zona de Paracas. Son los
        más antiguos de la costa. El Comercio, Lima, May 7, 1964, 1,
        (not seen).

ENGSTRAND, L.   See: Sellstedt, Engstrand and Gejvall.

ENLOW, D. H.
1966   A comparative study of facial growth in Homo and Macaca. Amer.
        Jour. Phys. Anthrop., 24, 293—307, 8 figs., 2 pls.

ENNOUCHI, EMILE
1963B. L'homme du J. Ihroud. Etude de paléontologie humaine. Hespéris
        Tamuda, 4, 229—230.
1965   La teneur en fluor des fossiles sert-elle d'horloge géologique? Notes
        Mém. Serv. Géol. Maroc, 185, 69—70.
1966A. Le site du Jebel Irhoud (Maroc). Actas V Congr. Panafr. Prehist. Estud.
        Cuaternario, 1963:2, 53—59, 1 fig., 2 pls.
1966B. Essai de datation du gisement du Jebel Irhoud (Maroc). C. R. Soc.
        Geol. France, 1966, 405—406, 1 fig.
1968   Le deuxième crâne de l'homme d'Irhoud. Ann. Pal., Vert., 54, 115—
        128, 7 figs.

EPITASHVILI, V. D.
1964   [On the Lyrolepis beds of the southern limb of the Lechkhumi syncline.]
        In: Tsagareli, 1964, 313—321, (Russian; English summary).

EPPEL, FRANZ
1963   Stationen der ältesten Kunst. Wien, München: Schroll, 128 pp., 75
        figs., 131 pls.
        Rev.: Bleich in Mitt. Verband Deutschen Höhlen- und Karstforscher,
        München, 10, 47—48; Fordinal in Die Höhle, 15, 54—55.

EPSHTEÏN, S. V.   See: Ganeshin, Zubakov, et al.

EPSTEIN, JEREMIAH F.
1964   Towards the systematic description of chipped stone. Proc. Internat.
        Congr. Americanists, 1962:1, 155—169, 1 table.
1965   Terminal Pleistocene cultures in northeast Mexico and Texas. 7th
        Internat. Congr., Internat. Assoc. Quat. Res., Abs., 1965, 133,
        (abs.).
1966A. Terminal Pleistocene cultures in Texas and northeast Mexico. Quater-
        naria, 8, 115—123, (Spanish and German summaries).
1966B. Recent archaeological excavations in Nuevo Leon, Mexico. Texas Jour.
        Sci., 18, 124, (abs.).

ERBAEVA, MARGARITA ALEXANDROVNA (= Erbajeva, M. A., = Yerbayeva, M. A.)
1965   [Conditions of accumulation of small mammals remains in the upper
        stratum of middle beds of the Tologoĭ occurence (West Trans-
        baĭkalia) and specific features of fauna composition.] In: Saks,
        (ed.), 1965, 311—313, 1 table, (Russian).
1966   [New data for biostratigraphy of Quaternary deposits of western
        Transbaĭkalia.] Biull. Kom. Izuch. Chetvert. Perioda, 31, 93—
        103, 3 figs., (Russian).

ERBAEVA, M. A., and POKATILOV, A. G.
  1966   [New species of Eopleistocene gopher from Tologoĭ (West Transbaykalia).]
            Pal. Zhurnal, 1966:1, 162—164, 1 pl., (Russian).

ERBEN, HEINRICH K.
  1966   Otto Heinrich Schindewolf und sein Werk. Zu seinem 70. Geburtstag
            am 7.6. 1966. Forsch. u. Fortschr., 40:6, 186—188, portr.

ERDBRINK, D. P.
  1960   Algunas impresiones sobre las cuencas continentales terciarias de Teruel
            y de Calatayud. Teruel, no. 23, 197—203, 2 figs.
  1964   A fossil faunule with Homo from a prehistoric site along the Meuse
            in the Netherlands. Natuurhist. Maandbl., 53, 107—114, 10 figs.,
            (Dutch summary).
  1965   A quantification of the Dryopithecus-and other lower molar patterns in
            man and some of the apes. Zeit. Morph. Anthrop., 57, 70—108,
            6 figs., 10 tables, (German summary).
  1967A.   New finds of fossil bears from The Netherlands. Lutra, 9, 17—41, 1
            fig., 4 tables, 6 pls., (Dutch summary).
            Rev.: Ehrenberg om Zbl. Geol. Pal., Teil 2, 1968:6, 663—664.
  1967B.   A collection of mammalian fossils from S. E. Shansi, China. I. Publs.
            Natuurhistor. Genootschap, Limburg, 17, 31—42, (Dutch sum-
            mary).

ERDBRINK, D. P., and VAN HEEKEREN, H. R.
  1965   The presence of supposedly primitive human tools along the upper
            reaches of the Kizil Irmak in Anatolia. Eiszeit. u. Gegenwart.,
            16, 78—87, 4 figs., (German summary).

ERDNIEV, U. E.
  1956   [Rock drawings near Ust'-Pisanaĩa village.]   Priroda, 1956:6, 107—109,
            2 figs., (Russian).

ERICH, ROBERT W., (ed.)
  1965   Chronologies in Old World archaeology. Illinois.: Univ. Chicago Press,
            596 pp., (not seen).

ERICKSON, B. R.
  1966   Mounted skeleton of Triceratops prorsus. Sci. Publ. Sci. Mus., St. Paul,
            Minn., 1, 1—16, (not seen).

ERICSON, DAVID B., and WOLLIN, G.
  1964   The deep and the past. New York: Knopf, xiv + 292 pp., + i—ix, 29
            figs., 16 pls.
            Rev.: Anon. in Discovery, 27:8, 56;   Compton in Stones and Bones
            Newsletter, April 1965, 6;   Dyson in Amer. Sci., 53, 131A;
            Hogan in This World, S. F. Chronicle, 11/15/64, 51.
  1966   The deep and the past. London: Jonathan Cape, 292 pp., illustr.
            Rev.: Coryndon in Ann. Mag. Nat. Hist., 9, 319—320.
  1968   Pleistocene climates and chronology in deep-sea sediments. Science,
            162, 1227—1234, 6 figs.

ERMOLAEV, D. I.   See: Voropinov and Ermolaev.

ERMOLOVA, N. M.
1968   [Found in the Paleolithic of Eniseĭ R.]   Priroda, 1968:2, 58, (Russian).

ESCALON DE FONTON, MAX   See: Fonton, Max Escalon de.

ESCH, MAX
1966   Die altsteinzeitlichen Funde von Albersdorf. IPEK, 21, 19–20, 3 pls.

ESTABROOK, GEORGE   See: Rogers, D. J., Fleming and Estabrook.

ESTERAS, MANUEL, and AGUIRRE, EMILIANO
1964   Parelephas trogontherii Pohlig en una terraza media de Teruel. Teruel,
           32, 235–241, 2 pls.

ESTERHUYSE, D. J.   See: Hoffman and Esterhuyse.

ESTES, RICHARD
1960   Change of name for a Cretaceous chimaeroid. Jour. Pal., 34, 1054.
1964   Fossil vertebrates from the Late Cretaceous Lance formation, eastern
           Wyoming. Univ. Calif. Publ. Geol. Sci., 49, 1–180, 73 figs.,
           5 pls., 7 tables.
           Rev.: Hotton in Jour. Pal., 39, 511–512;   Weiler in Zbl. Geol. Pal.,
           Teil 2, 1965, 221–223.
1965A.   Fossil salamanders and salamander origins. Amer. Zool., 5, 319–334,
           7 figs., 1 table.
           Abs.: Westphal in Zbl. Geol. Pal., Teil 2, 1966, 294.
1965B.   A new fossil salamander from Montana and Wyoming. Copeia, 1965,
           90–95, 4 figs.
           Abs.: Westphal in Zbl. Geol. Pal., Teil 2, 1966, 294.
1965C.   Notes on some Paleocene lizards. Copeia, 1965, 104–106.
1966   Anatomy and relationships of the primitive fossil snake Dinilysia. Year
           Book, Amer. Philos. Soc., 1966, 334–336.

ESTES, R., HECHT, M., and HOFFSTETTER, R.
1967   Paleocene amphibians from Cernay, France. Amer. Mus. Novit., 2295,
           1–25, 7 figs., 3 tables.
           Rev.: Westphal in Zbl. Geol. Pal., Teil 2, 1968, 201.

ESTES, R., and TIHEN, J. A.
1964   Lower vertebrates from the Valentine formation of Nebraska. Amer.
           Mid. Nat., 72, 453–472, 5 figs.
           Abs.: Westphal in Zbl. Geol. Pal., Teil 2, 1966, 294–295.

ETHERIDGE, RICHARD
1964   Late Pleistocene lizards from Barbuda, British West Indies. Bull. Flor-
           ida State Mus., Biol. Sci., 9, 43–75, 5 figs.
1965   Fossil lizards from the Dominican Republic. Quart. Jour. Florida Acad.
           Sci., 28, 83–105, 3 figs.
1966A.   Pleistocene lizards from New Providence. Quart. Jour. Florida Acad.
           Sci., 28, 349–358.
1966B.   An extinct lizard of the genus Leiocephalus from Jamaica. Quart.
           Jour. Florida Acad. Sci., 29, 47–59, 1 fig.
1967   Lizard caudal vertebrae. Copeia, 67, 699–720, 4 figs., 1 table.

EUFROSIN, C.
1960   La présence du genre Paleoniscus en association avec la flore autunienne
            de Valea Berzavita, à l'W de Resita-Banat (Carpathes méridionales).
            Ann. Comit. Geol. Republ. Popul. Romine, 29–30, 195–196,
            2 pls., (not seen).

EVANGELISTA, ALFREDO E.
1964   Philippines. Asian Perspectives, 7, 52–56, 1 pl.

EVANS, CLIFFORD
1964   Lowland South America. In: Jennings and Norbeck, (eds.), 1964A,
            419–450, 1 fig.
            See: Meggers and Evans.

EVANS, J. D.   See: Daniel, G. and Evans.

EVANS, P. R.
1964   The age of the Precipice Sandstone. Austral. Jour. Sci., 26, 323–324.

EVERNDEN, JACK F.   See: Curtis and Evernden.

EVERNDEN, J. F., and CURTIS, G. H.
1963   The time-scale of man. Abs. 62nd Ann. Meeting Amer. Anthrop.
            Assoc., 1963, 16–17, (abs.).
1965   The potassium-argon dating of Late Cenozoic rocks in East Africa and
            Italy. With comments. Current Anthrop., 6, 343–385, 3 + 1
            figs.
            Abs.: Anon. in Anthropos, 61, 319.

EVERNDEN, J. F., SAVAGE, D. E., CURTIS, G. H., and JAMES, G. T.
1964   Potassium-argon dates and the Cenozoic mammalian chronology of
            North America. Amer. Jour. Sci., 262, 145–198, 7 tables.

EVERNDEN, J. H.   See: Leakey, Evernden and Curtis.

EWER, ROSALIE F.
1964   The dating of the Australopithecinae: faunal evidence. In: Lasker,
            G. W., (ed.), 1964, 96–101, 4 tables, (reprint with editorial
            comment).
1965A.   Preliminary note on the large Carnivora of Beds I and II. In: Leakey,
            et al., 1965, 19–22.
1965B.   The fundamental mystery of man? S. Afr. Archaeol. Bull., 20:79,
            137–138.
1965C.   The anatomy of the thecodont reptile Euparkeria capensis Broom.
            Philos. Trans. Roy. Soc. London, Ser. B, 248, 379–435, 19 figs.,
            pls. 31–34.
1967A.   The fossil hyaenids of Africa – a reappraisal. Discussion. In: Bishop,
            W. W., and Clark, J. D., (eds.), 1967A, 109–123, 7 figs., 1 table,
            (French summary).
1967B.   Professor Tobias' new nomenclature. S. African Jour. Sci., 63, 281.

EWER, R. F. and COOKE, H. B. S.
1964   The Pleistocene mammals of Southern Africa. In: Davis, D. H. S.,
            ed., 1964, 35–48, 1 fig., 2 tables.

EWERS, J. C.

1960   Selected references on the Plains Indians. Washington: Smithsonian Institution, (Smithsonian Anthropological Bibliographies, no. 1), 36 pp.

EWING, G. H.   See: Armelagos, et al.; Greene, D. L., Ewing and Armelagos; Kelso and Ewing.

EWING, J. F.

1963   Correction in Amer. Jour. Phys. Anthrop., 24, 275.

EYLES, V. A.

1965   John Woodward, F. R. S. (1665 - 1728). Nature, 206, 868–870.

1966   The history of geology: suggestions for further research. Hist. Sci., 5, 77–86.

EYNOR, O. I.

1966   Problems of paleobiogeography and paleontology in lithological-paleogeographical atlas of U.S.S.R. Abstract by V. P. Sokoloff. Internat. Geol. Rev., 8, 331–335, 3 figs.

EYO, EKPO

1966   Rop rock shelter, Nigeria. W. Afr. Archaeol. Newsletter, no. 5, 12, (discussion, 21–22).

F., D.

1960   Um das Kinn des Homo sapiens. Urania, 23, 377.
1961A.   Riesige Fundstätte von Dinosaurier-Eiern. Urania, 24, 12.
1961B.   Uran in fossilen Knochen. Urania, 24, 53.

F., K.

1967   Et fossil i beste velgaende. Naturen, 91, 121, (Norwegian).

FABRE, FRED

1964   Les paléo-climats en Brasse-Provence du Magdalénien V anciens à l'Azilien ancien. Bull. Mus. Hist. Nat., Marseille, 24, 165–176, 2 figs.

1965   Les collections de la salle de préhistoire du Muséum d'Histoire Naturelle de Marseille. Bull. Mus. Hist. Nat. Marseille, 25, 49–56, 7 figs.

FACCHINI, FIORENZO

1968   Sur l'apport de Pierre Teilhard de Chardin à la paleoanthropologie et à l'étude de l'évolution humaine. Rev. Questions Sci., 29, 167–189.

FAGAN, BRIAN MURRAY

1967   Malawi. In: Oakley, K. P., and Campbell, B. G., (eds.), 1967A, 31–32.
        See: Clark, J. D. and Fagan.

FAGG, A. E.   See: Higgs, Vita-Finzi, et al.

FAHLBUSCH, KLAUS
1966   Eine Pteraspiden-Fauna aus dem Unterdevon von Alken an der Mosel.
            Senck. Lethaea, 47, 165—191, 24 figs., pls. 17—20.
1967   Chemische und physikalische Vorgänge bei der Aufbereitung von
            Gesteinen mit Fossilien aus Calciumphosphat. Neues Jahrb.
            Geol. Pal., Abh., 129, 207—221, 3 pls., (English summary).

FAHLBUSCH, VOLKER
1964   Die Cricetiden (Mamm.) der Oberen Süsswasser-Molasse Bayerns. Abh.
            Bayer. Akad. Wiss., Math.-Nat. Kl., 118, 136 pp., 67 figs., 7 pls.
            Abs.: Dehm in Sitz.-Ber. Bayer. Akad. Wiss., Math.-Naturwiss. Abt.,
            1964, 9*—10*;   Hünermann in Zbl. Geol. Pal., Teil 2, 1966,
            329—331.
1966   Cricetidae (Rodentia, Mamm.) aus der mittelmiocänen Spaltenfüllung
            Erkertshofen bei Eichstätt. Mitt. Bayer. Staatssamml. Pal. hist.
            Geol., 6, 109—131, 6 figs., 1 pl.
            Rev.: Fahlbusch in Zbl. Geol. Pal., Teil 2, 1967, 519—520.
1967A.   Über einen Potamotherium-Kiefer (Carnivora, Mammalia) aus dem
            Obermiozän von Reichenstetten bei Regensburg. Mitt. Bayer.
            Staatssamml. Pal. Hist. Geol., 7, 193—200.
1967B.   Die Beziehungen zwischen einigen Cricetiden (Mamm., Rodentia) des
            nordamerikanischen und europäischen Jungtertiärs. Pal. Zeit.,
            41:3—4, 154—164, 2 pls., (English summary).

FAIDER-FEYTMANS, S.   See: Danthine and Faider-Feytmans.

FAIRBANKS, CHARLES H.
1952   Creek and pre-Creek. In: Griffin, J. B., (ed.), 1952A, 285—300.
1964   The early occupations of northwestern Florida. Bull. Southeast.
            Archaeol. Confer., 1, 27—30.
            See: Lazarus, Fairbanks and Bullen.

FAIRBRIDGE, RHODES W.
1963   Nile sedimentation above Wadi Halfa during the last 20,000 years.
            Kush, 11, 96—107, pls. 17—18.

FAIRSERVIS, JAN   See: Comfort 1964.

FALCON, N. L.   See: Savage, R. J. G. 1965B.

FALKENBACH, CHARLES H.   See: Schultz, C. B. and Falkenbach; Schultz, C. B.,
            Falkenbach and Vondra.

FALKENBURGER, F.
1960   Die Urbevölkerung Amerikas. Urania, 23, 381—386, 5 figs.

FALLOW, WALLACE
1964   Cylindracanthus from the Eocene of the Carolinas. Jour. Pal., 38,
            128—129, 1 fig.

FALLS, DARRYL LEE   See: Cramer and Falls.

FANGE, RAGNAR   See: Brodal and Fange.

FARB, PETER
1962   The story of life. Plants and animals through the ages. Illustrated by
          Kathleen Elgin. New York: Harvey House, 126 pp., illustr.,
          (grade and high school).

FARINE, B.
1963   Sites préhistoriques gabonais. Libreville: Min. Inform. Gabon, s.d.,
          64 pp., 31 figs., (not seen).
          Rev.: Mauny in Bull. Inst. Franç. Afr. Noire, sér. B, 25, 478–479.

FARINHA DOS SANTOS, MANUEL
1964   Vestigos de pinturas rupestres descobertos na gruta de Escoural. O
          Arqueol. Port., n.s., 5, 48 pp., 15 pls., maps, (not seen).
          Rev.: [Beltrán] in Caesaraugusta, 23–24, 143–144.
          See: Glory, Vaultier and Farinha dos Santos.

FARMER, MALCOLM F.
1964   The Arctic-North Atlantic as prehistoric migration route. Anthrop.
          Jour. Canada, 2:4, 2–4.
          See: Brace 1964.

FARNDEN, T. H. G.
1966   Excavation of a Late Stone Age shelter at New Amalfi, East Griqualand.
          S. Afr. Archaeol. Bull., 21, 122–124, 2 figs., 1 table.
1967   Preliminary notes on prehistoric material from the Umgeni Valley near
          Cato Ridge, Natal. S. Afr. Archaeol. Bull., 21, 187–190, 2 figs.

FARQUHAR, R. M.   See: Hamilton, E. I. and Farquhar.

FARRAND, William R.
1968   Paleoclimate determined from prehistoric rockshelter sediments (Abri
          Pataud, France). Program, 1968 Ann. Meetings, Geol. Soc.
          Amer., 1968, 94, (abs.).

FARRAR, R. A. H., (ed.)
1968   Upper Palaeolithic artifacts from Portland. Proc. Dorset Nat. Hist.
          Archaeol. Soc., 89, 117–119, 1 fig.

FAUGÈRES, LUCIEN
1966   Découverte d'une molaire d'Elephas antiquus dans le bassin de Kozani-
          Ptolémaïs (Macédoine occidentale). C. R. Soc. Geol. France,
          1966, 184–185, 1 fig.

FAURE, HUGUES, and HUGOT, H.-J.
1966   Chronologie absolue du Quaternaire en Afrique de l'Ouest. Bull. Inst.
          Franç. Afr. Noire, Ser. A, 28, 384–397, 1 table.

FAURE, H., and ROUBET, C.
1968   Découverte d'un biface acheuléen dans les calcaires marins du golfe
          pléistocène de l'Afar (Mer Rouge, Ethiopie). C. R. Acad. Sci.
          Paris, Sci. Nat., 267, 18–21, 1 pl.

FAURE-MURET, ANNE   See: Choubert, G., and Faure-Muret, A.

FAVATI VANNI, VIRGINIA
1964   Studio antropologico dello scheletro d'un bambino del Paleolitico
         superiore, rinvenuto nella grotta Maritza presso Avezzano. Atti
         Soc. Toscana Sci. Nat. Mem., Ser. A, 71, 475—487, 1 fig., (French
         summary).

FEDOROV, G. B., (ed.)
1951   [On the traces of ancient civilizations.] Moscow: Goskul'tprosvet Press,
         270 pp., 60 figs., 52 pls., (Russian).

FEDOROV, P. V.
1957   [Stratigraphy of Quaternary deposits and the history of the development
         of the Caspian Sea.]   Trudy Geol. Inst., 10, 297 pp., 129 figs.,
         10 tables, (Russian).
1961   [New representations of fish from Paleolithic sites of European SSSR.]
         Krat. Soob. Inst. Ist. Mat. Kult. SSSR, 82, 140—142, (Russian).

FEDOSEEVA, S. A.   See: Mochanov and Fedoseeva.

FEDUCCIA, J. ALAN
1967A.   A new swallow from the Fox Canyon local fauna (Upper Pliocene) of
         Kansas. Condor, 69, 526—527, 1 fig.
1967B.   Ciconia maltha and Grus americana from the Upper Pliocene of Idaho.
         Wilson Bull., 79, 316—318.

FEDUCCIA, J. A., and WILSON, R. L.
1967   Avian fossils from the Lower Pliocene of Kansas. Occ. Pap. Mus. Zool.,
         Univ. Mich., 655, 1—6, 2 figs., 1 table.

FEJFAR, OLDŘICH
1962   Die Erforschung fossiler Wirbeltiere auf dem Gebiet der ČSSR. Zprávy
         Geol. Vyzk., 1961, 248—250, (Czech, not seen).
1964A.   The Lower Villafranchian vertebrates from Hajnačka near Filákovo in
         Southern Slovakia. Roz. Ustred. Ustav. Geol., 30, 115 pp., 58
         figs., 19 pls., 1 map, tables.
         Abs.: Hünermann in Zbl. Geol. Pal., Teil 2, 1965, 267—268.
1964B.   Vyzkum fosilních obratlovců ČSSR v roce 1963. Zprávy Geol. Vyzku-
         mech Roce, 1, 350—351.
1965   Die unter-mittelpleistozäne Mikromammalier-Fauna aus Dobrkovice,
         Südböhmen. Ber. Geol. Ges. Deutsch. Demokratischen Republ.,
         10, 6 figs.
1966A.   [New finds of Tertiary and Pleistocene mammals in Czechoslovakia.]
         Lynx, 6, 23—30, (Czech; German summary).
1966B.   Die plio-pleistozänen Wirbeltierfaunen von Hajnačka und Ivanovce
         (Slowakei), ČSSR V. Allosorex stenodus n.g.n.sp. aus Ivanovce A.
         Neues Jahrb. Geol. Pal., Abh., 123:3, 221—248, 14 figs., 5 pls.,
         5 tables.
         Abs.: Hünermann in Zbl. Geol. Pal., Teil 2, 1966, 324—325.
1966C.   Über zwei neue Säugetiere aus dem Altpleistozän von Böhmen. Neues
         Jahrb. Geol. Pal., Monatsh., 1966:11, 680—691, 2 figs., 2 tables.
         Rev.: Fahlbusch in Zbl. Geol. Pal., Teil 2, 1967, 520.
         See: Buday, et al.; Čtyroky, Fejfar and Holy; Daxner and Fejfar.

FELGENHAUER, FRITZ
1956-
  1959   Rev.: Gábori in Archaeol. Ért., 87, 253—254, (Hungarian).
  1962   Das niederösterreichische Freilandpaläolithikum. Mitt. Österreich.
             Arbeitsgemeinschaft Ur- und Frühgesch., 13, 1—16, (not seen).
  1966   Das "Oberflächenpaläolithikum" von Klein-Wilfersdorf, p. B. Korneuburg,
             NÖ. Archaeol. Austriaca, 40, 3—12, 4 pls.

FELIX, ROGER
1966   Glanes pour servir à la connaissance de la préhistoire dans le Nord.
             Bull. Soc. Préhist. Franç., C. R. séances mens., 63, 297—306,
             3 pls.

FELS, G.
1965   Abstammungslehre dargestellt anhand von Quellentexten. Stuttgart:
             Ernst Klett Verlag, Klett Studienbücher Bd. 1, 48 pp.
             Rev.: Kurth in Naturwiss. Rundschau, 19:5, 212.

FELTEN, H.
1965   Robert Mertens 70 Jahre. Säugetierkundl. Mitt., 13, 42, portr.

FENART, R.   See: Delattre and Fenart.

FENART, RAPHAËL, and HEIM, JEAN-LOUIS
1968   La posture des Néandertaliens d'après l'orientation vestibulaire du crâne.
             C. R. Acad. Sci. Paris, Sci. Nat., 267:23, 1968—1971, 2 figs.

FENART, ROBERT, and ANTHONY, J.
1967   La mandibule des singes platyrhiniens. Données ostéométriques et
             orientation vestibulaire. Ann. Pal., Vert., 53, 201—233, 8 figs.,
             6 tables.

FENIKSOVA, V. V.
1960   [Quaternary deposits in the Eniseĭ river valley from the city of Kras-
             noĭarsk to the mouth of the Big Pit river.] In: Ragozin, L. A.
             (ed.), 1960, 149—167, 6 figs., (Russian).
1961   [On the problem of development of the southern part of Ob'-Eniseĭ
             interfluve in Late Cenozoic.] Izv. Vyssh. Uch. Zav., Geol. i
             Razv., 1961:6, 21—35, 4 figs., (Russian).
1964   [Structure of the Neogene-Quaternary cover on the extra-glacial zone
             of West Siberian low-lands.] Vestnik Mosk. Univ., ser. IV, geol.,
             1964:6, 3—19, 3 maps, 1 table, (Russian).
1965   [New finds of mammalian fauna in Anthropogene (Quaternary) deposits
             of Chulym R. valley.] Geol. i Geof., 1965:3, 156—158, 2 figs.,
             (Russian).
1966   [Quaternary deposits in the south-east of Western Siberia.] In: Khain,
             (ed.), 1966, 185—211, 6 figs., (Russian).

FENTON, CARROLL LANE
1965   Tales told by fossils. [High School and layman.] New York: Double-
             day, 182 pp., illustr.
             Rev.: Batten in Nat. Hist., 75:9, 66.

FENTON, C. L., and FENTON, M. A.
1962B.   Giants of geology (the story of great geologists). Garden City, N. Y.:
             Doubleday, Dolphin Books, 318 pp., (pb. ed.).

FEREMBACH, DENISE
1959A.   Rev.: Genovés in Cuad. Inst. Hist., Ser. Antrop., no. 6, 9—14.
1962   La deuxième molaire déciduale inférieure de la grotte de Salemas (Por-
            tugal). Com. Serv. Geol. Portugal, 46, 177—186, 2 pls.
            Abs.: Anon. in Internat. Jour. Spel., 2:3, 21.
1964   La masculinité (sex-ratio) chez les hommes modernes et chez les hommes
            fossiles. Anthrop., 2:1, 27—40.
1965A.   Les ossements humains de Salemas (Portugal). Com. Serv. Geol. Portu-
            gal, 48, 165—184, 7 figs., 1 pl.
1965B.   La molaire humaine inférieure moustérienne de Bombarral (Portugal).
            Com. Serv. Geol. Portugal, 48, 185—190, 2 pls.
            Rev.: Vallois in L'Anthrop., 71:5—6, 539.
1965C.   Les restes humains de l'abri Lachaud. Préhist., 16, 97—114, 6 figs.
1965D.   Diagrammes craniens sagittaux et mensurations individuelles des squelettes
            ibéromaurusiens de Taforalt (Maroc Oriental). Travaux Centre
            Rech. Anthrop. Préhist. Ethnogr. Algérie, 124 pp., 26 figs., tables.
            Paris: Arts et Métiers Graphiques Press.
            Rev.: Sauter in Arch. Suiss. Anthrop. Gen., 31, 56—57.

FERGUSON, MAX
1968   Digging for sharkteeth. Desert Mag., 31:4, 10—11, 3 figs.

FERGUSSON, G. J.   See: Berger, R., Fergusson and Libby.

FERGUSSON, G. J., and LIBBY, W. F.
1964   UCLA radiocarbon dates III. Radiocarbon, 6, 318—339.

FERNÁNDEZ de AVILÉS, A.
1963   Joaquin Sánchez Jiménez (*1891 - †1962). Zephyrus, 13, 113—114,
            portr.

FERNANDEZ-GALIANO, DIMAS
1958   Descubrimiento de restos de dinosaurios en Galve. Teruel, no. 20, 201—
            203.
1959   Sobre una posible Sala de Geología en el Museo Provincial. Teruel, no.
            22, 307—313.

FERNÁNDEZ MEDRANO, D.   See: Barandiarán and Fernández Medrano.

FERNOW, LEONARD R.
1965   Paris basin. GeoTimes, 10:4, 9—13, 4 figs.

FERRUSQUIA, V. I. See: Alvarez, S. T., and Ferrusquia.

FERU, M., RĂDULESCU, C., and SAMSON, P.
1965   Contribution à la connaissance d'une faune de Mammifères villafranchiens
            dans la parte occidentale de la Dépression Gétique. Lucrarile
            Inst. Spel. "Emil Racovita", Bucuresti, 4, 285—297, 6 figs., (Ru-
            manian; French summary).
            Abs.: Semaka in Zbl. Geol. Pal., Teil 2, 1966, 317.

FEUSTEL, RUDOLF
1957   Rev.: Müller-Beck in L'Anthrop., 68, 598.
1960   Eiszeitliche Kunstwerke. Urania, 23, 300.
1965   Das Aurignacien vom Zoitzberg bei Gera. Alt-Thüringen, 7, 15—39,
            18 figs.

1968   Die Australopithecinen und das Problem der "Osteodontokeratic culture".
            (Zusammenfassung). Discussion. 7th Internat. Congr. Anthrop.
            Ethnol. Sci., Moscow, 1964, 3, 475—478.

FEUSTEL, R., TEICHERT, M., and UNGER, K. P.
1963   Die Magdalénienstation Lausnitz in der Orlasenke. Alt-Thüringen, 6,
            57—103, 17 figs., pls. 4—8.
            Rev.: Vencl in Archeol. Roz., 16, 466, (Czech).

FICAT, CHARLES
1964   Le crâne de renne fossile du Musée de Foix. Préhist. Spéléol. Ariégeoises,
            19, 53—57, 2 pls.

FICCARELLI, G., and TORRE, D.
1967   Il mustelide Enhydrictis galictoides del Pleistocene della Sardegna.
            Palaeont. Ital., 63:4, 139—160, 11 figs., pls. 20—24, (English
            summary).
            Rev.: Albanesi in Riv. Ital. Pal., 74:4, 1321.

FIDELI, G. FRANCO   See: Fussi and Fideli.

FIDLER, J. HAVELOC   See: Wagstaffe and Fidler.

FIEGE, KURT
1951   Abs.: Raabe in Zbl. Geol. Pal., Teil 2, 1964, 781—782.

FIELD, HENRY
1964   Stone Age man in southwestern Asia. In: Ripoll Perelló, E., (ed.),
            1964A, 423—429, (Spanish summary).
1966A.   Introduction. In: Beregovaia, N. A., Islamov, U., and Kalandadze,
            A. N., 1966, xi + xv.
1966B.   Petroglyphs from Syr-Darya. In: Beregovaia, N. A., Islamov, U., and
            Kalandadze, A. N., 1966, 149—154, 5 figs.
            See: Beregovaia, et al.; Kalandadze 1966.

FIENNES, RICHARD
1965   Man's role in the evolution of the dog. Comments by James Robertson-
            Justice. New Sci., 25, 84—86, 26, 48, 50, illustr.

FIERSTINE, HARRY L.
1966   Swollen dorsal fin elements in living and fossil Carangidae (Pisces:
            Teleostei). Program, 62nd Ann. Meeting, Geol. Soc. Amer.,
            Cordilleran Sect., 1966, 37, (abs.). Also: Spec. Pap. Geol. Soc.
            Amer., 101, 305—306, (abs.).
1968   Swollen dorsal fin elements in living and fossil Caranx (Teleostei:
            Carangidae). Contrib. Sci., Los Angeles Co. Mus., no. 137, 1—10,
            5 figs.

FIERSTINE, H. L., and APPLEGATE, S. P.
1968   Billfish remains from Southern California with remarks on the impor-
            tance of the predentary bone. Bull. S. Calif. Acad. Sci., 67,
            29—39, 2 figs., 3 tables.

FILIP, JAN
1961A.   Zemřel profesor Karel Absolon Archeol. Roz., 13, 121—122, (Czech;
            German summary).

1961B.   Jaroslav Petrbok [1881 - 1960]. Archeol. Roz., 13, 404, 433, portr,
            (Czech).
1963   Zemřel akademik Jaroslav Böhm (*8. III. 1901, Holešov − † 6. XII.
            1962, Praha). Archeol. Roz., 15, 133.
1966   et al. Enzyklopädisches Handbuch zur Ur- und Frühgeschichte Europas.
            Band I (A-K). Stuttgart Berlin Köhln Mainz: W. Kohlhammer
            Verlag, 664 pp., illustr., 40 pls.
            Rev.: Engelmayer in Mitt. Anthrop. Ges. Wien, 96–97, 384–385;
            Kühn in IPEK, 22, 146.
1967   Le VII-e Congrès International des sciences préhistoriques et protohisto-
            riques à Prague en 1966. Archeol. Roz., 19:1, 3–30, 15 pls.,
            (Czech and French text).

FILIPPOV, A. K.   See: Praslov and Filippov.

FILZER, PAUL
1965   Beiträge zur Problematik der Pollenanalyse kulturführender Lehme.
            Fundber. Schwaben, 17, 214–223, 1 fig., 1 table.
1966   Vegetation und Klima des Letzten Interglazials im nördlichen Alpen-
            vorland. Forsch. u. Fortschr., 40, 70–73.

FINASHINA, G. N.   See: Churakov, et al.

FINCH, RICHARD C.
1964   Cotton-pickin' bone-pickers. Nashville Speleonews, Oct., 51–52, (not
            seen).

FINDLAY, G. H.
1968A.   On the structure of the skin in Uranocentrodon (Rhinesuchus) seneka-
            lensis, van Hoepen. Pal. Africana, 11, 15–21, 5 figs.
1968B.   On the scaloposaurid skull of Olivieria parringtoni, Brink with a note
            on the origin of hair. Pal. Africana, 11, 47–59, 7 figs.

FINDLEY, JAMES S.
1964   Paleoecologic reconstruction: vertebrate limitations. Discussion. Publ.
            Fort Burgwin Res. Center, no. 3, 23–25.
1967   Insectivores and dermopterans. In: Anderson, S., and Jones, (eds.),
            1967, 87–108, figs. 8–12.
            See: Harris, A. H. and Findley.

FINE, MARY D.
1964   An abnormal P2 in Canis cf. C. latrans from the Hagerman fauna of
            Idaho. Jour. Mammal., 45, 483–485, 1 fig., 1 table.

FINZEL, ERIKA
1964   Plesiosaurusfund in der Unterkreide. Aufschluss, 15, 307.

FIRBY, JEAN B.
1966A.   The Irvington locality. In: [Savage, D. E., (ed.)], 1966B, 4 pp., map.
1966B.   The short-faced bears of America. Program, 62nd Ann. Meeting, Geol.
            Soc. Amer., Cordilleran Sect., 1966, 38, (abs.). Also: Spec.
            Pap. Geol. Soc. Amer., 101, 306, (abs.).
1967   New additions to the Irvington fauna of California. Program, 63rd
            Ann. Meeting, Geol. Soc. Amer., Cordilleran Sect., 34, (abs.).
            Also: Spec. Pap. Geol. Soc. Amer., 115, 324, (abs.).

1968   Fauna of the type Irvingtonian mammal age. Program, 1968 Ann. Meetings, Geol. Soc. Amer., 1968, 96, (abs.).

FIRSHSTEIN, B. V.   See: Popova and Firshstein.

FIRST, M.
1964   Skull fractures in suid fossils from Makapansgat. Leech, 34, 13—16, (not seen).

FIRST, R.   See: Morison, et al.

FIRU, P.
1963   Aspects de stomatologie anthropologique. Probl. Antrop., 7, 145—158, (Rumanian; Russian and French summaries).

FISCHER, FRANZ, and KIMMIG, W.
1965   Festschrift für Gustav Riek. Fundber. Schwaben, 17, xiii + 249 pp., figs., 49 pls.
             Rev.: Bleich in Mitt. Verband Deutschen Höhlen- und Karstforscher, München, 11, 120.

FISCHER, HANS
1963   Bernhard Peyer (1885 - 1963). Vierteljahreschr- Naturf. Ges. Zurich, 108, 467—469, portr.
1965   Conrad Gessner (26. März 1516 — 13. Dezember 1565). Leben und Werk. Viertel. Jahreschr. Naturf. Ges. Zürich, 110, 152 pp., 39 figs.

FISCHER, KARLHEINZ
1962   Abs.: I., K., in Jour. Ornithol., 105, 370;   Kuhn in Zbl. Geol. Pal., Teil 2, 1966, 312.
1963   Panzerplattenabrücke von Cotylosauriern aus dem Rotliegenden des Thüringer Waldes. Hallesches Jahrb. Mitteldeutch Erdgeschichte, 5, 44—46, pls. 3—6.
             Abs.: Rosenfeld in Zbl. Geol. Pal., Teil 2, 1964, 790—791.
1964   Die tapiroiden Perissodactylen aus der eozänen Braunkohle des Geiseltales. Geologie, Beiheft, 45, 101 pp., 22 figs., 10 pls., 15 tables. (English, French, and Russian summaries).
1965   Bisonreste (Bison schoetensacki voigtstedtensis ssp. n.) aus den altpleis- tozänen Tonen von Voigtstedt in Thüringen. Pal. Abh., Abt. A, 2, 363—378, 5 figs., pls. 8—12, (Russian and English summaries).
1967   Zur systematischen Stellung des Chasmotherium Rütimeyer, 1862 (Mam- malia, Perissodactyla). Ber. Geol. Ges. Deutsch. Demokratischen Republ., A 12:5, 595—600.
          See: Howorka and Fischer.

FISCHER, T.
1962   Dryopithecus-Muster und Zahngrössen an unteren Molaren bei Melanesiern. Basil: Diss. Zahnheilkd., 20 pp., (not seen).

FISHER, DONALD W.
1955   Prehistoric mammals of New York. N. Y. State Conservationist, 9:4, 18—22.
1963   An ancient beachhead. Devonian plants trigger animal conquest of the land. N. Y. State Conservationist, 17:3, 22—27, 41.
          See: Trimm and Fisher.

FISHER, JAMES
1966   The shell bird book. London: Ebury Press and Michael Joseph, 344
pp., 150 illustr., 20 pls., 9 maps., (not seen).
Rev.: M. D. L. in Ibis, 109, 449–450.

1967A.   Fossil birds and their adaptive radiation. In: Harland, W. B., et al.,
(eds.), 1967A, 133–156, 1 fig.

1967B.   Aves. In: Harland, W. B., et al., (eds.), 1967A, 733–762, 2 figs.
Rev.: Kuhn in Zbl. Geol. Pal., Teil 2, 1969:3, 290.

FISKE, TIMOTHY
1964   University of Manitoba field work. Manitoba Archaeol. Newsletter, 1:4,
3–6.

FITCH, JOHN E.
1964   The fish fauna of the Playa del Rey locality, a Southern California
marine Pleistocene deposit. Contrib. Sci., Los Angeles Co. Mus.,
82, 3–35, 49 figs., 1 table.
Abs.: Weiler in Zbl. Geol. Pal., Teil 2, 1965, 223–224.

1966   Additional fish remains, mostly otoliths, from a Pleistocene deposit at
Playa del Rey, California. Contrib. Sci., Los Angeles Co. Mus.,
no. 119, 16 pp., 12 figs., 2 tables.
Rev.: Weiler in Zbl. Geol. Pal., Teil 2, 1967, 495.

1967   The marine fish fauna, based primarily on otoliths, of a Lower Pleistocene deposit at San Pedro, California (LACMIP 332, San Pedro
sand). Contrib. Sci., Los Angeles Co. Mus., no. 128, 1–23,
31 figs.
Rev.: Weiler in Zbl. Geol. Pal., Teil 2, 1968:6, 644–645.

FITCH, J. E., and REIMER, R. D.
1967   Otoliths and other fish remains from a Long Beach, California Pliocene
deposit. Bull. S. Calif. Acad. Sci., 66, 77–91, 22 figs., 1 table.
Rev.: Weiler in Zbl. Geol. Pal., Teil 2, 1968:6, 645; Weiler in Zbl.
Geol. Pal., Teil 2, 1969:3, 283–284.

FITTE, PAUL   See: Bordes and Fitte.

FITTING, JAMES E.
1965A.   A quantitative examination of Virginia fluted points. Amer. Antiq.,
30, 484–491, 13 tables.

1965B.   Effect of sample preparation measurements of natural radioactivity.
In: Jelinek, A. J., and Fitting, J. E., (eds.), 1965, 8–13, 3 tables.

1965C.   Methodology. In: Jelinek, A. J., and Fitting, J. E., (eds.), 1965, 4–7.

1965D.   A gamma ray analysis of fossil bone from Blackwater Draw, Number 1,
Locality. In: Jelinck, A. J., and Fitting, J. E., (eds.), 1965,
77–88, 10 figs.

1965E.   A study of natural radioactivity in osteological materials from the
Blackwater Draw, Locality Number 1, Roosevelt County, New
Mexico. In: Jelinek, A. J., and Fitting, J. E., (eds.), 1965,
64–76, 11 tables, 2 charts.

1965F.   Internal variation in radioactivity of a standard sample. In: Jelinek,
A. J., and Fitting, J. E., (eds.), 1965, 23–27, 2 tables.

1965G.   Papers in honor of Emerson F. Greenman. Mich. Archaeol., 11, 79–
196, illustr.
Rev.: Binford in Amer. Anthrop., 68:4, 1067–1068.

1965H.   Observations on Paleo-Indian adaptive and settlement patterns. Mich.
Archaeol., 11, 103–109.

1966A. The archeology explosion in Michigan. Bull. Eastern States Archeol. Fed., no. 25, 10, (abs.).

1966B. Part I: the Holcombe site. In: Fitting, J. E., DeVisscher, J., and Wahla, E. J., 1966, 1–81, 15 figs., 38 tables.

1966C. Part III: the Paleo-Indian occupation of the Holcombe Beach. In: Fitting, J. E., DeVisscher, J., and Wahla, E. J., 1966, 109–140, 9 tables.

1966D. (ed.) Edge area archaeology. Mich. Archaeol., 12, 141–248, illustr. Rev.: Hurley in Amer. Antiq., 33, 395–396.

1967   Early man in the Upper Great Lakes region. Bull. Eastern States Archeol. Fed., no. 26, 12, (abs.).
See: Jelinek, A. and Fitting.

FITTING, J. E., DeVISSCHER, J., and WAHLA, E. J.
1966   The Paleo-Indian occupation of the Holcombe Beach. Anthrop. Papers, Univ. Mich., no. 27, vi + 147 pp., 20 figs., 49 tables, 12 pls. Rev.: MacDonald in Amer. Antiq., 32, 407–408; Richards in Totem Pole, 49, 45; Stoltman in Wisc. Archeol., 47, 214–218.

FITZSIMONS, VIVIAN F. M.
1962   Snakes of Southern Africa. London: Macdonald, 423 pp., illustr.

FITZWATER, ROBERT
1967   Localities 3 and 4A (C1–246, C1–250), Tule Springs, Nevada. In: Wormington, and Ellis, (eds.), 1967, 353–364, 3 pls., 4 maps.

FITZWATER, R. J. See: Butler, B. R. and Fitzwater.

FLAHIVE, MARY E.
1964   Valley geology. Explorer, 6:4, 5–8, illustr.

FLANDERS, S. E.
1962   Did the caterpillar exterminate the giant reptile? Jour. Res. Lepidoptera, 1, 85–88.

FLANDRIN, JACQUES
1963   Remarques stratigraphiques, paléontologiques et structurales sur la région de Séderon. Bull. Serv. Carte Géol. France, 59:272, 815–845, 1 map.

FLANDRIN, J., MEIN, P., and TRUC, G.
1968   Données paléontologiques et stratigraphiques nouvelles sur le Miocène continental du bassin d'Eoulx, au Sud de Castellane (Basses-Alpes). C. R. Acad. Sci. Paris, Sci. Nat., 267:17, 1351–1354, 1 fig.

FLANNERY, KENT V.
1967   Vertebrate fauna and hunting patterns. In: Byers, D. S., (ed.), 132–177, 7 figs., 6 tables.
See: Hole and Flannery.

FLEISCH, HENRI
1966   Notes de préhistoire libanaise. Bull. Soc. Préhist. Franç., C. R. séances mens., 63, 239–242.

FLEISCHER, ROBERT L.
1965   Application of fission track dating to anthropology. Publ. Nation. Acad. Sci., <u>1469</u>, 62–64.

FLEISCHER, R. L., LEAKEY, L. S. B., PRICE, P. B., and WALKER, R. M.
1965   Fission track dating of Bed I, Olduvai Gorge. Science, <u>148</u>, 72–74, 1 fig. Also in: Current Anthrop., <u>6</u>, 389–390; and Genovés, S., et al., (eds.), 1967, 92–96, with comment by Andrew P. Wilson.
          Rev.: J. C. In Bull. Soc. Préhist. Franç., C. R. séances mens., <u>1965</u>:6, cxcviii.

FLEISCHHACKER, H.
1955   Atlanthropus, ein neur Urmenschenfund aus Afrika. Umschau, <u>55</u>, 692–694, 2 figs.

FLEMING, HENRY S.   See: Rogers, D. J., Fleming and Estabrook.

FLEROV, K. K.
1953   [Unicorn – Elasmotherium.] Priroda, <u>1953</u>:9, 110–112, 4 figs., (Russian).
1965A.   [On the origin of Canadian fauna in connection with the history of Bering land-bridge.] In: Gromov, V. I., et al., (eds.), 1965, 121–128, (Russian; English summary).
1965B.   On the origin of the Canadian fauna in connection with the history of the Bering land-bridge. 7th Internat. Congr., Internat. Assoc. Quat. Res., Abs., <u>1965</u>, 140, (abs.).
1967   On the origin of the mammalian fauna of Canada. In: Hopkins, D. M., (ed.), 1967D, 271–280.
          See: Vangengeim and Flerov; Zablotsky and Flerov.

FLEROV, K. K., and SHEVYREVA, N. S.
1965   Pseudalces, Pliocene deer from Ciscaucasus. (Translation of Flerov and Shevyreva, 1963.) Internat. Geol. Rev., <u>7</u>, 931–934, 3 figs.

FLEROV, K. K., and TROFIMOV, B. A.
1966   [Iurii Aleksandrovich Orlov (1893 - 1966).] Pal. Zhurnal, <u>1966</u>:4, 3–7, portr., (Russian).

FLEURE, H. J.
1965   Renato Biasutti: 1878 - 1965. Man, <u>65</u>, 79.

FLIGHT, COLIN
1967   A note on problems of cultural taxonomy. W. Afr. Archaeol. Newsletter, no. <u>7</u>, 27–30, (French summary).

FLINT, RICHARD FOSTER
1959   Abs.: Ebers in Zbl. Geol. Pal., Teil 2, <u>1961</u>, 405.
1965   Introduction. In: Rankama, (ed.), <u>1965</u>, xi–xxii, 1 table.
1967   Introduction to part II. [Stratigraphical considerations.] In: Bishop, W. W., and Clark, J. D., (eds.), 1967A, 187–189.

FLORENSOV, N. A.
1960   [Mesozoic and Cenozoic depressions of Baĭkal region.] Trudy Vost.-Sib. Fil., ser. geol., <u>19</u>, 258 pp., 59 figs. and maps, (Russian).

FLORIS, SØREN
1964   Krokodillefundet fra Fakse. Meddel. Dansk Geol. Foren., 15, 435–436,
            (abs.).

FLORU, EUGEN   See: Nicolaescu-Plopşor, D. and Floru.

FLÜCKIGER, WALTER   See: Andrist, D., et al.

FLÜGEL, ERIK   See: Zapfe, et al.

FLÜGEL, E., and KOLLMANN, H.
1964   Verzeichnis der wichtigsten Objekte der Geologisch-Paläontologischen
            Sammlung (Rotpunkt-Verzeichnis). Veröff. Naturhist. Mus.
            Vienna, N. F. no. 5, 148–156.

FLUGEL, H.
1964   Ein Myliobatis-Fund im Leithakalk (Tortonium) von Leibnitz (Stmk).
            Anz. Akad. Wiss. Wien, 101, 417–418, 1 table.
            Rev.: Kühn in Zbl. Geol. Pal., Teil 2, 1967, 100.

FLÜKIGER, WALTER
1965   Burgäschi, Bez. Kriegstetten, SO. Jahrb. Schweiz. Ges. Urgesch., 51,
            71–86, 15 figs.

FOCHLER-HAUKE, GUSTAV
1955   Höhlenmalereien und Felszeichungen in Patagonien. Umschau, 55, 598–
            600, 4 figs.

FOCK, GERHARD J.
1965A.   Die Verbreitung vorgeschichtlicher Kulturen in der Nördlichen Kapprovinz,
            Südafrika. Fundber. Schwaben, 17, 11–20, 3 figs.
1965B.   J. H. Power 1884 - 1964. S. Afr. Archaeol. Bull., 20:78, 74, portr.;
            correction in 20:80, 166.

FOKANOV, V. A.
1964   [On the history of forming of the rodent fauna in the Badkhyz (South
            Turkmenistan) in the Holocene.] Bull. Mosk. Obshch. Prirody,
            Otd. Biol., 69:4, 51–56, 2 tables, (Russian).

FOLLETT, W. I.
1965   Fish remains in the archeological context. Pap. Sacramento Anthrop.
            Soc., 3, 36–52, 5 pls.

FOLSOM, FRANKLIN
1956   Exploring American caves. New York: Crown, x + 280 pp., illustr.
            Rev.: Ilming in Die Höhle, 16, 115.
1962   Exploring American caves. 2nd rev. ed. New York: Collier, 319 pp.,
            21 pls.
            Rev.: Siegel in Die Höhle, 16, 115.
1966   Science and the secret of man's past. Illustrated by Ursula Koering.
            Irvington-on-Hudson, N. Y.: Harvey House, 192 pp., illustr.,
            (junior high).
            Rev.: L. F. in Masterkey, 40, 158;   Meighan in Amer. Antiq., 32,
            403;   Stoltman in Wisc. Archeol., 49, 106–108.

FOLSTER, H.
1968   Stratigraphy of slope deposits at Asejire. W. Afr. Archaeol. Newsletter,
             no. 8, 35—37, 1 fig., (French summary).

FOMIN, I. N.   See: Barabashev, et al.

FONTON, MAX ESCALON DE
1956   Préhistoire de la Basse-Provence. Préhist., 12, viii + 162 pp., 110 figs.
1963B.   Recherches sur la Préhistoire dans le Midi de la France. Rapport pré-
             liminaire sur la campagne de fouilles 1962. Cahiers Ligures
             Préhist. Archéol., 12:2, 221—229, 8 figs.
1964A.   La Séquence climatique würmienne du gisement paléolithique de la
             Salpêtrière (Remoulins, Gard). Bull. Soc. Géol. France, 5, 555—
             561, 6 figs., 1 table.
1964B.   Un nouveau faciès du Paléolithique supérieur dans la grotte de la Sal-
             petrière (Remoulins, Gard). In: Ripoll Perelló, E., (ed.), 1964A,
             405—421, 9 figs., 1 pl., (Spanish summary).
1966A.   Du Paléolithique supérieur au Mésolithique dans le Midi méditérranéen.
             Bull. Soc. Préhist. Franç., Étud. et Trav., 63:1, 66—180, 73 figs.,
             10 pls., 1 chart.
             Rev.: Ripoll Perelló in Ampurias, 28, 159—161.
1966B.   Le campement romanellien de La Valduc à Istres (Bouches-du-Rhône).
             L'Anthrop., 70, 29—44, 10 figs., 1 table.

FOOTE, LEONARD J.   See: Meighan, et al.

FORBES, DUNCAN
1959   Life before man: the story of fossils. London: Black, 64 pp., 125
             figs., (elemen. school).

FORBIS, RICHARD G.   See: Wormington and Forbis.

FORD, JOE
1968   Early site in McLean County, Kentucky. Cent. States Archaeol. Jour.,
             15, 12—13, 2 figs.

FORD, NORMAN L.
1966   Fossil owls from the Rexroad fauna of the Upper Pliocene of Kansas.
             Condor, 68, 472—475, 1 fig.

FORD, N. L., and MURRAY, B. G., JR.
1967   Fossil owls from the Hagerman local fauna (Upper Pliocene) of Idaho.
             Auk, 84, 115—117, 1 fig., 1 table.

FORD, RICHARD
1967   Hampshire's age of crocodiles. Illustr. London News, 250:6660, 18—21,
             illustr.

FORD, T. D.
1964   A new fish bed in the Carboniferous limestone of Derbyshire. Mercian
             Geologist, 1, 3—9, (not seen).

FORMOZOV, A. A.
1956B.   [Exploration of a buried cave in Crimea.] Priroda, 1956:7, 102—104,
             3 figs., (Russian).

1957C.	[Can the Stone Age tools serve as ethnic characteristics?] Sov. Arkheol., 1957:4, 66—74, (Russian).
1958C.	[About the "Kapsian character" of the Paleolithic in the Caucasus.] Krat. Soob. Inst. Etnogr. SSSR, 30, 159—165, (Russian).
1959A.	[Investigations of the Stone Age in the Crimea in 1956.] Krat. Soob. Inst. Mat. Kult., 73, 39—47, 4 figs., (Russian).
1959B.	[Ethno-cultural provinces on the territory of the European part of USSR in the Stone Age.] Moscow: Akad. Nauk SSSR Press, 126 pp., 21 figs., (Russian).
1959C.	[Sergeĭ Nikolaevich Zamiatnin (4-21-1899 — 11-5-1958).] Sov. Arkheol., 1959:2, 143—147, portr., (Russian).
1960	[Investigations of Stone Age relics in the northern Caucasus in 1957.] Krat. Soob. Inst. Ist. Mat. Kult. SSSR, 78, 3 figs., (Russian).
1961	[The image of man in the prehistoric art on the territory of USSR.] Vest. Ist. Mir. Kult., 1961:6, 103—112, (Russian; French summary).
1962	[Relative chronology of Ancient Paleolithic in the Kuban' region.] Sov. Arkheol., 1962:4, 17—27, 5 figs., 1 table, (Russian).
1964	[Paleolithic sites in the caves of the Kuban' region.] Krat. Soob. Inst. Ist. Mat. Kult. SSSR, 98, 9—17, 3 figs., (Russian).
1965A.	[Stone Age and Eneolithic of Kuban' region.] Moscow; "Nauka" Press, 160 pp., 66 figs., 2 tables, (Russian).
1965B.	[60 years of Georgiĭ Franfsevich Debefs.] Sov. Arkheol., 1965:4, 242—244, portr., (Russian).
1967	[M. M. Gerasimov's 60 years.] Sov. Archeol., 1967:3, 212—214, portr., (Russian).
	See: Gvozdover and Formozov; Nasedkin and Formozov.

FOROVA, V. S.   See: Cherdynfsev, Alekseev, et al.

FORSTEN, A. M.

1968	Revision of the Palearctic Hipparion. Acta Zool. Fenn., 119, 134 pp., 42 figs., 4 pls., 27 tables. Rev.: Thenius in Zbl. Geol. Pal., Teil 2, 1969:6, 518.

FOSBROOKE, JOHN

1820	Geological description of the hills which pursue the course of the Wye, from Ross to Chepstow, with remarks upon the characteristics of the Herefordshire formations, and an outline of the stratifications of the Forest of Dean, and the opposite shores of the Severn. Quart. Jour. Sci. Lit. Arts, 9, 35—48.

FOSTER, HELEN L.   See: Whitmore and Foster.

FOSTER, I. L., and DANIEL, G.

1965	(eds.) Prehistoric and early Wales. New York: Humanities Press; London: Routledge and Kegan Paul, xii + 256 pp., 27 figs., 27 pls. Rev.: Hencken in Science, 151, 681; Rodden in Amer. Anthrop., 68, 1572.

FOSTOR, J. BRISTOL

1965	The evolution of the mammals of the Queen Charlotte Islands, British Columbia. Occ. Pap., Brit. Columbia Provincial Mus., no. 14, 130 pp., 13 figs., 2 tables.

FOTHERGILL, P. G.
Pierre Teilhard de Chardin — some aspects of his thought. Proc., Univ. Newcastle upon Tyne Philos. Soc., 1:3, 24—34.

FOTHERINGHAM, AUGUSTUS C.
1966   Eoörnis pterovelox gobiensis. 6th printing. "London: The Buighleigh Press", 34 pp., 38 figs. 6th printing by James Heath (1666 Willowmont Ave., San Jose, Calif.) and Ellis L. Yochelson (12505 Killian Lane, Bowie, Maryland). $1.10.
Rev.: Whitmore in Jour. Pal., 41, 1302—1303.

FOUQUET, MELLE
1966   Inventaire sommaire des collections préhistoriques présentées au public par la Société Académique de Saint-Quentin (Departement de l'Aisne). Cahiers Archéol. Nord-Est, 9, 12—17, 11 figs.

FOURIE, S.
1968   The jaw articulation of Tritylodontoideus maximus. S. African Jour. Sci., 64, 255—265, 4 figs.

FOWLER, JEAN HODGES
1967   Projectile point with Transitional traits? Jour. Ala. Archeol., 13, 64—65, 2 figs.

FOWLER, M. L.
1959   Summary report of Modoc Rock Shelter 1952, 1953, 1955, 1956. Ill. State Mus. Rept. Invest., no. 8, 72 pp., frontispiece, 20 figs., 19 tables.
1965   10,000 to 2,000 B. C. in central North America. 7th Internat. Congr., Internat. Assoc. Quat. Res., Abs., 1965, 147—148, (abs.).

FOWLER, WILLIAM S.
1964A.   Contributions to the advance of New England archaeology. Bull. Massachusetts Archaeol. Soc., 25, 50—69, 13 figs.
1964B.   Paleo evidence in New England. New World Antiq., 11, 15—19.

FOWLIE, JACK A.
1965   The snakes of Arizona. Their derivation, speciation, distribution, description, and habits. — A study in evolutionary herpeto-zoogeographic phylogenetic ecology. Fallbrook, Calif.: Azúl Quinta Press, 8 + lv + 164 pp., illustr.

FOX, RICHARD C.
1962   Abs.: Huene in Zbl. Geol. Pal., Teil 2, 1964, 168.
1964   The adductor muscles of the jaw in some primitive reptiles. Univ. Kansas Publ. Mus. Nat. Hist., 12:15, 657—680, 11 figs.
1965   Chorda tympani branch of the facial nerve in the middle ear of tetrapods. Univ. Kansas Publ. Mus. Nat. Hist., 17:2, 15—21.

FOX, R. C., and BOWMAN, M. C.
1966   Osteology and relationships of Captorhinus aguti (Cope) (Reptilia: Captorhinomorpha). Univ. Kans. Pal. Contrib., 41, 1—79, 38 figs., 1 table.
Rev.: Huene in Zbl. Geol. Pal., Teil 2, 1967, 509—510.

FOX, WILLIAM, and WELLES, S.
1965   From bones to bodies. First Cadmus ed. Eau Claire, Wisc.: E. M.
            Hale, 118 pp., illustr.

FRADKIN, E. E.
1965   [New Paleolithic materials at the Museum for Anthropology and Ethno-
            graphy of the Acad. Sci. U.S.S.R.] Sovetskaia Etnografiia, 1965:4,
            176—179, (Russian).

FRADKIN, G. S., NAKHABTSEV, Iu. S., and SHCHERBAKOV, O. I.
1967A.   [On the Devonian deposits of the west of Viliui syneclise.] In: Soko-
            lov, B. S., (ed.), 1967, 144—146, (Russian).
1967B.   [On the Lower Carboniferous in the west of Viliui syneclise.] In:
            Sokolov, B. S., (ed.), 1967, 197—198, (Russian).

FRANCH, JOSE ALCINA
1965   Manual de Arqueologia Americana. Madrid: Aguilar, S. A. Press, 821
            pp., 561 figs., 36 maps, 26 tables.
            Rev.: Ford in Amer. Antiq., 32, 245—246; Kidder in Amer. Anthrop.,
            68, 1557—1559; Piña Chan in An. Antropol., Mexico, 4, 221—
            224; Proulx in Amer. Jour. Archaeol., 72:1, 89—90.

FRANCIS, EDWARD HOWEL, and WOODLAND, A. W.
1964   The Carboniferous period. In: Harland, W. B., et al., (eds.), 1964,
            221—232, 1 fig., 2 tables.

FRANCIS, J. C., and MONES, A.
1965A.   Sobre el hallazgo de Cardiatherium talicei n. sp. (Rodentia, Hydrochoeri-
            dae) en la playa de Kiyú, Departamento de San José, República
            Oriental del Uruguay. Kraglieviana, 1:1.
1965B.   Sobre el hallazgo de Kiyutherium orientalis n.g., n. sp. (Rodentia,
            Hydrochoeridae) en la formación Kiyú, de las barrancas de San
            Gregorio, Departamento de San José, República Oriental del
            Uruguay. Kraglieviana, 1:2, 45—52.

FRANCISCOLO, M. E.   See: Bordes, Comas and Franciscolo.

FRANÇOIS, Y.
1967   Structures vertébrales des actinoptérygiens. Collog. Internat. Cent. Nation.
            Recherch. Sci., 163, 155—172, 13 figs., 2 pls., (English summary).

FRANK, HANS   See: Binder, et al.

FRANK, RUBEN M.
1965   A summary of vertebrate paleontology in the caves of Texas. Bull.
            Nat. Spel. Soc., 27, 59—60, (abs.).

FRANKE, HERBERT W.
1962   Rev.: Binder in Mitt. Verband Deutschen Höhlen- und Karstforscher,
            München, 9, 32; Trimmel in Die Höhle, 14, 24; Viete in
            Ber. Geol. Ges. Deutsch. Demokratischen Republ., Sonderheft 2,
            117—120.
1963   Kopie eines Höhlengemäldes aus Altamira in München. Die Höhle, 14,
            21.
1966   Der Mensch stammt doch von Affen ab. München: Kindler Verlag,
            420 pp., 16 figs., (not seen).

Rev.: K. T. in Universum, Natur u. Tech., 1967:4, II.

FRANKFORTER, W. D.
1966   Some recent discoveries of Late Pleistocene fossils in western Michigan.
              Papers Mich. Acad. Sci., 51, 209–220, 2 pls., 2 tables.
              See: Agogino and Frankforter.

FRANKOWSKA-LENARTOWSKA, MARIA   See: Ziółkiewicz, et al.

FRANZ, E.
1967   Tilly Edinger (1897 - 1967). Natur u. Mus., 97, 425–426, portr.

FRANZ, LEONHARD
1965   Aus der Geschichte der Ur- und Frühgeschichtlichen Bodenforschung
              in Österreich. In: Franz, L., and Neumann, A. R., (eds.), 1965,
              209–227.

FRANZ, L., and NEUMANN, A. R., (eds.)
1965   Lexikon ur- und frühgeschichtlicher Fundstätten Österreichs. Wien:
              Verlag Brüder Hollinek, xii + 244 pp.
              Rev.: Fordinal in Die Höhle, 16, 87–88.

FRAZIER, KENNETH
1968   Fossil vertebrates on the Southern California coast. Rocks and Minerals,
              43, 614–615, 2 figs.

FRAZZETTA, THOMAS   See: Estes, et al.

FRECHKOP, SERGE
1964A.   Remarques concernant l'histoire et la génétique du cheval. Bull. Inst.
              Royal Sci. Nat. Belg., 40:13, 33 pp., 19 figs., 2 color pls.
1964B.   Concernant l'histoire et la génétique du cheval. Bull. Soc. Zool.,
              France, 89, 196–201.
1965A.   Notes sur les mammiferes. LI. Remarques au sujet des antilopes
              Tragelaphus et Limnotragus. Bull. Inst. Royal Sci. Nat. Belg.,
              41:10, 11 pp., 3 figs.
1965B.   Notes sur les mammiferes. LII. Au sujet d'un caractère dentaire des
              Cervidés. Bull. Inst. Royal Sci. Nat. Belg., 41:25, 10 pp., 8 figs.,
              2 tables.
1965C.   Au sujet de l'histoire et de la génétique du cheval. Bull. Soc. Roy.
              Belge Anthrop. Préhist., 75, 33–39.
1965D.   La specifite du cheval de Prjewalsky. Bull. Inst. Royal Sci. Nat. Belge,
              41:29, 17 pp., 5 figs., 2 pls., 1 table.
1965E.   Notes sur les mammiferes. LIII. De la main du Koala, Phascolarctos
              cinereus (Goldfuss). Bull. Inst. Royal Sci. Nat. Belge, 41:38,
              3 pp., 1 fig.
1967   La distribution géographique et les nombres spécifiques de chromosomes
              des equidés. Mammalia, 31, 295–299.

FREDERIKS, G. N.
1934C.   [Concerning the article by A. N. Mazarovich "Stratigraphy of conti-
              nental Permian deposits of Volga and Viatka basin".] Biull.
              Mosk. Obshch. Ispyt. Prirody, Otd. Geol., 42, 545–550, (Russian).

FREEDMAN, LEONARD
1965   Fossil and subfossil primates from the limestone deposits at Taung, Bolt's Farm and Witkrans, South Africa. Pal. Africana, 9, 19–48, 15 figs., 4 tables.
1967   Skull and tooth variation in the genus Perameles. Part I: anatomical features. Rec. Austral. Mus. 27, 147–166, 7 figs., 8 pls.

FREEDMAN, L., and JOFFE, A. D.
1967A.   Skull and tooth variation in the genus Perameles. Part 2: metrical features of P. nasuta. Rec. Austral. Mus., 27, 183–195, 1 fig., 4 pls., 7 tables.
1967B.   Skull and tooth variation in the genus Perameles. Part 3: metrical features of P. gunnii and P. bougainville. Rec. Austral. Mus., 27, 197–212, 3 pls., 10 tables.

FREEMAN, LESLIE   See: Clark, J. D., Ascher, Freeman, et al.

FREEMAN, L. G., JR.
1965   The Middle Acheulean station of Torralba (Spain): a progress report. 7th Internat. Congr., Internat. Assoc. Quat. Res., Abs., 1965, 149, (abs.).
1966   The nature of Mousterian facies in Cantabrian Spain. In: Clark, J. D., and Howell, F. C., (eds.), 1966A, 230–237.

FREEMAN, L. G., JR., and BUTZER, K. W.
1966   The Acheulean station of Torralba (Spain): a progress report. Quaternaria, 8, 9–21, 1 fig., (German and French summaries).

FREEMAN, R. B.
1965   The works of Charles Darwin. An annotated bibliographical handlist. London: Dawsons of Pall Mall, x + 81 pp., frontispiece, illustr. Rev.: de Beer in Ann. Sci., 20, 243.

FREISING, HANS
1962   Neues zur Altsteinzeit Nordwürttembergs. Fundber. Schwaben, 16, 12–21, 7 figs.

FREĬZON, V. M.   See: Mazarovich, O. A., et al.

FRESNE, G.
1963   Höhle von Lascaux schon geschlossen. Kölnische Rundschau, no. 92, 20, (not seen).

FREUDENTHAL, M.
1963B.   Entwicklungsstufen der miozänen Cricetodontinae (Mammalia, Rodentia) Mittelspaniens und ihre stratigraphische Bedeutung. [Same as Freudenthal 1963A.] Wageningen: Ponsen & Looijen Ed., 107 pp., 38 figs., 1 pl., (English and French summaries).
1965   Betrachtungen über die Gattung Cricetodon. Proc. K. Nederl. Akad. Wet., Ser. B, 68, 293–305, 3 figs.
1966   On the mammalian fauna of the Hipparion-beds in the Calatayud-Teruel Basin (prov. Zaragoza, Spain). Part I. The genera Cricetodon and Ruscinomys (Rodentia). Proc. K. Nederl. Akad. Wet., Ser. B, 69, 296–317, 5 figs., 2 pls.

1967 On the mammalian fauna of the Hipparion-beds in the Calatayud-Teruel
     Basin. III. Democricetodon and Rotundomys (Rodentia). Proc.
     K. Nederl. Akad. Wet., Ser. B, 70, 298—315, 4 figs., 2 pls.

1968 On the mammalian fauna of the Hipparion-beds in the Calatayud-Teruel
     Basin. IV. The genus Megacricetodon (Rodentia). Proc. K.
     Nederl. Akad. Wet., Ser. B, 71:1, 57—72, 3 figs., 1 pl.

    See: Crusafont Pairó 1965M.

FREUDENTHAL, M., and SONDAAR, P. Y.
1964 Les faunes à Hipparion des environs de Daroca (Espagne) et leur valeur
     pour la stratigraphie du néogene de l'Europe. Proc. K. Nederl.
     Akad. Wet., Ser. B, 67, 473—490, 2 figs.

    Rev.: Crusafont-Pairó in Proc. K. Nederl. Akad. Wet., Ser. B, 68, 121—
      126, 1 fig.

FREUND, GISELA
1956B. Probleme des Paläolithikums in Jugoslawien. Mem. Serv. Invest. Arqueol.
     Asturias, 1, 65—94, 2 figs., 2 pls., (Spanish summary).
1960A. Rev.: Monreal Agustí in Ampurias, 24, 359—361.
1963C. Die ältere und mittlere Steinzeit in Bayern. Jahresb. Bayer. Boden-
     denkmalpflege, 4, 84 pp.

    Rev.: Klima in Quartär, 17, 220—222.
1965 Die Exkursion der Hugo Obermaier-Gesellschaft 1963 in die Provence.
     Quartär, 15—16, 177—182, pl. 9.

FREUND, G., and NABER, F. B.
1965 Die 10. Tagung der Hugo Obermaier-Gesellschaft 1964 in Säckingen
     mit Exkursionen ins Hoch- und Oberrheingebiet Sowie ins Birstal.
     Quartär, 15—16, 183—206.

FREUND, RUDOLF See: Huxley, T. H. 1967.

FREY, DAVID G.
1964 Remains of animals in Quaternary lake and bog sediments and their
     interpretation. Ergebn. Limnologie, 2, 114 pp., 2 pls.

    Rev.: Feyling-Hanssen in Norsk Geol. Tidsskrift, 45, 361; Livingstone
      in Ecology, 46, 216; Pennak in Amer. Mid. Nat., 73, 506;
      Swain in Jour. Pal., 39, 298—301.

    See: Wright, H. E. and Frey.

FREYBERG, BRUNO
1964 Zur Archaeopteryx — Bibliographie. Geol. Bl. No-Bayern, 14:3, p. 122—3,
     (German).
1965 Die Keupersammlung Kehl. Geol. Bl. No-Bayern, 15:3, p. 151—166,
     12 pls., (German).

FREYTAG, I. B.
1964 Reptilian vertebral remnants from Lower Cretaceous strata near Ood-
     nadatta. Quart. Geol. Notes, Geol. Surv. S. Austral., no. 10,
     1—2, 2 figs.

FREYTET, PIERRE
1965 Données nouvelles sur l'âge des Grès à Reptiles de St.-Chinian (Hérault).
     C. R. Soc. Geol. France, 1965, 127—128.

FRIANT, MADELEINE
1962D.   De l'évolution des molaires chez les ruminants. (Ongulés artiodactyles
          sélénodontes.) Bull., Groupement Internat. Recherch. Sci.
          Stomat., 5, 108—117, 4 figs.
1962E.   Sur les dents tubulées des mammifères. Bull., Groupement Internat.
          Recherch. Sci. Stomat., 5, 379—390, 7 figs., (English and German
          summaries).
1963C.   Le Rhinocéros (Tichorhinus) antiquitatis Blum. Recherches anatomiques
          sur la tête osseuse et la dentition. Ann. Soc. Geol. Nord, 83,
          15—21, 3 figs., 2 pls., (English summary).
1963D.   Le Trechomys, rongeur de l'Eocène Supérieur d'Europe. Caractéristiques
          de ses dents jugales. Bull. Groupement Internat. Recherch. Sci.
          Stomatol., 6, 43—58, 15 figs., (English, German and Spanish sum-
          maries).
1964A.   A propos de l'Haramyia, l'un des plus anciens mammiferes. Bull. Group-
          ement Internat. Recherch. Sci. Stomatol., 7, 265—271, 3 figs.,
          (English and German summaries).
1964B.   An European Castor of the Quaternary era, Castor plicidens F. Maj.
          Jour. Pal. Soc. India, 4, 75—77, 2 figs., 1 table.
1964C.   La régression des molaires temporaires chez les Musaraignes (Soricidae)
          d'Europe. Rev. Mens. Suisse Odonto-stomatol., 74, 1109—1115,
          (not seen).
1965A.   Sur les molaires temporaires des Soricidae (Musaraignes). Acta Anat.,
          60, 277—284, 4 figs., (English and German summaries).
1965B.   Sur les dents jugales du Dendrohyrax (Daman). Acta Zool., 46, 109—
          117, 3 figs., (English summary).
1966A.   Vue d'ensemble sur l'évolution du "Cartilage de Meckel" de quelques
          groupes de mammifères. Acta Zool., 47, 67—80, 8 figs., (En-
          glish summary).
1966B.   A propos des dents jugales d'un rongeur africain, le Thryonomys. Ann.
          Soc. Roy. Zool. Belg., 95, 97—104, 3 figs., (English summary).
1967   La morphologie des molaires chez les ruminants (Ongulés. artiodactyles
          sélénodontes) d'Europe. Son évolution phylogénique. Acta Zool.,
          48, 87—101, 11 figs., (English summary).

FRICK, CHILDS, and TAYLOR, B. E.
1968   A generic review of the stenomyline camels. Amer. Mus. Novit., 2353,
          1—51, 15 figs., 7 tables.

FRICK, HANS
1965   Probleme und Ergebnisse der vergleichenden Anatomie heute. Naturwiss.
          Rund., 18, 227—237, 14 figs.
          See: Ax, 1964.

FRIDENBERG, E. O.
1966   [Cave deposits of the southern slopes of northwestern Caucasus.] Biull.
          Mosk. Obshch. Ispyt. Prirody, Otd. geol., 41:5, 153—156, (Rus-
          sian).
          See: Autlev, et al.

FRIDRICH, J.
1961   Station paléolithique près de Lužná en Bohême. Archeol. Roz., 13,
          153—161, figs. 72—73, (Czech; French summary).
1964   Die Abbildung eines Fisches in der paläolithischen Kunst der böhmischen
          Länder. Archeol. Roz., 16, 716—738, 741, figs. 218—223, (Czech;
          German summary).

1965   Die paläolithische Fundstelle in Lužná — Krásná dolina. Archeol. Roz.,
         17, 25—31, figs. 17—18, (Czech; German summary).
1966   Ein Faustkeilfund in Mutějovice, Kr. Rakovník. Archeol. Roz., 18,
         189—193, figs. 72—74, (Czech; German summary).
1968   [Late Paleolithic site at Mutějovice (Lok. 30), Rakovník district.]
         Archeol. Roz., 20:4, 417—429, 8 figs., 1 table, (Czech; German
         summary).

FRIDRICH, J., KLIMA, B., and VALOCH, K.
1968   [Systematics of the concept "culture" in Paleolithic.]   Archeol. Roz.,
         20:3, 308—311, 1 fig., (Czech; German summary).

FRIDRICH, J., and SKLENAŘ, K.
1966   [Isolated finds of Middle Paleolithic tools in the Mělník region.]   Archeol.
         Roz., 18:5, 581—584, 4 figs., (Czech; French summary).

FRIEDLANDER, JONATHAN S.   See: Bailit and Friedlander.

FRIEDMANN, HERBERT
1965A.   Changes in the Los Angeles County Museum. Curator, 8, 269—286,
         17 figs.
1965B.   The little known research associates. Quart. Los Angeles Co. Mus. Nat.
         Hist., 3:3, 16—19, illustr.

FRIEND, JAMES P.   See: Walton, A., Trautman and Friend.

FRIEND, PETER FURNEAUX, and HOUSE, M. R.
1964   The Devonian period. In: Harland, W. B., et al., (eds.), 1964, 233—
         236, 1 fig., 1 table.

FRISCH, JOHN ERNEST
1965   Trends in the evolution of the hominoid dentition. Bibliotheca Pri-
         matologica, 3, 130 pp., 27 figs., 35 tables.
         Rev.: Brace in Human Biol., 37, 327—330;   Firbas in Mitt. Anthrop.
         Ges. Wien, 96—97, 354;   Haltenorth in Säugetierkundl. Mitt.,
         14, 148;   Hanihara in Jour. Anthrop. Soc. Nippon, 72, 174—175,
         (Japanese);   Knussmann in Homo, 17:2, 121;   Krogman in
         Amer. Jour. Phys. Anthrop., 23, 201—202;   Stęślicka in Przeglad.
         Zool., 12:1, 117—118, (Polish);   Turner in Amer. Anthrop., 67,
         1343—1344;   Welsch in Anthrop. Anz., 30, 74—75.

FRIZZELL, DON L.
1965A.   Otoliths of new fish (Vorhisia vulpes, n. gen., n. sp., Siluroidei?) from
         Upper Cretaceous of South Dakota. Copeia, 1965, 178—181,
         3 figs.
         Abs.: Weiler in Zbl. Geol. Pal., Teil 2, 1966, 277.
1965B.   Otoliths. In: Kummel and Raup, (eds.), 1965, 125—127.
1965C.   Otolith-based genera and lineages of fossil bonefishes (Clupeiformes,
         Albulidae). Senck. Lethaca, 46a, 85—110, 2 figs., pl. 4.
         Abs.: Weiler in Zbl. Geol. Pal., Teil 2, 1966, 276—277.

FRIZZELL, D. L., and DANTE, J. H.
1965   Otoliths of some Early Cenozoic fishes of the Gulf Coast. Jour. Pal.,
         39, 687—718, 2 figs., pls. 86—88.
         Abs.: Weiler in Zbl. Geol. Pal., Teil 2, 1966, 275—276.

FRIZZELL, D. L., and LAMBER, C. KURT
    1962A.   Abs.: Weiler in Zbl. Geol. Pal., Teil 2, 1964, 150.
    1962B.   New genera and species of Lower Cenozoic otoliths allied to Myripristis
               (Pisces, Beryciformes, Holocentridae). Bol. Soc. Geol. Peru, 38,
               147–148, (Spanish).

FROLOV, B. A.
    1965   [Use of numeration in the Paleolithic and the problem of the origin of
               mathematics.] Izv. Sib. Otd. Akad. Nauk SSSR, Ser. Obshch.
               Nauk, 3:9, 97–104, 6 figs., (Russian).
    1966A.   [Numeration in the life of Late Paleolithic man.] Biull. Mosk. Obshch.
               Ispyt. Prirody, otd. biol., 71:5, 157–158, (Russian).
    1966B.   [Foreign literature on the contents of Paleolithic art (1952–1964).]
               Sov. Arkheol., 1966:1, 297–305, (Russian).

FROST, BRUNO H.
    1956   A child's book of prehistoric animals. Text by John H. Ostrom. New
               York: Maxton Publ., 29 pp., color illustr., (pre-and elemen.
               school).

FROST, HAROLD M.
    1964   (ed.) Bone biodynamics. Boston: Little, Brown, xvi + 687 pp., illustr.
               Henry Ford Hospital Internat. Symposium, Detroit, Mich., March
               20–22, 1963.
    1966A.   Morphometry of bone in palaeopathology. In: Jarcho, S., (ed.), 1966,
               131–150, 9 figs.
    1966B.   The bone dynamics in osteoporosis and osteomalacia. Springfield, Ill.:
               Chas. C. Thomas, xv + 176 pp., (not seen).
               Rev.: Angel in Amer. Jour. Phys. Anthrop., 27, 223–224.

FROST, S. H. See: Langenheim, et al.

FROST, WINIFRED See: Pennington and Frost.

FRY, WILLIAM G.
    1965   Methods in taxonomy. Nature, 207, 245–246.

FRYE, JOHN C. See: Munson and Frye.

FRYXELL, ROALD
    1962   Early or pre-Wisconsin mammoth remains from the "Palouse Loess"
               near St. John, Washington. Rept. Invest., Wash. State Univ.,
               Lab. Anthrop., no. 17, (abs.), (not seen).

FRYXELL, R., and DAUGHERTY, R. D.
    1963   Late glacial and post glacial geological and archaeological chronology
               of the Columbia Plateau, Washington: an interim report to the
               National Science Foundation. Rept. Invest., Wash. State Univ.,
               Lab. Anthrop., no. 23, (not seen).

FUCHS, HERMAN
    1966   [New remains of Myliobatis from Eocene of Cluj environs.] Studia
               Univ. Babeş-Bolyai, ser. geol.-geogr., 11:1, 109–113, 8 figs.,
               (Rumanian; Russian and French summaries).

FUCHS, STEPHEN
1963   The origin of man and his culture. Bombay, London, New York:
              Asia Publishing House, vi + 300 pp.
              Rev.: Anon. in Discovery, 25:2, 46—47;   Befu in Amer. Anthrop.,
              67, 170—171;   Bouteiller in L'Anthrop., 68, 622—623;   Kant
              in E. Anthrop., 17, 64—65;   Kurth in Homo, 16, 121;   Sauter
              in Arch. Suiss. Anthrop. Gén., 29, 81.

FUCHS, YVES See: Ellenberger, F. and Fuchs.

FUENTES, VIDARTE CAROLINA
1966   Estudio de dos cráneos de Elephas meridionalis Nesti, de la Vega de
              Granada. Bol. R. Soc. Españ. Hist. Nat., Sec. Biol., 64:3, 277—
              313, 16 figs., 5 tables, (English summary).

FUHN, J. E., and VANCEA, S.
1961   [Die Fauna der rumänischen Volksrepublik. Reptilia. XIV. Eidechsen.
              Schlangen.] Bucuresti: Acad. Rep. Popul. Romin., 352 pp.,
              (Rumanian, not seen).

FUJIWARA, TAKAYO
1962   Palaeobiochemical studies on the organic substance remaining in various
              sorts of fossils. Misc. Rept. Res. Inst. Nat. Res., Tokyo, 58—59,
              139—149, 3 tables.

FUJIYAMA, CHIKAKO   See: Yamasaki, et al.

FULLER, W. A., and BAYROCK, L. A.
1965   Late Pleistocene mammals from Central Alberta, Canada. Vert. Pal. in
              Alberta, Univ. of Alberta, 1965, 53—63, figs. 14—19, 4 tables.

FUNK, ROBERT E.
1967   A Paleo-Indian site in the Hudson Valley. Bull. Eastern States Archeol.
              Fed., no. 26, 9—10, (abs.).

FUNK, R. E., and JOHNSON, R. A.
1964   A probable Paleo-Indian component in Greene County, New York. Penn.
              Archaeol., 34, 43—46, 1 pl.

FUNNELL, BRIAN MICHAEL
1964   The Tertiary period. In: Harland, W. B., et al., (eds.), 1964, 179—191,
              3 tables.
              See: Cutbill and Funnell.

FÜRER-HAIMENDORF, ELIZABETH VON
1964   An anthropological bibliography of South Asia, together with a directory
              of anthropological field research. Vol. II, 1955—59. Paris and
              The Hague: Mouton, 459 pp.
              Rev.: McCormack in Amer. Anthrop., 68, 567—568.

FURON, RAYMOND
1959   Rev.: Patrizi in Boll. Soc. Geog. Ital., ser. 9, 2, 515—517.
1963   Rev.: W. J. P. in Liverpool and Manchester Geol. Jour., 4:1, vi—vii.
1966   Manuel de préhistoire générals. Paris: Payot, 498 pp., 161 figs., 6
              tables, (not seen).

Rev.: Jovet in Rev. Gen. Sci., <u>74</u>, 58—59.

FUSSI, FERDINANDO
1962   Il metodo del fluoro applicato all'indagine di reperti paletnologici. Rass.
              speleol. italiana, <u>14</u>, 49—51.

FUSSI, FERNANDO, and FIDELI, G. F.
1967   Metodi di indagine della quota proteica nei reperti fossili. Atti Soc.
              Ital. Mus. Civico Milano, <u>106</u>:2, 158—166, (English summary).

FUSTE, MIGUEL
1966   Los Australopithecinos, un grupo de primates fosiles. Zoo, no. <u>5</u>, 13—15,
              illustr.

FYLES, J. G. See: Dyck, Fyles and Blake.

GABASHVILI, E. G.   See: Burchak-Abramovich, N. I. and Gabashvili; Burchak-
              Abramovich, N. O. and Gabashvili.

GABASHVILI, E. G., and GABUNIĨA, L. K.
1958   [On remains of <u>Dinotherium</u> from Udabno (East Georgia).]   Soob. Akad.
              Nauk Gruz. SSR, <u>21</u>, 151—154, 3 figs., (Russian).

GABE, M.
1967   Le squelette. Cartilage, tissu osseux et ostéogenèse. In: Grasse, (ed.),
              1967, Traite de Zool., <u>16</u>:1, 235—333, figs. 107—146, 4 tables.

GABEL, CREIGHTON
1964A.   (ed.) Man before history. Englewood Cliffs, N. J.: Prentice-Hall, vi +
              184 pp., 1 fig.
              Rev.: Cole in Man, <u>65</u>, 163;   Griffin in Amer. Antiq., <u>31</u>, 763;   Rouse
              in Amer. Anthrop., <u>67</u>, 1048—1049.
1964B.   The study of prehistoric man. In: Gabel, Creighton, (ed.), 1964A,
              1—10.
1965   African prehistory. In: Siegel, B. J., (ed.), 1965, 40—83.
1967A.   Analysis of prehistoric economic patterns. New York, etc.: Holt, Rine-
              hart and Winston, viii + 69 pp., 3 tables.
              Rev.: Fagan in Man, Jour. Roy. Anthrop. Inst., <u>2</u>, 468;   Renfrew in
              Antiq., <u>41</u>, 328—329.
1967B.   Archaeology in the western Copperbelt. S. Afr. Archaeol. Bull., <u>22</u>,
              3—14, 5 figs.

GABIE, VIVIAN
1965   The origin of mammals. S. African Jour. Sci., <u>61</u>, 37—42, 1 fig.

GABIS, RENEE V.
1964   Capacite cranienne relative des singes cynomorphes. C. R. Acad. Sci.
              Paris, <u>258</u>, 3530—3532, 1 fig.

GABORI, MIKLOS
1960   Rev.: Kozlowski in L'Anthrop., <u>68</u>, 145—146.

1960B.   Compte rendu d'un voyage d'étude en Mongolie. Archaeol. Ért., <u>87</u>,
           83–86, 2 figs., (Hungarian; French summary).
1962B.   Compte rendu de mon voyage en Mongolie en 1961. Archaeol. Ért.,
           <u>89</u>, 101–108, 7 figs., (Hungarian).
1963   Rev.: Vaufrey in L'Anthrop., <u>69</u>, 313–314.
1964A.   Beiträge zum Paläolithikum des Donauknie-Gebietes. Acta Archaeol.
           Hung., <u>16</u>, 171–186, 6 figs.
1964B.   New data on Palaeolithic finds in Mongolia. Asian Perspectives, <u>7</u>, 105–
           112, 1 fig.
1964C.   A késöi Paleolitikum Magyarországon. Régészeti Tanulmányok, Akad.
           Kiadó, Budapest, <u>3</u>, 85 pp., 19 pls., (not seen).
           Rev.: Bánesz in Sloven. Archeol., <u>13</u>, 250–252, (Czech); E. in Föld.
           Közlöny, <u>95</u>, 103–104.
1965   Der zweite paläolithische Hausgrundriss von Ságvár. Acta Archaeol.
           Hung., <u>17</u>, 111–127, 3 figs., 4 pls.

GÁBORINÉ CSÁNK, VERONIKA
1960   La détermination de l'âge absolu de la station de Ságvár. Archaeol.
           Ért., <u>87</u>, 125–129, 1 fig., (Hungarian; French summary).

GABUNIĨA, LEO K. (= Gabounia, Léo)
1954B.   [On Hipparion fauna from Arkneti.] Nauchn. Sess. Inst. Paleobiol. AN
           Gruz. SSR, <u>1</u>, 28, (Georgian and Russian).
1954C.   [On the problem of progressive evolution in the phylogenesis of mam-
           mals.] Trudy Inst. Paleobiol. Akad. Nauk Gruz, SSR, <u>2</u>, 137–157,
           7 figs., (Russian; Georgian summary).
1955G.   [Oligocene fauna of terrestrial vertebrates from Benara (southern Georgia).]
           Nauchn. Sess. Inst. Paleobiol. AN Gruz. SSR, <u>2</u>, 27–29, (Russian).
1956E.   [Significance of fossil remains of mammals for parallelization of con-
           tinental Neogene deposits.] Nauchn. Sess. Inst. Paleobiol. AN
           Gruz. SSR, <u>3</u>, 23–28, 1 table, (Russian).
1958E.   [Dinosaur tracks.] Moscow: Akad. Nauk SSSR Press, 72 pp., 19 figs.,
           (Russian).
1958F.   [On the problem of the limit between Miocene and Pliocene.] Nauchn.
           Sess. Inst. Paleobiol. AN Gruz. SSR, <u>6</u>, 3–4, (Russian).
1959C.   [On the horse from Sagvardzhile (West Georgia).] In: Gamkrelidze,
           (ed.), 1959, 263–271, 6 figs., 8 tables, (Russian).
1959D.   [First finding of a listriodon in the Miocene of USSR.] Soob. Akad.
           Nauk Gruz. SSR, <u>22</u>, 55–56, (Russian).
1961B.   [On the problem of origin and territorial expansion of anthracothes
           (family Anthracotheriidae).] Nauchn. Sess. Inst. Paleobiol. AN
           Gruz. SSR, <u>7</u>, 8–10, (Georgian and Russian).
1961C.   [Obailian fauna – the most ancient complex of fossil mammals in the
           USSR.] Soob. Akad. Nauk Gruzinskoi SSR, <u>27</u>:6, 711–713,
           2 figs., (Russian).
1962C.   [Oligocene landscape and climate in southern Georgia (mainly according
           to terrestrial vertebrates).] Nauchn. Sess. Inst. Paleobiol. AN
           Gruz. SSR, <u>8</u>, 14–15, (Russian).
1963   [Extinction of dinosaurs.] Nauchn. Sess. Inst. Paleobiol. AN Gruz.
           SSR, <u>9</u>, 7–8, (Russian).
1964A.   A propos de la correlation des faunes à Hipparion des régions méditer-
           ranéenne et ponto-caspienne. Cursillos y Confer. Inst. "Lucas
           Mallada", <u>9</u>, 187–189, 1 table.
1964B.   Sur la corrélation des faunes de mammifères de l'Oligocène d'Europe
           et d'Asie. Mém. Bur. Rech. Géol. Min., <u>28</u>:2, 979–983, 1 table.

1964C.   [Evolutionary progress in the history of mammals.]   Nauchn. Sess.
             Inst. Paleobiol. AN Gruz. SSR, 10, 21–23, (Georgian and Rus-
             sian).
1964D.   [Benara fauna of Oligocene vertebrates.]   Tbilisi: "Metsniereba" Press,
             267 pp., 94 figs., 12 plates, 23 tables, (Russian; French and
             Georgian summaries).
1966A.   Sur les mammifères oligocènes du Caucase. Bull. Soc. Géol. France,
             8, 857–869, 11 figs.
1966B.   Sur les Mammifères oligocènes du Caucase. C. R. Soc. Géol. France,
             1966, 372, (abs.).
1966C.   [On the age of continental deposits of Iagludzha mountain.]   Soob.
             Akad. Nauk Gruz. SSR, 43:1, 129–132, 1 fig., (Georgian; Rus-
             sian summary).
1967   Sur un lophiodontide de Hoogbutsel et de Hoeleden. Bull. Inst. Royal
             Sci. Nat. Belg., 43:5, 1–7, 1 pl.
             See: Gabashvili and Gabuniia.

GABUNIIA, L. K., and BELIAEVA, E. I.
1964   [On a representative of Anchitheriinae from Oligocene of Kazakhstan.]
             Soob. Akad. Nauk Gruz. SSR, 35:1, 125–132, 6 figs., 1 table,
             (Russian; Georgian summary).

GABUNIIA, L. K., and MELADZE, G. K.
1965   [Intraspecific variations of Hipparion.]   Nauchn. Sess. Inst. Paleobiol.
             AN Gruz. SSR, 11, 20–21, (Georgian and Russian).

GABUNIIA, L. K., and RUBINSHTEIN, M. M.
1964   [On the correlation of Neogene and Late Paleogene deposits of the
             Old and New Worlds (according to data on fossil mammals and
             absolute age).] In: Tsagareli, (ed.), 1964, 331–337, 1 table,
             (Russian; English summary).

GABUNIIA, L. K., and TROFIMOV, B. A.
1964   [Connections between Tertiary mammals of Europe and Asia.]   In:
             Orlov, (ed.), 1964C, 7–13, (Russian; English summary).

GABUNIIA, L. K., and VEKUA, A. K.
1963   [Fossil elephant from Taribana.]   Tbilisi: Ac. Sci. Press, 69 pp., 14
             figs., 6 pls., (Georgian; Russian and French summaries).
1966A.   [A peculiar representative of damans from East Georgian Upper Pliocene.]
             Soob. Akad. Nauk Gruz. SSR, 42:3, 643–647, 3 figs., (Georgian;
             Russian summary).
1966B.   [Fossil daman in Akchagylian of Eastern Georgia.]   In: Davitashvili,
             (ed.), 1966B, 93–100, 4 figs., (Russian; Georgic summary).
1966C.   [On the new find of southern elephant in the North Caucasus.]   In:
             Davitashvili, (ed.), 1966B, 101–103, 1 fig., (Russian; Georgic
             summary).

GADOMSKA, STEFANIA   See: Domoslawska-Baraniecka and Gadomska.

GADZHIEV, D. V.
1957   [Small antelope (Gazella sp.) in the Eldar hipparion faunal complex.]
             Dokl. Akad. Nauk Azerbaid. SSR, 13:11, 1177–1182, 1 fig.,
             1 table, (Russian; Azerbaidzhani summary).

1959   [New materials on El'dar Hipparion fauna.]   Izv. Akad. Nauk Azer-
            baĭdzhan. SSR, Ser. Geol.-Geogr. Nauk, 1959:4, 55—66, (Rus-
            sian; Azerbaijanian summary).
            See: Burchak-Abramovich, N. I. and Gadzhiev; Gadzhiev, G. V. and
            Gadzhiev.

GADZHIEV, D. V., and ALIEV, S. D.
    1965   [Remains of gigantic deer in Azerbaijan.]   Uch. zapiski Azerb. med.
                inst., 17, 43—62, (Russian).
    1966   [Fossil remains of Chiroptera from Taglar cave.]   Uch. zapiski Azerb.
                med. inst., 19, 17—23, (Russian).

GADZHIEV, G. V., and GADZHIEV, D. V.
    1954   [Deforming spondylitis in fossil Quaternary wolf.]   Dokl. Akad. Nauk
                Azerbaĭd. SSR, 10, 183—187, 2 figs., (Russian; Azerbaidjan
                summary).

GAGE, CARL   See: Wade, et al.

GAGLIANO, SHERWOOD M.
    1964A.   A preliminary report on the archaeology of Avery Island. Bull. South-
                east. Archaeol. Confer., 1, 12—13, 2 figs.
    1964B.   Post-Pleistocene occupations of southeastern Louisiana terrace lands.
                Bull. Southeast. Archaeol. Confer., 1, 18—26.

GAGLIANO, S., GREGORY, P., and WEBB, C. H.
    1965   The Paleo-Indian era: distribution of finds. Louisiana. Bull. South-
                east Archaeol. Confer., 2, 1—6.

GAGNIÈRE, SYLVAIN   See: Lumley, Gagnière and Pascal.

GAHERTY, GEOFFREY
    1968   Human skeletal material and its analysis. W. Afr. Archaeol. Newsletter,
                no. 8, 21—23, (French summary).

GAIDUK, I. M.   See: Adamenko and Gaiduk.

GAILLI, RENÉ, ROBERT, R., BELTRAN, A., and NOUGIER, L.-R.
    1966   Nouvelles découvertes d'art pariétal magdalénien dans la grotte de
                Bédeilhac: "Le diverticule aux bisons". Préhist. Spéléol. Arié-
                geoises, 21, 19—26, 6 figs.

GAINES, JOSEPH J.
    1955   Stalling's Island components on the upper Savannah and Broad Rivers.
                Bull. Georgia Acad. Sci., 13:2, 53.

GALABALA, R. O.
    1967   [On the glaciation on the right bank of the lower Lena R. course.]
                Izv. Vyssh. Uch. Zav., Geol. i Razv., 1967:12, 23—29, 3 figs.,
                (Russian).

GALABALA, R. O., and LEONOV, B. N.
    1967   [Stratigraphy of Quaternary deposits in the lower course of Lena R.]
                In: Collected Papers, 1967D, [Stratigraphy of the Mesozoic
                and Cenozoic of Middle Siberia], 177—183, (Russian).

GALBREATH, EDWIN C.
1962B.   Abs.: Westphal in Zbl. Geol. Pal., Teil 2, 1964, 199.
1962C.   Abs.: Westphal in Zbl. Geol. Pal., Teil 2, 1964, 190.
1964A.   A dire wolf skeleton and Powder Mill Creek Cave, Missouri. Trans. Ill. Acad. Sci., 57:4, 224—242, 4 figs., 3 tables.
            Abs.: Anon. in Internat. Jour. Spel., 2:3, 23.
1964B.   A corvid from the Miocene of Colorado. Trans. Ill. Acad. Sci., 57:4, 282.
1966   A record of Democricetodon (Order Rodentia) from the Late Tertiary of northeastern Colorado. Trans. Ill. Acad. Sci., 59, 212—213, 1 fig., 1 table.
1967A.   A skeleton of the geomyoid rodent, Gregorymys curtus (Matthew) from the Early Miocene of South Dakota. Trans. Ill. Acad. Sci., 60, 272—281, 1 fig., 1 table.
1967B.   An aid for drawing small objects. Trans. Ill. Acad. Sci., 60, 322—323, 1 fig.
1967C.   A large Bison occidentalis from South Dakota. Trans. Ill. Acad. Sci., 60, 436—437, 1 fig., 1 table.

GALBREATH, E. C., and STEIN, H.
1962   Abs.: Westphal in Zbl. Geol. Pal., Teil 2, 1964, 205.

GÁLGANO, MARIO
1963   Gioacchino Leo Sera. Arch. Antrop. Etnol., 93:2, 7—25, portr.

GALIBERTI, ATTILIO
1964   Giacimenti preistorici all'aperto sul promontorio di Piombino. Atti Soc. Toscana Sci. Nat. Mem., Ser. A, 71, 17—32, 7 figs.

GALLAY, ALAIN
1965   Inventaria Archaeologica Africana. Arch. Suiss. Anthrop. Gen., 30, 85.

GALLOWAY, ALEXANDER
1959   The skeletal remains of Bambandyanalo. Foreword by R. A. Dart. Johannesburg: Witwatersrand Univ. Press, xxii + 154 pp., 46 figs., 24 tables.

GALLOWAY, E.   See: Agogina and Galloway.

GAL'TSEV-BEZIÛK, S. D.
1964   [On connection between Sakhalin, the continent, and Hokkaido I. during the Quaternary time.] Izv. Akad. Nauk, Ser. Geograf., 1964:1, 56—62, (Russian).

GALUSHA, M. J.   See: Stucker, Galusha and McKenna.

GALUSHA, TED
1966   The Zia Sand formation, new Early to Medial Miocene beds in New Mexico. Amer. Mus. Novit., no. 2271, 12 pp., 4 figs.

GAMBAROV, K. M.   See: Burchak-Abramovich, N. I. and Gambarov.

GAMBASSINI, P.   See: Palma di Cesnola and Gambassini.

GAMKRELIDZE, P. D.
1959   (ed.) [Collection of works dedicated to A. I. Dzhanelidze.] Tbilisi: Akad. Nauk Gruz. SSR Press, 490 pp., illustr., (Georgian and Russian).

GAMOV, GEORGE
1963   A planet called Earth. New York: Viking Press, x + 257 pp., 99 figs.,
          (high school and laymen).

GANESHIN, G. S.
1959   [Stratigraphy of Upper Tertiary and Quaternary sediments of Sikhote-
          Alin' and the Maritime Province.]   Materialy Geol. Inst. (VSEGEI),
          Nov. Ser. Chetv. Geol. i Geomorf., 27, 77—87, 1 table, (Russian).

GANESHIN, G. S., and OKLADNIKOV, A. P.
1956   [On some archeologic remains of Maritime Province, and on their geo-
          logical significance.]   Materialy Geol. Inst. (VSEGEI), Nov. Ser.
          Geol. i Pol. Iskop., 15, 50—57, 3 figs., (Russian).

GANESHIN, G. S., ZUBAKOV, V. A., POKROVSKAÍA, I. M., SELIVERSTOV, ÍU. P.,
CHEMEKOV, ÍU. F., EPSHTEÍN, S. V., and ÍAKOVLEVA, S. V.
1961   [Volume, contents and nomenclature of stratigraphic subdivisions of the
          Quaternary system.]   Sov. Geol., 1961:8, 3—15, 1 table, (Russian;
          English summary).

GANÍA, I. M., and KETRARU, N. A.
1964   [Some data on ornithofauna from the Paleolithic cave Starye Duruitory.]
          Izv. Akad. Nauk Moldav. SSR, ser. Biol. i Khim. Nauk, 1964:1,
          45—48, 1 table, (Russian; Moldavian summary).
1965   [Fossil ornithofauna from Paleolithic site Brynzeny I.]   Izv. Akad.
          Nauk Moldav. SSR, 1965:5, 98—105, 2 figs., 4 tables, (Russian;
          Moldavian summary).

GANÍA, I. M., and KUROCHKIN, E. N.
1967   [Results and prospects of the research on the Neogene avifauna of the
          southwestern regions of the European part of SSSR.]   In: Col-
          lected Papers, 1967A, [Place and significance of fossil mammals
          of Moldavia in the Cenozoic of USSR], 105—109, (Russian).

GANS, CARL
1964   Vertebrate hard tissues. Science, 144, 323—324.
1966A.   The functional basis of the retroarticular process in some fossil reptiles.
          Jour. Zool., London, 150, 273—277, 2 figs.
1966B.   Locomotion without limbs. Nat. Hist., 75:2, 10—17, 8 figs., 1 color
          pl.; 75:3, 36—41, 9 figs.
          See: Schmalhausen 1968.

GANS, C., and PARSONS, T. S.
1966   On the origin of the jumping mechanism in frogs. Evolution, 20:1,
          92—99.
          Rev.: Anon. in Naturwiss. Rundschau, 19:11, 473.

GANSSER-BURCKHARDT, A.
1955   Italienische Parallelen zum Alpinen Paläolithikum der Schweiz. Ur-
          Schweiz, 19, 41—48, figs. 31—32.

GAPONOV, ÍU. A. (= Gaponov, E. A.)
1957C.   [New find of a tooth of Elasmotherium in the Kuíal'nik liman valley
          near Odessa.]   Trudy Odessk. Univ., Ser. Geol. Geogr., 147:4,
          115—120, 2 figs., (Ukrainian; Russian summary).

1957D.   [Lower jaw of <u>Dinotherium</u> from Meotic deposits of Veliki Kuial'nik
            valley.] Trudy Odessk. Univ., Ser. Geol. Geog., 147:5, 125–131,
            1 pl., (Ukrainian; Russian summary).
1962A.   [Teeth of the left part of upper jaw of <u>Dinotherium</u> from Raskoshnoe
            village.] Trudy Odessk. Univ., Ser. Geol. Geogr., 152:8, 7–16,
            1 pl., 2 tables, (Russian).
1962B.   [Upper jaw teeth of <u>Dinotherium</u> from the northern parts of Odessa
            region.] Trudy Odessk. Univ., Ser. Geol. Geogr., 152:8, 17–22,
            1 pl., 1 table, (Russian).
1967   [Jaw of deinothere from Nishkany.] Pal. Sborn., 4:1, 125–129, (Rus-
            sian; English summary).

GARBOE, AXEL
1964   Et Steno-Monument. Meddel. Dansk Geol. Foren., 15, 372–373, 1 fig.,
            (English summary).

GARCÍA, JULIO   See: Crusafont Pairó, Aguirre and García.

GARCÍA GUINEA, MIGUEL ANGEL
1962B.   Los recientes descubrimientos de pinturas rupestres levantinas en Nerpío
            (Albacete). Las Ciencias, 27:6, 458–469, 6 figs., (not seen).
            Rev.: Sonneville-Bordes in L'Anthrop., 69, 109–110.
1963C.   Le nouveau et important foyer de peintures levantines à Nerpio (Albacete,
            Espagne). Bull. Soc. Préhist. Ariège, 18, 55 pp., 28 figs., 4 pls.
            Rev.: Sonneville-Bordes in L'Anthrop., 69, 109–110.
1968   Los grabados de la Peña del Cuco en Castro Urdiales y de la cueva de
            Cobrantes (Valle de Aras). Santander: Patronato Cuevas Pre-
            históricas de la Provincia. Diputación Provincial, III. Illustr.
            Rev.: H.-P. in Bol. Soc. Españ. Hist. Nat., Sec. Geol., 66:2, 188.
            See: González-Echegaray and Garcia Guinea.

GARCÍA GUINEA, M. A., and GONZÁLEZ-ECHEGARAY, J.
1966   Découverte de nouvelles représentations d'art rupestre dans la grotte
            Del Castillo. Préhist. Spéléol. Ariégeoises, 21, 27–34, 6 figs., 1 map.

GARCÍA GUINEA, M. A., and KRAPOVICKAS, P.
1959   Rev.: Sonneville-Bordes in L'Anthrop., 69, 109–110.

GARCIA SANCHEZ, M.
1960   Rev.: Preuschoft in Anthrop. Anz., 26, 47.

GARDINER, BRIAN GEORGE
1966   Catalogue of Canadian fossil fishes. Contrib. Roy. Ont. Mus., Life Sci.
            Div., 68, 1–154.
            Rev.: Dineley in Canadian Field Nat., 81, 77.
1967A.   Further notes on palaeoniscoid fishes with a classification of the
            Chondrostei. Bull. Brit. Mus. (Nat. Hist.), Geol., 14:5, 145–206,
            24 figs., 3 pls.
1967B.   The significance of the preoperculum in actinopterygian evolution. In:
            Patterson, C., and Greenwood, P. H., (eds.), 1967, 197–209, 8 figs.
            See: Andrews, S. M., et al.

GARDNER, MARTIN
1957   Fads and fallacies in the name of science. 2nd ed., (formerly published
            under the title In the name of science). New York: Dover, 363 pp.

GAREVSKI, RISTO
1964   [Remains of a rodent from Makarovec II in the vicinity of T. Veles.]
        Fragmenta Balcanica, 5:10, 55–60, 2 figs., (Serbian; German
        summary).
        Abs.: Đ. in Bull. Sci., Zagreb, Sec. A, 10, 163.

GARIAINOV, V. A.   See: Ochev, Shishkin, et al.

GARIAINOV, V. A., and OCHEV, V. G.
1964   [On the stratigraphy of Triassic sediments of Orenburg region of the
        Urals.] Izv. Vyssh. Uch. Zav., Geol. i Razv., 1964:4, 16–22,
        2 figs., (Russian).

GARN, STANLEY M.
1964   (ed.) Culture and the direction of human evolution. Detroit, Mich.:
        Wayne State Univ. Press, iii + 98 pp., illustr.
        Rev.: Alekseev in Voprosy Antrop., 28, 186–187;   Anderson in Human
        Biol., 37, 400–402;   Hughes in Man, Jour. Roy. Anthrop. Inst.,
        1, 247;   Napier in Jour. Anat., 100, 415;   Sarkar in E. Anthrop.,
        19, 87–89;   Schwidetzky in Homo, 16, 127.
1965   Human races. 2nd edition. Springfield: Charles C. Thomas, xiv +
        155 pp., 26 figs.
        Rev.: Sarkar in E. Anthrop., 19, 259–260;   Valentine in Amer. An-
        throp., 68, 1582–1583.
1966   et al. Cusp number, occlusial groove pattern and human taxonomy.
        Nature, 210, 224–225, 1 table.

GARN, S. M., LEWIS, A. B., and KEREWSKY, R. S.
1964   Relative molar size and fossil taxonomy. Amer. Anthrop., 66, 587–592,
        1 fig. Also in: Genovés, S., et al., (eds.), 1966, 109–115, with
        comment by David L. Greene.

GARRABRANT, W. A.   See: Müller, E. H. 1965.

GARROD, DOROTHY A. E., and CLARK' J. G. D.
1965   Primitive man in Egypt, Western Asia and Europe. Cambridge: Uni-
        versity Press, 61 pp., 15 figs., 1 table, 1 map.
        Rev.: Czarnetzki in Anthrop. Anz., 30, 213;   Engelmayer in Mitt.
        Anthrop. Ges. Wien, 96–97, 338–339.

GARTLAN, J. S.   See: Crook, J. H. and Gartlan.

GARUTT, WADIM E. (= V. E.)
1964   Das Mammut. Mammuthus primigenius (Blumenbach). Wittenberg
        Lutherstadt: Ziemsen Verlag (Neue Brehm-Bücherei 322), 140 pp.,
        82 figs. and maps, (not seen).
        Rev.: Guenther in Schrift. Naturwiss. Ver. Schleswig-Holstein, 35,
        114–115, 2 figs.;   Haltenorth in Säugetierkundl. Mitt., 14, 53;
        Heintz in Naturen, 89, 118–120, (Norwegian);   Zapfe in Mitt.
        Geol. Ges. Wien, 57, 651–652.
1965   [Fossil elephants from Siberia.] Trudy Inst. Geol. Arktiki, 143, 106–
        130, 7 figs., 1 table, (Russian; English summary).
1966   [Eopleistocene mammals of Western Transbaikalia. Order Proboscidea.]
        Trudy Geol. Inst., 152, 47–58, 4 figs., 2 tables, (Russian).
        See: Alekseeva and Garutt; Dubinin and Garutt; Geints and Garutt;
        Heintz, A. E. and Garutt.

GARUTT, V. E., and ĪŪR'EV, K. B.
1966   [Mummified remains of a wild horse from the permafrost of Indigirka
            R. basin.] Bĭull. Kom. Izuch. Chetvert. Perioda, 31, 86–92,
            4 figs., 1 table, (Russian).

GARUTT, V. E., and SAFRONOV, I. N.
1965   [Discovery of a skeleton of the southern elephant Archidiskodon meri-
            dionalis (Nesti) near Georgievsk (Northern Caucasus).] Bĭull. Kom.
            Izuch. Chetvert. Perioda, Akad. Nauk SSSR, no. 30, 79–88, 5 figs.,
            2 tables, (Russian).

GASC, JEAN-PIERRE
1966A.   Définition des termes anatomiques. In: Lavocat, R., (ed.), 1966, 84–
            105, figs. 7–19.
1966B.   Les reptiles. In: Lavocat, R., (ed.), 1966, 470–474, pl. 136.
1966C.   Les amphibiens. In: Lavocat, R., (ed.), 1966, 475–478, pl. 137.
1967A.   Retentissement de l'adaptation à la locomotion apode sur le squelette
            des Squamates. Colloq. Internat. Cent. Nation. Recherch. Sci.,
            163, 373–394, 16 figs., (English summary).
1967B.   Squelette hyobranchial. In: Grassé, (ed.), 1967, Traité de Zool., 16:1,
            550–583, figs. 281–327, 2 tables.
            See: Hoffstetter and Gasc.

GASPARD, MARCEL
1964   La région de l'angle mandibulaire chez les Canidae. Mammalia, 28,
            249–349, 24 figs.

GASPARINI, ZULMA B. De
1968   Nuevos restos de Rhamphostomopsis neogaeus (Burm.) Rusconi 1933,
            (Reptilia, Crocodilia) del "Mesopotamiense" (Plioceno medio-
            superior) de Argentina. Ameghiniana, 5:8, 299–311, 1 fig.,
            2 pls., 2 tables, (English summary).

GASULL, LUIS, and ADROVER, R.
1966   Fauna malacológica y mastológica del yacimiento cuaternario de Es
            Bufador. Boll. Soc. Hist. Nat. Baleares, 12:1–4, 141–148.

GATEHOUSE, C. G.   See: Plane and Gatehouse.

GATEHOUSE, R. R.
1965   Human evolution and the arched foot. S. Afr. Archaeol. Bull., 20, 28.

GAUDANT, JEAN
1965   Lycoptera wangi nov. sp. (Poisson téléostéen) dans le Jurassique des
            environs de Hêngshan (Shensi, China). C. R. Soc. Géol. France,
            1965, 337–339, 2 figs.
            Rev.: Radig in Zbl. Geol. Pal., Teil 2, 1967, 101.
1966A.   Les actinoptérygiens du Mésozoïque continental d'Asie centrale et
            orientale et le problème de l'origine des Téléostéens. C. R. Soc.
            Géol. France, 1966, 142, (abs.).
1966B.   Sur la nécessité d'une subdivision du genre Anaethalion White (Poisson
            Téléostéen). C. R. Soc. Géol. France, 1966, 308–310, 1 fig.
1967   Les Actinoptérygiens du Mésozoïque continental d'Asie central et
            orientale et le problème de l'origine des Téléostéens. Bull. Soc.
            Géol. France, 8, 107–113, 4 figs.

1968   Recherches sur l'anatomie et la position systématique du genre <u>Lycoptera</u> (poisson Téléostéen). Mém. Soc. Géol. France, <u>109</u>, 41 pp., 18 figs., 6 pls., 2 tables.

GAUSSEN, JEAN
1960   Nouvelles fouilles dans la grotte de Gabillou. Bull. Soc. Hist. Archéol. Périgord, <u>87</u>, 58—65, 1 fig.
1964   La grotte ornée de Gabillou. With prefaces by F. Bordes and Léon Pales. Publ. Inst. Préhist. Univ. Bordeaux, Mem. <u>3</u>, 68 pp., 69 pls.
         Rev.: [Beltrán] in Caesaraugusta, <u>23—24</u>, 147—148;   L.-R. N. in Toulouse, Univ., Inst. d'Art Préhist., Trav., <u>7</u>, 207—209;   Sonneville-Bordes in L'Anthrop., <u>69</u>, 111—113;   Sonneville-Bordes in Soc. Préhist. Fr., Bull., C. R., <u>66</u>:9, 265.

GAUTHIER, J.
1956   Observations sur des restes humains en provenance de la caverne du Placard (Charente). Procès-Verbaux, Soc. Linn. Bordeaux, <u>96</u>, 62—65.

GAUTIER, ALBERT
1965   Relative dating of peneplains and sediments in the Lake Albert rift area. Amer. Jour. Sci., <u>263</u>, 537—547.
1966   <u>Camelus thomasi</u> from the northern Sudan and its bearing on the relationship <u>C</u>. <u>thomasi</u> — <u>C</u>. <u>bactrianus</u>. Jour. Pal., <u>40</u>, 1368—1372, 6 tables.
1967   New observations on the Later Tertiary and Early Quaternary in the Western Rift: the stratigraphic and paleontological evidence. Discussion. In: Bishop, W. W., and Clark, J. D., (eds.), 1967A, 73—87, 1 fig., 1 table, (French summary).
         See: Bishop, Gautier and de Heinzelin; Hooijer 1963D.

GAUTIER, FRANCIS   See: Crusafont Pairó, Gautier and Ginsburg.

GAVAUDAN, P.
1967   Sélection naturelle, origine et évolution des êtres vivants et pensants. L'Ann. Biol., <u>6</u>, 509—535.

GAVELA, BRANKO
1963   Abs.: P. in Bull. Sci., Zagreb, Sec. A, <u>10</u>, 296.

GAVRIÚSHENKO, P. P.   See: Abetekov, <u>et al.</u>

GAWNE, CONSTANCE ELAINE
1968   The genus <u>Proterix</u> (Insectivora, Erinaceidae) of the Upper Oligocene of North America. Amer. Mus. Novit., <u>2315</u>, 1—26, 11 figs., 1 table.

GAYRARD, Y.   See: Hoffstetter and Gayrard.

GAZIN, C. LEWIS
1965A.   Early Eocene mammalian faunas and their environment in the vicinity of the Rock Springs uplift, Wyoming. Guidebk. Wyo. Geol. Assoc., <u>1965</u>, 171—180, 1 fig.
1965B.   A study of the early Tertiary condylarthran mammal <u>Meniscotherium</u>. Smithson, Misc. Coll., <u>149</u>:2, iv + 98 pp., 9 figs., 11 pls., 1 chart.

1965C.   An endocranial cast of the Bridger Middle Eocene primate, <u>Smilodectes</u>
           <u>gracilis</u>. Smithson Misc. Coll., <u>149</u>:4, 14 pp., 2 pls.
1968A.   A new primate from the Torrejon Middle Paleocene of the San Juan
           Basin, New Mexico. Proc. Biol. Soc. Wash., <u>81</u>, 629—634, 3 figs.
1968B.   A study of the Eocene condylarthran mammal <u>Hyopsodus</u>. Smithson.
           Misc. Coll., <u>153</u>:4, 1—90, 10 figs., 13 pls.

GEBHARDS, JOHN H.
1965   Paleolithic pictographs at Escoural, Portugal. Mo. Archaeol. Soc. News-
           letter, no. <u>191</u>, 9.

GEDIGA, BOGUSŁAW
1965   Les Sudetes polonaises à l'âge de la pierre et dans les phases initiales
           de l'âge du bronze. Acta Archaeol. Carpathica, <u>5</u>, 163—167,
           4 figs., (Polish; French summary).

GEERTZ, CLIFFORD
1964   The transition to humanity. In: Tax (ed), 1964, 37—48.
1965   <u>et al.</u> Summary: next steps in research. In: DeVore, P. L., (ed.),
           1965, 138—148.

GEEVSKAĨA, E. A.
1963   [When stones speak.] Priroda, <u>1963</u>:1, 85—89, 4 figs., (Russian).

GEHLBACH, FREDERICK R.
1964   Reptiles and amphibians (Herpetozoa) in the North American Pliocene
           and Pleistocene epochs. Texas Jour. Sci., <u>16</u>, 495, (abs.).
1965   Amphibians and reptiles from the Pliocene and Pleistocene of North
           America: A chronological summary and selected bibliography.
           Texas Jour. Sci., <u>17</u>, 56—70, 2 tables.

GEHLEN, ARNOLD
1964   Urmensch und Spätkultur. Philosophische Ergebnisse und Aussagen.
           2nd rev. ed. Frankfurt am Main, Bonn: Athenäum, 271 pp.,
           5 pls.
           Rev.: Bernhard in Homo, <u>16</u>, 127.

GEHLEN, KURT VON
1959   Erzmikroskopische Beobachtungen an einem Saurierknochen aus dem
           Feuerletten. Geol. Bl. NO-Bayern, <u>9</u>, 32—35, (not seen).
           Abs.: Schnitzer in Zbl. Geol. Pal., Teil 2, <u>1964</u>, 597.

GEINTS, A. E., and GARUTT, V. E.
1964   Determination with radioactive carbon C^{14} of the absolute age of
           fossil remains of mammoth and woolly rhinoceros found in
           permanently frozen ground of Siberia. C. R. Acad. Sci. SSSR,
           <u>154</u>, 1367—1370, 2 figs., (Russian).

GEIST, OTTO WILLIAM
1951   Collecting Pleistocene fossils in Alaska. Proc. 2nd Alaskan Sci. Confer.,
           1951, 171—172.

GEJVALL, N. G.   See: Sellstadt, Engstrand and Gejvall.

GEKKER, R. F.
1959   [On orientation and methods of paleoecological research on marine
          faunas.] Izv. Vyssh. Uch. Zav., Geol. i Razv., 1959:1, 3—12,
          (Russian).
1966   (ed.) [Organism and environment in the geological past.]   Moscow:
          "Nauka" Press, 268 pp., ill., (Russian).
1967   [Nikolaĭ Nikolaevich Iakovlev (1870 - 1966).]   Pal. Zhurnal, 1967:1,
          155—156, portr., (Russian).

GELLER, M. Kh.
1967   [Mammoth corpse on Taĭmyr.]   Zool. Zhurnal, 46:6, 964—966, 1 fig.,
          (Russian; English summary).

GELVIN, BRUCE
1966   A sampling of points from the Ginn site.   Mo. Archaeol. Soc. News-
          letter, no. 201, 3—10, illustr.

GEMEINHARDT, M. See: Kummer, G. and Gemeinhardt.

GENET-VARCIN, EMILIENNE
1963   Rev.: Bone in Anthropologica, n. s., 6, 257—260;   ev. in Archeol.
          Roz., 18, 728;   Fiasson in Bull. Soc. Linn., Lyon, 33, 291;
          Goustard in L'Ann. Biol., 5, 206;   Haltenorth in Säugetierkundl.
          Mitt., 14, 234;   Knussmann in Homo, 17:1, 62;   M. in Arch.
          Suiss. Anthrop. Gén., 29, 74;   Preuschoft in Zbl. Geol. Pal.,
          Teil 2, 1965, 293—294;   Schaeuble in Zeit. Morph. Anthrop.,
          55, 384;   Simons in Amer. Jour. Phys. Anthrop., 24, 127;
          Steslicka-Mydlarska in Przeglad Zool., 14:1, 149—150.
1965   Anthropodus rouvillei.   Ann. Pal., Vert., 51, 209—219, 4 figs.
1966A.   Étude des dents permanentes provenant du gisement moustérien de la
          Croze del Dua (Lot).   Ann. Pal., Vert., 52:1, 89—114, 5 figs.
1966B.   Conjectures sur l'allure générale des Australopithèques.   Bull. Soc. Pré-
          hist. Franç., C. R. séances mens., 63, 106—107.
1966C.   L'Homme. In: Lavocat, R., (ed.), 1966, 110—160, figs. 20—52.
1966D.   Représentations de poissons dans l'art Paléolithic supérieur. In: Piveteau,
          J., (ed.), 1966B, Traité de Paléo., 4:3, 421—434, 11 figs.
1967   De quelques problèmes posés par les Australopithèques.   Colloq. Internat.
          Cent. Nation. Recherch. Sci., 163, 649—653, 1 fig., (English
          summary).
          See: Arambourou and Genet-Varcin.

GENET-VARCIN, E., and MIQUEL, M.
1967   Contribution à l'étude du squelette Magdalénien de l'abri Lafaye, à
          Bruniquel (Tarn-et-Garonne).   L'Anthrop., 71:5—6, 467—478,
          4 figs., 1 table.

GENING, V. F.
1968   [Works in middle Irtysh area.]   In: Rybakov, (ed.), 1968, 139—140,
          (Russian).

GENOVÉS TARAZAGA, SANTIAGO
1961   Los llamados "neandertales tropicales" (Broken Hill, Saldanha y Ngandong).
          Homenaje a Pablo Martínez del Río, 187—192.
1962A.   Rev.: Marquer in L'Anthrop., 69:5—6, 562—563.
1962B.   Sobre unos comentarios en el campo de la Antropología Física a un
          trabajo del arqueólogo Ibarra Grasso.   Khana, 1:36—37, 165—168,
          (not seen).

1962C.   Introducción al diagnóstico de la edad y del sexo en restos óseos pre-
              históricos. Publ. Inst. Hist., Univ. Nacion. Autónoma Mex.,
              no. 7, 137 pp., 9 pls.
              Rev.: Bass in Amer. Jour. Phys. Anthrop., 22, 207–208;   Chapman in
              An. Antrop., México, 1965, 2, 224–226.
1965A.   Problemas relativos al origen del hombre en America. An. Antrop.,
              México, 2, 121–129.
1965B.   Studies and advances in physical anthropology during 1963. Yearbook
              Phys. Anthrop., 11, 1–100.
1965C.   (ed.) Homenaje a Juan Comas en su 65 aniversario. Volume II. An-
              tropología física. Mexico: Editorial libros de México, S. A.
              (Av. Coyoacán 1035. México 12, D.F.), 413 pp., illustr.
              Rev.: Castro Faria in An. Antropol., México, 4, 274–277;   H. V. V.
              in L'Anthrop., 71:1–2, 160–161;   Hoyme in Human Biol.,
              40:1, 102–103.
1967   Some problems in the physical anthropological study of the peopling
              of America [with comments]. Current Anthrop., 8, 297–312.
              See: Brace 1964.

GENOVÉS T., S., et al., (eds.)
1966   Yearbook of physical anthropology 1964. Yearbook Phys. Anthrop.,
              12, 290 pp., illustr.
              Rev.: Angel in Amer. Jour. Phys. Anthrop., 26, 374–376;   Comas in
              An. Antropol., México, 4, 220–221;   Hughes in Amer. Anthrop.,
              70, 638–639;   M. R. S. in Arch. Suiss. Anthrop. Gen., 31,
              58–59;   Vallois in L'Anthrop., 72, 153–154.
1967   Yearbook of physical anthropology 1965. Yearbook Phys. Anthrop.,
              13, 280 pp., illustr.
              Rev.: Benfer in Amer. Anthrop., 71, 982–988;   Buettner-Janusch in
              Amer. Jour. Phys. Anthrop., 27, 403–405;   Schwidetzky in
              Homo, 18:4, 265.

GENOVÉS T., S., and COMAS, J.
1964   La antropología física en México: 1943-1964. Inventario bibliográfico.
              Cuad. Inst. Hist., Ser. Antrop., no. 17, 55 pp.

GENTNER, W. See: Koenigswald, Gentner and Lippolt.

GENTRY, ALAN WILLIAM
1965   New evidence on the systematic position of Hippotragus niro Hopwood,
              1936 (Mammalia). Ann. Mag. Nat. Hist., 8, 335–338, 1 fig.
1966   Fossil Antilopini of East Africa. Brit. Mus. (Nat. Hist.), Fossil Mamm.
              Afr., no. 20, 45–106, 15 figs., 9 pls. (Also: Bull., Brit. Mus.
              (Nat. Hist.), Geol., 12:2.)
              Rev.: Hünermann in Zbl. Geol. Pal., Teil 2, 1969:2, 210.
1967   Pelorovis oldowayensis Reck, an extinct bovid from East Africa. Fossil
              mammals of Africa no. 22. Bull. Brit. Mus. (Nat. Hist.), Geol.,
              14:7, 245–299, 40 figs., 6 pls.
1968   Historical zoogeography of antelopes. Nature, 217, 874–875.

GEORGE, ANDRÉ   See: Mortier and Aboux.

GEORGE, J. C., and BERGER, A. J.
1966   Avian myology. New York and London: Academic Press, xii + 500 pp.,
              illustr.

GEORGE, WILMA
1964   Biologist philosopher. A study of the life and writings of Alfred Rus-
            sel Wallace. New York: Abelard-Schuman, xiv + 320 pp., illustr.
            Rev.: G. G. Simpson in Science, 144, 1209—1210.

GEPTNER, V. G.   See: Vereshchagin, Geptner and Stroganova.

GERASIMOV, I. P.
1955   (ed.) [Problems of geomorphology and paleogeography of Asia.]
            Moscow: Akademiiâ Nauk SSSR, Institut Geografii, 255 pp.,
            45 figs., (Russian).
            See: Armand, et al.

GERASIMOV, I. P., SEREBRIÂNNYĬ, L. R., and CHEBOTAREVA, N. S.
1959   [Anthropogene (Pleistocene) of Northern Europe and its stratigraphic
            components.] Izv. Akad. Nauk, Ser. Geograf., 1959:6, 3—21,
            5 figs., 1 table, (Russian).

GERASIMOV, M. M.
1958,
1964A.   [The Mal'ta Palaeolithic site 1956-1957 excavations.] Sov. Etnog., 3,
            28—52. Translation, In: Michael, H. N., (ed.), 1964, 3—32,
            22 figs.
1961   [Round dwelling at Mal'ta site.] Krat. Soob. Inst. Ist. Mat. Kult. SSSR,
            82, 128—134, 3 figs., (Russian).
1964B.   [Men of the Stone Age.] Moscow: "Nauka" Press, 169 pp., illustr.,
            (Russian).

GERBOVA, V. G.
1959   [Some material on the stratigraphy of Quaternary formations in the
            delta of the Selenga river.] Trudy Geol. Inst., 32, 79—98, 3 figs.,
            1 table, (Russian).
            See: Nikiforova, Gerbova and Konstantinova; Ravskiĭ, Alexandrova,
            et al.

GERSBACH, EGON
1965   Bemerkungen zur Topographie altpaläolithischer Freilandsiedlungen im
            Hochrheintal. Fundber. Schwaben, 17, 21—28, 2 figs., 1 map.

GERSON, DONALD E.   See: Burr and Gerson.

GETZ, L. L., and HIBBARD, C. W.
1965   A molluscan faunule from the Seymour formation of Baylor and Knox
            Counties, Texas. Papers Mich. Acad. Sci., 50, 275—297, 1 fig.
            Abs.: Westphal in Zbl. Geol. Pal., Teil 2, 1966, 295.

GEYER, OTTO FRANZ
1962   (ed.) Festschrift Hermann Aldinger. Zur Vollendung des 60. Lebens-
            jahres am 1. Februar 1962 herausgeg. von seinen Schülern.
            Stuttgart: Schweizerbart, 214 pp., 32 figs., 11 pls., 8 enclosures,
            (not seen).

GEYER, O. F., and GWINNER, M. P.
1964   Einführung in die Geologie von Baden-Württemberg. Stuttgart: E.
            Schweizerbart'sche Verlagsbuchhandlung, viii + 223 pp., 73 figs.,
            11 pls., 7 tables.

Rev.: Medwenitsch in Mitt. Geol. Ges. Wien, 57, 652—653;   Staesche
in Jahresh. Ver. Vaterland. Naturk. Württemberg, 120, 301—302.

GÈZE, BERNARD
1965   La spéléologie scientifique. Paris: Editions du Seuil, 192 pp., (not seen).
Rev.: Moore in NSS News, 23, 82, 87;   Wójcik in Przegl. Geol., 1966,
189, (Polish).

GEZELISHVILI, I. A.   See: Bugianashvili, et al.

GHENEA, C., and RADULESCO, C.
1964   [Contributions à la connaissance d'une faune villafranchienne dans le Sud
du Plateau Moldave.]   Dări de seamă Comit. Inst. Geol., 50:1,
165—171, 1 fig., 1 pl., 1 table, (Rumanian;   French and Russian
summaries).
Abs.: Semaka in Zbl. Geol. Pal., Teil 2, 1966, 263—264.

GHEORGHIU, MARIA   See: Huică and Gheorghiu.

GHICA, M.   See: Dumitresco, et al.

GHOSH, ASOK KUMAR
1961B.   Occurrence of Upper Paleolithic implements in Mandla, M. P.   Proc.
Indian Sci. Congr., 48, 447, (abs.).
1963   Notes. Ancient India, 18—19, 1—3, 2 pls.
1965   The problem of laterite and associated palaeoliths in the Quaternary
deposits of eastern India. 7th Internat. Congr., Internat. Assoc.
Quat. Res., Abs., 1965, 165, (abs.).
See: Sen and Ghosh.

GIBBES, ROBERT W.
1847C.   Memoir on the fossil genus Basilosaurus;   with a notice of specimens
from the Eocene Green Sand of South Carolina. (Privately printed.)
Philadelphia: Merrihew and Thompson, Printers, i—ii, 1—13, 4 pls.
(Title page carries the date of 1847, "Republished" from the
Jour. Acad. Nat. Sci. Philadelphia, ser. 2, vol. I.)

GIBSON, CHARLES R.
1925   The great ball on which we live: an interestingly written description
of our world, the mighty forces of nature, and the wonderful
animals which existed before man, all described in simple language.
London: 249 pp., illustr., (not seen).

GIBSON, M. A.
1967   The histology of two samples of fossilized bone. Canadian Jour. Zool.,
45, 582, 1 pl.

GIDDINGS, JAMES LOUIS, JR.
1951C.   Problems of Early Man in Alaska. Proc. Alaskan Sci. Confer., 1950, 50.
1966   Cross-dating the archeology of northwestern Alaska. Science, 153, 127—
135, 12 figs.
1967   Ancient men in the Arctic. New York: Alfred A. Knopf, 391 pp.,
illustr.;   London: Secker and Warburg, 408 pp., (not seen).
Rev.: Anon. in Interamer., 14:5, 8;   Campbell in Sci. Jour., London,
4:4, 88—89;   Harp in Amer. Anthrop., 70, 1018—1019;   Peterson
in Minn. Archaeol., 29, 52—53.

GIEDION, SIEGFRIED
1962   The eternal present: a contribution to constancy and change. The
              beginnings of art. New York: Pantheon (Bollingen Series 25,
              6:1), xxi + 588 pp., 351 figs., 20 color pls., 5 maps.
          Rev.: Acanfora in Bull. Paletnol. Ital., n.s. 15, 73, 198—199;   [Beltrán]
              in Caesaraugusta, 23—24, 148—149;   Clark in Proc. Prehist. Soc.
              Cambridge, 30, 431—433;   Goldman in Nat. Hist., 71:2, 11—12;
              Leroi-Gourhan in Amer. Anthrop. Special Publ., 65, 1180—1181;
              Taus in Archaeol. Austriaca, 35, 123—124.
1964A.   Abbé Breuil from the point of view of art history. In: Ripoll Perelló,
              E., (ed.), 1964A, 431—434, (Spanish summary).
1964B.   Ewige Gegenwart — die entstehung der Kunst. Köln: DuMont-Schauberg,
              433 pp., 350 figs., 20 color pls., 5 maps, (not seen).
          Rev.: Felgenhauer in Archaeol. Austriaca, 35, 124—125;   Freund in
              Bayer. Vorges., 32:1—2, 206—209;   Rothermel in Mitt. Verband
              Deutschen Höhlen- und Karstforscher, München, 10, 115—116.

GIERS, RUDOLF
1964   Die Grossfauna der Mukronatenkreide (unteres Obercampan) im östlichen
              Münsterland. Fortschr. Geol. Rheinland u. Westfalen, 7, 213—294,
              10 figs., 8 pls., 3 tables.

GIESELER, W.
1967   Der wiedergefundene Neandertalerschädel von Le Moustier. Anthrop.
              Anz., 30, 95—96.

GILARDONI, SILVANO
1964   I sauri del Monte San Giorgio. Cooperazione, Sept. 26, no. 39, [2] +
              7 pp., illustr.

GILES, EUGENE
1966   Statistical techniques for sex and race determination. Some comments
              in defense. Amer. Jour. Phys. Anthrop., 25, 85—86.

GILL, EDMUND D.
1963   Abs.: Anon. in Anthropos, 59, 653;   Sch. in Naturwiss. Rund., 17,
              483.
1964   Age and origin of the Gisborne cave. Proc. Roy. Soc. Victoria, 77,
              532—533.
1965   Palaeontology of Victoria. Victorian Year Book 1965, no. 79, 1—24,
              (not seen).
1966   The paleogeography of Australia in relation to the migrations of mar-
              supials and men. Trans. N. Y. Acad. Sci., 28, 5—14.

GILL, W. D.   See: Savage, R. J. G. 1965B.

GILLET, SUZETTE, LORENZ, H. G., and WOLTERSDORF, F.
1965   Introduction à l'étude du Miocène supérieur de la région de Baccinello
              (environs de Grosseto, Italie). Bull. Serv. Carte Géol. Alsace-
              Lorraine, 18, 31—42, 2 pls., 1 map, (English, German and Rus-
              sian summaries).

GILLIAM, CHARLES EDGAR
1958A.   Folsomoid projectile points. Quart. Bull. Archeol. Soc. Virginia, 12:3,
              (not seen).

1958B. Type Early Man graver, Williamson site, Dinwiddie County. Quart. Bull.
        Archeol. Soc. Virginia, 13:1, (not seen).
1961   The Williamson Early Man workshop. Source of chert. Quart. Bull.
        Archeol. Soc. Virginia, 16, 10—11.

GILLULY, JAMES, WATERS, A. C., and WOODFORD, A. O.
1968   Principles of geology. Third edition. San Francisco, London: W. H.
        Freeman, 687 pp., illustr.
        Rev.: Shea in GeoTimes, 14:3, 30—31.

GILMORE, IRIS   See: Talmadge and Gilmore.

GILOT, E., ANCION, N., and CAPRON, P. C.
1965   Louvain natural radiocarbon measurements III. Radiocarbon, 7, 118—122.

GIMÉNEZ REYNA, SIMEÓN
1964   La cueva de Doña Trinidad, en Ardales. In: Ripoll Perelló, E., (ed.),
        1964A, 435—447, 13 figs., 1 pl., (French summary).

GIMBUTAS, MARIJAS   See: Ehrich and Gimbutas.

GINSBURG, LÉONARD
1961E. Plantigradie et digitigradie chez les Carnivores Fissipèdes. Mammalia,
        25, 1—21, 6 figs., (English summary).
1964A. Sur l'âge des faunules de Vertébres découvertes dans le Miocène con-
        tinental d'Aups (Var), (Feuille de Salernes au 50.000e). Bull.
        Mus. Hist. Nat. Paris, 35, 644—647.
1964B. Nouvelle découverte de pliopithèque dans les faluns helvétiens de l'Anjou.
        Bull. Mus. Hist. Nat. Paris, 36, 157—159, 1 fig.
1964C. Les mammifères fossiles récoltés à Sansan au cours du XIXe siècle.
        Bull. Soc. Géol. France, 5, 3—15, 4 figs.
1964D. Les régressions marines et le problème du renouvellement des faunes au
        cours des temps géologique. Bull. Soc. Géol. France, 6, 13—22.
        Rev.: M. C. in Fossilia, 1965:3—4, 50—51.
1964E. Découverte d'un scélidosaurien (Dinosaure ornithischien) dans le Trias
        Superieur du Basutoland. C. R. Acad. Sci. Paris, 258, 2366—2368,
        1 fig.
1964F. Les hipparions de l'ouest de la France. Cursillos y Confer. Inst. "Lucas
        Mallada", 9, 181—182.
1965   L'"Amphicyon" ambiguus des Phosphorites du Quercy. Bull. Mus. Hist.
        Nat. Paris, 137, 724—730, 3 figs.
1966   Les amphicyons des Phosphorites du Quercy. Ann. Pal., Vert., 52:1,
        23—64, 21 figs., 1 pl.
        Rev.: Fahlbusch in Zbl. Geol. Pal., Teil 2, 1967, 513—514.
1967A. Une faune de mammifères dans l'Helvétien marin de Sos (Lot-et-Garonne)
        et de Rimbez (Landes). Bull. Soc. Géol. France, 9, 5—18, 8 figs.,
        1 table.
1967B. Sur les affinités des mésosaures et l'origine des Reptiles euryapsides.
        C. R. Acad. Sci. Paris, ser. D, 264, 244—246.
1967C. Une faune de Mammifères dans l'Helvétien marin de Sos (Lot-et-Garonne)
        et de Rimbez (Landes). C. R. Soc. Géol. France, 1967, 17,
        (abs.).
1967D. L'âge relatif des gisements de mammifères de la Limagne d'Auvergne.
        C. R. Soc. Géol. France, 1967, 325.
1967E. Les problèmes de la classification des reptiles. Colloq. internat. Cent.
        Nation. Recherch. Sci., 163, 315—327, (English summary).

1968A.   L'évolution des fosses temporales chez les reptiles. C. R. Acad. Sci.
           Paris, Sci. Nat., 266, 761–763.
1968B.   L'évolution des Pliopithèques et l'âge de la faune de Sansan. C. R.
           Acad. Sci. Paris, Sci. Nat., 266, 1564–1566.
    See: Crusafont Pairo, Gautier and Ginsburg; Crusafont Pairo, Ginsburg
           and Truyols; Ellenberger, F. and Ginsburg; Ellenberger, P. and
           Ginsburg; Toutin, Damotte and Ginsburg.

GINSBURG, L., and COPPENS, Y.
1961   [Principaux gisements de Mammifères en] Afrique. In: Piveteau, J.,
           (ed.), 1961A, Traité de Paléo., 6:1, 496–498, fig. 9.

GINSBURG, L., and HEINTZ, E.
1966   Sur les affinités du genre Palaeomeryx (Ruminant du Miocène européen).
           C. R. Acad. Sci. Paris, Sci. Nat., 262, 979–982, 1 fig.

GINSBURG, L., LAPPARENT, A. F. de, LOIRET, B., and TAQUET, P.
1966   Empreintes de pas de vértébres tétrapodes dans les séries continentales
           à l'Ouest d'Agadès (République du Niger). C. R. Acad. Sci.
           Paris, 263, 28–31, 1 fig.

GINSBURG, L., LAPPARENT, A. F. de, and TAQUET, P.
1968   Piste de Chirotherium dans le Trias du Niger. C. R. Acad. Sci. Paris,
           Sci. Nat., 266, 2056–2058, 1 fig.

GINSBURG, L., MONTENAT, C., and POMEROL, C.
1965   Découvert d'une faune de mammifères terrestres dans les couches
           marines de l'Auversien (Bartonien inférieur) du Guépelle (Seine-
           et-Oise). C. R. Acad. Sci. Paris, 260, 3445–3446.

GINSBURG, L., and TELLES ANTUNES, M.
1967   Considérations sur les mastodontes du Burdigalien de Lisbonne et des
           sables de l'Orléanais (France). Rev. Fac. Ciên. Lisboa, ser. C,
           14:2, 135–150, 1 fig., 4 pls.
1968   Amphicyon giganteus, carnassier géant du Miocène. Ann. Pal., Vert.,
           54, 1–35, 31 figs., 1 pl.
           Rev.: Thenius in Zbl. Géol. Pal., Teil 2, 1970:3/4, 239.

GINSBURG, L., and ZBYSZEWSKI, G.
1965   Découverte de vertébrés paléogènes dans la falaise de Feligueira Grande
           entre S. Pedro de Muel et Nazaré. Com. Serv. Géol. Portugal,
           48, 97–108, 3 figs.

GINTER, BOLESŁAW
1964   Sprawozdanie z badań wykopaliskowych przeprowadzonych na schylkowo
           paleolitcznych stanowiskach w Wapienniku, pow. Klobuck i
           Trzebcy, pow. Pajeczno. Wyniki Badań Wykopaliskowych, 1964,
           12–15, (not seen).
1966   [Upper Paleolithic site of Wójcice, Grodków district.] Mat. Archeol.,
           7, 59–69, 1 fig., 4 pls., (Polish; French summary).
1967   Les materiaux en silex du Tertre de Krakus à Cracovie. Mat. Archeol.,
           8, 85–87, 1 pl., (Polish; French summary).

GINZBURG, VULF VENIAMINOVICH
1957   [About the hip-bone fragment from Aman- Kutan.] Krat. Soob. Inst.
           Etnogr. SSSR, 27, 60–63, 2 figs., (Russian).

1959   [Basic problems of the paleoanthropology of Central Asia in connection
              with the study of the ethnogenesis of its peoples.]   Krat. Soob.
              Inst. Etnogr. SSSR, 31, 27—35, 1 fig., (Russian).

GISIN, HERMANN
1966   Signification des modalités de l'évolution pour la théorie de la systéma-
              tique. Zeit. Zool. Syst. Evolut.-Forsch., 4:1—2, 1—12, 2 figs.
              (English and German summaries).

GITERMAN, R. E.   See: Alekseev, M. N., Giterman, et al.

GIURGEA, P.   See: Bandrabur and Giurgea.

GIVENS, R. DALE   See: Brace 1964.

GLADILIN, V. N.
1965   [New finds on Derkula R.]   Arkheologiîâ, 18, 171—177, 2 figs.,
              (Ukrainian;   Russian summary).
1966A.   [Discovery of a Mousterian site in Donetŝ region.]   Arkheologiîâ, 20,
              135—142, 4 pls., (Ukranian;   Russian summary).
1966B.   [Different types of Mousterian stone industry of the Russian Plain and
              Crimea, and their position in the Early Paleolithic of USSR.]
              In: Rybakov, (ed.), 1966, 14—17, (Russian).

GLADKOV, I. I., MNUSHKIN, L. B., and KHAĬRUTDINOV, D. Kh.
1955   [Some new data on stratigraphy of Tertiary deposits of Mangyshlak
              peninsula.]   Izv. Akad. Nauk Kazakh. SSR, Ser. Geol., 19, 51—58,
              (Russian;   Kazakh summary).

GLAESSNER, M. F.
1963   "Intrusive" vertebrate fossils in the Miocene of Victoria.   A correction.
              Austral. Jour. Sci., 25, 411—412.

GLASS, BENTLEY
1966   Evolution of hairlessness in man.   Science, 152, 294.

GLASS, B., TEMKIN, O., and STRAUS, W. L., JR.
1968   Forerunners of Darwin: 1745 - 1859.   Baltimore: Johns Hopkins
              Press, xxii + 471 pp., 5 pls.
              Rev.: Vogel in Anthropol. Anz., 31:4, 297—298.

GLIEWE, F.
1962   Ein Fisch aus dem Lias von Gadderbaum bei Bielefeld.   Ber. Naturw.
              Ver. Bielefeld u. Umgegend, 16, 196, pl. 8.

GLIKMAN, L. S. (= Glückman)
1956   [On the phylogenetic evolution of the genus Anacorax.]   Doklady
              Akad. Nauk SSSR, 109, 1049—1052, 2 figs., 1 table, (Russian).
1959   [Directions of evolutionary development and the ecology of some
              groups of Cretaceous elasmobranchs.]   Trudy Vses. Paleont.
              Obshch., II sess., 56—62, 6 figs., (Russian).
1963B.   [Sharks, origin and evolution.]   Priroda, 52:12, 58—62, 6 figs., (Russian).
1964A.   [Subclass Elasmobranchii.]   Osnovy Pal., [Agnathes. Pisces], [11],
              195—237, 39 figs., 6 pls., (Russian).
1964B.   [Sharks of Paleogene and their stratigraphic significance.]   Moskow-
              Leningrad: "Nauka" Press, 229 pp., 76 figs., 31 plates, 12 tables,
              (Russian).

GLIKMAN, L. S., and ISHCHENKO, V. V.
1967   [Marine Miocene deposits in Central Asia.]   Doklady Akad. Nauk SSSR,
         177:3, 662–665, 1 fig., (Russian).

GLIKMAN, L. S., and STOLIAROV, A. S.
1966   [Upper Eocene stratigraphy of Mangyshlak according to paleoichthyo-
         logical data.]   Izv. Akad. Nauk SSSR, Ser. Geol., 1966:11, 130–
         138, 2 figs., (Russian).

GLORY, ANDRÉ (ABBÉ)
1964A.   La stratigraphie des pigments, appliquée aux peintures de Lascaux.
         Bull. Soc. Préhist. Franç., C. R. séances mens., 1964:3, LXII,
         (Abs. and discussion).
1964B.   Datation des peintures de Lascaux par le radio-carbone. Bull. Soc.
         Préhist. Franç., C. R. séances mens., 1964:5, cxiv–cxviii, (Discus-
         sion: cxi–cxii).
1964C.   La Grotte de Rocadour (Lot). Bull. Soc. Préhist. Franç., C. R. séances
         mens., 1964:7, clxvi–clxix, illustr.
1964D.   La stratigraphie des peintures à Lascaux (France). In: Ripoll Perelló,
         E., (ed.), 1964A, 449–455, 1 pl., (English and Spanish summaries).
1965   Nouvelles découvertes de dessins rupestres sur le Causse de Gramat (Lot).
         Bull. Soc. Préhist. Franç., Etud. et Trav., 62:3, 528–538, 9 figs.,
         1 map.

GLORY, A., and PIERRET, B.
1960   Rev.: Joly in Bull. Soc. Préhist., Paris, 57, 658.

GLORY, A.,   VAULTIER, M., and FARINHA DOS SANTOS
1965   La grotte ornée d'Escoural (Portugal). Bull. Soc. Préhist. Franç., Etud.
         et Trav., 62:1, 110–117, 4 figs.

GOBERT, E. G.
1963   Bibliographie critique de la préhistoire tunisienne. Cahiers de Tunisie,
         no. 41–42, 37–77.

GODINA, A. IA.
1964A.   [Some problems in the evolution of Giraffidae.]   Biull. Mosk. Obshch.
         Ispyt. Prirody., Otd. Geol., 39:5, 146–147, (Russian).
1964B.   [On the evolutional trends in the Giraffidae family.]   In: Orlov, (ed.),
         1964C, 51–57, 1 table, (Russian; English summary).
1964C.   [On finds of giraffe of the genus Palaeotragus from Sarmatian of Mol-
         davia.]   Izv. Akad. Nauk Moldav. SSR, ser. Biol. i Khim. Nauk,
         1964:7, 68–69, (Russian; Moldavian summary).
1966   [Fossil giraffes on the territory of USSR.]   Biull. Mosk. Obshch. Ispyt.
         Prirody Otd. Biol., 71:6, 150–151, Author's summary, (Russian).
1967A.   [On the evolution of the extremities of the giraffe (Giraffidae).]   Biull.
         Mosk. Obshch. Ispyt. Prirody, Otd. Biol., 72:6, 107–119, 2 figs.,
         1 table, (Russian; English summary).
1967B.   [Neogene giraffes of Moldavia.]   In: Collected Papers, 1967A, [Place
         and significance of fossil mammals of Moldavia in the Cenozoic
         of USSR], 41–46, (Russian).
1968   [On the stages of evolution of the genus Palaeotragus.]   Biull. Mosk.
         Obshch. Ispyt. Prirody, Otd. Geol., 43:3, 150–151, (Russian).

GODINA, A. Ia., and DUBINSKIĬ, A. A.
1963   [First find of a fossil giraffe in Turkmeniia.]   Bull. Mosk. Obshch. Ispyt. Prirody, Otd. Geol., 68:1, 155–157, 2 figs., (Russian). Abs.: Stoltenberg in Zbl. Geol. Pal., Teil 2, 1965, 281–282.

GODINA, A. Ia., and KHUBKA, A. N.
1968   [On the giraffe of the genus Palaeotragus from the Baltic suite of Moldavia.]   Biull. Mosk. Obshch. Ispyt. Prirody, Otd. Geol., 43:2, 86–89, 1 fig., (Russian).

GOETZMANN, WILLIAM H.
1965   Army exploration in the American West, 1803–1863. New Haven and London: Yale Univ. Press, xx + 489 pp., 27 pls., 16 maps, (pb. ed.).
1966   Exploration and Empire. The explorer and scientist in the Winning of the American West. New York: Alfred A. Knopf. xxvii + 656 + xviii pp., 45 maps, pls.

GOFSHTEĬN, I. D.
1953   [On Meletta scales from black shales of Transcarpathia.]   Trudy Lvov. Geol. Obshch., 1953:2, 99–110, 2 figs., 3 pls., 1 table, (Russian).
1961   [Teeth of Plesiosaurus and fish from Podol Senoman deposits.]   Pal. Sbornik, 1, 127–130, 1 fig., (Russian; English summary).
1965   [Materials on fossil whales of the Geological Museum AN USSR in Kiev.]   Pal. Sborn., 2:1, 25–29, 1 table, (Russian; English summary.

GOGGIN, JOHN M.
1964   Indian and Spanish selected writings. Hialeah: Advercolor Press, 1964, 329 pp., illustr.

GOHARA, YASUMA
1963   Late Pleistocene tephrochronology of Kyushu region, Japan. Quat. Res., 3, 123–138, 4 figs., 1 table, (Japanese; English summary).

GOIN, COLEMAN J., and GOIN, O. B.
1962B.   Introduction to herpetology. San Francisco: W. H. Freeman, 341 pp., illustr.

GÖKE, GERHARD
1964   Drepanaspis gemündenensis Schlüter. Aufschluss, 15, 334, 1 fig.
1967   Die Konservierung von Fossilien und Grabungsfunden mit PVC. Aufschluss, 18:1, 5–6.

GOKHMAN, I. I.
1962   [Some problems of method of conservation and packing of paleo-anthropological materials in the field.]   Krat. Soob. Inst. Etnogr. SSSR, 36, 100–102, (Russian).
1964   The 60th anniversary of Vulf Veniaminovich Ginzburg. Voprosy Antrop., 18, 157–162, portr., (Russian).
1966A.   [Georgiĭ Frantsevich Debets. (60th birthday).]   Sov. Etnog., 1966:2, 136–139, (Russian).
1966B.   [Fossil Neoanthrops.]   Trudy Inst. Etnog. Akad. Nauk SSSR, 92, 227–272, 11 figs., 3 tables, (Russian).

GOLDBY, F.
1940   Recent discoveries of human fossils. Mankind, 2:9, 330.

GOLDING, WILLIAM
1955   The inheritors. London: Faber and Faber, 233 pp.
              Rev.: Lehiste in Current Anthrop., 6, 232.

GOLDRING, WINIFRED
1960   Handbook of paleontology for beginners and amateurs. Ithaca: New
              York Museum, Handbook no. 9, (not seen).

GOLDSTEIN, MARCUS S.
1963B.   Human paleopathology. Jour. Nation. Med. Assoc., 55, 100–106, 3 figs.

GOLPE, JUANA MARIA   See: Crusafont Pairo, Adrover and Golpe; Crusafont Pairo,
              Rosell Sanuy, Golpe and Renzi.

GOLSON, J.
1964   (ed.) COWA surveys and bibliographies. Area 22 – Australia. COWA
              Surv. and Bibliog., Area 22, no. 3, 10 + 11 pp.
              See: Polach and Golson; Polach, Stipp, Golson and Lovering.

GOLUBEVA, L. V.   See: Ravskiĭ, Alexandrova, et al.

GÓMEZ MILLAS, JUAN
1960   En Choukoutien, la morada del Hombre de Pekín. Bol. Univ. Chile,
              no. 11, 46–48, 1 fig.

GOMILA, JACQUES   See: Thoma 1965.

GÖMÖRY, ISTVÁN
1963   Preparation of fossils by freezing. Föld. Közlöny, 93, 390–391,
              (Hungarian; English summary).

GONCHAROV, V. F.
1967   [Stratigraphy of Quaternary deposits of Kular gold-bearing region.]
              Geol. i Geof., 1967:4, 102–108, 4 figs., 2 tables, (Russian;
              English summary).

GONZÁLES, ALBERTO REX   See: Rex Gonzáles, Alberto.

GONZÁLES-ECHEGARAY, JOAQUIN
1956C.   Pinturas rupestres en la Cueva de la Cullalvera. Mem. Serv. Invest.
              Arqueol. Asturias, 1, 171–178, 1 fig., 2 pls.
1964A.   Excavaciones en la terraza de "El Khiam" (Jordania). I, Estudio del
              yacimiento y los niveles paleoliticos. Bib. Praehist. Hispana, 5,
              160 pp., 58 figs., 6 pls., 1 table, 29 graphs., (not seen).
              Rev.: Sonneville-Bordes in L'Anthrop., 69, 115–117.
1964B.   Nuevos grabados y pinturas en las Cuevas del Monte-Castillo. Zephyrus,
              15, 27–35, 2 figs., 8 pls.
              See: Cheynier and Gonzáles-Echegaray; Garcia Guinea and Gonzáles-
              Echegaray.

GONZÁLEZ-ECHEGARAY, J., and GARCIA GUINEA, M. A.
1963   Guía del Museo Provincial de Prehistoria y Arqueologia de Santander.
              Madrid: Ediciones de la Direccion General de Bellas Artes, 81 pp.,
              64 pls., 1 map, (not seen).

Rev.: Orellana Rodríguez in Antropología, 2:1, 125.

GONZÁLEZ-ETCHEGARAY, P. J., GARCIA GUINEA, M. A., BEGINES RAMIREZ, A., and MADARIAGA DE LA CAMPA, B.
1963 Cueva de La Chora (Santander), la campaña financiada por la Excma. Diputación Provincial de Santander. Madrid: Ministère de l'éducation nationale (Excavaciones arqueologicas en España, 26), 80 pp., 24 figs., 7 pls., 2 maps, (not seen).
    Rev.: Sauter in Arch. Suiss. Anthrop. Gén., 29, 80.

GOODING, ANSEL M., and OGDEN, J. G., III
1965 A radiocarbon dated pollen sequence from the Wells Mastodon site near Rochester, Indiana. Ohio Jour. Sci., 65, 1–11, 4 figs., 1 table.

GOODMAN, MORRIS
1966 Phyletic position of tree shrews. Science, 153, 1550.

GOODY, PETER C.
1968 The skull of Enchodus faujasi from the Maastricht of Southern Holland. I and II. Proc. K. Nederl. Akad. Wet., Ser. B, 71:3, 209–221; 222–231, 9 figs.

GOORIS, RAYMOND J. See: Skinner, M. F., Skinner and Gooris; Skinner, S. M. and Gooris.

GORBACH, L. P.
1961C. [On some Pelagic fishes in the Carpathian Oligocene.] Pal. Sbornik, 1, 131–136, 2 pls., (Russian; English summary).
1967 [First find of mosasaur remains in Crimea.] Geol. Zhurnal, 27:1, 93–96, 2 figs., (Ukrainian).

GORCE, MAXIME
1965 Les pré-écritures de la préhistoire. C. R. Acad. Inscript. Belles-Lettres, 1964, 298–305.

GORDON, NORMA S. See: Donohue and Gordon.

GOREGLIAD, V. N. See: Okladnikov and Goregliad.

GORENSTEIN, SHIRLEY
1965 Introduction to archaeology. New York: Basic Books, 175 pp., illustr.
    Rev.: Longacre in Science, 151, 1210; Snow in Amer. Jour. Phys. Anthrop., 24, 382.
1967 Museo Nacional de Antropología de México. Photographs by Lee Boltin. Nat. Hist., 76:7, 34–45, illustr.

GORETSKIĬ, G. I.
1959 [Concerning more precise geological dating of the Paleolithic of the Russian plain.] Trudy Geol. Inst., 32, 22–44, 1 table, (Russian).
1966 [Formation of the Volga R. valley during Early and Middle Anthropogene. Alluvium of Paleo-Volga.] Moscow: "Nauka" Press, 412 pp., 102 figs., 63 tables, (Russian).

GORGAS, KARIN
1967 Vergleichende Studien zur Morphologie, mikroskopischen Anatomie und Histochemie der Nebennieren von Chinchilloidea und Cavioidea

(Caviomorpha Wood 1955). Zeit. Wiss. Zool., 175, 54—236, 118 figs., 6 tables, (English summary).

GORGAS, MICHAEL
    1967   Vergleichend-anatomische Untersuchungen am Magen-Darm-Kanal der Sciuromorpha, Hystricomorpha und Caviomorpha (Rodentia). Eine Studie über den Einfluss von Phylogenie, Spezialisation und funktioneller Adaptation auf den Säugetierdarm. Zeit. Wiss. Zool., 175:3:4, 237—404, 77 figs., (English and Russian summaries).

GORIACHEVA, R. I. See: Arendt and Goriacheva.

GORSHKOV, S. P.
    1960   [A contribution to the study of the terraces of the Eniseĭ river, in the sector from the city of Krasnoĭarsk to the mouth of the Kan river.] In: Ragozin, L. A. (ed.), 1960, 115—121, 2 figs., (Russian).
    1967   [On the structure and formation conditions of Samarovo accumulative plain of the extra-glacial zone of Eniseĭ region of Siberia.] Biull. Kom. Izuch. Chetvert. Perioda, 33, 113—120, 1 fig., (Russian).

GOSLINE, WILLIAM A.
    1965   Teleostean phylogeny. Copeia, 1965, 186—194, 1 fig.

GOTTFRIED, HELMUT
    1964   Aus den Sammlungen unserer Mitglieder: Zahn eines Lungenfisches (Ceratodus). Aufschluss, 15, 330, 1 fig.

GOULD, CHARLES
    1886   Mythical monsters. London: Allen, 407 pp., 93 figs., color frontispiece.

GOULD, L. M.   See: Simpson, G. G. 1965H.

GOULD, RICHARD A.
    1968   Chipping stones in the outback. Nat. Hist., 77:2, 42—49, illustr.
             See: Brown, Jack and Gould.

GOULD, STEPHEN JAY
    1966   Allometry and size in ontogeny and phylogeny. Biol. Rev., 41, 587—640, 6 figs., 3 tables.
    1967   Evolutionary patterns in pelycosaurian reptiles: A factor-analytic study. Evolution, 21, 385—401, 8 figs., 6 tables.
             See: Szalay and Gould.

GOUSTARD, M., and GRAPIN, P.
    1964   Quelques acquisitions récentes en primatologie. L'Ann. Biol., Ser. 4, 3, 495—543.

GOWDA, SOMANAHALLI SAMBE
    1964   Fossil fish ossiculiths from the Cenomanian of South India. Eclog. Geol. Helvetiae, 57, 743—746, 3 figs.
             Abs.: Weiler in Zbl. Geol. Pal., Teil 2, 1966, 278.
    1967A.   The first fossil otolith from India. Bull. Geol. Soc. India, 4, 15—17, 2 figs.

Rev.: Weiler in Zbl. Geol. Pal., Teil 2, 1967, 495—496.

1967B. On a new fossil fish known from an otolith from the South Indian
Cenomanian. Jour. Geol. Soc. India, 8, 119—129, 2 figs., pl. 12,
1 chart.

Rev.: Weiler in Zbl. Geol. Pal., Teil 2, 1968:6, 646.

GOŹDZIEWSKI, STANISŁAW
1959 Rasy paleolitu starszego. Przegląd Antrop., 25, 235—246.

GOZHIK, P. F., and CHEPALYGA, A. L.
1964 [On synchronization of Dnestr and Pruth terraces.] Izv. Akad. Nauk
Moldav. SSR, ser. Biol. i Khim. Nauk, 1964:7, 22—25, (Russian;
Moldavian summary).

GRABAU, AMADEUS W. See: Black, D. and Grabau.

GRADWOHL, DAVID M.
1967 Prehistoric archaeology in the Red Rock Reservoir, Iowa, 1966. Plains
Anthrop., 12, 208, (abs.).

GRAHAM, AL
1963 Down with dinosaurs! A Mesozoic melange. Illustr. by Tony Palazzo.
New York: Duell, Sloan & Pearce, 61 pp., illustr., (not seen).

GRAHAM, RICHARD E.
1960 A fossil Bassariscus from Hanging Gardens Cave, California. Cave Notes,
2, 20—21, fig. 3.
1962 Porcupine cave dens in California. Cave Notes, 4:1, 1—4, 1 fig.

GRAHAM, SYLVIA F.
1967 Moles of the Samwel Cave fossil deposits: additions to the Pleistocene
fauna of Samwel Cave, California II. Caves and Karst, 9:6, 49,
(abs.).

GRAHMANN, R., and MÜLLER-BECK, H.
1967 Urgeschichte der Menschheit. 3rd ed. Stuttgart: 416 pp., 143 figs.,
8 pls., 1 table.
Rev.: Czarnetzki in Anthropol. Anz., 31:1—2, 108—109; Eibner in
Archaeol. Austriaca, 43, 145; Klima in Quartär, 19, 408—409;
Lippert in Mitt. Anthrop. Ges. Wien, 96—97, 380; Preuschoft
in Zbl. Geol. Pal., Teil 2, 1968, 219—221; Reitinger in Jahrb.
Oberosterreich. Musealver, 112, 281; Valoch in Archeol. Roz.,
21:2, 260—261, (Czech).

GRAMANN, FRANZ
1964 L'Oligocène de la dépression Hessoise en sa qualité d'élément formant
la jonction entre le Bassin de la Mer du Nord et le Fossé de la
Vallée du Rhin. Mém. Bur. Rech. Géol. Min., 28:2, 565—570.
1966 Das Oligozän der Hessischen Senke als Bindeglied zwischen Nordseebecken
und Rheintalgraben. Zeit. Deutsche. Geol. Ges., 115, 497—514,
1 fig., (English summary).

GRAMBAST, LOUIS, MARTINEZ, M., MATTAUER, M., and TALER, L.
1967 Perutherium altiplanensis nov. gen., nov. sp., premier Mammifère
mésozoïque d'Amérique du Sud. C. R. Acad. Sci. Paris, Sci.
Nat., 264, 707—710, 1 fig., 1 pl.

GRAMBERG, I. S.   See: Saks, et al.

GRAMM, M. N.
1959   [A scheme for subdivision of Tertiary continental deposits of Fergana
         depression.] Uzbek. Geol. Zhurnal, 1959:6, 13—22, 1 fig., 1 table,
         (Russian; Uzbek summary).
         Abs.: Mirtsching in Zbl. Geol. Pal., Teil 2, 1962, 552—553.

GRAND, P. M.
1967   Prehistoric art. Paleolithic painting and sculpture. Greenwich, Conn.:
         New York Graphic Society, 103 pp., illustr., (not seen).
         Rev.: Levine in Science, 161, 150—152.

GRANGE, ROGER T., JR.
1964   A Clovis point from Nebraska. Plains Anthrop., 9, 64, 1 fig.

GRANGEON, PIERRE   See: Elhai and Grangeon.

GRANIER, JACQUES
1965   Nouveaux documents faunistiques sur les loess de Collias et de Remoulins
         (Gard). Bull. Soc. Linn. Lyon, 34, 51—56, 1 table.
         See: Cappetta, Granier and Ledoux.

GRANT, CAMPBELL
1967   Rock art of the American Indian. New York: Crowell, xiv + 178 pp.,
         illustr.
         Rev.: Gregory in Minn. Archaeol., 29, 99—100;   Krieger in Science, 159,
         293—294, 1 fig.;   McCarthy in Amer. Anthrop., 71, 969—970.

GRANT, VERNE
1963   Rev.: Detling in Ecology, 45, 425—426;   Mayr in Evolution, 19, 134—
         136;   G. G. Simpson in Amer. Scholar, 34, 500—502.

GRAPIN, P.   See: Goustard and Grapin.

GRASSÉ, PIERRE-P.
1967   (ed.) Traité de Zoologie. Tome XVI, 1. Mammifères. Téguments et
         squelette. Paris: Masson, 1162 pp., 863 figs.
         Rev.: Cavier in Rev. Gén. Sci., 74, 316—317;   Dorst in Mammalia,
         31, 670—671;   Ginet in Bull. Soc. Linn. Lyon, 36, 268—269;
         Kowalski in Przeglad Zool., 12:2, 238, (Polish);   MacIntyre in
         Quart. Rev. Biol., 42, 518—520;   Snyder in Science, 158, 625—
         626;   Young in Endeavour, 27:101, 104.

GRASSÉ, P.-P., et al.
1966   Biologie générale. Paris: Masson, viii + 998 pp., 598 figs.

GRASSÉ, P.-P., and DEVILLERS, C.
1965   Précis de sciences biologique. Zoologie. II. Vertébrés. Paris: Masson,
         1129 pp., 995 figs., 22 in color.
         Rev.: E. M.-C. in Rev. Questions Sci., 27, 444—446;   Ewer in S.
         African Jour. Sci., 62, 248;   Joly in L'Ann. Biol., 5, 412—414;
         Templado in Arbor, 256, 148—149.

GRATTAN-BELLEW, P. See: Rudner and Grattan-Bellew.

GRAVES, KATHLEEN E.
1958   The rarest animal in the world. Walkabout, 24:4, 15—16, illustr.

GRAVES, W., and WALDREN, W. H.
1966   El yacimiento de Myotragus balearicus en las cuevas de Son Muleta y
              su relación con los niveles arqueológicos de Mallorca. Bol. Soc.
              Hist. Nat. Baleares, 12:1—4, 51—58.

GRAY, ASA
1963   Darwiniana. Essays and reviews pertaining to Darwinism. [Reprint of
              1876 ed.] Edited and with introduction by A. Hunter Dupree.
              Cambridge, Mass.: Harvard Univ. Press; London: Oxford Univ.
              Press, xxiii + 327 pp.
              Rev.: Beer in New Sci., 21, 367;   Zirkle in Science, 144, 724—725.

GRAY, JAMES
1968   Animal locomotion. London: Weidenfeld and Nicolson, xii + 479 pp.,
              illustr.
              Rev.: Martof in Bio-Science, 19:8, 751;   Simons in Austral. Nat. Hist.,
              16:4, 128.

GRAY, PETER
1961   (ed.) Encyclopedia of the biological sciences. New York: Reinhold
              Publ. Co., xxi + 1119 pp., illustr.

GRAY, ROBERT S.
1965   Late Cenozoic geology in the San Pedro Valley near St. David, Arizona.
              Int. Res. Rept., Geochron. Lab., Univ. Ariz., 8, 1—32, 11 figs.,
              3 tables.

GRAY, STEPHEN WOOD, and CRAMER, H. R.
1961   A tapir mandible from a northwest Georgia cave. Bull. Georgia Acad.
              Sci., 19:4, 83—90, 4 figs.

GRAZIOSI, PAOLO
1962C.   Rev.: Almagro in Ampurias, 24, 367—368;   [Zotz] in Quartär, 15—16,
              209—210.
1964A.   Signes linéaires paléolithiques gravés dans l'Abri du Romito (Calabre).
              In: Ripoll Perelló, E., (ed.), 1964A, 457—466, 4 pls., (Spanish
              summary).
1964B.   Prehistoric research in northwestern Punjab. Anthropological researches
              in Chitral. Italian expeditions to the Karakorum (K2) and
              Hindu Kush V. Prehistory and anthropology. Leiden: Brill,
              249 pp., 151 pls., 2 maps, (not seen).
              Rev.: Allchin in Man, Jour. Roy. Anthrop. Inst., 1, 111;   Balout in
              l'Anthrop., 72, 138—141;   Bernhard in Homo, 17:3—4, 233;
              Movius in Amer. Anthrop., 68, 584—585;   Roth-Lutra in Zeit.
              Ethnol., 92:1, 130—131;   Vaufrey in L'Anthrop., 69, 118—119.
1965   Papsidero (Prov. di Cosenza). Riv. Sci. Preist., 19, 301—302.
1966   Les gravures paléolithiques de l'Abri du Romito, en Calabre, Italie.
              IPEK, 21, 21—22, 2 pls.

GREEN, MORTON
1961   Abs.: Dietrich in Zbl. Geol. Pal., Teil 2, 1964, 138.

1962D.   An arthritic grizzly bear from South Dakota. Proc. S. Dakota Acad.
          Sci., 41, 37–40.
1965   New late Miocene locality in South Dakota. Jour. Pal., 39, 103–107,
          1 fig., pl. 18B.

GREEN, M., and LILLEGRAVEN, J. A.
1965   Significance of Rangifer in the Herrick formation of South Dakota.
          Proc. S. Dakota Acad. Sci., 44, 48–51, 1 fig.

GREEN, M., and MARTIN, H.
1967   Exhibit of micro-fossils from a fissure deposit. Proc. S. Dakota Acad.
          Sci., 46, 61–63, 1 fig.

GREEN, R. C.
1966   Prehistory at the Eleventh Pacific Science Congress. Jour. Polynesian
          Soc., 75, 498–501.

GREENE, ANN M.
1967   T. Dale Stewart: "Recent studies of fossil man in the Near East:
          Shanidar Neanderthals in Iraq." Bull. Phila. Anthrop. Soc., Feb-
          ruary 1967, 4, (abs.).

GREENE, CLIFFORD F., JR.
1967   John Witthoft . . . the lithology and technology of flint tools. Bull.
          Phila. Anthrop. Soc., February 1967, 3, (abs.).

GREENE, DAVID L.   See: Armelagos, et al.

GREENE, D. L., EWING, G. H., and ARMELAGOS, G. J.
1967   Dentition of a Mesolithic population from Wadi Halfa, Sudan. Amer.
          Jour. Phys. Anthrop., 27, 41–55, 5 figs., 8 tables.

GREENE, JOHN C.
1961   Rev.: Gruber in Hist. Sci., 3, 115–123;   Heberer in Naturwiss. Rund.,
          17, 490.

GREENMAN, EMERSON F.
1958   Prehistoric Detroit. Mich. Archaeol., 4, 81–98, 3 figs.
1963   Rev.: Bordes, Comas, and Franciscolo, with reply by Greenman, in
          Current Anthrop., 5, 321–324.
          See: Bordes, Comas and Franciscolo; Fitting 1965G.

GREENWOOD, M.   See: Butler, P. M. and Greenwood.

GREENWOOD, P. HUMPHRY
1963   A history of fishes. (2nd ed. J. R. Norman, 1931). London: Ernest
          Benn, xxxi + 398 pp., 7 pls., 148 illustr.
1967   Blind cave fishes. Studies in Spel., 1, 262–274, 3 figs., 2 pls., 1 table.
1968   Professor J. L. B. Smith. Nature, 217, 690–691.
          See: Norman, J. R. and Greenwood.

GREENWOOD, P. H., and PATTERSON, C.
1967   A fossil osteoglossoid fish from Tanzania (East Africa). In: Patterson,
          C., and Greenwood, P. H., (eds.), 1967, 211–223, 3 figs., 3 pls.

GREENWOOD, P. H., ROSEN, D. E., WEITZMAN, S. H., and MYERS, G. S.
1966   Phyletic studies of teleostean fishes, with a provisional classification of
            living forms. Bull. Amer. Mus. Nat. Hist., 131:4, 339–456,
            9 figs., pls. 21–23, 32 charts.
            Rev.: Applegate in Copeia, 1967, 693–694;   Hubbs in Quart. Rev.
            Biol., 40–41.

GREER, JOHN W.
1965   A typology of burin facets on projectile points. El Palacio, 72:2, 34–37,
            1 fig.

GREER, PHILIP F. C.
1963   Preliminary report on the find of Pleistocene bear remains in Floyd
            County, Georgia. Bull. Georgia Acad. Sci., 21, 12–13, (abs.).
1964   A Pleistocene bear in northwest Georgia. Bull. Georgia Acad. Sci.,
            22:1, 13–14.

GREGG, CLIFFORD C.
1964   Memorial to Elmer S. Riggs (1869 - 1963). Bull. Geol. Soc. Amer.,
            75, P129–P131, portr.

GREGG, D. R.
1966   New dates for Pyramid Valley moas. New Zealand Archaeol. Assoc.
            Newsletter, 9, 155–159, 1 fig.

GREGOR, ARTHUR S.
1966A.   Charles Darwin. New York: Dutton, illustr., (juv.), (not seen).
1966B.   The adventure of man. New York: Macmillan, (juv.), (not seen).
            Rev.: Turnbull in Nat. Hist., 76:9, 29.

GREGORY, JOSEPH T.
1962A.   Abs.: Huene in Zbl. Geol. Pal., Teil 2, 1964, 169–170.
1962B.   Abs.: Huene in Zbl. Geol. Pal., Teil 2, 1964, 169.
1964A.   Microsaurs and the origin of captorhinomorph reptiles. Amer. Zool.,
            4, 379, (abs.).
1964B.   Triassic vertebrate fauna of the Redonda formation in northeastern
            New Mexico. Program, 60th Ann. Meeting, Geol. Soc. Amer.,
            Cordilleran Sect., 36, (abs.).
1965   Microsaurs and the origin of captorhinomorph reptiles. Amer. Zool.,
            5, 277–286, 4 figs., (comments by Robert L. Carroll).
            Abs.: Westphal in Zbl. Geol. Pal., Teil 2, 1966, 295.

GREGORY, PETE   See: Gagliano, Gregory and Webb.

GREGORY, WILLIAM KING
1939D.   The extinct anthropoid apes and the origin of the human dentition.
            Mankind, 2:7, 223.
1963   Our face from fish to man: a portrait gallery of ancient ancestors
            and kinsfolk together with a concise history of our best features.
            Foreword by W. Beebe. Reprint of 1929 ed. New York:
            Hafner, xl + 295 pp., 118 figs., 1 pl., (not seen).
            Rev.: Preuschoft in Anthrop. Anz., 27, 47.
1965   Our face from fish to man. Foreword by W. Beebe. Reprint. New
            York: Capricorn, xl + 295 pp., 118 figs.
            See: Nelson, N. C., McGregor and Gregory.

GREKHOVA, L. V.
1968   [Excavations in Timonovka village.]   In: Rybakov, (ed.), 1968, 27–28,
            (Russian).

GRELAUD, F.
1963   Nomogramme de classification des bifaces. Bull. Soc. Prehist., Paris,
            60, 153.

GREMIÁTSKIĬ, M. A.
1961B.   [Morphological features of a fossil bone of Paleolithic man in relation
            to the problem of the origin of sapient type man.]   Internat.
            Assoc. Quat. Res., Abs. Pap., 6th Congr., 136–137, (abs., Rus-
            sian).
1966   [Megagnathic Pleistocene forms of higher fossil primates.]   Trudy Inst.
            Etnogr. Akad. Nauk SSSR, 92, 121–142, 14 tables, (Russian).
1968   [Principles of systematics of fossil hominids.]   7th Internat. Congr.
            Anthrop. Ethnol. Sci., Moscow, 1964, 3, 358–364, (Russian).

GREMINGER, HENRY   See: Sciscenti and Greminger.

GRENET, PAUL
1965   Teilhard de Chardin. The man and his theories. Translated by R. A.
                Rudorff. London: Souvenir Press, 176 pp., 15 illustr., (not seen).
            Rev.: Sumner in Nature, 207, 1120.

GREW, EDWIN SHARPE
1909   The romance of modern geology. London, Philadelphia: Lippincott,
            307 pp., 25 pls.

GREY, DONALD C.   See: Haynes, Damon and Grey; Haynes, Grey, Damon and
            Bennett; Haynes and Grey.

GRIÁZNOV, M. P.   See: Gromov, V. I., Griáznov, et al.

GRICHUK, V. P., et al.
1966   (eds.) [Upper Pleistocene. Stratigraphy and absolute geochronology.]
            Moscow: "Nauka" Press, 284 pp., ill., (Russian).

GRICHUK, V. P., and MARKOVA, K. K.
1954   (eds.) [Materials on paleogeography.]   Moscow: Moscow University
            Press, issue 1, 206 pp., illustr., (Russian).

GRICHUK, V. P., SAMMET, E. ÎU., CHEBOTAREVA, N. S., and SHIK, S. M.
1961   [Stratigraphic scheme of Quaternary deposits.]   In: Markov, K. K.,
            (ed.), 1961B, 222–232, 4 tables, (Russian).

GRIFFIN, JAMES B.
1952A.   (ed.) Archeology of eastern United States. Chicago, London: Univ.
            Chicago Press, x + 392 pp., 205 figs.
1952B.   Culture periods in eastern United States archeology. In: Griffin, J. B.,
            (ed.), 1952A, 352–364.
1952C.   Radiocarbon dates for the eastern United States. In: Griffin, J. B.,
            (ed.), 1952A, 365–370.
1961B.   Ecologie post-glaciaire et changements culturels dans la région des
            Grands Lacs de l'Amérique du Nord. Internat. Assoc. Quat.
            Res., Abs. Pap., 6th Congr., 136, (abs.).

1964   The northeast Woodlands area. In: Jennings and Norbeck, (eds.), 1964A, 223–258, 5 figs.

1965   Late Quaternary prehistory in the northeastern Woodlands. In: Wright, H. E., and Frey, D. G., (eds.), 1965, 655–667, 1 fig.

1967   Eastern North American archaeology: a summary. Science, 156, 175–191, 7 figs.

See: Crane, H. R. and Griffin.

GRIFFIN, JOHN W.

1952   Prehistoric Florida: a review. In: Griffin, J. B., (ed.), 1952A, 322–334.

GRIFFITHS, I. See: Casamiquela 1965D.

GRIFONI, RENATA

1962   Rinvenimento di industria litica alla foce del fiume Foro (Abruzzo). Atti Soc. Toscana Sci. Nat. Mem., Ser. A, 69, 9–16, 3 figs., (English summary).

1964   La collezione di oggetti preistorici della Toscana esistente al Museo L. Pigorini di Roma. Atti Soc. Toscana Sci. Nat. Mem., Ser. A, 71, 51–82, 8 figs.

1966   Contributi alla conoscenza della preistoria Toscana. Industria di tipo Paleolitico superiore dell'Isola di Pianosa esistente al Museo Civico di Reggio Emilia. Atti Soc. Toscana Sci. Nat., Mem. Ser. A, 73, 49–61, 3 figs., (French summary).

GRIFONI, R. and RADMILLI, A. M.

1965   La Grotta Maritza e il Fucino prima dell'età romana. Riv. Sci. Preist., 19, 53–127, 25 figs., (French and English summaries).

GRIGELIS, A. A.

1963   [A detailed stratigraphic scheme of Upper Cretaceous deposits of South Baltic region based on foraminifera, and the problem of stratigraphy of Lower Cretaceous deposits of this region.] In: Grigelis, et al., (eds.), 1963, 479–496, 1 fig., 1 table, (Russian; Lithuanian and English summaries).

GRIGELIS, A., and KARATAJŪTE-TALIMAA, V.

1963   (eds.) [Problems of Lithuanian Geology.] Vilnius: Acad. Sci. Lithuanian SSR, Geol. and Geogr. Inst., 627 pp., illustr., (Russian; Lithuanian and English summaries).

GRIGGS, CLAYTON D. See: Semken and Griggs.

GRIGORENKO, B. G. See: Larichev and Grigorenko.

GRIGOR'EV, A. V. See: Shevchenko, A. I., and Grigor'ev.

GRIGOR'EV, G. P.

1963A.   [Szeletian and Kostenkovo-Streletskian culture.] Sov. Arkheol., 1963:1, 3–11, 1 fig., (Russian).

1963B.   [The problem of the origin of Aurignacian culture in France.] Voprosy Antrop., 14, 25–39, 18 figs., 1 table, (Russian).

1965A.   Migrations, indigenous development and diffusion in the Upper Paleolithic. Arctic Anthrop., 3, 116–121, (Trans. from the Russian by G. H. Clark).

1965B.   [Early Upper Paleolithic relics from Near East and the problem of
                migration of Homo sapiens to Europe.]   Voprosy Antrop., 21,
                96–110, 2 figs., 1 table, (Russian).
1967   A new reconstruction of the above-ground dwelling of Kostenki I.
                Current Anthrop., 8, 344–349, 3 figs.
                See: Ostrovskiĭ and Grigor'ev.

GRIGOR'EV, V. M.,   GROSHIN, S. I., and PAK SEN UK
1960   [Fundamental features of the geology of Korea.]   Izv. Vyssh. Uch.
                Zav., Geol. i Razv., 1960:1, 3–17, 1 map, 1 table, (Russian).

GRIGOR'EVA, G. V.
1963   [Functional determination of the tools at the Balukin station (Kostenki
                XIX).]   In: Boriskovskiĭ, P. I., 1963, (Appendix I), 192–200,
                figs. 135–139, (Russian).
1964   [New Paleolithic site Kokorevo VI on the Eniseĭ river.]   Krat. Soob.
                Inst. Ist. Mat. Kult. SSSR, 101, 64–68, 2 figs., (Russian).
1966A.   [Local variations of Late Paleolithic culture in the south of USSR,
                (Steppe zone).]   In: Rybakov, (ed.), 1966, 36–37, (Russian).
1966B.   [Late Paleolithic relics of Odessa region.]   Sborník Národního Musea v
                Praze.   Rada A: Historie, 20:1–2, 17–20, 1 pl., (Russian).
1967   [Bol'shaia Akkarzha and its place among Late Paleolithic monuments
                of the South of USSR.]   Krat. Soob. Inst. Arkheol. Akad.
                Nauk SSSR, 111, 86–90, 1 table, (Russian).

GRIGOR'EVA, G. V.,   KOROBKOVA, G. F.,   MARKEVICH, V. I.,   PASSEK, T. S.,
POPOVA, T. A., and CHERNYSH, E. K.
1968   [Results of the Moldavian expedition.]   In: Rybakov, (ed.), 1968,
                288–290, 1 fig., (Russian).

GRIMM, HANS
1961B.   Einführung in die Anthropologie. Jena: G. Fischer Verlag, 107 pp.,
                51 figs., 5 tables.
                Rev.:   Alekseev in Sovetskaia Etnografiia, 1964:5, 173–175, (Russian).

GRIMM, H. and ULLRICH, H.
1965   Ein jungpaläolithischer Schädel und Skelettreste aus Döbritz, Kr. Pöss-
                neck. Alt-Thüringen, 7, 50–89, 15 figs., pls. 4–22.
                Rev.:   Gerhardt in Homo, 18:4, 275.

GRIPP, KARL
1964   Erdgeschichte von Schleswig-Holstein. Neumunster: Wachholtz, 412 pp.,
                63 figs., 57 pls., 3 maps.
                Rev.:   Hagel in Kosmos (Stuttgart), 61, *380, *382;   Illies in Aufschluss,
                16, 48–49;   Schäfer in Natur u. Mus., 95, 121.

GRISHCHENKO, M. N.
1961B.   [On the geological age of open relics of Moustierian culture from the
                South of the European part of USSR.]   Internat. Assoc. Quat.
                Res., Abs. Pap., 6th Congr., 137, (abs.;   Russian).
1965   [Geology of Sukhaia Mechetka Volgograd site on the Volga and Rozhok
                I site in the Azov Sea area.]   In: Bader, O. N., et al., (eds.),
                1965, 141–156, 8 figs., 1 table, (Russian).
1968   [On the possibility of using the collagen method for determination of
                the absolute age of Anthropogene deposits.]   Prirodn. Obstan. i
                Fauny Proshl., 4, 137–140, 1 fig., (Russian).

GRISHCHENKO, V. A.
1968   [Find of armored fishes in northern Tian-Shan.]   Doklady Akad. Nauk
            SSSR, 179:3, 666–667, (Russian).

GRISON, MICHEL
1960B.   Geheimnis der Schopfung.   Was sagen Naturwissenschaft, Philosophie und
            Theologie vom Ursprung der Welt, der Lebewesen und der Menschen?
            Translated by Josef Rüttimann and Hans Güntert.   Luzern:
            Schweizer Volks-Buchgemeinde, 334 pp., illustr., (not seen).

GROMOV, IGOR MICHAILOVITCH
1961C.   [Using the fossil faunas of Late Quaternary rodents to ascertain the
            landscape-geographical changes.]   Internat. Assoc. Quat. Res.,
            Abs. Pap., 6th Congr., 127–128, (abs.; Russian).
1967   [Quaternary history of modern rodent fauna of USSR. (Facts and some
            research problems).]   Zool. Zhurnal, 46:10, 1566–1584, 3 figs.,
            (Russian; English summary).

GROMOV, I. M., BIBIKOV, D. I.,   KALABUKHOV, N. I., and MEĬER, M. N.
1965   [Fauna of the USSR. Mammals, vol. 3, issue 2. Marmotinae.]   Akad.
            Nauk SSSR, Zool. Inst., nov. ser. no. 92, 467 pp., 102 figs.,
            18 tables, (Russian).

GROMOV, VALERIAN INNOKENTIEVICH
1945C.   [Paleontological and archeological bases of stratigraphy of continental
            Quaternary deposits.]   Referaty Nauchno-Issl. Rab., 1947, 28,
            (Russian).
1960   [Concerning the scheme of subdividing the (Anthropogene) Quaternary
            system on the territory of the USSR and abroad.]   Trudy Geol.
            Inst., 26, 3–10, 1 chart, (Russian).
1961B.   [Questions of dispute in geological age determinations of the Paleolithic.]
            In: Gromov, V. I., et al., (eds.), 1961, 44–46, (Russian and
            English).
1961C.   [Controversial problems in the geological age determination of the Paleo-
            lithic (Anthropogene).]   Internat. Assoc. Quat. Res., Abs. Pap.,
            6th Congr., 137–138, (abs.; Russian).
1961D.   [The geological age of the Stalingrad site.]   Krat. Soob. Inst. Ist. Mat.
            Kult. SSSR, 82, 42–48, 1 table, (Russian).
1964   [Stratigraphy and periodization of the Paleolithic (A Symposium in
            Moscow).]   Vestnik Akad. Nauk SSSR, 1964:3, 124–125, (Rus-
            sian).
1967A.   [Bison (?) bone fractured by man.]   Biull. Kom. Izuch. Chetvert.
            Perioda, 33, 154–155, 1 fig., (Russian).
1967B.   [Symposium on Szeletian in Hungary.]   Biull. Kom. Izuch. Chetvert.
            Perioda, 34, 150–155, 2 figs., (Russian).
            See: Aliman, M.-H. 1960B; Bader, O. N., Gromov, and Sukachev;
            Sukachev, Gromov and Bader.

GROMOV, V. I., et al.
1965   Correlation scheme of Anthropogene deposits in Northern Eurasia.
            7th Internat. Congr., Internat. Assoc. Quat. Res., Abs., 1965,
            177–178, (abs.).

GROMOV, V. I., ALEKSEEV, M. N.,   VANGENGEIM, E. A.,   KIND, N. V.,
NIKIFOROVA, K. V., and RAVSKIĬ, E. I.
1965   [Correlation scheme for Anthropogene deposits of northern Eurasia.]

In: Nikiforova, (ed.), 1965A, 5–33, 2 tables, (Russian; English summary).

GROMOV, V. I., GRIAZNOV, M. P., IESSEN, A. A., POKROVSKAIA, I. M., and ZAKLINSKAIA, E. D.
1944   [Paleontological-stratigraphic study of lower Chusovaia R. terraces.] Referaty Nauchno-Issl. Rab., 1945, 19, (Russian).

GROMOV, V. I., IVANOVA, I. K., MARKOV, K. K., NEISHTADT, M. I., and RAEVSKII, E. I. (editors).
1965   [Quaternary period and its history, for VII congress of INQUA (USA, 1965).] Moscow: "Nauka" Press, 224 pp., 34 figs., 5 pls., 2 maps, 12 tables, (Russian; English summaries).

GROMOV, V. I., KRASNOV, I. I., NIKIFOROVA, K. V., and SHANTSER, E. V.
1961A.   [State of the problem on the lower boundary and the stratigraphic subdivision of the Anthropogene (Quaternary) system.] In: Gromov, V. I., et al., (eds.), 1961, 7–19, 1 table, (Russian; English summary).
1961B.   [State of the problem on the lower limit and on the stratigraphic subdivision of Anthropogene (Quaternary) system.] Izv. Akad. Nauk, Ser. Geograf., 1961:4, 33–41, 1 table, (Russian).

GROMOV, V. I., and NIKIFOROVA, K. V.
1965   Über die Grenze zwischen dem Unter- und dem Mittelpleistozän. Ber. Geol. Ges. Deutsch. Demokratischen Republ., 10, 13–18.

GROMOV, V. I., NIKIFOROVA, K. V., and SHANTSER, E. V.
1961   (eds.) [Problems of Anthropogene geology. (For the sixth Congress of INQUA in Warsaw in 1961).] Moscow: Akad. Nauk SSSR Press, 224 pp., illustr., (Russian; English table of contents and summaries).

GROMOV, V. I., VANGENGEIM, E. A., and NIKIFOROVA, K. V.
1963   [Stages of development of Anthropogene mammalian fauna as reflecting stages in the evolution of the Earth.] Izv. Akad. Nauk SSSR, Ser. Geol., 1963:1, 46–65, 3 figs., 3 tables, (Russian). English trans. in Internat. Geol. Rev., 7, 47–61, 3 figs.
1965   [Boundary between Lower and Middle Anthropogene.] In: Gromov, V. I., et al., (eds.), 1965, 25–40, (Russian; English summary).

GROMOVA, VERA I.
1963   [On the skeleton of tarpan (Equus caballus gmelini Ant.) and other wild horses.] Trudy Mosk. Obshch. Ispyt. Prirody, otd. biol., 10, 10–61, 21 figs., 28 tables, (Russian).
1964   [About methods of study of the teeth of fossil elephants.] Biull. Kom. Izuch. Chetvert. Perioda, Akad. Nauk SSSR, no. 29, 165–167, (Russian).
1965   [A short review of Quaternary mammals of Europe. (Essay on correlation).] Moscow: "Nauka" Press, 143 pp., 8 tables, (Russian).
1967A.   [Letter to the Editor: on the significance of mammals for the stratigraphy of Quaternary deposits.] Biull. Kom. Izuch. Chetvert. Perioda, 33, 173–175, (Russian).
1967B.   [New in the systematics and the history of Quaternary rhinoceroses.] Biull. Kom. Izuch. Chetvert. Perioda, 34, 145–149, (Russian).

1968   (ed.) Fundamentals of paleontology. A manual for paleontologists
            and geologists of the USSR. Vol. XIII. Mammals. [Chief editor:
            J. A. Orlov.] Translated from Russian. Jerusalem: Israel Pro-
            gram for Scientific Translations, vi + 585 pp., illustr. Available
            from the U. S. Department of Commerce.
        Rev.: Kermack in Nature, 222, 701—702; Thenius in Zbl. Geol. Pal.,
            Teil 2, 1969:6, 514—515.

GROSHIN, S. I.   See: Grigor'ev, V. M., et al.

GROSS, HUGO
1965   Die geochronologischen Befunde der Bärenoder Tischoferhöhle bei
            Kufstein am Inn. Quartär, 15—16, 133—141, (English summary).
1966   Der Streit um die Geochronologie des Spätpleistozäns und sein Ausgang.
            Forsch. u. Fortschr., 40:6, 165—168, 1 fig.
1967   Eine ganz ungewöhnlich voltständige Fernkonnektierung letzteiszeitlicher
            Schichtenfolgen von Nordamerika nach Europa. Quartär, 18,
            157—161, 1 table.

GROSS, WALTER
1962B.   Rev.: Rossi Ronchetti in Riv. Ital. Pal., 70, 624.
1964A.   Wilhelm Otto Dietrich (1881 - 1964). Neues Jahrb. Geol. Pal., Monatsh.,
            1964, 385—387, portr.
1964B.   Über die Randzähne des Mundes, die Ethmoidalregion des Schädels und
            die Unterkiefersymphyse von Dipterus oervigi n. sp. Pal. Zeit.,
            38, 7—25, 3 figs., 3 pls.
1964C.   Polyphyletische Stämme im System der Wirbeltiere? Zool. Anz., 173,
            1—22, 6 figs.
1965A.   Über die Placodermen-Gattungen Asterolepis und Tiaraspis aus den
            Devon Belgiens und einen fraglichen Tiaraspis-Rest aus dem Devon
            Spitzbergens. Bull. Inst. Roy. Sci. Nat. Belg., 41:16, 1—19, 4
            figs., 2 pls.
1965B.   Bothriolepis cf. panderi Lahusen in einem Geschiebe von Travemünde
            bei Lübeck. Mitt. Geol. Staatsinst. Hamburg, 34, 138—141, 2 figs.
1965C.   Über einen neuen Schädelrest von Stensiöella heintzi und Schuppen
            von Machaeracanthus sp. indet. aus dem Hunsrückschiefer.
            Notizbl. Hess. Landesamt. Bodenforsch., 93, 7—18, 3 figs., pls. 1—2.
1965D.   Über den Vorderschädel von Ganorhynchus splendens Gross (Dipnoi,
            Mitteldevon). Pal. Zeit., 39, 113—133, 7 figs., pl. 19.
1965E.   Onychodus jaekeli Gross (Crossopterygii, Oberdevon), Bau des Symphy-
            senknochens und seiner Zähne. Senck. Lethaea, 46a, 123—132,
            2 figs., pl. 5.
1966   Kleine Schuppenkunde. Neues Jahrb. Geol. Pal., Abh., 125, Festband,
            29—48, 7 figs., portr.
1967A.   Bemerkungen zum System und zur Phylogenie der Agnathen und Fische.
            Colloq. Internat. Cent. Nation. Recherch. Sci., 163, 73—79, 2
            figs., (French summary).
1967B.   Über das Gebiss der Acanthodier und Placodermen. In: Patterson, C.,
            and Greenwood, P. H., (eds.), 1967, 121—130, 2 figs., (English
            summary).
1967C.   Über Thelodontier-Schuppen. Palaeontogr., Abt. A, 127:1—2, 1—67,
            15 figs., 7 pls.
1968A.   Fragliche Actinopterygier-Schuppen aus dem Silur Gotlands. Lethaia,
            1, 184—218, 14 figs., (English summary).
1968B.   Juri Aleksandrowitsch Orlov. 13.6.1893 — 2.10.1966. Pal. Zeit., 42:1—2,
            3—4.

1968C.   Beobachtungen mit dem Elektronenraster-Auflichtmikroskop an den Siebplatten und dem Isopedin von Dartmuthia (Osteostraci). Mit einem Beitrag "Untersuchungsmethode" von Johanna Vahl und Willi Ziegler. Pal. Zeit., 42:1—2, 73—82, 1 fig., 3 pls., (English summary).

1968D.   Porenschuppen und Sinneslinien des Thelodontiers Phlebolepis elegans Pander. Pal. Zeit., 42:3—4, 131—146, 3 figs., 2 pls., (English summary).

GROSSET, H. E., DINESMAN, L. G., and ZALKIN, V. I.
1965   [On ancient distribution of the steppe marmot.]   Biull. Mosk. Obshch. Prirody, Otd. Biol., 70:2, 34—46, 2 figs., (Russian; English summary).

GROSSMAN, MARY LOUISE, and HAMLET, J.
1964   Birds of prey of the world. New York: Clarkson N. Potter, 496 pp., illustr.
Rev.: Cade in Wilson Bull., 77, 302—305;   P. R. E. in Ibis, 108, 637.

GROSSO, GERALD H.
1967   Cave life on the Palouse. Nat. Hist., 76:2, 38—43, illustr.

GROUBE, ROSEMARY
1966   (ed.) Salvage archaeology and site protection in New Zealand. New Zealand Archaeol. Assoc. Newsletter, 9, 77—140.

GRUBE, FRIEDRICH   See: Rust and Steffens.

GRUBE, GEORGE E.
1964   Introductory ornithology. Dubuque, Iowa: Brown, x + 294 pp., 108 figs.
Rev.: Lancaster in Wilson Bull., 71, 206—209.

GRUET, MICHEL
1964   Les terrasses du confluent Loir-Sarthe et leurs industries. Bull. Soc. Géol. France, 5, 458—463, 3 figs.

GRUET, M., and JAOUEN, P.
1964   Le gisement moustérien, et aurignacien du Bois Milet. Les Moutiers-en-Retz (Loire-Atlantique). L'Anthrop., 67, 429—458, 11 figs.

GRUJINSCHI, C.   See: Panin, Lăzărescu and Grujinschi.

GRYBA, EUGENE M.
1968   A possible Paleo-Indian and Archaic site in the Swan Valley, Manitoba. Plains Anthrop., 13, 218—227, 6 figs., 3 pls., 1 table.

GU, LAN-PO
1965   [Find of skull bones of Sinanthropus lantianensis Woo, and description of site.]   Kexue tongbao, 1965:6, 477—481, (Chinese).

GUENTHER, EKKE W.
1956D.   Die geologische Altersdatierung der fossilen Menschenfunde von Steinheim an der Murr und von Ehringsdorf. Ber. Tagung Deutsch. Ges. Anthrop., 5, 57—61, 1 fig.

1959 Abs.: Ebers in Zbl. Geol. Pal., Teil 2, 1962, 576.

1960C. Abs.: Ebers in Zbl. Geol. Pal., Teil 2, 1962, 571—572.

1961B. Abs.: Dietrich in Zbl. Geol. Pal., Teil 2, 1964, 205.

1961C. Abs.: Dietrich in Zbl. Geol. Pal., Teil 2, 1964, 199.

1962A. Abs.: Dietrich in Zbl. Geol. Pal., Teil 2, 1964, 205—206.

1962B. Abs.: Dietrich in Zbl. Geol. Pal., Teil 2, 1964, 186.

1964A. Säugetierreste aus eiszeitlichen Ablagerungen von Schleswig-Holstein. Lauenburgische Heimat, 45, Juni/Juli 1964, (not seen).

1964B. Zur Altersdatierung der "Homo"-Fundschicht von Ehringsdorf bei Weimar. Zeit. Morph. Anthrop., 56, 23—32, 3 figs., (English summary).

1965 Die Biber (Trogontherium cuvieri Fisch. und Castor fiber L.) der altpleistozänen Fundstelle von Voigtstedt in Thüringen. Pal. Abh., Abt. A, 2, 565—583, 3 figs., pls. 36—37, 8 tables, (Russian and English summaries).

1967 Ausgrabungen einer eiszeitlichen Tierwelt im Valsequillo (Hochland von Mexiko). Quartär, 18, 163—172, 2 figs., 1 pl.

GUENTHER, E. W., and TIDELSKI, F.

1964 Fauna und Flora im Pleistozän-Profil von Murg bei Säckingen und ihre Aussage zur Altersdatierung. Eiszeit. u. Gegenwart, 15, 164—180, 3 figs., 4 tables, (English summary).

GUÉRIN, CLAUDE

1965 Gallogoral (nov. gen.) meneghinii (Rütimeyer, 1878), un rupicapriné du Villafranchien d'Europe occidentale. Doc. Lab. Géol. Fac. Sci., Lyon, 11:1—2, 353 pp., 70 pls.

1966A. Les ruminants du gisement quaternaire des "Abîmes de La Fage" à Noailles (Corrèze). C. R. Soc. Géol. France, 1966, 340—341.

1966B. Diceros douariensis n. sp., un rhinoceros du Mio-Pliocène de Tunisie du nord. Doc. Lab. Géol. Fac. Sci. Lyon, 16, 1—50, 12 figs., 4 tables, (English summary).

GUERRI, MARA

1964A. L'industria litica delle stazioni di superficie sulla Maielletta. Atti. Soc. Toscana Sci. Nat. Mem., Ser. A, 70, 244—261, 5 figs.

1964B. Manufatti della "Pebble culture" nel Fezzan. Riv. Sci. Preist., 18, 255—260, 1 fig., (French and English summaries).

1964C. Su alcuni nuclei del Paleolitico antico garcanico. Riv. Sci. Preist., 18, 271—278, 2 figs., (French and English summaries).

GUICHARD, JEAN

1964 Note préliminaire sur l'étude des limons quaternaires du Bergeracois (Dordogne). Bull. Soc. Géol. France, 5, 489—494, 3 figs.

1965 Un faciès original de l'Acheuléen: Cantalouette (commune de Creysse, Dordogne). L'Anthrop., 69:5—6, 413—464, 34 figs., 3 tables, (English summary).

GUICHARD, J. and G.

1965 The Early and Middle Paleolithic of Nubia: a preliminary report. In: Wendorf, Fred, (ed.), 1965A, 57—116, 29 figs., 10 tables.

GUILDAY, JOHN E.

1960A. Mouse bones. Netherworld News, 8:1, 3—5.

1960B. Of microtines and men. Netherworld News, 8:8, 127—129.

1961C. Jaguar (old style). Netherworld News, 9:3, 41—43, cover photo.

1961D.   The pterosaur and the lemming. Netherworld News, 9:8, 142–144.
1962B.   The comings and goings of squirrels. Netherworld News, 10:5, 67–70, 1 fig.
1963A.   Abs.: Nicholas in Internat. Jour. Spel., 1, 566.
1963C.   The faunagraph record. Carnegie Mag., 37, 233–237, 3 figs.
1965A.   The Ice Age heffalump trap. Canadian Audubon, 27, 110–114, 11 figs.
1965B.   Differential extinction during Late Pleistocene/Recent times. 7th Internat. Congr., Internat. Assoc. Quat. Res., Abs., 1965, 181–182, (abs.).
1966   Rangifer antler from an Ohio bog. Jour. Mammal., 47, 325–326, 1 fig., 1 table.
1967A.   The climatic significance of the Hosterman's Pit local fauna, Centre County, Pennsylvania. Amer. Antiq., 32, 231–232, 1 table.
1967B.   Notes on the Pleistocene big brown bat [Eptesicus grandis (Brown).] Ann. Carnegie Mus., 39:7, 105–114, 3 figs., 2 tables.
1967C.   Differential extinction during Late-Pleistocene and Recent times. In: Martin, P. S., and Wright, H. E., (eds.), 1967, 121–140, 2 figs.
1968A.   Archaeological evidence of caribou from New York and Massachusetts. Jour. Mammal., 49, 344–345.
1968B.   Fauna of the Little Box Elder Cave, Converse County, Wyoming. Pleistocene zoogeography of the lemming Dicrostonyx. Univ. Colorado Studies, Ser. Earth Sci., 6, 61–71, 1 fig., 1 table.
            See: Hibbard, Ray, et al.; McCrady and Guilday; Martin, P. S., and Guilday.

GUILDAY, J. E., and ADAM, E. K.
1967   Small mammal remains from Jaguar Cave, Lemhi County, Idaho. Tebiwa, 10:1, 26–36, 1 fig., 6 tables.

GUILDAY, J. E., HAMILTON, H. W., and ADAM, E. K.
1967   Animal remains from Horned Owl Cave, Albany County, Wyoming. Contrib. Geol., Univ. Wyoming, 6, 97–99, 1 table.

GUILDAY, J. E., HAMILTON, H. W., and McCRADY, A. D.
1966   The bone breccia of Bootlegger Sink, York County, Pa. Ann. Carnegie Mus., 38, 145–163, 4 figs., 1 table.

GUILDAY, J. E., and HANDLEY, C. O., JR.
1967   A new Peromyscus (Rodentia: Cricetidae) from the Pleistocene of Maryland. Ann. Carnegie Mus., 39:6, 91–103, 2 figs., 4 tables.

GUILDAY, J. E., and IRVING, D. C.
1967   Extinct Florida spectacled bear Tremarctos floridanus (Gidley) from central Tennessee. Bull. Nat. Spel. Soc., 29, 149–162, 16 figs., 7 tables.
            Rev.: Ehrenberg in Zbl. Geol. Pal., Teil 2, 1969:3, 292.

GUILDAY, J. E., and McCRADY, A. D.
1966   Armadillo remains from Tennessee and West Virginia caves. Bull. Nat. Spel. Soc., 28, 183–184, 1 fig.
1968   Vertebrate fossils from Appalachian caves and their implications to Pleistocene geology. Spec. Pap. Geol. Soc. Amer., 101, 437, (abs.).

GUILDAY, J. E., MARTIN, P. S., and McCRADY, A. D.
1964   New Paris No. 4: a Late Pleistocene cave deposit in Bedford County, Pennsylvania. Bull. Nat. Spel. Soc., 26, 121–194, 34 figs., 2 maps.

Rev.: Holman in Copeia, 1965, 259–260.
Abs.: Nicholas in Internat. Jour. Spel., 1, 566.

GUILLIEN, YVES
1961   Les gisements préhistoriques de la vallée des Eaux-Claires. IV. – Mous-
            térien charentais et chronologie glaciarie. Mem. Soc. Archéol.
            Hist. Charente, 1960, 121–126.
1964   Les gisements préhistoriques de la vallée des Eaux-Claires. VIII. – De
            quelques maxillaires de jeunes rennes trouvés au Petit-Puymoyen
            (Charente). Fouilles de L. Duport. Mem. Soc. Archéol. Hist.
            Charente, 1962-1963, 111–122, 5 pls.
1965A.   Geomorphologie et préhistoire au sud d'Angouleme. I. Le Petit-Puymoyen.
            Bull. Assoc. Franç. Etude Quat., 1965:3–4, 185–187, 2 figs.
1965B.   La Basse-Tardoire. Formations lacustres, formations fluviales, et paléo-
            sols du Reuvérien à l'Holocène. Bull. Assoc. Franç. Etude Quat.,
            1965:3–4, 205–210.
1965C.   Geomorphologie et préhistoire au sud d'Angouleme II. Le renne,
            l'homme et le probleme de la sedentarite. Bull. Assoc. Franç.
            Etude Quat., 1965:3–4, 187–188.
1965D.   Dépôts de Pente, terrasses, remblaiements Holocènes entre Angouleme
            et Mansle. Bull. Assoc. Franç. Etude Quat., 1965:3–4, 251–256,
            2 figs.
            See: Brigot, et al.; David, P., Duplaix and Guillien.

GUILLIEN, Y., and DUPORT, L.
1960   Les gisements préhistoriques de la vallée des Eaux-Claires. II. – Les
            falaises et la Grotte du Petit-Puymoyen. Mem. Soc. Archéol.
            Hist. Charente, 1959, 47–59, 3 figs., 2 pls.

GUILLIER, M. T.   See: Delibrias, Guillier and Labeyrie.

GUINCHAT, C.   See: Narr 1964B.

GULIAMOV, IA. G.
1966   Archeological investigaions in Uzbekistan, 1963–64. Translated by
            Eugene V. Prostov. In: Beregovaia, N. A., Islamov, U., and
            Kalandadze, A. N., 1966, 125–126.

GULIĀMOVA, E., DAVIDOVICH, E. A., LITVINSKIĬ, B. A., and RANOV, V. A.
1956   [Archeological and numismatic collections of the Institute of History,
            Archeology, and Ethnography of the Acad. of Sci., of Tadzhik
            SSR.] Stalinabad: Ak. Nauk Tadzh. SSR Press, 36 pp., 11 pls.,
            (Russian).

GUMERMAN, GEORGE J.
1966   A Folsom point from the area of Mishongovi, Arizona. Plateau, 38,
            79–80, 1 fig.

GUMILEVSKIĬ, N. I., and KOROBKOV, I. I.
1967   [A site of Stone Age monuments near Kheïvani village.] Krat. Soob.
            Inst. Arkheol. Akad. Nauk SSSR, 111, 91–100, 4 figs., 1 table,
            (Russian).

GUNDERSON, HARVEY L.
1965   (ed.) Items of interest. Mus. Notes, Univ. Neb. State Mus., no. 26,
            [4].

1967   Eck Frank Schramm [Sept. 7, 1883 - Feb. 28, 1967]. Mus. Notes,
Univ. Neb. State Mus., no. 33, [p. 12].

GUNSTONE, A. J. H.   See: Thomas, N. and Gunstone.

GÜNTERT, HANS   See: Grison 1960B.

GÜNTHER, KLAUS
1964   Die altsteinzeitlichen Funde der Balver Höhle. Bodenaltertümer West-
falens, Band 8, Münster, 165 pp., 13 figs., 54 pls., 18 tables,
(not seen).
Rev.: Feustel in Ethnogr.-Archäol. Z., 9:2, 194—196;   Kernd'l in
in Berliner Jahrb. Vor- und Frühgesch., 6, 233—234;   Krüger
in Quartär, 18, 240—246;   Narr in Germania, 45, 161—164;
Woldstedt in Eiszeit. u. Gegenwart, 16, 249—250.
1967   Zur Geschichte der Abstammungslehre. Mit einer Erörterung von Vor-
und Nebenfragen. In: Heberer, (ed.), 1967A, 3—60.

GUPTA, B. B.
1966   Skeleton of Erethizon and Coendou. Mammalia, 30, 495—497.

GUPTA, S.-P.
1965   Les industries du Paléolithique supérieur de l'Inde. Bull. Soc. Préhist.
Franç., Etud. et Trav., 61, 28—31.
1968   [A review of the present state of Ancient Indian archeology in the
light of new discoveries in Middle Asia.]   Sovetskaia Etnografiia,
1968:4, 110—114, (Russian).

GUPTA, V. J.
1966   Fish remains from the Middle Paleozoic of the Kashmir Himalayas.
Current Sci., 35, 95—96, 2 figs.

GUPTA, V. J., and DENISON, R. H.
1966   Devonian fishes from Kashmir, India. Nature, 211, 177—178, 2 figs.

GURBA, JAN
1965   [On Paleolithic research in Urals.]   Acta Archaeol. Carpathica, 7:1—2,
113—115, 1 fig., (Polish;   French summary).

GUREEV, A. A.
1964   [Fauna of the USSR. Mammals, vol. 3, issue 10. Lagomorpha.]   Akad.
Nauk SSSR, Zool. Inst., nov. ser. no. 87, 276 pp., 129 figs.,
3 tables, (Russian).

GUREEV, A. A., and KON'KOVA, N. I.
1967   [New genus and species of hare from Pliocene of Moldavian SSR.]
Pal. geol. polezn. iskop. Moldavii, 2, 156—159, 2 figs., (Russian).

GURINA, N. N.
1965   [New data on the Stone Age of northwestern Belorussiia.]   Mat. Issled.
Arkheol. SSSR, no. 131, 141—203, 28 figs., (Russian).
Rev.: Briusov in Sov. Arkheol., 1966:3, 267—269, (Russian).

GUSEĬNOV, M. M.
1963   [Azykh cave — a large karst and the oldest site in Azerbaijan.]   Dokl.
Akad. Nauk Azerbaĭd. SSR, 19:11, 75—80, 1 fig., 2 pls., (Russian;   Azerbaijani summary).

GUSEV, A. I.
1956   [Mammoth horizon.]   Materialy Geol. Inst. (VSEGEI), Nov. Ser. Chetv.
            Geol. i Geomorf., 17, 169–177, 6 figs., (Russian).

GUSLITSER, B. I., and KANIVETS, V. I.
1962B.   [Caves of Pechora region as a source for the study of Quaternary
            Period.] Izv. Komi Fil. Vses. Geogr. Obshch., 7, 45–59, 4 figs.,
            1 table, (Russian).
1965   [Paleolithic sites on the Pechora.]   In: Bader, O. N., et al., (eds.),
            1965, 86–103, 5 figs., 1 table, (Russian).

GUSLITSER, B. I.,   KANIVETS, V. I., and TIMOFEEV, E. M.
1965   [Byzovaia site – a Paleolithic monument at the Polar Circle.]   Sov.
            Arkheol., 1965:2, 135–141, 3 figs., (Russian).

GUTH, CHRISTIAN
1961   [Principaux gisements de Mammifères en] Asie. In: Piveteau, J., (ed.),
            1961A (Traité de Paléo., 6:1), 480–484, fig. 6.
1964A.   Sinus veineux et veines de l'arrièrecrâne de quelques carnivores fossiles.
                Ann. Pal., Vert., 50, 31–43, 6 figs.
1964B.   À propos de Miacis exilis des Phosphorites du Quercy. Mammalia, 28,
            359–365, 1 fig., pls. 15–16, (English summary).
1967   Au sujet du temporal des Néanderthaliens. Colloq. Internat. Cent.
                Nation. Recherch. Sci., 163, 655–657, 1 fig., (English summary).
            See: Brunet, M. and Guth; Carbonnel and Guth.

GUTHE, ALFRED K.
1964A.   Two early projectile points from Greene County. Tenn. Archaeol.,
            20, 47, illustr.
1964B.   A reworked Clovis point. Tenn. Archaeol., 20, 83, 1 fig.
1964C.   The Tip Bowden collection. Tenn. Archaeol., 20, 84–86, illustr.
1964D.   Points from east Tennessee. Tenn. Archaeol., 20, 86–88.
1965A.   Paleo-Indian projectile points. Tenn. Archaeol., 21, 28–33, 11 figs.
1965B.   Paleo-Indian points from east Tennessee. A reworked Cumberland
                point. Tenn. Archaeol., 21, 72–74, 6 figs.
1965C.   A reworked Clovis from west Tennessee. Tenn. Archaeol., 21, 75, 1 fig.
1966A.   These four Paleo-Indian points or fragments of points were found on
                three different sites in Humphreys County, Tennessee. Tenn.
                Archaeol., 22, 46, 1 fig.
1966B.   Tennessee's Paleo-Indian. Tenn. Archaeol., 22, 67–77, 5 figs.
1967   The Paleo-Indian of Tennessee. Bull. Eastern States Archeol. Fed.,
                no. 26, 11, (abs.).

GUTHRIE, DANIEL ALBERT
1965   The mammals of the Eocene Lysite member, Wind River formation of
                Wyoming. Diss. Abst., 26, 2389, (abs.).
1966   A new species of dichobunid artiodactyl from the Early Eocene of
                Wyoming. Jour. Mammal., 47, 487–490, 1 fig., 1 table.
1967A.   Paeneprolimnocyon, a new genus of Early Eocene Limnocyonid (Mam-
                malia, Creodonta). Jour. Pal., 41, 1285–1287, 1 fig., 1 table.
1967B.   The mammalian fauna of the Lysite member, Wind River formation,
                (Early Eocene) of Wyoming. Mem. S. Calif. Acad. Sci., 5,
                vi + 53 pp., 36 figs., 29 tables.
1968   The tarsus of Early Eocene artiodactyls. Jour. Mammal., 49, 297–301,
                4 figs.

GUTHRIE, MEARL R.
    1964   I visited Hell Gap. Ohio Archaeol., 14, 132—133, 2 figs.

GUTHRIE, RUSSELL D.
    1965   Variability in characters undergoing rapid evolution, an analysis of
                Microtus molars. Evolution, 19, 214—233, 6 figs.
    1966A.   The extinct wapity of Alaska and Yukon Territory. Canadian Jour. Zool.,
                44, 47—57, 4 figs.
    1966B.   Pelage of fossil bison — a new osteological index. Jour. Mammal., 47,
                725—727, 1 fig.
    1966C.   Bison horn cores — character choice and systematics. Jour. Pal., 40,
                738—740.
    1967   Differential preservation and recovery of Pleistocene large mammal re-
                mains in Alaska. Jour. Pal., 41, 243—246, 5 figs.

GUTIÉRREZ, F.   See: Termier 1966.

GUTMANN, WOLFGANG FRIEDRICH
    1966A.   Die Funktion der Myomerie in phylogenetischer Sicht. (Vorläufige
                Mitteilung). Senckenberg. biol., 47, 155—160, 2 figs., (English
                summary).
    1966B.   Coelomgliederung, Myomerie und die Frage der Vertebraten-Antezedenten.
                Zeit. Zool. Syst. Evolut.-forsch., 4:1—2, 13—56, 8 figs., (English
                summary).
    1967A.   Das Dermalskelett der fossilen "Panzerfische" funktionell und phylo-
                genetisch interpretiert. Senck. Lethaea, 48:3—4, 277—283, 2 figs.,
                (English summary).
    1967B.   Nachtrag zur "Wurmtheorie" der Vertebraten-Evolution. Zeit. Zool.
                Syst. Evolut.-forsch., 5, 314—332, 4 figs., (English summary).

GUTOVA, L. N.
    1963   [On the stratigraphy of Jurassic deposits of the Irkutsk coal-basin.]
                Trudy Inst. Zemn. Kory SO AN SSSR, 15, 92—99, 1 table,
                (Russian).

GVOZDOVER, M. D.
    1959   [Archaeological surveys of the Palaeolithic on the Lower Don in
                1957 - 1958.] Izv. Rostovskogo Muz. Kraevedeniiă, no. 1:3,
                8—10, (not seen).
    1961B.   [Specific characteristics of the flint collection from the Avdeevo Paleo-
                lithic site.]   Krat. Soob. Inst. Ist. Mat. Kult. SSSR, 82, 112—119,
                3 figs., (Russian).
    1964   [Late Paleolithic sites of lower Don R.] In: Boriskovskiĭ and Praslov,
                1964 (Arkheol. SSSR, 14), 37—41, illustr., (Russian).
    1967   [Cultural elements of Late Paleolithic finds on the lower Don R.]
                Voprosy Antrop., 27, 82—101, 2 figs., 4 pls., 1 table, (Russian).

GVOZDOVER, M. D., and FORMOZOV, A. A.
    1960   Utilisation d'os dans la station moustérienne de Staroselié en Crimée.
                Archeol. Roz., 12, 390—393, 397—403, figs. 146, 149, 152—153,
                (Russian; French summary).

GWINNER, MANFRED P.   See: Geyer and Gwinner.

H., S. E.
1965   Obit.: [Frederick Everard Zeuner,   - 1963.]   Proc. Geol. Soc. London, no. 1618, 122—123.

HAAG, WILLIAM G., HAAS, G., and HÜRZELER, J.
1962   (eds.) Evolution und Bibel. Luzern and Munich: Rex Press.

HAARLÄNDER, WILHELM and HELLER, F.
1964   Anfänge geologischer Sammlungen im Gebiet der ehemaligen Reichsstadt Nürnberg. Geol. Bavarica, 53, 209—250, 16 figs.

HAAS, ADOLF
1963   Origen de la vida y del hombre. Madrid: La Editorial Católica, "Biblioteca de Autores Cristianos", xxviii + 552 pp., (not seen). Rev.: L. de C. in Brotéria, Sér. Mensal, 79, 240.

HAAS, GEORG
1963C.   Abs.: Huene in Zbl. Geol. Pal., Teil 2, 1964, 520.
1963E.   Excavation of earliest Pleistocene deposits of the Jordan River. Amer. Philos. Soc., Year Book, 1963, 329—330.
1963F.   The Ubeidiya fauna. S. Afr. Jour. Sci., 59, 126.
1965   Pleistocene of the Jordan Valley. Amer. Philos. Soc. Yearbook, 1964, 273—274.
1967   On the vertebral centra of nothosaurs and placodonts from the Muschelkalk of Wadi Ramon, Negev, Israël. Colloq. Internat. Cent. Nation. Recherch-Sci., 163, 329—334, 2 figs., (French and German summaries).
1968   On the fauna of Ubeidiya. Proc. Israel Acad. Sci., Sect. Sci., no. 7, 1—14.
     See: Haag, Haas and Hürzeler; Stekelis and Haas.

HAAS, N.   See: Anati, and Haas.

HACKETT, C. J.
1967   The human treponematoses. In: Brothwell, Don, and Sandison, A. T., (eds.), 152—169, 8 figs.

HADLEIGH-WEST, FREDERICK
1967   The Donnelly Ridge site and the definition of an early core and blade complex in central Alaska. Amer. Antiq., 32, 360—382, 10 figs.

HADLEIGH-WEST, F., and BANDI, H.
1965   The Campus Site and the problem of Epi-Gravettian infiltrations from Asia to America. 7th Internat. Congr., Internat. Assoc. Quat. Res., Abs., 1965, 185, (abs.).

HADŽI, JOVAN
1955   (ed.) Congrès Yougoslave de Spéléologie, Première Session. Ljubljana, Slovenian Academy of Sciences Press, 125 pp., (Yugoslavian; French, German or English summaries).

HAECK, J.
1964   La grotte du Mont Falise à Antheit, vallée de la Méhaigne, province de Liège. Bull. Soc. Roy. Belge Anthrop. Préhist., 74, 43—58, 21 figs.

HAGEL, JÜRGEN
    1965   Sehenswerte Sammlungen. Niedersächsisches Landesmuseum. Kosmos
                (Stuttgart), 61, *492, illustr.

HAGGERTY, JAMES J.   See: Stever, Haggerty and Editors of Life.

HAGUE, RENÉ   See: Cuénot 1965.

HAHN, KATHLEEN V.   See: Thomson, K. S., and Hahn.

HAHN, KENNETH
    1964   Dedication of Vertebrate Paleontology Laboratory Nov. 6, 1963. Quart.
                Los Angeles Co. Mus. Nat. Hist., 2:3, 12—13, illustr.

HAHN, PAUL
    1965   The Paleo-Indian era: distribution of finds. Mississippi. Bull. South-
                east. Archaeol. Confer., 2, 18.

HAHN, MRS' RICHARD N.
    1966A.   New Dalton-Big Sandy distribution. Jour. Ala. Archeol., 12, 70—71,
                1 fig.
    1966B.   Interesting Blountsville site. Jour. Ala. Archeol., 12, 160, 1 fig.

HAIGHT, MARION, and WRIGHT, N. L.
    1966   Reworked Palaeo artifacts. Ohio Archaeol., 16, 74, 3 figs.

HAILMAN, JACK P.   See: Brace, et al.

HALBOUTY, MICHEL T.
    1965   Geology for human needs. GeoTimes, 10:4, 14—17.

HALDANE, JOHN BURDON SANDERSON
    1960   The theory of natural selection today. Proc. Cent. Bicent. Congr. Biol.,
                Singapore, 1958, 1960, 1—8.
    1966   The causes of evolution. Reprint of 1932 ed. Ithaca, N. Y.: Cornell
                Paperbacks, Cornell Univ. Press, vii + 235 pp., illustr.
                Rev.: Caren in Bio-Science, 17, 424.

HALDEMANN, E. G.   See: Howell, Cole, et al.

HALL, E. and M.
    1964A.   An early dinosaur. Cambridge, Mass.: Mus. Comp. Zool., Harvard Univ.,
                26—27, 1 fig.
                Abs.: Huene in Zbl. Geol. Pal., Teil 2, 1965, 248.
    1964B.   Kronosaurus, ruler of the seas. Cambridge, Mass.: Mus. Comp. Zool.,
                Harvard Univ., 8—10, 1 fig.
                Abs.: Huene in Zbl. Geol. Pal., Teil 2, 1965, 248.

HALL, E. RAYMOND
    1967   (ed.) Henry Higgins Lane (1878 - 1965). Biographical data. Univ.
                Kansas Mus. Nat. Hist., Misc. Publ., 48, 1—8, portr.

HALL, ROBERT L.
    1965   Current research. Northern Mississippi Valley. Amer. Antiq., 30, 535—
                541.

1966   Current research: northern Mississippi Valley. Amer. Antiq., 31, 604–
             608.

HALLAM, ANTHONY
1967   The bearing of certain palaeozoogeographic data on continental drift.
             Palaeogeog., Palaeoclimatol., Palaeoecol., 3, 201–241, 12 figs.
             See: Craig, G. Y. 1966B, C.

HALTENORTH, THEODOR
1965   Bernhard Rensch 65 Jahre. Säugetierkundl. Mitt., 13, 44, portr.

HAMADA, TATSUJI   See: Yamasaki, et al.

HAMBLETON, H. J.
1967   The concept of geologic time. Sci. on the March, 47, 34–35, 1 fig.

HAMILTON, E. I.
1965   Applied geochronology. New York: Academic Press, 283 pp., 53 figs.,
             52 tables.
             Rev.: Faul in Science, 152, 955–956;   R. in Current Sci., 34, 703;
             Smith in New Sci., 28, 55;   Wedepohl in Naturwiss. Rund, 19,
             208–209.

HAMILTON, E. I., and FARQUHAR, R. M.
1968   (eds.) Radiometric dating for geologists. New York: Interscience Pub-
             lishers, 506 pp., (not seen).
             Rev.: Hurley in GeoTimes, 14:2, 32–34.

HAMILTON, HAROLD W.   See: Guilday, Hamilton and McCrady.

HAMILTON, T. H.
1967   Process and pattern in evolution. New York: Macmillan, 118 pp.,
             (not seen).
             Rev.: Johnston in Syst. Zool., 16, 262.

HAMLET, JOHN   See: Grossman and Hamlet.

HAMMACK, LAURENS C.
1965   Archaeology of the Ute Dam and Reservoir, northeastern New Mexico.
             Papers Anthrop. Mus. New Mex., no. 14, 69 pp., 27 figs., 4
             tables.

HAMMOND, PETER B.
1964   (ed.) Physical anthropology and archaeology; selected readings. New
             York: Macmillan, xi + 397 pp., illustr.
             Rev.: Angel in Amer. Jour. Phys. Anthrop., 23, 197–198.

HAMON, J. HILL
1962B.   Osteology and paleontology of the passerine birds of the Reddick Pleis-
             tocene. Diss. Abst., 22, 3784, (abs.).
1964   Osteology and paleontology of the passerine beds of the Reddick,
             Florida, Pleistocene. Bull. Florida Geol. Surv., no. 44, vii +
             210 pp., 13 figs.

HAN, DE-FEN   See: Li, Y.-h., Han and Hsu; Wu, et al.

HANDLEY, CHARLES O., JR.   See: Guilday and Handley.

HÄNEL, WOLFGANG
1965   Gewinnung und erste Bearbeitung der Solnhofener Plattenkalke. Aufsch-
            luss, 16, 237—242, 4 figs.

HANIHARA, KAZURO
1965   Some crown characters of the deciduous incisors and canines in Japanese-
            American hybrids. Jour. Anthrop. Soc. Nippon, 72, 135—145,
            3 figs., 5 tables, (Japanese summary).

HANIHARA, K., KUWASHIMA, T., and SAKAO, N.
1964   The deflecting wrinkle on the lower molars in recent man. Jour. Anthrop.
            Soc. Nippon, 72, 1—8, 10 figs., 1 table, (Japanese summary).

HANIHARA, K., and MINAMIDATE, T.
1965   Tuberculum accessorium mediale internum in the human deciduous
            lower second molars. Jour. Anthrop. Soc. Nippon, 73, 9—19,
            1 fig., 7 tables, (Japanese summary).

HANKINS, ROBERT O.
1967   Fluted point find of the year. Ohio Archaeol., 17, 107, 1 fig.

HANSEN, MICHAEL C.
1968   The Upper Paleozoic genus Petalodus (Bradyodonti) from North America.
            Proc. Neb. Acad. Sci., 78th Ann. Meeting, 1968, 19—20, (abs.).

HANSEN, RUSSELL F.
1967   A study of two bogs, II. Fern Lake. Explorer, 9:1, 9—11, illustr.

HANSEN, SIGURD
1965   The Quaternary of Denmark. In: Rankama, (ed.), 1965, 1—90, 16
            figs., 18 tables.

HANSEN, WALLACE R.
1965   Geology of the Flaming Gorge area, Utah — Colorado — Wyoming.
            U. S. Geol. Surv., Prof. Pap., 490, viii + 196 pp., 68 figs., 2 pls.,
            7 tables.

HANSON, EARL D.
1965   Die Entstehung der Formen. Entfaltung der Tierwelt in Zeit und Raum.
            Stuttgart: Franckh'sche Verlagshandlung (Kosmos-Mitglieder),
            135 pp., 57 figs., 1 pl., (not seen).
            Rev.: Heberer in Anthrop. Anz., 30, 210; Kurth in Naturwiss. Rund,
            19, 121; Zänkert in Kosmos (Stuttgart), 61, *498—*499.

HANTKE, RENÉ
1966   Der 7. Kongress der Internationales Assoziation für Quartärforschung
            (INQUA). Geog. Helvetica, 1966:1, 32—35.

HANULÍK, M. See: Adrik, et al.

HAPGOOD, CHARLES H.
1960   The mystery of the frozen mammoths. Coronet, 48:5, 70—78, illustr.
1966   Maps of the ancient sea kings: evidence of advanced civilization in the
            Ice Age. Philadelphia and New York: Chilton Books, 315 pp.,
            100 figs., color frontispiece.

HARČÁR, JÁN, and SCHMIDT, Z.
1965 [Quaternary deposits in the environs of Strekova (Hron Hills).] Geol.
Práce, Ustr. Ústav Geol., Bratislava, 34, 143–151, 1 pl., 2 tables,
(Slovakian; German summary).

HARDY, ALISTER
1965 The living stream. A restatement of evolution theory and its relation
to the spirit of man. London: Collins, 292 pp., 75 figs.
Rev.: LeGros Clark in Nature, 211, 909; Pinner in Naturwiss. Rund,
19, 204.

HARDY, W. G.
1967 (ed.) Alberta. A natural history. Edmonton, Alberta: M. G. Hurtig,
343 pp., illustr.
Rev.: Lister in Canadian Audubon, 29, 124.

HARE, RONALD
1967 The antiquity of diseases caused by bacteria and viruses, a review of the
problem from a bacteriologist's point of view. In: Brothwell,
Don, and Sandison, A. T., (eds.), 1967, 115–131.

HARINGTON, C. R., and IRVING, W. N.
1967 Some Upper Pleistocene middens near Old Crow, Yukon Territory.
Ottawa: National Museum of Canada, 10 pp., (not seen).

HARKSEN, J. C.
1966 Pteranodon sternbergi, a new fossil pterodactyl from the Niobrara Cretaceous of Kansas. Proc. S. Dakota Acad. Sci., 45, 74–77, 2 figs.

HARLAND, W. B. See: Buchan, et al.

HARLAND, W. B., et al.
1967A. (eds.) The fossil record. A symposium with documentation jointly
sponsored by the Geological Society of London and the Palaeontological Association. London: Geol. Soc. London, xii + 827 pp.,
illustr.
Rev.: Sornay in C. R. Soc. Géol. France, 1968:7, 234.
1967B. Introduction. In: Harland, W. B., et al., (eds.), 1967A, 1–11, 1 table.

HARLAND, W. B., SMITH, A. G., and WILCOCK, B.
1964 (eds.) The Phanerozoic time-scale. A symposium dedicated to Professor
Arthur Holmes. London: Geol. Soc. London, (Quart. Jour.
Geol. Soc. London, suppl. 120), viii + 458 pp., illustr.
Rev.: Armstrong in Amer. Jour. Sci., 264, 751–752; Faul in Science,
149, 292–293; Rand in Endeavor, 24, 171; Uytenbogaardt
in Geol. en Mijn., 44, 369.

HARMANN, GAY L. See: Arata and Harmann.

HARRINGTON, HORACIO J.
1965 Space, things, time, and events — an essay on stratigraphy. Bull. Amer.
Assoc. Petrol. Geolog., 49, 1601–1646, 7 figs.

HARRIS, ARTHUR H., and FINDLEY, J. S.
1964 Pleistocene-Recent fauna of the Isleta Caves, Bernalillo County, New
Mexico. Amer. Jour. Sci., 262, 114–120, 1 fig., 3 tables.

HARRIS, D. R.   See: Higgs, Vita-Finzi, et al.

HARRIS, E. M., and ROBERTS, U. G., JR.
1967   A multiple component site in north Alabama. Jour. Ala. Archeol., 13, 69—93, 12 figs., 12 tables.

HARRIS, JOHN M.
1967   Toxotherium (Mammalia: Rhinocerotoidea) from western Jeff Davis County, Texas. Pearce-Sellard Ser., Texas Mem. Mus., 9, 1—7, 1 fig., 1 table.

HARRIS, R. K., and HARRIS, I. M.
1968   Cyrus N. Ray [1880 - June 21, 1966], bibliography and contributions to Texas archaeology. Bull. Texas Archeol. Soc., 38, 130—134.

HARRISON, DAVID L.   See: Loberg and Harrison.

HARRISON, G. A., WEINER, J. S., TANNER, J. M., and BARNICOT, N. A.
1964   Human biology. An introduction to human evolution, variation and growth. New York: Oxford Univ. Press, xvi + 536 pp., illustr.
         Rev.: Anon. in Advance. Sci., 22, 159;   M. C. C. in L'Anthrop., 69, 124—125;   Comas in An. Antrop., Mexico, 1966, 3, 255—256; Damon in Science, 149, 621;   Hughes in Man, Jour. Roy. Anthrop. Inst., 1, 247—248;   Novak in Human Biol., 38, 74—77; Schwidetzky in Homo, 15, 246;   Terada in Jour. Anthrop. Soc. Nippon, 73, 64, (Japanese).

HARRISSON, BARBARA
1966   Malaysian Borneo. Asian Perspectives, 8:1, 92—97.

HARRISSON, TOM
1960   Alfred Russell Wallace and a century of evolution in Borneo. Proc. Cent. Bicent. Congr. Biol., Singapore, 1958, 1960, 25—38.
1964A.   Borneo caves with special reference to Niah Great Cave. Studies in Spel., 1, 26—32, pls. 4—5.
         Rev.: Anon. in Helictite, 3, 40.
         Abs.: Anon. in Internat. Jour. Spel., 2:3, 29—30.
1964B.   100,000 years of Stone Age culture in Borneo. Trans. Roy. Soc. Arts, 112, 174—191, (not seen).
1966   William Pengelly, 1864, and the Niah Caves, 1965. Studies in Spel., 1, 228—232.

HARTENBERGER, JEAN-LOUIS
1965A.   Les rongeurs fossiles de Can Llobatéres (Espagne). I. Cricetidae. C. R. Soc. Géol. France, 1965, 106, (abs.).
1965B.   Gliravus robiacensis n. sp., nouveau rongeur (Gliridae) de l'Eocène supérieur du Languedoc. C. R. Soc. Géol. France, 1965, 326—327, 1 fig.
         Rev.: Fahlbusch in Zbl. Geol. Pal., Teil 2, 1967, 520;   Radig in Zbl. Geol. Pal., Teil 2, 1967, 119.
1966A.   Les Cricetidae (Rodentia) de Can Llobatéres (Néogène d'Espagne). Bull. Soc. Géol. France, 7, 487—498, 3 figs., pl. 10, 3 tables.
         Rev.: Fahlbusch in Zbl. Geol. Pal., Teil 2, 1967, 119—120;   H.-P. in Bol. Soc. Espan. Hist. Nat., Sec. Geol., 64:3—4, 303.
1966B.   Les rongeurs du Vallésien (Miocène supérieur) de Can Llobatéres (Sabadell, Espagne): Gliridae, Romyidae. C. R. Soc. Géol. France, 1966, 237, (abs.).

1967A.   Les rongeurs du Vallésien (Miocène Supérieur) de Can Llobatéres
          (Sabadell, Espagne): Gliridae et Eomyidae. Bull. Soc. Géol.
          France, 8, 596—604, 5 figs.
          Rev.: Fahlbusch in Zbl. Geol. Pal., Teil 2, 1969:3, 297;   H.-P. in Bol.
          Soc. Españ. Hist. Nat., Sec. geol., 65, 280—281.
1967B.   Contributions à l'étude de l'anatomie crânienne des Rongeurs. I. Prin-
          cipaux types de Cricétodontinés. Palaeovertebrata, 1, 47—64,
          2 figs., 4 pls., 1 table, (German and English summaries).
          Rev.: Fahlbusch in Zbl. Geol. Pal., Teil 2, 1969:3, 297—298.
1968   Les Pseudosciuridae (Rodentia) de l'Eocène moyen et le genre Masillamys
          Tobien. C. R. Acad. Sci. Paris, Sci. Nat., 267, 1817—1820, 1 fig.
          See: Crusafont Pairo, Hartenberger and Heintz;   Ledoux, et al.

HARTENBERGER, J.-L.,   MICHAUX, J., and THALER, L.
1967   Remarques sur l'histoire des Rongeurs de la faune à Hipparion en Europe
          sud-occidentale.   Colloq. Internat. Cent. Nation. Recherch. Sci.,
          163, 503—513, 1 fig., 2 tables.

HARTENBERGER, J.-L.,   SIGÉ, B., and SUDRE, J.
1968   Nouveaux gisements de vertébrés dans l'Eocène continental du Minervois.
          C. R. Soc. Géol. France, 1968:1, 22—23, 1 fig.

HARTLINE, D. and E.
1963   Grotto briefs. NSS News, 21, 24—25.

HARY, A., and MULLER, Ad.
1967   Zur stratigraphischen Stellung des Bonebeds von Medernach (Luxemburg).
          Neues Jahrb. Geol. Pal., Monatsh., 1967:6, 333—341, 6 figs.,
          1 table, (French summary).

HASEGAWA, YOSHIKAZU
1964A.   Short note on pathologic bones of toad. Sci. Rept. Yokohama Nation.
          Univ., Sect. II, no. 11, 69—70, pl. 6.
          Abs.: Westphal in Zbl. Geol. Pal., Teil 2, 1966, 295.
1964B.   Preliminary report on the Gansuiji formation and its fauna. Sci. Rept.
          Yokohama Nation. Univ., Sect. II, 71—78, 3 figs., (Japanese;
          English summary).
1966A.   Horizons yielding human bones. Jour. Anthrop. Soc. Nippon, 74, 153—
          154, 175—176, (Japanese; English summary).
1066B.   Quaternary smaller mammalian fauna from Japan. Kaseki, 11, 31—40,
          1 table, (Japanese).
1968A.   On the buried valley and the cetacean bone in Kurihama Bay, Yokosuka.
          Sci. Rept. Yokosuka City Mus., no. 14, 12—19, 2 figs., pl. 6,
          (Japanese; English summary).
1968B.   [On fossil elk in Japan.] Shizen kagaku to Hakubutsu-kan, 35:1—2,
          8—20, (Japanese).
          See: Shikama and Hasegawa; Shikama, Hasegawa and Okafuji; Takai
          and Hasegawa.

HASEGAWA, Y., and MATSUSHIMA, Y.
1968A.   Fossil vertebrae of humpback whale from alluvial deposits in Yokohama
          City. Bull. Kanagawa Prefec. Mus., 1:1, 29—36, 2 figs., 1 pl.
1968B.   First discovery of fossil elk deer antler from Japan. Bull. Nation. Sci.
          Mus. Tokyo, 11:1, 77—84, 3 figs., 1 pl.

HASEGAWA, Y., YAMAUTI, H., and OKAFUJI, G.
1968   A fossil assemblage of <u>Macaca</u> and <u>Homo</u> from Ojikdo-Cave of Hiraodai
         karst Plateau, northern Kyushu, Japan. Trans. Proc. Pal. Soc.
         Japan, <u>69</u>, 218—229, pl. 26, 1 table, (Japanese summary).

HASSALL, GERALDINE I.   See: Callow, Baker and Hassall.

HASSLER, R., and STEPHAN, H.
1966   (eds.) Evolution of the forebrain. Phylogenesis and ontogenesis of the
         forebrain. A symposium held in Frankfurt and Sprendlingen,
         Germany, August 1965. Stuttgart: Thieme, viii + 464 pp., illustr.;
         New York: Plenum Press, 472 pp., illustr.
         Rev.: Noback in Amer. Jour. Phys. Anthrop., <u>27</u>, 108—109;   Noback
         in Science, <u>157</u>, 1027—1028;   Shriver in Quart. Rev. Biol., <u>43</u>:4,
         469;   Vallois in L'Anthrop., <u>72</u>, 156—157;   Vogel in Zeit.
         Morph. Anthrop., <u>58</u>, 321—323;   Wetzig in Anat. Anz., <u>120</u>,
         534—535.

HATAI, KOTORA
1959B.   Discovery of Miocene elephant molar from the Sen-Nan district, Miyaga
           prefecture, northeast Japan. Saito Ho-On Kai Mus. Res. Bull.,
           <u>28</u>, 1—5, 1 pl.
1965A.   Some fish otoliths from northeast Honshu, Japan. Sci. Repts. Tohoku
           Univ., Sendai, <u>37</u>:1, 63—77, pl. 15.
           Abs.: Weiler in Zbl. Geol. Pal., Teil 2, <u>1966</u>, 278—279.
1965B.   Some Pliocene fish otoliths from Japan. Senck. Lethaea, <u>46a</u>, 133—145,
           pl. 6.
1966   Cenozoic fish otoliths and their stratigraphical significance. Kaseki, <u>11</u>,
           19—29, 5 figs., (Japanese).

HATAI, K., and KOTAKA, T.
1963   Abs.: Weiler in Zbl. Geol. Pal., Teil 2, <u>1965</u>, 225—226.

HATAI, K., MURATA, M., and MASUDA, K.
1965   A sting ray and eagle ray from the Tatsunokuchi formation (Pliocene)
         in Sendai City, Miyagi Prefecture, Japan. Trans. Proc. Pal. Soc.
         Japan, <u>57</u>, 34—37, 1 fig.
         Abs.: Weiler in Zbl. Geol. Pal., Teil 2, <u>1966</u>, 278.

HATCHER, EVELYN   See: Johnson, E. and Hatcher.

HATT, ROBERT T.
1963   The mastodon of Pontiac. News Letter, Cranbrook Inst. Sci., <u>32</u>:6,
         62—64, (not seen).
1965   The organization of museum exhibits. Mus. News, <u>44</u>:4, 17—20.

HATTIN, DONALD E., and COBBAN, W. A.
1965   Guidebook for field trip no. 2. Upper Cretaceous stratigraphy, paleon-
         tology, and paleoecology of western Kansas. Lawrence, Kans.:
         State Geol. Surv. Kans., 69 pp., illustr., (not seen).
         Rev.: Cohee in GeoTimes, <u>10</u>:7, 28.

HAUBOLD, HARTMUT
1966A.   Eine Pseudosuchier-Fährtenfauna aus dem Buntsandstein Südthüringens.
           Hallesches Jahrb. Mitteldeutsche Erdgeschichte, <u>8</u>, 12—48, 18 figs.,
           7 pls., 10 tables, (English and Russian summaries).

1966B.   Therapsiden-und Rhynchocephalen-Fährten aus dem Buntsandstein Süd-
          thüringens. Hercynia, 3:2, 147—183, 16 figs., 6 tables, (English
          summary).
          Rev.: Huene in Zbl. Geol. Pal., Teil 2, 1967, 97.

HAUGHTON, SIDNEY HENRY
1963A.   Rev.: Lepersonne in Bull. Soc. Belge Geol. Pal. Hydrologie, 72, 274—276.
1963C.   Abs.: Huene in Zbl. Geol. Pal., Teil 2, 1964, 990.
1965A.   Report of the honorary director for the year ended March 31, 1965.
          Pal. Africana, 9, i—vi.
1965B.   The Rubidge collection of fossil Karroo vertebrates. Pal. Africana, 9,
          1—17.
1967A.   Report of the honorary scientific director for the year ended March 31,
          1966. Pal. Africana, 10, i—v.
1967B.   Report of the honorary director for the year ending March 31, 1967.
          Pal. Africana, 10, vi—ix.
1968   Report of the honorary director for the remainder of the year 1967.
          Pal. Africana, 11, i—v.

HAUTECOEUR, G.   See: Bronowski and Hautecoeur.

HAVESSON, ÎA. I.
1950   [Camels of the genus Paracamelus.] Doklady Akad. Nauk SSSR, 70:5,
          917—920, 2 figs., 2 tables, (Russian).

HAWKES, JACQUETTA
1958B.   Palaeolithic art. Hist. Today, 8, 10—16, 98—102, illustr.
1963   Rev.: Ashbee in Proc. Prehist. Soc. Cambridge, 32, 359;   Lamberg-
          Karlovsky in Amer. Anthrop., 68:4, 1078—1080.

HAWKES, J., and WOOLLEY, L.
1963   Rev.: Chowdhury in Man in India, 44, 88—89;   Bose in Man in India,
          44, 359—360;   Evans in Archaeol. Jour., 121, 206—207;   Narr
          in Anthropos, 61, 328—329.
1965   History of mankind, cultural and scientific development. Vol. 1, Part I:
          prehistory. New York: New American Library (Mentor), 478 pp.,
          paper, (not seen).
          Rev.: J. M. L. in Minn. Archaeol., 28, 64—66.

HAWKINS, STEWART   See: Payne, J. C. and Hawkins.

HAWKSLEY, OSCAR
1965   Short-faced bear (Arctodus) fossils from Ozark caves. Bull. Nat. Spel.
          Soc., 27, 77—92, 9 figs., 3 tables.
          Abs.: Anon. in Internat. Jour. Spel., 2:3, 30.
1966   Pleistocene bear fossils from a "bear bed" in Perkins Cave, Missouri.
          Bull. Nat. Spel. Soc., 28, 96, (abs.).

HAWKSLEY, O., REYNOLDS, J., and McGOWAN, J.
1963   The dire wolf in Missouri. Missouri Speleology, 5, 63—72, (not seen).

HAWLEY, J. W., and GILE, L. H.
1965   Tortugas gravel pit, [New Mexico]. Guidebk., 7th Inqua Congr., H,
          74—76, 1 fig.

HAY, RUTH J.   See: Ogden and Hay,

HAY, RICHARD L.
1963B.   Reprint in Current Anthrop., 6, 386–388. Comments on this article
           by several authors included in Evernden and Curtis, 1965, with
           reply by Hay.
1965A.   Preliminary notes on the stratigraphy of Beds I–IV, Olduvai Gorge,
           Tanganyika. In: Leakey, et al, 1965, 94–100.
1965B.   Hominid-bearing deposits of Olduvai Gorge. Publ. Nation. Acad. Sci.,
           1469, 30–42, 6 figs.
1967   Revised stratigraphy of Olduvai Gorge. Discussion. In: Bishop, W. W.,
           and Clark, J. D., (eds.), 221–228, 1 fig., 1 table, (French sum-
           mary).

HAYAMI, ITARU   See: Kobayashi, T., Takai and Hayami.

HAYASAKA, ICHIRO
1964   Ontogeny, phylogeny and evolution in paleontology. Kaseki, 8, 87–93,
           (Japanese).

HAYDEN, JULIAN D.
1965   Fragile-pattern areas. Amer. Antiq., 31, 272–276, 4 figs.

HAYES, WILLIAM C.
1964A.   Most ancient Egypt. Chapter I. The formation of the land. Jour. Near
           East. Studies, 23, 74–114.
1964B.   Most ancient Egypt. Chapter II. Paleolithic man in Egypt. Jour. Near
           East. Studies, 23, 145–192.

HAYNES, C. VANCE, JR.
1964A.   The geologist's role in Pleistocene paleoecology and archaeology. Dis-
           cussion. Publ. Fort Burgwin Res. Center, no. 3, 61–66.
1964B.   Fluted projectile points: their age and dispersion. Science, 145, 1408–
           1413, 2 figs., cover photo.
1965   The Hell Gap site, Wyoming. Geological sketch. Wyo. Archaeol., 8:2,
           35.
1966A.   Geochronology of Late Quaternary alluvium. Int. Res. Rept., Geochron.
           Lab., Univ. Ariz., 10, 1–35, 4 figs., 2 tables.
1966B.   Elephant-hunting in North America. Sci. Amer., 214:6, 104–112, illustr.
1967A.   Carbon-14 dates and early man in the New World. In: Martin, P. S.,
           and Wright, H. E., (eds.), 1967, 267–286, 5 figs., 1 table.
1967B.   Quaternary geology of the Tule Springs area, Clark County, Nevada.
           In: Wormington and Ellis, (eds.), 1967, 15–104, 21 figs., 13 pls.,
           7 tables.
1968   Radiocarbon: analysis of inorganic carbon of fossil bone and enamel.
           Science, 161, 687–688, 1 table.
           See: Damon, Haynes and Long; Mehringer and Haynes.

HAYNES, C. V., and AGOGINO, G. A.
1965   Prehistoric springs and geochronology of Blackwater no. 1 locality, New
           Mexico. Spec. Pap. Geol. Soc. Amer., 87, 285–286, (abs.).

HAYNES, C. V., JR.,   DAMON, P. E., and GREY, D. C.
1966   Arizona radiocarbon dates VI. Radiocarbon, 8, 1–21.

HAYNES, C. V., JR., DOBERENZ, A. R., and ALLEN, J. A.
1966   Geological and geochemical evidence concerning the antiquity of bone
              tools from Tule Springs, Site 2, Clark County, Nevada. Amer.
              Antiq., 31, 517–521, 3 figs.

HAYNES, C. V., et al.
1965   Lehner site. Guidebk., 7th Inqua Congr., H, 55–58, 2 figs.

HAYNES, C. V., JR., and GREY, D. C.
1965   The Sister's Hill site and its bearing on the Wyoming postglacial alluvial
              chronology. Plains Anthrop., 10, 196–207, 4 figs.

HAYNES, C. V., JR., GREY, D. C., DAMON, P. E., and BENNETT, R.
1967   Arizona radiocarbon dates VII. Radiocarbon, 9, 1–14.

HAYNES, C. V., JR., and HEMMINGS, E. T.
1968   Mammoth-bone shaft wrench from Murray Springs, Arizona. Science,
              159, 186–187, 1 fig.

HAYS, H. R.
1963   In the beginnings: early man and his gods. New York: Putnam, 575
              pp., illustr.
              Rev.: Dyson in Nat. Hist., 74:1, 8–9; Oehler in Archaeol., 18, 244;
              Wax in Amer. Anthrop., 66, 1184–1185.

HAZZARD, R. T.   See: Maxwell, R. A., et al.

HEALD, WELDON F.
1963   Nevada's state parks. Travel, 120:3, 40–42, illustr.

HEATH, G. ROSS   See: Van Andel, et al.

HEBERER, GERHARD
1956G.   Bericht über die Bergung der Skelettreste von Combe Capelle und Le
              Moustier aus dem Brandschutt des Berliner Museums für Vor-
              und Frühgeschichte. Ber. Tagung Deutsch. Ges. Anthrop., 5,
              67–72, 4 figs.
1956H.   Zum Neanderthal-Jubiläum 1856 - 1956. Festschr. Deutsch. Biol. Ham-
              burg, 1956, 40–47, 3 figs., (not seen).
1958F.   Zum Problem der additiven Typogenese. Uppsala Univ. Årsskrift, 1958:6,
              40–47, 3 figs.
1959K.   (ed.) Abs.: Schindewolf in Zbl. Geol. Pal., Teil 2, 1962, 313–314.
1962A.   Abs.: Kuhn-Schnyder in Zbl. Geol. Pal., Teil 2, 1964, 223.
1963D.   Der Schädelfund von Saldanha in Südafrika. Umschau, 63, 176–179,
              8 figs.
1963E.   Huxley, Thomas Henry. Zeugnisse für die Stellung des Menschen in
              der Natur. (Übersetzung von V. Carus 1863). Stuttgart: G.
              Fischer Verl., 181 pp., 1 portr., 32 figs.
              Rev.: Altehenger in Anthropos, 61, 306–317.
1964A.   Neue Funde zur ältesten Menschheitgeschichte. Kosmos (Stuttgart), 60,
              *210.
1964B.   Fortschritte in der Erforschung der Stammesgeschichte des Menschen
              seit 1954. Kosmos (Stuttgart), 60, 555–560, 6 figs.
1964C.   Fünfzehn Jahre Fortschritte in der Erforschung der Stammesgeschichte.
              Das Neutige Bild vom Ursprung des Menschen. Umschau, 64,
              135–139, 8 figs.

1964D.   "Homo habilis" — Eine neue Menschenform aus der Oldoway-Schlucht?
            Umschau, 64, 685—687, 3 figs.

1965A.   (ed.) Menschliche Abstammungslehre. Fortschritte der Anthropogenie
            1863—1964. Stuttgart: Gustav Fischer, viii + 481 pp., 212 figs.
            Rev.: Buettner-Janusch in Quart. Rev. Biol., 43:1, 116—117;   Ehgart-
            ner in Mitt. Anthrop. Ges. Wien, 95, 372—373;   Haltenorth in
            Säugetierkundl. Mitt., 14, 352;   Helms in Ber. Deutsch. Ges.
            Geol. Wiss., Reihe A, 11:6, 749—751;   Marinelli in Verh. Zool.-
            Bot. Ges. Wien, 105—106, 189;   Mertens in Natur u. Mus., 96,
            85—86;   G. N. in Bonner Zool. Beitr., 17, 151;   Portmann in
            Umschau, 66, 448;   Preuschoft in Zbl. Geol. Pal., Teil 2, 1967,
            523—524;   Roth-Lutra in Anthropos, 61, 909—913;   Sauter in
            Arch. Suiss. Anthrop. Gen., 30, 88;   Scharf in Gegenbaurs
            Morph. Jahrb., 109, 633—634;   Thenius in Mitt. Geol. Ges.
            Wien, 58, 273—274;   H. V. V. in L'Anthrop., 70:1—2, 169—172;
            Vogel in Zeit. Morph. Anthrop., 57, 313;   Zapfe in Ann. Natur-
            hist. Mus. Wien, 70, 521.

1965B.   Zur Geschichte der Evolutionstheorie, besonders in ihrer Anwendung
            auf den Menschen. In: Heberer, (ed.), 1965A, 1—19, 2 figs.

1965C.   Über den systematischen Ort und den physisch-psychischen Status der
            Australopithecinen. In: Heberer, (ed.), 1965A, 310—356, 35 figs.,
            6 tables.

1965D.   Olorgesailie — zehntausend Faustkeile. Naturwiss. Rund., 18, 1, cover
            illustr.

1966   Über die osteodontokeratische "Kultur" der Australopithecinen. Quartär,
            17, 21—50, 6 figs., pls. 3—11, tables.
            Rev.: Schwidetzky in Homo, 18:1, 66.

1967A.   (ed.) Die Evolution der Organismen. Ergebnisse und Probleme der Ab-
            stammungslehre. Band 1, 3rd ed. Stuttgart: Gustav Fischer,
            754 pp., 265 figs., 8 tables, portr.
            Rev.: Fleischhacker in Anthropol. Anz., 31:4, 293—297;   Heymer in
            Atomes, 257, 501;   Kaltenbach in Mitt. Anthrop. Ges. Wien,
            96—97, 345;   Kamptner in Ann. Naturhist. Mus. Wien, 72,
            715—716;   Knussmann in Homo, 18:4, 271;   Kurth in Natur-
            wiss. Rund., 21, 131;   Niethammer in Bonner Zool. Beitr., 18,
            338;   Romer in Quart. Rev. Biol., 44:1, 75;   Roth-Lutra in
            Anat. Anz., 124, 230—231;   Sauter in Arch. Suiss. Anthropol.
            Gén., 32, 142—143;   Schindewolf in Zbl. Geol. Pal., Teil 2,
            1968:6, 566—568;   Thenius in Mitt. Geol. Ges. Wien, 60, 160—161;
            Vallois in L'Anthrop., 72, 155—156.

1967B.   Ernst Haeckel und die Phylogenie der Primaten. In: Starck, D., Schneider,
            R., and Kuhn, H. J., (eds.), 1967, 8—14, 3 figs.

1967C.   Zur Erforschung der tertiären Vorgeschichte der Hominiden. Naturwiss.
            Runschau, 20:9, 385.

1968   Der Ursprung des Menschen. Unser gegenwärtiger Wissensstand. Stuttgart:
            Gustav Fischer, 43 pp., 21 figs., (not seen).
            Rev.: Gieseler in Anthropol. Anz., 31:4, 303;   Hemmer in Zeit. Säuge-
            tierk., 34:4, 255;   Hughes in Man, Jour. Roy. Anthrop. Inst.,
            3, 489;   Knussmann in Umschau, 68, 510;   Marinelli in Verh.
            Zool.-Bot. Ges. Wien, 108/109, 182;   Vallois in L'Anthrop.,
            73:1—2, 113—114;   Vogel in Zeit. Morph. Anthrop., 60:3, 333.
            See: Colbert 1965H; Dobzhansky 1966A; Huxley, T. H. 1963;
            Mayr, E. 1967B.

HEBERER, G., and KURTH, G.
1966   Die (Eu) Hominien vom Mittelpleistozän bis ins mittlere Jungpleistozän. In: Narr, (ed.), 209—223, 3 figs., 2 pls.

HEBERER, G., KURTH, G., and SCHWIDETZKY-ROESING, I.
1959   Rev.: Anon. in Acta Praehist., 1966, 5—7, 288.

HECHT, MAX K.   See: Casamiquela 1965C; Dobzhansky, Hecht and Steere; Estes, et al.; Wassersug and Hecht.

HECHT, M., HOFFSTETTER, R., and VERGNAUD, C.
1961   Le gisement de vertébrés miocènes de Beni Mellal (Maroc). Amphibiens. Notes Mém. Serv. Géol. Maroc, 155, 103.

HECKER, ROBERT (= Gekker)   See: Strel'nikov and Hecker.

HECKER, ROBERT THEODOR
1965   Ein Volksbild des Mammuts. Natur u. Mus., 95:5, 212—216, 1 pl.

HECKER, ROMAN FEDOROVICH (=Gekker, R. F.)
1961   Emma Richter, 1888 - 1956. Rudolph Richter, 1881 - 1957. Pal. Sbornik, 1, 159—162, (Russian).
1965   Introduction to paleoecology. Translated from the Russian, edited and prepared for publication by M. K. Elias and R. C. Moore, in cooperation with Scripta Technica. New York: American Elsevier, 166 pp., 31 figs., 17 pls.
         Rev.: Ager in Palaeogeog., Palaeoclimatol., Palaeoecol., 2, 75—77; Anon. in Discovery, 27:1, 50; Horowitz in Jour. Pal., 40, 1411; Law in Austral. Jour. Sci., 29, 150; Lawrence in Amer. Sci., 53, 498A—499A; Martinsson in Geol. Fören. Förh., 87, 568; Nestler in Geologie, 17:1, 104—105; Oliver in GeoTimes, 10:3, 37;' M. J. S. R. in Geol. Mag., 103, 470; Rhoads in Amer. Jour. Sci., 264, 671; van Voorthuysen in Geol. en Mijn., 44, 410.

HEGLAR, R.   See: Spuhler and Heglar.

HEIM, JEAN-LOUIS
1963   Les apophyses geni, étude anthropologique et classification. C. R. Acad. Sci. Paris, 257, 3216—3219.
1968   Les restes néandertaliens de la Ferrassie. Nouvelles données sur la stratigraphie et inventaire des squelettes. C. R. Acad. Sci. Paris, Sci. Nat., 266, 576—578, 1 fig.
         See: Fenart and Heim.

HEIMBACH, WOLFGANG   See: Benda, et al.

HEINEN, WERNER
1962   Woher stammt der Mensch? Fackelbucherei, Olten, Bd. 54. Stuttgart, Salzburg: Fackelverlag, 160 pp., 30 figs., 6 pls., 2 maps, (not seen).
         Rev.: Heberer in Homo, 14, 184; Kurth in Kosmos (Stuttgart), 60, *49.

HEINTZ, ANATOL
1962D.   Abs.: Dietrich in Zbl. Geol. Pal., Teil 2, 1964, 213.

1962E.   Nye mammutfun i Norge. Årbok Norsk. Vidensk.-Akad., <u>1961</u>, 28—29.
1963   Phylogenetic aspects of myxinoids. In: Brodal and Fänge, (eds.), 1963,
            9—21, 4 figs.
1964A.   Den første mammutrekonstrukjon. Naturen, <u>88</u>, 185—187, 1 fig.
1964B.   Nye funn av fossile hominider. Naturen, <u>88</u>, 259—274, 8 figs.
1964C.   Mer om <u>Gigantopithecus</u>. Naturen, <u>88</u>, 298—300, 1 fig.
1964D.   Et nytt mammut-funn ved Kvam i Gudbrandsdalen. Naturen, <u>88</u>, 444—
            445, 1 fig.
1965A.   Kari Joten, som fant den første mammuttann. Naturen, <u>89</u>, 250—255,
            2 figs.
1965B.   Småstykker. Antropologiske notiser I. Naturen, <u>89</u>, 505—507.
1965C.   A new mammoth-find from Norway and a determination of the age of
            the tusk from Toten by means of C14. Norsk Geol. Tidsskrift,
            <u>45</u>, 227—230, 1 fig.
1966A.   Pattedyrene erobrer verden. Naturen, <u>90</u>, 97—110, 7 figs.
1966B.   Vår egen stamme. Naturen, <u>90</u>, 111—127, 8 figs.
1966C.   Antropologiske notiser II. Er "<u>Homo habilis</u>" en myte? Naturen, <u>90</u>,
            248—251.
1966D.   New radio carbon (C14) age determinations of some mammal remains
            from the permafrost of Siberia. Norsk Geol. Tidssk., <u>46</u>, 215—217.
1967A.   Some remarks about the structure of the tail in cephalaspids. Collog.
            Internat. Cent. Nation. Recherch. Sci., <u>163</u>, 21—35, 7 figs., 2 pls.,
            (French summary).
1967B.   A new tremataspidid from Ringerike, South Norway. In: Patterson,
            C., and Greenwood, P. H., (eds.), <u>1967</u>, 55—68, 6 figs., 2 pls.
1967C.   Det trettende Mammutfunn fra Norge. Naturen, <u>91</u>, 483—489, 3 figs.,
            (Norwegian).
            See: Moore, R. and Editors of Life 1964B.

HEINTZ, A. E., and GARUTT, V. E.
1964A.   [Absolute age determination of fossil remains of mammoth and woolly
            rhinoceros from Siberian permafrost by means of radioactive
            carbon (C14).] Doklady Akad. Nauk SSSR, <u>154</u>:6, 1367—1370,
            2 figs., (Russian).
1964B.   C14 dating of mammoth and woolly rhinoceros remains from the perma-
            frost of Siberia. Dokl. Acad. Sci. USSR, Earth Sci. Sect., <u>154</u>,
            168—170, 2 figs.
1965   Determination of the absolute age of the fossil remains of mammoth
            and woolly rhinoceros from the permafrost of· Siberia by the
            help of radio carbon (C14). Norsk Geol. Tidsskrift, <u>45</u>, 73—79,
            2 figs.

HEINTZ, ÉMILE
1963B.   Complément d'étude sur <u>Oioceros atropatenes</u> (Rod. & Weith.), antilope
            du Pontien de Maragha (Iran). C. R. Soc. Géol. France, <u>1963</u>,
            81, (abs.).
1964A.   Complément d'étude sur <u>Oioceros atropatenes</u> (Rod. et Weith.), antilope
            du Pontien de Maragha (Iran). Bull. Soc. Géol. France, <u>5</u>, 109—
            116, 1 fig., 2 tables.
            Abs.: Lotze in Zbl. Geol. Pal., Teil 2, <u>1964</u>, 692.
1964B.   Un nouveau Rupicaprinae fossile du gisement villafranchien de Saint-
            Vallier. C. R. Soc. Géol. France, <u>1964</u>, 373—374, 1 fig.
1966A.   La présence de <u>Gazellospira torticornis</u> Aym. (Ruminant) dans le gise-
            ment villafranchien de Saint-Vallien (Drome). Essai de répartition
            géographique et stratigraphique. C. R. Soc. Géol. France, <u>1966</u>,
            32, (abs.).

Rev.: Radig in Zbl. Geol. Pal., Teil 2, <u>1967,</u> 121.

1966B.   Caractères distinctifs entre Cervidés et Bovidés actuels et quaternaires. Phalange II. Mammalia, <u>30</u>, 138–141, 1 fig., (English and German summaries).

1967A.   La présence de <u>Gazellospira</u> <u>torticornis</u> Aymard (Ruminant) dans le gisement villafranchien de Saint-Vallier (Drôme). Essai de répartition géographique et stratigraphique. Bull. Soc. Géol. France, <u>8,</u> 25–30, 2 figs., pl. 1.

1967B.   Données préliminaires sur les cervidés villafranchiens de France et d'Espagne. Colloq. Internat. Cent. Nation. Recherch. Sci., <u>163,</u> 539–552, 1 fig., 1 table, (English summary).

1968   Principaux résultats systématiques et biostratigraphiques de l'étude des cervidés villafranchiens de France et d'Espagne. C. R. Acad. Sci. Paris, Sci. Nat., <u>266</u>, 2184–2186, 1 table.

See: Crusafont Pairo, Hartenberger and Heintz;   Ginsburg and Heintz.

HEINTZ, NICOLE

1966A.   L'arcade alvéolaire antérieure de la mandibule des Hominidés. Croissance, variabilité, évolution. Ann. Pal., Vert., <u>52</u>:1, 67–86, 10 figs.

Rev.: Vallois in L'Anthrop., <u>71</u>:3–4, 313–314.

1966B.   La courbure des os de la voûte du crâne chez les Hominidés: évolution, variabilité. C. R. Acad. Sci. Paris, Sci. Nat., <u>262</u>, 1523–1526, 3 figs.

1967A.   Évolution de la hauteur maximale du frontal, du pariétal et de occipital chez les Hominidés. Ann. Pal., Vert., <u>53</u>, 49–75, 12 figs.

1967B.   Deux nouveaux indices craniomandibulaires et l'évolution des Hominidés. C. R. Acad. Sci. Paris, Sci. Nat., <u>264</u>, 2737–2740, 1 fig., 1 table.

1968   Interprétation phylogénétique de la croissance du crâne chez les Hominoidea. Discussion. 7th Internat. Congr. Anthrop. Ethnol. Sci., Moscow, 1964, <u>3</u>, 467–474, 6 figs.

HEINZELIN DE BRAUCOURT, JEAN DE

1961C.   More upon Upper Paleolithic archaeology. Current Anthrop., <u>2</u>, 5.

1962C.   Manuel de typologie des industries lithiques. Bruxelles: Institut Royal des Sciences Naturelles de Belgique, 74 pp., 50 pls.

1962D.   Comptages typologique par catégories. Extension aux industries Eurafricaines. Proc. 4th Panafrican Congr. Prehist., sec. <u>3,</u> 113–127, 2 figs., 4 pls., 2 tables, (discussion).

1963C.   Moustérien à Terhagen. Helinium, <u>3</u>, 225–228, 3 figs.

1965   Cailloutis de Wissant, capture de Marquise et percée de Warcove. Bull. Soc. Belge Géol. Pal. Hydrologie, <u>73</u>, 146–161, 7 figs., 1 pl.

1966   Connaissance de la faune quaternaire en Belgique (avec mention de problèmes connexes). Naturalistes belges, <u>47</u>:8, 373–389, ill.

1967   Pleistocene sediments and events in Sudanese Nubia. In: Bishop, W. W., and Clark, J. D., (eds.), 1967A, 313–328, 3 figs., (French summary; discussion, 478–479).

See: Anciaux de Faveaux, 1962; Bishop, Gautier and de Heinzelin; Mortelmans 1962B; Wendorf, Shiner, Marks, <u>et</u> <u>al.</u>

HEINZELIN, J. DE, and PAEPE, R.

1965   The geological history of the Nile Valley in Sudanese Nubia: preliminary results. In: Wendorf, Fred, (ed.), 1965A, 29–56, 15 figs., 4 maps.

HEINZELIN, J. DE, and TWIESSELMANN, F.

1967   Congo. In: Oakley, K. P., and Campbell, B. G., (eds.), 1967A, 9–11.

HEIZER, ROBERT F.
1959   (ed.) Rev.: Ray in Man in India, 44, 364.
1964   The western coast of North America. In: Jennings, D., and Norbeck,
           E., (eds.), 1964A, 117–148, 1 fig.
           Rev.: Meighan in Amer. Antiq., 30, 501.
1965   Problems in dating Lake Mojave artifacts. Masterkey, 39, 125–134, 2 figs.
           See: Baumhoff and Heizer; Cook, S. F. and Heizer; Hole and Heizer.

HEIZER, R. F., and BROOKS, R. A.
1965   Lewisville — ancient campsite or wood rat houses? Southwestern Jour.
           Anthrop., 21, 155–165.

HELLER, FLORIAN
1959D.   Abs.: Schnitzer in Zbl. Geol. Pal., Teil 2, 1964, 150–151.
1960B.   Rev.: Ehrenberg in Die Höhle, 12, 158–159.
1960C.   Rev.: Ehrenberg in Die Höhle, 12, 158–159.
           Abs.: Schnitzer in Zbl. Geol. Pal., Teil 2, 1964, 413.
1961C.   Abbé Henri Breuil zum Gedachtnis. Mitt. Verband Deutschen Höhlen-
           und Karstforscher, München, 7, 65.
1962B.   Englische Naturwissenschaftler des 18. und 19. Jahrhunderts und ihre
           Beziehungen zu den frankischen Knochenhöhlen. Die Höhle, 13,
           53–59, (French summary).
1964   Eine fossilführende Karstschlotte mit Jung-Mammut-Resten bei Langenalt-
           heim/Mfr. Geol. Bavarica, 53, 102–127, 5 pls., 1 table.
1966   Die Fauna von Hunas (Nördliche Frankenalb) im rahmen der deutschen
           ˙ Quartärfaunen. Eiszeit. u. Gegenwart, 17, 113–117, 1 fig., (Eng-
           lish summary).
           Rev.: Fahlbusch in Zbl. Geol. Pal., Teil 2, 1967, 521.
1967A.   Die Wühlmäuse (Arvicolidae Gray 1821) der altpleistozänen Säugetier-
           fauna von Schernfeld bei Eichstätt in Bayern. Mitt. Bayer.
           Staatssamml. Pal. Hist. Geol., 7, 201–203.
1967B.   Die Altersstellung des Villafranchium und seiner Fauna. Quartär, 18,
           9–23, 3 tables.
           See: Haarländer and Heller.

HELLER, F., and BRUNNACKER, K.
1966   Halsbandlemming-Reste aus einer Oberen Mittelterrasse des Rheins bei
           Niederaussem. Eiszeit. u. Gegenwart, 17, 97–112, 3 figs., (Eng-
           lish summary).

HELLER, WOLFGANG
1966   Untersuchungen zur sogenannten Hauterhaltung bei Ichthyosauriern aus
           dem Lias epsilon Holzmadens (Schwaben). Neues Jahrb. Geol.
           Pal., Monatsh., 1966:5, 304–317, 1 fig., 2 tables.
1967   Methodische Untersuchungen zur Darstellung der Kollagenstruktur des
           fossilen und rezenten Knochens. Neues Jahrb. Geol. Pal., Abh.,
           129, 222–230, 1 fig., 2 pls.

HELLMAN, GEOFFREY T.
1964   Blazing the trail for the alpha and omega. The New Yorker, Dec. 5,
           1964, 97–98, 100, 103–104, 106, 111–112, 114, 116, 118,
           121–123, 126, 128, 131–132, 134, 136, 138, 143–144, 146,
           149–150, 152, 155.
1968   The American Museum. 1, and 2. The New Yorker, Nov. 30, 1968,
           68–150; Dec. 7, 1968, 65–136.

HELMS, JOCHEM
1961   Saurierskelette des Museums für Naturkunde in Berlin. Natur und
            Heimat, 403–405, 5 figs., (not seen).

HELMUTH, HERMANN
1968   Körperhöhe und Gliedmassenproportionen der Australopithecinen. Zeit.
            Morph. Anthrop., 60, 147–155, 2 figs., 1 table, (English summary).

HELTNE, PAUL G. See: Singer and Heltne.

HELWIG, JAMES
1964   Stratigraphy of detrital fills of Carroll Cave, Camden County, Missouri.
            Missouri Speleology, 6, 1–15, 3 figs., 1 pl., 2 tables.

HELWIN, HELLMUT
1967   Ein Porträt aus dem Paläolithikum. Nova Acta Leop., 33, 197–208,
            18 figs.

HEMLEBEN, JOHANNES
1966   Teilhard de Chardin. In Selbstzeugnissen und Bilddokumenten, Rowohlts
            Monographien, herausgegeben von K. Kusenberg. Reinbek bei
            Hamburg: Rowohlts Taschenbuch Verlag, 180 pp., 75 figs.
            Rev.: Engelmayer in Mitt. Anthrop. Ges. Wien, 96–97, 337–338;
            Gieseler in Anthrop. Anz., 30, 192; Schaeuble in Zeit. Morph.
            Anthrop., 58, 212.

HEMMER, HELMUT
1964A.   Homo habilis – eine neue Hominidenart aus Ostafrika. Homo, 15,
            106–109.
1964B.   Über allometrische Beziehungen zwischen Hirnschädelkapazität und
            Hirnschädelwölbung im Genus Homo. Homo, 15, 218–224, 2 figs.
1964C.   Nachrichten. China. Homo, 15, 256.
1965A.   Der phylogenetische Gestaltwandel des Hominidenschädels in allometrischer
            Betrachtung. Ber. Tagung Deutsch. Ges. Anthrop., 9, 139–143,
            3 figs.
1965B.   Die Aussage der Säugetierfaunen für die Ökologie pleistozäner Hominiden.
            Homo, 16, 95–109, (English and French summaries).
1965C.   Studien an "Panthera" schaubi Viret aus dem Villafranchien von Saint-
            Vallier (Drôme). Neues Jahrb. Géol. Pal., Abh., 122, 324–336,
            4 figs., pl. 31, 4 tables.
1965D.   Zur Nomenklatur und Verbreitung des Genus Dinofelis Zdansky, 1924
            (Therailurus Piveteau, 1948). Pal. Africana, 9, 75–89, figs. 35–38,
            (English abstract).
1965E.   Abstammung des Nebelparders. Umschau, 65, 155.
1966   Untersuchungen zur Stammesgeschichte der Pantherkatzen (Pantherinae).
            I. Teil. Veröff. Zool. Staatssammlung München, 11, 1–21, 24 pls.
            Rev.: Berg in Zbl. Geol. Pal., Teil 2, 1968, 213.
1967A.   Allometrie – Untersuchungen zur Evolution des menschlichen Schädels
            und seiner Rassentypen. Fortschritte der Evolutionsforschung,
            3, vi + 98 pp., 80 figs., 26 tables.
            Rev.: Blume in Gegenbaurs Morph. Jahrb., 113:1, 157–158; Delattre
            in L'Anthrop., 73:5–6, 428–430; Grimm in Biol. Zbl., 88:3,
            389–390; Hunt in Amer. Jour. Phys. Anthrop., 31, 243–244;
            MacConnaill in Man, Jour. Roy. Anthrop. Inst., 3, 136; Preuschoft
            in Zbl. Geol. Pal., Teil 2, 1969:2, 210–212; Roth-Lutra in Anat.

Anz., 124, 465–466;   Sauter in Arch. Suiss. Anthropol. Gén.,
32, 147–148;   Schliemann in Zeit. Säugetierk., 34:6, 380;
Vogel in Zeit. Morph. Anthrop., 60, 224–225.

1967B.   Wohin gehört "Felis" palaeosinensis Zdansky, 1924 in systematischer
Hinsicht? Neues Jahrb. Geol. Pal., Abh., 129:1, 83–96, 9 figs.,
3 pls., 3 tables.

1967C.   Fossilbelege zur Verbreitung und Artgeschichte des Löwen, Panthera leo
(Linne, 1758). Säugetierkundl. Mitt., 15, 289–300, 9 figs., 3
tables, (English summary).
Rev.: Thenius in Zbl. Geol. Pal., Teil 2, 1970:3/4, 240.

1968   Der Tiger — Panthera tigris palaeosinensis (Zdansky, 1924) — im Jungpleistozän Japans. Neues Jahrb. Geol. Pal., Monatsh., 1968:10,
610–618, 3 figs., 3 tables.
Rev.: Thenius in Zbl. Geol. Pal., Teil 2, 1970:3/4, 240.

HEMMER, H., and KOENIGSWALD, G. H. R. von
1964   Fossile Nebelparder (Neofelis) aus dem Pleistozän Südchinas und Javas.
Proc. K. Nederl. Akad. Wet., Ser. B, 67, 1–16, 1 fig., 1 pl.

HEMMINGS, E. THOMAS   See: Haynes and Hemmings.

HENDEY, Q. B.
1967   A specimen of "Archidiskodon" cf. transvaalensis from the south-western
Cape Province. S. Afr. Archaeol. Bull., 22, 53–56, 2 figs., 1 pl.,
1 table.

HENDY, B. Q.   See: Inskeep and Hendy.

HENKEL, SIEGFRIED
1966   Methoden zur Prospektion und Gewinnung kleiner Wirbeltierfossilien.
Neues Jahrb. Geol. Pal., Monatsh., 1966:3, 178–184, 2 figs.

HENNIG, EDWIN
1964   Dr. phil. Werner Janensch 85 Jahre. Ber. Geol. Ges. Deutsch. Demokratischen Republ., 9, 711–717, 4 figs.

1965   Wilhelm Otto Dietrich. Paläontologischer Forscher. [July 30, 1881 –
March 26, 1964.] Jahresh. Ver. Vaterland. Naturk. Württemberg,
120, 55–58, portr.

HENNIG, WILLI
1966   Phylogenetic systematics. Translated from the German by D. Dwight
Davis and Rainer Zangerl. Urbana, Ill., and London: Univ.
Illinois Press, 271 pp., 69 figs.
Rev.: Bock in Evolution, 22:3, 646–648;   Byers in Syst. Zool., 18:1,
105–107;   Cain in Nature, 216, 412–413;   Horowitz in Jour.
Pal., 41, 1569;   Roth-Lutra in Anat. Anz., 125, 470–471;
Sokal in Science, 156, 1356.
See: Ax 1964.

HENNING, DALE R.
1961   Archaeological research in the proposed Joanna Reservoir, Missouri.
Missouri Archaeol., 23, 132–183, 11 figs.
See: Spier, Henning and Vincent.

HENRI-MARTIN, GERMAINE
1964   La dernière occupation moustérienne de la Quina (Charente). Datation
        par le radiocarbone. C. R. Acad. Sci. Paris, <u>258</u>, 3533—3535.
1965A. Géomorphologie et préhistoire au sud d'Angouleme. V. La Quina.
        Bull. Assoc. Franç. Étude Quat., <u>1965</u>:3—4, 198—204, 3 figs.,
        (English summary).
1965B. La Basse-Tardoire grottes et abris paleolithiques. A. Fontechevade. Le
        Grotte de Fontechevade. Bull. Assoc. Franç. Étude Quat., <u>1965</u>:3—4,
        211—216, 4 figs., (English summary).
1966   Découverte d'un temporal humain néandertalien dans le Moustérien de
        la Quina, Charente. C. R. Acad. Sci. Paris, Sci. Nat., <u>262</u>, 1937—
        1939, 1 fig.

HENRIQUES DA SILVA, G.
1961   Sobre una fauna ictiológica do Miocénico do Farol das Lagostas (Luanda,
        Angola). Mem. Not. Univ. Coimbra, Mus. Min. Geol., <u>52</u>, 75—84,
        4 pls., (English and French summaries).
1963   O género <u>Anacorax</u> no Cretácico superior de Angola. Mem. Not. Univ.
        Coimbra, Mus. Min. Geol., <u>55</u>, 25—41, (Portuguese; French and
        English summaries).

HENRIQUES DA SILVA, G., and PERREIRA SOARES, A.
1961   Contribucao para o conhecimento de fauna miocenica de S. Pedro de
        Barra e do Forol des Lagostas (Luanda, Angola). Garcia de Orta,
        <u>9</u>, 721—736, 8 pls., (not seen).

HENRY, JOHN, and NICHOLS, A.
1963   Paleo-points from Vermillion County, Illinois. Bull. Ill. Archaeol. Surv.,
        <u>4</u>, 119—125, figs. 50—53.

HENRY, VERNON J., and HOYT, J. H.
1965   Late Pleistocene fluvial and estuarine deposits at Savannah, Georgia.
        Bull. Georgia Acad. Sci., <u>23</u>, 67—68, (abs.).

HENSCHEN, FOLKE
1966A. Der menschliche Schädel in der Kulturgeschichte. Berlin, Heidelberg,
        New York: Springer Verlag (Verständliche Wissenschaft, Natur-
        wissenschaftliche Abteilung, 89), 117 pp., 81 figs.
        Rev.: Sauter in Arch. Suiss. Anthrop. Gen., <u>31</u>, 73.
1966B. The human skull. A cultural history. With an introduction by Kenneth
        P. Oakley. London: Thames and Hudson, 168 pp., 22 figs.,
        76 pls.
        Rev.: Barnicot in Man, Jour. Roy. Anthrop. Inst., <u>2</u>, 307; St. Hoyme
        in Amer. Anthrop., <u>70</u>, 168—169.

HENSEL, WITOLD
1958   Poznań à l'aube de l'histoire. Polskie Towarzystwo Archeol., Popular-
        nonaukowa Biblioteka Archeol., Nr. <u>2</u>, 197 pp., 101 figs., (Polish;
        French summary).
        Rev.: Hásek in Archeol. Roz., <u>11</u>, 435, (Czech).

HERMENS, R. DE BAYLE DES
1965   Note sur un éclat de basalte trouvé aux environs de Saint-Julien-Chapteuil
        (Haute-Loire). Bull. Soc. Préhist. Franç., C. R. séances mens.,
        <u>1965</u>:6, ccvii—ccix, illustr.

HERNÁNDEZ-PACHECO, EDUARDO
1956   Observaciones respecto a métodos y resultados del estudio de los yaci-
              mientos prehistóricos del solar hispano. Mem. Serv. Invest. Arqueol.
              Asturias, 1, 35–46.

HERNÁNDEZ-PACHECO, FRANCISCO
1965   Las reproducciones del techo de Altamira. Bol. Soc. Espan. Hist. Nat.,
              Sec. Geol., 63, 87–88.

HERNÁNDEZ-PACHECO, F., and CRUSAFONT-PAIRÓ, M.
1960   Primera caracterizacion paleontologica del Terciario de Extremadura.
              Bol. Soc. Espan. Hist. Nat., Sec. Geol., 58, 275–282, pl. 5.

HERRE, WOLF
1964   Zum Abstammungsproblem von Amphibien und Tylopoden sowie über
              Parallelbildungen und zur Polyphyliefrage. Zool. Anz., 173,
              66–91, 7 figs.

HERSHKOVITZ, PHILIP
1966   Mice, land bridges and Latin American faunal interchange. In: Wenzel
              and Tipton, 1966, 725–751, 4 figs.
            Rev.: Fahlbusch in Zbl. Geol. Pal., Teil 2, 1968, 28.
            See: Brace, et al.

HERTLEIN, LEO G.
1964   From the Academy collections. Acad. Newsletter, Calif. Acad. Sci.,
              no. 293, [4], 1 fig.
1966   Pliocene fossils from Rancho El Refugio, Baja California, and Cerralvo
              Island, Mexico. Proc. Calif. Acad. Sci., 30:14, 265–284, 17 figs.
            Rev.: Jaworski in Zbl. Geol. Pal., Teil 2, 1968, 453–454.

HESSE, HENRIKE
1966   Zum Schicksal des Neandertaler-Fundes von Le Moustier, (Homo mous-
              teriensis Hauseri). Forsch. u. Fortschr., 40:11, 347–348, 1 fig.

HESTER, A., JR.   See: Maggowan, K. and J. and Hester.

HESTER, JAMES J.
1964   Introduction. In: Hester, J. J., and Schoenwetter, J., (eds.), 1964,
              2–3.
1965   The agency of man in animal extinction. 7th Internat. Congr., Internat.
              Assoc. Quat. Res., Abs., 1965, 210–211, (abs.).
1966A.   Late Pleistocene environments and early man in South America. Amer.
              Nat., 100, 377–388, 4 figs.
1966B.   Origins of the Clovis culture. Proc. Internat. Congr. Americanists, 1,
              129–142, 7 figs.
1967   The agency of man in animal extinctions. In: Martin, P. S., and
              Wright, H. E., (eds.), 1967, 169–192, 1 fig., 3 tables.

HESTER, J. J., and SCHOENWETTER, J.
1964   (eds.) The reconstruction of past environments. Proceedings of the
              Fort Burgwin Conference on Paleoecology: 1962. Publ. Fort
              Burgwin Res. Center, no. 3, 89 pp., 28 figs., 9 tables.
            Rev.: Baerreis in Amer. Antiq., 31, 128–129.

HESTER, JOSEPH A., JR.
  1964   Kenneth Macgowan, 1888 - 1963. Amer. Antiq., 29, 376–378, portr.

HESTER, THOMAS ROY
  1968   Folsom points from southwest Texas. Plains Anthrop., 13, 117, 1 fig.

HEUER, R. E. See: Langenheim, et al.

HEWES, GORDON W.
  1964   Hominid bipedalism: independent evidence for the food-carrying theory.
                  Science, 146, 416–418.
  1965   Prehistoric cultures of the west bank of the Nile, Second Cataract region,
                  Republic of the Sudan. 7th Internat. Congr., Internat. Assoc.
                  Quat. Res., Abs., 1965, 215, (abs.).
                See: Arkell, A. J., and Hewes.

HEWES, G. W., IRWIN, H., PAPWORTH, M., and SAXE, A.
  1964   A new fossil human population from the Wadi Halfa area, Sudan.
                  Nature, 203, 341–343, 3 figs.

HEYERDAHL, THOR
  1964   Feasible ocean routes to and from the Americas in pre-columbian times.
                  Proc. 35th Internat. Congr. Americanists, Mexico 1962, 1, 133–142,
                  2 maps.
  1966   Discussions of transoceanic contacts: isolationism, diffusionism, or a
                  middle course? Anthropos, 61, 689–707.

HEYLER, DANIEL
  1965   Vertébrés de l'Autunien et du Saxonien de Lodève (Hérault). C. R.
                  Soc. Géol. France, 1965, 69–70, 1 fig.
  1967   Quelques points nouveaux au sujet d'Aeduella Westoll. Discuss. Colloq.
                  Internat. Cent. Nation. Recherch. Sci., 163, 81–88, 5 figs.,
                  (English summary).
                See: Blot and Heyler.

HEYLER, D., and LESSERTISSEUR, J.
  1963   Abs.: Huene in Zbl. Geol. Pal., Teil 2, 1964, 41.

HEYWOOD, V. H., and McNEILL, J.
  1964   (eds.) Phenetic and phylogenetic classification. London: Systematics
                  Association, Publ. no. 6, xi + 164 pp.
                Rev.: Kesling in Jour. Pal., 39, 516–517; Simpson in Science, 148,
                  no. 3673, 1078.

HIBBARD, CLAUDE W.
  1962A.   Abs.: Dietrich in Zbl. Geol. Pal., Teil 2, 1964, 199.
  1963B.   Abs.: Dietrich in Zbl. Geol. Pal., Teil 2, 1964, 199–200.
  1964   A contribution to the Saw Rock Canyon local fauna of Kansas. Papers
                  Mich. Acad. Sci., 49, 115–127, 3 figs., 1 table.
  1967   New rodents from the Late Cenozoic of Kansas. Papers Mich. Acad.
                  Sci., 52, 115–131, 5 figs.
                See: Getz and Hibbard.

HIBBARD, C. W., and DALQUEST, W. W.
  1966   Fossils from the Seymour formation of Knox and Baylor Counties, Texas,
                  and their bearing on the Late Kansan climate of that region.
                  Contrib. Mus. Pal. Univ. Mich., 21:1, 1–66, 8 figs., 5 pls., 3 tables.

HIBBARD, C. W.,   RAY, D. E.,   SAVAGE, D. E.,   TAYLOR, D. W., and
GUILDAY, J. E.
1965   Quaternary mammals of North America. In: Wright, H. E., and Frey,
            D. G., (eds.), 1965, 509–525, 9 figs., 4 tables.

HIBBARD, C. W., and ZAKRZEWSKI, R. J.
1967   Phyletic trends in the Late Cenozoic microtine, Ophiomys gen. nov.,
            from Idaho. Contrib. Mus. Pal. Univ. Mich., xxi, 255–271, 2 figs.
            1 table.

HIBBEN, FRANK C.
1960A.   Rev.: Yarus in Quart. Bull. Archeol. Soc. Virginia, 16, 5–6.
1967   Early man in southern Tanzania. Archaeol., 20, 247–253, illustr.
1968   The lost Americans. Revised and updated. New York: Thomas Y.
            Crowell, xiii + 187 pp., illustr.
            Rev.: Camp in Jour. of the West, 8, 293;   Gell in Archaeol., 23:3,
            260–261;   Wilmsen in Amer. Anthrop., 71, 1206–1207.

HICKS, VERBY   See: Wade, et al.

HIERNAUX, JEAN
1963A.   Origine et l'homme. Texte complete de la conférence enregistré au
            magnetophone revu et corrigé par l'auteur. Bruxelles: Cercle
            d'Education, 32 pp., (not seen).
            Rev.: [Stloukal] in Anthrop., 2:3, 93.
1963B.   Nature et origine des races humaines. Texte complet de la conférence,
            revu et corrigé par l'auteur. Bruxelles: Cercle d'Education
            Populaire, 31 pp., (not seen).
            Rev.: [Stloukal] in Anthrop., 2:3, 93.
            See: Van Noten and Hiernaux.

HIGGINS, C. G.
1964   Report on the First International Speleological Congress in Greece, 1963.
            NSS News, 22, 5–7.

HIGGS, E. S.
1964   A hand axe from Greece. Antiq., 38, 54–55, 1 fig., pl. 12.
1965   Search for Greece of the Stone Age. Nat. Hist., 74:9, 18–25, 11 figs.
1967A.   Faunal fluctuations and climate in Libya. In: Bishop, W. W., and
            Clark, J. D., (eds.), 1967A, 149–163, 4 figs., 2 tables, (French
            summary).
1967B.   Environment and chronology: the evidence from mammalian fauna.
            In: McBurney, C. B. M., 1967B, 16–44, 10 figs., 6 tables.
1967C.   Greece and Paleolithic man. Listener, 77:1983, 425–427, illustr.

HIGGS, E. S., and VITA-FINZI, C.
1966   The climate, environment and industries of Stone Age Greece: Part II.
            Proc. Prehist. Soc. Cambridge, 32, 1–29, 15 figs., 1 table, 5 pls.

HIGGS, E. S.,   VITA-FINZI, C.,   HARRIS, D. R., and FAGG, A. E.
1967   The climate, environment and industries of Stone Age Greece: Part III.
            Proc. Prehist. Soc. Cambridge, 33, 1–29, 13 figs.

HIGUCHI, RYOJI,   KITAME, T., and OZAKI, H.
1965   On the Uppermost Pleistocene cultures found at Tsukizaki, Iizaka,
            Fukushima City. Bull. Nation. Sci. Mus. Tokyo, 8:2, 193–218,
            12 pls.

HILL, CHRISTOPHER
1967   The Pengelly Centre museum. Studies in Spel., 1, 233—236, 1 fig., 2 pls.

HILL, D., PLAYFORD, G., and WOODS, J. T.
1965   Triassic fossils of Queensland. Brisbane: Queensland Paleont. Soc.,
        32 pp., 15 pls., 1 table.
        Rev.: Scott in Jour. Pal., 42, 863—864.
1966   Jurassic fossils of Queensland. Brisbane: Queensland Paleont. Soc.,
        32 pp., 15 pls., 1 table.
        Rev.: Scott in Jour. Pal., 42, 863—864.

HILL, LOREN GILBERT
1963   Castoroides ohioensis (Rodentia) in Arkansas. Southwest. Nat., 8, 150—
        153, 1 fig.

HILL, W. C. OSMAN
1966   Primates: Comparative anatomy and taxonomy. Vol. 6. Catarrhini:
        Cercopithecoidea (Cercopithecinae). New York: Wiley, 806 pp.,
        illustr.
        Rev.: Ashton in Nature, 212, 1021;   Dandelot in Mammalia, 30, 687—
        688;   Freedman in Amer. Anthrop., 70, 645—647;   Haltenorth
        in Säugetierkundl. Mitt., 15, 182;   Kittel in Gegenbaurs Morph.
        Jahrb., 109, 638—639;   MacConaill in Man, Jour. Roy. Anthrop.
        Inst., 1, 561—562;   Napier in Jour. Anat., 101, 597;   Schön
        in Science, 155, 308—309;   Schultz in Folia Primatologica, 5,
        315—316;   Vallois in L'Anthrop., 71:1—2, 163—164;   Zucker-
        man in Endeavour, 26:97, 58.

HILLABY, JOHN
1965A.   A geography of Genesis. New Sci., 25, 798—800, 2 figs.
1965B.   Naming our ancestors. New Sci., 28, 915, illustr.

HILLERUD, J. M.
1966   Blowfly puparia in a fossil bison skull. Proc. Neb. Acad. Sci., 76th
        Ann. Meeting, 1966, 14—15, (abs.).

HILTERMANN, HEINRICH   See: Arnold, et al.

HINDLE, EDWARD
1964   Prof. Victor Van Straelen. [— Feb. 29, 1964.] Nature, 202, 1058-1059.

HINZ, H.
1963   (ed.) Jahresbericht des staatlichen Vertrauensmannes für kulturgeschicht-
        liche Bodenaltertümer vom 1. Januar bis 31. Dezember 1961.
        Bonner Jahrb., 163, 498—570, 40 figs., 1 map.

HÎRJOABA, I.
1962   Über einen Bos sp. aus der Schottern von Brăhășești — Rayon Tecuci.
        Natura (Bucharest), 14:1, 42—43, 1 fig., (not seen).
        Abs.: Semaka in Zbl. Geol. Pal., Teil 2, 1964, 206.

HIRSCHFELD, SUE E.
1968   Mastication in ground sloths. Program, 1968 Ann. Meetings, Geol. Soc.
        Amer., 1968, 137—138, (abs.).

HIRSCHFELD, S. E., and WEBB, S. D.
    1968   Plio-Pleistocene megalonychid sloths of North America. Bull. Florida
                State Mus., Biol. Sci., 12:5, 213—296, 22 figs., 13 tables.

HLADY, WALTER M.
    1960   The occurrence of Plainview type projectile points in west central Canada.
                Winnipeg: Manitoba Museum, 4 pp.
    1964   Fieldwork by the Manitoba Archaeological Society — 1964. Manitoba
                Archaeol. Newsletter, 1:4, 6—8.

HLAVIN, WILLIAM J.
    1965A.   Interstate Ohio 71 fossil dig. Third of a series about the Natural
                Science Museum's I-71 fossil salvage program. Part II: Some
                preliminary notes on the I-71 discoveries. Explorer, 7:5, 8—11,
                illustr.
    1965B.   Report on the paleontological salvage operation on Interstate Route 71
                in Cuyahoga County, Ohio. News Bull., Soc. Vert. Pal., 74, 58.
    1966   A preliminary note on some significant fossil finds from the Interstate
                Route 71 paleontological salvage operation. News Bull., Soc.
                Vert. Pal., no. 76, 49—50.

HO, TO YOU
    1965   "Coulpo culture" — The Paleolithic site in Korea. Translated by Chang
                Han Dog. Jour. Archaeol. Soc. Nippon, 50, [207 - 213], 5 figs.,
                (Japanese).

HO, TONG-YUN
    1965   The amino acid composition of bone and tooth proteins in Late Pleis-
                tocene mammals. Proc. Nation. Acad. Sci., 54, 26—31, 3 tables.
    1968   Estimation of body temperature of fossil mammals by hydroxyproline
                content in collagen. Spec. Pap. Geol. Soc. Amer., 101, 94, (abs.).

HOARE, R. D.
    1964   Radiocarbon date on Pleistocene peccary find in Sandusky County, Ohio.
                Ohio Jour. Sci., 64, 427.

HOARE, R. D., COASH, J. R., INNIS, C., and HOLE, T.
    1964   Pleistocene peccary Platygonus compressus LeConte from Sandusky
                County, Ohio. Ohio Jour. Sci., 64, 207—214, 9 figs.

HOCKETT, CHARLES F., and ASCHER, R.
    1964   The human revolution. With comments. Current Anthrop., 5, 135—168.

HODGES, HENRY
    1964   Artifacts. An introduction to primitive technology. New York: Fre-
                derick A. Praeger, 248 pp., 51 figs., 5 tables, 9 diagrams.
                Rev.: Wineberg in Archaeol., 19, 294—297.

HOEBEL, E. ADAMSON
    1966   Anthropology: the study of man. 3rd ed. New York: McGraw-Hill,
                xii + 591 pp., illustr.
                Rev.: Krogman in Amer. Jour. Phys. Anthrop., 25, 339—340; Mathur
                in E. Anthrop., 19, 253—254; Whiteford in Amer. Anthrop.,
                70, 366—367.
                See: Jennings and Hoebel.

HOFER, HELMUT

1960   Das Gestaltungsproblem des Schädels der Säuger. Mitt. Naturf. Ges. Bern, N.F., 18, 81–87, 3 figs.

1962   Abs.: Kuhn-Schnyder in Zbl. Geol. Pal., Teil 2, 1964, 223–224.

1963   Die Situation und die Bedeutung der Primatologie. Zeit. Morph. Anthrop., 53, 2–5.

1964   Die Evolution des Gehirnes der Primaten und die Interpretation der Schädelform des Menschen. Ann. Soc. Roy. Zool. Belg., 94, 97–115, 6 figs.

1965   Die morphologische Analyse des Schädels des Menschen. In: Heberer, (ed.), 1965A, 145–226, 23 figs.

HOFER, H. O., and WILSON, J. A.

1967   An endocranial cast of an early Oligocene primate. Folia Primatologica, 5, 148–152, 3 figs.

HOFFMAN, A. C.

1965   On the discovery of a new thecodont from the Middle Beaufort beds. Navors. Nasion. Mus. Bloemfontein, 2, 33–40, 5 figs.
             Abs.: Huene in Zbl. Geol. Pal., Teil 2, 1966, 304.

1966   A gigantic plesiosaur from the South African Cretaceous. S. African Jour. Sci., 62, 138–140, 3 figs.

HOFFMAN, A. C., and ESTERHUYSE, D. J.

1965   Preliminary report on archaeological, palaeontological and anthropological field expeditions in the Orange River area. Navors. Nasion. Mus. Bloemfontein, 2, 21–27, 2 figs.

HOFFMEISTER, DONALD F.

1967   Tubulidentates, proboscideans, and hyracoideans. In: Anderson, S., and Jones, (eds.), 1967, 355–365, figs. 60–61.

HOFFSTETTER, ROBERT

1961E.   [Principaux gisements de Mammifères en] Amérique du Sud. In: Piveteau, J., (ed.), 1961A, (Traité de Paléo., 6:1), 492–495, fig. 8.

1961F.   Le gisement de vertébrés miocènes de Beni Mellal (Maroc). Squamates. Notes Mém. Serv. Géol. Maroc, 155, 95–101.

1964A.   Les glyptodontes du Pléistocène de Tarija (Bolivie). I. Genres Hoplophorus et Panochthus. Bull. Soc. Géol. France, 5, 126–133, 2 figs., pl. 10.
             Abs.: Lotze in Zbl. Geol. Pal., Teil 2, 1964, 718.

1964B.   Les serpents du Néogène du Pakistan (couches des Siwaliks). C. R. Soc. Géol. France, 1964, 294, (abs.).

1964C.   Les Squamates du Paléogène. Mém. Bur. Rech. Géol. Min., 28:2, 967–976.

1964D.   Les Sauria du Jurassique supérieur et spécialement les Gekkota de Bavière et de Mandchourie. Senck. Biologica, 45, 281–324, 3 figs., pls. 3–10, (German summary).

1965A.   Les serpents du Néogène du Pakistan (couches des Siwaliks). Bull. Soc. Géol. France, 6, 467–474, 5 figs.

1965B.   Les Sauria (=Lacertilia) du Jurassique supérieur du Montsech (Espagne). C. R. Soc. Géol. France, 1965, 204, (abs.).

1966A.   Les Sauria (=Lacertilia) du Jurassique supérieur du Montsech (Espagne). Bull. Soc. Géol. France, 7, 549–557, 2 figs., pls. 14–15.

1966B.   À propos des genres Ardeosaurus et Eichstaettisaurus (Reptilia, Sauria, Gekkonoidea) du Jurassique supérieur du Franconie. C. R. Soc. Géol. France, 1966, 190–191, (abs.).

1967A. À propos des genres <u>Ardeosaurus</u> et <u>Eichstaettisaurus</u> (Reptilia, Sauria, Gekkonoidea) du Jurassique supérieur de Franconie. Bull. Soc. Géol. France, <u>8</u>, 592–595, 1 fig.

1967B. Remarques sur les dates d'implantation des différents groupes de Serpents terrestres en Amérique du Sud. C. R. Soc. Géol. France, <u>1967</u>, 93–94.

1967C. Observations additionnelles sur les serpents du Miocène de Colombie et rectification concernant la date d'arrivée des Colubridés en Amérique du Sud. C. R. Soc. Géol. France, <u>1967</u>:5, 209–210.

1967D. Coup d'oeil sur les sauriens (=lacertiliens) des couches de Purbeck (Jurassique supérieur d'Angleterre). (Résumé d'un mémoire). Colloq. Internat. Cent. Nation. Recherch. Sci., <u>163</u>, 349–371, 13 figs., (English summary).

1968A. Un gisement de mammifères déséadiens (Oligocène inférieur) en Bolivie. C. R. Acad. Sci. Paris, Sci. Nat., <u>267</u>, 1095–1097.

1968B. Un gisement de vertébrés tertiaires à Sacaco (Sud-Pérou), témoin néogène d'une migration de faunes australes au long de la côte occidentale sudaméricaine. C. R. Acad. Sci. Paris, Sci. Nat., <u>267</u>, 1273–1276.

1968C. Sur la répartition géographique des Macraucheniidae (Mammifères, Litopternes) au Pléistocène. C. R. Soc. Géol. France, <u>1968</u>:3, 85–86.

1968D. A contribution to the classification of snakes. [Review of book by that title by Garth Underwood, 1967.] Copeia, <u>1968</u>:1, 201–213.

See: Branisa and Hoffstetter; Estes and Hoffstetter; Hecht, Hoffstetter and Vergnaud.

HOFFSTETTER, R., CRUSAFONT, M., and AGUIRRE, E.
1965   Note préliminaire sur la présence de sauriens (=lacertiliens) dan le Jurassique supérieur du Montsech (Espagne). C. R. Soc. Géol. France, <u>1965</u>, 53–55, 1 fig.

HOFFSTETTER, R., and GASC, J.-P.
1968   Observations sur le squelette cervical et spécialement sur les hypapophyses des sauriens varanoïdes actuels et fossiles. Bull. Mus. Hist. Nat. Paris, <u>1967</u>:6, 1028–1043, 3 figs.

HOFFSTETTER, R., and GAYRARD, Y.
1964   Observations sur l'ostéologie et la classification des Acrochordidae (Serpentes). Bull. Mus. Hist. Nat. Paris, <u>36</u>, 676–696, 6 figs.

HOFFSTETTER, R., and PASKOFF, R.
1966   Présence des genres <u>Macrauchenia</u> et <u>Hippidion</u> dans la faune pléistocène du Chili. Bull. Mus. Hist. Nat. Paris, <u>38</u>:4, 476–490, 3 figs.

HOFSTÄTTER, HANS H., and PIXA, H.
1962   Vergleichende Weltgeschichte. Band 1: Von der Urzeit bis um 2500 v. Chr. Baden-Baden: Holle, 194 pp., illustr.

HOGAN, THOMAS W.
1959   Dental plate of eagle ray found in Georgia cave. NSS News, <u>17</u>, 41–42.

HOGG, MARGARET E.
1962   A biology of man. Vol. I. Man's development as a species and an individual. London, Melbourne, Toronto: Heinemann, xi + 266 pp., 110 figs., 16 pls.

HOKKAIDO UNIV. ARCHAEOL. TEAM
1960 On the prehistoric remains excavated at Shirataki. Studies from Res. Inst. for North. Culture, Hokkaido Univ., 15, 207—270, (Japanese; English summary; not seen).

HOLDEN, RAYMOND PECKHAM
1966 Famous fossil finds: great discoveries in paleontology. Illustrated by John Martinez. New York: Dodd, Mead, 100 pp., illustr.

HÖLDER, HELMUT
1960 Rev.: Anon. in Bull. Acad. Soc. Lorraine Sci., 5:1, 104; Daber in Ber. Geol. Ges. Deutsch. Demokratischen Republ., 7, 443—444; Bleich in Mitt. Verband Deutschen Höhlen- und Karstforscher, München, 8, 24; Fischer in Aufschluss, 13, 80.
1964 Jura. (Band IV of the Handbuch der stratigraphischen Geologie.) Stuttgart: Ferdinand Enke, xii + 603 pp., 158 figs.
Rev.: Anon. in Bull. Acad. Soc. Lorraine Sci., 5:2, 240; Bachmayer in Universum; Natur u. Tech., 20:7, II; Hallam in Nature, 209, 440; Sittig in Aufschluss, 16, 52—54; Trimmel in Die Höhle, 16, 86—87.

HÖLDER, H., and STEINHORST, H.
1964 Lebendige Urwelt, Flora und Fauna der Vorzeit. Stuttgart: Spectrum, 135 pp., 155 figs., (not seen).
Rev.: Metz in Aufschluss, 16, 293.

HOLE, FRANK, and FLANNERY, K. V.
1967 The prehistory of southwestern Iran: a preliminary report. Proc. Prehist. Soc. Cambridge, 33, 147—206, 13 figs., 4 tables, 17 pls.

HOLE, F., and HEIZER, R. F.
1965 An introduction to prehistoric archeology. New York: Holt, Rinehart and Winston, x + 306 pp., 28 figs.
Rev.: Anon. in Anthropologica, 8, 151—154; Anon. in Bull. Archaeol. Soc. Virginia, no. 14, 4; Anon. in Mo. Archaeol. Soc. Newsletter, no. 193, 7; Baerreis in Wisc. Archeol., 46, 246—248; Cornwall in Man, 65, 200; Griffin in Science, 150, 874—875. Hutto in West Va. Archeol., no. 18, 45—46; Jelks in Amer. Antiq., 31, 584—585; Kühn in IPEK, 22, 149; Megaw in Archaeol., Phys. Anthrop. in Oceania, 1, 81; Narr in Anthropos, 62:1/2, 261—262; Piggott in Antiq., 39, 311—312; Schwartz in Amer. Anthrop., 67, 1336—1337; Swartz in Amer. Sci., 53, 338A—339A.

HOLE, THORNTON See: Hoare, et al.

HÖLKER, HERBERT
1960 Die Charlottenhöhle bei Hürben. Jahresh. für Karst- und Höhlenkunde, 1, 23—34, 8 figs.

HOLLAND, HORACE J.
1963 The Holland site (HJH 255), (University of Alabama site 1 Ct 140). Jour. Ala. Archaeol., 9, 62—71, 5 figs.
1965 Early lithic artifacts from north Alabama. Jour. Ala. Archeol., 11, 151, 1 fig.

HOLLINGWORTH, S. E.
1965   Frederick Everard Zeuner [- 1963]. Proc. Geol. Soc. London,
                   1618, 122–123.

HOLLITSCHER, W.
1964   [The origin of man. Truth, delusions, falsification.]   Priroda, 53:12,
                   51–58, illustr., (Russian).

HOLLOWAY, RALPH L., JR.
1966A.   Cranial capacity, neural reorganization, and hominid evolution: a search
                   for more suitable parameters. Amer. Anthrop., 68, 103–121.
1966B.   Structural reduction through the "probable mutation effect". A critique
                   with questions regarding human evolution. Amer. Jour. Phys.
                   Anthrop., 25, 7–11.
1967   Tools and teeth: some speculations regarding canine reduction. Amer.
                   Anthrop., 69, 63–67.

HOLLOWAY, R. L., JR., and TOBIAS, P. V.
1965   Cranial capacity of the hominine from Olduvai Bed I. Nature, 208,
                   205–206.
1966   Cranial capacity of the Olduvai Bed I hominine. Nature, 210, 1108–1110,
                   1 table.

HOLM, S. E.
1966   Bibliography of South African pre-and proto-historic archaeology. Pre-
                   toria: J. L. Van Schaik, Publication Series No. 16, xxv + 144 pp.
                   Rev.: Krogman in Amer. Jour. Phys. Anthrop., 27, 225.

HOLMAN, J. ALAN
1959C.   Birds and mammals from the Pleistocene of Williston, Florida. Bull.
                   State Mus., 5, 1–24, 2 pls., 11 tables.
1964A.   Pleistocene amphibians and reptiles from Texas. Herpetologica, 20,
                   73–83, 4 figs.
1964B.   Osteology of gallinaceous birds. Quart. Jour. Florida Acad. Sci., 27,
                   230–252, 3 pls.
1964C.   Fossil snakes from the Valentine formation of Nebraska. Copeia, 1964,
                   631–637, 3 figs.
1965A.   Pleistocene snakes from the Seymour formation of Texas. Copeia, 1965,
                   102–104, 1 fig.
1965B.   Early Miocene anurans from Florida. Quart. Jour. Florida Acad. Sci.,
                   28, 68–82, 2 figs.
1965C.   A small Pleistocene herpetofauna from Houston, Texas. Texas Journal
                   of Science, 17, 418–423.
1965D.   A Late Pleistocene herpetofauna from Missouri. Trans. Ill. Acad. Sci.,
                   58, 190–194.
1966A.   A huge Pleistocene box turtle from Texas. Quart. Jour. Florida Acad.
                   Sci., 28, 345–348, 1 fig.
1966B.   Some Pleistocene turtles from Illinois. Trans. Ill. Acad. Sci., 59, 214–216,
                   1 fig.
1966C.   A small Miocene herpetofauna from Texas. Quart. Jour. Florida Acad.
                   Sci., 29, 267–275, 1 fig.
1967   Additional Miocene anurans from Florida. Quart. Jour. Florida Acad.
                   Sci., 30, 121–140, 4 figs.

HOLMES, LOWELL D.
1965   Anthropology: an introduction. New York: The Ronald Press Co.,
                   ix + 384 pp., illustr., 5 tables.

	Rev.: Holzinger in Amer. Anthrop., 68, 1516−1517.
1967	Shoestring museum of man. Curator, 10, 261−266, 8 figs.

HOLTON, CHARLOTTE
1966	Bibliography of vertebrate paleontology and related subjects. 1964−1965. The Society of Vertebrate Paleontology, no. 20, 74 pp.
See:	McKenna and Holton.

HOLÝ, FRANTIŠEK See: Čtyroký, Fejfar and Holý.

HOLZ, HERMANN
1965	Zur innerartlichen Variabilität und phylogenetischen Stellung des afrikanischen Hyänenhundes Lycaon pictus. Zool. Anz., 174, 362−395, 28 figs., 7 tables.

HOLZSCHNEIDER, HANS
1962	Geschichte und Aufgaben der rheinischen Höhlenforschung. Mitt. Verband Deutschen Höhlen- und Karstforscher, München, 8, 1−5, 2 pls.

HONEA, KENNETH
1965	A morphology of scrapers and their method of production. Southwestern Lore, 31, 25−40, 12 figs.
1966	Evolution in lithic traditions of the Southwest. El Palacio, 72:4, 32−36.

HONEY, JAMES See: Wade, et al.

HOOD, DORA
1964	Davidson Black. A biography. Toronto: Univ. Toronto Press, xii + 145 pp., portr., 8 pls.
	Rev.: Heberer in Homo, 15, 253; Koenigswald in Amer. Anthrop., 67, 518; Krogman in Amer. Jour. Phys. Anthrop., 22, 211.

HOOIJER, DIRK ALBERT
1961C.	Middle Pleistocene mammals from Latamne, Orontes Valley, Syria. Ann. Archeol. Syrie, 11, 117−132, 24 figs., 9 tables.
1962G.	Abs.: Dietrich in Zbl. Geol. Pal., Teil 2, 1964, 194.
1963D.	Miocene Mammalia of Congo. (With a chapter by A. Gautier and J. Lepersonne.) Ann. Mus. Roy. Afr. Cent., ser. in 8º, Sci. Geol., no. 46, x + 77 pp., 8 figs., 10 pls., 11 tables.
1963E.	Mammalian remains from an Indian site on Curaçao. Studies on the fauna of Curaçao and other Caribbean islands, no. 64, 119−122.
1964A.	On two milk molars of a pygmy stegodont from Ola Bula, Flores. Bull. Geol. Surv. Indonesia, 1, 49−52, 1 fig., 1 table.
1964B.	The lower boundary of the Pleistocene in Java and the age of Pithecanthropus. In: Lasker, G. W., (ed.), 1964, 102−108, 1 table, (reprint with editorial comment).
1964C.	Preliminary identification of some fossil mammals from Narmada Valley, India. Riv. Sci. Preist., 18, 20.
1964D.	The snout of Paulocnus petrifactus (Mammalia, Edentata). Zool. Meded. Leiden, 39, 79−84, 1 fig., pl. 10, 2 tables.
1964E.	Pleistocene vertebrates from Celebes. XII. Notes on pygmy stegodonts. Zool. Meded. Leiden, 40, 37−44, 1 pl.
1964F.	New records of mammals from the Middle Pleistocene of Sangiran, central Java. Zool. Meded. Leiden, 40, 73−88, 1 fig., 1 pl.
1965A.	Pleistocene vertebrates of the Netherlands Antilles. 7th Internat. Congr., Internat. Assoc. Quat. Res., Abs., 1965, 221, (abs.).

1965B.   Note on Coryphomys bühleri Schaub, a gigantic murine rodent from
            Timor. Israel Jour. Zool., 14, 128–133, 1 pl., 1 table.
1966A.   Fossil mammals of the Netherlands Antilles. Arch. Néerland. Zool.,
            16, 531–532.
1966B.   Miocene rhinoceroses of East Africa. Brit. Mus. (Nat. Hist.), Fossil
            Mamm. Afr., no. 21, 117–190, 15 pls., 51 tables. (Also: Bull.,
            Brit. Mus. (Nat. Hist.), Geol., 13:2.)
1967A.   The Dicerorhinus hemitoechus (Falconer) at Yabroud. Ann. Archéol.
            Arabes Syrienne, 16:2, 155–156.
1967B.   Preliminary notes on the animal remains found at Bouqras and Ramad
            in 1965. Ann. Archéol. Arabes Syrienne, 16:2, 193–196.
1967C.   Indo-Australian insular elephants. Genetica, 38:2, 143–162, 3 figs., 5
            tables.
1967D.   Pleistocene vertebrates of the Netherland Antilles. In: Martin, P. S.,
            and Wright, H. E., (eds.), 1967, 399–406, 3 figs.
1967E.   The status of Aceratherium leakei Deraniyagala. Zool. Meded. Leiden,
            42, 121–123.
1968A.   Games paleontologists play. News Bull., Soc. Vert. Pal., no. 82, 66–67.
1968B.   Evidence for a pentadactyl manus in Brachyodus aequitorialis Macinnes
            from the East African Miocene. Proc. K. Nederl. Akad. Wet.,
            Ser. B, 71:1, 91–97, 2 figs., 1 table.
1968C.   A Cretaceous dinosaur from the Syrian Arab Republic. Proc. K. Nederl.
            Akad. Wet., Ser. B, 71:2, 150–152, 1 table.
1968D.   A note on the mandible of Aceratherium acutirostratum (Deraniyagala)
            from Moruaret Hill, Turkana District, Kenya. Zool. Meded.
            Leiden, 42:21, 231–235, 1 table.
1968E.   A rhinoceros from the Late Miocene of Fort Ternan, Kenya. Zool.
            Meded. Leiden, 43:6, 77–92, 3 pls., 13 tables.

HOOIJER, D. A., and RAY, C. E.
    1964   A metapodial of Acratocnus (Edentata: Megalonychidae) from a cave
                in Hispaniola. Proc. Biol. Soc. Wash, 77, 253–258, 1 fig.

HOOPER, A. B., III
    1966   The Clod Site, Madison County, Alabama. Anthrop. Jour. Canada, 4:3,
                15–16, 3 figs.
    1968   Pebble tools: Lively Complex duplicated in Bear Creek Watershed.
                Jour. Ala. Archeol., 14, 1–16, 6 figs., 3 tables.

HOOVER, B. REED   See: Slaughter and Hoover.

HOOYKAAS, REIJER
    1959   Natural law and divine miracle. A historical-critical study of the prin-
                ciple of uniformity in geology, biology and theology. Leiden:
                E. J. Brill, xiii + 237 pp.
                Abs.: Schindewolf in Zbl. Geol. Pal., Teil 2, 1962, 310–311.
    1963   Natural law and divine miracle. The principle of uniformity in geology,
                biology and theology. Leiden: E. J. Brill, Publ., 2nd impression,
                237 pp.
                Rev.: Albritton in GeoTimes, 12:8, 35–36.

HOPGOOD, JAMES F.
    1965   An archaeological survey of Portage Open Bay. Mo. Archaeol. Soc.
                Newsletter, no. 195, 9–10, illustr.

HOPKINS, DAVID M.
1967A.   Introduction. In: Hopkins, D. M., (ed.), 1967D, 1—6.
1967B.   Quaternary marine transgressions in Alaska. In: Hopkins, D. M., (ed.),
             1967D, 47—90, 5 figs., 2 tables.
1967C.   The Cenozoic history of Beringia — a synthesis. In: Hopkins, D. M.,
             (ed.), 1967D, 451—484, 4 figs.
1967D.   (ed.) The Bering land bridge. Based on a symposium held at the
             Seventh Congress of the International Association for Quaternary
             Research, Boulder, Colorado, Aug.—Sept. 1965. Stanford, Calif.:
             Stanford Univ. Press, 511 pp., illustr.
   Rev.:   Benson in Jour. Pal., 42, 1318—1319;   Dionne in Nat. Canadien,
             95:2, 601—602;   Gusinde in Anthropos, 62:5/6, 962;   Irving
             in Amer. Anthrop., 70, 816—817;   H. C. K. in Archeol. Soc.
             N. J., News., 82, 9;   Lehmann in Biol. Zbl., 88:2, 252—253;
             Lundman in Anthropos, 62:5—6, 962;   Martin in Science, 158,
             1168;   Olson in Quart. Rev. Biol., 43:4, 454—455;   Petter, F.
             in Mammalia, 32:1, 135;   Pinot in Rev. Géogr. Phys. Géol. Dyn.,
             11:4, 459—462;   Price in Nature, 1187;   Whitmore in Amer.
             Sci., 56, 150A, 152A;   Wilmsen in Amer. Jour. Archaeol., 72:2,
             198—200.
   See: Péwé and Hopkins;   Repenning, Hopkins and Rubin.

HOPKINS, D. M., MacNEIL, F. S., MERKLIN, R. L., and PETROV, O. M.
1965   Quaternary correlations across Bering Strait. Science, 147, 1107—1114.

HOPKINS, MARIE L.
1963   Appendix A: comparisons [for vertebrate fossils from the Nevada
             Northern Pipeline]. In: Tuohy, D. R., 1963A, 79—81, 3 tables.

HOPKINS, M. L., and MACDONALD, J. R.
1963   Appendix A: identification of vertebrate fossils. In: Tuohy, D. R.,
             1963A, 77—79.

HOPPE, WALTER
1965   The fossils of the Red Triassic Sandstone of Thuringia and their strati-
             graphical and ecological importance. Geologie, 14, 272—323,
             6 pls., 3 tables, map, (German;   English and Russian summaries).
   See: Pichardo del Barrio, et al.

HOPSON, JAMES A.
1964A.   Pseudodontornis and other large marine birds from the Miocene of
             South Carolina. Postilla, no. 83, 19 pp., 3 figs.
             Abs.: Kuhn in Zbl. Geol. Pal., Teil 2, 1965, 258.
1964B.   The braincase of the advanced mammal-like reptile Bienotherium. Pos-
             tilla, no. 87, 30 pp., 8 figs.
1964C.   Tooth replacement in cynodont, dicynodont and therocephalian reptiles.
             Proc. Zool. Soc. London, 142, 625—654, 9 figs.
1966   The origin of the mammalian middle ear. Amer. Zool., 6, 437—450,
             11 figs.
1967A.   Mammal-like reptiles and the origin of mammals. Discovery, Yale, 2:2,
             25—33, 7 figs.
1967B.   Comments on the competitive inferiority of the Multituberculates. Syst.
             Zool., 16, 352—355.

HORIOT, RENÉ
1965   Les "alènes" de Viry. Bull. Soc. Préhist. Franç., C. R. séances mens.,
            1965:6, cic—ccvi, 4 figs.

HORN, K. F.   See: Stokes, Smith and Horn.

HORNEY, AMOS G.   See: Berger, R., Horney and Libby.

HORR, DAVID A.
1959   (ed.) [COWA surveys and bibliographies.]   Area 19 — Southeast Asia.
            COWA Surv. and Bibliog., Area 19, no. 1, 6 + 6 pp.

HOSKINS, DONALD M.
1961   Stratigraphy and paleontology of the Bloomsburg formation of Penn-
            sylvania and adjacent states. Bull. Penn. Geol. Surv., G36, 1—
            124, 6 figs., 7 pls.
1964   Fossil collecting in Pennsylvania. Illustr. by A. Van Olden. Bull.
            Pennsylvania Geol. Surv., G40, 1—126, illustr.
            Rev.: Anon. in Rocks and Miner., 45:3, 197.

HOSSFELD, PAUL S.
1965A.   Patination or weathering? Mankind, 6:6, 269—274, 2 pls.
1965B.   Radiocarbon dating and palaeoecology of the Aitape fossil human re-
            mains. Proc. Roy. Soc. Victoria, 78, 161—165, 2 figs.

HOTTON, NICHOLAS, III
1965   Tetrapods. In: Kummel and Raup, (eds.), 1965, 119—125.
1967   Stratigraphy and sedimentation in the Beaufort series (Permian-Triassic),
            South Africa. In: Teichert, and Yochelson, (eds.), 1967, 390—
            428, 3 figs., 6 tables.
1968   The evidence of evolution. New York: American Heritage, 160 pp.,
            illustr.
            See: Crompton and Hotton.

HOUSE, MICHAEL ROBERT
1965   Dorset natural history reports, 1964. Geology. Proc. Dorset Nat. Hist.
            Archaeol. Soc., 86, 38—40.
            See: Friend and House.

HOUSTON, ROBERT S.
1962   Non-paleontological methods of correlation of rocks of Tertiary age in
            Wyoming. Part 1 — Heavy elements in bone fragments. Contrib.
            Geol., Univ. Wyoming, 1, 3—5, 1 fig., 1 table.

HOUSTON, R. S., and TOOTS, H.
1963   Variation in the content of heavy elements in bone fragments of Ter-
            tiary age in Wyoming. Spec. Pap. Geol. Soc. Amer., 73, 87, (abs.).

HOUSTON, R. S., TOOTS, H., and KELLEY, J. C.
1966   Iron content of fossil bones of Tertiary age in Wyoming correlated
            with climatic change. Contrib. Geol., Univ. Wyoming, 5:2, 1—18,
            3 figs., 9 tables.

HOUSTON, TERRY   See: Mincham 1966.

HOWARD, HILDEGARDE

1962F.   Fossil birds with especial reference to the birds of Rancho La Brea. Revised. Sci. Ser., Los Angeles Co. Mus., no. 17, Paleont. no. 10, 44 pp., 22 figs.

1964A.   A new species of the "pigmy goose", Anabernicula, from the Oregon Pleistocene, with a discussion of the genus. Amer. Mus. Novit., no. 2200, 14 pp., 2 figs.
Abs.: Kuhn in Zbl. Geol. Pal., Teil 2, 1966, 313.

1964B.   A fossil owl from Santa Rosa Island, California. With comments on the eared owls of Rancho La Brea. Bull. S. Calif. Acad. Sci., 63:1, 27—31, 1 fig., 1 table.

1964C.   Fossil anseriformes. In: Delacour and Scott, 1964, 4, 233—326, 5 figs., 10 pls., 5 tables.

1965A.   A new species of cormorant from the Pliocene of Mexico. Bull. S. Calif. Acad. Sci., 64, 50—55, 1 fig., 1 table.
Abs.: Kuhn in Zbl. Geol. Pal., Teil 2, 1966, 313.

1965B.   Further discoveries concerning the flightless "diving geese" of the genus Chendytes. Condor, 66, 372—376, 1 fig., 2 tables.
Abs.: Kuhn in Zbl. Geol. Pal., Teil 2, 1966, 312—313.

1965C.   First record of avian fossils from the Eocene of California. Jour. Pal., 39, 350—354, pl. 49.
Abs.: Kuhn in Zbl. Geol. Pal., Teil 2, 1966, 313.

1966A.   Pliocene birds from Chihuahua, Mexico. Contrib. Sci., Los Angeles Co. Mus., 94, 3—12, 1 fig., 2 tables.
Rev.: Kuhn in Zbl. Geol. Pal., Teil 2, 1967, 107—108.

1966B.   A possible ancestor of the Lucas auk (family Mancallidae) from the Tertiary of Orange County, California. Contrib. Sci., Los Angeles Co. Mus., 101, 1—8, 1 fig., 2 tables.
Rev.: Kinzelbach in Jour. Ornithol., 110:1, 118; Kuhn in Zbl. Geol. Pal., Teil 2, 1967, 108.

1966C.   Two fossil birds from the Lower Miocene of South Dakota. Contrib. Sci., Los Angeles Co. Mus., 107, 1—8, 1 fig., 2 tables.

1966D.   Additional avian records from the Miocene of Sharktooth Hill, California. Contrib. Sci., Los Angeles Co. Mus., no. 114, 1—11, 1 fig., 6 tables.
Rev.: Huene in Zbl. Geol. Pal., Teil 2, 1968, 211; Kinzelbach in Jour. Ornithol., 110:1, 118; Kuhn in Zbl. Geol. Pal., Teil 2, 1967, 511.

1968A.   Tertiary birds from Laguna Hills, Orange County, California. Contrib. Sci., Los Angeles Co. Mus., 142, 1—21, 2 figs.
Rev.: Kuhn in Zbl. Geol. Pal., Teil 2, 1969:3, 291.

1968B.   Limb measurements of the extinct vulture, Coragyps occidentalis, with a description of a new subspecies. Pap. Archaeol. Soc. N. Mex., 1, 115—128, tables 3—11.
Rev.: Kuhn in Zbl. Geol. Pal., Teil 2, 1969:3, 290—291.

1968C.   A preliminary report on Pleistocene birds of Central Mexico. Program, 1968 Ann. Meetings, Geol. Soc. Amer., 1968, 142, (abs.).

HOWARD, M. MAITLAND   See: Cole, S. 1966B; Cornwall 1968.

HOWARTH, MICHAEL KINGSLEY

1964   The Jurassic period. In: Harland, W. B., et al., (eds.), 1964, 203—205, 2 tables.

HOWE, BRUCE, (ed.)

1957   COWA surveys and bibliographies. Area 10 — northwest Africa. COWA Surv. and Bibliog., Area 10, no. 1, 7 + 18 pp.

1960   COWA surveys and bibliographies. Area 10 – northwest Africa. COWA
          Surv. and Bibliog., Area 10, no. 2, 9 + 22 pp.

HOWE, JOHN A.
1962B.   The Pleistocene horses of Nebraska. Diss. Abst., 22, 2754, (abs.).
1966A.   Observations on changes in the conformation and enamel pattern of
          horse teeth due to wear. Compass Sigma Gamma Epsilon, 44:1,
          10–18.
1966B.   The Oligocene rodent Ischyromys in Nebraska. Jour. Pal., 40, 1200–1210,
          3 figs., 3 tables.
          Rev.: Fahlbusch in Zbl. Geol. Pal., Teil 2, 1968, 215.

HOWELL, F. CLARK
1959C.   (ed.) COWA surveys and bibliographies. Area 12 – Equatorial Africa.
          COWA Surv. and Bibliog., Area 12, no. 1, 2 + 10 pp.
1962E.   Torralba: an open-air Acheulian occupation site in northern Spain.
          Abs. 61st. Ann. Meeting Amer. Anthrop. Assoc., 1962, 18, (abs.).
1963C.   Early Acheulian occupation sites in northern Spain. Abs. 62nd Ann.
          Meeting Amer. Anthrop., Assoc., 1963, 30, (abs.).
1964A.   Observations on European Middle Acheulian tool-kits. Abs. 63rd Ann.
          Meeting Amer. Anthrop. Assoc., 1964, 29–30, (abs.).
1964B.   The hominization process. In: Tax (ed.), 1964, 49–59.
1966   Observations on the earlier phases of the European Lower Paleolithic.
          In: Clark, J. D., and Howell, F. C., (eds.), 1966A, 88–201,
          28 figs., 15 tables.
1967A.   Later Cenozoic studies in Africa and palaeoanthropology: a post-confer-
          ence appraisal. In: Bishop, W. W., and Clark, J. D., (eds.),
          1967A, 903–922, 3 figs.
1967B.   Recent advances in human evolutionary studies. Quart. Rev. Biol., 42,
          471–513, 4 figs., 2 tables.
          See: Brace 1964; Clark, J. D., and Howell.

HOWELL, F. C., and BOURLIÈRE, F.
1963   (eds.) Rev.: Ascher in Amer. Sci., 52, 418A–419A;   Comas in An.
          Antrop., Mexico, 1965, 2, 194–196;   Ehgartner in Mitt. Anthrop.
          Ges. Wien, 95, 366–367;   Heberer in Homo, 15, 249;   Hugot
          in Ann. Geog., 75, 362–364;   Kleindienst in Amer. Anthrop.,
          68, 268–270;   Martin in Ecology, 45, 671;   Pilbeam in Human
          Biol., 37, 330–333;   Römer in Quart. Rev. Biol., 40, 84–85;
          Vallois in L'Anthrop., 69, 336–337.

HOWELL, F. C., BUTZER, K. W., and AGUIRRE, E.
1963   Noticia preliminar sobre el emplazamiento acheulense de Torralba (Soria).
          Exc. Arqueol. en España, 10, (not seen).
          Rev.: Jordá Cerdá in Zephyrus, 14, 141–142.

HOWELL, F. C., COLE, G. H., KLEINDIENST, M. R., and HALDEMANN, E. G.
1962   Isimila – an Acheulian occupation site in the Iringa Highlands, Southern
          Highlands Province, Tanganyika. Proc. 4th Panafrican Congr.
          Prehist., sec. 3, 43–80, 5 figs., 2 tables.

HOWELL, F. C., and EDITORS OF LIFE
1965   Early man. New York: Time Inc. (Life Nature Library), 200 pp., illustr.
          Rev.: Gabel in Amer. Anthrop., 68, 1581–1582;   Krogman in Amer.
          Jour. Phys. Anthrop., 23, 445;   McBryde in Mankind, 6, 525–
          527;   Vallois in L'Anthrop., 70:1–2, 132–133.

HOWELL, F. CLARK, and SCHANFIELD, S.
1959   (eds.) COWA surveys and bibliographies. Area 13 − South Africa.
            COWA Surv. and Bibliog., Area 13, no. 1, 5 + 16 pp.

HOWELL, THOMAS R.
1968   A Pleistocene vertebrate fauna from Nicaragua. Program, 1968 Ann.
            Meetings, Geol. Soc. Amer., 1968, 143−144, (abs.).

HOWELLS, WILLIAM WHITE
1954   Rev.: Goodwin in Wyo. Archaeol., 7:3, 10.
1962   Rev.: Genovés in An. Antrop., Mexico, 1964, 1, 229−230;   White in
            S. Afr. Archaeol. Bull., 19, 48.
1963   Die Ahnen der Menschheit. Der Werdegang des Menschen nach dem
            heutigen Kenntnisstand allgemeinverständlich dargestellt. Transl.
            by G. Kurth. Zürich, Stuttgart, Wien: Müller, 544 pp., 89 figs.,
            (not seen).
            Rev.: Altehenger in Anthropos, 59, 657−658;   Ax in Naturwiss. Rund.,
            18, 123−124;   Haltenorth in Säugetierkundl. Mitt., 13, 138;
            Zapfe in Universum: Natur u. Tech., 19, 480.
1965   Some present aspects of physical anthropology. Ann. Amer. Acad.
            Political Social Sci., 357, 127−133.
1967   Mankind in the making. The story of human evolution. Rev. ed. New
            York: Doubleday, 384 pp., 8 pls., illustr.
            Rev.: Hulse in Amer. Jour. Phys. Anthrop., 27, 397−398;   Lamb in
            Amer. Anthrop., 70, 637−638;   Vallois in L'Anthrop., 73:1−2,
            114−115.
            See: Brace 1964;   Patterson, B. and Howells.

HOWELLS, W. W., et al.
1965   Synthesis and evolution. In: DeVore, P. L., (ed.), 1965, 124−137.

HOWORKA, H., and FISCHER, K.-H.
1964   Über eine neue Abformung des Urvogels (Archaeopteryx lithographica
            H. v. Meyer). Geologie, 13:9, 1131−1141, 5 pls., (English and
            and Russian summaries).

HOYT, JOHN H.   See: Henry, V. H. and Hoyt.

HSIA NAI
1963   La arqueología en China. Zephyrus, 14, 63−73, 9 figs.

HSIEH, HSIANG-HSU
1960A.   Reprinted in Chinese in Paleovert. et Paleoanthrop., 2:2.
1960C.   Discovery of Tertiary mammalian fossils in Lintung, Shensi. Acta Pal.
            Sinica, 8, 200−204, 3 figs., (Chinese; English summary).
1964   Mammalian fossils from the Pleistocene of Huituipo, Tungchuan, Shensi.
            Vert. Palasiatica, 8:4, 387−397, 2 figs., 2 pls., (Chinese, English
            summary).
            See: Liu, H.-t. and Hsieh.

HSU, CHUN-HUA   See: Li, Y.-h., Han and Hsu.

HSU, JEN
1966A.   The climatic conditions in North China during the time of Sinanthropus.
            Coll. Pap. on the Quat., 4:1, 77−83, (Chinese).

1966B.   The climatic condition in North China during the time of <u>Sinanthropus.</u>
            Sci. Sinica, <u>15,</u> 410–414, 1 fig.
        See: Yin, Chow and Hsu.

HU, CHANG-KANG
    1962C.   Abs.: Dietrich in Zbl. Geol. Pal., Teil 2, <u>1964,</u> 206.
    1964   <u>Archaeotherium</u> <u>ordosius</u> from the Oligocene of Inner Mongolia.   Vert.
                Palasiatica, <u>8</u>:3, 312–317, 1 fig., 1 pl., 1 table, (Chinese;   English
                summary).
        See: Chow, M., Hu and Lee.

HU, SHOW-YUNG
    1963   Abs.: Huene in Zbl. Geol. Pal., Teil 2, <u>1964,</u> 990.
    1964   Carnosaurian remains from Alashan, Inner Mongolia.   Vert. Palasiatica,
                <u>8,</u> 42–63, 14 figs., 2 pls., (Chinese and English).
                Abs.: Huene in Zbl. Geol. Pal., Teil 2, <u>1965,</u> 248.

HUANG, EN-BAN   See: Li, T.-w. and Huang.

HUANG, TUNYOW
    1965   A new species of a whale tympanic bone from Taiwan, China.   Trans.
                Proc. Pal. Soc. Japan, no. <u>61,</u> 183–187, 2 figs., pl. 22.

HUANG, WAN-PO   See: Chang, Y. <u>et</u> <u>al.</u>;   Chow, M., Huang, <u>et</u> <u>al.</u>

HUANG, W.-P., and CHANG, Y.-P.
    1966   The Quaternary mammalian fossil localities of Lantian district, Shensi.
                Vert. Palasiatica, <u>10,</u> 35–46, 2 figs., 4 tables, (Chinese;   English
                summary).

HUANG, WEI-LUNG   See: Liu, H.-t., Su, <u>et</u> <u>al.</u>

HUANG, WEI-WEN
    1964   On a collection of palaeoliths from Sanmen area in western Honan.
                Vert. Palasiatica, <u>8,</u> 162–181, 20 figs., 4 pls., (Chinese;   English
                summary).

HUANG, XUE-SHIH   See: Chow, M., Huang, <u>et</u> <u>al.</u>

HUANG, ZHENWEI and MENG, Z.
    1964   New localities of fossil mammals of West Zhejiang.   Vert. Palasiatica,
                <u>8,</u> 92–94, 4 figs., (Chinese).

HUARD, PAUL
    1962   Archéologie et zoologie: Contribution à l'étude des singes au Sahara
                oriental et central.   Bull. Inst. Franç. Afr. Noire, sér. B, <u>24,</u>
                86–104, 2 figs.

HUBACH, ENRIQUE
    1957B.   Estratigrafia de la Sabana de Bogota y alrededores.   Inst. Geol. Nac.
                Colombia, <u>1957</u>:5, 1 map, 1 fig., 143–144, (Spanish).

HUBBS, CARL L.
    1964   David Starr Jordan.   Syst. Zool., <u>13,</u> 195–200, portr.

HUBBS, C. L., BIEN, G. S., and SUESS, H. E.
1965   La Jolla natural radiocarbon measurements IV. Radiocarbon, 7, 66–117.

HUCKRIEDE, REINHOLD, and JACOBSHAGEN, V.
1963   Eine Faunenfolge aus dem jungpleistozänen Löss bei Bad Wildungen.
              2. Die Fundschichten. Abh. Hess. Landesamt. Bodenforsch.,
              44, 93–105, pls. 12–14.

HUCKRIEDE, R., and WIESEMANN, G.
1968   Der jungpleistozäne Pluvial-See von El Jafr und weitere Daten zum
              Quartär Jordaniens. Geologica et Palaeontologica, 2, 73–96, 6 figs.,
              3 pls., 1 map, (English summary).

HUDDLESTON, LEE ELDRIDGE
1967   Origins of the American Indians. European concepts, 1492–1729.
              Austin: Univ. of Texas Press, x + 179 pp.
              Rev.: Jennings in Science, 161, 560–561; Soday in Man, Jour. Roy
              Anthrop. Inst., 3, 678; Wilmsen in Amer. Antiq., 34, 488.

HUDSON, J. D.
1966   Hugh Miller's reptile bed and the Mytilus Shales, Middle Jurassic, Isle
              of Eigg, Scotland. Scottish Jour. Geol., 2, 265–281, 2 figs., 1 pl.

HUEBER, F. M.   See: Dorofeyev 1966.

HUENE, FRIEDRICH FRHR. VON
1950B.   Abs.: Raabe in Zbl. Geol. Pal., Teil 2, 1964, 797.
1951B.   Abs.: Raabe in Zbl. Geol. Pal., Teil 2, 1964, 803.
1951D.   Abs.: Raabe in Zbl. Geol. Pal., Teil 2, 1964, 799–800.
1964   Neue Gedanken über die Herkunft der Ichthyosaurier. Pal. Zeit., 38,
              26–27.
              Abs.: Huene in Zbl. Geol. Pal., Teil 2, 1964, 984.
1966A.   Ein sehr junger und ungewöhnlicher Ichthyosaurier aus dem oberen
              Lias von Holzmaden. Neues Jahrb. Geol. Pal., Abh., 124, 53–55,
              2 figs., pl. 7.
              Abs.: Huene in Zbl. Geol. Pal., Teil 2, 1966, 304.
1966B.   Ein Megalosauriden-Wirbel des Lias aus norddeutschem Geschiebe. Neues
              Jahrb. Geol. Pal., Monatsh., 1966:5, 318–319, 2 figs.
              See: Nikolov and Huene.

HUGEDÉ, NORBERT
1966   Le cas Teilhard de Chardin. Preface by Jean Rostand. Paris: Fischbacher,
              220 pp.
              Rev.: Huard in Rev. Synthèse, 88, 74–75.

HUGHES, D. R., and BROTHWELL, D. R.
1966   The earliest populations of man in Europe, W. Asia and N. Africa
              (Fascicle No. 50). London: Cambridge Univ. Press, 19 pp.,
              (not seen).
              Rev.: Bhattacharya in E. Anthrop., 20, 287–289.

HUGHES, JACK T.   See: Dalquest and Hughes.

HUGOT, HENRI J.
1960A.   Congrès. Union Internationale des Sciences Préhistoriques et Proto-
              historiques — 5e Session. Hambourg 24-30 août 1958. Libyca,
              6–7, 277–278.

1960B.   Les missions Berliet au Sahara. Libyca, 8, 323–335, 5 figs.
1963   Recherches préhistoriques dans L'Ahaggar nord-occidental, 1950–1957.
              Mém. Cent. Recherch. Anthrop. Préhist., Ethnog., Algiers, 1,
              206 pp., 59 figs., 24 pls.
              Rev.: Marti Jusmet in Ampurias, 28, 321–322;   Vaufrey in L'Anthrop.,
              68, 416–417.
1964   État des recherches préhistoriques dans l'Afrique de l'Ouest, 1964–1965.
              W. Afr. Archaeol. Newsletter, no. 1, 4–7, (English summary).
1965   Données récentes sur la question atérienne au Sahara méridional. Qua-
              ternaria, 7, 79–89, 4 figs., (Italian and German summaries).
1966A.   Limites méridionales de l'Atérien. Acta V Congr. Panafr. Prehist. Estud.
              Cuaternario, 1963:2, 95–108, 2 figs., 1 pl., 3 tables.
1966B.   Présence d'un faciès archaïque du Paléolithique inférieur à Dakar. Bull.
              Inst. Franç. Afr. Noire, Ser. A, 28, 415–416.
1967   Le Paléolithique terminal dans l'Afrique de l'ouest. Discussion. In:
              Bishop, W. W., and Clark, J. D. (eds.), 1967A, 529–555, 6 figs.,
              8 pls., 5 tables, (English summary).
              See: Faure and Hugot.

HUGUENEY, MARGUERITE
1965   Les chiroptères du Stampien supérieur de Coderet-Branssat (Allier). Doc.
              Lab. Géol. Fac. Sci. Lyon, 9, 97–127, 10 pls.
              C. R. Soc. Géol. France, 1965, 80, (abs.).
1967   Les Gliridés (Mammalia, Rodentia) de l'Oligocène supérieur de Coderet-
              Branssat (Allier). C. R. Soc. Géol. France, 1967, 91–92, 1 fig.
              Rev.: Fahlbusch in Zbl. Géol. Pal., Teil 2, 1968, 216.

HUGUENEY, M., and MEIN, P.
1965   Lagomorphes et Rongeurs du Néogène de Lissieu (Rhône). Trav. Lab.
              Géol. Univ. Lyon, no. 12, 109–123, 3 pls.
1966   Les rongeurs pliocènes du Rousillon dans les collections Lyonnaise.
              Trav. Lab. Géol. Univ. Lyon, 13, 243–266, 19 figs., pl. 16.
              Rev.: Fahlbusch in Zbl. Géol. Pal., Teil 2, 1968, 215–216.

HUICĂ, I., and GHEORGHIU, M.
1962   Abs.: Weiler in Zbl. Géol. Pal., Teil 2, 1966, 279–280.

HULL, DAVID L.
1967   Certainty and circularity in evolutionary taxonomy. Evolution, 21,
              174–189.

HULSE, DAVID C.   See: Cambron and Hulse.

HULSE, FREDERICK S.
1963A.   Objectives and methods. In: Mandelbaum, D. G., Lasker, G. W., and
              Albert, E. M., (eds.), 1963, 69–79.
1963B.   The human species. An introduction to physical anthropology. New
              York: Random House, xxii + 504 pp., 78 figs., photographs.
              Rev.: Genovés in An. Antrop., Mexico, 1964, 1, 230–231;   Jay in
              Amer. Anthrop., 66, 1452–1453;   Johnston in Human Biol., 36,
              201–203;   MacConaill in Man, 64, 57;   Saran in Man in India,
              45, 325;   Sauter in Arch. Suiss. Anthrop. Gén., 29, 73;   Schwidetzky
              in Homo, 15, 110.

HULSE, F. S., and LAMB, N. P.
1963   Trends in physical anthropology. In: Siegel, Bernard J., (ed.), 1963, 146—177.

HUMBARD, R. A.
1967   Quartzite pebble tools. Jour. Ala. Archeol., 13, 52—55, 2 figs.

HUMPHREY, ROBERT L., JR.
1967   The Eurasian Paleolithic and the fluted point tradition: new evidence from the American arctic. Abs. 66th Ann. Meeting Amer. Anthrop. Assoc., 1967, 39, (abs.).

HÜNERMANN, KARL ALBAN
1964   Der Schädel eines Microbunodon (Mammalia, Artiodactyla, Anthracotheriidae) aus dem Chattium von Ebnat, Kt. St. Gallen. Eclog. Geol. Helvetiae, 57, 823—824.
1965   Die Suiden-Reste (Artiodactyla, Mammalia) des Altpleistozäns von Voigtstedt in Thüringen. Pal. Abh., Abt. A, 2, 427—432, pl. 23, (Russian and English summaries).
1966   Der Bau des Biber-Prämolaren und seine Verwendbarkeit für die Systematik der Castoridae (Rodentia, Mammalia). Neues Jahrb. Geol. Pal., Abh., 125, Festband, 227—234, 29 figs., portr.
       Rev.: Fahlbusch in Zbl. Geol. Pal., Teil 2, 1967, 522.
1967   Der Schädel von Microbunodon minus (Cuvier) (Artiodactyla, Anthracotheriidae) aus dem Chatt (Oligozän). Eclog. Geol. Helvetiae, 60, 661—688, 11 figs., 3 tables, (English summary).

HUNT, EDWARD E., JR.
1967   Reply [to reviews of "The living races of man"]. Current Anthrop., 8, 125.
       See: Coon and Hunt.

HUNTER, H. A., and LANGSTON, W., JR.
1965   Odontoma in a northern mammoth. Paleontol., 7, 674—681, 1 fig., pl. 101.

HUNYADI, L.
1962   Abs.: Bogsch in Zbl. Geol. Pal., Teil 2, 1964, 993.

HUPPERT, D.
1964   Otolithen, evolutionäre Wegweiser? Naturwiss. Rund., 17, 448—449.

HURLEY, WILLIAM M.
1965   Archaeological research in the projected Kickapoo Reservoir, Vernon County, Wisconsin. Wisc. Archeol., 46, 1—114, 20 figs.

HURT, WESLEY R.
1964   Recent radiocarbon dates for central and southern Brazil. Amer. Antiq., 30, 25—33, 1 fig.
1966   The altithermal and the prehistory of the Northern Plains. Quaternaria, 8, 101—114, 1 fig., 1 table, (French and German summaries).

HÜRZELER, JOHANNES
1962B.   Die Tatsache der biologischen Evolution. In: Haag, Haas, and Hürzeler, (eds.), 1962, 103—132, 5 figs.

1967   Nouvelles découvertes de mammifères dans les sédiments fluviolacustres
            de Villafranca d'Asti. Colloq. Internat. Cent. Nation. Recherch.
            Sci., 163, 633–636, (English summary).
            Rev.: Albanesi in Riv. Ital. Pal., 75:2, 456.

1968   Questions et réflexions sur l'histoire des Anthropomorphes. Ann. Pal.,
            Vert., 54:2, 195–233, 27 figs.
            See: Haag, Haas and Hürzeler; Schaub, S. and Hürzeler.

HUSCHER, HAROLD A.
1967   Post-Pleistocene climatic change in the southeastern United States. Bull.
            Southeast Archaeol. Confer., no. 5, 3–10.

HUSSAIN, S. T., and SONDAAR, P. Y.
1968   Some anomalous features in Euroasiatic Hipparion dentition. Proc. K.
            Nederl. Akad. Wet., 71:2, 137–143, 2 pls.
            Rev.: Thenius in Zbl. Geol. Pal., Teil 2, 1970:3/4, 245.

HUSTED, WILFRED M.
1965   Early occupation of the Colorado Front Range. Amer. Antiq., 30,
            494–498, 1 fig.
            See: Wedel, Husted and Moss.

HUTCHINSON, G. E.
1966   The sensory aspects of taxonomy, pleiotropism, and the kinds of manifest
            evolution. Amer. Nat., 100, 533–539.

HUTCHINSON, P. A. See: Bush 1966.

HUTCHISON, JOHN HOWARD
1965   Evolution and regional endemism of the talpid Scapanus (sensu lato).
            Program, Sec. E (Geol., Geog.), Amer. Assoc. Advanc. Sci., Meet-
            ing Dec. 26–31, 1965, 12, (abs.).

1966A.   Notes on some Upper Miocene shrews from Oregon. Bull., Mus. Nat.
            Hist., Univ. Oregon, no. 2, 23 pp., 17 figs., 7 tables.
            Rev.: Hünermann in Zbl. Geol. Pal., Teil 2, 1967, 112.

1966B.   Two aquatic insectivores from North America. Program, 62nd Ann.
            Meeting, Geol. Soc. Amer., Cordilleran Sect., 1966, 46, (abs.).
            Also: Spec. Pap. Geol. Soc. Amer., 101, 314, (abs.).

1966C.   Evolution and regional endemism of the talpid Scapanus (sensu lato).
            Spec. Pap. Geol. Soc. Amer., 87, 312, (abs.).

1967   A Pleistocene vampire bat (Desmodus stocki) from Potter Creek Cave,
            Shasta County, California. Paleo Bios, 3, 1–6, 2 figs., 1 table.

1968A.   Fossil Talpidae (Insectivora, Mammalia) from the later Tertiary of Oregon.
            Bull. Mus. Nat. Hist., Univ. Oregon, 11, 1–117, 98 figs., 28 tables.

1968B.   Order Insectivora. In: Shotwell, 1968, 17–20, fig. 10A-H, table 6.
            See: Arata and Hutchison.

HUXLEY, JULIAN S.
1960C.   Darwin und der Gedanke der Evolution. In: Heberer, and Schwanitz,
            (eds.), 1960, 1–10.

1963   Rev.: Montalenti in Scientia, 101, 285, 288; Spanner in Faith and
            Thought, 93, 196–199.

1964A.   (ed.) Der evolutionäre Humanismus. Zehn Essays über die Leitgedanken
            und Probleme. München: Beck, 267 pp., (not seen).
            Rev.: Spindler in Anthrop. Anz., 28, 137–138.

1964B. Essays of a humanist. New York: Harper and Row, 288 pp.
        Rev.: Anon. in Discovery, 25:7, 44; Anon. in Sci. Amer., 211:4,
        135—138; Bodmer in New Sci., 23, 177; Deevey in Science,
        145, 147.

HUXLEY, J., and KETTLEWELL, H. B. D.
1965   Charles Darwin and his world. London: Thames and Hudson, 144 pp.,
        128 figs.
        Rev.: Anon. in La Nature, no. 3370, 79; Anon. in Rev. Soc. Mexicana
        Hist. Nat., 26, 267—268; Anon. in Sci. Amer., 214:5, 144;
        Cannon in Isis, 56, 391—392; Johnston in Amer. Jour. Phys.
        Anthrop., 29, 111; King-Hele in Discovery, 26:7, 51—52.

HUXLEY, THOMAS H.
1963   Zeugnisse für die Stellung des Menschen in der Natur. Introduction
        by V. Carus. Translated by G. Heberer. Stuttgart: Fischer,
        187 pp., 32 figs., (not seen).
        Rev.: Firbas in Mitt. Anthrop. Ges. Wien, 95, 350; Knussman in
        Homo, 15, 115; Křizenecký in Anthrop., 2:2, 81; Kruytzer
        in Natuurhist. Maandbl., 54, 14—16, (Dutch); Preuschoft in
        Umschau, 65:16, VI; Preuschoft in Zbl. Geol. Pal., Teil 2, 1965,
        294—295; M. R. S. in Arch. Suiss Anthrop. Gen., 30, 87.
1967   On a piece of chalk. Edited with an introduction and notes by Loren
        Eiseley. Illustrated by Rudolf Freund. New York: Scribners,
        90 pp., illustr., portrs.
        Rev.: White in GeoTimes, 30.

HUYGHE, RENÉ, (ed.)
1962   Rev.: Kubler in Amer. Anthrop. Special Publ., 65, 1181—1182.

HYATT, BOB
1967   Ghost Ranch Museum. Desert Mag., 30:7—8, 18—20, illustr.

HYDE, JESSE E.
1965   Interstate Ohio 71 fossil dig. Second of a series about fossil salvage —
        an historic review of earlier days. Explorer, 7:4, 28—31, illustr.,
        [Reprint of Hyde, 1928].

ÎABLOKOV, A. V. (=Yablokov, A. V.)
1964   Is there a convergence or a parallelism in the evolution of Cetacea?
        Pal. Zhurnal, 1964:1, 97—106, 2 figs., 1 table, (Russian).
1965   Convergence or parallelism in the evolution of cetaceans. (Translation
        of Yablokov, 1964.) Internat. Geol. Rev., 7, 1461—1468, 2
        figs., 1 table.

ÎAKHIMOVICH, N. N.
1960   [Concerning the find of remains of Parelephas trogontherii (Pohl.) on
        the River Sukhaïla.] Voprosy Geol. Vost. Okrainy Russk. Plat.,
        1960:5, 133—138, 2 figs., (Russian).

ÎAKHIMOVICH, V. L.
1960A. [Concerning the problem of the lower boundary of the Quaternary
        (Anthropogene) system.] Voprosy Geol. Vost. Okrainy Russk.
        Plat., 1960:5, 7—13, 1 table, (Russian).

1960B.   [On the problem of the age of high river terraces and denudation sur-
           faces in Bashkirian Urals region (Sakmara-Belaiä interfluvium).]
           Voprosy Geol. Vost. Okrainy Russk. Plat., 1960:5, 195–201,
           1 fig., (Russian).

1965   (ed.) [Quaternary of South Urals.] Moscow: "Nauka" Press, 280 pp.,
           illustr., (Russian).

IAKIMOV, V. P. (=Yakimov, V. P.)

1947D.   [Gigantic fossil anthropoids (Hominidae?).] Priroda, 1947:12, 68–70,
           3 figs., (Russian).

1961B.   Rev.: Drozdowski in Przegląd Antrop., 29, 318–319, (Polish).

1961C.   [The problem of anthropological varieties in the Late Paleolithic popu-
           lation of Europe.] Internat. Assoc. Quat. Res., Abs. Pap., 6th
           Congr., 148–149, (abs.; Russian).

1963   [At the cradle of mankind. (Principal problems of man's evolution).]
           Moscow: Moscow Univ. Ed., 318 pp., illustr.
           et al. Rev.: Roginskiĭ, J. J., in Voprosy Antrop., 1965, 19, 149–152,
           (Russian).

1964   [Principal trends of adaptive radiation of the apes close to the end of
           the Tertiary and at the beginning of the Quaternary Periods.]
           In: Nesturkh, (ed.), 1964C, 179–189, 1 fig., (Russian; English
           summary).

1966   [Australopithecidae (Australopithecinae).] Trudy Inst. Etnog. Akad.
           Nauk SSSR, 92, 43–89, 17 figs., 14 tables, (Russian).

1967A.   [New study on the skulls of the so-called "Grimaldi negroids".] Voprosy
           Antrop., 26, 152–157, 5 figs., (Russian).

1967B.   [Finding of another skullcap of Pithecanthropus on Java.] Voprosy
           Antrop., 26, 181–182, (Russian).

1968   Adaptational radiation of the apes in the Tertiary and at the beginning
           of the Quaternary periods. 7th Internat. Congr. Anthrop. Ethnol.
           Sci., Moscow, 1964, 3, 407–412.

IAKOVLEV, S. A.

1959   [Conference on elaboration of a unified stratigraphic scheme for Siberia.]
           Materialy Geol. Inst. (VSEGEI), Nov. Ser. Chetv. Geol. i Geomorf.,
           27, 20–27, 1 table, (Russian).

IAKOVLEV, V. N. (=Yakovlev, Jakovlev)

1965A.   [Geological distribution of the genus Lycoptera and the problem of the
           limit between Jurassic and Cretaceous in Eastern Asia.] Izv.
           Akad. Nauk SSSR, ser. Geol., 1965:8, 110–115, (Russian).
           Rev.: Stoltenberg in Zbl. Geol. Pal., Teil 2, 1968, 200–201.

1965B.   [Taxonomy of the family Lycopteridae.] Pal. Zhurnal, 1965:2, 80–92,
           3 tables, (Russian).

1966A.   Systematics of the family Lycopteridae. Internat. Geol. Rev., 8, 71–80,
           2 tables.

1966B.   [Functional evolution of fish skeleton.] Pal. Zhurnal, 1966:3, 3–12,
           2 figs., (Russian).

1967A.   [Adaptations to swimming in armored Agnatha of the subclass Heterostraci.]
           Doklady Akad. Nauk SSSR, 173:3, 722–724, 3 figs., (Russian).

1967B.   [Mesozoic and Cenozoic fresh-water fishes and their stratigraphic signi-
           ficance.] In: Martinson, (ed.), 1967A, 92–96, (Russian).

1967C.   Functional evolution of the fish skeleton. Translation of Iakovlev, V. N.,
           1966B. Internat. Geol. Rev., 9, 525–532, 2 figs.

1967D.   [Soviet paleoichthyology for 50 years.] Voprosy Ikhtiol., 7:5, 751–756,
           (Russian).

See: Danil'chenko and Îakovlev.

ÎAKOVLEVA, S. V.   See: Ganeshin, Zubakov, et al.

ÎAKUSHOVA, A. F.   See: Bogdanov, et al.

ÎAMPOL'SKIĬ, Z. I.
1968   [On the primitive art.]   Doklady Akad. Nauk Azerb. SSR, 24:6, 77–79, (Russian; Azerbaĭdzhani summary).

ÎANIN, V. L.   See: Avdusin and Îanin.

ÎANOV, E. N.
1959   [Devonian stratigraphy of Kyzyl-Shin R. basin (High Altaĭ).]   Informatsionnyĭ Sbornik, 6, 37–45, 1 fig., 1 table, (Russian).

ÎANOVSKAÎA, N. M.
1953C.   [New titanotherium from Mongolia.]   Priroda, 1953:8, 107–109, 2 figs., (Russian).

ÎANSHIN, A. L.
1953   [Geology of North Aral region. Stratigraphy and history of geologic evolution.]   Moscow: Mosk. Obshch. Ispyt. Prirody Press, 736 pp., 80 figs., 22 tables, (Russian).

ÎARKOVAÎA, R. I.
1967   [Fossil animals on the territory of Riazan' Province.]   Biull. Mosk. Obshch. Ispyt. Prirody, Otd. Biol., 72:6, 144–145 (author's summary; Russian).

ÎARMAK, G. A.
1957   [First finds of Paleolithic tools in Southern Kazakhstan.]   Vestnik Akad. Nauk Kazakh. SSR, 1957:7, 104–108, 21 figs., (Russian).

ÎATSKO, I. ÎA.
1962B.   [Traces of diseases on fossil skeletons of camels from karst caves near Odessa.]   Trudy Odessk. Univ., Ser. Geol. Geogr., 152:8, 34–45, 2 pls., (Russian).
1964   [On Unionidae and mammals in Upper Pliocene deposits of Moldavian SSR.]   Izv. Akad. Nauk Moldav. SSR, ser. Biol. i Khim Nauk, 1964:7, 26–37, 2 tables, (Russian; Moldavian summary).

IBARRA GRASSO, DICK EDGAR
1955   Hallazgo de puntas paleolíticas en Bolivia.   Proc. Internat. Congr. Americanists, 1954, 561–568, 1 pl.
1964A.   Las culturas paleolíticas suramericanas.   Amerindia, 2, 21–36, 1 pl.
1964B.   Las primeras industrias líticas en América del Sur y su relación con las de América del Norte.   Proc. Internat. Congr. Americanists, 1962:1, 193–199.

IBRAGIMOV, A. KH., and TURDUKULOV, A. T.
1965   [On the stratigraphy of Tertiary (Paleogene-Neogene) continental deposits of Chu depression.]   In: Korolev, (ed.), 1965, 173–187, (Russian).

IBRAGIMOV, I. M., and TALIPOV, M. A.
1965   [Questions of stratigraphy of Cenozoic deposits of the Issyk-Kul' depression.] In: Korolev, (ed.), 1965, 188–199, 1 table, (Russian).

ICOLARI, DANIEL   See: Klein, B. and Icolari.

IESSEN, A. A.
1965   [Historical past of Mil'-Karabakh steppe.] Mat. Issled. Arkheol. SSSR., no. 125, 10–36, 16 figs., 2 pls., 2 tables, (Russian; French summary).
     See: Gromov, V. I., Griâznov, et al.

IGLESIAS, DOLORES, and MENEGHEZZI, M. DE L.
1964   Bibliografia e índice da geologia do Brasil 1960–1961. Serv. Geol. Min. Brasil, Bol. no. 220, 71 pp.

IKAWA, FUMIKO
1964   The continuity of non-ceramic to ceramic cultures in Japan. Arctic Anthrop., 2:2, 95–119, 7 figs., 1 chart.
1965   Grinding stones from pre-Jomon Japan. Abs. 64th Ann. Meeting Amer. Anthrop. Assoc., 1965, 34, (abs.).

IKEBE, N., and CHIJI, M.
1964   The distribution and age of the Late Cenozoic Proboscidea in the Kinki District, central Japan. Rept. 22nd Internat. Geol. Congr., 1964, 118, (abs.).

IKEBE, N., CHIJI, M., and ISHIDA, S.
1966   Catalogue of the Late Cenozoic Proboscidea in the Kinki District, Japan. Jour. Inst. Polytech., Osaka City Univ., Geosci., 9:3, (not seen).

IKEBE, N., ISHIDA, S., and CHIJI, M.
1965   Stratigraphical distribution of fossil elephants in Kinki District, central Japan. Kaseki, 9, 1–12, 4 figs., 2 tables, (Japanese).

ILIOU, JOSEPH   See: Bassoullet and Iliou.

IMAIZUMI, Y.
1966   Origin of the Japanese mammalian fauna. Kaseki, 11, 50–51, (Japanese).

IMANISHI, K.
1968   Evolution toward human societies. 7th Internat. Congr. Anthrop. Ethnol. Sci., Moscow, 1964, 3, 423–424.

IMBRIE, JOHN, and NEWELL, N. D., (eds.)
1964   Approaches to paleoecology. New York: Wiley, 432 pp., illustr.
     Rev.: F. T. B. in Liverpool and Manchester Geol. Jour., 4, xviii; Craig in Nature, 206, 332; Deevey in Science, 147, 592–593; Gaetani in Riv. Ital. Pal., 72, 252–253; Hart in S. African Jour. Sci., 62, 164–165; Hemmer in Homo, 17:1, 72; Henningsmoen in Norsk Geol. Tidsskrift, 45, 169; Kukal in Čas. Min. Geol., 1966, 11, 73–74, (Czech); Martin in Jour. Pal., 39, 737–738; Mcalester in Amer. Jour. Sci., 263, 824; Royment in Geol. Fören. Förh., 87, 168–169; Skinner in Tulane Studies Geol., 4, 47–48; Steininger in Mitt. Geol. Ges. Wien, 57, 654–655; Van Valen in Amer. Sci., 53, 352A; Voorthuysen in Geol. en Mijn., 27, 100–101, (Dutch).

IMPERATORI, LEO
1964   Cuándo apareció el hombre. Consideraciones sobre el amuleto muste-
            riense de Perales del Rio. Bol. Soc. Españ. Hist. Nat., Sec. Geol.,
            62, 241–244, 2 figs.
            Rev.: M. in Notas Comun. Inst. Geol. Min., 77, 306.

INGER, ROBERT F., and MARX, H.
1965   The systematics and evolution of the Oriental colubrid snakes of the
            genus Calamaria. Fieldiana: Zool., 49, 1–364, 73 figs., 63 tables.

INNIS, CHARLES   See: Hoare, et al.

INOUE, MORIAKI   See: Shimoda, Endo, Inoue and Ozaki.

INSINNA, MICHAEL   See: Whitaker and Meyers.

INSKEEP, R. R.
1962   The age of the Kondoa rock paintings in the light of recent excavations
            at Kisese II rock shelter. Proc. 4th Panafrican Congr. Prehist.,
            sec. 3, 249–256, 1 fig., 2 pls., (discussion by H. N. Chittick,
            L. S. B. Leakey, and J. D. Clark).
1964   Homo habilis at Olduvai Gorge. S. Afr. Archaeol. Bull., 19, 25–26.
1965   Earlier Stone Age occupation at Amanzi: a preliminary investigation.
            S. African Jour. Sci., 61, 229–242, 8 figs.
1967   The Late Stone Age in southern Africa. Discussion. In: Bishop, W. W.,
            and Clark, J. D., (eds.), 1967A, 557–582, 2 tables, (French sum-
            mary).

INSKEEP, R. R., and HENDY, B. Q.
1966   An interesting association of bones from the Elandsfontein fossil site.
            Discussion. Actas V Congr. Panafr. Prehist. Estud. Cuaternario,
            1963:2, 109–124, 4 figs., 2 pls., 2 tables.

IOGANZEN, B. G.
1959   [To the centenary of the publication of Ch. Darwin's "On the Origin
            of Species by means of Natural Selection or the Preservation of
            Favoured Races in the Struggle for Life".] Nauchn. Dokl. Vyssh.
            Shkoly, Biol. Nauki, 1959:3, 7–15, (Russian).

IONKO, V. I.
1954   [Discovery of fossil fishes in Lower Sarmatian of MSSR.] Sborn. Geol.-
            Geogr. Fak. Odessa Univ., 2, 109–119, 1 pl., (Russian).

IORDANSKIĬ, N. N.
1967   [Peculiarities of the crocodilian skull related to the feeding function
            and orogin of Gavialidae.] Zool. Zhurnal, 46:4, 567–575, 2 figs.,
            1 table, (Russian; English summary).

IRISH, E. J. W.
1965   Geology of the Rocky Mountain foothills, Alberta (between latitudes
            53° 15' and 54° 15'). Canada Dept. Mines, Geol. Surv., Mem.
            334, 241 pp., 7 figs., 7 pls., 7 tables.

IRVING, DAVID C.   See: Guilday and Irving.

IRVING, E., and BROWN, D. A.
    1964   Abundance and diversity of the labyrinthodonts as a function of paleo-
                latitude. Amer. Jour. Sci., 262, 689–708, 4 figs., 3 tables,
                addendum: 264, 496.
                Rev.: Stehli in Amer. Jour. Sci., 264, 481–487, 3 figs.
    1966   Reply to Stehli's discussion of labyrinthodont abundance and diversity.
                Amer. Jour. Sci., 264, 488–496, 3 figs.

IRVING, MARY B.   See: Robbins and Irving.

IRWIN, CYNTHIA C.   See: Irwin, Irwin and Agogino.

IRWIN, HENRY T.
    1965   Stratigraphic and chronological sequence of Paleo-Indian complexes on
                the Great Plains of North America. 7th Internat. Congr., Internat.
                Assoc. Quat. Res., Abs., 1965, 232, (abs.).
                See: Hewes, et al.; Irwin-Williams, Agogino and Irwin; Wheat and Irwin.

IRWIN, H. T., IRWIN, C. C., and AGOGINO, G. A.
    1965   The Hell Gap site. Archaeological sketch. Wyo. Archaeol., 8:2, 35–39.

IRWIN, H. T., IRWIN-WILLIAMS, C., and AGOGINO, G.
    1966   Resumé of cultural complexes at the Hell Gap site, Guernsey, Wyoming.
                Wyo. Archaeol., 9:2, 11–13.

IRWIN, H. T., and WHEAT, J. B.
    1965   Report of the Palaeolithic Section, University of Colorado Nubian Ex-
                pedition. Kush, 13, 17–23, 2 figs.

IRWIN-WILLIAMS, CYNTHIA
    1965   Early man in the Valsequillo region, Puebla, Mexico. 7th Internat.
                Congr., Internat. Assoc. Quat. Res., Abs., 1965, 233, (abs.).
    1967   Associations of early man with horse, camel and mastodon at Hueyatlaco
                Valsequillo (Puebla, Mexico). In: Martin, P. S., and Wright,
                H. E., (eds.), 1967, 337–347, 1 fig., 1 pl.
                See: Agogino, Rovner and Irwin-Williams; Irwin, Irwin-Williams and
                Agogino.

IRWIN-WILLIAMS, C., AGOGINO, G., and IRWIN, H.
    1965   New data from Hell Gap on early man on the High Plains. Plains
                Anthrop., 10, 46, (abs.).

ISAAC, GLYNN Ll.
    1965A.   The stratigraphy of the Peninj beds and the provenance of the Natron
                australopithecine mandible. 7th Internat. Congr., Internat. Assoc.
                Quat. Res., Abs., 1965, 234–235, (abs.).
    1965B.   The stratigraphy of the Peninj beds and the provenance of the Natron
                australopithecine mandible. Quaternaria, 7, 101–130, 3 figs.,
                6 pls., 1 table, (German and French summaries).
    1966A.   The geological history of the Olorgesailie area. Actas V Congr. Panafr.
                Prehist. Estud. Cuaternario, 1963:2, 125–133, 1 fig.
    1966B.   New evidence from Olorgesailie relating to the character of Acheulean
                occupation sites. Discussion. Actas V Congr. Panafr. Prehist.
                Estud. Cuaternario, 1963:2, 135–145, 2 figs., 3 pls.

1967A.   The stratigraphy of the Peninj Group — Early Middle Pleistocene forma-
          tions west of Lake Natron, Tanzania. Discussion. In: Bishop,
          W. W., and Clark, J. D., (eds.), 1967A, 229—257, 3 figs., 4 tables,
          3 maps, (French summary; discussion continued, 447).

1967B.   Towards the interpretation of occupation debris: some experiments
          and observations. Kroeber Anthrop. Soc. Papers, no. 37, 31—57,
          4 figs., 4 pls., 2 tables.

      See: Clark, J. D., Cole, et al.; Leakey, Tobias and Isaac.

ISAEV, S. A.   See: Sultanov, Khalifa-Zade and Isaev.

ISETTI, GIUSEPPE   See: Lumley and Isetti.

ISETTI, G., and CHIARELLI, B.
    1965   Nota preliminare su un deposito musteriano nella Grotta "Ciotta Ciara"
              vicino a Borgosesia. Natura, Riv. Sci. Nat., 56, 135—142, 2 figs.

ISETTI, G., and LUMLEY, H. DE
    1962A.   L'industria litica della caverna delle Fate. Riv. Ingauna e Intemelia,
              27, 15—29, 13 figs.
    1962B.   Osservazioni sulla stazione paleolitica di Pietra Ligure. Riv. Ingauna e
              Intemelia, 27, 30—32, 4 figs.

ISETTI, G., LUMLEY, H. DE, and MISKOVSKY, J. C.
    1962   Il giacimento musteriano della grotta della Madonna dell'Arma presso
              Bussana (Sanremo). Riv. Studi Liguri, 28, 5—116, 93 figs.
              Rev.: Bonifay in L'Anthrop., 70:1—2, 156—158.

ISHAM, LAWRENCE B.
    1965   Preparation of drawings for paleontologic publication. In: Kummel
              and Raup, (eds.), 1965, 459—468, 4 figs.

ISHCHENKO, V. V.   See: Glikman and Ishchenko.

ISHIDA, SHIRO
    1959   The Cenozoic strata of Noto, Japan. Mem. College Sci. Univ. Kyôto,
              Ser. B, 26, 83—101, 8 figs., 2 pls.
      See: Ikebe, Chiji and Ishida; Ikebe, Ishida and Chiji.

ISHII, SHINNOSUKE   See: Matsumoto, Ishii, et al.

ISHNAZAROV, N. I.
    1965   [Stratigraphy of Devonian deposits of Chatkal mountain system.]   Uzbek.
              Geol. Zhurnal, 1965:4, 17—28, 1 fig., 1 table, (Russian; Uzbek
              summary).
    1967   [Findings of Devonian placoderm fishes in Mal'guzar Mts. (Tian-Shan).]
              Doklady Akad. Nauk Uzb. SSR, 1967:5, 36—37, 1 fig., (Russian;
              Uzbek summary).

ISKIUL', N. V., and TALDYKINA, K. S.
    1962   [Guide to the A. P. Karpinskii Geological Museum of the U.S.S.R.
              Academy of Sciences. (History of Earth and Life).]   Moscow-
              Leningrad: Akad. Nauk SSSR Press, 97 pp., 27 figs., (Russian).

ISLAMOV, O. I.   See: Okladnikov and Islamov.

ISLAMOV, U.   See: Beregovaia, Islamov and Kalandadze.

ISSAWY, BAHAY   See: Said and Issawy.

ISTRATE, GH.   See: Litiănu, Pricăjan, et al.

ITO, Y.   See: Akiyama, Ito and Sasaki.

IUDIN, K. A. (=Judin)
1964   (Obit.)   [Ivan Ivanovich Schmal'gauzen [=Schmalhausen], necrology,
             1963.]   Trudy Zool. Inst. Akad. Nauk SSSR, 33, 349–352, photo,
             (Russian).

IUNUSALIEV, M.
1967   [Research on Stone Age in Kirgizia.]   Izv. Akad. Nauk Kirgiz. SSR,
             1967:4, 90–96, (Russian).

IUNUSALIEV, M. B.   See: Abetekov, et al.

IUR'EV, A. A.
1961   [On the problem of Quaternary (Anthropogene) Stratigraphy of Uzbekis-
             tan.]   Doklady Akad. Nauk Uzb. SSR, 1961:7, 31–35, 1 table,
             (Russian; Uzbek summary).

IUR'EV, K. B.   See: Garutt and Iur'ev; Khozatskiĭ and Iur'ev.

IURINA, A. L.   See: Mazarovich, O. A., et al.

IUROVSKAIA, V. Z.
1964   [Ontogenetic changes in musculature of the pelvic-femoral joint of man
             in comparison with a quadruped mammal.]   Voprosy Antrop.,
             16, 41–50, 9 figs., 2 tables, (Russian).

IVAN'EV, L. N.
1958   [Bones of fossil bison from Oka river valley.]   Trudy Vost.-Sib. Fil,
             Ser. Geol., 14, 186–191, 2 figs., 2 tables, (Russian).
1959   [Lower jaw of Elephas trogontherii Pohl. from Cenozoic sediments of
             Gusinoe Lake (West Transbaĭkalia).]   Kratk. Soobshch. BKNII
             SO AN SSSR, 1, 89–92, 2 figs., 1 table, (Russian).
1964   [Stratigraphical and paleogeographical significance of fossil ostrich remains
             in Western Transbaĭkalia.]   Geol. i Geof., 1964:6, 108–116, 1 fig.,
             1 table, (Russian).
1965   [A tooth of Elephas wüsti (M. Pav.) from Angara R., and a discussion
             of this species of fossil elephants in USSR.]   Izv. Vost.-Sib. Otd.
             Geogr. Obshch. SSSR, 63, 193–200, 1 fig., 1 table, (Russian).
1966A.   [New subspecies of fossil marmot (tarbagan) from Tertiary deposits of
             Western Transbaĭkalia.]   Izv. Vost.-Sib. Otd. Geogr. Obshch. SSSR,
             65, 173–175, 2 figs., 1 table, (Russian).
1966B.   [New Paleolithic sites on Chikoĭ R. and their stratigraphic significance.]
             Mater'iăly Ist. Sibiri, Drevn. Sibir', 2, 15–22, 8 figs., (Russian).
             See: Egorov, A. G. and Ivan'ev.

IVANOV, A. KH.
1962 [Stratigraphy of the Borotala R. basin in Dzungarian Alatau.] Sov. Geol., 1962:9, 126—132, (Russian).

IVANOVA, IRINA KONSTANTINOVNA
1961D. [Geology and fauna of Paleolithic and Neolithic of the Dnestr.] In: Gromov, V. I., et al., (eds.), 1961, 67—84, 5 figs., (Russian; English summary).
1961E. [Role of geology and paleogeography in the settlement of ancient man (example of Dnestr R. basin).] Internat. Assoc. Quat. Res., Abs. Pap., 6th Congr., 138, (abs.; Russian).
1962 [Problems of Paleolithic geology and of the history of fossil man on the 6th Congress of the International Association for the Study of the Quaternary Period (INQUA) in Poland.] Biull. Mosk. Obshch. Ispyt. Prirody, Otd. Geol., 37:5, 3—35, 6 figs., 2 tables, (Russian).
1965A. [Stratigraphic position of Moldova Paleolithic sites on Middle Dnestr in the light of general problems of stratigraphy and absolute age chronology of the Upper Pleistocene in Europe.] In: Bader, O. N., et al., (eds.), 1965, 123—140, 2 figs., 1 table, (Russian).
1965B. [The significance of fossil hominid finds and of their culture to the stratigraphy of the Quaternary period.] In: Gromov, V. I., et al., (eds.), 1965, 41—58, 2 figs., (Russian; English summary).
1965C. [On the duration of Quaternary Period according to data of paleoanthropology and absolute geochronology.] In: Saks, V. N., (ed.), 1965, 16—29, 1 fig., 2 tables, (Russian).
1965D. The significance of fossil hominid finds and of their culture for the stratigraphy of the Quaternary period. 7th Internat. Congr., Internat. Assoc. Quat. Res., Abs., 1965, 237—238, (abs.).
1965E. [Geological age of fossil man. (For the seventh congress of INQUA, U.S.A., 1965).] Moscow: "Nauka" Press, 192 pp., 68 figs., 13 tables, (Russian; English table of contents).
Rev.: Kochetkova in Voprosy Anthrop., 31, 173—174, (Russian); Ložek in Věstník Ústřed. Úst. Geol., 41:2, 148, (Czek); Nesturkh in Biull. Mosk. Obshch. Ispyt. Prirody, Otd. Geol., 43:4, 127—129, (Russian).
1966A. [On the antiquity of fossil men.] In: Collected Papers, 1966F, (Materials of the IV conference of pathologists-anatomists of Latviia), 343—350, (not seen).
1966B. [On the geological age of fossil hominids in the light of their absolute chronological dating.] Trudy Inst. Etnog. Akad. Nauk SSSR, 92, 5—42, 2 figs., 2 tables, (Russian).
1967 The significance of fossil hominids and their culture for the stratigraphy of the Quaternary period. Translated by R. G. Klein. Ed. by Hansjürgen Müller-Beck. Arctic Anthrop., 4:2, 212—223, 3 figs.
See: Alekseev, V. A., Ivanova, et al.; Bader, O. N., Ivanova, and Velichko; Gromov, V. I., Ivanova, et al.

IVANOVA, I. K., and CHERNYSH, A. P.
1963 Absolute age of Upper Paleolithic artifacts (Solutrean, Gravettian-type) from the Dniester region based on radiocarbon data. Dokl. Acad. Sci. SSSR, Earth Sci. Sect., 1481, 1—6.
1965 The Paleolithic site of Malodova V on the Middle Dnestr (USSR). Quaternaria, 7, 197—217, 10 figs., (German and French summaries).

IVANOVA, I. K., KIND, N. V., and CHERDYNTSEV, V. V.
    1963   [Absolute geochronology of Quaternary period.]   Moscow: Akad.
                Nauk SSSR Press, 159 pp., 27 figs., 1 map, 40 tables, (Russian).

IVANOVA, I. K., and PRASLOV, N. D.
    1963   [Concerning the find of a Mousterian nucleus on the north coast of the
                Sea of Azov.]   Bull. Mosk. Obshch. Ispyt. Prirody, Otd. Geol.,
                68:4, 97—100, 2 figs., (Russian).

IVANOVA, N. S.   See: Aliman, M.-H., 1960B.

IVASIK, V. M.
    1968   [On the center of expansion of carp and of its parasite fauna.]   Voprosy
                Ikhtiol., 8:2, 342—349, 1 fig., 1 table, (Russian).

IVES, PATRICIA   See: Levin, B., et al.

IVES, P. C., LEVIN, B., OMAN, C. L., and RUBIN, M.
    1967   U. S. Geological Survey radiocarbon dates IX. Radiocarbon, 9, 505—529.

IVES, P. C., LEVIN, B., ROBINSON, R. D., and RUBIN, M.
    1964   U. S. Geological Survey radiocarbon dates VII. Radiocarbon, 6, 37—76.

IWASAKI, C.   See: Tokunaga and Iwasaki.

IZIRI, S.   See: Takai, Shikama and Iziri.

JABLONSKYTE-RIMANTIENE, R.
    1964   [Some questions concerning the Paleolithic in Lithuania.]   Darbai, Lietuvos
                TSR, Ser. A, 16, 35—51, 7 figs., (Lithuanian; Russian summary).

JACKSON, CRAWFORD G., JR.
    1964   The status of Deirochelys floridana Hay with comments on the fossil
                history of the genus. Tulane Studies Geol., 2, 103—106, 2 figs.,
                1 pl.
                See: Arata and Jackson.

JACKSON, GEORGE F.
    1965   Defense Cave — its geology, paleontology and biology. NSS News, 23,
                88—90, 4 figs.

JACKSON, HARTLEY H. T.
    1967   Published writings of Arthur Holmes Howell (1872 - 1940). Univ.
                Kansas Mus. Nat. Hist., Misc. Publ., 47, 1—15, portr.

JACKSON, J. WILFRID
    1953   British caving: an introduction to speleology. VIII. Archaeology and
                palaeontology. In: Cullingford, C. H. D., (ed.), 1953, 170—246.
    1962   British caving: an introduction to speleology. 2nd rev. ed. VIII.
                Archaeology and palaeontology. In: Cullingford, C. H. D., (ed.),
                1962, 252—346, pl. xvi, e-f.

JACOB, TEUKU
   1964   A new hominid skull cap from Pleistocene Sangiran. Anthropologica,
               n.s., 6, 97—104, 3 pls., (French summary).
   1966   The sixth skull cap of Pithecanthropus erectus. Amer. Jour. Phys.
               Anthrop., 25, 243—259, 1 fig., 3 pls., 8 tables.
   1967   Fossil finds: recent Pithecanthropus finds in Indonesia. Current Anthrop.,
               8, 501—504, 6 figs., 1 table.
   1968   A human Wadjakoid maxillary fragment from China. Proc. K. Nederl.
               Akad. Wet., Ser. B, 71:3, 232—235, 2 figs., 1 pl.

JACOBI, BERNHARD
   1963   Saurierfährten in der Oberhöfer Schichten bei Friedrichroda in Thüringen.
               Hallesches Jahrb. Mitteldeutsche Erdgeschichte, 5, 75.
               Abs.: Rosenfeld in Zbl. Geol. Pal., Teil 2, 1964, 790.

JACOBSHAGEN, EDUARD
   1963   Eine Faunenfolge aus dem jungpleistozänen Löss bei Bad Wildungen.
               1. Die Faunen und ihre Bindung an Klima und Umwelt. Abh.
               Hess. Landesamt. Bodenforsch., 44, 5—92, 9 figs., pls. 1—11.

JACOBSHAGEN, VOLKER   See: Huckriede and Jacobshagen.

JACOBSON, DANIEL A.
   1963   The story of man. New York: Home Library Press, 56 pp., illustr.,
               (not seen).

JACOBSON, KARL W.
   1965   Jerry Long Cave (Ral-001). Missouri Speleology, 7, 10, 13, 22, 1 map,
               1 table.

JACZEWSKI, TADEUSZ
   1960   The work of Charles Darwin and the aims of modern zoological research.
               Przeglad Zool., 4, 15—24, (Polish; English summary).
   1961   The new director of the Zoological Museum in Cambridge, Mass., USA.
               Przeglad Zool., 5, 401, (Polish).

JAGER, S. DE See: Schroevers-Kommandeur and Jager.

JAGHER, ANTON   See: Schaub, S. and Jagher.

JAHN, MELVIN E., and WOOLF, D. J.
   1963   Rev.: Degen in Naturwiss. Rund., 17, 284; Frängsmyr in Lychnos,
               1963—1964, 415—417, (Swedish); Roscoe in Amer. Mid. Nat.,
               71, 250—251; Tomkeieff in Nature, 202, 1148—1149.

JAIN, SOHAN LALL
   1964   A new vertebrate fauna from the Triassic of the Deccan, India. Proc.
               Geol. Soc. London, 1612, 2.
   1968   Vomerine teeth of Ceratodus from the Maleri formation (Upper Triassic,
               Deccan, India). Jour. Pal., 42, 96—99, 3 figs.

JAIN, S. L., ROBINSON, P. L., and CHOWDHURY, T. K. R.
   1964   A new vertebrate fauna from the Triassic of the Deccan, India. Quart.
               Jour. Geol. Soc. London, 120, 115—124, 5 figs.
               Abs.: Huene in Zbl. Geol. Pal., Teil 2, 1964, 170, 980—981.

JAKOWLEW, W. N.
1965   Rev.: Stoltenberg in Zbl. Geol. Pal., Teil 2, 1967, 200–201.

JAKUBOWSKI, GWIDON
1967   [New location of forest elephant.]   Przegl. Geol., 1967:3, 137–138,
             3 figs., (Polish).

JAKWAY, GEORGE E., and CLEMENT, J. T.
1967   An endocranial cast of the Miocene dog Tomarctus, from the fossil beds
             of Barstow, California.   Bull. S. Calif. Acad. Sci., 66, 39–45, 1
             fig., 3 tables.

JAMES, E. O.
1965   From cave to cathedral.   Temples and shrines of prehistoric, classical,
             and early Christian times.   New York: Praeger, 404 pp., illustr.

JAMES, GIDEON T.   See: Evernden, Savage, Curtis and James.

JAMKA, R., (ed.)
1964   [Archaeological research in Upper Silesia in 1963.]   Katowice: Vydal
             Śląski Instytut Naukowy, 136 pp., (Polish, not seen).
             Rev.: Sp. in Archeol. Roz., 17, 557, (Czech).

JAMME, ALBERT   See: Van Beck, Cole and Jamme.

JANEKOVIĆ, ÐURO   See: Basler and Janeković.

JANKUHN, HERBERT, (ed.)
1963   Neue Ausgrabungen und Forschungen in Niedersachsen I.   Hildesheim:
             Lax (Arbeitsgemeinschaft der Ur- und Frühgeschichtsforscher in
             Niedersachsen), xii + 277 pp., 96 figs., 36 pls., (not seen).
             Rev.: Rochna in Germania, 42, 360–362.

JÁNOSSY, DÉNES
1962B.   Abs.: Bogsch in Zbl. Geol. Pal., Teil 2, 1964, 867.
1962D.   Vorläufige Ergebnisse der Ausgrabunger in der Felsnische Rejtek 1.
             (Bükkgebirge, Gem. Répáshuta).   Karst- és Barlangkutatás, 3, 49–58,
             4 figs., (Russian summary).
1964A.   Evolutionsvorgänge bei pleistozänen Kleinsäugern.   Zeit. Säugetierk., 29,
             285–289, 3 figs., (English summary).
1964B.   Letztinterglaziale Vertebraten-Fauna aus der Kálmán Lambrecht-Höhle
             (Bükk-Gebirge, No-Ungarn) II.   Acta Zool., Budapest, 10, 139–197,
             6 figs., 2 pls., 11 tables, (German; Russian summary).
             Abs.: Anon. in Internat. Jour. Spel., 2:3, 33, 34.
1965A.   Vertebrate microstratigraphy of the Middle Pleistocene in Hungary.
             Acta Geol. Hung., 9, 145–152, 5 figs., (Russian summary).
1965B.   Nachweis einer jungmittelpleistozänen Kleinvertebratenfauna aus der
             Felsnische Uppony I, (Nordungarn).   Karszt- és Barlangkutatás, 4,
             55–68, (Russian summary).
             Rev.: Bogsch in Zbl. Geol. Pal., Teil 2, 1968, 211.
1965C.   Vogelreste aus den altpleistozänen Ablagerungen von Voigtstedt in Thü-
             ringen.   Pal. Abh., Abt. A, 2, 335–361, 8 figs., pls. 6–7, 6 tables,
             (Russian and English summaries).
             Abs.: Kuhn in Zbl. Geol. Pal., Teil 2, 1966, 313.
1965D.   Die Insectivoren-Reste aus dem Altpleistozän von voigtstedt in Thüringen.
             Pal. Abh., Abt. A, 2, 663–679, 2 figs., pl. 40, 2 tables, (Russian
             and English summaries).

1965E.   Fossile Vogelfauna aus den Mousterien-Schichten der Curată-Höhle —
              Rumänien. Vert. Hungarica, 7, 101—116, 1 fig., 1 table, (Hun-
              garian summary).

JÁNOSSY, D., and DARNAY-DORNYAI, B.
1961   Die subfossile Fauna der Sikaliktya-Höhle (Keszthely-Gebirge). Vert.
              Hungarica, 3, 119—122, (Hungarian; German summary).

JANOT, CÉCILE
1966   Amia russelli nov. sp., nouvelle amiidé (Poisson holostéen) du Thanétien
              de Berru, près de Reims. C. R. Soc. Géol. France, 1966, 142—143,
              1 fig.
              Rev.: Weiler in Zbl. Geol. Pal., Teil 2, 1968:6, 646.
1967   A propos des Amiidés actuels et fossiles. Collog. Internat. Cent. Nation.
              Recherch. Sci., 163, 139—153, 5 figs., 12 pls., (English summary).
              .Rev.: Weiler in Zbl. Geol. Pal., Teil 2, 1968:6, 646—647.

JANSKY, L.
1967   Evolutionary adaptations of temperature regulation in mammals. Zeit.
              Säugetierk., 32:3, 167—172, 6 figs., (German summary).

JANSSEN, A. W.   See: Bosch and Janssen.

JANSSENS, P.
1960   La transition du harpon magdalénien au harpon azilien. Bull. Soc. Roy.
              Belge Anthrop. Préhist., 71, 47—54, 15 figs.
1961   Considérations médicales sur les figurations préhistoriques de mains
              humaines mutilées. Bull. Soc. Roy. Belge Anthrop. Préhist., 72,
              121—128, 4 figs.

JAOUEN, P.   See: Gruet and Jaouen.

JARCHO, SAUL, (ed.)
1966   Human palaeopathology. New Haven, London: Yale Univ. Press, xiii +
              182 pp., 29 figs.
              Rev.: Brothwell in Human Biol., 39, 469—472; Hengen in Anthropol.
              Anz., 31:1—2, 127—128; Hughes in Amer. Antiq., 32, 247—248;
              Hughes in Nature, 212, 1021; Krogman in Amer. Jour. Phys.
              Anthrop., 25, 99—100; Merbs in Amer. Anthrop., 69, 537—539;
              ms in Archeol. Roz., 20, 110; Vallois in L'Anthrop., 71:1—2,
              167—168; Wells in Man, Jour. Roy. Anthrop. Inst., 1, 562—563.

JARDEL, E., and ROUSSOT, A.
1967   L'Abri Jardel 11. Commune de Peyzac-le-Moustier (Dordogne). Bull.
              Soc. Hist. Archéol. Périgord, 94, 21—31, 5 figs.

JARVIK, ERIK
1964A.   Specializations in early vertebrates. Ann. Soc. Roy. Zool. Belg., 94,
              11—95, 28 figs., (French summary).
1964B.   Paleozoologiska avdelningen. K. Svenska Vetenskapsakad. Årsbok,
              1963, 297—300.
1965A.   On the origin of girdles and paired fins. Israel Jour. Zool., 14, 141—172,
              11 figs.
1965B.   Die Raspelzunge der Cyclostomen und die pentadactyle Extremität der
              Tetrapoden als Beweise für monophyletische Herkunft. Zool.
              Anz., 175, 101—143, 10 figs.

1967A.   Remarks on the structure of the snout in <u>Megalichthys</u> and certain other
          rhipidistid crossopterygians. Ark. Zool., <u>19</u>, 41–98, 19 figs., 5 pls.

1967B.   The homologies of frontal and parietal bones in fishes and tetrapods.
          Colloq. Internat. Cent. Nation. Recherch. Sci., <u>163</u>, 181–213,
          13 figs., 4 pls., (French summary).
          Rev.: Westphal in Zbl. Geol. Pal., Teil 2, <u>1969</u>:1, 50–51.

1967C.   On the structure of the lower jaw in dipnoans: with a description of
          an early Devonian dipnoan from Canada, <u>Melanognathus</u> <u>canadensis</u>
          gen. et sp. nov. In: Patterson, C., and Greenwood, P. H., (eds.),
          <u>1967</u>, 155–183, 9 figs., 6 pls.

JASCHKE, ADOLF
1965   Mammutzahn aus dem Kiesbett des Neckars, gefunden bei Wernau/Neckar.
          Aufschluss, <u>16</u>, 46, 1 fig.

JAUZEIN, A.   See: Coque and Jauzein.

JAUZION, GEORGES
1962   La grotte Papy. Spelunca, Bull., <u>2</u>:1, 28–30, 1 fig.

JAWAD, A. J.   See: Heekeren and Jawad.

JAY, PHYLLIS C.   See: Washburn and Jay.

JAYET, ADRIEN
1965   Quelques remarques au sujet des recherches dans le domaine du quater-
          naire régional. Arch. Sci. Geneva, <u>18</u>, 321–326.

JAZDZEWSKI, KONRAD
1956   Report on the scientific activity of the Łódz Archaeological Centre du-
          ring the 1945–1955 period. Prace Mat. Muz. Archeol. Etnog.
          Łódzi, Ser. Archeol., no. <u>1</u>, 9–27, 187–193, 7 pls., (Polish;
          English summary).

1962   (ed.) Glossarium archaeologicum. Bonn: Rudolf Habelt Verlag, and
          Warsaw: Editions Scientifiques de Pologne. Published by Union
          Internationale des Sciences Pré- et Protohistoriques (24 languages),
          (not seen).
          Rev.: Barandiarán in Munibe, <u>17</u>, 133–134.

1965A.   Prehistoria de Polonia. Caesaraugusta, <u>23–24</u>, 7–21.

1965B.   Poland. Ancient peoples and places, vol. <u>45</u>. London: Thames and
          Hudson, 240 pp., 33 figs., 77 pls.
          Rev.: Klindt-Jensen in Antiq., <u>40</u>, 77–78; Nandris in Bull. London
          Univ. Inst. Archaeol., no. <u>6</u>, 135.
          See: Kostrzewski, Chmielewski and Jazdzewski.

JEANNEL, RENÉ
1962   L'abbé Henri Breuil, biospéléologue. Ann. Spél., <u>17</u>, 5–9, portr.

JEFFERIES, R. P. S.
1967   Some fossil chordates with echinoderm affinities. Symp. Zool. Soc.
          London, <u>20</u>, 163–208.

1968   Subphylum Calcichordata (Jefferies 1967). Primitive fossil Chordates
          with echinoderm affinities. Bull. Brit. Mus. (Nat. Hist.), Geol.,
          <u>16</u>:6, 243–339, 27 figs., 10 pls.

JEFFRIES, M. D. W.
1965A.   The hand bolt. Man, 65, 153–154, 3 figs.
1965B.   Flying Buck. S. Afr. Archaeol. Bull., 20:78, 105–106.

JEHL, JOSEPH R., JR.
1966A.   Subspecies of Recent and fossil birds. Auk, 83, 306–307.
1966B.   Fossil birds from the Sand Draw local fauna (Aftonian) of Brown County, Nebraska. Auk, 83, 669–670.
1967   Pleistocene birds from Fossil Lake, Oregon. Condor, 69, 24–27, 1 fig., 2 tables.

JELETZKY, J. A.
1962   Abs.: Bartenstein in Zbl. Geol. Pal., Teil 2, 1964, 824–825.

JELETSKY, J. A., and CLEMENS, W. A.
1965   Comments on Cretaceous Eutheria, Lance Scaphites, and Inoceramus? ex gr. Tegulatus. Jour. Pal., 39, 952–959.

JELINEK, ARTHUR J.
1965A.   Lithic Technology Conference, Les Eyzies, France. Amer. Antiq., 31, 277–279.
1965B.   The Upper Paleolithic revolution and the peopling of the New World. Mich. Archaeol., 11, 85–88.
1966   An artifact of possible Wisconsin Age. Amer. Antiq., 31, 434–435, 1 fig.
1967   Man's role in the extinction of Pleistocene faunas. In: Martin, P. S., and Wright, H. E., (eds.), 1967, 193–200.

JELINEK, A. J., and FITTING, J. E., (eds.)
1965   Studies in the natural radioactivity of prehistoric materials. Anthrop. Papers, Univ. Mich., no. 25, iii + 97 pp., illustr.
     Rev.: Bowie in Amer. Antiq., 32, 248; Dumond in Amer. Anthrop., 68, 1556; Moll in Mich. Archaeol., 12, 107–108.

JELINEK, ELOISE KERLIN
1965   Introduction [Emerson Frank Greenman]. Mich. Archaeol., 11, 83–84.

JELÍNEK, JAN
1962?   Der Unterkiefer von Ochoz; ein Beitrag zu seiner phylogenetischen Stellung. 20 pp., 6 figs., 2 pls., (not seen).
     Rev.: Vallois in L'Anthrop., 68, 405–406.
1964A.   Nový nález neandertalského skeletu v Palestine. Anthrop., 2:1, 59.
1964B.   Betrachtungen über die Verwandtschaft der anthropologischen Funde Dolní Věstonice, Abri Pataud und Markina Gora. Zeit. Morph. Anthrop., 56, 18–22, 1 table, (English summary).
1965   Der Kiefer aus der Šipkahöhle. Anthropos, Brno, 135–178, 8 pls., 6 tables, (Czech; German summary).
     Rev.: H. V. V. in L'Anthrop., 71:5–6, 539–540.

JELKS, EDWARD B. See: Nunley, Duffield and Jelks.

JEN, PING-HUEI
1965   Mammalian fossils from an Upper Cenozoic section at Puchen, Shensi. Vert. Palasiatica, 9, 298–301, 1 fig., 1 pl., (Chinese; English summary).
     Abs.: Sci. Abs. China, Earth Sci., 4, 12–13.

JENKINS, F. A., JR. See: Crompton and Jenkins.

JENNINGS, JESSE D.
1955   The archeology of the Plains: an assessment. Salt Lake City: Univ. of
            Utah and Nation. Park Service, ix + 180 pp., illustr., (not seen).
1964   The Desert West. In: Jennings and Norbeck (eds.), 1964A, 149–174,
            3 figs.
            Rev.: Meighan in Amer. Antiq., 30, 503–504.
1965   Early Americans. 7th Internat. Congr., Internat. Assoc. Quat. Res.,
            Abs., 1965, 247, (abs.).
1966   Early man in the desert west. Quaternaria, 8, 81–89, (Spanish and
            German summaries).
            See: Spencer and Jennings.

JENNINGS, J. D., et al.
1956   The American Southwest: a problem in cultural isolation. In: Wauchope,
            R., (ed.), 1956, 59–127, 3 figs., 3 tables.

JENNINGS, J. D., and HOEBEL, E. A.
1966   Readings in anthropology. 2nd edition. New York: McGraw-Hill,
            viii + 489 pp., illustr.
            Rev.: Van Horn in Amer. Jour. Phys. Anthrop., 25, 342.

JENNINGS, J. D., and NORBECK, E., (eds.)
1964A.   Prehistoric man in the New World. Chicago: Univ. Chicago Press,
            x + 633 pp., illustr.
            Rev.: Anon. in Amer. Antiq., 30, 500–512; Bosch-Gimpera in An.
            Antrop., Mexico, 1965, 2, 235–244; Bushnell in Antiq., 39,
            75–76; Carluci in Humanitas, 1965, 5:2, 93–95; Clark in
            Proc. Prehist. Soc. Cambridge, 31, 380–381; Coe in Amer.
            Jour. Sci., 263, 632; Fleischhacker in Anthrop. Anz., 30, 308–309;
            Ford in Amer. Anthrop., 67, 157–159; Gilman Guillen in Am-
            purias, 28, 322–323; Griffin in Mich. Archaeol., 10, 66; Gruhn
            in Man, Jour. Roy. Anthrop. Inst., 1, 108; Haberland in Homo,
            18:1, 72; Kerby in Bull. Archaeol. Soc. Virginia, no. 12, 4;
            Parsons in Wisc. Archeol., 45, 146–148; Stirling in Science,
            144, 1326–1327; Woodbury in Amer. Jour. Archaeol., 69, 92–93;
            Wormington in L'Anthrop., 70:1–2, 162–168.
1964B.   Introduction. In: Jennings and Norbeck (eds.), 1964A, 3–10.

JENSEN, DAVID E.
1966A.   The ichthyosaurs of Holzmaden. Bull., Ward's Nat. Sci. Estab., 6:38, 4.
1966B.   Megatherium roundup. Our readers report. Bull., Ward's Nat. Sci.
            Estab., 6:38, 4–5, 10 figs.

JENSEN, JAMES A.
1966   Helpful hints. News Bull., Soc. Vert. Pal., no. 76, 50.
1968A.   Withdrawing an old deposit from a national treasury. Our Public Lands,
            18:1, 14–17, 4 figs.
1968B.   Discovery of extensive dinosaur egg materials in the Upper and Lower
            Cretaceous of Utah. Program, 21st Ann. Meeting, Geol. Soc.
            Amer., Rocky Mt. Sect., 45–46, (abs.).
            See: Romer and Jensen.

JEPSEN, GLENN L.
    1962D.   [Letter to Senator Joseph C. O'Mahoney.] Wyo. Archaeol., 5:3, 2—4.
    1962E.   Ancient buffalo hunters. Wyo. Archaeol., 5:3, 5—7.
    1964A.   Riddles of the terrible lizards. Amer. Sci., 52, 227—246, 8 figs.
    1964B.   Dinosaurs: The myths and the mysteries. Nation. Observer, 3:22, 18, (not seen).
    1964C.   Princeton University Museum of Natural History. Princeton, N. J.: Princeton Univ. Mus., 19 pp. + Appendices A—G, (mimeographed).
    1965   Time, strata, and fossil: comments and recommendations. Publ. Nation. Acad. Sci., 1469, 88—97.
    1966   Early Eocene bat from Wyoming. Science, 154, 1333—1338, 2 figs., cover pl., 4 tables.
        Rev.: Fahlbusch in Zbl. Geol. Pal., Teil 2, 1967, 512—513; Loory in New York Times, Dec. 9, 1966, on 2 pp., 2 figs.
    1967   Notable geobiologic moments. GeoTimes, 12:6, 16—18, illustr.

JERISON, HARRY J.
    1968   Brain evolution and Archaeopteryx. Nature, 219, 1381—1382, 2 figs.

JERZMAŃSKA, ANNA
    1962   Abs.: Weiler in Zbl. Geol. Pal., Teil 2, 1964, 151.
    1964   Ichthyofauna from the Jaslo Shales of Sobniow. Sci. Publ. Foreign Cooperl. Center of Cent. Inst. Sci., Tech., Econ. Inform., Warsaw, 1—51, 14 figs., 6 pls., (English translation of Jermanska, 1960).
        Abs.: Weiler in Zbl. Geol. Pal., Teil 2, 1966, 280.
    1967   Argentinidés (poissons) fossiles de la série ménilitique des Karpates. Acta Pal. Polonica, 12, 195—211, 10 figs., 1 pl., 2 tables, (Polish summary).
        Rev.: Weiler in Zbl. Geol. Pal., Teil 2, 1968:6, 647.

JERZMANSKA, A., and JUCHA, ST.
    1963   Abs.: Weiler in Zbl. Geol. Pal., Teil 2, 1965, 226—227.

JERZMANSKA, A., and KOTLARCZYK, J.
    1968   Ichthyofaunal assemblages in the Menilite beds of the Carpathians as indicators of sedimentary environment. Ann. Soc. Géol. Pologne, 38, 39—66, 6 figs., pls. 13—14, 2 tables, (Polish; English summary).
        Rev.: Weiler in Zbl. Geol. Pal., Teil 2, 1970:3/4, 224.

JESSEN, HANS L.
    1966A.   Die Crossopterygier des Oberen Plattenkalkes (Devon) der Bergisch-Gladbach-Paffrather Mulde (Rheinisches Schiefergebirge) unter Berücksichtigung von amerikanischem und europäischem Onychodus-Material. Ark. Zool., 18, 305—391, 15 figs., 22 pls., (English summary).
    1966B.   Struniiformes. In: Piveteau, 1966B, (Traité de Paléo., 4:3), 387—398, figs. 84—88.
    1967   The position of the Struniiformes Strunius and Onychodus among the Crossopterygians. Colloq. Internat. Cent. Nation. Recherch. Sci., 163, 173—180, 1 fig., 4 pls., (French summary).

JHINGRAN, A. G., et al., (eds.)
    1965   Dr. D. N. Wadia Commemorative Volume. Calcutta: Mining, Geol., Metal. Inst. India, xxiv + 834 pp., illustr.
        Rev.: Collins in New Zealand Jour. Geol., 9, 362—364.

JISL, LUMIR
1965   [New archeological findings in Mongolian mountains.]   Acta Archaeol.
            Carpathica, 7:1—2, 117—124, 13 figs., (Polish;   French summary).

JOFFE, A. D.   See: Freedman and Joffe.

JOFFE, JOYCE
1967   The 'dwarf' crocodile of the Purbeck formation, Dorset: a reappraisal.
            Palaeontol., 10, 629—639, 2 figs.

JOHNSON, DAVID H.
1961   Animal and bird bones.   In: Lambert, M. F., and Ambler, J. R., 1961,
            88—90.

JOHNSON, ELDEN
1963   The prehistory of Red River Valley.   Minn. Archaeol., 25, 146—155,
            6 figs.
            See: Spencer and Johnson.

JOHNSON, E., and HATCHER, E.
1965   Manual for introductory anthropology: prehistoric man and culture.
            Minneapolis: Burgress, iii + 82 pp., 24 figs., 16 charts.
            Rev.:   Van Horn in Amer. Jour. Phys. Anthrop., 24, 283.

JOHNSON, FREDERICK
1956   Chronology and development of early cultures in North America.   Andover,
            Mass., (not seen).
1967   Radiocarbon dating and archeology in North America.   Science, 155,
            165—169.

JOHNSON, F., and RAUP, H. M.
1964   Investigations in southwest Yukon: geobotanical and archaeological
            reconnaissance.   Pap. Robert S. Peabody Found. Archaeol., 6,
            ix—xvii, 1—198, 54 figs., 2 tables.
            Rev.:   Bushnell in Antiq., 40, 78;   Campbell in Science, 148, no. 3646,
            1451;   Mayer-Oakes in Amer. Antiq., 31, 596—597.

JOHNSON, GARY D.
1966   Small mammals of the Middle Oligocene of the Big Badlands of South
            Dakota.   Proc. S. Dakota Acad. Sci., 45, 78—83.
            See: Vondra and Johnson.

JOHNSON, GERALD H.   See: Cuffey, Johnson and Rasmussen.

JOHNSON, HORTON A.
1965   Teilhard's convergence principle.   Perspectives Biol. Med., 8, 394—402.

JOHNSON, I. W.   See: MacNeish, Nelken-Terner and Johnson.

JOHNSON, JERALD JAY
1967   The archeology of the Camanche Reservoir Locality, California.   Pap.
            Sacramento Anthrop. Soc., 6, xvi + 346 pp., 47 figs., 2 maps,
            23 tables, 23 pls.
            Rev.:   King in Amer. Antiq., 34, 339—340.

JOHNSON, PAUL
    1964   Cherokee Cave. Missouri Speleology, 6, 72—78, 2 pls., 1 map.

JOHNSON, R. ARTHUR   See: Funk and Johnson.

JOHNSON, RALPH G.
    1968   The amazing fossils of Mazon Creek. Program, 1968 Ann. Meetings,
                  Geol. Soc. Amer., 1968, 151—152, (abs.).

JOHNSON, R. ROY   See: Jones, J. K. and Johnson.

JOHNSON, SELINA T.
    1962   Mastodon dig spurs museology. Museologist, no. 85, 12—15, cover
                  photo.

JOHNSON, WALTER
    1912   Wimbledon Common. London, (not seen).

JOHNSTON, FRANCIS E.
    1964   Racial taxonomies from an evolutionary perspective. Amer. Anthrop.,
                  66, 822—827.

JOHNSTONE, ROBERT W.   See: Pearson, F. J., Davis, Tamers and Johnstone.

JOLLIE, M.
    1962   Chordate morphology. New York: Reinhold, 478 pp., illustr.

JOLLIFFE, PERCEVAL
    1910   Acton and its history. Ealing, (not seen).

JOLLY, ALISON
    1966   Lemur social behavior and primate intelligence. Science, 153, 501—506, 4 fig

JOLLY, R. G. W.   See: Murdock and Jolly.

JOLY, R. DE
    1961   Grotte de Villars (Dordogne). Bull. Soc. Préhist., Paris, 57, 658.

JONES, D. GARETH
    1967   The phenomenon of Teilhard de Chardin. Faith and Thought, 96,
                  55—74.

JONES, DANIEL J.
    1968   Thomas Jefferson and earth science. Program, 21st Ann. Meeting, Geol.
                  Soc. Amer., Rocky Mt. Sect., 46—47, (abs.).

JONES, J. KNOX, JR.
    1967   Monotremes. In: Anderson, S., and Jones, (eds.), 1967, 54—60, fig. 3.
                  See: Anderson, S., and Jones; Van Deusen and Jones.

JONES, J. K., JR., and JOHNSON, R. R.
    1967   Sirenians. In: Anderson, S., and Jones, (eds.), 1967, 366—373, fig. 62.

JONES, M. C.   See: Anon., 1964AW.

JONES, NEVILLE
1932   The Middle Stone Age of Rhodesia. Occ. Pap. Nation. Mus. S. Rho-
                desia, 1:1, 33—44, 3 figs., 1 chart.
1933   Excavations at Nswatugi and Madiliyangwa, and notes on new sites
                located and examined in the Matopo Hills, Southern Rhodesia, 1932.
                Occ. Pap. Nation Mus. S. Rhodesia, 1:2, 1—44, 14 figs., 8 pls.
1936   Note on the derivatives of the rostro-carinate implements from Hope
                Fountain, near Bulawayo. Occ. Pap. Nation Mus. S. Rhodesia,
                1:5, 64—69, 6 figs.
1938   The Bembesi industry. Occ. Pap. Nation. Mus. S. Rhodesia, 1:7, 7—31,
                15 figs., 1 pl.

JONES, RAYMOND
1965   Animals of long ago. Racine, Wis.: Whitman, 59 pp., illustr., (ages
                8—12).

JONES, RHYS
1967A.   Middens and man in Tasmania. Austral. Nat. Hist., 15, 359—364,
                illustr.
1967B.   From totemism to totemism in Palaeolithic art. Mankind, 6, 384—392,
                2 figs.

JONES, ROBERT E.
1967   A Hydrodamalis skull fragment from Montery Bay, California. Jour.
                Mammal., 48, 143—144, 1 fig.

JONES, WALDO H.
1965   Fantasy or geological facts? Rocks and Minerals, 40, 44—45.

JONET, SIMON
1963   Contribution à la connaissance de la faune ichthyologique crétacée.
                I. Note préliminaire sur la faune cénomanienne. Bol. Soc.
                Portugal, 15, 113—115.
                Abs.: Weiler in Zbl. Geol. Pal., Teil 2, 1965, 227.
1964A.   Note d'ichthyologie miocène. Bol. Mus. Lab. Min. Géol. Fac. Cien,
                Univ. Lisboa, 10, 129—149, 2 pls.
                Abs.: Weiler in Zbl. Geol. Pal., Teil 2, 1966, 280.
1964B.   Contribution à la connaissance de la faune ichthyologique crétacée. II.
                Eléments de la faune turonienne. Bol. Soc. Portugal, 15, 157—
                174, 2 figs., 2 pls.
                Abs.: Weiler in Zbl. Geol. Pal., Teil 2, 1965, 227.
1965-
1966A.   Notes d'ichthyologie miocènes. II. Les Carcharhinidae. Bol. Mus.
                Lab. Min. Géol. Fac. Cien, Univ. Lisboa, 10, 65—88, 4 pls.
                Rev.: Weiler in Zbl. Geol. Pal., Teil 2, 1967, 496.
1966B.   Sphyraenidés et Scrombridés du Miocène portugais. (Troisième note
                ichthyologique). Bull. Soc. Belge Géol. Pal. Hydrologie, 75:2,
                185—202, 2 pls.
                Rev.: Weiler in Zbl. Geol. Pal., Teil 2, 1968:6, 647.

JONG, JAN D. DE
1967   The Quaternary of the Netherlands. In: Rankama, K., (ed.), 1967,
                Vol. 2, 301—426, 36 figs., 3 tables.

JORDÁ CERDÁ, FRANCISCO

1956E.   La obra del Conde de la Vega del Sella y su proyección en la Prehistoria española. Mem. Serv. Invest. Arqueol. Asturias, 1, 15–33,
(not seen).

1963   Solutrense de facies iberica en Portugal. Zephyrus, 14, 80–86, 4 figs.

1964A.   Notas sobre arte rupestre del Levante español. Caesaraugusta, 21–22,
7–13.

1964B.   Préface. Préhist. Spéléol. Ariégeoises, 19, 5–8, portr., (Spanish).

1964C.   Sobre técnicas, temas y etapas del arte Paleolítico de la region Cantábrica.
Zephrys, 15, 5–25.

1965   Eduardo Hernandez-Pacheco 1872-1965. Zephrys, 16, 140–143.

JORDAN, DAVID STARR

1963   The genera of fishes and a classification of fishes. Reprinted with a
new foreword by George S. Myers and a comprehensive index
by Hugh M. Smith and Leonard P. Schultz. Stanford: Stanford
Univ. Press, xvi + 800 pp.
Rev.: Samuel in Current Sci., 33, 507–508.

JORDAN, RONALD E.   See: Kraus, B. and Jordan.

JORDAN, WILH.

1961   Zur Geschichte der paläontologischen Forschung. Zeit. Rhein. Naturf.
Ges. Mainz, 1, 29, 2 figs., (not seen).

JÖRG, ERWIN

1966   Eine Wand mit Versteinerungen aus dem Schwarzen Jura von Holzmaden
in den Landessammlungen für Naturkunde Karlsruhe. Aufschluss,
17:5, 122–126.

JORGENSEN, CLIVE D.   See: Wells, P. V. and Jorgensen.

JOSHI, RAMCHANDRA VINAYAK

1961   Rev.: Peuke in Wiss. Zeit. Halle Univ., Ges.-Sprachwiss. Reihe, 14, 516.

1961B.   Stone Age industries in the Upper Wainganga Basin, Maharashtra State.
Proc. Indian Sci. Congr., 48, 447, (abs.).

1964   Excavations in the pre-historic cave sites in France. Bull. Deccan Coll.
Res. Inst., 24, 21–25, 2 pls.

1966A.   Acheulian succession in Central India. Asian Perspectives, 8:1, 150–163,
7 figs., 2 pls., 1 table.

1966B.   Mohgaon Kalan: A Middle – and Late – Stone Age factory site in
central India. Jour. Maharaja Sayajirao Univ., 15:1, 49–55, 5 figs.

JOSHI, R. V., SALI, S. A., and BOPARDIKAR, B. P.

1966   Animal fossil and early Stone Age tools from Gangapur on the Godavari
River (Nasik dist., Maharashtra State). Current Sci., 35:13, 344,
1 fig.

JOSSELYN, DANIEL WADLEY

1961   Reprinted in Arkansas Archeologist, 4:2, 9–11.

1962   Another "Early Man" breakthrough? And exciting! Stones and Bones
Newsletter, Nov. 1962. Reprinted in: Arkansas Amateur, 2:2,
4–7.

1963B.   Discussion concerning projected method for classification of projectile
points. Parts 1–8. Anthrop. Jour. Canada, 1:1, 14–23, 1:2,
17–24, 1:3, 11–19, 1:4, 26–31, illustr.

1963C.   Depth and antiquity. Anthrop. Jour. Canada, 1:3, 10.
1964A.   Discussion concerning projected method for classification of projectile
              points. Part 9. Anthrop. Jour. Canada, 2:1, 18–21.
1964B.   Paleo-transitional projecticle points. North Alabama. New World Antiq.,
              11, 19–22, illustr.
1964C.   The Paleo in Alabama. New World Antiq., 11, 106–113.
1965A.   Seeing and reporting projectile point characteristics. Discussion con-
              cerning projected method for classification of projectile points:
              Part II. Anthrop. Jour. Canada, 3, 16–21, 1 fig.
1965B.   How to interpret Alaska's raised beaches? Anthrop. Jour. Canada, 3, 24–26.
1965C.   (ed.) The Lively complex [Lively and Josselyn papers]. D. W. Josselyn,
              408 Broadway, Edgewood, Birmingham, Alabama 35200; 70 pp.,
              42 figs., 59 pls.
1965D.   The Lively complex: discussion of some of the ABC's of this technology.
              In: Josselyn, D. W., (ed.), 1965C, 18 pp.
1965E.   America's "crude tools". Tenn. Archaeol., 21, 55–66, 4 figs., 1 pl.
1966A.   Announcing accepted American pebble tools: the Lively Complex of
              Alabama. Anthrop. Jour. Canada, 4:1, 24–31, 1 fig., 3 pls.
1966B.   One for the archaeological book! Anthrop. Jour. Canada, 4:2, 56.
1966C.   Projectile point traits or attributes. Jour. Ala. Archeol., 12, 59–63,
              4 figs.
1967A.   Does America have a "hand axe"? Anthrop. Jour. Canada, 5:1, 27–29,
              1 fig.
1967B.   Man gets closer to his roots. Anthrop. Jour. Canada, 5:2, 9.
1967C.   Pebble-tool terminology. Anthrop. Jour. Canada, 5:2, 14–15.
1967D.   The pebble tool explosion in Alabama. Anthrop. Jour. Canada, 5:3,
              9–12, 2 figs.
1967E.   The question of patination and age. Jour. Ala. Archeol., 13, 47–51,
              2 figs.
1967F.   More on America's 'crude tools". Tenn. Archaeol., 23, 1–11, 1 fig.,
              5 pls.
              See: Troup and Josselyn.

JOUFFROY, F. K., and LESSERTISSEUR, J.
    1967   Corrélations musculo-squelettiques de la ceinture scapulaire chez les
              reptiles et les mammifères. Remarques sur un problème de
              paléomyologie. Colloq. Internat. Cent. Nation. Recherch. Sci.,
              163, 453–473, 13 figs., 1 table, (German summary).

JOYCE, E. B.   See: Mulvaney and Joyce.

JUBB, R. A.
    1965   A new palaeoniscid fish from the Witteberg Series (Lower Carboniferous)
              of South Africa. Ann. S. Afr. Mus., 48, 267–272, 2 figs., 1 pl.

JUDD, NEIL M.
    1965   Alfred Vincent Kidder, a tribute. Amer. Antiq., 31, 272.

JUDE, P. E.   See: Arambourou and Jude.

JUDE, P. E., and ARAMBOUROU, R.
    1961   Le Périgordien ancien de Bourdeilles (Dordogne). Bull. Soc. Préhist.
              Paris, 58, 773–775, 1 fig.

JUHNKE, RICHARD
1952   Abs.: Raabe in Zbl. Geol. Pal., Teil 2, 1964, 851.

JULLIEN, ROBERT
1964   Micromammifères du gisement de l'Hortus. Bull. Mus. Anthrop. Pré-
          hist. Monaco, 11, 121–126, 1 fig.
1965A.   Micromammifères de la grotte du Lazaret, Locus VIII. Nice (A.-M.)
          Bull., Mus. Anthrop. Préhist. Monaco, 12, 103–114, 6 figs.
1965B.   Les hommes fossiles de la pierre taillée (Paléolithique et Mésolithique).
          Preface by G. Cordier. Paris: Éditions N. Boubée, 366 pp.,
          149 figs., 2 maps.
          Rev.: Alimen in Bull. Soc. Préhist. Franç., C. R. séances mens., 1965:4,
          cxxvi–cxxvii; Anon. in La Nature, 93, 198; Comes in An.
          Antrop., Mexico, 1966, 3, 258–261; Font in Ampurias, 26–27,
          375–379; Furon in Rev. Gén. Sci., 72, 349; Howell in Amer.
          Jour. Phys. Anthrop., 23, 453–454; Kochetkova in Voprosy
          Autrop., 25, 165–167, (Russian); Kurth in Homo, 16:4, 252;
          MacConaill in Man, 65, 163; L.-R. N. in Toulouse, Univ., Inst.
          d'Art Préhist., Trav., 7, 223–224; Roth-Lutra in Berliner Jahrb.
          Vor- und Frühgesch., 7, 345–347; Sauter in Arch. Suiss. Anthrop.
          Gen., 30, 89; P. E. L. Smith in Science, 148, 1583; H. V. V.
          in L'Anthrop., 70:1–2, 133–134.

JUNG, DIETER   See: Milojčić, et al.

JUNG, D., and SCHNEIDER, H.
1960,
1961   Neue Beobachtungen im ostthessalischen Quartär. Ann. Univ. Saravien-
          sis, Scientia, 9:3–4, 243–254, 7 figs., (French summary).

JUNGWIRTH, JOHANN
1966   Direktor Dr. Wilhelm Ehgartner. (1914 - 1965). Ann. Naturhist. Mus.
          Wien, 69, 1–5, portr.
          See: Blaha, et al.

JURCSÁK, T.   See: Terzea and Jurcsák.

JUX, ULRICH
1966   Entwicklungshöhe und stratigraphisches Lager des Mechernicher Stego-
          cephalen. Neues Jahrb. Geol. Pal., Monatsh., 1966:6, 321–325,
          1 fig.
          Rev.: Westphal in Zbl. Geol. Pal., Teil 2, 1967, 101–102.

KABANOV, K. A.
1959   [Burial of Jurassic and Cretaceous reptiles in Ul'ĩanovsk region.] Izv.
          Kazan. Fil. AN SSSR, Ser. geol., 7, 211–214, (Russian).

KABO, V. R.
1966   [Labyrinth motive in Australian art and the problem of ethnogenesis
          of Australians.] Sbornik Muz. Antrop. Etnogr., 23, 254–267,
          3 figs., 2 pls., (Russian).

KACHARAVA, I. V. (=Katscharava)
1964   [On the stratigraphy of the Middle Eocene deposits of the northern
        periphery of the Mediterranean basin.] In: Tsagareli, 1964,
        301—312, (Russian; English summary).

KAELAS, LILI
1967   Technical tips for the curator. Curator, 10, 79—82, 4 figs.

KAESTNER, A.   See: Ax, 1964.

KAHLKE, HANS DIETRICH
1960D.   Museum für Ur- und Frühgeschichte Thüringens, Weimar, Deutschland.
          Bol. Inform., Sabadell, 24—29, 59—61, (not seen).
1961E.   Revision der Säugetierfaunen der klassischen deutschen Pleistozän-
          Fundstellen von Süssenborn, Mosbach und Taubach. Internat.
          Assoc. Quat. Res., Abs. Pap., 6th Congr., 138—139, (abs.).
1962C.   Die chronologische Stellung der Faunen von Voigtstedt und Süssenborn
          und ihre Aquivalente innerhalb der pleistozänen Faunenfolge
          Südwest-Deutschlands. Exkursionsführer zur Herbsttagung Geol.
          Ges. Deutsch. Demokratischen Rep., Exkursion B3, 1962, (not
          seen).
1962D.   Das Pleistozän von Voigtstedt. Exkursionsführer zur Herbsttagung Geol.
          Ges. Deutsch. Demokratischen Rep., Exkursion B3, 1962, 133—
          138, (not seen).
1962E.   Die Kiese von Süssenborn. Exkursionsführer zur Herbsttagung Geol.
          Ges. Deutsch. Demokratischen Rep., Exkursion B3, 1962, 195—199,
          (not seen).
1963C.   Zur chronologischen Stellung der Choukoutien-Kultur. Alt-Thüringen,
          6, 22—41, 5 figs., pls. 1—3.
1964   Early Middle Pleistocene (Mindel/Elster) Praeovibos and Ovibos. A
          contribution to the systematics and phylogeny of the Ovibovini.
          Comment. Biol., Soc. Sci. Fennica, 26:5, 17 pp., 8 figs.
1965A.   Zur Grenze Unterpleistozän/Mittelpleistozän. Ber. Geol. Ges. Deutsch.
          Demokratischen Republ., 10, 5—6.
1965B.   Bericht über das Internationale Paläontologische Kolloquium vom 23.
          bis 28. September 1963 in Weimar Ber. Geol. Ges. Deutsch.
          Demokratischen Republ., 10, 95—97.
1965C.   Die chronologische Stellung der Choukoutien-Kultur. Ethnog.-Archäol.
          Zeit., 6, 35—38.
1965D.   On the earliest representatives of the genera Rangifer and Ovibos in the
          Old World. 7th Internat. Congr., Internat. Assoc. Quat. Res.,
          Abs., 1965, 253, (abs.).
1965E.   Upper Pliocene (Astium) and Lower Pleistocene (Villafranchian) verte-
          brate faunas of Europe, and the Pliocene-Pleistocene boundary.
          7th Internat. Congr., Internat. Assoc. Quat. Res., Abs., 1965,
          254, (abs.; German).
1965F.   Neue Funde von Urmenschen-Resten in Ostasien. Natur u. Mus., 95,
          109—115, 4 figs.
1965G.   Die Cerviden-Reste aus den Tonen von Voigtstedt in Thüringen. Pal.
          Abh., Abt. A, 2, 379—426, 35 figs., pls. 13—22, (Russian and
          English summaries).
1965H.   Die Rhinocerotiden-Reste aus den Tonen von Voigtstedt in Thüringen.
          Pal. Abh., Abt. A, 2, 451—519, 36 figs., pls. 24—31, (Russian
          and English summaries).
1965I.   Die stratigraphische Stellung der Faunen von Voigtstedt. Zur Grenze des
          kontinentalen Unterpleistozän/Mittelpleistozän im zentraleuropäischen
          Raume. Pal. Abh., Abt. A, 2, 691—692.

1965J.   Zur Grenze Unterpleistozän/Mittelpleistozän in Europa. Quaternaria, 7,
           235—237, (French and English summaries).
1966   Neue eiszeitliche Menschenreste in Ostasien. Umschau, 66, 84—87, 6 figs.

KAHN, JAMES STEVEN   See: Miller, R. L. and Kahn.

KAISER, HANS ELMAR
1964   Die Problematik des Abnormen in der Evolution. Ausgewählte Fragestel-
           lungen und Beispiele. Naturwiss. Rund., 17, 57—60.

KAKEBEEKE, A. D.
1961   Onze akkers. Brabants Heem, 13, 57—61, (not seen).

KALABIS, VLADIMIR
1960   Celed Sparidae Günther 1859 (Pisces) z Miocenu prostejovska a Hranica.
           Zpravy Vlastivedneho Ust. Olomouci, 91, 211—213, 1 fig., (Czech;
           not seen).

KALABUKHOV, N. I.   See: Gromov, I. M., et al.

KALANDADZE, A. K., and TUSHABRAMISHVILI, D. M.
1955   [New excavations in the Gvardzhilas-Klde cave.]   Krat. Soob. Inst.
           Arkheol. Akad. Nauk URSR, 4, 155—156, (Russian).

KALANDADZE, A. N.
1966   Paleolithic finds in Georgia. Translated from French by Henry Field.
           In: Beregovaia, N. A., Islamov, U., and Kalandadze, A. N., 1966,
           155—165, 3 figs.
           See: Beregovaia, Islamov and Kalandadze.

KALANDADZE, N. N.
1968   [New finds of vertebrates in Cisuralian Triassic.]   Author's summary.
           Biull. Mosk. Obshch. Ispyt. Prirody, Otd. Geol., 43:1, 151—152,
           (Russian).

KÄLIN, J. JOSEF
1956C.   Zur Morphogenese des Primaten-Schädels. Ber. Tagung Deutsch. Ges.
           Anthrop., 5, 28—33, 3 figs.
1961A.   Rev.: Preuschoft in Zbl. Geol. Pal., Teil 2, 1969:1, 55—59;   Vallois in
           L'Anthrop., 68, 159—160.
1962A.   Abs.: Kuhn-Schnyder in Zbl. Geol. Pal., Teil 2, 1964, 224.
1964   Zur evolutiven Deutung des Extremitäten-Typus bei Pongiden und
           Hominiden. Rev. Suisse Zool., 71, 601—602, (English and French
           summaries).
1965   Zur Ontogenese und Phylogenese des Schädels bei den höheren Primaten.
           Rev. Suisse Zool., 72, 594—603, 2 figs., 2 tables, (French and
           English summaries).
1966   Das Menschenbild der neuen Anthropologie. In: Narr, K. J., (ed.),
           1966B, 29—56, 12 figs.
           See: Remane 1964B.

KÁLLAI, L.   See: Bökönyi, et al.

KALLIES, HANS-BODO
1963   Gesteinsausbildung und Fossilführung an der Grenze Mittlerer/Oberer
            Buntsandstein in südlichen Niedersachsen. Geol. Jahrb., 80,
            367–436, pls. 5–10, (English and French summaries).

KALTWASSER P., JORGE   See: Orellana Rodriguez and Kaltwasser P.

KAMAKI, YOSHIMASA
1957B.   [The Ijima site in Kagawa Prefecture: microlith culture in Setouchi
            region.] Stone Age, no. 4, 1–11, (Japanese; not seen).
            See: Serizawa and Kamaki.

KAMAL, A. M.
1966   The single origin of the parachordal plate in Squamata. Zool. Anz.,
            176, 3–5, 2 figs.
            See: El-Toubi, Kamal and Mammouda.

KAMBARIDDINOV, R. K. (=Kambaritdinov)
1966   [Antilospira gracilis and Paracamelus cf. gigas from Pavlodar Irtysh
            region.] Doklady Akad. Nauk Uzb. SSR, 1966:9, 50–52, 2 figs.,
            (Russian; Uzbek summary).
1968   [On the correlation of faunistic complexes of Middle Asia with local
            stratigraphic schemes of Anlthropogene deposits.] Uzbek. Geol.
            Zhurnal, 1968:3, 69–73, 1 table, (Russian; Uzbek summary).

KAMBARIDDINOV, R. K., TETÍUKHIN, G. F., and SHUMAKOV, ÍU. F.
1968   [On the age of Quaternary deposits of Zirabulak-Ziaetdin Mts.] Doklady
            Akad. Nauk Uzb. SSR, 1968:8, 35–37, (Russian; Uzbek sum-
            mary).

KAMEI, TADAO
1964   On some proboscidean fossils from sea bottom of the Ariake Bay.
            Kyushu, Japan. Misc. Rept. Res. Inst. Nat. Res., Tokyo, 62,
            109–120, 2 pls., (Japanese; English summary).
1966   Notes on Elephas shigensis (Matsumoto and Ozaki) from the Osaka
            Group and the Paleo-Biwa Group. Mem. College Sci. Univ. Kyoto,
            ser. B, 32:4, Geol. Min., 381–399, 1 fig., pls. 12–14, 4 tables.
            See: Kobatake and Kamei.

KAMENOV, BL.
1965   [Pliocene-Pleistocene limit in Sofia Basin.] Spisanie Bŭlg. Geol. Druzh.,
            26:1, 112–114, (Bulgarian; German summary).

KAMER, B. L.
1954   Book of big beasts. Los Angeles, Calif.: Melmont, 21 pp., illustr.,
            (ages 5–6).

KANAMORI, H.   See: Takeuchi, Uyeda and Kanamori.

KANAMORI, KEIKO See: Takeuchi, et al.

KANISHCHEV, A. D.
1963   [On the uplift of Mergen'skiĭ and Asinskiĭ ranges above the Chikoĭ
            depression level at the end of the Quaternary Period.] Zapiski
            Zabaĭkal'. Otd. Geogr. Obshch. SSSR, 22, 137–139, 1 fig., (Russian).

KANIVETS, V. I.
1962   [First results of excavation in the Un'inskaĭa Cave.]   Materialy Arkh.
                Evrop. Sev.-Vost., 1, 103–144, 12 figs., 11 pls., 1 table, (Russian).
1967   [Archeological research on Pechora R.]   In: Rybakov, B. A., (ed.),
                1967, 5–6, (Russian).
                See: Guslitser and Kanivets; Guslitser, Kanivets and Timofeev; Timofeev
                and Kanivets.

KANSU, ŞEVKET AZIZ
1963B.   Note préliminaire sur le Paléolithique inférieur de la région égéenne
                (İzmir). Bell. Türk. Tarih Kurumu, 27, 485–490, 5 figs., (French
                and Turkish).
1963C.   Recherches préhistoriques dans la région de Marmara et en Thrace. Bell.
                Türk. Tarih Kurumu, 27, 657–705, 59 figs., 1 map, (Turkish;
                French summary).
1964   Sur l'Anatolie du Sud-Est et l'industrie du "Chopper", "Chopping-Tools".
                Bell. Türk. Tarih Kurumu, 28, 161–163, 7 figs., (Turkish).

KAO, FU-TSING
1962   Abs.: Dietrich in Zbl. Geol. Pal., Teil 2, 1964, 138.
                See: Ting, M.-l, et al.

KAPELIST, K. V.   See: Put' and Kapelist.

KAPICA, ZDZISLAW, and WIERCIŃSKI, A.
1966   [Anthropological analysis of human skeletal remains from Maszycka Cave,
                Olkusz District, of Magdalenian age, Upper Paleolithic epoch.]
                Archeol. Polski, 11, 313–354, 16 figs., 12 tables, (Polish; Eng-
                lish summary).

KAPLAN, A. A.
1964   [On Pärnu beds of Middle Devonian of the North-West of Russian Plat-
                form.]   In: Karatajūte-Talimaa and Narbutas, (eds.), 1964, 57–63,
                (Russian).

KAPLAN, NATHAN O.   See: Salthe and Kaplan.

KAPLAN, R. W.
1967   Probleme der Lebensentstehung und der frühesten Evolution. In:
                Heberer, G., (ed.), 1967A, 511–550, 4 figs.

KAPLIANSKAĬA, F. A.
1962   [On the climatic conditions of the Tobol Inter-glacial.]   Informatsion-
                nyĭ Sbornik, 53, 31–47, (Russian).

KAPLIANSKAĬA, F. A., and TARNOGRADSKIĬ, V. D.
1961   [On the Pleistocene stratigraphy of Lower Irtysh R.]   In: Rostovtsev,
                (ed.), 1961, 400–411, 1 table, (Russian).

KAPLIANSKAĬA, F. A., TARNOGRADSKIĬ, V. D., and VANGENGEĬM, É. A.
1964   [On the possibility of distinguishing Tazov strata in the cross-section
                of periglacial deposits of the Tobol Traus-Urals.]   Biull. Kom.
                Izuch. Chetvert. Perioda, Akad. Nauk SSSR, no. 29, 189–195,
                3 figs., (Russian).

KAPP, RONALD O.   See: Oltz and Kapp.

KARAGEORGIEV, IL.
   1952   [The "geometric progression of multiplication" in Darwin's doctrine.]
                  Godishnik Sof. Univ., 47:1—2, 59-82, (Bulgarian; Russian sum-
                  mary).

KARANDEEVA, M. V.
   1952   [Problems of paleogeography of the western part of Precaspian lowlands.]
                  Uchen. Zap. Mosk. Univ., 160, 5—30, 8 figs., 1 table, (Russian).

KARASZEWSKI, W.
   1966   Reptile tracks and dragging traces on the Roethian sandstone surface
                  observed in Jarugi near Ostrowiec Swcietokrzyski (Central Poland).
                  Kwart. Geol., 10:2, 327—333, (Polish; Russian and English sum-
                  maries).

KARATAJŪTĖ, V. N. (=Karatajute-Talimaa, V.)
   1958A.   [The stratigraphic distribution of the asterolepids in the Soviet Union.]
                  Darbai Lietuvos TSR, Ser. B, 1958:4, 143—150, 1 table, (Russian;
                  Lithuanian summary).
   1958B.   [On the mode of life of the representatives of the family Asterolepididae
                  (subclass Pterichthyes).] Moksliniai Pranešimai, Geol.-Geogr., 8,
                  258—270, (Russian; Lithuanian and English summaries).
   1960A.   The Devonian of Lithuania. Collectanea Acta Geol. Lithuanica, 79—91,
                  1 table, (English and Russian; Lithuanian summary).
   1960B.   Byssacanthus dilatatus (Eichw.) from the Middle Devonian of the U.S.S.R.
                  Collectanea Acta Geol. Lithuanica, 293—305, 3 figs., 3 pls.,
                  (English and Russian; Lithuanian summary).
   1962   [Description of remains of Downtonian ichthyo-fauna from Lithuania.]
                  Moksliniai Pranešimai, Geol.-Geogr., 14, 45—58, 2 figs., 1 pl.,
                  1 table, (Russian; Lithuanian and English summaries).
   1964   [Data on Lower Devonian stratigraphy of southern Baltic region.] In:
                  Karatajūte-Talimaa and Narbutas, (eds.), 1964, 21—39, 10 figs.,
                  3 tables, 2 pls., (Russian).
   1966   [Bothriolepids from the Shviantoĭ horizon of Baltic region.]   Pal. i
                  Strat. Pribalt. Belorus., 1, 191—279, 16 figs., 24 pls., (Russian;
                  English summary).
                  See: Grigelis and Karatajūte-Talimaa; Obruchev, D. V. and Karatajūte-
                  Talimaa.

KARATAJŪTE-TALIMAA, V. N., and NARBUTAS, V. V., (eds.)
   1964   [Problems of stratigraphy and paleogeography of Baltic Devonian.]
                  Vilnius; "Mintis" Press, 147 pp., 31 figs. and maps, 8 tables,
                  5 pls., (Russian).

KARLOV, N. N.
   1961   New data on the geological dating and interrelation of certain Paleolithic
                  industries in the Ukraine. Doklady Akad. Nauk USSR, 141:5,
                  1183—1186.
                  Rev.: Lee in Anthrop. Jour. Canada, 2:3, 15.
   1963   [Hand chopper from Middle Dnepr region.] Sov. Arkheol., 1963:3,
                  207—209, 1 fig., (Russian).
                  See: Nakel'skiĭ and Karlov.

KARLOV, N. N. and NAKEL'SKIĬ, S. K.
1963 [Late Paleolithic pendants of belemnite rostra and Caspian shells from Samara R.] Sov. Arkheol., 1963:1, 273–278, 1 fig., (Russian).
1966A. [Laurel-leaf shaped blade from Crimea.] Bíull. Kom. Izuch. Chetvert. Perioda, 31, 136–138, 1 fig., (Russian).
1966B. [Remains of turkmenian elephant in the Ukraine.] Pal. Sborn., 3:1, 75–77, 1 fig., (Russian; English summary).

KARPOFF, R. See: Alimen, Chavaillon, and Karpoff.

KARRER, CHRISTINE See: Deckert and Karrer.

KARVE-CORVINUS, GUDRUN
1967 Chirki, a Palaeolithic site on the Pravara River in the Upper Godavari Basin in India. Current Sci., 36, 268–269.

KAS'IANENKO, V. G.
1959 [Significance of function analysis of extremities joints of modern mammals for elucidation of the extremities functions of ancient forms.] Trudy Vses. Paleont. Obshch., II sess., 158–161, (Russian).
1968 [Ideas of evolutionary morphology in the works of Vladimir Kovalesvskiĭ.] Vestnik Zoologii, 1968:5, 84–86, (Russian).

KASILOVA, O. L. See: Aliman, M.-H. 1960B.

KASYMOV, M. R.
1960 [A new Paleolithic site near Brichmulla village.] Izv. Akad. Nauk Uz. SSR, ser. obshch. nauk, 1960:3, 51–52, (Russian).
1964 [New data on Stone Age workshops in Karatau region.] Istoriiã Mater. Kul't. Uzbekistana, 5, 12–20, 4 figs., (Russian).
1968 [Archeological works in Uzbekistan.] In: Rybakov, (ed.), 1968, 326–332, 3 figs., (Russian).
See: Okladnikov, Kasymov and Konopliã.

KASZAP, A.
1968 Korynichnium sphaerodactylum (Pabst) Einzelfährte im Perm von Balatonrendes (Transdanubien). Föld. Közlöny, 98:3–4. 429–433, 1 fig., (Hungarian; German summary).

KATS, A. I. (=Katz, A. I.)
1968 Formation de l'acte du lancement chez les singes inférieurs et sa signification pour l'anthropogenèse. 7th Internat. Congr. Anthrop. Ethnol. Sci., Moscow, 1964, 3, 425–432, 2 tables.

KATSCHARAVA, I. V. See: Kacharava, I. V.

KATSUI, YOSHIO, and KONDO, Y.
1965 Dating of stone implements by using hydration layer of obsidian. Jap. Jour. Geol. Geog., 16, 45–60, 6 figs., 1 pl., 5 tables.

KATZ, HERBERT, and KATZ, M.
1965 Museums, U. S. A. Garden City, N. Y.: Doubleday, xii + 395 pp., illustr., (not seen).
Rev.: Bedini in Science, 149, 173–174; Reekie in Nat. Hist., 74:10, 8.

KAUFFMAN, ERLE G.
1965   Collecting in concretions, nodules, and septaria. In: Kummel and Raup,
            (eds.), 1965, 175–184.

KAUFMANN, E. G., and McCULLOCH, D. S.
1965   Biota of a late glacial pond. Bull. Geol. Soc. Amer., 76, 1203–1232,
            5 figs., 2 pls., 5 tables.

KAUFFMAN, JOHN   See: Cottler 1966.

KAUFFMANN DOIG, FEDERICO
1961   Descubrimientos pre-Chavin en la arqueología Peruana y necesidad de
            distinguir dos periodos en la llamada epoca "Pre-Ceramica".
            Peruanistica, Ser.: Antrop., no. 2, 23 pp.
1963   Origen de la cultura peruana (aloctonismo de Chavín). Peruanistica, Ser:
            Antrop., no. 5, 74 pp., illustr.

KAY, MARSHALL, and COLBERT, E. H.
1965   Stratigraphy and life history. New York: John Wiley & Sons, 736 pp.,
            illustr.
      Rev.: Amos in Asoc. Geol. Argent., Rev., 20:3, 396;   Davidson in
            Nature, 207, 1022;   Dons in Norsk Geol. Tidsskrift, 45, 549–550,
            (Norwegian);   Jones in Science, 148, no. 3669, 488–489;   de
            Jong in Geol. en Mijn., 45, 86–87;   Kesling in Jour. Pal., 39,
            517–518;   Martinsson in Geol. Fören. Förh., 88, 120–121;
            Portmann in Ann. Guébhard, 41, 62;   Rossi Ronchetti in Riv.
            Ital. Pal., 72, 497–498; Westphal in Zbl. Geol. Pal., Teil 2, 1966,
            2–3;   Wheeler in Amer. Sci., 53, 464A, 466A.

KAYE, R. H.   See: Brouwer 1967.

KAZANTSEVA, A. A.
1964   [Subclass Actinopterygii.]   Osnovy Pal., [Agnathes. Pisces.], [11], 323–
            335, 21 figs., (Russian).
      See: Berg, L. S., Kazantseva and Obruchev; Obruchev, D. V. and
            Kazantseva.

KAZARINOV, V. P.
1958   [Mesozoic and Cenozoic deposits of Western Siberia.]   Moscow:
            Gostoptekhizdat Press, 324 pp., 26 figs., 56 tables, (Russian).

KEENAN-SMITH, D.
1966   South African Archaeological Society — 21st anniversary exhibition and
            lecture series. S. Afr. Archaeol. Bull., 21, 99–100.

KEHOE, ALICE B.
1962   Hunters of the buried years. The prehistory of the prairie provinces.
            Regina, Toronto: Schools Aids and Text Book Publ. Co. Ltd.,
            94 pp., illustr.
      Rev.: Gruhn in Amer. Antiq., 32, 549;   Hlady in Manitoba Archaeol.
            Newsletter, 1:2, 6–8;   Mayer-Oakes in Blue Jay, 21, 159–160;
            Rogers in Anthropologica, n. s., 6, 247–248;   Taylor in Canadian
            Geog. Jour., 67:4, V.

KEHOE, THOMAS F.
1961   Stone tipi rings. Antiq. 35, 145–147.

1965A.   "Buffalo stones": an addendum to "The folklore of fossils". Antiq.,
                39, 212–213, pl. 42.
1965B.   Fluted points in Saskatchewan. 7th Internat. Congr., Internat. Assoc.
                Quat. Res., Abs., 1965, 261, (abs., Spanish).
1966   The distribution and implications of fluted points in Saskatchewan.
                Amer. Antiq., 31, 530–539, 4 figs.
1967   Studies of bison remains at archaeological sites. Proc. Neb. Acad. Sci.,
                77th Ann. Meeting, 1967, 4, (abs.).

KEIL, ALBERT
1966   Grundzüge der Odontologie. 2nd Ed. Berlin-Nikolassee: Gebrüder
                Borntraeger, 278 pp., 251 figs., 4 color pls.
                Rev.: Mohr in Naturwiss. Rundschau, 20:4, 179; Schliemann in Zeit.
                Säugetierk., 32:6, 381–382; Thenius in Mitt. Geol. Ges. Wien,
                59:2, 300; Vogel in Zeit. Morph. Anthrop., 59, 107.

KELLAR, JAMES H.
1966   Glenn A Black, 1900 - 1964. Amer. Antiq., 31, 402–405, portr.

KELLEY, A. R.   See: Waring and Kelley.

KELLEY, A. R., and AYRES, H.
1966   An early Archaic site at Carter's Dam, Murray Co., Georgia. Bull.
                Georgia Acad. Sci., 24:2, 72.

KELLEY, HARPER
1965   Outils levalloisiens de grande taille. Bull. Soc. Préhist. Franç., Étud. et
                Trav., 62:1, 31–47, 12 figs.

KELLEY, JAMES C. See: Houston, Toots and Kelley.

KELLEY, JANE HOLDEN
1964   Comments on the archeology of the Llano Estacado. Bull. Texas Archeol.
                Soc., 35, 1–17, 2 figs.

KELLOGG, REMINGTON
1965   Fossil marine mammals from the Miocene Calvert formation of Maryland
                and Virginia. 1. A new whalebone whale from the Miocene
                Calvert formation. 2. The Miocene Calvert sperm whale
                Orycterocetus. Bull. U. S. Nation. Mus., 247, 1–63, 31 figs.,
                32 pls.
1966   Fossil marine mammals from the Miocene Calvert formation of Maryland
                and Virginia. Part 3. New species of extinct Miocene Sirenia.
                Part 4. A new odontocete from the Calvert formation of Mary-
                land. Bull. U. S. Nation. Mus., 247:3, 65–98, figs. 32–38, pls.
                33–43; 247:4, 99–101, pls. 44–45.
1968   Fossil marine mammals from the Miocene Calvert formation of Maryland
                and Virginia. Bull. U. S. Nation. Mus., 247:5–8, 103–201, 98
                figs., pls. 46–67.

KELLY, ARTHUR R.
1949   An early flint industry in southwest Georgia. Bull. Georgia Acad. Sci.,
                7:1, 21.
1951   Age measurements on decomposed flint. Bull. Georgia Acad. Sci., 9:1,
                17–18.

1952   Archaeology and the sciences. Bull. Georgia Acad. Sci., 10:1, 17.

KELSO, ALEC J.
    1966   The subdivisions of physical anthropology. Comments. Current Anthrop.,
                7, 315—319.

KELSO, JACK, and EWING, G.
    1962   Introduction to physical anthropology, laboratory manual. Boulder,
                    Colo.: Pruett Press, vii + [91] pp., illustr.
                Rev.: MacIntosh in Mankind, 6:1, 41;   Saul in Amer. Anthrop. Special
                    Publ., 65, 1200.

KELSO, J., and LASKER, G. W. (eds.)
    1964   Yearbook of physical anthropology, 1962. Yearbook Phys. Anthrop.,
                    10, x + 373 pp., illustr.
                Rev.: Hunt in Amer. Anthrop., 68:4, 1083—1084;   Singer in Amer.
                    Jour. Phys. Anthrop., 23, 442—443;   Vallois in L'Anthrop., 69:5—6,
                    563—564.

KELSO, J., LASKER, G. W., and BROOKS, S. T., (eds.)
    1965   Yearbook of physical anthropology — 1963. Yearbook Phys. Anthrop.,
                    11, ix + 300 pp., illustr.
                Rev.: Angel in Amer. Jour. Phys. Anthrop., 24, 281—282;   Fry in
                    Human Biol., 38, 334—336;   Hunt in Amer. Anthrop., 68:4,
                    1083—1084;   Romano in An. Antrop., Mexico, 1966, 3, 272—274.

KELSO, LEON   See: Schmalhausen 1968.

KENDRICK, G. W.   See: Douglass, Kendrick and Merrilees.

KENNEDY, KENNETH A. R. See: Ehrhardt and Kennedy.

KENNEDY, MARIE
    1966   Flint Hills fossils. Rocks and Minerals, 41, 15—18, illustr.

KENNINGTON, GARTH S.   See: Brace, et al.

KENNY, MICHAEL J.
    1966   Teach yourself evolution. London: English Universities, ix + 180 pp.,
                line drawings, (not seen).

KENT, BARRY C.   See: Kinsey and Kent.

KENT, DOUGLAS C.
    1967   Citellus kimballensis, a new Late Pliocene ground squirrel. Proc. Neb.
                State Mus., 6, 17—26, 3 figs., 1 table.

KENT, G. C., JR.
    1965   Comparative anatomy of the vertebrates. St. Louis: C. V. Mosby,
                x + 457 pp., 344 figs.

KENT, P. E.
    1967   Professor H. H. Swinnerton. Nature, 213, 20.

KENYON, KATHLEEN M.
1961   Beginning in archaeology. New York: Praeger, 228 pp., 24 illustr.

KENYON, W. A., and CHURCHER, C. S.
1965   A flake tool and a worked antler fragment from Late Lake Agassiz.
              Canadian Jour. Earth Sci., 2, 237—246, 4 figs., 1 table.

KERBY, MERLE D.
1965   Earliest migrations into North America. Quart. Bull. Archeol. Soc.
              Virginia, 19, 54—62.

KEREWSKY, R. S.   See: Garn, Lewis and Kerewsky.

KERLEY, ELLIS R.
1965   The microscopic determination of age in human bone. Amer. Jour.
              Phys. Anthrop., 23, 149—163.
              See: Blumberg and Kerley.

KERLEY, E. R., and BASS, W. M.
1967   Paleopathology: meeting ground for many disciplines. Science, 157,
              638—644, 10 figs.

KERMACK, DORIS M.   See: Patterson, C. and Greenwood.

KERMACK, D. M., KERMACK, K. A., and Mussett, F.
1968   The Welsh pantothere, Kuehneotherium praecursoris. Jour. Linn. Soc.
              London, Zool., 47, 407—423, 11 figs., 3 pls.

KERMACK, KENNETH ALEXANDER
1965A.   Problems of collecting from fissures. In: Kummel and Raup, (eds.),
              1965, 203—206.
1965B.   The origin of mammals. Sci. Jour., London, 1:7, 66—72, illustr.
              Rev.: M. C. in Fossilia, 1965:3—4, 56.
1967A.   The interrelations of early mammals. In: Patterson, C., and Greenwood,
              P. H., (eds.), 1967, 241—249, 1 fig.
1967B.   Molar evolution in Mesozoic mammals. Jour. Dental Res., 46, 792—795,
              illustr., (not seen).
1967C.   The Aegialodontidae — a new family of Cretaceous mammals. Proc.
              Geol. Soc. London, no. 1640, 146.
              See: Appleby, et al.; Kermack, D. M., Kermack and Mussett; Moss,
              M. L. and Kermack.

KERMACK, K. A., LEES, P. M., and MUSSETT, F.
1965   Aegialodon dawsoni, a new trituberculosectorial tooth from the Lower
              Wealden. Proc. Roy. Soc. London, 162, 534—554, 6 figs., pls.
              55—58.

KEROHER, GRACE C.
1967   Some uses of fossil names in the evolution of stratigraphic nomenclature
              in the midcontinent. In: Teichert, and Yochelson, (eds.), 1967,
              21—48, 8 figs.

KEROHER, G. C., et al.
1966   Lexicon of geologic names of the United States for 1936—1960. 3 vols.
              Bull. U. S. Geol. Surv., 1200, 4431 pp.

KERR, HANK
1964   The Bartow mammoth site, Oklahoma River Basin Surveys, Woodward
            County Salvage Project — Wd-13. Newsletter Okla. Anthrop.
            Soc., 12:5, 4—8, 1 fig.

KERR, WARWICK E., and SILVA, M. N.
1962   Evoluçao do homen. Anhembi, 48, 4—12, illustr.

KERRICH, J. E., and CLARKE, D. L.
1967   Notes on the possible misuse and errors of cumulative percentage fre-
            quency graphs for the comparison of prehistoric artefact assem-
            blages. Proc. Prehist. Soc. Cambridge, 33, 57—69, 5 figs., 3 tables.

KETRARU, N. A.
1964   [Archeological prospecting in the Chugur R. valley.] In: Zelenchuk
            et al. (eds.), 1964, 255—272, 13 figs., (Russian).
1965A.   [Paleolithic site Chutuleshty—I.] Izv. Akad. Nauk Moldav. SSR, 1965:12,
            53—61, 4 figs., (Russian).
1965B.   [Paleolithic station in the grotto Starye Duruitory. (Preliminary infor-
            mation).] Krat. Soob. Inst. Ist. Mat. Kult. SSSR, 1965:105,
            79—84, 2 figs., (Russian).
            See: Gania and Ketraru; Rafalovich and Ketraru.

KETTLEWORTH, H. B. D.   See: Huxley, J. and Kettleworth.

KETTNER, RADIM
1964   Hanns Bruno Geinitz (*1814, †1900). Čas. Min. Geol., 9, 249—250,
            portrait.

KHAIN, V. E., (ed.)
1966   [Problems of geology and paleogeography of Anthropogene.] Moscow:
            University Press, 228 pp., ill., (Russian).

KHAIRUTDINOV, D. KH.   See: Gladkov, et al.

KHAKIMOV, F.   See: Zakharov and Khakimov.

KHALIFA-ZADE, CH. M.   See: Sultanov, Khalifa-Zade and Isaev.

KHALILOV, A. G., et al.
1961   [Concerning a find of a Lower Cretaceous ichthyosaur from the south-
            eastern Caucasus.] Dokl. Akad. Nauk Azerbaid. SSR, 17, 1049—
            1051, 3 figs., (Russian; Azerbaijani summary).

KHAN, EHSANULLAH
1966   Ovibos pallantis rhenanus nov. subsp., an extinct Ovibos of Weinheim,
            Rhine Valley, Germany. Mitt. Bayer. Staatssamml. Pal. Hist.
            Geol., 6, 133—142, 2 pls., (English summary).
            See: Sahni and Khan.

KHATRI, A. PRAKASH
1961B.   Stone Age and Pleistocene chronology of the Marmada Cilley (central
            India.) Proc. Indian Sci. Congr., 48, 447—448, (abs.).
1961C.   Research of the Early Man in India. Proc. Indian Sci. Congr., 48, 448,
            (abs.).

1964   Recent explorations for the remains of early man in India. Asian Perspec-
                tives, 7, 160–182, 6 figs., 4 pls., 5 maps.

KHLOBYSTIN, L. P.
1964A.   [Concerning the ancient seal-cult at Baĭkal.]   Krat. Soob. Inst. Ist. Mat.
                Kult. SSSR, 101, 35–37, 1 fig., (Russian).
1964B.   [Work of sectors of Inst. Archeol. of Acad. of Sciences of USSR in
                1962. 1. Paleolithic sector.] Krat. Soob. Inst. Ist. Mat. Kult.
                SSSR, 97, 135–137, (Russian).
1965   [The oldest relics from Baĭkal.]   Mat. Issled. Arkheol. SSSR, no. 131,
                252–279, 8 figs., 1 table, (Russian).

KHOREVA, I. M.
1959   [New data on Quaternary stratigraphy of Aldan R. valley.]   Izv. Akad.
                Nauk SSSR, ser. geol., 1959:9, 80–89, 3 figs., (Russian).
        See: Alekseev, M. N., Giterman, et al.; Alekseev, M. N., Kuprina,
                et al.; Chebotareva, Kuprina and Khoreva.

KHOSBAĬAR, P.
1966   [Geological characterization of ancient fossils sites in Gurilin Gobi.]
                Mongol orny gazarzuĭn assudluud, 1966:6, 13–23, map, (Mongo-
                lian; Russian summary).

KHOZATSKIĬ, LEV I.
1957   [Fresh-water tortoises from Upper Cretaceous of Fergana.]   Doklady
                Akad. Nauk Tadzhik. SSR, 1957:22, 19–21, (Russian).
1959A.   [The doctrine of life forms of extinct and modern organisms.]   Trudy
                Vses. Paleont. Obshch., II sess., 145–157, 5 figs., (Russian).
1959B.   [Paleontological significance of fossil turtle remains.] Trudy Vses. Paleont.
                Obshch., III sess., 104–107, (Russian).
1965   [Phylogenetic significance of turtle armor structure.]   Ezhegodnik Vses.
                Pal. Ob., 17, 196–227, 3 pls., (Russian).
1966   [On a gigantic Mesozoic representative of trionychids and on some
                peculiarities in their armor.] Pozuon. zhiv. Sredn. Azii, 150–157,
                2 figs., (Russian).
1967   [Cenozoic land reptiles from the Asiatic part of the USSR.] In: Mar-
                tinson, G. G., (ed.), 1967A, 215–218, (Russian).
        See: Rozhdestvenskiĭ and Khozatskiĭ.

KHOZATSKIĬ, L. I., and ALEKPEROV, A. M.
1957   [Turtle armors from archeological excavations in Mingechaure.]   Uch.
                zapiski Azerb. Un., 1957:12, 101–112, (Russian; Azerbeidjani
                summary).

KHOZATSKIĬ, L. I., and IUR'EV, K. B.
1964A.   [Family Mosasauridae (=Pythonomorpha).] Osnovy Pal., [Amphibians,
                Reptiles, and Birds.], [12], 475–481, 10 figs., (Russian).
1964B.   [Superorder Pterosauria.] Osnovy Pal., [Amphibians, Reptiles, and
                Birds.], [12], 589–603, 10 figs., (Russian).

KHOZATSKIĬ, L. I., and MLYNARSKI, M.
1966   Fossil tortoises of the genus Geoemyda Gray, 1834 (s. lat.) of Europe.
                Acta Zool. Crac., 11, 398–421, 7 figs., pls., 29–33, 1 map,
                (Polish and Russian summaries).

KHRISANFOVA, E. N.
1964   [Taxonomic significance of the medullary index for long bones of the
            hominids.] In: Nesturkh, M. F., (ed.), 1964C, 169–178, 2
            tables, (Russian; English summary).
1965   [The thigh-bone of a Palaeoanthrope from Romankovo.] Voprosy
            Antrop., 20, 80–89, 3 tables, (Russian).
1966   [Skeleton of the trunk and of the extremities (long bones).] Trudy
            Inst. Etnog. Akad. Nauk SSSR, 92, 383–423, 1 fig., (Russian).
1967   [On the non-uniformity of the morphological evolution of hominids.]
            Voprosy Antrop., 26, 3–21, 3 tables, (Russian).

KHUBKA, A. N.
1965   [Essay of subdivision of continental deposits of Sarmatian of the Central
            part of MSSR.] Izv. Akad. Nauk Moldav. SSR, 1965:8, 52–56,
            1 table, (Russian).
See: Godina and Khubka.

KHUDÍAKOV, G. I.
1966   [Finds of Pleistocene vertebrates in the Irtysh and Tara valleys.] Geol.
            i Geof., 1966:5, 150–155, 3 figs., (Russian).

KIDDER, ALFRED, II
1964   South American high cultures. In: Jennings and Norbeck, (eds.),
            1964A, 451–486, 17 figs.

KIDDER, J. EDWARD   See: Chang, Kwang-chih and Kidder.

KIEFER, R.   See: Kindler and Kiefer.

KIELAN-JAWOROWSKA, ZOFIA
1965A.   Polish-Mongolian palaeontological expeditions to the Gobi Desert in
            1963 and 1964. Bull. Acad. polon. sci. Sér. Sci. biol., 13, 175–
            179, 1 fig.
1965B.   Expeditions of the Palaeozoological Department of the Polish Academy
            of Sciences to the Gobi Desert. Przegl. Geol., 1965, 30–32, 3
            figs., cover photo, (Polish).
1966A.   Third (1965) Polish-Mongolian paleontological expedition to the Gobi
            Desert and Western Mongolia. Bull. Acad. polon. sci. Sér. sci.
            biol., 14, 249–252, (Russian summary).
1966B.   Third (1965) Polish-Mongolian paleontological expedition to Mongolia.
            News Bull., Soc. Vert. Pal., no. 76, 47–48, 1 fig.
1966C.   Third expedition of the Palaeozoology Department of the Polish Acad-
            emy of Sciences to the Gobi Desert. Przegl. Geol., 1966, 108–
            110, 2 figs., cover photo, (Polish; English and Russian sum-
            maries).
1967   Les résultats des expéditions paléontologiques polono-mongoles (1963–
            1965) dans le désert de Gobi et en Mongolie Occidentale. Collog.
            Internat. Cent. Nation. Recherch. Sci., 163, 419–425, 4 pls.,
            1 map, (English summary).

KIETZKE, KENNETH K.   See: Clark, John, Beerbower and Kietzke; Clark, John
            and Kietzke.

KIGOSHI, KUNIHIKO
1967   Gakushuin natural radiocarbon measurements VI. Radiocarbon, 9, 43–62.

KIGOSHI, K., and KOBAYASHI, H.
1965   Gakushuin natural radiocarbon measurements IV. Radiocarbon, 7, 10–
              23.

KIGOSHI, K., LIN, D.-H., and ENDO, K.
1964   Gakushuin natural radiocarbon measurements III. Radiocarbon, 6, 197–
              207.

KILMER, FRANK H.
1965   A Miocene dugongid from Baja California, Mexico. Bull. S. Calif. Acad.
              Sci., 64, 57–74, 2 figs.

KIMMIG, WOLFGANG
1965   Gustav Riek zum 65. Geburtstag am 23. Mai 1965. Fundber. Schwaben,
              17, ix–xii, portr.
              See: Fischer, F. and Kimmig.

KIND, N. V.
1965   [Absolute chronology of the mainstages of last glaciation and post-glacial
              period in Siberia (according to radiocarbon data).] In: Gromov,
              V. I., et al., (eds.), 1965, 157–174, 2 figs., 2 tables, (Russian;
              English summary).
1967   Radiocarbon chronology in Siberia. In: Hopkins, D. M., (ed.), 1967D,
              172–192, 2 figs., 3 tables.
              See: Alekseev, V. A., et al.; Cherdyntsev, Alekseev, et al.; Gromov,
              V. I., et al.; Ivanova, Kind and Cherdyntsev.

KINDLER, W., and KIEFER, R.
1963   Röntgenologische Studien über Stirnhöhlen und Warzenfortsätze beim
              Neandertaler im mitteleuropäischen Raum (II. Teil). Zeit. Laryngol.
              Rhinol. Otol., 42, 752, (not seen).

KING, B. C.   See: Dineley 1966B.

KING, RUTH REECE, et al.
1964   Bibliography of North American geology, 1960. U. S. Geol. Surv. Bull.,
              1196, 777 pp.

KING-HELE, DESMOND
1964   Darwin and natural selection. New Sci., 21, 365.
1968   The essential writings of Erasmus Darwin. London: MacGibbon and
              Kee, 223 pp., 16 photographs.
              Rev.: Basalla in Science, 164, 686–687; Crowther in Nature, 219,
              655; Desmond in Endeavor, 28:105, 155.

KINGMAN, GRACE
1966   Report on the Campbell lithic collection. Masterkey, 40, 72–74.

KINGSBURY, EDITH C.
1961   Rocks that captured history. Boston: Beacon Press, Beacon Sci. Ser.,
              30 pp., illustr., (elemen. school and teachers).

KINSEY, W. FRED, III
1966   Observations on the archeology of the Tocks Island Reservoir area in
              Pennsylvania. Bull. Eastern States Archeol. Fed., no. 25, 15, (abs.).

KINSEY, W. F., III, and KENT, B. C.
   1965   The Tocks Island Reservoir survey in Pennsylvania: a preliminary state-
             ment. Penn. Archaeol., 35, 118–133, 5 figs.

KINZEY, W. G.
   1967   Preface [to symposium on primate locomotion]. Amer. Jour. Phys.
             Anthrop., 26, 115–118.

KIRCALDY, J. F.
   1967   Fossils in colour. London: Blanford Press, 223 pp., 40 figs., 79 col-
             oured pls., (not seen).
             Rev.: R. M. B. in Geol. Mag., 105, 201.

KIRCHNER, H., (ed.)
   1964   Ernst Wahle. Tradition und Auftrag prähistorischer Forschung. Berlin,
             München: Duncker und Humblot, 502 pp., (not seen).
             Rev.: Gerhardt in Homo, 16, 193.

KIRIAKOFF, SERGIUS G.
   1965   Some remarks on Sokal and Sneath's Principles of numerical taxonomy.
             Syst. Zool., 14, 61–64.

KIRILLOV, I. I.   See: Okladnikov and Kirillov.

KIRIUSHINA, M. T.
   1959   [The Anabar massif and the Anabar-Khatanga interfluvial area.]   In:
             Strelkov, S. A., et al., 1959. Quaternary deposits of the Soviet
             Arctic, 144–164, 2 figs., (Russian).

KIRK, RUTH
   1968   The discovery of Marmes man. Nat. Hist., 77:10, 56–59, illustr.

KIRKALDY, J. F.   See: Wells, A. K. and Kirkaldy.

KIRKLAND, DOUGLAS WRIGHT
   1964   Paleoecology of the varved Rita Blanca lake deposits, Hartley County,
             Texas. Diss. Abst., 24, 3691.

KIRPICHNIKOV, A. A.
   1964   [On the origin of the Caspian seal.]   Bull. Mosk. Obshch. Prirody, Otd.
             Biol., 69:5, 136–139, (Russian).

KISNERIUS, J.
   1960   Cretaceous deposits of Lithuania. Collectanea Acta Geol. Lithuanica,
             117–126, 1 fig., (English and Russian; Lithuanian summary).

KITAME, TANEYOSHI   See: Higuchi, et al.; Matsumoto, Mori, et al.

KITCHING, JAMES W.
   1963A.   Abs.: Anon. in Internat. Jour. Spel., 2:3, 37.
             Rev.: Angel in Amer. Jour. Phys. Anthrop., 23, 320;   Howell in
             Science, 149, 292;   Preuschoft in Anthrop. Anz., 27, 236–237.
   1963B.   Abs.: Huene in Zbl. Geol. Pal., Teil 2, 1964, 990.
   1963C.   Abs.: Huene in Zbl. Geol. Pal., Teil 2, 1964, 994.
   1965   A new giant hyracoid from the Limeworks Quarry, Makapansgat, Pot-
             gietersrus. Pal. Africana, 9, 91–96, figs. 39–40, 2 tables.

1968   On the Lystrosaurus zone and its fauna with special reference to some
               immature Lystrosauridae. Pal. Africana, 11, 61–76, 5 figs.

KITTLEMAN, LAURENCE, R., et al.
1965   Cenozoic stratigraphy of the Owyhee region, southeastern Oregon. Bull.,
               Mus. Nat. Hist., Univ. Oregon, no. 1, 4 + 45 pp., 11 figs., 9 pls.

KITTS, DAVID B.
1964   Aelurodon, an addition to the Durham local fauna, Roger Mills County,
               Oklahoma. Okla. Geol. Notes, 24, 76–78, 1 fig.
1965   Geology of the Cenozoic rocks of Ellis County, Oklahoma. Circ. Oklaho-
               ma Geol. Surv., 69, 1–30, 5 figs., 1 pl.
1966   Geologic time. Jour. Geol., 74, 127–146, 1 fig., 1 table.

KLAFS, GERHARD
1965   Zur Formenkenntnis von Bos primigenius Boj. nach Hornzapfenfunden
               im Mittelelbe-Gebiet. Zeit. Tierzüchtung Züchtungsbiol., 81,
               297–313, 7 figs., (English summary).

KLAGES, OTTO
1962   Aufschlüsse im Subherzynischen Becken. Aufschluss, 13, 113–118, 6
               figs.
1963   Das Oberpliocän von Willershausen. Aufschluss, 14, 16–19, 3 figs.

KLAPCHUK, M. N.
1964   [First Paleolithic finds in Central Kazakhstan.] Sov. Arkheol., 1964:3,
               268–271, 1 fig., (Russian).
1965   [Archeological finds in Karaganda region in 1962.] Sov. Arkheol.,
               1965:3, 212–217, 4 figs., 1 table, (Russian).
1967   [Archeological research in Nura R. and Sarysu R. basins.] In: Rybakov,
               (ed.), 1967, 300–302, 1 fig., (Russian).
1968   [New archeological finds in the Nur and Sarysu rivers basins.] In:
               Rybakov, (ed.), 1968, 321–322, (Russian).

KLASSEN, R. W., DELORME, L. D., and MOTT, R. J.
1967   Geology and paleontology of Pleistocene deposits in southwestern Manitoba.
               Canadian Jour. Earth Sci., 4, 433–447, 6 figs.

KLAUSEWITZ, WOLFGANG
1965A.   Die Bewegungsweise der Geigenrochen aus funktioneller und stammes-
               geschichtlicher Sicht. Natur u. Mus., 95, 97–108, 14 figs.
1965B.   Über die ungewöhnliche Ausbildung des Schädelaches von Pomadasys
               hasta. Senck. Lethaea, 46a, 161–176, 1 fig., pls. 7–10, (Eng-
               lish summary).

KLEBANOVA, I. M.
1964   A new occurrence of Eocene mammals in East Kazakhstan. Trans. of
               Klebanova, 1963A. Internat. Geol. Rev., 6, 1855–1857.
1965   [New locality of Middle Oligocene mammals in the Kyzyl-Kak site.]
               Pal. Zhurnal, 1965:4, 99–102, 1 fig., (Russian).
1966   [Andarak (Kirgizia) – a new locality of Eocene vertebrates.] Pal.
               Zhurnal, 1966:4, 101–103, 1 fig., (Russian).

KLEEMAN, GEORG
1962   Schwert und Urne. Ausgrabungen in Deutschland, Methoden und Funde.
               Stuttgart: Franckh'sche Verlagshandlung, 277 pp., 60 figs., 67
               pls., (not seen).

Rev.: Anon. in Jahrb. Schweiz. Ges. Urgesch., 50, 108.

1964A.   Die Heidelberger Kultur. Europas älteste Steingeräte. Kosmos (Stuttgart), 60, 154–157, illustr.

1964B.   Die ältesten Feuerstellen der Menschheit entdeckt. Kosmos (Stuttgart),
60, *282.

KLEIN, BERNARD, and ICOLARI, D., (eds.)

1967   Reference encyclopedia of the American Indian. New York: B. Klein
and Co., 544 pp., (not seen).
Rev.: Hoffman in Plains Anthrop., 13, 76–78.

KLEIN, HOWARD KENNETH

1965   My best friends are dinosaurs. Pictures by Windrow. New York: David
McKay, 28 pp., illustr., (not seen).

KLEIN, J. F.

1968   Fossilen-Museum im Pfarrhaus. Kosmos, 64, 198–199, 2 figs.

KLEIN, RICHARD G.

1965   The Middle Palaeolithic of the Crimea. Arctic Anthrop., 3, 34–68, 12
figs., 1 map.

1966A.   Early man and Upper Pleistocene stratigraphy in the Dnestr Basin.
Abs. 65th Ann. Meeting Amer. Anthrop. Assoc., 1966, 35–36,
(abs.).

1966B.   Chellean and Acheulean on the territory of the Soviet Union; a critical
review of the evidence as presented in the literature. In: Clark,
J. D., and Howell, F. C., (eds.), 1966A, 1–45, 10 figs., 5 maps.

1967   Radiocarbon dates on occupation sites of Pleistocene age in the U.S.S.R.
Arctic Anthrop., 4:2, 224–226.
See: Bader, O. N., 1965A; Beregovaia, et al.; Ivanova 1967.

KLEINDIENST, MAXINE R.

1962   Components of the East African Acheulian assemblage: an analytic
approach. Proc. 4th Panafrican Congr. Prehist., sec. 3, 81–112,
6 figs., 2 tables.

1967   Questions of terminology in regard to the study of Stone Age industries
in Eastern Africa: "cultural stratigraphic units". Discussion.
In: Bishop, W. W., and Clark, J. D., (eds.), 1967A, 821–859,
(French summary).
See: Clark, J. D., Cole, et al.; Howell, Cole, et al.

KLEINENBERG, S. E.

1958   [On the origin of cetaceans.] Doklady Akad. Nauk SSSR, 122:5, 950–
952, 1 fig., (Russian).

KLEINPELL, ROBERT M.

1968   Memorial to Ruben Arthur Stirton (1901 - 1966). Proc. Geol. Soc.
Amer. for 1966, 1968, 393–400, portr.

KLEINSCHMIDT, ADOLF

1964A.   Die Beziehungen zwischen Walther Bacmeister und Otto Kleinschmidt.
Jahresh. Ver. Vaterland. Naturk. Württemberg, 118–119, 355–358.

1964B.   Ohrengeieri im Diluvium Mitteleuropas. Jour. Ornithol., 105, 241–242,
(abs.).

1965   Die Mechanik der Sedimentbewegung in Kleinen Flussrinnen. Ein Beifrag
zur analytischen Sediment-Gefügekunde (Stratonomie). Jahresh.
Ver. Vaterland Naturk. Württemberg, 120, 126–184, 35 figs.

1966   Zur Geschichte des Pferdes. Zeit. Rhein. Naturf. Ges. Mainz, 4, 46–52.

KLEIWEG DE ZWAAN, JOHANNES PIETER
1956   Is the Neanderthal race extinct? Kon. Ned. Aardrijk. Genoot. Tijd-
               schrift, 73, 348–355, (Dutch; English summary).

KLEJN, L. N.
1960   [Ergebnisse einer Untersuchung der Otolithen aus pliozänen und post-
               pliozänen Ablagerungen der Prikurinsk Niederung Aserbajdshans.]
               Trudy Azerbaid. Inst. po dobyche nefti, 10, 101–121, 1 pl.,
               (Russian; not seen).
           Abs.: Weiler in Zbl. Geol. Pal., Teil 2, 1966, 280–281.

KLEMMER, KONRAD, (ed.)
1964   Festschrift zum 70. Geburtstag von Prof. Dr. Robert Mertens. Senck.
               Biologica, 45, 193–612, illustr.
           Rev.: Rabb in Copeia, 1965, 394–395.

KLIMA, BOHUSLAV
1961F.   L'état actuel des problèmes de l'aurignacien et du gravettien. Archeol.
               Roz., 13, 84–121, figs. 57–71, (Czech; French summary).
1961G.   Station paléolithique de Pavlov II. Archeol. Roz., 13, 461–464, figs.
               173, 182–184, (Czech; French summary).
1963B.   Rev.: [Zotz] in Quartär, 15–16, 211–212. ·
1964   Die paläolithische Reliefplastik einer Löwin von Pavlov. Památky
               Archeol., 55, 82–90, 6 figs., (Czech; German summary).
1965A.   Erforschung der paläolithischen Station Borsice in Mähren im J. 1964.
               Archeol. Roz., 17, 469–482, figs. 133–139, (Czech; German
               summary).
1965B.   Eine neue paläolithische Ritzzeichnung aus der Pekárna-Höhle in Mähren.
               Quartär, 15–16, 167–172, 1 fig., pl. 8.
1966A.   Die materielle Kultur des europäischen Jungpaläolithikums. In: Narr,
               (ed.), 1966B, 241–268, 4 figs.
1966B.   [Professor Dr. Josef Skutil (1904 - 1965).] Pamatky Archeol., 57:1,
               328–332, portr., (Czech).
1966C.   Josef Skutil †. Quartär, 17, 183–185, portr., pl. 14.
           See: Fridrich, Klíma and Valoch.

KLIMA, VON MILAN
1967   Die Entwicklung des Brustbeinkammes bei den Fledermäussen. Zeit.
               Säugetierk., 32, 276–284, 10 figs., (German and English sum-
               maries).

KLINGENER, DAVID
1966   Dipodoid rodents from the Valentine formation of Nebraska. Occ.
               Papers Mus. Zool. Univ. Mich., no. 644, 9 pp., 2 figs.

KLUGE, ARNOLD G.
1966   A new pelobatine frog from the Lower Miocene of South Dakota with
               a discussion of the Scaphiopus-Spea complex. Contrib. Sci., Los
               Angeles Co. Mus., no. 113, 26 pp., 8 figs., 5 tables.
1967   Higher taxonomic categories of gekkonid lizards and their evolution.
               Bull. Amer. Mus. Nat. Hist., 135:1, 59 pp., 8 figs., 5 pls., 3 tables,
               2 maps.

KN., R.
1964   Neue Menschenfossilien aus Nordafrika. Umschau, 64, 569, 1 fig.

KNEBERG, MADELINE
1952   The Tennessee area. In: Griffin, J. B., (ed.), 1952A, 190–198.

KNEUPER, G.
1964   Paul Guthörl [1895 - 1963]. Jahresb. Mitt. Oberrhein. Geol. Ver., 46,
            xx–xxii.

KNOROZOV, IU. V. See: Wauchope 1966B.

KNUSSMANN, RAINER
1965A.   Die Aussagen des Armskeletts zur Frage eines brachiatorischen Stadiums
            in der Stammesgeschichte des Menschen. Ber. Tagung Deutsch.
            Ges. Anthrop., 9, 133–139, 3 figs.
1965B.   Drei mittelpaläolithische menschliche Schädelfragmente von der Wildscheuer
            bei Steeden an der Lahn (Limburg). Ber. Tagung Deutsch. Ges.
            Anthrop., 1963, 230–237, 7 figs.
1967   Das proximale Ende der Ulna von Oreopithecus bambolii und seine
            Aussage über dessen systematische Stellung. Zeit. Morph. Anthrop.,
            59:1, 57–76, 19 figs., 2 tables, (English summary).

KOBATAKE, NOBUO, and KAMEI, T.
1966   The first discovery of fossil crocodile from Central Honshû, Japan.
            Proc. Japan Acad., 42, 264–269, 2 figs.

KOBAYASHI, HIROMI   See: Kigoshi and Kobayashi.

KOBAYASHI, KUNIO
1963   Pleistocene tephras in the central region of Japan. Quat. Res., 3, 110–
            122, 6 figs., (Japanese; English summary).
1964   [The radiocarbon dates for the Jomon and non-ceramic cultures.] Kagaku,
            34:2, 96–97, (Japanese).

KOBAYASHI, TEIICHI, (ed.)
1964A.   Geology and palaeontology of southeast Asia. Volume 1. Tokyo:
            Univ. Tokyo Press, 289 pp., illustr.
1964B.   Palaeontology of Thailand, 1916–62. In: Kobayashi, T., (ed.), 1964A,
            17–29, 2 tables, 1 map.
1967   Japanese palaeontology and palaeontologists in last three decades. Kaseki,
            no. 13, 1–16, 6 tables, (Japanese).

KOBAYASHI, T., TAKAI, F., and HAYAMI, I.
1963   On some Mesozoic fossils from the Khorat series of east Thailand and
            and a note on the Khorat series. Jap. Jour. Geol. Geog., 34,
            181–192, pl. 11.
1964   On some Mesozoic fossils from the Khorat series of East Thailand and
            a note on the Khorat series. In: Kobayashi, T., (ed.), 1964A,
            119–133, pl. 11, 2 tables.

KOBUSIEWICZ, MICHAL
1967   Materialien der Steinzeit im Kreis Oborniki. Fontes Archaeol. Posnanien-
            ses, 18, 1–28, 25 figs., 12 pls., (Polish).

KOBY, FRÉDÉRIC-EDOUARD
1964A.   Die Tierreste der drei Bärenhöhlen. Acta Bernensia, 3, 149—160, fig.
         31, pl. 16.
1964B.   Altérations dentaires extraordinaires chez un ours des cavernes. Eclog.
         Geol. Helvetiac, 57, 825—828, 1 fig.
1964C.   La faunule de la grotte de Néron à Soyons (Ardèche). In: Ripoll
         Perelló, E., (ed.), 1964A, 473—486, 2 pls., (Spanish summary).
1964D.   Ostéologie de Rupicapra pyrenaica d'après les restes de la caverne de
         la Vache. Prehist. Spéléol. Ariégeoises, 19, 13—31, 10 figs.
1964E.   Nouvelles constations de traces d'ostéolyse intra vitam sur des ossements
         fossiles. Verh. Naturf. Ges. Basel, 75, 78—85, 6 figs.

KOBY, F.-E., and BRÖCKELMANN, ST.
1967   Mandibule tératologique d'ours des cavernes. Eclog. Geol. Helvetiae,
         60, 657—660, 1 fig.

KOBY, F.-E., and SCHAEFER, H.
1961   Abs.: Ehrenberg in Zbl. Geol. Pal., Teil 2, 1964, 194—195.
         Rev.: Heller in Mitt. Verband Deutschen Höhlen- und Karstforscher,
         München, 9, 30—31.

KOBY, F.-E., and SCHEIDEGGER, S.
1964   Osteodystrophia deformans Paget bei Höhlenbären. Verh. Naturf. Ges.
         Basel, 75, 86—90, 3 figs.
         Abs.: Ehrenberg in Zbl. Geol. Pal., Teil 2, 1965, 273.

KOCH, JOHN G.   See: Camp, C. L. and Koch.

KOCH, J. G., and CAMP, C. L.
1966   Late Jurassic ichthyosaur from Sisters Rocks, coastal southwestern Oregon.
         Ore Bin, 28, 65—68, 3 figs. [Same as Camp and Koch, 1966.]

KOCH, NEIL C.
1967   Disappearance of the dinosaurs. Jour. Pal., 41, 970—972, 1 table.

KOCH, WILHELM   See: Arnold, et al.

KOCHANSKY-DEVIDÉ, V.
1962   Razvoj paleontologije u Hrvatskoj od 1951. do 1961. Geol. Vjesnik,
         15, 27—32.
1964   Paleozoologija. Zagreb: Udžbenici Zagrebačkog sveučilišta. Školska
         knjiga, xii + 452 pp., 552 figs., (not seen).
         Rev.: Kochansky-Devidé in Geol. Vjesnik, 18, 211—212.

KOCHENOV, A. V.   See: Mstislavskiĭ and Kochenov.

KOCHERÉZHKIN, V. G.
1967   [Evolutionary biochemistry and the origin of life.] Izv. Akad. Nauk
         SSSR, ser. biol., 1967:2, 310—313, (Russian).

KOCHETKOVA, V. I. (=Kotchetkova)
1961B.   [Evolution of specifically human cortex areas in hominids.] Voprosy
         Antrop., 7, 14—22, 6 figs., (Russian).
1964   [Mold of the cerebral cavity of the Cro-Magnon III fossil man.] In:
         Nesturkh, (ed.), 1964C, 111—135, 10 figs., 7 tables, (Russian;
         English summary).

1965   [Brain volume of the Paleolithic man from "Markina Gora" station.]
             Voprosy Antrop., 20, 99–101, (Russian).
1966A.   [Comparative characteristics of the endocrania of hominids in Paleoneu-
             rological aspect.]   Trudy Inst. Etnog. Akad. Nauk SSSR, 92,
             457–496, 13 figs., 13 tables, (Russian).
1966B.   [Structure of endocranium Pavlov I in paleoneurological aspect.]   Voprosy
             Antrop., 24, 64–76, 6 figs., 5 tables, (Russian).
1967   [Principal stages in the evolution of brain and material culture in ancient
             man.]   Voprosy Antrop., 26, 22–40, 4 pls., (Russian).
1968   Les particularités de la macrostructure de l'encephale de l'homme du
             Paléolithique supérieur.   Discussion.   7th Internat. Congr. Anthrop.
             Ethnol. Sci., Moscow, 1964, 3, 462–466.

KODAMA, SHINOBU   See: Miyasaka, et al.

KOEHLER, OTTO VON
    1960   Darwin und wir.   In: Heberer and Schwanitz, (eds.), 11–31.

KOENIG, JOHN W.
    1965   The Ro-Tap as an aid in sample preparation.   In: Kummel and Raup,
                 (eds.), 1965, 275–276.

KOENIGSWALD, GUSTAV HEINRICH RALPH VON
    1956J.   100 Jahre Neandertaler.   Umschau, 56, 513–515, 6 figs.
    1960C.   Rev.: Trimmel in Die Höhle, 13, 103.
    1961   Abs.: Dietrich in Zbl. Geol. Pal., Teil 2, 1964, 194.
    1962B.   Abs.: Kuhn-Schnyder in Zbl. Geol. Pal., Teil 2, 1964, 224–225.
    1962C.   Abs.: Dietrich in Zbl. Geol. Pal., Teil 2, 1964, 225.
    1963A.   Abs.: Langer in Zbl. Geol. Pal., Teil 2, 1964, 673.
    1963C.   Abs.: Dietrich in Zbl. Geol. Pal., Teil 2, 1964, 225.
    1963D.   Australopithecus und das Problem der Geröllkulturen. Ber. 7. Tagung
                 Deutsch. Ges. Anthrop., 1961, 139–152, 7 figs.
                 Abs.: Dietrich in Zbl. Geol. Pal., Teil 2, 1964, 225.
    1964A.   Potassium-Argon dates for the Upper Tertiary. Cursillos y Confer. Inst.
                 "Lucas Mallada", 9, 275–276.
    1964B.   [Some remarks on the early history of mankind.]   In: Nesturkh, (ed.),
                 1964C, 99–110, 9 figs., (Russian; English summary).
    1964C.   Die Göttin ohne Gesicht.   In: Ripoll Perelló, E., (ed.), 1964A, 487–494,
                 2 figs., (French summary).
    1964D.   Early Man: Facts and fantasy. Jour. Roy. Anthrop. Inst., 94, 67–79.
    1965A.   Die phylogenetische Stellung der Australopithecinen. Anthrop. Anz.,
                 27, 273–277.
    1965B.   Das Alter der Hominiden. Anthrop. Anz., 29, 163–170.
    1965C.   Dating by potassium-argon technique.   In: Leakey, et al., 1965, 89–90.
    1965D.   Begegnungen mit dem Vormenschen.   München: Deutscher Taschenbuch
                 Verlag, 185 pp.
                 Rev.: Knussman in Homo, 16, 190.
    1965E.   Critical observations upon the so-called higher primates from the Upper
                 Eocene of Burma.   Proc. K. Nederl. Akad. Wet., Ser. B, 68,
                 165–167.
    1966A.   Evolution of man. Geol. en Mijn., 45, 85, (abs.).
                 Rev.: MacIntosh in Mankind, 6:2, 88–89.
    1966B.   Fossil Hyracoidea from China. Proc. K. Nederl. Akad. Wet., Ser. B,
                 69, 345–356, 5 figs.
    1967A.   Neue Dokumente zur menschlichen Stammesgeschichte. Eclog. Geol.
                 Helvetiae, 60, 641–655, 5 figs.

1967B.	Die Fossilgeschichte der rezenten Anthropoiden. In: Starck, D., Schneider, R., and Kuhn, H. J., (eds.), 1967, 19–24, (English summary).
1967C.	75 Jahre Pithecanthropus. Ein Beitrag zur Stammesgeschichte des Menschen I, II. Natur u. Mus., 97:4, 131–138, 7 figs.; 97:5, 153–164, 9 figs.
1967D.	An Upper Eocene mammal of the family Anthracotheriidae from the Island of Timor, Indonesia. Proc. K. Nederl. Akad. Wet., Ser. B, 70, 529–533, 3 figs.
1968A.	The pattern of the upper molar in cercopithecoid primates. Discussion. 7th Internat. Congr. Anthrop. Ethnol. Sci., Moscow, 1964, 3, 327–332, 3 figs.
1968B.	Observations upon two Pithecanthropus mandibles from Sangiran, Central Java. Proc. K. Nederl. Akad. Wet., Ser. B, 71:2, 99–107, 2 figs., 2 pls.
See:	Brace 1964; Hemmer and Koenigswald; Tobias and Koenigswald.

KOENIGSWALD, G. H. R. VON, GENTNER, W., and LIPPOLT, H. J.
1965   Dating by potassium-argon technique. Age of the basalt flow at Olduvai, East Africa. In: Leakey, et al., 1965, 87–89.

KOERING, URSULA   See: Folsom 1966.

KOESTLER, ARTHUR
1965   Biological and mental evolution: an exercise in analogy. Nature, 208, 1033–1036.

KÖKTEN, İ. KILLIÇ
1963A.   Anadolu Ünye'de eskitaş Devrine (Paleolitik) ait yeni buluntular. Ankara Üniv. Dil. ve Tarih-Coğr. Fak Derg., 20, 275–276, 2 pls., (Turkish).
1963B.   İstanbul batisinda eskitaş (Paleolitik) Devrine Alt yeni buluntular. Ankara Üniv. Dil ve Tarih-Coğr. Fak. Derg., 20, 277–278, 1 pl., (Turkish).

KOLCHIN, B. A., (ed.)
1965   [Archeology and natural sciences.] Moscow: "Nauka" Press, 346 pp., illustr., (Russian).

KOLESNIKOV, CH. M.
1961   [Stratigraphy of Mesozoic continental deposits of Buriatsk ASSR (Western Transbaikal area).] Izv. Akad. Nauk SSSR, Ser. Geol., 1961:4, 59–73, 3 figs., (Russian).

KOLLMANN, HEINZ   See: Flügel, E. and Kollmann; Zapfe, et al.

KOLOSOV, IU. G.
1959   [Undescribed flint implements from the Chokurcha grotto in the Crimea.] Krat. Soob. Inst. Arkheol. Akad. Nauk URSR, 9, 47–51, 2 figs., (Russian).
1960   [The stratigraphy of the Romankov Paleolithic site.] Krat. Soob. Inst. Arkheol. Akad. Nauk URSR, 10, 11–12, 1 fig., (Russian).
1964   [Some Late Paleolithic sites of Dnepr Rapids region.] In: Boriskovskiĭ and Praslov, 1964, (Arkheol. SSSR), 14, 42–49, illustr., (Russian).
1965A.   [The problem of Stone Age habitation on Crimean îaĭlas.] Arkheologiia, 19, 14–21, 4 figs., (Ukrainian; Russian summary).
1965B.   [Research on Paleolithic of the Desna R. middle course basin.] In: Bondarchuk and Shelkoplîaś, (eds.), 1965, 321–328, 7 figs., (Russian; English summary).

1966   [Levalloisian and pseudo-levalloisian points from Crimea and their functional destination.] Arkheologiiă, 20, 6–14, 3 figs., (Ukranian;
Russian summary).

KOLPAKOV, V. V.
1966   [Paleogeography of Quaternary Period on the lower course of Lena R.]
Izv. Vyssh. Uch. Zav., Geol. i Razv., 1966:5, 41–48, 1 fig.,
(Russian).

KOMATSU, ISAO
1962   The Japanese people. Origins of the people and the language. Tokyo:
Kokusai Bunka Shinkokai (The Society for International Cultural
Relations), xxii + 64 pp., illustr.
Rev.: Pearson in Asian Perspectives, 9, 176.

KONDO, YUKO   See: Katsui and Kondo.

KÖNING, MARIE E. P.
1961B.   Das Problem der geistigen Entwicklung des paläolithischen und mesolith-
ischen Menschen. Internat. Assoc. Quat. Res., Abs. Pap., 6th
Congr., 140, (abs.).

KONIZESKI, R. L.   See: Wood, A. E., and Konizeski.

KON'KOVA, N. I.
1957   [On the distribution of terrestrial vertebrate fauna in the Upper Miocene
of Moldavian SSR.] Izv. Moldav. fil. Akad. Nauk SSSR, 1957:10,
37–50, illustr., (Russian; Moldavian and English summaries).
See: Burchak-Abramovich, N. I. and Kon'kova; Gureev and Kon'kova.

KONNERTH, A.
1966   Tilly bones. Oceanus, 12:2, 6–9, illustr.

KONOPLIĂ, P. T.
1959   [Traces of Stone Age men in southern Kirgizia.] Izv. Akad. Nauk
Kirgiz. SSR, ser. Obshch. Nauk, 1:1, 41–47, 3 figs., (Russian).
See: Okladnikov, Kasymov and Konopliă.

KONSTANTINOVA, N. A.
1963   Terraces of the lower Prut and the lagoons of the Danube Delta. Dokl.
Acad. Sci. S.S.S.R., Earth Sci. Sect., 149, 1–6.
1964   [About the geological age of the terraces of the lower reaches of the
Prut and Danube.] Biŭll. Kom. Izuch. Chetvert. Perioda, Akad.
Nauk SSSR, no. 29, 67–80, 1 chart, (Russian).
1965A.   [Archidiskodon gromovi Garutt et Alexeeva from lower Levantine
(lower Porat) deposits of the south-eastern part of the territory
of USSR.] Biŭll. Kom. Izuch., Chetvert. Perioda, Akad. Nauk
SSSR, no. 30, 171–175, 1 fig., (Russian).
1965B.   [On a possible correlation of continental Eopleistocene deposits in the
south of the European part of the USSR.] In: Nikiforova,
(ed.), 1965A, 46–55, (Russian; English summary).
1965C.   [Geological conditions of small mammal occurrences in the Eopleistocene
of South Moldavia and South-West Ukraine.] In: Nikiforova,
(ed.), 1965B, 60–97, 1 map, 1 chart, (Russian; English summary).
1967A.   [Anthropogene of southern Moldavia and southwestern Ukraine.] Trudy
Geol. Inst., 173, 139 pp., 45 figs., 2 tables, (Russian).

1967B.   [Stratigraphy of Anthropogene deposits of lower Prut and Danube
              rivers.] Pal. geol. polezn. iskop. Moldavii, 2, 183—191, (Russian).
        See: Nikiforova, Gerbova and Konstantinova; Rengarten and Kons-
              tantinova.

KONZHUKOVA, E. D. (=Konjukova)
    1963   The first discovery of Phyllospondyli in the Upper Palaeozoic of Ka-
              zakhstan. Pal. Zhurnal, 1963:4, 141.
    1964A.   [Subclass Apsidospondyli.] Osnovy Pal., [Amphibians, Reptiles, and
              Birds.], [12], 60—133, 94 figs., 2 tables, (Russian).
    1964B.   [Subclass Batrachosauria.] Osnovy Pal., [Amphibians, Reptiles, and
              Birds.], [12], 133—144, 15 figs., 1 table, (Russian).
    1964C.   [Superorder Crocodilia.] Osnovy Pal., [Amphibians, Reptiles, and Birds.],
              [12], 506—523, 30 figs., (Russian).
    1964D.   Senile individual of a melosaur from the Upper Permian of Vjatka. Pal.
              Zhurnal, 1964:4, 122—126, 4 figs., (Russian).
    1965A.   First discovery of Phyllospondyli in Upper Paleozoic of Kazakhstan.
              Internat. Geol. Rev., 7, 1074.
    1965B.   A new Parotosaurus from the Triassic of Cisuralia. Pal. Zhurnal, 1965:1,
              97—104, 4 figs., (Russian).

KOOPMAN, KARL F.
    1967   Artiodactyls. In: Anderson, S., and Jones, (eds.), 1967, 385—406,
              figs. 65—70.

KOOPMAN, K. F., and COCKRUM, E. L.
    1967   Bats. In: Anderson, S., and Jones, (eds.), 1967, 109—150, figs. 13—23.

KOPLIN, JAMES R.   See: Baldwin, P. H. and Koplin.

KORBEL, A.   See: Pawlicki, Korbel and Kubiak.

KORENEVA, E. V.   See: Arkhipov, et al.

KORENHOF, C. A. W.
    1962   The enamel-dentine border. A new factor in the study of the phylo-
              genetic interpretation of the morphologic details in the human
              dentition. Abs. 61st. Ann. Meeting Amer. Anthrop. Assoc.,
              1962, 20, (abs.).

KORN, NOEL, and SMITH, H. R., (eds.)
    1959   Rev.: Pulianos in Voprosy Antrop., 15, 153, (Russian).

KORN, N., and THOMPSON, F. W., (eds.)
    1967   Human evolution. Readings in physical anthropology. 2nd ed. New
              York and London: Holt, Rinehart and Winston, xiii + 466 pp.
              Rev.: Angel in Amer. Jour. Phys. Anthrop., 28, 231—233; Chamla
              in L'Anthrop., 72:5—6, 581—582; Day in Man, Jour. Roy.
              Anthrop. Inst., 3, 317—318; Sauter in Arch. Suiss. Anthropol.
              Gén., 32, 145; G. G. Simpson in Nature, 216, 309.

KORNIETS, N. L.
    1959D.   [New locality of Late Paleolithic fauna in Ukraine.] Trudy Inst. Zool.
              AN URSR, 15, 126—127, (Ukrainian; Russian summary).

KOROBKOV, I. I.

1962   [Exploratory work in the Khostinskiĭ caves in 1961.] Krat. Soob. Inst. Ist. Mat. Kult. SSSR, 92, 44—50, 4 figs., (Russian).

1963A.   [On methods of determining cores.] Sov. Arkheol., 1963:4, 10—19, 2 figs., (Russian).

1963B.   [New data on Neanderthal skeletons from Shanidar Cave (Iraq).] Voprosy Antrop, 15, 123—138, 4 figs., 3 tables, (Russian).

1964   [New find of hand-chopper on Ĭashtukh.] Krat. Soob. Inst. Ist. Mat. Kult. SSSR, 101, 77—80, 1 fig., (Russian).

1965A.   [The cores from Ĭashtukh.] Mat. Issled. Arkheol. SSSR, no. 131, 76—110, 10 figs., (Russian).

1965B.   [New Paleolithic findings on Ĭashtukh.] Sov. Arkheol., 1965:3, 91—99, 1 fig., 1 table, (Russian).

1967   [Results of five years research on Ĭashtukh Paleolithic site.] Sov. Arkheol., 1967:4, 194—206, 3 figs., (Russian).
    See: Gumilevskii and Korobkov.

KOROBKOVA, G. F. See: Grigor'eva, et al.

KOROLEV, V. G., (ed.)

1965   [New data on the stratigraphy of Tian-Shan.] Frunze: "Ilim" Press, 216 pp., illustr., (Russian).

KOROTKEVICH, E. L.

1957   [Giraffes in Hipparion fauna of Berislav.] Trudy Inst. Zool. AN URSR, 14, 129—140, 4 tables, (Ukrainian; Russian summary).

1961A.   [New discoveries of Hipparion and rhinoceros from the Middle Sarmatian of Moldavia.] Zbirn. Prats Zool. Muz. URSR, 30, 114—121, 4 figs., 4 tables, (Ukrainian, Russian summary).

1961B.   [On the study of the Hipparion fauna in the valley of the Kuyalink River.] Zbirn. Prats' Zool. Muz. Akad. Nauk URSR, 30, 122—129, 5 figs., (Ukrainian; Russian summary).

1964A.   [New finds of Pliocene roe-deer of the genus Procapreolus in the south of the USSR.] Dopovidi Akad. Nauk URSR, Kiev, 1964:3, 382—386, 2 figs., 2 tables, (Ukrainian; Russian and English summaries).

1964B.   [A new species of fossil Muntiacus from the Pliocene deposits of the south of the USSR.] Dopovidi Akad. Nauk URSR, Kiev, 1964:6, 807—810, 1 fig., 1 table, (Ukrainian; Russian and English summaries).

1965A.   [A new species of roe deer from Ukrainian Meotian.] Pal. Zhurnal, 1965:4, 60—67, 3 figs., 1 table, (Russian).

1965B.   [On deer from the Pliocene of the Kuchurgan R. valley and on their paleogeographical significance.] Prirodn. Obstan. i Fauny Proshl., 2, 102—119, 4 figs., 3 tables, (Russian).

1966   [New finds of Late Pliocene mammals in Ukraine.] Dopovidi Akad. Nauk URSR, 1966:4, 529—532, 3 figs., 2 tables, (Ukrainian; Russian and English summaries).

1967A.   [The first find of fossil tapir in the Ukraine.] Dopovidi Akad. Nauk URSR, ser. B, 1967:12, 1074—1076, 1 fig., (Ukrainian; Russian and English summaries).

1967B.   [Fauna of large mammals from the Pliocene deposits of Kuchurgan R. valley.] In: Collected Papers, 1967A. [Place and significance of fossil mammals of Moldavia in the Cenozoic of USSR], 77—84, (Russian).

1968   [On the problem of taxonomic position of Miocene gazelles in the south of USSR.] Vestnik Zoologii, 1968:4, 42—50, 5 figs., 1 table, (Russian; English summary).

See: Burchak-Abramovich, M. O. and Korotkevich.

KORTENBOUT VAN DER SLUIJS, G. See: Raaf, et al.

KORTENBOUT VAN DER SLUIJS, G., and ZAGWIJN, W. H.
1962 An introduction to the stratigraphy and geology of the Tegelen clay-pits.
Meded. Geol. Sticht., n. ser., 15, 31—37, 4 figs., pls. 2A, 2B, 3.
Abs.: Dietrich in Zbl. Geol. Pal., Teil 2, 1964, 15.

KORTLANDT, ADRIAAN
1967 Reply [to Washburn and Jay: "More on tool-use among primates"].
Current Anthrop., 8, 255—257.

KORZHUEV, S. S.
1961 [The structure of the middle Lena valley and the history of its evolu-
tion during Quaternary.] Mat. Vses. Sov. po Izuch. Chetvert.
Perioda, 3, 203—208, (Russian).
Abs.: Mirtsching in Zbl. Geol. Pal., Teil 2, 1964, 702—703.
See: Armand, et al.

KOŞAY, HÂMIT ZÜBEYR
1966 Cérémonie de célébration au Smithsonian Institute de Washington. Bell.
Türk Tarih Kurumu, 30, 165—171, 7 figs., (Turkish).

KOSSWIG, C. See: Ax, 1964.

KOSTENKO, N. N.
1964A. [Cenozoic stratigraphy of southeastern Kazakhstan.] Izv. Akad. Nauk
Kazakh. SSR, ser. geol., 1964:2, 3—17, 1 fig., (Russian).
1964B. [Continental Cenozoic deposits of South Kazakhstan.] Nauchn. Trudy
Tashkent. Gos. Un., Nov. ser., vyp. 249, geol. nauki, kn. 21,
164—184, (Russian).
See: Bazhanov and Kostenko; Biriukov and Kostenko.

KOSTENKO, N. N., and ALPYSBAEV, KH. A.
1966 [Paleolithic in the Turlan Pass region of Karatau Range.] Vestnik
Akad. Nauk Kazakh. SSR, 1966:8, 66—69, 3 figs., (Russian).

KOSTENKO, N. P., NESMEIANOV, S. A., and RANOV, V. A.
1961 [On the discovery of Paleolithic tools on the Ak-Dzhar heights (southern
Tadzhikistan).] Doklady Akad. Nauk Tadzhik. SSR, 4:6, 29—34,
2 figs., (Russian; Tadzhik summary).

KOSTRZEWSKI, J., CHMIELEWSKI, W., and JAŻDŻEWSKI, K.
1965 Préhistoire de la Pologne. Wydanie II, poprawione i uzupełnione.
Wrocłae, Warszawa, Kraków: Ossolineum, 428 pp., 111 figs.,
25 pls., (Polish; French summary; not seen).
Rev.: [Filip] in Archeol. Roz., 17, 564—566.

KOTLARCZYK, JANUSZ See: Jermanska and Kotlarczyk.

KOTOVICH, V. G.
1964 [The Stone Age of Dagestan.] Makhachkala: Dagestan. fil. AN SSSR
Press, 225 pp., 50 figs., 5 tables, (Russian).

KOTTEK, A.
1964   Fischreste aus dem griechischen Lias. Quenstedt's Kloake auf Leukas.
            Praktika Akad. Athenon, 39, 175—181, 2 figs., 1 pl., (Greek
            summary).

KOVACHEV, D.   See: Nikolov and Kovachev.

KOVACS, ALEXANDRU   See: Rădulescu and Kovacs; Rădulesco, Samson, Mihăilă
            and Kovacs; Samson and Kovács.

KOVACS, I.   See: Brabant and Kovacs.

KOVALEV, V. A.
1967   [Thorium in fossil bones.]   Dokl. Akad. Nauk BSSR, 11:8, 717—718,
            1 table, (Russian).

KOVALEVSKAĨA (DEOPIK), V. B.
1965   [Use of statistical methods in research on mass archeological material.]
            In: Kolchin, (ed.), 1965, 286—301, 6 figs., (Russian).

KOVALEVSKIĬ, S.
1966   [V. V. Bogachev. (Necrology).]   Izv. Akad. Nauk SSSR, 1966:7, 132—
            133, (Russian).

KOVANDA, JIŘÍ
1963   Zur biostratigraphischen Erforschung des tschechoslowakischen Quartärs
            im Jahre 1962. Zprápy Geol. Vyzk., 1962, 279—280, (Czech,
            not seen).
1964   Zpráva o mapování kvartéru na listu Beroun v roce 1963. Zprávy Geol.
            Vyzkumech Roce, 1, 311—312.

KOVESHNIKOV, V. G.
1966   [A new modification of diagraph: the craniograph.]   Voprosy Antrop.,
            22, 165—167, 4 figs., (Russian).

KOWALSKI, KAZIMIERZ
1958C.   Abs.: M. M. in Bull. Sci. Zagreb, 1962, 7:1—2, 22.
1961D.   The problem of the faunal relations between Europe and North America
            in the light of new zoological and paleontological investigations.
            Przeglad Zool., 5, 29—33, (Polish; English summary).
1961E.   Fauna pliocenśka z Wężów koło Działoszyna. Wszechświat, 7—8, 157—
            161, (not seen).
1964A.   Palaeoecology of mammals from the Pliocene and early Pleistocene of
            Poland. Acta Theriologica, 8, 73—88, 2 tables, (Polish; English
            summary).
1964B.   Paleozoological dating of cave sediments. Vert. Palasiatica, 8, 64—74,
            4 figs., (Chinese).
1965A.   Vor den Toren der Gobi. Die polnisch-mongolische paläontologische
            Gobi-Expedition 1964. Kosmos (Stuttgart), 61, 426—433, 8 figs.
1965B.   Cave studies in China today. Studies in Spel., 1, 75—81, fig. 7, pls.
            12—13.
1966A.   The stratigraphic importance of rodents in the studies on the European
            Quaternary. Folia Quaternaria, 22, 1—16, (Polish and Russian
            summaries).
            Rev.: Fahlbusch in Zbl. Geol. Pal., Teil 2, 1968, 216—217.

1966B. [New studies on the evolution of mammals.] Wszechświat, 1966:7—8, 168—170, (Polish).

1967A. Rodents from the Miocene of Opole. Acta Zool. Crac., 12, 1—18, 10 figs., 7 pls., (Polish and Russian summaries).
Rev.: Fahlbusch in Zbl. Geol. Pal., Teil 2, 1968, 217—218.

1967B. Lagurus lagurus (Pallas, 1773) and Cricetus cricetus (Linnaeus, 1758) (Rodentia, Mammalia) in the Pleistocene of England. Acta Zool. Crac., 12, 111—122, 24 figs., 1 table, (Polish and Russian summaries).
Rev.: Fahlbusch in Zbl. Geol. Pal., Teil 2, 1968, 217.

1967C. The Pleistocene extinction of mammals in Europe. In: Martin, P. S., and Wright, H. E., (eds.), 1967, 349—364, 6 figs.

KOWALSKI, K., et al.
1967   A study of the deposits of the rock-shelters in Żytnia Skała (Bębło, Kraków district.). Folia Quaternaria, 25, 1—49, 15 figs., 1 pl., (Polish; English and Russian summaries).

KOWALSKI, K., KOZŁOWSKI, J. K., KRYSOWSKA, M., and WIKTOR, A.
1965   Investigation of sediments of the Puchacza Skała Cave in Prądnik Czajowski, Olkusz District. Folia Quaternaria, 20, 44 pp., 13 figs., (Polish; English and Russian summaries).

KOWALSKI, K., and SYCH, L.
1967   Studies on the deposits of Koziarnia Cave at Sąspów in the Olkusz District. Fauna Kopalna. Folia Quaternaria, 26, 21—32, table 2, (Polish; English summary).

KOWALSKI, STANISŁAW
1964   Sprawozdanie z prac wykopaliskowych prowadzonych w Jaskini Ciemnej w Ojcowie w roku 1964. Wyniki Badań Wykopaliskowych, 1964, 8—11, (not seen).

1967A. Une importante trouvaille paléolithique dans la rue de Kopernik à Cracovie. Mat. Archeol., 8, 33—37, 1 fig., (Polish; French summary).

1967B. Les matériaux intéressants paléolithiques d'après les récentes recherches dans la grotte Ciemna à Ojców, distr. de Olkusz (1963—1965). Mat. Archeol., 8, 39—46, 1 fig., 2 pls., (Polish; French summary).

1967C. Les premiers résultats des recherches archéologiques dans la grotte Mamutova, faites en 1957—1964. Mat. Archeol., 8, 47—60, 6 pls., (Polish; French summary).

KOZHAMKULOVA, B. S.
1967A. [On similarity between Quaternary faunas of Kazakhstan and Moldavia.] In: Collected Papers, 1967A, [Place and significance of fossil mammals of Moldavia in the Cenozoic of USSR], 64—76, (Russian).

1967B. [Complexes of Quaternary mammals of Kazakhstan.] Izv. Akad. Nauk Kazakh. SSR, ser. Geol., 1967:3, 44, 1 chart, (Russian).
See: Bazhanov and Kozhamkulova.

KOZHEMIAKO, P. P.   See: Abetekov, et al.

KOZHOMBERDIEV, I. K.   See: Abetekov, et al.

KOZLOVA, E. V.
1960   [New fossil birds from southeastern Gobi.]   Trudy probl. temat. soveshch.
            Zool. Inst., 9, 323–329, 2 figs., (Russian).

KOZLOWSKI, JANUSZ KRZYZTAF
1959C.   Beiträge zur Kenntnis des Paläolithikum von Zagłębie Dąbrowski.   Ar-
            cheol. Polski, 4, 239–255, 5 figs., (Polish; German summary).
1961F.   Das Paläolithikum in Oberschlesien.   Internat. Assoc. Quat. Res., Abs.
            Pap., 6th Congr., 141, (abs.).
1962B.   Rev.: Vaufrey in L'Anthrop., 69, 310–311.
1962C.   Rev.: V [aufrey] in L'Anthrop., 68, 407–408.
1963B.   Rev.: Vaufrey in L'Anthrop., 69, 311–312.
1963C.   A propos de la datation des vestiges archéologiques de type levalloisien
            en Haute-Silésie.   Munera Archaeol. Iosepho Kostrzewski, 1963,
            60–69, (not seen).
1963D.   Niektore zagadnienia systematyki kulturowej paleolitu.   Referaty i
            Komunikaty, I Sympozjum Paleolityczne, Kraków, 1963:1, 21–
            26, (not seen).
1964A.   Quelques problèmes de la subdivision chronologique du Magdalénien en
            Europe Centrale.   Archaeol. Polona, 7, 180–192, 4 figs.
1964B.   [Le problème des relations entre l'Aurignacien et le Szélétien.]   Archeol.
            Polski, 9:2, 314–324, 5 figs., (Polish; French summary).
1964C.   Paleolitna Górnym Sląsku.   Wrocław, Warszawa, Kraków: 224 pp., 88
            pls., 3 maps, (not seen).
            Rev.: Vencl in Archeol. Roz., 17, 566.
1965A.   Etudes sur la différentiation de la culture dans le Paléolithique supérieur
            de l'Europe centrale.   Prace Archeol., 7, 155 pp., 12 figs., 2 pls.,
            2 tables, (Polish; French summary).
1965B.   An Upper Palaeolithic site at Dzierżysław I, Głubczyce district, Upper
            Silesia, in the light of the 1962 excavation.   Wiadomości Archeol.,
            30, 461–477, 11 figs., 4 pls., (Polish; Russian and English sum-
            maries).
1966A.   [Some remarks on the hypothesis of a West European local origin of
            Aurignacian industry.]   Archaeol. Polona, 9, 225–233, (Russian).
1966B.   Remarques sur l'Aurignacien en Poland.   Folia Quaternaria, 24, 1–37,
            17 figs., (Polish; French and Russian summaries).
            Rev.: Chavaillon in Bull. Soc. Préhist. Franç., C. R. séances mens., 63,
            257.
1967A.   Deux stations paléolithiques à Cracovie-Przegorzały.   Mat. Archeol., 8,
            61–74, 6 figs., 4 pls., 2 tables, (Polish; French summary).
1967B.   Le problème des ateliers de transformation du silex du Paléolithique
            supérieur.   Prace Archeol., Krakow, 8, 7–22, 5 figs., 2 pls., 1
            map, 1 table, (Polish; French summary).
1967C.   [Remarks on the Upper Paleolithic backed blade industries on the
            Polish territory.]   Wiadomości Archeol., 32:3–4, 265–278, 14
            figs., (Polish; Russian and English summaries).
            See: Kowalski, K., Kozłowski, et al.

KOZŁOWSKI, J. K., and SCHILD, R.
1964   Über den Stand der Erforschung des späten und des ausgehenden
            Paläolithikums in Polen.   Archaeol. Austriaca, 36, 83–105, 9
            pls.

KOZŁOWSKI, STEFAN KAROL
1964A.   [Remarques sur le Paléolithique tardif et le Mésolithique de la partie
            orientale de la vallée de Sandomierz.]   Archeol. Polski, 9:2,
            325–350, 7 tables, 1 map, (Polish; French summary).

1964B.   Badania w jaskini Maszyckiej w r. 1962-3. I Symp. Paleolityczne, Kraków, (not seen).

1964C.   Matériaux paléolithiques trouvés à la station des dunes de Tokary-Rąbierz, Gostynin, district de — (industrie du type Tokary). Swiatowit, 15, 253—269, 6 pls., (Polish; French summary).

1965   Matériaux paléolithiques, mésolithiques et néolithiques de environs de Przemyśl. Acta Archaeol. Carpathica, 5, 49—53, 2 figs., (Polish; French summary).

1966   [Some remarks on the stratigraphic position and dating of human remains from the Maszycka Cave, Olkusz District.] Archeol. Polski, 11, 307—312, 1 fig., (Polish; English summary).

KRAATZ, WALTER C.   See: Smith, Alan 1965.

KRADER, LAWRENCE   See: Dunn, S. P. 1966.

KRAGLIEVICH, JORGE LUCAS
1959A.   Contribución al conocimiento de la geología cuartaria de la Argentina. IV. Nota acerca de la geología costera en la desembocadura del arroyo Malacara (Provincia de Buenos Aires). Com. Mus. Argent. Cien. Nat., Geol., 1:17, 1—9.
     Rev.: Parodi Bustos in Rev. Fac. Cien. Nat. Salta, 1:3, 86—88.

1959B.   Rectificacion acerca de los supuestos "molares humanos fosiles" de Miramar (Prov. de Buenos Aires). Rev. Inst. Antrop., Univ. Nacion. Litoral, Rosario, 1, 223—236, 5 figs., 1 table.

1965   Spéciation phylétique dans les rongeurs fossiles du genre Eumysops Amegh. (Echimyidae, Heteropsomyinae). Mammalia, 29, 258—267, 5 figs., (English summary).

KRAĬNOV, D. A.
1960A.   [Excavations at the Bakhchisaraĭ Mousterian site in 1957.] Krat. Soob. Inst. Ist. Mat. Kult. SSSR, 78, 4 figs., (Russian).

1960B.   [The cave-site Tash-Air I as a basis for periodization of post-Late Paleolithic Crimean cultures.] Mat. Issled. Arkheol. SSSR, 91, 190 pp., 19 figs., 17 tables, 55 pls., (Russian).

1960C.   [100 years since the date of birthday of V. A. Gorodtsov.] Sov. Arkheol., 1960:1, 119—124, portr., (Russian).

1963   [60th birthday of Otto Nikolaevich Bader.] Sov. Arkheol., 1963:4, 126—128, portr., (Russian).

1964   [Some controversial aspects of the earliest history of the Volga-Oka basin.] Krat. Soob. Inst. Ist. Mat. Kult. SSSR, 97, 3—19, 3 figs., (Russian).

KRAĬNOV, D. A., and KRAĬNOV, A. A.
1968   [Man and human society in the making. (Symposium in Moscow).] Vestnik Akad. Nauk SSSR, 1968:7, 117—120, (Russian).

KRAJEWSKI, STANISLAW, and URBANIAK, J.
1964   [The localities with fauna in the Northern Flysch Carpathians. Part I. Metazoans.] Biul. Panstowowy Inst. Geol., 179, [Geological Research in the Carpathians, vol. VIII], 236 pp., 1 map, (Polish; Russian and English summaries).

KRÄMER, FRIEDRICH, and KUNZ, H.
1964   Fährtenfunde von Chirotherium barthi Kaup in der untersten Solling-Folge (Oberer Buntsandstein). Naturwiss., 51, 11.

1966   Chirotherium, das "unbekannte" Tier. Natur u. Mus., 96:1, 12–19,
                 2 figs., 2 tables.

KRANTZ, GROVER S.
1967   Winter survival of classic Neanderthals. Abs. 66th Ann. Meeting Amer.
                 Anthrop. Assoc., 1967, 47, (abs.).

KRAPIVNER, R. B.
1961   [The problem of the connection of the Kama, Vychegda, and Pechora
                 basins during the Quaternary period, and the periglacial deposits
                 of the Kama river basin.] Biull. Mosk. Obshch. Ispyt. Prirody,
                 Otd. Geol., 36:2, 81–101, 6 figs., 2 tables, (Russian; English
                 summary).

KRASHENINNIKOV, V. A., and PONIKAROV, V. P.
1964   [Stratigraphy of Mesozoic and Paleogene of Egypt.] Sov. Geol., 1964:2,
                 42–71, 2 figs., (Russian).

KRASKOVSKIĬ, V. I.
1962   [Prospecting for Late Paleolithic and Epipaleolithic in Odessa region.]
                 Sov. Arkheol., 1962:1, 257–262, 2 figs., (Russian).
              See: Boriskovskiĭ and Kraskovskiĭ.

KRASNENKOV, R. V.
1967   [Pliocene terraces of middle Don R.] In: Collected Papers, 1967B,
                 [Lower Pleistocene of glaciated regions of the Russian Plain],
                 157–167, (Russian).

KRASNOV, I. I.   See: Gromov, V. I., Krasnov, et al.; Zubakov and Krasnov.

KRASNOV, I. I., LUR'E, M. L., and MASAĬTIS, V. L.,(eds.)
1966   [Geology of Siberian Platform.] Moscow: "Nedra" Press, 447 pp.,
                 40 figs. and maps, 27 tables, (Russian).

KRASNOV, V. I., and PREDTECHENSKIĬ, N. N.
1967   [Devonian of the eastern part of the Saĭan-Altaĭ province.] In: Sokolov,
                 B. S., (ed.), 1967, 126–130, 1 table, (Russian).

KRASNOVIDOVA, S. S.
1964   [Australopithecines. Concerning the ancestors of man.] Arch. Russ.
                 Anat. Histol. Embryol., 66:5, 94–103, fig. 3, pl. 2, (Russian,
                 not seen).
              Rev.: Drozdowski in Przegląd Antrop., 31, 174–175, (Polish).

KRAUS, BERTRAM S.
1964   The basis of human evolution. New York: Harper and Row, xii +
                 384 pp., illustr.
              Rev.: Capell in Mankind, 6, 327–328;   Carter in Man, 65, 198;
                 Haviland in Amer. Jour. Phys. Anthrop., 23, 202–204;   Kurth
                 in Homo, 16, 57;   Shapiro in Jour. Polynesian Soc., 76, 247;
                 Slatis in Science, 147, 389–390.

KRAUS, B. S., and JORDAN, R. E.
1965   The human dentition before birth. Philadelphia: Lea and Febiger,
                 218 pp., 128 figs., 1 in color.

Rev.: Biggerstaff in Amer. Jour. Phys. Anthrop., <u>23</u>, 450—451.

KRAUS, OTTO
1964A. Victor van Straelen: 1889 — 1964. Natur u. Mus., <u>94</u>, 217, portr.
1964B. Mittelamerika — Bindeglied zweier Faunenreiche? Umschau, <u>64</u>, 718—
        722, 6 figs.

KRAUSKOPF, KONRAD B.
1967 The president's letter. Geologist, <u>2</u>:2, 1—2.

KRAUSS, ADAM
1957 [Report on archeological excavations at Kurdwanow near Cracow in
       1954—1955.] Sprawozdania Archeol., <u>1957</u>:4, 90—99, 8 figs.,
       (Polish; Russian and English summaries).

KREBS, BERNARD
1962   Abs.: Huene in Zbl. Geol. Pal., Teil 2, <u>1964</u>, 520.
1963B. Abs.: Huene in Zbl. Geol. Pal., Teil 2, <u>1964</u>, 520—521.
1965   E. Kuhn-Schnyder und B. Peyer †: Die Triasfauna der Tessiner Kalkalpen.
        XIX. <u>Ticinosuchus ferox</u> nov. gen. nov. sp. Schweiz. Pal. Abh.,
        <u>81</u>, 140 pp., 68 figs., 3 pls., frontispiece, 9 tables.
        Abs.: Huene in Zbl. Geol. Pal., Teil 2, <u>1966</u>, 304—305; <u>1967</u>, 510—511.
1966   Zur Deutung der <u>Chirotherium</u> — Fährten. Natur u. Mus., <u>96</u>, 389—396,
        5 figs.
        Rev.: Huene in Zbl. Geol. Pal., Teil 2, <u>1968</u>, 205.
1967A. Zwei <u>Steneosaurus</u>-Wirbel aus den Birmenstorfer Schichten (Ober-Oxford)
        vom "Weissen Graben" bei Mönthal (Kt. Aargau). Eclog. Geol.
        Helvetiae, <u>60</u>, 689—695, 2 figs., 1 table, (French and English
        summaries).
1967B. Der Jura-Krokodilier <u>Machimosaurus</u> H. v. Meyer. Pal. Zeit., <u>41</u>:1—2,
        46—59, 4 figs., (French and English summaries).
        Rev.: Huene in Zbl. Geol. Pal., Teil 2, <u>1968</u>, 205.

KREMMETER, ANTON-FRANZ
1967 Teilhard de Chardin und die moderne Biologie. Fortsch. u. Fortschr.,
       <u>41</u>, 1—3.

KRETZOI, MIKLÓS
1962E. Arvicolidae oder Microtidae? Vert. Hungarica, <u>4</u>, 171—175, (Hungarian
        summary).
1963   Zur Entfaltung der Wirbeltier fauna im Karpatenbecken. Vert. Hungarica,
        <u>5</u>, 195—217, (Hungarian; German summary).
1964A. A gerinces állatok története (Evolution of vertebrate animals). In:
        A természet világa, Gondolat, Publ., 351—545, (not seen).
1964B. Mammal faunae and the continental geology of India. Acta Geol. Hung.,
        <u>8</u>, 301—312.
        Abs.: Bogsch in Zbl. Geol. Pal., Teil 2, <u>1966</u>, 317—318.
1964C. Die Wirbeltierfauna des Travertinkomplexes von Tata. In: Vértes, L.,
        (ed.), 1964A, 105—126.
1964D. Über einige homonyme und synonyme Säugetiernamen. Vert. Hungarica,
        <u>6</u>, 131—138, (Hungarian summary).
1965A. Die <u>Hipparion</u>-Fauna von Györszentmárton in NW-Ungarn. Ann. Hist.-
        Nat. Mus. Nation. Hungarica, <u>57</u>, 127—143, 1 pl., 1 diagram.
1965B. Die Amphibien aus der altpleistozänen Fundstelle Voigtstedt in Thü-
        ringia. Pal. Abh., Abt. A, <u>2</u>, 323—333, (Russian and English
        summaries).

Rev.: Westphal in Zbl. Geol. Pal., Teil 2, 1967, 102.

1965C.   Die Nager und Lagomorphen von Voigtstedt in Thüringen und ihre
             chronologische Aussage. Pal. Abh., Abt. A, 2, 585–661, 2 figs.,
             pls. 38–39, 7 tables, (Russian and English summaries).

1965D.   Drepanosorex – neu definiert. Vert.Hungarica, 7, 117–129, 3 figs.,
             (Hungarian summary).

1965E.   Pannonicola brevidens n.g. n. sp., ein echter Arvicolide aus dem ungarischen
             Unterpliozän. Vert. Hungarica, 7, 131–139, 4 figs., (Hungarian
             summary).

1965F.   [Identification of the main faunal elements from Paleolithic localities.]
             In: Vértes, L. 1965F, 276–279, (Hungarian).
             See: Bertalan and Kretzoi; Vértes, Kretzoi and Bertalan.

KRETZOI, M., and VÉRTES, L.
1964A.   Die Ausgrabungen der mindel-zeitlichen (Biharian-) Urmenschensiedlung
             in Vértesszöllös. Acta Geol. Hung., 8, 313–317.
             Abs.: Bogsch in Zbl. Geol. Pal., Teil 2, 1966, 340.

1964B.   Zusammenfassung. In: Vértes, L. (ed.), 1964A, 251–253, 1 fig.

1965A.   The role of vertebrate faunae and Palaeolithic industries of Hungary
             in Quaternary stratigraphy and chronology. Acta Geol. Hung.,
             9, 125–144, (Russian summary).

1965B.   Upper Biharian (Intermindel) pebble-industry occupation site in western
             Hungary. Current Anthrop., 6, 74–87, 7 figs.

1965C.   Lower Palaeolithic hominid and pebble-industry in Hungary. Nature,
             208, 205.
             Abs.: Anon. in La Nature, no. 3371, 110.

KRIEGER, ALEX D.
1964A.   Early man in the New World. In: Jennings and Norbeck, (eds.), 1964A,
             23–81, 6 figs.
             Rev.: Bell in Amer. Antiq., 30, 500–501; Bird in Amer. Antiq., 31,
             262–272, 6 figs., with reply by Krieger; Orellana Rodríguez
             in Antropología, 2:2, 97–98.

1964B.   Terminology of chipped-stone artifacts in America. Proc. Internat.
             Congr. Americanists, 1962:1, 171–180.

KRIGER, N. I. (=Krieger, N. I.)
1962B.   [Quaternary deposits of Africa and the Near East.] Moscow: Akad.
             Nauk Press, 143 pp., illustr., (Russian).

1965   [On the geological age of Middle and Upper Paleolithic in the basins
             of the Volga, Don, and Dnepr.] In: Bader, O. N., et al., (eds.),
             1965, 157–165, 1 table, (Russian).
             See: Aliman, M.-H. 1960B.

KRIVOLAP, G. I.
1964   [Mousterian finds in Belgorod-Dnestrovskiĭ.] Arkheologiia, 17, 211–212,
             1 fig., (Ukrainian; Russian summary).

KRIZENECKY, J.
1965   Gregor Johann Mendel 1822–1884. Leipzig: J. A. Barth Verlag, 198 pp.,
             20 figs., 6 portrs.
             Rev.: Degen in Naturwiss. Rundschau, 19:12, 516; Kaltenbach in
             Mitt. Anthrop. Ges. Wien, 96–97, 344–345.

KROKOS, V.
1922 [What the excavations in the Ukraine have given.] Peoples Library no. 9. Odessa: Vseukrainskoe Gosudarstvennoe Izdatel'stvo Press, 68 pp., 25 figs., (Russian).

KROMER, KARL See: Blaha, et al.

KRÖMMELBEIN, KARL
1966 Probleme des Gondwanalandes. Zool. Anz., 177:1, 1—50, 19 figs. See: Ax, 1964.

KROMMENHOEK, W., and SLOB, A.
1967A. Variabiliteit in aantal en vorm van de alveolen der molaren uit de bovenkaak bij de bosmuis, Apodemus sylvaticus (L.). Lutra, 9, 41—51, 3 figs., 1 table, (Dutch; French summary).
1967B. De waarde van een tweetal kenmerken van de onderkaak bij het onderscheiden van Microtus arvalis (Pallas) en M. agrestis (L.). Lutra, 9, 51—56, 3 figs., (Dutch; English summary).

KRÖSCHE, O.
1963 Die Moa-Strausse, Neuseelands ausgestorbene Riesenvögel. Die Neue Brehm-Bücherei, no. 322, 148 pp., 14 figs.; Wittenberg Lutherstadt: A. Ziemsen Verlag, (not seen).
Rev.: E. in Ibis, 106, 542; Wolters in Bonner Zool. Beitr., 17, 153.
Abs.: Kuhn in Zbl. Geol. Pal., Teil 2, 1965, 258—259.

KRUCKOW, THORWALD
1962 Eine echte Bernstein-Eidechse. Aufschluss, 13, 267—270, 2 figs.
1965 Die Elasmobranchier des tertiären Nordseebeckens im nordwestdeutschen Bereich. Senck. Lethaea, 46a, 215—256, 7 tables, (English, French and Russian abstracts).

KRUEGER, HAROLD W., and WEEKS, C. F.
1965 Geochron Laboratories, Inc., radiocarbon measurements I. Radiocarbon, 7, 47—53.

KRÜGER, HERBERT
1959 Abs.: Ebers in Zbl. Geol. Pal., Teil 2, 1962, 284.
1962 Altsteinzeit-Forschung in Hessen. Fundber. Hessen, 2:6, 43, (not seen).
1964A. Zwei Paläolith-Artefakte aus dem Oberen Wettertal von Niederbessingen, Kr. Giessen. A. Die bogenschaberartige Spitze aus Brauneisenerz von den "Strassenäckern". B. Die Levallois-Spitze aus Basalt von den "Rabelsäckern". Fundber. Hessen, 4, 11—18, (not seen).
1964B. Eine spätalt- oder mittelsteinzeitliche Schlagstätte "In den Raupern" bei Langenaubach, Dillkreis. Fundber. Hessen, 4, 144—149, (not seen).
1964C. Ein diskoider Rundschaber im "Jungpaläolithikum" von Heddesheim, Kreis Kreuznach, als Zeugnis für ein selbständiges mittelpaläolithisches "Heddesheim 2". Mainzer Zeit, 59, 26—34, 5 figs.
1965 Zwei Blattspitzen unterschiedlicher Morphologie aus dem Palaolithikum Oberhessens. Quartär, 15—16, 155—166, 2 figs., (English summary).

KRUGER, W.
1958 Der Bewegungsapparat. Handb. der Zool. (Kükenthal), 8:13—14, 176 pp., 110 figs.

KRUKOFF, SERGE
1967   Reconstitution de la largeur bipariétale totale d'un crâne à partir d'un
            os pariétal isolé. C. R. Acad. Sci. Paris, Sci. Nat., 264, 1260—
            1262, 3 figs.

KRUMBIEGEL, GÜNTER
1959C.   Geologie und Paläontologie der Braunkohlenlagerstätte Geiseltal bei
            Halle/Saale, DDR. Geol. Práce, Bratislava, Zprávy 16, 105—113,
            2 figs., pls. 7—8, (German and Czech).
1963   Abs.: Lotze in Zbl. Geol. Pal., Teil 2, 1964, 676—677;   Westphal in
            Zbl. Geol. Pal., Teil 2, 1965, 249—250.
1964   Die Braunkohle des Geiseltales und ihre tropische Lebewelt. "Du und
            Dein Werk" NR, 3, 16—21, (not seen).
1966   Neue Fossilien aus der Braunkohle des Geiseltales. Natur u. Mus., 96:3,
            109—116, 5 figs.
            See: Matthes, H. W. and Krumbiegel.

KRUPÍNSKI, TADEUZ, KUBICZEK, T., STACHOWIAK, W., and STEŚLICKA, W.
1958   An attempt to reconstruct the skull of Paranthropus robustus. Przeglad
            Antrop., 24, 484—495, 10 figs., (Polish; English summary).

KRUPNOV, E. I.
1964   [Some unsolved problems concerning the primitive archeology of the
            Caucasus.]   Krat. Soob. Inst. Ist. Mat. Kult. SSSR, 98, 3—8,
            (Russian).
1966   [The Caucasus in the most ancient history of our country.]   Voprosy
            istorii, no. 5, 27—40, (Russian; not seen).
            Abs.: Dunn and Dunn in Current Anthrop., 8, 420.

KRUTZSCH, WILFRIED
1965   Das geologische Profil von Voigtstedt in Thüringen. Pal. Abh., Abt. A,
            2, 235—248, 10 figs., (Russian and English summaries).

KRUTZSCH, W., and LOTSCH, D.
1964   Contribution à la question de la subdivision du Tertiaire en deux systèmes
            indépendants: le Paléogène et le "Néogène". Mém. Bur. Rech.
            Géol. Min., 28:2, 931—936.

KRUYSEN, B.
1961   Blitterswijk (Limburg). Nieuws-Bull. Koninklijke Ned. Oudheidk. Bond,
            6e s., 14, 58, (not seen).

KRUYTZER, E. M.
1962A.   Schedels van ijstijdmensen bij Roermond. Natuurhist. Maandbl., 51,
            42—43.
1962B.   J. T. Binkhorst van den Binkhorst, burgemeester en geoloog. 1810 - 1876.
            Natuurhist. Maandbl., 51, 166—178, portr., (French summary).
1963A.   J. Bosquet, apotheker en paleontoloog. 1814 - 1880. Natuurhist.
            Maandbl., 52, 95—103, portr., (French summary).
1963B.   De mammoet. Natuurhist. Maandbl., 52, 162—163, illustr.
1964A.   Les Mosasauriens du Crétacé supérieur du Limbourg méridional, Pays-
            Bas. Natuurhist. Maandbl., 53, 150—156, 4 figs., (Dutch; French
            summary).
1964B.   Niels Stensen, anatoom en geoloog. 1638 - 1686. Natuurhist. Maandbl.,
            53, 173—188, portr., 1 fig., (English summary).

1966   On the definition of fossil and subfossil. Natuurhist. Maandbl., 55, 9—12, (Dutch; English summary).

KRYLKOV, IU. V., and RANOV, V. A.
1959   [Archeological finds of Moustierian time on the Kara-Bura heights, and their geological interpretation.] Doklady Akad. Nauk Tadzhik. SSR, 2:5, 3—8, 2 figs., (Russian; Tadzhik summary).

KRYLOVA, A. A.
1959   [New Paleolithic sites in eastern Kazakhstan.] Krat. Soob. Inst. Ist. Mat. Kult., 76, 28—32, 3 figs., (Russian).
1961   [Stone Age findings in Eastern Kazakhstan.] Trudy Inst. Ist. Arkheol. Etnogr. Akad. Nauk Kazakh. SSR, 12, 87—91, 3 figs., (Russian).

KRYLOVA, A. A., and PAVLIUCHENKO, I. M.
1962   [Stone Age implements in Mountain Altai.] Krat. Soob. Inst. Ist. Mat. Kult. SSSR, 92, 61—64, 2 figs., (Russian).

KRYLOVA, A. K.
1962   [Devonian stratigraphy and brachiopoda of the Siberian Platform.] Trudy Vses. Neft. Nauchn.-Issl. Geologorazv. Inst. (VNIGRI), 200, 108 pp., 2 figs., 15 pls., 2 tables, (Russian).

KRYSIAK, KAZIMIERZ
1956   Les restes d'animaux de l'abri sous roche près de Podlesice (distr. de Zawiercie). Prace Mat. Muz. Archeol. Etnog. Lódzi, Ser. Archeol., no. 1, 41—47, 199, 3 figs., (Polish; French summary).

KRYSOWSKA, MARIA
1965   Petrographic research on the Dzierżysław loess soils, Głubczyce district. Wiadomości Archeol., 30, 478—480, 1 fig., (Polish; Russian and English summaries).
        See: Kowalski, K., Kozłowski, et al.

KRZAK, ZYGMUNT
1965   [Temporary characteristic of flint mine in Świeciechów.] Archeol. Polski, 10:1, 217—233, 23 figs., (Polish; English summary).

KUBASIEWICZ, MARIAN
1965   Skeleton fragments of Bos primigenius Bojanus, 1827, from the vicinity of Szczecin. Przeglad. Zool., 9, 65—69, 3 figs., 3 tables, (Polish; English summary).

KUBIAK, HENRYK
1965A.   The fossil elephants of South Poland. Folia Quaternaria, 19, 1—43, 10 figs., pls. 1—9, 1 table, (Polish; English and Russian summaries).
1965B.   Examples of abnormalities in the dentition of fossil elephants. Folia Quaternaria, 19, 45—61, pls. 10—25, (Polish; English and Russian summaries).
        See: Pawlicki, Korbel and Kubiak.

KUBICZEK, TEODOR   See: Krupínski, et al.

KUDERINA, L. D.
1967   [On the age of Kyzyl-Kainar valley in northern Balkhash region.] Izv. Akad. Nauk Kazakh. SSR, ser. Geol., 1967:3, 69—72, 4 figs., (Russian).

KUDRIN, L. M.
    1961   [On a finding of mammoth bones in the environs of L'vov.]   Nauk.
                Zap. Nauk.-pryr. Muz., $\underline{9}$, 29—30, (Ukrainian; Russian summary).

KUDRIN, L. N., SIVKOVA, A. S., and MARTYNOVA, S. S.
    1962   Fluorine, phosphorus and minor elements in the bones of fossil fishes
                and dolphins. Dokl. Acad. Sci. U.S.S.R., $\underline{142}$, 160—161, 1 table.

KUDRIN, L. N., and TATARINOV, K. A.
    1965   [On Miocene dolphins of western Ukraine.]   Pal. Zhurnal, $\underline{1965}$:4, 68—
                74, 3 figs., (Russian).
    1966   Miocene dolphins of West Ukraine. Internat. Geol. Rev., $\underline{8}$, 976—981,
                3 figs.

KUGLER, H. G., and BOLLI, H. M.
    1967   Cretaceous biostratigraphy in Trinidad, W. I. Bol. Inform., Assoc.
                Venezolana Geol., Min., Petrol., $\underline{10}$, 209—236, 4 tables.

KUHN, HANS-JÜRG
    1967   Zur systematik der Cercopithecidae. In: Starck, D., Schneider, R.,
                and Kuhn, H. J., (eds.), 1967, 25—46, 2 figs.
            See: Starck, Schneider and Kuhn.

KUHN, HERBERT
    1962   Rev.: La Baume in Praehist. Zeit., $\underline{42}$, 207—210;   Nougier in Toulouse,
                Univ., Inst. d'Art Préhist., Trav., $\underline{5}$, 158—159.
    1965   Eiszeitkunst. Die Geschichte ihrer Erforschung. Göttingen: Muster-
                schmidt-Verlag, 336 pp., 58 figs., 48 pls.
            Rev.: Crémieux in L'Anthrop., $\underline{70}$:5—6, 553—554;   M. G. in Anthropos,
                $\underline{61}$, 959;   Gieseler in Anthrop. Anz., $\underline{30}$, 215;   La Baume in
                Praehist. Zeit., $\underline{43/44}$:3—4, 371—372;   Schlette in Ethnogr.-
                Archäol. Z., $\underline{10}$:1, 112—114;   Taus in Archaeol. Austriaca, $\underline{40}$,
                283.
    1966A.   Erwachen und Aufstieg der Menschheit. Frankfurt a. M., Hamburg:
                Fischer-Bücherei, 392 pp., (not seen).
            Rev.: Kurth in Kosmos (Stuttgart), $\underline{62}$, *277;   J. M. in Anthropos,
                $\underline{62}$:3/4, 617;   Taus in Archaeol. Austriaca, $\underline{40}$, 282—283.
    1966B.   Die Eiszeit-Gravierung im Schulerloch. IPEK, $\underline{21}$, 94—105, 4 pls.
    1966C.   Wenn Steine reden. Die Sprache der Felsbilder. Wiesbaden: F. A.
                Brockhaus, 288 pp., 75 figs., 65 pls.
            Rev.: Lippert in Mitt. Anthrop. Ges. Wien, $\underline{96-97}$, 380; · J. M. in
                Anthropos, $\underline{62}$:3/4, 617.

KUHN, OSKAR
    1955B.   Abs.: Raabe in Zbl. Geol. Pal., Teil 2, $\underline{1964}$, 795.
    1961D.   Abs.: Huene in Zbl. Geol. Pal., Teil 2, $\underline{1962}$, 331.
    1961H.   Rev.: Martinsson in Geol. Fören. Förh., $\underline{88}$, 120;   Seilacher in Zbl.
                Geol. Pal., Teil 2, $\underline{1962}$, 305;   v. V. in Geol. en Mijn, $\underline{43}$, 133,
                (Dutch).
    1962   Abs.: Huene in Zbl. Geol. Pal., Teil 2, $\underline{1964}$, 160.
    1963B.   Rev.: Huene in Zbl. Geol. Pal., Teil 2, $\underline{1964}$, 170.
    1963E.   Die Tierwelt des Solnhofener Schiefers. Die neue Brehm-Bücherei, Nr.
                318. Wittenberg Lutherstadt: A. Ziemsen, 36 pp., 115 figs.
            Rev.: Kruckow in Aufschluss, $\underline{14}$, 221—222;   Seilacher in Zbl. Geol.
                Pal., Teil 2, $\underline{1964}$, 5;   Skoglund in Geol. Fören. Förh., $\underline{86}$, 504—
                505;   Staesche in Jahresh. Ver. Vaterländ. Naturk. Württemberg,
                $\underline{118-119}$, 444—445.

1964A. Ornithischia (Supplementum I). Fossilium Catalogus. I: Animalia,
        Pars 105, 1–80.

1964B. Testudines. Fossilium Catalogus. I. Animalia, 107, 299 pp.
        Abs.: Staesche in Zbl. Geol. Pal., Teil 2, 1965, 248–249.

1964C. Umgelöste Probleme der Stammesgeschichte der Amphibien und Reptilien.
        Jahresh. Ver. Vaterländ. Naturk. Württemberg, 118–119, 293–325,
        14 figs.
        Abs.: Huene in Zbl. Geol. Pal., Teil 2, 1964, 981.

1964D. Geologie von Bayern. 3rd rev. and enlarged ed. München: BLV Ver-
        lagsgesellschaft, 165 pp., 113 figs., (not seen).
        Rev.: Möbus in Ber. Geol. Ges. Deutsch. Demokratischen Republ., 10,
        385–386.

1964E. Umfrangreiche Polyphylie der Amphibien und Reptilien. Neues Jahrb.
        Geol. Pal., Monatsh., 1964, 169–176, 2 figs.
        Abs.: Huene in Zbl. Geol. Pal., Teil 2, 1964, 981.

1964F. Cyrtura Jaekel aus dem Solnhofener ist ein Nachzügler der Temnospondyli
        (Amphibia, Labyrinthodontia). Neues Jahrb. Geol. Pal., Monatsh.,
        1964, 659–664, 1 fig.
        Abs.: Huene in Zbl. Geol. Pal., Teil 2, 1965, 240–241.

1964G. Die Tierwelt des Mansfelder Kupferschiefers. Neue Brehm-Bücherei Nr.
        333. Wittenberg Lutherstadt: Ziemsen, 58 pp., 44 figs.
        Rev.: Häntzschel in Zbl. Geol. Pal., Teil 2, 1965, 211; Heintz in
        Naturen, 89, 117–118, (norwegian); Staesche in Jahresh. Ver.
        Vaterland. Naturk. Württemberg, 120, 303–304; Weber in
        in Hallesches Jahrb. Mitteldeutsche Erdgeschichte, 1967, 8, 121;
        Zapfe in Mitt. Geol. Ges. Wien, 57, 656–657.

1965A. Saurischia. (Supplementum I.) Fossilium Catalogus I: Animalia, Pars
        109, 94 pp.
        Abs.: Berg in Zbl. Geol. Pal., Teil 2, 1966, 305.

1965B. Therapsida. (Supplementum I.) Fossilium Catalogus I: Animalia,
        Pars 110, 220 pp.

1965C. Der Stammbaum der Wirbeltiere und die Macroevolution. Jahresh. Ver.
        Vaterland Naturk. Württemberg, 120, 268–290, 17 figs.

1965D. Die fossilen Vögel. Osteologie, Stammesgeschichte und System der 42
        Ordnungen. Krailling vor München: Verlag Oeben, 42 pp., 15
        figs.
        Abs.: Kuhn in Zbl. Geol. Pal., Teil 2, 1965, 259–260.
        Rev.: Staesche in Jahresh. Ver. Vaterland. Naturk. Württemberg, 120,
        304–305; Steinbacher in Natur u. Mus., 99:3, 134.

1965E. Die Amphibien. System und Stammesgeschichte. Krailling b. München:
        Oeben, 102 pp., 34 figs. ["Berichtigungen und Nachträge" on
        page 153 of Kuhn 1966.]
        Rev.: Berg in Salamandra, 4:2–3, 98; Hellmich in Kosmos, 63, 316;
        Mertens in Natur u. Mus., 95, 409; Staesche in Jahresh. Ver.
        Vaterländ. Naturk. Württemberg, 122, 173; Westphal in Zbl.
        Geol. Pal., Teil 2, 1968, 201.

1965F. Die Abstammungslehre, Tatsachen und Deutungen. Krailling bei München:
        Verlag Oeben, 61 pp., 9 figs., (not seen).
        Rev.: Haltenorth in Säugetierkundl. Mitt., 15, 184.

1966   Die Reptilien. System und Stammesgeschichte. Krailling b. München:
        Oeben, 154 pp., 32 figs.
        Rev.: Berg in Salamandra, 4:2–3, 98; Büllow in Kosmos, 64, 143;
        Haltenorth in Säugetierkundl. Mitt., 17:3, 277–278; Mertens
        in Natur u. Mus., 96, 342; Staesche in Jahresh. Ver. Vaterländ.
        Naturk. Württemberg, 122, 173; Westphal in Zbl. Geol. Pal.,
        Teil 2, 1968, 205.

1967A.   Die fossile Wirbeltierklasse Pterosauria. Krailling: Oeben-Verlag, 52 pp.,
          26 figs.
          Rev.: Westphal in Zbl. Geol. Pal., Teil 2, 1968, 205—206.
1967B.   Namensänderungen bei einigen höheren Taxa der Amphibia und Reptilia.
          Neues Jahrb. Geol. Pal., Monatsh., 1967:3, 185—187.
1967C.   Amphibien und Reptilien. Katalog der Subfamilien und höheren Taxa
          mit Nachweis des ersten Auftreten. Stuttgart: Gustav Fischer,
          viii + 124 pp., (not seen).
          Rev.: Bachmayer in Ann. Naturhist. Mus. Wien, 72, 720—721;   Felten
          in Natur u. Mus., 99:4, 171;   Mertens in Salamandra, 4, 35;
          Preuschoft in Anthropol. Anz., 31:1—2, 133;   Rossi Ronchetti
          in Riv. Ital. Pal., 74:2, 658;   Thenius in Mitt. Geol. Ges. Wien,
          60, 163—164; Westphal in Zbl. Geol. Pal., Teil 2, 1968, 200.
1968   Die Grossgliederung der Amphibien und Reptilien. Neues Jahrb. Geol.
          Pal., Monatsh., 1968:9, 513—521, 1 fig.
          Rev.: Westphal in Zbl. Geol. Pal., Teil 2, 1968:6, 638.

KÜHNE, WALTER GEORG
    1950B.   Abs.: Raabe in Zbl. Geol. Pal., Teil 2, 1964, 804.
    1961D.   Abs.: Radig in Zbl. Geol. Pal., Teil 2, 1961, 375—376.
    1967   Ursprung und Entwicklung der Säugetiere. Umschau, 1967:9, 288—289,
              1 fig.
    1968   Kimeridge mammals and their bearing on the phylogeny of the Mammalia.
              In: Drake, E. T., (ed.), 1968, 109—123, 8 figs., 1 table.
              See: Ax, 1964.

KUHN-SCHNYDER, EMIL
    1962A.   Abs.: Huene in Zbl. Geol. Pal., Teil 2, 1964, 170;   Huene in Zbl.
              Geol. Pal., Teil 2, 1965, 249.
    1962B.   Abs.: Huene in Zbl. Geol. Pal., Teil 2, 1964, 170—171.
    1962D.   Das Paläontologische Institut und Museum der Universität Zürich. Viertel
              jahrsschr. Naturf. Ges. Zürich, 107, 263—268.
    1963B.   Abs.: Huene in Zbl. Geol. Pal.. Teil 2, 1964, 521.
    1963C.   I sauri del Monte San Giorgio. Archivio storico ticenese, no. 16, Dec.
              1963, 811—854, (not seen).
    1963D.   The saurians of Monte San Giorgio. Panorama, Dec. 1963, 15, 4 figs.,
              cover photo.
    1963E.   Das Paläontologische Institut und Museum der Universität Zürich. Viertel-
              jahrsschr. Naturf. Ges. Zürich, 108, 447—451, 1 fig.
    1964A.   Das Paläontologische Institut und Museum der Universität Zürich.
              Forschung. Vierteljahrsschr. Naturf. Ges. Zürich, 109, 477—479,
              1 fig.
    1964B.   Die Wirbeltierfauna der Trias der Tessiner Kalkalpen. Geol. Rund., 53,
              393—412, 7 figs., pls. 23—24, (English, French, and Russian
              summaries).
              Abs.: Huene in Zbl. Geol. Pal., Teil 2, 1964, 981—982;   Weiler in
              Zbl. Geol. Pal., Teil 2, 1965, 228.
              Rev.: Rossi Ronchetti in Riv. Ital. Pal., 71, 976—977.
    1965A.   Das Paläontologische Institut und Museum der Universität Zürich.
              Forschung. Vierteljahrsschr. Naturf. Ges. Zürich, 110, 500—502,
              2 figs.
    1965B.   Der Typus-Schädel von Cyamodus rostratus (Muenster 1839). Senck.
              Lethaea, 46a, 257—289, 6 figs., pls. 16—18, (French and English
              summaries).
              Abs.: Huene in Zbl. Geol. Pal., Teil 2, 1966, 305—306.

1965C.	Sind die Reptilien stammesgeschichtlich eine Einheit? Umschau, 65, 149–155, 8 figs., portr.
1966A.	Der Schädel von Paranothosaurus amsleri Peyer aus dem Grenzbitumenhorizont der anisisch-ladinischen Stufe der Trias des Monte San Giorgio (Kt. Tessin, Schweiz). Eclog. Geol. Helvetiae, 59:1, 517–540, 2 figs., 2 pls., (French and English summaries). Rev.: Huene in Zbl. Geol. Pal., Teil 2, 1967, 106.
1966B.	Bericht über die Jahresversammlung der Paläontologischen Gesellschaft in Zürich vom 21. bis 28. September 1965. Pal. Zeit., 40:1–2, 1–13.
1966C.	Paläontologische Forschung in der Trias des Monte San Giorgio (Kt. Tessin, Schweiz). Umschau, 66, 96.
1966D.	Das Paläontologische Institut und Museum der Universität Zürich. Vierteljahrsschr. Naturf. Ges. Zürich, 111, 384–392, 5 figs.
1967A.	Das Problem der Euryapsida. Colloq. Internat. Cent. Nation. Recherch. Sci., 163, 335–348, 11 figs., 1 pl., 2 tables, (French and English summaries).
1967B.	Paläontologie als stammesgeschichtliche Urkundenforschung. In: Heberer, (ed.), 1967A, 238–419, 128 figs., 8 tables.
1968	Präparation von Fossilien mit dem Sandstrahlapparat. Umschau, 1968:4, 122, 1 pl.

KUMMEL, BERNHARD

1961	Rev.: Lotze in Zbl. Geol. Pal., Teil 2, 1961, 313–314.
1965A.	Bibliography on paleontological techniques. In: Kummel and Raup, (eds.), 1965, 709–764.
1965B.	Compilation of bibliographies of use to paleontologists and stratigraphers. In: Kummel and Raup, (eds.), 1965, 767–832.

KUMMEL, B., and RAUP, D., (eds.)

1965	Handbook of paleontological techniques. San Francisco and London: Freeman, xiii + 852 pp., illustr. Rev.: Baird in Amer. Sci., 53, 509A; Barnard in Sci. Progress, 54, 117–118; A. J. R. in Liverpool and Manchester Geol. Jour., 5, viii; Bergström in Geol. Fören. Förh., 88, 292–293; Browne in Austral. Jour. Sci., 28, 400; Donovan in Nature, 208, 968; Gaetani in Riv. Ital. Pal., 72, 498; Heizer in Amer. Antiq., 31, 451; In Geol. Soc. Jap., J., 74:3, 194, (Japanese); Rietschel in Umschau, 67, 134, 136; Rixon in Mus. Jour., London, 66, 58–59; Simpson in Science, 148, no. 3668, 354; Steininger in Mitt. Geol. Ges. Wien., 58, 278–280; Teichert in Jour. Pal., 39, 1040–1041; Van Valen in Quart. Rev. Biol., 41, 56; Volkheimer in Asoc. Geol. Argent., Rev., 21:2, 162.

KUMMER, BENNO

1953	Untersuchungen über die Entwicklung der Schädelform des Menschen und einiger Anthropoiden. Abh. Exact. Biol., 3, 5–44, 14 figs., 3 tables.
1965	Das mechanische Problem der Aufrichtung auf die Hinterextremität im Hinblick auf die Evolution der Bipedie des Menschen. In: Heberer, (ed.), 1965A, 227–248, 18 figs.

KUMMER, G., and GEMEINHARDT, M., (eds.)

1964	Beiträge zur Abstammungslehre. Berlin: Volk u. Wissen Press.

KUNZ, HEINRICH   See: Krämer and Kunz.

KÜPPER, HEINRICH
1964   Eduard Suess — Abgeordneter und Wissenschaftler. Verh. Geol. Bunde-
              sanst., 1964, 2–4.

KUPRINA, N. P.
1966   [Stratigraphy of Quaternary sediments of Central Kamchatkan depression
              and some questions of Anthropogene paleogeography of Kamchatka.]
              Izv. Akad. Nauk SSSR, ser. Geol., 1966:1, 125–139, 1 fig., (Rus-
              sian).
         See: Alekseev, M. N., Giterman, et al.; Alekseev, M. N., Kuprina,
              et al.; Chebotareva, Kuprina and Khoreva.

KUPRINA, N. P., and VTIURIN, B. I.
1961   [Stratigraphy and cryogenic peculiarities of Quaternary deposits in Yana
              valley.] Izv. Akad. Nauk SSSR., Ser. Geol., 1961:5, 76–87,
              4 figs., (Russian).

KURAZHSKOVSKIĬ, IŪ. M.   See: Pidoplichko and Kurazhskovskiĭ.

KURISU, KOJIRO
1967   Anthropological study on the human skeletal remains from Usu shell-
              mound in Hokkaido. Jour. Anthrop. Soc. Nippon, 75:755, 103–
              119, 3 figs., 4 pls., 6 tables.

KUROCHKIN, E. N. (=Kurotchkin)
1966   [Alden H. Miller (1906–1965).] Pal. Zhurnal., 1966:4, 124, (Russian).
1968A.   [New Oligocene birds from Kazakhstan.] Pal. Zhurnal, 1968:1, 92–101,
              5 figs., (Russian).
         Rev.: Kuhn in Zbl. Geol. Pal., Teil 2, 1968:6, 657.
1968B.   [On a collection of egg shells of reptiles and birds.] Pal. Zhurnal, 1968:1,
              156, (Russian).
         See: Ganiā and Kurochkin.

KURTÉN, BJÖRN
1963F.   Abs.: Ehrenberg in Zbl. Geol. Pal., Teil 2, 1965, 273.
1964A.   The evolution of the polar bear, Ursus maritimus Phipps. Acta Zool.
              Fennica, 108, 30 pp., 4 figs., 4 pls.
         Abs.: Ehrenberg in Zbl. Geol. Pal., Teil 2, 1965, 273–274.
1964B.   Population structure in paleoecology. In: Imbrie and Newell, (eds.),
              1964, 91–106, 13 figs.
1965A.   The Carnivora of the Palestine caves. Acta Zool. Fennica, 107, 74 pp.,
              11 figs., 4 pls.
1965B.   On the evolution of the European wild cat, Felis silvestris Schreber.
              Acta Zool. Fennica, 111, 1–29, 9 figs., 3 pls., 4 tables.
1965C.   Die untere Grenze des Mittleren Pleistozäns. Ber. Geol. Ges. Deutsch.
              Demokratischen Republ., 10, 7–11, (German and English).
1965D.   The Pleistocene Felidae of Florida. Bull. Florida State Mus., Biol. Sci.,
              9, 215–273, 17 figs., 31 tables.
1965E.   Evolution in geological time. In: Moore, J. A., (ed.), 1965, 327–354,
              21 figs.
1966A.   Pleistocene bears of North America. 1. Genus Tremarctos, spectacled
              bears. Acta Zool. Fennica, 115, 120 pp., 64 figs., 24 pls., 37 tables.
         Rev.: Ehrenberg in Zbl. Geol. Pal., Teil 2, 1967, 114–115, 514–515;
              Lundelius in Quart. Rev. Biol., 42, 537.

1966B.   Holarctic land connexions in the Early Tertiary. Comment. Biol., Soc.
         Sci. Fennica, 29:5, 5 pp., 1 fig.

1966C.   A Late-Glacial find of Arctic fox (Alopex lagopus L.) from southwestern
         Finland. Comment. Biol., Soc. Sci. Fennica, 29:6, 7 pp., 1 fig.,
         3 tables, (Finnish and German summaries).

1966D.   Pleistocene mammals and the Bering bridge. Comment. Biol., Soc. Sci.
         Fennica, 29:8, 7 pp.

1967A.   Pleistocene bears of North America. 2. Genus Arctodus, short-faced
         bears. Acta Zool. Fennica, 117, 60 pp., 30 figs., 30 tables.

1967B.   Präriewolf und Säbelzahntiger aus dem Pleistozän des Valsequillo, Mexiko.
         Quartär, 18, 173—178, 2 figs., 2 tables.

1968A.   The age of the dinosaurs. London: Weidenfeld and Nicolson, 255 pp.,
         illustr., (World Univ. Library).
         Rev.: Cox in Nature, 220, 515;   Swinton in Man, 4:1, 138.

1968B.   Pleistocene mammals of Europe. London: Weidenfeld and Nicolson,
         viii + 317 pp., 111 figs., 15 tables.
         Rev.: Baldwin in Man, Jour. Roy. Anthrop. Inst., 3, 490;   Butler in
         Nature, 218, 502;   Butzer in Amer. Anthrop., 71, 562—563;
         Guilday in Ecology, 50:3, 531;   Klingener in Jour. Mammal.,
         50:2, 387—388;   Koopman and MacIntyre in Quart. Rev. Biol.,
         45:1, 61—62;   Kowalski in Jour. Animal Ecol., 38:1, 236—237;
         Reed in Science, 164, 1387—1388;   Thenius in Zbl. Geol. Pal.,
         Teil 2, 1970:3/4, 235—236;   Yochelson in Syst. Zool., 18:1,
         109—110.

KURTH, GOTTFRIED

1962K.   (ed.)   Abs.: Westphal in Zbl. Geol. Pal., Teil 2, 1962, 315—317.
         Rev.: Bruna in Natuurhist. Maandbl., 51, 56;   Ehgartner in Naturwiss.,
         51, 72;   Frick in Umshau, 66, 514;   Henschen in Naturwiss.,
         56:11, 580;   Roth-Lutra in Zeit, Ethnol., 89, 101.

1962L.   Australopithecinen jetzt auch in der Sahara belegt. Umschau, 62, 88—89.

1964A.   Ein Neandertaler aus Griechenland. Naturwiss. Rund., 17, 29.

1964B.   Homo habilis vor 1, 8 Millionen Jahre? Naturwiss. Rund., 17, 235.

1965A.   Die Rassenpolygenie Carleton Coons im Lichte der Fossilbelege. Ber.
         8. Tagung Deutsch. Ges. Anthrop., 1963, 224—230, 3 figs.

1965B.   Die (Eu) Homininen. Ein Jeweilsbild nach dem Kenntnisstand von
         1964. In: Heberer, (ed.), 1965A, 357—425, 33 figs., 4 tables.

1966A.   Die Neanthropinen des Endpleistozäns. In: Narr, (ed.), 1966B, 423—
         434, 1 fig.

1966B.   Neue (Eu) Homininenfunde aus dem unteren Mittelpleistozän. Natur-
         wiss. Rund., 19:5, 197.
         See: Brace 1964; Heberer and Kurth; Howells 1963.

KURTH, G., and MARSKY, KL.

1967   Versuchsergebnisse mit plastischen Endokranialausgüssen. In: Starck,
         D., Schneider, R., and Kuhn, H. J., (eds.), 1967, 140—144, 4 figs.

KUSS, SIEGFRIED E.

1958   Abs.: Huene in Zbl. Geol. Pal., Teil 2, 1964, 171—172.

1963   Ein Beitrag zur Korrelierung des sudwestdeutschen Aquitans. Neues
         Jahrb. Geol. Pal., Monatsh., 1963, 11—18, 4 figs.

1965A.   Über Cynelos rugosidens vireti n. ssp. und Hemicyon stehlini Hürzeler
         1944 (Carnivora, Mamm.). Ber. Naturf. Ges. Freiburg, 55:1,
         227—241, 20 figs.

1965B.   Eine pleistozäne Säugetierfauna der Insel Kreta. Ber. Naturf. Ges. Freiburg,
         55:2, 271—348, 6 figs., 6 pls., 3 tables, (English summary).

Abs.: Hünermann in Zbl. Geol. Pal., Teil 2, <u>1966</u>, 318—319.

1965C.   Revision der europäischen Amphicyoninae (Canidae, Carnivora, Mamm.) ausschliesslich der voroberstampischen Formen. Sitz.-Ber. Akad. Wiss. Heidelberg, <u>1965</u>, 1—168, 90 figs., 3 pls.
        Rev.: M. C. P. in Fossilia, <u>1965</u>:2, 46—47.

1966   Beiträge zur Pleistozän-Fauna der Insel Kreta. I. Die von D. Bate 1904 gesammelten Elephanten- und Cerviden-Reste. Ber. Naturf. Ges. Freiburg, <u>56</u>:2, 169—181, 4 figs., (English summary).

KUSS, S. E., and MISONNE, X.
1968   Pleistozäne Muriden der Insel Kreta. Neues Jahrb. Geol. Pal., Abh., <u>132</u>:1, 55—69, 8 figs.

KUSS, S. E., and SCHREINER, A.
1963   Mastodonten vom Schienerberg. Ber. Naturf. Ges. Freiburg, <u>53</u>, 213—223, 3 figs.

KUTSCHER, FRITZ
1966   Der Bundsandstein in Hessen. Zeit. Deutsche. Geol. Ges., <u>115</u>, 692—714.
1967   Zum <u>Chirotherium</u>—Problem. Notizbl. Hess. Landesamt. Bodenforsch., <u>95</u>, 227—231, 1 fig.

KUWASHIMA, TOSHIMITSU   See: Hanihara, Kuwashima and Sakao.

KUZ'MINA, I. E.
1966   [The history of the teriofauna in North Urals and Priurals in Upper Anthropogene.] Biull. Mosk. Obshch. Prirody, Otd. Biol., <u>71</u>:3, 91—102, 2 figs., 2 tables, (Russian).

KUZNETSOV, B. B. See: Biriukov, <u>et</u> <u>al.</u>

KUZNETSOV, V. V. See: Bakirov and Kuznetsov.

KUŹNICKI, L., and URBANEK, A.
1967   [Principles of Evolution.] Warsaw: Panstwowe Wydawnictwo Naukowe Press, 617 pp., 304 figs., (Polish).
        Rev.: Ryziewicz in Przeglad Zool., <u>11</u>:4, 449—450, (Polish).

KWANGTUNG PROVINCIAL MUSEUM
1960   The palaeoliths of Tunghsing, Kwangtung. Paleovert. et Paleoanthrop., <u>2</u>:1, 61—62, (Chinese, not seen).

KYRLES, GEORG See: Ehrenberg 1962E.

KYZLASOV, L. R.
1958   [Stages in the ancient history of Tuva (a brief report).] Vestnik Mosk. Univ., <u>13</u>:4, 71—99, 3 tables, (Russian).

L., E.
1966   Housing subdivision vs. Florissant fossils. Trail and Timberline, no. <u>573</u>, 162, 1 map.

LA BAUME, WOLFGANG
    1959   Der Ur in der Darstellung der steinzeitlichen Kunst. In: Müller, A. von,
            and Nagel, (eds.), 1959, 78—88, 1 pl.

LABEYRIE, J.   See: Delibrias, Guillier and Labeyrie.

LABHART, WALTER, and RUDIN, K.
    1964   Archäologischer Fundbericht. Altsteinzeit und Mittelsteinzeit. Jahrb.
            Schweiz. Ges. Urgesch., 50, 55—60, figs. 1—8.

LABORDE, A.   See: Bayle des Hermens and Laborde.

LACAILLE, A. D.
    1966   Two contrasting palaeoliths from Buckinghamshire. Antiq. Jour., 46,
            333—335, 2 figs.

LACASSAGNE, HENRI   See: Bourdier and Lacassagne.

LACHASTRE, JEAN
    1964A.   Découverte de peintures préhistoriques à Domme (Dordogne). Bull.
             Soc. Hist. Archéol. Périgord, 91, 19—24, 6 figs.
    1964B.   La Grotte la Martine. (Domme, Dordogne). Spelunca, Bull., 4:4, 19—23,
             2 figs.

LADD, H. S.
    1939   Land animals from the sea. Regional Review, 3:3, 7 pp., illustr.

LADYGINA-KOTS, N. N.
    1964   [Tool activity of apes and the problem of anthropogenesis.] In:
            Nesturkh, (ed.), 1964C, 136—150, 1 fig., (Russian; English sum-
            mary).

LAEMMELEN, MANFRED
    1960   Die Aufteilung der Hersfelder Gruppe des Mittleren Buntsandsteins.
            Zeit. Deutschen Geol. Ges., 112, 491—512, 3 figs., 1 pl., 3 tables.

LAFOND-GRELLETY, JACQUES
    1963   Les otolithes de l'helvétien de Sallespisse (Basses-Pyrénées). Procès-
            Verbaux, Soc. Linn. Bordeaux, 100, 140—158, 2 pls., 1 table.

LAFOND-GRELLETY, J., and VIGNEAUX, M.
    1964A.   Considérations paléoécologiques sur les otolithes de l'Helvétien de Sal-
             lespisse (Basses-Pyrénées). C. R. Acad. Sci. Paris, 258, 2138—
             2140.
    1964B.   Interprétation stratigraphique des otolithes du Miocène inférieur et
             moyen du bassin aquitain occidental. C. R. Soc. Géol. France,
             1964, 28—30.

LAL, B. B.
    1964A.   India. Asian Perspectives, 7, 27—38, 3 figs., 6 pls.
    1964B.   A decade of prehistoric and protohistoric archaeology in India, 1951—
             1960. Asian Perspectives, 7, 144—159, 6 figs., 6 pls.
    1966   India. Asian Perspectives, 8:1, 76—86, 5 pls.

LAMAKIN, V. V.
1957   [Vladimir Afanas'evich Obruchev — scientist and traveler.]   Izv. Geogr.
        Obshch., 89, 293–307, portr., (Russian).
1961   [Quaternary geology of Baĭkal depression and of its mountain frame.]
        In: Gromov, V. I., et al., (eds.), 1961, 152–165, 1 table, (Rus-
        sian; English summary).
1965   [Fish bones in talus deposits.]   Vestnik nauchn. inform. Zabaĭk. otd.
        Geogr. Obshch., 1965:1, 18–19, (Russian).

LAMARCK, J. B.
1964   Hydrogeology. Translated from the French (Paris, 1802) by Albert V.
        Carozzi. Urbana, Ill.: Univ. Illinois Press, viii + 152 pp., illustr.
        Rev.: Rappaport in Science, 148, 67–68.
        See: Brien 1967.

LAMB, N. P.   See: Hulse and Lamb.

LAMBER, C. KURT   See: Frizzell and Lamber.

LAMBERT, MARJORIE F., and AMBLER, J. R.
1961   A survey and excavation of caves in Hidalgo County, New Mexico.
        Monog. Sch. Amer. Res., Santa Fe, no. 25, xvi + 107 pp., 55
        figs., 21 tables.
        Rev.: Jennings in Amer. Antiq., 31, 586–587;   Schroeber in El Palacio,
        72:4, 38–39.

LAMBRECHT, FRANK L.
1964   Aspects of evolution and ecology of tsetse flies and Trypanosomiasis
        in prehistoric African environment. Jour. Afr. Hist., 5, 1–24,
        5 figs. Also in: Genovés, S., et al., (eds.), 1966, 84–108, with
        comment by Alice M. Brues.
1967   Trypanosomiasis in prehistoric and later human populations, a tentative
        reconstruction. In: Brothwell, Don, and Sandison, A. T., (eds.),
        1967, 132–151, 5 figs.
1968   Notions concerning the evolution of communicable diseases in man.
        S. African Jour. Sci., 64, 64–71, 1 table.

LAMBRECHT, K.
1964   Handbuch der Palaeoornithologie. [Reprint of 1933B.] Berlin: Stechert
        and Hafner, 2 vols.

LAMING, D. J. C.
1965   Age of the New Red Sandstone in South Devonshire. Nature, 207, 624–
        625.

LAMING, ANNETTE (=Laming Emperaire)
1959   Rev.: Davies in NSS News, 17, 73;   Kühn in IPEK, 22, 160–161.
1962   Rev.: [Beltrán] in Caesaraugusta, 23–24, 149–150;   Clark in Proc.
        Prehist. Soc. Cambridge, 30, 433–435;   Comas in An. Antrop.,
        Mexico, 1964, 1, 231–237;   Jordá Cerdá in Zephyrus, 13, 121–
        122;   Kühn in IPEK, 22, 160–161;   Pelichet in Ur-Schweiz,
        28:4, inside back cover.
1963   Rev.: L.-R. N. in Toulouse, Univ., Inst. d'Art Préhist., Trav., 6, 268–269.
1964   Origines de l'archéologie préhistorique en France: des superstitions
        médiévales à la découverte de l'homme fossile. Paris: Picard,
        243 pp., 25 figs.

Rev.: Bibby in Amer. Anthrop., <u>68</u>, 572—573; L.-R. N. in Toulouse,
Univ., Inst. d'Art Préhist., Trav., <u>7</u>, 211—216.
See: Leroi-Gourhan, Bailloud, <u>et</u> <u>al.</u>

LAMMERS, GEORGE E.
1964   Reptile tracks and the paleoenvironment of the Triassic Moenkopi of
Capitol Reef National Monument, Utah. Bull, Mus. No. Ariz.,
no. <u>40</u>, 49—55, 2 figs., cover photo.
1968   The Plio-Pleistocene fauna from the San Pedro Valley, Cochise County,
Arizona. Program, 64th Ann. Meeting, Geol. Soc. Amer., 75,
(abs.).

LAMPEL, GEROLF
1966   Josef Kälin. Säugetierkundl. Mitt., <u>14</u>, 143—144.

LANCASTER, JANE B.   See: Slobin, Lancaster and Diebold.

LANCE, JOHN F.
1965   Zoogeographic significance of capybaras in Arizona. Program, Sect. E
(Geol., Geog.), Amer. Assoc. Advanc, Sci., Meeting Dec. 26—31,
<u>1965</u>, 13, (abs.).
1966   Zoogeographic significance of capybaras in Arizona. Spec. Pap. Geol.
Soc. Amer., <u>87</u>, 313, (abs.).

LANCE, J. F., DOWNEY, J. S., and ALFORD, M.
1962   Cenozoic sedimentary rocks of Tonto Basin. Guidebk., New Mexico
Geol. Soc., 13th Field Confer., <u>1962</u>, 98—99.

LANDMANN, MICHAEL
1965   Der Mensch als Evolutionsglied und Eigentypus. In: Heberer, (ed.),
1965A, 426—443.

LANDRY, STUART O., JR.
1965   The status of the theory of the replacement of the Multituberculata
by the Rodentia. Jour. Mammal., <u>46</u>, 280—286, 2 tables.
1967   Disappearance of multituberculates. Syst. Zool., <u>16</u>, 172—173.

LANE, EDWARD A., and RICHARDS, A. M.
1963   The discovery, exploration and scientific investigation of the Wellington
Caves, New South Wales. Helictite, <u>2</u>, 1—53, 8 pls., 1 map.
Abs.: Nicholas in Internat. Jour. Spel., <u>1</u>, 568.
1966   Hand paintings in caves, with special reference to aboriginal hand sten-
cils from caves on the Nullarbor Plain, southern Australia. Helictite,
<u>4</u>, 33—50, 1 pl.

LANE, N. GARY
1966   New Harmony and pioneer geology. GeoTimes, <u>11</u>:2, 18—20, 22, 3 figs.

LANFRANCO, G. G.
1955   Reptiles, amphibians of the Maltese Islands. Malta Year Book, <u>1955</u>,
198—203, (not seen).

LANG, DAVID MARSHALL
1966   The Georgians. (Vol. 51, Ancient Peoples and Places.) London: Thames
and Hudson, 244 pp., 49 figs., 74 photos, 1 table, 4 maps.

Rev.: Nersessian in Antiq., 41, 319–320.

LANG, JEAN, and LAVOCAT, R.
1968   Première découverte d'une faune de vertébrés dans le tertiaire d'Afgan-
            istan et datation de la série de Bamian. C. R. Acad. Sci. Paris,
            Sci. Nat., 266, 79–82, 2 figs.

LANG, W. D.
1944B.   Report on Dorset natural history, 1943. Geological notes. Proc. Dorset
            Nat. Hist. Archaeol. Soc., 65, 147–149.
1945   Three letters by Mary Anning, "Fossilist," of Lyme. Proc. Dorset Nat.
            Hist. Archaeol. Soc., 66, 169–173.
1950   More about Mary Anning, including a newly-found letter. Proc. Dorset
            Nat. Hist. Archaeol. Soc., 71, 184–188, 1 pl.
1953   Mary Anning and the fire at Lyme. Proc. Dorset Nat. Hist. Archaeol.
            Soc., 74, 175–177.

LANGE, BRIGITTE
1967   Créodontes des Phosphorites du Quercy. Apterodon gaudryi. Ann.
            Pal., Vert., 53, 79–90, 5 figs., 1 table.

LANGE, D. DE   See: Chardin 1962F.

LANGE, SIEGFRIED P.
1968   Zur Morphologie und Taxonomie der Fischgattung Urocles aus Jura und
            Kreide Europas. Palaeontogr., Abt. A, 131:1–4, 1–78, 13 figs.,
            5 pls., 2 tables.

LANGENHEIM, R. L., JR., FROST, S. H., and HEUER, R. E.
1966   Paleocene through Pliocene sequence in the Ixtapa-Soyalo region, Chiapas,
            Mexico. Spec. Pap. Geol. Soc. Amer., 87, 93–94, (abs.).

LANGER, W.
1961   Abs.: Langer in Zbl. Geol. Pal., Teil 2, 1962, 546–547.

LANGSTON, WANN, JR.
1960A.   Rev.: Huene in Zbl. Geol. Pal., Teil 2, 1968, 206.
1963   Abs.: Huene in Zbl. Geol. Pal., Teil 2, 1964, 161.
1965A.   Oedaleops campi (Reptilia: Pelycosauria), new genus and species from
            the Lower Permian of New Mexico, and the family Eothyrididae.
            Bull. Texas Memorial Mus., 9, 1–47, 6 figs., 1 pl.
1965B.   Fossil crocodilians from Colombia and the Cenozoic history of the
            Crocodilia in South America. Univ. Calif. Publ. Geol. Sci., 52,
            vi + 169 pp., 48 figs., 5 pls., (Spanish summary).
            Abs.: Westphal in Zbl. Geol. Pal., Teil 2, 1965, 250.
            Rev.: Estes and Sill in Quart. Rev. Biol., 41, 311–312;   Patterson in
            Copeia, 1965, 392–393.
1965C.   Pre-Cenozoic vertebrate paleontology in Alberta: Its past and future.
            Vert. Pal. in Alberta, Univ. of Alberta, 1965, 9–31, figs. 1–4,
            1 table.
1966A.   Mourasuchus Price, Nettosuchus Langston, and the family Nettosuchidae
            (Reptilia: Crocodilia). Copeia, 1966:4, 882–885, 1 fig.
            Rev.: Huene in Zbl. Geol. Pal., Teil 2, 1968, 206–207.
1966B.   Limnosceloides brachycolis (Reptilia: Captohinomorpha), a new species
            from the Lower Permian of New Mexico. Jour. Pal., 40, 690–
            695, 3 figs.

Rev.: Huene in Zbl. Geol. Pal., Teil 2, <u>1967</u>, 106.

1966C. The Onion Creek mosasaur. Mus. Notes, Texas Mem. Mus., no. <u>10</u>, 24 pp., 7 figs.

1967 The thick-headed ceratopsian dinosaur <u>Pachyrhinosaurus</u> (Reptilia: Ornithischia), from the Edmonton formation near Drumheller, Canada. Canadian Jour. Earth Sci., <u>4</u>, 171—186, 6 figs., 2 pls.

Rev.: Huene in Zbl. Geol. Pal., Teil 2, <u>1968</u>, 207.

1968 A further note on <u>Pachyrhinosaurus</u> (Reptilia: Ceratopsia). Jour. Pal., <u>42</u>, 1303—1304, 1 fig.

See: Hunter and Langston.

LANGSTON, W., and OSCHINSKY, L.

1963 Notes on Taber "early man" site. Anthropologica, n.s. <u>5</u>, 147—150, 1 pl.

LANNING, EDWARD P.

1963B. Archaeology of the Rose Spring site, INY-372. Univ. Calif. Publ. Amer. Archaeol. Ethnol., <u>49</u>, 237—336, 5 figs., 13 pls., 2 maps.

Rev.: Byers in Amer. Antiq., <u>30</u>, 120—122.

1965A. Preceramic archaeology of the Andes. 7th Internat. Congr., Internat. Assoc. Quat. Res., Abs., <u>1965</u>, 281—282, (abs.).

1965B. Early Man in Peru. Sci. Amer., <u>213</u>:4, 68—76, illustr.

1966 Preceramic archaeology of the Andes. Quaternaria, <u>8</u>, 133—138, (French and Spanish summaries).

LANTIER, RAYMOND

1961C. La vie préhistorique. 4th ed. Paris: Presses Universitaires de France Coll. Que sais-je? no. <u>335</u>.

1965 Avec l'abbé Breuil sur les routes d'Espagne. In: Ripoll Perelló, E., (ed.), 1965B, 1—4, (Spanish summary).

See: Breuil and Lantier.

LAPLACE, GEORGES

1962C. Solutréen et foyers solutréens. Essai de typologie analytique sur le phénomène de Solutréanisation. Munibe, <u>14</u>:3/4, 414—455, 2 figs., 2 tables.

1964 Essai de typologie systématique. Ann. Univ. Ferrara, Sez. 15, <u>1</u>: suppl. 2, 85 pp., 8 figs., (Italian and English summaries).

Rev.: Bánesz in Sloven. Archeol., <u>15</u>:1, 260—264.

1965 Le niveau de Châtelperron de la grotte de la Chèvre à Bourdeilles (Dordogne). Analyse typologique et statistique de l'outillage. In: Ripoll Perelló, E., (ed.), 1965B, 5—30, 4 figs., 4 tables, (Italian summary).

1966A. Recherches sur l'origine et l'evolution des complexes leptolithiques. L'École française de Rome, Mélanges d'Archéologie et d'Histoire, Suppléments 4, xii + 586 pp., 8 figs., 23 diagr., 48 pls., (Paris: Boccard).

Rev.: Broglio in Quaternaria, <u>9</u>, 417—418; Delporte in L'Anthrop., <u>71</u>:3—4, 291—301; Delporte in Soc. Préhist. Fr., Bull., C. R., <u>64</u>:7, 199—200; Howell in Amer. Jour. Archaeol., <u>72</u>:3, 289—290; Müller-Beck in Germania, <u>46</u>:2, 335—343; Pittioni in Archaeol. Austriaca, <u>43</u>, 148—149; Sonneville-Bordes in Quartär, <u>18</u>, 233—237; Valoch in Archeol. Roz., <u>20</u>:3, 367—369; Waechter in Man, Jour. Roy. Anthrop. Inst., <u>2</u>, 310.

1966B. Les niveaux Castelperronien, Protoaurignaciens et Aurignaciens de la grotte Gatzarria à Suhare en Pays Basque. Quartär, <u>17</u>, 117—140, 4 figs., 5 tables, (German summary).

1966C.   Études de typologie analytique des complexes leptolithiques de l'Europe
                centrale, I. Les complexes aurignacoïdes de la Basse Autriche.
                II. Les complexes gravettiens de la Basse Autriche-Willendorf II.
                Riv. Sci. Preistor., 21, 61–121 and 303–364.
                See: Broglio, Laplace and Zorzi.

LAPORTE, LÉO F.
    1968   Ancient environments. Englewood Cliffs, N. J.: Prentice-Hall, 116 pp.,
                illustr., (paper).
                Rev.:   Coates in Jour. Pal., 42, 1322–1323;   Heusser in Geog. Rev.,
                59:4, 637–638;   Johnson in Jour. Geol., 77:4, 501.

LAPPARENT, ALBERT F. DE
    1960D.   Los dos dinosaurios de Galve (provincia de Teruel, España). Teruel, no.
                24, 177–197, 11 figs., 3 pls., (French summary).
    1966   Nouveaux gisements de reptiles mésozoiques en Espagne. Notas Comun.
                Inst. Geol. Min., 84, 103–110, 1 fig., (Spanish summary).
                See: Bessonnat, et al.;   Ginsburg, Lapparent, Loiret and Taquet;   Gins-
                burg, Lapparent and Taquet;   Larsonneur and Lapparent.

LAPPARENT, A. F. DE, and BLOT, J.
    1963   Ammonites et poissons dans la partie moyenne du Portlandien du Pays
                de Bray. Ann. Soc. Géol. Nord, 83, 201–202.

LAPPARENT, A. F. DE, LE JONCOUR, M., MATHIEU, A., and PLUS, B.
    1965   Découverte en Espagne d'empreintes de pas de Reptiles mésozoïques.
                Bol. Soc. Españ. Hist. Nat., Sec. Geol., 63:2–3, 225–230, 3 figs.,
                1 pl., (Spanish summary).

LAPPARENT, A. F. DE, and MONTENAT, C.
    1967   Les empreintes de pas de Reptiles de l'Infralias du Veillon (Vendée).
                C. R. Soc. Géol. France, 1967, 33, (abs.).
                Rev.:   Huene in Zbl. Geol. Pal., Teil 2, 1969:4, 328.
    1967B.   Les empreintes de pas de reptiles de l'Infralias du Veillon (Vendée).
                Mém. Soc. Géol. France, 107, 1–41, 18 figs., 13 pls.

LAPPARENT, A. F. DE, MONTENAT, C., and DESPARMET, R.
    1966   Nouvelles pistes de dinosauriens dans l'Infralias de Vendée. C. R. Soc.
                Géol. France, 1966, 20–21, 1 fig.

LAPPARENT, A. F. DE, and OULMI, M.
    1964   Une empreinte de pas de dinosaurien dans le Portlandien de Chassiron
                (île d'Oléron). C. R. Soc. Géol. France, 1964, 232–233, 1 fig.

LAPPARENT, A. F. DE, and STCHEPINSKY, V.
    1968   Les Iguanodons de la région de Saint-Dizier (Haute-Marne). C. R. Acad.
                Sci. Paris, Sci. Nat., 266, 1370–1372.

LARGE, N. F.   See: Savage, R. J. G. and Large.

LARICHEV, V. E.
    1963   [Discovery of Lower Paleolithic in Central Asia.] Vestnik Akad. Nauk
                SSSR, 1963:4, 89–94, 3 figs., (Russian).
    1964A.   [On the problem of local cultures of Lower Paleolithic in East and
                Central Asia.] In: Avrorin, (ed.), 1964, 123–146, 11 figs.,
                2 tables, (Russian).

1964B.   [Most ancient anthropomorphic apes and hominids of South China, and
           their significance in the evolution of East Asiatic man.]   In:
           Avrorin, (ed.), 1964, 190–214, 4 figs., (Russian).

1964C.   [The oldest monuments of Mongolian culture.]   Priroda, 53:4, 94–98,
           illustr., (Russian).

1968A.   [Ways and time of the first settlement of Japan by Paleolithic man.]
           Izv. Sib. Otd. Akad. Nauk SSSR, ser. Obshch. Nauk, 1968:1,
           87–94, (Russian).

1968B.   [A. P. Okladnikov is 60 years old.]   Izv. Sib. Otd. Akad. Nauk SSSR,
           ser. Obshch. Nauk, 11:3, 146–147, portr., (Russian).

           See: Okladnikov and Larichev.

LARICHEV, V. E., and GRIGORENKO, B. G.
    1967   [Discovery of Paleolithic in Korea (Kul'pkho Culture).]   Izv. Sib. Otd.
             Akad. Nauk SSSR, Ser. Obshch. Nauk, 1:1, 98–104, 3 figs.,
             (Russian).

LARICHEV, V. E., and VOLKOV, V. V.
    1964   [Moustierian and Neolithic relics from South Gobi (Solonker-somon,
             Sulat Khereobo).]   In: Avrorin, (ed.), 1964, 147–189, (Russian).

LARICHEVA, I. P.
    1966A.   [North American Paleolithic and the problem of its relationship with
             the Siberian Stone Age.]   Izv. Sib. Otd. Akad. Nauk SSSR, Ser.
             Obshch. Nauk, 5:2, 94–103, 2 figs., (Russian).

    1966B.   [Most ancient relics of North American culture.]   Materialy Ist. Sibiri,
             Drevn. Sibir', 2, 52–74, 9 figs., (Russian).

    1967   [Generalization works in the domain of Paleolithic and Mesolithic of
             North America.]   Izv. Sib. Otd. Akad. Nauk SSSR, Ser. Obshch.
             Nauk, 1:1, 126–130, (Russian).

LARINA, N. I.
    1958   [On the evolutionary significance of geographic changes and on inter-
             specific hybridization among rodents.]   Nauchn. Dokl. Vyssh.
             Shkoly, Biol. Nauki, 1958:4, 37–49, 4 figs., 2 tables, (Russian).

    1965   [Directions of geographical variability of bodily dimensions in homotherm
             animals and conditions of origin and dispersion of species.]   In:
             Shvarts, (ed.), 1965, 97–108, 3 figs., 2 tables, (Russian).

LA RIVERS, IRA
    1962   Fishes and fisheries of Nevada.   Nevada State Fish and Game Commission.
             Carson City: State Printer, 782 pp., 270 figs., 3 color pls.

    1964   A new trout from the Barstovian (Miocene) of western Nevada.   (Iso-
             spondyliformes, Salmonoidei, Salmonidae.)   Occ. Pap. Biol. Soc.
             Nevada, no. 3, 1–4, 1 fig.

    1966   Paleontological miscellanei. I. A new cyprinid fish from the Esmeralda
             (Pliocene) of southeastern Nevada . . . II. A new trout from the
             Esmeralda (Pliocene) of southeastern Nevada . . . III. A new
             frog from the Nevada Pliocene . . . Occ. Pap. Biol. Soc. Nevada,
             no. 11, 1–7, 3 figs.

LA ROCQUE, AURÈLE, (ed.)
    1964A.   1. Biographies of geologists. Vol. 1. Ohio State Univ., Dept. Geol.,
             Contrib. Hist. of Geol., iv + 130 pp., + Suppl. 1, (unpaged),
             Suppl. 2, 27 pp.

1964B.   2. Bibliography of the history of geology. Vol. 2. Ohio State Univ.,
            Dept., Geol., Contrib. Hist. of Geol., 86 + 7 + 11 pp.

1964C.   3. Biographic index. Vol. 3. Ohio State Univ., Dept. Geol., Contrib.
            Hist. of Geol., 217 pp.

LARREA, CARLOS MANUEL
1966   Notas sobre la antigüedad del hombre en el Ecuador y acerca del in-
            forne del Dr. Robert E. Bell de sus excavaciones en "El Inga."
            Humanitas, 6:1, 221–230.

LARSEN, HELGE
1966   James Louis Giddings, Jr., 1909–1964. Amer. Antiq., 31 , 398–401.

LARSONNEUR, CLAUDE
1961-   Faciès, faune et flore du Keuper supérieur–Rhétien dans la région
1962   d'Airel (Manche) (Bordure sud du Bassin de Carentan). Bull.
            Soc. Sci. Nat. Math., Cherbourg, 50, 73–118, 7 figs., 3 pls.,
            (not seen).
1964   Semionotus normannie du Trias supérieur de Basse-Normandie
            (France). Ann. Pal., Vert., 50, 101-117, 4 figs., 2 pls.

LARSONNEUR, C. and LAPPARENT, A. F. de
1966   Un dinosaurien carnivore, Halticosaurus, dans le Rhétien d'Airel
            (Manche). Bull. Soc. Linn. Normandie, 7, 108-117, 5 figs., 2 pls.

LASKER, GABRIEL W.
1959   Recent advances in physical anthropology. In: Siegel, Bernard J., (ed.),
            1959, 1-36.
1961   Rev.: Abbie in Mankind, 6:3, 140–141;   Vincent in Sci. of Man,
            2, 33.
1963B.   The introductory course. In: Mandelbaum, D. G., Lasker, G. W.,
            and Albert, E. M., (eds.), 1963, 99–110.
1963C.   Advanced courses. In: Mandelbaum, D. G., Lasker, G. W., and Albert,
            E. M., (eds.), 1963, 111–121.
1964   (ed.) Physical anthropology 1953-1961. Yearbook Phys. Anthrop., 9,
            322 pp., illustr.
           See: Kelso and Lasker; Mandelbaum, Lasker and Albert.

LATHAM, NYDINE SNOW
1966   Thumbnail sketch. (Leonard C. Bessom.) Quart., Snow Mus. Nat. Sci.,
            1:9, p. 4.

LAUDET, R.   See: Daumas, J.-C. and Laudet.

LAUGHLIN, W. S.
1965   Human migrations and permanent occupation in the Bering Sea area:
            A North American view. 7th Internat. Congr., Internat. Assoc.
            Quat. Res., Abs., 1965, 283, (abs.).
1967   Human migration and permanent occupation in the Bering Sea area.
            In: Hopkins, D. M., (ed.) 1967D, 409-450, 11 figs.
           See: Black, R. F. and Laughlin.

LAUGHLIN, W. S., and AIGNER, J. S.
1966   Preliminary analysis of the Anangula unifacial core and blade industry.

In: Laughlin, W. S., and Reeder, W. G., (eds.), 1966, 41-56, 13 figs.

LAUGHLIN, W. S., and REEDER, W. G., (eds.)
1966   Studies in Aleutian-Kodiak prehistory, ecology and anthropology. Arctic Anthrop., 3:2, 240 pp., illustr.

LAUKHIN, S. A.
1966   [An interesting find of Bison priscus Boj. remains from Chadobets river.] Vestnik Mosk. Univ., ser IV, Geol., 1966:4, 96-97, (Russian).
1967A.   [Mammalian fauna sites and the paleogeography of Chadobets R. basin (northern Angara region) at the end of Pleistocene.] Biull. Kom. Izuch. Chetvert. Perioda, 33, 130-139, 2 figs., (Russian).
1967B.   [Fauna and age of alluvial deposits of the 1-st terrace above flood plain of rivers in the southwestern part of the Siberian Platform.] Biull. Kom. Izuch. Chetvert. Perioda, 34, 140-144, 1 table, (Russian).

LAUKHIN, S. A. and SADIKOVA, M. B.
1966   [On the history of development of Enisei and Angara valleys in the Angara river mouth area.] Vestnik Mosk. Univ., ser. IV, Geol., 1966:3, 67–80, 5 figs., 3 tables, (Russian).

LAUR-BELART, RUDOLF
1956   Theodor Schweizer †. 1893–1956. Ur-Schweiz, 20, 2–5, portr.
1958   Theophil Nigg (1880-1957). Ur-Schweiz, 22, 1-4, fig. 1, portr.
1960   Prof. Dr. Otto Tschumi, 1878-1960. Ur-Schweiz, 24, 45-48, portr.

LAURENT, P.
1964   La tête humaine gravée sur bois de renne de la grotte du Placard (Charente). L'Anthrop., 67, 563-569, 2 figs.
1966   Découvertes récentes de Paléolithique dans le Nord du département du Lot. L'Anthrop., 70:3-4, 255-268, 5 figs.

LAVILLE, HENRI
1964   Recherches sédimentologiques sur le paléoclimatologie du Wurmien récent en Périgord. L'Anthrop., 68, 1–48, 219–252, 25 figs.

LAVOCAT, RENÉ
1961A.*   Le gisement de vertébrés miocènes de Beni Mellal (Maroc). Étude systématique de la faune de mammifères et conclusions générales. Notes Mém. Serv. Géol. Maroc, 155, 29-94 and 109-145, 25 figs., 1 map, 12 pls.
1961C.   [Principaux gisements de Mammifères en] Amérique du Nord. In: Piveteau, J., (ed.), 1961A (Traité de Paléo., 6:1), 484-492, fig. 7.
1964A.   Sur l'importance stratigraphique des rongeurs dans le Paléogène. Mém. Bur. Rech. Géol. Min., 28:2, 977–978.
1964B.   Fossil rodents from Fort Ternan, Kenya. Nature, 202, 1131, 1 fig.
1964C.   On the systematic affinities of the genus Delanymys Hayman. Proc. Linn. Soc. London, 175, 183-185, 1 fig.
1965   Rodentia and Lagomorpha. In: Leakey, et al., 1965, 17–19.
1966   (ed.) Atlas de préhistoire. Vol. III. Faunes et flores préhistoriques de l'Europe occidentale. Preface by J. Piveteau. Paris: Boubée, 486 pp., 64 figs., 137 pls., 33 tables.

Rev.: Alimen in L'Anthrop., 71:1–2, 145–149;   Petter in Mammalia, 30, 691–692;   Ripoll Perelló in Ampurias, 28,
320–321;   Sauter in Arch. Suiss. Anthrop. Gen., 31,
61–62.

1967A.   Observations sur la région auditive des rongeurs théridomorphes. Colloq.
Internat. Cent. Nation. Recherch. Sci., 163, 491-501, 2 figs.,
2 pls., (English summary).

1967B.   Les microfaunes du Néogène d'Afrique orientale et leurs rapports avec
celles de la région paléarctique. Discussion. In: Bishop, W. W.,
and Clark, J. D., (eds.), 1967A, 57-66, 1 fig., (English summary).

1967C.   Les microfaunes du Quaternaire ancien d'Afrique orientale et australe.
Discussion. In: Bishop, W. W., and Clark, J. D., (eds.), 1967A,
67-72, 1 fig., (English summary).

1967D.   A propos de la dentition des rongeurs et du problème de l'origine des
muridés. Mammalia, 31, 205-216.

See: Lang, J. and Lavocat.

LAVOCAT, R., and MICHAUX, J.
1966   Interprétation de la structure dentaire des Rongeurs africains de la
famille des Pédétidés. C. R. Acad. Sci. Paris, Sci. Nat., 262,
1677-1679, 2 figs.
Rev.: Fahlbusch in Zbl. Geol. Pal., Teil 2, 1968, 218.

LAVROV, V. V.
1955   [On the stratigraphic position of Kushuk beds in the Turgaĭ depression.]
Izv. Akad. Nauk Kazakh. SSR, Ser. Geol., 19, 59-65, 1 fig.,
(Russian; Kazakh summary).

1956B.   [Tertiary deposits of northern Kazakhstan.] Izv. Akad. Nauk Kazakh.
SSR, Ser. Geol., 25, 3-19, 1 fig., (Russian; Kazakh summary).

1959   [Continental Paleogene and Neogene of Aralo-Siberian plains.] Alma-
Ata: Akad. Nauk Kazakh. SSR Press, 231 pp., 41 figs., 43
tables, (Russian).

LAVRUSHIN, ĬU. A.
1962   [Stratigraphy and some specific features in the formation of Quaternary deposits in the lower reaches of the river Indigirka.] Izv.
Akad. Nauk SSSR, Ser. Geol., 1962:2, 73–87, 4 figs., 1 table,
(Russian).

1963   [Alluvium of plain rivers in the subarctic belt and in periglacial areas
of continental glaciations.] Trudy Geol. Inst., 87, 266 pp., 97
figs., 15 tables.

See: Arkhipov, et al.

LAWRENCE, BARBARA
1967   Early domestic dogs. Zeit. Säugetierk., 32:1, 44–59, 6 figs., 3 tables.
1968   Antiquity of large dogs in North America. Tebiwa, 11:2, 43-49, 2 figs.,
2 tables.

LAWRENCE, JUDITH ANN   See: Silverberg 1964

LAWRIE, JAMES
1964   Hugh Miller: geologist and man of letters. Proc. Roy. Instn. Gt. Britain, 40, 92-103, 3 pls.

LAWSON, NANCY
1964   'New' fossil man found. Discovery in East Africa of fossils of a primitive human being nearly two million years old resembling modern man may upset basic anthropological theories. Sci. News Letter, 85, 242-244, illustr., cover photo.

LAYNE, JAMES N.
1967   Lagomorphs. In: Anderson, S., and Jones, (eds.), 1967, 192–205, figs. 29-30.

LĂZĂRESCU, V.   See: Panin, Lăzărescu and Grujinschi.

LAZARUS, WILLIAM, FAIRBANKS, C. H., and BULLEN, R.
1965   The Paleo-Indian era: distribution of finds. Florida. Bull. Southeast. Archaeol. Confer., 2, 10-13.

LAZELL, JAMES D., JR.
1965   An Anolis (Sauria, Iguanidae) in amber. Jour. Pal., 39, 379-382, pl. 54.

LAZUKOV, G. I.
1957B.   [Natural environment in Upper Paleolithic of Kostenkovo-Borshev region.] Sov. Arkheol., 1957:3, 84-104, 4 figs., 8 tables, (Russian).
1965   [Quaternary mammalian fauna and man on the territory of the USSR.] In: Markov, et al., 1965B, 258–412, 34 figs., 7 tables, (Russian).
         See: Markov, K. K., Lazukov and Nikalaev.

LAZURKIN, D. V., and OCHEV, V. G.
1968   [First find of sauropterygian remains in the Triassic of the USSR.] Pal. Zhurnal, 1968:2, 141-142, 1 fig., (Russian).

LEAKEY, LOUIS SEYMOUR BAZETT
1960E.   Olduvai Gorge. Cambridge: Cambridge University Press.
1961B.   Rev.: Smolla in Zeit. Ethnol., 89, 124–125; Strouhal in Anthrop., 2:1, 84, (Czech); White in S. Afr. Archaeol. Bull., 19, 48.
1962I.   Man's African origin. Ann. N. Y. Acad. Sci., 96, 495-503, (discussion by Solecki and Buettner-Janusch).
1964A.   Coryndon Museum Centre for Prehistory and Palaeontology. Honorary Director's report. Ann. Rept. Coryndon Mem. Mus., 1963-1964, 30-40.
1964B.   The earliest human link: the skull of a female of the Homo habilis type, compared with a modern African skull. Illustr. London News, 244, 560, 1 fig.
1964C.   The new Olduvai hominid discoveries and their geological and faunal setting. Discussion. Proc. Geol. Soc. London, 1617, 104-109.
1964D.   Gamble's Cave, Kenya. A field museum in a cave. Studies in Spel., 1, 22-25, 1 fig.
1965A.   Honorary director's report. National Museum Centre for prehistory and palaeontology. Ann. Rept. Nairobi Nation. Mus., 1965, 25-31.
1965B.   Facts instead of dogmas on man's origin. Discussion. In: DeVore, P. L., (ed.), 1965, 3-19.
1966A.   Honorary director's report. Centre for prehistory and palaeontology. Ann. Rept. Nairobi Nation. Mus., 1966, 25-34.

1966B.   Homo habilis, Homo erectus and the australopithecines. Nature, 209,
            1279—1281, 6 figs., 1 table.
1966C.   Africa and Pleistocene overkill? Nature, 212, 1615—1616.
1967A.   Centre for prehistory and palaeontology. Ann. Rept. Nairobi Nation.
            Mus., 1967, (for 1966—1967), 25—37.
1967B.   Olduvai. Antiq., 41, 227—228.
1967C.   Notes on the mammalian faunas from the Miocene and Pleistocene of
            East Africa. Discussion. In: Bishop, W. W., and Clark, J. D.,
            (eds.), 1967A, 7—29, 2 tables, (French summary).
1967D.   Editor's note. In: Leakey, L. S. B., et al., 1967A, xv.
1967E.   An Early Miocene member of Hominidae. Nature, 213, 155—163, 6
            figs., 2 tables.
1967F.   Overkill at Olduvai Gorge. Nature, 215, 213.
1968A.   Pleistocene overkill — a criticism. Nat. Hist., 77:1, 73—74.
1968B.   Lower dentition of Kenyapithecus africanus. Nature, 217, 827—830,
            3 figs., 1 table.
1968C.   Upper Miocene primates from Kenya. Nature, 218, 527—528.
1968D.   Bone smashing by Late Miocene Hominidae. Nature, 218, 528—530,
            5 figs.
            See: Anciaux de Faveaux 1962; Fleischer, Leakey, et al.; Napier
            1964A.

LEAKEY, L. S. B., et al.
1965   Olduvai Gorge 1951—61. Vol. 1. A preliminary report on the geology
            and fauna. Foreword by G. G. Simpson. Cambridge: Univ.
            Press, xiv + 118 pp., 2 figs., 97 pls., 1 map., frontis. in color.
            Rev.: Anon. in Scientia, 100, (Libri ricevuti), 101;   Bauer in
            Mitt. Anthrop. Ges. Wien, 95, 355—356;   Boné in Rev. Questions
            Sci., 26, 446—447;   Bourlière in Terre et Vie, 112, 305;   Cole
            in Man, 65, 165;   Cooke in Science, 149, 1361—1362;   Dart in
            S. African Jour. Sci., 61, 226—228;   Davis in Nature, 206, 858—
            859;   R. W. H. in Geol. Mag., 103, 187;   Hemmer in Homo,
            16, 190;   Hendey in S. Afr. Archaeol. Bull., 20:80, 218—219;
            Howell in Amer. Jour. Phys. Anthrop., 23, 314—319;   McBurney
            in Antiq., 41, 73—75;   L. and M. Milne in Quart. Rev. Biol.,
            41, 416—417;   Patterson in Amer. Sci., 53, 334A, 336A;   Pilbeam
            in Proc. Prehist. Soc. Cambridge, 33, 457—462;   Pittioni in Ar-
            chaeol. Austriaca, 38, 107—108;   Robinson in Amer. Anthrop.,
            67, 1588—1589;   Sankalia in E. Anthrop., 21, 106—107;   Shapiro
            in Nat. Hist., 75:3, 19;   R. V. in L'Anthrop., 70:3—4, 352—354.
1967A.   Olduvai Gorge. Volume 2. The cranium and maxillary dentition of
            Australopithecus (Zinjanthropus) boisei, by P. V. Tobias. Fore-
            word by W. E. LeGros Clark. Cambridge: University Press,
            xvi + 264 pp., 39 figs., 42 pls., 49 tables.
1967B.   Kenya. In: Oakley, K. P., and Campbell, B. G., (eds.), 1967A, 21—28.

LEAKEY, L. S. B., EVERNDEN, J. H., and CURTIS, G. H.
1965   Dating by potassium-argon technique. Age of Bed 1, Olduvai Gorge,
            Tanganyika. In: Leakey, et al., 1965, 86—87.

LEAKEY, L. S. B., and LEAKEY, M. D.
1964   Recent discoveries of fossil hominids in Tanganyika: at Olduvai and
            near Lake Natron. Nature, 202, 5—7, 7 figs. Reprint: Current
            Anthrop., 6, 422—424.

LEAKEY, L. S. B., PROTSCH, R., and BERGER, R.
1968   Age of Bed V, Olduvai Gorge, Tanzania. Science, 162, 559—560, 1
            table.

LEAKEY, L. S. B., TOBIAS, P. V., and ISAAC, G. L.
1967   Tanzania. In: Oakley, K. P., and Campbell, B. G., (eds.), 1967A, 105—
            118.

LEAKEY, L. S. B., TOBIAS, P. V., and NAPIER, J. R.
1964   A new species of the genus Homo from Olduvai Gorge. Nature, 202,
            7—9. Reprint: Current Anthrop., 6, 424—427.

LEAKEY, MARY D.
1965   Personnel during the 1960—1 season . . . Descriptive list of the named
            localities in Olduvai Gorge. In: Leakey, et al., 1965, xiv, 101—
            107.
1966A.   A review of the Oldowan culture from Olduvai Gorge, Tanzania. Nature,
            210, 462—466, 1 fig.
1966B.   Primitive artefacts from Kanapoi Valley. Nature, 212, 579—581, 2 figs.,
            1 table.
1967   Preliminary survey of the cultural material from Beds I and II, Olduvai
            Gorge, Tanzania. Discussion. In: Bishop, W. W., and Clark,
            J. D., (eds.), 1967A, 417—446, 5 figs., 1 table, (French sum-
            mary).

LEAKEY, M. D., et al.
1967   Discussions on terminology. In: Bishop, W. W., and Clark, J. D.,
            (eds.), 1967A, 861—875, 1 table.

LEASON, PERCY A.
1938   A new view of Quaternary cave art. Mankind, 2:6, 181.

LEBEDEV, V. D.
1960B.   [Quaternary freshwater ichthyofauna of the European part of the USSR.]
            Moscow: MGU Press, 404 pp., 97 figs., 174 tables, (Russian).

LEBEDEVA, NATAL'IÂ ALEKSEEVNA
1961   [Stratigraphy of Neogene-Quaternary deposits of Kuban' foredeep.] In:
            Gromov, V. I., et al., (eds.), 1961, 117—128, (Russian; English
            summary).
1963   [Continental Anthropogene deposits of the Azov-Kuban' depression
            and their relation to marine strata.] Trudy Geol. Inst., 84, 105
            pp., 29 figs., 1 table, (Russian).
1965   [Geological conditions of occurrence of small mammals in Azov sea
            region Anthropogene.] In: Nikiforova, (ed.), 1965B, 111—140,
            8 figs., (Russian; English summary).
1966   [The position of Tamanian and Tiraspolian mammalian complexes in
            the section of marine sediments of Azov region.] Doklady Akad.
            Nauk SSSR, 171:3, 686—689, 1 fig., (Russian).

LEBEDKINA, N. S.
1964A.   [Development of nasal bones in caudate amphibians.] Doklady Akad.
            Nauk SSSR, 159:1, 219—222, 3 figs., (Russian).
1964B.   [The development of the dermal bones of the basement of the skull
            in Urodela (Hynobiidae).] Trudy Zool. Inst. Akad. Nauk SSSR,
            33, 75—172, 40 figs., 6 tables, (Russian).

LEBEUF, JEAN-PAUL
    1964   Prehistory, protohistory and history of Chad. Transl. by C. L. Patterson.
                Proc. 1st Internat. Congr. Africanists, 1962, 72—81.

LECOINTRE, G.
    1965   Le Quaternaire marin de l'Afrique du nord-ouest. Quaternaria, 7, 9—28,
                6 tables, (Italian and English summaries).

LeDANOIS, EDOUARD, and LeDANOIS, Y.
    1963   L'Ordre des Scombres. Mem. Inst. Franç. Afr. Noire, no. 68, 153—192,
                19 figs.

LeDANOIS, YSEULT
    1966   Remarques anatomiques sur la région céphalique de Gonorhynchus
                gonorhynchus (Linné, 1766). Bull. Inst. Franç. Afr. Noire, Ser.
                A, 28, 283—342, 33 figs.

LEDOUX, JEAN-CLAUDE   See: Cappetta, Granier and Ledoux.

LEDOUX, J. C., HARTENBERGER, J.-L., MICHAUX, J., SUDRE, J., and THALER, L.
    1966   Découverte d'un Mammifère dans le Crétacé supérieur à dinosaures de
                Champ-Garimond près de Fons (Gard). C. R. Acad. Sci. Paris,
                Sci. Nat., 262, 1925—1928, 2 figs.

LEE, MERLIN RAYMOND
    1960   Montane mammals of southeastern Utah, with emphasis on the effects
                of past climates upon occurrence and differentiation. Diss. Abst.,
                20, 4759—4766, (abs.).

LEE, R. B.
    1963   Rev.: Vaufrey in L'Anthrop., 68, 418—419.

LEE, THOMAS E.
    1963B.   Dr. George Carter. Anthrop. Jour. Canada, 1:2, 2, portr.
    1963C.   Daniel W. Josselyn. Anthrop. Jour. Canada, 1:2, 16, portr.
    1964A.   Sheguiandah: workshop or habitation? Anthrop. Jour. Canada, 2:3,
                16—24, 3 figs.
    1964B.   Early man in Canada. New World Antiq., 11, 54—70.
    1965   An unfluted Cumberland (Beaver Lake) point. Anthrop. Jour. Canada,
                3:3, 38, 1 fig.
    1966   Archaeological traces at Fort Chimo, Quebec, 1964. Anthrop. Jour.
                Canada, 4:1, 33—44, 2 figs.

LEE, YU-CHING   See: Chow, M., Hu and Lee.

LEEPER, G. W., (ed.)
    1962   Rev.: Roth-Lutra in Anat. Anz., 116, 306—307.

LEES, PATRICIA M.
    1964   A flotation method of obtaining mammal teeth from Mesozoic bone-
                beds. Curator, 7, 300—306, 2 figs.
                See: Kermack, K. A., Lees and Mussett.

LEFELD, J.
    1965   The age of mammal containing beds at Bain-Dzak northern Gobi Desert.
                Bull. Acad. polon. sci. ser. sci. biol., 13, 81—83, 1 fig.

LEFFLER, SANFORD R.
1964   Fossil mammals from the Elk River formation, Cape Blanco, Oregon.
              Jour. Mammal., 45, 53–61, 2 figs.

LE GALLIC, G. P.
1964   Application des lois générales de la paléontologie aux types australopithèque
              et oréopithèque. Bull. Mém. Soc. Anthrop., ser. 11, 6, 477–492.

LEGOUX, P.
1966   Détermination de l'âge dentaire de fossiles de la lignée humaine. Paris:
              Librairie Maloine S. A., 306 pp., illustr., 85 tables.
              Rev.: Billy in L'Anthrop., 71:3–4, 312–313;   Krogman in Amer.
              Jour. Phys. Anthrop., 25, 100.

LEHMAN, JEAN-PIERRE
1961A.   Abs.: Huene in Zbl. Geol. Pal., Teil 2, 1964, 161–162.
1962A.   Rev.: M. C. P. in Fossilia, 1965:2, 44.
1962D.   (ed.) Rev.: Glaessner in Austral. Jour. Sci., 27, 269–270;   Dietrich
              in Zbl. Geol. Pal., Teil 2, 1964, 136–137;   Musil in Čas. Min.
              Geol., 10, 192.
1963B.   A propos de quelques Arthrodires et Ichthyodorulites sahariens. Mem.
              Inst. Franç. Afr. Noire, no. 68, 193–200, 2 figs., 5 pls.
1964A.   Etude d'un saurichthyidé de la région d'Oden (Espagne). Ann. Pal.,
              Vert., 50, 23–30, 1 pl.
1964B.   Les techniques en paléontologie des vertébrés. In: Piveteau, (ed.),
              1964C, (Traité de Paléo., 4:1), 46–77, 17 figs.
1964C.   L'origine des vertébrés. Le milieu des premiers vertébrés. In: Piveteau,
              (ed.), 1964C (Traité de Paléo., 4:1), 78–91, 8 figs.
1965   Les progrès récents de la paleontologie des vertébrés du Trias au sud
              de la Méditerranée. Israel Jour. Zool., 14, 173–184, (English
              summary).
1966A.   Nouveaux stégocéphales de Madagscar. Ann. Pal., Vert., 52, 115–139,
              9 figs., 6 pls.
              Rev.: Westphal in Zbl. Geol. Pal., Teil 2, 1967, 102.
1966B.   Actinopterygii. In: Piveteau, (ed.), 1966B (Traité de Paléo., 4:3), 1–242,
              211 figs., 9 pls.
1966C.   Dipnoi et Crossopterygii. In: Piveteau, (ed.), 1966B (Traité de Paléo.,
              4:3), 243–387, 398–412, 126 figs., pls. 10–11.
1966D.   Brachiopterygii. In: Piveteau, (ed.), 1966B (Traité de Paléo., 4:3),
              413–420, 4 figs.
1966E.   L'origine des membres des Vertébrés terrestres. La Nature, no. 3369,
              24–25, 2 figs.
1967A.   Remarques concernant l'évolution des labyrinthodontes. Colloq. Internat.
              Cent. Nation. Recherch. Sci., 163, 215–222, 4 figs., (English
              summary).
              Rev.: Westphal in Zbl. Geol. Pal., Teil 2, 1969:1, 51.
1967B.   Quelques remarques concernant Drepanaspis gemuendenensis Schlüter.
              In: Patterson, C., and Greenwood, P. H., (eds.), 1967, 39–43,
              2 figs., 3 pls., (English summary).
1967C.   Quelques réflexions à propos de l'évolution. L'Ann. Biol., 6, 537–544.
1968   Compte rendu de la séance consacrée à la paléontologie des Vertébrés
              (2 décembre 1968). C. R. Soc. Géol. France, 1968:9, 289–292.
            See: Stensiö 1964.

LEHMANN, ERNST VON
   1967   Fund eines Stangenfragmentes von <u>Cervus</u> (<u>Eucladocerus</u>) <u>ctenoides</u>
             Nesti, 1841 bei Bergheim/Erft. Zeit. Säugetierk., <u>32</u>:3, 182–185,
             2 figs., 1 table.

LEHMANN, ULRICH
   1964   Paläontologisches Wörterbuch. Stuttgart: Enke, iv + 335 pp., 102 figs.,
             3 pls., (not seen).
             Rev.: Anon. in Umschau, <u>66</u>:5, 170–171;   Haltenorth in Säugetier-
             kundl. Mitt., <u>14</u>, 151;   Jaeger in Geologie, <u>16</u>:10, 1183–1184;
             Kullmann in Zbl. Geol. Pal., Teil 2, <u>1968</u>, 9;   Lazar in Ber.
             Geol. Ges. Deutsch. Demokratischen Republ., <u>10</u>, 387–388;
             Martinsson in Geol. Fören. Förh., <u>87</u>, 171;   Reinig in Kosmos,
             <u>61</u>, *106;   Shimanskiĭ in Pal. Zhurnal, <u>1967</u>:2, 135–136, (Rus-
             sian);   Sittig in Aufschluss, <u>15</u>, 340–341;   Staesche in Jahresh.
             Ver. Vaterland. Naturk. Württemberg, <u>120</u>, 305–306;   Struve
             in Natur u. Mus., <u>94</u>, 531;   Teichert in Jour. Pal., <u>41</u>, 272–273;
             Thenius in Mitt. Geol. Ges. Wien, <u>57</u>, 657–658;   Westphal in
             Naturwiss. Rund., <u>18</u>, 124;   Zapfe in Die Höhle, <u>16</u>, 28–29.
   1966   Die Boviden. In: Ehrenberg, (ed.), 1966A, 83–88, 1 pl.
             Rev.: Hünermann in Zbl. Geol. Pal., Teil 2, <u>1967</u>, 122.

LEHNER, ROBERT E.
   1962   Cenozoic history of the Jerome region, Yavapai County, Arizona.
             Guidebk., New Mexico Geol. Soc., 13th Field Confer., <u>1962</u>, 94–97,
             1 fig.

LEICH, HELMUT
   1964A.   Ein <u>Rhamphorhynchus</u>-Rest mit wohlerhaltener Flughaut. Aufschluss,
             <u>15</u>, 41–43, 4 figs.
   1964B.   Aus den Sammlungen unserer Mitglieder: <u>Belonostomus</u> <u>tenuirostris</u> Ag.
             Aufschluss, <u>15</u>, 169, 1 fig.
   1965   Zu den Sammlungen im Solnhofener Plattenkalkgebiet. Aufschluss, <u>16</u>,
             320.

LEIGHLY, JOHN (ed.)
   1963   Land and life: a selection from the writings of Carl Ortwin Sauer.
             Berkeley and Los Angeles: Univ. of California Press, vi + 435 pp.,
             portr., 7 maps and figs.
             Rev.: Carter in Quart. Rev. Biol., <u>39</u>, 118;   Cornwall in Man, <u>65</u>,
             168–169;   Evans in Geog. Rev., <u>54</u>, 596–597;   Jackson in
             Science, <u>143</u>, 945;   Jones in Amer. Antiq., <u>30</u>, 369–370.

LEJARDS, J.
   1965   Contribution à l'étude du Paléolithique inférieur et moyen dans le Nord-
             Agenais (région comprise entre le Lot et la Dordogne). Bull.
             Soc. Préhist. Franç., Étud. et Trav., <u>62</u>:1, 77–83, 4 figs.

LeJONCOUR, MICHEL   See: Lapparent, LeJoncour, <u>et</u> <u>al.</u>

LEMON, R. R. H.
   1965   Fossils in Ontario. Roy. Ontario Mus. Ser., no. <u>4</u>, 16 pp., illustr.

LENGYEL, IMRE
   1964   Contribution à l'analyse histologique, sérologique et chimique combinée
             des os et des dents en archéologie. Bull. Groupement Internat.
             Rech. Sci. Stomatol., <u>7</u>, 182–206, 7 figs., 1 table, (English and
             German summaries).

LEONARDI, A.
1966   L'ittiofauna cenomaniana di Floresta-Messina. Palaeontogr. Ital., 60,
            33—67, pls. 10—15, (English summary).
            Rev.: Weiler in Zbl. Geol. Pal., Teil 2, 1967, 497—499.

LEONARDI, PIERO
1956G.   Il Paleolitico dell'Italia Padana. Atti I. Conv. Interr. Padano Paletnol.,
            13—40, (not seen).
1957F.   La evolución biológica. Adaptación y prólogo de Bermudo Meléndez.
            Madrid: Ediciones Fax, 405 pp., (not seen).
1958   Sulle grotte con industria gravettiana dei Colli Berici. Atti. VIII Congr.
            Naz. Spel., 4, (not seen).
1959G.   Una lettera inedita di Carlo Darwin. Ann. Univ. Ferrara (n.s.), Sez.
            9, Sci. Geol. Pal., 3:4, 71—74, 1 fig., (French, English, and
            German summaries).
1961A.   (ed.) L'evoluzione. Venezia: San Giorgio Maggiori, 3, 16/17, 1959,
            xii + 165 pp.
1961B.   Nuove scoperte e nuevi problemi di paleontologia umana. In: Leonardi,
            P., (ed.), 1961A, 105—165, with discussion.
1963A.   Il Paleolitico nel versante meridionale della Alpi. Rend. Soc. Cult.
            Preistor. Trentina, no. 1, 62—85, 16 figs.
1963B.   Il contributo dei Veneti alla conoscenza della preistoria e protostoria
            delle Venezie. Studi Etruschi, 31, 331—350.
1964   Giorgio Dal Piaz [1872 - 1962]. Bull. Soc. Geol. Ital., 38:3, 19—30,
            portr.
            See: Broglio and Leonardi.

LEONARDI, P., ALLEGRANZI, A., and BROGLIO, A.
1965   Grotta del Broion (Colli Berici, Prov. di Vicenza). Riparo del Prunno
            (Altopiano di Asiago, Prov. di Vicenza). Riv. Sci. Preist., 19,
            296—297.

LEONARDI, P., ANNIBALDI, G., BROGLIO, A., and BARTOLOMEI, G.
1965   Monte Conero (Prov. di Ancona). Riv. Sci. Preist., 19, 298.

LEONARDI, P., BARTOLOMEI, G., and BROGLIO, A.
1965   Grotta Minore di San Bernardino (Colli Berici, Prov. di Vicenza). Riv.
            Sci. Preist., 19, 296—297.

LEONARDI, P., and BROGLIO, A.
1962A.   Rev.: Anon. in Acta Praehist., 1966, 5—7, 308—309; Ehrenberg in
            Die Höhle, 14, 27—28.
1963B.   Il deposito della Grotta del Broion. Atti IX Congr. Naz. Spel., 1963,
            1—12 (of separate), 11 figs.
1965   Il Paleolitico del Veneto. In: Ripoll Perelló, E., (ed.), 1965B, 31—73,
            33 figs., (Spanish summary).

LEONARDI, P., BROGLIO, A., and BOSELLINI, A.
1964   Nuovi contributi alla conoscenza del Paleolitico inferiore e medio delle
            marche. Emilia Preroma, no. 5, 93—106, 9 figs.

LEONHARDY, FRANK C.
1964   Lake Ellsworth mammoth discovery. Newsletter Okla. Anthrop. Soc.,
            12:5, 2.
1965   New radiocarbon dates for the Domebo site. Newsletter Okla. Anthrop.
            Soc., 13:6, 2.

1966A. (ed.) Domebo: A Paleo-Indian mammoth kill in the Prairie-Plains.
Contrib. Mus. Great Plains, Okla., 1, x + 53 pp., 36 figs., 2 tables.
Rev.: Anon. in Southwestern Lore, 32, 88; Biberson in L'Anthrop.,
72:3—4, 358—359; Bottoms in Chesopiean, 4:5—6, 136—137;
Irwin-Williams in Amer. Antiq., 32, 406—407; Martin in Science,
154, 1635; KV in Archeol. Roz., 22:3, 363.

1966B. Late Pleistocene research at Domebo: a summary and interpretation.
In: Leonhardy, (ed.), 1966A, 51—53.
Abs.: Anon. in Plains Anthrop., 11, 168—169.

LEONHARDY, F. C., and ANDERSON, A. D.
1966 The archaeology of the Domebo site. In: Leonhardy, (ed.), 1966A,
14—26, 13 figs.

LEONOV, B. N. See: Galabala and Leonov.

LEONOV, N. I. See: Okladnikov and Leonov.

LÉON-PORTILLA, MIGUEL, et al.
1965 Homenaje a Juan Comas en su 65 aniversario. 2 vols. Mexico, D. F.:
Instituto Indigenista Interamericano, (not seen).
Rev.: Clegg in Man, Jour. Roy. Anthrop. Inst., 1, 434—435.

LEONT'EV, L. N.
1956 [A short geological sketch of Tuva.] Trudy Tuvin. Kompl. Eksp., 4,
80 pp., 17 figs., (Russian).

LE PAIGE, GUSTAVO
1964 The preceramic in the Cordillera of Atacama and the cemeteries of the
Ceramic-Agricultural Period of San Pedro de Atacama. An. Univ.
Norte, no. 3, 275 pp., 160 pls., (not seen).

LEPERSONNE, J. See: Hooijer 1963D.

LERMAN, ABRAHAM
1965 On rates of evolution of unit characters and character complexes.
Evolution, 19, 16—25, 3 figs., 3 tables.

LEROI-GOURHAN, ANDRÉ
1961B. Préhistoire. In: Devambez, P., (ed.), 1961, 1—92, 35 pls.
1962B. Sociétés primitives. In: Daumas, M., (ed.), 1962, 9—53, figs. 1—21,
pls. 1—4.
1964A. Le site magdalénien de Pincevent (Seine-et-Marne). Bull. Assoc. Franç.
Étude Quat., 1, 59—64, 2 figs.
1964B. Le site préhistorique de Pincevent (Varennes-sur-Seine, Seine-et-Marne).
Bull. Soc. Préhist. Franç., C. R. séances mens., 1964:5, cix—cx,
(discussion).
1964C. Découvertes paléolithiques en Élide. Bull. Correspondence Hellén., 88,
1—8, 5 figs.
1964D. Le geste et la parole. Technique et langage. Paris: Albin Michel,
323 pp., 105 figs.
Rev.: Kennedy in Amer. Anthrop., 67, 1337—1338; Millot in Objets
et Mondes, 5, 61; Valoch in Archeol. Roz., 18:5, 604—605,
(Czech).
1964E. Les religions de la préhistoire (Paleolithique). Paris: Presses Universitaires de France, 154 pp., illustr.

Rev.: Anon. in Bull. Soc. Préhist. Franç., C. R. séances mens., 1964:7, clxiii; Jorda Cerdá in Zephyrus, 15, 147—150; Kühn in IPEK, 22, 159; Laming-Emperaire in Amer. Anthrop., 68, 573—574; Sauter in Arch. Suiss. Anthrop. Gen., 29, 65—68; G. V. in Spelunca, Bull., 5:4, 72—73; Valoch in Archeol. Roz., 18:5, 605—606, (Czech).

1965A. Sur les formes primaires de l'outil. Basler Beiträg Geog. Ethnol., Ethnol. Reihe, 2, 257—262.

1965B. Le Châtelperronien: probleme ethnologique. In: Ripoll Perelló, E., (ed.), 1965B, 75—81, (Spanish summary).

1965C. Préhistoire de l'art occidental. Paris: Mazenod, 483 pp., 700 figs. incl. 120 in color.

Rev.: Anon. in Caesaragusta, 25—26, 141—144; Banesz in Sloven. Archeol., 14:1, 229—231, (Slovakian); Camps in Libyca, 13, 392—394; Clark in Proc. Prehist. Soc. Cambridge, 31, 382—384; Frolov in Sov. Arkheol., 1966:3, 269—275, (Russian); Jorda Cerdá in Zephyrus, 16, 157—158; Laming-Emperaire in Bull. Soc. Préhist. Franç., C. R. séances mens., 63, 193—199; Levine in Amer. Anthrop., 68, 1568—1572; Millot in Objets et Mondes, 5, 207; L.-R. N. in Toulouse, Univ., Inst. d'Art Préhist., Trav., 7, 225—226; Nieuwenhoven in Natuurhist. Maandbl., 55, 3—5, (Dutch); Ucko in Man, Jour. Roy. Anthrop. Inst., 1, 563—564; R. V. in L'Anthrop., 69:5—6, 541—545; Vila in Spelunca, Bull., 5:3, 66—67; Zotz in Quartär, 17, 203—207.

1965D. Le geste et la parole. La mémoire et les rythmes. Paris: Albin Michel, 285 pp., 153 figs.

Rev.: Anon. in Scientia, 100 (Libri ricevuti), 123; Sauter in Arch. Suiss. Anthrop. Gen., 31, 54—55; Thiry in Rev. Questions Sci., 26, 456.

1966 Réflexions de méthode sur l'art paléolithique. Bull. Soc. Préhist. Franç., Étud. et Trav., 63:1, 35—49.

1967 Treasures of prehistoric art. New York: Abrams, 544 pp., illustr.

Rev.: Britt in Ohio Archaeol., 18, 71; Goldman in Nat. Hist., 77:3, 71—72, 1 fig.; Levine in Science, 161, 150—152.

1968A. The art of prehistoric man in western Europe. London: Thames and Hudson, 543 pp., 739 figs., 56 charts, (not seen).

Rev.: Coles in Antiq., 42, 152—155.

1968B. The evolution of Paleolithic art. Sci. Amer., 218:2, 58—70, illustr.

Rev.: Anon. in Interamer., 15:2, 8.

LEROI-GOURHAN, A., BAILLOUD, G., CHAVAILLON, J., LAMING-EMPERAIRE, A., et al.

1966 La Préhistoire. Paris: Presses Universitaires de France, 366 pp., 54 figs., tables.

Rev.: Anon. in Amer. Anthrop., 70, 808; De Laet in Helinium, 7, 276—277; Fujimoto in Jour. Archaeol. Soc. Nippon, 52:2, 61—66; Furon in Rev. Gén. Sci., 73, 255; Kühn in IPEK, 22, 156; Sauter in Arch. Suiss. Anthrop. Gen., 31, 62—63; Valoch in Archeol. Roz., 19, 275—276; Vila in Spelunca, Bull., 6:2, 149—150.

LEROI-GOURHAN, A., and CHAVAILLON, J. and N.

1963A. Paleolithique du Péloponese. Bull. Soc. Préhist., Paris, 60, 249—265, 5 figs.

1963B. Premiers résultats d'une prospection de divers sites préhistoriques en Élide occidentale. Ann. Géol. Pays Hellén., 14, 324—329, pls. 35—37.

LEROI-GOURHAN, ARLETTE
1961B.   Analyse pollinique de la grotte de Shanidar. Internat. Assoc. Quat.
                    Res., Abs. Pap., 6th Congr., 141–142, (abs.).
                    See: Solecki and Leroi-Gourhan.

LEROI-GOURHAN, A., and LEROI-GOURHAN, A.
1964   Chronologie des grottes d'Arcy-sur-Cure (Yonne). Gallia-Préhist., 7, 1–
                    64, 28 figs.
                    Rev.: Sonneville-Bordes in L'Anthrop., 70:1–2, 139–141.

LEROY, JEAN F.
1966   Charles Darwin et la théorie moderne de l'évolution. Paris: Éditions
                    Seghers, 209 pp., 16 pls., (not seen).
                    Rev.: Furon in Rev. Gén. Sci., 73, 374.

LEROY, PIERRE
1965   L'Institut de Géobiologie à Pékin, 1940–1946. Les dernières années
                    du P. Teilhard de Chardin en Chine. L'Anthrop., 69, 360–367.

LESLIE, VERNON
1963   Rev.: Josselyn in Anthrop. Jour. Canada, 2:4, 28.
1964A.   The Palaeo and the Archaic in the Upper Delaware Valley. Chesopiean,
                    2:4, 69–85, 8 pls.
1964B.   Some problems of the Pre-Archaic. New World Antiq., 11, 2–15.
                    See: Wilkison and Leslie.

LESLIE, V., and SYKES, E.
1964   Arthur George Smith, M. Arch., F. I. I. [1891-1964]. New World
                    Antiq., 11, 129.

LESSERTISSEUR, JACQUES
1961   La paléontologie et les trois images de l'anthropogénèse. Bull. Trimestriel
                    Dept. Serv. Inform. Géol., France, no. 51, 6–10.
1967   L'angle ilio-sacré des reptiles aux mammifères, son interpretation, son
                    intérêt paléontologique. Colloq. Internat. Cent. Nation. Recherch.
                    Sci., 163, 475–481, 4 figs. 1 pl., 1 table, (German summary).
                    See: Jouffroy and Lessertisseur.

LESSERTISSEUR, J., and SABAN, R.
1967A.   Généralités sur le squelette. In: Grassé, (ed.), 1967 (Traité de Zool.,
                    16:1), 334–404, figs. 147–206, 8 tables.
1967B.   Squelette axial. In: Grassé, (ed.), 1967 (Traité de Zool., 16:1), 584–
                    708, figs. 328–464, 6 tables.
1967C.   Squelette appendiculaire. In: Grassé, (ed.), 1967 (Traité de Zool.,
                    16:1), 709–1078, figs. 465–851, 15 tables.

LESSERTISSEUR, J., and SIGOGNEAU, D.
1965   Sur l'acquisition des principales caractéristiques du squelette des Mam-
                    mifères. Mammalia, 29, 95–168, 35 figs., pls. 8–11, (English
                    and German summaries).
                    Rev.: M. C. in Fossilia, 1965:5–6, 67.

LETTICK, BIRNEY   See: Pfeiffer 1966.

LEVENKO, A. I.
1960   [Devonian of Central and South Tuva.] Moscow: Akad. Nauk Press,
            158 pp., 34 figs., 5 tables, (Russian).
1967   [Materials for stratigraphy of Devonian deposits of the Tuva Basin.]
            In: Sokolov, B.S., (ed.), 1967, 148—150, (Russian).

LEVIN, BETSY   See: Ives, Levin, Oman and Rubin; Ives, Levin, Robinson and
                    Rubin.

LEVIN, B., IVES, P. C., OMAN, C. L., and RUBIN, M.
1965   U. S. Geological Survey radiocarbon dates VIII. Radiocarbon, $\underline{7}$, 372—
            398.

LEVIN, M. G.
1960   [Sketches on the history of anthropology in Russia.] Moscow: Akad.
            Nauk SSSR Press, 176 pp., (Russian).
            Rev.: Adler and Schwidetzky in Homo, $\underline{16}$, 60.
            See: Roginskiĭ and Levin.

LEVIN, M. G., and POTAPOV, L. P., (eds.)
1964   The peoples of Siberia. Chicago and London: Univ. Chicago Press, viii +
            948 pp., illustr., 1 fold-out map.
            Rev.: Dunn in Amer. Anthrop., $\underline{68}$, 519—521; Fischer in Anthrop. Anz., $\underline{27}$,
            238—239; Piggott in Antiq., $\underline{39}$, 235—236.

LEVIN, V. N.
1967   [The comparative anatomy of aural bones of primates.] Voprosy
            Anthrop., $\underline{27}$, 152—159, 10 figs., 5 tables, (Russian).

LEVORSEN, A. I.
1964   Vertress Lawrence Vander Hoof (1904—1964). Bull. Amer. Assoc.
            Petrol. Geolog., $\underline{48}$, 1954—1955, portr.

LEVORSEN, JAMES K.   See: Takeuchi, et al.

LEWIS, A. B.   See: Garn, Lewis and Kerewsky.

LEWIS, GEORGE EDWARD
1964A.   Barnum Brown (1873—1963). Bull. Amer. Assoc. Petrol. Geolog., $\underline{48}$,
            1595—1597.
1964B.   Memorial to Barnum Brown (1873—1963). Bull. Geol. Soc. Amer.,
            $\underline{75}$:2, pp. P19—P28, portr.
1964C.   Miocene vertebrates of the Barstow formation in Southern California.
            U. S. Geol. Surv. Prof. Pap. $\underline{475—D}$, 18—23.
1966   American Tritylodontidae from the Kayenta formation of Arizona.
            Spec. Pap. Geol. Soc. Amer., $\underline{87}$, 96—97, (abs.)

LEWIS, G. E., and VAUGHN, P. P.
1965   Early Permian vertebrates from the Cutler formation of the Placerville
            area, Colorado. With a section on footprints from the Cutler
            formation by Donald Baird. U. S. Geol. Surv. Prof. Pap., $\underline{503C}$,
            pp. i—iv, C1—C50, 14 figs., 1 table.
            Abs.: Westphal in Zbl. Geol. Pal., Teil 2, $\underline{1966}$, 264.

LEWIS, O. J.
1964 The homologies of the mammalian tarsal bones. Jour. Anat., 98, 195–208, 4 figs.

LHOTE, HENRI
1963B. The fertile Sahara: Men, animals and art of a lost world. In: Bacon, E., (ed.), 1963, 11–32, illustr.

LI, CHIA-LIN See: Ting, M.-L., et al.

LI, CHUAN-KUEI
1965 Eocene leporids of North China. Vert. Palasiatica, 9, 23–36, 1 pl., 1 table, (Chinese and English).
 See: Chow, M. and Li.

LI, C.-K., and CHI, T.
1964 Pontian mammals of Wenquan, Sinkiang. Vert. Palasiatica, 8, 288–300, 2 pls., (Chinese; English summary).

LI, TSAI-WAN, and HUANG, E.-B.
1966 [Finding of fossil fishes in the Middle Silurian of northwestern part of Kiang Si Province.] Ti chih lun-ping, 24:2, 159, (Chinese).

LI, YIU-HENG See: Pei and Li.

LI, Y.-H., HAN, D.-F., and HSU, C.-H.
1966 Preliminary observation on some coprolites from Choukoutien. Vert. Palasiatica, 10, 73–81, 4 figs., 2 pls., (Chinese; English summary).

LIANG, C. T.
1960 An observation on the stone implements of Hsichiaoshan, Kwangtung. Paleovert. et Paleoanthrop., 2:1, 63, (not seen).

LIARSKAIA, L. A.
1966 [On the problem of the limit between Middle and Upper Devonian in Latvia.] Pal. i Strat. Pribalt. Belorus., 1, 281–286, 1 fig., (Russian; English summary).
1967 [Biofacies zoning of Late Narovian, Arukiulian, and Burtniekian time on Latvian territory.] In: Collected Papers, 1967E (Problems of geology of Middle and Upper Paleozoic of Baltic regions], 26–35, (Russian).

LIBBY, W. F. See: Berger, R., Fergusson and Libby; Berger, R., Horney and Libby; Berger, R. and Libby; Fergusson and Libby.

LIEBUS, ADALBERT
1930B. Neue Schildkrötenreste aus den tertiärn Süsswassertonen von Preschen bei Bilin in Böhmen. Rozp. Stát. Geol. Ceskosl. Republ. (later changed to: Roz. Ustred. Ustav. Geol.), 4, 57 pp., 1 fig., 4 pls., (German and Czech).

LIEM, KAREL F.
1963 The comparative osteology and phylogeny of the Anabantoidei (Teleostei, Pisces). Ill. Biol. Monog., no. 30, 149 pp., 104 figs.

LIEPIŅSH, P. (=Liepiņ's)
1964   [On the unified subregional scheme of Devonian stratigraphy of the
            North-East of Russian Platform.]   Latv. PSR Zinat. Akad. Vestis,
            1964:1, 21—26, 1 fig., (Russian; German summary).
1966   [Some traits of fauna and flora ecology of Devonian basins in the
            eastern part of the Main Devonian Field.]   In: Gekker, (ed.),
            1966, 129—135, 1 fig., 1 table, (Russian).

LIERL, HANS JÜRGEN
1964   Aus den Sammlungen unserer Mitglieder: Leptolepis? knorri Blainv.
            Aufschluss, 15, 308, 1 fig.
1965   Museen im Solnhofener Plattenkalkgebiet. Comment by Leich. Auf-
            schluss, 16, 225—229, 6 figs., 320.

LIFE, EDITORS
1963   Het epos van de Mens. Netherland ed. by G. Messelaar. Amsterdam,
            Brussel: Elsevier, 308 pp., 300 photos, 59 color pls.
            Rev.: K. in Natuurhist. Maandbl., 53, 28.

LIGERON, J.-M.
1965   Faune quaternaire du Departement des Ardennes. Le Bos brachyceros.
            Bull. Soc. Hist. Nat. Ardennes, 54, 75.

LIGON, J. DAVID
1965   A Pleistocene avifauna from Haile, Florida. Bull. Florida State Mus.,
            Biol. Sci., 10:4, 127—158, 3 figs., 5 tables.
            Rev.: Kuhn in Zbl. Geol. Pal., Teil 2, 1967, 108.

LIKHAREV, B. K., (ed.)
1966   [The Permian system.] In: Nalivkin, (ed.), 1963, [vol. 5], 536 pp.,
            62 figs., 12 portrs.; suppl.: 3 maps, 20 tables, (Russian).

LILLE, ODETTE   See: Riche and Lille.

LILLEGRAVEN, JASON A.
1967   Bison crassicornis and the ground sloth Megalonyx jeffersoni in the
            Kansas Pleistocene. Trans. Kansas Acad. Sci., 69, 295—300, 2
            tables.
            See: Green, M. and Lillegraven.

LIM, S. S.   See: Loziev and Lim.

LIN, C. C.
1964   Geology and ecology of Taiwan prehistory. Asian Perspectives, 7, 203—
            213, 9 figs., 1 table.

LIN, DER-HWANG   See: Kigoshi, Lin and Endo.

LIN, YI-PU   See: Pei, Yuan, et al.

LINCK, O.
1964   Bedeutende eiszeitliche Funde im Löss von Neckarwestheim. Zabergäu-
            Ver., 1964:3, 1—3, (not seen).

LINDBERG, G. U.
1963   On an attempt to correct the spelling of generic names in the 'classifi-
            cation of fishes, both recent and fossil' by L. S. Berg. Zool.
            Jour. Moscow, 42, 1105—1107, (Russian; English summary).

LINDBERG, GENE
1962   Top U. S. archaeologists heading for Nevada dig. Newsletter Okla.
            Anthrop. Soc., 10:8, 3–4.

LINDEROTH-WALLACE, BIRGITTA, and SWAUGER, J. L.
1966   A collection of prehistoric artifacts from the Danish Isles. Ann. Carne-
            gie Mus., 38, 165–231, 24 figs.

LINDHOLM, W. A.
1931   Über eine angebliche Testudo-Art aus Südchina. Zool. Anz., 97, 27–30.

LINDNER, HERBERT
1965   Über die Patina altsteinzeitlicher Artefakte. Ein Versuch zur Klärung.
            Quartär, 15–16, 1–26, (French summary).

LINDSAY, EVERETT
1966   Small mammal fossils in the Upper Barstow formation, Mojave Desert.
            Program, 62nd Ann. Meeting, Geol. Soc. Amer., Cordilleran Sect.,
            1966, 50–51, (abs.). Also: Spec. Pap. Geol. Soc. Amer., 101,
            319, (abs.).
1967   Cricetid rodents from the Barstow syncline, Mojave Desert, California.
            Program, 63rd Ann. Meeting, Geol. Soc. Amer., Cordilleran Sect.,
            46–47, (abs.). Also: Spec. Pap. Geol. Soc. Amer., 115, 337,
            (abs.).
1968A.   Rodents from the Hartman Ranch local fauna, California. PaleoBios,
            6, 1–22, 5 figs., 2 tables.
1968B.   Rodents from the Hartman Ranch local fauna, California. Program,
            64th Ann. Meeting, Geol. Soc. Amer., 76, (abs.).

LINDSAY, GEORGE E.
1964   Report of the director. Ann. Rept. Calif. Acad. Sci., 33 pp., illustr.
1965   A fossil hunt. Pac. Discovery, 18:6, 18–24, illustr.

LINDSAY, H. A.
1966   Australia's extinct fauna. Walkabout, 32:3, 36–37, illustr.

LINDSLEY, PETE
1966   Project under the hill. NSS News, 24, 201–202.
1967   Project under the hill. NSS News, 25, 78–79, 3 photos.

LINTZ, JOSEPH, JR., and SAVAGE, D. E.
1966   Stegomastodon from Reno, Nevada. Program, 62nd Ann. Meeting, Geol.
            Soc. Amer., Cordilleran Sect., 1962, 51–52, (abs.). Also: Spec.
            Pap. Geol. Soc. Amer., 101, 320, (abs.).

LIPPOLT, H. J.   See: Koenigswald, Gentner and Lippolt.

LIPPS, JERE H.
1964   Late Pleistocene history of West Anacapa Island, California. Bull. Geol.
            Soc. Amer., 75, 1169–1176, 4 figs., 2 tables.
1968   Climatic regulation of factors controlling otariid pinniped origins and
            diversification. Program, 1968 Ann. Meetings, Geol. Soc. Amer.,
            1968, 176, (abs.).
            See: Mitchell, E. D. and Lipps.

LIPPS, J. H.,   VALENTINE, J. W., and MITCHELL, E.
1968   Pleistocene paleoecology and biostratigraphy, Santa Barbara Island,
              California. Jour. Pal., 42, 291—307, 7 figs.

LIPPS, LEWIS   See: Ray and Lipps.

LIPPS, L., and RAY, C. E.
1967   The Pleistocene fossiliferous deposit at Ladds, Bartow County, Georgia.
              Bull. Georgia Acad. Sci., 25:3, 113—119, 2 figs.

LIPSCOMB, RICHARD
1964   The museum: a new dimension in discovery. Quart. Los Angeles Co.
              Mus. Nat. Hist., 3:1, 10—13, illustr.

LIPTÁK, PAUL
1961   On the problems of historical anthropology (paleoanthropology). Acta
              Biol., Acta Univ. Szeged., 7:3—4, 175—183.
1965   On the taxonomic method in paleoanthropology (historical anthropo-
              logy). Acta Biol., Acta Univ. Szeged., 11, 169—183, 2 tables.
              Rev.: H. V. V. in L'Anthrop., 70:5—6, 559—560.

LISKUN, I. G.   See: Deviatkin and Liskun; Deviatkin, Liskun and Chumakov; Deviatkin,
                 Zazhigin and Liskun.

LISONBEE, L. K.
1965A.   Galileo, Darwin, and Mr. Moore. Ariz. Acad. Sci., 3, 199, (not seen).
1965B.   Thwarting the anti-evolution movement in Arizona. Sci. Teacher, 32,
              35, (not seen).

LISOWSKI, F. P.
1967   Angular growth changes and comparisons in the primate talus. Folia
              Primatologica, 7, 81—97, 6 figs., 9 tables.

LITIANU, EMIL I.
1962   Abs.: Semaka in Zbl. Geol. Pal., Teil 2, 1963, 907—908.

LITIANU, E.,   MIHAILA, N., and BANDRABUR, T.
1962   Contribution à l'étude stratigraphique du Quarternaire dans le bassin
              moyen de l'Olt (bassin de Baraolt). Studii şi Cercetari Geol., 7,
              485—511, 4 figs., (Rumanian; Russian and French summaries).

LITIANU, E.,   PRICĂJAN, A.,   ANDREESCU, I., and ISTRATE, GH.
1967   [Stratigraphic sequence of Cotmean Platform (RSR).]   Studii şi cerc.
              geol., geofiz, geogr., Ser. geol., 12:1, 183—192, 261, (Rumanian;
              German summary).

LITVINSKII, B. A.
1954   [Archeological study of Tadzhikistan by Soviet science.]   Trudy Akad.
              Nauk Tadzhik. SSR, 26, 83 pp., (Russian; Tadzhik summary).
              See: Guliamova, et al.

LITVINSKII, B. A.,   OKLADNIKOV, A. P., and RANOV, V. A.
1962   [Antiquities of the Kairak-Kum.]   Trudy Akad. Nauk Tadzhik. SSR,
              Inst. Istorii, 33, 405 pp., illustr., (Russian).

LITVINTSEV, G. G., and TARAKANOVA, G. I.
1967   [New data on stratigraphy and lithology of Tertiary deposits in the
         south of Siberian Platform.] In: Collected Papers, 1967D
         [Stratigraphy of the Mesozoic and Cenozoic of Middle Siberia],
         156—166, (Russian).

LIU, HSIEN-T'ING
1964   A new coelacanth from the marine Lower Triassic of N. W. Kwangsi,
         China. Vert. Palasiatica, 8, 211—215, 1 pl., (Chinese and English).
         Rev.: M. C. in Fossilia, 1965:5—6, 64—65.

LIU, H.-T., and HSIEH, H.-H.
1965   The discovery of bradyodont from Yangsin series, the Lower Permian
         of Liangshan, Shensi. Vert. Palasiatica, 9, 280—283, 1 pl., (Chi-
         nese; English abstract).

LIU, H.-T., SU, T., HUANG, W., and CHANG, K.
1963   Lycopterid fishes from North China. Inst. Vert. Pal. Paleoanthrop.,
         Acad. Sinica, Mem., Ser. A, 6, 53 pp., 11 figs., 19 pls., (Chinese;
         English summary).

LIU, H.-T., and TSENG, H.-Y.
1964   Note on a Permian Dorypterus of Hsinhua, Central Hunan. Vert. Pal-
         asiatica, 8:3, 318—321, 1 pl., (Chinese; English summary).

LIU, H.-T., and WANG, T.-K.
1961   A new pholidophorid fish from Sinkiang, China. Acta Pal. Sinica, 9,
         266—271, 1 pl., (Chinese and English).

LIU, H.-T., and ZHOU, J.-J.
1965   A new sturgeon from the Upper Jurassic of Liaonning, North China.
         Vert. Palasiatica, 9, 237—247, 4 figs., 4 pls., 1 table, (Chinese
         and English).

LIU, HOU-YI See: Chang, H. and Liu.

LIU, HUNG-YÜN
1962   [Paleogeographic atlas of China.] Moscow: Inostr. Liter. Press, 119 pp.,
         20 maps, (Russian. Translated from Chinese 1959 ed.).

LIU, SUN-CHIU
1966   New finds of vertebrate fossils. "China Reconstructs", 15:6, 33—34,
         4 figs.

LIU, YÜ-HAI
1965   New Devonian agnathans of Yunnan. Vert. Palasiatica, 9, 125—134,
         4 pls., (Chinese and English).
         Abs.: Sci. Abs. China, Earth Sci., 4, 11.

LIUBIN, V. P.
1958   [Investigations into the Paleolithic of southern Ossetia.] Krat. Soob.
         Inst. Ist. Mat. Kult., 71, 28—40, 4 figs., (Russian).
1959A.   [High altitude cave site Kudaro I (South-Osetia).] Izv. Geogr. Obshch.,
         91, 173—183, 6 figs., 1 table, (Russian).
1959B.   [The first lower Paleolithic find in the Stavropol area.] Krat. Soob.
         Inst. Ist. Mat. Kult., 73, 33—38, 2 figs., (Russian).

1961B.	[Upper-Acheulean workshop Dzhraber (Armenia).] Krat. Soob. Inst. Ist. Mat. Kult SSSR, 82, 59–67, 3 figs., (Russian).
1962B.	[New material on the Lower Paleolithic in northern Ossetiia.] Krat. Soob. Inst. Ist. Mat. Kult. SSSR, 92, 29–36, 2 figs., (Russian).
1964	[Lower Paleolithic in the region Dakka-Koshtamna.] In: Piotrovskii, (ed.), 1964, 32–68, 9 figs., 12 tables, (Russian).
1965	[The problem of methods in the study of Lower Paleolithic stone implements.] Mat. Issled. Arkheol. SSSR., no. 131, 7–75, 18 figs., 2 tables, (Russian).
1967A.	[Prospections for Paleolithic in the mountains of Black Sea region.] In: Rybakov, (ed.), 1967, 64–65, (Russian).
1967B.	[Mousterian spear head from northern Osetia.] Sov. Arkheol., 1967:4, 286–287, 1 fig., (Russian).
1968	[Research on Paleolithic in the mountains of western Caucasus.] In: Rybakov, (ed.), 1968, 71–72, (Russian).

LIUBIN, V. P., BADER, N. O., and MARKOVIN, V. I.
| 1962 | [First locations of Stone Age implements in Checheno-Ingushetiia.] Krat. Soob. Inst. Ist. Mat. Kult. SSSR, 92, 51–53, 1 fig., (Russian). |

LIUBIN, V. P., and PETRAKOV, I. I.
| 1964 | [The Mousterian site Zolotarikha near Belev (Tula Region).] Biull. Kom. Izuch. Chetvert. Perioda Akad. Nauk SSSR, no. 29, 171–174, 2 figs., (Russian). |

LIUBIN, V. P., and SHCHELINSKII, V. E.
| 1967 | [Investigation of the Navalishino Cave in 1965.] Krat. Soob. Inst. Arkheol. Akad. Nauk SSSR, 111, 73–79, 2 figs., 3 tables, (Russian). |

LIUBISHCHEV, A. A.
| 1965 | [Systematics and evolution.] In: Shvarts, (ed.), 1965, 45–57, (Russian). |

LIVELY, MATTHEW
| 1965A. | The Lively Complex: preliminary report on a pebble tool complex in Alabama. In: Josselyn, D. W., (ed.), 1965C, 14 pp. |
| 1965B. | The Lively Complex: announcing a pebble tool industry in Alabama. Jour. Ala. Archeol., 11, 103–122, 17 figs. |

LIVEROVSKAIA, E. V.
| 1960 | [Tertiary sediments of Mangyshlak.] Trudy Vses. Neft. Nauchno-Issl. Geologorazv. Inst. (VNIGRI), 151, 142 pp., 20 figs., 3 tables, (Russian). |

LIVINGSTONE, FRANK B.
| 1965 | Controversy regarding Gigantopithecus. Amer. Anthrop., 67, 1283–1284. |
| 1967 | Evolution due to selection for quantitative characteristics determined by several loci. Abs. 66th Ann. Meeting Amer. Anthrop. Assoc., 1967, 53, (abs.). |

LLONGUERAS CAMPAÑÁ, M.
1964-
1965	Sobre la industria del Paleolítico inferior del yacimiento de Pinedo
(Toledo). Ampurias, 26–27, 205–210.

LLOYD, HENRY
1964	Cheyenne chapter visits Hell Gap archaeological Site. Wyo. Archaeol.,
7:3, 7–9, illustr.

LOBANOV, M. F.
1957	[The geological structure of the Novosibirsk Islands.]	Trudy Inst. Geol.
Arktiki, 81, 484–503, (Russian).

LOBERG, MARY, and HARRISON, D. L.
1967	The terrible lizards: a pop-up book. Illustrated by Robert S. Robison.
Japan: Hallmark Cards, 39 pp., illustr., (juv.).

LOCHMAN-BALK, CHRISTINA
1964	Lexicon of stratigraphic names used in Lincoln County, New Mexico.
Guidebk., New Mexico Geol. Soc., 15th Field Confer., 1964, 57–61.
1965	Lexicon of stratigraphic names used in southwestern New Mexico.
Guidebk., New Mexico Geol. Soc., 16th Field Confer., 1965, 93–
111.

LOEHR, MAX	See: Beardsley, Chang and Loehr.

LOEWENBERG, BERT JAMES
1965	Darwin and Darwin studies, 1959-63. Hist. Sci., 4, 15–54.

LOGAN, ALAN
1968	Permian faunas of western Canada. Program, 1968 Ann. Meetings, Geol.
Soc. Amer., 1968, 179, (abs.).

LOGAN, A., and McGUGAN, A.
1968	Biostratigraphy and faunas of the Permian Ishbel Group, Canadian Rocky
Mountains. Jour. Pal., 42, 1123–1139, 3 figs., pls. 141–144.

LOIRET, BERNARD	See: Ginsburg, Lapparent, Loiret and Taquet.

LOLLINI, D.
1965	Ponte di Pietra di Arcevia (Prov. di Ancona). Grotta del Prete di Genga
(Prov. di Ancona). Riv. Sci. Preist., 19, 297–298.

LOMI, CESARE
1963	La fauna di foresta del Pleistocene antico nella breccia ossifera della cava
di Bristie presso Santa Croce di Trieste. Atti Mus. Civico Storia
Nat. Trieste, 23, 119–146, 12 figs.

LOMIZE, M. G.	See: Alekseeva, and Lomize.

LOMONOVICH, M. I.
1963	[V. A. Obruchev's letters on loess.]	Izv. Akad. Nauk Kazakh. SSR, Ser.
Geol., 1963:6, 10–17, (Russian; Kazakh summary).

LONG, A. G., JR.
1965A.   The Lively complex: plates for the Lively and Josselyn papers. In:
             Josselyn, D. W., (ed.), 1965C, 22 pp., 59 pls.
1965B.   Jackson County projectile points. Jour. Ala. Archeol., 11, 152–155, 8
             figs.
1965C.   How important is America's "Early Man". President Long opens our
             1965 fund drive. Stones and Bones Newsletter, April 1965, 1–3.

LONG, AUSTIN
1965   Smithsonian Institution radiocarbon measurements II. Radiocarbon, 7,
             245–256.
             See: Damon, Haynes and Long.

LONG, A., and MIELKE, J. E.
1966   Smithsonian Institution radiocarbon measurements III. Radiocarbon, 8,
             413–422.
1967   Smithsonian Institution radiocarbon measurements IV. Radiocarbon, 9,
             368–381.

LONG, CHARLES A.
1964   Taxonomic status of the Pleistocene badger, Taxidea marylandica. Amer.
             Mid. Nat., 72, 176–180.

LONG, J. C.   See: Carmichael and Long.

LONG, WILLIAM E.   See: Doumani and Long.

LONSDALE, J. T.   See: Maxwell, R. A., et al.

LOOK, AL
1967   1,000 million years on the Colorado Plateau. Illustrations by Jean Look
             Comiskey. Denver, Colo.: Bell Publications, xiii + 300 pp.,
             illustr.

LORAH, WILLIAM E.
1968   Basal fragment of a Clovis fluted point. Ohio Archaeol., 18, 91–92,
             2 figs.

LORANDI, A. M.   See: Rex González and Lorandi.

LORBLANCHET, MICHEL
1965   Découverte de peintures et d'une gravure préhistoriques dans la grotte
             des Escabasses (commune de Thémines, Lot). Bull. Soc. Préhist.
             Franç., C. R. séances mens., 1965:7, 240–251, 5 figs.
1966   Une nouvelle grotte ornée sur le causse de Gramat (Lot). Bull. Soc.
             Préhist. Franç., C. R. séances mens., 63, 108–111, 1 fig., 2 pls.
1967   A propos de la grotte ornée des Escabasses (Thémines, Lot). Spelunca,
             Bull., 7:2, 130–132.

LORENZ, HANS G.   See: Gillet, et al.

LORENZ, KONRAD
1965   Evolution and modification of behavior. Chicago: Univ. Chicago Press,
             121 pp.
1966   Rev.: Blest in Nature, 212, 564.

LORENZO, JOSÉ LUIS
1961   Un buril de la cultura precerámica de Teopisca, Chiapas. Homenaje a
         Pablo Martínez del Río, 75–90, 8 figs.
1964   Dos puntas acanaladas en la región de Chapala, México. Bol. Inst. Nac.
         Anthrop., 18, 1–6, 2 figs., 1 map.
1965   Early man in Mexico: Review and prospect. 7th Internat. Congr.,
         Internat. Assoc. Quat. Res., Abs., 1965, 298, (abs.).

LORGIN, J.
1963   La station préhistorique du Cap Ténès. Libyca, 9–10, 9–57, 13 figs.,
         8 pls., 2 tables.

LORRAIN, DESSAMAE   See: Dibble and Lorrain.

LOS, F. J.
1966   The prehistoric ethnology of Palestine. Mankind Quart., 7, 53–59.

LOSKUTOV, V. V.,   MELAMED, ÍA. R.,   RAFIEV, A.,   TROFIMOV, A. K., and
CHEDÍÍA, O. K.
1965   [On the age of Kuliab series of Tadzhikistan depression.] Doklady
         Akad. Nauk Tadzhik. SSR, 8:4, 28–30, (Russian; Tadzhik sum-
         mary).

LOTH, EDWARD
1957   Eugenic characters in the human body build. Przeglad Antrop., 23,
         313–317, 42 figs., (Polish; English and Russian summaries).

LOTSCH, D.   See: Krutzsch and Lotsch.

LOUIS, PIERRE
1963   Mammifères de l'Éocène inférieur des environs de Reims et d'Epernay.
         Rés. Com. LXXX Congr. Assoc. Franç. Avance. Sci., Reims,
         1961, 85–90, (not seen).
1966   Note sur un nouveau gisement situé à Conde-en-Brie (Aisne) et renfer-
         mant des restes de mammifères de l'Éocène inférieur. Ann.
         Assoc. rég. étude et rech. sci., 4:3, 108–118, illustr.
         See: Russell, D. E., Louis and Poirier; Russell, D. E., Louis and
         Savage; Savage, D. E., Russell and Louis.

LOUIS, P., and MICHAUX, J.
1962   Présence de Mammifères sparnaciens dans les sablières de Pourcy (Marne).
         C. R. Soc. Géol. France, 1962, 170–172.

LOUW, J. T.
1960   Prehistory of the Matjes River Rock Shelter. Mem. Nasion. Mus.
         Bloemfontein, no. 1, 143 pp., 59 figs., 7 pls.

LOVERING, J. F.   See: Polach, Stipp, Golson and Lovering.

LOZAN, M. N.
1967   [Preliminary data on small mammal remains from Voronkovo Cave in
         Moldavian SSR.] In: Collected Papers, 1967A [Place and
         significance of fossil mammals of Moldavia in the Cenozoic of
         USSR], 37–40, (Russian).

LOŽEK, VOJEN
1960   Aux problemes actuels de la stratigraphie des loess pléistocènes-récents
        et de la classification chronologique du paléolithique supérieur.
        Archeol. Roz., 12, 560—579, (Czech; French summary).
1962   Životni prostředí praveke společnosti [w:] Referaty o pracovních výsledcích
        československych archeologù za rok 1961. Smolenice, 1, 40—48,
        (not seen).
1964   Die Umwelt der urgeschichtlichen Gesellschaft nach neuen Ergebnissen
        der Quartär geologie in der Tschechoslowakei. Jahresschrift
        Mitteldeutsch. Vorgesch., 48, 7—24, 3 figs., 2 pls., 2 tables.

LOZIEV, V. P., and LIM, S. S.
1962   [On the finding of fossils of Ili faunistic complex in the northeastern
        part of Kafirnigan and Iliak interfluve.] Doklady Akad. Nauk
        Tadzhik. SSR, 5:5, 39—40, (Russian; Tadzhik summary).

LU, QIN-WU   See: Wu, et al.

LUCAS, A. T.   See: Barley and Lucas.

LÜDICKE, MANFRED
1962   Ordnung der Klasse Reptilia, Serpentes. Handb. der Zool. (Kükenthal),
        7:1:5, 1—128, 132 figs.

LÜDIN, CARL
1964   Die Silexartefakte aus dem Spätmagdalenien der Kohlerhöhle. Jahrb.
        Schweiz. Ges. Urgesch., 50, 33—42, 8 figs.

LUDOVICI, L. J.
1963   The great tree of life. Paleontology: the natural history of living
        creatures. A science survey book. Illustrated by Frank Aloise.
        New York: Putnam's, 191 pp., illustr., (junior high and laymen).

LUDWIG, W.
1960   Die heutige Gestalt der Selektionstheorie. (Der Evolutionsmechanismus).
        In: Heberer and Schwanitz, (ed.), 1960*, 45—80, 9 figs., 3 tables.

LUFKIN, JAMES M.
1964   The extinction of the giant mammals of the Pleistocene. Minn. Archaeol.,
        26, 108—132, 15 figs.

LUKASHEV, K. I.
1959   [Main problems of Quaternary geology and paleogeography.] Minsk:
        Akad. Nauk BSSR Press, 287 pp., 24 figs., 27 tables, (Russian).

LUMLEY, HENRY DE
1962B. Paleolithique ancien et moyen en Vaucluse. Note préliminaire. Bull.
        Soc. Étud. Sci. Nat. Vaucluse, 1957—1962, 29—79, 21 figs.,
        (not seen).
        Rev.: E. B. in L'Anthrop., 68, 400—401.
1964   Les niveaux quaternaires marins des Alpes-Maritimes. Corrélations avec
        les industries préhistorique. Bull. Soc. Géol. France, 5, 562—579,
        8 figs., 1 table.

1965A.   La grande revolution raciale et culturelle de l'Inter-Wurmien II-III. Cahiers Ligures Préhist. Archéol., 14:2, 133–135.
1965B.   L'abri Breuil, Vallée du Verdon (Montmeyan-Var). In: Ripoll Perelló, E., (ed.), 1965B, 119–134, 10 figs., (Spanish summary).
1967   Découverte d'habitats de l'Acheuléen ancien, dans des dépôts mindéliens, sur le site de Terra Amata (Nice, Alpes-Maritimes). C. R. Acad. Sci. Paris, Sci. Nat., 264, 801–804.
        See: Barrière, J., et al.; Isetti and Lumley; Ripoll Perelló and Lumley.

LUMLEY, H. DE, et al.
1963   Rev.: Bonifay in L'Anthrop., 68, 402–403.

LUMLEY, H. DE, and BERARD, G.
1964   Les industries moustériennes du bassin de Cabasse (Vallée de l'Issole, Var). Bull. Mus. Anthrop. Préhist. Monaco, 11, 81–119, 20 figs.

LUMLEY, H. DE, GAGNIÈRE, S., and PASCAL, R.
1963   La regression post-pliocène, la transgression calabrienne et la regression villafranchienne d'après le remplissage de la grotte du Vallonnet (Roquebrune-Cap Martin). Cahiers Ligures Préhist. Archeol., 12:2, 219–220, 3 figs.

LUMLEY, H. DE, and ISETTI, G.
1965   Le Moustérien à denticulés tardif de la station de San Francesco (San Remo) et de la grotte Tournal (Aude). Cahiers Ligures Préhist. Archéol., 14:1, 5–30, 10 figs., 1 table.

LUND, RICHARD
1966   Intermuscular bones in Pholidophorus bechei from the Lower Lias of England. Science, 152, 348–349, 2 figs.
1967A.   An analysis of the propulsive mechanisms of fishes, with reference to some fossil actinopterygians. Ann. Carnegie Mus., 39:15, 195–218, 12 figs.
1967B.   Fishing in old Pennsylvania. Carnegie Mag., 41, 89–92, 4 figs.
        See: Doberenz and Lund.

LUNDBERG, JOHN G.
1967   Pleistocene fishes of the Good Creek formation, Texas. Copeia, 1967, 453–455, 1 fig.

LUNDELIUS, ENREST L., JR.
1963   Abs.: R. in Helictite, 3, 41–42.
1964   The use of vertebrates in paleoecological reconstructions. Discussion. Publ. Fort Burgwin Res. Center, no. 3, 26–31.
1965   Late Pleistocene and Holocene faunal history of central Texas. 7th Internat. Congr., Internat. Assoc. Quat. Res., Abs., 1965, 303, (abs.).
1966   Marsupial carnivore dens in Australian caves. Studies in Spel., 1, 174–180, 1 fig., 1 pl., 1 table.
1967   Late-Pleistocene and Holocene faunal history of Central Texas. In: Martin, P. S., and Wright, H. E., (eds.), 1967, 287–319, 11 figs., 1 table.
        See: Turnbull, W. and Lundelius; Turnbull, W., Lundelius and McDougall.

LUNDELIUS, E. L., JR., and TURNBULL, W. D.
1967   Pliocene mammals from Victoria, Australia. 39th Congr., ANZAAS,
            Melbourne, 1967, Sec. C, p. K9, (abs.).

LUNDQUIST, G.
1964   Henrik Vilhelm Munthe * 1.11.1860 † 15.8.1958. Invald 25.10.1928.
            K. Svenska Vetenskapsakad. Årsbok, 1963, 367—502, 6 figs.

LUNDQVIST, JAN
1965   The Quaternary of Sweden. In: Rankama, (ed.), 1965, 139—198, 18
            figs., 2 tables.

LUNGU, A. N.
1962   [New data on Middle Sarmatian carnivores from the vicinity of the
            village Kalfa MSSR.] Trudy Odessk. Univ., Ser. Geol. Geogr.,
            152:8, 31—33, (Russian).
1967A.   [On deer from Moldavian Middle Sarmatian.] Izv. Akad. Nauk Moldav.
            SSR, 1967:4, 29—33, 2 figs., 1 table, (Russian).
1967B.   [Conditions of burial of Middle Sarmatian mammals in the environs of
            Kalfa village Moldavian SSR.] Pal. geol. polezn. iskop. Moldavii,
            2, 89—95, (Russian).
1968   [Conditions of life and peculiarities of specific composition of the hip-
            parion fauna of Moldavian Middle Sarmatian.] Izv. Akad. Nauk
            Moldav. SSR, ser. Biol. i Khim. Nauk, 1968:3, 30—36, 1 table,
            (Russian).

LUNGU, A. N., and TARABUKIN, B. A.
1966   [New data on vertebrate fauna from Moldavian Neogene.] Okhrana
            Prirody Moldavii, 4, 156—162, 1 map, (Russian).

LUR'E, M. L.   See: Kransov, I. I., Lur'e and Masaĭtis.

LÜTTIG, GERD
1960   Neue Ergebnisse quartärgeologischer Forschung im Raume Alfeld-Hameln-
            Elze. Geol. Jahrb., 77, 337—390, 11 figs., 3 pls., 5 tables, (Eng-
            lish summary).
            Abs.: Ebers in Zbl. Geol. Pal., Teil 2, 1962, 573.
1966   Prinzipielles zur Quartär-Stratigraphie. Geol. Jahrb., 82, 177—202, 1 fig.,
            (English and French summaries).

LUTTROPP, A.
1962   Ein Beitrag zum Levalloisien an Hand der Funde im nordhessischen
            Kreise Ziegenhain. Fundber. Hessen, 2, 54—59, (not seen).

LÜTTSCHWAGER, JOHANNES
1961   Die Drontevögel. Die Neue Brehm-Bücherei 276. Wittenberg Lutherstadt:
            Ziemsen, 60 pp., 34 figs.
            Abs.: Kuhn in Zbl. Geol. Pal., Teil 2, 1965, 260.

LUZGIN, B. K., and RANOV, V. A.
1966   [First discoveries of Paleolithic in Central Kopet-Dag.] Biul. Kom.
            Izuch. Chetvert. Perioda, 32, 87—95, 3 figs., (Russian).

LVOVA, A.   See: Egorov, M. E. and Lvova.

LWOFF, STÉPHANE
1963   Homomorphie cyclique ou cyclo-homomorphie de l'outillage préhistorique. Bull. Soc. Préhist., Paris, 60, 211—235, 11 pls.

LYNCH, BARBARA, and LYNCH, T. F.
1968   The beginnings of a scientific approach to prehistoric archaeology in 17th and 18th century Britain. Southwestern Jour. Anthrop., 24, 33—65.

LYNCH, JOHN D.
1964   Additional hylid and leptodactylid remains from the Pleistocene of Texas and Florida. Herpetologica, 20, 141—142.
1965   The Pleistocene amphibians of Pit II, Arredondo, Florida. Copeia, 1965, 72—77, 4 figs.

LYNCH, THOMAS F.
1966   The "Lower Perigordian" in French archaeology. Proc. Prehist. Soc. Cambridge, 32, 156—198, 8 figs.
1967A.   Quishqui Puncu: A preceramic site in Highland Peru. Science, 158, 780—783, 3 figs.
1967B.   The nature of the Central Andean preceramic. Occ. Pap. Idaho State Univ. Mus., no. 21, 98 pp.

LYNSENKO, N. I.
1960C.   [Concerning the find of remains of Equus süssenbornensis Wüsti in the terrace deposits of the mountainous area of Crimea.] Bull. Mosk. Obshch. Ispyt. Prirody, Otd. Geol., 65:2, 123—124, 2 figs., (Russian; brief English summary).
1962   [Mastodont (Tetralophodon aff. longirostris Caup) from the Pliocene deposits of the Crimea.] Zbirn. Prats' Zool. Mus. Akad. Nauk URSR, 31, 52—55, 2 figs., (Ukrainian; Russian summary).
1965   [About the stratigraphy of ancient Quaternary gravel beds of the Crimean steppes.] Biull. Kom. Izuch. Chetvert. Perioda Akad. Nauk SSSR, no. 30, 72—78, 3 figs., (Russian).
       See: Bachinskii, Dublianskii, and Lysenko.

M., B.
1960   Rouffignac nebo bitva mamutu. Archeol. Roz., 12, 759—761.

M., P.
1967   Obituary. Alden H. Miller, 1906 - 1965. Ibis, 109, 280.

M., W.
1966   Der Schadel des Homo mousteriensis Hauseri wieder in Berlin. Praehist. Zeit., 43/44:1—2, 1, 1 fig.

MACADIE, C. I.
1966   The use of flexible fiber light guides in preparative palaeontology. Mus. Jour., London, 66, 215—216.
1967   Ultrasonic probes in palaeontology. In: Patterson, C., and Greenwood, P. H., (eds.), 1967, 251—253, 1 fig.

McALESTER, A. LEE
1968   The history of life. Englewood Cliffs, N. J.:   Prentice-Hall, 152 pp., illustr., (paper).

Rev.:   Coates in Jour. Pal., 42, 1322—1323; Johnson in Jour. Geol., 77:4, 500; Rhodes in Nature, 220, 1255; Tonkin in Earth Sci. J., 2:2, 184—185.

MacALLISTER, D. E.
1968   The evolution of branchiostegals and associated opercular, gular, and hyoid bones and the classification of teleostome fishes, living and fossil. Bull. Nation. Mus. Canada, 221, xiv + 239 pp., 2 figs., 21 pls., 2 tables, 2 charts.

Rev.:   Anon. in Nature, 219, 11.

MACAROVICI, NICOLAE
1962   Abs.: Semaka in Zbl. Geol. Pal., Teil 2, 1964, 995.
1963   Nouvelles contributions à la connaissance d'Alces palmatus Ham. Smith dans le Quaternaire de la Roumanie. An. Ştiinţ. Univ. Cuza (n.s.), Sect. 2 (Ştiinţe Nat.), a. Biol., 9, 65—74, 4 pls., (French; Rumanian and Russian summaries).
1965   [Entwicklung der quartären Säugerfaunen Rumäniens.]   Natura (Biolog.), 1, 30—40, 4 pls., (Rumanian).

Abs.: Semaka in Zbl. Geol. Pal., Teil 2, 1966, 318.

MACAROVICI, N., MARINESCU, FL., and MOTAŞ, I. C.
1965   [On the Upper Neogene and Pontic s.s. from Dacian Basin.]   Studii şi cercetări geol., geofiz., geogr., Ser. geol., 10:2, 313—323, (Rumanian).

MACAROVICI, N., and MOTAŞ, I.
1965   [On a Trionyx sp. found in the Upper Sarmatian of Vrancea Mts.] An. ştiinţ. Univ. Cuza (n.s.), sect. 2 (ştiinţ. nat.), b. Geol.-Geog., 11, 93—96, 1 pl. (Rumanian; Russian and French summaries).

Abs.: Semaka in Zbl. Geol. Pal., Teil 2, 1966, 306.

MACAROVICI, N., MOTAŞ, I., and CONTESCU, L.
1963   Quelques observations stratigraphiques et sédimentologiques sur le Pliocène de la courbure des Carpathes Orientales Roumaines. 6th Congr. Assoc. Geol. Carpato-Balkanique, (not seen).

MACAROVICI, N., and PAGHIDA, N.
1964   Ein Endocranial-ausguss von Hipparion sebastopolitanum aus dem Sarmat von Păun-Iaşi (Rumänien). Sitz.-Ber. Akad. Wiss. Wien, 173:5—7, 219—230, 4 pls.

Abs.: Semaka in Zbl. Geol. Pal., Teil 2, 1966, 333.

Rev.: Simionescu in An. Ştiinţ. Univ. Cuza (n.s.), sect. 2 (Ştiinţe Nat.), b. Geol.-Geog., 13, 207—208.

MACAROVICI, N., and ZAHARIA, N.
1963   Mamutul (E. trogontherii Pohlig) de la Holboca (Iasi). Com. Geol., Bucuresti, 2, 155—170, 2 pls., (not seen).

Abs.: Semaka in Zbl. Geol. Pal., Teil 2, 1964, 995.

McAVOY, JOSEPH M.
1965   An early chert assemblage in Chesterfield Co., Virginia. Quart. Bull. Archeol. Soc. Virginia, 20, 48—51, 3 figs., 1 table.

1967A.   Distinctive lithic materials preferred by early man in Virginia for pro-
               duction of chipped tools and projectile points. Part I – large-
               grain quartzite. Chesopiean, 5, 61–63, 1 fig.
1967B.   The J. G. Pritchard Clovis. Chesopiean, 5, 136–137, 1 fig.
1968   A descriptive study of tools and projectile points of two early hunter
               camp sites on the Atlantic coastal plain. Chesopiean, 6, 62–75,
               4 figs., 2 tables.

McAVOY, J. M., and BOTTOMS, E.
1965   The Hopewell Paleo-Indian workshop site. Chesopiean, 3:6, 146–150,
               illustr.

McBURNEY, CHARLES BRIAN MONTAGU
1960B.   Rev.: Allchin in Jour. Afr. Hist., 2, 153–154; Da Silva in Brotéria,
               Sér. Mensal, 79, 114–115; Strouhal in Anthrop., 2:1, 85,
               (Czech).
1961C.   Aspects of Palaeolithic art. Antiq., 35, 107–114.
1964   Preliminary report on Stone Age reconnaissance in north-eastern Iran.
               Proc. Prehist. Soc. Cambridge, 30, 382–399, 6 figs., pls. xxvii–
               xxxiii, 6 tables.
1965   The Old Stone Age in Wales. In: Foster, I. L., and Daniel, G., (eds.),
               1965, 17–34, figs. 1–3.
1967A.   Libya. In: Oakley, K. P., and Campbell, B. G., (eds.), 1967A, 29–30.
1967B.   The Haua Fteah (Cyrenaica) and the Stone Age of the south-east Medi-
               terranean. Foreward by Grahame Clark. London: Cambridge
               Univ. Press, xv + 387 pp., 139 figs., 38 pls., 88 tables, inven-
               tory sheets, (French summary).
           Rev.: Bort in Man, Jour. Roy. Anthrop. Inst., 3, 491–492; Butzer
               in Amer. Jour. Phys. Anthrop., 29, 453–454; Coles in Antiq.,
               42, 162–163; Hawkes in Nature, 218, 1181–1182; Howell
               in Amer. Anthrop., 70, 1227–1231; Smith in Science, 164,
               705–708; KV in Archeol. Roz., 21:4, 561, (Czech).

MACCAGNO, A. M.
1966   Nuovi ritrovamenti di resi elefantini nel Villafranchiano .della Conca
               aquilana. Boll. Soc. Nat. Naples, 74, 231–242, 3 figs., 7 pls.,
               (English summary).
           Rev.: Albanesi in Riv. Ital. Pal., 72, 494–495.

McCALL, G. J. H., BAKER, B. H., and Walsh, J.
1967   Late Tertiary and Quaternary sediments of the Kenya Rift Valley. Dis-
               cussion. In: Bishop, W. W., and Clark, J. D., (eds.), 1967A, 191–
               220, 6 figs., 10 tables, (French summary).

McCALLUM, K. J., and WITTENBERG, J.
1965   University of Saskatchewan radiocarbon dates IV. Radiocarbon, 7, 229–
               235.

MacCALMAN, H. R.
1962   The Middle Stone Age in South West Africa. Part I: Gungams, an
               Early Middle Stone Age site in the Windhoek District. Cimbe-
               basia, no. 3, 2–13, 4 figs., 3 tables.
1963   The Middle Stone Age in South West Africa. Part II: The Neuhof-
               Kowas Middle Stone Age, Windhoek District. Cimbebasia, no. 7,
               42–54, 5 figs., 3 tables.

1964   First Intermediate or Middle Stone Age? S. Afr. Archaeol. Bull., 19, 20.

1967   Peperkorrel, a factory site of Lupemban affinities from central South
            West Africa. S. Afr. Archaeol. Bull., 22, 41—50, 6 figs.

McCARTHY, FREDERICK D.

1959   Methods and scope of Australian archaeology. Mankind, 5:7, 297—316.

1965   The Aboriginal past: archaeological and material equipment. In: Berndt,
            R. M., and Berndt, C. H., (eds.), 1965, 71—100, 10 pls.

1966   Australia. Asian Perspectives, 8:1, 102—111.
            See: Mulvaney 1963.

McCARTNEY, ALLEN P.

1964   A summary of available sources on the study of human bone. Arkan-
            sas Archeologist, 5, 74—78.

McCARTNEY, A. P., and TURNER, C. G. II

1966   Stratigraphy of the Anangula unifacial core and blade site. In: Laughlin,
            W. S., and Reeder, W. G., (eds.), 1966, 28—40, 7 figs., 1 table.

McCARY, BEN C.

1958   Survey of Virginia fluted points. Quart. Bull. Archeol. Soc. Virginia,
            13:1, (not seen).

1961A.   Survey of Virginia fluted points, numbers 282—293. Quart. Bull. Archaeol.
            Soc. Virginia, 15:3, 27—31, (not seen).

1961B.   Cores from the Williamson Site. Quart. Bull. Archeol. Soc. Virginia, 16,
            7, 8 figs.

1963A.   The archaeology of the western area of the Dismal Swamp in Virginia.
            Quart. Bull. Archeol. Soc. Virginia, 17, 40—48, illustr., 1 map.

1963B.   Survey of Virginia fluted points, numbers 294—314. Quart. Bull.
            Archeol. Soc. Virginia, 18, 25—29, illustr.

1965   Survey of Virginia fluted points, numbers 315—347. Quart. Bull. Archeol.
            Soc. Virginia, 20, 53—60, illustr.

1968   Survey of Virginia fluted points, numbers 348—384. Quart. Bull. Archeol.
            Soc. Virginia, 23, 2—10, illustr.

McCAUGHEY, WILLIAM F. See: Wyckoff, R. W. G., Doberenz and McCaughey;
            Wyckoff, R. W. G., McCaughey and Doberenz.

McCLURE, WILLIAM L. See: Slaughter and McClure.

McCLURE, W. L., and MILSTEAD, W.

1967   Terrapene carolina triunguis from the Late Pleistocene of southeast
            Texas. Herpetologica, 23, 321—322.

MacCORD, H. A.

1964   Late Pleistocene remains found in Virginia. Quart. Bull. Archeol. Soc.
            Virginia, 18, 61—62.

MacCORD, H. A., SR., and PEPLE, C.

1963   The Sloan Site, Chesterfield County, Virginia. Quart. Bull. Archeol.
            Soc. Virginia, 17, 73—76, 2 figs., 2 tables.

McCOY, JOHN J.

1960   The fossil birds of the Itchtuknee River, Florida. Diss. Abst., 20, 4760,
            (abs.).

McCRADY, ALLEN D.
1961   New Paris progress report. Netherworld News, 9:12, 208–209.
1962   Preliminary report on vertebrate fossils of Robinson Cave, Tennessee.
               Netherworld News, 10:9, 155–160, cover photo.
1963   Preliminary report on the Pleistocene fauna of Robinson Cave, Overton
               County, Tennessee. NSS News, 21, 163, (abs.).
1964   Preliminary report on the Pleistocene fauna of Robinson Cave, Overton
               County, Tennessee. Bull. Nat. Spel. Soc., 26, 73.
               See: Guilday, Hamilton and McCrady; Guilday and McCrady; Guilday,
               Martin and McCrady.

McCRADY, A. D., and GUILDAY, J. F.
1963   Final report — Late Pleistocene fauna of New Paris No. 4 (Lloyds Rock
               Hole). Netherworld News, 11:9, 153–162, 2 pls., 3 tables.

McCRADY, A. D., and SCHMIDT, V.
1963   Second interim report — Late Pleistocene fossils from Robinson Cave,
               Tennessee. Netherworld News, 11:2, 19–27, 2 maps.

McCRONE, A. W., et al.
1965   Stone artifacts: Identification problems. Science, 148, no. 3667, 167–
               168.

McCULLOCH, BEVERLY
1968   Interim report on an archaeological survey of the Weka Pass area. New
               Zealand Archaeol. Assoc. Newsletter, 11, 76–85, 5 figs.

McCULLOCH, D. S.
1967   Quaternary geology of the Alaskan shore of Chukchi Sea. In: Hopkins,
               D. M., (ed.), 1967D, 91–120, 3 figs., 1 table.
               See: Kauffman and McCulloch.

McCULLOUGH, DALE R.
1965   Elk deposit on the San Francisco peninsula. Jour. Mammal., 46, 347–
               348.

MACURDA, DONALD B., JR., (ed.)
1968   Paleobiological aspects of growth and development. A symposium.
               Pal. Soc. Mem. 2, 119 pp., illustr.

MACDONALD, DOUGLAS J.
1965   Fossil hunters of the "worselands". Quart. Los Angeles Co. Mus. Nat.
               Hist., 3:4, 14–18, illustr.

MacDONALD, GEORGE F.
1965   The technology and settlement pattern of a Paleo-Indian site at Debert,
               Nova Scotia. 7th Internat. Congr., Internat. Assoc. Quat. Res.,
               Abs., 1965, 309–310, (abs.).
1966   The technology and settlement pattern of a Paleo-Indian site at Debert,
               Nova Scotia. Quaternaria, 8, 59–74, 11 figs., (Italian and French
               summaries).
1968   Debert: a Paleo-Indian site in central Nova Scotia. Anthrop. Pap.,
               Nation. Mus. Canada, no. 16, x + 207 pp., 26 figs., 24 pls.,
               16 tables.
               Rev.: Salwen in Amer. Anthrop., 70, 1231–1233.

McDONALD, JAMES E.
    1966   Evolution in Arizona. Science, 151, 632, 634.

MACDONALD, JAMES REID
    1964A.   Stereo use urged. GeoTimes, 8:8, 26.
    1964B.   A plea for fossil vertebrates. Min. Inform. Serv., 17:12, 232–233.
                    Reprinted: Northrop Ventura Rockhound News, 4:13, 5–7; The Vista Rockorder 6:10, 5–7; California Highways & Public Works, 45:7–8, 13–15, (1966).
    1964C.   Barstovian mammal fauna from Camp Creek, Nevada. Program, 60th Ann. Meeting, Geol. Soc. Amer., Cordilleran Sect., 41, (abs.).
    1964D.   Geolabis wolffi, a new fossil insectivore from the Late Oligocene of South Dakota. Contrib. Sci., Los Angeles Co. Mus., 88, 3–6, 1 fig.
    1965   Barstovian mammal fauna from Camp Creek, Nevada. Spec. Pap. Geol. Soc. Amer., 82, 261, (abs.).
    1966A.   What to do when bulldozer meets mastodon. Constructor Mag., 48:6, 32–34, 4 figs.
    1966B.   The Barstovian Camp Creek fauna from Elko County, Nevada. Contrib. Sci., Los Angeles Co. Mus., 92, 3–18, 7 figs., 2 tables.
    1966C.   Electronic data processing methods in vertebrate paleontology catalogues. News Bull., Soc. Vert. Pal., no. 77, 44–45.
    1966D.   The search for the king of the tyrant lizards. Quart. Los Angeles Co. Mus. Nat. Hist., 4:3, 18–22, illustr.
    1966E.   Fossils are for digging. Quart. Los Angeles Co. Mus. Nat. Hist., 4:4, 37–40, illustr.
    1966F.   The bulldozer and the mastodon. Quart. Los Angeles Co. Mus., 5:1, 10–12, illustr.
    1966G.   Dig that horseheaven. Quart. Los Angeles Co. Mus. Nat. Hist., 5:2, 12–14, 2 figs.
    1967A.   A new species of Late Oligocene dog, Brachyrhynchocyon sesnoni, from South Dakota. Contrib. Sci., Los Angeles Co. Mus., 126, 5 pp., 2 figs., 1 table.
    1967B.   A new species of Late Oligocene dog, Sunkahetanka sheffleri, from South Dakota. Contrib. Sci., Los Angeles Co. Mus., 127, 5 pp., 2 figs., 1 table.
    1967C.   A plea for fossil vertebrates. Museologist, 102, 8–10.
    1967D.   The Tyrannosaurus search goes on. Quart. Los Angeles Co. Mus., 5:3, 12–14, 2 figs.
    1968   What is a curator? Quart. Los Angeles Mus. Nat. Hist., 6:4, 2 pp.
                    See: Hopkins, M. L. and Macdonald; Tordoff and Macdonald.

MACDONALD, J. R., and MACDONALD, D. J.
    1967   A return to the worselands. Quart. Los Angeles Co. Mus., 5:4, 16–20, 2 figs.

McDOUGALL, IAN   See: Turnbull, W. D., Lundelius and McDougall.

McDOWELL, SAMUEL BOOKER, JR.
    1964   Partition of the genus Clemmys and related problems in the taxonomy of the aquatic Testudinidae. Proc. Zool. Soc. London, 143, 239–279.

MacFALL, RUSSELL P.
    1963   Collecting rocks, minerals, gems and fossils. New York: Hawthorne, 156 pp., (not seen).

Rev.: Gaal in Quart. Los Angeles Co. Mus. Nat. Hist., 3:1, 22.

McGEARY, DAVID F. R.   See: Van Andel, et al.

McGINNIS, HELEN J.
1964   Phlegethontia, a snake like Permian and Pennsylvanian amphibian. Pro-
            gram, 60th Ann. Meeting, Geol. Soc. Amer., Cordilleran Sect.,
            43, (abs.).
1965   Phlegethontia, a snake-like Permian and Pennsylvanian amphibian. Spec.
            Pap. Geol. Soc. Amer., 82, 263, (abs.).
1967   The osteology of Phlegethontia, a Carboniferous and Permian aistopod
            amphibian. Univ. Calif. Publ. Geol. Sci., 71, 46 pp., 13 figs.,
            1 pl., 4 tables.
            Rev.: Hotton in Jour. Pal., 42, 1321;   Westphal in Zbl. Geol. Pal.,
            Teil 2, 1968, 202.
            See: Camp, C. L., Allison, Nichols and McGinnis.

McGOWAN, J.   See: Hawksley, Reynolds and McGowan.

MACGOWAN, K., and HESTER, J. A., Jr.
1962   Rev.: Roth-Lutra in Zeit. Ethnol., 89, 312–313.

MacGREGOR, ALEXANDER B.
1964   The Le Moustier mandible: an explanation for the deformation of the
            bone and failure of eruption of a permanent canine tooth. Man,
            64, 151–152, 4 figs.

McGREGOR, JOHN C.
1941   Southwestern archaeology. New York, London: John Wiley and Sons,
            Chapman and Hall, 403 pp., illustr.
1965   Southwestern archaeology. 2nd rev. ed. Urbana: Univ. Illinois Press,
            vii + 511 pp., illustr.
            Rev.: Wissler in Jour. West, 4:4, 599–600; Woodbury in Amer. Anthrop.,
            68:3, 813–814.

McGREGOR, JOHN H.   See: Nelson, N. C., McGregor and Gregory.

McGUGAN, ALAN   See: Logan and McGugan.

McINTOSH, JOHN S.
1965   Marsh and the dinosaurs. Discovery, Yale, 1:1, 31–37, 2 figs.
            See: Ostrom and McIntosh.

MACINTOSH, N. W. G.
1952   The Cohuna cranium: history and commentary from November, 1925
            to November, 1951. Mankind, 4:8, 307–329.
1965   The physical aspect of man in Australia. In: Berndt, R. M., and
            Berndt, C. H., (eds.), 1965, 29–70, 2 pls.
1967   Fossil man in Australia with particular reference to the 1965 discovery
            at Green Gully near Keilor, Victoria. Austral. Jour. Sci., 30,
            86–98, 3 figs.

MacINTYRE, GILES TERNAN
1966   The Miacidae (Mammalia, Carnivora). Part 1. The systematics of
            Ictidopappus and Protictis. Bull. Amer. Mus. Nat. Hist., 131,
            115–210, 21 figs., 20 pls., 12 tables.

Rev.: Clemens in Quart. Rev. Biol., 304;   Fahlbusch in Zbl. Geol. Pal.,
Teil 2, 1967, 115.

1967   Foramen pseudovale and quasi-mammals. Evolution, 21, 834—841, 3
figs.

MACKAY, J. R.,   MATHEWS, W. H., and MacNEISH, R. S.
1961   Geology of the Engigstciak archaeological site, Yukon Territory.   Arctic,
14, 25—52, 10 figs.

McKENNA, MALCOLM C.
1964   Mining for fossils in Wyoming.   Nat. and Sci., 1:16, 10—11, 4 figs.
1965A.   Stratigraphic nomenclature of the Miocene Hemingford group, Nebraska.
Amer. Mus. Novit., no. 2228, 1—21, 1 fig.
1965B.   Paleontology and the origin of the primates.   Folia Primatologica, 4,
1—25, 10 figs.
Rev.: M. C. in Fossilia, 1965:5—6, 63.
1965C.   Collecting microvertebrate fossils by washing and screening.   In: Kummel and Raup, (eds.), 1965, 193—203, 2 figs.
1965D.   Speculations on endemism in terrestrial West Coat Paleogene mammals.
Program, Sect. E (Geol., Geog.), Amer. Assoc. Advanc. Sci., Meeting Dec. 26—31, 1965, 14—15, (abs.).
1966A.   Synopsis of Whitneyan and Arikareean camelid phylogeny.   Amer. Mus.
Novit., no. 2253, 11 pp., 1 fig., 1 table.
1966B.   Speculations on endemism in terrestrial West Coast Paleogene mammals.
Spec. Pap. Geol. Soc. Amer., 87, 314—315, (abs.).
1967A.   Frick laboratory.   Ann. Rept. Amer. Mus. Nat. Hist., 98, 62—63.
1967B.   Classification, range, and deployment of the prosimian primates.   Colloq. Internat. Cent. Nation. Recherch., 163, 603—609, 1 fig.,
(French summary).
1968   Leptacodon, an American Paleocene nyctithere (Mammalia, Insectivora).
Amer. Mus. Novit., 2317, 12 pp., 4 figs., 1 table.
See: Clemens, McKenna, et al.;   Stucker, Galusha and McKenna;   Van
Valen, Butler, et al.

McKENNA, M. C., and HOLTON, C. P.
1967   A new insectivore from the Oligocene of Mongolia and a new subfamily
of hedgehogs. Amer. Mus. Novit., 2311, 11 pp., 2 figs., 1 table.

McKERN, THOMAS W.
1966A.   (ed.) Readings in physical anthropology.   Englewood Cliffs, New Jersey:
Prentice-Hall, vii + 199 pp.
Rev.: Bass in Amer. Anthrop., 69, 544;   Van Horn in Amer. Jour.
Phys. Anthrop., 25, 181.
1966B.   Prehistoric medicine.   Texas Jour. Sci., 18, 125, (abs.).
See: Clark, W. E. L. 1966;   Robinson, J. T. 1964B.

McKERROW, W. S.
1966   The rise and fall of fossil organisms.   New Sci., 29, 23—24, illustr.

McKUSICK, MARSHALL
1963   Identifying Iowa projectile points.   Jour. Iowa Archeol. Soc., 12:3—4,
36 pp., 17 figs.
1964   Men of ancient Iowa as revealed by archeological discoveries.   Ames,
Iowa: Iowa State Univ. Press, xix + 260 pp., illustr.
Rev.: Agogino in Amer. Antiq., 31, 123—124;   Bastian in Great Plains
Jour., 4, 63—64;   Fowler in Amer. Jour. Archaeol., 70, 213—
214;   Hagge in Mich. Archaeol., 12, 47—48;   Wedel in Amer.
Anthrop., 67, 1063—1065.

McLAREN, A.   See: Barnett, S. A. and McLaren.

McLAUGHLIN, CHARLES A.
1966   Of elephants and their ancestors.   Quart. Los Angeles Co. Mus. Nat.
             Hist., 4:4, 27–31, illustr.
1967   Aplodontoid, sciuroid, geomyoid, castoroid, and anomaluroid rodents.
             In: Anderson, S., and Jones, (eds.), 1967, 210–225, figs. 31–33.

MacLEOD, ROY M.
1965   Evolutionism and Richard Owen, 1830–1868:   an episode in Darwin's
             century.   Isis, 56, 259–280, 3 figs., portr.

McMICHAEL, E. V.
1963   Introduction to West Virginia archaeology.   W. Virginia Geol. and Econ.
             Surv.   Educational Ser., 1963, 49 pp., 21 figs., 7 maps.

McMURRY, JIM
1966   Human evolution in Africa.   Newsletter Kansas Anthrop. Assoc., 11:6,
             2–6.

McNEILL, J.   See: Heywood and McNeill.

MacNEISH, RICHARD STOCKTON
1961   First annual report of the Tehuacan Archaeological-Botanical Project.
             Andover, Mass.:   Robert S. Peabody Foundation for Archaeology,
             32 pp., frontis., 15 figs.
1962A.   Second annual report of the Tehuacan Archaeological-Botanical Project.
             Andover, Mass.:   Robert S. Peabody Foundation for Archaeology,
             42 pp., frontis., 16 figs.
             Rev.:   Coe in Amer. Antiq., 29, 525.
1962B.   Recent finds in the Yukon Territory of Canada.   In: Campbell, J. M.,
             (ed.), 1962A, 20–26.
1963   The early peopling of the New World as seen from the southwestern
             Yukon.   Anthrop. Pap. Univ. Alaska, 10:2, 93–106, 3 figs.
1964A.   Investigations in southwest Yukon: archaeological excavations, com-
             parisons, and speculations.   Pap. Robert S. Peabody Found.
             Archaeol., 6, i–xiii, 201–488, 95 figs., 26 tables.
             Rev.:   Bushnell in Antiq., 40, 78;   Campbell in Science, 148, no. 3676,
             1451;   Mayer-Oakes in Amer. Antiq., 31, 596–597.
1964B.   The peopling of the New World as seen from northwest America.   Proc.
             Internat. Congr. Americanists, 1962:1, 121–132.
1964C.   Ancient Mesoamerican civilization.   Science, 143, 531–537, 8 figs.
             Abs.:   Due Rojo in Notas Comun. Inst. Geol. Min., no. 75, 265–270,
             (Spanish).
1964D.   The origins of New World civilization.   Sci. Amer., 211:5, 29–37,
             illustr.
1967A.   An interdisciplinary approach to an archaeological problem.   In: Byers,
             D. S., (ed.), 1967, 14–24, 1 fig.
1967B.   A summary of the subsistence.   In: Byers, D. S., (ed.), 1967, 290–
             309, 3 figs., 3 tables.
1967C.   Mesoamerican archaeology.   In: Siegel, B. J., and Beals, A. R., (eds.),
             1967, 306–331.
             See: Mackay, Mathews and MacNeish.

MacNEISH, R. S., NELKEN-TERNER, A., and JOHNSON, I. W.
1967 The prehistory of the Tehuacan Valley. Vol. II. Nonceramic artifacts.
  In: Byers, (ed.), vol. II, 1967, xiii + 258 pp.

MacNEISH, R. S., and PETERSON, F. A.
1962 The Santa Marta rock shelter, Ocozocoautla, Chiapas, Mexico. New World
  Archaeol. Foundation, Publ. 10 (Paper no. 14), iv + 46 pp., 5 figs.,
  6 pls., 12 tables.

MacNIEL, F. S. See: Hopkins, D. M., et al.

McNULTY, CHARLES L., JR.
1964 Hypolophid teeth from the Woodbine formation, Tarrant County, Texas.
  Eclog. Geol. Helvetiae, 57, 537–539, 1 pl.
1965 ? Hypolorhus sylvestris White from the Woodbine formation of northeast
  Tarrant County, Texas. Spec. Pap. Geol. Soc. Amer., 82, 305–6,
  (abs.).

McNULTY, C. L., and SLAUGHTER, B. H.
1962A. Abs.: Weiler in Zbl. Geol. Pal., Teil 2, 1965, 229.
1962B. Abs.: Huene in Zbl. Geol. Pal., Teil 2, 1964, 172.
1963 Abs.: Weiler in Zbl. Geol. Pal., Teil 2, 1965, 229–230.
1964A. A protostegid turtle ramus from the Upper Cretaceous of Texas. Copeia,
  1964, 454, 1 fig.
1964B. Rostral teeth of Ischyrhiza mira Leidy from northeast Texas. Texas Jour.
  Sci., 16, 107–112, 1 pl.

MACORRA, L. (=Macorra Revilla, Louis de la)
1960 Repercussión de la oclusión dental en la forma nasal. Bol. Colegio Oficial
  Odontol. y Estomatol., 1a R., 1, 13–26.
1963 El factor dental y su importancia en la evolución del mentón en la especie
  humana. Rev. Española Estomatol., 11, 91–110.
1967 Importancia del factor dental en la aparición del mentón en el hombre.
  Discussion. 7th Internat. Congr. Anthrop. Ethnol. Sci., Moscow,
  1964, 2, 361–364.
  See: Aguirre and Macorra.

MADARIAGA DE LA CAMPA, BENITO
1963 Estudio zootécnico de la pinturas rupestres en la región cantábrica.
  Zephyrus, 14, 29–45, 12 figs., 3 pls.
1964 El mar y el hombre préhistorico. Zephyrus, 15, 37–45, 4 figs., 2 pls.,
  (English summary).
  See: González-Etchegaray, et al.

MADAULE, JACQUES
1963 Initiation à Teilhard de Chardin. Paris: Cerf, 142 pp.
  Rev.: Maia in Brotéria, Sér. Mensal, 79, 608.

MADERSON, PAUL F.
1967 A comment on the evolutionary origin of vertebrate appendages. Amer.
  Nat., 101, 71–78.

MADSEN, JAMES H., JR. See: Stokes, Anderson and Madsen.

MAGALHÃES MACEDO, ANTONIO CARLOS   See: Souza Cunha and Magalhães
        Macedo.

MAGGOWAN, KENNETH and J., and HESTER, A., JR.
    1962   Early man in the New World. New York: Doubleday & Co., 334 pp.,
                95 figs.
                Rev.: Lippert in Mitt. Anthrop. Ges. Wien, 96–97, 335.

MAGGS, T., and SPEED, E.
    1967   Bonteberg shelter. S. Afr. Archaeol. Bull., 22, 80–93, 6 figs., 4 tables.

MAGLIO, VINCENT JOSEPH
    1966   A revision of the fossil selenodont artiodactyls from the Middle Miocene
                Thomas Farm, Gilchrist County, Florida. Breviora, no. 255, 27 pp.,
                4 figs., 4 tables.

MAGRE, F.   See: Adams and Magre; Adams, Magre and Munger.

MAGUIRE, BRIAN
    1965   Foreign pebble pounding artefacts in the breccias and the overlying veg-
                etation soil at Makapansgat Limeworks. S. Afr. Archaeol. Bull.,
                20:79, 117–130, 9 figs.
    1968   The lithic industry in the Makapansgat Limeworks breccias and overlying
                surface soil. Pal. Africana, 11, 99–125, 4 figs., 1 table.

MAHÉ, JOËL
    1965A.   Un gisement nouveau de subfossile à Madagascar. C. R. Soc. Géol. France,
                1965, 66.
    1965B.   Les subfossiles malgaches (collection de l'Académie malgache). Rev.
                Madagascar, 29, 51–58, (not seen).
    1966   Le crâne de Testudo grandidieri Vaillant 1885. Bull. Soc. Géol. France,
                7, 124–128, 3 figs.
                Rev.: Radig in Zbl. Geol. Pal., Teil 2, 1967, 107.

MAHON, JUNE   See: Baer, 1964.

MAHONEY, J. A.
    1964   The taxonomic status of Dasyurus affinis McCoy [1865] (Dasyuridae)
                and Hypsiprymnus trisulcatus McCoy [1865] (Macropodidae),
                two marsupials from a Holocene cave deposit near Gisborne, Vic-
                toria. Proc. Roy. Soc. Victoria, 77, 525–532, 2 figs., pls. 77–78,
                3 tables.

MAINARDI, DANILO, and TAIBEL, M. A.
    1962   Filogenesi dei Galliformi. Rend. Ist. Lombardo, Sci. Biol. Med., B 96,
                118–130, 2 figs., (English summary).

MAIS, KARL
    1962A.   Über Lochungsversuche an einem rezenten Braunbärenwirbel. Archaeol.
                Austriaca, 32, 24–26, 1 fig.
    1962B.   Nachweis des Höhlenbären(Ursus spelaeus Rosenm.) in der Köhlerwand-
                höhle bei Lehenrotte (N.-Ö.). Die Höhle, 13, 68.
                See: Ehrenberg and Mais.

MAITRE, C.
1965   Inventaire des hommes fossiles de Columnata (Tiaret). Déposés au C.R.
            A.P.E. Libyca, 13, 9—26, 3 figs.

MAITRE, J.-P.
1965   Inventaire préhistorique de l'Ahaggar. I. Libyca, 13, 127—138, 1 table.
            See: Cinquabre and Maitre.

MAJEWSKI, ERAZM
1957   [Professor Przedpotopowicz.] Warsaw: "Czytelnik" Press, 248 pp., illustr.,
            (Polish).

MAJOROS, GYÖRGY
1964   Reptilian footprint from the Permian of Balatonrendes. Föld. Közlony,
            94:2, 243—245, 3 figs.
            Abs.: Bogsch in Zbl. Geol. Pal., Teil 2, 1966, 306.

MAKARENKO, D. E., and ROTMAN, R. N.
1966   [New data on Paleocene of the northeastern part of Ukrainian shield.]
            Geol. Zhurnal, 26:1, 42—51, 1 table, (Ukrainian; Russian summary).

MAKEEV, P. S.
1963   [On the problem of natural conditions during the Paleolithic, according
            to archeologic data.] Prirodn. Obstan. i Fauny Proshl., 1, 31—65,
            1 map, 1 table, (Russian).

MAKHNACH, N. A.   See: Ts'apenko and Makhnach.

MAKHOTIN, A. A.
1964   [Ivan Ivanovich Schmalhausen.] Zool. Jour. Moscow, 43:2, 297—302,
            portr., (Russian).

MAKSIMOV, A. V.
1960   [On the age of Sheshor horizon of East Carpathians.] Dopovidi Akad.
            Nauk USSR, Kiev, 1960:1, 69—71, (Ukrainian; Russian and
            English summaries).

MALAHAN, BERNARD J.
1967   The terrible lizards of Rocky Hill. Yankee, 31:6, 78—79, 168—171, illustr.

MALAN, BAREND DANIEL
1962B.   The stone industry of the site at Elandsfontein, Hopefield, South Africa.
            Proc. 4th Panafrican Congr. Prehist., Sec. 3, 225—232, 5 figs.,
            (discussion by R. R. Inskeep, and others).

MALARODA, ROBERTO
•1963   Cenni commemorativi di Costantino Socin (1913-1962). Boll. Soc. Geol.
            Ital., 38:1, 5—9, portr.
            See: Dal Piaz and Malaroda.

MAL'CHEVSKAĨA, T. M., and ROMANOVSKAĨA, L. V.
1966   [Catalogue of monographic paleontological collections, kept in T͡s NIGR
            Museum.] Leningrad: "Nedra" Press, 176 pp., (Russian; English
            summary).

MALDE, HAROLD E.
1964   Environment and man in arid America. Science, 145, 123–129, 1 fig.

MALDONADO-KOERDELL, MANUEL
1961   Semblanza y obra de un prehistoriador [Pablo Martínez del Río]. Ho-
            menaje a Pablo Martínez del Río, 9–15.
1964   Geohistory and paleogeography of Middle America. In: Wauchope,
            (ed.), 1964, 3–32, 11 figs.

MALDONADO-KOERDELL, M., and BORGONIO, G.
1961   Obra y bibliografía de don Pablo Martínez del Río. Homenaje a Pablo
            Martínez del Río, 23–28.

MALEEV, E. A.
1964A.   [Suborder Younginiformes.]   Osnovy Pal., [Amphibians, Reptiles, and
            Birds.], [12], 446–447, 2 figs., (Russian).
1964B.   [Suborder Choristodera.]   Osnovy Pal., [Amphibians, Reptiles, and
            Birds.], [12], 453–455, 1 fig., (Russian).
1964C.   [Family Prolacertidae.]   Osnovy Pal., [Amphibians, Reptiles, and Birds.],
            [12], 458–459, 1 fig., (Russian).
1964D.   [Family Tangasauridae.]   Osnovy Pal., [Amphibians, Reptiles, and
            Birds.], [12], 459, 1 fig., (Russian).
1964E.   [Family Thalattosauridae.]   Osnovy Pal., [Amphibians, Reptiles, and
            Birds.], [12], 460, 1 fig., (Russian).
1964F.   [Superorder Thecodontia.]   Osnovy Pal., [Amphibians, Reptiles, and
            Birds.], [12], 497–506, 14 figs., (Russian).
1964G.   [Suborder Theropoda. Carnivorous Dinosaurs.]   Osnovy Pal., [Amphib-
            ians, Reptiles, and Birds.], [12], 529–540, 20 figs., (Russian).
1964H.   [Family Compsognathidae.]   Osnovy Pal., [Amphibians, Reptiles, and
            Birds.], [12], 531–533, 3 figs., (Russian).
1964I.   [Family Coeluridae (=Coelurosauridae).]   Osnovy Pal., [Amphibians,
            Reptiles, and Birds.], [12], 533, 1 fig., (Russian).
1964J.   [Family Ornithomimidae.]   Osnovy Pal., [Amphibians, Reptiles, and
            Birds.], [12], 533–535, 2 figs., (Russian).
1964K.   [Family Megalosauridae.]   Osnovy Pal., [Amphibians, Reptiles, and
            Birds.], [12], 537, 3 figs., (Russian).
1964L.   [Family Ceratosauridae.]   Osnovy Pal., [Amphibians, Reptiles, and
            Birds.], [12], 537–538, 1 fig., (Russian).
1964M.   [Family Spinosauridae.]   Osnovy Pal., [Amphibians, Reptiles and
            Birds.], [12], 538, 1 fig., (Russian).
1964N.   [Family Deinodontidae (= Tyrannosauridae).]   Osnovy Pal., [Amphib-
            ians, Reptiles, and Birds.], [12], 538–540, 3 figs., (Russian).
1964O.   [Suborder Stegosauria.]   Osnovy Pal., [Amphibians, Reptiles, and
            Birds.], [12], 572–573, 3 figs., (Russian).
1964P.   [Suborder Ankylosauria.]   Osnovy Pal., [Amphibians, Reptiles, and
            Birds.], [12], 574–578, 9 figs., (Russian).
1965   [On the brain of carnivorous dinosaurs.]   Pal. Zhurnal, 1965:2, 141–
            143, 2 figs., (Russian).

MALEEVA, A. G.
1966   [Taphonomy of localities of fossil and sub-fossil remains of small mam-
            mals in connection with some problems of the rodent fauna
            history in the deserts of northwestern Caspian region.] Biull.
            Kom. Izuch. Chetvert. Perioda, 32, 75–86, 2 figs., 3 tables,
            (Russian).

MALENFANT, MICHEL   See: Bocquet and Malenfant.

MALEY, JEAN
1966   Remarques sur quelques sites préhistoriques de la vallée du Nil (Deuxième
     Cataracte). Bull. Soc. Préhist. Franç., C. R. séances mens., <u>63</u>,
     71—72, 1 fig.
     See: Chavaillon, J. and Maley.

MALEZ, MIRKO
1957C.   [Paleontological research in the Veternica Cave in 1955.] Ljetopis
     Jugoslav. Akademije Znanosti i Umjetnosti, <u>62</u>, 280—294, 4 figs.,
     6 pls., (Jugoslavian).
1958B.   Abs.: M. M. in Bull. Sci. Zagreb, 1962, <u>7</u>:1—2, 22.
1959E.   Dr. Otokar Kadić [1876 - 1957]. Geol. Vjesnik, <u>12</u>, 280—281, portr.
1960G.   [Die Höhlen der Cicarija-Gegend und des Učka-Gebirges in Istrien.]
     Acta Geol., Zagreb, <u>2</u>, 163—260, 47 figs., 4 pls., (Serbo-Croatian;
     German summary).
1961G.   Abs.: Herak in Zbl. Geol. Pal., Teil 2, <u>1964</u>, 414.
1961H.   Pećina Veternica Kao paleolitsko nalazište s tragovima Kulta medvjeda.
     Drugi Jug. Speleol. Kongr., Split i Dal. zagora, <u>1958</u>, 123—138,
     4 figs., 4 pls.
1962E.   Erster Fund des Rotwolfes (<u>Cuon</u> <u>alpinus</u> <u>europaeus</u> Bourguignat) im
     oberen Pleistozän der Balkanhalbinsel. Bull. Sci. Zagreb, <u>7</u>, 97—98,
     1 fig., 1 table.
1963B.   Paleontološka i speleološka istraživanja u 1960. godini. Ljetopsis
     Jugoslav. Akademije Znanosti i Umjetnosti, <u>67</u>, 250—269, 1 fig.,
     8 pls.
1963C.   Istraživanje pleistocenske stratigrafije i faune u 1962. godini. Ljetopsis
     Jugoslav. Akademije Znanosti i Umjetnosti, <u>69</u>, 305—313, 6 pls.
     Abs.: Malez in Bull. Sci., Zagreb, Sec. A, <u>10</u>, 200, (German).
1963D.   Die Quartäre Fauna der Höhle Veternica (Medvednica — Kroatien). Pal.
     Jugoslavica, <u>5</u>, 198 pp., 12 figs., 40 pls., 34 tables, 1 map, (Ger-
     man summary).
     Rev.: Brodar in Arheološki Vest., <u>17</u>, 517—522; Dulic in Säugetier-
     kundl. Mitt., <u>13</u>, 140.
     Abs.: Herak in Zbl. Geol. Pal., Teil 2, <u>1966</u>, 43—44; Malez in Bull.
     Sci., Zagreb, Sec. A, <u>10</u>, 84—85.
1963E.   Stratigraphische und paläontologische Untersuchungen diluvialer Fundorte
     in der Veternica-Höhle (Medvednica). Bull. Sci., Zagreb, <u>8</u>, 141,
     (abs.).
1964A.   Der erste Fund der grossen Höhlenkatze — <u>Panthera</u> <u>spelaea</u> (Goldf.) —
     im Pleistozän von Bosnien und Herzegowina. Bull. Sci. Zagreb,
     <u>9</u>, 2—3.
1964B.   Šandalja bei Pula — ein neuer und wichtiger paläolitischer Fundort in
     Istrien. Bull. Sci. Zagreb, <u>9</u>, 154—155, 2 figs.
1965A.   [Die Höhle Veternica in der Medvednica. I. Allgemeine speläologische
     Übersicht. II. Stratigraphie der quartären Ablagerungen.] Acta
     Geol., Zagreb, <u>5</u>, 175—237, 28 figs., 1 chart, 14 pls., 2 tables,
     (Serbo-Croatian; German summary).
     Rev.: Brodar in Arheološki Vest., <u>17</u>, 517—522.
     Abs.: M. S. in Bull. Sci., Zagreb, Sec. A, <u>11</u>:4—6, 148—149.
1965B.   [Sites of fossil hominids in Croatia.] Geol. Vjesnik, <u>18</u>:2, 309—324,
     (Serbo-Croatian; German summary).
     Rev.: Brodar in Arheološki Vest., <u>17</u>, 522; Kochansky-Devidé in Zbl.
     Geol. Pal., Teil 2, <u>1969</u>:1, 59.
     Abs.: M. M. in Bull. Sci., Zagreb, sec. A, <u>11</u>:7—9, 217.
1965C.   Die Höhlen von Cernovac. Izdanja Speleol. društva Hrvatske, Zagreb,
     <u>1</u>, 1—44.

	Abs.: M. M. in Bull. Sci., Zagreb, sec. A, 11:4—6, 150—151.
1965D.	Druška peć auf der Ucka — ein neuer Fundort der Fauna des oberen Pleistozäns in Istrien. Bull. Sci., Zagreb, Sec. A, 10, 65—66, 1 fig.
1965E.	Crvena Stijena in Montenegro, eine bedeutende paleontologische Lokalität aus der Balkanhalbinsel. Bull. Sci., Zagreb, Sec. A, 10, 145—147, 1 table.
1965F.	Über das Paläolithikum der Höhle Velika pećina auf der Ravna Gora in Nordwest-Kroatien. Bull. Sci., Zagreb, Sec. A, 10, 325, (abs.).
1965G.	Der altpleistozäne Fundort Dubci in Mitteldalmatien. Bull. Sci., Zagreb, Sec. A, 10, 418—420, 1 fig.
1965H.	Erster Fund der Gattung Mastodon (Bunolophodon) grandincisivus Schlesinger im Pliozän von Slawonien. Bull. Sci., Zagreb, Sect. A, 10, 420—421, 1 fig.
1965I.	Neue allgemeine Schwankungsbreite der Art Ursus spelaeus. Rosenm. und Heinroth. Geol. Vjesnik, 18, 130—133, 3 tables, (Croatian; German summary).
	Rev.: Ehrenberg in Zbl. Geol. Pal., Teil 2, 1967, 515.
	Abs.: Herak in Zbl. Geol. Pal., Teil 2, 1966, 328.
1965J.	Roter Alpenwolf und Vielfrass—zwei interessante Eiszeit-Mammalien aus unseren Höhlen. Priroda (Zagreb), 52, 135—139.
	Abs.: M. M. in Bull. Sci., Zagreb, Sec. A, 11:4—6, 150.
1965K.	Fossil-Menschen in Kroatien. Priroda (Zagreb), 52, 162—163.
	Abs.: M. M. in Bull. Sci., Zagreb, Sec. A, 11:4—6, 150.
1966	Die Gattung Ochotona Link, 1795 (Lagomorpha Brandt 1855) in Jugoslawien. Bull. Sci., Zagreb, Sect. A, 11, 5—6, 1 fig.
1968	Ochotona pusilla (Pallas) in the Upper Pleistocene of Central Bosnia. Bull. Sci., Zagreb, Sec. A, 13:1—2, 2—3, 1 fig.
	See: Basler, Malez and Brunnacker.

MALEZ, M., and BOŽIČEVIĆ, S.
1964	Medvjeđa pećina (Bärenhöhle) auf der Insel Lošinj als eine Beweis für postwürmsche Transgression im nördlichen Teile des Adriatischen Meeres. Bull. Sci., Zagreb, 9, 105—106, 1 fig.

MALEZ, M., and CRNOLATAC, I.
1966	Two new Paleolithic sites at Sinai. Bull. Sci., Zagreb, Sec. A, 11:4—6, 102—105, 3 figs.

MALEZ, M., and SLIŠKOVIĆ, T.
1964	Neue Fundorte tertiärer Wirbeltiere in Bosnien und Herzegowina. Bull. Sci., Zagreb, 9, 3—4, 1 fig.

MALICH, N. S.
1967	[On the Devonian stratigraphy of the northwest of the Siberian Platform.] In: Sokolov, B. S., (ed.), 1967, 143—144, (Russian).

MALIK, S. C.
1964	Levels in Indian prehistory. Current Anthrop., 5, 204—205.
1966	The Late Stone Age industries from excavated sites in Gujarat, India. Artibus Asiae, 28, 162—174, 7 figs., 2 tables.
	See: Wainwright and Malik.

MALINOVSKAÎA, S. P.   See: Mazarovich, O. A., et al.

MALINOWSKI, TADEUSZ
1964   Exposition permanente du Musée Archéologique à Poznań. Fontes
            Archaeol. Posnanienses, 15, 206—229, 35 figs., (Polish).

MALLORCA SYMPOSIUM
1966   Symposium de Deya (Mallorca) sobre Myotragus balearicus Bate, julio
            1965. Bol. Soc. Hist. Nat. Baleares, 12:1—4, 3—160.

MALOLETKO, A. M.
1959   [On the stratigraphy of Quaternary deposits of the Pre-Altaic part of
            Western Siberia.] Izv. Vyssh. Uch. Zav., Geol. i Razv., 1959:8,
            53—58, 1 fig., 1 table, (Russian).
1963   [Paleogeography of the Altai plain in the Quaternary period.] Trudy
            Kom. Chet. Period., 22, 165—182, 4 figs., 3 tables, (Russian).

MALTHUS, R. S.   See: Trotter and Malthus.

MALUQUER DE MOTES, J.
1965   La estratigrafía del covacho de Berroberría (Urdax, Navarra). In: Ripoll
            Perelló, E., (ed.), 1965B, 135—140, (French summary).

MALZ, HEINZ
1964   Kouphichnium walchi, die Geschichte einer Fährte und ihres Tieres.
            Natur u. Mus., 94, 81—97, 15 figs.
            Abs.: Häntzschel in Zbl. Geol. Pal., Teil 2, 1964, 876.
1967   "Branchiosaurus", ein problematisches Ur-Amphib aus dem Perm. Natur
            u. Mus., 97, 397—406, 8 figs.
            Rev.: Westphal in Zbl. Geol. Pal., Teil 2, 1968, 201—202.

MALZAHN, ERICH
1963   Lepidotus elvensis Blainville aus dem Posidonienschifer der Dobbertiner
            Liasscholle mit speziellen Untersuchungen zur Histologie des
            Operculums. Geol. Jahrb., 80, 539—560, pls. 40—45, (English
            and French summaries).
1968   Über neue Funde von Janassa bituminosa (Schloth.) im niederrheinischen
            Zechstein. Ein Beitrag zur Histologie der Zähne, Haut und Lebens-
            weise. Geol. Jahrb., 85, 67—96, 1 fig., 5 pls., (English and French
            summaries).

MALZAHN, E., and RABITZ, A.
1962   Ein Aufschluss in Zechstein-Randfazies im Hünxer Graben bei Bottrop
            und seine Fauna. Fortschr. Geol. Rheinld. u. Westf., 6, 239—
            244, 1 fig.
            Abs.: Hiltermann in Zbl. Geol. Pal., Teil 2, 1964, 24.

MAMEDOV, E.   See: Vakturskaĭa, Vinogradov and Mamedov.

MAMMOUDA, H. G.   See: El-Toubi, Kamal and Mammouda.

MAMONOVA, N. N.
1968   [The determination of the length of bones based on their fragments.]
            Voprosy Antrop., 29, 171—177, 5 figs., 2 tables, (Russian).

MANCA, V.   See: Zei and Manca.

MANDELBAUM, DAVID G., LASKER, G. W., and ALBERT, E. M., (eds.)
1963   The teaching of anthropology. Mem. Amer. Anthrop. Assoc., 94, xxvi +
          611 pp.
          Rev.: Kaufmann in Arch. Suiss. Anthrop. Gén., 29, 72-73;
          Spaulding in Amer. Anthrop., 69, 746-747.

MANDERA, H. E.
1963   Die ältere Steinzeit. Schrift. Städt. Mus. Wiesbaden, 5, 42 pp., illustr.,
          (not seen).

MANGERUD, JAN
1965   Drift in some tributary valleys of Gudbrandsdalen (Central Norway),
          with remarks on the Norwegian mammoth finds. Norsk. Geol.
          Tidsskrift, 45, 199-226, 14 figs., (Norwegian; English summary).

MANGIN, JEAN PHILIPPE
1962A.   Abs.: Häntzschel in Zbl. Geol. Pal., Teil 2, 1964, 43.
1962B.   Les cycles de dépôt des alluvions anciennes aux abords de Dijon et en
          Quelques points de Côte-d'Or. (Observations préliminaires.) Bull.
          Sci. Bourgogne, 21, 151-157, 1 fig.

MANGUS, MARLYN See: Schaeffer, B. and Mangus.

MANIA, DIETRICH
1963   Archäologische Studien in der zentralen Mongolei. Wiss. Zeit. Halle
          Univ., Ges.-Sprachwiss. Reihe, 12, 847-888, 29 pls.
1967   Der ehemalige Ascherslebener See (Nordharzvorland) in spät-und post-
          glazialer Zeit. Hercynia, 4:2, 199-260, 13 figs., 4 pls., 4 tables.

MANNAĬ-OOL, M. KH.
1964   [Archeological relics of Tuva.] Kyzyl: Tuva Press, 45 pp., 16 figs.,
          (Russian).

MANNINO, GIOVANNI
1960   Nuove incisioni rupestri in una grotta del Pizzo Muletta (Capaci – prov.
          di Palermo). Rass. speleol. italiana, 12, 183-190, 2 figs., 3 pls.
1962B.   Nuove incisioni rupestri nel trapanese. Rass. mensile della Prov. (Trapani),
          7 (9), 3-7.
          Rev.: Dell'Oca in Rass. speleol. italiana, 14, 376.
1965   Sicilia. Riv. Sci. Preist., 19, 302-303.

MANSFIELD, RAY
1967   A survey of British caving periodicals. Studies in Spel., 1, 285-294.

MANZIĬ, S. F.
1962   [Adaptation of vertebrates to terrestrial locomotion.] Trudy Inst. Zool.
          AN URSR, 18, 12-19, 5 figs., (Ukrainian; Russian summary).

MARÇAIS, JEAN
1966A.   Sur l'attribution du Prix Prestwich à M. Georges Choubert. [Choubert's
          reply.] C. R. Soc. Géol. France, 1966, 214-216.
1966B.   Sur l'attribution du Prix Lamothe à M. Marcel Gigout. [Gigout's reply.]
          C. R. Soc. Géol. France, 1966, 220-221.

MARCHAL, ANATOLE F.
    1965   O enigma dos dinossáurios fulminados. Brotéria, Sér. Mensal, 81, 129–
                130.

MARCHESSEAU, J.
    1966   Sur la découverte d'un gisement à industrie paléolithique dans le Nord-
                Ouest du Dahomey. Bull. Inst. Franç. Afr. Noire, 28, 575–594,
                1 fig., 19 pls., map.

MARCHIANDO, P. J.
    1966   Observations on the archeology of the Tocks Island Reservoir area in
                New Jersey. Bull. Eastern States Archeol. Fed., no. 25, 15, (abs.).

MARCOZZI, VITTORIO
    1965A.   I renvenimenti di Olduvai Gorge e le origini dell'Uomo. Gregorianum,
                46, 595–604.
    1965B.   Relazione di un viaggio nelle regioni degli Australopitecidi. Observazioni
                sui più recenti rinvenimenti. Riv. Antrop., 52, 43–74, 13 figs.,
                9 pls., 10 tables, (English summary).

MARCUS, LESLIE F.   See: Stirton and Marcus.

MARCUZZI, GIORGIO
    1959   Nuovi orientamenti in biogeografia. Monitore Zool. Ital., 66:4, 251–258.

MARDEN, LUIS
    1967   Madagascar, island at the end of the earth. Nation. Geog. Mag., 132,
                443–487, illustr.

MAREK, KURT W., (ed.) (pseud., Ceram, C. W.)
    1966   Hands on the past. New York: Knopf, 434 pp., illustr., (not seen).

MARELLI, CARLOS A.
    1953   Las grandes especies de mamiferos australes llamados notoungulados.
                "Gallardodon inexcussus" nuevo genero y nueva especie de
                ungulado fosil de la Argentina. Anales Museo Nahuel Huapi, 3,
                149–154, 3 pls.

MARGAIN, CARLOS
    1965   The desert and archeology. Desert Mag., 28:6, 33, 1 fig.; 28:7, 32.

MARGOS, ARA   See: Dzhambazov and Margos.

MARINESCU, FL.   See: Macarovici, Marinescu and Motaş.

MARINGER, JOHANNES
    1956D.   Einige faustkeilartige Geräte von Gongenyama (Japan) und die Frage
                des japanischen Paläolithikums. Anthropos, 51, 175–179.
    1962   Los dioses de la prehistoria. Las religiones de Europa durante el Paleo-
                lítico. Prologue by E. Ripoll Perelló. Barcelona: Editorial Des-
                tino, 279 pp., 63 figs., 53 pls., 3 color pls., (not seen).
                Rev.: Llongueras Campañá in Ampurias, 24, 365–367; Vidart in Bol.
                Bibliog. Cien. Hombre, no. 2, 7–8.

MARINOV, N. A.
1957   [Stratigraphy of Mongolian People's Republic.]   Moscow: Akad. Nauk
               SSSR Press, 268 pp., 24 figs. and maps, 9 tables, (Russian).
1966   (ed.) [Materials on geology of the Mongolian People's Republic.]   Moscow:
               "Nedra" Press, 287 pp., illustr., (Russian).

MARK, ELGA IŪ. (= Mark-Kurik, E. Ĭu.)
1963   [On the spinal plate of the Middle Devonian Arthrodire Homostius.]
               Uurimused Eesti NSV Tead. Akad. Geol. Inst., 13, 189–200, 7
               figs., 1 pl., (Russian; Esthonian and English summaries).
1964   [On the individuality of upper and lower parts of Tartu beds, and on
               their nomenclature.]   In: Karataĭute-Talimaa and Narbutas, (eds.),
               1964, 64–66, (Russian).
1966   [On injuries of the exoskeleton of psammosteids (Agnatha).]   In:
               Gekker, (ed.), 1966, 55–60, 5 figs., 3 pls., (Russian).
1968   New finds of psammosteid (Heterostraci) in the Devonian of Estonia
               and Latvia. Toimetised Eesti NSV Tead. Akad., ser. chem. geol.,
               17:4, 409–424, 11 figs., (Estonian and Russian summaries).
         See: Obruchev, D. V. and Mark-Kurik;   Verte and Mark-Kurik.

MARK-KURIK, E. IŪ., and TAMME, A.-L. E.
1964   [On the limit between Narova and Arukĭul' horizons in Esthonian SSR.]
               In: Karataĭute-Talimaa and Narbutas, (eds.), 1964, 67–73, 2
               tables, (Russian).

MARKEVICH, V. I.   See: David, A. I. and Markevich;   Grigor'eva, et al.

MARKOV, F. G.,   RAVICH, M. G., and VAKAR, V. A.
1957   [The geological structure of the Taĭmyr Peninsula.]   Trudy Inst. Geol.
               Arktiki, 81, 313–387, (Russian).

MARKOV, G.
1963   Abs.: Ehrenberg in Zbl. Geol. Pal., Teil 2, 1964, 993–994.

MARKOV, K. K.
1960   [Synthesis of Baltic Sea history.]   Izv. Akad. Nauk, Ser. Geograf.,
               1960:1, 105–117, 6 figs., (Russian).
1961B.   (ed.) [Relief and stratigraphy of Quaternary deposits of the northwest
               of Russian Plain. Publication for the Sixth Congress of INQUA
               in Warsaw, 1961.] Moscow: Akad. Nauk SSSR Press, 252 pp.,
               illustr., (Russian; English summary).
         See: Gromov, V. I., Ivanova, et al.

MARKOV, K. K.,   LAZUKOV, G. I., and NIKOLAEV, V. A.
1965A.   [The Quaternary Period (Glacial Period — Anthropogene Period). Vol. I.
               The territory of the USSR. (For the VII INQUA Congress).]
               Moscow: University Press, 371 pp., 126 figs., 31 tables, (Russian).
1965B.   [The Quaternary Period (Glacial Period — Anthropogene Period). Vol.
               II. The territory of the USSR. (For the VII INQUA Congress).]
               Moscow: University Press, 435 pp., 116 figs., 1 chart, 14 tables,
               (Russian).

MARKOVA, K. K.   See: Grichuk and Markova.

MARKOVA, N. G.   See: Vinogradov, A. P., et al.

MARKOVICH-MAR'ĪANOVICH, ELENA
1966   [Loess stratigraphy of Susak island in the northern part of the Adriatic Sea.] Bı͡ull. Kom. Izuch. Chetvert. Perioda, 31, 32—41, 4 figs., (Russian).

MARKOVIN, V. I.
1964   [New materials on the archeology of northern Ossetia and Chechnı͡a.] Krat. Soob. Inst. Ist. Mat. Kult. SSSR, 98, 81—89, 3 figs., (Russian).
        See: Lı͡ubin, Bader and Markovin.

MARKOVSKIĬ, B. P. See: Nalivkin and Markovskiĭ.

MARKS, ANTHONY E.
1964   The prehistory of Nubia. Dallas (Texas): Southern Methodist Univ., (not seen).
        See: Wendorf, Shiner and Marks; Wendorf, Shiner, Marks, et al.

MARKUS, MILES B.
1964   Premaxillae of the fossil Passer predomesticus Tchernov and the extant South African Passerinae. Ostrich, 35, 245—246.
        Abs.: W. in Jour. Ornithol., 106, 235.

MAROCHKIN, N. I. (ed.)
1962   [Discussion of "Volume, content and terminology of Stratigraphic subdivisions of Quaternary deposits".] Informat͡sionnyĭ Sbornik, 58, 91 pp., 9 tables, (Russian).

MARQUER, PAULETTE
1967   Morphologie des races humaines. Paris: Armand Colin, 222 pp., illustr., maps, (not seen).
        Rev.: Billy in L'Anthrop., 72:3—4, 365—366; Ducommun in Ann. Guébhard, 42/43, 147; MacConaill in Man, Jour. Roy. Anthrop. Inst., 2, 467; Tétry in L'Ann. Biol., 8:1—2, 141—142.

MÁRQUEZ TRIGUERO, ESTEBAN
1965A.   Nuevos yacimientos del Paleolítico en Vallecas (Madrid). Notas Comun. Inst. Geol. Min., 77, 175—186, 7 figs., (French and English summaries).
1965B.   Sobre un nuevo yacimiento del Paleolítico en Coslada (Madrid). Notas Comun. Inst. Geol. Min., 78, 77—83, 6 figs., (French and English summaries).

MARS, P.
1963   Les faunes et la stratigraphie du Quaternaire méditerranéen. Bull., Rec. Trav. Stat. Mar. Endoume, 28:43, 61—97, 6 figs., 3 tables.

MARSHACK, ALEXANDER
1964   Lunar notation on Upper Paleolithic remains. Science, 146, 743—745, 3 figs., cover photo.
        Abs.: Anon. in Naturwiss. Rund, 18, 166.
        Rev.: [Beltrán] in Caesaraugusta, 23—24, 155.

MARSHALL, DICK
1965   The Paleo-Indian era: distribution of finds. Missouri. Bull. Southeast. Archaeol. Confer., 2, 22—23.

MARSHALL, LAURISTON C.   See: Berkner and Marshall.

MARSHALL, P. M., and BUTLER, P. M.
1966   Molar cusp development in the bat, Hipposideros beatus, with reference
to the ontogenetic basis of occlusion. Arch. Oral Biol., 11, 949–
965, 12 figs., 1 pl., (French and German summaries).

MARSKY, KL.   See: Kurth and Marsky.

MARTEL SAN GIL, M., and AGUIRRE, E.
1964   Coleccion Rodrigo Botet del Museo Paleontológico Municipal de Valencia.
Publ. del Arch. Mun. de Valencia, ser. 1, 2.
Rev.: M. C. P. in Fossilia, 1965:2, 47–48.

MARTIN, CHRISTOPHER
1964   The wonders of prehistoric man. New York: Putnam, 128 pp., illustr.,
(not seen).

MARTIN, E. CRAIG
1965   Who begat whom? Newsletter Kansas Anthrop. Assoc., 11:2, 3–6.

MARTIN, GERALD P. R.
1965A.   Conrad Gesner (1516–1565). Natur u. Mus., 95:12, 483–494, 6 figs.,
portr.
1965B.   Berichtigung zur Arbeit Martin & Weiler 1965. Senck. Lethaea, 46,
481–482, table 3.
1965C.   Schriften von Prof. Dr. Wilhelm Weiler (Worms). Senck. Lethaea, 46a,
491–498.
1966A.   Ein "Diskussionsbeitrag" Eduard Mörike's zum Chirotherium-Problem.
Natur u. Mus., 96:1, 9–11, 1 fig.
1966B.   Robert Dick 1811 - 1866. Ein Scottischer Naturforscher. Natur u.
Mus., 96, 491–500, 4 figs., portr.

MARTIN, G. P. R., and WEILER, H.
1963   Der Wealden in der Gegend von Barnstorf (Kreis Grafschaft Diepholz,
Niedersachsen.) Neues Jahrb. Geol. Pal., Abh., 118, 30–64, 4 figs.,
6 pls.
Abs.: Bartenstein in Zbl. Geol. Pal., Teil 2, 1964, 648–649.

MARTIN, G. P. R., and WEILER, W.
1965   Neue Untersuchen an Fish-Otolithen aus dem älteren Jura NW-Deutsch-
lands. Senck. Lethaea, 46, 35–71, pls. 2–4, 3 tables.
Abs.: Weiler in Zbl. Geol. Pal., Teil 2, 1966, 282–283.

MARTIN, HAROLD   See: Green, M. and Martin.

MARTIN, LARRY D.
1966   Tooth replacement in Hyracodon. Proc. Neb. Acad. Sci., 76th Ann.
Meeting, 1966, 15, (abs.).
1967   X-ray techniques for the study of fossil vertebrates. Compass Sigma
Gamma Epsilon, 44:2, 101–103, 3 pls.
See: Tanner and Martin.

MARTIN, L. D., and TATE, J., Jr.
1966   A bird with teeth. Mus. Notes, Univ. Neb. State Mus., no. 29, 1–2, 1 fig.

MARTIN, PAUL SIDNEY
1963   The last 10,000 years. A fossil pollen record of the American Southwest. Tucson: Univ. of Arizona Press, viii + 87 pp., 37 figs., 14 pls.
           Rev.: Gell in Kiva, 31, 99–101; Hansen in Ecology, 46, 216–217; Maher in Amer. Jour. Sci., 263, 191–192; Wright in Science, 144, 715.
1965   Prehistoric overkill. 7th Internat. Congr., Internat. Assoc. Quat. Res., Abs., 1965, 323–324, (abs.).
1966   Africa and Pleistocene overkill. Nature, 212, 339–342, 1 fig., 4 tables.
           Rev.: KSM in Naturwiss. Rundschau, 20:9, 392–393.
1967A.   Preface. In: Martin, P. S., and Wright, H. E., (eds.), 1967, v–viii.
1967B.   Prehistoric overkill. In: Martin, P. S., and Wright, H. E., (eds.), 1967, 75–120, 4 figs., 6 tables.
1967C.   Pleistocene overkill. Nat. Hist., 76:10, 32–38, illustr.
1967D.   Overkill at Olduvai Gorge. Nature, 215, 212–213, 1 table.
1968   Pleistocene overkill – in rebuttal. Nat. Hist., 77:1, 74–75.
           See: Guilday, Martin and McCrady.

MARTIN, P. S., and GUILDAY, J. E.
1967   A bestiary for Pleistocene biologists. In: Martin, P. S., and Wright, H. E., (eds.), 1967, 1–62, 31 figs.

MARTIN, P. S., SABELA, B. E., and SHUTLER, D.
1961   Rev.: Graham in Cave Notes, 3, 7–8.

MARTIN, P. S., and WRIGHT, H. E., JR., (eds.)
1967   Pleistocene extinctions. The search for a cause. New Haven, Conn.: Yale Univ. Press, 453 pp., illustr. (Vol. 6 of Proc. 7th Inqua Congr.).
           Rev.: Anon. in Earth Sci. Jour., 2:2, 189; Anon. in GeoTimes, 13:4, 34; Cooke in Amer. Anthrop., 71, 161–163; Corbet in Jour. Animal Ecol., 38:1, 238; Dawson in Jour. Pal., 43:5, 1299–1300; Godwin in Nature, 219, 1285–1287; Guthrie in Arctic, 22, 82–84; Hibbard in GeoTimes, 14, 30; MacConaill in Man, Jour. Roy. Anthrop. Inst., 3, 665–666; Martin in Jour. Mammal., 50:1, 164–165; G. F. Mitchell in Antiq. Jour., 49:2, 397–398; Prufer in Science, 162, 1110–1112; Reed in Ecology, 50:2, 343–346; Wilmsen in Amer. Jour. Archaeol., 73:1, 99–101.

MARTIN, R.
1966   Le glouton de Villereversure. Doc. Lab. Géol. Fac. Sci. Lyon, 21, 71–100, 7 figs., 7 tables, (English abs.).

MARTIN, RICHARD A.
1966   Eternal spring: man's 10,000 years of history at Florida's Silver Springs. St. Petersburg, Fla.: Great Outdoors Publ. Co., 264 pp., illustr.

MARTIN, ROBERT A.
1967   A comparison of two mandibular dimensions in Peromyscus, with regard to identification of Pleistocene Peromyscus from Florida. Tulane Studies Zool., 14, 75–79, 5 figs.
1968A.   Late Pleistocene distribution of Microtus pennsylvanicus. Jour. Mammal., 49, 265–271, 2 figs., 1 table.
1968B.   Aquatic rodents of the Florida Pleistocene. Plaster Jacket, 8, 2–7, 5 figs., 1 table.

MARTIN, R. D.
1966   Sind Spitzhörnchen wirklich Vorfahren der Affen? Umschau, 66, 437–
438, 2 figs., 2 pls.
1968   Towards a new definition of primates. Man, Jour. Roy. Anthrop. Inst.,
3, 377–401, 4 figs.

MARTIN AGUADO, MAXIMO
1963A.   Recientes hallazgos prehistóricos en las graveras de Toledo. Est. Geol.
Inst. Invest., Lucas Mallada, 18, 139–154, 31 figs., (English summary).
1963B.   El yacimiento prehistórico de Pinedo (Toledo) y su industria triédrica.
Publ. Inst. Prov. de Invest. y Estud. Toledanos, 2nd ser., 1, (not
seen).
Rev.: H.-P. in Bol. Soc. Españ. Hist. Nat., Sec. Geol., 62, 136.
1966   Sobre el pobliamiento de la cuenca del Tajo en el Paleolítico inferior,
a partir de las costas Atlánticas de Marruecos. Actas V Congr.
Panafr. Prehist. Estud. Cuaternario, 1963:2, 179–186, 4 figs.

MARTINEZ, F.
1964   Resultados de una campaña de exploración paleontológica en Tenerife.
Publ. Cat. Paleont. Univ. Barcelona, 1.
1965   Nueva campaña paleomastológica en Tenerife. Fossilia, 1965:3–4, 9–12.

MARTINEZ, JOHN   See: Holden 1966.

MARTINEZ, MAXIMO   See: Grambast, et al.

MARTINEZ DEL RIO, PABLO
1931   El cráneo de Pekín. Univ. Méx., 1:4, 357–358, (not seen).
1933   Los cazodores del mamut. El Libro y el Pueblo, 11, 52–58, illustr.

MARTINI, ERLEND
1964   Ein Otolithen-Pflaster im Stettiner Gestein. Natur u. Mus., 94, 53–59,
3 figs.
Abs.: Weiler in Zbl. Geol. Pal., Teil 2, 1965, 228.
1965   Die Fischfauna von Sieblos Rhön (Oligozän). 1. Smerdis-Skelette mit
Otolithen in situ. 2. Fischreste aus Koprolithen. Senck. Lethaea,
46a, 291–314, 19 figs., pls. 19–21, 1 table.
Abs.: Weiler in Zbl. Geol. Pal., Teil 2, 1966, 281–282.
1967A.   Die oligozäne Fossilfundstätte Sieblos an der Wasserkuppe. Natur u.
Mus., 97:1, 1–8, 11 figs.
Rev.: Weiler in Zbl. Geol. Pal., Teil 2, 1967, 499.
1967B.   Pararallus hassenkampi n. sp., eine neue Rallen-Art (Aves) aus dem
Oligozän von Sieblos/Rhön. Neues Jahrb. Geol. Pal., Abh., 127:3,
288–292, 1 fig., 1 pl.
Rev.: Kuhn in Zbl. Geol. Pal., Teil 2, 1967, 511.

MARTINSON, G. G.
1958   [Origin of Baĭkal fauna.] Kraevedcheskii Sborn., 3, 37–41, (Russian).
1967A.   (ed.) [Stratigraphy and paleontology of Mesozoic and Paleogene-Neogene
continental deposits of the Asiatic part of the USSR.] Leningrad:
"Nauka" Press, 282 pp., ill., (Russian).
1967B.   [The problem of the origin of the Baĭkal Lake fauna.] Zool. Zhurnal,
46:10, 1594–1598, (Russian; English summary).

MARTINSSON, ANDERS
    1966   Beyrichiacean ostracodes associated with the earliest Silurian vertebrates
                from Gotland. Geol. Fören. Förh., 88, 327—339, 8 figs.
    1968   Towards a new style in palaeontological publishing. Lethaia, 1, i—ii,
                1 fig.

MARTIROSIÁN, A. A.
    1968   [Archeological discoveries in Armenia.] In: Rybakov, (ed.), 1968, 308—
                313, 2 figs., (Russian).

MARTYN, JOHN
    1967   Pleistocene deposits and new fossil localities in Kenya. Nature, 215,
                476—479, 2 figs.

MARTYNOV, V. A.
    1961   [Essay of correlating the Quaternary deposits of the southern part of
                West Siberian Lowlands.] In: Rostovtsev, (ed.), 1961, 412—428,
                1 fig., 1 table, (Russian).
    1962   [On the lower limit of Quaternary in the southern part of West Siberian
                lowlands.] Trudy SNIIGGIMS, 24, 182—197, 2 figs., (Russian).

MARTYNOV, V. A., MIZEROV, B. V., and STRELKOV, S. A.
    1964   [Stratigraphy of Quaternary (Anthropogene) deposits of Western Siberia.]
                Biull. Kom. Izuch. Chetvert. Perioda, Akad. Nauk, SSSR, no. 29,
                3—14, 1 fig., 1 table, (Russian).

MARTYNOVA, S. S. See: Kudrin, L. N., Sivkova and Martynova.

MARX, HYMEN   See: Inger and Marx.

MAS ALÓS, JOSÉ
    1967   Síntesis biográfica de la labor científica de Carlos Rusconi. Rev. Mus.
                Hist. Nat. Mendoza, 19:1—4, 23—139, portr., 2 figs.

MASAÏTIS, V. L.   See: Krasnov, I. I., Lur'e and Masaïtis.

MASHARSKIĬ, E. A.
    1967   [The functional role of the zygomatic arch.] Voprosy Antrop., 27,
                160—162, 4 figs., (Russian).

MASLANKIEWICZOWA, ZOFIA
    1965   Semionotus cf. bergeri Agassiz from the Lias of the Holy Cross Moun-
                tains, Poland. Acta Pal. Polonica, 10, 57—68, 2 figs., 2 pls., 2
                tables.

MASLINKOV, D.   See: Boev and Maslinkov.

MASON, J. ALDEN
    1966A.   Nels Christian Nelson, 1875 - 1964. Amer. Antiq., 31, 393—397, portr.
    1966B.   Pre-Folsom estimates of the age of man in America. With comments
                by John L. Cotter. Amer. Anthrop., 68, 193—198.

MASON, REVIL J.
    1962C.   Rev.: Heberer in Naturwiss., 52, 24; Summers in Amer. Anthrop.,
                67, 839—840.

1965A.   The Abbé H. Breuil in South Africa (1929 - 1950). In: Ripoll Perelló,
E., (ed.), 1965B, 141–147, 3 pls., (Spanish summary).

1965B.   Makapansgat Limeworks fractured stone objects and natural fractures in
Africa. S. Afr. Archaeol. Bull., 20, 3–16, 4 figs., 4 pls.

1966   The excavation of Doornlaagte Earlier Stone Age camp. Kimberley district. Actas V Congr. Panafr. Prehist. Estud. Cuaternario, 1963:2,
187–188.

1967A.   Analytical procedures in the Earlier and Middle Stone Age cultures in
southern Africa. In: Bishop, W. W., and Clark, J. D., (eds.),
1967A, 737–764, 18 figs., 5 tables, (French summary).

1967B.   Questions of terminology in regard to the study of Earlier Stone Age
cultures in South Africa. Discussion. In: Bishop, W. W., and
Clark, J. D., (eds.), 1967A, 765–769.

MASON, R. J., and BEAUMONT, P. B., (eds.)
1962   COWA surveys and bibliographies. Area 13 — South Africa. COWA
Surv. and Bibliog., Area 13, no. 2, 4 + 8 pp.

MASON, SHIRLEY L.   See: Mather and Mason.

MASSIP, SALVADOR
1961   La espeleología, ciencia de las cavernas. In: Núñez Jiménez, (ed.), 1961A,
181–199, illustr.

MASSON, M. E.
1940   [Termez archeological composite expedition.] Krat. Soob. Inst. Ist. Mat.
Kult. SSSR, 8, 113–116, (Russian).

MASSON, V.
1965   [80 years of Sergeĭ Ivanovich Rudenko.] Sov. Arkheol., 1965:4, 237–
241, portr., (Russian).

MASSON, V. M., (ed.)
1966   [Middle Asia at the epoch of stone and bronze.] Moscow-Leningrad:
"Nauka" Press, 290 pp., 54 figs., 10 pls., 1 table, (Russian).
Rev.: Vinogradov and Itina in Sov. Arkheol., 1968:1, 286–295, (Russian).

MASUDA, KUICHIRO   See: Hatai, Murata and Masuda.

MATE, M. S.   See: Misra, V. N. and Mate.

MATHER, KIRTLEY F., and MASON, S. L., (eds.)
1964   A source book in geology. Reprint of 1939 ed. New York: Stechert-
Hafner, xii + 702 pp., 41 figs.
Rev.: Summerson in Ohio Jour. Sci., 66, 350.

MATHESON, COLIN
1962   The roe deer in Wales. Rept. Trans. Cardiff Nat. Soc., 89, 5–8, 1 pl.
1964   George Brettingham Sowerby the First and his correspondents. Jour.
Soc. Bibliog. Nat. Hist., 4, 214–225, pls. 3–4.

MATHEW, GERVASE   See: Oliver and Mathew.

MATHEWS, W. H.   See: Mackay, Mathews and MacNeish.

MATHIEU, ALAIN   See: Lapparent, Le Joncour, et al.

MATOLCSI, J.   See: Bökönyi, et al.

MATSON, FREDERICK R., (ed.)
1957   COWA surveys and bibliographies. Area 15 — western Asia. COWA
Surv. and Bibliog., Area 15, no. 1, 12 + 22 pp.
1960   COWA surveys and bibliographies. Area 15 — western Asia. COWA
Surv. and Bibliog., Area 15, no. 2, 10 + 28 pp.

MATSUI, V. M.   See: Bazhanov, Matsui and Mos'kina.

MATSUMOTO, HIKOSHICHIRÔ, et al.
1966   On paleoliths from the gravels at Hagurodô and Hatatate, Yamada, Sendai
City. Bull. Nation. Sci. Mus., Tokyo, 9, 219—246, 1 fig., 5 pls.
1967   On the Middle Pleistocene paleoliths found at Hagurodô Hill, Yamada,
Sendai City. Bull. Nation. Sci. Mus. Tokyo, 10, 91—122, 1 fig.,
7 pls.

MATSUMOTO, H., ISHII, S., MORI, H., CHIBA, S., and OZAKI, H.
1964A.   On some pre-Neolithic worked stones from the Loam Formation in the
Tama Hills, Hachiôji City, Tokoyo. Bull. Nation. Sci. Mus. Tokyo,
7:1, 97—106, 8 pls.
1964B.   On two remarkable stone-tools from the pre-Neolithic site at Iwajuku,
near Kiryû City, Gumma Prefecture. Bull. Nation. Sci. Mus.
Tokyo, 7:1, 107—110, 1 pl.
1964C.   On some paleoliths from Kanagi, Kitatsugaru District, Aomori Prefecture.
Bull. Nation. Sci. Mus. Tokyo, 7:2, 179—192, 21 pls.

MATSUMOTO, H., MORI, H., and CHIBA, S.
1963   On an equid fossil from the coast of the Inawashiro Lake, Konan village,
Azaka district, Fukushima Perfecture. Bull. Nation. Sci. Mus.,
Tokyo, 6:4, (53), 423—427, illustr. (Japanese; English summary).

MATSUMOTO, H., MORI, H., MARUI, K., CHIBA, S., KITAME, T., and OZAKI, H.
1965   Paleoliths from the gravels and sand in the vicinities of Sendai City,
with a consideration of the antiquity of the Mukaiyama Fossil
Valley. Bull. Nation. Sci. Mus. Tokyo, 8:3, 407—436, 8 pls.

MATSUSHIMA, YOSHIAKI   See: Hasegawa and Matsushima.

MATTAUER, MAURICE   See: Grambast, et al.

MATTER, P., III   See: Doberenz and Matter.

MATTHES, HORST WERNER
1962A.   Abs.: Dietrich in Zbl. Geol. Pal., Teil 2, 1964, 187.
1963A.   Tektonik und die Geschichte der Säuger. Hallesches Jahrb. Mitteldeutche
Erdgeschichte, 5, 71, (abs.).
1963B.   Neue Ergebungen der Ausgrabungen des Geologisch-Paläontologischen
Institutes Halle im Eozän des Geiseltales. Hercynia, 1, 3—15, 7
figs.
1964   Aus der Geschichte der Tiere. In: Kummer, and Gemeinhardt, (eds.),
1964, Teil I, 98—127, 26 figs., 1 table.
1967A.   Eine neue Creodontier-Art aus der eozänen Geiseltalfauna. Ber. Geol.
Ges. Deutsch. Demokratischen Republ., A 12:6, 659—665.

1967B.   Erstmaliger Nachweis eines Vertreters der Oxyaeninae Trouessart 1885
                (Creodonta) in Europa. Geologie, 16:4, 452–456, 4 figs., (Eng-
                lish and Russian summaries).
                Rev.: Fahlbusch in Zbl. Geol. Pal., Teil 2, 1968, 214.
1967C.   Ein neuer Creodontier: Prodissopsalis theriodis Van Valen 1965 aus der
                eozänen Braunkohle des Geiseltales. Hallesches Jahrb. Mitteldeutsche
                Erdgeschichte, 8, 7–11, 2 pls., 1 table.

MATTHES, H. W., and KRUMBIEGEL, G.
1967   Bericht über Museum für Mitteldeutsche Erdgeschichte für die Jahre
                1959 bis 1965. Hallesches Jahrb. Mitteldeutsche Erdgeschichte,
                8, 100–108, 2 tables.

MATTHES, WALTER
1966   Die Entdeckung der Kunst des älteren und mittleren Paläolithikums in
                Norddeutschland. IPEK, 21, 1–18, 9 pls.

MATTHESS, GEORG
1966   Zur Geologie des Ölschiefervorkommens von Messel bei Darmstadt. Abh.
                Hess. Landesamt. Bodenforsch., 51, 1–87, 11 figs., 10 tables,
                (English and French summaries).

MATTHEWS, J. M.
1966   The Hoabinhian affinities of some Australian assemblages. Archaeol.,
                Phys. Anthrop. in Oceania, 1, 5–22, 6 figs., 13 tables.

MATTHEWS, WILLIAM HENRY, III
1964   Exploring the world of fossils. Illustr. by Corinne and Robert Borja.
                [For elementary to high school.]   Chicago: Children's Press,
                157 pp., illustr., (not seen).
                Rev.: Imbrie in Nat. Hist., 74:9, 12;   Matthews in GeoTimes, 10:6, 39.
1965   Teacher's manual. An introduction to fossils. Six filmstrips in color.
                Rochester, N. Y.:   Ward's Natural Science Establishment, Inc.

MATTHEWS, W. H., and CURTIS, G. H.
1966   Date of the Pliocene-Pleistocene boundary in New Zealand. Nature,
                212, 979–980, 1 table.

MATTIAT, BERNHARD
1968   Sedimentpetrographie. In: Sickenberg, 1968, 38–42, 1 fig.
                See: Benda, et al.

MATTOS, A.
1961   O homem das cavernas de Minas Gerães. Belo Horizonte: Editora
                Yatiaia, (not seen).

MATVEEV, B. S.
1963   [On the origin of heterodont dental system of mammals according to
                data of ontogenesis.]   Trudy Mosk. Obshch. Ispyt. Prirody, otd.
                biol., 10, 62–74, 2 pls., (Russian).
1967   [Progress and regress in evolution.]   Priroda, 1967:5, 71–78, 4 figs.,
                2 tables, (Russian).
1968   [Present state of A. N. Severtsov's doctrine on progress and regress in
                evolution.]   Zool. Zhurnal, 47:1, 5–19, 7 figs., (Russian; Eng-
                lish summary).

MATVEEVA, A. L.   See: Vorob'eva and Matveeva.

MAUBEUGE, PIERRE L.
1961   Le gisement paléontologique et préhistorique Acheuléen de Vassincourt
              (Meuse). Avec quelques remarques sur le Paléolithique en Lorraine.
              Bull. Soc. Lorraine Sci., 1, 166–173.
1965A.   Quelques documents ichnologiques du Trias et Jurassique, lorrains et
              suisses. Bull. Acad. Soc. Lorraine Sci., 5:1, 97–103, 2 pls.
1965B.   Un contact Rhétien-Hettangien dans le Grand Duché de Luxembourg.
              Bull. Acad. Soc. Lorraine Sci., 5:3, 123–127.

MAUNY, RAYMOND
1962   Les industries paléolithique de la région El-Beyyed-Tazazmout (Adrar
              de Mauritanie). Proc. 4th Panafrican Congr. Prehist., sec. 3, 179–
              193, 6 figs.

MAURIN, VIKTOR
1962   Oberbaurat Dipl.-Ing. Hermann Bock 80 Jahre alt. Die Höhle, 13, 91–
              95, portr.

MAUSER, PETER FLORIAN
1965   Die Interpretation steinzeitlicher Silexwerkzeuge nach modernen tech-
              nologischen Gesichtspunkten. Fundber. Schwaben, 17, 29–42,
              3 figs.

MAWBY, JOHN E.
1964,
1965A.   Species groups of the canid genus Aelurodon. Program, 60th Ann.
              Meeting, Geol. Soc. Amer., Cordilleran Sect., 43, (abs.). Also:
              Spec. Pap. Geol. Soc. Amer., 82, 263, (abs.).
1965B.   Machairodonts from the Late Cenozoic of the Panhandle of Texas.
              Jour. Mammal., 46, 573–587, 5 figs., 3 tables.
1967A.   Fossil vertebrates of the Tule Springs Site, Nevada. In: Wormington,
              and Ellis, (eds.), 1967, 105–128, 10 figs., 2 tables.
1967B,
1968A.   Dipodomys-like teeth from the Miocene and early Pliocene. Program,
              63rd Ann. Meeting, Geol. Soc. Amer., Cordilleran Sect., 49, (abs.).
              Also: Spec. Pap. Geol. Soc. Amer., 115, 339, (abs.).
1968B.   Megabelodon minor (Mammalia, Proboscidea), a new species of masto-
              dont from the Esmeralda formation of Nevada. PaleoBios, 4,
              1–10, 2 figs., 1 table.
1968C.   Megahippus and Hypohippus (Perissodactyla, Mammalia) from the
              Esmeralda formation of Nevada. PaleoBios, 7, 1–13, 2 figs., 2
              tables.

MAWHINNEY, BRIAN S.
1966   Man – his origin, his nature and his God. Faith and Thought, 95:2,
              54–71.

MAXIA, C.
1966   Man and his environment in Sardinian pre- and proto-history. Quater-
              naria, 8, 23–31, (French and German summaries).

MAXWELL, M. S.
1952   The archeology of the lower Ohio Valley. In: Griffin, J. B., (ed.),
              1952A, 176–189.

MAXWELL, ROSS A., LONSDALE, J. T., HAZZARD, R. T., and WILSON, J. A.
   1967   Geology of Big Bend National Park. Univ. Texas Publ. 6711, 320 pp., 152 figs., 11 pls.

MAY, GLYN
   1966   Dinosaur footprints. Frontiers, 30, 83, illustr.

MAY [DIKTY], JULIAN
   1965   They turned to stone. Illustrated by Jean Zallinger. New York: Holiday House, 39 pp., illustr., (elemen. school).

MAYER, GASTON
   1963A.   Muschelkalkaufschüsse im südlichen Kraichgau IV. Kieselbronn. Aufschluss, 14, 275—277, 2 figs.
   1963B.   Die Geologen-Familie Würtenberger aus Dettighofen/Baden (1818 - 1956). Ber. Naturf. Ges. Freiburg, 53, 241—257, 6 figs.
   1963C.   Das den Kraichgau betreffende geologische, mineralogische, und paläontologische Schrifttum. Erste Fortsetzung, Nachtrage und Ergänzungen. Jahresh. Geol. Landesamt. Baden-Württemberg, 6, 601—622.
   1964   Muschelkalkaufschüsse im südlichen Kraichgau. VI. Ubstadt. Aufschluss, 15, 328—329, 1 fig.
   1965   Muschelkalkaufschlüsse im südlichen Kraichgau. VII. Pforzheim. Aufschluss, 16, 246—254, 7 figs.

MAYER-OAKES, WILLIAM J.
   1963B.   Manitoba's earliest settlers. Image, Manitoba Hydro Commission, 6—10, (not seen).
   1966   El Inga projectile points — surface collections. Amer. Antiq., 31, 644—661, 18 figs., 3 tables.
   1967   (ed.) Life, land and water: proceedings of the 1966 Conference on Environmental Studies of the Glacial Lake Agassiz Region. Occ. Pap. Dept. Anthrop. Univ. Manitoba, 1, xvi + 414 pp., illustr., (not seen).
          Rev.: Irving in Man, Jour. Roy. Anthrop. Inst., 3, 668—669; Wilmsen in Amer. Antiq., 34, 333—334.

MAYR, ERNST
   1963B.   Rev.: Cain in Auk, 82, 654—657; Clement in Audubon Mag., 66, 129—130; Hecht in Ecology, 45, 902; Herre in Zeit. Tierzüchtung Züchtungsbiol., 80, 300; Inger in Copeia, 1964, 245—247; Spurway in Jour. Bombay Nat. Hist. Soc., 61, 671—675; Westphal in Zbl. Geol. Pal., Teil 2, 1964, 5—6.
   1964A.   Museum of Comparative Zoology. Report of the director. Ann. Rept. Dir. Mus. Comp. Zool. Harvard, 1962—1963, 7—20.
   1964B.   Introduction. In: Darwin, C., 1964, vii — xxvii.
   1964C.   Evolutionary theory today. McGraw-Hill Yearbook Sci. Tech., 1964, 86—95, 4 figs.
   1964D.   Systematics and the origin of species. New York: Dover, xviii + 334 pp.
          Rev.: Anon. in Quart. Rev. Biol., 40, 286; Hughes in Austral. Jour. Sci., 28, 208.
   1964E.   Inferences concerning the Tertiary American bird faunas. Proc. Nation. Acad. Sci., 51, 280—288, 1 fig., 2 tables.
   1965A.   Classification and phylogeny. Amer. Zool., 5, 165—174.

1965B.   Museum of Comparative Zoology. Report of the Director. Ann. Rept.
           Dir. Mus. Comp. Zool. Harvard, 1963 - 1964, 7—27, illustr.
1965C.   Evolution at the species level. In: Moore, J. A., (ed.), 1965, 313—325.
1965D.   Selektion und die gerichtete Evolution. Naturwiss., 52, 173—180, 6 figs.
1965E.   Avifauna: turnover on islands. Science, 150, 1587—1588, 2 figs.
1965F.   What is a fauna? Zool. Jahrb., Abt. Syst. Ökol. Geog. Tiere, 92, 473—
           486.
1966   Report of the director. Ann. Rept. Dir. Mus. Comp. Zool., Harvard,
           1964 - 1965, 1—41.
1967A.   Research. Ann. Rept. Dir. Mus. Comp. Zool. Harvard, 1965 - 1966,
           10—30, 2 figs.
1967B.   Artbegriff und Evolution. Translation by Gerhard Heberer. Hamburg
           and Berlin: Verlag Paul Parey, 617 pp., 65 figs., 42 pls.
           Rev.: Bohlken in Umschau, 68, 384; Dorst in Mammalia, 33:1, 164;
           Grau in Anthropol. Anz., 31:1—2, 132—133; Kühnelt in Verh.
           Zool.-Bot. Ges. Wien, 108/109, 184—185; Kurth in Naturwiss.
           Rund., 21, 270; Niethemmer in Jour. Ornithol., 109:3, 367—
           369; Peters in Natur u. Mus., 99:1, 40—41; Reese in Zeit.
           Morph. Anthrop., 60, 223—224; Reinig in Kosmos, 64, 220;
           Rieger in Biol. Zbl., 88:2, 258—259.
1968   Theory of biological classification. Nature, 220, 545—548.
           See: Darwin 1964; Parkes 1964.

MAYR, FRANZ X.
1967   Paläobiologie und Stratinomie der Plattenkalke der Altmühlalb. Erlanger
           Geol. Abh., 67, 40 pp., 6 figs., 16 pls.

MAYR, HELMUT, and SCHINDLMAYR, W.-E.
1967   Über eine neue Spaltenfüllung bei Schelklingen im Schwäbischen Jura.
           Mitt. Bayer. Staatssamml. Pal. Hist. Geol., 7, 327—329.

MAZAROVICH, A. N.
1934   [Stratigraphy of continental Permian deposits of Volga and Viatka
           basin.] Biull. Mosk. Obshch. Ispyt. Prirody, Otd. Geol., 42,
           32—110, 21 figs., 2 tables, (Russian; French summary).

MAZAROVICH, O. A., MALINOVSKAIA, S. P., OBRUCHEVA, O. P., FREIZON, V. M.,
and IURINA, A. L.
1966   [On Devonian stratigraphy of Sarysu-Teniz watershed (Central Kazakhstan).]
           Vestnik Mosk. Univ., ser. IV Geol., 1966:1, 3—18, 2 figs., (Rus-
           sian).

MAZET, JEAN   See: Méroc and Mazet.

MAZHUGA, P. M.
1961   [Some morphological skeletal indices for the Mammalia and their use
           in rating the limb functions in fossil forms.] Zbirn. Prats' Zool.
           Muz. Akad. Nauk URSR, 30, 21—28, 2 figs., 1 table, (Ukrainian;
           Russian summary).
1962   [Onto-and phylogenesis of principal vascular system of the pectoral
           limb of mammals.] Trudy Inst. Zool. AN URSR, 18, 20—49,
           7 figs., (Ukrainian; Russian summary).

MAZONOWICZ, DOUGLAS
1965   Prehistoric cave paintings in Spain. Mus. News, 43:7, 11—19, illustr.

1966   Rock shelter paintings of eastern Spain. Mus. News, 45:1, 11–16, illustr.

1968   Spain's prehistoric rock shelter paintings. Pac. Discovery, 21, 18–25, illustr.

MAZURCZAK, L.

1968   Diesmal fossil: Fisch im Fischmaul steckengeblieben. Kosmos, 64, *14, 1 fig.

MCHEDLIDZE, G. A.

1959   [A fossil dolphin (Imerodelphis thabagarii) from Sarmatian in the vicinity of Zestafoni.] Soob. Akad. Nauk Gruz. SSR, 23, 687–694, 5 figs., 2 tables, (Russian).

1964A.   [Some problems of biology and evolution of cetaceans.] In: Orlov, (ed.), 1964C, 37–46, 9 figs., (Russian; English summary).

1964B.   [On the problem of progress in the phylogenesis of Cetacea.] Nauchn. Sess. Inst. Paleobiol. AN Gruz. SSR, 10, 23–24, (Georgian and Russian).

1964C.   [Fossil cetaceans of Caucasus.] Tbilisi: "Metsniereba" Press, 145 pp., 34 figs., 20 pls., 35 tables, (Russian; Georgian and English summaries).

1964D.   [Remains of proboscideans from Middle Miocene sediments of western Georgia.] Soob. Akad. Nauk Gruz. SSR, 35:2, 333–338, 3 figs., (Georgian; Russian summary).

1967   [Some general features of the history of Tertiary cetaceans.] In: Collected Papers, 1967A, [Place and significance of fossil mammals of Moldavia in the Cenozoic of USSR], 99–104, (Russian; not seen).

MEDIANTSEV, A. I. See: Alekseev, M. N., Giterman, et al.; Alekseev, M. N., Kuprina, et al.

MEDOEV, A. G.

1961   [Ancient relics of pictorial art in domain of Kalmakzhatkan-Karashat.] Vestnik Akad. Nauk Kazakh. SSR, 1961:2, 100–101, 3 figs., (Russian).

1962   [Preliminary data on Paleolithic in the Turanga R. valley (Northern Balkhash region).] Izv. Akad. Nauk Kazakh. SSR, seriia ist., arkheol. i etnogr., 1962:2, 94–105, 5 figs., (Russian; Kazakh summary).

1964   [Stone Age of Sary-Arka in the light of latest research.] Izv. Akad. Nauk Kazakh. SSR, ser. Obshch. Nauk, 1964:6, 90–98, 5 figs., (Russian; Kazakh summary).

1965A.   [On the sources of Ancient Paleolithic of Sary-Arka.] Izv. Akad. Nauk Kazakh. SSR, ser. Obshch. Nauk, 1965:4, 78–81, 3 figs., (Russian).

1965B.   [Topography of Stone Age sites in Northern Balkhash Region.] Vestnik Akad. Nauk Kazakh. SSR, 1965, no. 5, 85–88, 2 figs., (Russian).

MEDVEDEV, G. I.

1968   [New data on the Paleolithic and Mesolithic of upper Angara area.] In: Rybakov, (ed.), 1968, 162–164, 2 figs., (Russian).

          See: Aksenov and Medvedev.

MEDWAY, DAVID G.

1967   Avian remains from new caves in the Taumatamaire district. Notornis, 14, 158–160, pl. 27.

MEDWAY, GATHORNE (LORD)
1964A. Niah bone cave — VII. Size changes in the teeth of two rats, Rattus sabanus Thomas and R. muelleri Jentink. Sarawak Mus. Jour., 11, 616—623, 6 tables.
1964B. Post-Pleistocene changes in the mammalian fauna of Borneo. Studies in Spel., 1, 33—37.
Abs.: Anon. in Helictite, 3, 39—40.
1965 Niah Cave bone. VIII. Rhinoceros. Sarawak Mus. Jour., 12, 77—82, pl. 21, 1 table.

MEESTER, J. See: Brain and Meester.

MEFFERD, DOROTHY
1965 Memorial to Ralph L. Mefferd. [9-9-1909 — 12-25-1964.] Bull. Geol. Soc. Amer., 76, P181.

MEGAW, A. H. S., et al.
1968 British archaeology abroad, 1967. Antiq., 42, 88—102.

MEGAW, J. V. S.
1967 Art.styles and analysis. Mankind, 6, 393—402, 4 figs.

MeGAW, VINCENT
1966 Australian archaeology — how far have we progressed? Mankind, 6, 306—312.

MEGGERS, BETTY J., and EVANS, C., (eds.)
1963 Aboriginal cultural development in Latin America: an interpretative review. Smithson. Misc. Coll., 146:1, vi + 145 pp., illustr.

MEHL, M. G.
1959 Mo. caves and Ice Age vertebrates. NSS News, 17, 93—94.
1966 The Domebo mammoth: vertebrate paleomorphology. In: Leonhardy, Frank C., (ed.), 1966A, 27—30, 4 figs.

MEHRINGER, PETER J., JR.
1964 Pollen analysis and Late Pleistocene vegetation change in the Mohave Desert. Jour. Arizona Acad. Sci., 3, 108, (abs.).
1965A. The environment of extinction of the Late Pleistocene megafauna in the southwestern United States. 7th Internat. Congr., Internat. Assoc. Quat. Res., Abs., 1965, 339, (abs.).
1965B. Late Pleistocene vegetation in the Mohave Desert of southern Nevada. Jour. Arizona Acad. Sci., 3, 172—188, 11 figs.
1966 Some notes on the Late Quaternary biogeography of the Mohave Desert. Int. Res. Rept., Geochron. Lab., Univ. Ariz., 11, 1—17, 6 figs.
1967 The environment of extinction of the Late-Pleistocene megafauna in the arid southwestern United States. In: Martin, P. S., and Wright, H. E., (eds.), 1967, 247—266, 8 figs., 3 tables.

MEHRINGER, P. J., and HAYNES, C. V., JR.
1965 The pollen evidence for the environment of early man and extinct mammals at the Lehner mammoth site, southeastern Arizona. Amer. Antiq., 31, 17—23, 8 figs.

MEHTA, R. N.
1967   Stone-age sites in Valia Taluka and Mangrol Taluka of Broach and
            Surat Districts. Jour. Orient. Inst., 17, 142–148, 1 fig.

MEĬER, M. N. See: Gromov, I. M., et al.

MEIGHAN, CLEMENT W.
1963   Pre-milling stone cultures. Nevada State Mus. Anthrop. Pap., 9, 78–81.
1965   Pacific Coast archaeology. In: Wright, H. E., and Frey, D. G., (eds.),
            1965, 709–720, 6 figs.
1966   Archaeology; an introduction. San Francisco: Chandler, xiii + 197,
            104 figs., 8 tables.
            Rev.: Ackerman in Amer. Anthrop., 70, 154–155;   Allen in Mankind,
            6, 445–446;   Fagan in Amer. Antiq., 33, 394;   E. S. R. in
            Archeol. Soc. N. J., News., 83, 9–10;   Simpson in Man, Jour.
            Roy. Anthrop. Inst., 2, 134.

MEIGHAN, C. W., FOOTE, L. J., and AIELLO, P. V.
1968   Obsidian dating in West Mexican archeology. Science, 160, 1069–1075,
            5 figs., 2 tables.

MEIJER, W. C. PH.
1962   Das Balirind. Die neue Brehm-Bücherei no. 303. Wittenberg Lutherstadt:
            Ziemsen, 59 pp., 98 figs., (not seen).
            Rev.: K. in Natuurhist. Maandbl., 52, 44, (Dutch).

MEIN, PIERRE
1965A.   Chiroptera (Miocène) de Lissieu (Rhone). C. R. 89e Congr. Nation.
            Soc. Savantes, Sec. Sci., Sci. Terre Biol. Méd., 1964, 237–253,
            18 figs.
1965B.   Rotundomys, nouveau genre de Cricetidae (Mammalia, Rodentia) de la
            faune néogène de Montredon (Aude). C. R. Soc. Géol. France,
            1965, 106, (abs.).
1966   Rotundomys, nouveau genre de Cricetidae (Mammalia, Rodentia) de la
            faune néogène de Montredon (Hérault). Bull. Soc. Géol. France,
            7, 421–425, 2 figs.
            Rev.: Fahlbusch in Zbl. Geol. Pal., Teil 2, 1967, 120.
1967   Détermination de l'humérus de quelques Cricetidae fossiles. Colloq.
            Internat. Cent. Nation. Recherch. Sci., 163, 515–521, 2 pls.,
            1 table, (English summary).
            See: Ballesio, et al.; Bruijn and Mein; Flandrin, Mein and Truc;
            Hugueney and Mein; Viret, David, Mein and Battetta.

MEIN, P., RUSSO, P., and VIRET, J.
1961   Abs.: Doc. Lab. Géol. Fac. Sci. Lyon, no. 1, 36.

MEIN, P., and TRUC, G.
1966   Faciès et association faunique dans le Miocène supérieur continental
            du Haut-Comtat Venaissin. Trav. Lab. Géol. Univ. Lyon, 13,
            273-276.

MEISCHNER, DIETER
1964   Präparation von Wirbeltierknochen aus tonigen Sedimenten mittels
            Wasserstoffperoxyd. Pal. Zeit., 38, 235–236.

MELADZE, G. K.

1963 [On the extinction of Sivatheria.] Nauchn. Sess. Inst. Paleobiol. AN
  Gruz. SSR, 9, 9—10, (Russian).

1964A. [On the phylogeny of Sivatheriinae.] In: Orlov, (ed.), 1964C, 47—50,
  1 fig., (Russian; English summary).

1964B. [About the paleobiological study of Sivatheriinae.] Soob. Akad. Nauk
  Gruz. SSR., 33:3, 597—600, (Georgian; Russian summary).

1967 [Hipparion fauna of Arkneti and Bazaleti.] Tbilisi: "Mefsniereba"
  Press, 201 pp., 28 figs., 32 pls., 1 table, (Russian; English summary).

 See: Gabuniiã and Meladze.

MELAMED, IÃ. R.

1964 [The limit between Neogene and Quaternary periods in Tadzhikistan
  depression.] Doklady Akad. Nauk Tadzhik. SSR, 7:9, 18—20,
  (Russian; Tadzhik summary).

1966 [Types of sections and the stratigraphy of Neogene deposits in South
  Tadzhikistan.] Izv. Vyssh. Uch. Zav., Geol. i Razv., 1966:5,
  10—19, 2 figs., 1 table, (Russian).

 See: Loskutov, et al.

MELENDEZ, BERMUDO

1959B. Abs.: Radig in Zbl. Geol. Pal., Teil 2, 1962, 305.

1964 Paleontología y evolución. Atlantida, Madrid, 10, 366—378, 6 figs.

MELENTIS, JOHANN K.

1960 Studien über fossile Vertebraten Griechenlands. I. Ein Beitrag zug
  Kenntnis der Verbreitung von Elephas (Archidiskodon) meridionalis
  archaicus Deperet und Mayet 1923. Ann. Géol. Pays Hellén.,
  11, 266—284, 4 figs., pl. 37, (Greek summary).

1961 Abs.: Davis in Zbl. Geol. Pal., Teil 2, 1964, 214—215.

1963 Abs.: Davis in Zbl. Geol. Pal., Teil 2, 1964, 215.

1964A. Uber Equus abeli aus dem Mittelpleistozän des Beckens von Megalopolis
  im Peloponnes (Griechenland). Praktika Akad. Athenon, 38,
  507—519, 2 figs., 2 pls., 1 table, (Greek summary).

1964B. Die pleistozänen Cerviden des Beckens von Megalopolis im Peloponnes.
  Praktika Akad. Athenon, 38, 555—564, 4 pls., 1 table, (Greek;
  German summary).

1964C. Die fossilen Rhinocerotiden, Hippopotamiden und andere Säugetiere aus
  dem Becken von Megalopolis im Peloponnes. Praktika Akad.
  Athenon, 39, 388—400, 4 figs., 1 pl., (Greek; German summary).

1966A. Erster Fund von Palaeoloxodon antiquus germanicus in den jungpleis-
  tozänen Ablagerungen des Beckens von Megalopolis (Peloponnes).
  Praktika Akad. Athenon, 40, 197—207, 1 fig., 1 pl., 2 tables,
  (Greek; German summary).

1966B. Archidiskodon meridionalis proarchaicus n. ssp., die geologisch ältesten
  Elephantenreste aus Griechenland. Praktika Akad. Athenon, 40,
  310—314, 2 figs., 1 pl., (Greek; German summary).

1966C. Der erste Nachweis von Brachyodus onoideus (Mammalia, Anthraco-
  theriidae) aus Griechenland und die Datierung der Fundschichten.
  Praktika Akad. Athenon, 40, 406—423, 5 figs., 2 pls., 2 tables,
  (Greek summary).

1966D. Neue Schädel- und Unterkieferfunde von Pliohyrax graecus aus dem Pont
  von Pikermi (Attica) und Halmyropotamos (Euböa). Praktika
  Akad. Athenon, 40, 424—459, 10 figs., 7 pls., 4 tables, (Greek
  summary).

1966E.   Studien über fossile Vertebraten Griechenlands. 5. Über Hippopotamus
              antiquus Desmarest aus dem Mittelpleistozän des Beckens von
              Megalopolis in Peloponnes (Griechenland). Ann. Géol. Pays
              Hellén., 16, 403—435, 6 figs., 3 pls., 7 tables.
1967A.   Über Coelodus münsteri Ag. (Pisces) aus dem Cenoman von Griechen-
              land. Praktika Akad. Athenon, 42, 115—122, 1 fig., 1 pl., 1 table.
1967B.   Orthogonoceros verticornis aus dem Altpleistozän des Beckens von
              Haliakmon (Griechenland). Praktika Akad. Athenon, 42, 79—87,
              2 figs., 2 pls., 2 tables.

MELENTIS, J. K., and TOBIEN, H.
1967   Paläontologische Ausgrabungen auf der Insel Chios (eine vorläufige Mit-
              teilung). Praktika Akad. Athenon, 42, 147—151.

MELESHCHENKO, V. S.   See: Rzhonsnit-Skaía and Meleshchenko.

MELICHAR, H.
1966   Japanese archaeological terms with English and German equivalents.
              Asian Perspectives, 8:2, 111 pp.

MELLARS, P. A.
1965   Sequence and development of Mousterian traditions in south-western
              France. Nature, 205, 626—627, 1 fig.

MELLETT, JAMES S.
1968   The Oligocene Hsanda Gol formation, Mongolia: A revised faunal list.
              Amer. Mus. Novit., 2318, 16 pp., 4 figs., 2 tables.
              See: Van Valen and Mellett.

MELLINK, MACHTELD J.
1964   Archaeology in Asia Minor. Amer. Jour. Archaeol., 68, 149—166, 2 figs.

MEL'NIKOVA, N. N.   See: Vereshchagin and Mel'nikova.

MELTON, WILLIAM G., JR.
1964   Glyptodon fredericensis (Meade) from the Seymour formation of Knox
              County, Texas. Papers Mich. Acad. Sci., 49, 129—146, 3 figs.,
              3 pls., 4 tables.

MENDREZ, CHRISTIANE
1965   Sur les affinités des Whaitsiidae (Therocephalia). C. R. Acad. Sci. Paris,
              261, 1044—1045.
1966   On Equus (Hippotigris) cf. burchelli (Gray) from 'Sterkfontein extension',
              Transvaal, South Africa. Ann. Transvaal Mus., 25:5, 92—97,
              2 figs.
1967   Sur quelques critères de distinction entre thérocéphales et cynodontes.
              Colloq. Internat. Cent. Nation. Recherch. Sci., 163, 431—437,
              figs. A—G, (English summary).

MENEGHEZZI, MARIA DE LOURDES   See: Iglesias and Meneghezzi.

MENESINI, E.
1967A.   I Pesci miocenici delle "Arenarie di Ponsano". Atti Soc. Tosc. Sci.
              Nat., Mem., (A), 74:1, 1—22, 3 pls., 2 tables, 1 map, (English
              summary).

Rev.: Albanesi in Riv. Ital. Pal., 74:3, 989.
1967B.   Ittioliti pliocenici di Porto Craulo (Otranto). Atti Soc. Tosc. Sci. Nat., Mem., (A), 74, 221–231, 1 fig., 1 pl., (French summary).
Rev.: Albanesi in Riv. Ital. Pal., 74:3, 990–991.

MENG, C. Y.
1961   The well preserved fossil bones first discovered from Taiwan. Shih Yu Tung Hsin, no. 220, 2–4, 7 figs., (Chinese; not seen).

MENG, ZIJIANG   See: Huang, Z. and Meng.

MENGHIN, OSVALDO F. A.
1958   Rev.: Gasperi in Rev. Inst. Antrop., Univ. Litoral, Rosario, 1, 367–368.
1963   Industrias de morfologia protolitica en Sudamerica. An. Univ. Norte, 2, 11 pp., (not seen).
See: Cardich 1959.

MENNER, V. V.
1961   [The stratigraphy of Devonian deposits in the northern section of the Tungus syneclise.] Trudy Inst. Geol. Arktiki, 125, 3–19, 2 figs., (Russian).
1967A.   [Valentin Aleksandrovich Teriaev (1891 - 1966).] Biull. Mosk. Obshch. Ispyt. Prirody, Otd. Geol., 42:1, 163–166, portr., (Russian).
1967B.   [Devonian of the Siberian Platform.] In: Sokolov, B. S., (ed.), 1967, 121–125, (Russian).
1968   [New data on the Devonian of Siberian Platform.] In: Collected Papers, 1968 [Materials on the regional geology of Siberia], 34–37, (Russian).

MENON, A. G. K.
1964   Catalogue and bibliography of fossil fishes of India. Jour. Pal. Soc. India, 4, 51–60.

MERBS, CHARLES F.   See: Simons and Pilbeam.

MERCADO, A.   See: Terent'ev 1965B.

MERCENIER, J. and L.
1962A.   Noduwez. Arch., 1962, 12–13, (not seen).
1962B.   Orp-le-Grand "Champ de la Bruyère". Arch., 1962, 47, (not seen).

MERCER, J. R.   See: Tarlo, L. B. H. and Mercer.

MERKEL, DALTON E.
1966,
1967   The roadrunner – a feathered character. Mus. Talk, Santa Barbara Mus. Nat. Hist., 41, 65–68, 1 fig.

MERKLIN, R. L.   See: Hopkins, D. M., et al.

MERLIN, SAMUEL   See: Wilf and Merlin.

MÉROC, LOUIS
1963A.   La préhistoire des Petites-Pyrénées garonnaises. Actes 18º Congr. Féder. Soc. Acad. et Sav. Languédoc, Pyrénées, Gascogne à St. Gaudens, 3–9, (not seen).

1963B.   Les éléments de datation de la mandibule de Montmaurin (Haute-Garonne).
           C. R. Soc. Géol. France, 1963, 163, (abs.).
           Rev.: Bonifay in L'Anthrop., 69:5—6, 540—541.
1964   Les éléments de datation de la mandibule humaine de Montmaurin
           (Haute-Garonne). Bull. Soc. Géol. France, 5, 508—515, 6 figs.
1965   Le Languedocien de la Haute et de la Moyenne Vallée de la Garonne.
           In: Ripoll Perelló, E., (ed.), 1965B, 149—172, 7 figs., (Spanish
           summary).

MÉROC, L., and MAZET, J.
1964   Cougnac grotte peinte. 2nd ed. Preface by H. Breuil. Stuttgart: 72
           pp., 12 figs., 4 color pls., 18 black and white pls., (not seen).
           Rev.: [Beltrán] in Caesaraugusta, 23—24, 145—147, 1 fig.

MERPERT, N. ÎA., and SHELOV, D. B.
1961   [The antiquities of our land.]   Moscow, Akad. Nauk SSSR Press, 240
           pp., 95 figs., 1 map, (Russian).

MERPERT, N. ÎA., and SMIRNOV, K. F.
1961   [Archeological work in the area of the construction of the Stalingrad
           hydroelectric station.]   Krat. Soob. Inst. Ist. Mat. Kult. SSSR,
           84, 3—11, 3 figs., (Russian).

MERRIAM, DANIEL F.
1967   Computer use in Europe. GeoTimes, 12:9, 14—16.

MERRILEES, DUNCAN
1965A.   Two species of the extinct genus Sthenurus Owen (Marsupialia, Macro-
           podidae) from south-eastern Australia, including Sthenurus gilli
           sp. nov. Jour. Roy. Soc. W. Australia, 48, 22—32, 8 figs., 4
           tables.
1965B.   Fossil wombat from Fremantle. Western Australian Nat., 9, 197.
1965C.   Time and the marsupial. Wildlife in Australia, 3:1, 20—23, 7 figs.
1967A.   South-western Australia occurrences of Sthenurus (Marsupialia, Macro-
           podidae), including Sthenurus brownei n. sp. Jour. Roy. Soc.
           W. Australia, 50, 65—79, 8 figs., 6 tables.
1967B.   Fossil bandicoots (Marsupialia, Peramelidae) from Mammoth Cave,
           western Australia, and their climatic implications. Jour. Roy.
           Soc. W. Australia, 50, 121—128, 1 fig., 3 tables.
1968   Man — the destroyer: late Quaternary changes in the Australian mar-
           supial fauna. Jour. Roy. Soc. W. Australia, 51, 1—24, 3 figs.
           See: Colbert and Merrilees; Douglass, Kendrick and Merrilees.

MERRILEES, D., and RIDE, W. D. L.
1965   Procoptodon goliah (Macropodidae, Marsupialia) from western Eyre
           Peninsula, South Australia. Trans. Roy. Soc. S. Australia, 89,
           139—142, 1 pl.

MERRILL, GEORGE PERKINS
1964   The first one hundred years of American geology. Reprint. New York:
           Stechert-Hafner, xxi + 773 pp., 130 figs., 36 pls., 1 map, (not
           seen).

MERTENS, ROBERT
1960   Von der statischen zur dynamischen Systematik in der Zoologie. In:
           Heberer, G., and Schwanitz, F., (eds.), 1960*, 186—202, 7 figs.

1965   Elaphe Fitzinger 1833, nicht Elaphis Bonaparte 1831 (Reptilia, Serpentes). Senck. Biologica, 46, 193–194.

1966   Aus der Welt der bedrohten Amphibien und Reptilien. Mitt. Naturf. Ges. Bern, 23, 1–19, 4 figs., 8 pls.

MESHCHERÎAKOV, ÎU. A.   See: Armand, et al.

MESÎATS, V. A.
1962A.   [Finds of Lower Paleolithic implements in the Zhitomir area.] Krat. Zoob. Inst. Ist. Mat. Kult, SSSR, 92, 54–55, 1 fig., (Russian).
1962B.   [Zhitomir Lower Paleolithic site.] Krat. Soob. Inst. Arkheol. Akad. Nauk URSR, 12, 53–56, 1 fig., (Russian).

MESSELAAR, G.   See: Life, editors 1963.

MESSERI, PIERO
1961   L'evoluzione morfologica del cranio umano nel profilo sagittale. Arch. Anthrop. Etnol. Ital., 90, 241–264, illustr.
1966   Une théorie sur la morphogénese du crâne humain. L'Anthrop., 70:3–4, 309–318, 4 figs.
        See: Palmadi Cesnola and Messeri.

MESTON, A. L.
1937   Tasmanian stone implements. Mankind, 2:4, 80–82.

MESZOELY, CHARLES A. M.
1965   North American fossil cryptobranchid salamanders. Amer. Mid. Nat., 75, 495–515, 6 figs., 4 tables.
        Abs.: Westphal in Zbl. Geol. Pal., Teil 2, 1966, 295–296.
1967   A new cryptobranchid salamander from the Early Eocene of Wyoming. Copeia, 1967, 346–349, 3 figs.
        Rev.: Westphal in Zbl. Geol. Pal., Teil 2, 1968, 202.

METRESS, JAMES F., JR.
1967   On the subdivision of physical anthropology. Current Anthrop., 8, 352.

METTLER, FRED A.
1956   Culture and the structural evolution of the neural system. James Arthur Lecture on the Evol. of the Human Brain, Amer. Mus. Nat. Hist., 1955, 57 pp., 6 figs., 9 tables.

MEURS, A. P. H. van   See: Bruijn and Meurs.

MEYER, JOACHIM D.
1967   Geology of the Ahuachapan area, western El Salvador, Central America. Tulane Studies Geol., 5, 195–215, 12 figs.

MEYERS, JOAN   See: Whitaker and Meyers.

MEZHLUMÎAN, S. K.
1965   [Large cattle from the Eneolithic settlement Shengavit and Bronze Age burials of Lchashen (Armenian SSR).] Izv. Akad. Nauk Armîan. SSR, Ser. Biol.-Ist.-Kh., 18:3, 64–74, 3 figs., 3 tables, (Russian; Armenian summary).

MEZHZHERIN, V. A.
1965   [An essay on Quaternary history and origin of the modern fauna of
        shrews (genus Sorex, Insectivora, Mammalia).] In: Bondarchuk
        and Shelkopliãs, (eds.), 1965, 164–174, 1 table, (Russian; Eng-
        lish summary).

MEZHZHERIN, V. A., and SVISTUN, V. I.
1966   [A new subspecies of fossil Sorex araneus praetetragonurus subsp. nova
        (Insectivora, Mammalia).] Dopovidi Akad. Nauk URSR, Kiev,
        1966:8, 1071–1074, 2 figs., 4 tables, (Ukrainian; Russian and
        English summaries).

MEZZALIRA, SÉRGIO
1966   Considerações sôbre novas ocorrências fossilíferas no estado de São Paulo.
        An. Acad. brasil. ciênc., 38:1, 65–72, 2 figs., map, (English sum-
        mary).

MEZZENA, FRANCO
1965   Oggetti d'arte mobiliare del Paleolitico scoperti al Riparo Tagliente in
        Valpantena (Verona). (Ricerche 1962 - 63). Riv. Sci. Preist.,
        19, 175–187, 3 figs., 1 pl., (French and English summaries).
        See: Pasa and Mezzena.

MIART, E.-J.
1967   Excursion dans la region de Reims 19 June 1966. Bull. Soc. Hist. Nat.
        Ardennes, 56, 17–22.

MICHA, FRANZ JOSEF
1965   Zur Geschichte der australischen Eingeborenen. Saeculum, 16, 317–342.

MICHAEL, HENRY N.
1964A.   Maksim Grigorevich Levin, 1904 - 1963. Amer. Antiq., 29, 480–482,
        portr.
1964B.   (ed.) The archaeology and geomorphology of northern Asia: selected
        works. Anthrop. of the North, no. 5, xvi + 512 pp., illustr.
        Rev.: Klein in Amer. Anthrop., 68:5, 1302–1303; Preuschoft in
        Anthrop. Anz., 28, 154; Sauter in Arch. Suiss. Anthrop. Gen.,
        31, 64–65; Thompson in Man, Jour. Roy. Anthrop. Inst., 1,
        255–256.
1965   (ed.) The Soviet Far East in antiquity: an archaeological and historical
        study of the Maritime Region of the U.S.S.R. A. P. Okladnikov.
        Anthrop. of the North, no. 6, v + 280 pp., 52 figs.
        Rev.: Klein in Amer. Anthrop., 68:5, 1302–1303.
        See: Okladnikov 1965.

MICHAUX, JACQUES
1963   Abs.: Lotze in Zbl. Geol. Pal., Teil 2, 1964, 677.
1964A.   Age des sables à unios et térédines (Eocène inférieur) d'Avenay (Marne)
        et leurs relations avec les sables du même nom des gisements
        classiques du Sud d'Epernay (Marne). C. R. Soc. Géol. France,
        1964, 103–104.
1964B.   Diagnoses de quelques paramyidés de l'Eocène inférieur de France. C.
        R. Soc. Géol. France, 1964, 153–154, 1 fig.
1965   Découverte d'un remplissage karstique à micromammifères d'âge Pliocène
        terminal à Seynes (Gard). C. R. Soc. Géol. France, 1965, 218–220.

1966 Sur deux faunules de micromammifères trouvées dans des assises termi-
     nales du Pliocène en Languedoc. C. R. Soc. Géol. France, <u>1966,</u>
     343–345, 1 fig.
     Rev.: Fahlbusch in Zbl. Geol. Pal., Teil 2, <u>1968,</u> 31.

1967 Origine du dessin dentaire "Apodemus" (Rodentia, Mammalia). C. R.
     Acad. Sci. Paris, Sci. Nat., <u>264,</u> 711–714, 7 figs.
     Rev.: Fahlbusch in Zbl. Geol. Pal., Teil 2, <u>1968,</u> 218–219.

1968 Les Paramyidae (Rodentia) de l'Eocène inférieur du Bassin de Paris.
     Palaeovertebrata, <u>1</u>:4, 135–193, 4 figs., 10 pls., 2 tables.
   See: Chaline and Michaux; Barrière and Michaux; Hartenberger,
     Michaux and Thaler; Lavocat and Michaux; Ledoux, <u>et al.</u>;
     Louis and Michaux.

MICHEL, F.
1964 Ein Flusspferdzahn im alluvialen Lehm der Leimen von Herbligen bei
     Oderdriessbach? [? Jahresb.] Hist. Mus. Schloss, Thun, <u>1963,</u>
     1–7, (not seen).

MICHEL, J. P.
1964 La gravière de Chelles. Bull. Assoc. Franç. Étude Quat., <u>1,</u> 42–45, 1
     fig., 1 table.

MICHELS, JOSEPH W.
1967 Archeology and dating by hydration of obsidian. Science, <u>158,</u> 211–
     214, 1 table.

MICHIE, JIM
1965 Fluted point types of South Carolina. Chesopiean, <u>3</u>:5, 107–113, 4 pls.
1967 South Carolina Dalton points and their variants. Chesopiean, <u>5,</u> 15–18,
     2 pls.
1968 The Edgefield scraper. Chesopiean, <u>6,</u> 30–31, 1 fig.

MIELE, FRANK
1966 The race concept. Mankind Quart., <u>7,</u> 78–85.

MIELKE, JAMES E. See: Long, Austin and Mielke.

MIGUET, R.
1967 Observations nouvelle sur les chiroptères des Phosphorites du Quercy.
     Trav. Lab. Géol. Univ. Lyon, <u>14,</u> 101–114, 5 figs., 3 tables.

MIHĂILĂ, N. See: Litianu, Mihăilă and Bandrabur; Patrulius and Mihăilă; Rădulesco,
     Samson, Mihăilă and Kovacs.

MIIATEV, KR., and MIKOV, V., (eds.)
1961 Studia in memoriam Karel Škorpil. Sofia: Bŭlg. Akad. Nauk Press,
     437 pp., illustr., (Bulgarian; French summaries).

MIKHANKOV, IU. M.
1960 [Stratigraphic scheme of Quaternary deposits in southern Ob' R. region.]
     Informatsionnyi Sbornik, <u>39,</u> 33–40, 1 fig., (Russian).

MIKLIN, A. M.
1967 [Is the concept of "unlimited" progress anthropocentric?] Voprosy
     Filosofii, <u>1967</u>:9, 137–146, (Russian).

MIKOV, V.   See: Miïatev and Mikov.

MIKOV, V., and DŽHAMBAZOV, N.
1960   La grotte de Devetaki. Sofia: Acad. Sci. Bulgarie, 199 pp., 140 figs.,
1 pl., (Russian; French summary).
Rev.: Vencl in Archeol. Roz., 13, 595—596.

MIKULA, EDWARD J.
1964   Evidence of Pleistocene habitation by woodland caribon in southern
Michigan. Jour. Mammal., 45, 494—495.

MIKUŤSKIĬ, S. P.
1960   [Stratigraphy of Pre-Upper Paleozoic deposits in the Eniseĭ area of Siberian Platform.] Trudy SNIIGGIMS, 13, 90—108, 1 map, 2 charts,
1 table, (Russian).

MILANOVSKIĬ, E. E.
1956   [Concerning the Neogene and Anthropogene vulcanism in the Lesser
Caucasus.] Izv. Akad. Sci. USSR., Geol. Ser., 10, 42—66, 5 figs.,
(Russian).
Abs.: Stoltenberg in Zbl. Geol. Pal., Teil 2, 1962, 335—336.

MILDENBERGER, GERHARD
1959   Rev.: Mossler in Die Höhle, 11, 83.

MILES, A. E. W., (ed.)
1967   Structural and chemical organization of teeth. New York and London:
Academic Press, xvi + 525 pp., illustr.

MILES, A. E. W., and POOLE, D. F. G.
1967   The history and general organization of dentition. In: Miles, A. E. W.,
(ed.), 1967, 3—44, 41 figs., 2 charts.

MILES, CHARLES
1964   Upper Chehalis Valley artifacts. Screenings, 13:5, 2—3, 5 figs.

MILES, ROGER S.
1964   A reinterpretation of the visceral skeleton of Acanthodes. Nature, 204,
457—459, 2 figs.
1965A.   Some features in the cranial morphology of acanthodians and the relationships of the Acanthodii. Acta Zool., 46, 233—255, 2 figs.
1965B.   Description of the fish plate. Antarctic Res. Ser., 6, 273—274, pl. 18.
1965C.   On some coccosteomorph arthrodires from the Devonian of Arizona.
Ark. Zool., 16, 427—460, 15 figs., 2 pls.
1965D.   A large arthrodire plate from Chautauqua County, New York. Ark.
Zool., 16, 545—550, 1 fig., 1 pl.
1965E.   The ventral thoracic neuromast lines of placoderm fishes. Nature, 206,
524—525, 2 figs.
1966A.   The acanthodian fishes of the Devonian Plattenkalk of the Paffrath
Trough in the Rhineland. With an appendix containing a classification of the Acanthodii and a revision of the genus Homala-
canthus. Ark. Zool., 18, 147—194, 18 figs., 10 pls.
1966B.   Protitanichthys and some other coccosteomorph arthrodires from the
Devonian of North America. K. Svenska Vetenskapsakad. Handl.,
10:3, 1—49, 30 figs., 8 pls.

1966C.   The placoderm fish <u>Rachiosteus</u> <u>pterygiatus</u> Gross and its relationships.
          Trans. Roy. Soc. Edinburgh, <u>66</u>:15, 377—392, 5 figs., 1 pl.
1967A.   The cervical joint and some aspects of the origin of the Placodermi.
          Colloq. Internat. Cent. Nation. Recherch. Sci., <u>163</u>, 49—71, 5 figs.,
          (French summary).
1967B.   Observations on the ptyctodont fish, <u>Rhamphodopsis</u> Watson. In:
          Patterson, C., and Greenwood, P. H., (eds.), 1967, 99—120, 20
          figs., 6 pls.
          See: Andrews, S. M., <u>et</u> <u>al.</u>

MILES, R. S., and WESTOLL, T. S.
1968   The placoderm fish <u>Coccosteus</u> <u>cuspidatus</u> Miller ex Agassiz from the
          Middle Old Red Sandstone of Scotland. Part 1. Descriptive
          morphology. Trans. Roy. Soc. Edinburgh, <u>67</u>:9, 373—476, 51
          figs., pls. 1—12, 1 table.

MILLER, ALDEN H.
1966A.   An evaluation of the fossil anhingas of Australia. Condor, <u>68</u>, 315—320,
          2 tables.
1966B.   Animal evolution on islands. In: Bowman, R. I., (ed.), 1966, 10—16.
1966C.   The fossil pelicans of Australia. Mem. Queensland Mus., <u>14</u>:5, 181—190,
          1 fig., 1 table.

MILLER, B. B.   See: Semken, Miller and Stevens.

MILLER, CARL
1965   The Paleo-Indian era: distribution of finds. Alabama. Bull. Southeast
          Archaeol. Confer., <u>2</u>, 16A—18.

MILLER, CHIP and ART
1965   A Buffalo River survey. Tenn. Archaeol., <u>21</u>, 1—13, 13 figs.

MILLER, GEORGE J.
1968   On the age distribution of <u>Smilodon</u> <u>californicus</u> Bovard from Rancho
          La Brea. Contrib. Sci., Los Angeles Co. Mus., <u>131</u>, 1—17, 11
          figs., 6 tables.
          Rev.: Thenius in Zbl. Geol. Pal., Teil 2, <u>1970</u>:3/4, 241.

MILLER, HALSEY W., JR.
1963   New faunal elements from the Cretaceous Arizona. Jour. Arizona Acad.
          Sci., <u>2</u>, 191, (abs.).
1964   Cretaceous dinosaurian remains from southern Arizona. Jour. Pal., <u>38</u>,
          378—384, 2 figs., pls. 61—62.
1967   Cretaceous vertebrates from Phoebus Landing, North Carolina. Proc.
          Acad. Nat. Sci. Phila., <u>119</u>, 219—239, 4 pls.

MILLER, JOHN A.
1967   Problems of dating East African Tertiary and Quaternary volcanics by
          the potassium-argon method. Discussion. In: Bishop, W. W.,
          and Clark, J. D., (eds.), 1967A, 259—272, 1 fig., (French sum-
          mary).

MILLER, LOYE
1965   Bird remains from an archaeological site in the Beaverhead Mountains
          of southeastern Idaho. Tebiwa, <u>8</u>, 17—20.

1966   An eddition to the bird fauna of the Barstow Miocene. Condor, <u>68</u>, 397.

MILLER, ROBERT L., and KAHN, J. S.
1962   Statistical analysis in the geological sciences. New York and London:
            John Wiley and Sons, xiv + 483 pp., illustr., tables.
            Rev.: Evans in Bull. London Univ. Inst. Archaeol., no. <u>6</u>, 131.

MILLER, ROBERT RUSH
1957   Utilization of X-rays as a tool in systematic zoology. Syst. Zool., <u>6</u>,
            29—40, 4 figs.; erratum 150.
1965   Quaternary freshwater fishes of North America. In: Wright, H. E.,
            and Frey, D. G., (eds.), <u>1965</u>, 569—581, 3 figs., 1 table.
            See: Uyeno and Miller.

MILLER, R. R., and SMITH, G. R.
1967   New fossil fishes from Plio-Pleistocene Lake Idaho. Occ. Pap. Mus.,
            Univ. Mich., <u>654</u>, 1—24, 9 figs.

MILLER, WADE E.
1966   Late Pleistocene mammals from Palos Verdes, California. Program, 62nd
            Ann. Meeting, Geol. Soc. Amer., Cordilleran Sect., <u>1966</u>, 55,
            (abs.). Also: Spec. Pap. Geol. Soc. Amer., <u>101</u>, 323—324, (abs.).
1968   Occurrence of a giant bison, Bison latifrons, and a slender-limbed camel,
            Tanupolama, at Rancho LaBrea. Contrib. Sci., Los Angeles Co.
            Mus., <u>147</u>, 9 pp., 6 figs., 1 table.

MILLOT, JACQUES, and ANTHONY, J.
1965   Anatomie de Latimeria chalumnae. Tome 2. Système nerveux et or-
            ganes des sens. Paris: Centre National Recherche Scientifique,
            130 pp., 57 figs., 76 pls.
            Rev.: Starck in Naturwiss., <u>54</u>, 75.

MILLOT, J., NIEUWENHUYS, R., and ANTHONY, J.
1964   Le diencéphale de Latimeria chalumnae Smith (Poisson Coelacanthide).
            C. R. Acad. Sci. Paris, <u>258</u>, 5051—5055, 2 figs.

MILLS, J. R. E.
1964   The dentitions of Peramus and Amphitherium. Proc. Linn. Soc. London,
            <u>175</u>, 117—133, 6 figs., 2 pls.
1966   The functional occlusion of the teeth of Insectivora. Jour. Linn. Soc.
            London, <u>46</u>:308, 1—25, 22 figs., 2 pls.
1967   Development of the protocone during the Mesozoic. Jour. Dental Res.,
            <u>46</u>:5, Part 1, 787—791.

MILOJČIĆ, V., BOESSNECK, J., JUNG, D., and SCHNEIDER, H.
1965   Paläolithikum um Larissa in Thessalien. Beitr. Ur- und Frühgesch.
            Archäol. Mittelmeer-Kulturr., <u>1</u>, 65 pp., 42 pls.

MILOJEVIĆ, B. D.
1966   [Petronijevic's interpretation of Archaeopteryx.] Glas Acad. Serbe
            Sci., Classe Sci. Math. et Nat., <u>265</u>:29, 199—205, (Serbian;
            German summary).
            Abs.: G. P. in Bull. Sci., Zagreb, Sec. A, <u>12</u>:5—6, 152, (German).
1967   Die Petronievics'sche Deutung der Archaeopteryx. Bull. Acad. Serbe
            Sci., <u>11</u>, 121.

MILSTEAD, WILLIAM W.
1965 Notes on the identities of some poorly known fossils of box turtles (Terrapene). Copeia, 1965, 513–514.
1967 Fossil box turtles (Terrapene) from central North America, and box turtles of eastern Mexico. Copeia, 1967, 168–179, 3 figs., 2 tables.
  See: Auffenberg and Milstead; McClure and Milstead.

MILSTEAD, W. W., and TINKLE, D. W.
1967 Terrapene of western Mexico, with comments on the species groups in the genus. Copeia, 1967, 180–187, 1 fig., 1 table.

MINAMIDATE, TADAYOSHI See: Hanihara and Minamidate.

MINCHAM, HANS
1966 Vanished giants of Australia. Illustr. by Terry Houston. Adelaide: Rigby Ltd., 84 pp., illustr., (juv.).
  Rev.: Elkin in Archaeol., Phys. Anthrop. in Oceania, 2, 79; Thorne in Mankind, 6, 364.

MINIKH, M. G. (= Minch) See: Vorob'eva and Minikh.

MINIS-VAN DE GEYN, W.
1962 De oudste sporen van de mens. Natuurhist. Maandbl., 51, 136–137.

MIGUEL, M. See: Genet-Varcin and Miguel.

MIRAMBELL S., LORENA
1964 Estudio microfotográfico de artefactos líticos. Publ. Dep. Prehist., México, 14, 17 pp., 6 phots., 2 pls.

MIROSHNIKOV, L. D.
1962 [On the homology of Korvunchana and Ilemorovo suites, and on the convergence of sedimentary series.] Trudy Vses. Neft. Nauchn.-Issl. Geologorazv. Inst. (VNIGRI), 190, 244–251, (Russian).

MIRTSCHING
1965 Mammutfund in Nordsibirien. Ost-Europa Naturw., 9, 138, (not seen).

MISHIN, A. V.
1965 [About the period and reasons for the fluctuations in level of Lake Issyk-Kul' in the Anthropogene.] Biull. Kom. Izuch. Chetvert. Perioda Akad. Nauk SSSR, no. 30, 145–153, (Russian).

MISKOVSKY, J. C. See: Isetti, Lumley and Miskovsky.

MISONNE, XAVIER See: Kuss and Misonne; Quinet and Misonne.

MISRA, K. S., and SAXENA, R. S.
1964 A new fossil fish, Jhingrania roonwali, from the Rajmahal Hills, India. Jour. Pal. Soc. India, 4, 30–32, 2 pls., 1 table.

MISRA, UMA SHANKER
1967 Vertebrate fossils from the Dera-Gopipur Tehsil District, Kangra, (Punjab). Current Sci., 36, 211, 1 table.

MISRA, V. N.
1964   Palaeoliths from District Udaipur, south Rajasthan.   Jour. Asiatic Soc.,
            Bombay, 36—37, 55—59, 6 pls.
1965   Seminar on prehistory and proto-history of India.   Current Anthrop.,
            6, 330—331.

MISRA, V. N., and MATE, M. S., (eds.)
1965   Indian prehistory: 1964.   Poona: Deccan College Postgraduate and
            Research Institute, xxii + 266 pp., (not seen).
            Rev.: Allchin in American Anthrop., 69, 251—252;   Clark in Proc.
            Prehist. Soc. Cambridge, 32, 370—371;   Fairservis in Asian Perspec-
            tives, 9, 177;   Sen in E. Anthrop., 19, 260—262.

MISZKIEWICZ, BRUNON
1964   Wazniejsze publikacje o Janie Czekanowskim.   Mat. Prace Antrop., 70,
            29—31.

MITCHELL, CLARENCE B.
1960   Through the halls.   Chicago: Chicago Nat. Hist. Mus., 39 pp., color
            illustr.

MITCHELL, DONALD H.
1965   Preliminary excavations at a cobble tool site (DjRi7) in the Fraser
            Canyon, British Columbia.   Anthrop. Pap., Nation. Mus. Canada,
            10, 1—20, 14 figs., 11 pls., 3 tables.
            Rev.: Carlson in Anthropologica, 9, 106—107.

MITCHELL, EDWARD D., JR.
1961   Abs.: Dietrich in Zbl. Geol. Pal., Teil 2, 1964, 195.
1962   Abs.: Dietrich in Zbl. Geol. Pal., Teil 2, 1964, 195.
1964   Pachyostosis in desmostylids.   Spec. Pap. Geol. Soc. Amer., 76, 214,
            (abs.).
1965A.   History of research at Sharktooth Hill, Kern County, California.   Bakers-
            field: Special Publ. Kern Co. Hist. Soc. and County of Kern
            through its Museum, vi + 46 pp., illustr., maps.
            Rev.: Camp in Jour. West, 5, no. 1, 147.
1965B.   Morphology of a Miocene sea lion.   Geol. Soc. Amer. Cordilleran Sect.,
            Pal. Soc., Pac. Coast Sect., Prog. 61st Ann. Meeting, 1965, 38,
            (abs.).
1965C.   Biostratonomy of a Miocene bone bed at Sharktooth Hill, California.
            Geol. Soc. Amer., Cordilleran Sect., Pal. Soc. Pac. Coast Sect.,
            Prog. 61st Ann. Meeting, 1965, 37—38, (abs.).
1966A.   Northeastern Pacific Pleistocene sea otters.   Jour. Fisheries Res. Board,
            Canada, 23, 1897—1911, 6 figs.
1966B.   Faunal succession of extinct North Pacific marine mammals.   Restora-
            tions by Bonnie Dalzell. Norsk Hvalf. Tid., no. 3, 47—60, 19 figs.
1966C.   Biostratonomy of a Miocene bone bed at Sharktooth Hill, California.
            Spec. Pap. Geol. Soc. Amer., 87, 217—218, (abs.).
1966D.   Morphology of a marine sea lion.   Spec. Pap. Geol. Soc. Amer., 87,
            218, (abs.).
1966E.   The Miocene pinniped Allodesmus.   Univ. Calif. Publ. Geol. Sci., 61,
            1—105, 29 pls., 2 tables.
            Abs.: B. B. in Przegl. Geol., 1967:3, 149.
            Rev.: Fahlbusch in Zbl. Geol. Pal., Teil 2, 1967, 115—116;   Repen-
            ning in Jour. Pal., 41, 812—813.

1967A.   [Faunal succession of extinct North Pacific marine mammals.]   [News
          Letters, Whales Research Inst., no. 186, Feb. 1967, 11–22, 19
          figs.]   (Japanese, translated by M. Nishiwaki. Transl. of 1966B.)
1967B.   Controversy over diphyly in pinnipeds. Syst. Zool., 16, 350–351.
1968   The Mio-Pliocene pinniped Imagotaria. Jour. Fisheries Res. Board, Canada,
          25, 1843–1900, 16 figs., 5 tables.
          Rev.: Thenius in Zbl. Geol. Pal., Teil 2, 1970:3/4, 241–242.
          See: Lipps, J. H., Valentine and Mitchell.

MITCHELL, E. D., JR., and LIPPS, J. H.
1964   Miocene marine vertebrates from San Clemente Island, California   Spec.
          Pap. Geol. Soc. Amer., 76, 214–215, (abs.).
1965   Fossil collecting on San Clemente Island. Pac. Discovery, 18:3, 2–8,
          illustr.

MITCHELL, GEORGE FRANCIS
1965A.   Quaternary deposits of the Ballaugh and Kirkmichael districts, Isle of
          Man. Proc. Geol. Soc. London, no. 1622, 70–71.
1965B.   The Quaternary deposits of the Ballaugh and Kirkmichael districts, Isle
          of Man. Quart. Jour. Geol. Soc. London, 121, 359–381, 3 figs.,
          pls. 32–33.

MITSCHA-MARHEIM, HERBERT
1964   Eduard Beninger [1897 - 1963]. Archaeol. Austriaca, 35, 111–116.

MITT, K. L.
1963   [New data, based on paleobotany and paleontology; regarding the
          stratigraphy of Quaternary deposits of the Anabaro-Olenensk de-
          pression.]   Trudy Inst. Geol. Arktiki, 136, 75–98, 13 figs.,
          (Russian).

MITZOPOULOS, MAXIMOS K.
1964   Über das Vorkommen von Archidiskodon meridionalis archaicus im
          Becken von Ptolemais (Griechisch-Mazedonien). Praktika Akad.
          Athenon, 39, 381–388, 1 map, 2 pls., (Greek; German summary).
1967   Zygolophodon borsoni und Anancus (Bunolophodon) arvernensis aus
          dem Oberpliozän von Griechenland. Ann. Géol. Pays Hellén., 18,
          436–446.

MITZOPOULOS, M. K., and ZAPFE, H.
1963   Fossile Hyäniden-Koprolithen aus Pikermi. Ann. Géol. Pays Hellén.,
          14, 405–407, pl. 47, (Greek summary).

MIYASAKA, EIICHI, KODAMA, S., and MIYASAKA, T.
1965   Report on the excavation of the pre-pottery site at Waribashi, Daimon-
          Tōge, Nagano-ken. Jour. Archaeol. Soc. Nippon, 50, 50–59,
          9 figs.

MIYASAKA, TORAJI   See: Miyasaka, E., et al.

MIZEROV, B. V.   See: Martynov, Mizerov and Strelkov.

MLYNARSKI, MARIAN
1961D.   Faune postglaciale de serpents (Colubridés) de Giebułtow près Cracovie,
          Pologne. Internat. Assoc. Quat. Res., Abs. Pap., 6th Congr., 129,
          (abs.).

1964A.   Die jungpliozäne Reptilienfauna von Rebielice Królewskie, Polen. Senck.
Biologica, 45, 325–347, 43 figs.

1964B.   Find of the tortoise Emys orbicularis (Linnaeus, 1758) in Early Pleis-
tocene fill of Cave C718 at Zlatý Kuň near Koněprusy. Věst.
Stát. Geol. Ceskosl. Republ., 39, 449–453, 1 fig., 1 pl., (Czech;
English summary).

1966   Die fossilen Schildkröten in den ungarischen Sammlungen. Acta Zool.
Crac., 11:8, 223–288, 15 figs., 7 pls., (Polish and Russian sum-
maries).
See: Khozatskiĭ and Młynarski.

MNUSHKIN, L. B.   See: Gladkov, et al.

MOCHANOV, IŪ. A.
1966A.   [Paleolithic of Aldan R.]   In: Rybakov, (ed.), 1966, 68–71, (Russian).
1966B.   [Most ancient civilizations of America.]   Sovetskaiă Etnografiiă, 1966:4,
83–99, (Russian;   English summary).

MOCHANOV, IŪ. A., and FEDOSEEVA, S. A.
1968   [Paleolithic site Ikhine in Iakutia.]   Sov. Arkheol., 1968:4, 244–248,
5 figs., (Russian).

MÖCKEL, J. R.   See: Regteren Altena and Möckel.

MODDERMAN, P. J. R.
1964   On a survey of Palaeolithic sites near Hama. Ann. Archéol. Syrie, 14,
51–66, 7 figs.

MOESCHLER, PIERRE
1966   A propos de l'influence du climat sur les caractères anthropologiques.
Bull. Schweiz. Ges. Anthrop. Ethnol., 42, 6–7.

MOGOŞANU, FLOREA
1967   [Presence of Dufour lamellae in Acropaleolithic sites of Banat.]   Studii
şi Cercetări de Ist. Veche, 18, 141–146, 2 figs., (Rumanian;
French summary).
See: Nicolăescu-Plopşor, C. S., Păunescu and Mogoşanu.

MOGOŞANU, F., and STRATAN, I.
1966   [New Paleolithic finds in Banat.]   Studii şi Cercetări de Ist. Veche, 17,
335–344, 4 figs., (Rumanian;   French summary).

MOHAPATRA, GOPAL CHANDRA
1962   Rev.: Sen in Man in India, 44, 84–88.
1964   Middle Stone Age industries of Orissa. Jour. Pal. Soc. India, 4, 35–50,
31 figs., 4 pls.

MOHAPATRA, G. C., BHATIA, S. B., and SAHU, B. K.
1963   The discovery of a Stone Age site in the Indian desert. Res. Bull. Punjab
Univ., 14, 215–223, 6 pls.

MOHAPATRA, M. R.
1964   The first record of small flake tools and polished stone celts in Kangra
district, E. Punjab. Current Sci., 33, 178–180, 12 figs.

MØHL-HANSEN, U.
1954   Først sikre spor af mennesker fra interglacialtid i Danmark: maruspaltede knogler fra diatoméjorden ved Hollerup. Aarboger for Nordisk Oldkyndighed og Historie, 1954, 101—126, 6 figs.

MOHR, CHARLES E.
1964   Exploring America underground. Nation. Geog. Mag., 125, 803—837, illustr.

MOHR, C. E., and POULSON, T. L.
1967   The life of the cave. New York: McGraw-Hill, 232 pp., illustr., (not seen).
           Rev.: Sloane in NSS News, 25, 24—25.

MOHR, ERNA
1959   Das Urwildpferd. Die Neue Brehm-Bücherei Nr. 249. Wittenberg-Lutherstadt: Ziemsen, 144 pp., 87 figs., (not seen).
1965   Altweltliche Stachelschweine. Die Neue Brehm-Bücherei 350. Wittemberg Lutherstadt: A. Ziemsen Verlag (Kosmos-Verlag, Stuttgart), 164 pp., 115 figs., (not seen).
           Rev.: Haltenorth in Kosmos (Stuttgart), 62, *204—*205.

MOÏSIDIS, G.
1967   La grotte de Petralona (Grèce). Spelunca, Bull., 7:4, 324—325.

MOJSKI, J. E. (= Moĭskiĭ, Iu. E.)
1967   [On the stratigraphy of loess in Poland.] Biull. Kom. Izuch. Chetvert. Perioda, 33, 41—56, 3 figs., 1 table, (Russian).

MOLIĂVKO, G. I.
1963   [On the problem of natural environment in southern Ukraine during the Pliocene.] Prirodn. Obstan. i Fauny Proshl., 1, 97—101, (Russian).
           See: Pidoplichko and Moliăvko.

MOLIĂVKO, G. I., and PIDOPLICHKO, I. G.
1952   [Terrestrial vertebrates from Upper Sarmatian of southern URSR.] Zbirn. Prats Zool. Mus. Akad. Nauk URSR, 25, 79—83, 1 map, (Ukrainian; Russian summary).

MOLIN, V. A.
1965   [New localities of vertebrate finds in Permian and Triassic deposits of western Timan region.] Izv. Komi Fil. Vses. Geogr. Obshch., 10, 103—106, 1 fig., (Russian).

MOLNAR, STEPHEN   See: Brace and Molnar.

MONES, A.   See: Francis, J. C. and Mones.

MONGAĬT, ALEXANDRE L.
1955   [Archeology in USSR.] Moscow: Akad. Nauk SSSR Press, 436 pp., 180 figs., 7 maps, (Russian).
1957   [Soviet archeological research.] Vest. Ist. Mir. Kult., 1957:5, 69—91, 2 pls., 2 maps, (Russian; English summary).
1958   [Gordon Child (1892 - 1957).] Sov. Arkheol., 1958:3, 284—287, portr., (Russian).

1961B.   Archaeology in the U.S.S.R. Baltimore: Penguin, 320 pp., (not seen).
          Rev.: J. M. L. in Minn. Archaeol., 28, 66.

MONMÉJEAN, E., BORDES, F., and SONNEVILLE-BORDES, D. DE
1964   Le Périgordien supérieur à burins de Noailles du Roc de Gavaudun (Lot-
          et-Garonne). L'Anthrop., 68, 253–316, 33 figs., 4 tables.

MONOD, THEODORE
1963B.   Achille Valenciennes et l'Histoire Naturelle des Poissons. Mém. Inst.
          Franç. Afr. Noire, no. 68, 9–45, 6 figs., 2 portrs.
1967   Le complexe urophore des Téléostéens: typologie et évolution. (Note
          préliminaire). Colloq. Internat. Cent. Nation. Recherch. Sci., 163,
          111–131, 16 figs., (English summary).

MONSEN, LILY
1966   The casting of fossil-models at the Palaeontological Museum in Oslo.
          Mus. Jour., London, 66, 212–215, figs. 30–32.

MONTAGU, MONTAGU FRANCIS ASHLEY
1960   Rev.: Genovés in An. Antrop., Mexico, 1964, 1, 238–240;   Sen in
          Man in India, 44, 89–91.
1962B.   (ed.) Rev.: Schwidetzky in Homo, 16, 127;   Tappen in Amer. Jour.
          Phys. Anthrop., 23, 437–438.
1963B.   A new theory concerning the origin of speech. Jour. Amer. Med. Assoc.,
          185, 1017–1018.
1964A.   Natural selection and man's relative hairlessness. Jour. Amer. Med. Assoc.,
          187, 356–357.
1964B.   (ed.) The concept of race. New York: Free Press of Glencoe, xviii +
          270 pp.
          Rev.: Johnston in Amer. Jour. Phys. Anthrop., 23, 205–207;   Miele
          in Mankind Quart., 6, 178–180;   S. in Archeol. Roz., 18, 81,
          (Czech);   Schwidetzky in Homo, 16, 63.
1964C.   On Coon's The Origin of Races. In: Montagu, M. F. A., (ed.), 1964B,
          228–241.
1965   The human revolution. Cleveland, New York: World Publishing Co.,
          224 pp., 31 figs., 5 tables.
          Rev.: Dobzhansky in Amer. Anthrop., 68:4, 1084–1085;   Fry in Amer.
          Jour. Phys. Anthrop., 24, 381–382.
1967   Letters to the editor. Perspectives Biol. Med., 10, 314–315.
          See: Brace 1964; Brace and Montagu.

MONTAGU, M. F. A., and TOBIAS, P. V.
1965   Homo habilis. Science, 149, 918.

MONTANE, JULIO
1968   Paleo-Indian remains from Laguna de Tagua Tagua, central Chili. Science,
          161, 1137–1138, 1 fig.

MONTEIL, VINCENT
1965A.   Hommage au Proffesseur Théodore Monod. Bull. Inst. Franç. Afr. Noire,
          27, 411.
1965B.   Hommage au Proffesseur Théodore Monod. Notes Africaines, 105, 1.

MONTENAT, CHRISTIAN   See: Arambourg and Montenat; Bessonnat, et al.; Gins-
          burg, Montenat and Pomerol; Lapparent and Montenat; Lapparent,
          Montenat and Desparmet.

MONTOCCHIO, H.,
1965   Précis de paléontologie humaine, suivi d'une introduction à l'anthropologie. Paris: Soc. d'Edition d'Enseignement Supérieur, 136 pp.
              Rev.: Béthune in Rev. Questions Sci., 27, 300; Furon in Rev. Gén. Sci., 73, 126; Kurth in Homo, 18:1, 64; Vallois in L'Anthrop., 70:5–6, 557–558.

MOODIE, ROY L.
1967   General considerations of the evidences of pathological conditions found among fossil animals. In: Brothwell, D., and Sandison, A. T., (eds.), 1967, 31–46, 2 figs., 1 table.

MOODY, J. W. T.
1964   Erasmus Darwin, M. D., F. R. S.: a biographical and iconographical note. Jour. Soc. Bibliog. Nat. Hist., 4, 210–213, pls. 1–2.

MOODY, R. T. J.
1968   A turtle, Eochelys crassicostata (Owen) from the London Clay of the Isle of Sheppey. Proc. Geol. Assoc. London, 79, 129–140, 4 figs., 3 pls., 2 tables.

MOOK, CHARLES C.
1964   New species of Goniopholis from the Morrison of Oklahoma. Okla. Geol. Notes, 24, 283–287, 2 figs.
1967   Preliminary description of a new goniopholid crocodilian. Kirtlandia, no. 2, 1–10, 5 figs.

MOONEY, CHRISTOPHER F.
1964   Teilhard de Chardin and the mystery of Christ. New York: Harper and Row, 288 pp., bibliog.

MOORE, CLYDE H., JR.
1964   Stratigraphy of the Fredericksburg Division, south-central Texas. Univ. Texas Bur. Econ. Geol., Rept. Inv., no. 52, 48 pp., 12 figs., 19 pls.

MOORE, DAVID R.
1967   Island clues to aboriginal prehistory. Austral. Nat. Hist., 15, 418–422, 2 figs.

MOORE, JOHN A., (ed.)
1965   Ideas in modern biology. Proc., 16th Internat. Congr. Zool., 6, x + 563 pp., illustr.

MOORE, RUTH, and EDITORS OF LIFE
1964A.   Die Evolution. Nederland: Time-Life International, N. V., 191 pp., (not seen).
              Rev.: Krogman in Amer. Jour. Phys. Anthrop., 28, 110; Preuschoft in Umschau, 65:15, 488.
1964B.   Utviklingens gåte. Transl. by Anatol Heintz. Oslo: Life-Gyldendals naturbibliotek, 188 pp., (not seen).
              Rev.: [Faegri] in Naturen, 88, 511.

MOORE, R. C. See: Hecker 1965A.

MOORE, R. C., COMMEMORATIVE VOLUME   See: Teichert and Yochelson, (eds.),
          1967.

MOORE, T. C.   See: Van Andel, et al.

MOORSEL, HENDRIK VAN   See: Mortelmans 1962B; Ploey and Moorsel.

MOOSER BARENDUN, C.
      1964   Una nueva especie de equido del genero Protohippus del Plioceno medio
               de la Mesa Central de México. An. Inst. Biol. Mex., 35, 157–158,
               2 figs.

MOOSER BARENDUN, OSWALDO
      1964   Neohipparion monias n. sp., equido fosil del Plioceno de la Mesa Central
               de México. An. Inst. Biol., Mex., 34:1–2, 393–396, 1 fig.

MOREL, JEAN
      1966   Le Paléolithique inférieur dans la région de la Calle (Algérie). Ses rela-
               tions avec les formations du Quaternaire ancien et moyen. Bull.
               Soc. Préhist. Franç., Étud. et Trav., 63:3, 613–630, 10 figs.

MORET, LÉON
      1965   Manuel de paléontologie animale. 5th ed., completed with addenda.
               Paris: Masson, 782 pp., 274 figs.
               Rev.: Furon in Rev. Gén. Sci., 73, 375–376;   Zapfe in Mitt. Geol.
               Ges. Wien, 58, 285–286.

MORGAN, RICHARD G.
      1952   Outline of cultures in the Ohio region. In: Griffin, J. B., (ed.), 1952A,
               83–98.

MORGAN, THOMAS HUNT
      1916   A critique of the theory of evolution. Princeton: Princeton University
               Press, 197 pp., 95 figs., 1 table.

MORI, FABRIZIO
      1961   Aspetti di cronologia sahariana alla luce dei ritrovamenti della V Missione
               paletnologica nell'Acacus (1960 - 61). La Ric. Sci., Parte I:
               Riv., 1, 204–215, 11 figs.

MORI, HAJIME   See: Matsumoto, Ishii, et al.; Matsumoto, Mori, et al.

MORIARTY, JAMES ROBERT
      1966   Culture phase divisions suggested by typological change coordinated with
               stratigraphically controlled radiocarbon dating at San Diego.
               Anthrop. Jour. Canada, 4:4, 20–30, 3 figs., 1 table.
      1967   Transitional pre-desert phase in San Diego County, California. Science,
               155, 553–556, 2 figs.

MORISON, S., FIRST, R., and PARTRIDGE, T. C.
      1965   Preliminary investigations of the surface of the breccia in the central
               excavation area, Limeworks. S. Afr. Archaeol. Bull., 20:79, 159–
               160, 2 figs.

MORLAN, RICHARD E.
- 1967A.   The preceramic period of Hokkaido: an outline. Arctic Anthrop., 4:1, 164—220, 32 figs., 2 tables.
- 1967B.   Chronometric dating in Japan. Arctic Anthrop., 4:2, 180—211, 10 figs., 4 tables.

MORLET, A.
- 1962   Glozel. Tome II. Mâcon: Ed. Buguet-Comptour, 126 pp., 65 figs., (not seen).
Rev.: R. V. in L'Anthrop., 69, 119—120.

MOROZOV, G. V.   See: Shelkoplias and Morozov.

MOROZOVA, V. F.   See: Bersenev, et al.

MORRIS, DESMOND
- 1967A.   The naked ape. Life, 63:25, 94—98, 100, 102, 104, 106—108, illustr.
- 1967B.   The naked ape. New York: McGraw-Hill, 252 pp.
Rev.: Anon. in Interamer., 15:2, 4; Anon. in Time, 91:4, 80, 82; Campbell in Advance. Sci., 24, 361; Chance in Man, Jour. Roy. Anthrop. Inst., 3, 138; B. D. M. in Frontiers, 32:4, 31—32; Postgate in Sci. Jour., 3:11, 92—93; Singer in Nat. Hist., 77:2, 64—67, 2 figs.; Tuttle in Amer. Anthrop., 70, 1238—1240; Williams in Nat. Hist., 77:2, 67—68.

MORRIS, P. A.   See: Corbet and Morris.

MORRIS, RAMONA and DESMOND
- 1966   Men and apes. New York: McGraw-Hill, viii + 271 pp., frontispiece, illustr.
Rev.: Hallowell in Amer. Anthrop., 69, 783; Schultz in Folia Primatologica, 5, 316; Tiger in Man, Jour. Roy. Anthrop. Inst., 2, 307.

MORRIS, WILLIAM J.
- 1965   Graphic analysis of some Miocene horse astragali from California. Jour. Pal., 39, 657—662, 4 figs.
- 1966A.   Fossil mammals from Baja California: New evidence on Early Tertiary migrations. Science, 153, 1376—1378, 1 fig., 1 table.
- 1966B.   Correlation of new Tertiary mammals from Baja California with North American provincial ages. Program, 19th Ann. Meeting, Geol. Soc. Amer., Rocky Mountain Sect., 1966, 42—43, (abs.). Also: Spec. Pap., Geol. Soc. Amer., 101, 410—411, (abs.).
- 1967A.   Late Cretaceous vertebrates from Baja California. Program, 63rd Ann. Meeting, Geol. Soc. Amer., Cordilleran Sect., 51, (abs.). Also: Spec. Pap. Geol. Soc. Amer., 115, 341, (abs.).
- 1967B.   Baja California: Late Cretaceous dinosaurs. Science, 155, 1539—1541, 1 fig.
- 1968   Late Cretaceous dinosaurs from Baja California. Program, 1968 Ann. Meetings, Geol. Soc. Amer., 1968, 209, (abs.).

MORRISON, ROGER B.   See: Hunt, C. B. and Morrison.

MORROW, CLIFFORD J., JR.
- 1967   Ottmar F. von Fuehrer. Carnegie Mag., 41, 238—241, illustr.

MORSE, DAN
1965   The Paleo-Indian era: distribution of finds. Tennessee. Bull. Southeast.
            Archaeol. Confer., 2, 20–22.
1967   Tuberculosis. In: Brothwell, D., and Sandison, A. T., (eds.), 1967,
            249–271, 7 figs., 6 tables.

MORSE, D. and P.
1964   Archaeological survey of the J. Percy Priest Reservoir, Tennessee. Jour.
            Ala. Archaeol., 10, 1–2, 3 figs.

MORSE, D. F., and P. A., and WAGGONER, J., Jr.
1964   Fluted points from Smith County, Tennessee. Tenn. Archaeol., 20, 16–
            34, 1 fig., 7 pls.

MORTELMANS, GEORGES
1962B.   Vue d'ensemble sur la préhistoire du Congo occidental. Proc. 4th Pan-
            african Congr. Prehist., Sec. 3, 129–164, 2 tables, (discussion by
            J. de Heinzelin, and H. van Moorsel).

MORTIER, JEANNE, and ABOUX, M.-L., (eds.)
1966A.   Teilhard de Chardin album. Compiled from the publications and letters
            of Pierre Teilhard de Chardin, and from papers preserved at the
            Fondation Teilhard de Chardin. Preface by André George. New
            York and Evanston: Harper and Row, 223 pp., illustr.
1966B.   Pierre Teilhard de Chardin images et paroles. Préface d'André George.
            Paris: Editions du Seuil, 223 pp., illustr.

MORTINE, WAYNE A.
1965   Florida's Ice Age clues found. Ohio Archaeol., 15, 46–49, 2 pls.
1968   The Keiser site: a Paleo-Indian site in Tuscarawas County. Ohio Archaeol.
            18, 12–16, 6 figs.

MORTINE, W. A., and DRIVE, S.
1965   Paleo artifacts from the Newcomerstown area. Ohio Archaeol., 15, 134–
            135, 1 fig.

MOSER, FRANK   See: Dorr and Moser.

MOS'KINA, O. D.
1968   [Small mammals from Neogene and Quaternary of Rudnyĭ Altaĭ.]   Pal.
            Zhurnal, 1968:1, 141–144, 1 fig., (Russian).
            See: Bazhanov, Matsui and Mos'kina.

MOSKVITIN, ALEKSANDR I.
1944   [Geomorphology, unconsolidated deposits and placers of southwestern
            Altaĭ.]   Referaty Nauchno-Issl. Rab., 1945, 19–20, (Russian).
1952   [A scheme of Pleistocene paleogeography of the European part of USSR
            on the basis of new ideas on the stratigraphy of Quaternary de-
            posits.] Mat. Chetvert. Period. SSSR, 3, 130–144, 5 figs., 1
            table, (Russian).
1958   [Quaternary deposits and history of the formation of the valley of the
            middle fork of the Volga R.]   Trudy Geol. Inst., 12, 209 pp.,
            66 figs., 24 tables, (Russian).
1960   [An attempt to apply a single stratigraphic scheme to the Quaternary
            deposits of western Siberia.]   Trudy Geol. Inst., 26, 11–36, 8
            figs., 9 tables, (Russian).

1961B. [Comparative stratigraphic review of Pleistocene cross-sections from European part of USSR, Poland, and Czechoslovakia, which contain traces of sojourn of Paleolithic man.] Internat. Assoc. Quat. Res. Abs. Pap., 6th Congr., 142, (abs.; Russian).

1961C. [Comparative stratigraphic review of Pleistocene sections of the European part of the USSR, Poland, and Czechoslovakia, containing traces of the Paleolithic man.] In: Gromov, V. I., et al., (eds.), 1961, 47—63, 9 figs., (Russian; English summary).

1962A. [On the subdivisions of the Wurm and its Middle and Upper Paleolithic levels arrangement in Europe.] Izv. Akad. Nauk SSSR, Ser. Geol., 1962:7, 35—44, 4 figs., (Russian).

1962B. [Pleistocene of the lower Volga region.] Trudy Geol. Inst., 64, 263 pp., 80 figs., 21 tables, (Russian).

1965   [Pleistocene in the European part of the USSR.] Trudy Geol. Inst., 123, 180 pp., 15 figs., 5 tables, (Russian).

1967   [Pleistocene stratigraphy of the European part of the USSR.] Trudy Geol. Inst., 156, 238 pp., 77 figs., 7 tables, (Russian).

MOSLEY, S. A.
1959   The Nebo Hill site, an early-man site near Decatur, Alabama. Jour. Ala. Archaeol., 5, 55—70, 5 pls.

MOSS, JOHN H.
1968   The geologic history of Mummy Cave — an early man site in the Absaroka Mountains west of Cody, Wyoming. Program, 21st Ann. Meeting, Geol. Soc. Amer., Rocky Mt. Sect., 52, (abs.).
        See: Wedel, Husted and Moss.

MOSS, MELVIN L.
1961   The initial phylogenetic appearance of bone. An experimental hypothesis. Trans. N. Y. Acad. Sci., 23, 495—500, 4 figs.

MOSS, M. L., and KERMACK, K. A.
1967   Enamel structure in two Triassic mammals. Jour. Dental Res., 46, 745—747, illustr., (not seen).

MOSS, M. L., and YOUNG, R. W.
1964   A functional approach to craniology. In: Lasker, G. W., (ed.), 1964, 278—290, 8 figs., (reprint with editorial comment).

MOSTECKÝ, VLASTIMIL
1961C. Pleistocene Mammalia of the "Chlupač-Grotto" in the Kobyla-Hill at Koněprusi (Beroun region). Čas. Národ. Musea, Odd. Prirod., 130, 22—25, 1 fig., (Czech; English summary).

1964   Pleistozäne Säugetiere aus dem Steinbruch aus "Chlum" (Mittelböhmen, unweit von Beroun, Späteres Würmstadial). Acta. Mus. Nat. Pragae, 20B, 153—188, 5 figs., 4 pls., 18 tables.

1966   Rhinocerotidae aus der Höhle "Chlupačova Sluj" bei koněprusy. Acta Mus. Nat. Pragae, 22, 143—161, 6 figs., 3 pls., 5 tables.

MOTAS, C., (ed.)
1964   Emil Racoviţa. Opere alese. Bucharest: Academia Republicii Populare Romîne Press, 812 pp., illustr., (Rumanian).

MOTAŞ, IONEL C.   See: Macarovici, Marinescu and Motaş; Macarovici and Motaş; Macarovici, Motas and Contescu.

MOTT, I. M.
1964   Dorcatherium aus dem unteren Sarmat von St. Stefan im Lavanttal.
         Carinthia II, 74, 22–24.

MOTT, R. J.   See: Klassen, Delorme and Mott.

MOTTL, MARIA
1964   Bärenphylogenese in Südost-Österreich mit besonderer Berücksichtigung
         des neuen Grabungsmaterials aus Höhlen des mittelsteirischen
         Karstes. Mitt. Mus. Bergbau, Geol. Tech., 26, 55 pp., 6 pls., 8
         tables.
         Abs.: Ehrenberg in Zbl. Geol. Pal., Teil 2, 1965, 274–275.
1966A.   Ein vollständiger Hyotherium palaeochoerus-Schädel aus dem Altpliozän
         (Pannon) Südost-Österreichs. Mitt. Mus. Bergbau, Geol. Tech.,
         28, 73–100, 4 pls., (not seen).
         Rev.: Kühn in Zbl. Geol. Pal., Teil 2, 1967, 512.
1966B.   Eine neue unterpliozän Säugetierfauna aus der Steiermark, SO-Österreich.
         Mitt. Mus. Bergbau, Geol. Tech., 28, 103–132, pl. 5, (not seen).
         Rev.: Kühn in Zbl. Geol. Pal., Teil 2, 1967, 512.
1966C.   Anthracotherium aus dem Sarmat der Steiermark. Mitt. Mus. Bergbau,
         Geol. Tech., 28, 133–135, pls. 6–7, (not seen).
         Rev.: Kühn in Zbl. Geol. Pal., Teil 2, 1968, 219.
1966D.   Ergebnisse der paläontologischen Untersuchung der Knochenartefakte
         aus der Tischoferhöhle in Tirol. Quartar, 17, 153–163.
1967A.   Neuer Beitrag zum Hystrix-Horizont Europas. Ann. Naturhist. Mus.
         Wien, 71, 305–327, 5 figs., 2 pls.
1967B.   Neue Schildkrötenreste aus dem Mittelmiozän SW – Österreichs. Carin-
         thia II, 77, 169–182, 1 fig., 3 pls.
         See: Schauberger, et al.

MOULIN, P.   See: Rozhdestvenskiĭ 1960C.

MOUNTAIN, EDGAR D.
1966   Footprints in calcareous sandstone at Nahoon Point. S. African Jour.
         Sci., 62, 103–111, 2 figs., 7 pls.

MOUNTFORD, CHARLES P., and EDWARDS, R.
1964   Rock engravings in the Red Gorge, Deception Creek, northern South
         Australia. Anthropos, 59, 849–859, 7 figs., 2 .pls.

MOURER-CHAUVIRÉ, C.
1964   Les oiseaux du Locus VIII de la grotte du Lazaret à Nice (A.-M.). Bull.
         Mus. Anthrop. Préhist. Monaco, 11, 61–80, 5 figs., 4 pls., 4 tables.

MOUSSA, MOUNIR T.
1968   Fossil tracks from the Green River formation (Eocene) near Soldier
         Summit, Utah. Jour. Pal., 42, 1433–1438, 1 fig., pls. 177–178.

MOVIUS, HALLAM L., JR.
1960B.   Rev.: Müller-Beck in Current Anthrop., 2, 439–444;   Pei in Vert.
         Palasiatica, 1961:2, 172–179, (Chinese).
1962   Preliminary results of the Abri Pataud excavations, Les Eyzies (Dordogne).
         Abs. 61st. Ann. Meeting Amer. Anthrop. Assoc., 1962, 25, (abs.).
1964   Upper Périgordian and Aurignacian hearths at the Abri Pataud, Les
         Eyzies (Dordogne). Abs. 63rd. Ann. Meeting Amer. Anthrop.
         Assoc., 1964, 41–42, (abs.).

1965	Upper Périgordian and Aurignacian hearths at the Abri Pataud, Les Eyzies (Dordogne). In: Ripoll Perelló, E., (ed.), 1965B, 181–196, 6 pls., (French summary).
	Rev.: Il in Archeol. Roz., 20, 278–279.
1966A.	L'histoire de la reconnaissance des burins en silex et de la découverte de leur fonction en tant qu'outils pendant le Paléolithique supérieur. Bull. Soc. Préhist. Franç., Etud. et Trav., 63:1, 50–65.
1966B.	The hearths of the Upper Périgordian and Aurignacian horizons at the Abri Pataud, Les Eyzies (Dordogne), and their possible significance. In: Clark, J. D., and Howell, F. C., (eds.), 1966A, 296–325, 14 pls.

MSTISLAVSKIĬ, M. M., and KOCHENOV, A. V.

1961	[On conditions controlling the accumulation of fish remains in Maĭkop deposits.] Izv. Vyssh. Uch. Zav., Geol. i Razv., 1961:3, 3–15, (Russian).

MUIR-WOOD, H. M.   See: Oakley and Muir-Wood.

MUKERJEE, RADHAKAMAL

1963	The dimensions of human evolution. A bio-philosophical interpretation. London: Macmillan, xiii + 217 pp.

MULLER, ADOLPHE

1964	Untersuchungen über das Rät in Luxemburg. Publ. Serv. Géol. Luxembourg, 14, 255–282, (French summary).
	See: Hary and Muller.

MÜLLER, ARNO HERMANN

1962A.	Abs.: Hantzschel in Zbl. Geol. Pal., Teil 2, 1964, 420–421.
1966	Lehrbuch der Paläozoologie. Band III. Vertebraten. Teil 1. Fische im weiteren Sinne und Amphibien. Jena: Gustav Fischer, xvi + 638 pp., 698 figs.
	Rev.: Bachmayer in Universum; Natur u. Tech., 1967:4, II; Boné in Rev. Questions Sci., 28, 285; Haltenorth in Säugetierkundl. Mitt., 15, 187; Heberer in Anthrop. Anz., 30, 216; Kollman in Ann. Naturhist. Mus. Wien, 68, 707; Kollmann in Ann. Naturhist. Mus. Wien, 70, 525; Rode in Homo, 18:4, 266; Romer in Quart. Rev. Biol., 43:1, 68–69; Rossi Ronchetti in Riv. Ital. Pal., 73, 1050; Struve in Natur u. Museum, 98:7, 286–287; 99:8, 393; Westphal in Zbl. Geol. Pal., Teil 2, 1967, 99–100; Zapfe in Mitt. Geol. Ges. Wien, 59:2, 304–305.
1968A.	Lehrbuch der Paläozoologie. Band III. Vertebraten. Teil 2. Reptilien und Vögel. Jena: Gustav Fischer, xvi + 657 pp., 728 figs.
	Rev.: Bachmayer in Ann. Naturhist. Mus. Wien, 72, 721; Fantini Sestini in Riv. Ital. Pal., 75:3, 684–685; Haltenorth in Säugetierkundl. Mitt., 17:2, 196; Heberer in Anthropol. Anz., 31:3, 227–228; Hölder in Biol. Zbl., 88:5, 666–667; Kinzelbach in Jour. Ornithol., 110:2, 228–229; Romer in Quart. Rev. Biol., 45:1, 64; Westphal in Zbl. Geol. Pal., Teil 2, 1968:6, 639–640; Zapfe in Mitt. Geol. Ges. Wien, 61, 211.

MULLER, A. H., and ZIMMERMANN, H.

1962	Rev.: Bachmayer in Universum; Natur u. Tech., 20:12, IV; Beyer in Aufschluss, 14, 137; Bogsch in Föld. Közlöny, 95, 111, (Hungarian).

MÜLLER, ARNT
1967 Die Geschichte der Familie Dimylidae (Insectivora, Mamm.) auf Grund der Funde aus tertiären Spaltenfüllungen Süddeutschlands. Abh. Bayer. Akad. Wiss., Math.-Nat. Kl., 129, 3–93, 29 figs., 3 pls., 42 tables.
 Rev.: Fahlbusch in Zbl. Geol. Pal., Teil 2, 1968:6, 660–661.

MÜLLER, A. VON, and NAGEL, W., (eds.)
1959 Gandert-Festschrift zum sechzigsten Geburtstag von Otto-Friedrich Gandert. Berliner Beit. Vor- und Frühgesch., 2, 178 pp., portr., 47 pls., figs. in text.

MÜLLER, ERNEST H.
1965 Bibliography of New York Quaternary geology. With historical note on studies of New York Quaternary geology by E. H. Muller and W. A. Garrabrant. Bull. N. Y. State Mus. and Sci. Serv., no. 398, vi + 116 pp., 2 figs.

MÜLLER, ERNST
1964 Pollenanalytische Untersuchungen in den drei Bärenhöhlen. Acta Bernensia, 3, 146–148, fig. 30.

MÜLLER, H. H.
1962 Bibliographie zur prähistorischen Zoologie und Geschichte der Haustiere: 1958 - 1961. Berlin: Institut für Vor- und Frühgeschichte der Deutschen Akademie der Wissenschaften, (not seen).
1963 Bibliographie zur prähistorischen Zoologie und Geschichte der Haustiere: 1961 - 1962. Berlin: Institut für Vor- und Frühgeschichte der Deutschen Akademie der Wissenschaften, (not seen).
1964 Bibliographie zur prähistorischen Zoologie und Geschichte der Haustiere: 1962 - 1963. Berlin: Institut für Vor- und Frühgeschichte der Deutschen Akademie der Wissenschaften, (not seen).

MÜLLER, KARL See: Binder, et al.

MÜLLER, WOLFGANG
1965 Lias ∈ im Flussbett der Apfelstädt bei Wechmar (Messtischblatt Gotha). Hallesches Jahrb., 6, 18–20, pls. 2–4.

MÜLLER-BECK, HANSJÜRGEN
1959 Bemerkungen zur Stratigraphie des mitteleuropäischen Jungpleistozäns. Eiszeit. u. Gegenwart, 10, 144–160, 3 figs., (English summary).
 Abs.: Ebers in Zbl. Geol. Pal., Teil 2, 1962, 569–570.
1961B. More on Upper Palaeolithic archaeology. Current Anthrop., 2, 439–444.
1961C. Zum Problem kultureller Beziehungen zwischen Nordeurasien und Nordamerika vor dem Würm-Maximum. Internat. Assoc. Quat. Res., Abs. Pap., 6th Congr., 142–143, (abs.).
1965A. Eine "Wurzel-Industrie" des Vogelherd-Aurignaciens. Fundber. Schwaben, 17, 43–51, 2 figs., pls. 7–13, 1 table.
1965B. Non-projectile point stone industries in America and the problem of their Eurasiatic origins (roots). 7th Internat. Congr., Internat. Assoc. Quat. Res., Abs., 1965, 354–355, (abs.).
1965C. 10,000 Jahre steinzeitliche Sammler und Jäger in Südamerika. Umschau, 65, 568–572, 5 figs.
1966A. Sondierungen in der paläolithisch-mesolithischen Freilandstation "Speckberg". Bayer. Vorges., 31, 1–33, 29 figs.

1966B.   Paläolitische Spuren aus dem Rixdorfer Horizont? Berliner Jahrb. Vor-
           und Frühgesch., 6, 71—83, 3 figs., 1 table.

1966C.   Die frühe und mittlere Altsteinzeit in Europa, Nordafrika und Vorderasien.
           In: Narr, (ed.), 1966B, 134—157, 9 figs., 1 table.

1966D.   Jäger- und Sammelkulturen Nordasiens und Amerikas. In: Narr, (ed.),
           1966B, 382—403, 9 figs.

1966E.   Paleohunters in America: origins and diffusions. Minn. Archaeol., 28,
           37—56, 21 figs.

1966F.   Paleohunters in America: Origins and diffusion. Science, 152, 1191—
           1210, 21 figs.

1967   On migrations of hunters across the Bering Land Bridge in the Upper
           Pleistocene. In: Hopkins, D. M., (ed.), 1967D, 373—408, 12
           figs.

           See: Brace 1964; Grahmann and Müller-Beck; Ivanova 1967.

MÜLLER-KARPE, HERMANN
     1966   Handbuch der Vorgeschichte. Band I. Altsteinzeit. München: Beck'sche
               Verlagsbuchhandlung, 389 pp., 3 figs., 274 pls., 1 table.
     Rev.:   Bánesz in Sloven. Archeol., 17:1, 260; Bosinski in Bonner Jahrb.,
               168, 515—520; T. Dobosi in Archaeol. Ért., 97:1, 142; Felgen-
               hauer in Archaeol. Austriaca, 43, 144—145; Fock in S. Afr.
               Archaeol. Bull., 23, 2; Gersbach in Anthrop. Anz., 30, 217—219;
               Prost in L'Anthrop., 71:3—4, 301—303.

MULLOY, WILLIAM
     1952   The northern Plains. In: Griffin, J. B., (ed.), 1952A, 124—138.

MULVANEY, D. J.
     1962   Advancing frontiers in Australian archaeology. Oceania, 33, 135—138.
     1963   Prehistory. Commentary by F. D. McCarthy. In: Sheils, H., (ed.),
               1963, 33—56.
     1964A.   The Pleistocene colonization of Australia. Antiq., 38, 263—267, 1 fig.,
               pls. 43—44.
     Rev.:   R. V. in L'Anthrop., 69:5—6, 558—559.
     1964B.   Australian archaeology 1929 - 1964: problems and policies. Austral.
               Jour. Sci., 27, 39—44, 2 figs.
     1964C.   Prehistory of the basalt plains. Proc. Roy. Soc. Victoria, 77, 427—432.
     1966A.   Fact, fancy and aboriginal Australian ethnic origins. Mankind, 6, 299—
               305.
     1966B.   The prehistory of the Australian aborigine. Sci. Amer., 214:3, 84—93,
               illustr.
     See: Bowler, et al.

MULVANEY, D. J., and JOYCE, E. B.
     1965   Archaeological and geomorphological investigations on Mt. Moffatt
               Station, Queensland, Australia. Proc. Prehist. Soc. Cambridge,
               31, 147—212, 25 figs., pls. 22—31, 3 maps, 6 tables.

MUMFORD, LEWIS
     1965   Technics and the nature of man. Nature, 208, 923—928.
     1967   The myth of the machine. Technics and human development. New
               York: Harcourt, Brace and World, viii + 342 pp., illustr.
     Rev.:   Steward in Science, 158, 105—106.

MUNGER, P.   See: Adams, Magre and Munger.

MUNN, A. C.
1966   The 1965 Livingstone School of Archaeology. S. Afr. Archaeol. Bull.,
          21, 55.
1967   Archaeological school. S. Afr. Archaeol. Bull., 22, 19.

MUNRO, ELISABETH   See: Prufer and Munro.

MUNRO, TOM   See: Anderson, J. E. 1962.

MUNSON, PATRICK J., and FRYE, J. C.
1965   Artifact from deposits of Mid-Wisconsin age in Illinois. Science, 150,
          1722—1723, 2 figs.

MUNTANER DARDER, A.
1966   Distribución en Baleares del Myotragus balearicus Bate. Bol. Soc. Hist.
          Nat. Baleares, 12:1—4, 25—28.

MUNTHE, HENRIK VILHELM
1956   On the development of the Baltic herring in the light of the Late-
          Quaternary history of the Baltic. Ark. Zool., Ser. 2, 9, 333—341,
          5 figs.

MURATA, MASAFUMI   See: Hatai, Murata and Masuda.

MURATOV, V. M.   See: Autlev, et al.

MURDOCK, C. J., and JOLLY, R. G. W.
1967   An excavation at Opito Bay. New Zealand Archaeol. Assoc. News-
          letter, 10, 157—166, 2 figs., 2 pls., 3 tables.

MURPHY, JAMES L., and PICKING, L.
1967   A new marine member in the Conemaugh Group of Ohio. Kirtlandia,
          no. 1, 1—7.

MURPHY, JOHN A.
1964   Department of Geology. Ann. Rept. Denver Mus. Nat. Hist., 1963,
          19—20, 1 fig.
1965   Department of Geology. Ann. Rept. Denver Mus. Nat. Hist., 1964,
          15.

MURRAY, BERTRAM G., JR.
1967   Grebes from the Late Pliocene in North America. Condor, 69, 277—
          288, 3 figs., 3 tables.
          See: Ford, N. and Murray.

MURRAY, MARIAN
1967   Hunting for fossils. New York: Macmillan, xxvi + 348 pp., illustr.

MURZAEV, E. M.
1956   [Vladimir Afanas'evich Obruchev.] Izv. Akad. Nauk SSSR, ser. geogr.,
          1956:5, 4—8, (Russian).
1966   [V. A. Obruchev and the Central Asia.] Izv. Akad. Nauk SSSR, ser.
          geograf., 1966:5, 113—118, (Russian).
          See: Armand, et al.

MUSAKULOVA, L. T.
1967 [Remains of a new species of the genus Dicrocerus Lartet (1837) from Miocene deposits of Kazakhstan.] In: Collected Papers, 1967A [Place and significance of fossil mammals of Moldavia in the Cenozoic of USSR], 85—89, (Russian; not seen).

MUSCHALEK, H.
1963 Urmensch — Adam. Die Herkunft des menschlichen Leibes in natur-wissenschaftlicher und theologischer Sicht. Berlin: Morus, 255 pp., 21 figs., 8 pls., (not seen).
Rev.: Knussman in Homo, 15, 115; Kurth in Naturwiss. Rund., 17, 160; Preuschoft in Anthrop. Anz., 27, 234.

MUSIL, RUDOLF
1962A. Abs.: Dietrich in Zbl. Geol. Pal., Teil 2, 1964, 187.
1964 Die Braunbären aus dem Ende des letzten Glazials. Čas. Morav. Mus. Brně, 49:1, 83—102, 4 pls., (Czech summary).
1965A. Wertung der früheren paläontologischen Funde aus der Šipka-Höhle. Anthropos, Brno, 17, 127—134, 1 table, (Czech; German summary).
1965B. Die Bärenhöhle Pod Hradem. Die Entwicklung der Höhlenbären im letzten Glazial. Anthropos, Brno, 18, 9—92, 38 figs., 14 pls., 21 tables.
Rev.: Ehrenberg in Zbl. Geol. Pal., Teil 2, 1967, 515—517.
1965C. Die Equiden-Reste aus dem Altpleistozän von Voigtstedt in Thüringen. Pal. Abh., Abt. A, 2, 433—449, 5 figs., pl. 23, 1 table, (Russian and English summaries).
1966A. Holštejn, eine neue altpleistozäne Lokalität in Mähren. Čas. Morav. Mus. Brně, Sci. Nat., 51, 133—168, 13 figs., 1 table, (Czech. summary).
1966B. [Influence of climatic oscillations during Pleistocene on morphological and metric changes.] Lynx, 6, 115—119, (Czech; German summary).
1967 Die interglaziale Fauna aus der Höhle Nr. 4 in Vratíkov. Čas. Morav. Mus. Brně. Sci. Nat., 52, 93—120, 10 figs., 4 pls., (Czech summary).
1968 Die Mammutmolaren von Predmostí (ČSSR). Pal. Abh., Abt. A., 3:1, 1—192, 71 figs., 44 pls., 44 tables, (English and Russian summaries).
Rev.: Bohlin in Geol. Fören. Förh., 90:4, 564; Fejfar in Čas. Mineral. Geol., 15:2, 122; Guenther in Quartär, 19, 413—415.

MUSIL, R., et al.
1965 Die Erforschung der Höhle Pod Hradem 1956 - 1958. Anthropos, Brno, 18, 152 pp., 49 figs., 16 pls., 1 col. chart, 43 tables.
Rev.: Gross in Quartär, 17, 222—224.

MUSSETT, FRANCES See: Kermack, D. M., Kermack and Mussett; Kermack, K. A., Lees and Mussett.

MUTHER, LUCY W. See: Collin and Stoiber.

MUTO, A. See: Okutsu and Muto.

MYERS, ARTHUR J.
1965 Late Wisconsinan date for the Bar M local fauna. Okla. Geol. Notes, 25, 168—170.

MYERS, DON
    1965   Okotipi Cave (Ral-018). Missouri Speleology, 7, 15.

MYERS, GEORGE S.
    1966   Derivation of the freshwater fish fauna of Central America. Copeia,
                1966, 766–773.
                See: Greenwood, et al.; Jordan, D. S. 1963.

MYERS, ROLLO   See: Chailley 1965.

MYRON, ROBERT
    1964   Prehistoric art. New York, Toronto, London: Pitman Publishing Co.,
                94 pp., illustr.

N.
    1960   Les origines de l'Homme, biologie et culture. Cahiers Étud. Biol., no.
                6–7, 204 pp., illustr., (not seen).
                Rev.: [Vallois] in L'Anthrop., 66, 136–137.

NABER, FRIEDRICH B.   See: Freund and Naber.

NADER, IYAD A.
    1962   Shanidar Cave, Irbil Liwa, Iraq. Summary of literature with emphasis
                on animal remains. Cave Notes, 4:4, 25–32, 1 fig.

NAGARAJA RAO, M. S.   See: Rao, Nagaraja M. S.

NAGASAWA, JOJI
    1967   On the fossil equine teeth from Kuzuu, Tochigi Prefecture and Tokyo
                City. Trans. Proc. Pal. Soc. Japan, no. 66, 83–91, 1 fig., pl. 10,
                3 tables, (Japanese summary).

NAGEL, W.   See: Müller, A. von and Nagel.

NAIRN, A. E. M., (ed.)
    1964   Problems in palaeoclimatology. Proceedings of the NATO Palaeoclimates
                Conference held at the University of Newcastle upon Tyne, Jan-
                uary 7–12, 1963. London, New York: Interscience (Wiley),
                xiv + 705 pp., illustr.
    1965   Rev.: Anon. in C. R. Soc. Géol. France, 1965, 83–84;   Bryson in
                GeoTimes, 10:2, 25, 27;   Davidson in Nature, 207, 7;   Dim-
                bleby in Bull. London Univ. Inst. Archaeol., no. 6, 131–132;
                De Jong in Geol. en Mijn., 44, 264;   Manten in Palaeogeog.,
                Palaeoclimatol., Palaeoecol., 1, 176–179;   Martinsson in Geol.
                Fören. Förh., 87, 173;   Stehli in Science, 148, no. 3671, 806–
                808;   Volkheimer in Asoc. Geol. Argent., Rev., 21:2, 162–164.
    1966   Earth Science Reviews. International magazine for geo-scientists. Palaeo-
                geog., Palaeoclimatol., Palaeoecol., 2, 77–78.

NAKAGAWA, HISAO
    1962   Sea-level and altitude of land bridges during the continental stages of
                Japan. Some problems on land connection. Quat. Res., 2,
                154–158, 1 fig., (Japanese; English summary).
                See: Serizawa and Nakagawa.

NAKAMURA, KAZUAKI   See: Serizawa, Nakamura and Aso.

NAKAZAWA, K.
1966   Fossil fish scales from the Bessho formation. Kaseki, 11, 30, (Japanese).

NAKEL'SKIĬ, S. K.   See: Karlov and Nakel'skiĭ.

NAKEL'SKIĬ, S. K., and KARLOV, N. N.
1965   [On the geological age and on the significance of the remains of fossil
            Palaeolithic man discovered in the middle Dnepr region.]   Voprosy
            Antrop., 20, 75–79, 1 pl., (Russian).
1966   [Remains of fossil Paleolithic man in Middle Dnepr region.]   Sov. Arkheol.,
            1966:1, 258–263, 2 figs., 1 table, (Russian).

NAKHABTSEV, IU. S.   See: Fradkin, et al.

NALETOV, P. I.
1961   [Catalogue of localities of fossil fauna, flora, pollen and spores of the
            central part of Buriat ASSR.]   Moskow: Gosgeoltekhizdat Press,
            63 pp., 1 map, (Russian).

NALIVKIN, D. V.
1962   [Geology of USSR.]   Moscow-Leningrad: Akad. Nauk Press, 813 pp.,
            285 figs. and maps, 58 tables, (Russian).
1963   (ed.) [Stratigraphy of the U.S.S.R., in 14 volumes.]   Moscow: "Nedra"
            Press.

NALIVKIN, D. V., and MARKOVSKIĬ, B. P., (eds.)
1962   [Decisions of the first plenary session of the permanent stratigraphic
            commission on the Devonian of U.S.S.R.]   Biulleten' Mezh.
            Strat. Kom., 4, 79 pp., (Russian).

NANIA, ION
1964   [A new find of Lower Paleolithic in the Argeş region.]   Studii şi Cer-
            cetări de Ist. Veche, 15, 517–521, 1 fig., (Rumanian;   Russian
            and French summaries).

NAORA, NUBUO
1959   [On the fossils found in Hanaizumi, Iwate Prefecture.]   Daiyonki
            Kenkyu, 1, 118–124, 4 figs., 1 pl., 1 map, (Japanese;   English
            summary, not seen).
            Abs.:   in Befu, Chard and Okada, 1964, 34.
1963   Life of the prehistoric man.   Tokyo: 249 pp.

NAPIER, JOHN R.
1962A.   Reprint in Current Anthrop., 6, 412–414.
1964A.   Five steps to man.   Discovery, 25:6, 34–36, figs. 2–3.   Discussion.
1964B.   Genesis of bipedalism in hominids.   Jour. Anat., 98, 297, (abs.).
1964C.   Profile of early man at Olduvai.   New Sci., 22, 86–89, 5 figs.
1964D.   The evolution of bipedal walking in the hominids.   Proc. 2nd Internat.
            European Anat. Congr., (not seen).
            Rev.:   H. V. V. in L'Anthrop., 71:1–2, 164–165.
            See: Campbell, B. G. 1964A;   Davis, P. R., Day and Napier;   Day and
            Napier;   Leakey, Tobias and Napier.

NAPIER, J. R., and DAVIS, P. R.
1959A.   Rev.: Preuschoft in Anthrop. Anz., 28, 151–152.

NAPIER, J. R., and WALKER, A. C.
1967   Vertical clinging and leaping in living and fossil primates. In: Starck,
D., Schneider, R., and Kuhn, H. J., (eds.), 1967, 66–69, 2 figs.,
1 pl.

NARBUTAS, V. V.
1964A.   [Some problems of actuality on stratigraphy and nomenclature of Baltic
Devonian.] In: Karataiūte-Talimaa and Narbutas, (eds.), 1964,
8–20, 1 table, (Russian).
1964B.   [Stratigraphy and lithology of early Frasnian sediments of Polish-Lithuan-
ian syneclise in the light of facies zones of Frasnian basin in the
North-West of Russian Platform.] In: Karataiūte-Talimaa and
Narbutas, (eds.), 1964, 89–103, 4 maps, (Russian).
See: Karatajūte and Narbutas.

NARR, KARL J.
1960D.   Weibliche Symbol-Plastik der älteren Steinzeit. Antaios, 2, 132–157,
10 figs., pls. 3–4.
Rev.: [Filip] in Archeol. Roz., 13, 149–150, (Czech).
1961   Rev.: Anon. in Ur-Schweiz, 26, 81; Maringer in Anthropos, 59, 948–
949; Schobinger in An. Arqueol. Etnol., Univ. Nac. Cuyo,
17–18, 220–222; Solheim in Asian Perspectives, 8:1, 132;
Trimmel in Die Höhle, 14, 25.
1963   Rev.: Angeli in Ann. Naturhist. Mus. Wien, 67, 724–725; Angeli in
Mitt. Anthrop. Ges. Wien, 93–94, 162–163; B. in Universum;
Natur u. Tech., 21:2, II; Butzer in Zeit. Ethnol., 92:1, 129–
130; Herre in Zeit. Säugetierk., 30, 191; K. in Natuurhist.
Maandbl., 53, 74–75; Kurth in Kosmos (Stuttgart), 61, *329–
*330; Preuschoft in Anthrop. Anz., 28, 53; Preuschoft in
Zbl. Geol. Pal., Teil 2, 1964, 523–524; Roth-Lutra in Anat.
Anz., 116, 523–524; Sauter in Arch. Suiss. Anthrop. Gen.,
31, 63–64; Schobinger in An. Arqueol. Etnol., Univ. Nac. Cuyo,
17–18, 223–224; Woldstedt in Eiszeit. u. Gegenwart, 16, 249.
1964A.   Das jungpleistozäne Bering-Land und die Erstbesiedlung Amerikas.
Forsch. u. Fortschr., 38, 277–282, 4 figs.
1964B.   A la recherche de la préhistorire. Translated by C. Guinchat. Paris:
Payot, 199 pp.
1966A.   El fenómeno cultural y la noogénesis, la obra de Teilhard de Chardin.
Acta Praehist., 5–7, 216–222.
1966B.   (ed.) Handbuch der Urgeschichte. Band I. Ältere und mittlere
Steinzeit. Jäger- und Sammelkulturen. Bern und München:
Francke Verlag, 516 pp., 104 figs., 22 pls.
Rev.: David in Quartar, 18, 237–240; T. Dobosi in Archaeol. Ért.,
96:1, 134–135; Engelmayer in Mitt. Anthrop. Ges. Wien,
96–97, 341; Gersbach in Anthropol. Anz., 31:4, 307–308;
Thompson in Antiq. Jour., 48:2, 312–314.
1966C.   Älteste Spuren der Kultur. In: Narr, (ed.), 1966B, 68–84, 4 figs.
1966D.   Die frühe und mittlere Altsteinzeit Süd- und Ostasiens. In: Narr,
(ed.), 1966B, 113–133, 7 figs., 2 tables.
1966E.   Geistiges Leben in der frühen und mittleren Altsteinzeit. In: Narr,
(ed.), 1966B, 158–168.
1966F.   Religion und Magie in der jüngeren Altsteinzeit. In: Narr, (ed.),
1966B, 298–320, 5 figs.

1966G.   Miolithische Kulturen von Westafrika bis Ostasien. In: Narr, (ed.), 1966B, 349—367, 9 figs.

       See: Brace 1964; Uslar and Narr.

NASEDKIN, V. V., and FORMOZOV, A. A.
1965   [Volcanic glass from Stone Age sites of Krasnodar area and Checheno-Ingushetia.] In: Kolchin, (ed.), 1965, 167—170, 1 fig., 2 tables, (Russian).

NASH, DAVID F.
1968   Occurrence of a new large crocodile from Utah. Program, 21st Ann. Meeting, Geol. Soc. Amer., Rocky Mt. Sect., 55, (abs.).

NASH, DIANE
1968   A crocodile from the Upper Triassic of Lesotho. Jour. Zool., London, 156, 163—179, 7 figs., 3 tables.

NASRETDINOV, KH. K.
1964   [Obirakhmat cave.] Istoriiā Mater. Kul't. Uzbekistana, 5, 21—27, 4 figs., (Russian).

NATIONAL ACADEMY OF SCIENCE
1965   Time and stratigraphy in the evolution of man. A symposium sponsored by the Division of Earth Sciences, National Academy of Sciences, National Research Council, October 16, 1965, Washington, D. C. Publ. Nation. Acad. Sci., 1469, 6 + 97 pp., illustr.

NEAL, ARMINTA, and AKERLEY, R. L.
1964   Department of Graphic Design. Ann. Rept. Denver Mus. Nat. Hist., 1963, 36—40, illustr.
1965   Department of Graphic Design. Ann. Rept. Denver Mus. Nat. Hist., 1964, 25—28, illustr.

NEALE, J. W. See: Pokorný 1965.

NEAVE, SHEFFIELD AIREY
1966   Nomenclatur zoologicus; a list of the names of genera and subgenera in zoology from the tenth edition of Linnaeus, 1758, to the end of 1935. London: Zool. Soc. London, 6, xii + 329 pp.

NECRASOV, OLGA
1962   Sur les particularités morphologiques d'un bourgeon dentaire, appartenant à l'Homme fossile (Homo sapiens fossilis), découvert dans le Grotte "La Adam" (Dobrogea). An. Ştiinţ. Univ. Cuza (n.s.), Sect. 2 (Ştiinţe Nat.), a. Biol, 8, 187—192, 1 pl., (Rumanian and Russian summaries).
       Abs.: Jelínek in Anthrop., 2:1, 83.
       Rev.: Malinowski in Przegląd Antrop., 30, 316, (Polish).
1964   Sur la signification de certains caractères morphologiques de Equus (Asinus) hydruntinus Reg. Rev. Roumaine Biol., 9:3, 141—149, 2 pls.

NECRASOV, O., and CRISTESCU, M.
1965   Données anthropologiques sur les populations de l'âge de la pierre en Roumanie. Homo, 16, 129—161, 28 figs., 7 tables, (German and English summaries).

Abs.: Anon. in Anthropos, <u>61</u>, 320–321.
Rev.: H. V. V. in L'Anthrop., <u>71</u>:3–4, 318–319.

NEGADAEV-NIKONOV, K. N.
1964   [Paleontological finds in Moldavia.]   Vestnik Akad. Nauk SSSR, <u>34</u>:10,
            122–125, 3 figs., (Russian).
1965   [Paleontological research in Moldavia in relation to problems of geo-
            chronology, paleogeography, and the laws of evolution of orga-
            nisms.]   Izv. Akad. Nauk Moldav. SSR, <u>1965</u>:8, 3–6, 2 tables,
            (Russian).
1967   [On biostratigraphic subdivision of the Quaternary deposits of Moldavia.]
            Pal. geol. polezn. iskop. Moldavii, <u>2</u>, 234–241, table, (Russian).
            See: Bukatchuk, Burdenko, et al.;   Bukatchuk and Negadaev-Nikonov.

NEGADAEV-NIKONOV, K. N., and ARAPOV, A. A.
1964   [On terraces of Pruth valley of Central Moldavia.]   Izv. Akad. Nauk
            Moldav. SSR, ser. Biol. i Khim. Nauk, <u>1964</u>:7, 3–11, 3 figs.,
            (Russian; Moldavian summary).

NEGREA, ALEXANDRINA, BOTOŞĂNEANU, L., and NEGREA, Ş.
1967   Documents pour servir à la connaissance de la faune de mammifères
            des grottes du Banat (Roumanie). Internat. Jour. Spel., <u>2</u>:4,
            341–353, (English summary).

NEGREA, ŞTEFAN   See: Negrea, et al.

NEILL, WILFRED T.
1961   Giant rattlesnakes – past and present. Florida Wildlife, <u>15</u>:1, 10–13,
            illustr.
1964   The association of Suwannee points and extinct animals in Florida.
            Florida Anthrop., <u>17</u>, 17–32, 5 figs.
1966   An Eden-like projectile point from South Carolina. Florida Anthrop.,
            <u>19</u>, 143–144, 1 fig.

NEĬMYSHEV, M. V.
1965   [Stratigraphy of Neogene deposits in Kochkor depression in the light
            of new paleontological data.]   In: Korolev, (ed.), 1965, 167–
            172, 3 figs., (Russian).

NEISHTADT, M. I.   See: Gromov, V. I., Ivanova, et al.

NEKHOROSHEV, V. P.
1958   [Geology of Altaĭ.]   Moscow: Gosgeoltekhizdat Press, 262 pp., (Rus-
            sian).

NELKEN-TERNER, A.   See: MacNeish, Nelken-Terner and Johnson.

NELSON, BRYCE
1968   Smithsonian: Innovative leadership carries new programs to inner city.
            Science, <u>161</u>, 30–32, 2 figs.

NELSON, G. J.
1967   Epibranchial organs in lower teleostean fishes. Proc. Zool. Soc. London,
            <u>153</u>, 71–89, 3 figs., 1 pl., 2 tables.

NELSON, NELS C.
1915 European caves and Early Man. Amer. Mus. Jour., 15, 237–247.
1919 Human culture: its probable place of origin on the earth and its mode of distribution. Nat. Hist., 19, 131–140.
1921 Recent activities of European archaeologists. Nat. Hist., 21, 537–541.
1924 European prehistory, with special reference to the work of the American Museum. Nat. Hist., 24, 665–672.
1927 The Jacob's Cavern mastodon again. Science, 66, 258–259.

NELSON, N. C., McGREGOR, J. H., and GREGORY, W. K.
1929 The Hall of the Age of Man. Amer. Mus. Nat. Hist., Guide Leaflet Ser., no. 57.

NELSON, PAULA R.
1964 North American man's oldest home? Bull. Chicago Nat. Hist. Mus., 35:11, 2–4, 3 figs.
1965 Australian expedition discovers landmark fossil site. Bull. Chicago Nat. Hist. Mus., 36:4, 4–6, illustr.

NELSON, ROBERT H.
1965 New locality for dinosaur tracks in Connecticut. Rocks and Minerals, 40, 5–7, 4 figs.

NEMESKÉRI, JÁNOS
1963 Az ember-őslénytan fogalma, tárgya, modszere [Concept, subjects and methods of human paleontology]. Budapest: Világnézeti Nevelésünk Természettudományos Alapjai [The scientific foundations of our ideological education], (not seen).

NEMOTO, H.
1936 A desmostylid excavation trip to Hatsuyukizawa, Keton, Saghalien. Warera-no-Kobutsu, 5, 10–18.

NENQUIN, JACQUES
1964A. Inventaria Archaeologica Africana. Jour. Afr. Hist., 5, 449–453, 1 fig.
1964B. The Magosian industry of Rutonde, Rwanda. S. Afr. Archaeol. Bull., 19, 83–90, 6 figs.
1965 Inventaria Archaeologica Africana. Amer. Anthrop., 67, 499–502, 1 fig.
1966 Recent excavations in Rwanda and Burundi. Discussion. Actas V Congr. Panafr. Prehist. Estud. Cuaternario, 1963:2, 205–212, 4 pls.
1968 Inventaria Archaeologica Africana. Antiq., 42, 131–132.

NESMEĬANOV, S. A.
1964 [On new finds of a southern elephant in Molasse of northwestern Fergana.] Doklady Akad. Nauk Tadzhik. SSR, 7:5, 36–38, 1 map, (Russian; Tadzhik summary).
 See: Kostenko, N. P., Nesmeĭanov and Ranov.

NESMEĬANOV, S. A., and RANOV, V. A.
1962 [Paleolithic finds at Shakhristan.] Doklady Akad. Nauk Tadzhik. SSR, 5:6, 26–30, 2 figs., 1 table, (Russian; Tadzhik summary).
1964 [On the geological age of the Upper Paleolithic site Khodzha-Gor (South Fergana).] Trudy Akad. Nauk Tadzhik. SSR, 42, 125–127, 1 fig., (Russian).

NESTURKH, M. F. (= Nestourkh, M. F.)
1954   [Fossil gigantic anthropoids of Asia, and Weidenreich's orthogenetic
                hypothesis of anthropogenesis.] Uchen. Zap. Mosk. Univ., 166,
                29—46, 7 figs., 2 tables, (Russian).
1964A.   [Victor Valerianovich Bunak.] In: Nesturkh, (ed.), 1964C, 9—18,
                portr., (Russian).
1964B.   [Some factors of hominization and extinction of fossil Pliocene and
                Pleistocene anthropoids.] 7th Internat. Congr. anthrop. ethnogr.
                sci., Moscow, (Russian).
1964C.   (ed.) [Modern anthropology.] Trudy Mosk. Obshch. Ispyt. Prirody,
                otd. biol., 14, 303 pp., illustr., (Russian; English summaries).
                Rev.: Schwidetzky in Homo, 16, 53.
1968A.   Quelques facteurs de l'hominisation et de l'extinction des Anthropoïdes
                fossiles du Pliocène et du Pleistocène. 7th Internat. Congr.
                Anthrop. Ethnol. Sci., Moscow, 1964, 3, 365—370.
1968B.   [Progress of primatology in USSR.] Voprosy Antrop., 28, 3—20, (Rus-
                sian).

NETO, M.   See: Mascarenhas Neto, M.

NETTING, M. GRAHAM
1965   Amid interminable reaches of time. Carnegie Mag., 39, 336—338, illustr.
1966   Museum summer activities. Carnegie Mag., 40, 199, 201, 203, 2 figs.
1967   Vertebrate fossils. Ann. Rept. Carnegie Mus., 1966, 14—16.

NEUMAN, ROBERT W.
1965   Current research. Plains. Amer. Antiq., 30, 529—535.
1967A.   Radiocarbon-dated archaeological remains on the northern and central
                Great Plains. Amer. Antiq., 32, 471—486, 4 figs., 1 table.
1967B.   Bone uprights: their description, suggested function and distribution.
                Plains Anthrop., 12, 210, (abs.).
1968   Additional annotated references: an archeological bibliography of the
                central and northern Great Plains prior to 1930. Plains Anthrop.,
                13, 100—102.

NEUMANN, A. R.   See: Franz, L. and Neumann.

NEUMANN, ERIK ARNULF
1964   Post-glacial ecology and prehistoric settlement patterns in the central
                states area. Proc. Indiana Acad. Sci., 73, 47—55.

NEUMANN, GEORG K.
1952B.   Archeology and race in the American Indian. In: Griffin, J. B., (ed.),
                1952A, 13—34, 1 table.

NEUMANN, GOTTHARD
1933   Eine Freilandsiedlung des Hochmagdalénien. Beitr. Geol. Thüringen, 3,
                362—364, 1 fig., (not seen).
1936   Ein Mammutstosszahn von Wichmar, Kreisabteilung Camburg. Spaten-
                forscher 1, Folge 1, 2—4, 2 figs., (not seen).

NEURATH, MARIE
1955   The wonder world of long ago. New York: Lothrop, Lee and Shipard,
                36 pp., illustr., (ages 5—7).

NEUSTUPNY, JIRI
1967   A new approach to an archeological exhibit. Curator, <u>10</u>, 211–220,
            5 figs.

NEUSTUPNY, J., et al.
1962   En marge de la discussion sur les problèmes de la préhistoire tchécos-
            lovaque. Archeol. Roz., <u>14</u>, 218–265, (Czech; French summary).

NEVES, R., and TARLO, L.B.H.
1965   Isolation of fossil osteocytes. Jour. Roy. Microsc. Soc., <u>84</u>, 217–219,
            1 fig.

NEVO, EVIATAR
1964   Fossil urodeles in Early Lower Cretaceous deposits of Makhtesh Ramon,
            Israel. Nature, <u>201</u>, 415–416, 1 fig.
            Abs.: Huene in Zbl. Geol. Pal., Teil 2, <u>1964</u>, 984.

NEWCOMB, W.W., JR.
1961   Rev.: Shiras in Arkansas Archeologist, <u>3</u>, 19.

NEWELL, NORMAN D.
1964   Raymond C. Moore, first Palentological Society medalist. Jour. Pal.,
            <u>38</u>, 178–179, portr.
1965   Mass extinctions at the end of the Cretaceous period. Science, <u>149</u>,
            922, 924.
1966   Problems of geochronology. Proc. Acad. Nat. Sci. Phila., <u>118</u>, 63–89,
            5 figs.
            See: Imbrie and Newell.

NEWMAN, B. H.
1968   The Jurassic dinosaur <u>Scelidosaurus</u> <u>harrisoni</u>, Owen. Palaeontol., <u>11</u>,
            40–43, pls. 7–8.

NEWSOME, A. E., and ROCHOW, K. A.
1964   Vertebrate fossils from Tertiary sediments in central Australia. Austral.
            Jour. Sci., <u>26</u>, 352.

NICHOLAS, BROTHER G., F. S. C.
1965   French cave hand prints. NSS News, <u>23</u>, 141.

NICHOLS, AL   See: Henry, J. and Nichols.

NICHOLS, RACHEL H.   See: Camp, C. L., Allison and Nichols; Camp, C. L.,
            Allison, Nichols and McGinnis.

NICOLĂESCU-PLOPŞOR, C. S. (=Nikolaescu-Plopsor, C. S.)
1962B.   [Research on Rumanian Paleolithic.] Sov. Arkheol., <u>1962</u>:3, 116–133,
            10 figs., (Russian).
1964A   Nouvelles données sur la possibilité de l'existence de protohominiens
            dans le Villafranchien de Roumanie. Dacia, <u>8</u>, 47–53.
1964B   [New data concerning the beginning and the end of Paleolithic in
            Rumania.] Studii şi Cercetări de Ist. Veche, <u>15</u>, 307–320,
            (Rumanian; Russian and French summaries).
1965   [On Paleolithic stratigraphy and periodization in Rumania.] In:
            Bader, O. N., et al., (eds.), 1965, 28–33, (Russian).

1966 [New research on the Paleolithic of Bucarest region.] Studii şi Cerce-
tǎri de Ist. Veche, 17, 311–318, 4 figs., (Rumanian; French
summary).

NICOLǍESCU-PLOPŞOR, C. S., and NICOLǍESCU-PLOPŞOR, D.
1963 The possible existence of the proto-hominids in Rumania's Villafranchian.
Dacia, 7, 9–25, 9 figs.
1968 Sur la présence du Prépaléolithique en Roumanie. L'une des premières
étapes du processus d'hominisation. Discussion. 7th Internat.
Congr. Anthrop. Ethnol. Sci., Moscow, 1964, 3, 371–380, 1
table.

NICOLǍESCU-PLOPŞOR, C. S., PǍUNESCU, and MOGOŞANU, F.
1966 Le Paléolithique de Ceahlǎu. Dacia, 10, 5–116, 72 figs., 24 tables.

NICOLǍESCU-PLOPŞOR, DARDU
1963 La contribution de la paleó-anthropologie à la recherche archéologique.
Probl. Antrop., 7, 263–272.
1968 Les hommes fossiles découverts en Roumanie. 7th Internat. Congr.
Anthrop. Ethnol. Sci., Moscow, 1964, 3, 381–386.

NICOLǍESCU-PLOPŞOR, D., and FLORU, E.
1963 Le matériel paléo-anthropologique – source des recherches pour l'histoire
de la médecine. Probl. Antrop., 7, 169–174, (Rumanian; Rus-
sian and French summaries).

NIELSEN, EIGIL
1962 The Thai Danish prehistoric expedition 1960 - 1962. Jour. Siam Soc.,
50, 7–14, 2 pls.
1964A. On the post-cranial skeleton of Eosphargis breineri Nielsen. Meddel.
Dansk Geol. Foren., 15, 281–328, 19 figs., 13 pls.
1964B. Om Tupilakosaurus og lidt om stereospondyle labyrinthodonter. Medel.
Dansk Geol. Foren., 15, 434, (abs.).
1967 New observations on the skull-roof of the holotype of Tupilakosaurus
heilmani Nielsen. In: Patterson, C., and Greenwood, P. H.,
(eds.), 1967, 225–229, 3 figs.

NIEUWENHUYS, RUDOLF
1965 The forebrain of the crossopterygian Latimeria chalumnae Smith. Jour.
Morphol., 117, 1–23, 1 fig., 1 pl.
See: Millot, Nieuwenhuys and Anthony.

NIKIFOROVA, KSENIÍÂ VLADIMIROVNA (=Nikiforowa, K. W.)
1960 [The Cenozoic of Golodnaiâ Step' in central Kazakhstan.] Trudy
Geol. Inst., 45, 254 pp., 63 figs., 3 tables, (Russian).
1961A [On the stratigraphic position of Astian.] Internat. Assoc. Quat. Res.,
Abs. Pap., 6th Congr., 130–131, (abs.; Russian).
1961B [On the stratigraphic position of Astian.] In: Gromov, V. I., et al.,
(eds.), 1961, 20–30, (Russian; English summary).
1965A (ed.) [Correlation of Anthropogene deposits of Northern Eurasia.
(For the Seventh Congress of INQUA in USA in 1965).] Moscow:
"Nauka" Press, 114 pp., 16 figs., 2 pls., 3 tables, (Russian; English title, table of contents, and summaries).
1965B (ed.) [Stratigraphic importance of small mammalian Anthropogene fauna.
(To the VII INQUA Congress in USA in 1965).] Akad. Nauk

SSSR, Geolog. Inst. Moscow; "Nauka" Press, 172 pp., illustr., (Russian; English title, table of contents, and summaries).

1965C   [Correlation of Quarternary deposits on paleomagnetic data.]   In: Saks, (ed.), 1965, 11–15, 1 table, (Russian).

1965D   Stratigraphische Equivalente des Villafranchiens in der Sowjetunion. Proc. K. Nederl. Akad. Wet., Ser. B, <u>68</u>, 237–248, 1 table.

1967   [International Paleontological Colloquium in the German Democratic Republic.] Bïull. Kom. Izuch. Chetvert. Perioda, <u>34</u>, 166–172, (Russian).

     See: Gromov, V. I., et al.; Gromov, V. I., Krasnov, et al.; Gromov, V. I. and Nikiforova; Gromov, V. I., Nikiforova and Shantser; Gromov, V. I., Vangengeym and Nikiforova.

NIKIFOROVA, K. V., and ALEKSEEVA, L. I.

1959   [Concerning the boundary between the Tertiary and Quartering systems on the basic of mammalian faunal data.] Trudy Geol. Inst., <u>32</u>, 7–21, 2 tables, (Russian).

1961   [On the limit between Neogene and Anthropogene in connection with the problem of Pliocene subdivision.] Mat. Vses. Sov. po Izuch. Chetvert. Perioda, <u>1</u>, 33–40, (Russian);

     Abs.: Mirtsching in Zbl. Geol. Pal., Teil 2, <u>1964</u>, 669.

NIKIFOROVA, K. V., GERBOVA, V. G., and KONSTANTINOVA, N. A.

1960   [Stratigraphy of continental Cenozoic deposits of Central Kazakhstan in comparison with those of the Ural, Turgaĭ, northern Aral region and southern west-Siberian lowland.] Trudy Geol. Inst., <u>26</u>, 204–247, 13 figs., 1 table, (Russian).

NIKIFOROVA, K. V., RAVSKIĬ, E. I., and DEVIATKIN, E. V.

1967   [Neogene and Eopleistocene stratigraphy of Kazakhstan and South Siberia.] In: Martinson, (ed.), 1967A, 195–200, (Russian).

NIKIFOROVA, O. I., and OBUT, A. M.

1965   (eds.) [The silurian system.] In: Nalivkin, (ed.), 1963-, [vol. 3] and suppl., 531 pp., 120 figs., 3 col. maps, 13 tables, (Russian).

NIKISHIN, V. I.

1962   [On the so-called Ĭasnopolĭanskiĭ substage and on the limit of Tournaisian and Visean of the Volga-Urals oil-bearing province.] Izv. Vyssh. Uch. Zav., Geol. i Razv., <u>1962</u>:8, 65–71, 1 table, (Russian).

NIKITENKO, M. F. (=Nikitsenka, M. F.)

1964   [Ways and factors of progressive evolution of brain in vertebrates.] Nauchn. Sess. Inst. Paleobiol. AN Gruz. SSR, <u>10</u>, 25–27, (Georgian and Russian).

1965   [Brain, evolution, and systematics of the mammals.] In: Shvarts, (ed.), 1965, 119–136, 2 tables, (Russian).

1966   [Morphological rules of brain evolution in vertebrates. III. Development of brain in amphibians in relation to their phylogeny and ecology.] Vestsi Akad. Navuk BSSR, ser. biĭal. Navuk, <u>1966</u>:3, 101–109, 1 table, (Belorussian; Russian summary).

NIKITIUK, B. A.

1966A   [The facial skeleton, its upper part.] Trudy Inst. Etnog. Akad. Nauk SSSR, <u>92</u>, 310–339, 5 figs., 13 tables, (Russian).

1966B   [Lower jaw.]   Trudy Inst. Etnog. Akad. Nauk SSSR, 92, 340–359,
             9 figs., 6 tables, (Russian).
1967   Some peculiarities of cranial suture obliteration in Hominides from com-
             parative anatomy point of view. Discussion. 7th Internat. Congr.
             Anthrop. Ethnol. Sci., Moscow, 1964, 2, 354–357.

NIKOLAEV, V. A.   See: Markov, K. K., Lazukov and Nikolaev.

NIKOLAEVA, T. V.
1959   [New data on Quaternary stratigraphy of Komsomol'sk district.]   Sov.
             Geol., 1959:11, 135, (Russian).

NIKOLOV, IVAN
1965   [New finds of Pliocene and Pleistocene mammals in Biăla Slatina region.]
             Trudove Vŭrkhu Geol. Bŭlg., Ser. Pal., 7, 225–259, 2 figs., 9
             pls, 1 table, (Bulgarian; Russian and German summaries).
1967   Neue obereozäne Arten der Gattung Elomeryx. Neues Jahrb. Geol. Pal.,
             Abh., 128:2, 205–214, 2 figs., 2 pls., 1 table.
             See: Bakalov and Nikolov; Tsankov and Nikolov.

NIKOLOV, I. and HUENE, F. V.
1966   Neue Vertebratenfunde in der Wüste Gobi. Neues Jahrb. Geol. Pal.,
             Monatsh., 1966:11, 691–694, 6 figs.

NIKOLOV, I. and KOVACHEV, D.
1966   [Pliocene mammalian fauna from Asenovgrad region.]   Trudove Vŭrkhu
             Geol. Bŭlg., Ser. Pal., 8, 131–142, 2 figs., 4 pls., 1 table, (Bul-
             garian; Russian and German summaries).

NIKOLOV, I., and THENIUS, E.
1967   Schizochoerus (Suidae, Mammalia) aus dem Pliozän von Bulgarien.
             Ann. Naturhist. Mus. Wien, 71, 329–340, 4 figs., (English sum-
             mary).

NIKOLOVA, IA., and ANGELOV, N.
1961   [Excavations at Emen cave.]   Izv. na Arkheol. Inst., 24, 297–316,
             24 figs., (Bulgarian; French summary).

NIKOL'SKIĬ, G. V.
1945   [A short review of fossil Quaternary fauna of fresh-water fishes of
             USSR.]   Izv. Geogr. Obshch., 77, 289–292, (Russian).

NIKONOV, A. A., and NIKONOVA, K. I.
1965   [On mammoth remains in Fennoscandia and their paleogeographic sig-
             nificance.]   Izv. Geogr. Obshch., 97, 276–279, 1 fig., (Russian).

NIKONOVA, K. I.   See: Nikonov and Nikonova.

NILSSON, E.
1964   Pluvial lakes and glaciers in East Africa. Stockholm Contrib. Geol.,
             11, 21–57, 14 figs., 2 tables.

NISHIWAKI, M.
1966   On the classification of the Cetacea. Kaseki, 11, 2–11, 4 tables, (Japanese).
            See: Mitchell, E. D. 1967A.

NOBACH, CHARLES R.
1959   The heritage of the human brain. James Arthur lecture. New York: Amer. Mus. Nat. Hist., 30 pp., 5 illustr., 1 chart.

NODA, HIROSHI
1965   Some fossil Anadara from southwest Japan. Trans. Proc. Pal. Soc. Japan, no. 59, 92–109, 4 figs., pls. 10–11, 2 tables.

NODA, KOICHIRO
            See: Shikama and Noda.

NOGAR, RAYMOND J.
1963   The wisdom of evolution. New York: Doubleday, 408 pp., illustr., (not seen). Rev.: Frisch in Sci. Digest, 55:2, 44.

NOGUER, SANTIAGO ALCOBE'
            See: Crusafont Pairo 1964D.

NOGUERA, EDUARDO
1963   La historia, la arqueología y métodos para computar el tiempo. Cuad. Inst. Hist., Ser. Hist., no. 8, 32 pp., 5 figs.

NOLTE, H. J., WOLFRAM, H. J., and WOLLNER, H.
1965   Zur Entdeckungsgeschichte des Altpleistozänvorkommens von Voigtstedt in Thüringen. Technische Daten und Fündpläne. Pal. Abh., Abt. A, 2, 229–234, 6 figs., 2 maps.

NOLTE Y ARAMBURU, E.
1963   Rev.: Dessulemoustier in Die Höhle, 14, 120.

NORBECK, EDWARD
            See: Jennings and Norbeck.

NORDMANN, VALDEMAR JOHN HEINRICH
1936C   Abemanden og Pekingmanden. Ledetråd ved Folkelig Universitetsundervisning, no. 42, (not seen).
1939   Nyere Undersøgelser af de aeldste Mennesketyper. Naturens Verden, 1939, 289–303, (not seen).
1941   Bison-Kranier fra Danmark. Naturens Verden, 1941, 193–206, (not seen).
1943A   Elefant-Levninger fundne i Danmark. Naturens Verden, 1943, 97–116, (not seen).
1943B   Et nyt Bison-Fund fra Als. Naturens Verden, 1943, 232–234, (not seen).
1946   Pekingmennesket er forsvundet. Avisudkl. Berlingske Aftenavis, 23:3, (not seen).

NORMAN, J. R., and GREENWOOD, P. H.
1963   A history of fishes. 2nd ed. London: Benn, xxxi +398 pp., 147 figs., 7 pls.

NORMAN, ROBERT R., and NORMAN, LARRY, Jr.
1964   The molars of Moab. Desert Mag., 27:4, 17–18, 2 figs.

NORTHROP, STUART A.
1964   Census of New Mexico Paleozoic, Mesozoic, and Early Cenozoic faunas
            and floras. Spec. Pap. Geol. Soc. Amer., 76, 287, (abs.).

NOTZ, F.-W.
1964   Von der Herkunft, Verbreitung und Geweihbildung des Damwildes.
            Deutsch. Jägerzeitung, 1964:6, 118–121, (not seen).

NOUGAREDE, F.   See: Claracq and Nougarede.

NOUGIER, LOUIS-RENÉ
1959B.   Rev.: Patrizi in Boll. Soc. Geog. Ital., ser. 9, 2, 415–417.
1963   La préhistoire. Essai de paléosociologie religieuse. Paris: Blond et
            Gay (Religions du Monde), 144 pp., illustr., (not seen).
            Rev.: [Filip] in Archeol. Roz., 17, 125–126, (Czech);   Sauter in Arch.
            Suiss. Anthrop. Gén., 29, 65–68.
1966   L'art préhistorique. Paris: Presses Universitaires de France, 186 pp.,
            40 figs., 39 pls., (not seen).
            Rev.: Jordá Cerdá in Zephyrus, 18, 157–158;   Kühn in IPEK, 22,
            157–158;   Vila in Spelunca, Bull., 6:3, 222.
            See: Gailli, et al.

NOUGIER, L.-R., and BARRIÈRE, C.
1965   La nouvelle grotte préhistorique des Fieux et ses mains "négatives".
            La Nature, 93, 81–86, 9 figs.

NOUGIER, L.-R., and ROBERT, R.
1961   Abbé Henri Breuil, 1877–1961. Préhist. Spéléol. Ariégeoises, 15, 5–6,
            portr.
1965A.   Bouquetins affrontés, dans l'art mobilier magdalénien de la grotte de La
            Vache, à Alliat. In: Ripoll Perelló, E., (ed.), 1965B, 197–205,
            1 pl., (Spanish summary).
            Rev.: Sonneville-Bordes in L'Anthrop., 69:5–6, 535–536.
1965B.   Les félins dans l'art quaternaire. Préhist. Spéléol. Ariégeoises, 20, 17–
            84, illustr.
1966A.   Les félins dans l'art quaternaire. Préhist. Spéléol. Ariégeoises, 21, 35–
            46, illustr.
1966B.   Bouquetin gravé d'une scène animalière Magdalénien final de la grotte
            de La Vache (Alliat, Ariège). Préhist. Spéléol. Ariégeoises, 21,
            75–79, 1 fig., 1 pl.

NOVIKOV, G. A.
1961   [Boris Stepanovich Vinogradov (1891 - 1958).]   Trudy Zool. Inst. Akad.
            Nauk SSSR, 29, 7–21, portr., (Russian).

NOVITŠKAIA, L. I. (=Novitskaya, L. I.)
1961   Abs.: Weiler in Zbl. Geol. Pal., Teil 2, 1966, 283–284.
1965   [Microstructure of some Psammosteida.]   In: Obruchev, D. V., and
            Mark-Kurik, E. Iu., 1965, 257–282, 29 figs., (Russian).

NOVITŠKAIA, L. I., and OBRUCHEV, D. V.
1964   [Class Acanthodei.]   Osnovy Pal., [Agnathes. Pisces.], [11], 175–194,
            25 figs., 1 pl., (Russian).

NOVOTNÝ, B.
1964   Bibliografia slovenskej archeológie za rok 1960. Bratislava: Philosophische
        Fakultät der Komenský-Universität, 64 pp., (not seen).
        Rev.: Sp. in Archeol. Roz., 17, 126.

NOVOZHILOV, NESTOR (=Novojilov)
1964A. [Order Sauropterygia.] Osnovy Pal., [Amphibians, Reptiles, and Birds.],
        [12], 309–332, 41 figs., (Russian).
1964B. [Superfamily Pistosauroidea.] Osnovy Pal., [Amphibians, Reptiles, and
        Birds.], [12], 317–318, 2 figs., (Russian).
1964C. [Superfamily Plesiosauroidea (=Dolichodeira).] Osnovy Pal., [Amphi-
        bians, Reptiles, and Birds.], [12], 318–327, 24 figs., (Russian).
1964D. [Superfamily Pliosauroidea (=Brachydeira).] Osnovy Pal., [Amphibians,
        Reptiles, and Birds.], [12], 327–332, 10 figs., (Russian).

NUGLISCH, KLAUS See: Toepfer and Nuglisch.

NÚÑEZ JIMÉNEZ, ANTONIO (ed.)
1961A. 20 años explorando a Cuba. Historia de la Sociedad Espeleológica de
        Cuba. La Habana: [Impr. del INRA], 384 pp., illustr.
1961B. Nueve años explorando a Cuba. In: Núñez Jiménez (ed.), 1961A,
        175–180.

NUNLEY, JOHN P., DUFFIELD, L. F., and JELKS, E. B.
1965   Excavations at Amistad Reservoir, 1962 season. Misc. Pap. Texas Archeol.
        Salvage Project, no. 3, 129 pp., 40 figs., 6 tables.

NURSALL, J. R.
1964   The jaws of pycnodonts (Holostei: Pycnodontiformes). Amer. Zool.,
        4, 395, (abs.).

NURUMOV, T. N.   See: Biriŭkov, et al.

NYBELIN, ORVAR
1965   Essai d'interprétation de "la Licorne" de Lascaux. Bull. Soc. Préhist.
        Franç., C. R. séances mens., 1965:8, 276–279, 1 pl.
1966   On certain Triassic and Liassic representatives of the family Pholido-
        phoridae s. str. Bull. Brit. Mus. (Nat. Hist.), Geol., 11:8, 353–
        432, 16 figs., 15 pls.
1967A. Versuch einer taxonomischen Revision der Anaethalion-Arten des Weiss-
        jura Deutschlands. Acta Reg. Soc. Sci. Litt. Gothob., Zool., 2,
        1–51, 5 figs., 8 pls., 1 table.
1967B. Notes on the reduction of the sensory canal system and of the canal-
        bearing bones in the snout of higher actinopterygian fishes.
        Ark. Zool., 19, 235–246, 4 figs.

O., V. V.
1958   [V. A. Obruchev in memoriam.] Izv. Geogr. Obshch., 90, 490–491,
        (Russian).

OAKESHOTT, GORDON B.
1966   San Francisco Bay area, its geologic setting. GeoTimes, 11:3, 11–19,
        illustr.

OAKLEY, KENNETH PAGE
   1961D.   Appendix II: radiometric assays. Publ. Fort Burgwin Res. Center, no.
            1, 136, 1 table.
   1963D.   Fluorine, uranium, and nitrogen dating of bone. In: Pyddoke, E., (ed.),
            1963, 111–119.
   1963E.   Man – the tool-maker. 5th edition. London: British Mus. (Nat. Hist.),
            98 pp., 41 figs., 2 pls., (not seen).
            Rev.: Burchard in Mus. Jour., London, 64, 173.
   1964A.   The problem of man's antiquity: an historical survey. Bull. Brit. Mus.
            (Nat. Hist.), Geol., 9, 85–155, 43 figs., 3 pls.
            Rev.: Cuffey in Jour. Pal., 42, 604–606; Daniel in Antiq., 38, 166–
               169; Freeman in Amer. Anthrop., 67, 171–172; Hawkes in
               Nature, 204, 952–953; Koenigswald in Man, 65, 163; Narr
               in Anthropos, 62:5/6, 961–962; Schaeuble in Zeit. Morph.
               Anthrop., 55, 385.
   1964B.   Frameworks for dating fossil man. Chicago: Aldine; London: Weiden-
            feld and Nicolson, x + 355 pp., 83 figs., 2 maps, 4 charts.
            Rev.: Bordaz in Nat. Hist., 75:1, 10–11; Campbell in Discovery, 26:2,
               58; Clark in Science, 148, no. 3671, 800–801; Coles in
               Antiq., 39, 308–309; Genovés in An. Antrop., Mexico, 1966,
               3, 263–265; Haltenorth in Saügetierkundl. Mitt., 14, 152–153;
               Howell in Amer. Anthrop., 67, 1043–1048; Jelinek in Mich.
               Archaeol., 11, 71; Koenigswald in Nature, 207, 796–797;
               Kühn in IPEK, 22, 152–153; Kurth in Naturwiss. Rund., 18,
               295–296; Lacaille in Antiq. Jour., 46, 109–110; Lisowski
               in New Sci., 25, 517; McBurney in Proc. Prehist. Soc. Cam-
               bridge, 32, 367; Pittioni in Archaeol. Austriaca, 38, 107;
               Preuschoft in Zbl. Geol. Pal., Teil 2, 1965, 295; Seddon in S.
               Afr. Archaeol. Bull., 20:79, 162–163; Smith in Anthropologica,
               8, 156–158; Stewart in Quart. Rev. Biol., 40, 380–381; Vaufrey
               in L'Anthrop., 70:1–2, 131–132; Yochelson in Jour. Pal., 39,
               515–516.
   1965A.   Folklore of fossils. Antiq., 39, 9–16, figs. 1–7, pls. 1–2; 117–
            120, figs. 8–11, pls. 21–26.
   1965B.   The antiquity of the new Kom Ombo skull. Man, 65:96, 104.
   1966A.   Frameworks for dating fossil man. 2nd ed. London: Weidenfeld &
            Nicolson, x + 355 pp., illustr., (not seen).
            Rev.: Dimbleby in Nature, 212, 565; Kennedy in Man, Jour. Roy.
               Anthrop. Inst., 1, 561; Lippert in Mitt. Anthrop. Ges. Wien,
               96–97, 377.
   1966B.   The problem of man's antiquity – an historical survey. New York, London:
            Johnson Reprint Corp.; (reprint of Bull. Brit. Mus. (Nat. Hist.),
            Geol., 9:5, 83–155, 44 figs., 3 pls. 1964A).
            Rev.: Anon. in Arch. Suiss. Anthropol. Gen., 32, 155.
   1966C.   Discovery of part of skull of Homo erectus with Buda industry at
            Vértesszöllos, north-west Hungary. Proc. Geol. Soc. London,
            1630, 31–34.
   1967   Appendix 2. Chemical analyses of Haua Fteah hominid mandibles.
            In: McBurney, C. B. M., 1967B, 353.
            See: Henschen 1966B; Napier 1964A.

OAKLEY, K. P., and CAMPBELL, B. G., (eds.)
   1967A.   Catalogue of fossil hominids. Part I: Africa. London: Trustees of
            the British Museum (Natural History), xv + 128 pp., frontispiece,
            1 map.

Rev.: Day in Nature, 218, 301; Krogman in Amer. Jour. Phys. Anthrop., 27, 405; T. M. in Studies in Spel., 1, 295–296; Preuschoft in Zbl. Geol. Pal., Teil 2, 1969:2, 212; Roberts in Man, Jour. Roy. Anthrop. Inst., 3, 318–319; Roth-Lutra in Anat. Anz., 125, 462–463.

1967B.   Introduction. [Catalogue of fossil hominids. Part I: Africa.]. In: Oakley, K. P., and Campbell, B. G., (eds.), 1967A, ix–xv, 1 map.

1967C.   (eds.) Mali. In: Oakley, K. P., and Campbell, B. G., (eds.), 1967A, 33–34.

1967D.   (eds.) Niger. In: Oakley, K. P., and Campbell, B. G., (eds.), 1967A, 45–46.

OAKLEY, K. P., and MUIR-WOOD, H. M.

1962   The succession of life though geological time. 5th ed. London: British Museum (Natural History), 94 pp., illustr., (not seen).

Rev.: Lerman in Quart. Rev. Biol., 39, 195.

OBA, TOSHIO, and CHARD, C. S.

1962   On the age determination for the prehistoric culture in Hokkaido. Jour. Archaeol. Soc. Nippon, 48, 49–53, (Japanese; English summary).

OBORIN, V. A.   See: Denisov and Oborin.

OBRHEL, J.   See: Obrhelova and Obrhel.

OBRHELOVÁ, NADĚŽDA

1966   Die Karpfenfisch-Faunen der nord- und westböhmischen Braunkohlenbecken. Čas. Min. Geol., 11, 401–407.

Rev.: Weiler in Zbl. Geol. Pal., Teil 2, 1968:6, 650.

1967   Cyprinoidei (Pisces) aus dem Hangenden des miozänen Braunkohlenflözes Nordböhmens. Palaeontogr., Abt. A, 126, 141–179, 27 figs., pls. 28–35, 8 tables.

Rev.: Weiler in Zbl. Geol. Pal., Teil 2, 1968:6, 650–651.

OBRHELOVÁ, N., and OBRHEL, J.

1965   Die Paläontologische Erforschung der Cypris-Serie im Cheb-Becken. Čas. Národ. Musea, Odd. Prirod., 134:3, 142–146, 2 figs., (Czech; German summary).

O'BRIEN, T. P.

1966   The Levalloisian flake industry of Nsongezi. Uganda Jour., 30, 207.

OBRUCHEV, DIMITRI VLADIMIROVICH

1961B.   [Devonian ichthyofauna.] Trudy SNIIGGIMS, 20, [Paleozoic biostratigraphy of Saian-Altaĭ mountain region, v. 2], 296–300, (Russian).

1961C.   [Class Ostracodermi.] Trudy SNIIGGIMS, 20, [Paleozoic biostratigraphy of Saian-Altaĭ mountain region, v. 2], 560–561, 1 fig., 1 pl., (Russian).

1962A.   [Carboniferous fishes.] Trudy SNIIGGIMS, 21, [Paleozoic biostratigraphy of Saian-Altaĭ mountain region, v. 3], 75–76, (Russian).

1962B.   [Class Acanthodei.] Trudy SNIIGGIMS, 21, [Paleozoic biostratigraphy of Saian-Altaĭ mountain region, v. 3], 212, 1 pl., (Russian).

1962C.   [Class Chondrichthyes.] Trudy SNIIGGIMS, 21, [Paleozoic biostratigraphy of Saian-Altaĭ mountain region, v. 3], 213–215, 1 pl., (Russian).

1962D.   [Permian fishes.]   Trudy SNIIGGIMS, 21, [Paleozoic biostratigraphy of ·
Saĩan-Altaỹ mountain region, v. 3], 440–442, 1 pl., (Russian).

1964A.   (ed.) Osnovy Paleontologii. [Fundamentals of paleontology. Agnathes,
Pisces.], [11], 522 pp., 197 figs., 14 pls. + figs. [Principal ed.
of series: J. A. Orlov.] Moscow: "Nauka", 522 pp., illustr.,
(Russian).

Rev.: Branson in Okla. Geol. Notes, 25, 170–172;   McAllister and
Dineley in Canadian Field Nat., 80, 112–113;   Nikol'skiĩ in
Voprosy Ikhtiol., 7:1, 197–199, (Russian);   Weiler in Zbl. Geol.
Pal., Teil 2, 1965, 230–232.

1964B.   [Type Chordata.]   Osnovy Pal. [Agnathes. Pisces.] [11], 15–33, 19
figs., (Russian).

1964C.   [Branch Agnatha.]   Osnovy Pal., [Agnathes. Pisces.], [11], 34–116,
138 figs., 9 pls., (Russian).

1964D.   [Branch Gnatostomi. Superclass Pisces. Class Placodermi.]   Osnovy Pal.,
[Agnathes. Pisces.], [11], 118–174, 84 figs., 6 tables, (Russian).

1964E.   [Subclass Holocephali. Chimeras.]   Osnovy Pal., [Agnathes. Pisces.],
[11], 238–266, 4 pls., (Russian).

1965A.   [Fishes and Agnatha.]   In: Nikiforova and Obut, (eds.), 1965, 456–
458, (Russian).

1965B.   [Fishes. In: Development and replacement of marine organisms on the
limit of Paleozoic and Mesozoic.]   Trudy Pal. Inst. Akad. Nauk
SSSR, 108, 85–87, (Russian).

1965C.   [Order Bradyodonti. In: Development and replacement of marine
organisms on the limit of Paleozoic and Mesozoic.]   Trudy Pal.
Inst. Akad. Nauk SSSR, 108, 266–267, 1 fig., 1 pl., (Russian).

1966   [Fossil egg capsules of Chimaerae.]   Pal. Zhurnal, 1966:3, 117–123,
1 pl., (Russian).

1967A.   On the evolution of the Heterostraci. Colloq. Internat. Cent. Nation.
Recherch. Sci., 163, 37–43, 3 figs., (French and German summaries).

1967B.   Fossil chimaera egg capsules. Translation of Obruchev, D. V., 1966.
Internat. Geol. Rev., 9, 567–573, 1 pl.

1967C.   [In memoriam of Ĩu. A. Orlov (13.VI.1893 – 2.X.1966).] Izv. Akad.
Nauk SSSR, ser. biol., 1967:1, 157–159, (Russian).

1967D.   (ed.) Fundamentals of paleontology. A manual for paleontologists and
geologists of the USSR. Vol. 11. Agnatha, Pisces. [Chief editor:
J. A. Orlov.] Translated from the Russian. Jerusalem: Israel
Program for Scientific Translations, x + 825 pp., illustr. Available
from the U. S. Department of Commerce.

Rev.: Patterson in Nature, 220, 514.

See: Berg, L. S., Kazanfseva and Obruchev; Berg, L. S. and Obruchev;
Novitskaya and Obruchev; Vorob'eva and Obruchev.

OBRUCHEV, D. V., and KARATAJŪTE-TALIMAA, V.
1967   Vertebrate faunas and correlation of the Ludlovian-Lower Devonian in
eastern Europe. In: Patterson, C., and Greenwood, P. H., (eds.),
1967, 5–14, 12 figs., 2 pls., 2 tables.

OBRUCHEV, D. V., and KAZANTSEVA, A. A.
1964A.   [Superorder Chondrostei.] Osnovy Pal., [Agnathes. Pisces.], [11], 371–
375, 7 figs., (Russian).

1964B.   [Superorder Polypteri (Cladistia, Brachiopterygii).] Osnovy Pal., [Agnathes.
Pisces.], [11], 376–377, 2 figs., (Russian).

OBRUCHEV, D. V., and MARK-KURIK, E. IŪ.

1965   [Devonian psammosteids (Agnatha, Psammosteidae) of USSR.]   Tallinn:
            Inst. Geol. Akad. Nauk Eston. SSR Press, 400 pp., 228 figs.,
            94 pls., 2 tables, (Russian; Esthonian and English summaries).

1968   On the evolution of the psammosteids (Heterostraci).   Toimetised Eesti
            NSV Tead. Akad., ser. chem. geol., 17:3, 279—284, 4 figs.,
            (Esthonian and Russian summaries).

OBRUCHEV, D. V., and SERGIENKO, A. A.

1961   [Class Placodermi.]   Trudy SNIIGGIMS, 20, [Paleozoic biostratigraphy
            of Saiān-Altaĭ mountain region, v. 2], 561—564, 1 fig., 3 pls.,
            (Russian).

OBRUCHEV, V. A.

1946   [Sketches of my life.]   Izv. Geogr. Obshch., 78, 261—272, portr., (Rus-
            sian).

1965A.   [Diverting geology.]   Moscow: "Nauka" Press, 344 pp., 285 figs., (Rus-
            sian).

1965B.   [Travels into past and future.]   Moscow: "Nauka" Press, 243 pp., portr.,
            (Russian).

OBRUCHEV, V. V.   See: Churakov, et al.

OBRUCHEVA, O. P.

1959B.   [Stratigraphic distribution of coccosteids and dinichthyids in the Devo-
            nian of USSR.]   Izv. Vyssh. Uch. Zav. Geol. i Razv., 1959:8,
            43—47, 1 table, (Russian).

1962A.   [Fishes of the central Devon region.]   Biull. Mosk. Obshch. Ispyt. Priro-
            dy, Otd. Geol., 37:3, 129, (Russian).

1962B.   [New data on the structure of the central portion of the skull roof of
            Plourdosteus (Arthrodira).]   Biull. Mosk. Obshch. Ispyt. Prirody,
            Otd. Geol., 37:6, 133—134, (Russian).

1963   [New material on Coccosteidae of Baltic region.]   Biull. Mosk. Obshch.
            Ispyt. Prirody, Otd. Geol., 68:3, 150, (Russian).

1966   [New data on the coccosteids (armored fishes) from the Baltic Devonian.]
            Pal. i Strat. Pribalt. Belorus., 1, 151—189, 10 figs., 4 pls., 2 tables,
            (Russian; English summary).

            See: Drushits and Obrucheva; Mazarovich, O. A., et al.

OBUT, A. M.   See: Nikiforova, O. I. and Obut.

OCHEV, V. G.

1960A.   [On continental stratigraphical break between Paleozoic and Mesozoic
            in the east of the European part of USSR.]   Izv. Vyssh. Uch.
            Zav., Geol. i Razv., 1960:3, 32—36, 1 table, (Russian).

1960B.   [On the climate of the Triassic period of the southeast of the European
            part of USSR.]   Izv. Vyssh. Uch. Zav., Geol. i Razv., 1960:6,
            18—22, (Russian).

1962B.   [New occurrences of Triassic vertebrates in the southern Pre-Ural region.]
            Izv. Vyssh. Uch. Zav., Geol. i Razv., 1962:4, 24—28, (Russian).

1964   [Evolution of Mesozoic reptiles.]   Priroda, 1964:12, 60—62, 3 figs.,
            (Russian).

1966A.   [On the problem of the stratigraphic scheme of continental Triassic
            deposits of Russian Platform and Ural region.]   Doklady Akad.
            Nauk SSSR, 171:3, 698—701, 1 table, (Russian).

1966B.   [Vertebrates.]   In: Likharev, (ed.), 1966, 440–446, (Russian).
1966C.   [Systematics and phylogeny of capitosauroid labyrinthodonts.]   Saratov:
             University Press, 184 pp., 8 figs., (Russian).
             Rev.: Westphal in Zbl. Geol. Pal., Teil 2, 1968, 202.
1967A.   [Some principles of land vertebrates burial in Permian and Triassic de-
             posits of the eastern part of European USSR.]   In: Collected
             Papers, 1967C [Problems of paleogeographical regionalization in
             the light of paleontological data], 93–101, (Russian).
1967B.   [On the classification of sites of fossil terrestrial vertebrates.]   In: Col-
             lected Papers, 1967F [Problems of geology of South Urals and
             Povolzh'e], 3:1, 205–216, (Russian).
1967C.   [New genus of Procolophonidae from Triassic of Donskaia Luka.]   Izv.
             Vyssh. Uch. Zav., Geol. i Razv., 1967:2, 15–20, 3 figs., (Russian).
1968   [A new representative of Triassic procolophonids from Bashkiria.]
             Ezhegod. Vses. Pal. Obshch., 18, 298–301, (Russian).
       See: Dubeikovskiĭ and Ochev; Goriainov and Ochev; Lazurkin and
             Ochev; Rykov and Ochev; Shishkin, M. A. and Ochev.

OCHEV, V. G., and POLUBOTKO, I. V.
1964   [New finds of ichthyosaurs in northeastern USSR.]   Izv. Vyssh. Uch.
             Zav., Geol. i Razv., 1964:7, 50–55, 3 figs., (Russian).

OCHEV, V. G., and RYKOV, S. P.
1968   [New genus of small reptile from Triassic of Donskaia Luka.]   Pal.
             Zhurnal, 1968:1, 140–141, 1 fig., (Russian).

OCHEV, V. G., and SHISHKIN, M. A.
1967   [Cemetery of ancient amphibians in Orenburg region.]   Priroda, 1967:1,
             79–85, 4 figs., (Russian).

OCHIROV, TS. O.
1960   [Quaternary bone-bearing deposits of Tugnuĭ depression.]   Kratk.
             Soobshch. BKNII SO AN SSSR, 2, 38–41, (Russian).

OCTOBON, F. C. E.
1965   Grotte du Lazaret, Nice (A.-M.). Huitième étude sur les fouilles ex-
             écutées dans le locus VIII de cette grotte (ancienne grotte
             Lympia). Bull., Mus. Anthrop. Préhist. Monaco, 12, 23–101,
             22 figs., 8 pls.

ODA, SHIZUO   See: Aso and Oda.

ODHNER, KNUT
1964   Sosialt liv hos de første mennesker. Naturen, 88, 360–371.

ODINTSOV, I. A.
1962   [Pliocene fauna in karst caves near Odessa.]   Trudy Odessk. Univ.,
             Ser. Geol. Geogr., 152:8, 100–110, 2 figs., (Russian).
1965   [Vulpes praecorsac Kormos from Pliocene of Odessa.]   Pal. Sborn.,
             2:2, 57–64, 1 fig., 1 pl., 2 tables, (Russian; English summary).
1967   [New species of a Pliocene carnivore Vulpes odessana sp. nov. from
             karst caves of Odessa.]   Pal. Sborn., 4:1, 130–137, 2 pls.,
             (Russian; English summary).
1968   [On methods of studying the lower jaws of some carnivores.]   Ezhegod.
             Vses. Pal. Obshch., 18, 369–371, (Russian).

ODUM, HILMAR
1964 Valdemar Johan Heinrich Nordmann. 23. februar 1872 - 31. januar 1962. Meddel. Dansk Geol. Foren., 15, 374—387, 2 portrs.

OERTEL, GERHARD See: Craig, G. Y. and Oertel.

OESCH, RONALD D.
1965 A preliminary report on the fossil Pleistocene mammals from Perry County caves. Missouri Speleology, 7, 77—81, 6 figs.
1966 Pleistocene bone remains from caves in Perry County, Missouri. Bull. Nat. Spel. Soc., 28, 95—96, (abs.).
1967 A preliminary investigation of a Pleistocene vertebrate fauna from Crankshaft Pit, Jefferson County, Missouri. Bull. Nat. Spel. Soc., 29, 163—185, 13 figs., 8 tables.

OESCHGER, H., and RIESEN, T.
1965 Bern radiocarbon dates IV. Radiocarbon, 7, 1—9.

OGDEN, J. GORDON, III
1964 More on the mastodon. Explorer, 6:6, 11.
  See: Gooding and Ogden.

OGDEN, J. G., III, and HAY, R. J.
1965 Ohio Wesleyan University natural radiocarbon measurements II. Radiocarbon, 7, 166—173.
1967 Ohio Wesleyan University natural radiocarbon measurements III. Radiocarbon, 9, 316—332.

OGOSE, SUNAO
1953 On some fundamental geological problems suggested from the study on the Mizunami Group. (Part 1.). Jour. Geol. Soc. Japan, 59, 15—23, 3 figs., (Japanese; English summary).

ÔI, HARUO
1963 Report on excavation of the Tasishô site at Kitami-shi, Hokkaidô. Jour. Archaeol. Soc. Nippon, 49, [75—90], 1, 8 figs., (Japanese; English summary).

OKADA, ATSUKO See: Befu, et al.

OKADA, A., OKADA, H., and CHARD, C. S.
1967 An annotated bibliography of the archaeology of Hokkaido. Arctic Anthrop., 4:1, 1—163.

OKADA, HIROAKI See: Okada, A., Okada and Chard.

OKAFUJI, GORÔ See: Hasegawa, Yamauti and Okafuji; Shikama, Hasegawa and Okafuji; Shikama and Okafuji.

OKLADNIKOV, ALEXEI P.
1939C. [Mousterian site in Teshik-Tash grotto in Uzbekistan.] Krat. Soob. Inst. Ist. Mat. Kult. SSSR, 2, 8, (Russian).
1940F. [Amir-Temir, a new relic of the Stone Age in the Baĭsum-tau mountains (Uzbekistan).] Krat. Soob. Inst. Ist. Mat. Kult. SSSR, 6, 67—69, 2 figs., (Russian).

1955B.   [Iäkutia before annexation to Russia.]   In: Potapov, (ed.), 1955,
          History of Iäkutian ASSR, 1, 432 pp., 104 figs., 5 pls., (Rus-
          sian).

1956A.   [Provisional report on the study of Stone and Bronze Age relics in
          Tadzhikistan in summer of 1954.]   Trudy Akad. Nauk Tadzhik.
          SSR, 37, 5—18, 10 figs., (Russian).

1956B.   [Research of Stone Age relics in the Syr-Dar'iä R. basin in autumn
          of 1955.]   Trudy Akad. Nauk Tadzhik. SSR, 63, 5—15, 3
          figs., (Russian).

1957   [Results and cardinal problems of the 40 years study of Paleolithic
          in U.S.S.R.]   Sov. Arkheol., 1957:4, 12—27, (Russian).

1958C.   [Earliest cultures of the Maritime area in the light of investigations
          1953—1956.]   In: Tikhomirov, M. N., (ed.), 1958, 5—80,
          24 figs., (Russian).

1959D.   [Stone Age of Tadzhikistan, summary and problems.]   In: Collected
          Papers, 1959 [Materials of the second conference of archeologists
          and ethnographers of Central Asia, Stalinabad, 1956], 158—184,
          16 figs., (Russian).

1959E.   [Research on Stone Age relics of northern and southern Tadzhikistan
          in 1956.]   Trudy Akad. Nauk Tadzhik. SSR, 91:4, 7—21,
          (Russian).

1959F.   [The distant past of the Maritime region.]   Vladivostok: "Primor-
          skoe Knizhnoe Izdatelstvo", 291 pp., 84 figs., (Russian).

1961B.   [The Khodzhikent cave — a new Mousterian relic in Uzbekistan.]
          Krat. Soob. Inst. Ist. Mat. Kult. SSSR, 82, 68—76, 3 figs.,
          (Russian).

1961C.   [Archeological finds at the great construction sites in the East.]
          Vestnik Akad. Nauk SSSR, 31:8, 71—77, 5 figs., (Russian).

1963   Palaeolithic finds in the region of Lake Orok-Nor.   Arctic Anthrop.,
          3, 142—145, 3 figs., (Trans. by W. W. Workman from Trudy
          Buriat. Kompleks. Nauch.-Issled. Inst., 1962, 8, 169—175).

1964A.   Ancient population of Siberia and its culture.   In: Levin, M. G.,
          and Potapov, L. P., (eds.), 1964, 13—98, illustr.

1964B.   Paleolithic remains in the Lena River Basin.   Translation of Okladnikov
          1953B.   In: Michael, H. N., (ed.), 1964B, 33—79, 18 figs.

1965   The remote past of the Maritime region.   (Notes on the ancient
          and medieval history of the Maritime Kray).   Translation of
          1959F.   Edited by H. N. Michael.   Anthrop. of the North,
          no. 6, v + 280 pp., 52 figs.
          Rev.:   Sauter in Arch. Suiss. Anthrop. Gen., 31, 64—65.

1966A.   [Paleolithic and Mesolithic of Middle Asia.]   In: Masson, V. M., (ed.),
           1966, 11—75, 12 figs., 2 pls., (Russian).
1966B.   [Ancient settlement on Tadusha R. near Ustinovka, and the problem
           of the Far East Mesolithic.]   In: Saks, (ed.), 1966, 352—372,
           1 fig., 8 pls., (Russian).
1966C.   [Archeology of Zeia R. and Middle Amur valleys.]   Sov. Arkheol.,
           1966:1, 32—41, 5 figs., (Russian).
1967   [Central-Asiatic focus of primitive art.]   Vestnik Akad. Nauk SSSR,
           1967:1, 96—104, 7 figs., 3 pls., (Russian).
1968A.   [Marxism and the problem of the origin of art.]   Izv. Sib. Otd.
           Akad. Nauk SSSR, ser. Obshch. Nauk, 6:2, 3—12, 1 fig., (Rus-
           sian).
1968B.   [Archeology of Siberia.]   Vestnik Akad. Nauk SSSR, 1968:6, 66—80,
           13 figs., (Russian).
           See: Ganeshin and Okladnikov;   Litvinskiĭ, Okladnikov and Ranov;
           Michael 1965.

OKLADNIKOV, A. P., and ADAMENKO, O. M.
1966   [First finding of Levallois-Mousterian blade in Middle Pleistocene de-
           posits of Siberia.]   In: Saks, (ed.), 1966, 373—382, 3 figs.,
           (Russian).

OKLADNIKOV, A. P., and GOREGLIAD, V. N.
1958   [New data on the earliest culture of the Stone Age in northern
           Japan.]   Sov. Arkheol., 1958:3, 246—250, 3 figs., (Russian).

OKLADNIKOV, A. P., and ISLAMOV, O. I.
1961   [Paleolithic finds at Shuralisaĭ (Bozsu-2).]   Istoriia Mater. Kul't. Uz-
           bekistana, 2, 51—60, 3 pls., (Russian).

OKLADNIKOV, A. P.,   KASYMOV, M. R., and KONOPLIA, P. T.
1964   [Kapchigaĭ Paleolithic workshop.]   Istoriia Mater. Kul't. Uzbekistana,
           5, 5—11, 2 figs., (Russian).

OKLADNIKOV, A. P., and KIRILLOV, I. I.
1968   [Paleolithic settlement at Sokhatino (Titovskaia sopka).]   Izv. Sib.
           Otd. Akad. Nauk SSSR, ser. Obshch. Nauk, 6:2, 111—114,
           3 figs., (Russian).

OKLADNIKOV, A. P., and LARICHEV, V. E.
1963   [Archeological research in Mongolia in 1961—1962. (A brief report
           on the activity of soviet-mongolian expedition for the study
           of the Stone Age in Central Asia).]   Izv. Sib. Otd. Akad.
           Nauk. SSSR, Ser. Obshch. Nauk, 1:1, 78—89, (Russian).
1964   [Discoveries of Siberian archeologists.]   Vestnik Akad. Nauk SSSR,
           1964:6, 71—78, 3 figs., (Russian).

OKLADNIKOV, A. P., and LARICHEV, V. E.
1967   [Archeological research in Mongolia in 1964 and 1966.]   Izv. Sib. Otd.
Akad. Nauk SSSR, ser. Obshch. Nauk, 6:2, 80–91, (Russian).
1968   [Archeological research in Mongolia in 1967.]   Izv. Sib. Otd. Akad.
Nauk SSSR, ser. Obshch. Nauk, 11:3, 104–115, 5 figs., (Russian).

OKLADNIKOV, A. P., and LEONOV, N. I.
1961   [First discoveries of the Stone Age in Fergana.]   Krat. Soob. Inst. Ist.
Mat. Kult. SSSR, 86, 36–42, 3 figs., (Russian).

OKLADNIKOV, A. P., and RANOV, V. A.
1962   [Paleolithic of the Kairak-Kum.]   In: Litvinskiĭ, et al., 1962, 29–88,
34 pls., 2 tables, (Russian).

OKLADNIKOV, A. P., and TROITSKIĬ, S. L.
1967   [Research on Quaternary deposits and on Paleolithic of Mongolia.]
Biull. Kom. Izuch. Chetvert. Perioda, 33, 3–30, 14 figs., (Russian).

OKLADNIKOV, A. P.,   VERESHCHAGIN, N. K., and OVODOV, N. D.
1968   [Discovery of Paleolithic cave in the Maritime Province.   Vestnik Akad.
Nauk SSSR, 1968:10, 54–62, 4 figs., (Russian).

OKUTSU, H., and MUTO, A.
1959   On the stratigraphy of the Eostegodon fossil locality and lowland deposits in Funaoka near Sendai.   Saito Ho-On Kai Mus. Res. Bull.,
28, 58–60, 2 figs.

OLARU, VLADIMIR   See: Apostal and Olaru.

OLBY, ROBERT C.
1967   Charles Darwin.   London: Oxford Univ. Press, 64 pp.
Rev.:   Jameson in BioScience, 18, 821.

OLDEN, A. VAN   See: Hoskins 1964.

OLDFIELD, FRANK
1964   Late Quaternary environments and early man on the southern High
Plains.   Antiq., 38, 226–229, 1 fig.

OLIVER, DOUGLAS L.
1964   Invitation to anthropology.   Garden City: Natural History Press, xvi +
102 pp., illustr.
Rev.:   Hopgood in Missouri Archaeol. Soc. Newsletter, no. 182, 9.

OLIVER, ROLAND, and MATHEW, G., (eds.)
1963   History of East Africa.   Volume 1.   Oxford: Clarendon Press, xiii +
500 pp., 16 maps.
Rev.:   Wrigley in Jour. Afr. Hist., 5, 299–304.

OLIVIER, GEORGES
1965A.   Teilhard de Chardin et le transformisme.   Bull. Mém. Soc. Anthrop.,
7:4, 351–359, 1 fig., portr.
1965B.   L'évolution et l'homme.   Paris: Petite Bibliothèque Payot, no. 78,
181 pp., 12 figs.

Rev.: Anon. in La Nature, no. 3373, 200;   Dorst in Mammalia, 30,
687;   Furon in Rev. Gén. Sci., 73, 63;   Genovés in An. Antrop.,
Mexico, 1966, 3, 265—268;   Kurth in Homo, 17:2, 121;   Pauly-
Kloiber in Mitt. Anthrop. Ges. Wien, 96—97, 365—366;   Sauter
in Arch. Suiss. Anthrop. Gén., 31, 57—58;   Schaeuble in Zeit.
Morph. Anthrop., 58, 105;   Smithgall in Amer. Jour. Phys.
Anthrop., 24, 286—287;   Vogel in Anthrop. Anz., 30, 79—80.

1965C.   Anatomie anthropologique. Paris: Vigot Frères, 488 pp., 150 figs.
Rev.: Firbas in Mitt. Anthrop. Ges. Wien, 95, 362—363;   Gerhardt in
Homo, 16, 120;   Ludwig in Acta Anat., 61, 478—479;   Mac-
Conaill in Man, 65, 199;   Roth-Lutra in Anat. Anz., 120, 538.

1967A.   Les pommettes et l'aplatissement facial des hommes fossiles. C. R.
Acad. Sci. Paris, Sci. Nat., 264, 2382—2385, 2 figs.

1967B.   Mesure du torus sus-orbitaire des hommes fossiles. C. R. Acad. Sci.
Paris, Sci. Nat., 264, 2563—2565, 1 fig.

OLSEN, STANLEY J.

1960A.   Abs.: Dietrich in Zbl. Geol. Pal., Teil 2, 1964, 195—196.
1964A.   The stratigraphic importance of a Lower Miocene vertebrate fauna from
north Florida. Jour. Pal., 38, 477—482, 2 figs., pls. 68—70.
1964B.   Vertebrate correlations and Miocene stratigraphy of north Florida fossil
localities. Jour. Pal., 38, 600—604, 3 figs.
1964C.   Geology and paleontology exhibits in a small museum. Southeastern
Mus. Conf. Notes, 9, 50—51, illustr.
1966   The importance of fragmentary vertebrate remains in archaeological
collections. Southwestern Lore, 32, 82—84, 1 fig.
1967   A note in regard to osteological field manuals. Amer. Antiq., 32, 231.
1968A.   Bulldozers uncover hidden treasures. Mo. Archaeol. Soc. Newsletter,
no. 218, 3 pp., 5 figs., (reprinted from Rock Products, May, 1965).
1968B.   Miocene vertebrates and North Florida shorelines. Spec. Pap. Geol.
Soc. Amer., 115, 491—492, (abs.).

OL'SHANSKAÍA, O. L.

1965   [Ichthyofauna of the river Piasina.]   Voprosy Ikhtiol., 5:2 (35), 262—
278, 1 map, 6 tables, (Russian).

OLSON, ALAN P.

1964   An unfinished Clovis point from Houck, Arizona. Plateau, 36, 123—124,
1 fig.

OLSON, EVERETT C.

1962B.   Abs.: Huene in Zbl. Geol. Pal., Teil 2, 1964, 139—141.
Rev.: Romer in Copeia, 1964:1, 250—253;   Van Valen in Quart. Rev.
Biol., 40, 83.
1962C.   Continental and mammalian evolution — Tertiary and Pleistocene of
South America. Abs. 61st Ann. Meeting Amer. Anthrop. Assoc.,
1962, 26, (abs.).
1962D.   The osteology of Captorhinikos chozaensis Olson. Okla. Geol. Surv.,
Circ. 59, 49—68, figs. 10—15.
Abs.: Huene in Zbl. Geol. Pal., Teil 2, 1964, 172.
1963D.   Community structure and the origin of mammals. Spec. Pap. Geol.
Soc. Amer., 73, 212, (abs.).
1964A.   The geology and mammalian faunas of the Tertiary and Pleistocene of
South America. Amer. Jour. Phys. Anthrop., 22, 217—225, 2 figs.
1964B.   Relationships of Diadectes, Seymouria and Chelonia. Amer. Zool., 4,
379, (abs.).

1964C.   Morphological integration and the meaning of characters in classification systems. Publ. Syst. Assoc., no. 6, 123–156, 8 figs.

1965A.   Evolution and relationships of the Amphibia: introductory remarks. Amer. Zool., 5, 263–265, 1 fig.

1965B.   Relationships of Seymouria, Diadectes and Chelonia. Comments by R. L. Carroll. Amer. Zool., 5, 295–307, 6 figs.

1965C.   The evolution of life. London: Weidenfeld and Nicolson; New York: New American Library (Mentor Book), xii + 300 pp., 61 figs. (P. b. reprint.)
       Rev.: Anon. in Mankind Quart., 6, 175–176; Baumann in Homo, 17:1, 58; deBeer in Nature, 206, 331–332.

1965D.   New Permian vertebrates from the Chicksha formation in Oklahoma. Circ. Oklahoma Geol. Surv., 70, 1–70, 5 figs., 8 pls., 2 tables.

1965E.   Zatrachys serratus Cope (Amphibia: Labyrinthodontia) from McClain County, Oklahoma. Okla. Geol. Notes, 25, 91–97, 3 figs., 1 table.

1965F.   Summary and comment. Syst. Zool., 14, 337–342.

1966A.   The middle ear — morphological types in amphibians and reptiles. Amer. Zool., 6, 399–419, 9 figs.

1966B.   The role of paleontology in the formulation of evolutionary thought. BioScience, 16, 37–40.

1966C.   Community evolution and the origin of mammals. Ecology, 47, 291–302, 5 figs.

1966D.   Relationships of Diadectes. Fieldiana, Geol., 14:10, 199–227, figs. 99–109.

1967   Early Permian vertebrates. Circ. Oklahoma Geol. Surv., 74, 1–111, 12 figs., 3 pls.

1968A.   Dialectics in evolutionary studies. (Essay review of Davitaschvili, 1966A.) Evolution, 22, 426–436.

1968B.   The family Caseidae. Fieldiana: Geol., 17:3, 223–349, 24 figs., 5 pls., 4 tables.

OLSON, E. C., and BARGHUSEN, H.
    1962   Abs.: Huene in Zbl. Geol. Pal., Teil 2, 1964, 138–139.

OLSON, E. C., and MILLER, R. L.
    1958   Abs.: Schindewolf in Zbl. Geol. Pal., Teil 2, 1962, 311–313.

OLSON, WALTER S.   See: Brace, et al.

OLTZ, DONALD F., JR., and KAPP, R. O.
    1963   Plant remains associated with mastodon and mammoth remains in central Michigan. Amer. Mid. Nat., 70, 339–346, 2 figs.

OMAN, CHARLES L.   See: Ives, Levin, Oman and Rubin; Levin, B., et al.

ONDRIAS, JOHN C.
    1961   Comparative osteological investigations on the front limbs of European Mustelidae. Ark. Zool., 13, 311–320, 4 figs., 4 tables.

ONODERA, SHINGO, ONUMA, D., and SIGA, M.
    1966   [New find of Stegodon in Higashiyama-te and Higashiivai-gun, Ivate Prefecture.] Jour. Geol. Soc. Japan, 72:7, 354–355, (Japanese).

ONUMA, DJENKICHI   See: Onodera, Onuma and Siga.

OPARIN, A. I.
1967   L'état actuel du problème de l'origine de la vie et ses perspectives.
            L'Ann. Biol., 6, 545–550, 1 fig.

OPPÉ, ERNEST F.
1954   Through to Swanage. Poole: privately printed, (not seen).
1965   The Isle of Purbeck: sunny spaces and dinosaur traces. Bournemouth:
            privately printed, 1–31, 7 pls.

OPPENHEIMER, A.
1964   Tool use and crowded teeth in Australopithecinae. Current Anthrop.,
            5, 419–421, 6 figs.

ORLINS, ROBERT   See: Brooks, R. H., Orlins and Williams.

ORELKIN, V. S.   See: Solov'ev and Orelkin.

ORELLANA RODRIGUEZ, MARIO
1961   Acerca de la arqueología del desierto de Atacama. Bol. Univ. Chile,
            no. 27, 41–43, illustr.
1962   [Descripción de artefactos líticos de Ghuatchi.] Notas Mus. Antrop.,
            Univ. Nac. La Plata. 79, 76–123, 9 plates, 1 map.
1963   El preceramico en el desierto de Atacama (Chile). Trab. Seminario
            Hist. Primitiva Hombre Univ. Madrid y Inst. Españ. Prehist. Con-
            sejo Superior Invest. Cien., 9, 35 pp., 10 pls., 1 map, 1 table.
1965   El metodo critico de Teilhard de Chardin. Bol. Univ. Chile, 55, 57–60,
            portr.

ORELLANA RODRIGUEZ, M., and KALTWASSER P., J.
1964   Las industrias líticas del departamento de El Loa. Antropología, Chile,
            2:2, 37–76, 13 pls., 2 maps, 10 tables.

ORLOV, ÍŪRII ALEKSANDROVICH (=Orlov, J. A.)

ORLOV, J. A. (gen. ed.)
1958D–
  1964A.   (gen. ed.) Osnovy Paleontologii. [Fundamentals of Paleontology.] Osnovy Pal.,
            15 vols., ill., (Russian). Moscow: Nauka.
            Rev.: Branson in Okla. Geol. Notes, 25, 5; Fantini Sestini in Riv.
            Ital. Pal., 75:1, 196; Lerman in Quart. Rev. Biol., 41, 55–56;
            Menner in Vestnik Akad. Nauk SSSR, 1966:6, 118–126, (Rus-
            sian); v. V. in Geol. en Minj., 43, 67–68, (Dutch).
  1959B.   [Aleksei Petrovich Bystrov. (1899 - 1959).] Pal. Zhurnal, 1959:4, 157–
            158, portr., (Russian).
  1960B.   Les dinocéphales rapace de la faune d'Isheevo (Titanosuchia). Transla-
            tion from Russian by Mme. Stretovich, of Orlov, J. A., 1958B.
            Paris: Bur. Recherch. Geol. Min., no. 2244, 113 pp., 55 figs.,
            1 table.
  1964B.   Some palaeontological problems of continental deposits of Asia. Jour.
            Pal. Soc. India, 4, 1–5.
  1964C.   (ed.) [Tertiary mammals.] [International Geological Congress XXII session,
            1964: Reports of soviet paleontologists. Problem 8.] Moscow:
            "Nauka" Press, 1964, 57 pp., illustr., (Russian; English summaries).
  1964D.   On one problem of vertebrate palaeontology in the U.S.S.R. Pal. Zhur-
            nal, 1964:1, 131–132, (Russian).

1964E.   Letter to the editors. Vert. Palasiatica, 8, 219, (Chinese summary).
1965   Vertebrate paleontology in the U.S.S.R. (Translation of Orlov, 1964C.)
            Internat. Geol. Rev., 7, 1487–1488.
1967   Quelques données sur les vertébrés du Pliocène supérieur d'Odessa.
            Colloq. Internat. Cent. Nation. Recherch. Sci., 163, 553–556.
1968   [In the world of ancient animals.] 2nd edition. Moscow: "Nauka"
            Press, 211 pp., 82 figs., 42 pls., 8 col. pls., 3 portrs., 1 table,
            (Russian).
            See: Kozhdestvenskiĭ and Tatarinov.

ORLOV, V. N.
1960   [The changes in the molars in the genus Equus as a function of age
            and evolution.] Nauchn. Dokl. Vyssh. Shkoly., Biol. Nauki,
            1960:4, 66–69, 1 fig., (Russian).

ORMEA, F.
1963   Pierre Teilhard de Chardin. Torino: Contessa, 168 pp., (not seen).
            Rev.: Boné in Rev. Questions Sci., 25, 148.

ORNANO, MICHELD'
1967   La myoglobine: une hémoglobine fossile? Atomes, 240, 119–121, 4 figs.

ORR, KENNETH G.
1952   Survey of Caddoan area archeology. In: Griffin, J. B., (ed.), 1952A,
            239–255.

ORR, PHIL CUMMINGS
1962C.   On new radiocarbon dates from the California Channel Islands. Obser-
            vations, no. 8, 7 pp.
1964   Pleistocene chipped stone tool on Santa Rosa Island, California. Science,
            143, 243–244, 1 fig.
1968   Prehistory of Santa Rosa Island. Foreword by Rainer Berger. Santa
            Barbara, Calif.: Santa Barbara Mus. Nat. Hist., xxi + 253 pp.,
            frontispiece, 79 figs., 34 tables.
            Rev.: deSaussure in Caves Karst, 11:1, 3–4.

ORTEGA, ENRIQUE J.
1967   Descripción de los restos de un Scelidotheriinae (Edentata, Mylodontidae)
            de edad Huayqueriense. Algunas consideraciones en torno a la
            filogenia de los Scelidotheriinae. Ameghiniana, 5:3, 109–120,
            1 pl., (English summary).
            See: Pascual, Pisano and Ortega.

ORTON, GRACE L.
1957   The bearing of larval evolution on some problems in frog classification.
            Syst. Zool., 6, 79–86.

ØRVIG, TOR
1961D.   Neuere Untersuchungen über die Fisch-Fauna des skandinavischen Devons.
            Svenska Naturvetenskap., Stockholm, 14, 267–269, (not seen).
1965   Palaeohistological notes. 2. Certain comments on the phyletic significance
            of acellular bone tissue in early lower vertebrates. Ark. Zool.,
            16, 551–556, 1 fig.
1967A.   Histologic studies of ostracoderms, placoderms and fossil elasmobranchs.
            2. On the dermal skeleton of two late Palaeozoic elasmobranchs.
            Ark. Zool., 19, 1–39, 6 figs., 5 pls.

1967B.   Phylogeny of tooth tissues: evolution of some calcified tissues in early
              vertebrates. In: Miles, A. E. W., (ed.), 45—110, 53 figs.
1967C.   Some new acanthodian material from the Lower Devonian of Europe.
              In: Patterson, C., and Greenwood, P. H., (eds.), 1967, 131—153,
              5 figs., 4 pls.

ORVIKU, K. K., (ed.)
1958   [Review of Paleozoic and Quaternary stratigraphy of Esthonian SSR.]
              Akad. Nauk Eston. SSR, Inst. Geol., Tallin: "Iukhiselu" Press,
              46 pp., illustr., (Russian).

OSABA Y RUIZ DE ERENCHUM, BASILIO
1964   Catálogo arqueológico de la provincia de Burgos. Noticiario Arqueólo-
              gico Hispánico, 6:1—3, 227—277.

OSBORN, F.   See: Burger 1965.

OSBORNE, P. J.   See: Shotton, Osborne and Sylvester-Bradley.

OSCHINSKY, LAWRENCE
1962   Facial flatness and cheekbone morphology in Arctic Mongoloids: a case
              of morphological taxonomy. Anthropologica, n.s., 4, 349—377,
              15 pls., 6 tables, (French summary).
1963A.   A critique of "The origin of races" by C. S. Coon. Anthropologica,
              n.s. 5, 111—116, 4 pls.
1963B.   The problem of parallelism in relation to the subspecific taxonomy of
              Homo sapiens. Anthropologica, n.s. 5, 131—145, 1 pl., (French
              summary).
              See: Langston and Oschinsky.

OSCHINSKY, L., GALL, P., MacDONALD, J., NIEMAN, L., SPENCE, M., and
WILSON, S.
1964   Parallelism, homology and homoplasy in relation to hominid taxonomy
              and the origin of Homo sapiens. Anthropologica, n.s., 6, 105—
              117, (French summary).

OSMÓLSKA, HALSZKA
1966   [Third Polish-Mongolian paleontological expedition in Mongolia (1965).]
              "Kosmos" (Poland), A15:1, 69—74, (Polish).

OSOLE, FRANC
1963   Abs.: P. in Bull. Sci., Zagreb, Sec. A, 10, 296.
1965A.   Le gravettien tardif en Slovenie. Bull. Sci., Zagreb, Sec. A, 10, 325—326.
1965B.   [Excavations on the Paleolithic site Ovčja Jama near Prestranek.]   Geol.
              Razpr. Poročila, 8, 139—159, 12 figs., 2 tables, (Slovenian; French
              summary).
1965C.   Les stations paléolithiques dans des grottes en Yougoslavie. Naše Jame,
              7, 33—40, 1 map, (Slovenian summary).
              Rev.: ll in Archeol. Roz., 1967, 19, 553, (Czechoslovakian).

OSTOYA, PAUL
1965   Entrée en scène du Tchadanthrope. La Nature, 93, 277, 1 fig.

OSTROM, JOHN H.
1962   Abs.: Huene in Zbl. Geol. Pal., Teil 2, 1964, 172.

1962B.	Cranial morphology of the North American Hadrosauridae. Diss. Abst., 22, 4321—4322, (abs.).
1963B.	Abs.: Huene in Zbl. Geol. Pal., Teil 2, 1965, 250—251.
1963C.	Vertebrate paleontology. Kline Geol. Lab., Yale Univ., 3 pp.
1964A.	A reconsideration of the paleoecology of hadrosaurian dinosaurs. Amer. Jour. Sci., 262, 975—997, 1 fig., 4 tables.
	Abs.: Westphal in Zbl. Geol. Pal., Teil 2, 1965, 251.
1964B.	The systematic position of Hadrosaurus (Ceratops) paucidens Marsh. Jour. Pal., 38, 130—134, 2 figs.
	Abs.: Huene in Zbl. Geol. Pal., Teil 2, 1964, 990—991.
1964C.	The strange world of dinosaurs. Illustrated by Joseph Sibal. New York: Putnam's, 128 pp., illustr., (elemen., junior high school).
1964D.	A functional analysis of jaw mechanics in the dinosaur Triceratops. Postilla, no. 88, 35 pp., 10 figs., 2 tables.
1965	Cretaceous vertebrate faunas of Wyoming. Guidebk. Wyo. Geol. Assoc., 1965, 35—41, 2 figs.
1966A.	A study in dinosaur evolution. Discovery, Yale, 1:2, 9—15, 9 figs.
1966B.	A dinosaur flies to Germany. Discovery, Yale, 2:1, 23—26, 10 figs.
1966C.	Functional morphology and evolution of the ceratopsian dinosaurs. Evolution, 20, 290—308, 12 figs., 1 table.
1967	Peabody paleontologists assist new dinosaur-track park. Discovery, Yale, 2:2, 21—24, 2 figs., cover.
	See: Frost, B. H. 1956.

OSTROM, J. H., and McINTOSH, J. S.
1966   Marsh's dinosaurs. The collections from Como Bluff. New Haven and
                 London: Yale Univ. Press, xiv + 388 pp., 13 figs., 155 pls.
              Rev.: Camp in Science, 155, 309, 1 fig.;   Jepsen in Amer. Sci., 55,
                 318A, 320A;   L. S. Russell in Jour. Pal., 41, 1029—1030;
                 Van Valen in Quart. Rev. Biol., 42, 536;   Whitmore in GeoTimes,
                 12:4, 34—36.

OSTROMECKI, ANDRZEJ
1967   [New cave in the Śnieżnik Kłodzki Massif.]   Przegl. Geol., 15:7, 335—
                 337, 3 figs., (Polish;   English and Russian summaries).

OSTROVSKIĬ, M. I., and GRIGOR'EV, G. P.
1966   [Lipa Paleolithic culture.]   Sov. Arkheol., 1966:4, 3—13, 2 figs., (Rus-
                 sian).

OSTROWSKI, JANUSZ   See: Ziołkiewicz, et al.

OTORBAEV, K.
1963   [Academician L. S. Berg.]   (1876 - 1950). Izv. Kirgiz. Filiala Vses.
                 Geogr. Obsh., 4, 7—8, portr., (Russian).

OTSUKA, HIROYUKI
1966A.   On a new species of Rusa from western Kyushu. Kaseki, 11, 43—49,
                 2 figs., 1 table, (Japanese).
1966B.   Pleistocene vertebrate fauna from Kuchinotsu Group of West Kyushu.
                 Part 1. A new species of Cervus (Rusa). Mem. Kyushu Univ.,
                 Ser. D, Geol., 17:3, 251—269, 10 figs., pls. 27—29.
1967   Pleistocene vertebrate fauna from the Kuchinotsu Group of West Kyushu.
                 Part 2. Two new species of fossil deer. Mem. Kyushu Univ.,
                 Ser. D, Geol., 18:2, 277—312, 13 figs., pls. 3—14.

1968   A new species of <u>Elaphurus</u> from the Akashi formation in Hyogo Pre-
       fecture, Japan. Rept. Faculty Sci., Kagoshima Univ., no. <u>1</u>, 121–
       129, 1 fig., 1 pl.

OTTO, H.
1959   Professor Dr. h. c. Ernst Haase zum Gedächtnis. *21.10.1871 † 13.12.1959.
       Ber. Geol. Ges. Deutsch. Demokratischen Republ., <u>4</u>, 368–370,
       portr.

OULEHLA, V. See: Skutil and Oulehla.

OULMI, MOHAMED See: Lapparent and Oulmi.

OVERHAGE, PAUL
1963   Die Evolution des Lebendigen. I. Das Phänomen. (Quaestiones Dis-
       putatae 20/21). Freiburg, Basel, Wien: Herder, 262 pp., 26 figs.
       Rev.: Heberer in Anthropol. Anz., <u>31</u>:4, 299–300; Kroeger in Homo,
       <u>16</u>, 189.
1964   Zur Frage einer Evolution der Menschheit während des Eiszeitalters, III.
       Teil. Acta Biotheoret., <u>17</u>, 1–32, (English and French summaries).

OVEY, CAMERON D., (ed.)
1964   The Swanscombe skull. A survey of research on a Pleistocene site.
       Occ. Pap., Roy. Anthrop. Inst. Great Britain and Ireland, no. <u>20</u>,
       215 pp., 68 figs., 25 pls., 21 tables.
       Abs.: Preuschoft in Zbl. Geol. Pal., Teil 2, <u>1966</u>, 340–341.
       Rev.: Comas in An. Antrop., Mexico, 1966, <u>3</u>, 270–272; Koenigswald
       in Man, Jour. Roy. Anthrop. Inst., <u>1</u>, 106–107; Kurth in Homo,
       <u>16</u>, 57; McBurney in Proc. Prehist. Soc. Cambridge, <u>32</u>, 367–368;
       Roth-Lutra in Berliner Jahrb. Vor- und Frühgesch., <u>8</u>, 225–228;
       H. V. V. in L'Anthrop., <u>69</u>:5–6, 564–566.

OVODOV, N. D. See: Okladnikov, Vereshchagin and Ovodov; Vereshchagin and
       Ovodov.

OWEN, DAVID
1964   Care of type specimens. Mus. Jour., London, <u>63</u>, 288–291.

OWENS, W. A. See: Case, G. R. and Owens.

OXNARD, CHARLES E.
1967   The functional morphology of the primate shoulder as revealed by
       comparative anatomical osteometric and discriminant function
       techniques. Amer. Jour. Phys. Anthrop., <u>26</u>, 219–240, 9 figs.,
       5 tables.
       See: Zuckerman, <u>et al.</u>

OYENUGA, KUNLE, and OZANNE, P.
1968   Excavation at Asejire. W. Afr. Archaeol. Newsletter, no. <u>8</u>, 32–34, 1
       fig., (French summary).

OZAKI, HIROSHI See: Higuchi, <u>et al.</u>; Matsumoto, Ishii, <u>et al.</u>; Matsumoto, Mori,
       <u>et al.</u>; Shikama and Ozaki; Shimoda, Endo, Inove and Osaki.

OZANNE, PAUL See: Oyenuga and Ozanne.

OZANSOY, FIKRET
1964   Le niveau du Sannoisien et sa faune mammalienne de la Thrace Orient-
            ale (Turquie) dans le systeme de l'Oligocene d'Europe. Mem. Bur.
            Rech. Geol. Min., 28:2, 991–999.
1965   Étude des gisements continentaux et des mammiféres du Cénozoïque de
            Turquie. Mém. Soc. Géol. France, (n.s.), no. 102, 1–92, 13 figs.,
            10 pls., 5 tables. Rev.: M. C. in Fossilia, 1965:5–6, 69.

PAAVER, K. L.
1964   [On the variation in time of the subfossil populations of mammals in
            the Baltic countries.]   Biull. Mosk. Obshch. Prirody, Otd. Biol.,
            69:2, 83–95, 4 tables, (Russian; English summary).

PACCARD, MAURICE
1964   L'abri no. 1 de Chinchon (Commune de Saumanes-de-Vaucluse). Cahiers
            Ligures Préhist. Archéol., 13:1, 3–67, 36 figs., 1 table.

PACKARD, ROBERT L.
1967   Octodontoid, bathyergoid, and ctenodactyloid rodents. In: Anderson,
            S., and Jones, (eds.), 1967, 273–290, figs., 42–44.

PACKARD, R. L., and ALVAREZ, T.
1965   Description of a new species of fossil Baiomys from the Pleistocene of
            central Mexico. Acta Zool. Mex., 7:4, 4 pp., 1 fig., (Spanish sum-
            mary).

PAÇO, ALFONSO DO
1966   Paleolítico de Abrantes. Bróteria, 83:7, 101–105, 3 figs.
1967   Paleolítico de Coruche. Bróteria, 84:2, 245–248, 2 figs.

PADBERG, WOLFGANG
1967   Annidation und hominisation. Ethnog.-Archäol. Zeit., 8, 1–14, (Rus-
            sian and English summaries).

PADDAYYA, K.
1967   Hunsiholi: a Late Stone Age site in Krishna Valley. E. Anthrop., 20,
            71–78, 2 figs.

PAEPE, ROLAND   See: Heinzelin and Paepe.

PAGE, CATHERINE   See: Abramova 1967A.

PAGE, IRVINE H.
1965   Why bibliography? Science, 149, 8.

PAGHIDA, NATALIA
1962   [Otoliths from the Buglovian of Moldavian Plateau.] An. Şţiinţ. Univ.
            Cuza (n.s.), Sect. 2 (Şţiinţe Nat.), a Biol., 8, 13–20, 1 fig., 2 pls.,
            (Rumanian; French and Russian summaries).
            Abs.: Weiler in Zbl. Geol. Pal., Teil 2, 1965, 232; 1966, 284.
            See: Macarovici and Paghida.

PAINTER, FLOYD E.

1959 The Chesopean site. Quart. Bull. Archeol. Soc. Virginia, 13:3, (not seen).

1964A. Paleo-Indian projectile points of Indiana. Cent. States Archaeol. Jour., 11, 132—134, figs. 89—90.

1964B. The Meherrin River Cache. Chesopiean, 2:1, (not seen).

1964C. Paleo-Indian projectile points of Georgia. Chesopiean, 2:3, 46—48, illustr.

1965A. Paleo-Indian projectile points of Tennessee and Kentucky. Chesopiean, 3:3, 72, illustr.

1965B. Paleo-Indian projectile points from Ohio. Ohio Archaeol., 15, 67—69, 1 pl.

1965C. The Cattail Creek fluting tradition. Chesopiean, 3:1, 11—18.

1967 Workshop debris or crude tools??? Chesopiean, 5, 23—25.

1968 Latest news on early man. Chesopiean, 6, 83—86.

 See: Bottoms and Painter.

PAKHTUSOVA, N. A.

1966 [On the stratigraphy of Upper Permian deposits in the north of Russian Platform.] In: Collected Papers, 1966D "Materials on geology and economic ores of the Northwest of RSFSR," 5, 30—86, (Russian).

PAK SEN UK See: Grigor'ev, V. M., et al.

PALAZZO, TONY See: Graham, Al. 1963.

PALES, LÉON See: Graham, Al. 1963.

PALES, L., and TASSIN DE SAINT PÉREUSE, M.

1964 Une scène gravée magdalénienne. Grotte de La Marche, Magdalénien III. Objets et Mondes, 4, 77—106, 12 figs.

 Abs.: Anon. in Anthropos, 59, 646.

 Rev.: Vaufrey in L'Anthrop, 69, 307—308.

1965 En compagnie de l'abbé Breuil devant les bisons gravés magdaléniens de la grotte de La Marche. In: Ripoll Perelló, E., (ed.), 1965B, 217—250, 2 figs., 10 pls., (Spanish summary).

 Rev.: Vaufrey in L'Anthrop., 70:1—2, 141—142.

PALMA DI CESNOLA, ARTURO

1961B. Gli scavi nel Riparo Zampieri presso Verona. Mem. Mus. Civico Storia Nat. Verona, 9, 273—290, 5 figs., 1 table.

1963B. Su alcune stazioni musteriane del Promontorio del Garganico. Mem. Mus. Civ. Storia Nat. Verona, 11, 155—177, 6 figs., 4 photos, 1 table.

1964A. Prima campagna di scavi nella Grotta del Cavallo presso Santa Caterina (Lecce). Riv. Sci. Preist., 18, 41—74, 8 figs., (French and English summaries).

1964B. Nuovi reperti del Paleolitico Superiore nella Grotta delle Campane (Lucca). Rev. Sci. Preist., 18, 279—285, 1 fig., (French and English summaries).

1965A. Seconda campagna di scavi nella Grotta del Cavallo presso Santa Caterina (Lecce). Riv. Sci. Preist., 19, 23—39, 6 figs., (French and English summaries).

1965B. Marina di Camerota (Prov. di Salerno). Riv. Sci. Preist., 19, 299.

PALMA DI CESNOLA, A., and BORZATTI VON LÖWENSTERN, E.
1965   Santa Caterina (Nardò, Prov. di Lecce). Galliano del Capo (Prov. di
         Lecce). Riv. Sci. Preist., 19, 300.

PALMA DI CESNOLA, A., and GAMBASSINI, P.
1965   Lama delle Grotte (Ruvo, Prov. di Bari). Riv. Sci. Preist., 19, 300–301.

PALMA DI CESNOLA, A., and MESSERI, P.
1967   Quatre dents humaines paléolithiques trouvées dans des cavernes de
         l'Italie Méridionale. L'Anthrop., 71:3–4, 249–261, 4 figs.

PALMA DI CESNOLA, A., and ZORZI, F.
1961   Il giacimento preistorico alla foce del torrente Romandato, presso Rodi
         Garganico. Mem. Mus. Civico Storia Nat. Verona, 9, 291–344,
         20 figs., 2 pls., 4 tables.

PALMER, EPHRAIM LAURENCE
1965   Fossils. Boston, London, Toronto: D. C. Heath, xii +124 pp., 216 figs.,
         (pb. ed.; for amateurs).

PALMER, EVE
1967   The plains of Camdeboo. New York: Viking Press, 320 pp., illustr.

PALMER, HARRIS A.   See: Reed, C. A. and Palmer.

PALMOWSKI, JOACHIM, and WACHENDORF, H.
1966   Eine unteroligozäne Wirbeltierfauna aus einer Spaltenfüllung in Herrlingen/
         Blau (Württ.) Mitt. Bayer. Staatssamml. Pal. Hist. Geol., 6, 229–
         245, 2 figs., 1 pl., 1 table, (English summary).
         Rev.: Fahlbusch in Zbl. Geol. Pal., Teil 2, 1967, 489.

P'AN, KIANG
1964   Some Devonian and Carboniferous fishes from South China. Acta Pal.
         Sinica, 12, 159–168, 8 pls.

PANĂ, IOANA
1965   Otolitele pliocene diu reginuea de Cubură a Carpaţilor. Studii şi Cercetari
         Geol., 10, 3–14, 3 figs., 4 pls., 1 table, (Rumanian).
         Abs.: Weiler in Zbl. Geol. Pal., Teil 2, 1966, 284–285.

PANCHEN, A. L.
1964   The cranial anatomy of two Coal Measure anthracosaurs. Philos. Trans.
         Roy. Soc. London, Ser. B, 247, 593–637, 19 figs, pl. 10.
         Abs.: Huene in Zbl. Geol. Pal., Teil 2, 1965, 241.
1966   The axial skeleton of the labyrinthodont Eogyrinus attheyi. Jour. Zool.,
         London, 150, 199–222, 10 figs.
1967A.   The nostrils of choanate fishes and early tetrapods. Biol. Rev., 42,
         374–420, 11 figs., 1 table.
         Rev.: Westphal in Zbl. Geol. Pal., Teil 2, 1968, 203.
1967B.   The homologies of the labyrinthodont centrum. Evolution, 21, 24–33,
         6 figs.
         Rev.: Westphal in Zbl. Geol. Pal., Teil 2, 1968, 203.
1967C.   Amphibia. In: Harland, W. B., et al., (eds.), 1967A, 685–694, fig. 27A.
         Rev.: Westphal in Zbl. Geol. Pal., Teil 2, 1969:1, 51.

PANCHEN, A. L., TILLEY, E. H., and STEEL, C. A. B.
1967   Discovery of an anthracosaur skull in the Durham Coal Measures. Nature, 214, 1001, 1 fig.
              Rev.: Westphal in Zbl. Geol. Pal., Teil 2, 1968, 203.

PANICHKINA, M. Z.
1959A.   [About two types of Upper Paleolithic cores (so-called core-scrapers and gigantoliths).] Krat. Soob. Inst. Ist. Mat. Kult., 75, 57—62, 2 figs., (Russian).
1959B.   [About two types of Upper Paleolithic cores II. Gigantoliths.] Krat. Soob. Inst. Ist. Mat. Kult., 76, 3—9, 1 fig., (Russian).
1961   [New Paleolithic finds on the river Psekups (Kuban').] Krat. Soob. Inst. Ist. Mat. Kult. SSSR, 82, 49—58, 4 figs., (Russian).

PANICHKINA, M. Z., and VEKILOVA, E. A.
1962   [Investigation of Akhshtyr Cave in 1961.] Krat. Soob. Inst. Ist. Mat. Kult. SSSR, 92, 37—43, 3 figs., (Russian).

PANIN, N.
1961   Sur quelques traces mécaniques et organiques du Miocéne au confluant de la Punta et de la Zabala. Studii şi Cercetari Geol., 6, 63—73, 11 figs. including 3 pls., (Rumanian; Russian and French summaries).

PANIN, N., and AVRAM, E.
1962   Nouvelles empreintes de vértébrés dans le Miocene de la zone subcarpathique roumaine. Studii şi Cercetari Geol., 7:3—4, 455—484, 12 figs., 10 pls., (Rumanian; French and Russian summaries).
              Abs.: Semaka in Zbl. Geol. Pal., Teil 2, 1964, 982.

PANIN, N., LĂZĂRESCU, V., and GRUJINSCHI, C.
1966   Un nou sector ichno-fosilifer în depozitele miocene din Carpaţii Orientali. Bul. Inst. petrol, gaze şi geol., 13:2, (not seen).

PANIN, N., and STEFĂNESCU, M.
1968   Un nou punct ichno-fosilifer în molasa miocena din Carpaţii Orientali. Studii şi Cercetari Geol., 13:2, 521—525, 4 figs., (French summary).

PANIŪTINA, L. B.   See: Tikhomirov, V. V. and Paniŭtina.

PAOLI, A. R. J.
1961   Consideraciones sobre Paleopatología. Holmbergia, 6:17, 45—66, (English summary).

PAPWORTH, M. L.   See: Armelagos, et al.; Hewes, Irwin, et al.

PARADISI, UMBERTO
1965   Prehistoric art in the Gebel el-Akhdar (Cyrenaica). Antiq., 39, 95—100, 4 figs., pls. 17—20 (with note by C.B.M. McBurney).

PARASKEVAIDIS, I.
1961   Neue Funde quartärer Wirbeltierreste in Attika. Ann. Geol. Pays Hellén., 12, 149—152, 1 fig., pls. 20—21, (Greek; German summary).

PARENT, RENÉ, and SAVY M.
1963   Un gisement Levalloiso-Moustérien à Ronchères (Aisne). Bull. Soc. Préhist., Paris, 60, 205–214, 6 figs.

PARENTI, RAFFAELLO
1965   Professor Renato Biasutti [1878–1965]. Mankind Quart., 6, 79–80.

PARET, OSCAR
1961   Rev.: Anon. in Ur-Schweiz, 26, 79–80.

PĂRIZKOVÁ, J.   See: Prokopec and Pǎrizková.

PARKER, BERTHA MORRIS
1949   Life through the ages. Evanston, Ill.:   Row, Peterson, 36 pp., color illustr., (junior high).
1966   Dinosaurs. They had their day. Golden Mag., 3:1, 48–55, color illustr., (elemen. school).

PARKER, J. R.   See: Buchan, et al.

PARKER, RONALD B.
1966   Electron microprobe analysis of fossil bones and teeth. Program, 19th Ann. Meeting, Geol. Soc. Amer., Rocky Mountain Sect., 1966, 47–48, (abs.).

PARKES, KENNETH C.
1964   Special review, Animal species and evolution, by Ernst Mayr. Wilson Bull., 76, 193–203.

PARKES, K. C., and CLARK, G. A., JR.
1966   An additional character linking ratites and tinamous, and an interpretation of their monophyly. Condor, 68, 459–471, 7 figs.

PARMALEE, PAUL W.
1967A.   Castoroides and Cervalces from Central Illinois. Trans. Ill. Acad. Sci. 60, 127–130, 2 figs.
1967B.   Additional noteworthy records of birds from archaeological sites. Wilson Bull., 79, 155–162, 1 table.

PARODI BUSTOS, RODOLFO
1960   Darwin en la Argentina, sus descubrimientos e impresiones. Rev. Fac. Cien. Nat. Salta, 1:2, 51–56.
1962   Los anuros cretácicos de Puente Morales (Salta) y sus vinculaciones con Shelania pasquali Casamiquela (Chubut) y E. reuningi Haughton, de Africa del Sur. Rev. Fac. Cien. Nat. Salta, 1:3, 81–85.

PARRINGTON, FRANCIS REX
1967A.   The origins of mammals. Advance. Sci., 24:120, 165–173, 5 figs.
1967B.   The vertebrae of early tetrapods. Colloq. internat. Cent. Nation. Recherch. Sci., 163, 269–279, 4 figs., (French summary).
             Rev.: Westphal in Zbl. Geol. Pal., Teil 2, 1969:1, 51.
1967C.   The identification of the dermal bones of the head. In: Patterson, C., and Greenwood, P. H., (eds.), 1967, 231–239, 5 figs.

PARRIS, DAVID C.
1968   Morphology and relationships of the Prosciurinae. Program, 21st Ann.
            Meeting, Geol. Soc. Amer., Rocky Mt. Sect., 57, (abs.).

PARSCH, KARL O. A.
1962   Palaozoische und mesozoische Fischfunde aus Alberta (Kanada). In:
            Geyer, O. F., (ed.), 1962, 125—130, 2 figs. (not seen).
1963   Die oberkretazischen "Dinosaurier" von Alberta, Kanada. Stuttgarter
            Beitr. z. Naturk., no. 119, 16 pp., 2 figs., 6 pls.
            Abs.: Huene in Zbl. Geol. Pal., Teil 2, 1964, 991.

PARSONS, THOMAS S.
1968   Variation in the choanal structure of Recent turtles. Canadian Jour.
            Zool., 46, 1235—1263, 13 figs., 5 pls., 3 tables.
            See: Bellairs and Parsons; Gans and Parsons; Tihen 1965.

PARTRIDGE, T. C.
1965   A statistical analysis of the Limeworks lithic assemblage. S. Afr. Arch-
            aeol. Bull., 20:79, 112—116, 4 figs., 3 pls.
            See: Morison, et al.

PARTRIDGE, T. C., et al.
1964   A Middle Stone Age and Iron Age site at Waterval, north west of Johannes-
            burg. S. Afr. Archaeol. Bull., 19, 102—110, 4 figs, 1 pl.

PASA, A., and MEZZENA, F.
1965   Riparo Tagliente (Grezzana, Prov. di Verona). Stazione della Neve (Fumane,
            Prov. di Verona). Riv. Sci. Preist., 19, 295—296.

PASCAL, RENÉ   See: Lumley, Gagnière and Pascal.

PASCUAL, ROSENDO (=Pasqual, R.)
1958   Rev.: Parodi Bustos in Rev. Fac. Cien. Nat. Salta, 1:2, 83.
1965A.   Un nuevo Condylarthra (Mammalia) de edad Casamayorense de Paso de
            los Indios (Chubut, Argentina). Breves consideraciones sobre la
            edad Casamayorense. Ameghiniana, 4, 57—65, 2 figs., map, (Eng-
            lish summary).
1965B.   Los Toxodontidae (Toxodonta, Notoungulata) de la formación Arroyo
            Chasico (Pliocene inferior) de la Provincia de Buenos Aires. Ca-
            racterísticas geológicas. Ameghiniana, 4, 101—132, 12 figs., 3 pls.,
            (English summary).
1967   Los roedores Octodontoidea (Caviomorpha) de la formación Arroyo
            Chasico (Plioceno inferior) de la provincia de Buenos Aires. Rev.
            Mus. La Plata, (n.s.), sec. Pal., 5:35, 259—282, 1 pl., 3 tables,
            (English summary).
            See: Patterson, B. and Pascual.

PASCUAL, R., and BONDESIO, P.
1968   Los Cardiatheriinae (Rodentia, Caviomorpha) de la formación Arroyo
            Chasico (Plioceno inferior) de la Provincia de Buenos Aires. Ame-
            ghiniana, 5:7, 237—251, 2 pls., 3 tables, (English summary).

PASCUAL, R., PISANO, J., and ORTEGA, E. J.
1965   Un nuevo Octodontidae (Rodentia, Caviomorpha) de la formación Epecuén
            (Plioceno Medio) de Hidalgo (Provincia de la Pampa). Ameghiniana,
            4, 19—30, 1 pl., (English summary).

PASKOFF, ROLAND   See: Hoffstetter and Paskoff.

PASSEK, T. S.   See: Grigor'eva, et al.

PASTERNAK, JAROSLAV
1961   Rev.: Kalinová in Archeol. Roz., 17, 436–437, (Czech).

PASTERNAK, S. I.
1962   [Pavlo Pavlovich Balabaĭ (1904 - 1961).]   Nauk. Zap. L'viv. prirod.
         Muz., 10, 128–130, portr., (Ukrainian).
         See: Vialov and Pasternak.

PASTERNAK, S. I., and TATARINOV, K. A.
1952   [New findings of Quaternary mammals in western Podolia.]   Zbirn.
         Prafs Zool. Mus. Akad. Nauk URSR, 25, 89–93, 1 table, (Ukrain-
         ian;   Russian summary).

PASTEUR, GEORGES
1964   Recherches sur l'évolution des lygodactyles, lézards Afro-Malgaches
         actuels.   Trav. Inst. Sci. Cherifien. Sér. Zool., no. 29, 160 pp.,
         30 figs., 12 pls., 1 chart.
         Rev.: Williams in Quart. Rev. Biol., 51–52.
         See: Dobzhansky 1966B.

PATERSON, T. T., and DRUMMOND, H. J. H.
1962   Soan, the Palaeolithic of Pakistan.   Mem. Dept. Archaeol. Pakistan, 2,
         171 pp., 59 figs., 4 pls.
         Rev.: Valoch in Archeol. Roz., 19, 276–277.

PATRULIUS D., and MIHĂILĂ, N.
1966   Stratigrafia depozitelor cuaternare din imprejurimle Branului şi neotectonica
         depresiunii Bîrsei.   Ann. Comit. Geol. Republ. Popul. Romine,
         35, 259–298, (Romanian;   English and French summaries).

PATTE, ÉTIENNE
1960B.   Rev.: Rätzel in Bonner Jahrb., 163, 573–574.
1961A.   Rev.: Genet-Varcin in L'Ann. Biol., ser. 4, 2, 395–396.
1962C.   Présence de l'Halitherium dans l'Oligocène du Poitou.   C. R. Soc. Géol.
           France, 1962, 241, (abs.).
1964A.   Quelques mammifères des alluvions de la Charente.   Ann. Pal., Vert.,
           50, 45–79, 12 figs., 1 pl.
1964B.   Restes d'un enfant et dents du Magdalénien et du Mésolithique de
           Saint-Rabier (fouilles Cheynier).   L'Anthrop., 67, 513–524, 7 figs.
1966   De l'importance de l'évolution parallèle dans l'étude de l'origine et de
         l'évolution de l'homme.   L'Anthrop., 70:5–6, 545–552.
1967   La basse terrasse de Sempigny (Oise):   ses industries osseuses et lithiques,
         sa faune.   L'Anthrop., 71:5–6, 401–434, 14 figs., 2 tables.
1968   L'homme et la femme de l'Azilien de Saint-Rabier.   Mem. Mus. Nation.
         Hist. Nat. Paris, ser. C, 19:1, 1–56, 36 figs., 2 pls.

PATTERSON, BRYAN
1964   The geologic history of non-hominid primates in the Old World.   In:
         Lasker, G. W., (ed.), 1964, 46–66, 3 figs., 1 table, (reprint with
         editorial comment).
1965A.   The auditory region of the borhyaenid marsupial Cladosictis.   Breviora,
           no. 217, 9 pp., 2 figs.

1965B.   The fossil elephant shrews (family Macroscelididae). Bull. Mus. Comp.
            Zool. Harvard, 133:6, 297–335, 7 figs., 1 pl.
            Rev.: Fahlbusch in Zbl. Geol. Pal., Teil 2, 1967, 112–113.
1965C.   Alfred Sherwood Romer, president-elect. Science, 147, 891–892, photo.
1966   A new locality for Early Pleistocene fossils in north-western Kenya.
            Nature, 212, 577–578, 1 fig.
            See: Van Valen, Butler, et al.

PATTERSON, B., and HOWELLS, W. W.
1967   Hominid humeral fragment from Early Pleistocene of northwestern Kenya.
            Science, 156, 64–66, 1 fig., 1 table.
            Rev.: Vallois in L'Anthrop., 72:5–6, 611–613, 1 fig..

PATTERSON, B., and OLSON, E. C.
1961   Abs.: Huene in Zbl. Geol. Pal., Teil 2, 1964, 188–189.

PATTERSON, B., and PASCUAL, R.
1963   The extinct land mammals of South America. Program 16th Internat.
            Congr. Zool., 138–148, (not seen).

PATTERSON, COLIN
1964   A review of Mesozoic acanthopterygian fishes, with special reference to
            those of the English Chalk. Philos. Trans. Roy. Soc. London,
            Ser. B, 247, 213–482, 103 figs., pls. 2–5.
            Rev.: Savage in Nature, 204, 735–736.
1965A.   Phylogeny of the chimaeroids. Nature, 207, 1240.
1965B.   The phylogeny of the chimaeroids. Philos. Trans. Roy. Soc. London,
            Ser. B, 249, 101–219, 44 figs., pls. 22–28.
1966   British Wealden sharks. Bull. Brit. Mus. (Nat. Hist.), Geol., 11:7, 283–
            350, 31 figs., 5 pls., 2 tables.
1967A.   New Cretaceous berycoid fishes from the Lebanon. Bull., Brit. Mus.
            (Nat. Hist.), Geol., 14:3, 67–110, 11 figs., 4 pls., 2 tables.
1967B.   A second specimen of the Cretaceous teleost Protobrama and the rela-
            tionships of the sub-order Tselfatioidei. Ark. Zool., 19, 215–234,
            8 figs., 1 table.
1967C.   Are the teleosts a polyphyletic group? Colloq. Internat. Cent. Nation.
            Recherch. Sci., 163, 93–109, 11 figs., (French summary).
1968   The caudal skeleton in Lower Liassic pholidophorid fishes. Bull. Brit.
            Mus. (Nat. Hist.), Geol., 16:5, 203–240, 12 figs., 5 pls.
            See: Andrews, S. M., et al.; Greenwood and Patterson.

PATTERSON, C., and GREENWOOD, P. H., (eds.)
1967   Fossil vertebrates. Papers presented to Dr. Errol I. White . . . London:
            Academic Press, vi + 260 pp., illustr. (Also: Jour. Linnean Soc.
            London, Zool., 47:311.)
            Rev.: Bellairs in Jour. Anat., 103:2, 381;   Cox in Nature, 217, 1187;
            Cruikshank in S. Afr. J. Sci., 64, 363–364;   Fischer in Ber.
            Deutsch. Ges. Geol. Wiss., Reihe A, 14:3, 357–360;   Gill in
            Earth-Sci. Rev., 4:4, A299–A300;   Hotton in Science, 160, 178;
            Jenkins in Amer. Sci., 56, 177A–178A;   Lehmann in Palaeogeog.,
            Palaeoclimatol., Palaeoecol., 5, 318–319;   Müller in Biol. Zbl.,
            88:3, 386;   Romer in BioScience, 18, 996;   R. J. G. S. in Geol.
            Mag., 105, 205–206;   Thenius in Naturwiss., 56:3, 151.

PATTERSON, C. L.   See: Lebeuf 1964.

PATTERSON, O. F., III   See: Baird and Patterson.

PATTERSON, RICHARD P.
1966   A Pleasant Ridge site. Ohio Archaeol., 16, 88—90, 2 figs.

PATTON, THOMAS H.
1964   The Thomas farm fossil vertebrate locality. Guidebk., Soc. Vert. Pal.
             1964 field trip., Fla., 1964, 12—20, 1 fig.
1965   A new genus of fossil microtine from Texas. Jour. Mammal., 46, 466—
             471, 3 figs.
1966A.   Occurrence of fossil vertebrates on Cayman Brac, B. W. I. Carib. Jour.
             Sci., 6, 181.
1966B.   Revision of the selenodont artiodactyls from Thomas Farm. Quart. Jour.
             Florida Acad. Sci., 29, 179—190.
1967A.   Fossil vertebrates from Navassa Island, W. I. Quart. Jour. Florida Acad.
             Sci., 30, 59—60.
1967B.   Reevaluation of Hay's artiodactyl types from the Miocene of the Texas
             Gulf Coastal Plain. Texas Jour. Sci., 19, 35—40.

PAULA COUTO, CARLOS DE
1959B.   Uma preguiça terrícola do Alto Amazonas, Colombia. An. Acad. Brasil.
             Ciên., 31, XIX—XX.
1961B.   Marsupiais fósseis do Paleoceno do Brasil. An. Acad. Brasil. Cien., 33,
             IX—X.
1961C.   Didelfídeos fósseis do Paleoceno do Brasil. An. Acad. Brasil. Cien., 33,
             XXIX—XXX.
1961D.   Considerações sôbre o Pleistoceno sul-americano. Rev. Bras. Geog., 23,
             569—574.
1962A.   Explorações paleontológicas no Pleistoceno do Nordeste. An. Acad.
             Brasil. Cien., 34, XIX.
1962B.   Didelfideos fosiles del Paleoceno de Brasil. Rev. Mus. Argent. Cien.
             Nat., Cien. Zool., 8, 135—166, 14 figs.
1963B.   Um Trigonostylopidae do Paleoceno do Brasil. An. Acad. Brasil. Cien.,
             35, i, (abs.).
1964   Desdentados do Pleistoceno das Antilhas. An. Acad. Brasil. Cien., 36,
             242—243, (abs.).
1965   Sôbre a nomenclatura de dois gliptodontes. Notas Prelim. Estud. Div.
             Geol. Min., no. 125, 1—6, (Portuguese and English).
1967   Pleistocene edentates of the West Indies. Amer. Mus. Novit., 2304,
             55 pp., 26 figs., 3 tables.

PĂUNESCU, ALEXANDRU
1966   [Paleolithic research.] Studii şi Cercetări de Ist. Veche, 17, 319—333,
             7 figs., (Rumanian; French summary).
1968   [Oriental Gravettian site in northern Moldavia.] Studii şi Cercetări de
             Ist. Veche, 19, 31—39, 5 figs., (Rumanian; French summary).
             See: Nicolaescu-Plopşor, C. S., Păunescu and Mogoşanu.

PAVLIŬCHENKO, I. M.   See: Krylova, A. A., and Pavliŭchenko.

PAVLOVA, M. V.
1933C.   Les restes des Dauphins provenant des bords de la Mer Noire. Biŭll.
             Mosk. Obshch. Ispyt. Prirody, Otd. Geol., 41, 40—45, 5 figs.

PAVLOVIĆ, MILORAD, and ĆIPOVIĆ, V.
1964   [On fossil mammals from the Tertiary basin of Kriva Reka near Bujanovac
            (Servia).] Ann. Geol. Pen. Balkan., 31, 147—160, 7 figs., 3 tables,
            (Serbian; German summary).

PAVLOVIĆ, M., and ĐURKOVIĆ, R.
1962   [Miocene mammals from "Jankova Klisura" mine in Toplice Basin (Servia).]
            Ann. Geol. Pen. Balkan., 29, 77—87, 3 figs., 1 table, (Serbian;
            German summary).
            Abs.: Semaka in Zbl. Geol. Pal., Teil 2, 1966, 319.

PAVLOVIĆ, M., and THENIUS, E.
1965   Eine neue Hyäne (Carnivora, Mammalia) aus dem Miozän Jugoslawiens
            und ihre phylogenetische Stellung. Anz. Akad. Wiss. Wien, no.
            9, 177—185, 1 fig.
            Rev.: Kühn in Zbl. Geol. Pal., Teil 2, 1967, 517.

PAVLOVSKIĬ, E. N. See: Severtsov 1950.

PAWLICKI, R., KORBEL, A., and KUBIAK, H.
1966   Cells, collagen fibrils and vessels in dinosaur bone. Nature, 211, 655—
            657, 3 figs.
            Abs.: Anon. in Sci. News Letter, 90, 127.

PAWLOWSKA, KAZIMIERA
1963   Abs.: Weiler in Zbl. Geol. Pal., Teil 2, 1965, 232.

PAWLOSKI, JOHN A.
1968   Dinosaur State Park, Rocky Hill, Connecticut. Rocks and Minerals,
            43, 424—425, 4 figs.

PAYNE, JOAN CROWFOOT, and HAWKINS, S.
1963   A surface collection of flints from Habarut in southern Arabia. Man,
            63, 185—188, 4 figs.

PAYNE, MELVIN M.
1965   The Leakeys of Africa: family in search of prehistoric man. Nation.
            Geog. Mag., 127, 194—231, illustr.

PAYNE, M. M., and SCHERSCHEL, J. J.
1966   Preserving the treasures of Olduvai Gorge. Nation. Geog. Mag., 130,
            700—709, illustr.

PAYZANT, CHARLES See: Shannon 1962.

PEAKE, E. C. See: Beer 1964E.

PEARSON, F. J., JR. See: Tamers and Pearson; Tamers, Pearson and Davis.

PEARSON, F. J., JR., DAVIS, E. M., TAMERS, M. A., and JOHNSTONE, R. W.
1965   University of Texas radiocarbon dates III. Radiocarbon, 7, 296—314.
1966   University of Texas radiocarbon dates IV. Radiocarbon, 8, 453—466.

PEARSON, RONALD
1964   Animals and plants of the Cenozoic Era: some aspects of the faunal
            and floral history of the last sixty million years. London:
            Butterworths, vii + 236 pp., 36 figs.

Rev.: Haltenorth in Säugetierkundl. Mitt., 14, 153;   Macnae in S.
African Jour. Sci., 61, 155;   Mitchell in Nature, 205, 218–219;
Rossi Ronchetti in Riv. Ital. Pal., 71, 978–979;   Van Valen in
Quart. Rev. Biol., 41, 416.

PECK, RODNEY M.
1968   The Elys Ford pentagonal point type. Chesopiean, 6, 87–88, 1 fig.

PECK, STEPHAN R.   See: Bova 1964.

PECORA, WILLIAM T., and RUBIN, M.
1965   Absolute dating and the history of man. Publ. Nation. Acad. Sci.,
1469, 43–56, 4 figs.

PEGETA, V. P.
1968   [Enchondral ossification in Latimeria chalumnae Smith.]   Dopovidi
Akad. Nauk URSR, ser. B, 1968:7, 653–656, 1 fig., (Ukrainian;
Russian and English summaries).

PEI, WEN-CHUNG
1930B.   W. C. Pei tells his own story. Peking Leader Reprints, no. 51, 10–11.
1960E.   The living environments of Chinese primitive men. Paleovert. et Paleoanthrop., 2:1, 9–21, (Chinese, not seen).
1962B.   Abs.: Dietrich in Zbl. Geol. Pal., Teil 2, 1964, 196.
1965A.   Professor Henri Breuil, pioneer of Chinese Palaeolithic archaeology and
its progress after him. In: Ripoll Perelló, E., (ed.), 1965B,
251–271, 11 figs., 1 pl., 1 table, (French summary).
1965B.   Excavation of Liucheng Gigantopithecus cave and exploration of other
caves in Kwangsi. Inst. Vert. Pal. Palanthrop., Acad. Sinica,
Mem., Ser. A, iv + 54 pp., illustr., (Chinese and English).
1965C.   More on the problem of augmentation and diminution in size of Quaternary mammals. Vert. Palasiatica, 9, 37–46, (Chinese and
English).
Rev.: M. C. in Fossilia, 1965:5–6, 70.
1965D.   On a new Trilophodon tooth from Wufeng of Hupeh Province. Vert.
Palasiatica, 9, 209–216, 1 pl., (Chinese; English summary).

PEI, W.-C., and LI, Y.
1964   Some tentative opinions on the problem of "Sjara-osso-gol Series".
Vert. Palasiatica, 8, 99–118, 11 figs., (Chinese; English summary).

PEI, W.-C., YUAN, C.-S., LIN, Y.-P., CHANG, Y.-Y., and TSAO, C.-T.
1965   Discovery of Palaeolithic chert artifacts in Kuan-yin-Tung Cave in
Chien-hsi-hsien of Kweichow Province. Vert. Palasiatica, 9, 270–
279, 7 figs., (Chinese; English abstract).
Abs.: Sci. Abs. China, Earth Sci., 4, 13.

PEIPER, ALBRECHT
1963   Der Aufstieg zum Menschen. Abh. Sächs. Akad. Wiss., Math.-Naturwiss.
Kl., 47:5, 26 pp., 18 figs.
Rev.: Preuschoft in Anthrop. Anz., 26, 270–271.

PELLETIER, H.   See: Dorsser and Pelletier.

PELOSSE, J. L.
1968   Les 60 ans de l'homme de Heidelberg. Atomes, 252, 190—191, 2 figs.

PEÑA BASURTO, LUIS
1959   El "oreophitecus", ? Hóminido de hace diez milliones de años? Munibe,
             11:1—2, 85—87, 1 fig.
1964   La transformación del Museo de San Telmo, de San Sabastian. La sala
             "Prehistoria I". Caesaraugusta, 21—22, 157—167, 4 pls.

PENDERGAST, JAMES F.
1963   Canadian archaeology and history in 1962. Canadian Geog. Jour., 66,
             132—139, illustr.

PENNIMAN, T. K.
1965   A hundred years of anthropology. (With contributions by Beatrice
             Blackwood and Dr. J. S. Weiner.) 3rd ed., rev. London: Gerald
             Duckworth, 397 pp.
             Rev.: Fortes in Nature, 208, 215—216;   Lundman in Lychnos, 1967,
             (for 1965-1966), 464—466, (Swedish);   Mathur in E. Anthrop.,
             19, 250—251.

PENNINGTON, WINIFRED, and FROST, W. E.
1961   Fish vertebrae and scales in a sediment core from Esthwaite Water
             (English Lake district). Hydrobiol., 17, 183—190, 2 figs., 1 pl.

PEPLE, CHARLES   See: MacCord and Peple.

PEPPER, JACK
1965   Bones of Baja. Desert Mag., 28:1, 24—25, 36—37, illustr.

PÉQUART, MARTHE ET SAINT-JUSTE
1960   Rev.: Cheynier in Bull. Soc. Préhist. Franç., C. R. séances mens., 63,
             160—162.

PERICOT GARCIA, LUIS
1962A.   Profesor Mendes Correa (1888 - 1959). Ampurias, 24, 348—349.
1962B.   Profesor Alberto-Carlo Blanc (1906 - 1960). Ampurias, 24, 350.
1962C.   Philippe Héléna (1898 - 1961). Ampurias, 24, 354—355, portr.
1962D.   El tipo de punta de muesca levantino. Homenaje al profesor Cayetano
             de Mergelina, 727—731, 2 figs.
1962E.   América Indigena. I. El hombre americano, los pueblos de América.
             2nd ed. Madrid: Salvat Editores, S. A., xxiv + 1182 pp., 300
             figs., 8 color pls., 61 maps.
1963A.   El V Congreso Panafricano de Prehistoria y de Estudios del Cuaternario.
             Zephyrus, 14, 103—107.
1963B.   Philippe Héléna (*1898 - † 1961). Zephyrus, 14, 132.
1963C.   A. A. Mendes Correa (*1888 - † 1959). Zephyrus, 14, 133—134.
1963D.   Alberto Carlos Blanc (*1906 - † 1960). Zephyrus, 14, 136—137.
1965A.   Intervención del Dr. D. Luis Pericot en la Sesión Cientifica del Museo
             Canario, Las Palmas. Actas V Congr. Panafr. Prehist. Estud.
             Cuaternario, 1963:1, 97—100.
1965B.   El abate Breuil y España: algunos recuerdos personales. In: Ripoll
             Perelló, E., (ed.), 1965B, 273—280, (English summary).
1965C.   Au sujet de la contribution française à la connaissance de la Préhistoire
             Hispanique. Préhist. Spéléol. Ariégeoises, 20, 85—91.

PERICOT GARCIA, L., and TARRADELL, M.
1962   Manual de prehistoria africana. Madrid: Consejo Superior de Investi-
            gaciones Cientificas, 347 pp., 110 figs.
            Rev.: Jordá Cerdá in Zephyrus, 13, 118–121; Souville in Hespéris
            Tamuda, 4, 235–236.

PÉRINET, GUY
1964   Détermination par diffraction X de la température de cuisson d'un
            ossement calciné. Application au matériel préhistorique. C. R.
            Acad. Sci. Paris, 258, 4115–4116.

PERINO, GREGORY
1965A.   The Paleo-Indian era: distribution of finds. Arkansas. Bull. Southeast.
            Archaeol. Confer., 2, 18.
1965B.   Early man in Arkansas. Cent. States Archaeol. Jour., 12, 131–135, 4 figs.
1966   A comment on projectile points. Newsletter Okla. Anthrop. Soc., 14:3,
            5–6, illustr.
1968   Clovis fluted points from Arkansas, Missouri and Illinois. Chesopiean,
            6, 14–15, 2 pls.

PERKINS, CAROL MORSE
1965   The shattered skull: a safari to man's past. New York: Atheneum,
            59 pp., illustr., (not seen).
            Rev.: Anon. in Sci. Amer., 213:6, 121; Metraux in Nat. Hist., 75:9,
            24.

PERKINS, DEXTER, JR.
1960   The faunal remains of Shanidar Cave and Zawi Chemi Shanidar: 1960
            season. Sumer, 16, 77–78.
1965   Three faunal assemblages from Sudanese Nubia. Kush, 13, 56–61.

PERREIRA SOARES, A.   See: Henriques da Silva and Perreira Soares.

PERSHINA, A. I.
1962   [Silurian and Devonian sediments of Chernyshev Range.] Moscow-
            Leningrad: Akad. Nauk SSSR Press, 122 pp., 20 figs., 7 charts,
            2 tables, (Russian).
1965   [Stratigraphy and facies of Devonian deposits in the southern part of
            Pechora Urals.] Trudy Inst. Geol., Komi fil. AN SSSR, 5, 21–
            30, 1 fig., (Russian).
1966   [Silurian and Devonian deposits of the western slope of North Urals.]
            In: Chalyshev, (ed.), 1966A, 3–34, 3 figs., (Russian).

PERSSON, PER OVE
1961A.   Abs.: Huene in Zbl. Geol. Pal., Teil 2, 1964, 174.
1962   Abs.: Huene in Zbl. Geol. Pal., Teil 2, 1964, 173.
1963A.   Abs.: Huene in Zbl. Geol. Pal., Teil 2, 1964, 172–173.
1963B.   Abs.: Huene in Zbl. Geol. Pal., Teil 2, 1964, 173–174.
1967   New finds of plesiosaurian remains from the Cretaceous of Scania. Geol.
            Fören. Förh., 89, 67–73, 4 figs.

PERU, DONALD V.
1965   The distribution of fluted points in the counties of Kent and Allegan,
            Michigan. Mich. Archaeol., 11, 1–8, 1 map, 1 pl.

PESCHEL, KARL
1963   Bibliographie Gotthard Neumann 1923 - 1961. Alt-Thüringen, 6, 661–
              673, frontispiece.

PETERS, E.
1931   Altsteinzeitliche Höhlenfunde. Nachrichtenblatt für Deutschen Vorzeit,
              7, 176.

PETERS, JAMES A., and COLLETTE, B. B.
1968   The role of time-share computing in museum research. Curator, 11, 65–
              75, 4 figs.

PETERSON, FREDRICK   See: MacNeish and Peterson.

PETERSON, R. L.
1965   A well-preserved grizzly bear skull recovered from a Late Glacial deposit
              near Lake Simcoe, Ontario. Nature, 208, 1233–1234, 1 fig.

PETIT, GEORGES, and THEODORIDES, J.
1962   Histoire de la Zoologie des origines à Linné (Histoire de la pensée VIII).
              Paris: Hermann, xii + 360 pp., 24 pls., (not seen).
              Rev.: Monod in Bull. Inst. Franç. Afr. Noire, ser. A, 25, 656–665;
              Montalenti in Scientia, 101, 285, 287.

PETIT, R.   See: Agache, Bourdier, and Petit.

PETRAKOV, I. I.   See: Liubin and Petrakov.

PETRÁNEK, J.
1967   New geochronological scale for the Phanerozoic (Paleozoic, Mesozoic
              and Cainozoic). Čas. Min. Geol., 12, 381–383, 1 table, (Czech).

PETRBOK, J.
1959   Le paléolithique de la grotte de Sudslavice, Bohême méridionale. Ar-
              cheol. Roz., 11, 106–107, (Czech; French summary).

PETRICHENKO, N. F.
1963   [Late Paleolithic station Bila on Prut R.] Sov. Arkheol., 1963:3, 215–
              218, 2 figs., (Russian).

PETROCHILOS, JEAN
1961   Découverte de lits de Mammifères dans la région de Patraloma (Chalkidiki).
              Die Höhle, 12, 93, (abs.). Reprinted in Actes 3ème Congr.
              Internat. Spéléol., A, 61.
1965   Découverte de restes de mammifères du Quaternaire moyen dans la
              région de Petralona en Chalkidiki. 3. Internat. Kongress Spel.,
              4, 37–39, 2 pls., 1 map.

PETRONIJEVIĆ, ŽIVADIN M.
1967   [Middle Miocene and Lower Sarmatian (Steier) mammalian fauna of
              Servia.] Pal. Jugoslavica, 7, 160 pp., 5 figs., 5 maps, 2 charts,
              24 pls., 29 tables, (Serbo-Croatian and German).
              Rev.: Kochansky-Devidé in Zbl. Geol. Pal., Teil 2, 1969:1, 52–53.

PETRONIJEVIĆ, Ž., and THENIUS, E.
    1958B.   Über das Vorkommen von Indricotherien (Baluchitherien) im Tertiär von
                Ivangrad (Berane) in Montenegro. Glas Acad. Serbe Sci., 231,
                Classe Sci. Math. Nat., 14, 61–74, 2 figs., (Serbian and German).
        Abs.: Dietrich in Zbl. Geol. Pal., Teil 2, 1960 (1961), 383–384.

PETROV, G. I.
    1940A.   [Find of remains of Neanderthal man on Monte Circeo (Italy).]   Krat.
                Soob. Inst. Ist. Mat. Kult. SSSR, 7, 102–105, 1 fig., (Russian).
    1940B.   [New data on Pithecanthropus.]   Krat. Soob. Inst. Ist. Mat. Kult. SSSR,
                6, 93–95, 1 fig., (Russian).

PETROV, O. M.   See: Hopkins, D. M., et al.

PETRUN', V. F.
    1956   [On the problem of the age of river terraces of southern Maritime
                Province.]   Materialy Geol. Inst. (VSEGEI), Nov. Ser. Geol. i
                Pol. Iskop., 15, 58–73, 4 pls., (Russian).

PETRUN', V. F., and BILOKRIS, L. S.
    1962   [New Stone Age finds in Crimea.]   Arkheologiia, 14, 167–183, 10 figs.,
                (Ukrainian).

PETTER, F.
    1967   Particularités dentaires des Petromyscinae Roberts 1951 (rongeurs,
                Cricétidés).   Mammalia, 31, 217–224, 7 figs.

PETTER, GERMAINE
    1963A.   Rev.: A., Hno. R., in Teruel, no. 30, 246–247.
    1964A.   Étude de quelques Viverridés (Mammifères, Carnivores) du Pléistocène
                inférieur du Tanganyika (Afrique orientale). Bull. Soc. Géol.
                France, 5, 265–274, 2 figs., pl. 12.
    1964B.   Deux mustélidés nouveaux du Pontien d'Espagne orientale. Bull. Mus.
                Hist. Nat. Paris, 36, 270–278, 2 figs., 1 pl.
    1964C.   Origine du genre Otocyon (Canidae africain de la sousfamille des
                Otocyoninae). Mammalia, 28, 330–344, 3 figs., (English sum-
                mary).
    1965   Viverridae. In: Leakey, et al., 1965, 22–23.
    1966   Cynodictis, Canidé Oligocène d'Europe. Région tympanique et affinités.
                Ann. Pal., Vert., 52:1, 3–19, 5 figs.
                Rev.: Fahlbusch in Zbl. Geol. Pal., Teil 2, 1967, 517–518.
    1967A.   Mustélidés nouveaux du Vallésien de Catalogne. Ann. Pal., Vert., 53,
                91–114, 1 fig., 2 pls., 2 tables.
                Rev.: Fahlbusch in Zbl. Geol. Pal., Teil 2, 1969:3, 292–293.
    1967B.   Paragale hürzeleri nov. gen., nov. sp. Mustélidé nouveau de l'Aquitanien
                de l'Allier. Bull. Soc. Géol. France, 9, 19–23, 1 pl., 1 table.
    1967C.   Paragale hürzeleri nov. gen., nov. sp. Mustélidé nouveau de l'Aquitanien
                de l'Allier. C. R. Soc. Géol. France, 1967, 17, (abs.).
    1967D.   Petits carnivores villafranchiens du Bed I d'Oldoway (Tanzanie). Colloq.
                Internat. Cent. Nation. Recherch. Sci., 163, 529–538, 6 figs.,
                1 table, (English summary).

PETTIT, CHARLES A.
    1968   A typological and cultural analysis of artifacts from a Clarksville, Vir-
                ginia, site. Chesopiean, 6, 16–21, 1 fig.

PÉWÉ, T. L., and HOPKINS, D. M.
  1967   Mammal remains of pre-Wisconsin age in Alaska. In: Hopkins, D. M.,
              (ed.), 1967D, 266–270.

PEYER, BERNHARD
  1963   Rev.: Gabe in L'Ann. Biol., ser 4, 4, 287–288;   K. in Natuurhist.
              Maandbl., 52, 84;   Keil in Umschau, 64, 446;   Meyer in Natur-
              wiss., 51, 279;   Schaeuble in Zeit. Morph. Anthrop., 54, 356;
              Strenger in Verh. Zool.-Bot. Ges. Wien, 103–104, 244.
  1968   Comparative odontology. Translated and edited by Rainer Zangerl.
              Chicago: Univ. Chicago Press, 472 pp., illustr.
              Rev.: Butler in Nature, 220, 407;   Denison in Evolution, 22:4, 842–
              843;   Haltenorth in Säugetierkundl. Mitt., 18:1, 90–91.

PEYRONY, ELIE
  1959   Les Eyzies, and the Vézère valley. Montignac: Imprimerie de la Vézère,
              63 pp., illustr.

PFEIFFER, JOHN
  1966   Man – through time's mists. Paintings by Birney Lettick. Sat. Eve.
              Post, Dec. 3, 1966, 40–44, 46, 48–50, 52, 65, 2 color illustr.

PFLUG, H. D., and STRÜBEL, G.
  1968   Umwandlungen in Wirbeltierknochen während der Fossilisation. Umschau,
              1968:13, 405.

PHILIP, JEAN, and TRONCHETTI, G.
  1966   Présence d'un poisson Pycnodontiforme dans le Turonien provençal.
              C. R. Soc. Géol. France, 1966, 29–30, 1 fig.
              Rev.: Radig in Zbl. Geol. Pal., Teil 2, 1967, 101.

PHILLIPS, ALLAN R.
  1968   Geologic age of Ciconia maltha. Auk, 85, 315.

PHILLIPS, E. D.
  1964   The Greek vision of prehistory. Antiq., 38, 171–178.

PHILLIPSON, D. W.
  1964   The 1963 Livingstone School of Archaeology. S. Afr. Archaeol. Bull.,
              19, 21.

P'IANKOV, V. P.
  1965   [Mammoths and the climate riddle.]   Priroda, 1965:10, 86–94, illustr.,
              (Russian).

PICARD, LEO
  1965   The Pleistocene of the Jordan Rift Valley. 7th Internat. Congr., Inter-
              nat. Assoc. Quat. Res., Abs., 1965, 379, (abs.).

PICARD, L., and BAIDA, U.
  1966   Stratigraphic position of the Ubeidiya formation. Proc. Israel Acad.
              Sci., Sect. Sci., no. 4, 3 pls.

PICCOLI, GIULIANO
  1966   Segnalazione di un frammento di sirenio (Prototherium) nello stratotipo
              del Priaboniano. Boll. Soc. Geol. Ital., 85, 349–353, 1 fig.

PICCOLI, G., and DEL PUP, G.
    1967   I resti di elefante nano Elephas falconeri della grotta "Luparello" (Palermo) conservati nell'Instituto Geologico di Padova. Atti Mem. Accad. Patavina Sci. Let. Arti, Mem. Cl. Sci. Mat. Nat., 79:2, 243–266, 11 figs., 2 pls.
        Rev: Albanesi in Riv. Ital. Pal., 73, 1389.

PICHARDO DEL BARRIO, M., BONILLA LUNA, J., and HOPPE, W.
    1961   El mamut posiblemente más antiquo de la Cuenca de Mexico, con algunas consideraciones paleoecológicas y geocronológicas. Homenaje a Pablo Martinez del Rio, 113–124, 2 figs.

PICKING, LARRY   See: Murphy, J. L. and Picking.

PIDOPLICHKO, IVAN G.
    1946–1956   [On the Glacial Period.] Kiev: 4 vols. V.1 "KGU" Press, 1946, 172 pp., (Russian; English summary). V.2, Akad. Nauk USSR Press, 1951, 264 pp., 35 figs., (Russian). V.3, 1954, 220 pp., 11 figs., (Russian). V.4, 1956, 336 pp., 72 figs., (Russian).
    1955C.   [The results of the study of Paleolithic fauna during the last few years.] Krat. Soob. Inst. Arkheol. Akad. Nauk URSR., 4, 163–164, (Rusian).
    1959C.   [Significance of vertebrate phylogeny for geochronology and stratigraphy.] Trudy Vses. Paleont. Obshch., II sess., 223–229, 1 fig., (Russian.)
    1960   [About the geological age of the ornamented metapod of a wild ass from the village of Romankov.] Krat. Soob. Inst. Arkheol. Akad. Nauk. URSR, 10, 16, (Russian).
    1961A.   [Paleontological investigations in the area of the Kakhov reservoir.] Arkheol. Pam. URSR, 10, 197–203, 1 fig., 3 tables, (Ukrainian).
    1961B.   [Study of ancient vertebrates of Ukraine for the last 40 years.] Trudy Vses. Paleont. Obshch., IV sess., 84–91, (Russian).
    1963A.   [Contemporary problems and aims in the study of the history of faunas and their habitat.] Prirodn. Obstan. i Fauny Proshl., 1, 9–30, (Russian).
    1963B.   [Development of anti-glacial theory in recent years.] Prirodn. Obstan. i Fauny Proshl., 1, 102–118, (Russian).
    1965   [On the problem of geochronology in connection with the evolution of man and of the Quaternary organic world.] Prirodn. Obstan. i Fauny Proshl., 2, 58–73, 2 tables, (Russian).
    1967A.   [Again on Anthropogene chronology.] Prirodn. Obstan. i Fauny Proshl., 3, 133–140, 1 table, (Russian).
    1967B.   [Actual tasks in vertebrate research for the solution of problems of paleogeography and stratigraphy.] In: Collected Papers: 1967A [Place and significance of fossil mammals of Moldavia in the Cenozoic of USSR], 5–10, (Russian).
        See: Moliavko and Pidoplichko.

PIDOPLICHKO, I. G., and KURAZHSKOVSKIĬ, IŪ. M.
    1956   [Paleogeographical significance of dipnoan vertebrates.] Zbirn. Prats' Zool. Mus. Akad. Nauk URSR, 27, 144–153, 2 figs., (Ukrainian; Russian summary).

PIDOPLICHKO, I. G., and MOLĪAVKO, G. I.
    1965   [On the problem of paleogeography of Ukraine during Neogene and Quaternary in the light of fossil organisms.] Prirodn. Obstan. i Fauny Proshl., 2, 16–40, 7 figs., (Russian).

PIEL, GERARD
1963   Last words from the dinosaur. Explorer, 5:6, 14—19, illustr.

PIERRET, BERNARD
1960   La caverne préhistorique de Villars. Bull. Soc. Hist. Archéol. Périgord, 87, 210—212.
1961A.   Grottes et abris aménagés du Périgord. Spelunca, Bull., 1:3, 11—13.
1961B.   Monte-Castillo. Spelunca, Bull., 1:3, 19—20.

PIETSCH, ERICH, and PIETSCH, G.
1964   Altamira y la prehistoria de la tecnología química. Madrid: 86 pp., illustr., (not seen).
         Rev.: [Beltrán] in Caesaraugusta, 23—24, 145; Franke in Die Höhle, 15, 21—22.

PIGGOTT, STUART, (ed.)
1961C.   Rev.: Anon. in Ur-Schweiz, 27, 69.
1962B.   Prehistoric India to 1000 B. C. London: Cassell, 295 pp., 32 figs., 8 pls., 2 tables.
1963   El despertar de la Civilización. (Transl. from 1961 ed.) Barcelona: Labor Press, 403 pp., 859 figs., 137 col. pls.
         Rev.: Vidart in Amerindia, 3, 92—96.
         See: Clark, J. G. D. 1967; Clark, J. G. D. and Piggott.

PILBEAM, DAVID R.
1964   Hominoids and hominids — the problem of variation and the meaning of taxonomic statements. Abs. 63rd. Ann. Meeting Amer. Anthrop. Assoc., 1964, 46, (abs.).
1966A.   Notes on Ramapithecus, the earliest known hominid, and Dryopithecus. Amer. Jour. Phys. Anthrop., 25, 1—5.
1966B.   Primate fossils in the Fayum. Eugen. Rev., 58:1, 4—5.
         Rev.: Preuschoft in Zbl. Geol. Pal., Teil 2, 1969:1, 55—59.
1968A.   The earliest hominids. Nature, 219, 1335—1338, 1 table.
1968B.   Human origins. Advance. Sci., 24, 368—378, 5 figs.
         See: Simons and Pilbeam.

PILBEAM, D. R., et al.
1965   Classification as synthesis. In: DeVore, P. L., (ed.), 39—51.

PILBEAM, D. R., and SIMONS, E. L.
1965   Some problems of hominid classification. Amer. Sci., 53, 237—259, 3 figs. Also in: Genovés, S., et al., (eds.), 1967, 97—120, with comment by A. T. Steegman, Jr.

PILBEAM, D., and WALKER, A.
1968   Fossil monkeys from the Miocene of Napak, north-east Uganda. Nature, 220, 657—660, 3 figs., 1 table.

PILL, A. L.
1963   The caves of Hartle Dale. I. Cave Sci., 5, 25—35, (not seen).

PILLERI, G.
1967   Considérations sur le cerveau et le comportement du Delphinus delphis. Rev.: Suisse Zool., 74, 665—676, 3 figs., 2 tables, 5 pls., (German and English summaries).

PILZ, ROMAN
  1962   Georg Lahner—neunzig Jahre. Die Höhle, 13, 96–98, portr.

PINEAU, HENRI   See: Delmas and Pineau.

PINEAU, H., and DELMAS, A.
  1966   Poids des vertèbres présacrées et orthogenèses rachidiennes, chez les Mam-
              mifères. C. R. Acad. Sci. Paris, 262, 2449–2452, 5 figs.

PINNA, GIOVANNI
  1964   La gita della Società Italiana di Scienze Naturali a Leffe, Pianico ed alle
              incisioni della Valcamonica. Natura, Riv. Sci. Nat., 55, 211–219,
              5 figs.
  1965   La sala di ≪ Introduzione alla Paleontologia ≫ del Museo Civico di storia
              Naturale di Milano. Natura, Riv. Sci., Nat., 5–60, 33 figs.
  1967   La collezione di rettili triassici di Besano (Varese) del Museo Civico di
              Storia Naturale di Milano. Natura, 58:3, 177–192, (English summary).

PINNER, ERNA
  1966   Neue Erwägungen zur Geschichte der Evolution. Naturwiss. Rundschau,
              19:5, 204.

PINSON, WILLIAM H., JR.
  1949   A criticism of Gondwana land bridges. Bull. Georgia Acad. Sci., 7:1,
              23.

PINTAUD, ROLAND C.
  1961   Sondages à Montgaudier. Mem. Soc. Archéol. Hist. Charente, 1960,
              133–149, 10 pls.

PIOTROVSKIĬ, B. B., (ed.)
  1964   [Ancient Nubia.]   Inst. Arkheologii, Akad. Nauk SSSR. Moscow: "Nauka"
              Press, 261 pp., illustr., (Russian).

PIRKER, RUDOLF
  1961   Gedanken zur paläolithischen Höhlenwandkunst. Die Höhle, 12, 94, (abs.),
              Reprinted in Actes 3ème Congr. Internat. Spéléol., A, 62.
  1963   Rudolf Saar zum Gedächtnis. Höhlenkundliche Mitt., 19:6. Reprinted
              in Mitt. Verband Deutschen Höhlen- und Karstforscher, 9, 51–52.
  1965   Gedanken zur paläolithischen Höhlenwandkunst. 3. Internat. Kongress
              Spel., 4, 41–45.

PISANO, JUAN A.
  1964   Un nuevo y significativo caso de adición prismática observado en el
              premolar cuarto (p4) inferior de un ejemplar del género Cavia
              (Rodentia, Caviidae). Ameghiniana, 3, 169–172, 2 figs., (English
              summary).
              See: Pascual, Pisano and Ortega.

PISCHEDDA, BRUNA
  1954   Fossili miocenici di Pischinappiu (Sardegna). Rend. Semin. Fac. Sci.
              Univ. Cagliari, 24:1–2, 128–144, 1 fig., 2 pls.

PISCOPO, G., and RADMILLI, A. M.
1966   Sul rinvenimento di due veneri Paleolitiche a Parabita (Lecce). Atti Soc.
              Toscana Sci. Nat., Mem., Ser. A, 73, 148−156, 3 figs.

PISHVANOVA, L. S.   See: Tkachenko, O. F., Pishvanova and Shvareva.

PITSKHELAURI, K. N.   See: Bugianashvili, et al.

PITTARD, EUGENE
1960   Une gravure de Cro-Magnon (Dordogne) exilée à Neuchâtel (Suisse). Bull.
              Soc. Hist. Archéol. Perigord, 87, 213−216, 1 fig.

PITTIONI, RICHARD
1962   Italien Urgeschichtliche Kulturen. Stuttgart: Pauly−Wissowa: Real-
              encyclopädie der classischen Altertums Wissenschaft−Supplement
              Band IX, columns 106−371, (not seen).
              Rev.: Barfield in Antiq., 41, 248−250.
1964   Vom Faustkeil zur Eisenschwert. Eine kleine Einführung in die Urgesch-
              ichte Niederösterreichs. Horn: Berger, 116 pp., 80 pls., (not seen).
              Rev.: Moucha in Archeol. Roz., 18, 219, (Czech).

PIVETEAU, JEAN
1957B.   (ed.) Rev.: Comas in Cuad. Inst. Hist., Ser. Antrop., no. 6, 15−27;
              Gregory, J. T. in Amer. Jour. Sci., 262, 557−560.
1958B.   (ed.) Rev.: Gregory, J. T. in Amer. Jour. Sci., 262, 557−560.
1961A.   (ed.) Rev.: Gregory, J. T. in Amer. Jour. Sci., 262, 557−560.
1961V.   Les gisements préhistoriques de la vallée des Eaux-Claires. VI−L'astragale
              humain de la grotte Simard. Mem. Soc. Archéol. Hist. Charente,
              1960, 129−131, 1 pl.
1962E.   L'origine de L'homme. L'homme et son passé. Paris: Hachette, 207
              pp., 29 figs.
              Rev.: Lefebvre in Libyca, 11, 313−314; Roth-Lutra in Anat. Anz.,
              116, 526−527; Uryson in Voprosy Antrop., 24, 151−155, (Rus-
              sian).
1963C.   Notice nécrologique sur Bernhard Peyer, Correspondant pour la Section
              de Géologie. C. R. Acad. Sci. Paris, 257, 4087−4089.
1963D.   Des premiers Vertébrés à l'Homme. Paris: Albin Michel (Coll. Sci.
              d'aujourd'bin), 212 pp., 59 figs.
              Rev.: Furon in Rev. Gén. Sci., 71, 127; Khrisanfova in Voprosy An-
              trop., 21, 192, (Russian); Montalenti in Scientia, 101, 285, 289;
              Vaufrey in L'Anthrop., 69, 104.
1964A.   La Grotte de Regourdon (Dordogne). Paléontologie humaine. (Suite).
              Ann. Pal., Vert., 50, 155−194, figs. 12−32, (cont. from Piveteau,
              1963A.).
1964B.   Le Père Teilhard de Chardin, savant. Paris: Fayard, Collection Bilan de
              la Science, no. 11, 142 pp., (not seen).
              Rev.: M. C. in Fossilia, 1965:3−4, 53−54; Vaufrey in L'Anthrop., 69,
              303−304.
1964C.   (ed.) Traité de paléontologie. Tome IV, vol. 1. L'origine des vertébrés, leur
              expansion dans les eaux douces et le milieu marin. Vertébrés (gén-
              éralités). Agnathes. Paris: Masson, 387 pp., 201 figs., 19 in color.
              Rev.: Anon. in C. R. Soc. Géol. France, 1965, 24; Anon. in La Nature,
              93, 368; M. C. in Fossilia, 1965:3−4, 54−55; Chaline in Rev.

Questions Sci., <u>28</u>, 281; Furon in Rev. Gén. Sci., <u>72</u>, 157—158;
Gortani in Scientia, <u>101</u>, 280; Romer in Quart. Rev. Biol., <u>41</u>,
205—206; Rossi Ronchetti in Riv. Ital. Pal., <u>71</u>, 978; Westphal
in Zbl. Geol. Pal., Teil 2, <u>1965</u>, 212.

1964D.   Caractères généraux des vertébrés. In: Piveteau; Traité de Paléo. 1964C.,
<u>4</u>:1, 25—35, 6 figs.

1964E.   Classification des vertébrés. In: Piveteau; Traité de Paléo., 1964C., <u>4</u>:1,
36—45, 1 fig.

1964F.   Les découvertes d'Oldoway (Tanganyika) et le problème des origines
humaines. La Nature, <u>92</u>, 457—462, 10 figs.

1965   La paleontologie humaine de Charente. Bull. Assoc. Franç. Étude Quat.,
<u>1965</u>:3—4, 177—183, 3 figs., (German summary).

1966A.   La Grotte de Regourdou (Dordogne). Paléontologie humaine. (Suite.)
Ann. Pal., Vert., <u>52</u>:2, 163—194, figs. 33—52, (cont. from Piveteau,
1964A.).

1966B.   Traité de paléontologie. Tome IV, vol. 3. Actinoptérygiens, Crossoptéry-
giens, Dipneustes. Paris: Masson, 442 pp., 357 figs., 11 pls.
Rev.: M. C. in Fossilia, <u>1965</u>:5—6, 61; Furon in Rev. Gén. Sci., <u>73</u>,
189—190; Romer in Quart. Rev. Biol., <u>41</u>, 310—311; Rossi
Ronchetti in Riv. Ital. Pal., <u>72</u>, 875; van Voorthuysen in Geol.
en Mijn., <u>45</u>, 453; Westphal in Zbl. Geol. Pal., Teil 2, <u>1966</u>, 289.

1966C.   Raymond Vaufrey... Quaternaria, <u>8</u>, 319.

1967A.   Un pariétal humain de la Grotte du Lazaret (Alpes-Maritimes). Ann. Pal.,
Vert., <u>53</u>, 165—199, 19 figs., 2 tables.

1967B.   La définition de l'homme et la paléontologie. L'Ann. Biol., <u>6</u>, 551—556.

1968   Quelques aspects de la paléontologie humaine depuis la mort du Père
Teilhard. In: Chardin, et al., <u>1968</u>, 68—76.
See: Lavocat 1966.

PIXA, HANNES   See: Hofstätter and Pixa.

PLA BALLESTER, ENRIQUE
1965   El abate Breuil y Valencia. In: Ripoll Perelló, E., (ed.), 1965B, 281—286,
(French summary).

PLANE, MICHAEL DUDLEY
1965   Late Tertiary lake deposits and a mammal fauna from New Guinea. Geol.
Soc. Amer. Cordilleran Sect.. Pal. Soc., Pac. Coast Sect., Prog. 61st
Ann. Meeting, <u>1965</u>, 43, (abs.).

1966   Late Tertiary lake deposits and a mammal fauna from New Guinea. Spec.
Pap. Geol. Soc. Amer., <u>87</u>, 223, (abs.).

1967A.   Two new diprotodontids from the Pliocene Otibanda formation, New
Guinea. Bull. Australian Bur. Min. Res., no. <u>85</u>, 105—128, 8 figs.,
2 tables.

1967B.   The stratigraphy and vertebrate fauna of the Otibanda formation, New
Guinea. Bull. Australian Bur. Min. Res., no. <u>86</u>, 1—64, 15 figs.,
6 pls.

1967C.   A new vertebrate fauna from the tertiary of the Northern Territory. 39th
Congr., ANZAAS, Melbourne, <u>1967</u>, Sec. C, p. K8, (abs.).
See: Stirton, Woodburne and Plane.

PLANE, M. D., and GATEHOUSE, C. G.
   1968   A new vertebrate fauna from the Tertiary of Northern Australia. Austral. Jour. Sci., 30, 272–273, 1 fig.

PLANQUAERT, J.
   1962   Sous les taillis de l'Enclus. Arch., Publ. Cercle Recherch. Préhist. Renaisis, 3, 19–20, (not seen).

PLATE, ROBERT
   1964   The dinosaur hunters: Othniel C. Marsh and Edward D. Cope. New York: MacKay, vi +281 pp.
           Rev.: Imbrie in Nat. Hist., 73:9, 10.

PLATEL, R.
   1967   Contribution 'a l'étude du nucleus olfactorius anterieor des reptiles. Colloq. Internat. Cent. Nation. Recherch. Sci., 163, 441–451, 2 figs., 2 pls., (English summary).

PLATZ, HOWARD, and PLATZ, K.
   1967   "Quigley points" (A new variety?). Mo. Archaeol. Soc. Newsletter, no. 208, 8–10, illustr.

PLAYFORD, G.   See: Hill, D., et al.

PLAZIAT, JEAN-CLAUDE
   1964   Pistes d'oiseaux et remaniements synsédimentaires dans le Lutétien du détroit de Carcassonne (Aude). C. R. Soc. Géol. France, 1964, 149, (abs.).
   1965   Pistes d'oiseaux et remaniements synsédimentaires dans le Lutétian du détroit de Carcassone (Aude). Bull. Soc. Géol. France, 6, 289–293, 2 figs., 1 text pl.
           Abs.: Kuhn in Zbl. Geol. Pal., Teil 2, 1966, 313.

PLEDGE, N. S.
   1967   Fossil elasmobranch teeth of South Australia and their stratigraphic distribution. Trans. Roy. Soc. S. Australia, 91, 135–160, 6 figs., 4 pls., 1 table.

PLEINER, R.   See: Soudský and Pleiner.

PLOEY, JAN DE
   1965   Position géomorphologique, génèse et chronologie de certains dépôts superficiels au Congo occidental. Quaternaria, 7, 131–154, 17 figs., (English and German summaries).

PLOEY, J. DE and MOORSEL, H. van
   1963   Contributions 'a la connaissance chronologique et paléogéographique des gisements préhistoriques des environs de Léopoldville. Studia Univ. "Lovanium", Fac. Sc., no. 19, (not seen).
   1966   Chronologie préhistorique des environs de Léopoldville. Actas V Congr. Panafr. Prehist. Estud. Cuaternario, 1963:2, 219–224, 3 figs., 1 pl.

PLUMSTEAD, EDNA P.
   1966   Congresses on Gondwanaland and drifting continents. S. African Jour. Sci., 62, 185–186.

PLUS, BERTRAND   See: Lapparent, LeJoncour, et al.

POBEDINA, B. M.
1954   Abs.: Weiler in Zbl. Geol. Pal., Teil 2, 1966, 286.

POEL, HILDA van de   See: Twiesselmann and Poel.

POHLE, HERMANN
1966   Knochenartefakte aus dem Rixdorfer Horizont. Berliner Jahrb. Vor-
              und Frühgesch., 6, 85—87, 1 pl.

POIRIER, MAX   See: Russell, D. E., Louis and Poirier.

POKATILOV, A. G.
1966A.   [Complexes of small mammals of Transbaĭkalian Pliocene and Quaternary
              deposits.] Geol. i Geof., 1966:8, 65—73, (Russian; English sum-
              mary).
1966B.   [Fossil remains of "micromammalia" from Neogene and Anthropogene of
              Transbaĭkalia.] In: Saks, (ed.), 1966, 340—343, (Russian).
              See: Erbaeva and Pokatilov; Yerbayeva and Pokatilov.

POKORNÝ, VLADIMÍR
1965   Principles of zoological micropalaeontology. Vol. 2. Translated by K.
              A. Allen. Edited by J. W. Neale. Oxford, London, Edinburgh,
              New York, Paris, Frankfurt: Pergamon Press ix + 465 pp., 1077
              figs.
              Rev.: Rhodes in Quart. Rev. Biol., 54.

POKROVSKAĬĀ, I. M. (ed.)
1954   [Contributions to palynology and stratigraphy.] Moscow: Gosgeoltekhiz-
              dat Press, Coletanea, Trudy VSEGEI, 202 pp., illustr., (Russian).
              See: Boĭsova and Pokrovskaĭā; Ganeshin, Zubakov, et al; Gromov, V. I.,
              Griāznov, et al.

POLACH, H. A., and GOLSON, J.
1966   Collection of specimens for radiocarbon dating and interpretation of re-
              sults. Manual Austral. Inst. Aboriginal Studies, no. 2, 42 pp., 3
              tables.
              Rev.: Barker in Man, Jour. Roy. Anthrop. Inst., 2, 469;   Clark in
              Proc. Prehist. Soc. Cambridge, 33, 467—468;   Jansen in Man-
              kind, 6:11, 604;   Jones in Archaeol., Phys. Anthropol. Oceania,
              3:2, 159—160.

POLACH, H. A., STIPP, J. J., GOLSON, J., and LOVERING, J. F.
1967   ANU radiocarbon date list 1. [Australian National University.]   Radio-
              carbon, 9, 15—27.

POLGÁR, LADISLAUS
1965   Internationale Teilhard-Bibliographie 1955—1965. Freiburg/Br.—München:
              Karl Alber, 94 pp., (not seen).
              Rev.: Gieseler in Anthropol. Anz., 31:1—2, 111;   Schaeuble in Zeit
              Morph. Anthrop., 59, 218.

POLGAR, STEVEN
1964   Evolution and the ills of mankind. In: Tax (ed.), 1964, 200—211.

POLIAKOVA, L. M.   See: Cherdyntsev, Strashnikov, et al.

POLIANSKIĬ, V. I., and POLIANSKIĬ, IŬ. I., (eds.)
1966   [History of evolution doctrines in biology.] Moscow: "Nauka" Press,
            324 pp., 43 figs., portrs., (Russian).

POLIKARPOVICH, K. M.
1955   [A new Mousterian find on the territory of Belorussia.] Krat. Soob.
            Inst. Arkheol. Akad. Nauk URSR., 4, 161−162, (Russian).
1957   [The problem of Mousterian culture in Upper Dnepr region.] Trudy
            Inst. Istorii AN BSSR, 1, 30−44, (Russian).

POLUBOTKO, I. V.   See: Ochev and Polubotko.

POMEROL, CHARLES   See: Ginsburg, Montenat and Pomerol.

PONIKAROV, V P.   See: Krasheninnikov and Ponikarov.

POOLE, D. F. G.
1967   Phylogeny of tooth tissues: enameloid and enamel in Recent vertebrates,
            with a note on the history of cementum. In: Miles, A. E. W.,
            (ed.), 111−149, 40 figs.
            See: Miles, A. E. W. and Poole.

POPESCU, ADRIAN   See: Apostal and Popescu.

POPESCU, DORIN
1963   Les fouilles archéologiques dans la République Populaire Roumaine en
            1962. Dacia, 7, 569−587, 1 map.

POPOV, A. I.
1959   [The Taĭmyr mammoth and the problem of preservation of mammoth
            fauna remains in the Quaternary deposits of Siberia.] In: Markov
            and Popov, Ice Age in the European section of the USSR and
            in Siberia, 259−275, 5 figs., (Russian).

POPOV, IŬ. N.
1947A.   [On present glaciation of North-East Asia in connection with the pro-
            blem of ancient glaciation.] Izv. Geogr. Obshch., 79, 280−288,
            (Russian).
1947B.   [Find of a fossil bison in permafrost.] Priroda, 1947:8, 68, (Russian).
1948   [New finds of Pleistocene mummified animals in Northeastern USSR.]
            Priroda, 1948:3, 75−76, 1 fig., (Russian).
1956   [Finds of fossil animals in permafrost areas.] Priroda, 1956:9, 40−48,
            6 figs., (Russian).

POPOV, I. V., (ed. in-chief)
1962   [Materials of the scientific conference for the study of karst.] Moscow:
            Akad. Nauk Press., 3 vols., (Russian).

POPOV, V. V.
1960   [Stratigraphy of the Anthropogene of Tian'-Shan'.] Trudy Geol. Inst.,
            26, 116−126, 1 table, (Russian).

POPOVA, T. A.   See: Grigor'eva, et al.

POPOVA, T. A., and FIRSHSTEIN, B. V.
1965   The exhibition "The Origin of Man and the Development of Primitive
          Society" at the Anthropological and Ethnographical Museum of
          the Academy of Sciences of the USSR. Anthrop., 2:3, 76–83,
          6 figs., (Russian and English).

PORSHNEV, B. F.
1958   [The problem of the origin of human society and human culture.]
          Vest. Ist. Mir. Kult., 1958:2, 25–44, (Russian; English summary).

PORTA, JAIME DE
1960   Rev.: Parodi Bustos in Rev. Fac. Cien. Nat. Salta, 1:3, 88.
1965   Nota preliminar sobre la fauna de vertebrados hallada en Curití (De-
          partamento de Santander, Colombia). Bol. Geol., Univ. Ind.
          Santander, S. A., 19, 111–114, 2 figs.

PORTER, STEPHEN C.
1964   Antiquity of man at Anaktuvuk Pass, Alaska. Amer. Antiq., 29, 493–
          496, 2 figs.

PORTMANN, ADOLF
1961   La imagen de la naturaleza y la fe cristiana: el caso Teilhard de Chardin.
          Bol. Univ. Chile, no. 26, 38–43.
1965A.   Vom Ursprung des Menschen. Ein Querschnitt durch die Forschungs-
          ergebnisse. 5th rev. ed. Illustr. by S. Bousani-Baur. Basel:
          Verlag Friedrich Reinhardt, 66 pp., (not seen).
          Rev.: Kurth in Kosmos (Stuttgart), 62, *277;   Preuschoft in Umschau,
          66:12, xvii.
1965B.   Einführung in die vergleichende Morphologie der Wirbeltiere. 3rd ed.
          Basel, Stuttgart: Schwabe, 344 pp., 271 figs.
          Rev.: Bauer in Mitt. Anthrop. Ges. Wien, 95, 357;   Preuschoft in
          Anthrop. Anz., 28, 149–150;   Schaueble in Zeit. Morph. Anthrop.,
          57, 317–318;   Scherf in Naturwiss. Rund, 19, 77–78;   Ulrich
          in Homo, 18:1, 63.
1965C.   Der Pfeil des Humanen. Über P. Teilhard de Chardin. 6th ed. Freiburg
          and München: Karl Alber, 61 pp.
1966   Prof. Dr. Joseph Kälin (Fribourg). 1903–1965. Bull. Schweiz. Ges.
          Anthrop. Ethnol., 42, 37–38.
1967   Sobre las restricciones de la lucha mortal y sobre la conservación de la
          especie en los animales. Bol. Univ. Chile, 76–77, 20–24.

PORTMANN, J.-P.
1962   Louis Agassiz, pionnier de la glacialogie. Ann. Guébhard, 38, 239–248,
          1 pl.

PÖRTNER, RUDOLF
1961   Rev.: Bleich in Mitt. Verband Deutschen Höhlen- und Karstforscher,
          München, 8, 53–54.

POSIN, DANIEL Q.
1961   What is a dinosaur? Illustrated by Maidi Wiebe. Chicago: Benefic
          Press, 48 pp., color illustr., (pre- and elemen. school).

POSNANSKY, MERRICK
1962   Recent Paleolithic discoveries in Uganda. Proc. 4th Panafrican Congr.
          Prehist., sec. 3, 207–214, 1 fig., 1 pl., 1 table.

1966   (ed.) Prelude to East African history: a collection of papers given at the first East African vacation school in pre-European African history and archaeology in Dec. 1962. London, Ibadan, Nairobi: Oxford Univ. Press, xi + 186 pp., 10 figs., 18 pls., 2 tables, 5 maps.
Rev.: Fagan in Man, Jour. Roy. Anthrop. Inst., 2, 311; Lewis in Amer. Anthrop., 70, 155—156.

POSTUPAL'SKAĨA, M., and ARDASHNIKOVA, S.
1963   [Obruchev.] Moscow: Ser. "Zhizn' zamechatel'nykh liŭdeĩ", "Molodaĩa Gvardiĩa" Press, 430 pp., illustr., (Russian).

POTAPOV, L. P., (ed.)
1955   [History of Ĩakutian ASSR.] Moscow-Leningrad: Akad. Nauk SSSR Press, (Russian).
1964   [The history of Tuva: Vol. I.] Moscow: "Nauka" Press, 410 pp., illustr., (Russian).
See: Levin, M. G. and Potapov.

POTOĨSKIĨ, S. P.
1962   [Traces of the most ancient man in Moscow according to latest data.] Biŭll. Mosk. Obshch. Ispyt. Prirody, Otd. Geol., 37:6, 148—149, (Russian).

POTTER, MARTHA A.
1964   Some Paleo-Indian artifacts from Miami County, Ohio. Ohio Archaeol., 14, 8—10, 5 figs., errata pg. 65.
See: Baby and Potter.

POTTER, STEPHEN R.
1968   A report on some Paleo-Indian projectile points from Virginia and nearby States. Quart. Bull. Archeol. Soc. Virginia, 23, 11—19, 9 figs.

POULAIN-JOSIEN, THÉRÈSE
1960   Étude de la faune provenant d'un dépotoir de la Tène à Larena-Chatelans (Isere). Rhodiana, 36, 51—63, (not seen).

POULSON, THOMAS L. See: Mohr, C. E. and Poulson.

POURADE, RICHARD F., (ed.)
1966   Ancient hunters of the Far West. San Diego: Copley Press, 208 pp., illustr., some in color.
Rev.: Anon. in Desert Mag., 30:1, 4; Anon. in Southwestern Lore, 32, 89; Cornwall in Man, Jour. Roy. Anthrop. Inst., 2, 138; Moriarty in Amer. Antiq., 32, 548—549.

POVOLNY, DALIBOR
1966   The fauna of Central Europe: its origin and evolution. Syst. Zool., 15, 46—53.

POWELL, BERNARD W.
1967   Curvilinear designs on northeast paintstones: a second find. Chesopiean, 5, 131—134, 1 fig.

POWELL, JON S.
1968   Reptilian fossils and geology of uppermost Cretaceous deposits of the
             San Juan Basin, New Mexico. Program, 64th Ann. Meeting, Geol.
             Soc. Amer., 97, (abs.).

POWELL, T. G. E.
1966   Prehistoric art. London: Thames and Hudson, 284 pp., illustr.
             Rev.: Ashbee in Proc. Prehist. Soc. Cambridge, 33, 470–471;   Gruber
             in Archaeol., 21, 228–230;   Rudner in S. Afr. Archaeol. Bull.,
             22, 52;   Sandars in Antiq., 41, 76–77;   Thomas in Archaeol.
             Jour., 123, 227–228.

POWERS, RICHARD M.
1963   The cave dwellers in the Old Stone Age. Educ. consultant: Rosemary
             Daly. New York: Coward-McCann, 62 pp., illustr.
             Rev.: Sutton in GeoTimes, 9:5, 24.

PRADEL, LOUIS
1961C.   Place pour le Gravétien. Bull. Soc. Préhist., Paris, 57, 657.
1963C.   Les enseignements ethnographiques du Moustérien de Fontmaure. Bull.
             Soc. Amis Grand-Pressigny, 1–8, (not seen).
1964A.   Notation de coups de burin successifs sur une même pièce. Bull. Soc.
             Préhist. Franç., C. R. séances. mens., 1964:3, lxiv–lxv, 1 pl.
1964B.   Moustérien et Paléolithique supérieur à Vicq-Exemplet (Indre). Bull.
             Soc. Préhist. Franç., C. R. séances mens., 1964:5, cxvii–cxix, 2 figs.
1965A.   Burins "d'angle et plan" et le type du Raysse. Bull. Soc. Préhist. Franç.,
             C. R. séances mens., 1965:2, liv–lviii, 2 figs.
1965B.   Choix du materiau et destination de l'outil. Bull. Soc. Préhist. Franç.,
             C. R. séances mens., 1965:8, 275–276.
1965C.   L'outillage au Paléolithique. Caractères et méthodes d'étude quantitatives.
             Bull. Soc. Préhist. Franç., Étud. et Trav., 62:1, 3–21, 5 figs.
1965D.   L'abri aurignacien et périgordien des Roches, commune de Pouligny-
             Saint-Pierre (Indre). L'Anthrop., 69, 219–236, 9 figs., 3 tables.
1966A.   A propos du burin du Raysse. Bull. Soc. Préhist. Franç., C. R. séances
             mens., 63:2, 47–49, 1 fig.
1966B.   Pièces moustériennes à bord fracturé et aminci. Bull. Soc. Préhist.
             Franç., C. R. séances mens., 63, 112–116, 2 figs.
1966C.   La station paléolithique de Fontmaure vient de disparaître. Bull. Soc.
             Préhist. Franç., C. R. séances mens., 63, 293.
1966D.   Classification des burins avec notation chiffrée. Bull. Soc. Préhist.
             Franç., Étud. et Trav., 63:3, 485–500, 3 figs., 2 tables.
1966E.   Transition from Mousterian to Perigordian: skeletal and industrial.
             Comments. Current Antrop., 7, 33–50, 2 + 1 figs.
1966F.   Quelques précisions sur la pointe moustérienne et la pointe des Cottés.
             L'Anthrop., 70:5–6, 602–605.
1967   La grotte des Cottés, commune de Saint-Pierre-de Maillé (Vienne);
             Moustérien-Périgordien-Aurignacien. Datation par le radiocarbone.
             L'Anthrop., 71:3–4, 271–277, 1 fig.

PRADEL, L., and J. H.
1966   La station paléolithique du Raysse, commune de Brive (Corrèze).
             L'Anthrop., 70:3–4, 225–254, 11 figs., 3 tables.
             Abs.: Anon. in Anthropos, 61, 893–894.
1967   L'abri solutréen de Monthaud, commune de Chalais (Indre). L'Anthrop.,
             71:1–2, 49–74, 10 figs., 4 tables.

PRAHL, EARL J.
1966   The Muskegon River survey: 1965 and 1966. In: Fitting, James E.,
               (ed.), 1966D, 183—209, 4 figs.

PRASAD, K. N.
1961A.   Fossil primates from Siwaliks. Indian Min., 15, 295, (abs.).
1961B.   Fossil primates from Haritalyangar, Himachal Pradesh, India. Indian
               Min., 15, 436, (abs.).
1962B.   Fossil primates from Haritalyangar, Himachal Pradesh, India. Indian
               Min., 16, 73—74.
1963A.   Middle Siwalik fauna from Haritalyangar, Bilaspur district, Himachal
               Pradesh. Indian Min., 16, 305, (abs.).
1963B.   Fossil anthropoids from the Siwalik beds of Haritalyangar, Himachal
               Pradesh. Indian Min., 16, 425, (abs.).
1963C.   The fossil Carnivora from the Haritalyangar area, Himachal Pradesh,
               India. Indian Min., 17, 95.
1964A.   Miocene vertebrates from Cutch District, Gujarat, India. Bull. Geol.
               Soc. India, 1:2, 9—12, 2 figs.
1964B.   Upper Miocene anthropoids from the Siwalik beds of Haritalyangar,
               Himachal Pradesh, India. Palaeont., 7, 124—134, pl. 20, 2 tables.

PRASAD, K. N., and RAY, D. K.
1964   The classification of the Siwalik system and nomenclature. Rept. 22nd
               Internat. Geol. Congr., 1964, 123, (abs.).

PRASAD, K. N., and SATSANGI, P. P.
1962   Fossil hoof of a bovid from the Nagri beds of Haritalyangar. Indian
               Min., 16, 180.
1963A.   Fossil tragulids from Nagri beds of Haritalyangar. Indian Min., 16, 307—
               308, (abs.).
1963B.   A note on the mandible of Hexaprotodon sivalensis from the Siwaliks
               of Punjab. Indian Min., 16, 308, (abs.).
1963C.   On a new species of chelonian from the Siwalik beds of Himachal
               Pradesh. Indian Min., 16, 424—425.

PRASAD, K. N., and SINGH, V. P.
1963   Fossil Proboscidea from the Siwalik beds of Haritalyangar, Himachal
               Pradesh. Indian Min., 17, 194.

PRASAD, K. N., and VERMA, K. K.
1967   Occurrence of dinosaurian remains from the Lameta Beds of Umrer,
               Nagpur district, Maharashtra. Current Sci. (India), 36:20, 547—548.

PRASLOV, N. D.
1963   [Paleolithic station Iugino in Azov region.] Sov. Arkheol., 1963:3,
               218—220, 1 fig., (Russian).
1964A.   [Field-work on Paleolithic relics in the Azev and Kuban' region in
               1963.] Krat. Soob. Inst. Ist. Mat. Kult. SSSR, 101, 74—76, (Rus-
               sian).
1964B.   [Gimelin site at Kostenki.] Krat. Soob. Inst. Ist. Mat. Kult. SSSR, 97,
               59—63, 2 figs., (Russian).
1964C.   [Paleolithic relics of the Lower Don and north-eastern cis-Azov region
               and their stratigraphic significance.] Biull. Kom. Izuch. Chetvert.
               Perioda Akad. Nauk SSSR, no. 29, 51—66, 5 figs., (Russian).
1967A.   [Search of Paleolithic in the Volga-Don interfluve.] Biull. Kom. Izuch.
               Chetvert. Perioda, 34, 120—126, 4 figs., (Russian).

1967B.   [Paleolithic finds in eastern Crimea.]   In: Rybakov, (ed.), 1967, 185–
187, 1 fig., (Russian).
See: Boriskovskiĭ and Praslov;   Ivanova and Praslov.

PRASLOV, N. D., and FILIPPOV, A. K.
1967   [First find of Paleolithic art in South Russian steppes.]   Krat. Soob.
Inst. Arkheol. Akad. Nauk SSSR, 111, 24–30, 3 figs., (Russian).

PRAT, FRANÇOIS
1956   Le grand équidé des brèches ossifères de Montoussé (Hautes Pyrénées).
Proces-Verbaux, Soc. Linn. Bordeaux, 96, 83–94, 3 figs.
1964   Contribution à la classification des Équidés villafranchiens.   Procès-Verbaux, Soc. Linn. Bordeaux, 101, 14–32, 2 pls., 3 tables.
1966A.   Les équidés.   In: Lavocat, R., (ed.), 1966, 194–215, figs. 55–56, pls.
10–17, table 14.
1966B.   Les capridés.   In: Lavocat, R., (ed.), 1966, 278–322, figs. 61–63, pls.
48–66, table 18.
1966C.   Les antilopes.   In: Lavocat, R., (ed.), 1966, 323–336, fig. 64, pls.
67–68.
See: Bordes and Prat;   David, P. and Prat.

PRAUS, ALEXIS A.
1964   Bibliography of Michigan archaeology.   Anthrop. Papers, Univ. Mich.,
no. 22, iv + 77 pp.
Rev.: Hays in Mich. Archaeol., 10, 44.

PREBLE, J. W., JR.
1967   Early elephant hunters.   Ohio Archaeol., 17, 101–102.

PREDTECHENSKIĬ, N. N.
1958   [Main stratigraphic features of Devonian deposits of Tuva.]   Informatsionnyĭ Sbornik, 5, 19–27, 1 fig., (Russian).
1967   [Stratigraphy of Devonian deposits of Tuva and Western Saĭan.]   Trudy
Vses. n.-i. geol. Inst., nov. ser., 120, 34–61, 5 figs., (Russian).
See: Krasnov, V. I. and Predtechenskiĭ.

PRENANT, ANDRÉ   See: Elhaï and Prenant.

PRESLEY, JAMES   See: Scopes and Presley.

PRESTON, ROBERT E.
1966   Turtles of the Gilliland faunule from the Pleistocene of Knox County,
Texas. Papers Mich. Acad. Sci., 51, 221–239, 6 figs., 1 pl.,
3 tables.

PREUSCHOFT, HOLGER
1961   Pliopithecus, ein Menschenaffe aus dem europäischen Tertiär.   Umschau,
61, 179.

PRICĂJAN, A.   See: Litiănu, Pricăjan, et al.

PRICE, JAMES
1965   Fossil beds of the Calicos.   Desert Mag., 28:2, 10–11, 3 figs.

PRICE, LLEWELLYN IVOR
1959B.   Dentes de Theropoda num testemunho de sonda no Estado do Amazonas. An. Acad. Brasil. Ciên., 31, xiv.
1961   Sôbre os dinosáurios do Brasil. An. Acad. Brasil. Ciên., 33, xxviii–xxix.
1963   Sôbre o crânio de um grande crocodilídeo extinto do Alto Rio Juruá, Estado do Acre. An. Acad. Brasil. Ciên., 35, xxvi, (abs.).
1964   Sôbre o crânio de um grande crocodilídeo extinto do Alto Rio Juruá, Estado do Acre. An. Acad. Brasil. Ciên., 36, 59–66, 1 fig., (English summary).
    Abs.: Huene in Zbl. Geol. Pal., Teil 2, 1965, 251–252.
    See: Stovall, Price and Romer.

PRICE, P. B.   See: Fleischer, Leakey, Price and Walker.

PRIKHOD'KO, ÎU. N.
1962   [Conditions of burial of Lower Permian vertebrates' skin in the Intinskiĭ coal deposit.] Izv. Komi Fil. Vses. Geogr. Obshch., 7, 115–119, 1 fig., (Russian).

PRINGLE, J. W. S.
1965   (ed.) Essays on physiological evolution. Oxford, London, etc.: Pergamon Press.
    Rev.: Pollitzer in Amer. Jour. Phys. Anthrop., 25, 188–190.
1967   Journal for taxonomists. Nature, 215, 332.

PRITCHARD, DAPHNE H.   See: Callow, Baker and Pritchard.

PRITCHARD, JAMES G.
1964   Quail Spring Paleo occupation site Princess Anne County, Virginia. Chesopiean, 2:3, 60–61, illustr.

PROKOPEC, M., and PAŘIZKOVÁ, J.
1965   Der 7. Internationale Kongress der Anthropologischen und Ethnologischen Wissenschaften in Moskau 1964 (Physische Anthropologie). Anthrop., 2:3, 83–88.

PROSHEK, FRANTIŠEK (=Prošek)
1959   [New type of Paleolithic hearth from Shanov-Kout II station near Gostim village.] Sov. Arkheol., 1959:1, 243–245, 2 figs., (Russian).

PROST, J. H., (ed.)
1964   Readings on human evolution. New York: Selected Academic Readings, College Division, articles separately paged, illustr.
    See: Dart 1964A; Simons 1964C.

PROSTOV, EUGENE V.   See: Beregovaîa, et al.; Guliamov 1966.

PROT, EMILE, and COUSTÉ, R.
1961   Bâton percé et aiguilles du gisement de Vidon (commune de Juillac, Gironde). Bull. Soc. Préhist., Paris, 57, 672–674, 1 fig.

PROTSCH, REINER   See: Leakey, Protsch and Berger.

PRUFER, OLAF H.
   1962C.   Survey of Ohio fluted points. No. 7. Cleveland, Ohio: Cleveland
                 Museum of Natural History, 10 pp., illustr.
   1962D.   Survey of Ohio fluted points. No. 8. Cleveland, Ohio: Cleveland
                 Museum of Natural History, 15 pp., illustr.
   1963B.   Ice Age overkill. Explorer, 5:6, 7–13, illustr.
   1963C.   Survey of Ohio fluted points. No. 9. Cleveland, Ohio: Cleveland
                 Museum of Natural History, 15 pp., illustr.
   1964A.   Pleistocene megafauna extinctions: the human factor. Abs. 63rd. Ann.
                 Meeting Amer. Anthrop. Assoc., 1964, 48–49, (abs.).
   1964B.   Survey of Ohio fluted points. No. 10. Cleveland, Ohio: Cleveland
                 Museum of Natural History, 24 pp., illustr.
   1964C.   The Ross County point, a comment. Tenn. Archaeol., 20, 80–81.
   1966   The Mud Valley site: a Late Palaeo-Indian locality in Holmes County,
                 Ohio. Ohio Jour. Sci., 66, 68–75, 4 figs.

PRUFER, O. H., and BABY, R. S.
   1963   Rev.: Bryan in Man, 65, 169–170;   Kinsey in Penn. Archaeol., 33,
                 196, 198.

PRUFER, O. H., and MUNRO, E. C.
   1961   Survey of Ohio fluted points. No. 5. Cleveland, Ohio: Cleveland
                 Museum of Natural History, 15 pp., illustr.

PRUFER, O. H., and SOFSKY, C.
   1965   The McKibben Site (33 TR-57), Trumbull County, Ohio: a contribu-
                 tion to the Late Paleo-Indian and Archaic phases of Ohio. Mich.
                 Archaeol., 11, 9–40, 5 figs.

PRUVOST, PIERRE
   1965   Sur l'attribution du prix Gaudry à M. Paul Fourmarier. [Fourmarier's
                 reply.]   C. R. Soc. Géol. France, 1965, 186–189.

PUISSEGUR, J.-J.
   1962   Les mollusques et leur signification climatique dans le gisement paléo-
                 lithique de Genay (Côte-d'Or). Bull. Sci. Bourgogne, 21, 159–
                 170, pl. 4, 2 tables.

PULIANOS, A. N.
   1963   [New Paleolithic finds in Greece.]   Sov. Arkheol., 1963:2, 227–229,
                 2 figs., (Russian).
   1965   [The place of Petralonian among Paleoanthropoids.]   Sov. Etnog.,
                 1965:2, 91–99, 5 figs., 1 table, (Russian; English summary).

PURI, HARBANS S., and VERNON, R. O.
   1964   Summary of the geology of Florida and a guidebook to the classic
                 exposures. Spec. Publ., Fla. Geol. Surv., no. 5, 1–175, 37 +
                 36 figs., 11 pls.

PUT', A. L.
   1952   [Find of a lophodont mastodon in the environs of Krivoĭ Rog.]   Zbirn.
                 Prafs Zool. Mus. Akad. Nauk URSR, 25, 84–86, 2 figs., (Uk-
                 rainian; Russian summary).

PUT', A. L., and KAPELIST, K. V.
1961   [A fauna of fossil Mammalia from the Malo-Kachnovoskogo quarry in
            the vicinity of Kremenchuga.]   Zbirn. Prats' Zool. Muz. Akad.
            Nauk URSR, 30, 130–133, 1 fig., (Ukrainian; Russian summary).

PUTNAM, WILLIAM C.
1964   Geology. New York: Oxford Univ. Press, xiv + 480 pp., illustr.
            Rev.: Snyder in GeoTimes, 8:8, 30.

PUTSCHAR, WALTER G. J.
1966   Problems in the pathology and palaeopathology of bone. Discussion
            by H. L. Jaffe, L. C. Johnson, and H. Hamperl. In: Jarcho,
            S., (ed.), 1966, 57–83, 2 figs.

PYCRAFT, WILLIAM P.
1912   The beasts of pre-historic Britain. Chatterbox, 1912, 116–118, 165–
            166, 212–214, 251–252, 283–285, 333–334, 363–364, 403–
            404, illustr.

PYDDOKE, EDWARD
1961   Rev.: Atkinson in Archaeol. Jour., 119, 362–363;   Deacon in S. Afr.
            Archaeol. Bull., 18, 184;   Rajguru in Bull. Deccan Coll. Res.
            Inst., 23, 106–107.
1963   (ed.) The scientist and archaeology. London: Phoenix House; New
            York: Roy, 208 pp., 32 figs., 24 pls.
            Rev.: Aitken in Antiq. Jour., 45, 144;   Anon. in Discovery, 25:3,
            46;   Bimson in New Sci., 22, 112;   Bisset in Mus. Jour., Lon-
            don, 64, 170–171;   [Filip] in Archeol. Roz., 16, 450, (Czech);
            Wailes in Man, 65, 199–200.

QI, TAO   See: Wu, et al.

QUENSTEDT, WERNER
1963   Rev.: Häntzschell in Zbl. Geol. Pal., Teil 2, 1964, 8.

QUERNER, JUTTA   See: Stebbins 1968.

QUIMBY, GEORGE I.
1952   The archeology of the upper Great Lakes area. In: Griffin, J. B.,
            (ed.), 1952A, 99–107.
1960   Rev.: Bushnell in Antiq., 35, 168–169.

QUINET, GUY-ELIE
1964A.   Morphologie dentaire des mammifères éocènes de Dormaal. Bull. Group-
            ement Internat. Recherch. Sci. Stomatol., 7, 272–294, 7 figs.,
            (English and German summaries).
1964B.   Plioplatecarpus (Dollo, 1882), animal plongeur des grandes profondeurs?
            Bull. Inst. Royal Sci. Nat. Belg., 40:7, 29 pp., 3 figs.
1965A.   Un condylarthre de Hoogbutsel. Bull. Inst. Roy. Sci. Nat. Belg., 41:15,
            1–5, 1 pl.
1965B.   Myotis misonnei n. sp. Chiroptère de l'Oligocène de Hoogbutsel. Bull.
            Inst. Royal Sci. Nat. Belge, 41:20, 11 pp., 1 pl.

1966A.   Teilhardina belgica, ancêtre des Anthropoidea de l'ancien monde. Bull.
              Inst. Royal Sci. Nat. Belg., 42:1, 14 pp., 1 pl.
1966B.   Le gradient morphogénétique responsable de la formule dentaire mamma-
              lienne. Bull. Inst. Royal Sci. Nat. Belg., 42:2, 13 pp., 1 pl.
1966C.   Le mesiostylide generateur du mesioconide chez eutheriens. Bull. Inst.
              Royal Sci. Nat. Belg., 42:3, 7 pp., 1 pl.

QUINET, G. E., and MISONNE, X.
1965   Les insectivores zalambdodontes de l'Oligocène inférieur Belge. Bull. Inst.
              Royal. Sci. Nat. Belge, 41:19, 15 pp., 2 pls.
1967   Les Marsupiaux de Hoogbutsel et de Hoeleden. Bull. Inst. Royal Sci. Nat.
              Belg., 43:2, 1–26, 2 figs., 3 pls., 2 tables.

R., A.
1967   Peut-on connaître la température des vertebrés fossiles? Atomes, 249,
              742–743, 2 figs.

R., R.
1956   Necrologi: Carlo Petrocchi. Boll. Soc. Geog. Ital., 93, 37.

RAAB, M.
1963   Abs.: Weiler in Zbl. Geol. Pal., Teil 2, 1965, 232–233.

RAAF, J. F. M. DE, BEETS, C., and KORTENBOUT VAN DER SLUIJS, G.
1965   Lower Oligocene bird-tracks from Northern Spain. Nature, 207, 146–148,
              1 fig.
              Abs.: Kuhn in Zbl. Geol. Pal., Teil 2, 1966, 314.

RABIELA DE GORTANI, RAQUEL   See: Boiteau 1964.

RABITZ, ALBRECHT
1966   Der marine Katharina-Horizont (Basis des Westfal B) im Ruhrrevier und
              seine Fauna. Fortschr. Geol. Rheinland u. Westfalen, 13:1, 125–194,
              40 figs., 9 pls., 5 tables, (French and English summaries).
              See: Malzahn and Rabitz.

RACHITSKIĬ, V. I.
1958   [Correlation of Tatarian deposits of the Russian Platform with corresponding
              deposits of other parts of the USSR and of foreign countries.] Izv.
              Vyssh. Uch. Zav., Geol. i Razv., 1958:3, 46–56, 1 table, (Russian).
1960   [Lower Triassic of Kuĭbyshev-Orenburg Trans-Volga region, and its relation
              to Tatarian stage.] Izv. Vyssh. Uch. Zav., Geol. i Razv., 1960:6, 23–
              27, 1 fig., (Russian).

RADE, J.
1964   Upper Devonian fish from the Mt. Jack area, New South Wales, Australia.
              Jour. Pal., 38, 929–932, pl. 149.

RADFORD, RICHARD D.   See: Cambron and Radford.

RADINSKY, LEONARD B.
1964A.   Paleomoropus, a new early Eocene chalicothere (Mammalia, Perissodactyla),
              and a revision of Eocene chalicotheres. Amer. Mus. Novit., no. 2179,
              28 pp., 3 figs.

1964B.   Notes on Eocene and Oligocene fossil localities in Inner Mongolia. Amer.
          Mus. Novit., no. 2180, 11 pp., 2 figs.
1965A.   Early Tertiary Tapiroidea of Asia. Bull. Amer. Mus. Nat. Hist., 129, 185–
          263, 41 figs., 4 pls.
1965B.   Evolution of the tapiroid skeleton from Heptodon to Tapirus. Bull. Mus.
          Comp. Zool., 134, 69–106, 23 figs., 3 pls.
1966A.   The adaptive radiation of the phenacodontid condylarths and the origin of
          the Perissodactyla. Evolution, 20, 408–417, 5 figs.
1966B.   The families of the Rhinocerotoidea (Mammalia, Perissodactyla). Jour.
          Mammal., 47, 631–639, 3 figs.
1966C.   Pataecops, new name for Pataecus Radinsky, 1965. Jour. Pal., 40, 222.
1966D.   A new genus of Early Eocene tapiroid (Mammalia, Perissodactyla). Jour.
          Pal., 40, 740–742, 1 fig.
1967A.   Hyrachyus, Chasmotherium, and the early evolution of helaletid tapiroids.
          Amer. Mus. Novit. 2313, 23 pp., 4 figs., 5 tables.
1967B.   A review of the rhinocerotoid family Hyracodontidae (Perissodactyl). Bull.
          Amer. Mus. Nat. Hist., 136, 1–46, 25 figs., 1 pl., 6 figs.
1967C.   Relative brain size: a new measure. Science, 155, 836–837, 1 fig., 1 table.

RADISCH, JINDŘICH, and ŽEBERA, K.
1964   Zpráva o geologickém mapování a výzkumu na listech Mělník a Lužec nad
          Vltavou. Zprávy Geol. Výzkumech Roce, 1, 305–307.

RADLEY, J.
1964   Late Upper Palaeolithic and Mesolithic surface sites in South Yorkshire.
          Trans. Hunter Archaeol. Soc., 9:1, (not seen).

RADMILLI, ANTONIO MARIO
1959B.   Apprenti di preistoria Marsicana: gli scavi nella grotta La Punta – Territorio
          del Fuceno. Atti. Soc. Tosc. Sci. Nat., Mem., ser. A, 66:2, 422–432,
          1 fig.
1962   Rev.: Dessulemoustier in Die Höhle, 14, 24–25.
1963C.   La preistoria d'Italia alla luce delle ultime scoperte. Firenze: Istituto Geo-
          grafico Militare, 364 pp., illustr., (not seen).
          Rev.: Pinna in Boll. Soc. Geog. Ital., ser. 9, 4, 645–647.
1963D.   Le prime età dell'uomo – popoli e civiltà. Illustr. by Savina Amodeo.
          Firenze: Sansoni, 142 pp., illustr., (not seen).
          Rev.: Grottanelli in Riv. Antrop., 50, 315–316.
1964   Il paleolitico superiore nel riparo Maurizio. Contributo per una datazione
          del detrito di falda nel Fucino. Atti Soc. Toscana Sci. Nat. Mem.,
          Ser. A, 70, 220–243, 12 figs., (English summary).
1965   Conca Peligna (Prov. di Chieti). Riv. Sci. Preist., 19, 299.
          See: Demangeot and Radmilli; Grifoni and Radmilli; Piscopo and Rad-
          milli.

RADMILLI, A. M., et al.
1964   Scoperte e scavi in Italia durante il 1963 Paleolitico. Riv. Sci. Preist., 18,
          307–316;

RADOVSKIĬ, M. I.
1963   [The first Russian woman paleontologist.] Priroda, 1963:5, 88–89, portr.,
          (Russian).

RADULESCO, COSTIN   See: Dumitresco, et al.; Feru, Rădulesco and Samson; Alimen,
          Rădulesco and Samson; Ghenea and Rădulesco; Samson and Rădulesco.

RĂDULESCO, C., and KOVÁCS, A.
1966   [Contribution to the knowledge of fossil mammalian fauna from Baraolt
        Basin (Braşov depression).] Lucrările Inst. Spel. "Emil Racovita",
        Bucureşti, 5, 233–250, illustr., tables, (Rumanian; French summary).

RĂDULESCO, C., and SAMSON, P.
1959   Abs.: Ebers in Zbl. Geol. Pal., Teil 2, 1962, 578.
1962A. Abs.; Dietrich in Zbl. Geol. Pal., Teil 2, 1964, 206.
1965   Sur la présence de Hydruntinus hydruntinus (Regàlia) en Roumanie. Qua-
        ternaria, 7, 219–234, 5 figs., 5 tables, (Italian and English summaries).
1967A. Sur un nouveau cerf mégacérin du Pléistocène moyen de la dépression de
        Brasov (Roumanie). Geol. Romana, 6, 317–344, 4 figs., 3 pls., 3
        tables, (English summary).
1967B. Sur la signification de certains Equidés du Pléistocène inférieur et moyen de
        Roumanie. Neues Jahrb. Geol. Pal., Abh., 127:2, 157–178, 3 figs.,
        6 tables.
1967C. Contributions à la connaissance du complexe faunique de Măluşteni–Bereşti
        (Pléistocène inférieur), Roumanie. I. Ord. Lagomorpha, Fam. Leopo-
        ridae. Neues Jahrb. Geol. Pal., Monatsh., 1967:9, 544–563, 3 figs.,
        2 tables.
        Rev.: Fahlbusch in Zbl. Geol. Pal., Teil 2, 1969:3, 295–296.

RĂDULESCO, C., SAMSON, P., MIHĂILĂ, N., and KOVÁCS, AL.
1965   Contributions à la connaissance des faunes de mammifères pleistocènes de
        la Dépression de Brasov (Roumanie). Eiszeit. u. Gegenwart, 16,
        132–188, 17 figs., 9 tables, (German and English summaries).

RĂDULESCO, C., and SAMSON, P.-M.
1967   Observations sur les Castoridés du Villafranchien inférieur de Roumanie.
        C. R. Acad. Sci. Paris, Sci. Nat., 265, 591–594, 2 figs.

RADWANSKI, ANDRZEJ
1965   A contribution to the knowledge of Miocene Elasmobranchii from Pińczów,
        (Poland). Acta Pal. Polonica, 10, 267–276, 2 pls., 1 table, (Polish
        and Russian summaries).
        Abs.: Weiler in Zbl. Geol. Pal., Teil 2, 1966, 287.

RAEVSKIĬ, E. I. See: Gromov, V. I., Ivanova, et al.

RAFALOVICH, I. A., and KETRARU, N. A.
1966   [From the history of Moldavian archeology and local lore.] Problemy geo-
        grafii Moldavii, 1, 93–111, (Russian).

RAFIEV, A. See: Loskutov, et al.

RAFTER, B. B. See: Breuil and Lantier.

RAGHUNATH, S. N.
1966   Late Stone Age sites near Madurai and Pudukkottai (Madras State). E.
        Anthrop., 19, 81–84, 1 fig.

RAGOZIN, L. A., (ed.)
1960   [A collection of materials on the geology of the Krasnoiarsk region.] Mos-
        cow: Universitet. Geologicheskiĭ fakultet. 1960. 186 pp., 26 figs.,
        20 plates (Russian).

RAINEY, FROELICH
1965   J. Louis Giddings (1909-1964). Amer. Anthrop., 67, 1503–1507, portr.

RAINEY, F., and RALPH, E. K.
1966   Archeology and its new technology. Science, 153, 1481–1491, 8 figs., 1
            table.

RAJCHEL, ZBIGNIEW
1965   Reconstruction of the skull of a woman from Steinheim. Przeglad Anthrop.,
            31, 275–284, 9 figs., 2 tables, (French and English summaries).

RAKOV, N. V.
1963   [Possible causes in variation of number of saigas in Crimean Paleolithic.]
            Prirodn. Obstan. i Fauny Proshl., 1, 147–151, (Russian).

RAKOVEC, IVAN
1963   Abs.: Rakovee in Bull. Sci., Zagreb, Sec. A, 10, 200.
1965A.   [Zygolophodon turicensis (Schinz) aus Kraljevci NW Jugoslawien.]   Acta
            Geol., Zagreb., 5, 61–72, 1 pl., 1 table, (Serbo-Croatian; German summary).
            Rev.: Kochansky-Devide in Zbl. Geol. Pal., Teil 2, 1969:1, 54.
            Abs.: M. S. in Bull. Sci., Zagreb., Sec. A., 11:4–6, 147.
1965B.   Pleistocene mammalian fauna from Risovača near Arandjelovac (Serbia).
            Razpr. Slovenska Akad. Ljubljana, 8, 223–317, 7 pls., 31 tables, (Eng-
            lish summary).
            Abs.: Rakovec in Bull. Sci., Zagreb., Sect. A, 11, 24.

RAKOVETS, O. A., and SHMIDT, G. A.
1963   [About Quaternary glacial periods of Mountain Altai.] Trudy Kom. Chet.
            Perioda, 22, 5–31, 7 figs., 1 chart, (Russian).

RALPH, ELIZABETH K.   See: Rainey and Ralph; Stuckenrath, Coe and Ralph.

RAMENDO, L.
1963A.   Le site 51. (Collection préhistoriques du C.R.A.P.E.) Libyca, 9–10, 81–101,
            10 figs., 2 tables.
1963A.   Les galets aménagés de Reggan (Sahara). Libyca, 11, 43–73, 17 figs., 4
            tables.
1964   Note sur un galet aménagé de Reggan. Libyca, 12, 43–45, 2 figs.
1965   Les industries préhistorique de Djidjelli-site ouest. Libyca 13, 29–58, 14
            figs., 4 tables.

RAMISHVILI, R. M.   See: Bugianashvili, et al.

RAMPLIN, MORGAN
1967   The Glacial Lake Agassiz survey, 1966. Plains Anthrop., 12, 220–221, (abs.).

RANALDI, FRANCESCO
1966   Unique prehistoric cave art found in Italian mountains. Illustr. London News,
            248:6598, 27, illustr.

RAND, AUSTIN L.
1967   Ornithology. An introduction. New York: Norton, 311 pp., illustr., (World
            Naturalist series).
            Rev.: Friedmann in Science, 159, 617–618.

RANDAL, J. M., and SCOTT, G. H.
    1967   Linnaean nomenclature: an aid to data processing. Syst. Zool., 16, 278–281.

RANDALL, ARTHUR G.
    1966   Geologic dating of selected archaeological sites in the Rocky Mountain re-
                  gion. Wyo. Archaeol., 9:4, 13–22, 3 figs., 1 table.

RANEY, A. H.
    1963   The Conard Fissure. Arkansas Amateur, 2:10, 5–6.

RANKAMA, KALERVO, (ed.)
    1965   The geologic systems. The Quaternary. Vol. 1. New York, London, Sidney:
                  John Wiley, xxii +300 pp., illustr.
              Rev.: Fink in Mitt. Geol. Ges. Wien, 58, 288–290; de Jong in Geol.
                  en Mijn., 44, 264; G. F. M. in Liverpool and Manchester Geol.
                  Jour., 5, vii–viii; Péwé in GeoTimes, 10:7, 35–36; Porter in
                  Amer. Jour. Sci., 265, 71–72.
    1967   The Quaternary. Vol. 2. The Quaternary of the British Isles, France, Germany,
                  and The Netherlands. New York, London, Sydney: Interscience (Wiley),
                  viii + 477 pp., 117 figs.;
              Rev.: Elhai in Rev. Géogr. Phys. Géol. Dyn., 11:2, 237–239;
                  Lundquist in Geol. Fören. Förh., 90, 136; Tanner in Jour.
                  Geol., 76:6, 726; Wiggers in Geol. en Mijn., 47, 221;
                  Wright in Science, 160, 868–869.

RANOV, V. A.
    1956   [Results of Stone Age research in 1955. (Hissar ridge and Kaĭrak-Kum).]
                  Trudy Akad. Nauk Tadzhik. SSR, 63, 17–25, 3 figs., (Russian).
    1958   [Stone Age findings in Alaĭ valley.] Trudy Inst. Istorii Kirg. SSR, 4, 103–
                  110, 3 figs., (Russian).
    1959A.   [Results of Stone Age research in 1956. (Shor-Kul' and eastern Pamir).]
                  Trudy Akad. Nauk Tadzhik. SSR, 91:4, 23–37, 5 figs., (Russian).
    1959B.   [Results of Stone Age research in 1957. (Lower Vakhsh R. and eastern
                  Pamir).] Trudy Akad. Nauk Tadzhik. SSR, 103:5, 21–42, 6 figs.,
                  (Russian).
    1961A.   [On the correlation of archeological data with the stratigraphy of Quaternary
                  deposits of Tadzhikistan.] Izv. Akad. Nauk Tadzhik. SSR, otd. Obshch.
                  Nauk, 1961:1(24), 89–109, 1 fig., 3 tables, (Russian; Tadzhik sum-
                  mary).
    1961B.   [Archeological explorations on Kara-Bura upland in 1959.] Trudy Akad.
                  Nauk Tadzhik. SSR, Inst. Istorii, 31, 16–29, 7 figs., (Russian).
    1962   [Two new Stone Age relics in South Tadzhikistan.] Trudy Akad. Nauk Tad-
                  zhik. SSR, 34, 130–138, 3 figs., (Russian).
    1964   [Results of prospecting for Stone Age remains in East Pamir (1956–1958).]
                  Mat. Issled. Arkheol. SSSR, 124, 7–50, 23 figs., 2 tables (Russian).
    1965   [Main problems in the study of Paleolithic of Middle Asia.] In: Saks, (ed.),
                  1965, 393–406, 2 tables, (Russian).
    1966   [Pebble tools and their role in Central Asia Paleolithic.] In: Rybakov,
                  (ed.), 1966, 3–4, (Russian).
    1967   [New works on Stone Age in West Pakistan.] Voprosy Antrop., 25, 140–146,
                  (Russian).
    1968A.   [On the possibility of distinguishing local cultures in the Paleolithic of Cen-
                  tral Asia.] Izv. Akad. Nauk Tadzhik. SSR, otd. obshch. nauk, 1968:3
                  (53), 3–11, (Russian; Tadzhik summary).
    1968B.   [Some remarks on S. P. Gupta's article "A review of the present state of An-
                  cient Indian archeology in the light of new discoveries in the Middle

Asia".] Sovetskaia Etnografiia, <u>1968</u>:4, 114–117, (Russian).
See: Guliamova, <u>et al</u>; Kostenko, N. P., Nesmeianov and Ranov;
Krylkov and Ranov; Litvinskii, Okladnikov and Ranov; Luzgin and
Ranov; Nesmeianov and Ranov; Okladnikov and Ranov; Zadneprov-
skii and Ranov.

RANSOM, JAY ELLIS
1964   Fossils in America. New York, Evanston, and London: Harper and Row,
        xii +402 pp., illustr.
        Rev.: Anon. in GeoTimes, <u>9</u>:1, 24; Anon. in Mineralogist, <u>32</u>:3, 39–40;
        Burden in Pac. Discovery, <u>18</u>:2, 32; Huston in Frontiers, <u>29</u>, 94;
        Kier in Science, <u>144</u>, 671; Richardson in Quart. Rev. Biol., <u>40</u>, 378.

RAO, C. NAGESWARA, and SHAH, S. C.
1963   On the occurrence of Pterosaur from the Kota–Maleri beds of Chanda dis-
        trict, Maharashtra. Rec. Geol. Surv. India, <u>92</u>:2, 315–318.

RAO, C. R. NARAYAN, and SESHACHAR, B. R.
1927   A short note on certain fossils taken in the Ariyalur area (S. India). Half-Year.
        Jour. Mysore Univ., <u>1</u>, 144–152, 9 figs.

RAO, M. S. NAGARAJA
1964   Archaeological remains of the Dharwar District – a review. Jour. Asiatic
        Soc. Bombay, <u>38</u>, 154–164, 4 figs., 7 pls., 1 map.

RAPPAPORT, RHODA
1964   Problems and sources in the history of geology, 1749–1810. Hist. Sci., <u>3</u>,
        60–78.

RASETTI, FRANCO
1965   Photography of fossils. In: Kummel and Raup, (eds.), 1965, 423–430.

RASMUSSEN, DONALD L.   See: Cuffey, Johnson and Rasmussen.

RASTSVETAEV, L. M.   See: Birman, <u>et al.</u>

RAT, PIERRE
1960   Empreintes fossilisées. Bull. Sci. Bourgogne, <u>19</u>, 10–11, (abs.).
1965   La succession stratigraphique des mammifères dans l'Eocène du bassin de
        Paris. C. R. Soc. Géol. France, <u>1965</u>, 88.
1966   La succession stratigraphique des mammifères dans l'Eocène du bassin de
        Paris. Bull. Soc. Géol. France, <u>7</u>, 248–256, pl. 3, 1 table.

RATAJ, J.
1960   Neue Installation im Museum in Benátsky nad Jizerou. Archeol. Roz., <u>12</u>,
        758–759, (Czech; German summary).

RATCLIFF, J. D.
1965   How man began. Reader's Digest, <u>Oct. 1965</u>, 129–133, illustr.

RATEKHIN, E. O.
1966   [Find of a rhinoceros in the Pliocene deposits of Southwestern Crimea.]
        Visnik Kiivs'k. Univ., ser. geol. geogr., <u>7</u>, 16–18, 2 figs., 1 table,
        (Ukrainian; Russian summary).

RATKEVICH, RON
    1968   New Mexico ["shovel-jawed" mastodon] . Rocks and Minerals, 43, 56, 1 fig.

RÄTZEL, WILHELM
    1964A.   Die Verhaltensweisen des Rentiers in der Kunst des Magdalenien. Bonner
                  Jahrb., suppl. 10:1, 50—67, 5 figs., 1 pl.
    1964B.   Die Verhaltensweisen des Rentiers in der Kunst des Magdaléniens. In: Uslar
                  and Narr, (eds.), 1964, 50—67, 5 figs.
    1965   Bemerkungen über einige Capriden-Darstellungen in der palä̈olithischen Kunst.
                  In: Ripoll Perelló, E., (ed.), 1965B., 287—295, 7 figs., (Spanish sum-
                  mary).

RAUNICH, LEO
    1961   L'evoluzione nel regno animale. In: Leonardi, 1961, 70—91, with discussion.

RAUP, DAVID   See: Kummel and Raup.

RAUP, HUGH M.   See: Johnson, F., and Raup.

RAUSHENBAKH, V. M.
    1967   [In memoriam Aleksandr Iakovlevich Briŭsov.] Sov. Arkheol., 1967:2, 117—
                  119, portr., (Russian).

RAUTENBACH, G. B.
    1967   A Late Stone Age shelter in the Clarens District, O. F. S. S. Afr. Archaeol.
                  Bull., 21, 183—186, 3 figs.

RAVDONIKAS, V. I.
    1940   [Archeological relics of western part of Karelo—Finnish SSR.] Krat. Soob.
                  Inst. Ist. Mat. Kult. SSSR, 7, 11—21, 2 figs., (Russian).

RAVICH, M. G.   See: Markov, G., Ravich and Vakar.

RAVIELLI, ANTHONY
    1965   Elephants, the last of the land giants. New York: Parents' Mag. Press, 45
                  unnumbered pp., color illustr., (juv.).

RAVIKOVICH, A. I.   See: Tikhomirov, V. V. and Ravikovich.

RAVOUX, GEORGES
    1966   La grotte magdalénienne de la Roque (Hérault). (Fouilles Gimon). Bull. Soc.
                  Préhist. Franç., Étud. et Trav., 63:2, 239—250, 7 figs.

RAVOUX, G., and BAZILE, F.
    1964   La station moustérienne du moulin de Lautier à Calvisson, Gard. Bull. Soc.
                  Préhist. Franç., C. R. séances mens., 1964:1, XIII—XVI, 2 pls.
    1965   La station moustérienne du pied de l'oppidum à Nages (Gard). Bull. Soc.
                  Préhist. Franç., C. R. séances mens., 1965:4, CXXXVIII—CXL, 2 figs.

RAVSKIĬ, É. I.
    1960   [Concerning the stratigraphy of Quaternary (Anthropogene) deposits of the
                  south and east of the Siberian platform.] Trudy Geol. Inst., 26, 37—
                  95, 20 figs., 1 chart, (Russian).
    1961   [Periglacial phenomena and periglacial zones of Eastern Siberian Pleistocene.]
                  In: Gromov, V. I., et al., (eds.), 1961, 141—151, 3 figs., (Russian; Englis

summary).

See: Alekseev, M. N., Ravskiǐ, and Tseitlin; Gromov, V. I., et al.; Nikiforova, K. V., Ravskiǐ and Deviatkin.

RAVSKIǏ, E., I., ALEXANDROVA, L. P., VANGENGEIM, E. A., GERBOVA, V. G., and GOLUBEVA, L. V.
1964   [Anthropogene deposits in the south of eastern Siberia.]   Trudy Geol. Inst.
            105, 280 pp., 73 figs., 29 tables, (Russian).

RAVSKIǏ, E. I., and TSEITLIN, S. M.
1965A.   [Geology of Enisei Paleolithic.] In: Bader, et al., (eds.), 1965, 200–228,
            12 figs., 1 table, (Russian).
1965B.   [Geological periodization of Siberian Paleolithic.] In: Saks, (ed.), 1965,
            387–392, 1 table, (Russian).

RAY, CLAYTON E.
1961   The monk seal in Florida. Jour. Mammal. 42, 113.
1964A.   A new capromyid rodent from the Quaternary of Hispaniola. Breviora, no.
            203, 4 pp., 1 fig.
1964B.   The taxonomic status of Heptaxodon and dental ontogeny in Elasmodontomys
            and Amblyrhiza (Rodentia: Caviomorpha). Bull Mus. Comp. Zool.
            Harvard., 131, 109–127, 2 figs.
1964C.   A small assemblage of vertebrate fossils from Spring Bay, Barbados. Jour.
            Barbados Mus. Hist. Soc., 31, 11–22, 3 figs.
1964D.   The jaguarundi in the Quaternary of Florida. Jour. Mammal, 45, 330–332,
            1 fig., 1 table.
1964E.   Tapirus copei in the Pleistocene of Florida. Quart. Jour. Florida Acad. Sci.,
            27, 59–66, 1 fig., 2 tables.
1965A.   An assemblage of Pleistocene vertebrates and mollusks from Bartow County,
            Georgia. Bull. Georgia Acad. Sci., 23, 67, (abs.).
1965B.   A new chipmunk, Tamias aristus, from the Pleistocene of Georgia. Jour.
            Pal., 39, 1016–1022, 1 fig., 2 tables.
1965C.   The relationships of Quemisia gravis (Rodentia: ?Heptaxodontidae). Smithson.
            Misc. Coll., 149:3, 12 pp., 2 figs., 1 pl.
1965D.   A glyptodont from South Carolina. Charleston, Mus. Leaflet, no. 27, 3–12,
            4 pls., 1 table.
1966A.   The identity of Bison appalachicolus. Not. Nat. Acad. Nat. Sci. Phila., no.
            384, 1–7, 2 figs.
1966B.   The status of Bootherium brazosis. Pearce-Sellards Ser. no. 5, 7 pp., 2 figs.
1967   Pleistocene mammals from Ladds, Bartow County, Georgia. Bull. Georgia
            Acad. Sci., 25, 120–150, 5 figs., 9 tables.
            See: Hooijer and Ray; Lipps, L. and Ray; Yerbayeva and Pokatilov.

RAY, C. E., COOPER, B. N., and BENNINGHOFF, W. S.
1967   Fossil mammals and pollen in a Late Pleistocene deposit at Saltville, Virginia. Jour. Pal., 41, 608–622, 4 figs., pls. 65–66, 6 tables.

RAY, C. E., and LIPPS, L.
1965   An assemblage of Pleistocene vertebrates and mollusks from Bartow County,
            Georgia. Bull. Georgia Acad. Sci., 23, 67, (abs.).

RAY, D. E. See: Hibbard, Ray, et al.

RAY, D. K. See: Prasad and Ray.

RAY, LOUIS L.   See: Schultz, C. B., Tanner, et al.

RAZNIT͡SYN, V. A.
    1966   [On some features of Mesozoic sediments of Timan and adjacent region.]
                      In: Chalyshev, (ed.), 97–104, 2 figs., 1 table, (Russian).

RAZUMOVA, V. N., and CHERNI͡AKHOVSKIĬ, A. G.
    1964   [Mesozoic and Tertiary sediments of Karatau Range in southern Kazakhstan.]
                      Bi͡ull. Mosk. Obshch. Ispyt. Prirody, Otd. Geol., 39:1, 88–108, 6 figs.,
                      map, 4 tables, (Russian).

REBER, GROTE
    1965   Aboriginal carbon dates from Tasmania. Mankind, 6:6, 264–268.

REDFIELD, ALDEN
    1962   Progress report on the archaeological survey for preceramic sites in the alluvial
                      valley of the Mississippi River. Arkansas Archeologist, 3, 11–12.

REED, ALMA M.
    1966   The ancient past of Mexico. New York: Crown, xii +388 pp., illustr.
                      Rev.: Kubler in Nat. Hist., 75:7, 10.

REED, CHARLES A.
    1962   Shimon Angress: March 14, 1924-March 30, 1958. In: Angress and Reed,
                      1962, 5–7.
    1965   A human frontal bone from the Late Pleistocene of the Kom Ombo Plain,
                      Upper Egypt. Man, 65:95, 101–104, 3 figs.
    1966   The Yale University Prehistoric Expedition to Nubia, 1962–1965. Discovery,
                      Yale, 1:2, 16–23, 8 figs.
    1967   The generic allocation of the hominid species habilis as a problem in system-
                      atics. S. African Jour. Sci., 63, 3–5, 1 fig.
                      See: Angress and Reed; Turnbull, W. D. and Reed.

REED, C. A., and PALMER, H. A.
    1964   A Late Quaternary goat (Capra) in North America? Zeit. Säugetierk., 29,
                      372–378, 6 figs., (German summary).

REED, C. A., and SCHAFFER, W.
    1966   Evolutionary implications of cranial morphology in the sheep and goats
                      (Caprini, Simpson 1945). Amer. Zool., 6, 565, (abs.).

REED, C. A., and TURNBULL, W. D.
    1965   The mammalian genera Arctoryctes and Cryptoryctes from the Oligocene and
                      Miocene of North America. Fieldiana, Geol., 15:2, 95–170, 33 figs.,
                      4 tables.
                      Rev.: Hünermann in Zbl. Geol. Pal., Teil 2, 1967, 113.

REED, ERIK K.
    1964   The greater southwest. In: Jennings and Norbeck, (eds.), 1964, 175–191,
                      1 fig.
    1965   Human prehistory in southwestern New Mexico. Guidebk., New Mexico
                      Geol. Soc., 16th Field Confer., 1965, 228–229.

REEDER, W. G. See: Laughlin and Reeder.

REEKIE, GORDON
1964   Expositions, exhibits and today's museums. Nat. Hist., 73:6, 20–29,
            illustr.
            See: Colbert and Reekie.

REGÖLY-MÉREY, GY.
1962   Az ösemberi és késöbbi emberi maradványok rendszeres korbonctana
            [Systematic pathological anatomy of primitive and more recent
            human remains.] Budapest: Országos Orvostörténeti Könyvtár
            kiadása, (not seen).

REGTEREN ALTENA, CAREL OCTAVIUS VAN, and MÖCKEL, J. R.
1965   Mineralen en fossielen in Teyler's Museum. Haarlem: Teyler's Museum,
            37 pp., illustr., 2 maps, (not seen).
            Rev.: [Kruytzer] in Natuurhist. Maandbl., 55, 15–16; van Voorthuysen
            in Geol. en Mijn., 44, 465.

REICHEL-DOLMATOFF, GERARDO
1965   Colombia. Ancient peoples and places, no. 44. New York: Praeger,
            231 pp., 70 figs., 65 pls.
            Rev.: Bray in Antiq., 40, 155–156; Lathrap in Science, 152, 923–
            924; Meggers in Amer. Jour. Archaeol., 70, 307–308; Mendieta
            in Amer. Antiq., 32, 404–405.

REIFE, WINFRIED
1965   Das Alter der Sauerwasserkalke von Stuttgart-Münster-Bad Canstatt-
            Untertürkheim. Jahresb. Mitt. Oberrheim. Geol. Ver., 47, 111–
            134, 3 figs.

REIG, OSVALDO A.
1961C.   La paleontologia de vertebrados en la Argentina. Retrospeccion y pros-
            pectiva. Holmbergia, 6:17, 67–127, (English summary).
1964   El problema del origen monofilético o polifilético de los anfibios, con
            consideraciones sobre las relaciones entre anuros, urodelos y
            ápodos. Ameghiniana, 3, 191–211, (English summary).
            Abs.: Westphal in Zbl. Geol. Pal., Teil 2, 1965, 241–242.
1967   Archosaurian reptiles: a new hypothesis on their origins. Science, 157,
            565–568, 1 fig.

REĬMAN, V. M.
1958   [On geological terms "Anthropogene" and "Syneclise".] Izv. Akad.
            Nauk Tadzhik. SSR, Otd. Estestv. Nauk, 2 (26), 53–58, (Russian;
            Tadzhik summary).
1964   (ed.) [Paleontology of Tadzhikistan.] Dushanbe: Akad. Nauk Tadzhik
            SSR Press, 143 pp., 14 figs., 26 plates, 25 tables, (Russian;
            Tadzhik summaries).

REIMER, ROGER D. See: Fitch and Reimer.

REIS, J.
1961   Lições da vida de Darwin. Anhembi, 43, 181–186.

REMANE, ADOLF
1962   Abs.: Kuhn-Schnyder in Zbl. Geol. Pal., Teil 2, 1964, 226.
1963   Zur Metamerie, Metamerismen und Metamerisation bei Wirbeltieren.
            Zool. Anz., 170:11–12, 489–502, 3 figs. (Discussion: Riedl, Starck).

1964A.   Zum Problem der Radiationen. Zool. Anz., 173, 92—95.
1964B.   Das Problem Monophylie-Polyphylie mit besonderer Berucksichtigung
                  der Phylogenie der Tetrapoden. With comments by J. Kalin.
                  Zool. Anz., 173, 22—51, 6 figs.
1965   Die Geschichte der Menschenaffen. In: Heberer, (ed.), 1965A, 249—309,
                  41 figs.
1967   Die Geschichte der Tiere. In: Heberer, (ed.), 1967A, 589—677, 27 figs.

REMY, JEAN ALBERT
1965   Un nouveau genre de paleotheride (Perissodactyla) de l'Eocene superieur
                  du Midi de la France. C. R. Acad. Sci. Paris, 260, 4362—4364,
                  1 fig.
             Rev.: M. C. in Fossilia, 1965:3—4, 49.
1967   Les Paleotheridae (Perissodactyla) de la faune de mammiferes de Fons 1
                  (Eocene superieur). Palaeovertebrata, 1, 1—46, 20 figs., 8 pls.,
                  12 tables, (German and English summaries).
             Rev.: Thenius in Zbl. Geol. Pal., Teil 2, 1970:3/4, 245.

REMY, J. A., and THALER, L.
1967   Une faune de vertebres de l'Oligocene Superieur dans les phosphorites
                  du groupe d'Uzes (Gard). C. R. Soc. Geol. France, 1967:4, 161—
                  163.
             Rev.: Fahlbusch in Zbl. Geol. Pal., Teil 2, 1968, 211—212.

RENGARTEN, N. V., and KONSTANTINOVA, N. A.
1965   [Role of facies-mineralogical analysis in the reconstruction of Anthropogen
                  climate. (On the example of southern Moldavia and south-western
                  Ukraine).] Trudy Geol. Inst., 137, 123 pp., 45 figs., 6 plates,
                  1 table (Russian).

RENSBERGER, JOHN M.
1964   Subdivisions of the John Day fauna: preliminary report. Program,
                  60th Ann. Meeting, Geol. Soc. Amer., Cordilleran Sect., 52—53,
                  (abs.).
1966   Evidence for the synonymy of Palustrimus and the gopher genus Entoptychus.
                  Program, 62nd Ann. Meeting, Geol. Soc. Amer., Cordilleran Sect.,
                  1966, 61, (abs.). Also: Spec. Pap. Geol. Soc. Amer., 101, 329—
                  330, (abs.).
             See: Stirton and Rensberger.

RENSBERGER, J. M., and BERRY, W. B. N.
1967   An automated system for retrieval of museum data. Curator, 10, 297—
                  317, 7 figs.

RENSCH, BERNHARD
1959B.   Rev.: Guinea in Bol. R. Soc. Espan. Hist. Nat., Sec. Biol., 59, 256.
1965   Homo sapiens. Vom Tier zum Halbgott. 2nd enlarged ed. Gottingen:
                  Vandenhoeck and Ruprecht, 224 pp., 1 map, illustr., (not seen).
             Rev.: Keiter in Homo, 16, 53.
1966   Evolution above the species level. 2nd edition. New York: Wiley,
                  Science Edition Paperback, (not seen).
             Rev.: Johnston in Amer. Jour. Phys. Anthrop., 25, 100—101.
1967   The evolution of brain achievements. In: Dobzhansky, et al., (eds.),
                  1967, 26—68, 5 figs., 2 tables.

RENZI, M. DE   See: Crusafont Pairo, Rosell, Golpe and Renzi.

REPENNING, CHARLES A.
1965A.   Palearctic-Nearctic mammalian dispersal during the Late Cenozoic. 7th Internat. Congr., Internat. Assoc. Quat. Res., Abs., 1965, 390, (abs.).
1965B.   An extinct shrew from the early Pleistocene of South Africa. Jour. Mammal., 46, 189–196, 3 figs.
1966   Santa Cruz area. In: Savage, D. E., (ed.) 1966A, 6 pp., cover illustr.
1967A.   Palearctic-Nearctic mammalian dispersal in the Late Cenozoic. In: Hopkins, D. M., (ed.), 1967D, 288–311, 9 tables.
1967B.   Miocene-Pliocene boundary correlations based upon vertebrate fossils. Program, 63rd Ann. Meeting, Geol. Soc. Amer., Cordilleran Sect., 1967, 58–59, (abs.). Also: Spec. Pap. Geol. Soc. Amer., 115, 349, (abs.).
1967C.   Subfamilies and genera of the Soricidae. U. S. Geol. Surv., Prof. Pap., 565, iv + 74 pp., 42 figs.
    Rev.: Fahlbusch in Zbl. Geol. Pal., Teil 2, 1968:6, 661–662.

REPENNING, C. A., HOPKINS, D. M., and RUBIN, M.
1964   Tundra rodents in a Late Pleistocene fauna from the Tofty placer district, central Alaska. Arctic, 17, 177–197, 7 figs., 1 table.

RESHETOV, IÚ. G.
1963   [Is it a man? (Lewis Leakey's findings in East Africa).] Priroda, 1963:4, 81–84, 1 fig., (Russian).
1964A.   [The find of Australopithecus bones in W. Africa.] Voprosy Antrop., 16, 139–140, (Russian).
1964B.   [Once more on "Prezinjanthropus" L. Leakey.] Voprosy Antrop., 16, 140–141, (Russian).
1965   [On a little known discovery of a fossil anthropoid in Turkey.] Voprosy Antrop., 20, 156–158, 1 table, (Russian).
1966   [The nature of the Earth and the origin of man.] Moscow: "Mysl'" Press, 274 pp., (Russian).
    Rev.: Uryson in Voprosy Antrop., 31, 175–178, (Russian); Uryson in Priroda, 1967:10, 122–123, (Russian).

REX GONZÁLEZ, ALBERTO
1959   Nuevas fechas de la cronología arqueológica argentina obtenidas por el método de radiocarbon. Cien. Invest., 15:6, (not seen).
1960   Rev.: Sacchero in An. Arqueol. Etnol., Univ. Nac. Cuyo, 17–18, 233–235.
1963   Cultural development in northwestern Argentina. Smithson. Misc. Coll., 146:1, 103–117.
1964   Las culturas paleoindias o paleolíticas sudamericanas: resumen y problemática actual. Proc. Internat. Congr. Americanists, Actas y Memorias 36th Congreso Internacional de Americanistas, España, 1964, 1, 15–41, 7 figs.

REX GONZÁLEZ, A., and LORANDI, A. M.
1959   Restos arqueológicos hallados en las orillas del Río Carcarañá, Provincia de Santa Fe. Rev. Inst. Antrop., Univ. Nacion. Litoral, Rosario, 1, 161–222, 44 figs.

REY, ROGER
1963   A propos d'une faune à Hipparion de l'Ouest de la France. Mém. Soc. Belge Géol. Pal. Hydrol., no. 6, 137–146, (not seen).

1964   Précisions stratigraphiques sur un gisement à Hipparion peu connu, du
              Massif Central. Cursillos y Confer. Inst. "Lucas Mallada", 9,
              183–185.

REYMENT, R. A.
1961   [Biostratigraphy of Cretaceous and Tertiary deposits of Nigeria and
              contiguous parts of Cameroon.] Biull. Mosk. Obshch. Ispyt.
              Prirody, Otd. Geol., 36:6, 26–36, 1 map, (Russian; English sum-
              mary).

REYMOND, J.
1964   Nouveaux gisements préhistoriques dans le Bugey. Bull. Soc. Linn. Lyon,
              33, 139–147, 2 figs.

REYNOLDS, ALBERT E.
1966   Two elephantine teeth from the Mill Creek drainage area. Proc. Indiana
              Acad. Sci., 75, 293–298, 3 figs.

REYNOLDS, G. M.   See: Dilks and Reynolds.

REYNOLDS, J.   See: Hawksley, Reynolds and McGowan.

REYNOLDS, VERNON
1966   Open groups in hominid evolution. Man, Jour. Roy. Anthrop. Inst., 1,
              441–452.
1967A.   Open groups in hominid evolution. Man, Jour. Roy. Anthrop. Inst., 2,
              302–303.
1967B.   The apes: their scientific and natural history. New York: Dutton, 296
              pp., illustr.
1967C.
1968   The apes: the gorilla, chimpanzee, orang-utan, and gibbon – their history
              and their world. New York: E. P. Dutton; London: Cassell,
              296 pp., 15 figs., 110 pls.
              Rev.: Tuttle in Amer. Anthrop., 70, 1239–1340;   Washburn in Man,
              Jour. Roy. Anthrop. Inst., 3, 661–662.

RHODES, FRANK HAROLD TREVOR
1966   The course of evolution. Proc. Geol. Assoc., London, 77, 1–53, 4 figs.

RHOZATSKII, L. I.   See: Birman, et al.

RIBA, ORIEL   See: Crusafont Pairo, Riba and Villena; Crusafont Pairo, Truyols
              Santonja and Riba.

RIBEIRO, O.   See: Breuil 1962B.

RICE, DALE W.
1967   Cetaceans. In: Anderson, S., and Jones, (eds.), 1967, 291–324, figs.
              45–50.

RICE, HARVEY
1967   University of Oregon: Museum of Natural History: its own story. Bull.,
              Mus. Nat. Hist., Univ. Oregon, 7, 16 pp., illustr.

RICH, T. HEWITT
1966 Second specimen of <u>Alzadasaurus pembertoni</u>. Program, 62nd Ann. Meeting, Geol. Soc. Amer., Cordilleran Sect., <u>1966</u>, 61–62, (abs.). Also: Spec. Pap. Geol. Soc. Amer., <u>101</u>, 330, (abs.).

RICHARD, LUCIEN
1961A. Restes de Mammifères pleistocènes trouvés recemment à Alicay (Eure). Rev. Soc. Sav. Haute-Normandie, Préhist.-Archéol., <u>22</u>, 7–9, (not seen).
1961B. Ossements d'equidé et de bovidé trouvés dans une briqueterie à Oissel (Seine-Marit.) Rev. Soc. Sav. Haute-Normandie, Préhist.-Archéol., <u>22</u>, 11–14, 1 fig., (not seen).

RICHARDS, A. M. See: Lane, E. A., and Richards.

RICHARDS, DARREL J.
1962 Paleo points. Totem Pole, <u>45</u>:3, 6 pp., illustr.

RICHARDS, HORACE G.
1953B. Georgia's geology and the life of its past. Bull. Georgia Acad. Sci., <u>11</u>:2, 26–31.
1966 Philadelphia's fossils. Dinosaurs in your backyard. Frontiers, <u>31</u>, 36–41, illustr.

RICHARDSON, PENELOPE, and DUDLEY, M.
1967 Social science research in New Guinea 1965. Current Anthrop., <u>8</u>, 424–440.

RICHE, JACQUES, and LILLE, O.
1962 Bibliographie marocaine 1952 - 1953. Hespéris Tamuda, <u>3</u>, 157–591.

RICHMOND, NEIL D.
1964 Fossil amphibians and reptiles of Frankstown Cave, Pennsylvania. Ann. Carnegie Mus., <u>36</u>, 225–228.
1965 Perhaps juvenile dinosaurs were always scarce. Jour. Pal., <u>39</u>, 503–505.

RICQLÈS, ARMAND DE
1967A. L'origine des dinosaures. Atomes, <u>242</u>, 258–260, 5 figs.
1967B. La paléontologie de Terrain: un bilan international. Atomes, <u>243</u>, 337–341, 10 figs.
1968A. Recherches paléohistologiques sur les os longs des Tétrapodes. I.-Origine du tissu osseux plexiforme des Dinosauriens Sauropodes. Ann. Pal., Vert., <u>54</u>:2, 133–145, 2 figs., 1 pl.
1968B. Quelques observations paléohistologiques sur le Dinosaurien Sauropode <u>Bothriospondylus</u>. Ann. Univ. Madagascar, <u>6</u>, 157–209, (not seen).
1968C. Ethiopie: la découverte du paraustralopithèque. Atomes, <u>251</u>, 125–126, 4 figs.
1968D. La phylogénie des Reptiles est remise en cause. Atomes, <u>253</u>, 253–255, 3 figs.
1968E. Les reptiles mammaliens d'Amérique du Sud et la dérive des continents. Atomes, <u>258</u>, 603–605, 5 figs.

RIDDELL, FRANCIS A., (ed.)
1967A. Current research. Amer. Antiq., <u>32</u>, 417–430.
1967B. Current research. Amer. Antiq., <u>32</u>, 560–574.

RIDE, WILLIAM DAVID LINDSAY
1964A.   A list of mammals described from Australia between the years 1933
           and 1963 (comprising newly proposed names and additions to
           the Australian faunal list). Bull. Austral. Mammal. Soc., no. 7:
           suppl., 1–15, (not seen).
1964B.   A review of Australian fossil marsupials. Jour. Roy. Soc. W. Australia,
           47:4, 97–131, 13 figs., 2 tables.
           See: Merrilees and Ride.

RIEDL, RUPERT, et al.
1963   Fauna und Flora der Adria. Hamburg and Berlin: Parey, 640 pp.,
           2590 figs., 2 pls., (not seen).
           Rev.: Zapfe in Verh. Geol. Bundesanst., 1964, 378–400.

RIEK, GUSTAV
1930   Ein neuer Höhlenschlupf des alt- und jungsteinzeitlichen Menschen am
           Papierfels bei Wiesensteig. Blätter Schwäbisch Albver., 42, 227–
           230, (not seen).
1931B.   Eine mittel- und jungpaläolithische Freilandstation am Randecker Maar.
           Nachrichtenblatt für Deutschen Vorzeit, 7, 175–176.
1932B.   Paläolithische Station mit Tierplastiken und menschlichen Skelettresten
           bei Stetten ob Lontal. Germania, 16, 1–8, 3 figs., 1 pl.
1932C.   Altsteinzeitliche Funde aus der Vogelherdhöhle bei Stetten ob Lontal.
           Schwäbische Mus., 8, 40–48, (not seen).
1933B.   Der Stand der paläolithischen Forschung in Württemberg. Korrespond-
           enzblatt Gesamtver. Deutch. Ges.- und Altertumsver., 81, 18–30.
1934   Altsteinzeitkulturen am Vogelherd bei Stetten ob Lontal (Württemberg).
           Ipek, 1932-33, 1–26, 2 pls.
1938A.   Feststellung des Hochsolutréen in Württemberg. Fortsch. u. Fortschr.,
           14, 147–148, 1 fig.
1938B.   Ein Beitrag zur Kenntnis des süddeutschen Solutréen. Germania, 22,
           147–150, pl. 28.
1938C.   Die Altsteinzeit und die Mittelsteinzeit im Kreis Heidenheim. Heiden-
           heimer Heimatbuch, 1938, 259–267, (not seen).
1962   Fundschau. Altsteinzeit. Fundber. Schwaben, 16, 199–200.
1964A.   Der Mensch zur Eiszeit bei Blaubeuren. Blätter Schwäbisch. Albver.,
           70, 78–79, (not seen).
1964B.   Spuren eiszeitlicher Rentierjäger in der Brillenhöhle bei Blaubeuren.
           Monatsschrift Baden-Württemberg, 6, 8–13, (not seen).

RIEL, STANLEY J.
1964   A new oreodont from the Cabbage Patch local fauna, western Montana.
           Postilla, no. 85, 10 pp., 2 figs., 2 pls., 1 table.

RIEMER, WILLIAM J., (ed.)
1963   et seq. Catalogue of American amphibians and reptiles. Amer. Soc.
           Ichthyologists and Herpetologists, loose-leaf sheets with distribu-
           tion maps.

RIESEN, T.   See: Oeschger and Riesen.

RIFKIND, KENNETH M.   See: Dumont and Rifkind.

RIGBY, J. KEITH, and CLARK, D. L.
1965   Casting and molding. In: Kummel and Raup, (eds.), 1965, 389–413,
           2 figs.

RIGGS, ELMER SAMUEL
1903D.   The use of pneumatic tools in the preparation of fossils. Science, n.s.
            17, 747—749, 1 fig.
1928   Work accomplished by the Field Museum Paleontological Expeditions
            to South America. Science, 67, 585—587.
1929   Koehring dragline encounters bones of mastodon. Pickups and Throw-
            overs, 5:10, (not seen).

RIKMAN, E. A.   See: Zelenchuk, Rikman and Smirnov.

RINGEADE, MICHEL   See: Cappetta, Ringeade and Thaler.

RINGOT, R.
1965   Vestiges lithiques de la période finale du Paléolithique moyen en Ardrésis
            (P.-de-C.). Bull. Soc. Préhist. Franç., Étud. et Trav., 62:1, 70—76,
            3 figs.

RINGUELET, RAUL A.
1961   Florentino Ameghino (1854 - 1911). Holmbergia, 6:17, 3—6, portr.

RIOULT, M.
1964   Victor Van Straelen (1889 - 1964). Bull. Soc. Linn. Normandie, ser.
            10, 5, 12—19.

RIOUMINE, A. V.
1961   Peintures pariétales de caverne du paléolithique récent dans l'Oural
            meridional. Archeol. Roz., 13, 712—732, figs. 247—258, (Rus-
            sian; French summary).

RIPINSKY, MICHAEL M.
1967   Taxonomic implications of immunochemical analysis with reference to
            the Hominidae. Mankind Quart., 7, 171—179, 1 table.

RIPLEY, S. DILLON
1965   The Smithsonian Institution: a great museum center. Mus. Jour.,
            London, 65, 89—97, figs. 21—25.

RIPLEY, S. D., and EDITORS OF LIFE
1964   The land and wild life of tropical Asia. New York: Time Inc., 200 pp.,
            illustr.
1967   The leaping of langurs: a problem in the study of locomotor adaptation.
            Amer. Jour. Phys. Anthrop., 26, 149—170, 12 figs.

RIPOLL PERELLÓ, EDUARDO
1962A.   Abate Henri Breuil (1877 - 1961). Ampurias, 24, 353—354, portr.
1962B.   La cronología relativa del "Santuario" de la cueva de La Pileta. Homenaje
            al profesor Cayetano de Mergelina, 739—751, 6 figs.
1963   Pinturas rupestres de la Gasulla (Castellón). Monog. de Arte Rupestre.
            Arte Levantino, no. 2, 60 pp., 34 figs., 35 pls., (not seen).
            Rev.: Llongueras Campaña in Ampurias, 28, 325—327;   H.-P. in Bol.
            Soc. Españ. Hist. Nat., Sec. Geol., 62, 273—274.
1964   (ed.) Miscelánea en homenaje al Abate Henri Breuil (1877 - 1961).
            Tomo I. Barcelona: Diputación Provincial de Barcelona, Instituto
            de Prehistoria y Arqueología, xix + 496 pp., illustr.
            Rev.: Beltrán in An. Antropol., Mexico, 4, 246—250; [Beltrán] in
            Caesaraugusta, 23—24, 151—154;   Kühn in IPEK, 22, 151;   Millot
            in Objets et Mondes, 5, 64.

1964B.   Vida y obra del Abate Henri Breuil, Padre de la Prehistoria. In: Ripoll
              Perelló, E., (ed.), 1964A, 1–69, 8 figs., 25 pls.
              Rev.: G. in Bol. Soc. Castell. Cult., 41, 199–200.
1964C.-
1965A.   Solutrense de tipo ibérico en Portugal. Ampurias, 26–27, 210–213.
1965B.   (ed.) Miscelánea en homenaje al Abate Henri Breuil (1877 - 1961).
              Tomo II. Barcelona: Diputación Provincial de Barcelona, Instituto
              de Prehistoria y Arqueología, xxiii + 450 pp., illustr.
              Rev.: Beltrán in An. Antropol., Mexico, 4, 246–250;   Clark in Proc.
              Prehist. Soc. Cambridge, 33, 466–467;   Millot in Objets et Mondes,
              5, 207;   Ripoll Perelló in Ampurias, 28, 269–280.
1965C.   Una pintura de tipo paleolítico en la sierra del Montsía (Tarragona) y
              su posible relación con los orígines del arte levantino. In: Ripoll
              Perelló, E., (ed.), 1965B, 297–305, 2 figs., 3 pls., (French summary).
1965D.   Une peinture de type paléolithique sur le litoral mediterranéen de Tar-
              ragone (Espagne). Riv. Sci. Preist., 19, 189–194, 3 figs.
              See: DeLaet 1960.

RIPOLL PERELLÓ, E., and LUMLEY, H. DE
1964-
1965   El Paleolítico medio en Cataluña. Ampurias, 26–27, 1–70, 51 figs.,
              2 pls.
              Rev.: Valoch in Archeol. Roz., 20, 260–261.

RIQUET, R.
1962   Les crânes d'Urtiaga en Iziar (Guipúscoa). Munibe, 14:1/2, 84–104,
              7 figs., 6 tables.

RISTO, GAREVSKI
1960   Neuer Fund von Mastodon in den Diatomeenschichten bei Barobo
              (Kavadarci) Mazedonien. Fragmenta Balcanica, 3:16, 133–144.

RITCHIE, ALEXANDER
1964   New light on the morphology of the Norwegian Anaspida. Norske
              Videns.-Akad. Oslo, Mat.-Nat. Kl., Skrifter, no. 14, 1–33, 3 figs.,
              6 pls.
1967   Ateleaspis tessellata Traquair, a non-cornuate cephalaspid from the
              Upper Silurian of Scotland. In: Patterson, C., and Greenwood,
              P. H., (eds.), 1967, 69–81, 3 figs., 4 pls.
1968   New evidence on Jamoytius Kerwoodi White, an important ostracoderm
              from the Silurian of Lanarkshire, Scotland. Palaeontol., 11,
              21–39, 2 figs., pls. 3–6.

RITCHIE, WILLIAM A.
1965   The archaeology of the State of New York. Garden City, N. Y.:
              Natural History Press, 379 pp., 12 figs., 113 pls.
              Rev.: Anon. in Chesopiean, 3:5, 124;   Bass in Amer. Jour. Phys.
              Anthrop., 24, 277–278;   Brennan, et al, in Bull. N. Y. State
              Archeol. Assoc., no. 36, 1–17;   Fitting in Mich. Archaeol.,
              12, 104–105;   Gould in Nat. Hist., 75:6, 59–60;   Griffin in
              Amer. Mid. Nat., 75, 251–252;   Johnston in Plains Anthrop.,
              12, 236–238;   Mayer-Oakes in Amer. Anthrop., 68:3, 811–
              813;   Spaulding in Science, 151, 677–678;   Wright in Amer.
              Antiq., 31, 749–750.
1966   Early Transatlantic contacts between the Old and New Worlds: fact
              or fiction? Proc. Internat. Congr. Americanists, 1, 107, (abs.).

RITZENTHALER, ROBERT
1966   The Kouba site: Paleo-Indians in Wisconsin. Wisc. Archeol., 171–187,
                16 figs.
1967A.   A probable Paleo-Indian site in Wisconsin. Amer. Antiq., 32, 227–229,
                4 figs.
1967B.   Prehistoric Indians of Wisconsin. Rev. ed. Milwaukee Public Museum,
                Popular Science Handbook Series No. 4, (not seen).
                Rev.: Anon. in Interamer., 14:8, 4.
1967C.   A cache of Paleo-Indian gravers from the Kouba site. Wisc. Archeol.,
                48, 261–262, 1 fig.

RIVERO, FRANCES CHARLTON DE
1962A.   Necrología del Dr. José Royo y Gómez (1895 - 1961). Geos, Esc. Geol.,
                Min. Met., Univ. Cent. Venezuela, no. 8, 7–12, 2 portrs.
1962B.   Curriculum vitae del profesor José Royo y Gómez. Geos, Esc. Geol.,
                Min. Met., Univ. Cent. Venezuela, no. 8, 13–20.

RIVET, PAUL
1957   Rev.: Pericot in Bol. Amer., 1, 115–116.

RIXON, A. E.
1965   The use of new materials as temporary supports in the development
                and examination of fossils. Mus. Jour. London, 65, 54–60,
                figs. 18–19.

RIZDVIÁNSKIĬ, K. F.   See: Belokrys and Rizdviánskiĭ.

ROBBINS, MAURICE
1964A.   A preliminary report of the Wapanucket No. 8 site, Middleboro, Mas-
                sachusetts. Bull. Eastern States Archeol. Fed., no. 23, 13, (abs.).
1964B.   A preliminary report of the Wapanucket No. 8 site. New World Antiq.,
                11, 79–94.

ROBBINS, M., and AGOGINO, G. A.
1964   The Wapanucket No. 8 site: a Clovis-Archaic site in Massachusetts.
                Amer. Antiq., 29, 509–513, 2 figs.

ROBBINS, M., and IRVING, M. B.
1966   The amateur archaeologist's handbook. New York: Crowell, 273 pp.,
                illustr.
                Rev.: Green in Mo. Archaeol. Soc. Newsletter, no. 200, 7;   Hayes in
                Amer. Antiq., 32, 246–247;   J. M. L. in Minn. Archeol., 28,
                57–62, illustr.;   Metraux in Nat. Hist., 75:9, 24;   Sanger in
                Amer. Anthrop., 69, 252–253.

ROBERT, ROMAIN   See: Beltrán, Robert and Vézian; Gailli, et al.; Nougier and
                Robert.

ROBERT, R., and NOUGIER, L.-R.
1965   Protome de cheval en relief des Pyrénées. Caesaragusta, 25–26, 39–41,
                1 fig.

ROBERTS, AUSTIN
1951   The mammals of South Africa. South Africa: Publ. by Trustees of
                "The mammals of South Africa" book fund, xlviii + 701 pp.,
                54 black and white, 23 color pls., 138 tables.

ROBERTS, FRANK HAROLD HANNA, JR.
1960   Seventy-sixth annual report of the Bureau of American Ethnology to the Secretary of the Smithsonian Institution. Ann. Rept. Bur. Amer. Ethnol., 76, 41 pp., 4 pls.
1961B.   Seventy-seventh annual report of the Bureau of American Ethnology to the Secretary of the Smithsonian Institution. Ann. Rept. Bur. Amer. Ethnol., 77, 35 pp., 2 pls.
1962B.   Seventy-eighth annual report of the Bureau of American Ethnology to the Secretary of the Smithsonian Institution. Ann. Rept. Bur. Amer. Ethnol., 78, 33 pp., 2 pls.
1963B.   Seventy-ninth annual report of the Bureau of American Ethnology to the Secretary of the Smithsonian Institution. Ann. Rept. Bur. Amer. Ethnol., 79, 29 pp., 2 pls.
1964   Eightieth annual report of the Bureau of American Ethnology to the Secretary of the Smithsonian Institution. Ann. Rept. Bur. Amer. Ethnol., 80, 33 pp., 2 pls.

ROBERTS, U. G., JR.   See: Harris, E. M., and Roberts. .

ROBERTSON-JUSTICE, JAMES   See: Fiennes 1965.

ROBINEAU, DANIEL   See: Anthony, J. and Robineau.

ROBINS, P. A., and SWART, E. R.
1964   Southern Rhodesian radiocarbon measurements I. Radiocarbon, 6, 31–36.

ROBINSON, DONALD H.
1961   Archeological aspects of Blue Ridge Parkway. Quart. Bull. Archeol. Soc. Virginia, 15:4, (not seen).

ROBINSON, JOHN TALBOT
1961A.   Rev.: Vallois in L'Anthrop., 68, 417–418.
1962D.   Artifacts and australopithecines at Sterkfontein. Abs. 61st. Ann. Meeting Amer. Anthrop. Assoc., 1962, 28, (abs.).
1963B.   Australopithecines, culture and phylogeny. Amer. Jour. Phys. Anthrop., 21, 595–605.
1964A.   The affinities of the new Olduvai australopithecine. In: Lasker, G. W., (ed.), 1964, 90–95, 1 fig., (reprint with editorial comment).
1964B.   Some critical phases in the evolution of man. S. Afr. Archaeol. Bull., 19, 3–12. Also in: Genovés, S., et al., (eds.), 1966, 73–83, with comment by Thomas W. McKern.
1965A.   Homo 'habilis' and the australopithecines. Nature, 205, 121–124.
1965B.   Relationships and trends in hominid evolution. Publ. Nation. Acad. Sci., 1469, 22–29, 1 fig.
1966   The distinctiveness of Homo habilis. Nature, 209, 957–960, 1 fig.
1967A.   On the locomotor habit of early hominids. Amer. Jour. Phys. Anthrop., 27, 246, (abs.).
1967B.   Variation and the taxonomy of the early hominids. In: Dobzhansky, Hecht, and Steere, (eds.), 1967, 69–100, 5 figs., 7 tables.
    See: Sigmon and Robinson.

ROBINSON, J. T., and ALLIN, E. F.
1966   On the Y of the Dryopithecus pattern of mandibular molar teeth. Amer. Jour. Phys. Anthrop., 25, 323–324, 2 figs.

ROBINSON, K. R.
1964   Dombozanga rock shelter, Mtetengwe River Beit Bridge, Southern Rhodesia. Excavation results. Arnoldia, 1:7, 1–14, 4 figs.
See: Cooke, C. K. and Robinson; Cooke, C. K., Summers and Robinson.

ROBINSON, PAMELA LAMPLOUGH
1962   Abs.: Huene in Zbl. Geol. Pal., Teil 2, 1964, 174–175, 1967, 107.
1965   The Gondwanas of the Pranhita-Godavari valley. Proc. Geol. Soc. London, no. 1622, 67–70, (discussion).
1967A.   The evolution of the Lacertilia. Colloq. Internat. Cent. Nation. Recherch. Sci., 163, 395–407, 3 figs., (French summary).
1967B.   Triassic vertebrates from lowland and upland. Sci. and Culture, 33, 169–173.
See: Jain, Robinson and Chowdhury.

ROBINSON, PETER
1957B.   Age of Galisteo formation, Santa Fe County, New Mexico. Bull. Amer. Assoc. Petrol. Geolog., 41, 757.
1963   Rev.: Hünermann in Zbl. Geol. Pal., Teil 2, 1967, 109.
1963B.   Fused cervical vertebrae from the Bridger formation (Eocene) of Wyoming. Univ. Colorado Studies, Ser. Geol., no. 1, 6–9.
Rev.: Hünermann in Zbl. Geol. Pal., Teil 2, 1967, 116.
1966A.   Fossil Mammalia of the Huerfano formation, Eocene of Colorado. Bull. Peabody, Mus. Nat. Hist., 21, viii +95 pp., 9 figs., 10 pls, 35 tables.
1966B.   Fossil occurrence of murine rodent (Nesokia indica) in the Sudan. Science, 154, 264, 1 fig.
Rev.: Fahlbusch in Zbl. Geol. Pal., Teil 2, 1967, 522.
1966C.   Paleontology and geology of the Badwater Creek area, central Wyoming, Part 3. Late Eocene Apatemyidae (Mammalia; Insectivora) from the Badwater area. Ann. Carnegie Mus., 38:15, 317–320, 1 fig.
Rev.: Fahlbusch in Zbl. Geol. Pal., Teil 2, 1967, 512.
1967   The mandibular dentition of ?Tetonoides (Primates, Anaptomorphidae). Ann. Carnegie Mus., 39:13, 187–191, 1 fig.
1968A.   Talpavus and Entomolestes (Insectivora, Adapisoricidae). Amer. Mus. Novit., 2339, 7 pp., 1 fig., 1 table.
1968B.   The paleontology and geology of the Badwater Creek area, central Wyoming. 4. Late Eocene primates from Badwater, Wyoming, with a discussion of material from Utah. Ann. Carnegie Mus., 39:19, 307–326, 24 figs., 7 tables.

ROBINSON, P., BLACK, C. C., and DAWSON, M. R.
1964   Late Eocene multituberculates and other mammals from Wyoming. Science, 145, 809–811, 1 fig.
Rev.: Hünermann in Zbl. Geol. Pal., Teil 2, 1967, 109–110.

ROBINSON, RICHARD D. See: Ives, Levin, Robinson and Rubin.

ROBINSON, W. W.
1961   Beasts of the tar pits. 3rd ed. Los Angeles, Calif.; Ward Ritchie Press, 49 pp., illustr., (age 10 to laymen).

ROBISON, RICHARD A.
1965   Use of the vibro-tool for mechanical preparation of fossils. In: Kummel and Raup, (eds.), 1965, 267–270, 1 fig.

ROBISON, ROBERT S.   See: Loberg, and Harrison 1967.

ROCHE, JEAN
   1965A.   Représentation humaine bisexuée trouvée à la grotte de Taforalt (Maroc). In: Ripoll Perelló, E., (ed.), 1965B., 307—308, 1 fig., (English summary).
   1965B.   Le Paléolithique supérieur portugais. Bilan de nos connaissances et problemes. Bull. Soc. Préhist. Franç., Étud. et Trav., 61, 11—27, 4 figs.
            Rev.: Ripoll Perelló in Ampurias, 28, 162.
            See: Arambourg, Biberson, et al.; Breuil 1962B.

ROCHE, J., CAMARATE FRANÇA, J., and VEIGA FERREIRA, O. DA
   1961   Rev.: J. R. in L'Anthrop., 69:5—6, 552—553.

ROCHE, J., CAMARATE FRANÇA, J., VEIGA FERREIRA, O. DA., and ZBYSZEWSKI, G.
   1962   Le paléolithique supérieur de la grotte de Salemas (Ponte de Lousa). Com. Serv. Geol. Portugal, 46, 187—207, 9 figs.
            Rev.: J. R. in L'Anthrop., 69:5—6, 552—553.

ROCHOW, K. A.   See: Newsome and Rochow.

RODENDORF, B. B.
   1959   [Problems of paleozoological systematics.]   Pal. Zhurnal, 1959:3, 15—26, (Russian).
   1964   [Research on the system and phylogenesis of animals.] Biull. Mosk. Obshch. Ispyt. Prirody, Otd. Geol., 39:3, p. 156, (Russian).

RODNICK, DAVID
   1966   An introduction to man and his development. New York: Appleton-Century-Crofts, xiv + 433 pp., maps.
            Rev.: Coon in Amer. Anthrop., 69, 385—386.

RODRIGUES, ADRIANO VASCO
   1961   Arqueologia da Península Hispânica do Paleolítico à Romanização. Lisboa: Porto Editora, 487 pp., 245 figs., 1 color pl., 17 maps.

RODRÍGUEZ COWAN, FRANCISCO
   1961   De entre los grandes. Bol. Grupo Explor. Cien., 1, 49—54, 1 fig.

ROE, D. A.
   1964   The British Lower and Middle Palaeolithic: Some problems, methods of study and preliminary results. Proc. Prehist. Soc. Cambridge, 30, 245—267, 21 figs., pl. XXVII.

ROE, NOEL   See: Shawcross and Roe.

ROGACHEV, A. N.
   1959   [Excavations of Paleolithic sites and burial places.]   Izv. na Arkheol. Inst., 22, 3—13, (Russian).
   1961D.   [Anosovka II — new many-layered site at Kostenki.]   Krat. Soob. Inst. Ist. Mat. Kult. SSSR, 86—96, 6 figs., (Russian).
   1962A.   [About the Anosovka-Mezin type of Paleolithic dwellings on the Russian plain.] Krat. Soob. Inst. Ist. Mat. Kult. SSSR, 92, 12—17, 1 fig., (Russian).

1962B.   [Basic results and objectives in the study of the Paleolithic of the Russian plain.]   Krat. Soob. Inst. Ist. Mat. Kult, SSSR, <u>92</u>, 3–11, (Russian).

1967   Appendix: schematic animal carvings from Kostenki. In: Abramova, Z. A., 101–104.

1968   [Triangular spear heads at Kostenki.] In: Rybakov, (ed.), 29–30, 1 fig., (Russian).

ROGERS, DAVID J., FLEMING, H. S., and ESTABROOK, G.

1967   Use of computers in studies of taxonomy and evolution. In: Dobzhansky, et al., (eds.), 169–196.

ROGERS, MALCOLM JENNINGS

1966   Ancient hunters of the Far West: Copley Press in cooperation with San Diego Museum of Man, 208 pp., illustr., (not seen). Rev.: Leonhardy in Amer. Anthrop., <u>70</u>, 164–165.

ROGERS, S. L.

1966   The need for a better means of recording pathological bone proliferation in joint areas. Amer. Jour. Phys. Anthrop., <u>25</u>, 171–176, 2 figs.

ROGINSKIĬ, ĬA. ĬA.

1957B.   [On some general problems of the theory of anthropogenesis.]   Voprosy Filosofii, <u>1957</u>:2, 110–116, (Russian).

1959   [The problem of "presapiens" in contemporary literature.]   Sov. Etnog., <u>1959</u>:6, 173–179, (Russian).

1964   [The problem of the place of origin of man of modern type.]   Nauka i Chelovechestvo, <u>3</u>, 36–51, 11 figs., 1 map, portr., (Russian).

1965   [Research on Paleolithic art and anthropology.] Voprosy Antrop., <u>21</u>, 151–156, (Russian).

1966A.   [Palestinian hominids and related forms.]   Trudy Inst. Etnog. Akad. Nauk SSSR, <u>92</u>, 182–204, 10 figs., 1 table, (Russian).

1966B.   [Extra-European paleoanthrops.]   Trudy Inst. Etnog. Akad. Nauk SSSR, <u>92</u>, 205–226, 11 figs., 5 tables, (Russian).

ROGINSKIĬ, ĬA. ĬA., and LEVIN, M. G.

1955   [Fundamentals of Anthropology.] Moscow: Moscow University Press, 502 pp., 238 figs., 44 tables, 7 pls., (Russian).

1963   [Anthropology.] 2nd edition, corrected and completed. Moscow: "Vysshaia Shkola" Press, 495 pp., illustr. Rev.: Schwidetzky in Homo, <u>15</u>:4, 246.

ROIG DE LEUCHSENRING, EMILIO

1961   La Sociedad Espeleológica de Cuba. In: Núñez Jiménez (ed.), 1961A., 45–64, illustr.

ROKHLIN, D. G.

1965   [Diseases of ancient men. (Bones of men of various epochs normal and pathologically changed).] Moscow–Leningrad: "Nauka" Press, 303 pp., 131 figs., (Russian; English title, contents, and summary). Rev.: S. in Archeol. Roz., <u>18</u>, 88–89, (Czech).

ROLFE, W. D. IAN

1958   A recent temporary section through Pleistocene deposits at Ilford. Essex Nat., <u>30</u>:2, 93–103, (not seen).

1965A.   Uses of infrared rays. In: Kummel and Raup, (eds.), 1965, 344–350,
              2 figs.
1965B.   Uses of ultraviolet rays. In: Kummel and Raup, (eds.), 1965, 350–360,
              2 figs.
1966   Woolly rhinoceros from the Scottish Pleistocene. Scottish Jour. Geol.,
              2, 253–258, 2 figs., 1 pl.

ROLINGSON, MARTHA ANN
1964   Paleo-Indian culture in Kentucky. A study based on projectile points.
              Kentucky Univ. Studies in Anthrop., no. 2, viii + 85 pp., 47 figs.,
              14 tables.
              Rev.: Bryan in Man, 65, 169–170; Guthe in Amer. Anthrop., 67,
              162–163; Fitting in Mich. Archaeol., 12, 41; Leonhardy in Amer.,
              Antiq., 31, 131; Vallois in L'Anthrop., 69, 348; Wood in Mo.
              Archaeol. Soc. Newsletter, no. 191, 7.

ROLINGSON, M. A., and SCHWARTZ, D.
1964   Paleo-Indian problems in Kentucky. Bull. Southeast. Archaeol. Confer., 1,
              42–48.
1966   Late Paleo-Indian and Early Archaic manifestations in Western Kentucky.
              Lexington: University Kentucky Press, 168 pp.
              Rev.: Bass in Amer. Jour. Phys. Anthrop., 24, 382; Bushnell in Antiq.,
              40, 311; Cotter in Penn. Archaeol., 36, 72; Fowler in Amer. Antiq.,
              32, 248–249; Honea in El Palacio, 73:3, 42–43; Mason in Amer.
              Anthrop., 69, 102–103; Sykes in New World Antiq., 13, 56–57.

ROMANOVSKAIÂ, L. V.   See: Mal'chevskaiâ and Romanovskaiâ.

ROMER, ALFRED SHERWOOD
1959B.   Rev.: Nowak in Przeglad Zool., 7, 178–179, (Polish); Schindewolf in
              Zbl. Geol. Pal., Teil 2, 1962, 305–306.
1959E.   Fossil skeleton reconstructed after 100 million year delay. Discovery, 20,
              464, 1 fig.
1962F.   La evolucion explosiva de los rhynchosaurios del Triasico. Rev. Mus.
              Argent. Cien. Nat., Cien., Zool., 8, 1–14, 3 figs.
1963B.   Abs.: Huene in Zbl. Geol. Pal., Teil 2, 1964, 521.
1963C.   Foreward. In: Davenport, G., 1963, vii – x.
1964A.   The braincase of the Paleozoic elasmobranch Tamiobatis. Bull. Mus. Comp.
              Zool. Harvard, 131, 89–105, 4 figs., 1 pl.
1964B.   The skeleton of the Lower Carboniferous labyrinthodont Pholidogaster
              pisciformis. Bull. Mus. Comp. Zool. Harvard, 131, 131–159, 5
              figs., 1 pl.
              Abs.: Westphal in Zbl. Geol. Pal., Teil 2, 1966, 296
1964C.   Late Permian terrestrial vertebrates, U. S. A. and U. S. S. R. [Review of
              E. C. Olson, 1962B.] Copeia, 1964, 250–253.
1964D.   Diadectes an amphibian? Copeia, 1964, 718–719.
1964E.   Vertebrate Paleontologists Society. GeoTimes, 8:6, 22–24, illustr.
1964F.   Bone in early vertebrates. In: Frost, H. M., (ed.), 1964, 13–37, 10 figs.,
              (discussion, 38–40).
1964G.   Problems in early amphibian history. Jour. Animal Morph. Physiol., 11,
              1–20, 3 figs.
              Abs.: Westphal in Zbl. Geol. Pal., Teil 2, 1966, 296–297.
              Rev.: M. C. in Fossilia, 1965:3–4, 50.
1964H.   Cope versus Marsh. Syst. Zool., 13, 201–207, 2 portr.
1964I.   Thomas Barbour. Syst. Zool., 13, 227–234.

1965A. Early Triassic reptiles in Argentina. News Bull., Soc. Vert. Pal., 74, 59—60.

1965B. Possible polyphylety of the vertebrate classes. Zool. Jahrb., Abt. Syst. Ökol. Geog. Tiere, 92, 143—156.

1966A. The Chañares (Argentina) Triassic reptile fauna. 1. Introduction. Breviora, 247, 1—14.

1966B. Letter from the president. Bull. AAAS, Sept. 1966, 1—2, portr.

1966C. Vertebrate paleontology. 3rd ed. revised. Chicago: Univ. Chicago Press, [x] + 468 pp., 443 figs., 4 stratigraphic tables.
Rev.: Bergström in Geol. Fören. Förh., 89, 388; Camp in Science, 156, 794—795; Dorr in GeoTimes, 12:5, 34; Estes in Copeia, 1967:4, 873—876; Fantini Sestini in Riv. Ital. Pal., 74:2, 655; George in Nature, 214, 1167; Haltenorth in Säugetierkundl. Mitt., 15, 257; Hotton in BioScience, 17, 422—423; Langston in Jour. Pal., 41, 1305—1307; Manten in Earth-Sci. Rev., 3:4, A241—A243; Olson in Quart. Rev. Biol., 297—299; F. R. P. in Geol. Mag., 104, 204—205.

1966D. Vergleichende Anatomie der Wirbeltiere, 2nd ed. Hambourg: Verlag Paul Parey, 548 pp., 407 figs.
Rev.: Dorst in Mammalia, 30, 689; Haltenorth in Säugetierkundl. Mitt., 15, 189; Herre in Zeit. Säugetierk., 32, 382; Knussmann in Homo, 18:1, 63; Preuschoft in Anthropol. Anz., 31:1—2, 133—134; Steffan in Naturwiss. Rundschau, 20:1, 38; K. T. in Universum; Natur u. Tech., 1967:1, ii; Vogel in Zeit. Morph. Anthrop., 59, 222—223; Westphal in Zbl. Geol. Pal., Teil 2, 1967, 100.

1966E. Las capas triasicas del "Gondwana" en la historia de la evolucion de los vertebrados. (Traduccion de Guillermo del Corro). Rev. Mus. Argent. Cien. Nat., Pal., 1:5, 115—131, illustr.

1967A. George Howard Parker. 1864—1955. A biographical memoir. Biog. Mem. Nation. Acad. Sci., 39, 359—390, portr.

1967B. The Chañares (Argentina) Triassic reptile fauna. III. Two new gomphodonts, Massetognathus pascuali and M. teruggii. Breviora, 264, 25 pp., 10 figs.

1967C. Early reptilian evolution re-viewed. Evolution, 21, 821—833, 3 figs.

1967D. How we put the romance back in fossil-hunting. Harvard Alumni Bull., 69:13, 14—18 illustr.

1967E. Tilly Edinger, 1897—1967. News Bull., Soc. Vert. Pal., 81, 51—53, portr.

1967F. Major steps in vertebrate evolution. Science, 158, 1629—1637, 4 figs.

1968A. Notes and comments on vertebrate paleontology. Chicago: Univ. Press, 304 pp.
Bellairs in Jour. Anat., 105:2, 415; Black in Jour. Mammal., 50:3, 655; Cox in Nature, 222, 497—498; Denison in Jour. Geol., 77:6, 738—739; Hotton in Science, 163, 1440—1441; Kuhn-Schnyder in Naturwiss., 56:6, 339; Müller in Biol. Zbl., 89:2, 262; Olson in Quart. Rev. Biol., 44:3, 297; Roth-Lutra in Anat. Anz., 127:1, 127—128; Whitmore in GeoTimes, 14:9, 33.

1968B. An ichthyosaur skull from the Cretaceous of Wyoming. Contrib. Geol., Univ. Wyoming, 7, 27—41, 9 figs.
See: Davenport 1963; Stovall, Price and Romer; Van Valen, Butler, et al.

ROMER, A. S., and COX, C. B.
1962   Abs.: Huene in Zbl. Geol. Pal., Teil 2, 1964, 521—522.

ROMER, A. S., and JENSEN, J. A.
1966   The Chañares (Argentina) Triassic reptile fauna. II. Sketch of the geo-

logy of the Rió Chañares Gualo region. Breviora, no. 252, 1–20, 2 figs.

ROMER, A. S., WRIGHT, N. E., EDINGER, T., and FRANK, R. v.
1962   Rev.: Edinger in Zbl. Geol. Pal., Teil 2, 1964, 141–144; Huene in Zbl. Pal., Teil 2, 1964, 141–144.

ROMER, MARGARET
1964   The story of Los Angeles. Part V. Jour. of the West, 3, 1–39, illustr.

RÖMISCH-GERMANISCHES ZENTRALMUSEUM, MAINZ, (ed.)
1966   COWA surveys and bibliographies. Area 3 — Western Europe: Part II. COWA Surv. and Bibliog., Area 3, no. 3, 3 + 15 pp.

ROMODANOVA, A. P., and SHEVCHENKO, A. I.
1959   [A new find of mammalian fossil remains of the Middle Pleistocene period in the Ukraine.] Geol. Zhurnal, Kiev, 19:4, 70–78, 4 figs., 3 tables, (Ukrainian; Russian summary).

RONEN, AVRAHAM
1964   Grattiors carénés à encoche de l'Aurignacien. Bull. Soc. Préhist. Franç., C. R. séances mens, 1964:6, CXLVII–CL, 2 figs., 1 table.
1965   Observations sur l'Aurignacien. L'Anthrop., 69:5–6, 465–485, 3 figs., 7 tables.
             Abs.: Anon. in Anthropos, 61, 319.

RONKINA, Z. Z.   See: Saks, et al.

ROOSA, WILLIAM B.
1965   Some Great Lakes fluted point types. Mich. Archaeol., 11, 89–102, 1 pl.

ROSE, FRANCIS L.   See: Weaver and Rose.

ROSE, L., and WEAVER, W. G., JR.
1967   Two new species of Chrysemys (=Pseudemys) from the Florida Pliocene. Tulane Studies Geol., 5, 41–48, 5 figs.

ROSE, G.
1965   Triassic rocks of the Sydney district. Austral. Nat. Hist., 15, 22–28, illustr.

ROSE, M. D.   See: Walker, Alan and Rose.

ROSELL SANUY, JUAN   See: Crusafont Pairo and Rosell Sanuy; Crusafont Pairo, Rosell Sanuy, et al.; Villalta and Rosell Sanuy.

ROSEN, DONN E.   See: Greenwood, et al.

ROSEN, ERIC VON
1957   Un mundo que se va. Exploraciones y aventuras entre las altas cumbres de la Cordillera de los Andes. Translated by Carlos F. Stubbe. Opera Lilloana, no. 1, xxiii +307 pp., 307 figs., 45 pls., 1 map.

ROSENFELD, ANDRÉE
1964A.   Excavations in the Torbryan Caves, Devonshire, II. Three Holes Cave.
            Trans. Devon Archaeol. Explor. Soc., no. 22, (not seen).
1964B.   The study and interpretation of archaeological deposits in caves. Studies
            in Spel., 1, 44—50.
1965   The inorganic raw materials of antiquity. New York: Praeger, xiii
            +245 pp., 30 figs., 26 pls, 7 tables.
            Rev.:   Anon. in Mankind Quart., 7, 128; Manning in Antiq., 40, 246—
            247; Matson in Amer. Anthrop., 68, 1557.
            See: Ucko and Rosenfeld.

ROSHCHIN, A. D.
1962   [Findings of fossil ostrich eggs in the south of Ukraine.] Trudy Odessk.
            Univ., Ser. Geol. Geogr., 152:8, 26—30, 3 figs, 1 table, (Russian).

ROSIŃSKI, BOLESŁAW
1958   Jerzy Dąmbski. 21 VII 1919 R.- 22 X 1956 R. Przeglad Antrop., 24,
            247—250, portr., (Polish; English summary).

ROSS, D. M.
1964   Vertebrate palaeontology in Alberta. Nature, 201, 768—769.
1965   Discussion held at the University of Alberta, Calgary. Vert. Pal. in Al-
            berta, Univ. of Alberta, 1965, 64—76.

ROSS, HERBERT H.
1962   Rev.: Blair in Quart. Rev. Biol., 40, 80—81.
1967   Understanding evolution. Englewood Cliffs, N. J.: Prentice Hall, 175
            pp., illustr., (not seen).
            Rev.: Cain in Nature, 216, 207; Clarke in Sci. Jour. 3:5, 128; Shapiro
            in Nat. Hist., 76:6, 68—71; Steffan in Naturwiss. Rund., 21, 87—88;
            Tidd in Ohio Jour. Sci., 67, 255; Williams in Quart. Rev. Biol.,
            42, 532—533.

ROSTAND, JEAN   See: Hugede 1966.

ROSTOVTSEV, N. N., (ed.)
1961   [Resolutions and transactions of the interdepartmental conference on com-
            pletion and precision of the unified and correlational stratigraphic
            schemes of the West Siberian Lowlands (Novosibirsk, 15-20 February,
            1960).] Leningrad: Gostoptekhizdat Press, 465 pp., illustr., (Rus-
            sian).

ROTHAUSEN, KARLHEINZ
1968A.   Die Squalodontidae (Odontoceti, Mamm.) im Oligozän und Miozän Italiens.
            Mem. Ist. Geol. Min. Univ. Padova, 26, 1—19, (of sep.), 1 fig.,
            2 pls., (Italian summary).
1968B.   Die systematische Stellung der europäischen Squalodontidae (Odontoceti,
            Mamm). Pal. Zeit., 42:1—2, 83—104, 3 figs., 2 pls., 1 table, (Eng-
            lish summary).

ROTH-LUTRA, K. R.
1965   Röntgenanthropologie: der Röntgenbefund als Hilfe der kombinierten
            Altersbestimmung. Anthrop. Anz., 27:3—4, 278—288, 6 figs.
            Rev.: Engel in L'Anthrop., 71:1—2, 167.

ROTMAN, R. N.   See: Makarenko and Rotman.

ROUBERT, COLETTE See: Faure and Roubert.

ROUQUETTE, DANIEL
1966   Nouveau gisement Moustérien dans l'Hérault. Bull. Soc. Préhist. Franç.,
              C. R. séances mens., 63:2, 51.

ROUSE, IRVING
1958B.   (ed.) COWA surveys and bibliographies. Area 11 – West Africa. COWA
              Surv. and Bibliog., Area 11, no. 1, 5 + 8 pp.
1961   (ed.) COWA surveys and bibliographies. Area 11 – West Africa. COWA
              Surv. and Bibliog., Area 11, no. 2, 3 + 11 pp.
1964A.   The Caribbean area. In: Jennings and Norbeck (eds.), 1964A., 389–417,
              6 figs.
1964B.   Prehistory of the West Indies. Science, 144, 499–513, 20 figs.
1965A.   The Paleo- and Meso-Indians of the Caribbean area. 7th Internat. Congr.,
              Internat. Assoc. Quat. Res., Abs., 1965, 399–400, (abs.).
1965B.   The place of "peoples" in prehistoric research. Jour. Roy. Anthrop.
              Inst., 95, 1–15.
1966   Paleo- and Meso-Indians of the Caribbean area. Quaternaria, 8, 125–132,
              (French and Spanish summaries).
1967   Early man in the Caribbean area. Bull. Eastern States Archeol. Fed.,
              no. 26, 13, (abs.).
              See: Cruxent and Rouse.

ROUSE, I., and CRUXENT, J. M.
1963   Venezuelan archaeology. New Haven and London: Yale Univ. Press,
              xiii + 179 pp., 34 figs., 55 pls.
              Rev.: Blackwood in New Sci., 23, 177–178; Bray in Archaeol. Jour.,
              120, 306–307; Bushnell in Man, 64, 190–191; Meggers and
              Evans in Amer. Antiq., 30, 227–228; Sanoja in Amer. Anthrop.,
              66, 1218–1220.

ROUSSEAU, MICHEL
1965   "Chefs-d'oeuvre du Musée de l'Homme". La Nature, 93, 263–268,
              12 figs.

ROUSSELIÈRE, G. M.
1964   Palaeo-Eskimo remains in the Pelly Bay region, N. W. T. Nation. Mus.
              Canada, Bull., Anthrop., Ser., Bull. 193. Series 61, 162–183, 9
              figs., 1 pl.

ROUSSOT, ALAIN
1961   Hommage à l'abbé Breuil. Bull. Soc. Hist. Archéol. Périgord, 88, 177–
              179.
1962A.   Notes de préhistoire en Périgord. I. Bull. Soc. Hist. Archéol. Périgord,
              89, 67–69, 1 fig.
1962B.   Le gisement paléolithique de Reignac, commune de Tursac (Dordogne).
              Premier fouille – Couche A. 1962. Bull. Soc. Hist. Archéol. Péri-
              gord, 89, 145–156, 5 pls.
1964   Le gisement paléolithique de Reignac (suite), commune de Tursac (Dor-
              dogne). Bull. Soc. Hist. Archéol. Périgord, 91, 63–70, 3 figs.
1966A.   Une lettre de l'abbé Breuil sur la découverte de la grotte des Combarelles
              aux Eyzies. Bull. Soc. Hist. Archéol. Périgord, 93, 199–202.

1966B.   Le film de la découverte de la grotte peinte de Lascaux près Montignac
              (Dordogne). Bull. Soc. Hist. Archéol. Périgord, 93, 203.
1966C.   Deux lissoirs aurignaciens identiques, à l'abri du Poisson (Les Eyzies)
              et à Castelmerle (Sergeac). L'Anthrop., 70:3—4, 343—346, 1 pl.
1966D.   Réflexions sur l'étude de l'art pariétal franco-cantabrique. L'Anthrop.,
              70:3—4, 384—387.
              See: Jardel and Roussot.

ROUSSOT, A., ANDRIEUX, C., and CHAUFFRIASSE, A.
1966   La grotte Nancy, commune de Sireuil (Dordogne). L'Anthrop., 70:1—2,
              45—62, 11 figs.

ROUX, GEORGES
1964   Ancient Iraq. London: George Allen and Unwin, 431 pp., 33 pls.,
              5 maps.
              Rev.: Penniman in Nature, 203, 802.

ROVNER, I.   See: Agogino and Rovner; Agogino, Rovner and Irwin-Williams.

ROWLANDS, M. J.   See; Beer, et al.

ROY, B. C.
1964   General report of the Geological Survey of India for the year 1960-61.
              VI. Technical sections at headquarters: Palaeontological Division.
              Rec. Geol. Surv. India, 95:1, 264—270.

ROY CHOWDHURY, T.   See: Chowdhury, T. Roy.

ROYER, RUSSELL
1963   A fluted point from Luzerne County, Pennsylvania. Penn. Archaeol.,
              33, 140—141, 1 fig.

ROYO Y GÓMEZ, JOSÉ
1960E.   Glaciarismo pleistoceno en Venezuela. Geos, Esc. Geol., Min. Met.,
              Univ. Cent. Venezuela, no. 4, 43—62, illustr.

ROZHDESTVENSKIĬ, A. K. (=Rojdestvenski, A. K. =Roshdestwenski, A. K.)
1960   Chasse aux dinosaures dans le désert de Gobi. Traduit du russe par
              P. Moulin. Paris: Libr. Arthème Fayard, 301 pp., 13 figs., 1
              map, 1 table.
1961B.   [Some results of the study in USSR of ancient amphibians, reptiles,
              and birds (1917 - 1957).] Trudy Vses. Paleont. Obshch., IV
              sess., 71—83, (Russian).
1964A.   [New data on dinosaur occurrences in Kazakhstan and Central Asia.]
              Nauchn. Trudy Tashkent. Gos. Un., Nov. ser. 234, geol. nauki,
              kn. 20, 227—241, 5 figs., (Russian).
1964B.   [Class Reptilia. General part.] Osnovy Pal., [Amphibians, Reptiles,
              and Birds.], [12], 191—213, 9 figs., (Russian).
1964C.   [Subclass Archosauria.] Osnovy Pal., [Amphibians, Reptiles, and Birds.],
              [12], 493—603, 153 figs., 1 table, (Russian).
1965   [Age differences and some questions on taxonomy of Asiatic dinosaurs.]
              Pal. Zhurnal, 1965:3, 95—109, 4 figs., 1 table, (Russian).
1966A.   [New iguanodonts from Central Asia. Phylogenetic and taxonomic
              relationships between late Iguanodontidae and early Hadrosauridae.]
              Pal. Zhurnal, 1966:3, 103—116, 4 figs., 1 table, (Russian).

1966B.   [Evgeniĭ Aleksandrovich Maleev (1915 - 1966).]   Pal. Zhurnal, 1966:3, 148—149, portr., (Russian).

1966C.   [Encounters with dinosaurs.]   Moscow: "Znanie" Press, 60 pp., illustr., (Russian).
Rev.: Ĭanovskaiâ in Priroda, 1967:10, 120—121, (Russian).

1967   New iguanodonts from Central Asia. Translation of Rozhdestvenskiĭ, A. K., 1966A. Internat. Geol. Rev., 9, 556—566, 4 figs., 2 tables.

1968A.   [New data on localities containing the remains of Tertiary mammals in Kazakhstan and Central Asia.]   Ezhegod. Vses. Pal. Obshch., 18, 302—321, table, (Russian).

1968B.   [Find of a gigantic dinosaur.]   Priroda, 1968:2, 115—116, 2 figs., (Russian).

ROZHDESTVENSKIĬ, A. K., and KHOZAT͡SKIĬ, L. I.
1967   [Late Mesozoic land vertebrates from the Asiatic part of the USSR.]   In: Martinson, (ed.), 1967A, 82—92, (Russian).

ROZHDESTVENSKIĬ, A. K., and TATARINOV, L. P., (eds.)
1964   Osnovy Paleontologii. [Fundamentals of paleontology. Amphibia, Reptilia, Aves.], [12], 722 pp., 703 figs. [Principal ed. of series: Ĭu. A. Orlov.]   Moscow: Nauka, 722 pp., illustr., (Russian).
Rev.: Huene in Zbl. Geol. Pal., Teil 2, 1964, 982—983;   Huene in Zbl. Geol. Pal., Teil 2, 1966, 364—365.

RUBANOV, I. V.
1959   [On Neogene fluviatile deposits of Brich-Mullin depression.]   Uzbek. Geol. Zhurnal, 1959:3, 44—52, 4 figs., (Russian; Uzbek summary).

RUBIN, MEYER   See: Ives, Levin, Oman and Rubin; Ives, Levin, Robinson and Rubin; Levin, B., et al.; Pecora and Rubin; Repenning, Hopkins and Rubin.

RUBIN, M., and BERTHOLD, S. M.
1961   U. S. Geological Survey radiocarbon dates VI. Radiocarbon, 3, 86—98.

RUBINSHTEIN, M. M.   See: Gabuniiâ and Rubinshtein.

RUCHHOLZ, KURT
1963   Professor Dr. Hans Wehrli 60 Jahre. Ber. Geol. Ges. Deutsch. Demokratischen Republ., 8, 474—480, portr.

RÜCKERT-ÜLKÜMEN, NERIMAN
1960   Trakya ve Çanakkale mintakalarinda bulunan Neojen Balikli formasyonlari hakkinda. [Tertiäre Fische aus Thrakien und den Dardanellen.]   Monogr. Istanbul Üniv. Fen Fak., 16, 1—80, 19 figs., 35 pls., 3 maps, (Turkish; German summary).
Abs.: Weiler in Zbl. Geol. Pal., Teil 2, 1965, 233—234.

1965   Fossile Fische aus dem Sarmat von Pinarhisar (Türkisch Thrakien). Senck. Lethaea, 46a, 315—361, 2 figs., pls. 22—29.
Abs.: Weiler in Zbl. Geol. Pal., Teil 2, 1966, 287—288.

RUDEL, A.   See: Bouchud 1965B.

RUDENKO, S. I., (ed.)
1963   [New methods in archeological research.]   Moscow-Leningrad: Institut Arkheologii Akad. Nauk SSSR, Akad. Nauk SSSR Press, 241 pp., illustr., (Russian).

RUDIN, KURT   See: Labhart and Rudin.

RUDINSKIĬ, M. ÍÀ.
1959   [Concerning the question of ancient Paleolithic implements of quart-
            zite.]   Krat. Soob. Inst. Ist. Mat. Kult., 73, 126—132, 1 fig.,
            (Russian).

RUDNER, J., and GRATTAN-BELLEW, P.
1964   Archaeological sites along the southern coast of southwest Africa. S.
            African Jour. Sci., 60, 67—79, 6 figs.

RUDORFF, R. A.   See: Grenet 1965.

RUFFIÉ, JACQUES
1967A.   Paléontologie biochimique et l'évolution des Primates supérieurs. Colloq.
            Internat. Cent. Nation. Recherch. Sci., 163, 637—648, 7 figs.,
            (English summary).
1967B.   Biologie moderne et origine de l'homme. L'Anthrop., 71:5—6, 493—513,
            7 figs.
            Rev.: Comas in An. Antropol., Mexico, 6, 324—325.

RUKHIN, L. B.
1957   [Climates of the past and biostratigraphy.]   Trudy Vses. Paleont. Obshch.,
            I sess., 25—41, 1 fig., 1 map, 1 table (Russian).

RUNDLE, A. J.
1967   The occurrence of Upper Liassic otoliths at Hollwell, Leicestershire.
            Mercian Geologist, 2, 63—72, 6 figs.
            Rev.: Weiler in Zbl. Geol. Pal., Teil 2, 1967, 500.

RUNYON, JOHN   See: Smith, Calvin, Runyon and Agogino.

RUPPÉ, REYNOLD J.
1966   The archaeological survey: a defense. Amer. Antiq., 31, 313—333, 2
            figs., 4 tables.

RUPRECHT, ANDRZEJ LECH
1965   Skulls of fossil brown bear, Ursus arctos L., from the environs of
            Ciechocinek. Przeglad. Zool., 9, 422—426, 2 figs., (English sum-
            mary).

RUSANOV, B. S.
1968   [Pleistocene horses of Yakutia.]   Kolyma, 1968:3, 36—38, (Russian).

RUSCONI, CARLOS
1959A.   Rev.: Parodi Bustos in Rev. Fac. Cien. Nat. Salta, 1:3, 89—90.
1964A.   Un viaje hacia el Cajón Grande (Malalhue). Rev. Mus. Hist. Nat. Men-
            doza, 16, 21—44, 5 figs.
1964B.   Hombres fósiles y otras cuestiones. Rev. Mus. Hist. Nat. Mendoza, 16,
            99—109.
1964C.   Anteproyecto de ley para la conservación de los yacimientos paleonto-
            lógicos y antropológicos de Mendoza. Rev. Mus. Hist. Nat. Men-
            doza, 16, 111—117.
1965   Carlos Ameghino. Rasgos de su vida y su obra. Rev. Mus. Hist. Nat.
            Mendoza, 17, 1—162, 9 figs.

Abs.: Westphal in Zbl. Geol. Pal., Teil 2, <u>1966</u>, 4.

1966   Provincias biológicas argentinas. Rev. Mus. Hist. Nat. Mendoza, <u>18</u>, 105–
         120, 1 fig., (English summary).

1967   Animales extinguidos de Mendoza y de la Argentina. Mendoza: Edicion
         Oficial, 489 pp., 276 figs., 46 pls., 3 tables.

RUSELL CORTEZ, F.
1963   Viana (Abel Gonçalves Martins) (*1896 - † 1964). Zephyrus, <u>14</u>, 138–
         139.

RUSKE, RALF
1965   Zur petrographischen Ausbildung und Genese der "Lehmzone" von
         Voigtstedt in Thüringen. Pal. Abh., Abt. A, <u>2</u>, 249–258, 3 figs.,
         (Russian and English summaries).

RUSSELL, DALE A.
1964   Intracranial mobility in mosasaurs. Postilla, no. <u>86</u>, 19 pp., 8 figs.
         Abs.: Westphal in Zbl. Geol. Pal., Teil 2, <u>1965</u>, 252.

1967A.   Systematics and phylogeny of American mosasaurs. (Reptilia, Sauria).
         Bull. Peabody Mus. Nat. Hist., <u>23</u>, viii + 241 pp., 99 figs., 2 pls.,
         7 charts, 3 tables, (Russian and French summaries).

1967B.   The dinosaurs of Canada. Canadian Geog. Jour., <u>75</u>:2, 44–51, illustr.

1967C.   Cretaceous vertebrates from the Anderson River, N. W. T. Canadian
         Jour. Earth Sci., <u>4</u>, 21–38, 12 figs., 4 pls., 4 tables.

1967D.   Cretaceous vertebrates from Arctic Canada. Colloq. Internat. Cent.
         Nation. Recherch. Sci., <u>163</u>, 439, (French summary).
         Rev.: Kuhn in Zbl. Geol. Pal., Teil 2, <u>1968</u>:6, 657.

1967E.   A census of dinosaur specimens collected in western Canada. Nat. Hist.
         Pap., Nation. Mus. Canada, <u>36</u>, 1–13.

RUSSELL, D. A., and CHAMNEY, T. P.
1967   Notes on the biostratigraphy of dinosaurian and microfossil faunas in
         the Edmonton formation (Cretaceous), Alberta. Nat. Hist. Pap.,
         Nation. Mus. Canada, <u>35</u>, 1–22, 6 figs.

RUSSELL, DONALD E.
1964   Les mammifères paléocènes d'Europe. Mem. Mus. Nation. Hist. Nat.
         Paris, Ser. C, <u>13</u>, 324 pp., 73 figs., 16 pls.
         Abs.: Hünermann in Zbl. Geol. Pal., Teil 2, <u>1966</u>, 319–321.

1967   Sur <u>Menatotherium</u> et l'âge paléocène du gisement de Menat (Puy-de-
         Dôme). Colloq. Internat. Cent. Nation. Recherch. Sci., <u>163</u>,
         483–490, 3 pls., (English summary).

1968   Succession, en Europe, des faunes mammaliennes au début du Tertiaire.
         Colloque sur l'Éocène, I. Mém. Bur. Rech. Géol. Min., <u>58</u>, 291–
         296, 1 chart, 1 map, (English, German, and Russian summaries).
         See: Clemens, McKenna, et al.; Crusafont Pairo and Russell; Savage,
         D. E., Russell and Louis.

RUSSELL, D. E., LOUIS, P., and POIRIER, M.
1966A.   Gisements nouveaux de la faune cernaysienne (Mammifères paléocènes
         de France). C. R. Soc. Géol. France, <u>1966</u>, 310, (abs.).

1966B.   Gisements nouveaux de la faune cernaysienne (Mammifères paléocènes
         de France). Bull. Soc. Géol. France, <u>8</u>, 845–856, 1 fig., pls.
         20–21.

RUSSELL, D. E., LOUIS, P., and SAVAGE, D. E.
1967   Primates of the French Early Eocene. Univ. Calif. Publ. Geol. Sci., 73,
            vi + 46 pp., 14 figs., (French summary).
            Rev.: Preuschoft in Zbl. Geol. Pal., Teil 2, 1969:1, 60—61.

RUSSELL, D. E., and McKENNA, M. C.
1961   Abs.: Dietrich in Zbl. Geol. Pal., Teil 2, 1964, 206.

RUSSELL, D. E., and SIGOGNEAU, D.
1965   Etude de moulages endocrâniens de mammifères paléocènes. Mem. Mus.
            Nation. Hist. Nat. Paris, ser. C, 16:1, 1—36, 3 figs., 3 pls.
            Rev.: M. C. in Fossilia, 1965:5—6, 70.

RUSSELL, GEORGE E.
1967A.   Projectile point sequences in the southeast. Anthrop. Jour. Canada,
            5:4, 23—29, 4 figs.
1967B.   Similar impact flutes on recent and early points. Jour. Ala. Archeol.,
            13, 66—67, 1 fig.

RUSSELL, LORIS S.
1933B.   The Cretaceous-Tertiary transition of Alberta. Trans. Roy. Soc. Canada,
            ser. 3, 26:4, 121—156, 2 figs., 5 pls., 2 tables.
1964   Cretaceous non-marine faunas of northwestern North America. Life
            Sci. Contrib., Roy. Ont. Mus., 61, 24 pp.
1965A.   The problem of the Willow Creek formation. Canadian Jour. Earth
            Sci., 2, 11—14.
1965B.   Body temperature of dinosaurs and its relationships to their extinction.
            Jour. Pal., 39, 497—501.
            Abs.: Huene in Zbl. Geol. Pal., Teil 2, 1966, 306.
1965C.   The mastodon. Roy. Ontario Mus. Ser., no. 6, 16 pp., illustr.
1965D.   Tertiary mammals of Saskatchewan. Part I: The Eocene fauna. Roy.
            Ontario Mus., Univ. of Toronto, Life Sci., Contrib., 67, 33 pp.,
            7 pls.
1965E.   The continental Tertiary of western Canada. Vert. Pal. in Alberta,
            Univ. of Alberta, 1965, 41—52, figs. 10—13.
1966A.   A Paleocene conglomerate in west-central Alberta. Canadian Jour.
            Earth Sci., 3, 127—128.
1966B.   Dinosaur hunting in western Canada. Contrib. Roy. Ont. Mus., Life
            Sci. Div., 70, 37 pp., illustr.
            Rev.: D. A. Russell in Canadian Field Nat., 81, 218.
1966C.   The changing environment of the dinosaurs in North America. Advance.
            Sci., 23:110, 197—204, 3 figs.
1967A.   Palaeontology of the Swan Hills area, north-central Alberta. Contrib.
            Roy. Ont. Mus., 71, 1—31, 1 pl.
1967B.   Comment on the above. [cys, 1967B] Jour. Pal., 41, 267.
1968   A dinosaur bone from Willow Creek beds in Montana. Canadian Jour.
            Earth Sci., 5:2, 327—329, 1 pl.
            See: Clemens and Russell.

RUSSELL, ROBERT J.
1968   Evolution and classification of the pocket gophers of the subfamily
            Geomyinae. Univ. Kansas Publ. Mus. Nat. Hist., 16:6, 473—579,
            9 figs., 1 table.

RUST, ALFRED
1965A.   Zeltwälle und Gruben im jungpaläolithischen Wohnbau. Fundber.
           Schwaben, 17, 52–60, 3 figs., pl. 31.
1965B.   Über Waffen- und Werkzeugtechnik des Altmenschen. Neumünster:
           Wachholtz, 68 pp., 5 pls., many figs., (not seen).
           Rev.: Kurth in Kosmos (Stuttgart), 62, *277.

RUST, A., and STEFFENS, G.
1962   Die Artefakte der Altonaer Stufe von Wittenbergen. Eine mittelpleisto-
           zäne Untergruppe der Heidelberger Kulturen. With contribution
           by Friedrich Grube. Neumünster: Wachholtz, 80 pp., 12 figs.,
           78 pls.
           Rev.: Felgenhauer in Archaeol. Austriaca, 33, 115–116;   Vencl in
           Archeol. Roz., 15, 667, (Czech).

RUTTE, ERWIN
1962   Abs.: Weiler in Zbl. Geol. Pal., Teil 2, 1964, 151–153.
1964   Neue Fossilien im limnischen Jungtertiär Süddeutschlands. Natur u.
           Mus., 94, 452, (abs.).
1966   Die Schlundzähne von Cypriniden. Neue Dokumente in Süsswasser-
           Sedimenten. Umschau, 66, 347–350, 6 figs.

RUTTEN, P.   See: Barrière, J., et al.

RÜTTIMANN, JOSEF   See: Grison 1960B.

RUYER, RAYMOND
1967   Evolution et cybernétique. L'Ann. Biol., 6, 557–572.

RUZHENTSEV, V. E.
1965   [Changes in organic world on the limit of Paleozoic and Mesozoic.]
           Trudy Pal. Inst. Akad. Nauk SSSR, 108, 117–134, (Russian).

RYASINA, V. YE.
1962   New finds of Quaternary mammalian fossils in the upper Ob' region.
           Dok. Acad. Sci. USSR, Earth Sci. Sect., 142:1, 80–81.

RYBAKOV, B. A., (ed.)
1966   [The 7th International Congress of historians and protohistorians. Re-
           ports and communications of URSS archeologists.] Moscow:
           "Nauka" Press, 268 pp., (Russian).
1967   [Archeological discoveries of 1966.] Moscow: "Nauka" Press, 350 pp.,
           illustr., (Russian).
1968   [Archeological discoveries of 1967.] Moscow: "Nauka" Press, 369 pp.,
           illustr., (Russian).

RYKOV, S. P.   See: Ochev and Rykov.

RYKOV, S. P., and OCHEV, V. G.
1966   [On localities of Triassic vertebrates in Donskaiā Luka.] In: [Probl.
           geol. South Urals and Pouolg'e], no. 3, part 2, 58–62, (Russian;
           not seen).

RYZIEWICZ, ZBIGNIEW
1955B.   [Present state of research on Pleistocene mammals in Poland.] Biul.
           Panstwowy Inst. Geol., 70, 71–76, (Polish; Russian and English
           summaries).

1961C.   Finding of a third specimen of <u>Archaeopteryx</u>. Przeglad Zool., <u>5</u>, 122–
126, 2 figs., 2 pls., (Polish; English summary).

RZHONSNITSKAÎA, M. A., and MELESHCHENKO, V. S., (eds.)
1955   [Field atlas of fauna and flora of Devonian sediments of Minusinsk
basin.] Moscow: Gosgeoltekhizdat Press, 140 pp., 1 chart, 36
pls., (Russian).

S., C.
1964   Orang-Utans schlafen auch in Höhlen. Mitt. Verband Deutschen Höhlen-
und Karstforscher, München, <u>10</u>, 120.

S., G.
1959   La genealogía del perro actual. Munibe, <u>11</u>:1–2, 80–83, 4 figs.

SABAN, ROGER
1963   Contribution à l'étude de l'os temporal des primates. Mém. Mus. Nat.
Hist. Nat., Paris, n.s. A. Zool., <u>29</u>, 377 pp., 84 figs., 30 pls.
Rev.: Dorst in Mammalia, <u>28</u>, 527–528.
1964   Aspects modernes de la théorie vertébrale du crâne. Ann. Pal., Vert.,
<u>50</u>, 1–21, 4 figs., 3 tables.
Abs.: Westphal in Zbl. Geol. Pal., Teil 2, <u>1965</u>, 212.
1967   Enderostes. In: Grassé, (ed.), Traité de Zool., <u>16</u>:1, 1079–1087, figs.
852–863.
See: Lessertisseur and Saban.

SABBAGH, SUZANNE KATHLEEN BORAM
1964   A preliminary study of fossils as stratigraphic indicators. Diss. Abst.,
<u>25</u>, 1150–1151.

SACCHI, DOMINIQUE
1964   Adaptation particulière de deux nuclei "livre de beurre" du Grand-
Pressigny. Bull. Soc. Préhist. Franç., C. R. séances mens., <u>1964</u>:8,
clxxxv–clxxxviii, 2 figs.

SACCHI VIALLI, G.
1962   Ricerche sulla flourescenza dei fossili; I. Osservazioni sullo smalto dei
denti di alcuni vertebrati. Atti Ist. Geol. Univ. Pavia, <u>13</u>, 23–53,
4 figs., pl. 3 (in color), (French, English, and German summaries).
1964A.   Le sostanze organiche nei fossili. Loro derivazione e significato. Limiti
e possibilità attuali della loro ricerca. Atti Ist. Geol. Univ. Pavia,
<u>14</u>, 20–68, 4 tables, (French, English, and German summaries).
1964B.   Ricerche sulla fluorescenza dei fossili. III: Osservazioni comparative
chimiche e di fluorescenza sulla costituzione dei denti di <u>Carcharodon
megalodon</u> Ag., in condizioni naturali e sperimentali. Atti Ist.
Geol. Univ. Pavia, <u>15</u>, 89–145, 25 figs., (French, English, and
German summaries).

SACKETT, JAMES R.
1964   Statistical applications in Upper Palaeolithic systematics. Abs. 63rd.
Ann. Meeting Amer. Anthrop. Assoc., <u>1964</u>, 52, (abs.).
1966   Quantitative analysis of Upper Paleolithic stone tools. In: Clark, J. D.,
and Howell, F. C., (eds.), 1966A, 356–394, 5 figs., 15 tables.

1967   Solvieux: an Upper Paleolithic open site in southwestern France. Abs.
            66th. Ann. Meeting Amer. Anthrop. Assoc., 1967, 71, (abs.).

SADEK, HIND
    1965   Appendix: distribution of the bird remains at Jaguar Cave. Tebiwa,
                8, 20–28.

SADIKOVA, M. B.   See: Laukhin and Sadikova.

SADOVSKIĬ, A. I.
    1962   [New data on the stratigraphy of Cenozoic deposits of the lower course
                of Kolyma R. and East-Siberian Sea Shore.] Geol. i Geof., 1962:5,
                120–125, 2 figs., (Russian).

SAEKI, M.
    1966   Morphological study on the Primates with special reference to monkey
                teeth. Kaseki, 11, 52–53, (Japanese).

SAFRONOV, I. N.   See: Garutt and Safronov.

SAHEKI, SHIRÔ
    1928   [An occurrence of Desmostylus in Saghalin.] Jour. Geol. Soc. Japan,
                35, 569, 1 fig., (Japanese).

SAHLY, ALI
    1963   Diagnosis 30,000 years later. Spelunking French physician turns medical
                detective in attempt to determine etiology of mutilated hand
                prints left by Pyrenees cave men. Med. World News, Oct. 25,
                1963, 118–119, 5 figs.
    1965   Essai de synthèse de la civilisation languedocienne (d'après les échanges
                de correspondances avec l'abbé Breuil). In: Ripoll Perelló, E.,
                (ed.), 1965B, 309–317, 1 fig., 3 pls., (Spanish summary).
            See: Barrière, C. and Sahly; Brabant and Sahly.

SAHNI, M. R., and KHAN, E.
    1962   Recent finds of Shivalik vertebrates. 4. On the skull of a young Equus
                sivalensis. Res. Bull. Punjab Univ., n.s., Sci., 12, 263–264, 1 pl.
    1964   Stratigraphy, structure and correlation of the Upper Shivaliks east of
                Chandigarh. Jour. Pal. Soc. India, 4, 61–74, 4 figs., 4 pls.

SAHU, B. K.   See: Mohapatra, G. C., et al.

SAĬADIĂN, IŬ. V.
    1966   [Stratigraphic division of Anthropogene lake and lacustrine-fluviatile
                sediments in the Leninakan basin.] Sov. Geol., 1966:2, 141–145,
                2 figs., (Russian).
    1967   [Lithology and history of development of Quaternary lacustrine and
                fluvio-lacustrine deposits of Shirak basin.] Izv. Akad. Nauk Armian.
                SSR, Nauki o Zemle, 20:1–2, 127–135, 1 fig., (Russian; Arme-
                nian summary).

SAID, RUSHDI   See: Wendorf and Said.

SAID, R., and ISSAWY, B.
    1965   Preliminary results of a geological expedition to Lower Nubia and to
                Kurkur and Dungul Oases, Egypt. In: Wendorf, Fred, (ed.),
                1965A, 1–28, 12 figs.

SAI-HALÁSZ, A.
1967   Das Problem der Extinktion im Lichte der neuroendokrinen Forschungen.
        Neues Jahrb. Geol. Pal., Monatsh., 1967:4, 231—237.

SAINSBURY, C. L.
1967   Quaternary geology of western Seward Peninsula, Alaska. In: Hopkins,
        D. M., (ed.), 1967D, 121—143, 11 figs., 2 tables.

SAINT-MATHURIN, S. DE
1965   Les rapports probables des industries de la région de Fontainebeau avec
        celles de la plaine du Nord-Est de l'Europe (Federmesser-Gruppen).

SAINT-PÉRIER, COMTESSE DE
1962D.   Le Professeur Pittard [- 1962]. Bull. Soc. Hist. Archéol. Périgord.,
         89, 107—109, portr.
1965   Réflexions sur le paléolithique supérieur d'Isturitz. In: Ripoll Perelló,
         E., (ed.), 1965B, 319—325, 2 figs., (Spanish summary).

SAINT-SEINE, PIERRE DE, and CASIER, E.
1962   Abs.: Weiler in Zbl. Geol. Pal., Teil 2, 1964, 154—155.

SAKAO, NOBUYOSHI   See: Hanihara, Kuwashima and Sakao.

SAKS, V. N. (=Sachs, V. N.)
1959   [Some controversial aspects of the history of the Quaternary period in
        Siberia.] Trudy Inst. Geol. Arktiki, 96, 151—163, 1 table, (Rus-
        sian).
1965   (ed.) [Principal problems of study of Quaternary Period. (For the
        seventh congress of INQUA in U.S.A., 1965).] Moscow: "Nauka"
        Press, 496 pp., illustr., (Russian; English table of contents).
1966   (ed.) [Quaternary Period of Siberia.] Moscow: "Nauka" Press, 514 pp.,
        illustr., (Russian).

SAKS, V. N., GRAMBERG, I. S., RONKINA, Z. Z., and APLONOVA, E. N.
1959   [Mesozoic deposits of the Khatanga depression.] Trudy Inst. Geol.
        Arktiki, 99, 225 pp., 22 figs., (Russian).

SALI, S. A.   See: Joshi, et al.

SALLER, KARL
1961   Zur Menschwerdung. Um den neuen Fund Oldoway (Ostafrika). Urania,
        24, 321—324, 3 figs., cover illustr.
1964A.   Die Nachfolge Martins. Anthrop. Anz., 27, 137—142.
1964B.   [Correlative variability of size characters of the cranium, its significance
         for the structure of racial types and for race genesis.] In:
         Nesturkh, (ed.), 1964C, 244—261, 6 figs., 4 tables, (Russian;
         English summary).
1964C.   Leitfaden der Anthropologie. 2nd rev. ed. Stuttgart: Fischer, viii +
         550 pp., 398 figs.
         Rev.: Gerhardt in Homo, 16, 53—54;   Jungwirth in Mitt. Anthrop.
         Ges. Wien, 93—94, 136;   Roth-Lutra in Anthrop. Anz., 30,
         66—67;   S. in Archeol. Roz., 17, 128, (Czech);   Sauter in
         Arch. Suiss. Anthrop. Gen., 30, 89—90.

SALMANOVICH, M. ÍA.
    1965   [Sergeǐ Aleksandrovich Tokarev. (65th anniversary).]   Sovetskaiă Etno-
                grafiiă, 1965:3, 152—153, (Russian).

SALTHE, STANLEY N., and KAPLAN, N. O.
    1966   Immunology and rates of evolution in the Amphibia in relation to the
                origins of certain taxa. Evolution, 20, 603—616, 3 figs.

SALUKVADZE, N. SH.
    1965   [On the age of the horizon with Lirolepis caucasica Rom. and adjacent
                foraminifera marls of Central Abkhazia.]   Izv. Geol. Obshch.
                Gruzii, 4:2, 61—64, (Russian).

SALUN, S. A. See: Bersenev, et al.

SAMARIN, V. G.   See: Chernov, A. A. and Samarin.

SAMMET, E. ÍU.   See: Grichuk, Sammet, et al.

SAMPSON, C. G.
    1965   A preliminary report on the Luano Spring deposits, Northern Rhodesia.
                S. Afr. Archaeol. Bull., 20, 29—33, 3 figs.
    1967A.   Coarse granulometric analysis of the Haua Fteah deposits. In: McBurney,
                C. B. M., 1967B, 50—54, 2 figs.
    1967B.   Excavations at Zaayfontein shelter, Norvalspont, North Cape. Navors.
                Nasion. Mus. Bloemfontein, 2:4, 41—124, 51 figs., 3 pls., 6 tables.
    1967C.   Excavations at Glen Elliot shelter, Colesburg District, North Cape.
                Navors. Nasion. Mus. Bloemfontein, 2:5—6, 125—210, 59 figs.,
                1 pl., 6 tables.
    1967D.   Zeekoegat 13: A Later Stone Age open-site near Venterstad, Cape.
                Navors. Nasion. Mus. Bloemfontein, 2:5—6, 211—237, 15 figs.,
                4 tables.

SAMSON, PETRE   See: Dumitresco, et al.; Feru, Rădulesco and Samson; Alimen,
                Rădulesco and Samson; Rădulesco and Samson.

SAMSON, P., and KOVÁCS, A.
    1967   [Felis spelaea Goldfuss in the Upper Pleistocene of Sf. Gheorghe basin
                (Broşov depression).] Lucrările Inst. speol., 6, 211—220, (Ro-
                manian; French summary).

SAMSON, P., and RĂDULESCO, C.
    1959   Beiträge zur Kenntnis der Chronologie des "Jüngeren Lösses" in der
                Dobrudscha (Rumänische Volksrepublik). Eiszeit. u. Gegenwart,
                10, 199—204, 1 pl.
                Abs.: Ebers in Zbl. Geol. Pal., Teil 2, 1962, 578.
    1964   [The Paleolithic of the "La Adam" cave in Dobrogea.] Biull. Kom
                Izuch. Chetvert. Perioda Akad. Nauk SSSR, no. 29, 156—164,
                4 figs., (Russian).
    1965   Die Säugetierfaunen und die Grenzen Pliozän/Pleistozän und Unter-
                pleistozän/Mittelpleistozän in Rumänien. Ber. Geol. Ges. Deutsch.
                Demokratischen Republ., 10, 67—76, 1 fig., 2 tables.
    1966A.   Sur la présence de Hydruntinus hydruntinus (Regàlia) dans le Post-glaciaire
                de Dobrogea. Lucrarile Inst. Spel. "Emil Racovita", Bucuresti,
                5, 251—260, tables, illustr., (Romanian; French summary).

1966B.   Sur la présence des Girafidés dans le Villafranchien supérieur de Rou-
            manie. Neues Jahrb. Geol. Pal., Monatsh., 1966:10, 588–594,
            1 fig., 1 table.

SAMSON, PIERRE-MICHEL   See: Rădulesco and Samson.

SAMSON, P.-M., and RĂDULESCO, C.
1963   Rev.: Bonifay in L'Anthrop., 68, 404–405.

SANDER, DAN
1964   Lithic material from Panama — fluted points from Madden Lake. Proc.
            Internat. Congr. Americanists, 1962:1, 183–192, 2 figs., 5 pls.

SANDERS, JOHN C. See: Brinkmann 1960.

SANDERSON, IVAN T.
1960B.   The riddle of the quick-frozen mammoths. [Condensed from 1960A.]
            Reader's Digest, 76:456, 121–125, illustr.

SANDFORD, KENNETH STUART
1965   The Reverend Charles Overy [1882 - 1963]. Proc. Geol. Soc. London,
            1618, 117-118.
            See: Arkell, A. J., and Sandford.

SANDISON, A. T.   See: Brothwell and Sandison.

SANDISON, A. T., and WELLS, C.
1967   Endocrine diseases. In: Brothwell, Don, and Sandison, A. T., (eds.),
            1967, 521–531, 7 figs.

SANKALIA, HASMUKH DHIRAJLAL
1962E.   Rev.: Fairservis in Amer. Anthrop. Special Publ., 65, 1186.
1963   Rev.: Allchin in Man, Jour. Roy. Anthrop. Inst., 1, 111;   Sunder Rajan
            in Jour. Maharaja Sayajirao Univ., 13, 83–87.
1964A.   Stone Age tools: their techniques, names and probable functions.
            Deccan College Building Centenary and Silver Jubilee, Ser., 1,
            xviii + 114 pp., 132 figs.
            Rev.: Bose in Sci. and Culture, 30, 499;   Das in Man in India, 44,
            369–370.
1964B.   Middle Stone Age culture in India and Pakistan. Science, 146, 365–375,
            7 figs.
1965   Early Stone Age in Saurashtra, Gujarat. In: Ripoll Perelló, E., (ed.),
            1965B, 327–346, 8 figs., 4 pls., (Spanish summary).
1966   Subbarao and his work. Jour. Maharaja Sayajirao Univ., 15, 3–8, portr.

SANOJA, MARIO
1963   Cultural development in Venezuela. Smithson. Misc. Coll., 146:1, 67–76.

SANTA, S.
1960   Essai de reconstitution de paysages végétaux quaternaires d'Afrique du
            Nord. Libyca, 6–7, 37–77.

SANTIANA, ANTONIO
1960   El Paleoindio en el Ecuador. II. Los cráneos de Punín y Paltacalo.
            In: Santiana and Carluci de Santiana, 1960B, 43–57, 2 pls.,
            Reprinted in: Humanitas, 3:2, 29–45, 3 pls., 3 tables.

SANTIANA, A., and CARLUCI DE SANTIANA, M. A.
    1960A.   Dos horizontes nuevos en la prehistoria ecuatoriana. Humanitas, 2:1,
                    85—93, illustr.
    1960B.   El Paleoindio en el Ecuador. Inst. Panamer. Geog. Hist., Plan Piloto
                    del Ecuador, Sec. Antrop., 1960, 1—57, 8 figs., 7 pls. Reprinted
                    in Humanitas, 3:2, 5—45, 7 figs., 3 pls., 1 map, 3 tables.
                    Rev.: Menghin in Acta Praehist., 3—4, 210.

SANZ FUENTES, E.   See: Crusafont Pairo, Valenciano Horta and Sanz Fuentes.

SANZ PAREJA, ALBERTO
    1961   El yacimiento de Concud, y la fauna terciaria de la cuenca de Teruel.
                    Teruel, no. 25, 205—237, 3 pls.

SARAIMAN, AUREL
    1966   [Mastodon longirostris Kaup from Meotian of Central Moldavian Plateau.]
                    An. şţiinţ. Univ. Iaşi, sec. 2b, 12, 123—132, 10 figs., (Romanian;
                    French and Russian summaries).
                    Rev.: Semaka in Zbl. Geol. Pal., Teil 2, 1968, 219.

SARAIMAN, A., and CǍPITANU, V.
    1964   Sur la présence de Elephas meridionalis Nesti dans la deuxième terrasse
                    de la Bistriţa (Racova — Buhuşi). An. Ştiinţ. Univ. Cuza (n.s.),
                    Sect. 2 (Ştiinţe Nat.), b. Geol.-Geog., 9, 79—84, 1 fig., 4 pls.,
                    (Rumanian, Russian and French summaries).
                    Abs.: Semaka in Zbl. Geol. Pal., Teil 2, 1966, 336.
    1965   [The presence of Mastodon arvernensis Croizet et Jobert in the 160 m.
                    terrace of Bistritsa R.]   An. Ştiinţ. Univ. Cuza (n.s.), sect. 2
                    (ştiinţ. nat.), b. Geol.-Geog., 11, 97—100, 2 pls., (Rumanian;
                    Russian and French summaries).

SARBADHIKARI, TIMIR RANJAN
    1966   The growth of palaeontological studies in India. Sci. and Culture, 32,
                    221—229, 6 figs.

SARGA, JOHN
    1965   Ancient society. Anthrop. Jour. Canada, 3:3, 22—34.
    1966   Totemic society. Anthrop. Jour. Canada, 4:3, 17—33.

SARICH, VINCENT
    1967A.   Man's place in nature. Abs. 66th. Ann. Meeting Amer. Anthrop. Assoc.,
                    1967, 74—75, (abs.).
    1967B.   Evolutionary rates and selective pressures in primate albumins. Amer.
                    Jour. Phys. Anthrop., 27, 244, (abs.).

SARKAR, S. S.
    1964   On the rates of evolution of some mammals from India and Pakistan.
                    Rept. 22nd. Internat. Geol. Congr., 1964, 125, (abs.).

SARTONO, S.
    1961   Notes on a new find of Pithecanthropus mandible. Pub. Tek., Ser.
                    Pal., Bandung, no. 2, 1—51, 10 figs., 11 pls., 11 tables.
    1963   [New discovery of a lower jaw of Pithecanthropus.]   Sov. Etnog.,
                    1963:3, 181—184, 3 figs., 1 table, (Russian).
    1964   On a new find of another Pithecanthropus skull. Bull. Geol. Surv.
                    Indonesia, 1, 2—5, 2 figs.

1967 An additional skull cap of a <u>Pithecanthropus.</u> Jour. Anthrop. Soc. Nippon, 75:754, 83—93, 12 figs., 2 tables.

SARYCHEVA, T. G.
1950B. [Against the pragmatism of certain American paleontologists, and on practical problems of Soviet paleontology.] Izv. Akad. Nauk SSSR, Ser. Geol., 1950:5, 8—15, (Russian).

SASAKI, S. See: Akiyama, Ito and Sasaki.

SASSI, P.
1964 Storia dei Dinosauri. Milan: series "Il Periscopio Minore", Massimo Press, 262 pp., numerous figs., 48 pls.
    Rev.: Franchi in Arch. Antrop. Etnol., 95, 273—274.

SATO, TATSUO See: Yamanouchi and Sato.

SATO, T., KOBAYASHI, T., and SAKAGUCHI, Y.
1962 Rev.: Anon. in Acta Praehist., 1966, 5—7, 315.

SATPAEV, K. I., and BOK, I. I.
1963 [Academician Vladimir Afanas'evich Obruchev.] Izv. Akad. Nauk Kazakh., SSR, Ser. Geol., 1963:6, 3—6, portr., (Russian; Kazakh summary).

SATSANGI, P. P.
1964 A note on <u>Chasmatosaurus</u> from the Panchet series of Raniganj coalfield, India. Current Sci., 33, 651—652, 3 figs.
    See: Prasad and Satsangi; Tripathi and Satsangi.

SAUER, E. G. FRANZ
1966A. Fossil eggshell fragments of a giant struthious bird (<u>Struthio oshanai</u>, sp. nov.) from Etosha Pan, South West Africa. Cimbebasia, no. 14, 2—51, 28 figs., (German summary).
1966B. Zwischenartliches Verhalten und das Problem der Domestikation. South West Afr., Sci. Soc., 20, 5—17, (English summary).

SAUSER, GUSTAV
1965 Von der Gestalt der Venus von Willendorf. Anthrop. Anz., 29, 205—208, 1 fig.

SAUTER, MARC-R.
1964 Eugène Pittard (1867—1962). Jahrb. Schweiz. Ges. Urgesch., 50, 127—128.
1965 Contrastes Esquimaux. Arch. Suiss. Anthrop. Gen., 30, 85—87.
1966A. Manuels et traités d'anthropologie. Arch. Suiss. Anthrop. Gen., 31, 48—50.
1966B. Nouvelles perspectives de l'art paléolithique. Arch. Suiss. Anthrop. Gen., 31, 50—54.

SAVAGE, C. N. See: Bowers and Savage.

SAVAGE, DONALD ELVIN
1965 Early Eocene continental mammalian fauna of Europe and North America. Spec. Pap. Geol. Soc. Amer., 82, 275, (abs.).

1966A.   (ed.) Society of Vertebrate Paleontology field trip no. 1. November 19, 1966. Mimeographed, Univ. Calif., Berkeley, 1966, 7 pp., illustr.

1966B.   (ed.) Society of Vertebrate Paleontology field trip, no. 2. November 20, 1966. Mimeographed, Univ. Calif., Berkeley, 1966, 16 pp., illustr.

See: Evernden, Savage, Curtis and James; Hibbard, Ray, et al.; Lintz and Savage; Russell, D. E., Louis and Savage.

SAVAGE, D. E., RUSSELL, D. E., and LOUIS, P.

1964   Early Eocene continental mammalian fauna of Europe and North America. Program, 60th Ann. Meeting, Geol. Soc. Amer., Cordilleran Sect., 55, (abs.).

1965   European Eocene Equidae (Perissodactyla). Univ. Calif. Publ. Geol. Sci., 56, 94 pp., 42 figs., 1 pl.

Abs.: Hünermann in Zbl. Geol. Pal., Teil 2, 1966, 333–335.

Rev.: Bohlin in Geol. Fören. Förh., 88, 415.

1966   Ceratomorpha and Ancylopoda (Perissodactyla) from the Lower Eocene Paris Basin, France. Univ. Calif. Publ. Geol. Sci., 66, 1–38, 28 figs., (French summary).

Abs.: B. B. in Przegl. Geol., 1967:3, 149.

SAVAGE, JAY MATHERS

1963C.   Evolution. New York: Holt, Rinehart and Winston, vii + 126 pp., illustr.

Rev.: Slatis in Science, 143, 1318.

1966   Evolution. München–Basel–Wien: Landwirtschaftsverlag, 139 pp., 38 figs., 9 tables, (not seen).

Rev.: Kurth in Naturwiss. Rundschau, 20:11, 492–493; Peters in Biol. Zbl., 89:1, 129.

SAVAGE, ROBERT JOSEPH GAY

1962B.   Rhaetic exposure at Emborough. Proc. Bristol Nat. Soc., 30, 275–278, 3 tables.

1963B.   Martin Alister Campbell Hinton. 1883–1961. Biog. Mem. Roy. Soc., 9, 155–170, portr.

1964A.   Recent reviews of fossil fishes. Nature, 204, 735–736.

1964B.   Martin Alister Campbell Hinton [–1961]. Proc. Linn. Soc. London, 175, 92–93.

1965A.   Fossil mammals of Africa:19. The Miocene Carnivora of East Africa. Bull. Brit. Mus. (Nat. Hist.), Geol., 10:8, 239–316, 62 figs., 5 pls., 12 tables. (Brit. Mus. Nat. Hist., Fossil Mamm. Afr., 19).

1965B.   Two mammal faunas from the early Tertiary of central Libya. Proc. Geol. Soc. London, no. 1623, 89–91, (discussion by N. L. Falcon and W. D. Gill).

1966   Irish Pleistocene mammals. Irish Nat. Jour., 15, 117–130, 1 table.

1967   Early Miocene mammal faunas of the Tethyan region. Publ. Syst. Assoc., 7, 247–282, 3 figs., 10 tables.

See: Smith, J. M. and Savage.

SAVAGE, R. J. G., and DONOVAN, D. T.

1962 The British Pleistocene Mammalia. Table of contents and index. Pal. Soc. Monog. London, 116, v + 7 pp.

SAVAGE, R. J. G., and LARGE, N. F.

1966   On Birgeria acuminata and the absence of labyrinthodonts from the Rhaetic. Palaeontol., 9, 135–141, pl. 20.

SÁVE-SÖDERBERGH, TORGNY
    1962   Preliminary report of the Scandinavian Joint Expedition. Kush, 10, 76–105, 13 figs., pls. 18–28.
    1963   Preliminary report of the Scandinavian Joint Expedition. Archaeological investigations between Faras and Gemai, November 1961–March 1962. Kush, 11, 47–69, 8 figs., pls. 7–12.
    1964   Preliminary report of the Scandinavian Joint Expedition. Archaeological investigations between Faras and Gamai, November 1962–March 1963. Kush, 12, 19–39, 9 figs., pls. 3–7.

SAVICH, V. P.
    1968   [Studies on Late Paleolithic site Lipa I in Volyn'.] In: Rybakov, (ed.), 203–204, (Russian).

SAVINOV, P. F.   See: Biriukov, et al.; Stogov and Savinov.

SAVORY, THEODORE
    1962   Naming the living world. An introduction to the principles of biological nomenclature. London: The English Universities Press Ltd., 128 pp.

SAVVAITOVA, L. S.
    1968   [On the limit Devonian Carboniferous in Latvia.] Izv. Vyssh. Uch., Zav., Geol. i Razv., 1968:5, 22–30, 4 figs., (Russian).

SAVY, MARCEL   See: Parent and Savy.

SAWICKI, LUDWIK (=Savitskii)
    1957   [Report on research on Paleolithic sites Zwierzyniec I and Piekary II performed in 1955.] Sprawozdania Archeol., 1957:4, 11–22, 1 fig., 4 pls., (Polish; Russian and English summaries).
    1960   [Magdalenian open station Antoniów Mały.] Biul. Panstwowy Inst. Geol., 150, 171–216, 15 figs., 8 pls., (Polish; Russian and English summaries).
    1964   Problèmes stratigraphiques et chronologiques des stations paléolithiques de Kostenki et de Borsevo. Archaeol. Polona, 7, 7–71, 14 figs., 17 tables.
    1965A.   [Problems of stratigraphy and geological age of Paleolithic sites Kostenki and Borshevo.] In: Bader, et al., (eds.), 1965, 166–199, 8 figs., 13 tables, (Russian).
    1965B.   Stations archéológiques de dune de l'industrie de Chwalibogowice à Chwalibogowice (Voyévodie Kielce). In: Ripoll Perelló, E., (ed.), 1965B., 347–354, 2 pls., (Polish; French summary).

SAXE, A.   See: Hewes, et al.

SAXENA, R. S.   See: Misra, K. S. and Saxena.

SAYLES, E. B.
    1965   Late Quaternary climate recorded by Cochise culture. Amer. Antiq., 30, 476–480, 3 figs.

SCHADÉ, J. P.   See: Bargmann and Schadé.

SCHAEFER, HANS
    1966   Die pontische Säugetierfauna von Charmoille (Jura bernois). I. Einleitung.

Rodentia.   Verh. Naturf. Ges. Basel, 77:1, 87—96, 6 figs., 1 table.

SCHAEFER, ULRICH
1964   Homo neanderthalensis (King). II.   E-Schädel-Fragment, Frontal F1 und
            Torus-Fragment 37,2 von Krapina.   Zeit. Morph. Anthrop., 54,
            260—271, 4 figs., pls. 22—25, 3 tables, (English summary).
            Rev.:   H. V. V. in L'Anthrop., 71:3—4, 314—315.
1968   Hans Weinert, 1887—1967. Anthrop. Anz., 30, 315—316.

SCHAEFFER, BOBB
1962   Abs.:   Weiler in Zbl. Geol. Pal., Teil 2, 1965, 234.
1963A.   Abs.:   Weiler in Zbl. Geol. Pal., Teil 2, 1965, 234—236.
1964   The rhipidistian-amphibian transition.   Amer. Zool., 4, 379, (abs).
1965A.   The rhipidistian-amphibian transition.   Comments by T. H. Eaton.   Amer.
            Zool., 5, 267—276, 6 figs.
1965B.   Fishes.   In: Kummel and Raup, (eds.), 1965, 110—118.
1965C.   (Obit.:)   Louis Hussakof [1883—1965].   News Bull., Soc. Vert. Pal., no.
            75, 52.
1965D.   The evolution of concepts related to the origin of the Amphibia.   Syst.
            Zool., 14, 115—118.
1965E.   The role of experimentation in the origin of higher levels of organization.
            Syst. Zool., 14, 318—336, 9 figs.
1967A.   Department of Vertebrate Paleontology.   Ann. Rept. Amer. Mus. Nat.
            Hist., 98, 57—61, 1 fig.
1967B.   Late Triassic fishes from the western United States.   Bull. Amer. Mus.
            Nat. Hist., 135:6, 285—342, 18 figs., pls. 8—30.
1967C.   Osteichthyan vertebrae.   In: Patterson, C., and Greenwood, P. H., (eds.),
            1967, 185—195, 3 figs., 1 pl.
1968A.   Merger of the Frick Laboratory with the Department of Vertebrate Paleon-
            tology.   News Bull., Soc. Vert. Pal., 83, 12—13.

SCHAEFFER, B., and MANGUS, M.
1965   Fossil lakes from the Eocene.   Nat. Hist., 74:4, 10—21, illustr.

SCHAEFFER, O. A., and ZÄHRINGER, J., (eds.)
1966   Potassium argon dating.   New York: Springer—Verlag, xii + 234 pp.,
            65 figs.
            Rev.:   Hebeda in Geol. en Mijn., 47, 220—221.

SCHÄFER, WILHELM
1962A.   Rev.:   Bachmayer in Universum; Natur u. Tech., 20:2, II.
1964A.   Aus dem Schaumuseum: Überregionali-tät.   Natur u. Mus., 94, 72—75,
            2 figs.
1964B.   Aktuopaläontologische Beobachtungen.   3.   Ein Säugerskelett am Pazifik-
            Boden.   Natur u. Mus., 94, 255—258, 1 fig.
            Abs.:   Häntzschel in Zbl. Geol. Pal., Teil 2, 1965, 12.
1964C.   Robert Mertens zum 70. Geburtstag.   Natur u. Mus., 94, 455—458,
            portr.
1966   Aktuopaläontologische Beobachtungen.   6.   Otolithen—Anreicherungen.
            Natur u. Mus., 96, 439—444, 4 figs.

SCHAFFER, WILLIAM   See: Reed, C. A. and Schaffer.

SCHANFIELD, SALLY   See: Howell and Schanfield.

SCHAUB, HANS
1964   Bericht über das Basler Naturhistorische Museum für das Jahr 1963.
                Verh. Naturf. Ges. Basel, 75, 1–27.
1965   Bericht über das Naturhistorische Museum für das Jahr 1964. Verh.
                Naturf. Ges. Basel, 76, 1–28.

SCHAUB, SAMUEL
1940D.   Ein Ratitenbecken aus dem Bohnerz von Egerkingen. Verh. Schweiz.
                Naturf. Ges., 120, 154–155.
1941B.   Hans Georg Stehlin †1870–1941. Nationalzeitung Basel, (not seen).
1941C.   Die kleine Hirschart aus dem Oberpliocaen von Seneze. Verh. Schweiz.
                Naturf. Ges., 121, 139.
1942F.   Das Naturhistorische Museum eröffnet einen neuen Saal. Nationalzeitung
                Basel, (not seen).
1942G.   Der Abschluss eines glucklichen Lebens. Dr. Fritz Sarasin. Nationalzei-
                tung Basel, (not seen).
1949B.   Elomeryx minor (Deperet), ein Bothriodontine aus dem schweizerischen
                Aquitanien. Eclog. Geol. Helvetiae, 41, 340–347, 3 figs., pl. 13.

SCHAUB, S., and HÜRZELER, J.
1949   Die Säugetierfauna des Aquitanien vom Wischberg bei Langenthal. Eclog.
                Geol. Helvetiae, 41, 354–366, 4 figs.

SCHAUB, S., and JAGHER, A.
1945   Höhlenbär und Höhlenhyäne im unteren Birstal. Verh. Schweiz. Naturf.
                Ges., 125, 156–157.

SCHAUBERGER, O., MOTTL, M., BAUER, F., and TRIMMEL, H.
1961   Guide of excursions. Actes 3eme Congr. Internat. Spéléol., B, 47–90,
                (German, French and English).

SCHAURTE, WERNER T.
1964   Darstellung eines Elasmotherium in der Felsmalerei von Rouffignac. Natur
                u. Mus., 94, 354–356, 3 figs.

SCHEELE, WILLIAM E.
1965A.   Interstate Ohio 71 fossil dig. First of a series about fossil salvage in a
                classic collecting locality. Explorer, 7:3, 5–8, illustr., cover photo.
1965B.   Interstate Ohio 71 fossil dig. Third of a series about the Natural Science
                Museum's I-71 fossil salvage program. Part I: Some comments on
                the dig. Explorer, 7:5, 4–7, illustr.
1965C.   The museum and the community it serves. Explorer, 7:6, 4–5, illustr.

SCHEFFER, V. B.
1965   Marine mammals and the history of Bering Strait. 7th Internat. Congr.,
                Internat. Assoc. Quat. Res., Abs., 1965, 408, (abs).
1967   Marine mammals and the history of Bering Strait. In: Hopkins, D. M.,
                (ed.), 350–363, 2 tables.

SCHEIDEGGER, S.
1963   Palaeopathologische Befunde an Knochen. Verh. Deutsche Pathol. Ge-
                sellsch., 47, 198–202, (not seen).
        See: Koby and Scheidegger.

SCHENDEL, J. A. A. VAN
    1965   Het Leudal. Natuurreservaat en recreatiegebied van het Staatsbosbeheer.
                Natuurhist. Maandbl., 54, 46–48, 1 fig.

SCHERBAKOV, D. I.
    1964   Scale of absolute geologic time. Jour. Pal. Soc. India, 4, 26–29, 1 table.

SCHERF, H.
    1967   Zur Stammesgeschichte der Hyänen. Naturwiss. Rundschau, 20:1, 29.

SCHERSCHEL, JOSEPH J.   See: Payne, M. M. and Scherschel.

SCHERZ, E. R.
    1965   Der Abbé H. Breuil besucht die Weisse Dame im Brandberg 1947. In:
                Ripoll Perelló, E., (ed.), 1965B, 355–362, 4 pls., (Spanish summary).

SCHERZ, GUSTAV
    1962   Niels Stensen, Bildbuch. Würzburg: Echter Verlag; New York: Stechert-
                Hafner, 48 pp., 72 pls.
                Rev.: J. G. de Ll. in Bol. Soc. Españ. Hist. Nat., Sec. Geol., 63:2–3,
                251–253; G. de Ll. in Notas Comun. Inst. Geol. Min., 79, 269.
    1963   Pionier des Wissenschaft. Niels Stensen in seinen Schriften. Copenhagen:
                Munksgaard, 348 pp., figs., 12 pls.
                Rev.: Hölder in Zbl. Geol. Pal., Teil 2, 1964, 386; Hooykaas in Lychnos,
                1963–1964, 387–389; Nickel in Aufschluss, 15, 88.
    1964   Niels Stensen. Denker und Forscher im Barock. 1638-1686. Grosse
                Naturforscher, Band 28. Stuttgart: Wissenschaftliche Verlagsgell-
                schaft, 275 pp., 16 figs., frontispiece.
                Rev.: Ankel in Naturwiss. Rund., 18, 122.

SCHEUENPFLUG, LORENZ
    1965   Ein Zufallsfund: Unterkiefer eines Halbpanzernashorns in einer Baugrube.
                Aufschluss, 16, 311–313, 1 fig.

SCHEYGROND, A.
    1965   In memoriam Dr. A. B. Van Deinse. Lutra, 7, 1–4, portr., (Dutch;
                English summary).

SCHIERL, MARGARET   See: Augusts and Burian, 1963B, 1964C.

SCHILD, ROMUALD
    1961   The chronology of the Masovian cycle. Internat. Assoc. Quat. Res.,
                Abs. Pap., 6th Congr., 145–146, (abs.).
    1963   Z zagadnień systematyki kulturowej paleolitu. I Symp. Paleolityczne,
                Kráków, 1963:1, 14–21, (not seen).
    1965A.   Remarques sur les principes de la systematique culturelle du Paléolithique
                (Surtout du Paléolithique final). Archaeol. Polona, 8, 67–81.
    1965B.   [A new industry of Magdalenian cycle in Poland.] Archeol. Polski, 10:1,
                115–150, 17 figs., (Polish; French summary).
    1966   [Le Paléolithique final de Crimée et le cycle Mazovien.] Archeol. Polski,
                10:2, 431–473, 7 figs., 6 pls., 1 table, (Polish; French summary).
                See: Kowłowski, J. K. and Schild.

SCHINDEWOLF, OTTO H.
    1962   Neokatastrophismus? Zeit. Deutsche Geol. Ges., 114, 430–435, 3 figs.

1964 Erdgeschichte und Weltgeschichte. Abh. Akad. Wiss. u. Lit., Math-naturw. Kl., Mainz, 1964, 55–104, 9 figs.
   Rev.: Daber in Geologie, 18:4, 508; Struve in Natur u. Museum, 98:7, 284.

SCHINDLMAYR, WULF-EIKE See: Mayr, H. and Schindlmayr.

SCHLESIER, KARL-HEINZ
1964A. Vorbericht über die Erste Deutsche Archäologische Brooks-Range-Expedition, Nord-Alaska, 1964. Anthropos, 59, 911–917, 2 pls.
1964B. Die Bering-Landbrücke und die frühen amerikanischen Spitzen-Traditionen. Saeculum, 15, 207–213.
1965 Geschichte der Besiedlung Nordamerikas von den Anfängen bis zum Beginn der christlichen Zeitrechnung. Saeculum, 16, 29–41, 3 figs.
1966 Sedna Creek: Abschlussbericht über eine archäologische Feldarbeit in Nord-Alaska. Zeit. Ethnol., 91:1, 5–39, 15 pls., 1 map, 1 table.
1967 Sedna Creek: report on an archaeological survey on the Arctic slope of the Brooks Range. Amer. Antiq., 32, 210–222, 3 figs., 1 table.

SCHLOSSER, MAX See: Zittel 1964B.

SCHMALHAUSEN, IVAN I.
1947 [New in modern darwinism.] Priroda, 1947:12, 31–44, 4 figs., (Russian).
1959B. [Concerning monophyletism and polyphyletism in relation to the problem of the origin of land vertebrates.] Biull. Mosk. Obshch. Prirody, Otd. Biol., 64:4, 15–33, 14 figs., (Russian).
1964A. [The position of Urodela among the lower terrestrial Vertebrata.] Trudy Zool. Inst. Akad. Nauk SSSR, 33, 5–33, 20 figs., (Russian).
1964B. [Origin of terrestrial vertebrates.] Moscow: "Nauka" Press, 272 pp., 167 figs., (Russian).
   Rev.: Matveev in Zool. Jour. Moscow, 1965, 44:10, 1582–1585, (Russian).
1968 Origin of terrestrial vertebrates. Translated from Russian by Leon Kelso. Edited by Keith Stewart Thomson. Preface by Carl Gans. New York and London: Academic Press, xxii + 314 pp., 165 figs.
   Rev.: Bellairs in Jour. Anat., 104:1, 164; Cox in Nature, 219, 1395; Eaton in Amer. Sci., 57:2, 140A–141A; Haltenorth in Säugetier-kundl. Mitt., 17:2, 198; Koenigswald in Naturwiss., 56:1, 47; Olson in Quart. Rev. Biol., 44:4, 416; Romer in Science, 162, 250–251; Westphal in Zbl. Geol. Pal., Teil 2, 1969:4, 327–328.
   See: Severtsov 1945, 1948.

SCHMID, ELISABETH
1958 Rev.: Trimmel in Die Höhle, 11, 24–25.
1964A. Ergebnisse der Untersuchung von Sediment–folgen in den drei Bärenhöhlen. Acta Bernensia, 3, 131–145, fig. 29.
1964B. Eine neu erkannte paläolithische Frauenstatuette vom Petersfels bei Engen (Baden). Bonner Jahrb., suppl. 10:1, 45–49, 1 fig., 1 pl.
1964C. Eine neu erkannte paläolithische Frauenstatuette vom Petersfeld bei Engen (Baden). In: Uslar and Narr, (eds.), 1964, 45–49, 1 fig., 1 pl.
1964D. Remarques au sujet d'une représéntation de bouquetin à Niaux. Préhist. Spéléol. Ariégeoises, 19, 33–39, 4 figs.
1965 Ueber gerundete Knochenbruchstücke aus dem romischen Strassenkies von Augusta Raurica. Basler Beiträge Geog. Ethnol., Ethnol. Reihe, 2, 333–338, fig. 83.
1966 Höhlenbären im Bärenloch bei Tecknau BL. Ur-Schweiz, 30, 1–2, 1 fig.

SCHMIDT, ALFRED A.
1965   Professor Dr. Robert Mertens zum 70. Geburtstag. Salamandra, 1, 2–6, portr.

SCHMIDT, HERMANN
1963   Abs.: Huene in Zbl. Geol. Pal., Teil 2, 1964, 421.
1966   Eine Entwicklungsreihe bei Schildkröten Gattung Chelydra. Neues Jahrb. Geol. Pal., Abh., 125, Festband, 19–28, 3 figs., portr.

SCHMIDT, V.   See: McCrady and Schmidt.

SCHMIDT, WOLFGANG
1959   Rev.: Chlupač in Věstnik Ústřed. Úst. Geol., 34, 60, (Czech).
1965   Der erste Nachweis einer ökologisch bedeutsamen Fisch-Gruppe (Haplole-pidae, Palaeoniscoidea) im Oberkarbon von Nordrhein-Westfalen. Neues Jahrb. Geol. Pal., Abh., 121:3, 254–263, 1 fig., 1 pl.

SCHMIDT, W. J.
1964   Über eine fossile Schwanen-Eischale. Jour. Ornithol., 105, 326–333, 5 figs.
1967   Struktur des Eischalenkalkes von Dinosauriern. Zeit. Zellforsch., 82:1, 136–155, 13 figs., (English summary).

SCHMIDT, ZOLTÁN
1964   [On the find of a Pleistocene deer (Cervus megaceros germanicus Pohl.) in eastern Slovakia.]   Sborn. Vychodosloven. múzea Košieiach, ser. A, 5, 35–38, (Slovakian; Russian, English, and German summaries).
1965A.   [Metric characteristics of fossil vertebrates from the collection of the Regional Museum at Spisska Nová Ves.]   Sborn. Vychodosloven. múzea v Košiciach, ser. A, 6, 119–133, 9 pls., 1 table, (Slovakian; Russian, English, and German summaries).
1965B.   [Find of fossil footprints of Cervidae and Equidae at Vyšné Ružbachy village.]   Sborn. Vychodosloven. múzea v Košiciach, ser. A, 6, 136, 1 fig., (Slovakian).
See: Harčár and Schmidt.

SCHMITTER, EDUARDO   See: Aveleyra Arroyo de Anda, 1965.

SCHMITZ-MOORMANN, K.
1966   Das Weltbild Teilhard de Chardins. Teil I. Physik, Ultraphysik, Metaphysik. Untersuchungen zur Terminologie Teilhard de Chardin. Köln and Opladen: Westdeutscher Verlag. 204 pp., 16 figs., (not seen). Rev.: Jürgens in Zeit. Morph. Anthrop., 58, 324–325; Spindler in Anthrop. Anz., 30, 294–295.

SCHNEIDER, HORST   See: Jung and Schneider; Milojčić, et al.

SCHNEIDER, R.
1966   Zur Kenntnis der innerartlichen Ausformung des Schmelzmusters bei Equidenzähnen. Zool. Anz., 176, 71–97, 25 figs. See: Starck, Schneider and Kuhn.

SCHOBINGER, JUAN
1959C.   Estudios recientes sobre el "Presapiens". Rev. Inst. Antrop., Univ. Nacion. Litoral, Rosario, 1, 237–247, 1 fig.

1962   Consideraciones terminológicas acerca del precerámico en Sudamérica y
            sus formas culturales. Ampurias, 24, 165—168.
1964   El 35º Congreso Internacional de Americanistas (México, 19-25 de
            Agosto 1962). An. Arqueol. Etnol., Univ. Nac. Cuyo, 17—18,
            203—207.
1966   El análisis de sedimentos. Una técnica moderna al servicio de la datación
            del "Paleolítico Alpino". Acta Praehist., 5—7, 223—239.

SCHOCH, ERHARD OTTO
1963B.   Die Olduwan-Werkzeuge vom Monte Gargano und Werkzeuge des Heidel-
            bergers. Ber. 7. Tagung Deutsch. Ges. Anthrop., 1961, 153—155.

SCHÖDUBE, WILHELM, and STEINBACKER, J.
1967   Aus der 150 jährigen Geschichte der Senckenbergischen Naturforschenden
            Gesellschaft zu Frankfurt am Main. Natur u. Mus., 97, 431—489,
            illustr.

SCHOENWETTER, JAMES   See: Hester, J. J., and Schoenwetter.

SCHOLZ, HEINZ
1963   Interessante Fischversteinerung aus dem Weissen Jura. Natur, 71, *5,
            1 fig., (not seen).
            Abs.: Lotze in Zbl. Geol. Pal., Teil 2, 1963, 881.

SCHÖNWÄLDER, MAX A.   See: Augusta and Burian, 1962D, 1964A.

SCHOTT, L.
1962B.   Zur Stellung von Oreopithecus bambolli Gervais innerhalb der Hominoid-
            systems. 5. Biologiai vándorgyülés elöadásainak ismertetése
            Budapest, 1962, 52, (not seen).
            Abs.: Anon. in Anthrop., 2:1, 68.

SCHRADER, K.   See: Cott and Schrader.

SCHREIBER, THEO
1962   Die Blätterkohle von Rott (2. Teil). Aufschluss, 13, 165—173, 23 figs.

SCHREIDER, EUGÈNE
1965   Biométrie et Évolution. In: Genovés, S., (ed.), 1965C, 319—336.

SCHREINER, A.   See: Kuss and Schreiner.

SCHROEVERS-KOMMANDEUR, H., and JAGER, S. DE
1966   De Henkeput. Opgravingen en determinatie van dierlijke resten. Natuur-
            hist. Maandbl., 55:7—8, 117—128, (English summary).

SCHUBERTH, CHRISTOPHER J.
1967   The Hudson's six geologies. Nat. Hist., 76:1, 46—55, illustr.

SCHUHL, P.-M., et al., (eds.)
1964   Bulletin signalétique 22. Histoire des sciences et des techniques Centre
            Nation. Recherch., Sci., 17:1, [3] + xxxix + pp. 309—369.

SCHULTZ, ADOLPH H.
1965   Die rezenten Hominoidea. In: Heberer, (ed.), 1965A, 56—102, 34 figs.,
            10 tables.

1967   Notes on diseases and healed fractures of wild apes. In: Brothwell,
                Don, and Sandison, A. T., (eds.), 47–55, 3 figs.

SCHULTZ, C. BERTRAND
    1934B.   The Pleistocene mammals of Nebraska. Bull. Univ. Neb. State Mus.,
                1:41, 359–393, 1 table.
    1960   Nebraska's changing climate. Mus. Notes, Univ. Neb. State Mus., no. 12,
                1–3.
    1961C.   Ice Age migrants from Asia. Mus. Notes, Univ. Neb. State Mus., no. 15,
                1–4, 4 figs.
    1963B.   The Late Pleistocene faunal sequence at Big Bone Lick, Kentucky.
                Amer. Philos. Soc., Year Book, 1963, 348–350.
    1965A.   The Bison of the Great Plains region. 7th Internat. Congr., Internat.
                Assoc. Quat. Res., Abs., 1965, 414, (abs.).
    1965B.   The stratigraphic distribution of vertebrate fossils in Quaternary eolian
                deposits in the midcontinent region of North America. 7th
                Internat. Congr., Internat. Assoc. Quat. Res., Abs., 1965, 415,
                (abs.).
    1965C.   The story of a Nebraska sea serpent. Mus. Notes, Univ. Neb. News,
                no. 27, [1–3], 4 figs.
    1966   The Agate Springs fossil quarries. Mus. Notes, Univ. Neb. State Mus.,
                no. 30, 1–7, 13 figs.
    1967   Erwin Hinkley Barbour (1856 - 1947), geologist, paleontologist, naturalist,
                humanitarian. Proc. Neb. Acad. Sci., 77th Ann. Meeting, 1967,
                28–29, (abs.).
                See: Eisele and Schultz; Stout and Schultz.

SCHULTZ, C. B., et al.
    1965   Big Bone Lick. Guidebook for field conference G, Great Lakes – Ohio
                River Valley. Guidebk., 7th INQUA Congr., 1965, 60–61.

SCHULTZ, C. B., and FALKENBACH, C. H.
    1968   The phylogeny of the oreodonts. Parts 1 and 2. Bull. Amer. Mus. Nat.
                Hist., 139, 498 pp., 56 figs., 19 tables, 23 charts.

SCHULTZ, C. B., FALKENBACH, C., and VONDRA, C. F.
    1965   The Brule-Gering contact in the Tertiary deposits of western Nebraska.
                Proc. Neb. Acad. Sci. 75, 15, (abs.).
    1967   The Brule-Gering (Oligocene-Miocene) contact in the Wildcat Ridge area
                of western Nebraska. Bull. Neb. State Mus., 6, 43–58, 7 figs.

SCHULTZ, C. B., and SMITH, H. T. U., (eds.)
    1965A.   Guidebook for field conference C, Upper Mississippi Valley. Guidebk.,
                7th INQUA Congr., 1965, 126 pp., illustr.
    1965B.   Guidebook for field conference D, central Great Plains. Guidebk., 7th
                INQUA Congr., 1965, 128 pp., illustr.
    1965C.   Guidebook for field conference I, Northern Great Basin and California.
                Guidebk., 7th INQUA Congr., 1965, 165 pp., illustr.

SCHULTZ, C. B., TANNER, L. G., WHITMORE, F. C., JR., RAY, L. L., and
CRAWFORD, E. C.
    1967   Big Bone Lick, Kentucky. A pictorial story of the paleontological ex-
                cavations at this famous fossil locality from 1962 to 1966. Mus.
                Notes, Univ. Neb. State Mus., no. 33, 12 pp., illustr.

SCHULTZ, C. B., WHITMORE, F. C., JR., and TANNER, L. G.
1966   Pleistocene mammals and stratigraphy of Big Bone Lick State Park, Kentucky. Spec. Pap. Geol. Soc. Amer., 87, 262—263, (abs.).

SCHULTZ, GERALD E.
1965A.   Four superimposed Late Pleistocene vertebrate faunas from southwest Kansas. 7th Internat. Congr., Internat. Assoc. Quat. Res., Abs., 1965, 416, (abs.).
1965B.   Pleistocene vertebrates from the Butler Spring local fauna, Meade County, Kansas. Papers Mich. Acad. Sci., 50, 235—265, 5 figs.
1966   Late Pleistocene microvertebrates from southwest Kansas. Texas Jour. Sci., 18, 101—102, (abs.).
1967   Four superimposed Late-Pleistocene vertebrate faunas from southwest Kansas. In: Martin, P. S., and Wright, H. E., (eds.), 1967, 321—336, 5 figs.

SCHULTZ, GWEN M.
1964   Was the Ice Age really so bad? Frontiers, 28, 149—152, illustr.

SCHULTZ, LEONARD P.   See: Jordan, D. S. 1963.

SCHULTZE, HANS-PETER
1966   Morphologische und histologische Untersuchungen an Schuppen mesozoischer Actinopterygier (Übergang von Ganoid-zu Rundschuppen). Neues Jahrb. Geol. Pal., Abh., 126:3, 232—314, 61 figs., 5 pls.
    Rev.: Weiler in Zbl. Geol. Pal., Teil 2, 1967, 500—504.
1968   Palaeoniscoidea-Schuppen aus dem Unterdevon Australiens und Kanadas und aus dem Mitteldevon Spitzbergens. Bull. Brit. Mus. (Nat. Hist.), Geol., 16:7, 343—370, 19 figs., 4 pls.

SCHUMACHER, GERT-HORST
1964   Richard Nikolaus Wegner 80 Jahre. Säugetierkundl. Mitt., 12, 185—186, portr.

SCHUTZ, FRED
1967   Identification of bison skulls. Blue Jay, 25, 191—192, 1 table.

SCHÜZ, ERNST
1967   175 Jahre Staatliches Museum für Naturkunde in Stuttgart. Jahresh. Ver. Vaterländ. Naturk. Württemberg, 122, Appendix, 1—40, 27 figs.

SCHÜZ, E., and STAESCHE, K.
1963   Sammel- und Forschungsreisen aus dem Bereich des Staatlichen Museums für Naturkunde in Stuttgart. Stuttgarter Beitr. z. Naturk., no. 112, 11 pp.

SCHWARTZ, DOUGLAS W.
1960   Rev.: Anon. in NSS News, 18, 135.
1965   The Paleo-Indian era: distribution of finds. Kentucky. Bull. Southeast. Archaeol. Confer., 2, 6—9.
1968   Conceptions of Kentucky prehistory: a case study in the history of archeology. Lexington: Univ. of Kentucky Press, (Studies in Anthropology, No. 6), ix + 133 pp., 39 figs.
    Rev.: Dunnell in Amer. Anthrop., 70, 1019—1020;   Soday in Man, Jour. Roy. Anthrop. Inst., 3, 667—668.
    See: Rolingson and Schwartz.

SCHWARZBACH, M.
1963   Rev.: d. J. in Geol. en Mijn, 43, 207, (Dutch).

SCHWEIZER, ROLF
1963   Bernhard Peyer [1885 - 2-23-1963]. Jahresb. Mitt. Oberrhein. Geol.
            Ver., 45, L11.
1964   Die Elasmobranchier und Holocephalien aus den Nusplinger Plattenkalken.
            Palaeontogr., Abt. A, 123, 58–110, 15 figs., pls. 7–12.
1966   Ein Coelacanthide aus dem Oberen Muschelkalk Göttingens. Neues Jahrb.
            Geol. Pal., Abh., 125, Festband, 216–226, 5 figs., 1 pl., portr.,
            (English summary).

SCHWIDETZKY, I.
1963   Europide und Mongolide in Russisch-Asien seit dem Jungpaläolithikum.
            Homo, 14, 151–167.
1965   Egon Freiherr von Eickstedt. 10.4.1892 - 20.12.1965. Homo, 16:4,
            197–200, portr.
            See: Arambourg 1965B.

SCISCENTI, JAMES V., and GREMINGER, H. C.
1962   Archaeology of the Four Corners power projects. New Mexico Pap.
            Anthrop., no. 5, 130 pp., (not seen).

SCOPES, JOHN T., and PRESLEY, J.
1967   Center of the storm: Memoirs of John T. Scopes. New York: Holt,
            Rinehart & Winston, 277 pp., (not seen).
            Rev.: Anon. in Time, 89:7, 102, E7.

SCOTT, G. H. See: Randal and Scott.

SCOTT, GLENN R.
1963   Quaternary geology and geomorphic history of the Kassler quadrangle,
            Colorado. U. S. Geol. Surv., Prof. Pap. 421A, 70 pp., 27 figs.,
            1 pl.

SCOTT, P.   See: Delacour and Scott.

SCOTTI, PIETRO
1965   Recherches de Spéléologie humaine. 3. Internat. Kongress Spel., 4, 57–59.

SEARS, PAUL B.
1964   The goals of paleoecological reconstruction. Discussion. Publ. Fort
            Burgwin Res. Center, no. 3, 4–6.

SEARS, WILLIAM H.
1964   The southeastern United States. In: Jennings and Norbeck, (eds.),
            1964, 259–287, 5 figs.

SEDDON, J. DAVID
1966A.   Communications in archaeology. S. Afr. Archaeol. Bull., 21, 1–2.
1966B.   The Early Stone Age at Bosman's Crossing, Stellenbosch. S. Afr.
            Archaeol. Bull., 21, 133–137, 4 figs., 1 table.
1967   Some Early Stone Age surface sites around Stellenbosch, S. W. Cape.
            S. Afr. Archaeol. Bull., 22, 57–59, 1 fig.

SEELEY, H. G.
1967   Dragons of the air: an account of extinct flying reptiles. (With a new
            introduction by Edwin H. Colbert.) Reprint of 1901 ed. New
            York: Dover Publ., xxi + 239 + 3 pp., illustr.
            Rev.: Okulitch in Quart. Rev. Biol., 42, 424.

SEEMANN, WALTER
1965   Fischreste aus dem Lettenkeuper von Rottweil. Aufschluss, 16, 14.

SEGEDIN, R. A.
1966   [Paleocene deposit on Tykbutak R. in Primugodzhar'e.] In: Collected
            Papers, 1966A, [Materials on the geology and economic ores of
            western Kazakhstan], 57—64, (Russian).

SEGERBLOM, CLIFF, and GENE
1965   About an old town and an old fish! Desert Mag., 28:10, 26—27, 2 figs.

SEGMEN, PATRICIA K.
1965   Junior notes and news: Ancient Elephant Trail. Sci. on the March,
            45, 33, illustr.

SEGRE, ALDO G.
1961   Remplissages pleistocènes dans les grottes du Monte Argentorio en pro-
            vince de Grosseto (Toscane, Italie). Die Höhle, 12, 117—118,
            (abs.; French and German). Reprinted in Actes 3ème Congr.
            Internat. Spéléol., A, 85—86.

SEIDEL, G., and WAGENBRETH, O.
1966   Walter Hoppe zum 70. Geburtstag. Geologie, 15, 391—395, portr.

SEITZ, HERMANN JOSEF
1966   Ein paläolithischer Grossschaber aus Wittislingen. Quartär, 17, 171—175,
            1 pl.

SEKI, M.   See: Tanaka and Seki.

SEKYRA, JOSEF
1967   [The Quaternary-geological conditions of the eastern Labe area.] Sborn.
            Geol. Věd, Rada A: Antropozoikum, 4, 97—124, 10 figs., 1 table,
            (Czech; English summary).

SELANDER, ROBERT K.
1965   Avian speciation in the Quaternary. In: Wright, H. E., and Frey, D. G.,
            (eds.), 1965, 527—542, 6 figs.
            Rev.: R. E. M. in Ibis, 109, 468.

SELIVERSTOV, IŪ. P.
1961   [On the stratigraphy of Quaternary formations of northeastern Kazakhstan
            and Altaǐ.] Materialy Geol. Inst. (VSEGEI), Nov. Ser. Chetv. Geol.
            i Geomorf., 42, 115—138, 2 tables, (Russian).
            See: Ganeshin, Zubakov, et al.

SELLSTEDT, H., ENGSTRAND, L., and GEJVALL, N. G.
1966   New application of radiocarbon dating to collagen residue in bones.
            Nature, 212, 272—274, 4 figs.

SELSAN, MILLICENT E.
1964   The voyage of the Beagle. Nat. and Sci., 1:16, 12—14, 3 figs.

SELTIN, RICHARD J.
1963   Evolution of the reptiles and amphibians from the early Permian red
                   beds of Texas. Amer. Philos. Soc., Year Book, 1963, 350—351.
1965   Evolution of the reptiles and amphibians in the Early Permian. Amer.
                   Philos. Soc. Yearbook, 1964, 295—297.

SEMENOV, IŪ. I.
1965   [On division of primeval history into periods.] Sovetskaiā Etnografiiā,
                   1965:5, 74—93, (Russian; English summary).
1966   [How has mankind originated?] Moscow: Izdatel'stvo Nauka, 576 pp.,
                   (Russian).
                   Rev.: Dobzhansky in Man, Jour. Roy. Anthrop. Inst., 3, 136—138;
                   Klein in Amer. Anthrop., 71, 343—344.
1967A.   Über die Periodisierung der Urgeschichte. Ethnog.-Archäol. Zeit., 8,
                   15—38, (Russian and English summaries).
1967B.   [New American editions of "Ancient Society" by L. H. Morgan.]
                   Sovetskaiā Etnografiiā, 1967:5, 182—185, (Russian).

SEMENOV, S. A.
1957D.   [Prehistoric technology.] Mat. Issled. Arkheol. SSSR, 54, (Russian).
                   Moscow-Leningrad, 240 pp., 106 figs. and pls.
                   Rev.: Guryev in Vest. Ist. Mir. Kult., 1958:3, 225—230;   Neustupny in
                   Antiq. 35, 161—163.
1958   [Concerning the stone implements of Australopithecus.] Sov. Arkheol.,
                   1958:3, 244—246, 1 fig., (Russian).
1959B.   [Experimental research on primeval technique.] Sov. Arkheol., 1959:2,
                   35—46, 12 figs., (Russian).
1960C.   [The question of the origin of facial and body hair of contemporary
                   man.] Trudy Inst. Etnograf., 50, 210—231, 2 figs., 1 table, (Rus-
                   sian).
1961A.   [Traces of work on implements and proof that Neanderthal men worked
                   right-handed.] Krat. Soob. Inst. Ist. Mat. Kult. SSSR, 84, 12—18,
                   2 figs., (Russian).
1961B.   [The origin of abrasive technique and its significance in ancient economy.]
                   Krat. Soob. Inst. Ist. Mat. Kult SSSR, 86, 3—10, 4 figs., (Russian).
1964A.   [Flint tools from Khor-Daud.] In: Piotrovskiĭ, (ed.), 1964, 178—179,
                   (Russian).
1964B.   Prehistoric technology: an experimental study of the oldest tools and
                   artifacts from traces of manufacture and wear. Transl. with
                   preface by M. W. Thompson. London: Cory, Adams and Mackay;
                   New York: Barnes and Noble, 211 pp., 105 figs.
                   Rev.: Honea in El Palacio, 71, 47—48; Irwin in Amer. Sci., 52, 466A;
                   Lacaille in Antiq. Jour., 45, 115—116; Sheldon in Bull. London
                   Univ. Inst. Archaeol., no. 6, 132; Witthoft in Penn. Archaeol.,
                   34, 7, 46.
1965   [Experimental method for studying primitive techniques.] In: Kolchin,
                   (ed.), 1965, 216—222, 2 figs., (Russian).
1968A.   [Labor and intellect in the early stages of evolution.] Discussion. 7th
                   Internat. Congr. Anthrop. Ethnol. Sci., Moscow, 1964, 3, 417—422,
                   (Russian).
1968B.   [Tools for straightening spear-shafts from Paleolithic epoch.] Voprosy
                   Antrop., 28, 166—176, 9 figs., (Russian).

SEMKEN, HOLMES A., JR.
1960 Vertebrate fossils from Longhorn Caverns, Burnet County, Texas. NSS News, 18, 71, (abs.).
1966 Stratigraphy and paleontology of the McPherson Equus beds (Sandahl local fauna), McPherson County, Kansas. Contrib. Mus. Pal. Univ. Mich., 20:6, 121–178, 7 figs., 1 map.
1967 Mammalian remains from Rattlesnake Cave, Kinney County, Texas. Pearce-Sellards Ser., Texas Mem. Mus., 7, 1–11, 1 fig., 1 table.

SEMKEN, H. A., and GRIGGS, C. D.
1965 The long-nosed peccary, Mylohyus nasutus, from McPherson County, Texas. Papers Mich. Acad. Sci., 50, 267–274, 2 figs.

SEMKEN, H. A., MILLER, B. B., and STEVENS, J. B.
1964 Late Wisconsin woodland musk oxen in association with pollen and invertebrates from Michigan. Jour. Pal., 38, 823–835, 2 figs., pls. 129–132, 4 tables.

SEN, D., and GHOSH, A. K.
1964 Lithic culture-complex in the Pleistocene sequence of the Narmada Valley, central India. Riv. Sci. Preist., 18, 3–23, 6 figs., (Italian and French summaries).
1966 (eds.) Studies in prehistory: Robert Bruce Foote memorial volume. Calcutta: Mukhopadhyay, viii + 195 pp., illus., pl., maps, (not seen).
  Rev.: Malan in S. Afr. Archaeol. Bull., 22, 67; Movius in Amer. Anthrop., 70, 157–159; Narr in Anthropos, 62:1/2, 269–270; Penniman in Man, Jour. Roy. Anthrop. Inst., 2, 138.

SENGHOR, LÉOPOLD SÉDAR
1968 Hommage à Pierre Teilhard de Chardin pour le 10ᵉ anniversaire de sa mort. In: Chardin, et al., 1968, 29–35.

SENYÜREK, MUZAFFER
1960C. The relative size of the permanent incisors in the suborder Anthropoidea. Anatolia, 5, 47–85, 2 tables.

SERA, GIOACHINO LEONE
1954C. Posizione zoologica del Pyrotherii. Monitore Zoologico Italiano, 62, 42–44, (English summary).

SEREBRIÁNNYĬ, LEONID RUVIMOVICH
1961 [Radiocarbon method and its use for the study of paleogeography of the Quaternary period.] Moscow: Akad. Nauk Press, 226 pp., 5 figs., 5 tables, (Russian; English summary).
1965 [Use of radiocarbon method in Quaternary geology.] Moscow: "Nauka" Press, 271 pp., 11 figs., 9 tables, (Russian).
  See: Gerasimov, I. P., Serebriánnyĭ, and Chebotareva.

SERGEEV, E. M. See: Bogdanov, et al.

SERGI, SERGIO
1961 Paleoantropologia. Enciclopedia Treccani, Appendice III, (not seen).
1964 Il protoantropo di Olduvai del Tanganica. Riv. Antrop., 51, 169–171, 2 figs., (French, English and German summaries).

SERGIENKO, A. A.
1961A.   [On the find of <u>Grossilepis</u> aff. <u>tuberculata</u> (Gross) in Upper Devonian
            sediments of Minusinsk basin.]   Trudy SNIIGGIMS, <u>15</u>, 135–137,
            1 pl., (Russian).
1961B.   [New species <u>Bothriolepis</u> <u>extensa</u> sp. nov. from the deposits of Tuba
            suite in Minusinsk basin.]   Trudy SNIIGGIMS, <u>15</u>, 139–140, 1 pl.,
            (Russian).
1961C.   [Class Osteichthyes.]   Trudy SNIIGGIMS, <u>20</u>, [Paleozoic biostratigraphy
            of Saián-Altaÿ mountain region, v. 2], 564–567, 1 fig., 2 pls.,
            (Russian).
1965   [Finds of fishes in Lower Devonian of Altaÿ.]   Trudy SNIIGGIMS, <u>34</u>:1,
            182, (Russian).
            See: Obruchev, D. V. and Sergienko.

SERIZAWA, CHŌSUKE
1960   The Stone Age of Japan.   Tokyo: Tsukiji Shokan, (Japanese;   not seen).
            Rev.:   Izumi and Okada in Jap. Jour. Ethnol., <u>26</u>, 88–89, (Japanese);
            Kamaki in Jour. Archaeol. Soc. Nippon, <u>46</u>, 153–155, (Japanese).
1962   [Problems of the Palaeolithic Age in Japan.]   Nihon rekishi koza, <u>1</u>,
            79–107, (not seen).
1963   Archeological materials from volcanic ash layers.   Quat. Res., <u>3</u>, 67–71,
            5 tables, (Japanese;   English summary).
            See: Sugihara, Yoshida and Serizawa.

SERIZAWA, C., and KAMAKI, Y.
1965   The rock-shelter of Fukui, Nagasaki.   Mem. Tokyo Archaeol. Soc., <u>3</u>:1,
            1–14, (not seen).

SERIZAWA, C., and NAKAGAWA, H.
1965   New evidence for the Lower Palaeolithic from Japan: a preliminary
            report on the Sozudai site, Kyushu.   In: Ripoll Perelló, E., (ed.),
            1965B, 363–371, (Spanish summary).

SERIZAWA, C., NAKAMURA, K., and ASO, M.
1959   [Kamiyama: excavation report of the Kamiyama site, Tsunan-machi,
            Nakauonuma-gun, Niigata Prefecture.]   Tsunan-machi Board of
            Education.

SERONIE-VIVIEN, R.
1964   Résultat provisoires des fouilles à la Grotte de la Bergerie à Caniac (Lot).
            Procès-Verbaux, Soc. Linn. Bordeaux, <u>101</u>, 35.

SERVAIS, JEAN
1961   Outils paléolithiques de l'Élide.   Bull. Correspondence Hellén., <u>85</u>, 1–9,
            5 figs.

SERVENTY, VINCENT
1960   Footprints in the sand.   Walkabout, <u>26</u>:5, 11, illustr.

SERVICE, ELMAN R.
1965   Lithic patina as an age criterion.   Mich. Archaeol., <u>11</u>, 110–114.

SESHACHAR, B. R.   See: Rao, C. R. N. and Seshachar.

SEVERTSOV, A. N.
1945   [Collected works. I. I. Schmalhausen, ed. Vol. III. General problems of evolution.] Moscow: Akad. Nauk SSSR Press, 530 pp., 161 figs., 6 pls., (Russian).
1948   [Collected works. I. I. Schmalhausen ed. Vol. IV. Origin and evolution of lower vertebrates.] Moscow: Akad. Nauk SSSR Press, 400 pp., 148 figs., 18 pls., 4 tables, (Russian).
1950   [Collected works. E. N. Pavlovskiĭ, ed. Vol. II. The origin and evolution of limbs.] Moscow: Akad. Nauk SSSR Press, 406 pp., 182 figs., 6 pls., tables, (Russian).

SEXTON, R. T.
1965   Caves of coastal areas of South Australia. Helictite, 3, 45—59, 3 figs.

SHACKELFORD, JOHN M., and WYCKOFF, R. W. G.
1964   Collagen in fossil teeth and bones. Jour. Ultrastruct Res., 11, 173, 11 figs.

SHAFER, HARRY J. See: Story and Shafer.

SHAFER, H. J., SUHM, D. A., and SCURLOCK, J. D.
1964   An investigation and appraisal of the archeological resources of Belton Reservoir, Bell and Coryell Counties, Texas: 1962. Misc. Pap., Texas Archeol. Salvage Project, no. 1, 113 pp., 24 figs., 7 tables.

SHAH, S. C. See: Rao, C. N. and Shah.

SHAMSUTDINOV, V. KH.
1966   [New Upper Paleolithic station in Transbaĭkalia.] Biul. Kom. Izuch. Chetvert. Perioda, 32, 128—133, 2 figs., (Russian).

SHAMSUTDINOV, V. KH., and BARABASHEV, E. V.
1963   [New archeological sites of Transbaikalia.] Zapiski Zabaĭkal'. Otd. Geogr. Obshch. SSSR, 22, 164—166, (Russian).

SHANNON, TERRY
1962   Stones, bones and arrowheads. Illustrated by Charles Payzant. Chicago: Whitman, 31 pp., color illustr., (elem. school).

SHANTSER, E. V.
1961A.   [Actual state of the problem on the limit between Neogene and Quaternary (Anthropogene) systems.] Mat. Vses. Sov. po Izuch. Chetvert. Perioda, 1, 10—19, (Russian).
1961B.   [A discussion of the question of the boundary between the Neogene and Quaternary systems.] Vestnik Akad. Nauk SSSR, 31:8, 113—115, (Russian).
      See: Gromov, V. I., Krasnov, et al.; Gromov, V. I., Nikiforova and Shantser.

SHAPP, MARTHA, and CHARLES
1968   Let's find out about animals of long ago. New York: Franklin Watts, 47 pp., illustr., (for young readers).

SHARASHIDZE, V. A.
1968   [On the history of formation of modern ichthyofauna in the inland waters of Georgia.] Soob. Akad. Nauk Gruz. SSR, 52:1, 223—227, 1 table, (Russian; Georgian summary).

SHARIPOVA, L. KH.
   1966   New finds of stone tools in Bukhara Oblast. Translated by Edith M.
                 Shimkin. In: Beregovaia, N. A., Islamov, U., and Kalandadze,
                 A. N., 131–134, 1 fig.

SHAROV, A. G.
   1965   Evolution and taxonomy. Zeit. Zool. Syst. Evolut.-Forsch., 3:3/4, 349–
                 358, 2 figs.
   1966   [Unique finds of reptiles from Mesozoic of Central Asia.] Biull. Mosk.
                 Obshch. Ispyt. Prirody, Otd. Geol., 41:2, 145–146, (Russian).

SHARP, ANDREW
   1956   The prehistory of the New Zealand Maoris. Some possibilities. Jour.
                 Polynesian Soc., 65, 155–160.

SHARROCK, FLOYD W.
   1966   Prehistoric occupation patterns in south-west Wyoming and cultural
                 relationships with the Great Basin and Plains culture areas. Ap-
                 pendices by Armand J. Eardley, and J. Desmond Clark. Anthrop.
                 Pap. Univ. Utah, 77, xii + 215 pp., 97 figs., 9 tables.
                 Rev.: Mulloy in Amer. Antiq., 32, 412–413;   Wedel in Amer. Anthrop.,
                 70, 161.

SHATSKIĬ, N. S.
   1960   [Geology in the researches of Charles Darwin.] Biull. Mosk. Obshch.
                 Ispyt. Prirody, Otd. Geol., 65:1, 3–24, (Russian; brief English
                 summary).
   1965   [Selected works. Vol. 4. History and methodology of geological science.]
                 Moscow: "Nauka" Press, 398 pp., portr., (Russian).

SHAVIAKOU, B. V. See: Shcheglova and Shaviakou.

SHAW, ALAN B.
   1964   Time in stratigraphy. New York: McGraw-Hill, xi + 365 pp., illustr.,
                 tables.
                 Rev.: Dutro in Jour. Pal., 39, 735–736;   Rossi Ronchetti in Riv.
                 Ital. Pal., 70, 910;   Schindewolf in Zbl. Geol. Pal., Teil 2, 1965,
                 2–3;   Simpson in Nature, 205, 221;   Toots in Contrib. Geol.,
                 Univ. Wyoming, 4, 41–42.

SHAW, THURSTON
   1966   Recent archaeological work in Nigeria. W. Afr. Archaeol. Newsletter,
                 no. 5, 9–11, (discussion, 21–22).
   1967   Nigeria. In: Oakley, K. P., and Campbell, B. G., (eds.), 1967A, 47–48.

SHAWCROSS, WILFRED, and ROE, N.
   1966   A note on the Houhora excavations. New Zealand Archaeol. Assoc.
                 Newsletter, 9, 47–48.

SHAY, CREIGHTON T.
   1965   1964 field report on the Itasca Bison Site. Plains Anthrop., 10, 46,
                 (abs.).

SHCHEGLOVA, V. V.
   1958B.   [On large-horned deer (genus Megaloceros) on the USSR territory.]
                 Uch. Zapiski Belorus. Univ., 43, 173–188, (Russian).

1961C.   [Concerning anthropogene mammalian fauna in Belorussia.]   Pal. i Stratig.
           BSSR, Minsk, 4, 216—248, 6 figs., 12 tables, 1 chart, (Russian).

1965   [The problem of the "small mammoth" and the subspecies of the Elisee-
           vichi mammoth.]   Dokl. Akad. Nauk BSSR, 9:11, 752—754, 2
           tables, (Russian).

SHCHEGLOVA, V. V., and SHAVIAKOU, B. V.
1959   [A find of mammoth remains in White Russia.]   Vesci Akad. Navuk BSSR,
           Ser. fiz.-Tckh. Navuk, 1959, 127—130, (Russian; not seen).

SHCHELINSKIĬ, V. E.   See: Liŭbin and Shchelinskiĭ.

SHCHERBAKOV, D. I.
1963   [A great scientist and traveler. (100 years birth date of V. A. Obruchev).]
           Vestnik Akad. Nauk SSSR, 1963:10, 116—119, portr., (Russian).

SHCHERBAKOV, O. I.   See: Fradkin, et al.

SHCHERBAKOVA, E. M.
1954A.   [On conditions of life of mammoth and rhinoceros in Angara R. basin.]
           In: Grichuk and Markova, (eds.), 1954, 82—85, 2 figs., (Russian).
1954B.   [A new find of screw-horned antelope in SSSR.]   In: Grichuk and Mar-
           kova, (eds.), 1954, 86—88, 1 table, (Russian).

SHCHUKINA, E. N.
1945   [Post-Paleozoic history of Urals in connection with the formation of con-
           tinental Mesozoic and Cenozoic deposits and related gold, platinum,
           and diamond placers.]   Referaty Nauchno-Issl. Rab., 1947, 34—35,
           (Russian).
1959   [Continental Tertiary deposits of the Central Urals.]   Trudy Geol. Inst.,
           17, 190 pp., 49 figs., 16 tables, (Russian).

SHEILS, HELEN, (ed.)
1963   Australian Aboriginal studies. A symposium of papers presented at the
           1961 research conference. Melbourne: Oxford University Press
           (Australian Institute of Aboriginal Studies), xx + 505 pp.
           Rev.: Brown in Man, Jour. Roy. Anthrop. Inst., 1, 126—127.

SHELKOPLĬAS, V. N.   See: Bondarchuk and Shelkoplĭas.

SHELKOPLĬAS, V. N., and MOROZOV, G. V.
1965   [Determination of the relative age of Quaternary deposits of the middle
           part of Dnepr basin by the method of thermoluminiscence.]   In:
           Saks, (ed.), 1965, 462—469, 2 figs., 1 table, (Russian).

SHELKOVNIKOV, S. S. (=Schelkovnikov)
1964   [The origin of labour as a factor of antropogenesis.]   Biull. Mosk. Obshch.
           Prirody, Otd. Biol., 69:4, 126—132, (Russian).

SHELLSHEAR, J. L.
1937   Recent advances in the prehistory of the Far East. Mankind, 2:3, 64—65.

SHELOV, D. B.   See: Merpert and Shelov.

SHEPHERD, WALTER
1962   Wealth from the ground. Illustrated by Gaynor Chapman and Clifford
             Bayly. New York: John Day, 48 pp., color illustr., (elemen.
             school).
1964   Rocks, minerals and fossils. New Rochelle, N. Y.: Sportshelf, 142 pp.,
             illustr., (not seen).

SHEPPARD, J. G., and SWART, E. R.
1967   Rhodesian radiocarbon measurements III. Radiocarbon, 9, 382–386.

SHER, A. V.
1967A.   [Fossil saiga in the northeastern Siberia and in Alaska.]   Biull. Kom.
             Izuch. Chetvert. Perioda, 33, 97–112, 2 figs., 2 tables, (Russian).
1967B.   [Early Quaternary mammals of northeastern USSR, and the problem of
             continental connections between Asia and America.]   Doklady
             Akad. Nauk SSSR, 1967:6, 1430–1433, (Russian).
1968   [Contribution to the history of musk oxen in northern Eurasia and
             America.]   Biull. Mosk. Obshch. Ispyt. Prirody, Otd. Geol., 43:2,
             157, (Russian).

SHERSTIŪKOV, N. M.
1968A.   [A new find of a tusk of the fossil meridional elephant in Checheno-
             Ingushskaiã ASSR.]   Trudy Groznen. Neft. n.–i. Inst., 29, 103–105,
             (Russian).
1968B.   [On the finding of horn-cores of fossil oxen in Checheno-Ingushskaiã
             ASSR.]   Trudy Groznen. Neft. n.–i. Inst., 29, 106–108, (Russian).

SHEVCHENKO, A. I. (=Schevtschenko)
1962   [Washing out and sifting as methods of extracting bone remains of small
             vertebrates from Cenozoic deposits.]   Geol. Zhurnal, Kiev, 22:3,
             66–74, 1 fig., 2 tables, (Ukrainian; Russian summary).
1965A.   [Some problems of biostratigraphic research on Anthropogene.]   In:
             Bondarchuk and Shelkoplias, (eds.), 1965, 99–103, 1 table, (Russian;
             English summary).
1965B.   [Key complexes of small mammals from Pliocene and Lower Anthropogene
             in the southwestern part of the Russian plain.]   In: Nikiforova,
             (ed.), 1965B, 7–59, 35 figs., 1 table, (Russian; English summary).
          See: Romadanova and Shevchenko.

SHEVCHENKO, A. I., and GRIGOR'EV, A. V.
1967   [Upper Pleistocene deposits of the northern Azov Sea area. (Kulikov strato-
             typic horizon).]   Dopovidi Akad. Nauk URSR, ser. B., 1967:8,
             681–684, 1 fig., (Ukrainian; Russian and English summaries).

SHEVCHENKO, IŪ. G. (=Chevtchenko, Y.)
1967   [Basic trends in brain development in Primates.]   Voprosy Antrop., 27,
             3–31, 12 figs., 1 chart, 1 table, (Russian).
1968   Etapes générales de l'évolution du cerveau des Primates. 7th Internat.
             Congr. Anthrop. Ethnol. Sci., Moscow, 1964, 3, 455–461.

SHEVYREVA, N. S.
1960   [The change in the distribution of the stag (Cervus elaphus L.) in the Anthro-
             pogene on the territory of the USSR.]   Biull. Mosk. Obshch. Ispyt.
             Prirody, Otd. Geol., 65:4, 152–153, (Russian).
1965   New Oligocene hamsters of the U.S.S.R. and Mongolia. Pal. Zhurnal,
             1965:1, 105–114, 3 fig., (Russian).

1966 [On the evolution of rodents from Middle Oligocene of Kazakhstan.]
     Biull. Mosk. Obshch. Ispyt. Prirody, Otd. Geol., 41:6, 143, (Russian).

1967 [Hamsters of the genus Cricetodon from Middle Oligocene of Central
     Kazakhstan.] Pal. Zhurnal, 1967:2, 90—98, 2 figs., (Russian).

1968A. [Rodents and Lagomorpha from Neogene of the southern part of Zaĭsan
     Basin.] Biull. Mosk. Obshch. Ispyt. Prirody, Otd. Geol., 43:4,
     156—157, (Russian).

1968B. [New genus of rodents of the family Ctenodactylidae from Middle Oligo-
     cene of Kazakhstan and Mongolia.] Author's summary. Biull.
     Mosk. Obshch. Ispyt. Prirody, Otd. Geol., 43:1, 154—155, (Russian).
   See: Birman, et al.; Flerov and Shevyreva.

SHIDLOVSKIĬ, M. V. See: Vekua and Shidlovskiĭ.

SHIK, S. M. See: Grichuk, Sammet, et al.

SHIKAMA, TOKIO

1962 Quaternary land connections of Japanese Islands with continent from
     viewpoints of paleomammology. Quat. Res., 2, 146—153, 1
     table, (Japanese; English summary).

1963A. Abs.: Huene in Zbl. Geol. Pal., Teil 2, 1964, 522.

1964A. Cervid antler from Akishima City, Tokyo. Sci. Rept. Yokohama Nation.
     Univ., Sect. II, no. 11, 55—58, 1 fig., pl. 3.

1964B. [Index fossils of Japan.] Tokyo: The Asakura Publishing Co., Ltd.;
     New York: W. A. Benjamin, Inc., 287 pp., 32 figs., 80 pls., 35
     tables, (Japanese).
     Rev.: Douglass in Jour. Pal., 41, 1301—1302.

1965 On some elephant teeth from Hiroshima and Yamaguchi Prefectures.
     Sci. Rept. Yokohama Nation. Univ., Sect. II, no. 12, 27—36, 9
     figs., pl. 1.

1966A. On some desmostylian teeth in Japan, with stratigraphical remarks on
     the Keton and Izumi desmostylids. Bull. Nation. Sci. Mus. Tokyo,
     9, 119—169, 8 figs., 6 pls., 16 tables.

1966B. Study on the skeletons of Japanese desmostylids (excluding the skull).
     Kaseki, 11, 41—42, (Japanese).

1966C. Postcranial skeletons of Japanese Desmostylia. Limb bones and sternum
     of Desmostylus and Paleoparadoxia, with considerations on their
     evolution. Spec. Pap. Pal. Soc. Japan, no. 12, 1—202, 116 figs.,
     12 pls., 31 tables.

1968 Additional notes on the postcranial skeletons of Japanese Desmostylia.
     Sci. Rept. Yokohama Nation. Univ., Sect. II, no. 14, 21—28, 5
     figs., pls. 3—6.
   See: Takai, Shikama and Iziri; Tan and Shikama.

SHIKAMA, T., and HASEGAWA, Y.

1962B. Abs.: Westphal in Zbl. Geol. Pal., Teil 2, 1964, 163.

1965A. Fossil suid from Kurihama, Kanagawa Prefecture. Sci. Rept. Yokohama
     Nation. Univ., sect. II, no. 12, 37—43, 2 figs., pls. 2—3.

1965B. On a new fossil cervid antler from western Japan. Sci. Rept. Yokohama
     Nation. Univ., Sect. II, no. 12, 45—47, pl. 4.

SHIKAMA, T., HASEGAWA, Y., and OKAFUJI, G.

1967 On a rhinocerid skull from Isa, Yamaguchi Prefecture, Japan. Bull.
     Nation. Sci. Mus. Tokyo, 10:4, 455—462, 1 pl.

SHIKAMA, T., and NODA, K.
1968   On an elephant tooth gained from off Cape Yozu, Kôchi Prefecture. Sci. Rept. Yokohama Nation. Univ., Sect. II, no. 14, 7-11, 1 pl.

SHIKAMA, T., and OKAFUJI, G.
1964   On a new Cyclemys from Akiyoshi, Japan. Sci. Rept. Yokohama Nation. Univ., Sect. II, no. 11, 59-67, 3 figs., pls. 4-5.
Abs.: Huene in Zbl. Geol. Pal., Teil 2, 1966, 306.

SHIKAMA, T., and OZAKI, H.
1966   On a reptilian skeleton from the Palaeozoic formation of San [São] Paulo, Brazil. Trans. Proc. Pal. Soc. Japan, no. 64, 351-358, 2 figs., pls. 38-39.

SHIMKIN, EDITH M.   See: Beregovaia, et al.; Sharipova 1966.

SHIMODA, NOBUO, ENDO, S., INOUE, M., and OZAKI, H.
1964   The fluorine and manganese contents in the fossil bones and their concentration-mechanism. Bull. Nation. Sci. Musc. Tokyo, 7:3, 225-233, illustr., (Japanese; English summary).

SHINER, JOEL L.   See: Wendorf, Shiner and Marks; Wendorf, Shiner, Marks, et al.

SHIPEROVICH, V. ÍA.
1962   [A stone tool from Borĭsovki in the Altaĭ region.] Sov. Arkheol., 1962:2, 201-203, 2 figs., (Russian).

SHIPPEE, J. M.
1966   The archaeology of Arnold Research Cave, Callaway County, Missouri. Missouri Archaeol., 28, v + 40 pp., illustr.

SHIPPEN, KATHERINE B.
1963   Men, microscopes, and living things. New York: Grosset and Dunlap, 191 pp., illustr., (pb. ed.).

SHIRATAKI, DANTAI KENKYUKAI
1963   [The study of the Shirataki site.] Tokyo Chigaku Dantai Kenkyu Kai, (English summary; not seen).

SHIRINOV, N. SH.
1966   [Geomorphological dating of Azykh cave site of Paleolithic man.] Izv. Akad. Nauk Azerb. SSR, ser. Nauk o Zemle, 1966:5, 67-74, (Russian; Azerbaijanese summary).

SHIRLEY, J. See: Dineley 1966B.

SHISHKIN, M. A.
1961   Abs.: Huene in Zbl. Geol. Pal., Teil 2, 1964, 162-163.
1964   [Suborder Stereospondyli.] Osnovy Pal., [Amphibians, Reptiles, and Birds.], [12], 83-122, 62 figs., (Russian).
1966   [A brachyopidian labyrinthodont from the Triassic of Russian Platform.] Pal. Zhurnal, 1966:2, 93-108, 8 figs., (Russian).
Rev.: Westphal in Zbl. Geol. Pal., Teil 2, 1967, 102-103.
1967A.   A brachyopid labyrinthodont from the Triassic of the Russian Platform. Translation of Shishkin, M. A., 1966. Internat. Geol. Rev., 9, 310-322, 8 figs.

1967B.   [Plagiosauria in the Triassic of the USSR.] Pal. Zhurnal, 1967:1, 92—99,
          4 figs., (Russian).
          Rev.: Westphal in Zbl. Geol. Pal., Teil 2, 1967, 509.
1968   [Irreversibility of evolution and factors of morphogenesis.] Pal. Zhurnal,
          1968:3, 3—11, (Russian).
          See: Ochev and Shishkin; Ochev, Shishkin, et al.

SHISHKIN, M. A., and OCHEV, V. G.
1966   [On the problem of endocranium evolution in ancient amphibia.] Dok-
          lady Akad. Nauk SSSR, 169:5, 1167—1170, 2 figs., (Russian).
1967A.   Evolution of the endocranium of ancient amphibians. Dokl. Acad. Sci.,
          U.S.S.R., Earth Sci. Sect., 169, 213—216, 2 figs.
1967B.   [Land vertebrates fauna as a basis of stratigraphy of continental Triassic
          deposits of the USSR.] In: Martinson, (ed.), 1967A, 74—82,
          (Russian).

SHISHKIN, V. A.
1961   [Uzbekistan Archeological Expedition AN UZSSR. (Field work 1956—
          1959).] Istoriĭa Mater. Kul't. Uzbekistana, 2, 18—50, 5 figs.,
          (Russian).
1962   [Field works of Uzbekistan Archeological Expedition in 1960.] Istorriĭa
          Mater. Kul't. Uzbekistana, 3, 5—18, (Russian).

SHLYGIN, E. D.
1963   [V. A. Obruchev and the problem of origin and oil-bearing of Central
          and Middle Asiatic depressions.] Izv. Akad. Nauk Kazakh. SSR,
          Ser. Geol., 1963:6, 7—9, (Russian; Kazakh summary).

SHMIDT, E. A.   See: Zaverniĭaev and Shmidt.

SHMIDT, G. A.
1940   [Charles Darwin's theory of sexual selection.] Priroda, 1940:7, 36—49,
          (Russian).
1947   [On the spiral march of evolution.] Priroda, 1947:7, 29—41, (Russian).
          See: Rakovets and Shmidt.

SHOKUROV, A. P., and BADER, O. N.
1960   [A Paleolithic site on the Belaĭa river.] Voprosy Geol. Vost. Okrainy
          Russk. Plat., 1960:5, 139—144, 5 figs., 1 table, (Russian).

SHORT, LESTER L., JR.
1966   A new Pliocene stork from Nebraska. Smithson. Misc. Coll., 149:9, 11
          pp., 1 pl.

SHORYGINA, L. D.
1960   [Stratigraphy of Cenozoic deposits of western Tuva.] Trudy Geol.
          Inst., 26, 165—203, 24 figs., 1 table, (Russian).
1961B.   [Quaternary deposits of western Tuva.] In: Gromov, V. I., et al., (eds.),
          1961, 166—174, (Russian; English summary).

SHOTTON, F. W.
1965   The President presented the Wollaston medal to Professor D. M. S. Watson,
          Proc. Geol. Soc. London, no. 1625, 128—129, (reply by D. M. S.
          Watson).

SHOTTON, F. W., OSBORNE, P. J., and SYLVESTER-BRADLEY, P. C.
1965   The fauna of the Hoxnian Interglacial deposits of Nechells, Birmingham.
         With appendix on Cytherissa lacustris and other ostracods at Ne-
         chells. Philos. Trans. Roy. Soc. London, Ser. B, 248, 353–378,
         7 figs., pl. 30.

SHOTWELL, J. ARNOLD
1964   Community succession in mammals of the Late Tertiary. In: Imbrie
         and Newell, (eds.), 1964, 135–150, 4 figs.
1967A.   Peromyscus of the Late Tertiary in Oregon. Bull., Mus. Nat. Hist., Univ.
         Oregon, 5, 4 + 35 pp., 11 figs., 11 tables.
         Rev.: Fahlbusch in Zbl. Geol. Pal., Teil 2, 1968:6, 664–665.
1967B.   Late Tertiary geomyoid rodents of Oregon. Bull., Mus. Nat. Hist., Univ.
         Oregon, 9, 51 pp., 28 figs., 4 tables.
         Rev.: Fahlbusch in Zbl. Geol. Pal., Teil 2, 1968:6, 664–665.
1968   Miocene mammals of southeast Oregon. Bull. Mus. Nat. Hist., Univ.
         Oregon, 14, 1–67, 33 figs., 19 tables.

SHOTWELL, J. A., et al.
1963   Rev.: Johnson in Jour. Geol., 72, 881.

SHOVKOPLIÂS, I. G.
1955B.   [Excavations of a Late Paleolithic site on the Supoe River.]   Krat. Soob.
         Inst. Arkheol. Akad. Nauk URSR., 4, 152–154, 1 fig., (Russian).
1955C.   [Paleolithic expedition of 1954.]   Krat. Soob. Inst. Arkheol. Akad. Nauk
         URSR., 5, 3–12, 8 figs., (Russian).
1957   [Some results of the study of Late Paleolithic settlement Mezin during
         1954–1956.]   Sov. Arkheol., 1957:4, 99–115, 14 figs., 2 pls.,
         (Russian).
1959C.   [The lower stratum of the Mezin Paleolithic site.]   Krat. Soob. Inst.
         Arkheol. Akad. Nauk URSR., 8, 92–103, 12 figs., (Russian).
1961   [Periodization of Late Paleolithic of Middle Dnepr basin.]   Internat.
         Assoc. Quat. Res., Abs. Pap., 6th Congr., 143–144, (abs.; Rus-
         sian).
1964   [The Paleolithic site at Radomyshl.]   Arkheologiiâ, 16, 89–102, 11 figs.,
         (Ukrainian; Russian summary).
1965A.   [Radomyshl' site, a relic of the early stage of Late Paleolithic.]   In:
         Bader, O. N., et al., (eds.), 1965, 104–116, 7 figs., (Russian).
1965B.   [On the nature of relations of Late Paleolithic population.]   In: Bon-
         darchuk and Shelkopliâs, (eds.), 1965, 312–320, (Russian; Eng-
         lish summary).
1965C.   [Mezin site. On the history of Middle Dnepr basin in Late Paleolithic
         epoch.]   Kiev: "Naukova Dumka" Press, 328 pp., 61 figs., 56
         pls., 3 tables, (Russian).
         Rev.: Banesz in Sloven. Archeol., 14:1, 232–234, (Slovakian).; Valoch
         in Archeol. Roz., 18:5, 610–611, (Czech).
1966   [On local differences in the Late Paleolithic culture development. (On
         materials from Ukraine and neighbour territories).] In: Rybakov,
         (ed.), 1966, 41–43, (Russian).
1967   [A new Late Paleolithic site in Chernigov region.]   In: Rybakov, (ed.),
         1967, 187–189, (Russian).

SHRAMKO, B. A.
1962   [Antiquities of northern Donefŝ.]   Khar'kov: State University Press, 404
         pp., 150 figs., (Russian).
         Rev.: Pletneva in Sov. Arkheol., 1964:3, 340–344, (Russian).

SHTEINBERG, D. M.
1954 [On the history of formation of fauna in the area between Volga and Ural rivers.] Trudy Zool. Inst. Akad. Nauk SSSR, 16, 15–29, (Russian).

SHTENGELOV, E. S. See: Bachinskii, Dublïanskii, and Shtengelov.

SHUL'TŜ, P. N., (ed.)
1957 [History and archeology of ancient Crimea.] Kiev; Akad. Nauk USSR Press, 336 pp., illustr., (Russian).
Rev.: Dashevskaïa in Sov. Arkeol., 1961:2, 282–288, (Russian).

SHUMAKOV, ÎU. F. See: Kambariddinov, et al.

SHUTLER, MARY ELIZABETH, and SHUTLER, R., JR.
1967 Origins of the Melanesians. Archaeol., Phys. Anthrop. in Oceania, 2, 91–99.

SHUTLER, RICHARD, JR.
1965 Tule Springs Expedition. Current Anthrop., 6, 110–111.
1967A. Introduction, acknowledgements, staff and advisory committee. In: Wormington, and Ellis, (eds.), 1967, 1–13, 6 figs.
1967B. Archaeology of Tule Springs. In: Wormington, and Ellis, (eds.), 1967, 297–303.
1967C. Cultural chronology in southern Nevada. In: Wormington and Ellis, (eds.), 1967, 303–308.

SHUTTLESWORTH, DOROTHY E.
1966 The wildlife of South America. New York: Hastings House, illustr., (juv.), (not seen).
Rev.: Shaw in Nat. Hist., 76:9, 78–79.

SHVAREVA, N. ÎA. See: Tkachenko, O. F., Pishvanova and Shvareva.

SHVARTŜ, S. S.
1965 (ed.) [Intraspecific variability of terrestrial vertebrate animals and micro-evolution. Transactions of All-Union conference.] Sverdlovsk: Ural. Fil. Akad. Nauk SSSR, Inst. Biol., 374 pp., illustr., (Russian).
1967 [Contemporary problems of the theory of evolution.] Voprosy Filosofii, 1967:10, 143–153, (Russian; English summary).

SIBAL, JOSEPH See: Ostrom 1964C.

SIBLEY, GRETCHEN
1963 Science and history docent program. Quart. Los Angeles Co. Mus. Nat. Hist., 2:1, 5–7, illustr.
1967 La Brea story. Illustr. by Mary Butler. Los Angeles: Los Angeles County Mus., 48 pp., illustr.

ŠIBRAVA, VLADIMIR
1966 [7th INQUA Congress in Boulder (U.S.A.).] Věstník Ústřed. Úst. Geol., 41:2, 149–151, 2 pls., (Czech).

SICKENBERG, OTTO
1961 Das wiedergefundene Typus-Exemplar vom Meereskrokodil aus Sachsenhagen. Ber. Naturhist. Ges. Hannover, 105, 5–6.

1962B.   Abs.:   Dietrich in Zbl. Geol. Pal., Teil 2, 1964, 187–188.
1964   Neue Säugetierfunde aus dem Gipskarst von Osterrode/Harz.   Mitt. Geol.
               Inst. T. H. Hanover, 1964:2, 12–21, (not seen).
1965   Dama clactoniana (Falc.) in der Mittelterrasse der Rhume-Leine bei Edesheim
               (Landkreis Northeim). Geol. Jahrb., 83, 353–396, 7 figs., pls.
               45–46, 4 tables, (English and French summaries).
1966   Die Wirbeltierfauna der Höhle bei Petralona (Griechenland). Eiszeit. u.
               Gegenwart, 17, 214–215.
1968   Die pleistozänen Knochenbrekzien von Volax (Griech.-Mazedonien). Geol.
               Jahrb., 85, 33–54, 2 figs., 3 pls., (English and French summaries).

SIEBER, RUDOLF, and WEINFURTER, E.
1967   Otolithen aus tiefen Gosauschichten Österreichs. Ann. Naturhist. Mus.
               Wien, 71, 353–361, 1 pl., (English summary).

SIEGEL, BERNARD J., (ed.)
1959   Biennial review of anthropology, 1959. Stanford: Stanford Univ. Press,
               vi + 273 pp.
1962   Biennial review of anthropology, 1961. Stanford: Stanford Univ. Press,
               338 pp.
1963   Biennial review of anthropology, 1963. Stanford: Stanford Univ. Press,
               315 pp.
1965   Biennial review of anthropology, 1965. Stanford: Stanford Univ. Press,
               305 pp.
               Rev.: Ehrich in Amer. Anthrop., 68, 1515–1516; Khare in E. Anthrop.,
               19, 251–253.

SIEGEL, B. J., and BEALS, A. R., (eds.)
1967   Biennial review of anthropology, 1967. Stanford: Stanford Univ. Press,
               vi + 368 pp.
               Rev.: Bohannan in Science, 161, 260.

SIEGFRIED, PAUL
1960   Ein Arthrodire aus dem Mitteldevon von Balve/Westfalen. Decheniana,
               113, 319–322, 2 pls., (not seen).
1962   Der Fund eines Wisentskelettes im Quartär von Gladbeck. Zeit. Deutsche.
               Geol. Ges., 113, 603–604.
1965   Anomotherium langewieschei n.g. n. sp. (Sirenia) aus dem Ober-Oligozän
               des Dobergs bei Bünde/Westfalen. Palaeontogr., Abt. A, 124,
               116–150, 30 figs., pls. 10–16, 1 table.
1966   Zur Osteologie der Gattung Dercetis Agassiz (Teleostei, Pisces). Pal.
               Zeit., 40, 205–217, 6 figs., 3 pls.
1967   Das Femur von Eotheroides libyca (Owen) (Sirenia). Pal. Zeit., 41:3–4,
               165–172, 2 figs., 1 pl.

SIEVEKING, ANN and GALE
1962   Rev.: Anon in NSS News, 21, 14; [Beltrán] in Caesaraugusta, 23–24,
               150–151; Daniel in Archaeol. Jour., 119, 357; Fordinal in Die
               Höhle, 15, 55.

SIGA, MASANORI   See: Onodera, Onuma and Siga.

SIGÉ, BERNARD
1966   Les chiroptères fossiles de Bouzigues (Hérault), recherches anatomiques
               sur Pseudorhinolophus bouziguensis n.s.p. Thèse de 3e Cycle, Univ.
               Paris, fasc. 1, 248 pp., fasc. 2, pls. 1–38.

1967   Les Chiroptères oligocènes de Saint-Victor-la-Coste (Gard). Etude préliminaire. C. R. Soc. Géol. France, 1967:4, 163–164, 1 fig.
     Rev.: Fahlbusch in Zbl. Geol. Pal., Teil 2, 1968, 211–212.

1968A.   Dents de micromammifères et fragments de coquilles d'oeufs de dinosauriens dans la faune de vertébrés du Crétacé supérieur de Laguna Umayo (Andes péruviennes). C. R. Acad. Sci. Paris, Sci. Nat., 267, 1495–1498.

1968B.   Les chiroptères du Miocène inférieur de Bouzigues. Palaeovertebrata, 1:3, 65–133, 28 figs., 10 tables, (German and English summaries).

SIGMON, B. A., and ROBINSON, J. T.
1967   On the function of m. Gluteus maximus in apes and in man. Amer. Jour. Phys. Anthrop., 27, 245–246, (abs.).

SIGNEUX, JEANNE
1959A.   Poissons et reptiles marins. In: Arambourg, Dubertret, et al., 1959, 223–228, 1 pl.

1959B.   Poissons et reptiles du Maëstrichtien et de l'Eocène inférieur des environs de Rutbah (Irak). In: Arambourg, Dubertret, et al., 1959, 235–241, 1 pl.

1959C.   Poissons de l'Eocène de la cimenterie de Doumar (Syrie). In: Arambourg, Dubertret, et al., 1959, 241–248, 3 pls.

1964   Additions à la faune ichthyologique du Crétacé supérieur de Bolivie. Deuxième partie. Gasteroclupea branisai, clupéidé nouveau du Crétacé supérieur de Bolivie. Bull. Mus. Hist. Nat. Paris, 36, 290–297, 1 pl.

     See: Arambourg, Dubertret, et al.

SIGOGNEAU, DENISE
1963A.   Abs.: Huene in Zbl. Geol. Pal., Teil 2, 1964, 991.

1968A.   On the classification of the Gorgonopsia. Pal. Africana, 11, 33–46.

1968B.   Le genre Dremotherium (Cervoidea). Anatomie du crâne, denture et moulage endocranien. Ann. Pal., Vert., 54, 37–113, 33 figs., 6 pls.

     See: Lessertisseur and Sigogneau; Russell, D. E. and Sigogneau.

SIKORA, P.
1967   Casimir Stolyhwo. L'Anthrop., 71:5–6, 561–562, portr.

SILER, WALTER L.
1964   A middle Eocene sirenian in Alabama. Jour. Pal., 38, 1108–1109.

SILINSKIĬ, P. P., (ed.)
1963   [In memoriam V. A. Obruchev (centenary of birthday).] Izv. Vost.-Sib. Otd. Geogr. Obshch. SSSR, 61, 66 pp., portrs., (Russian).

SILL, WILLIAM D.
1967   Proterochampsa barrionuevoi and the early evolution of the Crocodilia. Bull. Mus. Comp. Zool., Harvard, 135, 415–446, 10 figs., 9 pls., 2 tables.
     Rev.: Huene in Zbl. Geol. Pal., Teil 2, 1968, 207.

1968   The zoogeography of the Crocodilia. Copeia, 68:1, 76–88, 5 figs., 1 table.
     Rev.: Berg in Zbl. Geol. Pal., Teil 2, 1969:2, 210.

SILVA, ANGEL B.
1968   Pleistocene vertebrate faunas of the Mexican Plateau. Program, 1968
               Ann. Meetings, Geol. Soc. Amer., 1968, 279, (abs.).

SILVA, MARIA NEYSA   See: Kerr, W. E. and Silva.

SILVA, P. H. D. H. DE
1966A.   Les musées de Ceylon. Mus. UNESCO, 19, 219—224, 7 figs.
1966B.   Museums in Ceylon. Mus. UNESCO, 19, 225—229, 3 figs.

SILVA SANTOS, RUBENS DA
1961   Peixes fosseis do Devoniano Inferior de Picos, Estado do Piaui. An.
               Acad. Brasil. Ciên., 33, XXXII.
1962   Peixes cretacicos do Rio Grande do Norte. An. Acad. Brasil. Ciên.,
               34, XXXIV.

SILVA SANTOS, R. DA., and DUARTE, L.
1961   Fósseis do Arenito Açu. An. Acad. Brasil. Cien., 33, XXVII—XXVIII.

SILVERBERG, ROBERT
1964   Man before Adam. The story of man in search of his origins. Illustr.
               by Judith Ann Lawrence. Philadelphia: Macrae Smith, 253 pp.,
               illustr.
1965   Hoaxes and half-truths. Nat. Hist., 74:3, 62—65.

SILVERZWEIG, STANLEY   See: Whipple and Silverzweig.

SILVESTER, NORMAN L.
1963   Flint implements: Is patination any indication of age? Anthrop. Jour.
               Canada, 1:4, 12—16, 3 figs.

SIMAK, CLIFFORD D.
1966   Trilobite, dinosaur and man: the earth's story. [Junior and high school
               and layman.] New York: St. Martins, 306, pp., illustr.
          Rev.: Batten in Nat. Hist., 75:9, 66; H. E. W. in Irish Nat. Jour., 15:12,
               364.

SIMMONS, DAVID JAY
1965   The non-therapsid reptiles of the Lufeng Basin, Yunnan, China. Fieldiana,
               Geol., 15, 1—93, 12 figs., 20 tables.

SIMON, K. H.
1964   Pater semper incertus—Lücken im menschlichen Stammbaum. Naturwiss.
               Rund., 17, 356—357.

SIMONE, S.   See: Barral and Simone.

SIMONETTA, ALBERTO
1957C.   Sull'esistenza di giunti cinetici nel cranio di alcuni insettivori (Myosorex,
               Talpa) e sul loro possibile significato. (Nota preliminare). Monitore
               Zool. Ital., 64, 172—180, 3 figs., (English, French and German
               summaries).

SIMONS, ELWYN LAVERNE
1959   Rev.: Preuschoft in Zbl. Geol. Pal., Teil 2, 1969:1, 55—59.

1960C.	Abs.: Dietrich in Zbl. Geol. Pal., Teil 2, 1964, 206–208.
1961A.	Rev.: Preuschoft in Zbl. Geol. Pal., Teil 2, 1969:1, 55–59.
1962D.	Abs.: Dietrich in Zbl. Geol. Pal., Teil 2, 1964, 226; Rev.: Preuschoft in Zbl. Geol. Pal., Teil 2, 1969:1, 55–59.
1962E.	Division of vertebrate paleontology. Ann. Rept. Yale Peabody Mus. Nat. Hist., 1962, no. 3, 30–33.
1962F.	A new ancestor? The Listener, Apr. 5, 1962, 589.
1962G.	An expedition to the Egyptian desert. Yale Sci. Mag., March 1962.
1963F.	Abs.: Simon in Naturwiss. Rund., 17, 356–357.
1963H.	Vertebrate paleontology. Kline Geol. Lab., Yale Univ., 2 pp.
1963I.	A new phylogeny of Oligocene catarrhines. In: Walton, M. S., (ed.), 1963, 2 pp., illustr.
1964A.	New evidence on the origin of Hominoidea. Abs. 63rd Ann. Meeting Amer. Anthrop. Assoc., 1964, 54, (abs.).
1964B.	Division of vertebrate paleontology. Ann. Rept., Yale Peabody Mus. Nat. Hist., 1964, no. 5, 25–28.
1964C.	On the mandible of Ramapithecus. Proc. Nation. Acad. Sci., 51, 528–535, 3 figs. Also in: Genovés, S., et al., (eds.), 1966, 17–25, with comment by J. H. Prost.
	Rev.: M. C. in Fossilia, 1965:3–4, 56.
1964D.	The early relatives of man. Sci. Amer., 211:1, 50–62, illustr.
1965A.	The hunt for Darwin's third ape. Medical Opinion and Review, 1:2, 74–81, 1 fig., (not seen).
1965B.	New fossil apes from Egypt and the initial differentiation of Hominoidea. Nature, 205, 135–139, 4 figs. Also in: Genovés, S., et al., (eds.), 1967, 86–91, with comment by A. T. Steegmann, Jr.
	Rev.: Preuschoft in Zbl. Geol. Pal., Teil 2, 1969:1, 55–59.
1966	In search of the missing link. Discovery, Yale, 1:2, 24–30, 3 figs.
1967A.	Fossil primates and the evolution of some primate locomotor systems. Amer. Jour. Phys. Anthrop., 26, 241–253, 1 table.
1967B.	The significance of primate paleontology for anthropological studies. Amer. Jour. Phys. Anthrop., 27, 307–332, 9 figs., 1 table.
1967C.	Review of the phyletic interrelationships of Oligocene and Miocene Old World Anthropoidea. Colloq. Internat. Cent. Nation. Recherch. Sci., 163, 597–601, 4 pls. (French Summary).
	Rev.: Preuschoft in Zbl. Geol. Pal., Teil 2, 1969:1, 55–59.
1967D.	Order Pantodonta Cope 1873. In: Harland, W. B., et al., (eds.), 1967A, 778.
1967E.	New evidence on the anatomy of the earliest catarrhine primates. In: Starck, D., Schneider, R., and Kuhn, H. J., (eds.), 1967, 15–18.
	Rev.: Preuschoft in Zbl. Geol. Pal., Teil 2, 1969:1, 55–59.
1967F.	Unraveling the age of earth and man. Nat. Hist., 76:2, 52–59, illustr.
1967G.	A fossil Colobus skull from the Sudan (Primates, Cercopithecidae). Postilla, 111, 1–12, 3 figs.
1967H.	The earliest apes. Sci. Amer., 217:6, 28–35, illustr.
	Rev.: Preuschoft in Zbl. Geol. Pal., Teil 2, 1969:1, 55–59.
1968A.	Part I. African Oligocene mammals: introduction, history of study, and faunal succession. In: Simons, and Wood, 1968, 1–21, 1 section.
1968B.	A source for dental comparison of Ramapithecus with Australopithecus and Homo. S. African Jour. Sci., 64, 92–112, 7 figs.
	See: Pilbeam and Simons.

SIMONS, E. L., and ALEXANDER, H. L., JR.

1964	Age of the Shasta ground sloth from Aden Crater, New Mexico. Amer. Antiq., 29, 390–391.

SIMONS, E., and PILBEAM, D. R.
1965   Preliminary revision of the Dryopithecinae (Pongidae, Anthropoidea).
              Folia Primatologica, 3, 81—152, 1 table. Also in: Genovés, S.,
              et al., (eds.), 1967, 13—85, with comment by Charles F. Merbs.
              Abs.: Preuschoft in Zbl. Geol. Pal., Teil 2, 1966, 339—340.

SIMONS, E. L., and WOOD, A. E.
1968   Early Cenozoic mammalian faunas Fayum Province, Egypt. Part I.
              Elwyn L. Simons. Part II. Albert E. Wood. Bull. Peabody Mus.
              Nat. Hist., 28, vi + 105 pp., 17 figs., 11 tables.

SIMOONS, FREDERICK J.
1966   The mithan (Bos frontalis) in culture and history. Spec. Pap. Geol. Soc.
              Amer., 87, 317, (abs.).

SIMPSON, GEORGE GAYLORD
1964A.   Science v. the humanities. Nat. Hist., 73:6, 4, 6.
1964B.   This view of life: The world of an evolutionist. New York: Harcourt,
              Brace & World, 308 pp.
              Rev.: Anon. in Sci. Amer., 211:4, 139—140;   Beer in Science, 143,
              1311—1312, 1317;   Glass in Quart. Rev. Biol., 40, 176—178;
              Hardin in Saturday Rev., Mch. 28, 1964, 44;   Roofe in Evolution,
              19, 266—267;   Straus in Amer. Sci., 53, 79A.
1964C.   Los mamiferos Casamayorenses de la coleccion Tournouër. Rev. Mus.
              Argent. Cien. Nat., Pal., 1:1, 1—21, 3 figs.
1964D.   The nonprevalence of humanoids. Science, 143, 769—775;   144, 613—614.
1964E.   Organisms and molecules in evolution. Science, 146, 1535—1538. Also,
              In: Protides of the biological fluids, H. Peeters, (ed.). Amsterdam:
              Elsevier, sect. A Phylogeny, 29—35.
1964F.   Species density of North American recent mammals. Syst. Zool., 13:2,
              57—73, 5 figs.
1965A.   Note on the Fort Ternan beds of Kenya. Amer. Jour. Sci., 263, 922.
1965B.   The meaning of evolution. A study of the history of life and of its
              significance for man. Calcutta: Oxford and IBH Publ. Co., 364
              pp., 38 illustr. Indian edition of Simpson 1949 G.
1965C.   A review of masterometry. Evolution, 19, 249—255.
              Rev.: J. M. G. in Fossilia, 1965:5—6, 68;   Ja. Ma. G. in Fossilia, 1965
              1965:3—4, 46.
1965D.   Foreword. In: Leakey, et al., 1965, ix—x.
1965E.   Description of Galago senegalensis E. Geoffroy, 1796. In: Leakey,
              et al., 1965, 15—16.
1965F.   Zoology. In: Love, A., and Childers, J. S., (eds.), 1965, 121—139.
1965G.   The geography of evolution: collected essays. Philadelphia and New
              York: Chilton Books, x + 249 pp., 45 figs.
              Rev.: deBeer in Science, 150, 1706—1707;   MacArthur in Amer. Sci.,
              54, 106A—107A;   Oliver in Jour. Pal., 40, 1247.
1965H.   Attending marvels. A Patagonian journal. Modified reprint, with a
              new introduction by L. M. Gould. New York: Time Reading
              Program, Time Inc., xxv + 289 pp., illustr.
1965I.   New record of a fossil penguin in Australia. Proc. Roy. Soc. Victoria,
              79, 91—93, 1 fig.
1965J.   Long abandoned views. Science, 147, 1397.
1965K.   End of an era in biology. Science, 150, 1142—1143.
1966A.   Naturalistic ethics and the social sciences. Amer. Psych., 21, 27—35.
1966B.   [German version of remarks on Father Teilhard.]   In: Hemleben, 1966,
              166—167.

1966C. [The biological nature of man.] Japan-America Forum, 12, 45–63, (Japanese).

1966D. Mammals around the Pacific. The Thomas Burke Memorial Lecture. Memorial Washington State Museum, (not seen).

1966E. Die Evolution des Pferdes. Naturwiss. und Med., no. 14, 349, (not seen).

1966F. Mammalian evolution on the Southern Continents. Neues Jahrb. Geol. Pal., Abh., 125, Festband, 1–18, portr., (German summary).

1966G. This view of life. The world of an evolutionist. New York: Harcourt, Brace and World, vii–ix, 3–308. Harbinger Book series, paperback.

1966H. Tempo and mode in evolution. Reprint. New York: Stechert-Hafner, 237 pp., illustr.

1966I. Ages of experimental animals. Science, 151, 517; 152, 16.

1966J. The biological nature of man. Science, 152, 472–478.

1966K. Interpretations of DNA. Science, 154, 1120.

1967A. The beginning of the Age of Mammals in South America. Part 2. Bull. Amer. Mus. Nat. Hist., 137, 1–259, 54 figs., 46 pls., 79 tables. Rev.: Coryndon in Nature, 218, 1087–1088; Olson in Quart. Rev. Biol., 44:2, 216.

1967B. The Tertiary lorisiform primates of Africa. Bull. Mus. Comp. Zool., 136:3, 39–61, 2 pls., 5 tables.

1967C. The Ameghinos' localities for Early Cenozoic mammals in Patagonia. Bull. Mus. Comp. Zool., 136:4, 63–76, 3 maps.

1967D. Evolution. In: Merit Encyclopedia, vol. 6, 501–510.

1967E. La vida en el pasado. (Spanish version of Life of the past.) Madrid: Alianza Editorial.

1967F. The meaning of evolution. Revised edition. New Haven: Yale Univ. Press, 364 pp., (paperback), 38 figs.

1967G. The major features of evolution. New York: Simon and Schuster, 434 pp., (Clarion Books, paperback reprint).

1968A. The meaning of evolution. Revised edition. New Haven: Yale Univ. Press, 368 pp., (hardback).

1968B. Life of the past. An introduction to paleontology. New York: Bantam Books, 194 pp., (slightly modified paperback).

1968C. A didelphid (Marsupialia) from the Early Eocene of Colorado. Postilla, no. 115, 1–3, 1 fig., 1 table.

1968D. Premature citations of zoological nomina. Science, 161, 75–76.

1968E. The cochlea in multituberculates. Syst. Zool., 17, 98. See: Leakey, et al. 1965.

SIMPSON, G. G., and BECK, W. S.
1965   Life. An introduction to biology. 2nd ed., revised. New York, Chicago, Burlingame: Harcourt, Brace and World, xviii + 869 pp., illustr.

SIMPSON, RUTH DE ETTE
1964   The archeological survey of Pleistocene Manix Lake (an early lithic horizon). Proc. Internat. Congr. Americanists, 1962:1, 5–8.

SIMPSON, WILLIAM KELLY, (ed.)
1959   COWA surveys and bibliographies. Area 9 – northeast Africa. COWA Surv. and Bibliog., Area 9, no. 1, 11 + 28 pp.

SIMPSON, W. K., and CARTER, T. H., (eds.)
1962   COWA surveys and bibliographies. Area 9 – northeast Africa. COWA Surv. and Bibliog., Area 9, no. 2, 11 + 35 pp.

SIMS, JACK R., JR., and DANIEL, D. S.
1967   A lithic assemblage near Winslow, Arizona. Plateau, 39, 175—188, 1 fig.,
         2 pls.

SINGER, RONALD
1962A.   Abs.: Kuhn-Schnyder in Zbl. Geol. Pal., Teil 2, 1964, 226.
1964   Evolution and man. In: Lasker, G. W., (ed.), 1964, 67—78, 3 figs.,
         (reprint with editorial comment).
         See: Boné and Singer.

SINGER, R., and BONÉ, E. L.
1966   Hipparion in Africa. Quaternaria, 8, 187—191, (French and German
         summaries).

SINGER, R., and HELTNE, P. G.
1966   Further notes on a bone assemblage from Hopefield, South Africa.
         Actas V Congr. Panafr. Prehist. Estud. Cuaternario, 1963:2, 261—
         264.

SINGH, V. P.   See: Prasad and Singh.

SINITSYN, VASILIĬ MIKHAĬLOVICH
1959   [Central Asia.] Moscow: Gos. Izd. Geogr. Lit. 456 pp., 38 figs., 50
         maps, (Russian).
1965   [The ancient climates of Eurasia. Part I. Paleogene and Neogene.]
         Leningrad: Leningrad Univ. Press, (not seen).
         Rev.: Anon. in Internat. Geol. Rev., 7, 376.
1967   [Climates of Eurasia in Paleogene and Neogene.] In: Martinson, (ed.),
         1967A, 201—208, (Russian).

SINOTO, Y. H.   See: Yawata and Sinoto.

SIRKS, M. J., and ZIRKLE, C.
1964   The evolution of biology. New York: Ronald Press, vi + 376 pp.,
         64 figs.

SIROTO, LEON
1963   Concerning Livingstone's "Reconstructing man's Pliocene pongid ancestor".
         Amer. Anthrop., 65, 912—913.

SIRUGUE, FRANÇOIS   See: Dughi and Sirugue.

SITTLER, CLAUDE
1965   La sédimentation argileuse fluvio-lacustre à la limite du Crétacé et de
         l'Éocène en Provence et au Languedoc. Rapport avec le problème
         de la disparition des Dinosauriens. Bull. Serv. Carte Géol. Alsace-
         Lorraine, 18, 3—14, 1 fig., (English, German and Russian sum-
         maries).

SIVKOVA, A. S.   See: Kudrin, L. N., Sivkova and Martynova.

SIZIKOV, A. I.   See: Barabashev, et al.

SJÖDIN, ÅKE
1965   Nordic anthropological bibliography 1926 - 1955. Ymer, 1964: suppl.,
         90 pp.

SKARLAND, IVAR
1964   Otto William Geist, 1888 - 1963. Amer. Antiq., 29, 484–485, portr.

SKEELS, M. A.
1962A.   Abs.: Weiler in Zbl. Geol. Pal., Teil 2, 1965, 236.

SKINNER, B. F.
1966   The phylogeny and ontogeny of behavior. Science, 153, 1205–1213.

SKINNER, MORRIS F.
1957   Appendix D. Horse bones. In: Jennings, J. D., et al., 1957, 307–308, 1 fig.
1968   A Pliocene chalicothere from Nebraska, and the distribution of chalicotheres in the Late Tertiary of North America. Amer. Mus. Novit., 2346, 24 pp., 4 figs., 2 tables.

SKINNER, M. F., SKINNER, S. M., and GOORIS, R. J.
1968   Cenozoic rocks and faunas of Turtle Butte, south-central South Dakota. Bull. Amer. Mus. Nat. Hist., 138:7, 379–436, 16 figs., pls. 20–25, 7 tables.

SKINNER, M. F., and TAYLOR, B. E.
1967   A revision of the geology and paleontology of the Bijou Hills, South Dakota. Addendum: Rodent identification, by Thompson M. Stout. Amer. Mus. Novit., no. 2300, 53 pp., 12 figs., 5 tables.

SKINNER, SHIRLEY M., and GOORIS, R. J.
1966   A note on Toxotherium (Mammalia, Rhinocerotoidea) from Natrona County, Wyoming. Amer. Mus. Novit., no. 2261, 12 pp., 5 figs., 1 table.

SKLENÁŘ, K.   See: Fridrich and Sklenář.

SKORKOWSKI, EDWARD
1960   The Przewalski horse. Przeglad Zool., 4, 287–291, (Polish; English summary).
1964   Phenomena and correctnesses revealed by statistical methods. Mat. Prace Antrop., 70, 287–290, (Polish; English summary).
1967   Das Auftreten des Pferdes im alten Orient. Säugetierkundl. Mitt. 15, 1–6, 2 figs., (English summary).

SKRAMOVSKY, B. M.   See: Beer, et al.

SKROTZKY, NICOLAS
1964   L'Abbé Breuil. Paris: Éditions Seghers (Collection savants du monde entier), 187 pp., 13 pls.
    Rev.: Gerhard in Homo, 15, 253.

SKUTIL, JOSEF
1962B.   "Dolina", première station paléolithique en plein air à Ostrov près Macocha. Archeol. Roz., 14, 564–566, (Czech; French summary).
1963B.   Další stopy pobytu paleolitického člověka v Hulíně. Zprávy Oblastního Musea v Gottwaldově, 1963–64: sec. 1–4, 29, (not seen).

SKUTIL, J., and OULEHLA, V.
1961   Station solutréenne de Dukovany près de Moravský Krumlov. Archeol.
         Roz., 13, 8–12, fig. 20, (Czech; French summary).

SLABÝ, OTTO
1962   Historie a dnešní stav názorů na původa a vývoj končetin obratlovců.
         Československá Morfologie, 10, 372–390, 16 figs., (Russian and
         English summaries).

SLAUGHTER, BOB H.
1963B.? An ecological interpretation of the Brown Sand Wedge local fauna,
         Blackwater Draw, New Mexico, and a hypothesis concerning Late-
         Pleistocene extinction, 37 pp., (mimeographed preprint).
1964A.   Geological survey and appraisal of the paleontological resources of the
         Cooper Reservoir Basin, Delta and Hopkins Counties, Texas.
         Fondren Sci. Ser., S. Methodist Univ., 6, 1–11, 1 map.
1964B.   Cave with a past. Texas Caver, 9, 89–92, 2 figs.
1965A.   Preliminary report on the paleontology of the Livingston Reservoir
         Basin, Texas. Fondren Sci. Ser., S. Methodist Univ., 10, 1–12,
         1 map.
1965B.   "Out of step" mating as a possible cause of extinction. 7th Internat.
         Congr., Internat. Assoc. Quat. Res., Abs., 1965, 435, (abs.).
1965C.   Simple reproduction of enamel patterns of equine teeth. Jour. Pal., 39,
         165, 1 fig.
1965D.   A therian from the Lower Cretaceous (Albian) of Texas. Postilla, no.
         93, 18 pp., 6 figs.
1966A.   Platygonus compressus and associated fauna from the Laubach Cave of
         Texas. Amer. Mid. Nat., 75, 475–494, 7 figs., 3 tables.
1966B.   The vertebrates of the Domebo local fauna, Pleistocene of Oklahoma.
         Contrib. Mus. Great Plains, no. 1, 31–35, figs. 29–30, 1 table.
1966C.   The Moore Pit local fauna: Pleistocene of Texas. Jour. Pal., 40, 78–
         91, 6 figs.
1966D.   New fossil evidence concerning which is the primary cusp of the talonid
         on mammalian molars. Texas Jour. Sci., 18, 132–133, (abs.).
1967   Animal ranges as a clue to Late-Pleistocene extinctions. In: Martin,
         P. S., and Wright, H. E., (eds.), 1967, 155–167, 2 figs.
1968A.   The neglected angle in descriptive and interpretive vertebrate paleontology.
         Jour. Pal., 42, 1311–1312, 1 fig.
1968B.   Earliest known marsupials. Science, 162, 254–255, 1 fig.
1968C.   Earliest known eutherian mammals and the evolution of premolar occlusion.
         Texas Jour. Sci., 20, 3–12, 2 figs.
         See: Cheatum and Slaughter; McNulty and Slaughter; Welles and
         Slaughter.

SLAUGHTER, B. H., and HOOVER, B. R.
1965   An antler artifact from the Late Pleistocene of northeastern Texas.
         Amer. Antiq., 30, 351–352, 1 fig.

SLAUGHTER, B. H., and McCLURE, W. L.
1965   The Sims Bayou local fauna: Pleistocene of Houston, Texas. Texas
         Jour. Sci., 17, 403–417, 4 figs., 1 table.

SLAUGHTER, B. H., and STEINER, M.
1968   Notes on rostral teeth of ganopristine sawfishes, with special reference
         to Texas material. Jour. Pal., 42, 233–239, 4 figs.

SLAUGHTER, B. H., and THURMOND, J. T.
1965A.   Geological and paleontological survey of the Forney Reservoir Basin,
          Kaufman and Rockwall counties, Texas. Fondren Sci. Ser., S.
          Methodist Univ., 7, 1—11, 1 map.
1965B.   Geological and paleontological survey of the Bardwell Reservoir Basin,
          Ellis County, Texas. Fondren Sci. Ser., S. Methodist Univ., 8,
          1—10, 1 map.

SLIJPER, E. J.
1965   Vijftig jaren walvisonderzoek een jubileum van Dr. A. B. Van Deinse.
          Lutra, 7, 5—7, (Dutch).

SLIŠKOVIC, T.   See: Malez and Sliškovic.

SLOAN, ROBERT E.
1964   Paleoecology of the Cretaceous-Tertiary transition in Montana. Science,
          146, 430.
1966   Paleontology and geology of the Badwater Creek area, central Wyoming.
          Part 2. The Badwater multituberculate. Ann. Carnegie Mus.,
          38:14, 309—315, 6 figs., 1 table.
          See: Clemens, McKenna, et al.; Van Valen and Sloan.

SLOAN, R. E., and VAN VALEN, L.
1965   Cretaceous mammals from Montana. Science, 148, no. 3667, 220—227,
          6 figs., 1 table.

SLOB, A.   See: Krommenhoek and Slob.

SLOBIN, DANIEL, LANCASTER, J. B., DIEBOLD, A. R., et al.
1965   Language and communication. In: DeVore, P. L., (ed.), 1965, 71—88.

SLOTKIN, J. S., (ed.)
1965   Readings in early anthropology. Chicago: Aldine, Viking Fund Publi-
          cations in Anthropology, edited by Sol Tax, no. 40, xvii + 530 pp.
          Rev.: Fischer in Anthrop. Anz., 30, 194—195.

SM.
1960   Ein neuer afrikanischer Schädelfund — ältester menschlicher Skelettrest?
          Umschau, 60, 119—120.

SMAIL, WILLIAM
1951B.   Fluted points from Missouri. Missouri Archaeol., 13:1, 18—20, illustr.

SMIGIELSKA, TERESA
1966A.   Otoliths of fishes from the Tortonian of Southern Poland. Ann. Soc.
          Géol. Pologne, 36, 205—275, 10 figs., pls. 12—19, 4 tables.
          Rev.: Weiler in Zbl. Geol. Pal., Teil 2, 1968:6, 652—653.
1966B.   [Fish otoliths from Tortonian of southern Poland.] Roczn. Polsk.
          towarz. geol., 36:3, 205—275, (Polish and English).

SMIRNOV, E. S.
1959   [Philosophy of zoology of G. Lamarck (1809 - 1959).] Nauchn. Dokl.
          Vyssh. Shkoly, Biol. Nauki, 1959:3, 16—25, (Russian).

SMIRNOV, G. D.   See: Zelenchuk, Rikman and Smirnov.

SMIRNOV, K. F.   See: Merpert and Smirnov.

SMITH, ALAN
1965   Were dinosaurs a failure? With comment by W. C. Kraatz. Sci. Digest,
             58:3, 86–89, 58:6, 95–96, illustr.

SMITH, ALLEN
1966   A Lake Mohave point from the Uncompahgre Plateau. Southwestern
             Lore, 32, 23–24, 1 fig.

SMITH, ARTHUR GEORGE
1964A.   A primitive bark boat. Anthrop. Jour. Canada, 2:3, 11.
1964B.   Sheer speculation. New World Antiq., 11, 132–134.
1967A.   Waterworn artifacts from Late Pleistocene lake beaches in northern Ohio.
             Ohio Archaeol., 17, 56–59, 1 fig.
1967B.   The very first Ohioans. Ohio Archaeol., 17, 82–83, 1 pl.
1967C.   Onondaga chert in northern Ohio. Ohio Archaeol., 17, 159–162, 1 pl.
             See: Harland, Smith and Wilcock.

SMITH, CALVIN, RUNYON, J., and AGOGINO, G.
1966   A progress report on a pre-ceramic site at Rattlesnake Draw, eastern
             New Mexico. Plains Anthrop., 11, 302–313, 2 figs., 5 pls.

SMITH, C. LAVETT
1964   Fishes and climates. Nat. Hist., 73:2, 34–39, illustr.

SMITH, DENYS BARKER
1964   The Permian period. In: Harland, W. B., et al., (eds.), 1964, 211–220,
             1 fig., 1 table.

SMITH, GERALD R.
1966   Distribution and evolution of the North American catostomid fishes of
             the subgenus Pantosteus, genus Catostomus. Misc. Publ. Mus.
             Zool., Univ. Mich., 129, 1–132, 22 figs., 1 pl.
             Rev.: Smith in Quart. Rev. Biol., 42, 533.
             See: Miller, R. R. and Smith; Stokes, Smith and Horn.

SMITH, HOBART M.
1960   Evolution of chordate structure. New York: Holt, Rinehart and
             Winston, 529 pp., illustr.

SMITH, HUGH M.   See: Jordan, D. S. 1963.

SMITH, H. T. U.   See: Schultz, C. B. and Smith.

SMITH, JOHN MAYNARD
1965   Prof. J. B. S. Haldane, F. R. S. [1892 - 1964]. Nature, 206, 239–240.

SMITH, J. M., and SAVAGE, R. J. G.
1956   Some locomotory adaptations in mammals. Jour. Linn. Soc. London,
             Zool., 42:288, 603–622, 14 figs., 3 tables.

SMITH, LEAH M.
1966   Second-graders study dinosaurs. Earth Sci., Midwest Fed. Min. Soc.,
             19, 270, illustr.

SMITH, MALCOLM ARTHUR
1931   The fauna of British India, including Ceylon and Burma. Reptiles and
        Amphibia. Vol. 1.-Loricata, Testudines. London: Taylor and
        Francis, xxviii + 185 pp., 42 figs., 2 pls.

SMITH, PH.   See: Bordes and Smith.

SMITH, PHILIP E. L.
1962B.   The Abbe' Henri Breuil and prehistoric archaeology. Anthropologica,
          n.s., 4, 199—208.
1964A.   New data for the Late Paleolithic of northeastern Africa. Abs. 63rd
          Ann. Meeting Amer. Anthrop. Assoc., 1964, 56, (abs.).
1964B.   Expedition to Kom Ombo. Archaeol., 17, 209—210, illustr.
1964C.   The Solutrean culture. Sci. Amer., 211:2, 86—94, illustr.
1964D.   Radiocarbon dating of a Late Paleolithic culture from Egypt. Science,
          145, 811.
          Abs.: Anon. in Naturwiss. Rund., 18, 32.
1965A.   A new style of prehistoric rock art from North Africa. Abs. 64th Ann.
          Meeting Amer. Anthrop. Assoc., 1965, 64, (abs.).
1965B.   Some Solutrean problems and suggestions for further research. In:
          Ripoll Perello', E., (ed.), 1965B, 389—408, (Spanish summary).
1966A.   Le Solutréen en France. Publ. Inst. Préhist. Univ. Bordeaux, Mém. no.
          5, 450 pp., 81 figs., 3 pls., 21 graphs., 4 maps, 6 tables.
          Rev.: Jorda' Cerda' in Zephyrus, 17, 143—148; Valoch in Archeol.
          Roz., 19, 408.
1966B.   Le Solutréen en France. Translated into French by François Bordes.
          Bordeaux, France: Laboratory of Prehistory, Univ. Bordeaux,
          465 pp., illustr., paperback, (not seen).
          Rev.: Freeman in Science, 156, 787—789; Sackett in Amer. Anthrop.,
          70, 629—630.
1966C.   The Late Paleolithic of Northeast Africa in the light of recent research.
          In: Clark, J. D., and Howell, F. C., (eds.), 1966A, 326—355,
          4 figs., 1 table.
1966D.   New prehistoric investigations at Kom Ombo (Upper Egypt). Zephyrus,
          17, 31—45, 6 figs.
          See: Young, T. C. and Smith.

SMITH, ROBERT LEO
1966   Ecology and field biology. New York and London: Harper and Row,
        xiv + 686 pp., illustr.
        Rev.: Birch in Science, 153, 1234.

SMITH, SHIRLEY, and AGOGINO, G.
1966   A comparison of whole and fragmentary Paleo-Indian points from Black-
        water draw. Plains Anthrop., 11, 201—203.

SMOLLA, GÜNTER
1962   Steingeraete vom Tendaguru. Proc. 4th Panafrican Congr. Prehist., sec.
        3, 243—247, 3 pls.
1965   Höhlenprobleme. Fundber. Schwaben, 17, 61—68.
1966   Die frühe und mittlere Altsteinzeit südlich der Sahara. In: Narr, (ed.),
        1966B, 97—112, 10 figs., 1 table.

SNEATH, PETER H. A.   See: Sokal and Sneath.

SNEED, PAUL G.
    1967   An archaeological reconnaissance of the Craters of the Moon National
                Monument. Tebiwa, 10:1, 37–52, 5 figs.
                See: Swanson and Sneed.

SNELLING, NORMAN JOHN
    1964   A review of recent Phanerozoic time-scales. In: Harland, W. B., et al.,
                (eds.), 1964, 29–36, 1 fig.

SNOW, CLYDE C.   See: Brues and Snow.

SNYDER, RICHARD C.
    1967   Adaptive values of bipedalism. Amer. Jour. Phys. Anthrop., 26, 131–134.

SOERGEL, ELSBETH
    1960   Abstammung der Vögel. In: Berndt, R., and Meise, W., (eds.), 1960,
                6–17.
                Abs.: Kuhn in Zbl. Geol. Pal., Teil 2, 1966, 310–311.
    1966   Die Vogelreste. In: Ehrenberg, (ed.), 1966A, 93–107, 1 table.

SOETENS, J.
    1960   Le gisement paléolithiques d'Ottignies. Ottignies: 12 pp., (not seen).
    1963   Aperçu archéologique et préhistorique d'Israël. Bull. Soc. Roy. Belge
                Anthrop. Préhist., 73, 139–144.

SOFSKY, CHARLES   See: Prufer and Sofsky.

SOHN, I. G.
    1968   Premature citations and zoological nomenclature. Science, 159, 441–442.

SOHRE, HELMUT
    1964   Dem Pferde verschworen. Stuttgart: Franckh'sche Verlagshandlung,
                134 pp., 14 pls., (not seen).
                Rev.: Zänkert in Kosmos (Stuttgart), 61, *330.

SOKAL, ROBERT R., and SNEATH, P. H. A.
    1963   Principles of numerical taxonomy. San Francisco, London: Freeman,
                xvi + 359 pp., illustr.
                Rev.: Anon. in Jour. Mammal., 46, 111–112; James in Evolution,
                18, 513; Kiriakoff in Syst. Zool., 14, 61–64; Lerman in
                Quart. Rev. Biol., 39, 374–375; Ross in Syst. Zool., 13, 106–
                108; Simpson in Science, 144, 712–713; Stefan in Naturwiss.
                Rund., 18, 378.

SOKHIN, V. K.   See: Bersenev, et al.

SOKOLOFF, V. P.   See: Eynor 1966.

SOKOLOV, B. S.
    1965   Professor Roman Kozlowski: seventy-fifth birthday. Internat. Geol.
                Rev., 7, 1616–1621.
    1967   (ed.) [Paleozoic stratigraphy of Middle Siberia.] Novosibirsk: "Nauka"
                Press, 253 pp., 5 figs., 24 tables, (Russian).

SOKOLOV, D. S., (ed.)
1960   [Regional stratigraphy of China. Vol. 1. Translated from Chinese.]
            Moscow: IL Press, 659 pp., 1 map, (Russian).
1963   [Regional stratigraphy of China. Vol. 2. Translated from Chinese.]
            Moscow: IL Press, 274 pp., 1 map, (Russian).

SOKOLOV, I. I.
1965   [On some principles and methods in systematics.] Trudy Zool. Inst.
            Akad. Nauk SSSR, 35, 16–42, 8 figs., (Russian).

SOKOLOV, I. I., and VEKUA, A. K.
1966   [A screw-horned antelope (? Sinoreas sp.) from Lower Pleistocene de-
            posits of Akhalkalaki.]   Soob. Akad. Nauk Gruz. SSR, 43:1,
            147–150, 1 fig., (Russian; Georgian summary).

SOKOLOV, M. I.
1965   [Teeth evolution of some genera of Cretaceous sharks and reconstruction
            of their dentition.]   Biull. Mosk. Obshch. Ispyt. Prirody, Otd.
            Geol., 40:4, 133–134, (Russian).

SOKOLOV, V. N.
1957   [The geological structure of the northern section of the western-Siberian
            depression.]   Trudy Inst. Geol. Arktiki, 81, 105–132, (Russian).

SOKOLOVA, P. N.   See: Bersenev, et al.

SOKOLOVSKIĬ, I. L.
1958   [Loess of the western part of URSR.] Trudy Inst. Geol. Nauk AN URSR,
            ser. geomorf. ta chetvert. geol., 2, 99 pp., 12 figs., 20 tables,
            (Russian).

SOLBRIG, OTTO THOMAS
1966   Evolution and systematics. New York: Macmillan, 122 pp., illustr.,
            (not seen).

SOLECKI, RALPH S.
1961D.   Rev.: [Jelínek] in Anthrop., 2:3, 91–92.
1963   (ed.) Preliminary statement of the prehistoric investigations of the
            Columbia University Nubian Expedition in Sudan, 1961-62.
            Kush, 11, 70–92, 6 figs.

SOLECKI, R., and LEROI-GOURHAN, A.
1966   [Paleoclimatology and archeology of the Near East.]   In: Collected
            Papers, 1966C [Solar activity and changes of climate], 354–367,
            (Russian).

SOLECKI, R., and WAGLEY, C.
1963   William Duncan Strong. 1899 - 1962. Amer. Anthrop. Special Publ.,
            65, 1102–1111, portr., bibliog.

SOLECKI, ROSE LILIEN
1961   Zawi Chemi Shanidar, a post-Pleistocene village site in northern Iraq.
            Internat. Assoc. Quat. Res., Abs. Pap., 6th Congr., 144–145, (abs.).

SOLER GARCIA, JOSE MARIA
1956   La Cueva Grande de la Huesa-Tacaña. Estación paleolítica en Villena (Alicante). Mem. Serv. Invest. Arqueol. Asturias, 1, 123–131, 4 figs.

SOLHEIM, WILHELM G., II.
1960B.   (ed.) COWA surveys and bibliographies. Area 20 – Indonesia. COWA Surv. and Bibliog., Area 20, no. 2, 3 + 6 pp.
1963B.   Prehistoric archaeology in Thailand. Abs. 62nd Ann. Meeting Amer. Anthrop. Assoc., 1963, 62, (abs.).
1964   Formosan relationships with southeast Asia. Asian Perspectives, 7, 251–260.
1966A.   Prehistoric archaeology in Thailand. Antiq., 40, 8–16, 1 fig.
1966B.   Eastern Asia and Oceania. Asian Perspectives, 8:1, 1–9.
1966C.   (ed.) COWA surveys and bibliographies. Area 19 – Southeast Asia. COWA Surv. and Bibliog., Area 19, no. 3, 9 + 7 pp.

SOLLBERGER, J. B.
1968   The Paleo type flake knife. Bull. Texas Archeol. Soc., 38, 45–46.

SOLONEVICH, GEORGE   See: Craig, M. J. 1965.

SOLOV'EV, L. N., and ORELKIN, V. S.
1961   [Find of human bones in the Khupynishakhva cave (Cold cave) in Abkhazia.] Voprosy Antrop., 6, 143–145, 2 figs., (Russian).

SOMMER, FRIEDRICH WILHELM, and SOUZA CUNHA, F. L. DE
1962   Uma nova localidade fossiliferar – pleistocenica no norte de Minas-Geraes. An. Acad. Brasil. Cien., 34, xxxiv–xxxv.

SONDAAR, PAUL Y.
1968A.   A peculiar Hipparion dentition from the Pliocene of Saloniki (Greece). Proc. K. Nederl. Akad. Wet., ser. B, 71:1, 51–56, 2 pls.
    Rev.: Thenius in Zbl. Geol. Pal., Teil 2, 1970:3/4, 246.
1968B.   The osteology of the manus of fossil and Recent Equidae with special reference to phylogeny and function. Verh. Ned. Akad. Weten., ser. 1, 25:1, 1–76, 25 figs., 5 pls., 18 tables.
    Rev.: Thenius in Zbl. Geol. Pal., Teil 2, 1969:6, 519.
    See: Boekschoten and Sondaar; Crusafont Pairó 1965M; Freudenthal and Sondaar; Hussain and Sondaar.

SONDAAR, P. Y., and BOEKSCHOTEN, G. J.
1967   Quaternary mammals in the south Aegean Island arc; with notes on other fossil mammals from the coastal regions of the Mediterranean. I and II. Proc. K. Nederl. Akad. Wet., ser. B, 70, 556–576, 2 figs., 5 pls.

SONNEVILLE-BORDES, DENISE DE
1960A.   Rev.: Chmielewska in Archeol. Polski, 12, 172–177, (Polish); Jordá Cerdá in Zephyrus, 13, 117–119.
1961C.   Rev.: Jordá Cerdá in Zephyrus, 13, 116–117; Orellana Rodríguez in Antropología, 2:1, 124–125.
1963A.   Rev.: Vaufrey in L'Anthrop., 69, 306–307.
1965A.   Géomorphologie et préhistoire au sud d'Angoulême. IV. L'Abri de la Chaire-a-Calvin, Mouthiers (Charente). Bull. Assoc. Franç. Etude Quat., 1965:3–4, 193–197, 2 figs.

1965B.   Observations statistiques sur l'Aurignacien du Vogelherd, Lonetal,
           Würtemberg. fouilles G. Riek. Fundber. Schwaben, 17, 69–75,
           2 figs., 1 table.
1965C.   Deux gisements paléolithiques du Sud-Ouest de la France: le Trou de
           la Chèvre (Dordogne) et Pair-non-Pair (Gironde). L'Anthrop.,
           69:1–2, 169–175.
1965D.   Les religions de la préhistoire. L'Anthrop., 69, 381–385.
1965E.   Stations acheuléennes de la Vieille-Castille: Torralba et Ambrona.
           L'Anthrop., 69:5–6, 600–601.
1965F.   Le Paléolithique en Grèce. L'Anthrop., 69:5–6, 603–606.
1966A.   L'évolution du Paléolithique supérieur en Europe Occidentale et sa sig-
           nification. Bull. Soc. Préhist. Franç., Étud. et Trav., 63:1, 3–34.
1966B.   Le Solutréen en France. L'Anthrop., 70:5–6, 595–602.
           See: Barandiarán and Sonneville-Bordes; Bordes and Sonneville-Bordes;
           Monméjean, et al.

SOPER, R. C.
1966   A report on preliminary collections of Palaeolithic material from parts
           of Northern Nigeria. Actas V Congr. Panafr. Prehist. Estud.
           Cuaternario, 1963:2, 265–269.

SORNAY, J.   See: Arambourg, Dubertret, et al.

SOROKIN, V. S.
1967   [On the distribution of ichthyofauna in Snetogorskii (Lower Pliavin'skii)
           beds of the Latvian depression.] In: Collected Papers. 1967E
           [Problems of geology of Middle and Upper Paleozoic of Baltic
           regions], 85–105, (Russian).

SOSNOVSKII, G. P.
1935C.   [Settlement on the Afontova hill.] Izvestiia Gosud. Akad. Ist. Mater.
           Kult. N. Y. Marra, 118, 125–151, (Russian).
1940D.   [New Paleolithic sites in southern Siberia.] Krat. Soob. Inst. Ist. Mat.
           Kult. SSSR, 7, 86–90, 2 figs., (Russian).

SOUBEYRAN, MICHEL
1966   Station de Raymonden, à Chancelade. Résumé de thèse soutenue à
           l'École du Louvre. Bull. Soc. Hist. Archéol. Périgord, 93, 54–
           67, 5 pls.

SOUDSKÝ, B., and PLEINER, R.
1961   Aux problèmes de la préhistoire tchécoslovaque. Archeol. Roz., 13,
           520–570, (Czech; French summary).

SOUNDARA RAJAN, K. V.
1961A.   Rev.: Peuke in Wiss. Zeit. Halle Univ., Ges.-Sprachwiss. Reihe, 14, 516.
1962   [Obit.]: Dr. B. Subba Rao. Jour. Orient. Inst., 11, 304–305.

SOURLOCK, J. DAN   See: Shafer, Suhm and Sourlock.

SOUVILLE, GEORGES
1956B.   Atlas préhistorique de l'Algérie. Preface by L. Balout. Libyca, 4, 213–
           261, (map in Libyca, 6–7).
1956C.   La préhistoire au Maroc (1955 - 1956). Libyca, 4, 351–355, 1 map.
1960C.   La préhistoire au Maroc (1957 - 1958). Libyca, 6–7, 271–275, 1 map.

1960D.   La préhistoire au Maroc (1959-1960). Libyca, 8, 319—321.
1963   La préhistoire au Maroc (1961-1962). Libyca, 11, 291—294.

SOUZA CUNHA, FAUSTO LUIS DE
1960   Sobre o Hippidion da Lapa Mortuária de Confins, Lagoa Santa, Minas
              Gerais; estudos geo-paleontológicos baseados na Lapa Mortuária
              e na coleção "Padberg—Drenkpol" do Museu Nacional. Rio de
              Janeiro, 54 pp., illustr., (not seen).
1961   Sôbre a ocorrência de cavalos fósseis nos Estados do Ceará e Rio Grande
              do Norte. An. Acad. Brasil. Ciên, 33:3—4, xxxi — xxxii.
              See: Sommer and Souza Cunha.

SOUZA CUNHA, F. L., and DIAS DE ÁVILA PIRES, F.
1959   Cervídeos fósseis do Brasil. An. Acad. Brasil. Ciên., 31, XLIV.

SOUZA CUNHA, F. L. DE, and MAGALHÃES MACEDO, A. C.
1963   Novas ocorrências pleistocênicas no município de Curaçá, Bahia. An.
              Acad. Brasil. Ciên., 35, XX — XXI.

SOVA, P. P.
1964   [Paleolithic sites in Uzhgorod.] Arkheologiĭa, 180—187, 5 figs., (Ukrain-
              ian; Russian summary).

SPARKS, B. W.   See: West, R. G. and Sparks.

SPAULDING, ALBERT C., (ed.)
1959   COWA surveys and bibliographies. Area 14 — East Africa. COWA
              Surv. and Bibliog., Area 14, no. 1, 4 + 8 pp.

SPEED, E.   See: Maggs and Speed.

SPÉLÉO—CLUB DE BERGERAC
1966   La Grotte préhistorique des Fieux. Spelunca, Bull., 6:2, 106—108, 1 fig.

SPENCE, SAM ED
1964   Alibates, the prehistoric treasure. Desert Mag., 27:8, 30—31, 1 fig.

SPENCE, T. F.   See: Zuckerman, et al.

SPENCER, H. E. P.
1964   The contemporary mammalian fossils of the Crags. Trans. Suffolk. Nat.
              Soc., 12, 333—334.

SPENCER, ROBERT F., JENNINGS, J. D., et al.
1965   The native Americans. New York, London: Harper and Row, xi + 539
              pp., illustr.
              Rev.: Bhattacharya in E. Anthrop., 19, 268—270; Byers in Amer. Antiq.,
              31, 582—584; Haberland in Homo, 18:1, 72; Hillaby in New.
              Sci., 28, 292, 294; R. H. L. in Minn. Archaeol., 28, 62—63; Ritz-
              enthaler in Amer. Anthrop., 68:5, 1286—1288; Thatcher in Mich.
              Archaeol., 12, 102—103; Underhill in Man, Jour. Roy. Anthrop.
              Inst., 1, 121; Woodbury in Amer. Jour. Archaeol., 70, 87.

SPENCER, R. F., and JOHNSON, E.
1960   Atlas for anthropology. Dubuque, Iowa: W. C. Brown, iii + 52 pp.,
              15 maps.

Rev.: Smith in Plains Anthrop., 9, 58.

SPENDLOVE, EARL
1968   When dinosaurs trod Utah's Vermilion Cliffs. Desert Mag., 31:8, 22—25, 3 figs.

SPERANSKIĬ, V. S.
1967   [Phyloontogenetic classification of non constant sutures of cerebral skull.] Discussion. 7th Internat. Congr. Anthrop. Ethnol. Sci., Moscow, 1964, 2, 486—490, 2 tables, (Russian).

SPERRY, OWEN
1967   A sketch of Folsom man. Newsletter Kansas Anthrop. Assoc., 12:5, 2—3.

SPIEGEL, Z.   See: DeBrine, Spiegel and William.

SPIER, R. F. G., HENNING, D. R., and VINCENT, J. R.
1961—62   Graphic teaching aids in basic anthropometry. Columbia, Mo.: Missouri Archaeological Society, 28 pp., 20 illustrs. (Available from Missouri Archaeological Soc., 15, Switzler Hall, Univ. of Missouri, Columbia, Missouri).
            Rev.: Saul in Amer. Anthrop. Special Publ., 65, 1200.

ŠPINAR, ZDENĚK V.
1963   Der vorläufige Bericht über einige Ergebnisse des Studiums von Fröschen der Familie Palaeobatrachidae Cope, 1889. Věstnik Ústred. Úst. Geol., 38:3, 201—204, 2 pls., 2 tables, (Czech abstract).
            Abs.: Huene in Zbl. Geol. Pal., Teil 2, 1964, 984—985.
1966   Some further results of the study of Tertiary frogs in Czechoslovakia. Čas. Min. Geol., 11, 431—440, 5 figs., (Czech summary).
1967A.   Neue Kenntnisse über den stratigraphischen Bereich der Familie Palaeobatrachidae Cope 1885. Věstnik Ústred. Úst. Geol., 42:3, 217—218, 1 fig., (Czech summary).
            Rev.: Prantl in Zbl. Geol. Pal., Teil 2, 1967, 509.
1967B.   Familie Palaeobatrachidae Cope, 1865, ihre taxonomische Einreihung und Bedeutung für die Phylogenie der Frösche. Věstnik Ústred. Úst. Geol., 42:5, 375—379, 1 fig., (Czech summary).
1968   Obituary. Josef Augusta. [1903—1968] News Bull., Soc. Vert. Pal., 83, 39, portr.

SPIRKIN, ALEXANDRE G.
1959   The origin of language. Cahiers Hist. Mond., 5, 293—309.

SPIRU, ION
1965   [Some Paleolithic and Neolithic finds in Alexandria region.]   Studii şi Cercetări de Ist. Veche, 16, 307—309, 2 figs., (Rumanian; Russian and French summaries).

SPIVAK, MORRIS J.
1961   The cosmic dance of Lascaux, a new theory on Paleolithic art and religion. Montignac-sur-Vézère: printed by author, 14 pp., (not seen).
            Rev.: Roussot in Bull. Soc. Hist. Archeol. Perigord, 89, 37—40, illustr..

SPJELDNAES, N.
1967   The palaeoecology of the Ordovician vertebrates of the Harding formation

(Colorado, U. S. A.)   Colloq. Internat. Cent. Nation. Recherch. Sci., 163, 11—20, 1 fig., (French summary).

SPRAGUE, RODERICK
1967   A preliminary bibliography of Washington archaeology. Rept. Invest., Wash. State Univ., Lab. Anthrop., no. 43, iv + 88 pp.

SPREEN, BARRY
1965   Additional notes on Cherokee Cave, City of St. Louis. Missouri Speleology, 6, 107.

SPRINGER, VICTOR G.
1964   A revision of the carcharhinid shark genera Scoliodon, Loxodon and Rhizoprionodon. Proc. U.S. Nation. Mus., 115, 559—632, 14 figs., 17 tables.

SPUHLER, J. N.
1954B   (ed.) Yearbook of physical anthropology, 1952. Yearbook Phys. Anthrop., 8, viii + 394 pp., illustr.
1964   Somatic paths to culture. In: Lasker, G. W., (ed.), 1964, 16—29, 2 tables, (reprint with editorial comment).

SPUHLER, J. N., and HEGLAR, R.
1962   Advances in physical anthropology. In: Siegel, B. J., (ed.), 1962, 250—278.

SRIVASTAVA, SATISH K.
1967   Palynology of Late Cretaceous mammal beds, Scollard, Alberta (Canada). Palaeogeog., Palaeoclimatol., Palaeoecol., 3, 133—150, 2 figs., 3 pls.

STACH, JAN
1956   [Discovery of rhinoceros at Wadowice.]   Biul. Panstowowy Inst. Geol., 100, 233—236, 1 pl., (Polish; Russian and English summaries).

STACHOWIAK, WŁADYSŁAW   See: Krupinski, et al.

STAESCHE, KARL
1964A.   Wilhelm Otto Dietrich, 1881—1964. Jahresb. Mitt. Oberrhein. Geol. Ver., 46, XXII—XXIV.
1964B.   Zum 100. Geburtstag von Eberhard Fraas. Jahresh. Ver. Vaterländ. Naturk. Würtemberg, 118—119, 53—56.
1964C.   Funktionsmorphologie als Stammesgeschichte? Bemerkungen zu einem Aufsatz R. Schubert-Soldern's über den Schildkrötenpanzer. Neues Jahrb. Geol. Pal., Monatsh., 3, 176—183.
1964D.   Übersicht über die Fauna des deutschen Rotliegenden (Unteres Perm). C. Wirbeltiere. Stuttgart. Beitr. Naturk., 135, 1—12, 1 table.
          Abs.: Westphal in Zbl. Geol. Pal., Teil 2, 1966, 265.
1966   Bericht des Staatlichen Museums für Naturkund in Stuttgart für 1965. D. Abteilung für Geologie, Palaontologie und Mineralogie. Jahresh. Ver. Vaterland. Naturk. Würtemberg, 121, 19—21.
          See: Schüz and Staesche.

STAINES, H. R. E., and WOODS, J. T.
1964   Recent discovery of Triassic dinosaur footprints in Queensland. Austral. Jour. Sci., 27, 55, 1 fig.

STAINS, HOWARD J.
1967   Carnivores and pinnipeds. In: Anderson, S., and Jones, (eds.), 1967, 325–354, figs. 51–59.

STALEY, ROBERT N.   See: Dahlberg and Staley.

STALEY, R. N., and BARNHART, G. W.
1966   A new silicone rubber duplicating material advantageous for teaching and research in physical anthropology. Amer. Jour. Phys. Anthrop., 25, 325–333, 9 figs.

STAMP, L. DUDLEY
1965   Some aspects of paleoecology. In: Jhingran, A. G., et al., (eds.), 1965, 14–16.

STAMPFLI, HANS RUDOLF
1959B.   Die "Kastelhöhle" in Kaltbrunnental, Gemeinde Himmelried (Solothurn). IV. Die Tierfunde. Jahrb. Solothurn. Gesch., 32, 62–82, 5 tables.

STAN, IONIŢĂ
1963   Le gisement de mamifères de Reghin-Vransea et son importance stratigraphique. 5th Congr. Assoc. Géol. Carpato-Balkanique, 3:1, 199–213, (Rumanian; French summary).
        Abs.: Semaka in Zbl. Geol. Pal., Teil 2, 1965, 268.
1964   Vestiges d'Hipparion dans le Vindobonien d'Andreiaşu (Vrancea). Dǎri de seamǎ Comit. Inst. Geol., 50:2, 407–414, 2 figs., 1 pl., (Rumanian; French and Russian summaries).

STANDING CONFERENCE ON LIBRARY MATERIALS ON AFRICA
1964   Theses on Africa accepted by universities in the United Kingdom and Ireland. Cambridge: W. Heffer, x + 74 pp.
        Rev.: R. O. in Jour. Afr. Hist., 6, 136.

STANNARD, CLIVE
1965   A report on preliminary excavations in Tarzan's Cave, Simonstown. S. Afr. Archaeol. Bull., 20:78, 91–93, 1 fig., 1 pl., 1 table.

STARCK, DIETRICH
1962A.   Abs.: Kuhn-Schnyder in Zbl. Geol. Pal., Teil 2, 1964, 226–227.
1963A.   Die Metamerie des Kopfes der Wirbeltiere. Zool. Anz., 170:11–12, 393–429, 12 figs., 5 tables. (Discussion: Kälin, Riedl).
1963B.   "Freiliegendes Tectum mesencephali" ein Kennzeichen des primitiven Säugetiergehirns? Zool. Anz., 171:9–10, 350–359, 3 figs.
1964   Über das Entotympanicum der Canidae und Ursidae (Mammalia, Carnivora, Fissipedia). Acta Theriologica, 8, 181–188, 4 figs.
1965   Die Neencephalistion. (Die Evolution zum Menschenhirn). In: Heberer, (ed.), 1965A, 103–144, 10 figs., 1 table.
1966A.   Internationaler Primatologen Kongress in Frankfurt am Main vom 26 bis 30 Juli 1966. Natur u. Mus., 96:7, 261–262.
1966B.   Laudatio für G.H.R. von Koenigswald anlässlich der Verleihung des Werner Reimers-Stiftungspreises 1966. Natur u. Mus., 96:7, 257–260, portr.
1967A.   Le crâne des mammifères. In: Grassé, (ed.), Traité de Zool., 16:1, 405–549, figs. 207–280, 1 table.
1967B.   Opening address. In: Starck, D., Schneider, R., and Kuhn, H. J., (eds.), 3–4.

STARCK, D.,   SCHNEIDER, R.,   and KUHN, H. J., (eds.)
1967   Neue Ergebnisse der Primatologie. Progress in primatology. First Congress
         of the International Primatological Society, Frankfurt, July, 1966.
         Stuttgart: Gustav Fischer, viii + 446 pp., illustr.
   Rev.:   MacConaill in Man, Jour. Roy. Anthrop. Inst., 3, 138—139; Preus-
         choft in Zbl. Geol. Pal., Teil 2, 1968, 221—222; Schultz in Folia
         Primatologica, 8, 315—316; Straus in Science, 160, 1441; Tuttle
         in Evolution, 22:4, 843—844; Vallois in L'Anthrop., 72, 158—159;
         Vogel in Zeit. Morph. Anthrop., 60:3, 329—331.

STAROSTIN, V. I.
1962   [On lower Miocene deposits of the northwestern scarps of Ustiurt.]   Izv.
         Vyssh. Uch. Zav., Geol. i Razv., 1962:10, 37—42, 4 figs., (Russian).

STARRETT, ANDREW
1967   Hystricoid, erethizontoid, cavioid, and chinchilloid rodents. In: Anderson,
         S., and Jones, (eds.), 1967, 254—272, figs. 39—41.

STCHEPINSKY, VLADIMIR   See: Lapparent and Stchepinsky.

STEBBINS, G. LEDYARD
1966   Processes of organic evolution. Englewood Cliffs, N. J.: Prentice-Hall,
         xiv + 191 pp., illustr.
   Rev.:   Hemmer in Homo, 18:1, 62; Simpson, G. G. in Science, 152,
         1364; Washburn in Amer. Jour. Phys. Anthrop., 27, 224—225.
1968   Evolutionsprozesse. Einzelvorgänge im Wandel der Organismen. Trans-
         lated by Jutta Querner. Stuttgart: Gustav Fischer, viii + 188
         pp., 75 figs., (not seen).
   Rev.:   Hanelt in Biol. Zbl., 88:5, 673—674; Peters in Natur Mus., 100:3,
         147; Schindelwolf in Zbl. Geol. Pal., Teil 2, 1969:4, 303—304;
         Thenius in Mitt. Geol. Ges. Wien, 61, 217.

STECHER, ROBERT M.
1964   The Darwin-Innes letters. Ann. Sci., 17, 201—258.
1966   Przewalski's horse, its history, its nature and its threatened survival. Ex-
         plorer, 8, 12—15, 5 figs.

STEEGMANN, A. T., JR.   See: Simons 1965B.

STEEL, C. A. B.   See: Panchen, Tilley and Steel.

STEERE, W. G.   See: Dobzhansky, Hecht and Steere.

STEFĂNESCU, M.   See: Panin and Stefănescu.

STEFANOV, S.
1966   Fischreste aus der Trias Bulgariens. Trudove Vŭrkhu Geol. Bŭlg., Ser.
         Pal., 8, 123—130, 1 fig., 2 pls.

STEFFENS, GUSTAV   See: Rust and Steffens.

STEHLI, FRANCIS G.
1966   Labyrinthodont abundance and diversity. Amer. Jour. Sci., 264, 481—
         487, 3 figs.

STEIN, WALTER T.
1967   Locality 1 (C1−244), Tule Springs, Nevada. In: Wormington, and
            Ellis, (eds.), <u>1967</u>, 309−329, 8 figs., 2 pls.

STEINBACHER, JOACHIM   See: Schödube and Steinbacher.

STEINBRING, JACK
1966   A Scottsbluff projectile point from Manitoba. Wisc. Archaeol., <u>47</u>, 1−7,
            3 figs.

STEINER, GEROLF   See: Stümpke 1967.

STEINER, HANS
1956   Gedanken zur Initialgestaltung der Chordaten. Rev. Suisse Zool., <u>63</u>,
            330−341, 1 fig., 1 table.

STEINER, MAUREEN   See: Slaughter and Steiner.

STEINER, UTE
1965   Zum Auftreten der Heidelberger Kulter in Sülzfeld. Alt-Thüringen, <u>7</u>,
            7−14, 3 figs.

STEINHORST, H.   See: Hölder and Steinhorst.

STEININGER, FRITZ
1965   Ein bemerkenswerter Fund von <u>Mastodon</u> (<u>Bunolophodon</u>) <u>longirostris</u>
            Kaup 1832 (Proboscidea, Mammalia) aus dem Unterpliozän (Pannon)
            des Hausruck-Kobernausserwald-Gebietes in Oberösterreich. Jahrb.
            Geol. Bundesanst., <u>108</u>, 195−212, 2 figs., 6 pls., 2 tables, (English
            summary).
1966   Zur Kenntnis fossiler Euselachier-Eikapseln aus dem Ober-Oligozän von
            Mitteleuropa. Mitt. Bayer. Staatssamml. Pal. Hist. Geol., <u>6</u>, 37−49,
            2 pls., 1 table, (English summary).
            Rev.: Weiler in Zbl; Geol. Pal., Teil 2, <u>1968</u>:6, 653.
1967   Ein weiterer Zahn von <u>Dryopithecus</u> (<u>Dry</u>.) <u>fontani</u> <u>darwini</u> Abel, 1902
            (Mammalia, Pongidae) aus dem Miozän des Wiener Beckens. Folia
            Primatologica, <u>7</u>, 243−275, 1 fig., 4 pls., (English summary).

STEININGER, F., and THENIUS, E.
1963B.   Abs.: Ehrenberg in Zbl. Geol. Pal., Teil 2, <u>1964</u>, 227; Kühn in Zbl.
            Geol. Pal., Teil 2, <u>1964</u>, 995−996.
1965   Eine Wirbeltierfauna aus Sarmat (Ober-Miozän) von Sauerbrunn (Burgenland).
            Mitt. Geol. Ges. Wien, <u>57</u>, 449−467, 4 figs.

STEKELIS, M.
1960A.   Rev.: Tixier in Libyca, <u>8</u>, 341−342.
1964   Archaeology: excavations. Kabara Cave. Israel Explor. Jour., <u>14</u>, 277.

STEKELIS, M., and BAR YOSEF, O.
1965   Un habitat du Paléolithique supérieur a Ein Guev (Israël). Note prelimin-
            aire. L'Anthrop., <u>69</u>:1−2, 176−183, 4 figs.

STEKELIS, M., BAR-YOSEF, A., and TCHERNOV, A.
1966   A preliminary report on a prehistoric site near En Gev. Yediot, Tel-Aviv,
            <u>30</u>, 5−22.

STEKELIS, M., PICARD, L., SCHULMAN, N., and HAAS, G.
1960   Rev.: Tixier in Libyca, 8, 342—343.

STELCK, CHARLES R.
1967   The record of the rocks. In: Hardy, (ed.), 1967, 21—51, illustr.

STELLER, DOROTHY LA LONDE
1964   Pleistocene Equus sp. from Sandusky Co., Ohio. Ohio Jour. Sci., 64,
              423—427, 10 figs., 1 table.

STENSIÖ, ERIK A.
1963   The brain and the cranial nerves in fossil, lower craniate vertebrates.
              Skrift. Norsk. Videnskaps—Akad., Oslo, (Math.—Nat. Kl.) n.s., 13,
              1—120, 54 figs.
1964   Les cyclostomes fossiles ou Ostracodermes. In: Piveteau; Traité de
              Paléo., 4:1, 96—382, 125 figs. [French translation from the English
              of Stensiö, by J.— P. Lehman.]

STEPANIÁN, L. S.
1964   [Fragments of history of the palearctic mountain avifauna.]   Nauchn.
              Dokl. Vyssh. Shkoly, Biol. Nauki, 1964:1, 31—36, (Russian).

STEPANOV, D. L.
1965   [Past, present, and future of paleontology (150 years of paleontology).]
              Ezhegodnik Vses. Pal. Ob., 17, 13—29, 4 figs., (Russian).

STEPANOV, V. V.
1961   Abs.: Mirtsching in Zbl. Geol. Pal., Teil 2, 1964, 699.

STEPHAN, H. See: Bauchot and Stephan; Hassler and Stephan.

STEPHENS, E. A.
1966   Geological account of the northwest coast of Lake Malawi, between Kar-
              onga and Lion Point, Malawi. In: Clark, J. D., and Howell, F. C.,
              (eds.), 1966A, 50—58, 2 figs.
              See: Clark, J. D., Stephens and Coryndon.

STEPHENS, JOHN J.
1964   Ophiacodon from Ohio. Ohio Jour. Sci., 64:3, 217—220, 5 figs.
              Abs.: Huene in Zbl. Geol. Pal., Teil 2, 1965, 252.

STEPHENSON, N. G.
1964   On fossil giant wombats and the identity of Sceparnodon ramsayi. Proc.
              Zool. Soc. London, 142, 537—546, 2 figs., 4 pls.

STEPHENSON, ROBERT L.
1965   Quaternary human occupation of the Plains. In: Wright, H. E., and
              Frey, D. G., (eds.), 1965, 685—696, 3 figs.
1967   Frank H. H. Roberts, Jr., 1897—1966. Amer. Antiq., 32, 84—94, portr.,

STERNBERG, CHARLES M.
1964   Function of the elongated narial tubes in the hooded hadrosaurs. Jour.
              Pal., 38, 1003—1004.
1965   New restoration of hadrosaurian dinosaur. Nation. Mus. Canada, Nat.
              Hist. Papers, no. 30, 1—5, 2 figs.
              Abs.: Huene in Zbl. Geol. Pal., Teil 2, 1966, 307.

1966   Canadian dinosaurs. Second edition. Bull. Nation. Mus. Canada, 103, Geol., Ser. 54, 28 pp., illustr.

STĘŚLICKA, WANDA
1957   Jan Mydlarski, 1892—1956. Przeglad Antrop., 23, 54—98, 2 portr., (Polish; English and Russian summaries).
1959   Human fossil remains from Siemonia, Będzin Admin. District. Archeol. Polski, 4, 231—237, 7 figs., (Polish; English summary).
1962   Fossile Menschenreste aus Polen. Mitt. Arbeitsgruppe Anthrop. Biol. Ges. Deutsch. Demokratischen Rep., 2, 21—23, (not seen).
     Abs.: Anon. in Anthrop., 2:1, 71.
1963B. Polish reconstruction of fossil hominoids. Przegląd Antrop., 29, 67—75, 9 figs., (Polish; French and English summaries).
1964A. The endocranial casts of the fossils from Siemonia and Janisławice. Mat. Prace. Antrop., 70, 75—82, 5 figs., 2 tables, (Polish; English summary).
1964B. Development of primates in geological times. Przegląd Antrop., 30, 105—113, (Polish).
1965   [Oligocene ancestral forms of catarrhines.] "Kosmos" (Poland), A14:4, 405—406, (Polish).
     See: Krupiński, et al.

STEVENS, J. B. See: Semken, Miller and Stevens.

STEVENS, MARGARET SKEELS
1964   Thoracic armor of a new arthrodire (Holonema) from the Devonian of Presque Isle county, Michigan. Papers Mich. Acad. Sci., 49, 163—175, 2 figs., 1 pl.
1965   A new species of Urocyon from the Upper Pliocene of Kansas. Jour. Mammal., 46, 265—269, 2 figs.
1966   The osteology and relationships of the Pliocene ground squirrel, Citellus dotti Hibbard, from the Ogallala formation of Beaver County, Oklahoma. Pearce-Sellards Ser. no. 4, 1—24, 6 figs., 3 tables.

STEVENSON, JOHN S., and STEVENSON, L. S.
1966   Fluorine content of microsaur teeth from the Carboniferous rocks of Joggins, Nova Scotia. Science, 154, 1548—1550, 2 figs.

STEVER, H. GUYFORD, HAGGERTY, J. J., and THE EDITORS OF LIFE
1966   Flight. New York: Time, Inc., 200 pp., illustr.

STEWART, R. H. See: Whitmore and Stewart.

STEWART, THOMAS DALE
1960B. Abs.: Anon. in NSS News, 18, 135.
1962B. Abs.: Kuhn-Schnyder in Zbl. Geol. Pal., Teil 2, 1964, 227.
1963B. Shanidar skeletons IV and VI. Sumer, 19, 8—26, 18 figs.
1964   The scapula of the first recognized Neanderthal skeleton. Bonner Jahrb., 164, 1—14, 12 figs., 5 tables.
1965   Chronometric dating and taxonomic relationships. Publ. Nation. Acad. Sci., 1469, 17—21.
     See: Greene, A. M. 1967.

STINTON, FREDERICK CHARLES
1962   Teleostean otoliths from the Upper Tertiary strata of Sarawak, Brunei and North Borneo. Ann. Rept. British Borneo, Geol. Serv. Dept., 1962, 75—92, 18 figs., 1 table, 3 maps.

Abs.: Weiler in Zbl. Geol. Pal., Teil 2, 1965, 236–237.

1965 Teleost otoliths from the Lower London Tertiaries. Senck. Lethaea,
     46a, 389–425, pls. 31–33.

     Abs.: Weiler in Zbl. Geol. Pal., Teil 2, 1966, 288–289.

1966 Otolithes des poissons du London Clay. Appendice. In: Casier, 1966A,
     404–464, pls. 66–68.

     Rev.: Weiler in Zbl. Geol. Pal., Teil 2, 1968:6, 653–655.

1968 On the study of Tertiary fish otoliths. Mém. Bur. Rech. Géol. Min.,
     58, 153–162, 1 pl., (French, German, and Russian abstracts).

     See: Casier 1966A.

STINTON, F. C., and TORRENS, H. S.

1968 Fish otoliths from the Bathonian of Southern England. Palaeontol., 11,
     246–258, 14 figs.

     Rev.: Weiler in Zbl. Geol. Pal., Teil 2, 1969:3, 287–288.

STIPP, J. J. See: Polach, Stipp, Golson and Lovering.

STIRTON, RUBEN A.

1958B. Paleontology in the University of California. Symposium on physical and
     earth sciences, Univ. Calif., 1958, 66–78.

1959A.-
1963B. Rev.: Bülow in Geologie, 14, 118.

1962 A Middle Tertiary vertebrate fauna from Australia. Bull. Amer. Assoc.
     Petrol. Geol., 46, 280–281, (abs.).

1963C. Abs.: Dietrich in Zbl. Geol. Pal., Teil 2, 1964, 189.

1964 Relationships of Early Pliocene beavers. Spec. Pap., Geol. Soc. Amer.,
     76, 226, (abs.).

1965A. New genus of protoceratid artiodactyl and relationships of the Protocera-
     tidae. Geol. Soc. Amer., Cordilleran Sect., Pal. Soc. Pac. Coast
     Sect., Prog. 61st Ann. Meeting, 1965, 51, (abs.).

1965B. Cranial morphology of Castoroides. In: Jhingran, A. G., et al., (eds.),
     1965, 273–289, 4 figs.

1966 New genus of protoceratid artiodactyl and relationships of the Protocera-
     tidae. Spec. Pap. Geol. Soc. Amer., 87, 231, (abs.).

1967A. The Diprotodontidae from the Ngapakaldi fauna, South Australia. Bull.
     Australian Bur. Min. Res., no. 85, 1–44, 10 figs., 4 pls., 6 tables.

1967B. A diprotodontid from the Miocene Kutjamarpu fauna. Bull. Australian
     Bur. Min. Res., no. 85, 45–51, 1 fig., 1 table.

1967C. A new species of Zygomaturus and additional observations on Meniscolophus,
     Pliocene Palan-Karinna fauna, South Australia. Bull. Australian
     Bur. Min. Res., no. 85, 129–147, 5 figs., 3 tables.

1967D. Relationships of the protoceratid artiodactyls and description of a new
     genus. Univ. Calif. Publ. Geol. Sci., 72, 35 pp., 3 figs., 3 pls.,
     1 table.

STIRTON, R. A., and MARCUS, L. F.

1966 Generic and specific diagnoses in the gigantic macropodid genus Procoptodon.
     Rec. Austral. Mus., 26, 349–359, 10 figs.

     Rev.: Hünermann in Zbl. Geol. Pal., Teil 2, 1967, 111–112.

STIRTON, R. A., and RENSBERGER, J. M.

1964   Occurrence of the insectivore genus Micropternodus in the John Day formation of central Oregon. Bull. S. Calif. Acad. Sci., 63:2, 57–80, 2 figs., 1 table.

STIRTON, R. A., TEDFORD, R. H., and WOODBURNE, M. O.

1964   New Tertiary fauna from the Tirari Desert, South Australia. Program, 60th Ann. Meeting, Geol. Soc. Amer., Cordilleran Sect., 61–62, (abs.).

1965   New Tertiary fauna from the Tirari Desert, South Australia. Spec. Pap. Geol. Soc. Amer., 82, 281–282, (abs.).

1967A.   Review of Tertiary mammal-bearing deposits in Australia. 39th Congr., ANZAAS, Melbourne, 1967, Sec. C, pp. K6–K7, 1 table, (abs.).

1967B.   A new Tertiary formation and fauna from the Tirari Desert, South Australia. Rec. S. Austral. Mus., 15, 427–462, 12 figs., 1 table.

1968   Australian Tertiary deposits containing terrestrial mammals. Univ. Calif. Publ. Geol. Sci., 77, 30 pp., 2 figs., 1 chart.

STIRTON, R. A., and WOODBURNE, M. O.

1964   Revision of the Oligocene and Miocene peccaries. Program, 60th Ann. Meeting, Geol. Soc. Amer., Cordilleran Sect., 61, (abs.).

1965   Revision of the Oligocene and Miocene peccaries. Spec. Pap. Geol. Soc. Amer., 82, 281, (abs.).

STIRTON, R. A., WOODBURNE, M. O., and PLANE, M. D.

1967   A phylogeny of the Tertiary Diprotodontidae and its significance in correlation. Bull. Australian Bur. Min. Res., no. 85, 149–160, 1 fig.

ST. JEAN, JOSEPH

1967   Some observations and impressions on paleontology in the Soviet Union. Jour. Pal., 41, 515–522.

STODUTI, PIERO

1964   Un giacimento del Paleolitico Medio scoperto nella valle del torrente Popogna presso Livorno. Riv. Sci. Preist., 18, 261–270, 3 figs., (French and English summaries).

1965A.   Nuovi ritrovamenti preistorici sulle colline Livornesi. Atti. Soc. Tosc. Sci. Nat., 72, Ser. A, fasc. 1, 254–269, 6 figs., 6 pls., 1 map, (English, French, Italian summaries).

1965B.   Industrie del Paleolitico Superiore rinvenute nella zona di S. Cataldo (Sicilia). Riv. Sci. Preist., 19, 289–294, 2 figs., (French and English summaries).

STOGOV, I. I., and SAVINOV, P. F.

1965   [New species of Soricidae from a Hipparion fauna site.] Vestnik Akad. Nauk Kazakh. SSR, 1965:11, 91–94, 3 figs., (Russian).

STOHL, GÁBOR

1957   [The position of Lagomorpha in the system of mammals.] Ann. Inst. Biol. (Tihany) Hungaricae Acad. Sci., 24, 51–57. (Hungarian; German summary, not seen).

STOIBER, G. ALLEN   See: Collin and Stoiber.

STOKES, WILLIAM LEE
1964   Fossilized stomach contents of a sauropod dinosaur. Science, 143, 576—
            577, 1 fig.
            Abs.: Anon. in New Sci., 22, 106.
1966   Mountain sheep: a link with the Pleistocene. Spec. Pap. Geol. Soc.
            Amer., 87, 302—303, (abs.).

STOKES, W. L., ANDERSON, M., and MADSEN, J. H., JR.
1966   Fossil and sub-fossil bison of Utah and southern Idaho. Proc. Utah
            Acad. Sci., 43, 37—39.

STOKES, W. L., SMITH, G. R., and HORN, K. F.
1964   Fossil fishes from the Stansbury level of Lake Bonneville, Utah. Proc.
            Utah Acad. Sci., 41, 87—88.

STOLIÂR, A. D.
1964   [On the role of "natural model" as the initial form of figurative art.]
            Arkheol. Sbornik, Leningrad, 6, 20—52, 9 figs., (Russian).
1965   [On the evolution of elementary techniques of representing animals in
            European Paleolithic art.] Soobshch. Gosud. Ermitazha, 26, 24—
            28, 1 fig., (Russian; English summary).
1966A.   [The problem of the origin of figurative art of Eurasia.] Biull. Mosk.
            Obshch. Ispyt. Prirody, Otd. Biol., 71:5, 155—156, (Russian).
1966B.   [On the first stages of figurative activity in the culture of the European
            Paleolithic.] Soobshch. Gosud. Ermitazha, 27, 44—47, 1 fig., (Rus-
            sian).

STOLIÂROV, A. S.   See: Glikman and Stoliârov.

STOLTMAN, JAMES B.   See: Williams, S. and Stoltman.

STOŁYHWO, EUGENIA
1965   The important findings of fossil remnants of Hominidae and related forms
            in the last 20 years. Przeglad Zool., 9, 333—339, (English summary).

STORCK, W.
1964   Zur Altsteinzeit in der Pfalz. Die funde der Klagschen Sammlung in Bo-
            landen (II). Pfälzer Heimat, 15, 41, 1 fig., (not seen).

STORER, TRACY I., and USINGER, R. L.
1965   General zoology. 4th ed. New York: McGraw-Hill, vi + 741 pp., illustr.

STØRMER, LEIF
1966A.   Fra urfisk til øgle. Naturen, 90, 47—62, 7 figs.
1966B.   Dinosauriens tidsalder. Naturen, 90, 63—81, 9 figs.

STORY, DEE ANN
1965   The archeology of Cedar Creek Reservoir, Henderson and Kaufman Counties,
            Texas. Bull. Texas Archeol. Soc., 36, 163—257, 27 figs.

STORY, D. A., and SHAFER, H. J.
1965   1964 excavations at Waco Reservoir, McLennan Co., Texas: the Baylor
            and Britton sites. Misc. Pap., Texas Archeol. Salvage Project, no.
            6, 140 pp., 49 figs., 5 tables.

STOUT, THOMPSON M.
1964   The early geological and paleontological explorations in Nebraska and adjacent regions. Proc. Neb. Acad. Sci., 74, 16—17, (abs.).
See: Skinner, M. F. and Taylor.

STOUT, T. M., and SCHULTZ, C. B.
1968   Summary of the stratigraphy of the Marsland formation (Miocene) of Nebraska. Proc. Neb. Acad. Sci., 78th Ann. Meeting, 1968, 22—23, (abs.).

STOVALL, J. WILLIS, PRICE, L. I., and ROMER, A. S.
1966   The postcranial skeleton of the giant Permian pelycosaur Cotylorhynchus romeri. Bull. Mus. Comp. Zool. Harvard, 135:1, 1—30, 17 figs., 1 table.

ST. PIERRE, SHIRLEY
1967   Cave studies in Nordland, Norway. Studies in Spel., 1, 275—284, 3 figs., 2 pls.

STRACHAN, ISLES
1964   The Silurian period. In: Harland, W. B., Smith, A. G. and Wilcock, B., (eds.), 1964, 237—240, 2 tables.

STRAIN, WILLIAM SAMUEL
1965   Blancan mammalian fauna and Pleistocene formations, Hudspeth County, Texas. Diss. Abst., 25, 5216, (abs.).
1966   Blancan mammalian fauna and Pleistocene formations, Hudspeth County, Texas. Bull. Texas Memorial Mus., 10, 1—55, 8 figs., 13 pls., 5 tables.

STRASHNIKOV, N. S.   See: Cherdyntsev, Strashnikov, et al.

STRATON, I.   See: Mogoşanu and Straton.

STRAUS, WILLIAM L., JR.
1962A.   Abs.: Kuhn-Schnyder in Zbl. Geol. Pal., Teil 2, 1964, 227—228.
1965   Nature of the problem and the evidence. Publ. Nation. Acad. Sci., 1469, 1—17, 11 figs.
See: Glass, Temkin and Straus.

STRAUS, W. L., and CAVE, A. J. E.
1964   Pathology and the posture of Neanderthal man. In: Lasker, G. W., (ed.), 1964, 133—148, 7 figs., 1 table, (reprint with editorial comment).

STRAUSS, F.
1964A.   Zum Andenken an Hans Bluntschli: 1877-1962. Acta Anat., 58, 1—25, portr.
1964B.   Hans Bluntschli. 1877-1962. Mit. Naturf. Ges. Bern, 20, 79—82.

STRAWN, MARY
1965   Appendix A: Notes on the geography and Late Quaternary geology of the Lake Channel region. Tebiwa, 8, 21—28, 2 figs.

STRELCZENIA, VÍCTOR B. and ZETTI, J.
1964   Apéndice. In: Zetti, J. 1964, 263—265.

STRELKOV, A. A.   See: Vereshchagin 1968A.

STRELKOV, S. A.
1959   [The Verkhoiãnsk range and adjacent plains.] In: Strelkov, S. A., et al,
            1959. Quaternary deposits of the Soviet Arctic; 184–199, 2 figs.,
            (Russian).
        See: Martynov, Mizerov and Strelkov.

STRELKOV, S. A., et al.
1959   [Quaternary deposits of the Soviet Arctic.] Trudy Inst. Geol.
            Arktiki, 91, 220 pp., 21 figs., 4 tables, 1 map, (Russian).

STRELKOVSKIĬ, V. I.
1963A.   Origin and pre-Darwinian development of the ideas of the relationships
            between ontogenesis and phylogenesis. Trudy Inst. Paleobiol. Akad.
            Nauk Gruz, SSR, 8, 3–27, (Russian; Georgian and English summaries).
1963B.   [Specialization and the problem of extinction.] Nauchn. Sess. Inst. Paleo-
            biol. AN Gruz. SSR, 9, 3–4, (Russian).
1964   [Darwin, Müller, and Haeckel and their contributions to the knowledge
            of the biogenetical law.] Obshchie Vopr. Evoliũĩs. Paleobiol., 1,
            19–57, (Russian; Georgian and English summaries).
1966   [Specialization and the problem of extinction.] Obshchie Vopr. Evoliũĩs.
            Paleobiol., 2, 5–59, (Russian; Georgian summary).
1967   [The problem of progress in the living nature.] Obshch. Vopr. Evoliũĩs.
            Paleobiol., 3, 27–58, (Russian; Georgian and English summaries).

STREL'NIKOV, I. D.
1959   [On thermoregulation in modern, and on thermal regime in Mesozoic
            reptiles.] Trudy Vses. Paleont. Obshch., II sess., 129–144, 2 figs.,
            (Russian).
1966   [From the history of paleontology in Russia.] In: Gekker, (ed.), 7–13,
            portr., (Russian).

STRELNIKOV, I., and HECKER, R.
1968   Vladimir Kowalevsky's sources of ideas and their importance for his work
            and for Russian evolutionary palaeontology. Lethaia, 1:3, 219–229,
            3 portrs.

STRETOVICH, MME. See: Orlov 1960B.

STROGANOVA, A. S. See: Vereshchagin, Geptner and Stroganova.

STROUHAL, EVŽEN
1959A.   Oreopithecus bamboli Gervais. Archeol. Roz., 11, 112–113, (Czech).
1959B.   Kongress der tschechoslowakischen Anthropologen im Jahre 1958. Archeol.
            Roz., 11, 426–428, (Czech; German summary).
1961B.   Australopitekové a výroba nástroju. Archeol. Roz., 13, 268–271.
1964   Nové nálezy L. S. B. Leakeye v Olduvajské rokli v Tanganice. Anthrop.,
            2:1, 59–60.

STROUHAL, HANS
1961   In memoriam Univ.-Prof. Dr. phil. Karl Absolon. Die Höhle, 12, 24–28,
            portr.

STRÜBEL, G. See: Pflug and Strübel.

STRUVE, WOLFGANG
1967　Zur Geschichte der Paläozoologisch-Geologischen Abteilung des Natur-
Museums und Forschungs-Instituts Senckenberg. Teil 1: Von 1763
bis 1907. Senck. Lethaea, 48:A, 23—191, 34 figs., 3 tables.

STUBBE, CARLOS F. See: Rosen 1957.

STUBBLEFIELD, C. J.
1965　Victor-Emile Van Straelen [1889-1964]. Proc. Geol. Soc. London, 1618,
119—120.

STUBBS, FRANCIS L.
1950　A preliminary report of the Mill Creek area of Andrew County, Missouri.
Missouri Archaeol., 12, 1—48, 11 figs., 6 tables.

STUCKENRATH, R., JR.
1965　The Debert archaeological project: radiocarbon dating. 7th Internat. Congr.,
Internat. Assoc. Quat. Res., Abs., 1965, 450, (abs.).
1966　The Debert archaeological project, Nova Scotia. Radiocarbon dating.
Quaternaria, 8, 75—80, 2 figs., 1 table, (French and Italian summaries).

STUCKENRATH, R., COE, W. R., and RALPH, E. K.
1966　University of Pennsylvania radiocarbon dates IX. Radiocarbon, 8, 348—385.

STUCKER, GILBERT F., GALUSHA, M. J., and McKENNA, M. C.
1965　Removing matrix from fossils by miniature sandblasting. In: Kummel
and Raup, (eds.), 1965, 273—275.

STUIVER, MINZE, and SUESS, H. E.
1966　On the relationship between radiocarbon dates and true sample ages.
Radiocarbon, 8, 534—540, 1 fig., 1 table.

STÜMPKE, HARALD, pseud.
1962　Rev.: Théodoridès in L'Ann. Biol, ser. 4, 2, 97—98; Weber in Hallesches
Jahrb., 6, 106—107.
1967　The snouters. Translation by Leigh Chadwick of exerpt from Stümpke, H.,
1962. Epilogue by Gerolf Steiner. Nat. Hist., 76:4, 8—13, 4 figs.,
(fantasy).

STURANI, C.
1965　Présence de Palaeotherium et de Pulmonés dans l'Éocene continental du
Lauzanier (couverture sédimentaire de l'Argentera, Basses-Alpes).
Trav. Lab. Géol. Fac. Sci. Univ. Grenoble, 41, 229—246, 3 figs.,
(Italian summary).
Rev.: Gaetani in Riv. Ital. Pal., 72, 246—247.

STÜRMER, W.
1965　Röntgenaufnahmen von einigen Fossilien aus dem Geologischen Institut
der Universität Erlangen-Nürnberg. Geol. Bl. NO-Bayern, 15, 217—
223, 7 pls.
Rev.: Häntzschel in Zbl. Geol. Pal., Teil 2, 1966, 465.

SU, TE—TSAO　See: Liu, H.—t., Su, et al.

SUCHÝ, JAROSLAV
 1960   Die Bedeutung der Dokumente der Entwicklung der Menschheit aus der
          Tschechoslowakei und ihre Wertung. Przegląd Antrop., 25, 473–
          502, 7 figs., 7 tables, (Polish; German summary).

SUDRE, JEAN   See: Ledoux, et al.

SUESS, HANS E.   See: Hubbs, et al.; Stuiver and Suess.

SUGGS, ROBERT C.
 1965   The archaeology of San Francisco. New York: Thomas Y. Crowell,
          148 pp., illustr.
 1966   The archaeology of New York. New York: Crowell, 158 pp., illustr.
          Rev.: White in Amer. Anthrop., 69, 779.

SUGIHARA, SŌSUKE
 1956B.   The Stone Age remains found at Iwajuku, Gumma Prefecture, Japan.
          Rept. Res. Fac. Literature Meiji Univ., Archaeol., no. 1, (not seen).
 1962   The IVth Ice Age and Japanese preceramic age. Quat. Res., 2, 100–102,
          2 figs., (Japanese; English summary).

SUGIHARA, S., and TOZAWA, M.
 1960   Pre-ceramic age in Japan. Acta Asiatica, 1, 1–28, 6 figs.

SUGIHARA, S., YOSHIDA, I., and SERIZAWA, C.
 1959   [Knife-blade implements from Kanto loam bed at Moro, Tokyo.]   Sundai
          Shigaku, no. 9, 84–104, (English summary; not seen).

SUHM, DEE ANN   See: Shafer, Suhm and Sourlock.

SUKACHEV, V. N.   See: Bader, O. N., Gromov, and Sukachev.

SUKACHEV, V. N., GROMOV, V. I., and BADER, O. N.
 1966   [Upper Paleolithic Sungir' site.]   Trudy Geol. Inst., 162, 140 pp., 43
          figs., 19 pls., 21 tables, (Russian).

SUKHANOV, V. B.
 1964   [Subclass Testudinata.]   Osnovy Pal., [Amphibians, Reptiles, and Birds.],
          [12], 354–438, 91 figs., 1 table, (Russian).

SUKHOV, V. P.
 1967   [The discovery of remains of the representatives of genus Prosiphneus in
          the Bashkirian Cisuralia, and certain problems of the taxonomy of
          the family Myospalacidae.]   Doklady Akad. Nauk SSSR, 177:3,
          695–698, 1 fig., (Russian).

SULEĬMANOV, RUSTAM KHAMIDOVICH
 1966   Abi–Rakhmat rock shelter in Uzbekistan. In: Beregovaia, N. A., Islamov,
          U., and Kalandadze, A. N., 1966, 145–148, 3 figs.
 1968   [History of Obi-Rakhmat cave and its significance for the chronology of
          Middle Asian Paleolithic.] Biull. Kom. Izuch. Chetvert. Perioda,
          Akad. Nauk SSSR, 35, 192–197, 3 figs., (Russian).

SULERZHITSKII, L. D.   See: Cherdyntsev, Alekseev, et al.

SULIMSKI, ANDRZEJ

1964   Pliocene Lagomorpha and Rodentia from Węże 1 (Poland). Acta Pal.
Polonica, 9, 149–244, 24 figs., 16 pls., (Polish and Russian summaries).

1968   Remains of Upper Cretaceous Mosasauridae (Reptilia) of Central Poland.
Acta Pal. Polonica, 13, 243–251, 1 fig., 2 pls., (Polish and Russian summaries).

SULLIVAN, WALTER

1965   The cave man gets a new look. Sci. Digest, 57:1, 58–60, illustr.

SULTANOV, K. M.

1961   [A short paleontological dictionary.] Baku: Akad. Nauk Azerbaĭdzh.
SSR Press, 210 pp., illustr., (Russian).
See: Burchak-Abramovich, N. I. and Sultanov.

SULTANOV, K. M., KHALIFA-ZADE, CH. M., and ISAEV, S. A.

1966   [Some questions of biochemical research on marine organisms.] Uch.
Zap. Azerb., Univ., Ser. Geol.-Geogr. Nauk, 1966:1, 3–12, (Russian).

SUMMERS, ROGER

1944–

1955B.   Rock carvings at Bumbuzi. Occ. Pap. Nation. Mus. S. Rhodesia, 2:16,
343–351, 1 fig., 2 pls.

1957B.   Notes on the possible origin of Magosian cultures in Africa. Occ. Pap.
Nation. Mus. S. Rhodesia, 3:21A, 56–60, 1 map.

1964A.   Professor F. E. Zeuner, D. Sc., Ph. D., FSA, FZS, FGS. S. Afr. Archaeol. Bull., 19, 16.

1964B.   Handaxes in dune sands. S. Afr. Archaeol. Bull., 19, 78.

1967   Terminology in African archaeology. S. Afr. Archaeol. Bull., 22, 33,
See: Cooke, C. K., Summers and Robinson.

SUMMERS, ROGER, et al.

1958   Rev.: Mathew in Jour Afr. Hist., 1, 151–153.

SUN, AI-LIN

1962   Abs.: Huene in Zbl. Geol. Pal., Teil 2, 1964, 176.

1963   Abs.: Huene in Zbl. Geol. Pal., Teil 2, 1964, 175–176.

1964   Preliminary report on a new species of Lystrosaurus of Sinkiang. Vert.
Palasiatica, 8, 216–217, 1 fig., (Chinese and English).
Abs.: Huene in Zbl. Geol. Pal., Teil 2, 1965, 252–253.

ȘURARU, NICOLAE, and ȘURARU, MARIA

1966   [On some remains of Eocene fishes from Transylvanian basin.] Studia
Univ. Babeș-Bolyai, ser. geol.-geogr., 11:1, 69–77, 2 pls., (Rumanian and French summaries).
Rev.: Semaka in Zbl. Geol. Pal., Teil 2, 1967, 101; Weiler in Zbl.
Geol. Pal., Teil 2, 1967, 504–505.

SURRARRER, T. C.

1964   Mastodon record in Lorain County. Ohio Jour. Sci., 64, 375.

SUTCLIFFE, ANTHONY J.

1960B.   Mammalian remains from Selsey. Appendix 2 to: West, R. G., and
Sparks, B. W., 1960, Philos, Trans. Roy. Soc. London, ser. B,
243:701, 95–133, 13 figs., pl. 16.

1961   The prehistory of Caldey. Part 2. Appendix I. Report on animal bones
        from Pleistocene deposit, Daylight rock fissure, Caldey Island.
        Archaeol. Cambrensis, 1961, 64—66.

1965   Planning England's first cave studies centre. Studies in Spel., 1, 106—124,
        figs., 10—14, pls. 18—21.

SUVEIZDIS, P.
1963   [Upper Permian sediments of Polish—Lithuanian syneclise.]   In: Grigelis,
        et al., (eds.), 1963, 225—371, 63 figs., 14 pls., 4 tables, (Russian;
        Lithuanian and English summaries).

SUZUKI, HISASHI
1964   On the skull of Amud Man. Notes on the Amud Man and his cave
        site, Israel. The first season, 1961. Tokyo: Tokyo University
        Scientific Expedition to Western Asia, 4—6, (not seen).

1965   A Palaeoanthropic man from the Amud Cave, Israel. Preliminary report.
        Com. 7th Internat. Congr. Anthrop. Ethnol. Sci., Moscow, 1—8,
        6 figs.

1966   Skeletal remains of Hamakita man. Jour. Anthrop. Soc. Nippon, 74,
        119—136, 172—174, figs., 4 pls., tables, (Japanese; English summary).

1968   A Palaeoanthropic fossil man from Amud Cave, Israel. Discussion. 7th
        Internat. Congr. Anthrop. Ethnol. Sci., Moscow, 1964, 3, 305—316,
        9 figs.

SUZUKI, H., and ENDO, B.
1966   Site of Nekata. Jour. Anthrop. Soc. Nippon, 74, 101—118, 172, figs.,
        3 pls., (Japanese; English summary).

SVIATENKO, A. P.
1966   [On the possible use of the so-called "bâtons de commandement".]   Voprosy
        Antrop., 23, 153—157, 3 figs., (Russian).

SVISTUN, V. I.
1965   [On diagnostic signs of skulls in subspecies of the genus Megaloceros.]
        Dopovidi Akad. Nauk USSR, Kiev, 8, 1085—1087, 2 tables, (Ukrain-
        ian; Russian and English summaries).

1966   [Occurrence of Anthropogene vertebrates in the vicinity of the Kanev
        Hydroelectric Station construction site.] Dopovidi Akad. Nauk
        URSR, 1966:2, 253—256, 1 table, (Ukrainian; Russian and English
        summaries).

1968   [Fauna of Late Anthropogene mammals of the Romankovo alluvial de-
        posit.] Prirodn. Obstan. i Fauny Proshl., 4, 3—56, 26 figs., 34
        tables, (Russian).
        See: Mezhzherin and Svistun.

SVISTUN, V. I., and DIDKOVSKIĬ, V. ĨA.
1964   [A new find of Dinotherium remains in the Ukraine.] Dopovidi Akad.
        Nauk URSR, Kiev, 12, 1635—1637, 1 fig., (Ukrainian; Russian
        and English summaries).

SWADESH, MAURICIO
1965   Origen y evolución del lenguaje humano. An. Antrop., Mexico, 2, 61—88.

SWANSON, EARL H., JR.
1964   Geochronology of the DjRi3 site, British Columbia, 1959. Tebiwa, 7,
            42—52, 4 figs.
1966   Ecological communities in northwest prehistory. Quaternaria, 8, 91—99,
            1 fig., (Spanish and Italian summaries).

SWANSON, E. H., JR., and BRYAN, A. L.
1964   Birch Creek Papers No. 1. An archaeological reconnaissance in the Birch
            Creek Valley of eastern Idaho. Occ. Pap. Idaho State Univ. Mus.,
            No. 13, ii + 20 pp., 6 figs., 1 map.
            Rev.: Osborne in Amer. Anthrop., 68, 577—579.

SWANSON, E. H., JR., BUTLER, B. R., and BONNICHSEN, R.
1964   Birch Creek papers No. 2. Natural and cultural stratigraphy in the Birch
            Creek Valley of eastern Idaho. Occ. Pap. Idaho State Univ. Mus.,
            14, 120 pp., 40 figs., 10 tables, 1 map.

SWANSON, E. H., JR., and DAYLEY, J.
1968   Hunting at Malad Hill in southeastern Idaho. Tebiwa, 11:2, 59—69, 5
            figs., 2 tables.

SWANSON, E. H., JR., and SNEED, P. G.
1967   An archaeological reconnaissance of Railroad Ranch in eastern Idaho, 1966.
            Tebiwa, 10:1, 53—59, 3 figs.

SWART, E. R. See: Robins and Swart; Sheppard and Swart.

SWARTZBAUGH, RICHARD GREY
1967   Man and tools, race and culture. Mankind Quart., 7, 164—170.

SWAUGER, JAMES L.
1968   Carnegie Museum foreign visitor programs. Museologist, no. 107, 9—11.
            See: Lindroth-Wallace and Swauger.

SWAUGER, J. L., and WALLACE, B. L.
1964   An experiment in skinning with Egyptian Paleolithic and Neolithic stone
            implements. Penn. Archaeol., 34, 1—7, 7 pls.

SWIFT, CAMM, and WING, E.
1968   Fossil bony fishes from Florida. Plaster Jacket, 7, 2—11, 8 figs.

SWIFT, DONALD J. P.   See: Whitmore, Emery, et al.

SWIFT, ELLSWORTH R.
1961   Washington landscapes: past, present and future. Atlantic Nat., Apr.-
            June 1961, 93—101, 6 figs.

SWINTON, WILLIAM ELGIN
1962D.   Dinosaurs. London: Brit. Mus. (Nat. Hist), 44 pp., 6 figs., 11 pls and
            frontispiece.
1962E.   Digging for dinosaurs. New York: Doubleday; (not seen).
1964A.   Fossil birds. In: Thomson, A. L., (ed.), 1964, 322—324.
1964B.   Origin of birds. In: Thomson, A. L., (ed.), 1964, 559—562, 1 fig.
1964C.   Dinosaurs. 2nd ed. London: Brit. Mus. (Nat. Hist.), xii + 44 pp., 6
            figs., 11 pls.

1965A.   Fossil birds. 2nd ed. London: Brit. Mus. (Nat. Hist.), 65 pp., 25 figs.,
              11 pls., color frontisp.
1965B.   Dinosaurs of Canada. Roy. Ontario Mus. Ser., no. 5, 16 pp., illustr.

SWITSUR, V. R.
1967   Radioactive dating and low-level counting. Science, 157, 726—727.

SYCH, LUCJAN
1965   Fossil Leporidae from the Pliocene and Pleistocene of Poland. Acta
              Zool. Crac., 10, 1—88, 30 figs., 7 pls., 21 tables, (Polish and Rus-
              sian summaries).
1966A.   Correlation of tooth measurements in leporids. On the significance of the
              coefficient of correlation in the studies of macroevolution. Acta
              Theriologica, 11, 41—54, 20 figs., 2 tables, (Polish summary).
1966B.   Were the ungulated mammals ancestors of the hare? Przeglad Zool., 10,
              65—71, 6 figs., (Polish; English summary).
1967A.   Unworn teeth of Hypolagus brachygnathus Kormos (Leporidae, Mammalia).
              Acta Zool. Crac., 12, 19—26, 1 fig., pl. 8, (Polish and Russian sum-
              maries).
1967B.   Fossil endocranial cast of Hypolagus brachygnathus Kormos (Leporidae,
              Mammalia). Acta Zool. Crac., 12, 27—30, pls. 9—10, (Polish and
              Russian summaries).
              See: Kowalski, K. and Sych.

SYCHEVSKAĨA, E. K.
1966   [Esociformes of Western Siberia.] Biull. Mosk. Obshch. Ispyt. Prirody,
              Otd. Geol., 41:6, 142—143, (Russian).

SYKES, E.   See: Leslie and Sykes.

SYLVESTER-BRADLEY, P. C.
1967A.   Towards an International Code of Stratigraphic Nomenclature. In: Tei-
              chert, and Yochelson, (eds.), 1967, 49—56.
1967B.   Evolution versus entropy. Proc. Geol. Assoc. London, 78, 137—147, 1 fig.
              See: Shotton, Osborne and Sylvester-Bradley.

SZALAY, FREDERICK S.
1965   First evidence of tooth replacement in the subclass Allotheria (Mammalia).
              Amer. Mus. Novit., no. 2226, 12 pp., 6 figs.
1966   The tarsus of the Paleocene leptictid Prodiacodon (Insectivora, Mammalia).
              Amer. Mus. Novit., no. 2267, 13 pp., 4 figs.
              Rev.: Fahlbusch in Zbl. Geol. Pal., Teil 2, 1968, 212.
1967   The affinities of Apterodon (Mammalia, Deltatheridia, Hyaenodontidae).
              Amer. Mus. Novit., 2293, 17 pp., 10 figs.
1968   The beginnings of primates. Evolution, 22, 19—36, 5 figs.
              See: Van Valen, Butler, et al.

SZALAY, F. S., and GOULD, S. J.
1966   Asiatic Mesonychidae (Mammalia, Condylarthra). Bull. Amer. Mus. Nat.
              Hist., 132:2, 129—173, pls. 9—21, 11 tables.

SZARSKI, KAZIMIERZ W.
1957   The vicissitudes of the theory of paired limbs. Przeglad Antrop., 23,
              7—33, 20 figs., (Polish; Russian and English summaries).
1960   Charles Darwin. Przeglad Zool., 4, 5—15, portr, (Polish; English summary).

SZLACHETKO, KRYSTYNA
1966 [Odontological analysis of human teeth from Maszycka Cave, Olkusz District, of Upper Paleolithic age.] Archeol. Polski, 11, 355–362, 3 figs., 3 tables, (Polish; English summary).

TABASTE, NICOLE
1963 Étude des restes de poissons du Crétacé saharien. Mélanges ichthyologiques à la mémoire d'Achille Valenciennes. Mém. Inst. Franç. Afr. Noire, no. 68, 437–485, 5 figs., 13 pls., 4 tables.

TADLOCK, W. LEWIS
1966 Certain crescentic stone objects as a time marker in the Western United States. Amer. Antiq., 31, 662–675, 4 figs., 1 table.

TAIBEL, M. ALULAH See: Mainardi and Taibel.

TAKAI, FUYUJI
1937B. Odontoma in a fossil elephant from the Inland Sea of Japan. Jour. Geol. Soc. Japan, 44, 444–446, 1 pl., (Japanese; English summary).
1968 The geological age of the Amud man and the associated mammalian fauna. 7th Internat. Congr., Anthrop. Ethnol. Sci., Moscow, 1964, 3, 317–319, 1 fig., 1 table.
See: Kobayashi, T., Takai and Hayami.

TAKAI, F., and HASEGAWA, Y.
1966 Vertebrate fossils from the Gansuiji formation. Jour. Anthrop. Soc. Nippon, 74, 155–167, 176, 4 pls., 1 table, (Japanese; English summary).

TAKAI, F., SHIKAMA, T., and IZIRI, S.
1952 [Re-excavation of Desmostylus and its horizon in Doki District, Gihu Prefecture.] Jour. Geol. Soc. Japan, 58, 144, (Japanese).

TAKAI, F., and TSUCHI, R.
1963A. The Neogene. In: Takai, F., Matsumoto, T., and Toriyama, R., (eds.), 1963*, 141–172, fig. 13, chart 13.
1963B. The Quaternary. In: Takai, F., Matsumoto, T., and Toriyama, R., (eds.), 1963*, 173–196, fig. 14, chart 14.

TAKEDA, H.
1953 The Poronai formation (Oligocene, Tertiary) of Hokkaido and South Sakhalin and its fossil fauna. Stud. Coal Geol. no. 3. Geol. Sec. Hokkaido Assoc. Coal. Min. Technologists.

TAKEUCHI, H., UYEDA, S., and KANAMORI, H.
1967 Debate about the earth. Approach to geophysics through analysis of continental drift. Translated by Keiko Kanamori. Illustrated by James K. Levorsen. San Francisco: Freeman, Cooper, 253 pp., illustr.

TALAR, ANTONI
1967 L'atelier de silex du Paléolithique final à Durdy, distr. de Tarnobrzeg. Mat. Archeol., 8, 75–83, 1 fig., 4 pls., (Polish; French summary).

TALBOT, F. H.
1966   The coelacanth, living relic of 50 million years ago. Austral. Nat. Hist.,
            15, 137—140, 3 figs.

TALDYKINA, K. S.   See: Iskiul' and Taldykina.

TALENT, J. A. See: Warren, J. W. and Talent.

TALIPOV, M. A. See: Ibragimov and Talipov.

TALMADGE, MARIAN, and GILMORE, I.
1965   Adventure in an underground wonderland: Grand Canyon Caverns.
            Arizona Highways, 41:10, 4—10, illustr.

TAMERS, M. A.
1966   Istituto Venezolano de Investigaciones cientificas natural radiocarbon measure-
            ments II. Radiocarbon, 8, 204—212.
            See: Pearson, F. J., Davis., Tamers and Johnstone; Pearson, F. J., Davis
            and Tamers.

TAMERS, M. A., and PEARSON, F. J., JR.
1965   Validity of radiocarbon dates on bone. Nature, 208, 1053—1055, 3 tables.

TAMERS, M. A., PEARSON, F. J., JR., and DAVIS, E. M.
1964   University of Texas radiocarbon dates II. Radiocarbon, 6, 138—159.

TAMME, A.—L.E. See: Mark and Tamme.

TAN, KEINOSUKE, and SHIKAMA, T.
1965   On Desmostylus teeth from Tashiro, Akita Prefecture. Sci. Rept. Yokohama
            Nation. Univ., Sect., II, no. 12, 49—55, 1 fig., pls. 5—6, (Japanese;
            English summary).

TANABE, GIICHI
1966   Fluorine contents of human bones from Pleistocene deposits of Hamakita.
            Jour. Anthrop. Soc. Nippon, 74, 168—171, 176, 1 fig., 1 table,
            (Japanese; English summary).

TANAKA, K., and SEKI, M.
1962   A Desmostylus-like marine mammal found from Toyoshina-cho. Shinano
            Kyoiku, no. 912, 55—65.

TANG, YING—JUN See: Chang, Y. et al; Chow, M., Huang, et al.

TANG, ZIN and CHOW, M.
1964   A review of vertebrate bearing Lower Tertiary of South China. Vert. Pal-
            asiatica, 8, 119—133, 1 map, (Chinese; English summary).
1965   The vertebrate-bearing early Tertiary of South China: A review. (Trans-
            lation of Tang and Chow, 1964). Internat. Geol. Rev., 7, 1338—
            1352, 1 fig., 2 tables.

TANNER, J. M.   See: Harrison, et al.

TANNER, LLOYD G.
1967A.   A new species of rhinoceros, Aphelops kimballensis, from the latest Pliocene
            of Nebraska. Bull. Neb. State Mus., 6, 1—16, 1 fig., 5 pls., 2 tables.

1967B.   Citellus kimballensis, a new Late Pliocene ground squirrel. Bull. Neb. State. Mus., 6, 17–26, 3 figs., 1 table.

    See: Schultz, C. B., Tanner, et al; Schultz, C. B., Whitmore and Tanner.

TANNER, L. G., and MARTIN, L. D.

1968   Notes on Lower Oligocene hyracodontids. Proc. Neb. Acad. Sci., 78th Ann. Meeting, 1968, 23, (abs.).

TAPALOV, E. D.

1966   [Quaternary deposits of southern Mugodzhary and surrounding country.] In: Collected Papers: 1966A. ["Materials on geology and economic ores of Western Kazakhstan,"] Alma-Ata: "Nauka" Press, 71–77.

1967   [On the stratigraphic position of fossil mammals on the Emba R.] Vestnik Akad. Nauk Kazakh. SSR, 1967:7, 60–65, 4 figs., (Russian).

TAPPEN, NEIL C.

1966   Some basic science approaches to problems of human evolution. Abs. 65th Ann. Meeting Amer. Anthrop. Assoc., 1966, 66, (abs.).

TAPTYKOVA, M. F.   See: Bukatchuk, Burdenko, et al.

TAQUET, PHILIPPE

1967   Découvertes paléontologiques récentes dans le Nord du Niger. Colloq. Internat. Cent. Nation. Recherch. Sci., 163, 415–418, 1 map, 1 table, (English summary).

    See: Broin and Taquet; Ginsburg, Lapparent, Loiret and Taquet; Ginsburg, Lapparent and Taquet.

TARABUKIN, B. A.

1968   [On the excavation of a Deinotherium skeleton in the Rezin region of Moldavian SSR.] Izv. Akad. Nauk Moldav. SSR, ser. Biol. i. Khim. Nauk, 1968:3, 37–42, 4 figs., (Russian).

    See: David, A. I. and Tarabukin; Longu and Tarabukin.

TARAKANOVA, G. I.   See: Litvintsev and Tarakanova.

TARASHCHUK, V. I.

1957   [Remains of Pagellus (fam. Sparidae, Pisces) from Neogene deposits of Ternopol' Province.] Dopovidi Akad. Nauk URSR, 1957:5, 619–623, 2 figs., (Ukrainian; Russian and English summaries).

1965   [Cold-blooded vertebrates from Pliocene deposits of Zaporozh'e province.] Prirodn. Obstan. i Fauny Proshl., 2, 74–101, 8 figs., 5 tables, (Russian).

1967   [Fossil pike perches from Ukraine.] Voprosy Ikhtiol., 7:1, 33–45, 5 figs., 4 tables, (Russian).

TARASOV, L. M.

1961   [Uglianskiĭ Paleolithic site (Kostenki XVI).] Krat. Zoob. Inst. Ist. Mat. Kult. SSSR, 85, 38–47, 4 figs., (Russian).

1962   [New excavations at the Gagarino site.] Krat. Soob. Inst. Ist. Mat. Kult. SSSR, 92, 56–60, 2 figs., (Russian).

1963   [New Paleolithic statuette from Gagarino.] Sov. Arkheol., 1963:4, 179–183, 1 fig., (Russian).

1964   [Construction of Paleolithic dwelling at Gagarino.] Krat. Soob. Inst. Ist. Mat. Kult. SSSR, 97, 20–24, 2 figs., (Russian).

1965   [Paleolithic station Gagarino. (Excavation of 1962).]   Mat. Issled. Arkheol.
                 SSSR, no. 131, 111–140, 15 figs., 1 pl., (Russian).
1967A.   [Excavations at Gagarino.]   In: Rybakov., (ed.), 1967, 26–27, (Russian).
1967B.   [On dating of the Paleolithic site Gagarino.]   Krat. Soob. Inst. Arkheol.
                 Akad. Nauk SSSR, 111, 31–37, 2 figs., (Russian).
1968   [Excavations at Gagarino settlement.]   In: Rybakov, (ed.), 1968, 30–31,
                 (Russian).

TARJÁN, R. See: Bökönyi, et al.

TARLO, BERYL J., and TARLO, L. B. H.
     1963   The origin of tooth replacement. Jour. Anat., 97, 472, (abs.).
     1964   The origin of tooth succession. Roy. Dent. Hosp. Mag., n.s., 1:4, 4–7,
                       (not seen).
     1965   The origin of teeth. Discovery, 26:9, 20–26, 7 figs.

TARLO, LAMBERT BEVERLY HALSTEAD
     1963   Aspidin: the precursor of bone. Nature, 199, 46–48.
     1964A.   The origin of bone. Discussion. In: Blackwood, H. J. J., (ed.), 1964,
                       3–17, 8 figs.
     1964B.   Tooth replacement in the mammal-like reptiles. Nature, 201, 1081–1082.
     1964C.   Psammosteiformes (Agnatha)–A review with descriptions of new material
                       from the Lower Devonian of Poland. I. General part. Pal. Pol-
                       onica, 13, viii + 135 pp., 32 figs., 14 pls.
     1965   Psammosteiformes (Agnatha)–A review with descriptions of new material
                       from the Lower Devonian of Poland. II. Systematic part. Pal.
                       Polonica, 15, x + 168 pp., 48 figs., 19 pls.
     1967A.   Biochemical evolution and the fossil record. In: Harland, W. B., et al.,
                       (eds.), 1967A, 119–132, 4 figs.
     1967B.   Vertebrata. Agnatha. In: Harland, W. B., et al., (eds.), 1967A, 628–636.
     1967C.   The tessellated pattern of dermal armour in the Heterostraci. In: Patter-
                       son, C., and Greenwood, P. H., (eds.), 1967, 45–54, 5 figs.
     1967D.   Triassic reptiles from the shores of Tethys. Publ. Syst. Assoc., 7, 103–109.
                   See: Appleby, et al.; Armstrong, W. G., and Tarlo; Neves and Tarlo;
                       Wells, C. 1964B, C; Whiting and Tarlo.

TARLO, L. B. H., and MERCER, J. R.
     1966   Decalcified fossil dentine. Jour. Roy. Microsc. Soc., 86, 137–140.

TARLO, L. B. H., and TARLO, B. J.
     1963A.   The origin of tooth cusps. Roy. Dental Hospital Mag., n.s., 1:1, 4–8,
                       5 figs., (not seen).
     1963B.   Convergent evolution in teeth. Roy. Dental Hospital Mag., n.s., 1:2,
                       18–19, 1 fig., (not seen).

TARLO, L. B. H., and WHITING, H. P.
     1965   A new interpretation of the internal anatomy of the Heterostraci (Agnatha).
                       Nature, 206, 148–150, 1 fig.

TARNOGRADSKIĬ, V. D. See: Kaplianskaia and Tarnogradskiĭ; Kaplianskaia, Tarno-
                 gradskiĭ, and Vangengeĭm.

TARRADELL, MIGUEL See: Pericot García and Tarradell.

TASCH, KARL-HEINZ See: Arnold and Tasch.

TASHKENBAEV, N. KH.
1966   [On the find of a Levalloisian core near Obi-Rakhmat cave.] Obshch. nauki Uzbek., 1966:1, 56−57, (Russian).

TASNÁDI−KUBACSKA, ANDRÁS
1962   Rev.: Bogsch and Seilacher in Zbl. Geol. Pal., Teil 2., 1964, 856−859; Gieseler in Anthropol. Anz., 31:1−2, 133; K. in Natuurhist. Maandbl., 51, 130−131; Krogman in Amer. Jour. Phys. Anthrop., 27, 227.
1963   [Paläophysiologische und paläopathologische Notizen.] Orsz. Orvostörténeti Könyvtár Közleményei, 29, 73−88, 10 figs., (Hungarian).
    Abs.: Bogsch in Zbl. Geol. Pal., Teil 2, 1964, 858−859.
1964   Present state and progress of palaeopathology. Acta Geol. Hung., 8, 193−201.
    Abs.: Bogsch in Zbl. Geol. Pal., Teil 2, 1966, 17.

TASSIN DE SAINT PÉREUSE, MARIE See: Pales and Tassin de Saint Péreuse.

TATARINOV, K. A.
1956   [Material concerning the study of the Anthropogene mammalian fauna of the western regions of the USSR.] Zbirn. Prats' Zool. Muz. Akad. Nauk URSR, 27, 177−180, (Ukrainian; Russian summary).
1960   [On the occurrence of Sicista subtilis in Ukraine.] Dopovidi Akad. Nauk URSR, Kiev., 1960:4, 532−535, (Ukrainian; Russian and English summaries).
1964   [Supplementary information on Podolian caves and their fossil fauna.] Biull. Mosk. Obshch. Ispyt. Prirody, Otd. Geol., 39:3, 157−158, (Russian).
1965A.   [Pleistocene mammals from Nizhnekrivchansk cave (Podolia).] Pal. Sborn., 2:1, 30−37, 2 figs., 1 table, (Russian; English summary).
1965B.   [Some cave localities of fossil vertebrates in western areas of Ukraine.] Biull. Mosk. Obshch. Ispyt. Prirody, Otd. Geol., 40:6, 158−159, (Russian).
1966A.   [Pleistocene vertebrates from Podolia and Ciscarpathia.] Biull. Kom. Izuch. Chetvert. Perioda, 32, 51−62, 1 map, 1 table, (Russian).
1966B.   [Fossil giants.] Priroda, 1966:6, 39−44, 5 figs., 1 table, (Russian).
1967   [Correlation of Pliocene-Quaternary mammalian faunas of Podolia with corresponding therio-complexes of adjacent territories.] In: Collected Papers: 1967A[Place and significance of fossil mammals of Moldavia in the Cenozoic of USSR.] 57−63, (Russian).
    See: Bachinskii and Tatarinov; Kudrin, L. N. and Tatarinov; Pasternak, S. I. and Tatarinov.

TATARINOV, L. P.
1962   Abs.: Westphal in Zbl. Geol. Pal., Teil 2, 1965, 242.
1964A.   Functioning of the sound-conducting mechanisms of the labyrinthodonts. (Translation of Tatarinov, 1962.) Internat. Geol. Rev., 6, 1596-1603, 3 figs.
1964B.   [Class Amphibia. General Part.] Osnovy Pal., [Amphibians, Reptiles, and Birds.], [12], 25−59, 12 figs., (Russian).
1964C.   [Superfamily Colosteoidea.] Osnovy Pal., [Amphibians, Reptiles, and Birds.], [12], 67−69, 2 figs., (Russian).
1964D.   [Superfamily Cochleosauroidea.] Osnovy Pal., [Amphibians, Reptiles, and Birds.], [12], 70, 2 figs., (Russian).
1964E.   [Family Zatrachydidae.] Osnovy Pal., [Amphibians, Reptiles, and Birds.], [12], 80−81, 1 fig., (Russian).

1964F. [Order Plesiopoda.] Osnovy Pal., [Amphibians, Reptiles, and Birds.], [12], 123–124, 1 fig., (Russian).

1964G. [Superorder Salientia. Leaping, or tailless.] Osnovy Pal., [Amphibians, Reptiles, and Birds.], [12], 125–133, 6 figs, 1 table, (Russian).

1964H. [Family Gephyrostegidae.] Osnovy Pal., [Amphibians, Reptiles, and Birds.], [12], 138, 1 fig., (Russian).

1964I. [Family Chroniosuchidae.] Osnovy Pal., [Amphibians, Reptiles, and Birds.], [12], 142–143, 1 fig., (Russian).

1964J. [Family Waggoneriidae.] Osnovy Pal., [Amphibians, Reptiles, and Birds.], [12], 144, 1 fig., (Russian).

1964K. [Subclass Lepospondyli.] Osnovy Pal., [Amphibians, Reptiles, and Birds.], [12], 144–164, 16 figs., 1 table, (Russian).

1964L. [Amphibia incertae sedis, Order Microsauria.] Osnovy Pal., [Amphibians, Reptiles, and Birds.], [12], 164–171, 7 figs, 1 table, (Russian).

1964M. [Order Therapsida.] Osnovy Pal., [Amphibians, Reptiles, and Birds.], [12], 246–298, 84 figs., (Russian).

1964N. [Superfamily Diarthrognathoidea.] Osnovy Pal., [Amphibians, Reptiles, and Birds.], [12], 286, 1 fig., (Russian).

1964O. [Superfamily Tritylodontoidea.] Osnovy Pal., [Amphibians, Reptiles, and Birds.], [12], 273–275, 2 figs., (Russian).

1964P. [Subclass Synaptosauria (=Euryapsida).] Osnovy Pal., [Amphibians, Reptiles, and Birds.], [12], 299–338, 53 figs., 1 table, (Russian).

1964Q. [Suborder Nothosauria.] Osnovy Pal., [Amphibians, Reptiles and Birds.], [12], 310–316, 5 figs., (Russian).

1964R. [Suborder Plesiosauria.] Osnovy Pal., [Amphibians, Reptiles, and Birds.], [12], 316–332, 36 figs., (Russian).

1964S. [Subclass Ichthyopterygia.] Osnovy Pal., [Amphibians, Reptiles, and Birds.], [12], 338–354, 17 figs., 1 table, (Russian).

1964T. [Subclass Lepidosauria.] Osnovy Pal., [Amphibians, Reptiles and Birds.], [12][, 439–493, 62 figs., 1 table, (Russian).

1964U. [Family Polyglyphanodontidae.] Osnovy Pal., [Amphibians, Reptiles, and Birds.], [12], 461–462, 1 fig., (Russian).

1964V. [Superfamily Scincoidea.] Osnovy Pal., [Amphibians, Reptiles and Birds.], [12], 467, (Russian).

1964W. [Superfamily Xantusioidea.] Osnovy Pal., [Amphibians, Reptiles, and Birds.], [12], 467, (Russian).

1964X. [Family Elachistosuchidae.] Osnovy Pal., [Amphibians, Reptiles, and Birds.], [12], 499, (Russian).

1964Y. [Family Scleromochlidae.] Osnovy Pal., [Amphibians, Reptiles, and Birds.], [12], 501, 1 fig., (Russian).

1964Z. [Superfamily Coeluroidea (=Coelurosauria).] Osnovy Pal., [Amphibians, Reptiles, and Birds.], [12], 530–535, 9 figs., (Russian).

1964AA. [Superfamily Deinodontoidea (=Carnosauria).] Osnovy Pal., [Amphibians, Reptiles, and Birds.], [12], 535–540, 11 figs., (Russian).

1964AB. [A new locality of Permian seymouriamorphs in the U. S. S. R.] Pal. Zhurnal, 1964:1, 139–141, (Russian).

1964AC. Barnum Brown (1873–1963). Pal. Zhurnal, 1964:1, 150, (Russian).

1964AD. Bernhard Peyer (1885–1963). Pal. Zhurnal, 1964:1, 150, (Russian).

1964AE. [On the anatomy of the Therocephalian head (vessels, nerves, and glands of Moschowhaitsia).] Pal. Zhurnal, 1964:2, 72–84, 2 figs., (Russian).

1965A. New Late Permian Therocephalian. (Translation of Tatarinov 1963B.) Internat. Geol. Rev., 7, 1094–1109, 6 figs.

1965B. A new occurrence of Permian seymouriamorphs. (Translation of Tatarinov, 1964AB). Internat. Geol. Rev., 7, 1492–1494.

1965C. [On the formation of mammalian characters in the higher theriodonts.] Pal. Zhurnal, 1965:1, 3–12, (Russian).

1965D. [New data on <u>Ulemosaurus</u>.] Pal. Zhurnal, <u>1965</u>:2, 93–108, 5 figs., (Russian).

1965E. [The origin of Amphibia.] Priroda, <u>1965</u>:12, 25–31, 3 figs., (Russian).

1966A. [Recent data on the formation in Theriodontia of a supplementary maxillary articulation corresponding to the mammal type.] Doklady Akad. Nauk SSSR, <u>166</u>:3, 749–752, 3 figs., (Russian).

1966B. [New data on the veinous system of the brain of fossil therapsids.] Doklady Akad. Nauk SSSR, <u>169</u>:2, 449–452, 2 figs., (Russian).

1966C. [Basipterygoid articulation and vidian canal of therapsids.] Pal. Zhurnal, <u>1966</u>:1, 101–115, 6 figs., (Russian).

1966D. [On the parasphenoid of the theriodonts.] Pal. Zhurnal, <u>1966</u>:2, 131–133, 3 figs., (Russian).

1967A. More facts on the vein system of the brain of fossil therapsids. Dokl. Acad. Sci. U. S. S. R., Earth Sci. Sect., <u>169</u>, 206–208, 2 figs.

1967B. [Development of the system of labial (vibrissal) vessels and nerves in theriodonts.] Pal. Zhurnal, <u>1967</u>:1, 3–17, 8 figs., (Russian).

1968 Morphology and systematics of the northern Dvina cynodonts (Reptilia, Therapsida; Upper Permian). Postilla, <u>126</u>, 1–51, 8 figs.

See: Rozdestvenskiĭ and Tatarinov.

TATARINOV, L. P., and TROFIMOV, B. A.

1964 Ivan Ivanovich Schmalhausen (1884–1963). Pal. Zhurnal, <u>1964</u>:2, 169–173, portr., (Russian).

1965 Commemorative biography of Academician Ivan Ivanovich Shmal'gauzen (Schmalhausen). (Translation of Tatarinov and Trofimov, 1964). Internat. Geol. Rev., <u>7</u>, 1682–1686.

TATE, JAMES, JR See: Martin, L. D. and Tate.

TATE, ROBERT B.

1968 The Anceney local mammal fauna. Program, 21st Ann. Meeting, Geol. Soc. Amer., Rocky Mt. Sect., 79, (abs.).

TATISHVILI, K. G.

1968 [New outcrops of the Karatubani horizon deposits in Akhalt͡sikh area.] Soob. Akad. Nauk Gruz. SSR, <u>51</u>:3, 703–705, (Russian; Georgian summary).

TATTAR, A. V.

1961 [Die Veränderungen der Nager- und Vogel-Fauna im S der europäischen URSS während des Holozäns.] "Voprosy golocena", Vilnjus Inst. Geol. Akad. Nauk Litovsk, 359–370, (Russian; English summary).

TATTERSALL, IAN

1968 A mandible of <u>Indraloris</u> (Primates, Lorisidae) from the Miocene of India. Postilla, <u>123</u>, 1–10, 2 figs., 1 table.

TAUGOURDEAU, PHILIPPE

1965 <u>Podocnemys eremberti</u> nov. sp., chélonien pleurodire du Lutétien de St-Germain-en-Laye (Seine-et-Oise). C. R. Soc. Géol. France, <u>1965</u>, 165, (abs.).

TAURISSON, P. See: Coussy and Taurisson.

TAUTE, WOLFGANG

1965 Retoucheure aus Knochen, Zahnbein und Stein von Mittelpaläolithikum bis zum Neolithikum. Fundber. Schwaben, 17, 76–102, 2 figs., pls. 14–22, 32, 1 table.

TAVERA, JUAN
   1968   Ambiente sedimentario, condiciones de yacimiento y edad geológica de los restos de Megatherium hallados en Conchali. Bol. Univ. Chile, 85–86, 31–33, 1 fig.

TAVOSO, ANDRÉ
   1968   Découverte d'un Abbevillien évolué du type de Terra Amata dans la Vallée du Fresquel (Aude). C. R. Acad. Sci. Paris, Sci. Nat., 267, 1567–1569, 1 fig.

TAX, SOL
   1962B.   (ed.) Anthropology today: selections Reissue, (biographical data updated). Chicago: Univ. Chicago Press, viii + 481 pp.
   1964   (ed.) Horizons of anthropology. Chicago: Aldine, 288 pp.
               Rev.: Anon. in Mankind Quart., 6, 170; Heberer in Anthrop. Anz., 30, 69; Jennings in Amer. Anthrop., 66, 1187–1188; M. S. in Archeol. Roz., 17, 271–272, (Czech); Sachchidananda in E. Anthrop., 19, 86–87.
   1965   Introduction to the symposium. In: DeVore, P. L., (ed.), 1965, 1–2.

TAX, S., and CALLENDER, C., (eds.)
   1960   Rev.: Chaudhuri in Man in India, 44, 371–372.

TAYLOR, ALAN
   1968   A Manukau coastal site. New Zealand Archaeol. Assoc. Newsletter, 11, 125, 1 fig.

TAYLOR, BERYL E. See: Frick, C. and Taylor; Skinner, M. F. and Taylor.

TAYLOR, D. W. See: Hibbard, Ray, et al.

TAYLOR, FRANK A., and CARMICHAEL, L.
   1964   Report on the United States National Museum. Ann. Rept. Smithson. Instn., 1963, 27–63.

TAYLOR, MICHAEL E. See: Williams, J. S. and Taylor.

TAYLOR, M. S.
   1968   North Cape notes. New Zealand Archaeol. Assoc. Newsletter, 11, 39–49, 3 figs.

TAYLOR, R. M. S.
   1937   The dentition of the Piltdown man (Eoanthropus Dawsoni) from a new aspect. Mankind, 2:4, 95.

TCHERNOV, A. See: Stekelis, Bar Yosef and Tchernov.

TCHERNOV, EITAN
   1968A.   Peregrine falcon and purple gallinule of Late Pleistocene age in the Sudanese Aswan Reservoir area. Auk, 85, 133.

TEALE, EDWIN WAY
   1965   In the valley of Ice Age wildlife. Audubon Mag., 67, 286–291, 11 illustr.

TEDFORD, RICHARD H.

1965 Late Tertiary mammal succession. Mojave Desert region, Southern California. Program, Sect. E (Geol., Geog.), Amer. Assoc. Advance. Sci., Meeting Dec. 26–31, 1965, 18, (abs.).

1966A. Clarendonian faunal succession, Ricardo formation, Kern County, California. Spec. Pap., Geol. Soc. Amer., 87, 174, (abs.).

1966B. A review of the macropodid genus Sthenurus. Univ. Calif. Publ. Geol. Sci., 57, 1–72, 20 figs., 10 tables.
Rev.: Whitmore in Jour. Pal., 41, 815.

1966C. Late Tertiary mammal succession, Mojave Desert region, Southern California. Spec. Pap. Geol. Soc. Amer., 87, 318, (abs.).

1967A. Fossil mammals from the Carl Creek limestone, northwestern Queensland. Bull. Australian Bur. Min. Res., no. 92, 217–237, 6 figs. (Also: Palaeontological Papers, 1966.)

1967B. The fossil Macropodidae from Lake Menindee, New South Wales. Univ. Calif. Publ. Geol. Sci., 64, 156 pp., 32 figs., 4 pls., 58 tables.
Rev.: Clemens in Syst. Zool., 16, 343–344; Whitmore in Jour. Pal., 41, 1303–1304.
See: Stirton, Tedford and Woodburne.

TEDFORD, R. H., and DOWNS, T.

1965 Age of the Punchbowl Formation, Los Angeles and San Bernardino Counties, California. Geol. Soc. Amer. Cordilleran Sect., Pal. Soc. Pac. Coast Sect. Prog., 61st Ann. Meeting, 1965, 54, (abs.).

TEICHERT, CURT

1967 International symposium on Gondwana stratigraphy and paleontology. GeoTimes, 12:10, 10–11.

TEICHERT, C., and YOCHELSON, E. L., (eds.)

1967 Essays in paleontology and stratigraphy. R. C. Moore Commemorative Volume. Univ. Kans. Dept. Geol. Spec. Publ., 2, [vi] + 626 pp;. illustr.
Rev.: Kauffman in Jour. Pal., 42, 864–866; A. A. M. in Earth–Sci. Rev., 4, A72; Tröger in Geologie, 18:4, 508–510.

TEICHERT, MANFRED See: Feustel, Teichert and Unger.

TEICHMÜLLER, MARLIES

1962 Die Oreopithecus-führende Kohle von Baccinello bei Grosseto (Toskana/Italien). Geol. Jahrb., 80, 69–110, 3 figs., pls. 11–19, (English and French summaries).
Rev.: Spadea in Riv. Ital. Pal., 71, 334–335.

TEIXEIRA, CARLOS

1958 Note paléontologique sur le Karroo de la Lunda, Angola. Bol. Soc. Geol. Portugal, 12:3, 83–91, 2 pls.

1963 A paleontologia e a origem do homen. Angra do Heroísmo: sep. do Livro da II semana de Estudos Açorianos, 40 pp., (not seen).
Rev.: M., D., in Brotéria, Sér. Mensal, 80, 541–542.

1965 José Camarate Andrade França (1923-1963). Com. Serv. Geol. Portugal, 48, 283–288, portr.

TELBERG, V. G., (comp.)

1966 Russian-English dictionary of paleontological terms. New York: Telberg Book Corp., 168 pp.

TELLES ANTUNES, MIGUEL
1960B.   Notes sur la géologie et la paléontologie du Miocène de Lisbonne. I.
            Stratigraphie et faunes de mammifères terrestres. Bol. Soc. Geol.
            Portugal, 13:3, 257-268, 1 pl., 1 table, (English summary).
1961E.   Tomistoma lusitanica, crocodilien du Miocène du Portugal. Rev. Fac.
            Ciên. Lisbon, ser. 2, 9:1, 5-88, 13 figs., 12 pls., 2 tables, (Eng-
            lish summary).
1963   Sur quelques requins de la faune Néogène de Farol das Lagostas (Luanda,
            Angola). Leurs relations avec les formes Récentes. Mém. Inst.
            Franç. Afr. Noire, no. 68, 47-55, 4 pls.
1964A.   Notes sur la géologie et la paléontologie du Miocène de Lisbonne. IV.
            Présence de Triceromeryx pachecoi Vill., Crus. and Lavocat (Gir-
            affoidea, Triceromerycidae). Bol. Soc. Geol. Portugal, 15, 123-128,
            1 pl.
1964B.   Les Tomistoma (reptiles) et leur évolution. Cursillos y Confer. Inst.
            "Lucas Mallada", 9, 171-173.
1964C.   O Neocretácico e o Cenozóico do litoral de Angola. Lisboa: Junta de
            Investigações do Ultramar, 234 + [5] pp., 25 figs., 27 pls., 1 table,
            (French summary).
1964D.   Présence du genre Palaeotherium Cuv. (Equoidea, Mammalia) dans les
            argiles de Côja (Arganil). Considérations sur l'âge et l'extension des
            formations éocènes au Portugal. Rev. Fac. Ciên. Lisbon, ser. 2,
            12:1, 103-122, 1 fig., 1 pl.
1965   Sur la faune de vertébrés du Pléistocène de Leba, Humpata (Angola). Actas
            V Congr., Panafr. Prehist. Estud. Cuaternario, 1963:1, 127-128.
1967A.   Sur quelques caractères archaïques des crocodiliens, à propos d'un méso-
            suchien du Lias supérieur de Tomar (Portugal). Remarques sur
            l'origine des Crocodilia. Colloq. Internat. Cent. Nation. Recherch.
            Sci., 163, 409-414, 1 pl, (English summary).
1967B.   Um Mesosuquiano do Liásico de Tomar (Portugal). Considerações sobre
            a origem dos crocodilos. Mém. Serv. Géol. Portugal, 13, 1-66,
            10 figs., 6 pls., (French summary).
            Rev.: Berg in Zbl. Geol. Pal., Teil 2, 1969:6, 512.
1967C.   Dépôts paléogènes de Côja: nouvelles données sur la paléontologie et la
            stratigraphie. Comparaison avec d'autres formations paléogènes. Rev.
            Fac. Ciên. Lisbon, Ser. 2, 15:1, 69-111, 1 fig., 3 pls., 1 table.
            See: Ginsburg and Telles Antunes.

TEMKIN, O   See: Glass, Temkin and Straus.

TEMNIUK, F. P.
1965   [On a new find of fish fauna at the sources of Uzh river and on the age
            of the deposits in which the fauna was found.] Dopovidi Akad.
            Nauk USSR, Kiev, 8, 1076-1078, 1 fig., (Ukrainian; Russian and
            English summary).

TERENT'EV, PAVEL V.
1961   [Herpetology] Moscow: "Vysshaia Shkola" Press, 336 pp., 68 figs., 2
            pls., (Russian).
1965A.   [Methodological considerations on the study of intraspecific geographical
            variability.] In: Shvarts, (ed.), 1965, 3-20, 10 figs., (Russian).
1965B.   Herpetology. A manual on amphibians and reptiles. Translated by A.
            Mercado. Edited by O. Theodor. Jerusalem: Israel Program for
            Scientific Translations, v + 313 pp., 68 figs. (Available from U.S.
            Dept. of Commerce.)
            Rev.: Pozzi in Natura, Riv. Sci. Nat., 57, 285; Thomas in Salamandra,
            5:1-2, 80.

TERĪAEV, V. A.

1967   [From forgotten paleontological findings of last century.] Izv. Vyssh. Uch. Zav., Geol. i Razv., 1967:9, 36–41, 6 figs., (Russian).

1968   [Mammoth looked differently.] Priroda, 1968:12, 69–71, 5 figs., (Russian).

TERMIER, HENRI, and TERMIER, GENEVIÈVE

1960A.   Rev.: Patrizi in Boll. Soc. Geog. Ital., ser. 9, 2, 424.

1960B.   Rev.: Schindewolf in Zbl. Geol. Pal., Teil 2, 1962, 306–308.

1961   La trame géologique de l'histoire humaine. Paris: Masson, 186 pp., 38 figs., 16 pls., (not seen).

Rev.: Sauter in Arch. Suiss. Anthrop. Gen., 29, 79–80.

1964A.   Les temps fossilifères. I. Paléozoïque inférieur. Paris: Masson, v + 690 pp., 441 figs., 124 pls.

Rev.: Anon in Scientia, 100 (Libri ricevuti), 119; Elhai in Ann. Geog., 75, 306; Williams in Nature, 208, 614–615.

1964B.   Les échelles de l'évolution organique. Scientia, 99, 237–242.

1966   Trama geológica de la historia humana. Translation by F. Gutiérrez. Original title: La trama géologique de l'histoire humain. Barcelona-Madrid: Editorial Labor, S. A., (not seen).

Rev.: Anon. in Bol. Soc. Espan. Hist. Nat., Sec. Geol., 65, 268–269.

TERRA, HELMUT DE

1950   Radiocarbon age measurements and fossil man in Mexico. Ciencia, 10:7–8, 209–210, (not seen).

1963   Teilhard als reisgenoot. Baarn: Het Wereldvenster, 118 pp., (not seen).

Rev.: von Koenigswald in Geol. en Mijn., 43, 26, (Dutch).

1964   Memories of Teilhard de Chardin. Translated by J. Maxwell Brownjohn. New York: Harper and Row; London: Collins, 142 pp.

1965   Mes voyages avec Teilhard. Paris: Seuil, (not seen).

TERRY, R.

1965   Hingabe und Vollendung (Darts Werk oder Australopithecinen-Funde in Südafrika). Südafr. Panaroma, 1965:10, 18–24, (not seen).

TERS, MIREILLE

1964   Les alluvions de la Seine à Moisson. Bull. Assoc. Franç. Étude Quat., 1, 28–32, 2 figs.

See: Bessonnat, et al.

TERZEA, ELENA

1964   Considérations sur la dentition lactéale de Crocuta spelaea (Goldfuss). Rev. Roumaine Biol., 9:3, 151–162, 8 figs.

1965   Panthera spelaea (Goldf.) dans le Pléistocène supérieur de Roumanie. Lucrarile Inst. Spel. "Emil Racovita", Bucuresti, 4, 251–283, 7 figs., 7 tables, (Rumanian; French summary).

Abs.: Semaka in Zbl. Geol. Pal., Teil 2, 1966, 328.

1966   [Morphological particularities of cave bear, and its distribution on Rumanian territory.] Lucrarile Inst. Spel. "Emil Racovita", Bucuresti, 5, 195–231, (Rumanian; French summary).

Rev.: Ehrenberg in Zbl. Geol. Pal., Teil 2, 1969:3, 294.

See: Dumitresco, et al.

TERZEA, E., and JURCSÁK, T.

1967   [On a new fossilferous site discovered at Betfia.] Lucrarile Inst. Spel. "Emil Racovita", 6, 193–209, (Rumanian; French summary).

TESSMAN, NORMAN
1966   Cenozoic sharks of Florida. Plaster Jacket, no. 1, 7 pp., 2 figs.
            See: Webb, S. D. and Tessman.

TETÍUKHIN, G. F. See: Kambariddinov, et al.

TÉTRY, ANDRÉE
1967   Les "incertitudes" de l'évolution biologique. L'Ann. Biol., 6, 573-578.

TEWARI, A. P.
1962   Abs.: Huene in Zbl. Geol. Pal., Teil 2, 1964, 985.

THALER, LOUIS
1964A.   Un gisement de micro-mammifères du Miocène inférieur en Languedoc
            Méditerranéen, Bouzigues (Hérault). Cursillos y Confer. Inst. "Lucas
            Mallada", 9, 289-291.
1964B.   Sur l'utilisation des mammifères dans la zonation du Paleogène de France.
            Mém. Bur. Rech. Géol. Min., 28:2, 985-989.
1965A.   Une échelle de zones biochronologiques pour les Mammifères du Tertiaire
            d'Europe. C. R. Soc. Géol. France, 1965, 118.
            Rev.: M. C. in Fossilia, 1965:3-4, 49-50.
1965B.   Les oeufs des Dinosaures du Midi de la France livrent le secret de leur
            disparition. La Nature, 93, 41-48, 11 figs.
1966A.   Pairomys crusafonti nov. gen., nov. sp., rongeur énigmatique de l'Oligocène
            inférieur d'Espagne. C. R. Soc. Géol. France, 1966, 164-166,
            1 fig.
            Rev.: H.-P. in Bol. Soc. Espan. Hist. Nat., Sec. Geol., 64:2, 173-174.
1966B.   Les rongeurs fossiles du Bas-Languedoc dans leurs rapports avec l'histoire
            des faunes et la stratigraphie du Tertiaire d'Europe. Mém. Mus.
            Nation. Hist. Nat. Paris, ser. C, 17, 1-296, 25 figs., 27 pls., 15
            tables.
            Rev.: Fahlbusch in Säugetierkundl. Mitt., 15, 191; Fahlbusch in Zbl.
            Geol. Pal., Teil 2, 1967, 120-121; Van Valen in Quart. Rev. Biol.,
            43:2, 191.
            See: Cappetta, Ringeade and Thaler; Grambast, et al.; Hartenberger,
            Michaux and Thaler; Ledoux, et al; Remy and Thaler.

THALER, L., CRUSAFONT, M., and ADROVER, R.
1965   Les premiers micromammifères du Pliocène d'Espagne; précisions chro-
            nologiques et biogéographiques sur la faune d'Alcoy. C. R. Acad.
            Sci. Paris, 260, 4024-4027, 1 table.
            Rev.: J. M. G. in Fossilia, 1965:5-6, 68-69.

THENIUS, ERICH
1951F.   Abs.: Raabe in Zbl. Geol. Pal., Teil 2, 1964, 845-846.
1956D.   Abs.: Hermaden in Zbl. Geol. Pal., 1961:2, 221-222.
1960H.   Die jungeiszeitliche Säugetierfauna aus der Tropfsteinhöhle von Griffen
            (Kärnten). Carinthia II, Naturwiss. Beitr. Heimatk. Kärntens, 70,
            43-46, 1 pl.
1961F.   Paläozoologie und Prähistoire (Die Bedeutung der Paläozoologie als Hilfs-
            wissenschaft für die Urgeschichte). Mitt. U. A. G. Wien, 3-4, 39-
            61, (not seen).
1962C.   Niederösterreich im Wandel zer Zeiten. 2nd ed. Wien: G. A. Neumann,
            (not seen).
1963C.   Rev.: Gortani in Scientia, 101, 182, 184; K. in Natuurhist. Maandbl.,
            52, 176; Kühnelt in Verh. Zool.-Bot. Ges. Wien, 103-104, 234;

Schmidt in Naturwiss, <u>52</u>, 504; Zapfe in Die Höhle, <u>15</u>, 21.

1964A. Die Verbreitungsgeschichte der Rüsseltiere. Kosmos (Stuttgart), <u>60</u>, 235–242, 4 figs.

1964B. Entwicklungsgeschwindigkeit und Aussterben — zwei Probleme der Evolution. Umschau, <u>64</u>, 389–393, 4 figs.

1964C. Nur mehr Fossilien. Wie ist das Aussterben vorzeitlicher Tiere und Pflanzen zu erklären? Universum; Natur u. Tech., <u>19</u>, 71–75, 1 fig.

1964D. Herkunft und Entwicklung der südamerikanischen Säugetierfauna. Zeit. Säugetierk., <u>29</u>, 267–284, 3 figs., (English and French summaries).

1965A. Über das Vorkommen von Streifenhyänen (Carnivora, Mammalia) im Pleistozän Niederösterreichs. Ann. Naturhist. Mus. Wien, <u>68</u>, 263–268, 1 fig., (English summary).

1965B. Die Carnivoren-Reste aus dem Altpleistozän von Voigtstedt bei Sangerhausen in Thüringen. Pal. Abh., Abt. A, <u>2</u>, 537–564, 57 figs., (Russian and English summaries).

1965C. Ein Primaten-Rest aus dem Altpleistozän von Voigtstedt in Thüringen. Pal. Abh., Abt. A, <u>2</u>, 681–686, 1 fig., (Russian and English summaries).

1965D. Lebende Fossilien. Zeugen vergangener Welten. Stuttgart: Kosmos-Bibliothek, <u>246</u>, 88 pp., illustr.

Rev.: Backhaus in Salamandra, <u>1</u>, 80; Haltenorth in Säugetierkundl. Mitt., <u>14</u>, 242.

1966A. Die Cervidae und Perissodactyla (Equidae, Rhinocerotidae). In: Ehrenberg, (ed.), 1966A, 61–82, 5 pls., 4 tables.

1966B. Die Wildrinder. Ihre Herkunft und ihre Verbreitungsgeschichte. Kosmos (Stuttgart), <u>62</u>, 62–67, 2 figs.

1966C. Ergebnisse und Probleme der Wirbeltier paläontologie. Naturwiss., <u>53</u>, 261–268, 5 figs.

1966D. Grundlagen, Methoden und wissenschaftliche Bedeutung der Palökologie. Umschau, <u>66</u>, 213–219, 4 figs.

1966E. Die Vorgeschichte der Einhufer. Zeit. Säugetierk., <u>31</u>, 150–171, 13 figs.

1966F. Zur Stammesgeschichte der Hyänen (Carnivora, Mammalia). Zeit. Säugetierk., <u>31</u>, 293–300, 1 fig., (English summary).

1967A. Säugetierfährten aus dem Rohrbacher Konglomerat (Pliozän) von Niederösterreich. Ann. Naturhist. Mus. Wien, <u>71</u>, 363–379, 3 figs., 4 pls., (English summary).

1967B. Die Giraffen und ihr Vorfahren. Kosmos (Stuttgart), <u>63</u>:4, 160–164, 2 figs.

1967C. Zur Phylogenie der Feliden (Carnivora, Mamm.). Zeit. Zool. Syst. Evolut.-forsch., <u>5</u>, 129–143, 1 fig., (English summary).

See: Ax, 1964; Daxner and Thenius; Nikolov and Thenius; Pavlović and Thenius; Petronijevic and Thenius; Steininger and Thenius.

THÉOBALD, N.

1965 Deux dents de proboscidiens fossiles trouvées dans la Sablière de Marnay (Haute–Saône). Ann. Sci. Univ. Besançon, Ser. 3, Géol., <u>1</u>, 73–75, (German and English summaries).

THEODOR, O See: Terent'ev 1965B.

THEODORIDES, J. See: Petit and Theodorides.

THÉVENIN, A.

1965 L'outillage Paléolithique et Mésolithique du Bassin supérieur de la Saône. Ann. Sci. Univ. Besançon, ser. 3, Géol., <u>1</u>, 13–61, 21 pls.

THIBAULT, G.
1965   A propos de la pointe à cran solutréenne de Sabres (Landes) et des sables
          des Landes de Gascogne. L'Anthrop., 69, 377—380, 1 fig.

THIEULOY, JEAN-PIERRE
1965   Sur des centrums vertébraux d'Ichthyosauriens du Valanginien vocontien.
          C. R. Soc. Géol. France, 1965, 288—290, 1 fig.
          Rev.: Radig in Zbl. Geol. Pal., Teil 2, 1967, 107.

THOMA, ANDOR
1962   Rev.: Schaeuble in Zeit. Morph. Anthrop., 55, 384; Stloukal in Anthrop.,
          1:3, 96, (Czech).
1963   The dentition of the Subalyuk Neanderthal child. Zeit. Morph. Anthrop.,
          54, 127—150, pl. 17, 1 table., (German summary).
          Rev.: Chamla in L'Anthrop., 69:5—6, 566—567.
1964   Die Entstehung der Mongoliden. Homo, 15, 1—22, 11 figs., (English sum-
          mary).
          Rev.: Vallois in L'Anthrop., 69, 330—331.
1965   La définition des Néandertaliens et la position des hommes fossiles de
          Palestine. L'Anthrop., 69:5—6, 519—534. Also in: Genovés, S.,
          et al., (eds.), 1967, 121—145, with comment by Jacques Gomila,
          and English translation.
1966   L'occipital de l'homme mindélien de Vértesszöllös. L'Anthrop., 70:5—6,
          495—534, 8 figs., 6 tables.
          Rev.: Anon. in Naturwiss. Rundschau, 20:4, 175; Comas in An. Antropol.,
          Mexico, 5, 263—265.
1967   Human teeth from the Lower Palaeolithic of Hungary. Zeit. Morph.
          Anthrop., 58, 152—180, 4 figs., pl. 8, 3 tables.
          Rev.: Vallois in L'Anthrop., 72, 165—166.
          See: Brace 1964.

THOMAS, HORACE D.
1963   Samuel Howell Knight. Contrib. Geol., Univ. Wyoming, 2, 1—6, 5 figs.

THOMAS, H. L. See: DeLaet and Thomas.

THOMAS, MARGARET C.
1965   Let's find fossils on the beach. Venice, Fla.: Sunshine Press, 51 pp.,
          20 pls.
1968   Fossil vertebrates. Venice, Fla. Paper, 72 pp. Wholesale quantities avail-
          able from the author at 519 Harbor Dr., Venice, Fla. 33595. Single
          copies $2.00 from Smithsonian Institution museum bookshop, Wash-
          ington, D. C. 20560.
          Rev.: Anon. in Rocks and Minerals, 44:3, 233.

THOMAS, NICHOLAS
1960   Rev.: Ashbee in Archaeol. Jour., 116, 264—265.

THOMAS, N., and GUNSTONE, A. J. H.
1964   An introduction to the prehistory of Staffordshire. Archaeol. Jour., 120,
          256—262, 1 fig.

THOMAS, STANLEY
1965   Pre-Roman Britain. London: Studio Vista; New York: Graphic Society,
          191 pp., 320 pls.
          Rev.: Ashbee in Antiq. Jour., 46, 347; Megaw in Amer. Jour. Archaeol.,
          70, 306—307.

THOMPSON, FRED W. See: Korn and Thompson.

THOMPSON, M. W. See: Semenov, S. A. 1964B.

THOMSON, A. LANDSBOROUGH, (ed.)
1964 A new dictionary of birds. New York, and London: McGraw Hill, and Nelson, 928 pp., figs., 48 pls.

THOMSON, JACK
1961 Preliminary archaeological survey of the Pilchuck River and South Fork of the Stillaguamish River. Wash. Archaeol., 5:3, 4–10, (not seen).

THOMSON, KEITH STEWART
1964A. The comparative anatomy of the snout in rhipidistian fishes. Bull. Mus. Comp. Zool. Harvard, 131, 315–357, 10 figs.
1964B. Revised generic diagnoses of the fossil fishes Megalichthys and Ectosteorhachis (Family Osteolepidae). Bull. Mus. Comp. Zool. Harvard, 131, 285–311, 7 figs., 1 pl.
1964C. The ancestry of the tetrapods. Sci. Progress, 52, 451–459, 2 figs.
1965A. Gyroptychius (Rhipidistia, Osteolepidae) from the Middle Devonian of Scotland. Ann. Mag. Nat. Hist., 7, 725–732, 4 figs., 1 table.
1965B. The endocranium and associated structures in the Middle Devonian rhipistian fish Osteolepis. Proc. Linn. Soc. London, 176, 181–195, 7 figs.
1965C. On the relationships of certain Carboniferous Dipnoi; with descriptions of four new forms. Proc. Roy. Soc. Edinburgh, Sec. B, 69, 221–245, 8 figs., 4 pls.
1965D. The nasal apparatus in Dipnoi, with special reference to Protopterus. Proc. Zool. Soc. London, 145, 207–238, 12 figs., 1 pl.
1966A. The evolution of the middle ear in the rhipidistian-amphibian transition. Amer. Zool., 6, 379–397, 8 figs.
1966B. Quaternary fish fossils from west of Lake Rudolf, Kenya. Breviora, 243, 1–10, 1 fig.
1966C. Megalichthys and Rhizodus (Pisces, Rhipidistia): proposal for the stabilization of these generic names. Bull. Zool. Nomen., 23, 117–120.
1966D. The history of the coelacanth. Discovery, Yale, 2:1, 27–32, 3 figs.
1966E. Glyptolepis from the Middle Devonian of Scotland. Postilla, no. 99, 10 pp., 5 figs.
1966F. Intracranial mobility in the coelacanth. Science, 153, 999–1000, 1 fig.
1967A. Mechanisms of intracranial kinetics in fossil rhipidistian fishes (Crossopterygii) and their relatives. Jour. Linn. Soc. London, Zool., 46, 223–253, 17 figs.
1967B. Notes on the relationships of the rhipidistian fishes and the ancestry of the tetrapods. Jour. Pal., 41, 660–674, 3 figs.
1967C. A new genus and species of marine dipnoan fish, from the Upper Devonian of Canada. Postilla, no. 106, 1–6, 1 fig.
1968A. Further note on the structure of rhipidistian fishes. Jour. Pal., 42, 243.
1968B. A new Devonian fish (Crossopterygii: Rhipidistia) considered in relation to the origin of the Amphibia. Postilla, 124, 1–13, 14 figs.
 Rev.: Westphal in Zbl. Geol. Pal., Teil 2, 1969:3, 289.
 See: Schmalhausen 1968.

THOMSON, K. S., and HAHN, K. V.
1968   Growth and form in fossil rhipidistian fishes (Crossopterygii). Jour. Zool.,
London, 156, 199-223, 16 figs., 4 pls., 3 tables.

THOMSON, VIRGIL   See: Chailley 1965.

THORNDIKE, ELIZABETH E.
1968   Milwaukee gains new perspective on the emergence of man. Curator,
11, 53-57, 3 figs.

THORSLUND, PER
1966   Nytt fynd av Mammut i Sverige. Geol. Fören. Förh., 88, 208-212, 2
figs., (English summary).

THORSTEINSSON, R.
1967   Preliminary note on Silurian and Devonian Ostracoderms from Cornwallis
and Somerset Islands, Canadian Arctic Archipelago. Colloq. Internat.
Cent. Nation. Recherch. Sci., 163, 45-47, (French summary).

THURMOND, JOHN T.
1968   A new polycotylid plesiosaur from the Lake Waco formation (Cenomanian)
of Texas. Jour. Pal., 42, 1289-1296, 4 figs., 3 tables.
See: Slaughter and Thurmond.

THURRELL, R. G.
1961   The sub-Cretaceous rocks of Norfolk. Geol. of Norfolk, 1961, 277-278,
(not seen).

THURSTON, WILLIAM
1968   In Prague: 1. International Geological Congress. 2. International Union
of Geological Sciences. GeoTimes, 13:9, 10-14.

TIDELSKI, FRITZ   See: Guenther and Tidelski.

TIDWELL, W. A.
1960   The Beshers site: cross section of the Piedmont Potomac. Bull. Eastern
States Archeol. Fed., no. 19, 11, (abs.).

TIHEN, JOSEPH A.
1964A.   Evolutionary trends in frogs. Amer. Zool., 4, 386-387.
1964B.   Tertiary changes in the herpetofaunas of temperate North America. Senck.
Biologica, 45, 265-279, 4 figs.
1965   Evolutionary trends in frogs. Comments by T. S. Parsons. Amer. Zool.,
5, 309-318.
See: Estes and Tihen.

TIKHOMIROV, B. A.(=Tichomirow, B. A.)
1958B.   [On natural environment and on vegetation of mammoth epoch in North
Siberia.] Problemy Severa, 1958:1, 156-172, 8 figs., 1 table,
(Russian).
Abs.: Mirtsching in Zbl. Geol. Pal., Teil 2, 1962, 581.

TIKHOMIROV, MIKHAIL NIKOLAEVICH
1958   (ed.) Sbornik Statei po Istorii Dal'nego Vostoka. Moscow: Akad. Nauk
SSSR, 351 pp., illustr.

TIKHOMIROV, V. G. See: Borina and Tikhomirov.

TIKHOMIROV, V. V., and PANIŪTINA, L. B.
1967A.   [Evgeniĭ Aleksandrovich Maleev. (1915–1966).] Izv. Akad. Nauk SSSR,
                  ser. Geol., 1967:6, 115, (Russian).
1967B.   [Iŭriĭ Aleksandrovich Orlov. (1893–1966).] Izv. Akad. Nauk SSSR, ser.
                  Geol., 1967:6, 118–119, (Russian).

TIKHOMIROV, V. V., and RAVIKOVICH, A. I.
1968   History of geological sciences in the USSR. GeoTimes, 13, 19–22.

TIKHOMIROV, V. V., and VOSKRESENSKAĬA, N. A.
1961A.   [175 years since the date of birth of Jean de Charpentier.] Sov. Geol.,
                  1961:11, 166–167, portr., (Russian).
1961B.   [100 years since the date of birth of the French paleontologist P. M.
                  Boule.] Sov. Geol., 1961:11, 167–168, (Russian).
1961C.   [100 years since the date of birth of N. I. Andrusov.] Sov. Geol., 1961:11,
                  168–169, portr., (Russian).
1963A.   [100 years since the date of publication of Charles Lyell's "The geological
                  evidences of the antiquity of man".] Sov. Geol., 1963:5, 143–144,
                  (Russian).
1963B.   [25 years since the death of A. K. Alekseev.] Sov. Geol., 1963:7, 153,
                  portr., (Russian).
1963C.   [100 years since the date of birth of V. A. Obruchev.] Sov. Geol.,
                  1963:10, 129–131, portr., (Russian).
1964   [25 years since the death of M. V. Pavlova.] Sov. Geol., 1964:1, 150,
                  portr., (Russian).
1965   [50 years since the death of Adolf Könen.] Sov. Geol. 1965:10, 157-
                  158, portr., (Russian).

TILLEY, EILEEN H. See: Panchen, Tilley and Steel.

TILLSON, DAVID S.
1966   On recent misuse of nomenclature in Hominoidea. Reply by G. A.
                  Agogino. Current Anthrop., 7, 87–88.

TIMOFEEV, E. M. See: Guslit͡ser, Kanivet͡s and Timofeev.

TIMOFEEV, E. M., and KANIVET͡S, V. I.
1968   [Two-layered Paleolithic site Krutai͡a Gora in Pechora subpolar area.]
                  In: Rybakov, (ed.), 1968, 11–12, 1 fig., (Russian).

TIMUSH, A. V.
1966   [On the stratigraphy of continental Oligocene of Betpak–Dala.] Izv.
                  Akad. Nauk Kazakh. SSR, ser. Geol., 1966:3, 65–67, (Russian).

TINDALE, NORMAN B.
1964   Radiocarbon dates of interest to Australian archaeologists. Austral. Jour.
                  Sci., 27, 24.
1965   Stone implement making among the Nakako, Ngadadjara and Pitjandjara
                  of the Great Western Desert. Rec., S. Austral. Mus., 15, 131–164,
                  23 figs.

TING, MENG-LIN, KAO, F.-T., AN, T.-S., CHU, X.-T., and LI, C.-L.
1965   Late Pleistocene mammalian fossils of Kingyang, Kansu. Vert. Palasiatica,
                  9, 89–108, 1 fig., 5 pls., 11 tables, (Chinese and English).

TING, SU-YIN   See: Chang, Y. et al.

TING, W. S.
1966   Animal names in the oracle bone inscriptions and their paleontological
            identities. Chinese Language, Univ. Taiwan, 21, 22, 68 pp., (not
            seen).

TINKLE, DONALD W.   See: Milstead and Tinkle.

TIPTON, VERNON J.   See: Wenzel and Tipton.

TITIEV, MISCHA
1963   The science of man. An introduction to anthropology. Revised and
            enlarged. New York: Holt, Rinehart and Winston, xiv + 668
            pp., illustr.
            Rev.:   Narr in Anthropos, 59, 283—284.

TIXIER, JACQUES
1967   Procédés d'analyse et questions de terminologie concernant l'études des
            ensembles industriels du Paléolitique récent et de l'Épipaléolithique
            dans l'Afrique du Nord -- Ouest. Discussion. In: Bishop, W. W.,
            and Clark, J. D., (eds.), 1967A, 771—820, 15 figs., 2 tables, 4
            maps, (English summary).
            See: Balout, Biberson and Tixier.

TKACHENKO, BV., et al.
1957   [The geological structure of the northern section of the central—Siberian
            plateau.] Trudy Inst. Geol. Arktiki, 81, 133—242, 2 tables, (Rus-
            sian).

TKACHENKO, O. F.,   PISHVANOVA, L. S., and SHVAREVA, N. ĨA.
1967   [Tracks of birds and of a carnivore in "Guka" beds on Rybnitsa R. in
            Ciscarpathia.] Biull. Mosk. Obshch. Ispyt. Prirody, Otd. Geol.,
            42:4, 125—128, 4 figs., (Russian).

TOBIAS, PHILLIP V.
1959B.   Some developments in South African physical anthropology 1938-1958.
            In: Galloway, A., 1959, 129—154.
1963   Rev.:   Genovés in An. Antrop., Mexico, 1964, 1, 246—248; Reprint in
            Current Anthrop., 6, 414—417.
1964A.   The Olduvai Bed I hominine with special reference to its cranial capacity.
            Nature, 202, 3—4, 2 figs., Reprint in Current Anthrop., 6, 421—422.
1964B.   Dart and Taung forty years after. S. African Jour. Sci., 60, 325—329,
            4 figs.
1965A.   New discoveries in Tanganyika: their bearing on hominid evolution. With
            comments. Current Anthrop., 6, 391—411, 2 figs., 1 + 2 tables.
1965B.   Homo habilis: last missing link in Hominine phylogeny? In: Genovés,
            S., (ed.), 1965C, 377—390, 5 figs., 3 tables.
1965C.   Zinjanthropus returns to Tanzania. S. Afr. Archaeol. Bull., 20, 1—2.
1965D.   Australopithecus, Homo habilis, tool-using and tool-making. S. Afr. Archaeol.
            Bull., 20:80, 167—192, 14 figs., 9 tables.
1965E.   Early man in East Africa. Science, 149, 22—33, 12 figs., 4 tables. Also
            in Jennings, J. D., and Hoebel, E. A., 1966, 92—104.
            Abs.:   Preuschoft in Zbl. Geol. Pal., Teil 2, 1965, 297—300.
1966A.   The distinctiveness of Homo habilis. Nature, 209, 953—957, 2 figs., 3
            tables.

1966B.   Fossil hominid remains from Ubeidiya, Israel. Nature, 211, 130–133,
          4 figs., 2 tables.
1966C.   [Finds of the most ancient man in Africa.] Nauka i Chelovechestvo,
          5, 84–93, illustr., (Russian).
1966D.   A re-examination of the Kedung Brubus mandible. Zool. Meded. Leiden,
          41, 307–320, 1 fig., 1 pl.
1967A.   The cranium and maxillary dentition of Australopithecus (Zinjanthropus)
          boisei. In: Leakey, L. S. B., et al., 1967A, XVI, 1–264, 39 figs.,
          42 pls., 49 tables.
          Rev.: Anon in Interamer., 14:9, 8; Ashton in Jour. Anat., 103:2, 381;
          Campbell in Advance. Sci., 24, 361–362; Campbell in Sci. Jour.,
          3:11, 97–98; Ferembach in An. Antropol., Mexico, 6, 325–330;
          Ferembach in L'Anthrop., 73:5–6, 426–427; Howells in Amer.
          Jour. Phys. Anthrop., 28, 230–231; Iàkimov in Voprosy Antrop.,
          32, 203–204, (Russian); Jungwirth in Mitt. Anthrop. Ges. Wien,
          96–97, 337; Kennedy in Human Biol., 40:3, 420–421; Koenigswald
          in Quaternaria, 9, 418–419; Kühn in IPEK, 22, 185; Pilbeam in
          Proc. Prehist. Soc. Cambridge, 33, 457–462; Pittioni in Archaeol.
          Austriaca, 43, 146–147; Preuschoft in Zbl. Geol. Pal., Teil 2,
          1969:1, 61–63; Robinson in Nature, 219, 981–982; Roth-Lutra
          in Anat. Anz., 125, 230–232; Sauter in Arch. Suiss. Anthropol.
          Gen., 32, 144–145; Schaeuble in Zeit., Morph., Anthrop., 60,
          120; Simons in Science, 160, 672–675, 2 figs., (essay review);
          Singer in Folia Primatol., 9:1, 77–80; Stęslicka-Mydlarska in
          Przegląd Zool., 14:1, 148–149; Tattersall, in Amer. Sci., 56,
          187A-188A; Tiwari in E. Anthropol., 21:3, 342–344; Washburn
          in Quart. Rev. Biol., 43:3, 318; Wells in Antiq., 42, 60.
1967B.   Appendix 1B. The hominid skeletal remains of Haua Fteah. In: McBurney,
          C. B. M., 1967B, 338–352, 1 fig., 4 tables.
1967C.   Pleistocene deposits and new fossil localities in Kenya. Nature, 215,
          479–480, 2 figs., 1 table.
1967D.   Cultural hominization among the earliest African Pleistocene hominids.
          Proc. Prehist. Soc. Cambridge, 33, 367–376, 4 pls.
          Abs.: Anon. in Anthropos, 62:5–6, 949.
1967E.   General questions arising from some Lower and Middle Pleistocene hominids
          of the Olduvai Gorge, Tanzania. S. African Jour. Sci., 63, 41–48,
          1 fig.
1968A.   The early hominid remains from Tanganyika: Australopithecus and Homo.
          7th Internat. Congr. Anthrop. Ethnol. Sci., Moscow, 1964, 3, 333–
          341, 3 tables.
1968B.   Homage to Emeritus Professor R. A. Dart on his 75th birthday. S.
          African Jour. Sci., 64, 42–50.
1968C.   Cranial capacity in anthropoid apes, Australopithecus and Homo habilis,
          with comments on skewed samples. S. African Jour. Sci., 64,
          81–91, 1 fig., 3 tables.
          See: Brace 1964; Holloway and Tobias; Leakey, et al. 1967A; Leakey,
          Tobias and Isaac; Leakey, Tobias and Napier; Montagu and Tobias;
          Napier 1964A.

TOBIAS, P. V., and KOENIGSWALD, G. H. R. VON
1964   A comparison between the Olduvai hominines and those of Java and some
          implications for hominid phylogeny. Nature, 204, 515–518, 3
          figs. Reprint in Current Anthrop., 6, 427–430.

TOBIAS, P. V., and WELLS, L. H.
  1967   South Africa. In: Oakley, K. P., and Campbell, B. G., (eds.), 1967A,
                 49–100.

TOBIEN, HEINZ
  1961A.   Abs.: Dietrich in Zbl. Geol. Pal., Teil 2, 1964, 208–209.
  1961B.   Abs.: Dietrich in Zbl. Geol. Pal., Teil 2, 1964, 208.
  1961C.   [Principaux gisements de Mammifères en] Allemagne. In: Piveteau:
                 Traité de Paléo., 6:1, 472–476, fig. 4.
  1962B.   Abs.: Dietrich in Zbl. Geol. Pal., Teil 2, 1964, 189–190.
  1962C.   Abs.: Dietrich in Zbl. Geol. Pal., Teil 2, 1964, 215–216.
  1962E.   Ein Lophiodon-Fund (Tapiroidea, Mamm.) aus den niederhessischen Braun-
                 kohlen. Zeit. Deutsche. Geol. Ges., 113, 622.
  1963A.   Abs.: Hantzschel in Zbl. Geol. Pal., Teil 2, 1965, 6; Holder in Zbl.
                 Geol. Pal., Teil 2, 1966, 5.
  1963D.   Paläontologische Forschungen mit radiologischen Methoden. Deutscher
                 Röntgenkongress, Baden Baden, April 1963, Teil A, 11–22, 9 figs.,
                 (not seen).
  1964   Early zygodont mastodonts of Western North America and their European
                 relatives. Program, 60th Ann. Meeting, Geol. Soc. Amer. Cordilleran
                 Sect., 64, (abs.).
  1965A.   Early zygodont mastodonts of Western North America and their European
                 relatives. Spec. Pap. Geol. Soc. Amer., 82, 284, (abs.).
  1965B.   Insekten-Frass spuren an tertiären und pleistozänen Säugetier-Knochen.
                 Senck. Lethaea, 46a, 441–451, pls. 35–36, (English and French
                 summaries).
  1966   Ein Entelodon-Molar (Artiodactyla, Mamm.) aus dem Alt-Tertiär von Nord-
                 hessen. Notizbl. Hess. Landesamt. Boden-forsch., 94, 9–18, 2 figs.,
                 1 table, (English and French summaries).
  1968A.   Paläontologie. (Tier- und Pflanzenwelt der Vorzeit). In: "Das Wissen
                 unserer Zeit", Band I, 407–440, 49 figs. Frankfurt am Main-Wien-
                 Zürich: Büchergilde Gutenberg.
  1968B.   Paläontologische Ausgrabungen nach jungtertiären Wirbeltieren auf der
                 Insel Chios (Griechenland) und bei Maragheh (NW–Iran). Jahrb.
                 Verein. "Freunde der Universität Mainz", 1968, 51–58, 7 figs.
  1968C.   Mammifères éocènes du Bassin de Mayence et de la partie orientale du
                 fossé Rhénan. Colloque sur l'Éocène, I. Mém. Bur. Rech. Géol.
                 Min., 58, 297–307, 1 fig., 1 table, (German, English and Russian
                 summaries).
  1968D.   Das biostratigraphische Alter der mitteleozänen Fossilfundstätte Messel
                 bei Darmstadt (Hessen). Notizbl. Hess. Landesamt. Bodenforsch.,
                 96, 111–119, 1 fig., 2 tables, (English summary).
  1968E.   Tilly Edinger, 13.11.1897–27.5.1967. Pal. Zeit., 42:1–2, 1–2.
  1968F.   Ein Katalog der tertiären Säuger-Fundorte in der Schweiz. Pal. Zeit.
                 42:1–2, 127–129.
              See: Melentis and Tobien.

TOCHILENKO, G. IA.
  1967A.   [On climatic conditions during Quaternary Period in the zone of subtropical
                 deserts of the Arabian peninsula.] Izv. Geogr. Obshch., 99:3, 234–
                 237, (Russian).

1967B.   [Problem of natural environment in Anthropogene in the subtropical desert
           zone of Arabian Peninsula.] Prirodn. Obstan. i Fauny Proshl., 3,
           84—89, (Russian).

TOEPFER, VOLKER
1961F.   Das Altpaläolithikum im Saale-und Mittelgebiet. Internat. Assoc. Quat.
           Res., Abs. Pap., 6th Congr., 146, (abs.).
1963B.   Rev.: Bauer in Mitt. Anthrop. Ges. Wien, 93—94, 145—146; [Filip] in
           Archeol. Roz., 17, 131, (Czech); Haimovici in An. Ştiinţ. Univ.
           Cuza (n.s.), Sect. 2 (Ştiinţe Nat.), a. Biol., 10, 389, (Rumanian);
           Heberer in Anthrop. Anz., 27, 134—135; Matthes in Hallesches
           Jahrb. Mitteldeutsche Erdgeschichte, 7, 126; Thenius in Zeit. Säuge-
           tierk., 30, 128.
           Abs.: Westphal in Zbl. Geol. Pal., Teil 2, 1964, 872.
1963C.   Bemerkungen zum geologischen Alter und zu den Kernsteinen paläolithischer
           Kultur aus dem Eem-Interglazial in Mitteldeutschland. Alt-Thüringen,
           6, 42—56, 2 figs.
1964A.   Ein Saiga-Hornzapfen aus dem saaleeiszeitlichen Zeuchfelder Sander bei
           Freyburg (Unstrut). Geologie, 13:1, 110—113, 2 figs., 1 table.
1964B.   Das Magdeburger Elbgebiet zur Altsteinzeit. Varia Archaeol., 1964, 1—8,
           (not seen).
1965A.   Paläolithische Fundstätten am ehemaligan Aschersleboner-Gaterslebener
           See. Ausgrab. u. Funde, 10, 3—10, 3 figs.
1965B.   Drei spätpaläolithische Frauenstatuetten aus dem Unstruttal bei Nebra.
           Fundber. Schwaben, 17, 103—111, 2 figs., pl. 33.
1966   Westeregeln-ein klassischer Fundplatz für die Forschungsgeschichte des
           mitteldeutschen Pleistozäns. Jahresschrift Mitteldeutsch. Vorgesch.,
           50, 1—20, 3 figs., 2 pls.
1967A.   Steinzeitliche Funde aus den Rübeländer Höhlen im Harz. Überblick aus
           Anlass des Entdeckungsjubiläums der Baumanns- und Hermannshöhle.
           Ausgrabung. u. Funde, 12:1, 1—3.
1967B.   Ein Faustkeil vom oberen Nieplitztal im Fläming. Ausgrabung. u. Funde,
           12:3, 131—135, 1 fig., 2 pls.
1967C.   Die alt- und mittelsteinzeitliche Besiedlung der Altmark. Jahresschrift
           Mitteldeutsch. Vorgesch., 51, 5—52, 18 figs.
1968   Das Clactonien im Saale-Mittelgebiet. Jahresschrift Mitteldeutsch. Vorgesch.,
           52, 1—26, 5 figs., 1 table.

TOEFFER, V., and NUGLISCH, K.
1962   Paläolithikum und eiszeitliche Tierwelt im Flussgebiet der Elster und
           Saale sudwestlich Leipzig. Exkursionsführer zur Herbsttagung Geol.
           Ges. Deutsch. Demokratischen Rep., Exkursion B5, 1962, 155—
           168, (not seen).

TOKAREV, S. A.
1961B.   [On the significance of feminine figurines of the Paleolithic epoch.] Sov.
           Arkheol., 1961—2, 12—20, 5 figs., (Russian).

TOKUNAGA, S., and IWASAKI, C.
1914   [Notes on Demostylus japonicus.] Jour. Geol. Soc. Japan, 21, 33,
           (Japanese).

TOLMACHEV, A. I.
1959A.   [Geographical principles of evolution in the near and remote geological
           past.] Trudy Vses. Paleont. Obshch., II sess., 25—55, (Russian).

1959B.   [Significance of biocenotic conditions as a factor in evolution.]   Trudy
                Vses. Paleont. Obshch., III sess., 18–34, (Russian).

1961   (ed.)   [Forty years of soviet paleontology. (1917-1957).]   Trudy Vses.
                Paleont. Obshch., 4, 211 pp., (Russian).

1968   [Principles of biological taxonomy and their application in paleontology.]
                Vestnik Leningrad. Univers., 3, 5–18, (Russian; English summary).

TOLMACHEV, I. P.
1931   [Lower Carboniferous fauna of Kuznetsk coal basin.]   Moscow-Leningrad:
                GGRU Press, 2 vols, 663 pp., 23 pls., 1 map, (Russian; extensive
                French summary).

TOLOCHKO, P. P.
1968   [Research in Ukraine.]   In: Rybakov, (ed.), 1968, 186–198, 4 figs.,
                (Russian).

TOLSTOV, S. P.
1968   [Khoresmian archeological–ethnographic expedition.]   In: Rybakov,
                (ed.), 1968, 332–333, (Russian).

TOLSTOY, PAUL, (ed.)
1958   COWA surveys and bibliographies.   Area 8–European Russia. COWA
                Surv. and Bibliog., Area 8, no. 1, 14 + 11 pp.

TOMASSON, R. and J.
1964   Le gisement du Paléolithique moyen de la Côte d'Ossignoux, Vallentigny
                (Aube). Bull. Soc. Préhist., Paris, 60, 489–511, 10 figs., (English,
                German, and Italian summaries).

TOMIMASU, KENJI   See: Tozawa and Tomimasu.

TOMIMASU, K., and TOZAWA, M.
1962   [Microliths from the vicinity of Karatsu.]   Kokogaku Techo, no. 16,
                5–7, (not seen).

TOMKINS, JERRY R.,
1965   (ed.) D–Days at Dayton. Reflections on the Scopes trial. Baton Rouge, La.
                Louisiana State Univ. Press, xii + 173 + 8 pp., pls.
                Rev.: G. G. Simpson in Nature, 210, 1194–1195.

1966   'Monkey' law unconstitutional. Arkansas' anti-evolution law forbidding
                the teaching of Darwin's theory of the origin of man has been
                declared unconstitutional. Sci. News Letter, 89, 461.

TONG, MARVIN E., JR.
1962   Hunting elephants in Oklahoma. Arkansas Amateur, 1:5, 5–7.

TOOMBS, H. A.
1967   The published works of Dr. E. I. White, F. R. S. In: Patterson, C.,
                and Greenwood, P. H., (eds.), 1967, 1–4.

TOOTS, HEINRICH
1963B.   Helical burrows as fossil movement patterns. Contrib. Geol., Univ. Wyoming,
                2, 129–134, 4 pls.

1965A.   Sequence of disarticulation in mammalian skeletons. Contrib. Geol., Wyo-
                ming, 4, 37–39, 3 pls.
                Rev.: Hantzschel in Zbl. Geol., Pal., Teil 2, 1966, 462–463.

1965B.   Random orientation of fossils and its significance. Contrib. Geol., Univ.
          Wyoming, 4, 59–62, 1 fig.
          Rev.: Häntzschel in Zbl. Geol. Pal., Teil 2, 1966, 462.
1965C.   Orientation and distribution of fossils as environmental indicators. Guidebk.
          Wyo. Geol. Assoc., 1965, 219–229, 6 figs., 2 tables.
          See: Houston and Toots; Houston, Toots, and Kelley.

TOOTS, H., and VOORHIES, M. R.
1965   Strontium in fossil bones and the reconstruction of food chains. Science,
          149, 854–855, 1 table.
          Rev.: Häntzschel in Zbl. Geol. Pal., Teil 2, 1966, 463.

TOPACHEVSKIĬ, V. A.
1952   [Note on vertebrate fauna from Pliocene gravels of Bug liman.]   Zbirn.
          Prats. Zool. Mus. Akad. Nauk URSR, 25, 87–88, (Ukrainian; Rus-
          sian summary).
1957C.   [New species of marmot from the Upper Pliocene deposits of the Azov
          region of the Ukrainian SSR.] Dopovidi Akad. Nauk URSR, Kiev,
          2, 204–208, 1 fig., 1 table, (Ukrainian; Russian and English sum-
          maries).
1957D.   [Late Pleistocene and Holocene fauna of mammals from recent alluvial
          deposits of lower Dnepr.] Trudy Inst. Zool. AN URSR, 14, 113–
          128, 1 fig., 3 tables, (Ukrainian; Russian summary).
1957E.   [A study of Late Pliocene and Early Quaternary vertebrate fauna from
          ancient alluvial deposits of southern URSR.] Trudy Inst. Zool.
          AN URSR, 14, 141–147, 3 tables, (Ukrainian; Russian summary).
1965A.   [New species of the genus Ellobius Fischer (Rodentia, Microtidae) from
          Upper Pliocene deposits of the Southern Ukraine and Crimea.] Dopo-
          vidi Akad. Nauk URSR, Kiev, 4, 515–518, 2 figs., (Ukrainian; Rus-
          sian and English summaries).
1965B.   [Remains of voles of the genus Promimomys Kretzoi (Rodentia, Micro-
          tidae) from the Pliocene deposits of Southern Ukrainian SSR.]
          Dopovidi Akad. Nauk URSR, Kiev, 1965:6, 777–781, 1 fig., 1
          table, (Ukrainian; Russian and English summaries).
1965C.   [Insectivora and Rodentia of Nogaĭsk Late Pliocene fauna.]   Kiev: Inst.
          Zool. AN SSSR, "Naukova Dumka" Press, 164 pp., 38 figs., 25
          tables, (Russian).
1966   [New genus of white-toothed shrew (Insectivora, Soricidae) from South
          Ukrainian Pliocene deposits.] In: Voinstvenskiĭ, M. A., (ed.),
          1966, 90–96, 1 fig., (Ukrainian; Russian summary).

TOPÁL, GY.
1964   The subfossil bats of the Vass Imre Cave. Vert. Hungarica, 6, 109–120,
          2 tables, (Hungarian summary).

TORGERSEN, JOHAN
1965   Kropp og hjerne. Naturen, 89, 489–504.

TORRE, D.
1967   I cani villafranchiani della Toscana. Palaeontogr. Ital., 63:3, 113–138,
          6 figs., pls. 10–19, 2 tables, (English summary).
          Rev.: Albanesi in Riv. Ital. Pal., 74:4, 1320–1321.
          See: Ficcarelli and Torre.

TORRE ENCISO, EUGENIO
1962   Abs.: Radig in Zbl. Geol. Pal., Teil 2, 1964, 851–852.

TORRENS, H. S. See: Stinton and Torrens.

TOURAINE, FERNAND
1961B.   Abs.:   Brill in Zbl. Geol. Pal., Teil 2, 1964, 841–842.
1966   Découverte de l'Oligocène à Montmeyan et dans les bassins tertiaries du
            Var. C. R. Soc. Geol. France, 1966, 66–67, 2 figs.

TOUTIN, NADÈGE,   DAMOTTE, R., and GINSBURG, L., et al.
1965   Etude paléontologique et sédimentologique du Bartonien inférieur (=Auver-
            sien) dans la localité-type du Guépelle (Seine-et-Oise). C. R. Soc.
            Géol. France, 1965, 89, (abs.).

TOVELL, WALTER M., and DEANE, R. E.
1966   Grizzly bear skull: site of a find near Lake Simcoe. Science, 154, 158.

TOWARNICKI, ROBERT
1961   Evolutionism and Darwinism of Jósef Nusbaum. Przeglad Zool., 5, 83–96,
            portr., (Polish; English summary).

TOZAWA, MITSUNORI   See: Sugihara and Tozawa; Tomimasu and Tozawa.

TOZAWA, M., and TOMIMASU, K.
1962   [Artifacts from the Hara site, Saga Prefecture: Microliths in the vicinity
            of Karatsu.] Kokogaku Techo, no. 14, 1–3, (not seen).

TOZER, EDWARD TIMOTHY
1964   The Triassic period. In: Harland, W. B., et al., (eds.), 1964, 207–209,
            1 table.

TOZZI, CARLO
1962   Scavi nella grotta di Santa Lucia (Toirano). Riv. Studi Liguri, 28, 221–
            242, 10 figs.
1965   L'Industria litica dei Terrazzi Zannini (Chieti). Atti. Soc. Tosc. Sci. Nat.,
            72, ser. A, fasc. 1, 271–279, 3 figs., (French and Italian summaries).
1967   Giacimenti paleolitici di superficie sulle montagne Abruzzesi. Atti Soc.
            Toscana Sci. Nat., Mem., ser. A, 74:1, 107–119, 3 figs., (French
            summary).

TRATMAN, E. K.
1960   Gough's Old Cave, Cheddar, Somerset. Proc. Spelaeol. Soc. Univ. Bristol,
            9, 7–12, 4 figs.
1968   Pleistocene bone caves with special reference to the Mendips, Somerset.
            Trans. Cave. Res. Group, Great Britain, 10:1, 5–10.

TRAUTMAN, MILTON A.
1964   Isotopes, Inc., radiocarbon measurements IV. Radiocarbon, 6, 269–279.
            See: Walton, A., Trautman and Friend.

TRAUTMAN, M. A., and WILLIS, E. H.
1966   Isotopes, Inc. radiocarbon measurements V. Radiocarbon, 8, 161–203.

TRAVER, JEROME D.
1963B.   Paleo artifacts from northeastern North Carolina. Quart. Bull. Archeol.
            Soc. Virginia, 18, 35–36, illustr.
1964   The Pasquotank Site; North Carolina's easternmost Paleo site. Chesopean,
            2:1, (not seen).

TRÉCOLLE, G. See: Bouvier, J.–M. and Trécolle.

TREGANZA, ADAN E.
1964   An ethno-archaeological examination of Samwel Cave. Cave Studies, no.
            12, v + 29 pp., 2 figs., 4 pls., frontispiece.

TREMAINE, MARIE
1962   Arctic bibliography. Arctic, 15, 246—250, portr.

TREVOR, J. C., and WELLS, L. H.
1967   Appendix 1A. Preliminary report on the second mandibular fragment from
            Haua Fteah, Cyrenaica. In: McBurney, C. B. M., 1967B, 336—337,
            1 table.

TRIGGER, BRUCE G.
1965   Coon's theory on The Origin of Races. Anthropologica, n.s., 7, 179—187,
            (French summary).
1966   Sir Daniel Wilson: Canada's first anthropologist. Anthropologica, 8:1,
            3—28.

TRIMM, H. WAYNE
1964   Twentieth Century dinosaurs. N. Y. State Conservationist, 19:1, 28—29,
            illustr.

TRIMM, H. W., and FISHER, D. W.
1964   Dinosaurs, relatives of our reptiles, reminders of a lost world. N. Y.
            State Conservationist, 19:1, 23—27, illustr.

TRIMMEL, HUBERT
1954   Internationale Bibliographie für Speläologie, Jahr 1950. Wiss. Beihefte
            Zeit. "Die Höhle", no. 2, 61 pp.
1955   Internationale Bibliographie für Speläologie, (Karst- u. Höhlenkunde).
            Jahr 1951. Wiss. Beihefte Zeit. "Die Höhle", no. 3, 72 pp.
1958A.   Internationale Bibliographie für Speläologie (Karst- u. Höhlenkunde).
            Jahr 1952. Wiss. Beihefte Zeit. "Die Höhle", no. 4, 72 pp.
1958B.   Internationale Bibliographie für Speläologie (Karst- u. Höhlenkunde).
            Jahr 1953. Wiss. Beihefte Zeit. "Die Höhle", no. 5, 80 pp.
1959   Internationale Bibliographie für Speläologie (Karst- u. Höhlenkunde).
            Jahr 1954. Wiss. Beihefte Zeit. "Die Höhle", no. 6, 95 pp.
1962   Internationale Bibliographie für Speläologie (Karst- u. Höhlenkunde).
            Jahr 1955. Wiss. Beihefte Zeit. "Die Höhle", no. 7, 92 pp.
1963A.   Internationale Bibliographie für Speläologie (Karst- u. Höhlenkunde).
            Jahr 1956. Wiss. Beihefte Zeit. "Die Höhle", no. 8, 126 pp.
1963B.   Internationale Bibliographie für Speläologie (Karst- u. Höhlenkunde).
            Jahr 1957. Wiss. Beihefte Zeit. "Die Höhle", no. 9, 112 pp.
1964   Internationale Bibliographie für Speläologie (Karst- u. Höhlenkunde).
            Jahr 1958. Wiss Beihefte Zeit. "Die Höhle", no. 10, 128 pp.
1965   Im Jahre 1964 in Österreich unter Schutz gestellte Höhlen. Die Höhle,
            16, 16—18, (French summary).
            See: Schauberger, et al.

TRIMPE BURGER, J. A. See: DeLaet and Trimpe Burger.

TRINGHAM, RUTH
1967   A Russian conference. Antiq., 41, 218—220.

TRIPATHI, C.
1961A.   Fossil labyrinthodonts from the Panchet Series of the Raniganj Coalfield. Indian Min., 15, 198—199, (abs.).
1961B.   A note on the geology and vertebrate fossils around Nevasa, Ahmadnagar District. Indian Min., 15, 436—437.
1963   Critical concentration of the Kota-Maleri beds, Andhra Pradesh. Indian Min., 16, 305, (abs.).

TRIPATHI, C., and CHANDRA, P. R.
1961   Fossils from the Karewas around Nichahom, Kashmir. Indian Min., 15, 438, (abs.).

TRIPATHI, C., and SATSANGI, P. P.
1963   Lystrosaurus fauna of the Panchet series of the Raniganj coalfield. Pal. Indica, 37, 1—54, 13 pls.
     Rev.: Huene in Zbl. Geol. Pal., Teil 2, 1968, 207—208.

TRIPP, GEORGE W.
1966   A Clovis point from central Utah. Amer. Antiq., 31, 435—436, 1 fig.

TRIVEDY, A. N.
1966   A note on the finding of vertebrate fauna in the Surma Series of Tripura and its bearing on the stratigraphy of the area. Current Sci., 35, 68—69.

TROFIMOV, A. K. See: Loskutov, et al.

TROFIMOV, B. A.
1964A.   [Phylogenesis of mammals and some regularities in evolution.] Biull. Mosk. Obshch. Ispyt. Prirody, Otd. Geol., 39:3, 156—157, (Russian).
1964B.   Samuel Schaub (1882—1962). Pal. Zhurnal, 1964:1, 150, (Russian).
     See: Beliaeva and Trofimov; Flerov and Trofimov; Gabuniia and Trofimov; Tatarinov, L. P. and Trofimov.

TROITSKIĬ, S. L.
1966   [Quaternary deposits and relief of the coastal plains of the Enisei Bay and adjacent part of Byrranga Mts.] Moscow: "Nauka" Press, 207 pp., 38 figs., 15 tables, (Russian).
     See: Okladnikov and Troitskiĭ.

TRONCHETTI, GUY See: Philip and Tronchetti.

TROPIN, N. N.
1968   [Concerning the history of rodent fauna formation of the natural Volga-Ural plague focus.] Zool. Zhurnal, 47:1, 111—115, 4 figs., (Russian; English summary).

TROSHKINA, O. B.
1966   [On the use of F/P_2O_5 ratio for determining the geological age of Quaternary deposits.] Geol. Zhurnal (Kiev), 26:6, 87—91, (Ukrainian).

TROTTER, MICHAEL M.
1966A.   Recording and rescue work in Canterbury and North Otago. In: Groube, Rosemary, (ed.), 1966, 119—126.
1966B.   Consolidated ash from North Otago archaeological sites. New Zealand Archaeol. Assoc. Newsletter, 9, 48—52, 2 figs.

1967A.   Excavation at Hampden Beach, North Otago. New Zealand Archaeol.
Assoc. Newsletter, 10, 56–61, 1 fig.

1967B.   Radiocarbon dates from North Otago. New Zealand Archaeol. Assoc.
Newsletter, 10, 137–142.

1968A.   On the reliability of charcoal for radiocarbon dating New Zealand archaeological sites. New Zealand Archaeol. Assoc. Newsletter, 11,
86–87.

1968B.   North Otago archaeological sites. New Zealand Archaeol. Assoc. Newsletter, 11, 94–102, 2 figs.

TROTTER, M. M., and MALTHUS, R. S.
1967   Fluorine analysis in New Zealand archaeology. New Zealand Archaeol.
Assoc. Newsletter, 10, 151–157, 2 figs.

TROUP, CHARLES E., and JOSSELYN, D. W.
1967   Pebble tools from the Weiss Reservoir. Jour. Ala. Archeol., 13, 56–60,
3 figs.

TROUT, COTE
1963   Early man in northeast Yoakum County. Bull. S. Plains Archeol. Soc.,
1, 32–36, 8 figs.

TRUC, GEORGES See: Flandrin, Mein and Truc; Mein and Truc.

TRUE, W. P., (ed.)
1960   Smithsonian treasury of science. New York: Simon and Schuster, 3
vols., 1208 pp., illustr.

TRUNDLE, JOHN
1614   True and wonderful: a discourse relating to a strange and monstrous
serpent or dragon lately discovered and yet living, to the great
annoyance and divers slaughters both of men and cattell, by his
strong and violent poison. In Sussex, two miles from Horsham,
in a wood called St. Leonard's Forest, and thirtie miles from London, this present month of August 1614. London: privately
printed, illustr., (not seen).

TRUSOV, S. A.
1940   [Conference on the study of the Paleolithic.] Krat. Soob. Inst. Ist.
Mat. Kult. SSSR, 3, 44–52, (Russian).

TRUYOLS SANTONJA, J. See: Crusafont Pairo and Truyols Santonja; Crusafont
Pairo, Truyols Santonja and Riba.

TRYLICH, C., and BAYROCK, L. A.
1966   Bison occidentalis Lucas found at Taber, Alberta, Canada. Canadian
Jour. Earth Sci., 3, 987–995, 2 figs., 1 pl., 1 table.

TRZECIAKOWSKI, JAN
1964   Geological conditions of occurrence of fossil elephant skeleton discovered
in Warsaw. Przegl. Geol., 1964, 460–461, 1 fig., (Polish).

TSAGARELI, A. A., (ed. in-chief)
1964   Problems of the geology of Georgia. For the XXII session of International
Geological Congress (1964–Delhi). Tbilisi: "Metsniereba" Press,
477 pp., illustr., (Russian; English summaries).

TŜALKIN, V. I. (=Zalkin)
1962   [Mammals of ancient Moldavia.] Bíull. Mosk. Obshch. Ispyt. Prirody,
         Otd. Biol., 67:5, 36—49, 3 figs., 4 tables, (Russian; English summary).
1965   [The grey steppe cattle and Bos primigenius.] Bíull. Mosk. Obshch. Prirody,
         Otd. Biol., 70:5, 79—92, 6 tables, (Russian; English summary).

TŜANKOV, V., and DACHEV, D.
1966   [Fossil fishes from Upper Cretaceous and Paleogene of Bulgaria.] Godishnik
         Sof. Univ., 59, 1—22, 7 pls., (Bulgarian; French summary).

TŜANKOV, V., and NIKOLOV, IV.
1966A.   [Dinotherium near Ezerovo, Asenovgrad region.] Priroda i znanie, 15:4,
         3—6, (Bulgarian).
1966B.   [Fossil proboscideans and new finds in Bulgaria.] Priroda i znanie, 19:5,
         16—18, (Bulgarian).

TSAO, CHIEH-TIEN See: Pei, Yuan, et al.

TŜAPENKO, M. M., and MAKHNACH, N. A.
1959   [Anthropogene deposits of Belorussia.] Minsk: Akademiiá Nauk Beloruss-
         koĭ SSR, Inst. Geologicheskikh Nauk, 225 pp., 62 figs., 15 tables,
         1 map, 1 chart, (Russian).

TŜEĬTLIN, S. M. (=Zeitlin)
1964A.   [New Paleolithic sites in the valley of the Yenisei R.] Bíull. Kom. Izuch.
         Chetvert Perioda Akad. Nauk SSSR, no. 29, 175—182, 6 figs., (Rus-
         sian).
1964B.   [Comparison of Quaternary deposits in the glacial and extra-glacial zones
         of Central Siberia. (Nizhniaiá Tunguska Basin).] Trudy Geol. Inst.,
         100, 187 pp., 74 figs., 14 tables, (Russian).
1965   [Geology of the area of Upper Paleolithic Sungir' locality in Vladimir
         province.] In: Bader, et al., (eds.), 1965, 66—85, 8 figs., (Rus-
         sian).
         See: Aleksandrova and Tŝeitlin; Alekseev, M. N., Ravskiĭ, and Tŝeitlin;
         Ravskiĭ and Tŝeitlin.

TSING, H.—Y. See: Liu, H.—T. and Tsing.

TSUCHI, RYUICHI See: Takai and Tsuchi.

TSUI, CHEN-YAO
1962   [Some peculiarities of the upper part of facial skeleton in relation to its
         flatness.] Bíull. Mosk. Obshch. Ispyt. Prirody, Otd. Biol., 67:5,
         155—156, (Russian).

TSUNODA, BUNEI
1962   [The Nyu site, Oita Prefecture.] Kodai Bunka, 8:4, 74—92.

TUAEV, N. P.
1963   [On the stratigraphy of Dzhungaria.] Sov. Geol., 1963:5, 76—92, 2 figs.,
         1 table, (Russian).

TUCA ALSINA, L.
1965   Evolución y morfología dental. Fases de la reducción dentaria desde el
         mamífero ancestral hasta el hombre. Rev. española Estomatología,
         12:3, (not seen).

Rev.: M. C. in Fossilia, 1965:5–6, 72.

TUFTY, BARBARA
1965   New life for museums. Sci. News Letter, 88, 122–123, illustr, cover
              photo.
1967   The ascent of man. Out of the past, Dr. Leakey looks to the future.
              Sci. News Letter, 91, 188–189, 2 figs.

TUNG, TI-CHENG
1962   Abs.: Dietrich in Zbl. Geol. Pal., Teil 2, 1964, 228.

TUNG, YUNG-SHENG See: Chow, M. and Tung.

TUOHY, DONALD R.
1963A.   Archaeological survey in southwestern Idaho and northern Nevada.
              Anthrop. Pap., Nev. State Mus., 8, 136 pp., 4 figs., 39 pls., 3 tables,
              5 maps.
1963B.   Vertebrate fossils from the Nevada Northern pipeline. Introduction. In:
              Tuohy, D. R. 1963A, 76, pl. 2C.
1965   Nevada's prehistoric heritage. Nev. State Mus. Pop. Ser., no. 1, 14 pp.,
              illustr.
1967   Locality 5, (c1–248), Tule Springs, Nevada. In: Wormington, and Ellis,
              (eds.), 1967, 371–393, 4 figs., 11 pls.

TURDAKOV, F. A.
1963   [Reminiscences on L. S. Berg.] Izv. Kirgiz. Filiala Vses. Geogr. Obsh.,
              4, 33–37, portr., (Russian).

TURDUKULOV, A. T. See: Ibragimov and Turdukulov.

TURNBULL, LUCY, (ed.)
1960   COWA surveys and bibliographies. Area 7–Balkans. COWA Surv. and
              Bibliog., Area 7, no. 2, 13 + 11 pp.

TURNBULL, PRISCILLA
1967   Bones of Palegawra. Bull. Field Mus. Nat. Hist., 38, 4–5, illustr.

TURNBULL, WILLIAM D.
1968   A fossil comes to life. Bull. Field Mus. Nat. Hist., 39:1, 6–7, 5 figs.
              See: Lundelius and Turnbull; Reed, C. A. and Turnbull.

TURNBULL, W. D., and LUNDELIUS, E. L.
1967   Fossil vertebrate potential at Smeaton, Victoria. 39th Congr., ANZAAS,
              Melbourne, 1967, Sec. C, pp. K10–K11, 1 fig., (abs.).

TURNBULL, W. D., LUNDELIUS, E. L. and McDOUGALL, I.
1965   A potassium-argon dated Pliocene marsupial fauna from Victoria, Australia.
              Nature, 206, 816, 1 table.

TURNBULL, W. D., and REED, C. A.
1967   Pseudochrysochloris, a specialized burrowing mammal from the Early Oligo-
              cene of Wyoming. Jour. Pal., 41, 623–631, 5 figs.

TURNER, C. G., II See: McCartney and Turner.

TURNER, DONALD L.
1968   K–AR dating of Tertiary foraminiferal stages and their correlation with
          North American mammalian ages. Program, 1968 Ann. Meetings,
          Geol. Soc. Amer., 1968, 300, (abs.).

TURNER, FREDERICK
1922   History and antiquities of Brentford. Brentford, (not seen).

TURNER, M. D.   See: Dort, Zeller, Turner and Vaz.

TUSHABRAMISHVILI, D. M.
1960   [Paleolithic remains in Gvardzhilas-Klde cave.]   Tbilisi; (Georgian; Russian
          summary).
1968   [Result of works in the Kvirili gorge.]   In: Rybakov, (ed.), 1968, 298–
          299, (Russian).
          See: Kalandadze and Tushabramishvili.

TUTTLE, RUSSELL H.
1965   The functional morphology and evolution of hominoid hands. Amer.
          Jour. Phys. Anthrop., 23, 333, (abs.).
1966   Knuckle-walking and the problem of brachiation. Abs. 65th Ann. Meeting
          Amer. Anthrop. Assoc., 1966, 67–68, (abs.).
1967   Knuckle-walking and the evolution of hominoid hands. Amer. Jour. Phys.
          Anthrop., 26, 171–206, 12 figs., 6 tables.

TVERDOKHLEBOV, V. P.
1967   [New data on stratigraphy of Lower and Middle Triassic deposits of Pre-
          duralian foredeep in the limits of Orenburg and Bashkiria Priurl'e.]
          In: Collected Papers: 1967F [Problems of geology of South Urals
          and Povolzh'e] , 3:2, 3–24, tables, (Russian).
          See: Ochev, Shishkin, et al.

TVERDOKHLEBOVA, G. I.
1967   [On the remains of the genus Chroniosuchus from Permian of Orenburg
          Urals region.] Izv. Vyssh. Uch. Zav., Geol. i Razv., 1967:9, 31–35,
          1 fig., (Russian).

TWENTER, F. R.
1962   New fossil localities in the Verde formation, Verde Valley, Arizona. Guidebk.
          New Mexico Geol. Soc., 13th Field Confer., 1962, 109–114, 4 figs.

TWIESSELMANN, FRANÇOIS
1965   Description de deux dents molaires humaines d'âge paléolithique supérieur,
          provenant de la brèche ossifère de Kakontwe (Katanga). Bull. Soc.
          Roy Belge Anthrop. Préhist., 75, 107–119, 2 pls., 6 figs.
          See: Brabant and Twiesselmann; Heinzelin and Twiesselmann.

TWIESSELMANN, F., and POEL, H. VAN DE
1967   A propos des dents inférieures chez l'homme et les Anthropomorphes.
          L'Anthrop., 71:3–4, 239–247, 5 figs., 1 table.

TWISS, P. C.   See: Wilson, J. A., et al.

TYCHSEN, P. C., and VORHIS, R. C.
1955   Reconnaissance of geology and ground water in the Lower Grand River
          Valley, South Dakota. U.S. Geol. Surv. Water Supply Pap., no.
          1298, 33 pp., 3 figs., 1 map.

TYLER, CYRIL
1957   Some chemical, physical and structural properties of moa egg shells. Jour.
            Polynesian Soc., 66, 110–130, 6 figs., 4 tables.

UCHIDA, K.
1964   Ontogeny and evolution of the fishes. Kaseki, 8, 33–36, 4 figs., (Japanese).

UCHUPI, E.
1964   Unusual hauls from Georges Bank. Oceanus, 10:4, 20–22, illustr.

UCKO, P. J., and ROSENFELD, A.
1966   L'art paléolithique. (Translation from English). Paris: Hachette ed.,
            256 pp., 106 figs.
            Rev.: Lhote in L'Anthrop., 71:5–6, 515–520.
1967   Palaeolithic cave art. New York, Toronto: McGraw–Hill, 256 pp., illustr.
            Rev.: Blum in Amer. Sci., 57:1, 58A–59A; Jordá Cerdá in Zephyrus,
                18, 153–154; Kühn H., in IPEK, 22, 158–159; Levine in Science,
                161, 150–152; Movius in Amer. Anthrop., 70, 808–809; Waechter
                in Man, Jour. Roy, Anthrop. Inst., 3, 319.

UGGLA, ARVID HJALMAR
1957   Linnaeus. Stockholm: Swedish Institute, 18 pp., 16 pls.

ULLRICH, HERBERT
1966A.   Kritische Bemerkungen zur plastischen Rekonstruktionsmethode nach
            Gerasimov auf Grund persönlicher Erfahrungen. Ethnog.–Archäol.
            Zeit., 7, 111–123, 14 figs.
1966B.   Trepanationen: Jahrtausendealte Schädeloperationen. Urania, 1966:7,
            22–23, 2 figs.
            See: Grimm and Ullrich.

UNDERWOOD, GARTH
1967   A contribution to the classification of snakes. Publ. British Mus. (Nat.
            Hist.), 653, x + 179 pp., illustr.
            Essay rev.: Hoffstetter in Copeia, 1968:1, 201–213.
            See: Hoffstetter 1968D.

UNDERWOOD, LEON
1965   "Le bâton de commandement". Man, 65, 140–143, 5 figs.

UNGARO, SERGIO
1966   Prima segnalazione del Miocene superiore nella Peninsola Salentina. Mem.
            Mus. Civ. Stor. Nat., Verona, 435–448, 6 figs., 3 pls., 1 table.

UNGER, KURT PAUL   See: Feuster, Teichert and Unger.

UPDIKE, JOHN
1968   The naked ape. [A poem.] New Republic, 158:5, 28.

URBANEK, A.   See: Kuźniki and Urbanek.

URBANIAK, JADWIGA   See: Krajewski and Urbaniak.

URIST, MARSHALL R.
1962   The bone-body fluid continuum: calcium and phosphorus in the skeleton
            and blood of extinct and living vertebrates.   Perspectives Biol. Med.,
            6, 75—115, 10 figs., 6 tables.
1964   The origin of bone.   Discovery, 25:8, 13—19, 7 figs. Discussion: Tarlo,
            26:1, 57;   Urist. 26:2, 64.

URLICHS, MAX
1966   Zur Fossilführung und Genese des Feuerlettens, der Rat—Lias—Grenzschicten
            und des unteren Lias bei Nürnberg.   Erlanger Geol. Abh., 64, 42
            pp., 12 figs., 4 pls., 1 table.

URQUIOLA DE DE CARLI, MARIA JOSEFINA, and ARAMAYO, S. A.
1967   Descripción del craneo y mandibula de un nuevo ejemplar de Scelidotherium
            sp. Ameghiniana, 5:2, 65—90, 15 figs., (English summary).

URYSON, M. I.
1963   [Maksim Grigor'evich Levin (1904—1963).]   Voprosy Antrop., 15, 143—
            146, portr., (Russian).
1964A.   [Mikhail Antonovich Gremiâtskiĭ (1887—1963).]   Voprosy Antrop., 17,
            144—147, portr., (Russian).
1964B.   [New discoveries of fossil Hominidae and higher primates in Africa and
            the Near East.]   Voprosy Antrop., 18, 144—149, 2 figs., (Russian).
1965A.   [At the cradle of the human race.]   Priroda, 1965:2, 59—61, (Russian).
1965B.   [Some aspects of modern theory of Man's origin.]   Voprosy Antrop., 19,
            27—38, (Russian).
1965C.   [Mikhail Fedorovich Nesturkh. (70th birthday anniversary).]   Voprosy
            Antrop., 20, 149—153, portr., (Russian).
1966A.   [Pithecanthropus, Sinanthropus and related hominid forms.]   Trudy Inst.
            Etnog. Akad. Nauk SSSR, 92, 90—120, 13 figs., 7 tables, (Russian).
1966B.   [Fossil hominid from the Tchad Republic, and the problem of frontier
            forms between Australopithecines and oldest men.]   Voprosy Antrop.,
            22, 77—85, 2 figs., 1 table, (Russian).
1966C.   [New finds of bone remains of fossil hominids in East Asia.]   Voprosy
            Antrop., 24, 143—144, (Russian).
1967   [New method of cranial capacity computation on the basis of external
            diameters.]   Voprosy Antrop., 26, 174—177, 1 table, (Russian).

USCHMANN, G.
1960   Der dritte Urvogel-Fund.   Urania, 23, 435—437, 3 figs.

USHKO, K. A.
1959   [Likhvin (Chekalin) cross-section of interglacial lacustrine deposits.]   In:
            Markov and Popov, 1959*, 148—226, 15 figs., 7 tables, (Russian).

USINGER, ROBERT L.   See: Storer and Usinger.

USLAR, RAFAEL VON
1956   Der Neandertaler.   Führer des Rheinischen Landes museums in Bonn, Nr.
            1. Bonn: 48 pp., 28 figs., (not seen).
            Rev.: V., E., in Archeol. Roz., 11, 753—754 (Czech).

USLAR, R. VON, and NARR, K. J., (eds.)
1964   Studien aus Alteuropa.   Bonner Jahrb., suppl. 10:1, 283 pp., 69 figs.,
            22 pls.

USPENSKAĨÂ, N. ĨÛ.
1933 [Maikop series of Caucasus.] Inform. Sbornik Vses. Geol. Inst., 1933, 85–97, (Russian).

UYEDA, S. See: Takeuchi, Uyeda and Kanamori.

UYENO, TERUYA
1966 Evolution of the freshwater fish fauna in the Cenozoic Era. Kaseki, 11, 12–18, 2 figs., (Japanese).
1967A. A Miocene alepisauroid fish of a new family, Polymerichthyidae, from Japan. Bull. Nation. Sci. Mus. Tokyo, 10, 383–391, 3 figs., 1 table.
1967B. Pleistocene cyprinid fish from Tochiga Prefecture, Japan. Misc. Rept. Res. Inst. Nation. Res., 69, 131–134, 1 fig., pl. 11, 1 table, (Japanese; English summary).

UYENO, T., and MILLER, R.
1962A. Abs: Weiler in Zbl. Geol. Pal., Teil 2, 1964, 153.
1962B. Abs: Weiler in Zbl. Geol. Pal., Teil 2, 1964, 153–154.
1965 Middle Pliocene cyprinid fishes from the Bidahochi formation, Arizona. Copeia, 1965, 28–41, 8 figs.

VACHER, G., and VIGNARD, ED.
1965 Le Protomagdalénien I à rachettes des "Ronces" dans les Gros Monts de Nemours. Bull. Soc. Préhist. Franç., Etud. et Trav., 61, 32–44, 3 figs.
See: Beraud, et al.; Vignard and Vacher.

VACHOLD, J. See: Valšik and Vachold.

VADÁSZ, ELEMÉR
1964 Vorewort. In: Vértes; 1964A, 7–8.

VAKAR, V. A. See: Markov, G., Ravich and Vakar.

VAKHRUSHEV, G. V.
1960A. [On the discovery of fish imprints in Pliocene deposits of Bashkirian Urals region.] Voprosy Geol. Vost. Okrainy Russk. Plat., 1960:5, 87–92, 1 fig., 1 table, (Russian).
1960B. [On origin and age of some boulder-pebble deposits of Bashkirian Urals region.] Voprosy Geol. Vost. Okrainy Russk. Plat., 1960:5, 187–194, 1 fig., (Russian).

VAKTURSKAĨÂ, N. N., VINOGRADOV, A. V., and MAMEDOV, E.
1968 [Archeological-geographic research in southwestern Kyzylkumy.] In: Rybakov, (ed.), 1968, 333–334, (Russian).

VALENCIANO HORTA, M. See: Crusafont Pairo, Valenciano Horta and Sanz Fuentes.

VALENTINE, JAMES W. See: Lipps, J. H., Valentine and Mitchell.

VALLESPI, E. J.
1957 Las prospecciones y excavaciones arquelógicas de D. Lorenzo Pérez Temprado (1865-1954). Tervel, nos. 17–18, 353–356.

VALLOIS, HENRI VICTOR
1958A.	Rev.: Gevovés in Cuad Inst. Hist., Ser. Antrop., no. 6, 37–45.
1962A.	Abs.: Kuhn-Schnyder in Zbl. Geol. Pal., Teil 2, 1964, 228.
1964	The social life of early man: the evidence of skeletons. In: Lasker, G. W., (ed.), 1964, 109–131, 6 tables, (reprint with editorial comment).
1965A.	Le sternum néandertalien du Regourdou. Anthrop. Anz., 29, 273–289, 4 figs., 6 tables.
1965B.	La Basse-Tardoire grottes et abris paléolithiques. A. Fontechevade. L'Homme de Fontechevade. Bull. Assoc. Franç. Étude Quat., 1965:3–4, 217.
1965C.	Nouveaux Pithécanthropes. L'Anthrop., 69:5–6, 595–596.
1965D.	Des Hommes mindéliens en Hongrie. L'Anthrop., 69:5–6, 596–597.
1965E.	Un nouveau crâne de Sinanthrope. L'Anthrop., 68, 647–649, 2 figs.
1965F.	Point final au squelette de Galley Hill. L'Anthrop., 69, 368–369.
1966A.	Egon Freiherr von Eickstedt. L'Anthrop., 70:1–2, 191–193.
1966B.	Nouvelles découvertes d'Hommes de Néandertal en Tchécoslovaquie. L'Anthrop., 70:1–2, 204–206.
1967A.	Ethiopia. In: Oakley, K. P., and Campbell, B. G., (eds.), 1967A, 19–20.
1967B.	Mort du professeur R. Vaufrey. L'Anthrop., 71:1–2, 189.
1967C.	Il n'y a pas d'Australopithèque à Ubeidiya. L'Anthrop., 71:1–2, 189–191.
1967D.	La réapparition du crâne de Moustier. L'Anthrop., 71:1–2, 191.

VALLOIS, H. V., and BILLY, G.
1965	Nouvelles recherches sur les Hommes fossiles de l'abri de Cro-Magnon. L'Anthrop., 69, 47–74, 10 figs., 3 tables; 249–272, 14 figs., 16 tables.
	Rev.: Comas in An. Antropol., Mexico, 4, 217–220.

VALOCH, KAREL (=Valokh, K.)
1961F.	Contribution à la stratigraphie du pléistocène superieur. Archeol. Roz., 13, 571–580, (Czech; French summary).
1962B.	Rev.: Grigoriew in Archeol. Polski, 13:1, 232–239.
1963	Professor Frederick Everard Zeuner. Ph.D., D. Sc., F.S.A., F.G.S., F.Z.S. [–1963] Anthrop., 1:3, 87, portr.
1964A.	Entwicklungsfragen des Paläolithikums in der Tschechoslowakei. Archaeol. Austriaca, 36, 106–113.
1964B.	Borky II, eine Freilandstation des Aurignacien in Brno-Malomerice. Cas. Morav. Mus. Brně, Sci. Social., 49, 5–48, 1 fig., 16 pls., 1 table, (French summary).
	Rev.: Grigoriew in Archeol. Polski, 13:1, 232–239.
1964C.	Über das Vorkommen der Blattspitzen in Paläolithikum Mährens. Germania, 42, 239–244, 1 fig.
1965A.	Geröllgeräte aus Dolní Véstonice in Submähren. Alt-Thüringen, 7, 40–49, 5 figs., pls. 1–3.
1965B.	Die Höhlen Šipka und Certova Díra bei Stramberk. Anthropos, Brno, 17, 5–125, 16 figs., 1 table, 46 pls., (Czech; German summary).
1965C.	Die altsteinzeitlichen Begehungen der Höhle Pod hradem. Anthropos, Brno, 18, 95–106, 4 pls.
1965D.	Altsteinzeitliche Funde aus Brno und Umgebung. Cas. Morav. Mus. Brně, Sci. Social., 50, 21–30, 5 pls., 1 map, (Czekoslovakian summary).
1965E.	Prof. Dr. Josef Skutil. (1904-1965). Cas. Morav. Mus. Brně, Sci. Social., 50, 335–336, portr., (Czekoslovakian).

| 1965F. | [Population of Czechoslovakia during Middle Paleolithic.] In: Bader, et al., (eds.), 1965, 12–14, (Russian). |

1965F.   [Population of Czechoslovakia during Middle Paleolithic.] In: Bader, et al., (eds.), 1965, 12–14, (Russian).

1965G.   [Paleolithic findings from Rytiřské cave in Moravian Karst.] Sborn. Geol. Věd., Rada A: Antropozoikum, 3, 141–155, 7 pls., (Czech; German and Russian summaries).

1966A.   Zwei anthropomorphe Darstellungen aus dem Magdalénien Mährens. IPEK, 21, 23–24, 1 pl.

1966B.   Die Quarzitindustrie aus der Byčí Skala-Höhle in Mähren. Quartär, 17, 51–89, 17 figs., 1 table.

1967   Le Paléolithique moyen en Tchécoslovaquie. L'Anthrop., 71:1–2, 135–143, 4 figs.
            See: Fridrich, Klíma and Valoch.

VALŠIK, J., and VACHOLD, J.

1960   [The origin and evolution of organic nature and man.] Bratislava: "Osveta" Press, 66 pp., illustr., (Slovakian).

VALVERDE, J. A.

1963   Rev.: M. C. in Fossilia, 1965:5–6, 66.

VAN ANDEL, TJEERD H., HEATH, G. R., MOORE, T. C., and McGREARY, D. F. R.

1967   Late Quarternary history, climate and oceanography of the Timor Sea, northwestern Australia. Amer. Jour. Sci., 265, 737–758, 10 figs., 2 tables.

VAN BEEK, GUS W., COLE, G. H., and JAMME, A.

1964   An archeological reconnaissance in Hadhramaut, South Arabia — a preliminary report. Ann. Rept. Smithson. Instn., 1963, 521–545, 3 figs., 8 pls.

VANCEA, S. See: Fuhn and Vancea.

VANDEBROEK, G.

1964   Recherches sur l'origine des mammifères. Ann. Soc. Roy. Zool. Belg., 94, 117–160, 28 figs., (English summary).

1966   Plans dentaires fondamentaux chez les rongeurs. Origine des murides. Ann. Mus. Roy. Afr. Cent., Ser. in 8°. Sci. Zool., no. 144, 115–152, 22 figs., (English summary).

VAN DER HAMMEN, T.

1965   The age of the Mondoñedo formation and the Mastodon fauna of Mosquera (Sabana de Bogotá.) Geol. en Mijn., 44, 384–390, 4 figs., 1 table.

VANDERHOOF, VERTRESS LAWRENCE

1937A.   Abs.: Anon. in Current Sci., 8, 391.

VANDER KLAAUW, C. J.

1966   Introduction to the philosophic backgrounds and prospects of the supraspecific comparative anatomy of conservative characters in the adult stages of conservative elements of Vertebrata with an enumeration of many examples. Verh. Ned. Akad. Weten., Sect. 2, 57:1, 196 pp.

VANDERMEERSCH, BERNARD

1965   Position stratigraphique et chronologie relative des restes humains de Paléolithique moyen du sud-ouest de la France. Ann. Pal., Vert., 51:1, 67–126, 14 figs., 2 tables.
         Rev.: Vaufrey in L'Anthrop., 70:3–4, 347–348.

1966A.   Nouvelles découvertes de restes humains dans les couches Levalloiso-Moustériennes du gisemont de Qafzeh (Israel). C. R. Acad. Sci. Paris, Sci. Nat., 262, 1434–1436.

1966B.   L'industrie Moustérienne de Larikba. L'Anthrop., 70:1–2, 123–130, 4 figs., 1 table.

1968A.   Deux squelettes d'âge moustérien en Israël. Atomes, 252, 188–189, 3 figs.

1968B.   La paléontologie humaine en France. Atomes, 257, 532–533, 3 figs.
         See: Duport and Vandermeersch.

VANDERPOOL, EUGENE

1965   News letter from Greece. Amer. Jour. Archaeol., 69, 353–357, pls. 83–86.

VAN DEUSEN, HOBART M., and JONES, J. K., JR.

1967   Marsupials. In: Anderson, S., and Jones, (eds.), 1967, 61–86, figs. 4–7.

VANGENGEĬM, E. A. (=Vangengeym, E. A.)

1957B.   [On mammal fauna from Quaternary of lower Aldan R. area.] Izv. Akad. Nauk SSSR, ser. Geogr., 1957:3, 72–74, (Russian).

1960B.   [Quaternary mammalian fauna of the south-east and east of the Siberian platform.] Trudy Geol. Inst., 26, 96–115, 4 figs., 5 tables, (Russian).

1961   [Paleontological basis for the stratigraphy of Anthropogene deposits of the north of eastern Siberia. (On the evidence of mammalian fauna).] Trudy Geol. Inst., 48, 183 pp., 76 figs., 2 plates, 37 tables, (Russian).

1966A.   [Description of remains of horse Equus caballus cf. taubachensis Freudenberg from the Upper Paleolithic site Sungir'.] In: Sukachev, Gromov, and Bader, 1966, 118–135, 1 fig., 4 pls., 13 tables, (Russian).

1966B.   [Eopleistocene mammals of Western Transbaĭkalia. A review of the research on Eopleistocene fauna of Western Transbaĭkalia.] Trudy Geol. Inst., 152, 7–9, (Russian).

1966C.   [Eopleistocene mammals of Western Transbaĭkalia. Short geological characterization of Eopleistocene fauna sites.] Trudy Geol. Inst., 152, 10–22, 5 figs., 3 tables, (Russian).

1966D.   [Eopleistocene mammals of Western Transbaĭkalia. Order Carnivora.] Trudy Geol. Inst., 152, 44–46, 1 fig., 1 table, (Russian).

1966E.   [Eopleistocene mammals of Western Transbaĭkalia. Order Perissodactyla. Family Equidae.] Trudy Geol. Inst., 152, 59–92, 15 figs., 17 tables, (Russian).

1966F.   [Eopleistocene mammals of Western Transbaĭkalia. Order Artiodactyla. Subfamily Bovinae.] Trudy Geol. Inst., 152, 153–155, 1 fig., (Russian).

1966G.   [Eopleistocene mammals of Western Transbaĭkalia. Conclusions.] Trudy Geol. Inst., 152, 156–158, (Russian).

1967   The effect of the Bering Land Bridge on the Quaternary mammalian faunas of Siberia and North America. In: Hopkins, D. M., (ed.), 1967D, 281–287.
         See: Bakun and Vangengeĭm; Gromov, V. I., et al.; Gromov, V. I., Vangengeim and Nikiforova; Kaplianskaĭa, Tarnogradskiĭ and Vangengeĭm; Ravskiĭ, Alexandrova, et al.

VANGENGEĬM, É. A., and CHUMAKOV, I. S.
1963   [About the discovery of the remains of Knobloch's camel in the Rudnyi Altai.] Trudy Kom. Chet. Perioda, <u>22</u>, 147–149, 1 fig., 1 table, (Russian).

VANGENGEĬM, É. A., and FLEROV, K. K.
1965   [The broad-browed elk (<u>Alces latifrons</u>) in Siberia.] Biŭll. Izuch. Chetvert. Perioda, Akad. Nauk SSSR, no. <u>30</u>, 166–170, 2 figs., (Russian).

VANGENGEĬM, É. A., and ZAZHIGIN, V. S.
1965   [Some results of the research on Quaternary mammal fauna of West Siberia.] In: Saks, (éd.), <u>1965</u>, 301–310, 1 table, (Russian).

VANGEROW, E. F.
1967   Erdatmosphäre und Stammesgeschichte. Naturwiss. Rundschau, <u>20</u>:4, 152–154, 1 fig., 1 table.

VAN HEEKEREN, H. R. See: Erdbrink and Van Heekeren.

VAN HEEKEREN, H. R., <u>et al.</u>
1967   Archaeological excavations in Thailand. I, Sai-yok: Stone Age settlements. Copenhagen: Munsgaard, (not seen).
    Rev.: Chang in Amer. Anthrop., <u>70</u>, 1027–1028; Penniman in Man, Jour. Roy. Anthrop. Inst., <u>3</u>, 496.

VAN HEEKEREN, H. R., and JAWAD, A. J.
1966   An archeological report on the stone implements from the Fezzan Desert, Libya. Anthropos, <u>61</u>, 767–775, 2 pls., 5 tables.

VAN HOETER, F.
1963   A propos du centenaire de la publication par Boucher de Perthes de <u>De l'homme antédiluvien et des oeuvres.</u> Bull. Soc. Roy. Belge Anthrop. Préhist., <u>73</u>, 144–153.

VAN HORN, RICHARD N.
1966   The skillful hand. Abs. 65th Ann. Meeting Amer. Anthrop. Assoc., <u>1966</u>, 69, (abs.).

VAN METER, ELENA C.
1967   A continuing look: federal aid to museums. Mus. News, <u>45</u>:10, 35–38.

VAN NOORDEN, L. P.
1963   Werking van het onderkaaksgewricht van de <u>Mosasaurus</u>. Natuurhist. Maandbl., <u>52</u>, 3.

VAN NOTEN, F. L.
1967   Le Tjongerien en Belgique. Bull. Soc. Roy. Belge Anthrop. Prehist., <u>78</u>, 197–236, 5 figs.

VAN NOTEN, F., and HIERNAUX, J.
1967   The Late Stone Age industry of Mukinanira, Rwanda. S. Afr. Archaeol. Bull., <u>22</u>, 151–154, 2 figs.

VAN ROY, A.
1966   Découverte des restes <u>d'Equus caballus</u> à la carrière Delid à Villers-la-Tour (Hainaut). Bull. Soc. Belge Geol. Pal. Hydrologie, <u>75</u>:3, 390–391, 1 fig.

VAŇURA, JAROMÍR
  1965   [First find of sable in the Pleistocene of Czekoslovakia.]   Čas. Min. Geol.,
             10:4, 437–439, 1 fig., 1 pl., 1 table, (Czech; Russian summary).

VAN VALEN, LEIGH
  1963C.   Selection in natural populations: Merychippus primus, a fossil horse.
             Nature, 197, 1181–1183.
  1964A.   Age in two fossil horse populations. Acta Zool. Stockholm, 45, 93–106,
             2 figs.
  1964B.   Relative abundance of species in some fossil mammal faunas. Amer. Nat.,
             98, 109–116, 5 figs.
             Rev.: M. C. in Fossilia, 1965:3–4, 47.
  1964C.   A possible origin for rabbits. Evolution, 18, 484–491, 3 figs.
             Rev.: M. C. in Fossilia, 1965:3–4, 47.
  1964D.   Nature of the supernumerary molars of Otocyon. Jour. Mammal., 45,
             284–286.
  1965A.   Morphological variation and width of ecological niche. Amer. Nat., 99,
             377–390, 1 table.
  1965B.   Treeshrews, primates and fossils. Evolution, 19, 137–151, 1 fig.
  1965C.   The study of morphological integration. Evolution, 19, 347–349, 1 fig.,
             3 tables.
  1965D.   Selection in natural populations. III. Measurements and estimation.
             Evolution, 19, 514–528, 5 figs., 3 tables.
  1965E.   Paroxyclaenidae, an extinct family of Eurasian mammals. Jour. Mammal.,
             46, 388–397, 4 figs.
  1965F.   A Middle Palaeocene primate. Nature, 207, 435–436, 1 fig., 1 table.
  1965G.   Some European Proviverrini (Mammalia, Deltatheridia). Palaeontol., 8,
             638–665, 6 figs., 2 tables.
             Rev.: Fahlbusch in Zbl. Geol. Pal., Teil 2, 1968:6, 658.
  1966A.   Deltatheridia, a new order of mammals. Bull. Amer. Mus. Nat. Hist.,
             132:1, 126 pp., 17 figs., 8 pls., 26 tables.
             Rev.: Clemens in Quart. Rev. Biol., 42, 536–537; Fahlbusch in Zbl.
             Geol. Pal., Teil 2, 1968:6, 658–659.
  1966B.   On discussing human races. Perspectives, 9, 377–383, 1 fig.
  1967A.   The first discovery of a Cretaceous mammal. Amer. Mus. Novit., 2285,
             4 pp.
  1967B.   New Paleocene insectivores and insectivore classification. Bull. Amer.
             Mus. Nat. Hist., 135:5, 221–284, 7 figs., pls. 6–7, 7 tables.
             Rev.: Fahlbusch in Zbl. Geol. Pal., Teil 2, 1968:6, 658–659.
  1967C.   Prototomus viverrinus Cope, 1874 (Mammalia): Proposed designation of
             a neotype under the plenary powers together with grant of pre-
             cedence to Palaeonictiolae over Ambloctonidae. Bull. Zool. Nomen.,
             124, 93–94.
  1967D.   Letters to the editor. Perspectives Biol. Med., 10, 315–317.
  1968   Monophyly or diphyly in the origin of whales. Evolution, 22, 37–41.
             See: Clemens, McKenna, et al.; Sloan and Van Valen.

VAN VALEN, L., BUTLER, P. M., McKENNA, M. C., SZALAY, F. S., PATTERSON,
  B., and ROMER, A. S.
  1967   Galeopithecus Pallas, 1783 (Mammalia): Proposed validation under the
             plenary powers. Bull. Zool. Nomen., 124, 190–191.

VAN VALEN, L., and MELLETT, J. S.
  1968   Familial position of Oxyaenoides (Mammalia: Deltatheridia). Jour. Pal.,
             42, 1302.

VAN VALEN, L., and SLOAN, R. E.
1965   The earliest primates. Science, 150, 743–745, 1 fig., 1 table.
1966   The extinction of the multituberculates. Syst. Zool., 15, 261–278, 5
            figs., 2 tables.

VAN WIJNGAARDEN, A.
1966   De bever, Castor fiber L., in Nederland. Lutra, 8, 34–52, 3 figs., (English
            summary).

VAN ZINDEREN BAKKER, E. M.
1964   Pollen analysis and its contribution to the palaeoecology of the Pleistocene
            in Southern Africa. In: Davis, D. H. S., ed., Ecol. studies in So.
            Afr., 1964, 24–34, 1 fig., 1 table.
            See: Clark, J. D. and Van Zinderen Bakker.

VAPTSAROV, IV.
1963   [On the presence of Upper Miocene in Plovdiv and Khaskovo districts.]
            Spisanie Bŭlg. Geol. Druzh., 24:2, 204–206, (Bulgarian; French
            summary).

VARAGNAC, ANDRÉ See: Chollot 1964.

VARGAS, JOSÉ MARÍA
1958   Paul Rivet. Vida y obra de un americanista. Humanitas, 1:1, 84–87.

VARIOUS AUTHORS
1965   Time and stratigraphy in the evolution of man. A symposium sponsored
            by the Division of Earth Sciences, National Academy of Sciences,
            National Research Council, October 16, 1965, Washington, D. C.
            Publ. Nation. Acad. Sci., 1469, 6 + 97 pp., illustr.

VARNER, DUDLEY M.
1968   The nature of non-buried archeological data: problems in northeastern
            Mexico. Bull. Texas Archeol. Soc., 38, 51–65, 3 figs.

VASILENKO, V. K.
1961   [Geological history of Zaĭsan depression.] Trudy Vses. Neft. Nauchn.-
            Issl. Geologorazv. Inst. (VNIGRI), 162, 276 pp., 55 figs., maps
            and charts, 55 tables, (Russian).

VASIL'EV, IU. M. (=Wassiljew, Ju. M.)
1961   [Anthropogene of the southern trans-Volga region.] Trudy Geol. Inst.,
            49, 127 pp., 77 figs., (Russian).
1962   [Inter-relation of marine and continental upper Pliocene deposits in the
            Caspian and Ergeneĭ area.] Izv. Akad. Sci. USSR, Geol. Ser., 12,
            72–84, 6 figs., (Russian).
            Abs.: Stoltenberg in Zbl. Geol. Pal., Teil 2, 1964, 417.

VASIL'EV, IU. M., and ALEKSANDROVA, L. P.
1965   [New finds of fossil rodents (Rodentia, Microtinae) in the Anthropogene
            deposits of Dnepr and Don rivers basins.] In: Nikiforova, (ed.),
            1965, 141–148, 7 figs., (Russian; English summary).

VASIL'EV, V. G.
1960   [Geological structure and oil and gas presence in Iakutian ASSR.] Moscow:
            Gostoptekhizdat Press, 478 pp., illustr., (Russian).

VASILIAUSKAS, V.   See: Žeiba and Vasiliauskas.

VAS'KOVSKIĬ, A. P.
1959A.   [A short sketch of vegetation, climate, and chronology of Quaternary
             period in the upper courses of Kolyma and Indigirka rivers and
             on the northern shore of Okhotsk sea.] In: Markov and Popov,
             (eds.), 1959, 510–555, 1 map, 5 pls., (Russian).
             English translation in: Michael, H. N., (ed.), 1964, 464–512, 1 fig.,
             5 pls.
1959B.   [Early Quaternary beaver on Kolyma.] Kolyma, 1959:7, 45–46, (Russian).
1966   [Middle Quaternary elk in Kamchatka.]   Kraevedch. zapiski, Magadan,
             1966:6, 153–154, (Russian).

VAUFREY, RAYMOND
1965   Stratigraphie de la grotte de la Cotte, Saint-Brelade (Jersey). L'Anthrop.,
             69, 385.

VAUGHN, PETER PAUL
1963A.   Rev.: Huene in Zbl. Geol. Pal., Teil 2, 1964, 519.
1964A.   Vertebrates from the Organ Rock Shale of the Cutler Group, Permian
             of Monument Valley and vicinity, Utah and Arizona. Jour. Pal.,
             38, 567–583, 2 figs., pls. 93–94.
             Rev.: Huene in Zbl. Geol. Pal., Teil 2, 1964, 983.
1964B.   Evidence of aestivating lungfish from the Sangre de Cristo formation,
             Lower Permian of northern New Mexico. Contrib. Sci., Los Angeles
             Co. Mus., no. 80, 8 pp., 1 fig.
1965   Frog-like vertebrae from the Lower Permian of southeastern Utah. Con-
             trib. Sci., Los Angeles Co. Mus., no. 87, 1–18, 1 fig.
             Rev.: Huene in Zbl. Geol. Pal., Teil 2, 1966, 297.
1966A.   Comparison of the Early Permian vertebrate faunas of the Four Corners
             region and north-central Texas. Contrib. Sci., Los Angeles Co.
             Mus., 105, 1–13, 1 fig.
             Rev.: Huene in Zbl. Geol. Pal., Teil 2, 1967, 489–490.
1966B.   Seymouria from the Lower Permian of southeastern Utah, and possible
             sexual dimorphism in that genus. Jour. Pal., 40, 603–612, 1 fig.,
             pl. 74.
             Rev.: Huene in Zbl. Geol. Pal., Teil 2, 1967, 107; Westphal in Zbl. Geol.
             Teil 2, 1966, 297.
1967   Evidence of ossified vertebrae in actinopterygian fish of Early Permian
             age, from southeastern Utah. Jour. Pal., 41, 151–160, 2 figs.
             See: Lewis, G. E. and Vaughn.

VAULTIER, MAXIME   See: Breuil 1962B; Glory, Vaultier and Farinha dos Santos.

VAZ, J. E.   See: Dort, Zeller, Turner and Vaz.

VÉGH, ANNA, and VICZIÁN, I.
1964   Petrographische Untersuchungen an den Silexwerkzeugen. In: Vértes,
             1964, 129–131, 1 fig.

VEIGA FERREIRA, O. DA   See: Breuil 1962B; Roche, et al.; Zbyszewski and Veiga
             Ferreira.

VEKILOVA, E. A.
1967   [Short summary of Akhshtyr' Cave excavations in 1961–1965.] Krat.
             Soob. Inst. Arkheol. Akad. Nauk SSSR, 111, 80–85, 2 figs., (Rus-
             sian).

See: Panichkina and Vekilova.

VEKLICH, M. F.
1958   [Quaternary deposits of the right bank region of middle Dnepr.]   Trudy
            Inst. Geol. Nauk AN URSR, ser. geomorf, ta chetvert. geol., 3,
            3—200, 71 figs., 14 tables, (Ukrainian).

VEKUA, A. K.
1958B.   [Akhalkalaki fauna of Quaternary mammals and its correlation with
            corresponding faunas of Eurasia.]   Nauchn. Sess. Inst. Paleobiol.,
            AN Gruz. SSR, 6, 4—6, (Russian).
1962B.   [On paleogeography and climatic conditions of southern Georgia at the
            beginning of Quaternary Period (according to fossil mammals).]
            Nauchn. Sess. Inst. Paleobiol. AN Gruz. SSR, 8, 15—16, (Russian).
1963   Contributions to the study of the Paleolithic of Georgia.   Trudy Inst.
            Paleobiol. Akad. Nauk Gruz, SSR, 8, 109—131, 4 figs., tables,
            (Georgian;   Russian and English summaries).
1968   [Screw-horned antelope in Georgian Pliocene.]   Soob. Akad. Nauk Gruz.
            SSR, 51:3, 707—710, 2 figs., (Georgian;   Russian summary).
            See: Gabuniia and Vekua;   Sokolov, I. I. and Vekua.

VEKUA, A. K., and SHIDLOVSKIĬ, M. V.
1958   [First find of a pika (Ochotona) in the Paleolithic of Caucasus.]   Soob.
            Akad. Nauk Gruz. SSR, 21, 285—288, 1 fig., 2 tables, (Russian).

VELICH, R.
1961   Note on mammals from Nebraska and southwestern Iowa.   Jour. Mammal.,
            42, 92—94.

VELICHKO, ANDREĬ ALEKSEEVICH
1960   [Notes on working conference on the principles of periodization and
            stratigraphy of East European Paleolithic.]   Izv. Akad. Nauk SSSR,
            ser. geograf., 1960:2, 139—142, (Russian).
1961C.   [Prehistoric man sites.]   In: Markov, (ed.), 1961, 211—219, 1 fig., 1
            table, (Russian).
1961D.   [Mammalian fauna.]   In: Markov, (ed.), 1961, 219—221, 1 table, (Rus-
            sian).
1961E.   [Geology and stratigraphic position of Upper Paleolithic sites of the Rus-
            sian Plain.]   Internat. Assoc. Quat. Res., Abs. Pap., 6th Congr.,
            146—147, (abs.;   Russian).
1961F.   [The geological age of the Upper Paleolithic of the central part of the
            Russian plain.]   Moscow: Akademiia Nauk SSSR, Inst. Geogr.,
            296 pp., 75 figs., (incl. maps), 5 tables, 8 charts, (Russian).
            See: Bader, O. N., Ivanova, and Velichko.

VELIKOVSKAIA, E. M.
1960   [Upper Pliocene continental deposits in the Kuban' depression.]   Biull.
            Mosk. Obshch. Ispyt. Prirody, Otd. Geol., 65:5, 83—96, (Russian;
            brief English summary).
1961   [Pliocene red-beds and their distribution on the territories of USSR,
            China, and neighboring countries.]   Uchen. Zap. Mosk. Univ., 192,
            89—112, 1 map, (Russian).
1964   [Main features of the continental Neogene sediments of the northern foot-
            hills of western Caucasus.]   Biull. Mosk. Obshch. Ispyt. Prirody,
            Otd. Geol., 39:2, 52—69, 1 table, (Russian).

VENCL, SLAVOMIL
1962   Contribution à la connaissance du peuplement magdalénien de la Bohême.
            Archeol. Roz., 14, 517–541, figs. 170, 176–184, (Czech; French
            summary).
1964A.   Jungpaläolithische und mesolithische Station in Libín (Gemeinde Šárovcova
            Lhota) bei Jičín. Archeol. Roz., 16, 3–10, 49, figs., 1–4, 22,
            (Czech; German summary).
1964B.   Magdalénien-Funde aus Náchod. Archeol. Roz., 16, 161–164, fig. 56,
            (Czech; German summary).
1964C.   Ein Versuch über die Klassifizierung der spätglazialen und altholozänen
            Siedlungen in der Umgebung von Režabinec. Památky Archaeol.
            55, 233–245, 7 figs., (Czech; German summary).
1966   [The Ostroměř group (a new Late Paleolithic group in Bohemia).] Archeol.
            Roz., 18:3, 309–340, 16 figs., (Czech; French summary).
1968   [On Late Paleolithic settlement in Plzeň District.] Archeol. Roz., 20,
            77–79, (Czech; German summary).
            See: Vokolek and Vencl.

VENZO, SERGIO
1964   [Boundary between Pliocene and Pleistocene in Italy.] Biull. Kom. Izuch.
            Chetvert. Perioda Akad. Nauk SSSR, no. 29, 15–34, 7 figs., 1 table,
            (Russian).

VERBITSKAĨA, N. P.
1959   [Stratigraphy and lithology of alluvial deposits in diamantiferous regions
            of the western slopes of Middle Urals.] Materialy Geol. Inst.
            (VSEGEI), Nov. Ser. Chetv. Geol. i Geomorf., 27, 96–113, 2 figs.,
            2 tables, (Russian).

VERBRUGGE, A. R.
1964   [Report on] "Symposium international Pierre Teilhard de Chardin."
            Bull. Soc. Préhist. Franç., C. R. séances mens., 1964:7, CLXIV–
            CLXV.

VERESHCHAGIN, N. K.
1951C.   [Carnivora from Bingady asphalt.]   Trudy Estestv.-Istor. Muzeiã Zardabi,
            4, 28–140, 48 figs., 13 pls., 47 tables, (Russian; Azerbaijan sum-
            mary).
1953   [Great "cemeteries" of animals in the river valleys of Russian Plain.]
            Priroda, 1953:12, 60–65, 5 figs., (Russian).
1959C.   [Mammals of Caucasus. History of development of fauna.]   Moscow,
            Leningrad: Akad. Nauk S.S.S.R., 703 pp., 218 figs., 23 diagrams,
            97 charts, 115 tables, (Russian).
1967A.   Primitive hunters and Pleistocene extinction in the Soviet Union. In:
            Martin, P. S., and Wright, H. E., (eds.), 1967, 365–398, 16 figs.,
            2 tables.
1967B.   [Results and prospects of studying the history of Quaternary faunas.]
            Zool. Zhurnal, 46:9, 1298–1310, 1 fig., (Russian; English summary).
1968A.   The mammals of the Caucasus. A history of the evolution of the fauna.
            Translated from the Russian. Edited by A. A. Strelkov. Jerusalem:
            Israel Program for Scientific Translations, iii + 816 pp.
            Rev.: Coryndon in Nature, 220, 1360.
1968B.   [A fossil river.] Priroda, 1968:2, 53–54, 1 fig., (Russian).
            See: David, A. I. and Vereshchagin; Okladnikov, Vereshchagin and
            Ovodov.

VERESHCHĨAGIN, N. K., and BATYROV, B.
1967 [Fragments of the history of Middle Asia mammalian fauna.] Biull. Mosk. Obshch. Ispyt. Prirody, Otd. Biol., 72:4, 104—115, 1 fig., 1 table, (Russian; English summary).

VERESHCHAGIN, N. K., GEPTNER, V. G., and STROGANOVA, A. S.
1959 [On time and causes of the extinction of the Caucasian marmot.] Nauchn. Dokl. Vyssh. Shkoly, Biol. Nauki, 1959:2, 36—38, 2 figs., (Russian).

VERESHCHAGIN, N. K., and MEL'NIKOVA, N. N.
1958 [Zoogeographical discoveries of the archeologists in eastern Kazakhstan and in Altaĭ region.] Izv. Geogr. Obshch., 90, 385—387, 3 figs., (Russian).

VERESHCHAGIN, N. K., and OVODOV, N. D.
1968 [History of the fauna of Maritime Province.] Priroda, 1968:9, 42—49, 7 figs., 2 portrs., (Russian).

VERESHCHAGIN, N. K., and ZAKHARENKO, L. V.
1967 [Tracks millions of years old.] Priroda, 1967:12, 99, 1 fig., (Russian).

VERGNAUD-GRAZZINI, COLETTE
1966 Les amphibiens du Miocène de Beni—Mellal. Notes et mém. Serv. géol. Maroc., 194, 43—74, 34 figs., 2 pls.
Rev.: Westphal in Zbl. Geol. Pal., Teil 2, 1968, 203—204.
1968 Amphibiens pléistocènes de Bolivie. C. R. Soc. Géol. France, 1968:9, 309. See: Hecht, Hoffstetter and Vergnaud.

VERHEY, C. J. See: Deinse and Verhey.

VERHEYEN, RENÉ
1960 Les nandous (Rheiformes) sont apparentés aux tinamous (Tinamidae/Galliformes). Gerfaut, 50, 289—293, (English summary).
1961A. Tendances évolutives et ornithosystematique. Bull. Inst. Royal Sci. Nat. Belg., 37:5, 27 pp.
1961B. A new classification for the non-passerine birds of the world. Bull. Inst. Royal Sci. Nat. Belg., 37:27, 36 pp.

VERHEYLEWEGHEN, JEAN and FERNANDE
1961 A propos de "rites de chasse" pratiqués par les derniers chasseurs de renne du Paléolithique supérieur (Comparisons avec les Esquimaux... caribous). Bull. Soc. Roy. Belge. Anthrop. Prehist., 72, 159—174, 1 table.

VERHOEVEN, THEODOR
1964 Stegodon-Fossilien auf der Insel Timor. Anthropos, 59, 634, 2 pls.

VÉRIN, P. See: Battistini and Vérin.

VERMA, K. K.
1962 Chelydosaurus marahomensis n. sp., a new fossil labyrinthodont from the Lower Gondwanas near Marahon, Anantnag District, Kashmir. Indian Min., 16, 180—182, pl. 5.
1965A. Note on a new species of fossil frog from the Intertrappean Beds of Malabar Hill, Bombay. Current Sci., 34, 182—183.

1965B.   On fossil shark teeth from the Bagh Beds of the Amba Dongar area, Gu-
                jarat State. Current Sci., 34, 289–290, 20 figs.
                See: Prasad and Verma.

VERNON, ROBERT O.   See: Puri and Vernon.

VERTE, A. I., and MARK, E. IŨ.
1957   [On the stratigraphic position of Piärnu horizon (D₂a₁[1]) in Esthonian SSR.]
                Eesti NSV Teaduste Akademia, Toimitised, 1957:4, 392–393, (Rus-
                sian).

VÉRTES, LÁSZLÓ (=Vertesh, L.)
1959B.   Abs.: Ebers in Zbl. Geol. Pal., Teil 2, 1962, 286–287.
1960F.   Churinga de Tata (Hongrie). Bull. Soc. Préhist. Franç., 56, 1959. LeMans,
                1960 ?, 604–611, 3 figs.
                Rev.: Anon. in Acta Praehist., 1966, 5–7, 313.
1963C.   The Upper Palaeolithic site on Mt. Henye at Bodrogkeresztur. Acta Archaéol.
                Hung., 18:1, 1–14, 9 figs., 10 pls.
1964A.   (ed.) Tata. Eine mittelpaläolithische Travertin-Siedlung in Ungarn. Archaéol.
                Hungarica, 43, 284 pp., illustr.
                Rev.:   G. B. in Bull. Soc. Préhist. Franç., C. R. séances mens.,
                1964:7, CLXII–CLXIII.; Bandi in Bonner Jahrb., 167, 482–483;
                Bánesz in Sloven. Archeol., 13, 248–250, (Czech); Brodar in
                Arheološki Vest., 17, 522–524; Brunnacker in Bayer. Vorges.,
                29, 268; Ehrlich in C. R. Soc. Géol. France, 1964, 290; Filip
                in Archeol. Roz., 16, 765–766, (Czech); Freund in Quartär, 15–16,
                225–229; Gábori in Archaeol. Ért., 1966, 93:1, 123–126, (Hun-
                garian); Gross in Eiszeit. u. Gegenwart, 15, 236–237; Ivanova in
                Biull. Kom. Izuch. Chetvert. Perioda, 1966, 31, 144–147, (Russian);
                Krenn in Mitt. Anthrop. Ges. Wien, 93–94, 138–139; Ložek in
                Cas. Min. Geol., 1966, 11, 196, (Czech); Mania in Geologie, 1967:1,
                122–124; Narr in Anthropos, 59, 303–305; Valoch in Anthrop.,
                2:3, 89–90, (Czech); Zebera in Věstník Ústřed. Úst. Geol., 41:1,
                43–44, (Czech).
1964B.   Die Geschichte der Freilegung. In: Vertes, 1964A, 9–12.
1964C.   Die Ausgrabung und die Archäologischen Funde. In: Vertes, 1964A,
                133–249, 48 figs., 28 pls., 54 tables, 3 inserts.
1965A.   Discovery of Homo erectus in Hungary. Antiq., 39, 303.
1965B.   [Researches on the transition from the Moustierian to Upper Paleolithic
                on the basis of Hungarian material.] In: Bader, et al., (eds.),
                1965, 24–27, (Russian).
1965C.   Das Jungpaläolithikum von Arka in Nord-Ungarn. Quartär, 15–16, 79–132,
                30 figs., pls. 6–7, (English summary).
1965D.   Typology of the Buda industry, a pebble-tool industry from the Hungarian
                Lower Paleolithic. Quaternaria, 7, 185–195, 2 pls., (German and
                French summary).
1965E.   "Lunar calendar" from the Hungarian Upper Paleolithic. Science, 149,
                855–856, 1 fig.
1965F.   [Handbook of Hungarian archeology I: Monuments of Early Stone Age
                and Middle Stone Age in Hungary.] Budapest: Akademiai Kiado,
                385 pp., 76 figs., 75 pls., tables, (Hungarian).
                Rev.: Bogsch in Zbl. Geol. Pal., Teil 2, 1968:6, 669–670;
                Harmatta in Acta Archaeol. Hung., 20, 373–374.
                See: Kretzoi and Vertes.

VÉRTES, L., KRETZOI, M., and BERTALAN, K.
1962 Jungpleistozäne Funde aus einer Felsnische bei Görömböly-Tapolca. Karszt- és barlangkutatás, 4, 81—85, illustr., (German; Russian summary).
1965 Rev.: Bogsch in Zbl. Geol. Pal., Teil 2, 1968, 31—32.

VESEY, DESMOND I. See: Bastian, H. 1964.

VÉZIAN, JEAN See: Beltrán, Robert and Vézian.

VIA BRADA, L. See: Villalta and Via Brada.

VIALETTES, ABBÉ
1964 Note sur un biface du Quercy-Blanc. Bull. Soc. Préhist. Franç., C. R. séances mens., 1964:6, CLVIII—CLX, 2 figs.

VIALLI, VITTORIO
1966 Sul renvenimento di dinoterio (Deinotherium cf. hobleyi Andrews) nelle ligniti di Adi Ugri (Eritrea). Giorn. geol., 33:2, 447—458, map, 1 pl., (English summary).
 Rev.: Cita in Riv. Ital. Pal., 74:3, 994.

VIALOV, O. S.
1966 [Traces of life activity of organisms and their paleontological significance.] Kiev: "Naukova Dumka" Press, 219 pp., 51 figs., 53 pls., 4 tables, (Russian).

VIALOV, O. S., and PASTERNAK, S. I.
1961 Bronislava S. Kokoshinskaia, 1897—1959. Pal. Sbornik, 1, 157—158, portr., (Russian).

VIBERT, EDITH M.
1964 The Albert Morgan Chapter, Hartford. Conn. News, no. 89, 11.

VICZIÁN, I. See: Végh and Viczián.

VIDAL, NEY
1959 Abs.: Putzer in Zbl. Geol. Pal., Teil 2, 1962, 299.

VIDAL, PIERRE
1967 Grottes et abris ornés de la vallée de la Vézère (Dordogne). Spelunca, Bull., 7:3, 194—201, 3 figs.

VIDART, DANIEL
1965 Boletín bibliográfico de las ciencias del hombre, no. 2. Antropología e historia. Bol. Bibliog. Cien. Hombre, no. 2, 30 pp.

VIENNE, P. H.
1965 Une école à ciel ouvert dans le site archéologique de Pincevent. Touring Plein Air, 15—2, no. 200, 125—127, (not seen).

VIERECK, A.
1964 An examination of patina on stone tools with regard to possible dating. S. Afr. Archaeol. Bull, 19, 36—37.

VIGNARD, EDMOND
1964A.   Le protomagdalénien I.....Bull. Soc. Préhist. Franç., C. R. séances mens,
               1964:3, LX–LXI (Abs. and discussion); 1964:4, LXXIX–LXXX.
1964B.   Le gisement composite de Ballancourt-sur-Essonnes (S.-et-O.) Bull. Soc.
               Préhist. Franç., C. R. séances mens., 1964:4, LXXXIII (abs.).
1964C.   La Palafitte de Lannoy, près d'Ercheu (Somme). Bull. Soc. Préhist. Franç.,
               C. R. séances mens., 1964:6, CXXXVIII–CXLII, 3 figs.
1964D.   A propos du Carbone 14 dans nos climats. Bull. Soc. Préhist. Franç.,
               C. R. séances mens., 1964:8, CLXXXII–CLXXXIII, (Discussion:
               CLXXVIII–CLXXIX).
               See: Beraud, et al.; Delarue and Vignard; Vacher and Vignard.

VIGNARD, ED., and VACHER, G.
1965A.   Altérations des silex paléolithiques de Nemours sous l'influence des climats
               que se sont succédés du Périgordien Gravettien au Tardenoisien
               locaux. Bull. Soc. Préhist. Franç., Étud. et Trav., 61, 45–55.
1965B.   Quinze années de fouilles dans les Gros Monts des Beauregards de Nemours
               (Seine-et-Marne). Bull. Soc. Préhist. Franç., Étud. et Trav., 62:1,
               84–97, 1 map.

VIGNATI, MILCIÁDES ALEJO
1959   Rev.: Santiana in Humanitas, 2:2, 102–104.
1963   Estudios de paleontología humana argentina, I–VII. Acta Geol. Lilloana,
               4, 65–101, 2 figs., 6 pls.

VIGNEAUX, MICHEL   See: Lafond-Grellety and Vigneaux.

VIGNERON, J.   See: Barrière, J. et al.

VILAR FIOL, R.
1965   Le facteur déterminant de la verticalisation. Discussion by Le Gallic,
               Delattre, Schweich. Bull. Mém. Soc. Anthrop., 7:4, 381–406,
               12 figs.

VILARASAU DE EGOZCUE, M.   See: Egozcue and Vilarasau de Egozcue.

VILASECA, SALVADOR
1961   La estacion taller de silex de l'Areny (termino de Vilanova d'Escornalbou,
               provincia de Tarragona). [With letter by Georges Laplace-Jauretche]
               Trab. Seminario Hist. Primitiva Hombre Univ. Madrid y Inst. Españ.
               Prehist. Consejo Superior Invest. Cien., 3, 53 pp., 20 figs., 7 pls.

VILLALTA COMELLA, JOSÉ F. DE
1963   Las aves fósiles del Mioceno español. Bol. Soc. Españ. Hist. Nat., Sec.
               Geol., 61, 263–285, 5 pls., (French and English summaries).
               Abs.: Kuhn in Zbl. Geol. Pal., Teil 2, 1966, 314.
1964   Datos para un catálogo de las aves fósiles del Cuaternario Español. Speleón.,
               15, 79–102, (French summary).
               See: Crusafont Pairó and Villalta Comella.

VILLALTA COMELLA, J. F. DE, and ROSELL SANUY, J.
1964   Nota sobre la estratigrafía del Eoceno en el extremo W. del Valle de Ager
               (prov. Lérida). Est. Geol. Inst. Invest., Lucas Mallada, 19, 137–142,
               2 figs., (French and English summaries).
1966   Una formación turbosa rissiense en el subsuelo de Vilanova y La Geltrú.
               Mem. y Com., Sec. Geomorf., 2 ser., t.I, (not seen).

Rev.: H.−P. in Bol. Soc. Español. Hist. Nat., sec. Geol., 64:3−4, 299.

VILLALTA, J. F. DE, and VIA BRADA, L.
1966   Un nuevo celacántido en el Triásico español. Acta Geol. Hispanica, 1:2,
              21−23, 2 figs.
              Rev.: H.−P. in Bol. Soc. Español. Hist. Nat., Sec. Geol., 64:3−4, 304.

VILLATTE, JULIETTE
1966   Découverte de fragments de coquilles d'oeufs d'Oiseaux dans l'Éocène
              inférieur de l'Aude. C. R. Soc. Géol. France, 1966, 345−346.

VILLENA, JOAQUIN See: Crusafont Pairó, Riba and Villena.

VILLOUTREYS, OLIVIER DE
1965   Présence d'Echinides de l'Helvétien sarde à Roquebrune−Cap Martin (Alpes-
              Maritimes). C. R. Soc. Géol. France, 1965, 43−44.

VINCENT, J. R. See: Spier, Henning and Vincent.

VINEYARD, JERRY
1966   Missouri bone find. NSS News, 24, 195.

VINKEN, P. J.
1963   Pieter Harting en de afstamming van de mens. Proc. K. Nederl. Akad.
              Wet., Ser. C., 66, 383−389, (English summary).
              Rev.: [Jelínek] in Anthrop., 2:3, 93.

VINNICOMBE, PATRICIA
1966   The early recording and preservation of rock paintings in South Africa.
              Studies in Spel., 1, 153−162, 4 figs., 4 pls.
1967   Rock-painting analysis. S. Afr. Archaeol. Bull., 22, 129−141, 7 figs.

VINOGRADOV, A. P., DEVIRTS, A. L., DOBKINA, E. I., and MARKOVA, N. G.
1966   Radiocarbon dating in the Vernadsky Institute I−IV. Radiocarbon, 8,
              292−323.

VINOGRADOV, A. V.
1964   [Sebilian culture in the region of Dakka.] In: Piotrovskiǐ, (ed.), 1964,
              69−82, 9 figs., (Russian).
              See: Vakturskaiǎ, Vinogradov and Mamedov.

VIRET, JEAN
1955P.   Introduction à l'étude des mammifères fossiles. Paris: Centre de Docu-
              mentation Universitaire, 155 pp., illustr., (not seen).
              Rev.: [Brouwer] in Geol. en Mijn., 18, 284.

VIRET, J., DAVID, L., MEIN, P., and BATTETTA, J.
1962   Sur quelques trouvailles paléontologiques récentes faites à Lyon dans le
              sous-sol de la Croix-Rousse. Bull. Soc. Linn. Lyon, 31, 68−69.
              Abs.: Doc. Lab. Géol. Fac. Sci. Lyon, no. 1, 35−36.

VISHNEVSKIǏ, B. N.
1948   [The oldest man on Lena.] Priroda, 1948:4, 85, (Russian).

VITA–FINZI, CLAUDIO

1966 The Hasa formation: an alluvial deposition in Jordan. Man, Jour. Roy. Anthrop. Inst., 1, 386–390.

1967 Late Quaternary alluvial chronology of northern Algeria. Man, Jour. Roy. Anthrop. Inst., 2, 205–215, 2 figs., 2 pls., 2 tables.

See: Higgs and Vita-Finzi; Higgs, Vita-Finzi, et al.

VITTEK, J. See: Andrik, et al.

V'IUSHKOV, B. P. (=Vjuschkov)

1953 [Oldest poisonous reptile.] Priroda, 1953:11, 108–109, (Russian).

1964A. [Subclass Synapsida. (Thermorpha).] Osnovy Pal., [Amphibians, Reptiles, and Birds.], [12], 230–298, 106 figs., 1 table, (Russian).

1964B. [Suborder Deinocephalia.] Osnovy Pal., [Amphibians, Reptiles, and Birds.], [12], 246–258, 16 figs., (Russian).

1964C. [Suborder Theriodontia.] Osnovy Pal., [Amphibians, Reptiles, and Birds.], [12], 258–286, 46 figs., (Russian).

1964D. [Superfamily Galeopsoidea (=Dromasauria),] Osnovy Pal., [Amphibians, Reptiles, and Birds.], [12], 289–290, 3 figs., (Russian).

1964E. [Superfamily Dicynodontoidea.] Osnovy Pal., [Amphibians, Reptiles and Birds.], [12], 290–297, 15 figs., (Russian).

1964F. [Anomodontia incertae sedis. Family Dimacrodontidae.] Osnovy Pal., [Amphibians, Reptiles and Birds.], [12], 297–298, (Russian).

1964G. [Subclass Proganosauria.] Osnovy Pal., [Amphibians, Reptiles and Birds.], [12], 298–299, 1 fig., (Russian).

1964H. Discovery of Triassic theriodonts in the U.S.S.R. Pal. Zhurnal, 1964:2, 158–160, 1 fig., (Russian).

VLČEK, EMANUEL

1958B. L'homme de Néandertal à Spiš. Przeglad Antrop., 24, 138–159, 18 figs., (Polish; French summary).

1959A. František Prošek [1922–1958]. Archeol. Roz., 11, 261–262, figs., 119–120 (Czech: German summary).

1959B. Internationale Konferenz über den Fund des Neandertalers in Gánovce bei Poprad in der Slowakei. Archeol. Roz., 11, 361–378, figs. 157–158, (Czech; German summary).

1962B. Morphologie der orbitalen Partie des Endokraniums in der Phylogenese und Ontogenese des Menschen. Mitt. Arbeitsgruppe Anthrop. Biol. Ges. Deutsch. Demokratischen Rep., 2, 25–27, (not seen).

Abs.: Anon. in Anthrop., 2:1, 71.

1963A. Die Ausgrabungen und der Funde eines Neanderthalers in Gánovce. Ber. 7. Tagung Deutsch. Ges. Anthrop., 1961, 163–179, 15 figs.

1963B. [New find of a Neanderthaloid in Czekoslovakia.] Voprosy Antrop., 14, 99–102, 1 fig., (Russian).

1964A. Neuer Fund eines Neandertalers in der Tschechoslowakei. Anthrop. Anz., 27, 162–166, 3 figs.

1964B. [Morphological changes of the orbital part of human endocranium in onto- and phylogenesis.] In: Nesturkh, (ed.), 1964C, 92–98, 4 figs., (Russian; English summary).

1964C. Einige in der Ontogenese des modernen Menschen untersuchte Neandertal-merkmale. Zeit. Morph. Anthrop., 56, 63–83, 22 figs., 3 pls., (English summary).

1965A. Zur Problematik des Durchschneidens des bleibenden Gebisses bei den Neandertaler Menschen. Acta Univ. Carolinae, Biol. Suppl., 79–88, 5 figs.

1965B.   Rassendiagnose der aurignacienzeitlichen Bestattungen in der Grotte des Enfants bei Grimaldi. Anthrop. Anz., 29, 290—300, 8 figs., pls. 21—22.

1967   Die Sinus frontales bei europäischen Neandertalern. Anthrop. Anz., 30, 166—189, 14 figs., 3 pls., 2 tables.
    Rev.: Vallois in L'Anthrop., 73, 119.

1968   Une nouvelle trouvaille du type Homo neanderthalensis en Tchecoslovaquie. 7th Internat. Congr. Anthrop. Ethnol. Sci., Moscow, 1964, 3, 342—346, 2 figs.

VOGEL, CHRISTIAN

1966A.   Morphologische Studien am Gesichtsschädel Catarrhiner Primaten. Bibliotheca Primat., 4, 226 pp., 43 figs., 5 tables.

1966B.   Die Bedeutung der Primatenkunde für die Anthropologie. Naturwiss. Rundschau, 19, 415—421, 1 fig.

1968   Konstruktionstypen des Gesichtsschädels Catarrhiner Primaten. 7th Internat. Congr. Anthrop. Ethnol. Sci., Moscow, 1964, 3, 413—416.

VOGEL, J. C., and WATERBOLK, H. T.

1964   Groningen radiocarbon dates V. Radiocarbon, 6, 349—369.

1967   Groningen radiocarbon dates VII. Radiocarbon, 9, 107—155.

VOGEL, J. C., and ZAGWIJN, W. H.

1967   Groningen radiocarbon dates VI. Radiocarbon, 9, 63—106.

VOGELTANZ, RUDOLF

1965   Austrocknungsstrukturen bei Koprolithen. Neues Jahrb. Geol. Pal., Monatsh., 1965, 362—371, 12 figs., (English summary).

1967   Ergänzende Mitteilung über Koprolithen - Untersuchungen aus dem Unteroligozän von Nebraska. Neues Jahrb. Geol. Pal., Monatsh., 1967:3, 188—191, 1 table, (English summary).
    Rev.: Hantzschel in Zbl. Geol. Pal., Teil 2, 1968, 245.

VOGT, CARL

1858   Naturliche Geschichte der Schöpfung des Weltalls, der Erde und der auf ihr Befindlichen Organismen. Leipzig, (not seen).

VOIGT, ERHARD

1960B.   Über einen mutmasslich fossilen Harnstein (Urolith) aus der Oberen Kreide. Mitt. Geol. Staatsinst. Hamburg, 29, 85—94, 2 figs., pls. 5—8.

VOINSTVENSKĬI, M. A.

1966   (ed.) [Ecology and history of Ukrainian vertebrate fauna.] Kiev: "Naukova Dumka" Press, 204 pp., illustr., (Ukrainian; Russian summaries).

1967   [Fossil ornithofauna of Ukraine.] Prirodn. Obstan. i Fauny Proshl., 3, 3—76, (Russian).

VOJKFFY, GRAF CH.

1962   Grosswild und Jagd in der späteren Altsteinzeit. Vorzeit am Bodensee, 1961—62, 1—4, (not seen).

VOKOLEK, V., and VENCL, SL.

1961   Industrie taillée en procelanite en Boheme. Archeol. Roz., 13, 464—472, figs. 174—176, (Czech; French summary).

VOLKOV, V. V.   See: Larichev and Volkov.

VOLKOVA, V. S.
1966   [Quaternary deposits of Lower Irtysh R. and their biostratigraphic characterization.] Novosibirsk: "Nauka" Press, 174 pp., 35 figs., 16 tables.,
(Russian).

VOLLMAYR, THEODOR
1966   Oberoligozäne Gliridae (Rodentia, Mammalia) aus der suddeutschen Falten-
molasse. Mitt. Bayer. Staatssamml. Pal. Hist. Geol., 6, 65–107,
1 fig., 3 pls., 1 table, (English summary).
Rev.: Fahlbusch in Zbl. Geol. Pal., Teil 2, 1967, 522–523.

VOLLMER, CONRAD
1964   Funde, Forscher und Frühmenschen. 2nd ed. Leipzig: Prisma-Verlag,
236 pp., 33 pls.

VOLOCHKOVICH, K. L.
1961   [Stratigraphy and tectonics of the extreme North-East of Mongolia (region
of Tsagan-Shibetu, Kharkhira-Nuru, and Saïliúgem ridges).] Biull.
Mosk. Obshch. Ispyt. Prirody, Otd. Geol., 36:1, 3–23, 2 figs., (Russian; English summary).
Abs.: Stoltenberg in Zbl. Geol. Pal., Teil 2, 1964, 16–18.

VOLPE, E. P.
1967   Understanding evolution. Dubuque, Iowa: W. C. Brown, 160 pp., illustr.
Rev.: Leigh in Amer. Sci., 55, 493A–494A.

VÖLZING, H.
1964   Lammerspiel, ein Beitrag zum Paläolithikum des Rhein-Main-Gebietes.
Fundber. Hessen, 4, 1–11, (not seen).

VONDRA, CARL F.   See: Schultz, C. B., Falkenbach and Vondra.

VONDRA, C. F., and JOHNSON, G. D.
1968   Stratigraphy of the Siwalik deposits of the sub-Himalayan Gumber-Sakarghat
fault block in Himachal Pradesh, India. Program, 1968 Ann. Meetings,
Geol. Soc. Amer., 1968, 308, (abs).

VOORHIES, M. R.
1965   The Carnivora of the Trail Creek fauna. Contrib. Geol., Univ. Wyoming,
4, 21–25, 3 figs., 2 tables.
1966   Growth stages in Merycodus furcatus and their bearing on the taxonomy
of Miocene-Pliocene merycodonts. Spec. Pap. Geol. Soc. Amer., 87,
304–305, (abs.).
1967   Evidence of seasonal growth in Tertiary vertebrate fossils. Program, 1967
Ann. Meeting, Geol. Soc. Amer., 1967, 230, (abs.).
1968   Evidence of seasonal growth in Tertiary vertebrate fossils. Pal. Soc. Mem.
2, 119, (abs.).
See: Toots and Voorhies.

VORHIS, R. C.   See: Tychsen and Vorhis.

VOROB'EVA, EMILIÏA IVANOVNA (=Vorobyeva, E. I.)
1967   [Triassic ceratodus from South Fergana and some remarks on the systematics
and phylogeny of Ceratodontidae.] Pal. Zhurnal, 1967:4, 102–111,
5 figs., 1 table, (Russian).

VOROB'EVA, E. I., and MATVEEVA, A. L.
1962   [Class Osteichthyes.] Trudy SNIIGGIMS, 21, [Paleozoic biostratigraphy of Saiân-Altaĭ mountain region, v. 3], 215–220, 4 figs., 3 pls., (Russian).

VOROB'EVA, E. I., and MINIKH, M. G.
1968   [An attempt at a biometrical study of the tooth plates of ceratodontids.] Pal. Zhurnal, 1968:2, 76–87, 3 figs., 1 pl., 4 tables, (Russian).

VOROB'EVA, E. I., and OBRUCHEV, D. V.
1964   [Subclass Sarcopterygii.] Osnovy Pal., [Agnathes. Pisces.], [11], 268–321, 67 figs., 5 pls., (Russian).

VORONTSOV, N. N.
1963B.   [On the mechanism of masticatory movements of rodents and on the evolution of jaw apparatus of hamsteriformes (Cricetidae).] Trudy Mosk. Obshch. Ispyt. Prirody, otd. biol., 10, 75–104, 21 figs., (Russian).
1964   Aralomys glikmani – a new species of hamster (Cricetidae). [English translation of Vorontzov, 1963A.] Internat. Geol. Rev., 6, 2249–2252, 2 figs.

VOROPINOV, V. S., and ERMOLAEV, D. I.
1966   [Flora and fauna of Ust'-Baleĭ Jurassic.] Geol. i Geof., 1966:5, 30–38, 4 figs., (Russian; English summary).

VOSKOBOINIKOV, M. E.   See: Biriŭkov, et al.

VOSKRESENSKAIÂ, N. A.   See: Tikhomirov, V. V. and Voskresenskaiâ.

VOSKRESENSKIĬ, S. S.
1959   [Main features of the Quaternary history of Southwestern Baikal region.] In: Markov and Popov, (eds.), 1959, 422–441, 2 figs., 2 tables, (Russian).
1964   Main features of the Quaternary history of Southwestern Baikal region. English translation. In: Michael, H. N., (ed.), 1964B, 372–393, 3 figs., 2 tables.

VOSS-FOUCART, M. F.
1968   Paléoprotéines des coquilles fossiles d'oeufs de Dinosauriens du Crétacé supérieur de Provence. Compar. Biochem. Physiol., 24:1, 31–36, (English summary).

VOZIN, V. F.
1968   [Egg capsules of chimaeras from Triassic of Iâkutia.] Geol. i Geof., 1968:8, 67–77, 2 pls., 1 table, (Russian; English summary).

VRIES, H. DE, and WAARD, H. DE
1964   Die Untersuchungen des C14-Laboratoriums zu Groningen. In: Vértes, (ed.), 1964A, 35–36.

VTIURIN, B. I.   See: Kuprina and Vtiurin.

VUILLEUMIER, FRANÇOIS
  1965   Relationships and evolution within the Cracidae (Aves, Galliformes).
            Bull. Mus. Comp. Zool. Harvard, 135, 1—27, 21 figs.
  1967   Phyletic evolution in modern birds of the Patagonian forests.   Nature,
            215, 247—248.

VULLIAMY, C. E.
  1930   The archaeology of Middlesex and London.   London: Methuen, xx +
            308 pp., 41 figs., 11 pls., 1 map.

VYEZZHEV, R. I.
  1955   [Archeological investigations on the territory of the Ukrainian SSR in
            1954.]   Krat. Soob. Inst. Arkheol. Akad. Nauk URSR, 5, 55—63,
            (Russian).

WAARD, H. DE   See: Vries and Waard.

WACHENDORF, HORST   See: Palmowski and Wachendorf.

WADDELL, EUGENE G.
  1965A.   The Paleo—Indian era: distribution of finds.   South Carolina.   Bull.
            Southeast. Archaeol. Confer., 2, 14—15.
  1965B.   South Carolina fluted points.   Bull. Southeast. Archaeol. Confer., 2,
            52—54, 4 figs., 1 table.

WADDINGTON, C. H.
  1966   Die biologischen Grundlagen des Lebens.   Braunschweig: Vieweg and
            Sohn, "Die Wissenschaft" Bd. 121, 119 pp., 10 figs.
            Rev.: Steffan in Naturwiss. Rundschau, 19:12, 517.

WADE, ROBERT E., ALEXANDER, J., GAGE, C., HICKS, V., and HONEY, J.
  1968   Museum model making.   Quart. Los Angeles Co. Mus., 7:2, 37—44, illustr.

WADIA COMMEMORATIVE VOLUME   See: Jhingran, A. G., et al., (eds.).   Dr. D. N.
                             Wadia Commemorative Volume.   Calcutta: Mining, Geological
                             and Metallurgical Institute of India, LXXII + 834 pp., illustr., 1965.

WAECHTER, J. D'A., et al.
  1964   The excavation of Gorham's Cave, Gibraltar, 1951—54.   Bull. London
            Univ. Inst. Archaeol., no. 4, 189—221, 9 figs., 2 charts.

WAECHTER, JOHN
  1965   A preliminary report on four epi-Levallois sites.   In: Wendorf, Fred.,
            (ed.), 1965A, 117—145, 14 figs.
            See: Wendorf, Daugherty and Waechter.

WAGENBRETH, OTFRIED
  1965   Bernhard von Cotta, sein geologisches und philosophisches Lebenswerk an
            Hand ausgewählter Zitate.   Ber. Geol. Ges. Deutsch. Demokratischen
            Republ., A 12, Sonderheft 3, 172 pp., 27 figs., portr.
            See: Seidel and Wagenbreth.

WAGER, LAWRENCE RICKARD
  1964   The history of attempts to establish a quantitative time-scale.   In:
            Harland, W. B., et al., (eds.), 1964, 13—28, 6 figs., 2 tables.

WAGGONER, J., JR. See: Morse, Morse and Waggoner.

WAGLEY, CHARLES See: Solecki and Wagley.

WAGSTAFFE, REGINALD, and FIDLER, J. H.
   1968   The preservation of natural history specimens. Vol. 2. New York:
          Philosophical Library, 404 pp., illustr.

WAHLA, EDWARD J.
   1967   Holcombe caribou people in the light of studies of similar surviving
          hunters. Totem Pole, 50:1, 3–8, illustr.
        See: DeVisscher and Wahla; Fitting, DeVisscher and Wahla.

WAHLERT, GERD VON
   1966   Teilhard de Chardin und die moderne Theorie der Evolution der Organismen.
          Stuttgart: Fischer, vi + 45 pp., (not seen).
        Rev.: Gutmann in Natur u. Museum, 98:8, 350–351; Haltenorth in
          Säugetierkundl. Mitt., 14, 355; Kurth in Kosmos (Stuttgart), 62,
          *203; Sauter in Arch. Suiss. Anthrop. Gen., 31, 56; Schaeuble
          in Zeit. Morph. Anthrop., 58, 212; Schindewolf in Zbl. Geol.
          Pal., Teil 2, 1966, 458–459; Thenius in Mitt. Geol. Ges. Wien,
          58, 294–295.

WAINWRIGHT, G. J., and MALIK, S. C.
   1967   Recent field research on problems of archaeology and Pleistocene chrono-
          logy in Peninsular India. Proc. Prehist. Soc. Cambridge, 33, 132–
          146, 4 figs., 2 tables.

WAKE, DAVID B.
   1966   Comparative osteology and evolution of the lungless salamanders, family
          Plethodontidae. Mem. S. Calif. Acad. Sci., 4, viii + 111 pp., 33
          figs., 2 tables.
        Rev.: Freytag in Salamandra, 6:1/2, 71; Rabb in Copeia, 1967, 494–
          496.

WAKE, D. B., and DRESNER, I. G.
   1967   Functional morphology and evolution of tail autotomy in salamanders.
          Jour. Morphol., 122, 265–306, 24 figs., 8 pls., 2 tables.

WALCZAK, WOJCIECH
   1963   New traces of Paleolithic man in Sudet. Man in Time and Space, 6:1,
          (not seen).

WALDMAN, MICHAEL
   1967   Mesozoic fish from Koonwarra, Victoria. 39th Congr., ANZAAS, Mel-
          bourne, 1967, Sec. C, pp. K2–3, (abs.).

WALDREN, WILLIAM H.
   1966   Myotragus balearicus. Frontiers, 30, 105–107, illustr.
        See: Graves, W. and Waldren.

WALENSKY, NORMAN AARON
   1964   A re-evaluation of the mastoid region of contemporary and fossil man.
          Anat. Rec., 149, 67–72, 3 figs.

WALKER, A. C. See: Napier and Walker.

WALKER, A. D.
1964   Triassic reptiles from the Elgin area: Ornithosuchus and the origin of
              carnosaurs. Philos. Trans. Roy. Soc. London, Ser. B, 248:744,
              53–134, 18 figs.
              Abs.: Huene in Zbl. Geol. Pal., Teil 2, 1965, 253.
1966   Elachistosuchus, a Triassic rhynchocephalian from Germany. Nature,
              211, 583–585, 5 figs.
              Rev.: Huene in Zbl. Geol. Pal., Teil 2, 1969:1, 51–52.
1968   Protosuchus, Proterochampsa, and the origin of phytosaurs and crocodiles.
              Geol. Mag., 105, 1–14, 4 figs.
              Rev.: Huene in Zbl. Geol. Pal., Teil 2, 1969:1, 52.

WALKER, ALAN
1964   The giant lemurs of Madagascar. Human Biol., 36, 72, (abs.).
1967   Patterns of extinction among the subfossil Madagascan lemuroids. In:
              Martin, P. S., and Wright, H. E., (eds.), 1967, 425–432, 2 figs.
              See: Pilbeam and Walker.

WALKER, A., and ROSE, M. D.
1968   Fossil hominoid vertebra from the Miocene of Uganda. Nature, 217,
              980–981, 1 fig., 1 table.

WALKER, C. A.
1966   Podocnemis somaliensis, a new pleurodiran turtle from the Middle Eocene
              of Somalia. Palaeontol., 9, 511–516, 5 figs., pl. 80.

WALKER, ERNEST P.
1964   Mammals of the world. 3 vols. Baltimore: Johns Hopkins Press, 1500
              pp., illustr.

WALKER, G. F.
1967   The use of a mathematical model and a computer to predict cranial
              contents from skull fragments. Amer. Jour. Phys. Anthrop., 27,
              238, (abs.).

WALKER, HELEN
1968   San Bernardino's fossil beds. Desert Mag., 31:6, 6, 8, 1 fig.

WALKER, M. V.
1967   Revival of interest in the toothed birds of Kansas. Trans. Kansas Acad.
              Sci., 70, 60–66.

WALKER, R. M.   See: Fleischer, Leakey, Price and Walker.

WALLACE, BIRGITTA L.   See: Swauger and Wallace.

WALLACE, WILLIAM J.
1965   Current research: Great Basin. Amer. Antiq., 31, 301–302.

WALSH, J.   See: McCall, Baker and Walsh.

WALTER, HUBERT
1962   Die Entstehung der Menschheit in den Mythen der Völker. Kosmos
              (Stuttgart), 58, 122–125, 1 fig.

WALTON, ALAN
1967   Radioactive dating and methods of low-level counting. Antiq., 41, 317–318.

WALTON, A., TRAUTMAN, M. A., and FRIEND, J. P.
1961   Isotopes, Inc. radiocarbon measurements I. Radiocarbon, 3, 47–59.

WALTON, M. S., (ed.)
1963   A brochure published at the dedication of the Klein Geology Laboratory. New Haven: Yale Univ. Press.

WAMSER, W.
1959   Professor Dr. Hans Wehrli. Rektor der Ernst-Moritz-Arndt-Universität Greifswald. Ber. Geol. Ges. Deutsch. Demokratischen Republ., 4, 265.

WANG, AN-CHOU
1960   [Quaternary research in China.] Izv. Akad. Nauk SSSR, ser. geograf., 1960:2, 123–127, (Russian).

WANG, BAN-YUE
1965   A new Miocene aceratherine rhinoceros of Shanwang, Shantung. Vert. Palasiatica, 9, 109–113, 2 pls., (Chinese and English). See: Chow, M. and Wang.

WANG, CHIEN   See: Chia, Wang and Wang.

WANG, T. F.
1964   New techniques for cleaning fossils. Acta Pal. Sinica, 12, 536, 1 fig., (Chinese).

WANG, TSIANG-K'E   See: Liu, H.–T. and Wang.

WANG, TZE-YI   See: Chia, Wang and Wang.

WANG, T.–Y., and WANG, C.
1960   On the discovery of the palaeoliths at Gujiao, Shansi. Paleovert. et Paleoanthrop., 2:1, 59–60, (not seen).

WANKE, ADAM
1964A.   Sixty years of research work of Jan Czekanowski. Mat. Prace Antrop., 70, 7–27, (Polish and English).
1964B.   (ed.) Papers in honour of the sixty-years of Jan Czekanowski's research work. Mat. Prace Antrop., 70, 294 pp., illustr.
1965   Kongres Antropologiczno-Etnologiczny w Moskwie. Przegląd Antrop., 31, 192–196.

WARBURTON, F. E., and DENMAN, N. S.
1961   Larval competition and the origin of tetrapods. Evolution, 15, 566.

WARD, DEDERICK C.
1967   Geologic reference sources. Univ. Colorado Studies, Ser. Earth Sci., 5, xii + 114 pp.

WARGA, WAYNE
1966   The day the Bible beat the monkeys. Life, 61:24, 97–98, 4 figs.

WARING, A. J., and KELLEY, A. R.
    1965   The Paleo—Indian era: distribution of finds. Georgia. Bull. Southeast
               Archaeol. Confer., 2, 14.

WARNICA, JAMES M.
    1966   New discoveries at the Clovis site. Amer. Antiq., 31, 345—357, 9 figs.

WARREN, J. W.
    1965   Description of a fossil humerus (Marsupialia) from the Lower Pliocene
               of Victoria, Australia. Proc. Roy. Soc. Victoria, 79, 147—151, 1
               fig., pl. 20.

WARREN, J. W., and TALENT, J. A.
    1967   Lower Devonian fish from Buchan, Victoria. 39th Congr., ANZAAS,
               Melbourne, 1967, Sec. C, p. K1, (abs.).

WARREN, LYMAN O.
    1964   Possibly submerged oyster shell middens of Upper Tampa Bay. Florida
               Anthrop., 17, 227—230.
    1966   A possible Paleo-Indian site in Pinellas County. Florida Anthrop., 19,
               39—41, 1 pl.

WASHBURN, SHERWOOD L.
    1961B.   Rev.: Semenov in Voprosy Antrop., 14, 117—121, (Russian).
    1963A.   Rev.: Ascher in Amer. Sci., 52, 418A—419A; Haltenorth in Säugetier-
               kundl. Mitt., 14, 355; Heberer in Homo, 15, 249.
    1963C.   The curriculum in physical anthropology. In: Mandelbaum, D. G.,
               Lasker, G. W., and Albert, E. M., (eds.), 1963, 39—47.
    1964   The origin of races: Weidenreich's opinion. Amer. Anthrop., 66, 1165—
               1167, 1 fig.
               Rev.: Livingstone in Amer. Anthrop., 67, 1283—1284.
    1965   An ape's eye-view of human evolution. Discussion. In: DeVore, P. L.,
               1965, (ed.), 89—107.
    1966   Summary of design for man. Abs. 65th. Ann. Meeting Amer. Anthrop.
               Assoc., 1966, 71, (abs.).
    1967   An ape's eye-view of human evolution. Abs. 66th Ann. Meeting Amer.
               Anthrop. Assoc., 1967, 86, (abs.).

WASHBURN, S. L., and DeVORE, I.
    1964   Social behavior of baboons and early man. In: Lasker, G. W., (ed.),
               1964, 30—45, (reprint with editorial comment).

WASHBURN, S. L., and JAY, P. C.
    1964   Skill and the evolution of locomotion. Abs. 63rd. Ann. Meeting Amer.
               Anthrop. Assoc., 1964, 60, (abs.).
    1967   More on tool-use among primates. Current Anthrop., 8, 253—254.

WASSERSUG, R. J., and HECHT, M. K.
    1967   The status of the crocodylid genera Procaimanoidea and Hassiacosuchus
               in the New World. Herpetologica, 23, 30—34, 1 table.
               Rev.: Berg in Zbl. Geol. Pal., Teil 2, 1968:6, 656—657.

WATANABE, HITOSHI
    1964   Les "éclats et lames à Chanfrein" et la technique de fracturation transversale
               dans un horizon paléolithique en Palestine. Bull. Soc. Préhist.
               Franç., C. R. séances mens., 1964:4, LXXXIV—LXXXVIII, 2 figs.,

(Discussion, LXXXII—LXXXIII).

1965   Amud Cave. Israel Explor. Jour., 15:4, 246.

1968   A Palaeolithic industry from the Amud Cave, Israel. 7th Internat. Congr.
Anthrop. Ethnol. Sci., Moscow, 1964, 3, 320—326, 1 map, 4 pls.,
(46 figs.).

WATANABE, K.
1953   Some considerations on the geological horizons of desmostylids from the
Chichibu Basin, Saitama Prefecture and from other localities of
Honshu, Japan. Res. Bull. Chichibu Nat. Sci. Mus., no. 3, 43—60.

WATANABE, NAOTSUNE
1959   [The discovery of Zinjanthropus boisei.]   Jour. Anthrop. Soc. Nippon,
67, 296—299, 2 figs., (Japanese).

WATERBOLK, H. T.   See: Vogel, J. C. and Waterbolk.

WATERS, AARON C.   See: Gilluly, et al.

WATERS, SPENCER A.
1959   Red Hill, a Dalton site. Jour. Ala. Archaeol., 5, 77—81, pls. 12—13.

WATSON, DAVID MEREDITH SEARES
1962   Abs.: Huene in Zbl. Geol. Pal., Teil 2, 1964, 163—164.

WATSON, J. B., (ed.)
1964   New Guinea: the Central Highlands. Amer. Anthrop. Special Publ.,
66:4, ix + 329 pp., illustr.

WATSON, P. J.
1965   The chronology of North Syria and North Mesopotamia from 10,000 B.C.
to 2,000 B.C. The terminal food-collecting, incipient food-producing,
and earliest established food-producing settlements of North Syria
and North Mesopotamia. In: Ehrich, R. W., (ed.), 1965, 61—100.

WAUCHOPE, ROBERT
1956   (ed.) Seminars in archaeology: 1955. Mem. Soc. Amer. Archaeol.,
no. 11, ix + 158 pp., illustr.

1964   (ed.) Handbook of Middle American Indians. Vol. I. Natural environment and early cultures. Austin: Univ. Texas Press, viii + 570
pp., illustr.

1965   Alfred Vincent Kidder, 1885-1963. Amer. Antiq., 31, 149—171, portr.

1966A.   Archaeological survey of northern Georgia with a test of some cultural
hypotheses. Mem. Soc. Amer. Archaeol., no. 21, xxxii + 482 pp.,
258 figs., 52 tables.

1966B.   [Sunken continents and mysteries of lost tribes.] Transl. by E. V. Zibert.
Iu. V. Knorozov, (ed.). Moscow: "Mir" Press, 152 pp., illustr.,
(Russian).
Rev.: Afanas'ev in Sov. Etnog., 1968:6, 160—163, (Russian).

WEATHERSBEE, R. D.
1966   A collection of implements after top soil disturbance. Journal of the
Anthropological Society of South Australia, 4:4, 5—8.

WEAVER, W. G., JR.
1967   A re-evaluation of fossil turtles of the Chrysemys scripta group. Tulane

Studies Geol., 5, 53–66, 10 figs., 2 tables.
See: Rose, F. L. and Weaver.

WEAVER, W. G., JR., and ROSE, F. L.
1967   Systematics, evolution, and fossil record of the genus Chrysemys. Tulane
              Studies Zool., 14, 63–73, 12 figs., 1 table.

WEBB, CLARENCE H.
1968   James Alfred Ford, 1911–1968. Bull. Texas Archeol. Soc., 38, 135–146,
              bibliog.
              See: Gagliano, Gregory and Webb.

WEBB, G. L.
1965   Notes on some chalicothere remains from Makapansgat. Pal. Africana,
              9, 49–73, figs. 16–34, 2 pls.

WEBB, S. DAVID
1964A.   Stratigraphic position and phylogeny of the equid genus Calippus. Program,
              60th Ann. Meeting, Geol. Soc. Amer., Cordilleran Sect., 67, (abs.).
1964B.   The Alachua formation. Guidebk., Soc. Vert. Pal. 1964 field trip, Fla.,
              1964, 22–29, 4 figs., 1 table.
1965A.   Stratigraphic position and phylogeny of the equid genus Calippus. Spec.
              Pap. Geol. Soc. Amer., 82, 287, (abs.).
1965B.   New World origins of Old World camels. Program, Sect. E (Geol, Geog.),
              Amer. Assoc. Advanc. Sci., Meeting Dec. 26–31, 1965, 20–21, (abs.).
1965C.   The osteology of Camelops. Bull. Los Angeles Co. Mus., Science, no. 1,
              54 pp., 22 figs., 12 tables.
1966A.   A relict species of the burrowing rodent, Mylagaulus, from the Pliocene
              of Florida. Jour. Mammal., 47, 401–412, 3 figs., 2 tables.
1966B.   New World origins of Old World camels. Spec. Pap. Geol. Soc. Amer.,
              87, 320–321, (abs.).
1967A.   Fossil proboscideans of Florida. Plaster Jacket, 4, 2–11, 5 figs., 1 table.
1967B.   Reconnaissance in Central America. Plaster Jacket, 6, 8, 1 fig.

WEBB, S. D., and TESSMAN, N.
1967   Vertebrate evidence of a low sea level in the Middle Pliocene. Science,
              156, 379, 1 table.

WEBB, S. D., and WOODBURNE, M. O.
1966   The beginning of continental deposition in the Mount Diablo area. In:
              Savage, D. E., (ed.), 1966B, 9 pp., illustr.

WEBBER, E. LELAND
1966   Field Museum again. Name change honors Field family. Bull. Field Mus.
              Nat. Hist., 37:3, 2–3, 3 figs.

WEBER, EMIL
1951   Eine neue Lattorfium–Spaltenfüllung von Hagau bei Wemding–Ries. Neues
              Jahrb. Geol. Pal., Monatsh., 1951, 119–124, 1 fig.
              Abs.: Raabe in Zbl. Geol. Pal., Teil 2, 1964, 841.

WEBER, ROBERT H.
1963   Human prehistory of Socorro County. Guidebk., New Mexico Geol.
              Soc., 14th Field Confer., 1963, 225–233, 1 pl.

WEBER, T. J.
1963   A fluted point from Casper Mountain. Wyo. Archaeol., 6:4, 2—4, 1 fig.
1964   The more important archaeological sites in Wyoming. Wyo. Geol. Assoc.
             Guidebk., Highway Geol. Wyo., 1964, 1—7, 2 figs. Reprinted in
             Wyo. Archaeol., 8:1, 9—18, 2 figs.

WEBSTER, DAVID
1964A.   A history of Cherokee Cave, St. Louis, Missouri. Missouri Speleology,
             6, 53—63, 4 pls.
1964B.   Cherokee Cave bone deposit. Missouri Speleology, 6, 79—86, illustr.

WEBSTER, GARY D. See: Weide and Webster.

WECKLER, J. E. See: Brace 1964.

WEDEL, WALDO R.
1964A.   The Great Plains. In: Jennings and Norbeck (eds.), 1964A, 193—220,
             2 figs.
             Rev.: Baerreis in Amer. Antiq., 30, 504—505.
1964B.   Prehistoric man on the Great Plains. Norman: Univ. Oklahoma Press,
             xviii + 355 pp., 25 figs., 28 pls.
1967   Salvage archeology in the Missouri River basin. Science, 156, 589—597,
             9 figs.

WEDEL, W. R., HUSTED, W. M., and MOSS, J. H.
1968   Mummy cave: prehistoric record from Rocky Mountains of Wyoming.
             Science, 160, 184—186, 1 fig.

WEDLAKE, A. L. and D. J.
1963   Some palaeoliths from the Doniford gravels on the coast of West Somerset.
             Proc. Somersetshire Archaeol. Nat. Hist. Soc., 107, (not seen).

WEEKS, C. FRANCIS See: Krueger and Weeks.

WEGNER, H.
1965   Der Fossiliensammler. Eine Anleitung zum Sammeln, Präparieren und
             Aufbewahren von Versteinerungen. Thun and München: Ott,
             160 pp., 32 figs., 12 pls.
             Rev.: Rietschel in Umschau, 65:22, III; Sittig in Aufschluss, 16, 116.

WEI, CHENG-YI
1964   New discovery of Quaternary mammal fossils from the Sungary-Liaoning
             Plain. Vert. Palasiatica, 8:3, 322—323, illustr., (Chinese).

WEIDE, DAVID L., and WEBSTER, G. D.
1967   Ammonium chloride powder used in the photography of artifacts. Amer.
             Antiq., 32, 104—105, 2 figs.

WEIGEL, R. D.
1962B.   Fossil vertebrates of Vero, Florida. Diss. Abst., 22, 2922, (abs.).
1967   Fossil birds from Miller's Cave, Llano Co., Texas. Texas Jour. Sci., 19,
             107—109.

WEILER, WILHELM
1961A.   Abs.: Weiler in Zbl. Geol. Pal., Teil 2, 1964, 155.

1961E.   Abs.: Bartenstein in Zbl. Geol. Pal., Teil 2, 1962, 262.

1962F.   Hautplatten eines Selachiers aus dem Miozän der Tongrube von Todtglüsingen,
            Krs. Harburg. Geol. Jahrb., 80, 237–238, 1 fig.
            Abs.: Weiler in Zbl. Geol. Pal., Teil 2, 1964, 155.

1962G.   Fisch-Otolithen aus dem oberen Mittelmiozän von Twistringen, Bez.
            Bremen (NW-Deutschland). Geol. Jahrb., 80, 277–294, 2 figs.,
            (English and French summaries).
            Abs.: Hiltermann in Zbl. Geol. Pal., Teil 2, 1964, 156.

1963   Abs.: Weiler in Zbl. Geol. Pal., Teil 2, 1964, 157–159.

1965   Die Fischfauna des interglazialen Beckentons von Bilshausen bei Göttingen.
            Neues Jahrb. Geol. Pal., Abh., 123:2, 202–219, 19 figs., 2 pls.

1966A.   Die Fischfauna des Helvets von Ivančice (Eibenschitz) in Mähren. Pal.
            Zeit., 40:1–2, 118–143, 50 figs.
            Rev.: Weiler in Zbl. Geol. Pai., Teil 2, 1967, 505.

1966B.   Die Bedeutung der Fischfunde im Rupelton der Tongrube Frauenweiler
            bei Wiesloch südlich Heidelberg. Zeit. Rhein. Naturf. Ges. Mainz,
            4, 17–25, 9 figs., (not seen).
            Abs.: Weiler in Zbl. Geol. Pal., Teil 2, 1966, 289–290.
            See: Albers and Weiler.

WEINBURGER, L.
1960   Der Mastodonfund von Mettmach. Die Heimat. Heimatkalender Beil.
            "Rieder Volkz.", no. 11, 1–2, (not seen).

WEINER, J. S.
1964   The pattern of evolutionary development of the genus Homo. In: Lasker,
            G. W., (ed.), 1964, 79–89, 4 figs., (reprint with editorial comment).
            See: Baker, P. T. and Weiner; Day 1965; Harrison, et al.; Penniman
            1965.

WEINERT, HANS
1956   Das Problem der Hominiden–Abzweigung von den Anthropoiden. Ber.
            Tagung Deutsch. Ges. Anthrop., 5, 36–38.

WEINFURTE, E. See: Bachmayer and Weinfurte.

WEINFURTER, EMIL
1967   Die miozäne Otolithenfauna von St. Veit an der Triesting, NÖ. Ann.
            Naturhist. Mus. Wien, 71, 381–393, 2 pls., (English summary).
            Rev.: Weiler in Zbl. Geol. Pal., Teil 2, 1968:6, 655.
            See: Sieber and Weinfurter.

WEITZ, JOSEPH L.
1966   Your future in geology. New York: Rosen, 192 pp., illustr., (not seen).

WEITZMAN, STANLEY H.
1960A.   The systematic position of Piton's presumed characid fishes from the
            Eocene of Central France. Stanford Ichthyol. Bull., 7:4, 114–123,
            2 figs.
            Rev.: Weiler in Zbl. Geol. Pal., Teil 2, 1969:3, 288–289.

1960B.   Further notes on characid fossils. Stanford Ichthyol. Bull., 7:4, 215–
            216.

1960C.   The phylogenetic relationships of Triporthens, a genus of South American
            characid fishes. Stanford Ichthyol. Bull. 7:4, 239–244, 1 fig.

1967   The origin of the stomiatoid fishes with comments on the classification
            of salmoniform fishes. Copeia, 1967, 507–540, 18 figs.

See: Greenwood, et al.

WELLER, J. MARVIN
1964   Paleontology collections of the University of Chicago. Jour. Pal., 38,
            1007.
1965A.   Palaeontology, evolution and taxonomy. In: Jhingran, A. G., et al.,
            (eds.), 1965, 217—225.
1965B.   Presidential address: The status of paleontology. Jour. Pal., 39, 741—
            749.
1968   Evolution of mammalian teeth. Jour. Pal., 42, 268—290, 20 figs.

WELLES, SAMUEL P.
1962   Abs.: Huene in Zbl. Geol. Pal., Teil 2, 1964, 176.
1967   Arizona's giant amphibians. Pac. Discovery, 20:4, 10—15, illustr.
            See: Fox, W. and Welles.

WELLES, S. P., and COSGRIFF, J.
1964   Description of a new species of Parotosaurus from the Wupatki member
            of the Moenkopi formation of northern Arizona. Program, 60th
            Ann. Meeting, Geol. Soc. Amer., Cordilleran Sect., 67, (abs.).
1965A.   Description of a new species of Parotosaurus from the Wupatki member
            of the Moenkopi formation of northern Arizona. Spec. Pap. Geol.
            Soc. Amer., 82, 287, (abs.).
1965B.   A revision of the labyrinthodont family Capitosauridae and a description
            of Parotosaurus peabodyi, n. sp. from the Wupatki member of the
            Moenkopi formation of northern Arizona. Univ. Calif. Publ. Geol.
            Sci., 54, 1—148, 48 figs., 1 pl., 3 tables.
            Rev.: Hotton in Jour. Pal., 41, 269.
            Abs.: Westphal in Zbl. Geol. Pal., Teil 2, 1966, 297—298.

WELLES, S. P., and SLAUGHTER, B. H.
1963   Abs.: Huene in Zbl. Geol. Pal., Teil 2, 1964, 522.

WELLNHOFER, P.
1968   Uber Pterodactylus kochi (Wagner 1837). Neues Jahrb. Geol. Pal., Abh.,
            132:1, 97—126, 7 figs., 2 pls., 2 tables, (English summary).

WELLS, A. K., and KIRKALDY, J. F.
1966   Outline of historical geology. 5th rev. ed. London: Thomas Murby,
            503 pp., 133 figs.
            Rev.: deJong in Geol. en Mijn., 45, 361; W.S.M. in Geol. Mag., 103,
            376—377.

WELLS, CALVIN
1964A.   Bones, bodies and disease. Evidence of disease and abnormality in early
            man. Ancient peoples and places Vol. 37. London: Thames and
            Hudson, 288 pp., 41 figs., 88 pls.
            Rev.: Anon. in Sci. Amer., 212:5, 145—146; Armelagos in Amer. Anthrop.,
            68:5, 1309; Armelagos in Southwestern Lore, 31:3, inside back
            cover; Brothwell in Mus. Jour., London, 64, 340—341; Duggan
            in Antiq., 38, 311—312; Goff in Amer. Jour. Phys. Anthrop., 22,
            493—494; Gould in New Sci., 22, 633; Janssens in Helinium, 4,
            282—284; Roberts in Man, 65, 164; S. in Archeol. Roz., 18,
            95, (Czech); Stewart in Science, 145, 568—569; Taylor in New
            Zealand Archaeol. Assoc. Newsletter, 9, 39; Thomson in Antiq.
            Jour., 44, 275—276; V[allois] in L'Anthrop., 68, 605—606;

Warwick in Archaeol. Jour., 121, 215–216.

1964B.   Anomalous elephant tooth from the Forest Bed deposit near Corton,
Suffolk. Discussion by E. I. White and L. B. Tarlo. Proc. Geol.
Soc. London, 1615, 52–55, 1 fig.

1964C.   Pathological epipodials and tarsus in Stretosaurus macromerus from the
Kimmeridge Clay, Stretham, Cambridgeshire, (abs.). Discussion by
Tarlo, with reply by Wells. Proc. Geol. Soc. London, 1615, 55–57.
Abs.: Huene in Zbl. Geol. Pal., Teil 2, 1964, 991.

1964D.   Pathological epipodials and tarsus in Stretosaurus macromerus from the
Kimmeridge Clay, Stretham, Cambridgeshire. Quart. Jour. Geol. Soc.
London, 120, 299–304, pl. 13.

1967   Pseudopathology. In: Brothwell, D. and Sandison, A. T., (eds.), 1967,
5–19, 8 figs.
See: Sandison and Wells.

WELLS, JOHN W.
1964   The antiarch Asterolepis in the Upper Devonian of New York. Jour.
Pal., 38, 492–495, pls. 73–74.

WELLS, LAWRENCE HERBERT
1963D.   The end of an old song: the age of the Galley Hill skeleton. S. Afr.
Archaeol. Bull., 18, 183–184.

1964A.   A large extinct antelope skull from the "Younger Gravels" at Sydney-on-
Vaal, C. P. S. African Jour. Sci., 60, 88–91, 3 figs.

1964B.   The Vaal River "Younger Gravels" faunal assemblage: a revised list. S.
African Jour. Sci., 60, 91–93.

1965   Antelopes in the Pleistocene of southern Africa. Zool. Afr., 1, 115–120.

1967   Antelopes in the Pleistocene of southern Africa. Discussion. In: Bishop,
W. W., and Clark, J. D., (eds.), 1967A, 99–107, 1 table, (French
summary).
See: Tobias and Wells; Trevor and Wells.

WELLS, PHILIP V.
1966   Late Pleistocene vegetation and degree of pluvial climatic change in the
Chihuahuan Desert. Science, 153, 970–975, 2 figs., 1 table.

WELLS, P. V., and BERGER, R.
1967   Late Pleistocene history of coniferous woodland in the Mojave Desert.
Science, 155, 1640–1647, 3 figs., 1 table.

WELLS, P. V., and JORGENSEN, C. D.
1964   Pleistocene wood rat middens and climatic change in Mohave Desert: a
record of juniper woodlands. Science, 143, 1171–1174, 2 figs.

WELSCH, ULRICH
1967   Tooth wear of upper prosimian molars. In: Starck, D., Schneider, R.,
and Kuhn, H. J., (eds.), 1967, 137–139, 1 fig.

WEN
1966   Field activity of IVPP in 1965. Vert. Palasiatica, 10, 88–89.

WENDEL, CLARENCE A.
1967   Dinosaur for Turkey. GeoTimes, 12:6, 6, 8.

WENDORF, FRED

1965A.   (ed.) Contributions to the prehistory of Nubia. Publ. Fort Burgwin Research Center, no. 4, 200 pp., illustr.

    Rev.: Kleindienst in Man, Jour. Roy. Anthrop. Inst., 2, 135—136; Lister in Science, 151, 1074; Shinnie in Jour. Afr. Hist., 7, 536—537; Smith in Amer. Anthrop., 68:4, 1074—1075.

1965B.   Preface. In: Wendorf, Fred., (ed.), 1965A, iii — vi.

1965C.   Pre-pottery horizons of the Great Plains. 7th Internat. Congr., Internat. Assoc. Quat. Res., Abs., 1965, 498, (abs.).

1966   Early man in the New World. Problems of migration. Amer. Nat., 100, 253—270, 7 figs., 2 tables.

    See: Albritton and Wendorf.

WENDORF, F., DAUGHERTY, R. D., and WAECHTER, J.

1964   The Museum of New Mexico—Columbia University Nubian Expedition. The 1962-63 field programme. Kush, 12, 12—18, 1 fig., pls. 1—2.

WENDORF, F., and SAID, R.

1967   Palaeolithic remains in Upper Egypt. Nature, 215, 244—247, 1 fig.

WENDORF, F., SHINER, J. L., and MARKS, A. E.

1965   Contributions to the prehistory of Nubia, introduction. Summary of the 1963-1964 field season. In: Wendorf, Fred., (ed.), 1965A, ix — xxxv, 11 figs.

WENDORF, F., SHINER, J. L., MARKS, A. E., HEINZELIN, J. DE, and CHMIELEWSKI, W.

1965   The Combined Prehistoric Expedition: summary of 1963-64 field season. Kush, 13, 28—55, 12 figs.

WENDT, G. G. See: Ax, 1964.

WENDT, HERBERT

1963   Op zoek naar de eerste mens. Antwerp: W. De Haan, Zeist, van Loghum Slaterus, Arnhem en Standaard Boekhandel, viii + 316 pp., illustr., (not seen).

    Rev.: K. in Natuurhist. Maandbl., 52, 114—116.

1965A.   Ehe die Sintflut kam. Forscher entdecken die Urwelt. Oldenburg, Hamburg: Gerhard Stalling Verlag, 392 pp., illustr., (not seen).

    Rev.: Kurth in Naturwiss. Rund, 19, 79; Thenius in Kosmos (Stuttgart), 62, *277.

1965B.   Ich suchte Adam. Die Entdeckung des Menschen. rororo Taschenbuch Nr. 707—709. Rowohlt: Hamburg-Reinbek, 503 pp., 67 figs., 26 pls., (not seen).

    Rev.: Felgenhaur in Archaeol. Austriaca, 38, 113—114; Preuschoft in Anthrop. Anz., 28, 138—139; Schaueble in Zeit. Morph. Anthrop., 57, 313—314.

1968   Before the deluge. Translated from German by R. and C. Winston. London: Victor Gollancz Publ., and New York: Doubleday, 419 pp., illustr.

    Rev.: Schneer in GeoTimes, 14:2, 31—32.

WENINGER, MARGARETE

1962   Der Wandel der Kopfform im Laufe der Menschheitgeschichte. Umschau, 62, 263—265, 4 figs.

WENZ, SYLVIE
1964   Étude d'un nouveau Notagogus de la province de Lerida (Espagne). Bull.
            Soc. Géol. France, 6, 269–272, 1 fig., pl. 12b.
            Rev.: M. C. in Fossilia, 1965:5–6, 66; H.–P. in Bol. Soc. Espan. Hist.
            Nat., Sec. Geol., 63:2–3, 264.
1965A.   Les poissons Albiens de Vallentigny (Aube). Ann. Pal., Vert., 51:1, 1–23,
            5 figs., pls. 1–2.
1965B.   Sur un nouveau Furo, F. normandica, poisson holostéen du Toarcien de
            la Caine (Calvados). C. R. Soc. Géol. France, 1965, 145–146, 1
            fig.
1967A.   Remarques sur les transformations des os dermiques du museau chez les
            Actinoptérygiens. Colloq. Internat. Cent. Nation. Recherch. Sci.,
            163, 89–92, 3 figs., (English summary).
1967B.   Compléments à l'étude des poissons actinoptérygiens du Jurassique français.
            Paris: Cahiers de Paléontologie, Eds. C.N.R.S., 276 pp., 110 figs.,
            48 pls.
            Rev.: Lund in Quart. Rev. Biol., 44:4, 405; Waldman in Can. Field-Natur.
            84:3, 323–325.
1968A.   Contribution à l'étude du genre Metriorhynchus. Crâne et moulage endo-
            cranien de Metriorhynchus superciliosus. Ann. Pal., Vert., 54:2,
            149–183, 11 figs., 4 pls.
1968B.   Note préliminaire sur la faune ichthyologique du Jurassique supérieur du
            Montsech (Espagne). Bull. Soc. Géol. France, 10, 116–119, 1 pl.

WENZEL, RUPERT L., and TIPTON, V. J., (eds.)
1966   Ectoparasites of Panama. Chicago: Field Mus. of Nat. Hist., xii + 861
            pp., illustr., (not seen).

WERMUTH, HEINZ
1964   Die Wandelbarkeit des Schildkrötenpanzers. Schrift. Ver. Verbreitung
            Naturwiss. Kenntnisse Wien, 104, 97–117, 5 figs.

WERNER, DAVID J.
1964   Vestiges of Paleo-Indian occupation near Port Jervis, N. Y. New World
            Antiq., 11, 30–52, 5 figs. Reprinted in Chesopiean, 2:5, 98–113,
            1964.

WERNER, YEHUDAH L.
1965   Georg Haas, on the occasion of his sixtieth birthday. Israel Jour. Zool.,
            14, 5–6, portr.

WERNERT, PAUL
1961B.   Les boules de loess d'Achenheim et les "little mirr" – Essai d'ethno-
            graphie comparée. Cahiers Alsaciens Archéol. Art Hist., 5, 5–18,
            (not seen).
            Rev.: Anon. in Riv. Studi Liguri, 28, 291.
1963   Les boules de loess d'Achenheim et les "lhitte mirr". Essai de paléo-
            ethnographie comparée. Cahiers, Alsaciens Archéol. Art Hist.,
            7, 5–18, 4 figs.
            Rev.: Anon. in Acta Praehist., 1966, 5–7, 313.

WESCOTT, ROGER W.
1966A.   The evolution of language: reopening a closed subject. Abs. 65th Ann.
            Meeting Amer. Anthrop. Assoc., 1966, 72, (abs.).
1966B.   Neanderthal Man and the origin of speech. Program, Sixth Ann. Meeting
            Northeastern Anthrop. Assoc., 12.

1967   The exhibitionistic origin of human bipedalism. Man, Jour. Roy. Anthrop.
      Inst., 2, 630.

WESLEY, WILLIAM H.
1967   Site report 40GL−1, Giles County, Tennessee. Tenn. Archaeol., 23,
      45−57, 6 figs., 4 pls., 1 table.

WEST, FREDERICK HADLEIGH
1963   Leaf-shaped points in the western Arctic. Anthrop. Pap. Univ. Alaska,
      10:2, 51−62, 3 figs.
1966   Ivar Skarland, 1899-1965. Amer. Anthrop., 68, 132−133, portr.

WEST, ROBERT C., (ed.)
1964   Handbook of Middle American Indians. Vol. I. Natural environment and
      early cultures. Austin: University of Texas Press, 570 pp., illustr.
      Rev.: Hester in Amer. Antiq., 31, 445−446; Meggers in Amer. Jour.
      Archaeol., 69, 386−387.

WEST, R. G.
1967   The Quaternary of the British Isles. In: Rankama, K., (ed.), 1967, Vol.
      2, 1−87, 25 figs., 10 tables.
1968   Pleistocene geology and biology with especial reference to the British
      Isles. London: Longmans, xiii + 377 pp., figs., 16 pls., tables.
      Rev.: Anon. in Earth Sci. J., 2:2, 194; Bishop in Nature, 220, 718;
      deJong in Geol. en Mijn., 48:6, 578−579; Wright in Science, 164,
      539.

WEST, R. G., and SPARKS, B. W.
1960   Coastal Interglacial deposits of the English Channel. Philos. Trans. Roy.
      Soc. London, Ser. B., 243:701, 95−133, 13 figs., pl. 16.

WEST, W. D.
1964   The Geological Survey of India. Sci. and Culture, 30, 211−212.
1965   D. N. Wadia − an appreciation. In: Jhingran, A. G., et al., (eds.), 1−9,
      portr.

WESTERMANN, G. E. G.
1967   Last notice International Paleontological Union. Jour. Pal., 41, 1034.

WESTGATE, J. A.
1965   The Pleistocene stratigraphy of southeastern Alberta, Canada. 7th Internat.
      Congr., Internat. Assoc. Quat. Res., Abs., 1965, 500−501, (abs.).

WESTOLL, THOMAS STANLEY
1967   Radotina and other tesserate fishes. In: Patterson, C., and Greenwood,
      P. H., (eds.), 1967, 83−98, 3 figs.
      See: Miles, R. S. and Westoll.

WESTPHAL, FRANK
1962C.   Der Übergang vom Reptil zum Säugetier. Natur, 70, 77−83, 6 figs.,
      (not seen).
1963A.   Abs.: Huene in Zbl. Geol. Pal., Teil 2, 1964, 522−523.
1963C.   Ein fossilführendes Jungtertiar-Profil aus dem Randecker Maar (Schwabische
      Alb). Jahresb. Mitt. Oberrhein. Geol. Ver., 45, 27−44, 7 figs.,
      1 pl.
1965   Ein neuer Krokodil-Fund aus dem Plattenkalk des Oberen Malms von
      Eichstätt (Bayern). Neues Jahrb. Geol. Pal., Abh., 123, 105−114,
      2 figs., pls. 7−8.

Abs.: Huene in Zbl. Geol. Pal., Teil 2, 1966, 307.

1967A.   Erster Nachweis des Riesensalamanders (Andrias, Urodela, Amphibia) im
europäischen Jungpliozän. Neues Jahrb. Geol. Pal., Monatsh., 1967:9,
67–73, 1 fig., (English summary).
Rev.: Westphal in Zbl. Geol. Pal., Teil 2, 1967, 509.

1967B.   Eine Fledermaus (Tadarida, Chiroptera) aus dem Obermiozän des Randecker
Maars (Schwäbische Alb). Neues Jahrb. Geol. Pal., Monatsh 1967:9,
564–570, 5 figs.

1968   Fossile Fledermäuse im Tertiär von Württemberg. Umschau, 1968:5, 148,
1 fig.

WETMORE, ALEXANDER
1967   Re-creating Madagascar's giant extinct bird. Nation. Geog. Mag., 132:4,
488–493, illustr.

WETTSTEIN-WESTERSHEIMB, OTTO
1966   Kleinere Wirbeltiere. In: Ehrenberg, (ed.), 1966A, 89–92, 1 table.

WETZEL, W.
1966   Marine Zwergfische im Jungmesozoikum und Alttertiär, ein besonderes
Kapitel der Mikropaläontologie. Neues Jahrb. Geol. Pal., Monatsh.,
1966:5, 293–304, 15 figs.
Rev.: Weiler in Zbl. Geol. Pal., Teil 2, 1967, 506.

WHEAT, JOE BEN
1963   Prehistoric people of the northern Southwest. 3rd ed. Bull. Grand
Canyon Nat. Hist. Assoc., no. 12, iv + 39 pp., 11 pls., 2 maps.

1966   Final report on the Olsen-Chubbuck site. Plains Anthrop., 11, 170, (abs.).
See: Irwin and Wheat.

WHEAT, J. B., and IRWIN, H. T.
1965   Results of the University of Colorado excavations of Palaeolithic and
Mesolithic sites in Nubia. 7th Internat. Congr., Internat. Assoc.
Quat. Res., Abs., 1965, 503–504, (abs.).

WHEELER, WALTER H. See: Dorr and Wheeler.

WHIPPLE, HAROLD E., and SILVERZWEIG, S., (eds.)
1962   The relations of man: modern studies of the relation of the evolution
of nonhuman primates to human evolution. Ann. N. Y. Acad.
Sci., 102, 183–514.

WHISTLER, DAVID P.
1966   New Hemingfordian (Middle Miocene) mammalian fauna from Boron,
California, and its stratigraphic implications within the western
Mojave Desert. Program, 62nd Ann. Meeting, Geol. Soc. Amer.,
Cordilleran Sect., 1966, 76, (abs.). Also: Spec. Pap. Geol. Soc.
Amer., 101, 344–345, (abs.).

1967   Oreodonts of the Tick Canyon formation, Southern California. PaleoBios,
1, 1–14, 2 figs., 2 tables.

WHITAKER, GEORGE O., and MEYERS, J.
1965   Dinosaur hunt. Photographs by G. O. Whitaker and drawings by Michael
Insinna. New York: Harcourt, Brace and World, Inc., 94 pp.,
illustr.

Rev.: Anon. in Rocks and Minerals, 42, 362; Imbrie in Nat. Hist., 74:9, 13; Matthews in GeoTimes, 10:6, 38—39; Whitmore in GeoTimes, 10:6, 36—37.

WHITAKER, J. H. McD.
1966   Geology for the blind. Mus. Jour., London, 65, 299—300.

WHITE, ALEXANDER M.
1966   Ninety-seventh annual report of the president. Ann. Rept. Amer. Mus. Nat. Hist., 97, 3—8.

WHITE, CARMEL
1967   Early stone axes in Arnhem Land. Antiq., 41, 149—152, 1 fig., 2 tables. See: Calaby and White.

WHITE, ERROL IVOR
1944   The genus Phialaspis and the 'Psammosteus Limestones.' Abs. Proc. Geol. Soc. London, 1407, 6—10, (not seen).
1950D.   A fish from the Bunter near Kidderminster. Trans. Worcs. Nat. Club, 10, 185—189.
1954   [Note on a tooth of Hybodus grossiconus Agassiz from the Great Oolite of Salperton, Glos.] Proc. Cotteswold Nat. Fld. Club, 31, 123.
1955B.   The earliest reference to fossil fishes. News Bull. Soc. Vert. Pal., 43, 6.
1960B.   The coelacanth fishes. In: True, W. P., (ed.), 2, 610—622.
1965   The head of Dipterus valenciennesi Sedgwick and Murchison. Bull. Brit. Mus. (Nat. Hist.) Geol., 11:1, 1—45, 51 figs., 3 pls.
1966   Presidential address: A little on lung-fishes. Proc. Linn. Soc. London, 177, 1—10, 5 figs., 2 pls.
See: Casier 1966A; Croft and White; Dineley 1966B; Patterson, C. and Greenwood; Wells, C. 1964B.

WHITE, JOHN A.
1964   Kangaroo rats (family Heteromyidae) of the Vallecito Creek Pleistocene. Program, 60th Ann. Meeting, Geol. Soc. Amer., Cordilleran Sect., 68—69, (abs.).
1965   Kangaroo rats (family Heteromyidae) of the Vallecito Creek Pleistocene of California. Spec. Pap. Geol. Soc. Amer., 82, 288—289, (abs.).
1966   A new Peromyscus from the Late Pleistocene of Anacapa Island, California, with notes on variation in Peromyscus nesodytes Wilson. Contrib. Sci., Los Angeles Co. Mus., 96, 1—8, 4 figs., 1 table.
1967   The Hagerman zebra and other wildlife. Idaho Yesterdays, 11:1, 20—21.
1968   A new porcupine from the Middle Pleistocene of the Anza-Borrego Desert of California. With notes on mastication in Coendou and Erethizon. Contrib. Sci., Los Angeles Co. Mus., 136, 1—15, 8 figs., 2 tables.
See: Downs and White.

WHITE, THEODORE E.
1967   Dinosaurs at home. New York: Vantage, 232 pp., illustr., (for 12—16 age group).
Rev.: C. B. in Nat. Hist., 77:8, 82.

WHITEHEAD, G. KENNETH
1964   The deer of Great Britain and Ireland. An account of their history, status and distribution. London: Routledge and Kegan Paul, xv + 597 pp., 95 figs., 15 maps, 40 tables.
Rev.: Haltenorth in Säugetierkundl. Mitt., 13, 144.

WHITING, H. PHILIP
    1964   Arthrodiran anatomy. Nature, 203, 1023.
                See: Tarlo, L. B. H. and Whiting.

WHITING, H. P., and TARLO, L. B. H.
    1965   The brain of the Heterostraci (Agnatha). Nature, 207, 829–831, 2 figs.

WHITMORE, FRANK C., JR.
    1960   Fossil mammals from Ishigaki-Shima. Ryūkyū-Rettō. Prof. Pap., U.S.
                Geol. Surv., 400B, B372–B374.
    1967A.   Presentation of the Paleontological Society medal to Alfred S. Romer.
                Response by Alfred S. Romer. Jour. Pal., 41, 817–819, portr.
    1967B.   Elephants under the sea. Sci. Digest, 61:4, 15–16, 3 figs.
                See: Schultz, C. B., Tanner, et al.; Schultz, C. B., Whitmore and Tanner.

WHITMORE, F. C., JR., EMERY, K. O., COOKE, H. B. S., and SWIFT, D. J. P.
    1967   Elephant teeth from the Atlantic continental shelf. Science, 156, 1477–
                1481, 3 figs., 1 table.

WHITMORE, F. C., JR., and FOSTER, H. L.
    1967   Panthera atrox (Mammalia: Felidae) from central Alaska. Jour. Pal.,
                41, 247–251, 1 fig., 1 table.

WHITMORE, F. C., JR., and STEWART, R. H.
    1965   Miocene mammals and Central American seaways. Science, 148, no.
                3667, 180–185, 2 figs.

WHITTINGTON, HARRY BLACKMORE See: Cooper, G. A. and Whittington.

WHITTINGTON, H. B., and WILLIAMS. A.
    1964   The Ordovician period. In: Harland, W. B., et al., (eds.), 241–254, 1
                table.

WHITWORTH, THOMAS
    1965   Artifacts from Turkana, northern Kenya. S. Afr. Archaeol. Bull., 20:78,
                75–78, 17 figs.
    1966   A fossil hominid from Rudolf. S. Afr. Archaeol. Bull., 21, 138–150,
                3 figs., 1 pl., 4 tables.

WHYTE, LANCELOT LAW
    1965   Internal factors in evolution. New York: George Braziller, 128 pp.
                London: Tavistock, XXIII + 81 pp.
                Rev.: Bauchau in Rev. Questions Sci., 28, 287–288.

WICHLER, GERHARD
    1963   Charles Darwin. Der Forscher und der Mensch. München and Basel:
                Reinhardt, 240 pp., 22 figs., (not seen).
                Rev.: Ax in Naturwiss. Rund., 17, 284; Heberer in Naturwiss, 51,
                324; Kurth in Kosmos, (Stuttgart), 61, *494–*495; Magdefrau
                in Homo, 15, 253; Mertens in Natur u. Mus., 94, 214.

WICKLER, W.
    1960   Die Stammesgeschichte typischer Bewegungsformen der Fischbrustflosse.
                Zeits. Tierpsychologie, 17, 31–66, 19 figs., (English summary).

WICKMAN, FRANS E.
1968   How to express time in geology. Amer. Jour. Sci., <u>266</u>, 316–318.

WIDMER, BRUNO
1966   Ein Elefanten-Backenzahn aus der Kiesgrube Witzberg bei Pfäffikon (Kanton Zürich). Vierteljahrsschr. Naturf. Ges. Zürich, <u>111</u>:1, 125–140, 4 figs., 1 pl., 5 tables, (French and English summaries).

WIEBE, MAIDI   See: Posin 1961.

WIEDENROTH, KURT
1962   Der Lias ∈ im nördlichen Vorharzgebiet. Aufschluss, <u>13</u>, 121–124, 3 figs., cover photo.

WIERCIŃSKI, ANDRZEJ
1959B.   Le problème des fouilles sytématiques à Gánovce (Slovaquie). Przegląd Antrop., <u>25</u>, 111–122, 4 tables, (Polish; French summary).
1961   The problem of evolutionary rate of craniometric traits in Hominidae. Internat. Assoc. Quat. Res., Abs. Pap., 6th Congr., 147–148, (abs.).
     See: Kapica and Wierciński.

WIESEMANN, GERD   See: Huckriede and Wiesemann.

WIKTOR, ANDRZEJ   See: Kowalski, K., Kozłowski, <u>et al.</u>

WILCOCK, B.   See: Harland, Smith and Wilcock.

WILDIERS, N. M.
1964   Teilhard de Chardin, een inleiding in zijn denken. Antwerpen-Amsterdam: N. V. Standaard-Boekhandel, 184 pp., (not seen).
     Rev.: Huybens in Rev. Questions Sci., <u>26</u>, 319.

WILF, ALEXANDER, and MERLIN, S.
1964   The ascent of man. Foreword by S. Hugo Bergman. New York: Yoseloff, 193 pp., (not seen).

WILIMOVSKY, NORMAN J., <u>et al.</u>
1964   Contribution to a bibliography on the osteology of fishes. Reprint of Circ., Nat. Hist. Mus., Stanford Univ., <u>1</u>, 1956. Mimeographed, 103 pp.; suppl., 56 pp.

WILKIE, LEIGHTON
1965   Tools...creator of civilization. (The development of man as revealed by the discoveries of Dr. Raymond A. Dart.) Des Plaines, Illinois: Edit. Leighton Wilkie, (not seen).
     Rev.: M. C. in Fossilia, <u>1965</u>:5–6, 61–62.

WILKISON, ELIZABETH M.
1966   Paleo-Indian components of the Flint Run Jasper Quarry Site 44–WC–1 Shenandoah Valley of Virginia. Chesopian, <u>4</u>:4, 90–110, 6 pls., 1 table.

WILKISON, E., and LESLIE, V.
1967   The Limeton point – a Shenandoah Valley notched-base triangle. Chesopian, <u>5</u>, 8–12, 2 pls.

WILLCOX, A. R.
1963   The rock art of South Africa. Foreword by J. Desmond Clark. Johannes-
        burg, Melbourne, Toronto, Paris: Thomas Nelson, xiv + 96 pp., 42
        figs., 37 colour pls., xxiv black and white pls.
        Rev.: Fagan in Jour. Afr. Hist., 5, 459–461.

WILLEY, GORDON R.
1966   An introduction to American archaeology. Vol. I. North and Middle
        America. Englewood Cliffs, N. J.: Prentice-Hall, 540 pp., illustr.
        Rev.: Anon. in West Va. Archeol., no. 18, 46; Bernal in Man, Jour.
        Roy. Anthrop. Inst., 2, 636–637; Bray in Antiq., 42, 150–151;
        Bushnell in Proc. Prehist. Soc. Cambridge, 33, 468–470; Caldwell
        in Plains Anthrop., 13, 74–75; Fairbanks in Florida Anthrop., 19,
        155; Griffin in Amer. Antiq., 33, 106–109; MacNeish in Amer.
        Anthrop., 69, 532–533; Rouse in Amer. Jour. Archaeol., 72:1,
        88–89; Stirling in Science, 156, 789–790; Wood in Archaeol.,
        20, 307–308; Wormington in Amer. Sci., 55, 349A–350A.

WILLIAM, D. See: DeBrine, Spiegel and William.

WILLIAMS, ALWYN See: Whittington and Williams.

WILLIAMS, ERNEST See: Estes, et al.

WILLIAMS, GEORGE C.
1966   Adaptation and natural selection. A critique of some current evolutionary
        thought. Princeton, N. J.: Princeton Univ. Press, 307 pp., 4 figs.
        Rev.: Alvarado in Bol. R. Soc. Espan. Hist. Nat., Sec. Biol., 65:1–2,
        167; Bleibtreu in Amer. Anthrop., 71, 356–357; Kuttner in
        Mankind Quart., 7, 119–120; Lewontin in Science, 152, 338–339.

WILLIAMS, J. STEWART, and TAYLOR, M. E.
1964   The Lower Devonian Water Canyon formation of northern Utah. Contrib.
        Geol., Univ. Wyoming, 3, 38–53, 3 pls.

WILLIAMS, KENNETH L., and WILSON, L. D.
1967   A review of the colubrid snake genus Cemophora Cope. Tulane Studies
        Zool., 13, 103–124, 6 figs., 5 tables.

WILLIAMS, PATRICIA M.
1968   The Burnham plan and Field Museum. Bull. Field Mus. Nat. Hist., 39:5,
        8–12, 7 figs.

WILLIAMS, PETE See: Brooks, R. H., Orlins and Williams.

WILLIAMS, STEPHEN
1963   Report of the 20th Southeastern Conference. Southeast. Archaeol. Confer.
        Newsletter, 9:2, 15–18.
1965   The Paleo-Indian era: distribution of finds. Lower Mississippi Valley.
        Bull. Southeast. Archaeol. Confer., 2, 9–10.
1966   Antonio J. Waring, Jr., 1915-1964. Amer. Antiq., 31, 552–554, portr.

WILLIAMS, S., and STOLTMAN, J. B.
1965   An outline of southeastern United States prehistory with particular em-
        phasis on the Paleo-Indian era. In: Wright, H. E., and Frey, D. G.,
        (eds.), 1965, 669–683, 6 figs., 2 tables.

WILLIAMS, WESLEY
    1964   The first agnostic. Explorer, 6:1, 18—22, illustr.

WILLIAMS—ELLIS, A.
    1966   Darwin's moon. A biography of Alfred Russel Wallace. London and
                Glasgow: Blackie and Son, x + 261 + 5 pp., 25 pls.
                Rev.: Eiseley in Nature, 212, 14.

WILLIS, ERIC H. See: Trautman and Willis.

WILMETH, ROSCOE
    1967   Archaeological survey in south western Alberta, 1966. Plains Anthrop.,
                12, 199—200, (abs.).

WILMSEN, EDWIN N.
    1964   Flake tools in the American Arctic: some speculations. Amer. Antiq.,
                29, 338—344, 3 figs.
    1965   An outline of Early Man studies in the United States. Amer. Antiq.,
                31, 172—192.
    1968   Lithic analysis in paleoanthropology. Science, 161, 982—987, 3 figs.,
                2 tables.

WILSON, A. C. See: Arnheim, et al.

WILSON, JOHN ANDREW
    1966   A new primate from the earliest Oligocene, West Texas, preliminary
                report. Folia Primatologica, 4, 227—248, 9 figs.
                Rev.: Preuschoft in Zbl. Geol. Pal., Teil 2, 1967, 123.
    1967   Early Tertiary mammals. In: Maxwell, et al., 1967, 157—169, figs.
                107—122, table 10.
    1968   Additions to El Gramal local fauna, Nejapa, Oaxaca, Mexico. Program,
                1968 Ann. Meetings, Geol. Soc. Amer., 1968, 322, (abs.).
                See: Hofer, H. O. and Wilson; Maxwell, R. A., et al.

WILSON, J. A., TWISS, P. C., DeFORD, R. K., and CLABAUGH, S. E.
    1968   Stratigraphic succession, potassium-argon dates, and vertebrate faunas,
                Vieja group, Rim Rock Country, Trans-Pecos Texas. Amer. Jour.
                Sci., 266, 590—604, 2 figs., 4 tables.

WILSON, LARRY DAVID See: Williams, K. L. and Wilson.

WILSON, REX L.
    1965   Excavations at the Mayport mound, Florida. Gainesville: University
                Florida, 33 pp., 4 figs., 8 pls., (not seen).

WILSON, RICHARD LELAND
    1965   Techniques and materials used in the preparation of vertebrate fossils.
                Curator, 8, 135—143, 1 fig.
    1967   The Pleistocene vertebrates of Michigan. Papers Mich. Acad. Sci., 52,
                197—234, 5 figs., 4 tables.
    1968   Systematics and faunal analysis of a Lower Pliocene vertebrate assemblage
                from Trego County, Kansas. Contrib. Mus. Pal. Univ. Mich., 22:7,
                75—126, 17 figs., 19 tables.
                Rev.: Weiler in Zbl. Geol. Pal., Teil 2, 1970:3/4, 226.
                See: Feduccia and Wilson.

WILSON, R. L., and ZUG, G. R.
1966   A fossil map turtle (Graptemys pseudogeographica) from central Michigan. Copeia, 1966, 368–369.

WILSON, ROBERT W.
1964   Late Cretaceous mammals from South Dakota. Proc. S. Dakota Acad. Sci., 43, 210, (abs.).
1965   Type localities of Cope's Cretaceous mammals. Proc. S. Dakota Acad. Sci., 44, 88–90.
1967   Fossil mammals in Tertiary correlations. In: Teichert, and Yochelson, (eds.), 1967, 590–606, 2 tables.

WIMAN, CARL
1935C.   Über Schildkröten aus der Oberen Kreide in New Mexico. Nova Acta Soc. Sci. Upsala, ser. 4, 9:5, 1–35, 12 figs., 6 pls.

WINCIERZ, JOSEF
1967   Ein Steneosaurus-Fund aus dem nordwestdeutschen Oberen Lias. Pal. Zeit., 41:1–2, 60–72, 4 figs., 2 pls.

WING, ELIZABETH
1966   Fossil skates and rays of Florida. Plaster Jacket, no. 2, 7 pp., 4 figs. See: Swift, C. and Wing.

WINNER, ANNA K.
1964   Taxonomic nomenclature in palaeoanthropology. Current Anthrop., 5, 119–122.

WINTER, HANNS KURT
1960   Interessant Versteinerungen aus den Vicentinischen Alpen. Aufschluss, 11, 197–200, 3 figs.

WIRTH, CONRAD L.
1966   Today in our National Parks. The mission called 66, Nation. Geog. Mag., 130, 6–47, illustr.

WISE, WILLIAM
1963   In the time of dinosaurs. New York: Putnam's, 64 pp., illustr, (ages 5–7).
1965   The world of giant mammals. New York: Putnam's, 64 pp., illustr;. (ages 5–7).

WISZNIOWSKA, TERESA
1967   [A new paleontological find in the Sudety Mountains.] Przeglad Zool., 11:4, 430–433, 1 fig., 2 pls., (Polish; English summary).

WITTENBERG, J.   See: McCallum and Wittenberg.

WITTHOFT, JOHN
1956   Paleo-Indian cultures in eastern and southeastern North America. In: Johnson, F., 1956, (not seen).
1967   The art of flint chipping. Jour. Archaeol. Soc. Maryland, 3, 123–144B, illustr.
1968   Stone hammers. A preliminary report. Jour. Archaeol. Soc. Maryland, 4, 5–13.
See: Greene, C. F. 1967.

WOJCIK, ZBIGNIEW
1961A.   The Triassic cave and bone-breccia with <u>Nothosaurus</u> near Olkusz (Krakaw-
           Gestochowa Jurassic). Die Höhle, <u>12</u>, 103, (abs.; English and
           German). Reprinted in Actes 3ème Congr. Internat. Spéléol., <u>A</u>.,
           71.
1961B.   Bone-bed sedimentation in the Tatra Mountains. Die Höhle, <u>12</u>, 103—
           104, (abs.; English and German). Reprinted in Actes 3ème
           Congr. Internat. Spéléol., <u>A</u>, 71—72.

WOLAŃSKI, NAPOLEAN
1957A.   Further observations on sudden changes in the evolution of human forms
           and unevenness in the rate of development. Przeglad Antrop.,
           <u>23</u>, 441—445, (Polish; English summary).
1957B.   [Some problems on the mechanism and factors of human evolution.]
           Sov. Etnogr., <u>1957</u>:6, 3—8, 3 figs., (Russian).
1958   The problem of the stages in the evolution of human forms. Przeglad
           Antrop., <u>24</u>, 308—333, 7 figs., (Polish; English summary).

WOLANSKY, DORA
1962   Das Geologische Museum des Ruhrbergbaues zu Bochum. Aufschluss,
           <u>13</u>, 230—241, 6 figs.
           See: Arnold, <u>et al.</u>

WOLDSTEDT, PAUL
1965   Das Eiszeitalter. Grundlinien einer Geologie des Quartärs. Vol. 3. Afrika,
           Asien, Australien und Amerika im Eiszeitalter. Stuttgart: Ferdinand
           Enke, viii + 328 pp., 97 figs., 18 tables.
           Rev.: Firbas in Mitt. Anthrop. Ges. Wien., <u>95</u>, 362; Kurth in Naturwiss.
           Rund., <u>18</u>, 422; Lundquist in Geol. Fören. Förh., <u>88</u>, 118; G.F.M.
           in Geol. Mag., <u>104</u>, 198—199; Meinig in Aufschluss, <u>16</u>, 262—263;
           Reinig in Kosmos (Stuttgart), <u>62</u>, *203; Schwarzbach in Eiszeit.
           u. Gegenwart, <u>16</u>, 251; Solle in Umschau, <u>66</u>:2, 68—III; Struve
           in Natur u. Mus., <u>95</u>, 408; Trimmel in Die Höhle, <u>16</u>, 85—86;
           L.Z. in Quartär, <u>17</u>, 211—213.
1966   Der Ablauf des Eiszeitalters. Eiszeit. u. Gegenwart, <u>17</u>, 153—158, 1 fig.,
           1 chart, (English summary).
1967   The Quaternary of Germany. In: Rankama, K., (ed.), 1967, Vol. 2,
           239—300, 23 figs., 4 tables.

WOLF, JOSEF
1963   A contribution to the problem of the origin of human society in Africa.
           Przegląd Antrop., <u>29</u>, 152—155.

WOLFRAM, H. J.   See: Nolte, Wolfram and Wöllner.

WOLLIN, GOESTA   See: Ericson and Wollin.

WÖLLNER, H.   See: Nolte, Wolfram and Wöllner.

WOLPOFF, M. H.
1966   The status of "<u>Telanthropus</u>" as an example of sympatric hominid speciation.
           Amer. Jour. Phys. Anthrop., <u>25</u>, 204—205.

WOLTERSDORF, FRITZ   See: Gillet, <u>et al.</u>

WONG, WEN-HAO
    1930   Fossils will remain in China. Peking Leader Reprints, no. 51, 15—16.

WOO, JU-KANG
    1960C.   New discoveries of palaeanthropology in China. Sci. Rec., China, n.s.,
                4, 120—125, (not seen).
    1961C.   On the systematic position and evolutionary significance of the Giganto-
                pithecus. Internat. Assoc. Quat. Res., Abs., Pap., 6th Congr., 139—
                140, (abs.).
    1962A.   Abs.: Dietrich in Zbl. Geol. Pal., Teil 2, 1964, 228—229.
    1964A.   Mandible of Sinanthropus lantianensis. Antiq., 38, 294, pl. 55.
    1964B.   Discovery of ape-man fossil at Lantian. China Pictorial, 1964:2, 5—7,
                illustr.
    1964C.   Mandible of Sinanthropus lantianensis. Current Anthrop., 5, 98—101,
                8 figs.
    1964D.   Discovery of mandible of Sinanthropus lantianensis in Shensi Province,
                China. Homo, 15, 103—106, 5 figs.
    1964E.   [On the systematics of hominids.] In: Nesturkh, (ed.), 1964C, 161—168,
                1 fig., (Russian; English summary).
    1964F.   A newly discovered mandible of the Sinanthropus type — Sinanthropus
                lantianensis. Sci. Sinica, 13, 801—811, 2 figs., 5 pls.
    1964G.   Mandible of the Sinanthropus-type discovered at Lantian, Shensi — Sinan-
                thropus lantianensis. Vert. Palasiatica, 8, 2—17, 2 figs., 5 pls.,
                (Chinese; English summary).
    1964H.   The present status and prospects of the main theoretical problems on
                human evolution. Vert. Palasiatica, 8:4, 362—373, 1 table, (Chinese).
                Rev.: M. C. in Fossilia, 1965:5—6, 64.
    1965A.   Ape-man mandible and skull found in Lantian (Prov. Shensi, China).
                Acta Archaeol. Carpathica, 7:1—2, 125—129, 5 figs., (English;
                Polish summary).
    1965B.   Descubrimiento de una mandibula del Sinanthropus lantianensis en la
                provincia de Shensi, China. Bol. Inst. antropol. Univ. Antioquia,
                3:9, 128—130.
    1965C.   The skull of Lantian man. China Pictorial, 7, 28—31, illustr.
                Rev.: M. C. in Fossilia, 1965:5—6, 73.
    1965D.   Recent advances of paleoanthropology in China. In: Genovés, S., (ed.),
                1965C, 403—413.
    1965E.   Scoperta della mandibola del Sinanthropus lantianensis nella provincia
                dello Shensi in Cina. Riv. Sci. Preist., 19, 277—280, 2 figs., (French
                and English summaries).
    1965F.   Preliminary report on a skull of Sinanthropus lantianensis of Lantian,
                Shensi. Sci. Sinica, 14, 1032—1035, 1 pl., 1 table.
    1965G.   Skull-cap of ape-man found in Lantian, Shensi Province. Vert. Palasiatica,
                9:1, 124.
    1965H.   El cráneo del hombre de Lantián. Zephyrus, 16, 131—133, 2 pls.
    1966A.   The skull of Lantian Man. Current Anthrop., 7, 83—86, 6 figs., 2 tables.
    1966B.   Der Schädel des Lantien—Menschen. Neuer Fund eines Frühmenschen in
                China. Universum; Natur u. Tech., 21, 388—391, 4 figs.
    1966C.   The hominid skull of Lantian, Shensi. Vert. Palasiatica, 10, 1—22, 6 pls.,
                4 tables, (Chinese; English summary).

WOO, J. K., and BAI, H.-Y.
    1965   Attrition of molar teeth in relation to age in northern Chinese skulls.
                Vert. Palasiatica, 9, 217—222, 3 figs., 4 tables, (Chinese; English
                summary).

WOO, J.-K., and CHEBOKSAROV, N. N.
1959   [Continuity of evolution of the physical type of economic activity and
             of the culture of men of the Paleolithic epoch in the territory of
             China.] Sov. Etnog., 1959:4, 3—25, 1 map, (Russian; English
             summary).

WOOD, ALBERT ELMER
1962B.   Rev.: Van Valen in Quart. Rev. Biol., 40, 83—84.
1965A.   Grades and clades among rodents. Evolution, 19, 115—130, 4 figs.
1965B.   Small rodents from the early Eocene Lysite Member, Wind River formation
             of Wyoming. Jour. Pal., 39, 124—134, 4 figs., 5 tables.
1968   Part II. The African Oligocene Rodentia. In: Simons, and Wood, 1968,
             23—105, 17 figs., 11 tables. (German, French, and Russian sum-
             maries).
             See: Clark, J. B., Dawson and Wood; Simons and Wood.

WOOD, A. E., and KONIZESKI, R. L.
1965   A new eutypomyid rodent from the Arikareean (Miocene) of Montana.
             Jour. Pal., 39, 492—496, 2 figs., 2 tables.

WOOD, HORACE E., 2nd
1960   Abs.: Dietrich in Zbl. Geol. Pal., Teil 2, 1964, 209.
1964   Rhinoceroses from the Thomas Farm Miocene of Florida. Bull. Mus.
             Comp. Zool. Harvard, 130:5, 361—386, 2 figs., 5 pls., 5 tables.

WOOD, PAUL ALAN
1963   Pleistocene fauna from 111 Ranch area, Graham County, Arizona. Diss.
             Abst., 23, 3322, (abs.).

WOOD, ROGER C.
1967   A review of the Clark Fork vertebrate fauna. Breviora, no. 257, 30 pp.,
             3 figs., 3 tables.

WOOD, W. RAYMOND
1961   The Pomme de Terre Reservoir in Western Missouri prehistory. Missouri
             Archaeol., 23, 1—131, 23 figs., 20 tables.

WOODALL, J. NED
1968   The use of statistics in archaeology—a bibliography. Bull. Texas Archeol.
             Soc., 38, 25—38.

WOODBURNE, MICHAEL O.
1965A.   Evolutionary changes in the cranial myology of the mid-Tertiary Tayassui-
             dae. Geol. Soc. Amer. Cordilleran Sect., Pal. Soc. Pac. Coast Sect.,
             Prog. 61st Ann. Meeting, 1965, 59, (abs.).
1965B.   Northern California. The University of California at Berkeley. News
             Bull., Soc. Vert. Pal., no. 73, 46—47, 2 figs.
1966A.   Equid remains from the Sonoma volcanics, California. Bull. S. Calif.
             Acad. Sci., 65, 185—189, 1 fig.
1966B.   Evolutionary changes in the cranial myology of the mid-Tertiary Tayassui-
             dae. Spec. Pap. Geol. Soc. Amer., 87, 239, (abs.).
1967A.   Three new diprotodontids from the Tertiary of the Northern Territory,
             Australia. Bull. Australian Bur. Min. Res., no. 85, 53—103, 8 figs.,
             20 tables.
1967B.   The Alcoota fauna, central Australia: An integrated paleontological and
             geological study. Bull. Australian Bur. Min. Res., no. 87, 1—187,
             34 figs., 6 pls., 27 tables.

1968   The cranial myology and osteology of Dicotyles tajacu, the collared pec-
          cary, and its bearing on classification. Mem., S. Calif. Acad. Sci.,
          7, 1—48, 13 figs., 7 pls., 14 tables.
          See: Stirton, Tedford and Woodburne; Stirton and Woodburne; Stirton,
          Woodburne and Plane; Webb, S. D. and Woodburne.

WOODBURY, RICHARD B.
1962   New World archaeology. In: Siegel, B. J., (ed.), 1962, 79—119.

WOODFORD, A. O.
1965   Historical geology. San Francisco: W. H. Freeman and Co., 512 pp.
          Rev.: Anon. in Discovery, 27:1, 51; Bambach in Amer. Jour. Sci., 265,
          175—176; Hambleton in Sci. on the March, 46, 32; M.R.H. in
          Geol. Mag., 103, 183—184; Martinsson in Geol. Fören. Förh, 88,
          121—122; Toots in Contrib. Geol., Univ. Wyoming, 5:2, 46—47;
          Woodring in Science, 151, 187—188.
          See: Gilluly, et al.

WOODLAND, AUSTIN WILLIAM   See: Francis, E. H. and Woodland.

WOODS, JACK T.
1968   The identity of the extinct marsupial genus Nototherium Owen. Mem.
          Queensland Mus., 15, 111—116, pl. 13.
          See: Hill, D., et al.; Staines and Woods.

WOODWARD, ARTHUR SMITH   See: Zittel 1964A, B.

WOODWARD, JOHN A., and WOODWARD, A. F.
1966   The carbon—14 dates from Lake Mojave. Masterkey, 40, 96—102, 2 figs.,
          2 pls.

WOOLDRIDGE, S. W., and CORNWALL, I. W.
1964   A contribution to a new datum for the pre-history of the Thames Valley.
          Bull. London Univ. Inst. Archaeol., no. 4, 223—232, pl. 14 (270).

WORKMAN, WILLIAM B.   See: Chard and Workman.

WORKMAN, W. W.   See: Okladnikov 1963.

WORMINGTON, HANNAH MARIE
1961A.   Prehistoric cultural stages of Alberta, Canada. Homenaje a Pablo Martínez
          del Río, 163—171.
1961B.   Un exposé de la préhistoire américaine pendant le Pleistocène et le début
          de l'Holocène. Internat. Assoc. Quat. Res., Abs. Pap., 6th Congr.,
          148, (abs.).
1963   The Paleo-Indian and Meso-Indian stages of Alberta, Canada. Anthrop.
          Pap. Univ. Alaska, 10:2, 107—114.
1964A.   Department of Archaeology. Ann. Rept. Denver Mus. Nat. Hist., 1963,
          16—17.
1964B.   The problems of the presence and dating in America of flaking techniques
          similar to the Palaeolithic in the Old World. Minn. Archaeol., 26,
          133—143.
1964C.   Supplementary comments on Tule Springs. Minn. Archaeol., 26, 145.
1964D.   Problems relating to Palaeolithic flaking techniques in the New World.
          Proc. Internat. Congr. Americanists, 1962:1, 9—10.

1965 Department of Archaeology. Ann. Rept. Denver Mus. Nat. Hist., <u>1964</u>, 11—13.

1966 New developments in North American prehistory. Proc. Internat. Congr. Americanists, <u>1</u>, 3—14.

WORMINGTON, H. M., and ELLIS, D., (eds.)

1967 Pleistocene studies in southern Nevada. Anthrop. Papers Nev. State Mus., <u>13</u>, 411 pp., illustr.

  Rev.: Wallace in Amer. Anthrop., <u>71</u>, 796—798.

WORMINGTON, H. M., and FORBIS, R. G.

1965 An introduction to the archaeology of Alberta, Canada. Proc. Denver Mus. Nat. Hist., no. <u>11</u>, xx + 248 pp., 90 figs., 1 table.

  Rev.: Hlady in Manitoba Archaeol. Newsletter, <u>2</u>:4, 3—4; Kehoe in Plains Anthrop., <u>13</u>, 75—76; Wheeler in Amer. Antiq., <u>33</u>, 256—257.

WORTHINGTON, H. M.

1965 New developments in North American prehistory. Jour. Colo.—Wyo. Acad. Sci., <u>5</u>:6, 9.

WRESCHNER, E.

1964 Archaeology: excavations. Geulah Cave, Haifa. Israel Explor. Jour., <u>14</u>, 277—278.

WRIGHT, BILL

1968 Cyrus N. Ray, 1880—1966. Bull. Texas Archeol. Soc., <u>38</u>, 126—129.

WRIGHT, GARY A.

1966 Eastern edge survey: 1965 season. In: Fitting, James E., (ed.), <u>1966D</u>, 151—168, 1 fig.

1967 On Late Pleistocene chronology. Current Anthrop., <u>8</u>, 353.

WRIGHT, H. E., JR. See: Cushing and Wright.

WRIGHT, H. E., JR., and FREY, D. G., (eds.)

1965 The Quaternary of the United States. Princeton, N. J.: Princeton Univ. Press, 922 pp., illustr.

  Rev.: Elson in Amer. Jour. Sci., <u>265</u>, 72—74; Hunt in Science, <u>150</u>, 47—50; Jopling in Geog. Rev., <u>57</u>, 145—147; Leighton in Jour. Geol., <u>74</u>, 939—946; Livingstone in Ecology, <u>47</u>, 337—338; Lucke in Amer. Sci., <u>54</u>:4, 467A—469A; Müller-Beck in Amer. Anthrop., <u>68</u>:4, 1065—1067; Olsen in Amer. Mid. Nat., <u>75</u>, 542—544; Pewe in GeoTimes, <u>10</u>:7, 30, 32, 35; Shotton in Nature, <u>210</u>, 454—455; Van Valen in Quart. Rev. Biol., <u>41</u>, 205.

WRIGHT, HENRY T.

1966 A note on a Paleolithic site in the southern desert. Sumer, <u>22</u>, 101—106, 3 figs.

WRIGHT, NORMAN L.

1964 A selection of flint artifacts in the collection of John Hogue, Coshocton, Ohio. Ohio Archaeol., <u>14</u>, 111, 1 fig.

  See: Haight and Wright.

WU, XIN-ZHI, YUAN, Z.—X., HAN, D.—F., QI, T., and LU, Q.—W.

1966 Report of the excavation at Lantian man locality of Gongwangling in

1965. Vert. Palasiatica, 10, 23—29, 1 fig., (Chinese; English summary).

WUNDERLY, J., ADAM, W., KEBLE, R. A., MACPHERSON, H., and MAHONY, D. J.
1943   Rev.: Anon. in Mankind, 3:5, 139.

WUNNENBERG, CURT
1950   Abs.: Raabe in Zbl. Geol. Pal., Teil 2, 1964, 816—817.
1961   Saurierfunde im Ölschiefer des norddeutschen Lias Epsilon. Aufschluss, 12, 293—297, 3 figs.

WURSTER, PAUL
1964   Geologie des Schilfsandsteins. Mitt. Geol. Staatsinst. Hamburg, 33, 140 pp., 57 figs., 4 pls., 15 maps, (French, English and Russian summaries).

WURTZINGER, H. See: Bubeník and Wurtzinger.

WYCKOFF, DON G.
1964   The cultural sequence at the Packard site, Mayes County, Oklahoma. Archaeol. Site Rept., Oklahoma River Basin Surv. Project, no. 2, vi + 126 pp., 5 figs., 23 pls., 2 graphs, (not seen).
        Rev.: Mason in Amer. Antiq., 30, 365—366.

WYCKOFF, RALPH W. G.
1964A.   Application de méthodes physico-chemiques à l'étude de fossiles. Bull. Soc. Franç. Min. Crist., 87, 235—240, 9 figs.
1964B.   Proteins from Rancho La Brea fossils. Quart. Los Angeles Co. Mus., Sci. Hist., 2, 2 pp., 3 figs.
        See: Doberenz and Wyckoff; Shackelford and Wyckoff.

WYCKOFF, R. W. G., and DOBERENZ, A. R.
1965A.   Le collagène dans les dents Pléistocènes. Jour. Micros., 4, 271—274, 2 pls.
1965B.   The electron microscopy of Rancho La Brea bone. Proc. Nation. Acad. Sci., 53, 230—233, 4 figs.
1968   The strontium content of fossil teeth and bones. Acta, Geochim. Cosmochim., 32, 109—115, 3 tables.

WYCKOFF, R. W. G., DOBERENZ, A. R., and McCAUGHEY, W. F.
1965   The amino acid composition of proteins from desert-dried bone. Biochimica et Biophysica Acta, 107, 389—390, 1 table.

WYCKOFF, R. W. G., MCCAUGHEY, W. F., and DOBERENZ, A. R.
1964   The amino acid composition of proteins from Pleistocene bones. Biochimica et Biophysica Acta, 93, 374—377, 1 table.

X
1959   Neer (Limburg). Nieuws-Bull. Koninklijke Ned. Oudheidk. Bond, 6ᵉ s., 12, 60, (not seen).

XU, YU-XUAN
1962   Abs.: Dietrich in Zbl. Geol. Pal., Teil 2, 1964, 209.

1965   A new genus of amynodont from the Eocene of Lantian, Shensi. Vert. Palasiatica, <u>9</u>, 83—86, 2 pls., 2 tables, (Chinese and English).

1966   Amynodonts of Inner Mongolia. Vert. Palasiatica, <u>10</u>, 123—190, 15 pls., tables, (Chinese; English summary).

See: Chow, M. and Xu; Chow, M., Xu and Zhen.

Y, L. M.

1967   Representations of extinct animals in Ohio hieroglyphs. New World Antiq., <u>14</u>, 7.

YALDWYN, J. C.

1966   Moas and man in New Zealand. Austral. Nat. Hist., <u>15</u>, 184—189, 5 figs.

YAMANOUCHI, SUGAO, et al., (eds.)

1964   Nippon Genshi Bijutsu, vol. 1, Tokyo: Kodansha, (not seen).

YAMANOUCHI, S., and SATO, T.

1964   [Paleolithic Age.] In: Yamanouchi, et al., (eds.), 135—137, (not seen).

YAMASAKI, FUMIO, HAMADA, T., and FUJIYAMA, C.

1966   Riken natural radiocarbon measurements II. Radiocarbon, <u>8</u>, 324—339.

YAMAUTI, HIROSHI   See: Hasegawa, Yamauti and Okafuji.

YANG, LIN

1965   How the Lantian ape-man fossils were found. Peking Rev., <u>8</u>:13, 22—24, illustr.

YAPLE, DENNIS D.

1967   Paleo-Indians in Kansas. Newsletter Kansas Anthrop. Assoc., <u>13</u>:1, 9—11.

1968   Preliminary research on the Paleo-Indian occupation of Kansas. Newsletter Kansas Anthrop. Assoc., <u>13</u>:7, 1—9, 2 figs.

YAPP, WILLIAM BRUNSDON

1965   Vertebrates their structure and life. London, N. Y.: Oxford, vii + 525 pp., illustr.

Rev.: Hünermann in Zbl. Geol. Pal., Teil 2, <u>1967</u>, 97—99.

YAWATA, I., and SINOTO, Y. H. (eds.)

1968   Prehistoric culture in Oceania. A symposium of the 11th Pacific Science Congress, Tokyo, 1966. Honolulu: Bishop Mus. Press, 179 pp., illustr., (not seen).

Rev.: C. S. Smith in Science, <u>162</u>, 1378—1379; McBryde in Man, <u>4</u>:2, 300.

YEATMAN, HARRY C.

1964   Surface material from Maury County, Tennessee. Tenn. Archaeol., <u>20</u>, 59—79, 13 pls.

YEH, HSIANG-K'UEI

1961   The first discovery of a box-turtle in China. Vert. Palasiatica, <u>5</u>, 58—64, 1 fig., 1 pl.

1962   Abs.: Huene in Zbl. Geol. Pal., Teil 2, 1964, 176–177.
1963A.   Abs.: Huene in Zbl. Geol. Pal., Teil 2, 1964, 992.
1963B.   Fossil turtles of China. Pal. Sinica, n. ser. C, no. 18, iv + 112 pp.,
              34 figs., 21 pls., 7 tables, (Chinese and English).
              Abs.: Huene in Zbl. Geol. Pal., Teil 2, 1964, 991–992.
1965   New materials of fossil turtles of Inner Mongolia. Vert. Palasiatica, 9,
              47–70, 4 figs., 8 pls., 5 tables, (Chinese and English).
1966   A new Cretaceous turtle of Nanhsiung, northern Kwangtung. Vert. Pal-
              asiatica, 10, 191–206, 3 figs., 3 pls., (Chinese; English summary).

YIN, TSAN-HSUN, CHOW, M.–C., and HSU, J.
    1965   Progress of palaeontology in China. Nature, 205, 646–649, 5 figs.

YIZRAELI, TAMAR
    1967   A Lower Paleolithic site at Holon. Israel Explor. Jour., 17, 144–152.

YOCHELSON, ELLIS L.
    1965   Paleontological Society. GeoTimes, 9:7, 10–12, illustr.
    1967A.   Announcement by International Commission on Zoological Nomenclature.
              Jour. Pal., 41, 1308.
    1967B.   "Raising the dead." Science and Children, 4:6, 10–14, illustr.
              See: Teichert and Yochelson.

YOSHIDA, ITERU See: Sugihara, Yoshida and Serizawa.

YOSHIKAWA, TETSUO
    1963   Sulcus musculi zygomaticomandibularis, a new characteristic in the recon-
              struction of the human fossil skull. Jour. Anthrop. Soc. Nippon,
              71, 117–120, 1 fig., (Japanese; English summary).

YOUNG, CHUNG-CHIEN
    1930C.   Animal neighbors of "Peking man." Peking Leader Reprints, no. 51,
              16–19.
    1963A.   Abs.: Huene in Zbl. Geol. Pal., Teil 2, 1964, 177.
    1963B.   Abs.: Huene in Zbl. Geol. Pal., Teil 2, 1964, 992–993.
    1963C.   Abs.: Huene in Zbl. Geol. Pal., Teil 2, 1964, 985.
    1964A.   The pseudosuchians in China. Pal. Sinica, n.s.C., no. 19, no. 151, 205
              pp., 64 figs., 10 pls., 27 tables, (Chinese and English).
              Abs.: Huene in Zbl. Geol. Pal., Teil 2, 1965, 253–254.
    1964B.   On a new pterosaurian from Sinkiang, China. Vert. Palasiatica, 8:3,
              221–256, 11 figs., 2 pls., 1 table, (Chinese and English).
              Abs.: Huene in Zbl. Geol. Pal., Teil 2, 1965, 255–256.
    1964C.   New fossil crocodiles from China. Vert. Palasiatica, 8, 189–210, 6 figs.,
              2 pls., (Chinese and English).
              Abs.: Huene in Zbl. Geol. Pal., Teil 2, 1965, 255.
    1964D.   On a new Lagomeryx from Lantian, Shensi. Vert. Palasiatica, 8:4, 329–
              340, 1 fig., (Chinese and English).
    1964E.   Note on dinosaurian fossils collected by Yuan from Sinkiang and Inner
              Mongolia. Vert. Palasiatica, 8:4, 398–401.
    1965A.   On the first occurrence of fossil salamanders from the Upper Miocene
              of Shantung, China. Acta Pal. Sinica, 13, 457–459, 3 pls.
              Abs.: Westphal in Zbl. Geol. Pal., Teil 2, 1966, 298.
    1965B.   Fossil eggs from Nanhsiung, Kwangtung and Kanchou, Kiangsi. Vert.
              Palasiatica, 9, 141–170, 19 pls., 7 tables, (Chinese and English).
    1965C.   Note on the reptilian remains from Nanhsiung, Kwangtung. Vert. Pal-
              asiatica, 9, 292–297, 2 figs., (Chinese and English).

Abs.: Huene in Zbl. Geol. Pal., Teil 2, <u>1966</u>, 307—308.

1965D. On the new nothosaurs from Hupeh and Kweichou, China. Vert. Pal-
asiatica, <u>9</u>, 315—356, 14 figs., 9 pls., 2 tables, (Chinese and English).
Abs.: Huene in Zbl. Geol. Pal., Teil 2, <u>1966</u>, 308; Sci. Abs. China,
Earth Sci., <u>4</u>, 11—12.

1965E. On a revised determination of a fossil reptile from Jenhui, Kweichou
with note on a new ichthyosaur probably from China. Vert. Palasiatica, <u>9</u>, 368—375, 2 figs., 1 pl., (Chinese and English).
Abs.: Huene in Zbl. Geol. Pal., Teil 2, <u>1966</u>, 308; Sci. Abs. China,
Earth Sci., <u>4</u>, 12.

1966A. On the first discovery of capitosaurid from Sinkiang. Vert. Palasiatica,
<u>10</u>, 58—63, 2 figs., 1 pl., (Chinese and English).

1966B. On a new locality of the <u>Lufengosaurus</u> of Yunnan. Vert. Palasiatica,
<u>10</u>, 64—67, 1 fig.

1966C. Two footprints from the Jiaoping coal mine of Tungchuan, Shensi. Vert.
Palasiatica, <u>10</u>, 68—72, 1 pl., 1 table, (Chinese and English).

YOUNG, C.—C., and CHOW, M.
1962 Abs.: Huene in Zbl. Geol. Pal., Teil 2, <u>1964</u>, 177.

YOUNG, C.—C., and YEH, H. K.
1963 Abs.: Huene in Zbl. Geol. Pal., Teil 2, <u>1964</u>, 993.

YOUNG, HARVEY R.
1966 Proboscidean molars from Manitoba. Canadian Field Nat., <u>80</u>, 95—98,
6 figs.

YOUNG, J. Z.
1962 Rev.: Musil in Čas. Min. Geol., 1966, <u>11</u>, 468, (Czech).

YOUNG, RICHARD W. See: Moss, M. L. and Young.

YOUNG, T. CUYLER, JR., and SMITH, P. E. L.
1966 Research in the prehistory of Central Western Iran. Science, <u>153</u>, 386—
391, 1 fig.
Rev.: KHS in Naturwiss. Rundschau, <u>19</u>:12, 512.

YOUNGQUIST, WALTER
1967 Fossil systematics. In: Teichert, and Yochelson, (eds.), <u>1967</u>, 57—62.

YUAN, CHEN-SIN See: Pei, Yuan, <u>et al.</u>

YUAN, ZHEN-XIN See: Wu, <u>et al.</u>

Z., M.
1964 News from IVPP. Vert. Palasiatica, <u>8</u>, 97—98, (Chinese and English).

ZABLOTSKY, M. A. (=Zablotskiĭ), and FLEROV, K. K.
1963 [The past of the bisons.] Priroda, <u>52</u>:7, 92—95, illustr., (Russian).

ZABORSKI, J.
1965A. Quaco man — a Canadian representative of the Miolithic Llano culture.
7th Internat. Congr., Internat. Assoc. Quat. Res., Abs., <u>1965</u>, 519,
(abs.).

1965B.   Miolithic protohouse of Siberia and its peripheral survivals. 7th Internat.
           Congr., Internat. Assoc. Quat. Res., Abs., 520, (abs.).

ZADNEPROVSKIĬ, IU. A., and RANOV, V. A.
1966   [New finds of Stone Age in southern Kirgizia.] Biul. Kom. Izuch. Chetvert.
           Perioda, 32, 125–128, 2 figs., (Russian).

ZAGORSKAIA, N. G.
1959   [The Novosibirsk islands.] In: Strelkov, S. A., et al., 1959, 200–211,
           2 figs., (Russian).

ZAGWIJN, W. H. See: Kortenbout van der Sluijs and Zagwijn; Vogel, J. C. and Zagwijn.

ZÄHRINGER, J. See: Schaeffer, O. A. and Zähringer.

ZAIDOVA, S. L.
1964   [Concerning the history of the study of fossil representatives of Erinaceidae
           of Azerbaidzhan and U. S. S. R.] Izv. Akad. Nauk. Azerbaidzhan.
           S.S.R., 1964:1, 119–126, 1 table, (Russian; Azerbaidzhan sum-
           mary).

ZAKHARENKO, L. V. See: Vereshchagin and Zakharenko.

ZAKHAROV, S. A. (=Zagharow)
1964   [On a Cenomanian dinosaur, whose tracks were found in the Shirkent
           R. valley.] In: Reĭman, (ed.), 1964, 31–35, 2 figs., (Russian;
           English and Tadzhik summaries).

ZAKHAROV, S. A., and KHAKIMOV, F.
1963   [On foot-prints of a Cenomanian dinosaur in Western Tadzhikistan.]
           Doklady Akad. Nauk Tadzhik. SSR, 6:9, 25–27, 1 fig., (Russian;
           Tadzhik summary).

ŻAKI, ANDRZEJ
1964   Sinanthropus lantianensis. Acta Archaeol. Carpathica, 6:1–2, 125–127,
           4 figs., (Polish; French summary).

ZAKLINSKAIA, E. D. See: Gromov, V. I., Griaznov, et al.

ZAKRZEWSKI, RICHARD J.
1967A.   The systematic position of Canimartes? from the Upper Pliocene of Idaho.
           Jour. Mammal., 48, 293–297, 2 tables.
1967B.   The primitive vole, Ogmodontomys, from the Late Cenozoic of Kansas
           and Nebraska. Papers Mich. Acad. Sci., 52, 133–150, 5 figs.,
           3 tables.
           See: Hibbard and Zakrzewski.

ZALESSKIĬ, IU. M.
1947   [First find of a branchiosaur in the Urals.] Priroda, 1947:11, 79–80,
           1 fig., (Russian).

ZALKIN, V. I. See: Grosset, et al.

ZALKIND, N. G.
1963   [The opening of a new exposition "The Origin of Man" in the Institute
           and Museum of Anthropology named after D. N. Anuchin.] Voprosy

Antrop., 14, 110–112, 2 figs., (Russian).

ZALLINGER, JEAN See: May 1965.

ZAL'TSMAN, I. G.
1958   [Stratigraphy of Tertiary deposits of the southern part of West Siberian lowlands.] Materialy Geol. Zap. Sibiri, 61, 112–135, 1 chart, (Russian).
1967   [Tertiary continental deposits of the southern regions of West Siberian lowlands.] In: Martinson, (ed.), 189–194, (Russian).

ZAL'TSMAN, I. G., et al.
1960   [Project of unified and correlational stratigraphic schemes for continental Paleogene and Neogene deposits.] In: Rostovtsev, (ed.), 1961, 59–66, (Russian).

ZAMIATNIN, S. N.
1958   [Researches on Stone Age in Azerbaidzhan in autumn of 1953.] Trudy Inst. Ist. Azerbaidzhan, 13, 5–19, 3 figs., (Russian; Azerbaidzhan summary).
1960   [Certain problems in the study of the economy in the Paleolithic.] Trudy Inst. Etnog., 54, 80–108, 10 figs., (Russian).
1961A.   [Studies of the Paleolithic.] Moscow-Leningrad: Akademiia Nauk SSSR, 1961, 175 pp., 16 figs., 53 pls., 4 tables., 1 fold-out map, (Russian).
          Rev.: Vencl in Archeol. Roz., 16, 137–138, (Czech).
1961B.   [The Stalingrad Paleolithic site.] Krat. Soob. Inst. Ist. Mat. Kult, SSSR, 82, 5–36, 20 figs., 1 pl., (Russian).

ZAMORII, P. K.
1961   [Quaternary stratigraphy of Ukraine.] Mat. Vses. Sov. po Izuch. Chetvert. Perioda, 1, 53–64, 2 figs., 1 map, 1 table, (Russian).

ZAMYSLOVA, E. A.
1967   [Ancient man in North America (a review of the literature).] Biull. Kom. Izuch. Chetvert. Perioda, 34, 107–119, 4 figs., 1 table, (Russian).

ZANDRINO, M. A.
1959   Determinación del fluor en el fechado relativo de huesos fosiles. Rev. Inst. Antrop., Univ. Nacion. Litoral, Rosario, 1, 271–281, 1 fig.

ZANGERL, RAINER
1960A.   Rev.: Huene in Zbl. Geol. Pal., Teil 2, 1968, 208.
1963B.   Preliminary results of a restudy of Corosaurus alcovensis Case, the only known New World nothosaur. Contrib. Geol., Univ. Wyoming, 2, 117–123, 7 pls.
          Rev.: Huene in Zbl. Geol. Pal., Teil 2, 1968, 208–209.
1964   The ancient fish traps of Mecca. Bull. Chicago Nat. Hist. Mus., 35:2, 2–3, 8, 2 figs.; 35:3, 3–4, 8, 1 fig.
1965A.   The new anatomy of the geology department. Bull. Chicago Nat. Hist. Mus., 36:2, 4–6, illustr.
1965B.   Radiographic techniques. In: Kummel and Raup, (eds.), 1965, 305–320, 8 figs.
1965C.   Galvanoplastic reproduction of fossils. In: Kummel and Raup, (eds.), 1965, 413–420, 3 figs.

1966   A new shark of the family Edestidae, Ornithoprion hertwigi from the
        Pennsylvanian Mecca and Logan Quarry shales of Indiana. Field-
        iana, Geol., 16, 1—43, 26 figs.
        Rev.: Weiler in Zbl. Geol. Pal., Teil 2, 1967, 506—508.
1967   X-rays find fossils. Bull. Field Mus. Nat. Hist., 38:7, 2—3, 3 figs.
        See: Bardack and Zangerl; Hennig, W. 1966; Peyer 1968.

ZANGERL, R., and SLOANE, R. E.
1960   Rev.: Huene in Zbl. Geol. Pal., Teil 2, 1968, 209.

ZAPFE, HELMUTH
1960B.   Rev.: Burchak-Abramovich in Voprosy Antrop., 17, 154—157, (Russian).
          Abs.: Ehrenberg in Zbl. Geol. Pal., Teil 2, 1964, 229—231.
1960D.   Placochelys, ein eigenartiges Meeresreptil in der alpinen Obertrias. Veröff.
          Naturhist. Mus. Vienna, N. F. No. 3, 13—15, 3 figs.
1960E.   Mammutherde in der eiszeitlichen Landschaft von Wien. Ein Grossgemälde
          in der Geologisch-Paläontologischen Schausammlung. Veröff. Natur-
          hist. Mus. Vienna, N. F. No. 3, 24—26, 1 fig.
1964A.   Eduard Suess zum 50. Todestag. Ann. Naturhist. Mus. Wien, 67, 169—
          173.
1964B.   Das Meer der alpinen Trias. Seine organismenwelt und seine Ablagerungen.
          Veröff. Naturhist. Mus. Vienna, N. F. No. 5, 82—94, figs. 92—110.
1964C.   Das Meer der alpinen Gosauformation. Veröff. Naturhist. Mus. Vienna,
          N. F. No. 5, 111—117, figs. 137—146.
1964D.   Die jungtertiäre und eiszeitliche Landtierwelt in der Gegend von Wien.
          Veröff. Naturhist. Mus. Vienna, N. F. No. 5, 130—142, figs. 163—
          183.
1964E.   Aus der Arbeit der Geologisch-Paläontologischen Abteilung. Veröff. Na-
          turhist. Mus. Vienna, N. F. No. 5, 142—148, figs. 184—197.
1966A.   Die Höhlenbärenreste. In: Ehrenberg, (ed.), 1966A, 15—22.
1966B.   Die übrigen Carnivoren (ausser Höhlenhyäne und Höhlenbär). In: Ehren-
          berg, (ed.), 1966A, 23—38, 2 figs., 7 tables.
1966C.   Lebensspuren. In: Ehrenberg, (ed.), 1966A, 109—122, 2 figs., 4 pls.
1967A.   Ancylotherium im Obermiozän des Wiener Beckens. Ann. Naturhist.
          Mus. Wien, 71, 401—411, 2 figs., 1 pl., (English summary).
1967B.   Donau und Urdonau. Universum; Natur u. Tech., 1967:1, 20—23, 3
          figs.
          See: Bachmayer and Zapfe; Mitzopoulos and Zapfe.

ZAPFE, H., BACHMAYER, F., KOLLMAN, H., and FLÜGEL, E., (eds.)
1964   Schätze im Boden. Bilder aus Österreichs geologischer Vergangenheit.
        Veröff. Naturhist. Mus. Vienna, N. F. No. 5, 160 pp., 199 figs.,
        1 map.

ZAUNICK, RUDOLPH
1963   Aus dem Leben und Wirken des Dresdner Kupferstechers Moritz Müller
        genannt Steinla (1791 bis 1858), insbesondere von seinem paläon-
        tologischen Sammeln und Forschen. Jahrb. Staatl. Mus. Mineral.
        Geol. Dresden, 1962, 265—326, 10 figs., (not seen).
        Abs.: Häntzschel in Zbl. Geol. Pal., Teil 2, 1964, 389—390.

ZAUROVA, E. Z. See: Abetekov, et al.

ZAVADSKIĬ, K. M.
1967   [The problem of progress in Living Nature.] Voprosy Filosofii, 1967:9,
        124—136, (Russian; English summary).

1968   [Species and speciation.] Leningrad: "Nauka" Press, 404 pp., 8 figs., 14 portrs., 10 tables, (Russian).
          Rev.: Shvarts in Zh. Obshch. Biol., 30:1, 111—114, (Russian); Skripchinskiĭ in Biull. Mosk. Obshch. Ispyt. Prirody, Otd. Biol., 74:4, 154—157.

ZAVADSKIĬ, K. M., and BERMAN, Z. I.
1966   [On one form of antidarwinism.] Vestnik Leningrad Univers., 9, 5—22, (Russian; English summary).

ZAVERNIAEV, F. M., and SHMIDT, E. A.
1961   [New find of Lower Paleolithic on Upper Desna R.] Sov. Arkheol., 1961:1, 243—247, 5 figs., (Russian).

ZAZHIGIN, V. S.
1966A.   [Stratigraphic significance of small mammals fauna from West Siberian Eopleistocene.] Biul. Kom. Izuch. Chetvert. Perioda, 32, 46—50, (Russian).
1966B.   [Eopleistocene mammals of Western Transbaikalia. Order Lagomorpha.] Trudy Geol. Inst., 152, 23—26, 1 fig., 3 tables, (Russian).
1966C.   [Preliminary results of the research on Eopleistocene faunas of small mammals from West Siberia.] Geol. Inst. AN SSSR, Reports of the IV Conf. of junior coll. and researchers, 17—19, (Russian).
1966D.   [Eopleistocene mammals of Western Transbaikalia. Order Rodentia.] Trudy Geol. Inst., 152, 27—43, 9 figs., 9 tables, (Russian).
          See: Adamenko and Zazhigin; Deviatkin, Zazhigin and Liskun; Vangengeim and Zazhigin.

ZAZVORKA, VLASTISLAV
1966   [New find of crocodile tooth in the Miocene of northern Bohemia.] Cas. Narod. Muzea, Odd. Prirod., 135:1, 46—48, 1 pl., (Czech, Esperanto summary).

ZBYSZEWSKI, GEORGES
1953A.   Note sur l'apparition d'ossements de mammifères dans les argiles de Coja (Arganil). Bol. Soc. Geol. Portugal, 11, 59—64, 2 pls.
1953B.   Note sur une mandible d'Isocetus trouvée à Mutela. Bol. Soc. Geol. Portugal, 11, 91—92, 1 pl.
1962A.   L'Abbé H. Breuil et sa contribution à l'étude de la préhistoire portugaise. Com. Serv. Geol. Portugal, 46, 41—51, 1 pl.
1962B.   Considérations sur la position stratigraphique de l'Aquitanien portugais. Com. Serv. Geol. Portugal, 46, 297—316.
1964A.   L'Aquitanien du Portugal et sa place stratigraphique. Cursillos y Confer. Inst. "Lucas Mallada", 9, 9—12.
1964B.   Les rapports entre les milieux miocènes marins et continentaux au Portugal. Cursillos y Confer. Inst. "Lucas Mallada", 9, 103—108, 1 table.
1967   Le Mastodonte du "Pliocène" de Santarem. Com. Serv. Geol. Portugal, 52, 11—15, 3 pls.
          See: Breuil 1962B; Ginsburg and Zbyszewski; Roche, et al.

ZBYSZEWSKI, G., et al.
1961   Rev.: J. R. in L'Anthrop., 69:5—6, 552—553.

ZBYSZEWSKI, G., and VEIGA FERREIRA, O. DA
1967A.   Découverte de vertébrés fossiles dans le Miocène de la région de Leiria. Com. Serv. Geol. Portugal, 52, 5—10, 6 pls.

1967B.   Le Paléolithique des terrasses du Sorraia à l'Est de Benavente. Com. Serv.
          Geol. Portugal, 52, 95—107, 8 pls.
1967C.   Une nouvelle station paléolithique de style microlusitanien: Le gisement
          du promontoire de Môrro 'a l'Ouest de Sesimbra. Com. Serv. Geol.
          Portugal, 52, 109—116, 2 pls.

ŽEBERA, KAREL
1964   Zpráva o geologickém výzkumu kvartéru v Předmosti'u Přerova na Moravě
          a v jeho bezprostřednim. okoli. Zprávy Geol. Výzkumech Roce, 1,
          333—335.
1965   Das "Bohémien", eine Geröllindustrie als Voläufer des mitteleuropäischen
          Moustériens. ᵥQuartär, 15—16, 47—60, 6 figs., 5 pls.
          See: Rädisch and Žebera.

ZECCHINI, M.
1967   Contributo alla conoscenza della preistoria dell'isola d'Elba dal Paleolitico
          all'Età del Bronzo. Atti Soc. Toscana Sci. Nat., Mem., Ser. A,
          74:2, 470—501, 5 figs., (French summary).

ZEEMAN, J. P.   See: Anon., 1964 BR.

ZEI, M., and MANCA, V.
1965   Stazione di superficie del Paleolitico Medio in territorio di Anghiari
          (Arezzo). Atti Soc. Toscana Sci. Nat., Mem., ser. A, 72:2, 431—
          436, 2 pls.

ŽEIBA, S., and VASILIAUSKAS, V.
1958   [Some data from the study of Švétés beds of Upper Devonian.]   Moksliniai
          Pranešimai, Geol.-Geogr._8, 207—217, 1 fig., 1 table, (Lithuanian;
          Russian and English summaries).

ZEITNER, JOHN CULP
1967   Is it legal? A discussion of land laws and regulations. Lapidary Jour.,
          20:11, 1282—1291.

ZELENCHUK, V. S., RIKMAN, E. A., and SMIRNOV, G. D., (eds.)
1964   [Materials and studies on archeology and ethnography of Moldavian SSR.]
          Kishinev: "Kartiã Moldoveniaske" Press, 287 pp., 131 figs., 6 pls.,
          2 maps, 2 tables, (Russian).

ZELLER, E. J.   See: Dort, Zeller, Turner and Vaz.

ZEMLIAKOV, B. F.
1939A.   [About the representation of a mammoth from "Mammoth grotto" of
          Kamennaiã Mogila at Melitopol'shchina.]   Krat. Soob. Inst. Ist.
          Mat. Kult. SSSR, 2, 33—36, 2 figs., (Russian).
1939B.   [Results of the study of the "Arctic Paleolithic" during the period of
          1935—1938 on the territory of the USSR.]   Krat. Soob. Inst. Ist.
          Mat. Kult. SSSR, 2, 12—13, (Russian).
1940D.   [The excursion by the participants of the Kiev archeological conference
          into the Desna river basin.]   Krat. Soob. Inst. Ist. Mat. Kult. SSSR,
          3, 52—53, (Russian).
1940E.   [The geological history of the Karelo—Finnish republic during the Quater-
          nary Period in connection with the question of the settling of the
          North of Europe.]   Krat. Soob. Inst. Ist. Mat. Kult. SSSR, 7, 21—
          27, 3 figs., (Russian).

ZENKER, ADOLF
1965   Die pathologischen Veränderungen am Unterkiefer von <u>Megaladapis edwardsi</u> G. Grandidier. Folia Primatologica, <u>3</u>, 75—80, 3 figs.

ZERRIES, O.
1956   Neue Funde ältester Monschheits-Spuren in Nordamerika. Umschau, <u>56</u>, 659.

ZERVOS, CHR.
1959   Rev.: R. V. in L'Anthrop., <u>69</u>:5—6, 541—543.

ZETTI, JORGE
1964   El hallazgo de un Megatheriidae en el "Médano Invasor" del SW de Toay, provincia de La Pampa. Ameghiniana, <u>3</u>:9, 257—265, 3 figs., 1 table, (English summary).
1967   Sobre la presencia del genero <u>Marmosa</u> (Didelphidae, Marsupialia), en sedimentos de la formacion Epecuén (Plioceno medio). Ameghiniana, <u>5</u>, 169—173, 1 fig., (English summary).
See: Strelczenia and Zetti.

ZEUNER, FREDERICK EVERARD
1963   Rev.: Jaczewski in Przeglad Zool., <u>7</u>, 353—354, (Polish); Ryder in Proc. Prehist. Soc. Cambridge, <u>31</u>, 379—380.
1964   Soils and shorelines as aids to chronology. Bull. London Univ. Inst. Archaeol., no. <u>4</u>, 233—249, 3 figs., 2 tables.
See: Biberson 1965A.

ZEUNER, F. E., and BRAVO, T.
1966   The first fossil mammal from the Canary Islands. The beds of fossil rats in the Canary Islands. Actas V Congr. Panafr. Prehist. Estud. Cuaternario, <u>1963</u>:2, 289—298, 3 figs.

ZHAI, REN-JIE
1964   <u>Leptarctus</u> and other Carnivora from the Tung Gur formation, Inner Mongolia. Vert. Palasiatica, <u>8</u>, 18—32, 1 fig., 2 pls., (Chinese; English summary).

ZHEGALLO, V. I.
1966   [On the history of Pliocene hipparion faunas of Mongolia and Central Asia.] Biull. Mosk. Obshch. Ispyt. Prirody, Otd. Geol., <u>41</u>:6, 144, (Russian).
See: Birman, <u>et al.</u>

ZHEMKOVA, Z. P.
1965   [On the origin of Cetacea.] Zool. Jour. Moscow, <u>44</u>:10, 1546—1552, 2 pls., (Russian; English summary).

ZHEN, SHUO-NAN   See: Chow, M., Xu and Zhen.

ZHIRMUNSKIĬ, A. M.
1957   [Progress in the study of the Anthropozoic Era in Czechoslovakia.] Pal. i Stratig. BSSR, Minsk, <u>2</u>, 240—241, (Russian).

ZHIROV, NICHOLAS
1960   Cave paintings in the Urals. New World Antiq., <u>7</u>, 40—41.

ZHITENEVA, L. D.
    1968   [Fishes from Novgorod-Severskiǐ Upper Paleolithic site.]   Voprosy Ikhtiol.,
                8:2, 363–365, 1 fig., (Russian).
                Rev.: Weiler in Zbl. Geol. Pal., Teil 2, 1969:3, 289.

ZHIZHCHENKO, B. P.
    1964   [On the stratigraphy and extent of Lower Miocene.]   Sov. Geol., 1964:4,
                40–60, 2 figs., 1 table, (Russian).

ZHOU, JIA-JIAN See: Liu, H.–T. and Zhou.

ZHOU, MING-ZHEN =Chow, Minchen.

ZHUKOV, P. I.
    1965   [Distribution and evolution of fresh-water lampreys in BSSR.]   Voprosy
                Ikhtiol., 5:2(35), 240–244, 1 fig., 1 table, (Russian).

ZIBERT, E. V. See: Wauchope 1966B.

ZÍDEK, JIŘÍ
    1966   [New finds of sharklike fishes of the Order Xanacanthodii in the Lower
                Permian of Boskovicke basin in Moravia.]   Čas. Národ. Muzea, odd.
                přirod., 135:2, 74–80, 3 figs., 1 pl., (Czech; English summary).

ZIEGERT, HELMUT
    1964   Neue Ergebnisse fur die Klima- und Besiedlungs-Geschichte der zentralen
                Sahara. Umschau, 64, 712–715, 6 figs.
    1965   Climatic changes and Paleolithic industries in East Fezzan, Libya. Current.
                Anthrop., 6, 104–105, 5 figs.

ZIEGLER, ALAN C.
    1965   The role of faunal remains in archeological investigations. Pap. Sacramento
                Anthrop. Soc., 3, 47–93, 5 figs., 1 table.

ZIHLMAN, ADRIENNE L.
    1966   The bipedal pattern. Abs. 65th Ann. Meeting Amer. Anthrop. Assoc.,
                1966, 75, (abs.).
    1967   The question of size in Australopithecus. Abs. 66th Ann. Meeting Amer.
                Anthrop. Assoc., 1967, 90, (abs.).

ZILCH, A.
    1965   Die Typen und Typoide des Natur-Museums Senckenberg. 32: Fossile
                Fisch-Otolithen. Senck. Lethaea, 46a, 453–490, pl. 35.
                Abs.: Weiler in Zbl. Geol. Pal., Teil 2, 1966, 291.

ZIMERMANN-ROLLIUS, S.
    1967   Beiträge zur Schildkrötenfauna der mitteleozänen Braunkohle des Geiseltales.
                Hercynia, 4:1, 83–104, 5 figs., 1 map, 6 tables.

ZIMMERMAN, PAUL A., (ed.)
    1959   Darwin, evolution, and creation. St. Louis, Mo.: Concordia, 204 pp.,
                (not seen).

ZIMMERMANN, W.
    1960A.   Die Auseinandersetzung mit den Ideen Darwins. Der "Darwinismus" als
                ideengeschichtliches Phanomen. In: Herberer and Schwanitz, (eds.),
                290–354, 2 figs.

1960B. Unser heutiges Wissen von der Evolution. Mediz. Grundlagenforsch., 3, 655—704.

1960C. Über die Stammesgeschichte der Lebewesen. Schrift. Ver. Verbreit. natur-wiss. Kenntn., 100, 85—120.

1963   Gibt es ausser dem phylogenetischen System "natürliche" systeme der Organismen? Biol. Zentralbl., 82, 525—568.

1967   Methoden der Evolutionswissenschaft (=Phylogenetik). In: Heberer, (ed.), 1967A, 61—160, 11 figs.

ZIÓŁKIEWICZ, TADEUSZ, OSTROWSKI, J., FRANKOWSKA—LENARTOWSKA, M., and DRĄGOWSKA-ZIEMIAŃSKA, L.

1965   The goniac angle and the angle of opening of the mandible in the man in phylogenesis. Przegląd Antrop., 30, 161—168, 2 figs., 7 tables, (Polish; French and English summaries).

ZIRKLE, CONWAY See: Sirks and Zirkle.

ZITTEL, KARL A. VON

1964A. Text-book of palaeontology. Vol. II. Pisces, Amphibia, Reptila, Aves. Second revised edition. Translated and edited by C. R. Eastman, with additions by A. Smith Woodward. Reprint. New York: Stechert-Hafner, 464 pp., 533 figs.

1964B. Text-book of palaeontology. Vol. III. Mammalia. Revised by M. Schlosser. Translated under direction of C. R. Eastman, translation revised by A. Smith Woodward. Reprint. New York: Stechert-Hafner, 316 pp., 374 figs., (not seen).

ZÖBELEIN, H.—K.

1963   Zur Biostratigraphie der gefalteten Molasse (Chattien/Aquitanien) im Süden des Oberen Zürichsees. Bull. Ver. Schweiz. Petrol.-Geol., 29:77, 11—28, (not seen).
        Abs.: Hiltermann in Zbl. Geol. Pal., Teil 2, 1964, 15.

ZOL'NIKOV, V. G.

1961   [On the discovery of animal remains of the mammoth complex on the Suola R. in Megino-Kangalas region, Yakutian ASSR.] Izv. Akad. Nauk, Ser. Geograf., 1961:3, 81—85, 1 table, (Russian).

ZOLOTAREV, A. G.

1966   [Stratigraphy and paleogeographic conditions of Pliocene-Quaternary deposits formation of the central part of Baĭkal-Patoma uplands.] Geol. i Geof., 1966:11, 26—35, 2 figs., 1 chart, (Russian; English summary).

ZORZI, FRANCESCO

1959   Un'amigdala acheuleana scoperta a Lughezzano di Valpantena nel quadro del Paleolitico inferiore e medio veronese. Mem. Mus. Civ. Storia Nat. Verona, 7, 297—334, 15 figs., (French summary).

1961   Alberto Carlo Blanc. 1906—1961. Mem. Mus. Civ. Storia Nat. Verona, 9, 357—358.

1964   Palaeolithic discoveries in the Grotta Paglicci. Antiq., 38, 38—44, 5 figs., pls. 10—11.
        Note: Baumgartel in Antiq., 38, 139, pl. 23a.
        See: Broglio, Laplace and Zorzi; Palma di Cesnola and Zorzi.

ZOTZ, LOTHAR F.
1963C.   Rev.: Rozoy in Bull. Soc. Préhist. Franç., C. R. séances mens., 63, 129–
            130.
1964A.   Eine Stielspitze westeuropäischen Typs aus dem Altmühltal. Germania,
            42, 1–18, 4 figs.
1964B.   Mittelpaläolithikum. In: Uslar and Narr, (eds.), 1964, 36–44.
1965A.   Wichtige alt- und mittelpaläolithische Neufund aus Bayern. Bayer. Vorges.,
            30, 9–25, 5 figs.
1965B.   Ein Abschlag- Zweiseiter aus dem Manzanarestal bei Madrid. In: Ripoll
            Perelló, E., (eds.), 1965B, 443–447, 1 fig., (Spanish summary).
1965C.   Die Aurignac-Knochenspitzen aus der Tischoferhöhle in Tirol. Quartär,
            15–16, 143–153, 2 figs., (French summary).
1965D.   Zwei inhaltsgleiche sexual-mysteriöse Bilder aus dem französischen Magda-
            lenien. Quartär, 15–16, 173–176, 1 fig., (French summary).

ZUBAKOV, V. A.
1960   [Stratigraphic correlation of Quaternary deposits of the Eniseĭ region in
            Siberia.] In: Ragozin, L. A., (ed.), 1960, 131–135, (Russian).
1962   [New Paleolithic site in the Eniseĭ R. valley.] Informatsionnyĭ Sbornik,
            52, 113–120, 3 figs., (Russian).
1965A.   [The Pleistocene deposits of the Upper Eniseĭ valley in the Krasnoĭarsk-
            Angara region.] In: Gromov, et al., (eds.), 1965, 183–196, 2
            figs., 1 table, (Russian; English summary).
1965B.   [Glacial history of Alaska in the light of Pleistocene geochronology prob-
            lems.] Izv. Akad. Nauk, Ser. Geograf., 1965:3, 3–17, 1 fig., 2
            tables, (Russian).
1966   [Comparison of the radiometric scale of continental Pleistocene with chrono-
            logical scales of deep sea deposits and the curve of solar radiation.]
            Doklady Akad. Nauk SSSR, 171:3, 1153–1155, 1 fig., 1 table,
            (Russian).
            See: Ganeshin, Zubakov, et al.

ZUBAKOV, V. A., and KRASNOV, I. I.
1959   [Principles of stratigraphic division of Quaternary system and a project of
            a unified stratigraphic scale for this system.] Materialy Geol. Inst.
            (VSEGEI), Nov. Ser. Chetv. Geol. i Geomorf., 27, 28–71, 8 tables,
            (Russian).

ZUBOV, A. A.
1964   [On systematics of Australopithecinae.] Voprosy Antrop., 17, 99–105,
            (Russian).
1966A.   [Fundamentals of ethnic odontology.] Sov. Etnogr., 1966:1, 3–13, (Rus-
            sian; English summary).
1966B.   [Dental system.] Trudy Inst. Etnog. Akad. Nauk SSSR, 92, 360–382,
            9 figs., 4 tables, (Russian).
1967A.   [The cusp reduction order and the modification of the crown pattern in
            permanent lower molars of man in the passage from the five-cusp type
            into the three-cusp type.] Discussion. 7th Internat. Congr. Anthrop.
            Ethnol. Sci., Moscow, 1964, 2, 498–502, (Russian).
1967B.   [The distal trigonal ridge on the permanent lower human molars.] Voprosy
            Antrop., 26, 144–151, 6 figs., 1 table, (Russian).

ZUCKERMAN, SOLLY
1966   Myths and methods in anatomy. Jour. Roy. Coll. Surg., Edinburgh, 11,
            87–114.

ZUCKERMAN, S., ASHTON, E. H., OXNARD, C. E., and SPENCE, T. F.
   1967   The functional significance of certain features of the innominate bone in living and fossil primates. Jour. Anat., <u>101</u>, 608, (abs.).

ZUCKERMAN, S., ASHTON, E. H., and PEARSON, J. B.
   1962   Abs.: Kuhn—Schnyder in Zbl. Geol. Pal., Teil 2, <u>1964</u>, 231.

ZUÑIGA, NEPTALI
   1966   Localización de los primeros restos paleontológicos de la presidéncia de Quito. Juan de Larrea — Alejandro de Humboldt — Jorge Cuvier. Humanitas, <u>6</u>:1, 196—198.

ZYLL de JONG, C. G. VAN   See: Churcher and Zyll de Jong.

SUBJECT INDEX

SUBJECT INDEX

ACETIC ACID PREPARATION METHODS — See: technique.

ADAPTATIONS, ADAPTIVE RADIATION — See: aquatic adaptations; dentition; evolution; flight, origin, adaptations; general works; habits; paleobiology; paleomyology; paleophysiology; phylogeny; skeleton; skull.

AGE DETERMINATIONS, GEOLOGICAL DATINGS — See: correlation, paleochronology; technique.

AGE AND SEX DIFFERENCES — See: variation and heredity.

ANATOMY — See also: circulatory system; dentition; integumentary structures; paleomyology; paleonuerology; paleopathology; skeleton; skull.

GENERAL — Baer 1964 (comparative anat., verts.); Bjerring 1967 (muscle and cartilage); Bokhvardt 1966, 1967 (vertebral centra);
Denison 1966A (origin of lateral-line sensory system);
Eaton 1960C (comparative anat., verts.);
Fox 1965 (middle ear of tetrapods); Frick 1965 (current problems of comparative anat.);
Gabe 1967 (skeleton); Gans 1964 (vert. hard tissues); Gasc 1967B (hyobranchial skel.);
Jefferies 1968 (primitive fossil chordates);
Kent, G. C. 1965 (comparative anat., verts.);
Ørvig 1965 (bone tissue, verts.);
Parrington 1967C (dermal skull bones); Portmann, A. 1965B (vert. morphology);
Remane 1963 (vert. evol.); Romer 1966D (comp. anat., verts.);
Saban 1964 (skull and vertae.); Slabý 1962 (evol. of vert. limbs); Smith, Hobart M. 1960 (comparative anat., chordates); Stensiö 1963 (vert. brain);
Zuckerman 1966 (methods).

OSTRACODERMI — Dineley 1964A (pteraspids).

PISCES — Anthony and Robineau 1967 (Latimeria);
Balabai 1956B (Agnatha); Bardack 1965A (chirocentrid fishes); Bendix-Almgreen 1962, 1967 (edestids, E. Greenland); Blot 1968 (teleosteans); Blot and Heyler 1964 (palaeoniscoids, France); Brien 1964B (lung-fish);
Gardiner 1967B (preoperculum in fishes); Gaudant 1968 (Lycoptera);
Heintz, A. 1967A (cephalaspid tail);
Jarvik 1967A (structure of snout in Megalichthys and other rhipidistid crossopterygians), 1967B (skull bones in fishes and tetrapods), 1967C (lower jaw, dipnoans);
Karatajūte 1958B (asterolepids);
Lange, S. P. 1968 (Urocles, Europe); Le Danois 1966 (Gonorhynchidae); Lehman 1967B (Drepanaspis head-shield plates); Lund 1966 (Pholidophorus bechei intermuscular bones), 1967A (actinopterygian propulsive mechanisms);
MacAllister 1968 (teleost fishes); Mark-Kurik 1963 (arthrodire spinal plate); Miles, R. S. 1965E, 1967A (placoderms); Miles and Westoll 1968 (descriptive morphology of Coccosteus cuspidatus); Millot and Anthony 1965 (nervous system and sense organs of Latimeria); Monod 1967 (teleosts);
Nelson, G. J. 1967 (epibrancial organs in teleosts); Nieuwenhuys 1965 (Latimeria forebrain); Norman and Greenwood 1963 (hist. of fishes); Novitskaya 1965 (structure of Psammosteida plates); Nybelin 1967B (sensory canal system, actinopterygians);
Panchen 1967A (nostrils of choanate fishes); Pegeta 1968 (Latimeria);
Ritchie, A. 1964 (Anaspida), 1968 (Jamoytius);
Schaeffer, B. 1967C (osteichthyan vertae.); Siegfried 1966 (osteol., Dercetis);

Tarlo, L. B. H. 1963 (aspidin, precursor of bone), 1964A (origin of bone); Tarlo, L. B. H. and Whiting 1965 (Agnatha); Thomson, K. S. 1964A (osteolepid snout), 1965D (dipnoan nasal apparatus), 1966A (middle ear), 1966F (coelacanth), 1968A (rhipidistian fishes); Thomson and Hahn 1968 (rhipidistian fishes);

Weitzman 1967 (stomiatid fishes); Whiting 1964 (arthrodirans).

AMPHIBIA – Clairambault 1967 (Anura);

Lebedkina 1964A (development of nasal bones), 1964B (Hynobiidae skull dermal bones);

Olson 1966A (middle ear);

Panchen 1967A (nostrils of early tetrapods), 1967B (labyrinthodont centra); Parrington 1967B (vertae. of early tetrapods);

Špinar 1963 (frogs);

Tatarinov, L. P. 1964A (labyrinthodont ear bones); Thomson, K. S. 1966A (middle ear);

Wake 1966 (salamander osteology); Wake and Dresner 1967 (salamander tail).

REPTILIA – Anon. 1966BR (Dinilysia);

Bellairs and Parson 1968 (biol. of Reptilia);

Chudinov 1968 (skin structure of theromorphs); Cruickshank 1968B (dicynodont palates);

Estes 1966 (Dinilysia, Argentina); Ewer 1965C (Euparkeria);

Fox 1964 (jaw musculature);

Gans 1966A (synapsid skull);

Haas, G. 1967 (vertebral centra of Trias. reptiles, Israel);

Jouffroy and Lessertisseur 1967 (muscle-skel. correlation of scapular belt);

Kamal 1966 (parachordal plate in Squamata);

Lessertisseur 1967 (ilio-sacral angle); Lüdicke 1962 (snakes);

MacIntyre 1967 (foramen pseudovale and quasi-mammals);

Olson 1966A (middle ear); Ostrom 1962B (mandibular musculature, N. Amer. hadrosaurs), 1964D (Triceratops jaw mechanics);

Parsons 1968 (recent turtles); Platel 1967 (reptile brain);

Sternberg 1964 (hadrosaur narial tubes);

Tatarinov, L. P. 1964AE (therocephalian head), 1965C, 1966A, D, 1967B (theriodonts), 1966C (therapsid skull).

AVES – George and Berger 1966 (avian myology).

MAMMALIA – Bauchot and Stephan 1967 (endocranial casts, mammals); Bergmann 1965 (primate skull); Bökönyi, Kállai, Matolcsi and Tarján 1965 (metacarpus of cattle); Bonifay, M.-F. 1966B (mammal limb bones); Bunak 1966B (homminid braincase);

Chiarelli 1968A, B (primate chromosomes);

Danilova 1965 (evol. of the hand), 1966 (hand and foot of primates); Davis, D. D. 1964 (giant panda); Day 1967 (multivariate analysis of Olduvai hominid toe phalanx); Dumont and Rifkind 1968 (thoracic duct);

Edinger 1964A (mammal brain), 1966A (camel brain); Egozcue and Vilarasau de Egozcue 1967A (chromosome evol. in Cebidae), 1967B (primate chromosomes); Enlow 1966 (facial growth, Homo, Macaca);

Frechkop 1967 (equid chromosomes); Friant 1966A (Meckel's cartilage);

Gatehouse 1965 (arched foot in man); Gorgas, K. 1967 (rodents); Gorgas, M. 1967 (rodents); Grassé 1967 (mammals);

Heintz, Nicole 1968 (hominid skull); Hemmer 1966 (Pantherinae); Hill, W. C. O. 1966 (primates); Hopson 1966 (origin of middle ear);

Iurovskaia 1964 (musculature in man);

Jouffroy and Lessertisseur 1967 (muscle-skel. correlation of scapular belt);

Kälin 1964 (pongid and hominid limbs); Kas'ianenko 1959 (mammal limbs and
joints); Knussmann 1965A (primate arm bones); Krüger, W. 1958 (skel.,
muscles of mammals);

Lavocat 1967A (auditive region of rodents); Lessertisseur 1967 (ilio-sacral angle);
Levin, V. N. 1967 (ear-bones of primates); Lisowski 1967 (primate talus);
Loth 1957 (eugenic characters in man);

MacIntyre 1967 (foramen pseudovale and quasi-mammals); Martin, R. D. 1966
(tree shrews); Masharskiĭ 1967 (functional role of the zygomatic arch); Mazhuga 1961 (skel. indices for rating limb functions), 1962 (vascular system of
pectoral limb); Mchedlidze 1964C (cetaceans, Caucasus); Mein 1967 (cricetid humeri); Mitchell, E. D. 1964 (pachyostosis in desmostylids);

Notz 1964 (deer);

Olivier 1965C (primates); Ondrias 1961 (front limbs of European mustelids);
Oxnard 1967 (primate shoulder);

Patterson, B. 1965A (borhyaenid auditory region); Pineau and Delmas 1966 (vert.
column); Prat 1966A (osteol., equids), 1966B (osteol., bovids), 1966C (osteol.,
antilopes);

Saban 1963 (primate skull), 1967 (enderostes); Sigé 1966 (bats); Sigmon and
Robinson 1967 (primate leg muscles); 1968B (Dremotherium); Simonetta
1957C (kinetic insectivore skulls); Simons 1967E (early catarrhine primates);
Simpson, G. G. 1968E (multituberculates); Sondaar 1968B (osteol., equid manus);
Speranskiĭ 1967 (skull sutures in man); Starck 1963B (mammal brain), 1964 (dog
and bear skulls), 1967A (mammal skull); Stirton 1965B (cranial morphology,
Castoroides);

Toots 1965A (disarticulation of mammal skel.); Tsui 1962 (human facial skel.);
Vlček 1962B, 1964B (human skull); Vogel, Ch. 1966A, 1968 (primate skull);

Walenski 1964 (mastoid of early man); Webb, S. D. 1965C (osteol. of Camelops);
Weinert 1956 (apes and man); Weninger 1962 (human skull changes);

Ziolkiewicz et al. 1965 (human mandible); Zuckerman et al. 1967 (primate pelvis).

ANCESTRY — See: evolution; general works; paleoanthropology; phylogeny.

ANNIVERSARIES, ANNIVERSARY VOLUMES — See: biographies; museums, institutions
and congresses.

ANTHROPOLOGY — See: bibliographies; biographies; correlation; cultural remains; dentition, MAMMALIA; distribution; evolution; faunas, QUATERNARY and QUATERNARY
CAVE; general works; habits; history of paleontology and paleoanthropology; paleobiology; paleochronology; Paleolithic art; paleomyology; paleoneurology; paleopsychology;
phylogeny; skeleton, MAMMALIA; skull, MAMMALIA; technique; and (in the systematic Index) Hominidae, Mammalia, Primates, and the genera and species of man.

AQUATIC ADAPTATIONS — Iakovlev, V. N. 1967A (armored Agnatha);
Mchedlidze 1964A, B (cetaceans); Mitchell, E. D. 1964 (pachyostosis in desmosty-
lids), 1966E (Allodesmus, California);
Pilleri 1967 (dolphins);
Quinet 1964B (mosasaurs);
Russell, D. A. 1964 (mosasaur skulls);
Zangerl 1963B (nothosaur, N. Amer.).

ARCHAEOLOGY — See: anthropology.

ART — See: Paleolithic art.

ARTIFACTS — See: anthropology.

BEHAVIOR (see also: habits; Paleolithic; paleopsychology) — Clark, J. G. D. 1966 (pre-
hist. and human behavior);
DeVore, [B. I.] et al. 1965 (behavior as adaptation);
Hemmer 1966 (Pantherinae); Hockett and Ascher 1964 (evol. of human behav-
ior); Holloway 1966A (hominid evol.);
Jolly 1966 (lemurs);
Kats 1968 (throwing by monkeys); Kortlandt 1967 (primate tool use);
Ladygina-Kots 1964 (tool activity of apes); Leakey, L. S. B. 1968D (Mioc. hom-
inid bone smashing); Lorenz 1965 (evol. and behavior);
Martin, R. D. 1966 (tree shrews); Morris, D. 1967A, B (social development of
man);
Odhner 1964 (social life of Australopithecinae and Pithecanthropus);
Siroto 1963 (gorilla); Skinner, B. F. 1966 (evol. of behavior);
Washburn and DeVore 1964 (social behavior, apes, early man); Washburn and
Jay 1967 (primate tool use).

BIBLIOGRAPHIES, CATALOGUES and LISTS — Albritton 1964, 1966 (geol.); [Almela
Samper] 1963 (Dr. J. R. Bataller); Anderson, R. R. 1966 (N. Dakota archeol.);
Angress and Reed 1962 (origin of domestic animals); Anon. 1956BS, 1959BS,
1960CL, CM, 1963BY, BZ, 1964V, 1965AN (prehist., Maghreb-Sahara), 1960CQ
(paleontologists of world), 1964J, 1965Q (anthrop. institutions), 1964Y (Jan
Czekanowski), 1964AJ (paleont., USSR), 1965R (anthropologists), 1965AA, AC,
AE (geochronology), 1965AH, AI (Henri Breuil), 1965AJ (Geroge Haas), 1965AO
(Emerson F. Greenman), 1965BP (biol. and evol.), 1965CW (Bernhard Rensch),
1966S (geol.), 1967A (Spanish geol.); Arambourg and Balout 1967 (fossil hom-
inids, Algeria); Arambourg, Biberson et al. 1967 (fossil hominids, Morocco);
Arkell and Hewes 1967 (fossil hominids, Sudan); Arkell and Sandford 1967
(fossil hominids, Egypt); Aslanova 1963 (study of fossil cetaceans, USSR); Astre
1966A (Bull. Soc. Hist. Nat. Toulouse);
Banta 1966 (fossil amphibians, reptiles, Nevada); Barley and Lucas 1958, 1960
(COWA surveys—British Isles); Barradas 1967 (fossil hominids, Moçambique);
Barton 1968 (New Zealand archeol.); Beardsley 1962 (COWA surveys, Japan);
Beardsley, Chang and Loehr 1959 (COWA surveys, Far East); Beauchêne and
Hugon 1964 (Afr. anthrop.); Befu, Chard and Okada 1964 (Japanese archeol.);
Bell, R. E. 1965A, B (Oklahoma archeol.); Binder 1960, 1961A, 1962A (archeol., paleont., Germany); Birdsell 1959, 1962 (COWA surveys, Australia); Black
and Bisset 1894 (Grierson Mus., Scotland); Blake 1967 (vert. paleont.); Bonchev 1965 (Petŭr Nikolov Bakalov); Boss [1965] (archeol. periodicals); Bourdier 1962C (Quat., Rhône Valley); Bouvier 1889 (fossil whales); Brodkorb
1964A, 1967 (fossil birds); Broglio 1960B (French statistical studies of artifacts), 1961B (Mid. to Up. Pal. industries); Brown, D. F. 1959A, 1962 (COWA
surveys, W. Europe), 1959B, 1964 (COWA surveys, W. Mediterranean); Bülow
1962B (Johannes Walther);
Cahen 1966 (Arthur Holmes); Cahn 1962 (Etienne Geoffroy Saint-Hilaire); Calvocoressi 1965 (COWA surveys, W. Afr.); Camp, C. L. 1965A (V. L. Vander
Hoof); Camp, Allison and Nichols 1964 (fossil verts.); Camp, Allison, Nichols
and McGinnis 1968 (fossil verts.); Camp, Clemens, Gregory and Savage 1967
(Ruben Arthur Stirton); Campbell, B. G. 1968 (Australopithecus); Chang,
Kwang-chih 1961 (COWA surveys, Far East); Chang, Kwang-chih and Kidder
1964 (COWA surveys, Far East); Chard 1957, 1960B (COWA surveys, N. Asia);
Chollot 1964 (catalogue Piette collection Pal. art, Mus. Antiquités Nation., Paris);
Churakov, Obruchev and Finashina 1965 (Vladimir Afanas'evich Obruchev);
Clark, Janet 1967, 1968 (bibliog. vert. paleont.); Clark, J. D. 1962F, 1965C
(COWA surveys, Equatorial Afr.); 1962G, 1965D (COWA surveys, E. Afr.);

McBurney 1967A (fossil hominids, Libya); McCartney 1964 (sources on the study
of human bone); Malaroda 1963 (Constantino Socin); Mal'chevskaïa and Roma-
novskaïa 1966 (monographs on paleont. collections in TsNIGR Mus., USSR); Mal-
donado-Koerdell and Borgonio 1961 (Pablo Martínez del Rio); Malez 1959E
(Otokar Kadić), 1965B (hominid sites, Croatia); Mansfield 1967 (British caving
periodicals); Martin, G. P. R. 1965C (Wilhelm Weiler); Mason, J. A. 1966A
(Nels Christian Nelson); Mason and Beaumont 1962 (COWA surveys, S. Afr.);
Matson 1957, 1960 (COWA surveys, W. Asia); Maurin 1962 (Hermann Bock);
Mayer 1963C (geol., paleont. bibliog.); Menon 1964 (fossil fishes of India);
Michael 1964A (Maksim Grigorevich Levin); Miszkiewicz 1964 (papers on Jan
Czekanowski); Mitscha-Märheim 1964 (Eduard Beninger); Muller, E. H. 1965
(bibliog. of New York Quat. geol.); Müller, H. H. 1962, 1963, 1964 (bibliog.
of prehist., zoology, hist. of domestic animals);

Nader 1962 (Shanidar Cave, Iraq); Naletov 1961 (fossil localities, ASSR); Neave
1966 (zool. nomenclature); Nenquin 1964A 1965, 1968 (Inventaria Archaeologica Africana); Neuman 1968 (archeol., Great Plains); Northrop 1964 (Paleoz.,
Mesoz. and Cenoz. verts., New Mexico); Novotný 1964 (Slovakian archeol.,
1960);

Oakley and Campbell 1967A, B (catal. of fossil hominids, Afr.), 1967C (fossil hom-
inids, Mali), 1967D (fossil hominids, Niger); Ødum 1964 (Valdemar Johan
Heinrich Nordmann); Okada, Okada and Chard 1967 (archeol. of Hokkaido);
Osaba 1964 (archeol., Spain);

Page 1965 (preparation of bibliographies); Polgár, L. 1965 (P. Teilhard de Chardin)
Praus 1964 (Michigan archeol.);

Riche and Lille 1962 (prehist., Morocco); Riemer 1963 et seq. (Catal. Amer. amphibians and reptiles); Römisch-Germanisches Zentralmuseum 1966 (COWA surv.,
W. Europe); Rosiński 1958 (Jerzy Dąmbski); Rouse 1958B, 1961 (COWA
surveys, W. Afr.);

Schuhl et al. 1964 (geol., paleont., evol.); Sjödin 1965 (anthrop.); Solheim 1960B
(COWA surveys, Indonesia), 1966C (COWA surveys, S. E. Asia); Spaulding 1959
(COWA surveys, E. Afr.); Sprague, R. 1967 (Washington archeol.);

Tolstoy 1958 (COWA surveys, USSR); Toombs 1967 (E. I. White); Tremaine 1962
(Arctic); Trimmel 1954, 1955, 1958A, B, 1959, 1962, 1963A, B, 1964 (speleology); Turnbull, L. 1960 (COWA surveys, Balkans);

Vallespi 1957 (Pérez Temprado, L.); Vallois 1967A (fossil hominids, Ethiopia);
Vidart 1965 (anthrop.);

Ward 1967 (geol. reference sources); West, R. G. 1967 (Quat. faunas, British
Isles); White, E. I. 1955B (earliest reference to fossil fishes); Wilimovsky et
al. 1964 (osteol. of fishes); Williams, S. 1966 (Antonio J. Waring, Jr.); Woodall 1968 (statistics in archeol.);

Zhirmunskiǐ 1957 (Anthropozoic, Czechoslovakia).

BIOGRAPHIES, BIOGRAPHICAL NOTES, HONORS, MEMORIALS, ANNIVERSARY and MEMORIAL VOLUMES, PORTRAITS (See also: obituaries)

— Absolon, Karel
(Strouhal, H. 1961); Agassiz, Louis (Davenport 1963; Portmann, J. P. 1962;
Romer 1963C); Aldinger, Hermann (Geyer 1962); Alekseev, A. K. (Tikhom-
irov, V. V. and Voskresenskaïa 1963B.); Ameghino, Carlos (Rusconi 1965;
Simpson, G. G. 1967C.); Ameghino, Florentino (Ringuelet 1961; Simpson,
G. G. 1967C.); Anderson, Adrian (Anon. 1966AN.); Andrews, Roy Chapman
(Colbert 1968A.); Andrusov, N. I. (Tikhomirov, V. V. and Voskresenskaïa
1961C.); Angress, Shimon (Reed, C. A. 1962.); Anning, Mary (Bush 1966;
Lang, W. D. 1945, 1950, 1953; Matheson 1964.); Applegate, Shelton Pleasants
(Anon. 1963CL.); Artsykhovskii, Artemii Vladimirovich (Avdusin and Ianin.);
Bacmeister, Walther (Kleinschmidt, A. 1964A.); Bader, Otto Nikolaevich (Krainov
1963.); Bakalov, Petur Nikolov (Bonchev 1965.); Balabaǐ, Pavlo Pavlovich

(Pasternak 1962.); <u>Barbour, Erwin Hinkley</u> (Schultz, C. B. 1967.); <u>Barbour, Thomas</u> (Romer 1964I.); <u>Bataller, José Ramon</u> (Almela Samper, A. 1963.); <u>Beltran, Antonio</u> (D., J. 1964.); <u>Beninger, Eduard</u> (Mitscha-Märheim 1964); <u>Berg, Leo Simonovich</u> (Otorbaev 1963; Turdakov 1963.); <u>Beringer, Johann</u> (Cohen 1963.); <u>Bessom, Leonard C.</u> (Latham 1966.); <u>Biasutti, Renato</u> (Parenti 1965.); <u>Binkhorst van den Binkhorst, J. T.</u> (Kruytzer 1962.); <u>Black, Davidson</u> (Hood 1964.); <u>Black, Glenn A.</u> (Kellar 1966.); <u>Blanc, Alberto Carlo</u> (Anon. 1961CR, 1962CO; Blanc, E. 1966; Pericot García 1962B, 1963D.); <u>Bluntschli, Hans</u> (Strauss 1964A, B.); <u>Bock, Hermann</u> (Maurin 1962.); <u>Bogachev, Vladimir Vladimirovich</u> (Anon. 1966V; Eberzin 1966; Kovalevskiĭ 1966.); <u>Bonnet, Charles</u> (Glass, Temkin and Straus.); <u>Bosch Gimpera, Pedro</u> (Breuil 1963B.); <u>Bosquet, J.</u> (Kruytzer 1963A.); <u>Botet, Rodrigo</u> (Martel San Gil and Aguirre.); <u>Boule, P. M.</u> (Tikhomirov, V. V. and Voskresenskaia 1961B.); <u>Brace, C. Loring</u> (Anon. 1968P.); <u>Braidwood, Robert J.</u> (Anon. 1965P.); <u>Breuil, Henri</u> (Alonso del Real y Ramos 1964; Anciaux de Faveaux 1964; Anon. 1961CQ, 1965AI; Balout 1963, 1965; Baudet 1962B, 1964; Bouyssonie 1964; Boyle 1965; Breuil 1960D, 1964B, C, D, E; Burkitt 1964A; Combier, M. 1966; Dart, R. A. 1964B; Giedion 1964A; Jeannel 1962; Lantier 1965; Mason, R. J. 1965A; Méroc and Mazet; Pales and Tassin de Saint Péreuse 1965; Pei 1965A; Pericot García 1965B; Pla Ballester 1965; Ripoll Perelló 1962A, 1964A, B, 1965B; Roussot 1961, 1966A, D; Sahly 1965; Scherz, E. R. 1965; Skrotzky 1964; Smith, P. E. 1962B; Zbyszewski 1962A.); <u>Broom, Robert</u> (Colbert 1968A; Palmer, Eve 1967.); <u>Brown, Barnum</u> (Colbert 1968A; Lewis, G. E. 1964A, B.); <u>Buckland, William</u> (Boylan 1967B; Colbert 1968A.); <u>Buffon, Georges Louis Lelerc</u> (Glass, Temkin and Straus.); <u>Bülow, Kurd von</u> (Anon. 1965H.); <u>Bunak, Victor Valerianovich</u> (Nesturkh 1964A.); <u>Bystrov, Aleksei Petrovich</u> (Orlov 1959B.); <u>Camarate Andrade França, José</u> (Teixeira 1965.); <u>Camp, Charles L.</u> (Segerblom 1965.); <u>Carbonell, Virginia M.</u> (Dahlberg 1966.); <u>Carter, George</u> (Lee, T. E. 1963B.); <u>Chardin, Pierre Teilhard de</u> (Antunes, Manuel 1965; Barbour 1965A, B; Battetta 1966; Boné 1964A; Burkitt 1965; Campion 1965; Chauchard 1965; Collected Papers 1965B; Crusafont Pairó 1965A; Cuénot 1965; Delfgaauw 1964; Facchini 1968; Fothergill 1965; Grenet 1965; Hemleben 1966; Hugedé 1966; Huxley, J. 1964B; Johnson, H. 1965; Jones, D. G. 1967; Koenigswald 1965D; Kremmeter 1967; Leroy, P. 1965; Madaule 1963; Mooney 1964; Mortier and Aboux 1966A, B; Narr 1966A; Olivier 1965A; Orellana Rodriguez 1965; Ormea 1963; Piveteau 1964B; Portmann, A. 1961, 1965C; Schmitz-Moormann 1966; Senghor 1968; Simpson, G. G. 1966B; Terra 1963, 1964, 1965; Verbrugge 1964; Wahlert 1966; Wildiers 1964.); <u>Charpentier, Jean de</u> (Tikhomirov, V. V. and Voskresenskaia 1961A.); <u>Child, Gordon</u> (Mongaĭt 1958.); <u>Choubert, Georges</u> (Marçais 1966A.); <u>Clark, John Graham Douglas</u> (Anon. 1965P.); <u>Clark, Wilfrid Le Gros</u> (Anon. 1965BN.); <u>Colbert, Edwin Harris</u> (Anon. 1968N; Hellman 1964.); <u>Comas, Juan</u> (Leon-Portilla, et al. 1965); <u>Cope, Edward Drinker</u> (Colbert 1968A; Goetzmann 1965; Plate 1964; Romer 1964H.); <u>Correa, Mendes</u> (Pericot García 1962A.); <u>Cotta, Bernhard von</u> (Wagenbreth 1965.); <u>Crompton, A. W.</u> (Anon. 1967G.); <u>Cuvier, Georges</u> (Coleman 1964; Rodríguez Cowan 1961.); <u>Czekanowski, Jan</u> (Anon. 1964X; Miszkiewicz 1964; Wanke 1964A, B.); <u>Dal Piaz, Giorgio</u> (Leonardi, P. 1964.); <u>Dąmbski, Jerzy</u> (Rosiński 1958.); <u>Dart, Raymond A.</u> (Anon. 1964BI, 1964BT; Dart, M. 1968; Terry 1965; Tobias 1964B, 1968B.); <u>Darwin, Charles</u> (Anon. 1962CF; Barlow 1967; Beer 1962C, 1964A, E, 1966A; Beer, et al. 1967; Bell, P. R. 1964; Carreras 1960; Clark, R. E. D. 1967; Cramer 1959; Davitashvili 1960; Dibner, B. 1964; Gray, A. 1963; Gregor 1966B, Huxley, J. 1960C, 1964B; Huxley, J. and Kettlewell; Ioganzen 1959; Jaczewski 1960; King-Hele 1964; Koehler 1960; Leonardi, P. 1959G; Leroy, J. 1966; Lisonbee 1965A; Loewenberg 1965; Mayr 1964B; Mertens 1960; Olby 1967; Parodi Bustos 1960; Reis 1961; Rodríguez Cowan 1961; Selsan 1964;

Shatskiĭ 1960, 1965; Shippen 1963; Shmidt 1940; Stecher 1964; Strelkovskiĭ 1964; Szarski 1960; Wichler 1963; Zimmerman 1959; Zimmermann 1960A.); Darwin, Erasmus (King-Hele 1968; Moody, J. W. T. 1964.); Davis, D. Dwight (Anon. 1965O.); Debets, Georgiĭ Frantsevich (Editorial Staff 1966; Formozov 1965B; Gokhman 1966A.); Deevey, Edward S. (Anon. 1966BD.); Deinse, A. B. van (Slijper 1965.); Dick, Robert (Martin, G. P. R. 1966B.); Dietrich, Wilhelm Otto (Daber 1965; Gross, W. 1964A; Staesche 1964A.); Dobzhansky, Theodosius Grigorievich (Anon. 1967C.); Dollo, Louis (Colbert 1968A; Davitashvili 1956C; Edinger 1964C.); Douglass, Earl (Colbert 1968A.); Drennan, Matthew Robertson (Anon. 1966AY.); Dupree, Louis (Anon. 1968O.);

Edinger, Tilly (Anon. 1962CL; Franz, E. 1967; Tobien 1968E.); Efimenko, Petr Petrovich (Anon. 1959BU.); Ehgartner, Wilhelm (Jungwirth 1966.); Ehrenberg, Kurt (Anon. 1966AX.); Estes, Richard (Anon. 1966BR, BV.);

Flint, Richard F. (Anon. 1967N.); Foote, Robert Bruce (Ghosh 1963; Sen and Ghosh 1966.); Fourmarier, Paul (Pruvost 1965.); Fraas, Eberhard (Staesche 1964B.); Frick, Childs (Anthony H. 1966.); Fuehrer, Ottmar F. von (Morrow 1967.);

Gandert, Otto-Friedrich (Müller, A. von and Nagel.); Gates, Reginald Ruggles (Dart, R. A. 1966B.); Geinitz, Hanns Bruno (Kettner 1964.); Geist, Otto William (Skarland 1964.); Gerasimov, M. M. (Formozov 1967.); Gessner, Conrad (Fischer, H. 1965; Martin, G. P. R. 1965A.); Giddings, James Louis (Larsen 1966; Rainey 1965.); Gieseler, Wilhelm (Baitsch, 1965.); Gigout, Marcel (Marçais 1966B.); Gilmore, Charles W. (Colbert 1968A.); Ginzburg, Vulf Veniaminovich (Gokhman 1964.); Gladwin, H. S. (Anon. 1959BT.); Gorodtsov, V. A. (Krainov 1960C.); Granger, Walter (Colbert 1968A.); Greenman, Emerson F. (Fitting 1965G; Jelinek, E. K. 1965.); Guilday, John E. (Anon. 1965AR.); Guthörl, Paul (Kneuper 1964.);

Haas, George (Werner, Y. L. 1965.); Haase, Ernst (Otto 1959.); Haeckel, Ernst (Heberer 1967B; Strelkovskiĭ 1964.); Harrison, Tom (Anon. 1967U.); Harting, Pieter (Vinken 1963.); Heller, Florian (Binder 1965A; Ehrenberg 1965D.); Hinton, Martin Alister Campbell (Savage, R. J. G. 1964B.); Hitchcock, Edward (Colbert 1968A.); Holmes, Arthur (Cahen 1966; Harland, Smith and Wilcock.); Hoppe, Walter (Seidel and Wagenbreth); Hotton, Nicholas (Anon. 1964BR.); Howells, William White (Anon. 1967AY.); Huene, Friedrich von (Colbert 1968A.); Hürzeler, Johannes (Crusafont Pairo 1965B.); Huxley, Julian S. (Miklin 1967.); Huxley, Thomas H. (Colbert 1968A; Williams, W. 1964.);

Iakolev, Nikolai Nikolaevich (Arendt and Goriacheva, 1967.); Janensch, Werner (Anon. 1965H; Hennig, E. 1964.); Jefferson, Thomas (Jones, D. J. 1968.); Jordan, David Starr (Hubbs 1964.); Josselyn, Daniel W. (Lee, T. E. 1963C.); Joten, Kari (Heintz, A. 1965A.);

Kadic, Otokar (Malez 1959E.); Karpinskiĭ, A. P. (Shatskiĭ 1965.); Kidder, Alfred Vincent (Judd 1965; Wauchope 1965.); Kleinschmidt, Otto (Kleinschmidt, A. 1964A.); Knight, Samuel Howell (Thomas, H. D. 1963.); Koenigswald, Gustav Heinrich Ralph von (Anon. 1966W; Starck 1966B.); Konen, Adolf (Tikhomirov, V. V. and Voskresenskaia 1965.); Kovalevskiĭ, Vladimir (Kas'ianenko 1968; Strel'nikov 1966; Strel'nikov and Hecker.); Kozlowski, Roman (Sokolov, B. S. 1965.); Kühne, Walter G. (Anon. 1966I.);

Lahner, Georg (Pilz 1962.); Lamarck, G. (Smirnov 1959.); Lamarck, Jean Baptiste Pierre...(Glass, Temkin and Straus.); Lambe, Lawrence M. (Colbert 1968A); Lane, Henry Higgins (Hall, E. R. 1967.); Leakey, Louis Seymour Bazett (Anon. 1964Q, 1964BI, 1968AB; Payne, M. M. 1965; Tufty 1967.); Leidy, Joseph (Goetzmann 1965.); Levin, Maksim Grigorevich (Michael 1964A.); Linnaeus, Carolus (Uggla 1957.); Lull, Richard Swann (Colbert 1968A.); Lyell, Charles (Shatskiĭ 1965; Tikhomirov, V. V. and Voskresenskaia 1963A.);

Macdonald, James Reid (Anon. 1964BH.); Macgowan, Kenneth (Hester, J. A. 1964.); Mantell, Gideon (Colbert 1968A.); Marsh, Othniel C. (Colbert 1968A; Goetzmann

James (Carmichael and Long.); Socin, Costantino (Malaroda 1963.); Sowerby, George Brettingham (Matheson 1964.); Steno, Nicolaus (Becksmann 1939C; Garboe 1964.); Stensen, Niels (Kruytzer 1964B; Scherz, G. 1962, 1963, 1964.); Sternberg, Charles H. (Colbert 1968A.); Sternberg, Charles M. (Colbert 1968A.); Sternberg, George (Colbert 1968A.); Sternberg, Levi (Colbert 1968A.); Stirton, Ruben Arthur (Camp, C. L., Clemens, Gregory and Savage; Kleinpell 1968.); Stolyhwo, Casimir (Sikora 1967.); Suess, Eduard (Küpper 1964; Zapfe 1964A.); Tobias, Phillip V. (Anon. 1964BI.); Tokarev, Sergei Aleksandrovich (Salmanovich 1965.); Tschumi, Otto (Laur-Belart 1960.);

Valenciennes, Achille (Monod 1963B.); Vallisneri, Antonio (Dal Piaz 1962.); Vanderhoof, Vertress Lawrence (Camp, C. L. 1964, 1965A, B; Levorsen 1964.); Van Straelen, Victor (Anon. 1963CJ; Corin 1965; Rioult 1964; Stubblefield 1965.); Vaufrey, Raymond (Bordes and Sonneville-Bordes; Piveteau 1966C.); Vega del Sella, Conde de la (Jordá Cerdá 1956E.); Vinci, Léonard de (Buttin 1965.); Vinogradov, Boris Stepanovich (Novikov 1961.); V'iushkov, Boris Pavlovich (Efremov 1968.);

Wadia, D. N. (Jhingran, et al. 1965; West, W. D. 1965.); Wahle, Ernst (Kirchner 1964.); Wallace, Alfred Russell (Cottler 1966; Harrisson, T. 1960; George, W. 1964; Williams-Ellis 1966.); Walther, Johannes (Bülow 1962B.); Waring, Antonio J., Jr. (Williams, S. 1966.); Watson, David Meredith Seares (Shotton 1965.); Wegner, Richard Nikolaus (Schumacher 1964.); Wehrli, Hans (Anon. 1965H; Ruchholz 1963; Wamser 1959.); Weinert, Hans (Schaefer, U. 1968.); Weidenreich, Franz (Washburn 1964.); White, John A. (Friedmann 1965.); Wilson, Sir Daniel (Trigger 1966.); Woodward, John (Eyles 1965.); Würtenberger, Franz Joseph, Thomas, Oskar, Leopold, and Alexander (Mayer 1963B.);

Zeuner, Frederick Everard (Hollingsworth 1965.); Zhukov, B. S. (Bader, O. N., 1968C.).

BIOLOGY — See: anatomy; aquatic adaptations; behavior; circulatory system; coprolites; correlation; cultural remains; dentition; distribution; ecology; eggs; evolution; extinction; faunas; flight; general works; habits; ichnology; integumentary structures; legislation; occurrences; paleo-anthropology; paleobiology; paleochronology; Paleolithic art; paleomyology; paleoneurology; paleopathology; paleopsychology; paleophysiology; phylogeny; skeleton; skull; technique; terminology; variation and heredity.

BIOMECHANICS, PALEOBIOMECHANICS — See: paleomyology; skeleton; skull.

BIOMETRICS — See: craniometry; variations and heredity.

BIONOMICS — See: ecology.

BIOSTRATIGRAPHY — See: correlation; faunas.

BIOSTRATONOMY — See: ecology; occurrences; paleochronology.

BRAIN — See: anatomy; evolution; paleoneurology; skull.

CARBON–14, DATINGS AND METHODS — See: paleochronology; technique.

CASTS and MOLDS — See: economic and commercial paleontology; restorations; technique.

CATALOGUES — See: bibliographies.

CAVE and ROCK PAINTINGS — See: Paleolithic art.

CAVE FAUNAS and SPELEOLOGY — See: correlation; faunas; QUATERNARY CAVE; occurrences; Paleolithic art.

CHEMICAL COMPOSITION and ANALYSIS OF FOSSILS and SEDIMENTS — See: correlation; dentition; occurrences; skeleton; skull; technique.

CHEMICAL DATING OF FOSSILS and SEDIMENTS — See: paleochronology; technique.

CHONDROCRANIUM — See: paleoneurology; skull.

CHRONOLOGY — See: paleochronology.

CIRCULATORY SYSTEM, PALEOSEROLOGY, BLOOD GROUPS — Albrecht 1967
    (cranial arteries, turtles);
  Guth 1964A (fossil carnivores);
  Mazhuga 1962 (vascular system of mammal pectoral limb);
  Ornano 1967 (hemoglobine structure);
  Quinet 1964B (circulatory system of mosasaur head);
  Ruffié 1967A (primates); Russell, L. S. 1965B (dinosaurs);
  Sarich 1967B (primate albumins);
  Tatarinov, L. P. 1966B, 1967A (therapsid brain).

CLASSIFICATION — See: evolution; phylogeny; terminology; also: Systematic Index, and Table of Classification.

CLIMATOLOGY — See: paleoclimatology.

COMPARATIVE ANATOMY — See: anatomy.

CONGRESSES, CONFERENCES, and COLLOQUIA — See: museums, institutions, and congresses.

CONTINENTAL DRIFT — See: paleogeography.

COPROLITES, GASTROLITHS, VISCERAL CONTENTS, and CONCRETIONS — Adrover
    1964A (coprolites, Plioc., Spain); Arribas 1967 (gastroliths, Spain);
  Dorr 1966 (gastroliths and wind-polished stones);
  Li, Han and Hsu 1966 (coprolites, China); Lundelius 1966 (coprolites, Australian caves);
  Martini 1965 (coprolites, Germany); Mitzopoulos and Zapfe 1963 (hyaenid coprolites, Greece);
  Prasad and Verma 1967 (dinosaur coprolites, India);
  Thenius 1965B (carnivore coprolites, Germany);
  Vogeltanz 1965, 1967 (Olig. coprolites, Nebraska); Voigt 1960B (Cret. urinary calculus);
  Young, C.-C. 1964C (crocodilian coprolites, China);
  Zangerl 1964 (shark pellets and coprolites, Indiana).

CORRELATION, STRATIGRAPHIC and FAUNAL, BIOSTRATIGRAPHY, GEOLOGIC
  STUDIES and MAPS (see also: faunas) — Adam 1964, 1966C, (Pleist., cent. Europe);
  Adamenko 1963 (Pleist., USSR); Agassiz 1967 (glaciers); Aguirre 1964B (elephant-kill site, Spain), 1965 (Pleist. mammals, Spain); Alekseev, M. N. 1961A
  (Quat. USSR), 1961B (Quat., Lena R., USSR); Alekseev et al., 1961 (Quat. USSR); Alekseev et al. 1962 (Quat. N. E. Siberia); Alekseev et al. 1965, 1966
  (geochron., Siberia); Alimen 1964C (Quat., Sahara), 1964E (Pyrenees, France),

1966 (Quat., W. Europe), 1967 (Quat., France); Alimen, Radulesco and Samson 1968 (Pleist. correlation, Rumania); Alizade, K. A. 1967 (Azerbaidzhan); Aljter 1960 (Quat., USSR); Allen 1964 (Devonian, S. Wales); Allison 1966 (Fossil Lake, Oregon); Al'ter 1960 (Quat. deposits of Enisei R. valley, USSR); Anatol'eva 1960 (fishes, USSR); Anciaux de Faveaux 1962 (Plateau des Biano); Anon. 1964BL (geol. eras), 1967R (Afr. strat.), 1968AG (Gondwanaland); Arambourg 1963H (Europe and Afr., mammals); Arambourg et al. 1959 (Arabian peninsula); Arapov 1965 (Moldavia, USSR); Arkhipov 1960 (Siberia); Arkhipov, Koreneva and Lavrushin 1960 (Siberia); Arnold 1964A (Haltern ss., Germany); Arnold et al. 1964 (Germany); Astre 1964B (France);

Bachmayer and Cornelius-Furlani 1960 (fossil sites near Vienna); Bader, Ivanova and Velichko 1965 (Pal., E. and Cent. Europe); Badoux, M. H. 1964 (caves, France); Balout 1967A (Quat. strat., Tunisia); Banks 1965 (geol. and faunas, Tasmania); Baranova and Biske 1964 (mammals, E. Siberia); Barat 1960 (mammals, Rumania); Barta 1965A (Pleist. strat., Czechoslovakia); Bandet 1961C (Pleist., France); Bazhanov 1959B (stratigraphic significance of faunas); Bazhanov and Kostenko 1960 (Kazakhstan); Bazhanov and Kozhamkulova 1960 (Kazakhstan); Bazhanov, Mafsui and Mos'kina 1968 (USSR); Behm-Blancke 1967 (Ehringsdorf, Germany); Beliaeva 1961 (Elasmotheriinae); Belokrys 1959B (Zygolophodon); Benda, Heimbach and Mattiat 1962 (geol., N. W. Germany); Bersenev, et al. 1962 (Quat., USSR); Biberson 1965E (Mauritania), 1966 (Pleist., Morocco), 1967A (Quat., N. W. Afr.); Biriukov et al 1968 (Kazakhstan); Bishop 1959B (survey, Uganda), 1967B (fossil localities, E. Afr.); Biske 1964 (Quat. terraces, Siberia); Black and Dawson 1966B (paleont. and geol., cent. Wyoming); Bolotova 1966 (Mongolia); Bonaparte 1966E (Trias., Argentina); Bond, G. 1967 (S. Afr.); Bond, W. R. G. 1932, 1933 (Elephas ravine, England); Bonifay, E. 1964A (Plioc., Pleist., Mediterranean area), 1964B (Regourdou Cave, France); Bonnet, A. 1964 (Rhone Valley); Bosch 1964B (Mioc., North Sea Basin); Bosch and Janssen 1965 (Mioc., Netherlands); Bourdier 1961, 1962C (Quat., Rhone Valley); Bourdier and Lacassagne 1964 (Plioc., France); Bout 1964A, B (Quat., France); Bradley 1964 (Green River Form.); Brain 1965, 1967A (S. Afr. caves); Branson 1965A (Perm. site, Oklahoma); Bright 1967 (Pleist., Idaho); Brinkmann 1960 (geol. evol. of Europe); Brooks, R. H. 1967 (bone analysis, Tule Springs, Nevada); Brooks, Orlins and Williams 1967 (Tule Springs, Nevada); Bruijn and Meurs 1967 (lagomorphs, Spain); Brunet, J. 1967 (Tehuacan Valley, Mexico); Buchan et al. 1965 (Trias., Spitzbergen and Svalbard); Buday et al. 1964 (Up. Tert., W. Carpathians); Bukatchuk et al. 1967 (Plioc., USSR);

Chakravarti 1965 (elephants, India, Burma, Pakistan); Chalyshev 1966A (Paleozoic, N. Urals); Chang, Y.-p. et al. 1964 (Cenozoic, China); Chardin 1965A (Plio.-Pleist., S. E. Asia); Chavaillon, J. 1964, 1965A, 1966B, (Pleist. strat., Sahara); Chebotareva et al. 1957, 1959 (Quat., Lena and Aldan Rivers, USSR); Chepikov 1944, 1945 (Perm. red beds, USSR); Choubert and Faure-Muret 1961 (Mioc. verts., Marocco); Chow, M., Huang et al. 1965 (Cenoz., S. W. Shansi); Chumakov 1961A (Quat. micromammals), 1965 (Cenoz., USSR), 1967 (Plio., Pleist., Nile Valley); Chuvardinskii 1963 (Scandinavian glaciations); Clark, John 1962 (post-Silurian red beds), 1967A (Slim Buttes form.), 1967B (Brule form.), 1967C (Oligocene, S. Dakota); Clark and Beerbower 1967 (Chadron form.); Clark, Beerbower and Kietzke 1967 (Oligocene, S. Dakota); Clark and Kietzke 1967 (Brule form., S. Dakota); Colbert 1966D (erosion in Chinle form.); Colinvaux 1967 (Bering land bridge); Collected Papers 1966A (W. Kazakhstan), 1966B (E. Russian Platform), 1966D (N. W. RSFSR), 1966E (Russian Plain), 1967B (Low. Pleist., Russian Plain), 1967D (Mesoz., Cenoz., Siberia), 1967E (Paleoz., Baltic regions), 1967F (S. Urals and Povolzh'e), 1968 (Devon., Siberian Platform); Conolly 1965 (fishes, New South Wales); Conrad 1965 (Quat., Sahara); Cook, H. J. 1965 (Mioc. form., Nebraska); Cooke, H. B. S. 1967 (Pleist., S. Afr.);

(Cret., W. Kansas); Hay 1965A, B, 1967 (Olduvai Gorge, E. Afr.); Hayes 1964A
(geol. hist., Egypt); Haynes 1965 (geol. of Hell Gap site, Wyoming), 1967B
(Quat. geol. of Tule Springs, Nevada); Haynes and Grey 1965 (Sister's Hill site
and Wyoming postglacial alluvial chronol.); Heinzelin de Braucourt and Paepe
1965 (Nile Valley, Sudanese Nubia); Hoffstetter 1961E (mammal beds, S. Amer.);
Hölder 1964 (Jurassic); Hölker 1960 (Charlotten Cave, Germany); Hooijer 1964
(lower boundary of Pleist., Java); Hopkins, D. M. 1967B (Quat. marine transgressions, Beringia), 1967C (Cenoz. hist. of Beringia), 1967D (Bering land bridge);
Hopkins, D. M., et al. 1965 (Quat., Bering Str.); Hoskins 1961 (Silur., Pennsylvania
Hotton 1967 (Beaufort series, S. Afr.); House 1965 (geol., Dorset); Houston
1962 (Tert., Wyoming);

Iakhimovich, V. L. 1960A (lower boundary of Quat., Urals), 1960B (age of beds,
Urals), 1965 (Quat. of S. Urals); Iakovlev, S. A. 1959 (stratigraphic scheme for
Siberia); Iakovlev, V. N. 1967B (freshwater fishes, Mesoz., Cenoz.); Ianov 1959
(Devon., USSR); Ianshin 1953 (N. Aral region, USSR); Ibragimov and Turdukulov
1965 (Tert., USSR); Ibragimov and Talipov 1965 (Cenoz., USSR); Irish 1965
(Rocky Mt. foothills, Alberta); Isaac 1965A, B, 1967A (Pleist. Peninj beds, Tanzania), 1966A (Olorgesailie area, Kenya); Ishida 1959 (Mioc., Japan); Ishnazarov
1965 (Devon., USSR); Iur'ev 1961 (Quat., Uzbekistan); Ivan'ev 1964 (ostrich
remains, W. Transbaikalia); Ivanov 1962 (Plioc., Borotala R. basin, USSR); Ivanova 1961D, 1965A (Paleolithic, Dnestr, USSR), 1965B, D, 1967 (hominid stratig.);

Jackson, G. F. 1965 (Defense Cave, California); Jayet 1965 (Quat., Switzerland);
Johnson, P. 1964 (Cherokee Cave, Missouri); Jong 1967 (Quat. stratig., Netherlands);

Kahlke 1965A, I, J (Pleist., Europe), 1965E (Plioc.-Pleist. boundary, Europe); Kallies
1963 (Trias., Germany); Kambariddinov 1968 (faunistic complexes and Anthropo-
gene deposits, Middle Asia); Kamenov 1965 (Plioc.-Pleist. limit, Bulgaria); Kaplan,
A. A. 1964 (Devon., USSR); Kaplianskaia and Tarnogradskii 1961 (Pleist., USSR);
Kaplianskaia et al. 1964 (Tobol Trans-Urals); Karatajute 1958A (asterolepids, USSR
Karatajute-Talimaa 1960A, 1964 (Devon. fishes, Lithuania); Karatajute-Talimaa and
Narbutas 1964 (Baltic Devon.); Kay and Colbert 1965 (strat. and life hist.);
Kazarinov 1958 (Mesoz., Cenoz., W. Siberia); Keroher et al. 1966 (lexicon of
geol. names, U. S.); Khain 1966 (Anthropogene geol.); Khatri 1961B (Pleist.
chronol., cent. India); Khoreva 1959 (Quat., USSR); Khosbaiar 1966 (fossil sites,
Gobi Desert); Khubka 1965 (Mioc., Moldavia); Kiriushina 1959 (Quat., Soviet
Arctic); Kitching 1968 (Perm., S. Afr.); Kittleman et al. 1965 (Cenoz., Oregon);
Kitts 1965 (Cenoz., Oklahoma), 1966 (geol. time); Klages 1962 (geol. and fossils,
Germany); Klassen, Delorme and Mott 1967 (Pleist., S. W. Manitoba); Klein,
R. G. 1966A (Up. Pleist., Dnestr Basin, USSR); Kobayashi, T. 1964A (geol. and
paleont., S. E. Asia); Kolesnikov 1961 (Mesoz., W. Transbaikal); Konstantinova
1965B (Pleist., S. European USSR), 1965C (Pleist. small mammals, S. Moldavia,
S. W. Ukraine), 1967A (Anthropogene, S. Moldavia, S. W. Ukraine), 1967B (Anthro-
pogene, Prut and Danube Rs.); Korolev 1965 (Tian-Shan); Kortenbout van der
Sluijs and Zagwizn 1962 (Tegelen clay pits, Netherlands); Korzhuev 1961 (Quat.,
Lena valley); Kostenko 1964A, B (Cenoz., Kazakhstan); Kovanda 1963 (Czechoslovakia); Kowalski, K. 1966A (rodents, European Quat.); Kraglievich 1959A
(Quat., Argentina); Krainov 1964 (Volga-Oka basin, USSR); Krasheninnikov and
Ponikarov 1964 (Mesoz., Paleogene, Egypt); Krasnov, Lur'e and Masaitis 1966
(geol. of Siberian Platform); Kretzoi 1964B (mammals, India); Kretzoi and
Vértes 1965A (Quat., Hungary); Kriger 1962B (Quat., Afr., Near East); Krum-
biegel 1959C, 1964 (Eoc., Germany); Krutzsch and Lotsch 1964 (Paleogene
and Neogene); Krylova, A. K. 1962 (Dev., Siberia); Kugler and Bolli 1967
(Cret., Trinidad); Kuhn, O. 1963E (Solnhofen, Germany), 1964D (geol. of Bayern)
Kuprina 1966 (Quat., Kamchatka); Kuprina and Vtiurin 1961 (Quat., E. Siberia);
Kurten 1965C (divisions of Pleist.), 1966B (Tert. land connections); Kutscher
1966 (tracks in Trias. ss.);

Kazakhstan), 1961A, B (Plioc.-Quat.), 1965A (Anthropogene, N. Eurasia), 1965B (Anthropogene small mammal faunas), 1965D (Villafranchian, USSR); Nikiforova and Alekseeva 1959, 1961 (Neogene-Anthropogene boundary); Nikiforova, Gerbova and Konstantinova 1960 (Cenoz., cent. Asia); Nikiforova, Ravskiĭ and Deviatkin 1967 (Neogene, Eopleist., Kazakhstan, S. Siberia); Nikiforova and Obut 1965 (Silur. system); Nikishin 1962 (Carbonif., Volga-Urals oil-bearing province); Nikolaeva 1959 (Quat., USSR);

Oakeshott 1966 (geol. San Francisco Bay area); Obruchev and Karatajute-Talimaa 1967 (Ludlovian-Lower Devon. in E. Europe); Ochev 1960A (Paleoz.–Mesoz., USSR), 1966A (Trias., USSR), 1966B (Perm. verts., USSR); Ochev et al. 1964 (Trias., USSR); Ogose 1953 (Mizunami Group, Japan); Okutsu and Muto 1959 (Mioc., Japan); Olsen 1964A, B (Mioc. verts., Florida); Olson 1964A (mammals, S. Amer.), 1967 (Perm. localities, Oklahoma); Oppé 1965 (Juras. deposits with dinosaur tracks, Isle of Purbeck, England); Orlov, J. A. 1964B (continental deposits, Asia); Orviku 1958 (Paleoz., Quat., Esthonia); Ozansoy 1965 (Cenoz., Turkey);

Paktusova 1966 (Up. Perm., USSR); Panichkina and Vekilova 1962 (Quat. cave, USSR); Patterson, B. 1966 (Early Pleist., N. W. Kenya); Paula Couto 1961D (Pleist., S. Amer.), 1962A (Pleist., N. E. Brazil); Pei and Li 1964 (loess, Mongolia); Peru 1965 (Pleist., Michigan); Pichardo del Barrio et al. 1961 (Up. Pleist., Mexico); Pidoplichko 1946-1956 (Glacial Period), 1967B (vert. research); Plane 1967B (Plioc., New Guinea); Ploey 1965, Ploey and Moorsel 1963 (Quat., Congo); Pokrovskaiᾶ 1954 (palynology and stratigraphy); Popov, I. V. 1962 (Karst studies, USSR); Popov, V. V. 1960 (Quat. Cent. Asia); Prasad and Ray 1964 (Siwalik system); Predtechenskiĭ 1958, 1967 (Devon., Central Asia); Puri and Vernon 1964 (geol., Florida);

Rachitskiĭ 1958 (world wide Up. Perm.), 1960 (Low. Trias., USSR); Radinsky 1964B (Eoc., Olig. fossil localities, Mongolia); Rădulesco et al. 1965 (Quat. Transylvania, Rumania); Ragozin 1960 (geol. Krasnoiᾶrsk region, USSR); Rankama 1965 (Quat.), 1967 (Quat., Europe); Ranov 1961A (Quat., Cent. Asia); Rat 1965, 1966 (Eoc. mammals, Paris Basin); Ravskiĭ 1960, 1961, Ravskiĭ et al. 1964, Ravskiĭ and Tseĭtlin 1965A, B (Pleist., Siberia); Raznitsyn 1966 (Trias., Urals); Reife 1965 (Quat., Germany); Rensberger 1964 (John Day beds, Oregon); Repenning 1966 (Santa Cruz area, California), 1967B (Mioc.-Plioc. boundary); Reyment 1961 (Cret., Tert., Nigeria); Richards, H. G. 1953B (geol. Georgia); Ride, 1964B (Pleist., Australia); Robinson, P. 1957B (Eoc., New Mexico); Romer and Jensen 1966 (Trias., Argentina); Rose, G. 1965 (Trias., Australia); Rosen 1957 (Argentina); Rostovtsev 1961 (strat., W. Siberia); Rozhdestvenskiĭ 1968A (Tert. mammal sites, Cent. Asia); Rubanov 1959 (Neogene, USSR); Rukhin 1957 (biostrat., paleoclimatology); Rusconi 1966 (biol. provinces, Argentina); Russell and Chamney 1967 (Cret., Alberta); Russell, L. S. 1933B (Cret.-Tert., Canada), 1965A (Willow Creek form., Canada), 1965E (continental Ter., W. Canada), 1966A (Paleoc., Alberta); Ruzhentsev 1965 (Perm. to Trias. deposits);

Sabbagh 1964 (fossils as strat. indicators); Sahni and Khan 1964 (Siwaliks, India); Saiᾶdian 1967 (Quat., USSR); Sainsbury 1967 (Bering land bridge); Saks 1965 (Quat. period), 1966 (Quat., Siberia); Saks et al. 1959 (Mesoz., Soviet Arctic); Salukvadze 1965 (Eoc., USSR); Santa 1960 (Quat., N. Afr.); Sarycheva 1950B (atlases for field geologists); Schaeffer and Mangus 1965 (Eoc. Green R. form.); Schindewolf 1962 (faunal discontinuities); Schmid 1964A (sediments in bear caves); Schuberth 1967 (Hudson R., New Jersey); Schultz, C. B. 1965 (Quat. verts., U. S.); Schultz, C. B. et al. 1965, Schultz, Whitmore and Tanner 1966 (Big Bone Lick, Kentucky); Schultz, Falkenbach and Vondra 1965, 1967 (Tert., W. Nebraska); Scott, G. R. 1963 (Quat., Colorado); Sekyra 1967 (Quat., Czechoslovakia); Seliverstov 1961 (Quat. strat., USSR); Sexton 1965 (caves, S. Australia); Shantser 1961A, B (Neogene–Quat. boundary); Shaw, A. B. 1964 (time in stratigraphy); Shchukina 1959 (Tert., Urals); Shevchenko, A. I. 1965A (biostrat. research); Shevchenko and Grigor'ev 1967 (Quat., Azov Sea area); Simpson, G. G. 1965A (Mioc. mammal beds, Kenya); Sittler 1965 (Cret., Eoc., S. France); Skinner, M. F. and Taylor (Bijou Hills, S. Dakota); Slaughter 1964A (Texas); Slaughter and Thurmond 1965A, B (geol., paleont., Texas); Sokolov, B. S. 1967 (Paleoz., Siberia); Sokolov, D. S. 1960, 1963 (regional strat., China); Spreen 1965 (Cherokee Cave, St. Louis); Srivastava 1967 (Cret. mammal beds, Canada); Stein 1967 (Tule Springs, Nevada); Stephens, E. A. 1966 (Lake Malawi, S. Afr.); Stirton, Tedford and Woodburne 1968 (Australian Tert. mammal-bearing deposits); Stout and Schultz 1968 (Mioc., Nebraska); Strachan 1964 (Silurian); Strawn 1965 (Quat., Idaho); Strelczenia and Zetti 1964 (Pleist., Argentina); Strelkov et al. 1959 (strat., Soviet Arctic); Swanson 1964 (cultural site, B. C.).

Takai and Tsuchi 1963A (Neogene, Japan), 1963B (Quat., Japan); Tedford and Downs 1965 (Mioc., California); Teichert, C. 1967 (Gondwana strat.); Teichert, C. and Yochelson 1967 (strat.); Telles Antunes 1964D (clays of Côja, Portugal); Termier, H. and G. 1964A (Paleozoic of world); Ters 1964 (Quat., France); Thaler 1964B (mammal-bearing strat. zones, France), 1965A (mammal-bearing strat. zones, Tert. Europe); Timush 1966 (Olig., USSR); Tkachenko et al. 1957 (strat., Cent. Siberian Plateau); Tobien 1961C (mammal sites, Germany), 1968C, D (Eoc., Germany), 1968F (Tert., Switzerland); Touraine 1966 (Olig., France); Toutin et al. 1965 (Olig., France); Tratman 1968 (Pleist. bone caves, England); Tripathi 1963, Tripathi and Chandra 1961 (geol., India); Tsagareli 1964 (geol. of Georgia, USSR); Tsapenko and Makhnach 1959 (Quat., Belorussia); Tseĭtlin 1964B (Quat., cent. Siberia); Tuaev 1963 (Cent. Asia); Tverdokhlebov 1966 (Trias., USSR); Twenter 1962 (fossil localities, Arizona); Tychsen and Vorhis 1955 (Cret., South Dakota);

Valoch 1961F (Pleist., Czechoslovakia); Van Andel et al. 1967 (Timor Sea, Australia); Vangengeĭm 1960B, 1961 (Pleist., Siberia), 1966C (Pleist., USSR); Various authors 1965 (evol. of man); Vasil'ev, Iu. M. 1962 (marine and continental Plioc., USSR); Vasil'ev, V. G. 1960 (geol. structure, Iakutian ASSR); Vas'kovskiĭ, A. P. 1959A (Quat., USSR); Veklich 1958 (Quat., USSR); Velikovskaia 1961 (Plioc. red beds); Venzo 1964 (Plioc.-Pleist., Italy); Verbitskaia 1959 (Mid. Urals); Villalta Comella and Rosell Sanuy 1964 (Eoc., Spain); Vita-Finzi 1966 (archeol. site, Jordan), 1967 (Quat. Algeria); Volochkovich 1961 (N. E. Mongolia); Vondra and Johnson 1968 (Siwaliks, India); Vorob'eva and Matveeva 1962 (biostrat., USSR);

Wainwright and Malik 1967 (Pleist. archeol. and chronol., India); Wang, A.-C. 1960 (Quat., China); Watanabe, K. 1953 (desmostylid horizons, Japan); Webb, S. D. 1964A, 1965A (strat. position of Calippus), 1964B (Plioc., Florida); Webb and Woodburne 1966 (continental deposits, California); West, R. G. 1967, 1968 (Pleist., British Isles); West and Sparks 1960 (Pleist., England); Westgate 1965 (Pleist., Alberta); Williams, J. S. and Taylor 1964 (Devon., Utah); Wilson, J. A. et al. 1968 (Tert. verts, Texas); Wilson, R. W. 1967 (fossil mammals in Tert. correlations); Woldstedt 1965 (Ice Age, Afr., Asia, Aust., Amer.), 1967 (Quat. stratig., Germany); Wright, G. A. 1967 (Pleist.); Wu, Xin-zhi 1966 (Pleist. strat., China); Wurster 1964 (Trias., Germany);

Zal'tsman 1958, 1967 (Tert., W. Siberia); Zal'tsman et al. 1960 (Cenoz., USSR); Zamoriĭ 1961 (Quat., Ukraine); Zapfe 1964B (Trias. sea, Alps.); Zazhigin 1966A (Pleist., W. Siberia); Zbyszewski 1962B, 1964A, B (Mioc., Portugal); Zemliakov 1940E (Quat., N. W. USSR); Zeuner 1964 (Pleist. soils and shorelines); Zhizhchenko 1964 (Low Mioc.); Zöbelein 1963 (Mioc., Switzerland); Zolotarev 1966 (Quat., E. Siberia); Zubakov 1960 (Quat., Siberia), 1965A (Pleist., USSR), 1965B (Pleist., Alaska), 1966 (Pleist. geochron. stages); Zubakov and Krasnov 1959 (Quat.).

CRANIOMETRY — See: paleoanthropology; skull, MAMMALIA; technique.

CULTURAL REMAINS ASSOCIATED WITH FAUNAS (See also: faunas, QUATERNARY
CAVE; paleoanthropology; Paleolithic art) — Abramova, Z. A. 1964B (Siberia); Agogino
1963C (bison and Paleo-Indian); Agogino and Rovner 1965 (mammoths and
artifacts, New Mexico); Anon. 1963BR (mammal faunas and artifacts, France),
1967AA (mastodons and points, Missouri), 1967AM (mammals and points, Florida), 1967AZ (Ice Age animals and tools, Mexico), 1967BA (bones and artifacts,
Canada), 1968G (early man and mammoth, Oklahoma); Armillas 1964 (early
man and mammoth, N. Mesoamerica); Aveleyra Arroyo de Anda 1965 (carved
bone, Mexico);
  Binder, 1961B (Mousterian culture and Pleist. mammals, Great Cave, Germany);
    Blake-Palmer 1956 (Dinornis and artifacts, New Zealand); Boessneck 1967 (domes-
    tic and wild animals, Spain); Bouillon 1964 (Mousterian tools and Elephas, France);
  Cadeo 1965A (industry and mammals, Italy); Case and Owens 1966 (Suwanee and
    Bolen points with Pleist. mammals, Florida); Chiappella, G. 1965 (Up. Pal.
    industry and mammals, Italy); Chiappella, V. G. 1964 (Low. Pal. industires
    and mammals); Chow 1964B (mammals and Lantian man, China); Chow, M.,
    Hu, and Lee 1965 (mammals and Lantian man); Cleland 1965A (caribou and
    artifacts, Michigan); Cowles 1960 (artifacts, child burial and animal bones, Ore-
    gon);
  David and Prat 1962 (verts. and Mousterian implements, France); Demangeot 1964
    (industries and Ursus and Cervus, Apennines); Deraniyagala 1965 (mammals,
    hominids, and stone artifacts, Ceylon); Dunn, N. L. 1964 (clovis points and
    mammals, New Mexico);
  Egan and Agogino 1965 (bison and Paleo-Indian artifacts); Emery 1966B (Clovis
    points and proboscideans);
  Hammack 1965 (burned mammoth bones and flake tools, New Mexico); Haynes
    and Hemmings 1968 (mammoth skeleton and mammoth bone tool, Arizona);
    Howell, F. C. 1962E, 1963C, 1964A (mammals, early Acheulian industry, Spain);
    Howell, Cole, et al. 1962 (mammals and Acheulian industry, Tanzania);
  Irwin-Williams 1967 (mammals and early man artifacts, Mexico); Isetti and Lumley
    1962A, B (birds, mammals and Mousterian industry, Italy);
  Joshi, Sali and Bopardikar 1966 (Bos namadicus and Early Pal. tools, India); Jul-
    lien 1964 (micro-mammals and Mousterian industries, France); Jung and Schnei-
    der 1960-61 (Pleist. verts. and stone tools, Greece);
  Karlov 1961 (mammals and Pal. industries, Ukraine), 1963 (mammals and hand
    chopper, USSR); Karlov and Nakel'skiǐ 1966B (elephant and Acheulean arti-
    facts, Ukraine); Kenyon and Churcher 1965 (worked antler fragment and flake
    tool, Canada); Ketraru 1965B (mammals and Mousterian artifacts, Moldavia);
    Klíma, B. 1965A (mammals and Gravettian industry, Moravia); Kretzoi 1964C
    (verts. and Mousterian culture, Hungary), 1965F (birds and mammals at Pal.
    sites, Hungary);
  Lanning 1963B (sloth and projectile points, California); Leonhardy 1966A, B (Dom-
    ebo mammoth kill site, Oklahoma); Leonardy and Anderson 1966 (Domebo
    mammoth kill site, Oklahoma);
  Mackay, Mathews and MacNeish 1961 (verts. and flint artifacts, Yukon); MacNeish
    1967C (mammals and artifacts, Mesoamerica); Maldonado-Koerdell 1964 (mam-
    moth and stone artifacts, Mexico); Martin, P. S. 1963 (mammals and artifacts,
    American S. W.); Martín Aquado 1963A (mammals and Chelles-Acheulian cul-
    ture, Spain); Matthews, J. M. 1966 (Diprotodon nr. hearth, Australia); Mehl
    1966 (Domebo mammoth kill site, Oklahoma); Mehringer and Haynes 1965
    (mammoth and Clovis artifacts, Lehner site, Arizona); Montané 1968 (horse,
    mastodon and Paleo-Indian tools, Chile); Mortine 1965 (projectile point in sloth
    bone, Florida); Mottl 1964 (Pal. cultures and cave bears, Austria); Mourer-
    Chauviré 1964 (birds and Acheulian industry, France); Mulvaney 1964C (mar-
    supials and millstone, Australia);

Neill 1964 (elephants and Suwannee points, Florida);
Orr, P. C. 1964 (stone tool and mammoth skels., California), 1968 (mammals and
   bone tools, Santa Rosa Is., California); Osole 1965A, B (Gravettian mammals
   and tools); Ostrovskiĭ and Grigor'ev 1966 (mammals and flint artifacts, USSR);
Paccard 1964 (Up. Pal. verts. and artifacts); Painter 1968 (verts., artifacts and
   hearth, N. Amer.); Palma di Cesnola 1961B (mammals, fireplace and Mousterian
   artifacts, Italy), 1964A, 1965A (Pal. industries and mammals); Panichkina 1961
   (verts. and flint artifacts, USSR); Patte 1967 (mammals and stone and bone
   tools, France); Pei et al. 1965 (chert artifacts with "Stegodon-Ailuropoda fauna",
   S. China); Pendergast 1963 (copper spears with extinct horse, Canada); Peru
   1965 (fluted points, mammoths and mastodons, Michigan); Petrichenko 1963
   (Aurignacian flint artifacts and mammals, USSR); Picard 1965, 1966 (verts. and
   artifacts, Israel); Pintaud 1961 (bone artifacts and mammals, France); Piveteau
   1967A (Villafranchian fauna and stone artifacts, France); Polikarpovich 1957
   (Aurignacion artifacts and mammoth, USSR); Preble 1967 (early elephant hunters);
Reymond 1964 (Magdalenian lithic artifacts and verts., France); Riek 1931B (Mid.
   and Up. Pal. industries, with mammals, Middle Alps), 1932B, 1960*, 1962 (Stone
   Age industries and mammals, Germany);
Samson and Rădulesco 1959, 1964 (verts. and artifacts, Rumania); Schmid 1966
   (cave bear, hyena and flint tools); Segre 1961 (Villafranchian and Mousterian
   deposits with mammals, Italy); Sekyra 1967 (Gravettian, Aurignacian artifacts
   and mammals, Czechoslovakia); Seronie-Vivien 1964 (artifacts, hearth and verts.);
   Sharrock 1966 (bison and mountain sheep with unfluted lanceolate points); Shay
   1965 (bison and artifacts, Minnesota); Shawcross and Roe 1966 (artifacts and
   verts., New Zealand); Shovkoplias 1955B (mammoth bone dwellings, USSR),
   1955C, 1964, 1965C (cultural sites and mammals, USSR); Sonneville-Bordes
   1965A, C (Pal. industries and mammals, France), 1965E (Acheulean industry,
   elephants, Spain); Sosnovskiĭ 1940D (Pal. flint implements assoc. with verts.,
   USSR); Stampfli 1959B (Pleist. verts. and artifacts, Switzerland); Swanson
   and Dayley 1968 (hunting station, Idaho);
Takai 1968 (human bones, artifacts and mammals, Israel); Tedford 1967B (marsupials and artifacts, Australia); Toepfer 1967A (artifacts and bear skulls, Germany); Tomasson, R. and J. 1964 (tools and mammals, France); Tong 1962
   (mammoths, Oklahoma);
Vandermeersch 1965 (Mousterian industries and mammals, France); Vekilova 1967
   (Mousterian man and cave bear); Verhoeven 1964 (Stegodon, Timor, Asia);
   Vértes 1965F (verts. at Pal. sites, Hungary); Vulliamy 1930 (mammoth and im-
   plements, England);
Watanabe, H. 1964 (mammals and artifacts, Israel); Wedel et al. 1968 (verts. and
   artifacts, Wyoming); Wells, L. H. 1964B (industries and verts., S. Afr.);
Yizraeli 1967 (mammals, bone and stone artifacts);
Zamiatnin 1961B (verts. and artifacts, USSR).

CUSTOMS — See: habits; paleophysiology.

DATING — See: correlation; paleochronology; technique.

DEFINITIONS — See: terminology.

DENTITION — See also: skull.
   GENERAL — Anthony 1961B (comp. anat.),
      Dahlberg and Staley 1965 (diseases of dentition);
      Keil 1966 (odontology);
      Macorra 1960 (dental occlusion); Matveev 1963 (heterodont dental system); Miles,
         A. E. W. 1967 (structural and chemical organization); Miles and Poole 1967
         (history and general organization); Mills 1967 (development of the protocone

during Mesoz.);

Ørvig 1967B (tooth tissues);

Peyer 1968 (comparative odontology);   Poole 1967 (tooth tissues);

Sacchi Vialli 1962, 1964B (fluorescent study of teeth);   Shackelford and Wyckoff 1964 (collagen in fossil teeth);

Tarlo, B. J. and L. B. H. 1963 (tooth replacement), 1964 (tooth succession), 1965 (origin of teeth);   Tarlo, L. B. H. and Mercer 1966 (fossil dentine);   Tarlo, L. B. H. and B. J. 1963A (origin of tooth cusps), 1963B (convergent evol. in teeth);   Tuca 1965 (evol. and morphol);

Zubov 1966A (ethnic odontology).

PISCES — Applegate 1965B (Carcharias);

Berman 1967 (bradyodont);   Blot and Heyler 1964 (palaeoniscoids, France);

Case, G. R. 1967 (shark and fish teeth);   Case, J. 1964 (shark teeth, Maryland);   Coggi 1964 (Ptychodus, Sicily);   Converse 1967 (shark teeth, Ohio);   Cruickshank 1968A (tooth structure in Rhizodus);

Glikman 1956 (Anacorax), 1959 (Cret. elasmobranchs);   Glikman and Ishchenko 1967 (Mioc. sharks, Cent. Asia);   Gofshtein 1961 (fish, Ukraine);   Gottfried 1964 (Ceratodus);   Gross, W. 1967B (acanthodians and placoderms);

Jain 1968 (vomerine teeth of Ceratodus, India);

McNulty 1964, 1965 (hypolophid teeth, Texas);

Obruchev, D. V. 1965B (Helicampodus tooth structure);   Ørvig 1967A (elasmobranch teeth);

Radwanski 1965 (elasmobranchs, Poland);   Rutte 1966 (cyprinid teeth);

Slaughter and Steiner 1968 (sawfish rostral teeth);   Sokolov, M. I. 1965 (Cret. sharks);   Springer 1964 (carcharhinid sharks);

Telles Antunes 1963 (sharks, W. Afr.);   Tolmachev, I. P. 1931 (selachians, USSR);

Verma 1965B (Cret. sharks, India);   Vorob'eva and Minikh 1968 (ceratodontid tooth plates);

Weiler 1966A (fishes, Czechoslovakia).

AMPHIBIA — Chalyshev 1962B (stegocephalian, USSR);

Norman and Norman 1964 (labyrinthodont molars, Utah).

REPTILIA — Bakirov and Kuznetsov 1962 (cotylosaur, USSR);

Cox, C. B. 1964 (Endothiodon);

Edmund 1962 (crocodile tooth replacement);

Gofshtein 1961 (Plesiosaurus, Ukraine);

Hopson 1964C (tooth replacement);

Mendrez 1965 (Whaitsiidae), 1967 (therocephalians and cynodonts);

Ostrom 1962B (N. Amer. hadrosaurs);

Price, L. I. (theropod, Amazon);

Tarlo, L. B. H. 1964B (cynodont tooth replacement);

Zázvorka 1966 (crocodile, Bohemia).

MAMMALIA — Adam 1965B (hippo, Rhine Valley);   Alexandersen 1963 (human canines);   Alker 1966 (Eumys elegans);   Andrik, Hanulík and Vittek 1963 (modern man);   Anon. 1965CK (La Jolla people, California), 1967AQ (mammals, Wyoming), 1968AD (Mesozoic mammals);   Apostol 1957, 1962, 1965A (mammoths, Rumania);   Bailit and Friedlander 1965, 1966 (dental reduction in man);   Balsac 1966A, B (soricid insectivores);   Baudelot, L. 1964 (Cricetodon, France), Beaumont 1961D (Canis, France), 1965C (Cephalogale, France);   Belanger 1963 (hippo tooth, France);   Binford, S. R. 1966B (Neanderthal molar, Israel);   Biriukov et al. 1962 (Paraceratherium);   Black, C. C. 1968B (Mytonomys);   Boev and Maslinkov 1965 (human teeth, Bulgaria);   Brabant 1965, 1967 (early man);   Brabant and

Kovacs 1961 (taurodontism in man); Brabant and Sahly 1964 (Neanderthal
teeth, France); Brabant and Twiesselmann 1964 (early man, W. Europe); Brace
1965A, B (early man); Brace and Molnar 1967 (human tooth wear); Brues
1966 (evol. of hominid teeth and jaws); Bruijn and Meurs 1967 (lagomorphs,
Spain); Bubeník and Wurtzinger 1967 (Capreolus premolar); Butler, P. M.
1967A, B, C (human molars), 1967D (human tooth development);
Carbonell 1965 (Neanderthal child, Gibraltar); Chaline 1963 (Dicerorhinus, France),
1966A (dental variation in arvicolides); Churcher 1968 (mammoth molar,
Ontario); Colwell 1965 (Leontiniidae dentine tubules); Contreras 1964 (rodent
molar patterns); Crompton and Jenkins 1967 (molar morphology of Juras. symmetrodonts), 1968 (molar occlusion in Trias. mammals); Crusafont Pairó, Adrover
and Golpe 1964 (hippo, Spain); Cuffey, Johnson and Rasmussen 1964 (microtine rodent, Indiana);
Dahlberg and Carbonell 1961 (dentition of Cap Blanc female); Daxner and Fejfar
1967 (lagomorphs, Europe); Dietrich 1921B (proboscideans), 1965 (elephants,
Germany); Doben-Florin 1964 (tooth morphology, Soricidae); Dubrovo 1963D
(Archidiskodon teeth, USSR);
Elhai 1959B (Equus, Elephas and Rhino. teeth, Normandie); Erdbrink 1965 (molar
patterns, man and apes), 1967B (proboscideans, China); Esteras and Aguirre
1964 (Parelephas, Spain);
Fahlbusch, V. 1964 (Mioc. cricetids, Bavaria); Faugeres 1966 (Elephas molar, Macedonia); Ferembach 1962, 1965B (Mousterian molars, Portugal); Fine 1964 (Canis,
Idaho); Fischer 1962 (Dryopithecus); Frechkop 1965B (cervids); Freedman
1967 (variation in Perameles); Freedman and Joffe 1967A, B (metrical features,
Perameles); Friant 1962D, 1967 (Eoc. ruminant molars), 1962E (tubular mammal
molars), 1963C (rhino), 1963D (Trechomys, Europe), 1964A (Haramyia, Europe),
1964C, 1965A (insectivore molars), 1965B (hyraxes), 1966B (Thryonomys); Frisch
1965 (hominid dentition);
Gaponov 1957C (Elasmotherium USSR), 1962A, B (Deinotherium jaw, USSR); Garn
et al. 1966 (human molar pattern); Garn, Lewis and Kerewsky 1964 (relative
molar size in fossil man); Genet-Varcin 1965 (Anthropodus incisor), 1966A
(Mousterian teeth); Ginsburg and Telles Antunes 1967 (Trilophodon, France);
Goncharov 1967 (mammoth, N. E. Siberia); Greene, Ewing and Armelagos 1967
(Mesolithic population, Wadi Halfa, Sudan); Gregory, W. K. 1939D (origin of
human dentition); Gromova 1964 (elephants); Guthrie, R. D. 1965 (variability
and evol. in Microtus molars);
Hanihara 1965 (crown characters, Japanese-Americans); Hanihara, Kuwashima and
Sakao 1964 (primitive hominid character in Recent man); Hanihara and Mina-
midate 1965 (primitive hominid character in Recent man); Hatai 1959B (Mioc.
elephant molar, Japan); Hemmer and Koenigswald 1964 (Neofelis, China, Java);
Hendey 1967 ("Archidiskodon" molar, S. Afr.); Hibbard and Zakrzewski 1967
(microtine phyletic trends, Idaho); Hill, L. G. 1963 (giant beaver, Arkansas);
Holloway 1967 (hominid canine reduction); Howe, J. A. 1966A (horse teeth);
Hugueney and Mein 1965 (lagomorphs, rodents, France); Hünermann 1966
(beaver); Hussain and Sondaar 1968 (Hipparion);
Iakhimovich, N. N. 1960 (Parelephas, USSR);
Jakubowski 1967 (Paleoloxodon, Poland);
Kamei 1964, 1966 (proboscidean molars, Japan); Karlov and Nakel'skiǐ 1966B (elephant, Ukrain); Kermack 1967B (molar evol. in Mesoz. mammals); Kermack,
Lees and Mussett 1965 (mammal teeth, England); Koby and Brockelmann 1967
(cave bear); Koenigswald 1968A (Up. molar in cercopithecoids); Korenhof 1962
(enamel-dentine border, early man, Java); Kraglievich 1965 (Eumysops, Argentina); Kraus and Jordan 1965 (human dentition); Krommenhoek and Slob
1967A (Apodemus molars); Kubiak 1965A, B (elephants, S. Poland, USSR);
Lavocat 1964C (Delanymys), 1967D (rodents); Lavocat and Michaux 1966 (Afr.

rodents); Leakey, L. S. B. 1968B (Kenyapithecus); Leakey, L. S. B. et al.
1967A (Zinjanthropus, Olduvai Gorge); Legoux 1966 (dental age of fossil hominids);
MacIntyre 1966 (Ictidopappus and Protictis); McKenna 1968 (Leptacodon); Macorra 1963, 1967 (hominid dentition); Marelli 1953 (notoungulate molars, Argentina); Marshall and Butler 1966 (bat molars); Martin, L. D. 1966 (Hyracodon tooth replacement); Mawby 1967B, 1968A (Mioc.-Plioc. Dipodomys-like
teeth, California, Nevada); Medway, G. 1964A (rats, Niah Cave, Borneo); Mein
1965A (bats, France), 1966 (rodent, France); Melentis 1960 (elephant, Greece);
Merrilees and Ride 1965 (macropodid, Australia); Michaux 1967 (Apodemus);
Mills 1964 (pantotheres, England), 1966 (functional occlusion, Insectivora); Moss
and Kermack 1967 (enamel structure in Trias. mammals); Müller, Arnt 1967
(insectivores, S. Germany); Musil 1964 (brown bear, Czechoslovakia), 1966B
(variation in cave bear teeth), 1968 (mammoth, Czechoslovakia);
Nagasawa 1967 (equid, Japan); Necrasov 1962 (Up. Paleolithic child's tooth, France);
Oppenheimer 1964 (australopithecine tooth crowding); Orlov, V. N. 1960 (Equus
molars);
Palma di Cesnola and Messeri 1967 (Pal. human teeth, Italy); Paula Couto 1962B
(didelphids, Brazil); Pei 1965D (Trilophodon tooth, China); Petronijević and
Thenius 1958B (indricothere, Yugoslavia); Petter, F. 1967 (cricetid rodents);
Petter, G. 1964A (viverrids, E. Afr.), 1964B (mustelids, Spain), 1964C (canid,
E. Afr.); Pilbeam 1968A (hominids); Pisano 1964 (premolars, Caviinae); Pive-
teau 1967A (early man, France); Put' 1952 (mastodon, USSR);
Quinet 1964A (Eoc. mammals, Belgium), 1965A (condylarth, Belgium), 1966A
(Teilhardina, Belgium), 1966B (dental formulae), 1966C (eutherian lower pre-
molars and molars); Quinet and Misonne 1965 (zalambdodonts, Belgium);
Radinsky 1964A (chalicotheres, Wyoming), 1965A (tapiroids, Asia), 1966A (phenacodonts), 1966D (tapiroid, Wyoming); Radulesco and Samson, P. 1965 (Hydruntinus, Rumania); Rakovec 1965A (mastodon, Yugoslavia); Ratekhin 1966 (rhino,
Crimea); Ray, C. E. 1964A (capromyid, Dominican Repub.), 1964B (caviamorphs),
1964D (jaguarundi, Florida), 1964E (tapir, Florida), 1965B (chipmunk, Georgia),
1965C (capromyid, Haiti); Rensberger 1966 (geomyid); Repenning 1965B (shrew,
S. Afr.); Repenning et al. 1964 (tundra rodents, Alaska); Reynolds, A. E. 1966
(mammoth, Indiana); Ride 1964B (marsupials); Riel 1964 (oreodont, Montana);
Robinson, J. T. and Allin 1966 (Dryopithecus molar pattern); Robinson, P.
1957B (Coryphodon molar), 1967 (anaptomorphid, Wyoming);
Saeki 1966 (monkeys); Saraiman 1966 (mastodon, Moldavia); Senyürek 1960C
(anthropoid incisors); Sherstiukov 1968A (elephant tusk, USSR); Shikama 1966A
(desmostylid teeth, Japan); Shikama 1965, Shikama and Noda 1968 (elephant teeth,
Japan); Simons 1968B (primates); Slaughter 1965C (serial sectioning, equids),
1966D (molar cusps); Sondaar 1968A (Hipparion, Greece); Sych 1966A (leporid tooth measurements), 1967A (unworn leporid teeth); Szalay 1965 (Allotheria
tooth replacement); Szlachetko 1966 (Quat. human teeth, Poland);
Tan and Shikama 1965 (Desmostylus, Japan); Telles Antunes 1964D (Palaeotherium
molars, Portugal); Terzea 1964 (Crocuta milk dentition), 1965 (Panthera, Rumania), 1966 (evol. of cave bear dentition); Thaler 1966A (rodent, Spain); Thenius
1965B (carnivores, Germany); Théobald 1965 (elephant molars, France); Thoma
1963 (Neanderthal dentition), 1967 (human teeth, Hungary); Thorslund 1966
(mammoth, Sweden); Tobias 1965A (Homo habilis); Tobien 1962E (tapir, Germany), 1966 (Entelodon, Germany); Topachevskiǐ 1957C (marmot, Ukraine),
1965A (rodent, Ukraine), 1965B (voles, Ukraine), 1966 (insectivore, Ukraine);
Turnbull, Lundelius and McDougall 1965 (marsupial teeth, Australia); Twiesselmann 1965 (human molars, Congo); Twiesselmann and Poel 1967 (human and
anthropoid lower teeth);
Vandebroek 1966 (rodents); Vangengeǐm 1966A, E (Equidae, USSR), 1966D (canid,

USSR); Van Valen 1963C (horse teeth), 1964D (extra molars, Otocyon); Vértes 1965A (Homo erectus, Hungary); Vialli 1966 (Deinotherium, Ethiopia); Vignati 1963 (human, toxodont, Argentina);

Webb, G. L. 1965 (chalicotheres, S. Afr.); Webb, S. D. 1966A (Mylagaulus, Florida); Weller 1968 (evol. of mammalian teeth); Welsch 1967 (tooth wear of prosimian molars); Widmer 1966 (mammoth molar, Switzerland); Woo, Ju-Kang and Bai, Hui-ying 1965 (molar attrition and age of humans);

Young, H. R. 1966 (proboscidean, Canada);

Zbyszewski 1967 (mastodon, Portugal); Zenker 1965 (primate); Zubov 1966B (hominid dentition), 1967A, B (human molars).

DERMAL SKELETON — See: integumentary structures; skeleton; skull.

DESCENT — See: evolution; phylogeny.

DEVELOPMENT — See: evolution; paleoanthropology; phylogeny; variation and heredity.

DIGESTIVE SYSTEM — See: anatomy; coprolites, gastroliths, and visceral contents.

DINOSAUR EGGS — See: eggs and eggshells.

DISEASE — See: paleopathology.

DISTRIBUTION, DISPERSAL and MIGRATION, BIODYNAMICS (see also: paleogeography) — Afanas'ev 1960 (cent. Asia); Ahlén 1965A (red deer, Scandinavia); Altuna 1966A (Lezetxiki Cave, Spain); Amadon 1966 (birds); Anon. 1961CW, 1965CJ (Bering Straits land bridge); Appleby et al. 1967 (Reptilia); Arambourg, et al. 1959 (Arabian peninsula); Arata 1967 (geol. range of rodents); Auffenberg 1967A (box turtles, Florida);

Bain 1966 (Gondwanaland); Baird 1964A (Aïstopoda); Baker, R. H. 1967 (perissodactyls); Bandi 1965A (Bering bridge); Bardack 1965C (localities of Cret. verts., Kansas); Barlow, J. C. 1967 (edentates and pholidotes); Berg, D. E. 1964 (Tert. crocodiles, Europe); Bergounioux and Crouzel 1963 (Mioc. mastodons); Black, R. F. 1966 (Bering Straits); Boonstra 1968 (terrestrial reptiles, S. Afr.);

Carlquist 1965 (island life); Chard 1963D (migrations of man to New World); Colinvaux 1967 (Bering land bridge); Crane 1966 (Tert. radiation of viper-fishes); Crusafont Pairó and Truyols Santonja 1964A (mammals, Spain);

Darlington, P. J. 1965 (southern end of the world); Davitashvili 1955 (ecogenesis in the organic world); Dawson, M. R. 1967C (lagomorphs); Dorofeyev 1966 (Hipparion fauna);

Ebhardt 1967A (migration of horses), 1967B (Equus, Pleist. to Recent); Eĭkhgorn 1968 (Chimaerae, USSR);

Farmer 1964 (Arctic-N. Atlantic route); Flerov 1965A, B, 1967 (origin of Canadian fauna);

Gabuniia 1961B (anthracotheres); Giddings 1951C (early man across Bering Strait); Gill 1966 (migrations of marsupials and men, Australia); Godina 1966 (giraffes, USSR); Grigor'ev 1965A (Up. Paleolithic migrations), 1965B (migration of Homo sapiens to Europe); Grosset, Dinesman and Zalkin 1965 (steppe marmot); Guíllien 1965C (reindeer and hunters, France); Guthrie, R. D. 1966A (wapiti, Alaska, Yukon Territory);

Hershkovitz 1966 (Latin American faunal interchange); Heyerdahl 1964 (pre—Columbian ocean routes), 1966 (transoceanic contacts); Hibbard et al. 1965 (Quat. mammals, N. Amer.); Hoffstetter 1968C (Macrauchenia, S. Amer.); Hopkins, D. M. 1967A, C, D (Bering land bridge);

Iakovlev, V. N. 1965A (Lycoptera); Ikebe, Ishida and Chiji 1965 (fossil elephants,

Japan); Irving and Brown 1964, 1966 (labyrinthodonts);

Jelinek, A. J. 1965B (peopling of the New World); Josselyn 1962, 1965B (early
man across Bering Strait);

Kauffman Doig 1963 (man in the New World); Kerby 1965 (migrations of man
into N. Amer.); Kon'kova 1957 (terrestrial verts., Up. Mioc., Moldavia); Kurten
1966B (Tert. faunal interchange), 1966D (Pleist. mammals and Bering bridge);

Larina 1958, 1965 (rodents); Laughlin 1965, 1967 (human migrations across Bering
land bridge); Liem 1963 (Anabantoidei);

McKenna 1965D, 1966B (endemism of terrestrial W. coast Paleogene mammals),
1967B (prosimian primates); McLaughlin 1967 (rodents); MacNeish 1963, 1964A,
B (peopling of the New World); Martin, R. A. 1968A (Microtus, Pleist.);
Martin Aguado 1966 (Low. Pal. migration of man from Afr. to Europe); Mar-
tinson 1958, 1967B (origin of Lake Baikal fauna, Siberia); Mayr, E. 1964E
(Tert. Amer. bird faunas); Mehringer 1966 (migration path for big game hunters,
Mojave Desert); Meladze 1964B (Tert. Sivatheriinae); Mezhzherin 1965 (Plioc.,
Pleist. shrews, Europe); Miller, G. J. 1968 (age distribution of Smilodon at
Rancho La Brea); Miller, R. R. 1965 (N. Amer. Late Plioc. and Pleist. fishes);
Mitchell, E. D. 1966E (Allodesmus, California); Morris, W. J. 1966A, B (Tert.
mammals, Baja California and Rocky Mt. area); Müller, Arnt 1967 (insectivores,
S. Germany); Müller-Beck 1967 (Up. Pleist. migrations of hunters across Bering
bridge); Munthe 1956 (Baltic herring);

Nakagawa 1962 (land bridges, Japan); Narr 1964A (Pal. man across Bering bridge);
Neumann, G. K. 1952B (peopling of New World); Notz 1964 (deer);

Ol'shanskaia 1965 (Cenoz, teleosts, USSR); Olson 1962C (mammals, S. Amer.);

Rakov 1963 (antilopes, Crimea); Repenning 1965A, 1967A (Cenoz. mammals);
Ride 1964B (Pleist. marsupials, Australia); Ritchie, W. A. 1966 (transatlantic
contacts);

Sainsbury 1967 (Bering land bridge); Scheffer 1965, 1967 (marine mammals, N.
Pacific); Schlesier 1964B, 1965 (Bering land bridge); Schultz, C. B. 1961C
(migrants, Asia to N. Amer.); Shevyreva 1960 (Quat. deer, USSR); Shotwell
1964 (Tert. mammal communities); Shovkoplias 1965B (Paleolithic migrations);
Sill 1968 (Crocodilia); Simpson, G. G. 1964F (species density of N. Amer. mammals), 1965G (geography of evol.); Skinner, M. F. 1968 (chalicotheres, N. Amer.);
Smith, A. G. 1964B (Paleo-Indian migration); Smith, G. R. 1966 (N. Amer.
catostomid fishes); Szalay and Gould 1966 (Asiatic mesonychids);

Telles Antunes 1964B (distrib. of crocodiles); Terzea 1966 (cave bear); Thenius
1964A (Proboscidea), 1964D (S. Amer. mammals), 1966B (bovids);

Vuilleumier 1965 (Cracidae), 1967 (frogs);

Wendorf 1966 (early man, Amer.); Wenzel and Tipton 1966 (Latin Amer. faunal
interchange); Whitehead 1964 (deer, Great Britain, Ireland); Whitmore and
Stewart 1965 (mammals, Cent. and S. Amer.);

Zeuner and Bravo 1966 (Canary Islands); Zhukov 1965 (fresh water lampreys,
USSR).

DUNG, FOSSIL FECES — See: coprolites.

ECOLOGY, PALEOECOLOGY — Ahlen 1965C (red deer, Scandinavia); Aldinger 1965
(fish faunas, S. Germany); Alimen 1965C (Quaternary, N. W. Sahara);

Battistini and Vérin 1967 (prehist. Madagascar); Black, C. C. 1967 (Eoc. mammal
communities); Bresler 1966 (human ecology); Burchak-Abramovich 1967 (fossil primates, USSR);

Clark and Beerbower 1967 (Chadron formation); Clark, Beerbower and Krietzke
1967 (Oligocene, S. Dakota); Clark and Kietzke 1967 (Brule formation, S. Dakota); Cleland 1966 (animal ecology and ethnozoology, Great Lakes region);
Collected Papers 1962, 1965A (birds and mammals, Moldavia); Cooke, H. B. S.
1964 (Pleist., S. Afr.); Craig, G. Y. 1966A (concepts in paleoecology); Cushing

and Wright 1967 (Quat.);

Dakaris et al. 1964 (Stone Age Greece); Damon 1964 (geochemistry); Dart, R. A. 1964A (S. Afr. man-apes); Davis, D. H. S. 1964 (S. Afr.); Davitashvili 1955 (ecogenesis in the organic world); Degerbøl 1964 (verts., N. Europe); Dehm 1965 (Perm., Trias., S. Afr.); Dineley 1964A (pteraspids);

Efremov 1961 (biol. bases of paleozool.);

Findley 1964 (vert. data in paleoecol.); Fitting 1966D (Pleist. Mich archeol.); Fokanov 1964 (Quat. rodents, USSR);

Gabuniia 1962C (Olig., S. Georgia USSR), 1964D (Olig. verts., Benara); Gekker 1959 (research on marine faunas), 1966 (environment in the geol. past); Griffin, J. B. 1961B (Great Lakes region, N. Amer.); Gromov, I. M. 1961C (Quat. rodents and paleoecol.); Guilday 1960A (Pleist. mouse bones, Pennsylvania), 1960B (Pleist. microtine rodents, Pennsylvania);

Hattin and Cobban 1965 (Up. Cret., W. Kansas); Haynes 1964A (Pleist.); Hecker, R. F. 1965 (introduction to paleoecol.); Hemmer 1965B (biotopes of Pleist. hominids); Hester, J. J. 1964 (conf. on paleoecol.), 1966A (Pleist. environments and man in S. Amer.); Hester and Schoenwetter 1964 (reconstruction of past environments); Hossfeld 1965B (Aitape man, New Guinea);

Imbrie and Newell 1964 (approaches to paleoecol.);

Jong 1967 (Quat., Netherlands);

Kirkland 1964 (Rita Blanca lake deposits, Texas); Kowalski 1964A (Plioc.-Pleist. mammals of Poland); Kurtén 1964B (population structure);

Laporte 1968 (ancient environments); Lazukov 1957B (Up. Pal. environment of Kostenkovo-Borshev region, USSR); Lin 1964 (Quat., Taiwan); Lipps, Valentine and Mitchell 1968 (Pleist., Santa Barbara Is., Calif.); Lundelius 1964 (verts. as paleoecol. indicators);

Makeev 1963 (Paleolithic, Europe); Martinson 1958 (marine or fresh water origin of Lake Baikal, Siberia); Mayer-Oakes 1967 (environmental studies of Lake Agassiz region); Mehringer 1964, 1965B, 1966 (Quat., Mojave Desert); Mehringer and Haynes 1965 (Lehner mammoth site, Arizona);

Oldfield 1964 (early man sites, S. W. USA); Oltz and Kapp 1963 (plants with proboscideans, Pleist., Michigan); Ostrom 1964A (hadrosaurian dinosaurs);

Padberg 1967 (hominisation); Palmer, E. 1967 (fossils, ecology, S. Afr.); Pei 1960E (early man, China); Petronijević 1967 (Mid. Mioc. site, Serbia); Petter, G. 1967D (Olduvai, E. Afr.); Pidoplichko 1963A (hist. of faunas);

Reshetov 1966 (Tert. and Quat.); Russell, L. S., 1966C (Mesozoic, N. Amer.);

Sears, P. B. 1964 (paleoecol. reconstruction); Shcherbakova 1954A (Quat., USSR); Slaughter 1966E (Pleist., New Mexico); Sloan 1964 (Cret.-Tert., Montana); Smith, R. L. 1966 (ecol., field biol.); Spjeldnaes 1967 (Ordov. verts., Colorado); Stamp 1965 (India); Swanson 1966 (Pacific Northwest); Swift, E. R. 1961 (Washington landscapes);

Tarabukin 1968 (Deinotherium site, Moldavia); Tedford 1965, 1966C (Mojave Desert, California); Teichmüller 1962 (Oreopithecus fauna, Italy); Telles Antunes 1964B (crocodiles); Teriaev 1968 (mammoth); Thenius 1966D (methods and problems); Tikhomirov, B. A. 1958B (Pleist., N. Siberia); Tochilenko 1967B (Quat., Arabia); Toepfer 1966 (Late Pleist., Germany);

Van Zinderen Bakker 1964 (pollen analysis, S. Afr. Pleist.); Vaskovskii 1959A (Quat., USSR); Vértes 1965F (Stone Age, Hungary); Voinstvenskii 1966, 1967 (Cenoz., Ukraine); Volkova 1966 (Quat., USSR);

Welles 1967 (Trias., Arizona); Wells, P. V. 1966 (Pleist., Texas); Wells and Berger 1967 (Pleist., California); Wells and Jorgensen 1964 (Pleist.. California); Woldstedt 1965 (Ice Age, Afr., Asia, Aust., Amer.); Wurster 1964 (Trias., Germany).

ECONOMIC and COMMERCIAL ASPECTS —

EGGS, EGGSHELLS and EGG CAPSULES – An, Uzhi-shen 1964 (ostrich, N. China);
Anon. 1963BP (moas, New Zealand), 1963CH (dinosaur eggs), 1965CL (dino-
saur, S. China), 1966AK (reptile, Afr.), 1967AV (dinosaur, Utah);
Battistini 1965C (Aepyornis eggs); Bazhanov 1961C (ostriches, Asia), 1961D (dino-
saur, USSR); Burchak-Abramovich 1953C (ostriches, USSR); Burchak-Abramovich
and Kon'kova 1967 (ostriches, USSR);
Dughi and Sirugue 1964, 1965 (reptiles and birds); 1966 (fossilization of eggs),
1968 (Paleoc. bird eggs, France);
F., D. 1961A (dinosaur, France);
Ivan'ev 1964 (ostrich, W. Transbaĭkalia);
Jensen, J. A. 1968B (dinosaur, Utah);
Kurochkin 1968B (birds and reptiles);
Marchal 1965 (dinosaur); Marden 1967 (Aepyornis, Madagascar);
Obruchev, D. V. 1966, 1967B (Chimaerae egg capsules, Caucasus);
Roshchin 1962 (ostrich eggs, Ukraine);
Sauer 1966A (Struthio, S. W. Afr.); Schmidt, W. J. 1964 (swan egg, Pleist., Ger-
many), 1967 (structure of dinosaur egg shell); Sigé 1968A (dinosaur egg shell,
Peruvian Andes); Steininger 1966 (Olig. fishes, Bavaria);
Thaler 1965B (dinosaur, France); Tyler 1957 (moa);
Villatte 1966 (Eoc. birds, France); Voss-Foucart 1968 (Cret. dinosaur eggs, France);
Vozin 1968 (Trias. chimaeras, USSR);
Wetmore 1967 (Aepyornis egg, Madagascar);
Young, C.-c. 1965B (dinosaur, China).

ELECTRON-MICROSCOPY – See: anatomy; dentition; skeleton; skull; technique.

ENDOCRANIA, ENDOCRANIAL CASTS – See: circulatory system; paleoneurology; skull;
technique.

ENGRAVINGS – See: Paleolithic art.

ENVIRONMENTS – See: aquatic adaptations; ecology; evolution; habits and habitats;
occurrences; paleoanthropology; paleoclimatology; paleogeography.

ETHOLOGY – See: ecology.

EVOLUTION (see also: phylogeny) – Aguirre 1968 (skull); Albrecht 1967 (cranial arteries, turtles); Alekseev, V. P. 1968A (rate of evol. in Hominidae); Alekseeva and
Garutt 1965 (elephants); Amadon 1966 (birds); Anghi 1960 (Hungarian horse);
Anon. 1962CC, 1964M, 1965BU, BW (man), 1963CP (origin of man), 1964AR,
BS (S. Afr. dinosaurs), 1966AM (islands evol. traps), 1968W (marsupials); Antipchuk 1967 (lung evol. in reptiles); Appleby 1967 (Ichthyosauria); Ardrey 1966
(territorial imperative); Arnheim, Cocks and Wilson 1967 (hagfish); Augusta
and Burian n.d. (evol. plants and animals), 1960B (man); Axelrod 1967A (quantum evol.);
Babkin 1964 (reflexes of primates); Bailit and Friedlander 1965, 1966 (dental reduction in man); Baird 1966B (Lepospondyli); Baker, J. K. 1960 (plethodont
amphibians, Texas); Baker, P. T. 1967 (biol. race concept); Baker, R. H. 1967
(perissodactyls); Baldauf 1964B (Anura), 1965 (Lissamphibia); Ballesio et al.
1965 (Aceratherium); Balsac 1966A, B (soricid insectivores); Bardack 1965A
(chirocentrid fishes); Barghusen 1968 (therapsid jaw musculature); Barlow, N.
1967 (Darwin and Henslow); Barrett 1960 (Darwin notebook); Beer 1962C,
1966A (Darwin), 1964B (Archaeopteryx), 1964C (ratites), 1964D, 1965B (atlas
of evol.); Beer, Rowlands and Skramovsky 1967 (Darwin's notebooks); Berg,
Kazantseva and Obruchev 1964 (Palaeonisci); Berg and Obruchev 1964 (Ospiida);
Bergeijk 1966 (sense of hearing); Bergounioux and Crouzel 1967D (mammals);
Berkner and Marshall 1965 (oxygen and evol.); Berry 1968 (prehist. time scale);

biol. future); Dobzhansky, Hecht and Steere 1967 (evol. biology); Drake, E. T.
1968 (evol. and environment); Dumont and Rifkind 1968 (thoracic duct);
Edinger 1964A (mammal brain), 1966A (camel brain); Edwards 1967A (hominid
muzzle reduction); Egozcue and Vilarasau de Egozcue 1967A (chromosome evol.
in Cebidae), 1967B (primate chromosomes); El-Toubi, Kamal and Hammouda
1965 (origin of Ophidia); Estes 1965A (salamanders);
Ficcarelli and Torre 1967 (mustelid Enhydrictis); Fiennes 1965 (man's role in evol.
of dog); Findley 1967 (geol. range, insectivores, dermopterans); Fischer, K.
1964 (tapirs, Europe), 1967 (Chasmotherium); Fisher, J. 1967A (fossil birds);
FitzSimons 1962 (snakes of S. Afr.); Forsten 1968 (revision of Hipparion);
Fowlie 1965 (snakes of Arizona); Francis and Mones 1965A, B (hydrochoerid,
Uruguay); Frechkop 1964A, B, 1965C (horse), 1965D (Prjewalsky horse), 1967
(equid chromosomes); Freudenthal 1965 (cricetids, Europe); Friant 1962D,
1967 (Eoc. ruminant molars), 1962E (tubular mammal molars); Frick and
Taylor 1968 (stenomyline camels, N. Amer.); Frisch 1965 (hominid dentition);
Gabie 1965 (origin of mammals); Gabuniiā 1954C (equid brain), 1961B (anthracotheres), 1964C (mammals); Gabuniiā and Meladze 1965 (variations of Hipparion); Gardiner 1967B (preoperculum in fishes); Garutt, V. E. 1965 (origin
and evol. of elephants); Gavaudan 1967 (natural selection); Geertz 1964 (culture and evol. of man); Geertz et al. 1965 (anthrop. research); Ginsburg 1968B
(Pliopithecus); Gisin 1966 (quantum theory of taxonomy); Glass 1966 (hairlessness in man); Glikman 1956 (Anacorax), 1959, 1964A (elasmobranchs), 1963B
(sharks), 1964B (Paleogene sharks, USSR); Godina 1964A, B, 1966, 1967A
(Giraffidae), 1968 (Palaeotragus); Goin and Goin 1962B (herpetology); Gould,
S. J. 1966 (allometry and size), 1967 (pelycosaurs); Greenwood 1967 (blind
cave fishes); Greenwood et al. 1966 (teleostean fishes); Gregory, J. T. 1964A,
1965 (microsaurs); Gregory, W. K. 1963, 1965 (face, fish to man); Gromov,
I. M. 1967 (Quat. rodents, USSR); Gromov, I. M. et al. 1965 (Marmotinae,
USSR); Gromov, V. I., Vangengeĭm and Nikiforova 1963 (Anthropogene mammalian fauna); Gromova 1968 (mammals); Gross, W. 1964C (polyphyletic origin of verts.), 1965A (placoderms); Günther 1967 (evol. doctrine); Gureev
1964 (Lagomorpha, USSR); Guthrie, R. D. 1965 (variability in characters under-
going rapid evol.); Gutmann 1966A (fishes and early verts.), 1966B (early development of verts.), 1967A (dermal skel. of lower verts.), 1967B (metameric-
worm theory of evol. of verts.);
Haag, Haas and Hürzeler 1962 (evol. and the Bible); Haas, A. 1963 (origin of life
and man); Haldane 1960 (natural selection), 1966 (causes of evol.); Hambleton
1967 (geol. time); Hamilton, T. H. 1967 (process and pattern in evol.); Hanson
1965 (evol.); Hardy, A. 1965 (evol.); Harrison et al. 1964 (human evol.);
Hartenberger, Michaux and Thaler 1967 (rodents, S. W. Europe); Hassler and
Stephan 1966 (evol. of the forebrain); Hayasaka 1964 (ontogeny, phylogeny and
evol. in paleont.); Heberer 1958F ("Watson rule"), 1964C (evol. of man), 1967A
(evol. of the organism), 1968 (origin of man); Herre 1964 (origin of Amphibia,
Tylopoda); Hiernaux 1963A (origin of man), 1963B (origin of races); Hockett
and Ascher 1964 (human behavior); Hofer 1964 (primate brain); Hollitscher
1964 (origin of man); Holloway 1966A (parameters for evol. of hominid brain
and behavior), 1966B ("mutation pressure" and structural reduction in human
evol.); Hopson 1966 (origin of mammalian middle ear), 1967A (origin of mammals); Hotton 1968 (evol.); Howell, F. C. 1964B, 1967B (evol. of man);
Howells et al. 1965 (synthesis and evol.); Huene 1964 (ichthyosaurs); Huppert
1964 (evol. importance of otoliths); Hürzeler 1962B (biol. evol.); 1968 (anthropomorphs); Hutchinson 1966 (manifest evol.); Hutchison 1965, 1966C (fossorial
moles of cent. and W. N. Amer.); Huxley, J. 1964A (evolutionary humanism);
Iablokov 1964, 1965 (cetaceans); Iakimov 1963 (man's evol.), 1964, 1968 (adaptive radiation of Tertiary apes); Iakovlev, V. N. 1966B, 1967C (fish skeleton);

Imaizumi 1966 (origin of Japanese mammalian fauna); Inger and Marx 1965 (colubrid snakes); Iordanskiĭ 1967 (origin of Gavialidae);

Jánossy 1964A, 1965B (small mammals, Pleist.); Janot 1967 (<u>Amia</u>); Jansky 1967 (temp. regulation in mammals); Jarvik 1964A (specializations in early verts.), 1965A (origin of girdles and paired fins), 1965B (origin of cyclostomes), 1967A origin of tetrapods), 1967B (fishes and tetrapods); Jefferies 1968 (primitive fossil chordates); Jepsen 1965 (modes of primate evol.); Jordan, D. S. 1963 (fishes);

Kaiser 1964 (abnormalities and overspecialization); Kamal 1966 (single origin of parachordal plate in Squamata); Kaplan, R. W. 1967 (early forms of life); Karageorgiev 1952 (Darwin's "geometric progression of multiplication" concept); Kermack 1965B, 1967A, B (mammals); Kerr and Silva 1962 (man); Khozatskiĭ 1959A (life forms); Klima, Von M. 1967 (bats); Kluge 1967 (gekkonid lizards); Kocherëzhkin 1967 (origin of life); Kochetkova 1961B, 1967, 1968 (hominid brain); Koenigswald 1965B, 1966A (hominids); Koestler 1965 (biol. and mental evol.); Korn and Thompson 1967 (human evol.); Kowalski, K. 1966B (Mesoz. mammals); Kraus, B. S. 1964 (human evol.); Kretzoi 1964A (verts.); Kühn, H. 1966A (origin of man); Kuhn, O. 1964A (Ornithischia), 1964B (testundines), 1964E (amphibians and reptiles), 1965A (Saurischia), 1965B (Therapsida), 1965C (macroevolution), 1965D (fossil birds), 1965E (Amphibia), 1966 (Reptilia), 1967A (Pterosauria); Kühne 1968 (origin and hist. of mammalia); Kuhn-Schnyder 1965C (reptiles), 1967A (Euryapsida); Kurtén 1964A (polar bear), 1965B (European wild cat), 1965E (evol. in geol. time); Kurth 1965B (hominid species); Kuźnicki and Urbanek 1967 (principles of evol.);

Landmann 1965 (man and animal); Landry 1965, 1967 (multituberculates, rodents); Larina 1958 (rodents); Layne 1967 (lagomorphs); Leakey, L. S. B. 1965B (origin of man); Lehman 1964C (origin of verts.), 1966E (origin of terrestrial verts.), 1967A (labyrinthodonts), 1967C (evol.); Leonardi, P. 1957F (biol. evol.), 1961A (evol.); Lerman 1965 (rates of evol.); Leroi-Gourhan, André 1964D (evol. of man's techniques and language); Lipps, J. H. 1968 (origin of otariid pinnipeds); Lisonbee 1965A, B (anti-evol. movement, Arizona); Liubish-chev 1965 (systematics and evol.); Livingstone 1967 (hominid evol.); Lorenz 1965 (evol. and behavior); Ludwig 1960 (selection);

MacAllister 1968 (teleost fishes); Macurda 1968 (paleobiol. aspects of growth and development); McKenna 1965B (origin of primates), 1967B (prosimian primates); McKerrow 1966 (evol. explosion); McLaughlin 1966 (elephants); Maderson 1967 (origin of vert. appendages); Mainardi and Taibel 1962 (galliforms); Maleev 1964A (Younginiformes), 1964B (Choristodera), 1964C (Prolacertidae), 1964D Tangasauridae), 1964E (Tholattosauridae), 1964F (Thecodontia), 1964G (Theropoda), 1964H (Compsognathidae), 1964I (Coeluridae), 1964J (Ornithomimidae), 1964K (Megalosauridae), 1964L (Ceratosauridae), 1964M (Spinosauridae), 1964N (Deinodontidae), 1964O (Stegosauria), 1964P (Ankylosauria); Mallorca Symposium 1966 (<u>Myotragus</u>); Malz 1967 (<u>Branchiosaurus</u>); Marelli 1953 (notoungulate, Argentina); Martin, R. D. 1968 (new definition of primates); Matveev 1967, 1968 (progress and regress in evol.); Mawhinney 1966 (man's origin − evol. or devine creation); Mayr, E. 1964C (evol. theory today), 1964D (systematics and origin of species), 1965A (classif. and phylogeny), 1965C (species level), 1965D (natural selection), 1967B (species concept and evol.); Mchedlidze 1964A, B (cetaceans), 1964C (cetaceans, Caucasus), 1967 (Tertiary cetaceans); Meladze 1964A (Sivatheriinae); Melendez 1964 (paleont. and evol.); Mendrez 1967 (therocephalians and cynodonts); Merrilees 1965C (marsupials); Mezhzherin 1965 (Quat. shrews); Miklin 1967 (Huxley's concept of unlimited progress); Miles, R. S. 1967A (placoderms); Miller, A. H. 1966B (evol. on islands); Miller, R. R. 1965 (freshwater fishes, N. Amer.); Milojević 1966, 1967 (<u>Archaeopteryx</u> and non-correlative evol.); Milstead 1967 (box turtles, cent. N. Amer.

and E. Mexico);   Milstead and Tinkle 1967 (box turtles, W. Mexico);   Mitchell,
E. D. 1966E (Allodesmus, California), 1967B (diphyly in pinnipeds), 1968 (Imagotaria, California);   Mohr, E. 1959 (origin of wild horse);   Montagu 1963B
(origin of speech), 1964A (natural selection, hominids);   Moore and eds. of
Life 1964A, B (evol.);   Morgan, T. H. 1916 (critique of theory of evol.);   Motas
1964 (selected papers of Emil Racoviţa);   Müller, A. H. 1966 (fishes and amphibians), 1968 (reptiles and birds);   Myers, G. S. 1966 (origin of Cent. Amer. freshwater fishes);
N. 1960 (biol. and cultural origins of man);   Nesturkh 1954 (simians and hominids,
Asia);   Nikitenko 1964 (vert. brain), 1965 (mammal brain), 1966 (amphibian
brain);   Nobach 1959 (vert. brain);   Nogar 1963 (evol. and the Bible);   Notz
1964 (deer);   Novitskaya and Obruchev 1964 (Acanthodei);   Novozhilov 1964A
(Sauropterygia), 1964B (Pistosauroidea), 1964C (Plesiosauroidea), 1964D (Pliosauroidea);
Oakley and Muir-Wood 1962 (life through geol. time);   Obruchev, D. V. 1964A,
1967D (fishes), 1964B (Chordata), 1964C (Agnatha), 1964D (Placodermi), 1964E
Holocephali), 1965B (Paleoz. and Mesoz. fishes), 1967A (Heterostraci);   Obruchev
and Kazantseva 1964A (Chondrostei), 1964B (Polypteri);   Obruchev and Mark-
Kurik 1965, 1968 (psammosteids);   Obrucheva 1959B (Dev. fishes, USSR);
Ochev 1964 (Mesoz. reptiles), 1966C (capitosauroid labyrintodonts);   Olivier
1965B (evol. and man);   Olson 1962C (mammals, S. Amer.), 1963D, 1966C
(origin of mammals), 1965A (Amphibia), 1965C (evol. of life), 1965F (higher
levels of organization), 1966B (role of paleont. in evol.), 1968A (dialectics in
evol.), 1968B (Caseidae);   Oparin 1967 (origin of life);   Orlov, V. N. 1960 (Equus
molars);   Ortega 1967 (Scelidotheriinae);   Orton 1957 (frogs);   Ørvig 1967B
(tooth tissues);   Oschinsky 1963B (parallelism in Homo);   Oschinsky et al. 1964
(origin of Homo sapiens);   Ostrom 1964B (Hadrosaurus), 1966A, C (horned
dinosaurs);   Overhage 1963 (evol., vert. paleont.), 1964 (evol. of man);
Packard 1967 (rodents);   Panchen 1967C (Amphibia);   Parkes 1964 (evol.);   Parkes
and Clark 1966 (ratites and tinamous);   Parrington 1967A (origins of mammals);
Parris 1968 (prosciurids);   Pasteur 1964 (Afr. lizards);   Patte 1966 (parallel
evol.);   Patterson, B. 1964 (Old World non-hominid primates);   Patterson, C.
1964 (acanthopterygian fishes), 1965A, B (Holocephali), 1967C (teleosts);   Peiper
1963 (evol. of man);   Peña Basurto 1959 (Oreopithecus in hominid origins);
Petter, G. 1965 (Viverridae);   Pilbeam 1966A (Dryopithecinae), 1968B (origin
of man);   Pilbeam et al. 1965 (human origins);   Pinner 1966 (evol.);   Piveteau
1962E (origin of man), 1963D (evol., verts.), 1964C (Agnatha), 1964D (verts.),
1966B (fishes);   Portmann, A. 1967 ("struggle for existence");   Pringle 1965
(physiological evol.);   Prost 1964 (human evol.);
Radinsky 1965B (tapiroid skel.), 1966A (adaptive radiation of phenacodonts), 1967A
(tapiroids), 1967B (hyracodonts);   Rand 1967 (birds);   Ratcliff 1965 (origin
of man);   Raunich 1961 (verts.);   Reed, C. A. and Schaffer 1966 (caprini);
Reed, C. A. and Turnbull 1965 (moles);   Reig 1964 (land tetrapods), 1967
(Archosauria);   Remane 1963, 1964B, 1967 (verts.), 1964A (radiation), 1965
(apes);   Rensch 1966 (evol. above species level), 1967 (brain);   Reshetov 1966
(origin of man);   Reynolds, V. 1966, 1967A (man);   Rhodes 1966 (evol.);   Ricqlès
1967A (origin of dinosaurs), 1968E (mammal-like reptiles, S. Amer., S. Afr.);
Ripinsky 1967 (immunochemical analysis, Hominidae);   Ritchie, A. 1964 (Anaspida, Norway);   Robinson, J. T. 1964B, 1965B (hominids);   Robinson, P. L.
1967A (Lacertilia);   Rodnick 1966 (man);   Rodriguez, C. F. 1961 (man);   Rogers
et al. 1967 (computer analysis);   Romer 1964F (bone in early verts.), 1964G
(amphibians), 1965B (polyphylety of verts.), 1966C, D, 1967F, 1968A (vert.
paleont.), 1967C (early reptiles);   Ross, H. H. 1967 (evol.);   Rozhdestvenskiĭ
1964B (Reptilia), 1964C (Archosauria);   Ruffié 1967A (primates), 1967B (origin
of man);   Russell, D. A. 1964 (mosasaur skull);   Russell, R. J. 1968 (pocket gopher
Ruyer 1967 (cybernetics);

S., G. 1959 (types of prehist. dogs); Salthe and Kaplan 1966 (rates of evol. in Amphibia); Sarich 1967B (primate evol. rates); Sarkar 1964 (mammal evol. rates); Sassi 1964 (dinosaurs); Savage, J. M. 1963C, 1966 (evol.); Schaeffer, B. 1964, 1965A (tetrapod evol.), 1965D (origin of Amphibia), 1965E (levels of organization); Scheffer 1965, 1967 (marine mammals, N. Pacific); Schmalhausen 1947 (materialistic darwinism), 1959B, 1964B, 1968 (origin of land verts.), 1964A (Urodela); Schmidt, W. 1959* (pteraspids); Schreider 1965 (evol.); Scopes and Presley 1967 (Scopes evol. trial); Selander 1965 (Quat. avian speciation); Semenov, Iu. I. 1966 (origin of man); Sergienko 1961C (Osteichthyes); Severtsov 1945 (evol.), 1948 (verts.), 1950 (limbs); Sharashidze 1968 (origin of fish fauna, Georgia, USSR); Sharov 1965 (evol. and taxonomy); Shevyreva 1966 (Olig. rodents, Kazakhstan); Shikama 1966C (Desmostylus, Paleoparadoxia, Japan); Shishkin, M. A. 1964 (stereospondyli), 1968 (morphogenesis); Shishkin and Ochev 1966, 1967A (amphibian skull); Shmidt, G. A. 1940 (sexual selection), 1947 (spiral evol.); Shvarts 1965 (land verts.), 1967 (problems in evol.); Simon 1964 (pre-hominid primates); Simons 1964A (origin of man), 1964D, 1967A (primates), 1967D (Pantodonta); Simons and Pilbeam 1965 (Dryopithecinae); Simpson, G. G. 1964B, 1966G, H, 1967D, G (evol.), 1964D (extraterrestrial "humanoid" evol.), 1964E (molecules in evol.), 1965B, 1967F, 1968A (meaning of evol.), 1965C (masterometry), 1965G (geog. of evol.), 1965J (tupaiids), 1966E (horses), 1966F (mammals, S. continents); Singer 1964 Darwinism); Singer and Bone 1966 (Hipparion in Afr.); Slaby 1962 (vert. limbs); Smith, G. R. 1966 (N. Amer. catostomid fishes); Smith, Hobart M. 1960 (evol. of chordate structure); Smith, R. L. 1966 (ecol., field biol.); Soergel 1960 (origin of birds); Sohre 1964 (hist. of horse); Solbrig 1966 (evol. and systematics); Spinar 1967B (frogs); Spuhler 1964 (hominid evol.); Staesche 1964C (hist. of tortoises); Starck 1963A (vert. head metamery), 1965 (vert. brain), 1967B (primatology); Starrett 1967 (rodents); Stebbins 1966, 1968 (organic evol.); Steiner, H. 1956 (chordates); Stensiö 1964 (ostracoderms); Stepanian 1964 (hist. of mountain birds); Stęslicka 1964B (primates); Størmer 1966A (evol. through Paleoz.); Strelkovskii 1963A (parallelism), 1963B, 1966 (specialization and extinction), 1964 (biogenetics), 1967 (progressive evol.); Sukhanov 1964 (Testudinata); Swinton 1964A, 1965A (fossil birds), 1964B (origin of birds); Sych 1966B (origine of the hare); Sylvester-Bradley 1967B (evol. and time); Szalay, F. S. 1968 (earliest primates); Szalay and Gould 1966 (mesonychids); Szarski 1957 (origin of paired limbs); Tappen 1966 (human evol.); Tarlo, L. B. H. 1967B (Agnatha); Tatarinov, L. P. 1964B (Amphibia), 1964C (Colosteoidea), 1964D (Cochleosauroidea), 1964E (Zatrachydidae), 1964F (Plesiopoda), 1964G (Salientia), 1964H (Gephyrostegidae), 1964I (Chroniosuchidae), 1964J (Waggoneridae), 1964K (Lepospondyli), 1964L (Microsauria), 1964M (Therapsida), 1964N (Diarthrognathoidea), 1964O (Tritylodontoidea), 1964P (Synaptosauria), 1964Q (Nothosauria), 1964R (Plesiosauria), 1964S (Ichthyopterygia), 1964T (Lepidosauria), 1964U (Polyglyphanodontidae), 1964V (Scincoidea), 1964W (Xantusioidea), 1964X (Elachistosuchidae), 1964Y (Scleromochlidae), 1964Z (Coeluroidea), 1964AA (Deinodontoidea), 1965E (origin of Amphibia); Teixeira 1963 (origin of man); Telles Antunes 1964B (crocodiles); Termier, H. and G. 1961, 1966 (evol. of man), 1964B (organic evol.); Terzea 1966 (dentition, cave bear); Tétry 1967 (biol. evol.); Thenius 1964A (proboscideans), 1964B (evol.), 1964D (S. Amer. mammals), 1966B (bovids), 1966C (origin of mammals), 1966E (origin of horses), 1966F (hyenas), 1967B (giraffes), 1967C (felids); Thomson, K. S. 1964C (tetrapods), 1966A (middle ear); Thomson and Hahn 1968 (rhipidistian fishes); Tihen 1964A, 1965 (frogs); Tolmachev, A. I. 1959A (geog. principles), 1959B (biocenotic); Tomkins 1965 (Scopes trial), 1966 (anti-evol. law); Trofimov, B. A. 1964A (mammals); Tsankov and Nikolov 1966B (proboscideans); Tuttle 1965, 1967 (hominid hands); Uchida 1964 (fishes); Urist 1962 (origin of verts.), 1964 (origin of bone); Uyeno 1966 (Cenoz. freshwater fishes);

Vanderbroek 1964 (origin of mammals), 1966 (origin of murids); Van Deusen
and Jones 1967 (marsupials); Vangerow 1967 (oxygen and evol.); Van Valen
1963C (selection in natural populations), 1964A (age in horse populations),
1964B (species abundance), 1964C (origin of rabbits), 1965B (tupaiid-primate
affinities), 1965C (morphological integration), 1965D (measuring natural selection), 1965E (Paroxylaenidae), 1966A (Deltatheridia), 1968 (origin of whales);
Vereshchagin and Batyrov 1967 (Cent. Asian mammalian fauna); V'iushkov
1964A (Synapsida), 1964B (Deinocephalia), 1964C (Theriodontia), 1964D (Galeopsoidea), 1964E (Dicynodontoidea), 1964F (Anomodontia inc. sed.), 1964G
(Proganosauria); Voinstvenskiĭ 1966 (Ukrainian vert. fauna); Volpe 1967 (evol.);
Vorob'eva and Obruchev 1964 (Sarcopterygii); Voronŝov 1963B (rodent jaws);
Vuilleumier 1965 (Cracidae), 1967 (Patagonian forest birds);
Waddington 1966 (biol. and evol.); Wahlert 1966 (modern theories); Wake 1966
(salamanders); Wake and Dresner 1967 (salamander tail); Walker, A. D. 1968
(origin of phytosaurs, crocodiles); Warburton and Denman 1961 (origin of tetrapods); Washburn 1965, 1967 (human evol.), 1966 (biol. and evol.); Weaver
and Rose 1967 (Chrysemys); Webb, S. D. 1965B, 1966B (origin of camels),
1965C (Camelops); Weiner 1964 (evol. of man); Weinert 1956 (apes and man);
Weitzmann 1967 (stomiatoid fishes); Weller 1965A (paleont., evol., taxonomy),
1968 (mammal teeth); Welles and Cosgriff 1965B (labyrinthodonts); Wenz
1967A (Actinopterygia); Wermuth 1964 (origin and evol. of turtle shell); Westphal 1962C (origin of mammals); Whipple and Silverzweig 1962 (primates);
Whitehead 1964 (deer, Great Britain, Ireland); Whyte 1965 (selection in evol.);
Wierciński 1961 (hominid skull); Williams, G. C. 1966 (evol.); Williams, K. L.
and Wilson 1967 (colubrid snake, Cemophora); Wolański 1957A, B, 1958 (human
evol.); Woo, Ju-kang 1964H (human evol.); Wood, A. E. 1965A (rodents);
Zablotsky and Flerov 1963 (evol. of bisons); Zavadskiĭ 1967 (problem of progress
in nature), 1968 (theory of species); Zavadskiĭ and Berman 1966 (antidarwinism);
Zhemkova 1965 (origin of cetaceans); Zhukov 1965 (fresh water lampreys, USSR);
Zimmermann, W. 1960B (modern ideas).

EXHIBITS — See: museums; restorations; technique.

EXPEDITIONS, EXPLORATIONS, EXCURSIONS, EXCAVATIONS and SURVEYS —
Anderson, E. G. 1964 (Nullarbor expd., S. Australia); Anon. 1959BR (Uzbekistan
archeol. expd.), 1961CT (Pal. div., Geol. Surv., India), 1962CH (Movius in France),
1964I (Chicago Mus.), 1964BA (Shisha Pangma expd, Tibet), 1964BH (South
Dakota), 1964BO, 1966H (Yale Peabody Mus. to Egypt), 1964BZ (Hell Gap,
Wyoming), 1965BA, 1966AI, BN (Polish Pal. Expds., Gobi), 1966AB (Univ.
Nebraska), 1966AF (Yale Peabody Mus.), 1967M (Univ. Utah dinosaur dig),
1967AO (Florida underwater site); Arambourg 1967 (Omo expd.); Arkell 1959B
(British Ennedi Expd.); Attridge et al. 1964 (British expd. to Afr.); Auffenberg
et al. 1964 (field trip guide book, Florida);
Bader, O. N. 1968A (N. USSR); Bibikov 1963A, B (archeol., Ukraine); Black and
Dawson 1966B (paleont. and geol., cent. Wyoming); Bud'ko 1967C (Belorussian
archeol. expd.); Bush 1960 (Roy. Ontario Mus. Expd. to Peru);
Carlson 1967 (Univ. Colorado Nubian Expd.); Case, J. 1965A (fossil hunting, New
Jersey), 1965B (fossil hunting, Florida); Clemens 1965B (collecting Cret. mam-
mals, Alberta); Croft and White 1940 (Spitzbergen expd., 1939);
Devillers 1965 (dinosaur beds, Alberta);
Fernow 1965 (AGI Internat. Field Inst. trip); Fiske 1964 (Univ. Manitoba field
work); Freund 1965 (H. Obermaier Soc. trips, France); Freund and Naber 1965
(H. Obermaier Soc. trips, Rhine);
Grigor'eva et al. 1968 (Moldavian archeol expd.);
Hlady 1964 (Manitoba Archaeol. Soc.); Hoffman and Esterhuyse 1965 (Orange R.
area, Afr.); Hugot 1960B (Berliet archeol. expds., Sahara);

Irwin and Wheat 1965 (Univ. Colorado Nubian expd.);
Jisl 1965 (Czecho-Mongolian archeol. expd.);
Kielan-Jaworowska 1965A, B, 1966A, B, C, 1967 (Polish-Mongolian Gobi Expds.);
  Kowalski, K. 1965A (Polish-Mongolian Gobi Expd.);
Leakey, M. D. 1965 (Olduvai Gorge expd.); Lindberg 1962 (Tule Springs, Nevada);
  Lindsay, G. E. 1965 (California Acad. Sci. Baja expd.);
Macdonald, D. J. 1965 (S. Dakota fossil hunting expd.); Macdonald, J. R. 1966D,
  1967D (Los Angeles Co. Mus. Montana expd.); Macdonald, J. R. and D. J. 1967
  (Los Angeles Co. Mus. S. Dakota expd.); Martinez 1964 (paleont. explor. of
  Tenerife Is.); Masson, M. E. 1940 (Termez archeol. expd.); Miart 1967 (excur-
  sion in the region of Reims); Mitchell and Lipps 1965 (collecting on San Clements
  Is., California); Mori 1961 (5th Paletnol. Expd. to Acacus, Sahara);
Nelson, P. R. 1965 (Chicago Mus. Australian expd.); Nielsen 1962 (Thai Danish
  prehist. expd.);
Ochev and Shishkin 1967 (Soviet expd.); Okladnikov and Larichev 1963, 1967 (Sov-
  iet-Mongolian archeol expds.); Osmólska 1966 (Polish-Mongolian expd.);
Pinna 1964 (Soc. Ital. Sci. Nat.); Praslov 1964A (archeol., Ukraine);
Radinsky 1964B (Amer. Mus. expds. Eoc., Olig. fossil localities, Mongolia); Radmilli
  et al. 1964 (archeol. digs, Italy); Ramplin 1967 (Glacial Lake Agassiz Surv.);
  Redfield 1962 (archeol. surv., Mississippi Valley); Reed, C. A. 1966 (Yale Univ.
  Prehist. Expd., Nubia); Riggs 1928 (Field Mus. Paleont. Expd., S. Amer.); Romer
  1965A, 1966A, 1967D (Harvard Expds., Argentina); Rozhdestvenskiĭ 1960C,
  1966C (USSR Gobi expds.); Rusconi 1964A (Argentina expd.);
Said et al. 1965 (geol. expd. to Lower Nubia); Savage, D. E. 1966A, B (Soc. Vert.
  Pal. field trip); Säve-Söderberg 1962, 1963, 1964 (Scandinavian Nubian Expd.);
  Schauberger et al. 1961 (field guide, Austria); Schlesier 1964A (German Archeol.
  Expd., N. Alaska); Schultz, C. B. and Smith 1965A, B, C (Nebraska field conf.);
  Schüz and Staesche 1963 (Stuttgart Mus. expds.); Shishkin, V. A. 1961, 1962
  (Uzbekistan Archeol. Expd.); Sibrawa 1966 (INQUA Congr.); Simons 1962G
  (Yale Egyptian Expd.); Simpson, G. G. 1967C (S. Amer. localities); Smith,
  P. E. L. 1964B (Natl. Mus. Canada Egypt Expd.); Solecki, R. S. 1963 (Columbia
  Univ. Nubian Expd.); Stout 1964 (early paleont. work, Nebraska);
Tobien 1968B (expd. to Greece and Iran); Toepfer and Nuglisch 1962 (Excursion,
  Paleolithic, Germany); Tolstov 1968 (archeol. expd., Uzbekistan); Turnbull and
  Lundelius 1967 (Australian expd.);
Watanabe, H. 1965 (Tokyo Univ. Sci. Expd. W. Asia); Webb, S. D. 1967B (Cent.
  Amer. Expd.); Wendorf, Daugherty and Waechter 1964, Wendorf et al. 1965
  (Nubian expd.); Wheat and Irwin 1965 (Univ. Colo. Nubian expd.);
Zemliakov 1940D (archeol. excursion, USSR).

EXTINCTION — Afanas'ev 1960 (cent. Asia); Anon. 1968C (mammoths); Axelrod 1967B
  (Quat. mammals); Axelrod and Bailey 1968 (Cret. dinosaurs);
Beals 1966 (N. Amer. Pleist. mammals); Bramlette 1965 (Mesozoic biota); Budyko
  1967 (large mammals, Pleist.); Burchak-Abramovich 1963B (ratites), 1966B
  (unkeeled birds);
Cys 1967B (dinosaurs);
Deevey 1967 (elephants); Dreimanis 1967A (mastodons, Ontario), 1967B (mastodons,
  eastern N. Amer.); Due Rojo 1964 (mass extinctions);
Eaton 1963 (Cret. reptiles); Edwards 1966, 1967B (Pleist.);
Flanders 1962 (dinosaurs);
Gabuniia 1963 (dinosaurs); Ginsburg 1964D (evol. and extinction); Gould, C. 1886
  (prehist. animals); Guilday 1965B, 1967C (differential extinction, Pleist.-Recent);
  Gusev 1956 (mammoths, Siberia); Guthrie, R. D. 1966A (wapiti, Alaska and
  Yukon Territory);
Hester, J. J. 1965, 1967 (agency of man); Hopson 1967B (Multituberculates);

Jelinek, A. J. 1967 (agency of man, Pleist. faunas); Jepsen 1964A (dinosaurs);
Koch 1967 (dinosaurs); Kowalski, K. 1967C (Pleist. mammals, Europe);
Landry 1964, 1967 (multituberculates); Leakey, L. S. B. 1966C, 1967F, 1968A
(Pleist. overkill, Afr.); Lufkin 1964 (Pleist. mammals);
McKerrow 1966 (mass extinction); Marchal 1965 (dinosaurs); Martin, P. S.
1965, 1966, 1967B, C, 1968 (Pleist. overkill), 1967A (Pleist. extinction),
1967D (overkill at Olduvai Gorge, Tanzania); Martin and Wright 1967
Pleist.); Mayr, E. 1965E (island avifauna); Mehringer 1965A, 1967 (Pleist.
megafauna); Meladze 1963 (sivatheres); Merrilees 1968 (Australian Quat.
marsupials); Mertens 1966 (amphibians and reptiles); Mstislavskiĭ and
Kochenov 1961 (Maikop fish remains);
Nesturkh 1964B, 1968A (Plioc., Pleist. anthropoids); Newell 1965 (end of Cret.),
1966 (mass extinctions as geochronol. data);
Pidoplichko 1963B (anti-glacial theory); Prufer 1963B, 1964A (Pleist. overkill);
Russell, L. S. 1965B, 1967B (dinosaurs);
Sai-Halász 1967 (diminished fertility); Sassi 1964 (dinosaurs); Simpson, G. G.
(mammals, S. continents); Slaughter 1965B (causes), 1967 (animal ranges);
Smith, A. 1965 (dinosaurs); Strelkovskiĭ 1963B, 1966 (specialization);
Thaler 1965B (dinosaurs, France); Thenius 1964B, C (causes);
Van Valen and Sloan 1966 (multituberculates); Vereshchagin 1967A (Pleist., USSR);
Vershchagin, Geptner and Stroganova 1959 (Caucasian marmot);
Walker, A. 1967 (Madagascan lemuroids).

FAUNAS — GENERAL — Alizade, Asadov and Derzhavin 1951 (Azerbaidzhan);
Bannikov 1954 (origin mammalian fauna, Mongolia); Borovikov and Borsuk 1961
(verts., Kazakhstan);
Chmielewski, W. 1958A (cave animal bones, Poland); Chow 1965C (new finds,
China); Colbert 1964E (terrestrial faunas); Cooper, B. N. 1964 (fossil finds,
Virginia); Corr 1915 (fossils of Forfarshire, Scotland); Crusafont Pairó 1961E
(mammal sites, Spain), 1965F, O (fossil finds, Spain);
Dai and Chi 1964 (mammals, Lantian Co., China); Danilov 1960 (avifauna of
Urals); Daxner and Fejfar 1967 (lagomorphs, Europe); Dechaseaux 1964C
(chordates), 1964D (urochordates), 1964E (cephalochordates); Delair 1959
(new fossil finds); Dement'ev 1964 (Aves); Derzhavin 1951 (hist. of faunas,
Azerbaidzhan); Dineley 1965A (fossils, far north), 1966A (fossil verts., Canada);
Fejfar 1962 (fossil verts., Czechoslovakia); Fisher, D. W. 1955 (prehist. mammals,
N.Y.); Fisher, J. 1967B (fossil birds); FitzSimons 1962 (snakes of S. Afr.);
Flerov 1953 (Elasmotherium); Fowlie 1965 (snakes, Arizona); Fuhn and Vancea
1961 (reptiles, Rumania);
Garutt, W. E. 1964 (mammoth); Garutt, V. E. 1965 (elephants); Gentry 1968
(zoogeog. of antelopes); George and Berger 1966 (avian myology); Graves 1958
(Thylacinus, Tasmania); Greenwood 1963 (hist. of fishes), 1967 (blind cave
fishes); Gromova 1968 (mammals);
Harland et al. 1967A (the fossil record); Heintz, A. 1966A (fossil mammals);
Hoffmeister 1967 (tubulidentates, proboscideans, hyracoideans); Hoffstetter
1961E (mammal beds, S. Amer.); Hooijer 1963E (R. mammals, Curaçao);
Howard 1964C (anseriformes); Hürzeler 1968 (hist. of anthropomorphs);
Jerzmańska 1964 (fish fauna, ? Poland); Jessen 1966B, 1967 (Struniiformes);
Jones, J. K. 1967 (monotremes); Jones and Johnson 1967 (sirenians);
Kielan-Jaworowska 1965A, B, 1966A, B, C, 1967 (Polish-Mongolian Gobi expds.);
Klages 1962 (fossils of the Subherzynisch Basin, Germany); Klemmer 1964
(reptiles and amphibians); Koenigswald 1967B (fossil anthropoids); Kowalski,
K. 1961D (faunal relations, N. Amer. and Europe); Kraus, O. 1964B (verts.,
Cent. Amer.); Kretzoi 1963 (verts., Carpathians);

Gross, W. 1968A (rhombic fish scales, Gotland), 1968C (Dartmuthia), 1968D
(Phlebolepis scales, Oesel Island);
Heintz, A. 1967B (tremataspidid, S. Norway);
Li and Huang 1966 (fishes, China);
Martinsson 1966 (verts., Gotland);
Obruchev, D. V. 1965A (fishes and Agnatha, USSR);
Ritchie, A. 1967 (cephalaspid, Scotland), 1968 (Jamoytius, Scotland);
White, E. I. 1944 (Phialaspis, Europe).

FAUNAS — DEVONIAN — Anatol'eva 1960 (fishes, USSR); Anon. 1965CF (fishes,
Ohio), 1967AR (Bothriolepis, Canada); Atlasov 1960 (fishes, Siberia);
Balabaĭ 1959, 1960B (pteraspids, Ukraine), 1962 (cephalaspids, Ukraine); Borina
and Tikhomirov 1961 (fishes, Kazakhstan);
Campbell, K. S. W. 1965 (dipnoan, New S. Wales); Chang, Kuo-jui 1965 (antiarchs,
China); Conolly 1965 (fishes, New South Wales); Corr 1915 (fishes, Scotland);
Denison 1964A (armored fishes), 1964B (Cyathaspididae), 1966B (agnathan, Wyo-
ming), 1967B (Protaspis, Utah), 1968 (lung fishes, W. U. S.); Dineley 1964B
(ostracoderms, British Columbia), 1966C (pteraspids, Devon), 1967A (ostraco-
derms, Nova Scotia), 1967B (ostracoderms, fishes, Canada); Dunkle 1964B
(paleoniscid fish, Ohio);
Egiazarov 1957, 1958 (fishes, Soviet Arctic);
Fahlbusch, K. 1966 (pteraspids, Belgium); Flahive 1964 (fishes, Ohio); Fradkin,
Nakhabt̆sev and Shcherbakov 1967A (fishes, USSR);
Göke 1964 (agnathan, Germany); Grishchenko, V. A. 1968 (armored fishes, Tian-
Shan); Gross, W. 1964B (Dipterus, Bergisch Gladbach), 1965A (placoderms,
Belgium), 1965B (Bothriolepis, Lübech), 1965C (fishes, Germany), 1965D
(dipnoan, Ganorhynchus), 1965E (Onychodus, Germany); Gupta and Denison
1966 (fishes, Kashmir);
Hlavin 1965A, B, 1966 (fishes, Ohio);
Ishnazarov 1967 (fishes, Tian-Shan);
Jarvik 1967C (dipnoan, Canada); Jessen 1966A (crossopterygians, Germany);
Karatajute 1958A (asterolepids, USSR); Karatajute-Talimaa 1960A, 1962, 1964,
(fishes, Lithuania), 1960B (asterolepid, USSR), 1966 (bothriolepids, Baltic region);
Krasnov and Predtechenskiĭ 1967 (fishes, USSR);
Levenko 1960 (fishes, cent. Asia); Liu, Y.-h. 1965 (agnathans, China);
Mark-Kurik 1963 (arthrodire spinal plate), 1968 (psammosteids, Estonia, Latvia);
Mazarovich, O. A. et al. 1966 (fishes, Kazakhstan); Menner 1961, 1967B,
1968 (fishes, Siberia); Mikut̆skiĭ 1960 (fishes, Siberia); Miles, R. S. 1965B,
(placoderm, Antartica), 1965C (arthrodires, Arizona), 1965D (arthrodire, New
York), 1966A (Acanthodii, Germany), 1966B (arthrodires, N. Amer.), 1967B
(Rhamphodopsis, Scotland); Miles and Westoll 1968 (Coccosteus, Scotland);
Miroshnikov 1962 (fishes, USSR);
Narbutas 1964A (fishes, Baltic);
Obruchev, D. V. 1961B (fishes, USSR); Obruchev and Karatajute-Talimaa 1967
(verts., E. Europe); Obruchev and Mark-Kurik 1965 (psammosteids, USSR);
Obrucheva 1959B, 1962A (fishes, USSR), 1963, 1966 (coccosteids, Baltic region);
Ørvig 1961D (fishes, Scandinavia), 1967C (acanthodians, Europe); Orviku 1958
(fishes, Esthonia);
P'an 1964 (fishes, S. China); Pershina 1962 (fishes, USSR), 1965, 1966 (fishes,
Urals); Predtechenskiĭ 1958, 1967 (fishes, Cent. Asia);
Rabitz 1966 (fishes, Germany); Rade 1964 (fish, New S. Wales); Rzhonsnitskaiã
and Meleshchenko 1955 (verts., USSR);
Scheele 1965A, B (fishes, Ohio); Schultze 1968 (fish scales, Australia, Spitzbergen);
Sergienko 1961A, B, 1965 (fish, Siberia); Siegfried 1960 (arthrodire, Germany);
Silva Santos 1961 (fishes, Brazil); Stevens, M. S. 1964 (arthrodire, Michigan);

Tarlo, L. B. H. 1964C, 1965 (fishes, Poland); Thomson, K. S. 1965A (fish, Scotland), 1965B (Osteolepis), 1967C (dipnoan, Canada), 1968B (rhipidistian, Pennsylvania); Tkachenko et al. 1957 (fish, Siberia);

Verte and Mark 1957 (fishes, Esthonia); Volochkovich 1961 (fish, Mongolia);

Warren, J. W. and Talent 1967 (fishes, Australia); Wells, J. W. 1964 (antiarch, New York);

Żeiba and Vasiliauskas 1958 (fishes, Lithuania).

FAUNAS — CARBONIFEROUS — Alekseeva, L. I. 1959C (mammals, N. Caucasus); Altmeyer 1964 (Germany); Anon. 1968AA (reptiles and microsaurs);

Baird 1966A (labyrinthodont, Kansas); Baird and Carroll 1967B (oldest reptile, Nova Scotia); Bardack and Zangerl 1968 (lamprey, Illinois); Branson 1964C (Edestus, Oklahoma), 1965B (Petrodus, Oklahoma); Brough, M. C. and J. 1967 (microsaurs);

Carroll, R. L. 1964B (dissorophid amphibians), 1964C (reptiles, Nova Scotia), 1965B (lungfish burrows, Michigan), 1966 (microsaurs, Nova Scotia), 1967A (lepospondyl amphibian, Scotland), 1967B (labyrinthodonts, Nova Scotia), 1967C (cotylosaur, Nova Scotia); Carroll and Baird 1968 (microsaur Tuditanus and reptiles); Colbert 1966C (Rutiodon, Pennsylvania); Cramer and Falls 1966 (shark, Georgia, U.S.A.); Czygan 1963 (otoliths, Germany);

Dahm 1966 (fishes, Germany); Dorr and Moser 1964 (sharks, Michigan);

Ford, T. D. 1964 (fishes, England); Fradkin, Nakhabt̂sev and Shcherbakov 1967B (fishes, USSR);

Jubb 1965 (palaeoniscid fish, S. Afr.);

Leont'ev 1956 (fishes, cent. Asia); Lund 1967B (fishes, Pennsylvania);

McGinnis 1964, 1965, 1967 (aïstopod amphibian, Ohio, Illinois);

Obruchev, D. V. 1962A (fishes, USSR); Ørvig 1967A (Holmesella, Kansas);

P'an 1964 (fishes, S. China); Panchen 1964, Panchen, Tilley and Steel 1967 (anthracosaurs, England);

Romer 1964B (labyrinthodont, Scotland);

Schmidt, W. 1965 (fish, Germany);

Thomson, K. S. 1965C (Dipnoi); Tolmachev, I. P. 1931 (verts., USSR);

Vasil'ev, V. G. 1960 (verts., USSR);

Zangerl 1966 (shark, Indiana).

FAUNAS — PERMIAN — Anon. 1963BV (New Mexico);

Bendix-Almgreen 1962, 1967 (edestids, E. Greenland), 1966 (Helicoprion, Idaho); Berman 1968 (lungfish, Texas); Boonstra 1968 (terrestrial reptiles, S. Afr.); Borisenko 1966 (amphibian, USSR); Branson 1964A (helicoprion, China);

Carroll, R. L. 1964A (Parioxys), 1964B (dissorophid amphibians), 1968A (Pantylus), 1968C (? diapsid, Oklahoma); Chalyshev 1966B (N. Urals); Chase, J. N. 1965 (labyrinthodont, Texas); Chudinov 1964J, 1968B (Dinocephalia, Urals), 1965 (USSR);

Dalquest 1966 (paleoniscid, Texas); DeMar 1966A, 1967, 1968 (amphibians, Texas); Eufrosin 1960 (Paleoniscus, Carpathians);

Heyler 1965 (verts., France), 1967 (Aeduella, France); Hoffman 1965 (thecodont, S. Afr.);

Kitching 1968 (verts., S. Afr.); Konzhukova 1964D (melosaur); Kuhn, O. 1964F (labyrinthodont, U.S.A.), 1964G (verts., Germany);

Langston 1965A (pelycosaur, New Mexico), 1966B (captorhinomorph, New Mexico); Lewis and Vaughn 1965 (verts., Colorado); Liu and Hsieh 1965 (bradyodont, China); Liu and Tseng 1964 (fish, China); Logan 1968 (marine vert., W. Canada); Logan and McGugan 1968 (Helicoprion, W. Canada);

McGinnis 1964, 1965, 1967 (aïstopod amphibian, Oklahoma); Malzahn 1968 (Janassa, Lower Rhine); Molin 1965 (verts., USSR);

Obruchev, D. V. 1962D (fishes, USSR); Ochev 1966B (verts., USSR); Olson
1965D, 1967 (verts., Oklahoma), 1965E (Zatrachys, Oklahoma), 1966D (Dia-
dectes), 1968B (Caseidae); Orlov, J. A. 1960B (dinocephalians, USSR); Ørvig
1967A (Janassa, Germany);
Pakhtusova 1966 (verts., USSR);
Romer 1964C (terrestrial verts., USA and USSR);
Seltin 1963, 1965 (amphibians, reptiles, Texas); Shikama and Ozaki 1966 (reptile,
Brazil); Simmons 1965 (reptiles, China); Staesche 1964D (verts., Germany);
Stephens, J. J. 1964 (Ophiacodon, Ohio); Stovall, Price and Romer 1966 (pelyco-
saur, Oklahoma); Sun 1964 (Lystrosaurus, China); Suveizdis 1963 (fishes,
Poland);
Tatarinov, L. P. 1964AB, 1965B (seymouriamorphs, USSR), 1965A (therocephalian,
USSR), 1965C (theriodonts), 1968 (cynodonts, USSR); Teixeira 1958 (fishes,
W. Afr.); Tripathi and Satsangi 1963 (reptiles, India); Tverdokhlebova 1967
(amphibian, USSR);
Vasilenko 1961 (verts., USSR); Vasil'ev, V. G. 1960 (verts., USSR); Vaughn 1964A
(verts., Utah, Arizona), 1964B (lungfish, New Mexico), 1965 (amphibian, Utah),
1966A (verts., Utah, Texas), 1966B (Seymouria, Utah), 1967 (fish, Utah);
V'iushkov 1953 (poisonous reptile, S. Afr.);
Zalesskiĭ 1947 (branchiosaur, Urals); Zídek 1966 (fishes, Moravia).

FAUNAS — PALEOZOIC and MESOZOIC — Krasnov, Lur'e and Masaĭtis 1966 (verts.,
Siberia);
Misra and Saxena 1964 (fish, India);
Obruchev, D. V. 1965B (fishes), 1965C (Bradyodonti);
Parsch 1962 (fishes, Alberta).

FAUNAS — MESOZOIC — Anon. 1964BA (reptiles, Tibet), 1965G (dinosaurs, USSR),
1965CN (sharks, Israel);
Bodylevskiĭ 1958 (fishes, USSR);
Casier 1965 (fishes, Congo); Chao, Si-tszin' 1965 (dinosaur, China); Charrier 1965
(fish, Brazil); Cox, C. B. 1967A (changes in terrestrial faunas);
Dubeĭkovskiĭ and Ochev 1967 (plesiosaurs, USSR);
Fernandez-Galiano 1958 (dinosaurs, Spain);
Gaudant 1966A, 1967 (teleosts, Asia); Grambast et al. 1967 (Perutherium, Peru);
Kabanov 1959 (reptiles, USSR); Kermack, D. M. et al. 1968 (pantothere, Wales);
Kobayashi, Takai and Hayami 1963, 1964 (reptiles, Thailand); Kowalski, K.
1966B (mammals);
Lange, S. P. 1968 (Urocles, Europe); Lapparent 1966 (reptiles, Spain); Liu, Su,
Huang and Chang 1963 (lycopterids, China);
Nash, D. F. 1968 (crocodile, Utah);
Orlov, J. A. 1964D (mammals);
Patterson, C. 1964 (acanthopterygian fishes, England), 1966 (sharks, England);
Rozhdestvenskiĭ and Khozatskiĭ 1967 (land verts., Asiatic USSR);
Schultz, C. B. 1965C (plesiosaur, Nebr.); Sharov 1966 (reptiles, Kazakhstan);
Young. C.-c. 1964E (dinosaurs, China, Mongolia).

FAUNAS — TRIASSIC — Anon. 1964BS (dinosaur, S. Afr.), 1968AD (mammals);
Baird 1964B (reptile, New Mexico); Baird and Patterson 1967 (reptiles, N. Carolina); Banks 1965 (geol. and faunas, Tasmania); Barrett, Baillie and Colbert
1968 (amphibian, Antarctica); Blom 1966A, B (verts., USSR); Bonaparte 1963C,
D (cynodonts, Argentina), 1966A (Exaeretodon, Argentina), 1966B, C, D (therapsids, Argentina); Bond, G. 1955B, 1965 (dinosaurs, Rhodesia); Braga 1966
(fishes, Italy); Brink 1965A, B (cynodonts, S. Afr.), 1965C (bauriamorph, S.
Afr.), 1965D (ictidosuchid, S. Afr.); Buchan et al. 1965 (fishes, Spitzbergen
and Svalbard);

Campbell, J. D. 1965 (ichthyosaur, New Zealand); Casamiquela 1964B (pseudo-suchian, Argentina), 1964E (dinosaurs, Argentina), 1967A (ornithischian dino-saur, Argentina); Chalyshev 1962A (marina fauna, N. Urals), 1962B (stego-cephalian, USSR); Charig 1957 (archosaurs, Tanzania), 1967A (mammal, S. Afr.); Chatterjee 1967 (phytosaurs, India); Chowdhury 1965 (metoposaurid amphibian, India); Colbert 1964A (dinosaurs), 1965A (Rutiodon, New Jersey), 1966A (gliding reptile, New Jersey); Cosgriff 1965 (labyrinthodont, W. Aus-tralia), 1967 (labyrinthodonts, New. S. Wales); Cox, C. B. 1965 (dicynodonts, S. Amer.); Crompton 1964B (mammal, S. Afr.); Crompton and Jenkins 1968 (molar occlusion in mammals); Cruickshank 1964 (dicynodonts), 1965 (ano-modont, Tanzania), 1967 (dicynodont, Tanzania);

Dreyer 1962 (fishes, Germany); Dutuit 1964, 1966, 1967 (verts., Morocco), 1965 (dicynodonts, Morocco);

Eaton 1965 (phytosaur, Wyoming);

Friant 1964A (Haramyia, Europe);

Gariainov and Ochev 1964 (verts., Urals); Gilardoni 1964 (reptiles, Switzerland); Ginsburg 1964E (dinosaur, Basutoland); Gregory, J. T. 1964B (verts., New Mexico);

Hall, E. and M. 1964A (Plateosaurus, Germany); Hary and Muller 1967 (verts., Luxemburg); Hoppe 1965 (verts., Germany); Hopson 1964B (Bienotherium, China);

Jain 1964 (verts., India), 1968 (Ceratodus, India); Jain, Robinson and Chowdhury 1964 (verts., India); Jux 1966 (Parotosaurus, Germany);

Kalandadze, N. N. 1968 (reptiles, USSR); Konzhukova 1965B (capitosaurid, USSR); Krebs 1965 (Ticinosuchus ferox, Switzerland); Kuhn-Schnyder 1963C, D (saurians, Switzerland), 1964B, 1966C (verts., Switzerland), 1966A (nothosaur, Switzerland);

Larsonneur 1961-62 (verts., France), 1964 (fishes, France); Lazurkin and Ochev 1968 (sauropterygian, USSR); Lehman 1965 (verts., N. Afr., Israel); Lewis, G. E. 1966 (tritylodonts, Arizona); Liu, H.-t. 1964 (coelacanth, China);

Mayer 1963A, 1965 (verts., Germany), 1964 (fishes, Germany); Miroshnikov 1962 (fishes, USSR); Molin 1965 (verts., USSR); Moss and Kermack 1967 (enamel structure in mammals); Muller, Adolphe 1964 (fishes, Luxemburg);

Nash, D. 1968 (crocodile, S. Afr.); Nielsen 1964B, 1967 (labyrinthodont, Green-land); Nybelin 1966 (Pholidophoridae);

Ochev 1962B (verts., USSR), 1967C, 1968 (procolophonids, USSR); Ochev and Polubotko 1964 (ichthyosaurs, USSR); Ochev and Rykov 1968 (reptile, USSR); Ochev and Shishkin 1967 (amphibians, fish, USSR);

Robinson, P. L. 1967B (verts., India); Romer 1962F (rhynchosaurs), 1965A, 1966A (reptiles, Argentina), 1966E (transition faunas, S. Amer.), 1967B (gomphodonts, Argentina); Rose, G. 1965 (verts., Australia); Rykov and Ochev 1966 (verts., USSR);

Savage, R. J. G. 1962B (fishes, England); Savage, R. J. G. and Large 1966 (Bir-geria, England); Schaeffer, B. 1967B (fishes, W. U.S.); Schuberth 1967 (rep-tiles, New Jersey); Schweizer 1966 (coelacanth, Austria); Seeman 1965 (fishes, Germany); Shishkin, M. A. 1966, 1967A (labyrinthodont, USSR), 1967B (Plagiosauria, USSR); Shishkin and Ochev 1967B (verts., USSR); Sill 1967 (crocodile, Argentina); Stefanov 1966 (fishes, Bulgaria);

Tarlo, L. B. H. 1967D (reptiles);

Vasil'ev, V. G. 1960 (verts., USSR); Villalta Comella and Via Brada 1966 (coela-canth, Spain); V'iushkov 1964H (theriodonts, USSR); Vorob'eva 1967 (cerato-dontid, Siberia);

Walker, A. D. 1964 (reptiles, Scotland), 1966 (rhynchocephalian, Germany); Welles 1967 (giant amphibians, Arizona); Welles and Cosgriff 1964, 1965A (Parotosaurus, Arizona), 1965B (labyrinthodonts, Arizona); White, E. I. 1950D (fish, England);

Young, C.-c. 1964A (pseudosuchians, China), 1965D (nothosaurs, China), 1965E (ichthyosaur, China), 1966A (capitosaurid, China), 1966B (Lufengosaurus, China);

Zangerl 1963B (nothosaur, N. Amer.);   Zapfe 1960D (placodont, Alps).

FAUNAS – JURASSIC – Aldinger 1965 (fish faunas, S. Germany);   Anon. 1965T (sauropod, China), 1965BJ (dinosaur, China);   Astre 1967B (pycnodont fish, France);

Bocchino 1967 (fish, Argentina);   Bräm 1965 (turtles, Germany);

Camp and Koch 1966 (ichthyosaur, Oregon);   Casamiquela 1965D (Anura, Argentina);   Chaline 1963 (fissure faunas, France);   Cocude-Michel 1964, 1965 (Eichstättisaurus, Germany);   Crompton and Jenkins 1967 (Amer. symmetrodonts);

Desroches 1964 (fishes, France);

Evans, P. R. 1964 (labyrinthodonts, Australia);

Gaudant 1965 (Lycoptera, China);   Gliewe 1962 (fish, Germany);   Gutova 1963 (fishes, USSR);

Hill, Playford and Woods 1966 (verts., Queensland);   Hoffstetter 1964D (lizards, Europe and Asia), 1965B, 1966A (lizards, Spain), 1966B, 1967A (lizards, France), 1967D (lizards, England);   Hoffstetter, Crusafont and Aguirre 1965 (lizards, Spain);   Hudson 1966 (reptile beds, Scotland);   Huene 1966A (ichthyosaur, Germany), 1966B (megalosaur, Germany);

Jensen, J. A. 1968A (new dinosaur localities);   Joffe 1967 ("dwarf" crocodile, England);

Koch and Camp 1966 (ichthyosaur, Oregon);   Kottek 1964 (fishes, Greece);   Krebs 1967A (Steneosaurus, Switzerland), 1967B (crocodile, Portugal);   Kuhn, O. 1963E (verts., Solnhofen, Germany), 1964F (labyrinthodont, Germany);

Lapparent and Blot 1963 (fishes, France);   Lierl 1964 (fish from Solnhofen Plattenkalk, Bavaria);   Liu and Wang 1961 (fish, China);   Liu and Zhou 1965 (sturgeon, China);

Martin, G. P. R. 1965B (table ommitted from Martin and Weiler 1965);   Martin and Weiler 1965 (otoliths, Germany);   Maślankiewiczowa 1965 (Semionotus, Poland);   Mills 1964 (pantotheres, England);   Mook 1964, 1967 (crocodiles, Oklahoma, Colorado);

Newman 1968 (Scelidosaurus harrisoni);   Nybelin 1966 (Pholidophoridae);

Oppé 1954 (verts., Purbeck, England);

Patterson, C. 1968 (pholidophorid fishes);   Piel 1963 (dinosaur, Colorado);

Rao, C. N. and Shah 1963 (pterosaur, India);   Rozhdestvenskii 1968B (sauropod, Cent. Asia);   Rundle 1967 (otoliths, England);

Scholz 1963 (fishes);   Schweizer 1964 (fishes, Alps);   Stinton and Torrens 1968 (otoliths, S. England);

Telles Antunes 1967A, B (mesosuchian, Portugal);

Urlichs 1966 (verts., Germany);   Uschmann 1960 (Archaeopteryx);

Voropinov and Ermolaev 1966 (fishes, USSR);

Wellnhofer 1968 (Pterodactylus, Bavaria);   Wenz 1964 (Notagogus, Spain), 1965B, 1967B, 1968A (fishes, France), 1968B (fishes, Spain);   Westphal 1965 (crocodile, Germany);   White, E. I. 1954 (fish, England);   Wiedenroth 1962 (verts., Germany);   Wincierz 1967 (Steneosaurus, Germany);   Wojcik 1961A (Nothosaurus, Poland);   Wunnenberg 1961 (ichthyosaurs, Germany).

FAUNAS – CRETACEOUS – Albers and Weiler 1964 (fish fauna, Holland);   Anon. 1964BY (dinosaur, Spitzbergen), 1965AM (reptiles, Niger, W. Afr.), 1965AW (dinosaurs and primates, Montana), 1965CL (tortoise, S. China), 1966X (mammal, France), 1967AQ (mammal, Wyoming);   Applegate 1964A, 1965A (sharks, California);   Arambourg 1959 (pterosaur, Jordania), 1964B (Hadrodus, Morocco);   Arambourg et al. 1959 (Arabian peninsula);   Arnold 1964B, C (fishes, Germany);   Arnold and Tasch 1964 (fishes, Germany);   Arnold et al. 1964 (fishes, Germany);   Avnimelech 1966 (dinosaur, Israel);

Baird 1964D (sea-turtle, New Jersey), 1967 (birds, New Jersey);   Baird and Case 1966 (marine reptiles, New Jersey);   Baldwin, S. A. 1962 (dinosaur, Sussex);

Bardack 1965B (teleost, Texas), 1965C (localities, Kansas), 1967 (teleosts from
N. Amer. or Lebanon ?), 1968A (marine verts., Canada), 1968B (holostean,
Texas); Bartholomai 1966A (plesiosaurs, Australia); Bassoullet and Iliou 1967
(dinosaurs, Sahara); Bataller 1959 (Garumnian stage); Bezrukov 1934 (sharks,
Siberia); Bohn 1966 (turtle, Hungary); Braniša and Hoffstetter 1964 (fishes,
Bolivia); Broin and Taquet 1966 (crocodile, Sahara);

Case, G. R. 1965A, B (sawfish, Minnesota); Casier 1964 (fishes, Belgium); Chapman, J. J. 1964 (mosasaur, Arkansas); Chudinov 1966 (dinosaurs, Mongolia);
Clemens 1965B (mammals, Alberta), 1966 (marsupials, Wyoming), 1968A (Didelphodon, Montana); Clemens and Russell 1965 (mammals, Alberta); Coggi 1964
(Ptychodus, Sicily); Crusafont Pairó and Adrover 1965 (Parendotherium, Spain);

Dalinkevicius 1960 (fishes, Lithuania); Delair 1966B (reptiles, Dorset); Deloffre
1961 (otoliths, Pyrenees), 1964 (Leiodon, France);

Ejel and Dubertret 1966 (fishes, Libya); Estes 1964 (verts., Wyoming), 1965B
(salamander, Wyoming, Montana), 1966 (Dinilysia, Argentina);

Finzel 1964 (plesiosaur, Germany); Freytag 1964 (marine reptiles, Australia); Freytet 1965 (reptiles, France); Frizzell 1965A (otoliths, S. Dakota);

Giers 1964 (fishes, Germany); Gofshtein 1961 (Plesiosaurus and fish, Ukraine);
Goody 1968 (Enchodus, Holland); Gorbach 1967 (mosasaur, Crimea); Gowda
1964 (fish ossiculiths, India), 1967A, B (otolith, India); Gunderson 1965 (plesiosaur, Nebraska);

Hall, E. and M. 1964B (Kronosaurus, Australia); Harksen 1966 (Pteranodon, Kansas);
Henriques da Silva 1963 (shark, Angola, Afr.); Hoffman 1966 (plesiosaur, S.
Afr.); Hooijer 1968C (dinosaur, Syria); Hu, Show-yung 1964 (dinosaurs, Inner
Mongolia);

Jeletsky and Clemens 1965 (placental mammals); Jensen, J. A. 1968B (dinosaur
eggs, Utah); Jonet 1963, 1964B (fishes, Portugal);

Kermack, Lees and Mussett 1965 (Aegialodon, England); Khalilov et al. 1961
ichthyosaur, Caucasus); Khosbaiar 1966 (verts., Gobi Desert); Khozatskii 1957
(tortoises, cent. Asia), 1966 (Trionyx, Kazakhstan); Kisnerius 1960 (fishes,
Lithuania); Kruytzer 1964A (mosasaurs, Netherlands);

Langston 1967, 1968 (ceratopsian, Canada); Lapparent 1960D (dinosaurs, Spain);
Ledoux et al. 1966 (mammal, France); Lefeld 1965 (mammals, Gobi Desert);
Leonardi, A. 1966 (fishes, Italy);

McNulty 1964, 1965 (sting ray, Texas); McNulty and Slaughter 1964A (turtle,
Texas), 1964B (sawfish, Texas); Martin and Weiler 1963 (otoliths, Germany);
Melentis 1967A (fish, Greece); Miller, H. W. 1963 (verts., Arizona), 1964
(dinosaurs, Arizona), 1967 (verts., N. Carolina); Morris, W. J. 1967A, B, 1968
(dinosaurs, Baja California);

Nevo 1964 (urodeles, Israel); Nikolov and Huene 1966 (reptiles, Mongolia);
Ostrom 1965 (verts., Wyoming);

Parodi 1962 (anurans, Argentina); Parsch 1963 (dinosaurs, Alberta); Patterson, C.
1967A (fishes, Lebanon), 1967B (teleost Protobrama); Persson 1967 (plesiosaurs, Scania); Philip and Tronchetti 1966 (fish, France); Powell, J. S. 1968
(reptiles, New Mexico); Prasad and Verma 1967 (dinosaurs and turtles, India);
Price, L. I. 1959B (theropod, Amazon), 1961 (dinosaurs, Brazil);

Quinet 1964B (mosasaurs, Belgium);

Rao, C. R. N. and Seshachar 1927 (reptiles, India); Rich 1966 (plesiosaur, Montana); Romer 1959E (Kronosaurus, Australia), 1968B (ichthyosaur, Wyoming);
Rozhdestvenskii 1964A (verts., Cent. Asia), 1966A, 1967 (iguanadonts, Cent.
Asia); Russell, D. A. 1967C, D (verts., Arctic Canada); Russell, L. S. 1964
(non-marine verts., n.w. N. Amer.), 1968 (dinosaur, Montana);

Sickenberg 1961 (crocodile, Germany); Sieber and Weinfurter 1967 (otoliths, Aus-
tria); Sigé 1968A (micro-mammals, dinosaur egg shell, misc. verts., Peruvian
Andes); Signeux 1959A (fishes and reptiles, Syria), 1959B (fishes and reptiles,
Iraq), 1964 (fishes, Bolivia); Silva Santos 1962, Silva Santos and Duarte 1961

(fishes, Brazil); Slaughter 1965D (therian, Texas), 1968B (marsupial, Texas), 1968C (eutherians, Texas); Sloan and Van Valen 1965 (mammals, Montana); Sokolov, M. I. 1965 (shark teeth); Sulimski 1968 (mosasaurs, Poland); Tabaste 1963 (fishes, Sahara); Telles Antunes 1964C (verts., W. Afr.); Thieuloy 1965 (ichthyosaur, France); Thurmond 1968 (plesiosaur, Texas); Thurrell 1961 (pliosaur, England); Tsankov and Dachev 1966 (fishes, Bulgaria); Van Valen and Sloan 1965 (primates); Verma 1965B (sharks, India); Waldman 1967 (fishes, Australia); Wenz 1965A (fishes, France); Wilson, R. D. 1964 (mammals, South Dakota); Wiman 1935C (turtles, New Mexico); Yeh, Hsiang-k'uei 1966 (turtle, China); Young, C.-c. 1964B (pterosaur, China), 1964C (crocodile, China), 1965C (reptiles, China); Zapfe 1964C (reptiles, E. Austria).

FAUNAS – MESOZOIC and CENOZOIC – Krajewski and Urbaniak 1964 (verts., N. Carpathians); Marinov 1957 (verts., Mongolia); Martinson 1967A (verts., USSR); Razumova and Cherniakhovskii 1964 (verts., Kazakhstan); Wetzel 1966 (marine dwarf-fishes); Yeh, Hsiang-k'uei 1963B (turtles, China), 1965 (turtles, Mongolia).

FAUNAS – CENOZOIC – Anon. 1959BQ (Britain); Arata and Jackson 1965 (Gulf Coastal Plain); Bazhanov 1961C (ostriches, Asia); Casier 1966B (fishes, Barbados); Chakravarti 1965 (elephants, India, Burma, Pakistan); Chang, Y.-p. et al. 1964 (China); Chantell 1966 (hylids, Great Plains); Chumakov 1965 (Rudnyi Altai, USSR); Collected Papers 1967A (mammals, Moldavia); Davitashvili 1966B (verts., Georgia, USSR); Deviatkin and Liskun 1967 (verts., W. Mongolia); Dorr and Wheeler 1964 (verts., southwestern Montana); Downs and White 1965, 1966 (verts., S. California); Frizzell and Dante 1965 (otoliths, Gulf Coast, N. Amer.); Frizzell and Lamber 1962B (otoliths); Hatai 1966 (otoliths); Hibbard 1967 (rodents, Kansas); Hibbard and Zakrzewski 1967 (microtine, Idaho); Hoffstetter 1967B (snakes, S. Amer.); Ikebe and Chiji 1964 (Proboscidea, Japan); Ikebe, Chiji and Ishida 1966 (Proboscidea, Japan); Ivan'ev 1959 (Elephas, USSR); Jen 1965 (mammals, China); Khozatskii 1967 (land reptiles, Asiatic USSR); Kostenko 1964A, B (verts., Kazakhstan); Langston 1965B (crocodiles, Colombia); Mawby 1965B (machairodonts, Texas); Ol'shanskaia 1965 (fishes, USSR); Ozansoy 1965 (mammals, Turkey); Ride 1964B (marsupials, Australia); Simons and Wood 1968 (mammals, Egypt); Skinner, M. F. and S. M. and Gooris 1968 (mammals, S. Dakota); Smith, M. A. 1931 (verts., Siwaliks, India); Tanaka and Seki 1962 (marine mammal, Japan); Tessman 1966 (sharks, Florida); Tsankov and Nikolov 1966B (proboscideans, Bulgaria); Voinstvenskii 1967 (fossil birds, Ukraine).

FAUNAS – TERTIARY – Anon. 1965CB (Paleoparadoxia), 1965CQ (primates, Sahara); Arambourg 1965E (paleo-mediterranean fishes); Arata 1966 (proboscidean, Louisiana); Aslanova 1965B (Perekishkiul', USSR); Auffenberg 1964B (Stylemys), 1967C (snakes, Florida), 1967D (crocodilians, Florida); Bakalov and Nikolov 1962 (mammals, Bulgaria); Banks 1965 (geol. and faunas, Tasmania); Bauza Rullán 1964 (fishes, Majorca), 1966A (otoliths, Baleares Is.),

Newsome and Rochow 1964 (verts., Australia); Nikiforova 1960 (mammals, Kazakhstan);

Olson 1962C, 1964A (mammals, S. Amer.); Orlov, J. A. 1964C, 1965 (mammals);

Pavlović and Cipović 1964 (mammals, Serbia); Plane 1965, 1966 (mammals, New Guinea), 1967C, Plane and Gatehouse 1968 (verts., N. Australia); Pledge 1967 (elasmobranchs, S. Australia); Porta 1965 (verts., Colombia); Poulain-Josien 1960 (mammals, France); Prasad and Satsangi 1962 (bovid, India), 1963A (tragulids, India); Prasad and Singh 1963 (proboscideans, India); Pr. 1961 (Pliopithecus);

Quinet and Misonne 1967 (marsupials, Belgium);

Radinsky 1965A (tapiroids, Asia); Repenning 1966 (mammals, California); Rückert-Ülkümen 1960 (fishes, Turkey); Russell, D. E. 1968 (mammals, Europe); Rutte 1964 (verts., Germany);

Saheki 1928 (Desmostylus, Japan); Savage, R. J. G. 1965B (Low. Tert. verts., Libya); Schultz, C. B. and Falkenbach 1968 (oreodonts); Shevyreva 1968A (rodents, lagomorphs, USSR); Shotwell 1967A, B (rodents, Oregon); Simpson, G. G. 1967B (Lorisidae, Afr.); Skinner, M. F. and Taylor 1967 (mammals, S. Dakota); Skinner, S. M. and Gorris 1966 (Toxotherium, Wyoming); Slaughter 1965A (verts., Texas); Spinar 1966 (frogs, Czechoslovakia); Starostin 1962 (fishes, USSR); Stinton 1962 (fish otoliths, Borneo), 1966 (fish otoliths, England), 1968 (fish otoliths); Stirton 1962 (verts., Australia), 1967A (diprotodonts, Australia); Stirton, Tedford and Woodburne 1964, 1965 (verts., S. Australia), 1967A (mammals, Australia), 1967B (mammals, S. Australia); Stirton, Woodburne and Plane (diprotodonts); Strouhal 1959A (Oreopithecus); Svistun and Didkovskii 1964 (Deinotherium, Ukraine);

Tang and Chow 1964, 1965 (verts., S. China); Tarashchuk 1962 (fishes, Ukraine); Tedford 1965, 1966C (mammals, California), 1967A (verts., Australia); Telles Antunes 1964C (verts., W. Afr.); Thaler 1966B (rodents, France); Tihen 1964B (changes in N. Amer. herpetofauna); Tobien 1968F (mammals, Switzerland); Tsankov and Dachev 1966 (fishes, Bulgaria); Tuohy 1963B (verts., Idaho);

Uspenskaia 1933 (fishes, Caucasus);

Vasilenko 1961 (verts., USSR); Volochkovich 1961 (mammals, Mongolia); Vorontsov 1964 (cricetid, Aral Sea, USSR);

Weitzman 1960C (characid fish, S. Amer.); Westphal 1963C (verts., Germany); Wilson, J. A. 1967 (mammals, U.S.); Wilson, J. A. et al. 1968 (mammals, Texas); Woodburne 1967A (diprotodontids, Australia), 1967B (verts., Australia);

Xu, Yu-xuan 1966 (amynodonts, Mongolia);

Zaidova 1964 (hedgehogs, USSR); Zapfe 1964D (mammals, Austria).

FAUNAS — PALEOCENE — Anon. 1965CP (primate, E. Montana);

Bezrukov 1934 (sharks, Siberia); Brown, R. W. 1962 (verts., Rocky Mts. and Great Plains, U. S.);

Casamiquela 1964D (hadrosaurian, Argentina); Chow 1960C (Prodinoceras, China);

Estes 1965C (lizards, Wyoming); Estes, Hecht and Hoffstetter 1967 (amphibians, France);

Floris 1964 (crocodile, Denmark);

Gazin 1968A (primate, New Mexico);

Janot 1966 (fish, France);

MacIntyre 1966 (Ictidopappus and Protictis); McKenna 1968 (Leptacodon); Morris, W. J. 1966A (mammals, Baja California);

Paula Couto 1961B, C, 1962B (marsupials, Brazil), 1963B (Trigonostylops, Brazil);

Russell, D. E. 1964 (mammals, Europe), 1967 (primates, France); Russell, Louis and Poirier 1966A, B (mammals, France); Russell, L. S. 1967A (verts., Canada);

Segedin 1966 (sharks, USSR); Simpson, G. G. 1967A (mammals, S. Amer.);

Van Valen 1965F (primate, Montana), 1967B (insectivores); Van Valen and Sloan 1965 (primates);

Wood, R. C. 1967 (verts., Wyoming);
Young, C.-c. 1964C (crocodiles, China).

FAUNAS — EOCENE — Anon. 1965Z (sting ray, Wyoming); Avnimelech 1962C (Carcharodon, Israel);
Beaumont 1965B, 1966 (miacids, Switzerland), 1965C (Cephalogale, France); Berg,
D. E. 1965 (Diatryma, Germany), 1966 (crocodiles, Germany); Bjork 1967 (verts.,
South Dakota); Black, C. C. 1967 (mammal communities), 1968B (Mytonomys);
Black and Dawson 1966A (mammals, N. Amer.); Bocchino 1964 (fish, Argen-
tina); Bogachev 1965 (fishes, Crimea); Böger 1966 (fishes, Germany); Bonde
1966 (fishes, Denmark); Bonis 1964 (mammals, France); Bosch 1964C (sharks
and rays, N. Europe); Bradley 1964 (Green River Form.);
Casier 1966A (fishes, England), 1967 (fishes, Germany); Cavender 1966A (Leuciscus,
British Columbia); Chow 1964A (lemuroid primate, China), 1965B (mesonychids,
China); Chow and Chiu 1964 (giant rhino, China); Chow and Li 1965 (tapiroids,
China); Chow and Tung 1965 (coryphodont, China); Chow and Xu 1965
(amynodonts, China); Chow, Xu and Zhen 1964 (amynodonts, Yunnan); Crusa-
font Pairó 1964C, 1965M, 1966A Mammals, Spain), 1967B (prosimians, Spain);
Crusafont Pairó, De Renzi and Clavell 1968 (mammals, Europe); Crusafont Pairó
and Rosell Sanuy 1966 (verts., Spain); Crusafont Pairó, Rosell, Golpe and Renzi
1968 (mammals, Spain); Crusafont Pairó and Russell 1967 (condylarth, Spain);
Crusafont Pairó and Truyols Santonja 1964B (mammals, Spain);
Dawson, M. R. 1964 (rodents, Mongolia), 1966, 1968B (rodents, Utah); Dong 1965
(lizard, China);
Fallow 1964 (Cylindracanthus, Carolinas); Fischer, K. 1964 (tapirs, Europe); Friant
1963D (Trechomys, Europe); Fuchs, H. 1966 (Myliobatis, Rumania);
Gabuniiā 1961C (mammals, USSR); Gazin 1965A (mammals, Wyoming), 1968B
(Hyopsodus); Gibbes 1847C (Basilosaurus, S. Carolina); Ginsburg, Montenat and
Pomerol 1965 (mammals, France); Glikman and Stoliarov 1966 (sharks, Caspian
Peninsula); Grigor'ev, Groshin and Pak Sen Uk 1960 (mammals, Korea); Guthrie,
D. A. 1965, 1967B (mammals, Wyoming), 1966 (dichobunid, Wyoming), 1967A
(creodont, Wyoming);
Hartenberger 1965B (rodent, France), 1968 (rodents, Europe); Hartenberger, Sigé
and Sudre 1968 (verts., France); Hogan 1959 (eagle ray, Georgia, USA); Howard
1965C (bird, California);
Jepsen 1966 (bat, Wyoming);
Kacharava 1964 (fishes, Mediterranean); Klebanova 1964 (mammals, E. Kazakhstan),
1966 (verts., Asiatic USSR); Koenigswald 1965E (higher primates, Burma), 1967D
(anthracothere, Indonesia); Kruckow 1962 (lizard in amber); Krumbiegel 1959C,
1966 (verts., Germany);
Li, Chuan-kuei 1965 (leporids, N. China); Lindsay, E. 1968A, B (rodents, California);
Louis 1963 (mammals, France), 1966 (verts., France); Louis and Michaux 1962
(mammals, France);
Matthes, H. W. 1963B (Geisel Valley verts., Germany), 1967A, B, C (creodonts,
Germany); Maxwell, R. A. et al. 1967 (mammals, Texas); Meszoely 1967 (crypto-
branchid, Wyoming); Michaux 1964A (rodents, France), 1964B, 1968 (paramyids,
France); Miguet 1967 (bats, France); Moody, R. T. J. 1968 (turtle, England);
Nielsen 1964A (marine turtle, Denmark); Nikolov 1967 (Elomeryx, Bulgaria);
Pascual 1965A (condylarth, Argentina); Piccoli 1966 (sirenian, Italy);
Quinet 1964A (mammals, Belgium), 1966A (Teilhardina, Belgium);
Radinsky 1964A (chalicotheres, Wyoming), 1966D (tapiroid, Wyoming); Rat 1965,
1966 (mammals, Paris Basin); Remy 1965, 1967 (paleotheres, France); Robin-
son, P. 1963B (Edentates, Wyoming), 1966A (mammals, Colorado), 1966C (insecti-
vores, Wyoming), 1967 (anaptomorphid, Wyoming), 1968B (primates, Wyoming,
Utah); Robinson, P. et al 1964 (multituberculates, Wyoming); Russell, D. E.,

Louis and Savage 1967 (primates, France);   Russell, L. S. 1965D (mammals, Canada);

Savage, D. E. 1965 (land mammals, Europe, N. Amer.);   Savage, D. E. et al. 1964 (land mammals, Europe, N. Amer.), 1965 (equids, Europe), 1966 (perissodactyls, France);   Savage, R. J. G. 1965B (marine mammals, Libya);   Schaub, S. 1940D (ratite, Germany);   Siegfried 1967 (sirenian, Egypt);   Signeux 1959B (fishes and reptiles, Iraq), 1959C (fishes, Syria);   Siler 1964 (sirenian, Alabama);   Simpson, G. G. 1964C (mammals, Argentina), 1967A (mammals, S. Amer.), 1968C (didelphid, Colorado);   Sloan 1966 (multituberculate, Wyoming);   Špinar 1967A (frogs, Germany);   Sturani 1965 (Paleotherium, Italy);   Şuraru, N. and M. 1966 (fishes, Transylvania);   Szalay and Gould 1966 (mesonychids, Asia);

Taugourdeau 1965 (turtle, France);   Telles Antunes 1964D, 1967C (verts., Portugal);   Temniuk 1965 (fishes, USSR);   Tobien 1962E (tapir, Germany), 1968C (mammals, Germany);

Van Valen 1965G (Proviverrini, Europe);   Verma 1965A (frog, Bombay);

Walker, C. A. 1966 (pleurodiran turtle, Somalia);   Weitzman 1960A (characid fishes, France);   Winter 1960 (fishes, Italy);   Wood, A. E. 1965B (rodents, Wyoming);

Xu, Yu-xuan 1965 (amynodont, China);

Zimmermann-Rollius 1967 (turtles, Germany).

FAUNAS – OLIGOCENE – Alker 1968 (cricetines, N. Amer.);   Anon. 1967AC, BH, 1968A (primate, Fayum);   Arai, J. 1953 (desmostylid, Japan);   Astre 1964B (mammals, France), 1964C (Aceratherium, France);

Barbu 1964 (Anthracotherium, Rumania);   Beaumont 1964A (Amphicyon, France), 1968 (viverrids, France);   Black, C. C. 1965A (rodents, Montana), 1968A (Ischyromys);   Bogachev 1959 (cetacean, USSR);   Bonis 1966B, 1967 (Haplocyon), 1968 (mammals, France);   Borisoglebskaia 1967 (beaver, Kazakhstan);   Brunet and Guth 1968A (Ronzotherium, France);   Brzobohatý 1967A (fish otoliths, Moravia);

Cattoi 1962 (xenarthran, Argentina);   Clemens 1964 (Sinclairella);   Crusafont Pairo and Truyols Santonja 1964B (mammals, Spain);

Dashzeveg 1964 (hyaenodonts, Mongolia), 1965 (Entelodon, Mongolia);   Dawson, M. R. 1968A (rodents, Mongolia);   Dickson, M. R. 1964 (Prosqualodon, New Zealand);   Dzhafarova 1962 (fishes, Caucasus), 1963, 1964 (fishes, Shemakhih region), 1965, 1967 (fishes, Azerbaïdzhan), 1966 (fishes, USSR);

Emlong 1966 (cetacean, Oregon);

Ford, R. 1967 (verts., England);

Gabuniia 1955G, 1964D (verts., S. Georgia, USSR), 1966A, B (mammals, Caucasus);   Gabuniia and Beliaeva 1964 (anchithere, Kazakhstan);   Gawne 1968 (Proterix, N. Amer.);   Ginsburg 1965, 1966 (amphicyons, France);   Gorbach 1961C (fishes, Carpathia);   Gramann 1964 (verts., Rhine Valley), 1966 (mammals, Germany);   Greenwood and Patterson 1967 (osteoglossoid, Tanzania);

Hofer and Wilson 1967 (primate endocranial cast);   Hoffstetter 1968A (mammals, Bolivia);   Howe, J. A. 1966B (rodent, Nebraska);   Hu, Chang-kang 1964 (Archaeotherium, Inner Mongolia);   Hugueney 1965 (bats, France), 1967 (rodents, France);   Hünermann 1964, 1967 (anthracothere, Switzerland);

Ianovskaia 1953C (titanotherium, Mongolia);   Ivasik 1968 (carp, Eurasia);

Johnson, G. D. 1966 (small mammals, S. Dakota);

Klebanova 1965 (mammals, USSR);   Kozlova 1960 (birds, Mongolia);   Kurochkin 1968A (birds, Kazakhstan);   Kuss 1965A (canids);

Lange, B. 1967 (creodonts, France);

Macdonald, J. R. 1964D (insectivore, S. Dakota), 1967A, B (dogs, S. Dakota);   McKenna and Holton 1967 (insectivore, Mongolia);   Maksimov 1960 (fishes, E. Carpathians);   Martin, L. D. 1967 (X-ray study of vert. jaws);   Martini 1964 (otoliths, Germany), 1965 (fishes, Germany), 1967A (verts., Germany), 1967B (birds, Germany); Mayr and Schindlmayr 1967 (mammals, Germany); Mellett 1968 (verts., Mongolia);

Obrhelová 1966 (fishes, Bohemia); Ozansoy 1964 (mammals, Turkey);

Palmowski and Wachendorf 1966 (verts., Germany); Patte 1962C (Halitherium, France); Petronijević and Thenius 1958B (indricothere, Yugoslavia); Petter, G. 1966 (Cynodictis, Europe);

Quinet 1965A (condylarth, Belgium), 1965B (bats, Belgium); Quinet and Misonne 1965 (zalambdodont insectivores, Belgium);

Reed, C. A. and Turnbull 1965 (moles, N. Amer.); Remy and Thaler 1967 (verts., France); Rothausen 1968A (squalodonts, Italy);

Schreiber 1962 (fish, Germany); Shevyreva 1965 (hamsters, USSR, Mongolia), 1966 (rodents, Kazakhstan), 1967 (hamsters, Kazakhstan), 1968B (Kazakhstan, Mongolia); Siegfried 1965 (sirenian, Germany); Sigé 1967 (bats, France); Simons 1965B, 1967H (primates, Egypt), 1967C (anthropoids, Old World), 1968A (mammals, Afr.); Stęślicka 1965 (primates, Egypt); Stirton and Woodburne 1964, 1965 (peccaries); Sychevskaiā 1966 (fishes, W. Siberia);

Takeda 1953 (verts., Japan); Tanner, L. G. and Martin 1968 (hyracodontids, Nebraska); Tatishvili 1968 (verts., USSR); Thaler 1966A (rodent, Spain); Tobien 1966 (Entelodon, Germany); Turnbull and Reed 1967 (burrowing mammal, Wyoming);

Vollmayr 1966 (rodents, Germany);

Weber, E. 1951 (mammals, Germany); Weiler 1966B (fishes, Germany); Whistler 1966 (mammals, California), 1967 (oreodonts, California); Wilson, J. A. 1966 (primate, Texas); Wood, A. E. 1968 (rodents, Fayum).

FAUNAS — MIOCENE — Accordi and Leonardi 1959 (fishes, Sicily); Adrover 1968 (micromammals, Spain); Alf 1966 (mammals, Calif.); Anđelković 1962, 1963 (fishes, Turkey), 1964 (Clupea, Turkey), 1966 (Rhombus, Turkey); Anon. 1962CG (Proconsul, Africa), 1966P (bird, Virginia); Aoki, R. 1915 (Desmostylus); Apostol 1966 (Aceratherium, Rumania); Applegate 1964B (shark, California); Arambourg 1964A (suid, Libya), 1968A, B (suid, N. Afr.); Arambourg and Montenat 1968 (fishes, Spain); Arapov 1965 (Moldavia, USSR); Aslanova 1965A (seal, Azerbaijan); Astre 1965B (Brachyodus, France); Auffenberg 1964C (tortoise, Texas);

Bachmayer 1964A (bird feathers), 1966 (Trionyx, Vienna); Bachmayer and Weinfurte 1965 (fishes, Austria); Baudelot, S. 1965, 1966 (glirids, France), 1967 (soricids, France); Baudelot and de Bonis 1966 (glirids, France); Bauza Rullán 1968 (fishes, Spain); Beaumont 1965A (machairodont, France); Belokrys 1960D (Trilophodon, Ukraine); Belokrys and Rizdviānskiǐ 1958 (Trilophodon, USSR); Bergounioux 1964 (beavers, France); Bergounioux and Crouzel 1964, 1965A (Pliopithecus, France), 1965B (chelonians, France), 1965C (beavers, France), 1966A (mastodons, France), 1966B (Amphicyon, France), 1967A (suids, France), 1967B (mammals, France); Biriūkov et al. 1962 (Paraceratherium); Bishop 1964A (primates, Uganda), 1964B (mammals, Uganda); Boediharto 1964 (cent. Java); Bogachev 1960B (goat, Crimea); Bosch 1964A, B (sharks and rays, N. Europe); Bosch and Janssen 1965 (sharks, Netherlands); Bradley 1964 (Green River Form.); Bruijn 1966A, B (Gliridae, Spain); Brunet, J. 1961 (birds, Morocco); Brzobohatý 1965 (fish otoliths, Czechoslovakia); Burchak-Abramovich and Korotkevich 1966 (proboscideans, USSR); Burchak-Abramovich 1966C (Dinotherium, Caucasus); Butler, P. M. 1965A (chalicotheres, E. Afr.);

Caldwell, D. K. 1966 (needle fish, Jamaica); Cappetta, Granier and Ledoux 1967 (selachians, France); Case, J. 1966B (white shark localities); Chantell 1965 (hylid, Colorado); Chabot 1963 (fish, France); Chow and Wang 1964 (verts., China); Chumakov 1961C (mammals, USSR); Ćirić 1960, 1962B (mammals, Serbia), 1962A (mastodon, Serbia); Cole, S. 1964A (primates, E. Afr.); Crusa-

font Pairó 1964B (verts., Spain);   Crusafont Pairó, Aguirre and García 1968
(mammals, Spain);   Crusafont Pairó, Gautier and Ginsburg 1966 (verts., Spain);
Crusafont Pairó, Riba and Villena 1966 (verts., Spain);   Crusafont Pairó, Valenciano Horta and Sanz Fuentes 1968 (verts., Spain);   Čtyroký, Fejfar and Holý
1964A, B (mammals, Czechoslovakia);
David, L. 1967 (verts., France);   Dawson, M. R. 1965 (lagomorphs, W. U.S.);   Dehm
1964 (shrew "mouse", Germany);   Deinse 1963, 1964A (Cetacea, Netherlands);
Des Lauriers 1965 (tortoise, California);   Doben-Florin 1964 (shrews, Bavaria);
Estes and Tihen 1964 (verts., Nebraska);
Fahlbusch, V. 1964 (cricetids, Bavaria), 1966 (cricetids, Germany), 1967A (<u>Pota-
motherium</u>, Germany);   Fierstine and Applegate 1968 (billfish, S. California);
Flandrin, Mein and Truc 1968 (mammals, France);   Flügel 1964 (<u>Myliobatis</u>,
Austria);   Freudenthal 1963B (cricetids, Spain);
Gabashvili and Gabuniiá 1958 (<u>Dinotherium</u>, E. Georgia, USSR);   Gabuniiá 1959D
(listriodon, W. Georgia, USSR), 1966C (mammals, USSR);   Galbreath 1964B
(corvid, Colorado), 1967A (rodent, S. Dakota);   Ginsburg 1964A (verts., France),
1964B (<u>Pliopithecus</u>, France), 1964C, 1967A (mammals, France);   Ginsburg and
Telles Antunes 1967 (mastodons, France), 1968 (<u>Amphicyon giganteus</u>);   Glikman
and Ishchenko 1967 (sharks, Cent. Asia);   Godina 1964C (<u>Palaeotragus,</u> Moldavia);
Godina and Khubka 1968 (<u>Palaeotragus</u>, Moldavia);   Gofshteïn 1965 (whales,
USSR);   Green, M. 1965 (mammals, S. Dakota);
Hartenberger 1966B, 1967A (rodents, Spain);   Hatai 1959B (elephant, Japan);   Hecht,
Hoffstetter and Vergnaud 1961 (amphibians, Morocco);   Henriques dā Silva 1961
(fishes, Angola, Afr.);   Henriques dā Silva and Perreira Soares 1961 (verts., Angola);
Hernandez-Pacheco and Crusafont Pairó 1960 (rhino, Spain);   Hoffstetter 1961F
(squamates, Morocco), 1967C (snakes, Colombia);   Holman 1965B, 1967 (anurans,
Florida), 1966C (herpetofauna, Texas);   Hooijer 1963D (mammals, Congo), 1966B
(rhinos, E. Afr.), 1968B (<u>Brachyodus</u> manus, E. Afr.), 1968E (rhino, Kenya);
Hopson 1964A (marine birds, S. Carolina);   Howard 1966C (birds, S. Dakota),
1966D (birds, California);   Hutchison 1966A (shrews, Oregon), 1968B (insectivores,
Oregon);
Ionko 1954 (fishes, Moldavia);
Jakway and Clement 1967 (<u>Tomarctus,</u> California);   Jonet 1964A, 1965-1966A,
1966B (fishes, Portugal);
Kalabris 1960 (fishes);   Kellogg 1965, 1966, 1968 (marine mammals, Maryland,
Virginia);   Kilmer 1965 (dugongid, Mexico);   Klingener 1966 (rodents, Nebraska);
Kluge 1966 (frog, S. Dakota);   Kon'kova 1957 (terrestrial verts., Moldavia);
Korotkevich 1961A (mammals, Moldavia), 1965A (roe-deer, Ukraine), 1968
(gazelles, S. USSR);   Kowalski, K. 1967A (rodents, Poland);   Kudrin and Tatarinov
1965, 1966 (dolphins, W. Ukraine);   Kuss 1963 (<u>Amphicyon</u>, Germany), 1965A
(bears, Basel Mus.);   Kuss and Schreiner 1963 (mastodons, Germany);
Lafond-Grellety 1963 (otoliths, France);   Lafond-Grellety and Vigneaux 1964A, B
(otoliths, France);   LaRivers 1964 (trout, Nevada);   Lavocat 1961D (verts.,
Morocco), 1967B (micromammals, E. Afr.);   Leakey, L. S. B. 1967C (mammals,
E. Afr.), 1967E (<u>Kenyapithecus</u>), 1968C (primates, Kenya);   Lewis, G. E. 1964C
(verts., S. California);   Lindsay, E. 1966 (mammals, California), 1967 (rodents,
California);   Lungu 1962 (carnivores, USSR), 1967A (deer, Moldavia), 1968
(mammals, Moldavia);   Lungu and Tarabukin 1966 (mammals, Moldavia);
Macarovici, Marinescu and Motas 1965 (mammals, Rumania);   Macarovici and Paghida
1964 (<u>Hipparion</u>, Rumania);   Macdonald, J. R. 1964, 1965, 1966B (mammals,
Nevada);   Maglio 1966 (selenodonts, Florida);   Mchedlidze 1959 (dolphin, Georgia,
USSR), 1964D (proboscideans, Georgia, USSR);   Mein 1965A (bats, France);
Mein and Truc 1966 (verts., France);   Melentis 1966C (anthracothere, Greece);
Melentis and Tobien 1967 (mammals, Greece);   Menesini 1967A (fishes, Italy);
Miller, L. 1966 (birds, California);   Mitchell, E. D. 1965B, 1966D, E (<u>Allodesmus,</u>

California), 1968 (Imagotaria, California); Mitchell and Lipps 1964, 1965 (marine verts., California); Moliavko and Pidoplichko 1952 (verts., S. URSR); Morris, W. J. 1965 (horse astragali, California); Mott 1964 (Dorcatherium, Austria); Mottl 1966C (Anthracotherium, Austria), 1967B (tortoise, Austria); Musakulova 1967 (Dicrocerus, Kazakhstan);

Nemoto 1936 (desmostylid, Sakhalin);

Obrhelová 1967 (Cyprinidae, Bohemia); Obrhelova and Obrhel 1965 (fishes, Bohemia); Okutsu and Muto 1959 (Eostegodon, Japan); Olsen 1964A, B, 1968B (verts., Florida);

Paghida 1962 (otoliths, Moldavia); Patton 1964 (verts., Florida), 1966B (artiodactyls, Florida), 1967B (artiodactyls, Texas); Pavlović and Durković 1962 (mammals, Serbia); Pavlović and Thenius 1965 (hyaena, Yugoslavia); Petronijević 1967 (mammals, Serbia); Petter, G. 1967B, C (mustelid, France); Pilbeam and Walker 1968 (monkeys, Afr.); Pischedda 1954 (fishes, Sardinia); Prasad 1964A (verts., India), 1964B (primates, India); Price, J. 1965 (mammals, California); Put' 1952 (mastodon, USSR);

Radwanski 1965 (elasmobranchs, Poland); Rakovec 1965A (mastodon, Yugoslavia); Rao, C. R. N. and Seshachar 1927 (mammals, India); Reed, C. A. and Turnbull 1965 (moles, N. Amer.); Reshetov 1965 (anthropoid, Turkey); Rey 1963, 1964 (Hipparion fauna, France); Riel 1964 (oreodont, Montana); Rothausen 1968A (squalodonts, Italy); Rückert-Ülkümen 1965 (fishes, Turkey);

Sanz Pareja 1961 (mammals, Concud, Spain); Savage, R. J. G. 1965A (carnivores, E. Afr.), 1967 (mammals, Europe, Asia, Afr.); Schaub, S. 1949B (Elomeryx, Switzerland); Schaub and Hürzeler 1949 (mammals, Switzerland); Scheuenpflug 1965 (rhino, Germany); Shotwell 1968 (mammals, Oregon); Sigé 1968B (bats, France); Simons 1967C (anthropoids, Old World); Simpson, G. G. 1965I (penguin, Australia); Smigielska 1968A, B (otoliths, Poland); Stan 1963 (mammals, Rumania); Steininger 1967 (Dryopithecus, Germany); Steininger and Thenius 1965 (verts., Austria); Stirton 1967B (diprotodont, Australia), 1967D (Protoceratidae); Stirton and Rensberger 1964 (insectivore, Oregon); Stirton and Woodburne 1964, 1965 (peccaries);

Takai, Shikama and Iziri 1952 (Desmostylus, Japan); Tan and Shikama 1965 (Desmostylus, Japan); Tarashchuk 1957 (fish, Ukraine); Tate 1968 (local fauna, Montana); Tattersall 1968 (Indraloris, India); Telles Antunes 1960B, 1964A (mammals, Portugal), 1961E (crocodile, Portugal); Thaler 1964A (micromammals, France); Tokunaga and Iwasaki 1914 (Desmostylus, Japan); Trivedy 1966 (verts., India);

Ungaro 1966 (fish teeth, Italy); Uyeno 1967A (fish, Japan);

Vapt̃sarov 1963 (Gomphoterium); Vergnaud-Grazzini 1966 (amphibians, Morocco); Villalta Comella 1963 (birds, Spain); Villoutreys 1965 (fishes, France); Voorhies 1965 (carnivores, Wyoming);

Walker, A. and Rose 1968 (hominoid, Uganda); Walker, H. 1968 (verts., California); Wang, B.-y. 1965 (rhino, China); Weiler 1962F (sharks, Germany), 1962G (otoliths, Germany), 1966A (fishes, Czechoslovakia); Weinfurter 1967 (otoliths, Austria); Westphal 1967B, 1968 (bats, Germany); Whitmore and Stewart 1965 (mammals, Cent. and S. Amer.); Wilson, J. A. 1968 (mammals, Mexico); Wood and Konizeski 1965 (rodent, Montana); Wood, H. E. 1964 (rhinos, Florida);

Young, C.-c. 1964D (Lagomeryx, China), 1965A (salamanders, China);

Zapfe 1967A (chalicothere, Austria); Zázvorka 1966 (crocodile, Bohemia); Zbyszewski 1953B (cetacean, Portugal); Zbyszewski and Veiga Ferreira 1967A (verts., Portugal); Zhai 1964 (carnivores, Inner Mongolia).

FAUNAS — PLIOCENE — Adamenko 1967 (USSR); Adrover 1962 (Mastodon, Spain), 1963 (Spain); Alekperova 1959, 1964 (cervids, Caucasus), 1966 (history of deer, Caucasus); Anon. 1968E (Gigantopithecus, India); Auffenberg 1966B (Geochelone, Florida); Azzaroli 1964A (rhino, Italy), 1965 (Equus, Italy);

Bachmayer 1967 (Testudo, Greece); Baigusheva 1964 (Rostov region, USSR); Bakalov and Nikolov 1963 (Trilophodon, Bulgaria); Bakun and Vangengeym 1963 (USSR); Barrière, J. and Michaux 1968 (micromammals, France); Beaumont 1964B (Ictitherium, France); Belokrys 1959B (Zygolophodon), 1960E (mastodons, USSR); Berzi 1966 (bear, France); Birman et al. 1968 (USSR); Bogachev 1958B (fishes), 1960C (turtle, Crimea); Bolomey 1965A (mammals, Rumania); Bonifay, M.-F. 1966A (Villafranchian, Europe); Bonnet, A. 1965, 1966 (mastodon, France); Bourdier and Lacassagne 1964 (mammals, France); Brattstrom 1967 (snakes, high plains, U.S.); Brodkorb 1964C (teal, S. Dakota); Bruijn and Mein 1968 (Sciurinae, Spain); Brunet, J. 1968 (rhinos, Mexico); Bryant 1968 (mustelid, Washington); Bukatchuk et al. 1967 (verts., USSR); Bukatchuk and Negadaev-Nikonov 1968 (mammals, USSR); Burchak-Abramovich and Kon'kova 1967 (ostriches, USSR); Burchak-Abramovich, N. O. 1950 (Orycteropus, USSR);
Casamiquela 1967B (Bufo, Argentina); Chaline and Michaux 1966 (microcmammals, France); Chang, Hsi-chih 1964A (mastodons, China); Chang, Hsi-chih and Liu 1964 (Metailurus, China); Chiguriaeva 1960 (Sus scrofa, USSR); Chow and Chow 1965 (Villafranchian mammals, China); Chumakov 1961C (mammals, USSR), 1967 (Egypt); Clark, Dawson and Wood 1964 (mammals, Nevada); Collins, C. T. 1964 (ibises, Kansas); Crusafont Pairó 1962D (Indarctos, Spain), 1965P (Pontian mammals, Spain), 1966D (giraffe, Spain); Crusafont Pairó, Adrover and Golpe 1964 (hippo, Spain); Crusafont Pairó and Angel 1966 (Myotragus, Spain); Crusafont Pairó, Angel and Cuerda 1965A (Myotragus, Spain); Crusafont Pairó, Hartenberger and Heintz 1964 (mammals, Spain); Cuscani Politi 1963A (Megaceros, (Italy), 1963B, C (rhinos, Italy);
Dalquest and Hughes 1966 (mammals, Texas); Dalzell 1966 (salmonid fish, Oregon); David, A. I. 1967A (mammals, Moldavia); Daxner 1967 (rodents, Austria); DeBrine, Spiegel and William 1963 (mammals, New Mexico); Deviatkin 1963, 1965 (mammals, S. E. Altai); Deviatkin, Zazhigin and Liskun 1968 (small mammals, W. Mongolia); Dobie 1968 (turtle, Florida); Downs and White 1968 (verts., California); Dubrovo 1964B (Protelephas, USSR), 1967 (mammals, Urals);
Eisele 1965 (Leptarctus, Nebraska); Elhai and Grangeon 1964 (mammals, France); Feduccia 1967A (swallow, Kansas), 1967B (birds, Idaho); Feduccia and Wilson 1967 (birds, Kansas); Fejfar 1964A, 1966B (verts., Czechoslovakia); Feru, Radulescu and Samson 1965 (mammals, Rumania); Fitch and Reimer 1967 (fishes, S. California); Flerov and Shevyreva 1965 (Pseudalces, USSR); Ford, N. L. 1966 (owls, Kansas); Ford and Murray 1967 (owls, Idaho); Freudenthal 1966, 1967, 1968 (rodents, Spain); Freudenthal and Sondaar 1964 (mammals, Spain);
Gabashvili and Gabuniia 1958 (Dinotherium, E. Georgia, USSR); Gabuniia 1954B (mammals, USSR); Gabuniia and Vekua 1963, 1966C (Archidiskodon, USSR), 1966A, B (daman, E. Georgia, USSR); Gadzhiev and Aliev 1965 (deer, Caucasus); Ganeshin 1959 (mammals, USSR); Gaponov 1957C (Elasmotherium, USSR); Gasparini 1968 (crocodile, Argentina); Gehlbach 1964 (reptiles, amphibians, N. Amer.); Ghenea and Radulesco 1964 (mammals, Moldavia); Ginsburg 1964F (Hipparion, France), 1967C (mammals, France); Gromova 1967B (rhinos); Guérin 1965 (rupicaprine, Europe); Gureev and Kon'kova 1967 (hare, Moldavia);
Hatai 1965A, B (otoliths, Japan); Hatai, Murata and Masuda 1965 (rays, Japan); Havesson 1950 (Paracamelus, Asia); Heintz, E. 1963B, 1964A (antilope, Iran), 1964B, 1966A, 1967A (ruminants, France), 1967B, 1968 (cervids, France, Spain); Heller, F. 1967B (mammals, Europe); Hemmer 1965C ("Panthera," France); Hertlein 1966 (cetaceans, Mexico); Hibbard 1964 (mammals, Kansas); Hirschfeld and Webb 1968 (megalonychids, N. Amer.); Howard 1965A (cormorant, Mexico), 1966A (birds, Mexico); Huang, Tunyow 1965 (whale, Taiwan, China); Hugueney and Mein 1965 (lagomorphs and rodents, France), 1966 (rodents, France); Hürzeler 1967 (mammals, Italy); Hutchison 1965, 1966C (moles, Cent. and W. N. Amer.);
Iatsko 1964 (mammals, Moldavia); Ivan'ev 1966A, 1967 (marmot, W. Transbaikalia);

(verts., California);   Teichmüller 1962 (Oreopithecus fauna, Italy);   Telles Antunes
1963 (sharks, W. Afr.);   Thaler et al. 1965 (micromammals, Spain);   Topachevskiǐ
1952 (verts., Ukraine), 1957C (marmot, Ukraine), 1957E (verts., USSR), 1965A
(rodent, Ukraine), 1965B (voles, Ukraine), 1965C (insectivores, rodents, Ukraine),
1966 (shrew, Ukraine);   Tsankov and Nikolov 1966A (deinothere, Bulgaria);   Turnbull, Lundelius and McDougall 1965 (marsupials, Australia);
Uyeno and Miller 1965 (fishes, Arizona);
Vakhrushev 1960A (fishes, Urals);   Vekua 1968 (antelope, Georgia, USSR);   Velikov-
skaiā 1960 (mammals, USSR), 1964 (mammals, Caucasus);   Vereshchagin 1968B
(mammals, USSR);   Viret et al. 1962 (mammals, France);
Warren, J. W. 1965 (marsupial, Australia);   Webb, S. D. 1964B (verts., Florida), 1966A
(burrowing rodent, Florida), 1967A (proboscideans, Florida);   Westphal 1967A
(giant salamander, Germany);   Wilson, Ri. L. 1968 (verts., Kansas);   Woodburne
1966A (Plesippus, California);
Zakrzewski 1967B (vole, Kansas, Nebraska);   Zapfe 1967B (Austria);   Zbyszewski
1967 (mastodon, Portugal);   Zetti 1967 (marsupial, Argentina);   Zhegallo 1966
(Hipparion, Mongolia).

FAUNAS — QUATERNARY — Abramova, Z. A. 1962C, D, 1964A (Siberia);   Accordi
1963 (Elephas, Italy);   Adam 1964 (cent. Europe), 1965A (primates, Germany),
1965B (hippo, Rhine Valley), 1966A (Elephas, cent. Europe);   Adamenko 1963,
1966A, 1967 (Siberia);   Adamenko and Zazhigin 1965 (small mammals, S. Siberia);
Adams 1953 (mammals, Mississippi R.);   Adrover 1964 (hippo, Spain);   Adrover,
Rafael and Angel 1966 (mammals, Balearic Is.);   Agache, Bourdier and Petit
1964 (Somme Valley);   Agassiz 1967 (glaciers);   Aguirre 1964A (Metailurus, Spain),
1964B, 1965 (mammals, Spain);   Ahlén 1965A, B, C (red deer, Scandinavia);
Akhundov 1963 (pinnipeds, USSR);   Alekperova 1966 (history of deer, Caucasus);
Aleksandrova 1965A, 1966 (voles, Ukrania), 1965B (rodents, Volga), 1967 (ro-
dents, USSR);   Aleksandrova and Tseǐtlin 1965 (small mammals, USSR);   Alekseev,
M. N. 1961A (mammals, USSR), 1964 (mammals, E. Siberia, China);   Alekseev
et al. 1961 (mammals, USSR);   Alekseev et al. 1962 (N. E. Siberia);   Alekseeva,
L. I. 1961A, B, C, 1966 (mammals, USSR), 1964 (primates, USSR), 1965 (probos-
cideans, USSR), 1967A (mammals, Black Sea area), 1967B (mammals, Moldavia),
1967C (Bovinae, USSR);   Alekseeva and Lomize 1960 (mammals, Caucasus);
Alimen 1964B, D, 1967 (France), 1966 (W. Europe);   Almagro Basch 1960C
(Maltravieso cave, Spain);   Al'ter 1960 (mammals, USSR);   Altmeyer 1964 (Germany);   Altuna 1963A (mammals, Spain), 1963B (Gulo, Spain), 1966A (Lezetxiki
Cave, Spain), 1966B (cold faunas, Basque countries);   Alvarez 1966 (rodents,
Mexico);   Alvarez and Ferrusquia V. 1967 (marsupials, Mexico);   Ambrosetti
1963, 1964, 1965 (Elephas, Italy);   Anastas'eva 1957 (Bison, USSR);   Anderson,
E. 1967 (Equus, Wyoming);   Andrianov 1960 (mammals, TASSR);   Angel, Basilio
de la Salle 1962 (Myotragus, Majorca);   Anokhina 1965 (Mediterranean);   Anon.
1960CG (mammoth, Veracruz), 1963BP (moas, New Zealand), 1963CE (Oklahoma),
1964C (amphibians and reptiles, Pennsylvania and Tennessee), 19640, 1965W
(mastodon, Ohio), 1964AS (elephants, Essex), 1964BM (goose, California), 1964BX
(Paleoparadoxia, California), 1965I (mammoth, Canada), 1965J (mammoth tusk,
France), 1965AY (hippo, E. Devon), 1965BC (bison skulls, Oklahoma), 1965BD
(mastodons, Spain), 1965BI (Germany), 1966AE (mastodon, Missouri), 1966AJ
(relict marsupial, Burramys, Australia), 1966BO (frog, USSR), 1967J (mastodon
teeth, continental shelf), 1967V (Yukon), 1967AT (verts., Florida);   Aoki, N.
1967 (otoliths, Japan);   Apostol 1963, 1965B (elephants, Rumania), 1967A (bovids,
Rumania), 1967B (rhino, Rumania);   Apostol and Olaru 1966 (mammoth, Rumania);   Apostol and Popescu 1963 (mammoth, Rumania);   ApSimon and Boon
1960 (England);   Arambourg 1963H (mammals, Europe and Afr.);   Arambourg,
Chavaillon and Coppens 1967 (Omo, Ethiopia);   Arambourg and Choubert 1965

(mammals, Morocco); Arata and Harmann 1966 (<u>Euarctos</u>, Louisiana); Arata
and Hutchison 1964 (<u>Procyon</u>, N. Amer.); Arkhipov 1960 (Siberia); Arkhipov,
Koreneva and Lavrushin 1960 (Siberia); Arredondo 1958C (<u>Mesocnus</u>, Cuba),
1961 (new edentates, Cuba); Astakhov 1963 (Siberia); Astre 1964A, 1966D
(mammals, France), 1965A, 1967A (<u>Elephas</u>, France), 1966C (<u>Elephas</u>, Greece);
Atkinson 1966 (condor, California); Aubekerov 1967 (mammals, USSR); Auffenberg 1964A (Reddick cave, Florida), 1967A (box turtles, Florida), 1967B (tortoises, West Indies), 1967C (snakes, Florida), 1967D (crocodilians, Florida);
Auffenberg and Milstead 1965 (reptiles, N. Amer.); Augusta and Burian 1962B,
C (mammoths); Avakiân 1959 (mammals, Armenia); Avakiân and Alekseeva 1966
(<u>Palaeoloxodon</u>, Armenia);
Babaev 1962 (mammals, Tadzhik); Bader, O. N. 1959 (USSR); Badoux, D. M.
1966A (<u>Sus</u>, Netherlands), 1966B (woolly rhino, Netherlands); Bakalov and
Nikolov 1964 (mammals, Bulgaria); Baldwin and Koplin 1966 (relict owl, Colo-
rado); Balland 1964B (<u>Elephas</u>, France); Balland and Elhaï 1965 (mammals,
France); Bandrabur and Giurgea 1965 (<u>Archidiskodon</u>, USSR); Barandiaran
Maestu, I. 1965B (Spain); Baranova and Biske 1964 (mammals, E. Siberia);
Barat 1960 (mammals, Rumania); Bartholomai 1966C (revision of Macropodidae),
1967 (new macropodid), 1968 (new Koala, Queensland); Bartolomei 1964,
1965 (mammals, Italy); Bates and eds. of Life 1964 (mammals, S. Amer.);
Battistini 1965A, B (<u>Aepyornis</u>, Madagascar); Bayrock 1964 (amphibians, Alberta);
Bazarov 1965 (Selenga, USSR); Bazhanov and Kostenko 1960 (Kazakhstan);
Bazhanov, Matsuĭ and Mos'kina 1968 (USSR); Beaumont 1961D (<u>Canis</u>, France);
Behm-Blancke 1967 (Ehringsdorf, Germany); Beilekchi 1966 (Moldavia); Beliaeva
1966 (rhinos, Siberia); Berge 1967 (Scandinavia); Bersenev <u>et al.</u> 1962 (USSR);
Bertalan and Kretzoi 1962 (Hungary); Binford, L. R. 1965 (<u>Lepus</u>, Pennsylvania);
Biske 1964 (Siberia); Blake-Palmer 1956 (<u>Dinornis</u>, New Zealand); Blanc, A. C.
1959B (Italy); Boediharto 1964 (cent. Java); Boekschoten and Sondaar 1966
(hippo, Crete); Boessneck 1967 (domestic and wild animals, Spain); Bolotova
1966 (Mongolia); Bonadonna 1965A (hippo, Italy), 1965B (Italy), 1967 (<u>Elephas</u>,
Italy); Boné 1965 (<u>Hipparion</u>, Afr.); Bonfiglio 1964 (elephant, Italy); Bonifay,
M.-F. 1964 (<u>Equus</u>, France), 1966A (Villafranchian, Europe); Bonifay and Bonifay
1965 (mammals, France); Bonnet, A. 1964 (<u>Elephas</u>, Rhone Valley); Bonté
1966 (<u>Elephas</u>, France); Bordes and Prat 1965 (Dordogne); Borsuk-Białynicka
1966 (rhinos, Poland); Bottoms 1967 (mammoths, mastodons, Continental Shelf,
U.S.); Bouchud 1965A (<u>Cervus megaceros</u>, France), 1965B (mammals, France),
1966B (proboscideans), 1966C (rhinos), 1966D (artiodactyls), 1966E (cervids),
1967 (reindeer, France), 1968A (<u>Crocuta</u>, Cambodia), 1968B (cervids and equids,
France); Bourdier 1961 (Rhone Valley); Bout 1964A, B (mammals, France);
Brattstrom 1967 (snakes, high plains, U.S.); Brigot, Duport and Guillien 1962
(<u>Elephas</u>, France); Brodkorb 1964B (birds, Barbados); Brown, J. A. 1886B
(mammals, England); Bruemmer 1968 (muskoxen); Bruijn 1966C (Gliridae,
Malta, Mallorca); Brun 1960 (mammals, France); Brunet, J. 1967 (verts., Mex-
ico); Buachidze 1968 (voles, USSR); Burchak-Abramovich 1951D (terrestrial
verts., Azerbaidzhan), 1953C (ostriches, USSR), 1962B, 1965A, 1966A, D (birds,
USSR), 1965B (horned owl, USSR); Burchak-Abramovich and Dzhafarov 1965
(<u>Sus</u>, USSR); Burchak-Abramovich and Gadzhiev 1962 (beaver, USSR); Burchak-
Abramovich and Kon'kova 1967 (ostriches, USSR); Bush 1960 (tar pits, Peru);
Butler, P. M. 1965A, B (chalicotheres, E. Afr.);
Carbonnel and Guth 1968 (mammals, Cambodia); Carreck 1955 (verts., Dorset);
Castellanos 1965 (mammals, Corrientes, S. Amer.); Chaline 1965A (lemming,
France), 1965B (rodents, France), 1967 (<u>Microtus</u>, France); Chaline and Michaux
1966 (micromammals, France); Chang, Chik-kuo 1964 (mammals, China); Chang,
Hsi-chih 1964B (<u>Palaeoloxodon</u>, China); Chauviré 1962 (mammals, France), 1965B
(birds and mammals, France); Cheatum and Slaughter 1966 (mammals, Texas);

Chebotareva, Kuprina and Khoreva 1957, 1959 (mammals, USSR); Chemekov
1959 (mammals, USSR); Chernov and Samarin 1966 (proboscideans, N. Atlantic
shelf); Chou 1960 (faunas, China); Chow 1964B (mammals assoc. with Lantian
man, China); Chow, M., Hu and Lee 1965 (mammals assoc. with Lantian man,
China); Chumakov 1961A (micromammals), 1961C (mammals, Rudnyǐ Altaǐ,
USSR), 1967 (Egypt); Churcher 1965B (camelids, Peru), 1968 (mammoth, Ontario); Churcher and Zyll de Jong 1965 (skunk, Peru); Comaschi Caria 1965
(dwarf elephant, Sardinia); Cooke, H. B. S. 1963C, 1968 (mammals, Afr.);
Coppens 1965B, 1966C, 1967B, 1968 (proboscideans, Chad); Corbet and Morris
1967 (mammals, S. Turkey); Coryndon 1966 (verts., Malawi); Couturier 1961
(fossil goat, Capra); Cracraft 1968 (Meleagris, Mexico); Crossley 1964, 1965
(muskox, Manitoba); Crusafont Pairó 1959D (mammals, Spain), 1965H (variability of Myotragus, Mallorca); Crusafont Pairó, Angel and Cuerda 1965B (survival of Myotragus); Cuerda Barceló 1966 (Myotragus, Spain); Cuffey, Johnson
and Rasmussen 1964 (microtine rodent, Indiana); Curry-Lindahl 1964 (verts.,
Scandinavia); Cuscani Politi 1965, 1966 (hippos, Italy);
Dalquest 1964A (Equus scotti, Texas), 1964B, 1965A (mammals, Texas); Dalquest and
Hughes 1965 (small Equus, Texas); David, A. I. 1962B, 1965E, 1966, 1967B,
1968B (mammals, Moldavia), 1964 (horses, Moldavia), 1965A (carnivores, Moldavia), 1965B (antelope, Moldavia), 1965C (elephant, Moldavia), 1965D (Alces,
Moldavia); David and Markevich 1967 (mammals, Moldavia); David and Tarabukin 1967 (rhino, Moldavia); David and Vereshchagin 1967 (mammals, Moldavia); David, L. 1966 (mammals, S. W. France); David and Prat 1965 (verts.,
France); Daxner and Thenius 1965 (wild goats, Austria); Dechaseaux 1967B
(beaver, Europe); Deckert and Karrer 1965 (fishes, Germany); Deconinck 1962B
(mammoth, Belgium); Degerbøl 1964 (verts., N. Europe); Deinse and Verhey
1965 (Panthera, Netherlands); Demediuk 1966 (mammals, USSR); Deraniyagala
1965 (hominids and other mammals, Ceylon); Deviatkin 1965 (mammals, S. E.
Altai); Diaz Garcia 1961 (edentates, N. E. Caribbean); Dickenson 1968 (koala,
W. Australia); Dietrich 1928F (hippo, Dutch E. Afr.), 1965 (elephants, Germany),
1968 (Felidae, Europe, Afr.); Dmitrieva 1966 (gazelles, Transbaikalia); Domoslawska-Baraniecka et al. 1965 (Elephas, Poland); Donner 1965 (mammals, Finland); Dorsser and Pelletier 1965 (verts., France); Doughty 1966 (Megaceros,
Ireland); Douglas, Kendrick and Merrilees 1966 (carnivore's den, W. Australia);
Dove 1967 (mammals, Nevada); Downs 1965 (verts., Colorado Desert, California);
Downs and White 1968 (verts., California); Draper 1923 (mammals, England); Dru
1937 (mammoth, Hamper Hill, England); Dubinin and Garutt 1954 (mammoth, Ler
delta); Dubrovo 1964A (Archidiskodon, USSR), 1966A (Mammuthus, USSR), 1966
(mammals, Urals); Dubrovo and Alekseev 1964 (mammals, USSR); Dubrovo and B
usheva 1964 (elephants, USSR); Dubrovo and Chepalyga 1967 (elephants, USSR);
farov 1960 (rhinos, USSR), 1966 (birds and mammals, USSR);
Edmund 1965 (mammals, Ecuador); Egorov and Ivan'ev 1956 (sturgeon, USSR);
Egorov and Lvova 1962 (mammals, USSR); Elhaie 1965 (mammals, France);
Erbaeva 1966 (mammals, Transbaikalia); Erbaeva and Pokatilov 1966 (gopher,
Transbaikalia); Erdbrink 1964 (mammals and Homo, Neatherlands), 1967A (bears,
Netherlands), 1967B (proboscideans, China); Etheridge 1964 (lizards, British W.
Indies), 1965 (lizards, Dominican Republic), 1966A (lizards, Bahamas), 1966B (lizar
Jamaica); Ewer 1965A (carnivores, Olduvai, E. Afr.), 1967A (hyaenids, Afr.); Ewe
and Cooke 1964 (mammals, S. Afr.);
Faugères 1966 (Elephas, Macedonia); Fedorov, P. V. 1957 (mammals, USSR);
Fejfar 1964B, 1966B (verts., Czechoslovakia), 1965 (micromammals, Czechoslo-
vakia), 1966A (mammals, Czechoslovakia), 1966C (mammals, Bohemia); Feniksova
1960 (verts., Siberia), 1965, 1966 (mammals, Siberia); Feustel, Teichert and
Unger 1963 (mammals, Germany); Ficat 1964 (reindeer, France); Fierstine
and Applegate 1968 (billfish, S. California); Filzer 1966 (mammals, N. Alps);

Huckriede and Jacobshagen 1963 (verts., Germany); Hünermann 1965 (suid, Germany); Hutchison 1967 (vampire bat, California);
Iakhimovich, V. L. 1965 (mammals, S. Urals); Iarkovaia 1967 (mammals, USSR); Inskeep and Hendy 1966 (mammals, S. Afr.); Isaac 1966A (mammals, Kenya), 1967A (verts., Tanzania); Ivan'ev 1958 (bison, USSR), 1965 (Elephas wüsti, USSR);
Jackson, C. G. 1964 (turtle, Florida); Jacobshagen 1963 (verts., Germany); Jakubowski 1967 (Paleoloxodon, Poland); Janossy 1964A (small mammals), 1965B (small mammals, Hungary), 1965C (birds, Germany), 1965D (insectivores, Germany), 1965E (birds, Rumania); Jaschke 1965 (mammoth, Germany); Jehl 1966A (subspecies in fossil birds), 1967 (birds, Oregon); Johnson, S. T. 1962 (mastodon, New Jersey); Jolliffe 1910 (mammoth, England); Jones, Robert E. 1967 (sea cow, California); Jong 1967 (Netherlands); Jordan, Wilh 1961 (elephants); Jung and Schneider 1960-61 (verts., Greece);
Kahlke 1961E, 1962E (mammals, Germany), 1962C, D (verts., Germany), 1964 (Ovibovini), 1965D (Rangifer, Ovibos, Old World), 1965E (verts., Europe), 1965G (cervids, Germany), 1965H (rhinos, Germany); Kambariddinov 1966 (antilope, camel, USSR), 1968 (mammal complexes, Middle Asia); Kamei 1964, 1966 (proboscideans, Japan); Kanishchev 1963 (mammals, USSR); Kaplianskaia and Tarnogradskii 1961 (mammals, USSR); Karandeeva 1952 (mammals, USSR); Kauffman and McCulloch 1965 (verts., Colorado); Kennedy 1966 (mastodon, Kansas); Kerr 1964 (Bartow mammoth site, Oklahoma); Khan 1966 (Ovibos, Germany); Khoreva 1959 (mammals, USSR); Khudiakov 1966 (verts., USSR); Kiriushina 1959 (mammals, Soviet Arctic); Kitching 1965 (hyracoid, S. Afr.); Klafs 1965 (Bos, Europe); Kleinschmidt 1964B (vulture, Europe); Konstantinova 1963, 1964 (verts., Prut. R., Danube Delta), 1965C (small mammals, S. Moldavia, S.W. Ukraine); Korniets 1959D (mammals, Ukraine); Kortenbout van der Sluijs and Zagwijn 1962 (mammals, Tegelen clay pits, Netherlands); Kovanda 1964 (Equus, Czechoslovakia); Kowalski, K. 1966A (rodents, Europe), 1967B (rodents, England); Kozhamkulova 1967A, B (mammals, Kazakhstan and Moldavia); Krapivner 1961 (mammals, USSR); Krasnov, Lur'e and Masaitis 1966 (verts., Siberia); Kretzoi 1965B (amphibians, Germany), 1965C (rodents, lagomorphs, Germany), 1965F (birds, mammals, Hungary); Kretzoi and Vertes 1965A, B, C (verts., Hungary); Kriger 1962B (verts., Afr., Near East); Krutzsch 1965 (verts., Germany); Krysiak 1956 (mammals, Poland); Kubiak 1965A (elephants, S. Poland); Kuprina and Vtiurin 1961 (mammals, E. Siberia); Kurten 1964A (polar bears), 1965D (felids, Florida), 1966A (bears, N. Amer.), 1966C (Arctic fox, Finland), 1967A (short-faced bears, N. Amer.), 1967B (Canis and Smilodon, Mexico), 1968B (mammals, Europe); Kuss 1966 (mammals, Crete); Kuss and Misonne 1968 (murids, Crete);
Ladd 1939 (verts., S. Carolina coast); Lamakin 1965 (fishes, USSR); Lammers 1968 (verts., Arizona); Laukhin 1966 (Bison, USSR), 1967A, B (mammals, Siberia); Laukhin and Sadikova 1966 (mammals, Siberia); Lavocat 1966 (verts., W. Europe), 1967C (rodents, E. and S. Afr.); Lazukov 1965 (mammals and man, USSR); Leakey, L. S. B. 1967C (mammals, E. Afr.); Leakey, L. S. B. et al. 1965 (mammals, Olduvai Gorge, Afr.); Lebedev 1960B (fishes, USSR); Lebedeva 1963, 1965 (mammals, S. E. USSR); Leffler 1964 (mammals, Oregon); Leonhardy 1964 (mammoth, Oklahoma); Ligeron 1965 (Bos, France); Ligon 1965 (birds, Florida); Lillegraven 1967 (Bison and Megalonyx, Kansas); Linck 1964 (mammals, Germany); Lindholm 1931 (turtle, S. China); Lipps, J. H. 1964 (verts., Anacapa Is., California); Lipps and Ray 1967 (verts., Georgia, USA); Loskutov et al. 1965 (mammals, Tadzhikistan); Loziev and Lim 1962 (mammals, USSR); Lumley 1964 (mammals, Maritime Alps); Lundberg 1967 (fishes, Texas); Lundelius 1965, 1967 (verts., Texas); Lüttschwager 1961 (moas, Mauritius Is.; solitaires, Rodriguez Is.); Lynch, J. D. 1964, 1965 (amphibians, Texas, Florida); Lysenko 1960C (Equus, Crimea);

Macarovici 1963 (elk, Rumania), 1965 (mammals, Rumania); Macarovici and
Zaharia 1963 (mammoth, Rumania); Maccagno 1966 (elephants, Italy); McClure
and Milstead 1967 (box turtle, Texas); MacCord 1964 (mammals, Virginia);
McCoy 1960 (birds, Florida); McCrady 1961 (verts., Pennsylvania); McCrady
and Guilday 1963 (verts., Pennsylvania); McCrady and Schmidt 1963 (mammals,
Tennessee); McCullough 1965 (elk, California); Mahe 1965A, B (subfossil
verts., Madagascar), 1966 (subfossil turtle, Madagascar); Maleeva 1966 (rodents,
N. W. Caspian area); Malez 1962E (dog, Balkans), 1965J (arctic mammals, Balkans); Mangerud 1965 (mammoths, Norway); Mangin 1962B (Elephas, France);
Markus 1964 (passerines, Palestine); Martin and Guilday 1967 (verts.); Martin,
R. 1966 (glutton, France); Martin, R. A. 1967 (Peromyscus, Florida), 1968B
(aquatic rodents, Florida); Matheson 1962 (roe deer, Wales); Matsumoto, Mori
and Chiba 1963 (equid, Japan); Mawby 1967A (verts., Nevada); Mehl 1959
(verts., Missouri), 1966 (mammoth, Oklahoma); Meijer 1962 (Bos, Java); Melentis
1960 (elephant, Greece), 1964A (Equus, Greece), 1964B, 1967B (cervids, Greece),
1964C (mammals, Greece), 1966A (mammoth, Greece). 1966E (hippo, Greece);
Melton 1964 (glyptodont, Texas); Mendrez 1966 (equid, S. Afr.); Merkel 1966-67
(roadrunner, California); Merrilees 1965A (Sthenurus, Australia), 1965B (wombat,
Australia); Mezhlumian 1965 (Bos, Armenia); Mezhzherin and Svistun 1966
(shrew, USSR); Michel, F. 1964 (hippo, N. Europe); Michel, J. P. 1964 (mammals, France); Mikula 1964 (caribou, Michigan); Milanovskii 1956 (mammals,
Caucasus); Miller, A. H. 1966A (birds, Australia); Miller, G. J. 1968 (Smilodon,
Rancho La Brea); Miller, R. R. 1965 (freshwater fishes, N. Amer.); Miller and
Smith 1967 (fishes, Lake Idaho); Miller, W. E. 1966 (mammals, California),
1968 (bison, camel, Rancho La Brea); Milojcic et al. 1965 (mammals, Greece);
Milstead 1967 (box turtles, cent. N. Amer. and E. Mexico); Milstead and Tinkle
1967 (box turtles, W. Mexico); Mirtsching 1965 (mammoth, Siberia); Mishin
1965 (mammals, cent. Asia); Mitchell, E. D. 1966A (sea otters, N. E. Pacific);
Mitchell, G. F. 1965A, B (deer, Isle of Man); Mitt 1963 (verts., Soviet Arctic);
Mitzopoulos 1964 (Archidiskodon, Macedonia); Mlynarski 1961D (snakes, Poland);
Mochanov and Fedoseeva 1968 (mammals, USSR); Mos'kina 1968 (mammals,
USSR); Mostecky 1964 (mammals, Czechoslovakia); Muntaner Darder 1966
(Myotragus, Balearics); Munthe 1956 (Baltic herring); Murdock and Jolly 1967
(moa, New Zealand); Musil 1964 (brown bear, Czechoslovakia), 1965C (equids,
Germany), 1966A, 1967 (verts., Moravia), 1968 (mammoth, Czechoslovakia);
Nagasawa 1967 (equids, Japan); Naora 1959 (mammals, Japan); Necrasov 1964
(Equus); Negadaev-Nikonov 1964 (verts., Moldavia); Negadaev-Nikonov and
Arapov 1964 (mammals, Moldavia); Neill 1961 (rattlesnakes, Florida); Nelson,
N. C. 1927 (mastodon); Nesmeianov 1964 (elephant, Fergana); Nesturkh 1954
(giant anthropoids, Asia); Neumann, G. 1936 (mammoth tusk, Germany); Nicol-
aescu-Plopşor, C. S. 1965 (verts., Rumania); Nicolaescu-Plopşor, C. S., and D.
1963 (mammals, Rumania); Nicolaescu-Plopşor, Paunescu and Mogoşanu 1966
(mammals, Rumania); Nikiforova 1965B (small mammals, SSSR); Nikolov 1965
(mammals, Bulgaria); Nikol'skii 1945 (fresh water fishes, USSR); Nikonov and
Nikonova 1965 (mammoths, Scandinavia); Noda 1965 (mammals, Japan); Nolte,
Wolfram and Wöllner 1965 (mammals, Germany); Nordmann 1943A (elephant,
Denmark), 1943B (bison, Denmark);
Ochirov 1960 (mammals, USSR); Ogden 1964 (mastodon, Ohio); Okladnikov and
Adamenko 1966 (mammals, Siberia); Olson 1962C, 1964A (mammals, S. Amer.);
Onodera, Shingo, Onuma and Siga 1966 (Stegodon, Japan); Osole 1965A (mam-
mals, Slovenia); Ostrovskii and Grigor'ev 1966 (mammals, USSR); Otsuka 1966A
(Rusa, Japan), 1966B (fish, reptiles, Rusa, Japan), 1967, 1968 (deer, Japan);
Paccard 1964 (mammals, birds, fish, France); Packard and Alvarez 1965 (Baiomys,
Mexico); Paraskevaidis 1961 (mammals, Greece); Parmalee 1967A (mammals,
Illinois), 1967B (birds in archeol. sites, Iowa, Illinois, W. Virginia, Georgia);

Pasternak, S. I. and Tatarinov 1952 (mammals, USSR); Patrulius and Mihăilă 1966 (mammals, USSR); Patte 1964A, 1967 (mammals, France); Patterson, B. 1966 (mammals, Kenya); Patton 1965 (rodent, Texas), 1966A (verts., Cayman Is.), 1967A (verts., West Indies); Paula Couto 1962A (verts., Brazil), 1964 (mammals, Antilles), 1967 (edentates, West Indies); Pei 1965D (Trilophodon, China); Pennington and Frost 1961 (fishes, England); Perkins, D. 1960 (mammals, Iraq), 1965 (verts., Nubia); Peterson, R. L. 1965 (bear, Ontario); Petrichenko 1963 (mammals, USSR); Petrov, G. I. 1940A (mammals, Italy); Petter, G. 1964A (viverrids, E. Afr.), 1964C (canid, E. Afr.), 1967D (carnivores, Olduvai, E. Afr.); Pewe and Hopkins 1967 (mammals, Alaska); Phillips, A. R. 1968 (stork, Arizona); Picard and Baida 1966 (verts., Israel); Pichardo del Barrio et al. 1961 (mammoth, Mexico); Pidoplichko 1946-1956 (Glacial Period), 1955C (verts., Ukraine), 1961A (verts., USSR); Popov, Iu. N. 1947A, B, 1948 (verts., in permafrost, USSR); Popov, V. V. 1960 (mammals, Central Asia); Prat 1956 (equids, Pyrenees), 1964 (mammals, France); Preston 1966 (turtles, Texas); Put' and Kapelist 1961 (mammals, USSR);

Rădulesco and Kovacs 1966 (mammals, Rumania); Rădulesco and Samson, P. 1967A (deer, Rumania), 1967B (equids, Rumania), 1967C (lagomorphs and leporids, Rumania); Rădulesco et al. 1965 (mammals, Rumania); Rădulesco and Samson, P.-M. 1967 (beavers, Rumania); Rakovec 1965B (mammals, Serbia); Rakovets and Shmidt 1963 (mammals, Siberia); Ray, C. E. 1961 (monk seal, Florida), 1964B (Heptaxodon, Puerto Rico), 1964C (verts., Barbados), 1964D (jaguarundi, Florida), 1964E (tapir, Florida), 1965A (verts., Georgia), 1965B (chipmunk, Georgia), 1965D (glyptodont, S. Carolina), 1967 (mammals, Georgia); Ray, C. E. et al. 1967 (mammals, Virginia); Ray, C. E. and Lipps 1965 (verts., Georgia); Reed, C. A. and Palmer 1964 (goat, Iowa); Repenning 1965B (shrew, S. Afr.); Repenning et al. 1964 (tundra rodents, Alaska); Richard 1961A, B (mammals, France); Risto 1960 (mastodon, Macedonia); Robinson, P. 1966B (rodent, Sudan); Rolfe 1958 (mammals, England), 1966 (woolly rhino, Scotland); Romodanova and Shevchenko 1959 (mammals, Ukraine); Royo y Gómez 1960E (verts., Venezuela); Ruprecht 1965 (brown bear, Poland); Rusanov 1968 (horses, USSR); Ruske 1965 (verts., Germany); Ryasina 1962 (mammals, USSR); Ryziewicz 1955B (mammals, Poland);

Sadovskiĭ 1962 (mammals, Siberia); Saiadian 1966 (mammals, USSR); Saks 1959 (mammals, Siberia), 1966 (verts., Siberia); Samson and Kovács 1967 (cave lion, Rumania); Samson and Rădulesco 1965 (mammals, Rumania), 1966A (Hydruntinus, Rumania), 1966B (giraffes, Rumania); Saraiman and Căpitanu 1964 (elephant, Moldavia); Savage, R. J. G. 1966 (mammals, Ireland); Savage, R. J. G. and Donovan 1962 (mammals, Britain); Schmidt, Z. 1964 (deer, Slovakia), 1965A (mammals, Slovakia); Schultz, C. B. 1934B (mammals, Nebraska), 1961C (migrants, Asia to N. Amer.), 1965A (Bison, Great Plains), 1963B, Schultz, Whitmore and Tanner 1966 (mammals, Big Bone Lick, Kentucky); Schultz, G. E. 1965A, B, 1967 (verts., Kansas); Scott, G. R. 1963 (mammals, Colorado); Seliverstov 1961 (mammals, USSR); Semken 1966 (microverts., Kansas); Semken and Griggs 1965 (peccary, Texas); Semken et al. 1964 (musk ox, Wisconsin); Shcheglova 1958B (Megaloceros, USSR), 1961C (mammals, USSR), 1965, Shcheglova and Shaviakou 1959 (mammoths, USSR); Shcherbakova 1954A (mammoth and rhino, USSR), 1954B (antelope); Shchukina 1945 (mammals, Urals); Sher 1967A (saiga, Siberia and Alaska), 1967B (mammals, N. Asia, N. Amer.), 1968 (musk ox, Eurasia, N. Amer.); Sherstiukov 1968A (elephant tusk, USSR), 1968B (oxen horn-cores, USSR); Shevchenko 1965B (rodents, USSR); Shevyreva 1960 (Quat. deer, USSR); Shikama 1965, Shikama and Noda 1968 (elephant, Japan); Shikama and Hasegawa 1965A (suid, Japan), 1965B (cervid antler, Japan); Shikama and Okafuji 1964 (terrapin, Japan); Shorygina 1960, 1961B (verts., Cent. Asia); Shotton et al. 1965 (fishes, England); Sibley 1967 (Rancho La Brea, California);

Sickenberg 1965 (Dama, Germany), 1968 (mammals, Greece); Siegfried 1962 (bison, Germany); Silva, A. B. 1968 (verts., Mexico); Simons 1967G (monkey, Sudan); Simons and Alexander 1964 (ground sloth, New Mexico); Simpson, G. G. 1965E (Galago, Olduvai); Singer and Heltne 1966 (verts., S. Afr.); Slaughter 1965A, 1966C (verts., Texas), 1966B (verts., Oklahoma); Slaughter and McClure 1965 (mammals, Texas); Sokolov, I. I. and Vekua 1966 (antelope, USSR); Sokolov, V. N. 1957 (mammals, W. Siberia); Sokolovskiĭ 1958 (mammals, W. USSR); Sommer and Souza Cunha 1962 (mammals, Brazil); Sondaar and Boekschoten 1967 (mammals, Greece); Souza Cunha 1960 (Hippidion, Brazil), 1961 (horses, Brazil); Souza Cunha and Dias de A´vila Pires 1959 (deer, Brazil); Souza Cunha and Magalhães Macedo 1963 (mammals, Brazil); Spencer, H. E. P. 1964 (mammals, England); Stach 1956 (woolly rhino, Poland); Stein 1967 (mammals, Nevada); Steller 1964 (Equus, Ohio); Stephenson, N. G. 1964 (wombats, Australia); Stirton and Marcus 1966 (macropodid); Stokes 1966 (mountain sheep, N. Amer.); Stokes, Anderson and Madsen 1966 (bison, Utah, Idaho); Stokes, Smith and Horn 1964 (fishes, Utah); Strain 1965, 1966 (mammals, Texas); Strelkov 1959 (mammals, Soviet Arctic); Sukachev et al. 1966 (mammals, USSR); Surrarrer 1964 (mammoth, Ohio); Sutcliffe 1960B, 1961 (mammals, England); Suzuki 1965 (mammals, Israel); Svistun 1966 (verts., USSR), 1968 (mammals, USSR); Swift, C. and Wing 1968 (teleosts, Florida); Sych 1965 (leporids, Poland);
Takai and Hasegawa 1966 (verts., Japan); Tapalov 1966, 1967 (mammals, USSR); Tarashchuk 1962 (fishes, Ukraine); Tatarinov, K. A. 1956 (mammals, USSR), 1960 (rodent, Ukraine), 1966A (verts., Poland), 1967 (mammal faunas, Poland); Tattar 1961 (rodents and birds, USSR); Tavera 1968 (ground sloth, Chile); Taylor, M. S. 1968 (moas, N. Z.); Tchernov, E. 1968A (birds, Nubia); Tedford 1966B (Sthenurus, Australia), 1967B (marsupials, Australia); Telles Antunes 1965 (verts., W. Afr.); Ters 1964 (mammals, France); Thenius 1960H (mammals, Austria), 1965A (hyena, Austria), 1965B (carnivores, Germany), 1965C (primate, Germany), 1966A (deer, horses, rhinos); Théobald 1965 (elephant, France); Thomson, K. S. 1966B (fishes, Kenya); Thorslund 1966 (mammoth, Sweden); Ting et al. 1965 (mammals, China); Toepfer 1966 (verts., Germany); Topachevskiĭ 1957D (mammals, USSR), 1957E (verts., USSR); Torre, D. 1967 (canids, Italy); Tovell and Deane 1966 (bear, Ontario); Tripathi 1961B (verts., India); Troitskiĭ 1966 (mammoth, USSR); Tropin 1968 (rodents, USSR); Trylich and Bayrock 1966 (bison, Canada); Tsalkin 1962 (mammals, Moldavia); Tuohy 1967 (verts., Nevada);
Urquiola de de Carli and Aramayo 1967 (edentate, Argentina); Ushko 1959 (verts., USSR); Uyeno 1967B (fish, Japan);
Vakhrushev 1960B (mammals, Urals); Van der Hammen 1965 (mammals, Colombia); Vangengeĭm 1957B (mammals, USSR), 1960B, 1961 (mammals, Siberia), 1966A (Equus, Sungir'), 1966D, E, F, G (mammals, Transbaĭkalia); Vangengeĭm and Chumakov 1963 (camel, Kazakhstan); Vangengeĭm and Flerov 1965 (elk, Siberia); Vangengeĭm and Zazhigin 1965 (mammals, W. Siberia); Van Roy 1966 (Equus, France); Vañura 1965 (mammals, Czechoslovakia); Van Wijngaarden 1966 (beaver, Netherlands); Vasil'ev, Iu. M. 1961, 1962 (verts., USSR); Vasil'ev, Iu. M. and Aleksandrova 1965 (rodents, USSR); Vasil'ev, V. G. 1960 (verts., U.S.S.R.); Vas'kovskiĭ, A. P. 1959B (giant beaver, Siberia), 1966 (elk, USSR); Vekua 1958B (mammals, USSR), 1963 (mammals, Georgia, USSR); Vekua and Shidlovskiĭ 1958 (pika, Caucasus); Velich 1961 (bison, Nebraska, Iowa); Velichko 1961D (mammals, USSR); Vereshchagin 1951C (Carnivora, USSR); Vereshchagin and Mel'nikova 1958 (mammals, Kazakhstan); Vereshchagin and Ovodov 1968 (verts., Far East, USSR); Vergnaud-Grazzini 1968 (amphibians, Bolivia); Verhoeven 1964 (Stegodon, Timor, Asia); Villalta Comella 1964 (birds, Spain); Villalta Comella and Rosell Sanuy 1966 (mammals, Spain); Vineyard 1966 (mammals, Missouri); Volkova 1966 (fish and mammals, USSR); Voskresenskiĭ 1959, 1964 (mammals, USSR); Vulliamy 1930 (mammals, England);

Walker, A. 1964 (giant lemurs, Madagascar); Wang, A.-C. 1960 (mammals, China); Webb, G. L. 1965 (chalicotheres, S. Afr.); Webb, S. D. 1967A (proboscideans, Florida); Wei 1964 (mammals, China); Weigel 1962B (verts., Florida); Weiler 1965 (fishes, Germany); Weinberger 1960 (mastodon, Austria); Wells, L. H. 1964A, 1965, 1967 (antelopes, S. Afr.), 1964B (verts., S. Afr.); White, J. A. 1964, 1965 (kangaroo rats, California), 1966 (cricetid rodent, California), 1967 (Plesippus and other mammals, Idaho), 1968 (procupine, California); Whitmore 1960 (mammals, Japan); Whitmore and Foster 1967 (Panthera, Alaska); Widmer 1966 (mammoth, Switzerland); Wilson, Ri. L. 1967 (verts., Michigan); Wilson, Ri. L. and Zug 1966 (turtle, Michigan); Wo, Ju-kang 1964A, B, C, D, F, 1965B, C, G (mammals, China); Woldstedt 1967 (fishes, turtle, mammals, Germany); Wood, P. A. 1963 (verts., Arizona);

Yaldwyn 1966 (moas, N. Z.); Yeh, Hsiang-k'uei 1961 (box turtle, China); Young, 1930C (animals assoc. with Peking man); Young, H. R. 1966 (proboscidean, Canada);

Zagorskaiă 1959 (mammals, Soviet Arctic); Zaidova 1964 (hedgehogs, USSR); Zapfe 1964D (mammals, Austria), 1966B (carnivores, Austria); Zazhigin 1966A, C (small mammals, W. Siberia), 1966B (lagomorphs, Transbaĭkalia), 1966D (rodents, Transbaĭkalia); Zetti 1964 (sloth, Argentina); Zeuner and Bravo 1966 (verts., Canary Islands); Zol'nikov 1961 (mammals, USSR).

FAUNAS — QUATERNARY — cave faunas — Adrover 1966 (Son Muleta, Spain); Anderson, E. G. 1964 (Thylacinus, S. Australia); Anderson, E. 1968 (carnivores, Wyoming); Andrist, Flückiger and Andrist 1964 (Ursus, Germany); Angel, Basilio de la Salle 1966 (Myotragus); Annelli 1961 (mammals, Italy); Anon. 1958AZ (mammals, Italy), 1960CJ (Samwel Cave, N. California), 1964Z (mammals, Germany); d'Aramengo 1966 (Italy); Armstrong, M. H. 1965 (France and Spain); Auffenberg 1964A (Reddick Cave, Florida);

Bachinskiĭ 1965A (mammals, Odessa); Bachinskiĭ and Chernysh 1965 (Ukrainia); Bachinskiĭ and Dubliănskiĭ 1962, 1966, 1968 (Crimea); Bachinskiĭ, Dubiănskiĭ and Lysenko 1967 (Krasnaiă Cave, Crimea); Bachinskiĭ, Dubiănskiĭ and Shtengelov 1964 (Poland); Bachinskiĭ and Tatarinov 1966 (USSR); Bachmayer and Zapfe 1960A (Burgenland, Austria), 1960B (cave bear, Austria), 1964 (hyena, Austria); Badoux, M. H. 1964 (France); Baker, K. 1960 (Carlsbad Cavern, New Mexico); Balázs 1962 (early man, S. China); Balliot 1959 (cave bear, France); Barral and Simone 1965 (mammals, Italy); Bartolomei and Broglio 1964 (mammals, Italy); Bernstein 1965 (birds, Dominican Rep.); Bibikov 1940C (Pal. cave sites, S. Urals); Binder, Frank and Müller 1960 (Alpine caves, Germany); Binford, S. R. 1966B (Me'arat Shovakh, Israel); Blanc, G. A. 1958 (Romanelli Cave, Italy); Bliznetŝov 1964, 1968 (Urals); Bökönyi 1959 (wolverine, Hungary); Bonadonna 1964 (Elephas, Italy); Bonifay, E. 1965 (mammals, Rigabe Cave, France); Borzatti von Löwenstern 1964, 1965A (Uluzzo Cave, Sicily); Bostanci 1964 (Clemoutsi Cave, Greece); Brain 1967A (S. Afr. caves); Brattstrom 1964A (amphibians, reptiles, New Mexico); Butler, R. B. 1968 (Bison, Owl Cave, Idaho); Calaby and White 1967 (Tasmanian devil, Australia); Chaline 1961C, 1962, 1965C (fissure faunas, France), 1966B (micromammals); Chaline and Delingette 1965 (mammals, France); Chaviré 1963B (European owls), 1965A (rock shelter birds, France); Choate and Birney 1968 (Insectivora and Chioptera, Puerto Rico); Cleland 1965B (beta activity of bone samples, Reclau Cave, Spain); Cotter 1965B (mammals, Pennsylvania); Cranbrook 1967 (bats, Niah Cave); Cubillas Pérez 1961 (mammals, Cuba);

David, A. I. 1968A (large mammals, Moldavia); David and Prat 1962 (Equus, verts., France); DePorta 1965 (fissure verts., Colombia); Dumitresco et al. 1965 (mammals, Rumania); Duport 1959 (mammals, France); Dzhambazov 1957, 1959A, B, 1962, 1967A, B (mammals, Bulgaria);

and Dzhambazov 1960 (verts., Bulgaria); Miller, L. 1965 (birds, Idaho); Młynarski 1964B (tortoise, Poland); Moïsidis 1967 (mammals, Petralona Cave, Greece); Mostecky 1961C (mammals, Czechoslovakia), 1966 (rhinos, Czechoslovakia); Mottl 1964 (bears, Austria); Mourer-Chaviré 1964 (birds, France); Musil 1965A (mammals, Czechoslovakia), 1965B (birds and mammals, Czechoslovakia); Musil et al. 1965 (bear cave, Czechoslovakia);

Nader 1962 (verts., Shanidar Cave, Iraq); Negrea, Botoşǎneanu and Negrea 1967 (mammals, Rumania);

Octobon 1965 (verts., (France); Oesch 1965, 1966 (mammals, Missouri), 1967 (verts., Missouri); Okladnikov 1939C (verts., Uzbekistan); Ostromecki 1967 (cave bear, Poland);

Pei 1965B (mammals, Kwangsi caves, China); Perkins 1960 (mammals, Shanidar Cave, Iraq); Petrochilos 1961, 1965 (mammals, Greece); Pettus 1956* (lagomorphs, Texas); Piccoli and Del Pup 1967 (elephant, Italy); Pierret 1961A (Pal. caves, France); Pill 1963 (mammals, Hartle Dale); Pradel, L. and J. H. 1966 (verts., France); Prat 1956 (equids, Pyrenees);

Raney 1963 (Conard Fissure, Arkansas); Ray, C. E. 1964A (capromyid, Dominican Repub.), 1965C (capromyid, Haiti); Richmond 1964 (amphibians, reptiles, Pennsylvania); Ride 1964B (marsupials, Australia); Riek 1932B, 1934, 1938B (mammals, Germany); Roig de Leuchsenring 1961 (groundsloth, crocodile, Cuba);

Sadek 1965 (birds, Idaho); Schaub and Jagher 1945 (cave bear and hyena, Switzerland); Schroevers-Kommandeur and Jager 1966 (mammals, Netherlands); Semken 1960 (verts., Texas), 1967 (mammals, Texas); Sickenberg 1964 (mammals, Germany), 1966 (verts., Greece); Slaughter 1964B (mammals, Texas), 1966A (peccary, Texas); Soergel 1966 (birds, Austria); St. Pierre 1967 (mammals, Norway); Sutcliffe 1965 (mammals, England);

Tatarinov, K. A. 1964, 1965A (verts., Poland), 1965B (verts., Ukraine), 1966B (mammals preserved in ozocerite); Terzea 1965 (Panthera, Rumania), 1966 (cave bear, Rumania); Terzea and Jurcsák 1967 (mammals, Rumania); Topál 1964 (bats, Hungary); Tozzi 1962 (mammals, Italy); Tratman 1960 (mammals, England), 1968 (Pleist. bone caves); Treganza 1964 (mammals, N. California); Turnbull, P. 1967 (mammals, Iraq);

Waldren, W. H. 1966 (Myotragus, Majorca); Webster, D. 1964A, B (mammals, Missouri); Wedel et al. 1968 (birds and mammals, Wyoming); Weigel 1967 (birds, Texas); Wettstein-Westersheimb 1966 (small verts., Austria); Wiszniowska 1967 (mammals, Poland); Wojcik 1961B (mammals, Poland);

Young, C.-c. 1930C (animals assoc. with Peking man);

Zapfe 1966A (cave bear).

FLIGHT, ORIGIN and ADAPTATIONS – Albring 1967 (flight adaptations); Arambourg 1959 (pterosaur, Jordania);

Beer 1964B (Archaeopteryx);

Colbert 1966A (Trias. gliding reptile, New Jersey), 1967A (adaptations for gliding lizard Draco);

George and Berger 1966 (avian myology);

Leich 1964A (pterosaur, Germany);

Stever et al. 1966 (Archaeopteryx);

Teriaev 1967 (Rhamphorhynchus);

Wellnhofer 1968 (Pterodactylus, Bavaria).

FIELD WORK – See: expeditions; technique.

FOOTPRINTS – See: ichnology, tracks.

FOSSILIZATION – See: occurrences.

GASTROLITHS – See: coprolites and gastroliths.

GENERAL WORKS, POPULAR ITEMS, and TEXTBOOKS – Adam 1961C (fossil faunas,
    Europe); Alimen 1960B (prehist., Afr.), 1965B (atlas of prehist.); Allchin 1966
    (Stone Age hunters, Old World); Almagro Basch 1963 (prehist., archeol.); Ama-
    don 1966 (birds); Anderson, S. 1967A (primates), 1967B (rodents); Anderson
    and Jones 1967 (mammals of world); Andrews et al. 1967 (fishes); Anon. 1860
    (early man), 1957CC (dictionary of geol. terms), 1959BQ (Cǎenozoic fossils, Bri-
    tain), 1963BQ (Darwin and Huxley), 1963CA (field archeol.), 1964P (salvage
    operations, Ohio), 1964R, S (World Fair dinosaurs), 1964BP (review archeol.,
    biol.), 1965BR (fossil finds), 1965CS (anthrop. and archaeol.), 1966AH (fossil
    mammals), 1966BG (Aukland Is. rail discovered), 1967H (Homo habilis), 1967BK
    (geol., Denver, Colorado), 1968M (places to be notified of fossil discoveries),
    1968T (first fishes); Appleby 1967 (Ichthyosauria); Appleby et al. 1967 (Rep-
    tilia); Arambourg 1965C (origin of man); Arambourou and Jude 1964 (fossil
    goat, France); Asimov 1964A (hist. of biol.), 1964B (biol. sciences); Augusta
    and Burian n.d. (evol. plants and animals), 1962B, C (mammoths), 1962E, 1963B
    (prehist. reptiles and birds), 1964B, C (prehist. sea monsters);
Bachmayer 1964B (fossils); Bacon 1963 (vanished peoples); Bader, O. N. 1966C
    (archeol., Ural Mts.); Baldwin, G. C. 1963 (early man); Bargmann and Schade
    1964 (brain research); Barlow, J. C. 1967 (edentates and pholidotes); Barnard
    1954 (S. Afr. whales); Barnett and eds. of Life 1958 (prehist. animals); Barnett
    and McLaren 1964 (Penguin science survey); Barta 1965D (Stone Age, Czecho-
    slovakia); Bartosch 1962 (tetrapod tracks, Germany); Bastian, H. 1953, 1964
    (prehist. of earth); Basu 1963 (prehist. man); Bates 1967B (early man); Bayer
    1964 (Halzmaden quarries); Beals and Hoijer 1963, 1965 (anthrop.); Beebe
    1953 (fossil verts., New York); Beer 1964D, 1965B (atlas of evol.); Beerbower
    1965, 1968 (paleont.); Beiser and eds. of Life 1962 (the earth); Bellairs 1968
    (reptiles); Bellairs and Carrington 1966 (reptiles); Bellairs and Parson 1968
    (biol. of Reptilia); Beltrao 1966 (paleont. of Brazil); Bergamini and eds. of
    Life 1964 (fossils, Australia); Berka 1968 (Solnhofen); Berndt and Berndt
    1964, 1965 (early man, Australia); Berndt and Meise 1960 (birds); Berry 1968
    (prehist. time scale); Bestel 1967 (dinosaur bones); Biram 1960 (dinosaurs,
    juv.); Bishop 1967A (fossil vert. research); Blackwelder 1967 (taxonomy);
    Bleibtreu 1967 (physical anthrop.); Blîakher 1962 (animal morphology); Blot
    1967 (fish fauna, Italy); Boas 1965 (anthrop.); Boca 1961 (survey of anthrop.);
    Bodylevskiǐ 1962 (atlas of fossils); Boiteau 1964 (biology); Bormida 1960
    (paleont., Argentina); Bourdier 1967 (prehist., France); Bova 1962 (giants,
    juv.), 1964 (reptiles, juv.); Bowman 1966 (Galapagos Islands); Brace 1967
    (human evol.); Brace and Montagu 1965 (man's evol.); Breger 1963 (organic
    geochemistry); Bresler 1966 (human ecology); Brinkmann 1960 (geol. evol. of
    Europe); Bronowski 1965 (identity of man); Brouwer 1967 (gen. paleont.);
    Bublichenko 1961 (paleont. of Kazakhstan); Buettner-Janusch 1964 (biol. of
    primates), 1966 (origins of man); Burger 1965 (elephants, juv.); Burton, M.
    1966 (ichthyosaurs); Burton, V. L. 1962 (earth hist., juv.); Bush 1966 (Mary
    Anning, juv.); Butler, P. M., et al. 1967 (Mammalia); Butler and Greenwood
    1965 (insectivores, bats, E. Afr.); Butzer 1964 (Pleist. environment and archeol.);
Cailleux 1964B (prehist.); Caldwell, D. K. and M. C. 1965 (coelacanths); Caldwell,
    J. R. 1966 (archeol.); Camp, C. L. 1966 (stories of fossils, juv.); Camp, L. S.
    1964 (elephants); Camp, L. S. and C. C. 1968 (dinosaurs); Campbell, B. G.
    1966, 1967 (human evol.); Carlquist 1965 (island life); Carr 1966 (fossils,
    Georgia); Carrington 1965 (early man); Carroll, R. L. 1965A (comments on
    microsaur paper); Carroll and Baird 1967 (microsaurs and reptiles); Carter,
    G. S. 1967A, B (vert. evol.); Case, J. 1965C, 1966A (fossil finds); Chailley
    1965 (hist. of music); Chaline 1966C (lagomorphs and rodents), 1966D (insecti-
    vores), 1966E (bats); Chamberlain 1964 (fossils, Cape Cod); Chao, Si-ͭszin'

1965 (dinosaur, China); Chardin 1962F, 1964A, B (man), 1965C (letters during World War I), 1965D, 1968A, B (philosophy, religion, and science); Chardin et al. 1965, 1968 (evol. and religion); Charig 1967B (fossil fishes); Chernov 1959B (origin of modern reptiles, cent. Asia); Clark, D. L. 1968 (paleont. and evol.); Clark, J. D. 1967A (atlas Afr. prehist.); Clark, W. E. LeGros 1968 (exploration); Colbert 1964G (dinosaurs), 1965E (age of reptiles), 1965H (evol. of verts.); Cole, S. 1966B (animal ancestors); Collin and Stoiber 1962 (collecting fossils, juv.); Comfort 1964 (rocks and fossils); Cook, M. A. 1966 (prehist. and earth models); Coppens 1961B (developments in paleont.); Cornwall 1968 (prehistoric animals and hunters); Cottler 1966 (Alfred Wallace); Craig, M. J. 1965 (dinosaurs, juv.); Cramer 1959 (Darwin and paleont.); Craw 1967 (elephants); Crusafont Pairó 1965J (biometrics in evol.); Cullingford 1953, 1962 (British caving); Cutbill and Funnell 1967 (numerical analyses);

Dal Piaz and Malaroda 1966 (vert. paleont.); Daniel, G. 1966 (hist. of archeol.), 1967 (origin and growth of archeol.); Danil'chenko 1964A (Holostei), 1964B (Teleostei); Danil'chenko and Iakovlev 1964 (Pholidophorida); Dart, R. A. 1965F (origin of man); Dart and Craig 1962, 1963 (missing link); Darwin 1964 (1st. ed. facsimile, Origin of Species), 1966 (evol. of man); Daumas 1962 (hist. of techniques); Davidson 1950 (fossils); Davies, O. 1964 (Quat., Guinea); Davies, W. E. (earth sci. and speleology); Davis, L. W. 1965 (shark teeth, Kansas); Davitashvili 1956D (theoretical foundations of paleont.); Day 1965, 1968 (human paleont.); Dechaseaux 1964B (vert. paleont.), 1964C (chordates), 1964D (urochordates), 1964E (cephalochordates); Deetz 1967 (archeol.); Dehm 1967 (paleont.); Delacour and Scott 1954–1964 (waterfowl of world); De Laet 1960 (archeol.); Delair 1959 (new fossil finds); Delfgaauw 1965 (hist. of man); Dement'ev 1964 (Aves); De Rosnay 1965 (biochemical evol.); Devambez 1961 (hist. of art); DeVore, P. L. 1965, 1966 (origin of man); Dibner, B. 1964 (Darwin); Dickenson 1968 (Koalas); Dickinson 1962 (Stone Age man, juv.); Dineley 1965A (fossils, far north), 1966A (fossil verts., Canada); Dinsdale 1961 (Loch Ness monster); Dobzhansky 1964A, 1965B, 1966B (evol. of man), 1964B-1965A, 1966A (heredity in man); Dobzhansky, Hecht and Steere 1967 (evol. Biology); Doumani and Long 1962 (ancient life, Antarctica); Downs, 1968 (fossil verts., S. California); Drushits and Obrucheva 1962 (paleont.); Duarte 1961 (prehist.), Dubos 1965 (man adapting); Due Rojo 1964 (calculating weights of dinosaurs); Duges 1892 (paleont., Mexico); Dunbar 1966 (the earth); Durrell 1967 (prehist., W. Ohio); Duster 1967 (fossil hunting, Wyoming); Dyson, J. L. 1962 (frozen mammoths); Dyson, R. H. 1964 (hist. of domestic animals);

Eaton 1960C (comparative anat. verts.), 1964B (vert. pal.); Edinger 1966B (puzzles in bones), 1966C (ref. to "toadstones" in Shakespeare); Efremov 1961 (biol. bases of paleozool.); Ehrenberg 1963 (speleology in Austria), 1966A (paleont. of caves, Austria); Eimerl, DeVore and the eds. of Life 1965 (primates); Einor 1964 (geol. of USSR); Eisele 1964 (salvaging fossils, Nebraska); Eisentraut 1963 (verts., Cameroons); Eklund 1966 (fossil collecting in the Badlands); Ericson and Wollin 1964, 1966 (dating by deep sea cores);

F., K. 1967 (living Burramys, Australia); Farb 1962 (story of life); Fedorov, G. B. 1951 (Stone Age man, Siberia); Fejfar 1962 (fossil verts., Czechoslovakia); Fels 1965 (evolutionists); Fenton 1965 (fossils); Fenton, C. L. and M. A. 1962B (great geologists); Finch 1964 (speleology); Fisher, D. W. 1955 (prehist. mammals, N. Y.), 1963 (Devonian land animals); Fisher, J. 1966, 1967A, B (fossil birds); FitzSimons 1962 (snakes of S. Afr.); Flerov 1953 (Elasmotherium), 1965A, B, 1967 (origin of Canadian fauna); Flint 1965, 1967 (Quat. studies); Fokanov 1964 (Quat. rodents, USSR); Folsom 1956, 1962 (Amer. cave exploration), 1966 (early man); Forbes 1959 (fossils, juv.); Forsten 1968 (revision of Hipparion); Foster and Daniel 1965 (prehist. Wales); Fostor 1965 (Queen Charlotte Islands as habitat for land mammals); Fotheringham 1966 ("Eoörnis," a hoax);

Jackson, J. W. 1953, 1962 (speleology); Jacobson, D. A. 1963 (story of man, juv.);
Jazdzewski 1962 (archeol. glossary), 1965B (prehist., Poland); Jennings and Hoebel
1966 (readings in anthrop.); Jepsen 1964A, B (dinosaurs), 1967 (fish swallowed
fish); Jhingran et al. 1965 (Wadia commemorative volume); Johnson and Hatcher
1965 (introductory anthrop.); Jollie 1962 (chordate morphology); Jones, J. K.
1967 (monotremes); Jones and Johnson 1967 (sirenians); Jones, Raymond 1965
(reptiles to man, juv.); Jordan, D. S. 1963 (fishes); Jullien 1965B (fossil man);
Kamer 1954 (fossil animals, juv.); Katz, H. and M. 1965 (museums, U.S.A.); Kay
and Colbert 1965 (strat. and life hist.); Kazantseva 1964 (Actinopterygii); Kehoe,
A. B. (prehist. of the prairie provinces, Canada); Keil 1966 (odontology); Kelso
and Ewing 1962 (physical anthrop.); Kenny 1966 (evol.); Kent, G. C. 1965
(comparative anat. verts.); Kenyon 1961 (archeol.); Kingsbury 1961 (fossils,
juv.); Klein and Icolari 1967 (ref. encyclopedia of the Amer. Indian); Klein,
H. K. 1965 (dinosaurs, juv.); Kleinschmidt 1966 (horses); Kobayashi, T. 1964A
(geol. and paleont., S. E. Asia); Kochansky-Devidé 1962, 1964 (paleont., Yugoslavia); Koenigswald 1965D (early man), 1967B (fossil anthropoids); Kolchin
1965 (archeol. and nat. sciences); Komatsu 1962 (early man, Japan); Konzhukova
1964A (Apsidospondyli), 1964B (Batrachosauria), 1964C (Crocodilia); Koopman
1967 (artiodactyls); Koopman and Cockrum 1967 (bats); Korn and Thompson
1967 (human evol.); Kostrzewski, Chmielewski and Jazdzewski 1965 (prehist.,
Poland); Kraus, B. S. 1964 (human evol.); Kraus and Jordan 1965 (human
dentition); Krösche 1963 (moas); Kühn, H. 1966A (origin of man), 1966C
prehist. art); Kuhn, O. 1964D (geol. of Bayern); Kuhn-Schnyder 1967B (hist.
of paleont.); Kummel and Raup 1965 (paleont. techniques); Kummer and
Gemeinhardt 1964 (phylogeny); Kurtén 1968A (dinosaurs), 1968B (Pleist. mammals, Europe); Kuznicki and Urbanek 1967 (principles of evol.);
Lamarck 1964 (hydrogeology); Lambrecht, K. 1964 (paleoornithology); Lantier
1961C (prehist. life); Laporte 1968 (ancient environments); LaRivers 1962
(fossil fishes, Nevada); Lavocat 1966 (atlas of prehist.); Layne 1967 (lagomorphs);
Leakey, L. S. B. 1960E, 1967B (Olduvai Gorge); Lehmann, U. 1964 (paleont.
dictionary); Lemon 1965 (fossils in Ontario); Leonardi, P. 1957F, 1961A (evol.);
Leroi-Gourhan et al. 1966 (prehist.); Levin and Potapov 1964 (peoples of Siberia); Life 1963 (epic of man); Lindsay, H. A. 1966 (Australia's extinct fauna);
Loberg and Harrison 1967 (dinosaurs, juv.); Lorenz 1965 (evol. and behavior);
Lüdicke 1962 (anat. of snakes); Ludovici 1963 (paleont.);
McAlester 1968 (hist. of life); McBurney 1967B (Haua Fteah, Libya); McCartney
1964 (study of human bone); Macdonald, J. R. 1964B, 1967C (vandalism of
fossil verts.), 1968 (curators); MacFall 1963 (collecting fossils); Maggowan, K.
and J., and Hester 1962 (early man in the New World); Marcuzzi 1959 (biogeography); Marek 1966 (prehist.); Marinov 1966 (geol., Mongolia); Marquer 1967
(morphology of human races); Martin, C. 1964 (prehist. man, juv.); Martin and
Tate 1966 (Hesperornis); Massip 1961 (speleology); Mather and Mason 1964
(source book in geol.); Matthes, H. W. 1963A (paleobiogeog.), 1964 (hist. of
the earth); Matthews, W. H. 1964 (world of fossils, juv.), 1965 (teachers' manual — introduction to fossils); May [Dikty], J. 1965 (fossils, juv.); Mayer-Oakes
1967 (environmental studies of Lake Agassiz region); Mayr, E. 1965F (definition
of fauna), 1967B (species concept and evol.); Meighan 1966 (introduction to
archeol.); Merpert and Shelov 1961 (early man, E. Europe); Merrilees 1965C
(marsupials); Miles, A. E. W. 1967 (structural and chemical organization of
teeth); Miller and Kahn 1962 (statistical methods in geol. sciences); Mincham
1966 (Australian fossils); Mohr, C. E. 1964 (cave exploring, Amer.); Mohr and
Poulson 1967 (life of caves); Mongait 1955, 1961B (archeol., USSR); Montocchio
1965 (human paleont.); Moore, J. A. 1965 (modern biol.); Moore and eds. of
Life 1964A, B (evol.); Moret 1965 (manual of paleont.); Morris, R. and D.
1966 (men and apes); Müller, A. H. 1966 (fishes and amphibians), 1968 (reptiles
and birds); Müller-Karpe 1966 (Old World Paleolithic); Mumford 1967 (technics

(evol.), 1965B, 1967F, 1968A (meaning of evol.), 1965D (Olduvai Gorge, Tanzania), 1965F (zool.), 1965H (fossil collecting in Argentina), 1965K (biol.), 1966D (mammals around the Pacific), 1966K (DNA), 1967E, 1968B (paleont.); Simpson, G. G. and Beck 1965 (biol.); Sinitsyn 1959 (fossil verts., Cent. Asia); Sirks and Zirkle 1964 (biol.); Skorkowski 1960, 1967 (Przewalski horse); Slotkin 1965 (anthrop.); Smith, Hobart M. 1960 (comparative anat., Chordates); Smith, L. M. 1966 (dinosaurs, juv.); Sokal and Sneath 1963 (numerical taxonomy); Solbrig 1966 (evol. and systematics); Spencer, Jennings, et al. 1965 (early man, N. Amer.); Spencer and Johnson 1960 (anthrop. atlas); Springer 1964 (sharks); Stains 1967 (carnivores and pinnipeds); Standing Conference...on Afr. 1964 (paleont. theses); Starrett 1967 (rodents); Stebbins 1966, 1968 (organic evol.); Stecher 1966 (Przewalski horse); Stehli 1966 (labyrinthodonts); Stelck 1967 (geol., fossils); Stensiö 1964 (ostracoderms); Sternberg 1966 (Canadian dinosaurs); Stever et al. 1966 (flight); St. Jean 1967 (USSR paleont.); Storer and Usinger 1965 (gen. zool.); Størmer 1966B (dinosaurs); Stümpke, H., pseud. 1967 (fantasy); Suggs 1965 (archeol., San Francisco), 1966 (archeol., New York); Sukhanov 1964 (Testudinata); Sultanov 1961 (paleont. dictionary, in Russian); Swinton 1962D, E, 1964C (dinosaurs), 1964A, 1965A (fossil birds), 1965B (Canadian dinosaurs);

Takai and Tsuchi 1963A (Neogene, Japan), 1963B (Quat., Japan); Takeuchi, Uyeda and Kanamori 1967 (earth sci.); Talbot 1966 (coelacanth); Taquet 1967 (paleont., W. Afr.), Tarlo, L. B. H. 1967B (Agnatha); Tatarinov, L. P. 1964B (Amphibia), 1964C (Colosteoidea), 1964D (Cochleosauroidea), 1964E (Zatrachydidae), 1964F (Pleisopoda), 1964G (Salientia), 1964H (Gephirostegidae), 1964I (Chroniosuchidae), 1964J (Waggoneridae), 1964K (Lepospondyli), 1964L (Microsauria), 1964M (Therapsida), 1964N (Diarthrognathoidea), 1964O (Tritylodontoidea), 1964P (Synaptosauria), 1964Q (Nothosauria), 1964R (Plesiosauria), 1964S (Ichthyopterygia), 1964T (Lepidosauria), 1964U (Polyglyphanodontidae), 1964V (Scincoidea), 1964W (Xantusioidea), 1964X (Elachistosuchidae), 1964Y (Scleromochlidae), 1964Z (Coeluroidea), 1964AA (Deinodontoidea); Teale 1965 (Big Bone Lick, Kentucky); Teichert, C. and Yochelson 1967 (paleont. and strat.); Telberg 1966 (Russian-English paleont. dictionary); Terent'ev 1961, 1965B (herpetology); Termier, H. and G. 1964A (Paleozoic); Thenius 1961F (paleont., prehist.), 1962C (prehist., Austria), 1965D (living fossils); Thomas, M. C. 1965 (fossil hunting), 1968 (fossil verts.); Thomson, A. L. 1964 (dictionary of birds); Thomson, K. S. 1966D (coelacanth); Titiev 1963 (anthrop.); Tobien 1964, 1965A (zygodont mastodonts, N. Amer., Europe), 1968A (paleont.); Tozer 1964 (Triassic); Trimm and Fisher 1964 (dinosaurs); Trundle 1614 (dinosaurs, England); Turnbull, W. D. 1968 (living fossil marsupial, Australia);

Uchupi 1964 (fossils from continental shelf); Updike 1968 (the naked ape [poem]);

Van Deusen and Jones 1967 (marsupials); Van Noorden 1963 (mosasaurs); Van Valen 1965E (Paroxyclaenidae); Vereshchagin 1953 (bone "cemeteries", USSR), 1959C, 1968A (mammals, Caucasus); Viret 1955P (study of fossil mammals); V'iushkov 1964A (Synapsida), 1964B (Deinocephalia), 1964C (Theriodontia), 1964D (Galeopsoidea), 1964E (Dicynodontoidea), 1964F (Anomodontia inc. sed.), 1964G (Proganosauria); Vogt 1858 (origin of earth); Vollmer 1964 (early man); Vorob'eva and Obruchev 1964 (Sarcopterygii);

Waddington 1966 (biol. and evol.); Wagstaffe and Fidler 1968 (preservation of nat. hist. specimens); Walker, E. P. 1964 (mammals of the world); Walter 1962 (myths on origin of man); Warga 1966 (Scopes evol. trial); Wauchope 1966B (sunken continents); Wegner 1965 (fossil collecting and preparation); Weitz 1966 (geol.); Weller 1965B (status of paleont.); Wells, A. K. and Kirkaldy 1966 (hist. geol.); Wells, C. 1964A (disease, early man), 1967 (pseudopathology); Wendt, H. 1963, 1965B (early man), 1965A, 1968 (prehist.); Whitaker, G. O. and Mayers 1965 (dinosaur hunt, New Mexico); Whitaker 1966 (geol. for the blind); White, E. I. 1955B (fossil fishes), 1960B (coelacanths), 1966 (lungfishes);

White, T. E. 1967 (dinosaurs, juv.); Whitehead 1964 (deer of Great Britain and Ireland); Wilf and Merlin 1964 (early man); Wilson, R. W. 1965 (type loc. of Cope's Cret. mammals); Wing 1966 (fossil skates and rays, Florida); Wise 1963 (dinosaurs, juv.), 1965 (giant mammals, juv.); Woldstedt 1965 (Ice Age, Afr., Asia, Australia, Amer.); Woodford 1965 (hist. geol.); Wright, H. E. and Frey 1965 (Quat., United States);

Yaldwyn 1966 (moas, N.Z.); Yapp 1965 (verts.); Yin, Tsan-Hsun et al. 1965 (paleont., China); Yochelson 1967B (teaching paleont.);

Zablotsky and Flerov 1963 (evol. of bisons); Zapfe et al. 1964 (geol. and paleont. of Austria); Zittel 1964A, B (paleont. text).

GENETICS — See: evolution; general works; variation and heredity.

GEOCHRONOLOGY — See: correlation, paleochronology; technique.

GEOGRAPHIC DISTRIBUTION — See: distribution; paleogeography.

GEOGRAPHY — See: paleogeography.

GEOLOGY — See: bibliographies; correlation; distribution; expeditions; faunas; general works; history of paleontology; occurrences; paleochronology; paleoclimatology; paleogeography.

GROWTH CHANGES, RATES, and STAGES — See: variation and heredity.

HABITS and HABITATS, CUSTOMS, TECHNOLOGIES (see also: paleopsychology) —
Bates 1967A (man's eating habits); Bitiri 1965B (early man, Rumania);
Dineley 1964A (pteraspids); Dreimanis 1967A, B (mastodons, eastern N. Amer.);
Jefferies 1968 (primitive fossil chordates);
Karatajūte 1958B (asterolepids); Krämer and Kunz 1966 (Chirotherium habitat);
Krebs 1967A (Steneosaurus, Switzerland); Kruytzer 1964A (moasaurs, Netherlands);
Langston 1965B (crocodiles, Colombia); Lantier 1961C (prehist. life); Leon-Gourhan, André 1964D (evol. of hominid techniques and language);
Pidoplichko 1963A (hist. of faunas); Piel 1963 (dinosaur, Colorado);
S., C. 1964 (orangs sleep in caves); Sauer 1966B (domestication); Sternberg 1965 (hadrosaurs).

HEREDITY — See: variation and heredity.

HISTOLOGY, ELECTROMICROSCOPY — Ascenzi 1964 (fossil bone);
Blumberg and Kerley 1966 (bone); Bystrov 1959B (microstructure of arthrodire armor);
Carlström 1963 (crystallographic study of otoliths);
Doberenz and Lund 1966 (collagen in Jurassic bone); Deberenz and Wyckoff 1967A (microstructure of fossil teeth), 1967B (structure in fossil collagen);
Frost, H. M. 1966A (morphometry of bone);
Gibson, M. A. 1967 (histology of fossil bone); Gorgas, K. 1967 (rodents); Gross, W. 1966 (fish scale types), 1967C (ostracoderms), 1968C (Dartmuthia), 1968D (Phlebolepis scales);
Heller, W. 1967 (collagen structures);
Kerley 1965 (microscopic determination of age in bone); Kraus and Jordan 1965 (human dentition);
McNulty 1964, 1965 (sting ray teeth, Texas); Malzahn 1963 (Lepidotus operculum), 1968 (Janassa); Martin, L. D. 1966 (Hyracodon dentition); Moss, M. L. 1961 (processes of calcification);

Novitskaya 1965 (structure of Psammosteida plates);
Ørvig 1965 (bone tissue, verts.), 1967A (fossil fish teeth), 1967B (tooth tissues);
Parker, R. B. 1966 (fossil bones and teeth);
Ricqlès 1968A, B (dinosaur bone);
Schultze, H.-P. 1966 (fish scales);
Voss-Foucart 1968 (Cret. dinosaur eggs, France);
Wyckoff, R. W. G. and Doberenz 1965 (Rancho La Brea bone).

HISTORICAL GEOLOGY — See: geology.

HISTORY OF PALEONTOLOGY and PALEOANTHROPOLOGY — Agache 1958F (Pal.
    research, Somme, France); Alizade, K. A. 1967 (Azerbaidzhan); Anon. 1962CF
    (Darwin), 1967AL (Scopes evol. trial); Aslanova 1963 (study of fossil cetaceans,
    USSR);
Baker, J. R. 1968A (Cro-magnon man); Berry 1968 (prehist. time scale); Binder
    1962B (prehist., Germany), 1964 (cave research, Germany); Bliakher 1962
    (animal morphology); Bourdier 1960D (origin of life); Boyle 1965 (Altamira,
    Spain); Bublichenko 1961 (paleont. of Kazakhstan); Burton, M. 1966 (ichthyo-
    saurs);
Cahn 1962 (life and times of Geoffroy Saint-Hiliare); Carmichael and Long 1965
    the (Smithsonian story); Chin 1958 (prehist. of Thailand); Churcher 1966B
    (Dinobastis); Colbert 1964B (saurischian dinosaurs), 1968A (men and dinosaurs);
    Coleman 1964 (theory of evol.);
Daber 1960 (Berlin); Dal Piaz 1962 (Antonio Vallisneri); Dalquest 1961C (bison
    in N. Amer.); Daniel, G. 1965 (archeol. study in Wales); Danielsson 1965,
    1967 (Darwinism in Sweden); Darlington, C. D. 1964 (evolution); Davies, Wendy
    1964 (William Pengelly); Dechaseaux 1965B (Dichodon); Deinse 1964B (wal-
    ruses, Netherlands); Dietrich 1960 (paleont. collection, Humboldt Univ. Mus.,
    Berlin); Drake, E. T. 1966 (Yale Peabody Mus.); Duarte 1961 (prehist.); Du-
    binin and Garutt 1954 ("Adams" mammoth, Lena R.); Dyson, R. H. 1964
    (hist. of domestic animals);
Ehrenberg 1966B (Fuchsenlucken Cave, Austria); Eyles 1966 (hist. of geol.);
Franz 1965 (prehist., Austria);
Gardner 1957 (geol. vs. Genesis); Ghosh 1963 (paleoanthrop., India); Goetzmann
    1965, 1966 (exploration, early Amer. West); Gromov, V. I., Ivanova, et al.
    1965 (Quat.); Gunther 1967 (evol. doctrine);
Haarländer and Heller 1964 (early collections, Nürnberg); Halbouty 1965 (geol.);
    Harrison, T. 1966 (Niah Caves, Borneo); Heberer 1965B (theories of evol.);
    Heintz, A. 1963 (class. of armored fishes), 1965A (first mammoth find, Norway);
    Heller, F. 1962B (early English naturalists and Franconian bone caves); Hesse
    1966 (Neanderthal skull from Le Moustier); Hillaby 1965A (discovery of fossil
    man); Hofer 1963 (primatology); Holden 1966 (famous fossil finds); Holz-
    schneider 1962 (Rhine caves); Hooykaas 1959, 1963 (uniformity in geol. and
    paleont.); Huddleston 1967 (origins of Amer. Indians — European concepts);
    Hudson 1966 (reptile beds, Isle of Egg, Scotland); Hyde 1965 (fossil collect-
    ing, Ohio);
Iakovlev, V. N. 1967D (Soviet paleoichthyology);
Jensen 1966A (ichthyosaurs of Holzmaden, Germany), 1966B (Megatherium cast);
Keroher 1967 (fossil names in strat. nomenclature, N. Amer.); Kobayashi, T. 1964B
    (paleont., Thailand, 1916-62), 1967 (Japanese paleont. and paleontologists);
    Koenigswald 1956J (Neanderthal centenary), 1964D, 1967C (fossil man), 1965A
    (Australopithecinae); Kretzoi 1964C (paleont. of Tata, Hungary); Kühn, H.
    1965 (hist. of discovery of Pal. art, 1830-1960); Kuhn-Schnyder 1967B (hist.
    of paleont.);
Lamarck 1964 (hydrogeology); Laming-Emperaire 1964 (prehist. archeol., France);
    Lane and Richards 1963 (Wellington Caves, New S. Wales); Langston 1965C
    (vert. paleont. in Alberta); LaRocque 1964A (biogs. of geologists), 1964C (biog.

index of geologists); Lawrie 1964 (Hugh Miller); Lehman 1964C (origin of
verts.); Lessertisseur 1961 (paleont. and the three images of anthropogenesis);
Levin, M. G. 1960 (hist. of anthrop. in Russia); Lynch, B. and T. F. 1968
17th and 18th century prehist. archeol.);

Macintosh, N. W. G. 1952 (Cohuna cranium, Australia); Matheson 1964 (corres-
pondence of George Brettingham Sowerby); Matthes, H. W. 1963B (Geisel
Valley Eocene deposits, Germany); Mayr, E. 1965A (classif. and phylogeny);
Merrill 1964 (100 years of Amer. geol.); Mertens 1960 (influence of evol.
theory on taxonomy); Mitchell, E. D. 1965A (Sharktooth Hill, California);
Mongait 1957 (archeol., USSR); Movius 1966A (hist. of the study of burins);
Muschalek 1963 (hist. of paleoanthrop.);

Nesturkh 1968B (primatology in USSR);

Ostrom and McIntosh 1966 (hist. of paleont. at Como Bluff, Wyoming);

Penniman 1965 (hist. of anthrop.); Petit, G. and Theodorides 1962 (zool.); Phillips
E. D. 1964 (Greeks and prehist.); Pidoplichko 1961B (verts., Ukraine); Polianskii,
V. I. and Iu. I. 1966 (hist. evol.); Popov, Iu. N. 1956 (finds of animals in
permafrost);

Rafalovich and Ketraru 1966 (archeol., Moldavia); Rappaport 1964 (geol. and
paleont.); Reig 1961C (vert. paleont., Argentina); Ride 1964B (Australian
marsupials); Romer 1967C (reptile evol.); Romer, M. 1964 (Rancho La Brea);
Roussot 1966B (Lascaux Cave); Rozhdestvenskii 1961B (vert. pal., USSR);
Russell, L. S. 1966B (dinosaur hunting, Canada);

Sanz Pareja 1961 (Concud, Spain); Sarbadhikari 1966 (paleont. in India); Schultz,
C. B. et al. 1967 (Big Bone Lick, Kentucky); Scopes and Presley 1967 (Scopes
evol. trial); Selson 1964 (voyage of the Beagle, juv.); Sen and Ghosh 1964
(Narmada Valley paleoanthrop., India); Sexton 1965 (S. Australian caves);
Shippen 1963 (hist. of biol.); Silverberg 1965 (hoaxes); Simons 1966 (search
for early man), 1968A (mammals, Afr.); Sirks and Zirkle 1964 (biol.); Starck
1967A (mammal skull); Stepanov, D. L. 1965 (hist. of pal.); Stout 1964 (early
paleont. work, Nebraska); St. Pierre 1967 (cave studies, Norway);

Terent'ev 1961, 1965B (herpetology); Tikhomirov and Ravikovich 1968 (geol. sci.
in USSR); Tobias 1964B (Taung skull); Toepfer 1967A (German Paleolithic
caves); Tolmachev, A. I. 1961 (Soviet paleont.); Tomkins 1965 (Scopes trial);
Trundle 1614 (dinosaurs, England); Turner, F. 1922 (fossil mammals, England);

Vangengeim 1966B (Quat. mammals, USSR); Van Hoeter 1963 (early man); Van
Valen 1967A (first find of Cret. mammal); Vereshchagin 1967B (hist. of Quat.
faunas); Vertes 1964B (Tata site, Hungary), 1965F (Paleolithic research, Hungary);
Vinken 1963 (evol. in Netherlands);

Wager 1964 (time scale); Walker, M. V. 1967 (Kansas toothed birds); Webster, D.
1964A (Cherokee Cave, St. Louis, Missouri); Wendt, H. 1965A, 1968 (paleont.,
prehist.); Wilmsen 1965 (early man studies, U.S.);

Zuniga 1966 (early S. Amer. fossils found in Danish Zool. Mus.).

HONORS — See: biographies.

HORN — See: integumentary structures.

HUMAN PALEONTOLOGY — See: anthropology; paleoanthropology.

ICHNOLOGY, PALICHNOLOGY, TRACKS, TRACKWAYS and TRAILS (see also: faunas;
restorations; and, in the Systematic Index, Ichnites) — Anon. 1828 (antediluvian footsteps), 1961CY (camel, California), 1964AV (Megalosaurus), 1964BY (dinosaur,
Spitzbergen), 1965G (tetrapod tracks, USSR), 1965BF (dinosaur), 1965BV (dinosaur, Australia), 1967AP (dinosaur, Connecticut); Avnimelech 1966 (dinosaur,
Israel);

Baird 1964B (reptile, New Mexico), 1965B (Perm., Colorado); Bartholomai 1966B (dinosaur, Australia); Bartosch 1962 (tetrapod, Germany); Bessonnat et al. 1965 (Juras. reptiles, France); Bock, W. 1964 (Perm. and Trias.); Breed 1967 (amphibian trackway, Arizona);

Casamiquela 1964A (Mesoz., Patagonia), 1964C (Carbonif., Argentina), 1965B (Paleoz., Argentina), 1966 (gaits of saurischian dinosaurs); Cerveri 1964 (Nevada); Colbert 1964F (dinosaur, Spitzbergen), 1968A (dinosaurs); Colbert and Merrilees 1967 (Cret. dinosaur, Australia); Courel and Demathieu 1962 (Trias. tracks, France);

Deacon 1966 (dating Nahoon footprints); Delair 1966C (England), 1967 (Perm. footprints, England); Demathieu 1964, 1966 (Trias. footprints, France);

Ellenberger and Fuchs 1965 (Juras. verts., France); Ellenberger, P. 1965 (Mesoz. verts., France);

Fischer, K. 1963 (cotylosaur armor impressions);

Gabuniia 1958E (Cret. dinosaur, Georgia, USSR); Ginsburg, Lapparent, Loiret and Taquet 1966 (tetrapods, Nigeria); Ginsburg, Lapparent and Taquet 1968 (Chirotherium, Nigeria);

Haubold 1966A, B (Trias. tracks, Germany); Hill, Playford and Woods 1965 (Trias. tracks, Queensland);

Jacobi 1963 (reptile, Germany);

Karaszewski 1966 (reptile, Poland); Kaszap 1968 (cotylosaur, Hungary); Kircaldy 1967 (reptile); Krämer and Kunz 1964, 1966 (Chirotherium, Germany); Krebs 1966 (Chirotherium is Ticinosuchus ferox); Kutscher 1966 (tracks in Trias. ss.), 1967 (Chirotherium);

Laemmelen 1960 (Chirotherium); Lammers 1964 (Trias. reptile, Utah); Lapparent 1966 (Chirotherium, Spain); Lapparent et al. 1965 (Mesoz. reptiles, Spain); Lapparent and Montenat 1967A, B (reptiles, France); Lapparent, Montenat and Desparmet 1966 (dinosaurs, France); Lapparent and Oulmi 1964 (Juras. dinosaur, France); Lewis and Vaughn 1965 (verts., Colorado);

Majoros 1964 (Perm. reptile, Hungary); Malahan 1967 (dinosaur, Connecticut); Malz 1964 (Kouphichnium, Juras., Solnhofen); Martin, G. P. R. 1966A (Chirotherium); Maubeuge 1965A (Mesoz. tracks, France, Switzerland); May, G. 1966 (dinosaur, Australia); Mayr, F. X. 1967 (tracks on floors of Juras. lagoons); Mountain 1966 (human and bird tracks, S. Afr.); Moussa 1968 (Eoc. tracks, Utah);

Nelson, R. H. 1965 (dinosaur tracks, Connecticut);

Oppé 1965 (Juras. dinosaur, Isle of Purbeck, England); Ostrom 1967 (dinosaur, Connecticut);

Panin 1961, Panin and Avram 1962, Panin, Lăzărescu and Grujinschi 1966, Panin and Stefănescu 1968 (Mioc. tracks, Rumania); Pawloski 1968 (Dinosaur State Park, Connecticut); Plaziat 1964, 1965 (Eoc. shore birds, France);

Raaf et al. 1965 (Olig. bird, Spain); Rat 1960 (Oligo-Mioc. bird tracks, France); Rozhdestvenskii 1964A (Juras. dinosaurs, Cent. Asia);

Schmidt, Z. 1965B (deer and horse, Slovakia); Serventy 1960 (Juras. dinosaur, Australia); Spendlove 1968 (dinosaur, Utah); Staines and Woods 1964 (Trias. dinosaur, Australia); Stan 1964 (Hipparion, Mioc., Rumania);

Thenius 1967A (Plioc. mammals, Austria); Tkachenko, Pishvanova and Shvareva 1967 (bird and mammal, USSR);

Vereshchagin and Zakharenko 1967 (Mioc., Machairodus); Vialov 1966 (traces of life activity);

Young, C.-c. 1966C (dinosaur, China);

Zakharov 1964, Zakharov and Khakimov 1963 (Cret. dinosaur, USSR).

ILLUSTRATIONS — See: Paleolithic art.

INDUSTRIES — See: paleoanthropology.

INSTITUTIONS — See: museums.

INTEGUMENTARY STRUCTURES (skin, scales, horn, etc.) — Chudinov 1968A (skin structure of theromorphs);
  Findlay 1968A (labyrinthodont), 1968B (origin of hair);
  Gofshteĭn 1953 (fish scales, Transcarpathia); Grasse' 1967 (mammals); Gross, W.
    1966 (fish scale types), 1967C (ostracoderms), 1968A (rhombic fish scales),
    1968D (Phlebolepis scales); Guthrie, R. D. 1966B (pelage of fossil bison), 1966C
    (bison horn cores); Gutmann 1967A (dermal skel. of lower verts.);
  Hasegawa and Matsushima 1968B (elk antler, Japan); Heller, W. 1966 (ichthyosaur
    "skin");
  Khozatskiĭ 1959B, 1965 (turtle shells), 1966 (Trionyx armor); Khozatskiĭ and Alek-
    perov 1957 (turtle shells, USSR); Klafs 1965 (urus horn cores, Europe); Korot-
    kevich 1964B (Muntiacus, S. USSR);
  Lebedkina 1964B (amphibian skull dermal bones); Lehman 1967B (Drepanaspis
    head-shield plates); Lehmann, E. von 1967 (deer antler, Germany);
  Macarovici 1963 (elk horns, Rumania); McClure and Milstead 1967 (box turtle
    shell, Texas); Malzahn 1968 (Janassa); Mark-Kurik 1963 (arthrodire spinal
    plate); Miles, R. S. 1965B, (arctolepid placoderm plate, Antarctica), 1965C, D
    (arthrodire plates, U.S.), 1966A (Acanthodii scales, Germany); Miles and Westoll
    1968 (Coccosteus); Mitchell, E. D. 1966E (Allodesmus, California);
  Nakazawa 1966 (fossil fish scales, Japan); Novitskaya 1965 (structure of Psammos-
    teida plates);
  Ørvig 1967A (elasmobranch scales);
  Pennington and Frost 1961 (fish scales, England); Prasad and Satsangi 1962 (bovid
    hoof, India), 1963C (turtle shell, India); Prikhod'ko 1962 (mummified amphib-
    ian skin, USSR);
  Rao, C. N. and Shah 1963 (pterosaur skin ornamentation, India);
  Schmidt, H. 1966 (Chelydra skin imprints, Germany); Schmidt, W. 1965 (fish
    scales, Germany); Schultze 1966 (fish scales), 1968 (fish scales, Australia, Spitz-
    bergen); Semenov, S. A. 1960C (origin of human body hair); Stevens, M. S.
    1964 (arthrodire armor, Michigan);
  Tarlo, L. B. H. 1963 (aspidin, precursor of bone), 1964A (origin of bone), 1967C
    dermal armor in fishes); Taugourdeau 1965 (turtle shell, France);
  Vignati 1963 (glyptodon carapace, Argentina);
  Walker, A. D. 1964 (Ornithosuchus scutes, Scotland); Walker, C. A. 1966 (pleuro-
    diran turtle plastron and carapace, Somalia); Weiler 1962F (selachian skin plates);
    Wermuth 1964 (origin and evol. of turtle shell); Wilson, R. L. and Zug 1966
    (turtle shell, Michigan);
  Yeh, Hsiang-k'uei 1961, 1963B, 1966 (turtle shells, China), 1965 (turtle shells,
    Mongolia); Young, C.-c. 1964D (Lagomeryx horn, China), 1965A (salamander
    skin impression, China).

INVENTORIES — See: bibliographies; paleoanthropology.

LAND BRIDGES — See: paleogeography.

LEGISLATION, POLITICAL and THEOLOGICAL DOCTRINE and CONTROVERSY —
  Camp, L. S. de 1968 (Scopes evol. trial); Clark, J. M. 1964 (Genesis); Crusafont
    Pairó 1964E (proteognosis versus evol.);
  Haag, Haas and Hürzeler 1962 (evol. and the Bible); Hooykaas 1959, 1963 (prin-
    ciple of uniformity in geol. and theology);
  Lisonbee 1965A (anti-evol. movement, Arizona);
  McDonald, J. E. 1966 (anti-evol. movement, Arizona); Mawhinney 1966 (origin of
    man — evol. or divine creation); Mukerjee 1963 ((bio-philosophical aspects of

human evol.);   Muschalek 1963 (paleoanthrop. and the Bible);
Nogar 1963 (evol. and the Bible);
Olson 1968A (dialectics in evol.);
Pidoplichko 1963B (anti-glacial theory);   Porshnev 1958 (Marxist theory on evol.
of human culture and society);
Rusconi 1964C (conservation, Argentina);
Schmalhausen 1947 (materialistic darwinism);   Scopes and Presley 1967 (Scopes
evol. trial);
Tomkins 1965 (Scopes trial), 1966 (anti-evol. law);
Van Meter 1967 (federal aid to museums);
Warga 1966 (Scopes trial);
Zeitner 1967 (land laws).

LISTS — See: bibliographies.

LOCOMOTOR MECHANISMS — See: aquatic adaptations; flight; paleomyology; skeleton.

MAGIC — See: Paleolithic art; paleopsychology.

MAPS — See: bibliographies; correlation.

MEMORIALS, MEMORIAL VOLUMES, MONUMENTS — See: biographies, obituaries.

METHODS — See: correlation; ecology; evolution; expeditions; general works; history of
paleontology; paleoanthropology; paleochronology; paleoclimatology; phylogeny, methods
of study of; technique.

MICROPALEONTOLOGY, MICROFOSSILS, MICROVERTEBRATES — See: dentition;
integumentary structures (fish scales); (Otoliths, in Systematic Index).

MIGRATION — See: distribution.

MORPHOLOGY — See: anatomy; dentition; paleoanthropology; paleomyology; paleoneurology; skeleton; skull.

MUSCULATURE — See: paleomyology.

MUSEUMS, INSTITUTIONS, and CONGRESSES —
ORGANIZATION AND HISTORY — Adam 1966B (Stuttgart Mus.);   Agron 1965 (theft
of fossil fish, Rutgers Univ., N.J.);   Anon. 1961CT (Pal. div., Geol. Surv., India),
1967AN (Florida State Mus.), 1967AW (Agate Fossil Beds Nation. Monument
Assoc.), 1967BI (Fort Lamy pal. lab.);   Astre 1966B, 1967C (Soc. Hist. Nat.
Toulouse);
Balaša 1960 (Mus. Banská Bystrica);   Balout 1965D (Mus. Nation. Hist. Nat. Paris);
Barrera 1967 (Mus. Nat. Hist. Mexico City);   Bernal 1966A, B (Nation. Mus.
Anthrop., Mexico);   Bertram 1967 (fossil hall, Sydney Mus.);   Binder 1965
(Blaubeuren Mus.);   Blaha, Jungwirth and Kromer 1966 (Vienna Nat. Hist. Mus.);
Carmichael and Long 1965 (Smithsonian Inst.);   Colbert and Reekie 1965 (Canter-
bury Mus., New Zealand; Australian Mus., Sydney);   Cole, S. 1961B (British
Mus. forgeries);   Curl 1962 (Pengelly Cave Research Center, England);
Dart, R. A. 1964C, (S. Afr. Assoc. Sci. Tech. Soc.);   Dietrich 1960 (paleont. col-
lection, Humboldt Univ. Mus., Berlin);   Drake, E. T. 1966 (Yale Peabody Mus.);
Elkin 1966 (new Australian archeol. jour.);
Hill, C. 1967 (Pengelly Centre Mus., Devon);   Holmes 1967 (Mus. of Man, Kansas);
Katz, H. and M. 1965 (museums, U.S.A.);   Keenan-Smith 1966 (S. Afr. Archaeol.
Soc.);

Lane 1966 (New Harmony, Indiana);   Leroy, P. 1965 (Peking Inst. Geobiol.);
Netting 1965 (Paleozoic Hall, Carnegie Mus.);   Nuñez Jiménez 1961A, B (Soc.
    Espeleol. Cuba);
Ostrom and McIntosh 1966 (Marsh's dinosaurs at Yale);
Rataj 1960 (Benátsky Mus., Czechoslovakia);   Reekie 1964 (museums and exhibits);
    Rice, H. 1967 (Univ. Oregon Mus. Nat. Hist.);   Ripley 1965 (Smithsonian Inst.);
    Roig de Leuchsenring 1961 (Soc. Espeleol. Cuba);   Romer 1964E (Soc. Vert.
    Pal.), 1966B (Amer. Ass. Advanc. Sci.);
Schäfer 1964A (Senckenberg Mus.);   Schaeffer, B. 1968A (Amer. Mus. Nat. Hist.,
    N.Y.);   Schödube and Steinbacher 1967 (Senckenberg. Naturf. Gesell., Frankfurt
    am Main);   Schüz 1967 (Stuttgart Nat. Hist. Mus.);   Sibley 1963 (Los Angeles
    Co. Mus.);   Silva, P. H. D. H. 1966A, B (Ceylon museums);   Stirton 1958B
    (Univ. Calif. paleont.);   Struve 1967 (Senckenberg Nat. Hist. Mus.);   Sutcliffe
    1965 (Pengelly Cave Res. Center);
Teichert, C. 1967 (Gondwana symposium);   Tufty 1965 (museums);
Van Meter 1967 (federal aid to museums);
Walton, M. S. 1963 (Klein Geol. Lab., Yale Univ.);   Webber 1966 (Field Mus. Nat.
    Hist.);   Weller 1964 (Univ. Chicago paleont. dept.);   West, W. D. 1964 (Geol.
    Surv. India);   Williams, P. M. 1968 (Field Mus. Nat. Hist.);   Wong 1930 (Cenoz.
    Res. Lab., China);
Yochelson 1965 (Paleont. Soc.);
Zalkind 1963 (Moscow Univ. Mus.);   Zangerl 1965A (Field Mus. Nat. Hist.);   Zapfe
    1964E (Vienna Nat. Hist. Mus.).

REPORTS, NOTICES AND GUIDEBOOKS — Anon. 1960CH (Soc. for Amer. Archeol.),
    1961CS Soc. Espeleol., Cuba), 1962CI, 1965D (Field Mus. Nat. Hist., Chicago),
    1962CK (Munich Mus.), 1963CB (Neanderthal Mus., Düsseldorf), 1963CK, CM,
    1964BD, BE, BF, BG, 1966AV, 1968AF (Los Angeles Co. Mus.), 1964B, 1965B,
    C (ann rept. Carnegie Mus.), 1964D, 1965E (ann. rept. Santa Barbara Mus.),
    1964E (ann. rept. U.S. Nation. Mus.), 1964G (36th Internat. Congr. American-
    ists), 1964H (early man films, Univ. Nebraska), 1964BC, 1965Y (Univ. Bar-
    celona), 1965Q (anthrop. institutions), 1965V (congr. on prehist. and Quat.),
    1965AL (Stuttgart Mus.), 1965AR (NSF grant), 1965AT (ann. rept. Coryndon
    Mus.), 1965BL (Antrodemus, Los Angeles Co. Mus.), 1965BM (Brontotherium,
    Los Angeles Co. Mus.), 1965BO (Ratnapura Nation. Mus.), 1965BS, 1966AC
    (Santa Barbara Mus.), 1965CE (coelacanth, Univ. California, Los Angeles), 1966A
    (California Acadamy Sci.), 1966B (ann. rept. Smithsonian Inst.), 1966F (center
    for prehist., N. Italy), 1966K (dinosaur, Cleveland Mus.), 1966AN (Iowa State
    Archeol.), 1966AW (La Brea ground sloth, Oakland Mus.), 1966BQ (W. Afr.
    Archeol.), 1967B (Mus. Paleont., Univ. California, Berkeley), 1967Q (Nairobi
    Mus.), 1967X (E. New Mexico Univ.), 1968R (Mus. Comp. Zool., Harvard),
    1968Y (Univ. Reading Symposium);   Arambourg 1965A (Panafr. Congr. on Prehist.);
Bader, O. N. 1968B (symposium on Szeletian);   Balland 1964A (study courses on
    Pal.);   Biberson and Souville 1959 (5th INQUA Congr.);   Bishop and Clark
    1967A, B (Wenner Gren Symposium);   Black, D. 1930H (geol. meeting, Peking);
    Black and Grabau 1930 (Anglo-Amer. Assoc., Peking);   Bondarchuk and Shelkoplias
    1965 (7th INQUA Congr.);   Braslin 1967 (Yale Peabody Mus., electronic message
    system);   Brien 1964A (Roy. Zool. Soc. Belgium);   Bronowski and Hautecoeur
    1966A, B (Archeol. Folklore Mus., Belgium);   Bruce-Mitford 1961 (British Mus.);
Carmichael 1964 (Smithsonian Inst.);   Chollot 1964 (Piette collection Pal. Art, Mus.
    Antiquités Nation., Paris);   Chow 1965D (Inst. Vert. Pal. Palanthrop.);   Chudinov
    1964I (Soviet Meetings);   Clark, J. D. 1963D (5th Pan-Afr. Congr.), 1967C
    Confer. W. Afr. Archeol.);   Clarke, D. T. D. 1966 (Jewry Wall Mus., England);
    Colbert 1963F, 1964C, 1965B, C, 1966B (Amer. Mus. Nat. Hist.), 1968A (dino-
    saurs);   Collected Papers 1966F (conference of pathologists-anatomists, Latviia);

Conci 1966 (Milan Mus.);   Connah 1967A (Colloquim, Afr. archeol.);   Cook,
M. C. 1965, 1967, 1968 (Agate Fossil Beds Nation. Monument);   Crusafont
Pairo 1965A (Symposium, France), 1965I (Univ. Barcelona, Dept. Paleont.);
David, L. 1962, 1963, 1964 (Lyon Univ., Geol. Lab.);   Davies, O. 1967B (Burg-
Wartenstein Conf.);   Dragoo 1963 (archeol. conference, Carnegie Mus.);   Drake,
E. T. 1968 (Yale Peabody Mus. symposium);   Dunkle 1964A (Cleveland Nat.
Sci. Mus.);   Dutro 1968 (paleont. conferences);
Eisele and Schultz 1965 (mastodon, Univ. Nebraska Mus.);   Eller 1965A, B (Carnegie
Mus.);
Fabre 1965 (Mus. Hist. Nat. Marseille);   Fernandez-Galiano 1959 (Provincial Mus.,
Teruel, Spain);   Filip 1967 (7th Internat. Congr. Prehist., Protohist., Prague);
Flügel and Kollmann 1964 (Naturhist. Mus., Vienna);   Fradkin 1965 (USSR Mus.
Anthrop. Etnog.);   Freyberg 1965 (Keuper coll. of J. Kehl);   Friedmann 1965
(Los Angeles Co. Mus.);
Gofshtein 1965 (whales of the Geol. Mus. AN USSR, Kiev);   Gómez Millas 1960
(Choukoutien Mus., China);   González-Echegaray, J. and Garcia Guinea 1963
(Santander Prehist. Mus.);   Gorenstein 1967 (Mus. Nac. Antrop. Méx.);   Green,
R. C. 1966 (11th Pacific Sci. Congr.);   Gromov, V. I. 1964 (Paleolithic sympos-
ium, Moscow);   1967B (Early Up. Paleolithic symposium, Hungary);   Guliamova
et al. 1956 (Pal. artifacts of the Inst. Hist., Archeol., Ethnol., Acad. Sci., Tadzhik
SSR);
Hadži 1955 (Speleol. Congr., Jugoslavia);   Hagel 1965 (diorama of Iguanodon, Nieder-
sächsisches Mus.);   Hahn, K. 1964 (vert. paleont. lab., Los Angeles Co. Mus.);
Haldane 1960 (congr. on natural selection);   Hantke 1966 (INQUA);   Harland
et al. 1967A (symposium on the fossil record);   Harland, Smith and Wilcock
1964 (symposium on the Phanerozoic time scale);   Harrison, B. 1966 (archeol.
activities of Sarawak Mus.);   Haughton 1965A, 1967A, B, 1968 (reports, Bernard
Price Inst. Pal. Res., S. Afr.), 1965B (Rubidge Coll. Karroo verts., S. Afr.);   Heald
1963 (Ichthyosaur park, Nevada);   Heberer 1956H (Neanderthal centenary);
Hellman 1964, 1968 (Amer. Mus. Nat. Hist., N.Y.);   Helms 1961 (Berlin Nat.
Hist. Mus.);   Hertlein 1964 (Prionotropis branneri, Calif. Acad. Sci.);   Higgins
1964 (Internat. Speleol. Congr., Greece);   Hlavin 1965A, B, 1966 (Cleveland Nat.
Sci. Mus., fossil salvage program);   Hugot 1960A (Hamburg congr. prehist., 1958);
Hyatt 1967 (Ghost Ranch Mus.);
Iskiul and Taldykina 1962 (guide to the Karpinskii Geol. Mus., USSR);   Ivanova
1962 (INQUA, Poland);
Jarvik 1964B (Swedish Acad. Sci.);   Jazdzewski 1956 (Lódź Archaeol. Center, Po-
land);   Jelinek, A. J. 1965A (Lithic Technology Conf., France);   Jepsen 1964C
(Princeton Univ. Mus. Nat. Hist.);   Johnson, S. T. 1962 (mastodon dig at Bergen
Community Mus., New Jersey);
Kahlke 1960D (Thüringen Mus.), 1965B (Weimar Paleont. Coll.);   Katz, H. and M.
1965 (museums, U.S.A.);   Khlobystin 1964B (Inst. Archeol. Acad. Sci. USSR);
Klein, J. F. 1968 (Stuttgart State Mus. Nat. Hist.);   Kozay 1966 (Smithsonian
Inst., Washington);   Krauskoph 1967 (Geol. Soc. Amer.);   Kuhn-Schnyder 1962D,
1963E, 1964A, 1965A, 1966D (Univ. Zürich Paleont. Inst., Mus.), 1966B (Paleont.
Soc. Zürich);
L., E. 1966 (Florissant Natl. Mon., Colorado);   Lafond-Grellety 1963 (otoliths, Bor-
deaux Nat. Hist. Mus.);   Leakey, L. S. B. 1964A (Coryndon Mem. Mus.), 1964D
(Gamble's Cave Mus., Kenya), 1965A, 1966A, 1967A (Nairobi Nation. Mus.);
Lehman 1968 (vert. paleont. meeting);   Leich 1965 (verts. in Bavarian museums);
Lierl 1965 (Juras. verts. in Solnhofen Plattenkalk museums, Bavaria);   Lindsay,
G. E. 1964 (California Acad. Sci.);   Lipscomb 1964 (Los Angeles Co. Mus.);
Macdonald, J. R. 1966E (Los Angeles Co. Mus.), 1968 (curators);   McKenna 1967A
(Frick Lab., Amer. Mus. Nat. Hist.);   MacNeish 1961, 1962A (Tehuacan Archeol.-
Botan. Project, Mexico);   Malez 1963B, C (Yugoslav. Acad. Sci.);   Malinowski
1964 (Poznań Archeol. Mus.);   Martel San Gil and Aguirre 1964 (Mus. Pal. Mun.

Valencia); Matthes and Krumbiegel 1967 (Mus. Mitteldeutsche Erdges.); Mayr,
E. 1964A, 1965B, 1966, 1967A (Mus. Comp. Zool., Harvard); Megaw, A. H. S.
et al. 1968 (Brit. School Archaeol., Athens); [Mitchell, C. B.] 1960 (Chicago
Nat. Hist. Mus.); Młynarski 1966 (fossil turtles in Hungarian museums); Munn
1966 (Livingstone School of Archaeol., S. Afr.), 1967 (Bernard Price Inst. Paleont.,
S. Afr.); Murphy 1964, 1965 (Denver Mus. Nat. Hist.);
Neal and Akerley 1964, 1965 (Denver Mus. Nat. Hist.); Nelson, B. 1968 (new pro-
grams, Smithsonian Inst.); Nelson, N. C. 1924 (Amer. Mus. and European pre-
hist.); Nelson, McGregor and Gregory 1929 (Amer. Mus. Nat. Hist.); Netting
1966, 1967 (Carnegie Mus.); Neustupny 1967 (archeol. exhibit, Prague Nation.
Mus.); Nikiforova 1967 (Internat. Paleont. Colloquium);
Orlov, J. A. 1964C, 1965 (tertiary mammals, Internat. Geol. Congress, xxii. Session);
Pawloski 1968 (Dinosaur State Park, Connecticut); Peña Basurto 1964 (Munic. Mus.
San Telmo, San Sabastian); Pericot García 1963A (5th Panafr. Congr. Prehist.);
Phillipson 1964 (Livingstone School Archeol. and Prehist.); Pierret 1960 (Villars
Cave, France), 1961A (Pal. caves, France); Pinna 1965, 1967 (Mus. Civ. Sto. Nat.
Milano); Popova and Firshstein 1965 (Anthrop. Ethnog. Mus., USSR); Pringle
1967 (Jour. Nat. Hist.); Prokopec and Pařizková 1965 (7th Internat. Congr.
Anthrop. Ethnol., Moscow);
Regteren Altena and Möckel 1965 (Teyler's Mus., Netherlands); Ricqles 1967B
(Colloq. Internat. Paleont. Anat., Paris); Roberts, F. H. H. 1960, 1961B, 1962B,
1963B, 1964 (Bureau Amer. Ethnol.); Ross, D. M. 1964 (Univ. Alberta Field
Conference), 1965 (vert. paleont. in Canada, Univ. Alberta); Rousseau 1965
Mus. l'Homme, Paris); Roy 1964 (Geol. Surv. India); Rybakov 1966 (7th Inter-
nat. Congr. archeol.);
Schaeffer, B. 1967A (Amer. Mus. Nat. Hist., N.Y.); Schaub, H. 1964, 1965 (Basel
Nat. Hist. Mus.); Schaub, S. 1942F (Basel Nat. Hist. Mus.); Scheele 1965C
(Cleveland Nat. Hist. Mus.); Schobinger 1964 (35th Congr. Internac. Amer.);
Schultz, C. B. 1966 (Agate Spr. Nation. Mon., Nebraska); Segerblom, C. and
G. 1965 (Ichthyosaur State Mon., Nevada); Segman 1965 (Buffalo Mus. Sci.,
New York); Simons 1962E, 1964B (Yale Peabody Mus.), 1963H (Kline Geol.
Lab., Yale); Staesche 1966 (Stuttgart Nat. Hist. Mus.); Starck 1966A, Starck,
et al. 1967 (Internat. Primat. Congr.); Strouhal 1959B (Czech. Anthrop. Congr.);
Swauger 1968 (Carnegie Mus.);
Talmadge and Gilmore 1965 (Grand Canyon Caverns); Tax 1965 (anthrop. symposium);
Taylor, F. A. and Carmichael 1964 (U.S. Nation. Mus.); Thorndike 1968 (Mil-
waukee Public Mus.); Thurston 1968 (Internat. Geol. Congr.); Tobias 1965C
(Nat. Mus. Tanzania); Tringham 1967 (Russian Archeol. conf.); True 1960
(Smithsonian Inst.); Trusov 1940 (Ukrainian Inst. Archeol.);
Valsik and Vachold 1960 ("Slovenske Mus.", Bratislava, Czechoslovakia); Vlček
1959B (Internat. Neanderthal Conf.);
Wanke 1965 (Moscow Anthrop. Congr.); Wen 1966 (Inst. Vert. Paleont. Paleoanthrop.,
China); Wendel 1967 (Turkish Nat. Hist. Mus.); Westermann 1967 (Internat.
Paleont. Union); White, A. M. 1966 (Amer. Mus. Nat. Hist.); Williams, S.
1963 (S.E. Archeol. Conf.); Wirth 1966 (Dinosaur Nation. Park); Wolansky
1962 (Bochum Geol. Mus.); Wormington 1964A, 1965 (Denver Mus. Nat. Hist.);
Z., M. 1964 (Inst. Vert. Paleont. Paleoanthrop., China); Zapfe 1960E (diorama of
mammoth herd, Vienna Nat. Hist. Mus.); Zilch 1965 (Senckenberg Nat. Mus.);
Zuñiga 1966 (Copenhagen Zool. Mus.).

MUTATIONS — See: variation and heredity.

MYOLOGY — See: paleomyology.

NATURAL SELECTION — See: evolution; variation and heredity.

NEUROCRANIUM, NEUROLOGY – See: paleoneurology; skull.

NOMENCLATURE – See: terminology; Systematic Index.

OBITUARIES (see also: biographies) – Absolon, Karel (Filip 1961A; Strouhal, H. 1961.);
    Angress, Shimon (Reed, C. A. 1962.); Augusta, Josef (Špinar 1968.);
Bakalov, Petur Nikolov (Bonchev 1965.); Bataller, José Ramon (Almela Samper, A.
    1963.); Beninger, Eduard (Mitscha-Märheim 1964.); Biasutti, Renato (Fleure
    1965; Parenti 1965.); Black, Glenn A. (Kellar 1966.); Blanc, Alberto Carlo
    (Anon. 1961CR, 1962CO; Pericot García 1962B, 1963D; Zorzi 1961.); Blanc,
    Gian Alberto (Anon. 1967O.); Bluntschli, Hans (Strauss 1964A, B.); Bogachev,
    Vladimir Vladimirovich (Anon. 1966V.); Böhm, Jaroslav (Filip 1963.); Breuil,
    Henri (Agache, M. R. 1962; Anon. 1961CQ; Heller, F. 1961C; Nougier and
    Robert 1961; Ripoll Perelló 1962A; Roussot 1961.); Briusov, Aleksandr Iakovlevich
    (Raushenbakh 1967.); Brown, Barnum (Lewis, G. E. 1964A, B; Tatarinov, L. P.
    1964AC.);
Camp, Russell R. (Eaton 1968.); Camarate Andrade França, José (Teixeira 1965.);
    Carbonell, Virginia M. (Dahlberg 1966.); Cattoi, Noemi V. (Anon. 1965A.);
    Correa, Mendes (Pericot García, 1962A, 1963C.);
Dąmbski, Jerzy (Rosiński 1958.); Davis, D. Dwight (Anon. 1965O.); Dietrich,
    Wilhelm Otto (Daber 1965; Gross, W. 1964A; Hennig, E. 1965; Staesche 1964A.);
    Dollo, Louis (Bonté 1967.); Drennan, Matthew Robertson (Anon. 1966AY.);
Edinger, Tilly (Anon 1967P, AG; Romer 1967E.); Eickstedt, Egon Freiherr von
    Schwidetzky 1965; Vallois 1966A.); Engleheart, Francis Henry Arnold (Baden-
    Powell, 1965.);
Ford, James Alfred (Anon. 1968I; Webb, C. H. 1968.); Frick, Childs (Anthony, H.
    1966.);
Gaudron, Guy (Anon. 1965K.); Geist, Otto William (Skarland 1964.); Gessner,
    Conrad (Fischer, H. 1965.); Giddings, James Louis (Larsen 1966; Rainey 1965.);
    Glory, Abbé A. (L. B. 1967.); Gremiatskii, Mikhail Antonovich (Uryson 1964A.);
    Guthörl, Paul (Kneuper 1964.);
Haase, Ernst (Otto 1959.); Haldane, John Burdon Sanderson (Smith, J. M. 1965.);
    Heléna, Philippe (Pericot García 1962C, 1963B.); Hernández-Pacheco, Eduardo
    (Almagro Basch, M. 1964-65; Anon. 1965X, 1965BE; Crusafont Pairó 1965K;
    Jordá Cerdá 1965.); Hinton, Martin Alister Campbell (Savage, R. J. G. 1963B,
    1964B.); Holmes, Arthur (Anon. 1965AD; Cahen 1966.); Hussakof, Louis
    (Schaeffer, B. 1965C.);
Iakovlev, Nikolai Nikolaevich (Arendt and Goriacheva, 1967; Gekker 1967.);
Kadić, Otokar (Malez 1959E.); Kälin, Josef (Lampel 1966; Portmann, A. 1966.);
    Kudrin, Lavrentii Nikolaevich (Anon. 1966AU; Eberzin 1967.);
Lahner, Georg (Anon. 1963BS.); Lane, Henry Higgins (Hall, E. R. 1967.); Levin,
    Maksim Grigorevich (Michael 1964A; Uryson 1963.);
Macgowan, Kenneth (Hester, J. A. 1964.); Maleev, Eugenii Aleksandrovich (Rozhdest-
    venskii 1966B; Tikhomirov, V. V. and Paniutina 1967A.); Mefferd, Ralph L.
    (Mefferd 1965.); Mehl, Maurice G. (Anon. 1966O; Branson 1966; Ellison 1966.);
    Mennell, Frederick Philip (G. B. 1966.); Miller, Alden H. (D., J. 1965; Davis,
    J. 1967; Kurochkin 1966; M., P. 1967.); Mook, Charles Craig (Colbert 1968B.);
    Munthe, Henrik Vilhelm (Lundquist 1964.); Mydlarski, Jan (Stęślicka 1957.);
Nelson, Nels Christian (Mason, J. A. 1966.); Nigg, Theophil (Laur-Belart 1958.);
    Nordmann, Valdemar Johan Heinrich (Ødum 1964.);
Obruchev, Sergi Vladimirovich (Anon. 1965AK; Armand, et al. 1965.); Obruchev, Vladir
    Afanas'evich (Editorial Staff 1956; Murzaev 1956.); Obruchev, Vladimir Vladimiro-
    vich (Boiarkina, et al. 1966.); Orlov, Iurii Alexandrovich (Anon. 1967AF; Bog-
    danov, et al. 1966; Charig 1966; Flerov and Trofimov 1966; Obruchev, D. V. 1967C
    Tikhomirov, V. V. and Paniutina 1967B.); Overy, Charles (Sandford 1965.);
Pérez Temprado, Lorenzo (Vallespi 1957.); Petrbok, Jaroslav (Filip 1961B.);

Petrocchi, Carlo (R., R. 1956.); Peyer, Bernhard (Fischer, H. 1963; Piveteau 1963C; Schweizer 1963; Tatarinov, L. P. 1964AD.); Pittard, Eugene (Anon. 1963BW; Saint Périer 1962D; Sauter 1964.); Polikarpovich, K. M. (Anon. 1963 CQ.); Power, J. H. (Fock 1965.); Proshek, Frantishek (Boriskovskiĭ 1959D; Vlček 1959A.);

Ray, Cyrus N. (Harris, R. K. and Harris 1968; Wright, B. 1968.); Richter, Emma (Hecker 1961.); Richter, Rudolph (Hecker 1961.); Riggs, Elmer S. (Gregg, C. C. 1964.); Rivet, Paul (Anon. 1958BA.); Roberts, Frank H. H. (Anon. 1966Y; Stephenson 1967.); Royo y Gomez, José (Anon. 1962CJ; De Sola 1962; Rivero 1962.); Rudinskiĭ, M. Ĭa. (Danilenko 1959.); Ryan, Francis Joseph (Anon. 1964A.);

Saar, Rudolf (Pirker 1963.); Sánchez Jimenez, Joaquin (Fernández de Avilés 1963.); Schaub-Glück, Samuel (Crusafont Pairó 1964A; Trofimov 1964B.); Schmalhausen, Ivan Ivanovich (Ĭudin 1964; Makhotin 1964; Tatarinov, L. P. and Trofimov 1964, 1965.); Schramm, Eck Frank (Gunderson 1967.); Schweizer, Theodor (Laur-Belart 1956.); Skarland, Ivar (West, F. H. 1966.); Skutil, Josef (Barta 1966; Klíma, B. 1966B, C; Valoch 1965E.); Smith, Arthur George (Anon. 1964BV, 1965BH; Leslie and Sykes 1964.); Smith, Herschel C. (Davis, E. L. 1967B.); Smith, James L. B. (Anon. 1968AH; Greenwood 1968.); Socin, Costantino (Malaroda 1963.); Sorensen, Carl (Colbert 1965G.); Stehlin, Hans Georg (Schaub, S. 1941B.); Stekelis, M. (Anon. 1967AD.); Stirton, Ruben Arthur (Anon. 1966C; Camp, C. L., Clemens, Gregory and Savage 1967; Camp, C. L., Gregory and Savage 1967A, B; Kleinpell 1968.); Strong, William Duncan (Solecki and Wagley 1963.); Subba Rao, B. (Soundara Rajan 1962.); Swinnerton, Henry Hurd (Anon. 1967L; Kent 1967.);

Teriaev, Valentin Aleksandrovich (Menner 1967A.); Tikhomirov, M. N. (Alexandrov, V. A. 1965.); Tschumi, Otto (Laur-Belart 1960.);

Van Deinse, A. B. (Scheygrond 1965.); Vanderhoof, Vertress Lawrence (Anon. 1964AE; Camp, C. L. 1964, 1965A, B; Levorsen 1964.); Van Straelen, Victor (Corin 1965; Hindle 1964; Kraus, O. 1964A; Rioult 1964; Stubblefield 1965.); Vaufrey, Raymond (Bordes and Sonneville-Bordes 1967; Vallois 1967B.); Viana, Abel Gonçalves Martins (Russell Cortez 1963.);

Wade, Robert Theodore (Anon. 1968U.); Waring, Antonio, J., Jr. (Williams, S. 1966.); Weiler, Wilhelm (Anon. 1965CU.);

Yakovlev, Nikolai Nikolaevich (Anon. 1966R.);

Zamiatnin, Sergei Nikolaevich (Anon. 1961CU; Formozov 1959C.); Zeuner, Frederick Everard (H., S. E. 1965; Hollingsworth 1965; Summers 1964A; Valoch 1963.); Zhukov, B. S. (Bader, O. N. 1968C.); Zotz, Lothar F. (L. B. 1967.).

OCCURRENCES, MANNER OF BURIAL, PETRIFACTION, PRESERVATION, BIOSTRATONOMY, CHEMISTRY OF FOSSIL BONE — Abelson 1959A, B, 1963 (geochemistry); Akiyama, Ito and Sasaki 1968 (citric acid in fossil tusks); Anon. 1965CT (pseudofossils); Arata 1964 (mistaken rept. of peccary, Lousiana); Avnimelech 1962C (chalk cast fragment Carcharodon, Israel);

Bachinskiĭ 1965A (mammals, Odessa), 1965B (terrestrial vert.), 1966 (fossilization); Bachinskiĭ, Dublĭanskiĭ and Lysenko 1967 (Krasnaia cave, Crimea); Bachmayer 1964A (bird feathers, Austria); Benda, Heimbach and Mattiat 1962 (Keuper Bonebeds, N. W. Germany); Bilewicz 1960B (chem. of mammoth bones); Binford, L. R. 1965 (Lepus, Pennsylvania); Biske 1959 (Berezovka mammoth); Blackwood 1964 (bones and teeth); Blokh 1961 (Paleozoic fishes, USSR); Brain 1967C (bone weathering); Briggs, L. C. 1956B (human skeletons); Brooks, R. H. 1967 (bone analysis, Tule Springs, Nevada); Bush 1960 (tar pits, Peru);

Cappetta, Granier, and Ledoux 1967 (selachians, France); Carroll, R. L. 1965B (lungfish burrows, Michigan); Case, J. 1968 (fishes, New Jersey); Chmielewski, W. 1958A (cave animal bones, Poland); Chudinov 1968A (skin structure of theromorphs); Cleland 1965B (cave bones, Spain); Colbert 1968A (dinosaurs);

Crusafont Pairó 1961E (mammal sites, Spain);

Delair 1966A (ichthyosaur skull); Doberenz and Lund 1966 (collagen in Jurassic bone); Doberenz and Matter 1965 (nitrogen analysis of bone); Doberenz and Wyckoff 1967B (structure in fossil collagen); Drozdova and Blokh 1966 (amino-acids in bone); Dughi and Sirugue 1966 (fossilization of eggs); Dyson, J. L. 1962 (frozen mammoths);

Eaton 1964A (reptile predator and prey); Ennouchi 1965 (fluride in bone); Erbaeva 1965 (small mammals, Transbaĭkalia);

Fahlbusch, K. 1967 (fossils in calcium phosphate); Frey 1964 (Quat. lake and bog deposits); Frost, H. M. 1964, 1966B (bone biodynamics), 1966A (morphometry of bone); Fujiwara 1962 (biochemistry of fossils);

Gabe 1967 (skeleton); Garutt and Ĭur'ev 1966 (mummified horse, Siberia); Gehlen, K. v. 1959 (mineral content of Plateosaurus bone); Geller 1967 (mammoth, Siberia); Gibson, M. A. 1967 (histology of fossil bone); Glaessner 1963 ("intrusive" Pleist. verts. in Mioc., Australia); Göke 1967 (preservation of fossils); Gusev 1956 (frozen mammoths, Siberia); Guthrie, R. D. 1967 (large Pleist. mammals, Alaska);

Hapgood 1960 (frozen mammoths); Heller, W. 1966 (ichthyosaur "skin"), 1967 (conditions of preservation of collagen structures); Ho, Tong-yun 1965 (bone and tooth composition, Pleist. mammals), 1968 (collagen, body temp. of fossil mammals); Houston 1962, 1963 (heavy elements in Tert. bone); Houston, Toots and Kelley 1966 (iron content of Tert. bone);

Jacobson, K. W. 1965 (fissure, Missouri); Jelinek and Fitting 1965 (natural radioactivity); Johnson, R. G. 1968 (Mazon Creek soft-bodied marine faunas, Illinois);

Kabanov 1959 (burial of reptiles, USSR); Kauffman 1965 (concretions, nodules and septaria); Kauffman and McCulloch 1965 (verts. in glacial pond, Colorado); Kermack 1965A (fissure deposits); Kleinschmidt 1965 (mammals in stream deposits); Konnerth 1966 (swollen fish bones); Kovalev 1967 (thorium in fossil bone); Kruckow 1962 (lizard in amber); Kudrin, Sivkova and Martynova 1962 (chemistry of fossil fish, whale and dolphin bones);

Lazell 1965 (lizard in amber, Mexico); Lungu 1967B (conditions of burial of Mioc. mammals, Moldavia);

McCartney 1964 (study of human bone); Mazurczak 1968 (fossil fish swallowing another); Mchedlidze 1964C (cetaceans, Caucasus); Mehl 1966 (mammoth, Oklahoma); Mstislavskiĭ and Kochenov 1961 (Maikop fish remains);

Ochev 1967A (burial in Perm. and Trias., USSR); Odintsov 1962 (Plioc. karst cave fauna nr. Odessa);

Pawlicki, Korbel and Kubiak 1966 (dinosaur bone, Mongolia); Payne, M. M. and Scherschel 1966 (preservation of Olduvai); Pflug and Strübel 1968 (chemical composition of fossils); Popov, A. I. 1959 (Siberian mammoths); Popov, Ĭu. N. 1947A, B, 1948 (verts. in permafrost); Prikhod'ko 1962 (mummified amphibian skin);

Robinson, P. 1963B (fused cervical vertebrae, Wyoming); Romer 1964F (bone in early verts.);

Sacchi Vialli 1964A (organic substances in fossils); Sanderson 1960B (frozen mammoths); Schäfer 1964B (marine mammal skeletons), 1966 (otoliths); Schaeffer, B. 1965B (fishes); Schmid 1965 (rounded bone fragments); Shackelford and Wyckoff 1964 (collagen); Stevenson, J. S. and L. S. 1966 (fluorine in microsaur teeth); Stokes 1964 (sauropod stomach contents); Sultanov et al. 1966 (fossil fishes);

Tanabe 1966 (fluorine content of Pleist. human bone); Tarabukin 1968 (Deinotherium, Moldavia); Teichmüller 1962 (Oreopithecus fauna, Italy); Tobien 1965B (larval burrows in Pleist. bone); Toots 1963B (helical burrows), 1965A (disarticulation of mammal skel.), 1965B (random orientation), 1965C (orientation and distribution); Toots and Voorhies 1965 (strontium in bone); Troitskiĭ 1966 (preserved mammoth, USSR); Trzeciakowski 1964 (elephant, Poland);

Urist 1962 (chemistry of bone);

Vereshchagin 1951C (tarpits, USSR);

Whitmore 1967B, Whitmore et al. 1967 (elephants on continental shelf); Wyckoff, R. W. G. 1964B (collagen in vert. bones); Wyckoff and Doberenz 1965A (collagen in Pleist. teeth), 1968 (strontium in vert. fossils); Wyckoff, Doberenz and McCaughey 1965, Wyckoff, McCaughey and Doberenz 1964 (amino acids in Pleist. bone);

Zangerl 1964 (carbonif. fish traps, Indiana); Zapfe 1966C (traces on fossil bone).

ODONTOLOGY — See: dentition.

ONOMATOLOGY — See: terminology.

ONTOGENY — See: evolution; skeleton; skull.

OÖLITHS — See: eggs, eggshells.

ORIGINS — See: distribution; evolution; paleoanthropology; phylogeny.

ORNAMENTS — See: Paleolithic art.

ORTHOGENESIS — See: evolution; phylogeny.

OSTEOLOGY — See: dentition; paleoanthropology; paleopathology; skeleton; skull; variation and heredity.

OTOLITHS — See: faunas; skull (and Otolithu in Systematic Index).

PAINTINGS — See: Paleolithic art.

PALEOANTHROPOLOGY, PALEOLITHIC CULTURES, PHYSICAL ANTHROPOLOGY, PREHISTORY (see also: behavior; cultural remains associated with faunas; habits and habitats; Paleolithic art; paleopathology; paleopsychology; religion; restorations) — This section has been broken down in the following manner:

I GENERAL AND MISCELLANEOUS (including articles dealing exclusively with the the Old World)

II EUROPE

    A General

    B Western Europe

        1. General

        2. Alphabetical listing of countries

    C Central and eastern Europe

        1. General

        2. Alphabetical listing of countries

    D USSR

III ASIA

    A General

    B Near East (Asia Minor)

        1. General

        2. Alphabetical listing of countries

    C Southern and eastern Asia (including Indonesia and the Philippines)

        1. General

        2. Alphabetical listing of countries

IV AUSTRALIA AND NEW ZEALAND

PALEOANTHROPOLOGY – GENERAL AND MISCELLANEOUS – A., J. A. 1966 (prehist., protohist.); Alekseev, V. A. 1959 (origin of man); Alexandersen 1963 (human canines), 1967A (Neanderthals); Alimen 1965B (atlas of prehist.); Allchin 1966 (Stone Age hunters, Old World); Alpysbaev, Kh. A. 1966 (stone tools); Anderson, J. E. 1962 (human skel.); Angel, J. L. 1967 (palaeodemography); Angelov 1967 (Homo habilis); Angelroth 1961A (Up. Pal. scrapers); Anon. 1860, 1968X (early man), 1962CC, 1964M, 1965BU, BW (evol. of man), 1962CD (dates, Zinjanthropus), 1962CE (Zinganthropus and hominid evol.), 1963CP (origin of man), 1964AP (Homo habilis), 1964BN (uses of Stone Age knives), 1964BQ (man's ancestry), 1965AX (Stone Age glue), 1965BX (speech), 1965CC (new name for Homo habilis), 1966AG (nomenclature, early man), 1966AR (Homo erectus), 1967S (Afr. prehist.), 1967BF (unpalatable man), 1968D (dating ancestor of man and ape), 1968V (new developments); Arambourg 1963H (Pal. cultures, Afr. and Europe), 1965C (origin of man); Augusta and Burian 1960B (evol. of man), 1962D (ancient hunters), 1964A (campfires, Old Stone Age);

Babkin 1964 (reflexes of primates); Bacon 1963 (vanished peoples); Bailit and Friedlander 1965, 1966 (dental reduction in man); Baker and Weiner 1966 (human adaptability); Baldwin, G. C. 1963 (man's beginnings); Basu 1963 (prehist. man); Bates 1967B (early man); Beals and Hoijer 1963, 1965 (introduction to anthrop.); Beardsley et al. 1956 (community patterning); Bergner 1965 (modern theories on early man); Bilewicz 1960A (Sinanthropus); Binford, L. R. and S. R. 1966A (cultural levels), 1966B (variation of Mousterian); Binford, S. R. 1965 (Mousterian); Bliebtreu 1967 (physical anthrop.); Boas 1965 (general anthrop.); Boca 1961 (surv. of anthrop.); Bordes 1965A (utilization of Up. Pal. burins), 1965B, 1967 (typology and classif. of Pal. industries); Boriskovskiĭ 1961D (ancient digging tools); Bosinski 1965 (Mid. Pal. chips); Bourdier 1960C (human evol.); Brabant 1965, 1967 (evol. of hominid teeth); Brabant and Kovacs 1961 (taurodontism in man); Brace 1964, 1968 (Neanderthals), 1965A, B (early man dentition), 1967 (human evol.); Brace et al. 1966 (loss of hair in man); Brace and Molnar 1967 (human tooth weat); Brace and Montagu 1965 (man's evol.); Braun 1963 (anthrop. technique); Bresler 1966 (human ecology); Breuil and Lantier 1965 (men of the Old Stone Age); Briggs, L. C. 1956B (human skels.); Bronowski 1965 (identity of man); Brothwell 1962B (scientific revolution in archeol.); Brues 1966 (hominid teeth and jaws);

Brues and Snow 1965 (physical anthrop.); Bruna 1963 (early man); Buettner-Janusch 1966 (origins of man); Bugyi 1963 (paleoendocrinology); Bunak 1959C, 1966B, 1968 (human skull), 1959B, 1966C (origin and development of speech); Bunak et al. 1966 (fossil hominids and origin of man); Buttin 1965 (projectiles); Butzer 1964 (Pleist. environment and archeol.), 1967 (Late Pleist. chronol.);

Cailleux 1964A (dating prehist. industries); Caldwell, J. R. 1966 (archeol.); Campbell, B. G. 1964A (Homo habilis), 1966, 1967 (human evol.), 1968 (Australopithecus); Campbell and Goldby 1942 (finds of prehist. man); Carrington 1965 (early man); Chailley 1965 (history of music); Chalus 1963 (man and religion); Chardin 1962F, 1964B (human phenomenon), 1964A (future of man), 1965B (human evol.); Chardin et al. 1965, 1968 (evol. and religion); Chernysh 1967 (nomenclature of Late Pal. tools); Cheynier 1965A, 1967 (Stone Age man), 1963B (Perigordian not valid), 1966 (Magdalenian and Azilian industries); Childe 1965 (evol. of culture); Clark, Ascher, Freeman et al. 1965 (Pleist. culture and living sites); Clark and Howell 1966A, B (Old World paleoanthrop.); Clark, J. G. D. 1960, 1961 (archeol. and society), 1964 (world prehist.), 1966 (prehist. and human behavior), 1967 (Stone Age hunters); Clark and Piggott 1965 (prehist. societies); Clark, W. E. LeGros 1964A (human evol.), 1964B, 1966 (origin of man), 1965A (hist. of primates), 1965B (relation of sciences); Cliquet 1965 (anthrop.); Cole, S. 1966A (races of man); Coles 1966 (functional archeol.); Comas 1965, 1966 (physical anthrop.), 1967 (unity and variety in the human species), 1968 (definition of the human genus); Connah 1967B (use of the term "culture"); Cook, S. F. 1964 (charcoal from archeol. sites); Cook and Heizer 1965 (chemical analysis of archeol. sites); Coon 1961 (Neanderthals), 1967A, B (races of man); Coon and Hunt 1965 (living races of man); Coppens 1961B, 1966B (human paleont.); Cornwall 1964, 1966 (early man), 1968 (prehist. animals and hunters); Courville 1967 (cranial injuries in prehist. man); Crusafont Pairó 1964D (evol. of man), 1965G (Oreopithecus);

Dahr 1952 (Australopithecinae); Dąmbski 1957 (unity of human species); Daniel, G. 1966, 1967 (hist. and development of archeol.); Dart, R. A. 1965C (osteodontokeratic culture), 1965F (origin of man), 1965H (bone tool felled a tree), 1966C (bone artifacts, France, S. Afr.); Dart and Craig 1962, 1963 (missing link); Darwin 1966 (evol. of man); Dastugue 1967 (Cro-Magnon pathology); Daumas 1962 (hist. of techniques); Dawson, W. R. 1967 (evidence of disease in early hominids); Day 1965, 1968 (human paleont.); Debelmas 1963 (origin of man); Deetz 1967 (archeol.); De la Calle 1967 (human evol. on Cuban stamps); De Laet 1960 (archeol.); Delfgaauw 1965 (hist. of man); Dennis 1967 (museum program for high school students); Deuel 1966 (origin of man and culture); DeVore, I. 1964 (evol. of social life); DeVore, P. L. 1965 (origin of man); Dickinson 1962 (Stone Age man, juv.); Dietrich 1948C (origin of man); Diop 1963 (evol. of Negro); Dobzhansky 1964A, 1965B, 1966B (evol. of man), 1964B-1965A. 1966A (heredity), 1967 (man's future); Dragoo 1963 (archeol. conference, Carnegie Mus.); Duarte 1962 (prehist. art, magic); Dubos 1965 (man adapting); Ducros 1967 (occipital in man); Due Rojo 1965 (origin and evol. of Solutrean culture; origin of hominids);

Edwards 1965 (earliest hominids), 1967A (hominid muzzle reduction); Ehrenberg 1961B (cave bears and hunters); Ehrich 1965 (chronologies in Old World archeol.); Eiseley 1965 (man, past and future); Epstein 1964 (artifacts and tools); Erich 1965 (Old World archeol.); Ewer 1965B (bipedalism of man);

Fenart and Heim 1968 (Neanderthals); Ferembach 1964 (sex ratio of man); Feustel 1968 (protolithic and osteodontoceratic cultures); Filip 1967 (7th Internat. Congr. Prehist., Protohist., Prague); Firu 1963 (stomatology); Flight 1967 (cultural taxonomy); Follett 1965 (fish remains in archeol. sites); Folsom 1966 (early man); Formozov 1957C (Stone Age tools as ethnic characteristics); Franke 1966 (early man); Fridrich, Klíma and Valoch 1968 (systematics of "culture"

concept); Frisch 1965 (hominid dentition); Frolov 1965, 1966A (numeration
in the Pal. and origin of math.); Fuchs, S. 1963 (origin of man); Furon 1966
(manual of prehist.); Fusté 1966 (Australopithecinae);

Gabel 1964A, B (prehist. man), 1967A (prehist. economic patterns); Garn 1964
(culture and human evol.), 1965 (human races); Garn et al. 1966 (human molar
pattern and taxonomy); Garn, Lewis and Kerewsky 1964 (relative molar size
and fossil taxonomy); Garrod and Clark 1965 (early man, Egypt, Asia, Europe);
Gatehouse 1965 (human evol. and the arched foot); Geertz 1964 (culture and
evol. of man); Geertz et al. 1965 (anthrop. research); Genet-Varcin 1966B
(Plesianthropus), 1967 (Australopithecus); Genovés 1961 ("tropical Neanderthals"),
1962B (physical anthrop.), 1962C (determining age and sex), 1965B (physical
anthrop., 1963); Genovés et al. 1966 (yearbook physical anthrop., 1964), 1967
(yearbook physical anthrop., 1965); Gerasimov, M. M. 1964B (Stone Age men);
Giles 1966 (sex and race determination); Glass 1966 (hairlessness in man);
Gokhman 1966B (Late Pal. man); Goldby 1940 (recent discoveries of human
fossils); Golding 1955 (Pal. man, fiction); Gorenstein 1965 (introduction to
archeol.); Goustard and Grapin 1964 (Zinjanthropus); Goździewski 1959 (races
of Pal. man); Grahmann and Müller-Beck 1966 (early man); Greene, C. F.
1967 (lithology and technology of flint tools); Gregory, W. K. 1939D (origin
of human dentition); Grelaud 1963 (classification of hand axes); Gremiatskii
1961B (morphological features of bone of early man), 1966 (Meganthropus,
Gigantopithecus), 1968 (systematics of fossil hominids); Grigor'ev 1965A (Up.
Pal. migrations), 1965B (Near East and human migration to Europe); Grimm
1961B (anthrop. as part of biol.); Gromov, V. I. 1945C, 1960, 1964 (stratig.
of the Pal.), 1961B, C (Pal. age determinations);

Hammond 1964 (physical anthrop. and archeol.); Harrison et al. 1964 (human evol.);
Hawkes and Woolley 1965 (hist. of man); Haynes 1964A (paleoecol. and archeol.);
Heberer 1956H (Neanderthal centenary), 1964C (evol. of man), 1965A (100
years of anthrop.), 1965C (Australopithecinae), 1967C (Ramapithecus), 1968
(origin of man); Heberer and Kurth 1966 (Gigantopithecus), 1966B (evol. of man),
1962 (origin of man); Heintz, A. 1964C (Gigantopithecus), 1966B (evol. of man),
1966C (Homo habilis); Heintz, Nicole 1966A, B, 1967A, B (hominid skull –
evol., variability); Heinzelin de Braucourt 1961C (Up. Pal. archeol.), 1962C
(typology of lithic industries); Helmuth 1968 (australopithecine stature); Hemmer
1964B, 1965A, 1967A (allometric studies of hominid skulls), 1965B (biotops of
Pleist. hominids); Henschen 1966A, B (the human skull); Hewes 1964 (hominid
bipedalism); Heyerdahl 1964 (pre-Columbian ocean routes), 1966 (transoceanic
contacts); Hiernaux 1963A (origin of man), 1963B (origin of races); Hillaby
1965A (discovery of fossil man); Hockett and Ascher 1964 (evol. of human
behavior); Hodges 1964 (primitive technology); Hoebel 1966 (study of man);
Hofer 1964, 1965 (primate skull and brain); Hogg 1962 (biol. of man); Hole
and Heizer 1965 (prehist. archeol.); Hollitscher 1964 (origin of man); Holloway
1966A (parameters for evol. of hominid brain and behavior), 1966B ("mutation
pressure" and structural reduction in human evol.), 1967 (relation of canine reduction to tool-use and tool-making); Holmes 1965 (introduction to anthrop.);
Howell, F. C. 1964B (the hominization process), 1967B (recent advances in
human evol. studies); Howell and Editors of Life 1965 (early man); Howells
1963 (early man), 1965 (phys. anthrop.), 1967 (human evol.); Howells et al.
1965 (synthesis and evol.); Hughes and Brothwell 1966 (earliest populations
of man, Europe, W. Asia, N. Afr.); Hulse 1963A (teaching physical anthrop.),
1963B (introduction to physical anthrop.); Hulse and Lamb 1963 (trends in
physical anthrop.); Humbard 1967 (pebble tools); Hunt 1967 (living races of
man); Huxley, T. H. 1963 (man in nature);

Iakimov 1947D (Meganthropus, Gigantopithecus), 1963 (man's evol.), 1966 (Australopithecinae); Imanishi 1968 (evol. toward human societies); Ivanova 1965B,
D, 1967 (hominid stratig.), 1965C (paleoanthrop. and duration of Quat.), 1965E,

paleont.); Morris, D. 1967A, B (social development of man); Moss and Young
1964 (hominid craniology); Mukerjee 1963 (bio-philosophical aspect of human
evol.); Müller-Beck 1961B (Up. Pal. archeol.), 1961C, 1966D (Pal. cultures, N.
Eurasia and N. Amer.), 1966B ("artifacts" perhaps not man-made), 1966C (Pal.,
Europe, Afr., Asia); Müller-Karpe 1966 (Old World Pal.); Mumford 1965, 1967
(technics and the nature and development of man);

N. 1960 (biol. and cultural origins of man); Naora 1963 (life of prehist. man); Napier
1964B, D (bipedalism in hominds); Narr 1964B (prehist.), 1966B (Early, Mid.
Stone Age hunters and gatherers), 1966C (earliest traces of culture), 1966E (Pal.
social and religious life), 1966G (Pal. industries, Asia, Afr., Australia); National
Academy of Science 1965 (time and strat. in evol. of man); Nelson, N. C. 1919
(origin and distribution of human culture); Nemeskéri 1963 (human paleont.);
Nesturkh 1964B, 1968A (hominization), 1964C (modern anthrop.); Neuman
1967B (bone uprights); Nicolǎescu-Plopşor, D. 1963 (physical anthrop. and arch-
eol.); Nicolǎescu-Plopşor and Floru 1963 (paleoanthrop. and hist. of medicine);
Nikitiŭk 1967 (hominid cranial suture obliteration); Nordmann 1936C, 1946
(Peking man), 1939 (early man);

Oakley 1963E (man the tool-maker), 1964A, 1966B (man's antiquity), 1964B, 1966A
(dating fossil man); Odhner 1964 (social life of Australopithecinae and Pithecanthropus); Oliver 1964 (introductory anthrop.); Olivier 1965B (evol. and man),
1965C (primate anat.), 1967A, B (facial structure of fossil man); Olsen 1966,
1968A (verts. in archeol. collections), 1967 (osteology in archeol.); Oppenheimer
1964 (australopithecine tooth crowding); Oschinsky 1962 (racial groups of Homo),
1963A (human races), 1963B (parallelism in Homo); Oschinsky et al. 1964 (origin of Homo sapiens); Overhage 1964 (evol. of man);

Padberg 1967 (hominisation); Peiper 1963 (evol. of man); Peña Basurto 1959 (Oreopithecus); Penniman 1965 (hist. anthrop.); Pfeiffer 1966 (early man); Piggott
1963 (early man); Pilbeam 1966A (Dryopithecinae), 1968A (hominids); Pilbeam
et al. 1965 (human origins); Pilbeam and Simons 1965 (hominid classification);
Piveteau 1962E (origin of man), 1967B (definitions of man), 1968 (human paleont.);
Porshnev 1958 (origin of human culture); Portmann, A. 1965A (origin of man);
Powers 1963 (early man, juv.); Pradel, L. 1961C (cultures, Europe), 1965B (material for artifacts), 1965C (method for study of stone tools), 1966D (classification
of burins), 1966E (Mousterian to Perigordian), 1966F (pointed artifacts); Prost
1964 (human evol.); Puliànos 1965 (Petralon man); Pyddoke 1963 (scientific
methods in archeol.);

Radmilli 1963D (early man); Ratcliff 1965 (origin of man); Reed, C. A. 1967
(Homo habilis); Rensch 1965 (Homo sapiens); Reshetov 1966 (origin of man);
Robbins and Irving 1966 (archeol. handbook); Robinson, J. T. 1963B (australopithecines), 1964B, 1965B (evol. of man), 1965A, 1966 (Homo habilis); Rodnick
1966 (evol. of man), Roginskiĭ 1957B, 1964 (origin of man), 1959 (early man),
1966B (early man, USSR, China, Afr.); Roginskii and Levin 1955, 1963 (anthrop.);
Rokhlin 1965 (diseases of early man); Ronen 1965 (Aurignacian tools); Rosenfeld 1964B (archeol. of caves), 1965 (archeol.); Rouse 1965B (early man); Rudenkо
1963 (methods in archeol.); Ruffié 1967B (origin of man); Ruppé 1966 (archeol.
surveys); Rusconi 1964B (early man, Argentina); Russell, G. E. 1967B (projectile points); Rust 1965B (weapons and tools); Rybakov 1967 (archaeol., 1966),
1968 (archeol., 1967);

Sackett 1964, 1968 (statistical applications in stone tool analysis); Sahly 1965
(Languedocian culture); Saller 1964B (skull character and race), 1964C (phys.
anthrop.); Sankalia 1964A (Stone Age tools); Sarich 1967A (man's place in
nature); Sauter 1966A (anthrop.); Schott 1962B (Oreopithecus); Scotti 1965
(cave man); Seddon 1966A (archeol. centers); Semenov, Iu. I. 1965, 1967A
(cultural periods), 1966 (origin of man), 1967B (comments on "Ancient Society");
Semenov, S. A. 1957D, 1959B, 1961B, 1964B, 1965 (prehist. technology), 1958
(australopithecine tools), 1968A (tool-making and intellect), 1968B (prehist. tools);

Sen and Ghosh 1966 (prehist.); Sergi 1961 (paleoanthrop.); Shannon 1962 (Paleo-Indians, juv.); Shelkovnikov 1964 (origin of labor); Shovkoplias 1965B (Pal. migrations); Shutler, M. and R. 1967 (origin of Melanesians); Siegel 1959, 1962, 1963, 1965, Siegel and Beals 1967 (anthrop. rev.); Silverberg 1964 (early man); Silvester 1963 (flint implements); Simons 1967B (primate paleont.); Simpson, G. G. 1966A (human ethics), 1966C, J (biol. nature of man); Slobin et al. 1965 (language); Slotkin 1965 (early anthrop.); Smolla 1965 (use of caves by early man); Sollberger 1968 (flake knife); Spencer and Johnson 1960 (anthrop. atlas); Spier et al. 1961-62 (anthrop. teaching aids); Spirkin 1959 (origin of language); Spuhler 1954B, Spuhler and Heglar 1962 (phys. anthrop.); Spuhler 1964 (hominid evol.); Stolyhwo 1965 (human fossils); Straus and Cave 1964 (Neanderthal posture); Strouhal 1961B (australopithecines); Sviatenko 1966 (use of "batons"); Swadesh 1965 (origin of language); Swatzbaugh 1967 (man and tools); Swauger and Wallace 1964 (skinning tools);

Tappen 1966 (human evol.); Taute 1965 (bone and stone artifacts); Tax 1962B, 1964 (anthrop.); Teixeira 1963 (origin of man); Termier, H. and G. 1961, 1966 (evol. of man); Thoma 1964 (Mongoloid race), 1965 (Neanderthals); Titiev 1963 (anthrop.); Tixier 1967 (classification of stone tools); Tobias 1965D (tool-making Homininae); Tobias and Koenigswald 1964 (comparison of Afr. and Java hominids); Torgersen 1965 (early man); Trigger 1965 (origin of races);

Underwood, L. 1965 ("batons"); Uryson 1965B (origin of man), 1966A (Pithecanthropus);

Vallois 1964 (social life of early man), Van Horn 1966 (tool making); Various authors 1965 (evol. of man); Verheyleweghen, J. and F. 1961 (hunting weapons); Vlček 1964C, 1965A (Neanderthal); Vogel, Ch. 1966B (primatology); Vojkffy 1962 (Stone Age hunting); Vollmer 1964 (early man);

Walensky 1964 (mastoid of early man); Walter 1962 (myths on origin of man); Washburn 1964 (origin of races), 1965, 1967 (human evol.); Washburn and DeVore 1964 (social behavior, apes, early man); Wauchope 1956 (seminars in archeol.); Weiner 1964 (evol. of man); Wendt, H. 1963, 1965B (early man); Wescott 1966A (evol. of language), 1966B (Neanderthal man and the origin of speech); Wiercinski 1961 (hominid skull); Wilf and Merlin 1964 (early man); Wilkie 1965 (tools); Wilmsen 1968 (stone artifacts); Witthoft 1968 (stone hammers); Wolanski 1957A, B, 1958 (human evol.); Woo, Ju-kang 1964H (human evol.); Woodall 1968 (statistics in archeol.);

Yamanouchi et al. 1964, Yamanouchi and Sato 1964 (Pal.);

Zamiatnin 1960 (Pal. economy); Zihlman 1967 (size in Australopithecus); Zotz 1964B (Mid. Pal.).

PALEOANTHROPOLOGY — EUROPE

GENERAL — Badoux, D. M. 1965 (Neanderthal differentiation); Banesz 1965B (Aurig. in Europe); Baudet 1968 (peopling of Europe and problems of chronol.); Beer 1965A (genetics and prehistory);

Collins, D. M. 1965B (stone technology);

Del Real 1963 (Mousterian cultures);

Ehrenberg 1966E (osteodontokeratic culture, Makapansgat and Teufelslucken);

Felix 1966 (Up. Pal. artifacts); Filip et al. 1966 (European prehist.);

Howell, F. C. 1966 (earlier phases of Low. Pal.);

Iakimov 1961C (variety in Late Pal. populations); Ivanova 1962 (INQUA, Poland);

Jelinek, A. J. 1965A (Lithic Technology Conference); Jelinek, J. 1964B (early man relationships);

Kindler and Kiefer 1963 (X-ray studies of Neanderthal skulls); Klima, B. 1961F (Aurignacian and Gravettian, E. and Cent. Europe), 1966A (Late Pal. cultures); Kozłowski, J. K. 1964B (Aurignacian and Szeletian influences);

Laplace 1966C (analytical typology of lithic complexes, cent. Europe); Lumley 1965A (racial and cultural revolutions of Würm II - III);

Müller-Beck 1959 (Up. Pleist. archeol. sites, Mid. Europe), 1965A (Pal. cultures, Mid. Europe);

Nelson, N. C. 1915 (caves and early man), 1921 (recent archeol. activities), 1924 (European prehist. and the Amer. Mus.);

Schild 1961 (Masovian cycle), 1963, 1965 (prehist. cultures); Schobinger 1959C (Neanderthal man), 1966 (Alpine Paleolithic);

Uslar and Narr 1964 (prehist.);

Van Valen 1966B, 1967D (human races); Vlček 1967 (Neanderthal, Europe).

WESTERN EUROPE

GENERAL — Brabant and Twiesselmann 1964 (evol. of human teeth); Brown, D. F. 1959A, 1962 (COWA surveys, W. Europe), 1959B, 1964 (COWA surveys, W. Mediterranean);

Daniel and Evans 1967 (prehist., W. Mediterranean); De Laet and Thomas 1965 (COWA surveys, W. Europe); Diego 1962 (Pal. "perforated sticks" of Basque country);

Filzer 1966 (Pal. cultures, N. Alps);

Kozłowski, J. K. 1966A (origin of Aurignacian);

Lavocat 1966 (atlas of prehist. — Pleist. fauna and flora); Lumley 1964 (industries and mammal faunas, Maritime Alps);

Römisch-Germanisches Zentralmuseum, Mainz 1966 (COWA surv., W. Europe);

Schmid 1965 (rounded bone frags.); Schoch 1963B (bone tools, Germany, Italy); Smith, P. E. L. 1964C, 1965B (Solutrean culture); Sonneville-Bordes 1966A (Up. Pal. W. Europe);

Vallois 1965F (Galley Hill skel. rejected);

Waechter 1964 (artifacts, Gorham's Cave, Gibraltar).

AUSTRIA — Beninger 1936 (Pal., Drosendorf); Berg, F. 1966 (Up. Pal., Eggenberg);

Ehrenberg 1962D (bored cave bear vertae., Salzonfen Cave);

Felgenhauer 1962, 1966 (artifacts, Up. Pal. sites, Lower Austria); Franz and Neumann 1965 (archeol. sites);

Mottl 1966D (Aurignacian artifacts, Tirol);

Pittioni 1964 (prehist.);

Trimmel 1965 (Pal. caves);

Zotz 1965C (Aurignacian bone points, Tischoferhöhle, Tirol).

BELGIUM — Angelroth 1960A (flint blades, Faulx-les-Tambes), 1960B, 1961B, 1963 (industries, Goyet-Mozet);

Danthine and Faider-Feytmans 1963, 1966 (summary of current Paleo. research); Deconinck 1962A (Pal., Enclus Mt.); De Laet et al. 1963, 1964 (bibliog. archeol.); De Laet and Trimpe Burger 1964 (archeol., Zeeland); Dacquier-Huart 1961A (burin), 1961B (Up. Pal., Liège and Namur); Doize 1960 (Magdalenian harpoon, Verlaine);

Heinzelin de Braucourt 1963C (Mousterian, Rupel R.);

Schendel 1965 (Pal. site, Leudal); Soetens 1960 (Pal., Ottignies);

Van Noten 1967 (Tjongerien artifacts);

X. 1959 (Pal., Neer, Limburg).

DENMARK — Hansen, S. 1965 (Pal. cultures);

Linderoth-Wallace and Swauger 1966 (Pal. flint artifacts, Bromme);

Møhl-Hansen 1954 (deer bones split by man, Hollerup).

FRANCE — Agache 1958F (Pal. research, Somme); Agache, Bourdier and Petit 1964 (Pal., Somme Valley); Alimen 1964A (Pal., Hautes Bruyeres); Andrieu and Dubois 1966 (Noailles Cave); Anon. 1963BR (Lower-Mid. Pal., Meuse),

(Mousterian teeth, Lot);   Genet-Varcin and Miquel 1967 (Magdalenian skull, Bruniquel);   Grigor'ev 1963B (origin of Aurignacian culture);   Gruet 1964 (Pal. industries, Loir-Sarthe);   Gruet and Jaouen 1964 (Mousterian and Aurignacian artifacts, Bois Milet);   Guichard 1964 (Pal., Bergeracois Plateau), 1965 (Late Acheulian, Cantalouette);   Guillien 1965A (Mousterian occupation, Angouleme), 1965C (Pal. hunting, Angouleme), 1965D (Aurignacian industry, Angouleme and Mansle);   Guillien and Duport 1960 (Mousterian industry, Charente);
Haeck 1964 (Mont Falise Cave, Antheit);   Heim 1968 (Neanderthals, Dordogne); Henri-Martin 1964, 1965A (La Quina site, Charente), 1965B (Fontechevade Cave), 1966 (Neanderthal, La Quina site);   Hermens 1965 (Pal. industry, Haute-Loire); Hariot 1965 (microlithic Magdalenian industry, Viry);
Jardel and Roussot 1967 (Low. Magdalenian bone industry, Dordogne);   Joshi 1964 (Pal. cave sites);   Jude and Arambourou 1961 (Perigordian industry, Bourdeilles);
Kelley, H. 1965 (rare artifacts);
Lachastre 1964B (La Grotte la Martine, Dordogne);   Laming-Emperaire 1964 (hist. of archeol.);   Laplace 1965 (Châtelperronian industry, Chèvre Cave, Dordogne), 1966B (Pal. industries, Pays Basque);   Laurent 1966 (Pal. artifacts, Lot);   Lejards 1965 (Pal. artifacts, Nord-Agenais);   Leroi-Gourhan, André 1964A, B (Pincevent Magdalenian site, Siene-et-Marne), 1965B (Châtelperronian man and industry, Arey-sur-Cure, Yonne);   Leroi-Gourhan, A. and A. 1964 (chronol. of the caves of Arcy-sur-Cure;   Lumley 1962B (Pal., Vaucluse), 1965B (Mousterian industry, Abri Breuil), 1967 (Acheulian habitation site of Terra Amata, nr. Nice); Lumley and Berard 1964 (Mousterian industries of the Cabasse Basin);   Lumley, Gagnière and Pascal 1963 (Vallonnet Cave pebble culture, Cap Martin);   Lumley and Isetti 1965 (Mousterian industries at San Francesco, San Remo, and Tournal Cave, Aude);   Lwoff 1963 (bone needles from Up. Pal. sites);   Lynch, T. F. 1966 (the "Lower Perigordian");
MacGregor, A. B. 1964 (Le Moustier mandible, Dordogne);   Maubeuge 1961 (the Pal. in Lorraine);   Mellars 1965 (Mousterian sequence and development, S. W.); Méroc 1963A (prehist., Petites-Pyrénées), 1963B, 1964 (Montmaurin mandible, Haute-Garonne), 1965 (Languedocian industry, Haute and Moyenne Valley); Monméjean, Border and Sonneville-Bordes 1964 (Up. Perigordian culture, Lot-et-Garonne);   Morlet 1962 (Glozel);   Movius 1962, 1964, 1965, 1966B (Up. Perigordian and Aurignacian occupations, Abri Pataud, Les Eyzies), 1966A (hist. of the study of flint gravers);
Necrasov 1962 (Up. Pal. child's tooth, "La Adam" Cave, Dobrogea);
Octobon 1965 (Lazaret Cave, Nice);
Paccard 1964 (Up. Pal. artifacts, Chinchon);   Parent and Savy 1963 (Levalloisian-Mousterian culture, Rochères);   Patte 1964B (Magdalenian infant), 1967 (bone and stone tools, Sempigny), 1968 (Azilian man, Saint-Rabier);   Peyrony 1959 (tourist guide, Vézère);   Pintaud 1961 (Montgaudier Caves, Charente);   Piveteau 1961V (human astragalus, Simar Cave), 1964A, 1966A (early man, Regourdon Cave), 1965 (human fossils, Charente), 1967A (human fossils, Lazaret Cave); Planquaert 1962 (Mousterian, Enclus);   Pradel, L. 1963C (Mousterian, Fontmaure), 1964B (artifacts, Vicq-Exemplet), 1965A, 1966A (burins, Raysse), 1965D (artifacts, Pouligny-Saint-Pierre), 1966B (Mousterian artifacts), 1966C (Fontmaure site destroyed), 1967 (C—14 dates, Cotté caves, Saint-Pierre-de Maillé);   Pradel , L. and J. H. 1966 (Pal. artifacts, Raysse), 1967 (Solutrian artifacts, Monthaud); Puissegur 1962 (Mousterian climate, Genay);
Ravoux 1966 (Magdalenian industry, Roque Cave, Hérault);   Ravoux and Bazile 1964, 1965 (Mousterian artifacts, Gard);   Ringot 1965 (Mousterian, Ardrésis); Ronen 1964 (Aurignacian scrapers);   Rouquette 1966 (Mousterian artifacts, Montbazin cave, Hérault);   Roussot 1962A (prehist., Périgord), 1962B, 1964 (Magdalenian industry, Reignac), 1966C (Aurignacian artifacts, Poisson and Castelmerle);   Roussot et al. 1966 (Up. Pal. artifacts, Nancy Cave);
Sacchi, D. 1964 (artifacts, Grand-Pressigny);   Sackett 1967 (Up. Pal. site, Solvieux);

Saint-Mathurin 1965 (Aurignacian and Perigordian industries, Nemours); Saint-Périer 1965 (Up. Pal. industries, Isturitz Cave); Seronie-Vivien 1964 (Up. Pal. artifacts, hearth, Bergerie Cave, Caniac); Smith, P. E. L. 1966A, B (Solutrean culture); Sonneville-Bordes 1965A (Magdalenian industries, Chaire-a-Calvin, Charente), 1965C (Mousterian artifacts, S. W. France), 1966B (Solutrean); Soubeyran 1966 ("man of Chancelade"); Speléo-Club de Bergerac 1966 (Aurignacian artifacts, Fieux Cave); Sullivan 1965 (early man, Les Eyzies);

Tavoso 1968 (Abbevillean industry, Fresquel Valley, Aude); Thevenin 1965 (artifacts, Saone Valley); Thibault 1965 (Solutrean notched point); Tomasson, R. and J. 1964 (Mid. Pal. Tools, Côte d'Ossignoux);

Vacher and Vignard 1965 (artifacts, Nemours); Vallois 1965A (Neanderthal sternum, Regourdou Cave), 1965B (Fontechevade man); 1967D (lost Moustier skull found); Vallois and Billy 1965 (Cro-Magnon); Vandermeersch 1965, 1968B (Pal. industries, S. W.); Vialettes 1964 (biface, Quercy-Blanc); Vienne 1965 (Magdalenian site, Pincevent); Vignard 1964A (Protomagdalenian), 1964B (cultures, Ballancourt-sur-Essonnes), 1964C (Pal. artifacts, Ercheu, Somme); Vignard and Vacher 1965A (effect of climate on flints, Nemours), 1965B (Up. Pal. habitats and workshops, Nemours, Seine-et-Marne).

GERMANY – Adam 1965A (primates); Andrist, Flückiger and Andrist 1964 (pal. sites, Stimme R.); Anon 1961CV (Pal. research, Württemberg);

Binder 1960, 1961A, 1962A (bibliog. archeol. and paleont.); Binder, Frank and Müller 1960 (Pal., Alpine caves); Brandt 1966 (Aurignacian artifact), 1967 (Ursus calcanea as artifacts, Westphalia);

Diehl 1964 (Pal. site, Südhessen);

Feustel 1965 (Aurignacian culture, Elster Valley); Feustel, Teichert and Unger 1963 (Magdalenian industry, Lausnitz rock shelter); Freising 1962 (Pal. tools, N. Württemberg); Freund 1963C (prehist., Bavaria);

Gersbach 1965 (Pal. tools, camp sites, Upper Rhine Valley); Gieseler 1967 (skull of Neanderthal child, Berlin Mus.); Grimm and Ullrich 1965 (Homo skeleton, Urd Cave); Guenther 1956D (Steinheim man and Ehringsdorf man); Gunther 1964 (Balver Cave);

Heberer 1956G (attempts to recover skeletons of Combe and Le Moustier men from ashes of Berlin Mus.); Hesse 1966 (Neanderthal skull from Le Moustier); Hinz 1963 (archeol., Rheinland Paltinate, 1961);

Jamka 1964 (archeol. research in Up. Silesia, 1963); Jankuhn 1963 (archeol. research, Lower Saxonia);

Kahlke 1963C, 1965C (chronol. of Choukoutien culture); Kleeman 1962 (archeol.), 1964A (Heidelberg culture); Krüger, H. 1962 (Old Stone Age), 1964A, B (artifacts), 1964C (Mid. Pal. scrapers, Kreuznach district), 1965 (bifacial tools); Kruysen 1961 (Paleolithic);

Luttropp 1962 (Levalloisan industry);

M., W. 1966 (Neanderthal skull returned to Berlin Mus.); Mania 1967 (Late Pal. artifacts); Müller-Beck 1966A ("Speckberg" artifacts);

Neumann, G. 1933 (Magdalenian site);

Pelosse 1968 (Heidelberg man); Peters, E. 1931 (Cave finds); Pohle 1966 (Up. Pal. bone artifacts, Rixdorf);

Rajchel 1965 (Steinheim woman); Riek 1930 (shelter, Wiesensteig), 1932B, C, 1934 (industries, Vogelherd Cave), 1933B, 1938A (industries, Württemberg), 1938B (Solutrian industry, Haldenstein Cave), 1938C (industries, Heidenheim), 1962 (Blaubeuren and Rusenschloss, Württemberg), 1964A, B (early man, Blabueuren, Württemberg); Rust and Steffens 1962 (culture, N. Germany);

Seitz 1966 (Mousterian scraper, Wittislingen, Late Pleistoc. scraper, Dattenhausen); Sonneville-Bordes 1965B (Aurignacian industry, Vogelherd Cave, Lone Valley, Württemberg); Steiner, U. 1965 (Heidelberg-type stone artifacts, Sülzfeld, Thüringia);

Stewart, T. D. 1964 (Neanderthal scapula); Storck 1964 (Pal. site, Bolanden);
Toepfer 1963C, 1964B, 1965A (cultures), 1967B (hand-ax, Nieplitz valley, Fläming), 1967C, 1968 (Pal. artifacts);
Uslar 1956 (Neanderthal);
Völzing 1964 (Pal., Rhein-Main-Gebietes);
Woldstedt 1967 (Pleist. man and his cultures).
Zotz 1964A (artifacts, Dollnstein), 1965A (flaked points, Bayern).

GREAT BRITAIN – Anon. 1968Z (Swanscombe re-excavated), 1968AC (lithic industry, Suffolk); ApSimon and Boon 1960 (Pal. implements, Shirehampton);
Arkell 1951 (Pal. implements, Dorset);
Barley and Lucas 1958, 1960 (COWA surveys); Brown, J. A. 1887 (early man, Middlesex); Brown, J. C. 1957 (artifacts, Shirehampton district);
Daniel, G. 1965 (archeol. study in Wales);
Farrar 1968 (Up. Pal. artifacts, Isle of Portland); Foster and Daniel 1965 (prehist. Wales);
Lacaille 1966 (Acheulian flaked flint artifacts);
McBurney 1965 (early man, Wales);
Ovey 1964 (survey of research at Swanscombe);
Radley 1964 (early man, Yorkshire); Roe, D. A. 1964 (Low. and Mid. Pal.); Rosenfeld 1964A (archeol., Torbryan Caves, Devonshire);
Taylor, R. M. S. 1937 (Piltdown man); Thomas, N. and Gunstone 1964 (prehist., Staffordshire); Thomas, S. 1965 (Pal., Britain);
Vaufrey 1965 (Mousterian, Jersey); Vulliamy 1930 (archeol., Middlesex and London);
Wedlake, A. L. and D. J. 1963 (artifacts, Doniford gravels, West Somerset); Wells, L. H. 1963D (age of Galley Hill skel.); Woodridge and Cornwall 1964 (prehist., Thames Valley).

ITALY – Anon. 1964AC (Neanderthal, Grosseto); Arias 1964 (Levalloisian industry, Piano di Santa Maria di Arabona);
Bartolomei and Broglio 1964 (Mid. Pal., cave at San Bernardino); Bernabo'-Brea 1965A (Up. Pal., Sicily), 1965B (Up. Pal., Palike); Blanc, A. C. 1959B (Mousterian, Capo di Leuca); Blanc, G. A. 1958 (Up. Pal. industry, Romanelli Cave); Brozatti von Löwenstern 1964, 1965A (Uluzzo Cave, Salento), 1965B (flint tools, Santa Caterina, Lecce); Broglio 1964 (Mousterian industry, Broion Cave), 1965 (epi-Gravettian industry, R. Baltaglia rock shelter, Vincenza); Broglio, Laplace and Zorzi 1963 (Low. to Up. Pal. cave industries, Ponte di Veia); Broglio and Leonardi 1964 (Acheulian and Mousterian industries, Mt. Conero);
Cadeo 1961 (archeol., Lombarde Cave), 1965A (Low. Pal. industry and mammals, Lombardia), 1965B (Pal. industries, Fiume Nevola and Torrette di Fano); Charles 1963A (Grimaldi race); Chiappella, G. 1965 (Palidoro Up. Pal. site, Rome); Chiappella, V. G. 1964 (Low. Pal. industries, Venosa); Corazza 1964 (Pal. industries, Abruzzo); Correnti 1968 (human skulls, Sicily); Cremonesi 1964 (Low., Mid. Pal. tools, Abruzzo);
Demangeot 1964 (Pal. beds of Giumentina Valley, Apennines); Demangeot and Radmilli 1966 (Pal. of Giumentina Valley);
Favati Vanni 1964 (Up. Pal. human skeleton, Maritza Cave);
Galiberti 1964 (Pal. tools, Piombino); Gansser-Burckhardt 1955 (Neanderthal cave bear hunters); Graziosi 1965 (Romito Cave progress report); Grifoni 1962 (Low. Pal. artifacts, Foro R.), 1964, 1966 (Mus. collections of artifacts from Toscana); Grifoni and Radmilli 1965 (Up. Pal. artifacts from Maritza Cave, Abruzzi); Guerri 1964A (Mid. Pal. industry, Maielletta), 1964C (Early Pal. cores, Gargano);
Iakimov 1967A (skulls of the Grimaldi negroids); Isetti and Chiarelli 1965 (Mousterian industry, Ciotta Ciara Cave, Borgosesia); Isetti and Lumley 1962A (Mousterian industry, Liguria), 1962B (Pal. industry, Pietra Ligure); Isetti, Lumley and Miskovsky 1962 (Mousterian cave, Bussana);

Leonardi, P. 1956G (Pal., Padua), 1958 (Gravettian cave industry, Colli Berici), 1963A (Pal. industries, Alps), 1963B (prehist., Venezia); Leonardi, Allegranzi and Broglio 1965 (Gravettian industry, Vincenza); Leonardi, Annibaldi, Broglio and Batolomei 1965 (Acheulian, Mid. Pal. industries, Monte Conero); Leonardi, Bartolomei and Broglio 1965 (Minore Cave, San Bernardino); Leonardi and Broglio 1963B (Mousterian industry, Broion Cave), 1965 (Pal. of Veneto); Leonardi, Broglio and Bosellini 1964 (Low. and Mid. Pal.); Lollini 1965 (Pal. sites, Ancona);

Mannino 1965 (prehist. research, Sicily); Maxia 1966 (Neanderthal man and environment, Sardinia);

Palma di Cesnola 1961B, 1963B (Mousterian industry), 1964A, 1965A (industries, Cavallo Cave), 1964B (Up. Pal. industry, Cave delle Campane), 1965B (Mousterian industry, Camerota); Palma di Cesnola and Borzatti von Löwenstern 1965 (industries, Santa Caterina and Galliano del Capo); Palma di Cesnola and Gambassini 1965 (Mousterian); Palma di Cesnola and Messeri 1967 (Pal. human teeth); Palma di Cesnola and Zorzi 1961 (pebble culture); Pasa and Mezzena 1965 (cultures, Veneto); Petrov, G. I. 1940A (Neanderthal man, Monte Circeo); Pittioni 1962 (prehist. cultures);

Radmilli 1959B (artifacts, La Punta Cave), 1963C (prehist.), 1964 (Up. Pal. industry, Maurizio Cave), 1965 (Pal. industry, Conca Peligna);

Stoduti 1964, 1965A (Pal. industry, Leghorn Hills), 1965B (Up. Pal. industry, Sicily);

Tozzi 1962 (Mousterian industry, Santa Lucia Cave, Toirano), 1965 (industries, Terrazzi Zannini, Chieti), 1967 (industries, Aquila);

Vlček 1968 (Aurignacian man, Grotte des Enfants, near Grimaldi);

Zecchini 1967 (Mousterian, Elba Is.); Zei and Manca 1965 (Mousterian, Arezzo); Zorzi 1959 (Acheulian ax, Lughezzano di Valpantena, near Verona), 1964 (Pal. industry, Paglicci cave).

NETHERLANDS — Bohmers 1961B, C, D, E, F, G (Up. Pal. sites); Breuil 1965 (artifacts);

Dielis 1961 (Up. Pal.);

Elzinga 1960, 1961, 1962, 1963 (archeol.); Erdbrink 1964 (human skull cap, Limburg);

Knussmann 1965B (Neanderthals, Limburg); Kruytzer 1962A (Roermond man);

Mercenier, J. and L. 1962A, B (Mousterian artifacts).

NORWAY — Andersen, B. G. 1965 (Stone Age archeology).

PORTUGAL — Breuil 1962B (Pal. artifacts, Minho);

Do Paço and Cabaço 1964 (hand-axes, Caldas da Rainha);

Ferembach 1962 (milk molar, Salemas Cave), 1965A (Up. Pal. skeletal remains, Salemas), 1965B (Neanderthal molar, Bombarral);

Jordá Cerdá 1963 (Solutrean industries, Salemas Cave, Casa de Moura Cave);

Paço 1966 (Pal. artifacts, Abrantes), 1967 (Pal. artifacts, Coruche);

Ripoll Perelló 1964-1965A (Solutrian); Roche 1965B (prehist.); Roche et al. 1962 (Up. Pal. industries, Salemas Cave);

Zbyszewski and Veiga Ferreira 1967B (artifacts, Sorraia R., E. of Benavente), 1967C (artifacts, Môrro promontory, W. of Sesimbra).

SPAIN — Aguirre 1964B (elephant-kill site, Toledo); Aguirre and Butzer 1967 (artifacts, Louro Valley); Aguirre, Collins and Cuenca 1964 (Pal. cultures, Andalusia, Toledo, Galicia); Almagro Basch 1960C (Maltravieso cave); Almagro Basch and Arribas 1956 (Millares, Almeria);

Barandiarán, J. M. de 1955, 1960 (Urtiaga cave, Guipúzcoa Prov.), 1959, 1964B, C,

1965A (Lezetxiki and Kobatxo caves, Garagarza - Mondragón), 1961, 1962, 1963A, B, 1964A, 1965B (Aitzbitarte cave, Guipúzcoa Prov.); Barandiarán and Altuna 1965, 1966 (Lezetxiki cave, Mondragón); Barandiarán and Elósequi 1962 (Urtiaga cave, Guipúzcoa Prov.); Barandiarán and Fernández Medrano 1957, 1960, 1963, 1964 (Lezetxiki cave, Mondragón); Barandiarán and Sonneville-Bordes 1964 (Urtiaga cave, Guipúzcoa Prov.); Barandiarán Maestu 1964, 1965A, B (Pal., Guipúzcoa Prov.); Basabe 1966 (humerus, Lezetxiki cave); Biberson 1964C (Acheulian elephant-kill sites, Vieille Castille); Biberson and Aguirre 1965 (use of bones as tools, Torralba, Ambrona); Butzer 1965 (Acheulian occupation sites, Torralba and Ambrona);

Callejo 1958 (prehist. of Maltravieso Cave); Carbonell 1965 (teeth of Neanderthal child, Gibraltar); Cheynier and González-Echegaray 1964 (Valle Cave, Bilbao);

Do Paço 1963 (Low. Pal. pebble tools, Mérida);

Freeman, L. G. 1965 (Mid. Acheulian station of Torralba), 1966 (Mousterian facies in Cantabrian Spain); Freeman and Butzer 1966 (Acheulian station of Torralba);

González-Etchegaray, P. J. et al. 1963 (Magdalenian industry, Santander);

Hernandez-Pacheco 1956 (prehist. research and progress); Howell, F. C. 1962E, 1963C, 1964A (early Acheulian occupation sites, Torralba and Ambrona); Howell, Butzer and Aguirre 1963 (Acheulian of Torralba);

Janssens 1960 (harpoons, El Pendo Cave);

Llongueras Campaña 1964-65 (Low. Pal. industry of Pinedo, Toledo);

Madariaga de la Campa 1964 (fishing activities of prehist. men); Maluquer de Motes 1965 (Magdalenian cave, Navarra); Marquez Triguero 1965A (Early Pal. industries, Vallecas), 1965B (Low. Pal. sites, Coslada); Martín Aguado 1963A (Pal. industries, Toledo), 1963B (prehist. site, Pinedo);

Osaba 1964 (archeol. catalogue, Burgos);

Pericot García 1962D (notched points, Up. Pal. caves), 1965C (French contributions to study of Spanish prehist.); Pietsch, E. and G. 1964 (Altamira);

Ripoll Perelló and Lumley 1964-1965 (Mid. Pal. industry, Catalonia); Riquet 1962 (skulls, Iziar); Rodriguez, A. V. 1961 (archeol.);

Soler Garcia 1956 (Pal. industry, Grand Cave of Huesa-Tacaña, Villena); Sonneville-Bordes 1965E (Acheulian industry, Torralba and Ambrona);

Zotz 1965B (industry, Manzanares Valley, near Madrid).

SWITZERLAND – Degen 1965 (Pal. sites);

Flükiger 1965 (Magdalenian stone tools, Burgäschi);

Labhart and Rudin 1964 (summary of archeol. research); Lüdin 1964 (industries of Kohler Cave);

Stampfli 1959B (Magdalenian and Mousterian industries, "Kastel" Cave, Solothurn);

Vilaseca 1961 (Up. Pal. stone tools, l'Areny rock shelter, near Vilanova d'Escornalbou).

CENTRAL AND EASTERN EUROPE

GENERAL – Bader, Ivanova and Velichko 1965 (Pal. E. and cent. Europe); Bibikov 1959, 1961B (Pal. peopling of E. Europe);

Chmielewski, W. 1964 (Mid. Pal. traditions in Up. Pal. cultures);

Dokládal 1960 (anthrop., Balkans);

Ehrich 1959, 1962, 1966 (COWA surveys, Balkans), 1964 (COWA surveys, cent. Europe); Ehrich and Gimbutas 1957, 1960 (COWA surveys, cent. Europe);

Jisl 1965 (Czecho-Mongolian archeol. expd.);

Kozłowski, J. K. 1964A (chronol. subdivision of Magdalenian), 1965A (evol. of Up. Pal. cultures), 1967B (flint work shops);

Ložek 1960 (Up. Pal. chronol., cent. Europe);

Merpert and Shelov 1961 (early man, E. Europe); Moskvitin 1961B, C (comparative strat. of Pal. sites in European USSR, Poland and Czechoslovakia);

Rust 1965A (Pal. huts, cent. Europe and W. USSR).

artifacts in Epire and Élide, Acheulean artifacts in Macedonia);
Vanderpool 1965 (Pal. site, Asprochaliko, near Arta).

HUNGARY – Anon. 1966AZ (Homo erectus, Vértesszöllös), 1967T (Budapest skull);
Banner 1960, 1966 (préhist.);
Gábore 1964A, 1965 (Gravettian sites), 1964C (Late Pal.); Gáboriné Csánk 1960
(Gravettian industry, Ságvár site);
Gromov, V. I. 1967B (symposium on Early Up. Pal.);
Kleeman 1964B (hearth site); Kretzoi and Vértes 1964A, 1965B, C (Vértesszöllös
Pal. pebble-industry occupation site), 1964B (Pal. site, Tata), 1965A (Pal. indus-
tries, Quat stratig. and chronol.);
Oakley 1966C (Homo erectus and Buda industry, Vértesszöllös);
Thoma 1963 (juvenile Neanderthal dentition, Subalyuk), 1966 (Vértesszöllös skull),
1967 (pebble tools and human teeth, W. of Budapest);
Vadász 1964 (Tata site); Vegh and Viczián 1964 (flint artifacts, Tata); Vertes 1960F
(Mousterian industry, Tata), 1963C (Up. Pal. industry, Mt. Henye at Bodrogkereszt-
úr), 1964A (Mid. Pal. site, Tata), 1964B (hist. of Tata), 1964C (artifacts, Tata),
1965A (Homo erectus, Vértesszöllös), 1965B (industries), 1965C (Up. Pal. industries, Arka, Hernád V.), 1965D (pebble-tool industry, Vértesszöllös), 1965F (Stone
Age handbook); Vertes et al. 1962 (bone and stone industry, Görömböly-Tapolca).

POLAND – Anon. 1964AH (Mid.-Up. Pal. industries, Racibórz-Ocice); Arnette 1965
(prehist.);
Chmielewska, M. 1961C (Up. Pal. encampment, Lódz); Chmielewski, W. 1958B (Pal.
of the Czestochowa Plateau), 1961A (Tayacian industries), 1961B (Up. Pal. Jerz-
manowice culture), 1965A (Up. Pleist. archeol.), 1967 (archeol. of Koziarnia
Cave, Sąspów);
Gediga 1965 (survey Stone Age sites); Ginter 1964 (Pal. sites), 1966 (Wójcice Up.
Pal. site, Grodków), 1967 (Up. Pal. site, Krakus Hill);
Hensel 1958 (summary of Paleolithic);
Jażdżewski 1965A, B (prehist.);
Kapica and Wierciński 1966 (analysis of human skeletal remains, Maszycka Cave,
Olkusz District); Kobusiewicz 1967 (lithic industries); Kostrzewski, Chmielewski
and Jażdżewski 1965 (prehist.); Kowalski et al. 1967 (rock shelters in Żytnia
Skała); Kowalski, Kozłowski, Krysowska and Wiktor 1965 (Puchacza Skała Cave,
Olkusz District); Kowalski, S. 1964, 1967B (Pal., Ciemna Cave at Ojców), 1967A
(Pal. flint artifact, Cracovie), 1967C (archeol. of Mamutowa Cave, Wierzchowie);
Kozłowski, J. K. 1959C (industries), 1961F, 1964C, 1965B (Pal. sites, Silesia),
1966B (Aurignacian industries), 1967A (Pal. sites, Cracovie-Przegorzały), 1967C (Up
Pal. blade industries); Kozłowski and Schild 1964 (Magdalenian industries); Koz-
łowski, S. K. 1964A (Late Pal., valley of Sandomierz), 1964C (Late Pal. site
of Tokary-Rąbierz, Gostynin), 1965 (Up. Pal., Przemysl), 1966 (Magdalenian hom-
inids, Maszycka Cave, Olkusz District); Krauss 1957 (Early Pal. knife, Kurdwanow)
Krysowska 1965 (Up. Pal. site, Silesia); Krzak 1965 (flint mine, Swieciechów);
Sawicki 1960 (Magdalenian artifacts, Antoniów Maly), 1965B (industry, Chwalibogowic
Pińczów); Schild 1965B (Magdalenian industry, Grzybowa Gora, Kielce Prov.);
Steślicka 1959, 1962 (human fossils); Szlachetko 1966 (human teeth, Maszycka
Cave, Olkusz Dist.);
Talar 1967 (artifacts, Durdy, Tarnobrzeg Dist.);
Walczak 1963 (early man, Sudet).

RUMANIA – Anon. 1961CZ (Up. Pal. culture, Prahova Valley);
Bárta 1965B (Pal. summarized); Bitiri 1964, 1965A, B, C, 1967A, B (Pal. sites,
industries);
Mogoşanu 1967 (Aurignacian sites, Banat); Mogoşanu and Stratan 1966 (Aurignacian
artifacts, Banat);

Nania 1964 (Low. Pal., Arges region); Necrasov and Cristescu 1965 (Pal. hominid remains); Nicolăescu-Plopşor, C. S. 1962B, 1964B, 1965 (Pal. studies), 1964A (protohominid pebble-culture, Oltenia Province), 1966 (Pal., Bucarest); Nicolăescu-Plopşor, C. S. and D. 1963, 1968 (proto-hominid kill site, Grăunceanu Valley); Nicolăescu-Plopşor, Păunescu and Mogoşanu 1966 (Up. Pal. sites, Ceahlău); Nicolăescu-Plopşor, D. 1968 (fossil hominids);

Popescu, D. 1963 (archeol. excavations);

Samson and Rădulesco 1959 (industries, Dobrudscha), 1964 (Pal. "La Adam" cave, Dobrogea); Spiru 1965 (artifacts, Alexandria region).

YUGOSLAVIA — Basler 1962, 1963B (Pal., N. Bosnia); Basler and Janekovic' 1961 (Pal., Kulaši site); Basler, Malez and Brunnacker 1966 (Pal., Bileca); Benac 1964 (N.W. Balkans); Brodar, M. 1962 (rock shelter, Montenegro), 1965 (chronol. of Pal. cultures); Brodar, S. 1955D (Pal. industries, Betalov Cave), 1965 (Pal. man in Postojna Cave), 1966 (Mousterian and Up. Pal. artifacts, Postojnska Jama Cave); Freund 1956B (Pal. cave sites);

Malez 1964B (Gravettian industry and human skull fragments, Istria), 1965A (Mousterian cave, Veternica, Croatia), 1965B, K (hominid sites, Croatia), 1965C (Up. Pal. man in the Dinaric Karst region, Croatia), 1965E (Mousterian artifacts, Crvena Stijena rock shelter, Montenegro), 1965F (Pal. cultures, Velika Cave, Ravna Gora); Osole 1965A, B (Gravettian industries and artifacts, Slovenia), 1965C (Pal. caves); Schaefer, U. 1964 (Neanderthal, Krapina).

PALEOANTHROPOLOGY — USSR

Abetekov et al. 1968 (Mousterian, Kirgizia); Abramov 1964 (artifact, Ukrainia); Abramova, E. A. 1966 (Pal. cultures, Siberia); Abramova, Z. A. 1962C, D, 1964A, B, 1965, 1966B, 1967B, C, 1968 (Pal. sites, Siberia); Adamenko 1966B (Mousterian, Siberia); Adamenko and Gaĭduk 1967 (artifacts, Altai); Aksenov and Medvedev 1966 (Pal., Angara, Siberia); Aleksandrov, A. L. 1967 (Kirenga R., Siberia); Alekseev, V. A. et al. 1964 (C−14 dates, Moldova site); Alekseev, V. P. 1960 (Kiik-Koba man), 1964 (research, USSR), 1966A (research methods), 1966B (Neanderthal and Mousterian), 1968B (craniology); Alpysbaev, Kh. A. 1959A, 1960, 1961A, 1961B (Pal. sites, Kazakhstan), 1959B, 1962 (Pal., Karatau Mts., Kazakhstan); Alpysbaev, Kh. K. 1959 (Pal. flint implements, Kostenki II); Anisiutkin 1966, 1968 (Mousterian, middle Dnestr R.); Anon. 1959BR (Uzbekistan archeol. expedition), 1960CO (early C−14 dates), 1965G (Up. Pal. burial site, Vladmir), 1965BT (Pal. funeral, N. E. of Moscow), 1965CR (Neanderthal, Moldova site); Astakhov 1963, 1966A, B, 1967A, B, 1968 (artifacts, Siberia); Autlev 1964 (Mousterian, Caucasus); Autlev, Muratov and Fridenberg 1967 (Mousterian, Kuban' R. region);

Bader, N. O. 1961, 1964 (Pal., Crimea and Caucasus), 1965 (Up. Pal., Caucasus); Bader, O. N. 1940I (Mousterian, Crimea), 1959, 1961B, 1965B, 1967A (Pal., Sungir' site, central USSR), 1962B, 1966B (caves and rock shelters, archeol), 1964, 1965E, 1966A, 1967C, 1967D (Cro-Magnon burial, Sungir' site), 1965A, 1965C, 1966C (Pal., Urals); Bader, Gromov and Sukachev 1961A, B (Up. Pal., Sungir' site); Bader, Ivanova and Velichko 1965 (Pal., European USSR); Beĭlekchi 1966 (Moldavia); Berdzenishvili 1964 (Stone Age site, Tskhalfsitela canyon); Beregovaia 1966 (Pal. sites); Beregovaia, Islamov and Kalandadze 1966 (archeol.); Bibikov 1940C (Pal. cave sites, S. Urals), 1963A, B (archeol. 1960-61, Ukraine); Bibikova 1966 (bone tool, Kiev); Bliznetsov 1964, 1968 (artifacts in caves, Urals); Bodianskiĭ 1959 (Mousterian campsite, Orelcliff); Boriskovskiĭ 1955C, 1959B, C, 1960, 1961E, 1963 (Kostenski Late Pal. site, Ukraine), 1961C (flint workshops, Valuĭki), 1961F (Up. Pal. site near Odessa), 1964A (Late Pal. culture, Siberia), 1964B (Late Pal., N. W. Black Sea), 1965 (Pal. research in USSR); Boriskovskiĭ and Kraskovskiĭ 1961 (Pal., Black Sea region); Boriskovskiĭ and Praslov 1964 (Pal. of the Dnepr basin and Azov region); Bud'ko 1964 (mammoth bone dwellings, Berdyzh Pal. site), 1965 (mammoth bone dwellings, Eliseevichi), 1966 (Up. Pal., N. W. Russian Plain), 1967A, B (mammoth bone dwellings, Iudinovo Up. Pal. site), 1967C (Belorussian archeol. expd.), 1968 (Studeneŝ Up. Pal. site, Belorussia); Bugianashvili et al. 1968 (Mousterian artifacts, Alazan' R. Basin); Chard and Workman 1965 (Soviet archeol. C–14 dates); Chernysh 1955B, 1960C, 1965B, (Pal. sites, Dnestr region), 1959B, 1960B, 1961C, D, 1965A (Moldova sites, Ukraine), 1968A (Ataki site, Ukraine), 1968B (Oselivka site); Debeŝ 1939C (Neanderthal skull from Teshik-tash Cave, Uzbekistan), 1941 (early man, Siberia), 1955, 1961B (hominid remains, Kostenki), 1956 (early man, USSR), 1967 (Up. Pal. skeleton from Sungir' burial); Denisov and Oborin 1968 (Up. Pal. artifacts, Chusovaiâ R.); Dunn, S. P. 1966 (peoples of Siberia); Dzhavrishvili 1961 (man's use of caves, Georgia);

Ermolova 1968 (Up. Pal., Eniseǐ R.);

Fedorov, G. B. 1951 (Stone Age man, Siberia), Formozov 1956B, 1959A (Mousterian sites, Crimea), 1958C (culture variations, Caucasus), 1960 (Stone Age in N. Caucasus), 1962, 1964, 1965A (Pal. of the Kuban' region, Caucasus), 1959B (Stone Age cultural provinces); Fridenberg 1966 (Mousterian tools in cave deposits, N. W. Caucasus);

Gábori 1960B, 1962B, 1964B (archeol., Mongolia); Ganeshin and Okladnikov 1956 (Pal. artifacts, Maritime Province); Gening 1968 (Pal. site, Irtysh area); Gerasimov, M. M. 1958, 1964A (Malta Pal. dwelling site, Siberia), 1961 (reconstruction of round dwelling, Malta site); Gladilin 1965, 1966A (Mousterian artifacts, Ukraine), 1966B (Mousterian industries); Grekhova 1968 (Up. Pal., Timonovka Village); Grigor'ev 1963A (local cultural development), 1967 (reconstruction of Kostenki I dwelling); Grigor'eva 1963 (Kostenki tools), 1964 (Kokorevo VI Pal. site, Siberia), 1966A (Late Pal. culture variations, Steppe zone), 1966B (Late Pal. of Odessa region), 1967 (Late Pal. of Bol'shaiâ Akkarzha); Grishchenko, M. N. 1961B (Mousterian culture, S. European USSR), 1965 (Sukhaiâ Mechetka Volgograd and Rozhok I site); Gromov, V. I. 1961D (geol. age of Mousterian site near Stalingrad), 1967A (fractured bovid bone, Chernyǐ Iâr); Guliamov 1966 (archeol. in Uzbekistan, 1963-64); Guliâmova et al. 1956 (Pal. artifacts in the Inst. Hist., Archeol., Ethnol., Acad. Sci., Tadzhik SSR); Gumilevskiǐ and Korobkov 1967 (Pal. site, Kheǐvani); Gurba 1965 (Pal. research, Urals); Gurina 1965 (Up. Pal. artifacts, N. W. Belorussiiâ); Guseǐnov 1963 (Azykh Cave, Azerbaijan); Guslitŝer and Kanivetŝ 1962B, 1965 (Late Solutrean-Early Magdalenian caves, Pechora region); Guslitŝer, Kanivetŝ and Timofeev 1965 (Byzovaiâ Pal. cave site, Polar Circle, Pechora region); Gvozdover 1959, 1964, 1967 (Pal. sites, Lower Don R.), 1961B (flint collection from the Avdeevo Pal site); Gvozdover and Formozov 1960 (utilization of Equus bones, Mousterian cave, Crimea);

Iârmak 1957 (Pal. tools, S. Kazakhstan); Iessen 1965 (Pal. artifacts, Mil'-Karabakh steppe); Iûnusaliev 1967 (Stone Age Kirgizia); Ivan'ev 1966B (Up. Pal. sites, Chikoǐ R., nr. Mongolia); Ivanova 1961D, E, 1965A (Pal., Dnestr R.); Ivanova and Chernysh 1963, 1965 (Molodova V Up. Pal. site, Middle Dnester R.); Ivanova and Praslov 1963 (Mousterian nucleus, N. coast Sea of Azov);

Jablonskyte-Rimantiene 1964 (Pal. cultures, Lithuania);

Kalandadze, A. N. 1966 (Pal. camp sites, Georgia); Kalandadze and Tushabramishvili 1955 (Givardzhilas-Klde Cave, Caucasus); Kanivetŝ 1967 (mammoth bone houses and artifacts, Byzovskaiâ site); Karlov 1961 (Pal. industries, Ukraine), 1963 (Chellean hand chopper, Mid. Dnepr region); Karlov and Nakel'skiǐ 1966A (Solutrean blade, Crimea); Kasymov 1960 (Mousterian site, Turkestan), 1964 (Acheulian-Mousterian workshops, Karatau region), 1968 (Pal. sites, Uzbekistan); Ketraru 1964 (archeol. of the Chugur R. valley), 1965A (Chutuleshty-I Pal. site), 1965B (Pal. station in the grotto Starye Duruitory, Moldavia); Khlobystin 1965 (Pal. artifacts, Baǐkal); Klapchuk 1964 (Pal. finds in cent. Kazakhstan), 1965 (archeol. finds in Karaganda region), 1967, 1968 (archeol., Nura and Sarysu R. basins); Klein, R. G. 1965 (Mid. Pal., Crimea), 1966A (Mousterian, Up. Pal. sites, Dnestr Basin), 1966B (review of evidence for Chellean and Acheullian in USSR), 1967

(C—14 dates on Pleist. occupation sites); Kochetkova 1965 (brain volume of Pal. man from "Markina Gora"); Kolosov 1959 (flint artifacts, Chokurcha Pal. site, Crimea), 1960 (Mousterian site nr. Romankov, Ukraine), 1964 (Late Pal. sites, Dnepr Rapids region), 1965A (Stone Age occupation of Crimean ĭaĭlas), 1965B (Pal. sites, Desna R.), 1966 (Mousterian points, Shaĭtan-Koba cave, Crimea); Konopliả 1959 (Mousterian, Up. Pal. sites, Kirgizia); Korobkov 1962 (Khostinskiĭ caves, Caucasus), 1964 (Chellean hand-chopper, Ĭashtukh, Caucasus), 1965A (Pal. cores from Ĭashtukh), 1965B, 1967 (Ĭashtukh industries); Kostenko and Alpysbaev 1966 (pal. artifacts, Turlan Pass region of Karatau Range); Kostenko, Nesmeiảnov and Ranov 1961 (Mousterian artifacts, S. Tadzhikistan); Kotovich 1964 (Stone Age, Dagestan); Kraĭnov 1960A (Bokhchisaraĭ Mousterian site), 1960B (Up. Pal. cave site, Tash-Air I, Crimea), 1964 (Pal. sites of the Volga-Oka basin); Kraskovskiĭ 1962 (Late Pal. sites, Odessa); Krivolap 1964 (Mousterian flints, Belgorod-Dnestrovskiĭ); Krupnov 1964, 1966 (archeol., Caucasus); Krylkov and Ranov 1959 (Mousterian artifacts, Kara-Bura); Krylova, A. A. 1959, 1961 (Pal. sites, E. Kazakhstan); Krylova and Pavliủchenko 1962 (flint implements, Altaĭ); Kuderina 1967 (Mousterian artifacts, Kyzyl-Kaĭnar valley); Kyzlasov 1958 (prehist., Tuva);

Lang, D. M. 1966 (early man, Georgia); Larichev 1964C (Low. Pal. settlements, Gobi); Larichev and Volkov 1964 (Mousterian sites, S. Gobi); Laricheva 1966A (N. Amer. and Siberian Pal. cultures); Lazukov 1965 (Quat. mammals and man); Levin, M. G. 1960 (hist. of anthrop. in Russia); Levin and Potapov 1964 (peoples of Siberia); Litvinskiĭ 1954 (Tadzhikistan archeol.); Litvinskiĭ, Okladnikov and Ranov 1962 (archeol., Kaĭrak-Kum); Liubin 1958, 1959A, 1962B, 1967B (Pal. sites, Ossetia, Georgia), 1959B (Mousterian artifacts, Stavropol area), 1967A (Pal. in Black Sea region of Caucasus), 1968 (Mousterian artifacts, W. Caucasus); Liủbin, Bader and Markovin 1962 (Pal. implements, Checheno-Ingushetiiả, Caucasus); Liủbin and Petrakov 1964 (Zolotarikha Mousterian site, Up. Oka Basin); Liủbin and Shchelinskiĭ 1967 (Navalishino Cave, Black Sea area); Luzgin and Ranov 1966 (Pal., cent. Kopet-Dag);

Mania 1963 (archeol., cent. Mongolia), Mannaĭ-Ool 1964 (archeol. of Tuva); Markov 1961B (archeol., N. W. Russian Plain); Markov, Lazukov and Nikolaev 1965B (the Quat. period); Markovin 1964 (archeol. of N. Ossetia and Chechniả); Masson, V. M. 1966 (Mid. Asia at the epoch of stone and bronze); Medoev 1962, 1965B (Pal. sites, N. Balkhash region), 1964, 1965A (early cultures of Sary-Arka, Kazakhstan); Medvedev 1968 (Pal. artifacts, upper Angara area); Merpert and Smirnov 1961 (Mid. Pal. site nr. Stalingrad); Mesiats 1962A, B (Zhitomir Low. Pal. site, N. Ukraine); Michael 1965 (archeol. of the Soviet Far East); Mochanov 1966A (Pal. of the Aldan R.); Mochanov and Fedoseeva 1968 (Ikhine Pal. site, Ĭakutia); Mongaĭt 1955, 1957, 1961B (archeol.); Moskvitin 1962B (Volgograd Pal. site, Sukhaiả Mechetka R.);

Nakel'skiĭ and Karlov 1965, 1966 (Pal. cultural and hominid remains, mid. Dnepr. region); Nasedkin and Formozov 1965 (obsidian from Late Pal. sites, N. Caucasus); Nasretdinov 1964 (Low. Mousterian artifacts, Obirakhmat Cave, Tashkent Province); Negadaev-Nikonov and Arapov 1964 (Magdalenian and Mousterian sites, Moldavia); Nesmeiảnov and Ranov 1962 (Mousterian artifacts, Shakhristan), 1964 (Khodzha-Gor Up. Pal. site, S. Fergana);

Okladnikov 1939C (Teshik-Tash Mousterian site, Uzbekistan), 1940F (Amir-Temir Cave, Uzbekistan), 1955B (Ĭakutia), 1956A, 1959D, E (Stone Age of Tadzhikistan), 1956B (Stone Age of Syr-Dar'iả R. basin), 1957 (Pal. of USSR), 1959C, F, 1965 (early cultures of Maritime region), 1961B (Khodzhikent Cave, Mousterian site, Uzbekistan), 1961C, 1964A, 1968B (archeol. of Siberia), 1963 (Pal. of Lake Orok-Nor, Mongolia), 1964B (Pal. of Lena R. basin), 1966A (Pal. of Mid. Asia), 1966B (Levalloisian settlement, Tadusha R.), 1966C (archeol. of Zeiả R. and Mid. Amur valleys); Okladnikov and Adamenko 1966 (Levalloisian-Mousterian blade, Siberia); Okladnikov and Islamov 1961 (Mousterian and Up. Pal. artifacts at Shuralisaĭ); Okladnikov, Kasymov and Konopliả 1964 (Kapchigaĭ Pal. workshop,

Fergana); Okladnikov and Kirillov 1968 (Up. Pal. settlement at Sokhatino, Titovskaia sopka); Okladnikov and Larichev 1963, 1967, 1968 (archeol. research in Mongolia), 1964 (Siberian archeol.); Okladnikov and Leonov 1961 (Mousterian finds, Fergana); Okladnikov and Ranov 1962 (Pal. of the Kairak-Kum); Okladnikov and Troitskii 1967 (Pal. sites, Mongolia); Okladnikov, Vereshchagin and Ovodov 1968 (Up. Pal. cave, Maritime Province); Ostrovskii and Grigor'ev 1966 (Aurignacian sites and artifacts);

Panichkina 1959A, B (Up. Pal. cores), 1961 (flint artifacts, Kuban'); Panichkina and Vekilova 1962 (cave industries, Caucasus); Păunescu 1966 (artifacts Braşov, Moldova, Muntenia), 1968 (Gravettian site, Moldavia); Petrichenko 1963 (Aurignacian artifacts, Prut R.); Petrun' 1956 (artifacts, Maritime Province); Petrun' and Bilocris 1962 (artifacts, Crimea); Polikarpovich 1955 (Mousterian flints, Belorussia), 1957 (Mousterian and Aurignacian artifacts, Up. Dnepr); Potapov 1955 (prehist., Siberia), 1964 (prehist., Tuva); Pototskii 1962 (early man, Moscow); Praslov 1963, 1964A, 1964C (artifacts, Azov), 1964B (artifacts, Kostenki), 1967A (cultures, Volga-Don), 1967B (Mousterian artifacts, E. Crimea); Proshek 1959 (Pal. hearth, Shanov-Kout II);

Rafalovich and Ketraru 1966 (hist. archeol., Moldavia); Ranov 1956 (Mousterian artifacts, Kairak-Kum), 1958 (artifacts, Alai Valley), 1959A (Pal. artifacts, Shor-Kul' and E. Pamir), 1959B (Mousterian artifacts, Vakhsh Valley and E. Pamir), 1961B, 1962 (Mousterian artifacts, S. Tadzhikistan), 1964 (artifacts, E. Pamir); Ravdonikas 1940 (archeol., Karelo-Finnish SSR); Rogachev 1961D, 1962A, 1968 (artifacts, Kostenki, Don R. valley), 1962 (archeol., Russian plain); Rudinskii 1959 (Pal. quartzite tools, Ukraine);

Savich 1968 (Early Up. Pal. site, Volyn'); Sawicki 1957 (Solutrian artifacts), 1964, 1965A (Up. Pal. sites, Kostenki and Borševo); Schild 1966 (Up. Pal., Crimea); Schwidetzky 1963 (Up. Pal. human skulls, Afontova Gora and Mal'ta); Semenov, S. A. 1961A (Neanderthal flints, Stalingrad), 1964A (flint tools, Khor-Daud); Shamsutdinov 1966 (Up. Pal. site, Transbaikalia); Shamsutdinov and Barabashev 1963 (archeol. sites, Transbaikalia); Sharipova 1966 (stone tools, Bukhara Oblast, Uzbekistan); Shiperovich 1962 (stone tool, Altai region); Shokurov and Bader 1960 (Pal. site, Belaia R.); Shovkoplias 1955B (mammoth bone dwellings Dobranichevka, Supoe R.), 1955C, 1957, 1959C, 1964, 1965A, C, 1966 (cultures, Ukraine), 1961 (Late Pal., Middle Dnepr basin), 1967 (artifacts, Chernigov Prov.); Shramko 1962 (Pal., Donets); Shul'ts 1957 (archeol., Crimea); Solov'ev and Orelkin 1961 (human bones and artifacts, Khupynishakhva Cave, Abkhazia); Sosnovskii 1935C (settlement, Afontova hill), 1940D (Pal. sites, S. Siberia); Sova 1964 (Mousterian tools, Uzhgorod, Ukraine); Sukachev et al. 1966 (artifacts, Kliaz'ma R. near Vladimir); Suleimanov 1966 (rock shelter, Uzbekistan), 1968 (Mousterian sites, Cent. Asia);

Tarasov 1961 (artifacts, Uglianskii site, Kostenki), 1962, 1967A (artifacts, Gagarino, Up. Don R.), 1964 (dwellings, Gagarino), 1965, 1968 (dwellings, artifacts, Gagarino); Tashkenbaev 1966 (Levalloisian flint core, Obi-Rakhmat cave); Timofeev and Kanivets 1968 (artifacts, Soviet Arctic); Tolochko 1968 (settlement, Ukraine); Tseitlin 1964A (Pal. site, Yenisei R.), 1965 (Up. Pal. site, Sungir', Vladimir Province); Tushabramishvili 1960 (Pal. Gvardzhilas-Klde cave), 1968 (artifacts, Kvirili Gorge, Chiatury region);

Vakturskaia et al. 1968 (Mousterian, Uzbekistan); Vekilova 1967 (Mousterian man, Akhshtyr' Cave); Vishnevskii 1948 (archeol., Lena R.); Voskresenskii 1959, 1964 (artifacts, Baikal region); Vyezzhev 1955 (archeol., Ukraine);

Zaborski 1965B (artifacts, Siberia); Zadneprovskii and Ranov 1966 (Mousterian, Kirgizia); Zamiatnin 1958 (artifacts, Azerbaidzhan), 1961A (early man), 1961B (Mousterian site, near Stalingrad); Zaverniaev and Schmidt 1961 (Low. Pal. artifacts, Up. Desna R.); Zelenchuk et al. 1964 (archeol., Moldavia); Zemliakov 1939B (archeol., Arctic USSR), 1940E (archeol., Karelia); Zhiteneva 1968 (fish remains in archeol. sites, Desna R.); Zubakov 1962 (Pal. site, Enisei R. Valley).

PALEOANTHROPOLOGY – ASIA
GENERAL – Chard 1957, 1960B (COWA surveys, N. Asia), 1964A, B, 1966 (archeol.,
    N. E. Asia);
  Efimenko 1960 (cultural changes);
  Field 1966A (archeol., anthrop.);
  Ginzburg 1959 (paleoanthrop., Cent. Asia);
  Larichev 1963, 1964A (Low. Pal. cultures, E. and Cent. Asia);
  Michael 1964B (archeol., N. Asia);
  Narr 1966D (Pal. cultures, S. and E. Asia);
  Ranov 1965, 1968A, B (archeol., Cent. Asia), 1966 (pebble tools, Cent. Asia).

NEAR EAST
  GENERAL – Asmus 1965 (fossil hominids, Palestine);
  Field 1964 (Stone Age man);
  Grigor'ev 1965B (no human migration to Europe);
  Jelínek, J. 1964A (Neanderthal skel., Palestine);
  Los 1966 (prehist., Palestine);
  Matson 1957, 1960 (COWA surveys, W. Asia); Mellink 1964 (current research, Asia
    Minor);
  Roginskiĭ 1966A (fossil hominids);
  Uryson 1964B (new hominid finds);
  Watson, P. J. 1965 (early settlements, Syria and Mesopotamia).

  AFGANISTAN – Dupree 1964 (archeol. surveys and excavations).

  ARMENIA – Arakeliân 1961 (archeol.);
  Liubin 1961B (Up. Acheulian workshop, Dzhraber);
  Martirosiân 1968 (Pal. cave artifacts, Erevan).

  IRAN – Hole and Flannery 1967 (prehist. of S. W.);
  McBurney 1964 (Ké Aram Cave, Mazandaran province);
  Young, T. C. and Smith 1966 (prehist., Cent. W.).

  IRAQ – Anon. 1960CK, CP (Shanidar man);
  Charles 1963B (Shanidar man);
  Greene, A. M. 1967 (Neanderthals, Shanidar Cave);
  Korobkov 1963B (Shanidar Neanderthals);
  Leroi-Gourhan, Arlette 1961B (Shanidar Cave);
  Nader 1962 (Shanidar Cave – summary of literature);
  Roux 1964 (prehist.);
  Solecki, R. and Leroi-Gourhan 1966 (archeol. and paleoclim., Shanidar Cave); Solecki,
    R. L. 1961 (Shanidar Cave); Stewart, T. D. 1963B (Shanidar skeletons);
  Wright, H. T. 1966 (Pal. site, southern desert).

  ISRAEL – Anati and Haas 1967 (Homo erectus, Plain of Esdraelon);
  Bay 1966 (early artifacts); Binford, S. R. 1966A (excavations at Me'Arat Shovakh);
  Picard 1965 (early man, Jordan Rift Valley), Picard and Baida 1966 (early man,
    'Ubeidiya formation);
  Soetens 1963 (prehist.); Stekelis 1964 (Pal. cultures, Kabara Cave); Stekelis and
    Bar Yosef 1965, Stekelis, Bar Yosef and Tchernov 1966 (Up. Pal. site, En Gev);
    Suzuki 1964, 1965, 1968 (Amud man);
  Takai 1968 (Amud man); Tobias 1966B (fossil hominid, Ubeidiya);
  Vallois 1967C (Ubeidiya man); Vandermeersch 1966A, 1968A (human remains,
    Qafzeh cave), 1966B (Mousterian industry, Larikba, Judean Desert);
  Watanabe, H. 1964, 1965, 1968 (Amud Cave); Wreschner 1964 (archeol., Geulah
    Cave, Haifa);

Yizraeli 1967 (artifacts, Holon).

JORDAN — Anon. 1963CN (Mid. Pleist. artifacts and hominid remains, Jordan
    Valley);
González-Echegaray, J. 1964A (excavations at "El Khiam");
Huckriede and Wiesemann 1968 (Pal. artifacts, El Jafr Basin).

LEBANON — Fleisch 1966 (Acheulian site, Ard es-Saoude).

SYRIA — Anon. 1964AT (camp site, Latamne);
Modderman 1964 (Pal. sites near Hama).

SAUDI ARABIA — Anon. 1964AG (flint tools, Habarat);
Payne, J. C. and Hawkins 1963 (flints, handaxes, Habarut).

TURKEY — Bostanci 1965 (early man, Anatolia);
Erdbrink and Van Heekeren 1965 (pebble tools, Anatolia);
Kansu 1963B (Low. Pal., Izmir), 1963C (prehist. sites, Marmara and Thrace), 1964
    (choppers, S. E. Anatolia); Kökten 1963A (lithic industry, Black Sea coast),
    1963B (cave, Küçükçekmece area).

SOUTHERN AND EASTERN ASIA
    GENERAL — Anon. 1960A (Yeti as early man); Avrorin 1964 (prehist., Far East);
    Beardsley, Chang and Loehr 1959 (COWA surveys, Far East);
    Chang, Kwang-chih and Kidder 1964 (COWA surveys, Far East); Chard 1963D
        (migrations of man to New World); Chardin 1965A (Plio.-Pleist.); Conklin
        1957 (COWA surveys, Indonesia);
    Dales 1964 (COWA surveys, S. Asia); Dyson, R. H. 1958, 1960 (COWA surveys,
        S. Asia);
    Emory 1958, 1960, 1965 (COWA surveys, Pacific Islands);
    Fürer-Haimendorf 1964 (anthrop. bibliog., S. Asia, 1955-59);
    Horr 1959 (COWA surveys, S. E. Asia);
    Jacob 1967 (Pithecanthropus finds, Indonesia);
    Kahlke 1965F, 1966 (new hominid finds);
    Sartono 1961, 1963, 1964, 1967 (Pithecanthropus finds, Indonesia); Shellshear
        1937 (prehist., Far East); Solheim 1960B (COWA surveys, Indonesia), 1964
        (Formosa and S. E. Asia), 1966B (E. Asia and Oceania), 1966C (COWA surveys,
        S. E. Asia);
    Tikhomirov, M. N. 1958 (prehist., Far East);
    Uryson 1966C (East Asian hominids).

    BORNEO — Anon. 1965BY (Niah skull);
    Burkitt 1964B (Niah Cave, Sarawak);
    Harrisson, T. 1964A, B, 1966 (Niah Caves);
    Iakimov 1967B (Pithecanthropus skull cap, Java);
    Jacob 1964, 1966 (Pithecanthropus, Java);
    Koenigswald 1968B (Pithecanthropus, Java); Korenhof 1962 (dentition of human
        population at Sangiran, Java);
    Petrov, G. I. 1940B (Pithecanthropus, Java);
    Tobias 1966D (Kedung Brubus mandible);
    Vallois 1965C (Pithecanthropus, Java).

    CAMBODIA — Carbonnel and Biberson 1968 (evidence of Pleist. man, Phnom Loang
        Cave).

CEYLON — Deraniyagala 1960F, 1965 (hominids), 1964A (bibliog. of archeol., paleont.), 1964B (prehist. archeol.).

CHINA — An, Chin-min 1959 (survey, Yellow R.), 1961 (Stone Age cave, Anyang); Andrews, R. C. 1930 (Peking man); Anon. 1961CX (Lower—Mid. Pleist. artifacts, Shansi Province), 1962CN (Gigantopithecus, Kwangsi), 1963CG (mandible of "ape-man", Shensi Province), 1964AO (Sinanthropus lantianensis, Lantien Co.), 1964AX, BB, 1965U, BK, CO (Lantian man, Shensi Province), 1968J (early man jaw);
Balázs 1962 (early man, S. China); Basch 1964 (review of archeol.); Br. 1961 (Neanderthal, Mapa, S. China);
Chang, Kwang-chih 1966 (new sites; Pleist. primates), 1968 (early man and archeol. of China); Chardin 1930I (Sinanthropus); Chêng 1964 (prehist.); Chia, Wang and Wang 1964 (K'o Ho Pal. site, Shansi Province); Chow 1965A (Sinanthropus lantianensis), 1965C (new finds);
Dai 1966 (artifacts, Lantian man site); Dai and Bai 1966 (artifact, Shantung cave); Dai and Chi 1964 (paleoliths, Lantian);
Gu 1965 (Sinanthropus skull bones and site);
Heintz, A. 1965B (Sinanthropus, Lantien); Hemmer 1964C (Lantian man); Hsia 1963 (archeol. in China); Hsu 1966A, B (climatic conditions during time of Sinanthropus); Huang, Wei-wen 1964 (paleoliths, Sanmen area, W. Honan);
Jacob 1968 (Wadjakoid maxillary, Hong Kong);
Kowalski, K. 1965B (cave studies); Kwang-tung Provincial Museum 1960 (paleoliths of Tunghsing, Kwangtung);
Larichev 1964B (apes and hominids of S. China and evol. of E. Asiatic man); Liang 1960 (stone implements of Hsichiaoshan, Kwangtung);
Martínez del Rio 1931 (Peking man);
Pei 1930B (Sinanthropus), 1960E (living environments of early man), 1965A (Chinese Pal. archeol.), 1965B (Gigantopithecus cave, Kwangsi); Pei et al. 1965 (chert artifacts, Kuan-yin-tung Cave, Kweichow);
Vallois 1965E (Lantian man);
Wang, T. Y. and C. 1960 (paleoliths, Gujiao, Shansi); Woo, Ju-kang 1960C (new finds), 1961C (Gigantopithecus), 1964A, B, C, D, F, 1965A, B, C, E, F G, H, 1966A, B, C (Lantian man), 1965D (paleoanthrop.); Woo, Ju-kang and Cheboksarov 1959 (early man); Wu, Xin-zhi et al. 1966 (site of Lantian man);
Yang 1965 (Lantian man);
Zaki 1964 (Lantian man).

INDIA — Adyalkar 1961 (Pal. cultures); Allchin 1959 (Mid. Stone Age); Anon. 1964F (Indian prehist.), 1968E (Gigantopithecus);
Banerji 1964 (prehist., Rajasthan); Boriskovskiĭ 1967 (Pal. research);
Chand 1957 (Pal. of Orissa);
Due Rojo 1965 (dating, correlating Pal. industries);
Ehrhardt and Kennedy 1965 (human remains, Langhnaj);
Ghosh 1961B (microliths, Bahmni), 1963 (hist. of paleoanthrop.), 1965 (paleoliths, E. India); Graziosi 1964B (prehist. research, N. W. Punjab); Gupta, S. P. 1965 (Up. Pal. industries), 1968 (Early Low. Pal. cultures compared with those of Middle Asia);
Joshi 1961B (Pal. industries, Upper Wainganga Basin, Maharashtra), 1966A (Acheulian succession, Adamgarh site, central India), 1966B (Stone Age factory site, Mohgaon Kalan, central India); Joshi, Sali and Bopardikar 1966 (Early Pal. tools from Gangapur, Nasik);
Karve-Corvinus 1967 (Chirki Pal. site, Upper Godavari Basin); Khatri 1961B (Stone Age and Pleist. chronol., Narmada Cilley), 1961C, 1964 (early man research);
Lal 1964A, B, 1966 (archeol. research);
Malik 1964 (prehist. cultural levels), 1966 (Late Stone Age industries, Gujarat); Mehta

1967 (Stone Age sites, Valia Taluka and Mangrol Taluka); Misra, V. N. 1964 (paleoliths, Udaipur district, Rajasthan), 1965 (prehist.); Misra and Mate 1965 (prehist.); Mohapatra, G. C. 1964 (Mid. Stone Age industries, Orissa); Mohapatra, Bhatia and Sahu 1963 (Levallois industry, nr. Bap, Jodhpur district); Mohapatra, M. R. 1964 (flaked tools and polished stone celts, E. Punjab); Paddayya 1967 (Late Stone Age industries, Krishna Valley, Mysore); Piggott 1962B (prehist.); Raghunath 1966 (Late Pal. industry, Madura and Pudukkottai, Madras State); Rao, M. S. N. 1964 (Early Pal. stone tools, Dharwar district); Sankalia 1964B (Mid. Stone Age cultures), 1965 (Early Stone Age industry, Saurashtra, Gujarat); Sen and Ghosh 1964 (Abbevillean, Levalloisian cultures, Narmada Valley); Wainwright and Malik 1967 (Pleist. archeol.).

JAPAN — Aso and Oda 1966 (Pal. site, Shizuoka Prefecture); Beardsley 1962 (COWA surveys, Japan); Befu, Chard and Okada 1964 (bibliog. of archeol.); Chinzei 1966 (Nekata Cave site, Hamakita); Hasegawa 1966A (human bones, Gansuiji form.); Higuchi, Kitami and Ozaki 1965 (Up. Pleist. cultures, Tsukizaki, Iizaka, Fukushima City); Hokkaido Univ. Archaeol. Team 1960 (prehist. remains excavated at Shirataki); Ikawa 1964 (pre-ceramic to ceramic cultures), 1965 (grinding stones); Kamaki 1957B (microlith culture, Ijima site, Kagawa Prefecture); Komatsu 1962 (early man); Kurisu 1967 (human skel. remains, Hokkaido); Larichev 1968A (first Pal. settlement); Maringer 1956D (Levallois hand-axes, Gongeyama); Matsumoto et al. 1966, 1967 (paleoliths from Hagurodô and Hatatate, Yamada); Matsumoto, Ishii, et al. 1964A (paleoliths from the Tama Hills, Hachiôji City), 1964B (axe-heads from Iwajuku, Kiryû City), 1964C (paleoliths from Kanagi, Kitatsugaru District); Matsumoto, Mori, et al. 1965 (paleoliths of the Ashinokuchi Valley); Miyasaka, Kodama and Miyasaka 1965 (excavations at Waribashi, Daimon-Tōge, Nogano-ken); Morlan 1967A (pre-ceramic period of Hokkaido); Oba and Chard 1962 (chronol. for Hokkaido prehist.); Ôi 1963 (Tasishô site, Hokkaido); Okada, A. and H. and Chard 1967 (bibliog. of Hokkaido archeol); Okladnikov and Goregliăd 1958 (Early Stone Age, N. Japan); Serizawa 1960, 1962 (Stone Age), 1963 (stone artifacts, N. Kanto Plain, Fujiyama site); Serizawa and Kamaki 1965 (rock shelter, Fukui, Nagasaki); Serizawa and Nakagawa 1965 (Low. Pal. artifacts, Sozudai site, Kyushu); Serizawa et al. 1959 (Kamiyama site, Niigata); Shirataki 1963 (archeol.); Sugihara 1956B, Sugihara and Tozawa 1960 (Pre-ceramic cultures, Iwajuku, Gumma Prefecture); Sugihara 1962 (archeol.); Sugihara et al. 1959 (knives, Kanto loam bed, Moro); Suzuki 1966, Suzuki and Endo 1966 (Hamakita man); Tomimasu and Tozawa 1962 (microliths, Karatsu); Tozawa and Tomimasu 1962 (artifacts, Karatsu); Tsunoda 1962 (Nyu site, Oita Prefecture).

KOREA — Ho, To You 1965 ("Coulpo" Pal. culture); Larichev and Grigorenko 1967 (Kul'pkho culture, Khamgen prov.).

MONGOLIA — Dai et al. 1964 (Up. Pal. stone tools, Alashan desert).

NEW GUINEA — Hossfeld 1965B (paleoecology and dating of Aitape man); Richardson and Dudley 1967 (archeol.).

PAKISTAN — Dani 1964 (prehist.); Paterson and Drummond 1962 (Pal. Soan culture);

Ranov 1967 (archeol., Karakorum, Hindu-Kush and Sanghao Cave);
Sankalia 1964B (Mid. Stone Age culture).

PHILIPPINE ISLANDS — Beckett 1957 (occupied sites, Polynesia);
Evangelista 1964 (humain remains and flake tools, Tabon Cave).

THAILAND — Chin 1958 (survey of prehist.);
Heekeren et al. 1967 (Stone Age settlements, Sai-yok);
Nielsen 1962 (Pal. rock shelter, Sai-Yok);
Solheim 1963B, 1966A (prehist. archeol.).

VIETNAM — Boriskovskiǐ 1962A, B, 1966 (Stone Age, Mt. Do Pal. site).

PALEOANTHROPOLOGY — AUSTRALIA AND NEW ZEALAND
    Anon. 1963BX (antiquity of man), 1965AU (stone tools), 1966BB (human skel.),
       1967W (early man, Melbourne);
    Barton 1968 (bibliog. of archeol.); Berndt, R. M. and C. H. 1964, 1965 (early
       man); Birdsell 1959, 1962 (COWA surveys and bibliog.), 1967 (origin of Aus-
       tralian aborigines); Blake-Palmer 1956 (Otago coastal occupation site, N. Z.);
       Bowler et al. 1967 (human burial, Melbourne); Browne 1963 (time origin of
       aborigines); Bulmer, S. and R. 1964 (prehist. Australian New Guinea High-
       lands);
    Campbell, A. H. 1967 (legends and Aboriginal prehistory); Clegg 1965 (stone in-
       dustry, Queensland); Cooper, H. M. 1966 (stone artifacts, Kangaroo Island);
       Coutts 1966 (prehist. campsites, Australia); Crosby, E. 1968 (archeol. site sur-
       vey, Queensland);
    Daniels, J. R. S. 1966 (site recording, N. Z.);
    Elkin 1967 (aboriginal man); Emory 1958, 1960, 1965 (COWA surveys, Pacific
       Islands);
    Gill 1966 (migrations of men, Australia); Golson 1964 (COWA surveys, Australia);
       Gould, R. A. 1968 (chipping stones in the outback); Groube 1966 (archeol., N.Z.);
    Jones, Rhys 1967A (early man, Tasmania);
    McCarthy 1959, 1965, 1966 (Australian archeol.); McCulloch, B. 1968 (shelters,
       Weka Pass area, N. Z.); Macintosh, N. W. G. 1952 (hist. of Cohuna cranium),
       1965 (Australian human fossil material), 1967 (human bones at Green Gully,
       nr. Keilor, Victoria); Matthews, J. M. 1966 (Kartan pebble tool industries, S.
       Australia and Kangaroo Is.); MeGaw, V. 1966 (directions of Australian archeol.);
       Meston 1937 (Tasmanian stone culture); Micha 1965 (Australian aborigines);
       Moore, D. R. 1967 (aboriginal prehist., Australia); Mulvaney 1962, 1963, 1964A,
       B, C, 1966A, 1966B (Australian prehist.); Mulvaney and Joyce 1965 (archeol.
       of Kenniff Cave, The Tombs, and Marlong Plains Cave, Queensland);
    Sharp 1956 (prehist., N. Z.); Shawcross and Roe 1966 (artifacts and verts., Houhora,
       N.Z.); Sheils 1963 (Australian prehist.);
    Taylor, A. 1968 (cultural site, N. Z.); Tindale 1965 (stone tool making); Trotter
       1966A, B, 1967A, B, 1968B (moa-hunter sites, N. Z.);
    Watson, J. B. 1964 (prehist., New Guinea); Weathersbee 1966 (artifacts, Morphett
       Vale, Australia); White, C. 1967 (stone axes, Arnhem land);
    Yawata and Sinoto 1968 (prehist., Oceania).

PALEOANTHROPOLOGY — AFRICA
    GENERAL — Alimen 1960B (prehist.); Anon. 1963CO (australopithecines and Chad
       man), 1964AL (origin of man in Africa), 1966BP, 1967BJ (archeol. terminology),
       1966BQ (posts and training facilities, W. Afr.), 1967S (Afr. prehist.); Arambourg
       1965A (human evol. in Afr.);
    Beauchêne and Hugon 1964 (bibliog. Afr. archeol.); Bishop and Clark 1967A, B
       (evol. in Africa); Brien 1956 (human finds, 1856—1956);

Calvocoressi 1965 (COWA surveys, W. Afr.), 1967 (terminology in Afr. archeol.);
  Clark, J. D. 1962F, 1965C (COWA surveys, Equatorial Afr.), 1962G, 1965D
  (COWA surveys, E. Afr.), 1964A (Sangoan culture of Equatoria), 1964B (origins
  of Afr. cultures), 1965B, 1967A (atlas of Afr. prehist.), 1965E (later Pleist.
  cultures, Afr.), 1966A (Acheulian occupation sites), 1967C (W. Afr. Archeol.
  Resolutions on Terminology); Clark, Cole et al. 1966 (Afr. archeol.); Clark,
  W. E. LeGros 1967B (australopithecine types); Cole, S. 1963D, 1964B, 1965
  (prehist., E. Afr.); Connah 1967A (Colloquim, Afr. archeol.); Curtis et al.
  1965 (correlation of major Pleist. deposits);
Daniels, S. G. H. 1967 (terminology, W. Afr. prehist.); Dart, R. A. 1960G (Afr.
  and the emergence of civilization), 1961D (Afr. and the evol. of man), 1965A
  (australopithecine acceptance), 1965B (australopithecine cordage and thongs), 1968A
  (tool-makers); Davies, O. 1965, 1967C (prehist., W. Afr.), 1967B (Burg-Wartenstein Conf. — chronology); Debets 1962 (Aliman's L'Afrique préhistorique);
Folster 1968 (Mid. Stone Age site, Oshun R.);
Gabel 1965 (Afr. prehist.); Gaherty 1968 (human skeletal materials, W. Afr.);
  Gallay 1965 (Inventaria Archaeologica Africana);
Heberer 1966 (Australopithecus and osteodontokeratic culture); Heinzelin de Brau-
  court 1962D (industry typology); Howell, F. C. 1959C (COWA surveys, Equat-
  orial Afr.), 1967A (Later Cenozoic studies); Hugot 1964, 1967 (prehist., W.
  Afr.);
Kleindienst 1962 (Acheulian assemblage, E. Afr.), 1967 (terminology and Stone Age
  industries, E. Afr.);
Lambrecht, F. L. 1964, 1967, 1968 (influence of blood parasites on hominid evol.);
  Leakey, L. S. B. (man's Afr. origin), 1966B (hominid mandibles), 1967E (Early
  Mioc. hominids); Leakey, M. D. et al. 1967 (classif. of Afr. industrial complexes);
Marcozzi 1965B (Afr. hominids);
Nenquin 1964A, 1965, 1968 (Inventaria Archaeologica Africana);
Oakley and Campbell 1967A, B (catalogue of fossil hominids); Oliver and Mathew
  1963 (hist. of E. Afr.); Oyenuga, Kunle, and Ozanne 1968 (artifacts, W. Afr.);
Pericot Garcia and Tarradell 1962 (prehist., Afr.);
Reshetov 1964A (Australopithecus, W. Afr.); Rouse 1958B, 1961 (COWA surveys,
  W. Afr.);
Spaulding 1959 (COWA surveys, E. Afr.); Summers 1957B (Magosian cultures);
Tobias 1966C (early man), 1967D (Australopithecus);
Uryson 1964B (new hominid finds);
Watanabe, N. 1959 (Zinjanthropus, autralopithecines); Wolf 1963 (human cultures).

NORTH AFRICA AND THE SAHARAN REGION

GENERAL — Alimen 1964C, 1965C (Quaternary, Sahara), 1965A, 1968 (Acheulian,
  Sahara); Alimen and Chavaillon 1962 (pebble culture, N. W. Sahara); Alimen,
  Chevaillon and Karpoff 1963 (Pal., central Sahara); Anon. 1956BS, 1959BS,
  1960CL, CM, 1963BY, BZ (prehist., Maghreb-Sahara); Arkell 1959B (Ennedi
  Expd., Nile Valley); Armelagos et al. 1965 (prehist. man, Nile Valley);
Balout 1965E, F (Mousterian, N. Afr.); 1967B, C (industries and terminology, N.
  Afr.); Biberson 1965C, 1967B (Low. Pal., N. W. Afr.); Biberson and Souville
  1959 (Saharan archeol.);
Chavaillon, J. 1964, 1965A, B, 1966B (Pal. sites, industries, cultural chronology,
  Sahara); Chavaillon, N. 1964, 1965 (prehist., Saoura Valley); Claracq and Nou-
  garede 1959 (Acheulian sites, Erg Bourarhet);
Heinzelin de Braucourt 1967 (prehist., Nubia); Howe, B. 1957, 1960 (COWA sur-
  veys, N. W. Afr.); Hugot 1963 (prehist. research 1950-57, Sahara), 1965, 1966A
  (Aterian, Sahara);
Kn., R. 1964 (early man skulls);
Lhote 1963B (survey of Saharan archeol.);

Marks 1964 (prehist., Nubia);
Pericot Garcia 1965A (prehist., N. Afr.);
Ramendo 1963A (lithic industries, Tarf region), 1965 (Pal. industries, Djidjelli);
Simpson, W. K. 1959, Simpson and Carter 1962 (COWA surveys, N. E. Afr.);
Smith, P. E. L. 1966C (cultures, N. E. Afr.);
Van Beek et al. 1964 (archeol., S. Yemen).

ALGERIA — Arambourg 1965B (Ternifine man); Arambourg and Balout 1967
   (fossil hominids);
Balout 1956 (prehist.); Balout, Biberson and Tixier 1967 (Atlanthropus, Ternifine);
   Bayle des Hermens 1964, 1965A, B (Pal. industries, Tiaret);
Cadenat 1960 (prehist., Ammi-Moussa); Camps 1964 (Low. Pal. artifacts); Cin-
   quabre and Maitre 1964 (Pal. industry, In-Eker region);
Dedieu 1965 (lithic industry, djebel Zabaouine Cave);
Fleischhacker 1955 (Atlanthropus, Ternifine);
Lorgin 1963 (Cap Ténès, Orléansville);
Maitre, C. 1965 (fossil hominids of Columnata, Tiaret); Maitre, J.-P. 1965 (prehist.
   localities and industries, Ahaggar); Morel 1966 (Low. Pal. in the region of La
   Calle);
Souville 1956B (prehist. atlas).

CHAD — Bayle des Hermens 1966, 1967 (Pal. artifacts and sites);
Coppens 1963, 1965A, C, D, 1966C (Tchad man), 1967C (catalogue fossil hominids),
   1968 (paleont. and archeol., N. Chad); Courtin 1967 (developed Acheulian, N.
   Chad);
Kurth 1962L (australopithecine skull);
Lebeuf 1964 (prehist.);
Ostoya 1965 (Tchadanthropus);
Uryson 1966B (Tchad man).

DAHOMEY — Marchesseau 1966 (Pal. industry, N. W.).

EGYPT — Albritton and Wendorf 1967 (artifacts, Tushka archeol. site); Arkell and
   Sandford 1967 (fossil hominids);
Guichard, J. and G. 1965 (Early and Mid. Pal., Nubia);
Hayes 1964B (Pal. man);
Liubin 1964 (Mousterian-Levalloisian artifacts, Nubia);
Malez and Crnolatac 1966 (Pal. sites, Sinai);
Oakley 1965B (Kom Ombo skull);
Piotrovskii 1964 (prehist., Nubia);
Reed, C. A. 1965 (Kom Ombo skull fragment);
Simons 1964A (early hominoids, Fayum); Smith, P. E. L. 1964A (cultures), 1966D
   (Kom Ombo artifacts);
Vinogradov, A. V. 1964 (Up. Pal. Sebilian culture, Dakka region, Nubia);
Waechter 1965 (artifacts, Nubia); Wendorf 1965A (prehist., Nubia), 1965B (salvage
   archeol., Aswan Dam); Wendorf and Said 1967 (cultures, Up. Egypt); Wendorf,
   Shiner and Marks 1965 (prehist., Nubia).

ETHIOPIA — Anon. 1964AN (Melka Kontouré site, Awash Valley); Arambourg
   1967, Arambourg, Chavaillon and Coppens 1967, Arambourg and Coppens 1967,
   1968 (Paraustralopithecus aethiopicus, Omo);
Bailloud 1965 (Pal. artifacts, Melka-Kontouré);
Chavaillon, J. 1965C, 1966A (Melka Kontouré site, near Addis–Ababa);
Faure and Roubet 1968 (Acheulian biface, Red Sea);
Ricqlès 1968C (Paraustralopithecus jaw, Omo).

GABON — Beauchêne 1963 (prehist.);
Farine 1963 (prehist. sites and industries).

GHANA — Davies, O. 1961D (pebble tools), 1966 (Low. and Mid. Pal. tools, Volta R.).

GUINEA — Davies, O. 1964 (Pal. sites, industries).

LIBYA — Arkell 1964A (prehist. site, Salvador), 1964B (Wanyanga site);
Dupree 1965 (archeol., S. Tripolitania, N. Fezzan);
Guerri 1964B ("pebble culture", Fezzan);
Heekeren and Jawad 1966 (Low. Pal. stone tools, Fezzan Desert);
McBurney 1967A (fossil hominids, Haua Fteah), 1967B (Haua Fteah);
Ramendo 1963B, 1964 (pebble culture, Reggan);
Sampson 1967A (methods of study, Haua Fteah);
Tobias 1967B (Haua Fteah hominids); Trevor and Wells 1967 (Haua Fteah mandible);
Ziegert 1964, 1965 (Pleist. climate and cultures).

MALI — Charles 1966 (Ibalaghem man);
Oakley and Campbell 1967C (fossil hominids, Asselar).

MAURITANIA — Biberson 1964B, 1965B, E (Low. Pal., Adrar);
Mauny 1962 (Pal. industries of the El-Beyyed-Tazazmout).

MOROCCO — Anthony 1966 (endocranial casts Jebel Irhoud man); Arambourg 1963G, 1965D (Neanderthal skulls, Jebel Irhoud); Arambourg, Biberson et al. 1967 (fossil hominids);
Balout 1964 (Neanderthal industry, Djebel Irhoud); Berthélémy 1960 (Lavalloisian technique); Biberson 1964A, 1965D, 1966 (Pleist. chronol. and Pal. industries), 1965A (Pleist. geol. and prehist. of Tarfaïa);
Ennouchi 1963B, 1966A, B, 1968 (Neanderthal cave at Jebel Irhoud);
Ferembach 1965D (cranial diagrams, Taforalt);
Souville 1956C, 1960C, D, 1963 (prehist.).

NIGER — Beauchêne 1966 (prehist. and archeol.);
Oakley and Campbell 1967D (fossil hominids, Achegour).

NIGERIA — Eyo 1966 (Rop rock shelter);
Shaw, T. 1966, 1967 (archeol.); Soper 1966 (Pal. industries, N. Nigeria).

SENEGAL — Barbey and Descamps 1967 (lithic industries, Dakar);
Hugot 1966B (Acheulian industry, Cape Manual).

SUDAN — Arkell 1960 (prehist.); Arkell and Hewes 1967 (fossil hominids); Armelagos 1964 (human mandible and artifacts, Wadi Halfa);
Carlson 1967 (Pal., Khor Abu Anga and Nubia); Chavaillon and Maley 1966 (pebble industry, Nile Valley); Chmielewski, W. 1965B, 1966 (archeol., Nile R. Valley, N. Sudan);
Greene, Ewing and Armelagos 1967 (dentition of Mesolithic population, Wadi Halfa); Guichard, J. and G. 1965 (Early and Mid. Pal., Nubia);
Hewes 1965 (prehist. cultures, W. bank of Nile); Hewes, et al. 1964 (fossil hominids from Wadi Halfa);
Maley 1966 (Acheulian sites, 2nd. Cataract).

TUNISIA — Gobert 1963 (bibliog. of prehist.).

SOUTH OF THE SAHARA
  GENERAL — Anon. 1967H (Homo habilis);
  Clark, J. D. 1959D (prehist. cultural influences in S. W. Afr.), 1966B, C (prehist.
    sites, Malawi), 1967B (archeol., sub-Saharan Afr.); Clark, Stephens and Coryndon
    1966 (Malawi Rift); Cooke, C. K. 1967C (Wilton complex linked with cave
    art); Cooke, H. B. S. 1967 (Pleist. sequence);
  Deacon 1965 (COWA surveys, S. Afr.);
  Evernden and Curtis 1963 (time scale of man);
  Inskeep 1967 (the Late Stone Age in S. Afr.);
  Koenigswald 1963D (Australopithecus doubtful tool makers);
  Ostoya 1965 (E. Afr. hominids);
  Posnansky 1966 (prehist., E. Afr.);
  Rudner and Grattan-Bellew 1964 (archeol. sites, S. W. Afr.);
  Smolla 1966 (Early and Mid. Pal., S. of Sahara).

  ANGOLA — Almeida and Camarate França 1965 (Magosian industries);
  Breuil and Almeida 1962 (prehist.);
  Clark, J. D. 1965A, 1966D (distribution of prehist. culture).

  BURUNDI — Nenquin 1966 (excavations at Nyarunazi).

  KENYA — Anon. 1967AY (humerus, man-ape);
  F., D. 1960 (Pleist. hominid jaw);
  Heberer 1965D (Acheulian handaxes, Olorgesailie);
  Isaac 1966A, B, 1967B (Acheulian occupation sites, Olorgesailie);
  Josselyn 1967B (discovery of Kenyapithecus);
  Leakey, L. S. B. 1964D (Gamble's Cave), 1968B (Kenyapithecus mandible, Kathwan-
    ga, Rusinga Is.), 1968D (hominid bone smashing at Fort Ternan); Leakey, L. S. B.,
    et al. 1967B (catalogue of fossil hominids); Leakey, M. D. 1966B (primitive arti-
    facts, Kenapoi Valley);
  Martyn 1967 (hominid remains nr. Lake Baringo);
  Patterson, B. and Howells 1967 (hominid humerus, Lake Rudolf);
  Tobias 1967C (hominids);
  Whitworth 1965 (artifacts, Lake Rudolf), 1966 (hominid, Lake Rudolf).

  MALAWI — Fagan 1967 (catalogue of fossil hominids);
  Stephens, E. A. 1966 (Mid. Stone Age chopper, Chitimwe Beds).

  MOÇAMBIQUE — Barradas 1967 (catalogue fossil hominids).

  THE REPUBLIC OF CONGO — Breuil 1964B, C, D, E (Pal. sites and industries);
  Heinzelin de Braucourt and Twiesselmann 1967 (catalogue fossil hominids);
  Mortelmans 1962B (prehist. cultures of W. Congo);
  Ploey and Moorsel 1966 (Pal. industries, Leopoldville);
  Twiesselmann 1965 (human molars, Katanga).

  RHODESIA (see also: ZAMBIA) — Baker, J. R. 1968B (Broken Hill man - Homo
    rhodesiensis); Bond, G. 1957 (Khami Stone Age sites); Brain 1967B (Redcliff
    Stone Age cave site); Brain and Cooke 1967 (Redcliff site);
  Cooke, C. K. 1964A (artifacts, Shashi and Shashani Rivers), 1964C (intro. to pre-
    hist.), 1964D (artifacts, Inyanga), 1966A (Proto-Stillbay now Charama industry),
    1966B (archeol. of Mafungabusi area, Gokwe), 1967A (Stone Age of the Nata
    R., Botswana), 1967B (archeol. and excavation, Redcliff Stone Age site); Cooke
    and Robinson 1954 (Wilton and Stillbay industries, Amadzimba Cave); Cooke,
    Summers and Robinson 1966 (the Stone Age); Crawford, J. R. 1965 (Mid. Stone
    Age site, Umvukwes);

Jones, N. 1932 (Mid. Stone Age), 1933 (archeol., Nswatugi, Madiliyangwa; new sites in the Matopo Hills), 1936 (artifacts, Hope Fountain, Bulawayo), 1938 (Bembesi industry).

RWANDA — Nenquin 1964B (Magosian industry, Rutonde), 1966 (excavations at Campion and Rutonde);
Van Noten and Hiernaux 1967 (Late Stone Age industry, Mukinanira).

TANZANIA — Anon. 1961CM, 1965CG (hominids, Olduvai), 1961CP (Zinjanthropus, Olduvai), 1964K, L, AY, BJ, BK, BW, 1965CI (Homo habilis, Olduvai), 1964AM (primates, Olduvai), 1965BQ, CV (origin of man);
Bach 1960 (Zinjanthropus, Olduvai); Betts 1965A, B (Zinjanthropus, Homo habilis, Olduvai);
Clark, J. D. 1962H, 1964C (Kalambo Falls site); Clark, W. E. LeGros 1967A (Olduvai Gorge); Coppens 1964 (Homo habilis, Olduvai); Crusafont Pairó 1966B (Homo habilis, Olduvai); Curtis et al. 1965 (evaluation of Olduvai);
Dart, R. A. 1965G (Olduvai Gorge); Davis, P. R. 1964 (hominids, Olduvai Gorge); Davis, Day and Napier 1964 (hominid tibia and fibula, Olduvai Gorge); Day 1967 (Olduvai hominid 10); Day and Napier 1964, 1966 (hominid foot bones, Olduvai Gorge); Debets 1964 (pebble industry and Homo habilis); Drake, F. and K. 1964 (Zinjanthropus);
Hay 1965B (hominid-bearing deposits of Olduvai Gorge); Heberer 1964A, B, D (Homo habilis, Olduvai Gorge); Heintz, A. 1964B (Homo habilis); Hemmer 1964A (Homo habilis); Hibben 1967 (early man); Holloway and Tobias 1965, 1966 (cranial capacity of Olduvai hominid); Howell et al. 1962 (Isimila Acheulian occupation site, Iringa Highlands);
Inskeep 1964 (Homo habilis, Olduvai); Isaac 1965A, B, 1967A (stratig. of the Peninj site);
Lawson 1964 (discovery of Homo habilis); Leakey, L. S. B. 1960E, 1967B, D (Olduvai Gorge), 1964B (Homo habilis type skull), 1964C (Olduvai hominids); Leakey, L. S. B. et al. 1965 (geol. and fauna of Olduvai Gorge), 1967A (cranium and dentition of Zinjanthropus, Olduvai Gorge); Leakey, L. S. B. and M. D. 1964 (hominids, Olduvai Gorge and Lake Natron); Leakey, Tobias and Isaac 1967 (catalogue of fossil hominids); Leakey, Tobias and Napier 1964 (Homo habilis defined); Leakey, M. D. 1965 (named localities, Olduvai Gorge), 1966A (review of Oldowan culture, Olduvai Gorge), 1967 (cultural material from Beds I and II, Olduvai Gorge); Leakey, M. D. et al. 1967 (typology of the Oldowan);
McMurry 1966 (human evol., Olduvai Gorge); Marcozzi 1965A (Olduvai Gorge);
Napier 1964A (Olduvai hominids), 1964C (Homo habilis, Olduvai);
Perkins, C. M. 1965 (Olduvai Gorge, juv.); Piveteau 1964F (Homo habilis, Olduvai); Reshetov 1963 (Zinjanthropus), 1964B (hominids, Olduvai); Robinson, J. T. 1964A (Zinjanthropus);
Saller 1961 (Zinjanthropus); Sergi 1964 (Olduvai skull); Sm. 1960 (Zinjanthropus); Smolla 1962 (artifacts, Tendaguru); Strouhal 1964 (Olduvai Gorge);
Tobias 1964A, 1965C, 1967A (Zinjanthropus); 1965A, 1965B, 1966A (Homo habilis), 1965E, 1967E, 1968A (Olduvai Gorge hominids);
Uryson 1965A (Olduvai Gorge).

UGANDA — Bishop 1959B (survey of Pal. research);
Cole, G. H. 1965, 1967 (Acheulian and Sangoan, S. Uganda);
O'Brien 1966 (Levalloisian flake industry, Nsongezi);
Posnansky 1962 (Pal. industries).

UNION OF SOUTH AFRICA — Anderson, J. M. 1968B (rhino teeth and osteodonto-keratic culture, Makapansgat); Anon. 1964BT (Taungs skull);
Beater 1965, 1967 (Mid. Stone Age implements, Natal); Biggerstaff 1967 (age of

Taungs child); Brain 1967A (australopithecines in S. Afr. caves); Breitinger 1955C (Saldanha skull, Cape Prov.);

Daniels, S. G. H. 1968 (Stone Age, Transvaal); Daniels, S. 1967 (Mid. Stone Age sites, Transvaal); Dart, R. A. 1928 (big game of early man), 1962H (osteodontokeratic culture, Makapansgat), 1964A (ecology of S. Afr. man-apes), 1964B (osteodontokeratic culture), 1965D (stone pounding tools, Makapansgat), 1965E (recent discoveries, Makapansgat), 1966A (archeol. research), 1967A (antiquity of mining), 1967B (cranial chalices, Makapansgat), 1968B (Australopithecus africanus);

Farnden 1966 (Late Stone Age shelter, New Amalfi), 1967 (Acheulian industry and sites, Natal); Fock 1965 (Stone Age sites, N. Cape Province);

Galloway 1959 (skel. remains, early man);

Heberer 1963D (hominid skull cap, Saldanha Bay); Holm 1966 (bibliog. of pre- and proto-historic archeol.); Howell and Schanfield 1959 (COWA surveys, S. Afr.);

Inskeep 1965 (Early Stone Age occupation at Amanzi);

Keenan-Smith 1966 (S. Afr. Archaeol. Soc.);

Louw 1960 (Bushmen of Matjes River Rock Shelter);

MacCalman 1962, 1963, 1964 (Mid. Stone Age, S. W. Afr.), 1967 (factory sites, S. W. Afr.); Maggs and Speed 1967 (Bonteberg shelter); Maguire 1965, 1968 (Makapansgat Limeworks); Malan 1962B (Elandsfontein stone industry, Hopefield); Mason, R. J. 1965B (fractured pebbles from the Makapansgat Limeworks), 1966 (Acheulian culture, Doornlaagte site, Kimberley), 1967A (analytical procedure for Stone Age cultures), 1967B (terminology for Earlier Stone Age cultures); Mason and Beaumont 1962 (COWA surveys, S. Afr.); Morison, First and Partridge 1965 (Makapansgat Limeworks);

Partridge 1965 (Stone artifacts, Makapansgat Limeworks); Partridge et al. 1964 (industry, Waterwal);

Rautenbach 1967 (shelter, clarens district, O. F. S.); Robinson, J. T. 1962D (australopithecines, Sterkfontein);

Sampson 1967B (industries, Zaayfontein shelter, Norvalspont), 1967C (industries, Glen Elliot shelter, Colesburg District), 1967D (industry, Zeekoegat 13, Venterstad); Seddon 1966B, 1967 (Up. Pal. artifacts, Bosman's Crossing, Stellenbosch); Stannard 1965 (artifacts, Tarzan's Cave, Simonstown); Summers 1964B (artifacts in dunes);

Tobias 1959B (phys. anthrop., S. Afr.); Tobias and Wells 1967 (S. Afr. fossil hominids).

ZAMBIA (see also: RHODESIA) — Clark and Fagan 1967 (catalogue of fossil hominids); Clark and Van Zinderen Bakker 1964 (Kalambo Falls);

Gabel 1967B (archeol., W. Copperbelt);

Robinson, K. R. 1964 (rock shelter, Mtetengwe R. Beit Bridge);

Sampson 1965 (artifacts, Luano Spring deposits).

PALEOANTHROPOLOGY — NEW WORLD

GENERAL — Agogino, Rovner and Irwin-Williams 1964 (early man); Alcina 1965 (early cultures); Anon. 1960CH (new Paleo-Indian finds), 1964H (films on early man in N. Amer.);

Beatty 1967 (atlatl weights); Bernal 1964 (early man); Bordes, Comas and Franciscolo 1964 (Up. Pal.); Bosch-Gimpera 1968 (origin of Amer. hunters); Boss [1965] (bibliog. of archeol. periodicals); Brennan 1963B (Pal. choppers); Bushnell 1961 (New World chronol.); Byers et al. 1965 (Paleo-Indian conference);

Chard 1963D (migrations of man to New World); Comas 1961 (origin of man in Amer.); Compton 1960, 1963 (early man, Amer.);

Emanuel 1968 (Amer. "hand axe");

Falkenburger 1960 (prehist. man in Amer.); Franch 1965 (manual of Amer. Archeol.);

Genoves 1965A, 1967 (origin of man in Amer.); Gilliam 1958A (Folsomoid projectile points); Greer, J. W. 1965 (projectile points);

Haynes 1967A (C–14 dates and early man); Hester, J. J. 1966B (origins of Clovis culture); Huddleston 1967 (origins of Amer. Indians);

Jelinek, A. J. 1965B (peopling of the New World); Jennings 1955, 1964, 1965, 1966 (early man in the Great Plains); Jennings and Norbeck 1964A, B (prehist. man in the New World); Josselyn 1962 (entrance of early man);

Krieger 1964A (early man in the New World), 1964B (terminology of chipped-stone artifacts);

Leslie 1964B (projectile point cultures);

Maggowan, K. and J., and Hester 1962 (early man); Mochanov 1966B (ancient civilizations of Amer.); Müller-Beck 1965B (Eurasiatic origins of non-projectile point stone industries), 1966E, F (origins and diffusions of Paleohunters), 1967 (Up. Pleist. migrations of hunters across Bering bridge);

Narr 1964A (early man);

Pericot Garcia 1962E (early man, Amer.);

Riddell 1967A (archeol.);

Wendorf 1966 (early man); Willey 1966 (Amer. archeol.); Woodbury 1962 (archeol.); Wormington 1961B (prehist., Amer.), 1964B, D (flaking techniques, Amer.).

NORTH AMERICA

GENERAL — Bryan 1964, 1965, 1967 (early man);

Campbell, J. M. 1962A (cultural relations between Arctic and Temperate N. Amer.), 1965 (current research, Arctic); Carter, G. F. 1966B (pebble tools), 1967A (artifacts and naturifacts), 1967B (artifacts in Japan similar to Paleo-Indian); Cotter 1965A, B (Paleo-Indian sites, N. E. Amer.);

Daugherty 1966 (current archeol. research, northwest); Dolan 1966 (skeletal remains of Pleist. man); Dragoo 1967A (early man, eastern N. Amer.), 1967B (early man);

Emery 1966A (underwater archeol.), 1966B (early man and the Atlantic shelf); Emery and Edwards 1966 (archeol. of Atlantic continental shelf);

Fitting 1965H (Paleo-Indian adaptive and settlement patterns), 1967 (early man, Great Lakes area);

Giddings 1967 (early man in Arctic); Griffin 1961B (cultural changes, Great Lakes region), 1964, 1965 (N. E. Woodlands area), 1967 (summary E. N. Amer. archeol.);

Haynes 1964B (age and dispersion of fluted projectile points), 1966B (Clovis point culture); Hibben 1968 (early man); Hurt 1966 (prehist., N. Plains);

Irwin 1965 (Paleo-Indian complexes, Great Plains);

Jennings et al. 1956 (early man in the Southwest); Johnson, F. 1956, 1967 (chronol. and development of cultures); Josselyn 1963B, 1964A, 1965A, 1966C (classif. of projectile points), 1965E (crude lithic tools), 1967A (Amer. hand-axes);

Kehoe, T. F. 1961 (stone tipi rings, High Plains), 1965A ("buffalo stones"), 1967 bison kill sites); Kerby 1965 (migrations into N. Amer.);

Laricheva 1966A (Siberian influence on N. Amer. Pal.), 1966B, 1967 (Pal. cultures);

MacNeish 1964B (peopling of New World);

Neumann, G. K. 1952B (archeol. and racial hist. of Amer. Indian);

Painter 1968 (early man);

Quimby 1952 (archeol., Up. Great Lakes area);

Reed, E. K. 1964 (archeol., Southwest); Roosa 1965 (fluted points, Great Lakes);

Sauter 1965 (prehist., N. Amer.); Smith, A. G. 1964A (Paleo-Indian bark boat); Spencer, Jennings et al. 1965 (early man, N. Amer.); Sperry 1967 (Folsom man);

West, F. H. 1963 (leaf points, W. Arctic); Witthoft 1956 (Paleo-Indians, E. and S.E.); Wormington 1966 (prehist.); Worthington 1965 (prehist.);

Zamyslova 1967 (early man).

CANADA — Anon. 1967BA (early man artifacts), 1968L (early man remains, Alberta);

Bonham 1965 (projectile points, Niagara Peninsula); Borden 1960, 1961 (artifacts, archeol., Fraser Canyon, British Columbia); Borns 1965, 1966 (Debert site, Nova Scotia); Byers 1965, 1966 (Debert site, Nova Scotia);

Fiske 1964 (Univ. Manitoba field work);

Gryba 1968 (Paleo-Indian/Archaic site, Manitoba);

Harington and Irving 1967 (Up. Pleist. mammoth bone artifacts, Yukon Territory); Hlady 1960 (Plainview type projectiles, W. Canada), 1964 (Manitoba Archaeol. Soc. fieldwork, 1964);

Johnson and Raup 1964 (archeol., S. W. Yukon);

Kehoe, A. B. 1962 (prehist. of the prairie provinces); Kehoe, T. F. 1965B, 1966 (fluted points, Saskatchewan); Kenyon and Churcher 1965 (artifacts from Lake Agassiz, Ontario);

Langston and Oschinsky 1963 (Taber infant, Alberta); Lee, T. E. 1964A (Sheguiandah: workshop/habitation, Ontario), 1964B (early man in Canada), 1966 (archeol. at Fort Chimo, Quebec);

MacDonald, G. F. 1965, 1966, 1968 (Debert Paleo-Indian site, Nova Scotia); Mac-Neish 1962B, 1963, 1964A (archeol., Yukon); Mayer-Oakes 1963B (early man, Manitoba); Mitchell, D. H,. 1965 (cobble tool site, Fraser Canyon, B. C.);

Pendergast 1963 (Canadian archeol.);

Rousselière 1964 (Paleo-Eskimos, Pelly Bay, N. W. T.);

Steinberg 1966 (projectile point, Lake Agassiz, Manitoba); Stuckenrath 1965, 1966 (hearths, Nova Scotia);

Wilmeth 1967 (archeol., Alberta); Wormington 1961A, 1963 (Paleo-Indians, Alberta); Wormington and Forbis 1965 (archeol., Alberta);

Zaborski 1965A (Quaco man, New Brunswick).

UNITED STATES MAINLAND

GENERAL — Agogino 1960A (federal aid needed), 1960B (early man, cent. U.S.), 1963C (bison and Paleo-Indian), 1963D, 1966 (Paleo-Indian chronol. and cultural sequence), 1965A, 1967 (pre-projectile point cultures), 1964B (Paleo-Indians, High Plains); Agogino and Rovner 1964 (Paleo-Indian traditions); Anon. 1963CF (Paleo-Indian points), 1964AD (Dalton points), 1964M (early man, New England);

Bell, R. E. 1960C (Amer. Indian projectile points); Bennett 1952 (prehist., Mississippi Valley); Bottoms 1967 (early man occupation of Continental Shelf); Bottoms and Painter 1965 (Paleo-Indian projectile points);

Carter, G. F. 1964A (food storage pits, Colorado and Mohave deserts), 1964B (pre-Paleo-Indian coastal archeol.); Collins, H. B. 1965 (Paleo-Indian research);

Ewers 1960 (references on the Plains Indians);

Fowler, M. L. (early prehist. occupation, cent. N. Amer.); Fowler, W. S. 1964A, B (New England archeol.);

Griffin, J. B. 1952A, B (archeol., E. U.S.);

Hall, R. L. 1965, 1966 (current archeol. research, N. Mississippi Valley); Hayden 1965 (fragile-pattern areas); Honea 1965 (morphology of scrapers), 1966 (evol. of lithic traditions of the S. W.);

Josselyn 1963C (antiquity of E. Paleo-Indian artifacts), 1967C (pebble-tool terminology), 1967E (patination and age of pebble-tools); 1967F (crude tools);

McAvoy 1968 (tools and projectile points, Atlantic coastal plain); McGregor, J. C. 1941, 1965 (Southwestern archeol.); Malde 1964 (environment and early man, S.W.); Meighan 1963 (pre-Desert Culture, Great Basin), 1965 (early man, Pacific coast); Michie 1968 (the Edgefield scraper); Morgan, R. G. 1952 (cultures in the Ohio region); Mulloy 1952 (culture types and sequences, N. Plains);

Neuman 1965 (current archeol. research, Great Plains); Neumann, E. A. 1964

(Paleo-Indian occupation of the central States);

Oldfield 1964 (paleoecol. of Late Quat. sites, Llano Estacado);   Orr, K. G. 1952 (archeol., Caddoan area);

Prahl 1966 (Paleo-Indians, Muskegon R.);   Prufer 1964C (Ross Co. point);

Richards, D. J. 1962 (Paleo-Indian projectile points);   Riddell 1967B (archeol.); Rogers, M. J. 1966 (prehist. hunters, Far West);   Russell, G. E. 1967A (projectile points, S. E.);

Sciscenti and Greminger 1962 (archeol., S. W.);   Sears, W. H. 1964 (Paleo-Indians, S.E.);   Stephenson, R. L. 1965 (early man, Great Plains);

Tadlock 1966 (crescentic stone artifacts, W. U.S.);   Tidwell 1960 (artifacts, E. U.S.);

Wahla 1967 (Holcombe caribou hunters);   Wallace, W. J. 1965 (current archeol., Great Basin);   Wedel 1964A, B (Paleo-Indians, Great Plains);   Wendorf 1965C (cultures, Great Plains);   Wheat 1963 (Paleo-Indians, W. United States);   Williams S. 1965 (Paleo-Indians, L. Mississippi Valley);   Williams and Stoltman 1965 (Paleo-Indians, S. E.).

Alabama — Anon. 1965F (pebble-tools);

Brock 1967 (Paleo-Indian blades);   Brock and Clayton 1966 (Paleo-Indian sites and industries);   Burns 1967 (crude tools);

Cambron and Hulse 1964 (point types);   Cambron and Radford 1959 (Jacks site, Jackson Co.);   Clayton 1965, 1967 (Paleo-Indian bluff shelters);   Cornell 1964 (Cumberland point, Morgan Co.);

DeJarnette 1964 (rock shelter, Marshall Co.), 1967 (Lively Complex pebble-tools); Duncan and Brosemer 1964 (Late Paleo-Indian site, Jackson Co.);

Fowler, J. H. 1967 (transitional projectile point);

Hahn, Mrs. R. N. 1966A (Dalton-Big Sandy site, Helena Quad.), 1966B (Blountsville Paleo site);   Harris and Roberts 1967 (multiple component site, Marshall Co.);   Holland 1963 (the Holland site), 1965 (early lithic artifacts);   Hooper 1966 (Clod site, Madison Co.), 1968 (Lively Complex duplicated in Franklin Co.);

Josselyn 1964B, C (projectile points), 1965C, D, 1966A, B (the Lively Complex), 1967D (pebble-tool sites);

Lee, T. E. 1965 (Cumberland point);   Lively 1965A, B (Lively Complex pebble tools);   Long, A. G. 1965A (Lively Complex pebble tools), 1965B (projectile points, Jackson Co.), 1965C (early man in Alabama);

Miller, C. 1965 (distribution of Paleo-Indian finds);   Mosley 1959 (Nebo Hill early man site);

Painter 1967 (workshop debris, Lively Complex);

Troup and Josselyn 1967 (pebble tools, Weiss Reservoir);

Waters 1959 (artifacts, Red Hill, Lawrence Co.);

Alaska — Bandi 1965A, B, C (early man, Bering bridge);   Black, R. F. 1966 (migration of man, Bering Straits);   Black and Laughlin 1964 (oldest site, Aleutians);

Campbell, J. M. 1961, 1962B (Kogruk complex, Anaktuvuk Pass), 1962A (cultural relations between Arctic and Temperate N. Amer.), 1963 (Alaska and Pal. Europe);   Collins, H. B. 1951C (anthrop.), 1963 (Paleo-Indian artifacts), 1964 (prehist.);

Giddings 1951C (early man migrations), 1966 (dating archeol. of N. W. Alaska);

Hadleigh-West 1967 (Donnelly Ridge site and an early core and blade complex in cent. Alaska);   Hadleigh-West and Bandi 1965 (Campus site and "American Epi-Gravettian");   Humphrey 1967 (fluted points and European Up. Pal. blades, Utukok R. basin);

Josselyn 1962, 1965B (Bering Bridge in doubt);

Laughlin 1965, 1967 (migrations and occupation in the Bering Sea area); Laughlin and Aigner 1966 (Anangula core and blade industry); Laughlin and Reeder 1966 (Aleutian-Kodiak prehist.);
McCartney and Turner 1966 (Anangula site);
Porter 1964 (early man, Anaktuvuk Pass);
Schlesier 1964B, 1966, 1967 (artifacts, N. Alaska);
Wilmsen 1964 (flake tools, Arctic).

Arizona — Ascher, R. and M. 1965 (early man at Leupp); Ayres 1966 (Clovis point, Kayenta);
Gumerman 1966 (Folsom point, Mishongovi);
Haynes et al. 1965 (Lehner mammoth site); Haynes and Hemmings 1968 (mammoth bone tool, Murray Springs);
Nelson, P. R. 1964 (Desert Culture site, Snowflake);
Olson, A. P. 1964 (Clovis point, Houck);
Sims and Daniel 1967 (projectile points, Winslow).

Arkansas — Dickson, D. R. 1962 (prehist., Ozarks);
Perino 1965A, 1966 (projectile points), 1965B (Paleo-Indians), 1968 (Clovis points).

California - Anon. 1965CK (dentition La Jolla people);
Carter, G. F. 1967C (cultural chronol., La Jolla, Santa Rosa Island and Mission Bay);
Davis, E. L. 1964 (archeol. survey of Mono Lake Basin), 1967A (artifacts, L. Mojave); Donnan 1964 (early man sequence, E. Mojave Desert);
Heizer 1964 (early man locations), 1965 (dating L. Mojave artifacts);
Johnson, J. J. 1967 (archeol. of Camanche Reservoir Locality);
Kingman 1966 (Campbell lithic collection, early man sites);
Lanning 1963B (archeol. of Rose Spring site, Inyo Co.);
Moriarty 1966 (culture phase divisions, San Diego sites), 1967 (cultures, San Diego Co.);
Orr, P. C. 1964 (stone tool, Santa Rosa Island), 1968 (prehist., Santa Rosa Island);
Pourade 1966 (early man);
Simpson, R. D. 1964 (industry, Manix Lake); Suggs 1965 (archeol., San Francisco);
Treganza 1964 (Samwell Cave).

North and South Carolina — Anon. 1967BE (early point types);
Bottoms 1968 (oolitic quartzite utilization);
Caldwell, J. R. 1952 (projectile points); Coe 1952, 1964 (cultures, Carolina Piedpiedmont, 1965 (distribution of Paleo-Indian finds); Cooper, P. P. 1967 (early points, Upper Yadkin);
Michie 1965 (fluted point types, S. C.), 1967 (Dalton points, S. C.);
Neill 1966 (Eden projectile point, S. C.);
Traver 1963B, 1964 (artifacts, Pasquotank site);
Waddell 1965A, B (projectile points).

Colorado — Anderson, D. C. 1966 (burial, Gordon Creek);
Breternitz 1967 (early man);
Husted 1965 (Paleo-Indian occupation of the Rocky Mts.);
Smith, A. 1966 (Lake Mohave point, Uncompahgre Plateau);
Wheat 1966 (Olsen-Chubbuck bison-kill site).

Connecticut — Anon. 1965L, N (Clovis points);
Vibert 1964 (Milnesand point, Connecticut R.).

Florida — Brewer 1965 (Suwannee points);
Case and Owens 1966 (mound builders);
Fairbanks 1964 (early occupations);
Goggin 1964 (Paleo-Indian occupation); Griffin, J. W. 1952 (prehist. survey);
Lazarus, Fairbanks and Bullen 1965 (distribution of Paleo-Indian finds);
Martin, R. A. 1966 (early man, Silver Springs); Mortine 1965 (projectile point in sloth bone);
Warren, L. O. 1964 (shell middens, Tampa Bay), 1966 (Paleo-Indian site, Boot Ranch, Pinellas Co.); Wilson, Rex L. 1965 (archeol., Mayport mound).

Georgia — Caldwell, J. R. 1952 (projectile points); Chase, J. W. 1956 (early man, Halloka Creek site);
Fairbanks 1952 (early man tools);
Gaines 1955 (archeol., Upper Savannah and Broad Rivers);
Kelley and Ayres 1966 (Carter's Dam site, Murray Co.); Kelly 1949 (early flint industry);
Painter 1964C (projectile points);
Waring and Kelley 1965 (Paleo-Indians, Richmond and Burke counties); Wauchope 1966A (archeol., N. Georgia).

Idaho — Bowers and Savage 1962 (early man, Brown's Bench); Butler, B. R. 1964 (early man points, Snake River), 1965 (early man points, S.E. Idaho), 1968 (archeol., Pioneer Basin); Butler and Fitzwater 1965 (Clovis site, Big Camas Prairie);
Lawrence 1967 (early domestic dogs, Jaguar Cave);
Sneed 1967 (archeol. sites, Craters of Moon Nat. Mon.); Swanson and Bryan 1964, Swanson, Butler and Bonnichsen 1964 (cultures, Birch Creek Valley); Swanson and Dayley 1968 (hunting station, Malad Hill); Swanson and Sneed 1967 (artifacts, Railroad Ranch);
Tuohy 1963A (prehist., S. W.).

Illinois — Anon. 1965CH (Folsom point), 1966BC (stone artifact);
Fowler, M. L. 1959 (summary report of Modoc Rock Shelter);
Henry and Nichols 1963 (projectile points, Vermillion Co.);
Munson and Frye 1965 (artifact of Mid-Wisconsin age);
Perino 1968 (Clovis points).

Indiana — Dorwin 1966 (fluted points and Late Pleist. geochronology);
Painter 1964A (projectile points).

Iowa — Anon. 1965BB, 1967AH (Clovis points), 1967AI, AK (Sandia points), 1967AJ (projectile points);
Gradwohl 1967 (Paleo-Indian artifact forms);
McKusick 1963 (key to identification of projectile points), 1964 (early man).

Kansas — Yaple 1967?, 1968 (Paleo-Indians).

Kentucky — Anon. 1964AZ (fluted point);
Bottoms 1965 (projectile points);
Ford, J. 1968 (Paleo-Indian projectile points, McLean Co.);
Painter 1965A (Paleo-Indian projectile points);
Rolingson 1964, Rolingson and Schwartz 1964, 1966 (Paleo-Indians);
Schwartz 1965, 1968 (Paleo-Indians).

New Jersey — Marchiando 1966 (archeol. of Tocks Is. Reservoir area).

New Mexico — Agogino 1964A, 1965B (Blackwater Draw site); Agogino and
   Rovner (Blackwater Draw site); Anon. 1966AQ (Folsom man occupation
   site), 1966BA (Rio Rancho occupation site), 1967Y, 1968H (Mockingbird
   Clovis site);
Baker, K. 1960 (human occupation, Carlsbad Cavern);
Hammack 1965 (archeol. of Ute Dam and Reservoir); Haynes and Agogino 1965
   (Blackwater Draw site);
Kelley, J. H. 1964 (archeol. of the Llano Estacado);
Reed, E. K. 1965 (prehist., southwestern N. M.);
Smith, C. et al. 1966 (artifacts, Rattlesnake Draw); Smith, S. and Agogino 1966
   (Paleo-Indian points, Blackwater draw);
Warnica 1966 (Clovis site); Weber, R. H. 1963 (prehist., Socorro Co.).

New York — Anderson, A. J. 1965 (fluted points, Staten Is.);
Brennan 1966 (Paleo-Indians);
Funk 1967 (Paleo-Indian site, Hudson Valley); Funk and Johnson 1964 (Paleo-
   Indian site, Hudson Valley);
Ritchie, W. A. 1965 (archeol.);
Suggs 1966 (archeol.);
Werner, D. J. 1964 (Paleo-Indian zierdt site near Port Jervis).

North Dakota — Anderson, R. R. 1966 (bibliog. of archeol.).

Ohio — Anon. 1965BG, 1966AS, AT (fluted points);
Baby and Potter 1965 (fluted points); Britt 1968 (Paleo-Indian artifacts, Hop-
   kins sites);
Carskadden 1966 (Paleo-Indian points, Muskingum Co.); Converse 1963 (flint
   artifacts);
Haight and Wright 1966 (reworked Paleo artifacts); Hankins 1967 (fluted point,
   Scioto Co.);
Maxwell 1952 (Folsom-Yuma hunters, Ohio Valley); Mortine 1968 (Keiser site
   Paleo-Indian projectile points); Mortine and Drive 1965 (Paleo-Indian arti-
   facts, Newcomerstown);
Painter 1965B (Paleo-Indian projectile points); Patterson, R. P. 1966 (artifacts,
   Pleasant Ridge); Potter, M. A. 1964 (Paleo-Indian points, Miami Co.); Prufer
   1962C, D, 1963C, 1964B (fluted points), 1966 (Mud Valley Paleo-Indian
   site, Holmes Co.); Prufer and Munro 1961 (fluted points); Prufer and
   Sofsky 1965 (McKibben site, Trumbull Co.);
Smith, A. G. 1967A, B, C (artifacts);
Wright, N. L. 1964 (flint artifacts, Flint Ridge area, Licking Co.).

Oklahoma — Anon. 1963CD (Folsom point);
Bastian, T. 1965 (archeol., Wichita Mts.); Bell, R. E. 1965A, B (bibliog. of
   archeol.);
Leonhardy 1966A, B (mammoth kill site, Domebo); Leonhardy and Anderson
   1966 (Domebo site);
Wyckoff, D. G. 1964 (culture, Packard site, Mayes Co.).

Oregon — Arment 1965 (desert artifacts);
Cowles 1960 (Cougar Mt. Cave); Cressman 1964 (early man).

Pennsylvania — Carter, G. F. 1966A (mammoth engraving a hoax);
Dickson, J. A. 1967 (fluted point, Cumberland Valley);

Kinsey 1966 (archeol. sites, Tocks Is. Reservoir area); Kinsey and Kent 1965 (archeol. survey, Tocks Is. Reservoir);
Lorah 1968 (Clovis point);
Royer 1963 (fluted point, Luzerne Co.).

Tennessee — Anon. 1966BK, BL, 1967BD (Paleo-Indian points), 1967BB (flake tool), 1967BC (Cumberland points);
Cambron and Hulse 1961, 1963 (fluted points);
Dragoo 1965 (Paleo-Indian site, Stewart Co.);
Guthe 1964A, B, C, D, 1965A, B, C, 1966A (Paleo-Indian projectile points), 1966B, 1967 (Paleo-Indian occupation);
Kneberg 1952 (cultural sequences);
Miller, C. and A. 1965 (Cumberland point, Buffalo R.); Morse 1965 (distribution of Paleo-Indian finds); Morse, D. and P. 1964 (Paleo-Indian points, Percy Priest Reservoir); Morse, D. F. and P. A., and Waggoner 1964 (fluted points, Smith Co.);
Painter 1965A (Paleo-Indian projectile points);
Wesley 1967 (pebble tools, Giles Co.);
Yeatman 1964 (artifacts, Maury Co.).

Texas — Compton 1965 (Paleo-Indian sites); Crawford, D. D. 1965 (camp site, Granite Beach, Llano Co.); Crook 1964 (C—14 dates, Lewisville site);
Dibble and Lorrain 1965 (bison kill site, Val Verde Co.);
Epstein 1965, 1966A (terminal Pleist. cultures);
Heizer and Brooks 1965 (Lewisville site); Hester, T. R. 1968 (Folsom points, S. W.);
Jelinek, A. J. 1966 (crude artifact, Wichita Falls);
Kelley, J. H. 1964 (archeol. of the Llano Estacado);
Nunley, Duffield and Jelks 1965 (Paleo-Indian points, Amistad Reservoir);
Shafer et al. 1964 (Paleo-Indians, Belton Reservoir); Slaughter and Hoover 1965 (antler artifact, N. Sulphur R., Delta Co.); Spence, S. E. 1964 (Alibates flint quarries); Story 1965 (archeol., Cedar Creek Reservoir); Story and Shafer 1965 (archeol., Waco Reservoir);
Trout 1963 (early man, Yoakum Co.).

Utah — Tripp 1966 (Clovis point, Acord Lake, Sevier Co.).

Virginia — Bottoms 1964 (the "Dime" site), 1966 (the Richmond site), 1968 (oolitic quartzite utilization);
Carter, G. F. 1966C (Paleo-Indian components, Shenandoah Valley);
Fitting 1965A (statistical study of fluted points);
Gilliam 1958B, 1961 (Williamson early man site, Dinwiddie Co.);
McAvoy 1965 (chert assemblage, Chesterfield Co.), 1967A (quartzite tools), 1967B (Clovis point); McAvoy and Bottoms 1965 (Hopewell Paleo-Indian Workshop site); McCary 1958, 1961A, 1963B, 1965, 1968 (survey of fluted points), 1961B (cores from the Williamson site), 1963A (archeol. of W. area of Dismal Swamp); MacCord and Peple 1963 (Sloan site, Chesterfield Co.); McMichael 1963 (W. Virginia archeol.);
Painter 1959, 1964B (Paleo-Indians), 1965C (artifacts, Cattail Creek); Peck, R. M. 1968 (pentagonal points, Elys Ford); Pettit 1968 (artifacts, Clarksville); Potter, S. R. 1968 (projectile points); Pritchard, J. G. 1964 (artifacts, Princess Anne Co.);
Robinson, D. H. 1961 (archeol., Blue Ridge);
Wilkinson 1966 (Paleo-Indians, Flint Run Jasper Quarry); Wilkinson and Leslie 1967 (Limeton points, Shenandoah V.).

Washington — Anon. 1968K (needle, Marmes site), 1968AI (Marmes man);
Grosso 1967 (rock shelters, Palouse R.);
Kirk 1968 (Marmes man);
Miles, C. 1964 (Clovis point, Up. Chehalis Valley);
Thomson 1961 (archeol., Pilchuck R. and S. Fork of the Stillaguamish R.).

Wisconsin — Hurley 1965 (Paleo-Indian artifacts, Vernon Co.);
Ritzenthaler 1966, 1967A, C (Paleo-Indian artifacts, Kouba site), 1967B (Paleo-Indians).

Wyoming — Agogino 1964C, D (Cody Complex); Agogino and Frankforter 1964 (Paleo-Indian site, Brewster); Agogino and Galloway 1965 (Hell Gap points, Sister's Hill site); Anon. 1964BZ (Hell Gap expd.), 1966AO, AP (huts, Hell Gap site);
Belz 1963 (early man);
Carroll, W. B. 1964 ("Alberta" point, Casper);
Guthrie, M. R. 1964 (Hell Gap site);
Haynes 1965 (geol. of Hell Gap site); Haynes and Grey 1965 (Sister's Hill site); Irwin, H. T. and C. C. and Agogino 1965 (Hell Gap site); Irwin, Irwin-Williams and Agogino 1966 (resume of cultural complexes, Hell Gap site); Irwin-Williams, Agogino and Irwin 1965 (Hell Gap site and early man on the High Plains);
Jepsen 1962D, E (Cody Complex, Horner site);
Lloyd 1964 (Hell Gap site);
Moss, J. H. 1968 (Mummy Cave early man site);
Sharrock 1966 (Paleo-Indians and mammals, s. w. Wyoming);
Weber, T. J. 1963 (fluted points, Casper Mt.), 1964 (archeol. sites); Wedel et. al. 1968 (Mummy Cave).

MEXICO — Anon. 1960CI (incised mastodon bone, Valsequillo), 1967Z, AB (early man at Valsequillo), 1967AZ (early man artifacts); Aveleyra Arroyo de Anda 1964A, B (Paleo-Indian hunters), 1965 (carved bone, Tequixquiac);
Bernal 1961 (archeol. in 1960); Byers 1967 (prehist. of Tehuacán Valley);
Di Peso 1963 (evidence for Pleist. man, N. Mexico), 1965 (Clovis point from Timmy site, Chihuahua); Due Rojo 1964 (cultural sequence, Tehuacán Valley);
Epstein 1965, 1966A (terminal Pleist. cultures), 1966B (archeol. excavations, Nuevo Leon);
Flannery 1967 (Pleist. hunting, Tehuacán Valley);
Genovés and Comas 1964 (physical anthrop., 1943-1964);
Irwin-Williams 1965, 1967 (early man, Valsequillo region, Puebla);
Lorenzo 1961 (burin from Teopisca, Chiapas), 1964 (fluted points, Chapala), 1965 (early man);
MacNeish 1961, 1962A, 1964C, D, 1967A, B (archeol. of the Tehuacán Valley); MacNeish, Nelken-Terner and Johnson 1967 (prehist. of the Tehuacán Valley); MacNeish and Peterson 1962 (Santa Marta rock shelter, Chiapas);
Pepper 1965 (early man, Baja California);
Reed, A. M. 1966 (prehist.);
Terra 1950 (fossil man);
Varner 1958 (archeol., N. E. Mexico).

CENTRAL AMERICA — Armillas 1964 (prehist. man, N. Mesoamerica); Aveleyra Arroyo de Anda 1964A, B (Paleo-Indian hunters);
Borhegyi 1964 (Paleo-Indian period, Guatemala);
MacNeish 1967C (Mesoamerican archeol.);
Sander 1964 (artifacts, Panama);
Wauchope 1964 (Paleo-Indians); West, R. C. 1964 (Paleo-Indian cultures).

SOUTH AMERICA
  GENERAL — Cardich 1963 (cultural chronology, S. South Amer.);
  Evans, C. 1964 (prehist., lowland S. Amer.);
  Ibarra Grasso 1964A, B (Pal. cultures);
  Kidder 1964 (cultures);
  Lanning 1965A, 1966 (preceramic archeol., Andes); Lynch, T. F. 1967B (prehist.,
    Cent. Andes);
  Meggers and Evans 1963 (cultural development in Latin Amer.); Menghin 1963
    (industries); Müller-Beck 1965C (Stone Age cultures);
  Rex 1964 (early man); Rouse 1964B (prehist., West Indies).

  ARGENTINA — Chebataroff 1960 (early man site, Catalán Chico); Cigliano 1961
    (Ampajangian industry, Santa Maria Valley), 1962B (Tres Morros and Saladillo
    sites, Puna Jujeña);
  Orellana 1962 (artifacts, Ghuatchi);
  Rex 1963 (cultues, northwestern Arg.); Rex and Lorandi 1959 (archeol., Rio Carca-
    rena, Santa Fe Prov.); Rosen 1957 (early man);
  Vignati 1963 (human remains).

  BOLIVIA — Ibarra Grasso 1955 (Pal. points, Viscachani);
  Le Paige 1964 (prehist., Atacama);
  Rosen 1957 (early man).

  CHILE — Bird 1965 (pre-projectile point cultural stage);
  Montané 1968 (Paleo-Indian tools, Laguna de Tagua Tagua);
  Orellana 1961, 1963 (Ghatchi industry); Orellana and Kaltwasser 1964 (El Loa
    industry).

  COLOMBIA — Reichel-Dolmatoff 1965 (archeol.).

  ECUADOR — Carluci de Santiana 1961B (early man), 1963 (projectile points);
  Due Rojo 1964 (El Inga Pal. site);
  Larrea 1966 (early man);
  Mayer-Oakes 1966 (El Inga projectile points);
  Santiana 1960, Santiana and Carluci de Santiana 1960A, B (early man).

  PERU — Bird 1965 (pre-projectile point cultural stage); Bonavia 1966 (skel. remains,
    early occupation sites); Bushnell 1966 (early man, cent. Andes);
  Cardich 1959, 1964 (prehist. cultures, Lauricocha);
  Dollfus 1964 (climate and early human occupation);
  Engel 1964 (human skel., Paracas);
  Kauffmann Doig 1961 (the Lauricocha Horizon), 1963 (origin of Peruvian cultures);
  Lanning 1965B (early man); Lynch, T. F. 1967A (Quishaqui Puncu preceramic site).

  URUGUAY — Bórmida 1965 (lithic industries, Arroyo Catalán Chico, and Rio Cua-
    reim).

  VENEZUELA — Cruxent 1962 (Paleo-Indian lithic cultures compared with Cent.
    Afr. cultures); Cruxent and Rouse 1961 (archeol. chronology);
  Rouse 1964A, 1965A, 1966, 1967 (Caribbean cultures); Rouse and Cruxent 1963
    (archeol.);
  Sanoja 1963 (early man).

PALEOBIOCHEMISTRY — See: paleobiology.

PALEOBIOLOGY — Breger 1963 (organic geochemistry);
De Rosnay 1965 (biochemical evol.);
Khozatskiĭ 1959A (life forms); Kocherëzhkin 1967 (evol. biochemistry and origin of life);
Macurda 1968 (paleobiol. aspects of growth and development); Meladze 1964B (Tert. Sivatheriinae);
Richmond 1965 (juvenile dinosaurs);
Stepanov, D. L. 1965 (paleobiol. in paleont.);
Washburn 1966 (biol. and evol.);

PALEOBIOMECHANICS — See: paleomyology.

PALEOCHRONOLOGY, GEOCHRONOLOGY, POLLEN DATING, LEAD, HELIUM, C–14, FLUORINE and CHEMICAL DATING (see also: technique; correlation) —
Agogino 1968 (C–14 dating); Alessio, Bella and Cortesi 1964 (C–14 dates, Rome); Alessio, Bella, Bachechi and Cortesi 1965, 1966, 1967 (C–14 dates, Rome); Alimen 1967 (Quat., France); Anon. 1963BT (C–14 dating methods), 1964T (Phanerozoic time-scale), 1965S, AB (collagen dating), 1965AA, AC, AE (bibliog. geochronol.), 1965AV (glass dating), 1965CI (Homo habilis), 1966N (C–14 dating), 1968D (new evol. dating process); Arai, F. 1962 (Quat., Japan); Asmus 1965 (fossil hominids, Palestine);
Bachinskiĭ 1966 (fossilization); Barker 1961 (potassium argon); Barker, H. 1967, (C–14); Battistini 1965C (Aepyornis eggs), 1966 (C–14 dating, N. Madagascar); Baudet 1968 (chronol., Pal. Europe); Bender, Bryson and Baerreis 1965 (Univ. Wisconsin C–14 dates); Berger, Fergusson and Libby 1965 (UCLA C–14 dates); Berger, Horney and Libby 1964 (C–14 dating); Berger and Libby 1966, 1967 (UCLA C–14 dates); Berry 1968 (prehist. time scale); Bertalan and Kretzoi 1965 (geochronol., Hungary); Biggerstaff 1967 (age of Taungs child); Brothwell 1962B (dating techniques in archeol.); Brown and Gould 1964 (carbon migration); Browne 1963 (problems in dating, Australia); Bushnell 1961 (New World chronol.); Butomo 1965 (C–14 dating in archeol.); Butzer 1967 (Late Pleist. chronol.);
Cailleux 1964A (dating prehist. industries); Callow, Baker and Hassall 1965 (Nation. Phys. Lab. C-14 dates); Callow, Baker and Pritchard 1964 (Nation. Phys. Lab. C–14 dates); Casey 1964 (Cretaceous dates); Cayeux 1967 (prehist., France); Chard and Workman 1965 (Soviet archeol. C–14 dates); Cherdyntsev 1961 (dating Quat. bones); Cherdyntsev et al. 1964 (Soviet C–14 dates); Cherdyntsev et al. 1965 (Soviet C–14 dates); Cherdyntsev et al. 1961 (dating Quat. bones); Che̅ 1965A (dating artifacts in the Ukraine); Clark, J. D. 1962I (C–14 chronol., sub-Sahara); Cowie 1964 (Cambrian period); Crane and Griffin 1964, 1965, 1966 (Univ. Michigan C–14 dates); Crook 1964 (C–14 dates, Lewisville site, Texas); Curtis 1967 (Mioc.-Pleist. dates for paleont. sites); Curtis and Evernden 1965 (potassium-argon dating);
Damon, Haynes and Long 1964 (Ariz. C–14 dates); Dart, R. A. 1966A (S. Afr.); Deacon 1966 (Nahoon footprints); Delibrias, Guillier and Labeyrie 1964, 1965 (Saclay C–14 dates), 1966 (GIF C–14 dates); Due Rojo 1965 (Pleist. glacial chronol.); Dury 1964 (C–14 dates, Australia); Dyck 1967 (C–14 dating); Dyck, Fyles, and Blake 1965 (Geol. Surv. Canada C–14 dates);
Ennouchi 1965 (fluride in bone), 1966B (dating Irhoud man); Ericson and Wollin 1964, 1966 (dating by deep sea cores), 1968 (Pleist. climates and deep sea chronol.); Evernden and Curtis 1963 (K–A dates, S. Afr. Pleist.), 1965 (K–A dating, E. Afr., Italy); Evernden et al. 1964 (K–A dates for Cenozoic mammalian chronol., N. Amer.); Ewer 1964 (dating Australopithecinae);
F., D. 1961B (dating fossil bone); Faure and Hugot 1966 (C–14 dates, Quat., W.

McCallum and Wittenberg 1965 (Univ. Saskatchewan C–14 dates); Martin, P. S. 1963 (pollen dating the Amer. S. W.); Mason, J. A. 1966B (age of man in Amer.); Matthews and Curtis 1966 (Plioc.-Pleist. boundary, New Zealand); Meighan, Foote and Aiello 1968 (obsidian dating W. Mexican archeol.); Méroc 1963B, 1964 (Montmaurin mandible, France); Michels 1967 (dating by hydration of obsidian); Miller, J. A, 1967 (potassium-argon dating, E. Afr.); Morlan 1967B (chronometric dating, Japan); Müller, E. 1964 (pollen analysis of bear caves, Stimme Valley); Myers, A. J. 1965 (C–14 date for Pleist. fauna, Oklahoma); National Academy of Science 1965 (time and strat. in evol. of man); Neuman 1967A (C–14 dates for archeol. of Great Plains); Nikiforova 1965C (Quat., paleomagnetic data); Noguera 1963 (dating archeol. remains); Oakley 1961D (radiometric assays), 1963D (dating bone), 1964B, 1966A (dating fossil man), 1967 (Haua Fteah hominid mandibles); Oeschger and Riesen 1965 (Bern C–14 dates); Ogden 1964 (mastodon, Ohio); Ogden and Hay 1965, 1967 (Ohio Wesleyan Univ. C–14 dates); Oltz and Kapp 1963 (Pleist. pollen assoc-iated with proboscideans, C–14 dates); Orr, P. C. 1962C (C–14 dates for California Channel Islands); Pearson, F. J. et al. 1965 (Univ. Texas C–14 dates); Pearson, F. J. et al. 1966 (Univ. Texas C–14 dates); Pecora and Rubin 1965 (chronometric dating); Petra-nek 1967 (time scale); Pidoplichko 1959C (vert. phylogeny), 1965 (methods for dating Quat. bone); Pokrovskaía 1954 (palynology and stratigraphy); Polach and Golson 1966 (C–14 dating); Polach et al. 1967 (ANU C–14 dates); Pradel, L. 1967 (C–14 dates, France); Rainey and Ralph 1966 (new methods in archeol.); Randall 1966 (dating archeol. sites, Rocky Mt. region); Ray, C. E. et al. 1967 (Pleist. mammals and pollen, Virginia); Reber 1965 (C–14 dates, Tasmania); Rex 1959 (C–14 dates, Argen-tina); Robins and Swart 1964 (C–14 dates, S. Rhodesia); Rubin and Berthold 1961 (USGS C–14 dates); Schaeffer and Zähringer 1966 (potassium-argon dating); Scherbakov 1964 (time scale); Sellstedt et al. 1966 (C–14 dating); Serebriànnyĭ 1961, 1965 (C–14 dating); Service 1965 (lithic patina); Shelkoplias and Morozov 1965 (thermolu-minescence); Sheppardiand Swart 1967 (Rhodesian C–14 dates); Shimoda et al. 1964 (fluorine and manganese in fossil bone, dating applications); Shirinov 1966 (dating Quat. cave, USSR); Simons 1967F (dating methods); Simons and Alexander 1964 (C–14 dates, ground sloth, New Mexico); Smith, D. B. 1964 (Permian); Smith, P. E. L. 1964D (C–14 dating Egyptian culture); Snelling 1964 (time scales); Srivastava 1967 (pollen analysis, Cret. mammal beds, Canada); Stewart, T. D. 1965 (chronometric dating); Stuckenrath et al. 1966 (Univ. Penn. C–14 dates); Stuiver and Suess 1966 (C–14 dates); Switsur 1967 (radioactive dating); Tamers 1966 (C–14 measurements); Tamers and Pearson 1965 (C–14 dates on bone); Tamers, Pearson and Davis (Univ. Texas C–14 dates); Tarasov 1967B (dating Gagarino site, USSR); Tarlo, L. B. H. 1967A (dating methods); Terra 1950 (C–14 dates, Mexico); Tindale 1964 (C–14 dates, Australia); Tobien 1963D (C–14 dating); Tozer 1964 (Triassic); Trautman 1964, Trautman and Willis 1966 (Isotopes, Inc. C–14 dates); Troshkina 1966 (Quat. dating); Trotter 1968A, Trotter and Malthus 1967 (dating N.Z. archeol. sites); Turner, D. L. 1968 (dating N. Amer. mammal ages); Various authors 1965 (evol. of man); Velichko 1960 (geol. age of E. European Paleolithic), 1961F (geol. age of Russian Paleolithic); Viereck 1964 (patina on stone tools); Vignard 1964D (C–14 dating); Vinogradov, A. P. et al. 1966 (Vernadsky Inst. C–14 dates); Vogel, J. C. and Waterbolk 1964, 1967, Vogel and Zagwijn 1967 (Groningen C–14 dates); Vries and Waard 1964 (Groningen C–14 dates); Wager 1964 (time scale); Walton, A. 1967 (C–14 dating); Walton, A. et al. 1961 (Isotopes, Inc., C–14 dates); Wells, L. H. 1963D (age of Galley Hill skel., Eng-land); Whittington and Williams 1964 (Ordovician); Wickman 1968 (time in geol.); Wilson, J. A. et al. (potassium-argon dates, Texas); Woodward, J. A. and A. F. 1966 (Lake Mojave C–14 dates); Yamasaki et al. 1966 (Riken C–14 dates); Zandrino 1959 (fluorine dating).

PALEOCLIMATOLOGY – Alekseeva, L. I. 1967A (Quat. mammals, Black Sea area); Alimen 1964E (Pyrenees, France), 1965C (Quat., N. W. Sahara), 1966 (Quat. W. Europe); Axelrod 1967B (Quat. mammals); Axelrod and Bailey 1968 (Cret. dinosaurs);

Banerji 1964 (prehist., Rajasthan, India); Baumhoff and Heizer 1965 (West. U.S.); Blair 1965 (amphibian speciation); Bond, G. 1967 (S. Afr.); Bottema 1967 (Late Quat., N. W. Greece); Brain and Meester 1964 (S. Afr.);

Chavaillon, J. 1964 (Quat., N. W. Sahara); Clark, John 1964 (Utah), 1967C (Oligoc., S. Dakota); Clark and Beerbower 1967 (Chadron formation); Clark, Beerbower and Kietzke 1967 (Oligoc., S. Dakota); Colbert 1964D (paleont. data), 1964E (climatic zonation); Collected Papers 1966C (changes of climate); Combier, J. 1967 (prehist., Ardèche); Cooke, H. B. S. 1964, 1967 (Pleist. climate, S. Afr.); Coque and Jauzein 1966 (Quat., Tunisia);

Dakaris et al. 1964 (Stone Age Greece); Dehm 1965 (Perm., Trias., S. Afr.); Dollfus 1964 (Peru); Dorf 1959 (climatic changes); Dort 1968 (Pleist., Idaho); Dreimanis 1967A (mastodons, Ontario), 1967B (mastodons, eastern N. Amer.);

Ericson and Wollin 1968 (Pleist. climates and deep sea chronol.);

Fabre 1964 (Pleist., France); Fairbridge 1963 (Nile sedimentation); Farrand 1968 (prehist. rockshelter sediments, France); Filzer 1966 (Pleist., N. Alps);

Gabuniia 1962C (Olig., S. Georgia, USSR); Gill 1966 (Australia); Gromov and Nikiforova 1965 (Pleist., Europe); Guilday 1962B, 1967A (Pleist., Pennsylvania); Guilday and McCrady 1968 (Pleist., Appalachia); Guillien 1961 (Quat., Charente, France);

Hapgood 1960 (frozen mammoths); Hemmer 1965B (biotops of Pleist. hominids); Hibbard and Dalquest 1966 (Pleist., Texas); Higgs 1967A, B (faunal fluctuations, Haua Fteah and other Mediterranean faunas); Higgs and Vita-Finzi 1966 (Stone Age Greece); Higgs et al. 1967 (Stone Age Greece); Hopkins, D. M. 1967A, C, D (Bering land bridge); Hsu 1966A, B (Pleist., N. China); Huscher 1967 (post-Pleist., S. E. U.S.);

Kaplianskaia 1962 (Tobol Inter-glacial);

Laville 1964 (France); Lee, M. R. 1960 (effects of climates on mammals, Utah);

Makeev 1963 (Paleolithic, Europe); Malde 1964 (environment and early man, S.W. USA); Mehringer 1964, 1965B (Pleist., Mojave Desert); Moliàvko 1963 (Plioc., Ukraine); Müller-Beck 1959 (Pleist., Mid. Europe); Musil 1966B (Pleist., Europe);

Nairn 1964 (proceedings of NATO Paleoclim. Confer.); Nilsson 1964 (Pleist., E. Afr.);

Ochev 1960B (Trias., European USSR); Oyenuga, Kunle and Ozanne 1968 (Quat., W. Afr.);

Paula Couto 1961D (Pleist., S. Amer.); Pei 1965C (effect of climate on animal size); P'iankov 1965 (Pleist. Arctic); Pidoplichko 1946-1956 (Glacial Period), 1967B (vert. research); Puissegur 1962 (Mousterian, France);

Rengarten and Konstantinova 1965 (Anthropogene, USSR); Rukhin 1957 (biostrat. and paleoclimatology);

Santa 1960 (Quat., N. Afr.); Sayles 1965 (Quat., Arizona); Schultz, C. B. 1960 (Nebraska); Sinitsyn 1965, 1967 (Eurasia); Sittler 1965 (Cret., Eoc., S. France); Smith, C. L. 1964 (fishes as indicators); Solecki, R. and Leroi-Gourhan 1966 (Shanidar Cave, Iraq);

Tochilenko 1967A (Quat., Arabia);

Van Andel et al. 1967 (Timor Sea, Australi); Vas'kovskii 1959A (Quat., USSR); Vekua 1962B (Quat., S. Georgia, USSR); Vertes 1965F (Pleist., Hungary); Vignard and Vacher 1965A (effect of climate on flints); Volkova 1966 (Quat., USSR);

West, R. G. 1967 (Quat. glaciations, British Isles); Woldstedt 1965 (Ice Age, Afr.,
    Asia, Australia, Amer.), 1966 (Quat.), 1967 (Quat., Germany);
    Ziegert 1964, 1965 (Pleist., Lybia).

PALEOECOLOGY, PALEOETHOLOGY – See: ecology.

PALEOETHNOLOGY – See: habits; paleoanthropology; paleopsychology.

PALEOGEOGRAPHY – Anatol'eva 1960 (fishes, USSR); Apostol 1963 (Rumania);
    Bachinskiĭ and Dubliănskiĭ 1968 (verts., Crimea); Bain 1966 (Gondwanaland); Baird
    1964A (Aïstopoda); Bazhanov and Kozhamkulova 1960 (Kazakhstan); Benda,
    Heimbach and Mattiat 1962 (geol., paleogeog., N.W. Germany); Bonaparte 1966D
    (therapsids, Argentina), 1967 (Trias. transatlantic connection);
    Clark, John 1967B (Brule form); Collected Papers 1967C (paleont. data); Colom
    1966 (Tert., W. Mediterranean); Cooke, H. B. S. 1968 (Mesoz., Tert., Afr.);
    Creer 1964 (Paleoz. continents); Crusafont Pairó, Valenciano Horta and Sanz
    Fuentes 1968 (verts., Spain);
    Darlington, P. J. 1965 (southern end of the world); David, A. I. 1966 (mammals,
    (Moldavia); Devillers 1965 (dinosaur beds, Alberta);
    Eynor 1966 (USSR atlas);
    Gerasimov, I. P. 1955 (geomorph. and paleogeog. of Asia); Gill 1966 (migrations,
    Australia); Gorefskiĭ 1966 (Quat., USSR); Gorshkov 1967 (Quat., Siberia);
    Grichuk and Markova 1954 (field research, USSR);
    Hallam 1967 (paleozoogeog. data and continental drift); Hapgood 1966 (ancient
    maps); Hershkovitz 1966 (Latin Amer. faunal interchange); Hopkins, D. M.
    1967A, C. D. (Bering land bridge); Hopkins et al. 1965 (Quat. correlations
    across Bering Str.);
    Ivan'ev 1964 (ostrich remains, W. Transbaĭkalia);
    Jones, W. H. 1965 (Atlantis); Josselyn 1962, 1965B (submergence of Bering Bridge
    during Pleist.);
    Karandeeva 1952 (W. part of Precaspian lowlands); Karatajūte-Talimaa and Narbutas
    1964 (Baltic Devon.); Khain 1966 (Anthropogene paleogeog.); Kolpakov 1966
    (Quat., Lena R., USSR); Konstantinova 1967A (Anthropogene, S. Moldavia,
    S. W. Ukraine); Korotkevich 1965B (Plioc. deer, Kuchurgan R. valley, USSR);
    Krömmelbein 1966 (Gondwanaland); Kuprina 1966 (Anthropogene paleogeog.,
    Kamchatka); Kurtén 1966B (Tert. land connections);
    Larina 1958 (rodent evol.); Laukhin 1967A (N. Angara, Siberia); Lin 1964 (Quat.,
    Taiwan); Liu, H.-y. 1962 (atlas, China); Lukashev 1959 (Quat.);
    Maldonado-Koerdell 1964 (Middle Amer.); Maloletko 1963 (Quat., Altai plain);
    Markov, Lazukov and Nikolaev 1965A (Quat., USSR); Martinson 1967B (origin
    of Lake Baĭkal fauna, Siberia); Matthes, H. W. 1963A (geotektonic theories in
    paleobiogeog.); Moskvitin 1952 (Pleist., European USSR);
    Olsen 1968B (Mioc. shorelines, Florida);
    Paula Couto 1961D (Pleist., S. Amer.); Pidoplichko 1946–1656 (Glacial Period),
    1967B (vert. research); Pidoplichko and Kurazhskovskiĭ 1956 (Devon. dipnoans,
    Ukraine); Pidoplichko and Miliăvko 1965 (Neogene, Quat., Ukraine); Pinson
    1949 (Gondwana land bridges); Plumstead 1966 (Gondwanaland);
    Rachitskiĭ 1960 (Low. Trias., USSR); Reshetov 1966 (Tert. and Quat.); Ricqlès 1968I
    (mammal-like reptiles, S. Amer., S. Afr.); Robinson, P. L. 1965 (Indian Gond-
    wana);
    Saks 1966 (Quat., Siberia); Sekyra 1967 (Quat., Czechoslovakia); Shikama 1962
    (Japan); Simpson, G. G. 1965G (geog. of evol.);
    Teichert, C. 1967 (Gondwana); Thenius 1964D (Cenoz. S. Amer.);
    Van Andel et al. 1967 (Timor Sea, Australia); Vangengeĭm 1967 (Bering land

bridge); Vekua 1962B (Quat., S. Georgia, USSR);
Wauchope 1966B (sunken continents); Webb, S. D. and Tessmann 1967 (Plioc. low
sea level, Florida); Wenzel and Tipton 1966 (Latin Amer.); Whitmore and
Stewart 1965 (Cent. and S. Amer.).

PALEOHISTOLOGY — See: anatomy; dentition; skeleton; skull; technique.

PALEOLITHIC ART, CAVE and ROCK PAINTINGS, ENGRAVINGS, ORNAMENTS,
PETROGLYPHS, STATUETTES — Abramov 1960 (carved bone, Ukrainia); Abramova,
Z. A. 1957 (human sculptures, cent. and W. Europe), 1958 (cave lion), 1959
(feminine images), 1960 (E. Europe), 1961 (animal carvings, Don R.), 1962A, B,
1967D (sculptures, engravings, USSR), 1966A (representations of man, Eurasia),
1967A (USSR); Alarcao 1965 (cave paintings, Portugal); Almagro Basch 1960C
(Maltravieso cave, Spain), 1964 (dating Spanish cave painting), 1966 (rock art);
Anon. 1960CI (incised mastodon bone, Mexico), 1961CN (reproductions of Lascaux paintings), 1962CK, 1964N, 1964U, 1966BF (reproductions of Altamira
paintings), 1964AA (cave paintings, Germany), 1964AB (algae, Lascaux), 1964AF
(spotted horses), 1964AQ, 1965AP, CD, 1966AD (cave paintings, Portugal), 1964AW
(engravings), 1965AS (cave drawings, France), 1966BJ (hand imprints, Fieux cave,
France), 1968Q (Przewalski horse, Lascaux caves); Antoniewicz 1964 (primitive
art); Armstrong, M. H. 1963 (mutilated hands, Gargas), 1964 (fungus, Lascaux),
1965 (cave drawings, France and Spain); Astruc 1965 (new cave drawings, France);
Bader, O. N. 1961B (Pal. figure, Sungir' site, USSR), 1962A, 1963, 1965D, 1967B
(Kapovaia cave paintings, Urals); Bánesz 1961D (Pal. idol, Cejkov), 1961E (figurine fragment, Kašov); Barandiaran Maestu, I. 1966 (cave art, Basque country);
Barrière, C. 1961 (Rouffignac, Dordogne); Barrière and Sahly 1964 (hand and
foot prints, Lascaux); Barta 1959B (sculpture, Czechoslovakia); Baumgartel 1964
(hand prints); Beater 1967 (engraved tool, Natal); Behn 1962B (rock paintings);
Beltrán 1964A (new finds reviewed), 1964B, 1965 (cave paintings, Ariège and
and Dordogne), 1964C (fertility symbols, Ariège), 1964D (cave paintings, S. Urals);
Beltrán, Robert and Vézian 1965, 1966 (Le Portel Cave, Ariège); Bergounioux
1960B (Bara-Bahau cave, France); Biedermann 1966 (cave paintings); Blanc, G. A.
1958 (engraving, Romanelli Cave, Italy); Blanchard 1964 (representations of
deer); Bonavia 1966 (cave paintings, Peru); Bordes and Smith 1965 (Solutrean
sculpture, France); Bosch-Gimpera 1964A, B, 1968 (American and Asian rock
paintings); Bouvier and Trécolle 1966 (rock shelter, France); Bouyssonie 1966
(Lascaux, France); Breuil 1956G (Lascaux), 1962C (classification of Pal. art),
1964A (reindeer engraving);
Chabredier 1966 (reproduction of prehist. art); Chernysh 1957D (human figure,
Ukraine); Cheynier 1964A (engraved ivory, France); Chollot 1964 (Piette collection Pal. art, Mus. Antiquités Nation., Paris); Choppy, B. and J. 1964 (cave
paintings, N. Spain), 1966 (Salques Cave, France); Cigliano 1964 (pictographs
and petroglyphs, Argentina); Collins, D. 1965A (fertility symbols); Cooke, C. K.
1958 (weapons in S. Rhodesian rock art), 1964B (animals in S. Rhodesian rock
art), 1967C (S. Afr. cave art); Cooke and Robinson 1954 (Amadzimba Cave,
S. Rhodesia); Courtin 1967 ("Bovidian" rock engravings, Chad); Coussy and
Taurisson 1965 (Rocadour Cave, France); Cox, A. 1961 (Lascaux paintings);
Crosby, E. 1968 (cave paintings, Queensland);
Daniel 1963C (Lascaux); De Chabalier 1963 (Lascaux paintings); Delporte 1964A,
1965 (Up. Pal. Venus figure, Krasnii Iar, Siberia), 1964C (Pal. Venus figures, cen-
tral Russia); Devambez 1961 (hist. of art); Dobat 1963 (Lascaux); Duarte 1962
(prehist. art, magic); Due Rojo 1964 (Pal. art); Dupree 1968 (sculptured head,
Afganistan);
Ebhardt 1967A (horse painting, Libya); Eisenbud 1964 (symbolic carving, Calif.);
Eppel 1963 (cave art, France and Spain); Erdniev 1956 (rock drawings, USSR);
Esch 1966 (Mousterian sculptures, N. Germany);

Farinha dos Santos 1964 (Portugal);   Fedorov, V. V. 1961 (fish engravings, USSR);
Feustel 1960 (Up. Pal. art objects, Germany); Field 1966B (petroglyphs, Asia);
Fochler-Hauke 1955 (petroglyphs, Patagonia); Fromozov 1961 (images of man,
USSR); Franke 1963 (Altamira paintings copied); Fresne 1963 (Lascaux); Frid-
rich 1964 (fishes in Bohemian art); Frolov 1966B (Pal. art 1952-1964);
Gailli et al. 1966 (bison paintings, Bédeilhac Cave, France); García Guinea 1962B,
1963C (paintings, Albacete, Spain), 1968 (rock engravings, Spain); García Guinea
and Gonzales Echegaray 1966 (cave paintings, Spain); Gaussen 1960, 1964
(Gabillou Cave, France); Gebhards 1965 (pictographs, Portugal); Genet-Varcin
1966D (fishes in Up. Pal. art); Giedion 1962, 1964B (hist. of art); Giménez
Reyna 1964 (Doña Trinidad cave, Spain); Glory 1964A, D (Lascaux paintings),
1964B (dating Lascaux paintings), 1964C (Rocadour Cave, France), 1965 (Aurignacian paintings, France); Glory Vaultier and Farinha dos Santos 1965 (Aurignacian paintings, Portugal); González-Echegaray, J. 1956C (paintings in Cullalvera Cave, Spain), 1964B (Monte-Castillo Cave, Spain); Gorce 1965 ("pre-writing");
Grand 1967 (prehist. art); Grant, C. 1967 (Amer. Indian rock art); Graziosi
1964A, 1966 (engravings, Romito Cave, Italy);
Hawkes 1958B (Pal. art); Helwin 1967 (ivory portrait); Hernández-Pacheco 1965
(reproductions of Altamira paintings); Huard 1962 (monkey paintings, Sahara);
Iampol'skii 1968 (primitive art); Imperatori 1964 (Mousterian amulet, Spain); Inskeep 1962 (Kondoa rock paintings, Afr.);
James 1965 (evidence of religion and ritual); Janssens 1961 (mutilated hands); Joly
1961 (Villars Cave, Dordogne); Jones, Rhys 1967B (totemism); Jorda Cerda
1964A (Francocantabrian and Levantine art in Spain); 1964B, C (Pal. art in
Franco-Cantabrian region);
Kabo 1966 (Australian art); Karlov and Nakel'skii 1963 (pendants, USSR); Khlobyst
1964A (seal carvings, USSR); Klíma, B. 1964 (lion statuette, Moravia), 1965B
(engraved horse rib, Moravia); Koenigswald 1964C ("Venus" figures); Kühn,
H. 1965 (hist. of discovery of Pal. art, 1830-1960), 1966B (Magdalenian goat
engraving, Schulerloch Cave, Bavaria; Magdalenian engravings, Klause Caves,
Bavaria), 1966C (prehist. art);
La Baume 1959 (aurochs, France, Italy); Lachastre 1964A (Magdalenian paintings,
Dordogne); Lane and Richards 1966 (hand paintings, S. Australia); Lantier
1961C (Pal. art); Laurent 1964 (engraving, France); Leason 1938 (Quat. cave
art); Leroi-Gourhan, André 1961B, 1965C, 1966, 1967, 1968A, B (prehist.
art); Lorblanchet 1965, 1966, 1967 (cave paintings, France);
M., B. 1960 (cave painting, France); McBurney 1961C (Pal. art); McCulloch, B.
1968 (Moa Hunter drawings, New Zealand); Madariaga de la Campa 1963 (animals of Up. Pal. Cantabrican art); Mannino 1960 (rock incisions, Italy), 1962B
(rock incisions, Sicily); Marshack 1964 (Pal. notation of lunar observation);
Matthes, W. 1966 (Early and Mid. Pal. flint sculptures, N. Germany); Mazonowicz
1965 (cave paintings, Spain), 1966, 1968 (rock shelter paintings, Spain); Medoev
1961 (Late Pal. rock paintings, Kazakhstan); Megaw, J. V. S. 1967 (art styles and
analysis); Méroc and Mazet 1964 (cave paintings, France); Mezzena 1965 (engraved pebbles, Italy); Mountford and Edwards 1964 (rock engravings, S. Australia); Myron 1964 (prehist. art);
Narr 1960D (Pal. female representations); Nicholas 1965 (hand prints, France);
Nougier 1966 (prehist. art); Nougier and Barrière 1965 (hand impressions, France);
Nougier and Robert 1965A, 1966B (goat engravings, France), 1965B, 1966A (cats
in European Quat. art); Nybelin 1965 (Lascaux unicorn);
Oakley 1965A (fossil shell and tooth ornaments); Okladnikov 1967 (cave paintings,
Cent. Asia), 1968A (Marxism and the origin of art);
Pales and Tassin de Saint Péreuse 1964, 1965 (Magdalenian engravings); Paradisi
1965 (rock engravings, Cyrenaica); Petit, G. and Theodorides 1962 (hist. Pal.
art); Pidoplichko 1960 (engraved bone, USSR); Pierret 1960 (paintings, Villars
Cave, France), 1961A (Pal. caves, Périgord, France), 1961B (cave paintings, France);

Pintaud 1961 (engravings, France); Pirker 1961, 1965 (cave art); Piscopo and Radmilli 1966 (bone statuette, Italy); Pittard 1960 (engraved bone, France); Powell, B. W. 1967 (paintstones, northeastern N. Amer.); Powell, T. G. E. 1966 (prehist. art); Praslov and Filippov 1967 (Pal. engravings, Ukraine); Prot and Couste 1961 (engraved deer antler, France);

Ranaldi 1966 (cave paintings, rock and bone carvings, Italy); Rätzel 1964A, B (reindeer engravings), 1965 (ibex in prehist. art); Rautenbach 1967 (paintings, S. Afr.); Riek 1932B, 1960* (Aurignacian animal statuettes); Rioumine 1961 (Late Pleist. mammal paintings, S. Urals); Ripoll Perelló 1962B, 1963, 1965C, D (cave paintings, Spain); Robert and Nougier 1965 (horse head, Magdalenian bone carving, Pyrenees); Roche 1965A (pebble carving, Morocco); Rogachev 1967 (animal carvings, USSR); Roginskiĭ 1965 (research); Roussot 1966B (cave paintings, Lascaux); Roussot et al. 1966 (sculpture, engravings, France);

Sahly 1963 (mutilated hand prints, Pyrenees); Sarga 1965, 1966 (blood principle, totemism); Sauser 1965 (Venus statuette); Sauter 1966B (review of Pal. art books); Schaurte 1964 (Elasmotherium, France); Schmid 1964B, C (female figurine, Germany), 1964D (ibex, Niaux Cave); Smith, P.E.L. 1965A (rock art, N. Afr.); Sonneville-Bordes 1965C (Mousterian wall paintings, France); Soubeyran 1966 (Magdalenian artifacts, France); Spéléo-Club de Bergerac 1966 (cave paintings, France); Spivak 1961 (Lascaux); Stoliar 1964 (initial forms), 1965 (animals), 1966A (figurative art, Eurasia), 1966B (figurative art, Europe); Summers 1944-55B (rock carvings, Afr.);

Tarasov 1963, 1965, 1967A (ivory statuette, Gagarino, USSR); Toepfer 1965B (Venus figures, Germany); Tokarev 1961B (feminine figurines);

Ucko and Rosenfeld 1966, 1967 (Pal. cave art);

Valoch 1966A (bone sculpture, Czechoslovakia); Vértes 1965E (carving, Hungary); Vidal, P. 1967 (ornamented caves and shelters, France); Vinnicombe 1966 (preservation of S. Afr. rock paintings), 1967 (rock paintings);

Willcox 1963 (rock art, S. Afr.);

Y., L. M. 1967 (extinct animal drawings, Ohio);

Zamiatnin 1961A (Pal. art, USSR); Zemliakov 1939A (mammoth drawing, Ukraine); Zhirov 1960 (cave paintings, Urals); Zorzi 1964 (engravings, wall paintings, Italy); Zotz 1965D (engravings, France).

PALEOMYOLOGY, PALEOBIOMECHANICS, KINETICS, LIGAMENTS — Anon. 1965AZ (locomotion of bipedal dinosaurs);

Barghusen 1968 (jaw musculature of cynodont reptiles); Boonstra 1967A (therapsid girdles and limbs), 1967B (pareiasaurs and dicynodonts); Brown, L. 1968 (restoration of fossil animals);

Callison 1967 (cranial kinesis in mosasaurs); Casamiquela 1966 (gaits of saurischian dinosaurs); Crompton and Hotton 1967 (jaw mechanism of dicynodonts);

Davis, Day and Napier 1964 (tibia and fibula showing adaptation to bipedalism, Olduvai Gorge); Day 1967 (striding gait of Olduvai hominid); Day and Napier 1964, 1966 (plantigrade bipedalism of Olduvai hominid);

Frick 1965 (mammalian jaw articulation);

Gans 1966B (locomotion without limbs); Gans and Parsons 1966 (jumping mechanism, frogs); Gasc 1967A (limbless locomotion); Gray, J. 1968 (animal locomotion); Gutmann 1966A (fishes), 1966B (early development of verts.), 1967A (dermal skel. of lower verts.);

Hewes 1964 (hominid bipedalism); Hirschfeld 1968 (jaw mechanics, ground sloths);

Iakovlev, V. N. 1966B, 1967C (evol. of fish skel.);

Jarvik 1965A (origin of girdles and paired fins); Jouffroy and Lessertisseur 1967 (scapular belt in reptiles and mammals);

Kalin 1964 (pongid and hominid limbs); Kas'ianenko 1959 (mammal limbs and joints); Kinzey 1967 (primate locomotion); Klausewitz 1965A (locomotion of the Rhinobatoidei); Krüger, W. 1958 (skel., muscles of mammals); Kummer 1965 (bipedal position of verts.);

Lessertisseur and Saban 1967C (appendicular skel.); Lessertisseur and Sigogneau 1965 (evol. of principal characteristics of mammal. skel.); Lisowski 1967 (primate talus); Lund 1967A (fish locomotion);

Manziĭ 1962 (vert. terrestrial locomotion); Mazhuga 1961 (skel. indices for mammalian limb functions);

Napier 1964B, D (bipedalism in hominids); Napier and Walker 1967 (primate locomotor adaptations);

Ostrom 1964A (locomotion of hadrosaurian dinosaurs), 1964D (Triceratops jaw mechaics); Oxnard 1967 (primate shoulder and locomotion);

Parrington 1967B (locomotion in early tetrapods); Peiper 1963 (upright posture, man); Pilbeam 1968A (locomotion, hominids);

Ripley 1967 (primate locomotor adaptation); Robinson, J. T. 1967A (hominid locomotion);

Simonetta 1957C (insectivore skulls); Simons 1967A (locomotion in extinct primates); Smith, J. M. and Savage 1956 (locomotory adaptations); Snyder 1967 (bipedal locomotion); Straus and Cave 1964 (Neanderthal posture);

Thomson, K. S. 1966F (intracranial mobility, coelacanth), 1967A (intracranial kinetics in fossil fishes); Tuttle 1965 (hominoid hands), 1966, 1967 (knuckle-walking).

Vilar Fiol 1965 (upright posture); Vorontsov 1963B (rodent jaws);

Washburn and Jay 1964 (evol. of locomotion); Wescott 1967 (human bipedalism); White, J. A. 1968 (porcupine mastication); Wickler 1960 (fish locomotion); Woodburne 1965A, 1966B (Tayassuidae), 1968 (collared peccary);

Zihlman 1966 (human bipedalism).

PALEONEUROLOGY — Cobb and Edinger 1962 (emu brain);

Dechaseaux 1964A (natural endocast, insectivore), 1967B (beaver, Europe), 1967C, 1968A (mammal brain), 1968B (Archaeopteryx brain);

Edinger 1964B (recent advances);

Gazin 1965C (Smilodectes endocranial cast);

Hassler and Stephen 1966 (evol. of the forebrain); Hofer 1960 (orientation of brain to snout, mammals), 1964 (primate brain), 1965 (skull structure and brain development, primates); Hofer and Wilson 1967 (Olig. primate endocranial cast); Holloway 1966A (cranial capacity, neural reorganization and hominid evol.); Holloway and Tobias 1965, 1966 (cranial capacity of Olduvai hominid); Hopson 1964B (Bienotherium braincase);

Jakway and Clement 1967 (natural endocast, Tomarctus); Jerison 1968 (Archaeopteryx brain);

Kochetkova 1961B, 1966A, 1967, 1968 (evol. of hominid brain), 1964 (Cro-Magnon cranial mold), 1965 (brain volume of Pal. man from "Markina Gora"), 1966B (endocranium of Pal. man from Pavlov I, Czekoslovakia); Kurth and Marsky 1967 (endocranial molds);

Macarovici and Paghida 1964 (Hipparion endocranial cast, Rumania); Maleev 1965 (carnivorous dinosaurs); Mchedlidze 1964A, B, C (cetaceans); Meladze 1967 (Hipparion and Mirabilocerus endocranial molds); Mettler 1956 (evol. of human brain); Millot, Nieuwenhuys and Anthony 1964 (brain of Latimeria);

Nieuwenhuys 1965 (Latimeria forebrain); Nikitenko 1964 (vert. brain), 1965 (mammal brain), 1966 (amphibian brain); Nobach 1959 (vert. brain);

Pilleri 1967 (cetaceans); Platel 1967 (reptile brain);

Radinsky 1967C (mammal brain size); Romer 1964A (elasmobranch braincase); Russell and Sigogneau 1965 (endocranial casts, Paleoc. mammals);

Shevchenko, Iu. G. 1967, 1968 (primate brain); Sigogneau 1968B (Dremotherium); Starck 1963B (mammal brain), 1965 (vert. brain evol.); Stensiö 1963 (brain of lower verts.); Stęślicka 1964A (hominid endocranial casts); Sych 1967B (leporid endocranial cast);

Tatarinov, L. P. 1966B, 1967A (therapsid brain), 1967B (theriodont nerves); Thomson,

K. S. 1965B (Osteolepis endocranium); Tobias 1964A (Zinjanthropus cranial capacity), 1968C (cranial capacity of anthropoid apes and early man);

Wenz 1968A (fish endocranial mold); White, E. I. 1965 (Dipterus neurocranium); Whiting and Tarlo 1965 (heterostracan brain); Wierciński 1959B (hominid endocranial cast, Czechoslovakia).

PALEONTOGRAPHY – See: paleogeography.

PALEOÖRNITHOLOGY – See: anatomy, AVES; aquatic adaptations; faunas; flight; skeleton, AVES; skull, AVES.

PALEOPATHOLOGY – Alexandersen 1967A (Neanderthals), 1967B (Pleist. skulls); Anon. 1965BJ (dinosaur, China); Armelagos 1965 (human);

Bach 1962 (prehist. man); Bendix-Almgreen 1964 (fossil verts.); Blumberg and Kerley 1966 (bone); Boev and Maslinkov 1965 (human teeth, Bulgaria); Brabant 1967 (dental diseases, early man); Brothwell 1967 (human disease); Brothwell and Sandison 1967 (diseases in early man);

Courville 1967 (cranial injuries in prehist. man); Crain 1966 (population dynamics and disease);

Dahlberg and Staley 1965 (diseases of dentition); Dastugue 1967 (Cro-Magnon); Dawson, W. R. 1967 (hominid paleopath.);

First 1964 (skull fractures in suids, S. Afr.); Frost, H. M. 1966A (morphometry of bone), 1966B (bone dynamics);

Gadzhiev, G. V. and D. V. 1954 (spondylitis in Quat. wolf); Goldstein 1963B (human paleopath.); Green, M. 1962D (arthritic bear, S. Dakota); Greene, A. M. 1967 (Shanidar Neanderthals, Iraq);

Hackett 1967 (origin and spread of human treponematoses); Hare 1967 (antiquity of diseases); Hasegawa 1964A (bones of subfossil toad, Japan); Hunter and Langston 1965 (odontoma in mammoth);

Iatsko 1962B (camel skels., USSR);

Jarcho 1966 (human paleopath.);

Kerley 1967 (paleopath. and other disciplines); Koby 1964B (cave bear skull), 1964D (osteolysis in chamois, Pyrenees), 1964E (osteolysis in Pleist. mammals, Pyrenees); Koby and Bröckelmann 1967 (cave bear jaw); Koby and Scheidegger 1964 (bone disease in cave bear); Konnerth 1966 (swollen fish bones); Kubiak 1965B (elephant dentition);

Lambrecht, F. L. 1964, 1967, 1968 (influence of blood parasites on hominid evol. in Afr.);

MacGregor, A. B. 1964 (Le Moustier mandible); McKern 1966B (prehist. medicine); Mark-Kurik 1966 (exoskel. injuries of fishes); Mehl 1966 (Domebo mammoth, Oklahoma); Moodie 1967 (fossil animals); Morse 1967 (tuberculosis);

Nicolăescu-Plopşor and Floru 1963 (paleoanthrop. and hist. of medicine);

Paoli 1961 (hist. and bibliog.); Polgar, S. 1964 (ills of primitive man); Putschar 1966 (bone);

Regöly-Mérey 1962 (human remains); Rogers, S. L. 1966 (bone proliferation); Rokhlin 1965 (early man);

Sahly 1963 (mutilated hand prints, Pyrenees); Sandison and Wells 1967 (endocrine diseases); Scheidegger 1963 (cave bear); Schultz, A. 1967 (wild apes); Straus and Cave 1964 (Neanderthals);

Takai 1937B (elephant); Tasnádi-Kubacska 1963 (studies), 1964 (present state);

Ullrich 1966B (skull operations);

Wells, C. 1964A (disease, early man), 1964B (elephant tooth, England), 1964C, D (pliosaur, England), 1967 (pseudopathology); Woo, Ju-kang 1964B, F, G (Lantian man, China);

Zenker 1965 (lemur jaw).

PALEOPEDOLOGY, FOSSIL SOILS – See: paleochronology.

PALEOPHYSIOLOGY – Jansky, 1967 (temp. regulation in mammals); Jarvik 1964A (special-
　　　　izations in early verts.), 1965A (origin of girdles and paired fins), 1965B (tetrapods),
　　　　1967B (skull bones in fishes and tetrapods);
　　　R., A. 1967 (temp. of fossil verts.); Russell, L. S. 1965B (body temp. of dinosaurs);
　　　Strel'nikov 1959 (reptile thermoregulation);
　　　Tasnádi-Kubacska 1963 (studies);

PALEOPSYCHOLOGY, RELIGION, RITES, MAGIC
　　　PALEOETHNOLOGY – Anon. 1965BT (Pal. funeral, USSR); Ardrey 1966 (territorial
　　　　　imperative);
　　　　Bader, O. N. 1964, 1965E, 1966A, 1967C, D (Cro-Magnon burial, Sungir' site, USSR);
　　　　　Bergounioux 1966 (prehist. religions); Binford, S. R. 1968 (disposal of the dead);
　　　　　Bowler et al. 1967 (human burial, Australia);
　　　　Chalus 1963 (man and religion); Chardin 1965D (science and religion); Cox, A. 1961
　　　　　(Lascaux paintings);
　　　　Due Rojo 1964 (Pal. religion);
　　　　Ehrenberg 1967 (Neanderthal bear ceremony); Eickstedt 1964 (critical review);
　　　　Gehlen, A. 1964 (Pal. religion, magic);
　　　　Hays 1963 (early man and religion);
　　　　James 1965 (prehist. religion);
　　　　Lantier 1961C (prehist. life); Leroi-Gourhan, André 1964E (prehist. religions), 1965D
　　　　　(development of human society);
　　　　Malez 1961H (bear cult, Yugoslavia); Maringer 1962 (Pal. religions of Europe);
　　　　Narr 1966E, F (religion and magic); Nougier 1963 (prehist. religion);
　　　　Oakley 1965A (fossil shell and tooth ornaments);
　　　　Sarga 1965, 1966 (blood principle, totemic society); Sonneville-Bordes 1965D (prehist.
　　　　　religion);
　　　　Ting 1966 (Chinese oracle bones);
　　　　Wernert 1961B, 1963 (magic rituals).

PALEOSEROLOGY – See: circulatory system, blood groups.

PALEOSOCIOLOGY – See: ecology; habits; paleoanthropology; paleopsychology.

PALEOZOOLOGY – See: biology.

PALICHNOLOGY, PALEOICHNOLOGY – See: ichnology.

PALYNOLOGY, POLLEN DATING – See: paleochronology.

PETRIFACTION – See: occurrences.

PETROGLYPHS – See: Paleolithic art.

PHOTOGRAPHY – See: technique.

PHYLOGENY, PHYLOGENESIS, CLASSIFICATION (see also: evolution) – Ahlén 1965B
　　　　(red deer, Scandinavia); Alekseeva, L. V. 1968 (primates); Anderson, J. M. 1968A
　　　　(Procynosuchidae); Anon. 1961CO (Oreopithecus), 1965CC (new name for Homo
　　　　habilis), 1966AG (nomenclature, early man); Appleby et al. 1967 (Reptilia); Azzar-
　　　　roli 1964B (Rhinoceros hemitoechus), 1966A (elephants), 1966B (Pleist. and living
　　　　horses);
　　　　B., H. 1965 (Oreopithecus); Baird 1964A, 1965C (Aïstopoda), 1964C (Changisaurus a

turtle); Balabaĭ 1956A (Poraspis), 1956B, C (Agnatha); Baldauf 1964A (Anura);
Beaumont 1964C (Mustelidae), 1964D (Felidae), 1968 (viverrids, France); Beer
1964C (ratites); Bluntschli 1911 (fossil primates and man); Boné and Singer
1965 (Hipparion in Afr.); Boonstra 1965A (Deuterosaurus); Bouvier 1889 (fossil
whales); Branson 1964B (Edestus); Briggs, J. E. 1961 (fishes); Brodal and
Fänge 1963 (myxinoids); Brodkorb 1964A, 1965, 1967 (fossil birds), 1964D
(Fulica), 1964E (fossil turkeys); Brough, M. C. and J. 1967 (microsaurs); Bunak
1966A (hominids); Butler, P. M., et al. 1967 (Mammalia);
Campbell, B. G. 1964A (Homo habilis), 1964B (human evol.), 1965 (Hominidae);
Campbell, C. B. G. 1966 (tree shrews); Cantwell 1968 (Sigmodon); Carroll, R. L.
1964A (Parioxys); Carroll and Baird 1967, 1968 (microsaurs and reptiles); Carter,
G. S. 1957C (chordates); Casamiquela 1965D (Anura, Argentina), 1965E (Salientia); Cavender 1966A (Leuciscus, British Columbia), 1966B (teleosts); Chakravarti 1965 (elephants, India, Burma, Pakistan); Chang, Hsi-chih 1964B (Palaeoloxodon, China); Charig, Attridge and Crompton 1965 (Saurischia); Chudinov
1964A (Cotylosauria), 1964B (Eotitanosuchidae), 1964C (Estemmenosuchidae),
1964D (Venyukovioidea), 1964E (Iguania), 1964F (Scincomorpha), 1964G (Varanoidea), 1964H (Cholophidia); Churcher 1966A (Epieuryceros); Clark, John
1966B (Metacodon and Geolabis); Clemens et al. 1964 (Cimolestidae); Colbert
1964B (saurischian dinosaurs); Comas 1968 (definition of the human genus);
Cox, C. B. 1964 (Endothiodon); Crompton and Jenkins 1967 (symmetrodonts
and pantotheres), 1968 (Triassic mammals); Crusafont Pairó 1967B (prosimians,
Spain); Cuscani Politi 1967 (Hippopotamus);
Dahr 1952 (Australopithecinae); Davis, D. D. 1964 (giant panda); Davitashvili 1964
(assemblages of organic remains); Daxner and Thenius 1965 (wild goats, Austria);
Dechaseaux 1963C (Xiphodon); Delmas and Pineau 1966 (mammals); DeMar
1968 (Dissorophidae); Denison 1964B (Cyathaspididae), 1967B (Pteraspididae);
Dietrich 1949 (Equidae); Dineley 1964A (pteraspids); Doben-Florin 1964 (Sor-
icidae); Dubrovo 1965 (Elephas wüsti), 1966A (Mammuthus trogontherii chosa-
ricus);
Fahlbusch, V. 1967B (cricetids, N. Amer., Europe); Fischer, K. 1967 (Chasmotherium);
Forsten 1968 (revision of Hipparion); Fox and Bowman 1966 (Captorhinus);
Frechkop 1965A (antelopes), 1965B (cervids); Fuller and Bayrock 1965 (Late
Pleist. bisons);
Gardiner 1967A (Chondrostei); Gazin 1965B (Meniscotherium), 1968B (Hyopsodus);
Gentry 1965 (Hippotragus), 1966 (Antilopini), 1967 (Pelorovis); Ginsburg 1967E
(reptiles); Ginsburg and Heintz 1966 (Palaeomeryx); Gisin 1966 (quantum theory
of taxonomy); Glikman 1956 (Anacorax), 1964A (elasmobranchs), 1964B (Paleogene sharks, USSR); Gokhman 1966B (Late Paleolithic man); Goodman 1966
(tree shrews); Gorgas, K. 1967 (rodents); Gorgas, M. 1967 (rodents); Gosline
1965 (teleosts); Gould, S. J. 1967 (pelycosaurs); Greenwood et al. 1966 (teleostean fishes); Gremiatskiĭ 1968 (fossil hominids); Gromov, I. M., et al. 1965
(Marmotinae, USSR); Gromova 1967B (Quat. rhinos); Gross, W. 1964C (polyphyletic origin of verts.), 1965A (placoderms), 1966 (fish scales), 1967A (Agnatha
and Pisces); Gureev 1964 (Lagomorpha, USSR);
Havesson 1950 (Paracamelus); Hayasaka 1964 (ontogeny, phylogeny and evol. in
paleont.); Heberer 1965C (Australopithecinae), 1967B (primates); Heberer and
and Kurth 1966 (Homo); Heintz, A. 1963 (classif. of armored fishes), 1964C
(Gigantopithecus), 1966C (Homo habilis); Heintz, Nicole 1967B (primates), 1968
(Hominoidea); Hemmer 1965D (Dinofelis), 1966 (Pantherinae); Hennig, W. 1966
(phylogenetic systematics); Heywood and McNeill 1964 (phenetic and phylogenetic
classif.); Hill, W. C. O. 1966 (primates); Hirschfeld and Webb 1968 (megalonychids, N. Amer.); Hoffstetter 1968D (snakes); Hoffstetter and Gayrard 1964
(snakes); Holz 1965 (Lycaon); Hooijer 1967E (Aceratherium); Hull 1967 (taxonomy); Hürzeler 1968 (anthropomorphs); Hutchison 1968A (moles, N. Amer.);

Iakovlev, V. N. 1965B, 1966A (Lycopteridae); Inger and Marx 1965 (colubrid snakes);

Janot 1967 (Amia); Jefferies 1967, 1968 (subphylum Calcichordata); Jehl 1966A (subspecies in fossil birds); Jessen 1966B, 1967 (Struniiformes); Jolly 1966 (primates); Jordan, D. S. 1963 (fishes); Josselyn 1963B, 1964A, 1965A, 1966C (classif. of projectile points);

Kahlke 1964 (Ovibovini), 1966 (hominids); Kälin 1965 (primates), 1966 (prehominids, hominids); Kazantseva 1964 (Actinopterygii); Kermack, D. M. et al. 1968 (pantotheres); Kermack, K. A. 1965B (origin of mammals), 1967A (interrelations of early mammals), 1967B (molar evol. in Mesoz. mammals), 1967C (Aegialodontidae); Kerr and Silva 1962 (hominids); Khozatskiĭ 1965 (significance of turtle armor structure); Khozatskiĭ and Iur'ev 1964A (Mosasauridae), 1964B (Pterosauria); Khozatskiĭ and Mlynarski 1966 (Geoemyda, Europe); Khrisanfova 1964, 1967 (hominids); Kiriakoff 1965 (numerical taxonomy); Kirpichnikov 1964 (origin of the Caspian seal); Klausewitz 1965A (Rhynchobatidae, Rhinobatidae); Kleinenberg 1958 (origin of cetaceans); Kleinschmidt 1966 (horses); Klima, Von M. 1967 (bats); Kluge 1967 (gekkonid lizards); Knussmann 1967 (Oreopithecus); Koenigswald 1964B, 1966A, 1967A, C (early man); Konzhukova 1964A (Apsidospondyli), 1964B (Batrachosauria), 1964C (Crocodilia); Koopman 1967 (artiodactyls); Koopman and Cockrum 1967 (bats); Korotkevich 1968 (Mioc. gazelles, S. USSR); Kraglievich 1965 (Eumysops, Argentina); Kretzoi 1962E (Arvicolidae/Microtidae), 1965E (Arvicolidae); Kuhn, H.-J. 1967 (Cercopithecidae); Kuhn, O. 1964A (Ornithischia), 1964B (testudines), 1964C, E, 1967B, 1968 (Amphibia and Reptilia), 1965A (Saurischia), 1965B (Therapsida), 1965C (macroevol., phylogeny), 1965D (fossil birds), 1965E (Amphibia), 1965F (science of phylogeny), 1966 (Reptilia), 1967A (Pterosauria); Kühne 1967 (phylogenetic tree of mammals), 1968 (origin and history of Mammalia); Kuhn-Schnyder 1965C (reptiles), 1967A (Euryapsida); Kummer and Gemeinhardt 1964 (phylogeny); Kurtén 1964A (polar bear), 1966A (bears, N. Amer.); Kurth 1964B (Homo habilis), 1965B (hominid species); Kuss 1965C (European amphicyons);

Lange, S. P. 1968 (Urocles, Europe); Langston 1965B (crocodiles, S. Amer.), 1966A (Nettosuchidae); Lavocat 1964C (Delanymys); Leakey, L. S. B. 1965B (origin of man), 1966B (Homo habilis, H. erectus and the australopithecines), 1967E (Early Mioc. hominids); Leakey, Tobias and Napier 1964 (Homo habilis); Le Danois and Le Danois 1963 (Scombrida); Lehman 1966B (Actinopterygii), 1966C (Dipnoi and Crossopterygii), 1966D (Brachiopterygii); Liem 1963 (Anabantoidei); Lindberg, G. U. 1963 (generic names of fishes); Liubin 1965 (classif. of Low. Pal. stone tools); Long, C. A. 1964 (Taxidea marylandica);

MacAllister 1968 (teleost fishes); McDowell 1964 (Testudinidae); MacIntyre 1966 (Ictidopappus and Protictis); McKenna 1966A (Olig.-Mioc. camels), 1967B (prosimian primates), 1968 (Leptacodon); Mahoney 1964 (marsupials, Australia); Maleev 1964A (Younginiformes), 1964B (Choristodera), 1964C (Prolacertidae), 1964D (Tangasauridae), 1964E (Thalattosauridae), 1964F (Thecodontia), 1964G (Theropoda), 1964H (Compsognathidae), 1964I (Coeluridae), 1964J (Ornithomimidae), 1964K (Megalosauridae), 1964L (Ceratosauridae), 1964M (Spinosauridae), 1964N (Deinodontidae), 1964O (Stegosauria), 1964P (Ankylosauria); Martin, R. D. 1968 (new definition of primates); Mawby 1964, 1965A (Aelurodon); Mayr, E. 1964D (systematics and origin of species), 1965A (classif. and phylogeny), 1968 (biol. classif.); Meladze 1964A (Sivatheriinae), 1967 (Arkneti and Bazaleti faunas, USSR); Melentis 1966C (Anthracotherium now Brachyodus), 1966D (hyracoids); Mertens 1960 (influence of evol. theory on taxonomy); Miles, R. S. 1965A, 1966A (Acanthodii); Miles and Westoll 1968 (Coccosteidae); Milstead 1965 (box turtles); Monod 1967 (teleosts); Mottl 1964 (cave bears, Austria); Müller, A. H. 1966 (fishes and amphibians), 1968 (reptiles and birds); Müller, Arnt 1967 (insectivores, S. Germany);

Nielsen 1964B (Tupilakosaurus, Greenland); Nikitenko 1965 (mammal brain), 1966 (amphibian brain); Nishiwaki 1966 (Cetacea); Novitskaya and Obruchev 1964 (Acanthodei); Novozhilov 1964A (Sauropterygia), 1964B (Pistosauroidea), 1964C (Pleisosauroidea), 1964D (Pliosauroidea); Nybelin 1966 (Pholidophoridae), 1967A (Anaethalion);

Obruchev, D. V. 1961C (Ostracodermi), 1962B (Acanthodei), 1962C (Chondrichthyes), 1964A, 1967D (fishes), 1964B (Chordata), 1964C (Agnatha), 1964D (Placodermi), 1964E (Holocephali), 1965C (Bradyodonti), 1967A (Heterostraci); Obruchev and Kazantseva 1964A (Chondrostei), 1964B (Polypteri); Obruchev and Mark-Kurik 1965, 1968 (psammosteids); Obruchev and Sergienko 1961 (Placodermi); Ochev 1966C (capitosaurid labyrinthodonts), 1967B (classif. of fossil vert. sites, USSR), 1967C (Coelodontognathus); Olson 1964B, 1965B, 1966D (Batrachosauria, Chelonia), 1965A (Amphibia); Orlov, J. A. 1964E (Doliosuchus); Orton 1957 (frogs); Ørvig 1967B (tooth tissues); Oschinsky et al. 1964 (origin of Homo sapiens); Ostrom 1964B (Hadrosaurus);

Panchen 1967C (Amphibia); Parris 1968 (prosciurids); Parsons 1968 (recent turtles); Patterson, B. 1964 (Old World non-hominid primates), 1965B (fossil elephant shrews); Patterson, C. 1964 (acanthopterygian fishes), 1965A, B (Holocephali); Pilbeam 1964 (variation and taxonomy); Pilbeam et al. 1965, Pilbeam and Simons 1965 (hominids); Piveteau 1964E (verts.); Pradel, L. 1966D (classification of burins); Prat 1964 (Pleist. equids);

Radinsky 1964A (chalicotheres), 1966B (rhino families), 1967A (tapiroids), 1967B (hyracodonts); Ray, C. E. 1964B (Heptaxodon); Reed, C. A. 1967 (Homo habilis); Reig 1967 (Archosauria); Rensberger 1966 (geomyid); Repenning 1967C (Soricidae); Ricqlès 1968D (reptiles); Ride 1964B (Australian marsupials); Ripinsky 1967 (immunochemical analysis in hominid evolution); Robinson, J. T. 1963B (australopithecines), 1967B (early hominids); Robinson, P. 1968A (insectivores); Rodendorf 1959 (paleozool. systematics), 1964 (animals); Romer 1964B (labyrinthodont, Scotland), 1964D (Diadectes), 1964G (amphibians), 1966C, 1968A (vert. paleont.); Rothausen 1968B (European fossil squalodonts); Rozhdestvenskii 1965 (Asiatic dinosaurs), 1966A, 1967 (iguanadonts, Cent. Asia); Russell, D. A. 1967A (Amer. mosasaurs); Russell, R. J. 1968 (pocket gophers);

Sackett 1964 (stone tools); Scherf 1967 (hyena); Schmalhausen 1964A (Urodela); Schmidt, W. 1959* (pteraspids); Schultz, A. 1965 (Hominoidea); Schultz, C. B. and Falkenbach 1968 (oreodonts); Sera 1954C (Pyrotherium); Siegfried 1966 (Dercetis); Sigogneau 1968A (Gorgonopsia); Sill 1967, 1968 (Crocodilia); Simons 1963I (Oligocene catarrhines), 1967B (primate paleont.); Simons and Pilbeam 1965 (Dryopithecinae); Singer and Bone 1966 (Hipparion, Africa); Sokal and and Sneath 1963 (numerical taxonomy); Sokolov, I. I. 1965 (phylogenetic systematics); Spinar 1967B (frogs); Stensiö 1963 (lower verts.), 1964 (ostracoderms); Stirton 1964 (beavers), 1965A, 1966, 1967D (Protoceratidae); Stirton and Marcus 1966 (macropodid); Stirton, Woodburne and Plane 1967 (diprotodonts); Stohl 1957 (Lagomorpha); Straus 1965 (Hominidae); Szalai 1967 (Apterodon);

Tatarinov, L. P. 1965D (Ulemosaurus); Telles Antunes 1964B, 1967A (crocodiles); Terent'ev 1961, 1965B (amphibians and reptiles); Thenius 1967C (Felidae); Thomson, K. S. 1967B (rhipidistian fishes); Tobias 1965A, B (Homo habilis); Tolmachev, A. I. 1968 (biol. taxonomy);

Underwood, G. 1967 (snakes);

Vandebroek 1964 (mammals); Van Valen 1965G (Proviverrini, Europe), 1966A (Deltatheridia, new order), 1967B (insectivores), 1967C (Prototomus); Van Valen et al. 1967 (Galeopithecus); Van Valen and Mellett 1968 (Oxyaenoides); Verheyen 1960, 1961A, B (birds); Vialov 1966 (traces of life activity); Vuilleumier 1965 (Cracidae), 1967 (frogs);

Walker, A. D. 1964 (Carnosauria), 1966 (Elachistosuchus); Wassersug and Hecht 1967 (crocodiles); Weaver 1967, Weaver and Rose 1967 (Chrysemys); Webb, S. D. 1964A, 1965A (Calippus), 1965C (Camelops); Weinert 1956 (apes and man); Weitzman 1960A, B, C (characid fishes), 1967 (stomiatoid fishes); Weller

1965A (paleont., evol., taxonomy); Welles and Cosgriff 1965B (labyrinthodonts); Westoll 1967 (Radontina); Williams, K. L. and Wilson 1967 (colubrid
snake, Cemophora); Wolpoff 1966 (Telanthropus); Woo, Ju-kang 1964E (hominids); Woodburne 1968 (collared peccary);

Zakrzewski 1967A (Canimartes?); Zimmermann, W. 1960C (living things); Zubov
1964 (Australopithecinae).

PHYLOGENY, METHODS OF STUDY OF — Ax 1964 (polyphyletism and phylogenetic
systematics);

Bachinskiĭ 1965B (terrestrial vert.); Baker, P. T. 1967 (biol. race concept); Birch
and Ehrlich 1967B (phylogeny and taxonomy); Bonner 1968 (size change); Boyce
1964 (numerical taxonomy and hominid classif.); Brink 1967 (taxonomic groups);
Burr and Gerson 1965 (Venn diagrams and human taxonomy);

Fry 1965 (methods in taxonomy);

Gould, S. J. 1966 (allometry and size); Guthrie, R. D. 1966C (bison horn cores —
character choice and systematics);

Hennig, W. 1966 (phylogenetic systematics); Heywood and McNeill 1964 (phenetic
and phylogenetic classif.); Hünermann 1966 (dentition, Castoridae);

Kälin 1956C (primate skull prientation);

Lipták 1965 (taxonomic method in paleoanthrop.);

Mayr, E. 1965A (classif. and phylogeny), 1968 (theory of biol. classif.); Moss,
M. L. 1961 (the initial phylogenetic appearance of bone);

Olson 1964C (numerical taxonomic methods);

Ricqlès 1968D (reptiles); Ripinsky 1967 (immunochemical analysis in primates);
Rogers et al. 1967 (use of computers);

Sackett 1964 (stone tools); Sarycheva 1950B (phylogenetic classification);

Van der Klaauw 1966 (method of study);

White, E. I. 1965 (dipnoans);

Zimmermann, W. 1963 ("natural" system), 1967 (systems in evol.).

PHYSICAL ANTHROPOLOGY — See: paleoanthropology.

PHYSIOLOGY — See: habits; paleomyology; biomechanics; paleophysiology.

PICTOGRAPHS — See: Paleolithic art.

POLITICAL and THEOLOGICAL DOCTRINE and CONTROVERSY — See: legislation.

POLLEN DATING — See: paleochronology.

POPULAR WORKS — See: general works.

PORTRAITS — See: biographies; Paleolithic art.

PREHISTORY — See: paleoanthropology; Paleolithic art; paleopsychology.

PRESERVATION — See: occurrences; techniques.

PSYCHOLOGY — See: habits; paleopsychology.

RADIOCARBON DATING — See: paleochronology; technique.

RECONSTRUCTIONS — See: restorations; technique.

RELIGION, RITES, MAGIC — See: paleoanthropology; Paleolithic art; paleopsychology.

RESPIRATORY SYSTEM — See: anatomy; habits; paleophysiology; skeleton; skull.

RESTORATIONS, RECONSTRUCTIONS, CASTS, ILLUSTRATIONS and EXHIBITS —
Angell 1964 (animal restorations); Anon. 1964R, S (World Fair dinosaurs), 1965AF,
CB (Paleoparadoxia), 1966E (Megatherium skel.), 1966U (dinosaur dioramas —
juv.), 1966AW (La Brea ground sloth, Oakland Mus.); Augusta and Burian n.d.
(evol. plants and animals), 1960B (evol. of man), 1962B, C (mammoths), 1962E,
1963B (prehist. reptiles and birds), 1964A (campfires, Old Stone Age), 1964B,
C (prehist. sea monsters);
Bachmayer and Zapfe 1966 (Plioc. diorama, Austria); Ballesio et al. 1965 (Aceratherium); Barrera 1967 (replica of Diplodocus carnegiei, Mexico City); Bates
and eds. of Life (mammals, S. Amer.); Battetta 1964 (reconstructions); Beer
1964D, 1965B (atlas of evol.); Bergamini and eds. of Life 1964 (fossils, Australia); Bishop 1964B (Proconsul); Bourdier 1962C (Pleist. mammals, Rhone
Valley); Brown, L. 1968 (restoration of fossil animals); Bush 1960 (diorama
of Peru tar pits, Roy. Ontario Mus.);
Colbert 1968A (dinosaurs); Cole, S. 1966B (animal ancestors); Coon 1961 (Neanderthals); Crompton 1964A (Oligokyphus skull);
Davidson 1950 (fossils); Debets 1939C (Neanderthal); De la Calle 1967 (human
evol. on Cuban stamps); Delair 1954 (Wealden dinosaurs), 1955 (flying reptiles),
1956A (Pliosaurus), 1956B (sea reptiles); Denison 1964A (Dunkleosteus, Bothriolepis); Devillers 1965 (dinosaurs); Downs 1968 (fossil verts., S. California);
Flerov 1953 (Elasmotherium); Fox and Bowman 1966 (Captorhinus); Fox and
Welles 1965 (paleont. and restorations); Franke 1963 (Altamira paintings copied);
Gazin 1965B (Meniscotherium), 1968B (Hyopsodus); Gerasimov, M. M. 1961 (round
dwelling at Malta site, Siberia), 1964B (Stone Age men); Greene, A. M. 1967
(skulls of Shanidar man, Iraq); Grigor'ev 1967 (Kostenki I dwelling, USSR);
Grossman and Hamlet 1964 (birds of prey); Grube 1964 (birds);
Haubold 1966A (Scleromochlus), 1966B (Chelichnus walking); Heberer 1965C
(Australopithecines); Hecker, R. T. 1965 (early reconstruction of mammoth);
Heintz, A. 1964A (early reconstruction of mammoth), 1967B (tremataspidid, S.
Norway); Hesse 1966 (Neanderthal skull from Le Moustier); Hoare et al. 1964
(peccary, Ohio); Hoffman 1965 (thecodont, S. Afr.); Hopson 1967A (Thrina-
xodon);
Jorg 1966 (life in Jurassic sea);
Karatajūte-Talimaa 1966 (bothriolepids, Baltic region); Koenigswald 1956J (Neander-
thal); Krebs 1965 (Ticinosuchus ferox, Switzerland), 1966 (Chirotherium skel.),
1967B (Machimosaurus skull, Portugal); Krupinski et al. 1958 (Paranthropus skull);
Kuhn, O. 1964G (Mansfield Kupferschiefer fauna, Germany); Kuhn-Schnyder
1966A (nothosaur skull, Switzerland); Kurten 1966A (Tremarctos floridanus);
Kurth and Marsky 1967 (endocranial molds);
Larsonneur 1964 (Semionotus normannie); Larsonneur and Lapparent 1966 (Up.
Trias. carnivorous dinosaur, France); Lehman 1966A, 1967A (stegocephalian
skulls, Madagascar); Lindsay, H. A. 1966 (Thylacoleo and Diprotodon);
McLaughlin 1966 (elephants); Malzahn 1968 (Janassa); Martínez del Río 1933
(mammoth); Maslankiewiczowa 1965 (Semionotus, Poland); Merrilees 1965C
(Australian marsupials); Miles, R. S. 1966A (acanthodian fishes), 1966C (Rachio-
steus pterygiatus), 1967B (Rhamphodopsis); Miles and Westoll 1968 (head of
Coccosteus); Mitchell, E. D. 1966B, 1967A (N. Pacific marine mammals), 1966E
(Allodesmus, California);
Neill 1961 (Paleo-Indian fighting rattlesnake, Florida); Nielsen 1967 (Tupilakosaurus
skull); Nybelin 1966 (Pholidophoridae);
Obrhelova 1967 (Cyprinidae, Bohemia); Obruchev and Mark-Kurik 1968 (psammos-
teids); Obrucheva 1966 (coccosteid skulls); Olsen 1964C (exhibits in small
museums);
Panchen 1964 (anthracosaur skull musculature), 1966 (labyrinthodont axial skele-
ton); Parsch 1963 (dinosaurs, Alberta); Popova and Firshtein 1965 (fossil man);

Rajchel 1965 (skull, Steinheim woman); Ricqlès 1968E (Diademodon skel.); Ritchie,
A. 1964 (anaspid); Romer 1959E (Kronosaurus, Australia), 1964B (labyrinthodont, Scotland); Rosen 1957 (fossil mammals, Argentina); Rusconi 1967 (fossil
animals, Argentina); Russell, D. A. 1967B (dinosaurs, Canada); Russell and
Chamney 1967 (dinosaurs, Canada);

Schaurte 1964 (Elasmotherium, France); Schultz, A. 1955 (early man); Segerblom,
C. and G. 1965 (ichthyosaur skels, I. State Mon., Nevada); Sinitsyn 1959 (dinosaurs, mammals, Cent. Asia); Sternberg 1965 (hadrosaurs); Stęslicka 1963B
(fossil hominids); Stever et al. 1966 (Archaeopterix); Stovall, Price and Romer
1966 (pelycosaur, Oklahoma); Straus and Cave 1964 (Neanderthal skels, France);

Talbot 1966 (coelacanth); Teriaev 1968 (mammoth); Thenius 1964D (S. Amer.
mammals), 1966E (horses); Trimm 1964 (life-size dinosaurs);

Walker, A. D. 1966 (rhynchocephalian skull); Walker, C. A. 1966 (pleurodiran turtle,
Somalia); Wenz 1964 (Notagogus, Spain), 1965A, B (fishes, France); Wetmore
1967 (Aepyornis); White, E. I. 1965 (Dipterus); Woo, Ju-kang 1966B (skull,
Lantian man);

Yaldwyn 1966 (moas, N.Z.); Yoshikawa 1963 (human fossil skull); Young, C.-c.
1964A (pseudosuchians, China), 1964B (pterosaur, China);

Zapfe 1960D (placodont, Alps), 1960E (mammoth herd).

ROCK PAINTINGS — See: Paleolithic art.

SCALES, SCUTES — See: integumentary structures; skeleton.

SCULPTURE, STATUETTES, FIGURINES — See: Paleolithic art; paleopsychology.

SEDIMENTATION — See: correlation; cultural remains; faunas, Quaternary cave; ichnology;
occurrences.

SENSE ORGANS — See: anatomy; integumentary structures; skull.

SEX DIFFERENCES, DIMORPHISM — See: variation and heredity.

SKELETON — GENERAL — Borkhvardt 1966, 1967 (vertebral centra); Braun 1963 (anthrop
techniques);
Carlström 1963 (crystallographic study of otoliths);
Denison 1963B (hist. of vert. skel.);
Lavocat 1966 (osteol. of Pleist. fauna of W. Europe); Lessertisseur and Saban 1967B
(axial skel.), 1967C (appendicular skel.).

OSTRACODERMI — Denison 1964B (Cyathaspididae).

PISCES — Andelković 1966 (Rhombus, Turkey); Anon. 1967AS, AU (fishes, New Jer-
sey); Avnimelech 1962C (Carcharodon, Israel);
Blot 1966A (Platax), 1966B (palaeoniscoids, France), 1968 (teleosteans); Bogachev
1964 (Chaetodon), 1965 (fishes, Crimea); Bystrov 1959B (microstructure of
arthrodire armor);
Cavender 1966A (Leuciscus, British Columbia), 1966B (teleosts);
Dalquest 1966 (paleoniscid, Texas);
Fierstine 1966, 1968 (swollen fin elements, Carangidae); François 1967 (teleost
vertebrae);
Gross, W. 1964B (Dipterus), 1965B (Bothriolepis), 1967C (ostracoderms);
Heintz, A. 1967A (cephalaspid tail structure);
Iakovlev, V. N. 1966B, 1967C (evol. of fish skel.);
Karatajūte-Talimaa 1966 (bothriolepids, Baltic region);

Switzerland), 1967B (crocodile, Portugal); Kuhn-Schnyder 1963D (nothosaur, Switzerland);

Lapparent and Stchepinsky 1968 (iguanodonts, France); Leich 1964A (pterosaur, Germany);

Mottl 1967B (tortoise, Austria);

Nielsen 1964A (marine turtle, Denmark);

Olson 1962D (Captorhinikos), 1968B (Caseidae); Orlov, J. A. 1960B (dinocephalians, USSR);

Prasad and Satsangi 1963C (chelonian, India); Prasad and Verma 1967 (dinosaurs, India);

Rozhdestvenskiĭ 1968B (sauropod, Cent. Asia); Russell, D. A. 1967E (dinosaurs, W. Canada);

Satsangi 1964 (thecodont, India); Schmidt, H. 1966 (Chelydra, Germany); Schultz, C. B. 1965C (plesiosaur, Nebraska); Shikama and Okafuji 1964 (terrapin, Japan); Shikama and Ozaki 1966 (reptile, Brazil); Stovall, Price and Romer 1966 (pelycosaur, Oklahoma); Sun 1964 (Lystrosaurus, China);

Taugourdeau 1965 (turtle, France); Teriàev 1967 (Rhamphorhynchus wing bones); Thieuloy 1965 (ichthyosaur centra, France); Thurmond 1968 (plesiosaur, Texas);

Walker, A. D. 1964 (Ornithosuchus); Wellnhofer 1968 (Pterodactylus, Bavaria); Westphal 1965 (crocodile, Germany); Wincierz 1967 (crocodile, Germany);

Yeh, Hsiang-k'uei 1966 (turtle, China); Young, C.-c. 1964A (pseudosuchians, China), 1964B (pterosaur, China), 1964C (crocodile, China), 1964E (dinosaurs, China, Mongolia), 1965E (ichthyosaur, China);

Zangerl 1963B (nothosaur, N. Amer.).

AVES — Anon. 1966P (bird, Virginia), 1966BD (moa, New Zealand);

Beer 1964B (Archaeopteryx); Brunet, M. 1966 (birds); Burchak-Abramovich 1953C (ostriches, USSR); Burchak-Abramovich and Gambarov 1964 (Archaeopteryx); Chauviré 1963B (European owls);

Hamon 1962B, 1964 (passerine birds, Florida); Holman 1964B (gallinaceous birds); Kuhn, O. 1965D (osteol.);

Luttschwager 1961 (moas and solitaires);

Phillips, A. R. 1968 (stork, Arizona);

Ryziewicz 1961C (third Archaeopterix);

Schaub, S. 1940D (ratite, Germany);

Tchernov, E. 1968A (peregrine falcon and purple gallinule, Nubia).

MAMMALIA — Adam 1965A (primates, Germany); Ahlen 1965B (red deer, Scandinavia) Akhundov 1963 (pinnipeds, USSR); Anderson, J. E. 1962 (human skel.); Ankel 1965 (primates); Anon. 1960CP (Shanidar man, Iraq), 1964AC (Neanderthal, Italy), 1966BB (human skel., Australia), 1967AO (mammoth, Florida underwater site); Apostol 1965A (mammoth, Rumania); Asmus 1965 (fossil hominids, Palestine); Azzaroli 1965 (Equus, Italy);

Bergounioux and Crouzel 1966B (Amphicyon, France); Bogachev 1960B (goat, Crimea); Bökönyi 1959 (wolverine, Hungary); Bolomey 1965B (Pliotragus, Rumania); Bonifay, M.-F. 1964 (Equus, France), 1966B (mammal limb bones), 1966C (bovids), 1966D (carnivores); Bouchud 1966B (proboscideans), 1966C (rhinos), 1966D (artiodactyls), 1966E (cervids); Briggs, L. C. 1956B (human skeletons); Burchak-Abramovich and Dzhafarov 1951 (rhino metapodials);

Chaline 1966C (lagomorphs and rodents), 1966D (insectivores), 1966E (bats); Cheynier 1964C (Azilian man, France); Comaschi Caria 1965 (dwarf elephant, Sardinia); Crusafont Pairó 1965G (Oreopithecus), 1965H (variability of Myotragus);

Danilova 1965 (evolution of the hand), 1966 (hand and foot of primates); Dart, R. A. 1968B (Australopithecus africanus); Daumas and Laudet 1968 (cave bear); David and Prat 1962 (Equus, France); Davis, D. D. 1964 (giant panda); Day and Napier 1964, 1966 (hominid foot bones, Olduvai Gorge); Debets 1955

(Kostenki hominids, USSR), 1967 (Up. Pal. man from Sungir' burial, USSR);
Desmostylus Research Committee (DEREC) 1951 (Desmostylus, Japan); Domoslawska-Baraniecka et al. 1965 (Elephas, Poland); Dubinin and Garutt 1954
(mammoth, Lena R. delta);
Ehrenberg 1964A (cave bear, Germany); Elouard 1966 (Zeuglodon, Afr.);
Favati Vanni 1964 (Up. Pal. human infant, Italy); Ferembach 1965A (human skel-
eton, Portugal); Fischer, K. 1964 (tapirs, Europe); Frechkop 1965D (Prjewalsky
horse), 1965E (koala hand);
Gabuniia and Vekua 1963 (Archidiskodon, USSR); Gadzhiev 1957 (Gazella, Azerbaidzhan); Galbreath 1964A (dire wolf, Missouri); Garutt and Safronov 1965
(Archidiskodon, N. Caucasus); Gautier 1966 (Camelus, N. Sudan); Gazin 1965B
(Meniscotherium), 1968B (Hyopsodus); Genet-Varcin 1966B (Plesianthropus),
1966C (osteology of man); Ginsburg 1961E (fissipede carnivores); Godina 1967A
(Giraffidae); Gofshtein 1965 (whales, Geol. Mus. AN USSR); Grasse 1967 (mam-
mals); Grimm and Ullrich 1965 (Homo, Germany); Gromova 1963 (Equus); Gupta,
B. B. 1966 (Erethizon, Coendou); Guthrie, D. A. 1968 (Eoc. artiodactyl tarsus);
Hasegawa 1968A (whale vertae., Japan); Hasegawa and Matsuchima 1968A (whale
vertae., Japan); Heintz, E. 1966B (cervids and bovids); Hemmer 1966 (Pantherinae); Hooijer 1968B (Brachyodus manus, E. Afr.);
Jepsen 1966 (Eocene bat, Wyoming); Johnson, S. T. 1962 (mastodon, New Jersey);
Kahlke 1965H (rhinos, Germany); Kälin 1964 (pongid and hominid limbs); Kapica
and Wiercinski 1966 (analysis of Up. Pal. human skels., Poland); Kas'ianenko
1959 (mammal limbs); Khrisanfova 1964 (hominid long bones), 1965 (Palaeoanthropus, Palestine), 1966 (hominid postcranial skel.); Knussmann 1965A (primate arm bones), 1967 (Oreopithecus ulna); Korotkevich 1957 (giraffes, USSR);
Krüger, W. 1958 (skel., muscles of mammals); Kubasiewicz 1965 (Bos, Poland);
Kudrin 1961 (mammoth, Ukraine); Kurten 1967A (Arctodus, N. Amer.);
Lehmann, U. 1966 (Bison); Lessertisseur and Saban 1967A (mammalian skel.);
Lessertisseur and Sigogneau 1965 (evol. of principal characteristics of mammal
skel.); Lewis, O. J. (tarsal bones);
Mamonova 1968 (determination of bone length in hominids); Martin, R. D. 1966
(tree shrews); Mazhuga 1961 (skel. indices for limb functions); Mchedlidze 1959
(dolphin, Georgia, USSR), 1964A (skel. evol., cetaceans), 1964C (cetaceans, Caucasus); Mein 1967 (cricetid humeri); Mitchell, E. D. 1965B, 1966D, E (Allodesmus, California), 1968 (Imagotaria, California); Morris, W. J. 1965 (Mioc.
horse astragali);
Necrasov 1964 (Equus);
Ortega 1967 (mylodonts, Argentina); Oxnard 1967 (primate shoulder);
Patte 1968 (Azilian man, France); Patterson, B. and Howells 1967 (hominid humerus, Kenya); Paula Couto 1959B (groundsloth, Colombia); Pavlova 1933C (dolphins, Black Sea); Pichardo del Barrio et al. 1961 (mammoth, Mexico); Piveteau 1961V, 1966A (early man, France);
Radinsky 1965B (evol., tapiroid); Ratkevich 1968 (limb bones, shovel-jawed mastodon, New Mexico); Reed, C. A. and Turnbull 1965 (mole front limb, N. Amer.);
Robinson, P. (sections of fused cervical vertebrae, edentates, Wyoming);
Savage, R. J. G. 1965B (sirenians, Libya); Schaub, S. 1941C (deer, France); Schmid
1966 (cave bear, Switzerland); Sexton 1965 (Thylacoleo, Australia); Shikama
1966B, 1966C, 1968 (desmostylids, Japan); Siegfried 1962 (bison), 1965 (sirenian,
Germany), 1967 (sirenian, Egypt); Simons 1967A (post-cranial skeleton in primate evol.); Skinner, M. F. 1957 (horse phalanges); Sondaar 1968B (equid
manus); Soubeyran 1966 (complete Magdalenian human skeleton, France); Stach
1956 (woolly rhino, Poland); Stevens, M. S. 1966 (ground squirrel, Oklahoma);
Stewart, T. D. 1963B (human skeletons, Iraq), 1964 (Neanderthal scapula);
Surrarrer 1964 (mammoth, Ohio); Suzuki 1966 (Hamakita man, Japan); Svistun
and Didkovskii 1964 (Deinotherium, Ukraine); Szalay 1966 (leptictid tarsus);

Tanner, L. G. 1967A (rhino, Nebraska); Tarabukin 1963 (Deinotherium, Moldavia);
Tavera 1968 (ground sloth, Chile); Terzea 1965 (Panthera, Rumania), 1966
(cave bear, Rumania); Thenius 1965B (carnivores, Germany), 1965C (primate
phalanx, Germany); Tobias 1965A (Homo habilis); Trylich and Bayrock 1966
(bison, Canada); Tsalkin 1965 (bovids); Tsankov and Nikolov 1966A (deinothere,
Bulgaria), 1966B (proboscideans, Bulgaria);
Vallois 1965A (Neanderthal sternum, France); Vangengeim 1966A, E (Equidae,
USSR), 1966F (bovine, USSR); Vlček 1964C (Neanderthal);
Waldren 1966 (Myotragus, Majorca); Walker, A. and Rose 1968 (hominid vertebra,
Uganda); Warren, J. W. 1965 (marsupial humerus, Australia); Webb, G. L. 1965
(chalicotheres, S. Afr.); Westphal 1967B (bat, Germany); White, J. A. 1967
(complete Plesippus); Whitworth 1966 (hominid fragments, Kenya); Woodburne
1965B (Paleoparadoxia, California);
Zapfe 1966A (cave bear), 1967A (chalicothere, Austria); Zbyszewski 1953A (cervid,
Portugal); Zol'nikov 1961 (mammoth, USSR); Zuckerman et al. 1967 (primate
pelvis).

SKULL – GENERAL – Bock, W. J. 1963 (kinesis in early tetrapods);
Krukoff 1967 (parietal);
Masharskiĭ 1967 (functional role of the zygomatic arch);
Parrington 1967C (dermal skull bones in lower verts.).

OSTRACODERMI –

PISCES – Anon. 1966BH (Eusthenopteron "ear");
Campbell, K. S. W. 1965 (dipnoan, New S. Wales);
Dunkle 1965 (holocephalian fish);
Egorov and Ivan'ev 1956 (sturgeon, USSR);
Goody 1968 (Enchodus, Holland); Gross, W. 1965C (fishes, Germany), 1965D
(dipnoan, Ganorhynchus), 1965E (Onychodus, Germany);
Jarvik 1967A (structure of snout in Megalichthys and other rhipidistid crossoptery-
gians), 1967B (fishes and tetrapods), 1967C (lower jaw, dipnoans);
Klausewitz 1965B (Pomadasys hasta); Kottek 1964 (Leptolepis, Greece);
Le Danois 1966 (Gonorhynchidae); Lehman 1967B (Drepanaspis);
Miles, R. S. 1964 (Acanthodus);
Nursall 1964 (pycnodont jaws); Nybelin 1966 (Pholidophoridae), 1967B (sensory
canal system, actinopterygians);
Obrucheva 1962B (Plourdosteus skull roof);
Panchen 1967A (nostrils, choanates);
Romer 1964A (elasmobranch braincase);
Savage, R. J. G. and Large 1966 (Birgeria maxilla);
Thomson, K. S. 1964B, 1965B (osteolepid skulls), 1966E (Glyptolepis, Scotland),
1967C (dipnoan lower jaw, Canada);
White, E. I. 1965 (Dipterus);
Zangerl 1966 (shark, Indiana).

AMPHIBIA – Baldauf 1964A (Anura); Brough, M. C. and J. 1967 (microsaurs);
Chase, J. N. 1965 (labyrinthodont, Texas); Chowdhury 1965 (metoposaurid am-
phibian, India); Corsin 1967 (Urodela);
DeMar 1966A (dissorophid amphibian, Texas);
Lebedkina 1964A (development of nasal bones), 1964B (development of dermal
bones); Lehman 1967A (labyrinthodonts);
Nielsen 1967 (Tupilakosaurus skull-roof);
Olson 1964B, 1965B (Batrachosauria), 1965E (Zatrachys, Oklahoma);
Panchen 1964 (anthracosaurs, England), 1967A (nostrils, early tetrapods); Panchen,
Tilley and Steel 1967 (anthracosaur, England);

Shishkin and Ochev 1966, 1967A (endocranium evol.);

Vaughn 1966B (Seymouria, Utah); Verma 1962 (labyrinthodont, Kashmir);

Welles and Cosgriff 1964, 1965A (Parotosaurus, Arizona), 1965B (labyrinthodonts, Arizona);

Young, C.-c. 1965A (salamanders, China), 1966A (capitosaurid, China).

REPTILIA — Albrecht 1967 (cranial arteries, turtles); Anon. 1962CM (Mosasaurus);

Barghusen 1968 (cynodont lower jaw); Barry 1965 (therapsid), 1967 (Pristerodon); Bonaparte 1963C, D (cynodonts, Argentina), 1963E (Traversodontidae), 1963B, 1966A (Exaeretodon, Argentina), 1966C (therapsid, Argentina); Boonstra 1965A Deuterosaurus), 1965C (Struthiocephalus);

Callison 1967 (cranial kinesis in mosasaurs); Chudinov 1968B (dinocephalian, USSR); Cox, C. B. 1964 (Endothiodon); Crompton 1964A (Oligokyphus); Crompton and Hotton 1967 (jaw mechanism of dicynodonts); Cruickshank 1965 (anomodont, Tanzania), 1968B (dicynodont palates); Cys 1967A (Diadectes);

Delair 1966A (ichthyosaur skull); Dong 1965 (lizard, China);

El-Toubi, Kamal and Hammouda 1965 (Ophidia); Ewer 1965C (Euparkeria); Findlay 1968B (scaloposaurid); Fourie 1968 (Tritylodontoideus jaw articulation); Fox 1964 (jaw musculature);

Ginsburg 1968A (temporal fossae);

Hoffman 1965 (thecodont, S. Afr.); Hopson 1964B (Bienotherium braincase, China); Iordanskiĭ 1967 (crocodilian skull);

Jux 1966 (Parotosaurus);

Kobatake and Kamei 1966 (crocodile, Japan); Konzhukova 1965B (capitosaurid, USSR); Krebs 1965 (Ticinosuchus ferox, Switzerland), 1967B (crocodile, Portugal); Kuhn-Schnyder 1965B (Cyamodus), 1966A (nothosaur, Switzerland);

Langston 1965B (crocodilian cranial indices), 1967, 1968 (ceratopsian, Canada);

Mahé 1966 (subfossil turtle, Madagascar); Mook 1964, 1967 (crocodiles, Oklahoma, Colorado);

Nash, D. F. 1968 (crocodile, Utah);

Olson 1962D (Captorhinikos), 1964B, 1965B, 1966D (Batrachosauria, Chelonia), 1968B (Caseidae); Orlov, J. A. 1960B (dinocephalians, USSR); Ostrom 1962B (hadrosaurs, N. Amer.), 1964D (Triceratops jaw mechanics);

Price, L. I. 1963, 1964 (crocodile, Brazil);

Romer 1967B (gomphodonts, Argentina), 1968B (ichthyosaur, Wyoming); Russell, D. A. 1964 (mosasaur);

Sickenberg 1961 (crocodile, Germany); Sill 1967 (crocodile, Argentina); Sternberg 1964 (hadrosaur narial tubes); Sun 1964 (Lystrosaurus, China);

Tatarinov, L. P. 1965C (theriodonts), 1965D (Ulemosaurus), 1966A (theriodont jaws), 1966C (therapsid skull), 1966D (theriodont skull), 1968 (cynodonts, USSR); Telles Antunes 1961E (crocodile, Portugal), 1967A, B (mesosuchian, Portugal);

Walker, A. D. 1964 (Ornithosuchus), 1966 (Elachistosuchus);

Yeh, Hsiang-k'uei 1966 (turtles, China); Young, C.-c. 1964A (pseudosuchians, China), 1964B (pterosaur, China), 1964C (crocodile, China);

Zapfe 1960D (placodont, Alps).

AVES — Markus 1964 (passerines, Palestine).

MAMMALIA — Aguirre 1968 (fossil hominids); Aguirre and Macorra 1964 (fossil hominids); Alekperova 1966 (deer, Caucasus); Alekseev, V. P. 1968B (craniology); Ambrosetti, 1964 (Elephas, Italy); Anon. 1964AK (Cervus antler, Reuzehert), 1965BC (bison skulls, Oklahoma), 1965BY (Niah skull, Borneo), 1966L (giant pig), 1967AC (primate, Fayum), 1968E (Gigantopithecus, India); Apostol 1957, 1962 (mammoth mandibles and molars); Arambourg 1964A (Bunolistriodon); Arambourou and Genet-Varcin 1965 (human skull, France); Azzaroli 1964B (Rhinoceros hemitoechus), 1966A (elephants), 1966B (Pleist. and living horses);

Baker, J. R. 1968B (Broken Hill man — Homo rhodesiensis); Beaumont 1964A
(Amphicyon, France), 1965C (Cephalogale, France), 1968 (viverrids, France);
Bergmann 1965 (primate skull); Black, C. C. 1968A (Ischyromys); Bolomey
1965B (Pliotragus, Rumania); Bonadonna 1967 (Elephas, Italy); Bonis 1966A
(carnivores, France); Bouchud 1964, 1967 (reindeer, France); Breitinger 1955C
(Neanderthal, S. Afr.); Broers 1962 (tympanic region in mammals); Brues 1966
(hominid teeth and jaws); Brunet, M. 1968 (Microbunodon, France); Brunet
and Guth 1968A (Ronzotherium, France); Banuk 1959C, 1966B, 1968 (human
skull); Burchak-Abramovich and Gabashvili 1968 (ox, USSR); Burchak-Abramovich and Sultanov 1965 (beaver, Caucasus); Burchak-Abramovich, N. O. 1950
(Orycteropus, USSR);

Chang, Hsi-chih and Liu 1964 (Metailurus, China); Charig 1967A (Erythrotherium,
Basutoland);   Charles 1965A (Neanderthal, Greece), 1965B (Up. Pal. human
skulls, France), 1966 (Ibalaghem man, W. Afr.); Clemens 1968A (Didelphodon,
Montana); Correnti 1968 (human skulls, Sicily); Crompton 1964B (Erythrotherium, Basutoland); Crossley 1964, 1965 (muskox, Manitoba); Crusafont Pairó
and Angel 1966 (Myotragus, Spain); Crusafont Pairó, Angel and Cuerda 1965A
(Myotragus, Spain); Cuscani Politi 1963A (Megaceros, Italy);

Dahr 1952 (Australopithecinae); Dalquest 1961C (bison, Texas), 1964A (Equus
scotti, Texas); Dalquest and Hughes 1965 (small Equus, Texas); David and
Tarabukin 1967 (rhino, Moldavia); Debénath 1967 (human mandible, France);
Debeś 1939C (hominid from Teshik-tash cave, USSR), 1961B (Kostenki Cro-Mag-
non child, USSR); Dechaseaux 1965A (Cynohyaenodon), 1965B (Dichodon), 1967A
(Xiphodon), 1967B (beaver, Europe); Dehm 1966 (muskox); Delattre and Fen-
hart 1960 (hominization of primate skull); Dickson, M. R. 1964 (Prosqualodon,
New Zealand); Dokládal 1965 (skull shapes, primates); Doughty 1966 (Megaceros,
Ireland); Dubrovo 1966A (Mammuthus, USSR); Ducros 1967 (occipital in
man); Dzhafarova 1961 (Elephas, USSR);

Ehrenberg 1964A (cave bear, Germany); Enlow 1966 (facial growth, Homo, Macaca);
Ennouchi 1968 (human skull from Jebel Irhoud, Morocco); Erdbrink 1964 (human
skull cap, Netherlands), 1967A (bear, Netherlands);

Fenart and Anthony 1967 (primate mandibles); Fenart and Heim 1968 (Neanderthals); Ferembach 1965D (cranial diagrams); Ficat 1964 (reindeer, France);
First 1964 (skull fractures in suids, S. Afr.); Fischer, K. 1965 (bison, Germany);
Frechkop 1965A (antelopes); Freedman 1967 (variation in Perameles); Freedman
and Joffe 1967A, B (metrical features, Perameles); Friant 1963C (rhino); Fuentes
1966 (Elephas, Spain);

Gabashvili and Gabuniiá 1958 (Dinotherium, E. Georgia, USSR); Gabis 1964 (cranial
capacity, primates); Gabuniiá and Vekua 1966A, B (daman, E. Georgia, USSR);
Galbreath 1967C (bison, S. Dakota); Gaponov 1957D, 1967 (Deinotherium jaw,
USSR); Garevski 1964 (beaver, USSR); Gaspard 1964 (canid mandible); Gazin
1968A (primate, New Mexico); Genet-Varcin and Miquel 1967 (Magdalenian skull);
Gentry 1965 (Hippotragus horn core), 1967 (bovid, Olduvai); Gieseler 1967 (Neanderthal child); Gokhman 1966B (Late Paleolithic man); Gremiatskiǐ 1966 (jaw
size, Meganthropus, Gigantopithecus); Grimm and Ullrich 1965 (Homo, Germany);
Grosset, Dinesman and Zalkin 1965 (steppe marmot); Gu 1965 (Sinanthropus);
Guillien 1964 (reindeer, France); Guth 1964A (venous system, fossil carnivores),
1964B (Miacis, France), 1967 (Neanderthal tympanal);

Harris 1967 (Toxotherium, Texas); Hartenberger 1967B (rodents); Heim 1963 (human
apophyses geni); Heintz, Nicole 1966A, B, 1967A, B (hominids), 1968 (Hominoidea);
Hemmer 1964B, 1965A, 1967A (allometric studies of hominid skulls), 1965C
("Panthera," France), 1967B (Panthera, China), 1967C (Panthera, Europe, Afr.),
1968 (Panthera, Japan); Henschen 1966A, B (the human skull); Hesse 1966
(Neanderthal from Le Moustier); Hewes et al. 1964 (hominids from Wadi Halfa,
Sudan); Hill, L. G. 1963 (giant beaver, Arkansas); Hillerud 1966 (fossil bison);

1964 (goat horn cores, Iowa); Reed, C. A. and Schaffer 1966 (Caprini); Remy 1965 (paleothere maxilla, France); Repenning 1965B (shrew, S. Afr.); Reshetov 1965 (Indopithecus jaw, Turkey); Ricqlès 1968C (hominid jaw, Ethiopia); Ride 1964B (marsupials); Riek 1932B (Homo sapiens cranium and mandible, Germany); Riquet 1962 (hominids, Spain); Ruprecht 1965 (brown bear, Poland); Russell and Sigogneau 1965 (Paleoc. mammals);

Saban 1963 (temporal bone of primates); Saller 1964B (human skull character and race); Sartono 1961, 1963 (Pithecanthropus mandible, Indonesia), 1964, 1967 (Pithecanthropus skull, Indonesia); Savage, R. J. G. 1965B (sirenians, Libya); Schaefer, U. 1964 (Neanderthal fragments, Yugoslavia); Schaub, S. 1949B (Elomeryx, Switzerland); Scheumpflug 1965 (rhino mandible, Germany); Schmidt, Z. 1965A (mammals, Slovakia); Schutz 1967 (bison skulls); Schwidetzky 1963 (human skulls, USSR); Sergi 1964 (Olduvai skull); Shcherbakova 1954B (antelope, USSR); Sherstiukov 1968B (oxen horn-cores, USSR); Shikama et al. 1967 (rhino, Japan); Siegfried 1965 (sirenian, Germany); Sigogneau 1968B (Dremotherium); Simonetta 1957C (kinetic insectivore skulls); Simons 1964C (Ramapithecus mandible), 1967G (monkey, Sudan); Simpson, G. G. 1965E (Galago, Olduvai); Skinner, S. M. and Gooris 1966 (Toxotherium, Wyoming); Solov'ev and Orelkin 1961 (human skull, jaws, teeth, USSR); Stach 1956 (woolly rhino, Poland); Starck 1967A (mammal skull); Stęślicka 1959 (human calvaria, Poland); Stewart, T. D. 1963B (Neanderthals, Iraq); Stirton 1965B (Castoroides); Stokes, Anderson and Madsen 1966 (bison, Utah and Idaho); Suzuki 1964, 1965 (Amud man, Israel); Svistun 1965 (Megaloceros); Svistun and Didkovskiĭ 1964 (Deinotherium, Ukraine);

Tanner, L. G. 1967A (rhino, Nebraska); Tattersall 1968 (Indraloris mandible, India); Telles Antunes 1964D (Paleotherium mandible, Portugal); Terzea 1965 (Panthera, Rumania); Thenius 1965B (carnivores, Germany); Thoma 1966 (partial human skull, Hungary); Tobias 1964A, 1967A (Zinjanthropus, Tanzania), 1965A (Homo habilis, Tanzania), 1966D (Kedung Brubus mandible, Java), 1967B (hominid mandibles, Lybia), 1967C (hominid skull fragments, Kenya); Tobien 1962E (tapir jaw fragments, Germany); Toepfer 1964A (antelope horn core, Germany); Topachevskiĭ 1957C (marmot jaws, Ukraine), 1965B (lower jaw, voles, Ukraine), 1966 (lower jaw, shrew, Ukraine); Tovell and Deane 1966 (grizzly bear, Ontario); Trevor and Wells 1967 (hominid mandible, Lybia); Troitskiĭ 1966 (young mammoth jaw, USSR); Tsankov and Nikolov 1966A (deinothere, Bulgaria); Tsui 1962 (human facial skel.);

Urquiola de de Carli and Aramayo 1967 (edentate, Argentina);

Vallois 1965D (hominid skull, Hungary), 1967D (lost Moustier skull found); Vallois and Billy 1965 (Cro-Magnon skulls); Vangengeïm 1966D (canid jaw, USSR), 1966F (bovine skull fragments); Vañura 1965 (sable jaws, Neanderthal skull, Czechoslovakia); Vas'kovskiĭ 1959B (giant beaver, Siberia), 1966 (elk, USSR); Velich 1961 (bison, Nebraska, Iowa); Vértes 1965A (Homo erectus, Hungary); Vignati 1963 (human jaws, skull fragments, Argentina); Vlček 1958B, 1963A, 1963B, 1964A, 1968 (Neanderthal, Czechoslovakia), 1967 (Neanderthal, Europe); Vogel, Ch. 1966A, 1968 (primate skull); Voorhies 1966 (growth stages in Merycodus); Vulliamy 1930 (Homo, England);

Waldren 1966 (Myotragus, Majorca); Watanabe, H. 1964 (skull cap, Amud man); Webb, G. L. 1965 (chalicotheres, S. Afr.); Wells, L. H. 1964A (antelope, S. Afr.); Weninger 1962 (human skull changes); Westphal 1967B (bat, Germany); White, J. A. 1966 (Peromyscus mandibles and maxilla); Whitmore and Foster 1967 (Panthera mandible, Alaska); Whitworth 1966 (hominid, Kenya); Wilson, J. A. 1966 (primate, Texas); Woo, Ju-kang 1964A, B, C, D, F, G, 1965A, B, E (mandible, Lantian man, China), 1965C, F, G, H, 1966A, B, C (skull, Lantian man, China); Wood and Konizeski 1965 (Eutypomys jaw, Montana); Wood, H. E. 1964 (rhino skull, Florida); Woodburne 1965A, 1966B (Tayassuidae), 1968 (collared peccary);

Zaki 1964 (lower jaw, Lantian man, China); Zbyszewski 1953A (cervid jaw fragt., Portugal), 1953B (cetacean jaw, Portugal); Zetti 1967 (marsupial jaw fragt., Argentina); Zhai 1964 (carnivores, Mongolia); Ziolkiewicz et al. 1967 (human mandible).

SOFT PARTS — See: anatomy; circulatory system; coprolites; integumentary structures; Paleolithic art; paleomyology; paleoneurology.

SPECIATION, SPECIES QUESTIONS — See: evolution; variation and heredity.

SPELEOLOGY — See: correlation; faunas, QUATERNARY CAVE; occurrences; Paleolithic art.

STATISTICAL METHODS, MENSURATION — See: technique; variation and heredity.

STATUETTES — See: Paleolithic art.

STOMACH CONTENTS — See: coprolites, visceral contents and concretions.

STRATIGRAPHY, BIOSTRATIGRAPHY — See: correlation.

SURVEYS — See: expeditions; history of paleontology; museums.

SYMBOLISM IN ART — See: Paleolithic art.

SYNTHETIC THEORY — See: evolution.

SYSTEMATICS, CLASSIFICATION, TAXONOMY — See: phylogeny; Systematic Index; terminology.

TECHNIQUES — Agache 1961 (use of hydraulics in archeol.); Ager 1965 (serial grinding); Agogino 1968 (C–14 dating); Angell 1964 (animal restorations); Anon. 1961CN (reproductions of Lascaux paintings), 1962CK, 1966BF (reproductions of Altamira paintings), 1964AV (saw for fossil footprints), 1965AV (glass dating), 1965AX (Stone Age glue), 1966G (preparation of diprotodont), 1966M, 1967I (cleaning dinosaur skel.), 1967BG (ancient body temp.); Armstrong, W. G. 1966 (amino-acid analysis); Armstrong and Tarlo 1966 (amino-acid analysis); Auffenberg 1967E (plaster jackets);
Ballesio et al. 1965 (Aceratherium); Bass and Katzev 1968 (underwater archeol.); Battetta 1964 (reconstructions); Bouchud 1966A (collecting fossils); Braun 1963 (anthrop. techniques); Briggs, L. C. 1956B (human skeletons); Brooks, H. K. 1965 (underwater collecting); Brothwell 1965 (human remains in caves); Brothwell and Sandison 1967 (diseases in early man); Brown, L. 1968 (restoration of fossil animals); Bush 1960 (removal of tar from bones); Butts 1962 (photographing artifacts);
Campbell, B. G. 1964B (scientific methods and human evol.); Carlström 1963 (crystallographic study of otoliths); Cassidy 1964 (reinforced plastics); Chabredier 1966 (reproduction of prehist. art); Chao and Bi 1964 (replicas of tooth surfaces); Cherdyntsev 1961 (dating Quat. bones); Cherdyntsev et al. 1961 (dating Quat. bones); Chumakov 1961B (paleont. study of Anthropogene deposits); Clark, John 1962 (post-Silurian red beds), 1966A (ant hill collecting); Clemens 1965B (collecting Cret. mammals, Alberta); Colbert 1965D (collecting, preparing fossils), 1968A (dinosaurs); Coles 1966 (functional archeol.); Collin and Stoiber 1962 (collecting fossils, juv.); Cook and Heizer 1965 (chemical analysis of archeol. sites); Cooper and Whittington 1965 (acid preparation of fossils); Cott and Schrader 1966 (endocranial casts); Crabtree 1966 (making fluted points); Crabtree and Davis 1968 (manufacturing with stone tools); Craig, G. Y. 1966B

(computer experiments for size-frequency distribution of fossil populations);
Craig and Oertel 1966 (computer experiments for size-frequency distribution of
fossil populations); Crosby, J. L. 1967 (computers in the study of evol.);
Dalquest 1965B (microscope turntable); Daniels, J. R. S. 1966 (site recording);
Daniels, S. G. H. 1968 (multifactorial techniques); Dart, R. A. 1965H (bone
tool used as an axe); Davis, L. W. 1965 (shark teeth, Kansas); DeJarnette
1968 (polyethylene and stratigraphic profiles); De La Torre and Dysart 1966
(photographing small mammal teeth); Delattre and Fenhart 1960 (study of hominid skull); Destexhe-Jamotte 1964 (making and classifying burins); Dort 1965
(paleotemps. of caves); Downs 1967 (collecting microfossils, S. California);
Fitting 1965B, C, D, E, F (radioactivity measurements); Frizzell 1965B (otoliths);
Fussi 1962 (fluoride determination); Fussi and Fideli 1967 (proteins in equid
teeth);
Gabis 1964 (cranial capacity, primates); Gaherty 1968 (human skeletal material,
analysis, W. Afr.); Galbreath 1967B (drawing aid); Giles 1966 (sex and race
determination); Göke 1967 (preservation of fossils); Gokhman 1962 (preservation and packing); Gömöry 1963 (preparation by freezing); Green and Martin
1967 (exhibit of micro-fossils); Guthrie, R. D. 1967 (recovery of Pleist. large
mammal remains, Alaska);
Hatt 1965 (organization of mus. exhibits); Haynes 1968 (C–14 analysis); Henkel
1966 (collecting microverts.); Hernández-Pacheco 1965 (reproductions of Altamira paintings); Hester and Schoenwetter 1964 (reconstruction of past environments); Hotton 1965 (collecting tetrapods); Howorka and Fischer 1964 (molding delicate fossils);
Isham 1965 (prep. of drawings);
Jensen, J. 1966 (use of Gelva V-15);
Kaelas 1967 (Stone Age exhibit); Kälin 1956C (primate skull orientation); Katsui
and Kondo 1965 (dating stone implements); Kauffman 1965 (collecting in concretions, nodules and septaria); Kelly 1952 (archeol.); Kermack 1965A (collecting from fissures); Kerrich and Clarke 1967 (cumulative percentage frequency
graphs for artifacts); Kindler and Kiefer 1963 (X-ray studies of European Neanderthal skulls); Koby and Scheidegger 1964 (X-ray photos of bone disease in
cave bear); Koenig 1965 (Ro-Tap sieves); Koenigswald 1965C (potassium-argon
dating); Koenigswald, Gentner and Lippolt 1965 (potassium-argon dating); Korobkov 1963A (determining archeol. cores); Kovalevskaíà (Deopik) 1965 (statistical
methods in archeol.); Koveshnikov 1966 (craniograph); Kühne 1967 (study of
small Mesozoic mammals); Kuhn-Schnyder 1963D (X-rays and prep. of nothosaur
skel.), 1968 (sandblasting fossils); Kummel and Raup 1965 (paleont. techniques);
Kummer 1953 (primate skull form); Kurth and Marsky 1967 (endocranial molds);
Langston 1966C (prep. of Texas mosasaur); Lees 1964 (flotation method of obtain-
ing mammal teeth); Le Gallic 1964 (paleont. laws applied to hominids); Lehman
1964B (vert. paleont.), 1966A (plaster, plastic casts); Lengyel 1964 (teeth and
bones in archeol.);
Macadie 1966 (fiber light guides), 1967 (ultrasonic probes); Macdonald, J. R. 1964A
(Stereo-Tach), 1966A, F (bulldozers and fossils), 1966C (electronic data processing); Macintosh, N. W. G. 1967 (use of acetone); McKenna 1964, 1965C (washing technique for collecting fossils); Mamonova 1968 (determination of bone
length from fragments); Martin, L. D. 1967 (X-ray techniques); Martinsson
1968 (paleont. publishing); Mauser 1965 (making flint tools); Mazonowicz 1966
(screenprinting process for reproducing rock shelter art); Meighan, Foote and
Aiello 1968 (obsidian dating); Meischner 1964 (prep. of fossil bone); Merriam
1967 (computer uses, Europe); Miller, R. R. 1957 (use of X-rays in zool.);
Mirambell S. 1964 (microphotography of stone artifacts); Monsen 1966 (casting
fossils); Moss, M. L. 1961 (X-ray diffraction showing calcification process);
Neustupny 1967 (archeol. exhibit, Prague Nation. Mus.); Neves and Tarlo 1965
(isolation of osteocytes);

Oakley 1961D (radiometric assays), 1967 (chemical analysis of hominid mandibles); Odintsov 1968 (methods of studying carnivore jaws); Olsen 1964C (exhibits in small museums); Ostrom 1966B (packing a dinosaur skull); Owen 1964 (care of type specimens);

Panchen 1964 (preparation by solution in pyridine); Perinet 1964 (X-ray diffraction for determination of baking temperature of prehist. bone); Peters, J. A. and Collette 1968 (computer use); Pradel, L. 1964A (making burins), 1965C (study of stone tools); Pyddoke 1963 (scientific methods in archeol.);

Radinsky 1967C (measuring mammal brain size); Rainey and Ralph 1966 (new methods in archeol.); Randal and Scott 1967 (data processing); Rasetti 1965 (photography of fossils); Reekie 1964 (museums and exhibits); Rensberger and Berry 1967 (automated system for mus. data); Rigby et al. 1965 (casting and molding); Riggs 1903D (pneumatic tools); Rixon 1965 (fossil preparation); Robison, R. A. 1965 (vibro-tools for fossil preparation); Rogachev 1959 (archeol. field methods); Rogers et al. 1967 (computer analysis of evol.); Rolfe 1965A (infrared rays), 1965B (ultraviolet rays); Rosenfield 1965 (archeol.); Roth-Lutra 1965 (x-rays); Roussot 1966D (copying Paleolithic art); Rudenko 1963 (archeol. methods);

Sacchi Vialli 1962, 1964B (fluorescent study of teeth); Sackett 1964, 1966 (quantitative analysis of stone tools); Salthe and Kaplan 1966 (biochem. methods); Schaeffer, B. 1965B (fishes); Semenov, S. A. 1957D, 1959B, 1961B, 1964B, 1965 (prehist. tool-making); Shevchenko, A. I. 1962 (washing method); Simpson, G. G. 1965C (masterometry), 1966I (experimental animals); Skorkowski 1964 (statistical methods); Slaughter 1965C (serial sectioning), 1968A (measuring small teeth); Staley and Barnhart 1966 (new material for anthrop.); Stepanov, D. L. 1965 (new laboratory and field methods); Stucker et al. 1965 (sandblasting); Stürmer 1965 (x-rays of Archaeopterix); Swauger and Wallace 1964 (Stone Age skinning tools);

Ullrich 1966A (reconstruction method); Uryson 1967 (cranial capacity measurement); Wade et al. 1968 (mus. model making); Wagstaffe and Fidler 1968 (preservation of nat. hist. specimens); Walker, G. F. 1967 (math. model and computer); Wang, T. F. 1964 (cleaning fossils); Wegner 1965 (fossil collecting and preparation); Weide and Webster 1967 (photography of artifacts); Wilson, Ri. L. 1965 (prep. of vert. fossils); Witthoft 1967 (flint chipping); Woodall 1968 (statistics in archeol.); Wyckoff, R. W. G. 1964A (physico-chemical methods); Wyckoff, Doberenz and McCaughey 1965, Wyckoff, McCaughey and Doberenz 1964 (amino acid determination in Pleist. bone);

Zangerl 1965B (x-ray techniques), 1965C (galvanoplastic reproduction), 1967 (x-ray photography); Ziegler 1965 (faunal remains in archeol. study).

TEETH, ODONTOLOGY — See: dentition.

TERATOLOGY (anomalies, abnormalities) — See: paleopathology; variation and heredity.

TERMINOLOGY, ONOMATOLOGY, NOMENCLATURE — Anon. 1966BP, 1967BJ (archeol. terminology, Afr.), 1967R (strat. nomenclature, Afr.), 1967S (Afr. prehist.), 1968B (Quat. nomenclature); Applegate 1965B (tooth terminology, sharks); Ax 1964 (polyphyletism and phylogenetic systematics);

Bishop 1967C (Quat. strat. nomenclature, E. Afr.); Bishop and Heinzelin 1967 (strat. nomenclature, W. Rift, Afr.); Blackwelder 1967 (taxonomy); Boylan 1967A (rhinos);

Calvocoressi 1967 (Afr. archeol.); Campbell, B. G. 1965 (Hominidae), 1968 (Australopithecus); Campbell, C. B. G. (tree shrews); Chernysh 1967 (Late Pal. tools); Connah 1967B (use of the term "culture"); Crusafont Pairó 1965E (new name for Hesperoceras);

Daniels, S. G. H. 1967 (W. Afr. prehist.); Davies, O. 1967B (recommendations of Burg-Wartenstein conference); Davitashvili 1964 (assemblages of organisms and organic remains);

Estes 1960 (Cret. chimaeroid);   Ewer 1967B (new nomenclature);

Flight 1967 (cultural taxonomy);   Freudenthal 1965 (cricetids, Europe);   Fridrich, Klíma and Valoch 1968 (systematics of "culture" concept in Paleolithic);

Gasc 1966A (anatomical terms);   Gaudant 1966B (Anaethalion), 1968 (Lycoptera); Genet-Varcin 1967 (Australopithecus);

Haubold 1966A (track terminology);   Hillaby 1965B (fossil hominids);   Hossfeld 1965A (patination and weathering);

Josselyn 1967C (pebble-tool terminology);

Keroher 1967 (fossil names in strat. nomenclature, N. Amer.);   Keroher et al. 1966 (lexicon of geol. names of U.S., 1936-1960);   Kleindienst 1967 (Stone Age in-dustries, E. Afr.);   Kretzoi 1962E (Arvicolidae/Microtidae), 1964D (rodents and lagomorphs), 1965D (Drepanosorex);   Krieger 1964B (chipped-stone artifacts, Amer.);   Kruytzer 1966 (fossil and subfossil);

Leakey, M. D. et al. 1967 (Afr. Stone Age and industrial complexes);   Lindberg, G. U. 1963 (generic names of fishes);

McKenna 1965A (Mioc. strat. nomenclature, Nebraska);   Mason, R. J. 1967B (S. Afr. Earlier Stone Age cultures);   Melichar 1966 (Japanese archeol. terms); Mertens 1965 (Elaphe not Elaphis);   Nalivkin and Markovskiǐ 1962 (Devon. strat., USSR);

Narbutas 1964A (Devon. strat., Baltic);   Neave 1966 (zool. nomenclature);   Newman 1968 (Scelidosaurus harrisoni);

Paula Couto 1965 (glyptodonts);   Pidoplichko 1967A (Anthropogene chronology); Prasad and Ray 1964 (Siwalik system);

Radinsky 1966C (Pataecus);   Randal and Scott 1967 (data processing);   Ray, C. E. 1966A, B (musk ox);   Reǐman 1958 (geol. terms);   Remane 1963 (verts.); Ritchie, A. 1967 (Ateleaspis);   Robinson, P. 1968A (Adapisoricidae);

Savory 1962 (biol. nomenclature);   Schobinger 1962 (preceramic cultures, S. Amer.); Simpson, G. G. 1964D (exobiology, humanoids);   1968D (zool. nomina);   Sohn 1968 (zool. nomenclature);   Summers 1967 (Afr. archeol.);   Sylvester-Bradley 1967A (Internat. Code Stratig. Nomenclature);

Thomson, K. S. 1966C (fossil fish names);   Tillson 1966 (Hominoidea);   Tixier 1967 (classification of stone tools);

Winner 1964 (paleoanthrop.);   Woods 1968 (Nototherium);

Yochelson 1967A (Prototomus);   Youngquist 1967 (fossil systematics).

TEXTBOOKS – See: general works.

THEOLOGY, THEOLOGICAL CONTROVERSY – See: legislation.

THEORIES – See: distribution; evolution; general works; paleoanthropology; paleo-climatology; paleogeography; Paleolithic art; paleopsychology; phylogeny; restorations; techniques; terminology; variation and heredity.

TRACKS, TRACKWAYS, TRAILS – See: ichnology; restorations; and, in the Systematic Index, Ichnites.

ULTRAMICROSCOPY, ELECTRON-MICROSCOPY – See: histology; technique.

VARIATION and HEREDITY – Alexandersen 1963 (human canines);   Applegate 1965B (Carcharias);

Baker, J. K. 1960 (plethodont amphibians, Texas);   Beer 1966B (genetics);

Chaline 1966A (dental variation in arvicolides);   Colbert 1965F (adaptations of Trias. tetrapods), 1967C (adaptations of Trias. reptiles);   Comas 1967 (unity and variety of the human species);   Contreras 1964 (rodent molar patterns);   Crusa-font Pairó 1965H (variability of Myotragus);

SYSTEMATIC INDEX

SYSTEMATIC INDEX

aciedentatum (Smilerpeton)
Acinonyx Felidae
  jubatus Vereshchagin 1951C
Acipenser Acipenseridae
  eruciferus Estes 1964
  toliapicus Casier 1966A
Acipenseridae Acipenseriformes
  Acipenser
Acipenseriformes Chondrostei Lehman
        1966B (with Acipenseridae and
        Polyodontidae)
Acmeodon Palaeoryctidae
  secans Van Valen 1966A
Acoelohyrax Isotemnidae
  coalitus Simpson, G. G. 1967A (new
        comb.)
  coarctatus Simpson, G. G. 1967A (new
        comb.)
  complicatissimus Simpson, G. G. 1967A
  coronatus Simpson, G. G. 1967A
  sigma Simpson, G. G. 1967A (new
        comb.)
Acoelodus Oldfieldthomasiidae
  oppositus Simpson, G. G. 1967A
  proclivus Simpson, G. G. 1967A
  terminalis Simpson, G. G. 1967A
acontion (Alactagulus)
acoronatus (Cervus)
Acrania Chordata Obruchev, D. V. 1964B
Acratocnus Megalonychidae Hooijer and
        Ray 1964
  odontrigonus Paula Couto 1967
Acris Hylidae Chantell 1965; Wilson, R.
        L. 1968
  barbouri Holman 1967
  crepitans Chantell 1965; Wilson, R.
        Hibbard and Dalquest 1966 (cf.)
Acrocheilus Cyprinidae
  xestes Miller, R. R. and Smith 1967
Acrochordidae [Acrochordinae] Colubri-
        dae Hoffstetter 1964B p. 967
        (Henophidia= Booidea), 1965A
        p. 467 (related to Booidea); Hoff-
        stetter and Gayrard 1964 (os-
        teol.)
Acrochordus Colubridae
  dehmi Hoffstetter 1964B, 1965A
Acrodelphidae Delphinoidea
  Acrodelphis, Champsodelphis, Cyrto-
        delphis
Acrodelphis Acrodelphidae
  letochae Steininger and Thenius 1965
Acrodus Hybodontidae Albers and Weiler
        1964
  alexandrae LaRivers 1962

lateralis Dreyer 1962; Stefanov 1966
  minimus Dreyer 1962
  oreodontus LaRivers 1962
  substriatus Dreyer 1962; Stefanov 1966
Acrogaster Trachichthyidae
  anceps Patterson, C. 1964
  brevicostatus Patterson, C. 1964
  daviesi Patterson, C. 1964
  dayi Patterson, C. 1964
  heckeli Patterson, C. 1964
  parvus Patterson, C. 1964
Acropithecus Archaeopithecidae
  rigidus Simpson, G. G. 1967A
Acroplous Trimerorhachidae Chase, J. N.
        1965
Acrorhizamys Clethrionomys Topachevskiǐ
        1965C
Acrosaurus Pleurosauridae
  frischmanni Cocude-Michel 1967
Actinolepididae Arctolepidiformes Obruchev,
        D. V. 1964D (incl. Kujdano-
        wiaspididae)
  Actinolepis, Kujdanowiaspis
Actinolepis Actinolepididae Miles, R. S.
        1965C
Actinopterygii Teleostomi Kazantseva 1964;
        Lehman 1966B; MacAllister 1968
        (with "Groups" Chondrostei, Ho-
        lostei and Teleostei); Obruchev,
        D. V. and Kazantseva 1964A, B;
        Piveteau 1966B; Wenz 1967A, B
Actinistia Crossopterygii Lehman 1966C
        (with Coelacanthiformes)
aculeatus (Carcharhinus)
acuminata (Birgeria, Pattenaspis)
acuminatus (Saurichthys)
acutangulus (Ophidiidarum)
acuticosta (Pionaspis)
acutidens (Esthonyx, Etmopterus, Holcodus)
acutirostratum (Aceratherium)
acutissima (Carcharias)
acutus (Provaranosaurus)
adamsi (Cryptotis, Geomys)
Adapidae Adapoidea Crusafont Pairó 1967B
  Adapis, Anchomomys, Caenopithecus,
        Gesneropithex, Lantianius, Pely-
        codus, Pronycticebus, Protoada-
        pis
adapinus (Notopithecus, Notopithecus ada-
        pinus)
Adapis Adapidae Crusafont Pairó 1967B
  parisiensis Saban 1963
  priscus Crusafont Pairó 1965M
Adapisorex Adapisoricidae
  abundans Russell, D. E. 1964

gaudryi Russell, D. E. 1964
Adapisoricidae Erinaceoidea Van Valen
1967B
Adapisorex, Gypsonictops, Hyracoles-
tes, Opisthopsalis, Praolestes
Adapisoricinae, Creotarsinae, Geolabi-
dinae, Nyctitheriinae
Adapisoricinae Adapisoricidae Van Valen
1967B
Adapisoriculinae Tupaiidae Van Valen
1967B
Adapisoriculus Anagalidae Crusafont Pairó
1967B; Russell, D. E. 1964 (in
? Leptictidae)
germanicus Russell, D. E. 1964
minimus Russell, D. E. 1964
Adapoidea Palaeoprosimii
Adeloblarina Soricidae Repenning 1967C
berklandi Repenning 1967C
Adelogyrinidae Microsauria
Adelogyrinus, Dolichopareias
Adelogyrinus Adelogyrinidae
simnorhynchus Brough and Brough
1967
Adelomys Adelomys Thaler 1966B
Adelomys Pseudosciuridae Lavocat 1967A
crusafonti Thaler 1966B (subgen. Paradelomys)
depereti Thaler 1966B (subgen. Adelomys)
fontensis Thaler 1966B (subgen. ?Sciu-
roides)
ibericus Thaler 1966B
siderolithicus Thaler 1966B (subgen.
Sciuroides)
"vaillanti" Thaler 1966B (subgen. Adelomys)
Adelopithecus Cercopithecidae
hypsolephus Burchak-Abramovich, N.
1967
Adelospondyli Lepospondyli
Adelospondylus Lepospondyli incertae
sedis Carroll, R. L. 1967A
watsoni Carroll, R. L. 1967A
adichaster (Necromantis)
Adjidaumo Eomyidae
minimus Black, C. C. 1965A
quartzi Shotwell 1967B
admissadomus (Paeneprolimnocyon)
adnepos (Proplanodus)
Adocus Dermatemydidae
orientalis Yeh 1963B
adroveri (Baranogale, Indarctos atticus,
Parapodemus)
Adunator Leptictidae Russell, D. E. 1964;
Van Valen 1967B

lehmani Russell, D. E. 1964
aduncus (Galeocerdo)
Advenimus Ischyromyidae Dawson, M.
1964 (in ?Sciuravidae)
bohlini Dawson, M. 1964
burkei Dawson, M. 1964 (type)
adzalycensis (Struthiolithus)
Aechmophorus Podicipedidae
classon Murray, B. G. 1967
occidentalis Miller, L. 1966
Aeduella Aeduellidae
blainvillei Heyler 1967
Aeduellidae Palaeoniscoidei Heyler 1967;
Romer 1945D*
Aeduella, Bourbonnella, Decazella
Aeduelliformes Chondrostei Heyler 1967
Aegialodon Aegialodontidae Kermack, K.
A., Lees and Mussett 1965
dawsoni Kermack, K. A., Lees and
Mussett 1965
Aegialodontidae Pantotheria incertae sedis
Kermack, K. A. 1967C
Aegialodon
Aegypius Accipitridae
monachus Jánossy 1965E
aegyptiacus (Asteracanthus, Globidens)
aegyptius (Gaudeamus)
Aegyptopithecus Pongidae Simons, E. L.
1965B
zeuxis Simons, E. L. 1965B
Aelurodon Canidae Mawby 1964, 1965A
mortifer Kitts 1964 (cf.)
taxoides Dalquest and Hughes 1966 (cf.)
Aelurosauridae Titanosuchia
Aelurosaurinae
Aelurosaurinae Aelurosauridae Viushkov
1964C, p. 263 (wrongly assigned
to Broom 1903; of Gorgonopsidae)
Aelurosauropsidae Titanosuchia
Aelurosauropsinae
Aelurosauropsinae Aelurosauropsidae
Viushkov 1964C, p. 264 (as-
cribed to Watson and Romer
1956*; of Gorgonopsidae)
aeneus (Cricetops)
aenigmaticum ("Stenogenium")
Aenocyon Canis Galbreath 1964A
aeolamnis (Angistorhinus)
Aeoliscus Centriscidae
heinrichi Dzhafarova 1963
Aepycamelus Camelidae Macdonald 1966B;
Skinner, M. F., Skinner and
Gooris 1968; Webb, S. D. 1965C
Aepyornis Aepyornithidae Battistini 1965A,
B, C; Wetmore 1967 (rest.)

Aepyornithes [Aepyornithiformes]
    Neognathae Dement'ev 1964
Aepyornithidae Aepyornithiformes
    Aepynoris, Psammornis
Aepyornithiformes Neognathae
aeruginosus (Circus)
aequatorialis (Brachyodus, Palaeolama)
aerata (Psammolepis)
Aethalionopsis ?Leptolepididae Gaudant
    1966B
    robustus Gaudant 1966B
Aethia Alcidae
    rossmoori Howard, H. 1968A
aethiopicus (Paraustralopithecus, Stromer-
    ichthys)
Aethodontiformes Actinopterygii Lehman
    1966B
Aetiocetidae Archaeoceti Emlong 1966
    Aetiocetus
Aetiocetus Aetiocetidae Emlong 1966
    cotylalveus Emlong 1966
Aetobatis Myliobatidae Tsankov and
    Dachev 1966
    arcuatus Radwanski 1965
    irregularis Casier 1966A
Aëtosauridae Pseudosuchia
    Aëtosauroides, Desmatosuchus
Aëtosauroides Aëtosauridae
    scagliai Casamiquela 1964B
affine (Cricetodon, Neohipparion)
affinis (Cricetodon, Dasyurus, Democrice-
    todon, Isurus, Ortalis, Platecar-
    pus, Pseudocorax, Telmatornis,
    Triazeugacanthus)
africana (Loxodonta)
africanava (Loxodonta)
Africanomys Tataromyidae Lavocat 1961D
    (in Tataromyinae)
    incertus Lavocat 1961D
    pulcher Lavocat 1961D
africanum (Hipparion)
africanus (Ceratodus, Elephas, Kenyapithe-
    cus, Metailurus, Palaeothen-
    toides, Proconsul, Pterodon, Pul-
    tiphagonides, Rhinelles, Sorex
    dehmi)
Afropterus Chiroptera incertae sedis Lavo-
    cat 1961D
    gigas Lavocat 1961D
ageiensis (Paramys)
Agerina Necrolemuridae Crusafont Pairó
    1967B
    roselli Crusafont Pairó 1967B
agespensis (Araloselachus)
agilis (Rana, Varanodon)

agiloides (Rana)
Agispelaginae Leporidae Gureev 1964
Agispelagus Leporidae
    simplex Gureev 1964
    youngi Gureev 1964
Aglaocetus Cetotheriidae
    patulus Kellogg 1968
Aglossa [Opisthocoela] Salientia
Aglyptorhynchus Xiphiidae Casier 1966A
    sulcatus Casier 1966A
    venablesi Casier 1966A, 1967
Agnatha Craniata Balabai 1956B, C; Gross,
    W. 1967A; Jarvik 1964A; Obru-
    chev, D. V. 1964C, 1967D; Pive-
    teau 1964C; Tarlo, L. B. H. 1967B
    (incl. classes Diplorhina and Mon-
    orhina); Tarlo, L. B. H. and
    Whiting 1965; Whiting and Tarlo
    1965
agrestis (Microtus)
Agriocetus Squalodontidae
    incertus Rothausen 1968D
Agriocharis Phasianidae Brodkorb 1964A
    (in Meleagrinae)
    anza Brodkorb 1964E; Hibbard and
        Dalquest 1966
    progenes Brodkorb 1964A, E
Agriochoeridae Merycoidodontoidea
    Agriochoerus, Protagriochoerus, Proto-
        reodon
Agriochoerus Agriochoeridae Friant 1962D
    antiquus Clark, J. and Beerbower 1967
        (cf.)
aguilerai (Rogerbaletichnus)
aguti (Captorhinus)
Aigialosauridae Varanoidea
    Proaigialosaurus
Ailuraviinae Paramyidae Michaux 1968
Ailuravus Paramyidae Michaux 1968
Ailuropoda Procyonidae
    melanoleuca Davis, D. D. 1964
        fovealis Chow, M.-c., Hu and Lee
            1965 (cf.)
Aipichthyidae Dinopterygoidei Patterson,
    C. 1964
    Aipichthys
Aipichthys Aipichthyidae
    minor Patterson, C. 1964
    nuchalis Patterson, C. 1964
    pretiocus Patterson, C. 1964
    velifer Patterson, C. 1964 (rest.)
Aïstopoda Lepospondyli Baird 1964A,
    1965C
Aistopodidae [Aïstopoda] Lepospondyli
        Huene 1956D*, p. 24 (invalid)
aitkeni (Elonichthys)

akajei (Dasybatus)
Akidnognathidae Therocephalia
 Haughton and Brink 1954*, p. 136,
  (emend. of Nopcsa 1928B*)
akiyoshiensis (Cyclemys)
alabamae (Archaealbula)
alabamaensis (Globidens)
Alachtherium Odobenidae Deinse 1964B
Alacodon Didelphidae Quinet 1964A
 angularis Quinet 1964A
 gracilis Quinet 1964A
 latus Quinet 1964A
Alactagulus Dipodidae Topachevskii 1965C
 acontion Aleksandrova 1965B (cf.)
 kujalnikensis Shevchenko, A. I. 1965B
  (?)
alashanensis (Aspideretes)
alashanicus (Probactrosaurus)
alatus (Goniporus)
albanense (Trocharion)
albertense (Hipparion)
alberti (Gyrolepis)
Albertogaudrya Trigonostylopidae
 unica Simpson, G. G. 1967A
albertyni (Parotosaurus)
albicilla (Haliaeetus)
albiensis (Syllaemus)
albigense (Aceratherium)
Albula Albulidae
 oweni Casier 1966A
 vulpes Frizzell 1965C (otolith)
Albulidae Elopoidea Estes 1964
 Albula, Archaealbula, Dixonina, Eoalbula, Istieus, Metalbula, Palealbula, Prealbula
albus (Lagopus)
albyi (Bregmaceros)
Alca Alcidae Howard, H. 1968A
Alcae Charadriiformes Dement'ev 1964
 (ord.)
Alcelaphus Bovidae
 howardi Leakey, L. S. B. 1965
alces (Alces)
Alces Cervidae
 alces David, A. and Markevich 1967;
  Harčar and Schmidt 1965; Malez
  1963D; Svistun 1968; Tsalkin
  1962; Whitehead 1964
 latifrons David, A. 1965D; Kahlke
  1965G; Vangengeim 1960B, 1961
  postremus Vangengeim and Flerov
  1965; Vas'kovskii 1966
 palmatus Macarovici 1963
Alcidae Alcae
 Alca, Aethia, Cerorhinca

Alcodes Mancallidae Howard, H. 1968A
 ulnulus Howard, H. 1968A
alcootense (Pyramios)
alcovensis (Corosaurus)
aldanensis (Citellus undulatus)
aldeni (Miortyx)
Alectornis Phasianidae
 graeca Burchak-Abramovich, N. 1966D
Alegeinosaurus Dissorophidae
 aphthitos DeMar 1966B
alemanii (Platygonus)
Alepisauroidei Clupeiformes
alexanderi (Chasmatosaurus, Scaphiopus)
alexandrae (Acrodus, Liodontia)
alexejevi (Paracamelus, Procamelus, Struthiolithus)
alexi (Otionohyus)
Alilepini Leporinae Gureev 1964
Alilepus Leporidae Daxner and Fejfar 1967
 annectens Gureev 1964
 brachypus Gureev 1964
 lascarevi Gureev 1964
 ucrainicus Gureev 1964
Allacerops Rhinocerotidae Gabuniia 1964D;
  Radinsky 1967B (in Hyracodontidae)
Allactaga Dipodidae
 nogaiskiensis Topachevskii 1965C
 praejaculus Topachevskii 1965C
 saltator Zazhigin 1966D
  transbaicalicus Erbaeva 1966
 ucrainica Shevchenko, A. I. 1965B
Allaeovhelyinae Carettochelyidae
  Bergounioux 1952B*
allegheniensis (Petalodus)
allenae (Vernonaspis)
alleni (Geochelone, Kallostrakon)
Alligator Crocodylidae Hibbard and Dalquest 1966; Holman 1966C
 darwini Langston 1965B
 mississippiensis Edmund 1962
 parahybensis Langston 1965B (nomen
  vanum)
Alligatoridae [Alligatorinae] Crocodylidae
Alligatorinae Crocodylidae
allisoni (Halianassa)
Allocaenelaphus Cervidae Rădulesco and
  and Samson 1967A
 arambourgi Rădulesco and Samson 1967A
Allocricetulus Cricetidae Topachevskii 1965C
Allocryptaspis Cyathaspididae
 elliptica Denison 1964B
 flabelliformis Denison 1964B
 laticostata Denison 1964B
 utahensis Denison 1964B

Allodesminae Otariidae Mitchell, E. D.
1968
Allodesmus Otariidae Mitchell, E. D.
1965B, 1966B (rest.), D
Kelloggi Mitchell, E. D. 1966E
Allognathosuchus Crocodylidae
haupti Berg, D. E. 1966
riggsi Bjork 1967 (cf.)
Allomorone Serranidae See: Otolithus
Frizzell and Dante 1965
burlesonis Frizzell and Dante 1965
Allophaiomys Cricetidae
pliocaenicus Aleksandrova 1965A;
Buachidze 1968;
Shevchenko, A. I. 1965B (cf.)
Topachevskii 1965C
Allosorex Soricidae Fejfar 1966B (in Allo-
soricinae)
stenodus Fejfar 1966B; Repenning
1967C
Allosoricinae Soricidae Fejfar 1966B;
Repenning 1967C
Allotheria Mammalia Szalay 1965
Allothrissops Chirocentridae Bardack 1965A
Alluvisorex Soricidae Hutchison 1966A
(in Soricinae)
arcadentes Hutchison 1966A; Repenning
1967C
chasseae Repenning 1967C
Alopecocyan Mustelidae Beaumont 1964C
(in Broilianinae)
Alopecognathus Pristerognathidae Boonstra
1964
Alopex Canidae
lagopus Feustel, et al. 1963; Jacobshagen 1963; Kurtén 1966C;
Malez 1963D; Sukachev, et
al. 1966; Zapfe 1966B
Alopias Alopiidae
vulpinus Fitch 1964
Alopiidae Galeoidea
Alopias
Alosa Clupeidae
arcuata Rückert-Ülkümen 1960
baykali Rückert-Ülkümen 1965
brevis Rückert-Ülkümen 1965
crassa Rückert-Ülkümen 1965
elongata Rückert-Ülkümen 1965
fortipinnata Rückert-Ülkümen 1965
genuina Dzhafarova 1964
heterocerca Rückert-Ülkümen 1965
ovalis Rückert-Ülkümen 1965
pinarhisarensis Rückert-Ülkümen 1965
sagorensis Rückert-Ülkümen 1965
sculptata Anđelković 1963
weileri Rückert-Ülkümen 1960, 1965

alpha (Bathygenys)
Alphadon Didelphidae
lulli Clemens 1966
marshi Clemens 1966
rhaister Clemens 1966
alpherakyi (Vulpes vulpes)
alpinus (Cuon)
alstoni (Neotomodon)
alta (Weigeltaspis)
altageringensis (Pithecistes)
Althaspis Pteraspididae (Stensiö 1964 (pp.
193–4, 280, 323)
zychi Stensiö 1964
Althaspis Pteraspis Denison 1967B
Alticamelinae Camelidae Maglio 1966
alticeps (Laparon)
altidens (Apternodon, Didelphodus, Didymictis, Equus, Parmularius)
altiplanensis (Perutherium)
altirostre (Elassotherium)
altivelis (Urocles)
altmani (Meniscognathus)
altus (Miophasianus)
aluticus (Equus)
Alzadasaurinae Elasmosauridae Welles 1962*,
p. 4
Alzadasaurus Elasmosauridae
pembertoni Rice, T. H. 1966
amalphea (Pecoripeda)
amaltheus (Tragocerus)
amarorum (Eomoropus)
amazonensis (Mourasuchus)
ambadongarensis (Carcharias)
ambigua (Pantinomia)
ambiguus (Amphicyon, Dryomys, Pseudocyonopsis)
Amblycoptus Soricidae Repenning 1967C
Amblyopsiformes Paracanthopterygii
Amblypteridae [Palaeoniscidae] Palaeoniscoidei Romer 1945D*
Amblyrhiza Dinomyidae Ray, C. E. 1964B
inundata Ray, C. E. 1964B
Ambystoma Ambystomatidae Wilson, R. L.
1968
maculatum Holman 1965D
tigrinum Hibbard and Dalquest 1966 (cf.)
Ambystomatidae Ambystomatoidea
Ambystoma,
Wolterstorffiella
Ambystomatoidea Mutabilia
Ameghinichnidae Mammalia incertae sedis
Casamiquela 1964A
Ameghinichnus
Ameghinichnus Ameghinichnidae See:
Ichnites Casamiquela 1964A
patagonicus Casamiquela 1964A

Ameiva Teiidae
  griswoldi Etheridge 1964
  thoracica Etheridge 1966A
Amerhippus Equus Edmund 1965
americana (Americaspis, Grus, Martes,
      Squatirhina, Tarentola)
americanum (Mammut, Megatherium,
      "Myctophum")
americanus (Bothriodon, Bufo, Bufo ameri-
      canus, Eriptychius, Lepus,
      Rakomeryx, Ursus)
Americaspis Cyathaspididae
  americana Denison 1964B
  claypolei Denison 1964B
Amia Amiidae Estes and Tihen 1964;
      Janot 1967
  calva Wilson, R. L. 1968
  montesechensis Lange, S. P. 1968
  munieri Janot 1967
  russelli Janot 1966 (Paleoc., France)
  valenciennesi Janot 1967
Amiida Holostei Danil'chenko 1964A
      (order)
Amiidae Amiiformes Miller, H. W. 1964
  Amia, Amiidarum, Amiopsis, Kindleia,
      Lehmanamia, Protamia, Stylo-
      myleodon, Urocles
Amiidarum Amiidae See: Otolithus Lange,
      S. P. 1968
  mawsoni Lange, S. P. 1968
Amiiformes Holostei Lehman 1966B (with
      Furidae, Amiidae and Macro-
      semiidae)
Amioidei Amiiformes
Amiopsis Amiidae Wenz 1968B
ammon (Ovis)
Ammosauridae Palaeosauria Colbert 1964B
Ammospermophilus Sciuridae
  junturensis Gromov, I. M., et al. 1965
Amphekepubis Mosasauridae
  johnsoni Russell, D. A. 1967A
Ampheristus Scorpaenidae
  toliapicus Casier 1966A
Amphiaspida Pteraspidiformes
Amphiaspididae Amphiaspida
Amphibamus Dissorophidae
  calliprepes Carroll, R. L. 1964B
  lyelli Carroll, R. L. 1964B
  grandiceps Carroll, R. L. 1964B
Amphibia Tetrapoda Banta 1966 (Nev.);
      Blair 1965 (speciation); Cox,
      C. B. 1967B (origin); Gasc
      1966C; Herre 1964 (origin);
      Jarvik 1964A; Kuhn 1965E
      (classif.; incl. subclass Urodelo-
      morpha = Lepospondyli, and

Batrachomorpha = Apsido-
      spondyli), 1967B, C, 1968
      (classif.); Müller, A. H. 1966;
      Olson, E. 1965A; Panchen
      1967C (incl. subclasses Laby-
      rinthodontia and Lepospondyli);
      Parsons, T. S. and Williams
      1962* (Lissamphibia); Romer
      1964G; Salthe and Kaplan
      1966; Schaeffer, B. 1965D
      (origin); Tatarinov, L. P.
      1964B, 1965E (origin)
  Incertae sedis: Lasalidae
amphibius (Arvicola, Hippopotamus)
Amphicentridae Palaeoniscoidei Gardiner
      1967A; Moy-Thomas 1939B*
      (in Platysomida)
  Paraeurynotus
Amphichelydia Testudinata
Amphicoela Salientia Kuhn, O. 1967B
      (replaced by Archaeocoela)
Amphicoelidae [Teleosauridae+] Mesosuchia
      Nopcsa 1928C* p. 75 (invalid;
      includes most of the amphi-
      coelous Crocodilia)
Amphicyon Canidae Gabuniiä 1964D;
      Hooijer 1963D; Shotwell 1968
  ambiguus Beaumont 1964A; Ginsburg
      1965; Kuss 1965C
  giganteus Ginsburg and Telles Antunes
      1968 (in Ursidae); Kuss 1963
  major Bergounioux and Crouzel 1966B;
      Ginsburg 1964C; Kuss 1965C;
      Telles Antunes 1960A*
  eppelsheimensis Kuss 1965C
  grivensis Kuss 1965C
  gutmanni Kuss 1965C
  major Kuss 1965C
  robustus Kuss 1963
  steinheimensis Kuss 1965C
  bohemicus Kuss 1965C
  steinheimensis Kuss 1965C
amphicyonides (Bestiopeda)
Amphicyoninae Canidae Ginsburg 1966
      (in Ursidae); Kuss 1965C
Amphilaginae Palaeolagidae Gureev 1964
Amphilagus Palaeolagidae
  antiquus Gureev 1964
  fontannesi Gureev 1964
Amphilemur Amphilemuridae Crusafont
      Pairó 1967B (in Palaeoprosimii
      incertae sedis)
Amphilemuridae Erinaceoidea
  Amphilemur, Entomolestes,
  Tulpavus

Amphipithecus Pongidae
  mogaungensis Koenigswald 1965E,
    1967B; Simons, E. L. 1965B
Amphisbaenia Sauria
Amphisbaenidae Amphisbaenia
  Oligodontosaurus
Amphitheria Eupantotheria Kermack,
    D. M., Kermack and Mussett
    1968 (suborder)
Amphitheriidae Eupantotheria
  Amphitherium, Peramus
Amphitherium Amphitheriidae
  prevostii Mills 1964
Amphitragulus
  aurelianensis Crusafont Pairo, Valenciano
    Horta, et al. 1968 (cf.)
  elegans Crusafont Pairo, Valenciano
    Horta, et al. 1968 (cf.)
  gracilis Crusafont Pairo, Valenciano
    Horta, et al. 1968 (cf.)
Amphiuma Salamandridae
  means Holman 1965C
Amphorosteus Mosasauridae
  brumbyi Russell, D. A. 1967A (nomen
    vanum)
ampliatus (Diplodontops, Heterolophodon)
amplidens (Notopithecus)
amsleri (Paranothosaurus)
Amud man (Israel) [cf. Palaeoanthropus
    sp.] Hominidae Suzuki 1964,
    1965, 1968; Takai 1968
Amyda [Trionyx] Trionychidae
Amynodon Amydontidae
  lunanensis Chow, M.-c., Xu and Zhen
    1964
  mongoliensis Xu–1966
Amynodontidae Rhinocerotoidea Xu 1966
  Amynodon, Amynodontopsis, Giganta-
    mynodon, Lushiamynodon,
    Paracadurcodon, Sianodon
Amynodontopsis Amynodontidae
  bodei Bjork 1967
Amyzon Catostomidae
  mentalis La Rivers 1962
Anabantidae Anabantoidei
  Anabas
Anabantoidei Perciformes Liem 1963
Anabas Anabantidae Liem 1963
Anabernicula Anatidae Howard, H. 1964A
  gracilenta Howard, H. 1964A
  minuscula Howard, H. 1964A
  oregonensis Howard, H. 1964A
anacingularis (Paramys)
Anacodon Arctocyonidae
  ursidens Guthrie, D. A. 1967B
Anacorax Isuridae

faleatus Henriques da Silva 1963
  kaupi Henriques da Silva 1963
  pristodontus Glikman 1956; Henriques
    da Silva 1963; Tsankov and
    Dachev 1966
  yangaensis Henriques da Silva 1963
Anaethalion Leptolepididae Gaudant 1966B
Anaethalion Anaethalionidae Nybelin 1967A
?Anaethalionidae Leptolepidiformes Gaudant
    1967
  Anaethalion, Manchurichthys, Sinolycop-
    tera
Anagalidae Anagaloidea Crusafont Pairo
    1967B
  Adapisoriculus
Anagaloidea Palaeoprosimii
Anagonia Mammalia incertae sedis Simpson,
    G. G. 1967A (nomen dubium)
  insulata Simpson, G. G. 1967A
Anancus Gomphotheriidae
  arvernensis Alekseeva, L. I. 1965; Apos-
    tol 1965B; Apostol and Po-
    pescu 1963; Bakelov and Ni-
    kolov 1962; Feru, et al. 1965;
    Mitzopoulos 1966 (subgen.
    Bunolophodon), 1967; Niko-
    lov 1962*, 1965; Nikolov and
    Kovachev 1966; Radulesco,
    Samson, et al. 1965; Theobald
    1965
  yüsheensis Chang, H.-c. 1964A (Pentalo-
    phodon)
Ananogmius Thryptodontidae Bardack 1968A
Anapsida Cephalaspidomorpha
Anaptomorphidae Anaptomorphoidea Crusa-
    font Pairo 1967B
  Absarokius, Anemorphysis, Berruvius,
    Huerfanius, Microchoerus,
    Phenacolemur, Tetonoides,
    Tetonius, Trogolemur, Uinta-
    sorex
Anaptomorphoidea Palaeoprosimii
anarsius (Grangeria)
Anas Anatidae
  apscheronica Burchak-Abramovich, N. I.
    1966E
  bunkeri Howard, H. 1966A
  crecca Janossy, 1965C (cf.)
  penelope Janossy 1965C (cf.), E
  platyrhynchus Janossy, 1965C (cf.), E
anas (Anatipeda)
Anasinopa Hyaenodontidae Savage, R. J. G.
    1965A
  leakeyi Savage, R. J. G. 1965A
Anaspida Cephalaspidomorpha Stensiö 1964

Anaspidiformes Anaspida
Anatidae Anseres
  Anabernicula, Anas, Anser, Aythya,
    Branta, Bucephala, Chendytes,
    Cygnavus, Cygnopterus,
    Cygnus, Dendrocygna, Ere-
    mochen, ?Guguschia, Laornis,
    Mergus, Neochen, Nettion,
    Oxyura, Presbychen, Quer-
    quedula, Somateria, Tadorna,
    Wasonaka
  Paranyrocinae
Anatipeda Anatipedae Panin and Avram
    1962
  anas Panin and Avram 1962
Anatipedae Avipedia Panin and Avram
    1962
  Anatipeda
anatolicus (Gomphotherium)
Anatopus Ichnites Lapparent and Mon-
    tenat 1967B
  palmatus Lapparent and Montenat
    1967B
Anatosaurus Hadrosauridae Devillers, C.
    and J. 1965 (reconst.)
Ancanamunidae [Macropterygiidae] Lati-
    pinnati Kuhn, Oskar 1966A,
    p. 148 (credited to Rusconi
    1942B*)
anceps (Acrogaster, Mosasaurus, Tylosaurus)
Ancepsoides Plesiadapis Crusafont Pairó
    1967B; Russell, D. E. 1964
Anchilophus Equidae Savage, D. E., Rus-
    sell and Louis 1965
  desmaresti Savage, D. E., Russell and
    Louis 1965
  dumasi Remy 1967
  gaudini Remy 1967
  lusitanicus Ginsburg and Zbyszewski
    1965
Anchisauridae [Thecodontosauridae] Pro-
    sauropoda
Anchisauripus Ichnites
  hitchcocki Baird 1964B (coelurosaurian)
Anchitheriomys Castoridae
  wiedmani Bergounioux and Crouzel
    1965C
Anchitherium Equidae Whitmore and
    Stewart 1965
  aurelianensis Bergounioux and Crouzel
    1967B; Circí 1960, 1962B;
    Crusafont Pairó, Valenciano
    Horta, et al. 1968; Ginsburg
    1967A; Pavlović and Cipović
    1964; Pavlović and Durkovic
    1962; Petronijević 1967

Anchomomys Adapidae Crusafont Pairó
    1967B
Ancodonta Suiformes
Anconodon Ptilodontidae Russell, L. S.
    1967A
Ancylopoda Perissodactyla Radinsky 1964A
    (suborder)
Ancylotherium Chalicotheriidae Korotkevich
    1961B; Petronijević 1967;
    Zapfe 1967A
  hennigi Butler, P. M. 1965A
  pentelicum Bakalov and Nikolov 1962;
    Butler, P. M. 1965A
andersoni (Martes, Poebrotherium, Sthenur-
    us)
anderssoni (Struthio)
Andreolepis Pisces incertae sedis Gross, W.
    1968A
  hedei Gross, W. 1968A
Andrewsarchinae Mesonychidae Szalay and
    Gould 1966
Andrewsarchus Mesonychidae
  mongoliensis Szalay and Gould 1966
andrewsi (Gobiolagus, Hyaenodon, Phiomys)
Andrias Cryptobranchidae Meszoely 1965
  scheuchzeri Westphal 1967A
Androconus Periptychidae Quinet 1965A
  verlindeni Quinet 1965A
Androsorex Lepticidae Quinet 1964A
andrussovi (Lotella)
Anemorhysis Anaptomorphidae
  musculus Guthrie, D. A. 1967B
anfractuosa (Oldfieldthomasia)
angammensis (Loxodonta atlantica)
Angaraspis Olbiaspididae Obruchev, D. V.
    1964C
  urvanteevi Obruchev, D. V. 1964C
Angelosaurus Caseidae
  dolani Olson, E. 1968B
  greeni Olson, E. 1968B
  romeri Olson, E. 1965D, 1968B
Angistorhinus Phytosauridae
  aeolamnis Eaton 1965
Anglaspis Cyathaspididae
  elongata Denison 1964B (nomen nudum)
  expatriata Denison 1964B
  heintzi Denison 1964B
  insignis Denison 1964B
  macculloughi Denison 1964B
  platostriata Denison 1964B (nomen
    nudum)
Angolaichthys Semionotidae
  lerichei Teixeira 1958
Angolasaurus Mosasauridae Telles Antunes
    1964C
  locagei Telles Antunes 1964C

Anguidae Anguioidea
   Anguis, Gerrhonotus, Glyptosaurus,
       Haplodontosaurus, Melano-
       sauroides, Ophipseudopus,
       Ophisauriscus, Ophisaurus,
       Parapseudopus, Peltosaurus
Anguillida Teleostei Danil'chenko 1964A
   (order)
Anguilliformes Ostariophysi
Anguilloidei Anguilliformes
Anguimorpha Sauria
   Incertae sedis: Euposauridae, Litakis
Anguioidea Diploglossa
Anguis Anguidae
   fragilis Młynarski 1964A (cf.)
angularis (Alacodon)
anguliferus (Platecarpus)
angulorugatus (Scaloporhinus)
angulum (Bematherium)
angusta (Yukonaspis)
angustatus (Deirosteus)
angusticephalus (Rhyphodon)
angusticeps (Protospermophilus)
angustidens (Belesodon, Carcharodon,
       Cricetus, Gomphotherium,
       Humbertia, Isurus, Mammut,
       Mammut angustidens, Proto-
       adapis)
Angustidens Soricidae Repenning 1967C
   vireti Repenning 1967C
angustipes (Bucephala)
angustirostre (Itanzatherium)
angustirostris (Todus)
angustum (Percostoma)
angustus (Dissorophus)
Aniliidae Booidea
   Coniophis
Animalia
Anisolambda ?Proterotheriidae Simpson,
       G. G. 1967A (nomen vanum)
   nodulosa Simpson, G. G. 1967A (nomen
       vanum)
Anisorhizus Mammalis incertae sedis
   atriarius Simpson, G. G. 1967A
Anisotemnus Isotemnidae
   distentus Simpson, G. G. 1967A
Ankistrorhynchus Pristidae Casier 1964
       (Cret., Belgium)
   lonzeensis Casier 1964
Ankarapithecus Pongidae Ozansoy 1965
   meteai Ozansoy 1965
Ankylosauria Ornithischia Maleev 1964P;
       Simmons 1965
Ankylosauridae Ankylosauria
   Ankylosaurus

Ankylosaurus Ankylosauridae Devillers,
       C. and J. 1965 (reconst.)
ankyranum (Hipparion)
annectens (Alilepus, Ondatra, Plagiolophus)
anni (Hungkiichthys)
Anningia ?Millerettidae Watson 1957A*
       (possibly a sauropsid)
annulatum (Isotypotherium)
annulatus (Saurichthys)
Anogmius Thryptodontidae Leonardi, A.
       1966
Anolis Iguanidae Lazell 1965
   bimaculatus
      leachii Etheridge 1964
   carolinensis Etheridge 1966A
   chlorocyanus Etheridge 1965
   cybotes Etheridge 1965
   distichus Etheridge 1965, 1966A
   ricordii Etheridge 1965
   roquet Ray, C. E. 1964C
   sagrei Etheridge 1966A
Anomalomys Cricetidae
   gaillardi Hartenberger 1966A
   gaudryi Kowalski, K. 1967A; Mein 1967
anomalum (Campostoma)
Anomerycoidodon Merycoidodon Schultz,
       C. B. and Falkenbach 1968
Anomocoela Salientia
Anomodontia Therapsida Kuhn, Oskar
       1965B (bib. catalog, taxonomy;
       incl. infraorders, Tapinoceph-
       alia, Venyukovioidea, Droma-
       sauria and Dicynodontia);
   V'iushkov 1964F
Anomodontoidea [Dicynodontia] Anomo-
       dontia Nopcsa 1928B* (sub-
       order of order Chainosauria;
       incl. Endothiodontidae, Geiki-
       iidae and Dicynodontidae)
Anomoepus Ichnites Baird 1964B
Anomotherium Dugongidae Siegfried 1965
   langewieschei Siegfried 1965
Anoplotheriidae Anthracotherioidea
   Anoplotherium, Diplobune
Anoplotherium Anoplotheriidae
   commune Bonis 1964
   latipes Bonis 1964
   laurillardi Bonis 1964
Anosteira Carettochelyidae
   manchuriana Yeh 1963B
   maomingensis Yeh 1963B
   mongoliensis Yeh 1963B
Anourosorex Soricidae Repenning 1967C
Anourosoricodon Soricidae Topachevskii
       1966

Anurognathidae ? Rhamphorhynchoidea
    Kuhn, Oskar 1966A (incl. ?
    Batrachognathus), 1967A
Anurognathus, Batrachognathus
Anurognathus Anurognathidae Kuhn, O.
    1967A
anyangensis (Pseudocadia)
anyapahensis (Peromyscus)
anza (Agriocharis)
apachensis (Hypolagus)
Apatemyidae Apatemyoidea McKenna 1965B
    Apatemys, Eochiromys, Sinclairella
    Unuchiniinae
Apatemyoidea Menotyphla Van Valen
    1967B (in Proteutheria)
Apatemys Apatemyidae Robinson, Peter
    1966A
    hendryi Robinson, Peter 1966C
    whitakeri Guthrie, D. A. 1967B
Apateodus Enchodontidae Albers and
    Weiler 1964
Apatopodidae Ichnites
    Kuhn, Oskar 1966A (ascribed by error
        to Baird "1937", should be
        1957A; in Parasuchia)
Apatosaurinae Titanosauridae Romer 1957E*
apertosulcus (Leiocephalus)
Apertotemporalidae Pleurosternoidea
    Kuhn, Oskar 1966A (ascribed to Kuhn
        1937)
Aphaneramma Trematosauridae Lehman
    1966A; Stensio 1963 (brain
    rest.)
Aphataspis Ctenaspididae Obruchev, D. V.
    1964C (?)
    kiaeri Obruchev, D. V. 1964C
Aphelocoma Corvidae
    coerulescens Hamon 1964
Aphelops Rhinocerotidae Shotwell 1968
    kimballensis Tanner 1967A
Aphredoderidae Aphredoderoidei
    Trichophanes
Aphredoderoidei Amblyopsiformes
aphthitos (Alegeinosaurus)
apicalis (Aspidosaurus, Saurichthys, Strat-
        odus)
apiculata (Isurus)
apivorus (Pernis)
aplanatus ("Isolophodon")
Aplodinotus Sciaenidae
    grunnieus Hibbard 1964; Lundberg
        1967; Wilson, R. L. 1968 (cf.)
Aplodontidae Aplodontoidea
    Liodontia, Sciurodon

Aplodontoidea Sciuromorpha
Apodemus Muridae Shevchenko, A. I. 1965B;
    Thaler 1966B
    atavus Fejfar 1964A
    jeanteti Michaux 1967
    primaevus Hugueney and Mein 1965;
        Michaux 1967
    sylvaticus Jullien 1965A; Krommenhoek
        and Slob 1967A; Malez 1963D
Apodiformes Neognathae
apodus (Pycnodus)
Apostasella Sparidae
    sturi Rückert-Ülkümen 1965
appalachicolus (Bootherium)
appendiculata (Isurus, Lamna)
applanata (Sinochelys)
applanatus (Mugil)
aprica (Hirundo)
Aprionodon Carcharhinus Jonet 1965-66A
apscheronica (Anas)
apsheronicus (Canis lupus, Sus)
Apsidospondyli Amphibia Konzhukova
    1964A
Apsopelicidae Elopoidea
    Apsopelix
Apsopelix Apsopelicidae
    sauriformis Bardack 1968A
Apterodon Mesonychidae
    altidens Van Valen 1966A
    flanheimensis Lange, B. 1967 (subgen.
        Dasyurodon; syn. with A.
        gaudryi)
    gaudryi Lange, B. 1967; Szalay 1967
    macrognathus Van Valen 1966A
    minutus Van Valen 1966A
Apternodontidae Soricoidea
    Apternodus
Apterodontini Hyaenodontidae Szalay 1967
    (tribe)
Apternodus Apternodontidae Edinger 1964A
    (brain cast)
Apteryges [Apterygiformes] Neognathae
    Dement'ev 1964
Apterygiformes Neognathae
apthomasi (Trigonostylops)
aquatilis (Isoptychus)
Aquila Accipitridae
    chrysaëtus Malez 1963D (cf.)
    clanga Jánossy 1965E (cf.)
    minuta Villalta 1963 (cf.)
aquitanensis (Emys)
Archaeoceti Cetacea
Araeoscelidia Cotylosauria Tatarinov 1964P
    (Areoscelidia)
    Incertae sedis: ?Doniceps

Araeosceloidea Araeoscelidia Tatarinov
1964P (suborder Araeosceli-
doidei)
Araeoscelomorpha [Euryapsida] Reptilia
Kuhn, O. 1968 (incl.
Aracoscelidia, Trilopho-
sauria and Weigeltisauria)
araeum (Plagiodontia)
aragonensis (Armantomys, Armantomys
aragonensis, Cricetodon decedens)
aralensis (Carcharias)
Aralomys Cricetidae
glikmani Vorontsov 1964
Araloselachus Carchariidae Glikman 1964B
(in Odontaspididae)
agespensis Glikman 1964B
arambourgi (Allocaenelaphus, Goniocranion,
Hyaena, Ictitherium, Mylio-
batis, Priohybodus, Schizochoerus)
Aramichthys Scombridae Signeux 1959C
dammeseki Signeux 1959C
araneus (Sorex)
arankae (Lagurus)
arborea (Dendrocygna)
arcadentes (Alluvisorex)
arcanus (Molybdopygus)
Archaealbula Albulidae Frizzell 1965C
(otolith)
alabamae Frizzell 1965C
Archaeobatrachia Salientia
Archaeoceti Cetacea Aslanova 1963 (USSR)
Archaeohippus Equidae Whitmore and
Stewart 1965
equinanus Skinner, M. F., Skinner and
Gooris 1968
Archaeohyracidae Hegetotheria
Bryanpattersonia, Eohyrax, Pseudohyrax
Archaeoindris Indriidae
fontoynonti Saban 1963
Archaeolemur Archaeolemuridae
edwardsi Saban 1963
Archaeolemuridae Lemuroidea Crusafont
Pairo 1967B
Archaeolemur
Archaeomaenidae Pholidophoriformes
Wadeichthys
Archaeomys Theridomyidae
gervaisi Thaler 1966B
hürzeleri Thaler 1966B
laurillardi Lavocat 1967A; Thaler 1966B
Archaeonectrus Plesiosauridae Novozhilov
1964C
rostratus Novozhilov 1964C (for Plesio-
saurus rostratus)

Archaeopithecus Archaeopithecidae
fossulatus Simpson, G. G. 1967A
rogeri Simpson, G. G. 1967A
Archaeopithecidae Typotheria
Acropithecus, Archaeopithecus
Archaeopteryges [Archaeopterygiformes]
Archaeornithes Dement'ev
1964
Archaeopterygidae Archaeopterygiformes
Archaeopteryx
Archaeopterygiformes Archaeornithes
Archaeopteryx Archaeopterygidae Beer
1964B; Burchak-Abramovich,
N. and Gambarov 1964 (3rd
skel.); Dechaseaux 1968B
(brain); Edinger 1964A (brain
cast); Freyberg 1964; Jerison
1968; Kuhn, O. 1965D; Milo-
jevic 1966, 1967; Ryziewicz
1961C (3rd skel.); Stever, et
al. 1966; Stürmer 1965 (X-rays);
Uschmann 1960 (3rd skel.)
Archaeornithes Aves
Archaeosuchia Crocodilia Sill 1967 (subord.),
1968 (Archeosuchia)
Archaeotherium Entelodontidae Clark, J. and
Beerbower 1967
ordosius Hu, C.-k. 1964 (Olig., Mong.)
trippensis Skinner, M. F., Skinner and
Gooris 1968
archaicus (Elephas, Mammuthus meridionalis)
Archanthropinae Hominidae Dokládal 1965
(pithecanthropines); Genet-
Varcin 1966C (invalid)
Archegonaspis Cyathaspididae
drummondi Denison 1964B
integra Denison 1964B
lindstromi Denison 1964B
ludensis Denison 1964B
schmidti Denison 1964B
Archegosauridae Micropholoidea
Melosaurus
Archegosauroidea [Micropholoidea]
Rhachitomi
Archeolagini Leporinae Gureev 1964
Archeolagus Leporidae
acaricolus Gureev 1964
enninsianus Gureev 1964
macrocephalus Gureev 1964
primigenius Gureev 1964
Archegadus Gadidae See: Otolithus Stinton
1965
comptus Stinton 1965
Archemacroroides Coryphaenoididae See:
Otolithus Stinton 1965
ornatus Stinton 1965

Archengraulis Leptolepididae See: Oto-
lithus Stinton and Torrens
1968
productus Stinton and Torrens 1968
Archeriidae [Cricotidae] Embolomeri Kuhn,
Oskar 1945E (p. 70, ascribed
to "Romer")
Archerpeton Romeriidae Carroll, R. L.
1964C
anthracos Carroll, R. L. 1964C
Archidiskodon Elephas
Archidiskodon [Mammuthus] Elephantidae
Chow, M.-c. and Chow 1965;
Garutt 1966
Archoplites Centrarchidae
taylori Miller, R. R. and Smith 1967
Archosauria Diapsida Charig 1957; Reig
1967; Rozhdestvenskii 1964C
incertae sedis: Shimmelia
Arctamphicyon Canidae
depereti Kuss 1965C
tolsanus Kuss 1965C
eibiswaldensis Kuss 1965C
tolsanus Kuss 1965C
arctica (Jarvikia, Wijdeaspis)
arcticus (Rangifer)
Arctocyon Arctocyonidae Edinger 1964A
(brain cast)
matthesi Russell, D. E. 1964
primaevus Russell, D. E. 1964; Russell,
D. E. and Sigogneau 1965
(endocast)
Arctocyonides Arctocyonidae
arenae Russell, D. E. 1964; Russell, D.
E. and Sigogneau 1965 (endo-
cast)
trouessarti Russell, D. E. 1964
weigelti Russell, D. E. 1964
Arctocyonidae Condylarthra
Anacodon, Arctocyon, Arctocyonides,
Claenodon, Kelba, Landenoden,
Mentoclaenodon, Protungulatum, Thryptacodon
Oxyclaeninae
Arctodus Ursidae Firby 1966; Kurtén
1967A
bonariensis Kurtén 1967A (subgen.
Arctotherium)
brasiliensis Kurtén 1967A
pamparus Kurtén 1967A (subgen.
Arctotherium)
pristinus Hawksley 1965, 1966; Kurtén
1967A
simus Kurtén 1967A
Arctognathidae Gorgonopsia Watson and
Romer 1956* (emended:

Hartmann-Weinberg 1938*
Arctognathinae)
Arctognathoididae Gorgonopsia Watson and
Romer 1956*
Arctognathoidinae
Arctognathoidinae Arctognathoididae
Viushkov 1964C, p. 264 (as-
cribed to Watson and Romer
1956; of Gorgonopsidae)
Arctolepida Arthrodira
Arctolepidida [Arcto lepidiformes] Euarthro-
dira Obruchev, D. V. 1964D
Arctolepididae [Phlyctaenaspididae] Arctol-
epidiformes
Arctolepidiformes Euarthrodira
Arctolepis Phlyctaenaspididae Lehman 1963B;
Miles, R. S. 1965C
arctomyoides (Arctomyoides)
Arctomyoides Sciuridae
arctomyoides Gromov, I. M., et al. 1965
Arctoryctes Talpidae Reed, C. A. and Turn-
bull 1965
arctos (Ursus)
Arctotherium Arctodus Kurtén 1967A
arcuata (Alosa, Clupea)
arcuatum (Arkanserpeton)
arcuatus (Aetobatis, Gillicus)
Ardea Ardeidae
cinerea Jánossy, 1965C (cf.)
Ardeae Ardeiformes
ardei (Arvernoceros)
Ardeidae Ardeae Dekeyser 1962B
Ardea
Ardeiformes Neognathae
Ardeipeda Ardeipedae Panin and Avram 1962
egretta Panin and Avram 1962
gigantea Panin and Avram 1962
incerta Panin and Avram 1962
Ardeipedae Avipedia Panin and Avram 1962
Ardeipeda
Ardeosauridae Sauria incertae sedis Kuhn,
Oskar 1966A (in Gekkonoidea)
Ardeosaurus, Yabeinosaurus
Ardeosaurus Ardeosauridae Hoffstetter 1966B,
1967A
brevipes Hoffstetter 1964D
digitatellus Hoffstetter 1964D
ardeus (Pliotragus)
Ardiodus ? Scrombridae
marriotti Casier 1966A
Ardynia Hyracodontidae
plicidentata Gabuniia 1964D, 1966A
praecox Radinsky 1967B
Ardynomys Cylindrodontidae Dawson, M.
1968A

Ardynomys Cylindrodontidae Dawson, M.
1968A
arenae (Arctocyonides)
arenarum (Merychyus)
arenatus (Catostomus)
areolata (Nectaspis, Rana)
Arfia Hyaenodontidae Van Valen 1965G
argalus (Platybelone)
argentinensis (Kannemeyeria)
Argentinidae Salmonoidei
Glossanodon
argentonicum (Propalaeotherium)
Argillichthys Synodidae Casier 1966A
toombsi Casier 1966A
Argilloberyx Berycidae Casier 1966A
prestwichae Casier 1966A
Argillotherium Oxyaenidae
toliapicum Van Valen 1966A
argonautus (Otospermophilus)
Argyrohyus Tayassuidae Kraglievich 1959B
chapadmalensis Kraglievich 1959B
(syn. Homo chapadmalensis)
argyropuloi (Ochotonolagus)
Ariaspis Cyathaspididae
ornata Denison 1964B
aries (Ovis)
Arikarornis Accipitridae Howard, H.
1966C
macdonaldi Howard, H. 1966C
?Arisella Omomyidae Crusafont Pairó
1967B
capella Crusafont Pairó 1967B
Aristelliger Gekkonidae
lar Etheridge 1965
aristus (Tamias)
arizonae (Marmota)
arizonensis (Eldenosteus)
Arkanserpeton Dissorophidae
arcuatum Carroll, R. L. 1964B
arkelli (Taurotragus)
arknethensis (Phronetragus)
armaghensis (Menaspacanthus)
Armantomys Gliridae
aragonensis Bruijn 1966A
aragonensis Bruijn 1966A
armata (Menaspis)
armatus (Dercetis, Phanerorhynchus)
armigerus (Deltoptychius)
arnee (Bubalus)
arnensis (Canis)
Arnoglossus Bothidae See: Otolithus
miocenicus Weiler 1962G
Arretosauridae Iguania Kuhn, Oskar 1966A
arrodeus (Marmota)
arroyoensis (Broiliellus)
Arthrodira [Euarthrodira] Coccostei
Whiting 1964

Artibeus Phyllostomatidae
jamaicensis
jamaicensis Choate and Birney 1968
artica (Psammolepis)
Artiodactipedae Mammalipedia Panin and
Avram 1962
Pecoripeda
Pecoripedinae
Artiodactipedida Mammalipedia Vialov
1966 (order)
Artiodactyla Paraxonia Koopman 1967
Incertae sedis: Dierocerus, Phronetragus
artus (Ganosteus)
arvalinus (Microtus)
arvalis (Microtus)
arvalis-agrestis (Microtus)
arvaloides (Pitymys)
arvernensis (Anancus, Mammut, Tapirus)
arverniensis (Procharacinus)
Arvernoceros Cervidae Heintz, E. 1968
ardei Heintz, E. 1968
Arvicola Cricetidae
amphibius Jacobshagen 1963
bactonensis Fejfar 1965
greeni Fejfar 1965
sapidus Jullien 1965A
schermann Jullien 1965A
terrestris Malez 1963D
Arvicolidae [Microtinae] Cricetidae Chaline
1966A (dentition); Kretzoi
1962E
arzniensis (Citellus xanthoprymnus)
Asaphestera Tuditanidae
intermedium Carroll, R. L. 1966
asatkini (Schizosteus)
Ascaphidae Archaeobatrachia Estes 1964
Asellia Hipposideridae
vetus Lavocat 1961D
Asiacanthus Climatiidae
kaoi P'an 1964
suni P'an 1964
asiaticus (Struthio)
Asiatoceratodus Ceratodontidae Vorob'eva
1967
sharovi Vorob'eva 1967
Asiatosuchus Crocodylidae
germanicus Berg, D. E. 1966
nanlingensis Young, C.-c. 1964C
Asinus Equus Azzaroli 1966B
asio (Otus)
Asio Strigidae Ford, N. L. 1966
brevipes Ford, N. L. and Murray 1967
flammeus Brunet, J. 1961; Jánossy
1965E
priscus Howard, H. 1964B
asius (Vulpavus)

Askeptosauria [Askeptosauridae] Sauria
    Tarlo, L. B. H. in Appleby,
    et al. and Tarlo 1967
Askeptosauridae Sauria
asodes (Uintacyon)
aspalex (Myospalax)
asper (Psammosteus)
asphaltense (Diceratherium)
aspidephorus (Cacops)
Aspideretes Trionychidae Khozat'skii 1957;
        Miller, H. W. 1964
    alashanensis Yeh 1965
    beecheri Estes 1964
    impressus Yeh 1963B
    jaxarticus Riabinin 1938A*
    maortuensis Yeh 1965
    planicostatus Yeh 1963B
    sculptus Yeh 1963B
    sinuosus Yeh 1963B
Aspidichthys Holonematidae
    ingens Miles, R. S. 1965D
aspidiformis (Trionyx)
Aspidorhynchida Holostei Danil'chenko
        1964A (order)
Aspidorhynchidae Aspidorhynchiformes
    Belonostomus
Aspidorhynchiformes Holostei Lehman
        1966B
Aspidosaurus Dissorophidae
    apicalis DeMar 1966B
    crucifer DeMar 1966B
    glascocki DeMar 1966B
    novomexicanus Carroll, R. L. 1964B;
        DeMar 1966B
Aspius Cyprinidae
    laubei Obrhelová 1967 (reconst.)
Aspro Percidae
    nogaicus Tarashchuk 1965
assenzae (Neosqualodon)
assymmetrus (Astrapanotus)
Asteracanthus Hybodontidae
    aegyptiacus Tabaste 1963
    ornatissimus Tabaste 1963 (aff.)
Asterolepidinae Asterolepididae Gross, W.
        1965A
Asterolepididae Asterolepiformes Karatajūte
        1958A, B; Obruchev, D. V.
        1964D
    Asterolepis, Gerdalepis, Taeniolepis
    Asterolepidinae, Gerdalepidinae
Asterolepidiformes Pterichthyes Gross, W.
        1965A (incl. Asterolepididae,
        Remigolepididae, Microbrachi-
        idae, Sinolepididae)
Asterolepis Asterolepididae Gross, W.

        1965A; Karatajūte 1958B,
        1963*; P'an 1964
    chadwicki Wells, J. W. 1964
    dellei Karatajūte 1963*
    estonica Karatajūte 1963*
    ornata Gross, W. 1965A; Karatajūte
        1957* (listed under Trav.
        Acad. Sci. Lithuanie), 1963*
    radiata Karatajūte 1963*
    sinensis P'an 1964
Asterosteidae [Gemuendinidae] Gemuen-
        diniformes
asticus (Elomeryx)
Astraponotus Astrapotheriidae
    assymmetrus Simpson, G. G. 1967A
    dicksoni Simpson, G. G. 1967A
    dilatatus Simpson, G. G. 1967A
    holdichi Simpson, G. G. 1967A
    thompsoni Simpson, G. G. 1967A
Astrapotheria Protoungulata
    Incertae sedis: Blastoconus, Grypolopho-
        don, Notorhinus
Astrapotheriidae Astrapotherioidea
    Astraponotus, Seaglia
Astrapotherioidea Astrapotheria
Astraspida Pteraspidiformes
Astraspididae Astraspida
    Astraspis
Astraspis Astraspididae
    desiderata Denison 1967A
    splendens Denison 1967A
Astrodonius Brachiosauridae Kuhn, Oskar
        1964A, p. 324 (for Astrodon
        heidy preocc.)
Astrohippus Equidae Wilson, R. L. 1968
astutus (Bassariscus)
Astylolama Palaeolama Churcher 1965B
atavella (Louisina)
atavus (Apodemus, Orchesteropus, Sclero-
        rhynchus)
Ateleaspida [Aceraspida] Oligobranchiata
        Tarlo 1967B (Ateleaspidida;
        incl. Aceraspididae and Hemi-
        cyclaspididae of Group A of
        Aceraspida of Stensiö as well
        as the Hirellidae of Ortho-
        branchiata)
Ateleaspididae Osteostraci
    Ateleaspis, Ilemoraspis, Tuvaspis
Ateleaspis Ateleaspididae Ritchie, A. 1967
        (incl. Aceraspis)
    tessellata Ritchie, A. 1967
atheles (Tamias)
Atherina Atherinidae Dzhafarova 1963
    sarmatica Anđelković 1963; Ionko 1954

1964, 1965; Gania and
Kurochkin 1967; Kuhn, O.
1965D; Müller, A. H. 1968;
Rand 1967; Soergel 1960,
1966; Swinton 1964A, B
Avipeda Avipedia
  filiportatis Vialov 1966
  phoenix Vialov 1966
  sirin Vialov 1966
Avipedia Vertebratichnia Panin and Avram
        1962; Vialov 1961*, 1966
Avipelvia Ornithischia Avnimelech 1966
Avipelviens [Ornithischia] Dinosauria
        Lapparent and Lavocat 1955*
avitus (Ischyodus)
avonicola (Ischyrhiza)
Avunculus Palaeoryctidae Van Valen
        1966A
  didelphodonti Van Valen 1966A
avus (Parahippus, Protobrama)
Axelia Coelacanthidae Lehman 1966C
        (lateral line system)
Axis Cervidae
  rugosus Chow, M.-c. and Chow 1965
Axis Cervus Otsuka 1967
ayestarani (Calibarichnus)
aymardi (Hyaenodon)
Aythya Anatidae
  fuligula Jánossy 1965C (cf.)
  nyroca Jánossy 1965C (cf.), E

baardi (Hipparion albertense)
bacai (Paramerycoidodon)
bactonensis (Arvicola)
baderi (Hyla)
Baena Baenidae Estes 1964 (cf.)
  nodosa Wiman 1935C
Baenidae Baenoidea
  Baena, Chengyuchelys
Baenoidea Amphichelydia Romer 1957E*
baenoides (Chengyuchelys)
baghensis (Scapanorhynchus)
Bagridae Siluroidei
  Bucklandium, ?Claibornichthys
bahoensis (Sianodon)
baicherei (Lophiaspis)
baigubeki (Carcharias)
Baiomys Cricetidae
  intermedius Alvarez 1966 (Mex.);
        Packard and Alvarez 1965
bairdi (Lisserpeton)
Balaenidae Mysticeti
  Eschrichtius
Balaenoptera Balaenopteridae Hasegawa
        1968A

taiwanica Huang, T. 1965
Balaenopteridae Mysticeti
  Balaenoptera, Megaptera
Balanerodus Crocodylidae Langston 1965B
        (in Alligatoridae incertae sedis)
  logimus Langston 1965B
balangodensis (Homo sapiens)
balearicus (Myotragus)
Balistes Balistidae
  crassidens Bauza Rullan 1968
  lerichei Bauza Rullan 1968
Balistidae Balistoidei
  Balistes
Balistoidei Perciformes
ballaratensis (Glaucodon)
baltica (Pteraspis)
bambergi (Elaphrosaurus)
bamberi (Veronaspis)
bambolii (Oreopithecus)
bamiani (Kanisamys)
banksi (Cyathaspis)
Bantuchelys Pelomedusidae
  congolensis Telles Antunes 1964C
Baranogale Mustelidae
  adroveri Petter, G. 1964B
Baranomys Cricetidae Fejfar 1964A
  longidens Sulimski 1964
barbadiana (Neochen)
barbouri (Acris, Diceratherium, Paenemar-
        mota)
Barbourochoerus Paramerycoidodon
        Schultz, C. B. and Falkenbach
        1968
Barbourula Discoglossidae Estes 1964
Barbus Cyprinidae
  bispinosus Rückert-Ülkümen 1960
  bohemicus Obrhelová 1967 (reconst.)
Bargmannia Ambystomatidae Herre 1939*
Barornis Diatyma Baird 1967
barrionuevoi (Proterochampsa)
barroisi (Poraspis)
barthii (Chirotherium)
baryosteus (Pliolymbus)
Barysoma Kannemeyeriidae Cox, C. B.
        1965
  lenzii Cox, C. B. 1965
basanus (Hybodus)
bashiana (Metalbula)
Basilemys Dermatemydidae Estes 1964
  nobilis Wiman 1935C
basilicus (Leptonysson)
basilii (Martes)
Basilosauridae Archaeoceti
  Basilosaurus, Microzeoglodon, Zeuglodon
Basilosaurus Basilsauridae Gibbes 1847C;

belinkoi (Hadrodus)
bellunensis (Squalodon)
bellus (Dasypus)
Belodon Phytosauridae Hary and Muller
    1967; Kuhn, Oskar 1966A
    (substituted for Phytosaurus)
Belonida Teleostei Danil'chenko 1964B
    (order)
Belonidae Exocoetoidei
    Platybelone
Beloniformes Mesichthyes
Belonostomus Aspidorhynchidae Bardack
    1968B
    longirostris Estes 1964
    tenuirostris Leich 1964B
Bematherium Diprotodontidae Tedford
    1967A (in Nototheriinae)
    angulum Tedford 1967A
Benaratherium Perissodactyla incertae sedis
    Gabuniiā 1955G (nomen
    nudum), 1964D (in Indri-
    cotheriidae)
    callistrati Gabuniiā 1955G (nomen
    nudum), 1964D, 1966A
benarensis (Lophiomeryx)
benedeni (Isurus)
benedentatus (Oxydactylus)
Benneviaspida Orthobranchiata Tarlo
    1967B (Benneviaspidida, sub-
    order of Kiaeraspidiformes;
    incl. Boreaspididae and Hoel-
    aspididae)
bennisoni (Plotosaurus)
bensoni (Otospermophilus)
Benthosuchidae Capitosauroidea Ochev
    1966C
    Benthosuchus, Wantzosaurus
Benthosuchus Benthosuchidae Lehman
    1966A
    sushkini Stensiö 1963; Welles and
    Cosgriff 1965B
bequaerti (Dyrosaurus)
beremendensis (Pliolagus)
Beremendia Soricidae Fejfar 1964A; Re-
    penning 1967C
bergeri (Semionotus)
bergi (Acanthodes, Psammosteus, Yoglinia)
berislavicus (Palaeotragus)
berklandi (Adeloblarina)
bernissartensis (Iguanodon)
Berruvius Anaptomorphidae Crusafont
    Pairó 1967B; Russell,
    D. E., 1964
    lasseroni Russell, D. E. 1964; Russell,
    D. E., Louis and Savage 1967

Berycida Teleostei Danil'chenko 1964B
    (order)
Berycidae Beryciformes
    Argilloberyx
Beryciformes Acanthopterygii
    Incertae sedis: Brazosiella
Berycoidei Beryciformes Patterson, C.
    1964 (suborder)
    Incertae sedis: ?Beryx, Lobopterus,
    ?Cleidogonia
Berycopsis Polymixiidae
    elegans Patterson, C. 1964
    germanicus Patterson, C. 1964
    oblongus Patterson, C. 1964
Beryx ? Berycoidei incertae sedis
    dalmaticus Patterson, C. 1964
    subovatus Patterson, C. 1964
bessarabiensis (Cervavitus)
Bessoecetor Pantolestidae
    levei Russell, D. E., Louis and Poirier
    1966B
bessomi (Oxyura)
bestia (Bestiopeda)
Bestiopeda Ichnites Thenius 1967A; Vialov
    1966 (in Carnivoripedida)
    amphicyonides Thenius 1967A
    bestia Vialov 1966
    gracilis Vialov 1966
    guloides Thenius 1967A
    sanguinolenta Vialov 1966
betpakdalensis (Borissiakia)
Bettongia Macropodidae
    lesueuri Tedford 1967B
    penicillata Tedford 1967B
biarmicus (Deuterosaurus)
Biarmosaurus Eotitanosuchidae Chudinov
    1964J
    antecessor Chudinov 1964J
biauriculata (Isurus)
biauriculatus (Scyliorhinus)
Bibos Bos Meijer 1962
bicolor (Tiaris)
bicostatus (Hedralophus, Thelodus)
bicuspidens (Oxyaenoides)
bicuspis (Proterix)
bidens (Heptaxodon)
Bienotherium Tritylodontidae Hopson 1966
    yunnanense Hopson 1964B
bifidus (Cotimus, Pleurostylodon)
bifurcatus (Elaphurus)
bilolus (Prolagus)
bimaculatus (Anolis)
binagadensis (Bubo)
binckhorsti (Rhombodus)
bingadensis (Ursus arctos)

bohemicus (Amphicyon steinheimensis,
     Barbus, Gephyrostegus, Tri-
     onyx)
bohlini (Advenimus, Capra, Chodsigoa)
Boidae Booidea
     Eryx, Ogmophis, Python,
     Boinea, Erycinae, Madtsoiinae
Boidea
Booidea
Boii Tuditanidae Carroll, R. L. 1966
     crassidens Carroll, R. L. 1966
Boinae Boidae Holman 1964C
boisei (Australopithecus, Zinjanthropus)
boisvilletti (Trogontherium)
bollensis (Mystriosaurus, Ptycholepis,
     Steneosaurus)
bolli (Parioxys)
bombifrons (Erophylla, Erophylla, bombi-
     frons, Stegodon)
bonaerense (Chasichimys)
bonali (Hemitragus jemlahicus)
bonariensis (Arctodus)
bonasus (Bison)
bonythoni (Ngapakaldia)
Booidea Serpentes Hoffstetter 1955G*
     p. 649 (duplicates the name
     of the bovoid mammals),
     1964, p. 647 (Henophidia
     substituted for Booidea)
Bootherium Bovidae Ray, C. E., Cooper,
     et al. 1967
     appalachicolus Ray, C. E. 1966A
     brazosis Ray, C. E. 1966B
     sargenti Semken, Miller and Stevens
          1964
borbonicoides (Elomeryx)
borealis (Dromomeryx, Eotitanops, Homa-
     laspidella, Lasiurus, Protic-
     tops)
boreas (Bufo)
Boreosomidae Palaeonisciformes Gardiner
     1967A
     Boreosomus, ?Mesembroniscus
Boreosomus Boreosomidae Gardiner 1967A
Borhyaenidae Borhyaenoidea
     Cladosictis, Thylacosmilus
Borhyaenoidea Marsupicarnivora
boriei (Pachycynodon)
Borissiakia Chalicotheriidae Butler, P. M.
          1965A (for Moropus betpak-
          dalensis)
     betpakdalensis Butler, P. M. 1965A
bornemanni (Rhynchosauroides)

borsoni (Mammut)
Bos Bovidae Hîrjoaba 1962; Vekua 1958B
     brachyceros Ligeron 1965
     javanicus Meijer 1962 (subgen. Bibos)
     longifrons La Baume 1959 (to be drop-
          ped)
     primigenius Apostol 1967A; Bakalov and
          Nikolov 1964; Bökönyi, et
          al. 1965; Chang, C.-k. 1964;
          David, A. and Markevich 1967;
          Klafs 1965; Kubasiewicz 1965;
          La Baume 1959; Lomi 1963;
          Malez 1963D; Melentis 1964C;
          Milojčić, et al. 1965; Rakovec
          1965B; Svistun 1968; Ting,
          M.-l., et al. 1965; Tsalkin
          1962, 1965
     trochoceros Avakian 1959
bosniaskii (Clupea)
Bothidae Pleuronectoidea
     Arnoglossus, Rhombus
Bothriaspis Ctenaspididae Obruchev, D. V.
          1964C
     Kiaeri Obruchev, D. V. 1964C
Bothriodon Anthracotheriidae
     americanus Clark, J. and Beerbower
          1967 (cf.)
     velaunus Gabunia 1964D (ex. gr.)
Bothriolepididae Asterolepidiformes
     Bothriolepis, Dianolepis, Grossilepis,
     Yunnanolepis
     Bothriolepidinae, Yunnanolepidinae
Bothriolepidinae Bothriolepididae Gross,
     W. 1965A
Bothriolepiformes [Asterolepidiformes]
          Pterichthyes Gross, W. 1965A
          (incl. Bothriolepididae)
Bothriolepis Bothriolepididae Denison
          1964A (rest.); Dineley 1967B
          (rest.); Grishchenko 1968
     canadensis Gross, W. 1965A
     cellulosa Anatol'eva 1960 (cf.); Kara-
          tajūte 1966 (reconst.); Obru-
          chev, D. V. and Sergienko
          1961
     extensa Obruchev, D. V. and Sergienko
          1961; Sergienko 1961B
     kwangtungensis P'an 1964
     lochangensis P'an 1964
     maxima Karatajūte 1966
     obrutschewi Karatajūte 1966
     ornata Obruchev, D. V. and Sergienko
          1961
     panderi Gross, W. 1965B (cf.); Karata-
          jūte 1966

prima Karatajūte 1966
sibirica Anatol'eva 1960 (cf.); Obruchev, D. V. and Sergienko 1961
tuberculata Obruchev, D. V. and Sergienko 1961
tungseni Chang, K.-j. 1965
Bothrosauropodoidea [Brachiosauridae] Sauropoda Kuhn, Oskar 1965A (invalid)
bougainville (Perameles)
bounites (Aulolithomys)
Bourbonnella Aeduellidae
guilloti Heyler 1967
bouziguensis (Hipposideros, Muscardinus, Pseudorhinolophus)
Bovidae Bovoidea Bonifay, M.-F. 1966C; Heintz, E. 1966B; Lavocat 1961D
Alcelaphus, Antidorcas, Antilope, Antilospira, Beatragus, Bison, Bootherium, Bos, Bubalus, Capra, Damaliscus, Eotragus, Gallogoral, Gazella, Gazellospira, Gorgon, Helicotragus, Hemitragus, Hesperidoceras, Hippotragus, Leptobos, Limnotragus, Megalotragus, Myotragus, Nemorheodus, Oioceros, Olioceros, Ovibos, Ovis, Palaeoreas, Palaeoryx, Parastrepsiceros, Parmularius, Pelorovis, Phenacotragus, Pliotragus, Praeovibos, Procapra, Protoryx, Pseudalces, Pultiphagonides, Rupicapra, Saiga, Sinoreas, Spirocerus, Strepsiceros, Symbos, Taurotragus, Tragelaphus, Tragocerus, Udabnocerus, Xenocephalus
Antilopinae, Bovinae, Caprinae, Rupicaprinae
Bovinae Bovidae Alekseeva, L. I. 1967C (Pleist., USSR)
Bovipedidae Pecoripedoidei Vialov 1966
Bovoidea Pecora
bowerbanki (Paraberyx, Pycnodus, Sciaenurus)
boycei (Cyrbasiodon)
boyeri (Myotis)
Brachaucheniidae [Polycotylidae] Pliosauroidea Novozhilov 1964D; Persson 1963A (in Polycotylidae)

Brachiopterygii Pisces Lehmann 1966D (with two living genera, Polypterus and Calamiochthys); MacAllister 1968
Incertae sedis: Calamoichthys, Polypterus
Brachiosauridae Sauropoda Colbert 1964B (in Cetiosauria)
Camarasaurus, Oplosaurus, Tienshanosaurus
Brachiosaurinae
Brachiosaurinae Brachiosauridae Janensch 1929A
Brachipposideros Hipposideros Sigé 1968B
Brachipteraspis Pteraspididae
bryanti Balabaĭ 1961
heintzi Balabaĭ 1959
latissima Balabaĭ 1959
Brachycephalidae Procoela Quinquevertebron
brachycephalus (Platecarpus)
brachyceras (Palaeoreas)
brachyceros (Bos)
Brachychampsa Crocodylidae
montana Estes 1964
brachycolis (Limnosceloides)
Brachycrus Merycoidodontidae Macdonald 1966B (?);
buwaldi Schultz, C. B. and Falkenbach 1968
laticeps
mooki Schultz, C. B. and Falkenbach 1968
rusticus
riograndensis Schultz, C. B. and Falkenbach 1968 (geog. var.)
vaughani
rioosoensis Schultz, C. B. and Falkenbach 1968 (geog. var.)
Brachycyon Canidae Ginsburg 1966 (in Ursidae)
palaeolycos Ginsburg 1966
gaudryi Ginsburg 1966 (var.)
reyi Ginsburg 1966 (var.)
brachydactylus (Struthio)
Brachydegma Brachydegmidae Gardiner 1967A
Brachydegmidae Palaeonisciformes Gardiner 1967A
Brachydegma
Brachydiridae Pachyosteiformes
Brachyericinae Erinaceidae McKenna and Holton 1967 (new rank)
Brachygnathosuchus Crocodylidae
braziliensis Langston 1965B

brachygnathus (Hypolagus, Macroneomys,
        Panthera leo)
brachynatus (Hypolagus)
brachyodon (Megalagus)
Brachyodus Anthracotheriidae
    aequatorialis Hooijer 1963D (cf.), 1968B
    manchharensis Prasad 1964A
    onoideus Astre 1965B; Melentis 1966C
brachyodus (Eohyrax)
Brachyopidae Brachyopoidea Ochev
        1962A*
    Batrachosuchoides
    Eobrachyopinae
Brachypoidea Stereospondyli
Brachyphylla Phyllostomatidae
    cavernarum Choate and Birney 1968
Brachypotherium Rhinocerotidae
    brachypus Ginsburg 1967A
    heinzelini Hooijer 1963D, 1966B
Brachypsalis Mustelidae Shotwell 1968
brachypus (Alilepus, Brachypotherium)
Brachyrhinodontinae Sphenodontidae
            Huene 1948H* p. 100,
            (Bradyrhinodontinae, in
            error)
Bradyrhinodontinae [Brachyrhinodontinae]
        Sphenodontidae
Brachyrhynchocyon Canidae
    sesnoni Macdonald 1967A
Brachyspiza Fringillidae
    capensis Bernstein 1965
brachystephanus (Antepithecus)
Brachythoraci Arthrodira
Bradyodonti Elasmobranchii incertae sedis
brailloni (Dryomys, Megaderma, Peridyro-
        mys)
brama (Abramis)
Bramidae Percoidea
    Bramoides, Goniocranion
Bramoides Bramidae Casier 1966A
    brieni Casier 1966A
Brancasauridae [Elasmosauridae] Plesio-
            sauroidea Novozhilov 1964C
            (incl. subfamilies Branca-
            saurinae and Tremamesaclei-
            dinae)
Brancasaurinae Elasmosauridae Novozhilov
        1964C
branchialis (Rhinchorhinus)
Branchiosauridae Micropholoidea
    Branchiosaurus
Branchiosaurus Branchiosauridae Malz 1967
brancoi (Trilobodon)
Brandmayria Notoungulata incertae sedis
    simpsoni Simpson, G. G. 1967A

braneti (Leptochelys)
branisai (Gasteroclupea)
bransoni (Cotylorhynchus)
branssatensis (Hipposideros, Piezodus)
Branssatoglis Gliridae Hugueney 1967
    concavidens Hugueney 1967
Branta Anatidae
    ruficollis Jánossy 1965C (cf.)
Braunosteidae [Trematosteidae] Pachyostei-
        formes
    Braunosteus
braziliensis (Arctodus, Brachygnathosuchus,
        Purussaurus, Tadarida)
Brazilosaurus Reptilia incertae sedis Shikama
        and Ozaki 1966
    sanpauloensis Shikama and Ozaki 1966
brazosensis (Parbatmya)
brazosia (Stintonia)
Brazosiella Beryciformes incertae sedis See:
        Otolithus Frizzell and Dante
        1965
    kokeni Frizzell and Dante 1965
    moseleyi Frizzell and Dante 1965
brazosis (Bootherium)
bredai (Sciurus, Spermophilinus)
Bregmaceros Bregmacerotidae
    albyi Bachmayer and Weinfurte 1965
    catulus Weiler 1962G (cf.)
    troelli Frizzell and Dante 1965
Bregmacerotidae Gadiformes
    Bregmaceros
brehus (Protemnodon)
breineri (Eosphargis)
bressanus (Equus)
breve (Cricetodon, Lonchidion, Lonchidion
        breve)
brevicauda (Blarina)
breviceps (Clupea)
Brevicipitidae Neobatrachia
    Gastrophryne
brevicornis (Gazella, Procapra, Tragocerus)
brevicostatus (Acrogaster, Hybodus, Urocles)
brevidens (Pannonicola)
brevidontus (Merychippus)
Brevidorsum Dissorophidae Carroll, R. L.
        1964B
    profundum Carroll, R. L. 1964B (reconst.)
brevifacies (Pithecistes)
Breviodon Lophialetidae Radinsky 1965A
    acares Radinsky 1965A
    minutus Radinsky 1965A
brevior (Wetherellus)
brevipes (Ardeosaurus, Asio, Harpagolestes)
brevirostris (Acidorhynchus, Chalicotherium,
            Citellus undulatus, Hyaena,
            Promephitis, Zanclus)

brevirrostris (Neomesocnus)
brevis (Alosa, Broiliellus, Democricetodon
    minor, Palimphyes, Poraspis)
brevissimus (Diplomystus)
breviventralis (Capros)
breweri (Parascalops)
brewsteri (Siphonorhis)
brieni (Bramoides)
Brithopodidae Titanosuchia Chudinov
        1964J
    Chthomaloporus, Doliosauriscus, Dolio-
        saurus, Notosyodon, Syodon,
        Titanophoneus
brodiei (Macellodus, Sycosaurus)
brodkorbi (Pliopicus)
Broila Testudinidae
    denticulata Bergounioux and Crouzel
        1965B
    robusta Bergounioux and Crouzel
        1965B
Broiliana Mustelidae Beaumont 1964C (in
        Broilianinae)
Broilianinae Mustelidae Beaumont 1964C
Broiliellus Dissorophidae
    arroyoensis DeMar 1967
    brevis Carroll, R. L. 1964B (Tex.)
    olsoni DeMar 1967
    texensis DeMar 1966B
Broken Hill man (Homo rhodesiensis)
        Hominidae Baker, J. R.
        1968B
bronni (Acanthodes)
Brönnimanni (Tapirus)
Brontornithinae Phorusrhacidae Brodkorb
        1967 (new emendation)
Brontotheriidae Brontotherioidea
    Brontotherium, Diplacodon, Embolo-
        therium, Eotitanops, Lamb-
        dotherium, Menodus, Palaeo-
        syops, Teleodus
Brontotherium Brontotheriidae
    rumelicum Bakalov and Nikolov 1962
Brontotherioidea Hippomorpha
brookvalensis (Parotosaurus)
broomensis (Megalosauropus)
broomi (Parapapio)
Broomia Reptilia incertae sedis Watson
        1957A* (probably in Millero-
        sauria)
broomianus (Rhinesuchus)
Broomisauridae Titanosuchia
    Broomisaurinae
Broomisaurinae Broomisauridae Viushkov
        1964C, p. 265 (ascribed to
        Watson and Romer 1956*;
        in Gorgonopsidae)

Broomitherium Diarthrognathidae Huene
        1956D* (p. 345, invalid, cf.
    Diarthrognathus. No species is named.
        Proposed to include Broom's
        ictidosaurs "Forms A and B".)
Brotula Brotulidae
    longipinnata Andelkovic 1963 (?)
Brotulidae Ophidioidea
    Brotula, Fehmarnichthys
brotzeni (Weigeltaspis)
browni (Euskelosaurus, Merycoidodon cul-
        bertsonii, Mesocnus, Sthenurus,
        Toxochelys)
brownorum (Ceraunosaurus)
bruijni (Gliravus)
brumbyi (Amphorosteus)
brusinai (Chrysophrys)
Bryanictis Protictis MacIntyre 1966
Bryanpattersonia Archaeohyracidae Simpson,
        G. G. 1967A
    nesodontoides Simpson, G. G. 1967A
    sulcidens Simpson, G. G. 1967A
bryanti (Brachipteraspis, Cardipeltis, Mio-
        spermophilus, Vernonaspis)
Brychaetus Osteoglossidae
    muelleri Casier 1966A
Bubalus Bovidae Ting, M.-l., et al. 1965
    arnee Milojcic, et al. 1965 (cf.)
    nilssoni Nilsson 1964
Bubo Strigidae
    binagadensis Burchak-Abramovich 1965B
buccatus (Tretulias)
bucella (Rana)
Bucephala Anatidae
    angustipes Janossy 1965C
Bucerotes Coraciiformes
Buchanosteidae [Coccosteidae] Coccostei-
        formes
Buchanosteus Coccosteidae
    Obruchev, D. V. 1964D
    Romer 1966C
buchsowillanum (Lophiodon)
bucklandi (Cervus, Naupygus)
Bucklandium Bagridae
    diluvii Casier 1966A
Budamys Mus Kretzoi and Vertes 1965B
buffaloensis (Pristerodon)
bufo (Bufo)
Bufo Bufonidae Hibbard and Dalquest
        1966; Kretzoi 1965B; Verg-
        naud-Grazzini 1966
    americanus Richmond 1964 (cf.)
        americanus Guilday, Martin and
            McCrady 1964
        copei Guilday, Martin and McCrady
            1964

boreas Wilson, R. L. 1968
bufo
    japonicus Hasegawa 1964A
cognatus Bayrock 1964; Wilson, R. L.
        1968
hibbardi Estes and Tihen 1964 (cf.)
marinus Wilson, R. L. 1968
pisanoi Casamiquela 1967B
pliocompactilis Wilson, R. L. 1968
praevius Holman 1967
valentinensis Estes and Tihen 1964
viridis Jacobshegen 1963
vulgaris Malez 1963D
Bufonidae Procoela
    Bufo, Indobatrachus, Pliobatrachus
bühleri (Coryphomys)
Bukobaja Bukobajidae Ochev 1966C
    enigmatica Ochev 1966C
Bukobajidae Capitosauroidea Ochev 1966C
    Bukobaja, Meyerosuchus
bulgaricum (Dorcatherium)
bullatus (Otionohyus)
buloloensis (Protemnodon)
bunkeri (Anas)
Bunolistriodon Suidae
    massai Arambourg 1964A
Bunolophodon Anancus Mitzopoulos 1966
Bunolophodon Mammut Steininger 1965
Bunophorus Dichobunidae Guthrie, D. A.
        1966, 1968 (tarsus)
    etsagicus Guthrie, D. A. 1967B
    macropternus Guthrie, D. A. 1967A;
            Robinson, Peter 1966A (cf.)
    sinclairi Guthrie, D. A. 1966 (Eoc.,
            Wyo.), 1967B
burchelli (Equus)
burkei (Advenimus, Yoderimys)
burlesonis (Allomorone)
Burnetiidae Gorgonopsia Kuhn, Oskar
        1966A (in Titanosuchoidea)
Burramys Phalangeridae F., K. 1967
        (found living, Australia)
    parvus Ride 1964B; Turnbull 1968
bursauxi (Enchodus)
Buteo Accipitridae
    jamaicensis Brodkorb 1964B
    lagopus Jánossy 1965E (cf.)
butovi (Gyroplacosteus)
Butselia Butselidae Quinet and Misonne
        1965
    biveri Quinet and Misonne 1965
Butselidae Tenrecoidea Quinet and
        Misonne 1965
    Butselia
buwaldi (Brachycrus)

Byssacanthus Pterichthyodidae Gross, W.
        1965A (in Grossaspididae)
        Karatajūte 1958B, 1960B (in
        Asterolepididae); Obruchev,
        D. V. 1964B
    dilatatus Gross, W. 1965A; Karatajūte
            1958B, 1960B; Obruchev, D.
            V. 1964B
bystrowi (Psammosteus, Psephaspis)

caballus (Equus)
cabrerai (Tsamnichoria)
Cacops Dissorophidae
    aspidephorus DeMar 1966B
cadlei (Dicynodon)
caducus (Cricetodon)
cadurcensis (Cephalogale)
Caeciliomorpha [Gymnophiona] Amphibia
        Kuhn, O. 1968 (incl. Caecilia)
Caenognathi [Caenagnathiformes] ?Reptilia
        incertae sedis Dement'ev 1964
        (in Odontornithes)
Caenagnathiformes ?Reptilia incertae sedis
Caenolestoidea Marsupialia
Caenophidia Serpentes Hoffstetter 1964C
        (infraorder: =Colabroidea)
Caenopithecus Adapidae Crusafont Pairó
        1967B
Caenopus Rhinocerotidae
    mitis Clark, J. and Beerbower 1967
Caenotheriidae [Cainotheriidae] Cainother-
        oidea
Caenotherium [Cainotherium] Cainotherii-
        dae
caffii (Pholidophorus)
Caiman Crocodylidae
    lutescens Langston 1965B (cf.)
    neivensis Langston 1965B
    praecursor Langston 1965B
Cainotheriidae Cainotheroidea
    Cainotherium
Cainotherium Cainotheriidae Friant 1962D
        (Caenotherium)
    miocenicum Ginsburg 1967A
Cainotheroidea Tylopoda
calaminthus (Merychyus)
Calamoichthys Brachiopterygii incertae sedis
        Lehman 1966D (living genus)
Calcichordata Chordata Jefferies 1967
        (subphylym), 1968
calciculus (Heptodon)
calhouni (Puffinus)
Calibarichnus Ichnites Casamiquela 1964A
        (in Vertebrata inc. sed.)
    ayestarani Casamiquela 1964A

californica (Rhina, Sespia)
californicus (Eurypterygius, Lepus, Myliobatis, Smilodon, Tapirus)
californiensis (Protostrix)
Calippus Equidae Webb, S. D. 1964A, 1965A
 placidens Dalquest and Hughes 1966
 regulus Dalquest and Hughes 1966
Calligenethlon Cricotidae
 watsoni Carroll, R. L. 1967B
Callionymus Gobiidae
 macrocephalus Anđelković 1962
calliprepes (Amphibamus)
callistrati (Benaratherium)
Callorhynchus Chimaeridae
 rossicus Obruchev, D. V. 1966
Callospermophilus Ostospermophilus Gromov, I. M., et al. 1965
Calopomus Sparidae
 porosus Casier 1966A (nomen nudum)
Caloprymnus Macropodidae
 campestris Tedford 1967B (cf.)
calva (Amia)
calvertense (Hadrodelphis, Metaxytherium)
calvertensis (Pelocetus)
Calyptophilus Thraupidae
 frugivorus Bernstein 1965
Camarasaurus Brachiosauridae Jensen, J. A. 1968A
Camelidae Tylopoda McKenna 1966A (phylogeny); Webb, S. D. 1965B, 1966B
 Aepycamelus, Blickomylus, Camelops, Camelus, Eschiatius, Floridatragulus, Gigantocamelus, Hesperocamelus, Megatylopus, Nothokemas, Oxydactylus, Palaeolama, Paracamelus, Pegomylus, Pliauchenia, Poebrotherium, Procamelus, Rakomylus, Stenomylus, Tanupolama, Titanotylopus
 Alticamelinae, Floridatragulinae, Stenomylinae
Camelopardalis Giraffidae
 parva Bakalov and Nikolov 1962 (Cameliopardalis)
Camelops Camelidae Dalquest 1964B; Hibbard and Dalquest 1966; Webb, S. D. 1965C
 hesternus Webb, S. D. 1965C
 kansanus Schultz, G. E. 1965B
Camelus Camelidae Edinger 1966A (endocast); Hooijer 1961C
 knoblochi Avakian 1959; Vangengeim

and Chumakov 1963
 thomasi Gautier, A. 1966
camelus (Struthio)
campanicus (Chiromyoides)
campestris (Caloprymnus)
campi (Oedaleops, Tseajaia)
Campostoma Cyprinidae
 anomalum Lundberg 1967
Campylocynodon Parictis Clark, J. and Beerbower 1967
Campylognathoides Rhamphorhynchidae Kuhn, O. 1967A (in subfam. Nov. ?)
camtschatica (Marmota)
canadensis (Bothriolepis, Castor, Cervus elephus, Listraspis, Melanognathus, Pachyrhinosaurus, Palaeosaniwa, Plourdosteus, Ptomaspis)
canavus (Vulpavus)
cancellata (Ctenaspis)
cancellatum (Epitypotherium)
Canidae Canoidea Starck 1964
 Aelurodon, Alopex, Amphicyon, Arctamphicyon, Brachycyon, Brachyrhynchocyon, Canis, Cephalogale, Cuon, Cynelos, Cynodictis, Cynodon, Daphoenocyon, Daphoenus, Enhydrocyon, Gobicyon, Hadrocyon, Haplocyon, Hecubides, Hemicyon, Ischyrocyon, Lycaon, Megamphicyon, Metarctos, Nyctereuctes, Otocyon, Pachycynodon, Parahaplocyon, Parictis, Prototocyon, Pseudamphicyon, Pseudarctos, Pseudocyon, Pseudocyonopsis, Sarcocyon, Sunkahetanka, Tomarctus, Urocyon, Vulpes, Ysengrinia
 Amphicyoninae, Haplocyoninae, Hemicyoninae
Canimartes Mustelidae
 cookii Zakrzewski 1967A (assigned to Trigonictis)
 idahoensis Zakrzewski 1967A (assigned to Trigonictis)
canina (Grangeria)
caninus (Pachyrhizodus)
Canipeda Carnivoripedae Panin and Avram 1962
 longigriffa Panin and Avram 1962
Canipedinae Carnivoripedae Panin and Avram 1962

Canis Canidae Beaumont 1961D; Shotwell
      1968
   arnensis Torre 1967
   aureus Dal' 1954*; Hooijer 1961C
   dirus Galbreath 1964A (subgen.
      Aenocyon)
   etruscus Torre 1967
   falconeri Torre 1967
   latrans Anderson, E. 1968; Fine
      1964; Hibbard and Dalquest
      1966 (cf.); Kurtén 1967B
   lupaster Kurtén 1965A
   lupus Alekseeva, L. I. and Lomize
      1960 (cf.); Anderson, E.
      1968; David, A. and Marke-
      vich 1967; Feustel, et al.
      1963; Hibbard and Dalquest
      1966 (cf.); Koby 1964C;
      Kurtén 1965A; Lomi 1963;
      Malez 1963D; Rakovec
      1965B; Sukachev, et al.
      1966; Svistun 1968; Wisz-
      niowska 1967; Zapfe 1966B
   apsheronicus Gadzhiev, G. V. and
      Gadzhiev 1954; Vereshchagin
      1951C
   mosbachensis Thenius 1965B
   tengisii Vekua 1958B
   variabilis Vangengeïm 1961
Canoidea Fissipeda
Cantius Omomyidae Crusafont Pairó
      1967B
   eppsi Russell, D. E., Louis and Savage
      1967 (cf.)
cantotiana (Testudo)
canus (Picus)
caparti (Nycticonodon)
capella (Arisella)
capensis (Brachyspiza, Euparkeria,
      Rhinesuchus)
Capitosauridae Capitosauroidea
   Capitosaurus, Cyclotosaurus, Eryo-
      suchus, Karoosuchus, Kestro-
      saurus, Paracyclotosaurus,
      Parotosaurus, Stenotosaurus,
      Watsonisuchus, Wetlugasaurus
   Cyclotosaurinae, Paracyclotosaurinae,
      Wetlugasaurinae
Capitosauroidea Stereospondyli Ochev
      1966C; Welles and Cosgriff
      1965B (incl. Benthosuchidae,
      Capitosauridae and Masto-
      donsauridae)
Capitosaurus Capitosauridae Welles and
      Cosgriff 1965B (nomen
      vanum)

cappelensis (Mastodonsaurus)
Capra Bovidae
   bohlini Ozansoy 1965
   caucasica Alekseeva, L. I. and Lomize
      1960
   hircus Reed, C. A. and Palmer 1964
   ibex Bouchud 1965B; Couturier
      1961; Malez 1963D; Prat
      1966B; Zapfe 1964D
      (reconst.)
   pyrenaica Prat 1966B
   taurica Bogachev 1960B (Crimea)
capreolus (Capreolus)
Capreolus Cervidae Melentis 1964B
   capreolus Bubeník and Wurtzinger
      1967; Crusafont Pairó
      1959D; David, A. and
      Markevich 1967; Feustel,
      et al. 1963; Krysiak 1956;
      Malez 1963D; Matheson
      1964; Milojčić, et al. 1965;
      Rădulesco, Samson, et al.
      1965; Svistun 1968; Tsalkin
      1962; Whitehead 1964
   manchuricus Dai and Chi 1964
   süssenbornensis Kahlke 1965G
Caprimulgi Caprimulgiformes Dement'ev
      1964 (ord.)
Caprimulgidae Caprimulgi
   Siphonorhis
Caprimulgiformes Neognathae
Caprinae Bovidae
Caprini [Caprinae] Bovidae Reed, C. A.
      and Schaffer 1966
Caproberycinae Holocentridae Patterson,
      C. 1967A
Caproberyx Holocentridae
   pharsus Patterson, C. 1967A
   polydesmus Patterson, C. 1964
   superbus Patterson, C. 1964
Caproidae Zeiformes
   Capros
Caprolagus Leporidae
   sivalensis Gureev 1964 (subgen. sivali-
      lagus)
   veter Gureev 1964 (subgen. Poelagus)
Capromeryx Antilocapridae Hibbard and
      Dalquest 1966
Capromyidae [Myocastoridae] Octodon-
      toidea
Capros Caproidae
   breviventralis Rückert-Ülkümen 1960,
      1965
   longirostris Anđelković 1963
   radobojanus Anđelković 1962

Captorhinidae Captorhinoidea Lewis,
G. E. and Vaughn 1965
Captorhinikos, Captorhinus, Hypop-
nous, Rothia
Captorhinikos Captorhinidae
chozaensis Olson, E. 1962D (osteol.)
Captorhinoidea Captorhinomorpha
Captorhinomorpha Cotylosauria Gregory,
J. T. 1964A, 1965
Captorhinus Captorhinidae Barghusen
1968; Fox, R. C. 1964
aguti Baird and Carroll 1967A; Fox,
R. C. and Bowman 1966
(rest.)
captus (Otospermophilus beecheyi)
Caracara Falconidae
prelutosa Hibbard and Dalquest 1966
caraibaea (Isurus)
Carangidae Percoidea Fierstine 1966
Acanthonemus, Caranx, Zanclus
Caranx Carangidae Fierstine 1968
gracilis Rückert-Ülkümen 1960
haueri Andelković 1963; Rückert-
Ülkümen 1965
longipinnatus Rückert-Ülkümen 1965
Carapidae Ophidiodea
Carapus
Carapus Carapidae See: Otolithus
smithvillensis Frizzell and Dante 1965
carassius (Carassius)
Carassius Cyprinidae
carassius Deckert and Karrer 1965
carbo (Phalocrocorax)
Carbovelidae [Palaeoniscidae] Palaeonis-
coidei Romer 1945D*
Carcharhinidae Catuloidei
Carcharhinus, Galeocerdo, Galeo-
rhinus, Hemipristis, Hypo-
prion, Physodon, Scoliodon
Carcharhinus Carcharhinidae Fitch 1964;
Olsen 1964A
aculeatus Pledge 1967 (subgen.
Prionodon)
collatus Pledge 1967 (cf.)
gracilis Jonet 1965-66A (subgen.
Aprionodon)
lusttanicus Jonet 1965-66A (subgen.
Hypoprion)
macrorhiza Jonet 1965-66A (subgen.
Aprionodon)
malembeensis Henriques da Silva
1961
Carcharias Carchariidae Casier 1966B
(Odontaspis), 1967; Miller,
H. W. 1967

acutissima Ginsburg 1967A (Odontaspis); Henriques da Silva
1961 (Odontaspis); Mene-
sini 1967A; Rückert-
Ülkümen 1960 (Odontaspis);
Weiler 1966A (Odontaspis)
ambadongarensis Verma 1965B (subgen. Prionodon)
aralensis Glikman 1964B (Odontaspis)
baigubeki Glikman 1964B (Odontaspis)
contortidens Pischedda 1954 (Odontaspis); Pledge 1967
cuspidata Ginsburg 1967A (Odontaspis);
Pledge 1967; Rückert-Ülkü-
men 1960 (Odontaspis);
Signeux 1959C (Odontaspis)
dubius Pledge 1967
ensiculatus Pledge 1967
hopei Bosch 1964C (subgen. Synodontaspis; Odontaspis); Casier
1966A (subgen. Synodon-
taspis; Odontaspis)
macrorhiza Albers and Weiler 1964
(Odontaspis)
macrota Bosch 1964C (subgen. Synodontaspis; Odontaspis);
Casier 1966A (subgen. Synodontaspis; Odontaspis);
Signeux 1959B
macrotus Pledge 1967
maslinensis Pledge 1967
praecrassidens Glikman 1964B (Odontaspis)
robusta Casier 1966A (subgen. Synodontaspis; Odontaspis)
rutoti Pledge 1967
secundus Bosch 1964C (subgen. Physodon)
tamdensis Glikman 1964B (Odontaspis)
taurus Applegate 1965B
trigonalis Casier 1966A (subgen.
Synodontaspis; Odontaspis)
whitei
gigas Glikman 1964B (Odontaspis)
carcharias (Carcharodon)
Carchariidae Isuroidei
Araloselachus, Carcharias, Cretaspis,
?Jaekelotodus,
Scapanorhynchus
Carchariolamna Isuridae
heroni Pledge 1967
Carcharodon Isuridae Avnimelech 1962C
(Israel); Bauza Rullan 1966B
angustidens Rückert-Ülkümen 1960

auriculatus Pledge 1967; Signeux
    1959C
carcharias Fitch 1964; Pledge 1967
egertoni Ray, C. E. 1964C
megalodon Ginsburg 1967A; Hen-
    riques da Silva 1961; Mene-
    sini 1967A; Pischedda
    1954; Pledge 1967; Ray,
    C. E. 1964C
Carcharoides Isuridae
totuserratus Pledge 1967 (cf.)
Cardiatheriinae Hydrochoeridae Pascual
    and Bondesio 1968
Cardiatherium Hydrochoeridae
dubium Pascual and Bondesio
    1968(?)
    talicei Francis, J. C. and Mones
    1965A
Cardipeltida Cardipeltiformes
Cardipeltidae Cardipeltida
    Cardipeltis
Cardipeltiformes Pteraspidomorpha
Cardipeltis Cardipeltidae Stensiö 1964
    bryanti Denison 1966B
    richardsoni Denison 1966B
    wallacii Denison 1966B
Carettochelyidae Carettochelyoidea
    Anosteira, Leptochelys
    Allaeochelyinae
Carettochelyoidea Cryptodira
careyi (Shastasaurus)
carezi (Spaniella)
Cariamae Gruiformes Dement'ev 1964
    (order)
Cariamidae Cariamae
    Prophorhacinae
carinatus (Leiocephalus, Massospondylus)
carinidens (Periptychus)
carnifex (Thylacoleo)
Carnivora Ferae Bonifay, M.-F. 1966D;
    Stains 1967
Carnivoripedae Mammalipedia Panin and
    Avram 1962
    Canipeda, Felipeda
    Canipedinae, Felipedinae
Carnivoripedida Mammalipedia Vialov
    1966 (order)
Carnosauria Theropoda Charig, Attridge
    and Crompton 1965; Col-
    bert 1964B; Tatarinov,
    L. P. 1964AA (Deinodont-
    oidea); Walker, A. D. 1964
    (classif.)
Carodnia Carodniidae
    feruglioi Simpson, G. G. 1967A

Carodniidae Xenungulata
    Carodnia
carolina (Terrapene)
carolinae (Protoryx)
carolinense (Eremotherium)
carolinensis (Anolis, Gastrophryne,
    Rutiodon)
caroliniensis (Mosasaurus)
Caroloameghinia Caroloameghiniidae
    mater Simpson, G. G. 1964C, 1967A
Caroloameghiniidae Didelphoidea
    Caroloameghinia
Carolodarwinia Notoungulata incertae
    sedis
    pyramidentata Simpson, G. G. 1967A
Carolozittelia ?Pyrotheria incertae sedis
    eluta Simpson, G. G. 1967A (nomen
    dubium)
    tapiroides Simpson, G. G. 1967A
carpathicus (Pseudotheridomys)
carpio (Carpiodes)
Carpiodes Catostomidae
    carpio Lundberg 1967
Carpolestes Carpolestidae
    cygneus Russell, L. S. 1967A
Carpolestidae Anaptomorphoidea
    Crusafont Pairó 1967B
    Carpolestes, Saxonella
    Carpolestinae, Saxonellinae
Carpolestinae Carpolestidae Russell, D. E.
    1964 (Carpolestidés)
carri (Chrysemys)
carteri (Drepanaspis, Leithia)
cartieri (Chasmotherium, Protadelomys)
caruntorum (Megaloceros)
casei (Ctenospondylus)
Caseidae Edaphosauria Langston 1965A;
    Olson, E. 1968B
    Angelosaurus, Cotylorhynchus, Enna-
    tosaurus
casieri (Nycticonodon)
casimbae (Megalocnus rodens)
caspia (Clupea)
caspius (Echinorhinus)
castanops (Cratogeomys)
castellanosi (Ischyrodidelphis)
Castor Castoridae Topachevskiĭ 1965C
    canadensis Semken 1966
    fiber Bakalov and Nikolov 1964;
        Burchak-Abramovich, N. and
        Gadzhiev 1962; David, A.
        and Markevich 1967; Erd-
        brink 1964; Fejfar 1964A;
        Garevski 1964; Guenther
        1965; Malez 1963D; Melentis

cephalica (Eubaena)
Cephalogale Canidae
    cadurcensis Beaumont 1965C
    depereti Beaumont 1965C
    geoffroyi Beaumont 1965C (cf.)
    gracile Beaumont 1965C
    minor Beaumont 1965C
    meschethense Gabuniiā 1964D, 1966A
Céphaloxéniformes Actinopterygii Lehman
        1966B
cephalus (Eschrichtius)
Ceratodidae Ceratodiformes Lehman
        1966C
Ceratodiformes Dipnoi Lehman 1966C
        (with Ceratodidae)
Ceratodonti Dipnoi
Ceratodontida [Ceratodontiformes]
        Ceratodonti Andrews, S. M.
        Gardiner, Miles, and Patter-
        son 1967
Ceratodontidae Ceratodontiformes
    Asiatoceratodus, Ceratodus
Ceratodontiformes Ceratodonti
Ceratodus Ceratodontidae Gottfried
        1964; Jain 1968
    africanus Tabaste 1963
    donensis Vorob'eva and Minikh 1968
        donensis Vorob'eva and Minikh
        1968
        gracilis Vorob'eva and Minikh
        1968
    humei Tabaste 1963
    multicristatus Vorob'eva and Minikh
        1968
    parvus Dreyer 1962 (cf.)
    pectinatus Tabaste 1963
    protopteroides Tabaste 1963
    recticristatus Vorob'eva and Minikh
        1968
    tiguidiensis Tabaste 1963
    tuberculatus Tabaste 1963
Ceratomorpha Perissodactyla
    Incertae sedis: Toxotherium
Ceratopidae Ceratopsia
    Triceratops
ceratops (Purgatorius)
Ceratopsia Ornithischia Ostrom 1966A, C
Ceratosauridae Carnosauria Maleev 1964L
Ceraunosaurus Polycotylidae Thurmond
        1968
    brownorum Thurmond 1968
Cercomys Echimyidae
    primitiva Pascual 1967
Cercopithecidae Ceropithecoidea Chiarelli
        1968A; Kuhn, H. J. 1967

Adelopithecus, Cercopithecoides,
    Colobus, Dolichopithecus,
    Macaca, Mesopithecus,
    Moeripithecus, Papio, Para-
    papio
Cercopithecinae, Colobinae, Hylo-
    bathinae, Papinae
Cercopithecinae Cercopithecidae Chiarelli
    1968A
Cercopithecoidea Anthropoidei Hill, W.
    C. O. 1966
Cercopithecoides Cercopithecidae
    williamsi Freedman 1965
cernua (Acerina)
Cerorhinca Alcidae Howard, H. 1968A
Cerritosaurus ?Rhadinosuchidae Kuhn,
        Oskar 1966A, p. 73; Walker,
        A. D. 1968
Cervalces Cervidae Parmalee and Clark
        1967A; Ray, C. E., Cooper,
        et al. 1967

Cervavitus Cervidae
    bessarabiensis Lungu 1967A
Cervidae Cervoidea Bouchud 1966E;
        Frechkop 1965B; Heintz, E.
        1966B, 1967B
    Alces, Allocaenelaphus, Arvernoceros,
        Axis, Blastomeryx, Capreolus,
        Cervalces, Cervavitus, Cervus,
        Croizetoceros, Dama, Dicro-
        cerus, Dolichodoryceros,
        Dremotherium, Dromomeryx,
        Elaphurus, Eostyloceros,
        Epieuryceros, Eucladoceros,
        Euctenoceros, Heteroprox,
        Iberomeryx, Libralces, Long-
        irostromeryx, Machaeromeryx,
        Megaceros, Megaloceros, Mun-
        tiacus, Nesoleipoceros, Odocoi-
        leus, Orthogonoceros, Para-
        blastomeryx, Pliocervus,
        Praedama, Praemegaceros,
        Procapreolus, Procervulus,
        Psekupsoceros, Pseudaxis,
        Rakomeryx, Rangifer, Stephan-
        ocemas, Strongyloceros
    Cervinae, Odocoileinae
Cervinae Cervidae Heintz, E. 1968
cervinum (Dichodon)
Cervipeda Pecoripeda Vialov 1966
Cervoidea Pecora
cervulum (Lophiotherium)
Cervus Cervidae Alekperova 1964 (subgen.
        Rusa), 1966 (Caucasus);
        Avakiān 1959; Feru, et al.

Chameleontidae Iguania
  Tinosaurus
chamense (Meniscotherium)
Chamops Teiidae
  segnis Estes 1964
Champsodelphis Acrodelphidae
  fuchsii Mchedlidze 1964C (cf.)
  letechae Mchedlidze 1964C (cf.)
Champsosauridae Choristodera
  Champsosaurus
Champsosaurus Champsosauridae Estes
  1964
changhsingensis (Helicampodus, Sino-
  helicoprion)
changi (Galeaspis)
Changisaurus ?Thalassemyididae Baird
  1964C; Kuhn, Oskar 1966A
  ("Kein Lacertilier")
  microrhinus Baird 1964C (not a
  lizard)
Chanidae Chanoidei
  Parachanos
Chanoidei Clupeiformes
chapadmalensis (Argyrohyus)
chapalmalensis (Eumysops)
Characidae Cyprinoidei
  Triportheus
Characoidei [Cyprinoidei] Cypriniformes
Charactosuchus Crocodylidae Langston
  1965B
  fieldsi Langston 1965B
Charadrii Charadriiformes
Charadriidae Charadrioidea
  Squatarola, Tringa
Charadriiformes Neognathae
Charadriipeda Charadriipedae Panin and
  Avram 1962
  becassi Panin and Avram 1962
  disjuncta Panin and Avram 1962
  minima Panin and Avram 1962
  recurvirostrioidea Panin and Avram
  1962
Charadriipedae Avipedia Panin and
  Avram 1962
  Charadriipeda
Charadrioidea Charadrii
Charadrius Scolopacidae
  morinellus Burchak-Abramovich,
  N. I. 1966E (cf.)
Charangidae Percoidea
  Teratichthys
chardini (Postschizotherium)
Charitosomus Gonorhynchidae
  hakelensis Le Danois, Y. 1966
  lineolatus Le Danois, Y. 1966

Chasichimys Echimyidae Pascual 1967
  (in Heteropsomyinae)
  bonaerense Pascual 1967
chasicoense (Procardiatherium)
chasicoensis (Hemixotodon)
Chasicomys Octodontidae Pascual 1967
  (in Octodontinae)
  octodontiforme Pascual 1967
Chasmatosauridae Proterosuchia
  Chasmatosaurus
Chasmatosaurus Chasmatosauridae Satsangi
  1964
  alexanderi Hoffman 1965
  ultimus Young, C.-c. 1964A
  yuani Young, C.-c. 1964A
Chasmistes Catostomidae
  spatulifer Miller, R. R. and Smith 1967
Chasmotheriinae Helaletidae Radinsky
  1967A
Chasmotherium Helaletidae Fischer, K.
  1967; Radinsky 1967A
  cartieri Fischer, K. 1964
  hoeledense Gabounia 1967 (=Tongri-
  ceros hoeledenensis)
  minimum Fischer, K. 1964
Chauliodontidae Stomiatoidei
  Chauliodus
Chauliodus Chauliodontidae
  eximius Crane, J. M. 1966
Chaetodontidae Percoidei
  Pomacanthus
chantrei (Plesiodimylus)
chasseae (Alluvisorex)
cheganicus (Galeocerdo)
Cheiracanthidae Acanthodiformes Miles,
  R. S. 1966A
  Cheiracanthus, Protogonacanthus
Cheiracanthus Cheiracanthidae
  latus Miles, R. S. 1966A
Cheirodidae [Amphicentridae] · Palaeoni-
  scoidei Moy-Thomas 1939B*
  (in Platysomida)
Cheirolepididae Palaeoniscoidei
  Cheirolepis
Cheirolepis Cheirolepididae Dineley 1967B
  (rest.)
  trailli Wenz 1967A
Cheirostephanus Squalidae
  hurzeleri Casier 1966B
Chelichnoidae Therapsida See: Ichnites
  Haubold 1966B
  Chelichnus
Chelichnus Chelichnoidae
  geinitzi Haubold 1966B (reconst.)
chelkaris (Woodromys)

Laemmelen 1960; Lammers
1964 (Trias., Utah); Lap-
parent 1966; Martin, G.
P. R. 1966A
barthii Jux and Pflug 1958*; Krämer
and Kunz 1964, 1966
harrasense Haubold 1966A
praeparvum Haubold 1966A
sickleri Haubold 1966A
soergeli Haubold 1966A
chirotheroides (Shimmelia)
chitaiensis (Tienshanosaurus)
chiyuanensis (Sianodon)
Chlamytherium Dasypodidae
septentrionale Hibbard and Dalquest
1966
chlorocyanus (Anolis)
Chodsigoa Soricidae
bohlini Repenning 1967C
kastschenko Repenning 1967C
Choerolophodon Gomphotheriidae
pentelici Burchak-Abramovich, M.
and Korotkevich 1966
Choerolophodon Trilophodon
Choeropotamidae Dichobunoidea
Helohyus
Cholophidia [Palaeophididae] Serpentes
Chudinov 1964H
Chondrenchelyidae ?Bradyodonti incertae
sedis
Chondrenchelys, Eucentrurus
Chondrenchelyiformes [Chondrenchelyi-
dae] ?Bradyodonti incertae
sedis Patterson, C. 1965B
Chondrenchelys Chondrenchelyidae
problematica Patterson, C. 1965B
(reconst.)
Chondrichthyes [Elasmobranchii] Pisces
Obruchev, D. V. 1962C
Chondrostei Actinopterygi Gardiner
1967A (classification),
1967B; Obruchev, D. V.
and Kazantseva 1964A
Chondrosteiformes Actinopterygii Lehman
1966B
Chordata Animalia Carter, G. S. 1957C
(phylogeny); Dechaseaux
1964C, D, E; Obruchev,
D. V. 1964B
Choristodera Rhynchocephalia Kuhn,
Oskar 1966A (order of
Lepidosauria incl. Champ-
sosauridae and Pachystro-
pheidae); Maleev 1964B
chosaricus (Equus, Mammuthus trogontherii

chozaensis (Captorhinikos)
Chroniosuchidae Seymouriamorpha Tatarinov, L. P. 1964I
Chroniosuchus
Chroniosuchus Chroniosuchidae
mirabilis Tverdokhlebova 1967 (cf.)
chrysaëtus (Aquila)
Chrysemys Chelydridae Skinner, M. F.,
Skinner and Gooris 1968;
Weaver and Rose 1967;
Wilson, R. L. 1968 (cf.)
carri Rose and Weaver 1967
inflata Weaver 1967
platymarginata Weaver 1967
scripta
petrolei Weaver 1967
williamsi Rose and Weaver 1967
Chrysochloroidea Lipotyphla
Incertae sedis: ?Pseudochrysochloris
Chrysophrys Sparidae
aurata Menesini 1967A
brusinai Ionko 1954; Rückert-Ülkümen
1965
cincta Pischedda 1954
intermedia Rückert-Ülkümen 1965
Chthomaloporus Brithopodidae Chudinov
1964J
lenocinator Chudinov 1964J
chucuae (Schizotherium)
Chumashius Omomyidae Robinson, Peter
1968B (?)
chungkingensis (Plesiochelys)
chunyii (Eoalligator)
Ciconia Ciconiidae
maltha Feduccia 1967B (Plioc., Idaho);
Phillips, A. R. 1968
Ciconiae Ciconiiformes
Ciconiidae Ciconiae Dekeyser 1962B
Ciconia, Dissourodes
Ciconiiformes Neognathae
Cimexomys Ectypodidae Sloan and Van
Valen 1965
minor Sloan and Van Valen 1965
Cimolestes Palaeoryctidae Clemens, Mc-
Kenna, et al. 1964
incisus Clemens and Russell 1965;
Van Valen 1966A
magnus Clemens and Russell 1965
Cimolestidae [Palaeoryctidae] Creodonta
Clemens, McKenna, et al.
1964
Cimolichthys Enchodontidae Albers and
Weiler 1964
nepaholica Bardack 1968A
Cimolomyidae Taeniolaboidea
Meniscoessus

Cladoselachii Elasmobranchii
Cladosictis Borhyaenidae
    lustratus Patterson, B. 1965A
Claenodon Arctocyonidae Russell, L. S.
        1967A
    procyonoides Maxwell, R. A., et al.
        1967 (cf.); Wilson, J. A.
        1967 (cf.)
"Claenodon" ?Notoungulata incertae
        sedis
    patagonicus Simpson, G. G. 1967A
claibornensis (Eosolea)
Claibornichthys ?Bagridae See: Otolithus
        Frizzell and Dante 1965
    troelli Frizzell and Dante 1965
clanga (Aquila)
clappi (Thursius)
Clarazisauria Rhynchocephalia
clarki (Pseudacris, Rhynchocyon)
Clarkeosteus Coccosteidae Obruchev, D.
        V. 1964D
    halmodeus Miles, R. S. 1966B
classon (Aechmophorus)
claypolei (Americaspis)
Cleidogonia ?Berycoidei incertae sedis
        See: Otolithus Stinton and
        Torrens 1968
    antiqua Stinton and Torrens 1968
Clemensia Didelphidae Slaughter 1968B
    texana Slaughter 1968B
Clemmydopsinae Sakyidae Chkhikvadze
        1968
Clemmydopsis Testudinidae Chkhikvadze
        1968 (in Sakyidae)
    sopronensis Khozatskii and Mlynarski
        1966
Clemmys Testudinidae Gabuniia 1964D;
        McDowell 1964
    insculpta Richmond 1964
    rotundiformis Bergounioux and
        Crouzel 1965B
    schansiensis Yeh 1963B
Clethrionomys Clethrionomys Topachev-
        skii 1965C
Clethrionomys Cricetidae Oesch 1967
    glareolus Feustel, et al. 1963; Jacobs-
        hagen 1963; Malez 1963D
    iorensis Buachidze 1968
    sokolovi Topachevskii 1965C (sub-
        gen. Acrorhizamys)
Clidastes Mosasauridae
    congrops Russell, D. A. 1967A
        (nomen vanum)
    iguanavus Russell, D. A. 1967A
    liodontus Russell, D. A. 1967A
    propython Russell, D. A. 1967A

    sternbergi Russell, D. A. 1967A
clidastoides (Ectenosaurus)
clifti (Stegodon)
Climatiidae Climatiiformes Miles, R. S.
        1966A (in Climatioidei)
    Asiacanthus, Erriwacanthus, Nostolepis,
        Sincanthus
Climatiiformes Acanthodii
Climatioidei Climatiiformes Miles, R. S.
        1966A
clinderi (Cetotherium)
Clupavus Clupeidae
    neocomiensis Jonet 1964B
Clupea Clupeidae Śmigielska 1959*
    arcuata Rückert-Ülkümen 1965
    bonsniaskii Rückert-Ülkümen 1965
    breviceps Rückert-Ülkümen 1960
    caspia Vakhrushev 1960A (cf.)
    doljeana Andelković 1962 (subgen.
        Meletta), 1964; Rückert-
        Ülkümen 1960
    gorjensis Andelković 1964; Huică and
        Gheorghiu 1962*
    gregaria Rückert-Ülkümen 1965
    heterocerca Andelković 1964
    humilis Ionko 1954; Rückert-Ülkümen
        1960, 1965
    lanceolata Rückert-Ülkümen 1965
    maceki Andelković 1964
    melettaeformis Andelković 1962, 1964;
        Rückert-Ülkümen 1965
    sardinites Andelković 1964
    spinosa Rückert-Ülkümen 1965
    tenuissima Rückert-Ülkümen 1965
    trinacridis Rückert-Ülkümen 1965
    voinovi
        sarmatica Andelković 1962, 1964
    vukotinovici Andelković 1964
Clupeida Teleostei Danil'chenko 1964B
        (order)
Clupeidae Clupeoidea
    Alosa, Clupavus, Clupea, Diplomystus,
        Gasteroclupea, Jhingrania,
        Knightia, Meletta, Paraclupea,
        Sardinella
    Gasteroclupeinae
Clupeiformes Isospondyli Lehman 1966B
        (primitive Téléostéens; with
        suborders Lycopteroidei and
        Leptolepioidei)
Clupeoidea Clupeoidei Gosline 1965
Clupeoidei Clupeiformes
Clupeomorpha [Clupeiformes] Isospondyli
        Andrews, S. M., Gardiner,
        Miles and Patterson 1967
        (superorder of Teleostei)

Coelorhynchus Macrouridae See: Otolithus
toulai Weiler 1962G
Coeluridae Coelurosauria Colbert 1964B;
Maleev 1964I
Elaphrosaurus, Paronychodon, Saurornithoides
Coelurosauria Theropoda Charig, Attridge and Crompton 1965;
Colbert 1964B; Tatarinov,
L. P. 1964Z (Coeluroidea)
Coelurosauroidea Coelurosauria
Coendou Erethizontidae Gupta, B. B.
1966
stirtoni White, J. A. 1968
coerulescens (Aphelocoma)
cognathus (Bufo)
colhuehuapiensis (Isotemnus)
colei (Eocoelopoma)
Colhuapia ?Isotemnidae incertae sedis
rosei Simpson, G. G. 1967A (nomen
dubium)
Colhuelia ?Isotemnidae incertae sedis
fruhi Simpson, G. G. 1967A (nomen
dubium)
collatum (Cricetodon)
collatus (Carcharhinus)
collispannoni (Procapra)
collongensis (Hipposideros, Megacricetodon
minor)
Colobinae Cercopithecidae Chiarelli
1968A; Fejfar 1964A
Colobodus Perleididae
frequens Stefanov 1966
maximus Dreyer 1962; Stefanov 1966
Colobotis Citellus Kretzoi 1965C
Colobus Cercopithecidae
polykomos
abyssinicus Simons, E. L. 1967G
Colodon Helaletidae Gabuniia 1964D
grangeri Radinsky 1965A
hodosimai Radinsky 1965A
inceptus Radinsky 1965A
orientalis Radinsky 1965A
Coloeus Corvidae
monedula Jánossy 1965E; Mourer-
Chauviré 1964
colombianus (Gavialis)
coloradensis (Pseudotomus)
Colosteoidea Temnospondyli Tatarinov,
L. P., 1964C, p. 67
Colpodontosaurus Diploglossa incertae
sedis Estes 1964 (Cret.,
Wyo.)
cracens Estes 1964

Coltonia Recurvirostridae Hardy 1959*
recurvirostra Hardy 1959*
Coluber Colubridae
plioagellus Wilson, R. L. 1968 (?)
robertmertensi Młynarski 1964A
viridiflavus Młynarski 1964A (cf.)
Colubridae Colubroidea Holman 1966C;
Inger and Marx 1965
Acrochordus, Cemophora, Coluber,
Elaphe, Heterodon, Lampro-
peltis, Leimadophis, Natrix,
Paleoheterodon, Pituophis,
Thamnophis, Tropidoclonion
Colubroidea Serpentes Hoffstetter 1955G*
p. 649; 1964 p. 967 (Caeno-
phidia substituted for Colu-
broidea)
Columba Columbidae Mourer-Chauviré
1964
leucocephala Bernstein 1965
squamosa Bernstein 1965
Columbae Columbiformes Dement'ev 1964
(ord.)
columbianus (Neurotrichus)
Columbidae Columbae
Columba, Columbigallina,
Zenaidura
Columbiformes Neognathae
Columbigallina Columbidae
passerina Bernstein 1965
Columbomyinae Theridomyidae Thaler
1966B
Columbomys Theridomyidae
lavocati Thaler 1966B
Colymbiformes Neognathae
combesi (Mesodon)
comes (Synocnus)
Commentrya Palaeoniscidae
traquairi Blot 1966B
Commentryidae Palaeoniscoidei Gardiner
1963*
commune (Anoplotherium)
communis (Phocaena)
complanatus (Pleurostylodon, Pycnodus)
complicata (Irregulareaspis)
complicatissimus (Acoelohyrax)
complicatus (Microdyromys, Rohonosteus)
complicidens (Lagomeryx, Ochotonoides)
complicidents (Marmota)
Compressidens Mosasauridae Russell, D. A.
1967A
compressus (Antesorex, Elliptonodon,
Paraisurus, Platygonus, Trimylus)
Compsemys Dermatemydidae
victa Estes 1964

intermedia Frizzell and Dante 1965
pseudoradians Frizzell and Dante
1965
Corvus Corvidae
corone-cornix Jánossy 1965C
frugilegus
furgilegus Erdbrink 1964
coryphaenoides (Leptolepis)
Coryphaenoididae Gadoidei
Archemacruroides,
Latirhynchus
coryphaeus (Platecarpus)
Coryphodon Coryphodontidae Guthrie,
D. A. 1967B; Maxwell,
R. A., et al. 1967; Robin-
son, Peter 1966A; Wilson,
J. A. 1967
ninchiashanensis Chow, M.-c., and
Tung 1965
Coryphodontidae Pantodonta
Coryphodon, Eudonoceras
Coryphomys Muridae
bühleri Hooijer 1965B
Cosmacanthus Gyracanthidae
humboldtensis LaRivers 1962
Cosmoslepididae Palaeonisciformes
Gardiner 1967A
Cosmolepis
Cosmolepis Cosmolepididae Gardiner
1967A
Cosomys Mimomys Thaler 1966B
costatus (Thelodus)
costilloi (Leptotomus)
Cothurnocystidae Cornuta
Cothurnocystis
Cothurnocystis Cothurnocystidae
curvata Jefferies 1968
elizae Jefferies 1968
Cotimus Cricetidae Freudenthal 1965
bifidus Fahlbusch, V. 1964; Kowalski, K. 1967A
leemanni Hartenberger 1966A
medius Fahlbusch, V. 1964
cotteri (Pondaungia)
Cottoidei Perciformes
coturnix (Coturnix)
Coturnix Phasianidae
coturnix Burchak-Abramovich, N.
1966D; Jánossy 1965C (cf.)
miocenica Villalta 1963
cotylalveus (Aetiocetus)
Cotylorhynchus Caseidae
bransoni Olson, E. 1965D
romeri Stovall, Price and Romer
1966

Cotylosauria Anapsida Chudinov 1964A
Incertae sedis: Tseajaiidae
couchi (Scaphiopus)
couperi (Mosasaurus)
coutoi (Eobrasilia)
covensis (Pseudogenetochoerus)
covurluiensis (Zamolxifiber)
cracens (Colpodontosaurus)
Cracidae Galliformes Vuilleumier 1965
Ludiortyx, Ortalis, Palaeortyx, Para-
crax, Pirortyx
Gallinuloidinae, Filholornithinae
Cragievarus Diademodontidae Brink
1965A
kitchingi Brink 1965A
cragini (Ictidomys)
Craniata Chordata
Craspedochelys Plesiochelyidae
picteti Bräm 1965 (restor.)
craspedotum (Hyracotherium)
crassa (Alosa)
crassartus (Prognathodon)
crassicornis (Bison)
crassicostata (Eochelys)
crassicostatus (Stenopterygius)
crassidens (Balistes, Boii, Cynelos, Enhydrocyon, Isurus, Mosa-
saurus, Plesiotylosaurus,
Scombramphodon)
Crassigyrinidae [Anthracosauridae]
Anthracosauria Huene
1948A*
crassiramis (Pleurostylodon)
crassirostris (Smerdis)
crassum (Dorcatherium, Hipparium,
Palaeotherium)
crassus (Myliobatis)
Cratogeomys Geomyidae
cf. castanops Alvarez 1966 (Mex.)
crecca (Anas)
crenatidens (Homotherium)
Crenilabrus Labridae Ionko 1954
crenulata (Fadenia, Pholidophoroides)
Crenosteus Drepanaspididae Tarlo 1964C
levis Tarlo 1964C, 1965
crenulatum (Lonchidion breve)
Creodonta Ferae
Incertae sedis: Apternodus
Creotarsinae Adapisoricidae Van Valen
1967B
crepaturae (Saxonella)
crepitans (Acris)
Cressores [Ardeiformes] Neognathes
Dement'ev 1964
Cretaspis Carchariidae Sokolov, M. I. 1965

Cricetus Cricetidae
  angustidens Hugueney and Mein 1966;
    Mein 1967; Thaler 1966B
  cricetus David, A. and Markevich 1967;
    Kowalski, K. 1967B; Kret-
    zoi 1965C; Malez 1963D
  major Topachevskii 1965C (aff.)
  palaeoasovicus Topachevskii 1965C
cricetus (Cricetus)
Cricotidae Embolomeri
  Calligenthlon
Criorhynchidae Dsungaripteroidea Kuhn,
    O. 1967A
  Criorhynchus
Criorhynchus Criorhynchidae Kuhn, O.
    1967A
crispus (Elomeryx)
cristata (Deperetella, Hystrix)
cristatus (Fenhosuchus, Wetherellus)
cristifera (Gila)
croaticus (Auxis)
Crocidosorex Soricidae
  antiquus Repenning 1967C
  piveteaui Repenning 1967C
Crocidura Soricidae Repenning 1967C
  pavlodarica Stogov and Savinov 1965
Crocidurinae Soricidae Hutchison 1966A;
    Repenning 1967C
Crocodilia Archosauria Auffenberg 1967D
    (Fla.); Berg, D. E. 1964
    (distrib.); Konzhukova 1964C;
    Sill 1968 (classif.)
crocodolinus (Orycterocetus)
Crocodylidae Eosuchia Iordanskiĭ 1967
  Alligator, Allognathosuchus, Asiato-
    suchus, Balanerodus, Brachy-
    champsa, Brachygnathosuchus,
    Caiman, Charactosuchus,
    Crocodilus, Dinosuchus, Dip-
    locynodon, Eoalligator,
    Eocaiman, Eotomistoma,
    Hassiacosuchus, Leidyo-
    suchus, Mourasuchus,
    Notocaiman, Pristochampsus,
    Proalligator, Procaimanoidea,
    Purussaurus, Rhamphostom-
    opsis, Sebecus, Thoraco-
    saurus, Tomistoma, Weigel-
    tisuchus, Xenosuchus
  Alligatorinae, Crocodylinae, Gavialinae,
    Tomistominae
Crocodylus Crocodylidae Langston 1965B
    (Crocodilus); Signeux 1959A;
    Woodburne 1967B
  ebertsi Langston 1965B

paranensis Langston 1965B (nomen
    vanum)
  rugosus Miller, H. W. 1967
crocuta (Crocuta, Hyaena)
Crocuta Hyaenidae Vekua 1958B
  crocuta Hooijer 1961C; Melentis 1964C
    crocuta Kurtén 1965A
    debilis Kurtén 1965A
    dorotheae Kurtén 1965A
    sinensis Bouchud 1968A
    spelaea Jacobshagen 1963; Vere-
      schagin 1951C
  miriani Meladze 1967
  perrieri Fejfar 1964A (subgen. Plesio-
      crocuta)
  spelaea Alekseeva, L. I. and Lomize
      1960; Malez 1963D; Mostecký
      1964; Rakovec 1965B; Svistun
      1968; Terzea 1964
Croizetoceros Cervidae Heintz, E. 1968
  ramosus
    medius Heintz, E. 1968
    minor Heintz, E. 1968
    ramosus Heintz, E. 1968
Cro-Magnon [Homo sapiens] Hominidae
    Bader, O. N. 1965E, 1966B
    (burial, USSR); Baker, J. R.
    1968A; Dastugue 1967;
    Debets 1961B (Kostenki);
    Kochetkova 1964; Vallois
    and Billy 1965
cromis (Pogonias)
Crossopterygii [Sarcopterygii] Teleostoma
    Lehman 1966C (with Actin-
    ista and Rhipidistia); MacAl-
    lister 1969; Piveteau 1966B;
    Thomson, K. S. 1967A
Crotalidae [Crotalinae] Viperidae Bratstrom
    1964B
Crotalinae Viperidae
Crotalus Viperidae Richmond 1964
  horridus Holman 1965D
crouchi (Pteraspis)
crowcrofti (Rhizophascolonus)
Crucians (Haplocyon)
cruciferus (Acipenser)
cruciformis (Logania)
crusafonti (Adelomys, Ilerdaesaurus,
    Leptolepis, Megacricetodon,
    Megacricetodon crusafonti,
    Muscardinus, Pairomys,
    Praearmantomys)
Cryphiolepididae [Palaeoniscidae] Palaeo-
    niscoidei Moy-Thomas 1939B*
    (Cryphiolepidae)

1962E, 1963D, 1965J
curtum (Palaeotherium)
curtus (Eucastor, Gregorymys, Pachycormus)
curvata (Cothurnocystis)
curvatum (Eocoelopoma)
curvicuspidens (Protoadapis)
curvidens (Desmotochoerus, Megalonyx, Metasayimys)
curvirostris (Phascolonus, Smerdis)
curvistriatus (Taeniodus)
cusanus (Cervus, Procapreolus)
cuspidata (Carcharias, Eudaemonema)
cuspidatus (Coccosteus)
cutlerensis (Lasalia, Limnopus)
Cutleria Sphenacodontidae Lewis, G. E. and Vaughn 1965
    wilmarthi Lewis, G. E., and Vaughn 1965
Cuttysarkus ?Sauria incertae sedis Estes 1964 (Cret., Wyo.)
    mcnallyi Estes 1964
cuvieri (Deinotherium, Lophiodon, Marmoops blainvillii, Peratherium, Pseudoltinomys, Trogontherium)
Cuvieronius Gomphotheriidae Hibbard and Dalquest 1966
Cyamodus Placochelyidae
    rostratus Kuhn-Schnyder 1965B
cyanellus (Lepomis)
Cyathaspida Cyathaspidiformes
Cyathaspididae Cyathaspida Denison 1964B (revision)
    Allocryptaspis, Americaspis, Anglaspis, Archegonaspis, Ariaspis, Ctenaspis, Cyathaspis, Dikenaspis, Dinaspidella, Eoarchegonaspis, Homalaspidella, Irregulareaspis, Kiangsuaspis, Listraspis, Pionaspis, Poraspis, Ptomaspis, Sanidaspis, Seretaspis, Steinaspis, Tolypelepis, Vernonaspis
    Ctenaspidinae, Cyathaspidinae, Irregulareaspidinae, Poraspidinae, Tolypelepidinae
Cyathaspidinae Cyathaspididae Denison 1964B
Cyathaspidiformes Pteraspidomorpha
Cyathaspis Cyathaspididae
    acadia Denison 1964B
    banksi Denison 1964B
    miroshnikovi Denison 1964B

Cybiidae Scombroidea
    Cybium
Cybium Cybiidae
    proosti Casier 1966A (cf.)
    serralheiroi Jonet 1966B
cybotes (Anolis)
Cyclemys Testudinidae
    akiyoshiensis Shikama and Okafuji 1964
Cyclopidius Merycoidodontidae
    emydinus Schultz, C. B. and Falkenbach 1968
    simus Schultz, C. B. and Falkenbach 1968
Cyclostomata Agnatha Jarvik 1965B
Cyclotosauridae Capitosauroidea Shishkin, M. A. 1964
Cyclotosaurinae Capitosauridae Ochev 1966C
Cyclotosaurus Capitosauridae
    ebrachensis Welles and Cosgriff 1965B
    hemprichi Welles and Cosgriff 1965B
    mechernichensis Jux and Pflug 1958*
    mordax Welles and Cosgriff 1965B
    posthumus Welles and Cosgriff 1965B
    robustus Welles and Cosgriff 1965B
    stantonensis Welles and Cosgriff 1965B
Cyclura Iguanidae Etheridge 1966A
Cygnavus Anatidae Kurochkin 1968A
    formosus Kurochkin 1968A
cygneus (Carpolestes)
Cygnopterus Anatidae Kurochkin 1968A
    lambrechti Kurochkin 1968A
Cygnus Anatidae Jánossy 1965C
Cylindracanthus Blochiidae Fallow 1964
    rectus Casier 1966A, 1967; Signeux 1959C
cylindrica (Poraspis)
Cylindrodon Cylindrodontidae
    fontis Black, C. C. 1965A ·
Cylindrodontidae Ischyromyoidea
    Ardynomys, Cylindrodon, Pareumys, Pseudocylindrodon
Cymatorhiza Gymnarthridae
    kittsi Olson, E. 1965D (?)
Cymatosauridae Pistosauroidea Novozhilov 1964B
Cynariognathus Pristerognathidae Boonstra 1964
    platyrhinus Cys 1967C
Cynariopidae Gorgonopsia Watson and Romer 1956* (Cynariopsidae)
    Cynariopinae
Cynariopinae Cynariopidae Viushkov 1964C, p. 262 (Cynariopsinae,

granulatus Wenz 1967B
magnevillei Wenz 1967B
milloti Wenz 1967B
pholidotus Wenz 1967B
politus Wenz 1967B
punctatus Aldinger 1965; Wenz
        1967B; Wiedenroth 1962
Daphoenocyon Canidae
    dodgei Clark, J. and Beerbower
        1967
Daphoenus Canidae Clark, J. and
        Beerbower 1967
dares (Taphrosphys)
dartevellei (Palaeochoerus)
dartevelli (Diplomystus)
Dartmuthia Dartmuthiidae Gross, W.
        1968C
Dartmuthiidae Tremataspidoidea
    Dartmuthia, Tyriaspis
    Dartmuthiinae
Dartmuthiinae Dartmuthiidae Heintz, A.
        1967B
darwini (Alligator, Diplocynodon, Dryo-
        pithecus fontani)
Dasyatidae Rajiformes
    Dasyatis, Dasybatus, Hypolorhus,
        Myledaphus, Parapalaeo-
        bates, Rhombodus, Trygon
Dasyatis Dasyatidae
    davisi Casier 1966A
Dasybatus Dasyatidae
    akajei Hatai, Murata and Masuda
        1965 (cf.)
Dasypodidae Dasypodoidea
    Chlamytherium, Dasypus, Pampa-
        therium
Dasypodoidea Cingulata
Dasypus Dasypodidae
    bellus Guilday and McCrady 1966;
        Oesch 1967
Dasyuridae Dasyuroidea Plane 1967B
    Dasyurus, Glaucodon, Sarcophilus,
        Thylacinus
Dasyurodon Apterodon Lange, B. 1967
Dasyurodon Mesonychidae Van Valen
        1966A
Dasyuroidea Marsupicarnivora
Dasyurus Dasyuridae
    affinis Mahoney 1964
daubentonii (Myotis)
Daubentoniidae Lemuroidea Crusafont
        Pairó 1967B
daubrei (Platychoerops)
daurica (Ochotona)
dauricus (Citellus)

davidi (Lycoptera, Paracyclotosaurus)
daviesi (Acrogaster, Rhinoptera, Teleo-
        lophus)
davisi (Dasyatis, Eporeodon)
dawkinsi (Megaceros, Praemegaceros)
dawsoni (Aegialodon, Hylerpeton)
Dawsonia ?Trimerorhachidae Chase, J.
        N. 1965
Dawsonomys Ischyromyidae Wood, A. E.
        1965B (in Sciuravidae)
    minor Wood, A. E. 1965B
dayi (Acrogaster, Lissoberyx)
Dayohyus Merycoidodontidae Schultz,
        C. B. and Falkenbach 1968
    trigonocephalus Schultz, C. B. and
        Falkenbach 1968
    wortmani Schultz, C. B. and Falken-
        bach 1968
debequensis (Lophiparamys)
debilis (Crocuta crocuta)
debilitata (Oldfieldthomasia)
debruijni (Megacricetodon)
Decazella Aeduellidae
    vetteri Heyler 1967
decedens (Cricetodon)
dechaseauxi (Circamustela, Hipposideros)
dechemi (Xenacanthus)
decipicus (Coccosteus)
decipiens (Tamesichthys)
deckerti (Latvius)
decora (Leptauchenia)
decorus (Palaeogyrinus, Paramblypterus)
deflexus ("Interhippus")
"Degonia" Notoungulata incertae sedis
    sympathica Simpson, G. G. 1967A
degrooti (Otionohyus wardi)
dehiscus (Gopherus)
dehmi (Acrochordus, Peridyromys, Peri-
        dyromys dehmi, Pseudarctos
        bavaricus, Sorex)
dehneli (Pliosciuropterus, Sorex)
Deinodon Deinodontidae Kuhn, Oskar
        1965A (= ?Gorgosaurus,
        =Albertosaurus)
Deinodontidae Carnosauria Kuhn, Oskar
        1965A (p. 37, taxonomic
        note); Maleev 1964N
        (= Tyrannosauridae)
    Deinodon
Deinotheriidae Deinotherioidea
    Deinotherium
Deinotherioidea Proboscidea
Deinotherium Deinotheriidae Burchak-
        Abramovich and Korotkevich
        1966; Gabashvili and Gabuniia

deningeri (Ursus)
deningeroides (Ursus spelaea)
denisoni (Tesseraspis, Traquairaspis)
densa (Hadroleptauchenia)
densicingulata (Shikamainosorex)
dentalis (Copemys, Peromyscus)
dentata (Ctenaspis, Oniscolepis)
dentatus (Mahavisaurus, Scoliodon)
Dentex Sparidae See: Otolithus Wein-
        furter 1967
Denticipitidae Isospondyli incertae sedis
Denticipitoidei [Denticipitidae] Isospon-
        dyli incertae sedis Andrews,
        S. M., Gardiner, Miles and
        Patterson 1967 (suborder
        of Clupeiformes)
denticulata (Broïla)
denticulatus (Elonichthys, Leptochamops,
        Notorhinus)
de Pauwii (Isocetus)
depereti (Arctamphicyon, Cephalogale,
        Steneofiber)
depereita (Gazella)
Deperetella Deperetellidae
    biramicum Radinsky 1965A
    cristata Radinsky 1965A
    depereti Radinsky 1965A
    similis Radinsky 1965A
Deperetellidae Tapiroidea Radinsky
        1965A
    Deperetella, Teleolophus
depereti (Adelomys, Deperetella)
Deperetia Cervus Otsuka 1967
deploratus (Cricetodon)
depressifrons (Aulopopsis)
depressus (Knightomys, Plioplatecarpus)
Dercetidae Myctophiformes
    Dercetis, Kwangodercetis, Lepto-
        trachelus, Paradercetis,
        Rhynchodercetis, Stratodus
Dercetis Dercetidae
    armatus Siegfried 1966
    congolensis Casier 1965
    ornatissimus Casier 1965
    sagittatus Siegfried 1966
derjavini (Helodus)
Dermatemydidae Testudinoidea
    Adocus, Basilemys, Compsemys,
        Heishanemys, Peishanemys,
        Sinochelys, Tsaotanemys,
        Yümenemys
dermatorhinum (Hipparion)
Dermochelyidae Dermocheloidea
    Eosphargis
Dermocheloidea Cryptodira Romer
        1957E*

Dermodactylus Pterodactylidae Kuhn, O.
        1967A (inc. sed.)
Dermoptera Unguiculata Findley 1967
        (geol. range); Van Valen
        1967B (in Insectivora)
descendens (Sciurodon)
desiderata (Astrapis)
Desmana Talpidae
    moschata
        palaeoborysthenica Svistun 1968
    nehringi Fejfar 1964A
    thermalis Jánossy 1965D (cf.); To-
        pachevskiĭ 1965C
Desmaninae Talpidae
desmaresti (Anchilophus)
Desmatochoerus Merycoidodontidae Skin-
        ner, M. F., Skinner and
        Gooris 1968
    anthonyi Schultz, C. B. and Falken-
        bach 1968 (subgen. Para-
        desmatochoerus)
    curvidens
        gregoryi Schultz, C. B. and
            Falkenbach 1968
    macrosynaphus Riel 1964
Desmatolagus Ochotonidae Gureev 1964
        (in Palaeolagidae)
    gobiensis Gureev 1964
    robustus Gureev 1964
    schizopetrus Dawson, M. 1965
Desmatophoca Otariidae Mitchell, E. D.
        1966B (rest.)
Desmatophocinae Otariidae Mitchell, E.
        D. 1968
Desmatosuchus Aëtosauridae Colbert
        1967C (restor.)
desmatotheroides (Veragromovia)
Desmodus Desmodontidae
    magnus Hutchison 1967 (syn. with
        D. stocki)
    stocki Hutchison 1967
Desmostylia Paenungulata Shikama 1966B,
        1968
Desmostylidae Desmostyliformes
    Cornwallius, Desmostylos
Desmostyliformes Desmostylia Shikama
        1966B (skel.)
Desmostylus Desmostylidae Desmostylus
        Research Committee (DEREC)
        1951; Mitchell, E. D. 1966B
        (rest.); Saheki 1928; Takai,
        Shikama and Iziri 1952;
        Tan and Shikama 1965;
        Tanaka and Seki 1962
    hesperus Aoki, R. 1915
    japonicus Shikama 1966A, C;

Tokunaga and Iwasaki
1914
desori (Isurus)
Deuterosauridae Dinocephalia
Deuterosaurus
Deuterosaurus Deuterosauridae Kuhn,
Oskar 1965B (nomenclature)
biarmicus Boonstra 1965A
deutschi (Remiculus)
devauxi (Propotamochoerus)
diaboli (Pecoripeda)
Diacodexis Dichobunidae Guthrie, D. A.
1968 (tarsus)
chacensis Robinson, Peter 1966A
metsiacus Guthrie, D. A. 1967B
secans Robinson, Peter 1966A (cf.)
Diacodon Leptictidae Van Valen 1967B
minutus Russell, L. S. 1967A (cf.)
Diadecta [Diadectoidea] Diadectomorpha
Chudinov 1964A (suborder
p. 213)
Diadectes Diadectidae Cys 1967A; Olson,
E. 1964B, 1965B, 1966D;
Romer 1964D; Vaughn
1964A
sanmiguelensis Lewis, G. E. and
Vaughn 1965
Diadectidae Diadectoidea
Diadectes
Diadectoidea Diadectomorpha
Romer 1956F* (superfam.)
Diadectomorpha Cotylosauria
Diademodon Diademodontidae Ricqlès
1968E (reconst.)
Diademodontidae Cynodontia
Cragievarus, Diademodon, Exaereto-
don, Microconodon, Pas-
cualgnathus, Protacmon,
Trirachodon
Eudiademodontinae, Gomphodon-
tinae, Gomphodontoidinae
Dialipina Palaeoniscidae Schultze 1968
salgueiroensis Schultze 1968
Dianolepis Bothriolepididae Chang, K.-j.
1965
liui Chang, K.-j. 1965
diaphorus (Metarctos)
Diaphyodectes Leptictidae Russell, D. E.
1964; Van Valen 1967B
prolatus Russell, D. E. 1964
Diapsida Reptilia Carroll, R. L. 1968C
(?diapsid, Okla.)
Diarthrognathidae Ictidosauria Crompton
1958*
Diarthrognathus

Diarthrognathoidea [Ictidosauria] Therio-
dontia Tatarinov 1964N,
p. 286
Diarthrognathus Diarthrognathidae
Barghusen 1968; Kermack,
K. A. 1967A; Parrington
1967A
Diatryma Diatrymidae
regens Baird 1967 (subgen. Barornis)
steini Berg, D. E. 1965
Diatrymae [Diatrymiformes] Neognathae
Dement'ev 1964
Diatrymidae Gastornithes Brodkorb 1967
Diatryma
Diatrymiformes Neognathae Brodkorb
1967 (reduced to subord.)
Dibothrosuchus Ornithosuchidae Simmons
1965
elaphros Simmons 1965
dicei (Montanolagus)
Dicellopygidae Palaeoniscoidei Romer
1945D*
Diceratherium Rhincerotidae Whitmore
and Stewart 1965
asphaltense Schaub, S. and Hürzeler
1949
barbouri Wood, H. E. 1964 (subgen.
Menoceras)
pleuroceros Schaub, S. and Hürzeler
1949
Dicerorhininae Rhinocerotidae Beliaeva
1966 (Siberia)
Dicerorhinus Rhinocerotidae Beliaeva
1966; Boylan 1967A; Cìrcì
1962B; Feru, et al. 1965;
Korotkevich 1961A; Rakovec
1965B
etruscus Alekseeva, L. I. 1966 (cf.);
Babaev 1962; Crusafont Pairó
1959D; David, A. and Tarabukin 1967; Feru, et al.
1965; Kahlke 1965H; Rădulesco, Samson, et al. 1965
germanicus Scheuenpflug 1965
hemitoechus Hooijer 1961C (cf.),
1967A Melentis 1964C;
Milojćić, et al. 1965
kirchbergensis Malez 1963D; Mos-
teckÿ 1966
leakeyi Hooijer 1966B
megarhinus Fejfar 1964A; Rădulesco,
Samson, et al. 1965
mercki Bouchud 1966C; Chaline 1963;
Melentis 1964C
nipponicus Shikama, Hasegawa and
and Okafuji 1967

orientalis Ratekhin 1966 (cf.)
schleiermacheri Bakalov and Nikolov
    1962; Nikolov 1962*, 1965;
    Nikolov and Kovachev
    1966
Diceros Rhinocerotidae
    douariensis Guérin 1966B
Dichobunidae Dichobunoidea
    Antiacodon, Bunophorus, Diacodexis
Dichobunoidea Palaeodonta
Dichodon Xiphodontidae Friant 1962D
    cervinum Dechaseaux 1965B (cf.)
dichotomus (Procervulus)
dickinsonensis (Genetochoerus)
Dickosteus Coccosteidae
    threiplandi Miles, R. S. 1966B
dicksoni (Astraponotus)
Dicoryphochoerus Suidae
    fategadensis Prasad 1964A
    meteai Ozansoy 1965
Dicotyles Tayassuidae
    tajacu Woodburne 1968
dicroceroides (Pecoripeda)
Dicrocerus Cervidae Lungu 1967A
    elegans Círcí 1962B; Petronijević 1967
    parviceros Ginsburg 1967A
    lawrowi Musakulova 1967
    salomeae Meladze 1967
Dicrostonyx Cricetidae Fejfar 1965;
    Guilday 1962B (Penn.);
    Heller, F. and Brunnacker
    1966
    groenlandicus Repenning, et al. 1964
    henseli Jacobshagen 1963
    hudsonius Guilday 1968B; Guilday,
        Martin and McCrady 1964
    simplicior Fejfar 1966C
    torquatus Feustel, et al. 1963; Guil-
        day 1968B; Repenning, et
        al. 1964; Sukachev, et al.
        1966 (cf.)
Dicynodon Dicynodontidae
    cadlei Broom 1940A*
    macrodon Broom 1940A*
    nesemanni Broom 1940A*
    swierstrai Broom 1940C*
    whitsonae Toerien 1954* (invalid;
        proposed to replace Dicyno-
        don annae [anneae] Broom
        which under Broom's orig-
        inal spelling is not pre-
        occupied)

Dicynodontia Anomodontia Boonstra
    1966A, 1967B; Cox, C. B.
    1965 (classif.); Crompton
    and Hotton 1967; Cruick-
    shank 1968B (palates)
Dicynodontidae Dicynodontia
    Dicynodon
Dicynodontoidea [Dicynodontia] Ano-
    modontia Viushkov 1964E,
    p. 290 (incl. the usual di-
    cynodont families)
Didelphidae Didelphoidea
    Alacodon, Alphadon, Clemensia, Coöna,
        Didelphis, Didelphodus, Eo-
        brasilia, Glasbius, Ischyrodi-
        delphis, Marmosa, Marmo-
        sopsis, Minusculodelphis,
        Monodelphopsis, Peratherium,
        Protodidelphis, Xenodelphis
    Didelphinae, Glasbiinae, Microbio-
        theriinae
Didelphinae Didelphidae
Didelphodon Stagodontidae Clemens 1966
    vorax Clemens 1966, 1968A
didelphodonti (Avunculus)
Didelphodontinae Palaeoryctidae Van
    Valen 1966A
Didelphis Didelphidae Warren, J. W. 1965
    marsupialis Alvarez and Ferrusquia 1967
        (Mex.)
Didelphodus Didelphidae Guthrie, D. A.
    1967B (in Palaeoryctidae);
    Van Valen 1966A (in Palaeo-
    ryctidae)
    absarokae Van Valen 1966A
    altidens Van Valen 1966A
Didelphoidea Marsupicarnivora
Didermocerus Rhinocerotidae Boylan
    1967A
Didolodontidae Condylarthra
    Didolodus, Ernestokokenia, ?Oxybuno-
        therium
Didolodus Didolodontidae Leanza 1954*
    conidens Simpson, G. G. 1967A
    minor Simpson, G. G. 1964C (cf.),
        1967A
    multicuspis Simpson, G. G., 1964C,
        1967A
Didus Raphidae
    ineptus Lüttschwager 1961
Didymaspida [Didymaspidoidea] Acer-
        aspida Tarlo 1967B (Didymas-
        pidida)
Didymaspidoidea Aceraspida
Didymictis Miacidae Russell, L. S. 1967A

Diplacanthus Diplacanthidae Dineley
1967B (rest.)
Diplacodon Brontotheriidae Russell,
L. S. 1965D
Diplasiocoela Salientia
Diplobune Anoplotheriidae
bavaricum Palmowski and Wachendorf 1966
quercyi Weber, E. 1951
secundarium Bonis 1964; Telles
Antunes 1967C (secundar-
ia)
Diplocaulidae [Keraterpetontidae] Nectridia
Diplocaulinae Keraterpetontidae Beerbower 1963* (in Diplo-
caulidae)
Diplocercidida [Coelacanthiformes] Coelacanthi Andrews, S. M.,
Gardiner, Miles and Pat-
terson 1967
Diplocercidae Diplocercidoidei
Diplocercides, Nesides
Diplocercides Diplocercidae Lehman
1966C (endocranium)
Diplocercidoidei Coelcanthiformes Lehman 1966C
Diplocynodon Crocodylidae
darwini Berg, D. E. 1966; Zázvorka
1966
ebertsi Berg, D. E. 1966
gervaisi Berg, D. E. 1966
hallensis Berg, D. E. 1966
hantoniensis Berg, D. E. 1966
rateli Berg, D. E. 1966
stuckeri Berg, D. E. 1966
styriacus Berg, D. E. 1966; Ginsburg
1967A
Diplodactylinae Gekkonidae Kluge 1967
Diplodontops Mammalia incertae sedis
ampliatus Simpson, G. G. 1967A
Diploglossa Anguimorpha
Incertae sedis: Colpodontosaurus
Diplomeri Anthracosauria Romer 1964B,
G, 1966 (suborder; actually
a stage in vertebral evolution)
Diplomesodon Soricidae
fossorius Repenning 1965B, 1967C
Diplomystus Clupeidae Cavender 1966B
brevissimus Leonardi, A. 1966
dartevelli Casier 1965 (reconst.)
marmorensis Rückert-Ülkümen 1965
Diplorhina [Pteraspidomorpha] Ostracodermi Obruchev, D. V.
1964C; Tarlo 1967B

Diplurus Coelacanthidae Lehman 1966C
(lateral line system)
Dipneusti [Dipnoi] Crossopterygii Mac-
Allister 1968; Piveteau 1966B
Dipnoi Crossopterygii Jarvik 1964A,
1967C; Lehman 1966C; Pan-
chen 1967A; Thomson, K. S.
1965D
Incertae sedis: Melanognathus, Sunwapta
Dipnorhynchidae Dipteriformes Lehman
1966C
Dipnorhynchus, Griphognathus,
Uranolophus
Dipnorhynchus Dipnorhychidae
sussmilchi Campbell, K. S. W. 1965
Dipodidae Dipodoidea
Alactagulus, Allactaga, Megasminthus,
Paralactaga, ?Plesiosminthus,
Plioscirtopoda
Sicistinae
Dipodoidea Dipodomorpha
Dipodormorpha Rodentia Thaler 1966B
(suborder)
Dipodomys Heteromyidae Shotwell 1967B
Dipoides Castoridae
major Bakalov and Nikolov 1962
Diprionomys Heteromyidae
parvus Clark, J. B., Dawson and Wood
1964 (cf.); Shotwell 1967B
Diprotodon Diprotodontidae Bergamini
and editors of Life 1964
(rest.); Lane, E. A. and
Richards 1963
australis Lindsay, H. 1966 (rest.)
Diprotodonta Marsupialia Ride 1964B
(order; incl. Diprotodontidae,
Macropodidae, Phalangeridae,
Vombatidae and Wynyardii-
dae)
Diprotodontidae Phalangeroidea Stirton,
Woodburne and Plane 1967
(phylog.)
Bematherium, Diprotodon, Kolopsis,
Kolopsoides, Meniscolophus,
Neohelos, Ngapakaldia, Noto-
therium, Palorchestes, Piti-
kantia, Plaisiodon, Pyramios,
Sceparnodon, Zygomaturus
Diprotodontinae, Nototheriinae, Palor-
chestinae, Zygomaturinae
Diprotodontinae Diprotodontidae Stirton,
Woodburne and Plane 1967
(new rank)
Dipsalidictides Oxyaenidae Van Valen
1966A

Dipsalodon Oxyaenidae
matthewi Van Valen 1966A
Dipteri Dipnoi
Dipterida [Dipteriformes] Dipteri An-
drews, S. M., Gardiner,
Miles and Patterson 1967
Dipteridae Dipteriformes Lehman 1966C
Chirodipterus, Dipterus, Ganorhynchus,
Grossipterus, ?Rhinodipterus
Dipteriformes Dipteri Lehman 1966C
(with Dipnorhynchidae and
Dipteridae)
Dipteroidei [Dipteriformes] Dipteri
Andrews, S. M., Gardiner,
Miles and Patterson 1967
Dipterus Dipteridae Denison 1968; Leh-
man 1966C (dermocranium);
Säve-Söderbergh 1951*
oervigi Gross, W. 1964B
valenciennesi White, E. I. 1965
dirus (Canis)
Discoglossidae Opisthocoela Estes, Hecht
and Hoffstetter 1967
Barbourula, Discoglossus
Discoglossus Discoglossidae Vergnaud-
Grazzini 1966
discoides (Pycnosterinx)
discors (Podiceps, Querquedula)
discrepans (Soricella)
disjectus (Dolichopareias)
disjuncta (Charadriipeda)
Dissacus Mesonychidae Szalay and
Gould 1966
europaeus Russell, D. E. 1964
Dissopsalis Hyaenodontidae
pyroclasticus Savage, R. J. G. 1965A
Dissorophidae Eryopoidea
Alegeinosaurus, Amphibamus, Arkanserpeton, Aspidosaurus,
Brevidorsum, Broiliellus,
Cacops, Conjunctio, Dis-
sorophus, Fayella, Longiscitula, Platyhystrix, Ter-
somius
Dissorophus Dissorophidae
angustus Carroll, R. L. 1964B (reconst.)
multicinctus DeMar 1966B, 1968
Dissourodes Ciconiidae Short 1966
milleri Short 1966
distentus (Anisotemnus)
distichus (Anolis)
divesensis (Eustreptospondylus)
dividerus (Eucastor)
dixoni (Myliobatis)

Dixonina Albulidae
nemoptera Frizzell 1965C (otolith)
dixseptiensis (Lepidotus)
djali (Pecoripeda)
djurinensis (Cephalaspis)
Docodonta Eotheria
dodgei (Daphoenocyon)
dodogolica (Ochotona)
doelloi (Xenodelphis)
dohmi (Gerdalepis)
dolani (Angelosaurus)
doliata (Lampropeltis)
dolichanthereus (Floridatragulus)
Dolichodoryceros Cervidae
savini Rădulesco and Samson 1967A;
Rădulesco, Samson, et al.
1965
dolichognathus (Mongoloryx)
Dolichohippus Equus Azzaroli 1966B
Dolichopareias Adelogyrinidae Watson
1929K* (of Adelospondyli)
disjectus Brough and Brough 1967
Dolichopareiidae Microsauria Kuhn, Oskar
1965E (assigned to Watson
1929K*; but probably orig-
inates with Romer 1945D*,
p. 591)
Dolichopithecus Cercopithecidae
ruscinensis Alekseeva, L. I. 1964
Dolichorhynchopidae [Polycotylidae]
Pliosauroidea
Dolichorhynchops Polycotylidae
kirki Bardack 1968A
osborni Russell, D. A. 1967C
Dolichosomatites Phlegethontiidae Kuhn,
Oskar 1961A (p. 11, Do-
lichosomatides on p. 79)
Doliosauriscus Brithopodidae
yaushinovi Tatarinov, L. P. 1966C
Doliosaurus Brithopodidae Orlov, J. A.
1964E (preocc.)
doljeana (Clupea)
dolli (Paschatherium)
Dollosaurus Mosasauridae Russell, D. A.
1967A
Dolomys Cricetidae
gromovorum Aleksandrova 1966
hungaricus Shevchenko, A. I. 1965B;
Sulimski 1964 (cf.)
kretzoii Topachevskiĭ 1965C (subgen.
Pliomys)
milleri Aleksandrova 1965A; Shevchenko, A. I. 1965B
nehringi Sulimski 1964 (cf.)
dolorensis (Turseodus)

dominans (Melissiodon)
dominicus (Anthracothorax)
Domnina Soricidae
   gradata Repenning 1967C
   greeni Repenning 1967C
   thompsoni Repenning 1967C
Domninoides Talpidae Hutchison 1968A
   mimicus Wilson, R. L. 1968
   riparensis Clark, J. B., Dawson and
      Wood 1964 (cf.)
donensis (Ceratodus, Ceratodus donensis)
Dongusaurus Ericiolacertidae V'iushkov
     1964H
   schepetovi V'iushkov 1964H
Doniceps ?Araeoscelidia incertae sedis
     Ochev and Rykov 1968
   lipovensis Ochev and Rykov 1968
donnae (Protungulatum)
donnezani (Stephanomys)
dorab (Chirocentrus)
dorae (Progalago)
Doratorhynchus Pterodactylidae Kuhn,
     O. 1967A (inc. sed.)
Dorcabune Tragulidae
   anthracotherioides Prasad and
     Satsang 1963A
   hyaemoschoides Prasad and Satsang
     1963A
   nagrii Prasad and Satsang 1963A
dorcadoides (Gazella)
Doracatherium Tragulidae Hooijer 1963D
   bulgaricum Bakalov and Nikolov 1962
   crassum Mott, I. M. 1964
   vindobonense Petronijević 1967
Dorcopsis Macropodidae Plane 1967B (cf.)
Dorcopsoides Macropodidae Woodburne
     1967B
   fossilis Woodburne 1967B
dormaalense (Peratherium)
Dormaaliidae Tupaioidea Quinet 1964A
   Dormaalius
Dormaalius Dormaaliidae Quinet 1964A
   simonsi Quinet 1964A
   vandebroeki Quinet 1964A
dormitor (Cricetops)
dorotheae (Crocuta crocuta)
dorsalis (Homonotichthys)
dorsatum (Erethizon)
dorsetensis (Pholidolepis, Sphaeronchus)
Dorsetisauridae Anguioidea Hoffstetter
     1967D
   Dorsetisaurus
Dorsetisaurus Dorsetisauridae Hoffstetter
     1967D
   hebetidens Hoffstetter 1967D
   purbeckensis Hoffstetter 1967D

Doryaspididae Pteraspida
   Doryaspis
Doryaspis Doryaspididae Denison 1967B
     (preocc.; in Pteraspididae)
Dorygnathus Rhamphorhynchidae Kuhn,
     O. 1967A
Dorypteridae Platysomoidei
   Dorypterus
Dorypteriformes Actinopterygii Lehman
     1966B
Dorypterus Dorypteridae Liu, H.-t. and
     Tsing 1964
doryssus (Gasterosteus)
dotti (Citellus, Otospermophilus)
douariensis (Diceros)
douglassi (Ischyromys, Mimetodon)
downsi (Imagotaria)
Draco Lacertilia Colbert 1967A (Recent)
Dremotherium Cervidae
   feignouxi Sigoneau 1968B
Drepanaspida Pteraspidiformes
Drepanaspididae Drepanaspida (incl.
     Pycnosteidae and Weigeltas-
     pididae)
   Crenosteus, Drepanaspis, Ganosteus,
     Karelosteus, Psammolepis,
     Psammosteus, Psephaspis,
     Pycnolepis, Pycnosteus,
     Rohonosteus, Schizosteus,
     Tartuosteus, Weigeltaspis,
     Yoglinia
Drepanaspis Drepanaspididae
   carteri Tarlo 1965
   edwardsi Tarlo 1964C, 1965
   gemündenensis Göke 1964; Lehman
     1967B; Tarlo 1965
   jaegeri Tarlo 1964C, 1965
   lipperti Tarlo 1965
   schrieli Tarlo 1965
Drepanosorex Sorex Kretzoi 1965D;
     kretzoi Repenning 1967C
dreyeri (Kestrosaurus)
Dromasauria Theriodontia
Dromomeryx Cervidae
   borealis Shotwell 1968
drummondi (Archegonaspis)
dryas ("Halmaturus")
Drydenius Gonatodidae
   insignis Gardiner 1967A
   molyneuxi Gardiner 1967A
Dryolestidae Eupantotheria
   Parendotherium
Dryomys Gliridae Čtyroký, Fejfar and
     Holý 1964A
   ambiguus Lavocat 1961D
   brailloni Thaler 1966B

Ectopotamochoerus Suidae Leakey, L.
　　S. B. 1965
　dubius Leakey, L. S. B. 1965
Ectosteorhachis Osteolepidae Lehman
　　1966C (endocranium);
　　Thomson, K. S. 1964A,
　　B, 1967B
　nitida Stensiö 1963
Ectypodidae [Ectypodontidae] Ptilodon-
　　toidea Sloan and Van Valen
　　1965
　Cimexomys, Mesodma
Ectypodontidae Multituberculata Sloan
　　1966 (spelling corrected
　　from Ectypodidae)
　Parectypodus
Ectypodus Ptilodontidae Robinson,
　　Peter, Black and Dawson
　　1964
　cochranensis Russell, L. S. 1967A
　laytoni Russell, L. S. 1967A (cf.)
Edaphodon Chimaeridae Novokhatskiĭ
　　1954*
Edaphosauria Pelycosauria Kuhn, Oskar
　　1966A (ascribed to Romer
　　and Price 1940, by error)
edenensis (Scenopagus)
edensis (Hypolagus)
Edentata Unguiculata Barlow 1967
Edestidae Chimaeriformes Bendix-Alm-
　　green 1962, 1967
　Edestus, Fadenia, Ornithoprion
Edestiformes [Edestidae] Chimaeriformes
　　Patterson 1965 (order of
　　Holocephali)
Edestus Edestidae
　giganteus Branson 1964B
　vorax Branson 1963*, 1964C
edithae (Nesophontes)
Edmontosaurus Hadrosauridae Russell,
　　D. A. 1967B (reconst.);
　　Russell, D. A. and Chamney
　　1967 (rest.)
Edopidae Edopoidea
　Smilerpeton
Edopoidea Temnospondyli
Edvardocopeia Notoungulata incertae
　　sedis
　sinuosa Simpson, G. G. 1967A
Edvardotrouessartia Notostylopidae
　sola Simpson, G. G. 1967A
edvardsianus (Laornis)
edwardsi (Archaeolemur, Drepanaspis,
　　Megaladapis, Orthaspido-
　　therium, Palaeortyx, Pro-
　　gempylus, Scaptonyx)

egerkingiae (Prorhzaene)
egertoni (Aulopopsis, Carcharodon)
Egertonia Labridae Casier 1966A (in
　　Phyllodontidae); Miller, H.
　　W. 1967
　isodonta Casier 1966A
Eglonspida [Hibernaspidida] Pteraspidi-
　　formes
Eglonaspididae Hibernaspidida Obruchev,
　　D. V. 1964C
　Pelurgaspis
egloni (Helicampodus)
egretta (Ardeipeda)
ehrlichi (Patriocetus)
eibiswaldensis (Arctamphicyon tolsanus)
Eichstaettisauridae Gekkonoidea Cocude-
　　Michel 1964, 1965; Hoff-
　　stetter 1966B, 1967A (incl.
　　Ardeosauridae); Kuhn, Oskar
　　1966A (revised spelling)
　Eichstaettisaurus
Eichstaettisaurus Eichstaettisauridae
　　Cocude-Michel 1964, 1965;
　　Hoffstetter 1966B, 1967A
　　(in Ardeosauridae); Kuhn,
　　Oskar 1966A (revised spel-
　　ling)
　schroederi Hoffstetter 1964D
eifeliensis (Rhenonema)
eiseleyi (Hadroleptauchenia)
Ektopodon Ektopodontidae Stirton, Ted-
　　ford and Woodburne 1967B
　serratus Stirton, Tedford and Wood-
　　burne 1967B
Ektopodontidae ?Monotremata Stirton,
　　Tedford and Woodburne
　Ektopodon
Elachistosuchidae Pseudosuchia Tatarinov,
　　L. P. 1964X
Elachistosuchoidea Pseudosuchia Walker,
　　A. D. 1966 (discarded)
Elachistosuchus Sphenodontidae
　huenei Walker, A. D. 1966 (rest.)
Elaphe Colubridae Mertens 1965
　nebraskensis Holman 1964C
　situla Młynarski 1964A (cf.)
　vulpina Holman 1965D
elaphros (Dibothrosuchus)
Elaphrosaurus Coeluridae
　bambergi Avnimelech 1966 (ichnites)
Elaphurus Cervidae
　bifurcatus Chow, M.-c. and Chow 1965
　shikamai Otsuka 1968
elaphus (Cervus)
Elaphus Cervus Bakalov and Nikolov 1964
Elasmobranchii Pisces Glikman 1964A
　　(classification)

Eleutherodactylus Leptodactylidae Holman 1967
Eleutherornis Eleutherornithidae Schaub,
S. 1940D
helveticus Schaub, S. 1940D
Eleutherornithidae Struthioniformes
Eleutherornis
Eliomys Gliridae
intermedius Thaler 1966B
quercinus Jullien 1965A
elisabethae (Prolimnocyon)
elizae (Cothurnocystis)
ellenbergeri (Anthracomys)
elliotti (Hemirhabdorhynchus)
Elliotsmithia ?Millerettidae Watson
1957A* (possibly a sauro-
psid)
elliptica (Allocryptaspis)
ellipticus (Deltistes)
Elliptonodon Mosasauridae
compressus Russell, D. A. 1967A
(nomen dubium)
Ellobius Cricetidae
kujalnikensis Topachevskiĭ 1965A
palaeotalpinus Shevchenko, A. I.
1965B
talpinus Aleksandrova 1965B (cf.)
tancrei Topachevskiĭ 1965C
tauricus Topachevskiĭ 1965A
Elomeryx Anthracotheriidae
asticus Nikolov 1967
borbonicoides Gabuniiâ 1964D (ex.
gr.)
crispus Bonis 1964
minor Schaub, S. 1949B
palaeoponticus Nikolov 1967
elongata (Alosa, Anglaspis, Palaeochelys,
Poraspis, Pteraspis)
elongatum (Prodremotherium)
elongatus (Acestrus, Ifasaurus, Oölithes,
Trionyx, Urocles, Wantzo-
saurus)
Elonichthys Palaeoniscidae Lund 1967B;
Teixeira 1958
aitkeni Dahm 1966
denticulatus Dahm 1966
Elopidae Elopoidea Estes 1964
Elopoides, Elops, Esocelops, Holcolepis, Megalops, Promegalops,
Thrissopater
Elopoidea Clupeoidei
Elopoides Elopidae Wenz 1965A
tomassoni Wenz 1965A
Elopomorpha [Clupeoidei] Clupeiformes
Andrews, S. M., Gardiner,
Miles and Patterson 1967

(superorder of Teleostei)
Elops Elopidae Casier 1966A; Nybelin
1967B
Elpidophorus Mixodectidae
elegans Russell, L. S. 1967A
Elpistostegalia Temnospondyli Camp and
Allison 1961* (suborder)
elsanus (Prolagus)
eluta (Carolozittelia)
elvensis (Lepidotus)
Emballonuridae Emballonuroidea
Vespertiliavus
Emballonuroidea Microchiroptera
Embolomeri Anthracosauria Romer
1964B
Embolotherium Brontotheriidae
Iânovskaiâ 1953C
eminens (Palaeomeryx, Paracittelus)
eminus (Hyaenodon)
Emydidae [Testudinidae] Testudinoidea
Emydinae Testudinidae McDowell 1964
emydinus (Cyclopidius)
Emydops Endothiodontidae Crompton
and Hotton 1967
Emys Testudinidae Yeh 1963B (?)
aquitanensis Bergounioux and Crouzel
1965B
dumeriliana Bergounioux and Crouzel
1965B
orbicularis Młynarski 1964A (cf.), B
Enaliosuchus Metriorhynchidae
schröderi Sickenberg 1961 (lost type
found)
Enchodontidae Alepisauroidei
Apateodus, Cimolichthys, Enchodus
Rharbichthys
Enchodus Enchodontidae Albers and
Weiler 1964
bursauxi Signeux 1959A
elegans Jonet 1964B; Signeux 1959A,
B
faujasi Goody 1968
lamberti Tabaste 1963
lewesiensis Jonet 1964B
libycus Signeux 1959A
saevus Bardack 1968A
shumardi Bardack 1968A
venator Leonardi, A. 1966
encristadens (Sciuravus)
Endeiolepididae Anaspidiformes
Endeiolepis
Endeiolepis Endeiolepididae Dineley
1967B (rest.)
Endotherioidea Proteutheria Van Valen
1967B

piveteaui Ozansoy 1965
Eomoropidae Chalicotherioidea
    Eomoropus, Grangeria, Litolophus,
        Paleomoropus
Eomoropus Eomoropidae
    amarorum Radinsky 1964A
    quadridentatus Radinsky 1964A
Eomorphippus Notohippidae
    obscurus Simpson, G. G. 1967A
    pascuali Simpson, G. G. 1967A (?)
Eomuraena Muraenidae Casier 1967
    sagittidens Casier 1967
Eomuscardinus Muscardinus Hartenberger
        1967A
Eomyctophum Myctophidae
    koraensis Dzhafarova 1964
Eomyidae Geomyoidea
    Adjidaumo, Aulolithomys, Eomyidarum,
        Eomys, Gregorymys, Kera-
        midomys, Leptodontomys,
        Namatomys, Paradjidaumo,
        Pseudotheridomys, Yoder-
        imys
Eomyidarum Eomyidae Schaub, S. and
        Hürzeler 1949
Eomys Eomyidae
    catalaunicus Hartenberger 1967A
    schlosseri Thaler 1966B
Eonycteris Pteropidae
    spelaea Cranbrook 1967 (cf.)
Eopachyrucos ?Hegetotheria incertae
        sedis
    pliciformis Simpson, G. G. 1967A
Eopleistolagus Lagomorpha incertae sedis
    selengensis Pokatilov 1966B (nomen
        nudum)
Eoreptilia Tetrapoda Brough and Brough
        1967 (incl. Microsauria, Sey-
        mouriamorpha and Anthra-
        cosauria)
Eosauravidae [Tuditanidae] Captorhino-
        morpha Kuhn, Oskar 1961B*
        (=Sauravidae)
Eosolea Soleidae See: Otolithus Frizzell
        and Dante 1965
    claibornensis Frizzell and Dante 1965
    texana Frizzell and Dante 1965
Eosphargis Dermochelyidae
    breineri Nielsen 1964A
Eosqualodon Squalodontidae Rothausen
        1968B
    langewieschei Rothausen 1968A, B
    latirostris Rothausen 1968A, B
Eostegodon Elephantidae
    pseudolatidens Okutsu and Muto 1959

Eostylocerus Cervidae
    pidoplitshkoi Korotkevich 1964B, 1965B
Eosuchia Lepidosauria
    eotauricus (Sparnodus)
Eotheria Mammalia
Eotheroides Dugongidae
    libyca Siegfried 1967
Eothynnus Scombridae
    salmoneus Casier 1966A
Eothyrididae Ophiacodontia
    Oedaleops
Eotitanops Brontotheriidae
    borealis Robinson, Peter 1966A
    minimus Robinson, Peter 1966A
Eotitanosuchia [Phthinosuchia] Therio-
        dontia Boonstra 1963A*
Eotitanosuchidae Titanosuchia Chudinov
        1964B (in Titanosuchoidea),
        1964J
    Biarmosaurus, Eotitanosuchus
Eotitanosuchus Eotitanosuchidae
    olsoni Chudinov 1965
Eotomistoma Crocodylidae Young, C.-c.
        1964C
    multidentata Young, C.-c. 1964C
Eotragus Bovidae
    haplodon Petronijević 1967
    sansaniensis Circí 1960; Ginsburg 1964A,
        C, 1967A; Petronijević 1967
Eotrigonodon Trigonodontidae
    tabroumiti Tabaste 1963
Eoxenopodidae Opisthocoela
    Eoxenopoides, Shelania
Eoxenopoides Eoxenopodidae
    saltensis Parodi Bustos 1962
Epapheliscus Hyopsodontidae Van Valen
        1966A
    italicus Van Valen 1966A
Ephippidae Percoidei
    Laparon, Platax, Semiophorus, Whitep-
        hippus
Epiemys Testudinidae Yeh 1963B
    perfectus Yeh 1963B
Epieuryceros Cervidae Churcher 1966A
        (invalid)
    proximus Churcher 1966A
    truncus Churcher 1966A
Epigaulus Mylagaulidae
    minor Wilson, R. L. 1968
Epigenetochoerus Merycoidodontidae
        Schultz, C. B. and Falkenbach
        1968
    parvus Schultz, C. B. and Falkenbach
        1968
Epihippus Equidae Russell, L. S. 1965D
    intermedius Bjork 1967

hipparionoides Vekua 1958B
huanghoensis Chow, M.-c. and Chow
     1965
hydruntinus Azzaroli 1966B; Bonifay,
     M.-F. 1964; Dal' 1954*;
     Gromova 1963 (subgen.
     Asinus); Milojčić, et al. 1965
     (subgen. Asinus); Necrasov
     1964 (subgen. Asinus); Prat
     1966A; Rakovic 1965B;
     Thenius 1966A (subgen.
     ?Asinus)
idahoensis Strain 1966 (subgen. Plesip-
     pus)
mosbachensis David, A. 1964 (cf.);
     Rădulesco, Samson, et al.
     1965
przewalski Azzaroli 1966B; Dai and
     Chi 1964; Frechkop 1965D;
     Gromova 1963; Skorkowski
     1960, 1967; Stecher 1966;
     Ting, M.-l., et al. 1965
robustus Dubrovo 1967; Dubrovo and
     Alekseev 1964
sanmeniensis Chow, M.-c., Hu and Lee
     1965; Vangengeĭm 1960B,
     1966E
santae-elenae Edmund 1965 (cf.; sub-
     gen. Amerhippus)
scotti Dalquest 1964A; Hibbard and
     Dalquest 1966; Oesch 1965
simionesoui Rădulesco and Samson
     1967B
simplicidens Strain 1966 (subgen.
     Plesippus)
sivalensis Sahni and Khan 1962
somaliensis Gromova 1963
stehlini Azzaroli 1965, 1966B
stenonis Alekseeva, L. I. 1966 (cf.);
     Avakiàn 1959; Azzaroli
     1965, 1966B; Bolomey
     1965A; Korotkevich 1966;
     Loziev and Lim 1962;
     Ozansoy 1965; Prat 1966A
senezensis Prat 1964
vireti Prat 1964
sussenbornensis Crusafont Pairó 1959D;
     Lysenko 1960C; Vekua
     1958B (cf.)
Equus Equus Azzaroli 1966B
erectus (Homo, Homo erectus, Pithecan-
     thropus)
eremberti (Podocnemis)
Eremochen Anatidae
     russeli Howard, H. 1966A (cf.)
Eremotherium Megatheriidae
     carolinense Edmund 1965 (cf.)

Erethizon Erethizontidae Gupta, B. B.
     1966
     dorsatum Graham, R. E. 1962
Erethizontidae Erethizontoidea
     Coendou, Erethizon
Erethizontoidea Caviomorpha
ergassaminon (Helicoprion)
Ergilornis Ergilornithidae Kozlova 1960
     rapidus Kozlova 1960
Ergilornithidae Gruiformes Kozlova 1960
     Ergilornis, Proergilornis
erici (Peltostega)
Ericiolacertidae Bauriamorpha
     Cyrbasiodon, Dongusaurus
Erinaceidae Erinaceoidea Zaidova 1964
     Erinaceus, Exallerix, Galerix, Geolabis,
          Hemiechinus, Lantanotherium,
          Neurogymnurus, Palaeoerina-
          ceus, Protechinus, Proterix,
          Scenopagus, Talpavus
     Brachyericinae, Echinosoricinae, Erina-
          ceinae, Galericinae
Erinaceinae Erinaceidae Lavocat 1961D
Erinaceoidea Lipotyphla Van Valen 1967B
     (in Erinaceota)
Erinaceota Insectivora Van Valen 1967B
     (suborder, incl. Erinaceoidea
     and Soricoidea)
Erinaceus Erinaceidae Topachevskiĭ 1965C
     europaeus Malez 1963D; Rakovec 1965B
     priscus Schaub, S. and Hürzeler 1949
erinaceus (Microchoerus, Necrolemur)
Eriptychiidae Astraspida
     Eriptychius
Eriptychius Eriptychiidae
     americanus Denison 1967A
     orvigi Denison 1967A
erminea (Mustela)
Ernestokokenia Didolodontidae Simpson,
     G. G. 1964C, 1967A
Erophylla Phyllostomatidae
     bombifrons
          bombifrons Choate and Birney 1968
Erpetocephalus Dendrerpetontidae Chase,
     J. N. 1965
Erpetosuchidae Pseudosuchia
     Stegomosuchus
errans (Merluccius)
Erriwacanthus Climatiidae Ørvig 1967C
     falcatus Ørvig 1967C
erroli (Protaspis)
Erromenosteidae Pachyosteiformes
     Obruchev, D. V. 1964D
     Erromenosteus
Erromenosteus Erromenosteidae Romer
     1966C

Eudaemonema Mixodectidae
　　cuspidata Russell, L. S. 1967A (cf.)
Eudiademodontinae Gomphognathidae
　　Lehman 1961C*
Eudocimus Plataleidae Collins, C. T.
　　1964
Eudolops Polydolopidae Simpson, G. G.
　　1967A (incl. Promysops)
Eudonoceras Coryphodontidae
　　obailiensis Gabuniiā 1961C
euguii (Paratrigodon)
Eulagus Lepus David, A. and Markevich
　　1967
Euleptaspididae Coccosteiformes Obru-
　　chev, D. V. 1964D
Eumeces Scincidae Estes and Tihen
　　1964; Holman 1966C;
　　Wilson, R. L. 1968
Eumyarion Cricetodon Thaler 1966B
Eumys Cricetidae
　　elegans Alker 1966
Eumysops Capromyidae
　　cavoides Kraglievich 1965
　　chapalmalensis Kraglievich 1965
　　formosus Kraglievich 1965
　　laeviplicatus Kraglievich 1965
　　paravioides Kraglievich 1965
　　scalabrinianus Kraglievich 1965
Eupantotheria Pantotheria Kermack in
　　Butler, P. M., et al. 1967
　　(order)
Euparkeria Euparkeriidae
　　capensis Ewer 1965C
Euparkeriidae Pseudosuchia
　　Euparkeria, Wangisuchus
Euphanerida Anaspida Kuhn, O. 1965C
euphractus (Hoplophorus)
Euposauridae Anguimorpha incertae sedis
　　Williston Ms. in Camp
　　1923A* (Euposauridáe);
　　Kuhn, Oskar 1966A (in
　　Inguania)
　　Euposaurus
Euposaurus Euposauridae
　　lorteti Hoffstetter 1964D
～～～～（Ceoemyda）
Eureptilia Reptilia Ginsburg 1967E
　　(subclass)
Eurhinodelphidae Delphinoidea
　　Eurhinodelphis
Eurhinodelphis Eurhinodelphidae Mitchell,
　　E. D. 1966B (rest.)
euri (Lyrocephalus)
europaea (Talpa)
europaeus (Cuon alpinus, Dissacus, Erina-
　　ceus, Lepus, Ruscinomys)

Euryapsida Reptilia Ginsburg 1967B;
　　Kuhn-Schnyder 1967A;
　　Tatarinov, L. P. 1964P
　　(Synaptosauria)
Euryceros Megaceros Cuscani 1963A
Eurylambda Spalacotheriidae Crompton
　　and Jenkins 1967
Eurymylidae Lagomorpha
　　Eurymylus, Mimolagus
Eurymylus Eurymylidae Van Valen
　　1964C
　　laticeps Gureev 1964
euryodon (Hecubides)
Eurypterygius Macropterygiidae Camp,
　　C. L. and Koch 1966
　　(ichthyosaur); Campbell,
　　J. D. 1965 (ichthyosaur,
　　N. Z.)
　　californicus Koch, J. G. and Camp
　　1966 (Ichthyosaurus)
"Eurystephanodon" ?Isotemnidae incertae
　　sedis
　　modicus Simpson, G. G. 1967A
　　(nomen dubium)
Eurysternum Thalassemyidae
　　ignoratum Bräm 1965 (restor.)
Euselachii Oölithes
Euskelosaurus Melanorosauridae
　　browni Ellenberger, F. and Ginsburg
　　1966
Eusmilus Felidae Clark, J. and Beerbower
　　1967
Eusthenodon Rhizodontidae Thomson,
　　K. S. 1967B
Eusthenopteridae [Osteolepidídae] Osteo-
　　lepidiformes Berg 1955A*
Eusthenopteron Osteolepididae Dineley
　　1967B (rest.); Jarvik 1967A;
　　Lehman 1966C (endo-
　　cranium; in Rhizodontidae);
　　Thomson, K. S. 1967B
　　foordi Stensiö 1963; Thomson, K. S.
　　and Hahn 1968
Eustreptospondylus Megalosauridae Walker,
　　A. D. 1964 (for 'Strepto-
　　spondylus' cuvieri)
　　divesensis Walker, A. D. 1964
　　oxoniensis Walker, A. D. 1964
Eutamias Sciuridae Shotwell 1968
　　orlovi Sulimski 1964
Eutamias Tamias Gromov, I. M., et al.
　　1965
Euthacanthidae Climatioidei Miles, R. S.
　　1966A
Eutheria Theria Jeletsky and Clemens
　　1965

concolor Anderson, E. 1968;
　　Hibbard and Dalquest 1966
　　(cf.); Kurtén 1965D
issiodorensis Bolomey 1965A
　　(subgen. Lynx)
leo
　　spelaea Bouchud 1965B; Koby
　　　1964A; Lomi 1963
lynx
　　pardina Malez 1963D
ocreata Vereshchagin 1951C
onca
　　augusta Kurtén 1965D
ornata Dal' 1954*
pamiri Ozansoy 1965
pardalis Kurtén 1965D
pardus Hooijer 1964F; Koby 1964A,
　　C; Kurtén 1965A
rufus Anderson, E. 1968 (subgen.
　　Lynx)
　　floridanus Kurtén 1965D
　　koakudsi Kurtén 1965D
silvestris David, A. and Markevich
　　1967; Krysiak 1956; Kurtén
　　1965A, B; Malez 1963D
spelaea Samson and Kovács 1967;
　　Sukachev, et al. 1966;
　　Svistun 1968; Vangengeïm
　　1961; Vereshchagin 1951C
tigris Chow, M.-c. 1964B
　　groeneveldtii Hooijer 1964F
yagouaroundi Ray, C. E. 1964D
　　(subgen. Herpailurus)
Feloidea Fissipeda
Felsinotherium Dugongidae Kellogg
　　1966
fengshanensis (Sinocoelacanthus)
Fenhosuchus Stagonolepididae Young,
　　C.-c. 1964A (in ?Rauisuchi-
　　dae)
　　cristatus Young, C.-c. 1964A
Ferae Ferungulata
ferganicus (Teleolophus)
ferocior (Sphenacodon)
ferox (Rharbichthys, Sarcocyon,
　　Sphingopus, Ticinosuchus)
ferragus (Macropus)
ferreri (Notagogus)
ferrieri (Helicoprion)
ferrum (Rhinolophus)
feruglioi (Carodnia)
Ferungulata Eutheria
fiber (Castor)
fieldsi (Charactosuchus)

filholi (Lophiodon, Ronzotherium)
Filholornithinae Cracidae Brodkorb 1964A
filipescui (Romanocastor)
filiportatis (Avipeda)
finlayensis (Citellus)
1st Branch [Anagaloidea] Palaeoprosimii
　　Crusafont Pairó 1967B
fissacaudus (Sphenocephalus)
fissidens (Bathyopsis)
Fissipeda Carnivora Ginsburg 1961E
fissurae (Sciurus)
fissus (Helaletes)
flabelliformis (Allocryptaspis)
flammeus (Asio)
flanheimensis (Apterodon)
fletti (Watsonosteus)
Fleurantia Fleurantiidae Dineley 1967A
　　(rest.); Lehman 1966C
Fleurantiidae Scaumenaciformes Lehman
　　1966C
　　Fleurantia, Jarvikia, Oervigia
florencae (Pediomys)
Florentinoameghinia Mammalia incertae
　　sedis
　　mystica Simpson, G. G. 1967A
Floridaceras Rhinocerotidae Wood, H. E.
　　1964
　　whitei Wood, H. E. 1964
floridana (Dierochelys, Pandanaris,
　　Pseudemys)
floridanus (Blastomeryx, Felis rufus,
　　Nothokemas, Proheteromys,
　　Sylvilagus, Tremarctos)
Floridatragulinae Camelidae Maglio 1966;
　　Patton 1966B
Floridatragulus Camelidae
　　dolichanthereus Maglio 1966; Patton
　　1966B
fluviatilis (Perca)
fodiens (Neomys)
foina (Martes)
foliiformis (Pseudopachyrucos)
Folsom man [Homo sapiens] Hominidae
　　Sperry 1967
fontani (Dryopithecus)
fontanieri (Myospalax)
fontannesi (Amphilagus)
fontensis (Adelomys)
fontinalis (Palaeosyops)
fontis (Cylindrodon)
fontoynonti (Archaeoindris)
foordi (Eusthenopteron)
foratus (Procolpodon)
forcipata (Oxyaena)
formicarum (Procerberus)

Galeoidea Selachii
Galeopithecidae Plagiomenoidea
  Galeopithecus
Galeopithecoidea Dermoptera Van Valen
     1967B
Galeopithecus Galeopithecidae Van Valen,
     Butler, et al. 1967
Galeopoidea [Dromasauria] Theriodontia
     V'iushkov 1964D, p. 289
     (Galeopsoidea)
Galeorhinus Carcharhinidae
  formosus Signeux 1959B
  lefevrei Casier 1966A
  minor Casier 1966A
  pulchellus Jonet 1965-66A
  zyopterus Fitch 1964
Galerhinidae Gorgonopsia Watson and
     Romer 1956*
  Galerhininae
Galerhininae Galerhinidae V'iushkov
     1964C, p. 264 (ascribed to
     Watson and Romer 1956*;
     of Gorgonopsidae)
Galericinae Erinaceidae Van Valen
     1967B
galeritus (Hipposideros)
Galerix Erinaceidae
  exilis Petronijević 1967
Galesauridae Cynodontia
Galesuchidae Gorgonopsia Watson and
     Romer 1956* (reduced to
     subfam. by V'iushkov 1964,
     p. 262)
Galethylax Hyaenodontidae
  blainville Van Valen 1966A
galictoides (Enhydrictis)
Galkinia Oligopleuridae Gaudant 1967
     (in Galkiniidae)
  nuda Gaudant 1967
Gallarodon Homalodotheridae Marelli
     1953
  inexcussus Marelli 1953
Gallegosichnus Ichnites Casamiquela
     1964A (in Vertebrata inc.
     sed.)
  garridoi Casamiquela 1964A
Galli [Galliformes] Neognathae Dement'ev
     1964
gallica (Teilhardina)
gallicus (Libralces, Palaeoproteus)
Galliformes Neognathae Holman 1964B
     (osteol.); Mainardi and
     Taibel 1962
Gallinula Rallidae Jánossy 1965C
Gallinuloidinae Cracidae Brodkorb 1964A

Gallogoral Bovidae Guérin 1965 (in Ruca-
     prinae)
  meneghinii Guérin 1965
Gallus Phasianidae Brunet, J. 1961;
     Burchak-Abramovich, N.
     1966D
galushai (Blickomylus, Merycoidodon,
     Pliometanastes)
Gandakasia Mesonychidae
  potens Szalay and Gould 1966
ganesa (Stegodon)
Ganorhynchus Dipteridae
  splendens Gross, W. 1965D
Ganosteus Drepanaspididae
  artus Obruchev, D. V. and Mark-Kurik
     1965; Tarlo 1965
  obtusus Tarlo 1965
  stellatus Mark-Kurik 1966, 1968;
     Novitskaya 1965; Obruchev,
     D. V. and Mark-Kurik 1965;
     Tarlo 1965
gardneri (Paramys excavatus)
garedzicum (Hipparion)
garedziensis (Udabnopithecus)
gardimondi (Pachynolophus, Remys)
garjainova (Eryosuchus)
garridoi (Gallegosichnus)
Garrulus Corvidae Jánossy 1965C
  glandarius Malez 1963D
gastaldii (Neosqualodon, Neosqualodon
     gastaldii)
Gasteroclupea Clupeidae Signeux 1964
  branisai Signeux 1964
Gasteroclupeinae Clupeidae Signeux 1964
Gasterosteida Teleostei Danil'chenko 1964B
     (order)
Gasterosteidae Gasterosteiformes
  Gasterosteus
Gasterosteiformes Mesichthyes
Gasterosteus Gasterosteidae
  doryssus LaRivers 1962
Gastornithes Ralli
Gastrophryne Brevicipitidae
  carolinensis Holman 1965B (cf.)
gaudini (Anchilophus)
Gaudeamus Phiomyidae Wood, A. E.
     1968
  aegyptius Wood, A. E. 1968
gaudryi (Adapisorex, Anomalomys, Aptero-
     don, Brachycyon palaeolycos,
     Coöna, Cryptomeryx, Ga-
     zella, Orycteropus, Pholido-
     phorus, Pronycticebus, Pro-
     pachynolophus, Sciuropterus)
gaultinus (Xiphactinus)

Geolabidinae Adapisoricidae Van Valen
    1967B
Geolabis Erinaceidae Clark, John 1966B
    rhynchaeus Clark, John 1966B
    wolffi Macdonald 1964D
Geomorpha Rodentia Thaler 1966B
    (subord.)
Geomyidae Geomyoidea Russell, R. J.
    1968
    Cratogeomys, Entoptychus, Geomys,
        Griphomys, Thomomys
    Entoptychinae, Geomyinae
Geomyinae Geomyidae Russell, R. J.
    1968
Geomyini Geomyinae Russell, R. J.
    1968 (tribe)
Geomyoidea Geomorpha
Geomys Geomyidae
    adamsi Hibbard 1967
    jacobi Hibbard 1967
    minor Hibbard 1967 (subgen. Ner-
        terogeomys)
    paenebursarius Strain 1966
    smithi Hibbard 1967 (subgen. Nertero-
        geomys)
    tobinensis Hibbard and Dalquest 1966
georgei (Paramerycoidodon)
georgicus (Hippopotamus, Udabnocerus)
gephyrognathus (Hoplopteryx)
Gephyrostegidae Seymouriamorpha Tatar-
        inov, L. P. 1964H
    Gephyrostegus
Gephyrostegus Gephyrostegidae
    bohemicus Brough and Brough 1967
    watsoni Brough and Brough 1967
gerandianum (Cricetodon)
gerandianus (Pseudocyonopsis landesquei)
Geranoidinae Gruidae Brodkorb 1967
    (new rank)
Gerdalepidinae Asterolepididae Gross, W.
    1965A
Gerdalepis Asterolepididae
    dohmi Gross, W. 1965A
    rhenana Gross, W. 1965A
germaniae (Sclerorhynchus)
germanicum (Quinquevertebron)
germanicus (Adapisoriculus, Asiatosuchus,
        Berycopsis, Cervus mega-
        ceros, Dicerorhinus, Equus,
        Palaeoloxodon antiquus,
        Pholidophorus)
Germanodactylidae Pterodactyloidea
        Young, C.-c. 1964B
    Germanodactylus
Germanodactylus Germanodactylidae
        Young, C.-c. 1964B

kochi Young, C.-c. 1964B (for Ptero-
        dactylus kochi)
Germanomys Cricetidae
    helleri Fejfar 1964A
    parvidens Fejfar 1964A
    trilobodon Sulimski 1964
    weileri Sulimski 1964
Gerrhonotus Anguidae Estes 1964 (cf.);
        Estes and Tihen 1964
    mungerorum Wilson, R. L. 1968
Gerrhosauridae Cordyloidea Hoffstetter
    1967D
    Paramacellodus
gervaisi (Archaeomys, Diplocynodon)
Gesneropithex Adapidae Crusafont Pairó
    1967B
get (Kibenikhoria)
Getulocerus Sciuridae Lavocat 1961D
    tadlac Lavocat 1961D
getulus (Lampropeltis)
geygani (Genetochoerus)
gibberodon (Episoriculus)
gibberosus (Sciuropterus)
gidleyi (Blarina, Otospermophilus, Plesi-
        adapis)
Gigantamynodon Amynodontidae
    promisus Xu 1966
gigantea (Ardeipeda, Testudo)
giganteum (Deinotherium)
giganteus (Amphicyon, Edestus, Equus,
        Megaceros, Megamphicyon,
        Megaloceros, Megaloceros
        giganteus, Menodus, Sciurus,
        Spalax, Tartuosteus)
gigantissimum (Deinotherium)
Gigantobison Bison Stokes, Anderson and
        Madsen 1966
Gigantocamelus Camelidae Strain 1966
Gigantodontidae Holostei
    Stromerichthys
Gigantohyrax Procaviidae Kitching 1965
    maguirei Kitching 1965
Gigantopithecus ?Pongidae Frisch 1965;
        Gremiatskiĭ 1966; Heintz, A.
        1964C; Iakimov 1947D;
        Livingstone 1965; Pei 1965B;
        Tobias 1965D; Woo 1961C
    blacki Larichev 1964B; Nesturkh 1954
gigas (Afropterus, Carcharias whitei,
        Cretaspis, Eocoelopoma, Hip-
        potragus, Paracamelus,
        Placerias, Proochotona, Pycno-
        dus)
Gila Cyprinidae
    cristifera Uyeno and Miller 1965
    esmeralda La Rivers 1966

Glyptodontoidea Cingulata
Glyptolepidae [Holoptychiidae]
    Porolepidiformes
Glyptolepis Holoptychiidae Jarvik 1967A;
    Mark-Kurik 1966; Stensiö
    1963; Thomson, K. S.
    1967B
  paucidens Thomson, K. S. 1966E (cf.)
  remota Anatol'eva 1960
Glyptopomus Osteolepididae Jarvik 1967A;
    Lehman 1966C (dermo-
    cranium; in Osteolepidae);
    Thomson, K. S. 1967B
Glyptops Pleurosternidae Yeh, H.-k.
    1963B
Glyptosaurus Anguidae Skinner, M. F.,
    Skinner and Gooris 1968
Glyptotherium Glyptodontidae Strain
    1966
gmelini (Equus caballus, Ovis)
Gnathoberyx Trachichthyidae Patterson,
    C. 1967A
  stigmosus Patterson, C. 1967A (rest.)
Gnathostomata (Pisces + Tetrapoda)
    Craniata
Gnomomys Cricetidae Wilson, R. L.
    1968
  saltus Wilson, R. L. 1968
Gobicyon Canidae
  macrognathus Zhai 1964
gobiensis (Desmatolagus, Litolophus,
        Paludotona, Probactrosaurus)
Gobiesocida Teleostei Danil'chenko 1964B
    (order)
Gobiidae Gobioidea
  Callionymus, Gobius, Lepidocottus,
Gobioidea Gobioidei
Gobioidei Perciformes
Gobiolagus Leporidae Li, C.-k. 1965
  andrewsi Gureev 1964
  major Gureev 1964 (?)
  teilhardi Gureev 1964 (?)
  tolmachovi Gureev 1964
Gobius Gobiidae
  multipinnatus Weinfurter 1967
  pretiosus Weiler 1966A; Weinfurter
    1967
  telleri Weiler 1966A (cf.)
  vicinalis Weiler 1966A
godmani (Weigeltaspis)
goeriachensis (Sciurus)
goini (Hyla)
goldfussi (Chalicotherium, Pleurosaurus)
goletensis (Phalacrocorax)
goliah (Procoptodon)
gollcheri (Hypnomys)

Gomphodontinae Diademodontidae
Gomphodontoidinae Diademodontidae
    Kuhn, Oskar 1965B (p. 72,
    to replace Gomphodontoinae
    Lehman 1961*)
Gomphognathidae [Diademodontidae]
    Cynodontia
Gomphotheriidae Elephantoidea
    Anancus, Choerolophodon, Cuviero-
    nius, Eubelodon, Gompho-
    therium, Megabelodon,
    Stegomastodon, Tetralopho-
    don
Gomphotherium Gomphotheriidae
    Vaptsarov 1963 (Trilophodon)
  anatolicus Ozansoy 1965 (Trilophodon;
    subgen. Choerolophodon)
  angustidens Bakalov and Nikolov 1962
    (Trilophodon); Belokrys
    1960D (Trilophodon); Belo-
    krys and Rizdvianskii 1958
    (Trilophodon); Bergounioux
    and Crouzel 1966A (Trilo-
    phodon), 1967B; Ginsburg
    1967A (Trilophodon); Gins-
    burg and Telles Antunes
    1967 (Trilophodon); Hooijer
    1963D; Mchedlidze 1964D
    (Trilophodon); Nikolov 1962*
    (Trilophodon); Telles Antunes
    1960B
  pentelici Ozansoy 1965 (Trilophodon;
    subgen. Choerolophodon)
  pentelicus Bakalov and Nikolov 1962
    (Trilophodon), 1963 (Trilo-
    phodon, subgen. Choerolo-
    phodon)
  wufengensis Pei 1965D (Trilophodon)
Gonatodidae Palaeonisciformes Gardiner
    1967A
    Drydenius, Gonatodus, Pseudogonatodus
Gonatodus Gonatodidae
  punctatus Gardiner 1967A (rest.)
Goniocranion Bramidae Casier 1966A
  arambourgi Casier 1966A
Goniopholidae Mesosuchia
    Eutretauranosuchus, Goniopholis,
        Nannosuchus, Theriosuchus
Goniopholis Goniopholidae
  simus Joffe 1967
  stovalli Mook 1964
Goniporus Thelodontidae Gross, W.
    1967C
  alatus Gross, W. 1967C
Gonorhynchidae Gonorhynchoidei
    Charitosomus, Gonorhynchus, Notogoneus

Gonorhynchoidei Clupeiformes
Gonorhynchus Gonorhynchidae
    gonorhynchus LeDanois, Y. 1966
gonorhynchus (Gonorhynchus)
Gonostomatidae Gonostomatoidea
    Idrissia, Vinciguerria
Gonostomatoidea Stomiatoidei
goorisi (Megabathygenys)
Gopherus Testudinidae Hibbard and
        Dalquest 1966; Preston
        1966
    dehiscus Des Lauriers 1965
    huecoensis Strain 1966
Gorgon Bovidae Leakey, L. S. B. 1965
        (in Bovini)
    olduvaiensis Leakey, L. S. B. 1965
Gorgonognathidae Gorgonopsia Watson
        and Romer 1956*
Gorgonognathinae
Gorgonognathinae Gorgonognathidae
        V'iùshkov 1964C, p. 264
        (ascribed to Watson and
        Romer 1956*; of Gorgon-
        opsidae)
Gorgonopsia Theriodontia Boonstra
        1965B; Sigogneau 1968A
        (classif.)
    Incertae sedis: Lycaenops
Gorgosaurus Tyrannosauridae Miller,
        H. W. 1967 (?)
gorjensis (Clupea)
gortanii (Protriacanthus)
goyenechei (Delatorrichnus)
gracile (Cephalogale, Hipparion)
gracilenta (Anabernicula)
gracilia (Trionyx)
gracilidens (Nannosuchus, Sorex)
gracilis (Alacodon, Amphitragulus,
        Antilospira, Bestiopeda,
        Caranx, Carcharhinus,
        Ceratodus donensis, Demo-
        cricetodon minor, Gliru-
        dinus, Laidleri, Mimomys,
        Plegadis, Proviverra, Pycno-
        sterinx, Smilodectes, Steno-
        mylus, Viverravus)
graculus (Pyrrhocorax)
gradata (Domnina)
Gradientes [Neognathae, partum] Neor-
        nithes Dement'ev 1964
graeca (Alectornis)
graecus (Pliohyrax)
Grallator Ichnites
    maximus Lapparent and Montenat
        1967B
    olonensis Lapparent and Montenat
        1967B

    vairabilis Lapparent and Montenat
        1967B
gandaensis (Dulcidon)
grande (Chalicotherium)
grandiana (Ysengrinia)
grandiceps (Amphibamus, Sunwapta)
grandidieri (Testudo)
grandincisivus (Mammut, Tetralophodon)
grandipes (Palaeobatrachus)
grandis (Eptesicus, Eryops, Leptotomus,
        Livosteus, Mesohippus, Pro-
        camelus, Strepsiceros, Xyla-
        canthus)
grangerensis (Beckia)
grangeri (Colodon, Entomolestes, Phena-
        codus, Shamalagus, Trogosus)
Grangeria Eomoropidae
    anarsius Radinsky 1964A
    canina Radinsky 1964A
    major Radinsky 1964A
granulata (Hainbergia, Psammolepis)
granulatus (Dapedius, Metopacanthus)
Graptemys Testudinidae Bjork 1967
    pseudogeographica Wilson, R. L. and
        Zug 1966
graticulata (Corvaspis)
gratiosa (Hyla)
gratus (Nannippus)
gravis (Macropodosaurus, Quemisia)
grayi (Pseudaxis)
graziosii (Equus)
greeni (Angelosaurus, Arvicola, Cionichthys,
        Domnina, Nettion)
gregalis (Microtus)
gregaria (Clupea, Trionyx)
gregarium (Megacricetodon)
gregarius (Blainvillimys, Cricetodon, Demo-
        cricetodon, Megacricetodon,
        Megacricetodon gregarius)
gregoryi (Desmatochoerus curvidens,
        Sugrivapithecus)
Gregorymys Eomyidae
    curtus Galbreath 1967A
Gregoryochoerus Paramerycoidodon
        Schultz, C. B. and Falken-
        bach 1968
grewingki (Latvius)
grimmi (Sciuropterus)
grindrodi (Kallostrakon)
Griphippus Equidae Wilson, R. L. 1968
        (cf.)
Griphognathus Dipnorhynchidae Lehman
        1966C
Griphomys Geomyidae Lindsay, E.
        1968A
Grippidae ?Longipinnati
Grippidia [Grippidae] ?Longipinnati

Wiman 1933B (order of
Parapsida); Kuhn, Oskar
1966A (Grippida)
griseus (Notidanus)
grisigensis (Rajitheca)
griswoldi (Ameiva)
grivensis (Amphicyon major, Heteroxerus,
Miosorex, Rhinolophus,
Sorex)
groeneveldtii (Felis tigris)
Groenlandaspididae Arctolepidiformes
Obruchev, D. V. 1964D
Groenlandaspis
Groenlandaspis Groenlaspididae Rade
1964
mirabilis Miles, R. S. 1965C
groenlandica (Psammolepis, Soederberg-
hia)
groenlandicus (Dicrostonyx)
groensis (Isurus apendiculata)
gromovae (Hipparion sitifense)
gromovi (Citellus undulatus, Mammuthus,
Plioselevinia)
gromovorum (Dolomys)
Grossaspididae [Lepadolepididae] Astero-
lepidiformes Obruchev,
D. V. 1964D
grossi (Coccosteus)
grossiconus (Hybodus)
Grossilepis Bothriolepididae
tuberculata Obruchev, D. V. and
Sergienko 1961 (aff.);
Sergienko 1961A
Grossipterus Dipteridae Vorob'eva and
Obruchev 1964
Grues [Gruiformes] Neognathae De-
ment'ev 1964 (ord.)
Gruidae Grues
Grus, Urmiornis
Geranoidinae
Gruiformes Neognathae
Gruipeda Gruipedae Panin and Avram
1962
maxima Panin and Avram 1962
Gruipedae Avipedia Panin and Avram
1962
Gruipeda
Grumantaspis Pteraspididae Obruchev,
D. V. 1964C
lyktensis Obruchev, D. V. 1964C
grumosus (Latirhynchus)
grunnieus (Aplodinotus)
Grus Gruidae
americana Feduccia 1967B (Plioc.,
Idaho
grus Jánossy 1965C (cf.)

grus (Grus)
gryei (Pachycynodon)
Grypolophodon ?Astrapotheria incertae
sedis
imperfectus Simpson, G. G. 1967A
(nomen vanum)
morenoi Simpson, G. G. 1967A (nomen
vanum)
tuberculosis Simpson, G. G. 1967A
(nomen vanum)
Gryzajidae Otides Brodkorb 1967
Guerichosteidae Psammosteida Tarlo
1964C, 1965
Guerichosteus, Hariosteus
Guerichosteus Guerichosteidae Tarlo
1964C, 1965
kotanskii Tarlo 1964C, 1965
kozlowskii Tarlo 1964C, 1965
kulczyckii Tarlo 1964C, 1965
lefeldi Tarlo 1964C, 1965
guestfalicus (Leptosomus)
guettardi (Rangifer)
Guguschia ?Anatidae
nailii Burchak-Abramovich, N. I. 1966E
Guilielmoscottia Interatheriidae
plicifera Simpson, G. G. 1967A
guilloti (Bourbonnella)
gulo (Gulo)
Gulo Mustelidae
gulo Altuna 1963B (Spain); Bökönyi
1959; Malez 1963D, 1965J;
Martin, R. 1966; Sukachev,
et al. 1966; Zapfe 1966B
luscus Anderson, E. 1968
guloides (Bestiopeda)
gunni (Perameles)
guptai (Indolophus)
gureevi (Lepus europaeus)
gurejevi (Ochotona daurica)
gusevi (Notosyodon)
gutmanni (Amphicyon major)
gutturosum (Palaeobalistum)
gwyneddensis (Ryaneria)
Gymnarchoidea [Gymnarchidae] Mormyroidei MacAllister 1968
Gymnarthridae Microsauria
Cymatorhiza, Hylerpeton, Leiocephalikon, Pantylus, Sparodus,
Trachystegos
Gyps Accipitridae
himalayensis Stepanian 1964 (subgen.
Gyps)
Gyps Gyps Stepanian 1964
Gypsonictopinae Leptictidae Van Valen
1967B

hamadryas (Dryomys)
Hamakita man (Japan) [Homo sapiens]
          Hominidae Suzuki 1966
hamiltoni (Saurichthys)
hammeli (Gliravus)
hammeri (Fulmarus)
hammondi (Scaphiopus)
hantoniensis (Diplocynodon)
Hapalodectes Mesonychidae
    leptognathus Guthrie, D. A. 1967B
    lushiensis Chow, M.-c. 1965B
    serus Szalay and Gould 1966
Hapalodectinae Mesonychidae Szalay
          and Gould 1966
Haplocyon Canidae
    crucians Bonis 1966B, 1967 (subgen.
          Haplocyon)
    elegans Bonis 1966B, 1967 (subgen.
          Parhaplocyon)
Haplocyon Haplocyon Bonis 1966B, 1967
Haplocyoninae Canidae Bonis 1966B, 1967
haplodon (Eotragus)
Haplodontosaurus Anguidae
    excedens Estes 1965C
Haplolepiformes Actinopterygii Lehman
          1966B
Haplomeryx Xiphodontidae Friant 1962D
haplous (Protoclepsydrops)
Haptosphenus Teiidae Estes 1964 (Cret.,
          Wyo.)
    placodon Estes 1964
Haramyia Haramyidae Friant 1964A,
          1965A; Parrington 1967A
    antiqua Friant 1964A
    moorei Friant 1964A
    rhaetica Friant 1964A
Haramyidae [Microcleptidae] Mammalia
          incertae sedis Kuhn, Oskar
          1965B, p. 88 (taxonomic
          note)
Hariosteus Guerichosteidae Tarlo 1964C,
          1965
    kielanae Tarlo 1964C, 1965
    lobanowskii Tarlo 1964C, 1965
harlani (Paramylodon)
harmeri (Periphragnis)
harmonicus (Protobradys)
haroldcooki (Mammuthus imperator)
haroldi (Notorhinus)
Harpagolestes Mesonychidae
    brevipes Szalay and Gould 1966
    immanis Szalay and Gould 1966
    koreanicus Szalay and Gould 1966
    leotensis Szalay and Gould 1966
    macrocephalus Szalay and Gould 1966
    orientalis Szalay and Gould 1966

uintensis Szalay and Gould 1966
harrasense (Chirotherium)
harriesi (Massospondylus)
Harriotta ?Chimaerotheca Obruchev, D. V.
          1966
harrisi (Sarcophilus)
harrisoni (Scelidosaurus)
hartenbergeri (Eliomys, Rotundomys)
harundinea (Megagallinula)
haslachensis (Cordylodon)
harveyi (Leptauchenia)
hassenkampi (Pararallus)
Hassiacosuchus Crocodylidae
    kayi Wassersug and Hecht 1967 (syn.
          of Procaimanoidea)
hassiacum (Propalaeotherium)
hasta (Pomadasys)
hastalis (Isurus)
hatcheri (Pediomys)
haueri (Caranx)
haughtoni (Karoosuchus, Parotosaurus)
Haughtoniscus Scaloposauridae Kuhn, Oskar
          1965B (credited to Kuhn
          1937A*, by error)
haugi (Isotemnus)
haupti (Allognathosuchus)
hauseri (Homo mousteriensis)
haydeni (Palaeolagus)
haydenianus (Protictis)
headonensis (Geoemyda)
"Hebe" ?Rhinocryptidae Fisher, J. 1967
          (validity)
heberti (Prolates)
hebetidens (Dorsetisaurus)
hebetis (Honanodon)
heckeli (Acrogaster)
heckeri (Obruchevia)
Hecubides Canidae Savage, R. J. G. 1965A
    euryodon Savage, R. J. G. 1965A
    macrodon Savage, R. J. G. 1965A
hedei (Andreolepis)
hedlundae (Bathygenys alpha)
Hedralophus ?Trigonostylopidae incertae
          sedis
    bicostatus Simpson, G. G. 1967A (nomen
          dubium)
Hegetotheria Notoungulata
    Incertae sedis: ?Eohegetotherium,
          ?Eopachyrucos, ?Pseudo-
          pachyrucos
heidelbergensis (Homo)
heiligenstockiensis (Nesides)
heilmani (Tupilakosaurus)
heinrichi (Aeoliscus)
heinzelini (Brachypotherium)
heintzi (Anglaspis, Brachipteraspis, Pharyn-

golepis, Weigeltaspis)
Heishanemys Dermatemydidae Yeh 1963B
(?)
heiyuekouensis (Shansisuchus)
Helaletes Helaletidae
fissus Radinsky 1965A
mongoliensis Radinsky 1965A
nanus Robinson, Peter 1966A (cf.)
Helaletidae Tapiroidea
Chasmotherium, Colodon, Helaletes,
Heptodon, Hyrachyus, Selenaletes, Veragromovia
Chasmotheriinae, Helaletinae, Hyrachyinae
Helaletinae Helaletidae Radinsky 1966B
helbingi (Cynelos lemanensis)
helenae (Otionohyus hybridus)
Heleosaurus ?Millerittidae Watson 1957A
(possibly a millerittid)
helgolandicus (Parotosaurus)
Helicampodus Helicoprionidae Obruchev,
D. V. 1965B
changhsingensis Branson 1964A
egloni Obruchev, D. V. 1965C
kokeni Obruchev, D. V. 1965C
Helicoprion Helicoprionidae Logan and
McGugan 1968
ergassaminon Bendix-Almgreen 1966
ferrieri Bendix-Almgreen 1966
nevadensis LaRivers 1962
Helicoprioni Elasmobranchi Bendix-Alm-
green 1966 (superorder)
Helicoprionidae Helicoprioniformes
Helicampodus, Helicoprion, Sinoheli-
coprion, Syntomodus
Helicoprioniformes Helicoprioni Bendix-
Almgreen 1966 (order)
Helicotragus Bovidae
incarinatus Ozansoy 1965
major Ozansoy 1965
Heliscomys Heteromyidae
vetus Black, C. C. 1965A (cf.)
Helladotherium Giraffidae
duvernoyi Bakalov and Nikolov 1962;
Kretzoi 1965A
helleri (Germanomys)
Helochelydinae Pleurosternidae Kuhn,
Oskar 1966A (assigned to
Stromer 1934B)
Helodontidae Chimaerae incertae sedis
Patterson, C. 1965B (in
Helodontiformes); Romer
1966 (Bradyodonti incertae
sedis)
Helodus
Helodontiformes [Helodontidae] Chimaerae
incertae sedis Patterson, C.

1965B (order of Holocephali)
Helodus Helodontidae
derjavini Obruchev, D. V. 1962C;
Tolmachev, I. P. 1931
semenowi Tolmachev, I. P. 1931
simplex Obruchev, D. V. 1962C;
Patterson, C. 1965B (reconst.)
Helohyus Choeropotamidae
lentus Maxwell, R. A. et al. 1967 (cf.);
Wilson, J. A. 1967
helvetica (Humbertia, Rajitheca)
helveticum (Cricetodon, Propalaeotherium)
helveticus (Simamphicyon)
Hemiacodon Omomyidae
jepseni Robinson, Peter 1968B
Hemicalypterus Semionotidae Schaeffer, B.
1967B
weiri Schaeffer, B. 1967B (rest.)
hemicingularis (Paramys)
Hemicyclaspididae Aceraspidoidea
Hemicyclaspis
Hemicyclaspis Hemicyclaspididae
murchison Heintz, A. 1967A
Hemicyon Canidae Shotwell 1968(?)
sansaniensis Circí 1962B; Telles Antunes
1960
stehlini Kuss 1965A (in Ursidae)
Hemicyoninae Canidae Kuss 1965A (in
Ursidae)
Hemiechinus Erinaceidae Tropin 1968
hemionus (Equus)
Hemipristis Carcharhinidae
serra Casier 1966B; Henriques da Silva
1961; Pledge 1967; Radwanski
1965
Hemirhabdorhynchus Blochiidae
elliotti Casier 1966A
Hemisorex Soricidae Baudelot, S. 1967
robustus Baudelot, S. 1967
hemispherica (Sharemys)
hemitoechus (Dicerorhinus, Rhinoceros)
Hemitragus Bovidae
jemlahicus
bonali Daxner and Thenius 1965
Hemixotodon Toxodontidae
chasicoensis Pascual 1965B
hemprichi (Cyclotosaurus)
Hemprichisaurus [Cyclotosaurus] Capitosauridae Kuhn, Oskar 1939;
Welles and Cosgriff 1965B
hendryi (Apatemys)
hennigi (Ancylotherium)
Henophidia Serpentes Hoffstetter 1964C
p. 967 (infraorder, substituted
for Booidea)
henseli (Dicrostonyx)

Heosemys Geoemyda Khozatskiĭ and
    Mẏynarski 1966
Heptacodon Anthracotheriidae Clark,
    J. and Beerbower 1967
Heptaxodon Dinomyidae
    bidens Ray, C. E. 1964B (an immature
        Elasmodontomys obliquus)
Heptaxodontidae [Dinomyidae] Cavioidea
Heptodon Helaletidae Robinson, Peter
    1966A (?)
    calciculus Guthrie, D. A. 1967B
    niushanensis Chow, M.-c. and Li 1965
    posticus Radinsky 1965B (rest.)
herbstii (Vieraella)
heroni (Carchariolamna)
Herpailurus Felis Ray, C. E. 1964D
Herpestes Viverridae
    aurelianensis Petronijević 1967
    palaeogracilis Petter, G. 1964A
    palaeoserengetensis Petter, G. 1964A
Herpestides Viverridae Beaumont 1968
    (in Herpestinae)
    antiquus Beaumont 1968
Herpestinae Viverridae
herpestoides (Oödectes)
herrerei (Parendotherium)
herrlingensis (Sorex)
hertwigi (Ornithoprion)
Hesperocamelus Camelidae
    stylodon Macdonald 1966B
Hesperidoceras Bovidae Crusafont Pairó
    1965E (for Hesperoceras,
    preocc.)
    merlae Crusafont Pairó 1965E
Hesperolagomys Ochotonidae Clark, J. B.,
    Dawson and Wood 1964
    galbreathi Clark, J. B., Dawson and
        Wood 1964
Hesperoloxodon Elephantidae
    antiquus Kubiak 1965A, B
    falconeri Kuss 1966
Hesperornis Hesperornithidae
    regalis Bardack 1968A; Martin, L. D.
        and Tate 1966; Russell, D.
        A. 1967C
Hesperornithes [Hesperornithiformes]
    Odontognathae Dement'ev
    1964
Hesperornithidae Hesperornithiformes
    Hesperornis
Hesperornithiformes Odontognathae
Hesperosorex Soricidae
    lovei Repenning 1967C
Hesperotestudo Geochelone Auffenberg
    1966B
hesperus (Desmostylus)

hessei (Lambdoceras)
hessi (Marmota monax)
Hessolestes Mesonychidae Szalay and Gould
    1966
hesternus (Camelops)
heterocerca (Alosa, Clupea)
Heterodon Colubridae Wilson, R. L. 1968
    nasicus Hibbard and Dalquest 1966;
        Holman 1965A
heterodon (Lonchidion, Palaeocorax falea-
    tus, Sespia)
Heterodontidae Heterodontoidei
    Heterodontus, Synechodus
Heterodontiformes Selachoidii
Heterodontoidei Heterodontiformes
Heterodontosauridae Ornithopoda incertae
    sedis Kuhn, Oskar 1966A,
    p. 101
Heterodontus Heterodontidae
    falcifer Schweizer 1964
    rugosus Albers and Weiler 1964
    vincenti Casier 1966A
    wardenensis Casier 1966A
Heterofelis Machairodus Mawby 1965B
"Heterohominidae" Hominoidea Hürzeler
    1968
heterolepis (Schizosteus)
Heterolophodon Mammalia incertae sedis
    ampliatus Simpson, G. G. 1967A
Heteromyidae Geomyoidea White, J. A.
    1964, 1965
    Dipodomys, Diprionomys, Heliscomys,
        Parapliosaccomys, Peridiomys,
        Perognathus, Pliosaccomys,
        Prodipodomys, Proheteromys
Heteroprox Cervidae
    larteti Pavlović and Ćipović 1964; Petro-
        nijević 1967
Heteropsomyinae Echimyidae Pascual
    1967
Heterosaurus ?Iguanodontidae Lapparent
    and Stchepinsky 1968
    neocomiensis Lapparent and
        Stchepinsky 1968 (?)
Heterosorex Soricidae Hutchison 1966A
Heterosoricinae Soricidae Hutchison 1966A;
    Repenning 1967C
Heterosteidae Pachyosteiformes Obruchev,
    D. V. 1964D (Heterostiidae;
    =Ichthyosauroididae of
    Camp, et al)
Heterosteus Heterosteidae Obruchev, D. V.
    1964D
Heterostraci [Pteraspidomorpha] Ostra-
    codermi Iakovlev, V. N.
    1967A; Jarvik 1964A; Obru-
    chev, D. V. 1967A; Obru-
    chev, D. V. and

amphibius Bonadonna 1965A; Bouchud 1966D; Hooijer
1961C, 1963D
antiquus Adam, K. D. 1965B;
Milojčič, et al. 1965
major Cuscani 1965 (var.), 1966,
1967
primaevus Adrover 1964 (subgen. Hexaprotodon)
antiquus Melentis 1964C, 1966E
creutzburgi Boekschoten and Sondaar
1966 (reconst.)
georgicus Vekua 1958B
imaguncula Hooijer 1963D
primaevus Crusafont Pairó, Adrover
and Golpe 1964
sivalensis
soloensis Hooijer 1964F
Hipposideridae Rhinolophoidea
Asellia, Hipposideros, Palaeophyllophora, Pseudorhinolophus
Hipposideros Hipposideridae
beatus Marshall, P. M. and Butler
1966
bouziguensis Sigé 1968B (subgen.
Pseudorhinolophus)
branssatensis Hugueney 1965
collongensis Sigé 1968B (subgen.
Brachipposideros)
dechaseauxi Sigé 1968B (subgen.
Brachipposideros)
galeritus Cranbrook 1967 (cf.)
hipposideros (Rhinolophus)
Hippotigris Equidae
robustus Rădulesco and Samson
1967B
simplicidens Howe, J. A. 1966A
suessenbornensis Musil 1965C; Rădulesco, Samson, et al. 1965
stenonis Rădulesco, Samson, et al.
1965
Hippotigris Equus Azzaroli 1966B
Hippotragus Bovidae
gigas Leakey, L. S. B. 1965
niro Gentry 1966
hircus (Capra)
Hirundinidae Passeres
Hirundo, Petrochelidon
Hirundo Hirundinidae
aprica Feduccia 1967A (Plioc., Kan.)
hispanicus (Democricetodon minor, Muscardinus pliocaenicus)
Hispanotherium Rhinocerotidae
matritensis Hernández-Pacheco and
Crusafont Pairó 1960

hispidus (Perognathus)
hitchcocki (Anchisauripus)
hiwegi (Leakitherium)
hlavini (Kentuckia)
hobleyi (Deinotherium)
hochuanensis (Mamenchisaurus)
hodosimai (Colodon)
hoeledense (Chasmotherium)
hoeli (Irregulareaspis, Mimetaspis)
hoffmanni (Mosasaurus)
hoffstetteri (Palaeotragus)
holbrooki (Scaphiopus)
Holcodus Mosasauridae
acutidens Russell, D. A. 1967A (nomen
vanum)
Holcolepis Elopidae
lacostei Leonardi, A. 1966
holdichi (Astraponotus)
hollandi (Megoreodon)
Holmesella ?Mesacanthidae Ørvig 1967A
(an elasmobranch)
Holocentridae Berycoidei
Caproberyx, Kansius, Myripristis,
Naupygus, Paraberyx, Stichocentrus, Stintonia, Trachich-
thyoides
Caproberycinae
Holocephali Elasmobranchii Patterson, C.
1965A, B
Incertae sedis: ?Pseudodontichthys
Holonema Holonematidae Obruchev, D. V.
and Sergienko 1961; Rade
1964
farrowi Stevens, M. S. 1964
Holonematidae Arctolepidiformes Obruchev,
D. V. 1964D
Aspidichthys, Deirosteus, Glyptaspis,
Gyroplacosteus, Holonema,
Rhenonema
Holonemidae [Holonematidae] Arctolepidi-
formes
Holoptychiida [Porolepidiformes] Opteo-
lepides Andrews, S. M., Gardi-
ner, Miles and Patterson
1967
Holoptychiidae Porolepidiformes Warren,
J. W. and Talent 1967
Glyptolepis, Holoptychius
Holoptychioidea [Porolepidiformes] Osteo-
lepides Romer 1966C, p.
361 (Holoptychoidea =Poro-
lepiformes)
Holoptychius Holoptychiidae Dineley
1967B (rest.); Jarvik 1967A;
Panchen 1967A; Säve-Söder-
bergh 1951* (reconst.);

sapiens Reed, C. A. 1965; Straus
        1965
sinhaleyus Deraniyagala 1960F,
        1964B, 1965
steinheimensis Rajchel 1965 (reconst.)
Homo sapiens (local names)
    Cro-Magnon, Folsom man, Hamakita
        man, Kiik-Koba man, Mar-
        mes man, Petralon man,
        Swanscombe man
Homodontosauridae Sphenacodontia
        Kuhn, Oskar 1961A*
Homodontosaurus ?Pelycosauria Broom
        1949A*, Kuhn, Oskar 1965B
        (note)
    kitchingi Broom 1949A*
Homoeosaurus Sphenodontidae
    maximiliani Cocude-Michel 1967
Homogalax Isectolophidae
    wutuensis Chow, M.-c. and Li 1965
Homonotichthys Polymixiidae
    dorsalis Patterson, C. 1964
    pulchellus Patterson, C. 1964
    rotundus Patterson, C. 1964
Homopithecus Hominidae
    sinhaleyus Deraniyagala 1960F,
        1964B, 1965
Homostiidae Pachyosteiformes
    Homostius
Homostius Homostiidae Mark-Kurik 1963
Homotherium Felidae
    crenatidens Bolomey 1965A; Crusa-
        font Pairó 1959D
    moravicum Thenius 1965B
honanensis (Sianodon, Testudo)
Honanodon Mesonychidae Chow, M.-c.
        1965B
    hebetis Chow, M.-c. 1965B
    macrodontus Chow, M.-c. 1965B
hoogbutselense (Peratherium)
hopei (Carcharias)
Hoplophoneus Felidae Clark, J. and Beer-
        bower 1967
Hoplophorinae Glyptodontidae Paula
        Couto 1965
Hoplophorini Glyptodontidae Paula Couto
        1965 (tribe; =Sclerocalyptini
        Hoffstetter 1958E*)
Hoplophorus Glyptodontidae
    echazui Hoffstetter 1964A
    euphractus Hoffstetter 1964A; Paula
        Couto 1965
Hoplopteryx Trachichthyidae
    antiquus Patterson, C. 1964
    gephyrognathus Patterson, C. 1964

lewesiensis Patterson, C. 1964 (rest.)
lewisi Patterson, C. 1964
macracanthus Patterson, C. 1964
simus Patterson, C. 1964
spinulosus Patterson, C. 1964
syriacus Patterson, C. 1964
zippei Patterson, C. 1964
hopsoni (Mytonius)
hopwoodi (Eocoelopoma)
horribilis (Ursus, Ursus arctos)
horridus (Cretaspis, Crotalus)
hortulorum (Pseudaxis)
houfenense (Hipparion)
houghae (Longiscitula)
Hovacrex Rallidae Brodkorb 1965 (for
        Tribonyx)
    roberti Brodkorb 1965
Hovasaurus Tangasauridae Watson 1957A*
        (in Prolacertilia)
howardi (Alcelaphus)
howelli (Otospermophilus)
Howesia Mesosuchidae Watson 1957A*
        (in Rhynchosauria, derived
        from Prolacertilia)
hsandagolensis (Exallerix)
hsui (Platyognathus)
huanghoensis (Equus)
hudsonicus (Tamiasciurus)
hudsonius (Dicrostonyx)
hudspethensis (Sigmodon)
huecoensis (Gopherus)
huenei (Elachistosuchus)
huerfanensis (Antiacodon pygmaeus,
        Leptotomus, Paramys, Reith-
        roparamys)
Huerfanius Anaptomorphidae Robinson,
        Peter 1966A
    rutherfurdi Robinson, Peter
        1966A
hugii (Thalassemys)
hui (Keichousaurus)
huilensis (Sebecus)
Hulgana, Ischyromyidae Dawson, M. 1968A
        (Olig., Mongolia)
    ertnia Dawson, M. 1968A
Humbertia Miacidae Beaumont 1965B
        (in Viverravinae), 1966
        (replaced by Quercygale Kret-
        zoi 1945)
    angustidens Beaumont 1965B
    helvetica Beaumont 1965B
humboldtensis (Cosmacanthus)
humei (Ceratodus)
humilis (Clupea)
hungarica (Peté nyia)

baderi Lynch, J. D. 1965
cinerea Chantell 1964 (cf.); Wilson,
    R. L. 1968 (cf.);
goini Holman 1967
gratiosa Chantell 1964 (cf.), 1966;
    Wilson, R. L. 1968
miocenica Holman 1966C
miofloridana Holman 1967
squirella Chantell 1964 (cf.)
versicolor Chantell 1966
Hylaeobatis Ptychodontidae
    ornatus Patterson, C. 1966
Hylaeobatrachidae Proteida
Hylaeobatrachoidea [Hylaeobatrachidae]
    Proteida Huene 1931J
    (Hyaelobatrachoidea)
Hylerpeton Gymnarthridae
    dawsoni Carroll, R. L. 1966; Steven-
        son and Stevenson 1966
    longidentatum Carroll, R. L. 1966
Hylidae Procoela
    Acris, Hyla, Proacris, Pseudacris
Hylobathinae Cercopithecidae Chiarelli
    1968A
Hylonomus Romeriidae
    latidens Carroll, R. L. 1966
    lyelli Carroll, R. L. 1964C
    wymani Carroll, R. L. 1966
Hylopetes Sciuridae Thaler 1966B
Hyneria Rhizodontidae Thomson, K. S.
    1968B
    lindae Thomson, K. S. 1968B
Hynobiidae Caudata Lebedkina 1964B
Hyoboops Anthracotheriidae Gabuniia
    1964D
Hyopsodontidae Condylarthra
    Epapheliscus, Hyopsodus, Litolestes,
        Louisina, Parapheliscus,
        Paratricuspiodon, Paschather-
        ium, Tricuspiodon
Hyopsodus Hyopsodontidae Gazin 1968B
    (rest.)
    fastigatus Russell, L. S. 1965D
    miticulus Guthrie, D. A. 1967B
    paulus Robinson, Peter 1966A
    powellianus Guthrie, D. A. 1967B
    walcottianus Robinson, Peter 1966A
    wortmani Guthrie, D. A. 1967B;
        Robinson, Peter 1966A
Hyotheridium Palaeoryctidae Van Valen
    1966A
Hyotherium Suidae
    palaeochoerus Mottl 1966A
    soemmeringi Ginsburg 1967A
Hypacrosaurus Hadrosauridae Morris,
    W. J. 1967B

hypercostata (Testudo)
Hyperoarti [Cephalaspidomorpha +
        Petromyzontiformes] Agnatha
        Tarlo, L. B. H. 1967B
Hypertragulidae Hypertraguloidea
    Leptotragulus, Oromeryx
Hypertraguloidea Tragulina
Hypictops Leptictidae Van Valen 1967B
Hyponomys Gliridae
    gollcheri Bruijn 1966C
    morpheus Bruijn 1966C
Hypohippus Equidae Shotwell 1968
    nevadensis Mawby 1968C
Hypolagus Leporidae Dawson, M. 1965;
        Fejfar 1964A; Shotwell
        1968; Wilson, R. L. 1968
    apachensis Gureev 1964
    brachygnathus Sych 1965, 1967A, B
    brachynatus Gureev 1964; Sulimski
        1964
    edensis Gureev 1964
    fontinalis Clark, J. B. Dawson and
        Wood 1964; Gureev 1964
    furlongi Gureev 1964
    I. Gromovi Gureev 1964
    limnetus Gureev 1964
    oregonensis Gureev 1964
    parviplicatus Gureev 1964
    regalis Gureev 1964
    vetus Gureev 1964
Hypolophidae [Dasyatidae] Rajiformes
Hypolorhus Dasyatidae
    sylvestris McNulty 1964, 1965
Hypopnous Captorhinidae
    squaliceps Baird and Carroll 1967A
        (squalidens, in error; syn.
        of Captorhinus aguti); Eaton
        1964A
Hypoprion Carcharhinidae Casier 1966A
Hypoprion Carcharhinus Jonet 1965-66A
hypostylus (Mesohippus)
hypselus (Aboletylestes)
Hypsilophodontidae Ornithopoda Simmons
    1965
    Tatisaurus
hypsilophus (Stegodon)
Hypsiprymnodontinae Macropodidae Ted-
    ford 1967B
Hypsiprymnus Macropodidae
    trisulcatus Mahoney 1964
hypsodus (Ticholeptus)
Hypsohipparion Equidae Singer and Boné
    1966 (dropped)
hypsolephus (Adelopithecus)
Hypurostegi [Scombroidei] Perciformes
        LeDanois and LeDanois 1963*
        (order; classif.)

Hyrachyinae Helaletidae Radinsky 1966B
Hyrachyus Helaletidae Maxwell, R. A.,
    et al. 1967; Radinsky
    1965A, 1967A; Wilson,
    J. A. 1967
  intermedius Russell, L. S. 1965D
  minimus Fischer, K. 1967
  modestus Robinson, Peter 1966A
  stehlini Savage, D. E., Russell and
    Louis 1966
Hyracodon Hyracodontidae Martin, L. D.
    1966
  nebraskensis Radinsky 1967B
  priscidens Clark, J. and Beerbower
    1967 (cf.)
Hyracodontidae Rhinocertoidea Radinsky
    1967B
  Ardynia, Epitriplopus, Forstercooperia,
    Hyracodon, Prohyracodon,
    Triplopides, Triplopus,
    Urtinotherium
Hyracoida Protungulata Hoffmeister 1967
Hyracoidea [Hyracoida] Protungulata
Hyracolestes Adapisoricidae Van Valen
    1966A
Hyracotheriinae Equidae Savage, D. E.,
    Russell and Louis 1965
Hyracotherium Equidae Radinsky 1966A;
    Savage, D. E., Russell and
    Louis 1965
  craspedotum Guthrie, D. A. 1967B;
    Robinson, Peter 1966A
  index Guthrie, D. A. 1967B
  vasacciense Guthrie, D. A. 1967B;
    Maxwell, R. A., et al.
    1967; Robinson, Peter
    1966A; Wilson, J. A. 1967
Hystricidae Hystricoidea Mohr 1965
  Hystrix
Hystricognathi Rodentia
Hystricoidea Hystricomorpha
Hystricomorpha Hystricognathi Gorgas,
    M. 1967
Hystrix Hystricidae
  cristata Mottl 1967A
    minor Malez 1963D
  primigenia Hugueney and Mein 1966;
    Sulimski 1964
  vinogradovi Mottl 1966A
hysudricus (Elephas)
hysudrindicus (Elephas, Palaeoloxodon)

ianishevskyi (Ctenacanthus)
ibericum (Ictitherium, Phalacrocorax)
ibericus (Adelomys, Megacricetodon gre-
    garius, Pseudodryomys)

Iberomeryx Cervidae Gabuniia 1964D,
    1966A
  parvus Gabuniia 1964D
ibex (Capra)
Icaronycteridae Microchiroptera Jepsen
    1966
  Icaronycteris
Icaronycteris Icaronycteridae Jepsen 1966
  index Jepsen 1966, 1967
Icarosaurus Lacertilia Colbert 1966A
    (Trias., N.J.)
  siefkeri Colbert 1966A; Robinson,
    P.L. 1967B (in Kuehneo-
    sauridae)
Ichnites Craniata Alf 1966 (mammal,
    Calif.); Avnimelech 1966
    (dinosaur, Israel); Baird
    1964B (ornithischian, etc.),
    1965B (Perm., Colo.); Bar-
    tholomai 1966B (dinosaur,
    Australia); Bartosch 1962
    (Germany); Bessonnat, et al.
    1965 (reptile, France);
    Bock 1964 (Colo.); Breed
    1967 (Ariz.); Casamiquela
    1964A (Mesoz., Patagonia);
    Cerveri 1964 (Nev.); Colbert
    1964F (Spitzbergen); Courel
    and Demathieu 1962 (Trias.,
    France); Deacon 1966; Delair
    1966C (Eng.), 1967; De-
    mathieu 1964 (Trias., France);
    Ellenberger, F. and Fuchs
    1965 (Jur., France); Ellen-
    burger, P. 1965 (Mesoz.,
    France); Fischer, K. 1963
    (cotylosaur); Gabuniia 1958E
    (dinosaur, USSR); Ginsburg,
    Lapparent, Loiret and Taquet
    1966; Ginsburg, Lapparent,
    and Taquet 1968; György
    1964; Haubold 1966A; Hill,
    D. and Woods 1965 (Trias.,
    Austral.); Jacobi 1963 (rep-
    tile, Germany); Karaszewski
    1966; Kutscher 1966 (Trias.);
    Lapparent, LeJoncour, et al.
    1965; Lapparent and Mon-
    tenat 1967A, B; Lapparent,
    Montenat and Desparmet
    1966 (dinosaur, France);
    Lapparent and Oulmi 1964;
    Majoros 1964 (Perm. reptile);
    Malahan 1967 (Conn.); Malz
    1964 (Jur., Germany); May,
    G. 1966 (dinosaur); Mayr, F.X.

1967; Mountain 1966 (S. Afr.); Moussa 1968 (Eoc., Utah); Nelson, R. H. 1965 (Conn.); Oppé 1965; Ostrom 1967; Panin 1961; Panin and Avram 1962; Raaf, et al. 1965 (Olig. bird); Rat 1960; Sarjeant 1967 (Trias., Eng.); Schmidt, Z. 1965B; Serventy 1960; Spendlove 1968 (Utah; dinosaur); Staines and Wood 1964 (Trias., Australia); Stan 1964 (Hipparion); Thenius 1967A (Plioc. mammals); Tkachenko, O. F., et al. 1967; Vaughn 1964A; Vereshchagin and Zakharenko 1967 (felid); Vialov 1966 (classif.); Young, C.-c. 1966C; Zakharov and Khakimov 1963; Zapfe 1966C

Ameghinichnus, Anatopus, Anchisauripus, Anomoepus, Batrachopus, Bestiopeda, Calibarichus, Chitherioidea, Chirotherium, Deltorrichnus, Eubrontes, Gallegosichnus, Grallator, Iguanodon, Ingenierichnus, Kouphichnium, Limnopus, Macropodosaurus, Megalosauropus, Onychopoides, Orchesteropus, Palaciosichnus, Pecoripeda, Rhynchosauroides, Rogerbaletichnus, Rotodactylus, Ryaneria, Saltopoides, Sarmientichnus, Satapliasaurus, Sathapliasaurus, Shensipus, Shimmelia, Sphingopus, Talmontopus, Varanopus, Wildeichnus

Ichthyodectes Chirocentridae Cavender 1966B
   ctenodon Bardack 1965A, 1968A
   minor Bardack 1965A
Ichthyodectoidei Osteoglossiformes
Ichthyolestes Mesonychidae
   pinfoldi Szalay and Gould 1966
Ichthyophis ?Lepospondyli incertae sedis Kuhn, Oskar 1965E, p. 42 (probably not a gymnophionan)
Ichthyopterygia Reptilia Tatarinov, L. P. 1964S
Ichthyornithes Neornithes

Ichthyosauria Ichthyopterygia Burton, M. 1966; Huene 1966A; Jensen, D. E. 1966A (Holzmaden); Segerblom 1965 (Nevada)
Ichthyosauridae [Macropterygiidae] Latipinnati
Myopterygius
Ichthyosauroididae [Heterosteidae] Pachyosteiformes
Ichthyosaurus [Eurypterygius] Macropterygiidae Wiedenroth 1962
Ichthyostegalia Labyrinthodontia Romer 1964B (suborder)
Ictaluridae Siluriformes
   Ictalurus
Ictalurus Ictaluridae Estes and Tihen 1964
   lambda Wilson, R. L. 1968
   melas Hibbard and Dalquest 1966 (cf.)
   natalis Lundberg 1967
   punctatus Hibbard and Dalquest 1967
   vespertinus Miller, R. R. and Smith 1967
ictericus (Platecarpus)
Icteridae Passeres
   Pandanaris, Quiscalus
Ictidognathus [Ictidostoma] Ictidosuchidae Kuhn, Oskar 1965B, p. 113 (nomen vanum)
Ictidomys Otospermophilus Gromov, I. M., et al. 1965
Ictidomys Sciuridae
   cragini Gromov, I. M., et al. 1965
   meadensis Gromov, I. M., et al. 1965
   tayleri Gromov, I. M., et al. 1965
Ictidopappus Miacidae
   mustelinus MacIntyre 1966
Ictidosauria Theriodontia
Ictidosuchidae Ictidosuchoidea
   Olivieria
Ictidosuchops Nanictidopidae Barghusen 1968; Brink 1965D (in Ictidosuchidae)
Ictidosuchoidea Scaloposauria
Ictiobus Catostomidae Wilson, R. L. 1968
Ictitherium Hyaenidae Lavocat 1961D (?)
   arambourgi Ozansoy 1965
   hipparionum Beaumont 1964B; Ozansoy 1965
   ibericum Meladze 1967
   intuberculatum Ozansoy 1965
   orbignyi Bakalov and Nikolov 1962
   prius Ozansoy 1965
   robustum Bakalov and Nikolov 1962
idahoensis (Canimartes, Equus)
Idiornis Idiornithidae Brodkorb 1965 (for Orthocnemus, preoccup.)

ingens (Aspidichthys, Beerichthys, Koale-
    mus, Pseudocivetta)
Ingentisorex Soricidae Hutchison 1966A
    (in Heterosoricinae)
    tumididens Hutchison 1966A; Repen-
        ning 1967C
Iniopsis Delphinidae
    caucasica Mchedlidze 1964C
innexus (Antepithecus)
Inostranceviidae Gorgonopsia
    Sauroctonus
insculpta (Clemmys)
Insectivora Unguiculata Butler, P. M.
        and Greenwood 1965;
        Chaline 1966D; Findley
        1967 (geol. range); Hutchi-
        son 1968B; Mills 1966
    Incertae sedis: Pentacodontidae
insigne (Menatotherium, Plesiadapis)
insignis (Anglaspis, Drydenius, Halecop-
        sis, Merychippus, Stegodon)
insulata (Anagonia)
insiliens (Thescelus)
insuliferus (Promimomys)
integra (Archegonaspis)
Interatheriidae Typotheria
    Antepithecus, Guilielmoscottia, Noto-
        pithecus, Transpithecus
intercedens (Cordylodon)
"Interhippus" Notohippidae
    deflexus Simpson, G. G. 1967A
        (nomen dubium)
intermedia (Chrysophrys, Corvina, Por-
        aspis
intermedium (Asaphestera, Ocnerotherium,
        Omosoma, Paraentelodon,
        Postschizotherium)
intermedius (Baiomys, Cynodictis, Elio-
        mys, Epihippus, Euthynotus,
        Hyrachyus, Mammut, Mam-
        muthus primigenius, Mimo-
        mys, Platecarpus, Platinx,
        Potamochoerus, Tapirus)
interruptus (Ctenodus, Polyptychodon)
intrepidus (Pseudaelurus)
intricatus (Glasbius)
intuberculatum (Ictitherium)
inundata (Amblyrhiza)
irgisensis (Peloneustes, Strongylokrotaphus)
iorensis (Clethrionomys)
Irregulareaspidinae Cyathaspididae Denison
        1964B
Irregulareaspis Cyathaspididae
    complicata Denison 1964B (nomen
        nudum)
    hoeli Denison 1964B (nomen nudum)

prisca Denison 1964B (nomen nudum)
stensioi Denison 1964B
irregularis (Aetobatis, Myliobatis)
isabenae (Pivetonia)
Ischignathus Traversodontidae Bonaparte
        1963C
    sudamericanus Bonaparte 1963C
Ischigualastia Kannemeyeriidae
    jenseni Cox, C. B. 1965
Ischisaurus Thecodontosauridae Kuhn,
        Oskar 1965A (Ichisaurus;
        in Anchisauridae)
Ischnacathidae Ischnacanthiformes Miles,
        R. S. 1966A
    ?Acanthodopsis, Xylacanthus
Ischnacanthiformes Acanthodii Miles, R. S.
        1966A
Ischnodon Peramelidae
    australis Ride 1964B
Ischyodus Chimaeridae
    avitus Schweizer 1964
    schuebleri Schweizer 1964
Ischyrhiza Pristidae
    avonicola Casier 1964 (cf.); Estes 1964;
        Slaughter and Steiner 1968
    mira McNulty and Slaughter 1964B;
        Miller, H. W. 1967; Slaughter
        and Steiner 1968
    mira Slaughter and Steiner 1968
    schneideri Slaughter and Steiner
        1968
Ischyrictis Mustelidae
    zibethoides Ginsburg 1967A
Ischyrocyon Canidae Skinner, M. F.,
        Skinner and Gooris 1968
Ischyrodidelphis Didelphidae
    castellanosi Paula Couto 1962B
Ischyromyidae Ischyromyoidea Black,
        C. C. 1968A
    ?Advenimus, Dawsonomys, Hulgana,
        Ischyromys, Knightomys,
        Sciuravus, Titanotheriomys
    Sciuravinae
Ischyromyoidea Sciuromorpha
Ischyromys Ischyromyidae
    douglassi Black, C. C. 1968A
    parvidens Howe, J. A. 1966B
    pliacus Black, C. C. 1965A; Howe,
        J. A. 1966B
    typus Black, C. C. 1968A
    veterior Black, C. C. 1968A
Ischyrosmilus Felidae
    johnstoni Mawby 1965B
Isectolophidae Tapiroidea Radinsky 1965A
    Homogalax, Indolophus
Isistius Scymnorhinidae

italicus (Elephas antiquus, Epapheliscus,
          Megaceros, Palaeoloxodon
          antiquus)
itancinicus (Citellus, Citellus undulatus)
Itanzatherium Rhinocerotidae Beliaeva
          1966 (in Dicerorhininae)
    angustirostre Beliaeva 1966
iudei (Prolimnocyon)
ivoensis (Mosasaurus)
iwaniensis (Pteraspis)

jaccardi (Plesiochelys)
jacksoni (Eucrotaphus)
jacksonoides (Singida)
jacobi (Geomys)
Jacobulus Parasemionotidae
          novus Lehman 1966B
jaculus (Eryx)
jaegeri (Chalicomys, Drepanaspis, Masto-
          donsaurus, Steneofiber)
jaekeli (Acanthorhina, Onychodus,
          Trygon)
Jaekelotodus ?Carchariidae Glikman
          1964B (in Odontaspididae)
    karagiensis Glikman 1964B
Jagorina Jagorinidae
    pandora Stensiö 1963
Jagorinidae Gemuendiniformes
    Jagorina
jahni (Merychyus)
jamaicensis (Artibeus, Artibeus jamaicen-
          sis, Buteo, Leiocephalus)
Jamoytidae Anaspidiformes
    Jamoytius
Jamoytiiformes [Anaspidiformes] Ana-
          spida Tarlo, L. B. 1967B
          (order)
Jamoytius Jamoytidae
    kerwoodi Ritchie, A. 1968
Janassa Petalodontidae
    bituminosa Malzahn 1968; Ørvig
          1967A
janeti (Notogoneus)
Janimus ?Paramyidae Dawson, M. 1966
    rhinophilus Dawson, M. 1966
janossyi (Sminthozapus)
japonicus (Bufo bufo, Cervus, Desmosty-
          lus hesperus)
jarrovii (Pelycodus)
Jarvikia ?Fleurantiidae
    arctica Lehman 1966C
javanicus (Bos)
jaxarticus (Aspideretes, Plastomenus)
jeanneli (Listriodon)
jeanteti (Apodemus)
jebeli (Sayimys)

jeffersoni (Mammuthus, Megalonyx,
          Protosciurus)
Jefitchia Sciaenidae See: Otolithus
          Frizzell and Dante 1965
    copelandi Frizzell and Dante 1965
jemlahicus (Hemitragus)
jenseni (Ischigualastia)
jepseni (Hemiacodon, Miacis, Paleomoro-
          pus, Phenacolemur)
Jhingrania Clupeidae Misra, K. S. and
          Saxena 1964
    roonwali Misra, K. S. and Saxena
          1964
jigulensis (Citellus pygmaeus)
Jimuria [Jimusaria] Dicynodontidae
Jimusaria Dicynodontidae
johnsoni (Amphekepubis, Trionx)
johnstoni (Geochelone, Ischyrosmilus)
Jonkeria Jonkeriidae
    rossouwi Boonstra 1955B*
jonkeriidae Titanosuchia Boonstra 1954C
          (Jonkeridae)
    Jonkeria
Jordanomys ?Cricetidae Haas, G. 1968
          (nomen nudum)
Josepholeidya Proterotheriidae Simpson,
          G. G. 1964C, 1967A
joyneri (Catopsalis)
jubae (Idrissia)
jubatus (Acinonyx)
juergeni (Protogonacanthus)
julieni (Plesictis)
jullyi (Lemur)
jumae (Giraffa)
junturensis (Ammospermophilus)
juradoi (Marmosopsis)
jurensis (Synechodus)
Juxia Rhinocerotidae Chow, M.-c. and
          Chiu 1964
    sharamurenensis Chow, M.-c. and Chiu
          1964
Jynx Picidae
    torquilla Brunet, J. 1961 (cf.)

kacheticus (Kvabebihyrax)
kaisensis (Stegodon)
kaiseri (Metapterodon)
kalganensis (Testudo)
kalliokoskii (Tanaocrossus)
Kallostrakon Tesseraspididae
    alleni Tarlo 1964C, 1965
    grindrodi Tarlo 1964C, 1965
    macanuffi Tarlo 1964C, 1965
    podura Tarlo 1965
kamensis (Muraenosaurus)
kameruni (Proportheus)

kipalaensis (Paradercetis)
Kipalaichthys ?Bathyclupeidae Casier
        1965
    sekirskyi Casier 1965
kirchbergensis (Dicerorhinus)
kirgizica (Proochotona)
kiridus (Kritimys)
kirki (Dolichorhynchops)
kirkinskayae (Ilemoraspis)
Kislangia Cricetidae Topachevskii 1965C
Kislangia Mimomys Aleksandrova 1965A
Kistecephalidae Dicynodontia Kuhn,
        Oskar 1965B, p. 23, 184,
        (=Cistecephalidae)
kitchingi (Cragievarus, Homodontosaurus,
        Struthiocephalus)
kittsi (Cymatorhiza)
Kiyutherium Hydrochoeridae Francis, J.
        C. and Mones 1965B
    orientalis Francis, J. C. and Mones
        1965B
klatti (Protoadapis)
kneri (Pteraspis)
knightensis (Cynodontomys)
knightia Clupeidae Cavender 1966B
Knightomys Ischyromyidae Wood, A. E.
        1965B (in Sciuravidae)
    depressus Wood, A. E. 1965B
knoblochi (Camelus)
knorri (Leptolepis)
knoxensis (Tetrameryx)
kochi (Pterodactylus)
koakudsi (Felis rufus)
Koalemus Phalangeridae
    ingens Bartholomai 1968 (in Dipro-
        todontidae)
Koaliella Salamandridae Estes, Hecht
        and Hoffstetter 1967
kochi (Germanodactylus, Pterodactylus)
Kochictis Paroxyclaenidae Van Valen
        1966A
    centenii Van Valen 1965E
koenigswaldi (Hipparion, Microdyromys)
kokeni (Brazosiella, Helicampodus, Ursus
        thibetanus)
kolakovskii (Sakya)
Kolopsis Diprotodontidae Woodburne
        1967A
    rotundus Plane 1967A, B
    torus Woodburne 1967A, B
Kolopsoides Diprotodontidae Plane 1967A,
        B
    cultridens Plane 1967A, B
Kolymaspididae Kolymaspidiformes
Kolymaspidiformes Rhenanida

Komba Lorisidae Simpson, G. G. 1967B
    minor Simpson, G. G. 1967B
    robustus Simpson, G. G. 1967B
konwanlinensis (Sinomegaceros)
Kopidodon Paroxyclaenidae Van Valen
        1965E, 1966A
koraensis (Eomyctophum)
koreanicus (Harpagolestes)
kormosi (Blarinella)
korotorensis (Stegodon)
Korynichniidae Diadectoidea Lotze 1927A*
        (of Romer; Korynichnidae)
    Korynichnium
Korynichnium Korynichniidae See: Ich-
        nites
    sphaerodactylum Kaszap 1968
kotanskii (Guerichosteus)
kounoviensis (Sphaerolepis)
Kouphichnium Ichnites
    walchi Malz 1964
kowalskii (Pliomys)
kozlowskii (Guerichosteus)
kraglievichorum (Scaglia)
krejcii (Pediomys)
kretzoi (Drepanosorex)
kretzoii (Dolomys, Mimomys, Pliomys,
        Sorex)
Kritimys Muridae Kuss and Misonne
        1968
    catreus Kuss and Misonne 1968
    kiridus Kuss and Misonne 1968
Kronosaurus Pliosauridae Bergamini and
        editors of Life 1964 (restor.);
        Hall, E. and M. 1964B;
        Romer 1959E
kruckowi (Fehmarnichthys)
krugi (Masillamys)
krumbiegeli (Paratricuspiodon)
Kuehneosauridae Eolacertilia Romer 1966
        (in new infraorder Eolacer-
        tilia)
    Icarosaurus, Kuehneosaurus, Kuehneo-
        suchus
Kuehneosaurus Kuehneosauridae
    latus Robinson, P. L. 1967B
Kuehneosuchus Kuehneosauridae Robinson,
        P. L. 1967B
    latissimus Robinson, P. L. 1967B
Kuehneotheriidae Amphitheria Kermack,
        D. M., Kermack and Mussett
        1968
    Kuehneotherium
Kuehneotherium Kuehneotheriidae Ker-
        mack, D. M., Kermack and
        Mussett 1968

Lagurodon); Buachidze 1968
(subgen. Lagurodon); Shevchenko, A. I. 1965B; To-
pachevskii 1965C
lagurus Chaline 1965A; Jánossy
1960A*; Kowalski, K.
1967B; Sukachev, et al.
1966
luteus Aleksandrova 1965B (cf.);
Jullien 1965A; Tropin 1968
pannonicus Aleksandrova 1965A (cf.)
praeluteus Shevchenko, A. I. 1965B
praepannonicus Topachevskii 1965C
(subgen. Lagurodon)
simplicidens Zazhigin 1966D
sibiricus Erbaeva 1966 (subgen.
Eolagurus)
transiens Aleksandrova 1965A, B;
Shevchenko, A. I. 1965B
lagurus (Lagurus)
Laidleri ?Rhytidosteidae
gracilis Cosgriff 1965
lambda (Ictalurus)
Lambdaconus Mammalia incertae sedis
suinus Simpson, G. G. 1967A (nomen
vanum)
Lambdoceras Protoceratidae Stirton
1967D
hessei Stirton 1967D
Lambdotherium Brontotheriidae
popoagicum Robinson, Peter 1966A
Lambeosaurus Hadrosauridae Sternberg
1965 (rest.)
paucidens Ostrom 1964B (for Hadrosaurus paucidens)
lamberi (Bauzaia)
lamberti (Enchodus)
lambi (Merycoidodon)
lambrechti (Cygnopterus)
Lamna [Isurus] Isuridae
Lamnidae [Isuridae] Isuroidei
Lampridida Teleostei Danil'chenko 1964B
(order)
Lampropeltis Colubridae
doliata Holman 1965D
getulus Holman 1965D
similis Holman 1964C
lancensis (Exostinus)
lanceolata (Clupea, Morrhua)
landenensis (Eochiromys)
Landenoden Arctocyonidae Quinet 1966C
woutersi Quinet 1966C
landesquei (Pseudocyonopsis, Pseudocyonopsis landesquei)
langewieschei (Anomotherium, Eosqualodon)

langhae (Pliobatrachus)
langi (Tropidemys)
langshanensis (Sinolycoptera)
laniarius (Sarcophilus)
lankesteri (Rhyphodon)
Lantanotherium Erinaceidae Hutchison
1968B
lantaniensis (Homo erectus)
Lantian man [Sinanthropus lantianensis]
Hominidae Hemmer 1964C;
Kurth 1966B; Vallois 1965E;
Woo 1964A, B, C, D, F, G,
1965A, B, C, D, E, F, G, H,
1966A, B, C; Wu, Yuan, et
al. 1966; Yang 1965
lantianensis (Sinanthropus)
Lantianus Adapidae Chow, M.-c. 1964A
xiehuensis Chow, M.-c. 1964A
Laornis Anatidae
edvardsianus Baird 1967
Laparon Ephippidae Casier 1966A
alticeps Casier 1966A
lapis (Lepus)
lapparenti (Phenacolemur)
Lapparentophidae Serpentes incertae sedis
lar (Aristelliger)
Lari Charadriiformes Dement'ev 1964
(order)
Laridae Lari
sterna
larteti (Democricetodon, Heteroprox,
Myoglis, Testudo)
Lasalia Lasalidae Vaughn 1965
cutlerensis Vaughn 1965
Lasalichthys Redfieldiidae Schaeffer, B.
1967B
hillsi Schaeffer, B. 1967B (rest.)
Lasalidae Amphibia incertae sedis Vaughn
1965
Lasalia
lascarevi (Alilepus)
Lasicopus Prunella Stepanian 1964
Lasiurus Vespertilionidae
borealis
minor Choate and Birney 1968
laskarevi (Cricetodon helveticum)
lasseroni (Berruvius)
Lasticopus ?Rhytidosteidae Cosgriff 1965
lateralis (Acrodus)
laticeps (Brachycrus, Eurymylus, Pelosaurus, Piocormus)
laticostata (Allocryptaspis)
latidens (Cynodontomys, Galeocerdo,
Hylonomus, Isotemnus, Mesohippus, Meterix, Miacis, Myliobatis, Stegolophodon, Stegolophodon latidens)

latifrons (Alces, Bison, Kannemeyeria, Libralces)
latimanus (Scapanus)
latimarginalis (Plesiochelys)
Latimeria Coelacanthidae Anthony, J. and Robineau 1967; Caldwell, D. K. and Caldwell 1965; Thenius 1965D; Thomson, K. S. 1966F
  chalumnae Millot and Anthony 1965; Millot, Nieuwenhuys and Anthony 1964; Nieuwenhuys 1965; Pegeta 1968; Stensiö 1963
latipes (Anoplotherium, Equus caballus)
Latipinnati Ichthyosauria
latipons (Peishanemys)
Latirhynchus Coryphaenoididae See: Otolithus Stinton 1965
  grumosus Stinton 1965
latirostris (Eosqualodon)
latiscuta (Shansiemys)
latispinus (Platecarpus)
latissima (Brachipteraspis)
latissimus (Kuehneosuchus, Ptychodus)
latiusculus (Pholidophorus)
latrans (Canis)
latum (Palaeotherium)
latus (Alacodon, Cheiracanthus, Kuehneosaurus)
Latvius Osteolepididae
  deckerti Jessen 1966A
  grewingki Jessen 1966A
laubei (Aspius, Ptychogaster)
laurillardi (Anoplotherium, Archaeomys)
lautricense (Lophiodon)
laveirensis (Pycnodus)
lavocati (Columbomys, Cricetodon, Cricetulus, Mawsonia, Ruscinomys)
lawi (Chendytes)
Lawnia Lawniidae Gardiner 1967A
Lawniidae Palaeonisciformes Gardiner 1967A
  Lawnia
Lawrencia Vireonidae
  nana Bernstein 1965
lawrowi (Dicrocerus)
laytoni (Ectypodus)
leachi (Pteraspis)
leachii (Anolis bimaculatus)
leaderensis (Ticholeptus hypsodus)
leakeyi (Aceratherium, Anasinopa, Dicerorhinus, Propotto, Viverra)
Leakeymys ?Cricetidae Lavocat 1964B
  ternani Lavocat 1964B

Leakitherium Hyaenodontidae Savage, R. J. G. 1965A
  hiwegi Savage, R. J. G. 1965A
leari (Pantomimus)
leathensis (Pteraspis)
lednevi (Merluccius)
leemanni (Cotimus)
lefeldi (Guerichosteus)
lefevrei (Galeorhinus)
legetet (Limnopithecus)
Lehmanamia Amiidae Casier 1966A
  sheppeyensis Casier 1966A
lehmani (Adunator)
lehneri (Ginglymostoma)
Leiacanthus Hybodontidae
  falcatus Stefanov 1966
Leidyosuchus Crocodylidae Miller, H. W. 1967
  sternbergi Estes 1964
Leimadophis Colubridae
  perfuscus Ray, C. E. 1964C
Leiocephalikon Gymnarthridae
  problematicum Carroll, R. L. 1966
Leiocephalus Iguanidae
  apertosulcus Etheridge 1965
  carinatus Etheridge 1966A
  cuneus Etheridge 1964
  jamaicensis Etheridge 1966B
  personatus Etheridge 1965
leiopheurus (Proraniceps)
Leiosteidae Pachyosteiformes
Leithia Gliridae
  carteri Bruijn 1966C
  melitensis Bruijn 1966C
lemanense (Aceratherium)
lemanensis (Cynelos, Cynelos lemanensis, Plesictis)
lembronicus (Treridomys)
Lemmus Cricetidae
  lemmus Fejfar 1965 (aff.); Feustel, et al. 1963; Jacobshagen 1963
  sibiricus Repenning, et al. 1964
lemmus (Lemmus)
Lemur Lemuridae
  jullyi Saban 1963 (subgen. Pachylemur)
Lemuridae Lemuroidea Crusafont Pairó 1967B; Jolly, A. 1966
  Lemur, Pachylemur
Lemuriformes Prosimi
Lemuroidea Lemuriformes Crusafont Pairó 1967B
lemuroides (Paroxyclaenus)
lenensis (Rhinoceros)
lenki (Pliomys)
lennieri (Lepidotus)

lenocinator (Chthomaloporus)
lens (Sinemys, Sphaerodus)
lenticularis (Neohipparion)
lentus (Helohyus)
lenzii (Barysoma)
leo (Felis)
Leo Panthera Dietrich 1968
leonardi (Vernonaspis)
leonensis (Parahippus)
Leontiniidae Toxodontia Colwell 1965
leotensis (Harpagolestes)
Lepadolepididae Asterolepidiformes
    Obruchev, D. V. 1964D
    (=Grossaspididae Stensiö
    1959B* partim)
  Lepadolepis
Lepadolepis Lepadolepididae Gross, W.
    1965A (=Ceratolepis; in
    Grossaspididae)
lepersonnei (Stegolophodon)
Lepidocottus Gobiidae Ionko 1954
Lepidopleuroidea [Percoidea partim]
    Percoidei Le Danois and Le
    Danois 1963* (suborder of
    Hypurostegi)
Lepidopus Trichiuridae
  glarisianus Dzhafarova 1963
Lepidosauria Diapsida Reig 1967; Robin-
    son, P. L. 1967A; Tatarinov,
    L. P. 1964T
Lepidosirenoidei [Lepidosireniformes]
    Ceratodonti Andrews, S. M.,
    Gardiner, Miles and Patterson
    1967
Lepidosiren Lepidosirenidae Lehman
    1966C
Lepidosirenidae Lépidosiréniformes
    Lepidosiren, Propterus
Lepidosireniformes Ceratodonti Lehman
    1966C (Lepidosiren and
    Propterus)
Lepidotus Semionotidae Tabaste 1963
  dixseptiensis Silva Santos 1962
  elvensis Malzahn 1963; Wenz 1967A,
    B
  lennieri Wenz 1967B
lepidotus (Urocles)
Lepisosteidae Lepisosteiformes
    Lepisosteus
Lepisosteiformes Holostei Lehman 1966B
Lepisosteus Lepisosteidae Bjork 1967;
    Gosline 1965; Hibbard and
    Dalquest 1966; Lehman
    1966B (vertae.); Lundberg
    1967; Wilson, R. L. 1968
  occidentalis Estes 1964 (skull rest.)

Lepistosteida Holostei Danil'chenko
    1964A (order)
Lepomis Centrarchidae
  cyanellus Hibbard and Dalquest 1966
    (cf.); Lundberg 1967
Leporidae Lagomorpha Sych 1966A
  Agispelagus, Alilepus, Archeolagus,
    Caprolagus, Eulagus, Gobio-
    lagus, Hypolagus, Lepus,
    Litolagus, Lushilagus, Mega-
    lagus, Montanolagus, Mytono-
    lagus, Notolagus, Oryctolagus,
    Pliolagus, Pliopentalagus,
    Poelagus, Pratilepus, Procapro-
    lagus, Proeulagus, Serengeti-
    lagus, Shamolagus, Sivalilagus,
    Sylvilagus, Trischizolagus,
    Veterilepus
  Agispelaginae, Leporinae, Megalaginae,
    Mytonolaginae
leporides (Lagorchestes)
Leporinae Leporidae Gureev 1964
Leporini Leporinae Gureev 1964
Lepospondyli Amphibia Baird 1965A,
    1966B; Tatarinov, L. P.
    1964K
  Incertae sedis: Adelospondylus
leptacanthus (Eporeodon)
Leptacodon Leptictidae McKenna 1968
    (in ?Nyctitheriidae)
  tener Russell, L. S. 1967A
Leptarctus Mustelidae Eisele 1965
    (Plioc., Nebr.)
  neimenguensis Zhai 1964
  primus Skinner, M. F. and Taylor 1967
Leptauchenia Merycoidodontidae
  decora Schultz, C. B. and Falkenbach
    1968; Skinner, M. F., Skinner
    and Gooris 1968 (cf.)
  harveyi Schultz, C. B. and Falkenbach
    1968
  margeryae Schultz, C. B. and Falken-
    bach 1968
  martini Schultz, C. B. and Falkenbach
    1968
  parasimus Schultz, C. B. and Falkenbach
    1968
Leptaucheniinae Merycoidodontidae Schultz,
    C. B. and Falkenbach 1968
Leptaucheniini Leptaucheniinae Schultz,
    C. B. and Falkenbach 1968
    (tribe)
Lepterpetontidae Nectridia Romer 1945D*;
    see also Kuhn, Oskar 1965E,
    p. 23
leporinus (Noctilio)

Schreiber 1962
leucocephala (Columba)
Leucocrossuromys Cynomys Gromov, I.
     M., et al. 1965
leucodon (Spalax)
leucogaster (Onychomys)
leudersensis (Schaefferichthys)
levei (Bessoecetor)
levenkoi (Tannuaspis)
levis (Crenosteus, Psammosteus)
levius (Deinotherium)
lewesiensis (Enchodus, Hoplopteryx)
lewisi (Hoplopteryx, Merycoidodon)
lhemani (Wetlugasaurus)
lherminieri (Puffinus)
liaojaoshanensis (Polybranchiaspis)
libanica (Pateroperca)
libitum (McKennatherium)
Libralces Cervidae
     gallicus Heintz, E. 1968
     latifrons Whitehead 1964
libyca (Eotheroides)
libycus (Enchodus, Stephanodus)
Libycosuchinae [Libycosuchidae] Meso-
     suchia Nopcsa 1928B
     (Lybicosuchinae)
Libycosuchidae Mesosuchia
     Libycosuchinae
Libytherium Giraffidae
     maurusium Hooijer 1963D
licenti (Postschizotherium)
licinus (Strigosuchus)
ligniticus (Triportheus)
Ligulalepis Palaeoniscidae Schultze 1968
     toombsi Schultze 1968
limbata (Pholidophoroides)
Limicolae [Charadriiformes] Neognathae
     Dement'ev 1964
Limicorallus Rallidae Kurochkin 1968A
     saiensis Kurochkin 1968A
Limnerpeton Microbrachis Brough and
     Brough 1967
limnetus (Hypolagus)
Limnocyonidae Oxyaenoidea
     Prolimnocyon, Prototomus
Limnoecinae Soricidae Repenning 1967C
Limnoecus Soricidae Hutchison 1966A;
     Wilson, R. L. 1968
     micromorphus Dehm 1964; Doben-
          Florin 1964; Repenning
          1967C
     niobrarensis Repenning 1967C
     tricuspis Repenning 1967C
Limnopithecus Pongidae
     legetet Frisch 1965
     macinnesi Frisch 1965

Limnopus Ichnites
     cutlerensis Baird 1965B
Limnoscelididae Captorhinoidea Romer
     1945D* (Limnoscelidae)
     Limnosceloides, Limnoscelops, Limn-
          ostygis, Romeriscus
Limnosceloides Limnoscelididae
     brachycolis Langston 1966B
Limnoscelops Limnoscelididae Lewis, G.E.
     and Vaughn 1965
     longifemur Lewis, G. E. and Vaughn
          1965
Limnostygis Limnoscelididae Carroll,
     R. L. 1967C
     relictus Carroll, R. L. 1967C
Limnotragus Bovidae Frechkop 1965A
lindae (Hyneria)
lindermayeri (Palaeoreas)
lindstromi (Archegonaspis)
lineatum (Tropidoclonion)
lineolatus (Charitosomus)
Liodon Mosasauridae
     mosasauroides Deloffre 1964
     sectorius Russell, D. A. 1967A
Liodontia Aplodontidae
     alexandrae Shotwell 1968
liodontus (Clidastes)
liorhinus (Thrinaxodon)
Liotomus Ptilodontidae
     marshi Russell, D. E. 1964; Russell,
          D. E., Louis and Poirier
          1966B
Lipotyphla Insectivora
lipovensis (Doniceps)
lipperti (Drepanaspis)
liratus (Stichocentrus)
Lissamphibia Amphibia Baird 1965A;
          Baldauf 1965; Kuhn, O.
          1967B (to be dropped)
Lissemydinae Trionychidae Goin and
          Goin 1962*
Lissemys Trionychidae Smith, M. A. 1931
          (for Emyda Gray 1831)
Lisserpeton Scapherpetontidae Estes 1965B
          (Mont., Wyo.)
     bairdi Estes 1965B
Lissoberyx Trachichthyidae Patterson, C.
          1967A
     dayi Patterson, C. 1967A (rest.)
lissiensis (Glirulus, Rhinolophus grivensis)
Listraspis Cyathaspididae Denison 1964B
     canadensis Denison 1964B
Listriodon Suidae
     jeanneli Hooijer 1963D (cf.)
     lockharti Petronijević 1967

lautricense Fischer, K. 1964
leptorhynchum Fischer, K. 1964
parisiense Fischer, K. 1964
remensis Savage, D. E., Russell and
    Louis 1966
rhinocerodes Fischer, K. 1964
sardus Fischer, K. 1964
tapiroides Fischer, K. 1964
tapirotherium Fischer, K. 1964
thomasi Fischer, K. 1964
Lophiodonticulus Notoungulata incertae
    sedis
    patagonicus Simpson, G. G. 1967A
    retroversus Simpson, G. G. 1967A
Lophiodontidae Tapiroidea
Lophiaspis, Lophiodon
Lophiomeryx Tragulidae Friant 1962D
    benarensis Gabuniia 1964D, 1966A
Lophiotherium Equidae Savage, D. E.,
    Russell and Louis 1965
    cervulum Remy 1967 (aff.); Savage,
        D. E., Russell and Louis
        1965
    pygmaeum Savage, D. E., Russell and
        Louis 1965
    robiacense Savage, D. E., Russell and
        Louis 1965
Lophiparamys Paramyidae
    debequensis Wood, A. E. 1965B
Lorisidae Lorisioidea Crusafont Pairó
    1967B
    Indraloris, Komba, Mioeuoticus, Pro-
        galago, Propotto
Lorisioidea Neoprosimii Crusafont Pairó
    1967B
lorteti (Euposaurus, Pseudaelurus)
Lotella Moridae
    andrussovi Dzhafarova 1962
louisi (Meldimys, Reithroparamys)
Louisina Hyopsodontidae Russell, D. E.
    1964
    atavella Russell, D. E. 1964
    mirabilis Russell, D. E. 1964
lovei (Hesperosorex, Parectypodus)
Loveina Omomyidae
    zephyri Robinson, Peter 1966A
loxodon (Copemys)
Loxodonta Elephantidae
    africana Coppens 1965B
    africanava Coppens 1965B
    atlantica
        angammensis Coppens 1965B
    cretica Kuss 1966
    creutzburgi Kuss 1965B
loxodus (Prolagus)
lucioperca (Lucioperca)

Lucioperca Percidae
    lucioperca Tarashchuk 1965, 1967
    zaissanicus Tarashchuk 1965, 1967
        occidentalis Tarashchuk 1965, 1967
lucius (Esox)
luckhoffi (Notictosaurus)
ludensis (Archegonaspis)
Ludiortyx Cracidae Brodkorb 1964A (in
        Gallinuloidinae)
    blanchardi Brodkorb 1964A
ludlowiensis (Logania)
ludovicianus (Cynomys)
Lufengosaurus Plateosauridae
    magnus Young, C.-c. 1966B
Luganoiformes Actinopterygii Lehman
        1966B
lugdunensis (Parapodemus)
luhai (Tartuosteus)
Luisiella Dussumieriidae Bochinno, R.
        1967 (in Sprattelloidinae)
    inexcutada Bochinno, R. 1967
Lukousaurus Podokesauridae
    yini Simmons 1965
lulli (Alphadon, Indraloris)
lullianus (Pseudocyclopidius)
lunanensis (Amynodon, Testudo)
Lunania ?Chalicotherioidea incertae sedis
        Radinsky 1964A, 1965A
    youngi Radinsky 1964A (probably a
        chalicothere)
lunata (Onychogalea)
lundeliusi (Microsyops)
lundensis (Proserranus)
lungtêensis (Lycoptera)
lunulata (Ricardolydekkeria)
lupaster (Canis)
Lupeosauridae Edaphasuria Kuhn, Oskar
        1966A (ascribed to Romer
        1937, by error)
lupina (Oxyaena)
lupinus (Pseudamphicyon)
lupus (Canis)
Luscina Turdidae
    megarhyncha Brunet, J. 1961
luscus (Gulo gulo)
Lushiamynodon Amynodontidae Chow,
        M.-c. and Xu 1965
    menchiapuensis Chow, M.-c. and Xu
        1965
    obessus Chow, M.-c. and Xu 1965
    sharamurenensis Xu 1966
lushiensis (Hapalodectes)
Lushilagus Leporidae Li, C.-k. 1965
    lohoensis Li, C.-k. 1965
lusitanica (Tomistoma)
lustanicus (Anchilophus)

Machaeracanthus Acanthodii incertae
sedis Gross, W. 1965C;
Lehman 1963B
Machaeromeryx Cervidae
gilchristensis Maglio 1966; Patton
1966B
Machairodus Felidae Mawby 1965B
(subgen. Heterofelis)
schlosseri Bakalov and Nikolov 1962
machikanense (Tomistoma)
Machimosaurus Teleosauridae Krebs
1967B
macinnesi (Limnopithecus)
macintyri (Miacis)
macoveii (Spalax)
macracanthus (Hoplopteryx)
Macrauchenia Macraucheniidae Hoffstetter
and Paskoff 1966 (Pleist.,
Chili)
Macraucheniidae Litopterna Hoffstetter
1968C (distrib.)
Macrauchenia
Macrobaenidae Baenoidea Sukhanov
1964
macrocephala (Sinolepis, Tanupolama)
macrocephalus (Archeolagus, Callionymus,
Harpagolestes)
Macrochires [Apodiformes] Neognathae
Dement'ev 1964
Macroclemys Chelydridae
auffenbergi Dobie 1968 (Plioc., Fla.)
Macrocnemia [Macrocnemus] Sauria
incertae sedis (ascribed to
Kuhn 1946A as a suborder
by Tarlo in Appleby et al.
Tarlo 1967)
Macrocnemus Sauria incertae sedis
macrodactylus (Bavarisaurus)
Macrodon (Dicynodon, Hecubides)
macrodontus (Honanodon)
Macrognathomys Zapodidae Shotwell
1968
nanus Wilson, R. L. 1968
macrognathus (Apternodon, Gobicyon,
Pachypithecus, Sorex araneus)
macrolepidotus (Osteolepis)
macrolepis (Pseudogonatodus)
macromerus (Stretosaurus)
Macromesodon Gyrodontidae Lehman
1966B (reconst. of head)
Macroneomys Soricidae Fejfar 1966C
brachygnathus Fejfar 1966C
Macropetalichthyidae Macropetalichthyiformes
Macropetalichthys, Wijdeaspis

Macropetalichthyiformes Petalichthyida
Macropetalichthys Macropetalichthyidae
rapheidolabis Stensiö 1963
macrophtalmus (Sparodus)
Macropodidae Phalangeroidea Ride 1964B
Bettongia, Caloprymnus, Dorcopsis,
Dorcopsoides, Hadromas,
"Halmaturus," Hypsiprymnus,
Lagorchestes, Macropus,
Onychogalea, Procoptodon,
Propleopus, Protemnodon,
Sthenurus, Troposodon,
Wallabia
Hypsiprymnodontinae, Macropodinae,
Potoroinae, Sthenurinae
Macropodinae Macropodidae Tedford 1967B
Macropodosaurus Theropoda incertae sedis
See: Ichnites Zakharov 1964
gravis Zakharov 1964
Macropoma Coelacanthidae Lehman 1966C
(dermocranium)
macropomus (Scombrinus)
macropternus (Bunophorus)
macropterus (Platinx)
Macropterygiidae Latipinnati Huene 1948H*,
p. 72; Appleby 1967 (Ichthyosauridae)
Eurypterygius
Macropus Macropodidae
birdselli Tedford 1967B (subgen. Macropus)
faunus Bartholomai 1966C
ferragus Tedford 1967B (subgen. Macropus)
magister Bartholomai 1966C
pan Bartholomai 1966C
rufus Tedford 1967B (subgen. Megaleia)
Macropus Macropus Tedford 1967B
macrorhinus (Merycoidodon)
macrorhiza (Carcharhinus, Carcharias)
Macrorhizodon Isuridae Sokolov, M. I.
1965 (in Lamnidae)
macrorhizus Sokolov, M. I. 1965
priscus Sokolov, M. I. 1965
macrorhizus (Macrorhizodon, Paraisurus)
macrorhyncha (Pelurgaspis)
Macrosaurus Mosasauridae
impar Miller, H. W. 1967
Macroscelididae Macroscelidoidea
Elephantulus, Metoldobotes, Mylomygale,
Myohyrax, Palaeothentoides,
Protypotheroides, Rhynchocyon
Macroscelidinae, Mylomygalinae, Myohyracinae

Macroscelidinae Macroscelididae Patterson, B. 1965B
Macroscelidoidea Menotyphla Van Valen 1967B (Macroscelidea; in Insectivora)
Macrosemiidae Amioidei
   Notagogus, Ophiopsis, Propterus
macrosynaphus (Desmatochoerus)
macrota (Carcharias)
Macrotarsius Omomyidae
   siegerti Robinson, Peter 1968B
Macrotherium Chalicotheriidae Hooijer 1963D
Macrotus Phyllostomatidae
   waterhousii
      waterhousii Choate and Birney 1968
Macrurida Teleostei Danil'chenko 1964B (order)
Macrouridae Macrouroidei
   Coelorhynchus, Macrouridarum
Macrouridarum Macrouridae See: Otolithus Weiler 1962
   globosus Weiler 1962G
Macrouroidei Gadiformes
macrurus (Leuciscus)
maculata (Pholidophoropsis)
maculatum (Ambystoma)
maculatus (Notorhynchus)
madagascariensis (Trematosaurus)
Madtsoiinae Boidae Hoffstetter 1961A*; Kuhn, Oskar 1966 (Madtsoinae)
magister (Macropus, Schlosseria)
magistrae (Tricuspiodon)
magna ("Pehuenia", Poraspis)
magnifontis (Pliauchenia)
magnevillei (Dapedius)
Magnosaurus [Megalosaurus] Megalosauridae
   woodwardi Huene 1932C*
magnum (Aceratherium, Palaeotherium)
magnus (Cimolestes, Cochliodus, Desmodus, Lufengosaurus, Phascolonus, Pliosaccomys, Teleolophus, Watsonisuchus)
maguirei (Gigantohyrax)
Magyarosaurus [Titanosaurus] Titanosauridae Kuhn, Oskar 1965A (p. 68, note)
Mahavisaurus ?Rhinesuchoidea incertae sedis Lehman 1966A
   dentatus Lehman 1966A, 1967A
maicopicum (Cetotherium)
maior (Neosqualodon gastaldii)
maius (Tragocerus)

majmesculae (Tichvinskia)
major (Amphicyon, Amphicyon major, Cephalaspis, Citellus, Cricetus cricetus, Ctenacanthus, Dipoides, Gobiolagus, Grangeria, Helicotragus, Hippopotamus amphibius, Metailurus, Microstonyx, Neocnus, Paramerycoidodon, Peratherium hoogbutselense, Phyllonycteris, Pirortyx, Proconsul, Pseudocyclopidius, Rhinchorhinus, Sinolagomys, Ustatochoerus, Veronaspis)
majori (Anthracomys, Gliravus, Mimomys, Palaeoryx)
majusculus (Podilymbus)
malabaricus (Indobatrachus)
Malayemys Testudinidae Lindholm 1931 (for Damonia; incl. Emys subtrijuga)
maldani (Propachynolophus)
maldonadoi (Peromyscus)
malembeensis (Carcharhinus)
maleriensis (Metoposaurus)
malheurensis (Protospermophilus)
maltha (Ciconia)
malustensis (Geoemyda, Hipparion)
Mamenchisaurus Titanosauridae Kuhn, Oskar 1965A (Manenchisaurus)
   hochuanensis Chao, S.-t. 1965
Mammalia Tetrapoda Anderson, S. and Jones 1967 (families); Butler, P. M., et al. 1967; Gabie 1965 (origin); Gabuniiá 1964C; Grassé 1967; Kermack, K. A. 1967A; Kühne 1967, 1968; Lessertisseur and Sigogneau 1965 (skel.); Olson, E. 1963D (origin), 1966C; Parrington 1967A (origin); Tarlo, in Butler, P. M., et al. 1967 (classif.); Walker, E. P. 1964
   Incertae sedis: Ameghinichnus, Anagonia, Anisorhizus, Diplodontops, Eutrochodon, Florentinoameghinia, Heterolophodon, "Isolophodon," Lambdaconus, Pachypithecus, Picunia, Proplanodus, Prostylophorus, "Stenogenium," Trilobodon
   Haramyidae, Microcleptidae
Mammalipedia Ichnites Panin and Avram 1962; Vialov 1961*, 1966
mammilaris (Ptychodus)

mammillata (Tremataspis)
Mammonteus Elephas Adam, K. D. 1966A
Mammonteus [Mammuthus] Elephantidae
mammontoides (Phanagoroloxodon)
Mammut Mammutidae Thorslund 1966
   americanum Frankforter 1966; John-
      son, S. T. 1962; Ray, C. E.,
      Cooper, et al. 1967
   angustidens Circi 1962A (subgen.
      Bunolophodon; Mastodon);
      Pavlovic and Durkovic 1962
      (subgen. Bunolophodon);
      Petronijevic 1967
   angustidens Kuss and Schreiner
      1963 (Mastodon)
   tapiroides Kuss and Schreiner
      1963 (Mastodon)
   turicensis Kuss and Schreiner
      1963 (Mastodon)
   arvernensis Fejfar 1964A (Mastodon);
      Saraiman and Capitanu 1965
      (Mastodon)
   borsoni Alekseeva, L. I. 1965 (Masto-
      don); Bakalov and Nikolov
      1962 (Zygolophodon); Be-
      lokrys 1959B (Zygolopho-
      don); Fejfar 1964A (Masto-
      don); Mitzopoulos 1966,
      1967 (Zygolophodon); Niko-
      lov 1965; Nikolov and Ko-
      vachev 1966; Put' 1952
      (Mastodon); Radulesco, Sam-
      son, et al. 1965
   grandincisivus Malez 1965H (Mastodon;
      subgen. Bunolophodon)
   intermedius Chang, H.-c. 1964A
   longirostris Saraiman 1966 (Mastodon);
      Steininger 1965 (Mastodon;
      subgen. Bunolophodon);
      Zapfe 1964D (reconst.)
   pyrenaicus Bergounioux and Crouzel
      1966A (Zygolophodon)
   shansiensis Erdbrink 1967B (subgen.
      Zygolophodon)
   tapiroides Bakalov and Nikolov 1962
      (Zygolophodon)
   turicensis Rakovec 1965A (Zygolopho-
      don)
Mammuthus Elephantidae Pichard del
      Barrio, et al. 1961 (skel.)
   gromovi Alekseeva, L. I. 1965 (Archi-
      diskodon) Alekseeva, L. I.
      and Garutt 1965 (Archidis-
      kodon); Konstantinova 1965A
      (Archidiskodon)

imperator Leonhardy 1966A, B; Mehl
      1966
   haroldcooki Hibbard and Dalquest
      1966
jeffersoni Frankforter 1966
meridionalis Alekseeva, L. I. 1965
      (Archidiskodon); Apostol
      1965B (Archidiskodon);
      Bandrabur and Giurgea 1965
      (Archidiskodon); Bolomey
      1965A (Archidiskodon);
      Dubrovo 1963D (Archidisko-
      don), 1964A; Dubrovo and
      Alekseev 1964 (Archidisko-
      don); Gabuniia and Vekua
      1966C (Archidiskodon);
      Garutt and Safronov 1965
      (Archidiskodon); Radulesco,
      Samson, et al. 1965 (Archi-
      diskodon)
   archaicus Mitzopoulos 1964 (Archi-
      diskodon)
   meridionalis Gabuniia and Vekua
      1963 (Archidiskodon)
   proarchaicus Melentis 1966B (Archi-
      diskodon)
   tamanensis Dubrovo and Chepalyga
      1967
   taribanensis Gabuniia and Vekua
      1963 (Archidiskodon)
planifrons Chakravarti 1965 (Archidis-
      kodon)
primigenius Altmeyer 1964 (Elephas);
      Apostol 1957 (Mammonteus),
      1962; Apostol and Olaru
      1966; Chang, C.-k. 1964;
      Churcher 1968; Dubrovo and
      Chepalyga 1967; Feustel, et
      al. 1963; Garutt 1964, 1966;
      Goncharov 1967; Heller, F.
      1964 (Mammonteus); Hunter
      and Langston 1965; Jacob-
      shagen 1963 (Mammonteus);
      Kaplianskaia, Tarnogradskii
      and Vangengeim 1964; Kruy-
      tzer 1963B (Mammonteus);
      Kubiak 1965A, B; Musil 1968;
      Rakovec 1965B; Ray, C. E.,
      Cooper, et al. 1967; Svistun
      1968; Sukachev, et al. 1966;
      Theobald 1965; Troitskii 1966;
      Widmer 1966 (Mammonteus);
      Zol'nikov 1961
   intermedius Shcheglova 1961C
   transvaalensis Hendey 1967 ("Archidis-
      kodon")

trogontherii Apostol 1965A; David,
A. 1965C (subgen. Parele-
phas); Dietrich 1965; Du-
brovo and Chepalyga 1967;
Esteras and Aguirre 1964
(Parelephas); Iakhimovich,
N. N. 1960 (Parelephas);
Kubiak 1965A, B; Vekua
1958B (Mammonteus)
    chosaricus Dubrovo 1966A; Tapalov
1967
    wüsti Alekseeva, L. I. 1965 (Archidis-
kodon)
Mammuthus Elephas Bakalov and Nikolov
1964
Mammutidae Elephantoidea
    Mammut
Mancallidae Alcae
    Alcodes, Praemancalla
    Mancallinae
Mancallinae Mancallidae
manchharensis (Brachyodus)
manchouensis (Manchurochelys)
manchoukuoensis (Manchurochelys)
manchuriana (Anosteira)
Manchurichthys ?Anaethalionidae
    uwatokoi Gaudant 1967
manchuricus (Capreolus)
Manchurochelys Thalassemyididae Yeh
1963B (in Sinemyididae)
    manchoukuoensis Endo and Shikama
1942B*; Yeh 1963B
maniculatus (Peromyscus)
mantchurica (Marmota)
mantelli (Xiphactinus)
maomingensis (Anosteira)
maortuensis (Aspideretes, Chilantaisaurus)
maotaiensis (Mixosaurus)
maraghanus (Urmiornis)
marahomensis (Chelydosaurus)
maral (Cervus)
Marcetia Mustelidae Petter, G. 1967A
    santigae Petter, G. 1967A
Marckgrafia Pristidae
    nigeriensis Tabaste 1963
margaritae (Tuvaspis)
margeriei (Prostylophorus)
margeryae (Leptauchenia)
mariae (Blarinoides, Pithecistes)
marianae (Sespia)
marinus (Bufo)
maritimus (Ursus)
markae (Coccosteus, Psammosteus)
Marmes man [Homo sapiens] Hominidae
    Kirk 1968 (Wash.)

Marmoops Phyllostomatidae
    blainvillii
        cuvieri Choate and Birney 1968
marmorensis (Diplomystus)
Marmosa Didelphidae Zetti 1967
    mexicana Alvarez and Ferrusquia
1967 (cf.); (Mex.)
Marmosopsis Didelphidae Paula Couto
1962B
    juradoi Paula Couto 1962B
marmota (Marmota)
Marmota Sciuridae Alekseeva, L. I. and
Lomize 1960; Mostecký 1964
    arizonae Gromov, I. M., et al. 1965
    arrodeus Gromov, I. M., et al. 1965
    bobac Gromov, I. M., et al. 1965;
        Grosset, et al. 1965; Veresh-
        chagen, Geptner, et al. 1959
    palaeoplanicola Gromov, I. M., et al.
1965
    palaeorossica Gromov, I. M., et al.
1965
    camtschatica
        vaskovskii Gromov, I. M., et al. 1965
    caudata Gromov, I. M., et al. 1965
    complicidents Gromov, I. M., et al. 1965
    himalayana Gromov, I. M., et al. 1965
    longipes Gromov, I. M., et al. 1965;
        Vekua 1958B
    mantchurica Gromov, I. M., et al. 1965
    marmota Altuna 1966A; Malez 1965D
    primigenia Gromov, I. M., et al.
1965
    minor Gromov, I. M., et al. 1965
    monax
        hessi Gromov, I. M., et al. 1965
    oregonensis Gromov, I. M., et al. 1965
    sawrockensis Hibbard 1964
    siberica
        nekipelovi Erbaeva 1966
    tologoica Ivan'ev 1966A, 1967
    vetus Gromov, I. M., et al. 1965
Marmotinae Sciuridae Gromov, I. M., et al.
1965 (USSR)
Marmotini (partim) Marmotinae Gromov,
I. M., et al. 1965
marnocki (Syrrhophus)
maroccanus (Protostomias)
marplesi (Prosqualodon)
marrioti (Ardiodus)
marshi (Alphadon, Liotomus, Plioplatecarpus)
Marsupialia Metatheria Clemens 1965A,
1968B; Van Deusen and
Jones 1967 (geol. range)
    Incertae sedis: Notoryctidae, Progarzonia

marsupialis (Antidorcas, Didelphis)
Marsupicarnivora Marsupialia Ride 1964B
    (order; incl. Didelphoidea,
    Borhyaenoidea and Dasyu-
    roidea)
martes (Martes)
Martes Mustelidae Wiszniowska 1967
    americana Anderson, E. 1968
    andersoni Petter, G. 1967A (aff.)
    basilii Petter, G. 1964B
    foina David, A. and Markevich 1967;
        Kurtén 1965A; Malez 1963D
    martes Krysiak 1956; Lomi 1963;
        Malez 1963D; Thenius
        1965B (cf.); Zapfe 1966B
    muncki Ginsburg 1964C; Petronijević
        1967
    stirtoni Wilson, R. L. 1968
    zibellina
        zibellina Vaňura 1965
martinssoni (Logania)
maryanus (Strepsiceros)
marylandica (Taxidea)
mascallensis (Prodipodomys)
Masillamys Pseudosciuridae
    beegeri Hartenberger 1968; Thaler
        1966B
    krugi Hartenberger 1968
    tobieni Thaler 1966B
maslinensis (Carcharias)
massai (Bunolistriodon)
massetericus (Uintacyon)
Massetognathus Traversodontidae Romer
    1967B
    pascuali Romer 1967B
    teruggii Romer 1967B
Massospondylus Thecodontosauridae
    carinatus Bond, G. 1955B
    harriesi Bond, G. 1955B
Mastersoniidae Dinocephalia Kuhn, Oskar
    1966A (? in Titanosuchoi-
    dea)
mastivus (Noctilio leporinus)
Mastodon [Mammut] Mammutidae
Mastodonsauridae Capitosauroidea Ochev
    1966C; Welles and Cosgriff
    1965B
    Mastodonsaurus
Mastodonsaurus Mastodonsauridae
    cappelensis Welles and Cosgriff 1965B
    jaegeri Welles and Cosgriff 1965B
matachicensis (Otospermophilus)
mathisi (Megalonyx)
martini (Leptauchenia)
mater (Caroloameghinia)
matritensis (Hispanotherium)

matthesi (Rotodactylus)
matthesi (Arctocyon)
matthewi (Dipsalodon, Hipparion, Hyaeno-
    don, Megahippus, Megatylopus,
    Otospermophilus)
maurettei (Lophiaspis)
mauritanicus (Atlanthropus, Pagrus,
    Plesiosaurus)
maurusium (Libytherium)
mawsoni (Amiidarum, Meniscolophus)
Mawsonia Coelacanthidae
    lavocati Tabaste 1963
maxima (Bothriolepis, Gruipeda)
maximiliani (Homoeosaurus)
maximus (Colobodus, Elephas, Grallator,
    Mosasaurus, Palaeopropithecus,
    Procaprolagus, Tartuosteus,
    Tritylodontoideus)
Maxschlosseria Oldfieldthomasiidae
    consumata Simpson, G. G. 1967A
        (new comb.)
    expansa Simpson, G. G. 1967A (new
        comb.)
    minima Simpson, G. G. 1967A (new
        comb.)
    minuta Simpson, G. G. 1967A (new
        comb.)
    praeterita Simpson, G. G. 1967A
    rusticula Simpson, G. G. 1967A (new
        comb.)
    septa Simpson, G. G. 1967A (new
        comb.)
mayeri (Cetotherium)
Mayomyzon Petromyzontidae Bardack
    and Zangerl 1968
    pieckoensis Bardack and Zangerl 1968
mcgheei (Citellus)
mcgrewi (Phenacolemur)
mckayensis (Citellus)
Mckennatherium ?Paromomyidae Van
    Valen 1965F
    libitum Van Valen 1965F
mcnallyi (Cuttysarkus)
meadensis (Cryptotis, Cynomys, Ictidomys,
    Ophiomys)
meagherensis (Paramerycoidodon)
meandrinus (Psammosteus)
means (Amphiuma)
Meantes Caudata
mechernichensis (Cyclotosaurus, Paroto-
    saurus)
mediterraneum (Hipparion)
mediterraneus (Hipparion, Hipparion med-
    iterraneus)
medium (Palaeotherium)

mongoliensis Dashzeveg 1964
megalopteryx (Psammosteus)
Megalosauridae Carnosauria Charig, At-
	tridge and Crompton 1965;
	Colbert 1964B; Maleev
	1964K
	Chilantaisaurus, Eustreptospondylus,
		Megalosaurus, Metriacantho-
		saurus
Megalosauroidea Carnosauria Kuhn, Oskar
	1966A (credited to Walker,
	A. D. 1964, but see O. P.
	Hay, bibliog.); Walker, A. D.
	1964 (incl. Megalosauridae)
Megalosauropus Icnites Colbert and Mer-
	rilees 1967 (Cret., Australia)
	broomensis Colbert and Merrilees 1967
Megalosaurus Megalosauridae Huene 1966B
megalotis (Reithrodontomys)
Megalotragus Bovidae
	cucornutus Wells, L. H. 1964A
megamastoides (Nyctereuctes)
Megamphicyon Canidae Kuss 1965C
	giganteus Kuss 1965C
Megantereon Felidae Chow, M.-c., Hu and
	Lee 1965
	megantereon Bolomey 1965A
	nihowanensis Chow, M.-c. and Chow
		1965
	piveteaui Ozansoy 1965
megantereon (Megantereon)
Meganthropus Hominidae Gremiatskii
	1966; Iakimov 1947D; Nes-
	turkh 1954; Tobias 1965D
Megapedetes Pedetidae Lavocat 1961D;
	Lavocat and Michaux 1966
Megaptera Balaenopteridae
	expansa Kellogg 1968
	novaeanglidae Hasegawa and Matsu-
		shima 1968A (cf.)
megarhinus (Dicerorhinus, Rhinoceros)
megarhyncha (Luscina)
Megasespia Merycoidodontidae Schultz,
	C. B. and Falkenbach 1968
	middleswarti Schultz, C. B. and Falken-
		bach 1968
Megasminthus Dipodidae Klingener 1966
	(in Zapodinae)
	tiheni Klingener 1966
Megatheriidae Megalonychoidea
	Eremotherium, Megatherium
Megatylopus Camelidae Webb, S. D. 1965C
	matthewi Webb, S. D. 1965C
Megatherium Megatheriidae Jensen, D. E.
	1966B; Tavera 1968
	americanum Zetti 1964

Megazostrodon Triconodonta Crompton
	and Jenkins 1968
	rudnerae Crompton and Jenkins 1968
Megoreodon Merycoidodontidae
	hollandi Skinner, M. F., Skinner and
		Gooris 1968
meini (Cricetodon, Pentaglis)
meissneri (Palaeochoerus)
Melanognathus Dipnoi incertae sedis
	Jarvik 1967C
	canadensis Jarvik 1967C
melanoleuca (Ailuropoda)
Melanopelta Plagiosauridae Shishkin, M. A.
	1967B
	antiqua Shishkin, M. A. 1967B
Melanorosauridae Plateosauria Charig, At-
	tridge and Crompton 1965
	(in Prosauropoda); Colbert
	1964B
	Euskelosaurus
Melanosauridae [Necrosauridae] Varanoidea
	McDowell and Bogert 1954*
	(in Anguinomorpha (sic))
Melanosauroides Anguidae Kuhn, Oskar
	1940J*
melas (Ictalurus)
Meldimys Paramyidae Michaux 1968
	louisi Michaux 1968
Meleagrididae Phasianoidea
	Agriocharis
Meleagrinae Phasianidae Brodkorb 1964A
Meleagris Phasanidae
	gallopavo Cracraft 1968 (Mex. Pleist.)
meles (Meles)
Meles Mustelidae
	meles Dal' 1954*; David, A. and Marke-
		vich 1967; Jacobshagen 1963;
		Kurtén 1965A; Malez 1963D;
		Rakovec 1965B; Thenius
		1965B; Tsalkin 1962; Vekua
		1958B; Zapfe 1966B
	minor Vereshchagin 1951C (aff.)
Meletta Clupea Anđelkovic 1962
Meletta Clupeidae Gofshtein 1953
melettaeformis (Clupea)
Melinae Mustelidae
Melissiodon Cricetidae
	dominans Ctyroky, Fejfar and Holy
		1964A
melitensis (Elephas, Leithia)
mellali (Dubiomys)
Mellivorinae Mustelidae
Melosaurus Archegosauridae
	uralensis Konzhukova 1964D
melrosensis (Bauzaia)
menakiae (Lycoclupea)

osborni Schultz, C. B. and Falkenbach 1968
dani Schultz, C. B. and Falkenbach
1968 (subgen. Anomerycoi-
dodon)
forsythae Schultz, C. B. and Falkenbach 1968
galushai Schultz, C. B. and Falkenbach 1968 (subgen. Blickohyus)
lambi Schultz, C. B. and Falkenbach
1968 (subgen. Anomerycoi-
dodon)
lewisi Clark, J. and Beerbower 1967
lynchi Schultz, C. B. and Falkenbach
1968 (subgen. Blickohyus)
macrorhinus Schultz, C. B. and Falkenbach 1968
Merycoidodontidae Merycoidodontoidea
Schultz, C. B. and Falkenbach
1968
Barbourochoerus, Bathygenys, Brachycrus, Cyclopidius, Dayohyus,
Desmatochoerus, Epigenetochoerus, Eucrotaphus, Genetochoerus, Gregoryochoerus,
Hadroleptauchenia, Leptauchenia, Megabathygenys,
Megasespia, Megoreodon,
Merychyus, Merycochoerus,
Merycoidodon, Metoreodon,
Osbornohyus, Otionohyus,
Parabathygenys, Paradesma-
tochoerus, Paraeporeodon,
Paramerycoidodon, Pithe-
cistes, Pseudocylopidius,
Pseudogenetochoerus, Sespia,
Ticholeptus, Ustatochoerus
Desmatochoerinae, Eporeodontinae,
Leptaucheniinae, Merychyi-
nae, Merycochoerinae, Mery-
coidodontinae, Miniochoeri-
nae, Oreonetinae, Ticholep-
tinae
Merycoidodontinae Merycoidodontidae
Schultz, C. B. and Falken-
bach 1968
Merycoidodontoidea Oreodonta
Mesacanthidae Acanthodiformes Miles,
R. S. 1966A
?Holmesella, Mesacanthus, Triazeuga-
canthus
Mesacanthus Mesacanthidae
mitchelli Miles, R. S. 1966A
Mesaxonia Ferungulata
meschethense (Cephalogale)

meschetica (Testudo)
Meschotherium Rhinocerotidae Gabuniiä
1964D
meschethicum Gabuniiä 1964D, 1966A
Mesembrinibis ?Plataleidae
cayennensis Collins, C. T. 1964
Mesembroniscus ?Boreosomidae Gardiner
1967A
Mesenosauridae [Younginidae] Eosuchia
Romer 1956F*
Mesenosaurus
Mesenosaurus Younginidae Watson 1956B*
(related to Millerosaurus),
1957A* (in Millerosauria)
Mesichthyes Teleostei
Mesocetus Cetotheriidae
siphunculus Kellogg 1968
Mesoclupea Chirocentridae
Showchangensis Bardack 1965A; Gaudant 1967
Mesocnus Megalonychidae
browni Paula Couto 1967
torrei Arredondo 1958C; Paula Couto
1967
Mesocricetodon Megacricetodon Daxner
1967
Mesodma Ectypodidae
thompsoni Sloan and Van Valen 1965
Mesodon Pycnodontidae
combesi
var. ciricinus Astre 1967B
Mesohippus Equidae
celer Clark, J. and Beerbower 1967
grandis Clark, J. and Beerbower 1967
hypostylus Clark, J. and Beerbower
1967
latidens Clark, J. and Beerbower 1967
viejensis Clark, J. and Beerbower 1967
Mesoleptidae [Aigialosauridae] Varanoidea
Huene 1956D* p. 668 (incl.
Mesoleptos and Eidolosaurus.
Mesomephitis Mustelidae Petter, G. 1967A
medius Petter, G. 1967A
Mesonychidae Condylarthra
Andrewsarchus, Apterodon, Dasyurodon,
Dissacus, Gandakasia, Hapalodectes, Harpagolestes, Hessolestes, Honacodon, Ichthyolestes, Mesonyx, Microclaenodon, Mongolestes, Mongolonyx,
Olsenia, Pachyaena, Synoplotherium
Andrewsarchinae, Haplodectinae, Mes-
onychinae
Mesonyx Mesonychidae Szalay and Gould
1966

michali (Listriodon splendens)
Microbiotheriinae Didelphidae
Microbrachidae Microsauria
    Microbrachis
Microbrachis Microbrachidae
    mollis Brough and Brough 1967
    obtusatum Brough and Brough 1967
        (subgen. Limnerpeton)
    pelikani Brough and Brough 1967
Microbunodon Anthracotheriidae Hüner-
        mann 1964
    minimum Brunet, M. 1968
    minus Hünermann 1967
Microcavia Caviidae
    australis
        australis Contreras 1964
Microcephala (Ctenothrissa)
Microchampsa Protosuchidae
    scutata Simmons 1965; Young, C.-c.
        1964A
Microchiroptera Chiroptera
Microchoerus Necrolemuridae Crusafont
        Pairó 1967B
    erinaceus Crusafont Pairó 1965M
    ornatus Crusafont Pairó 1967B
Microclaenodon Mesonychidae Szalay
        and Gould 1966
Microcleptidae Mammalia incertae sedis
Microcnus Megalonychidae
    gliriformis Paula Couto 1967
Microconodon Diademodontidae Kuhn,
        Oskar 1965B (note)
microdon (Rhombodus)
microculus (Nanpanaspis)
Microdyromys Gliridae Bruijn 1966A
    complicatus Bruijn 1966A
    koenigswaldi Bruijn 1966A; Vollmayr
        1966
microlepidota (Cephalaspis)
microlestes (Protictis)
micromorphus (Limnoecus)
Micromyrus Echelidae Casier 1967
    fehmarnensis Casier 1967
Micromys Muridae
    praeminutus Sulimski 1964 (cf.)
Microparamyinae Paramyidae
Microparamys Paramyidae Robinson,
        Peter 1966A
    dubius Dawson, M. 1966
    lysitensis Wood, A. E. 1965B
    minutus Dawson, M. 1968B
    monspeliensis Thaler 1966B
    nanus Michaux 1968
    parvus Hartenberger 1968 (=Masilla-
        mys parvus)
    russelli Michaux 1964B, 1968

Microphocaena Phocaenidae Kudrin and
        Tatarinov 1965, 1966
    podolica Kudrin and Tatarinov 1965,
        1966
Micropholoidea Rhachitomi
microphtalmus (Spalax)
Micropternodontinae Palaeoryctidae Van
        Valen 1966A
Micropternodus Palaeoryctidae Van Valen
        1966A
    morgani Stirton and Rensberger 1964
Micropterus Centrarchidae
    punctulatus Wilson, R. L. 1968 (cf.)
microrhinus (Changisaurus)
Microsauria Lepospondyli Gregory, J. T.
        1964A, 1965; Tatarinov, L. P.
        1964L
    Incertae sedis: Novascoticus
Microsaurops ?Sauropoda Kuhn, Oskar
        1964C (for Microsaurus
        Hatcher, preocc.), p. 324;
        1965A (taxonomic note)
Microsorex Soricidae Repenning 1967C
Microstonyx Suidae Meladze 1967
    major Nikolov 1962*
Microsula Sulidae Howard, H. 1968A
Microsyopidae Prosimii incertae sedis
        McKenna 1965B
    Cynodontomys, Microsyops
Microsyops Microsyopidae
    lundeliusi Robinson, Peter 1966A
Microtidae [Microtinae] Cricetidae
        Kretzoi 1962E
Microtinae Cricetidae
Microtus Cricetidae Guthrie, R. D. 1965
    agrestis Krommenhoek and Slob 1967B;
        Malez 1963D
    arvalinus Buachidze 1968; Kretzoi
        1965C; Shevchenko, A. I.
        1965B
    arvalis Aleksandrova 1965A, B (cf.)
        Feustel, et al. 1963; Jacob-
        shagen 1963; Krommenhoek
        and Slob 1967B
    arvalis-agrestis Aleksandrova and
        Tseitlin 1965; Jullien 1965A
    conjungens Kretzoi and Vértes 1965B
    gregalis Aleksandrova 1965A, B (cf.)
        Jacobshagen 1963; Zazhigin
        1966D
    mediterraneus Chaline 1967
    mexicanus Alvarez 1966 (Mex.)
    miurus Repenning et al. 1964 (subgen.
        Stenocranius)
    nivalis Aleksandrova 1965A (cf.);
        Jacobshagen 1963

Proergilornis, Propotamo-
choerus provincialis, Proviverra, Sinolagomys, Spalax
microphtalmus, Squalus,
Troposodon, Varanopsis)
minotaurus (Mus)
mintoni (Proacris)
minus (Cricetodon, Democricetodon,
Microbunodon, Trogonther-
ium)
minuscula (Anabernicula)
Minusculodelphis Didelphidae Paula Couto
1962B
minimus Paula Couto 1962B
minuta (Aquila, Maxschlosseria)
minutus (Apternodon, Breviodon, Diacodon, Megacricetodon, Microparamys, Omomys, Phio-
cricetomys, Sorex, Steneofiber, Ulemosaurus)
minutissimus (Scyliorhinus)
miocaena (Palaeortyx)
miocaenicum (Potamotherium)
miocaenicus (Glirulus)
miocaenus (Physodon, Proalector)
miocea s (Palaeochenoides)
miocenica (Coturnix, Hyla, Percrocuta,
Rana)
miocenicum (Cainotherium)
miocenicus (Arnoglossus, Procynops)
Miocnus Megalonychidae
antillensis Paula Couto 1967
Mioeuoticus Lorisidae
bishopi Simpson, G. G. 1967B
miofloridana (Hyla)
Mionictis Mustelidae
dubia Petronijević 1967
Miophasianus Phasianidae
altus Villalta 1963
medius Villalta 1963
Miortyx Phasianidae
aldeni Howard, H. 1966C
Miosorex Soricidae
grivensis Repenning 1967C
Miospermophilus Sciuridae
bryanti Gromov, I. M., et al. 1965
wyomingensis Gromov, I. M., et al.
1965
Miosula ?Sulidae Howard, H. 1968A
mira (Ischyrhiza, Ischyriza mira, Olsenia)
mirabilis (Chroniosuchus, Euchambersia,
Groenlandaspis, Louisina,
Parapliohyrax, Parapodemus)
Mirabilocerus Tragocerus Meladze 1967
miriani (Crocuta)
mirificus (Stegomastodon)

mironovi (Plourdosteus)
miroshnikovi (Cyathaspis, Steinaspis)
mirus (Pugiodons)
mirzadi (Rhizomys)
misonnei (Myotis)
mississipensis (Corax)
mississippiensis (Alligator)
missouriensis (Mosasaurus)
mitchelli (Mesacanthus)
mitchilli (Mosasaurus)
miticulus (Hyopsodus)
Mitilanotherium Giraffidae Samson and
Rădulesco 1966B
inexspectatum Samson and Rădulesco
1966B
mitis (Caenopus)
mitra (Mitrocystites)
Mitrata Calcichordata
Mitrocystella Mitrocystitidae
incipiens
miloni Jefferies 1968
Mitrocystites Mitrocystitidae
mitra Jefferies 1968
Mitrocystitidae Mitrata
Mitrocystella, Mitrocystites
miurus (Microtus)
Mixocetus Cetotheriidae Mitchell, E. D.
1966B (rest.)
Mixodectidae ?Apatemyoidea McKenna
1965B
Elpidophorus, Eudaemonema, Remiculus
Mixosauridae Latipinnati Appleby 1967
Mixosaurus
Mixosaurus Mixosauridae
corvalianus Gilardoni 1964
maotaiensis Young, C.-c. 1965E
miyokoae (Stegolophodon)
mlokosiewicze (Tetrao)
mnaidriensis (Elephas)
mnaidvensis (Elephas)
modestus (Glirudinus, Hyrachyus)
modicus ("Eurystephanodon", Pleurostylodon, "Trigonolophodon")
Moeripithecus Cercopithecidae Simons,
E. L. 1967H (syn. with
Propliopithecus)
mogaungensis (Amphipithecus)
moldavicus (Promimomys)
moldaviensis (Pliopentalagus)
Molgophidae Microsauria
Palaeomolgophis
molidens (Litolagus)
mollis (Microbrachis)
Molossidae Vespertilionoidea Lavocat
1961D
Chaerophon, Molossus, Tadarida

anceps Signeux 1959A (cf.)
caroliniensis Russell, D. A. 1967A
    (nomen vanum)
conodon Baird and Case 1966; Russell,
    D. A. 1967A
couperi Russell, D. A. 1967A (nomen
    vanum)
crassidens Russell, D. A. 1967A (nomen
    dubium)
dekayi Russell, D. A. 1967A
hoffmanni Kruytzer 1964A
iembeensis Telles Antunes 1964C
impar Russell, D. A. 1967A (nomen
    dubium)
ivoensis Russell, D. A. 1967A
laevus Russell, D. A. 1967A (nomen
    vanum)
maximus Langston 1966C; Russell,
    D. A. 1967A
missouriensis Russell, D. A. 1967A
mitchelli Russell, D. A. 1967A (nomen
    vanum)
occidentalis Russell, D. A. 1967A
    (nomen nudum)
reversus Russell, D. A. 1967A (nomen
    dubium)
validus Russell, D. A. 1967A (nomen
    vanum)
mosbachensis (Canis lupus, Equus, Panthera
    leo, Praemegaceros)
moschata (Desmana)
moschatus (Ovibos)
Moschops Tapinocephalidae
    svijagensis Tatarinov, L. P. 1966C
Moschowhaitsia Whaitsiidae Tatarinov,
    L. P. 1965A, C
    vjuschkovi Tatarinov, L. P. 1964AE,
        1965A, 1966C, D
Moschowhaitsiinae Whaitsiidae Tatarinov,
    L. P. 1963B*, 1965A
Moschorhininae Whaitsiidae Tatarinov,
    L. P. 1963B*
moseleyi (Brazosiella)
mosensis (Stephanodus)
moseri (Thalassemys)
mossoczyi (Geoemyda)
Mourasuchus Crocodylidae Kuhn, Oskar
    1966A (Maurosuchus);
    Langston 1966A; Price,
    L. I. 1963, 1964
    amazonensis Price, L. I. 1963 (in Alli-
        gatorinae), 1964
mousteriensis (Homo)
moythomasi (Deltoptychius)
Moythomasia Palaeoniscidae Lehman 1966B

mucronata (Bauzaia, Raja)
mudgei (Platecarpus)
muelleri (Brychaetus, Protohippus, Rattus)
muensteri (Notidanus)
Mugil Mugilidae
    applanatus Weiler 1966A
    radobojanus Ionko 1954
Mugilida Teleostei Danil'chenko 1964B
    (order)
Mugilidae Mugiliformes
    Mugil
Mugiliformes Acanthopterygii
mukiri (Promesochoerus)
mukirii (Paradiceros)
multicinctus (Dissorophus)
multicrestatus (Peridyromys)
multicristatus (Ceratodus)
multicuspis (Didolodus)
multidens (Conjunctio, Novascoticus)
multidentata (Eotomistoma)
multifragum (Psittacotherium)
multipinnatus (Gobius)
Multituberculata Allotheria Hopson 1967B;
    Landry 1965, 1967; Simpson,
    G. G. 1968E; Van Valen and
    Sloan 1966 (extinction)
muncki (Martes)
mungerorum (Gerrhonotus)
Mungos Viverridae
    dietrichi Petter, G. 1964A
munieri (Amia)
münsteri (Coelodus)
Muntiacus Cervidae
    pliocaenicus Korotkevich 1965B
        (Muntjacus)
Muraenidae Anguilliformes
    Eomuraena
Muraenosauridae [Plesiosauridae] Plesio-
    sauroidea
Muraenosaurinae Plesiosauridae Kuhn, Oskar
    1966A (assigned to White, T.
    1940A, fam.); Novozhilov
    1964C
Muraenosaurus Plesiosauridae
    kamensis Dubeikovskii and Ochev 1967
murchison (Hemicyclaspis)
Muridae Muroidea
    Anthracomys, Apodemus, Coryphomys,
        Kritimys, Micromys, Mus,
        Nesokia, ?Palustrimus, Para-
        podemus, Progonomys, Rattus,
        Rhagapodemus, Stephanomys
murinus (Notostylops, Peridyromys)
Muroidea Myomorpha
muroii (Lycoptera)

murrayi (Lystrosaurus)
Mus Muridae
    minotaurus Kuss and Misonne 1968
    musculus Shevchenko, A. I. 1965B
        (cf.)
    synanthropus Kretzoi and Vértes
        1965B (subgen. Budamys)
Muscardinulus Muscardinus Hartenberger
        1967A; Thaler 1966B
Muscardinus Gliridae
    bouziguensis Thaler 1966B (subgen.
        Muscardinulus)
    crusafonti Hartenberger 1967A (sub-
        gen. Muscardinus)
    davidi Hugueney and Mein 1965
    pliocaenicus Sulimski 1964
      hispanicus Bruijn 1966B
    sansaniensis Baudelot, S. 1965, 1966
    thaleri Bruijn 1966A
    vallesiensis Hartenberger 1967A (sub-
        gen. Eomuscardinus)
    vireti Hugueney and Mein 1965
Muscardinus Muscardinus Hartenberger
        1967A
musceli (Glossanodon)
musculus (Anemorhysis, Mus)
musicoides (Citellus)
musicus (Citellus)
Mustela Mustelidae Oesch 1967; Para-
        skevaidis 1961; Shotwell
        1968
    erminea Malez 1963D; Zapfe 1966B
    eversmanni Thenius 1965B (subgen.
        Putorius); Zapfe 1966B
    frenata Anderson, E. 1968
    nigripes Anderson, E. 1968 (subgen.
        Putorius)
    nivalis Zapfe 1966B
    putorius Krysiak 1956; Malez 1963D
Mustelavus Mustelidae
    priscus Clark, J. and Beerbower 1967
Mustelidae Canoidea Lavocat 1961D (?)
    Alopecocyon, Baranogale, Beckia,
        Brachypsalis, Broiliana,
        Canimartes, Circamustela,
        Conepatus, Enhydra, En-
        hydrictis, Eomellivora,
        Gulo, Ischyrictis, Leptarctus,
        Lutra, Marcetia, Martes,
        Meles, Mephitis, Mesome-
        phitis, Mionictis, Mustela,
        Mustelavus, Paragale, Plesic-
        tis, Plesiogulo, Potamother-
        ium, Promephitis, Putorius,
        Simocyon, Stenoplesictis,
        Taxidea, Trigonictis, Tro-
        charion, Vormela

Broilianinae, Melinae, Mellivorinae,
    Mephitinae
mustelinus (Ictidopappus)
musteloides (Galea, Galea musteloides)
Mustelus Triakidae Pledge 1967
Mutabilia Caudata
mutabilis (Tesseraspis)
mutata (Semigenetta)
Mutica Eutheria
mutilus (Democricetodon affinis)
Mycterosaurus Nitosauridae
    smithae Lewis, G. E. and Vaughn
        1965
Myctophidae Myctophiformes
    Eomyctophum, Hygophus, Leptosomus,
        Myctophum, Rhinellus
Myctophiformes Mesichthyes
Myctophum Myctophidae See: Otolithus
    pulcher Weiler 1962G (?)
"Myctophum" ?Osteoglossidae See: Oto-
        lithus
    americanum Frizzell and Dante 1965
Mylagaulidae Aplodontoidea
    Epigaulus, Mylagaulus
Mylagaulus Mylagaulidae Stout in Skinner,
        M. F. and Taylor 1967
    kinseyi Webb, S. D. 1966A
    laevis Shotwell 1968 (cf.)
Myledaphus Dasyatidae
    bipartitus Estes 1964
Myliobatidae Myliobatoidea
    Aetobatis, Myliobatis, Rhinoptera
Myliobatis Myliobatidae Bauza Rullan
        1966B; Flügel, H. 1964;
        Fuchs, H. 1966; Hogan 1959;
        Olsen 1964A; Pledge 1967;
        Signeux 1959B; Şuraru and
        Şuraru 1966
    arambourgi Glikman 1964B
    californicus Fitch 1964
    crassus Menesini 1967A
    dixoni Casier 1966A; Tsankov and
        Dachev 1966
    irregularis Tsankov and Dachev 1966
    latidens Casier 1966A
    meridionalis Radwanski 1965
    sendaicus Hatai, Murata and Masuda
        1965
    toliapicus Casier 1966A
    varnensis Tsankov and Dachev 1966
Myliobatoidea Batoidea
Mylodontidae Megalonychoidea
    Elassotherium, Paramylodon, Scelido-
        therium
Mylohyus Tayassuidae
    nasutus Guilday, Martin and McCrady

1964; Semken and Griggs
1965
Mylomygale Macroscelididae
spiersi Patterson, B. 1965B
Mylomygalinae Macroscelididae Patterson,
B. 1965B
Mylopteraspis Pteraspididae Stensiö 1964
Mylostomatidae Pachyosteiformes
Myocastoridae Octodontoidea
Plagiodontia
Myocricetodon Cricetidae Lavocat 1961D
(in Myocricetodontinae)
cherifiensis Lavocat 1961D (corrected
from cherifiense)
Myocricetodontinae Cricetidae Lavocat
1961D
Myodes Cricetidae
glareolus Kretzoi 1965C
Myoglis Gliridae Baudelot, S. 1965, 1966
larteti Baudelot, S. 1965, 1966
Myohyracinae Macroscelididae Patterson,
B. 1965B
Myohyrax Macroscelididae
oswaldi Patterson, B. 1965B
Myomimus Gliridae
personatus Corbet and Morris 1967
Myomorpha Sciurognathi
Myopterygius Ichthyosauridae Thieuloy
1965
petersoni Romer 1968B
Myosorex Soricidae Simonetta 1957C
robinsoni Repenning 1967C
Myospalax Cricetidae
aspalax
wongi Zazhigin 1966D
fontanieri Chow, M.-c. 1964B; Chow,
M.-c. and Chow 1965
myotis (Myotis)
Myotis Vespertilionidae Sigé 1968B;
Wilson, R. L. 1968
bechsteini Topál 1964
boyeri Mein 1965A
daubentonii Malez 1963D
misonnei Quinet 1965B
myotis Malez 1963D (cf.)
nattereri Topál 1964
Myotragus Bovidae Angel 1962; Crusafont Pairó 1966C; Crusa-
font Pairó, Angel and
Cuerda 1965B; Cuerda Bar-
celó 1966; Gasull and
Adrover 1966; Graves, W.
and Waldren 1966
balearicus Angel 1966; Crusafont
Pairó 1965H; Mallorca

Symposium 1966; Muntaner
Darder 1966; Waldren 1966
batei Crusafont Pairó and Angel 1966
Myriacanthidae Myriacanthoidei
Metopacanthus, Myriacanthus
Myriacanthoidei Chimaeriformes Patterson,
C. 1965B (suborder)
Myriacanthus Myriacanthidae
paradoxus Patterson, C. 1965B (rest.)
Myripristis Holocentridae Frizzell and
Lamber 1962B
toliapicus Casier 1966A (nomen nudum)
Myrmecoboides Leptictidae Ride 1964B
Van Valen 1967B
mystica (Florentinoameghinia)
Mysticeti Cetacea
Mystipterus Mystipterus Hutchison 1968A
Mystipterus Talpidae
pacificus Hutchison 1968A (subgen.
Mystipterus)
vespertilio Hutchison 1968A (subgen.
Mystipterus)
Mystriosaurus Teleosauridae
bollensis Telles Antunes 1967A (cf.),
B
Mystriosuchus [Belodon] Phytosauridae
Mytoniinae Omomyidae Robinson, Peter
1968B
Mytonius Omomyidae Robinson, Peter
1968B
hopsoni Robinson, Peter 1968B
Mytonolaginae Leporidae Gureev 1964
Mytonolagus Leporidae
petersoni Gureev 1964; Russell, L. S.
1965D
wyomingensis Gureev 1964
Mytonomys Paramyidae
robustus Black, C. C. 1968B; Russell,
L. S. 1965D
Myxinoidea Pteraspidomorpha Stensiö
1964

nagrii (Dorcabune)
nagurai (Polymerichthys)
Naiadochelys Pelomedusidae Staesche
1929*
nailii (Guguschia)
namadicus (Elephas, Palaeoloxodon)
Namatomys Eomyidae Black, C. C. 1965A
fantasma Lindsay, E. 1968A
lloydi Black, C. C. 1965A
nana (Lawrencia)
Nanchangosauria Euryapsida Appleby,
Charig, Cox, Kermack and
Tarlo 1967 (in Sauropterygia)

Nectridia Lepospondyli
neglectus (Pseudocylindrodon)
nehringi (Desmana, Dolomys)
neimenguensis (Leptarctus, Trionyx)
neivensis (Caiman, Dinosuchus)
nekipelovi (Marmota siberica)
Neldasaurus Trimerorhachidae Chase,
        J. N. 1965 (Perm., Tex.)
    wrightae Chase, J. N. 1965
Nemacanthus Hybodontidae
    monilifer Dreyer 1962 (cf.)
nemoptera (Dixonina)
Nemopteryx Gadidae
    dubertreti Signeux 1959C
Nemorhoedus Bovidae
    meneghinii Heintz, E. 1964B
Neoanthropinae Hominidae Dokládal
        1965 (Homo sapiens fossilis)
Neobatrachia Anura
Neocathartoidea Cathartae
Neochen Anatidae
    barbadiana Brodkorb 1964B
Neocnus Megalonychidae Arredondo 1961
        (in Ortotheriinae, prov.)
    major Arredondo 1961 (Cuba)
    minor Arredondo 1961 (Cuba)
Neocometes Cricetidae
    similis Fahlbusch, V. 1966
neocomiensis (Clupavus, Heterosaurus,
        Palealbula)
Neofelis Felidae
    nebulosa
        primigenia Hemmer 1965E; Hem-
            mer and von Koenigswald
            1964
neogaeus (Rhamphostomopsis, Smilodon)
Neognathae Neornithes
Neohelos Diprotodontidae Stirton 1967B
    tirarensis Stirton 1967B
Neohipparion Equidae
    affine Wilson, R. L. 1968 (cf.)
    lenticularis Wilson, R. L. 1968 (cf.)
    monias Mooser Barendun, O. 1964A
    occidentalis Dalquest and Hughes
        1966; Wilson, R. L. 1968
        (cf.)
Neomesocnus Megalonychidae Arredondo
        1961 (in Ortutheriinae,
        prov.)
    brevirrostris Arredondo 1961 (Cuba);
        Paula Couto 1967
Neomyini Soricinae Repenning 1967C
Neomys Soricidae Jánossy 1965D; Re-
        penning 1967C
    fodiens Friant 1965A

Neoparacamelus Paracamelus Havesson
        1950
Neoplagiaulax Ptilodontidae
    copei Russell, D. E. 1964 (?)
    eocaenus Russell, D. E. 1964
Neoprosimii Prosimii Crusafont Pairó 1967B
        (infraord.)
Neornithes Aves
Neornithes [Neognathae] Neornithes
        Dement'ev 1964
Neosclerocalyptus Glyptodontidae Paula
        Couto 1965 (=Glyptodon,
        1845, nec. Glyptodon Owen,
        1838)
    ornatus Paula Couto 1965
Neosqualodon Squalodontidae
    assenzae Rothausen 1968B
    gastaldii Rothausen 1968B
        gastaldii Rothausen 1968A
        gemmellaroi Rothausen 1968A
        maior Rothausen 1968A
Neotoma Cricetidae
    magnodonta Alvarez 1966 (Mex.)
    quadriplicatus Hibbard 1967 (subgen.
        Paraneotoma)
    sawrockensis Hibbard 1967 (subgen.
        Paraneotoma)
    taylori Hibbard 1967 (subgen. Para-
        neotoma)
Neotomodon Cricetidae
    alstoni Alvarez 1966 (Mex.)
nepaeolicus (Tylosaurus)
nepaholica (Cimolichthys)
Nerterogeomys Geomys Hibbard 1967
nerviensis (Synechodus)
nesebricum (Hipparion)
nesemanni (Dicynodon)
Nesides Diplocercidae Lehman 1966C
        (endocranium)
    heiligenstockiensis Jessen 1966A
    schmidti Stensiö 1963
Nesiotites Soricidae Repenning 1967C
Nesodon Toxodontidae Leanza 1954*
    nesodontoides (Bryanpattersonia)
Nesokia Muridae
    indica Robinson, Peter 1966B
Nesoleipoceros Cervidae Rădulesco and
        Samson 1967A
    cazioti Rădulesco and Samson 1967A
Nesophontes Nesophontidae
    edithae Choate and Birney 1968
Nesophontidae Soricoidea
    Nesophontes
nestoris (Necromites)
Nestoritherium Chalicotheriidae

sinense Chow, M.-c., Hu and Lee
1965 (cf.)
sivalense Hooijer 1964F (cf.)
Nettion Anatidae
greeni Brodkorb 1964C
Nettosuchidae Eosuchia Langston 1965B,
1966A
Nettosuchus
Nettosuchus Nettosuchidae Langston
1965B, 1966A (syn. with
Mourasuchus)
atopus Langston 1965B
netzvetaevi (Otsheria)
neumayrianus (Trimylus, Trimylus neumayrianus)
Neurankylidae Baenoidea
Neurankylus, Thescelus
Neurankylus Neurankylidae
baueri Wiman 1935C
Neurogymnurus Erinaceidae
cayluxi Dechaseaux 1964A
Neurotrichus ?Talpidae
columbianus Hutchison 1968A
neuter (Scaphiopus)
nevadensis (Fundulus, Helicoprion, Hybodus, Hypohippus, Lepto-
lepis, Merycodus, Oreolagus,
Ustatochoerus profectus)
newtoni (Mimomys)
Ngapakaldia Diprotodontidae Stirton
1967A
bonythoni Stirton 1967A
tedfordi Stirton 1967A
nicoli (Signata)
Nielsenia Uronemidae
nordica Lehman 1966C
nigeriensis (Markgrafia)
nigripes (Mustela)
nihowanensis (Megantereon)
nilssoni (Bubalus)
Nimravus Felidae Gabuniia 1964D
ninchiashanensis (Coryphodon)
ninghsiaensis (Pinacosaurus)
niobrarensis (Limnoecus)
niobrarius (Cynomys)
nipponicus (Dicerorhinus)
niro (Hippotragus)
nitens (Entomolestes)
nitida (Ectostereorhachis, Homalaspidella,
Picunia, Sespia)
nitidus (Podocephalus, Talpavus)
Nitosauridae Edaphosauria Kuhn, Oskar
1966A (syn. of Glauco-
sauridae; ascribed to Romer
1937 by error);

Langston 1965A
Delorhynchus, Mycterosaurus
niushanensis (Heptodon)
nivalis (Microtus, Mustela)
njalilius (Tetragonius)
njarasensis (Panthera leo)
nobilis (Basilemys)
nocerai (Absarokius noctivagus)
Noctilio Noctilionidae
leporinus
mastivus Choate and Birney 1968
Noctilionidae Emballonuroidea
Noctilio
noctivagus (Absarokius)
nodosa (Baena)
Nodosauridae Ankylosauria Simmons 1965
Pinacosaurus
nodulosa (Anisolambda)
Noemacheilus Cyprinidae
tener Obrhelova 1967
nogaici (Citellus)
nogaicus (Aspro)
nogaiskiensis (Allactaga)
nombrevillae (Cricetodon decedens, Peridyromys)
norbeckensis (Genetochoerus)
nordensis (Pseudacris)
nordica (Nielsenia, Oervigia)
normandica (Furo)
normannie (Semionotus)
Nostolepis Climatiidae Karatajūte 1964
notabilis (Pleurostylodon, Sthenurus)
Notacanthida Teleostei Danil'chenko
1964B (order)
Notagogus Macrosemiidae
ferreri Wenz 1964, 1968B
Notemigonus Cyprinidae
crysoleucas Hibbard and Dalquest
1966
Notharctidae Adapoidea Crusafont Pairó
1967B
Notharctus, Smilodectes
Notharctus Notharctidae Saban 1963
nunienus Robinson, Peter 1966A
Nothokemas Camelidae
floridanus Maglio 1966; Patton 1966B
Nothosauravidae Sauropterygia Kuhn, Oskar
1964C, fig. 14
Nothosauria Euryapsida Haas, G. 1967;
Tatarinov, L. P. 1964Q
Nothosauridae Nothosauria Kuhn-Schnyder
1963D
Chinchenia, Nothosaurus, Paranothosaurus
Sanchiaosaurus
Nothosaurus Nothosauridae Colbert 1967C
(rest.); Dreyer 1962; Lazur-

kin and Ochev 1968;
　Wojcik 1961A
Nothrotherium Megalonychidae
　shastense Hibbard and Dalquest
　　1966 (cf.); Simons, E. L.
　　and Alexander 1964
Notictosaurus Thrinaxodontidae
　luckhoffi Brink 1965B
Notidanidae [Hexanchidae] Hexanchi-
　formes
Notidanus Hexanchidae Casier 1966A
　(in Notidanidae)
　griseus Menesini 1967B
　muensteri Schweizer 1964
　primigenius Radwanski 1965
　serratissimus Casier 1966A; Pledge
　　1967
　serratus Schweizer 1964
Notioprogonia Notoungulata
Notiosorex Soricidae Repenning 1967C
Notocaiman Crocodylidae
　stromeri Langston 1965B
Notochampsa Protosuchidae Walker,
　　A. D. 1968 (in Stegomo-
　　suchidae Huene 1922)
Notochampsidae [Protosuchidae] Proto-
　suchia
Notogoneus Gonorhynchidae
　janeti Le Danois 1966
Notohippidae Toxodonta
　Eomorphippus, "Interhippus"
Notolagus Leporidae
　lepusculus Gureev 1964
　velox Gureev 1964
Notophthalmus Salamandridae
　slaughteri Holman 1966C
Notopithecus Interatheriidae Simpson,
　　G. G. 1964C
　adapinus Simpson, G. G. 1967A (rest.)
　adapinus Simpson, G. G. 1967A
　reduncus Simpson, G. G. 1967A
　amplidens Simpson, G. G. 1967A
"Notopithecus" Notoungulata incertae
　sedis
　summus Simpson, G. G. 1967A
Notopteroidei Osteoglossiformes
Notorhinus ?Astrapotheria incertae sedis
　denticulatus Simpson, G. G. 1967A
　　(nomen vanum)
　haroldi Simpson, G. G. 1967A (nomen
　　vanum)
Notorhynchus Hexanchidae
　maculatus Fitch 1964
　pectinatus Applegate 1965A
Notoryctidae Marsupialia incertae sedis
　Ride 1964B

notostylopense (Progarzonia)
Notostylopidae Notioprogonia
　Edvardotrouessartia, Homalostylops,
　　Notostylops
Notostylops Notostylopidae Leanza
　　1954*
　murinus Simpson, G. G. 1964C,
　　1967A
Notosyodon Brithopodidae Chudinov
　　1968B
　gusevi Chudinov 1968B
Nototheriinae Diprotodontidae Stirton,
　　Woodburne and Plane 1967
　　(new rank)
Nototherium Diprotodontidae Woods 1968
　inerme Woods 1968
　watutense Plane 1967A, B
Notoungulata Protungulata
　Incertae sedis: Brandmayria, Carolo-
　　darwinia, "?Claenodon,"
　　"Degonia," Edvardocopeia,
　　Epitypotherium, Isotypo-
　　therium, Lophiodonticulus,
　　"Notopithecus," Ortholo-
　　phodon, Pleurostylops, Pro-
　　colpodon, Puelia, Tono-
　　stylops, "Ultrapithecus"
Notropis Cyprinidae Wilson, R. L. 1968
　　(?)
nougareti (Ctenopristis)
nouletti (Leptolophus)
novaeanglidae (Megaptera)
Novascoticus Microsauria incertae sedis
　　Carroll, R. L. 1966
　multidens Carroll, R. L. 1966
novomexicanus (Aspidosaurus)
novorossicus (Struthio)
novus (Jacobulus)
nuchalis (Aipichthys, Scombrinus)
Nucras Lacertidae Kruckow 1962
nuda (Galkinia)
nudus (Chirocentrus)
numidus (Onchopristis)
nunienus (Notharctus)
nürtingensis (Entoplastrites)
nyanzae (Proconsul, Pterodon)
Nyctereuctes Canidae
　megamastoides Bolomey 1965A
　sinensis Vangengeïm 1966D (cf.)
　vinetorum Kurtén 1965A
Nycticonodon ?Tupaiidae Quinet 1964A
　　(for Adapisoriculus)
　caparti Quinet 1964A
　casieri Quinet 1964A
Nyctitheriidae Soricoidea
　?Leptacodon, Nyctitherium

Nyctitheriinae Adapisoricidae Van Valen
1967B
Nyctitherium Nyctitheriidae
velox Robinson, Peter 1966A (cf.)
Nyctosaurinae Ornithocheiridae Kuhn, O.
1967A
Nyctosaurus Ornithocheiridae Kuhn, O.
1967A
nyroca (Aythya)
Nyssodon Palaeoryctidae
punctidens Van Valen 1966A

obailiensis (Eudonoceras)
oberndorferi (Platychelys)
obessus (Lushiamynodon)
obliqua (Isurus)
obliquidentatus (Onychodus)
obliquus (Elasmodontomys, Isurus)
oblongus (Berycopsis, Megalops, Pharyngolepis)
obruchevi (Pycnosteus)
Obruchevia Obrucheviidae
heckeri Tarlo, L. B. 1965
Obrucheviida Psammosteiformes Tarlo,
L. B. 1965 (subord.)
Obrucheviidae Obrucheviida Tarlo, L. B.
1964C, 1965 (to replace
Aspidosteidae Berg 1955)
Obruchevia, Traquairosteus
obrutschewi (Bothriolepis)
obscura (Vinciguerria)
obscurus (Eomorphippus)
obtentus (Transpithecus)
obtruncata (Tinca)
obtusatum (Microbrachis)
obtusidens (Mesonyx)
obtusus (Ganosteus, Saurillus)
Ocadia Testudinidae
perplexa Yeh 1963B
sansaniensis Bergounioux and Crouzel
1965B
sinensis Yeh 1963B
occidentale (Hipparion, Pampatherium)
occidentalis (Aechmophorus, Bison,
Coccosteus, Coragyps, Eporeodon, Lepisosteus, Lucioperca zaissanicus, Mosasaurus,
Neohipparion, Paraphiomys,
Petrodus, Sthenurus)
occitanicus (Lophiaspis)
occitanus (Peridyromys)
Oceanitidae [Hydrobatidae] Procellariiformes Fisher, J. 1967
Ochotona Ochotonidae Dai' 1954*;
Gureev 1964 (in Lagomyidae);

Malez 1963D, 1966; Vekua
and Shidlovskii 1958
antiqua Gureev 1964
daurica Zazhigin 1966B (cf.)
gurejevi Erbaeva 1966
dodogolica Erbaeva 1966
lagreli Gureev 1964
pricei Zazhigin 1966B (cf.)
pseudopusilla
schvtschenko Gureev 1964
pusillus Jacobshagen 1963; Malez 1968
tologoica Gureev 1964; Zazhigin 1966B
Ochotonidae Lagomorpha
Desmatolagus, Hesperolagomys, Lagopsis,
Ochotona, Oreolagus, Prolagus
Ochotonoides Lagomyidae
complicidens Gureev 1964
Ochotonolagus Lagomyidae
argyropuloi Gureev 1964
ochrogaster (Microtus, Pedomys)
ochropus (Tringa)
Ocnerotherium Toxodontidae
intermedium Pascual 1965B
ocreata (Felis)
octodontiforme (Chasicomys)
Octodontidae Octodontoidea
Chasicomys, Phtoramys
Octodontinae
Octodontinae Octodontidae Pascual 1967
Octodontoidea Caviomorpha
odessana (Vulpes)
odin ("Halmaturus")
Odobenidae Pinnipedia
Alachtherium, Odobenus
Odobeninae Otariidae Mitchell, E. D. 1968
Odobenus Odobenidae
huxleyi Deinse 1964B
Odocoileinae Cervidae Heintz, E. 1968
Odocoileus Cervidae Hibbard and Dalquest
1966; Strain 1966
salinae Edmund 1965 (cf.)
virginianus Dalquest 1964B
Odontaspidae [Carchariidae] Isuroidei
Odontaspididae [Carchariidae] Isuroidei
Odontaspis [Carcharias] Carchariidae
Odontoceti Cetacea
Incertae sedis: Hadrodelphis
Odontognathae Neornithes
Odontomysopidae Marsupialia Simpson,
G. G. 1967A (nomen vanum)
Odontomysops
Odontomysops Odontomysopidae Simpson,
G. G. 1967A (unidentifiable;
nomen vanum)
spiniferus Simpson, G. G. 1967A
(nomen vanum)

Odontopterygia Pelecaniformes
Odontorhynchus Rhamphorhynchidae
    Kuhn, O. 1967A
Odontornithes [Odontognathae] Neor-
    nithes Dement'ev 1964
odontrigonus (Acratocnus)
oeconomus (Microtus)
Oedaleops Eothyrididae Langston 1965A
    campi Langston 1965A
oehleri (Tatisaurus)
oeningensis (Prolagus)
oervigi (Dipterus)
Oervigia ?Fleurantiidae
    nordica Lehman 1966C
oeselensis (Procephalaspis)
Ogmodontomys Cricetidae
    poaphagus
        poaphagus Zakrzewski 1967B
        transitionalis Zakrzewski 1967B
    sawrockensis Hibbard 1964; Zakrzew-
        ski 1967B
Ogmophis Boidae
    kansasensis Wilson, R. L. 1968
ohioensis (Castoroides)
Oioceros Bovidae
    atropatenes Heintz, E. 1963B, 1964A
oiostolus (Lepus)
Olbiaspida Pteraspidiformes Obruchev,
        D. V. 1964C (order; in
        Heterostraci)
Olbiaspididae Olbiaspidida Obruchev,
        D. V. 1964C
    Angaraspis, Olbiaspis, Siberiaspis
Olbiaspis Olbiaspididae Obruchev, D. V.
        1964C
    coalescens Obruchev, D. V. 1964C
oldawayi (Struthio)
Oldfieldthomasia Oldfieldthomasiidae
        Simpson, G. G. 1964C
    anfractuosa Simpson, G. G. 1967A
    debilitata Simpson, G. G. 1967A
    parvidens Simpson, G. G. 1964C,
        1967A
    transversa Simpson, G. G. 1967A
Oldfieldthomasiidae Toxodonta
    Acoelodus, Kibenikhoria, Maxschlos-
        seria, Oldfieldthomasia,
        Paginula, Tsamnichoria,
        Ultrapithecus
oldowayensis (Pelorovis)
olduvaiensis (Gorgon)
Oligobranchiata Osteostraci
Oligodontosaurus Amphisbaenidae
    wyomingensis Estes 1965C
Oligokyphus Tritylodontidae Crompton
        1964A; Dreyer 1962
Oligopleuridae Pholidophoriformes

Galkinia
Olioceros Bovidae Meladze 1967
olisiponensis (Sphyraena)
Olivieria Ictidosuchidae Brink 1965D
    parringtonia Brink 1965D; Findlay
        1968B
olonensis (Grallator)
Olsenia Mesonychidae
    mira Szalay and Gould 1966 (?nomen
        dubium)
olsoni (Broiliellus, Eotitanosuchus)
Oltinomys Theridomyidae Thaler 1966B
Omo man [Paraustralopithecus aethiopi-
        cus] Hominidae
Omomyidae Anaptomorphoidea Crusafont
        Pairó 1967B
    ?Arisella, Cantius, Chumashius, Hemia-
        codon, Loveina, Macrotarsus,
        Mytonius, Omomys, Ourayi,
        Periconodon, Pivetonia,
        Pseudoloris, ?Rooneyia,
        Shoshonius
    Mytoniinae
Omomys Omomyidae
    minutus Guthrie, D. A. 1967B
Omosoma Polymixiidae
    intermedium Patterson, C. 1964
    monasteri Patterson, C. 1964
    pulchellum Patterson, C. 1964
    sahel-almae Patterson, C. 1964 (rest.)
    simum Leonardi, A. 1966; Patterson,
        C. 1964
Omphalosauridae Longipinnati
Omphalosauroidei [Omphalosauridae]
        Longipinnati Tatarinov
        1964S (p. 343)
Onager Equus Azzaroli 1966B
onca (Felis)
onchognathus (Halisaurus)
Onchopristis Pristidae
    dunklei Case, G. R. 1965A, B;
        Slaughter and Steiner 1968
    numidus Tabaste 1963
Onchosaurus Pristidae
    pharao Tabaste 1963
Onchus Diplacanthidae
    overathensis Ørvig 1967C
    rarus Liepiņsh 1959*
Ondatra Cricetidae
    annectens Hibbard and Dalquest 1966
    nebrascensis Semken 1966
Oniscolepis Tesseraspididae
    dentata Tarlo 1965
onoideus (Brachyodus)
Onychodontidae Osteolepides incertae sedis
        Jessen 1966A (in Struniiformes)

Onychodus, Strunius
Onychodus Onychodontidae
  jaekeli Gross, W. 1965E; Jessen
    1966A, 1967
  obliquidentatus Jessen 1966A, 1967
Onychogalea Macropodidae
  fraenata Tedford 1967B
  lunata Tedford 1967B
Onychomys Cricetidae Hibbard and
    Dalquest 1966
  leucogaster Schultz, G. E. 1965B
    (cf.)
Onychopoides Ichnites Kuhn, Oskar
    1958D*, p. 20 (for Onycho-
    pus Rühle von Lilienstern,
    preocc.)
Oödectes Miacidae
  herpestoides Robinson, Peter 1966A
Oölithes (eggs, eggshells and egg capsules)
    Gnathostomata Bazhanov
    1961D; Thaler 1965B; Tyler
    1957 (moa); Villatte 1966
    (Eoc. bird); Voss-Foucart
    1968 (Cret. dinosaur);
    Vozin 1968 (Trias. fish)
  elongatus Young, C.-c. 1965B
  nanhsiungensis Young, C.-c. 1965B
  rugustus Young, C.-c. 1965B
  spheroides Young, C.-c. 1965B
Ophiacodon Ophiacodontidae Lewis, G.
    E. and Vaughn 1965;
    Vaughn 1964A
  uniformis Stephens, J. J. 1964 (cf.)
Ophiacodontia Pelycosauria
Ophiacodontidae Ophiacodontia
  Ophiacodon
Ophiderpeton Ophiderpetontidae Baird
    1964A, 1965C
Ophiderpetontidae Aistopoda
  Ophiderpeton
  Ophiderpetontinae
Ophiderpetontinae Ophiderpetontidae
    Huene 1956D*, p. 25
Ophidia [Serpentes] Squamata El-Toubi,
    Kamal and Hammouda
    1965 (origin)
Ophidiidae Ophidioidea
  Bauzaia, Ophidiidarum, Ophidypterus,
    Preophidion, Signata
Ophidiidarum Ophidiidae See: Otolithus
  acutangulus Weiler 1962G
Ophidiiformes Acanthopterygii MacAllis-
    ter 1968 (order)
Ophidioidea Ophidioidei
Ophidioidei Perciformes
Ophidypterus Ophidiidae See: Otolithus

Stinton 1965
retusus Stinton 1965
Ophiomys Cricetidae Hibbard and Zakrzew-
    ski 1967 (in Microtidae)
  meadensis Hibbard and Zakrzewski
    1967
  parvus Hibbard and Zakrzewski 1967
  taylori Hibbard and Zakrzewski 1967
Ophiopsis Macrosemiidae
  montsechensis Wenz 1968B
Ophipseudopus Anguidae Kuhn, Oskar
    1940J*
Ophisauriscus Anguidae Kuhn, Oskar
    1940J*
Ophisaurus Anguidae
  pannonicus Młynarski 1964A
  ventralis Holman 1965D; Wilson, R. L.
    1968
Ophthalmosauridae Latipinnati Appleby
    1967
opimus (Rhombomys)
Opisthocoela Salientia Kuhn, Oskar
    1967B (replaced by Bom-
    binatorina)
Opisthocoelellidae [Discoglossidae] Aglossa
    Kuhn, Oskar 1945E (assigned
    to Kuhn 1941)
Opisthopsalis Adapisoricidae Van Valen
    1966A
Opisthotriton ?Plethodontidae
  kayi Estes 1964
Oplosaurus Brachiosauridae Kuhn, Oskar
    1965A (taxonomic note;
    = ?Pelorosaurus, and Hoplo-
    saurus hydekk. 1890)
oppositus (Acoelodus)
Oracanthus Menaspididae
  milleri Obruchev, D. V. 1962C
Orasius Giraffidae
  atticus Bakalov and Nikolov 1962
  speciosus Bakalov and Nikolov 1962
orbicularis (Emys)
orbignyi (Ictitherium)
Orchesteropus Ichnites
  atavus Casamiquela 1964C, 1965B
ordosianus (Sinomegaceros)
ordosius (Archaeotherium)
oreas (Sthenurus)
Orectolobidae Galeoidea
  Ginglymostoma, Squatirhina
oregonensis (Anabernicula, Hypolagus,
    Marmota, Parapliosaccomys,
    Peridiomys, Protospermo-
    philus)
oregoniana (Sinclairia)
orellaensis (Pseudocyclopidius)

orenburgensis (Parotosaurus)
Oreodonta Suiformes
oreodontus (Acrodus)
Oreolagus Ochotonidae Gureev 1964
    (in Lagomyidae)
    nebrascensis Dawson, M. 1965; Gureev
        1964
    nevadensis Gureev 1964
    wallacei Dawson, M. 1965
    wilsoni Dawson, M. 1965
Oreonetinae Merycoidodontidae Schultz,
    C. B. and Falkenbach 1968
Oreopithecidae Hominoidea
    Oreopithecus
Oreopithecoidea [Oreopithecidae] Ho-
    minoidea Koenigswald
    1964B
Oreopithecus Oreopithecidae B., H.
        1965; Crusafont Pairó
        1965G; Koenigswald 1964B;
        Peña Basurto 1959; Simons,
        E. L. 1964D; Teichmüller
        1962
    bambolii Knussmann 1967; Schott
        1962B; Strouhal 1959A
Oriensarctos Otariidae Mitchell, E. D.
        1968
    watasei Mitchell, E. D. 1968
orientalis (Adocus, Colodon, Dicero-
        rhinus, Entelodon, Harpa-
        golestes, Kiyutherium, Par-
        otosaurus, Psekupsoceros,
        Rhynchosaurus, Stegodon,
        Sthenurus)
orlovi (Eomellivora, Eutamias, Kyzylkak-
        hippus, Procaprolagus, Simi-
        lisorex, Tamias)
ornata (Ariaspis, Asterolepis, Bothrio-
        lepis, Felis, Hylaeobatis,
        Terrapene)
ornatissimus (Asteracanthus, Dercetis)
ornatus (Acestrus, Archemacruroides,
        Microcheorus, Neosclero-
        calyptus, Peritresius, Rohono-
        steus, Tartuosteus, Trachi-
        chthyoides)
Ornithischia Dinosauria Kuhn, Oskar
        1964A
Ornithocheira Pterosauria Kuhn, O. 1967A
Ornithocheiridae Pterodactyloidea Kuhn,
    O. 1966A (in Dsungaripteroidea)
    Nyctosaurus, Ornithocheirus, Ornitho-
        stoma, Pteranodon, Titano-
        pteryx
    Nyctosaurinae, Ornithocheirinae,
        Pteranodontinae

Ornithocheirinae Ornithocheiridae Kuhn,
    O. 1967A
Ornithocheirus Ornithocheiridae Kuhn,
    Oskar 1967A
Ornithodesmidae Dsungaripteroidea
    Ornithodesmus
Ornithodesmus Ornithodesmidae Kuhn,
    O. 1967A
Ornithomimidae Coelurosauria Colbert
        1964B; Maleev 1964J
    Ornithomimus
Ornithomimus Ornithomimidae Devillers,
        C. and J. 1965 (reconst.);
        Miller, H. W. 1967
Ornithopoda Ornithischia
Ornithoprion Edestidae Zangerl 1966
    hertwigi Zangerl 1966
Ornithostoma Ornithocheiridae Kuhn,
        Oskar 1967A
Ornithosuchia [Tyrannosauroidea] Carno-
        sauria Kuhn, Oskar 1966A
        (ascribed to Reig 1961*)
Ornithosuchidae Pseudosuchia Walker,
        A. D. 1964 (in Saurischia)
    Dibothrosuchus, Ornithosuchus, Strigo-
        suchus
Ornithosuchoidea Pseudosuchia Kuhn,
        Oskar 1966A, p. 93 (Tyran-
        nosauroidea, partim)
Ornithosuchus Ornithosuchidae
    longidens Walker, A. D. 1964 (rest.)
Oromerycidae Tylopoda
    Oromeryx, Protylopus
Oromeryx Oromerycidae Russell, L. S.
        1965D (?; in Hypertragulidae)
orri (Osteodontornis)
Ortalis Cracidae
    affinis Feduccia and Wilson 1967;
        Wilson, R. L. 1968
ortegense (Metaxytherium)
Orthacodidae Isuroidei
    Paraorthacodus
Orthacodontidae Galeoidea
    Sphenodus
Orthaspidotherium Meniscotheriidae
    edwardsi Russell, D. E. 1964
Orthobranchiata Osteostraci
Orthogonoceros Cervidae
    verticornis Hooijer 1961C; Melentis
        1967B
Ortholophodon Notoungulata incertae
        sedis
    prolongus Simpson, G. G. 1967A
Orthosuchus Protosuchidae Nash, Diane
        1968 (in Notochampsidae)
    stormbergi Nash, Diane 1968

cedrensis Schultz, C. B. and Falken-
    bach 1968 (subgen. Otaro-
    hyus)
hybridus Schultz, C. B. and Falken-
    bach 1968 (subgen. Otaro-
    hyus)
    helenae Schultz, C. B. and Falken-
        bach 1968 (subgen. Otaro-
        hyus)
vanderpooli Schultz, C. B. and Fal-
    kenbach 1968
wardi Schultz, C. B. and Falkenbach
    1968
    degrooti Schultz, C. B. and Falken-
        bach 1968
Otocratioidea [Colosteoidea] Temno-
    spondyli Tatarinov 1964C,
    p. 67
Otocyon Canidae Petter, G. 1964C; Van
    Valen 1964D
Otodus [Isurus] Isuridae
Otolithus Pisces Carlström 1963; Czygan
    1963; Deloffre 1961; Friz-
    zell 1965A, B, C; Frizzell
    and Dante 1965; Frizzell
    and Lamber 1962B; Gowda
    1967A (India); Lehman
    1966B
abbatiae (Argentina) Stinton 1965
aculeatus (Xenistius) Stinton 1966
acuminatus (Macruridarum) Paghida
    1962
acuminatus (Pereidarum) Pană 1965
acutangulus (Ophidiidarum) Brzobo-
    haty 1967A
acutum (Peristedion) Brzobohaty
    1967A; Smigielska 1966A
acutus (Conger) Stinton 1966
acutus (Scorpaenichthys) Stinton
    1966
affinis (Atherinops) Fitch 1964
aggregata (Cymatogaster) Fitch 1964
alabamae (Archaealbula) Frizzell
    1965C
alsheimensis (Umbrina) Pană 1965
    (cf.)
americanum ("Myctophum") Frizzell
    and Dante 1965
angulatus (Megalops) Stinton 1965
angulatus (Pterothrissus) Stinton 1966
angustus (Genypterus) Stinton 1966
antiqua (Cleidogonia) Stinton and
    Torrens 1968
antiquus (Pterothrissus) Stinton 1965
aomoriensis (Limanda) Hatai 1965B

approximatoides (Otolithus major)
    Brzobohaty 1967A
aquila (Sciaena) Lafond-Grellety 1963
arcuata (Pristipoma) Lafond-Grellety
    1963
argentea (Sphyraena) Fitch 1964
argutus (Dinematichthys) Stinton 1966
arthaberi (Macrurus) Smigielska 1966A
aurora (Sebastodes) Fitch 1964
balearica (Congermuraena) Smigielska
    1966A
balearicus (Eucitharus) Bauza Rullan
    1964
bashiana (Metalbula) Frizzell 1965C
bauzi (Arnoglossus) Bauza Rullan
    1964
biatlanticum (Myctophum) Brzobohaty
    1967A
biscaicum (Ophidium) Bauza Rullan
    1964
biscissus (Percidarum) Brzobohaty
    1967A
biscissus (Trachinus) Martini 1964
bognoriensis (Caesio) Stinton 1966
bognoriensis (Pagrus) Stinton 1966
brazosensis (Parbatmya) Frizzell and
    Dante 1965
brazosia (Stintonia) Frizzell and Dante
    1965
brevirostris (?Lycopteroidarum) Martin,
    G.P.R. and Weiler 1965
brevis (?Lycopteroidarum) Martin,
    G.P.R. and Weiler 1965
burlesonis (Allomorone) Frizzell and
    Dante 1965
californicus (Paralichthys) Fitch 1964
californiensis (Atherinopsis) Fitch 1964
carpaticus (Myctophidarum) Brzobo-
    haty 1965
casieri (Congermuraena) Bauza Rullan
    1964
catulus (Bregmaceros) Brzobohaty
    1964B, 1967A
chikagawaensis (Gadus) Hatai 1965B
circularis (Bathycongrus) Stinton
    1966
circularis (Eucitharus) Stinton 1966
circularis (Sphaeronchus) Stinton and
    and Torrens 1968
claibornensis (Eosolea) Frizzell and
    Dante 1965
cognatus (Merlangus) Smigielska 1966A
communis (Coelorhynchus) Brzobohaty
    1967A

laevis (Gobius) Paṅǎ 1965
lamberi (Bauzaia) Frizzell and Dante
    1965
latidens (Raniceps) Stinton 1966
latior (Dentex) Bauza Rullan 1964;
    Lafond-Grellety 1963;
    Smigielska 1966A
latirostratum (Myctophum) Smigiel-
    ska 1966A
lavis (Gobius) Lafond-Grellety 1963
leiopleurus (Proraniceps) Stinton
    1965
lemoinei (Trachichthodes) Stinton
    1966
lepidus (Lepidogobius) Fitch 1964
lineatus (Genyonemus) Fitch 1964
londinensis (Pterygotrigla) Stinton
    1966
longirostrum (Acanthochaetodon)
    Stinton 1966
longirostris (Myctophidarum kokeni)
    Brzobohaty 1967A
lozanoi (Apogon) Bauza Rullan 1964
lozanoi (Dentex) Bauza Rullan 1964
lucidus (Morone) Lafond-Grellety
    1963
macrocephalus macrocephalus (Gadus)
    Hatai 1965B
macrocephalus oshimai (Gadus) Hatai
    1965B
major (Ophidion) Smigielska 1966A
major (Otolithus) Brzobohaty 1967A
matoschi (Stintonia) Brzobohaty
    1967A
mediterraneum (Myctophum) Smigiel-
    ska 1966A
mediterraneus (Myctophidarum) Brzo-
    bohaty 1965
medius (Phrynorhombus) Smigielska
    1966A
melrosensis (Bauzaia) Frizzell and
    Dante 1965
menakiae (Lycoclupea) Gowda 1967B
meridiana (Eoalbula) Frizzell 1965C
minor (Pterothrissus) Martini 1964
minsterensis (Spicara) Stinton 1966
minusculoides (Gadus) Paghida 1962
miocaenicus (Trachinus) Lafond-Grel-
    lety 1963
moguntina (Morone) Paṅǎ 1965
moguntina (Sciaena) Paṅǎ 1965
mordax (Engraulis) Fitch 1964
moseleyi (Brazosiella) Frizzell and
    Dante 1965
mucronata (Bauzaia) Frizzell and
    Dante 1965

multipinnatus (Gobius) Brzobohaty
    1965; Smigielska 1966A
myriaster (Porichthys) Fitch 1964
myrus (Myrus) Lafond-Grellety 1963
negropinna (Lepophidium) Fitch 1964
nemoptera (Dixonina) Frizzell 1965C
neocomiensis (Palealbula) Frizzell
    1965C
nicoli (Signata) Frizzell and Dante
    1965
niger (Gobius) Paṅǎ 1965
nobilis (Cynoscion) Fitch 1964
noetlingi (Serranus) Martini 1964;
    Smigielska 1966A
notatus (Porichthys) Fitch 1964
notoensis (Gobius) Aoki, N. 1967
nuntius (Fierasfer) Bauza Rullan 1964
obliquus (Myctophidarum) Brzobohaty
    1965
oblongus (Percidarum) Brzobohaty
    1967A
obscura (Odontobutis) Hatai 1965B
obscura obscura (Odontobutis) Hatai
    1965B
obscura yuriagensis (Odontobutis)
    Hatai 1965B
obtusus (Neobythites) Stinton 1966
opinatus (Percidarum) Brzobohaty
    1967A (aff.)
ordinatus (Percidarum) Brzobohaty
    1967A
ornatus (Archemacruroides) Stinton
    1965
ornatus (?Lycopteroidarum) Martin,
    G. P. R. and Weiler 1965
ornatus (Malacocephalus) Brzobohaty
    1965
ornatus apicatus (Macrurus) Smigielska
    1966A
ostiolatus (Etelinus) Stinton 1966
ovalis (Epinephelus) Stinton 1966
ovalis (Gadophycis) Stinton 1965
ovalis (Macruridarum) Paghida 1962
ovalis (Pomadasys) Stinton 1966
ovalis (Uroconger) Brzobohaty 1967A
ovatus (Trigla) Bauza Rullan 1966A
pantanelli (Congermuraena) Bauza
    Rullan 1964; Brzobohaty
    1965
papillosus (Raniceps) Stinton 1966
paradoxicus (Pholidophorus) Stinton
    and Torrens 1968
parascorpius (Cottus) Lafond-Grellety
    1963
parvula (Argentina) Brzobohaty 1964B

stintoni (Preophidion) Frizzell and
Dante 1965
striatus (Epinephelus) Stinton 1966
subcirrhosa (Umbrina) Lafond-Grellety
1963
subdeltoideus (Gyrosteus) Stinton
and Torrens 1968
subdenudatum (Gonostoma) Brzobohaty 1967A
subglaber (Solea) Bauza Rullan 1964
subobtusus (Plectroplites) Stinton
1966
subrotunda (Monocentris) Brzobohaty
1967A
subsmilus (Ubrina) Lafond-Grellety
1963
subteres (Lepophidium) Stinton 1965
sulcifer (Amanses) Stinton 1966
sylvestris (Isacia) Stinton 1965
tankilensis (Gobius) Bauza Rullan
1964
taureri (Solea) Smigielska 1966A
tayleri (Otophidium) Fitch 1964
telleri (Gobius) Bauza Rullan 1964;
Pana 1965; Smigielska 1966A
tenue murbani (Myctophum) Smigielska 1966A
tenuicauda (Paralabrax) Stinton 1966
tenuirostris (Leptolepis) Stinton and
Torrens 1968
tenuis (Embiotoca) Stinton 1965
tenuis (Gobius) Paghida 1962; Pana
1965
tenuis (Leuresthes) Fitch 1964
tenuis (Phycis) Smigielska 1966A
texana (Eosolea) Frizzell and Dante
1965
texana (Genertina) Frizzell and
Dante 1965
thanetensis (Gadus) Stinton 1965
tietzei (Cantharus) Smigielska 1966A
toliapicus (Ampheristus) Stinton
1966
toulai (Coelorhynchus) Brzobohaty
1967A
transitus (Otolithus, Percidarum)
Sieber and Weinfurter 1967
triangularis (Gobius) Paghida 1962;
Pana 1965
triconus (Palaeogadus) Stinton 1965
tricrenulatus (Primaevomesus) Stinton
1965
triquetrus (Otolithus) Brzobohaty
1967A
troelli (Claibornichthys) Frizzell and
Dante 1965

tuberculosus (Raniceps) Martini
1964
umbonatus (Pterothrissus) Lafond-Grellety 1963
undata (Synanceia) Stinton 1966
undatus (Toxotes) Stinton 1966
undulatus (Elops) Stinton 1966
undulatus (Menticirrhus) Fitch 1964
undulatus (Micrometrus) Stinton 1966
upnoriensis (Raniceps) Stinton 1965
validus (Uroconger) Stinton 1966
varians (Citharichthys) Stinton 1966
vastus (Otolithus incertae sedis) Klejn
1960
veneris (Lates) Stinton 1965
vetulus (Parophrys) Fitch 1964
vincinalis (Gobius) Bauza Rullan 1964;
Paghida 1962; Pana 1965;
Smigielska 1966A
vulpes (Albula) Frizzell 1965C
weileri (Ceratoscopelus) Brzobohaty
1965
weileri (Beryx) Hatai 1965B
weileri (Clupea) Smigielska 1966A, B
weileri (Gobius) Bauza Rullan 1964
weileri (Prealbula) Frizzell 1965C
weinbergeri (otolithus) Sieber and
Weinberger 1967
Otospermophilini Marmotinae Gromov,
I. M., et al. 1965
Otospermophilus Otospermophilus
Gromov, I. M., et al. 1965
Otospermophilus Sciuridae
argonautus Gromov, I. M., et al. 1965
(subgen. Otospermophilus)
beecheyi
captus Gromov, I. M., et al. 1965
(subgen. Otospermophilus)
bensoni Gromov, I. M., et al. 1965
(subgen. Otospermophilus)
dotti Gromov, I. M., et al. 1965
(subgen. Callospermophilus)
fricki Gromov, I. M., et al. 1965
(subgen. Pliocitellus)
gidleyi Gromov, I. M., et al. 1965
(subgen. Otospermophilus)
howelli Gromov, I. M., et al. 1965
(subgen. Callospermophilus)
matachicensis Gromov, I. M., et al.
1965 (subgen. Pliocitelloides)
matthewi Gromov, I. M., et al. 1965
(subgen. Otospermophilus)
pattersoni Gromov, I. M., et al. 1965
primitivus Gromov, I. M., et al. 1965
rexroadensis Gromov, I. M., et al. 1965
(subgen. Ictidomys)

Pachyosteiformes Euarthrodira
Pachypithecus Mammalia incertae sedis
    macrognathus Simpson, G. G. 1967A
      (nomen dubium)
Pachypleurosauridae Nothosauria
    Pachypleurosaurus
Pachypleurosauroidea Nothosauria
Pachypleurosaurus Pachypleurosauridae
    Gilardoni 1964
Pachyrhinidae Gorgonopsia
    Pachyrhininae
Pachyrhininae Pachyrhinidae Viushkov
    1964C, p. 262 (of Gorgon-
    opsidae)
Pachyrhinosauridae Ankylosauria
    Pachyrhinosaurus
Pachyrhinosaurus Pachyrhinosauridae
    canadensis Langston 1967, 1968
Pachyrhizodontidae Elopoidea
    Pachyrhizodus
Pachyrhizodus Pachyrhizodontidae
    caninus Bardack 1968A
    minimus Bardack 1968A
Pachysaurops Teratosauridae Huene
    1959A* (=Pachysaurus
    Huene non Fitzinger 1843)
Pachysuchus Phytosauridae
    imperfectus Young, C.-c. 1964A
Pachytegos Endothiodontidae
    stockleyi Cox, C. B. 1964
Pachythrissops Chirocentridae Bardack
    1965A
    propterus Bardack 1965A
Pachyvaranidae ?Varanoidea
    Pachyvaranus
Pachyvaranus Pachyvaranidae
    Kuhn, Oskar 1966A ("Palaeovaranus",
    by error)
pacificus (Eporeodon, Mystipterus)
paenebursarius (Geomys)
Paenemarmota Sciuridae
    barbouri Gromov, I. M., et al. 1965
Paeneprolimnocyon Hyaenodontidae
    Guthrie, D. A. 1967A
    admissadomus Guthrie, D. A. 1967A
Paenungulata Ferungulata
pagei (Cephalaspis, Peromyscus, Pseudo-
    theridomys, Turina)
Pagellus Sparidae
    erythrinus Tarashchuk 1957
Paginula Oldfieldthomasiidae
    parca Simpson, G. G. 1964C, 1967A
Pagonomus Pantolestidae Russell, D. E.
    1964
    dionysi Russell, D. E. 1964

Pagrus Sparidae
    mauritanicus Menesini 1967B
painei (Palorchestes)
Pairomys Rodentia incertae sedis: Thaler
    1966A
    crusafonti Thaler 1966A
Palaciosichnus Ichnites Casamiquela 1964A
    (in Vertebrata inc. sed.)
    zetti Casamiquela 1964A
Palacrodontidae [Brachyrhinodontinae]
    Sphenodontidae
Palaeacanthaspididae Palaeacanthaspidi-
    formes
Palaeacanthaspidiformes Rhenanida
Palaeanodon Metacheiromyidae
    woodi Guthrie, D. A. 1967B
Palaeanodonta Edentata
Palaearctomys Sciuridae
    montanus Gromov, I. M., et al. 1965
Palaechameleontidae [Weigeltisauridae]
    Eosuchia
Palaeochelys Testudinidae
    elongata Yeh 1963B (?)
palaeformis (Pycnosteus)
Palaeictops Leptictidae Van Valen 1967B
    pineyensis Guthrie, D. A. 1967B (cf.)
Palaeoanthropinae Hominidae Dokládal
    1965 (Neanderthals)
Palaeoanthropus Hominidae Suzuki 1964,
    1965 (Amud man)
    neanderthalensis Alexandersen 1967A;
    Schaefer, U. 1964 (Homo)
Palaeoasovicus (Cricetus cricetus)
Palaeobalistum Pycnodontidae
    gutturosum Leonardi, A. 1966
Palaeobatrachidae Procoela Spinar 1967A,
    B
    Palaeobatrachus
Palaeobatrachus Palaeobatrachidae
    grandipes Spinar 1966, 1967A
Palaeobergia Gyrolepidotidae Gardiner
    1967A
palaeoborysthenica (Desmana moschata)
palaeocaspicus (Citellus pygmaeus)
Palaeochenoides ?Cyphornithidae
    mioceanus Hopson 1964A
palaeochoerus (Hyotherium)
Palaeochoerus Suidae
    dartevellei Hooijer 1963D
    meissneri Crusafont Pairó, Valenciano
    Horta, et al. 1968
Palaeociconiinae Phorushacidae Brodkorb
    1967
Palaeocorax Isuridae Glikman 1956
    faleatus Glikman 1956

Palaeorhynchidae Xiphioidea
    Enniskillenus
Palaeoryctes Palaeoryctidae
    puercensis Van Valen 1966A
    punctatus Van Valen 1966A
Paleoryctidae Palaeoryctoidea Clemens
        and Russell 1965 (in In-
        sectivora, sensu lato); Van
        Valen 1965G, 1966A
    Aboletylestes, Acmeodon, Avunculus,
        Cimolestes, Deltatheridium,
        Deltatheroides, Gelastops,
        Hyotheridium, Micropter-
        nodus, Nyssodon, Palaeo-
        ryctes, Paleotomus, Para-
        ryctes, Puercolestes, Sar-
        codon
    Deltatheridiinae, Didelphodontinae,
        Micropternodontinae,
        Palaeoryctinae
Palaeoryctinae Palaeoryctidae Van Valen
        1966A
Palaeortyx Cracidae
    edwardsi Villalta 1963
    miocaena Villalta 1963
Palaeoryctoidea Deltatheridia Van Valen
        1966A, 1967B (in Hyaeno-
        donta)
Palaeoryx Bovidae
    majori Bakalov and Nikolov 1962
    pallasii Bakalov and Nikolov 1962
Palaeosaniwa Varanidae
    canadensis Estes 1964
Palaeosauria Palaeopoda Colbert 1964B;
        Kuhn, O. 1967B (preoccup.)
Palaeosauridae Palaeosauria Colbert
        1964B
Palaeoscyllium Scyliorhinidae Schweizer
        1964
palaeoserengetensis (Herpestes)
palaeosinensis (Panthera tigris)
Palaeosinopa Pantolestidae
    simpsoni Van Valen 1967B
Palaeosyops Brontotheriidae
    fontinalis Robinson, Peter 1966A
palaeotalpinus (Ellobius)
Palaeotetrix Phasianidae Jehl 1967
        (syn. with Dendragapus)
    gilli Jehl 1967
Palaeothentoides Macroscelididae
    africanus Patterson, B. 1965B
Palaeotheriidae Equoidea
    Leptolophus, Palaeotherium, Plagio-
        lophus
Palaeotherium Palaeotheriidae Sturani
        1965

crassum Bonis 1964; Telles Antunes
        1964D (cf.), 1967C (cf.)
    curtum Bonis 1964
    duvali Bonis 1964; Remy 1967
    latum Bonis 1964
    magnum Bonis 1964
    medium Bonis 1964
Palaeotoxodon Toxodontidae
    nazari Pascual 1965B (?)
Palaeotraginae Giraffidae Godina 1967B
Palaeotragus Giraffidae Godina 1964C,
        1967B, 1968; Godina and
        Khubka 1968 (subgen.
        Achtiaria); Meladze 1967
    berislavicus Korotkevich 1957 (subgen.
        Achtiaria)
    hoffstetteri Ozansoy 1965
    rouenii Bakalov and Nikolov 1962
Palaeotragus Palaeotragus Godina 1967B,
        1968
Palaeotringa Scolopacidae
    vetus Baird 1967
Palaeourodeloidea ?Cryptobranchoidea
        Herre 1950A*
palankarinnica (Perikoala)
Palealbula Albulidae Frizzell 1965C
        (otolith)
    neocomiensis Frizzell 1965C
Palenochtha Paromomyidae Van Valen
        1965F
    minor Van Valen 1965F
Paleoheterodon Colubridae Holman 1964C;
        Wilson, R. L. 1968
    tiheni Holman 1964C
Paleomoropus Eomoropidae Radinsky
        1964A
    jepseni Radinsky 1964A
Paleonisciformes Actinopterygii Lehman
        1966B (Suborders Palaeo-
        niscoidei and Platysomoidei)
Paleoparadoxia Paleoparadoxidae Wood-
        burne 1965B
    tabatai Shikama 1966A, C
Paleoparadoxidae Desmostyliformes
        Paleoparadoxia
Paleostruthio Struthionidae Burchak-Abram-
        ovich, N. 1953C
    sternatus Burchak-Abramovich, N.
        1953C
Paleotomus Palaeoryctidae Van Valen
        1967B
    senior Van Valen 1967B
pales (Sthenurus)
Paleunycteris ?Rhinolophidae
    quercyi Miguet 1967 (aff.)
Palimphyes Euzaphlegidae
    brevis Gorbach 1961C

Paracaptorhinidae Captorhinomorpha
    Kuhn, Oskar 1966A (valid)
Paracentrophoridae [Semionotidae] Amii-
    formes Obruchev, D. V.
    1964A, p. 380
Paraceratherium Rhinocerotidae
    prochorovi Biriukov, Voskoboinikov,
    Kuznetsov and Nurimov
    1962
Parachanos Chanidae Leonardi, A. 1966
Paracittelus Paramyidae
    eminens Black, C. C. 1966 (transf.
    from Sciuridae); Gromov,
    I. M., et al. 1965
Paraclupea Clupeidae
    chetungensis Gaudant 1967
.Paracrax Cracidae Brodkorb 1964E
Paracricetodon Cricetidae Alker 1968
    (Nebr. Olig.); Thaler 1966B
Paracryptotis Soricidae
    rex Repenning 1967C
Paracyclotosaurinae Capitosauridae Ochev
    1966C
Paracyclotosaurus Capitosauridae
    davidi Welles and Cosgriff 1965B
Paradelomys Adelomys Thaler 1966B
Paradercetis Dercetidae Casier 1965
    kipalaensis Casier 1965
Paraderma Parasaniwidae Estes 1964
    (Cret., Wyo.)
    bogerti Estes 1964
Paradesmatochoerus Desmatochoerus
    Schultz, C. B. and Falken-
    bach 1968
Paradiceros Rhinocerotidae Hooijer
    1968E
    mukirii Hooijer 1968E
Paradjidaumo Eomyidae
    minor Black, C. C. 1965A
Paradomnina Soricidae Hutchison 1966A
    (in Heterosoricinae)
    relictus Hutchison 1966A; Repenning
    1967C
paradoxa (Psammolepis)
paradoxus (Dimylus, Eucentrurus, Myria-
    canthus)
Paraentelodon Entelodontidae Gabuniia
    1964D
    intermedium Gabuniia 1964D, 1966A
Paraeporeodon Eporeodon Schultz, C. B.
    and Falkenbach 1968
Paraeurynotus Amphicentridae
    chabakovi Obruchev, D. V. 1962D
Paragale Mustelidae Petter, G. 1967B, C
    hürzeleri Petter, G. 1967B, C

Parahippus Equidae Macdonald 1966B
    avus Shotwell 1968 (cf.)
    blackbergi Olsen 1964B
    leonensis Olsen 1964A, B
    parahybensis (Alligator)
Parailurus Procyonidae
    lungaricus Fejfar 1964A
Paraisurus Isuridae
    compressus Sokolov, M. I. 1965
    elegans Sokolov, M. I. 1965
    macrorhizus Sokolov, M. I. 1965
Paralactaga Dipodidae Topachevskii 1965C
paralpha (Parabathygenys)
Paramacellodus ?Gerrhosauridae Hoffstetter
    1967D
    oweni Hoffstetter 1967D
Paramblypteridae Palaeoniscoidei Blot
    1966B
Paramblypterus
Paramblypterus Paramblypteridae Blot
    1966B
    decorus Blot 1966B (restor.)
Paramerycoidodon Merycoidodontidae
    Schultz, C. B. and Falkenbach
    1968
    bacai Schultz, C. B. and Falkenbach
    1968 (subgen. Barbourochoe-
    rus)
    georgei Schultz, C. B. and Falkenbach
    1968
    major Schultz, C. B. and Falkenbach
    1968 (subgen. Barbouro-
    choerus)
    meagherensis Schultz, C. B. and Falken-
    bach 1968 (subgen. Gregoryo-
    cheorus)
    wanlessi Schultz, C. B. and Falkenbach
    1968 (subgen. Gregoryochoerus)
Paramyidae Ischyromyoidea Dawson, M.
    1964
    Ailuravus, Franimys, Janimus, Lepto-
    tomus, Lophiparamys, Mel-
    dimys, Microparamys, Myto-
    nomys, Paracittelus, Paramys,
    Prosciurus, Pseudotomus,
    Reithroparamys
    Ailuraviinae, Prosciurinae, Paramyinae,
    Microparamyinae, Pseudo-
    paramyinae, Reithropara-
    myinae
Paramyinae Paramyidae
Paramylodon Mylodontidae
    harlani Hibbard and Dalquest 1966;
    Schultz, G. E. 1965B
Paramys Paramyidae Russell, L. S. 1965D

Parechelus Parechelidae Casier 1967
    prangei Casier 1967
Parectypodus Ectypodontidae
    lovei Sloan 1966
Pareiasauria [Diadectomorpha] Cotylo-
        sauria Kuhn, Oskar 1966A
        (suborder of Diadectomor-
        pha); Watson 1957A* (deri-
        vation, skull)
Pareiasauridae Procolophonoidea Boonstra
    1967B
Pareiasauroidea [Pareiasauridae] Procolo-
        phonoidea Chudinov 1957B*
        (suborder); Kuhn, Oskar
        1966A (ascribed to Romer
        1956F)
Parelephas [Mammuthus] Elephantidae
Parelephas Mammuthus David, A. 1965C
Parendotherium Dryolestidae Crusafont
        Pairó and Adrover 1965
        (Cret., Spain)
    herrerei Crusafont Pairó and Adrover
        1965
Paremys Cylindrodontidae Lindsay, E.
    1968A
Parhaplocyon Haplocyon Bonis 1966B,
    1967
Parictis Canidae
    dakotensis Clark, J. and Beerbower
        1967 (subgen. Parictis)
    personi Clark, J. and Beerbower
        1967 (subgen. Campylo-
        cynodon)
Parictis Parictis Clark, J. and Beerbower
    1967
Parietobalaena Cetotheriidae
    palmeri Kellogg 1968
Parioxydae Eryopoidea
    Parioxys
Parioxys Parioxydae
    bolli Carroll, R. L. 1964A
parisiense (Lophiodon)
parisiensis (Adapis)
Parmularius Bovidae
    altidens Leakey, L. S. B. 1965
    rugosus Leakey, L. S. B. 1965
parnellii (Pteronotus)
Parocnus Megalonychidae
    serus Paula Couto 1967
Paromomyidae Adapoidea Crusafont
        Pairó 1967B; Robinson,
        Peter 1968B
    Ignacius, Mckennatherium, Palenochtha,
        Purgatorius, Torrejonia
    Purgatoriinae
Paronychodon ?Coeluridae

lacustris Estes 1964
paroperarius (Microtus)
Parotosaurus Capitosauridae Welles 1967;
        Welles and Cosgriff 1964,
        1965A
    albertyni Welles and Cosgriff 1965B
        (nomen vanum)
    augustifrons Welles and Cosgriff 1965B
    birdi Welles and Cosgriff 1965B
    brookvalensis Welles and Cosgriff 1965B
    haughtoni Welles and Cosgriff 1965B
    helgolandicus Welles and Cosgriff
        1965B
    mechernichensis Jox 1966
    nasutus Welles and Cosgriff 1965B
    orenburgensis Konzhukova 1965B
    orientalis Ochev 1966C; Shishkin and
        Ochev 1966, 1967A
    panteleevi Ochev 1966C
    peabodyi Welles 1967; Welles and Cos-
        griff 1965B
    semiclausis Welles and Cosgriff 1965B
    turfanensis Young, C.-c. 1966A
Paroxyclaenidae Leptictoidea
    Dulcidon, Kochictis, Kopidodon,
        Paroxyclaenus, Pugiodons,
        Russellites, Spaniella
Paroxyclaenus Paroxyclaenidae
    lemuroides Van Valen 1965E
parringtonia (Olivieria)
parringtoni (Erythrotherium)
parryii (Citellus)
partium (Lyrurus)
Parulidae Passeres
    Seiurus
parva (Camelopardalis, Cryptotis)
parviceros (Dicrocerus elegans)
parvidens (Germanomys, Hybodus, Ischy-
        romys, Oldfieldthomasia,
        Pseudogonatodus, Thelodus)
parviplicatus (Hypolagus)
parvivorus (Miacis)
parvula (Dinaspidella)
parvulum (Propalaeotherium)
parvulus (Lagomeryx, Pseudoloris, Pseudo-
        theridomys, Rhombus, Uinta-
        sorex)
parvus (Acrogaster, Burramys, Ceratodus,
        Cricetodon, Diprionomys,
        Epigenetochoerus, Felis,
        Homalostylops, Iberomeryx,
        Leptotomus, Microparamys,
        Ophiomys, Pataecus, Proto-
        reodon, Schizotheriodes,
        Xiphiorhynchus)
Parydrosorex Soricidae Wilson, R. L. 1968

concisus Wilson, R. L. 1968
Paschatherium Hyopsodontidae Russell,
        D. E. 1964
    dolli Russell, D. E. 1964; Quinet
        1964A
    petri Russell, D. E. 1964; Russell,
        D. E., Louis and Poirier
        1966B
    s'jongersi Quinet 1966C
Pascualgnathus Diademodontidae Bona-
        parte 1966B
    polanskii Bonaparte 1966B, D, 1967
pascuali (Eomorphippus, Massetognathus)
paskapooensis (Plesiadapis)
pasquali (Shelania)
Passer Ploceidae
    predomesticus Markus 1964
Passeres Passeriformes Dement'ev 1964
        (ord.)
Passeriformes Neognathae
passerina (Columbigallina)
Pataecops ?Lophialetidae Radinsky 1966C
        (for Pataecus, preocc.)
Pataecus ?Lophialetidae Radinsky 1965A,
        1966C (preocc.)
    parvus Radinsky 1965A
patagonicus (Ameghinichnus, "Claenodon,"
        Lophiodonticulus)
patellifrons (Woodwardella)
Pateroperca Aulolepidae
    libanica Patterson, C. 1964
Patriocetinae Squalodontidae
Patriocetus Squalodontidae
    ehrlichi Rothausen 1968A, B
Patriofelis Oxyaenidae
    ulta Robinson, Peter 1966A (cf.); Van
        Valen 1966A
Pattenaspis Cephalaspididae
    acuminata Stensiö 1963
Pattersomys Echimyidae Pascual 1967
        (in Heteropsomyinae)
    scagliai Pascual 1967
pattersoni (Otospermophilus, Pappother-
        ium, Pararyctes)
patulus (Aglaocetus)
paucidens (Glyptolepis, Hadrosaurus,
        Zinnosaurus)
Paucituberculata Marsupialia Ride 1964B
        (incl. Caenolestidae and
        Polydolopidae)
paulhiacensis (Heteroxerus)
pauli (Pycnosteus)
Paulocnus Megalonychidae
    petrifactus Hooijer 1964D; Paula
        Couto 1967
paulsoni (Basilosaurus)

paulus (Hyopsodus)
Paurodontidae Eupantotheria
Pauromys Cricetidae Dawson, M. 1968B
pavlodarica (Crocidura)
peabodyi (Parotosaurus)
Pecora Ruminantia
Pecoripeda Artiodactipedae Panin and
        Avram 1962 (=Pecorapeda
        Vialov 1961); Thenius
        1967A; Vialov 1966 (in
        Bovipedidae)
    amalphea Panin and Avram 1962;
        Panin and Stefănescu 1968;
        Vialov 1966 (subgen. Ga-
        zellipeda)
    gazella Panin and Avram 1962; Panin
        and Stefănescu 1968; Vialov
        1966 (subgen. Gazellipeda)
    diaboli Vialov 1966 (subgen. Ovipeda)
    dicroceroides Vialov 1966 (subgen.
        Cervipeda)
    djali Vialov 1966 (subgen. Ovipeda)
    satyri Vialov 1966 (subgen. Ovipeda)
Pecoripedinae Artiodactipedae Panin and
        Avram 1962
Pecoripedoidei Artiodactipedida Vialov
        1966
pectinatus (Ceratodus, Lobopterus, Noto-
        rhynchus, Psammosteus)
Pedetidae Sciurognathi incertae sedis
        Lavocat and Michaux 1966
        (dentition)
    Megapedetes
Pediomyidae Didelphoidea Clemens 1966
    Pediomys
Pediomys Pediomyidae
    cooki Clemens 1966
    elegans Clemens 1966
    florencae Clemens 1966
    hatcheri Clemens 1966
    krejcii Clemens 1966
Pedomys Cricetidae
    ilanensis Hibbard and Dalquest 1966
    ochrogaster Schultz, G. E. 1965B
Pegomylus Stenomylus Frick, C. and
        Taylor 1968
"Pehuenia" ?Isotemnidae incertae sedis
    magna Simpson, G. G. 1967A (nomen
        dubium)
peii (Spirocerus)
Peipiaosteidae Acipenseriformes Liu, H.-t.
        and Zhou 1965
    Peipiaosteus
Peipiaosteus Peipiaosteidae Liu, H.-t. and
        Zhou 1965
    pani Liu, H.-t. and Zhou 1965

Peishanemys Dermatemydidae
    latipons Yeh 1963B
pekingensis (Sinanthropus)
Peking man (Sinanthropus pekingensis)
        Hominidae Andrews, R. C.
        1930; Martínez del Río
        1931; Nordmann 1936C,
        1946
Pelecani Pelecaniformes
Pelecanidae Pelecanoidea
    Pelecanus
Pelecaniformes Neognathae
Pelecanoidea Pelecani
Pelecanus Pelecanidae
    tirarensis Miller, A. H. 1966C
pelikani (Microbrachis)
pellegrini (Prohydrocyon)
Pelobates Pelobatidae
    fuscus Jacobshagen 1963
Pelobatidae Anomocoela Estes 1964
    Palaeopelobates, Pelobates, Pelopati-
        nopsis, Scaphiopus
Pelocetus Cetotheriidae Kellogg 1965
    calvertensis Kellogg 1965
Pelomedusidae Trionychoidea
    Bantuchelys, Naiadochelys, Podocnemis,
        Taphrosphys
Pelopatinopsis Pelobatidae Kuhn, Oskar
        1941D*
    hinschei Kuhn, Oskar 1941D*
Pelorovis Bovidae
    oldowayensis Gentry 1967
Pelosaurus Eryopidae
    laticeps Konzhukova 1963
Peltopleuridae Pholidopleuriformes
Peltopleuriformes [Peltopleuridae] Phol-
        idopleuriformes Lehman
        1966B
Peltosaurus Anguidae
    piger Estes 1964
Peltostega Rhytidosteidae Cosgriff 1965
    erici Lehman 1966A
Pelurgaspis Eglonaspididae Obruchev,
        D. V. 1964C
    macrorhyncha Obruchev, D. V. 1964C
Pelycodus Adapidae Guthrie, D. A.
        1967B (in Notharctidae)
    frugivorus Guthrie, D. A. 1967B
    jarrovii Guthrie, D. A. 1967B
Pelycosauria Synapsida Gould, S. J.
        1967
    Incertae sedis: Protoclepsydrops
pembertoni (Alzadasaurus)
penai (Lagopsis)
penelope (Anas)
penicillata (Bettongia)

penniger (Chaetodon)
pennsylvanicus (Microtus)
Pentacodontidae Insectivora incertae sedis
        Van Valen 1967B (new rank)
Pentaglis Gliridae
    meini Bruijn 1966A
Pentalophodon [Anancus] Gomphotheriidae
pentelici (Choerolophodon, Gomphotherium,
        Mesopithecus)
pentelicum (Ancylotherium)
pentelicus (Gomphotherium)
Peraceras Rhinocerotidae
    superciliosus Dalquest and Hughes
        1966 (cf.)
Perameles Peramelidae Freedman 1967;
        Freedman and Joffe 1967A,
        B; Merrilees 1967B
    bougainville Freedman and Joffe 1967B
    gunnii Freedman and Joffe 1967B
    nasuta Freedman and Joffe 1967A
Peramelidae Perameloidea Merrilees 1967B
    Ischnodon, Perameles
Peramelina Marsupialia Ride 1964B (incl.
        Peramelidae)
Perameloidea Marsupialia
Peramuridae Eupantotheria Kermack in
        Butler et al. 1967, p. 766
        (attributed to Kretzoi)
Peramus Amphitheriidae
    tenuirostris Mills 1964
Peratherium Didelphidae Robinson, Peter
        1966A (?)
    comstocki Simpson, G. G. 1968C (cf.)
    cuvieri Bonis 1964; Telles Antunes
        1967C (cf.)
    dormaalense Quinet 1964A
    hoogbutselense Quinet and Misonne
        1967
        major Quinet and Misonne 1967
        minor Quinet and Misonne 1967
perbullatus (Eporeodon longifrons)
Perca Percidae
    floviatilis Deckert and Karrer 1965;
        Weiler 1965
Perchoerus Tayassuidae
    minor Clark, J. and Beerbower 1967
        (cf.)
Percida Teleostei Danil'chenko 1964B
        (order)
Percidae Percoidea
    Acerina, Aspro, Lucioperca, Perca
Perciformes Acanthopterygii
Percoidea Percoidei
Percoidei Perciformes
Percopsida Teleostei Danil'chenko 1964B
        (order)

Petalodontidae Petalodontes
    Janassa, Petalodus
Petalodus Petalodontidae
    allegheniensis Hansen, M. C. 1968
    shingkuoi Liu, H.-t. and Hsieh 1965
Petauria Sciuridae
    voigtstedtensis Kretzoi 1965C
Petaurinae Sciuridae Kretzoi 1965C (in
    Petauristidae)
Petauristidae [Sciuridae] Sciuroidea
Petauristinae Sciuridae Fejfar 1964A
Petényia Soricidae Repenning 1967C
    hungarica Fejfar 1964A
Petenyiella Soricidae Repenning 1967C
petersi (Trionyx)
petersoni (Myopterygius, Mytonolagus)
Petralon man [Homo sapiens] Hominidae
    Pulianos 1963, 1965
petri (Paschatherium, Rhynchosauroides)
petrifactus (Paulocnus)
Petrochelidon Hirundinidae
    fulva Bernstein 1965
Petrodus Hybodontidae
    occidentalis Branson 1965B
petrolei (Chrysemys scripta)
Petromyzon Petromyzontidae Stensiö
    1963
Petromyzontida Cephalaspidomorpha
    Stensiö 1964
Petromyzontidae Cyclostomata
    Mayomyzon, Petromyzon
petropolis (Preophidion)
Pezophaps Raphidae
    solitarius Lüttschwager 1961
Phaenicophilus Thraupidae
    palmarum Bernstein 1965
Phalacrocoracidae Suloidea
    Phalacrocorax
Phalacrocorax Phalacrocoracidae
    carbo Jánossy 1965C
    goletensis Howard, H. 1965A
    ibericum Villalta 1963
Phalangeridae Phalangeroidea Ride 1964B
    Burramys, Koalemus, Phascolarctos
Phalangeroidea Marsupialia
Phanagoroloxodon Elephantidae
    mammontoides Alekseeva, L. I. 1965
Phaneropleuridae Phaneropleuriformes
    Lehman 1966C
Phaneropleuriformes Dipteri Lehman
    1966C (with Phaneropleuri-
    dae)
Phaneropleuroidei [Phaneropleuriformes]
    Dipteri Andrews, S. M.,
    Gardiner, Miles and Patterson
    1967

Phanerorhynchida [Phanerorhynchiformes]
    Chondrostei Obruchev, D. V.
    1964A, p. 363
Phanerorhynchidae Phanerorhynchiformes
    Obruchev 1964 (ascribed to
    Stensiö 1932; in Phanero-
    rhynchida)
    Phanerorhynchus
Phanerorhynchiformes Chondrostei Leh-
    man 1966B
Phanerorhynchus Phanerorhynchidae
    armatus Gardiner 1967A (rest.)
pharao (Onchosaurus)
Pharmacichthyidae Dinopterygoidei Pat-
    terson, C. 1964
    Pharmacichthys
Pharmacichthys Pharmacichthyidae
    venenifer Patterson, C. 1964 (rest.)
pharsus (Caproberyx)
Pharyngolepididae Anaspida
    Pharyngolepis
Pharyngolepis Pharyngolepididae
    heintzi Ritchie, A. 1964
    oblongus Ritchie, A. 1964
Phascolarctidae [Phalangeridae] Diproto-
    donta
Phascolarctos ?Phalangeridae Dickenson
    1968
    cinereus Frechkop 1965E
    stirtoni Bartholomai 1968
Phascolomidae Phalangeroidea
    Phascolonus
Phascolonus Phascolomidae
    curvirostris Stephenson, N. G. 1964
    gigas Stephenson, N. G. 1964
    magnus Stephenson, N. G. 1964
    medius Stephenson, N. G. 1964
Phasianidae Phasianoidea
    Agriochoerus, Alectornis, Coturnix,
        Dendragapus, Gallus,
        Lyrurus, Meleagris, Miophasia-
        nus, Miortyx, Palaeoperdix,
        Palaeotetrix, Perdix, Proalector,
        Schaubortyx, Tetrao
    Meleagrinae, Phasianinae, Tetraoninae
Phasianinae Phasianidae
Phasianoidea Galliformes
Phenacodon Phenacodontidae Radinsky
    1966A
Phenacodontidae Condylarthra
    Ectocion, Phenacodon, Phenacodus,
        Tetraclaenodon
Phenacodus Phenacodontidae
    grangeri Maxwell, R. A., et al. 1967
        (cf.); Wilson, J. A. 1967

latiusculus Nybelin 1966 (rest.)
pusillus Nybelin 1966 (cf.; rest.)
retrodorsalis Wenz 1967B (?)
Pholidopleuriformes Chondrostei Leh-
    man 1966B
Pholidosauridae Mesosuchia
    Dyrosaurus, Sarcosuchus
Pholidosteidae Coccosteiformes Obruchev,
    D. V. 1964D
Pholidota Unguiculata Barlow 1967
pholidotus (Dapedius)
phonax (Prodissopsalis)
Phororhaci Gruiformes
Phorusrhacidae Cariamae
    Brontornithinae, Palaeociconiinae
Phreatosauridae [Phreatosuchidae] Synap-
        sida incertae sedis Kuhn, Oskar
    1966A (ascribed to Efremov
    1954A*; in Tapinocephaloidea
Phreatosuchidae Synapsida incertae sedis
        Kuhn, Oskar 1965B, p. 8
    (in Titanoschidae)
Phronetragus Artiodactyla incertae sedis
        Gabuniiᵃ 1954C (nomen
    nudum)
    arknethensis Gabuniiᵃ 1954C (nomen
        nudum); Meladze 1967 (in
        Bovidae)
    secundus Meladze 1967
Phrynosoma Iguanidae Estes and Tihen
    1964
Phthinosuchia Theriodontia
Phtoramys Octodontidae
    hidalguense Pascual, Pisano and Ortego
    1965
Phylctaenaspididae Arctolepidiformes
    Phylctaenaspis
Phylctaenaspis Phylctaenaspididae Leh-
    man 1963B
Phyllodontidae [Labridae] Labroidea
Phyllodus Labridae Casier 1966A (in
    Phyllodontidae)
    toliapicus Casier 1966A
Phyllolepida Coccostei Andrews, S. M.,
        Gardiner, Miles and Patter-
        son 1967 (order of Arthro-
        dira); Stensiö 1934A*
Phyllolepididae Phyllolepidiformes
    Phyllolepis
Phyllolepidiformes Petalichthyida
Phyllolepis Phyllolepididae Rade 1964
Phyllonycteris Phyllostomatidae
    major Choate and Birney 1968
Phyllospondyli [Rhachitomi] Temno-
        spondyli Konzhukova 1963

(suggests it be revived to
    incl. Pelosaurus and other
    branchisaurs), 1965A
Phyllostomatidae Phyllostomatoidea
    Artibeus, Brachyphylla, Erophylla,
        Macrotus, Marmoops, Mono-
        phyllus, Phyllonycteris,
        Pteronotus, Stenoderma
Phyllostomatoidea Microchiroptera
Phyllotillon Chalicotheriidae Gabuniiᵃ
    1964D
phyllurus (Rhamphorhynchus)
Physeteridae Physeteroidea
    Orycterocetus
Physeteroidea Odontoceti
Physodon Carcharhinidae
    miocaenus Jonet 1965-66A
    secundus Casier 1966A
    tertius Casier 1966A
Physodon Carcharias Bosch 1964C
Phytosauria Thecodontia Chatterjee 1967
    (Trias., India)
Phytosauridae Phytosauria Kuhn, Oskar
        1966A p. 79 (invalid since
        Phytosaurus "undefinierbar
        ist.")
    Angistorhinus, Belodon, Coburgosuchus,
        Mesorhinus?, Pachysuchus,
        Rutiodon
Piceoerpeton Cryptobranchidae Meszoely
    1967
    willwoodensis Meszoely 1967
Pici Piciformes Dement'ev 1964 (ord.)
Picidae Pici
    Jynx, Picus, Pliopicus
Piciformes Neognathae
picteti (Craspedochelys, Cretodus)
pictus (Lycaon)
Picunia Mammalia incertae sedis
    nitida Simpson, G. G. 1967A (nomen
        vanum)
Picus Picidae
    canus Jánossy 1965E
pidoplickai (Geoemyda)
pidoplitschkoi (Anourosoricodon)
pidoplitshkoi (Eostylocerus)
pieckoensis (Mayomyzon)
Piezodus Palaeolagidae
    branssatensis Gureev 1964
piger (Peltosaurus)
pigotti (Paraphiomys)
pilari (Scorpaena)
pilaris (Turdus)
pilgrimi (Chalicotherium, Geoemyda,
        Hyaenodon, Sivapithecus)

Pilosa Xenarthra
"Piltdown man" (fraudulent) [Homo
    sapiens] Hominidae Taylor,
    R. M. S. 1937
Pinacosaurus Nodosauridae
    ninghsiaensis Young, C.-c. 1964E
pinarhisarensis (Alosa)
pineyensis (Palaeictops)
pinfoldi (Ichthyolestes)
pinjorensis (Stegodon)
Pinnipedia Carnivora Stains 1967
Piocormus Sphenodontidae
    laticeps Cocude-Michel 1967
Pionaspis Cyathaspididae Denison 1964B
    acuticosta Denison 1964B
    planicosta Denison 1964B
Pipestoneomys Castoridae
    bisculatus Black, C. C. 1965A
Pipedae Opisthocoela
    Xenopus
pipiens (Rana)
Pirortyx Cracidae Brodkorb 1964A (in
    Gallinuloidinae)
    major Brodkorb 1964A
pisanoi (Bufo)
Pisanosauridae Ornithopoda Casamiquela
    1967A
    Pisanosaurus
Pisanosaurus Pisanosauridae Casamiquela
    1967A
    mertii Casamiquela 1967A
Pisces Craniata Andrews, S. M., et al.
    1967; Gardiner, B. G. 1966
    (classif.); Gross, W. 1967A;
    Müller, A. H. 1966; Tarlo
    1967B (incl. classes Acantho-
    dii, Placodermi, Crossoptery-
    gii, Dipnoi, Actinopterygii,
    Selachii and Holocephali)
    Incertae sedis: Andreolepis
pisinnus (Copemys)
Pistosauridae Pistosauroidea Novozhilov
    1964B
Pistosauroidea Plesiosauria Kuhn, Oskar
    1966A (assigned to Edinger
    1935A, probably should be
    Kuhn 1960A); Novozhilov
    1964B
Pithanotaria Otariidae Mitchell, E. D.
    1966B (rest.)
Pithecanthropus Hominidae Iakimov
    1967B; Koenigswald 1967C,
    1968B; Odhner 1964; Petrov
    1940B; Sartono 1961, 1963,
    1964, 1967; Uryson 1966A;
    Vallois 1965C

erectus Jacob 1964, 1966, 1967
robustus Nesturkh 1954
Pithecistes Merycoidodontidae
    altageringensis Schultz, C. B. and Fal-
      kenbach 1968
    brevifacies Schultz, C. B. and Falken-
      bach 1968
    copei Schultz, C. B. and Falkenbach
      1968
    mariae Schultz, C. B. and Falkenbach
      1968
    tanneri Schultz, C. B. and Falkenbach
      1968
Pitikantia Diprotodontidae Stirton 1967A
    dailyi Stirton 1967A
Pituophis Colubridae Wilson, R. L. 1968
    catenifer Holman 1965D
Pitymys Cricetidae
    arvaloides Aleksandrova 1965A; Buachi-
      dze 1968: Shevchenko, A. I.
      1965B
    hintoni Aleksandrova 1965A, B; Shev-
      chenko, A. I. 1965B
    piveteaui (Crocidosorex, Cynelos, Eomelli-
      vora, Equus caballus, Hyaen-
      ictis, Megantereon)
Pivetonia Omomyidae Crusafont Pairó
    1967B
    isabenae Crusafont Pairó 1967B
Placerias Kannemeyeriidae
    gigas Cox, C. B. 1965 (reconst.)
placidens (Calippus)
Placochelyidae Placodontia
    Cyamodus, Placochelys
Placochelys Placochelyidae
    stoppanii Zapfe 1960D, 1964B (re-
      const.)
Placodermi Pisces Denison 1964A; Gross,
    W. 1967B; Miles, R. S. 1967A;
    Obruchev, D. V. 1964D
placodon (Haptosphenus)
Placodontia Euryapsida Haas, G. 1967
Placodontidae Placodontia
    Placodus
Placodontoidea [Placodontidae] Placodontia
    Peyer and Kuhn-Schnyder
    1955A (suborder of Placo-
    dontia)
Placodontomorpha [Euryapsida] Reptilia
    Kuhn, O. 1968 (incl. Placo-
    dontia)
Placodus Placodontidae Colbert 1967C
    (rest.)
Placosauridae Anguioidea
    Placosauriops, Placosauroides, Placo-
    therium

Placosauriops Placosauridae Kuhn, Oskar
1940J*
Placosauroides Placosauridae Kuhn, Oskar
1940J*
Placotherium Placosauridae Kuhn, Oskar
1940J*
Plagiodontia Myocastoridae
araeum Ray, C. E. 1964A (?)
Plagiolophus Palaeotheriidae Sturani
1965
annectens Remy 1967
Plagiomenidae Galeopithecoidea Van
Valen 1967B
Plagiomeninae, Thylacaelurinae
Plagiomeninae Plagiomenidae Van Valen
1967B
Plagiomenoidea Dermoptera
Plagiosauridae Plagiosauroidea
Melanopelta
Plagiosauroidea Temnospondyli Kuhn,
Oskar 1965E, p. 59
Plaisiodon Diprotodontidae Woodburne
1967A
centralis Woodburne 1967A, B
plana (Siberiaspis)
planiceps (Rhinocephalus)
planicosta (Pionaspis)
planicostatus (Aspideretes)
planifrons (Elephas, Mammuthus, Platecarpus, Protelephas)
planoides (Trionyx)
Plastomenus Trionychidae Miller, H. W.
1964; Wiman 1935C
jaxarticus Riabinin 1938A*
Platacodon Sciaenidae
nanus Estes 1964 (rest.)
Plataleae Ciconiiformes
Plataleidae Plataleae Dekeyser 1962B
Eudocimus, ?Mesembrinibis, Phimosus,
Plegadis
Platax Epihippidae
papilio Lehman 1966B
plinianus Blot 1966A, 1967 (sp.
discarded)
subvespertilio Blot 1967
Platecarpus Mosasauridae Bardack 1968A
(Platycarpus)
affinis Russell, D. A. 1967A (nomen
vanum)
anguliferus Russell, D. A. 1967A
(nomen vanum)
brachycephalus Russell, D. A. 1967A
(nomen dubium)
coryphaeus Russell, D. A. 1967A
gladiferus Russell, D. A. 1967A
(nomen vanum)

ictericus Russell, D. A. 1967A, C
intermedius Russell, D. A. 1967A
latispinus Russell, D. A. 1967A (nomen
dubium)
minor Russell, D. A. 1967A (nomen
vanum)
mudgei Russell, D. A. 1967A (nomen
vanum)
planifrons Russell, D. A. 1967A (nomen
vanum)
ptychodon Signeux 1959A
somenensis Russell, D. A. 1967A
tectulus Russell, D. A. 1967A (nomen
vanum)
tympaniticus Russell, D. A. 1967A
Plateosauravidae [?Melanorosauridae]
Carnosauria Kuhn, Oskar
1965A (ascribed to Huene
1929)
Plateosauria [Prosauropoda] Theropoda
Colbert 1964B
Plateosauria Palaeopoda Colbert 1964B;
Kuhn, O. 1967B (preoccup.)
Plateosauridae Plateosauria Charig, Attridge and Crompton 1965
(in Prosauropoda; incl.
Teratosauridae remains);
Colbert 1964B
Lufengosaurus, Plateosaurus
Plateosaurus Plateosauridae Colbert 1967C
(rest.); Gehlen 1959
quenstedti Hall, E. and M. 1964A
Platinx ?Chirocentridae
intermedius Signeux 1959C
macropterus Bardack 1965A
platostriata (Anglaspis)
Platybelone Belonidae
argalus Caldwell, D. K. 1966 (cf.)
Platycephalichthys Sarcopterygia incertae
sedis Jarvik 1967A; Thomson,
K. S. 1967B
platycephalus (Elephas)
platyceps (Lystrosaurus)
Platychelyidae Amphichelyidia Bräm
1965
Platychelys
Platychelys Platychelyidae
oberndorferi Bräm 1965
Platychoerops Plesiadapidae Crusafont
Pairo 1967B; Russell, D. E.
1964
daubrei Russell, D. E., Louis and
Savage 1967
richardsoni Russell, D. E., Louis and
Savage 1967

Plesiosauroidea Plesiosauria Novozhilov
1964C
Plesiosaurus Plesiosauridae Hoffman
1966
elasmosaurus Finzel 1964
mauritanicus Signeux 1959A, B
Plesioserranus Serranidae Casier 1966A
wemmeliensis Casier 1966A (cf.)
Plesiosminthus ?Dipodidae Klingener
1966
promyarion Thaler 1966B
schaubi Thaler 1966B
Plesiosoricidae Soricoidea Van Valen
1967B
Plesiotylosaurus Mosasauridae
crassidens Russell, D. A. 1967A
Plesippus Equus Strain 1966; Woodburne 1966A
shoshonensis White, J. A. 1967
Plethodoidea Osteoglossoidei
plethodon (Coelodus, Monophyllus)
Plethodontidae Salamandroidea Baker,
J. K. 1960; Patterson, C.
1967B; Wake 1966
Enischnorhynchus, ?Opisthotriton,
Prodesmodon, Tselfatia
Pleuraspidotherium Meniscotheriidae
aumonieri Russell, D. E. 1964 (rest.);
Russell, D. E. and Sigogneau
1965 (endocast)
pleuroceros (Diceratherium)
Pleuronectida Teleostei Danil'chenko
1964B (order)
Pleuronectidae Pleuronectoidea
Hippoglossoides, Protopsetta
Pleuronectiformes Acanthopterygii
Pleuronectoidea Pleuronectoidei
Pleuronectoidei Pleuronectiformes
Pleuropholidae Pholidophoriformes
Pleuropholis
Pleuropholis Pleuropholidae Wenz 1968B
Pleurosauria [Pleurosauridae] ?Clarazi-
sauria Kuhn, Oskar 1967B
(replaced by Ascrosauria);
Tatarinov 1964P (in Araeo-
scelidia)
Pleurosauridae ?Clarazisauria
Acrosaurus, Pleurosaurus
Pleurosaurus Pleurosauridae
goldfussi Cocude-Michel 1967
Pleurosternidae Pleurosternoidea
Glyptops
Pleurosternoidea Amphichelydia
Pleurostylodon Isotemnidae Simpson,
G. G. 1964C

bifidus Simpson, G. G. 1967A
complanatus Simpson, G. G. 1967A
crassiramis Simpson, G. G. 1967A (?)
modicus Simpson, G. G. 1967A
notabilis Simpson, G. G. 1967A
recticrista Simpson, G. G. 1967A (?)
similis Simpson, G. G. 1967A
Pleurostylops Notoungulata incertae sedis
glebosus Simpson, G. G. 1967A
pliacus (Ischyromys)
Pliauchenia Camelidae Webb, S. D. 1965C
magnifontis Webb, S. D. 1965C
Plicagnathus Cryptobranchidae Meszoely
1965
plicata (Puelia)
plicatilis (Hybodus)
plicatus (Chaerophon)
plicidens (Castor)
plicidentata (Ardynia)
plicifera (Guilielmoscottia)
pliciformis (Eopachyrucos)
plinianus (Platax)
plioagellus (Coluber)
Pliobatrachus Bufonidae
lánghae Kretzoi 1965B
pliocaenica (Pliopetaurista)
pliocaenicus (Allophaiomys, Mimomys,
Muscardinus, Muntiacus)
pliocaenicus-polonicus (Mimomys)
pliocenicus (Peromyscus)
Pliocervus Cervidae
kutchurganicus Korotkevich 1965B
Pliocitelloides Otospermophilus Gromov,
I. M., et al. 1965
Pliocitellus Otospermophilus Gromov,
I. M., et al. 1965
pliocompactilis (Bufo)
Pliohippus Equidae Wilson, R. L. 1968
(cf.)
fossulatus Dalquest and Hughes 1966
Pliohyracidae [Pliohyracinae] Procaviidae
Pliohyracinae Procaviidae
Pliohyrax Procaviidae
graecus Melentis 1966D
Pliolagus Leporidae
beremendensis Gureev 1964
tothi Gureev 1964; Sych 1965
Pliolumbus Podicipedidae Murray, B. G.
1967
baryosteus Murray, B. G. 1967
Pliometanastes Megalonychidae Hirschfeld
and Webb 1968
galushai Hirschfeld and Webb 1968
protistus Hirschfeld and Webb 1968
Pliomys Cricetidae
episcopalis Aleksandrova 1965A;

Poelagus Caprolagus Gureev 1964
Pogonias Sparidae
    cromis Olsen 1964A
poirrieri (Rhizospalax)
polanskii (Pascualgnathus)
polaris (Poraspis)
politus (Dapedius)
polonicus (Citellus)
Polyacrodontidae Elasmobranchii Glikman
    1964A (in order Polyacro-
    dontida)
Polyacrodus Hybodontidae
    polycyphus Dreyer 1962
Polybranchiaspidae Polybranchiaspiformes
    Liu, Y.-h. 1965
Polybranchiaspis
Polybranchiaspiformes Pteraspidomorpha
    Liu, Y.-h. 1965
Polybranchiaspis Polybranchiaspidae Liu,
    Y.-h. 1965
    liaojaoshanensis Liu, Y.-h. 1965
Polycotylidae Pliosauroidea Kuhn, Oskar
    1966A (reinstated; incl.
    Dolichorhynchopidae and
    Trinacromerinae); Novozhilov
    1964D
    Ceraunosaurus, Dolichorhynchops,
        Polyptychodon, Strongylo-
        krotaphus
polycyphus (Polyacrodus)
polydesmus (Caproberyx)
Polydolopidae Caenolestoidea
    Eudolops, Polydolops
Polydolops Polydolopidae
    thomasi Simpson, G. G. 1964C, 1967A
polyglottos (Mimus)
Polyglyphanodontidae Sauria incertae
        sedis Kuhn, Oskar 1966A
        (in Teiidae); Tatarinov, L.
        P. 1964U
Polygonodon Mosasauridae
    rectus Miller, H. W. 1967
polygyrus (Ptychodus)
polykomos (Colobus)
Polymerichthyidae Alepisauroidei Uyeno
    1967A
    Polymerichthys
Polymerichthys Polymerichthyidae Uyeno
    1967A
    nagurai Uyeno 1967A
Polymixiidae Polymixioidei
    Berycopsis, Homonotichthys, Omo-
        soma, Pycnosterinx
Polymixioidei Beryciformes Patterson,
        C. 1964 (suborder)
Polyperca Serranidae See: Otolithus

Stinton 1965
serranoides Stinton 1965
Polypterei Actinopterygi Obruchev, D. V.
    and Kazantseva 1964B
Polypterus Brachiopterygii incertae sedis
    Lehman 1966D (living genus)
Polyptychodon Polycotylidae
    interruptus Gofshtein 1961
polyspondyla (Squaloraja)
polyspondylus (Lycoptera, Urocles)
Polysternidae [Pelomedusidae] Trionychoi-
        dea Bergounioux 1952*
Pomacanthus Chaetodontidae
    subarcuatus Lehman 1966B
Pomadasyidae Percoidei
    Pomadasys
Pomadasys Pomadasyidae
    hasta Klausewitz 1965B
Pomoxis Centrarchidae Wilson, R. L.
    1968
pompeckji (Poraspis)
Pondaungia Pongidae
    cotteri Koenigswald 1965E, 1967B
Pongidae Hominoidea Kälin 1964
    Aegyptopithecus, Amphipithecus,
        Ankarapithecus, ?Anthropodus,
        Dryopithecus, ?Gigantopithe-
        cus, Limnopithecus, Plio-
        pithecus, Pondaungia, Pro-
        consul, Propliopithecus,
        Ramapithecus, Sivapithecus,
        Sugrivapithecus, Udabnopithe-
        cus
    Dryopithecinae, Ramapithecinae
Ponginae Hominidae Chiarelli 1968A
pontica (Sakya)
ponticus (Abramis)
popi (Sciuravus)
popoagicum (Lambdotherium)
Poraspidida Cyathaspidiformes
Poraspidinae Cyathaspididae Denison 1964B
Poraspis Cyathaspididae Denison 1964B;
        Stensiö 1964 (brain and
        nerves, p. 333)
    barroisi Denison 1964B
    brevis Denison 1964B
    cylindrica Denison 1964B
    elongata Denison 1964B
    intermedia Denison 1964B
    magna Denison 1964B
    polaris Denison 1964B
    pompeckji Denison 1964B; Stensiö
        1963
    rostrata Denison 1964B
    sericea Denison 1964B
    siemiradzkii Denison 1964B

simplex Denison 1964B
sturi Balabaǐ 1956A, 1961; Denison
    1964B
subtilis Denison 1964B
Porolepididae Porolepidiformes
    Gyroptychius, Porolepis
Porolepidiformes Osteolepides
Porolepiformes Rhipidistia Lehman 1966C
    (with Porolepidae and Holo-
    ptychiidae)
Porolepis Porolepididae Jarvik 1967A;
    Karatajūte 1964; Liepiņsh
    1959*; Panchen 1967A;
    Thomson, K. S. 1967B
porosus (Calopomus)
portoricensis (Monophyllus redmani,
    Pteronotus parnellii)
porzana (Porzana)
Porzana Rallidae
    porzana Jánossy 1965C (cf.)
posthumus (Cyclotosaurus)
posticus (Heptodon)
postremus (Alces latifrons)
Postschizotherium Chalicotheriidae
    chardini Koenigswald 1966B
    intermedium Koenigswald 1966B
    licenti Koenigswald 1966B
Potamochoerus Suidae Hooijer 1963D (?)
    intermedius Leakey, L. S. B. 1965
Potamotherium Mustelidae
    miocaenicum Fahlbusch, V. 1967A
potens (Gandakasia, Thylacinus)
poteus (Titanophoneus)
Potoroinae Macropodidae Tedford 1967B
pottieri (Orycteropus)
pourcyensis (Paramys)
powellianus (Hyopsodus)
powriei (Cephalaspis)
Praearmantomys Gliridae
    crusafonti Bruijn 1966A
praecorsac (Vulpes)
praecox (Ardynia, Sciurotamias)
praecrassidens (Carcharias)
praecursor (Caiman, Cricetodon, Isurus,
    Oxybunotherium, Palaeo-
    corax. faleatus, Psammosteus)
praecursoris (Kuehneotherium)
Praedama Cervidae Kahlke 1965G
praefiber (Castor)
Praehomininae [Homininae] Hominidae
    Dokládal 1965 (australo-
    pithecines)
praehungaricus (Mimomys)
praejaculus (Allactaga)
praeluteus (Lagurus)

Praemancalla Mancallidae Howard, H.
    1966B
    lagunensis Howard, H. 1966B, 1968A
Praemegaceros Cervidae Kahlke 1965G
    dawkinsi Rădulesco and Samson 1967A
    mosbachensis Rădulesco and Samson
        1967A
    solilhacus Rădulesco and Samson
        1967A
    verticornis Kahlke 1965G; Rădulesco
        and Samson 1967A
praeminutus (Micromys)
praemurinus (Peridyromys)
praenipponicus (Cervus)
Praeovibos Bovidae Kahlke 1965D
    priscus Kahlke 1964
    schmidtgeni Kahlke 1964
praepannonicus (Lagurus)
praeparvum (Chirotherium)
praeraphiodon (Scapanorhynchus)
praerusticus (Eohyrax)
praeterita (Maxschlosseria)
praetetragonurus (Sorex araneus)
praeting (Prosiphneus)
praevius (Bufo)
prangei (Parechelus)
Praolestes Adapisoricidae Van Valen
    1966A
Pratilepus Leporidae
    kansasensis Gureev 1964
    progressus Gureev 1964
Prealbula Albulidae Frizzell 1965C
    (otolith)
    weileri Frizzell 1965C
precapensis (Serengetilagus)
precedens (Coniophis)
predomesticus (Passer)
prelucius (Ptychocheilus)
prelutosa (Caracara)
Preophidion Ophidiidae See: Otolithus
        Frizzell and Dante 1965
    petropolis Frizzell and Dante 1965
    stintoni Frizzell and Dante 1965
Presbychen Anatidae
    abavus Howard, H. 1966D, 1968A
Presbyornithinae Recurvirostridae Brodkorb
    1967 (new rank)
Prestosuchidae Pseudosuchia Charig 1967
    (excl. of Rauisuchus)
prestwichae (Argilloberyx)
pretiocus (Aipichthys)
pretiosus (Gobius)
prevostii (Amphitherium)
Priacanthidae Percoidea
    Priacanthus

Priacanthus Priacanthidae
  longispinus Dzhafarova 1962
pricei (Ochotona, Protocynodon)
prima (Bothriolepis, Dvinia, Platysepta,
    Putoranaspis, Radotina,
    Rhina)
Primaevomesus Osmeridae See: Otolithus
    Stinton 1965
  tricrenulatus Stinton 1965
primaevus (Apodemus, Arctocyon, Hip-
    popotamus, Hippopotamus
    amphibius, Phenacodus,
    Plioplatecarpus, Propygi-
    dium)
primarius (Promysops)
Primates Unguiculata Alekseeva, L. V.
    1968 (phylogeny); Ander-
    son, S. 1967A; Ankel 1965;
    Bergmann 1965 (skull);
    Buettner-Janusch 1964
    (biol.), 1967 (evol.); Clark,
    W. E. 1965A; Eimerl, De
    Vore and editors of Life
    1965; Kochetkova 1961B;
    Levin, V. N. 1967 (ear
    bones); McKenna 1965B
    (origin); Martin, R. D.
    1968; Oxnard 1967; Ruffie
    1967A; Shevchenko, Iu. G.
    1967, 1968 (brain); Simons,
    E. L. 1967A (evol.), B;
    Szalay 1968
  Incertae sedis: ?Menatotherium
primigenia (Hystrix, Marmota marmota,
    Neofelis nebulosa)
primigenius (Archeolagus, Bos, Citellus,
    Elephas, Hipparion, Mam-
    muthus, Notidanus)
primitiva (Cercomys, Hadroleptauchenia)
primitivus (Isotemnus, Megacricetodon
    primitivus, Megalagus)
primus (Leptarctus, Merychippus)
principialis ("Thomashuxleya")
Prinodon Carcharias Verma 1965B
Priohybodus Hybodontidae
  arambourgi Tabaste 1963
Prionochelys Toxochelyidae
  nauta Baird and Case 1966 cf.
Prionodon Carcharhinus Pledge 1967
prisca (Cestracion, Hyaena hyaena,
    Irregulareaspis)
priscidens (Hyracodon)
priscum (Eohegetotherium)
priscus (Adapis, Asio, Bison, Cretaspis,
    Erinaceus, Gliravus, Macro-
    rhizodon, Megalops, Muste-

lavus, Praeovibos, Procyon,
    Prospalax, Puffinus, Sceno-
    pagus, Scomber, Siphonoce-
    tus, Sphyraenodus, Telma-
    tornis, Ursus arctos, Xiphio-
    rhynchus)
Pristerodon Endothiodontidae
  buffaloensis Barry 1965, 1967
Pristerognathidae Eutheriodonta Boonstra
    1964
  Alopecognathus, Cynariognathus,
    Pristerognathoides, Pristero-
    gnathus, Ptomalestes, Scymno-
    saurus, Therioides, Zinno-
    saurus
Pristerognathoides Pristerognathidae
    Boonstra 1964
Pristerognathus Pristerognathidae Boonstra
    1964
  roggeveldensis Boonstra 1953G*
Pristerosauria [Theriocephalia] Theriodontia
    Kuhn, Oskar 1966A (assigned
    to Boonstra 1953)
Pristichampsus Crocodylidae
  rollinati Berg, D. E. 1966
Pristidae Rajiformes
  Ankistrorhynchus, Ctenopristis,
    Ischyrhiza, Marckgrafia, Oncho-
    pristis, Onchosaurus, Platy-
    spondylus, Pristis, Schizor-
    hiza, Sclerorhynchus)
pristinus (Arctodus)
Pristis Pristidae Bauza Rullan 1966B
  cudmorei Pledge 1967
pristodontus (Anacorax, Corax, Squali-
    corax)
prius (Ictitherium)
prjewalskii (Gazella)
Proacris Hylidae
  mintoni Holman 1967
Proaigialosaurus Aigialosauridae Tarlo,
    L. B. in Appleby et al.
    and Tarlo 1967 p. 705
    (a doubtful pleurosaurian)
  huenei Hoffstetter 1964D
Proalector Phasianidae Brodkorb 1964A
    (in Phasianinae)
  miocaenus Brodkorb 1964A
Proalligator Crocodylidae
  australis Langston 1965B
Proanura Salientia
proarchaicus (Mammuthus meridionalis)
proavum (Deinotherium)
proavus (Leptotragulus)
Probactrosaurus Iguanodontidae Rozdest-
    venskii 1966A

pusio Stirton and Marcus 1966
rapha Stirton and Marcus 1966
Procynodontidae Cynodontia Huene
　　1948H* (invalid)
Procynops Salamandridae Young, C.-c.
　　1965A
　　miocenicus Young, C.-c. 1965A
Procynosuchidae Cynodontia Anderson,
　　J. M. 1968A; Brink and
　　Kitching 1951B*; Kuhn,
　　Oskar 1966A (ascribed to
　　Broom 1937B*)
Permocynodon
Procyon Procyonidae Hibbard and Dal-
　　quest 1966
　　nanus Arata and Hutchison 1964
　　priscus Arata and Hutchison 1964
　　　(nomen nudum)
　　simus Arata and Hutchison 1964
Procyonidae Canoidea
　　Ailuropoda, Bassariscus, Parailurus,
　　　Procyon
procyonoides (Claenodon)
Prodesmodon Plethodontidae Estes 1964
　　(Cret., Wyo.)
　　copei Estes 1964
Prodiacodon Leptictidae Szalay 1966
　　(tarsus); Van Valen 1967B
Prodinoceras Uintatheriidae
　　turfanensis Chow, M.-c. 1960C
Prodipodomys Heteromyidae
　　mascallensis Shotwell 1967B (?)
Prodissopsalis Hyaenodontidae
　　eocaenicus Van Valen 1965G
　　phonax Van Valen 1965G
　　theriodis Matthes, H. W. 1967A, C;
　　　Van Valen 1965G
Prodremotherium Gelocidae
　　elongatum Palmowski and Wachendorf
　　　1966
　　trepidum Gabuniïa 1964D
productus (Archengraulis)
Proeriglornis Ergilornithidae Kozlova
　　1960
　　minor Kozlova 1960
Proeulagus Lepus Gureev 1964
Proexaeretodon Traversodontidae Bona-
　　parte 1963D
　　vincei Bonaparte 1963D
profectus (Ustatochoerus)
profundum (Brevidorsum)
Progalago Lorisidae Saban 1963 (in
　　Galagidae)
　　dorae Simpson, G. G. 1967B
　　songhorensis Simpson, G. G. 1967B

Proganochelydia [Triassochelyoidea] Amphi-
　　chelydia Appleby, Charig,
　　Cox, Kermack and Tarlo
　　1967 (incl. Proganochelys);
　　Romer 1966C
Proganochelyoidea Amphichelydia Romer
　　1957E*
Proganosauria Reptilia V'iu'shkov 1964G
Proganosauromorpha [Synapsida] Reptilia
　　Kuhn, Oskar 1968 (incl.
　　Mesosaurus)
Progarzonia ?Marsupialia incertae sedis
　　notostylopense Simpson, G. G. 1937A
　　　(unidentifiable)
Progempylus Gempylidae Casier 1966A
　　edwardsi Casier 1966A
progenes (Agriocharis)
Prognathodon Mosasauridae
　　crassartus Russell, D. A. 1967A
　　overtoni Russell, D. A. 1967A
　　rapax Russell, D. A. 1967A
Prognathodontini Plioplatecarpinae Russell,
　　D. A. 1967A (tribe)
Progonomys Muridae
　　cathalai Michaux 1967; Thaler 1966B
progressus (Monosaulax, Peromyscus,
　　　Pratilepus, Sauroctonus,
　　　Urocyon)
Proheteromys Heteromyidae
　　floridanus Olsen 1964A
Prohydrocyon Salmonidae
　　pellegrini Weitzman 1960A, B
Prohypogeophis Mollusca Kuhn, Oskar
　　1965E, p. 42 (a mollusc)
Prolacertilia Lepidosauria
Prolacertidae Prolacertoidea Maleev 1964C
Prolucertoidea Eosuchia partim Kuhn,
　　Oskar 1966A (ascribed to
　　Camp 1923; suborder incl.
　　Prolacertidae)
Prolaginae Lagomyidae Gureev 1964
Prolagus Ochotonidae Gureev 1964 (in
　　Lagomyidae)
　　bilolus Bruijn and Meurs 1967
　　elsanus Gureev 1964
　　loxodus Gureev 1964
　　oeningensis Bruijn and Meurs 1967;
　　　Ginsburg 1967A; Hugueney
　　　and Mein 1965 (cf.)
　　sardus Bruijn and Meurs 1967; Gureev
　　　1964
　　vasconiensis Bruijn and Meurs 1967;
　　　Gureev 1964
Prolates Serranidae
　　herberti Patterson, C. 1964

prolatus (Diaphyodectes)
Prolebias Cyprinodontidae Ionko 1954
Prolimnocyon Limnocyonidae Van Valen
    1966A (in Hyaenodontidae)
    elisabethae Guthrie, D. A. 1967B
    iudei Guthrie, D. A. 1967B
prolongus (Ortholophodon)
Promegalops Elopidae Casier 1966A
    sheppeyensis Casier 1966A
    signeuxae Casier 1966A
Promephitis Mustelidae
    brevirostris Meladze 1967
Promesochoerus Suidae Leakey, L. S. B.
    1965
    mukiri Leakey, L. S. B. 1965
Promimomys Cricetidae
    insuliferus Topachevskiĭ 1965B
    moldavicus Topachevskiĭ 1965B
promisus (Gigantamynodon)
Promoeritherium Pyrotheriidae
    australe Simpson, G. G. 1967A
promyarion (Plesiosminthus)
Promysops Polydolopidae Simpson, G. G.
    1967A (syn. of Eudolops)
    primarius Simpson, G. G. 1967A
    (nomen vanum)
Pronycticebus Adapidae Crusafont Pairó
    1967B
    gaudryi Saban 1963
Proochotona Lagomyidae
    eximia Gureev 1964
    gigas Gureev 1964
    kirgizica Gureev 1964
    kurdjukovi Gureev 1964
proosti (Cybium)
Propachynolophus Equidae Savage, D. E.,
    Russell and Louis 1965
    gaudryi Savage, D. E., Russell and
    Louis 1965
    maldani Savage, D. E., Russell and
    Louis 1965
Propalaeocastor Castoridae Borisogleb-
    skaia 1967
    habilis Borisoglebskaia 1967
    kazachstanicus Borisoglebskaia 1967
Propalaeotherium Equidae Savage, D. E.,
    Russell and Louis 1965
    argentonicum Savage, D. E., Russell,
    and Louis 1965
    hassiacum Savage, D. E., Russell and
    Louis 1965
    helveticum Savage, D. E., Russell and
    Louis 1965
    isselanum Savage, D. E., Russell and
    Louis 1965

messelense Savage, D. E., Russell and
    Louis 1965
    parvulum Savage, D. E., Russell and
    Louis 1965
Prophorhacinae Cariamidae Brodkorb
    1967
Proplanodus Mammalia incertae sedis
    adnepos Simpson, G. G. 1967A (nomen
    dubium)
Proplatyarthrus ?Megalonychoidea
    longipes Simpson, G. G. 1967A
Propleopus Macropodidae
    oscillans Tedford 1967B
Propliopithecus Pongidae Frisch 1965
    haeckeli Simons, E. L. 1965B
Proportheus Chirocentridae
    kameruni Bardack 1965A
Propotamochoerus Suidae
    devauxi Arambourg 1968A, B
    provincialis Rădulesco, Samson, et al. 1965
    minor Fejfar 1964A
Propotto Lorisidae Simpson, G. G. 1967B
    leakeyi Simpson, G. G. 1967B
propria (Gazella)
proptera (Pachythrissops)
Propterodon Hyaenodontidae Van Valen
    1966A
Propterus Lepidosirenidae Lehman 1966C
    vidali Wenz 1968B
Propygidium Pygidiidae Bocchino R. 1964
    primaevus Bocchino R. 1964
Propyrotherium Pyrotheriidae
    saxeum Simpson, G. G. 1967A
propython (Clidastes)
Proraniceps Gadidae See: Otolithus
    Stinton 1965
    leiopleurus Stinton 1965
Prorhzaene Hyaenodontidae
    egerkingiae Van Valen 1966A
proriger (Tylosaurus)
prorsus (Triceratops)
Prosauropoda [Plateosauria] Palaeopoda
    Charig, Attridge and Cromp-
    ton 1965 (in Sauropodo-
    morpha); Colbert 1964B
    (=Plateosauria)
Prosauropsis Pachycormidae
    elongatus Wenz 1967B
Proscalopinae Talpidae Van Valen 1967B
Proscapanus Talpidae
    sansaniensis Ginsburg 1967A
Prosciurinae Paramyidae Parris 1968
Prosciurus Paramyidae
    vetustus Black, C. C. 1965A
Proserranus Serranidae Patterson, C. 1964

lundensis Patterson, C. 1964 (for
    Hoplopteryx lundensis)
Prosimii Primates
    Incertae sedis: Microsyopidae
Prosiphneus Cricetidae Sukhov 1967
    praeting Zazhigin 1966D (cf.)
    selengensis Pokatilov 1966B (nomen
        nudum)
Prospalax Spalacidae
    priscus Fejfar 1964A; Sulimski 1964
prosper (Peridyromys)
Prosqualodon Squalodontidae
    marplesi Dickson 1964
Prosthenops Tayassuidae Shotwell 1968
Prostylophorus Mammalia incertae sedis
    margeriei Simpson, G. G. 1967A
Prosynthetoceras Protoceratidae
    francisi Patton 1967B
    texanus Patton 1966B, 1967B
Prosynthetoceras Synthetoceras Maglio
    1966
Protacanthopterygii [Salmonoidei +]
        Clupeiformes Andrews, S.
        M., Gardiner, Miles and
        Patterson 1967 (superorder
        of Teleostei)
Protacmon Diademodontidae Mendrez
    1967
Protadelomys Pseudosciuridae Harten-
        berger 1968
    cartieri Hartenberger 1968 (for
        "Adelomys" cartieri)
Protagriochoerus Agriochoeridae Friant
    1962D
Protalbula Albulidae Frizzell 1965C
        (otolith)
    sohli Frizzell 1965C
Protamia Amiidae Russell, L. S. 1967A
Protaspis Pteraspididae Denison 1967B
    erroli Denison 1967B (subgen. Pro-
        taspis)
Protaspis Protaspis Denison 1967B
Protechinus Erinaceidae Lavocat 1961A*
    salis Lavocat 1961A*
Proteida Caudata
Protelephas Elephantidae
    planifrons Dubrovo 1964B
Protemnodon Macropodidae Bergamini
        and editors of Life 1964
        (restor.)
    brehus Tedford 1967B
    bululoensis Plane 1967B
    otibandus Plane 1967B
protenus (Didymictis)
Protericini Erinaceinae Van Valen 1967B

Proterix Erinaceidae
    bicuspis Gawne 1968 (n. comb.)
    loomisi Gawne 1968
Proterochampsa Proterochampsidae Walker,
        A. D. 1968 (a primitive
        phytosaur)
    barrionuevoi Sill 1967
Proterochampsidae Archaeosuchia Sill
    1967
    Proterochampsa
Proterosuchia Thecodontia
Proterotheriidae Litopterna
    Anisolambda, Josepholeidya, Ricardo-
        lydekkeria
Protetraceros Procapra Kretzoi 1965A
Proteutheria Insectivora
Prothyracodon Hyracodontidae Gabuniia
        1964D, 1966A
Protictis Miacidae MacIntyre 1966 (new
        rank)
    haydenianus MacIntyre 1966 (subgen.
        Protictis)
    microlestes MacIntyre 1966 (subgen.
        Bryanictis)
    tenuis MacIntyre 1966 (subgen. Simp-
        sonictis)
    vanvaleni MacIntyre 1966 (subgen.
        Bryanictis)
Protictis Protictis MacIntyre 1966
Protictops Leptictidae
    borealis Russell, L. S. 1965D
protistus (Pliometanastes)
Protitanichthys Coccosteidae
    fossatus Miles, R. S. 1966B
    rockportensis Miles, R. S. 1966B
Protoadapis Adapidae Crusafont Pairó
    1967B
    angustidens Russell, D. E., Louis and
        Savage 1967
    curvicuspidens Russell, D. E., Louis
        and Savage 1967
    klatti Russell, D. E., Louis and Savage
        1967
Protobatrachidae [Triadobatrachidae] Proa-
        nura Kuhn, Oskar 1965E
        (ascribed to Piveteau 1937)
Protobradyidae Mammalia incertae sedis
        Simpson, G. G. 1967A (nomen
        vanum)
    Protobradys
Protobradys Protobradyidae Simpson, G.
        G. 1967A (nomen vanum)
    harmonicus Simpson, G. G. 1967A
        (nomen vanum)
Protobrama Tselfatiidae

Protypotheroides Macroscelididae
  beetzi Patterson, B. 1965B
Proumbra Umbridae Sychevskaia 1966
  (nomen nudum)
Provaranosaurus Parasaniwidae
  acutus Estes 1965C
provincialis (Propotamochoerus)
Proviverra Hyaenodontidae
  gracilis Van Valen 1965G
  minor Van Valen 1965G
  palaeonictides Van Valen 1966A
  typica Van Valen 1965G
Proviverrinae Hyaenodontidae Savage,
          R. J. G. 1965A; Van Valen
          1965G (reduced to tribe
          Proviverrini)
Proviverrini Hyaenodontidae Van Valen
          1965G (in Hyaenodontinae)
proximus (Epieuryceros, Thamnophis)
Prunella Prunellidae
  himalayana Stepanian 1964 (subgen.
          Lasicopus)
Prunellidae Passeres
  Laiscopus, Prunella
Prymnetes Chirocentridae
  longiventer Bardack 1965A
przwalski (Equus)
Psammodontidae Chimaerae incertae sedis
  Psammodus
Psammodontiformes [Psammodontidae]
          Chimaerae incertae sedis
          Patterson, C. 1965B (order
          of Holocephali)
Psammodus Psammodontidae
  rugosus Obruchev, D. V. 1962C
Psammolepis Drepanaspididae Mark-Kurik
          1966
  abavica Novitskaya 1965; Obruchev,
          D. V. and Mark-Kurik 1965;
          Tarlo 1965
  aerata Tarlo 1965
  alata Obruchev, D. V. and Mark-Kurik
          1965; Tarlo 1965
  artica Tarlo 1965
  granulata Tarlo 1965
  groenlandica Tarlo 1964C, 1965
  heteraster Obruchev, D. V. and Mark-
          Kurik 1965
  paradoxa Novitskaya 1965; Obruchev,
          D. V. and Mark-Kurik 1965;
          Tarlo 1965
  proia Obruchev, D. V. and Mark-Kurik
          1965; Tarlo 1965
  toriensis Mark-Kurik 1968
  undulata Novitskaya 1965; Obruchev,
          D. V. and Mark-Kurik 1965;

Tarlo 1965
  venyukovi Mark-Kurik 1968; Novits-
          kaya 1965; Obruchev, D. V.
          and Mark-Kurik 1965; Tarlo
          1965
Psammornis Aepyornithidae
  rothschildi Dughi and Sirugue 1964,
          1965
Psammosteida [Drepanaspida] Pteraspidi-
          formes Kiaer 1932*
Psammosteidae [Drepanaspididae] Drepan-
          aspida Obruchev, D. V. and
          Mark-Kurik 1965
Psammosteus Drepanaspididae
  asper Obruchev, D. V. and Mark-Kurik
          1965; Tarlo 1965
  bergi Mark-Kurik 1966, 1968; Obru-
          chev, D. V. and Mark-Kurik
          1965
  bystrowi Obruchev, D. V. and Mark-
          Kurik 1965
  cuneatus Obruchev, D. V. and Mark-
          Kurik 1965
  falcatus Novitskaya 1965; Obruchev,
          D. V. and Mark-Kurik 1965;
          Tarlo 1965
  kiaeri Tarlo 1964C, 1965
  levis Obruchev, D. V. and Mark-Kurik
          1965
  livonicus Mark-Kurik 1968; Novitskaya
          1965; Obruchev, D. V. and
          Mark-Kurik 1965
  markae Tarlo 1965
  meandrinus Novitskaya 1965; Obruchev,
          D. V. and Mark-Kurik 1965;
          Tarlo 1965
  megalopteryx Novitskaya 1965; Obru-
          chev, D. V. and Mark-Kurik
          1965; Tarlo 1965
  pectinatus Obruchev, D. V. and Mark-
          Kurik 1965; Tarlo 1965
  praecursor Mark-Kurik 1968; Novitskaya
          1965; Obruchev, D. V. and
          Mark-Kurik 1965; Tarlo
          1965
  tchernovi Obruchev, D. V. and Mark-
          Kurik 1965; Tarlo 1965
  tenuis Novitskaya 1965; Obruchev, D.
          V. and Mark-Kurik 1965
          (for P. grossi, preocc.)
  waltergrossi Tarlo 1965
Psekupsoceros Cervidae Rădulesco and
          Samson 1967A
  orientalis Rădulesco and Samson 1967A
Psephaspis Drepanaspididae
  bystrowi Tarlo 1964C, 1965

Pseudogonatodus Gonatodidae Gardiner
    1967A
  macrolepis Gardiner 1967A
  parvidens Gardiner 1967A
pseudolatidens (Eostegodon)
Pseudoloris Omomyidae Crusafont Pairó
    1967B
  parvulus Crusafont Pairó 1965M,
    1967B
  requanti Crusafont Pairó 1967B
Pseudoltinomys Theridomyidae
  cuvieri Thaler 1966B
  gaillardi Thaler 1966B
Pseudopachyrucos ?Hegetotheria incertae
    sedis
  foliiformis Simpson, G. G. 1967A
Pseudoparamyinae Paramyidae Michaux
    1964B
Pseudoparamys Paramyidae
  teilhardi Michaux 1964B, 1968
pseudopusilla (Ochotona)
pseudoradians (Corvina)
Pseudorhinolophus Hipposideridae
  bouziguensis Sigé 1966
  morloti Miguet 1967 (cf.)
Pseudorhinolophus Hipposideros Sigé
    1968B
Pseudosaurillus Cordyloidea incertae
    sedis Hoffstetter 1967B
  becklesi Hoffstetter 1967D
Pseudosciuridae Theridomyoidea
  Adelomys, Masillamys, Paradelomys,
    Protadelomys, Pseudosciurus,
    Sciuroides, Suevosciurus
Pseudosciurus Pseudosciuridae
  suevicus Palmowski and Wachendorf
    1966; Weber, E. 1951
pseudosiderolithicus (Theridomys)
Pseudosinopa Hyaenodontidae Van Valen
    1966A
Pseudosphaerodon Labridae
  antiquus Casier 1966A
Pseudosuchia Thecodontia Young, C.-c.
    1964A
  Incertae sedis: Ticinosuchus
Pseudotheridomys Eomyidae
  carpathicus Kowalski, K. 1967A
  pagei Shotwell 1967B
  parvulus Čtyroký, Fejfar and Holý
    1964A; Thaler 1966B
  pertesunatoi Hartenberger 1967A
    (subgen. Keramidomys)
Pseudotomus Paramyidae
  coloradensis Guthrie, D. A. 1967B
  robustus Dawson, M. 1968 (nr.)

Psittaci [Psittaciformes] Neognathae
    Dement'ev 1964
Psittaciformes Neognathae
Psittacotherium Stylinodontidae
  multifragum Maxwell, R. A., et al.
    1967; Wilson, J. A. 1967
    (cf.)
Pteranodon Ornithocheiridae Kuhn, O.
    1967A; Russell, D. A. 1967B
    (reconst.)
  sternbergi Harksen 1966 (Cret., Kan.)
Pteranodontinae Ornithocheiridae Kuhn,
    O. 1967A
Pteraspida Pteraspidiformes Kiaer 1932*
Pteraspididae Pteraspida Balabai 1960B;
    Dineley 1964A
  Althaspis, Belgicaspis, Brachipteraspis,
    Cyrtaspidichthys, Doryaspis,
    Grumantaspis, Mylopteraspis,
    Protaspis, Protopteraspis,
    Pteraspis, Rhinopteraspis,
    Simopteraspis, Zascinaspis
Pteraspidiformes Pteraspidomorpha
Pteraspidomorpha Ostracodermi Stensiö
    1964 (Pteraspidomorphi)
Pteraspis Pteraspida Denison 1967B;
    Karatajūte 1964
  baltica Liepiņsh 1959*
  crouchi Schmidt, W. 1959* (subgen.
    Belgicaspis)
  dunensis Fahlbusch, K. 1966 (subgen.
    Rhinopteraspis); Schmidt, W.
    1959* (subgen. Rhinopter-
    aspis)
  elongata Balabai 1959
  iwaniensis Balabai 1961
  kneri Balabai 1959, 1961
  leachi Schmidt, W. 1959* (subgen.
    Rhinopteraspis)
  leathensis Schmidt, W. 1959* (subgen.
    Protopteraspis)
  longirostra Balabai 1959
  podolica Balabai 1959, 1961
  zychi Balabai 1961
Pteraspis Pteraspis Denison 1967B
Pterichthyes Placodermi
Pterichthyidae [Pterichthyodidae] Astero-
    lepidiformes
Pterichthyodes Pterichthyodidae Gross,
    W. 1965A
  concatenatus Karatajūte 1958B (syn.
    of Byssacanthus dilatatus)
  milleri Gross, W. 1965A
  rugosus Obruchev, D. V. and Sergienko
    1961 (Pterichthys)

pulcher (Africanomys, Myctophum)
Pultiphagonides Bovidae Leakey, L. S. B.
    1965
    africanus Leakey, L. S. B. 1965
pumilio (Rhinolophus)
punctulatus (Micropterus)
punctatus (Dapedium, Gonatodus, Icta-
        lurus, Palaeoryctes)
punctidens (Nyssodon)
punjabicus (Dryopithecus, Ramapithecus)
punjabiensis (Giraffokeryx)
purbeckensis (Dorsetisaurus)
Purgatoriinae Paromomyidae Van Valen
        and Sloan 1965
Purgatorius Paromomyidae Van Valen
        and Sloan 1965
    ceratops Van Valen and Sloan 1965
    unio Van Valen and Sloan 1965
Purussaurus Crocodylidae
    braziliensis Langston 1965B
pusilliformis (Sorex)
pusillus (Eschrichtius, Ochotona, Pholido-
        phorus, Rhynchosauroides,
        Theriosuchus)
pusio (Procoptodon)
pustulatum (Lonchidion breve)
pustulatus (Deltasaurus, Traquairosteus)
pustulosus (Eastmanosteus)
Putoranaspis Ctenaspididae Obruchev,
        D. V. 1964C (?)
    prima Obruchev, D. V. 1964C
putorius (Mustela)
Putorius Mustela Thenius 1965B
Putorius Mustelidae
    eversmanni Jacobshagen 1963; Koby
        1964C; Svistun 1968
Pycnodontida Holostei Danil'chenko
        1964A (order)
Pycnodontidae Amiiformes
    Coelodus, Hadrodus, Mesodon, Palaeo-
        balistum, Pycnodus, Sphae-
        ronchus
Pycnodontiformes Actinopterygii Lehman
        1966B (with Gyrodontidae,
        Pycnodontidae and Cocco-
        dontidae)
Pycnodus Pycnodontidae
    apodus Lehman 1966B
    bowerbanki Casier 1966A
    complanatus Gofshtein 1961
    gigas Jonet 1964B
    laveirensis Jonet 1964B
    toliapicus Casier 1966A
Pycnolepis Drepanaspididae Tarlo 1964C,
        1965
    splendens Tarlo 1964C, 1965

Pycnosteidae [Drepanaspididae] Drepana-
        spida
Pycnosterinx Polymixiidae
    discoides Patterson, C. 1964
    dubius Patterson, C. 1964
    gracilis Patterson, C. 1964
    russeggerii Patterson, C. 1964
Pycnosteroides Pycnosteroididae
    levispinosus Patterson, C. 1964 (rest.)
Pycnosteroididae Dinopterygoidei Patter-
        son, C. 1964
    Pycnosteroides
Pycnosteus Drepanaspididae
    nathorsti Tarlo 1965
    obruchevi Tarlo 1964C, 1965
    palaeformis Novitskaya 1965; Obruchev,
        D. V. and Mark-Kurik 1965;
        Tarlo 1965
    pauli Mark-Kurik 1966; Novitskaya
        1965; Obruchev, D. V. and
        Mark-Kurik 1965; Tarlo
        1965
    tuberculatus Mark-Kurik 1966, 1968;
        Novitskaya 1965; Obruchev,
        D. V. and Mark-Kurik 1965;
        Tarlo 1965
Pygidiidae Siluriformes
    Propygidium
pygmaeum (Lophiotherium)
pygmaeus (Antiacodon, Citellus, Rhodo-
        pagus)
pygmea (Testudo)
pyramidentata (Carolodarwinia)
Pyramios Diprotodontidae Woodburne
        1967A
    alcootense Woodburne 1967A, B
pyrenaica (Capra, Rupicapra)
pyrenaicus (Mammut, Trilophomys)
pyroclasticus (Dissopsalis)
Pyrotheria Paenungulata
    Incertae sedis: Carolozittelia
Pyrotheriidae Pyrotheria
    Promoeritherium, Propyrotherium,
        Pyrotherium
Pyrotherium Pyrotheriidae Sera 1954C
        (a proboscidean)
Pyrrhocorax Corvidae
    graculus Jánossy 1965E
    pyrrhocorax Burchak-Abramovich, N.
        1966D
pyrrhocorax (Pyrrhocorax)
Python Boidae Hoffstetter 1964B, 1965A;
        Telles Antunes 1964C
Pythonomorphidae [Mosasauridae] Platy-
        nota Kuhn, Oskar 1966A
        (=Mosasauridae of Varanoidea.

Ascribed to Huene 1928
but probably Nopcsa 1923H*
of Hay)

quadeemae (Kelba)
quadratidens (Orycterocetus)
quadratus (Pseudocyclopidius)
quadridentatus (Eomoropus)
quadriplicatus (Neotoma)
quartzi (Adjidaumo)
quatalensis (Protospermophilus)
Quemisia ?Dinomyidae
     gravis Ray, C. E. 1965C
quenstedti (Plateosaurus)
quercensis (Pseudocyonopsis)
quercinus (Eliomys, Isoptychus)
Quercitherium Hyaenodontidae Van
     Valen 1966A
quercyi (Diplobune, Palaeophyllophora,
     Paleunycteris)
Quercymys Isoptychus Thaler 1966B
Querquedula Anatidae
     discors Hibbard and Dalquest 1966
Quinquevertebron ?Brachycephalidae
     Kuhn, Oskar 1941D*
     germanicum Kuhn, Oskar 1941D*
Quiscalus Icteridae
     quiscula Hamon 1964
quiscula (Quiscalus)

radians (Ctenothrissa)
radiata (Asterolepis)
radiatus (Enniskillenus)
radiplicatus (Plesiochelys)
radobojanus (Capros, Mugil)
Radotina Radotinidae Westoll 1967
     prima Westoll 1967
Radotinida [Radotiniformes] Rhenanida
     Andrews, S. M., Gardiner,
     Miles and Patterson 1967
     (credited to Gross 1950);
     Obruchev, D. V. 1964D
     (order of Rhenanida)
Radotinidae Radotiniformes Obruchev,
     D. V. 1964D (renamed)
     Radotina
Radotiniformes Rhenanida
Raja Rajidae Fitch 1964; Signeux
     1959A, B
     duponti Casier 1966A (cf.)
     mucronata Signeux 1959B
Rajidae Rajioidei
     Raja
Rajiformes Batoidii
Rajioidei Rajiformes Albers and Weiler
     1964

Rajitheca Euselachi Steininger 1966
     bavarica Steininger 1966
     grisigensis Steininger 1966
     helvetica Steininger 1966
rajurkari (Lystrosaurus)
raki (Rakomylus)
Rakomeryx Cervidae
     americanus Shotwell 1968 (cf.)
Rakomylus Camelidae
     raki Frick, C. and Taylor 1968
Rallidae Ralloidea
     Crex, Fulica, Gallinula, Hovacrex,
          Limicorallus, Megagallinula,
          Pararallus, Porzana, Telma-
          tornis
Ralloidea Grues
Ramapithecinae Pongidae Heberer 1967C
Ramapithecus Pongidae Heberer 1967C;
     Pilbeam 1966A, 1968A;
     Simons, E. L. 1968B
     punjabicus Pilbeam and Simons 1965
          (hominid); Simons, E. L.
          1964C
ramosus (Croizetoceros, Croizetoceros
     ramosus)
ramsayi (Sceparnodon)
Rana Ranidae Estes and Tihen 1964;
     Hibbard and Dalquest 1966;
     Klages 1963; Kretzoi 1965B;
     Richmond 1964; Vergnaud-
     Grazzini 1966
     agilis Malez 1963D
     agiloides Jacobshagen 1963
     areolata Wilson, R. L. 1968 (cf.)
     bucella Holman 1965B
     catesbeiana Lynch, J. D. 1965
     esculenta Jacobshagen 1963; Malez
          1963D
     miocenica Holman 1965B
     pipiens Holman 1965B (cf.), C, 1966C,
          1967; Lynch, J. 1965
     plax La Rivers 1966
     temporaria Jacobshagen 1963
Rangifer Cervidae Green, M. and Lille-
     graven 1965; Guilday 1966;
     Kahlke 1965D; Ray, C. E.,
     Cooper, et al. 1967
     arcticus Cleland 1965A; Mostecký 1964
     guettardi Bouchud 1967
     tarandus Bouchud 1965B, 1966E;
          Feustel, et al. 1963; Guilday
          1968A; Guillien 1964; Jacobs-
          hagen 1963; Koby 1964C;
          Krysiak 1956; Mikula 1964;
          Sukachev, et al. 1966; Svis-
          tun 1968; Thenius 1966A;

Whitehead 1964
Ranidae Diplasiocoela
    Ptychadena, Rana
rapax (Prognathodon, Scapanorhynchus)
rapha (Procoptodon)
rapheidolabis (Macropetalichthys)
Raphidae Columbae
    Didus, Pezophaps
Raphus [Didus] Raphidae
rapicaudus (Thecadactylus)
rapidus (Ergilornis)
rapiens (Thescelus)
raricostatus (Hybodus)
rarus (Onchus)
rateli (Diplocynodon)
Ratites [Neognathae, partim] Neornithes
    Beer 1964C; Parkes and
    Clark 1966
ratticepoides (Microtus)
Rattus Muridae
    muelleri Medway, G. 1964A
    rattus Malez 1963D
    sabanus Medway, G. 1964A
rattus (Rattus)
Rauisuchidae [Stagonolepididae] Pseudo-
    suchia
Rauisuchinae Stagonolepididae Huene
    1944F* (of Stagonolepidae)
recki (Elephas, Phenacotragus)
recticrista (Pleurostylodon)
recticristatus (Ceratodus)
rectus (Cylindracanthus, Polygonodon)
Recurvirostridae Charadrii
    Coltonia
    Presbyornithinae
recurvirostrioidea (Charadriipeda)
Redfieldiidae Redfieldoidei
    Cionichthys, Lasalichthys, Synorich-
        thys
Redfieldoidei Palaeonisciformes
redmani (Monophyllus)
reduncus (Notopithecus adapinus)
reevesii (Chinemys)
regalis (Hesperornis, Hypolagus)
regens (Diatryma)
regulus (Calippus)
reidi (Mimomys)
Reithrodontomys Cricetidae
    megalotis Schultz, G. E. 1965B (cf.)
    montanus Semken 1966 (cf.)
Reithroparamyinae Paramyidae
Reithroparamys Paramyidae
    atwateri Guthrie, D. A. 1967B
    huerfanensis Robinson, Peter 1966A
    louisi Michaux 1964B
    thaleri Michaux 1964B

relictus (Citellus, Limnostygis, Merychip-
    pus, Merychyus, Paradom-
    nina
remensis (Lophiodon)
Remiculus Mixodectidae Russell, D. E.
    1964; Russell, D. E., Louis
    and Poirier 1966B
    deutschi Russell, D. E. 1964
Remigolepididae Remigolepidiformes
    Remigolepis
Remigolepidiformes Pterichthyes
Remigolepis Remigolepididae Gross, W.
    1965A
remota (Glyptolepis)
Remys Theridomyidae
    garimondi Thaler 1966B
renieri (Rhadinichthys)
Reptilia Tetrapoda Antipchuk 1967 (lung
    evol.); Appleby, et al. 1967;
    Banta 1966 (Nev.); Barg-
    husen 1968; Bellairs 1968;
    Bellairs and Carrington
    1966; Bellairs and Parsons
    1968; Colbert 1965E; Gasc
    1966B; Ginsburg 1967E;
    Kuhn, O. 1966A (general
    review and classif.), 1967B,
    C, 1968 (classif.); Kuhn-
    Schnyder 1965C (origin);
    Müller, A. H. 1968; Rozh-
    destvenskiĭ 1964B; Watson
    1957A* (phylogeny and
    classif.)
    Incertae sedis: Broomia, Brazilosaurus,
        Caenagnathiformes
requanti (Pseudoloris)
requieni (Hyaenodon)
reticularia (Deirochelys)
retrodorsalis (Pholidophorus)
retroflexus (Isurus)
retroversus (Lophiodonticulus)
retrusum (Pseudhipparion)
retusus (Ophidypterus)
reversus (Mosasaurus)
rex (Paracryptotis)
rexroadensis (Otospermophilus)
reyi (Brachycyon palaeolycos)
Rhabdoderma Coelacanthidae
    elegans Dahm 1966
    tingleyense Dahm 1966
Rhachiosteidae [Coccosteidae] Coccostei-
    formes
Rhachiosteus Coccosteidae
    pterygiatus Miles, R. S. 1966C (rest.)
Rhachitomi Temnospondyli

schleiermacheri Viret, et al. 1962
sondaicus
    sivasondaicus Hooijer 1964F
    tichorhinus Bouchud 1966C
Rhinocerotidae Rhinocerotoidea Radin-
        sky 1966B
    Aceratherium, Allacerops, Aphelops,
        Benaratherium, Caenopus,
        Chilotherium, Coelodonta,
        Diceratherium, Dicerorhinus,
        Diceros, Didermocerus,
        Elasmotherium, Floridaceras,
        Hispanotherium, Indrico-
        therium, Itanzatherium,
        Juxia, Mescotherium, Para-
        ceratherium, Paradiceros,
        Peraceras, Plesiaceratherium,
        Rhinoceros, Ronzotherium,
        Teleoceras, Tichorhinus,
        Trigonias
    Dicerorhininae, Elasmotheriinae
Rhinocerotoidea Ceratomorpha
Rhinochimaera ?Chimaerotheca
    caucasica Obruchev, D. V. 1966,
        1967B
Rhinocryptidae Tyranni
Rhinodipterus Dipteridae Lehman 1966C
Rhinoidei Squaliformes
Rhinolophidae Rhinolophoidea
    ?Paleunycteris, Rhinolophus
Rhinolophoidea Microchiroptera
Rhinolophus Rhinolophidae
    cluzeli Hugueney 1965
    delphinensis Mein 1965A
    ferrum
        equinum Lavocat 1961A*; Malez
            1963D
    grivensis
        lissiensis Mein 1965A
    hipposideros Malez 1963D
    pumilio Miguet 1967
rhinophilus (Janimus)
Rhinoptera Myliobatidae
    daviesi Casier 1966A
Rhinopteraspis Pteraspididae Denison
        1967A
Rhinopteraspis Pteraspis Fahlbusch, K.
        1966; Schmidt, W. 1959*
Rhinosteidae [Pachyosteidae] Pachyostei-
        formes Obruchev, D. V.
        1964D
Rhipidistia Crossopterygii Lehman 1966C
    (with Porolépiformes and
    Ostéolépiformes); Panchen
    1967A; Thomson, K. S.
    1968A; Thomson, K. S.

and Hahn 1968
Rhipis Coelacanthidae
    moorseli Casier 1965
    tuberculatus Casier 1965
rhizion (Lonchidion)
Rhizodontidae Osteolepidiformes
    Eusthenodon, Hyneria, Rhizodopsis,
        Rhizodus, Tristicopterus
Rhizodopsis Rhizodontidae Jarvik 1967A;
        Lehman 1966C (endocra-
        nium); Thomson, K. S.
        1967B
    sauroides Dahm 1966
Rhizodus Rhizodontidae Thomson, K. S.
        1966C, 1967B
    hibberti Cruickshank 1968A
rhizoides (Katoporus)
Rhizomyidae Sciurognathi incertae sedis
    Rhizomys
Rhizomys Rhizomyidae
    mirzadi Lang, J. and Lavocat 1968
Rhizophascolonus Phalangeridae Stirton,
        Tedford and Woodburne
        1967B (in Phascolarctidae)
    crowcrofti Stirton, Tedford and Wood-
        burne 1967B
Rhizospalacidae Rodentia incertae sedis
        Thaler 1966B
    Rhizospalax
Rhizospalax Rhizospalacidae
    poirrieri Thaler 1966B (cf.)
rhodanicum (Chalicotherium grande)
rhodanicus (Cricetodon)
rhodesiensis (Homo)
Rhodopagus ?Lophialetidae Radinsky
        1965A
    minimus Radinsky 1965A (?)
    pygmaeus Radinsky 1965A
Rhomaleosauridae [Thaumatosauridae]
        Plesiasauroidea
rhombea (Mene)
Rhombodus Dasyatidae
    binckhorsti Albers and Weiler 1964;
        Signeux 1959A
    microdon Signeux 1959B
Rhombomys Cricetidae
    opimus Tropin 1968
Rhombus Bothidae
    parvulus Anđelković 1962
    serbicus Anđelković 1966
rhynchaeus (Geolabis)
Rhynchocephalia Lepidosauria
Rhynchocyon Macroscelididae
    clarki Patterson, B. 1965B
Rhynchodercetis Dercetidae
    yovanovitchi Leonardi, A. 1966

roonwali (Jhingrania)
roquet (Anolis)
rosadoi (Coelodus)
rosei (Colhuapia, Eohiodon)
roselli (Agerina)
rossicus (Callorhynchus)
rossmoori (Aethia)
rossouwi (Jonkeria)
rostrata (Poraspis, Thomashuxleya)
rostratus (Archaeonectrus, Cyamodus,
          Plesiosaurus)
Rothia Captorhinidae
     robusta Olson, E. 1965D
rothschildi (Psammornis)
Rotodactylidae Ichnites
     Rotodactylus
Rotodactylus Rotodactylidae
     matthesi Haubold 1966A (recons.)
rotundiformis (Clemmys)
Rotundomys Cricetidae Mein 1965B,
          1966
     hartenbergeri Freudenthal 1967
     montisrotundi Mein 1965B, 1966
rotundus (Homonotichthys, Kolopsis)
rouenii (Palaeotragus)
roumanei (Holosteus)
rouvillei (Anthropodus)
rubidgei (Aulacocephalodon)
Rubidginidae Phthinosuchia Kuhn, Oskar
          1965B (assigned by error
          to Haughton and Brink
          1954*), 1966A (Rubidginii-
          dae, assigned by error to
          Broom 1943)
rubricati (Heteroxerus)
Rucervus Cervus Shikama and Hasegawa
          1965B
rudnerae (Megazostrodon)
ruetimeyeri (Cynohyaenodon)
ruffi (Megaloceros giganteus)
ruficollis (Branta)
rufum (Stenoderma, Stenoderma rufum)
rufus (Felis, Macropus)
rugosidens (Cynelos, Cynelos rugosidens)
rugosum (Ginglymostoma)
rugosus (Axis, Crocodylus, Exostinus,
          Heterodontus, Parmularis,
          Platyhystrix, Psammodus,
          Pterichthyodes, Vasseuromys)
rugustus (Oölithes)
rumelicum (Brontotherium)
Ruminantia Artiodactyla
Rupicapra Bovidae
     pyrenaica Koby 1964D
     rupicapra Malez 1963D; Mostecký
          1964; Prat 1966B

rupicapra (Rupicapra)
Rupicaprinae Bovidae
rurestris (Tomarctus)
Rusa Cervus Otsuka 1966B
ruscinensis (Dolichopithecus)
Ruscinomys Cricetidae Freudenthal 1966
     europaeus Hugueney and Mein 1966;
          Thaler 1966B
     lavocati Hartenberger 1967B
     schaubi Mein 1967
     thaleri Hartenberger 1966A
rusinge (Kenialagomys)
rusingense (Chalicotherium)
russeggerii (Pycnosterinx)
russeli (Eremochen)
russelli (Amia, Anthracosaurus, Micro-
          paramys)
Russellites Paroxyclaenidae Van Valen
          1965E
     simplicidens Van Valen 1965E
rusticula (Maxschlosseria)
rusticus (Brachycrus, Eohyrax)
rutherfurdi (Huerfanius)
rutilans (Ultrapithecus)
Rutilus Cyprinidae Weiler 1966A
     frisii Tarashchuk 1965
     rutilus Deckert and Karrer 1965;
          Weiler 1965
rutilus (Rutilus)
rutimeyeri (Tricuspiodon)
Rutiodon Phytosauridae Colbert 1966C,
          1967C (restor.)
     carolinensis Colbert 1965A (N.J.)
rutoti (Carcharias)
Ryaneria Ichnites Bock 1964
     gwyneddensis Bock 1964

sabadellensis (Cricetulodon)
sabanus (Rattus)
sabrinus (Glaucomys)
sabulonis (Merycodus)
saevus (Enchodus)
Sagenodontidae Dipnoi
     Straitonia
sagittatus (Dercetis)
sagittidens (Eomuraena, Trichiurides)
sagorensis (Alosa)
sagrei (Anolis)
sahel-almae (Omosoma)
saiensis (Limicorallus)
Saiga Bovidae
     ricei Sher 1967A
     tatarica Erdbrink 1964; Milojčić, et.
          al. 1965; Prat 1966C; Suka-
          chev, et al. 1966 (cf.);
          Toepfer 1964A

Saurerpeton Saurerpetonidae Chase, J.
N. 1965
Saurerpetonidae Trimerorhachoidea
Chase, J. N. 1965
Saurerpeton
Sauria Squamata
Incertae sedis: Ardeosauridae, Poly-
glyphanodontidae, Tany-
stropheidae, Cuttysarkus,
Ilerdaesaurus, Macrocnemus,
Meyasaurus
Saurichthyidae Acipenseriformes Lehman
1964A
Acidorhynchus, Saurichthys
Saurichthyiformes Actinopterygii Lehman
1966B
Saurichthys Saurichthyidae Hary and
Muller 1967
acuminatus Dreyer 1962; Stefanov
1966
annulatus Stefanov 1966 (cf.)
apicalis Dreyer 1962; Stefanov 1966
hamiltoni Stensiö 1963
tenuirostris Stensiö 1963
sauriformis (Apsopelix)
Saurillus Cordyloidea incertae sedis
obtusus Hoffstetter 1967D
robustidens Hoffstetter 1967D
Sauripelvia Saurischia Avnimelech 1966
Saurischia Dinosauria Charig, Attridge
and Crompton 1965 (clas-
sif.); Colbert 1964B (classif.); Kuhn, O. 1965A
(bibliog., classif., nomenclature; incl. suborders
Theropoda and Sauropoda)
Sauriscus Scincidae Estes 1964 (Cret.,
Wyo.)
cooki Estes 1964
Sauroctonus Inostranceviidae
progressus Tatarinov, L. P. 1966C
sauroides (Rhizodopsis)
Saurolophidae [Saurolophinae] Hadrosauridae Huene 1956D*,
p. 542
Saurolophinae Hadrosauridae
Saurolophus Hadrosauridae Russell, D.
A. and Chamney 1967
(rest.)
Sauropoda Saurischia Charig, Attridge
and Crompton 1965 (in
Sauropodomorpha); Col-
bert 1964B; Kuhn, Oskar
1965A (bibliog., classif., review; incl. Bothrosauropodoidea and Homalosauro-

podoidea); Ostrom and
McIntosh 1966
Sauropodomorpha [Palaeopoda] Saurischia
Charig, Attridge and Cromp-
ton 1965
Sauropterygia [Euryapsida] Reptilia
Novozhilov 1964A
Sauropterygiomorpha [Euryapsida] Rep-
tilia Kuhn, O. 1968 (incl.
Sauropterygia)
Saurornithes [Archaeornithes] Aves
Dement'ev 1964
Saurornithoides ?Coeluridae Estes 1964
Saurostomus Pachycormidae
esocinus Wenz 1967B
Saurothera Cuculidae
longirostris Bernstein 1965
sauvagei (Urocles)
savagei (Paramys)
savini (Dolichodoryceros, Mimomys)
sawrockensis (Marmota, Neotoma, Ogmodontomys, Peromyscus)
saxeum (Propyrotherium)
Saxicola Turdidae
torquata Jánossy 1965C (cf.)
Saxonella Carpolestidae Crusafont Pairó
1967B; Russell, D. E. 1964
crepaturae Russell, D. E. 1964
Saxonellinae Carpolestidae Russell, D. E.
1964 (Saxonellinés)
saxonica (Geoemyda)
Sayimyinae Tataromyidae Lavocat 1961A*
Sayimys Tataromyidae
jebeli Lavocat 1961A*
Scaglia Astrapotheriidae
kraglievichorum Simpson, G. G. 1967A
scagliai (Aëtosauroides, Pattersomys, Sarmientichnus)
scalabrinianus (Eumysops)
Scalopini Talpinae Hutchison 1968A
Scalopoides Talpidae
isodens Hutchison 1968A
ripafodiator Hutchison 1968A
Scaloporhinus Silpholestidae
angulorugatus Boonstra 1953A*; Mendrez 1967
Scaloposauria Theriodontia
Scaloposauridae Bauriamorpha
Protocynodon
Scalopus Talpidae Hibbard and Dalquest
1966; Strain 1966
scanicus (Thoracosaurus)
Scanilepidae [Palaeoniscidae] Palaeoniscoidei Romer 1945D*
(Scanilepidae)
Scanisaurus ?Elasmosauridae

Schizotheriinae Chalicotheriidae
Schizotheriodes Perissodactyla incertae
    sedis
    parvus Radinsky 1964A
Schizotherium Chalicotheriidae
    chucuae Gabuniia 1964D, 1966A
schizurus (Labrax)
schleiermacheri (Dicerorhinus, Rhinoceros)
schlosseri (Cynelos rugosidens, Eomys,
        Gazella, Machairodus, Meta-
        cordylodon, Vespertiliavus)
schlosseria Lophialetidae
    magister Radinsky 1965A
schmidtgeni (Praeovibos)
schmidti (Archegonaspis, Lafkenia, Ne-
        sides, Thelodus)
schneideri (Ischyrhiza mira)
schoetensacki (Bison)
schreideri (Serengetilagus)
schrieli (Drepanaspis)
schröderi (Enaliosuchus)
schroederi (Eichstaettisaurus)
schucherti (Neanis)
schuebleri (Ischyodus)
schvtschenko (Ochotona pseudopusilla)
schweinfurthi (Pterosphenus)
Sciaena Sciaenidae
    similis Weiler 1966A
Sciaenidae Percoidea
    Aplodinotus, Corvina, Eokokenia,
        Jefitchia, Platacodon, Sciaena,
        Sciaenidarum, Umbrina
Sciaenidarum Sciaenidae See: Otolithus
        Weiler 1966A
Sciaenuropsis Sparidae Casier 1966A
    turneri Casier 1966A
Sciaenurus Sparidae
    bowerbanki Casier 1966A
Scincidae Scincoidea
    Eumeces, Sauriscus
Scincoidea Scincomorpha Hoffstetter
        1967D; Tatarinov, L. P.
        1964V
scincoides (Becklesisaurus)
Scincomorpha Sauria Chudinov 1964F
        (in Lacertilia)
    Incertae sedis: Becklesisaurus, Macel-
        lodus
Scincosauridae Nectridia Kuhn, Oskar
        1965E, p. 23
Sciuravidae [Sciuravinae] Ischyromyidae
Sciuravinae Ischyromyidae
Sciuravus Ischyromyidae
    encristadens Dawson, M. 1968B
    popi Dawson, M. 1966

Sciuridae Sciuroidea
    Ammospermophilus, Arctomyoides,
        Callospermophilus, Citellus,
        Colobotis, Csakvaromys,
        Cynomys, Eutamias, Getulo-
        cerus, Glaucomys, Heteroxerus,
        Hylopetes, Ictidomys, Leuco-
        crossoromys, Marmota, Mio-
        spermophilus, Otospermophil-
        us, Paenemarmota, Palaearc-
        tomys, Petauria, Pliocitellus,
        Pliocitelloides, Pliopetaurista,
        Pliopetes, Pliosciuropterus,
        ?Protosciurus, Protospermo-
        philus, Sciuropterus, Sciuro-
        tamias, Sciurus, Spermophi-
        lus, Stenocranius, Tamias,
        Tamiasciurus, Urocitellus,
        Xerus
    Marmotinae, Petauristinae, Sciurinae
Sciurinae Sciuridae Bruijn and Mein
        1968
sciurinus (Sciurotamias)
Sciurodon Aplodontidae
    descendens Ctyroky, Fejfar and Holy
        1964A
Sciurognathi Rodentia
    Incertae sedis: Pedetidae, Phiomyidae,
        Rhizomyidae, Spalacidae
Sciuroidea Sciuromorpha
Sciuroides Adelomys Thaler 1966B
Sciuromorpha Sciurognathi Gorgas, M.
        1967
Sciuromys Theridomyidae
    cayluxi Thaler 1966B
Sciuropterus Sciuridae Shotwell 1968
    gaudryi Black, C. C. 1966 (cf.)
    gibberosus Kowalski, K. 1967A
    grimmi Black, C. C. 1966
Sciurotamias Sciuridae
    praecox Gromov, I. M., et al. 1965
    sciurinus Gromov, I. M., et al. 1965
        (subgen. Csakvaromys)
Sciurus Sciuridae
    bredai Kowalski, K. 1967A; Petroni-
        jevic 1967
    fissurae Kowalski, K. 1967A
    giganteus Thaler 1966B (cf.)
    goeriachensis Kowalski, K. 1967A
    vulgaris Malez 1963D
    warthae Sulimski 1964
Sclerodontida [Tremataspidoidea] Acera-
        spida Tarlo 1967B
Scleromochlidae Scleromochloidea Tatar-
        inov, L. P. 1964Y

Scleromochloidea Pseudosuchia Young,
C.-c. 1964A p. 190 (also
as Scleromochlioidea, p.
92 incl. Scleromochidae, p.
90 =Sclermochlidae p. 91)
Sclerorhynchus Pristidae Signeux 1959B
atavus Slaughter and Steiner 1968
batavicus Albers and Weiler 1964
germaniae Albers and Weiler 1964
leptodon Casier 1964
Sclerothoracidae [Eryopidae] Eryopoidea
Ochev 1966C
Scolecophidia Serpentes Hoffstetter 1964C
p. 967 (infraorder)
Scoliodon Carcharhinidae Springer 1964
dentatus Jonet 1965-66A
longurio Fitch 1964
Scolopacidae Charadrioidea
Charadrius, Palaeotringa, Totanus
Scomber Scombridae
priscus Anđelković 1962
Scombramphodon Scombridae
crassidens Casier 1966A
sheppeyensis Casier 1966A
Scombridae Scombroidei
Aramichthys, Ardiodus, Auxis, Eo-
coelopoma, Eothynnus,
Scomber, Scombramphodon,
Scombrinus, Sphyraenodus,
Tamesichthys, Wetherellus,
Woodwardella
Scombrinus Scombridae
macropomus Casier 1966A
nuchalis Casier 1966A
Scombroidea [Scombroidei] Perciformes
Le Danois, E. and Le Danois 1963*
(subord. of Hypurostegi)
Scombroidei Perciformes Le Danois, E.
and Le Danois 1963*
scopaeus (Selenaletes)
Scopelida Teleostei Danil'chenko 1964B
(order)
Scorpaena Scorpaenidae
minima Anđelković 1963
pilari Rückert-Ülkümen 1965
Scorpaenidae Scorpaenoidea
Ampheristus, Scorpaena
Scorpaenoidea Cottoidei
scotica (Logania)
scoticus (Palaeomolgophis)
scotti (Equus)
scottianus (Cynodontomys)
scripta (Chrysemys, Pseudemys)
scrofa (Sus)
sculptata (Alosa)

sculptilis (Thelodus)
sculptus (Aspideretes)
scutata (Microchampsa)
Scutemys Testudinidae
tecta Yeh 1963B
Scylacocephalidae Gorgonopsia Watson
and Romer 1956*
Scylacocephalus
Scylacocephalinae
Scylacocephalinae Scylacocephalidae
Viushkov 1964C, p. 264
(ascribed to Watson and
Romer 1956*; of Gorgonop-
sidae)
Scylacocephalus Scylacocephalidae Broom
1940A*
watermeyeri Broom 1940A*
Scylacopidae Gorgonopsia Watson and
Romer 1956* (Scylacopsidae)
Scylacopinae
Scylacopinae Scylacopidae Viushkov
1964C, p. 264 (Scylacopsi-
nae, ascribed to Watson and
Romer 1956*; of Gorgonop-
sidae)
Scylacosauroidea [Therocephalia] Therio-
dontia Viushkov 1964C,
p. 275
Scyliorhinidae Galeoidea
Palaeoscyllium, Scyliorhinus, Scyllium
Scyliorhinoidei [Catuloidei] Isuriformes
Andrews, S. M., Gardiner,
Miles and Patterson 1967
Scyliorhinus Scyliorhinidae Signeux 1959B
biauriculatus Casier 1966A
gilberti Casier 1966A (cf.)
minutissimus Casier 1966A
Scyllium Scyliorhinidae Rückert-Ülkümen
1960
Scymnognathidae Gorgonopsia Watson and
Romer 1956*
Scymnognathinae
Scymnognathinae Scymnognathidae
Viushkov 1964C, p. 263
(credited to Watson and
Romer 1956*; of Gorgonop-
sidae)
Scymnorhinidae Squaloidei
Isistius
Scymnosaurus Pristerognathidae Boonstra
1964
Scytalopidae Tyranni
Neanis
sebastopolitanum (Hipparion mediter-
raneus)

Sebecus Crocodylidae Berg, D. E. 1966
(?n. sp.)
huilensis Langston 1965B
secans (Acmeodon, Diacodexis)
2nd Branch [Adapoidea] Palaeoprosimii
Crusafont Pairó 1967B
sectorius (Liodon)
secundarium (Diplobune)
secundus (Carcharias, Phronetragus,
Physodon)
sedgewicki (Euctenoceros)
sefvei (Hipparion)
Segisauridae Coelurosauria Colbert
1964B
segnis (Chamops)
Seiurus Parulidae
aurocapillus Bernstein 1965
sekirskyi (Kipalaichthys)
sekwiae (Veronaspis)
Selachii Elasmobranchii Glikman 1964B
(classif.)
Selachoidii Selachii
selachos (Lonchidion)
Selenaletes Helaletidae Radinsky 1966D
scopaeus Radinsky 1966D
selengensis (Eopleistolagus, Prosiphneus)
Selenosteidae [Pachyosteidae] Pachyosteiformes Obruchev, D. V.
1964D (=Pachyosteidae
Stensiö + Rhinosteidae
Stensiö)
Seleviniidae Gliroidea
Plioselevinia
semenovi (Psephodus)
semenowi (Helodus)
semiclausis (Parotosaurus)
Semigenetta Viverridae
mutata Petronijević 1967
Semionotidae Amiiformes
Angolaichthys, Dapedius, Hemicalypterus, Lepidotus, Semio-
notus
Semionotiformes Actinopterygii Lehman
1966B (with Semionotidae
and Dapediidae)
Semionotus Semionotidae Schaeffer, B.
1967B
bergeri Maślankiewiczowa 1965; Stefanov 1966
normannie Larsonneur 1964
Semiophorus Ephippidae
velicans Lehman 1966B
sendaicus (Myliobatis)
senegalensis (Galago)
senekalensis (Uranocentrodon)
senezensis (Equus stenonis, Eucladoceros,

Eucladoceros senezensis,
Euctenoceros)
senior (Paleotomus)
senni (Sphyraena)
Senonemys Testudinidae Bohn 1966
(in. Emyidae)
sümegensis Bohn 1966
senyüreki (Hyaena)
septa (Maxchlosseria)
septentrionale (Chlamytherium)
serengetense (Hipparion albertense)
Serengetilagus Leporidae
precapensis Gureev 1964
schreideri Gureev 1964
Seretaspis Cyathaspididae
zychi Denison 1964B
sericea (Poraspis)
Serpentes Squamata Auffenberg 1967C
(Fla.); Lüdicke 1962 (anat.);
Underwood, G. 1967 (classif.)
serpentina (Chelydra)
serra (Hemipristis)
serralheiroi (Cybium)
Serranidae Percoidea
Allomorone, Labrax, Morone, Percostoma, Platysepta, Plesioserranus, Polyperca, Prolates,
Proserranus, Serranopsis,
Smerdis
serranoides (Polyperca)
Serranopsis Serranidae Casier 1966A
londinensis Casier 1966A
serrata (Isurus)
serratissimus (Notidanus)
serratus (Ektopodon, Notidanus, Zatrachys)
serridens (Gillicus)
serus (Dinobastis, Hapalodectes, Parocnus,
Pseudocyon sansaniensis)
sesnoni (Brachyrhynchocyon)
Sespia Merycoidodontidae
californica Schultz, C. B. and Falkenbach 1968
heterodon Schultz, C. B. and Falkenbach 1968
marianae Schultz, C. B. and Falkenbach 1968
nitida Schultz, C. B. and Falkenbach
1968
Sespiini Leptaucheniinae Schultz, C. B.
and Falkenbach 1968 (tribe)
severskensis (Citellus)
seversus (Merychippus)
Seymouria Seymouriidae Olson, E. 1964B,
1965B
sanjuanensis Vaughn 1966B
Seymouriamorpha Anthracosauria Romer

1964B; Tatarinov, L. P.
1964AB, 1965B
Seymouriidae Seymouriamorpha Lewis,
G. E. and Vaughn 1965
Seymouria
Shamolagus Leporidae
grangeri Gureev 1964
medius Li, C.-k. 1965
shanafeltae (Hadroleptauchenia)
Shanidar man (Iraq) [Homo] Hominidae
Stewart 1963B
Shansiemys Testudinidae Chkhikvadze
1968 (in Sakyidae); Yeh
1963B (in Emydidae)
latiscuta Yeh 1963B
shansiensis (Mammut borsoni, Testudo)
Shansiodontidae Dicynodontia Cox, C.
B. 1965
Shansiodontinae [Shansiodontidae]
Dicynodontia Bonaparte
1966D
Shansisuchidae Proterosuchia Young,
C.-c. 1964A
Shanisuchus
Shansisuchus Shansisuchidae Young,
C.-c. 1964A
heiyuekouensis Young, C.-c. 1964A
shansisuchus Young, C.-c. 1964A
shansisuchus (Shansisuchus)
shanwangensis (Plesiaceratherium)
sharamurenensis (Juxia, Lushiamynodon)
sharanensis (Testudo)
Sharemys Testudinidae
hemispherica Yeh 1963B
sharovi (Asiatoceratodus)
Shastasauridae Ichthyosauria
Shastasauroidea [Longipinnati] Ichthyosauria Tatarinov 1964S
(p. 349, Shastosauroidea)
Shastasaurus Shastasauridae
careyi Ochev and Polubotko 1964
silversi Ochev and Polubotko 1964
shastense (Nothrotherium)
Shecenia ?Trigonostylopidae incertae sedis
ctirneru Simpson, G. G. 1967A
sheffleri (Sunkahetanka)
Shelania Eoxenopodidae Parodi Bustos
1962
pasquali Casamiquela 1965A
shensiensis (Testudo)
Shensipus Ichnites Young, C.-c. 1966C
tungchuanensis Young, C.-c. 1966C
sheppeyensis (Isurus, Lehmanamia, Promegalops, Scombramphodon)
sherwoodi (Phlyctaenaspis)
shigensis (Elephas)

shikamai (Elaphurus)
Shikamainosorex Soricidae
densicingulata Repenning 1967C
shimabarensis (Cervus)
Shimmelia Ichnites Casamiquela 1964A
(in Archosauria inc. sed.)
chirotheroides Casamiquela 1964A
shingkuoi (Petalodus)
Shingyisaurus Simosauridae Young, C.-c.
1965D
unexpectus Young, C.-c. 1965D
shoshonensis (Plesippus)
Shoshonius Omomyidae
cooperi Robinson, Peter 1966A
shotwelli (Otospermophilus, Tregomys)
showchangensis (Mesoclupea)
shufeldti (Fulica)
shultzi (Scapanus)
shumardi (Enchodus)
Sianodon Amynodontidae Xu 1965
bahoensis Xu 1965
chiyuanensis Chow, M.-c. and Xu 1965
honanensis Chow, M.-c. and Xu 1965
mienchiensis Chow, M.-c. and Xu 1965
sinensis Chow, M.-c. and Xu 1965
ulausuensis Xu 1966
Siberiaspis Olbiaspididae Obruchev, D. V.
1964C
plana Obruchev, D. V. 1964C
siberica (Marmota, Sanidaspis)
sibirica (Bothriolepis)
sibiricum (Elasmotherium)
sibiricus (Citellus erythrogenys, Lagurus
simplicidens, Lemmus)
sicarius (Viverravus)
sichuanensis (Sinohadrianus)
Sicista Zapodidae
subtilis Tatarinov, K. A. 1960
vinogradovi Topachevskii 1965C
Sicistinae Dipodidae
sickleri (Chirotherium)
sicula (Lacerta)
siderolithicus (Adelomys, Isoptychus)
sieblosensis (Smerdis)
siefkeri (Icarosaurus)
siegeri (Trionyx petersi)
siegerti (Macrotarsius)
siemiradzkii (Poraspis)
sierrai (Ingenierichnus)
sigma (Acoelohyrax)
Sigmodon Cricetidae Alvarez 1966 (Mex.);
Cantwell 1968 (Ariz.)
hudspethensis Strain 1966
Signata Ophidiidae See: Otolithus Frizzell
and Dante 1965

nicoli Frizzell and Dante 1965
stenzeli Frizzell and Dante 1965
signata (Zenaspis)
signeuxae (Promegalus)
signifer (Ctenothrissa)
silesiacus (Eryosuchus)
Silphedestidae Cynodontia Haughton and
     Brink 1954*
Silpholestidae Bauriamorpha Watson and
     Romer 1956*
     Scaloporhinus, Tetracynodon
Siluridae Siluroidei
     Parasilurus
Siluriformes Ostariophysi
Siluroidei Cypriniformes
silversi (Shastasaurus)
silvestris (Felis)
Simamphicyon Miacidae
     helveticus Beaumont 1966
similis (Democricetodon, Deperetella,
          Lampropeltis, Neocometes,
          Pleurostylodon, Sciaena)
Similisorex Soricidae Stogav and Savinov
     1965
     orlovi Stogov and Savinov 1965
similus (Megacricetodon)
Simimys Cricetidae Lindsay, E. 1968A
simionesoui (Equus)
simnorhynchus (Adelogyrinus)
Simocyon Mustelidae Beaumont 1964C
          (in Broilianinae); Korotke-
          vich 1961B; Meladze 1967
Simoliophidia [Lapparentophidae] Ser-
          pentes incertae sedis Tarlo,
          L. B. in Appleby, et al.
          and Tarlo 1967 (infraorder
          of Serpentes)
simonsi (Dormaalius, Paraphiomys)
Simopteraspis Pteraspididae Stensiö 1964
          (endocranium)
simorrensis (Conohyus, Conohyus simor-
          rensis)
Simosauridae Nothosauria
     ?Corosaurus, Shingyisaurus
Simosthenurus Sthenurus Tedford 1966B
simplex (Agispelagus, Ectoganus, Helodus,
          Poraspis)
simplicidens (Equus, Lagurus, Lutra,
          Pseudodryomys, Russellites,
          Scapanoscaptor)
simplicior (Dicrostonyx)
simpsoni (Austrolagomys, Brandmayria,
          Oxyaena, Palaeosinopa,
          Phenacolemur jepseni
          Puercolestes)
Simpsonictis Protictis MacIntyre 1966
          (new rank)

simum (Omosoma)
simus (Arctodus, Cyclopidius, Goniopho-
          lis, Hoplopteryx, Procyon)
Sinanthropus Hominidae Bilewicz 1960A;
          Chardin 1930I; Frisch 1965;
          Heintz, A. 1965B; Pei
          1930B, 1965A; Uryson 1966A
     lantianensis Chow, M.-c. 1965A; Gu
          1965; Kahlke 1965F, 1966;
          Woo 1964A, B, C, D, F, G,
          1965A, B, C, D, E, F, G, H,
          1966A, B. C; Zaki 1964
     pekingensis Andrews, R. C. 1930;
          Koenigswald 1967C
Sinaspideretes Trionychidae
     wimani Yeh 1963B
Sincanthus Climatiidae
     wuchangensis P'an 1964
Sinclairella Apatemyidae
     dakotensis Clemens 1964
sinclairi (Bunophorus)
Sinclairia Megalonychidae
     oregoniana Hirschfeld and Webb 1968
          (nomen dubium)
Sinemydidae Pleurosternoidea Yeh 1963B
     Manchurochelys, Sinemys
Sinemys Sinemydidae
     lens Yeh 1963B
sinense (Nestoritherium, Proboscidipparion)
sinensis (Asterolepis, Crocuta crocuta,
          Gazella, Indarctos, Lycoptera,
          Nyctereutes, Ocadia, Siano-
          don, Stegodon, Tapirus,
          Trionyx)
Singida Singididae Greenwood and Patter-
     son 1967
     jacksonoides Greenwood and Patterson
          1967
Singididae Osteoglossoidei Greenwood and
          Patterson 1967
     Singida
sinhaleyus (Hexaprotodon, Homo, Homo-
          pithecus)
Sinobison Bison Stokes, Anderson and
          Madsen 1966
Sinocastor Castoridae
     zhdansky Zazhigin 1966D
Sinochelys Dermatemydidae
     applanata Yeh 1963B
Sinocoelacanthus Coelacanthidae Liu, H.-t.
     1964
     fengshanensis Liu, H.-t. 1966
Sinoconodon Triconodontidae Edinger
          1964A (brain cast)
     rigneyi Crompton 1964B
Sinohadrianus Testudinidae

somonensis (Cervus)
sompoensis (Stegodon)
sondaicus (Rhinoceros)
songarus (Cricetiscus)
songhorensis (Progalago)
sopronensis (Clemmydopsis)
sorenseni (Chinlea)
Sorex Soricidae Jánossy 1965D; Repen-
        ning 1967C
    araneus Friant 1965A
        macrognathus Jánossy 1965B
        praetetragonurus Mezhzherin and
            Svistun 1966
    cinereus Guilday, Martin and McCrady
        1964; Hibbard and Dalquest
        1966; Oesch 1967; Schultz,
        G. E. 1965B; Semken 1966
    dehmi Baudelot, S. 1967; Petroni-
        jević 1967; Repenning 1967C
        africanus Lavocat 1961A*
    dehneli Repenning 1967C
    gracilidens Repenning 1967C
    grivensis Baudelot, S. 1967
    herrlingensis Palmowski and Wachen-
        dorf 1966
    hibbardi Repenning 1967C
    kretzoii Repenning 1967C
    minutus Friant 1965A
    pusilliformis Dehm 1964; Doben-
        Florin 1964; Repenning
        1967C
    stehlini Dehm 1964; Doben-Florin
        1964; Repenning 1967C
    tasnadii Kretzoi 1965D (subgen.
        Drepanosorex)
Soricella Soricidae Dehm 1964 (Mioc.,
        Germany); Doben-Florin
        1964
    discrepans Dehm 1964; Doben-
        Florin 1964; Repenning
        1967C
Soricidae Soricoidea Balsac 1966A, B;
        Friant 1964C, 1965A;
        Repenning 1967C
    Adeloblarina, Allosorex, Alluvisorex,
        Amblycoptus, Angustidens,
        Anourosorex, Anourosori-
        codon, Antesorex, Beremen-
        dia, Blarina, Blarinella,
        Blarinoides, Chodsigoa,
        Crocidosorex, Crocidura,
        Cryptotis, Diplomesodon,
        Domnina, Episoriculus,
        Hemisorex, Hesperosorex,
        Heterosorex, Ingentisorex,
        Limnoecus, Macroneomys,

Microsorex, Miosorex, Myo-
    sorex, Neomys, Nesiotites,
    Notiosorex, Paracryptotis,
    Paradomnina, Parydrosorex,
    Petényia, Petenyiella, Shi-
    kamainosorex, Smilisorex,
    Sorex, Soricella, Suncus,
    Trimylus, Zelceina
Allosoricinae, Crocidurinae, Heterosori-
    cinae, Limnoecinae, Soricinae
Soricinae Soricidae Hutchison 1966A;
    Repenning 1967C
Soricini Soricinae Repenning 1967C
Soricoidea Lipotyphia Van Valen 1967B
    (in Erinaceota)
soriculoides (Zelceina)
Spalacidae Sciurognathi incertae sedis
    Prospalax, Spalax
Spalacotheriidae Symmetrodonta
    Eurylambda, Tinodon
Spalax Spalacidae
    giganteus Bazhanov and Kozhamkulova
        1960
    leucodon Rakovec 1965B
    macoveii Topachevskii 1965C (aff.)
    microphtalmus
        minor Topachevskii 1957E, 1965C
Spaniella Paroxyclaenidae Crusafont Pairó
        and Russell 1967
    carezi Crusafont Pairó and Russell
        1967
Sparidae Percoidea
    Apostasella, Calopomus, Chrysophrys,
        Dentex, Pagellus, Pagrus,
        Podocephalus, Pogonias,
        Sciaenuropsis, Sciaenurus,
        Sparnodus, Sparus, Sphaero-
        dus
Sparnodus Sparidae
    eotauricus Bogachev 1965
Sparodus Gymnarthridae
    macrophtalmus Lehman 1966B
    validus Carroll, R. L. 1966
Sparus Sparidae
    cinctus Menesini 1967B
spatulatus (Woodwardosteus)
spatulifer (Chasmistes)
Spea Scaphiopus Estes and Tihen 1964
speciosa (Taeniolepis)
speciosus (Hippodon, Orasius)
spekei (Teratodon)
spelaea (Crocuta, Crocuta crocuta, Eonyc-
        terus, Felis, Felis leo,
        Hyaena crocuta, Panthera)
Spelaearctos Ursidae
    spelaeus Burchak-Abramovich, N. 1960*

spelaeus Svistun 1968
spelaeus (Spelaearctos, Spelaearctos
        spelaeus, Strongyloceros,
        Ursus)
Spenisciformes Impennes
Speotyto Strigidae
    megalopeza Ford, N. L. 1966; Ford,
        N. L. and Murray 1967
Spermophilus Sciuridae
    tephrus Shotwell 1968
    undulatus Repenning, et al. 1964
        (subgen. Spermophilus)
Spermophilus Spermophilus Repenning,
    et al. 1964
Spermophilinus Sciuridae Bruijn and
    Mein 1968
    bredai Bruijn and Mein 1968
    turolensis Bruijn and Mein 1968
sphaerica (Testudo)
Sphaerodactylinae Gekkonidae Kluge
    1967
sphaerodactylum (Korynichnium)
Sphaerodus Sparidae
    lens Pischedda 1954
    minimus Hary and Muller 1967
Sphaerolepis Trissolepididae
    kounoviensis Gardiner 1967A (rest.)
Sphaeronchus Pycnodontidae See: Oto-
    lithus Stinton and Torrens
    1968
    circularis Stinton and Torrens 1968
    dorsetensis Stinton and Torrens 1968
Sphenacodon Sphenacodontidae
    ferocior Vaughn 1964A (cf.)
Sphenacodontia Pelycosauria
Sphenacodontidae Sphenacodontia
    Ctenospondylus, Cutleria, Dimetro-
        don, Sphenacodon
Spheniscidae Sphenisciformes Simpson,
    G. G. 1965I (Mioc., Aus-
    tralia)
Sphenisciformes Impennes
Sphenocephalidae Polymixioidei Patter-
    son, C. 1964
    Sphenocephalus
Sphenocephalus Sphenocephalidae
    fissicaudus Patterson, C. 1964 (rest.)
Sphenodontia Rhynchocephalia
Sphenodontidae Sphenodontia
    Ctenosauriscus, Elachistosuchus,
        Homoeosaurus, Pio-
        cormus
    Brachyrhinodontinae, Monjuro-
        suchinae
Sphenodus Orthacodontidae
    macer Schweizer 1964
spheroides (Oölithes)

Sphingopus Ichnites
    ferox Demathieu 1966
Sphyraena Sphyraenidae Fitch 1964
    bognorensis Casier 1966A
    kugleri Casier 1966B
    olisiponensis Jonet 1966B
    senni Casier 1966B
Sphyraenidae Sphyraenoidei
    Sphyraena
Sphyraenodus Scombridae
    priscus Casier 1966A
Sphyraenoidei Mugiliformes
Sphyrna [Cestracion] Cestraciontidae
spiersi (Mylomygale)
Spinemys Geoemyda Khozatskii and
    Mlynarski 1966
spinifera (Trionyx)
spiniferus (Odontomysops)
spinosa (Clupea)
Spinosauridae Carnosauria Maleev 1964M
spinosus (Dinopteryx)
spinulosus (Hoplopteryx)
Spirocerus Bovidae
    kiakhtensis David, A. 1965B; Shcherba-
        kova 1954B; Ting, M.-l.,
        et al. 1965
    peii Vangengeim 1966F (cf.)
spissus (Tonostylops)
spizpiza (Cynomys)
splendens (Astraspis, Ganorhynchus,
        Listriodon, Pycnolepis,
        Schizosteus)
Spratelloidinae Dussumieriidae
squaliceps (Hypopnous)
Squalicoracidae Isuroidea Patterson, C. in
    Andrews, S. M., Gardiner,
    Miles and Patterson 1967,
    p. 671 (in Lamnoidei)
Squalicorax Isuridae
    falcatus Applegate 1964A; Bardack
        1968A
    pristodontus Miller, H. W. 1967
Squalidae Squaloidei
    Centrophorus, Centroscymnus,
        Cheirostephanus, Etmopterus,
        Squalus
Squaliformes Selachoidii
Squalodon Squalodontidae
    antverpiensis
        antverpiensis Rothausen 1968B
        papillatus Rothausen 1968B
    bellunensis Rothausen 1968A
    dalpiazi Rothausen 1968A
        kelloggi Rothausen 1968B
Squalodontidae Squalodontoidea
    Agriocetus, Eosqualodon, Neosqualodon,

Patriocetus, Prosqualodon,
Squalodon
Patriocentinae, Squalodontinae
Squalodontinae Squalodontidae Rothau-
sen 1968B
Squalodontoidea Odontoceti
Squaloidei Squaliformes
Squaloraja Squalorajidae
polyspondyla Patterson, C. 1965B
Squalorajidae Squalorajoidei
Squaloraja
Squalorajoidei Chimaeriformes Patterson,
C. 1965B
Squalus Squalidae
minor Casier 1966A
Squamata Lepidosauria Hoffstetter
1964C; Kamal 1966
squamosa (Columba)
Squatarola Charadriidae Jánossy 1965C
Squatina [Rhina] Rhinidae
Squatirhina Orectolobidae
americana Estes 1964
squirella (Hyla)
Stagodontidae Didelphoidea
Didelphodon
Stagonolepididae Pseudosuchia
Fenhosuchus
Episcoposaurinae, Rauisuchinae
Stahlekeriidae [Kannemeyeriidae] Dicyno-
dontia
Stahleckeriinae Kannemeyeriidae Kuhn,
Oskar 1965B, p. 184,
1966A (emend.)
Stanocephalosaurus Capitosauridae
birdi Welles and Cosgriff 1965B
(nomen vanum)
stantonensis (Cyclotosaurus)
"Staurodon" ?Trigonostylopidae incertae
sedis
supernus Simpson, G. G. 1967A
(nomen dubium)
Steganopodes [Pelecaniformes] Neognathae Dement'ev 1964
Stegocephalia [Labyrinthodontia] Apsidospondyli Chalyshev
1962B
Stegodon Elephantidae Hooijer 1964A;
Onodera, et al. 1966;
Verhoeven 1964
bombifrons Chakravarti 1965
clifti Chakravarti 1965
elephantoides Chakravarti 1965
ganesa Chakravarti 1965
hypsilophus Hooijer 1964F
insignis Chakravarti 1965
kaisensis Coppens 1965B

korotorensis Coppens 1965B
orientalis Chow, M.-c., Hu and Lee
1965 (cf.); Kamei 1964;
Shikama 1965
pinjorensis Chakravarti 1965
sinensis Erdbrink 1967B
sompoensis Hooijer 1964E
trigonocephalus Hooijer 1961C (cf.),
1964F
Stegodontinae Elephantidae Chakravarti
1965
stegodontoides (Stegolophodon latidens)
Stegolophodon Elephantidae
latidens Erdbrink 1967B (cf.)
var. latidens Chakravarti 1965
var. stegodontoides Chakravarti
1965
lepersonnei Hooijer 1963D
miyokoae Hatai 1959B
Stegomastodon Gomphotheriidae Lintz
and Savage 1966
mirificus Hibbard and Dalquest 1966
(cf.)
Stegomomuschidae Pseudosuchia Kuhn,
Oskar 1966A (in Chirother-
ioidea); Reig 1961B (valid);
Stegomosuchus Erpetosuchidae Walker,
A. D. 1968 (in Stegomo-
suchidae Huene 1968)
Stegosauria Ornithischia Maleev 1964O;
Ostrom and McIntosh 1966
Stegotrachelidae Palaeoniscoidei
Kentuckia
stehlini (Dimyloides, Equus, Gazella,
Hemicyon, Hyrachyus, Leptolophus, Mimomys, Sorex)
Steinaspis Cyathaspididae Obruchev, D.
V. 1964C
miroshnikovi Obruchev, D. V. 1964C
steindachneri (Chalcalburnus)
Steinheim man [Homo steinheimensis]
Hominidae Rajchel 1965
(reconst.)
steinheimensis (Amphicyon, Amphicyon
steinheimensis, Homo)
steini (Diatryma)
stellatus (Ganosteus)
Steneofiber Castoridae
depereti Bergounioux and Crouzel
1965C; Ginsburg 1967A
eseri Kowalski, K. 1967A
jaegeri Bergounioux and Crouzel
1965C; Kowalski, K. 1967A;
Petronijević 1967
minimus Bergounioux and Crouzel
1965C

minutus Bergounioux and Crouzel
1965C; Kowalski, K.
1967A
wenzensis Sulimski 1964
Steneosauridae ?Mesosuchia
Streptostylus
Steneosaurus Teleosauridae Krebs 1967A;
Westphal 1965
bollensis Wincierz 1967 (aff.)
Stenocranius Microtus Repenning, et al.
1964
Stenoderma Phyllostomatidae
rufum
anthonyi Choate and Birney 1968
rufum Choate and Birney 1968
stenodus (Allosorex)
"Stenogenium" Mammalia incertae sedis
aenigmaticum Simpson, G. G. 1967A
Stenomylus Camelidae
gracilis Frick, C. and Taylor 1968
(subgen. Stenomylus, n.
rank)
keelinensis Frick, C. and Taylor 1968
(subgen. Pegomylus)
Stenomylus Stenomylus Frick, C. and
Taylor 1968
stenonis (Equus, Hippotigris)
Stenoplesictis Mustelidae
cayluxi Palmowski and Wachendorf
1966 (aff.)
Stenopterygiidae Longipinnati
Stenopterygius
Stenopterygius Stenopterygiidae Delair
1966A
crassicostatus Wunnenberg 1961
(aff.)
Stenotosaurus Capitosauridae Welles and
Cosgriff 1965B (syn. of
Parotosaurus)
Stensiöella Stensiöellidae
heintzi Gross, W. 1965C
Stensiöellidae Stensiöelliformes
Stensiöella
Stensiöelliformes Rhenanida
stensioi (Irregulareaspis, Pteronisculus)
stenzeli (Signata)
stepanovi (Plioscirtopoda)
Stephanocemas Cervidae Young, C.-c.
1964D
Stephanodus Trigonodontidae Tabaste
1963
libycus Signeux 1959A, B; Tabaste
1963
mosensis Albers and Weiler 1964
Stephanomys Muridae
donnezani Hugueney and Mein 1966;

Thaler 1966B
Stereornithes [Phororhaci] Gruiformes
Dement'ev 1964
Stereospondyli Temnospondyli Shishkin,
M. A. 1964
Sterna Laridae Burchak-Abramovich, N. I.
1966E
sternatus (Paleostruthio)
sternbergi (Clidastes, Kansius, Leidyosuchus,
Platypeltis, Pteranodon)
stewarti (Nannospondylus, Synorichthys)
Sthenurinae Macropodidae Tedford 1967B
Sthenurus Macropodidae
andersoni Tedford 1966B (subgen.
Sthenurus), 1967B
antiquus Tedford 1966B (subgen.
Simosthenurus)
atlas Tedford 1966B (subgen. Sthenurus), 1967B
browni Merrilees 1967A
gilli Merrilees 1965A
notabilis Tedford 1966B (subgen.
Sthenurus)
occidentalis Merrilees 1967A; Tedford
1966B (subgen. Simosthenu-
rus)
oreas Tedford 1966B (subgen. Simosthenurus)
orientalis Tedford 1966B (subgen.
Simosthenurus)
pales Tedford 1966B (subgen. Simosthenurus)
tindalei Tedford 1966B (subgen. Sthenurus), 1967B
Sthenurus Sthenurus Tedford 1966B
Stichocentrus Holocentridae Patterson, C. 1967A
liratus Patterson, C. 1967A
stintoni (Preophidion)
Stintonia Holocentridae See: Otolithus
brazosia Frizzell and Dante 1965
stirtoni (Coendou, Martes, Phascolarctos)
stocki (Desmodus, Phoenicopterus)
stockleyi (Pachytegos)
Stomiatoidei Salmoniformes
stoppanii (Placochelys)
stormbergi (Orthosuchus)
stovalli (Goniopholis)
Straitonia Sagenodontidae Thomson, K. S.
1965C
waterstoni Thomson, K. S. 1965C
strangulatus (Pseudhyrax)
Stratodus Dercetidae
apicalis Signeux 1959A; Tabaste
1963
strausi (Chelydra)
strenua (Sinopa, Tritemnodon)

Strepsiceros Bovidae
    grandis Leakey, L. S. B. 1965
    maryanus Leakey, L. S. B. 1965
Streptostylus Steneosauridae Kuhn,
        Oskar 1965A (p. 32; in
        Crocodilia)
Stretosaurus Pliosauridae
    macromerus Wells, C. 1964C, D
Striacanthus ?Acanthodii incertae sedis
        Rade 1964
striatum (Lonchidion)
striatus (Schizosteus)
strictipes (Equus caballus)
Striges [Strigiformes] Neognathae De-
        ment'ev 1964
Strigidae Strigiformes
    Asio, Bubo, Otus, Speotyto, Strix
Strigiformes Neognathae
Strigosuchus Ornithosuchidae Simmons
        1965
    licinus Simmons 1965
Strix Strigidae
    nebulosa Jánossy 1965E (cf.)
Stromateidae Stromateoidei
Stromateoidei Perciformes
stromeri (Metoldobotes, Notocaiman,
        Schizorhiza)
Stromerichthys Gigantodontidae
    aethiopicus Tabaste 1963
Strongyloceros Cervidae
    spelaeus Whitehead 1964
Strongylokrotaphus Polycotylidae
        Novozhilov 1964D (in
        Trinacromeriidae)
    irgisensis Novozhilov 1964D (for
        Peloneustes irgisensis)
Struniiformes Osteolepides Jessen 1966A
        (order), B, 1967
Strunius Onychodontidae Jessen 1966A,
        B, 1967
    rolandi Jessen 1966A, B, 1967
    walteri Jessen 1966A, B, 1967
Struthio Struthionidae
    anderssoni An 1964 (eggs, China);
        Burchak-Abramovich, N.
        1953C
    asiaticus Burchak-Abramovich, N.
        1953C
    brachydactylus Burchak-Abramovich,
        N. 1953C
    camelus An 1964 (eggs, China);
        Burchak-Abramovich, N.
        1953C
    chersonensis Burchak-Abramovich, N.
        1953C

    indicus Burchak-Abramovich, N.
        1953C
    karatheodoris Burchak-Abramovich,
        N. 1953C
    mongolicus Bazhanov 1961C; Burchak-
        Abramovich 1953C
    novorossicus Burchak-Abramovich, N.
        1953C
    oldawayi Burchak-Abramovich, N.
        1953C
    oshanai Sauer 1966A
    wimani Burchak-Abramovich, N. 1953C
Struthiocephalus Tapinocephalidae
    kitchingi Boonstra 1965C
Struthiolithus Struthionidae
    adzalycensis Roshchin 1962
    alexejevi Roshchin 1962
Struthiones [Struthioniformes] Neognathae
        Dement'ev 1964
Struthionidae Struthioniformes
    Paleostruthio, Struthio, Struthiolithus
Struthioniformes Neognathae
Struthionops Tapinocephalidae Boonstra
        1952C* (by error listed as
        Struthiops in our 1949–53
        bibliog.)
stuckeri (Diplocynodon)
sturi (Apostasella, Poraspis)
Sturnidae Passeres
    Sturnus
Sturnus Sturnidae
    vulgaris Jánossy 1965E
Stygimys Eucosmodontidae Sloan and
        Van Valen 1965
    kuszmauli Sloan and Van Valen 1965
Stylemys Testudinidae Auffenberg 1964B
        (redefined)
Stylinodon Stylinodontidae Robinson,
        Peter 1966A
Stylinodontidae Taeniodonta
    Ectoganus, Psittacotherium, Stylinodon
stylodon (Hesperocamelus)
Stylohipparion Hipparion Boné and Singer
        1965
Stylomyleodon Amiidae Russell, L. S.
        1967A
Styracopteridae [Palaeoniscidae] Palaeo-
        niscoidei Moy-Thomas 1939B*
styriacum (Chalicotherium)
styriacus (Diplocynodon)
subarcuatus (Pomacanthus)
subaureus (Acanthonemus)
subcircularis (Platypeltis)
sublaevis (Hybodus, Poecilodus)
subovatus (Beryx)

subsequens (Trimylus neumayrianus)
subserrata (Isurus obliqua)
substriatus (Acrodus)
subtilis (Poraspis, Sicista)
subulatus (Todus)
subvespertilio (Platax)
suchovi (Bison)
sudamericanus (Ischignathus)
Sudidae Myctophiformes
    Holosteus
suessenbornensis (Hippotigris)
suevicus (Pseudosciurus)
Suevosciurus Adelomys Thaler 1966B
Suevosciurus Pseudosciuridae
    fraasi Palmowski and Wachendorf
        1966
Sugrivapithecus Pongidae
    gregoryi Prasad 1964B
suhaituensis (Paracadurcodon)
Suidae Suoidea
    Bunolistriodon, Conohyus, Dicory-
        phochoerus, Ectopotamo-
        choerus, Hyotherium,
        Listriodon, Microstonyx,
        Palaeochoerus, Potamo-
        choerus, Promesochoerus,
        Propotamochoerus, Schizo-
        cheorus, Sus
    Suinae
Suiformes Artiodactyla
Suina Suiformes
Suinae Suidae
suinus (Lambdaconus)
sulcatus (Acanthodes, Aglyptorhynchus,
        Cretodus, Democricetodon
        minor)
sulcidens (Bryanpattersonia)
sulcifera (Lafkenia)
Sulidae Suloidea
    Microsula,?Miosula, Morus
Suloidea Pelecani
sümegensis (Senonemys)
summus ("Notopithecus")
suncus Soricidae Repenning 1967C
Sungarichthys Chirocentridae
    longicephalus Gaudant 1967
sungi (Chinchenia)
suni (Asiacanthus)
Sunkahetanka Canidae
    sheffleri Macdonald 1967B
Sunwapta Dipnoi incertae sedis Thomson,
        K. S. 1967C
    grandiceps Thomson, K. S. 1967C
Suoidea Suina
superbus (Caproberyx)

superciliosus (Citellus, Citellus supercilio-
        sus, Metriorhynchus, Pera-
        ceras)
supernus ("Staurodon")
superstes (Periptychus)
Sus Suidae Hooijer 1963D (?)
    apscheronicus Burchak-Abramovich, N.
        and Dzhafarov 1965
    erymanthius Bakalov and Nikolov
        1962; Ozansoy 1965
    lydekkeri Chow, M.-c. 1964B; Shi-
        kama and Hasegawa 1965A
        (cf.)
    scrofa Badoux, D. 1966A; Bakalov
        and Nikolov 1964; Bouchud
        1966D; Chiguriaeva 1960;
        David, A. and Markevich
        1967; Harčar and Schmidt
        1965; Hünermann 1965;
        Krysiak 1956; Lomi 1963;
        Malez 1963D; Melentis
        1964C; Rakovec 1965B;
        Svistun 1968; Tsalkin 1962
sushkini (Benthosuchus, Permocynodon)
sussenbornensis (Capreolus, Equus, Ovibos
        moschatus)
sussmilchi (Dipnorhynchus)
svijagensis (Moschops, Ulemosaurus)
sviridenkoi (Citellus musicus)
Swanscombe man [Homo sapiens] Homi-
        nidae Ovey 1964
swierstrai (Dicynodon)
Sycosauridae Gorgonopsia
    Sycosaurus
    Sycosaurinae
Sycosaurinae Sycosauridae Viushkov 1964C,
        p. 264 (ascribed to Watson
        and Romer 1956*; of Gor-
        gonopsidae)
Sycosaurus Sycosauridae
    brodiei Broom 1941A*
Syllaemidae Clupeoidei
    Syllaemus
Syllaemus Syllaemidae
    albiensis Wenz 1965A
sylvaticus (Apodemus)
sylvestris (Hypolorhus)
Sylvilagus Leporidae
    auduboni Pettus 1956*
    floridanus Hibbard and Dalquest 1966
        (cf.); Pettus 1956*
Symbos Bovidae Ray, C. E., Cooper, et
        al. 1967
    cavifrons Frankforter 1966; Semken,
        Miller and Stevens 1964

Symmetrodonta Theria
symondsi (Traquairaspis)
sympathica ("Degonia")
synanthropus (Mus)
Synapsida Reptilia V'iushkov 1964A
Synaptomys Cricetidae Oesch 1967
    cooperi Guilday, Martin and McCrady
        1964
Synaucheniidae Pachyosteiformes
Synechodus Heterodontidae Albers and
        Weiler 1964 (in Palaeo-
        spinacidae)
    jurensis Schweizer 1964
    nerviensis Albers and Weiler 1964
        (cf.)
Syngnathidae Syngnathoidei
    Syngnathus
Syngnathiformes Mesichthyes
Syngnathida Teleostei Danil'chenko
        1964B (order)
Syngnathoidei Syngnathiformes
Syngnathus Syngnathidae Smigielska
        1959*
Synocnus Megalonychidae Paula Couto
        1967
    comes Paula Couto 1967
Synodidae ?Myctophiformes
    Argillichthys
Synodontaspis Carcharias Casier 1966A
Synoplotherium Mesonychidae Szalay
        and Gould 1966 (=Dromo-
        cyon)
Synorichthys Redfieldiidae Schaeffer, B.
        1967B
    stewarti Schaeffer, B. 1967B (rest.)
Synthetoceras Protoceratidae
    rileyi
        australis Maglio 1966 (subgen.
            Prosynthetoceras)
Syntomodus Helicoprionidae Obruchev,
        D. V. 1964E
    abbreviatus Obruchev, D. V. 1964E
Syodon Brithopodidae Barghusen 1968
syriacus (Hoplopteryx)
Syrrhophus Leptodactylidae
    marnocki Hibbard and Dalquest
        1966

tabroumiti (Eotrigonodon)
Tachystomata [Meantes] Caudata
Tadarida Molossidae Westphal 1967B,
        1968
    braziliensis
        antillularum Choate and Birney
            1968
tadlac (Getulocerus)

Tadorna Anatidae Jánossy 1965C
Taematosteidae [Coccosteidae] Coccostei-
        formes
Taematosteus Coccosteidae Obruchev, D.
        V. 1964D; Romer 1966C
taenia (Cobitis)
Taeniodonta Unguiculata
Taeniodus Theridomyidae
    curvistriatus Thaler 1966B
Taeniolabididae Taeniolabidoidea
    Catopsalis
Taeniolabidoidea Multituberculata Sloan
        and Van Valen 1965 (new
        rank)
Taeniolaboidea Multituberculata
Taeniolepis Asterolepididae
    speciosa Gross, W. 1965A
taiti (Logania)
taiwanica (Balaenoptera)
tajacu (Dicotyles)
talarae (Conepatus)
talicei (Cardiatherium)
talimaae (Tesseraspis)
Talmontopus Ichnites Lapparent and
        Montenat 1967B
    tersi Lapparent and Montenat 1967B
Talpa Talpidae Jullien 1965A; Simonetta
        1957C
    europaea Malez 1963D
Talpavus Erinaceidae
    nitidus Robinson, Peter 1966A (cf),
        1968A
Talpidae Soricoidea Hutchison 1968A
        (classif.)
    Achlyoscaptor, Arctoryctes, Crypto-
        ryctes, Desmana, Domninoi-
        des, Gaillardia, Mystipterus,
        ?Neurotrichus, Parascalops,
        Proscapanus, Scalopoides,
        Scalopus, Scapanoscaptor,
        Scapanus, Scaptonyx, Talpa
    Desmaninae, Gaillardinae, Proscalopinae,
        Talpinae, Uropsilinae
Talpinae Talpidae
talpinus (Ellobius)
tamanensis (Mammuthus meridionalis)
tamdensis (Carcharias)
Tamesichthys Scombridae Casier 1966A
    decipiens Casier 1966A
tamesis (Whitephippus)
Tamias Sciuridae Wilson, R. L. 1968
    aristus Ray, C. E. 1965B
    atheles Gromov, I. M., et al. 1965
        (subgen. Eutamias?)
    laevidens Gromov, I. M., et al. 1965
    nasutus Gromov, I. M., et al. 1965

orlovi Gromov, I. M., et al. 1965
  (subgen. Eutamias)
wimani Gromov, I. M., et al. 1965
  (subgen. Eutamias)
Tamiasciurus Sciuridae
  hudsonicus Oesch 1967
  tenuidens Guilday, Martin and
    McCrady 1964
Tamiini Marmotinae Gromov, I. M., et
    al. 1965
Tamiobatis Cladoselachidae
  vetustus Romer 1964A
tanaitica (Mimomys)
tanaiticus (Lepus)
Tanaocrossus Palaeonisciformes incertae
    sedis Schaeffer, B. 1967B
  kalliokoskii Schaeffer, B. 1967B
tancrei (Ellobius)
Tangasauridae Younginiformes Maleev
    1964D
Tangasaurus
Tangasaurus Tangasauridae Watson 1957A*
    (related to the Prolacertilia)
Taniwhasaurus Mosasauridae Russell, D.
    A. 1967A
tanneri (Pithecistes)
Tannuaspida [Tremataspidoidea] Acer-
    aspida Tarlo, L. B. 1967B
    (Tannuaspidida)
Tannuaspididae Tremataspidoidea Obru-
    chev, D. V. 1964C
Tannuaspis Cephalaspididae
  levenkoi Obruchev, D. V. 1961C
Tanupolama Camelidae Miller, W. E.
    1968; Strain 1966; Webb,
    S. D. 1965C
  blancoensis Hibbard and Dalquest
    1966 (cf.)
  macrocephala Oesch 1965
Tanystropheidae Sauria incertae sedis
    Camp 1945B* (Tanystro-
    phaeidae, in Trachelosauria
    of Protorosauria of Lepido-
    sauria); Romer 1945D* (in
    Protorosauria [=Araeosceli-
    dia])
Taphrosphys Pelomedusidae
  dares Miller, H. W. 1967
tapiacitis (Meniscotherium)
Tapinocephalidae Dinocephalia
  Moschops, Struthiocephalus, Struthio-
    nops, Ulemosaurus
  Mormosaurinae, Riebeekosaurinae
Tapiridae Tapiroidea
  Tapirus
Tapiroidea Ceratomorpha

tapiroides (Carolozittelia, Lophiodon,
    Mammut, Mammut angus-
    tidens)
tapirotherium (Lophiodon)
Tapirus Tapiridae Gray, S. W. and
    Cramer 1961
  arverensis Bakalov and Nikolov 1962;
    Fejfar 1964A; Korotkevich
    1967B; Rădulesco, Samson,
    et al. 1965
  brönnimanni Schaub, S. and Hürzeler
    1949
  californicus Leffler 1964 (cf.)
  copei Hibbard and Dalquest 1966;
    Ray, C. E. 1964E; Strain
    1966 (cf.)
  excelsus Oesch 1967 (cf.)
  intermedius
    robustus Schaub, S. and Hürzeler
    1949
  sinensis Chow, M.-c., Hu and Lee 1965
Tappenosauridae ?Sphenocodontia Kuhn,
    Oskar 1966A (? in Titano-
    suchoidea)
tarandus (Rangifer)
Tarentola Gekkonidae
  americana Etheridge 1966A
taribanensis (Mammuthus meridionalis)
Tarrasiiformes Actinopterygii Lehman
    1966B
Tarsiidae Tarsioidea Crusafont Pairó
    1967B
Tarsioidea Neoprosimii Crusafont Pairó
    1967B
Tartuosteus Drepanaspididae Mark-Kurik
    1966
  giganteus Obruchev, D. V. and Mark-
    Kurik 1965; Tarlo 1965
  luhai Obruchev, D. V. and Mark-Kurik
    1965 (?); Tarlo 1965
  maximus Mark-Kurik 1968; Obruchev,
    D. V. and Mark-Kurik 1965;
    Tarlo 1965
  ornatus Obruchev, D. V. and Mark-
    Kurik 1965 (?)
tashuikouensis (Chilantaisaurus)
tasnadii (Sorex)
tatalgolicus (Sinolagomys)
tatarica (Saiga)
Tataromyidae Ctenodactyloidea
  Africanomys, Metasayimys, Sayimys
  Sayimyinae, Tataromyinae
Tataromyinae Tataromyidae Lavocat
    1961A*
Tatisaurus Hypsilophodontidae
  oehleri Simmons 1965

tatsuensis (Plesiochelys)
Taucanamo Tayassuidae
    sansaniense Bergounioux and Crouzel
        1967A; Petronijević 1967
taurica (Capra)
tauricus (Ellobius)
Taurotragini Bovidae Leakey, L. S. B.
        1965
Taurotragus Bovidae
    arkelli Leakey, L. S. B. 1965
taurus (Carcharias)
Taxidea Mustelidae
    marylandica Long, C. A. 1964
    taxus Anderson, E. 1968 (in Melinae)
Taxoides (Aelurodon)
taxus (Taxidea)
Tayassuidae Suoidea Woodburne 1965A,
        1966B
    Argyrohyus, Dicotyles, Mylohyus,
        Perchoerus, Platygonus,
        Prosthenops, Taucanamo
taylori (Archoplites, Ictidomys, Merych-
        yus relictus, Neotoma,
        Ophiomys)
Tchad man [Tchadanthropus uxoris]
        Hominidae Coppens 1963,
        1965A, C, D, 1966C;
        Uryson 1966B
Tchadanthropus Hominidae Coppens
        1965C
    uxoris Coppens 1965C, 1966C; Ostoya
        1965
tchernovi (Psammosteus)
tecta (Scutemys)
tecton (Ennatosaurus)
tectulus (Platecarpus)
tectum (Scapherpeton)
tedfordi (Ngapakaldia)
Teiidae Lacertoidea
    Ameiva, Champs, Cnemidophorus,
        Haptosphenus, Leptochamps,
        Meniscognathus
teilhardi (Gobiolagus, Lagomeryx, Pseudo-
        paramys)
Teilhardina Teilhardidae Crusafont Pairó
        1967B; Quinet 1964A
    belgica Quinet 1964A, 1966A, C
    gallica Russell, D. E., Louis and
        Savage 1967
Teilhardidae Tarsiiformes Quinet 1964A
    Teilhardina
Telanthropus Hominidae Wolpoff 1966
Teleoceras Rhinocerotidae Skinner, M.
        F., Skinner and Gooris
        1968

Teleocrateridae Pseudosuchia Charig 1967
Teleodus Brontotheriidae
    thyboi Bjork 1967
Teleolophus Deperetellidae
    daviesi Radinsky 1965A (?)
    ferganicus Radinsky 1965A (?)
    magnus Radinsky 1965A
    medius Radinsky 1965A
Teleosauridae Mesosuchia
    Machimosaurus, Mystriosaurus, Steneo-
        saurus
Teleosteens Actinopterygii Lehman 1966B
Teleostei Actinopterygii Blot 1968;
        Danil'chenko 1964B (super-
        ord.); François 1967 (vertae.);
        Greenwood, Rosen, et al.
        1966 (classif.); MacAllister
        1968; Patterson, C. 1967C,
        1968
    Incertae sedis: Protriacanthus
Teleostomi Pisces
telleri (Gobius)
Telmatodon Anthracotheriidae Gabuniia
        1964D
Telmatornis Rallidae
    affinis Baird 1967
    priscus Baird 1967
temnospondyla (Cyrtura)
Temnospondyli Labyrinthodontia Romer
        1964B
temporaria (Rana)
tener (Dinodontosaurus, Noemacheilus)
tengisii (Canis)
Tenrecoidea Lipotyphla
Tenuidens (Tamiasciurus hudsonicus)
tenuirostris (Belonostomus, Peramus,
        Saurichthys)
tenuis (Protictis, Psammosteus, Scapano-
        rhynchus, Tetracynodon,
        Yabeinosaurus)
tenuissima (Clupea)
tenuistriatum (Eocoelopoma curvatum)
tephrus (Otospermophilus, Spermophilus)
Teratichthys Carangidae
    antiquitatis Casier 1966A
Teratodon Teratodontidae Savage, R. J. G.
        1965A
    enigmae Savage, R. J. G. 1965A
    spekei Savage, R. J. G. 1965A
Teratodontidae Oxyaenoidea Savage, R. J.
        G. 1965A
    Teratodon
Teratornithidae Cathartoidea
Teratornithinae [Teratornithidae] Cathar-
        toidea Brodkorb 1964A (of
        Cathartidae)

Nikolov and Kovachev 1966
longirostris Bakalov and Nikolov
1962; Belokrys 1960E;
Burchak-Abramovich, M.
and Korotkevich 1966;
Lysenko 1962; Nikolov
1962*; Nikolov and Kova-
chev 1966
Tetrameryx Antilocapridae
knoxensis Hibbard and Dalquest
1966
Tetrao Phasianidae
mlokosiewiczi Burchak-Abramovich, N.
1966D
tetrix Malez 1963D
urogallus Jánossy 1965E; Malez 1963D
Tetraonidae Phasianoidea
Lagopus
Tetraoninae Phasianidae Brodkorb 1964A
Tetrapoda Craniata Kuhn, O. 1967B
(preoccup.); Thomson, K.
S. 1964C (ancestry)
tetrix (Lyrurus, Tetrao)
Tetrodontida Teleostei Danil'chenko
1964B (order)
texana (Clemensia, Eosolea, Genartina)
texanus (Prosynthetoceras)
texensis (Atopomys, Broiliellus, Tersom-
ius)
thabagarii (Imerodelphis)
Thalassemyididae Pleurosternoidea
?Changisaurus, Eurysternum, Manchurochelys, Thalassemys, Tro-
pidemys
Thalassemys Thalassemyidae
hugii Bräm 1965 (restor.)
moseri Bräm 1965 (restor.)
Thalattosauria Prolacertilia Tarlo in
Appleby et al. and Tarlo
1967 (a separate order of
Lepidosauria)
Thalattosauridae Thalattosauria Maleev
1964E
thaleri (Muscardinus, Reithroparamys,
Ruscinomys)
Thamnophis Colubridae Hibbard and
Dalquest 1966; Holman
1965A; Wilson, R. L. 1968
proximus Holman 1965D (cf.)
Thaumatosauridae Plesiosauroidea Romer
1956F* (incl. Brancasaurus)
Termatosaurus
Thaumaturidae Salmonoidei
Thaumaturus
Thaumaturus Thaumaturidae See: Oto-
lithus Weinfurter 1967

Thecadactylus Gekkonidae
rapicaudus Etheridge 1964
Thecodontia Archosauria Maleev 1964F
Thecodontosauridae Plateosauria Charig,
Attridge and Crompton
1965 (in Prosauropoda; incl.
Gryponychidae ="Palaeo-
sauridae"); Colbert 1964B
Massospondylus, Thecodontosaurus
Thecodontosaurus Thecodontosauridae
skirtopodus Bond, G. 1955B
Thelodonti Ostracodermi Stensiö 1964
Thelodontida Thelodonti Stensiö 1964
Thelodontidae Thelodontida
Goniporus, Katoporus, Logania,
Thelodus, Turinia
Thelodontiformes [Thelodontida] Thelodonti Tarlo 1967B
Thelodus Thelodontidae Karatajūte 1964
bicostatus Gross, W. 1967C
costatus Gross, W. 1967C
laevis Gross, W. 1967C
parvidens Gross, W. 1967C
pugniformis Gross, W. 1967C
schmidti Gross, W. 1967C
sculptilis Gross, W. 1967C
traquairi Gross, W. 1967C
trilobatus Gross, W. 1967C
theotonicus (Chiniquodon)
Therapsida Synapsida Barghusen 1968;
Boonstra 1967A; Kuhn, Oskar
1965B (bibliog., catalog,
taxonomy; incl. suborders
Theriodontia and Anomodontia); Tatarinov, L. P. 1964M
Incertae sedis: Dinosaurus
Thereutherium Hyaenodontidae Van Valen
1966A
Theria Mammalia Ledoux, et al. 1966
Incertae sedis: Perutherium, Pappotherii-
dae
Theridomorpha [Theridomyomorpha]
Sciurognathi Thaler in Butler
et al. 1967 (ascribed to Lavo-
cat 1955)
Theridomyidae Theridomyoidea
Archaeomys, Blainvillimys, Columbomys,
Isoptychus, Issiodoromys,
Oltinomys, Pseudoltinomys,
Remys, Sciuromys, Taenio-
dus, Theridomys, Trechomys
Columbomyinae, Issiodoromyinae,
Theridomyinae
Theridomyinae Theridomyidae Thaler
1966B
Theridomyoidea Theridomyomorpha

Ticholeptus Merycoidodontidae
    hypsodus
        leadorensis Schultz, C. B. and
            Falkenbach 1968
        obliquidens Shotwell 1968 (cf.)
        rileyi Schultz, C. B. and Falkenbach
            1968
Tichorhinus Rhinoceros Friant 1963C
Tichorhinus Rhinocerotidae
    antiquitatis Mostecký 1964; Stach 1956
tichorhinus (Rhinoceros)
Tichvinskia Procolophonidae
    majmesculae Ochev 1968
Ticinosuchus Pseudosuchia incertae sedis
            Krebs 1965 (Trias., Switzer-
            land)
    ferox Krebs 1965, 1966
Tienfuchelys Plesiochelyidae
    tzuyangensis Yeh 1963B
Tienshanosaurus Brachiosauridae
    chitaiensis Young, C.-c. 1964E
tigrina (Paranguilla)
tigrinum (Ambystoma)
tigris (Felis, Panthera)
Tigris Panthera Hemmer 1967B
tiguidiensis (Ceratodus)
tiheni (Megasminthus, Paleoheterodon)
Tillodontia Unguiculata
timanica (Tolypelepis)
timanicus (Plourdosteus)
timidus (Lepus)
Tinca Cyprinidae Weiler 1966A
    obtruncata Obrhelová 1967 (reconst.)
    tinca Deckert and Karrer 1965
tinca (Tinca)
tindalei (Sthenurus)
tingleyense (Rhabdoderma)
tinnunculus (Falco)
Tinodon Spalacotheriidae Crompton and
            Jenkins 1967
Tinosaurus Chameleontidae
    lushihensis Dong 1965 (Eoc., China)
tirarensis (Neohelos, Pelecanus)
Titanichthyiidae Brachythoraci
    Titanichthys
Titanichthys Titanichthyiidae
    termieri Lehman 1963B
Titanomys Palaeolagidae
    visenoviensis Gureev 1964
Titanophoneidae [Brithopedidae] Titano-
            suchia Kuhn, Oskar 1965B,
            p. 8, (ascribed by error to
            "Romer 1950")
Titanophoneus Brithopodidae
    poteus Tatarinov, L. P. 1966C

Titanopteryx Ornithocheiridae Arambourg
            1959E
    philadelphiae Arambourg 1959E
Titanosauridae Sauropoda Colbert 1964B
    (in Cetiosauria)
    Mamenchisaurus, Titanosaurus
Titanosaurus Titanosauridae Colbert
            1964G
Titanosuchia Theriodontia
Titanosuchidae [Jonkeriidae] Titanosuchia
Titanotheriomys Ischyromyidae
    veterior Black, C. C. 1965A
Titanotylopus Camelidae Hibbard and
            Dalquest 1966; Webb, S. D.
            1965C
tobieni (Masillamys)
tobinensis (Geomys)
todei (Torgos tracheliotus)
Todidae Halcyones
    Todus
Todus Todidae
    angustirostris Bernstein 1965
    subulatus Bernstein 1965
tokunagai (Lycoptera)
toliapicum (Argillotherium)
toliapicus (Acipenser, Ampheristus,
            Myliobatis, Myripristis,
            Phyllodus, Pycnodus)
tolmachevi (Gobiolagus)
tologoica (Marmota, Ochotona)
tologoicus (Citellus)
tologoijensis (Coelodonta)
tolsanus (Arctamphicyon, Arctamphicyon
            tolsanus)
Tolypelepidida Cyathaspidiformes Tarlo
            1967B
Tolypelepidinae Cyathaspididae Denison
            1964B
Tolypelepis Cyathaspididae
    timanica Denison 1964B
    undulata Denison 1964B
tomanensis (Citellus)
Tomarctus Canidae Jakway and Clement
            1967
    kelloggi Shotwell 1968 (cf.)
    rurestris Shotwell 1968 (cf.); Voorhies
            1965
tomassoni (Elopoides)
Tomistoma Crocodylidae Telles Antunes
            1964B
    lusitanica Telles Antunes 1967E
    machikanense Kobatake and Kamei
            1966
Tomistominae Crocodylidae Young, C.-c.
            1964C

Tremamesacleidinae Elasmosauridae No-
        vozhilov 1964C
Tremarctos Ursidae
    floridanus Guilday and Irving 1967;
        Kurtén 1966A (rest.)
    mexicanus Kurtén 1966A (invalid)
Tremataspididae Tremataspidoidea
    Tremataspis
Tremataspidoidea Aceraspida
Tremataspis Tremataspididae
    mammillata Aaloe 1963 (Silurian,
        Saaremaa Is.); Stensiö 1963
Trematosauria Temnospondyli
    Incertae sedis: Lyrosaurus
Trematosauridae Trematosauroidea
    Aphaneramma, Ifasaurus, Lyrocephalus,
        Trematosaurus
Trematosauroidea Trematosauria
Trematosaurus Trematosauridae
    madagascariensis Lehman 1966A
Trematosteidae Pachyosteiformes Obru-
        chev, D. V. 1964D (incl.
        Braunosteidae)
trepidum (Prodremotherium)
Tretulias Cetotheriidae
    buccatus Kellogg 1968
Triadobatrachidae Proanura
Triakidae Galeoidea
    Mustelus
triangulus (Katoporus)
Triassochelyoidea Amphichelydia
Triazeugacanthus Mesacanthidae Miles,
        R. S. 1966A
    affinis Miles, R. S. 1966A (rest.)
tricavus (Katoporus)
Triceratops Ceratopidae Ostrom 1964D,
        1966B
    prorsus Erickson 1966 (skel.)
Triceromeryx ?Giraffidae
    pachecoi Telles Antunes 1964A
Trichiuridae Trichiuroidei
    Eutrichiurides, Lepidopus
Trichiurides Gadidae
    sagittidens Casier 1966A
Trichiuroidei Perciformes
Trichophanes Aphredoderidae
    hians La Rivers 1962
triconodens (Durotrigia)
Triconodonta Mammalia incertae sedis
    Megazostrodon
Triconodon Triconodontidae Edinger
        1964A (brain cast)
Triconodontidae Triconodonta
    Sinconodon, Triconodon
tricrenulatus (Primaevomesus)

tricuspidens (Plesiadapis)
Tricuspiodon Hyopsodontidae
    magistrae Russell, D. E. 1964
    rutimeyeri Russell, D. E. 1964
tricuspis (Limnoecus)
Triglyphus [Tritylodon] Tritylodontidae
        Kuhn, Oskar 1965B, p. 86
        (taxonomic note)
trigonalis (Carcharias)
Trigonias Rhinocerotidae
    osborni Clark, J. and Beerbower
        1967
Trigonictis Mustelidae Zakrzewski 1967A
Trigoniformes Neognathae
trigonocephalus (Dayohyus, Stegodon)
Trigonodontidae Tetradontiformes incertae
        sedis
    Eotrigonodon, Stephanodus
"Trigonolophodon" ?Isotemnidae incertae
        sedis
    modicus Simpson, G. G. 1967A
        (nomen dubium)
Trigonostylopidae Trigonostylopoidea
    Albertogaudrya, Trigonostylops
    Incertae sedis: Hedralophus, Shecenia,
        "Staurodon," "Trigonostylops"
Trigonostylopoidea Protungulata Simpson,
        G. G. 1967A (order; new
        rank)
Trigonostylops Trigonostylopidae
    apthomasi Paula Couto 1963B
    gegenbauri Simpson, G. G. 1967A
    wortmani Simpson, G. G. 1964C,
        1967A
"Trigonostylops" ?Trigonostylopidae
        incertae sedis
    duplex Simpson, G. G. 1967A
trilobatus (Thelodus)
trilobodon (Germanomys)
Trilobodon Mammalia incertae sedis
    brancoi Simpson, G. G. 1967A
Trilophodon [Gomphotherium] Gompho-
        theriidae
Trilophomys Cricetidae
    pyrenaicus Hugueney and Mein 1966;
        Sulimski 1964
Trilophosauria Cotylosauria Kuhn, O.
        1966A (order, related to
        Diadectomorpha); Romer
        1956F* (suborder of
        Protorosauria)
Trimerorhachidae Trimerorhachoidea Baird
        1966A

Acroplous, ?Dawsoni, Eobrachyops,
    Nannospondylus, Nelda-
    saurus, Trimerorhachis
Trimerorhachis Trimerorhachidae Chase,
    J. N. 1965
Trimerorhachoidea Rhachitomi
"Trimerostephanos" Isotemnidae
    ultimus Simpson, G. G. 1967A
    (nomen vanum)
Trimylus Soricidae Palmowski and
    Wachendorf 1966
    compressus Repenning 1967C
    neumayrianus Repenning 1967C
        neumayrianus Doben-Florin
            1964
            subsequens Dehm 1964; Doben-
                Florin 1964
        sansaniensis Petronijević 1967; Re-
            penning 1967C
trinacridis (Clupea)
Trinacromeriidae [Polycotylidae] Plio-
            sauroidea Novozhilov 1964D
Tringa Charadriidae
    ochropus Jánossy 1965C (cf.)
Trionychidae Trionychoidea
    Aspideretes, Lissemys, Plastomenus,
        Platypeltis, Sinaspideretes,
        Trionyx
    Lissemydinae
Trionychoidea Cryptodira
Trionyx Trionychidae Albrecht 1967;
            Bachmayer 1966; Khozatskii
            1957 (Amyda); Wilson,
            R. L. 1968
    aspidiformis Liebus 1930B
    bohemicus Liebus 1930B
    elongatus Liebus 1930B
    gracilia Yeh 1963B (Amyda)
    gregaria Yeh 1963B (Amyda)
    halophilus Miller, H. W. 1967
    johnsoni Yeh 1963B (Amyda)
    neimenguensis Yeh 1965 (Amyda)
    petersi
        siegeri Mottl 1967B (var.)
    planoides Kuhn, Oskar 1964B (for
            T. planus)
    pliopedemontana Macarovici and
            Motaş 1965 (cf.)
    richardii Bergounioux 1938C*
    sinensis Yeh 1963B (Amyda)
    spinifera Hibbard and Dalquest 1966;
            Holman 1966B; Preston
            1966
    zakhidovi Khozatskii 1966
trippensis (Archaeotherium)

Triplopides Hyracodontidae Radinsky
    1967B
    rieli Radinsky 1967B
Triplopus Hyracodontidae Radinsky
    1967B
Triportheus Characidae
    ligniticus Weitzman 1960C
Trirachodon Diademodontidae Barghusen
    1968
Trischizolagus Leporidae Rădulesco and
        Samson 1967C
    dumitrescuae Rădulesco and Samson
        1967C
triseriata (Pseudacris)
trispinatus (Rhamphodopsis)
Trissolepididae Palaeonisciformes
    Sceletophorus, Sphaerolepis
Tristicopterus Rhizodontidae Thomson,
        K. S. 1967B
tristis (Mineopterus)
trisulcatus (Hypsiprymnus)
Tritemnodon Hyaenodontidae
    strenua Guthrie, D. A. 1967B
triton (Cricetulus)
trituratus (Isistius)
Tritylodon Tritylodontidae
    longaevus Ellenberger, P. and Ginsburg
        1965
Tritylodontidae Ictidosauria Lewis, G. E.
        1966; Tatarinov, L. P.
        1964O
    Bienotherium, Oligokyphus, Tritylodon,
        Tritylodontoideus
Tritylodontoideus Tritylodontidae
    maximus Fourie 1968
triunguis (Terrapene carolina)
Trocharion Mustelidae
    albanense Petronijević 1967; Petter,
        G. 1967A
Trochili Apodiformes
Trochilidae Trochili
    Anthracothorax
trochoceros (Bos)
troelli (Bregmaceros, Claibornichthys)
Trogolemur Anaptomorphidae Robinson,
        Peter 1968B (?)
Trogones [Trigoniformes] Neognathae
        Dement'ev 1964
trogontherii (Elephas, Mammuthus)
Trogontherium Castoridae Hugueney and
        Mein 1966; Vas'kovskii
        1959B
    boisvilletti Dechaseaux 1967B
    cuvieri Burchak-Abramovich, N. 1964A;
            Burchak-Abramovich, N. and
            Sultanov 1965; Dubrovo and
            Alekseev 1964; Guenther
            1965; Topachevskii 1965C;

Vangengeim 1960B, 1961
minus Fejfar 1964A
Trogosus Esthonychidae
grangeri Robinson, Peter 1966A
tropicalis (Monachus)
Tropidemys Thalassemyidae
langi Bräm 1965 (rest.)
Tropidoclonion Colubridae
lineatum Hibbard and Dalquest 1966;
Holman 1965A
Troposodon Macropodidae Bartholomai
1967 (for Sthenurus minor)
minor Bartholomai 1967
trouessarti (Arctocyonides)
truncus (Epieuryceros)
trux (Cynohyaenodon)
Trygon Dasyatidae
jaekeli Bosch 1964C
Tsamnichoria Oldfieldthomasiidae
cabrerai Simpson, G. G. 1967A
Tsaotanemys Dermatemydidae Yeh
1963B
tschabukianii (Sathapliasaurus)
Tscherskia Cricetulus Zazhigin 1966D
Tseajaia Tseajaiidae Vaughn 1964A
campi Vaughn 1964A
Tseajaiidae Cotylosauria incertae sedis
Vaughn 1964A
Tseajaia
Tselfatia Plethodontidae Patterson, C.
1967B
Tselfatiidae Beloniformes
Protobrama
Tselfatioidei [Plethodoidea] Osteoglossoidei Patterson, C. 1967B
(incl. Plethodontidae and
Protobramidae)
Tubantia Trachichthyidae Patterson, C.
1964 (for Sphenocephalus
cataphractus)
cataphractus Patterson, C. 1964
(rest.)
tuberculata (Bothriolepis, Grossilepis)
tuberculatus (Ceratodus, Panochthus,
Pycnosteus, Rhipis)
tuberculosis (Grypolophodon)
Tubulidentata Protungulata Hoffmeister
1967
tuckeri (Plotosaurus)
Tuditanidae Microsauria
Asaphestera, Boii, Ricnodon, Tuditanus
Tuditanus Tuditanidae Carroll, R. L.
and Baird 1967, 1968
tuitus (Citellus)
Tulpavus Amphilemuridae Guthrie, D. A.
1967B

tumididens (Ingentisorex)
tungchuanensis (Shensipus)
tungi (Lycoptera)
tungseni (Bothriolepis)
Tungusichthyidae Ospiiformes
Tungusichthys
Tungusichthys Tungusichthyidae Berg
1941A*
acentrophoroides Berg 1941A*
Tungussogyrinidae [?Brachyopidae]
Brachyopoidea Kuhn, Oskar
1962* (not seen)
tunhuanensis (Testudo)
Tupaiidae Tupaioidea Campbell, C. B. G.
1966 (taxonomy); Crusafont
Pairó 1967B; McKenna 1965B;
Martin, R. D. 1966
?Nycticonodon
Adapisoriculinae
Tupaioidea Neoprosimii Crusafont Pairó
1967B; Goodman 1966;
Simpson, G. G. 1965J; Van
Valen 1967B (in Proteuther-
ia)
Tupilakosauridae Brachyopoidea
Tupilakosaurus
Tupilakosaurus Tupilakosauridae Nielsen
1964B
heilmani Nielsen 1964B, 1967
Turdidae Passeres
Luscina, Saxicola, Turdus
Turdus Turdidae
merula Malez 1963D
pilaris Jánossy 1965E
turfanensis (Parotosaurus, Prodinoceras)
turgaicus (Paraorthacodus)
turgidus (Megalagus)
turicensis (Mammut, Mammut angustidens)
Turinia Thelodontidae
pagei Gross, W. 1967C
Turiniida [Turiniidae] Drepanaspida
Turiniidae ?Drepanaspida Obruchev, D. V.
1964C
Turiniiformes [Drepanaspida] Pteraspidiformes
turkmenicus (Dalatias, Palaeoloxodon)
turnauensis (Pseudaelurus)
turneri (Richardsonius, Sciaenuropsis)
turolensis (Spermophilinus)
turpier (Dinodontosaurus)
Turseodus Palaeoniscidae
dolorensis Schaeffer, B. 1967B (rest.)
Tuvaspis Ateleaspididae
margaritae Obruchev, D. V. 1961C
Tverdochlebovi (Eryosuchus)
Tylopoda Artiodactyla Herre 1964 (origin)

Urocles Amiidae
  altivelis Lange, S. P. 1968
  "austeni" Lange, S. P. 1968
  brevicostatus Lange, S. P. 1968
  damoni Lange, S. P. 1968
  elegantissimus Lange, S. P. 1968
  elongatus Lange, S. P. 1968
  lepidotus Lange, S. P. 1968
  ovatus Lange, S. P. 1968
  polyspondylus Lange, S. P. 1968
  sauvagei Lange, S. P. 1968
  woodwardi Lange, S. P. 1968
Urocyon Canidae
  progressus Stevens, M. S. 1965
Urodela [Caudata] Lepospondyli Corsin
    1967 (skull); Schmalhausen
    1964A
  urodeloides (Vaughniella)
Urodelomorpha Amphibia Kuhn, Oskar
    1965E (subclass, =Lepo-
    spondyli)
urogallus (Tetrao)
Urolophidae Myliobatoidea
  Urolophus
Urolophus Urolophidae
  halleri Fitch 1964
Uronemidae Cténodontiformes Lehman
    1966C
  Nielsenia
Uropsilinae Talpidae
Urotrichini Talpinae Van Valen 1967B
Ursidae Canoidea Ginsburg 1966 (classi-
    fication; incl. Amphicyon-
    inae); Starck 1964
  Arctodus, Indarctos, Spelaearctos,
    Tremarctos, Ursus
ursidens (Anacodon)
ursinus (Papio)
ursulus (Megalocnus)
Ursus Ursidae Alekseeva, L. I. 1966;
    Lomi 1963; Vekua 1958B
  americanus Frankforter 1966; Greer
    1963, 1964
  arctos Bakalov and Nikolov 1964;
    Dal' 1954*; David, A. and
    Markevich 1967; Ehrenberg
    1965A, 1966D; Erdbrink
    1964, 1967A; Koby 1964A,
    C; Krysiak 1956; Kurtén
    1965A; Ruprecht 1965;
    Sukachev, et al. 1966;
    Tsalkin 1962
  bingadensis Vereshchagin 1951C
  horribilis Anderson, E. 1968;
    Peterson, R. L. 1965; Tovell
    and Deane 1966

priscus Mottl 1964; Musil 1964
  deningeri Thenius 1965B
  etruscus Crusafont Pairó 1959D
  horribilis Green, M. 1962D
  maritimus Kurtén 1964A
    tyrannus Kurtén 1964A
  minimus Berzi 1966 (skel.)
  spelaeus Andrist, et al. 1964; Bachmayer
      and Zapfe 1960B; Bakalov
      and Nikolov 1964; Balliot
      1959; Brandt 1967; Daumao
      and Laudet 1968; Ehrenberg
      1961B, 1962D, F, 1964A,
      B, 1966D; Ehrenberg and
      Mais 1967; Erdbrink 1967A;
      Gross, H. 1965; Koby 1964A,
      B, C; Koby and Bröckelmann
      1967; Koby and Scheidegger
      1964; Mais 1962B; Malez
      1957C, 1963D, 1965C, D, I;
      Ostromecki 1967; Paraske-
      vaidis 1961; Rakovec 1965B;
      Terzea 1966; Wiszniowska
      1967; Zapfe 1964D (reconst.),
      1966A
  deningeroides Mottl 1964
  thibetanus
    kokeni Chow, M.-c., Hu and Lee
        1965
Urtinotherium Hyracodontidae Radinsky
    1967B
urvanteevi (Angeraspis)
Ustatochoerus Merycoidodontidae
  major Schultz, C. B. and Falkenbach
      1968
  profectus
    nevadensis Schultz, C. B. and Fal-
        kenbach 1968 (geog. ssp.)
utahensis (Allocryptaspis)
uwatokoi (Manchurichthys)
uxoris (Tchadanthropus)

vagabundus (Morus)
"vaillanti" (Adelomys)
valenciennesi (Amia, Dipterus)
valensis (Peromyscus)
valentinensis (Bufo)
validus (Mosasaurus, Sparodus)
vallesensis (Schizochoerus)
vallesiensis (Muscardinus)
valliensis (Cervus philisi)
vancleveae (Didymictis)
vandebroeki (Dormaalius)
vanderpooli (Otionohyus)
vaningeni (Vernonaspis)
vanvaleni (Protictis)

Vieraella Salientia incertae sedis
  herbstii Casamiquela 1965D
Vieraellidae Amphicoela Kuhn, Oskar
  1965E (ascribed to Hecht
  1963)
vigoratus (Longirostromeryx)
Villanyia Cricetidae
  hungaricus Topachevskii 1965C (cf.)
vincei (Proexaeretodon)
vincenti (Heterodontus, Isurus)
vinceus ("Halmaturus")
Vinciguerria Gonostomatidae Weitzman
  1967
  obscura Dzhafarova 1964
vindobonensis (Dorcatherium, Pliopithecus)
vinetorum (Nyctereuctes)
vinogradovi (Hystrix, Sicista)
Viperidae Colubroidea Holman 1966C
  Crotalus
Vireonidae Passeres
  Lawrencia
vireti (Angustidens, Cynelos rugosidens,
  Equus stenonis, Euclado-
  ceros senezensis, Heteroxerus, Megaderma, Muscardinus, Parapodemus, Plesictis)
virginianus (Odocoileus)
viridescens (Diemictylus)
viridiflavus (Coluber)
viridis (Bufo, Lacerta)
visenoviensis (Titanomys)
vishnu ("Halmaturus")
Viverra Viverridae
  leakeyi Petter, G. 1964A
Viverravinae Miacidae
Viverravus Miacidae
  gracilis Guthrie, D. A. 1967B; Robinson, Peter 1966A
  lutosus Guthrie, D. A. 1967B
  sicarius Robinson, Peter 1966A
Viverridae Feloidea Petter, G. 1965
  Herpestes, Herpestides, Kichechia,
  Mungos, Pseudocivetta,
  Semigenetta, Viverra
  Herpestinae
viverrinus (Prototomus)
vjuschkovi (Moschowhaitsia)
voigtstedtensis (Bison schoetensacki, Elephas meridionalis, Petauria)
voinovi (Clupea)
voithi (Leptolepis)
Volantes [all flying birds] Aves Dement'ev
  1964
vorax (Didelphodon)

Vorhisia Vorhisiidae Frizzell 1965A (otolith)
  vulpes Frizzell 1965A
Vorhisiidae ?Siluroidei Frizzell 1965A
  Vorhisia
Vormela Mustelidae
  peregusna Dal' 1954*; Kurtén 1965A;
  Vereshchagin 1951C
vortmani (Phenacodus, Protospermophilus)
vukotinovici (Clupea)
vulgaris (Bufo, Sciurus, Sturnus)
Vulpavus Miacidae
  asius Robinson, Peter 1966A
  canavus Guthrie, D. A. 1967B
vulpecula (Prototomus)
Vulpes Canidae Alekseeva, L. I. 1966;
  Mostecký 1964
  corsae Vereshchagin 1951C
  odessana Odintsov 1967
  praecorsac Odintsov 1965
  velox Anderson, E. 1968
  vulpes Anderson, E. 1968; David, A.
  and Markevich 1967; Feustel,
  et al. 1963; Jacobshagen
  1963; Koby 1964A, C;
  Kurtén 1965A; Lomi 1963;
  Malez 1963D; Rakovec 1965B;
  Tsalkin 1962; Zapfe 1966B
  alpherakyi Vereshchagin 1951C
  (aff.)
vulpes (Albula, Vorhisia, Vulpes)
vulpina (Elaphe)
vulpinos (Alopias, Hyaenodon)
Vulturidae Neocathartoidea
  Coragyps, Plesiocathartes
  Teratornithinae

Wadeichthys Archaeomaenidae Waldman
  1967 (nomen nudum)
  oxyops Waldman 1967 (nomen nudum)
wadiai (Rhinesuchus)
wadleyi (Austropelor)
Waggoneriidae Seymouriamorpha Tatarinov,
  L. P. 1964J
Wagneria Hyaenidae Meladze 1967 (for
  Ictitherium orbignyi)
walbeckensis (Mentoclaenodon, Plesiadapis)
walchi (Kouphichnium)
walcottianus (Hyopsodus)
Wallabia Macropodidae Tedford 1967B
wallacei (Oreolagus)
wallacii (Cardipeltis)
walshi (Mentzichthys)
waltergrossi (Psammosteus)
walteri (Strunius)
wangi (Lycoptera)

Woodromys Ctenodactylidae Shevyreva
    1968B (nomen nudum)
  chelkaris Shevyreva 1968B
Woodwardella Scombridae Casier 1966A
  patellifrons Casier 1966A
woodwardi (Coccolepis, Lycoptera,
    Magnosaurus, Urocles)
Woodwardosteus Coccosteidae
  spatulatus Miles, R. S. 1966B
wortmani (Dayohyus, Hyopsodus,
    Oxyaenodon, Trigonostylops)
woutersi (Landenoden)
wrightae (Neldasaurus)
wuchangensis (Sincanthus)
wuchingensis (Nanhsiungensis)
Wudinolepidae Asterolepidiformes Chang,
    K.-j. 1965
  Wudinolepis
Wudinolepis Wudinolepidae Chang, K.-j.
    1965
  weni Chang, K.-j. 1965
wufengensis (Gomphoterium)
wurmi (Panthera leo)
wüsti (Elephas, Mammuthus)
wutuensis (Homogalax)
wymani (Hylonomus)
Wynyardia Wynyardiidae
  bassiana Ride 1964B
Wynyardiidae Diprotodonta Ride
    1964B
  Wynyardia
wyomingensis (Miospermophilus, Mytono-
    lagus, Oligodontosaurus,
    Parasaniwa, Uranolophus)

xanthognathus (Microtus)
xanthoprymnus (Citellus)
Xantusioidea Scincomorpha Tatarinov,
    L. P. 1964W
Xenacanthi Elasmobranchii
Xencanthidae Xenacanthiformes
  Xenacanthus
Xenacanthiformes Xenacanthi
Xenacanthus Xenacanthidae Olson, E.
    1965D
  decheni Zídek 1966
Xenarthra Edentata
Xenocephalus Bovidae Leakey, L. S. B.
    1965
  robustus Leakey, L. S. B. 1965
Xenocongridae Anguilloidei
  Paranguilla
Xenodelphis Didelphidae Paula Couto
    1962B
  doelloi Paula Couto 1962B

Xenodolamia Hexanchidae Casier 1966A
    (in Notidanidae)
  eocaena Casier 1966A
Xenopus Pipidae Vergnaud-Grazzini
    1966
Xenosauridae Anguioidea
  Exostinus
Xenosuchus Crocodylidae Langston 1965B
    (syn. of Caiman)
Xenungulata Paenungulata
Xeroscapanus Scapanus Hutchison 1968A
Xerus Sciuridae Thaler 1966B
xestes (Acrocheilus)
xiehuensis (Lantianus)
Xiphactinus Chirocentridae Cavender
    1966B
  audax Bardack 1965A, 1968A
  australis Bardack 1965A
  gaultinus Bardack 1965A
  mantelli Bardack 1965A
Xiphiidae Xiphioidea
  Acestrus, Aglyptorhynchus, Xiphio-
    rhincus
Xiphioidea Scombroidei
Xiphiorhynchus Xiphiidae
  parvus Casier 1966A
  priscus Casier 1966A
Xiphodon Xiphodontidae Dechaseaux
    1963C, 1967A; Friant 1962D
Xiphodontidae Tylopoda
  Dichodon, Haplomeryx, Pseudoamphi-
    meryx, Xiphodon
Xylacanthus Ischnacanthidae Ørvig 1967C
  grandis Ørvig 1967C

Yabeinosaurus Ardeosauridae Endo and
    Shikama 1942B* (in Yabeino-
    sauridae)
  tenuis Endo and Shikama 1942B*;
    Hoffstetter 1964D
  youngi Hoffstetter 1964D
yagouaroundi (Felis)
yangaensis (Anacorax)
yaushinovi (Doliosauriscus)
yavorskyi (Holuropsis)
yepomerae (Wasonaka)
yini (Lukousaurus)
yoderensis (Pseudochrysochloris)
Yoderimys Eomyidae
  burkei Black, C. C. 1965A
Yoglinia Drepanaspididae
  bergi Tarlo 1965
youngi (Agispelagus, Lunania, Lystrosaurus,
    Yabeinosaurus)
Younginidae Eosuchia
  Mesenosaurus

SYNOPSIS OF CLASSIFICATION

SYNOPSIS OF CLASSIFICATION

Consult the Systematic Index for citations to literature, also for names of subfamilies, tribes, subtribes, genera, subgenera and lower categories.

Kingdom ANIMALIA

Subkingdom METAZOA

Incertae sedis: CONODONTI (conodonts)

Phylum CHORDATA

Subphylum CALCICHORDATA

Subphylum ACRANIA

Subphylum CRANIATA (= Vertebrata)

Incertae sedis: NEURODONTIFORMES
(problematical craniates, doubtfully
including Archeognathus)

Ichnites (tracks, trackways, trails, burrows, finger prints)
Oölithes (eggs, egg shells, egg capsules)

Superclass AGNATHA
Class OSTRACODERMI
Subclass CEPHALASPIDOMORPHA
Superorder OSTEOSTRACI
Incertae sedis: Escuminaspis
Order Orthobranchiata
Benneviaspididae, Boreaspididae, Hirelidae, Hoelaspididae, Kiaeraspi-
didae, Mimetaspididae
Order Oligobranchiata
Suborder Zenaspida
Procephalaspididae, Zenaspididae
Suborder Aceraspida
Superfamily Aceraspidoidea
Aceraspididae, Pattenaspididae, Hemicyclaspididae
Superfamily Didymaspidoidea
Didymaspididae
Superfamily Tremataspidoidea
Dartmuthiidae, Oeselaspididae, Saaremaaspididae, Tannuaspididae,
Thyestidae, Tremataspididae
Order Nectaspidiformes
Nectaspididae
Superorder ANASPIDA
Order Anaspidiformes
Birkeniidae, Endeiolepididae, Euphaneropidae, Lasaniidae,
Pharyngolepididae, Pterolepididae, Rhyncholepididae
Suborder Euphanerida
Jamoytiidae

1091

Superorder GALEASPIDA
 Order Galeaspidiformes
  Galeaspidae
Subclass PTERASPIDOMORPHA (= Heterostraci)
  Incertae sedis: Gunaspis, Sanidaspis
 Order Pteraspidiformes
  Suborder Astraspida (incertae sedis)
   Astraspididae, Eriptychiidae (= Eriptychida)
  Suborder Obrucheviida
   Obrucheviidae
  Suborder Drepanaspida
   Drepanaspididae, Guerichosteidae, Pycnosteidae, Turiniidae,
    Weigeltaspididae
   Incertae sedis: Psephaspis
  Suborder Traquairaspida
   Traquairaspididae
  Suborder Pteraspida
   Doryaspididae, Pteraspididae
  Suborder Corvaspida
   Corvaspididae
  Suborder Amphiaspida
   Amphiaspididae
  Suborder Hibernaspidida
   Eglonaspididae
 Order Cyathaspidiformes
  Suborder Cyathaspida
   Cyathaspididae
  Suborder Cardipeltida
   Cardipeltidae
  Suborder Ctenaspida
   Ctenaspididae
  Suborder Paraspidida
   Poraspididae
  Suborder Olbiaspida
   Olbiaspididae
 Order Polybranchiaspiformes
  Polybranchiaspidae
Subclass THELODONTI
 Order Thelodontida (= Coelolepidiformes)
  Palaeodontidae, Thelodontidae (= Coelolepididae)
 Order Phlebolepida
  Phlebolepididae
Class CYCLOSTOMI
 Order Petromyzontiformes
  Petromyzontidae
 Order Myxiniformes
  Bdellostomatidae, Myxinidae
Superclass PISCES
  Ichthyodorulites (spines of fishes)
  Otolithus (ear stones of fishes)
Class PLACODERMI (= Aphetohyoidea)
 Subclass PTERICHTHYES (= Antiarchi)
  Order Remigolepidiformes
   Remigolepididae
  Order Asterolepidiformes

Asterolepididae, Bothriolepididae, Groenlandaspididae, Gross-
aspididae, Pterichthyodidae, Wudinolepidae
Subclass COCCOSTEI
Infraclass EUARTHRODIRA (= Arthrodira)
Incertae sedis: <u>Bungartius</u>, <u>Grazosteus</u>, <u>Tafilalichthys</u>
Order Arctolepidiformes (= Acanthaspida = Eolichothoraci)
Actinolepididae, Arctolepididae, Kujdanowiaspididae, Phlyctaen-
aspididae, Williamaspididae
Incertae sedis: <u>Wheathillaspis</u>
Order Coccosteiformes (= Brachythoraci)
Brachydeiridae, Braunosteidae, Buchanosteidae, Coccosteidae,
Dunkleosteidae, Erromenosteidae, Euleptaspididae, Hadros-
teidae , Holonemidae, Homostiidae, Hussakofiidae, Ichthyo-
sauroididae (= Teterostiidae), Leiosteidae, Leptosteidae,
Millerosteidae, Pachyosteidae, Pholidosteidae, Rhachiosteidae,
Rhinosteidae, Selenosteidae, Synaucheniidae, Taemasosteidae,
Titanichthyidae, Trematosteidae
Incertae sedis: <u>Malerosteus</u>, <u>Operchallosteus</u>, <u>Tomaiosteus</u>
Order Mylostomatiformes
Mylostomatidae
Order Ptyctodontiformes
Ptyctodontidae
Infraclass PHYLLOLEPIDA
Order Phyllolepidiformes
Phyllolepididae
Infraclass MACROPETALICHTHYES (= Anarthrodira)
Incertae sedis: <u>Ellopetalichthys</u>
Order Rhadotinida
Rhadotinidae
Order Macropetalichthyiformes (= Petalichthyida)
Macropetalichthyidae
Order Stensiöelliformes
Stensiöellidae, and doubtfully: Cratoselachidae (= Stegoselachii)
Subclass GEMUENDINIA
Order Gemuendiniformes (= Rhenanida, = Palaeacanthaspidiformes, = Acan-
thoraci)
Gemuendinidae (= Asterosteidae), Kolymaspididae, Palaeacanthas-
pididae
Order Jagoriniformes
Jagorinidae
Class ELASMOBRANCHII (= Chondrichthyes)
Incertae sedis: Polyacrodontidae
Subclass XENACANTHI (= Pleuracanthodii)
Order Xenacanthiformes
Xenacanthidae (= Pleuracanthidae)
Subclass CLADOSELACHII (= Pleuropterygii)
Order Cladoselachiformes
Cladoselachidae, Coronodontidae
Order Cladodontiformes
Cladodontidae, Tamiobatidae
Subclass SELACHII (= Euselachii, = Plagiostomi)
Superorder SELACHOIDII (= Pleurotremata)
Order Heterodontiformes
Suborder Ctenacanthoidei
Ctenacanthidae

Suborder Heterodontoidei (= Centracoidei, = Protoselachii)
Heterodontidae (= Centracionidae), Hybodonti-
dae, Palaeospinacidae, Tristychiidae
Order Hexanchiformes (= Notidanoidei)
Chlamydoselachidae, Hexanchidae (= Hexeptranchidae, = Noti-
danidae)
Order Isuriformes
Suborder Isuroidea
Carchariidae (= Mitsukurinidae, = Odontaspidae, = Scapano-
rhynchidae), Eugaleidae, Isuridae (= Cetorhinidae, = Halsydri-
dae, = Lamnidae), Orectolobidae (= Ginglymostomatidae,
= Hemiscylliidae, = Protospinachidae), Rhinocodontidae,
Vulpeculidae (= Alopiidae)
Suborder Catuloidei
Carcharhinidae (= Eulamiidae, = Galeolamnidae), Catulidae
(= Atelomycteridae, = Halaeluridae, = Scyliorhinidae, =
Scyllidae), Cestraciontidae (= Sphyrnidae)
Order Squaliformes (= Tectospondyli)
Suborder Squaloidei
Pristiophoridae, Squalidae (= Dalatiidae, = Scymnorhinidae,
= Spinacidae)
Suborder Rhinoidei
Rhinidae (= Squatinidae)
Superorder BATOIDII
Order Rajiformes
Suborder Rhinobatoidei
Pristidae, Rhinobatidae
Suborder Rajioidei
Rajidae
Suborder Dasyatoidei
Dasyatidae (= Trygonidae), Mobulidae, Myliobatidae, Ptycho-
dontidae
Order Narcacioniformes (= Torpediniformes)
Narcacionidae (= Torpedinidae)
Subclass HOLOCEPHALI (= Bradyodonti)
Incertae sedis: Pseudodontichthyidae
Superorder CHONDRENCHELYES
Order Chondrenchelyiformes
Chondrenchelyidae
Superorder CHIMAERAE
Incertae sedis: Chimaeropsidae, Copodontidae, Deltoptychidae, Helo-
dontidae, Psammodontidae, Radamantidae
Order Chimaeriformes
Acanthorhinidae, Calorhynchidae, Chimaeridae, Cochliodontidae,
Edestidae, Helicoprionidae, Menaspididae, Myriacanthidae,
Rhinochimaeridae, Squalorajidae
Superorder PETALODONTES
Order Petalodontiformes
Petalodontidae
Class TELEOSTOMI (= Osteichthyes)
Subclass ACANTHODII
Order Diplacanthiformes
Diplacanthidae
Order Climatiformes
Climatiidae, Euthacanthidae, Parexidae

Order Mesacanthiformes
    Mesacanthidae
Order Ischnacanthiformes
    Ischnacanthidae
Order Gyracanthiformes
    Gyracanthidae
Order Cheiracanthiformes
    Cheiracanthidae
Order Acanthodiformes
    Acanthodidae, Protodontidae
Subclass SARCOPTERYGII
    Incertae sedis: Panderichthys, Platycephalichthys
Infraclass DIPNOI
    Incertae sedis: Griphognathus, Paraceratodus
Superorder DIPTERI
Order Dipteriformes
    Dipnorhynchidae, Dipteridae
Order Rhynchodipteriformes
    Rhynchodipteridae
Order Phaneropleuriformes
    Fleurantiidae, Phaneropleuridae, Scaumenacidae
Order Uronemiformes
    Conchopomidae, Uronemidae
Order Ctenodontiformes
    Incertae sedis: Nielsenia
    Ctenodontidae
Order Soederberghiiformes
Superorder CERATODONTI
Order Ceratodontiformes
    Ceratodontidae
Order Lepidosireniformes
    Lepidosirenidae, Protopteridae
Infraclass CROSSOPTERYGII
Superorder RHIPIDISTIA (= Osteolepides)
Order Porolepidiformes
    Holoptychiidae, Porolepididae
Order Osteolepidiformes
    Megalichthyidae (= Ectosteorhachidae, = Parabatrachidae),
        Osteolepididae (= Glyptopomidae), Rhizodontidae (= Rhizo-
        dopseidae)
Superorder COELACANTHI (= Actinistia)
Order Coelacanthiformes
    Coelacanthidae (incl. Diplocercidae, Latimeriidae, and Laugiidae)
Order Struniiformes
    Onychodontidae, Struniidae
Subclass ACTINOPTERYGI
    Incertae sedis: ?Aphelolepis
Infraclass POLYPTEREI
Order Polypteriformes
    Polypteridae
Infraclass CHONDROSTEI
Order Terrasiiformes
    Terrasiidae
Order Palaeonisciformes
    Suborder Palaeoniscoidei

Aeduellidae, Amphicentridae, Atherstoniidae, Birgeriidae,
Boreosomidae, Brachydegmidae, Centrolepididae, Cheiro-
lepididae, Coccocephalichthyidae, Coccolepididae, Com-
mentryidae, Cornuboniscidae, Cosmolepididae, Cosmo-
ptychiidae, Dicellopygidae, Elonichthyidae, Gonatodidae,
Gyrolepidotidae, Holuridae, Lawniidae, Osorioichthyidae,
Palaeoniscidae, Paramblypteridae, Pygopteridae, Rhabdo-
lepidae, Stegotrachelidae, Thrissonotidae (= Oxygnathidae),
Urosthenidae
    Suborder Uropterygina
        Uropterygidae
  Order Gymnonisciformes
        Gymnoniscidae
  Order Luganoiiformes
        Luganoiidae
  Order Phanerorhynchiformes
        Phanerorhynchidae
  Order Dorypteriformes
        Dorypteridae
  Order Bobasatraniiformes
        Bobasatraniidae
  Order Redfieldiiformes (= Catopteriformes)
        Redfieldiidae (= Catopteridae, = Dictyopygidae)
  Order Perleidiformes
        Cleithrolepididae, Haplolepididae, Perleididae
  Order Pholidopleuriformes
        Habroichthyidae, Peltopleuridae, Pholidopleuridae
  Order Platysaigiformes
        Platysiagidae
  Order Cephaloxeniformes
        Cephaloxenidae
  Order Ospiiformes
        Ospiidae, Parasemionotidae, Tungusichthyidae
  Order Aetheodontiformes
        Aetheodontidae
  Order Ptycholepidiformes
        Ptycholepididae
  Order Saurichthyiformes
        Saurichthyidae (= Belonorhynchidae)
  Order Acipenseriformes
        Acipenseridae, Chondrosteidae, Peipiaosteidae, Polyodontidae
Infraclass HOLOSTEI
  Incertae sedis: Peltopleurus
  Order Amiiformes
        Amiidae, Furidae (= Eugnathidae, = Caturidae), Macrosemiidae,
        Pachycormidae, Pycnodontidae, Semionotidae
  Order Lepisosteiformes (= Ginglymodi, =Rhomboganoidei)
        Lepisosteidae
Infraclass HALECOSTOMI
  Incertae sedis: Ligulellidae
  Order Aspidorhynchiformes
        Aspidorhynchidae
  Order Pholidophoriformes
        Archaeomenidae, Ichthyokentemidae, Oligopleuridae, Pholido-
        phoridae, Pleuropholidae

Order Leptolepidiformes
    ?Anaethalionidae, Leptolepididae
Infraclass TELEOSTEI
    Incertae sedis: <u>Imboffius</u>
  Superorder ISOSPONDYLI (= Malacopterygii, = Thrissomorphi)
    Incertae sedis: Denticipitidae
  Order Clupeiformes
    Suborder Lycopteroidei
      Lycopteridae
    Suborder Clupeoidei
      Superfamily Clupeoidea
        Clupavidae, Clupeidae, Engraulidae, Pterothrissidae, Syllaemidae
      Superfamily Elopoidea
        Albulidae, Elopidae, Protelopidae, Pterothrissidae
      Superfamily Alepocephaloidea
        Alepocephalidae
    Suborder Cheirocentroidei
      Chirocentridae, Ichthyodectidae
    Suborder Saurodontoidei
      Saurodontidae
    Suborder Chanoidei
      Chanidae, Kneriidae, Phractolaemidae
    Suborder Cromerioidei
      Cromeriidae
    Suborder Salmonoidei
      Cyclolepididae, Haplochitonidae, Osmeridae, Plecoglossidae,
        Retropinnidae, Salangidae, Salmonidae, Thaumaturidae,
        Thymallidae
    Suborder Esocoidei (= Haplomi)
      Dalliidae, Esocidae, Palaeoesocidae, Umbridae
    Suborder Bathylaconoidei
      Bathylaconidae
    Suborder Stomiatoidei
      Incertae sedis: Tomognathidae
      Superfamily Gonostomatoidea
        Gonostomatidae, Sternoptychidae
      Superfamily Stomiatoidea
        Chauliodontidae, Stomiatidae
      Superfamily Astronesthoidea
        Astronesthidae, Idiacanthidae, Melanostomiatidae, Protostomiatidae
    Suborder Opisthoproctoidei
      Argentinidae, Bathylagidae, Macropinnidae, Microstomatidae,
        Opisthoproctidae
    Suborder Miripinnatoidei
      Miripinnidae, Taeniophoridae
    Suborder Gonorhynchoidei
      Gonorhynchidae
    Suborder Notopteroidei
      Hyodontidae, Notopteridae
    Suborder Osteoglossoidei
      Superfamily Plethodoidea
        Plethodidae
      Superfamily Osteoglossoidea
        Arampaimidae, Heterotidae, Osteoglossidae, Singididae
      Superfamily Pantodontoidea
        Pantodontidae

Suborder Alepisauroidei
Alepisauridae, Anotopteridae, Enchodontidae, Polymerichthyidae
Suborder Alepocephaloidei
Alepocephalidae
Order Bathyclupeiformes
Bathyclupeidae, Ctenothrissidae
Order Galaxiiformes
Aplochitomidae, Galaxiidae
Superorder OSTARIOPHYSI
Order Cypriniformes
Suborder Cyprinoidei
Superfamily Characinoidea
Anostomatidae, Characinidae, Citharinidae, Erythrinolepididae,
Gasteropelecidae, Hemiodontidae, Xiphostomatidae
Superfamily Gymnotoidea
Electrophoridae, Gymnotidae, Rhamphicthyidae, Sternarchidae
Superfamily Cyprinoidea
Catostomatidae, Cobitidae, Cyprinidae, Gyrinocheilidae, Homalo-
pteridae
Suborder Siluroidei
Ageniosidae, Akysidae, Amblycipitidae, Amiuridae, Amphiliidae,
Ariidae, Auchenipteridae, Bagridae, Bunocephalidae, Callich-
thyidae   , Chacidae, Clariidae, Doiichthyidae, Doradidae,
Helogenidae, Hypophthalmidae, Loricariidae, Malapteruridae,
Mochocidae, (= Synodontidae), Olyridae, Pimelodidae, Ploto-
sidae, Saccobranchidae, Schilbeidae, Siluridae, Sisoridae,
Trichomycteridae, ?Vorhisiidae
Suborder Anguillavoidei
Anguillavidae
Suborder Anguilloidei
Anguillidae, Congridae, Derichthyidae, Dysommidae, Echelidae
(= Myridae), Heterenchelyidae, Hypophidae, Moringuidae,
Muraenidae, Muraenesocidae, Mylomyridae, Myrocongridae,
Neenchelyidae, ?Nessorhamphidae, Nettastomatidae, Ophich-
thyidae   , Parachelidae, Simenchelyidae, Synaphobranchidae,
?Urenchelyidae, Xenocongridae
Suborder Nemichthyoidei
Avocettinopidae, Cyemidae, Nemichthyidae, Serrivomeridae
Order Synbrachiformes
Suborder Alabetoidei
Alabetidae
Suborder Synbranchoidei
Amphipnoidae, Synbranchidae
Superorder HETEROMI
Order Halosauriformes
Halosauridae
Order Notacanthiformes
Lipogenyidae, Notacanthidae
Superorder MESICHTHYES
Order Beloniformes (= Synentognathi)
Belonidae, Scomberesocidae, Tselfatiidae
Order Myctophiformes (= Iniomi, = Scopeliformes)
Aulopidae, ?Beerichthyidae, Cetomimidae, Chirothricidae,
Dercetidae (= Stratodontidae), Evermannellidae, Myctophidae,
Osmosudidae, Scopelarchidae, Sudidae, Synodontidae

Order Ateleopodiformes
    Ateleopodidae
Order Giganturiformes
    Giganturidae
Order Saccopharyngiformes
    Eurypharyngidae, Monognathidae, Saccopharyngidae
Order Mormyriformes
  Suborder Mormyroidei
    Gymnarchidae, Mormyridae
  Suborder Exocoetoidei
    Exocoetidae, Hemirhamphidae
Order Gadiformes
    Bregmacerotidae, Gadidae, Macrouroididae, Macruridae, Moridae, Muraenolepididae
Order Gasterosteiformes (= Thoracostei)
    Aulorhynchidae, Gasterosteidae, Indostomatidae, Protosyngnathidae
Order Syngnathiformes
  Suborder Syngnathoidei (= Lophobranchii)
    Solenostomatidae, Syngnathidae
  Suborder Aulostomatoidei
    Superfamily Aulostomatoidea
      Aulostomatidae, Fistulariidae
    Superfamily Centriscoidea (= Solenichthyes)
      Centriscidae, Macrorhamphoseidae
Order Tetraodontiformes (= Orbiculati, = Plectognathi)
    Incertae sedis: Eotrigonodontidae, Trigonodontidae
  Suborder Triodontoidei
    Triodontidae
  Suborder Ostracionoidei
    Ostracionidae
  Suborder Tetraodontoidei
    Diodontidae, Eodiodontidae, Tetraodontidae
  Suborder Moloidei
    Molidae
Order Cyprinodontiformes
  Suborder Amblyopsoidei
    Amblyopsidae
  Suborder Cyprinodontoidei
    Superfamily Cyprinodontoidea
      Adrianichthyidae, Cyprinodontidae
    Superfamily Poecilioidea
      Anablepidae, Goodeidae, Horaichthyidae, Jenynsiidae, Poeciliidae
Order Phallostethiformes
    Neostethidae, Phallostethidae
Order Percopsiformes
    Aphredoderidae, Percopseidae
Order Stephanoberyciformes
    Melamphaidae, Rondeletiidae, Stephanoberycidae
Superorder ACANTHOPTERYGII
  Order Beryciformes
    Anomalopidae, Berycidae, Caristidae, Caulolepididae, Dinopterygidae, Diretmidae, Gibberichthyidae, Korsogasteridae, Melamphaidae, Monocentridae, Ostracoberycidae
  Suborder Berycoidei
    Holocentridae, Trachichthyidae

Order Ctenothrissiformes
    Aulolepidae, Ctenothrissidae
  Suborder Polymixioidei
    Polymixiidae, Sphenocephalidae
  Suborder Dinopterygoidei
    Aipichthyidae, Dinopterygidae, Pharmacichthyidae,
      Pycnosteroididae
Order Zeiformes
    Caproidae, Grammicolepididae, Palaeocentrotidae, Zeidae
Order Mugiliformes
  Suborder Mugiloidei
    Atherinidae, Mugilidae
  Suborder Sphyraenoidei
    Sphyraenidae
Order Polynemiformes
    Polynemidae
Order Perciformes
    Incertae sedis: Ophioclinidae, Schinleriidae, <u>Tungtingichthys</u>
  Suborder Percoidei
    Incertae sedis: Oxudercidae
    Superfamily Percoidea
      Acanthoclinidae, Acropomidae, Amphistiidae, Apogonidae,
        Arripidae, Banjosidae, Bramidae, Carangidae, Centrarchidae,
        Centropomidae, Cichlidae, Chaetodontidae, Coryphaenidae,
        Dichistiidae, Drepanidae, Emmelichthyidae, Enoplosidae,
        Ephippidae, Formionidae, Girellidae, Glaucosomatidae,
        Histiopteridae, Hoplegnathidae, Inermiidae, Ioscionidae,
        Kuhliidae, Kyphosidae (= Cyphosidae), Labracoglossidae,
        Lactariidae, Latilidae, Lethrinidae, Lobotidae, Lutianidae,
        Maenidae, Malacanthidae, Menidae, Mullidae, Nandidae,
        Nematistiidae, Nemipteridae, Pempheridae, Percidae, Plesio-
        pidae, Polycentridae, Pomadasyidae, Priacanthidae, Pristo-
        lepididae, Psettidae, Pseudoplesiolepididae, Rachycentridae,
        Scatophagidae, Sciaenidae, Scombropidae, Scorpidae, Ser-
        ranidae, Sillaganidae, Sparidae, Theraponidae, Toxotidae
    Superfamily Cepoloidea
      Cepolidae
    Superfamily Labroidea
      Embiotocidae, Labridae, Odacidae, Pomacentridae, Scaridae
    Superfamily Gadopseoidea
      Gadopseidae
    Superfamily Cirrhitoidea
      Chilodactylidae, Chironemidae, Cirrhitidae, Naplodactylidae,
        Latridae
    Superfamily Tricodontoidea
      Trichodontidae
    Superfamily Trachinoidea
      Bathymasteridae, Bembropidae, Creediidae, Chlamarrichthyidae,
        Dactyloscopidae, Hemerocoetidae, Leptoscopidae, Limnichthyi-
        dae, Mugiloididae, Opisthognathidae, Owstoniidae, Percophidae,
        Trachinidae, Trichonotidae, Uranoscopidae, Zaproridae
    Superfamily Champsodontoidea
      Champsodontidae
    Superfamily Chiasmodontoidea
      Chiasmodontidae

Superfamily Notothenioidea
 Bathydraconidae, Bovichthyidae, Chaenichthyidae, Nototheniidae
Suborder Blennioidei
 Anarhichadidae, Blenniidae, Clinidae, Congrogadidae, Derepodich-
 thyidae, Lumpenidae, Lycodapodidae, Microdesmidae, Noto-
 graptidae, Ophioclinidae, Peronedyidae, Pholidae, Ptilichthyi-
 dae, Scytalinidae, Stichaeidae, Xenocephalidae, Xiphisteridae,
 Zoarcidae
Suborder Ophidioidei
 Superfamily Ophidioidea
  Brotulidae, Ophidiidae
 Superfamily Fierasferoidea
  Fierasferidae
Suborder Ammodytoidei
 Ammodytidae
Suborder Callionymoidei
 Callionymidae, Draconettidae
Suborder Siganoidei
 Siganidae
Suborder Acanthuroidei
 Acanthuridae, Zanclidae
Suborder Balistoidei
 Balistidae, Spinacanthidae, Triacanthidae
Suborder Trichiuroidei
 Gempylidae, Trichiuridae
Suborder Scombroidei
 Superfamily Scombroidea
  Cybiidae, Euzaphlegidae, Scombridae, Thunnidae
 Superfamily Xiphioidea
  Blochiidae, Histiophoridae, Makairidae, Palaeorhynchidae,
  Xiphiidae, Xiphiorhynchidae
Suborder Luvaroidei
 Luvaridae
Suborder Stromateoidei
 Nomeidae, Stromateidae, Tetragonuridae
Suborder Anabantoidei
 Anabantidae, Luciocephalidae
Suborder Kurtoidei
 Kurtidae
Suborder Rhamphosoidei
 Rhamphosidae
Suborder Ophicephaloidei
 Ophicephalidae
Suborder Gobioidei
 Incertae sedis: Kraemeriidae
 Superfamily Eleotroidea
  Eleotridae
 Superfamily Gobioidea
  Gobiidae, Periophthalmidae, Pirskeniidae
Suborder Cottoidei
 Superfamily Scorpaenoidea
  Anoplopomidae, Aploactidae, Caracanthidae, Congiopodidae,
  Hexagrammidae, Pataecidae, Platycephalidae, Scorpaenidae,
  Synancejeidae, Triglidae
 Superfamily Cottoidea

Agonidae, Comephoridae, Cottidae, Cottocomephoridae,
     Cottunculidae, Cyclopteridae, Icelidae, Normanichthyidae,
     Psychrolutidae
Order Dactylopteriformes
     Dactylopteridae
Order Pegasiformes
     Pegasidae
Order Pleuronectiformes
     Suborder Psettodoidei
          Joleaudichthyidae, Psettodidae
     Suborder Pleuronectoidei
          Superfamily Pleuronectoidea
               Bothidae, Pleuronectidae
          Superfamily Soleoidea
               Cynoglossidae, Soleidae
Order Icosteiformes
     Actotidae, Icosteidae
Order Chaudhuriiformes
     Chaudhuriidae
Order Mastacembeliformes
     Mastacembelidae
Order Echeneiformes
     Echeneidae, Opisthomyzonidae
Order Gobiesociformes
     Gobiesocidae
Order Batrachoidiformes
     Batrachoididae
Order Lampridiformes
     Suborder Lampridoidei
          Lamprididae
     Suborder Veliferoidei
          Lophotidae, Veliferidae
     Suborder Trachypteroidei
          Regalecidae, Trachypteridae
     Suborder Styleophoroidei
          Styleophoridae
Order Lophiiformes (= Pediculati)
     Suborder Lophioidei
          Lophiidae
     Suborder Antennarioidei
          Superfamily Antennarioidea
               Antennariidae, Brachionichthyidae, Chaunacidae
          Superfamily Oncocephaloidea
               Oncocephalidae (= Ogcocephalidae)
     Suborder Ceratioidei
          Caulophrynidae, Certiidae, Diceratiidae, Gigantactidae,
               Himantolophidae, Laevoceratiidae, Linophrynidae, Melanoce-
               tidae, Neoceratiidae, Oneirodidae, Photocorynidae
     Incertae sedis: Ischyrotherium
Superclass TETRAPODA
     Class AMPHIBIA
          Incertae sedis: Lasalidae
          Subclass APSIDOSPONDYLI (= Batrachosauria)

Superorder LABYRINTHODONTIA (= Stegocephalia)
    Incertae sedis: Yarengiidae, Erierpeton, Erpetobrachium,
        Otumnisaurus
  Order Temnospondyli
    Suborder Ichthyostegalia
        Acanthostegidae, Ichthyostegidae
    Suborder Elpistostegalia
        Colosteidae, Elpistostegidae, Otocratiidae
    Suborder Rhachitomi (incl. Phyllospondyli)
      Incertae sedis: Platyhystricidae, Platyopidae, Chalcosaurus, Jugosuchus,
        Micrerpeton
      Superfamily Loxommoidea
        Loxommidae
      Superfamily Edopoidea
        Cochleosauridae, Dendrerpetontidae, Edopidae, Zatracheidae
          (= Acanthostomatidae)
      Superfamily Rhytidosteoidea
        Rhytidosteidae
      Superfamily Trimerorhacheoidea
        Dvinosauridae, Peliontidae, Trimerorhacheidae
      Superfamily Micropholoidea
        Archegosauridae, Branciosauridae (= Lysipterygiidae), Micropho-
        lidae, Platyoposauridae
      Superfamily Eryopoidea
        Chenoprosopidae, Dissorophidae (= Amphibamidae, = Miobatrachi-
        dae), Eryopidae, Intasuchidae, Parioxydae, Trematopidae
        (= Achelomidae)
    Suborder Trematosauria
        Trematosauridae
    Suborder Stereospondyli
      Incertae sedis: Latiscopidae, Enosuchidae, Trigonosternum
      Superfamily Rhinesuchoidea
        Lydekkerinidae, Rhinesuchidae, Sclerothoracidae, Uranocentro-
        dontidae
      Superfamily Capitosauroidea
        Benthosuchidae, Capitosauridae, Odontosauridae
      Superfamily Brachyopoidea
        Brachopidae, Metoposauridae
  Order Plagiosauria
    Suborder Plagiosauri
        Plagiosauridae
    Suborder Peltobatrachi
        Peltobatrachidae
  Order Anthracosauria
      Incertae sedis: ?Eosaurus, Neopteroplax, Tupilakosaurus
    Suborder Embolomeri
      Incertae sedis: ?Eosaurus
        Anthracosauridae Cricotidae (= Atopteridae), Eogyrinidae,
        Palaeogyrinidae, Pholidogasteridae
    Suborder Seymouriamorpha (? intermediate between Anthracosauria and
        Diadectomorpha)
      Incertae sedis: Apateonidae, Waggoneriidae, ?Eosauravus, Eusauro-
        pleura, Holodectes, Tuditanus
        Bystrowianidae, Discosauriscidae, Gephyrostegidae, Kotlassiidae,
        Seymouriidae

Order Plesiopoda
  Hesperoherpetonidae
Superorder SALIENTIA (= Anura, = Euanura)
  Incertae sedis: Comobatrachus, Vieraella
Order Proanura (= Proanoura)
  Triadobatrachidae
Order Amphicoela (= Angusticoela)
  Leiopelmidae, Montsechobatrachidae
Order Opisthocoela
  Incertae sedis: ?Eobatrachus, ?Saltenia
  Discoglossidae, Pipidae, Rhinophrynidae
Order Anomocoela
  Pelobatidae, Pelodytidae, Scaphiopodidae
Order Procoela
  Brachycephalidae, Bufonidae, Hylidae, Leptodactylidae, Palaeo-
    batrachidae
Order Diplasiocoela
  Brevicipitidae, Polypedatidae, Ranidae, Rhacophoridae
Subclass LEPOSPONDYLI
  Incertae sedis: Broilisaurus
Order Microsauria (= Adelospondyli, = Micramphibia)
  Incertae sedis: Asaphestera
  Adelogyrinidae, Dolichopareiidae, Gymnarthridae, (= Cardio-
    cephalidae, =Pantylidae, = Pariotichidae), Lysorocephalidae,
    Microbrachidae, Ostodolepididae
Order Aistopoda
  Dolichosomatidae (= Phlegethontidae), Ophiderpetontidae, Palaeo-
    sirenidae, Steenisauridae
Order Nectridia
  Batrachiderpetontidae, Keraterpetontidae, Lepterpetontidae,
    Scincosauridae, Urocordylidae (= Sauropleuridae)
Order Caudata (= Urodela)
  Incertae sedis: Comonecturoides, Hemitrypus, Koaliella
  Suborder Mutabilia
    Superfamily Cryptobranchoidea
      Cryptobranchidae, Hynobiidae
    Superfamily Ambystomatoidea
      Ambystomatidae
    Superfamily Salamandroidea
      Amphiumidae, Plethodontidae, Salamandridae
  Suborder Proteida
    Necturidae, Proteidae
  Suborder Meantes
    Sirenidae
Order Gymnophiona (= Apoda, = Coecilia)
  Coeciliidae, Lysorophidae
Class REPTILIA
  Incertae sedis: Brazilosaurus, Caenagnathiformes, Caenagnathidae,
    Broomia
Subclass ANAPSIDA (= Reptiliomorphoidea)
  Incertae sedis: Bolosaurus, Nothosaurops
Order Cotylosauria
  Incertae sedis: Tseajaiidae
  Suborder Captorhinomorpha
    Incertae sedis: Eosauravus, Fritschia, Hylonomus, Leiocephalikon,
      Petrobates

Superfamily Captorhinoidea (ancestral to Synapsida)
    Captorhinidae, Limnoscelididae, Paracaptorhinidae, Romeriidae
Superfamily Millerettoidea (ancestral to Diapsida)
    ?Mesenosauridae, Millerettidae
Suborder Araeoscelidia
    Araeoscelidae, ? Petrolacosauridae, Trilophosauridae, Variodentidae
Suborder Diadectomorpha
    Superfamily Diadectoidea
        Diadectidae, Korynichniidae
Suborder Procolophomorpha
    Superfamily Procolophonoidea
        Nyctiphruretidae, Pareiasauridae, Procolophonidae, Rhipaeosauridae
    Incertae sedis: Lanthanosuchidae
Order Testudinata (= Chelonia)
    Incertae sedis: Archaeochelydium, Colossoemys, Yümenemys, Gaf-
        sachelys, Notoemys
Suborder Eunotosauria (incertae sedis)
    Eunotosauridae
Suborder Amphichelydia
    Superfamily Triassochelyoidea
        Triassochelyidae (= Proganochelyidae)
    Superfamily Pleurosternoidea
        Apertotemporalidae, Platychelidae, Plesiochelyidae, Pleurostemidae,
            Sinemydidae, Thalassemydidae
    Superfamily Baenoidea
        Baenidae, Eubaenidae, Meiolaniidae, Neurankylidae
Suborder Cryptodira
    Incertae sedis: Nanhsiungchelyidae, Tropidemys
    Superfamily Testudinoidea
        Chelydridae, Dermatemydidae, Kinosternidae, Sakyidae, Testu-
            dinidae
    Superfamily Chelonioidea
        Cheloniidae, Desmatochelyidae, ?Protostegidae, Toxochelyidae
    Superfamily Dermochelyoidea
        Dermochelyidae
    Superfamily Carettochelyoidea
        Carettochelyidae
    Superfamily Trionychoidea
        Trionychidae
Suborder Pleurodira
    Chelyidae, Eusarkiidae, Pelomedusidae
Subclass SYNAPSIDA
    Incertae sedis: Phreatosuchidae
Order Mesosauria (subclass uncertain, = Proganosauria)
    Mesosauridae
Order Pelycosauria
    Suborder Ophiacodontia
        Eothyrididae, Ophiacodontidae, Tetraceratopidae
    Suborder Sphenacodontia
        Ctenosauriscidae, Homodontosauridae, Sphenacodontidae,
            Varanopidae
    Suborder Edaphosauria
        Caseidae, Edaphosauridae, Lupeosauridae, Nitosauridae
Order Theraspida
    Incertae sedis: Protocynodon

Suborder Theriodontia
  Incertae sedis: Biarmosuchidae
  Infraorder Titanosuchia
    Anteosauridae, Brithopodidae, Eotitanosuchidae, Estemmeno-
    suchidae, Jonkeriidae
  Infraorder Gorgonopsia
    Incertae sedis: Aelurognathus, Alopecorhynchus, Alopsauroides,
    Lycaenops, Tetraodontonius
    Aelurosauridae, Aelurosauropsidae, Arctognathidae, Arctog-
    nathoididae, Broomisauridae, ?Burnetiidae, Cynariopidae,
    Galerhinidae, Galesuchidae, Gorgonognathidae, Gorgon-
    opidae, Ictidorhinidae, Inostranceviidae, Pachyrhinidae,
    Pthinosuchidae, Rubiogeidae, Scylacocephalidae, Scyla-
    copidae, Scymnognathidae, Sycosauridae
  Infraorder Cynodontia
    Incertae sedis: Luangwa
    Cynognathidae, Diademodontidae, Gomphodontosuchidae,
    Procynosuchidae, Silphedestidae, Thrinaxodontidae. Incertae
    sedis: Dromatherium
  Infraorder Ictidosauria (composite group)
    Diarthrognathidae (intermediate between reptiles and triconodont
    "mammals"), ? Trithelodontidae, and Tritylodontidae (not
    intermediate between reptiles and multiberculate mammals)
  Infraorder Therocephalia
    Incertae sedis: Cerdops, Cerdosuchoides, Cerdosuchus,
    Proalopecopsis
    Akidnognathidae, Annidae, Euchambersiidae, Pristerognathi-
    dae, Moschorhinidae, Trochosuchidae, Whaitsiidae
  Infraorder Bauriamorpha
    Incertae sedis: Haughtoniscus, Ictidochampsa, Ictidognathus,
    Ictidostoma, Polycynodon, Protocynodon
    Bauriidae, Ericiolacertidae, ?Ictidosuchidae, Lycideopidae,
    Nanictidopidae, ? Rubidginidae, Scaloposauridae, Silpholes-
    tidae
Suborder Anomodontia
  Infraorder Dinocephalia
    Deuterosauridae, Phreatosauridae, Tapinocephalidae
  Infraorder Venyukoviamorpha
    Dimacrodontidae, Venyukoviidae
  Infraorder Dromasauria
    Galechiridae, Galeopidae
  Infraorder Dicynodontia
    Incertae sedis: Digalodon, Haughtoniana
    Cistecephalidae, Dicynodontidae, Endothiodontidae, Geikiidae,
    Kannemeyeriidae, Lystrosauridae, Oudenodontidae
Subclass EURYAPSIDA (= Synaptosauria)
  Order Nothosauria
    Cymatosauridae, Keichousauridae, Nothosauridae, Nothosauravi-
    dae, Pachypleurosauridae, Simosauridae
  Order Placodontia
    Cyamodontidae, Helveticosauridae, Henodontidae, Paraplacodon-
    tidae, Placochelyidae, Placodontidae
  Order Plesiosauria
    Incertae sedis: Oligosimus, Orphosaurus, Uronautes
    ?Superfamily Pistosauroidea
      Pistosauridae

       Superfamily Plesiosauroidea
         Elasmosauridae, Plesiosauridae, Thaumatosauridae
       Superfamily Pliosauroidea
         Rhomaleosauridae, Leptocleididae, Pliosauridae, Dolichorhyncho-
         pidae
Subclass ICHTHYOPTERYGIA
    Order Ichthyosauria
       Suborder Latipinnati
         Mixosauridae, Macropterygiidae
       Suborder Longipinnati
         Californosauridae, Cymbospondylidae, Omphalosauridae, Shasta-
         sauridae, Stenopterygiidae
Subclass DIAPSIDA
 Infraclass LEPIDOSAURIA
  Superorder PROLACERTILIA
    Order Eosuchia (= Prolacertiformes)
       Incertae sedis: Paliguanidae, <u>Aenigmasaurus</u>, <u>Macronemus</u>, <u>Santai-</u>
         <u>saurus</u>
         Nettosuchidae, Palaeagamidae, Priceidae, Prolacertidae, Protoro-
         sauridae, Tangasauridae, Weigeltisauridae, Younginidae
    Order Thalattosauria
       Thalattosauridae
  Superorder RHYNCHOCEPHALIA
    Order Sphenodontia
       Monjurosuchidae, Sapheosauridae, Sphenodontidae
    Order Rhynchosauria
       Mesasuchidae, Rhynchosauridae
    Order Clarazisauria
       Claraziidae, ? Pleurosauridae
    Order Choristodera
       Champsosauridae
  Superorder SQUAMATA
       Incertae sedis: <u>Kuehneosaurus</u>
    Order Sauria (= Lacertilia)
       Incertae sedis: Ardeosauridae, Askeptosauridae, Kuehneosauridae,
         Tanystropheidae, Tholodontidae, Trachelosauridae, Zanclo-
         dontidae, <u>Bavarisaurus</u>, <u>Broilisaurus</u>, <u>Chamops</u>, <u>Francosaurophis</u>,
         <u>Macellodus</u>, <u>Macrocnemus</u>, <u>Pachyophis</u>, <u>Paliguana</u>, <u>Saurophis</u>
       Suborder Gekkota (= Nyctisauria)
         Pygopodidae. Incertae sedis: Dibamidae
       Superfamily Gekkonoidea
         Gekkonidae
       Suborder Iguania
         Agamidae, Arretosauridae, Bavarisauridae, Iguanidae. Incertae
         sedis: Eposauridae, <u>Macellodus</u>, <u>Teilhardosaurus</u>
       Suborder Rhiptoglossa
         Chamaeleontidae
       Suborder Scincomorpha (= Leptoglossa). Incertae sedis: Eichstätti-
         sauridae
       Superfamily Xantusioidea
         Eichstaettisauridae, Xantusiidae
       Superfamily Scincoidea
         Scincidae
       Superfamily Lacertoidea
         Cordylidae, Gerrhosauridae, Lacertidae, Teiidae

Suborder Amphisbaenia
  Amphisbaenidae
Suborder Auguimorpha
  Incertae sedis: <u>Euposaurus</u>
  Infraorder Diploglossa
    Superfamily Anguioidea
      Anguidea, Anniellidae, Dorsetisauridae, Xenosauridae
    Infraorder Platynota
      Superfamily Varanoidea
        Aigialosauridae, Dolichosauridae, Helodermatidae, Lanthanotidae,
          Pachyvaranidae, Parasaniwidae, Varanidae
      Superfamily Mosasauroidea
        Mosasauridae
Order Serpentes (= Ophidia)
  Incertae sedis: Anomalophididae, Archaeophididae,
      Lapparentophidae, Palaeophididae, <u>Cheilophis</u>, <u>Coniophis</u>,
      <u>Dunnophis</u>
  Superfamily Typhlopoidea (= Scolecophidia)
    Leptotphlopidae, Typhlopidae
  Superfamily Booidea
    Aniliidae, Boidae, Dinilysiidae, Pythonidae
  Superfamily Colubroidea
    Colubridae, Elapidae, Hydrophiidae, Viperidae, Xenopeltidae
Infraclass ARCHOSAURIA
Superorder THECODONTIA
  Order Proterosuchia
    Chasmatosauridae, Erythrosuchidae
  Order Pseudosuchia
    Aëtosauridae, Euparkeriidae, Ornithosuchidae, Pedeticosauridae,
      Pallisteriidae, Platyognathidae, Prestosuchidae, Scleromochlidae,
      Sphenosuchidae, Stagonolepididae, Stegomuschidae, Teleocra-
      teridae
    Incertae sedis: Garjainidae; <u>Elachistosuchus</u>, <u>Mamenchisaurus</u>
  Order Phytosauria (= Parasuchia)
    Phytosauridae
Superorder CROCODILIA
  Order Protosuchia
    Incertae sedis: Proterochampsidae
    Protosuchidae
  Order Mesosuchia
    Atoposauridae, Dyrosauridae, Goniopholidae, Pholidosauridae,
      Teleosauridae
  Order Eusuchia
    Crocodylidae, Hylaeochampsidae, Stomatosuchidae
  Order Sebecosuchia
    Baurusuchidae, Sebecidae
  Order Thalattosuchia
    Metriorhynchidae
Superorder DINOSAURIA
  Order Saurischia
    Incertae sedis: <u>Herrerasaurus</u>, <u>Ischisaurus</u>
    Suborder Theropoda
      Incertae sedis: <u>Troödon</u>
      Infraorder Coelurosauria
        Incertae sedis: <u>Lukousaurus</u>

Coeluridae (incl. Compsognathidae), Hallopodidae (incl. ? Procompsognathidae), Halticosauridae, Ornithomimidae, Podokesauridae, ? Segisauridae

Infraorder Carnosauria (= Megalosauroidea)

Incertae sedis: Chingkankousaurus, Torbosaurus

Antrodemidae, Megalosauridae (incl. Allosauridae, Bahariasauridae, Erectopodidae, and Spinosauridae), Poposauridae, Tyrannosauridae (incl. Aublysodontidae, and Deinodontidae)

Suborder Palaeopoda

Infraorder Palaeosauria

Ammosauridae, Palaeosauridae (incl. Gryponychidae), Teratosauridae (incl. Zanclodontidae)

Infraorder Plateosauria

Plateosauridae, Melanorosauridae (incl. Plateosauravidae), Thecodontosauridae

Suborder Sauropoda (= Opisthocoelia, = Cetiosauria)

Incertae sedis: Asiatosaurus, Mongolosaurus

Brachiosauridae, Titanosauridae

Order Ornithischia

Suborder Ornithopoda

Incertae sedis: Heterodontosaurus, Heterodontosauridae

Hadrosauridae (= Trachodontidae), Hypsilophodontidae (incl. Nanosauridae, and Thescelosauridae), Iguanodontidae (incl. Camptosauridae), Pachycephalosauridae (= "Troödontidae," sensu latu), Pisanosauridae, Psittacosauridae

Suborder Stegosauria

Stegosauridae

Suborder Ankylosauria (= Apredentalia, = Nodosauroidea)

Acanthopholidae, Nodosauridae, Syrmosauridae

Suborder Ceratopsia (= Ponderopoda, = Ceratopoidea)

Ceratopidae, Pachyrhinosauridae, Protoceratopidae

Superorder PTEROSAURIA

Order Pterodactyli

Superfamily Rhamphorhynchoidea

Dimorphodontidae, Rhamphorhynchidae, Scaphognathidae

Superfamily Pterodactyloidea

Aurognathidae, Dsungaripteridae, Germanodactylidae, Ornithocheiridae (= Pteranodontidae, = Nyctosauridae), Pterodactylidae, Pteromonodactylidae

Class AVES

Incertae sedis: Ornitholithus

Subclass ARCHAEORNITHES

Order Archaeopterygiformes

Archaeopterygidae

Subclass NEORNITHES

Superorder ODONTOGNATHAE

Order Hesperornithiformes

Hesperornithidae

Superorder ICHTHYORNITHES

Order Ichthyornithiformes

Apathornithidae, Ichthyornithidae

Superorder IMPENNES

Order Sphenisciformes

Spheniscidae

Superorder NEOGNATHAE
    Incertae sedis: Eremopezidae
        <u>Eobalearica</u>
Order Struthioniformes
    Eleutherornithidae, Struthionidae
Order Casuariformes
    Casuariidae, Dromiceiidae, Dromornithidae
Order Aepyornithiformes
    Aepyornithidae
Order Apterygiformes
    Emeidae, Apterygidae, Dinornithidae
Order Rheiformes
    Rheidae, Tinamidae, Opisthodactylidae
Order Gaviiformes
    Enaliornithidae, Gaviidae, Lonchodytidae
Order Colymbiformes
    Baptomithidae, Colymbidae, Podicipedidae
Order Procellariiformes
    Diomedeidae, Oceantidae, Pelecanoididae, Procellariidae
Order Pelecaniformes
    Incertae sedis: Cladornithidae, <u>Pliocarbo</u>
    Suborder Odontopteryges
        Odontopterygidae, Pseudodontornithidae
    Suborder Phaëthontes
        Phaëthontidae
    Suborder Pelecani
      Superfamily Pelecanoidea
        Cyphornithidae, Pelecanidae
      Superfamily Suloidea
        Anhingidae, Elopterygidae, Pelagornithidae, Phalacrocoracidae,
          Sulidae
    Suborder Fregatae
        Fregatidae
Order Ardeiformes
    Suborder Ardeae
        Ardeidae, Cochleariidae
    Suborder Balaenicipites
        Balaenicipitidae
    Suborder Ciconiae
      Superfamily Scopoidea
        Scopidae
      Superfamily Ciconioidea
        Ciconiidae
      Superfamily Threskiornithoidea
        Threskiornithidae
    Suborder Plataleae
        Plagodornithidae, Plataleidae
Order Phoenicopteriformes
    Agnopteridae, Phoenicopteridae, Palaelodidae, Scaniornithidae
Order Anseriformes
    Incertae sedis: <u>Brantadorna</u>, <u>Gallornis</u>
    Suborder Anhimae
        Anhimidae
    Suborder Anseres
        Anatidae, Paranyrocidae

Order Falconiformes
   Suborder Cathartae
      Superfamily Neocathartoidea (= Eocathartoidea)
         Neocathartidae
      Superfamily Cathartoidea
         Cathartidae, Teratornithidae
   Suborder Falcones
      Superfamily Sagittarioidea
         Sagittariidae
      Superfamily Falconoidea
         Accipitridae, Falconidae, Pandionidae
Order Galliformes
   Suborder Galli
      Superfamily Cracoidea
         Cracidae, Gallinuloididae, Megapodiidae
      Superfamily Phasianoidea
         Meleagrididae, Numididae, Phasianidae, Tetraonidae
   Suborder Opisthocomi
      Opisthocomidae
Order Gruiformes
   Incertae sedis: Ergilornithidae
   Suborder Mesitornithides
      Mesitornithidae
   Suborder Turnices
      Pedionomidae, Turnicidae
   Suborder Grues
      Superfamily Gruoidea
         Aramidae, Eogruidae, Geranoididae, Gruidae, Psophiidae
      Superfamily Ralloidea
         Idiornithidae, Rallidae
   Suborder Heliornithes
      Heliornithidae
   Suborder Rhynocheti
      Rhynochetidae
   Suborder Eurypygae
      Eurypygidae
   Suborder Phororhaci
      Brontornithidae, Cunampaiidae, Phororhacidae, Psilopteridae
   Suborder Cariamae
      Bathornithidae, Cariamidae, Hermosiornithidae
   Suborder Otides
      Gryzajidae, Otididae
Order Diatrymiformes
      Diatrymidae, Gastornithidae
Order Charadriiformes
   Suborder Charadrii
      Superfamily Jacanoidea
         Jacanidae
      Superfamily Charadrioidea
         Recurvirostridae, Rhegminornithidae, Rostratulidae, Scolopacidae
      Superfamily Dromadoidea
         Dromadidae
      Superfamily Burhinoidea
         Burhinidae
      Superfamily Glareoloidea
         Glareolidae

Superfamily Thinocoroidea
Thinocoridae
Superfamily Chionidoidea
Chionididae
Suborder Lari
Laridae, Stercorariidae
Suborder Alcae
Alcidae, Mancallidae
Order Columbiformes
Suborder Pterocletes
Pteroclidae
Suborder Columbae
Columbidae, Raphidae (= Dididae)
Order Psittaciformes
Psittacidae
Order Cuculiformes
Suborder Musophagi
Musophagidae
Suborder Cuculi
Cuculidae
Order Strigiformes
Protostrigidae, Strigidae, Tytonidae
Order Caprimulgiformes
Suborder Steatornithiformes
Steatornithidae
Suborder Caprimulgi
Aegothelidae, Caprimulgidae, Nyctibiidae, Podargidae
Order Apodiformes (= Micropodiformes)
Suborder Apodi (= Micropodi)
Aegialornithidae, Apodidae (= Micropodidae), Hemiprocnidae
Suborder Trochili
Trochilidae
Order Coliformes
Coliidae
Order Trogoniformes
Trogonidae
Order Coraciiformes
Suborder Alcedines
Superfamily Alcedinoidea
Alcedinidae
Superfamily Todoidea
Todidae
Superfamily Momotoidea
Momotidae
Suborder Meropes
Meropidae
Suborder Coracii
Brachypteraciidae, Coraciidae, Leptosomatidae, Phoeniculidae,
Upupidae
Suborder Bucerotes
Bucerotidae
Order Piciformes
Suborder Galbulae
Superfamily Galbuloidea
Bucconidae, Galbulidae

Superfamily Capitonoidea
Capitonidae, Indicatoridae
Superfamily Ramphastoidea
Ramphastidae
Suborder Pici
Picidae
Order Passeriformes (families not listed unless referred to)
Suborder Oscines
Palaeoscinidae
Suborder Eurylaimi
Suborder Tyranni
Suborder Menurae
Suborder Passeres
Corvidae, Fringillidae, Hirundinidae, Icteridae, Meliphagidae,
Mimidae, Troglodytidae

Class MAMMALIA
Incertae sedis: Microcleptidae, Ameghinichnidae, Acamana, Astro-
conodon
Subclass EOTHERIA
Order Docodonta
Docodontidae
Subclass PROTOTHERIA
Order Monotremata
? Ektopodontidae, Ornithorhynchidae, Tachyglossidae
Subclass ALLOTHERIA
Order Multituberculata
Incertae sedis: Paulchoffatia
Eucosmodontidae, Plagiaulacidae, Ptilodontidae, Taeniolabididae
Subclass THERIA
Incertae sedis: Pappotheriidae
Infraclass TRITUBERCULATA
Order Triconodonta
Amphilestidae, Morganucodontidae, Triconodontidae
Order Pantotheria
Aegialodontidae, Amphitheriidae, Dryolestidae, Kuehneotheriidae,
Paurodontidae
Order Symmetrodonta
Amphidontidae, Spalacotheriidae
Infraclass METATHERIA
Order Marsupialia
Superfamily Didelphoidea
Caroloameghiniidae, Didelphidae, Pediomyidae
Superfamily Borhyaenoidea
Borhyaenidae
Superfamily Dasyuroidea
Dasyuridae, Myrmecobiidae, Notoryctidae, Thylacinidae
Superfamily Perameloidea
Peramelidae
Superfamily Caenolestoidea
Caenolestidae, Groeberiidae, Necrolestidae, Polydolopidae
Superfamily Phalangeroidea
Diprotodontidae, Macropodidae, Phalangeridae, Phascolomidae,
Thylacoleonidae, Wynyardiidae
Infraclass EUTHERIA (= Monodelphia, = Placentalia)
Cohort UNGUICULATA

Incertae sedis: Anagalidae, Apheliscidae, Picrodontidae, Ceciliolemur,
Arctoryctes
Order Insectivora
Incertae sedis: Endotheriidae, Metacodontidae, Pentacodontidae,
Batodon, Telacodon
Suborder Lipotyphla
Superfamily Tenrecoidea
Butselidae, Nesophontidae, Potamogalidae, Solenodontidae,
Tenrecidae
Superfamily Chrysochloroidea
Chrysochloridae
Superfamily Erinaceoidea
Amphilemuridae, Dimylidae, Erinaceidae
Superfamily Soricoidea
Plesiosoricidae, Soricidae, Talpidae
Suborder Menotyphla
Incertae sedis: Metacodon
Superfamily Macroscelidoidea
Macroscelididae
Superfamily Tupaioidea
Anagalidae, Dormaaliidae, Tupaiidae
Superfamily Leptictoidea
Leptictidae, Pantolestidae, Zalamdalestidae
Superfamily Apatemyoidea
Apatemyidae, ? Mixodectidae
Order Dermoptera
Cynocephalidae, Plagiomenidae
Order Chiroptera
Suborder Megachiroptera
Pteropodidae
Suborder Microchiroptera
Incertae sedis: Cecilionycteris, Archaeonycteridae, Icaronycteridae,
Palaeochiropterygidae
Superfamily Emballonuroidea
Emballonuridae, Noctilionidae, Rhinopomatidae
Superfamily Rhinolophoidea
Hipposideridae, Megadermatidae, Nycteridae, Rhinolophidae
Superfamily Phyllostomatoidea
Desmodontidae, Phyllostomatidae
Superfamily Vespertilionoidea
Furipteridae, Molossidae, Mystacinidae, Myzopodidae, Natilidae,
Thyropteridae, Vespertilionidae
Order Primates
Incertae sedis: Microtarsioides
Suborder Prosimii (= Eteroprimates)
Incertae sedis: Carpolestidae, Microsyopidae, Phenacolemuridae
Infraorder Lemuriformes
Superfamily Lemuroidea
Adapidae, Galagidae, Indriidae, Lemuridae, Notharctidae,
Plesiadapidae
Superfamily Daubentonioidea
Daubentoniidae
Infraorder Lorisiformes
Lorisidae
Infraorder Tarsiiformes
Incertae sedis: Lushius

Anaptomorphidae, Omomyidae, Tarsiidae, Teilhardidae
Suborder Anthropoidei (= Euprimates, = Pithecoidea, = Simii)
Superfamily Ceboidea (= Arctopithecoidea = Platyrrhina)
Callitrichidae (= Hapalidae), Cebidae
Superfamily Cercopithecoidea (= Catarrhini)
Incertae sedis: Oligopithecus
Cercopithecidae (= Cinomorphidae, = Cynocephalidae, = Macadidae, = Papionidae)
Superfamily Hominoidea (= Anthropi, = Anthropomorpha)
Incertae sedis: Oreopithecidae, Kenyapithecus, Pondaungia
Hominidae (= Anthropidae), Parapithecidae, Pongidae (= Anthropomorphidae, = Simiidae)
Order Tillodontia
Incertae sedis: Kuanchuanius
Esthonychidae (= Tillotheriidae)
Order Taeniodontia
Stylinodontidae
Order Edentata (= Bruta)
Suborder Palaeanodonta
Epoicotheriidae, Metacheiromyidae
Suborder Xenarthra
Infraorder Pilosa
Superfamily Megalonychoidea
Incertae sedis: Chungchienia
Megalonychidae, Megatheriidae, Mylodontidae
Superfamily Myrmecophagoidea
Myrmecophagidae
Superfamily Bradypodoidea
Bradypodidae
Superfamily Entelopsoidea
Entelopsidae
Infraorder Cingulata (= Hicanodonta)
Superfamily Dasypodoidea
Dasypodidae, Peltephilidae
Superfamily Orophodontoidea
Orophodontidae
Superfamily Glyptodontoidea
Glyptodontidae
Order Pholidota
Manidae
Cohort GLIRES
Order Lagomorpha (= Duplicidentata)
Eurymylidae, Lepotidae, Ochotonidae
Order Rodentia
Suborder Sciurognathi
Incertae sedis: Pedetidae, Phiomyidae, Rhizomyidae, Spalacidae, Homocentrus
Infraorder Sciuromorpha
Superfamily Ischyromyoidea
Cylindrodontidae, Ischyromyidae, Paramyidae, Protoptychidae
Superfamily Aplodontoidea
Aplodontidae, Mylagaulidae
Superfamily Sciuroidea
Sciuridae
Infraorder Theridomyomorpha

Superfamily Theridomyoidea
    Pseudosciuridae, Theridomyidae
Superfamily Anomaluroidea
    Anomaluridae
Infraorder Castoromorpha
  Superfamily Castoroidea
    Castoridae, Eutypomyidae
Infraorder Myomorpha
  Incertae sedis: Gliroidea (incl. Gliridae and Seleviniidae)
  Superfamily Muroidea
    Cricetidae, Muridae
  Superfamily Geomyoidea
    Eomyidae, Geomyidae, Heteromyidae
  Superfamily Dipodoidea
    Dipodidae, Zapodidae
Suborder Hystricognathi
  Infraorder Caviomorpha (= Nototrogomorpha, = Orthohystricognathes)
    Superfamily Erethizontoidea
      Echimyidae, Erethizontidae
    Superfamily Cavioidea
      Caviidae, Dinomyidae, Eocardiidae, Hydrochoeridae
    Superfamily Octodontoidea
      Ctenomyidae, Cuniculidae, Myocastoridae, Octodontidae
    Superfamily Chinchilloidea
      Cephalomyidae, Chinchillidae, Perimyidae
  Infraorder Hystricomorpha (<u>sensu</u> <u>stricto</u>)
    Superfamily Hystricoidea
      Hystricidae
    Superfamily Thryonomoidea
      Thryonomyidae
    Superfamily Petromyoidea
      Petromyidae
    Superfamily Bathyergoidea
      Bathyergidae
    Superfamily Ctenodactyloidea
      Ctenodactylidae
Cohort MUTICA
  Order Cetacea (= Cete)
    Suborder Archaeoceti
      Incertae sedis: <u>Anglocetus</u>
      Aetiocetidae, Basilosauridae, Dorudontidae, Protocetidae
    Suborder Odontoceti
      Incertae sedis: <u>Araeodelphis, Pelodelphis</u>
      Superfamily Squalodontoidea
        Agorophiidae, Squalodontidae
      Superfamily Platanistoidea
        Plantanistidae
      Superfamily Physeteroidea
        Physeteridae, Ziphiidae
      Superfamily Delphinoidea
        Acrodelphidae, Delphinidae, Eurhinodelphidae, Hemisyntrachelidae,
          Monodontidae, Phocaenidae
    Suborder Mysticeti
      Balaenidae, Balaenopteridae, Cetotheriidae, Rhachianectidae
Cohort FERUNGULATA
Superorder FERAE

Order Carnivora
    Suborder Creodonta
        Incertae sedis: <u>Apternodus, Ardynictis, Didymoconus, Hyaenaelurus,</u>
            Creotarsidae, Kochictidae, Palaeoryctidae, Tshelkariidae
        Superfamily Oxyaenoidea (= Pseudocreodi)
            Hyaenodontidae, Limnocyonidae, Oxyaenidae, Teratodontidae
    Suborder Fissipeda
        Incertae sedis: <u>Progenetta</u>
        Superfamily Miacoidea
            Miacidae
        Superfamily Canoidea (= Arctoidea)
            Canidae, Mustelidae, Procyonidae, Ursidae
        Superfamily Feloidea (= Aeluroidea)
            Felidae, Hyaenidae, Viverridae
    Suborder Pinnipedia
        Odobenidae, Otariidae, Phocidae, Semantoridae
Superorder PROTUNGULATA
    Incertae sedis: Tricuspiodontidae
Order Condylarthra
        Didolodontidae, Hyopsodontidae, Meniscotheriidae, Periptychidae,
            Phenacodontidae
    Superfamily Arctocyonoidea
        Arctocyonidae
    Superfamily Mesonychoidea (= Acreodi)
        Mesonychidae
Order Hyracoida
    Suborder Procaviamorpha
        Procaviidae (Hyracidae)
    Suborder Pseudhippomorpha
        Geniohyidae, Myohyracidae
Order Litopterna
        Adianthidae, Macraucheniidae, Proterotheriidae
Order Notoungulata
    Suborder Notioprogonia
        Arctostylopidae, Henricosborniidae, Notostylopidae
    Suborder Toxodonta
        Archaeohyracidae, Archaeopithecidae, Homalodotheriidae, Iso-
            temnidae, Leontiniidae, Notohippidae, Oldfieldthomasiidae,
            Toxodontidae
    Suborder Typotheria
        Interatheriidae, Mesotheriidae (= Typotheriidae)
    Suborder Hegetotheria
        Hegetotheriidae
Order Astrapotheria
    Suborder Trigonostylopoidea
        Trigonostylopidae
    Suborder Astrapotheroidea
        Astrapotheriidae
Order Tubulidentata
        Orycteropodidae
Superorder PAENUNGULATA
    Order Xenungulata
        Carodniidae
    Order Pantodonta
        Incertae sedis: Pantolambdondontidae

Superfamily Coryphodontoidea
　　Coryphodontidae
Superfamily Pantolambdoidea
　　Barylambdidae, Pantolambdidae, Titanoideidae
Order Dinocerata
　　Uintatheriidae
Order Pyrotheria
　　Pyrotheriidae
Order Proboscidea
　Suborder Moeritherioidea
　　Moeritheriidae
　Suborder Elephantoidea
　　Elephantidae, Gomphotheriidae (= Bunomastodontidae, = Trilo-
　　phodontidae), Mammutidae (= Mastodontidae)
　Suborder Deinotherioidea
　　Deinotheriidae
　Suborder Barytherioidea
　　Barytheriidae
Order Embrithopoda (= Barypoda)
　　Arsinoitheriidae
Order Desmostylia
　Suborder Desmostyliformes
　　Desmostylidae, Paleoparadoxidae
Order Sirenia
　　Dugongidae, Protastomatidae, Protosirenidae, Trichechidae
　　(= Manatidae)
Superorder MESAXONIA
Order Perissodactyla
　Incertae sedis: Caucasotherium
　Suborder Hippomorpha
　　Superfamily Equoidea (= Hippoidea)
　　　Equidae, Palaeotheriidae
　　Superfamily Brontotherioidea
　　　Brontotheriidae
　Suborder Ceratomorpha
　　Incertae sedis: Toxotherium
　　Superfamily Tapiroidea
　　　Deperetellidae, Helaletidae, Isectolophidae, Lophiodontidae,
　　　Lophialetidae, Tapiridae
　　Superfamily Rhinocerotoidea
　　　Amynodontidae, Hyrachyidae, Hyracodontidae, Rhinocerotidae
　Suborder Ancylopoda
　　Superfamily Chalicotherioidea
　　　Chalicotheriidae, Eomoropidae
Superorder PARAXONIA
Order Artiodactyla
　Suborder Suiformes
　　Infraorder Palaeodonta (= Bunodonta)
　　　Superfamily Dicholbunoidea
　　　　Cebochoeridae, Choeropotamidae (= Helohyidae), Dichobunidae,
　　　　Leptochoeridae
　　　Superfamily Entelodontoidea
　　　　Entelodontidae
　　Infraorder Suina
　　　Superfamily Suoidea
　　　　Suidae, Tayassuidae

Infraorder Ancodonta
  Superfamily Anthracotherioidea
    Anoplotheriidae, Anthracotheriidae (= Hyopotamidae), Hippo-
      potamidae
  Superfamily Cainotherioidea
    Cainotheriidae
Infraorder Oreodonta
  Superfamily Merycoidodontoidea
    Agriochoeridae, Merycoidodontidae (= Oreodontidae)
Suborder Tylopoda
    Camelidae, Oromerycidae, Xiphodontidae
Suborder Ruminantia
  Infraorder Tragulina
    Superfamily Amphimerycoidea
      Amphimerycidae
    Superfamily Hypertraguloidea
      Hypertragulidae, Leptomerycidae, Protoceratidae
    Superfamily Traguloidea
      Gelocidae, Tragulidae
  Infraorder Pecora
    Superfamily Cervoidea
      Cervidae, Eumerycidae, Palaeomerycidae, Triceromerycidae
    Superfamily Giraffoidea
      Giraffidae (= Heladotheriidae), Lagomerycidae
    Superfamily Bovoidea
      Antilocapridae, Bovidae